Baseball America
2026 ALMANAC

BASEBALL AMERICA INC. · DURHAM, N.C.

Baseball America

ESTABLISHED 1981
P.O. BOX 12877, DURHAM, NC 27709 • PHONE (800) 845-2726

EDITOR IN CHIEF J.J. Cooper *@jjcoop36*
EXECUTIVE EDITOR Matt Eddy *@MattEddyBA*
CHIEF INNOVATION OFFICER Ben Badler *@benbadler*
VICE PRESIDENT, DESIGN & STRATEGY Seth Mates *@sethmates*
HEAD OF AUDIENCE DEVELOPMENT Mark Chiarelli *@Mark_Chiarelli*
DIRECTOR OF FINANCE AND REVENUE Mike Stewart
TECHNOLOGY DIRECTOR Steven Peters

EDITORIAL
SENIOR EDITOR Josh Norris *@jnorris427*
NATIONAL WRITERS Carlos Collazo *@CarlosACollazo*
Peter Flaherty *@PeterGFlaherty*
PROSPECT WRITER Geoff Pontes *@GeoffPontesBA*
NATIONAL COLLEGE WRITER Jacob Rudner *@JacobRudner*
STAFF WRITER Jesús Cano *@Jesus_Cano88*
SENIOR DIGITAL EDITOR Dan Malone
SPECIAL CONTRIBUTOR Tim Newcomb *@tdnewcomb*

BUSINESS
MARKETING/OPERATIONS COORDINATOR Angela Lewis
CUSTOMER SERVICE Melissa Sunderman

STATISTICAL SERVICE
MAJOR LEAGUE BASEBALL ADVANCED MEDIA

BASEBALL AMERICA ENTERPRISES
CHAIRMAN & CEO Gary Green
PRESIDENT Larry Botel
GENERAL COUNSEL Matthew Pace
DIRECTOR OF OPERATIONS Joan Disalvo
PARTNERS Stephen Alepa
Jon Ashley
Martie Cordaro
David Geaslen
Glenn Isaacson
Sonny Kalsi
Peter R. Riguardi
Ian Ritchie
Brian Rothschild
Beryl Snyder
Tom Steiglehner

PJL MEDIA
PRESIDENT Jonathan Segal
VICE PRESIDENT, OPERATIONS B.J. Schecter

BASEBALL AMERICA is published bimonthly, six double issues per year, by Baseball America Enterprises, LLC, 650 Fifth Avenue, Suite 2400, New York, NY 10019. Subscription rate is $109.99 for one year; Canada $112.99 (U.S. funds); all other foreign $125.99 per year (U.S. funds). Periodicals postage paid at New York NY, & additional mailing offices. Occasionally our subscriber list is made available to reputable firms offering goods and services we believe would be of interest to our readers. If you prefer to be excluded, please send your current address label and a note requesting to be excluded from these promotions to Baseball America Enterprises, LLC, PO Box 12877, Durhan, NC 27709, Attn: Privacy Coordinator. POSTMASTER: Send all UAA to CFS (See DMM 707.4.12.5); NONPOSTAL & MILITARY FACILITIES: send address corrections to Baseball America, P.O. Box 420235, Palm Coast, FL 32142-0235. CANADA POST: Return undeliverable Canadian addresses to IMEX Global Solutions, P.O. Box 25542, London, ON N6C 6B2. Please contact 1-800-381-1288 to start carrying Baseball America in your store.

© 2026 by Baseball America Enterprises, LLC. All Rights Reserved. Printed in the USA.

Baseball America
2026 ALMANAC

Editor
J.J. Cooper

Associate Editors
Carter Woodiel, Josh Norris, Matt Eddy

Contributing Editors
Jesús Cano, Carlos Collazo, Jacob Rudner

Design & Production
Seth Mates

Cover Photo
MAIN PHOTO: Cal Raleigh
PHOTO BY: Evan Bernstein/Getty Images

©2026 Baseball America Inc.
No portion of this book may be reprinted or reproduced without the written consent of the publisher.

For additional copies, visit our Website at
BaseballAmerica.com or call 1-800-845-2726 to order.
US $37.95 / CAN $50.95, plus shipping and handling per order. Expedited shipping available.
Distributed by Simon & Schuster.
ISBN-13: 979-8-9916170-3-1

Statistics provided by Major League Baseball Advanced Media and Compiled by Baseball America.

EDITOR'S NOTE: Major league statistics are based on final, unofficial 2025 averages.

» The organization statistics, which begin on Page 45, include all players who participated in at least one game during the 2024 season.

» Pitchers' batting statistics are not included, nor are the pitching statistics of position players who pitched in fewer than five games.

TABLE OF CONTENTS

Bobby Witt Jr.

MAJOR LEAGUES — 6

2025 IN REVIEW

Year In Review	7
Major League Player of the Year	10
Rookie of the Year	12
Organization of the Year	18
Major League All-Stars	20
Executive of the Year	21
Manager of the Year	21
Major League Debuts	23

AMERICAN LEAGUE

Standings	11
Club Batting, Pitching Statistics	24
Department Leaders	25
Year-By-Year Champions	32
Playoff Composite Box Scores	39

NATIONAL LEAGUE

Standings	13
Club Batting, Pitching Statistics	27
Department Leaders	28
Year-By-Year Champions	33
Playoff Composite Box Scores	41

POSTSEASON

Playoffs in Review	30
Year-By-Year Champions	34
World Series Box Scores	35

ORGANIZATION STATISTICS 43

Arizona Diamondbacks	44
Athletics	54
Atlanta Braves	64
Baltimore Orioles	73
Boston Red Sox	86
Chicago Cubs	96
Chicago White Sox	106
Cincinnati Reds	116
Cleveland Guardians	126
Colorado Rockies	135
Detroit Tigers	144
Houston Astros	155
Kansas City Royals	166
Los Angeles Angels	176
Los Angeles Dodgers	185
Miami Marlins	195
Milwaukee Brewers	206
Minnesota Twins	216
New York Mets	226
New York Yankees	237
Philadelphia Phillies	247
Pittsburgh Pirates	257
St. Louis Cardinals	268
San Diego Padres	277
San Francisco Giants	287
Seattle Mariners	297
Tampa Bay Rays	306
Texas Rangers	316
Toronto Blue Jays	327
Washington Nationals	338

MINOR LEAGUES 347

Year In Review	348
Player Of The Year	351
Executive Of The Year	353
Manager Of The Year	354
Classification All-Stars	355
Minor League All-Star Team	357
Team Of The Year	358
Department Leaders	359

TRIPLE-A

International League	361
Pacific Coast League	363

DOUBLE-A

Eastern League	365
Southern League	367
Texas League	369

HIGH CLASS A

Midwest League	371
Northwest League	373
South Atlantic League	375

LOW CLASS A

California League	377
Carolina League	379
Florida State League	381

ROOKIE

Arizona Complex League	383
Florida Complex League	385

LATIN AMERICA

Dominican Summer League	389

FALL LEAGUES

Arizona Fall League	391

INDEPENDENT LEAGUES 395

Year In Review	396
Player of Year	397
League Standings, Leaders and Statisitics	398

INTERNATIONAL 416

Year in Review	417

FOREIGN LEAGUES

Mexico	420
Japan	421
Italy	423
Netherlands	423
Korea	424
Taiwan	425
Cuba	426

WINTER LEAGUES

Winter Roundup	427

COLLEGE 429

Year in Review	430
RPI Rankings	434
All-America Team	435
NCAA Leaders	441
Top 25 Final Statistics	447
Conference Standings and Leaders	454
Small Colleges	471

SUMMER LEAGUES

Team USA	474
League Standings and Leaders	475

HIGH SCHOOL 485

Player of the Year	486
High School Top 50 Rankings	487
All-America Team	488

DRAFT 491

Year in Review	492
Top 100 Picks	498
Team by Team Selections	499

APPENDIX 504

Obituaries	505
Index	515

MAJOR LEAGUES

Baseball Thrilled In 2025

On a team filled with stars, ace Yoshinobu Yamamoto (center) stood out in the World Series. Yamamoto won Game 6 as a starter, and then won Game 7 as a reliever.

As manager Dave Roberts celebrated the Dodgers' National League Championship Series victory against the Milwaukee Brewers, he was interviewed by TBS while the microphone piped the sound through the Dodger Stadium public-address system.

"Before the season started, they said the Dodgers are ruining baseball," Roberts said, never identifying the antecedent to the pronoun 'they.' "Let's get four more wins and really ruin baseball."

The Dodger Stadium crowd roared. Los Angeles has emerged as baseball's model franchise, winning on the field with a team of international stars, developing prospects in the minors for MLB use and trade fodder, and becoming the new Evil Empire, early 2000s Yankees style, for opposing fans and salary cap-seeking media. They have emerged as the front-running favorite entering every major league season.

And of course they spend money, and they make money. The Dodgers' financial might draws the "ruining baseball" charge. Sports-business website Sportico reports the franchise crossed the $1 billion revenue threshold in 2024—when they won the World Series—joining the NFL's Dallas Cowboys and Spanish soccer clubs Barcelona and Real Madrid.

They signed two-way unicorn Shohei Ohtani for $700 million last offseason—$680 million of it deferred after the 10 years that he's guaranteed to play. They furthered their ties to Japan last offseason signing ace righty Yoshinobu Yamamoto and prior to 2025 by signing 23-year-old Japanese flamethrower Roki Sasaki. All that has made them bigger in Japan than bullet trains and body pillows.

And they spend lavishly on domestic free agents as well, last offseason signing two-time Cy Young Award winner Blake Snell (five years, $136.96 million), back-end relievers Tanner Scott (4/$72M), Blake Treinen (2/$22M) and Kirby Yates (1/$13M), as well as outfielder Michael Conforto (1/$17M) all to go with Ohtani, Yamamoto, future Hall of Famers Mookie Betts and Freddie Freeman, and the rest of the well-heeled gang.

The players who didn't live up to those contracts—especially Conforto, Scott and Yates—would have crippled other teams. The Dodgers' outsized revenue and payroll give them the cushion to absorb them, and gave Roberts as much ammunition as a manager could want. He used it to shepherd an injury-filled regular season roster to 93 wins and the 12th NL West division title in the last 13 seasons.

But ultimately, Roberts was proved wrong. The Dodgers didn't ruin baseball.

Instead, they elevated it, with a near-perfect run through three NL playoff rounds, then with a rousing, dramatic seven-game World Series tussle with the Toronto Blue Jays. Toronto had much of a nation rooting for it as Canada's Team, stars of its own such as Vladimir Guerrero Jr. and George Springer, and an accomplished offense that blended power and patience with a well below-average strikeout rate.

The Jays made a worthy foil, but in the end they were a footnote. The Dodgers rode Yamamoto's right arm—he won Game Six as a starter and returned the next evening to get the final eight outs of the Dodgers' 5-4, 11-inning Game Seven clincher—to win the ninth championship in franchise history and eighth since moving to Los Angeles in 1958.

It's the third World Series crown for the Dodgers in the last six seasons, joining in 2020 and 2024, and they became the first repeat World Series champs since the 1998-2000 Yankees won three in a row.

Asked after Game Seven whether the Dodgers are a dynasty, Roberts replied, "We've put together something pretty special. I do know that. I'm proud of the players, for the fans, scouting, player development, all the stuff. To do what we've done in this span of time is pretty remarkable. I guess let the pundits and all the fans talk about if it's a dynasty or not, but I'm pretty happy with where we're at."

A Classic Fall Classic

Every World Series crowns a champion. The 2025 edition made itself part of baseball history, in a way that few Series have before. It had a bit of everything and captivated viewing audiences in a way few Fall Classics have in the 21st century.

This World Series had star turns, such as the epic 18-inning Game Three, with Ohtani reaching base nine times, Dodgers rookie Will Klein throwing four innings of scoreless relief to forestall the use of a position player and Freddie Freeman's second straight Series with a walk-off homer. It had Toronto righthander Trey Yesavage, barely a year removed from being a first-round pick out of East Carolina, turning in arguably the best start ever by a rookie in World Series play, a 12-strikeout, no-walk, seven-inning gem in Game Five.

The 12 strikeouts broke Don Newcombe's 1949 mark (11) for strikeouts by a rookie in a Series game, and were the most ever in one Series game by a pitcher who didn't issue a walk. The Dodgers swung and missed 23 times against Yesavage, a record in the pitch-tracking era (2008) and became just the third starter to strike out every batter in an opposing starting lineup, joining Hall of Famers Randy Johnson (2001) and Bob Gibson (1968).

Yesavage's 6-1 Game Five win left the Jays a win away from their first World Series crown since they went back-to-back in 1992-93, but they couldn't keep the Dodgers from pulling their own back-to-back. LA had Yamamoto pitching it to a 3-1 victory in Game Six, with Tyler Glasnow—scheduled to start Game Seven—getting the save in the ninth inning as the Dodgers bullpen faltered.

That set up the Game Seven showdown with Ohtani starting on three days' rest, and the strain showed on baseball's greatest talent, as Bichette hit a three-run third-inning homer to send the Rogers Centre crowd into pandemonium. But the Jays couldn't quite put the Dodgers away, and with Ohtani lurking on deck, Toronto closer Jeff Hoffman hung a 3-2 slider with one out in the ninth on a full-count pitch to Miguel Rojas.

The 37-year-old Venezuelan hadn't started in the Series until Roberts played a hunch and inserted him in the lineup in Game Six. Now Rojas stepped to the forefront, sending Hoffman's slider into the left-field seats to tie the game at 4, and he turned in a key out in the bottom of the inning, forcing a runner at the plate on a groundout.

"Miggy Ro—I talk about the game honors you and right there the game honored him," Roberts said after Game Seven. "He does things the right way and he deserved that moment. And what Yoshi did tonight is unprecedented in modern day baseball.

"Just the young guys coming out there with the arms and just the big plays and—again, it's been a long season, man. We started out in Tokyo and ended up north of the border, so just proud of this group of guys."

Rookie Trey Yesavage debuted in September and then became an October ace.

Two innings later, as Yamamoto continued to quiet the crowd and Toronto's bats in extras, catcher Will Smith homered off Shane Bieber for what proved to be the final margin. Guerrero doubled off Yamamoto to open the bottom of the 11th, but with runners at first and third and one out, Yamamoto used a split-fingered fastball to induce Jays catcher Alejandro Kirk to hit into a Series-ending 6-3 double play, with Betts starting the celebration after the final out.

It capped a long season for the Dodgers, who started the regular season March 18 against the Cubs in a two-game series in Japan. Like any club, no matter the payroll, they went through cold stretches, falling behind the rival Padres in the NL West in August, and their bullpen never lived up to the expectations raised by the free-agent signings of Scott, Treinen (who re-signed after playing a key 2024 role) and Yates.

They also struggled offensively as Betts, who lost 15 pounds around the Japan trip due to illness, shifted at age 32 to being the everyday shortstop and was constantly catching up, by his own admission, to his pre-weight loss self. Max Muncy and his consistent grind-it-out offensive presence was sorely missed in a second half marred by injuries to his left knee and right oblique muscle, and Smith missed nearly all of September with a hairline fracture in his right hand.

Those factors and more tripped up the Dodgers from time to time, but nothing ruined them. When they needed a hero, they had Rojas, they had Smith, and they had Yamamoto, who emerged to become the first pitcher since Randy Johnson in 2001 to win Game Six as a starter and win Game Seven as a reliever.

"When I started (throwing) in the bullpen before I went in, to be honest, I was not really sure if I could pitch up there to my best ability," said Yamamoto, who earned Series MVP honors. "But as I started getting warmed up, because I started making a little bit of an adjustment, and then I started thinking I can go in and do my job."

A Ratings Winner

The Series did its job for FOX TV, as viewers turned out in droves. Game Seven drew 27,330,000 viewers according to FOX, making it the most-watched game since 2017's Game Seven between the Dodgers and Astros. It's a huge number especially when you compare Houston, the fourth-largest U.S. market, to Toronto, literally not in the U.S. and thus the only home market not watching on FOX. Game Seven peaked at 33,064,000 viewers just before midnight, up 16 percent from the last Game Seven, the 2019 Nationals-Astros tilt. The seven-game Series average of 15,709,000 viewers was the best complete average since '17 as well. It was even up 2 percent over the '24 series that featured the dream TV matchup of Dodgers vs. New York Yankees.

And according to MLB, Game Seven averaged 51 million viewers between the U.S., Canada and Japan, making it the most-watched MLB game in 34 years, back to the Jack Morris/John Smoltz Game Seven epic in the 1991 World Series.

Canada went all-in for the Jays, who had their best season since the Jose Bautista bat flip era of 2015-2016. (For more on the Blue Jays, see the Postseason story, p. 30). Game Seven in Canada garnered 10.9 million viewers, making it the most-watched English-language show in Canada since the 2010 Winter Olympics, which were held in Vancouver, B.C. Sportsnet, the Canadian broadcast home for the Series (which like the Blue Jays is owned by Rogers Communication), estimated that 23 million Canadians tuned in at some point in the seven games, out of a nation of 41 million.

It capped a good business year for MLB, both as content and at the gates. Attendance rose for the third straight year, the first time that's happened since 2005-07, as the 2025 season drew 71,409,42, surpassing the 70 million benchmark for a third straight season.

PLAYER OF THE YEAR

Judge Keeps Besting Himself

BY MATT EDDY

Aaron Judge has shown 80-grade power since his rookie season. He hit 52 home runs in 2017, establishing a since-broken rookie record.

That was just the tip of the iceberg. Since then, Judge has:

Hit 62 home runs in 2022 to establish a new American League single-season record.

Topped 50 home runs four times, including in each of the past two seasons.

Reached 300 home runs in just 955 games—the fastest pace in MLB history.

No hitter has more home runs or a higher slugging percentage than Judge since MLB resumed post-pandemic normalcy in 2021. Even more notable: In recent seasons, the 33-year-old Yankees superstar has become an 80-grade hitter.

Judge is one of three qualified hitters to carry a .300 batting average since 2021, as he trails only Luis Arraez and Freddie Freeman. Meanwhile, nobody can touch his .426 on-base percentage, either, not even Juan Soto, the king of walks.

Judge has always been selective at the plate, but in recent seasons, he has hit the ball harder and kept it off the ground at a higher rate. This has driven a high expected batting average—and a much higher actual batting average.

Judge hit .272 through 2020, followed by a .306 mark in the five seasons since.

As an 80 hitter with 80 power, Judge has reached a level of offensive dominance sel-

Aaron Judge has four 50-homer seasons.

dom seen.

For his incredible season—yet another one for the ages—he is the Baseball America Major League Player of the Year.

A Lot Of Black Ink

Judge batted .331/.457/.688 with 53 home runs and 114 RBIs this season. He led with a 1.144 OPS, 9.7 bWAR and 215 OPS+. His 124 walks trailed only Soto.

Judge might have challenged for additional counting categories had he not missed 10 games in late July with a flexor strain in his right elbow. The injury limited him to DH in August and the first half of September, which constrained his ability to add additional defensive value in right field.

Slash Stat Triple Crown

Rarely does a hitter lead the major leagues in the three slash stats. Doing so requires a player to rack up a lot of hits, take a lot of walks and hit a lot of home runs. Only the best hitters can truly excel in all three disciplines.

That describes Judge this season, as he led all MLB hitters in batting average, on-base percentage and slugging. That had been accomplished just five times in a non-strike-shortened season since World War II.

LAST 10 WINNERS

2015: Bryce Harper, OF, Nationals
2016: Mike Trout, OF, Angels
2017: Jose Altuve, 2B, Astros
2018: Mike Trout, OF, Angels
2019: Justin Verlander, RHP, Astros
2020: Freddie Freeman, 1B, Braves
2021: Shohei Ohtani, DH/RHP, Angels
2022: Aaron Judge, OF, Yankees
2023: Shohei Ohtani, DH/RHP, Angels
2024: Aaron Judge, OF, Yankees

Full list: search "Baseball America awards"

TV ratings were up across all MLB's partners and outlets according to MLB's communications arm. ESPN finished a 35-year run of Sunday Night Baseball by averaging 1.8 million viewers, up 21 percent from 2024. FOX (up 9%) and cable partner FS1 (10%) saw gains as well, as did league-run outlet MLB Network, whose showcase games gained 13 percent more viewers, while TNT's non-exclusive games gained a robust 29 percent.

It all comes as the collective bargaining agreement expires after the 2026 season, leading to fears of labor strife, but also as national broadcast contracts wind down with ESPN and other partners. The regional cable television model that proved lucrative for MLB and its clubs, and habit-forming for fans, is drawing down, leaving many fans scrambling for ways to watch their favorite teams in recent years.

The goal of commissioner Rob Manfred is to have more shared broadcast revenue for the entire sport, with expectations that ESPN will pivot to more local broadcasts while MLB adds new partners such as Netflix, which reportedly will become the new home of the Home Run Derby during the all-star break.

Speaking to the LA Times' Bill Shaikin during the NL Division Series, Manfred said, "I think there is a lot of acceptance within the industry that, given what's happened within the media environment, we need to be more national. The idea of centralizing, and getting more games available on national platforms, is really appealing to people. Now, we've got some cards to play, still. But I remain optimistic that it can happen."

Stars Come Out

The best card MLB has to play is a batch of star players who enjoyed amazing seasons in 2025, all of whom it was able to showcase in the postseason. Ohtani missed out on that experience in his first six seasons in the majors, coming from Japan to the Angels before becoming an even bigger star with the Dodgers.

In his first season in Dodger blue, he posted an unprecedented 50-50 season with 54 homers and 59 stolen bases as LA's DH. He re-incorporated pitching into his quiver in 2025 as he worked his way back from a second reconstructive elbow surgery and had another historic season, hitting .282/.392/.622 with 55 home runs, 20 steals and a league-high 146 runs scored. Oh by the way … he also posted a 2.87 ERA over 47 innings while striking out 62 on the mound.

While he ran hot and cold in the postseason, no one's "hot" can match Ohtani's, as he showed in an all-time performance in Game Four of the NLCS against the Brewers. He homered three times, including a 469-foot, 116.9 mph laser beam in the fourth inning off Chad Patrick that cleared the Dodger Stadium right-field pavilion, territory previously reached only by Hall of Famer Willie Stargell. Meanwhile, Ohtani tossed six scoreless innings on the mound, striking out 10. It was a one-game performance no one had seen before and likely never will again, unless it comes from Ohtani.

Ohtani was joined by his foil at the top of MLB in recent years, Aaron Judge, to become the seventh and eighth players to produce consecutive 50-homer seasons. Judge pushed his own bound-

AMERICAN LEAGUE STANDINGS

East	W	L	PCT	GB	Manager	Head Baseball Ops	Attendance	Average	Last Penn.
Toronto Blue Jays	94	68	.580	—	John Schneider	Ross Atkins	2,849,935	35,184	2025
New York Yankees	94	68	.580	—	Aaron Boone	Brian Cashman	3,392,659	41,884	2024
Boston Red Sox	89	73	.549	5	Alex Cora	Craig Breslow	2,776,496	34,277	2018
Tampa Bay Rays	77	85	.475	17	Kevin Cash	Erik Neander	786,750	9,712	2020
Baltimore Orioles	75	87	.463	19	Brandon Hyde/Tony Mansolino	Mike Elias	1,803,655	22,267	1983

Central	W	L	PCT	GB	Manager	Head Baseball Ops	Attendance	Average	Last Penn.
Cleveland Guardians	88	74	.543	—	Stephen Vogt	Chris Antonetti	2,051,360	25,325	2016
Detroit Tigers	87	75	.537	1	A.J. Hinch	Scott Harris	2,413,442	29,795	2012
Kansas City Royals	82	80	.506	6	Matt Quatraro	J.J. Picollo	1,748,808	21,590	2015
Minnesota Twins	70	92	.432	18	Rocco Baldelli	Derek Falvey	1,768,718	21,836	1991
Chicago White Sox	60	102	.370	28	Will Venable	Chris Getz	1,405,702	17,354	2005

West	W	L	PCT	GB	Manager	Head Baseball Ops	Attendance	Average	Last Penn.
Seattle Mariners	90	72	.556	—	Dan Wilson	Jerry Dipoto	2,538,053	31,333	Never
Houston Astros	87	75	.537	3	Joe Espada	Dana Brown	2,727,877	33,677	2022
Texas Rangers	81	81	.500	9	Bruce Bochy	Chris Young	2,397,071	29,593	2023
Athletics	76	86	.469	14	Mark Kotsay	David Forst	768,537	9,488	1990
Los Angeles Angels	72	90	.444	18	R. Washington/R. Montgomery	Perry Minasian	2,615,506	32,290	2002

Wild Card Series: Tigers defeated Guardians 2-1 and Yankees defeated Red Sox 2-1 in best-of-three. **Division Series:** Mariners defeated Tigers 3-2 and Blue Jays defeated Yankees 3-1 in best-of-five. **Championship Series:** Blue Jays defeated Mariners 4-3 in best-of-seven.

ROOKIE OF THE YEAR

Kurtz Speeds To MLB Stardom

BY JESÚS CANO

They were the four swings heard round the baseball world. Yet for Athletics first baseman Nick Kurtz, that July night when he became the first rookie—and one of just 21 players ever—to slug four home runs in one game still feels like a blur.

To the A's organization, it was something else entirely. The long-awaited light at the end of a dark, winding tunnel. A moment that didn't erase the pain of the firesales, the empty seats or the heartbreaking dislocation to Sacramento ahead of a planned relocation to Las Vegas.

For the A's fans who endured the chaos and stayed when others walked away, it offered something rare—hope. Hope to keep following, to keep caring, even when the times are tough.

As the A's embark on a new chapter, they do so with a new foundation. At its center is Kurtz, the Baseball America Rookie of the Year.

More than just a cornerstone of transition, he is rapidly becoming one of the game's most formidable young sluggers. Kurtz represents the promise of a future that finally feels possible.

"He's been a revelation," said A's assistant GM Billy Owens. "He was No. 1 on our (draft) board. The numbers were overwhelming, and the picturesque swing was amazing. I made sure, right after the draft, that it was on record in multiple interviews: Nick Kurtz was No. 1 on our board going into that season."

Kurtz authored one of the most dominant rookie seasons the game has ever seen. He slashed .291/.384/.613 with 33 home runs in 111 games. He led all rookies in homers. He led with 81 RBIs and 83 runs. His .998 OPS rank seventh-highest in history for a rookie with at least 450 plate appearances. His 168 wRC+ ranks fourth.

Kurtz's meteoric rise becomes even more remarkable when one considers where he was a year prior to his MLB debut, wearing a Wake Forest uniform on a quiet Tuesday night

Nick Kurtz dominated as a rookie.

road game at Elon. Twelve months later, he was anchoring a big league lineup, carrying the hopes of a franchise and proving why the Athletics made him the No. 4 pick in the 2024 draft.

It took some time for Kurtz to find his footing in the majors. The same dominance he showed at Triple-A didn't immediately translate, and he didn't hit his first home run until his 16th game. But once that ball left the yard, everything began to click.

And July? That was Kurtz's coming-out party.

It wasn't just a hot streak. It was a month in which raw potential became production. The rookie didn't just announce his arrival—he demanded attention. The four-homer game was the exclamation point.

"It's crazy how all that happened," Kurtz said. "A lot more people knew who I was after that game."

LAST 10 WINNERS

2015: Kris Bryant, 3B, Cubs
2016: Corey Seager, SS, Dodgers
2017: Aaron Judge, OF, Yankees
2018: Shohei Ohtani, RHP/DH, Angels
2019: Pete Alonso, 1B, Mets
2020: Tony Gonsolin, RHP, Dodgers
2021: Jonathan India, 2B, Reds
2022: Julio Rodriguez, OF, Mariners
2023: Corbin Carroll, OF, Diamondbacks
2024: Paul Skenes, RHP, Pirates

Full list: search "Baseball America awards"

aries at age 33, winning his first batting title and modern Triple Crown, posting a .331/.457/.688 line to lead in batting, on-base and slugging. At 6-foot-7, he's the tallest batting champ ever, and his 53 homers gave him his fourth 50-home run season. That ties the all-time mark held by Babe Ruth, Mark McGwire and Sammy Sosa. (See more on Judge in the Player of the Year story, page 10)

Amazingly, neither led their respective league in home runs. Phillies DH Kyle Schwarber had his best season—just in time to become a free agent—as he swatted 56 homers to lead the NL. His 132 RBIs led the majors, and 23 of his homers came as a lefthanded hitter off a lefty pitcher, a new MLB mark.

Seattle's Star Shone Bright

The AL home run champ, however, might have had the most memorable season of all. Mariners catcher Cal Raleigh had already established himself as one of the game's best catchers, with 91 homers in his three previous full seasons and a 2024 Gold Glove award. But no one was prepared for Raleigh's 2025 season, least of all Raleigh himself.

He became just the sixth player ever to swat 60 home runs in a single season, joining Judge (2022), Ruth (1927), McGwire (1998 ,'99), Sosa ('98, '99 and 2001), single-season record holder Barry Bonds ('01) and Roger Maris (1961). He set a new record for home runs by a catcher (48, Salvador Perez, 2021) and switch-hitter (54, Mickey Mantle, 1961). And he did it while leading the Mariners to their first AL West title since Ichiro Suzuki's rookie season in 2001.

Raleigh hit five more home runs in the Mariners'

run to the seventh game of the ALCS as well, and did it all while catching 121 games (fifth in the league), plus 12 more in the playoffs. Overall, he batted .247/.359/.589, leading the league with 125 RBIs, and scored 110 runs while stealing 14 bases.

And in the middle of July, Raleigh also won the Home Run Derby in Atlanta, shining as his father Todd threw for him and his younger brother Todd Jr. squatted behind him as the BP catcher.

"It's a dream come true," said his father Todd, who served as head coach at Tennessee and Western Carolina. "Anybody that's ever played baseball as a kid dreams of stuff like this. I dreamed of it. He dreamed of it. When you're a parent, you look at it differently because you want your kids to be happy.

"To do it as a family has been really special . . . When we involved the family, the complexion of it changed. It was all a family thing, and I thought, you know what? If he doesn't hit any home runs, we'll still be good."

Raleigh became the first catcher and first switch-hitter to win the Derby, part of a unique season that merited serious contention for AL MVP despite Judge's amazing performance.

The two significant Wins Above Replacement measures, websites Baseball-Reference and Fangraphs, had him behind Judge; he had 7.4 bWAR and 9.1 fWAR, which gives credit for a catcher's pitch framing, compared to 9.7 bWAR and 10.1 fWAR for Judge.

Minor Threats

Raleigh hit 28 of his 60 regular-season shots at Seattle's T-Mobile Park with 32 coming on the road. Only one of them was hit in Tampa Bay

NATIONAL LEAGUE STANDINGS

East	W	L	PCT	GB	Manager	Head Baseball Ops	Attendance	Average	Last Penn.
Philadelphia Phillies	96	66	.593	—	Rob Thomson	Dave Dombrowski	3,375,477	41,672	2022
New York Mets	83	79	.512	13	Carlos Mendoza	David Stearns	3,182,052	39,284	2015
Miami Marlins	79	83	.488	17	Clayton McCullough	Peter Bendix	1,156,228	14,274	2003
Atlanta Braves	76	86	.469	20	Brian Snitker	Alex Anthopoulos	2,903,167	35,841	2021
Washington Nationals	66	96	.407	30	Dave Martinez/Miguel Cairo	Mike Rizzo/Mike DeBartolo	1,916,768	23,663	2019
Central	**W**	**L**	**PCT**	**GB**	**Manager**	**Head Baseball Ops**	**Attendance**	**Average**	**Last Penn.**
Milwaukee Brewers	97	65	.599	—	Pat Murphy	Matt Arnold	2,650,089	32,717	1982 (AL)
Chicago Cubs	92	70	.568	5	Craig Counsell	Jed Hoyer	3,017,983	37,259	2016
Cincinnati Reds	83	79	.512	14	Terry Francona	Nick Krall	2,117,213	26,138	1990
St. Louis Cardinals	78	84	.481	19	Oliver Marmol	John Mozeliak	2,250,007	27,777	2013
Pittsburgh Pirates	71	91	.438	26	Derek Shelton/Don Kelly	Ben Cherington	1,525,025	18,827	1979
West	**W**	**L**	**PCT**	**GB**	**Manager**	**Head Baseball Ops**	**Attendance**	**Average**	**Last Penn.**
Los Angeles Dodgers	93	69	.574	—	Dave Roberts	Andrew Friedman	4,012,470	49,536	2025
San Diego Padres	90	72	.556	3	Mike Shildt	A.J. Preller	3,437,201	42,434	1998
San Francisco Giants	81	81	.500	12	Bob Melvin	Buster Posey	2,925,823	36,121	2014
Arizona Diamondbacks	80	82	.494	13	Torey Lovullo	Mike Hazen	2,393,973	29,555	2023
Colorado Rockies	43	119	.265	50	Bud Black/Warren Schaeffer	Bill Schmidt	2,404,623	29,686	2007

Wild Card Series: Cubs defeated Padres 2-1 and Dodgers defeated Reds 2-0 in best-of-three. **Division Series:** Dodgers defeated Phillies 3-1 and Brewers defeated Cubs 3-2 in best-of-five. **Championship Series:** Dodgers defeated Brewers 4-0 in best-of-seven.

MAJOR LEAGUES

The Nationals fired GM Mike Rizzo just before the 2025 MLB Draft. Interim GM Mike DeBartolo and his front office selected shortstop Eli Willits with the No. 1 pick.

and none came in six games against the division-rival Athletics, meaning he hit 59 of his 60 in big league ballparks. Those two teams, the Rays and A's, dragged MLB's attendance down as both teams played their home games in minor league stadiums.

One was planned, as the Athletics franchise ended its run in Oakland en route to a planned move to Las Vegas. Owner John Fisher has the A's scheduled to spend three seasons in Sacramento's Sutter Health Park, home of the Triple-A RiverCats of the Pacific Coast League, before a new park opens in Vegas. The park also hosted a full Triple-A slate and is scheduled to do so for two more seasons.

The Athletics' Sacramento residency allows them to continue to fulfill their lucrative NBC Sports California cable TV contract, but their first season in the state capital was uneven at best. Visiting pitchers such as Zack Wheeler and Joe Ryan roundly criticized the condition of the pitcher's mound, and so did A's righty Luis Severino, who signed a two-year, $45 million deal prior to the season to be the club's ace.

Severino struggled getting into a routine with the clubhouse at Sutter Health located in center field, making it inaccessible between innings, and went just 2-9, 6.01 at home compared to 6-2, 3.02 on the road. Severino, who previously played for the Mets and Yankees, flatly (and factually) told the Yankees' YES Network, "It's not a big league ballpark."

The A's meant to play in a minor league park;

the Rays had to. St. Petersburg's Tropicana Field, the Rays' home since their 1998 inaugural season, suffered significant damage from an October 2024 hurricane that ripped its roof to shreds.

The Yankees came to the rescue, allowing the Rays to use their Tampa spring training home, Steinbrenner Field, as a temporary home. The Rays and visiting teams had to play outdoors in Florida, which meant withering heat and humidity in the summer. Surprisingly, the team had no home games rained out and just 11 rain delays.

The Rays covered the Yankees' signage and were able to take advantage of big league facilities such as a new clubhouse and technology. It wasn't home, but it was as close as the Rays could get for 2025. As righthander Drew Rasmussen told BA correspondent Marc Topkin, "This has been a really good Plan B."

Topkin reported in November that the $60 million in repairs for Tropicana Field and its new roof were on schedule to be ready for Opening Day 2026.

The Rays out-drew the A's, averaging 9,712 while the A's averaged 9,487. In their last year in Oakland, the A's drew 11,528 per game, while the Rays averaged 16,515 per game in 2024 at the Trop.

Impactful Transactions

Even without a ballpark either now or set for the future, the Rays still sold for $1.7 billion. Primary owner Stuart Sternberg sold the franchise to a group headed up by Jacksonville, Fla., housing

ALL-ROOKIE TEAM 2025

Pos	Player, Team	Age	AB	HR	SB	AVG	OBP	SLG	wRC+	Summary
C	Drake Baldwin, Braves	24	405	19	0	.274	.341	.469	125	Started 85 G behind plate; one of best hitters at position
1B	Nick Kurtz, Athletics	22	420	36	2	.290	.383	.619	170	One of seven rookies ever with 1.000 OPS (min. 450 PA)
2B	Luke Keaschall, Twins	22	182	4	14	.302	.382	.445	134	All ingredients are present to become a Twins table setter
3B	Matt Shaw, Cubs	23	393	13	17	.226	.295	.394	93	Hit 11 of 13 HR in second half; has 20 HR, 20 SB potential
SS	Jacob Wilson, Athletics	23	486	13	5	.311	.355	.444	121	.311 AVG is 10th best for rookie in 30-team era (min. 500 PA)
OF	Roman Anthony, Red Sox	21	257	8	4	.292	.396	.463	140	Had .910 OPS with 6 of his 8 home runs in final 25 games
OF	Daylen Lile, Nationals	22	321	9	8	.299	.347	.498	132	His 132 wRC+ ranked fifth among rookies (min. 200 PA)
OF	Jakob Marsee, Marlins	24	209	5	14	.292	.363	.478	133	Got on base and stole bags; held onto power gains
DH	Colson Montgomery, White Sox	21	255	21	0	.239	.311	.529	129	Tied for second among rookies with 21 HR in just 71 G

Pos	Pitcher, Team	Age	IP	BB	SO	HR	ERA	WHIP	FIP	Summary
SP	Noah Cameron, Royals	25	138	43	114	18	2.99	1.10	4.18	Kept batters guessing w/ 5-pitch mix, lots of soft contact
SP	Cade Horton, Cubs	23	118	33	97	10	2.67	1.08	3.59	Hits spots like a veteran, shows quality breaking stuff
SP	Chad Patrick, Brewers	26	120	40	127	13	3.53	1.28	3.53	Resembles Lance Lynn with heavy dose of fastball types
SP	Cam Schlittler, Yankees	24	73	31	84	8	2.96	1.22	3.74	His 99 mph heat is a top whiff and putaway pitch
SP	Will Warren, Yankees	26	162	65	171	22	4.44	1.37	4.07	Uses a sinker/sweeper approach to neutralize RH batters
RP	Braydon Fisher, Blue Jays	24	50	19	62	4	2.70	1.02	3.02	Led rookie relievers with 31.6% SO rate (min. 50 IP)

developer Patrick Zalupski, a deal the other MLB owners approved in late September.

The price was close to the $1.725 billion what the Angelos family sold the Orioles for in January 2024. That was also reported to be the price the Pohlad family sought to sell the Twins, which the family has owned since Carl Pohlad purchased it from Calvin Griffith in 1984. While the Pohlads, who admitted they were $500 million in debt with the Twins, had the club on the market for nine months, they reconsidered and announced they were bringing on two limited minority partners in August, rather than selling the franchise.

"We've owned this franchise for 40 years," Twins executive chair Joe Pohlad told The Athletic. "It's a really difficult thing to part with. We feel we're the right people to lead this organization, to own this franchise."

Twins fans responded to the non-sale and to the club's on-field struggles by staying away in droves, as attendance dropped by 9.4 percent, from 1.95 million to 1.77 million. It was a lost season in Minneapolis as the Twins fell out of the playoff race despite a May 13-game winning streak. They sold more aggressively than any club at the July deadline, trading 10 big leaguers (plus one minor leaguer) in a three-day span, including five members of the big league bullpen. Minnesota wound up finishing 72-90, a record that cost manager Rocco Baldelli his job after seven seasons. He was replaced in the offseason by Derek Shelton, who had been the Twins' bench coach in 2018-19, the latter year coming under Baldelli.

Shelton left the Twins to manage the Pirates and was fired in May 2025, his sixth season, after Pittsburgh got off to a 12-26 start. Don Kelly replaced him and eventually got the job on a permanent basis. Shelton was the first of three in-season managerial dismissals.

It was a busy year for managerial firings and front-office changes overall. The Nationals held the No. 1 overall pick in the July draft and shocked the industry by firing GM Mike Rizzo and manager Davey Martinez on July 6, only a week before the draft. Rizzo had run the club since 2009 and Martinez had managed since 2018, and they both were crucial factors in Washington's 2019 World Series championship.

The Nats drafted Oklahoma prep shortstop Eli Willits (son of ex-big league outfielder Reggie) with that top pick at the direction of interim GM Mike DeBartolo, then replaced Rizzo on a permanent basis with Paul Toboni, a former scouting director and assistant GM of the Red Sox. Just 35, Toboni became the youngest head of baseball operations in MLB and hired the youngest manager in the game, Blake Butera (son of ex-MLB catcher Sal), to run the dugout.

The Rockies fired Bud Black 40 games into a 43-119 season (they were 7-33 under Black). Colorado posted the worst run differential, -424, since the infamous Cleveland Spiders in 1899, and they finished just two games better than the 2024 121-loss White Sox. The season cost general manager Bill Schmidt his post, as he resigned at season's end, and more than a month later, the Rockies stunned the industry by hiring Paul DePodesta as the new head of baseball operations. DePodesta, who spent the last nine years as chief strategy officer for the NFL's Cleveland Browns, was GM of the Dodgers for two seasons (2004-05) after rising to fame as Billy Beane's assistant GM with the "Moneyball" Oakland A's of the early 2000s. He also was VP of player development and scouting under Sandy Alderson with the Mets from 2011-2015.

Free agent signee Juan Soto made an instant impact for the Mets, as he led the National League with a .396 on-base percentage. More surprisingly, he also led the league with 38 stolen bases.

Several veteran managers exited the scene, led by Bruce Bochy, who stepped down as Rangers manager two years after leading Texas to a World Series championship, the club's first but his fourth as a manager. He returned to the Giants, whom he managed when they won Series titles in 2010, '12 and '14, but as a special assistant to club president Buster Posey. San Francisco did need a new manager, firing Bob Melvin after just two seasons, and Posey went bold, hiring Tony Vitello away from his job as head coach at the University of Tennessee.

Vitello had led the Vols to three College World Series trips and the program's first national championship in 2024 with a talent-laden roster and brash playing style that reflected Vitello's energy and confidence. The former Missouri player has never played, coached or managed in professional baseball, making him the first of his kind as a college coach directly jumping to the big leagues.

San Diego made it three of the five NL West teams to make a managerial change, their fourth in six years, after Mike Shildt stepped down after two seasons, both of them 90-win playoff teams. Former Padres reliever Craig Stammen, who had started the process interviewing prospective new managers in his special assistant role, wound up being hired for the job.

Stammen will manage several Padres that he played with in his last season in 2022. That's the same year Kurt Suzuki last played, and he was named as the Angels' new manager, signing only a one-year contract. Suzuki, a member of that 2019 Nationals title team, replaces Ron Washington, 73, who lasted 74 games in '25 before having to step away from the dugout due to health problems.

Gambling Losses

Ever since sports gambling laws started loosening around the country in the wake of a 2018 Supreme Court ruling, skeptics had warned that it was only a matter of time before gambling and pro sports became ensnared in tumult. And in 2025, MLB encountered its biggest in-game gambling scandal.

MLB's biggest brushes include Ohtani's translator and personal assistant, Ippei Mizuhara, being investigated and then sentenced to 57 months in federal prison for stealing nearly $17 million from Ohtani to pay off his gambling debts. MLB also dismissed umpire Pat Hoberg in Feb. 2025 for sharing legal sports betting accounts with a friend who bet on baseball and for intentionally deleting messages that were a focus of the investigation into his conduct. And in June 2024, five players were disciplined for gambling, with four suspended for one year and the fifth, infielder Tucupita Marcano, ruled permanently ineligible for betting on baseball, including 231 MLB-related bets.

The stakes rose in 2025, though, as the Cleveland Guardians lost a starter and their all-star closer to gambling-related investigations that first led to the players being placed by MLB on administrative leave, and then federal indictments coming down in November.

The effect on the Guardians proved ephemeral; in fact, Cleveland rallied down the stretch of the season, led by its pitching, and ran down Detroit in an epic American League Central comeback. The Guardians won the division after being 11 games behind the Tigers as late as Sept. 4.

They did it without closer Emmanuel Clase and fellow righthander Luis Ortiz, a starter whom the Guardians acquired in a three-team offseason trade prior to the 2025 season. The players were placed on leave separately in July—Ortiz last pitched at the end of June, while Clase lasted another month before his suspension—and indicted in November on charges including wire fraud and several conspiracy counts, alleging that the players schemed to rig pitches.

The players were charged to have communicated with bettors to wager that they would throw pitches out of the strike zone and below certain velocity thresholds, then threw such pitches on purpose and collected winnings themselves.

The indictment alleges that Clase started making illegal wagers in 2023, then encouraged Ortiz to join him after they became teammates in 2025.

The effect on baseball likely will be even more significant than it was for the Guardians. The ramifications started with MLB announcing new safeguards with its betting partners to limit the kind of pitch-by-pitch bets that Clase and Ortiz are alleged to have exploited. They also worked with sportsbooks to establish a nationwide $200 betting limit on individual pitches, as well as removing individual pitch bets from being included in parlays, in an attempt to limit in-game manipulation.

The Dodgers certainly didn't ruin baseball; gambling or an ill-timed work stoppage are much bigger threats.

Duly Noted

While MLB had a historically awful team for the second straight season as the Rockies followed the White Sox's 2024 futility, the last two seasons have not seen similar extremes at the top of the standings. For the second straight season, no team won 100 games in the regular season. That last time that happened was 2013-14. The Brewers led the majors with 97 victories, a franchise record, and after several seasons of postseason struggles, they won a five-game Division Series tussle with their biggest rivals, the Cubs. It was their first playoff series victory since 2018. However, Milwaukee

AMERICAN LEAGUE BEST TOOLS

A Baseball America survey of American League managers, conducted in August 2025, ranked players with the best tools.

Best Hitter
1. Aaron Judge, Yankees
2. Jose Ramirez, Guardians
3. Bobby Witt Jr., Royals

Best Power
1. Aaron Judge, Yankees
2. Cal Raleigh, Mariners
3. Junior Caminero, Rays

Best Bunter
1. Steven Kwan, Guardians
2. Daulton Varsho, Blue Jays
3. Kyle Isbel, Royals

Best Strike-Zone Judgment
1. Steven Kwan, Guardians
2. Vladimir Guerrero Jr., Blue Jays
3. Aaron Judge, Yankees

Best Hit-And-Run Artist
1. Steven Kwan, Guardians
2. Jacob Wilson, Athletics
3. Ernie Clement, Blue Jays

Best Baserunner
1. Bobby Witt Jr., Royals
2. Chandler Simpson, Rays
3. Byron Buxton, Twins

Fastest Baserunner
1. Chandler Simpson, Rays
2. Bobby Witt Jr., Royals
3. Byron Buxton, Twins

Most Exciting Player
1. Aaron Judge, Yankees
2. Bobby Witt Jr., Royals
3. Byron Buxton, Twins

Best Pitcher
1. Tarik Skubal, Tigers
2. Garrett Crochet, Red Sox
3. Jacob deGrom, Rangers

Best Fastball
1. Mason Miller, Athletics
2. Joe Ryan, Twins
3. Tarik Skubal, Tigers

Best Curveball
1. Hunter Brown, Astros
2. Framber Valdez, Astros
2. Nathan Eovaldi, Rangers

Best Slider
1. Jacob deGrom, Rangers
2. Griffin Jax, Twins/Rays
3. Matt Brash, Mariners

Best Changeup
1. Tarik Skubal, Tigers
2. Michael Wacha, Royals
3. Devin Williams, Yankees

Best Control
1. Tarik Skubal, Tigers
2. Jacob deGrom, Rangers
3. Bryan Woo, Mariners

Best Pickoff Move
1. Max Fried, Yankees
2. Gavin Williams, Guardians
3. Tanner Bibee, Guardians

Best Reliever
1. Josh Hader, Astros
2. Aroldis Chapman, Red Sox
3. Emmanuel Clase, Guardians

Best Defensive C
1. Alejandro Kirk, Blue Jays
2. Dillon Dingler, Tigers
3. Carlos Narvaez, Red Sox

Best Defensive 1B
1. Carlos Santana, Guardians
2. Vladimir Guerrero Jr., Blue Jays
3. Ty France, Twins/Blue Jays

Best Defensive 2B
1. Andres Gimenez, Blue Jays
2. Marcus Semien, Rangers
3. Ernie Clement, Blue Jays

Best Defensive 3B
1. Jose Ramirez, Guardians
2. Alex Bregman, Red Sox
3. Maikel Garcia, Royals

Best Defensive SS
1. Bobby Witt Jr., Royals
2. Jeremy Peña, Astros
3. Taylor Walls, Rays

Best Infield Arm
1. Carlos Correa, Twins/Astros
2. Addison Barger, Blue Jays
3. Maikel Garcia, Royals

Best Defensive OF
1. Ceddanne Rafaela, Red Sox
2. Daulton Varsho, Blue Jays
3. Byron Buxton, Twins

Best Outfield Arm
1. Addison Barger, Blue Jays
2. Julio Rodriguez, Mariners
3. Nolan Jones, Guardians

Best Manager
1. AJ Hinch, Tigers
2. Kevin Cash, Rays
3. Bruce Bochy, Rangers

came up very short against the Dodgers in the NLCS, scoring just four runs in the sweep after finishing third in the majors in runs scored during the regular season.

While many fans resented the Dodgers' largesse and success, the Mets technically had the largest

ORGANIZATION OF THE YEAR

Milwaukee Does More With Less

BY TODD ROSIAK

Big things are happening in baseball's smallest market.

The Milwaukee Brewers are experiencing an organizational renaissance that shows no signs of faltering as they continue to click off wins, clinch division titles and stack playoff appearances.

In many ways, the Brewers' 2025 season was their best yet. They won an MLB-best 97 games and claimed the top seed in the National League playoffs, all while operating with a bottom-third payroll.

Milwaukee achieved all this despite trading all-star closer Devin Williams in the offseason and making no free agent splashes. Their biggest import was veteran lefthander Jose Quintana, who signed midway through spring.

The Brewers had winning streaks of eight, 11 and 14 games, and in October they recorded their first postseason series victory since 2018 with a five-game Division Series triumph against the rival Cubs.

The good vibes ended rather abruptly in the NL Championship Series, when the Dodgers swept them in four games en route to repeating as World Series champions.

It was a performance that stung in the moment, but all that went right to get to that point should be noted and lauded.

A combination of acquisitions panned out better than expected, and the development of some of their homegrown talent set the stage for the Brewers to be named the Baseball America Organization of the Year.

"We're just trying to make good decisions, not just on their own, but throughout our process. It's a different soup every year," Brewers president of baseball operations and GM Matt Arnold said. "The good thing is—and I really do mean it—we have really good people here."

Jackson Chourio is one of a number of young Brewers' stars.

The 2025 season was a continuation of a run of success that first began in 2018, which was the last time the Brewers were honored as Organization of the Year. Milwaukee has won 90 or more games three straight seasons and in four of the last five. It has earned postseason berths in seven of the last eight seasons.

That territory is normally reserved for the sport's biggest spenders.

And since the Brewers' strategy entails doing no more than dabbling on the fringes of free agency, they need to be ahead of the curve in other ways. For example, by extending homegrown outfielder Jackson Chourio to a team-friendly deal prior to his 2024 MLB debut season.

"It's an extremely hard-working, creative and evolving front office," said Giants GM Zack Minasian, who worked in various roles in Milwaukee's front office for 14 years. "I don't think they're ever resting on just what has worked. They're always looking to get better." ∎

LAST 10 WINNERS

2015: Pittsburgh Pirates
2016: Chicago Cubs
2017: Los Angeles Dodgers
2018: Milwaukee Brewers
2019: Tampa Bay Rays
2020: Los Angeles Dodgers
2021: Tampa Bay Rays
2022: Seattle Mariners
2023: Texas Rangers
2024: San Diego Padres

Full list: search "Baseball America awards"

ACTIVE LEADERS

Career leaders among players who played in a game in 2025. Batters require 3,000 plate appearances and pitchers 1,000 innings to qualify for percentage titles.

BATTERS			PITCHERS		
AVG	Luis Arraez	.317	ERA	Clayton Kershaw	2.53
OBP	Juan Soto	.417	H/9	Jacob deGrom	6.86
SLG	Aaron Judge	.615	SO/9	Blake Snell	11.19
OPS	Aaron Judge	1.028	BB/9	Miles Mikolas	1.77
R	Freddie Freeman	1,379	HR/9	Clayton Kershaw	0.63
H	Freddie Freeman	2,431	W	Justin Verlander	266
2B	Freddie Freeman	547	L	Justin Verlander	158
3B	S. Marte/M. Trout	55	SV	Kenley Jansen	476
HR	Giancarlo Stanton	453	IP	Justin Verlander	3567.2
RBI	Freddie Freeman	1,322	SO	Justin Verlander	3,553
BB	Carlos Santana	1,330	BB	Justin Verlander	952
SO	Giancarlo Stanton	2,059	G	Kenley Jansen	933
XBH	Freddie Freeman	947	GS	Justin Verlander	555
SB	Starling Marte	361	HR	Justin Verlander	371

NATIONAL LEAGUE BEST TOOLS

A Baseball America survey of National League managers, conducted in August 2025, ranked players with the best tools.

Best Hitter
1. Freddie Freeman, Dodgers
2. Shohei Ohtani, Dodgers
3. Manny Machado, Padres

Best Power
1. Shohei Ohtani, Dodgers
2. Kyle Schwarber, Phillies
3. Eugenio Suarez, D-backs

Best Bunter
1. Jacob Young, Nationals
2. TJ Friedl, Reds
3. Victor Scott II, Cardinals

Best Strike-Zone Judgment
1. Juan Soto, Mets
2. Kyle Schwarber, Phillies
3. Kyle Tucker, Cubs

Best Hit-And-Run Artist
1. Luis Arraez, Padres
2. Nico Hoerner, Cubs
3. Xavier Edwards, Marlins

Best Baserunner
1. Elly De La Cruz, Reds
2. Pete Crow-Armstrong, Cubs
3. Trea Turner, Phillies

Fastest Baserunner
1. Pete Crow-Armstrong, Cubs
2. Elly De La Cruz, Reds
3. Trea Turner, Phillies

Most Exciting Player
1. Pete Crow-Armstrong, Cubs
2. Shohei Ohtani, Dodgers
3. Elly De La Cruz, Reds

Best Pitcher
1. Zack Wheeler, Phillies
2. Paul Skenes, Pirates
3. Logan Webb, Giants

Best Fastball
1. Zack Wheeler, Phillies
2. Paul Skenes, Pirates
3. Jacob Misiorowski, Brewers

Best Curveball
1. MacKenzie Gore, Nationals
2. Sonny Gray, Cardinals
3. Edward Cabrera, Marlins

Best Slider
1. Chris Sale, Braves
2. Dylan Cease, Padres
3. Paul Skenes, Pirates

Best Changeup
1. Cristopher Sanchez, Phillies
2. Logan Webb, Giants
3. Michael King, Padres

Best Control
1. Zack Wheeler, Phillies
2. Logan Webb, Giants
3. Sonny Gray, Cardinals

Best Pickoff Move
1. Matthew Boyd, Cubs
2. Robbie Ray, Giants
3. Merrill Kelly, D-backs

Best Reliever
1. Adrian Morejon, Padres
2. Randy Rodriguez, Giants
3. Edwin Diaz, Mets

Best Defensive C
1. Patrick Bailey, Giants
2. Will Smith, Dodgers
3. William Contreras, Brewers

Best Defensive 1B
1. Matt Olson, Braves
2. Freddie Freeman, Dodgers
3. Willson Contreras, Cardinals

Best Defensive 2B
1. Brice Turang, Brewers
2. Nico Hoerner, Cubs
3. Bryson Stott, Phillies

Best Defensive 3B
1. Matt Chapman, Giants
2. Ke'Bryan Hayes, Pirates/Reds
3. Manny Machado, Padres

Best Defensive SS
1. Masyn Winn, Cardinals
2. Dansby Swanson, Cubs
3. Nick Allen, Braves

Best Infield Arm
1. Elly De La Cruz, Reds
2. Masyn Winn, Cardinals
3. Matt Chapman, Giants

Best Defensive OF
1. Pete Crow-Armstrong, Cubs
2. Jacob Young, Nationals
3. Fernando Tatis Jr., Padres

Best Outfield Arm
1. Fernando Tatis Jr., Padres
2. Ronald Acuña Jr., Braves
3. Brenton Doyle, Rockies

Best Manager
1. Craig Counsell, Cubs
2. Pat Murphy, Brewers
3. Dave Roberts, Dodgers

---

payroll in MLB in 2025, boosted by landing Juan Soto in the offseason.

The outfielder signed with the Mets for 15 years at $765 million, shunning the Yankees after his one season in the Bronx that included New York's AL pennant since 2009.

After a somewhat slow start, Soto produced, hitting .263/.396/.525 with 43 home runs, and he led the league in OBP and walks (127) while tying for the NL lead with a career-best 38 stolen bases.

However, the Mets' pitching collapsed, leaving them reliant on three rookies in their rotation in September, and an infusion of bullpen arms acquired at the trade deadline failed to stem the tide. The Mets were 45-24 at one point but slowly crumbled, finishing 83-79 overall and missing out on a wild-card berth by losing the tiebreaker with the Cincinnati Reds.

Soto's 38 steals tied for the NL lead with Oneil Cruz, and he was one of seven players to read the 30-homer, 30-steals threshold, a record for 30-30 seasons in a season. Soto and shortstop Francisco Lindor became the third pair of teammates ever to go 30-30 in the same season, joining 1987 Mets Howard Johnson and Darryl Strawberry, and 1996 Rockies Dante Bichette (father of Bo) and Ellis Burks.

The five other 30-30 seasons were recorded by the Diamondbacks outfielder Corbin Carroll, Yankees second baseman Jazz Chisholm Jr., Cubs outfielder Pete Crow-Armstrong, Guardians third baseman Jose Ramirez and Mariners outfielder Julio Rodriguez.

For Ramirez, it was his third 30-30 season and second in a row. The only players with more 30-30 campaigns than Ramirez are Alfonso Soriano (four) and the Bonds family, both father Bobby and son Barry with five apiece.

The best single-game performance of the regular season came from a rookie. On July 25 in Houston, A's first baseman Nick Kurtz had a game

MAJOR LEAGUE ALL-STARS

SELECTED BY BASEBALL AMERICA

Seattle's Cal Raleigh had one of the best seasons ever seen from a catcher.

Pirates' righthander Paul Skenes has a 1.96 career ERA after two MLB seasons.

FIRST TEAM

Pos	Player, Team	Age	AVG	OBP	SLG	AB	R	HR	RBI	BB	SO	SB	wRC+	fWAR
C	Cal Raleigh, Mariners	28	.247	.359	.589	596	110	60	125	97	188	14	161	9.1
1B	Nick Kurtz, Athletics	22	.290	.383	.619	420	90	36	86	63	151	2	170	4.6
2B	Ketel Marte, D-backs	31	.283	.376	.517	480	87	28	72	64	83	4	145	4.6
3B	Jose Ramirez, Guardians	32	.283	.360	.503	593	103	30	85	66	74	44	133	6.3
SS	Bobby Witt Jr., Royals	25	.295	.351	.501	623	99	23	88	49	125	38	130	8.0
OF	Aaron Judge, Yankees	33	.331	.457	.688	541	137	53	114	124	160	12	204	10.1
OF	Julio Rodriguez, Mariners	24	.267	.324	.474	652	106	32	95	44	152	30	126	5.7
OF	Juan Soto, Mets	26	.263	.396	.525	577	120	43	105	127	137	38	156	5.8
DH	Shohei Ohtani, Dodgers	30	.282	.392	.622	611	146	55	102	109	187	20	172	7.5

Pos	Pitcher, Team	Age	W	L	ERA	G	IP	H	HR	BB	SO	WHIP	FIP	fWAR
SP	Hunter Brown, Astros	26	12	9	2.43	31	185	133	17	57	206	1.03	3.14	4.6
SP	Garrett Crochet, Red Sox	26	18	5	2.59	32	205	165	24	46	255	1.03	2.89	5.8
SP	Cristopher Sanchez, Phillies	28	13	5	2.50	32	202	171	12	44	212	1.06	2.55	6.4
SP	Paul Skenes, Pirates	23	10	10	1.97	32	188	136	11	42	216	0.95	2.36	6.5
SP	Tarik Skubal, Tigers	28	13	6	2.21	31	195	141	18	33	241	0.89	2.45	6.6
RP	Aroldis Chapman, Red Sox	37	5	3	1.17	67	61	28	3	15	85	0.70	1.73	2.6

SECOND TEAM

Pos	Player, Team	Age	AVG	OBP	SLG	AB	R	HR	RBI	BB	SO	SB	wRC+	fWAR
C	Will Smith, Dodgers	30	.296	.404	.497	362	64	17	61	64	89	2	153	4.1
1B	Vladimir Guerrero Jr., Blue Jays	26	.292	.381	.467	589	96	23	84	81	94	6	137	3.9
2B	Brice Turang, Brewers	25	.288	.359	.435	584	97	18	81	66	150	24	124	4.4
3B	Maikel Garcia, Royals	25	.286	.351	.449	595	81	16	74	62	84	23	121	5.6
SS	Geraldo Perdomo, D-backs	25	.290	.389	.462	597	98	20	100	94	83	27	138	7.1
OF	Byron Buxton, Twins	31	.264	.327	.551	488	97	35	83	41	148	24	136	5.0
OF	Corbin Carroll, D-backs	24	.259	.343	.541	564	107	31	84	67	153	32	139	6.5
OF	George Springer, Blue Jays	35	.309	.399	.560	498	106	32	84	69	111	18	166	5.2
DH	Kyle Schwarber, Phillies	32	.240	.365	.563	604	111	56	132	108	197	10	152	4.9

Pos	Pitcher, Team	Age	W	L	ERA	G	IP	H	HR	BB	SO	WHIP	FIP	fWAR
SP	Max Fried, Yankees	31	19	5	2.86	32	195	164	14	51	189	1.10	3.07	4.8
SP	Freddy Peralta, Brewers	29	17	6	2.70	33	177	124	21	66	204	1.08	3.65	3.6
SP	Logan Webb, Giants	28	15	11	3.22	34	207	210	14	46	224	1.24	2.60	5.5
SP	Zack Wheeler, Phillies	35	10	5	2.71	24	150	107	19	33	195	0.94	3.00	4.0
SP	Yoshinobu Yamamoto, Dodgers	26	12	8	2.49	30	174	113	14	59	201	0.99	2.94	5.0
RP	Jhoan Duran, Phillies	27	7	6	2.06	72	70	58	3	19	80	1.10	2.35	2.1

EXECUTIVE OF THE YEAR

After a decade of clawing to get there, Seattle in 2025 fell just one win short of their first World Series appearance.

But with a stacked rotation of homegrown starters and a lineup that features star players Julio Rodriguez, catcher Cal Raleigh and first baseman Josh Naylor, along with a loaded farm system, the Mariners are here to stay.

For his efforts, Dipoto is the 2025 Major League Executive of the Year.

Though it was devastating to fall short after coming so close to the World Series, Dipoto sees this past season as a sign that the organization's plans are coming together.

"It really was reaffirming that what we all believed was that through a foundation in scouting and player development—what we've been able to achieve in those areas—putting together a really strong foundation with our major league club," Dipoto said.

"This really should just be our coming out party of sorts." ■

Jerry Dipoto

LAST 10 WINNERS

2015: Sandy Alderson, Mets
2016: Chris Antonetti, Indians
2017: Brian Cashman, Yankees
2018: Dave Dombrowski, Red Sox
2019: Mike Rizzo, Nationals
2020: Andrew Friedman, Dodgers
2021: Farhan Zaidi, Giants
2022: Alex Anthopoulous, Braves
2023: Mike Elias, Orioles
2024: Matt Arnold, Brewers

Full list: search "Baseball America awards"

MANAGER OF THE YEAR

Pat Murphy calls the shots on the field for the Brewers. But he's also positively affecting lives.

"I've grown tremendously playing under the man for the last two seasons," said Jake Bauers, a six-year MLB veteran. "Not only as a baseball player, but as a man. He's changed my perspective on life a little bit. I feel like he's made me a better husband, made me a better father.

"That's something I'll never be able to repay, but I appreciate everything he's done for me."

The feeling is mutual for Murphy, who guided the Brewers to the team's first appearance in the NL Championship Series since 2018.

"I'm just part of the act," Murphy said. "You want to impact players. I'm hopeful that I can impact a lot of different players in my own little way. But there's a lot of other coaches on our staff who do that better than I do.

"I get far too much credit for things like this. Players win games." ■

Pat Murphy

LAST 10 WINNERS

2015: Joe Maddon, Cubs
2016: Terry Francona, Indians
2017: A.J. Hinch, Astros
2018: Bob Melvin, Athletics
2019: Craig Counsell, Brewers
2020: Brian Snitker, Braves
2021: Dusty Baker, Astros
2022: Brandon Hyde, Orioles
2023: Torey Lovullo, Dbacks
2024: Dave Roberts, Dodgers

Full list: search "Baseball America awards"

---

for the ages, going 6-for-6 with four home runs, becoming the first rookie in MLB history with a four-homer game and just the 20th player ever to accomplish the feat. He also singled and doubled in the game, tying the MLB record with 19 total bases, scored six runs and drove in eight. The 22-year-old was the fourth overall pick in the 2024 draft out of Wake Forest and had a monster first season, batting .290/.383/.619 with 36 homers in just 420 at-bats. The BBWAA's voters chose him unanimously as the AL's rookie of the year.

Braves catcher Drake Baldwin took home the NL award after hitting .274 with 19 home runs.

A's shortstop Jacob Wilson, their 2023 first-rounder, was the runner-up in a season in which he hit .311, good for third in the AL batting race behind Judge and Bo Bichette. Phillies shortstop Trea Turner hit .304 to lead the NL in a season in which he was the only player to hit .300 in the entire NL. It's the lowest batting average ever to lead the senior circuit, and the second-lowest league-leading mark ever, following Carl Yastrzemski's memorable .301 mark in the Year of the Pitcher, 1968. The overall batting average in MLB was just .248 in 2025.

When asked why averages are so low, Turner told reporters, "Everyone throws 100. Everyone has six pitches. Nobody knows where the ball's going. Defenses are way better than they've ever been." ■

HR Derby Gives NL The Win

BY J.J. COOPER

At any baseball game, there's always the hope to see something you've never seen before.

In the 2025 MLB All-Star Game in Atlanta, Ga. those wishes were met. A Bobby Witt Jr. RBI double followed by a Steven Kwan RBI single to score Witt gave the American League a ninth-inning comeback that tied the game.

When Aroldis Chapman retired the National League in order in the bottom of the ninth, it meant that the All-Star Game was once again tied after nine innings.

But unlike the 2002 All-Star Game, which ended in a tie when both teams ran out of pitching after 10 innings, this time there was a plan.

And so the first-ever All-Star tiebreaking Home Run Derby was immediately instituted.

Kyle Schwarber was the star of the Home Run Derby. He entered with the NL trailing 3-1, and he had three swings. He homered three times, giving the NL a 4-3 lead. That brought up Jonathan Aranda, who needed one homer to tie and two to give the AL the win. He went homerless, giving the National League a dramatic win.

Ketel Marte had doubled in a pair of runs in the first to give the NL an early lead. Pete Alonso extended the lead with a three-run homer in the sixth and Corbin Carroll added a solo homer later in the same inning.

With a bullpen of closers and a six-run lead, the National League looked to be in great shape, but Brent Rooker's three-run homer off Randy Rodriguez cut the lead in half, and Witt grounded out to score Royals teammate Maikel Garcia later in the seventh to cut the lead to two.

That set up Witt and Kwan's ninth-inning heroics. Wildly, because of the Home Run Derby tiebreaker, the official winning pitcher was the National League, and the loser was the American League.

The American League leads the All-Star Game with 48 wins to the National League's 45, with two ties, which is a stat we may not see again. ■

All-Star Game MVP Kyle Schwarber

2025 ALL-STAR GAME

JULY 15, 2025
NL 7, AL 6* (WON IN TIEBREAKER)

American	AB	R	H	RBI	National	AB	R	H	RBI
Torres, 2B	2	0	0	0	Ohtani, DH	2	1	1	0
Chisholm Jr., 2B	3	0	0	0	Schwarber, PH-DH	2	0	0	0
Greene, R, LF	3	0	0	0	Acuña Jr., RF	2	1	1	0
Kwan, LF	2	0	1	1	Tatis Jr., RF	2	1	0	0
Judge, RF	2	0	0	0	Marte, K, 2B	2	0	1	2
Arozarena, RF	3	0	0	0	Donovan, 2B	3	1	2	0
Raleigh, C	2	0	1	0	Freeman, F, 1B	1	0	0	0
Kirk, C	2	1	1	0	Alonso, 1B	2	1	1	3
Guerrero Jr., 1B	2	0	1	0	Olson, 1B	1	0	0	0
Aranda, 1B	1	1	1	0	Machado, M, 3B	2	0	0	0
O'Hearn, DH	2	0	0	0	Suárez, E, 3B	1	0	0	0
Rooker, PH-DH	1	1	1	3	Smith, W, C	2	0	0	0
McKinstry, PH-DH	1	0	0	0	Goodman, C	1	0	0	0
Caminero, 3B	2	0	1	0	Wood, PH	1	0	0	0
Garcia, M, 3B	1	1	0	0	Tucker, LF	2	0	0	0
Báez, C	2	0	0	0	Carroll, LF-CF	1	1	1	1
Buxton, CF	2	1	1	0	Lindor, SS	2	0	0	0
Wilson, J, SS	2	0	0	0	De La Cruz, E, SS	2	0	0	0
Witt Jr., SS	2	1	1	2	Crow-Armstrong, CF	2	0	1	0
AL, P	0	0	0	0	Stowers, LF	2	0	0	0
					NL, P	0	1	0	0
Totals	**37**	**6**	**9**	**6**	**Totals**	**35**	**7**	**8**	**6**

2B: Marte, K (1, Skubal); Crow-Armstrong (1, Rodón); Buxton (1, Suarez, Ro); Witt Jr. (1, Suarez, Ro). **HR:** Alonso (1, 6th inning off Bubic, 2 on, 0 out); Carroll (1, 6th inning off Mize, 0 on, 2 out); Rooker (1, 7th inning off Rodríguez, R, 2 on, 0 out). **SB:** Tatis Jr. (1, 2nd base off Bubic/Kirk); Garcia, M (1, 2nd base off Rodríguez, R/Goodman); Kwan (1, 2nd base off Díaz/Goodman). **E:** Goodman (1, throw); Olson (1, fielding).

American	IP	H	R	SO	National	IP	H	R	SO
Skubal	1	3	2	2	Skenes	1	0	0	2
Rodón	1	1	0	1	Kershaw	0.2	0	0	1
Woo	1	0	0	1	Adam (H, 1)	0.1	0	0	1
Ryan	1	0	0	2	Webb, L (H, 1)	1	1	0	0
Rasmussen	1	0	0	0	Peterson, D (H, 1)	1	2	0	1
Bubic	0.1	2	3	0	Gore (H, 1)	1	0	0	0
Mize	0.2	1	1	1	Abbott, A (H, 1)	1	0	0	0
Estévez	1	1	0	3	Morejon	0	1	2	0
Smith, S	0.1	0	0	0	Rodríguez, R	0.2	1	2	0
Muñoz, A	0.2	0	0	1	Megill (H, 1)	0.1	0	0	0
Chapman	1	0	0	1	Misiorowski (H, 1)	1	1	0	1
AL	0	0	1	0	Suarez, Ro (H, 1)	0.1	2	2	0
					Díaz (BS, 1)	0.2	1	0	1
Totals	**9**	**8**	**7**	**12**	**Totals**	**10**	**9**	**6**	**6**

MAJOR LEAGUE DEBUTS

ARIZONA DIAMONDBACKS
Tim Tawa .... Apr 5
Juan Morillo............ Apr 19
C. Montes De Oca....... Jun 7
Kyle Backhus .... Jun 8
Tristin English .... Jul 9
Taylor Rashi .... Aug 28
Philip Abner.......... Sep 19
Austin Pope .... Sep 25

ATHLETICS
Max Muncy .... Mar 27
Noah Murdock ...... Mar 29
Nick Kurtz............... Apr 23
Gunnar Hoglund ..... May 2
Elvis Alvarado .... May 9
Carlos Duran .... May 22
Denzel Clarke.......... May 23
Logan Davidson ... May 24
Willie MacIver .... May 25
Drew Avans............ May 27
Jack Perkins .... Jun 22
Colby Thomas .... Jun 30
Carlos Cortes .... Jul 23
Luis Morales .... Aug 1
Mason Barnett ..... Aug 30

ATLANTA BRAVES
Drake Baldwin....... Mar 27
Nathan Wiles.......... Apr 22
Didier Fuentes........ Jun 20
Hayden Harris......... Sep 2
Rolddy Muñoz .... Sep 2

BALTIMORE ORIOLES
Tomoyuki Sugano . Mar 30
Brandon Young....... Apr 19
Grant Wolfram....... Apr 26
Maverick Handley . Apr 29
Kade Strowd .... May 18
Yaramil Hiraldo..... May 27
Jeremiah Jackson ... Aug 1
Dylan Beavers....... Aug 16
Samuel Basallo..... Aug 17
Carson Ragsdale ... Sep 14

BOSTON RED SOX
Kristian Campbell . Mar 27
Hunter Dobbins ...... Apr 6
Marcelo Mayer..... May 24
Roman Anthony ..... Jun 9
Jhostynxon Garcia Aug 22
Payton Tolle .... Aug 29
Connelly Early........ Sep 9

CHICAGO CUBS
Matt Shaw............ Mar 18
Gage Workman..... Mar 29
Cade Horton .... May 10
Moisés Ballesteros May 13
Owen Caissie .... Aug 14

CHICAGO WHITE SOX
Mike Vasil .... Mar 31
Shane Smith .... Apr 1
Chase Meidroth .... Apr 11

CINCINNATI REDS
Edgar Quero.......... Apr 17
Caleb Freeman....... May 5
Tim Elko................ May 10
Kyle Teel .... Jun 6
Grant Taylor .... Jun 10
Wikelman González Jun 20
Jake Palisch .... Jun 21
Colson Montgomery...Jul 4

CINCINNATI REDS
Tyler Callihan .... Apr 30
Chase Petty........... Apr 30
Luis Mey .... May 1
Chase Burns.......... Jun 24
Will Banfield.......... Aug 23
Zach Maxwell .... Aug 23
Sal Stewart .... Sep 1

CLEVELAND INDIANS
Zak Kent .... Apr 23
Will Wilson .... Apr 23
Doug Nikhazy .... Apr 26
Nic Enright............ May 25
C.J. Kayfus .... Aug 2
Parker Messick..... Aug 20
George Valera .... Sep 1
Petey Halpin .... Sep 20

COLORADO ROCKIES
Chase Dollander ..... Apr 6
Zac Veen .... Apr 8
Braxton Fulford .... Apr 16
Zach Agnos .... Apr 20
Juan Mejia .... Apr 24
Ryan Rolison .... May 13
Carson Palmquist. May 16
Ryan Ritter .... May 21
Yanquiel Fernández ..Jul 2
Warming Bernabel Jul 26
Dugan Darnell .... Aug 1
Kyle Karros............ Aug 8
McCade Brown .... Aug 24

DETROIT TIGERS
Chase Lee .... Apr 22
Tyler Owens......... May 1
Dylan Smith.......... Jun 2
Troy Melton..........Jul 23
Drew Sommers......Aug 22

HOUSTON ASTROS
Cam Smith........... Mar 27
Ryan Gusto .... Mar 31
Logan VanWey...... Apr 11
AJ Blubaugh......... Apr 30
Colton Gordon ..... May 14
Jacob Melton .... Jun 1
Kenedy Corona ......Jul 7
Brice Matthews ..... Jul 11
John Rooney........ Aug 24
Jayden Murray ...... Sep 4
Zach Cole .... Sep 12

KANSAS CITY ROYALS
Tyler Tolbert.......... Mar 31
Evan Sisk.............. Apr 15

KANSAS CITY ROYALS
Noah Cameron ....Apr 30
John Rave............... May 26
Andrew Hoffmann. May 30
Jac Caglianone .... Jun 3
Luinder Avila .... Aug 13
Carter Jensen......... Sep 2

LOS ANGELES ANGELS
Ryan Johnson .... Mar 27
Garrett McDaniels.. Mar 31
Michael Darrell-Hicks Apr 11
José Fermin .... Apr 26
Matthew Lugo....... May 9
Christian Moore .... Jun 13
Chad Stevens..........Jul 3
Mitch Farris............ Sep 2
Denzer Guzman ... Sep 13

LOS ANGELES DODGERS
Jack Dreyer............. Mar 19
Roki Sasaki .... Mar 19
Hyeseong Kim ...... May 3
Dalton Rushing.......May 15
Jack Little .... Jun 19
Alex Freeland .... Jul 30
Justin Dean .... Aug 8

MIAMI MARLINS
Liam Hicks .... Mar 28
Luarbert Arias....... Mar 31
Patrick Monteverde. Apr 19
Cade Gibson........... Apr 20
Agustín Ramírez ... Apr 21
Ronny Simon .... Apr 21
Víctor Mesa Jr. ..... May 26
Heriberto Hernández May 30
Jack Winkler .... May 31
Robinson Piña ..... Jun 20
Josh Simpson .... Jun 21
Troy Johnston .... Jul 29
Jakob Marsee......... Aug 1
Maximo Acosta.... Aug 18
Christian Roa .... Sep 6

MILWAUKEE BREWERS
Chad Patrick .... Mar 29
Connor Thomas.... Mar 29
Caleb Durbin .... Apr 18
Logan Henderson . Apr 20
Craig Yoho .... Apr 21
Jacob Misiorowski Jun 12
Anthony Seigler....... Jul 2

MINNESOTA TWINS
Luke Keaschall ...... Apr 18
Ryan Fitzgerald... May 16
Carson McCusker.. May 18
Travis Adams ....Jul 5
Pierson Ohl............Jul 29
Cody Laweryson ... Sep 13

NEW YORK METS
Hayden Senger..... Mar 27
Justin Hagenman . Apr 16
Blade Tidwell......... May 4
Jonathan Pintaro ...Jun 25

NEW YORK YANKEES
J.C. Escarra.......... Mar 29
Jorbit Vivas .... May 2
Jayvien Sandridge ...Jul 5
Cam Schlittler.........Jul 9

PHILADELPHIA PHILLIES
Mick Abel .... May 18
Alan Rangel .... Jun 6
Otto Kemp .... Jun 7
Nolan Hoffman ..... Aug 18

PITTSBURGH PIRATES
Tom Harrington ...... Apr 1
Tsung-Che Cheng ... Apr 9
Matt Gorski .... Apr 24
Braxton Ashcraft .. May 26
Cam Sanders.......... Aug 5
Bubba Chandler .... Aug 22
Cam Devanney ..... Aug 31
Rafael Flores .... Sep 17
Hunter Barco .... Sep 23

ST. LOUIS CARDINALS
Matt Svanson .... Apr 17
Andre Granillo ...... Jun 12
Nathan Church..... Aug 17
Jimmy Crooks ...... Aug 29
César Prieto .... Aug 29
Nick Raquet .... Sep 8

SAN DIEGO PADRES
Omar Cruz .... Apr 1
Tirso Ornelas.......... Apr 19
Ryan Bergert .... Apr 26
David Morgan....... May 26
Bradgley Rodriguez .. May 31
Eduarniel Núñez ...... Jul 2

SAN FRANCISCO GIANTS
Christian Koss .... Apr 1
Carson Seymour ... Jun 29
Carson Whisenhunt Jul 28
Drew Gilbert.......... Aug 8
Joel Peguero........ Aug 21
Bryce Eldridge ...... Sep 15

SEATTLE MARINERS
Ben Williamson .... Apr 15
Sauryn Lao .... Apr 22
Logan Evans .... Apr 27
Rhylan Thomas..... May 2
Blas Castano .... May 28
Cole Young........... May 31
Juan Burgos ....Jul 1
Brandyn Garcia .... Jul 21
Harry Ford .... Sep 5

TAMPA BAY RAYS
Jake Mangum.......... Mar 30
Chandler Simpson .... Apr 19
Ian Seymour........... Jun 9
Paul Gervase......... Jun 21
Joe Rock .... Jun 28
Tristan Peters........ Aug 8
Bob Seymour........ Aug 15
Carson Williams ... Aug 22
Brian Van Belle .... Aug 24
Cole Wilcox........... Sep 19

TEXAS RANGERS
Blaine Crim............ May 2
Alejandro Osuna .. May 25
Cody Freeman....... Jul 18
Luis Curvelo ....Jul 31
Jose Corniell .... Sep 28

TORONTO BLUE JAYS
Alan Roden........... Mar 27
Mason Fluharty ...... Apr 1
Paxton Schultz...... Apr 20
Braydon Fisher..... May 11
Will Robertson...... Jun 15
Lazaro Estrada ....Jul 5
Trey Yesavage ...... Sep 15

WASHINGTON NATIONALS
Brad Lord........... Mar 30
Cole Henry............ Apr 13
Robert Hassell III . May 22
Daylen Lile........... May 23
Brady House .... Jun 16
Andry Lara............Jul 2
Shinnosuke Ogasawara. Jul 6
PJ Poulin.............. Aug 5
Andrew Alvarez .... Sep 1
CJ Stubbs .... Sep 1

AMERICAN LEAGUE 2025 STATISTICS

CLUB BATTING

	AVG	G	AB	R	H	2B	3B	HR	RBI	BB	SO	SB	OBP	SLG
Toronto	.265	162	5507	798	1461	294	13	191	771	520	1099	77	.333	.427
Boston	.254	162	5562	786	1414	324	24	186	748	518	1419	139	.324	.421
Athletics	.253	162	5547	733	1403	296	16	219	709	502	1406	80	.318	.431
Tampa Bay	.251	162	5470	714	1374	242	16	182	680	468	1397	194	.313	.401
New York	.251	162	5471	849	1371	255	20	274	820	639	1463	134	.332	.455
Houston	.250	162	5490	686	1372	247	12	182	655	471	1301	85	.315	.399
Kansas City	.247	162	5431	651	1342	292	22	159	638	435	1096	111	.309	.397
Detroit	.247	162	5456	758	1346	244	36	198	724	511	1454	61	.316	.413
Seattle	.244	162	5502	766	1345	234	9	238	734	544	1446	161	.320	.420
Minnesota	.238	162	5432	678	1295	249	20	191	643	495	1372	114	.310	.397
Baltimore	.235	162	5416	677	1273	251	19	191	643	484	1457	121	.305	.394
Texas	.234	162	5443	684	1275	245	15	175	658	486	1327	134	.302	.381
Chicago	.232	162	5377	647	1250	243	10	165	626	498	1364	85	.302	.373
Cleveland	.226	162	5310	643	1199	243	18	168	621	494	1344	129	.296	.373
Los Angeles	.225	162	5374	673	1209	212	17	226	649	484	1627	88	.298	.397

CLUB PITCHING

	ERA	G	CG	SHO	SV	IP	H	R	ER	HR	BB	SO	AVG
Texas	3.47	162	2	14	37	1443.0	1235	605	557	172	463	1344	.230
Cleveland	3.70	162	2	16	47	1442.0	1291	649	593	169	527	1381	.238
Boston	3.70	162	2	11	45	1448.1	1333	676	596	164	530	1361	.243
Kansas City	3.73	162	0	10	47	1436.2	1308	637	596	171	478	1271	.241
Houston	3.86	162	3	12	45	1442.0	1257	665	619	199	508	1504	.232
Seattle	3.87	162	0	11	43	1462.2	1331	694	629	192	454	1426	.241
New York	3.91	162	0	11	43	1439.2	1239	685	625	175	557	1440	.229
Tampa Bay	3.94	162	1	11	35	1431.1	1273	683	627	205	474	1416	.237
Detroit	3.95	162	1	17	40	1436.1	1309	691	630	187	485	1375	.241
Toronto	4.19	162	2	8	42	1438.0	1313	721	669	209	517	1430	.241
Chicago	4.26	162	0	9	25	1416.0	1336	742	671	189	595	1286	.248
Minnesota	4.55	162	1	10	28	1426.2	1411	773	721	194	459	1372	.253
Baltimore	4.60	162	1	7	38	1432.2	1433	788	733	217	523	1351	.259
Athletics	4.70	162	0	11	35	1437.2	1387	817	750	222	570	1323	.252
Los Angeles	4.89	162	0	8	38	1431.1	1429	837	777	223	620	1280	.260

CLUB FIELDING

	PCT	PO	A	E	DP		PCT	PO	A	E	DP
Texas	.991	4329	1364	51	122	Minnesota	.985	4280	1210	85	98
Kansas City	.989	4310	1437	62	132	Athletics	.984	4313	1212	88	109
Seattle	.988	4388	1355	69	118	New York	.984	4319	1389	94	105
Houston	.988	4326	1284	70	105	Los Angeles	.983	4294	1419	97	84
Detroit	.986	4309	1379	79	128	Cleveland	.983	4326	1330	99	121
Tampa Bay	.986	4294	1416	81	147	Chicago	.982	4248	1271	100	131
Toronto	.985	4314	1272	86	118	Boston	.980	4345	1461	116	131
Baltimore	.985	4298	1403	88	121						

INDIVIDUAL BATTING LEADERS

	AVG	G	AB	R	H	2B	3B	HR	RBI	BB	SO	SB
Aaron Judge, NYY	.331	152	541	137	179	30	2	53	114	124	160	12
Bo Bichette, TOR	.311	139	582	78	181	44	1	18	94	40	91	4
Jack Wilson, ATH	.311	125	486	62	151	26	0	13	63	27	39	5
George Springer, TOR	.309	140	498	106	154	27	1	32	84	69	111	18
Jeremy Peña, HOU	.304	125	493	68	150	30	2	17	62	35	93	20
Yandy Díaz, TB	.300	150	583	79	175	29	1	25	83	57	92	3
Bobby Witt Jr., KC	.295	157	623	99	184	47	6	23	88	49	125	38
Vladimir Guerrero Jr., TOR	.292	156	589	96	172	34	0	23	84	81	94	6
Maikel Garcia, KC	.286	160	595	81	170	39	5	16	74	62	84	23
Jose Ramírez, CLE	.283	158	593	103	168	34	3	30	85	66	74	44

INDIVIDUAL PITCHING LEADERS

	W	L	ERA	G	GS	CG	SV	IP	H	R	ER	BB	SO
Tarik Skubal, DET	13	6	2.21	31	31	1	0	195.1	141	55	48	33	241
Hunter Brown, HOU	12	9	2.43	31	31	1	0	185.1	133	55	50	57	206
Garrett Crochet, BOS	18	5	2.59	32	32	1	0	205.1	165	62	59	43	255
Max Fried, NYY	19	5	2.86	32	32	0	0	195.1	164	73	62	51	189
Bryan Woo, SEA	15	7	2.94	30	30	0	0	186.2	137	64	61	36	198
Jacob deGrom, TEX	12	8	2.97	30	30	0	0	172.2	122	57	57	37	185
Gavin Williams, CLE	12	5	3.06	31	31	0	0	167.2	130	62	57	83	173
Carlos Rodón, NYY	18	9	3.09	33	33	0	0	195.1	132	74	67	73	203
Brayan Bello, BOS	11	9	3.35	29	28	1	0	166.2	147	71	62	59	124
Joe Ryan, MIN	13	10	3.42	31	30	0	0	171.0	138	69	65	39	194

AWARD WINNERS

Selected by Baseball Writers Association of America

MOST VALUABLE PLAYER

Player	1st	2nd	3rd	Total
Aaron Judge, Yankees	17	13		355
Cal Raleigh, Mariners	13	17		335
José Ramírez, Guardians			19	224
Bobby Witt Jr., Royals			9	215
Tarik Skubal, Tigers			1	139
Julio Rodríguez, Mariners				136
George Springer, Blue Jays				125
Garrett Crochet, Red Sox				74
Junior Caminero, Rays			1	37
Jeremy Peña, Astros				32
Byron Buxton, Twins				30
Nick Kurtz, Athletics				29
Vladimir Guerrero Jr., Blue Jays				14
Cody Bellinger, Yankees				7
Maikel Garcia, Royals				7
Bo Bichette, Blue Jays				5
Riley Greene, Tigers				3
Aroldis Chapman, Red Sox				1
Yandy Díaz, Rays				1
Jacob Wilson, Athletics				1

CY YOUNG AWARD

Player	1st	2nd	3rd	Total
Tarik Skubal, Tigers	26	4		198
Garrett Crochet, Red Sox	4	26		132
Hunter Brown, Astros			24	80
Max Fried, Yankees		6		61
Bryan Woo, Mariners				26
Carlos Rodón, Yankees				5
Aroldis Chapman, Red Sox				4
Jacob deGrom, Rangers				2
Trevor Rogers, Orioles				1
Drew Rasmussen, Rays				1

ROOKIE OF THE YEAR

Player	1st	2nd	3rd	Total
Nick Kurtz, Athletics	30			210
Jacob Wilson, Athletics		23	4	107
Roman Anthony, Red Sox		3	15	72
Noah Cameron, Royals		3	7	54
Colson Montgomery, White Sox		1		23
Carlos Narváez, Red Sox			2	21
Jack Leiter, Rangers			1	6
Will Warren, Yankees			1	5
Luke Keaschall, Twins				3
Braydon Fisher, Blue Jays				2
Shane Smith, White Sox				2
Cam Smith, Astros				2
Chandler Simpson, Rays				1
Luis Morales, Athletics				1
Jasson Domínguez, Yankees				1

MANAGER OF THE YEAR

Player	1st	2nd	3rd	Total
Stephen Vogt, Guardians	17	8	4	113
John Schneider, Blue Jays	10	11	8	91
Dan Wilson, Mariners	2	9	13	50
Alex Cora, Red Sox	1		2	7
A.J. Hinch, Tigers		1	3	6
Joe Espada, Astros		1		3

GOLD GLOVE WINNERS

P-Max Fried, Yankees. C-Dillon Dingler, Tigers. 1B-Ty France, Blue Jays. 2B-Marcus Semien, Rangers. 3B-Maikel Garcia, Royals. SS-Bobby Witt Jr., Royals. LF-Steven Kwan, Guardians. CF-Ceddanne Rafaela, Red Sox. RF-Wilyer Abreu, Red Sox. UT-Mauricio Dubon, Astros. Guardians. 3B—Alex Bregman, Astros. SS—Bobby Witt Jr., Royals. LF—Steven Kwan, Guardians. CF—Daulton Varsho, Blue Jays. RF—Wilyer Abreu, Red Sox. UT—Dylan Moore, Mariners.

AMERICAN LEAGUE DEPARTMENT LEADERS

Julio Rodriguez

BATTING

GAMES
Brent Rooker, Athletics	162
Randy Arozarena, Seattle	160
Vinnie Pasquantino, KC	160
Julio Rodriguez, Seattle	160
Maikel Garcia, Kansas City	160

AT-BATS
Julio Rodriguez, Seattle	652
Brent Rooker, Athletics	626
Steven Kwan, Cleveland	625
Bobby Witt, Kansas City	623
Vinnie Pasquantino, KC	621

PLATE APPEARANCES
Julio Rodriguez, Seattle	710
Randy Arozarena, Seattle	709
Cal Raleigh, Seattle	705
Brent Rooker, Athletics	699
Jarren Duran, Boston	696

RUNS
Aaron Judge, NY Yankees	137
Cal Raleigh, Seattle	110
Julio Rodriguez, Seattle	106
George Springer, Toronto	106
Jose Ramirez, Cleveland	103

HITS
Bobby Witt, Kansas City	184
Bo Bichette, Toronto	181
Aaron Judge, NY Yankees	179
Yandy Diaz, Tampa Bay	175
Julio Rodriguez, Seattle	174

TOTAL BASES
Aaron Judge, NY Yankees	372
Cal Raleigh, Seattle	351
Junior Caminero, Tampa Bay	322
Bobby Witt, Kansas City	312
Julio Rodriguez, Seattle	309

DOUBLES
Bobby Witt, Kansas City	47
Bo Bichette, Toronto	44
Jarren Duran, Boston	41
Brent Rooker, Athletics	40
Maikel Garcia, Kansas City	39

TRIPLES
Jarren Duran, Boston	13
Zach McKinstry, Detroit	11
Byron Buxton, Minnesota	7
Bobby Witt, Kansas City	6
Four tied	5

EXTRA-BASE HITS
Aaron Judge, NY Yankees	85
Cal Raleigh, Seattle	84
Bobby Witt, Kansas City	76
Brent Rooker, Athletics	73
Junior Caminero, Tampa Bay	73

HOME RUNS
Cal Raleigh, Seattle	60
Aaron Judge, NY Yankees	53
Junior Caminero, Tampa Bay	45
Jo Adell, LA Angels	37
Riley Greene, Detroit	36
Nick Kurtz, Athletics	36
Taylor Ward, Angels	36

RUNS BATTED IN
Cal Raleigh, Seattle	125
Aaron Judge, NY Yankees	114
Vinnie Pasquantino, KC	113
Riley Greene, Detroit	111
Junior Caminero, Tampa Bay	110

SACRIFICES
Kyle Isbel, Kansas City	13
Myles Straw, Toronto	11
Nathan Lukes, Toronto	7
Ernie Clement, Toronto	7
J.P. Crawford, Seattle	6

SACRIFICE FLIES
Austin Wells, NY Yankees	11
Ramon Urias, Baltimore	10
Cody Bellinger, NY Yankees	9
Marcus Semien, Texas	9
Seven tied	7

HIT BY PITCHES
Randy Arozarena, Seattle	27
Ty France, Minnesota	21
Zach Neto, LA Angels	14
Victor Caratini, Houston	13
Jonathan India, Kansas City	13
Luke Raley, Seattle	13

WALKS
Aaron Judge, NY Yankees	124
Cal Raleigh, Seattle	97
Mike Trout, LA Angels	87
Gleyber Torres, Detroit	85
Trent Grisham, NY Yankees	82

STOLEN BASES
Jose Caballero, Tampa Bay	49
Jose Ramirez, Cleveland	44
Chandler Simpson, Tampa Bay	44
Bobby Witt, Kansas City	38
Luis Robert, Chi White Sox	33

STOLEN BASE PERCENTAGE
Byron Buxton, Minnesota	1.000
Trevor Story, Boston	.969
George Springer, Toronto	.947
Jeremy Pena, Houston	.909
Jose Ramirez, Cleveland	.863

STRIKEOUTS
Riley Greene, Detroit	201
Randy Arozarena, Seattle	191
Cal Raleigh, Seattle	188
Lawrence Butler, Athletics	179
Mike Trout, LA Angels	178

STRIKEOUT PERCENTAGE
Mike Trout, LA Angels	32.0
Riley Greene, Detroit	30.7
Lawrence Butler, Athletics	28.4
Jazz Chisholm, NY Yankees	27.9
Christian Walker, Houston	27.7

MULTI-HIT GAMES
Julio Rodriguez, Seattle	54
Bo Bichette, Toronto	53
Yandy Diaz, Tampa Bay	53
Vladimir Guerrero Jr., Toronto	51
Maikel Garcia, Kansas City	51
Aaron Judge, NY Yankees	51

ON-BASE PERCENTAGE
Aaron Judge, NY Yankees	.457
George Springer, Toronto	.399
Vladimir Guerrero, Toronto	.381
Yandy Diaz, Tampa Bay	.366
Jeremy Pena, Houston	.363

ON-BASE PLUS SLUGGING
Aaron Judge, NY Yankees	1.144
George Springer, Toronto	.959
Cal Raleigh, Seattle	.948
Byron Buxton, Minnesota	.878
Jose Ramirez, Cleveland	.863

PITCHING

WINS
Max Fried, NY Yankees	19
Carlos Rodon, NY Yankees	18
Garrett Crochet, Boston	18
Bryan Woo, Seattle	15
Casey Mize, Detroit	14

LOSSES
Jack Flaherty, Detroit	15
Michael Wacha, Kansas City	13
Shane Baz, Tampa Bay	12
Chris Paddack, Minnesota	12
Ryan Pepiot, Tampa Bay	12

GAMES
Brendon Little, Toronto	79
Gabe Speier, Seattle	76
Cade Smith, Cleveland	76
John Schreiber, Kansas City	74
Louie Varland, Minn./Toronto	74

GAMES STARTED
Yusei Kikuchi, LA Angels	33
Carlos Rodon, NY Yankees	33
Will Warren, NY Yankees	33
Four tied	32

GAMES FINISHED
Jeff Hoffman, Toronto	59
Carlos Estevez, Kansas City	57
Pete Fairbanks, Tampa Bay	48
Kenley Jansen, LA Angels	47
Andres Munoz, Seattle	47

COMPLETE GAMES
Tanner Bibee, Cleveland	2
Framber Valdez, Houston	2
11 tied with	1

SHUTOUTS
Nathan Eovaldi, Texas	1
Kevin Gausman, Toronto	1
Tarik Skubal, Detroit	1
Garrett Crochet, Boston	1
Tanner Bibee, Cleveland	1

INNINGS PITCHED
Garrett Crochet, Boston	205
Max Fried, NY Yankees	195

Judge

AMERICAN LEAGUE DEPARTMENT LEADERS

Hunter Brown

Carlos Rodon, NY Yankees	195
Tarik Skubal, Detroit	195
Kevin Gausman, Toronto	193

HITS ALLOWED
Yusei Kikuchi, LA Angels	180
Chris Bassitt, Toronto	174
Tomoyuki Sugano, Baltimore	173
Framber Valdez, Houston	171
Tanner Bibee, Cleveland	170

RUNS ALLOWED
Chris Paddack, Minnesota	98
Charlie Morton, Baltimore	94
Luis Severino, Athletics	93
Tanner Bibee, Cleveland	93
Kyle Hendricks, LA Angels	92

HOME RUNS ALLOWED
Tomoyuki Sugano, Baltimore	33
Chris Paddack, Minnesota	31
Bailey Ober, Minnesota	30
Tyler Anderson, LA Angels	28
Jeffrey Springs, Athletics	28

WALKS ALLOWED
Gavin Williams, Cleveland	83
Jose Soriano, LA Angels	78
Yusei Kikuchi, LA Angels	74
Carlos Rodon, NY Yankees	73
Charlie Morton, Baltimore	71

LOWEST WALKS PER NINE
Tarik Skubal, Detroit	1.52
Bryan Woo, Seattle	1.74
Jacob deGrom, Texas	1.93
Garrett Crochet, Boston	2.02
Joe Ryan, Minnesota	2.05

HIT BATTERS
Luis Severino, Athletics	16
Charlie Morton, Baltimore	14
Chris Bassitt, Toronto	13
Brayan Bello, Boston	13
Joe Ryan, Minnesota	12

STRIKEOUTS
Garrett Crochet, Boston	255
Tarik Skubal, Detroit	241
Hunter Brown, Houston	206
Carlos Rodon, NY Yankees	203
Bryan Woo, Seattle	198

STRIKEOUTS PER NINE
Garrett Crochet, Boston	11.18
Tarik Skubal, Detroit	11.10
Joe Ryan, Minnesota	10.21
Hunter Brown, Houston	10.00
Jacob deGrom, Texas	9.64

STRIKEOUTS PER NINE (Relievers)
Bryan Abreu, Houston	13.31
Devin Williams, NY Yankees	13.06
Josh Hader, Houston	12.99
Cade Smith, Cleveland	12.71
Aroldis Chapman, Boston	12.47

DOUBLE PLAYS
Jose Soriano, LA Angels	30
Framber Valdez, Houston	22
Shane Baz, Tampa Bay	19
Four tied	18

PICKOFFS
Max Fried, NY Yankees	7

WILD PITCHES
Ryan Pepiot, Tampa Bay	5
Jose Berrios, Toronto	4
Charlie Morton, Baltimore	4
Logan Allen, Cleveland	4
Seranthony Dominguez, Balt.	12
Michael Lorenzen, Kansas City	12
Framber Valdez, Houston	12
Logan Gilbert, Seattle	10
Jack Leiter, Texas	10

WHIP
Tarik Skubal, Detroit	0.89
Jacob deGrom, Texas	0.92
Bryan Woo, Seattle	0.93
Hunter Brown, Houston	1.03
Garrett Crochet, Boston	1.03

OPPONENT AVERAGE
Carlos Rodon, NY Yankees	.188
Jacob deGrom, Texas	.196
Tarik Skubal, Detroit	.200
Bryan Woo, Seattle	.200
Hunter Brown, Houston	.201

WORST ERA
Shane Baz, Tampa Bay	4.87
Kyle Hendricks, LA Angels	4.76
Luis Severino, Athletics	4.54
Will Warren, NY Yankees	4.44
Jose Soriano, LA Angels	4.26

FIELDING

PITCHER
PCT	Jose Berrios, Toronto	1.000
PO	Nathan Eovaldi, Texas	23
A	Max Fried, NY Yankees	39
DP	Bailey Ober, Minnesota	3
E	Sean Burke, Chi White Sox	5

CATCHER
PCT	Cal Raleigh, Seattle	.996
PO	Yainer Diaz, Houston	1064
A	Carlos Narvaez, Boston	58
E	Carlos Narvaez, Boston	9
	Alejandro Kirk, Toronto	9
CS	Carlos Narvaez, Boston	32
PB	Shea Langeliers, Athletics	9
	Carlos Narvaez, Boston	9

FIRST BASE
PCT	Ty France, Minn./Toronto	.996
PO	Christian Walker, Houston	1,100
A	Spencer Torkelson, Detroit	100
DP	Nolan Schanuel, Los Angeles	120
E	Nick Kurtz, Athletics	10

SECOND BASE
PCT	Marcus Semien, Texas	.996
PO	Gleyber Torres, Detroit	197
A	Jackson Holliday, Baltimore	331
DP	Brandon Lowe, Tampa Bay	86
E	Jazz Chisholm, NY Yankees	13

THIRD BASE
PCT	Maikel Garcia, Kansas City	.980
PO	Maikel Garcia, Kansas City	105
A	Jose Ramirez, Cleveland	235
DP	Junior Caminero, Tampa Bay	27
E	Junior Caminero, Tampa Bay	18

SHORTSTOP
PCT	Gunnar Henderson, Baltimore	.986
PO	Trevor Story, Boston	219
A	Trevor Story, Boston	397
DP	Trevor Story, Boston	89
E	Trevor Story, Boston	19
	Anthony Volpe, NY Yankees	19

OUTFIELD
PCT	Kyle Isbel, Kansas City	.997
PO	Julio Rodriguez, Seattle	431
A	Steven Kwan, Cleveland	13
DP	Nathan Lukes, Toronto	4
E	Steven Kwan, Cleveland	8

NATIONAL LEAGUE 2025 STATISTICS

CLUB BATTING

	AVG	G	AB	R	H	2B	3B	HR	RBI	BB	SO	SB	OBP	SLG
Philadelphia	.258	162	5517	778	1426	268	24	212	753	528	1337	124	.328	.431
Milwaukee	.258	162	5510	806	1423	265	18	166	750	564	1266	164	.332	.403
Los Angeles	.253	162	5481	825	1384	257	21	244	791	580	1353	88	.327	.441
San Diego	.252	162	5424	702	1369	254	18	152	663	510	1161	106	.321	.390
Arizona	.251	162	5480	791	1377	277	38	214	768	545	1316	121	.325	.433
Miami	.250	162	5543	709	1388	272	29	154	677	482	1247	138	.314	.393
Chicago	.249	162	5495	793	1371	267	29	223	771	554	1277	161	.320	.430
New York	.249	162	5457	766	1359	262	19	224	746	563	1325	147	.326	.427
St. Louis	.245	162	5433	689	1331	264	9	148	653	478	1321	89	.314	.379
Atlanta	.245	162	5508	724	1349	243	19	190	701	575	1371	82	.320	.399
Cincinnati	.245	162	5448	716	1333	250	23	167	677	527	1415	105	.315	.391
Washington	.242	162	5422	687	1313	258	28	161	657	443	1351	132	.304	.389
Colorado	.237	162	5408	597	1281	253	37	160	581	395	1531	87	.293	.386
San Francisco	.235	162	5375	705	1261	239	28	173	672	556	1380	68	.311	.386
Pittsburgh	.231	162	5375	583	1244	245	21	117	561	530	1422	115	.305	.350

CLUB PITCHING

	ERA	G	CG	SHO	SV	IP	H	R	ER	HR	BB	SO	AVG
Milwaukee	3.58	162	0	12	45	1442.0	1237	634	574	168	534	1432	.230
San Diego	3.63	162	2	17	49	1433.0	1197	621	578	178	535	1425	.225
Pittsburgh	3.76	162	1	19	36	1430.2	1267	645	598	153	473	1314	.236
Philadelphia	3.79	162	2	14	47	1440.1	1342	648	607	177	435	1471	.245
Chicago	3.79	162	0	15	44	1435.0	1284	649	605	202	405	1265	.239
San Francisco	3.82	162	1	9	41	1433.2	1353	684	609	143	506	1358	.248
Cincinnati	3.86	162	4	9	41	1435.0	1260	681	616	190	494	1380	.233
Los Angeles	3.95	162	0	10	46	1441.0	1250	683	633	175	563	1505	.232
New York	4.03	162	1	9	40	1432.0	1338	715	641	149	556	1387	.246
St. Louis	4.29	162	2	13	42	1432.0	1434	754	682	170	461	1209	.259
Atlanta	4.36	162	1	8	34	1438.0	1348	734	696	197	530	1416	.247
Arizona	4.49	162	0	9	42	1444.0	1403	785	721	196	500	1288	.252
Miami	4.60	162	0	11	40	1443.1	1376	798	737	199	507	1294	.248
Washington	5.35	162	0	9	37	1423.1	1491	899	846	214	566	1248	.268
Colorado	5.97	162	0	3	29	1407.1	1673	1021	933	251	554	1093	.296

CLUB FIELDING

	PCT	PO	A	E	DP		PCT	PO	A	E	DP
Atlanta	.991	4314	1367	54	109	New York	.986	4296	1475	79	119
Chicago	.989	4305	1342	60	117	Arizona	.986	4332	1437	84	125
Philadelphia	.989	4321	1383	62	105	Miami	.985	4330	1383	85	107
Los Angeles	.988	4323	1346	68	102	Cincinnati	.985	4305	1239	67	101
San Diego	.987	4299	1234	74	117	San Francisco	.984	4301	1523	96	134
Milwaukee	.987	4326	1297	76	122	Washington	.984	4270	1404	94	131
St. Louis	.987	4296	1557	80	124	Colorado	.981	4222	1465	110	155
Pittsburgh	.986	4292	1334	77	118						

INDIVIDUAL BATTING LEADERS

	AVG	G	AB	R	H	2B	3B	HR	RBI	BB	SO	SB
Turner, Trea, PHI	.304	141	589	94	179	31	7	15	69	43	107	36
Hoerner, Nico, CHC	.297	156	599	89	178	29	4	7	61	39	49	29
Freeman, Freddie, LAD	.295	147	556	81	164	39	2	24	90	60	128	6
Arraez, Luis, SD	.292	154	620	66	181	30	4	8	61	34	21	11
Perdomo, Geraldo, AZ	.290	161	597	98	173	33	5	20	100	94	83	27
Burleson, Alec, STL	.290	139	497	54	144	26	2	18	69	39	79	5
Frelick, Sal, MIL	.288	142	528	76	152	20	3	12	63	47	80	19
Turang, Brice, MIL	.288	156	584	97	168	28	2	18	81	66	150	24
Donovan, Brendan, STL	.287	118	460	64	132	32	0	10	50	42	67	3
Bohm, Alec, PHI	.287	120	464	53	133	18	3	11	59	29	82	2

INDIVIDUAL PITCHING LEADERS

	W	L	ERA	G	GS	CG	SV	IP	H	R	ER	BB	SO
Paul Skenes, PIT	10	10	1.97	32	32	1	0	187.2	136	45	41	42	216
Yoshinobu Yamamoto, LAD	12	8	2.49	30	30	0	0	173.2	113	53	48	59	201
Cristopher Sánchez, PHI	13	5	2.50	32	32	1	0	202.0	171	58	56	44	212
Freddy Peralta, MIL	17	6	2.70	33	33	0	0	176.2	124	54	53	66	204
Andrew Abbott, CIN	10	7	2.87	29	29	1	0	166.1	148	60	53	43	149
Nick Pivetta, SD	13	5	2.87	31	31	0	0	181.2	129	63	58	50	190
Matthew Boyd, CHC	14	8	3.21	31	31	0	0	179.2	154	69	64	42	154
Logan Webb, SF	15	11	3.22	34	34	0	0	207.0	210	82	74	46	224
Clay Holmes, NYM	12	8	3.53	33	31	0	0	165.2	150	74	65	66	129
Robbie Ray, SF	11	8	3.65	32	32	1	0	182.1	148	81	74	73	186

AWARD WINNERS
Selected by Baseball Writers Association of America

MOST VALUABLE PLAYER

Player	1st	2nd	3rd	Total
Shohei Ohtani, Dodgers	30			420
Kyle Schwarber, Phillies		23	5	260
Juan Soto, Mets		4	15	231
Geraldo Perdomo, Diamondbacks		3	7	196
Trea Turner, Phillies			1	102
Paul Skenes, Pirates				83
Corbin Carroll, Diamondbacks				83
Fernando Tatis Jr., Padres				78
Pete Crow-Armstrong, Cubs				63
Francisco Lindor, Mets				61
Pete Alonso, Mets			1	48
Christian Yelich, Brewers				34
Freddie Freeman, Dodgers			1	29
Brice Turang, Brewers				23
Cristopher Sánchez, Phillies				16
Michael Busch, Cubs				11
Manny Machado, Padres				11
Matt Olson, Braves				7
Nico Hoerner, Cubs				5
Seiya Suzuki, Cubs				3
Will Smith, Dodgers				3
Ketel Marte, Diamondbacks				2
Elly De La Cruz, Reds				1

CY YOUNG AWARD

Player	1st	2nd	3rd	Total
Paul Skenes, Pirates	30			210
Cristopher Sánchez, Phillies		30		120
Yoshinobu Yamamoto, Dodgers			16	72
Logan Webb, Giants			10	47
Freddy Peralta, Brewers			4	44
Nick Pivetta, Padres				7
Jesús Luzardo, Phillies				5
Andrew Abbott, Reds				4
Zack Wheeler, Phillies				1

ROOKIE OF THE YEAR

Player	1st	2nd	3rd	Total
Drake Baldwin, Braves	21	9		183
Cade Horton, Cubs	9	16	4	139
Caleb Durbin, Brewers		2	13	69
Isaac Collins, Brewers		2	9	62
Daylen Lile, Nationals			1	17
Agustín Ramírez, Marlins				10
Chad Patrick, Brewers			1	9
Jakob Marsee, Marlins			1	8
Jack Dreyer, Dodgers			1	4
Matt Shaw, Cubs			1	4
Jacob Misiorowski, Brewers				2
Nolan McLean, Mets				2
Heriberto Hernández, Marlins				1

MANAGER OF THE YEAR

Player	1st	2nd	3rd	Total
Pat Murphy, Brewers	27	2		141
Terry Francona, Reds	2	9	12	49
Rob Thomson, Phillies	1	7	6	32
Craig Counsell, Cubs		7	3	24
Clayton McCullough, Marlins		5	7	22
Torey Lovullo, Diamondbacks			1	1

GOLD GLOVE WINNERS
P—Logan Webb, Giants. C—Patrick Bailey, Giants. 1B—Matt Olson, Braves. 2B—Nico Hoerner, Cubs. 3B—Ke'Bryan Hayes, Reds. SS—Masyn Winn, Cardinals. LF—Ian Happ, Cubs. CF—Pete Crow-Armstrong, Cubs. RF—Fernando Tatis Jr., Padres. UT—Javier Sanoja, Marlins. 1B—Christian Walker, D-backs. 2B—Brice Turang, Brewers. 3B—Matt Chapman, Giants. SS—Ezequiel Tovar, Rockies. LF—Ian Happ, Cubs. CF—Brenton Doyle, Rockies. RF—Sal Frelick, Brewers. UT—Jared Triolo, Pirates.

NATIONAL LEAGUE DEPARTMENT LEADERS

BATTING

GAMES
Pete Alonso, NY Mets, 162	162
Matt Olson, Atlanta	162
Kyle Schwarber, Philadelphia	162
Elly De La Cruz, Cincinnati	162
Geraldo Perdomo, Arizona	161

AT-BATS
Francisco Lindor, NY Mets	644
Elly De La Cruz, Cincinnati	629
Pete Alonso, NY Mets	624
Matt Olson, Atlanta	624
Luis Arraez, San Diego	620
Heliot Ramos, San Fran.	620

PLATE APPEARANCES
Francisco Lindor, NY Mets	732
Shohei Ohtani, LA Dodgers	727
Matt Olson, Atlanta	724
Kyle Schwarber, Philadelphia	724
Geraldo Perdomo, Arizona	720

RUNS
Shohei Ohtani, LA Dodgers	146
Juan Soto, NY Mets	120
Francisco Lindor, NY Mets	117
Kyle Schwarber, Philadelphia	111
Fernando Tatis, San Diego	111

HITS
Luis Arraez, San Diego	181
Trea Turner, Philadelphia	179
Nico Hoerner, Chi Cubs	178
Geraldo Perdomo, Arizona	173
Francisco Lindor, NY Mets	172
Shohei Ohtani, LA Dodgers	172

TOTAL BASES
Shohei Ohtani, LA Dodgers	380
Kyle Schwarber, Philadelphia	340
Pete Alonso, NY Mets	327
Corbin Carroll, Arizona	305
Juan Soto, NY Mets	303

DOUBLES
Pete Alonso, NY Mets	41
Matt Olson, Atlanta	41
Freddie Freeman, LA Dodgers	39
Bryan Reynolds, Pittsburgh	38
James Wood, Washington	38

TRIPLES
Corbin Carroll, Arizona	17
Jung Hoo Lee, San Francisco	12
Daylen Lile, Washington	11
Shohei Ohtani, LA Dodgers	9
Mickey Moniak, Colorado	8

EXTRA-BASE HITS
Shohei Ohtani, LA Dodgers	89
Kyle Schwarber, Philadelphia	81
Pete Alonso, NY Mets	80
Corbin Carroll, Arizona	80
Matt Olson, Atlanta	72

HOME RUNS
Kyle Schwarber, Philadelphia	56
Shohei Ohtani, LA Dodgers	55
Juan Soto, NY Mets	43
Pete Alonso, NY Mets	38
Eugenio Suarez, Arizona	36

RUNS BATTED IN
Kyle Schwarber, Philadelphia	132
Pete Alonso, NY Mets	126
Juan Soto, NY Mets	105

Arraez

Seiya Suzuki, Chi Cubs	103
Christian Yelich, Milwaukee	103

SACRIFICES
Luis Arraez, San Diego	12
Jose Herrera, Arizona	11
Victor Scott, St. Louis	10
Jacob Young, Washington	9
Two tied	8

SACRIFICE FLIES
Pete Crow-Armstrong, Chi Cubs	12
Geraldo Perdomo, Arizona	11
Mookie Betts, LA Dodgers	10
Four tied	9

HIT BY PITCHES
Caleb Durbin, Milwaukee	24
Willson Contreras, St. Louis	23
Heliot Ramos, San Francisco	17
TJ Friedl, Cincinnati	16
Francisco Lindor, NY Mets	16

WALKS
Juan Soto, NY Mets	127
Shohei Ohtani, LA Dodgers	109
Kyle Schwarber, Philadelphia	108
Marcell Ozuna, Atlanta	94
Geraldo Perdomo, Arizona	94

STOLEN BASES
Oneil Cruz, Pittsburgh	38
Juan Soto, NY Mets	38
Elly De La Cruz, Cincinnati	37
Trea Turner, Philadelphia	36
Pete Crow-Armstrong, Chi Cubs	35

STOLEN BASE PERCENTAGE
CJ Abrams, Washington	.912
Xander Bogaerts, San Diego	.909
Juan Soto, NY Mets	.905
Brenton Doyle, Colorado	.900
Matt McLain, Cincinnati	.900

STRIKEOUTS
James Wood, Washington	221
Kyle Schwarber, Philadelphia	197
Shohei Ohtani, LA Dodgers	187
Elly De La Cruz, Cincinnati	181
Willy Adames, San Francisco	179

STRIKEOUT PERCENTAGE
James Wood, Washington	32.1
Oneil Cruz, Pittsburgh	32.0
Jordan Beck, Colorado	29.6
Matt McLain, Cincinnati	28.9
Kyle Schwarber, Phil.	27.2

MULTI-HIT GAMES
Nico Hoerner, Chi Cubs	52
Luis Arraez, San Diego	49
Trea Turner, Philadelphia	49
Freddie Freeman, LA Dodgers	48
Pete Alonso, NY Mets	47

ON-BASE PERCENTAGE
Juan Soto, NY Mets	.396
Shohei Ohtani, LA Dodgers	.392
Geraldo Perdomo, Arizona	.389
Kyle Tucker, Chi Cubs	.377
Ketel Marte, Arizona	.376

ON-BASE PLUS SLUGGING
Shohei Ohtani, LA Dodgers	1.014
Kyle Schwarber, Philadelphia	.928
Juan Soto, NY Mets	.921
Ketel Marte, Arizona	.893
Corbin Carroll, Arizona	.883

PITCHING

WINS
Freddy Peralta, Milwaukee	17
Jesus Luzardo, Philadelphia	15
Logan Webb, San Francisco	15
Matthew Boyd, Chi Cubs	14
Sonny Gray, St. Louis	14
Brady Singer, Cincinnati	14

LOSSES
Kyle Freeland, Colorado	17
German Marquez, Colorado	16
Mitchell Parker, Washington	16
Five tied	15

GAMES
Tyler Rogers, San Francisco	81
Tony Santillan, Cincinnati	80
Jeremiah Estrada, San Diego	77
Scott Barlow, Cincinnati	75

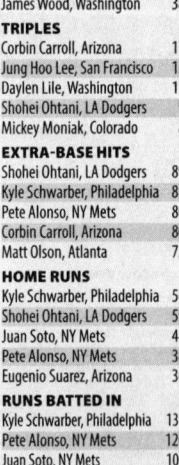

Turner

NATIONAL LEAGUE DEPARTMENT LEADERS

Peralta

Adrian Morejon, San Diego	75
Abner Uribe, Milwaukee	75

GAMES STARTED
Logan Webb, San Francisco	34
Zac Gallen, Arizona	33
Freddy Peralta, Milwaukee	33
Jake Irvin, Washington	33
Brandon Pfaadt, Arizona	33

GAMES FINISHED
Raisel Iglesias, Atlanta	57
Emilio Pagan, Cincinnati	56
Robert Suarez, San Diego	56
Edwin Diaz, NY Mets	48
Trevor Megill, Milwaukee	44

COMPLETE GAMES
Nick Lodolo, Cincinnati	2
12 tied with	1

SHUTOUTS
8 tied with	1

INNINGS PITCHED
Logan Webb, San Francisco	207
Cristopher Sanchez, Phila.	202
Zac Gallen, Arizona	192
Paul Skenes, Pittsburgh	188
Jesus Luzardo, Philadelphia	184

HITS ALLOWED
Logan Webb, San Francisco	210
Brandon Pfaadt, Arizona	198
Jake Irvin, Washington	195
Kyle Freeland, Colorado	193
Antonio Senzatela, Colorado	192

RUNS ALLOWED
Jake Irvin, Washington	120
Mitchell Parker, Washington	116
Zac Gallen, Arizona	109
Andre Pallante, St. Louis	109
Sandy Alcantara, Miami	107
Brandon Pfaadt, Arizona	107

HOME RUNS ALLOWED
Jake Irvin, Washington	38
Zac Gallen, Arizona	31
Shota Imanaga, Chi Cubs	31
Miles Mikolas, St. Louis	29
Brandon Pfaadt, Arizona	26

WALKS ALLOWED
Robbie Ray, San Francisco	73
Dylan Cease, San Diego	71

HIT BATTERS
Erick Fedde, St. Louis	67
Zac Gallen, Arizona	66
Clay Holmes, NY Mets	66
Freddy Peralta, Milwaukee	66

LOWEST WALKS PER NINE
Brandon Pfaadt, Arizona	1.88
Sonny Gray, St. Louis	1.89
Cristopher Sanchez, Phila.	1.96
Logan Webb, San Francisco	2.00
Paul Skenes, Pittsburgh	2.01

HIT BATTERS
Michael Soroka, Washington	15
Brady Singer, Cincinnati	14
Clay Holmes, NY Mets	13
Nick Lodolo, Cincinnati	13
Brandon Pfaadt, Arizona	12

STRIKEOUTS
Logan Webb, San Francisco	224
Jesus Luzardo, Philadelphia	216
Paul Skenes, Pittsburgh	216
Dylan Cease, San Diego	215
Cristopher Sanchez, Phila.	212

STRIKEOUTS PER NINE
Dylan Cease, San Diego	11.52
Jesus Luzardo, Philadelphia	10.58
Yoshinobu Yamamoto, LAD	10.42
Freddy Peralta, Milwaukee	10.39
Paul Skenes, Pittsburgh	10.36

STRIKEOUTS PER NINE (Relievers)
Jeremiah Estrada, SD	13.32
Edwin Diaz, NY Mets	13.30
Ronny Henriquez, Miami	12.08
Alex Vesia, LA Dodgers	12.07
Randy Rodriguez, SF	11.90

DOUBLE PLAYS
Logan Webb, San Francisco	22
David Peterson, NY Mets	20
Cristopher Sanchez, Phil.	20
Jake Irvin, Washington	19
Quinn Priester, Milwaukee	18

PICKOFFS
Matthew Boyd, Chi Cubs	11
Jesus Luzardo, Philadelphia	6
Robbie Ray, San Francisco	6
Colin Rea, Chi Cubs	6
Taijuan Walker, Philadelphia	5

WILD PITCHES
MacKenzie Gore, Washington	12
Andre Pallante, St. Louis	12

Shohei Ohtani, LA Dodgers	10
Antonio Senzatela, Colorado	9
Eury Perez, Miami	9

WALKS PLUS HITS PER INNING
Paul Skenes, Pittsburgh	0.95
Nick Pivetta, San Diego	0.99
Yoshinobu Yamamoto, LAD	0.99
Cristopher Sanchez, Phila.	1.06
Freddy Peralta, Milwaukee	1.08

OPPONENT AVERAGE
Yoshinobu Yamamoto, LAD	.183
Freddy Peralta, Milwaukee	.193
Nick Pivetta, San Diego	.195
Paul Skenes, Pittsburgh	.199
Robbie Ray, San Francisco	.221

WORST ERA
Jake Irvin, Washington	5.70
Mitchell Parker, Washington	5.68
Sandy Alcantara, Miami	5.36
Andre Pallante, St. Louis	5.31
Brandon Pfaadt, Arizona	5.25

FIELDING

PITCHER
PCT	David Peterson, NY Mets	1.000
PO	Yoshinobu Yamamoto, LAD	24
A	Logan Webb, San Francisco	34
DP	Five tied	3
E	Chase Dollander, Colorado	6

CATCHER
PCT	Carson Kelly, Chi Cubs	.998
PO	J.T. Realmuto, Philadelphia	1216
A	Patrick Bailey, SF Giants	57
E	Augustin Ramirez, Miami	10
DP	J.T. Realmuto, Philadelphia	10
CS	J.T. Realmuto, Philadelphia	30
PB	Augustin Ramirez, Miami	19

FIRST BASE
PCT	Luis Arraez, San Diego	.999
PO	Pete Alonso, NY Mets	1178
A	Matt Olson, Atlanta	145
DP	Pete Alonso, NY Mets	100
E	Pete Alonso, NY Mets	10
	Eric Wagaman, Miami	10

SECOND BASE
PCT	Ozzie Albies, Atlanta	.997
PO	Brice Turang, Milwaukee	245
A	Ozzie Albies, Atlanta	368
DP	Brice Turang, Milwaukee	83
E	Jake Cronenworth, San Diego	10

THIRD BASE
PCT	Ke'Bryan Hayes, Pitt./Cinc.	.987
PO	Manny Machado, San Diego	117
A	Ke'Bryan Hayes, Pitt./Cinc.	291
DP	Manny Machado, San Diego	34
E	Manny Machado, San Diego	16

SHORTSTOP
PCT	Masyn Winn, St. Louis	.994
PO	Gerardo Perdomo, Arizona	223
A	Willy Adames, San Francisco	398
DP	Gerardo Perdomo, Arizona	84
E	Elly De La Cruz, Cincinnati	26

OUTFIELD
PCT	Jacob Young, Washington	1.000
PO	Pete Crow-Armstrong, CHC	427
A	Jordan Beck, Colorado	12
DP	Andy Pages, LA Dodgers	5
E	Oneil Cruz, Pittsburgh	11
	Andy Pages, LA Dodgers	11

2025 POSTSEASON

Yoshinobu Yamamoto threw the first World Series complete game since 2015.

Dodgers Outlast Blue Jays In World Series For The Ages

Baseball's postseason has added layers over the years, from league championship series in 1969 to added wild cards in 1995, to the current 12-team setup, adopted for the 2022 season.

Skeptics point out that every new level devalues the regular season and makes baseball's ultimate champion more dependent on random chance than ever. The fact that the Yankees won four World Series in the first six years of the wild card era, including three in a row, may have masked the significance of randomness, but more than 20 years without a repeat World Series champion did well to reinforce it.

The 2025 postseason gave little ammunition to the skeptics, instead providing compelling play at every level and providing an October to remember—and a repeat champion.

Start with the best-of-three wild-card series. In the first three years of that round, just two series had failed to be a sweep. In 2025, only the Dodgers swept their series, and they were the only team to sweep a series in the postseason.

If every series runs to maximum, a postseason would contain 53 total games. The 2025 postseason had 47 games played, including an epic seven-game World Series with the Dodgers ending the Blue Jays with each of the last two games ending with Toronto hitting into double plays with the tying run in scoring position—a World Series first.

"I was with the Braves in 1991, and we lost the World Series in extra innings of Game Seven," Dodgers club president Stan Kasten said on The Athletic's "Starkville" podcast in an interview with

Jayson Stark. "I have said for 30-some years, that's the most painful any loss can be. And now . . . I think Toronto had that same kind of loss twice in this series, two nights in a row, Games Six and Seven.

"That's a kind of pain no one deserves, and I feel for them."

The World Series included an 18-inning Game Three thriller, tying for the longest Series game of all-time. The Blue Jays won the next two games in Los Angeles, including Game Five with an epic 12-strikeout performance by righthander Trey Yesavage—a Series record for a rookie. It came 15 months after the Jays had drafted Yesavage 20th overall in the first round of the 2024 draft.

In the end, the Dodgers had enough star power and grit to pull out the championship, their ninth all-time and eighth since moving to Los Angeles in 1958. Manager Dave Roberts pushed a lot of the right buttons en route to his third World Series ring. He inserted veteran Miguel Rojas into the starting lineup for Games Six and Seven, and he turned in two crucial plays in the finale. His solo homer with one out in the ninth inning off Toronto closer Jeff Hoffman tied that game at 4, and in the bottom of the ninth, he threw out the potential game-winning run on a force play at the plate, nipping pinch-runner Isiah Kiner-Falefa in a play that was replay reviewed.

Catcher Will Smith barely kept a cleat on the plate on that play, then two innings later hit the game- and Series-winning home run, in the 11th off righty Shane Bieber. Smith caught every inning of the Series and went 8-for-30 (.267) with a team-high six RBIs in the Series.

Dodgers star Shohei Ohtani started Games Four and Seven and was the Dodgers' most productive hitter, as only he can do. His Game Three effort was historic; he went 4-for-4 with a pair of home runs, including a game-tying solo shot in the seventh inning. For the next 11 innings, Toronto wouldn't let him beat them; he walked five times and reached base a Series-record nine times.

And in the end, there was Yoshinobu Yamamoto, the Japanese righthander who was in the second year of his record (for a pitcher) 12-year, $325 million contract. It takes a lot to outshine Ohtani, but Yamamoto did in earning MVP honors. He threw a complete game in a 5-1 Game Two victory, the first World Series CG since Johnny Cueto threw one for the Royals in 2015.

After warming up in the bullpen late in the Game Three marathon, he won Game Six with six quality innings before returning the next night to earn his third victory of the series. He wriggled out

Miguel Rojas was an unlikely hitting star, as his home run turned the series in Game 7.

of a ninth-inning jam, then pitched the 10th and 11th to finish the Series.

As Roberts recounted, "Even for the third (inning of work), he said, 'daijoubu.' It means, 'I'm OK.' And so for me, I just trusted him and he came up big."

Links To The Past

The Dodgers and Blue Jays franchises don't have much in common on the surface, but their rosters have some surprising links, especially internationally. Back in 2015, the Blue Jays sent two future major leaguers, righthander Chase De Jong and infielder Tim Locastro, to the Dodgers for more than $1 million in international bonus pool money to help them sign Vladimir Guerrero Jr. as an amateur. Guerrero has proved well worth the investment, becoming the face of the Jays' franchise and signing a 14-year, $500 million extension in April 2025.

The Blue Jays became sort of a punchline in the 2023 offseason for their pursuit of free agent Shohei Ohtani, when Jays fans obsessively tracked a flight that was erroneously reported to be bringing Ohtani to Toronto on Dec. 8, 2023, shortly after Ohtani had met with club officials at their spring-training complex in Dunedin, Fla.

Prior to the 2025 season, Toronto again pursued a Japanese free agent, this time Roki Sasaki, a flamethrowing righty who decided to leave Nippon Professional Baseball while still subject to international bonus pool rules. Again the Jays wheeled and dealed for more pool room, acquiring an extra $2 million from Cleveland in exchange for acquiring outfielder Myles Straw and his contract, with its remaining two years and $13 million.

Instead, Sasaki chose the Dodgers, and while his regular season included an early crash out, more than three months on the injured list and a late-September return in a relief role, Sasaki played an important postseason role for LA. He saved the first two games of the Division Series against the Phillies and threw three scoreless innings in the 11-inning 2-1 series clincher.

The Jays countered with an offense led by Guerrero, resurgent outfielder/DH George Springer, shortstop Bo Bichette and a host of role players both young and old. Guerrero was the unquestioned leader, Bichette his longtime wingman since their time in the minors, and Springer the free-agent addition in 2021 with the lengthy postseason resume from his time with Houston.

They all delivered in the postseason and they all had help. Guerrero dominated the Yankees in the Division Series, going 9-for-17 with three homers and nine RBIs. Toronto dominated the Yankees, scoring 23 runs in the first two games, then stifled the Bronx Bombers with eight pitchers in a bullpen game in the 5-2 Game Four clincher.

Toronto then outlasted its fellow 1977 expansion partner, Seattle, in a thrilling seven-game AL Championship Series. Guerrero earned ALCS MVP honors with three solo homers and a .385/.484/.846 line for the series. Springer, 36, fought off various injuries to post team-highs in runs and RBIs (seven apiece) and had the series' biggest hit, a three-run homer in the seventh inning of Game Seven off Seattle reliever Eduard Bazardo. It flipped a 3-1 deficit to a 4-3 lead that the Jays were able to hold.

Ernie Clement, primarily their third baseman, posted a historic postseason and embodied the Jays' high-contact offensive approach. Clement walked once in the entire postseason but used an aggressive approach and short swing to rack up 30 postseason hits, breaking the mark of 29 set by the Rays' Randy Arozarena in 2020. In the bottom of the ninth of Game Seven, he just missed being the Series hero, as his long drive to left-center field was snagged by LA center fielder Andy Pages, who trucked left fielder Kiké Hernandez in the process and held onto to send the game to extra innings.

Perilous Preliminaries

The Jays needed all hands on deck to dispatch the Mariners, who had stormed past the Astros in September to win the AL West and were seeded second behind Toronto entering the postseason. Seattle outlasted Tarik Skubal and the Tigers in a five-game Division Series, with three of the games finishing with 3-2 scores. That included the 11-inning opener, won by Detroit, and the 15-inning finale won by Seattle.

Skubal struck out 13 in six innings of Game Five, but pinch-hitter Leo Rivas drove in the tying

AMERICAN LEAGUE CHAMPIONS, 2000-2025

American League postseason results from 2000 to present, where (*) denotes wild card playoff entrant.

YEAR	CHAMPIONSHIP SERIES	ALCS MVP	DIVISION SERIES	DIVISION SERIES
2025	Toronto 4, Seattle 3	Vladimir Guerrero Jr., 1B, Toronto	Toronto 3, New York* 1	Seattle 3, Detroit* 2
2024	New York 4, Cleveland 1	Giancarlo Stanton, DH, New York	Cleveland 3, Detroit* 2	New York 3, Kansas City* 1
2023	Texas 4, Houston 3	Adolis Garcia, OF, Texas	Houston 3, Minnesota 1	Texas* 3, Baltimore 0
2022	Houston 4, New York 0	Jeremy Peña, SS, Houston	Houston 3, Seattle* 0	New York 3, Cleveland 2
2021	Houston 4, Boston 2	Yordan Alvarez, OF, Houston	Houston 3, Chicago 1	Boston* 3, Tampa Bay 1
2020	Tampa Bay 4, Houston 3	Randy Arozarena, OF, Tampa Bay	Tampa Bay 3, New York* 2	Houston* 3, Oakland 1
2019	Houston 4, New York 2	Jose Altuve, 2B, Houston	Houston 3, Tampa Bay* 2	New York 3, Minnesota 0
2018	Boston 4, Houston 1	Jackie Bradley Jr., OF, Boston	Boston 3, New York* 1	Houston 3, Cleveland 0
2017	Houston 4, New York 3	Justin Verlander, RHP, Houston	New York* 3, Cleveland 2	Houston 3, Boston 1
2016	Cleveland 4, Toronto 1	Andrew Miller, LHP, Cleveland	Toronto* 3, Texas 0	Cleveland 3, Boston 0
2015	Kansas City 4, Toronto 2	Alcides Escobar, SS, Kansas City	Kansas City 3, Houston* 2	Baltimore 3, Texas 2
2014	Kansas City 4, Baltimore 0	Lorenzo Cain, OF, Kansas City	Kansas City 3, Los Angeles 0	Baltimore 3, Detroit 0
2013	Boston 4, Detroit 2	Koji Uehara, RHP, Boston	Boston 3, Tampa Bay* 1	Detroit, 3, Oakland 2
2012	Detroit 4, New York 0	Delmon Young, OF, Detroit	New York 3, Baltimore* 2	Detroit 3, Oakland 2
2011	Texas 4, Detroit 2	Nelson Cruz, OF, Texas	Detroit 3, New York 2	Texas 3, Tampa Bay* 1
2010	Texas 4, New York 2	Josh Hamilton, OF, Texas	Texas 3, Tampa Bay 2	New York* 3, Minnesota 0
2009	New York 4, Los Angeles 2	C.C. Sabathia, LHP, New York	New York 3, Minnesota 0	Los Angeles 3, Boston* 0
2008	Tampa Bay 4, Boston 3	Matt Garza, RHP, Tampa Bay	Boston* 3, Los Angeles 1	Tampa Bay 3, Chicago 1
2007	Boston 4, Cleveland 3	Josh Beckett, RHP, Boston	Boston 3, Los Angeles 0	Cleveland 3, New York* 1
2006	Detroit 4, Oakland 0	Placido Polanco, 2B, Detroit	Detroit* 3, New York 1	Oakland 3, Minnesota 0
2005	Chicago 4, Los Angeles 1	Paul Konerko, 1B, Chicago	Chicago 3, Boston* 0	Los Angeles 3, New York 2
2004	Boston 4, New York 3	David Ortiz, DH, Boston	Boston* 3, Anaheim 0	New York 3, Minnesota 1
2003	New York 4, Boston 3	Mariano Rivera, RHP, New York	New York 3, Minnesota 1	Boston* 3, Oakland 2
2002	Anaheim 4, Minnesota 1	Adam Kennedy, 2B, Anaheim	Anaheim* 3, New York 1	Minnesota 3, Oakland 2
2001	New York 4, Seattle 1	Andy Pettitte, LHP, New York	Seattle 3, Cleveland 2	New York 3, Oakland* 2
2000	New York 4, Seattle 2	David Justice, OF, New York	New York 3, Oakland 2	Seattle* 3, Chicago 0

run in the seventh, and the two teams' bullpens traded scoreless innings until veteran Jorge Polanco singled home J.P. Crawford with the bases loaded in the bottom of the 15th.

The Mariners had only one day off after the lengthy Division Series clincher, flying cross-continent to Toronto for the ALCS, and won the first two games in Rogers Centre before the Jays stormed back. Trailing 2-0 in Game Three at T-Mobile Park, they rallied with three home runs off George Kirby en route to a 13-4 victory and tied the series behind 5 ⅔ innings from venerable righty Max Scherzer in Game Four. The clubs traded victories before Springer's Game Seven heroics, giving the Jays their first pennant since 1993.

The AL Wild Card series had drama as well. Cleveland chased down Detroit in September, winning 17 of 19 at one point to erase an 11-game deficit and win the division. The Guardians' reward? A three-game wild-card series against those same Tigers as the No. 3 and 6 seeds. Skubal, who won the AL Cy Young Award for the second straight season, struck out 14 in a Game One victory, and the Tigers scored four runs in the seventh en route to a 6-3 win in the clincher.

AL East rivals Boston and New York rekindled their postseason rivalry in the other Wild Card matchup. Garrett Crochet shackled the Yankees with 11 strikeouts in 7 ⅔ innings in a 3-1 Game One win, but the Yankees evened the series with a 4-3 Game Two victory.

That set up Massachusetts native and Northeastern alum Cam Schlittler, a rookie who made 14 regular-season starts, to make some Yankees postseason history. No franchise has more postseason history to try to surpass, but Schlitter hit 100 mph 11 times during eight scoreless innings, and his 12 strikeouts were the most ever by a Yankees pitcher in his first postseason start.

No Drama NL

The Brewers led the major leagues with 97 regular-season wins and claimed their first playoff series since reaching the 2018 NLCS by beating the Cubs in a five-game Division Series.

However, Milwaukee's bats went silent against the Dodgers, scoring only one run in each of the four NLCS losses. In the final loss, Ohtani authored perhaps the most impressive single-game performance in MLB history, striking out 10 in six scoreless innings while hitting three home runs.

The other bitter disappointment in the NL postseason was the second-seeded Phillies. The team swept the Reds in the Wild Card Series but fell to the Dodgers in the Division Series. The final game came down to a play that will haunt Philadelphia for years.

With the bases loaded and two outs in the 11th, Andy Pages hit a grounder to Orion Kerkering. The righty fielded the ball in front of the mound but threw wildly toward home, allowing the season-ending run to score.

NATIONAL LEAGUE CHAMPIONS, 2000-2025

National League postseason results from 2000 to present, where (*) denotes wild card playoff entrant.

YEAR	CHAMPIONSHIP SERIES	NLCS MVP	DIVISION SERIES	DIVISION SERIES
2025	Los Angeles* 4, Milwaukee 0	Shohei Ohtani, DH/RHP, Los Angeles	Milwaukee 3, Chicago* 2	Los Angeles* 3, Philadelphia 1
2024	Los Angeles 4, New York* 2	Tommy Edman, SS/OF, Los Angeles	New York* 3, Philadelphia 1	Los Angeles 3, San Diego* 2
2023	Arizona 4, Philadelphia 3	Ketel Marte, 2B, Arizona	Philadelphia* 3, Atlanta 1	Arizona* 3, Los Angeles 0
2022	Philadelphia 4, San Diego 1	Bryce Harper, OF, Philadelphia	Philadelphia* 3, Atlanta 1	San Diego* 3, Los Angeles 1
2021	Atlanta 4, Los Angeles 2	Eddie Rosario, OF, Atlanta	Atlanta 3, Milwaukee 1	Los Angeles* 3, San Francisco 2
2020	Los Angeles 4, Atlanta 3	Corey Seager, SS, Los Angeles	Los Angeles 3, San Diego* 0	Atlanta 3, Miami* 0
2019	Washington 4, St. Louis 0	Howie Kendrick, 2B, Washington	Washington* 3, Los Angeles 2	St. Louis 3, Atlanta 2
2018	Los Angeles 4, Milwaukee 3	Cody Bellinger, 1B/OF, Los Angeles	Los Angeles 3, Atlanta 1	Milwaukee 3, Colorado 0*
2017	Los Angeles 4, Chicago 1	Justin Turner, 3B/OF, L.A.	Los Angeles 3, Arizona* 0	Chicago 3, Washington 2
2016	Chicago 4, Los Angeles 2	Javier Baez, 2B/Jon Lester, LHP, Chicago	Chicago 3, San Francisco* 1	Los Angeles 3, Washington 2
2015	New York 4, Chicago 0	Daniel Murphy, 2B, New York	New York 3, Los Angeles 2	Chicago* 3, St. Louis 1
2014	San Francisco 4, St. Louis 1	Madison Bumgarner, LHP, San Francisco	San Francisco 3, Washington 1	St. Louis 3, Los Angeles 1
2013	St. Louis 4, Los Angeles 2	Michael Wacha, RHP, St. Louis	St. Louis 3, Pittsburgh* 2	Los Angeles 3, Atlanta 1
2012	San Francisco 4, St. Louis 3	Marco Scutaro, 2B, San Francisco	St. Louis* 3, Washington 2	San Francisco 3, Cincinnati 2
2011	St. Louis 4, Milwaukee 2	David Freese, 3B, St. Louis	St. Louis* 3, Philadelphia 2	Milwaukee 3, Arizona 2
2010	San Francisco 4, Philadelphia 2	Cody Ross, OF, San Francisco	Philadelphia 3, Cincinnati 0	San Francisco 3, Atlanta* 1
2009	Philadelphia 4, Los Angeles 1	Ryan Howard, 1B, Philadelphia	Los Angeles 3, St. Louis 0	Philadelphia 3, Colorado* 1
2008	Philadelphia 4, Los Angeles 1	Cole Hamels, LHP, Philadelphia	Los Angeles 3, Chicago 0	Philadelphia 3, Milwaukee* 1
2007	Colorado 4, Arizona 0	Matt Holliday, OF, Colorado	Arizona 3, Chicago 0	Colorado* 3, Philadelphia 0
2006	St. Louis 4, New York 3	Jeff Suppan, RHP, St. Louis	New York 3, Los Angeles* 0	St. Louis 3, San Diego 1
2005	Houston 4, St. Louis 2	Roy Oswalt, RHP, Houston	St. Louis 3, San Diego 0	Houston* 3, Atlanta 1
2004	St. Louis 4, Houston 3	Albert Pujols, 1B, St. Louis	St. Louis 3, Los Angeles 1	Houston* 3, Atlanta 2
2003	Florida 4, Chicago 3	Ivan Rodriguez, C, Florida	Florida* 3, San Francisco 1	Chicago 3, Atlanta 2
2002	San Francisco 4, St. Louis 1	Benito Santiago, C, San Francisco	San Francisco* 3, Atlanta 2	St. Louis 3, Arizona 0
2001	Arizona 4, Atlanta 1	Craig Counsell, SS, Arizona	Atlanta 3, Houston 0	Arizona 3, St. Louis* 2
2000	New York 4, St. Louis 1	Mike Hampton, LHP, New York	St. Louis 3, Atlanta 0	New York* 3, San Francisco 1

THE WORLD SERIES YEAR-BY-YEAR

Commissioner's Trophy

Year	Winner	Loser	Result
1903	Boston (AL)	Pittsburgh (NL)	5-3
1904	NO SERIES		
1905	New York (NL)	Philadelphia (AL)	4-1
1906	Chicago (AL)	Chicago (NL)	4-2
1907	Chicago (NL)	Detroit (AL)	4-0
1908	Chicago (NL)	Detroit (AL)	4-1
1909	Pittsburgh (NL)	Detroit (AL)	4-3
1910	Philadelphia (AL)	Chicago (NL)	4-1
1911	Philadelphia (AL)	New York (NL)	4-2
1912	Boston (AL)	New York (NL)	4-3-1
1913	Philadelphia (AL)	New York (NL)	4-1
1914	Boston (NL)	Philadelphia (AL)	4-0
1915	Boston (AL)	Philadelphia (NL)	4-1
1916	Boston (AL)	Brooklyn (NL)	4-1
1917	Chicago (AL)	New York (NL)	4-2
1918	Boston (AL)	Chicago (NL)	4-2
1919	Cincinnati (NL)	Chicago (AL)	5-3
1920	Cleveland (AL)	Brooklyn (NL)	5-2
1921	New York (NL)	New York (AL)	5-3
1922	New York (NL)	New York (AL)	4-0
1923	New York (AL)	New York (NL)	4-2
1924	Washington (AL)	New York (NL)	4-3
1925	Pittsburgh (NL)	Washington (AL)	4-3
1926	St. Louis (NL)	New York (AL)	4-3
1927	New York (AL)	Pittsburgh (NL)	4-0
1928	New York (AL)	St. Louis (NL)	4-0
1929	Philadelphia (AL)	Chicago (NL)	4-1
1930	Philadelphia (AL)	St. Louis (NL)	4-2
1931	St. Louis (NL)	Philadelphia (AL)	4-3
1932	New York (AL)	Chicago (NL)	4-0
1933	New York (NL)	Washington (AL)	4-1
1934	St. Louis (NL)	Detroit (AL)	4-3
1935	Detroit (AL)	Chicago (NL)	4-2
1936	New York (AL)	New York (NL)	4-2
1937	New York (AL)	New York (NL)	4-1
1938	New York (AL)	Chicago (NL)	4-0
1939	New York (AL)	Cincinnati (NL)	4-0
1940	Cincinnati (NL)	Detroit (AL)	4-3
1941	New York (AL)	Brooklyn (NL)	4-1
1942	St. Louis (NL)	New York (AL)	4-1
1943	New York (AL)	St. Louis (NL)	4-1
1944	St. Louis (NL)	St. Louis (AL)	4-2
1945	Detroit (AL)	Chicago (NL)	4-3
1946	St. Louis (NL)	Boston (AL)	4-3
1947	New York (AL)	Brooklyn (NL)	4-3
1948	Cleveland (AL)	Boston (NL)	4-2
1949	New York (AL)	Brooklyn (NL)	4-1
1950	New York (AL)	Philadelphia (NL)	4-0
1951	New York (AL)	New York (NL)	4-2
1952	New York (AL)	Brooklyn (NL)	4-3
1953	New York (AL)	Brooklyn (NL)	4-2
1954	New York (NL)	Cleveland (AL)	4-0
1955	Brooklyn (NL)	New York (AL)	4-3
1956	New York (AL)	Brooklyn (NL)	4-3
1957	Milwaukee (NL)	New York (AL)	4-3
1958	New York (AL)	Milwaukee (NL)	4-3
1959	Los Angeles (NL)	Chicago (AL)	4-2
1960	Pittsburgh (NL)	New York (AL)	4-3
1961	New York (AL)	Cincinnati (NL)	4-1
1962	New York (AL)	San Francisco (NL)	4-3
1963	Los Angeles (NL)	New York (AL)	4-0
1964	St. Louis (NL)	New York (AL)	4-3
1965	Los Angeles (NL)	Minnesota (AL)	4-3
1966	Baltimore (AL)	Los Angeles (NL)	4-0
1967	St. Louis (NL)	Boston (AL)	4-3
1968	Detroit (AL)	St. Louis (NL)	4-3
1969	New York (NL)	Baltimore (AL)	4-1
1970	Baltimore (AL)	Cincinnati (NL)	4-1

Year	Winner	Loser	Result
1971	Pittsburgh (NL)	Baltimore (AL)	4-3
1972	Oakland (AL)	Cincinnati (NL)	4-3
1973	Oakland (AL)	New York (NL)	4-3
1974	Oakland (AL)	Los Angeles (NL)	4-1
1975	Cincinnati (NL)	Boston (AL)	4-3
1976	Cincinnati (NL)	New York (AL)	4-0
1977	New York (AL)	Los Angeles (NL)	4-2
1978	New York (AL)	Los Angeles (NL)	4-2
1979	Pittsburgh (NL)	Baltimore (AL)	4-3
1980	Philadelphia (NL)	Kansas City (AL)	4-2
1981	Los Angeles (NL)	New York (AL)	4-2
1982	St. Louis (NL)	Milwaukee (AL)	4-3
1983	Baltimore (AL)	Philadelphia (NL)	4-1
1984	Detroit (AL)	San Diego (NL)	4-1
1985	Kansas City (AL)	St. Louis (NL)	4-3
1986	New York (NL)	Boston (AL)	4-3
1987	Minnesota (AL)	St. Louis (NL)	4-3
1988	Los Angeles (NL)	Oakland (AL)	4-1
1989	Oakland (AL)	San Francisco (NL)	4-0
1990	Cincinnati (NL)	Oakland (AL)	4-0
1991	Minnesota (AL)	Atlanta (NL)	4-3
1992	Toronto (AL)	Atlanta (NL)	4-2
1993	Toronto (AL)	Philadelphia (NL)	4-2
1994	NO SERIES		
1995	Atlanta (NL)	Cleveland (AL)	4-2
1996	New York (AL)	Atlanta (NL)	4-2
1997	Florida (NL)	Cleveland (AL)	4-3
1998	New York (AL)	San Diego (NL)	4-0
1999	New York (AL)	Atlanta (NL)	4-0
2000	New York (AL)	New York (NL)	4-1
2001	Arizona (NL)	New York (AL)	4-3
2002	Anaheim (AL)	San Francisco (NL)	4-3
2003	Florida (NL)	New York (AL)	4-2
2004	Boston (AL)	St. Louis (NL)	4-0
2005	Chicago (AL)	Houston (NL)	4-0
2006	St. Louis (NL)	Detroit (AL)	4-1
2007	Boston (AL)	Colorado (NL)	4-0
2008	Philadelphia (NL)	Tampa Bay (AL)	4-1
2009	New York (AL)	Philadelphia (NL)	4-2
2010	San Francisco (NL)	Texas (AL)	4-1
2011	St. Louis (NL)	Texas (AL)	4-3
2012	San Francisco (NL)	Detroit (AL)	4-0
2013	Boston (AL)	St. Louis (NL)	4-2
2014	San Francisco (NL)	Kansas City (AL)	4-3
2015	Kansas City (AL)	New York (NL)	4-1
2016	Chicago (NL)	Cleveland (AL)	4-3
2017	Houston (AL)	Los Angeles (NL)	4-3
2018	Boston (AL)	Los Angeles (NL)	4-1
2019	Washington (NL)	Houston (AL)	4-3
2020	Los Angeles (NL)	Tampa Bay (AL)	4-2
2021	Atlanta (NL)	Houston (AL)	4-2
2022	Houston (AL)	Philadelphia (NL)	4-2
2023	Texas (AL)	Arizona (NL)	4-1
2024	Los Angeles (NL)	New York (AL)	4-1
2025	Los Angeles (NL)	Toronto (AL)	4-3

WORLD SERIES BOX SCORES

GAME ONE October 24, 2025
TORONTO BLUE JAYS 11, L.A. DODGERS 4

	1	2	3	4	5	6	7	8	9	R	H	E
LA DODGERS	0	1	1	0	0	0	2	0	0	4	6	0
TORONTO	0	0	0	2	0	9	0	0	X	11	14	0

LA DODGERS	AB	R	H	RBI	BB	SO	LOB	AVG
Ohtani, DH	4	1	1	2	1	2	3	.222
Betts, SS	4	1	1	0	1	2	1	.289
Freeman, F, 1B	3	0	0	0	1	0	1	.214
Smith, W, C	3	0	1	1	1	0	1	.290
Hernández, T, RF	3	1	0	0	1	1	2	.250
Muncy, 3B	4	0	1	0	0	2	2	.219
Hernández, K, LF	4	0	1	1	0	3	1	.300
Edman, 2B	3	1	1	0	1	1	0	.289
Pages, A, CF	4	0	0	0	2	4	4	.077
TOTALS	32	4	6	4	6	13	15	.188

HR: Ohtani (6, 7th inning off Fisher, 1 on, 1 out). TB: Betts; Edman; Hernández, K; Muncy; Ohtani 4; Smith, W. RBI: Hernández, K (5); Ohtani 2 (11); Smith, W (3). Runners left in scoring position, 2 out: Ohtani 2; Muncy. Team RISP: 3-for-7. Team LOB: 7. DP: 2 (Freeman, F-Betts-Freeman, F; Muncy-Edman-Freeman, F).

TORONTO	AB	R	H	RBI	BB	SO	LOB	AVG
Springer, DH	5	1	2	0	0	0	3	.255
Schneider, LF	3	0	0	0	0	1	1	.154
b-Barger, PH-RF	2	1	2	4	0	0	0	.324
Guerrero Jr., 1B	4	1	2	0	1	0	1	.447
Bichette, 2B	2	0	1	0	1	0	1	.500
1-Kiner-Falefa, PR-2B	2	1	0	0	0	0	2	.217
Kirk, C	3	3	3	2	1	0	0	.271
Varsho, CF	3	2	1	2	0	0	3	.277
Clement, 3B	4	0	2	1	0	0	0	.435
Straw, RF	2	0	0	0	0	1	1	.182
a-Lukes, PH-LF	1	1	0	1	1	0	0	.325
Giménez, SS	4	1	1	1	0	2	1	.262
TOTALS	35	11	14	11	4	4	13	.400

a-Walked for Straw in the 6th. b-Homered for Schneider in the 6th. HR: Varsho (3, 4th inning off Snell, 1 on, 0 out); Barger (3, 6th inning off Banda, 3 on, 1 out); Kirk (4, 6th inning off Banda, 1 on, 2 out). TB: Barger 5; Bichette; Clement 2; Giménez; Guerrero Jr. 2; Kirk 6; Springer 2; Varsho 4. RBI: Barger 4 (8); Clement (8); Giménez (9); Kirk 2 (9); Lukes (8); Varsho 2 (10). 2-out RBI: Kirk 2. Runners left in scoring position, 2 out: Varsho 2. GIDP: Bichette; Schneider. Team RISP: 3-for-5. Team LOB: 5. Outfield assists: Straw (Freeman, F at 3rd base).

LA DODGERS	IP	H	R	ER	BB	SO	HR	ERA
Snell (L, 3-1)	5.0	8	5	5	3	4	1	2.42
Sheehan	0.1	2	3	3	1	0	0	17.18
Banda	0.2	3	3	3	0	0	2	8.10
Wrobleski	1.0	0	0	0	0	0	0	0.00
Klein	1.0	1	0	0	0	0	0	0.00
TOTALS	8.0	14	11	11	4	4	3	12.38

TORONTO	IP	H	R	ER	BB	SO	HR	ERA
Yesavage	4.0	4	2	2	3	5	0	4.26
Fluharty	0.2	1	0	0	0	1	0	5.40
Domínguez (W, 2-0)	1.1	0	0	0	0	2	0	3.38
Fisher	1.0	1	2	2	1	2	1	9.64
Bassitt	1.0	0	0	0	1	2	0	0.00
Lauer	1.0	0	0	0	1	1	0	6.75
TOTALS	9.0	6	4	4	6	13	1	4.00

HBP: Varsho (by Snell). Pitches-strikes: Snell 100-62; Sheehan 16-11; Banda 12-7; Wrobleski 14-11; Klein 14-12; Yesavage 80-44; Fluharty 17-12; Domínguez 13-8; Fisher 23-14; Bassitt 21-13; Lauer 17-9. Groundouts-flyouts: Snell 4-2; Sheehan 1-0; Banda 0-2; Wrobleski 2-1; Klein 0-3; Yesavage 5-1; Fluharty 0-1; Domínguez 0-1; Fisher 0-1; Bassitt 1-0; Lauer 0-0. Batters faced: Snell 24; Sheehan 4; Banda 5; Wrobleski 3; Klein 4; Yesavage 18; Fluharty 3; Domínguez 4; Fisher 5; Bassitt 4; Lauer 4. Inherited runners-scored: Sheehan 3-3; Banda 3-3; Domínguez 1-0. Umpires: HP: Will Little. 1B: Mark Wegner. 2B: John Tumpane. 3B: Alan Porter. LF: Adam Hamari. RF: Jordan Baker. Weather: 68 degrees, Roof Closed. Wind: 0 mph, None. First pitch: 8:14 PM. T: 3:13. Att: 44,353. Venue: Rogers Centre.

GAME TWO October 24, 2025
LOS ANGELES DODGERS 5, TORONTO BLUE JAYS 1

	1	2	3	4	5	6	7	8	9	R	H	E
LA DODGERS	1	0	0	0	0	0	2	2	0	5	6	0
TORONTO	0	0	1	0	0	0	0	0	0	1	4	0

Vladimir Guerrero Jr. hit .397/.494/.795 with eight home runs in 18 postseason games.

LA DODGERS	AB	R	H	RBI	BB	SO	LOB	AVG
Ohtani, DH	4	1	1	0	0	0	0	.224
Betts, SS	3	0	0	0	1	0	0	.271
Freeman, F, 1B	3	1	1	0	1	0	0	.222
Smith, W, C	4	1	2	3	0	0	0	.314
Hernández, T, RF	4	0	0	0	0	4	3	.229
Dean, CF	0	0	0	0	0	0	0	.000
Muncy, 3B	3	1	1	1	1	1	0	.229
Hernández, K, LF	4	0	0	0	0	1	1	.273
Edman, 2B	4	0	0	0	0	1	1	.262
Pages, A, CF-RF	4	1	1	0	0	1	1	.093
TOTALS	33	5	6	4	3	7	8	.185

2B: Freeman, F (5, Gausman). HR: Smith, W (1, 7th inning off Gausman, 0 on, 1 out); Muncy (2, 7th inning off Gausman, 0 on, 2 out). TB: Freeman F 2; Muncy 4; Ohtani; Pages, A; Smith, W 5. RBI: Muncy (2); Smith, W 3 (6). 2-out RBI: Smith, W; Muncy. Runners left in scoring position, 2 out: Hernández, T. Team RISP: 1-for-3. Team LOB: 4.

TORONTO	AB	R	H	RBI	BB	SO	LOB	AVG
Springer, DH	3	1	1	0	0	1	0	.259
Lukes, LF	4	0	1	0	0	2	1	.318
Guerrero Jr., 1B	4	0	1	0	0	1	2	.431
Kirk, C	3	0	0	1	0	1	2	.255
Varsho, CF	4	0	0	0	0	3	3	.255
Clement, 3B	3	0	1	0	0	0	0	.429
Barger, RF	3	0	0	0	0	1	1	.300
Kiner-Falefa, 2B	2	0	0	0	0	1	1	.200
a-Bichette, PH-2B	1	0	0	0	0	0	1	.333
Giménez, SS	3	0	0	0	0	1	1	.244
TOTALS	30	1	4	1	0	8	11	.277

a-Grounded out for Kiner-Falefa in the 7th. 2B: Springer (6, Yamamoto). TB: Clement; Guerrero Jr.; Lukes; Springer 2. RBI: Kirk (10). Runners left in scoring position, 2 out: Varsho. SF: Kirk. Team RISP: 1-for-4. Team LOB: 4.

LA DODGERS	IP	H	R	ER	BB	SO	HR	ERA
Yamamoto (W, 3-1)	9.0	4	1	1	0	8	0	1.57
TOTALS	9.0	4	1	1	0	8	0	6.35

TORONTO	IP	H	R	ER	BB	SO	HR	ERA
Gausman (L, 2-2)	6.2	4	3	3	0	6	2	2.55
Varland	0.2	2	2	2	1	0	0	4.63
Hoffman, J	0.2	0	0	0	1	1	0	1.13
Fisher	1.0	0	0	0	1	0	0	7.94
TOTALS	9.0	6	5	5	3	7	2	4.50

WP: Hoffman, J. IBB: Freeman, F (by Hoffman, J). HBP: Springer (by Yamamoto). Pitches-strikes: Yamamoto 105-73; Gausman 82-59; Varland 13-8; Hoffman, J 8-5; Fisher 14-7. Groundouts-flyouts: Yamamoto 11-3; Gausman 2-7; Varland 0-2; Hoffman, J 1-0; Fisher 0-2. Batters faced: Yamamoto 32; Gausman 24; Varland 4; Hoffman, J 3; Fisher 4. Inherited runners-scored: Hoffman, J 3-2. Umpires: HP: Adrian Johnson. 1B: John Tumpane. 2B: Alan Porter. 3B: Adam Hamari. LF: Jordan Baker. RF: Will Little. Weather: 68 degrees, Roof Closed. Wind: 0 mph, None. First pitch: 8:09 PM. T: 2:36. Att: 44,607. Venue: Rogers Centre.

GAME 3 October 27, 2025
LOS ANGELES DODGERS 6, TORONTO BLUE JAYS 5 (18)

	1	2	3	4	5	6	7	8	9	10	11	12
TORONTO	0	0	0	4	0	0	1	0	0	0	0	0
LA DODGERS	0	1	1	0	2	0	1	0	0	0	0	0

	13	14	15	16	17	18	R	H	E
TORONTO	0	0	0	0	0	5	5	15	0
LA DODGERS	0	0	0	0	1	6	6	16	2

TORONTO	AB	R	H	RBI	BB	SO	LOB	AVG
Springer, DH	3	0	0	0	0	2	1	.246
a-France, T, PH-DH	3	0	1	0	0	1	0	.333
3-Schneider, PR-DH	3	0	1	0	0	1	0	.188
Lukes, LF-RF	8	0	1	0	1	1	5	.288
Guerrero Jr., 1B	7	2	2	0	2	0	1	.414
Bichette, 2B	4	1	2	1	0	1	2	.429
1-Kiner-Falefa, PR-2B	4	0	0	0	1	2	2	.172
Varsho, CF	6	0	2	0	2	1	3	.263
Kirk, C	4	1	2	3	2	0	2	.273
4-Heineman, PR-C	3	0	0	0	0	1	3	.000
Barger, RF	4	1	2	0	0	1	2	.318
2-Straw, PR-LF	4	0	0	0	0	1	3	.133
Clement, 3B	8	0	1	0	0	1	5	.386
Giménez, SS	6	0	1	1	1	3	1	.235
TOTALS	67	5	15	5	9	16	32	.250

a-Struck out for Springer in the 7th. 1-Ran for Bichette in the 7th. 2-Ran for Barger in the 8th. 3-Ran for France, T in the 10th. 4-Ran for Kirk in the 12th. 2B: Lukes (4, Sheehan). HR: Kirk (5, 4th inning off Glasnow, 2 on, 1 out). TB: Barger 2; Bichette 2; Clement; France, T; Giménez; Guerrero Jr. 2; Kirk 5; Lukes 2; Schneider; Varsho 2. RBI: Bichette (1); Giménez (10); Kirk 3 (13). 2-out RBI: Bichette. Runners left in scoring position, 2 out: Straw; Springer; Kirk; Lukes 4; Heineman; Clement. SF: Giménez. Team RISP: 2-for-12. Team LOB: 19. PO: Bichette (1st base by Glasnow). Outfield assists: Barger (Freeman, F at home).

LA DODGERS	AB	R	H	RBI	BB	SO	LOB	AVG
Ohtani, DH	4	3	4	3	5	0	0	.283
Betts, SS	8	0	1	0	1	1	5	.250
Freeman, F, 1B	7	1	2	2	2	0	7	.231
Smith, W, C	6	0	1	0	1	4	2	.293
Muncy, 3B	7	0	0	0	1	3	3	.190
Hernández, T, RF	8	1	4	1	0	0	0	.268
Edman, 2B-CF	8	0	1	0	0	2	5	.240
Hernández, K, LF	5	1	2	0	0	3	0	.286
a-Rojas, M, PH-2B	2	0	0	0	0	0	2	.300
Pages, A, CF	5	0	0	0	0	0	1	.083
b-Call, PH-LF	3	0	1	0	0	0	1	.571
TOTALS	63	6	16	6	10	13	26	.219

a-Hit a sacrifice bunt for Hernández, K in the 13th. b-Popped out for Pages, A in the 13th. 2B: Ohtani 2 (2, Scherzer, Fluharty); Edman (2, Lauer). HR: Hernández, T (5, 2nd inning off Scherzer, 0 on, 1 out); Ohtani 2 (8, 3rd inning off Scherzer, 0 on, 1 out, 7th inning off Domínguez, 0 on, 1 out); Freeman, F (2, 18th inning off Little, B, 0 on, 0 out). TB: Betts; Call; Edman 2; Freeman, F 5; Hernández, K 2; Hernández, T 7; Ohtani 12; Smith, W. RBI: Edman (2); Hernández, T (12); Ohtani 3 (8); Freeman, F 2. 2-out RBI: Freeman, F. Runners left in scoring position, 2 out: Edman; Rojas, M; Smith, W; Freeman, F 3; Muncy; Betts. SAC: Rojas, M. Team RISP: 2-for-14. Team LOB: 18. SB: Freeman, F (1, 2nd base off Scherzer/Kirk). CS: Ohtani (1, 2nd base by Hoffman, J/Kirk). E: Edman (1, fielding); Betts (1, throw). Outfield assists: Hernández, T (Schneider at home). Pickoffs: Glasnow (Bichette at 1st base).

TORONTO	IP	H	R	ER	BB	SO	HR	ERA
Scherzer	4.1	5	3	3	1	3	2	4.50
Fluharty	0.1	2	1	1	0	0	0	6.75
Varland	1.1	2	0	0	0	2	0	4.15
Domínguez (BS, 1)	1.0	1	1	1	2	1	1	4.00
Bassitt	1.0	0	0	0	0	1	0	0.00
Hoffman, J	2.0	1	0	0	0	1	0	0.90
Fisher	1.1	1	0	0	0	1	0	6.43
Lauer	4.2	2	0	0	4	2	0	3.12
Little, B (L, 0-2)	1.0	2	1	1	1	1	1	11.25
TOTALS	17.0	16	6	6	10	13	4	3.86

LA DODGERS	IP	H	R	ER	BB	SO	HR	ERA
Glasnow	4.2	5	4	2	3	5	1	1.50
Banda	0.1	0	0	0	0	0	0	7.36
Wrobleski	1.2	0	0	0	0	2	0	0.00
Treinen	0.1	3	1	0	0	0	0	9.00
Dreyer	2.1	1	0	0	0	4	0	0.00
Sasaki	1.2	1	0	0	2	0	0	0.93
Sheehan	2.2	3	0	0	2	2	0	9.95
Kershaw	0.1	0	0	0	0	0	0	15.43
Henriquez, E	2.0	0	0	0	0	2	0	4.50
Klein (W, 1-0)	4.0	1	0	0	2	5	0	0.00
TOTALS	18.0	15	5	3	9	16	1	3.86

Little, B pitched to 1 batter in the 18th. WP: Klein. IBB: Giménez (by Sheehan); Ohtani 4 (by Hoffman, J, by Fisher, by Lauer, by Lauer); Betts (by Lauer). HBP: Varsho (by Henriquez, E); Smith, W (by Hoffman, J). Pitches-strikes: Scherzer 79-54; Fluharty 14-9; Varland 20-13; Domínguez 27-12; Bassitt 8-6; Hoffman, J 33-20; Fisher 19-15; Lauer 68-45; Little, B 29-15; Glasnow 85-56; Banda 3-2; Wrobleski 28-19; Treinen 15-12; Dreyer 5-5; Sasaki 29-13; Sheehan 37-24; Kershaw 5-2; Henriquez, E 30-23; Klein 72-49. Groundouts-flyouts: Scherzer 1-5; Fluharty 0-1; Varland 0-1; Domínguez 1-1; Bassitt 0-2; Hoffman, J 0-1; Fisher 0-1; Lauer 3-4; Little, B 1-0; Glasnow 3-5; Banda 0-0; Wrobleski 3-0; Treinen 1-0; Dreyer 1-1; Sasaki 3-1; Sheehan 2-1; Kershaw 1-0; Henriquez, E 2-2; Klein 3-1. Batters faced: Scherzer 18; Fluharty 3; Varland 5; Domínguez 6; Bassitt 3; Hoffman, J 8; Fisher 6; Lauer 20; Little, B 6; Glasnow 22; Banda 1; Wrobleski 6; Treinen 4; Dreyer 3; Sasaki 7; Sheehan 12; Kershaw 1; Henriquez, E 7; Klein 15. Inherited runners-scored: Fluharty 1-1; Varland 1-0; Banda 1-1; Kershaw 3-0. Umpires: HP: Mark Wegner. 1B: Alan Porter. 2B: Adam Hamari. 3B: Jordan Baker. LF: Will Little. RF: Adrian Johnson. Weather: 71 degrees, Clear. Wind: 9 mph, Varies. First pitch: 5:11 PM. T: 6:39. Att: 52,654. Venue: Dodger Stadium.

GAME 4 October 28, 2025
TORONTO BLUE JAYS 6, LOS ANGELES DODGERS 2

	1	2	3	4	5	6	7	8	9	R	H	E
TORONTO	0	0	2	0	0	0	4	0	0	6	11	0
LA DODGERS	0	1	0	0	0	0	0	1	2	6	0	

TORONTO	AB	R	H	RBI	BB	SO	LOB	AVG
Lukes, LF	3	1	2	0	0	0	0	.309
a-France, T, PH	1	0	0	0	0	0	1	.250
Straw, LF	1	0	0	0	0	1	2	.125
Guerrero Jr., 1B	4	2	2	2	1	1	1	.419
Bichette, DH	4	0	1	1	0	0	1	.364
Barger, RF	5	2	1	1	0	1	1	.327
Kirk, C	4	0	0	0	1	2	4	.254
Varsho, CF	5	1	1	0	0	2	2	.258
Clement, 3B	4	1	2	0	0	1	0	.393
Giménez, SS	3	1	1	0	1	0	1	.241
Kiner-Falefa, 2B	4	0	0	0	0	0	4	.152
TOTALS	38	6	11	6	3	9	16	.259

a-Grounded out for Lukes in the 7th. 2B: Clement (4, Ohtani). HR: Guerrero Jr. (7, 3rd inning off Ohtani, 1 on, 1 out). TB: Barger 2; Bichette; Clement 3; Giménez; Guerrero Jr. 6; Lukes 2; Varsho. RBI: Barger (9); Bichette (2); Fisher, T (1); Giménez (11); Guerrero Jr. 2 (14). 2-out RBI: Barger; Bichette. Runners left in scoring position, 2 out: Varsho; Straw 2; Kirk 2. Team RISP: 3-for-11. Team LOB: 9. DP: (Giménez-Kiner-Falefa-Guerrero Jr.).

LA DODGERS	AB	R	H	RBI	BB	SO	LOB	AVG
Ohtani, P-DH	3	0	0	0	1	2	0	.268
Betts, SS	4	0	1	0	0	1	2	.250
Freeman, F, 1B	4	0	2	0	0	1	2	.250
Smith, W, C	4	0	0	0	0	4	0	.267
Hernández, T, RF	3	1	1	0	1	0	0	.271
Muncy, 3B	3	1	1	0	1	1	2	.200
Edman, 2B	3	0	1	1	1	1	3	.245
Hernández, K, LF-CF	3	0	0	1	0	1	2	.269
Pages, A, CF	2	0	0	0	0	1	1	.080
a-Call, PH-LF	2	0	0	0	0	0	1	.444
TOTALS	31	2	6	2	4	7	16	.214

a-Struck out for Pages, A in the 7th. 2B: Muncy (2, Varland). TB: Betts; Edman; Freeman, F 2; Hernández, T; Muncy 2. RBI: Edman (7); Hernández, K (6). Runners left in scoring position, 2 out: Edman; Call. SF: Hernández, K. GIDP: Smith, W. Team RISP: 0-for-5. Team LOB: 7.

TORONTO	IP	H	R	ER	BB	SO	HR	ERA
Bieber (W, 2-0)	5.1	4	1	1	3	3	0	3.57
Fluharty (H, 1)	0.2	0	0	0	0	1	0	6.00
Bassitt	2.0	2	0	0	0	2	0	0.00
Varland	1.0	1	1	1	1	1	0	4.50
TOTALS	9.0	6	2	2	4	7	0	3.48

LA DODGERS	IP	H	R	ER	BB	SO	HR	ERA
Ohtani (L, 2-1)	6.0	6	4	4	1	6	1	3.50
Banda	0.2	1	2	2	1	2	0	10.38
Treinen	0.1	2	0	0	0	0	0	8.31
Dreyer	2.0	2	0	0	1	3	0	0.00
TOTALS	9.0	11	6	6	3	9	1	4.30

Balk: Varland. Disengagement violations: Varland. IBB: Guerrero Jr. (by Banda); Kirk (by Dreyer). HBP: Giménez (by Dreyer). Pitches-strikes: Bieber 81-48; Fluharty

Andy Pages' acrobatic catch was crucial to the Dodgers' Game 7 win.

4-4; Bassitt 20-14; Varland 20-11; Ohtani 93-60; Banda 15-9; Treinen 8-6; Dreyer 29-23. Groundouts-flyouts: Bieber 3-7; Fluharty 0-1; Bassitt 3-0; Varland 1-0; Ohtani 5-4; Banda 1-0; Treinen 0-0; Dreyer 2-0. Batters faced: Bieber 23; Fluharty 2; Bassitt 6; Varland 5; Ohtani 25; Banda 4; Treinen 3; Dreyer 10. Inherited runners-scored: Fluharty 2-0; Banda 2-2; Treinen 2-2. Umpires: HP: John Tumpane. 1B: Adam Hamari. 2B: Jordan Baker. 3B: Will Little. LF: Adrian Johnson. RF: Mark Wegner. Weather: 85 degrees, Clear. Wind: 9 mph, Varies. First pitch: 5:11 PM. T: 2:54. Att: 52,552. Venue: Dodger Stadium.

GAME 5 October 29, 2025

TORONTO BLUE JAYS 6, LOS ANGELES DODGERS 1

	1	2	3	4	5	6	7	8	9	R	H	E
TORONTO	2	0	0	1	0	0	2	1	0	6	9	0
LA DODGERS	0	0	1	0	0	0	0	0	0	1	4	0

TORONTO	AB	R	H	RBI	BB	SO	LOB	AVG
Schneider, LF	3	1	1	1	1	2	2	.211
Straw, LF	1	0	0	0	0	0	1	.118
Guerrero Jr., 1B	3	1	1	0	2	0	1	.415
Bichette, DH	5	0	1	1	0	1	1	.313
Kirk, C	4	0	1	0	1	1	1	.254
Varsho, CF	4	1	1	0	0	0	4	.258
Clement, 3B	3	1	1	1	0	0	0	.391
Barger, RF	3	1	2	0	1	0	1	.346
Kiner-Falefa, 2B	4	0	1	1	0	1	3	.162
Giménez, SS	3	1	0	1	2	3	.228
TOTALS	33	6	9	5	6	7	17	.261

3B: Varsho (1, Snell). HR: Schneider (1, 1st inning off Snell, 0 on, 0 out); Guerrero Jr. (8, 1st inning off Snell, 0 on, 0 out). TB: Barger 2; Bichette; Clement; Guerrero Jr. 4; Kiner-Falefa; Kirk; Schneider 4; Varsho 3. RBI: Bichette (3); Clement (9); Guerrero Jr. (15); Kiner-Falefa (2); Schneider (1). 2-out RBI: Bichette (3); Clement (9); Guerrero Jr. Team RISP: 2-for-7. Team LOB: 7. SB: Kiner-Falefa (1, 2nd base off Banda/Smith, W). CS: Varsho (1, 2nd base by Snell/Smith, W). DP: (Clement-Kiner-Falefa-Guerrero Jr.).

LA DODGERS	AB	R	H	RBI	BB	SO	LOB	AVG
Ohtani, DH	4	0	0	0	0	1	1	.250
Smith, W, C	4	0	1	0	0	2	0	.265
Betts, SS	4	0	0	0	0	2	1	.234
Freeman, F, 1B	3	0	0	0	0	3	1	.237
Hernández, T, RF	4	0	2	0	0	2	1	.286
Edman, 2B	3	0	0	0	0	1	3	.232
Muncy, 3B	3	0	0	0	0	1	0	.188
Hernández, K, CF	3	1	1	1	0	2	0	.273
Call, LF	2	0	0	0	1	1	0	.364
TOTALS	30	1	4	1	1	15	7	.201

HR: Hernández, K (1, 3rd inning off Yesavage, 0 on, 1 out). TB: Hernández, K 4; Hernández, T 2; Smith, W. RBI: Hernández, K (7). Runners left in scoring position, 2 out: Edman. GIDP: Edman. Team RISP: 0-for-1. Team LOB: 4. DP: (Snell-Edman-Freeman, F).

TORONTO	IP	H	R	ER	BB	SO	HR	ERA
Yesavage (W, 3-1)	7.0	3	1	1	0	12	1	3.46
Domínguez	1.0	0	0	0	1	1	0	3.60
Hoffman, J	1.0	1	0	0	0	2	0	0.82
TOTALS	9.0	4	1	1	1	15	1	3.06

LA DODGERS	IP	H	R	ER	BB	SO	HR	ERA
Snell (L, 3-2)	6.2	6	5	5	4	7	2	3.31
Henríquez, E	0.0	1	0	0	2	0	0	4.50
Banda	1.1	2	1	1	0	0	0	9.53
Treinen	1.0	0	0	0	0	0	0	6.75
TOTALS	9.0	9	6	6	6	7	2	4.58

Henríquez, E pitched to 3 batters in the 7th. WP: Snell 2; Henríquez, E; Banda. HBP: Freeman, F (by Yesavage). Pitches-strikes: Yesavage 104-71; Domínguez 13-9; Hoffman, J 22-13; Snell 116-69; Henríquez, E 15-4; Banda 20-15; Treinen 13-9. Groundouts-flyouts: Yesavage 4-1; Domínguez 2-0; Hoffman, J 0-1; Snell 7-1; Henríquez, E 0-0; Banda 2-1; Treinen 3-0. Batters faced: Yesavage 24; Domínguez 4; Hoffman, J 4; Snell 28; Henríquez, E 3; Banda 6; Treinen 3. Inherited runners-scored: Henríquez, E 2-2; Banda 3-0. Umpires: HP: Alan Porter. 1B: Jordan Baker. 2B: Will Little. 3B: Adrian Johnson. LF: Mark Wegner. RF: John Tumpane. Weather: 86 degrees, Clear. Wind: 10 mph, Out To RF. First pitch: 5:10 PM. T: 3:02. Att: 52,175. Venue: Dodger Stadium.

GAME 6 October 31, 2025

LOS ANGELES DODGERS 3, TORONTO BLUE JAYS 1

	1	2	3	4	5	6	7	8	9	R	H	E
LA DODGERS	0	0	3	0	0	0	0	0	0	3	4	1
TORONTO	0	0	1	0	0	0	0	0	0	1	8	0

LA DODGERS	AB	R	H	RBI	BB	SO	LOB	AVG
Ohtani, DH	3	1	1	0	1	1	0	.254
Smith, W, C	3	1	1	1	1	1	0	.269
Freeman, F, 1B	3	0	0	0	1	1	2	.226
Betts, SS	3	0	1	2	1	0	0	.239
Hernández, T, RF	4	0	0	0	0	3	5	.269
Pages, A, RF	0	0	0	0	0	0	0	.080
Muncy, 3B	4	0	0	0	0	2	0	.173
Hernández, K, LF	4	0	0	0	0	3	0	.254
Edman, CF	4	1	1	0	0	0	0	.233
Dean, CF	0	0	0	0	0	0	0	.000
Rojas, M, 2B	3	0	0	0	0	1	1	.231
TOTALS	31	3	4	3	4	12	8	.191

2B: Edman (3, Gausman); Smith, W (1, Gausman); Ohtani (3, Fluharty). TB: Betts; Edman 2; Ohtani 2; Smith, W 2. RBI: Betts 2 (8); Smith, W (7). 2-out RBI: Smith, W; Betts 2. Runners left in scoring position, 2 out: Hernández, T 3. Team RISP: 2-for-6. Team LOB: 5. E: Muncy (3, fielding). Outfield assists: Hernández, K (Barger at 2nd base). DP: 3 (Muncy-Rojas, M-Freeman, F; Rojas, M-Betts-Freeman, F; Hernández, K-Rojas, M).

TORONTO	AB	R	H	RBI	BB	SO	LOB	AVG
Springer, DH	4	0	2	1	0	0	0	.262
Lukes, LF	4	0	0	0	0	0	2	.288
Guerrero Jr., 1B	3	0	1	0	1	1	0	.412
Bichette, 2B	3	0	0	1	0	1	2	.316
Varsho, CF	4	0	0	0	0	1	5	.243
Kirk, C	3	0	0	0	0	2	0	.242
1-Straw, PR	0	0	0	0	0	0	0	.118
Barger, RF	4	1	2	0	0	1	0	.357
Clement, 3B	4	0	2	0	0	1	3	.397
Giménez, SS	4	0	1	0	0	1	5	.213
TOTALS	33	1	8	1	2	8	18	.258

2B: Barger 2 (4, Yamamoto, Sasaki); Guerrero Jr. (4, Yamamoto); Clement (5, Wroblewski). TB: Barger 4; Bichette; Clement 3; Guerrero Jr. 2; Springer 2. RBI: Springer (10). 2-out RBI: Springer. Runners left in scoring position, 2 out: Varsho; Giménez. GIDP: Guerrero Jr.; Varsho. Team RISP: 1-for-9. Team LOB: 8.

MAJOR LEAGUES

Will Smith's game-winning two-out 11th-inning home run in Game 7 gave the Dodgers back-to-back titles.

LA DODGERS	IP	H	R	ER	BB	SO	HR	ERA
Yamamoto (W, 4-1)	6.0	5	1	1	1	6	0	1.56
Wrobleski (H, 1)	1.0	1	0	0	0	2	0	0.00
Sasaki (H, 2)	1.0	2	0	0	1	0	0	0.84
Glasnow (S, 1)	1.0	0	0	0	0	0	0	1.42
TOTALS	9.0	8	1	1	2	8	0	4.06

TORONTO	IP	H	R	ER	BB	SO	HR	ERA
Gausman (L, 2-3)	6.0	3	3	3	2	8	0	2.93
Varland	1.1	0	0	0	0	1	0	4.11
Fluharty	0.1	1	0	0	1	0	0	5.68
Domínguez	0.1	0	0	0	1	1	0	3.48
Bassitt	1.0	0	0	0	0	2	0	0.00
TOTALS	9.0	4	3	3	4	12	0	3.05

Sasaki pitched to 2 batters in the 9th. IBB: Ohtani (by Gausman); Smith, W (by Fluharty). HBP: Kirk (by Sasaki). Pitches-strikes: Yamamoto 96-63; Wrobleski 16-12; Sasaki 33-18; Glasnow 3-2; Gausman 93-63; Varland 17-10; Fluharty 8-5; Domínguez 10-5; Bassitt 13-10. Groundouts-flyouts: Yamamoto 6-3; Wrobleski 1-0; Sasaki 1-1; Glasnow 0-0; Gausman 5-1; Varland 0-2; Fluharty 0-1; Domínguez 0-0; Bassitt 1-0. Batters faced: Yamamoto 25; Wrobleski 4; Sasaki 7; Glasnow 2; Gausman 23; Varland 4; Fluharty 3; Domínguez 2; Bassitt 3. Inherited runners-scored: Glasnow 2-0; Domínguez 2-0. Umpires: HP: Will Little. 1B: John Tumpane. 2B: Adrian Johnson. 3B: Mark Wegner. LF: John Tumpane. RF: Alan Porter. Weather: 72 degrees, Roof Closed. Wind: 0 mph, None. First pitch: 8:10 PM. T: 3:02. Att: 44,710. Venue: Rogers Centre.

GAME 7 November 1, 2025
LOS ANGELES DODGERS 3, TORONTO BLUE JAYS 1

	1	2	3	4	5	6	7	8	9	10	11	R	H	E
LA DODGERS	0	0	0	1	0	0	1	1	0	0	1	5	11	0
TORONTO	0	0	3	0	0	1	0	0	0	0	0	4	14	0

LA DODGERS	AB	R	H	RBI	BB	SO	LOB	AVG
Ohtani, P-DH	5	0	2	0	1	0	0	.265
Smith, W, C	6	2	2	1	0	1	4	.276
Freeman, F, 1B	6	0	1	0	0	0	4	.221
Betts, SS	3	1	0	0	2	0	3	.229
Muncy, 3B	4	1	3	1	1	1	0	.214
Hernández, T, RF	3	0	0	1	1	0	2	.257
Dean, CF	0	0	0	0	0	0	0	.000
Edman, 3B	3	0	0	1	0	2	0	.222
Pages, A, CF-RF	1	0	0	0	0	0	3	.078
Hernández, K, LF	5	0	1	0	0	2	3	.250
Rojas, M, 2B	5	1	2	1	0	1	2	.278
Kim, 2B	0	0	0	0	0	0	0	.000
TOTALS	41	5	11	5	5	5	23	.203

2B: Smith, W (2, Scherzer). HR: Muncy (3, 8th inning off Yesavage, 0 on, 1 out); Rojas, M (1, 9th inning off Hoffman, J, 0 on, 1 out); Smith, W (2, 11th inning off Bieber, 0 on, 2 out). TB: Freeman, F; Hernández, K; Muncy 6; Ohtani 2; Rojas, M 5; Smith, W 6. RBI: Edman (8); Hernández, T (13); Muncy (3); Rojas, M (2); Smith, W (8). 2-out RBI: Smith, W. Runners left in scoring position, 2 out: Edman; Rojas, M; Freeman, F; Betts. SF: Edman; Hernández, T. GIDP: Freeman, F. Team RISP: 1-for-11. Team LOB: 10. DP: (Smith, W-Rojas, M; Betts-Freeman, F).

TORONTO	AB	R	H	RBI	BB	SO	LOB	AVG
Springer, DH	6	1	3	0	0	3	2	.284

	AB	R	H	RBI	BB	SO	LOB	AVG
Lukes, LF	3	0	0	0	0	2	4	.274
Schneider, PH	1	0	0	0	0	1	1	.200
Straw, LF	1	0	0	0	0	0	0	.111
Guerrero Jr., 1B	5	1	1	0	1	1	4	.397
Bichette, 2B	4	1	2	3	1	1	0	.348
Kiner-Falefa, PR-2B	0	0	0	0	0	0	0	.162
Barger, RF	4	0	2	0	2	1	0	.367
Kirk, C	5	0	2	0	0	0	5	.254
Varsho, CF	5	0	0	0	0	2	8	.227
Clement, 3B	5	1	3	0	0	0	3	.411
Giménez, SS	4	0	1	0	1	0	4	.215
TOTALS	43	4	14	4	4	12	31	.269

2B: Giménez (2, Glasnow); Clement (6, Sheehan); Guerrero Jr. (5, Yamamoto). HR: Bichette (1, 3rd inning off Ohtani, 2 on, 1 out). TB: Barger 2; Bichette 5; Clement 4; Giménez 2; Guerrero Jr. 2; Kirk 2; Springer 3. RBI: Bichette 3 (6); Giménez (12). Runners left in scoring position, 2 out: Schneider; Guerrero Jr. 2; Giménez 2; Clement 2. SAC: Kiner-Falefa; Lukes. GIDP: Kirk. Team RISP: 3-for-17. Team LOB: 14. SB: Clement (1, 2nd base off Glasnow/Smith, W). CS: Springer (1, 2nd base by Ohtani/Smith, W). DP: (Guerrero Jr.-Giménez-Guerrero Jr.).

LA DODGERS	IP	H	R	ER	BB	SO	HR	ERA
Ohtani	2.1	5	3	3	2	3	1	4.43
Wrobleski	1.1	2	0	0	0	2	0	0.00
Glasnow	2.1	3	1	1	0	2	0	1.69
Sheehan	1.0	2	0	0	0	2	0	8.59
Snell	1.1	1	0	0	1	2	0	3.18
Yamamoto (W, 5-1)	2.2	1	0	0	1	1	0	1.45
TOTALS	11.0	14	4	4	4	12	1	3.95

TORONTO	IP	H	R	ER	BB	SO	HR	ERA
Scherzer	4.1	4	1	1	1	3	0	3.77
Varland	0.2	1	0	0	0	0	0	3.94
Bassitt (H, 2)	1.0	2	1	1	1	0	0	1.04
Yesavage (H, 1)	1.2	1	1	1	1	0	1	3.58
Hoffman, J (BS, 1)	1.1	1	1	1	0	2	1	1.46
Domínguez	1.0	1	0	0	2	0	0	3.18
Bieber (L, 2-1)	1.0	1	1	1	0	0	1	3.86
TOTALS	11.0	11	5	5	5	5	3	3.21

Sheehan pitched to 1 batter in the 8th. WP: Ohtani. IBB: Guerrero Jr. (by Ohtani). HBP: Giménez (by Wrobleski); Kirk (by Yamamoto). Pitches-strikes: Ohtani 51-31; Wrobleski 21-15; Glasnow 38-23; Sheehan 20-14; Snell 28-16; Yamamoto 34-21; Scherzer 54-34; Varland 9-7; Bassitt 26-16; Yesavage 21-13; Hoffman, J 22-13; Domínguez 27-13; Bieber 13-8. Groundouts-flyouts: Ohtani 1-1; Wrobleski 1-0; Glasnow 2-0; Sheehan 1-0; Snell 0-1; Yamamoto 4-2; Scherzer 2-5; Varland 0-2; Bassitt 2-1; Yesavage 3-1; Hoffman, J 1-1; Domínguez 2-1; Bieber 3-0. Batters faced: Ohtani 13; Wrobleski 7; Glasnow 10; Sheehan 5; Snell 6; Yamamoto 10; Scherzer 18; Varland 3; Bassitt 6; Yesavage 6; Hoffman, J 5; Domínguez 6; Bieber 4. Inherited runners-scored: Glasnow 2-0; Snell 1-0; Yamamoto 2-0; Varland 1-0. Umpires: HP: Jordan Baker. 1B: Adrian Johnson. 2B: Mark Wegner. 3B: John Tumpane. LF: Alan Porter. RF: Adam Hamari. Weather: 68 degrees, Roof Closed. Wind: 0 mph, None. First pitch: 8:10 PM. T: 4:07. Att: 44,713. Venue: Rogers Centre.

AMERICAN LEAGUE WILD CARD SERIES

DETROIT TIGERS VS. CLEVELAND GUARDIANS

DETROIT	AVG	G	AB	R	H	2B	3B	HR	RBI	BB	SO	SB
Báez, Javier	.455	3	11	1	5	1	0	0	1	0	1	0
Carpenter, Kerry	.400	3	10	2	4	1	0	0	1	4	3	0
Greene, Riley	.364	3	11	2	4	2	0	0	1	1	3	0
Meadows, Parker	.250	3	12	2	3	0	0	0	0	1	3	0
Torkelson, Spencer	.182	3	11	0	2	0	0	0	2	1	5	0
Torres, Gleyber	.154	3	13	0	2	0	0	0	0	3	0	0
Dingler, Dillon	.100	3	10	1	1	0	0	1	1	3	5	0
Pérez, Wenceel	.077	3	13	1	1	0	0	0	2	0	4	0
Ibáñez, Andy	.000	1	0	0	0	0	0	0	0	0	0	0
Jones, Jahmai	.000	1	1	0	0	0	0	0	0	0	1	0
Malloy, Justin-Henry	.000	1	1	0	0	0	0	0	0	0	0	0
McKinstry, Zach	.000	3	8	0	0	0	0	0	1	3	4	0
Totals	.218	3	101	9	22	4	0	1	9	13	33	0

DETROIT	W	L	ERA	G	GS	SV	IP	H	R	ER	BB	SO
Finnegan, Kyle	1	0	0.00	2	0	0	3.0	0	0	0	1	1
Holton, Tyler	0	0	0.00	2	0	0	3.1	2	0	0	0	2
Kahnle, Tommy	0	0	0.00	1	0	0	0.1	2	2	0	0	0
Vest, Will	0	0	0.00	2	0	1	3.0	1	0	0	0	2
Skubal, Tarik	1	0	1.17	1	1	0	7.2	3	1	1	3	14
Flaherty, Jack	0	0	1.93	1	1	0	4.2	3	1	1	2	4
Mize, Casey	0	0	3.00	1	1	0	3.0	1	1	1	2	1
Hurter, Brant	0	0	13.50	1	0	0	0.2	1	1	1	0	0
Melton, Troy	0	1	108.00	1	0	0	0.1	3	4	4	1	0
Totals	2	1	2.77	3	3	1	26.0	16	10	8	9	24

CLEVELAND	AVG	G	AB	R	H	2B	3B	HR	RBI	BB	SO	SB
Martínez, Angel	.333	1	3	1	1	0	0	0	0	0	2	0
Schneemann, Daniel	.333	3	3	1	1	1	0	0	1	0	1	0
Valera, George	.286	3	7	2	2	1	0	1	1	0	2	0
Ramírez, Jose	.250	3	8	1	2	0	0	0	1	4	2	0
Rocchio, Brayan	.222	3	9	2	2	0	0	1	1	3	0	0
Arias, Gabriel	.200	3	10	0	2	0	0	0	1	0	3	0
DeLauter, Chase	.167	2	6	0	1	0	0	0	0	1	1	0
Kayfus, C.J.	.167	3	6	0	1	0	0	0	0	1	0	0
Kwan, Steven	.167	3	12	2	2	2	0	0	0	0	1	0
Naylor, Bo	.125	3	8	1	1	0	0	1	3	0	1	0
Manzardo, Kyle	.091	3	11	0	1	0	0	0	0	1	3	0
Halpin, Petey	.000	2	0	0	0	0	0	0	0	0	0	0
Hedges, Austin	.000	1	1	0	0	0	0	0	0	2	1	0
Noel, Jhonkensy	.000	1	3	0	0	0	0	0	0	0	3	0
Rodriguez, Johnathan	.000	2	3	0	0	0	0	0	0	2	0	0
Totals	.178	3	90	10	16	4	0	3	8	9	24	0

CLEVELAND	W	L	ERA	G	GS	SV	IP	H	R	ER	BB	SO
Festa, Matt	0	0	0.00	1	0	0	0.2	0	0	0	1	1
Herrin, Tim	0	0	0.00	2	0	0	1.1	1	0	0	0	3
Junis, Jake	0	0	0.00	2	0	0	1.2	0	0	0	1	0
Smith, Cade	1	0	0.00	3	0	0	3.1	0	0	0	2	4
Williams, Gavin	0	1	0.00	1	1	0	6.0	5	2	0	1	8
Bibee, Tanner	0	0	1.93	1	1	0	4.2	5	1	1	3	6
Cantillo, Joet	0	1	3.38	1	0	0	2.2	2	1	1	2	3
Cecconi, Slade	0	0	3.86	1	1	0	2.1	2	1	1	1	3
Gaddis, Hunter	0	0	6.75	3	0	0	2.2	5	2	2	1	3
Sabrowski, Erik	0	0	10.80	3	0	0	1.2	2	2	2	1	2
Totals	1	2	2.33	3	3	0	27.0	22	9	7	13	33

SCORE BY INNINGS

DETROIT	1	0	1	1	0	1	5	0	0	9
CLEVELAND	1	0	0	2	0	0	7	0	10	

BOSTON RED SOX VS. NEW YORK YANKEES

BOSTON	AVG	G	AB	R	H	2B	3B	HR	RBI	BB	SO	SB
Masataka Yoshida	.571	3	7	0	4	0	0	0	2	0	1	0
Nate Eaton	.400	2	5	0	2	1	0	0	0	1	1	0
Trevor Story	.385	3	13	2	5	0	0	1	3	0	4	1
Nick Sogard	.333	2	6	1	2	1	0	0	0	0	1	0
Alex Bregman	.300	3	10	0	3	1	0	0	1	3	2	0
Nathaniel Lowe	.143	3	7	0	1	0	0	0	0	0	1	0
Romy Gonzalez	.111	3	9	0	1	0	0	0	0	0	3	0
Jarren Duran	.091	3	11	1	1	0	0	0	0	4	3	0
Carlos Narvaez	.000	3	8	0	0	0	0	0	3	4	0	0
Ceddanne Rafaela	.000	3	10	2	0	0	0	0	2	4	0	0
Rob Refsnyder	.000	2	5	0	0	0	0	0	1	2	0	0
Wilyer Abreu	.000	3	5	0	0	0	0	0	0	3	0	0
Totals	.198	33	96	6	19	3	0	1	6	10	30	1

BOSTON	W	L	ERA	G	GS	SV	IP	H	R	ER	BB	SO
Aroldis Chapman	0	0	0.00	2	0	1	2.1	4	0	0	0	5
Greg Weissert	0	0	0.00	1	0	0	1.0	0	0	0	0	0
Justin Wilson	0	0	0.00	1	0	0	1.2	0	0	0	0	0
Payton Tolle	0	0	0.00	1	0	0	0.1	0	0	0	0	0
Steven Matz	0	0	0.00	2	0	0	2.0	3	0	0	0	2
Zack Kelly	0	0	0.00	1	0	0	0.1	0	0	0	0	1
Garrett Crochet	1	0	1.17	1	1	0	7.2	4	1	1	0	11
Justin Slaten	0	0	4.50	2	0	0	2.0	1	1	1	1	1
Garrett Whitlock	0	1	5.40	1	0	0	1.2	3	1	1	2	3
Connelly Early	0	1	7.36	1	1	0	3.2	6	4	3	1	6
Brayan Bello	0	0	7.71	1	1	0	2.1	4	2	2	1	0
Totals	1	2	2.88	14	3	1	25.0	25	9	8	5	29

NY YANKEES	AVG	G	AB	R	H	2B	3B	HR	RBI	BB	SO	SB
Paul Goldschmidt	.600	2	5	0	3	0	0	0	0	0	1	0
Aaron Judge	.364	3	11	0	4	0	0	0	1	0	2	0
Anthony Volpe	.364	3	11	1	4	0	0	1	2	0	5	0
Ben Rice	.286	2	7	1	2	0	0	1	2	0	3	0
Cody Bellinger	.250	3	12	2	3	1	0	0	0	0	1	0
Jazz Chisholm	.250	3	8	2	2	0	0	0	0	3	3	0
Ryan McMahon	.250	2	4	0	1	0	0	0	0	1	2	0
Austin Wells	.222	3	9	0	2	0	0	0	2	1	3	0
Amed Rosario	.167	2	6	1	1	0	0	0	1	0	1	0
Trent Grisham	.167	3	12	1	2	1	0	0	0	1	5	1
Giancarlo Stanton	.091	3	11	1	1	1	0	0	0	1	2	0
Jose Caballero	.000	1	3	0	0	0	0	0	0	0	0	0
Totals	.194	35	62	3	12	1	0	0	3	5	15	1

NY YANKEES	W	L	ERA	G	GS	SV	IP	H	R	ER	BB	SO
Cam Schlittler	1	0	0.00	1	1	0	8.0	5	0	0	0	12
Devin Williams	1	0	0.00	2	0	0	2.0	1	0	0	1	1
Fernando Cruz	0	0	0.00	2	0	0	1.2	1	0	0	1	1
Luke Weaver	0	1	0.00	1	0	0	0.0	2	2	1	2	0
Max Fried	0	0	0.00	1	1	0	6.1	4	0	0	3	6
Tim Hill	0	0	0.00	1	0	0	0.1	0	0	0	0	0
David Bednar	0	0	3.38	3	0	1	2.2	2	1	1	1	4
Carlos Rodon	0	0	4.50	1	1	0	6.0	4	3	3	3	6
Totals	2	1	2.00	12	3	1	27.0	19	6	6	10	30

SCORE BY INNINGS

BOSTON	0	0	2	0	0	1	2	0	1	6
NY YANKEES	2	1	0	4	1	0	2	1	0	9

AMERICAN LEAGUE DIVISION SERIES

NEW YORK YANKEES VS. TORONTO BLUE JAYS

NY YANKEES	AVG	G	AB	R	H	2B	3B	HR	RBI	BB	SO	SB
Aaron Judge	.600	4	15	5	9	2	0	1	6	4	3	0
Amed Rosario	.500	2	4	1	2	1	0	0	0	0	0	0
Ryan McMahon	.300	4	10	2	3	0	0	1	0	0	0	0
Giancarlo Stanton	.267	4	15	0	4	1	0	0	4	2	4	0
Paul Goldschmidt	.250	3	4	1	1	0	0	0	0	1	0	0
Austin Wells	.231	4	13	1	3	0	0	0	1	0	3	0
Cody Bellinger	.188	4	16	2	3	1	0	1	4	2	4	0
Ben Rice	.182	4	11	1	2	1	0	0	2	2	5	0
Jazz Chisholm	.143	4	14	1	2	0	0	0	1	2	2	0
Trent Grisham	.118	4	17	3	2	1	0	0	0	2	5	0
Anthony Volpe	.067	4	15	1	1	0	0	0	0	0	11	0
Jasson Dominguez	.000	1	1	1	1	0	0	0	0	0	0	0
Jose Caballero	.000	2	1	0	1	0	0	0	0	0	0	0
Totals	.250	44	136	19	34	9	0	4	19	15	37	0

NY YANKEES	W	L	ERA	G	GS	SV	IP	H	R	ER	BB	SO
David Bednar	0	0	0.00	2	0	1	3.1	1	0	0	0	5
Devin Williams	0	0	0.00	2	0	0	2.0	2	0	0	1	3
Tim Hill	1	0	0.00	2	0	0	2.2	1	0	0	0	1
Camilo Doval	0	0	2.70	3	0	0	3.1	3	1	1	0	1
Cam Schlittler	0	1	2.84	1	1	0	6.1	8	4	2	0	2
Fernando Cruz	0	0	4.50	2	0	0	2.0	2	1	1	1	3
Luis Gil	0	1	6.75	1	1	0	2.2	4	2	2	0	2
Will Warren	0	0	11.57	1	0	0	4.2	7	6	6	1	4
Max Fried	0	1	21.00	1	1	0	3.0	8	7	7	2	1

Carlos Rodon	0	0	23.14	1	1	0	2.1	6	6	2	2
Paul Blackburn	0	0	27.00	1	0	0	1.1	6	4	0	0
Luke Weaver	0	0	81.00	2	0	0	0.1	2	3	3	1	0
Totals	1	3	8.47	19	4	1	34.0	50	34	32	8	24

TORONTO	AVG	G	AB	R	H	2B	3B	HR	RBI	BB	SO	SB
Ernie Clement	.643	4	14	5	9	1	0	1	5	0	0	0
Vladimir Guerrero	.529	4	17	5	9	0	3	9	2	1	0
Daulton Varsho	.438	4	16	7	7	3	0	2	4	1	3	0
Myles Straw	.400	3	5	2	2	0	0	0	1	1	1	0
Nathan Lukes	.333	4	12	0	4	2	0	0	5	0	1	0
Addison Barger	.333	3	12	0	4	1	0	0	0	0	4	0
Davis Schneider	.333	2	6	3	2	1	0	0	2	3	0
Andres Gimenez	.267	4	15	4	4	1	0	0	2	0	1	1
Alejandro Kirk	.222	4	18	4	4	1	0	2	3	0	1	0
Anthony Santander	.200	3	10	0	2	0	0	0	2	0	3	0
George Springer	.176	4	17	4	3	2	0	1	2	2	5	0
Isiah Kiner-Falefa	.000	3	6	0	0	0	0	0	0	1	0
Totals	.338	42	148	34	50	12	0	9	33	8	24	1

TORONTO	W	L	ERA	G	GS	SV	IP	H	R	ER	BB	SO
Seranthony Dominguez	1	0	0.00	3	0	0	3.1	0	0	0	3	3
Trey Yesavage	1	0	0.00	1	1	0	5.1	0	0	0	1	11
Yariel Rodriguez	0	0	0.00	2	0	0	1.2	0	0	0	1	0
Kevin Gausman	1	0	1.59	1	1	0	5.2	4	1	1	2	3
Brendon Little	0	0	3.38	3	0	0	2.2	3	1	1	2	1
Jeff Hoffman	0	0	3.86	2	0	1	2.1	2	1	1	1	2
Louie Varland	0	1	4.50	4	1	0	4.0	4	2	2	0	5
Braydon Fisher	0	0	5.40	3	0	0	1.2	4	1	1	1	3
Shane Bieber	0	0	6.75	1	1	0	2.2	5	3	2	1	2
Mason Fluharty	0	0	9.00	3	0	0	2.0	1	3	2	1	4
Eric Lauer	0	0	13.50	2	0	0	2.0	3	3	3	1	3
Tommy Nance	0	0	13.50	2	0	0	1.1	5	2	2	1	0
Justin Bruihl	0	0	54.00	1	0	0	0.1	3	2	2	0	0
Totals	3	1	4.37	28	4	1	35.0	34	19	17	15	37

SCORE BY INNING

NY YANKEES	1	0	3	3	2	4	5	0	1	19
TORONTO	4	3	7	6	2	1	6	5	0	34

DETROIT TIGERS VS. SEATTLE MARINERS

SEATTLE	AVG	G	AB	R	H	2B	3B	HR	RBI	BB	SO	SB
Cal Raleigh	.381	5	21	2	8	1	0	1	4	4	7	0
Leo Rivas	.333	1	3	0	1	0	0	0	1	1	2	0
J.P. Crawford	.263	5	19	3	5	0	0	1	2	1	5	0
Josh Naylor	.261	5	23	3	6	2	0	0	0	1	1	1
Mitch Garver	.200	4	5	0	1	0	0	0	1	1	2	0
Jorge Polanco	.182	5	22	3	4	0	0	2	3	2	8	0
Randy Arozarena	.174	5	23	3	4	1	0	0	1	1	8	1
Julio Rodriguez	.174	5	23	1	4	1	0	1	3	2	9	0
Dominic Canzone	.167	3	6	1	1	0	0	0	1	1	2	0
Victor Robles	.143	5	14	1	2	2	0	0	0	4	3	0
Eugenio Suarez	.095	5	21	2	2	0	0	1	1	1	9	0
Luke Raley	.000	3	4	1	0	0	0	0	0	0	2	0
Totals	.207	51	184	19	38	7	0	6	17	19	58	2

SEATTLE	W	L	ERA	G	GS	SV	IP	H	R	ER	BB	SO
Andres Munoz	0	0	0.00	4	0	1	5.1	0	0	0	2	5
Luis Castillo	1	0	0.00	2	1	0	6.0	1	0	0	4	4
Luke Jackson	0	0	0.00	1	0	0	1.0	0	0	0	0	0
Logan Gilbert	1	0	1.13	2	1	0	8.0	7	1	1	1	9
Matt Brash	1	0	1.93	4	0	0	4.2	1	2	1	2	7
George Kirby	0	0	2.70	2	2	0	10.0	9	3	3	1	14
Bryce Miller	0	0	4.15	1	1	0	4.1	4	2	2	0	2
Eduard Bazardo	0	0	4.50	5	0	0	6.0	6	3	3	1	4
Gabe Speier	0	1	6.75	4	0	0	4.0	4	3	3	1	4
Carlos Vargas	0	1	13.50	2	0	0	2.0	3	3	3	2	2
Caleb Ferguson	0	0	40.50	2	0	0	0.2	3	3	3	2	0
Totals	3	2	3.29	29	5	1	52.0	38	20	19	16	55

DETROIT	AVG	G	AB	R	H	2B	3B	HR	RBI	BB	SO	SB
Gleyber Torres	.286	5	21	2	6	2	0	1	3	7	0
Javier Baez	.238	5	21	2	5	1	0	1	4	1	2	1
Zach McKinstry	.238	5	21	2	5	0	0	0	2	1	6	1
Kerry Carpenter	.227	5	22	2	5	0	2	5	3	8	0
Dillon Dingler	.200	5	20	2	4	2	0	0	1	2	5	0
Spencer Torkelson	.190	5	21	3	4	3	0	0	4	2	6	0
Wenceel Perez	.167	3	6	1	1	0	0	0	0	3	0
Riley Greene	.136	5	22	2	3	0	0	1	1	1	6	0
Colt Keith	.067	5	15	0	1	0	0	0	0	1	5	0
Parker Meadows	.059	5	17	1	1	0	0	0	0	0	7	0
Andy Ibanez	.000	1	1	0	0	0	0	0	1	0	0
Jahmai Jones	.000	3	1	2	1	1	0	0	1	2	0	0
Jake Rogers	.000	1	1	1	0	0	0	0	0	0
Totals	.201	53	189	20	38	10	0	5	20	16	55	2

DETROIT	W	L	ERA	G	GS	SV	IP	H	R	ER	BB	SO
Will Vest	1	0	0.00	3	0	0	5.0	1	0	0	0	7
Troy Melton	1	0	1.13	3	1	0	8.0	5	1	1	3	8
Keider Montero	0	0	1.68	3	0	1	5.1	1	1	0	2	7
Tarik Skubal	0	0	2.08	2	2	0	13.0	7	3	3	1	22
Brant Hurter	0	0	3.00	3	0	0	3.0	1	1	1	0	1
Casey Mize	0	0	3.00	1	1	0	3.0	2	1	1	2	6
Tommy Kahnle	0	1	4.50	3	0	0	2.0	3	1	1	2	2
Jack Flaherty	0	1	5.06	2	1	0	5.1	4	4	3	6	8
Kyle Finnegan	0	1	6.23	4	0	0	4.1	7	3	3	1	2
Tyler Holton	0	0	6.75	3	0	0	1.1	3	1	1	1	0
Brenan Hanifee	0	0	18.00	1	0	0	1.0	2	2	2	0	0
Rafael Montero	0	0	inf	1	0	0	0.0	2	1	1	1	0
Totals	2	3	2.98	29	5	1	51.1	38	19	17	19	58

SCORE BY INNINGS

DETROIT	0	0	0	0	6	6	1	3	3	1	20
SEATTLE	0	2	2	5	1	3	1	2	2	1	19

AMERICAN LEAGUE CHAMPIONSHIP SERIES
SEATTLE MARINERS VS. TORONTO BLUE JAYS

TORONTO	AVG	G	AB	R	H	2B	3B	HR	RBI	BB	SO	SB
Vladimir Guerrero	.385	7	26	6	10	3	0	3	3	4	2	0
Nathan Lukes	.333	7	27	3	9	1	0	0	2	3	4	0
Isiah Kiner-Falefa	.333	4	15	3	5	2	0	0	1	0	0	0
Ernie Clement	.321	7	28	5	9	2	1	0	2	1	2	0
George Springer	.276	7	29	7	8	3	0	3	7	3	6	0
Andres Gimenez	.261	7	23	3	6	0	0	2	6	2	4	0
Addison Barger	.261	7	23	4	6	1	0	1	2	4	5	3	0
Alejandro Kirk	.222	7	27	3	6	1	0	1	4	4	6	0
Anthony Santander	.200	2	5	1	1	0	0	0	0	1	2	0
Daulton Varsho	.179	7	28	1	5	1	0	0	4	1	9	0
Myles Straw	.000	4	4	1	0	0	0	0	0	0	1	0
Davis Schneider	.000	2	4	0	0	0	0	0	0	1	1	0
Joey Loperfido	.000	1	1	0	0	0	0	0	0	0	0	0
Totals	.271	69	240	37	65	14	1	11	33	25	40	0

TORONTO	W	L	ERA	G	GS	SV	IP	H	R	ER	BB	SO
Chris Bassitt	0	0	0.00	2	0	0	2.2	0	0	0	0	3
Eric Lauer	0	0	0.00	1	0	0	1.0	1	0	0	0	2
Jeff Hoffman	0	0	0.00	4	0	1	5.0	1	0	0	1	0
Kevin Gausman	1	1	2.19	3	2	0	12.1	6	3	3	7	9
Louie Varland	0	0	2.57	6	0	0	7.0	4	2	2	1	8
Max Scherzer	1	0	3.18	1	1	0	5.2	3	2	2	4	5
Shane Bieber	1	0	3.72	2	2	0	9.2	11	4	4	2	13
Mason Fluharty	0	0	3.86	4	0	0	2.1	4	1	1	1	3
Trey Yesavage	1	1	6.52	2	2	0	9.2	10	7	7	6	11
Seranthony Dominguez	0	0	8.10	4	0	0	3.1	3	3	3	2	2
Braydon Fisher	0	0	9.00	2	0	0	2.0	3	2	2	0	3
Yariel Rodriguez	0	0	27.00	1	0	0	1.0	2	3	3	3	1
Brendon Little	0	1	81.00	2	0	0	0.1	2	3	3	0	1
Totals	4	3	4.35	35	7	1	62.0	50	30	30	29	71

SEATTLE	AVG	G	AB	R	H	2B	3B	HR	RBI	BB	SO	SB
Mitch Garver	.500	2	2	0	1	0	1	0	0	0	0
Josh Naylor	.417	7	24	4	10	0	0	3	5	3	5	1
Eugenio Suarez	.308	7	26	3	8	1	0	2	3	5	9	0
Julio Rodriguez	.240	7	25	5	6	1	0	3	6	5	10	0
Cal Raleigh	.240	7	25	6	6	1	0	4	4	10	0
Jorge Polanco	.231	7	26	6	6	1	0	1	5	2	4	0
Randy Arozarena	.200	7	25	7	5	0	0	1	1	3	11	4
J.P. Crawford	.143	7	21	0	3	1	0	0	2	3	2	0
Dominic Canzone	.091	7	22	0	2	0	0	0	0	8	0
Victor Robles	.077	4	13	0	1	0	0	0	0	3	4	0

NATIONAL LEAGUE WILD CARD SERIES

CINCINNATI REDS VS. LOS ANGELES DODGERS

CINCINNATI	AVG	G	AB	R	H	2B	3B	HR	RBI	BB	SO	SB
Gavin Lux	.500	2	6	2	3	0	0	0	0	0	1	0
Sal Stewart	.500	2	4	0	2	0	0	0	4	1	1	1
Spencer Steer	.375	2	8	0	3	0	0	0	1	0	2	0
Matt McLain	.286	2	7	1	2	1	0	0	0	1	5	0
Tyler Stephenson	.143	2	7	0	1	1	0	0	2	0	4	0
Austin Hays	.143	2	7	3	1	0	0	0	0	1	1	0
TJ Friedl	.125	2	8	0	1	0	0	0	0	2	3	0
Ke'Bryan Hayes	.000	2	6	0	0	0	0	0	0	0	1	0
Elly De La Cruz	.000	2	6	1	0	0	0	0	2	2	4	0
Miguel Andujar	.000	2	4	1	0	0	0	0	0	1	1	0
Noelvi Marte	.000	1	3	1	0	0	0	0	0	1	2	0
Will Benson	.000	1	1	0	0	0	0	0	0	1	1	0
Totals	.194	22	67	9	13	2	0	0	9	10	25	1

CINCINNATI	W	L	ERA	G	GS	SV	IP	H	R	ER	BB	SO
Chase Burns	0	0	0.00	1	0	0	1.2	0	0	0	0	1
Graham Ashcraft	0	0	0.00	1	0	0	1.0	2	0	0	0	0
Nick Lodolo	0	0	0.00	1	0	0	1.2	1	0	0	0	0
Scott Barlow	0	0	0.00	1	0	0	1.2	0	0	0	0	4
Brent Suter	0	0	6.75	1	0	0	1.1	4	2	1	0	2
Zack Littell	0	1	8.10	1	1	0	3.1	6	3	3	0	2
Tony Santillan	0	0	9.00	1	0	0	1.0	2	1	1	2	0
Hunter Greene	0	1	15.00	1	1	0	3.0	6	5	5	2	4
Connor Phillips	0	0	27.00	1	0	0	1.0	3	3	3	1	2
Nick Martinez	0	0	81.00	1	0	0	0.1	4	4	3	1	0
Totals	0	2	9.00	10	2	0	16.0	28	18	16	6	15

LA DODGERS	AVG	G	AB	R	H	2B	3B	HR	RBI	BB	SO	SB
Mookie Betts	.667	2	9	1	6	3	0	0	3	1	1	0
Miguel Rojas	.600	2	5	2	3	0	0	0	1	0	0	0
Enrique Hernandez	.500	2	8	3	4	1	0	0	1	0	1	0
Ben Rortvedt	.500	2	6	2	3	1	0	0	1	0	2	0
Teoscar Hernandez	.400	2	10	2	4	1	0	2	6	0	0	0
Shohei Ohtani	.333	2	9	3	3	0	0	2	4	1	3	0
Tommy Edman	.333	1	3	1	1	0	0	1	1	0	2	0
Freddie Freeman	.250	2	8	1	2	1	0	0	0	2	1	0
Max Muncy	.143	2	7	2	1	0	0	0	0	2	3	0
Andy Pages	.000	2	9	0	0	0	0	0	0	0	2	0
Alex Call	.000	1	1	1	1	0	0	0	0	0	0	0
Totals	.373	20	75	18	28	7	0	5	17	6	15	0

LA DODGERS	W	L	ERA	G	GS	SV	IP	H	R	ER	BB	SO
Blake Treinen	0	0	0.00	2	0	0	1.1	1	0	0	0	2
Jack Dreyer	0	0	0.00	1	0	0	0.2	0	0	0	1	1
Roki Sasaki	0	0	0.00	1	0	0	1.0	0	0	0	0	2
Yoshinobu Yamamoto	1	0	0.00	1	1	0	6.2	4	2	0	2	9
Blake Snell	1	0	2.57	1	1	0	7.0	4	2	2	1	9
Alex Vesia	0	0	18.00	2	0	0	1.0	1	2	2	2	2
Emmet Sheehan	0	0	54.00	1	0	0	0.1	2	2	2	2	0
Edgardo Henriquez	0	0	inf	1	0	0	0.0	1	1	1	2	0
Totals	2	0	3.50	10	2	0	18.0	13	9	7	10	25

SCORE BY INNINGS
CINCINNATI	2	0	0	0	0	0	2	5	0	9
LA DODGERS	1	0	5	2	1	6	3	0	0	18

SAN DIEGO PADRES VS. CHICAGO CUBS

SAN DIEGO	AVG	G	AB	R	H	2B	3B	HR	RBI	BB	SO	SB
Freddy Fermin	.364	3	11	0	4	2	0	0	0	0	1	0
Xander Bogaerts	.333	3	12	0	4	1	0	0	1	0	3	1
Jackson Merrill	.333	3	9	2	3	2	0	1	2	1	2	0
Ryan O'Hearn	.222	3	9	0	2	0	0	0	0	1	1	0
Luis Arraez	.182	3	11	0	2	0	0	0	0	0	1	1
Gavin Sheets	.167	3	6	0	1	0	0	0	0	0	1	0
Manny Machado	.100	3	10	1	1	0	0	1	2	2	3	0
Fernando Tatis	.083	3	12	2	1	0	0	0	0	1	4	1
Jake Cronenworth	.000	3	11	0	0	0	0	0	0	0	3	0
Bryce Johnson	.000	2	2	0	0	0	0	0	0	0	1	0
Jose Iglesias	.000	2	2	0	0	0	0	0	0	0	0	0
Totals	.189	31	95	5	18	5	0	2	5	5	20	3

SAN DIEGO	W	L	ERA	G	GS	SV	IP	H	R	ER	BB	SO
Adrian Morejon	1	0	0.00	3	0	0	4.1	2	0	0	0	2
David Morgan	0	0	0.00	1	0	0	1.0	1	0	0	0	2
Dylan Cease	0	0	0.00	1	1	0	3.2	3	0	0	1	5
Mason Miller	0	0	0.00	2	0	0	2.2	0	0	0	0	8
Michael King	0	0	0.00	1	0	0	1.0	1	0	0	0	3
Wandy Peralta	0	0	0.00	2	0	0	1.1	2	0	0	0	1
Jeremiah Estrada	0	0	3.38	2	0	0	2.2	2	1	1	2	2
Nick Pivetta	0	1	3.60	1	1	0	5.0	3	2	2	0	9
Robert Suarez	0	0	3.86	2	0	1	2.1	5	1	1	0	2
Yu Darvish	0	1	18.00	1	1	0	1.0	4	2	2	0	1
Totals	1	2	2.16	16	3	1	25.0	23	6	6	3	35

CHI CUBS	AVG	G	AB	R	H	2B	3B	HR	RBI	BB	SO	SB
Michael Busch	.400	3	10	1	4	0	0	1	1	1	0	0
Carson Kelly	.375	3	8	1	3	0	0	1	1	1	4	0
Nico Hoerner	.364	3	11	0	4	1	0	0	1	0	0	0
Pete Crow-Armstrong	.300	3	10	0	3	0	0	0	1	0	6	0
Seiya Suzuki	.273	3	11	3	3	2	0	1	1	0	5	0
Kyle Tucker	.273	3	11	1	3	0	0	0	0	2	0	0
Dansby Swanson	.222	3	9	1	2	0	0	0	1	1	6	0
Ian Happ	.091	3	11	0	1	1	0	0	0	0	6	0
Matt Shaw	.000	3	7	0	0	0	0	0	0	0	5	0
Moises Ballesteros	.000	1	1	0	0	0	0	0	0	0	0	0
Totals	.258	28	89	6	23	4	0	3	6	3	35	0

CHI CUBS	W	L	ERA	G	GS	SV	IP	H	R	ER	BB	SO
Caleb Thielbar	0	0	0.00	2	0	0	1.1	2	0	0	1	3
Colin Rea	0	0	0.00	1	0	0	1.2	1	0	0	0	1
Daniel Palencia	2	0	0.00	2	0	0	3.0	2	0	0	1	2
Drew Pomeranz	0	0	0.00	2	0	0	2.0	0	0	0	0	0
Jameson Taillon	0	0	0.00	1	0	0	4.0	2	0	0	0	4
Michael Soroka	0	0	0.00	1	0	0	0.2	0	0	0	0	0
Taylor Rogers	0	0	0.00	1	0	0	1.0	0	0	0	0	1
Matthew Boyd	0	0	2.08	1	1	0	4.1	4	1	1	1	2
Andrew Kittredge	0	1	3.38	3	1	1	2.2	1	1	1	0	2
Brad Keller	0	0	3.86	2	0	1	2.1	2	1	1	0	3
Shota Imanaga	0	0	4.50	1	0	0	4.0	3	2	2	2	3
Totals	2	1	1.67	17	3	2	27.0	18	5	5	5	20

SCORE BY INNINGS
SAN DIEGO	1	1	0	0	2	0	0	0	1	5
CHI CUBS	0	2	0	0	2	0	1	1	0	6

NATIONAL LEAGUE DIVISION SERIES

PHILADELPHIA PHILLIES VS. LOS ANGELES DODGERS

LA DODGERS	AVG	G	AB	R	H	2B	3B	HR	RBI	BB	SO	SB
Max Muncy	.444	4	9	1	4	1	0	0	0	1	1	0
Teoscar Hernandez	.250	4	16	2	4	0	0	1	3	1	7	0
Mookie Betts	.235	4	17	0	4	0	0	1	1	1	1	0
Tommy Edman	.235	4	17	2	4	0	0	1	2	0	3	0
Enrique Hernandez	.214	4	14	2	3	1	0	0	3	3	3	0
Freddie Freeman	.200	4	15	2	3	1	0	0	0	1	5	0
Will Smith	.154	4	13	1	2	0	0	0	2	1	6	0
Andy Pages	.067	4	15	1	1	0	0	0	0	0	4	0
Shohei Ohtani	.056	4	18	1	1	0	0	0	1	2	9	0
Miguel Rojas	.000	2	3	0	0	0	0	0	0	0	0	0
Alex Call	.000	2	2	0	2	0	0	0	0	2	0	0
Dalton Rushing	.000	1	1	0	0	0	0	0	0	0	1	0
Ben Rortvedt	.000	2	1	0	0	0	0	0	0	0	1	0
Justin Dean	.000	1	0	1	0	0	0	0	0	0	0	0
Hyeseong Kim	.000	1	0	0	0	0	0	0	0	0	0	0
Totals	.199	45	141	13	28	3	1	2	12	12	41	0

LA DODGERS	W	L	ERA	G	GS	SV	IP	H	R	ER	BB	SO
Alex Vesia	1	0	0.00	3	0	0	2.0	1	0	0	1	1
Anthony Banda	0	0	0.00	1	0	0	1.0	0	0	0	1	2
Blake Snell	1	0	0.00	1	1	0	6.0	1	0	0	4	9
Jack Dreyer	0	0	0.00	1	0	0	1.0	0	0	0	1	0
Roki Sasaki	0	0	0.00	3	0	2	4.1	1	0	0	0	3
Tyler Glasnow	0	0	0.00	2	1	0	7.2	3	0	0	5	10
Shohei Ohtani	1	0	4.50	1	1	0	6.0	3	3	3	1	9
Emmet Sheehan	0	0	6.00	2	0	0	3.0	4	2	2	0	2
Yoshinobu Yamamoto	0	1	6.75	1	1	0	4.0	6	3	3	1	2
Blake Treinen	0	0	18.00	2	0	0	1.0	3	2	2	0	0
Clayton Kershaw	0	0	18.00	1	0	0	2.0	6	5	4	3	0
Totals	3	1	3.32	18	4	2	38.0	28	15	14	17	38

MAJOR LEAGUES

PHILADELPHIA	AVG	G	AB	R	H	2B	3B	HR	RBI	BB	SO	SB
Harrison Bader	.500	3	2	0	1	0	0	0	1	0	1	0
Alec Bohm	.333	4	12	3	4	0	0	0	6	1	0	0
Edmundo Sosa	.333	2	3	0	1	0	0	0	0	1	0	0
J.T. Realmuto	.294	4	17	3	5	2	1	1	3	0	3	0
Trea Turner	.235	4	17	1	4	0	0	0	3	2	5	2
Bryce Harper	.200	4	15	1	3	1	0	0	0	3	3	0
Kyle Schwarber	.188	4	16	2	3	1	0	2	3	2	8	0
Max Kepler	.167	4	12	3	2	1	1	0	0	3	2	1
Bryson Stott	.154	4	13	0	2	0	0	0	0	0	4	1
Nick Castellanos	.133	4	15	1	2	2	0	0	3	0	3	0
Brandon Marsh	.077	4	13	1	1	0	0	0	1	1	5	0
Otto Kemp	.000	1	2	0	0	0	0	0	0	0	2	0
Totals	.204	42	137	15	28	7	2	3	14	17	38	4

PHILADELPHIA	W	L	ERA	G	GS	SV	IP	H	R	ER	BB	SO
Aaron Nola	0	0	0.00	1	1	0	2.0	1	0	0	0	3
Jhoan Duran	0	0	0.00	3	0	0	3.2	1	0	0	4	7
Tanner Banks	0	0	0.00	2	0	0	1.1	1	0	0	0	0
Ranger Suarez	1	0	1.80	1	1	0	5.0	5	1	1	1	4
Cristopher Sanchez	0	0	2.25	2	2	0	12.0	9	3	3	3	13
Jesus Luzardo	0	2	2.35	2	1	0	7.2	5	3	2	1	8
Matt Strahm	0	0	3.86	3	0	0	2.1	2	1	1	0	2
Orion Kerkering	0	0	6.75	4	0	0	2.2	1	2	2	2	3
Taijuan Walker	0	0	13.50	1	0	0	0.2	2	1	1	1	1
David Robertson	0	1	54.00	1	0	0	0.1	1	2	2	0	0
Totals	1	3	2.87	20	4	0	37.2	28	13	12	12	41

SCORE BY INNINGS

PHILADELPHIA	0	3	0	3	0	0	1	6	2	0	15
LA DODGERS	0	0	1	0	0	2	8	0	1	1	13

MILWAUKEE BREWERS VS. CHICAGO CUBS

MILWAUKEE	AVG	G	AB	R	H	2B	3B	HR	RBI	BB	SO	SB
Jake Bauers	.500	2	4	1	2	0	0	1	2	1	1	0
Jackson Chourio	.389	5	18	2	7	2	0	1	6	1	4	0
William Contreras	.300	5	20	5	6	1	0	2	3	1	3	0
Andrew Vaughn	.286	5	14	4	4	0	0	2	4	3	0	0
Christian Yelich	.263	5	19	3	5	1	0	0	3	2	0	0
Caleb Durbin	.250	5	16	1	4	0	0	0	2	2	3	1
Sal Frelick	.235	5	17	2	4	1	1	0	0	1	2	2
Blake Perkins	.214	5	14	1	3	1	0	0	1	2	5	0
Joey Ortiz	.154	5	13	1	2	0	0	0	0	2	3	0
Brice Turang	.150	5	20	2	3	1	0	1	2	1	8	0
Isaac Collins	.000	2	3	0	0	0	0	0	0	2	0	0
Brandon Lockridge	.000	1	2	0	0	0	0	0	0	1	0	0
Totals	.250	50	160	22	40	7	0	7	21	18	34	2

MILWAUKEE	W	L	ERA	G	GS	SV	IP	H	R	ER	BB	SO
Abner Uribe	0	0	0.00	2	0	1	3.0	0	0	0	1	3
Chad Patrick	0	0	0.00	4	0	0	4.2	0	0	0	0	6
Grant Anderson	0	0	0.00	1	0	0	2.0	1	0	0	0	2
Jose Quintana	0	0	0.00	1	0	0	3.0	2	0	0	1	2
Nick Mears	0	0	0.00	3	0	0	1.2	1	0	0	1	2
Trevor Megill	0	0	0.00	3	1	0	2.0	1	0	0	1	2
Jacob Misiorowski	2	0	1.29	2	0	0	7.0	4	1	1	2	7
Jared Koenig	0	0	3.38	3	0	0	2.2	3	1	1	0	1
Freddy Peralta	1	1	4.66	2	2	0	9.2	7	5	5	5	15
Aaron Ashby	0	0	5.79	4	1	0	4.2	5	4	3	4	4
Robert Gasser	0	0	9.00	1	0	0	2.0	5	2	2	1	0
Quinn Priester	0	1	54.00	1	1	0	0.2	3	4	4	2	1
Totals	3	2	3.35	27	5	1	43.0	32	17	16	18	46

CHI CUBS	AVG	G	AB	R	H	2B	3B	HR	RBI	BB	SO	SB
Justin Turner	.500	1	2	0	1	0	0	0	0	0	0	0
Nico Hoerner	.450	5	20	4	9	0	0	1	1	0	2	1
Kyle Tucker	.250	5	16	4	4	0	0	1	5	3	0	0
Michael Busch	.235	5	17	3	4	0	0	3	3	2	4	0
Seiya Suzuki	.200	5	20	2	4	1	0	2	4	1	5	0
Matt Shaw	.200	5	10	0	2	0	0	0	1	5	2	1
Dansby Swanson	.118	5	17	0	2	1	0	0	0	2	9	0
Pete Crow-Armstrong	.118	5	17	0	2	0	0	0	2	1	6	1
Ian Happ	.105	5	19	2	2	0	0	2	4	2	7	0
Carson Kelly	.100	5	20	1	2	0	0	0	0	0	8	0
Moises Ballesteros	.000	2	2	0	0	0	0	0	0	0	0	0
Totals	.200	48	160	17	32	2	0	9	16	18	46	3

CHI CUBS	W	L	ERA	G	GS	SV	IP	H	R	ER	BB	SO
Aaron Civale	0	0	0.00	1	0	0	4.1	3	0	0	0	3
Ben Brown	0	0	0.00	1	0	0	2.1	0	0	0	2	3
Brad Keller	0	0	0.00	3	0	1	3.1	0	0	0	2	2
Caleb Thielbar	0	0	0.00	3	0	0	2.1	0	0	0	2	2
Colin Rea	0	1	1.50	2	0	0	6.0	8	1	1	3	2
Drew Pomeranz	1	0	2.25	4	1	0	4.0	1	1	1	0	6
Matthew Boyd	0	1	3.38	2	2	0	5.1	6	6	2	4	7
Jameson Taillon	0	0	4.50	1	1	0	4.0	5	2	2	1	3
Daniel Palencia	1	0	5.79	4	0	0	4.2	3	3	3	1	1
Andrew Kittredge	0	0	7.71	2	0	0	2.1	3	2	2	1	1
Shota Imanaga	0	1	13.50	1	1	0	2.2	5	4	4	0	3
Michael Soroka	0	0	27.00	1	0	0	1.0	5	3	3	2	1
Totals	2	3	3.86	25	5	1	42.0	40	22	18	18	34

SCORE BY INNINGS

MILWAUKEE	11	3	1	5	0	0	2	0	0	22
CHI CUBS	0	1	2	1	0	7	3	6	3	17

NATIONAL LEAGUE CHAMPIONSHIP SERIES
LOS ANGELES DODGERS VS. MILWAUKEE BREWERS

LA DODGERS	AVG	G	AB	R	H	2B	3B	HR	RBI	BB	SO	SB
Will Smith	.400	4	15	3	6	0	0	0	0	2	4	0
Shohei Ohtani	.357	4	14	4	5	0	1	3	4	4	5	1
Tommy Edman	.333	4	15	0	5	1	0	0	3	1	7	0
Enrique Hernandez	.286	4	14	2	4	2	0	0	1	5	0	0
Freddie Freeman	.250	4	16	2	4	2	0	0	1	2	5	0
Teoscar Hernandez	.200	4	15	1	3	0	0	1	2	1	4	0
Andy Pages	.182	4	11	0	2	1	0	0	1	0	3	0
Mookie Betts	.133	4	15	1	2	1	0	0	0	2	2	0
Max Muncy	.083	4	12	2	1	0	0	1	4	2	0	0
Alex Call	.000	1	1	0	0	0	0	0	0	0	0	0
Justin Dean	.000	1	0	0	0	0	0	0	0	0	0	1
Totals	.250	38	128	15	32	7	1	6	14	17	37	2

LA DODGERS	W	L	ERA	G	GS	SV	IP	H	R	ER	BB	SO
Alex Vesia	1	0	0.00	2	0	0	1.2	1	0	0	0	1
Anthony Banda	0	0	0.00	2	0	0	1.2	0	0	0	0	1
Blake Snell	1	0	0.00	1	1	0	8.0	1	0	0	0	10
Shohei Ohtani	1	0	0.00	1	1	0	6.0	2	0	0	3	10
Yoshinobu Yamamoto	1	0	1.00	1	1	0	9.0	3	1	1	1	7
Tyler Glasnow	0	0	1.59	1	1	0	5.2	3	1	1	3	8
Roki Sasaki	0	0	3.38	3	0	1	2.2	2	1	1	2	1
Blake Treinen	0	0	6.75	3	0	1	1.1	1	1	1	2	3
Totals	4	0	1.00	14	4	2	36.0	14	4	4	11	41

MILWAUKEE	AVG	G	AB	R	H	2B	3B	HR	RBI	BB	SO	SB
Caleb Durbin	.308	4	13	2	4	2	1	0	0	1	5	2
Jake Bauers	.222	4	9	0	2	1	0	0	1	0	2	1
Jackson Chourio	.200	4	15	1	3	1	0	1	2	0	5	0
William Contreras	.143	4	14	0	2	0	0	0	0	2	4	0
Sal Frelick	.071	4	14	0	1	0	0	0	0	0	3	0
Christian Yelich	.071	4	14	0	1	0	0	0	0	2	7	1
Brice Turang	.067	4	15	0	1	0	0	0	1	1	6	0
Andrew Vaughn	.000	4	12	0	0	0	0	0	0	1	2	0
Joey Ortiz	.000	4	6	0	0	0	0	0	0	1	1	0
Isaac Collins	.000	4	6	1	0	0	0	0	0	1	5	0
Blake Perkins	.000	2	1	0	0	0	0	0	0	1	1	0
Andruw Monasterio	.000	1	0	0	0	0	0	0	0	0	0	0
Totals	.118	43	119	4	14	4	1	1	4	11	41	4

MILWAUKEE	W	L	ERA	G	GS	SV	IP	H	R	ER	BB	SO
Grant Anderson	0	0	0.00	1	0	0	0.2	0	0	0	0	0
Jared Koenig	0	0	0.00	3	0	0	4.0	1	0	0	2	6
Quinn Priester	0	0	0.00	1	0	0	4.0	3	0	0	3	1
Robert Gasser	0	0	0.00	1	0	0	0.2	1	0	0	1	2
Jacob Misiorowski	0	1	1.80	1	0	0	5.0	3	2	1	1	9
Chad Patrick	0	1	4.15	2	0	0	4.1	3	2	2	1	5
Aaron Ashby	0	0	4.50	3	2	0	2.0	3	1	1	2	3
Trevor Megill	0	0	4.50	2	0	0	2.0	2	1	1	0	3
Freddy Peralta	0	1	4.76	1	1	0	5.2	5	3	3	1	4
Abner Uribe	0	0	6.00	3	0	0	3.0	3	2	2	3	3
Jose Quintana	0	1	13.50	1	1	0	2.0	6	3	3	1	1
Tobias Myers	0	0	13.50	1	0	0	0.2	2	1	1	2	0
Totals	0	4	3.71	20	4	0	34.0	32	15	14	17	37

SCORE BY INNINGS

LA DODGERS	4	2	0	1	0	4	2	1	1	15
MILWAUKEE	1	1	0	0	0	0	0	1	1	4

ORGANIZATION STATISTICS

Arizona Diamondbacks

SEASON SYNOPSIS: The Diamondbacks rode the roller coaster, raising hopes in the offseason, sagging under the weight of crucial injuries, then riding a loaded top of the lineup into wild-card contention until the season's final weekend. Ultimately, an injury-depleted pitching staff proved too much to overcome, as Arizona lost its final five games and finished below .500 for the first time in three seasons.

HIGH POINT: Clinging to wild-card hopes, Arizona had won four out of five September series when it fell behind the Dodgers 4-0 in a series opener Sept. 23. It rallied against LA's bullpen and pulled out a 5-4 victory on Geraldo Perdomo's RBI single off Tanner Scott, pulling Arizona to within a game of the Mets in the wild-card standings. Perdomo extended his own hit streak to 12 games during a breakout season, as he batted .290/.389/.462 with 20 homers, 100 RBIs and 27 stolen bases.

LOW POINT: Corbin Burnes had looked every bit like an ace in May with a 1.67 ERA over 27 innings. But in a June 1 start against the Nationals, Burnes felt tightness in his forearm and walked off the mound after his velocity fell in the top of the fifth. He wound up requiring reconstructive UCL surgery, one of five D-backs pitchers—including top relievers Justin Martinez and A.J. Puk—who needed it in 2025.

NOTABLE ROOKIES: Tim Tawa played six positions and hit seven homers during a .201/.274/.347 campaign, while C/DH Adrian del Castillo (.242/.290/.392, 4 HR) provided some thump with less defensive value. Tyler Locklear, acquired from Seattle, got a shot at the first base job but didn't pass the audition (.175, 43 SO/103 AB). Rookies such as Josh Collmenter throw-a-like Taylor Rashi were among the league-record 17 D-backs pitchers to record a save as manager Torey Lovullo tried to piece together a bullpen after the Martinez and Puk injuries.

KEY TRANSACTIONS: Burnes' six-year, $210 million was the third big pitching deal the D-backs have handed out of late, and they shed one of them, trading Jordan Montgomery (another UCL injury victim) to the Brewers at the deadline in a cost-cutting deal that also included Shelby Miller. Believing it was out of the race at the July deadline, Arizona also dealt its corner infielders, Josh Naylor and team home runs leader Eugenio Suarez, in separate trades to the Mariners.

OPENING DAY PAYROLL: $195,294,235 (11th)

PLAYERS OF THE YEAR

MAJOR LEAGUE
Geraldo Perdomo
SS
.290/.389/.462
20 HR, 27 SB
98 R, 100 RBIs, 94 BB

MINOR LEAGUE
Ryan Waldschmidt
OF
(A+,AA)
.289/.419/.473
18 HR, 29 SB, 96 BB

ORGANIZATION LEADERS

Batting		*Qualifiers
MAJORS		
* AVG	Geraldo Perdomo	.290
* OPS	Ketel Marte	.893
HR	Eugenio Suarez	36
RBI	Geraldo Perdomo	100
MINORS		
* AVG	Tristin English, Reno/ACL D-backs	.324
* OBP	Ryan Waldschmidt, Amarillo/Hillsboro	.419
* SLG	Tristin English, Reno/ACL D-backs	.524
* OPS	Ryan Waldschmidt, Amarillo/Hillsboro	.892
R	Ryan Waldschmidt, Amarillo/Hillsboro	114
H	Gino Groover, Amarillo	145
TB	Ryan Waldschmidt, Amarillo/Hillsboro	229
2B	Tristin English, Reno/ACL D-backs	31
3B	Andy Weber, Reno/Amarillo	8
3B	Jansel Luis, Hillsboro/ACL D-backs	8
HR	A.J. Vukovich, Reno	22
RBI	Jose Fernandez, Amarillo	80
BB	Ryan Waldschmidt, Amarillo/Hillsboro	96
SO	Kristian Robinson, Reno/Amarillo	144
SB	Kristian Robinson, Reno/Amarillo	34

Pitching		#Qualifiers
MAJORS		
W	Zac Gallen	13
W	Brandon Pfaadt	13
# ERA	Zac Gallen	4.83
SO	Zac Gallen	175
SV	Shelby Miller	10
MINORS		
W	Dylan Ray, Reno/Amarillo	12
L	Casey Anderson, Reno/Amarillo/Hillsboro/Visalia	11
# ERA	Daniel Eagen, Amarillo/Hillsboro	2.99
G	Eli Saul, Amarillo/Hillsboro	53
G	Philip Abner, Reno/Amarillo/Hillsboro	53
GS	Dylan Ray, Reno/Amarillo	28
SV	Landon Sims, Amarillo	12
IP	Dylan Ray, Reno/Amarillo	140
BB	Roman Angelo, Reno/Amarillo	74
SO	Daniel Eagen, Amarillo/Hillsboro	153
# AVG	Daniel Eagen, Amarillo/Hillsboro	.189
	Roman Angelo, Visalia/Hillsboro	

2025 PERFORMANCE

General Manager: Mike Hazen. **Farm Director:** Chris Slivka. **Scouting Director:** Ian Rebhan.

Class	Team	League	W	L	PCT	Finish	Manager
Majors	Arizona Diamondbacks	National	80	82	.494	9 (15)	Torey Lovullo
Triple-A	Reno Aces	Pacific Coast	63	87	.420	9 (10)	Jeff Gardner
Double-A	Amarillo Sod Poodles	Texas	71	67	.514	4 (10)	Javier Colina
High-A	Hillsboro Hops	Northwest	60	71	.458	4 (6)	Mark Reed
Low-A	Visalia Rawhide	California	65	67	.492	5 (8)	Dee Garner
Rookie	ACL D-backs	Arizona Complex	31	29	.517	7 (15)	Juan Francia
Rookie	DSL Arizona Black	Dominican	24	32	.429	37 (52)	Vladimir Frias
Rookie	DSL Arizona Red	Dominican	34	22	.607	11 (52)	Izzy Alcantara
Overall 2025 Minor League Record			348	375	.481	20th (30)	

ORGANIZATION STATISTICS

ARIZONA DIAMONDBACKS
NATIONAL LEAGUE

Batting	B-T	Ht.	Wt.	DOB	AVG	OBP	SLG	G	PA	AB	R	H	2B	3B	HR	RBI	BB	HBP	SH	SF	SO	SB	CS	BB%	SO%
Alexander, Blaze	R-R	5-11	160	6-11-99	.230	.323	.383	74	266	230	31	53	12	1	7	28	22	10	3	1	86	4	6	8.3	32.3
Barrosa, Jorge	S-L	5-5	165	2-17-01	.141	.169	.225	33	77	71	8	10	3	0	1	7	2	1	0	3	22	0	0	2.6	28.6
Carroll, Corbin	L-L	5-10	165	8-21-00	.259	.343	.541	143	642	564	107	146	32	17	31	84	67	7	0	4	153	32	6	10.4	23.8
Del Castillo, Adrian	L-R	5-9	208	9-27-99	.242	.290	.392	44	131	120	9	29	6	0	4	17	8	1	0	2	47	0	0	6.1	35.9
English, Tristin	R-R	6-0	208	5-14-97	.091	.130	.136	7	23	22	0	2	1	0	0	1	1	0	0	0	8	0	0	4.4	34.8
Garcia, Aramis	R-R	6-1	228	1-12-93	.000	.000	.000	2	4	4	0	0	0	0	0	0	0	0	0	0	3	0	0	0.0	75.0
Grichuk, Randal	R-R	6-2	216	8-13-91	.240	.277	.457	70	188	175	25	42	15	1	7	22	10	0	0	3	39	0	1	5.3	20.7
Gurriel, Lourdes	R-R	6-4	215	10-10-93	.248	.295	.418	129	546	500	52	124	24	2	19	80	31	6	0	9	76	10	4	5.7	13.9
Hampson, Garrett	R-R	5-11	196	10-10-94	.167	.359	.167	18	41	30	10	5	0	0	0	0	9	0	2	0	10	2	1	22.0	24.4
Herrera, Jose	S-R	5-10	217	2-24-97	.187	.285	.259	58	204	166	21	31	6	0	2	17	23	1	11	3	47	0	0	11.3	23.0
Kaiser, Connor	R-R	6-3	195	11-20-96	.111	.158	.167	11	19	18	1	2	1	0	0	2	1	0	0	0	5	0	0	5.3	26.3
Lawlar, Jordan	R-R	6-1	190	7-17-02	.182	.257	.288	28	74	66	9	12	7	0	0	5	6	1	0	1	26	2	0	8.1	35.1
Locklear, Tyler	R-R	6-1	210	11-24-00	.175	.267	.262	31	116	103	11	18	0	0	3	6	10	3	0	0	43	3	1	8.6	37.1
Marte, Ketel	S-R	6-1	210	10-12-93	.283	.376	.517	126	556	480	87	136	28	0	28	72	64	9	0	3	83	4	2	11.5	14.9
McCann, James	R-R	6-3	235	6-13-90	.260	.324	.431	42	137	123	18	32	6	0	5	17	8	4	1	1	33	0	0	5.8	24.1
McCarthy, Jake	L-L	6-2	215	7-30-97	.204	.247	.345	67	222	206	18	42	7	5	4	20	10	2	3	1	40	6	0	4.5	18.0
Moreno, Gabriel	R-R	5-11	195	2-14-00	.285	.353	.433	83	309	277	44	79	12	1	9	40	29	1	0	2	53	2	2	9.4	17.2
Naylor, Josh	L-L	5-11	250	6-22-97	.292	.360	.447	93	394	349	49	102	19	1	11	59	37	2	0	4	49	11	2	9.4	12.4
Nelson, Ryne	R-R	6-3	184	2-1-98	1.000	1.000	1.000	34	1	1	1	1	0	0	0	0	0	0	0	0	0	0	0	0.0	0.0
Perdomo, Geraldo	S-R	6-2	203	10-22-99	.290	.389	.462	161	720	597	98	173	33	5	20	100	94	10	8	11	83	27	6	13.1	11.5
Smith, Pavin	L-L	6-2	208	2-6-96	.258	.362	.434	87	288	244	36	63	17	1	8	28	41	0	0	2	92	2	2	14.2	31.9
Suarez, Eugenio	R-R	5-11	213	7-18-91	.248	.320	.576	106	437	387	64	96	19	0	36	87	29	15	0	6	117	1	0	6.6	26.8
Tawa, Tim	R-R	5-10	196	4-7-99	.201	.274	.347	74	225	199	29	40	8	0	7	18	20	1	2	3	64	8	2	8.9	28.4
Thomas, Alek	L-L	5-11	175	4-28-00	.249	.289	.370	143	469	433	51	108	19	3	9	38	21	5	6	4	122	7	4	4.5	26.0
Vargas, Ildemaro	S-R	6-0	195	7-16-91	.270	.292	.383	38	121	115	12	31	2	1	3	19	2	2	1	1	15	0	0	1.7	12.4

Pitching	B-T	Ht.	Wt.	DOB	W	L	ERA	G	GS	SV	IP	Hits	Runs	ER	HR	BB	SO	AVG	OBP	SLG	SO%	BB%	BF
Abner, Philip	L-L	6-1	220	5-5-02	0	0	4.91	5	0	0	4	5	2	2	0	3	5	.333	.444	.467	27.8	16.7	18
Backhus, Kyle	L-L	6-4	185	1-31-98	0	3	4.62	32	0	2	25	28	14	13	3	8	22	.283	.348	.465	19.1	7.0	115
Beeks, Jalen	L-L	5-11	215	7-10-93	5	3	3.77	61	2	1	57	42	26	24	6	20	47	.202	.277	.341	20.4	8.7	231
Brigham, Jeff	R-R	6-0	195	2-16-92	0	0	8.10	4	0	0	3	7	3	3	1	1	3	.412	.444	.588	16.7	5.6	18
Burgos, Juan	R-R	6-0	155	12-22-99	1	1	8.10	9	0	0	7	10	7	6	2	6	6	.345	.457	.621	17.1	17.1	35
Burnes, Corbin	R-R	6-3	246	10-22-94	3	2	2.66	11	11	0	64	49	23	19	7	26	63	.210	.297	.356	23.8	9.8	265
Castillo, Jose	L-L	6-6	252	1-10-96	0	1	11.37	5	0	0	6	10	8	8	3	3	3	.370	.419	.778	9.7	9.7	31
Crismatt, Nabil	R-R	6-1	220	12-25-94	3	0	3.71	8	5	0	34	40	20	14	6	9	25	.282	.327	.465	16.3	5.9	153
Curtiss, John	R-R	6-5	290	4-5-93	3	2	3.93	30	0	1	37	29	18	16	5	5	24	.215	.243	.385	17.0	3.6	141
DeSclafani, Anthony	R-R	6-2	195	4-18-90	1	2	5.12	13	4	2	39	37	23	22	11	12	36	.250	.321	.527	21.3	7.1	169
Diaz, Yilber	R-R	6-0	190	8-19-00	0	0	9.00	1	0	0	3	4	3	3	0	3	1	.333	.467	.500	6.7	20.0	15
Feyereisen, J.P.	R-R	6-2	215	2-7-93	0	1	9.00	2	0	0	2	3	3	2	1	0	2	.333	.333	.889	22.2	0.0	9
Gallen, Zac	R-R	6-2	189	8-3-95	13	15	4.83	33	33	0	192	176	109	103	31	66	175	.239	.303	.426	21.5	8.1	813
Garcia, Brandyn	L-L	6-4	225	5-27-00	0	2	5.84	12	0	0	12	14	10	8	0	5	13	.286	.364	.327	23.6	9.1	55
Ginkel, Kevin	L-R	6-4	235	3-24-94	1	4	7.36	29	0	3	26	29	22	21	2	13	29	.284	.364	.412	24.0	10.7	121
Graveman, Kendall	R-R	6-2	200	12-21-90	1	0	7.13	19	0	0	18	23	14	14	2	12	9	.333	.439	.580	11.0	14.6	82
Henry, Tommy	L-L	6-3	205	7-29-97	0	0	4.05	2	0	0	7	6	3	3	1	8	.261	.320	.652	30.8	3.9	26
Herrera, Jose	S-R	5-10	217	2-24-97	0	0	4.50	2	0	0	2	4	1	1	0	0	0	.400	.400	.500	0.0	0.0	10
Hoffmann, Andrew	R-R	6-5	210	2-2-00	1	1	7.36	8	0	0	7	7	6	6	1	6	7	.241	.371	.448	20.0	17.1	35
Jameson, Drey	R-R	6-0	165	8-17-97	0	1	3.00	3	0	1	3	4	2	1	0	2	3	.400	.538	.600	0.0	23.1	13
Jarvis, Bryce	L-R	6-2	195	12-26-97	0	0	5.73	12	0	1	22	23	14	14	3	10	21	.267	.347	.465	21.4	10.2	98
Kelly, Casey	R-R	6-3	215	10-4-89	0	0	0.00	2	0	0	2	1	0	0	0	1	0	.200	.333	.200	0.0	16.7	6
Kelly, Merrill	R-R	6-2	202	10-14-88	9	6	3.22	22	22	0	129	98	53	46	14	38	121	.206	.267	.323	23.5	7.4	514
Mantiply, Joe	R-L	6-4	219	3-1-91	0	1	15.83	10	0	0	10	26	17	17	5	3	8	.481	.517	.833	13.8	5.2	58
Martinez, Justin	R-R	6-3	180	7-30-01	1	2	4.11	17	0	5	15	7	8	7	1	12	22	.135	.328	.231	32.8	17.9	67

ARIZONA DIAMONDBACKS

Pitcher	B-T	Ht.	Wt.	DOB	W	L	ERA	G	GS	SV	IP	H	R	ER	BB	SO	AVG	OBP	SLG	BB%	SO%	BF
McGough, Scott	R-R	5-11	190	10-31-89	0	0	6.43	7	0	0	7	6	5	5	1	6	5	.214	.371	.393	14.3	17.1	35
Mena, Cristian	R-R	6-2	170	12-21-02	1	0	1.35	3	0	0	7	3	1	1	1	3	8	.130	.231	.261	30.8	11.5	26
Miller, Shelby	R-R	6-3	225	10-10-90	3	3	1.98	37	0	10	36	24	11	8	3	11	40	.190	.266	.286	28.0	7.7	143
Montes De Oca, Christian	R-R	6-4	230	8-30-99	0	0	0.00	1	0	0	3	0	0	0	0	1	2	.000	.111	.000	22.2	11.1	9
Morillo, Juan	R-R	6-1	150	3-19-99	0	3	4.19	42	0	1	34	38	19	16	2	20	36	.297	.393	.430	23.7	13.2	152
Nelson, Kyle	L-L	6-1	175	7-8-96	0	0	9.00	3	0	1	2	1	2	2	1	4	2	.143	.455	.571	18.2	36.4	11
Nelson, Ryne	R-R	6-3	184	2-1-98	7	3	3.39	33	23	1	154	124	62	58	17	41	132	.217	.273	.381	21.3	6.6	619
Pfaadt, Brandon	R-R	6-4	220	10-15-98	13	9	5.25	33	33	0	177	198	107	103	26	37	147	.279	.323	.469	19.2	4.8	767
Pope, Austin	R-R	6-3	210	10-26-98	0	0	0.00	1	0	0	2	2	0	0	0	1	1	.250	.333	.250	11.1	11.1	9
Puk, A.J.	L-L	6-7	248	4-25-95	0	0	3.38	8	0	4	8	8	3	3	2	2	12	.250	.314	.531	34.3	5.7	35
Rashi, Taylor	R-R	6-4	220	1-15-96	0	1	4.41	10	0	2	16	16	8	8	0	8	22	.250	.333	.313	30.6	11.1	72
Richards, Trevor	R-R	6-2	205	5-15-93	0	0	3.38	2	0	0	3	4	1	1	0	0	3	.400	.400	.500	27.3	0.0	11
Rodriguez, Eduardo	L-L	6-2	231	4-7-93	9	9	5.02	29	29	0	154	178	94	86	25	60	143	.286	.347	.475	20.6	8.7	694
Saalfrank, Andrew	L-L	6-3	205	8-18-97	2	1	1.24	28	0	3	29	19	5	4	1	10	19	.188	.257	.257	16.8	8.9	113
Scott, Tayler	R-R	6-3	185	6-1-92	0	0	9.00	6	0	0	9	13	9	9	3	4	7	.325	.386	.675	15.9	9.1	44
Thompson, Ryan	R-R	6-5	210	6-26-92	3	2	3.92	48	0	1	41	42	21	18	4	13	36	.263	.326	.381	20.6	7.4	175
Woodford, Jake	R-R	6-4	215	10-28-96	0	4	6.44	22	0	3	36	45	28	26	3	13	23	.298	.363	.424	13.5	7.7	170

Fielding

Catcher	PCT	G	PO	A	E	DP	PB
Del Castillo	1.000	5	34	0	0	0	0
Garcia	1.000	2	11	1	0	0	0
Herrera	.994	57	472	16	3	2	1
McCann	.996	40	260	14	1	1	0
Moreno	.998	75	521	28	1	5	3

First Base	PCT	G	PO	A	E	DP
English	1.000	7	43	8	0	4
Locklear	.996	30	246	12	1	21
McCann	1.000	1	1	0	0	0
Naylor	.993	76	558	40	4	52
Smith	.996	36	230	22	1	19
Suarez	1.000	1	2	0	0	0
Tawa	.991	20	95	11	1	10
Vargas	1.000	12	62	4	0	5

Second Base	PCT	G	PO	A	E	DP
Alexander	1.000	14	26	47	0	14
Hampson	1.000	10	19	32	0	5
Kaiser	1.000	9	5	15	0	2
Lawlar	.913	5	9	12	2	2
Marte	.986	104	176	247	6	53
Tawa	.962	23	27	49	3	14
Vargas	1.000	13	17	38	0	8

Third Base	PCT	G	PO	A	E	DP
Alexander	.954	54	39	105	7	8
Hampson	1.000	1	1	3	0	0
Lawlar	.833	12	5	15	4	1
Suarez	.949	101	59	166	12	16
Tawa	1.000	3	0	5	0	2
Vargas	.889	7	1	7	1	1

Shortstop	PCT	G	PO	A	E	DP
Hampson	1.000	2	3	3	0	1
Lawlar	.667	1	0	2	1	0
Perdomo	.971	161	223	387	18	84
Vargas	.000	1	0	0	0	0

Outfield	PCT	G	PO	A	E	DP
Alexander	1.000	7	7	1	0	0
Barrosa	1.000	33	54	0	0	0
Carroll	.997	141	303	9	1	3
Grichuk	1.000	23	27	0	0	0
Gurriel	.986	118	211	6	3	1
Hampson	1.000	3	5	0	0	0
McCarthy	1.000	63	131	1	0	1
Tawa	1.000	35	43	0	0	0
Thomas	.991	139	325	3	3	0

RENO ACES — TRIPLE-A
PACIFIC COAST LEAGUE

Batting	B-T	Ht.	Wt.	DOB	AVG	OBP	SLG	G	PA	AB	R	H	2B	3B	HR	RBI	BB	HBP	SH	SF	SO	SB	CS	BB%	SO%
Alcantara, Sergio	S-R	6-4	151	7-10-96	.315	.435	.470	45	185	149	26	47	11	3	2	23	32	1	1	2	31	2	2	17.3	16.8
Alexander, Blaze	R-R	5-11	160	6-11-99	.284	.413	.479	54	241	194	41	55	12	1	8	41	38	6	1	2	59	11	1	15.8	24.5
Almora, Albert	R-R	6-2	190	4-16-94	.303	.378	.476	35	166	145	22	44	5	4	4	26	18	0	2	1	23	5	3	10.8	13.9
Barrosa, Jorge	S-L	5-5	165	2-17-01	.294	.378	.431	93	456	394	67	116	29	2	7	58	54	1	4	3	95	10	4	11.8	20.8
Boyd, Jermiah	R-R	5-10	225	7-1-00	.167	.444	.167	2	9	6	1	1	0	0	0	0	3	0	0	0	5	0	0	33.3	55.6
Brown, Seth	L-L	6-1	223	7-13-92	.291	.381	.544	26	118	103	17	30	6	1	6	21	14	1	0	0	28	0	1	11.9	23.7
Corniel, Juan	R-R	5-11	150	10-2-02	.234	.272	.338	22	84	77	12	18	5	0	1	9	3	1	3	0	16	0	1	3.6	19.1
Del Castillo, Adrian	L-R	5-9	208	9-27-99	.288	.386	.559	14	70	59	13	17	4	0	4	16	10	0	1	0	19	0	0	14.3	27.1
English, Tristin	R-R	6-0	208	5-14-97	.325	.368	.514	93	417	385	55	125	31	0	14	77	21	7	1	3	62	0	0	5.0	14.9
Garcia, Aramis	R-R	6-1	228	1-12-93	.266	.385	.481	70	296	241	56	64	10	0	14	44	45	5	0	5	81	0	0	15.2	27.4
Graham, Kevin	L-R	6-1	195	8-12-99	.137	.244	.205	25	86	73	9	10	2	0	1	9	10	1	0	2	25	1	0	11.6	29.1
Herrera, Jose	S-R	5-10	217	2-24-97	.278	.381	.417	11	42	36	4	10	2	0	1	7	6	0	0	0	4	0	0	14.3	9.5
Kaiser, Connor	R-R	6-3	195	11-20-96	.236	.345	.406	71	273	229	32	54	17	2	6	31	36	2	6	0	75	2	1	13.2	27.5
Kessinger, Grae	R-R	6-1	204	8-25-97	.235	.447	.324	11	47	34	6	8	3	0	0	3	13	0	0	0	12	1	1	27.7	25.5
Lawlar, Jordan	R-R	6-1	195	7-17-02	.313	.403	.564	63	300	259	52	81	22	5	11	50	36	3	0	2	70	20	3	12.0	23.3
Logan, Gavin	L-R	5-9	212	1-14-00	.366	.417	.659	12	48	41	10	15	3	0	3	11	3	2	0	2	16	0	0	6.3	33.3
Lopez, Nicky	L-R	5-11	195	3-13-95	.267	.303	.317	24	109	101	16	27	3	1	0	7	5	1	0	2	9	1	2	4.6	8.3
Mancini, Trey	R-R	6-3	230	3-18-92	.308	.373	.522	74	335	299	62	92	16	0	16	62	25	8	0	3	70	2	1	7.5	20.9
McCarthy, Jake	L-L	6-2	215	7-30-97	.314	.401	.440	49	237	207	43	65	15	4	1	16	24	6	0	0	33	12	3	10.1	13.9
Melendez, Ivan	R-R	6-3	225	1-24-00	.292	.347	.483	25	98	89	10	26	6	1	3	19	7	1	0	1	24	0	0	7.1	24.5
Mervis, Matt	L-R	6-2	225	4-16-98	.245	.320	.518	30	122	110	20	27	10	1	6	24	11	0	0	1	29	1	0	9.0	23.8
Moreno, Gabriel	R-R	5-11	195	2-14-00	.400	.478	.850	6	23	20	4	8	3	0	2	4	3	0	0	0	5	0	0	13.0	21.7
Osborn, Drake	R-R	5-9	190	7-22-98	.273	.360	.409	7	25	22	3	6	3	0	0	3	2	1	0	0	2	0	0	8.0	8.0
Pache, Cristian	R-R	6-2	215	11-19-98	.251	.351	.389	70	288	247	44	62	15	2	5	25	34	4	3	0	77	8	2	11.8	26.7
Perez, Michael	L-R	5-10	195	8-7-92	.273	.351	.424	19	74	66	4	18	4	0	2	9	6	2	0	0	17	0	0	8.1	25.7
Pinto, Rene	R-R	5-10	195	11-2-96	.268	.324	.517	54	225	205	44	55	18	0	11	42	18	0	0	2	69	2	0	8.0	30.7
Robinson, Kristian	R-R	6-3	190	12-11-00	.262	.393	.469	41	178	145	28	38	8	2	6	22	31	1	0	1	43	10	0	17.4	24.2
Smith, Dominic	L-L	6-2	208	2-6-96	.267	.333	.467	4	17	15	3	4	3	0	0	1	2	0	0	0	6	0	0	11.8	35.3
Tawa, Tim	R-R	5-10	196	4-7-99	.238	.359	.492	18	78	63	10	15	5	1	3	15	11	2	0	2	13	2	0	14.1	16.7
Troy, Tommy	R-R	5-10	197	1-17-02	.295	.381	.429	38	182	156	23	46	8	2	3	17	18	5	1	2	28	3	1	9.9	15.4
Valdez, Jesus	R-R	5-9	175	12-23-98	.284	.346	.373	37	139	127	18	36	7	0	2	20	9	4	0	0	36	0	1	7.2	25.9
Vargas, Ildemaro	S-R	6-0	195	7-16-91	.255	.328	.389	54	241	216	29	55	8	3	5	36	21	3	0	1	22	4	1	8.7	9.1
Vukovich, A.J.	R-R	6-2	210	7-20-01	.284	.355	.498	111	476	426	80	121	19	3	22	79	46	2	0	2	129	0	2	9.7	27.1
Weber, Andy	L-R	5-11	190	7-24-97	.310	.368	.434	97	404	364	60	113	19	7	4	43	35	0	2	3	56	0	5	8.7	13.9

Pitching	B-T	Ht.	Wt.	DOB	W	L	ERA	G	GS	SV	IP	Hits	Runs	ER	HR	BB	SO	AVG	OBP	SLG	SO%	BB%	BF
Abner, Philip	L-L	6-1	220	5-5-02	0	0	0.00	8	0	1	8	2	0	0	0	3	11	.071	.161	.071	35.5	9.7	31
Albright, Luke	R-R	6-4	215	12-13-99	0	1	13.50	2	0	0	4	7	7	6	1	6	4	.389	.542	.611	16.0	24.0	25
Almora, Albert	R-R	6-2	190	4-16-94	0	0	9.00	1	0	0	1	2	1	1	0	0	0	.500	.500	.750	0.0	0.0	4
Amendt, Kyle	R-R	6-5	237	4-5-00	0	1	3.03	27	0	2	30	26	11	10	1	19	42	.230	.341	.319	31.8	14.4	132
Anderson, Casey	R-R	6-4	185	8-31-00	0	0	43.20	1	0	0	2	9	9	8	1	2	1	.643	.706	.929	5.9	11.8	17
Angelo, Roman	R-R	6-5	220	5-17-00	1	1	6.19	4	4	0	16	17	14	11	3	14	13	.274	.403	.565	16.9	18.2	77
Backhus, Kyle	L-L	6-4	185	1-31-98	4	4	2.05	26	0	0	26	28	9	6	1	10	37	.275	.362	.382	31.6	8.6	117
Baker, Alec	R-R	6-3	202	12-4-99	0	0	6.00	1	0	0	3	5	2	2	0	1	3	.357	.400	.571	20.0	6.7	15
Beeks, Jalen	L-L	5-11	215	7-10-93	0	0	0.00	1	0	0	1	0	0	0	0	0	1	.000	.333	.000	33.3		3
Bielak, Brandon	L-R	6-2	208	4-2-96	1	0	2.79	2	2	0	10	3	3	3	2	5	5	.103	.235	.310	14.7	14.7	34
Brigham, Jeff	R-R	6-0	195	2-16-92	6	2	5.23	17	0	0	21	16	14	12	5	9	32	.213	.291	.493	37.2	10.5	86
Burgos, Juan	R-R	6-0	155	12-22-99	0	0	8.31	4	0	0	4	7	4	4	0	3	3	.368	.478	.474	12.5	12.5	24
Castillo, Jose	L-L	6-6	252	1-10-96	0	0	1.69	5	0	0	5	4	1	1	0	0	7	.222	.211	.333	36.8	0.0	19
Corcoran, Billy	R-R	6-8	220	8-21-99	2	3	10.55	5	5	0	21	36	26	25	4	7	18	.371	.410	.608	17.1	6.7	105
Crismatt, Nabil	R-R	6-1	220	12-25-94	0	0	0.00	1	1	0	2	1	0	0	0	0	2	.143	.143	.286	28.6	0.0	7
Curtiss, John	R-R	6-5	220	4-5-93	1	1	6.34	21	1	2	33	38	24	23	7	9	28	.295	.331	.550	19.7	6.3	142
Diaz, Yilber	R-R	6-0	190	8-19-00	1	3	11.63	21	8	0	41	39	55	53	9	64	49	.248	.471	.497	21.8	28.4	225
Drake, Kohl	L-L	6-5	220	7-17-00	1	2	9.18	4	4	0	17	24	18	17	3	8	19	.338	.407	.507	23.2	9.8	82
Durke, Hayden	R-R	6-1	206	5-1-02	0	2	9.53	19	0	1	17	17	19	18	1	18	20	.250	.422	.397	22.2	20.0	90
Endersby, Jimmy	R-R	6-1	194	1-16-98	0	1	2.57	2	0	0	7	6	2	2	0	3	5	.231	.310	.346	17.2	10.3	29
English, Tristin	R-R	6-0	208	5-14-97	0	1	6.75	2	0	0	1	1	1	1	0	1	1	.200	.333	.200	16.7	16.7	6
Feyereisen, J.P.	R-R	6-2	215	2-7-93	1	0	0.96	7	0	0	9	12	1	1	0	2	7	.324	.359	.405	18.0	5.1	39
Foster, Matt	R-R	6-2	215	1-27-95	2	2	3.89	31	0	2	35	37	18	15	5	12	42	.264	.327	.450	27.5	7.8	153
Garcia, Brandyn	L-L	6-4	225	5-27-00	1	1	3.27	6	0	0	11	7	5	4	2	8	13	.189	.362	.405	27.7	17.0	47
Giesting, Spencer	L-L	6-4	200	7-2-01	5	7	6.47	17	17	0	79	89	60	57	12	45	72	.284	.388	.521	19.3	12.1	373
Ginkel, Kevin	L-R	6-4	235	3-24-94	0	0	6.75	6	0	0	4	5	6	3	1	7	5	.294	.480	.529	20.0	28.0	25
Gomez, Cesar	L-R	6-3	195	7-9-98	1	2	7.43	11	4	0	27	37	23	22	6	13	21	.336	.411	.582	16.8	10.4	125
Gose, Anthony	L-L	6-0	200	8-10-90	0	3	5.14	14	0	0	14	14	11	8	2	9	16	.241	.343	.379	23.9	13.4	67
Graham, Kevin	L-R	6-1	195	8-12-99	0	0	9.00	1	0	0	1	1	1	1	0	0	0	.250	.250	1.000	0.0	0.0	4
Grammes, Conor	R-R	6-1	200	7-13-97	0	0	2.25	4	0	0	4	3	1	1	0	7	7	.214	.500	.286	31.8	31.8	22
Graveman, Kendall	R-R	6-2	200	12-21-90	0	0	0.00	2	0	0	2	1	0	0	0	0	1	.143	.143	.143	14.3	0.0	7
Henry, Tommy	L-L	6-3	205	7-29-97	2	6	8.12	11	11	0	54	76	51	49	7	21	51	.335	.392	.581	20.2	8.3	252
Hoffmann, Andrew	R-R	6-5	210	6-27-00	0	1	19.29	3	0	0	2	5	5	5	1	3	2	.417	.533	.667	13.3	20.0	15
Jameson, Drey	R-R	6-0	165	8-17-97	0	1	7.11	9	0	0	13	20	11	10	4	8	19	.345	.424	.621	28.8	12.1	66
Jarvis, Bryce	L-R	6-2	195	12-26-97	3	7	8.47	19	19	0	79	100	77	74	14	44	72	.314	.409	.550	19.1	11.7	377
Kelly, Casey	R-R	6-3	215	10-4-89	3	7	5.63	24	20	0	115	142	84	72	14	48	61	.306	.379	.483	11.5	9.0	531
Lin, Yu-Min	L-L	5-11	160	7-12-03	5	7	6.64	23	23	0	102	124	81	75	18	60	85	.303	.397	.509	17.7	12.5	481
Mantiply, Joe	R-L	6-4	219	3-1-91	2	0	5.56	10	0	0	11	14	9	7	4	3	11	.292	.333	.604	21.6	5.9	51
Martinez, Justin	R-R	6-3	180	7-30-01	0	0	0.00	1	0	0	1	1	0	0	0	0	0	.333	.333	.333	0.0	0.0	3
McGough, Scott	R-R	5-11	190	10-31-89	1	0	3.95	11	0	0	14	17	6	6	0	4	18	.309	.367	.345	30.0	6.7	60
Mena, Cristian	R-R	6-2	170	12-21-02	2	3	4.84	9	9	0	45	46	30	24	6	16	52	.264	.330	.454	27.1	8.3	192
Mercado, Logan	R-R	6-0	220	10-19-01	0	0	108.00	1	0	0	0	3	4	4	0	3	1	.750	.857	1.500	14.3	42.9	7
Mervis, Matt	L-R	6-2	225	4-16-98	0	0	12.00	2	0	0	3	5	4	4	1	1	0	.357	.400	.714	0.0	6.7	15
Montes De Oca, Christian	R-R	6-4	230	8-30-99	1	0	4.07	17	0	2	24	26	11	11	2	6	26	.274	.324	.400	25.5	5.9	102
Morillo, Alfred	R-R	6-3	190	11-14-01	1	0	5.59	20	0	0	29	33	18	18	1	20	23	.292	.403	.354	17.2	14.9	134
Morillo, Juan	R-R	6-1	150	3-19-99	1	1	2.57	21	0	2	21	18	7	6	1	9	20	.237	.341	.289	22.2	10.0	90
Nelson, Kyle	L-L	6-1	175	7-8-96	0	4	9.00	34	0	0	34	39	35	34	13	17	31	.277	.358	.603	19.5	10.7	159
Pope, Austin	R-R	6-3	210	10-26-98	0	3	4.60	25	1	0	29	34	19	15	2	10	34	.291	.346	.419	26.6	7.8	128
Rashi, Taylor	R-R	6-4	220	1-15-96	4	2	3.48	40	2	3	67	62	33	26	5	30	72	.242	.317	.359	24.7	10.3	292
Ray, Dylan	R-R	6-3	230	5-9-01	6	3	6.30	18	18	0	90	107	65	63	18	38	70	.300	.370	.538	17.3	9.4	405
Reid-Foley, Sean	R-R	6-3	230	8-30-95	0	1	5.79	16	0	1	14	13	11	9	1	19	15	.241	.447	.315	19.5	24.7	77
Rice, Jake	L-L	6-1	220	7-19-97	3	1	7.83	46	0	0	54	59	50	47	9	51	52	.288	.430	.493	19.2	18.8	271
Richards, Trevor	R-R	6-2	205	5-15-93	1	0	5.79	21	0	0	33	33	22	21	5	7	32	.256	.297	.488	23.2	5.1	138
Rodriguez, Elvin	R-R	6-3	160	3-31-98	0	0	12.60	4	0	0	5	10	7	7	1	1	6	.400	.423	.500	23.1	3.9	26
Saalfrank, Andrew	L-L	6-3	205	8-18-97	0	2	7.15	10	0	2	11	6	9	9	1	10	14	.162	.333	.243	28.6	20.4	49
Scott, Tayler	R-R	6-3	185	6-1-92	1	0	0.00	3	0	1	3	1	0	0	0	0	4	.100	.100	.100	40.0	0.0	10
Short, Avery	R-L	6-1	205	3-14-01	0	1	11.57	1	1	0	5	7	6	6	3	2	3	.404	.444	.773	11.1	7.4	27
Thompson, Ryan	R-R	6-5	210	6-26-92	0	0	0.00	2	0	0	2	1	0	0	0	0	0	.167	.167	.167	16.7	0.0	6
Valdez, Jesus	R-R	5-9	175	12-29-97	0	0	22.50	2	0	0	2	6	5	5	0	3	0	.600	.600	.600	0.0	20.0	15
Weber, Andy	L-R	5-11	190	7-24-97	0	0	9.64	5	0	0	5	11	10	5	5	0	1	.423	.407	1.038	3.7	0.0	27

Fielding

Catcher	PCT	G	PO	A	E	DP	PB
Boyd	.941	2	15	1	1	1	2
Del Castillo	.985	9	67	0	1	0	0
Garcia	.994	56	462	27	3	4	5
Herrera	1.000	11	99	3	0	1	0

	PCT	G	PO	A	E	DP
Logan	1.000	10	75	2	0	0	1
Moreno	1.000	4	25	2	0	0	1
Osborn	.982	6	53	1	1	0	1
Perez	.981	16	144	7	3	0	3
Pinto	.989	46	349	21	4	0	3

First Base	PCT	G	PO	A	E	DP
Brown	1.000	13	100	9	0	13
English	.996	32	205	20	1	24
Garcia	1.000	4	17	1	0	3
Kessinger	1.000	3	17	5	0	4

	PCT	G	PO	A	E	DP
Logan	1.000	1	11	1	0	1
Lopez	.750	2	3	0	1	0
Mancini	.991	60	428	33	4	55
Melendez	.990	17	97	6	1	12
Mervis	.976	16	111	12	3	18
Smith	1.000	4	38	6	0	5
Tawa	1.000	8	58	10	0	3
Valdez	1.000	4	21	1	0	1

Second Base	PCT	G	PO	A	E	DP
Alexander	.933	4	6	8	1	3
Corniel	.988	18	34	46	1	12
Kaiser	.976	8	16	25	1	8
Kessinger	1.000	2	1	3	0	3
Lawlar	.978	20	40	47	2	10
Lopez	1.000	7	7	16	0	2
Troy	.983	23	46	67	2	16
Valdez	1.000	2	4	10	0	2
Vargas	1.000	17	24	45	0	14
Weber	.986	54	88	126	3	36

Third Base	PCT	G	PO	A	E	DP
Alcantara	1.000	2	2	4	0	2
Alexander	.925	18	11	26	3	4
Corniel	1.000	2	4	1	0	0
English	.930	18	11	29	3	6
Kaiser	1.000	12	7	24	0	2
Kessinger	1.000	1	0	1	0	0
Lawlar	.926	20	14	36	4	2
Lopez	.857	7	3	9	2	0
Tawa	.857	4	2	4	1	1
Valdez	.912	21	7	24	3	2
Vargas	.930	25	15	38	4	2
Weber	.959	30	21	49	3	11

Shortstop	PCT	G	PO	A	E	DP
Alcantara	.959	43	62	103	7	29
Alexander	.966	16	17	39	2	8
Kaiser	.970	52	61	134	6	37
Kessinger	1.000	3	4	8	0	0
Lawlar	.963	20	35	43	3	20

	PCT	G	PO	A	E	DP
Lopez	1.000	3	1	3	0	0
Vargas	1.000	7	9	17	0	3
Weber	.957	10	16	29	2	8

Outfield	PCT	G	PO	A	E	DP
Alexander	1.000	10	15	0	0	0
Almora	1.000	33	76	2	0	0
Barrosa	.987	95	227	4	3	0
Brown	.913	12	21	0	2	0
English	.973	31	36	0	1	0
Graham	1.000	15	22	1	0	0
Lopez	1.000	6	10	1	0	0
Mancini	1.000	3	2	0	0	0
McCarthy	.971	48	100	2	3	0
Pache	.980	65	146	4	3	1
Robinson	.975	39	78	1	2	1
Tawa	1.000	5	7	1	0	0
Troy	.964	15	26	1	1	1
Vukovich	.983	89	163	10	3	1

AMARILLO SOD POODLES

DOUBLE-A

TEXAS LEAGUE

Batting	B-T	Ht.	Wt.	DOB	AVG	OBP	SLG	G	PA	AB	R	H	2B	3B	HR	RBI	BB	HBP	SH	SF	SO	SB	CS	BB%	SO%
Boyd, Jermiah	R-R	5-10	225	7-1-00	.333	.444	.800	5	18	15	3	5	1	0	2	7	3	0	0	0	6	0	0	16.7	33.3
Cerda, Christian	R-R	6-0	190	12-27-02	.237	.340	.449	93	383	321	44	76	14	0	18	49	51	2	4	5	67	1	0	13.3	17.5
Conticello, Gavin	L-R	6-4	195	6-11-03	.275	.369	.435	121	517	444	67	122	27	4	12	67	59	10	0	4	110	4	5	11.4	21.3
D'Orazio, J.J.	R-R	6-1	170	12-28-01	.223	.259	.302	39	147	139	14	31	5	0	2	12	6	1	0	1	37	1	0	4.1	25.2
Fernandez, Jose	R-R	6-3	165	9-22-03	.272	.321	.454	122	511	471	68	128	27	4	17	80	32	3	2	2	104	12	4	6.3	20.4
Franco, Junior	L-L	5-9	165	9-13-02	.160	.192	.160	6	26	25	2	4	0	0	0	2	1	0	0	0	3	1	0	3.9	11.5
Graham, Kevin	L-R	6-1	195	8-12-99	.175	.217	.281	15	60	57	3	10	3	0	1	4	3	0	0	0	21	0	0	5.0	35.0
Groover, Gino	R-R	6-2	212	4-16-02	.309	.399	.434	123	547	470	73	145	23	0	12	56	63	10	0	4	79	3	2	11.5	14.4
Hurley, Jack	L-R	6-0	185	3-13-02	.218	.273	.370	68	261	238	29	52	11	2	7	23	14	5	1	3	107	1	6	5.4	41.0
Logan, Gavin	L-R	5-9	212	1-14-00	.138	.219	.397	19	66	58	7	8	1	1	4	6	5	1	2	0	27	0	0	7.6	40.9
Martin, David	L-R	6-1	185	10-28-00	.333	.500	.333	1	4	3	1	1	0	0	0	0	1	0	0	0	1	0	0	25.0	25.0
McLaughlin, Ben	L-R	6-3	200	5-30-02	.343	.435	.556	28	115	99	17	34	9	0	4	26	14	2	0	0	24	0	0	12.2	20.9
Melendez, Ivan	R-R	6-3	225	1-24-00	.258	.348	.480	71	282	244	31	63	6	0	16	43	28	7	0	3	69	2	0	9.9	24.5
Osborn, Drake	R-R	5-9	190	7-22-98	.143	.229	.238	17	70	63	9	9	0	0	2	5	4	3	0	0	23	0	0	5.7	32.9
Pena, Manuel	R-R	6-1	170	12-5-03	.288	.326	.460	106	470	437	68	126	27	3	14	52	24	3	0	6	105	2	2	5.1	22.3
Roberts, Caleb	L-R	5-11	195	2-9-00	.237	.327	.388	104	437	379	58	90	21	3	10	57	45	8	0	5	103	8	3	10.3	23.6
Robinson, Kristian	R-R	6-3	190	12-11-00	.250	.359	.436	75	334	280	52	70	13	3	11	38	46	4	0	4	101	24	8	13.8	30.2
Torin, Cristofer	R-R	5-10	155	5-26-05	.381	.440	.571	5	25	21	5	8	4	0	0	2	3	0	0	1	3	1	0	12.0	12.0
Troy, Tommy	R-R	5-10	197	1-17-02	.286	.382	.461	87	399	343	56	98	20	2	12	47	49	5	1	1	70	21	4	12.3	17.5
Valdez, Jesus	R-R	5-9	175	12-29-97	.284	.364	.478	23	77	67	12	19	4	0	3	10	5	4	0	1	18	0	2	6.5	23.4
Waldschmidt, Ryan	R-R	6-1	205	10-7-02	.309	.423	.498	66	300	249	57	77	14	3	9	45	45	5	0	1	53	19	6	15.0	17.7
Walters, Sean	S-R	5-11	155	4-4-00	.305	.376	.466	60	220	194	25	46	11	2	4	28	18	1	7	0	50	2	2	8.2	22.7
Weber, Andy	L-R	5-11	190	7-24-97	.260	.321	.400	27	109	100	20	26	3	1	3	18	8	1	0	0	30	1	1	7.3	27.5

Pitching	B-T	Ht.	Wt.	DOB	W	L	ERA	G	GS	SV	IP	Hits	Runs	ER	HR	BB	SO	AVG	OBP	SLG	SO%	BB%	BF
Abner, Philip	L-L	6-1	220	5-5-02	3	1	4.21	34	0	1	36	35	24	17	5	7	42	.257	.299	.441	28.4	4.7	148
Albright, Luke	R-R	6-4	215	12-13-99	2	1	3.72	18	0	0	36	27	15	15	5	22	41	.208	.327	.400	26.3	14.1	156
Alvarez, Jhosmer	R-R	6-1	155	6-20-01	4	2	4.79	26	0	2	41	35	28	22	3	28	35	.232	.361	.338	19.0	15.2	184
Anderson, Casey	R-R	6-4	185	8-31-00	2	1	2.52	11	0	0	25	23	8	7	1	5	25	.245	.297	.340	24.5	4.9	102
Angelo, Roman	R-R	6-5	220	5-17-00	3	9	5.18	23	23	0	113	107	71	65	20	60	112	.248	.357	.439	22.0	11.8	510
Baker, Alec	R-R	6-3	202	12-4-99	3	4	5.72	27	15	0	83	102	59	53	17	33	61	.298	.360	.538	16.0	8.7	381
Barnes, Zach	R-R	6-0	180	4-10-99	2	0	2.57	16	0	1	14	7	4	4	1	13	10	.156	.361	.289	16.4	21.3	61
Bernal, Jonatan	R-R	6-1	194	6-29-02	4	3	5.57	14	8	1	53	64	35	33	8	19	38	.296	.356	.500	15.9	8.0	239
Boyd, Jermiah	R-R	5-10	225	7-1-00	0	0	9.00	1	0	0	1	1	1	1	0	0	0	.250	1.000	0.0	0.0	0	4
Bratt, Mitch	L-L	6-1	190	7-3-03	1	1	3.98	6	6	0	32	31	16	14	5	5	42	.242	.271	.461	31.6	3.8	133
Cabrera, Jose	R-R	6-3	190	5-30-02	9	6	4.92	26	26	0	135	153	79	74	16	50	118	.286	.354	.462	19.8	8.4	596
Chalas, Yordin	R-R	6-3	175	2-22-04	0	0	11.37	5	0	0	6	9	8	8	2	8	5	.346	.486	.654	14.3	22.9	35
Clayton, Logan	R-R	6-5	188	5-20-01	1	4	12.46	7	5	0	22	31	31	30	4	17	17	.330	.439	.606	14.9	14.9	114
Diaz, Yilber	R-R	6-0	190	8-19-00	0	0	6.43	13	0	0	14	16	10	10	0	9	16	.281	.388	.368	23.9	13.4	67
Durke, Hayden	R-R	6-1	206	5-1-02	0	1	2.31	11	0	4	12	4	4	3	0	6	18	.105	.261	.132	38.3	12.8	47
Eagen, Daniel	R-R	6-4	200	11-23-02	0	3	5.49	4	4	0	20	16	13	12	5	11	21	.216	.318	.473	24.7	12.9	85
Endersby, Jimmy	R-R	6-1	194	1-16-98	4	2	2.27	6	6	0	36	42	10	9	2	6	32	.290	.318	.372	21.2	4.0	151
Giesting, Spencer	L-L	6-4	200	7-2-01	3	2	3.67	10	10	0	56	53	27	23	6	19	59	.244	.311	.378	24.4	7.9	242
Gomez, Cesar	L-R	6-3	195	7-9-98	2	1	4.25	15	4	3	36	34	19	17	4	11	25	.260	.315	.412	17.0	7.5	147
Grammes, Conor	R-R	6-1	200	7-13-97	0	0	7.89	21	0	0	22	27	25	19	1	31	24	.300	.496	.389	18.9	24.4	127

	B-T	Ht.	Wt.	DOB																	
Gutierrez, Gerardo	R-R	6-0	177	9-15-98	2	3	5.15	24	0	0	37	41	23	21	3	16	34	.289	.360	.415	20.5	9.6	166
Kubiuk, Dan	R-R	6-1	220	9-30-95	2	1	9.53	13	0	1	11	19	13	12	2	7	6	.396	.456	.604	10.5	12.3	57
Morales, Victor	R-R	5-10	165	10-10-01	0	1	18.90	2	0	0	3	9	7	7	3	0	2	.474	.474	1.158	10.5	0.0	19
Morillo, Alfred	R-R	6-3	190	11-14-01	3	1	4.31	25	0	4	31	32	16	15	1	14	37	.269	.353	.353	27.0	10.2	137
Perez, Adonys	L-L	6-3	185	10-10-03	1	0	2.35	2	0	0	8	8	2	2	1	1	4	.276	.300	.448	13.3	3.3	30
Ray, Dylan	R-R	6-3	230	5-9-01	6	3	3.93	10	10	0	50	38	26	22	8	17	53	.205	.279	.368	25.5	8.2	208
Rey, Carlos	L-L	6-2	180	5-19-02	0	0	6.75	5	0	0	8	12	6	6	1	2	11	.364	.410	.545	28.2	5.1	39
Russell, Zane	R-R	6-2	196	6-12-02	1	8	4.14	48	0	4	54	40	31	25	8	24	54	.201	.284	.357	23.8	10.6	227
Saul, Eli	L-R	6-5	215	8-16-01	4	0	6.19	29	0	0	32	29	27	22	2	35	26	.242	.423	.375	16.0	21.5	163
Savino, Nate	L-L	6-3	210	1-24-02	1	1	10.24	15	0	0	29	38	36	33	4	26	19	.311	.444	.484	12.4	17.0	153
Short, Avery	R-L	6-1	205	3-14-01	4	6	4.41	21	21	0	98	91	50	48	13	35	72	.245	.314	.403	17.1	8.3	420
Sims, Landon	R-R	6-2	227	1-3-01	4	2	3.63	49	0	12	52	51	25	21	2	31	57	.256	.361	.322	24.5	13.3	233
Valdez, Jesus	R-R	5-9	175	12-29-97	0	0	0.00	1	0	0	1	0	0	0	0	0	0	.000	.250	.000	0.0	0.0	4
Walters, Jean	S-R	5-11	155	8-13-01	0	0	0.00	1	0	0	1	0	0	0	0	1	0	.000	.000	.000	33.3	0.0	3

Fielding

Catcher	PCT	G	PO	A	E	DP	PB
Boyd	1.000	3	24	0	0	0	0
Cerda	.995	75	594	44	3	2	7
D'Orazio	.996	34	261	22	1	1	7
Logan	.977	17	126	4	3	0	2
Martin	1.000	1	10	1	0	1	0
Osborn	1.000	13	107	7	0	0	1
Roberts	1.000	1	3	0	0	0	0

First Base	PCT	G	PO	A	E	DP
Fernandez	.984	9	62	1	1	9
Logan	1.000	1	1	0	0	0
McLaughlin	.994	20	157	16	1	18
Melendez	.991	43	291	28	3	28
Pena	.991	59	442	24	4	40
Roberts	.964	3	26	1	1	3
Valdez	1.000	5	38	1	0	4
Walters	1.000	2	11	1	0	0

Second Base	PCT	G	PO	A	E	DP
Groover	.000	1	0	0	0	0
Pena	1.000	9	16	16	0	4
Torin	1.000	4	5	12	0	2
Troy	.964	79	156	195	13	43
Valdez	.938	5	5	10	1	0
Walters	.990	46	78	127	2	35
Weber	.857	1	2	4	1	2

Third Base	PCT	G	PO	A	E	DP
Fernandez	.897	9	12	14	3	1
Groover	.938	113	78	150	15	14
McLaughlin	.000	1	0	0	0	0
Pena	.940	14	22	25	3	4
Valdez	.750	3	0	3	1	0
Walters	1.000	1	1	3	0	1

Shortstop	PCT	G	PO	A	E	DP
Fernandez	.944	104	139	233	22	51
Torin	1.000	1	4	7	0	3
Troy	1.000	1	0	1	0	0
Valdez	.857	2	1	5	1	2
Walters	1.000	11	10	26	0	6
Weber	.951	25	31	67	5	18

Outfield	PCT	G	PO	A	E	DP
Conticello	1.000	122	194	10	0	2
Franco	.909	6	10	0	1	0
Graham	.971	16	31	2	1	0
Hurley	.985	66	129	4	2	1
Pena	1.000	1	1	0	0	0
Roberts	.958	78	133	5	6	2
Robinson	.976	71	162	3	4	2
Troy	1.000	5	9	0	0	0
Waldschmidt	1.000	66	186	3	0	0

HILLSBORO HOPS — HIGH-A
NORTHWEST LEAGUE

Batting	B-T	Ht.	Wt.	DOB	AVG	OBP	SLG	G	PA	AB	R	H	2B	3B	HR	RBI	BB	HBP	SH	SF	SO	SB	CS	BB%	SO%
Boyd, Jermiah	R-R	5-10	225	7-1-00	.313	.333	.375	9	33	32	3	10	2	0	0	4	1	0	0	0	11	0	0	3.0	33.3
Caldwell, Slade	L-L	5-9	182	6-18-06	.238	.370	.311	66	300	244	43	58	16	1	0	18	47	6	0	3	76	12	4	15.7	25.3
Castillo, Kenny	R-R	6-2	170	5-13-04	.222	.267	.348	64	251	230	21	51	15	1	4	32	15	1	0	5	52	0	0	6.0	20.7
Corniel, Juan	S-R	5-11	150	10-2-02	.150	.190	.200	8	21	20	1	3	1	0	0	0	3	1	0	0	6	0	0	4.8	28.6
Crisantes, Demetrio	R-R	6-0	178	9-5-04	.252	.358	.415	34	151	123	18	31	8	0	4	29	21	2	0	5	19	6	1	13.9	12.6
De Leon, Adrian	R-R	5-7	180	2-4-04	.136	.260	.152	20	77	66	4	9	1	0	0	1	9	2	0	0	26	0	0	11.7	33.8
D'Orazio, J.J.	R-R	6-1	170	12-28-01	.273	.364	.338	23	88	77	6	21	3	1	0	9	9	2	0	0	20	0	1	10.2	22.7
Feltner, Jackson	R-R	6-2	225	9-19-01	.172	.318	.351	60	212	174	31	30	5	1	8	21	26	11	1	0	76	0	1	12.3	35.9
Franco, Junior	L-L	5-9	165	9-13-02	.300	.372	.470	73	260	230	35	69	14	2	7	31	25	2	0	1	33	10	5	9.6	12.7
Jones, Druw	R-R	6-4	180	11-28-03	.255	.335	.360	123	545	478	77	122	25	5	5	56	56	4	1	6	127	28	4	10.3	23.3
Logan, Gavin	L-R	5-9	212	1-14-00	.234	.336	.336	33	129	107	13	25	8	0	1	14	21	1	0	0	35	0	0	16.3	27.1
Luis, Jansel	S-R	6-0	170	3-6-05	.304	.342	.422	102	447	405	60	123	19	7	5	65	27	2	2	11	73	22	7	6.0	16.3
Marte, Modeifi	R-R	6-0	200	7-31-02	.276	.325	.397	43	169	156	12	43	11	1	2	27	9	3	0	1	21	2	2	5.3	12.4
Martin, David	L-R	6-1	185	10-28-00	.286	.412	.286	8	17	14	0	4	0	0	0	1	3	0	0	0	4	0	0	17.7	23.5
McLaughlin, Ben	L-R	6-3	200	5-30-02	.250	.378	.395	72	267	220	29	55	17	0	5	33	45	1	0	1	46	0	1	16.9	17.2
Ortiz, Angel	L-L	6-0	180	10-3-02	.266	.332	.420	117	494	433	58	115	26	4	11	64	46	3	0	12	96	3	3	9.3	19.4
Rodriguez, Adrian	R-R	6-0	170	10-21-03	.143	.217	.143	9	23	21	1	3	0	0	0	1	1	0	0	0	9	0	0	4.4	39.1
Rojas, Anderson	L-R	5-10	250	3-8-04	.232	.307	.300	116	474	413	58	96	19	3	1	38	47	0	8	6	76	19	8	9.9	16.0
Santana, Ruben	R-R	6-0	190	2-16-05	.141	.233	.188	21	73	64	5	9	3	0	0	6	8	0	0	1	23	1	0	11.0	31.5
Sim, Kevin	R-R	6-2	210	2-7-02	.214	.277	.262	39	157	137	21	27	3	0	1	9	7	4	0	0	36	4	1	5.1	26.3
Torin, Cristofer	R-R	5-10	155	5-26-05	.287	.381	.385	122	544	467	78	134	22	5	7	57	66	7	0	4	78	15	7	12.1	14.3
Waldschmidt, Ryan	R-R	6-1	205	10-7-02	.268	.415	.447	68	301	235	57	63	13	1	9	43	51	11	0	4	53	10	4	16.9	17.6
Walters, Jean	S-R	5-11	155	8-13-01	.203	.309	.237	20	69	59	8	12	2	0	0	4	9	1	0	0	13	0	0	13.0	18.8

Pitching	B-T	Ht.	Wt.	DOB	W	L	ERA	G	GS	SV	IP	Hits	Runs	ER	HR	BB	SO	AVG	OBP	SLG	SO%	BB%	BF
Abner, Philip	L-L	6-1	220	5-5-02	0	1	1.93	11	0	5	14	9	3	3	0	6	17	.184	.268	.224	30.4	10.7	56
Anderson, Casey	R-R	6-4	185	8-31-00	3	9	6.68	15	12	0	62	66	50	46	4	37	61	.275	.381	.396	21.3	12.9	287
Ayers, Kyle	L-R	6-2	200	3-3-03	0	0	4.91	2	0	0	4	3	2	2	0	2	5	.231	.313	.308	31.3	12.5	16
Brown, Dawson	R-R	6-1	198	6-28-01	1	0	3.46	22	0	1	26	19	10	10	0	20	22	.209	.378	.209	18.5	16.8	119
Chalas, Yordin	R-R	6-3	175	2-22-04	2	4	5.54	21	17	0	65	70	45	40	2	30	63	.294	.389	.381	21.4	10.2	295
Clayton, Logan	R-R	6-5	188	5-2-00	0	3	6.15	7	6	0	26	33	19	18	1	8	17	.317	.407	.404	13.6	10.4	125
Corniel, Juan	S-R	5-11	150	10-2-02	0	0	18.00	1	0	0	1	1	2	2	0	2	1	.250	.500	.250	16.7	33.3	6
Craig, Luke	L-L	6-2	205	8-6-01	1	0	0.00	6	0	2	6	3	0	0	0	3	9	.150	.292	.200	37.5	12.5	24
Durke, Hayden	R-R	6-1	206	5-1-02	3	0	0.89	15	0	5	20	3	2	2	0	11	36	.048	.213	.065	48.0	14.7	75
Eagen, Daniel	R-R	6-4	200	11-23-02	7	5	2.49	19	19	0	98	63	36	27	7	41	132	.184	.272	.286	34.1	10.6	387
Encarnacion, Lorenzo	R-R	5-11	175	11-9-01	0	4	13.22	7	4	0	16	29	24	24	4	13	16	.387	.489	.627	17.6	14.3	91

ARIZONA DIAMONDBACKS

Player	B-T	Ht	Wt	DOB																		
Fitzgibbons, Jake	L-L	5-11	175	3-21-02	0	0	3.00	12	0	0	18	12	7	6	1	14	17	.197	.359	.295	21.8	18.0	78
Gonzalez, Joangel	R-R	6-4	210	7-1-04	3	3	7.12	27	0	1	37	45	37	29	3	17	36	.302	.380	.443	21.1	9.9	171
Hagaman, David	R-R	6-4	185	4-16-03	1	0	3.15	5	5	0	20	11	7	7	3	4	27	.159	.237	.362	35.5	5.3	76
Hitt, Grayson	R-L	6-3	195	12-11-01	0	1	5.06	3	0	0	5	3	6	3	0	7	5	.188	.462	.250	19.2	26.9	26
Isea, Edgar	R-R	6-3	185	8-20-02	0	1	3.86	45	0	6	42	29	21	18	1	47	49	.196	.405	.257	23.9	22.9	205
Izzi, Ashton	R-R	6-3	165	11-18-03	1	2	3.58	6	6	0	28	27	15	11	3	7	26	.250	.291	.398	22.2	6.0	117
Knowlton, Sam	R-R	6-7	255	6-15-00	2	3	5.05	47	0	9	46	28	28	26	0	47	57	.181	.403	.239	26.3	21.7	217
Larrondo, Denny	R-R	6-2	180	5-31-02	3	4	7.58	9	6	0	30	36	29	25	5	20	35	.300	.415	.542	23.8	13.6	147
Liebano, Alexis	R-R	6-1	175	3-8-03	2	0	9.58	20	0	0	21	36	23	22	6	16	17	.396	.491	.681	15.7	14.8	108
Marriott, Mason	L-R	6-2	188	8-14-02	1	0	2.29	4	4	0	20	13	5	5	0	8	25	.188	.273	.232	32.5	10.4	77
Marte, Modeifi	R-R	6-1	200	7-31-02	0	0	27.00	1	0	0	1	3	3	3	0	3	0	.500	.667	.500	0.0	33.3	9
McLaughlin, Ben	L-R	6-3	200	5-30-02	0	0	0.00	3	0	0	4	1	0	0	0	1	1	.077	.143	.077	7.1	7.1	14
Mendez, Teofilo	R-R	5-11	170	10-8-01	0	1	9.82	3	0	0	4	5	4	4	2	2	357	.412	.357	11.1	11.1	18
Minyety, Jorge	R-R	6-1	170	1-4-03	3	0	10.29	20	0	0	28	25	33	32	1	28	17	.250	.447	.380	12.1	19.9	141
Morales, Victor	R-R	5-10	165	10-10-01	1	1	4.01	16	0	0	25	24	11	11	3	9	17	.255	.324	.383	16.2	8.6	105
Norris, Liam	L-L	6-4	215	8-13-01	1	1	8.67	22	0	0	27	23	32	26	6	50	47	.223	.484	.485	30.3	32.3	155
Nunez, Daniel	R-R	6-0	196	4-3-03	5	5	6.58	24	15	0	78	95	63	57	12	32	57	.300	.365	.508	15.7	8.8	364
Paredes, Wilkin	L-L	6-2	180	9-19-03	3	2	3.63	7	7	0	35	34	16	14	4	11	25	.258	.315	.409	17.1	7.5	146
Reid, Rocco	R-L	5-11	190	10-16-02	1	0	3.21	21	0	0	28	26	13	10	3	18	24	.245	.370	.358	18.9	14.2	127
Rey, Carlos	L-L	6-2	180	5-19-02	1	5	3.38	43	0	6	53	39	25	20	1	39	69	.206	.354	.270	28.9	16.3	239
Rodriguez, Adrian	R-R	6-0	170	10-21-03	0	0	0.00	2	0	0	1	3	0	0	0	1	0	.500	.571	.667	0.0	14.3	7
Sanchez, Junior	R-R	5-10	175	10-5-05	2	2	2.59	7	7	0	31	21	10	9	2	15	24	.191	.291	.282	18.9	11.8	127
Saul, Eli	L-R	6-5	215	8-16-01	1	3	3.23	24	1	1	31	26	14	11	3	21	31	.226	.357	.383	22.0	14.9	141
Savino, Nate	L-L	6-3	210	1-24-02	4	0	1.41	17	0	0	32	24	6	5	0	11	31	.209	.281	.252	24.0	8.5	129
Walters, Jean	S-R	5-11	155	8-13-01	0	0	0.00	1	0	0	1	0	0	0	0	2	0	.000	.000	.000	66.7	0.0	3
West, John	R-R	6-8	260	10-5-01	5	8	5.89	20	19	0	99	93	73	65	13	41	96	.245	.334	.406	22.2	9.5	432
Yan, Ricardo	R-R	6-4	180	11-14-02	3	3	5.22	32	3	1	71	56	43	41	5	55	71	.226	.391	.367	21.7	16.8	327

Fielding

Catcher	PCT	G	PO	A	E	DP	PB
Boyd	.985	8	59	6	1	1	3
Castillo	.985	54	505	29	8	3	14
De Leon	.994	19	147	10	1	1	5
D'Orazio	.984	18	170	15	3	1	6
Logan	.997	32	279	12	1	1	5
Martin	1.000	4	22	3	0	0	0

First Base	PCT	G	PO	A	E	DP
Feltner	.981	33	189	19	4	18
Marte	.982	36	244	33	5	27
Martin	1.000	2	2	0	0	0
McLaughlin	1.000	65	434	33	0	53
Santana	1.000	9	56	2	0	5
Sim	.968	6	25	5	1	0

Second Base	PCT	G	PO	A	E	DP
Corniel	.938	4	3	12	1	4

	PCT	G	PO	A	E	DP
Crisantes	.977	19	30	56	2	17
Luis	.962	52	71	132	8	17
Rodriguez	1.000	4	9	11	0	3
Rojas	.965	19	34	49	3	12
Torin	.986	18	23	49	1	8
Walters	.988	18	28	51	1	15

Third Base	PCT	G	PO	A	E	DP
Corniel	.000	2	0	0	0	0
Crisantes	.950	10	9	10	1	4
Luis	.932	27	26	42	5	5
Marte	.000	1	0	0	0	0
McLaughlin	1.000	1	0	2	0	0
Rodriguez	1.000	2	2	0	0	0
Rojas	.945	62	33	105	8	9
Santana	1.000	7	5	5	0	1
Sim	.967	30	19	39	2	3

Shortstop	PCT	G	PO	A	E	DP
Corniel	1.000	1	3	1	0	0
Luis	.957	18	22	44	3	11
Rodriguez	1.000	1	0	1	0	0
Rojas	.939	14	18	28	3	7
Torin	.966	100	138	229	13	56

Outfield	PCT	G	PO	A	E	DP
Caldwell	.992	63	122	1	1	0
Feltner	.000	2	0	0	0	0
Franco	1.000	44	85	1	0	1
Jones	.986	118	282	10	4	3
Marte	.917	5	11	0	1	0
Ortiz	.973	88	128	14	4	3
Rojas	.982	25	52	3	1	1
Waldschmidt	1.000	58	95	3	0	0

VISALIA RAWHIDE
CALIFORNIA LEAGUE — LOW-A

Batting	B-T	Ht.	Wt.	DOB	AVG	OBP	SLG	G	PA	AB	R	H	2B	3B	HR	RBI	BB	HBP	SH	SF	SO	SB	CS	BB%	SO%
Alpuria, Jose	S-R	6-2	160	2-12-05	.199	.323	.297	72	297	246	40	49	13	1	3	29	30	16	3	2	80	23	7	10.1	26.9
Barriga, Alberto	R-R	5-9	155	11-15-04	.199	.326	.296	99	410	341	50	68	19	1	4	32	53	12	2	2	118	16	4	12.9	28.8
Benua, Alexander	R-R	6-2	185	10-19-03	.250	.343	.378	54	204	172	23	43	7	3	3	23	23	3	2	3	53	6	1	11.3	26.0
Cabeza, Diosfran	S-R	5-10	155	5-13-03	.255	.358	.314	45	160	137	21	35	5	0	1	17	18	4	1	0	32	2	3	11.3	20.0
Caldwell, Slade	L-L	5-9	182	6-18-06	.294	.460	.454	48	216	163	40	48	13	2	3	20	44	7	1	1	62	13	6	20.4	28.7
Clark, Wallace	S-R	6-0	192	6-8-02	.120	.389	.120	8	36	25	3	3	0	0	0	3	10	1	0	0	4	1	0	27.8	11.1
Corniel, Juan	S-R	5-11	150	10-2-02	.230	.319	.302	45	164	139	22	32	8	1	0	17	18	1	4	2	42	7	7	11.0	25.6
Cunningham, Kayson	L-R	5-10	182	6-25-06	.255	.308	.277	11	52	47	2	12	1	0	0	4	3	1	0	1	15	1	1	5.8	28.9
De La Cruz, Abdias	R-R	6-3	175	11-3-04	.216	.312	.290	101	409	352	36	76	16	2	2	31	46	5	2	4	105	12	2	11.3	25.7
De Leon, Adrian	R-R	5-7	180	2-9-04	.180	.304	.284	62	240	194	21	35	11	0	3	30	32	5	3	6	74	2	1	13.3	30.8
Dix, JD	S-R	6-2	170	10-26-05	.261	.391	.335	50	230	188	34	49	7	2	1	17	38	3	0	1	51	19	4	16.5	22.2
Josepha, Jakey	L-R	6-2	135	5-15-04	.235	.342	.359	68	276	234	41	55	8	3	5	30	35	4	1	2	68	23	2	12.7	24.6
Luciano, Ivan	L-R	5-10	155	11-24-06	.286	.286	.357	3	14	14	2	4	1	0	0	2	0	0	0	0	5	0	0	0.0	35.7
Marte, Modeifi	R-R	6-1	200	7-31-02	.286	.359	.357	57	237	210	29	60	12	0	1	22	24	1	0	2	42	7	2	10.1	17.7
Nin, Yerald	R-R	6-3	180	8-8-05	.246	.331	.305	101	457	394	53	97	10	5	1	40	49	4	3	6	102	31	12	10.7	22.3
Perez, Enyervert	R-R	5-11	180	10-20-05	.248	.308	.295	27	117	105	11	26	2	0	1	12	9	1	0	2	32	1	0	7.7	27.4
Rodriguez, Adrian	R-R	6-0	170	10-21-03	.206	.318	.274	81	329	277	37	57	9	2	2	25	41	6	2	3	86	5	5	12.5	26.1
Santana, Ruben	R-R	6-0	180	4-28-05	.281	.358	.358	86	366	316	41	72	15	1	8	50	39	9	0	2	98	15	3	10.7	26.8
Soler, Yassel	R-R	5-11	185	1-26-06	.240	.342	.395	92	403	342	42	82	13	2	12	46	42	10	0	5	90	5	0	10.4	22.3
Virahonda, Carlos	R-R	5-11	180	12-12-05	.256	.362	.357	33	153	129	13	33	4	0	3	14	13	9	1	1	34	1	0	8.5	22.2
Youngblood, Trent	L-R	5-10	175	9-4-01	.266	.393	.332	84	355	274	36	73	6	0	4	35	62	1	9	9	57	25	2	17.5	16.1

Pitching	B-T	Ht.	Wt.	DOB	W	L	ERA	G	GS	SV	IP	Hits	Runs	ER	HR	BB	SO	AVG	OBP	SLG	SO%	BB%	BF
Anderson, Casey	R-R	6-4	185	8-31-00	0	1	2.16	2	1	1	8	8	3	2	0	1	6	.242	.278	.273	16.7	2.8	36
Ayers, Kyle	L-R	6-2	200	3-3-03	1	0	3.38	12	0	0	21	19	10	8	0	8	19	.232	.300	.280	21.1	8.9	90
Bernal, Jonatan	R-R	6-1	194	6-29-02	2	0	3.32	7	0	1	19	15	7	7	3	2	13	.211	.233	.352	17.8	2.7	73
Brown, Dawson	R-R	6-1	198	6-28-01	2	2	3.79	15	0	2	19	20	11	8	0	10	24	.270	.365	.392	28.2	11.8	85
Bruno, Ryan	L-L	6-3	221	1-4-02	4	1	3.66	20	0	3	32	19	14	13	1	28	42	.183	.360	.260	30.7	20.4	137
Cabeza, Diosfran	S-R	5-10	155	5-13-03	0	0	0.00	3	0	0	2	1	0	0	0	1	0	.143	.250	.143	0.0	12.5	8
Camejo, Jesus	R-R	6-0	180	2-20-01	0	0	7.50	4	0	0	6	7	5	5	0	4	4	.318	.448	.545	13.8	13.8	29
Ciprian, Junior	R-R	6-3	180	6-2-05	0	1	3.45	5	4	0	16	8	11	6	0	9	18	.140	.269	.175	26.9	13.4	67
Dominguez, Eric	L-L	6-3	180	1-12-03	0	1	22.24	5	0	0	6	9	14	14	4	8	6	.391	.529	.913	17.7	23.5	34
Encarnacion, Lorenzo	R-R	5-11	175	11-9-01	3	2	3.43	9	9	0	45	43	25	17	5	14	48	.250	.320	.413	24.7	7.2	194
Fell, Mervin	R-R	6-1	215	2-22-03	6	4	4.65	20	17	0	79	67	45	41	4	48	82	.235	.350	.358	24.1	14.1	340
Fitzgibbons, Jake	L-L	5-11	175	3-21-02	4	0	0.31	21	0	5	29	11	1	1	1	19	29	.118	.287	.161	25.2	16.5	115
Foley, Connor	R-R	6-5	230	7-14-03	0	2	7.07	5	5	0	14	13	11	11	0	15	20	.250	.420	.308	29.0	21.7	69
Fuerte, Abel	R-R	6-2	175	1-1-05	0	0	22.50	2	0	0	2	4	5	5	1	2	3	.400	.500	.800	25.0	16.7	12
Galvan, Alex	R-R	6-6	250	7-10-01	0	0	6.00	3	0	0	6	3	4	4	0	3	2	.200	.385	.200	15.4	23.1	13
Garnett, Travis	R-L	6-6	225	1-19-03	0	0	9.00	3	0	0	3	1	3	3	0	6	4	.100	.500	.100	22.2	33.3	18
Gonzalez, Joangel	R-R	6-4	210	7-1-04	0	2	2.89	14	0	6	19	14	8	6	0	9	22	.203	.304	.261	27.5	11.3	80
Guzman, Alvin	R-R	6-1	166	10-20-01	1	0	3.21	22	0	1	34	24	13	12	3	22	32	.202	.349	.319	21.5	14.8	149
Hawks, Sawyer	R-R	6-4	225	6-25-03	0	0	1.80	5	0	0	5	2	1	1	0	2	5	.118	.211	.118	26.3	10.5	19
Hitt, Grayson	R-L	6-3	195	12-11-01	2	3	4.25	28	6	1	59	58	39	28	2	48	69	.251	.395	.325	23.7	16.5	291
Huang, Chung-Hsiang	R-R	6-0	175	10-26-05	3	2	2.78	7	7	0	36	26	11	11	2	5	38	.200	.241	.300	27.7	3.7	137
Kelly, Jaitoine	R-R	6-3	257	6-29-07	0	0	6.00	1	1	0	3	4	3	2	0	1	2	.333	.385	.417	15.4	7.7	13
Larrondo, Denny	R-R	6-2	180	5-31-02	1	3	4.06	11	11	0	51	37	24	23	3	21	57	.204	.305	.320	27.0	10.0	211
Liebano, Alexis	R-R	6-1	175	3-8-03	1	1	4.88	17	0	1	24	20	14	13	5	14	19	.233	.343	.465	18.6	13.7	102
Marte, Modeifi	R-R	6-1	200	7-31-02	0	0	45.00	1	0	0	1	4	5	5	1	2	0	.571	.667	1.000	0.0	22.2	9
Mercado, Logan	R-R	6-0	220	10-19-01	3	1	3.10	15	4	2	41	25	15	14	4	20	46	.177	.282	.348	28.1	12.2	164
Minyety, Jorge	R-R	6-1	170	1-4-03	0	0	12.46	6	0	0	4	3	10	6	0	8	8	.176	.500	.235	28.6	28.6	28
Montiel, Tayler	L-L	6-2	210	7-5-02	0	1	5.40	5	0	0	5	6	3	3	0	2	8	.300	.364	.400	36.4	9.1	22
Morales, Victor	R-R	5-10	165	10-10-01	3	1	4.05	19	0	3	27	20	14	12	3	8	33	.208	.290	.354	30.6	7.4	108
Paredes, Wilkin	L-L	6-2	180	9-19-03	5	3	3.78	15	15	0	81	89	37	34	9	31	39	.278	.346	.413	11.0	8.7	355
Perez, Adonys	L-L	6-3	185	10-10-03	7	7	6.40	21	13	0	83	108	67	59	8	35	63	.315	.388	.446	16.1	8.9	392
Pinales, Darlin	R-R	6-4	240	8-28-02	1	3	5.90	35	0	4	40	31	30	26	2	32	56	.217	.383	.273	30.6	17.5	183
Quinn, Braden	L-L	6-3	210	6-24-03	4	2	5.13	18	0	0	40	50	32	23	5	31	23	.325	.432	.500	11.9	16.0	194
Ramirez, Gregori	R-R	6-3	170	9-12-04	0	0	9.00	2	0	0	3	2	3	2	1	2	2	.333	.455	.667	18.2	18.2	11
Reid, Rocco	R-L	5-11	190	10-16-02	1	0	2.60	10	0	0	17	14	8	5	0	10	26	.215	.333	.277	33.3	12.8	78
Reynoso, Erick	R-R	6-4	185	11-21-02	3	10	4.40	21	16	0	76	57	41	37	10	58	68	.213	.364	.377	20.2	17.2	337
Sanchez, Junior	R-R	5-10	175	9-16-05	4	1	2.32	15	13	0	74	62	21	19	4	23	64	.226	.287	.339	21.2	7.6	302
Santana, Sandro	L-L	5-10	155	3-7-05	2	4	3.38	21	0	3	48	39	25	18	3	28	47	.220	.333	.322	22.2	13.2	212
Savino, Nate	L-L	6-3	210	1-24-02	0	0	1.50	5	0	1	12	7	5	2	0	8	15	.175	.294	.250	29.4	15.7	51
Smith, Caswell	R-R	6-3	210	1-26-01	0	1	11.05	7	0	0	7	9	10	9	0	11	10	.321	.512	.429	24.4	26.8	41
Suarez, Josdanner	R-R	6-3	170	10-4-04	0	5	8.57	11	5	0	35	51	38	33	2	24	31	.345	.443	.493	17.3	13.4	179
Vasquez, Daury	R-R	6-2	170	4-17-06	1	3	3.72	5	5	0	19	17	8	8	2	14	19	.227	.363	.333	20.9	15.4	91
Zapata, Deyer	L-L	6-0	150	12-4-03	1	0	1.20	6	0	0	15	12	6	2	1	5	14	.211	.266	.298	21.9	7.8	64

Fielding

Catcher	PCT	G	PO	A	E	DP	PB
Barriga	.982	77	626	87	13	8	6
Cabeza	1.000	4	14	6	0	0	1
De Leon	.980	37	309	31	7	2	9
Luciano	.957	2	22	0	1	0	1
Virahonda	.989	19	162	14	2	3	3

First Base	PCT	G	PO	A	E	DP
Cabeza	.990	24	192	6	2	18
Marte	.988	35	227	27	3	23
Perez	.993	18	130	4	1	9
Santana	.991	58	428	31	4	36

Second Base	PCT	G	PO	A	E	DP
Cabeza	1.000	1	1	1	0	0
Corniel	.963	6	11	15	1	3

Dix	.974	46	88	139	6	28
Nin	.972	57	106	134	7	33
Rodriguez	.957	13	22	23	2	12
Youngblood	.957	12	20	24	2	5

Third Base	PCT	G	PO	A	E	DP
Clark	.944	8	2	15	1	0
Corniel	.889	6	2	14	2	2
Perez	.958	9	5	18	1	1
Rodriguez	.947	6	4	14	1	3
Santana	.965	26	15	40	2	5
Soler	.939	81	54	161	14	18

Shortstop	PCT	G	PO	A	E	DP
Corniel	.938	30	41	64	7	10
Cunningham	.897	11	18	17	4	4
Nin	.948	30	46	63	6	10
Rodriguez	.959	63	95	165	11	36

Outfield	PCT	G	PO	A	E	DP
Alpuria	.993	70	140	6	1	1
Benua	.937	48	83	6	6	1
Caldwell	1.000	46	102	4	0	1
De La Cruz	.981	94	146	5	3	0
Josepha	.994	68	158	9	1	4
Marte	1.000	15	26	2	0	0
Nin	.000	1	0	0	0	0
Youngblood	.968	67	115	5	4	2

ACL D-BACKS
ARIZONA COMPLEX LEAGUE — ROOKIE

Batting	B-T	Ht.	Wt.	DOB	AVG	OBP	SLG	G	PA	AB	R	H	2B	3B	HR	RBI	BB	HBP	SH	SF	SO	SB	CS	BB%	SO%
Alcala, Moises	S-R	5-9	155	2-10-03	.000	.333	.000	2	6	4	1	0	0	0	0	0	2	0	0	0	1	0	0	33.3	16.7
Alejos, Eliesbert	R-R	6-0	175	6-9-06	.241	.315	.302	56	226	199	21	48	9	0	1	25	9	13	4	1	35	9	2	4.0	15.5
Alpuria, Jose	S-R	6-2	160	2-12-05	.222	.391	.444	6	23	18	2	4	1	0	1	2	3	2	0	0	7	0	1	13.0	30.4

ARIZONA DIAMONDBACKS

Batting	B-T	Ht.	Wt.	DOB	AVG	OBP	SLG	G	PA	AB	R	H	2B	3B	HR	RBI	BB	HBP	SH	SF	SO	SB	CS	BB%	SO%	BF
Benua, Alexander	R-R	6-2	185	10-19-03	.200	.294	.250	22	68	60	9	12	3	0	0	2	5	3	0	0	20	1	1	7.4	29.4	
Blanco, Pedro	L-R	6-1	205	4-22-07	.238	.327	.385	37	150	130	15	31	10	3	1	18	16	2	0	2	51	0	1	10.7	34.0	
Carroll, Corbin	L-L	5-10	165	8-21-00	.000	.500	.000	1	4	2	0	0	0	0	0	0	2	0	0	0	0	0	0	50.0	0.0	
Castillo, Kenny	R-R	6-2	170	5-13-04	.000	.000	.000	1	5	4	0	0	0	0	0	0	1	0	0	0	1	0	0	0.0	0.0	
Catuy, Pedro	R-R	6-1	150	2-3-06	.221	.291	.329	44	158	140	18	31	7	1	2	22	12	3	0	3	42	5	1	7.6	26.6	
Cissell, Tytus	S-R	6-2	185	4-6-06	.201	.282	.304	53	206	184	23	37	6	2	3	20	17	4	0	1	76	9	1	8.3	36.9	
Del Castillo, Adrian	L-R	5-9	208	9-27-99	.313	.443	.667	14	61	48	14	15	4	2	3	11	10	2	0	1	17	0	0	16.4	27.9	
Dix, JD	S-R	6-2	170	10-12-05	.342	.421	.493	39	178	152	31	52	12	4	1	19	20	3	0	3	34	9	4	11.2	19.1	
English, Tristin	R-R	6-0	208	5-14-97	.300	.364	.900	3	11	10	2	3	0	0	2	2	1	0	0	0	2	0	0	9.1	18.2	
Hurley, Jack	L-R	6-0	185	3-13-02	.143	.260	.214	13	50	42	4	6	0	0	1	4	7	0	0	1	23	0	0	14.0	46.0	
Josepha, Jakey	L-R	6-2	135	5-15-04	.339	.388	.441	20	68	59	10	20	1	1	1	7	6	0	1	2	15	3	2	8.8	22.1	
Luciano, Ivan	L-R	5-10	185	11-24-06	.275	.398	.382	44	166	131	16	36	6	1	2	19	28	2	0	5	31	1	0	16.9	18.7	
Luis, Jansel	S-R	6-0	170	3-6-05	.500	.500	.750	4	16	16	5	8	2	1	0	2	0	0	0	0	1	2	0	0.0	6.3	
McLaughlin, Ben	L-R	6-3	200	5-30-02	.500	.500	.500	1	4	4	1	2	0	0	0	0	0	0	0	0	1	0	0	0.0	25.0	
Pena, Jefferson	R-R	5-8	160	1-13-04	.195	.307	.230	25	102	87	15	17	3	0	0	9	13	1	1	0	37	7	0	12.8	36.3	
Perez, Enyervert	R-R	5-11	200	5-11-06	.283	.383	.461	51	215	180	29	51	17	0	5	27	22	9	0	3	55	3	0	10.2	25.6	
Pinto, Rene	R-R	5-10	195	11-2-96	.167	.167	.333	2	6	6	0	1	1	0	0	0	0	0	0	0	1	0	0	0.0	16.7	
Rios, Alejandro	R-R	5-11	150	3-30-05	.222	.222	.222	4	9	9	0	2	0	0	0	1	0	0	0	0	3	0	0	0.0	33.3	
Sim, Kevin	R-R	6-2	210	2-7-02	.063	.211	.063	5	19	16	1	1	0	0	0	0	3	0	0	0	4	0	0	15.8	21.1	
Sinzza, Kyle	S-R	5-9	160	4-11-07	.350	.418	.500	17	67	60	9	21	7	1	0	8	5	2	0	0	13	2	3	7.5	19.4	
Virahonda, Carlos	R-R	5-11	180	12-12-05	.347	.464	.455	37	152	121	30	42	8	1	1	20	14	14	1	2	18	3	2	9.2	11.8	
Walker, Bo	R-R	6-3	180	3-14-06	.185	.336	.277	41	147	119	17	22	1	2	2	7	21	6	1	0	52	0	1	14.3	35.4	
Zapata, Gian	L-L	6-4	195	9-13-05	.284	.368	.459	24	87	74	19	21	3	2	2	14	10	0	0	2	24	5	0	12.6	27.6	

Pitching	B-T	Ht.	Wt.	DOB	W	L	ERA	G	GS	SV	IP	Hits	Runs	ER	HR	BB	SO	AVG	OBP	SLG	SO%	BB%	BF
Amparo, Jeffrey	R-R	6-3	175	9-24-04	0	0	67.50	1	0	0	1	4	5	5	0	2	1	.667	.750	.833	12.5	25.0	8
Ayers, Kyle	L-R	6-2	200	3-3-03	0	0	0.00	4	3	0	6	3	0	0	0	1	7	.158	.200	.211	35.0	5.0	20
Brea, Victor	L-L	6-4	170	10-8-02	0	0	1.80	3	0	0	5	4	1	1	0	2	4	.211	.286	.263	19.1	9.5	21
Brigham, Jeff	R-R	6-0	195	2-16-92	0	0	0.00	1	1	0	1	0	0	0	0	2	0	.000	.500	.000	0.0	50.0	4
Bruno, Ryan	L-L	6-3	221	1-4-02	0	0	0.00	4	0	0	5	1	0	0	0	2	10	.067	.222	.133	55.6	11.1	18
Calvo, Jeison	R-R	6-2	200	10-31-05	2	3	6.33	11	2	0	27	39	29	19	0	17	29	.345	.429	.407	21.8	12.8	133
Cardenas, Anderson	R-R	6-2	160	6-21-06	0	0	0.00	4	1	1	8	4	1	0	0	2	12	.143	.226	.179	38.7	6.5	31
Ciprian, Junior	R-R	6-3	180	6-2-05	2	1	4.62	12	8	1	39	32	21	20	4	22	33	.230	.347	.388	19.5	13.0	169
Diaz, Yilber	R-R	6-0	190	8-19-00	0	0	9.00	1	0	0	2	2	2	2	1	0	5	.250	.250	.625	62.5	0.0	8
Dominguez, Eric	L-L	6-3	180	1-12-03	0	0	3.65	7	0	0	12	8	7	5	1	8	14	.186	.352	.279	25.9	14.8	54
Escobar, Jesus	R-R	5-10	228	5-2-28-06	4	3	4.29	11	4	0	42	45	25	20	6	18	31	.274	.348	.470	16.6	9.6	187
Espinal, Jeury	R-R	5-11	165	1-5-07	2	1	4.50	15	2	1	38	33	20	19	4	19	31	.236	.331	.393	19.3	11.8	161
Fuerte, Abel	R-R	6-2	175	1-1-05	2	1	3.27	18	0	4	22	19	10	8	0	9	17	.238	.351	.275	17.9	9.5	95
Garnett, Travis	R-L	6-6	225	1-19-03	0	0	6.75	1	0	0	1	1	1	1	0	0	3	.429	.429	.571	42.9	0.0	7
Graveman, Kendall	R-R	6-2	200	12-21-90	0	0	0.00	2	2	0	2	4	0	0	0	1	2	.444	.500	.444	18.2	9.1	11
Guzman, Alvin	R-R	6-1	166	10-20-01	1	2	1.29	11	0	1	14	8	3	2	0	3	14	.163	.226	.224	26.4	5.7	53
Huang, Chung-Hsiang	R-R	6-0	175	10-26-05	1	1	4.41	9	8	0	33	24	20	16	2	10	40	.200	.281	.325	29.6	7.4	135
Jameson, Drey	R-R	6-1	187	8-17-97	0	1	6.75	2	2	0	1	2	1	1	0	1	3	.286	.375	.286	37.5	12.5	8
Jimenez, Onias	R-R	6-1	170	5-23-04	1	3	9.24	13	0	1	13	19	17	13	1	12	15	.358	.485	.453	22.1	17.7	68
Kelly, Jaitoine	R-R	6-3	257	6-29-07	1	1	4.81	5	4	1	24	24	13	13	1	7	15	.276	.326	.437	15.8	7.4	95
Martinez, Justin	R-R	6-3	180	3-21-01	0	0	0.00	1	1	0	1	0	0	0	0	1	0	.000	.000	.000	33.3	0.0	3
Mena, Walvin	R-R	6-1	195	9-30-05	1	2	3.77	10	2	0	14	11	6	6	1	8	15	.268	.391	.375	21.7	11.6	69
Mercado, Logan	R-R	6-0	220	10-19-01	0	1	3.00	3	2	0	12	11	6	4	1	6	14	.244	.364	.333	25.0	10.7	56
Mojica, Augie	R-R	6-2	180	8-30-04	3	1	4.76	6	2	0	17	16	11	9	3	9	15	.254	.360	.444	20.0	12.0	75
Nelson, Kyle	L-L	6-1	175	7-8-96	0	0	0.00	1	0	0	1	0	0	0	0	2	0	.000	.000	.000	66.7	0.0	3
Pope, Austin	R-R	6-3	210	10-26-98	1	0	3.52	6	3	0	8	8	4	3	1	1	9	.276	.300	.448	30.0	3.3	30
Ramirez, Gregori	R-R	6-3	170	9-12-04	0	2	7.71	9	0	5	7	8	7	6	0	7	4	.320	.457	.400	11.1	19.4	36
Rodriguez, Eduardo	L-L	6-2	231	4-7-93	0	1	5.79	1	1	0	5	3	4	3	1	9	.188	.235	.750	50.0	5.6	18
Rosario, Kelvin	L-L	6-2	140	8-28-06	4	0	4.10	14	1	1	26	25	14	12	4	22	26	.245	.384	.402	20.8	17.6	125
Saalfrank, Andrew	L-L	6-3	205	8-18-97	0	0	21.60	2	0	0	2	4	4	4	0	3	1	.500	.636	.875	9.1	27.3	11
Santana, Sandro	L-L	5-10	150	3-7-05	2	0	0.00	5	0	0	11	5	0	0	0	3	14	.143	.205	.229	35.9	7.7	39
Serda, Dawel	R-R	6-3	165	10-13-04	0	2	4.26	6	1	1	13	13	6	6	0	2	9	.265	.296	.327	16.7	3.7	54
Smith, Caswell	R-R	6-3	210	1-26-01	0	0	8.10	3	1	0	3	0	3	3	2	0	4	.000	.214	.000	28.6	14.3	14
Suarez, Josdanner	R-R	6-3	170	10-4-04	3	2	2.20	8	2	0	29	26	13	7	1	14	20	.260	.361	.380	16.8	11.8	119
Vasquez, Daury	R-R	6-2	170	4-17-06	1	1	3.83	11	7	0	45	36	21	19	1	23	61	.218	.326	.279	31.4	11.9	194

Fielding

C: Luciano 30, Virahonda 26, Del Castillo 2, Pinto 2, Rios 2, Alcala 1, Castillo 1. 1B: Perez 31, Blanco 26, English 2, McLaughlin 1, Rios 1, Sim 1. 2B: Dix 34, Sinzza 15, Cissell 10, Luis 1. 3B: Alejos 8, Perez 20, Sim 3, Luis 1. SS: Cissell 39, Alejos 18, Sinzza 2, Dix 1, Luis 1. LF: Pena 23, Walker 19, Benua 9, Josepha 7, Zapata 2, Alpuria 1, English 1. CF: Catuy 42, Hurley 14, Walker 5, Alpuria 3, Josepha 3, Zapata 2, Pena 1. RF: Zapata 19, Walker 15, Benua 10, Josepha 9, Hurley 5, Alpuria 1, Carroll 1, Catuy 1, Pena 1.

DSL ARIZONA RED   *ROOKIE*
DOMINICAN SUMMER LEAGUE

Batting	B-T	Ht.	Wt.	DOB	AVG	OBP	SLG	G	PA	AB	R	H	2B	3B	HR	RBI	BB	HBP	SH	SF	SO	SB	CS	BB%	SO%
Alvarez, Juan	S-R	6-1	190	3-3-06	.248	.320	.392	48	173	153	23	38	9	2	3	32	13	4	0	2	41	4	1	7.5	23.7
Ayena, Erickson	R-R	6-1	180	10-16-05	.133	.417	.133	12	24	15	4	2	0	0	0	1	6	2	0	1	7	3	3	25.0	29.2
Benzan, Alfredo	S-R	6-2	165	4-21-07	.329	.379	.494	22	89	79	16	26	4	3	1	9	6	1	2	1	15	6	3	6.7	16.9
De La Cruz, Erick	R-R	6-0	160	11-15-06	.350	.417	.400	6	24	20	3	7	1	0	0	3	2	1	0	1	4	4	1	8.3	16.7

Batting	B-T	Ht.	Wt.	DOB	AVG	OBP	SLG	G	PA	AB	R	H	2B	3B	HR	RBI	BB	HBP	SH	SF	SO	SB	CS	BB%	SO%
Encarnacion, Andy	R-R	6-1	160	1-18-05	.225	.349	.338	31	88	71	11	16	6	1	0	14	14	0	2	1	16	9	1	15.9	18.2
Fernandez, Johan	R-R	6-0	180	3-10-07	.230	.338	.410	24	72	61	12	14	2	0	3	12	8	2	1	0	17	1	0	11.1	23.6
Guanchez, Alfredo	S-R	6-0	150	10-17-05	.750	.875	1.250	3	8	4	3	3	0	1	0	1	4	0	0	0	1	0	1	50.0	12.5
Lantigua, Robert	L-R	5-9	175	5-24-07	.250	.250	.250	2	4	4	1	1	0	0	0	0	0	0	0	0	1	0	0	0.0	25.0
Lara, Jorge	S-R	5-6	145	10-24-05	.345	.483	.500	38	149	116	31	40	9	3	1	25	27	5	0	1	13	18	3	18.1	8.7
Liriano, Raily	R-R	6-2	160	1-9-07	.283	.355	.439	52	215	187	39	53	13	2	4	23	17	6	1	4	56	23	8	7.9	26.1
Mendez, Jeshua	R-R	6-0	175	12-19-07	.238	.379	.286	12	29	21	4	5	1	0	0	6	5	1	0	2	6	2	1	17.2	20.7
Montero, Daonil	R-R	6-0	165	11-11-07	.153	.231	.220	21	65	59	5	9	1	0	1	1	4	2	0	0	20	1	0	6.2	30.8
Peralta, Ramy	R-R	6-1	156	9-8-06	.225	.410	.350	34	105	80	17	18	2	1	2	14	22	3	0	0	27	2	0	21.0	25.7
Radney, Adriel	R-R	6-3	180	6-23-07	.266	.364	.401	54	209	177	33	47	7	4	3	37	25	4	0	3	37	18	3	12.0	17.7
Ramos, Santiago	L-R	5-10	170	1-3-07	.125	.462	.125	8	13	8	1	1	0	0	0	0	4	1	0	0	3	0	1	30.8	23.1
Rivera, Belfi	L-R	6-0	165	12-16-06	.175	.325	.206	22	77	63	10	11	2	0	0	4	14	0	0	0	21	4	2	18.2	27.3
Rodriguez, Jose	R-R	5-8	175	4-11-07	.200	.200	.400	3	5	5	1	1	1	0	0	1	0	0	0	0	2	0	0	0.0	40.0
Sanchez, Eybert	L-R	6-0	160	1-12-08	.287	.432	.316	54	221	174	47	50	3	1	0	23	43	2	1	1	27	17	8	19.5	12.2
Santana, Victor	R-R	6-2	180	2-23-08	.241	.328	.362	17	67	58	13	14	2	1	1	10	5	3	0	1	9	0	1	7.5	13.4
Sinzza, Kyle	R-R	5-9	160	4-11-07	.370	.437	.500	18	61	54	13	20	4	0	1	11	5	0	1	1	9	9	2	8.2	14.8
Suarez, Angel	R-R	5-9	155	8-9-08	.200	.448	.283	36	88	60	18	12	3	1	0	7	25	2	1	0	14	12	3	28.4	15.9
Suarez, Ronny	R-R	6-1	180	1-10-08	.231	.333	.269	11	30	26	4	6	1	0	0	0	3	1	0	0	9	3	1	10.0	30.0
Urbina, Jose	R-R	5-11	195	5-14-06	.186	.373	.265	42	150	113	21	21	4	1	1	14	25	10	0	2	27	0	0	16.7	18.0

Pitching	B-T	Ht.	Wt.	DOB	W	L	ERA	G	GS	SV	IP	Hits	Runs	ER	HR	BB	SO	AVG	OBP	SLG	SO%	BB%	BF
Almonte, Raminel	R-R	6-0	150	4-17-07	1	2	4.76	12	0	0	28	27	18	15	1	19	29	.255	.380	.321	22.5	14.7	129
Bello, Samuel	R-R	6-3	195	10-18-04	2	3	4.08	19	0	6	29	28	16	13	2	16	23	.259	.388	.370	17.2	11.9	134
Beltran, Angel	R-R	6-4	230	7-13-07	2	2	3.08	11	11	0	50	28	18	17	0	38	38	.172	.345	.209	18.5	18.5	206
Calcano, Johan	R-R	6-5	190	3-21-07	0	1	21.00	6	0	0	6	12	14	14	0	10	7	.429	.575	.464	17.5	25.0	40
Carrasco, Luis	L-L	6-1	175	1-22-05	3	2	6.06	9	1	0	16	23	11	11	2	9	10	.348	.434	.530	13.2	11.8	76
Castro, Jhossua	R-R	5-11	165	11-15-05	4	0	2.14	11	0	0	21	20	5	5	1	9	11	.263	.364	.329	12.4	10.1	89
Cepeda, Luis	L-L	6-1	170	8-23-07	1	0	4.50	5	2	0	14	13	9	7	0	11	13	.250	.397	.288	19.1	16.2	68
Encarnacion, Andy	R-R	6-1	160	1-18-05	0	0	0.00	0	0	0	1	0	0	0	0	0	2	.000	.000	.000	66.7	0.0	3
Fransua, Berlin	R-R	6-2	160	3-26-08	0	0	0.00	1	0	0	2	0	0	0	0	1	0	.667	.750	.667	25.0	0.0	4
Frias, Frederic	R-R	6-3	180	6-24-04	0	0	0.00	1	0	0	1	0	0	0	0	4	0	.000	1.000	.000	0.0	100.0	4
Gonzalez, Samuel	R-R	6-3	185	1-18-05	2	0	1.27	7	2	0	21	14	3	3	0	5	23	.194	.256	.278	29.5	6.4	78
Huizi, Estiven	R-R	6-3	195	2-24-07	1	0	3.00	2	0	0	3	2	1	1	0	3	2	.200	.385	.300	15.4	23.1	13
Jimenez, Yaury	R-R	6-3	175	7-13-06	3	2	3.92	12	8	0	39	35	19	17	5	19	23	.246	.367	.394	13.6	11.2	169
Kelly, Jaitoine	R-R	6-3	257	6-29-07	0	0	4.66	3	0	0	10	11	7	5	0	3	11	.289	.333	.342	26.2	7.1	42
Ledezma, Juan	R-R	6-2	200	12-3-04	1	0	6.75	12	0	3	12	13	10	9	1	9	14	.277	.404	.383	24.6	15.8	57
Lopez, Manuel	R-R	6-2	185	1-12-07	0	2	9.00	8	0	0	8	4	9	8	2	12	4	.148	.465	.407	9.3	27.9	43
Lugo, Alexander	L-L	6-1	160	8-29-06	0	0	8.00	7	0	0	9	8	8	8	1	10	9	.306	.469	.472	18.4	20.4	49
Mago, Yan	R-R	6-0	160	11-17-03	2	1	6.52	17	0	1	19	22	15	14	3	23	15	.293	.465	.453	14.9	22.8	101
Paredes, Luis	R-R	6-1	170	12-16-05	1	0	9.35	7	0	1	9	4	13	9	1	10	.133	.462	.267	19.2	38.5	52
Pena, Geremias	R-R	6-2	165	10-12-06	0	0	7.00	5	2	0	9	12	8	7	0	7	9	.316	.447	.342	19.2	14.9	47
Puello, Jose	R-R	6-4	155	5-24-07	2	1	1.59	6	6	0	28	21	14	5	2	18	16	.210	.339	.290	5.0	14.9	121
Quintana, Luis	R-R	6-1	190	11-26-06	0	0	81.00	2	0	0	1	3	3	3	0	5	0	.500	.857	.500	0.0	71.4	7
Ramirez, Gregori	R-R	6-3	175	9-12-04	2	0	0.00	6	0	0	11	3	4	0	0	6	17	.083	.250	.083	38.6	13.6	44
Rosario, Naimer	L-L	6-0	160	7-18-06	5	1	2.21	8	8	0	41	24	11	10	0	11	38	.171	.255	.250	24.2	7.0	157
Sanchez, David	R-R	6-1	165	2-14-07	0	0	0.00	2	0	0	4	3	0	0	0	1	3	.200	.250	.267	18.8	6.3	16
Sanchez, Gregory	L-L	5-9	170	1-13-05	0	0	9.00	1	0	0	1	1	1	1	0	2	1	.250	.500	.250	16.7	33.3	6
Terrero, Robert	R-R	6-4	300	1-8-07	1	1	11.57	4	2	0	7	6	10	9	2	13	4	.250	.538	.583	10.3	33.3	39
Torres, Isael	R-R	6-0	175	6-18-06	1	2	3.58	18	0	4	28	17	12	11	2	19	30	.173	.308	.276	25.0	15.8	120
Valdez, Miguel	L-L	5-11	195	9-1-06	0	0	81.00	1	0	0	1	6	9	9	1	1	1	.600	.636	1.200	9.1	9.1	11
Vargas, Modesto	R-R	6-2	195	12-14-04	0	1	6.23	8	4	0	9	4	8	6	0	18	8	.148	.500	.148	17.4	39.1	46

Fielding
C: Urbina 36, Fernandez 20, Ramos 6, Mendez 2, Rodriguez 2, Lantigua 1. 1B: Alvarez 36, Peralta 28, Lantigua 1. 2B: Lara 37, Sanchez 9, Sinzza 9, Suarez 8, De La Cruz 1. 3B: Suarez 27, Montero 17, Santana 15, Guanchez 2, Lara 2, Peralta 1, Sanchez 1. SS: Sanchez 46, Sinzza 9, Suarez 3, Montero 1, Peralta 1. LF: Encarnacion 18, Radney 15, Benzan 10, Rivera 10, Mendez 4, Ayena 3, Alvarez 1, De La Cruz 1, Guanchez 1, Liriano 1. CF: Liriano 34, Rivera 11, Benzan 8, Encarnacion 6, Mendez 1, Radney 1. RF: Radney 36, Liriano 12, Ayena 5, Suarez 5, Encarnacion 2, De La Cruz 1, Mendez 1.

DSL ARIZONA BLACK — ROOKIE
DOMINICAN SUMMER LEAGUE

Batting	B-T	Ht.	Wt.	DOB	AVG	OBP	SLG	G	PA	AB	R	H	2B	3B	HR	RBI	BB	HBP	SH	SF	SO	SB	CS	BB%	SO%
Ayena, Erickson	R-R	6-1	180	10-16-05	.462	.611	.538	6	18	13	5	6	1	0	0	4	4	1	0	0	6	1	1	22.2	33.3
Benzan, Alfredo	S-R	6-2	165	4-21-07	.302	.436	.387	32	135	106	22	32	5	2	0	20	25	1	2	1	18	9	2	18.5	13.3
Brima, Juan	S-R	6-0	180	9-14-07	.266	.398	.361	49	201	158	31	42	7	1	2	28	35	3	0	5	45	13	5	17.4	22.4
Bruno, Alam	L-R	6-4	180	4-16-08	.129	.275	.161	9	40	31	2	4	1	0	0	7	7	0	0	2	10	0	0	17.5	25.0
De La Cruz, Elian	R-R	6-1	195	9-25-07	.236	.373	.309	17	67	55	7	13	1	0	1	8	9	3	0	0	14	5	0	13.4	20.9
De La Cruz, Erick	R-R	6-0	160	11-15-06	.339	.414	.556	35	145	124	34	42	11	2	4	32	16	2	0	3	19	7	3	11.0	13.1
De La Rosa, Mayki	R-R	6-1	175	1-18-07	.277	.417	.455	34	127	101	22	28	8	2	2	14	21	4	0	1	34	12	3	16.5	26.8
Fernandez, Johan	R-R	6-0	180	3-10-07	.500	.500	.500	1	4	4	1	2	0	0	0	1	0	0	0	0	0	0	0	0.0	0.0
Gallegos, Alonso	R-R	5-9	150	2-23-07	.298	.402	.333	31	102	84	19	25	1	1	0	7	13	3	0	2	13	5	2	12.8	12.8
Genao, Feliz	L-R	6-3	200	1-19-08	.301	.444	.442	44	172	136	27	41	11	2	0	15	32	3	1	0	38	4	1	18.6	22.1
Gil, Santiago	R-R	5-10	160	5-29-08	.191	.325	.338	25	84	68	12	13	3	2	1	10	11	3	1	1	17	1	1	13.1	20.2
Gonzalez, Rodrigo	R-R	6-1	170	1-28-08	.242	.365	.263	35	115	95	17	23	2	0	0	11	17	2	0	1	23	11	1	14.8	20.0
Lantigua, Robert	L-R	5-9	175	5-24-07	.148	.313	.148	17	67	54	9	8	0	0	0	6	12	1	0	0	11	4	0	17.9	16.4
Lara, Jorge	S-R	5-6	145	10-24-05	.306	.447	.389	13	47	36	14	11	1	1	0	6	9	1	0	1	7	5	0	19.2	14.9

ARIZONA DIAMONDBACKS

	B-T	Ht.	Wt.	DOB	AVG	OBP	SLG	G	AB	R	H	2B	3B	HR	RBI	BB	SO	SB	CS	OPS	XBH%	K%
Medina, Albert	L-L	6-0	180	9-27-07	.295	.475	.364	22	59	44	15	13	3	0	0	8	13	2	0	0	15	0	0	22.0	25.4
Mejia, Ismael	R-R	6-1	180	7-15-08	.163	.305	.204	19	59	49	8	8	2	0	0	6	10	0	0	0	9	3	0	17.0	15.3
Mendez, Jeshua	R-R	6-0	175	12-19-07	.115	.303	.192	10	33	26	6	3	2	0	0	1	7	0	0	0	7	4	0	21.2	21.2
Montero, Daonil	R-R	6-0	165	11-11-07	.186	.255	.209	14	47	43	6	8	1	0	0	2	2	2	0	0	6	0	0	4.3	12.8
Pitre, Jose	L-L	6-1	185	11-6-07	.146	.333	.188	20	64	48	7	7	2	0	0	4	11	3	1	1	6	1	2	17.2	9.4
Ramos, Santiago	L-R	5-10	170	1-3-07	.000	.000	.000	1	1	1	0	0	0	0	0	0	0	0	0	0	0	0	0	0.0	0.0
Rivera, Belfi	L-R	6-0	165	12-16-06	.283	.397	.317	19	73	60	7	17	2	0	0	10	12	0	0	1	13	10	2	16.4	17.8
Rodriguez, Jose	R-R	5-8	175	4-11-07	.196	.378	.393	23	74	56	9	11	2	0	3	14	14	3	0	1	16	1	0	18.9	21.6
Santana, Victor	R-R	6-2	180	2-23-08	.319	.436	.389	35	141	113	22	36	5	0	1	18	22	3	0	2	13	0	0	15.6	9.2
Suarez, Ronny	R-R	6-1	180	1-10-08	.180	.306	.288	33	134	111	17	20	5	2	1	17	18	3	0	2	32	10	6	13.4	23.9

Pitching	B-T	Ht.	Wt.	DOB	W	L	ERA	G	GS	SV	IP	Hits	Runs	ER	HR	BB	SO	AVG	OBP	SLG	SO%	BB%	BF
Aquino, Francis	R-R	6-2	195	3-29-07	0	0	11.12	5	0	0	6	5	7	7	1	11	9	.227	.485	.409	27.3	33.3	33
Barrera, Reibert	R-R	6-2	180	8-28-07	1	0	10.97	6	2	0	11	13	13	13	1	20	9	.317	.541	.488	14.8	32.8	61
Calcano, Johan	R-R	6-5	190	3-21-07	0	1	12.91	6	4	0	8	7	11	11	0	9	7	.250	.463	.286	17.1	22.0	41
Carrasco, Luis	L-L	6-1	175	1-22-05	0	1	2.53	7	0	1	11	8	3	3	1	6	7	.235	.357	.412	16.7	14.3	42
Cepeda, Luis	L-L	6-1	170	8-23-07	1	1	2.84	7	5	0	25	17	11	8	0	15	28	.193	.327	.250	26.2	14.0	107
Frias, Frederic	R-R	6-3	180	6-24-04	1	0	23.82	6	0	0	6	7	15	15	0	15	8	.280	.571	.360	19.1	35.7	42
Gallegos, Alonso	R-R	5-9	150	2-23-07	0	0	9.00	1	0	0	1	1	2	1	0	0	.250	.250	1.000	0.0	0.0	4
Gonzalez, Samuel	R-R	6-3	185	1-18-05	2	0	0.71	5	0	0	13	7	3	1	0	1	18	.156	.255	.200	35.3	2.0	51
Huizi, Estiven	R-R	6-3	195	2-24-07	1	1	4.91	12	0	0	15	12	15	8	2	14	12	.222	.377	.426	17.4	20.3	69
Lopez, Manuel	R-R	6-2	185	1-12-07	1	1	6.00	6	0	1	9	9	8	6	0	10	10	.250	.417	.417	20.8	20.8	48
Lugo, Alexander	L-L	6-1	160	8-29-06	0	2	6.52	7	0	1	10	11	8	7	1	11	4	.306	.490	.500	8.0	22.0	50
Marcano, Alan	R-R	6-4	175	4-24-07	2	1	7.11	8	0	0	13	10	10	10	1	15	7	.227	.417	.341	11.7	25.0	60
Mejia, Bryant	R-R	6-3	190	9-17-03	0	1	14.81	11	0	0	10	12	18	17	0	20	5	.308	.576	.385	7.6	30.3	66
Mejia, Ismael	R-R	6-1	180	7-15-08	0	1	27.00	1	0	0	1	4	5	4	0	1	1	.500	.556	.625	11.1	11.1	9
Palacios, Neiker	R-R	6-1	170	11-4-06	0	1	10.53	13	2	0	20	24	26	23	3	17	19	.300	.440	.538	19.0	17.0	100
Paredes, Luis	R-R	6-1	170	12-16-05	0	0	0.00	1	0	0	0	3	3	0	3	0	.000	1.000	.000	0.0	100.0	3
Pena, Geremias	R-R	6-2	165	10-12-06	1	1	4.24	7	2	0	17	8	9	8	2	13	15	.136	.346	.237	19.2	16.7	78
Perez, Elquis	R-R	6-1	170	7-11-06	0	0	12.66	10	0	0	11	15	15	15	1	22	10	.349	.567	.512	14.7	32.4	68
Puello, Jose	R-R	6-4	155	5-24-07	2	0	4.19	5	2	0	19	19	10	9	1	8	7	.250	.329	.382	8.2	9.4	85
Quintana, Luis	R-R	6-1	190	11-26-06	1	0	1.42	3	1	0	6	3	1	1	0	5	8	.136	.296	.136	29.6	18.5	27
Rogers, Stiven	R-R	6-2	170	1-20-07	0	2	7.32	5	7	0	20	23	16	16	1	14	18	.303	.419	.434	19.4	15.1	93
Rosario, Naimer	L-L	6-0	160	7-18-06	0	1	3.72	4	4	0	19	13	8	8	1	5	26	.197	.274	.288	35.6	6.9	73
Sanchez, David	R-R	6-1	170	2-14-07	2	5	7.04	10	8	0	46	47	40	36	7	18	39	.261	.343	.461	19.0	8.8	205
Sanchez, Gregory	L-L	5-9	170	1-13-05	4	2	6.29	17	0	1	24	33	21	17	1	20	20	.333	.455	.444	16.3	16.3	123
Terrero, Robert	R-R	6-4	180	1-8-07	1	2	6.65	7	6	0	23	19	17	3	23	22	.264	.420	.425	19.6	20.5	112
Valdez, Miguel	L-L	5-11	165	9-1-06	1	2	7.40	17	0	2	24	29	25	20	4	19	23	.290	.405	.480	19.0	15.7	121
Vargas, Miguel	R-R	6-5	205	1-31-08	0	1	5.63	6	5	0	8	6	6	5	0	10	6	.214	.425	.393	15.0	25.0	40
Vargas, Modesto	R-R	6-2	195	12-14-04	2	1	1.80	9	0	1	10	8	5	2	0	11	11	.211	.423	.211	21.2	21.2	52
Vasquez, Keivan	L-L	6-3	165	10-3-07	1	4	7.88	11	10	0	38	40	35	33	2	35	27	.274	.422	.377	14.4	18.7	187

Fielding

C: Gil 24, Lantigua 15, Mendez 9, Rodriguez 9, Fernandez 1. 1B: Genao 37, Mejia 16, Lantigua 2, Rodriguez 2, Santana 2, Gallegos 1. 2B: Brima 46, Gallegos 9, Lara 3. 3B: Santana 31, Montero 12, Genao 7, Gallegos 4, Gonzalez 3, Lara 1, Benzan 1, Mejia 1. SS: Gonzalez 32, Gallegos 17, Bruno 8, Montero 2. LF: Medina 18, De La Rosa 14, Pitre 8, Benzan 6, Suarez 6, Erick De La Cruz 5, Elian De La Cruz 4, Rivera 3, Lara 2, Ayena 1. CF: Rivera 16, De La Cruz 15, Pitre 14, Benzan 11, Lara 4, De La Rosa 2, Suarez 1. RF: Suarez 18, De La Rosa 13, Benzan 12, Elian De La Cruz 10, Erick De La Cruz 6, Ayena 4

Athletics

SEASON SYNOPSIS: The Athletics began their scheduled three-year residency in Sacramento, and with the drama of their move from Oakland behind them, they went 76-86, including (perhaps predictably) a 40-41 road record. It was their most wins since 2021, driven by a young, powerful offense that ranked seventh in the majors with 219 home runs.

HIGH POINT: After stumbling out of the all-star break by losing five of six, the A's went to first-place Houston and turned their season around, sweeping the four-game set en route to a 35-29 second-half record. The key game was a 15-3 victory when rookie first baseman Nick Kurtz, already emerging as a team fulcrum, had one of the best games in major league history. He went 6-for-6 with four home runs (off four different pitchers) and a double, driving in eight. His 36 dingers led five A's with 20 or more homers, from OFs Lawrence Butler (21) and Tyler Soderstrom (25) to DH Brent Rooker (30) and C Shea Langeliers (31).

LOW POINT: The A's got off to a solid 22-20 start before their pitching fell apart in May and early June; they lost 21 of 22 games while giving up double-digit runs eight times. Veteran righty Luis Severino, signed in the offseason for $67 million over three seasons, gave up eight runs in two different home starts during the streak. He publicly complained about the A's current Sutter Health Park home, citing small crowds, lack of clubhouse air conditioning and other issues, and posted a 2-9, 6.01 mark at home while going 6-2, 3.02 on the road.

NOTABLE ROOKIES: The A's 2023 and '24 first-rounders, shortstop Jacob Wilson and Kurtz, quickly have become franchise cornerstones. Wilson (.311/.355/.444) earned an all-star nod and finished third in the majors in batting, while Kurtz (.280/.393/.619, 36 HR) had one of the best rookie seasons ever, ranking eighth all-time in home runs in a season and setting a record for the most in a first full pro season. CF Denzel Clarke dazzled defensively (13 Outs Above Average) in just 47 games. LHP Jacob Lopez (7-7, 4.08) used deception to rack up 11 K/9.

KEY TRANSACTIONS: The A's traded closer Mason Miller to the Padres for a large prospect package, including San Diego's top prospect, SS Leo De Vries, who finished the year in Double-A. LHP Sean Newcomb, whom the A's released in 2024, returned in May 2025 and anchored the bullpen after Miller was dealt, posting a 1.75 ERA in 51 A's innings.

OPENING DAY PAYROLL: $73,118,981 (29th)

PLAYERS OF THE YEAR

MAJOR LEAGUE
Nick Kurtz
1B
.290/.383/.619
36 HR, 26 2B, 86 RBIs
1.002 OPS as rookie

MINOR LEAGUE
Henry Bolte
OF
(AA,AAA)
.284/.385/.427
9 HR, 44 SB, 57 BB

ORGANIZATION LEADERS

Batting		*Qualifiers
MAJORS		
* AVG	Jacob Wilson	.311
* OPS	Shea Langeliers	.861
HR	Nick Kurtz	36
RBI	Tyler Soderstrom	93
MINORS		
* AVG	Darell Hernaiz, Las Vegas	.305
* OBP	Clark Elliott, Midland/Lansing	.395
* SLG	Colby Thomas, Las Vegas	.529
* OPS	Colby Thomas, Las Vegas	.894
R	Junior Perez, Las Vegas/Midland	87
H	Josh Kuroda-Grauer, Midland/Lansing	147
TB	Junior Perez, Las Vegas/Midland	232
2B	Cameron Leary, Lansing/Stockton	31
3B	Colby Halter, Midland/Lansing	8
HR	Junior Perez, Las Vegas/Midland	26
RBI	Junior Perez, Las Vegas/Midland	87
BB	Junior Perez, Las Vegas/Midland	87
SO	Junior Perez, Las Vegas/Midland	165
SB	Cameron Leary, Lansing/Stockton	56

Pitching		#Qualifiers
MAJORS		
W	Jeffrey Springs	11
# ERA	Jeffrey Springs	4.11
SO	Jeffrey Springs	138
SV	Mason Miller	20
MINORS		
W	Jack Cushing, Las Vegas	11
L	Kyle Robinson, Midland/Lansing	12
# ERA	Gage Jump, Midland/Lansing	3.28
G	Colton Johnson, Midland	50
GS	Kade Morris, Las Vegas/Midland	28
SV	Mark Adamiak, Midland/Lansing	21
IP	Kade Morris, Las Vegas/Midland	150
BB	Mason Barnett, Las Vegas	65
SO	Chen Zhong-Ao Zhuang, Midland	145
# AVG	Gage Jump, Midland/Lansing	.214

2025 PERFORMANCE

General Manager: David Forst. **Farm Director:** Ed Sprague. **Scouting Director:** Eric Kubota.

Class	Team	League	W	L	PCT	Finish	Manager
Majors	Athletics	American	76	86	.469	11 (15)	Mark Kotsay
Triple-A	Las Vegas Aviators	Pacific Coast	83	67	.553	3 (10)	Fran Riordan
Double-A	Midland RockHounds	Texas	66	72	.478	6 (10)	Gregorio Petit
High-A	Lansing Lugnuts	Midwest	62	70	.470	7 (12)	Darryl Kennedy
Low-A	Stockton Ports	California	57	75	.432	7 (8)	Javier Godard
Rookie	ACL Athletics	Arizona Complex	25	35	.417	12 (15)	Tim Esmay
Rookie	DSL Athletics	Dominican	35	20	.636	6 (52)	Wilkin Castillo
Overall 2025 Minor League Record			328	339	.492	18th (30)	

ORGANIZATION STATISTICS

ATHLETICS
AMERICAN LEAGUE

Batting	B-T	Ht.	Wt.	DOB	AVG	OBP	SLG	G	PA	AB	R	H	2B	3B	HR	RBI	BB	HBP	SH	SF	SO	SB	CS	BB%	SO%
Alexander, C.J.	L-R	6-3	215	7-17-96	.176	.176	.176	6	17	17	0	3	0	0	0	0	0	0	0	0	8	0	0	0.0	47.1
Andujar, Miguel	R-R	6-0	211	3-2-95	.298	.329	.436	60	231	218	22	65	10	1	6	27	11	0	0	2	30	1	0	4.8	13.0
Avans, Drew	L-L	5-9	195	6-13-96	.133	.133	.133	7	15	15	1	2	0	0	0	0	0	0	0	0	5	1	0	0.0	33.3
Bleday, JJ	L-L	6-2	205	11-10-97	.212	.294	.404	98	344	307	48	65	17	0	14	39	36	0	0	1	91	1	2	10.5	26.5
Brown, Seth	L-L	6-1	223	7-13-92	.185	.303	.262	38	76	65	6	12	2	0	1	3	9	2	0	0	23	1	0	11.8	30.3
Butler, Lawrence	L-R	6-3	210	7-10-00	.234	.306	.404	152	630	569	83	133	30	2	21	63	59	0	2	0	179	22	7	9.4	28.4
Clarke, Denzel	R-R	6-5	220	5-1-00	.230	.274	.372	47	159	148	18	34	8	2	3	8	6	3	2	0	61	6	0	3.8	38.4
Cortes, Carlos	L-S	5-7	197	6-30-97	.309	.323	.543	42	99	94	11	29	8	1	4	14	3	0	0	2	20	0	0	3.0	20.2
Davidson, Logan	S-R	6-3	185	12-26-97	.150	.261	.200	9	24	20	1	3	1	0	0	2	3	0	0	0	12	0	0	12.5	50.0
Gelof, Zack	R-R	6-2	205	10-19-99	.174	.230	.272	30	101	92	12	16	3	0	2	7	7	0	1	1	46	1	2	6.9	45.5
Harris, Brett	R-R	6-1	208	6-24-98	.274	.349	.342	32	84	73	11	20	5	0	0	5	7	2	1	1	21	1	0	8.3	25.0
Hernaiz, Darell	R-R	5-11	190	8-3-01	.231	.292	.306	51	197	173	17	40	5	1	2	16	17	0	2	5	24	3	4	8.6	12.2
Kurtz, Nick	L-L	6-6	230	3-11-03	.290	.383	.619	117	489	420	90	122	26	2	36	86	63	0	0	3	151	2	1	12.9	30.9
Langeliers, Shea	R-R	6-0	205	11-18-97	.277	.325	.536	123	523	481	73	133	32	0	31	72	36	1	0	5	103	7	1	6.9	19.7
MacIver, Willie	R-R	6-1	205	10-28-96	.186	.252	.324	33	111	102	7	19	5	0	3	9	7	2	0	0	27	3	0	6.3	24.3
Muncy, Max	R-R	6-1	180	8-25-02	.214	.259	.379	63	220	206	17	44	7	0	9	23	10	3	0	1	68	1	1	4.6	30.9
Pereda, Jhonny	R-R	6-1	202	4-18-96	.175	.283	.225	19	46	40	3	7	2	0	0	3	6	0	0	0	13	0	0	13.0	28.3
Rooker, Brent	R-R	6-4	225	11-1-94	.262	.335	.479	162	699	626	92	164	40	3	30	89	65	5	0	2	155	6	1	9.3	22.2
Schuemann, Max	R-R	5-11	186	6-11-97	.197	.295	.273	101	213	183	20	36	4	2	2	13	22	4	3	1	35	7	1	10.3	16.4
Soderstrom, Tyler	L-R	6-1	200	11-24-01	.276	.346	.474	158	624	561	75	155	34	1	25	93	55	6	0	2	141	8	3	8.8	22.6
Thomas, Colby	R-R	6-0	190	1-26-01	.225	.267	.417	49	132	120	20	27	5	0	6	19	7	1	1	3	49	2	1	5.3	37.1
Urias, Luis	R-R	5-10	202	6-3-97	.230	.315	.338	96	330	287	40	66	7	0	8	25	31	6	0	3	45	2	1	9.4	13.6
Urshela, Gio	R-R	6-0	215	10-11-91	.238	.287	.326	59	197	181	10	43	14	1	0	20	13	0	2	1	40	0	1	6.6	20.3
Wilson, Jacob	R-R	6-3	190	3-30-02	.311	.355	.444	125	523	486	62	151	26	0	13	63	27	7	2	1	39	5	2	5.2	7.5
Wynns, Austin	R-R	6-0	190	12-10-90	.222	.242	.444	22	67	63	7	14	5	0	3	10	2	0	1	1	20	0	0	3.0	29.9

Pitching	B-T	Ht.	Wt.	DOB	W	L	ERA	G	GS	SV	IP	Hits	Runs	ER	HR	BB	SO	AVG	OBP	SLG	SO%	BB%	BF
Alexander, Jason	R-R	6-2	227	3-1-93	0	0	18.00	4	0	0	6	12	13	12	3	5	5	.400	.486	.867	14.3	14.3	35
Alvarado, Elvis	R-R	6-4	183	2-23-99	1	1	3.19	37	0	0	42	34	17	15	6	22	50	.214	.317	.371	27.3	12.0	183
Barnett, Mason	R-R	6-0	218	11-7-00	1	1	6.85	5	5	0	22	26	18	17	3	11	18	.286	.365	.451	17.3	10.6	104
Basso, Brady	R-L	6-2	213	10-8-97	1	1	2.31	11	1	0	12	4	3	0	9	8	.255	.375	.298	14.3	16.1	56
Bido, Osvaldo	R-R	6-3	175	10-18-95	2	5	5.87	26	10	1	80	93	56	52	19	35	68	.297	.370	.537	18.7	9.6	363
Bowden, Ben	L-L	6-4	249	10-21-94	0	0	4.22	11	0	0	11	9	6	5	2	5	7	.225	.298	.550	14.9	10.6	47
Duran, Carlos	R-R	6-7	230	7-30-01	0	0	81.00	1	0	0	0	1	3	3	0	3	0	.500	.800	.500	0.0	60.0	5
Estes, Joey	R-R	6-2	190	10-6-01	0	2	9.82	3	2	0	11	16	12	12	4	6	6	.348	.418	.696	10.9	10.9	55
Ferguson, Tyler	R-R	6-4	225	10-5-93	4	2	4.66	56	0	2	58	43	32	30	4	34	54	.214	.332	.328	22.0	13.8	246
Ginn, J.T.	R-R	6-2	200	5-20-99	4	7	5.08	23	16	0	90	92	52	51	17	31	99	.260	.329	.472	25.3	7.9	392
Harris, Hogan	R-L	6-3	230	12-26-96	2	1	3.20	48	0	4	65	54	26	23	5	33	65	.226	.319	.339	23.5	11.9	277
Hoglund, Gunnar	L-R	6-4	220	12-17-99	1	3	6.40	6	6	0	32	38	23	23	10	11	23	.299	.353	.583	16.6	7.9	139
Holman, Grant	R-R	6-6	250	5-31-00	4	2	5.09	22	2	0	23	26	14	13	3	9	17	.280	.350	.409	16.5	8.7	103
Kelly, Michael	R-R	6-4	185	9-6-92	4	4	3.18	42	0	2	40	32	17	14	5	19	29	.224	.317	.378	17.5	11.5	166
Krook, Matt	L-L	6-4	225	10-21-94	0	0	5.40	3	0	0	3	5	2	2	0	1	3	.385	.429	.538	20.0	6.7	15
Leclerc, Jose	R-R	6-0	195	12-19-93	0	1	6.00	10	0	0	9	13	6	6	3	5	8	.317	.391	.634	17.4	10.9	46
Lopez, Jacob	L-L	6-4	220	3-11-98	7	7	4.08	21	17	0	93	81	47	42	15	37	113	.230	.317	.403	28.3	9.3	399
MacIver, Willie	R-R	6-1	205	10-28-96	0	0	0.00	2	0	0	2	4	0	0	0	0	0	.400	.400	.500	0.0	0.0	10
Maldonado, Anthony	R-R	6-4	220	6-8-93	0	0	12.00	6	0	0	6	10	8	8	3	5	7	.357	.455	.786	21.2	15.2	33
McFarland, T.J.	L-L	6-3	200	6-8-89	0	0	6.89	27	0	0	16	26	12	12	2	7	7	.377	.405	.609	9.5	4.1	74
McGough, Scott	R-R	5-11	190	10-31-89	0	0	7.00	6	0	0	9	12	7	7	3	1	11	.308	.325	.641	27.5	2.5	40
Miller, Mason	R-R	6-5	200	8-24-98	1	2	3.76	38	0	20	38	21	17	16	4	18	59	.163	.268	.370	39.1	11.9	151
Morales, Luis	R-R	6-1	200	9-24-02	4	3	3.14	10	9	0	49	38	17	17	8	18	43	.212	.286	.397	21.6	9.1	199
Murdock, Noah	R-R	6-8	205	8-29-98	1	1	13.24	14	0	0	17	26	25	25	0	20	21	.347	.490	.453	21.4	20.4	98
Newcomb, Sean	L-L	6-5	255	6-12-93	2	1	1.75	36	0	2	51	39	12	10	2	14	50	.214	.280	.297	24.9	7.0	201
Nunez, Eduarniel	R-R	6-2	170	6-7-97	1	0	9.00	6	0	0	8	9	8	8	1	7	9	.310	.462	.483	23.1	18.0	39

Player	B-T	Ht.	Wt.	DOB	AVG	OBP	SLG	G	PA	AB	R	H	2B	3B	HR	RBI	BB	HBP	SH	SF	SO	SB	CS	BB%	SO%
Otanez, Michel	R-R	6-4	218	7-3-97	0	0	13.50	6	0	0	5	7	8	8	2	5	6	.318	.464	.727	21.4	17.9	28		
Perdomo, Angel	L-L	6-8	265	5-7-94	0	0	5.40	4	0	0	3	2	2	2	0	3	2	.167	.375	.167	12.5	18.8	16		
Pereda, Jhonny	R-R	6-1	202	4-18-96	0	0	21.00	3	0	0	3	9	7	7	1	2	3	.529	.550	.941	15.0	10.0	20		
Perkins, Jack	R-R	6-1	220	12-26-99	3	2	4.19	12	4	3	39	27	18	18	4	18	37	.193	.292	.321	23.0	11.2	161		
Sears, JP	R-L	5-11	180	2-19-96	7	9	4.95	22	22	0	111	112	63	61	23	29	97	.258	.310	.491	20.6	6.1	472		
Severino, Luis	R-R	6-2	218	2-20-94	8	11	4.54	29	29	0	163	162	93	82	16	50	124	.257	.324	.389	17.6	7.1	705		
Spence, Mitch	R-R	6-1	185	5-6-98	3	6	5.10	32	8	1	85	96	57	48	16	26	66	.281	.337	.480	17.6	6.9	375		
Springs, Jeffrey	L-L	6-3	218	9-20-92	11	11	4.11	32	30	0	171	153	90	78	28	54	138	.236	.295	.422	19.4	7.6	713		
Sterner, Justin	R-R	6-1	215	8-29-96	4	3	3.18	59	1	0	65	47	24	23	10	21	70	.201	.283	.350	26.3	7.9	266		

Fielding

Catcher	PCT	G	PO	A	E	DP	PB
Langeliers	.991	108	890	40	8	3	9
MacIver	.989	31	255	10	3	1	2
Pereda	.990	15	100	2	1	0	1
Wynns	.993	20	126	9	1	0	1

First Base	PCT	G	PO	A	E	DP
Alexander	1.000	2	9	0	0	0
Andujar	.000	1	0	0	0	0
Davidson	1.000	4	19	1	0	1
Harris	1.000	5	13	1	0	2
Kurtz	.988	112	762	40	10	71
Soderstrom	.991	49	318	18	3	25
Urshela	1.000	2	15	2	0	2

Second Base	PCT	G	PO	A	E	DP
Davidson	1.000	1	0	2	0	0
Gelof	.991	30	46	64	1	15
Hernaiz	.976	14	17	23	1	5
Muncy	.950	23	34	42	4	8
Schuemann	.991	39	42	64	1	14
Urias	.985	87	104	162	4	33

Third Base	PCT	G	PO	A	E	DP
Alexander	1.000	2	3	3	0	0
Andujar	.977	32	12	30	1	3
Cortes	.000	1	0	0	0	0
Davidson	.875	3	2	5	1	1
Harris	.983	27	16	43	1	4
Hernaiz	.957	20	14	30	2	5
Muncy	.918	32	20	47	6	6
Schuemann	1.000	27	10	30	0	4
Urias	.875	9	1	6	1	0
Urshela	.972	56	26	77	3	6

Shortstop	PCT	G	PO	A	E	DP
Hernaiz	.984	23	26	37	1	6
Muncy	1.000	7	5	12	0	3
Schuemann	.956	24	27	38	3	9
Wilson	.979	124	139	239	8	46

Outfield	PCT	G	PO	A	E	DP
Alexander	1.000	2	2	0	0	0
Andujar	1.000	30	46	1	0	0
Avans	1.000	7	9	1	0	0
Bleday	.981	90	206	3	4	1
Brown	1.000	21	30	0	0	0
Butler	.995	151	366	4	2	1
Clarke	.983	47	173	1	3	0
Cortes	.974	29	37	1	1	0
Rooker	.978	28	43	2	1	1
Schuemann	1.000	13	6	0	0	0
Soderstrom	.992	108	231	11	2	2
Thomas	1.000	48	64	2	0	0

LAS VEGAS AVIATORS
PACIFIC COAST LEAGUE — TRIPLE-A

Batting	B-T	Ht.	Wt.	DOB	AVG	OBP	SLG	G	PA	AB	R	H	2B	3B	HR	RBI	BB	HBP	SH	SF	SO	SB	CS	BB%	SO%
Alexander, C.J.	L-R	6-3	215	7-17-96	.252	.348	.509	42	184	159	31	40	7	2	10	33	24	0	0	1	47	2	1	13.0	25.5
Andujar, Miguel	R-R	6-0	211	3-2-95	.222	.222	.333	5	18	18	2	4	0	1	0	0	0	0	0	0	3	0	0	0.0	16.7
Angeles, Euribiel	R-R	5-11	175	5-11-02	.288	.358	.342	43	165	146	25	42	8	0	0	14	14	2	3	0	17	4	1	8.5	10.3
Avans, Drew	L-L	5-9	195	6-13-96	.328	.414	.444	48	222	189	41	62	8	1	4	34	30	0	0	3	31	16	5	13.5	14.0
Bleday, JJ	L-L	6-2	205	11-10-97	.353	.409	.571	28	132	119	23	42	6	1	6	23	12	0	0	1	25	3	1	9.1	18.9
Bolte, Henry	R-R	6-3	195	8-4-03	.300	.404	.433	34	141	120	23	36	6	2	14	16	5	0	0	46	13	0	11.4	32.6	
Bowden, Ben	L-L	6-4	249	10-21-94	.000	.000	.000	31	1	1	0	0	0	0	0	0	0	0	0	0	0	0	0	0.0	0.0
Bowman, Cooper	R-R	6-0	205	1-25-00	.236	.326	.375	72	301	259	37	61	12	3	6	41	32	4	3	3	71	21	1	10.6	23.6
Brown, Seth	L-L	6-1	223	7-13-92	.500	.512	1.071	9	43	42	10	21	3	0	7	13	1	0	0	0	3	0	0	2.3	7.0
Clarke, Denzel	R-R	6-5	220	5-1-00	.280	.430	.411	32	135	107	26	30	8	3	0	21	23	5	0	0	30	7	1	17.0	22.2
Cortes, Carlos	L-S	5-7	197	6-30-97	.322	.414	.603	71	314	267	55	86	24	0	17	77	41	3	0	3	46	2	0	13.1	14.7
Davidson, Logan	S-R	6-3	185	12-26-97	.263	.412	.397	73	330	262	48	69	12	1	7	40	64	3	0	1	87	7	1	19.4	26.4
Gelof, Zack	R-R	6-2	205	10-19-99	.256	.371	.517	47	213	176	46	45	10	0	12	31	34	0	0	3	54	12	0	16.0	25.4
Gomez, Mario	L-R	5-10	185	12-30-02	.000	.000	.000	1	3	3	0	0	0	0	0	0	0	0	0	0	1	0	0	0.0	33.3
Halter, Colby	L-R	6-1	200	8-24-01	.203	.271	.364	34	133	118	16	24	6	2	3	16	9	3	0	3	46	6	1	6.8	34.6
Harris, Brett	R-R	6-1	208	6-24-98	.282	.369	.500	59	252	216	40	61	11	0	12	39	28	4	0	4	38	7	1	11.1	15.1
Hernaiz, Darell	R-R	5-11	190	8-3-01	.305	.383	.424	96	445	387	67	118	28	3	4	50	46	5	4	3	51	12	0	10.3	11.5
Kurtz, Nick	L-L	6-6	230	3-11-03	.321	.385	.655	20	97	84	18	27	7	0	7	24	10	0	0	2	26	0	0	10.3	26.8
Langeliers, Shea	R-R	6-0	205	11-5-97	.615	.615	.846	3	13	13	6	8	0	0	1	4	0	0	0	0	0	0	0	0.0	0.0
Lasko, Ryan	R-R	6-0	190	6-24-02	.256	.313	.349	13	48	43	5	11	1	0	1	4	3	0	0	1	10	2	0	8.3	20.8
Lavastida, Bryan	R-R	6-0	200	11-27-98	.348	.404	.562	23	100	89	10	31	3	2	4	17	9	0	0	1	12	4	0	9.0	12.0
Lopez, Alejo	S-R	5-8	170	5-5-96	.268	.365	.353	117	482	414	61	111	16	2	5	48	48	16	2	2	66	17	3	10.0	13.7
MacIver, Willie	R-R	6-0	205	10-24-95	.426	.541	.554	25	85	77	20	27	7	2	7	56	21	4	0	3	44	8	2	8.9	18.7
Mann, Luke	L-R	6-2	218	4-13-00	.200	.315	.489	14	54	45	9	2	1	3	7	3	8	0	0	1	19	1	0	14.8	35.2
Martini, Nick	L-L	5-11	205	6-27-90	.259	.383	.434	74	360	290	70	75	19	1	10	44	50	13	0	7	66	0	0	13.9	18.3
McGuire, Shane	L-R	5-10	195	4-25-99	.370	.392	.522	32	120	102	18	28	6	0	2	18	15	1	0	0	30	5	1	12.5	25.0
Milone, Brennan	R-R	6-1	198	5-6-01	.230	.367	.379	30	109	87	19	20	3	2	2	13	18	2	0	2	24	1	0	16.5	22.0
Muncy, Max	R-R	6-1	180	8-25-02	.325	.397	.504	31	141	123	24	40	11	1	3	22	11	5	0	2	32	1	3	7.8	22.7
Newton, Ben	S-R	5-10	170	6-11-02	.125	.125	.250	6	16	16	1	2	2	0	0	0	0	0	0	0	5	0	0	0.0	31.3
Pereda, Jhonny	R-R	6-1	202	4-18-96	.200	.440	.270	27	91	75	29	15	2	0	1	11	9	0	0	2	15	13	0	0	1	23	0	0	12.4	21.9
Perez, Junior	R-R	6-1	165	7-4-01	.298	.412	.642	42	182	151	37	45	14	1	12	34	30	0	1	0	49	11	3	16.5	26.9
Ruiz, Esteury	R-R	6-0	169	2-15-99	.375	.444	.375	2	9	8	3	3	0	0	0	1	1	0	0	0	2	1	0	11.1	22.2
Schuemann, Max	R-R	5-11	186	6-11-97	.400	.520	.700	5	25	20	4	8	3	0	1	6	4	1	0	0	4	0	0	16.0	16.0
Schwartz, Nick	R-R	5-11	290	3-7-01	.000	.000	.000	3	8	8	0	0	0	0	0	0	0	0	0	0	3	0	0	0.0	37.5
Susac, Daniel	R-R	6-4	218	5-14-01	.275	.349	.483	97	407	360	48	99	19	1	18	68	35	8	0	4	109	7	3	8.6	26.8
Swift, Drew	R-R	6-0	165	2-15-99	.318	.383	.417	41	169	151	24	48	9	0	2	21	16	0	2	0	45	5	1	9.5	26.6
Thomas, Colby	R-R	6-1	205	2-15-00	.266	.366	.529	82	358	313	66	97	21	2	18	74	32	11	0	7	103	7	4	8.3	26.8
Urshela, Gio	R-R	6-0	215	10-11-91	.500	.563	.857	4	16	14	5	7	2	0	0	5	2	0	0	0	0	0	0	12.5	25.0
Valenzuela, Sahid	S-R	5-7	165	9-16-97	.125	.125	.125	6	16	16	1	2	0	0	0	2	0	0	0	0	3	0	0	0.0	18.8
Wilson, Jacob	R-R	6-3	190	3-30-02	.214	.267	.500	4	15	14	3	3	1	0	1	1	0	0	0	0	0	0	0	6.7	0.0

ATHLETICS

Pitching	B-T	Ht.	Wt.	DOB	W	L	ERA	G	GS	SV	IP	Hits	Runs	ER	HR	BB	SO	AVG	OBP	SLG	SO%	BB%	BF
Alexander, Jason	R-R	6-2	227	3-1-93	1	0	1.27	5	5	0	21	17	6	3	1	8	21	.218	.295	.295	23.6	9.0	89
Alvarado, Elvis	R-R	6-4	183	2-23-99	2	1	3.38	25	0	8	29	20	13	11	3	13	34	.189	.283	.330	28.1	10.7	121
Barnett, Mason	R-R	6-0	218	11-7-00	6	2	6.13	25	23	0	119	125	81	81	17	65	124	.265	.360	.441	22.8	12.0	544
Basso, Brady	R-L	6-2	213	10-8-97	0	0	9.00	7	0	0	8	11	8	8	1	3	9	.314	.368	.457	23.7	7.9	38
Baum, Tyler	R-R	6-2	195	1-14-98	0	3	10.97	12	0	0	11	15	17	13	4	10	12	.319	.450	.617	20.0	16.7	60
Beers, Blake	R-R	6-4	215	7-15-98	0	2	6.59	12	5	0	29	41	23	21	6	10	32	.331	.390	.540	23.5	7.4	136
Bido, Osvaldo	R-R	6-3	175	10-18-95	2	0	5.71	4	3	0	17	24	11	11	3	9	18	.333	.407	.542	22.2	11.1	81
Bowden, Ben	L-L	6-4	249	10-21-94	1	1	1.36	31	0	2	40	27	10	6	1	18	41	.194	.281	.266	25.6	11.3	160
Brooks, Aaron	R-R	6-4	230	4-27-90	3	6	5.78	16	12	0	76	88	60	49	16	29	55	.286	.349	.506	16.0	8.4	344
Cushing, Jack	R-R	6-3	195	12-3-96	11	2	6.67	38	6	0	80	99	65	59	19	28	83	.306	.363	.531	22.8	7.7	364
Cusick, Ryan	R-R	6-6	235	11-12-99	1	0	6.75	13	0	0	15	15	13	11	4	13	11	.283	.433	.509	16.4	19.4	67
Dodson, Tanner	S-R	6-1	160	5-9-97	2	2	7.90	34	1	0	41	51	38	36	5	24	32	.305	.402	.473	16.5	12.4	194
Duran, Carlos	R-R	6-7	230	7-30-01	4	0	5.25	37	1	1	58	50	39	34	2	51	59	.234	.393	.313	21.5	18.6	275
Estes, Joey	R-R	6-2	190	10-8-01	4	4	5.51	17	15	0	80	84	51	49	17	20	67	.273	.320	.526	19.8	5.9	339
Ferguson, Tyler	R-R	6-4	225	10-5-93	0	1	0.90	9	0	1	10	8	6	1	0	3	11	.222	.282	.333	27.5	7.5	40
Floro, Dylan	L-R	6-2	203	12-27-90	1	2	7.04	16	0	0	15	23	13	12	3	5	12	.354	.400	.631	19.7	7.1	70
Ginn, J.T.	R-R	6-2	200	5-20-99	1	0	2.11	5	5	0	21	15	6	5	1	9	30	.203	.289	.297	35.7	10.7	84
Harris, Hogan	R-R	6-3	230	12-26-96	2	1	4.30	10	0	0	15	14	8	7	0	7	25	.246	.338	.333	37.9	10.6	66
Hoglund, Gunnar	L-R	6-4	220	12-17-99	1	2	2.43	6	6	0	30	24	9	8	3	7	30	.226	.287	.377	26.1	6.1	115
Holman, Grant	R-R	6-6	250	5-31-00	1	0	0.00	8	0	4	9	1	0	0	0	1	9	.036	.069	.036	31.0	3.5	29
Johnston, Will	L-L	6-3	215	12-12-00	1	0	12.19	9	0	0	10	16	15	14	4	10	6	.356	.473	.756	10.9	18.2	55
Krook, Matt	L-L	6-4	225	10-21-94	3	1	3.21	12	0	1	14	14	6	5	1	8	21	.264	.371	.358	33.3	12.7	63
Leal, David	L-L	6-5	250	4-22-97	2	1	4.14	33	1	1	37	33	18	17	7	21	35	.237	.346	.439	21.5	12.9	163
Lopez, Jacob	L-L	6-4	220	3-11-98	3	0	2.33	6	4	0	27	16	8	7	2	8	38	.167	.231	.281	36.5	7.7	104
Maldonado, Anthony	R-R	6-4	220	2-6-98	2	5	5.10	41	0	12	48	42	30	27	10	24	60	.233	.322	.450	29.0	11.6	207
McGough, Scott	R-R	5-11	190	10-31-89	4	0	3.00	19	0	1	27	24	11	9	3	9	22	.235	.304	.392	19.5	8.0	113
Morales, Luis	R-R	6-3	190	9-24-02	4	2	4.40	15	6	0	47	39	23	23	7	20	54	.224	.318	.297	27.1	10.1	199
Morris, Kade	R-R	6-3	170	6-21-01	2	7	5.22	19	19	0	98	112	59	57	14	37	80	.289	.360	.468	18.4	8.5	435
Nunez, Eduarniel	R-R	6-2	170	6-7-99	1	0	3.09	10	0	0	12	8	4	4	1	8	15	.205	.333	.282	30.6	16.3	49
Otanez, Michel	R-R	6-4	218	7-3-97	2	2	7.27	18	0	0	17	19	16	14	2	17	26	.279	.437	.412	29.9	19.5	87
Perdomo, Angel	L-L	6-8	265	5-7-94	1	1	5.52	12	0	0	15	14	9	9	4	13	13	.255	.397	.491	19.1	19.1	68
Perkins, Jack	R-R	6-1	220	12-26-99	3	2	2.86	9	9	0	44	25	14	14	3	20	68	.164	.282	.276	38.4	11.3	177
Robles, Domingo	L-L	6-2	170	4-29-98	0	0	6.75	1	0	0	1	1	1	1	1	2	1	.200	.429	.800	14.3	28.6	7
Rodriguez, Gustavo J.	R-R	6-3	160	1-6-01	2	1	2.27	26	0	5	32	20	9	8	2	21	36	.177	.314	.257	26.3	15.3	137
Shuster, Jared	L-L	6-3	210	8-3-98	0	2	8.53	10	0	0	13	18	13	12	1	7	7	.340	.410	.528	11.3	11.3	62
Spence, Mitch	R-R	6-1	185	5-6-98	0	1	6.21	8	7	0	29	41	21	20	3	12	31	.331	.391	.468	22.0	8.5	141
Taylor, Zane	R-R	6-0	200	6-1-02	0	0	0.00	1	1	0	2	1	1	0	0	2	4	.200	.375	.200	50.0	25.0	8
Tomioka, Shohei	R-R	6-0	190	2-29-96	0	2	8.31	8	0	0	9	17	8	8	3	3	12	.405	.444	.571	26.7	6.7	45
Tur, Yunior	R-R	6-6	200	8-9-99	0	1	6.39	5	3	0	13	11	10	9	1	6	13	.234	.333	.298	24.1	11.1	54
Waldichuk, Ken	L-L	6-4	220	1-8-98	2	6	8.65	16	15	0	51	63	52	49	13	42	64	.301	.419	.579	25.3	16.6	253
Walkinshaw, Jake	R-R	6-3	200	7-7-96	4	4	4.89	36	3	0	53	57	37	29	4	26	33	.273	.358	.368	13.8	10.8	240

Fielding

Catcher	PCT	G	PO	A	E	DP	PB
Langeliers	1.000	2	18	0	0	0	0
Lavastida	.992	14	112	6	1	1	1
MacIver	.987	31	284	11	4	2	3
McGuire	1.000	10	81	4	0	1	0
Newton	1.000	1	8	0	0	0	1
Pereda	.993	16	132	11	1	1	1
Schwartz	1.000	3	24	3	0	0	0
Susac	.990	81	721	40	8	5	6

First Base	PCT	G	PO	A	E	DP
Alexander	.984	14	108	13	2	12
Bowman	.991	15	99	10	1	11
Brown	1.000	6	46	2	0	8
Davidson	.990	35	267	19	3	29
Halter	1.000	13	83	5	0	8
Harris	1.000	6	49	3	0	1
Kurtz	.985	16	124	7	2	16
Lavastida	1.000	1	7	0	0	0
MacIver	.981	7	48	5	1	6
Mann	.980	11	90	7	2	6
McGuire	.982	16	100	12	2	13
Milone	.991	20	104	8	1	5
Pereda	1.000	4	11	1	0	1

Second Base	PCT	G	PO	A	E	DP
Angeles	.964	8	9	18	1	5
Bowman	.980	25	36	63	2	13
Davidson	.989	22	43	48	1	14

	PCT	G	PO	A	E	DP
Gelof	.980	42	78	120	4	26
Halter	.917	5	5	6	1	2
Harris	1.000	4	5	8	0	2
Hernaiz	.955	7	6	15	1	4
Lopez	.985	32	46	87	2	23
Milone	1.000	1	0	2	0	1
Muncy	1.000	4	8	10	0	5
Newton	1.000	1	6	0	0	0
Schuemann	1.000	3	4	7	0	0
Swift	1.000	2	2	3	0	1
Valenzuela	1.000	6	3	8	0	0

Third Base	PCT	G	PO	A	E	DP
Alexander	1.000	17	8	19	0	2
Andujar	.750	3	1	2	1	0
Angeles	.950	25	14	43	3	7
Bowman	.000	1	0	0	0	0
Davidson	1.000	11	10	12	0	2
Halter	.917	5	6	5	1	0
Harris	.981	45	28	76	2	12
Hernaiz	1.000	3	0	5	0	0
Lopez	.925	22	19	30	4	0
Mann	1.000	2	0	4	0	1
Muncy	.892	16	10	23	4	3
Newton	1.000	1	1	2	0	1
Schuemann	1.000	1	0	1	0	0
Swift	1.000	5	1	9	0	1
Urshela	1.000	2	0	1	0	0

Shortstop	PCT	G	PO	A	E	DP
Angeles	.946	11	10	25	2	5
Davidson	.905	5	10	9	2	2
Hernaiz	.965	87	106	228	12	45
Lopez	.979	14	18	29	1	7
Muncy	1.000	2	4	10	0	3
Schuemann	.833	1	1	4	1	0
Swift	.976	33	4	88	3	13
Wilson	.923	3	4	8	1	3

Outfield	PCT	G	PO	A	E	DP
Alexander	.900	7	9	0	1	0
Andujar	1.000	1	1	0	0	0
Avans	.990	50	97	3	1	0
Bleday	.964	27	52	2	2	0
Bolte	.953	33	61	0	3	0
Bowman	1.000	30	44	4	0	1
Brown	.857	3	6	0	1	0
Clarke	.986	31	65	4	1	0
Cortes	.990	55	90	6	1	1
Davidson	1.000	4	5	0	0	0
Lasko	1.000	13	28	1	0	0
Lopez	.973	40	69	3	2	0
Martini	.988	47	79	4	1	0
Milone	1.000	4	3	0	0	0
Perez	.978	42	85	3	2	1
Ruiz	1.000	1	2	0	0	0
Schuemann	1.000	1	1	0	0	0
Thomas	.987	80	144	6	2	1

MIDLAND ROCKHOUNDS
TEXAS LEAGUE
DOUBLE-A / ATHLETICS

Batting	B-T	Ht.	Wt.	DOB	AVG	OBP	SLG	G	PA	AB	R	H	2B	3B	HR	RBI	BB	HBP	SH	SF	SO	SB	CS	BB%	SO%
Aldrete, Carter	R-R	6-1	205	10-12-97	.216	.266	.348	58	222	204	26	44	10	1	5	28	15	0	0	3	54	0	2	6.8	24.3
Angeles, Euribiel	R-R	5-11	175	5-11-02	.288	.359	.400	86	359	320	43	92	21	0	5	47	32	4	2	1	39	13	4	8.9	10.9
Bolte, Henry	R-R	6-3	195	8-4-03	.278	.378	.424	80	347	295	43	82	14	4	7	42	41	8	0	3	95	31	2	11.8	27.4
Bowman, Cooper	R-R	6-0	205	1-25-00	.286	.500	.714	2	10	7	3	2	0	0	1	1	3	0	0	0	2	0	0	30.0	20.0
Buelvas, Brayan	R-R	5-11	155	6-8-02	.194	.271	.310	70	270	242	29	47	13	0	5	26	22	4	0	1	86	6	1	8.2	31.9
Conn, Cole	S-R	6-0	175	7-11-01	.224	.315	.288	48	178	156	17	35	6	2	0	12	17	4	0	1	45	4	2	9.6	25.3
De Vries, Leodalis	S-R	6-2	183	10-11-06	.281	.359	.551	21	103	89	17	25	7	1	5	16	10	2	0	2	20	2	1	9.7	19.4
Dickey, Jared	L-R	6-1	204	3-1-02	.309	.390	.366	33	146	123	14	38	7	0	0	21	18	1	0	4	21	1	1	12.3	14.4
Elliott, Clark	L-R	6-0	183	9-29-00	.259	.386	.425	75	316	259	41	67	13	3	8	32	48	7	0	2	67	9	1	15.2	21.2
Franco, Carlos	R-R	5-10	150	2-17-03	.104	.122	.104	12	49	48	4	5	0	0	0	4	1	0	0	0	8	0	0	2.0	16.3
Gomez, Mario	L-R	5-10	185	12-30-02	.200	.333	.400	8	18	15	2	3	1	1	0	3	1	2	0	0	5	0	0	5.6	27.8
Gouldsmith, Gunner	S-R	5-8	170	9-12-01	.400	.571	.400	2	7	5	1	2	0	0	0	2	0	0	2	0	0	0	0	28.6	28.6
Halter, Colby	L-R	6-1	200	8-24-01	.280	.381	.424	89	380	321	54	90	19	6	5	47	50	4	2	3	102	22	3	13.2	26.8
Kuroda-Grauer, Josh	R-R	6-0	185	1-31-03	.301	.372	.393	41	183	163	25	49	9	0	2	21	14	5	0	1	12	1	0	7.7	6.6
Lin, Lyle	R-R	6-1	200	6-26-97	.183	.284	.204	32	112	93	7	17	2	0	0	9	11	3	0	2	15	1	1	9.8	13.4
Mann, Luke	L-R	6-2	218	4-13-00	.197	.299	.340	111	462	391	54	77	19	2	11	66	52	9	0	10	139	8	1	11.3	30.1
McGuire, Shane	L-R	5-10	195	4-12-99	.265	.388	.365	57	241	200	26	53	8	0	4	26	36	4	1	0	47	2	1	14.9	19.5
Milone, Brennan	R-R	6-1	198	5-6-01	.246	.349	.405	88	395	338	57	83	18	0	12	49	51	4	0	2	89	5	2	12.9	22.5
Nankil, Nate	R-R	6-3	185	10-16-02	.243	.307	.303	36	166	152	24	37	7	1	0	12	11	3	0	0	32	3	2	6.6	19.3
Newton, Ben	S-R	5-10	170	6-11-02	.222	.417	.556	5	12	9	5	2	0	0	1	4	1	2	0	0	4	0	0	8.3	33.3
Perez, Junior	R-R	6-1	165	7-4-01	.201	.318	.398	95	405	339	50	68	15	5	14	53	57	3	3	3	116	16	3	14.1	28.6
Rodriguez, CJ	R-R	5-7	200	7-7-00	.071	.270	.071	10	37	28	3	2	0	0	0	2	7	1	0	1	8	0	0	18.9	21.6
Schofield-Sam, T.J.	L-R	6-1	185	6-20-01	.210	.258	.210	16	66	62	1	13	0	0	0	3	4	0	0	0	13	2	0	6.1	19.7
Swift, Drew	R-R	6-0	165	2-15-99	.205	.301	.253	80	291	249	34	51	8	2	0	21	33	2	5	2	71	15	2	11.3	24.4
Takayoshi, Thomas	S-R	6-1	190	3-20-01	.000	.000	.000	1	4	4	0	0	0	0	0	0	0	0	0	0	2	0	0	0.0	50.0
Trenkle, Caeden	L-L	5-10	179	6-29-01	.199	.274	.256	60	199	176	25	35	3	2	1	18	18	1	2	2	66	3	3	9.1	33.2
Valenzuela, Sahid	S-R	5-7	165	9-16-97	.262	.327	.324	42	159	145	19	38	4	1	1	12	9	5	0	0	25	1	2	5.7	15.7
White, Tommy	R-R	6-0	242	3-2-03	.311	.354	.387	27	113	106	11	33	5	0	1	15	7	0	0	0	17	0	1	6.2	15.0
Yamauchi, Casey	R-R	5-9	155	8-8-00	.474	.474	.789	4	19	19	3	9	1	1	1	4	0	0	0	0	2	0	0	0.0	10.5

Pitching	B-T	Ht.	Wt.	DOB	W	L	ERA	G	GS	SV	IP	Hits	Runs	ER	HR	BB	SO	AVG	OBP	SLG	SO%	BB%	BF
Adamiak, Mark	R-R	6-4	230	12-15-00	1	0	4.50	2	0	0	4	5	3	2	0	1	3	.313	.353	.375	17.7	5.9	17
Avant, Corey	R-R	6-4	225	11-6-01	0	0	17.36	2	1	0	5	10	9	9	3	2	3	.455	.500	.955	12.5	8.3	24
Baez, Henry	R-R	6-3	175	10-12-02	1	1	5.84	3	3	0	12	13	9	8	1	4	11	.260	.327	.420	20.0	7.3	55
Barrera, Diego	L-L	6-0	165	5-5-00	2	2	4.67	31	1	0	44	42	24	23	3	15	43	.258	.324	.411	22.9	8.0	188
Baum, Tyler	R-R	6-2	195	1-14-98	1	1	3.80	21	0	1	21	20	9	9	2	7	25	.244	.303	.378	28.1	7.9	89
Beers, Blake	R-R	6-4	215	7-15-98	1	2	2.70	7	7	0	30	23	13	9	2	12	24	.213	.290	.324	19.4	9.7	124
Brooks, Aaron	R-R	6-4	230	4-27-90	0	1	4.09	2	2	0	11	15	6	5	0	6	11	.333	.412	.378	21.2	11.5	52
Calderon, Yorlin	R-R	6-3	155	8-17-01	3	2	4.66	30	1	1	37	33	20	19	4	21	28	.237	.348	.381	16.9	12.7	166
Dallas, Micah	R-R	6-2	215	4-14-00	7	1	3.99	41	1	0	50	50	22	22	3	16	45	.265	.322	.381	21.6	7.7	208
Emanuels, Stevie	R-R	6-5	210	1-30-99	8	1	2.70	46	0	0	53	44	20	16	0	37	67	.221	.346	.271	27.9	15.4	240
Gonzalez, James	L-L	6-2	257	9-15-00	4	4	4.27	17	17	0	78	81	45	37	6	35	83	.273	.347	.384	24.4	10.3	340
Guante, Wander	R-R	6-1	180	6-15-00	1	1	5.40	10	0	0	15	11	9	9	2	7	13	.200	.308	.364	20.0	10.8	65
Johnson, Colton	L-L	6-4	222	7-28-98	2	2	2.98	50	0	0	48	49	19	16	3	27	33	.265	.365	.362	15.1	12.3	219
Johnston, Will	L-L	6-3	215	12-12-00	2	6	3.62	34	6	5	60	43	27	24	3	29	81	.203	.299	.297	32.9	11.8	246
Jump, Gage	L-L	6-0	185	4-12-03	5	6	3.64	20	19	0	82	69	41	33	6	29	86	.224	.297	.331	25.3	8.5	340
Leal, David	L-L	6-5	250	4-22-97	0	0	1.84	13	0	0	15	10	3	3	1	6	16	.185	.302	.259	25.4	9.5	63
Lin, Wei-En	L-L	6-2	179	11-4-05	0	0	4.05	2	2	0	7	4	3	3	1	4	8	.167	.286	.333	28.6	14.3	28
Morales, Luis	R-R	6-3	190	9-24-02	3	1	2.98	8	8	0	42	28	15	14	3	15	53	.187	.259	.293	31.7	9.0	167
Morris, Kade	R-R	6-3	170	6-21-02	2	3	2.79	9	9	0	52	42	22	16	2	11	48	.221	.288	.316	23.1	5.3	208
Myers, Mitch	R-R	6-2	200	1-8-99	1	1	1.99	17	2	2	23	18	5	5	2	3	19	.225	.253	.325	22.9	3.6	83
Nett, Braden	R-R	6-3	185	6-18-02	1	3	4.60	7	7	0	31	36	16	16	3	14	30	.293	.379	.415	21.3	9.9	141
Pelham, CD	R-L	6-6	238	2-21-95	3	4	3.43	41	0	0	39	36	20	15	3	15	47	.247	.327	.356	28.0	8.9	168
Peluse, Colin	R-R	6-3	230	6-11-98	4	1	2.64	47	0	0	58	52	20	17	3	12	54	.239	.282	.321	22.9	5.1	236
Robinson, Kyle	R-R	6-6	210	7-17-03	1	6	5.29	11	10	0	51	56	31	30	4	31	37	.286	.383	.408	16.1	13.5	230
Robles, Domingo	L-L	6-2	170	4-29-98	0	4	4.78	10	2	0	32	30	17	17	3	7	25	.246	.295	.393	18.8	5.3	133
Rodriguez, Gustavo J.	R-R	6-3	160	1-8-01	0	0	0.00	7	0	3	6	4	0	0	0	1	11	.231	.167	.167	42.3	3.9	26
Sanchez, Edgar	R-R	6-1	190	8-2-00	0	0	3.12	18	0	4	17	13	8	6	0	10	27	.194	.304	.254	33.8	12.5	80
Santos, Pedro	R-R	6-4	205	1-7-00	2	0	5.28	32	0	1	29	26	19	17	1	36	33	.241	.429	.380	22.5	24.5	147
Tomioka, Shohei	R-R	6-0	190	2-29-96	2	3	3.64	37	0	11	42	34	17	17	1	22	40	.225	.326	.318	22.7	12.5	176
Tur, Yunior	R-R	6-6	200	8-9-99	3	5	2.93	16	14	0	68	47	24	22	4	34	74	.197	.306	.280	26.3	12.1	281
Zhuang, Chen Zhong-Ao	R-R	6-1	190	8-25-00	6	11	4.08	28	26	0	146	151	79	66	22	35	145	.262	.305	.455	23.5	5.7	617

Fielding

Catcher	PCT	G	PO	A	E	DP	PB
Conn	.978	44	341	23	8	2	3
Franco	1.000	10	87	6	0	0	0
Gomez	1.000	5	22	1	0	0	0
Lin	.993	29	269	9	2	1	2
McGuire	.987	44	447	25	6	3	10
Newton	1.000	1	9	0	0	0	0

First Base	PCT	G	PO	A	E	DP
Aldrete	.996	36	230	17	1	24
Dickey	1.000	1	6	0	0	1
Franco	1.000	1	8	2	0	0
Mann	.997	39	287	24	1	31
Rodriguez	1.000	10	66	3	0	0	1

	PCT	G	PO	A	E	DP
McGuire	1.000	4	28	7	0	4
Milone	.991	43	299	19	3	29
Schofield-Sam	.991	13	106	6	1	9
Trenkle	1.000	3	19	0	0	1
White	1.000	4	38	0	0	2

Second Base	PCT	G	PO	A	E	DP
Angeles	.995	49	78	129	1	32
Bowman	.889	2	5	3	1	0
Conn	1.000	1	0	1	0	0
Gouldsmith	1.000	2	4	1	0	0
Halter	.956	40	58	93	7	25
Kuroda-Grauer	1.000	10	21	17	0	5
Mann	.947	6	6	12	1	4
Milone	1.000	1	2	0	0	0
Swift	1.000	7	8	15	0	1
Valenzuela	1.000	20	42	50	0	13
Yamauchi	.960	4	6	18	1	3

Third Base	PCT	G	PO	A	E	DP
Halter	.934	31	28	57	6	4
Kuroda-Grauer	.963	7	9	17	1	3
Mann	.939	56	27	112	9	16
Schofield-Sam	1.000	2	1	5	0	1
Swift	1.000	1	6	15	0	2
Valenzuela	1.000	18	12	35	0	3
White	.881	18	10	27	5	1

Shortstop	PCT	G	PO	A	E	DP
Angeles	.964	34	52	81	5	17
De Vries	.980	18	16	33	1	4
Kuroda-Grauer	.982	24	41	69	2	15
Swift	.974	62	72	156	6	25

Outfield	PCT	G	PO	A	E	DP
Aldrete	.000	1	0	0	0	0
Bolte	.973	72	138	7	4	3
Buelvas	.982	62	105	4	2	0
Conn	.000	1	0	0	0	0
Dickey	.974	25	38	0	1	0
Elliott	.985	71	126	2	2	0
Halter	.909	4	9	1	1	0
Milone	.947	24	35	1	2	1
Nankil	1.000	31	82	2	0	0
Perez	.995	88	187	9	1	1
Schofield-Sam	.000	1	0	0	0	0
Trenkle	.987	46	72	4	1	1
Valenzuela	1.000	3	3	0	0	0

LANSING LUGNUTS — HIGH-A
MIDWEST LEAGUE

Batting	B-T	Ht.	Wt.	DOB	AVG	OBP	SLG	G	PA	AB	R	H	2B	3B	HR	RBI	BB	HBP	SH	SF	SO	SB	CS	BB%	SO%
Butler, Jonny	L-R	6-1	200	2-12-99	.221	.361	.382	25	83	68	6	15	6	1	1	3	15	0	0	0	15	2	0	18.1	18.1
Camarillo, Ali	R-R	6-0	170	5-15-03	.260	.339	.280	15	57	50	4	13	1	0	0	2	6	0	1	0	6	3	2	10.5	10.5
Conn, Cole	S-R	6-0	175	7-11-01	.258	.387	.464	28	119	97	20	25	8	0	4	20	18	3	0	1	28	1	2	15.1	23.5
De Vries, Leodalis	S-R	6-2	183	10-11-06	.268	.338	.518	15	65	56	9	15	2	3	2	12	4	3	0	2	15	1	0	6.2	23.1
Diaz, Davis	R-R	5-11	186	3-2-03	.218	.310	.280	60	242	211	25	46	7	0	2	17	28	1	0	2	33	2	1	11.6	15.7
Dickey, Jared	L-R	6-1	204	3-1-02	.253	.363	.386	88	375	308	49	78	17	3	6	43	56	2	0	9	51	7	3	14.9	13.6
Elliott, Clark	L-R	6-0	183	9-29-00	.236	.413	.417	42	167	127	24	30	7	2	4	21	33	6	0	1	30	7	0	19.8	18.0
Franco, Cesar	L-R	6-1	190	4-6-02	.000	.000	.000	2	8	8	0	0	0	0	0	1	0	0	0	0	5	0	0	0.0	62.5
Gomez, Mario	L-R	5-10	185	12-30-02	.250	.316	.462	15	57	52	6	13	3	1	2	11	4	1	0	0	0	0	7.0	14.0	
Gouldsmith, Gunner	S-R	5-8	170	9-12-01	.211	.328	.263	18	67	57	8	12	3	0	0	1	9	1	0	0	12	2	2	13.4	17.9
Green, Rodney	L-L	6-3	190	4-12-03	.158	.279	.287	83	355	303	39	48	14	2	7	28	48	3	0	1	118	11	5	13.5	33.2
Kuroda-Grauer, Josh	R-R	6-0	185	1-31-03	.293	.353	.362	80	366	334	38	98	15	1	0	26	26	5	1	0	37	26	6	7.1	10.1
Lasko, Ryan	R-R	6-0	190	6-24-02	.241	.359	.339	72	312	257	44	62	8	1	5	35	41	9	0	5	73	12	5	13.1	23.4
Leary, Cameron	L-L	6-0	180	11-13-01	.275	.374	.358	33	134	109	14	30	4	1	1	14	16	3	3	3	32	12	3	11.9	23.9
Montero, Darlyn	S-R	6-2	170	11-5-02	.193	.273	.281	33	128	114	12	22	4	0	2	14	8	5	0	1	43	4	0	6.3	33.6
Nankil, Nate	R-R	6-3	185	10-16-02	.294	.382	.396	88	369	316	47	93	19	2	3	44	38	10	0	5	53	7	1	10.3	14.4
Newton, Ben	S-R	5-10	170	6-11-02	.239	.283	.291	32	129	117	12	28	4	1	0	5	7	1	2	2	41	1	1	5.4	31.8
Pacheco, Carlos	R-R	5-10	150	11-1-04	.089	.259	.089	18	60	45	5	4	0	0	0	4	10	1	1	2	13	3	0	16.7	21.7
Pineda, Pedro	R-R	6-1	170	9-6-03	.255	.306	.353	28	111	102	8	26	3	2	1	9	8	0	0	1	37	3	1	7.2	33.3
Pittaro, C.J.	L-R	6-1	195	10-16-01	.176	.222	.200	26	90	85	5	15	0	1	0	2	5	0	0	0	23	1	0	5.6	25.6
Rijo, Elvis	R-R	5-11	165	11-27-03	.081	.190	.135	14	43	37	2	3	2	0	0	2	5	0	1	0	16	0	0	11.6	37.2
Rodriguez, CJ	R-R	5-7	200	7-7-00	.189	.291	.254	37	142	122	9	23	5	0	1	11	16	2	1	2	28	0	0	11.3	19.7
Schofield-Sam, T.J.	L-R	6-1	185	2-18-00	.267	.401	.402	102	442	384	59	108	21	5	5	52	24	30	0	4	94	2	1	5.4	21.3
Schwartz, Nick	R-R	5-11	190	3-7-01	.255	.307	.340	28	104	94	12	24	3	1	1	10	7	0	1	0	30	1	0	6.7	28.9
Valenzuela, Sahid	S-R	5-7	165	9-16-97	.228	.306	.293	50	186	167	20	38	5	0	2	15	18	1	0	0	27	5	2	9.7	14.5
White, Tommy	R-R	6-0	242	3-2-03	.260	.326	.461	66	282	254	38	66	13	0	11	36	22	4	0	2	37	3	0	7.8	13.1
Yamauchi, Casey	R-R	5-9	155	8-8-00	.276	.328	.345	119	481	435	38	120	21	3	1	55	22	15	2	7	36	13	7	4.6	7.5

Pitching	B-T	Ht.	Wt.	DOB	W	L	ERA	G	GS	SV	IP	Hits	Runs	ER	HR	BB	SO	AVG	OBP	SLG	SO%	BB%	BF
Adamiak, Mark	R-R	6-4	230	12-15-00	4	1	2.94	44	0	21	49	49	21	16	3	13	41	.271	.323	.376	20.4	6.5	201
Avant, Corey	R-R	6-4	225	11-6-01	6	6	3.65	29	21	0	106	93	46	43	3	48	101	.239	.325	.326	22.4	10.7	450
Breault, Hunter	R-R	6-2	228	6-12-99	2	3	5.36	39	0	1	45	55	33	27	5	20	21	.296	.363	.462	9.9	9.4	212
Christianson, Jake	R-R	6-3	190	10-22-99	3	1	4.67	39	0	0	52	53	31	27	5	22	41	.261	.342	.433	17.6	9.4	233
Dettmer, Nathan	R-R	6-4	230	4-26-02	1	4	7.28	6	6	0	30	42	25	24	5	14	20	.339	.410	.516	14.2	9.9	141
Echavarria, Steven	R-R	6-1	180	8-6-05	3	7	4.59	26	25	0	104	106	57	53	8	42	88	.268	.342	.410	19.5	9.3	451
Garland, Jake	R-R	6-5	236	9-26-00	4	4	4.19	20	12	0	77	84	39	36	7	22	55	.287	.334	.451	17.0	6.8	324
Gomez, Henry	R-R	6-1	163	10-17-01	3	3	6.21	37	0	4	38	39	29	26	3	19	30	.264	.363	.419	17.5	11.1	171
Guante, Wander	R-R	6-1	180	6-15-00	2	3	3.65	32	0	2	37	31	17	15	3	12	37	.225	.288	.333	24.2	7.8	153
Huggins, Kenya	R-R	6-3	215	12-12-00	0	1	4.30	6	6	0	15	15	7	7	2	6	15	.263	.333	.421	23.8	9.5	63
Irvin, Garrett	L-L	6-0	185	2-18-99	0	1	17.18	4	0	0	4	8	7	7	0	4	7	.421	.522	.632	30.4	17.4	23
Judkins, Grant	L-R	6-3	200	8-6-97	8	9	4.73	24	24	0	124	123	75	65	20	42	103	.254	.313	.470	19.4	7.9	531
Jump, Gage	L-L	6-0	185	4-12-03	4	1	2.32	6	5	0	31	21	9	8	1	5	45	.186	.231	.283	37.2	4.1	121
Lin, Wei-En	L-L	6-2	170	11-14-05	3	1	3.26	11	1	0	30	17	11	11	3	12	40	.163	.244	.283	33.6	10.1	119
Magdic, Ryan	L-L	6-4	225	6-4-00	0	3	4.63	7	3	0	23	26	14	12	4	4	22	.286	.330	.473	22.0	4.0	100
Mahoney, Jack	L-L	6-8	230	5-5-99	3	3	5.29	20	0	0	34	38	25	20	1	21	34	.286	.394	.406	21.1	13.0	161
Pfennigs, Jake	R-R	6-7	215	9-9-99	0	0	6.83	24	0	0	29	41	23	22	4	14	24	.323	.387	.504	16.9	9.9	142
Pontes, Blaze	R-R	6-0	185	11-6-00	3	2	1.79	42	0	2	50	42	17	10	0	22	38	.222	.305	.270	17.5	10.1	177
Reisinger, Tom	R-R	6-3	215	3-17-01	4	2	6.27	32	0	0	47	53	47	33	7	33	31	.279	.394	.458	13.4	14.2	232
Robinson, Kyle	R-R	6-6	210	7-17-03	5	6	3.99	14	10	0	70	72	34	31	6	22	50	.268	.321	.390	17.0	7.5	294
Rodriguez, Gustavo J.	R-R	6-3	160	1-8-01	0	0	0.00	6	0	1	6	1	0	0	0	1	5	.053	.100	.053	25.0	5.0	20
Sanchez, Yehizon	R-R	6-2	170	11-16-00	2	0	4.14	39	0	0	41	31	24	19	3	22	67	.208	.313	.322	21.0	12.5	176
Schwartz, Nick	R-R	5-11	190	3-7-01	0	0	0.00	1	0	0	1	1	0	0	0	0	0	.250	.250	.250	0.0	0.0	4
Sha, Tzu-Chen	R-R	6-2	165	10-15-03	1	6	5.62	12	10	1	50	51	34	31	7	21	28	.267	.360	.503	12.4	9.3	225
Tur, Yunior	R-R	6-6	200	8-9-99	1	3	2.98	9	9	0	45	34	20	15	2	20	43	.234	.321	.351	21.9	10.2	196

Fielding

Catcher	PCT	G	PO	A	E	DP	PB
Conn	1.000	20	155	14	0	2	0
Diaz	.986	45	331	28	5	0	8
Gomez	1.000	12	84	2	0	0	1
Newton	.889	1	7	1	1	0	1
Rodriguez	.989	34	252	18	3	5	4
Schwartz	.988	22	157	11	2	1	5

First Base	PCT	G	PO	A	E	DP
Dickey	.977	10	77	8	2	6
Montero	.990	26	188	10	2	14
Pittaro	1.000	9	61	5	0	10
Schofield-Sam	.994	93	668	42	4	70
Schwartz	1.000	1	4	1	0	2

Second Base	PCT	G	PO	A	E	DP
Diaz	1.000	3	2	6	0	2
Gouldsmith	1.000	11	14	37	0	5
Rijo	.500	1	0	1	1	0
Valenzuela	.968	14	16	45	2	5
Yamauchi	.970	104	172	281	14	74

Third Base	PCT	G	PO	A	E	DP
Diaz	.963	11	9	17	1	3
Gouldsmith	.818	6	4	5	2	1
Newton	.923	28	25	35	5	3
Rijo	.950	11	10	9	1	2
Schofield-Sam	.750	4	1	2	1	0
Valenzuela	.958	17	9	37	2	2
White	.900	59	46	71	13	10
Yamauchi	.000	1	0	0	0	0

Shortstop	PCT	G	PO	A	E	DP
Camarillo	1.000	14	16	29	0	9
De Vries	.978	14	20	24	1	6
Kuroda-Grauer	.963	79	100	208	12	53
Valenzuela	.973	18	31	41	2	10
Yamauchi	.963	8	9	17	1	5

Outfield	PCT	G	PO	A	E	DP
Butler	.974	20	36	2	1	1
Dickey	.981	56	97	4	2	1
Elliott	.985	33	63	1	1	1
Franco	1.000	2	2	0	0	0
Green	.975	71	150	3	4	0
Lasko	.986	63	200	8	3	0
Leary	.987	30	77	0	1	0
Nankil	.987	77	146	5	2	1
Pacheco	1.000	16	43	1	0	0
Pineda	.984	26	60	2	1	0
Pittaro	1.000	16	22	1	0	0

STOCKTON PORTS
CALIFORNIA LEAGUE
LOW-A

Batting	B-T	Ht.	Wt.	DOB	AVG	OBP	SLG	G	PA	AB	R	H	2B	3B	HR	RBI	BB	HBP	SH	SF	SO	SB	CS	BB%	SO%
Andrade, Bryan	R-R	6-1	145	2-3-05	.233	.344	.287	41	152	129	18	30	4	0	1	21	21	1	1	0	28	1	0	13.8	18.4
Arendt, Bryan	R-R	6-2	210	4-5-03	.136	.271	.203	18	71	59	6	8	1	0	1	1	8	3	1	0	20	0	0	11.3	28.2
Blandford, Bobby	L-L	6-2	185	1-10-03	.248	.377	.448	28	130	105	21	26	4	1	5	20	19	4	0	2	38	1	2	14.6	29.2
Boser, Bobby	R-R	6-1	205	12-5-02	.202	.368	.298	32	144	114	18	23	3	1	2	15	22	8	0	0	42	1	1	15.3	29.2
Brooks, Michael	R-R	5-11	190	2-25-02	.208	.382	.247	23	103	77	15	16	3	0	0	6	23	0	1	2	18	1	2	22.3	17.5
Camarillo, Ali	R-R	6-0	170	5-15-03	.254	.329	.318	80	354	311	36	79	15	1	1	34	32	5	1	5	62	15	3	9.0	17.5
Diaz, Davis	R-R	5-11	186	3-2-03	.250	.384	.355	42	190	152	24	38	10	3	0	21	29	6	0	3	28	6	3	15.3	14.7
Durrington, Max	L-R	5-9	165	2-13-07	.225	.308	.283	49	197	173	21	39	4	0	2	15	19	2	2	1	33	6	1	9.6	16.8
Fernandez, Jesus	R-R	5-11	145	2-14-06	.181	.224	.208	20	77	72	4	13	2	0	0	6	3	1	1	0	11	1	1	3.9	14.3
Fien, Dylan	S-R	6-3	200	10-20-05	.234	.315	.315	73	337	295	35	69	11	2	3	38	27	10	0	5	70	0	0	8.0	20.8
Franco, Carlos	R-R	5-10	150	2-17-03	.242	.292	.338	61	250	231	20	56	11	1	3	38	15	2	0	2	43	1	0	6.0	17.2
Franco, Cesar	L-R	6-1	190	4-6-02	.105	.289	.163	28	114	86	16	9	3	1	0	12	22	2	0	4	38	0	0	19.3	33.3
Freitez, Luis	R-R	6-0	180	5-17-03	.193	.307	.273	55	219	187	23	36	7	1	2	15	27	4	1	0	56	2	1	12.3	25.6
Gomez, Mario	L-R	5-10	185	12-30-02	.000	.154	.000	3	13	11	1	0	0	0	0	0	1	1	0	0	5	0	0	7.7	38.5
Gonzalez, Cesar	R-R	6-2	165	1-13-05	.179	.261	.231	12	46	39	7	7	2	0	0	3	5	0	0	2	12	0	0	10.9	26.1
Gouldsmith, Gunner	S-R	5-8	170	9-12-01	.159	.268	.205	40	154	132	23	21	6	0	0	11	19	1	1	1	35	5	0	12.3	22.7
Green, Rodney	L-L	6-3	190	4-12-03	.275	.362	.496	36	153	131	24	36	7	2	6	29	16	3	0	2	31	5	0	10.5	20.4
Kurtz, Nick	L-L	6-6	230	3-11-03	.667	.750	1.667	1	4	3	2	2	0	0	1	3	1	0	0	0	0	0	0	25.0	0.0
Leary, Cameron	L-L	6-0	180	11-13-01	.266	.386	.433	93	422	349	66	93	27	2	9	52	66	4	0	3	98	44	5	15.6	23.2
Naylor, Myles	R-R	6-2	195	4-15-05	.185	.319	.307	81	345	287	51	53	12	1	7	37	53	4	0	1	137	10	2	15.4	39.7
Ortiz, German	S-R	6-2	195	8-2-04	.216	.298	.252	34	126	111	14	24	4	0	0	9	13	0	0	0	35	0	0	10.3	27.8
Pacheco, Carlos	R-R	5-10	150	11-1-04	.174	.326	.235	39	141	115	14	20	2	1	1	13	21	5	0	0	41	11	1	14.9	29.1
Pineda, Pedro	R-R	6-1	170	9-6-03	.253	.356	.458	53	222	190	35	48	5	2	10	37	27	4	0	1	65	2	1	12.2	29.3
Pittaro, C.J.	L-R	6-1	195	10-16-01	.246	.358	.323	92	413	350	46	86	16	4	1	36	52	10	0	1	85	6	3	12.6	20.6
Rodriguez, Joseph	R-R	6-1	165	1-4-03	.150	.190	.150	6	21	20	4	3	0	0	1	1	0	0	0	0	9	0	0	4.8	42.9
Sprague-Lott, Jared	R-R	6-1	190	10-10-01	.216	.383	.329	74	331	255	40	55	11	0	6	34	65	6	2	3	57	10	2	19.6	17.2
Superlano, Jesus	R-R	5-11	165	3-20-05	.245	.286	.340	18	57	53	9	13	5	0	0	2	3	0	1	0	14	1	0	5.3	24.6
Takayoshi, Thomas	S-R	6-1	190	3-20-01	.221	.287	.252	39	143	131	7	29	1	0	1	7	10	2	0	0	50	0	0	7.0	35.0
Taylor, Devin	L-R	6-0	194	1-6-04	.264	.388	.481	28	129	106	25	28	5	0	6	18	21	1	0	1	37	2	1	16.3	28.7
Turley, Gavin	R-R	6-2	200	11-12-03	.243	.336	.430	27	125	107	15	26	8	0	4	20	14	2	0	2	34	0	0	11.2	27.2

Pitching	B-T	Ht.	Wt.	DOB	W	L	ERA	G	GS	SV	IP	Hits	Runs	ER	HR	BB	SO	AVG	OBP	SLG	SO%	BB%	BF
Alvarado, Wilfred	R-R	6-3	190	11-20-05	0	2	3.79	22	0	1	40	40	21	17	3	19	37	.270	.360	.385	21.4	11.0	173
Anderson, Luke	R-R	6-2	205	8-5-98	0	1	16.88	5	0	0	3	3	6	5	0	5	3	.273	.500	.455	18.8	31.3	16
Barrera, Diego	L-L	6-0	165	5-5-00	0	0	0.00	5	0	1	6	1	0	0	0	2	3	.056	.150	.167	15.0	10.0	20
Basso, Brady	R-L	6-2	213	10-8-97	0	0	0.00	1	1	0	1	0	0	0	0	2	.250	.250	.250	50.0	0.0	4
Castro, Felix	R-R	6-3	180	2-16-04	1	3	4.19	37	1	2	54	53	35	25	3	38	63	.249	.383	.338	23.9	14.4	264
Conover, Drew	R-R	6-5	185	7-27-01	0	2	6.89	7	0	0	16	21	15	12	1	11	18	.323	.430	.477	22.8	13.9	79
Dettmer, Nathan	R-R	6-4	230	4-26-02	5	5	5.42	19	14	0	80	100	54	48	5	31	68	.308	.371	.415	18.7	8.5	364
Dicochea, Jose	R-R	6-3	180	3-21-01	5	10	4.86	25	13	1	91	98	59	49	11	39	95	.274	.352	.422	23.2	9.5	410
Dill, Jay	R-R	6-5	240	11-19-02	1	0	3.52	6	0	1	8	5	6	3	0	5	12	.179	.303	.214	36.4	15.2	33
Dutton, Samuel	R-R	5-11	185	5-5-03	0	0	3.52	5	3	0	8	7	3	3	1	2	13	.241	.290	.379	41.9	6.5	31
Fernandez, Richard	R-R	6-1	190	9-22-02	1	0	4.97	9	0	0	13	9	8	7	0	11	8	.214	.386	.238	14.0	19.3	57
Ferrer, Andinson	R-R	6-3	190	5-5-04	1	1	7.16	16	0	0	16	14	14	13	1	15	24	.222	.380	.317	30.0	18.8	80
Franco, Carlos	R-R	5-10	150	2-17-03	0	0	7.71	3	0	0	2	5	2	2	1	2	0	.455	.538	.818	0.0	15.4	13
Hammond, Blake	R-R	6-3	195	7-13-03	1	3	7.85	28	3	0	47	61	43	41	5	30	63	.311	.405	.474	27.0	12.9	233
Hernandez, Camilo	R-R	6-1	190	9-30-03	1	0	3.18	3	0	0	6	4	2	2	0	6	6	.250	.423	.350	22.2	22.2	27
Huge, Riley	L-L	6-4	235	5-14-02	2	4	5.24	43	0	7	55	40	35	32	5	37	77	.205	.343	.313	31.8	15.3	242
Jean, Jefferson	R-R	6-3	170	1-29-05	3	9	5.59	24	20	1	87	78	57	54	6	60	94	.241	.389	.359	22.9	14.6	411
Kirn, Griffin	L-L	6-3	215	4-19-02	2	0	1.13	6	0	0	8	6	1	1	0	4	12	.200	.294	.233	35.3	11.8	34

	B-T	Ht.	Wt.	DOB	G	AB	R	H	2B	3B	HR	RBI	BB	SO	SB	CS	OBP	SLG	AVG	OPS
Layton, Aidan	R-R	6-2	195	1-31-02	1	2	8.24	28	2	0	59	81	59	54	11	17	50	.321	.369	.516	17.9	6.1	280
Lin, Wei-En	L-L	6-2	179	11-4-05	1	4	3.96	13	10	0	50	49	27	22	5	6	69	.253	.281	.407	34.0	3.0	203
Magdic, Ryan	L-L	6-4	225	6-4-00	5	3	2.96	18	13	0	73	67	27	24	3	19	77	.241	.296	.338	25.4	6.3	303
Manzano, Alejandro	R-R	6-2	165	2-28-02	6	5	3.38	41	0	6	67	62	35	25	6	24	60	.244	.314	.409	20.8	8.3	288
McFarland, T.J.	L-L	6-3	200	6-8-89	0	0	9.00	1	0	0	1	2	1	1	1	0	1	.500	.500	1.250	25.0	0.0	4
Miller, Cole	R-R	6-6	225	5-2-05	1	2	1.56	11	9	0	40	33	14	7	1	8	36	.221	.267	.329	22.4	5.0	161
Novotny, Tucker	L-L	6-5	235	11-22-02	4	5	3.82	30	9	1	78	58	42	33	5	37	97	.201	.301	.288	29.0	11.1	334
Otanez, Michel	R-R	6-4	218	7-3-97	0	0	13.50	1	0	0	1	0	1	1	0	1	2	.000	.333	.000	66.7	33.3	3
Restituyo, Brayan	L-L	5-11	160	1-17-02	3	3	5.43	40	1	0	58	59	41	35	6	26	72	.254	.343	.392	26.8	9.7	269
Sha, Tzu-Chen	R-R	6-2	165	10-15-03	3	3	2.70	12	7	1	50	43	19	15	1	9	59	.231	.280	.296	29.2	4.5	202
Stuhr, Sam	R-R	6-0	195	8-8-02	5	8	6.59	25	16	0	96	111	75	70	10	47	92	.294	.384	.429	20.9	10.7	440
Troconis, Donny	R-R	6-4	180	10-12-05	5	0	1.24	11	9	0	51	24	9	7	0	17	39	.136	.215	.165	19.9	8.7	196
Waldichuk, Ken	L-L	6-4	220	1-8-98	0	0	0.00	1	1	0	3	1	0	0	0	0	4	.100	.182	.200	36.4	0.0	11

Fielding

Catcher	PCT	G	PO	A	E	DP	PB
Arendt	.992	12	116	12	1	2	1
Diaz	.989	27	245	16	3	0	7
Fien	.988	50	462	22	6	2	5
Franco	.984	29	292	18	5	1	1
Gomez	1.000	1	9	1	0	0	1
Takayoshi	.993	18	131	8	1	2	2

First Base	PCT	G	PO	A	E	DP
Andrade	.984	15	112	8	2	16
Arendt	1.000	6	51	5	0	4
Fien	1.000	9	68	3	0	12
Franco	1.000	7	37	6	0	4
Gonzalez	.990	11	95	2	1	10
Kurtz	1.000	1	6	0	0	1
Naylor	.929	3	25	1	2	3
Ortiz	.980	30	181	12	4	14
Pittaro	.991	48	322	16	3	24
Sprague-Lott	1.000	6	37	2	0	4
Superlano	.973	7	35	1	1	4
Takayoshi	1.000	2	17	0	0	1

Second Base	PCT	G	PO	A	E	DP
Andrade	1.000	5	8	10	0	2
Boser	1.000	3	6	8	0	2
Brooks	1.000	3	6	8	0	3
Camarillo	1.000	1	0	2	0	1
Diaz	.942	10	16	33	3	2
Durrington	.954	41	64	103	8	27
Fernandez	1.000	5	15	8	0	3
Gouldsmith	.984	15	24	38	1	8
Naylor	.964	6	8	19	1	3
Sprague-Lott	.937	39	86	77	11	20
Superlano	1.000	6	9	9	0	6

Third Base	PCT	G	PO	A	E	DP
Andrade	.911	22	9	32	4	2
Boser	.714	3	2	3	2	1
Brooks	.935	20	11	32	3	2
Camarillo	1.000	5	2	7	0	1
Diaz	1.000	3	2	8	0	0
Gouldsmith	1.000	3	1	5	0	0
Naylor	.891	52	31	84	14	8
Pittaro	.500	2	0	1	1	0

Shortstop	PCT	G	PO	A	E	DP
Sprague-Lott	.892	24	21	45	8	6
Superlano	.889	4	1	7	1	0
Boser	.959	27	41	75	5	24
Camarillo	.950	70	78	170	13	33
Fernandez	.920	15	16	30	4	4
Gouldsmith	.920	21	27	54	7	13
Superlano	.750	1	1	2	1	1

Outfield	PCT	G	PO	A	E	DP
Blandford	1.000	23	32	1	0	0
Durrington	1.000	5	10	0	0	0
Franco	.966	26	54	2	2	2
Freitez	.990	55	92	3	1	0
Green	.983	32	54	5	1	1
Leary	.993	85	138	3	1	0
Pacheco	.987	38	78	0	1	0
Pineda	.993	51	132	4	1	0
Pittaro	.984	44	60	3	1	0
Rodriguez	1.000	6	16	1	0	0
Taylor	.971	18	33	1	1	0
Turley	.944	23	32	2	2	0

ACL ATHLETICS
ARIZONA COMPLEX LEAGUE

ROOKIE

Batting	B-T	Ht.	Wt.	DOB	AVG	OBP	SLG	G	PA	AB	R	H	2B	3B	HR	RBI	BB	HBP	SH	SF	SO	SB	CS	BB%	SO%
Andrade, Bryan	R-R	6-1	145	2-3-05	.291	.359	.430	23	92	79	10	23	2	3	1	21	9	1	0	3	13	2	0	9.8	14.1
Beltran, Nelson	R-R	5-10	160	12-28-01	.217	.413	.274	41	143	106	19	23	3	0	1	17	27	9	0	1	40	4	2	18.9	28.0
Bowman, Cooper	R-R	6-0	205	1-20-00	.167	.267	.417	4	15	12	2	2	1	1	0	3	1	0	1	0	5	1	0	6.7	33.3
Buelvas, Brayan	R-R	5-11	155	6-8-02	.276	.323	.379	8	31	29	3	8	3	0	0	4	1	1	0	0	4	1	0	3.2	12.9
Butler, Jonny	L-R	6-1	200	2-12-99	.200	.316	.400	5	19	15	2	3	3	0	0	2	3	0	0	1	4	0	0	15.8	21.1
Camarillo, Ali	R-R	6-0	170	5-15-03	.111	.182	.111	3	11	9	1	1	0	0	0	2	1	0	0	1	5	0	0	9.1	45.5
De La Paz, Reynaldo	R-R	6-3	190	9-11-05	.158	.301	.257	38	123	101	17	16	2	1	2	8	18	3	0	1	42	1	0	14.6	34.2
Dume, Kevin	L-R	6-5	220	9-19-04	.200	.297	.375	24	91	80	13	16	5	0	3	14	10	1	0	0	30	0	0	11.0	33.0
Durrington, Max	L-R	5-9	165	2-13-07	.256	.359	.312	40	145	125	16	32	5	1	0	15	20	0	0	0	25	6	1	13.8	17.2
Fernandez, Darling	R-R	6-2	190	12-05-04	.294	.445	.403	42	155	119	23	35	4	3	1	14	32	2	0	2	35	4	2	20.7	22.6
Fernandez, Jesus	R-R	5-11	145	2-14-06	.178	.245	.200	18	49	45	9	8	1	0	0	1	4	0	0	0	23	0	0	8.2	4.1
Fien, Dylan	S-R	6-3	200	10-20-05	.321	.441	.393	9	34	28	4	9	2	0	0	4	6	0	0	0	7	2	1	17.7	20.6
Franco, Cesar	R-R	6-1	190	4-26-02	.253	.372	.343	33	121	99	14	25	4	1	1	12	19	1	0	2	30	1	2	15.7	24.8
Gomez, Mario	L-R	5-10	185	12-4-00	.225	.304	.300	12	46	40	4	9	0	0	1	5	4	1	0	1	7	0	2	8.7	15.2
Gonzalez, Cesar	R-R	6-2	195	1-13-05	.238	.356	.369	25	101	84	16	20	9	1	0	14	15	1	0	1	26	0	1	14.9	25.7
Gouldsmith, Gunner	S-R	5-8	170	9-12-01	.182	.397	.250	17	63	44	9	8	1	1	0	8	14	3	0	2	8	2	4	22.2	12.7
Harris, Brett	R-R	6-1	208	6-24-98	1.000	1.000	2.000	1	3	2	1	2	1	0	0	0	1	0	0	0	0	0	0	0.0	0.0
Landaeta, Ramon	R-R	6-2	180	4-19-06	.282	.385	.427	40	156	131	20	37	10	0	3	26	23	0	0	2	44	0	1	14.7	28.2
Lasko, Ryan	R-R	6-0	190	6-24-02	.250	.400	.417	4	15	12	3	3	2	0	1	2	2	1	0	0	3	0	0	6.7	20.0
Machado, Anderson	R-R	6-1	170	10-10-03	.125	.176	.176	13	34	32	3	4	1	0	0	0	1	1	0	0	12	0	0	2.9	35.3
Marinez, Luis	R-R	6-1	155	10-11-01	.188	.316	.438	9	19	16	2	3	1	0	1	4	3	0	0	0	10	0	0	15.8	52.6
Montero, Darlyn	S-R	6-2	170	5-11-02	.381	.364	.571	6	22	21	1	8	1	0	1	7	0	0	0	1	6	1	0	0.0	27.3
Morii, Jericho	L-R	6-0	190	12-06	.258	.399	.384	43	188	151	39	39	8	1	3	27	36	0	0	1	47	4	3	19.2	25.0
Newton, Ben	S-R	5-10	170	6-11-02	.327	.438	.462	16	65	52	5	17	5	1	0	14	10	1	1	1	13	0	1	15.4	20.0
Ortiz, German	S-R	6-2	195	8-2-04	.300	.370	.356	27	100	90	13	27	5	0	0	5	10	0	0	0	19	3	0	10.0	19.0
Pacheco, Carlos	R-R	5-10	150	11-11-04	.235	.460	.265	12	52	34	11	8	1	0	0	7	9	2	1	1	11	5	1	17.3	21.2
Pariguan, Javier	R-R	5-10	160	2-5-04	.182	.400	.455	9	15	11	4	2	0	0	1	0	1	2	0	0	4	0	0	13.3	26.7
Pineda, Pedro	R-R	6-1	170	9-6-03	.211	.348	.368	62	213	191	34	11	0	4	4	4	33	0	0	4	80	0	0	17.4	17.4
Rijo, Elvis	R-R	5-11	165	11-27-03	.100	.250	.100	6	12	10	0	1	0	0	0	0	2	0	0	0	1	0	1	0.0	8.3
Rodriguez, Joseph	R-R	6-1	165	1-4-03	.230	.299	.311	17	67	61	13	14	3	1	0	6	5	1	0	0	25	1	1	7.5	37.3
Superlano, Jesus	R-R	5-11	165	9-20-05	.283	.362	.342	54	210	184	31	52	6	1	2	23	19	5	0	2	59	11	0	9.1	28.1

ATHLETICS

Pitching

Pitching	B-T	Ht.	Wt.	DOB	W	L	ERA	G	GS	SV	IP	Hits	Runs	ER	HR	BB	SO	AVG	OBP	SLG	SO%	BB%	BF
Alvarado, Wilfred	R-R	6-3	190	11-20-05	0	1	1.88	11	0	0	14	12	7	3	0	6	25	.207	.281	.259	39.1	9.4	64
Baum, Tyler	R-R	6-2	195	1-14-98	0	0	0.00	3	1	0	4	4	1	0	0	2	8	.250	.333	.250	44.4	11.1	18
Beers, Blake	R-R	6-4	215	7-15-98	0	1	1.13	3	3	0	8	9	2	1	0	1	9	.273	.314	.394	25.7	2.9	35
Chacon, Paul	R-R	6-0	180	9-8-05	0	3	8.39	14	4	0	25	35	29	23	2	18	20	.324	.435	.556	15.3	13.7	131
Conover, Drew	R-R	6-5	185	7-27-01	4	3	4.02	13	9	0	54	57	25	24	2	26	41	.275	.375	.401	17.1	10.8	240
Cooke, Bjay	R-R	6-2	187	3-14-03	0	0	15.58	9	0	0	9	18	18	15	0	5	8	.400	.462	.533	15.4	9.6	52
Corro, Derek	L-L	5-11	145	11-19-04	3	1	4.38	9	0	0	12	6	8	6	0	11	17	.150	.358	.175	32.1	20.8	53
De Los Santos, Eliazar	R-R	6-4	220	8-15-02	0	2	19.85	11	1	0	11	21	25	25	1	14	8	.396	.548	.604	11.0	19.2	73
Fernandez, Richard	R-R	6-1	190	9-22-02	1	2	6.20	20	1	2	25	28	22	17	2	16	35	.283	.387	.424	29.4	13.5	119
Gouldsmith, Gunner	S-R	5-8	170	9-12-01	0	0	18.00	1	0	0	1	4	2	2	1	0	0	.571	.571	1.143	0.0	0.0	7
Hernandez, Camilo	R-R	6-1	190	9-30-03	4	1	4.07	23	0	4	24	22	12	11	1	9	24	.242	.314	.418	23.5	8.8	102
Irvin, Garrett	L-L	6-0	185	2-18-99	0	1	3.00	3	0	0	3	3	1	1	0	1	3	.273	.357	.273	21.4	7.1	14
Miller, Cole	R-R	6-6	225	5-2-05	0	2	3.09	4	3	0	12	12	5	4	0	3	9	.261	.306	.304	18.4	6.1	49
Nova, Alvin	R-R	6-4	170	5-5-05	1	0	2.81	4	3	0	16	12	5	5	0	6	15	.203	.314	.271	21.4	8.6	70
Parra, Josnier	R-R	6-1	170	10-15-01	3	4	6.65	12	9	0	47	61	37	35	1	14	28	.321	.379	.511	12.8	6.4	218
Perez, Manuel	R-R	6-2	180	8-29-05	1	4	6.14	14	11	0	56	73	46	38	0	22	47	.311	.375	.451	17.9	8.4	262
Pinto, Jose	R-R	6-1	180	8-4-02	2	1	6.88	14	0	1	17	21	16	13	1	16	7	.318	.452	.439	8.3	19.1	84
Puason, Robert	R-R	6-3	165	9-11-02	2	1	6.84	19	0	0	26	33	22	20	3	11	16	.320	.402	.544	13.0	8.9	123
Robles, Domingo	L-L	6-2	170	4-29-98	0	1	1.00	3	3	0	9	7	2	1	0	1	12	.219	.265	.281	34.3	2.9	35
Romeo, Josiah	R-R	6-3	195	1-11-06	1	5	8.81	13	11	0	48	76	51	47	1	23	33	.364	.426	.478	14.0	9.8	236
Santos, Pedro	R-R	6-4	205	1-7-00	0	0	0.00	4	1	0	5	1	0	0	0	6	6	.067	.067	.067	40.0	0.0	15
Silva, Yeferson	R-R	6-0	175	6-28-05	1	1	5.72	18	0	0	28	36	21	18	1	19	15	.319	.420	.442	10.9	13.8	138
Urdaneta, Roberto	R-R	6-2	190	9-22-05	2	1	4.62	19	0	0	25	21	13	13	0	12	23	.216	.304	.278	20.5	10.7	112

Fielding
C: Landaeta 39, Newton 7, Fien 6, Pariguan 6, Gomez 4, Marinez 4. **1B:** Gonzalez 24, Ortiz 23, Dume 13, Montero 5, Marinez 1. **2B:** Durrington 30, Gouldsmith 14, Morii 7, Superlano 4, Bowman 3, Newton 3, Andrade 1, Camarillo 1, Fernandez 1, Rijo 1. **3B:** Superlano 39, Andrade 17, Machado 11, Fernandez 1, Harris 1, Ortiz 1. **SS:** Morii 23, Fernandez 15, Superlano 11, Andrade 10, Rijo 5, Camarillo 2, Gouldsmith 2, Machado 1. **LF:** Beltran 24, Fernandez 14, Durrington 10, Rodriguez 8, Franco 5, Newton 4, Butler 3, Pacheco 3. **CF:** Franco 24, Beltran 14, Pacheco 11, Rodriguez 10, Buelvas 6, Pineda 5, Lasko 3. **RF:** De La Paz 38, Fernandez 23, Franco 6, Beltran 4.

DSL ATHLETICS — ROOKIE
DOMINICAN SUMMER LEAGUE

Batting

Batting	B-T	Ht.	Wt.	DOB	AVG	OBP	SLG	G	PA	AB	R	H	2B	3B	HR	RBI	BB	HBP	SH	SF	SO	SB	CS	BB%	SO%
Barazarte, Aiverson	R-R	6-1	180	1-27-08	.239	.421	.268	33	95	71	15	17	0	1	0	11	16	7	0	1	14	1	1	16.8	14.7
Cota, Brayan	L-R	6-1	170	5-14-07	.172	.341	.219	48	166	128	20	22	4	1	0	10	28	6	2	2	27	3	2	16.9	16.3
Cuevas, Luis	R-R	6-0	175	10-5-07	.174	.345	.174	18	29	23	7	4	0	0	0	2	6	0	0	0	11	4	0	20.7	37.9
De La Cruz, Reinaldo	R-R	6-2	170	1-12-06	.368	.478	.474	6	23	19	10	7	0	1	0	0	3	1	0	0	3	1	1	13.0	13.0
Diaz, Yorvit	R-R	6-0	185	10-27-07	.279	.361	.365	34	122	104	20	29	5	2	0	15	13	2	0	3	14	7	1	10.7	11.5
Gonzalez, Samuel	R-R	5-11	170	11-20-06	.247	.364	.324	50	206	170	35	42	8	1	1	26	24	9	0	3	24	12	5	11.7	11.7
Guedez, Breyson	L-R	5-11	170	9-28-07	.359	.395	.490	53	210	192	38	69	15	2	2	46	14	0	0	4	20	5	1	6.7	9.5
Johnson, Ayden	R-R	6-0	180	2-13-08	.257	.414	.321	39	140	109	29	28	5	1	0	13	23	7	0	1	38	15	2	16.4	27.1
Lopez, Jeison	R-R	6-1	170	4-6-06	.234	.315	.333	48	198	171	25	40	10	2	1	27	15	7	1	4	41	4	4	7.6	20.7
Montero, Edgar	R-R	6-2	190	11-21-06	.313	.484	.580	55	244	176	47	55	14	3	9	50	60	3	0	5	54	11	4	24.6	22.1
Ozuna, Darwing	R-R	6-3	185	3-24-08	.211	.301	.311	35	103	90	12	19	3	0	2	11	9	3	0	1	25	2	1	8.7	24.3
Pacheco, Azaeel	R-R	6-0	170	12-13-06	.500	.667	.500	2	3	2	1	1	0	0	0	1	1	0	0	0	0	0	0	33.3	0.0
Peralta, Jean	R-R	6-1	176	4-27-07	.000	.000	.000	2	2	2	0	0	0	0	0	0	0	0	0	0	1	0	0	0.0	50.0
Pereira, Alejandro	R-R	5-11	170	6-12-07	.218	.343	.272	48	178	147	20	32	8	0	0	19	16	13	0	2	24	4	0	9.0	13.5
Ramos, Jose	L-R	6-1	160	10-1-06	.303	.411	.441	43	176	136	26	44	11	3	1	25	24	4	1	2	33	10	5	13.6	18.8
Rojas, Sebastian	R-R	6-0	175	3-13-07	.190	.390	.305	37	141	105	24	20	6	0	2	9	21	14	0	1	31	8	2	14.9	22.0
Salmeron, Carlos	R-R	6-0	165	1-22-08	.154	.370	.179	26	55	39	8	6	1	0	0	4	8	6	1	1	7	3	0	14.6	12.7

Pitching

Pitching	B-T	Ht.	Wt.	DOB	W	L	ERA	G	GS	SV	IP	Hits	Runs	ER	HR	BB	SO	AVG	OBP	SLG	SO%	BB%	BF
Arends, Nathan	R-R	6-2	180	9-23-06	1	2	5.94	15	0	0	17	8	11	11	1	13	19	.143	.342	.250	26.0	17.8	73
Brea, Jhose	R-R	6-2	190	12-20-07	1	0	5.51	13	5	1	33	32	22	20	2	18	25	.271	.367	.381	17.6	12.7	142
Burgos, Yerlin	R-R	6-2	185	4-29-08	1	0	4.09	11	0	0	11	7	5	5	0	13	13	.206	.472	.235	24.5	24.5	53
Contreras, Yohandri	R-R	6-3	200	10-30-06	2	5	5.14	15	4	0	28	29	18	16	0	20	26	.266	.403	.339	19.1	14.7	136
Delgado, Jesus	R-R	6-2	170	11-7-05	1	2	3.41	12	7	0	34	26	16	13	2	17	26	.215	.345	.306	17.9	11.7	145
Gonzalez, Diomar	R-R	6-1	190	10-11-04	4	0	2.23	10	7	0	44	30	14	11	1	11	37	.185	.224	.272	21.1	6.3	175
Guzman, Freilyn	R-R	6-3	160	11-5-05	1	4	9.28	13	3	0	21	27	22	22	0	15	11	.314	.444	.395	10.2	13.9	108
Matos, Erick	R-R	6-4	195	1-20-07	5	0	2.84	12	5	0	32	27	14	10	1	15	18	.239	.341	.292	13.6	11.4	132
Medina, Amilcar	R-R	6-2	154	9-2-04	0	2	13.50	14	0	1	9	15	18	14	1	14	12	.349	.541	.465	19.7	23.0	61
Mendoza, Edwin	R-R	6-3	195	10-11-07	0	0	1.69	5	0	0	5	4	1	1	0	8	5	.235	.464	.353	17.9	28.6	28
Osorio, Ricardo	R-R	6-4	185	3-3-08	1	2	4.98	15	0	2	22	18	15	12	0	14	25	.222	.351	.309	25.8	14.4	97
Parra, Jose	L-L	5-11	175	12-30-05	3	0	2.64	11	8	0	44	27	14	13	1	23	52	.182	.305	.250	29.9	13.2	174
Plicet, Luis	R-R	6-4	160	4-2-07	2	1	0.77	15	0	0	12	3	1	1	0	16	16	.083	.377	.111	30.2	30.2	53
Polanco, Brayan	R-R	6-6	180	2-28-05	0	0	5.73	12	0	1	11	11	7	7	0	8	10	.282	.442	.308	15.1	18.9	53
Reyes, Francisco	R-R	6-2	175	5-21-08	3	2	2.45	12	5	0	33	27	11	9	1	14	26	.231	.350	.299	18.4	9.9	141
Rodriguez, Yordan	R-R	6-3	190	1-29-08	2	0	2.93	8	1	0	15	11	5	5	1	8	20	.208	.302	.283	31.8	12.7	63
Sirotti, Oliver	R-R	6-3	180	9-26-06	4	0	3.38	20	0	4	21	15	10	8	2	8	14	.197	.271	.316	16.3	9.3	86
Ventura, Raulin	R-R	6-2	185	5-4-07	0	0	11.57	9	0	0	2	5	3	3	0	5	2	.250	.538	.250	14.3	35.7	14
Vizcaino, Angel	R-R	6-2	168	12-20-05	0	0	0.90	11	0	0	10	7	1	1	0	3	7	.200	.263	.200	18.4	7.9	38
Zabaleta, Franco	L-L	6-2	165	10-12-06	4	0	0.51	11	8	0	53	31	9	3	0	14	44	.176	.242	.210	22.2	7.1	198

Fielding
C: Pereira 47, Barazarte 17, Ozuna 1, Pacheco 1. **1B:** Cota 47, Barazarte 18, Ozuna 2. **2B:** Gonzalez 49, Diaz 13. **3B:** Johnson 35, Diaz 20, Cuevas 4, Cota 1, De La Cruz 1. **SS:** Montero 54, Gonzalez 1, Johnson 1. **LF:** Guedez 31, Ramos 13, Salmeron 9, Ozuna 6, Lopez 4, De La Cruz 3, Johnson 1. **CF:** Lopez 32, Ramos 25, Rojas 1, Salmeron 1. **RF:** Rojas 25, Salmeron 13, Lopez 10, Ozuna 10, Guedez 4, Ramos 2.

Atlanta Braves

SEASON SYNOPSIS: The Braves lost their first seven games, and after seven consecutive winning seasons—including a 2021 World Series crown and six NL East titles—struggled offensively, had their lack of pitching depth exposed and posted their first losing season since 2017. It wound up being the final season for manager Brian Snitker, who stepped down at season's end after 49 years in the organization and 10 years as manager.

HIGH POINT: Atlanta spent one day above .500 all year, May 18, but quickly faded even after bringing Spencer Strider and Ronald Acuña Jr. off the injured list. Perhaps a 10-game September win streak will have some carry-over into 2026, as Strider and rookie righty Hurston Waldrep won twice apiece while 2023 all-star Bryce Elder continued a competent second half. Acuña had four multi-hit games and four homers during the streak as Atlanta played spoiler by sweeping reeling host Detroit.

LOW POINT: Pick an injury—Reynoldo Lopez, a 2024 all-star, made one start, March 28, and missed the rest of the season after April shoulder surgery, though he made progress in September. Staff workhorse Spencer Schwellenbach's elbow fracture ended his season in late June and signaled the end of Atlanta's chances to contend. AJ Smith-Shawver (May) and Grant Holmes (July) both had UCL injuries end their seasons; Smith-Shawver had Tommy John surgery while Holmes did not. The Braves scrounged the waiver wire and DFA trades for fill-ins, using 19 starters in all including castoffs such as Carlos Carrasco, Erick Fedde, Cal Quantrill and, in the final game of his career, returning 2021 World Series hero Charlie Morton.

NOTABLE ROOKIES: C Drake Baldwin (.274/.341/.469, 19 HR) emerged as a Rookie of the Year contender and future roster stalwart, sharing time with veteran Sean Murphy. The duo combined for 35 homers. Waldrep (6-1, 2.88) looks like a rotation keeper. 2B/3B Nacho Alvarez Jr. (.234/.296/.330) hit both of his homers in a comeback win in Detroit during the 10-game win streak.

KEY TRANSACTIONS: After losing Max Fried in free agency to the Yankees, Atlanta's biggest offseason move was signing Jurickson Profar to a three-year, $42 million deal to be the new left fielder. He was lost March 31 on an 80-game PED suspension, robbing the offense of a potential leadoff hitter; he posted a .787 OPS in the final 80 games. Adding reliever Tyler Kinley (5-0, 0.72 in 25 IP) from Colorado could boost the bullpen in '26 as well.

OPENING DAY PAYROLL: $217,290,000 (8th)

PLAYERS OF THE YEAR

MAJOR LEAGUE
Matt Olson
1B
.272/.366/.484
29 HR, 41 2B, 95 RBIs
162 G 4th yr in a row

MINOR LEAGUE
JR Ritchie
RHP
(A+,AA,AAA)
2.64 ERA in 140 IP
140 SO, 1.00 WHIP

ORGANIZATION LEADERS

Batting *Qualifiers

MAJORS
* AVG	Matt Olson	.272
* OPS	Matt Olson	.850
HR	Matt Olson	29
RBI	Matt Olson	95

MINORS
* AVG	David McCabe, Gwinnett/Columbus	.275
* OBP	David McCabe, Gwinnett/Columbus	.367
* SLG	Eddys Leonard, Gwinnett	.435
* OPS	David McCabe, Gwinnett/Columbus	.794
R	John Gil, Columbus/Augusta/FCL Braves	76
H	Carlos D. Rodriguez, Gwinnett/Columbus	131
TB	David McCabe, Gwinnett/Columbus	200
2B	David McCabe, Gwinnett/Columbus	27
3B	Isaiah Drake, Rome/Augusta	6
HR	Eddys Leonard, Gwinnett	20
RBI	David McCabe, Gwinnett/Columbus	71
BB	David McCabe, Gwinnett/Columbus	71
SO	Ambioris Tavarez, Columbus/Rome	160
SB	Patrick Clohisy, Columbus/Rome	79

Pitching #Qualifiers

MAJORS
W	Bryce Elder	8
# ERA	No qualifier	
SO	Chris Sale	165
SV	Raisel Iglesias	29

MINORS
W	Ian Mejia, Gwinnett/Columbus	12
L	Adam Maier, Gwinnett/Rome	12
L	Davis Daniel, Gwinnett	12
# ERA	JR Ritchie, Gwinnett/Columbus/Rome	2.64
G	Enoli Paredes, Gwinnett	46
GS	JR Ritchie, Gwinnett/Columbus/Rome	26
GS	Lucas Braun, Gwinnett/Columbus	26
SV	Wander Suero, Gwinnett	12
IP	Lucas Braun, Gwinnett/Columbus	150
BB	Herick Hernandez, Rome	68
SO	Lucas Braun, Gwinnett/Columbus	145
# AVG	JR Ritchie, Gwinnett/Columbus/Rome	.175

2025 PERFORMANCE

General Manager: Alex Anthopoulos. **Farm Director:** Ben Sestanovich. **Scouting Director:** Ronit Shah.

Class	Team	League	W	L	PCT	Finish	Manager
Majors	Atlanta Braves	National	76	86	.469	12 (15)	Brian Snitker
Triple-A	Gwinnett Stripers	International	63	87	.420	16 (20)	Kanekoa Texeira
Double-A	Columbus Clingstones	Southern	58	77	.430	7 (8)	Cody Gabella
High-A	Rome Emperors	South Atlantic	58	70	.453	8 (12)	Angel Flores
Low-A	Augusta GreenJackets	Carolina	67	62	.519	7 (12)	Wynston Sawyer
Rookie	FCL Braves	Florida Complex	21	37	.362	13 (15)	Nestor Perez
Rookie	DSL Braves	Dominican	22	31	.415	40 (52)	Maikol Gonzalez
Overall 2025 Minor League Record			**289**	**364**	**.443**	**29th (30)**	

ORGANIZATION STATISTICS

ATLANTA BRAVES
NATIONAL LEAGUE

Batting	B-T	Ht.	Wt.	DOB	AVG	OBP	SLG	G	PA	AB	R	H	2B	3B	HR	RBI	BB	HBP	SH	SF	SO	SB	CS	BB%	SO%
Acuna, Ronald	R-R	6-0	205	12-18-97	.290	.417	.518	95	412	338	74	98	12	1	21	42	71	3	0	0	102	9	1	17.2	24.8
Albies, Ozzie	S-R	5-8	165	1-7-97	.240	.306	.365	157	667	603	74	145	23	2	16	74	55	4	0	5	94	14	3	8.2	14.1
Allen, Nick	R-R	5-8	166	10-8-98	.221	.284	.251	135	416	371	32	82	11	0	0	22	31	3	8	3	99	8	7	7.5	23.8
Alvarez, Ignacio	R-R	5-11	190	4-11-03	.234	.296	.330	58	208	188	18	44	12	0	2	15	12	5	2	1	49	0	0	5.8	23.6
Arcia, Orlando	R-R	6-0	187	8-4-94	.194	.219	.226	14	32	31	1	6	1	0	0	1	1	0	0	0	8	0	0	3.1	25.0
Azocar, Jose	R-R	5-11	181	5-11-96	.000	.000	.000	2	1	1	0	0	0	0	0	0	0	0	0	0	0	0	0	0.0	0.0
Baldwin, Drake	L-R	6-0	210	3-28-01	.274	.341	.469	124	446	405	56	111	18	2	19	80	38	3	0	0	68	0	0	8.5	15.2
Brujan, Vidal	S-R	5-10	180	2-9-98	.268	.362	.317	24	47	41	8	11	2	0	0	5	5	1	0	0	9	0	0	10.6	19.1
De La Cruz, Bryan	R-R	6-2	175	12-16-96	.191	.240	.213	16	50	47	1	9	1	0	0	0	3	0	0	0	18	1	0	6.0	36.0
Fairchild, Stuart	R-R	6-0	205	3-17-96	.216	.273	.333	28	55	51	7	11	4	1	0	2	4	0	0	0	15	2	1	7.3	27.3
Fraley, Jake	L-L	6-0	206	5-25-95	.304	.333	.348	9	24	23	2	7	1	0	0	0	1	0	0	0	8	0	1	4.2	33.3
Harris, Michael	L-L	6-0	195	3-7-01	.249	.268	.409	160	641	611	55	152	26	6	20	86	16	3	4	7	128	20	6	2.5	20.0
Kelenic, Jarred	L-L	6-1	206	7-16-99	.167	.231	.300	23	65	60	7	10	2	0	2	2	5	0	0	0	23	0	1	7.7	35.4
Kim, Ha-Seong	R-R	5-9	168	10-17-95	.253	.316	.368	24	98	87	14	22	1	0	3	12	8	1	0	2	16	0	1	8.2	16.3
Leon, Sandy	S-R	5-10	235	3-13-89	.083	.083	.333	5	12	12	1	1	0	0	1	3	0	0	0	0	4	0	0	0.0	33.3
Murphy, Sean	R-R	6-3	228	10-4-94	.199	.300	.409	94	337	291	34	58	13	0	16	45	35	8	0	3	105	0	0	10.4	31.2
Olson, Matt	L-R	6-5	225	3-29-94	.272	.366	.484	162	724	624	98	170	41	2	29	95	91	4	0	5	176	1	0	12.6	24.3
Ornelas, Jonathan	R-R	6-0	196	5-26-00	.500	.500	.500	2	4	4	1	2	0	0	0	0	0	0	0	0	0	0	0	0.0	0.0
Ozuna, Marcell	R-R	6-1	225	11-12-90	.232	.355	.400	145	592	487	61	113	19	0	21	68	94	3	0	7	144	0	0	15.9	24.3
Profar, Jurickson	S-R	6-0	184	2-20-93	.245	.353	.434	80	371	318	56	78	16	1	14	43	48	5	0	0	59	9	2	12.9	15.9
Riley, Austin	R-R	6-3	240	4-2-97	.260	.309	.428	102	447	416	54	108	20	1	16	54	27	3	0	1	128	2	1	6.0	28.6
Rosario, Eddie	L-L	6-1	180	9-28-91	.000	.000	.000	3	4	4	1	0	0	0	0	0	0	0	0	0	2	0	0	0.0	50.0
Tromp, Chadwick	R-R	5-8	221	3-21-95	.000	.167	.000	2	6	5	0	0	0	0	0	0	1	0	0	0	2	0	0	16.7	33.3
Verdugo, Alex	L-L	6-0	192	5-15-96	.239	.296	.289	56	213	197	21	47	10	0	0	12	14	2	0	0	31	1	0	6.6	14.6
White, Eli	R-R	6-2	195	6-26-94	.234	.270	.406	105	271	256	43	60	8	3	10	35	11	2	1	1	70	10	1	4.1	25.8
Williams, Luke	R-R	6-0	186	8-9-96	.129	.176	.194	45	34	31	5	4	2	0	0	5	1	0	1	1	9	5	0	2.9	26.5
Wisely, Brett	L-R	5-10	290	5-8-99	.000	.333	.000	4	9	6	0	0	0	0	0	0	3	0	0	0	4	0	0	33.3	44.4

Pitching	B-T	Ht.	Wt.	DOB	W	L	ERA	G	GS	SV	IP	Hits	Runs	ER	HR	BB	SO	AVG	OBP	SLG	SO%	BB%	BF
Blewett, Scott	R-R	6-6	245	4-10-96	2	0	5.51	11	1	0	16	16	11	10	5	10	13	.267	.371	.517	18.1	13.9	72
Brebbia, John	L-R	6-1	200	5-30-90	0	1	7.71	3	0	0	5	6	5	4	2	1	6	.300	.364	.600	27.3	4.5	22
Brujan, Vidal	S-R	5-10	180	2-9-98	0	0	13.50	2	0	0	2	4	3	3	1	1	0	.400	.455	.700	0.0	9.1	11
Bummer, Aaron	L-L	6-3	215	9-21-93	3	2	3.81	42	2	0	54	51	27	23	3	17	51	.250	.336	.373	21.7	7.2	235
Carrasco, Carlos	R-R	6-4	224	3-21-87	0	0	9.88	3	3	0	14	22	15	15	3	7	9	.355	.414	.629	12.0	10.0	70
Chavez, Jesse	R-R	6-1	175	8-21-83	0	1	9.00	4	0	0	8	14	8	8	4	5	8	.368	.442	.789	18.6	11.6	43
Cox, Austin	L-L	6-4	235	3-28-97	0	0	8.86	13	1	0	21	30	21	21	9	7	22	.319	.363	.681	21.6	6.9	102
Daniel, Davis	R-R	6-1	190	6-11-97	0	1	5.40	3	2	0	10	9	6	6	1	7	9	.250	.370	.444	19.6	15.2	46
De Los Santos, Enyel	R-R	6-3	235	12-25-95	3	3	4.53	43	0	0	44	39	25	22	2	18	38	.231	.312	.343	20.1	9.5	189
Diaz, Alexis	R-R	6-2	224	9-28-96	0	0	10.13	3	0	0	3	0	4	3	0	5	5	.000	.429	.000	35.7	35.7	14
Dodd, Dylan	L-L	6-2	210	6-6-98	1	0	3.60	28	0	0	35	28	14	14	5	5	30	.219	.250	.391	22.1	3.7	136
Dunning, Dane	R-R	6-4	225	12-20-94	0	0	10.80	7	0	0	10	15	13	12	2	2	11	.333	.388	.511	22.4	4.1	49
Elder, Bryce	R-R	6-2	220	5-19-99	8	11	5.30	28	28	0	156	167	95	92	24	51	131	.271	.331	.446	19.3	7.5	679
Fedde, Erick	R-R	6-4	203	2-25-93	1	2	8.10	5	4	0	23	30	21	21	3	13	13	.316	.400	.516	11.7	11.7	111
Fuentes, Didier	R-R	6-0	170	6-17-05	0	3	13.85	4	4	0	13	23	20	20	6	6	12	.383	.449	.717	17.4	8.7	69
Harris, Hayden	L-L	6-0	186	3-2-99	0	0	3.38	3	0	0	3	3	1	1	0	2	0	.300	.417	.400	0.0	16.7	12
Herget, Kevin	L-R	5-10	185	4-3-91	0	0	0.00	1	0	0	1	0	0	0	0	2	0	.250	.500	.250	0.0	33.3	6
Hernandez, Daysbel	R-R	5-10	220	9-15-96	4	3	3.41	39	0	0	37	27	16	14	3	30	33	.206	.362	.313	20.1	18.3	164
Holmes, Grant	L-R	6-0	226	3-22-96	4	9	3.99	22	21	0	115	100	52	51	16	54	123	.238	.387	.25.0	11.0	492
Iglesias, Raisel	R-R	6-2	190	1-4-90	4	6	3.21	70	0	29	67	51	25	24	8	16	73	.206	.259	.352	27.4	6.0	266
Johnson, Pierce	R-R	6-2	202	5-10-91	3	3	3.05	65	0	1	59	52	21	20	8	19	59	.242	.303	.400	24.8	8.0	238
Kimbrel, Craig	R-R	6-0	215	5-28-88	0	0	0.00	1	0	0	1	0	0	0	0	1	0	.500	.667	.500	33.3	33.3	3
Kinley, Tyler	R-R	6-4	220	1-31-91	5	0	0.72	24	0	0	25	11	2	2	1	6	22	.126	.191	.172	23.4	6.4	94
Lee, Dylan	L-L	6-3	214	8-1-94	2	4	3.29	74	0	2	68	53	27	25	14	76	.213	.254	.398	28.6	5.3	266
Lopez, Reynaldo	R-R	6-1	225	1-4-94	0	0	5.40	1	1	0	5	9	3	3	1	2	1	.391	.440	.565	4.0	8.0	25

ATLANTA BRAVES

Player	B-T	Ht	Wt	DOB			ERA	G			IP	H	R	ER	HR	BB	SO	AVG	OBP	SLG	K/9	BB/9	AB
Montero, Rafael	R-R	6-0	190	10-17-90	0	1	5.50	36	0	0	34	27	22	21	3	21	34	.211	.320	.344	22.7	14.0	150
Morton, Charlie	R-R	6-5	215	11-12-83	0	0	0.00	1	1	0	1	2	0	0	0	1	1	.400	.500	.400	16.7	16.7	6
Munoz, Rolddy	R-R	6-2	183	4-14-00	0	0	12.27	3	0	0	4	4	5	5	1	5	5	.286	.524	.500	23.8	23.8	21
Neris, Hector	R-R	6-2	227	6-14-89	0	1	45.00	2	0	0	1	5	5	5	1	1	1	.714	.750	1.286	12.5	12.5	8
Payamps, Joel	R-R	6-2	217	4-7-94	0	0	3.38	2	0	0	3	2	1	1	1	0	2	.222	.222	.556	22.2	0.0	9
Petersen, Michael	R-R	6-7	195	5-16-94	0	0	4.05	4	0	0	7	7	3	3	1	2	5	.269	.321	.462	17.9	7.1	28
Quantrill, Cal	L-R	6-3	195	2-10-95	0	2	13.50	2	2	0	8	14	12	12	5	5	3	.368	.442	.842	7.0	11.6	43
Ruiz, Jose	R-R	6-1	245	10-21-94	0	0	13.50	2	0	0	2	2	3	3	0	3	3	.250	.455	.250	27.3	27.3	11
Sale, Chris	L-L	6-6	183	3-30-89	7	5	2.58	21	20	0	126	102	38	36	11	32	165	.220	.285	.341	32.4	6.3	510
Schwellenbach, Spencer	R-R	6-1	200	5-31-00	7	4	3.09	17	17	0	111	89	44	38	13	18	108	.217	.252	.366	24.9	4.1	434
Seabold, Connor	R-R	6-2	190	1-24-96	0	0	9.82	4	0	0	4	5	4	4	1	3	5	.313	.421	.563	26.3	15.8	19
Smith-Shawver, AJ	R-R	6-3	205	11-20-02	3	2	3.86	9	9	0	44	42	20	19	4	21	42	.249	.335	.379	21.9	10.9	192
Stratton, Hunter	R-R	6-4	225	11-17-96	1	1	2.20	12	0	1	16	13	5	4	2	5	15	.217	.294	.333	22.1	7.4	68
Strider, Spencer	R-R	6-0	195	10-28-98	7	14	4.45	23	23	0	125	124	63	62	20	51	131	.261	.340	.453	24.3	9.5	539
Suarez, Jose	L-L	5-10	225	1-3-98	2	0	1.86	7	1	1	19	15	5	4	1	10	16	.217	.313	.290	19.8	12.3	81
Suero, Wander	R-R	6-4	216	9-15-91	0	0	11.37	5	0	0	6	10	8	8	3	4	7	.357	.438	.714	21.9	12.5	32
Thompson, Zach	R-R	6-7	250	10-23-93	0	0	0.00	2	0	0	4	0	0	0	0	1	3	.000	.083	.000	25.0	8.3	12
Waldrep, Hurston	R-R	6-2	205	3-1-02	6	1	2.88	10	9	0	56	45	18	18	3	22	55	.222	.306	.305	24.0	9.6	229
Wentz, Joey	L-L	6-5	220	10-6-97	3	6	4.92	14	13	0	64	68	38	35	6	23	64	.270	.327	.393	23.0	8.3	278
Wiles, Nathan	R-R	6-4	228	7-2-98	0	0	27.00	1	0	0	1	4	3	3	0	0	1	.667	.571	.833	14.3	0.0	7
Williams, Luke	R-R	6-0	186	8-9-96	0	0	3.00	6	0	0	6	2	2	1	1	4	.250	.280	.417	16.0	4.0	25

Fielding

Catcher	PCT	G	PO	A	E	DP	PB
Baldwin	.995	97	745	32	4	3	3
Leon	1.000	5	34	0	0	0	0
Murphy	.997	76	644	32	2	4	2
Tromp	1.000	2	17	1	0	0	0

First Base	PCT	G	PO	A	E	DP
Olson	.996	162	1147	145	5	96
White	1.000	4	5	1	0	1

Second Base	PCT	G	PO	A	E	DP
Albies	.997	157	205	368	2	64
Allen	.933	5	6	8	1	2
Wisely	1.000	4	6	8	0	3

Third Base	PCT	G	PO	A	E	DP
Alvarez	.978	58	36	97	3	10
Brujan	1.000	6	1	8	0	1
Ornelas	1.000	1	0	1	0	0
Riley	.953	102	55	166	11	13
Williams	.889	4	4	4	1	0

Shortstop	PCT	G	PO	A	E	DP
Allen	.988	130	152	258	5	47
Arcia	1.000	13	7	17	0	6
Brujan	1.000	13	7	11	0	0
Kim	1.000	24	31	42	0	10
Ornelas	1.000	2	1	0	0	0
Williams	1.000	25	13	15	0	4

Outfield	PCT	G	PO	A	E	DP
Acuna	.988	91	164	5	2	2
Azocar	.000	1	0	0	0	0
Brujan	1.000	3	8	0	0	0
De La Cruz	1.000	14	21	1	0	1
Fairchild	1.000	20	33	3	0	0
Fraley	1.000	7	14	0	0	0
Harris	.998	160	402	1	1	0
Kelenic	.941	23	32	0	2	0
Profar	.994	79	164	0	1	0
Rosario	1.000	1	3	0	0	0
Verdugo	.978	54	88	1	2	0
White	.992	90	129	3	1	0

GWINNETT STRIPERS — TRIPLE-A
INTERNATIONAL LEAGUE

Batting	B-T	Ht.	Wt.	DOB	AVG	OBP	SLG	G	PA	AB	R	H	2B	3B	HR	RBI	BB	HBP	SH	SF	SO	SB	CS	BB%	SO%
Acuna, Ronald	R-R	6-0	205	12-18-97	.417	.632	.833	5	19	12	6	5	2	0	1	1	7	0	0	0	2	0	0	36.8	10.5
Alvarez, Eddy	L-R	5-8	178	1-30-90	.176	.323	.302	51	197	159	28	28	5	0	5	14	28	7	2	1	45	10	3	14.2	22.8
Alvarez, Ignacio	R-R	5-11	190	4-11-03	.254	.405	.349	18	79	63	10	16	3	0	1	7	11	5	0	0	15	0	1	13.9	19.0
Bastidas, Jesus	R-R	5-8	145	9-14-98	.259	.348	.388	37	159	139	20	36	6	0	4	15	19	0	1	0	40	4	1	11.9	25.2
Batten, Matthew	R-R	5-11	180	6-22-95	.192	.264	.328	114	399	360	32	69	14	1	11	36	34	2	2	1	104	12	3	8.5	26.1
Bunnell, Cade	L-R	5-11	190	5-14-97	.212	.295	.323	32	112	99	8	21	5	0	2	11	11	1	0	1	46	1	0	9.8	41.1
Campos, Elio	R-R	5-9	157	1-2-04	.000	.000	.000	1	0	0	0	0	0	0	0	0	0	0	0	0	0	0	0	0.0	0.0
Capel, Conner	L-L	6-1	185	5-19-97	.234	.314	.360	119	414	367	43	86	10	3	10	39	42	2	0	3	83	21	4	10.1	20.0
Conley, Cal	S-R	5-8	185	7-17-99	.250	.294	.313	5	17	16	2	4	1	0	0	0	1	0	0	0	5	0	0	5.9	29.4
Cooper, Garrett	R-R	6-5	235	12-25-90	.228	.312	.309	35	138	123	8	28	4	0	2	17	13	2	0	0	33	1	0	9.4	23.9
De La Cruz, Bryan	R-R	6-2	175	12-16-96	.200	.256	.225	11	43	40	1	8	1	0	0	1	3	0	0	0	14	0	0	7.0	32.6
Delay, Jason	R-R	5-11	200	3-7-95	.215	.282	.256	60	214	195	13	42	8	0	0	12	14	4	0	0	37	1	0	6.5	17.3
Devers, Jose	L-R	6-0	174	12-7-99	.286	.345	.356	29	110	98	10	28	5	3	0	9	7	0	2	1	15	1	1	8.2	13.6
Fairchild, Stuart	R-R	6-0	205	3-17-96	.417	.462	.500	3	13	12	3	5	1	0	0	0	1	0	0	0	3	1	0	7.7	23.1
Fletcher, David	R-R	5-9	185	5-31-94	.180	.213	.268	67	217	205	12	37	9	0	3	15	7	2	1	2	30	3	0	3.2	13.8
Jarvis, Jim	S-R	5-10	165	10-27-99	.400	.556	.3	10	9	3	2	2	0	0	2	0	1	0	0	2	0	0	0.0	0.0
Kelenic, Jarred	L-L	6-1	206	7-16-99	.213	.286	.309	95	399	362	40	77	17	3	4	29	36	1	0	0	110	11	8	9.0	27.6
Leblanc, Charles	R-R	6-3	195	6-3-96	.291	.394	.316	22	95	79	8	23	1	0	0	8	12	2	1	1	19	0	1	12.6	20.0
Leon, Sandy	S-R	5-10	235	3-13-89	.166	.245	.358	58	211	187	19	31	6	0	10	19	18	2	3	1	66	2	0	8.5	31.3
Leonard, Eddys	R-R	5-11	195	11-10-00	.239	.304	.435	126	494	439	48	105	18	4	20	61	36	9	5	9	95	11	5	7.3	19.2
Marisnick, Jake	R-R	6-4	220	3-30-91	.098	.178	.195	12	45	41	5	4	1	0	1	3	1	0	0	0	13	1	0	6.7	28.9
McCabe, David	S-R	6-3	230	3-25-00	.235	.321	.398	28	112	98	8	23	4	0	4	19	13	0	0	1	32	1	0	11.6	28.6
McCann, James	R-R	6-3	235	6-13-90	.274	.351	.493	41	160	148	19	44	11	0	6	30	9	0	0	3	45	0	0	5.6	25.6
Milligan, Cody	L-R	5-9	170	12-23-98	.211	.320	.282	50	169	142	17	30	4	3	0	10	23	1	0	3	45	12	3	13.6	26.6
Murphy, Sean	R-R	6-3	228	10-4-94	.200	.200	.500	3	10	10	1	2	0	0	1	2	0	0	0	0	1	0	0	0.0	10.0
Olsavsky, Joe	R-R	6-1	180	3-29-02	.000	.333	.000	1	3	2	0	0	0	0	0	0	1	0	0	0	2	0	0	0.0	66.7
Ornelas, Jonathan	R-R	6-0	196	5-26-00	.279	.325	.385	333	295	35	57	3	3	10	28	33	3	0	3	86	6	5	9.9	25.8
Profar, Jurickson	S-R	6-0	184	2-20-93	.333	.407	.583	13	59	48	7	16	3	0	3	9	8	0	0	3	6	0	0	13.6	10.2
Rodriguez, Carlos D.	L-L	5-8	186	12-7-00	.247	.317	.323	128	533	474	53	117	10	1	8	32	49	1	3	3	68	17	8	9.2	12.8
Sanchez, Luis	R-R	5-7	165	1-5-00	.500	.500	.500	1	4	3	0	1	0	0	0	0	1	0	0	0	0	0	2	25.0	0.0
Seagle, Chandler	R-R	5-10	190	5-23-96	.212	.241	.269	20	54	52	6	11	3	0	0	1	1	0	0	1	16	0	0	1.9	29.6
Verdugo, Alex	L-L	6-0	192	5-15-96	.207	.303	.448	9	33	29	8	6	1	0	2	4	4	0	0	0	4	1	0	12.1	12.1
Waddell, Luke	L-R	5-7	180	7-13-98	.272	.364	.340	91	380	324	34	88	17	1	1	30	46	4	1	5	47	5	2	12.1	12.4

ATLANTA BRAVES

Pitching	B-T	Ht.	Wt.	DOB	W	L	ERA	G	GS	SV	IP	Hits	Runs	ER	HR	BB	SO	AVG	OBP	SLG	SO%	BB%	BF
Williams, Luke	R-R	6-0	186	8-9-96	.114	.188	.125	24	96	88	4	10	1	0	0	2	7	1	0	0	32	3	0	7.3	33.3
Wisely, Brett	L-R	5-10	180	5-8-99	.375	.444	.500	2	9	8	0	3	1	0	0	0	1	0	0	0	1	0	0	11.1	11.1
Zebrowski, Adam	R-R	6-0	230	9-28-00	.200	.273	.300	3	11	10	1	2	1	0	0	1	1	0	0	0	3	1	0	9.1	27.3
Alvarez, Eddy	L-R	5-8	178	1-30-90	0	0	0.00	1	0	0	1	1	0	0	0	0	0	.250	.400	.500	0.0	0.0	5
Anderson, Ian	R-R	6-3	170	5-2-98	1	4	6.08	9	9	0	37	38	26	25	2	28	27	.273	.391	.396	16.0	16.6	169
Braun, Lucas	R-R	6-0	185	8-26-01	2	1	1.42	3	3	0	19	9	3	3	0	4	11	.150	.203	.183	17.2	6.3	64
Brebbia, John	L-R	6-1	200	5-30-90	1	1	1.89	15	0	2	19	18	6	4	1	3	21	.243	.269	.324	26.9	3.8	78
Burkhalter, Blake	R-R	6-0	204	9-19-00	2	2	3.77	18	2	1	31	28	13	13	3	16	23	.248	.336	.381	17.6	12.2	131
Carrasco, Carlos	R-R	6-4	224	3-21-87	2	2	5.80	7	7	0	36	43	23	23	2	12	30	.307	.368	.457	19.4	7.7	155
Chavez, Jesse	R-R	6-1	175	8-21-83	2	0	2.05	23	1	2	31	24	9	7	2	12	36	.214	.288	.330	28.8	9.6	125
Covey, Dylan	R-R	6-2	215	8-14-91	1	1	0.00	6	1	1	7	5	0	0	0	1	4	.241	.267	.345	13.3	3.3	30
Cox, Austin	L-L	6-4	235	3-28-97	0	3	4.61	20	1	1	27	35	17	14	2	11	18	.321	.382	.468	14.6	8.9	123
Daniel, Davis	R-R	6-1	190	6-11-97	6	12	5.60	25	17	0	101	102	66	63	15	44	81	.262	.338	.459	18.2	9.9	445
Diaz, Alexis	R-R	6-2	224	9-28-96	0	0	0.00	2	0	0	2	0	0	0	0	4	.286	.286	.429	57.1	0.0	7
Dodd, Dylan	L-L	6-2	210	6-6-98	2	1	4.26	24	0	0	25	27	12	12	4	3	32	.278	.307	.443	31.4	2.9	102
Dunning, Dane	R-R	6-4	225	12-20-94	2	1	5.09	6	3	0	23	27	16	13	1	5	16	.287	.323	.436	16.0	5.0	100
Elder, Bryce	R-R	6-2	220	5-19-99	0	2	8.76	3	3	0	12	16	12	12	3	6	16	.308	.390	.519	27.1	10.2	59
Farmer, Buck	L-R	6-4	243	2-20-91	1	0	7.71	5	0	0	5	7	5	4	0	4	7	.350	.458	.400	29.2	16.7	24
Fletcher, David	R-R	5-9	185	5-31-94	0	0	9.00	1	0	0	1	3	1	1	0	1	0	.600	.667	.600	0.0	16.7	6
Fuentes, Didier	R-R	6-0	170	6-17-05	1	1	3.63	5	5	0	22	20	9	9	3	4	29	.238	.270	.369	32.6	4.5	89
Gonzalez, Domingo	R-R	6-0	185	9-27-99	2	1	4.29	35	0	0	42	40	21	20	3	21	39	.252	.339	.377	21.4	11.5	182
Harris, Hayden	L-L	6-0	186	3-2-99	0	0	0.31	25	0	1	29	9	2	1	1	12	42	.097	.234	.161	37.8	10.8	111
Herget, Kevin	L-R	5-10	185	4-3-91	1	0	3.68	13	0	0	15	16	6	6	2	3	14	.276	.323	.448	22.6	4.8	62
Hernandez, Daysbel	R-R	5-10	220	9-15-96	0	0	2.25	8	0	3	8	3	2	2	2	3	11	.107	.194	.357	35.5	9.7	31
Ingram, Kolton	L-L	5-9	170	10-21-96	0	0	7.11	5	0	0	6	8	6	5	0	5	8	.333	.433	.500	26.7	16.7	30
Kimbrel, Craig	R-R	6-0	215	5-28-88	1	1	2.45	15	0	3	15	8	4	4	0	8	17	.157	.271	.216	28.8	13.6	59
Kuhl, Chad	R-R	6-3	207	9-10-92	0	3	6.55	7	3	0	22	26	17	16	2	12	18	.299	.385	.448	17.1	11.4	105
Lara, Jhancarlos	R-R	6-3	190	1-15-03	0	5	6.53	28	9	0	51	30	40	37	4	46	78	.169	.359	.292	33.8	19.9	231
Maier, Adam	R-R	6-0	203	11-26-01	0	1	7.20	1	1	0	5	3	4	4	2	2	5	.167	.250	.500	10.0	10.0	20
Mejia, Ian	R-R	6-3	205	1-31-00	0	1	4.50	1	1	0	4	5	4	2	1	4	3	.294	.429	.588	14.3	19.0	21
Moran, Brian	L-L	6-4	225	9-30-88	0	1	4.26	6	1	0	13	11	7	6	2	2	15	.239	.314	.435	29.4	3.9	51
Munoz, Rolddy	R-R	6-2	183	4-14-00	1	1	4.15	16	2	0	22	17	10	10	2	10	25	.215	.300	.329	27.8	11.1	90
Paredes, Enoli	R-R	5-11	171	9-28-95	2	3	4.40	46	0	3	57	57	31	28	4	30	72	.258	.363	.389	27.6	11.5	261
Petersen, Michael	R-R	6-7	195	5-16-94	0	0	3.13	20	0	0	23	25	8	8	2	7	26	.269	.327	.398	25.7	6.9	101
Pilar, Anderson	R-R	6-2	210	3-2-98	0	0	3.18	11	1	1	17	12	6	6	0	6	13	.200	.269	.233	19.4	9.0	67
Ragsdale, Carson	R-R	6-8	225	5-25-98	0	1	36.00	1	0	0	1	3	4	4	1	2	1	.500	.625	1.000	12.5	25.0	8
Ritchie, JR	R-R	6-2	185	6-26-03	3	2	3.02	11	11	0	60	38	24	20	5	27	61	.181	.288	.290	25.1	11.1	243
Ruiz, Jose	R-R	6-1	245	10-21-94	0	2	4.70	7	0	2	8	9	4	4	0	1	6	.300	.323	.367	19.4	3.2	31
Sale, Chris	L-L	6-6	183	3-30-89	0	1	2.53	3	3	0	11	10	3	3	0	3	11	.244	.295	.293	25.0	6.8	44
Seabold, Connor	R-R	6-2	190	1-24-96	0	1	3.12	6	0	0	9	6	3	3	1	3	7	.194	.297	.297	18.9	8.1	37
Seagle, Chandler	R-R	5-10	190	5-23-96	0	0	0.00	1	0	0	0	0	0	0	0	3	0	.000	.750	.000	0.0	75.0	4
Sears, Brett	R-R	6-0	205	5-2-00	0	2	10.24	2	2	0	10	11	11	7	2	6	29	.349	.892	14.0	4.7	43
Shreve, Chasen	L-L	6-4	180	7-12-90	1	2	5.60	5	4	0	18	21	15	11	3	5	12	.292	.346	.472	15.2	6.3	79
Smith-Shawver, AJ	R-R	6-3	205	11-20-02	0	1	4.82	2	2	0	9	9	5	5	0	4	13	.250	.325	.361	32.5	10.0	40
Stephens, Jackson	R-R	6-2	220	5-11-94	4	0	2.57	22	4	0	49	35	14	14	1	15	42	.205	.270	.287	22.2	7.9	189
Stratton, Hunter	R-R	6-4	225	11-17-96	1	1	1.59	10	0	0	11	7	3	2	1	3	11	.167	.222	.262	24.4	6.7	45
Strider, Spencer	R-R	6-0	195	10-28-98	1	0	1.32	3	3	0	14	5	2	2	0	5	27	.111	.216	.156	52.9	9.8	51
Suarez, Jose	L-L	5-10	225	1-3-98	3	1	3.53	9	8	0	43	42	20	17	4	9	50	.249	.294	.408	27.6	5.0	181
Suero, Wander	R-R	6-4	216	9-15-91	2	3	1.35	43	0	12	47	35	12	7	2	13	59	.203	.275	.279	31.2	6.9	189
Thompson, Zach	R-R	6-7	250	10-23-93	1	4	6.67	12	5	1	27	31	25	20	3	18	17	.292	.397	.453	13.5	14.3	126
Waldrep, Hurston	R-R	6-2	205	3-1-02	7	8	4.42	19	19	0	92	85	58	45	8	50	92	.244	.341	.350	22.5	12.3	408
Weems, Jordan	L-R	6-4	212	11-7-92	1	1	5.09	14	0	1	18	19	11	10	3	10	18	.288	.367	.470	22.5	12.5	80
Wiles, Nathan	R-R	6-4	228	7-2-98	6	8	3.04	25	19	1	113	106	42	38	14	34	105	.244	.297	.403	22.2	7.2	473
Willingham, Amos	R-R	6-4	217	8-21-98	1	1	4.91	7	0	0	11	15	9	6	3	3	10	.333	.367	.622	20.4	6.1	49

Fielding

Catcher	PCT	G	PO	A	E	DP	PB
Delay	.981	57	447	29	9	5	0
Leon	.993	42	386	20	3	0	1
McCann	.982	32	267	8	5	1	4
Murphy	.964	3	26	1	1	0	0
Seagle	.983	19	160	11	3	2	0
Zebrowski	1.000	3	22	2	0	0	0

First Base	PCT	G	PO	A	E	DP
Batten	.996	72	486	49	2	56
Bunnell	1.000	23	134	16	0	20
Capel	1.000	7	41	4	0	3
Cooper	.974	23	133	15	4	5
Leblanc	.967	7	52	7	2	6
Leonard	1.000	6	41	2	0	6
McCabe	1.000	17	129	12	0	8
McCann	1.000	1	4	0	0	1
Williams	1.000	2	12	0	0	0

Second Base	PCT	G	PO	A	E	DP
Alvarez N	1.000	7	7	20	0	5
Alvarez E	.974	10	19	18	1	7
Bastidas	1.000	16	26	40	0	7
Batten	1.000	4	4	4	0	0
Conley	1.000	5	9	15	0	1
Devers	.908	22	26	43	7	12
Fletcher	1.000	22	29	44	0	13
Leblanc	1.000	1	1	2	0	1
Leonard	.964	30	48	58	4	9
Milligan	1.000	8	11	21	0	8
Olsavsky	1.000	1	1	0	0	0
Waddell	.984	30	50	74	2	26
Williams	1.000	2	3	2	0	0

Third Base	PCT	G	PO	A	E	DP
Alvarez E	.950	8	3	16	1	3
Alvarez N	1.000	11	12	17	0	4
Bastidas	.750	2	3	1	0	
Batten	1.000	29	15	38	0	4
Bunnell	.778	4	3	4	2	1
Cooper	.000	1	0	0	0	0
Devers	.833	3	1	4	1	0
Fletcher	.939	26	19	43	4	8
Leblanc	.938	10	3	12	1	1
Leonard	.936	36	16	57	5	5
Ornelas	1.000	14	13	21	0	4
Sanchez	.667	1	0	2	1	0
Waddell	1.000	6	0	7	0	0
Williams	.913	10	10	11	2	2

Shortstop	PCT	G	PO	A	E	DP
Alvarez	.938	10	13	17	2	5
Bastidas	.981	14	20	31	1	9
Fletcher	1.000	19	38	46	0	12
Jarvis	1.000	3	1	2	0	0
Leonard	.000	1	0	0	0	0
Ornelas	.988	43	63	103	2	29
Waddell	.955	53	56	115	8	19
Williams	1.000	8	10	10	0	0

Outfield	PCT	G	PO	A	E	DP
Acuna	.857	3	5	1	1	0
Alvarez	.976	22	38	2	1	0
Batten	1.000	6	14	0	0	0
Capel	.983	96	171	6	3	2
De La Cruz	1.000	9	16	0	0	0
Fairchild	1.000	2	2	0	0	0
Wisely	1.000	2	1	4	0	1
Kelenic	.985	94	193	5	3	1
Leonard	1.000	21	33	1	0	1
Marisnick	1.000	10	13	1	0	0
Milligan	.988	41	83	2	1	1
Ornelas	.971	23	31	2	1	0
Profar	1.000	8	15	0	0	0
Rodriguez	.992	126	249	9	2	0
Verdugo	.846	8	11	0	2	0
Williams	1.000	2	2	0	0	0

COLUMBUS CLINGSTONES — DOUBLE-A
SOUTHERN LEAGUE

Batting	B-T	Ht.	Wt.	DOB	AVG	OBP	SLG	G	PA	AB	R	H	2B	3B	HR	RBI	BB	HBP	SH	SF	SO	SB	CS	BB%	SO%
Bunnell, Cade	L-R	5-11	190	5-14-97	.157	.280	.293	45	164	140	13	22	2	1	5	14	23	1	0	0	59	4	0	14.0	36.0
Clohisy, Patrick	L-L	5-10	190	12-6-01	.270	.328	.384	39	174	159	22	43	4	1	4	16	11	3	0	1	29	19	4	6.3	16.7
Compton, Drew	S-R	6-2	212	3-25-01	.251	.326	.341	112	448	399	38	100	22	1	4	33	45	1	0	3	117	2	0	10.0	26.1
Conley, Cal	S-R	5-8	185	7-17-99	.194	.253	.235	125	507	463	46	90	10	3	1	29	34	3	5	2	103	21	5	6.7	20.3
Delay, Jason	R-R	5-11	200	3-7-95	.114	.139	.257	8	37	35	4	4	2	0	1	2	1	0	0	0	12	0	0	2.7	32.4
Espinoza, Lizandro	R-R	5-7	158	11-20-02	.238	.353	.476	12	51	42	15	10	4	0	2	7	7	1	0	1	16	3	0	13.7	31.4
Exposito, E.J.	R-R	5-11	190	5-4-01	.220	.259	.332	62	232	214	20	47	7	1	5	31	10	3	0	5	56	6	2	4.3	24.1
Fletcher, David	R-R	5-9	185	5-31-94	.200	.302	.218	16	63	55	5	11	0	0	0	5	8	0	0	0	10	1	1	12.7	15.9
Gil, John	R-R	6-1	175	5-14-06	.174	.240	.174	6	25	23	2	4	0	0	0	1	2	0	0	0	7	4	0	8.0	28.0
Jarvis, Jim	L-R	5-10	185	11-6-00	.265	.344	.361	21	93	83	20	22	8	0	0	8	7	3	0	0	21	6	0	7.5	22.6
Kato, Kobe	R-R	6-1	170	3-19-99	.180	.314	.304	55	194	161	14	29	8	0	4	16	30	2	0	1	60	15	4	15.5	30.9
Kern, Kade	R-R	6-0	200	9-18-01	.300	.417	.400	4	12	10	1	3	1	0	0	0	1	1	0	0	3	1	0	8.3	25.0
Kilpatrick, Kevin	R-R	5-10	186	11-25-00	.214	.295	.259	99	353	313	34	67	7	2	1	24	31	6	0	3	85	22	9	8.8	24.1
Machado, Austin	L-R	6-1	205	6-11-01	.000	.000	.000	1	3	3	0	0	0	0	0	0	0	0	0	0	1	0	0	0.0	33.3
McCabe, David	S-R	6-3	230	3-25-00	.286	.379	.434	105	435	371	54	106	23	1	10	52	58	1	0	5	89	2	1	13.3	20.5
McCann, James	R-R	6-3	235	6-13-90	.667	.750	1.333	1	4	3	0	2	0	0	0	0	0	0	0	1	0	0	0	25.0	0.0
Milligan, Cody	L-R	5-9	170	12-23-98	.186	.323	.251	53	225	183	25	34	6	0	2	7	34	4	2	2	66	10	3	15.1	29.3
Ogans, Keshawn	R-R	5-8	180	8-26-01	.179	.298	.211	35	114	95	10	17	3	0	0	5	15	2	0	2	22	4	3	13.2	19.3
Paolini, Stephen	L-L	6-1	195	11-23-00	.195	.277	.317	40	137	123	10	24	3	0	4	10	13	1	0	0	48	16	2	9.5	35.0
Quintero, Geraldo	S-R	5-5	155	10-10-01	.212	.327	.358	102	399	335	43	71	11	4	10	41	52	7	0	4	87	29	11	13.0	21.8
Rodriguez, Carlos D.	L-L	5-8	186	12-7-00	.341	.404	.366	10	47	41	4	14	1	0	0	5	5	0	0	1	5	3	2	10.6	10.6
Seagle, Chandler	R-R	5-10	190	5-23-96	.144	.213	.198	34	122	111	4	16	6	0	0	14	6	4	0	1	42	1	1	4.9	34.4
Shockley, Dylan	R-R	5-9	195	4-10-97	.158	.264	.184	24	87	76	3	12	2	0	0	2	11	0	0	0	34	0	0	12.6	39.1
Tavarez, Ambioris	R-R	5-11	168	11-12-03	.178	.302	.200	15	53	45	5	8	1	0	0	3	7	1	0	0	21	6	2	13.2	39.6
Tolve, Tyler	L-R	6-0	200	7-16-00	.000	.000	.000	2	6	6	0	0	0	0	0	0	0	0	0	0	5	0	0	0.0	83.3
Workinger, Ethan	R-R	6-0	185	10-19-01	.224	.299	.385	120	493	441	56	99	19	2	16	70	43	5	0	2	90	12	5	8.7	18.3
Zebrowski, Adam	R-R	6-0	230	9-28-00	.231	.289	.349	87	349	321	29	74	11	0	9	42	23	4	0	1	109	3	1	6.6	31.2

Pitching	B-T	Ht.	Wt.	DOB	W	L	ERA	G	GS	SV	IP	Hits	Runs	ER	HR	BB	SO	AVG	OBP	SLG	SO%	BB%	BF
Abeyta, Blane	R-R	6-3	185	9-4-98	3	1	2.29	43	0	9	51	34	16	13	6	20	68	.187	.272	.324	32.9	9.7	207
Anderson, Ian	R-R	6-3	170	5-2-98	0	3	3.09	3	3	0	12	9	6	4	1	6	11	.214	.320	.310	22.0	12.0	50
Bourassa, Ryan	R-R	6-0	230	12-18-99	0	0	0.82	8	0	2	11	3	1	1	0	5	14	.088	.220	.088	33.3	11.9	42
Braun, Lucas	R-R	6-0	185	8-26-02	5	5	3.99	24	23	0	131	110	64	58	19	35	134	.225	.282	.381	25.1	6.6	533
Bunnell, Cade	L-R	5-11	190	5-14-97	0	0	0.00	1	0	0	0	0	0	0	0	0	0	.000	.000	.000	0.0	0.0	1
Burkhalter, Blake	R-R	6-0	204	9-19-00	2	5	3.13	14	14	0	72	63	28	25	1	29	65	.237	.319	.289	21.2	9.5	306
Cuas, Jose	R-R	6-3	195	6-28-94	2	1	3.22	18	0	1	22	17	9	8	0	18	23	.205	.350	.253	22.1	17.3	104
Frey, Riley	L-L	6-1	185	4-19-02	0	1	15.00	1	0	3	7	5	5	0	1	4	.438	.471	.563	23.5	5.9	17
Fuentes, Didier	R-R	6-0	170	6-17-05	0	5	4.98	5	5	0	22	21	13	12	1	7	24	.250	.333	.357	25.0	7.3	96
Gallegos, Isaac	R-R	6-3	215	9-17-02	0	0	0.00	1	0	0	2	1	0	0	0	0	2	.143	.143	.286	28.6	0.0	7
Hackenberg, Drue	R-R	6-2	220	4-1-02	2	8	6.99	18	18	0	66	72	60	51	9	52	56	.280	.405	.440	17.3	16.1	323
Halligan, Patrick	R-R	6-6	230	10-4-99	0	0	18.00	1	0	0	1	1	2	2	1	1	2	.250	.400	1.000	40.0	20.0	5
Harper, Landon	R-R	6-1	176	4-8-01	5	8	3.59	26	14	2	108	98	46	43	14	21	105	.236	.276	.393	23.9	4.8	439
Harris, Hayden	L-L	6-0	186	3-2-99	4	0	0.79	18	0	3	23	11	2	2	0	7	37	.147	.238	.187	43.5	8.2	85
Hughes, Jonathan	R-R	6-2	196	1-8-97	0	0	3.60	6	0	0	10	7	4	4	2	5	5	.206	.293	.382	11.9	11.9	42
Ingram, Kolton	L-L	5-9	170	10-21-96	0	0	4.26	5	0	0	6	5	4	3	1	6	5	.208	.367	.375	16.7	20.0	30
Joseph, Elison	R-R	6-0	170	1-24-01	1	4	4.31	37	0	6	40	32	20	19	2	0	41	57	.181	.371	.261	30.5	21.9	187
Juan, Jorge	R-R	6-8	200	3-6-99	0	1	9.00	6	0	0	5	3	7	5	1	6	9	.167	.444	.389	33.3	22.2	27
Kato, Kobe	L-R	6-1	170	3-19-99	0	0	0.00	1	0	0	0	0	0	0	0	0	0	.000	.316	.500	0.0	0.0	19
Kimbrel, Craig	R-R	6-0	215	5-28-88	0	0	0.00	3	0	0	3	0	0	0	0	1	6	.000	.091	.000	54.5	9.1	11
LaPorte, Tyler	R-R	6-1	175	4-9-97	2	3	4.23	21	0	1	28	26	14	13	1	16	27	.252	.352	.359	22.0	13.0	123
Lara, JhonCarlos	R-R	6-3	190	11-15-03	0	4	11.21	6	5	0	18	24	28	23	6	26	19	.319	.469	.611	27.1	19.8	96
McDonough, LJ	R-R	6-4	200	4-2-00	2	2	5.34	25	0	2	32	37	19	19	2	20	33	.298	.414	.411	21.7	13.2	152
McSteen, Jake	R-L	6-0	215	3-12-96	1	2	2.95	11	0	0	18	20	9	6	4	18	.290	.338	.377	23.4	5.2	77
Mejia, Ian	R-R	6-3	205	11-30-01	4	10	2.62	24	17	1	127	98	54	37	9	37	106	.214	.284	.348	21.0	7.3	504
Mejia, Samuel	R-R	6-1	160	6-17-02	0	0	0.00	1	1	0	5	0	0	0	0	0	7	.000	.158	.000	21.1	15.8	19
Moran, Brian	L-L	6-4	225	9-30-88	1	1	3.11	17	3	1	46	36	18	16	2	10	42	.218	.267	.309	23.9	5.7	176
Munoz, Rolddy	R-R	6-2	183	4-14-00	2	2	2.11	24	1	6	38	21	11	9	4	23	34	.206	.337	.324	20.5	13.9	166
Ritchie, JR	R-R	6-2	185	6-26-03	1	3	3.49	8	8	0	39	26	15	15	4	17	41	.181	.274	.324	22.7	9.4	181
Schanaman, Shay	R-R	6-0	195	8-12-99	3	2	7.06	25	0	0	29	33	25	23	2	25	.289	.421	.447	17.7	16.3	141
Sears, Brett	R-R	6-0	205	5-2-00	6	7	3.63	15	14	0	74	56	34	30	6	23	74	.204	.277	.325	24.1	7.5	307
Smith, Austin	R-R	6-4	210	6-22-99	0	3	5.40	18	0	4	20	16	14	12	3	11	21	.256	.348	.423	23.6	12.4	89

Stratton, Hunter	R-R	6-4	225	11-17-96	0	0	0.00	1	0	0	1	0	0	0	1	2	.000	.250	.000	50.0	25.0	4
Suarez, Jose	L-L	5-10	225	1-3-98	1	0	4.02	3	3	0	16	12	7	7	3	15	.211	.250	.421	24.6	4.9	61
Thompson, Zach	R-R	6-7	250	10-23-93	1	0	6.30	5	1	0	10	10	7	7	2	4	12	.256	.318	.513	27.3	9.1	44
Vargas, Luis	R-R	5-11	196	5-2-02	1	2	4.30	12	0	2	15	13	8	7	0	11	16	.250	.394	.288	23.9	16.4	67
Wall, Cory	R-R	6-4	230	3-14-00	0	0	3.46	8	1	0	13	9	6	5	1	7	15	.196	.327	.391	26.8	12.5	56
Willingham, Amos	R-R	6-4	217	8-21-98	1	1	5.08	22	3	0	39	42	28	22	7	12	45	.263	.318	.450	25.9	6.9	174

Fielding

Catcher	PCT	G	PO	A	E	DP	PB
Delay	.975	7	73	4	2	1	1
McCann	1.000	1	12	1	0	1	0
Seagle	.994	34	295	28	2	2	1
Shockley	.982	24	205	11	4	1	2
Tolve	1.000	2	10	3	0	0	0
Zebrowski	.968	68	598	38	21	2	11

First Base	PCT	G	PO	A	E	DP
Bunnell	1.000	18	113	18	0	8
Compton	.994	100	727	59	5	51
Exposito	1.000	11	66	6	0	6
McCabe	.977	7	41	1	1	5
Workinger	1.000	1	9	0	0	1

Second Base	PCT	G	PO	A	E	DP
Bunnell	.957	7	5	17	1	3
Conley	1.000	17	32	40	0	9
Exposito	.952	23	22	57	4	10

	PCT	G	PO	A	E	DP
Fletcher	1.000	7	13	13	0	3
Jarvis	1.000	2	1	6	0	0
Kato	.968	53	60	122	6	18
Milligan	.950	4	9	10	1	3
Ogans	.976	10	14	26	1	5
Quintero	1.000	4	3	6	0	0
Tavarez	1.000	12	23	20	0	8

Third Base	PCT	G	PO	A	E	DP
Bunnell	.935	12	6	23	2	1
Conley	.842	5	0	16	3	1
Exposito	.793	12	10	13	6	4
Fletcher	.957	9	10	12	1	0
Jarvis	1.000	4	4	12	0	0
McCabe	.938	70	46	105	10	13
Ogans	.983	24	19	39	1	2

Shortstop	PCT	G	PO	A	E	DP
Conley	.980	104	143	208	7	39
Espinoza	.926	8	10	15	2	3
Exposito	1.000	2	6	7	0	1
Gil	.929	6	9	17	2	3
Jarvis	.950	13	20	37	3	2
Tavarez	.917	3	5	6	1	1

Outfield	PCT	G	PO	A	E	DP
Bunnell	.000	1	0	0	0	0
Clohisy	.976	39	82	1	2	0
Espinoza	1.000	4	11	0	0	0
Kern	1.000	4	7	0	0	0
Kilpatrick	.973	97	218	1	6	1
Milligan	1.000	48	100	1	0	0
Paolini	.984	37	62	1	1	0
Quintero	.969	83	146	8	5	0
Rodriguez	1.000	10	12	0	0	0
Workinger	.969	84	150	4	5	3

ATLANTA BRAVES

ROME EMPERORS
SOUTH ATLANTIC LEAGUE

HIGH-A

Batting	B-T	Ht.	Wt.	DOB	AVG	OBP	SLG	G	PA	AB	R	H	2B	3B	HR	RBI	BB	HBP	SH	SF	SO	SB	CS	BB%	SO%
Arroyo, Carlos	R-R	5-9	170	7-11-01	.154	.195	.205	11	41	39	1	6	2	0	0	6	2	0	0	0	14	1	0	4.9	34.1
Braunschweig, Logan	L-R	6-1	195	11-29-02	.294	.406	.353	26	101	85	12	25	3	1	0	9	14	2	0	0	18	4	2	13.9	17.8
Clohisy, Patrick	L-L	5-10	190	12-6-01	.247	.338	.330	92	405	352	50	87	16	2	3	27	45	5	0	3	76	60	13	11.1	18.8
Devers, Jose	R-R	6-0	174	12-7-99	.167	.167	.333	2	6	6	0	1	1	0	0	1	0	0	0	0	1	0	0	0.0	16.7
Drake, Isaiah	L-R	5-10	185	7-15-05	.303	.336	.336	32	130	122	11	37	1	0	1	12	8	0	0	0	23	11	4	6.2	17.7
Dumitru, Titus	R-R	6-2	220	5-17-03	.231	.310	.319	64	281	251	27	58	9	2	3	36	26	3	0	1	71	13	3	9.3	25.3
Espinoza, Lizandro	R-R	5-7	158	11-20-02	.201	.261	.350	85	377	343	45	69	15	3	10	35	26	3	1	4	107	20	13	6.9	28.4
Exposito, E.J.	R-R	5-11	190	5-4-01	.269	.365	.485	37	156	134	23	36	6	1	7	17	16	5	0	1	42	5	0	10.3	26.9
Grady, Mason	S-R	5-11	182	5-25-01	.166	.262	.241	61	214	187	16	31	11	0	1	13	23	2	0	2	62	4	3	10.7	29.0
Guerra, Mason	R-R	6-3	195	8-28-02	.182	.262	.255	54	214	192	15	35	5	0	3	20	20	1	0	1	51	0	0	9.3	23.8
Guscette, Mac	R-R	6-0	200	2-14-02	.174	.236	.230	50	178	161	7	28	4	1	1	17	11	6	0	3	29	0	1	6.2	16.3
Horne, Bryson	L-R	5-10	220	3-6-99	.176	.245	.283	53	208	187	18	33	5	0	5	20	16	2	0	3	62	2	1	7.7	29.8
Janas, Justin	L-R	6-2	205	9-18-00	.252	.328	.329	91	354	313	29	79	9	3	3	40	22	15	0	4	60	10	3	6.2	16.9
Jones, Colby	R-R	5-11	180	9-30-03	.240	.308	.256	31	133	121	19	29	2	0	0	7	10	2	0	0	28	15	6	7.5	21.1
Kern, Kade	R-R	6-0	200	9-18-01	.000	.750	.000	1	4	1	0	0	0	0	0	0	3	0	0	0	0	5	0	75.0	0.0
Lodise, Alex	R-R	6-1	190	3-10-04	.252	.294	.398	25	109	103	11	26	10	1	1	9	5	1	0	0	42	2	1	4.6	38.5
Machado, Austin	L-R	6-1	205	6-11-01	.211	.400	.211	7	25	19	4	4	0	0	0	2	6	0	0	0	4	1	1	24.0	16.0
McIntyre, Dalton	L-L	6-3	175	7-17-03	.161	.278	.194	9	36	31	6	5	1	0	0	1	5	0	0	0	15	2	0	13.9	27.8
McMurray, Cooper	L-L	6-4	250	12-19-01	.132	.263	.235	21	80	68	7	9	1	0	2	9	8	4	0	0	29	0	0	10.0	36.3
Miller, Cody	R-R	5-11	185	7-1-04	.297	.357	.422	16	70	64	7	19	3	1	1	6	5	1	0	0	22	6	1	7.1	31.4
Ogans, Keshawn	R-R	5-8	180	8-26-01	.258	.355	.318	43	153	132	5	34	8	0	0	9	16	4	0	0	16	1	5	10.5	10.5
Olsavsky, Joe	R-R	6-1	180	3-29-02	.163	.311	.235	37	119	98	10	16	2	1	1	4	15	6	0	0	26	3	1	12.6	21.8
Owen, Harry	R-R	6-1	225	3-7-02	.174	.259	.231	38	136	121	7	21	4	0	1	7	10	4	1	0	24	0	0	7.4	17.6
Paolini, Stephen	L-L	6-1	195	11-23-00	.194	.318	.278	11	44	36	7	7	0	0	1	8	5	2	0	1	12	4	1	11.4	27.3
Pineda, Alen	R-R	5-10	180	11-4-04	.080	.080	.200	8	25	25	1	2	0	0	1	5	0	0	0	0	10	0	0	0.0	40.0
Sanchez, Luis	R-R	5-7	165	1-16-04	.170	.302	.170	20	63	53	5	9	0	0	0	1	9	1	0	0	10	1	1	14.3	15.9
Shockley, Dylan	R-R	5-9	195	4-10-97	.246	.362	.298	20	69	57	13	14	0	0	1	5	9	2	0	1	30	1	0	13.0	43.5
Smith, Tanner	R-R	5-11	210	9-26-02	.222	.417	.333	3	12	9	2	2	1	0	0	3	0	0	0	0	4	0	0	25.0	33.3
Steels, Jake	R-R	6-0	185	6-17-02	.238	.326	.300	29	95	80	10	19	2	0	1	5	9	3	0	3	16	0	1	9.5	16.8
Tavarez, Ambioris	R-R	5-11	168	11-12-03	.209	.319	.277	98	398	339	39	71	8	0	5	28	47	9	0	3	139	15	3	11.8	34.9
Tolve, Tyler	L-R	6-0	200	7-16-00	.101	.195	.116	21	77	69	3	7	1	0	0	3	7	1	0	0	39	0	0	9.1	50.6
Verdung, Will	R-R	6-2	200	6-8-03	.279	.375	.328	81	339	287	32	80	10	2	0	22	44	3	0	5	57	6	4	13.0	16.8
Waddell, Luke	L-R	5-7	180	7-13-98	.154	.241	.231	7	29	26	4	4	2	0	0	3	0	0	0	0	6	0	0	10.3	20.7

Pitching	B-T	Ht.	Wt.	DOB	W	L	ERA	G	GS	SV	IP	Hits	Runs	ER	HR	BB	SO	AVG	OBP	SLG	SO%	BB%	BF
Baumann, Garrett	R-R	6-8	245	8-15-04	6	9	3.40	23	23	0	114	110	48	43	10	31	108	.251	.308	.353	22.5	6.4	481
Bourassa, Ryan	R-R	6-0	230	12-18-99	1	4	2.95	30	0	3	43	30	14	14	4	23	62	.138	.259	.269	36.5	13.5	170
Buchanan, Trent	R-R	6-1	233	9-24-01	0	1	1.59	4	0	1	6	4	1	1	0	2	2	.222	.286	.222	9.5	9.5	21
De Grandpre, Cedric	R-R	6-2	210	1-25-02	5	11	3.74	13	13	0	53	35	24	22	1	41	66	.188	.349	.253	28.1	17.4	235
Diaz, Giomar	R-R	6-2	190	11-23-02	3	0	5.63	14	0	0	24	16	17	15	2	17	18	.235	.362	.353	17.1	16.2	105
Frey, Riley	L-L	6-1	185	4-19-02	2	3	4.14	19	6	1	67	55	34	31	8	20	69	.217	.275	.356	24.9	7.2	277
Fuentes, Didier	R-R	6-1	170	6-17-05	0	1	5.54	3	3	0	13	8	8	8	0	5	18	.186	.269	.326	34.0	9.4	53
Gallegos, Isaac	R-R	6-3	215	9-17-02	0	2	3.31	34	0	8	49	44	23	18	1	19	46	.235	.316	.332	21.7	9.0	212
Gomez, Jacob	R-L	5-10	190	10-27-01	1	2	2.73	20	2	0	30	18	9	9	0	18	35	.178	.308	.228	29.2	15.0	120

ATLANTA BRAVES

Batting																						
Griswold, Rob	R-R	6-1	185	7-13-98	3	3	4.65	33	0	1	50	65	30	26	4	14	25	.322	.384	.455	10.8	6.1	231
Hernandez, Herick	L-L	5-10	192	8-11-03	3	6	3.57	22	21	0	103	70	42	41	14	68	127	.193	.330	.365	28.7	15.3	443
Horne, Bryson	L-R	5-10	220	5-8-99	0	0	5.79	2	0	0	5	3	2	1	0	.417	.423	.667	0.0	3.8	26
Kroeger, Jacob	L-L	6-1	190	5-18-00	3	5	2.03	12	10	0	62	39	14	14	4	21	46	.177	.252	.277	19.0	8.7	242
LaPorte, Tyler	R-R	6-1	175	4-9-97	2	0	1.50	17	0	1	24	17	4	4	3	7	21	.202	.272	.345	22.8	7.6	92
Long, Justin	R-R	6-1	180	3-4-02	2	1	3.44	15	0	1	18	10	9	7	1	18	15	.177	.410	.263	17.9	21.4	84
Maier, Adam	R-R	6-0	203	11-26-01	4	11	5.76	22	19	0	95	93	65	61	9	44	72	.260	.352	.402	17.0	10.4	424
McDonough, LJ	R-R	6-4	200	4-2-00	1	2	3.00	14	0	1	15	14	7	5	1	7	18	.237	.313	.339	26.5	10.3	68
Murphy, Owen	R-R	6-1	190	9-27-03	3	0	1.32	6	6	0	27	15	6	4	1	6	29	.161	.218	.258	28.7	5.9	101
Niekro, J.J.	R-R	6-0	185	1-28-98	0	1	7.11	3	0	0	6	5	5	5	1	7	7	.227	.414	.455	24.1	24.1	29
Ritchie, JR	R-R	6-2	185	6-26-03	4	1	1.30	7	7	0	42	23	7	6	3	10	38	.161	.226	.245	24.2	6.4	157
Rodriguez, David	L-R	6-2	196	12-31-01	1	0	3.86	7	0	0	19	17	9	8	1	3	13	.236	.276	.333	17.1	3.9	76
Salinas, Royber	R-R	6-3	205	4-10-01	0	0	7.71	5	0	0	5	3	4	4	0	5	6	.176	.364	.235	27.3	22.7	22
Samuels, Logan	R-R	6-4	170	2-18-02	2	4	6.08	22	4	2	47	49	38	32	10	22	37	.265	.364	.470	17.3	10.3	214
Sears, Brett	R-R	6-0	205	5-2-00	2	1	2.00	3	3	0	18	10	5	4	2	17	.149	.186	.269	24.3	2.9	70
Shoemaker, Adam	L-L	6-2	205	8-24-02	1	0	2.70	5	0	0	7	5	4	2	0	8	10	.200	.382	.360	29.4	23.5	34
Silva, William	R-R	6-0	185	8-2-01	1	1	8.77	18	0	2	26	37	29	25	4	16	25	.333	.440	.523	18.7	11.9	134
Sinnard, Luke	R-R	6-8	250	10-21-02	2	4	4.19	9	9	0	43	36	22	20	2	15	45	.221	.293	.331	24.9	8.3	181
Smith, Austin	R-R	6-4	210	6-22-99	0	1	2.38	11	0	0	11	5	3	3	1	4	13	.139	.244	.250	31.7	9.8	41
Strickland, Samuel	R-L	6-2	218	3-26-99	3	2	2.87	22	2	1	38	31	14	12	3	4	41	.221	.253	.343	27.3	2.7	150
Suarez, Jose	L-L	5-10	225	1-3-98	1	0	0.00	1	0	0	3	1	0	0	0	0	4	.111	.111	.111	44.4	0.0	9
Vargas, Luis	R-R	5-11	196	5-2-02	0	0	2.57	5	0	1	7	4	2	2	1	2	13	.167	.222	.292	48.1	7.4	27
Wall, Cory	R-R	6-4	230	3-14-00	4	1	1.75	26	2	1	36	24	7	7	0	10	40	.183	.255	.237	27.6	6.9	145
Willingham, Amos	R-R	6-4	217	8-21-98	0	0	6.00	3	0	0	3	2	2	2	0	2	5	.182	.308	.182	38.5	15.4	13

Fielding

Catcher	PCT	G	PO	A	E	DP	PB
Guscette	.986	47	376	34	6	4	4
Machado	1.000	6	49	4	0	0	2
Owen	.988	36	315	14	4	1	2
Pineda	.957	6	43	2	2	0	0
Shockley	.984	16	119	5	2	0	1
Smith	1.000	3	30	1	0	0	0
Tolve	.994	21	171	9	1	1	4

First Base	PCT	G	PO	A	E	DP
Guerra	.989	36	263	17	3	27
Horne	.997	37	285	25	1	26
McMurray	.992	17	116	7	1	13
Olsavsky	1.000	5	27	4	0	1
Verdung	.996	34	234	19	1	15

Second Base	PCT	G	PO	A	E	DP
Arroyo	.964	9	7	20	1	1
Devers	1.000	2	6	1	0	0
Exposito	.958	6	7	16	1	2

	PCT	G	PO	A	E	DP
Jones	.972	10	12	23	1	8
Lodise	1.000	3	1	7	0	0
Miller	1.000	3	8	7	0	2
Ogans	1.000	3	3	3	0	0
Olsavsky	.921	10	10	25	3	3
Sanchez	.951	8	10	29	2	6
Tavarez	.974	58	93	135	6	29
Verdung	.961	17	25	49	3	10
Waddell	1.000	3	9	8	0	3

Third Base	PCT	G	PO	A	E	DP
Arroyo	1.000	1	1	3	0	0
Exposito	.919	29	21	47	6	7
Guerra	1.000	2	2	2	0	0
Jones	.947	13	16	20	2	2
Miller	.917	6	5	6	1	2
Ogans	.942	28	26	39	4	5
Olsavsky	.909	13	11	19	3	0
Sanchez	.955	11	5	16	1	1
Verdung	.985	27	26	41	1	2

Shortstop	PCT	G	PO	A	E	DP
Espinoza	.937	53	82	111	13	25
Jones	1.000	7	9	13	0	3
Lodise	.969	20	25	38	2	10
Miller	.947	6	6	12	1	3
Tavarez	.952	40	59	79	7	18
Waddell	1.000	2	3	1	0	0

Outfield	PCT	G	PO	A	E	DP
Braunschweig	1.000	27	40	5	0	0
Clohisy	.990	89	185	4	2	0
Drake	1.000	32	63	2	0	0
Dumitru	1.000	60	104	3	0	2
Espinoza	.975	32	112	3	3	0
Grady	.952	39	58	1	3	0
Janas	.982	66	110	2	2	0
Kern	1.000	1	1	0	0	0
McIntyre	1.000	8	12	1	0	0
Paolini	1.000	10	19	0	0	0
Steels	1.000	28	49	2	0	0

AUGUSTA GREENJACKETS — LOW-A
CAROLINA LEAGUE

Batting	B-T	Ht.	Wt.	DOB	AVG	OBP	SLG	G	PA	AB	R	H	2B	3B	HR	RBI	BB	HBP	SH	SF	SO	SB	CS	BB%	SO%
Burgess, Colin	R-R	5-8	195	11-10-00	.208	.277	.292	42	160	144	17	30	6	0	2	15	11	3	0	1	36	0	0	6.9	22.5
Campos, Elio	R-R	5-9	157	1-2-04	.211	.263	.278	26	99	90	13	19	1	1	1	10	6	1	0	2	10	8	0	6.1	10.1
Carey, Owen	L-L	6-0	185	7-22-06	.258	.330	.345	117	525	469	63	121	25	2	4	63	38	14	1	3	82	17	10	7.2	15.6
Drake, Isaiah	L-R	5-10	185	7-15-05	.260	.341	.364	84	364	319	41	83	6	6	5	47	39	2	0	4	82	35	9	10.7	22.5
Estevez, John	L-R	6-3	190	5-17-06	.174	.345	.174	8	29	23	3	4	0	0	0	2	6	0	0	0	5	0	0	20.7	17.2
Figueroa, Leiker	R-R	5-10	155	1-12-05	.242	.321	.333	46	135	120	17	29	3	1	2	11	10	4	1	0	32	3	3	7.4	23.7
Friese, Hayden	R-R	6-1	220	8-16-04	.239	.396	.239	24	91	71	12	17	0	0	0	9	18	1	0	1	24	1	0	19.8	26.4
Gil, John	R-R	6-1	175	5-14-06	.258	.352	.378	100	462	399	73	103	25	1	7	48	57	2	1	2	64	50	14	12.3	13.9
Glod, Douglas	R-R	5-9	185	1-20-05	.213	.343	.342	84	329	272	33	58	14	0	7	36	49	6	0	2	115	1	2	14.9	35.0
Guanipa, Luis	R-R	5-11	188	12-15-05	.269	.331	.324	29	118	108	16	29	0	1	0	13	9	1	0	0	14	2	1	7.6	11.9
Guerra, Mason	R-R	6-3	195	8-28-02	.240	.389	.473	47	185	146	25	35	5	1	9	27	33	4	0	2	49	0	0	17.8	26.5
Guscette, Mac	R-R	6-0	200	2-14-02	.293	.413	.453	23	92	75	14	22	7	1	1	16	14	2	0	1	15	0	1	15.2	16.3
Hartman, Eric	L-R	6-1	180	6-16-06	.248	.344	.374	83	370	318	56	79	17	4	7	41	37	11	1	3	85	44	5	10.0	23.0
Jones, Colby	R-R	5-11	180	9-30-03	.214	.350	.260	91	374	304	52	65	5	3	1	25	60	6	0	4	78	54	10	16.0	20.9
Macias, Dallas	S-R	6-0	190	10-28-03	.031	.184	.031	1	38	32	4	1	0	0	0	1	3	3	0	0	9	0	0	7.9	23.7
Mateo, Juan	S-R	6-0	165	5-22-07	.235	.299	.269	31	135	119	18	28	4	0	0	18	10	0	3	2	32	4	1	8.9	23.7
Miller, Cody	R-R	5-11	185	7-1-04	.372	.417	.488	10	48	43	8	16	2	0	1	11	3	1	0	1	10	4	2	6.3	20.8
Montenegro, Carlos	L-L	6-1	177	12-10-05	.115	.308	.131	19	78	61	7	7	1	0	0	7	10	0	0	0	25	0	0	21.8	30.8
Montgomery, Nicholas	R-R	6-4	200	11-7-05	.170	.272	.252	87	357	306	23	52	6	2	5	35	42	3	0	5	119	1	0	11.8	33.3
Niazoa, Roiber	R-R	6-0	175	12-23-04	.150	.220	.186	32	123	113	6	17	4	0	0	5	9	1	0	0	49	0	0	7.3	39.8
Olsavsky, Joe	R-R	6-1	180	3-29-02	.291	.439	.358	48	187	148	18	43	5	1	1	17	27	12	0	0	35	6	0	14.4	18.7
Orellana, Josnaider	R-R	5-11	175	9-26-04	.286	.333	.571	4	15	14	2	4	1	1	1	5	0	0	0	1	4	0	0	0.0	6.7	20.0
Pineda, Alen	R-R	5-10	180	11-4-04	.167	.318	.194	12	46	36	5	6	1	0	0	6	4	4	0	0	22	0	0	9.1	50.0
Sanchez, Luis	R-R	5-7	165	1-16-04	.224	.341	.272	44	173	147	13	33	5	1	0	20	24	2	0	0	23	0	0	13.9	13.3

ATLANTA BRAVES

Batting (cont.)	B-T	Ht.	Wt.	DOB	AVG	OBP	SLG	G	PA	AB	R	H	2B	3B	HR	RBI	BB	HBP	SH	SF	SO	SB	CS	BB%	SO%
Smith, Tanner	R-R	5-11	210	9-26-02	.150	.227	.500	5	22	20	5	3	1	0	2	4	2	0	0	0	8	1	0	9.1	36.4
Southisene, Tate	R-R	5-11	180	10-6-06	.219	.242	.297	15	66	64	10	14	3	1	0	6	1	1	0	0	27	3	0	1.5	40.9
Steels, Jake	R-R	6-0	185	6-17-02	.150	.175	.175	43	143	120	13	18	3	0	0	9	17	5	1	0	27	2	1	11.9	18.9
Williams, Dixon	L-R	6-1	200	12-19-03	.269	.395	.462	28	114	93	14	25	6	3	2	13	16	4	0	1	35	6	0	14.0	30.7

Pitching	B-T	Ht.	Wt.	DOB	W	L	ERA	G	GS	SV	IP	Hits	Runs	ER	HR	BB	SO	AVG	OBP	SLG	SO%	BB%	BF
Antonio, Rayven	R-R	6-1	190	3-2-06	7	4	4.15	21	20	0	93	81	47	43	6	36	95	.231	.312	.328	23.8	9.0	400
Arestigueta, Luis	R-R	6-3	175	10-14-05	0	3	4.85	12	10	1	43	39	28	23	2	24	36	.248	.381	.306	18.4	12.2	196
Bagwell, Ethan	R-R	6-4	230	2-24-06	1	4	2.88	10	10	0	50	34	19	16	3	15	30	.198	.280	.279	15.5	7.7	194
Beidelschies, Landon	L-L	6-3	230	3-28-04	0	1	7.11	2	2	0	6	11	7	5	2	2	8	.393	.433	.643	25.8	6.5	31
Buchanan, Trent	R-R	6-1	233	9-24-01	4	0	2.68	24	0	4	37	35	12	11	1	13	46	.255	.340	.350	29.3	8.3	157
Caminiti, Cam	L-L	6-2	200	8-8-06	2	3	2.08	13	13	0	56	43	16	13	1	26	75	.210	.311	.259	31.9	11.1	235
Christo, Drew	L-R	6-4	230	1-19-03	1	1	3.12	5	1	0	9	8	4	3	0	6	15	.235	.381	.265	35.7	14.3	42
Corona, Reibyn	R-R	5-11	175	11-13-01	5	1	3.60	22	1	1	45	39	22	18	2	29	44	.241	.357	.352	22.4	14.8	196
Dannelley, Jackson	R-R	5-10	195	8-23-01	4	3	5.51	30	0	2	51	48	36	31	5	26	48	.251	.350	.408	21.2	11.5	226
Figueroa, Leiker	R-R	5-10	155	1-12-05	0	0	6.75	3	0	0	3	5	2	2	0	1	0	.385	.467	.538	0.0	6.7	15
Forsythe, Logan	R-R	6-0	180	7-29-03	0	1	6.00	5	1	0	9	9	6	6	0	7	9	.265	.395	.412	20.9	16.3	43
Francique, Kendy	R-R	6-2	195	9-8-04	0	1	3.47	6	4	0	23	20	10	9	1	11	27	.233	.333	.349	27.3	11.1	99
Frey, Riley	L-L	6-1	185	4-19-02	2	0	2.70	2	2	0	10	6	4	3	0	4	10	.162	.262	.216	23.8	9.5	42
Garcia, Anthony	R-R	6-2	200	3-28-02	1	0	3.00	1	0	0	3	1	2	1	0	2	3	.091	.231	.182	23.1	15.4	13
Gomez, Jacob	R-L	5-10	190	10-27-01	1	2	2.95	13	1	2	21	15	10	7	2	11	32	.205	.314	.301	36.8	12.6	87
Hackman, Owen	R-R	6-1	185	11-2-01	3	5	3.68	24	17	1	95	94	44	39	10	19	96	.256	.295	.411	24.4	4.8	393
Juan, Jorge	R-R	6-8	260	3-6-99	0	0	0.00	1	0	0	1	1	0	0	0	2	2	.250	.250	.250	50.0	0.0	4
Keller, Seth	R-R	5-10	180	5-26-04	2	4	7.13	22	1	0	35	26	29	28	3	39	32	.213	.443	.361	18.3	22.3	175
Kroeger, Jacob	L-L	6-1	190	5-18-00	2	0	1.86	11	2	1	29	19	6	6	1	10	40	.186	.259	.235	35.7	8.9	112
Lawrence, Colson	R-R	6-5	210	3-3-02	0	1	15.19	6	0	0	5	3	9	9	1	8	6	.176	.462	.412	23.1	30.8	26
Long, Justin	R-R	6-1	180	3-4-02	2	0	1.56	14	0	0	17	8	3	3	0	9	21	.140	.269	.140	31.3	13.4	67
Lovasz, Carter	R-R	6-3	185	1-31-03	1	1	9.00	4	0	1	7	11	7	7	0	5	10	.333	.421	.455	26.3	13.2	38
Mejia, Samuel	R-R	6-1	160	6-17-02	6	5	4.68	23	4	3	67	47	39	35	6	28	77	.193	.288	.325	27.6	10.0	279
Militello, Justin	R-R	6-1	190	12-3-03	1	1	4.74	9	2	0	19	17	14	10	0	15	23	.239	.396	.352	15.3	16.5	91
Paden, Jaylen	R-R	5-10	195	2-2-02	0	1	3.00	4	0	0	6	8	5	2	0	2	6	.296	.345	.481	20.7	6.9	29
Pineda, Alen	R-R	5-10	180	11-4-04	0	0	0.00	1	0	0	1	0	0	0	0	0	0	.000	.000	.000	0.0	0.0	3
Reyes, Jeremy	R-R	6-1	170	1-11-06	3	6	2.71	18	18	0	76	47	30	23	2	49	84	.181	.331	.242	25.6	14.9	328
Rivas, Albert	R-R	6-0	155	2-18-03	6	1	3.62	27	0	4	50	43	23	20	4	22	46	.232	.316	.346	21.7	10.4	212
Rodriguez, David	L-R	6-2	196	12-31-01	5	2	2.34	18	4	1	50	31	17	13	4	14	42	.176	.242	.295	21.6	7.2	194
Samuels, Logan	R-R	6-4	170	2-18-02	0	1	1.93	6	2	1	23	17	5	5	1	6	23	.202	.264	.310	25.3	6.6	91
Sanchez, Juan	R-R	6-0	180	5-21-03	0	2	4.45	21	0	2	28	19	19	14	2	28	38	.184	.375	.262	27.7	20.4	137
Sears, Brett	R-R	6-0	205	5-2-00	2	1	1.93	5	2	0	19	15	6	4	1	4	31	.211	.273	.282	39.7	5.1	78
Shafer, Jacob	R-R	6-8	240	4-30-02	3	0	2.12	7	5	0	34	24	10	8	4	14	21	.195	.283	.333	15.1	10.1	139
Shoemaker, Adam	L-L	6-6	205	8-24-02	1	3	5.52	18	0	2	31	25	24	19	1	23	34	.221	.373	.301	23.8	16.1	143
Sifontes, Lewis	L-L	5-9	155	2-7-06	1	0	7.00	3	0	0	9	10	8	7	1	3	11	.286	.359	.429	28.2	7.7	39
Sinnard, Luke	R-R	6-8	250	10-21-02	0	2	0.92	7	7	0	29	22	7	3	1	12	41	.202	.279	.284	33.3	9.8	123
Steels, Jake	R-R	6-0	185	6-17-02	0	0	40.50	1	0	0	1	4	3	3	0	0	0	.800	.667	1.400	0.0	0.0	6
Taveras, Jhonly	R-R	6-1	180	12-16-04	1	2	8.10	7	0	0	13	11	13	12	0	15	12	.234	.406	.277	18.8	23.4	64
Woods, Kade	R-R	6-2	195	9-4-02	0	3	2.63	6	0	3	14	9	4	4	1	5	16	.196	.288	.326	30.8	9.6	52

Fielding

Catcher	PCT	G	PO	A	E	DP	PB
Burgess	.977	37	353	22	9	2	1
Guscette	.981	19	183	19	4	2	3
Montgomery	.978	66	582	40	14	5	12
Orellana	1.000	2	16	2	0	0	1
Pineda	1.000	3	20	1	0	0	0
Smith	1.000	5	45	2	0	0	1

First Base	PCT	G	PO	A	E	DP
Friese	.992	17	116	9	1	15
Guerra	.996	33	247	16	1	19
Monteverde	.976	18	112	10	3	9
Niazoa	.993	22	135	13	1	13
Olsavsky	.987	37	284	23	4	17
Pineda	1.000	5	37	2	0	4

Second Base	PCT	G	PO	A	E	DP
Campos	.960	13	18	30	2	5
Figueroa	1.000	1	0	3	0	0

(cont.)						
Hartman	.960	18	27	45	3	7
Jones	.990	46	74	118	2	15
Mateo	1.000	3	2	3	0	1
Olsavsky	1.000	2	2	4	0	0
Sanchez	.966	20	41	45	3	12
Southisene	1.000	4	7	10	0	2
Williams	1.000	24	36	66	0	14

Third Base	PCT	G	PO	A	E	DP
Campos	.917	12	10	23	3	3
Figueroa	.894	33	17	42	7	1
Gil	1.000	12	6	18	0	3
Guerra	1.000	5	2	6	0	1
Jones	.923	24	18	42	5	7
Mateo	.963	16	11	41	2	3
Miller	1.000	2	3	4	0	0
Olsavsky	.955	8	12	9	1	1
Sanchez	.875	23	24	32	8	7

Shortstop	PCT	G	PO	A	E	DP
Figueroa	1.000	1	1	0	0	0
Gil	.960	88	139	170	13	36
Jones	.971	23	23	44	2	4
Mateo	1.000	4	7	11	0	1
Miller	.933	8	11	17	2	4
Southisene	.929	9	8	18	2	2

Outfield	PCT	G	PO	A	E	DP
Carey	.975	102	192	5	5	1
Drake	.974	84	148	4	4	1
Estevez	.923	8	12	0	1	0
Friese	1.000	6	4	0	0	0
Glod	.966	55	82	4	3	2
Guanipa	1.000	20	45	2	0	0
Hartman	.982	59	106	5	2	0
Macias	1.000	11	18	3	0	0
Niazoa	1.000	7	13	0	0	0
Steels	.982	40	50	4	1	1

FCL BRAVES
FLORIDA COMPLEX LEAGUE — ROOKIE

Batting	B-T	Ht.	Wt.	DOB	AVG	OBP	SLG	G	PA	AB	R	H	2B	3B	HR	RBI	BB	HBP	SH	SF	SO	SB	CS	BB%	SO%
Acuna, Ronald	R-R	6-0	205	12-18-97	.333	.333	1.333	1	3	3	1	1	0	0	1	1	0	0	0	0	0	0	0	0.0	0.0
Alvarez, Ignacio	R-R	5-11	190	4-11-03	.000	.400	.000	2	5	3	1	0	0	0	0	0	2	0	0	0	0	0	0	40.0	0.0
Baez, Mario	R-R	5-9	175	8-25-06	.208	.368	.236	44	134	106	15	22	3	0	0	12	20	7	0	0	15	13	4	14.9	11.2
Batten, Matthew	R-R	5-11	180	6-22-95	.000	.333	.000	1	3	2	0	0	0	0	0	0	1	0	0	0	0	0	0	33.3	0.0

ATLANTA BRAVES

Batting	B-T	Ht.	Wt.	DOB	AVG	OBP	SLG	G	AB	R	H	2B	3B	HR	RBI	BB	HBP	SH	SF	SO	SB	CS	BB%	SO%
Benitez, Diego	R-R	6-0	180	11-19-04	.214	.353	.294	43	153	126	19	27	4	0	2	20	17	10	0	0	26	2	0	11.1	17.0
Campos, Elio	R-R	5-9	157	1-2-04	.300	.300	.300	3	10	10	2	3	0	0	0	0	0	0	0	0	3	0	0	0.0	30.0
Devers, Jose	L-R	6-0	174	12-7-99	.429	.733	.571	4	15	7	5	3	1	0	0	0	8	0	0	0	1	0	0	53.3	6.7
Dos Passos, Manuel	R-R	5-10	165	1-8-07	.222	.361	.325	41	155	126	22	28	10	0	1	13	22	6	0	1	34	4	2	14.2	21.9
Estevez, John	L-R	6-3	190	5-17-06	.181	.311	.260	43	152	127	13	23	5	1	1	14	23	1	1	0	32	3	3	15.1	21.1
Garcia, Junior	L-R	6-2	190	7-13-05	.200	.280	.331	43	161	145	16	29	8	1	3	13	15	1	0	0	39	2	1	9.3	24.2
Gil, John	R-R	6-1	175	5-14-06	.000	.500	.000	1	4	2	1	0	0	0	0	0	2	0	0	0	0	0	0	50.0	0.0
Gonzalez, Robert	L-R	5-10	175	12-22-04	.186	.326	.243	28	86	70	6	13	1	0	1	10	15	0	0	1	23	5	1	17.4	26.7
Guanipa, Luis	R-R	5-11	188	12-15-05	.222	.417	.333	6	24	18	4	4	2	0	0	2	5	1	0	0	6	0	0	20.8	25.0
Hartman, Eric	L-R	6-1	180	6-16-06	.100	.296	.100	6	27	20	4	2	0	0	0	1	5	1	0	1	7	4	1	18.5	25.9
Kern, Kade	R-R	6-0	200	9-18-01	.105	.244	.132	13	45	38	3	4	1	0	0	2	7	0	0	0	10	0	2	15.6	22.2
King, Will	R-R	5-9	190	9-2-03	.500	.714	.500	4	14	8	3	4	0	0	0	2	5	1	0	0	1	1	1	35.7	7.1
Martinez, Alexander	R-R	5-11	170	11-16-04	.138	.265	.172	24	68	58	9	8	2	0	0	3	8	2	0	0	8	0	0	11.8	11.8
Martinez, Michael	R-R	6-2	175	1-24-07	.237	.310	.474	11	42	38	8	9	3	0	2	9	1	3	0	0	7	1	0	2.4	16.7
Mateo, Juan	S-R	6-0	165	5-22-07	.277	.352	.319	51	210	188	22	52	8	0	0	18	21	1	0	0	34	10	7	10.0	16.2
McIntyre, Dalton	L-L	6-3	175	7-17-03	.260	.373	.291	37	150	127	22	33	2	1	0	10	23	0	0	0	30	17	2	15.3	20.0
Monteverde, Carlos	L-L	6-1	177	12-10-05	.202	.346	.260	35	127	104	10	21	3	0	1	16	19	4	0	0	30	1	0	15.0	23.6
Niazoa, Roiber	R-R	6-0	175	12-23-04	.444	.706	.778	5	17	9	4	4	0	0	1	2	5	3	0	0	4	1	0	29.4	23.5
Nieblas, Angel	R-R	5-8	170	9-4-05	.164	.247	.178	31	82	73	9	12	1	0	0	3	8	0	0	0	19	9	0	9.8	23.2
Orellana, Josnaider	R-R	5-11	175	9-26-04	.286	.429	.357	6	21	14	1	4	1	0	0	4	3	2	0	2	2	0	0	14.3	9.5
Parababire, Luis	R-R	5-10	195	4-8-06	.200	.400	.200	15	40	30	4	6	0	0	0	4	7	3	0	0	15	1	0	17.5	37.5
Perdomo, Jose	R-R	5-11	180	9-20-06	.223	.275	.270	54	233	215	20	48	7	0	1	18	14	2	0	2	45	4	2	6.0	19.3
Shockley, Dylan	R-R	5-9	195	4-10-97	.333	.417	.333	3	12	9	0	3	0	0	0	2	2	0	0	0	2	0	0	16.7	16.7
Tolve, Tyler	L-R	6-0	200	7-16-00	.278	.333	.278	6	21	18	2	5	0	0	0	2	2	0	0	1	9	0	0	9.5	42.9
Waddell, Luke	L-R	5-7	180	7-13-98	.333	.600	.667	2	5	3	2	1	1	0	0	0	1	2	0	0	0	0	0	40.0	0.0

Pitching	B-T	Ht.	Wt.	DOB	W	L	ERA	G	GS	SV	IP	Hits	Runs	ER	HR	BB	SO	AVG	OBP	SLG	SO%	BB%	BF
Bagwell, Ethan	R-R	6-4	230	2-24-06	0	2	4.00	3	2	0	9	8	6	4	1	4	15	.235	.316	.324	39.5	10.5	38
Beltran, Jeiki	R-R	5-11	170	10-11-03	0	0	10.66	12	0	0	13	14	20	15	0	22	10	.298	.545	.383	13.0	28.6	77
Caminiti, Cam	L-L	6-2	200	8-8-06	0	1	7.24	4	4	0	14	17	12	11	4	2	15	.298	.322	.526	25.0	3.3	60
Cedano, Edward	R-R	6-1	165	11-14-05	1	1	6.30	16	0	4	20	18	15	14	0	20	14	.247	.415	.288	14.7	21.1	95
Correa, Yoel	R-R	6-3	205	11-23-01	2	1	11.45	12	0	0	11	6	14	14	0	18	8	.162	.475	.189	13.6	30.5	59
De Grandpre, Cedric	R-R	6-2	210	1-25-02	0	0	0.00	2	2	0	7	6	0	0	0	2	13	.214	.313	.214	40.6	6.3	32
Francique, Kendy	R-R	6-2	195	9-8-04	4	2	1.81	10	6	0	45	34	13	9	2	19	37	.213	.302	.281	20.3	10.4	182
Goode, Cayman	R-R	6-1	190	7-11-05	2	1	3.57	9	7	0	35	33	18	14	2	16	25	.252	.344	.364	16.1	10.3	155
Guerra, Whilmer	R-R	6-2	160	10-14-05	2	1	4.61	13	0	1	27	21	14	14	2	20	23	.216	.364	.320	19.0	16.5	121
Hackenberg, Drue	R-R	6-2	220	4-1-02	0	1	5.40	3	3	0	8	9	5	5	0	2	11	.273	.314	.364	31.4	5.7	35
Lawrence, Colson	R-R	6-5	210	3-3-02	1	2	3.44	12	0	3	18	15	9	7	0	13	19	.221	.364	.265	21.6	14.8	88
Marquez, Noslen	R-R	6-0	165	6-27-05	1	1	3.66	12	0	0	20	16	14	8	2	14	6	.219	.389	.315	6.3	14.6	96
Militello, Justin	R-R	6-1	190	12-3-03	1	4	6.75	6	5	0	24	28	18	18	4	13	21	.217	.333	.325	21.2	13.1	99
Murphy, Owen	R-R	6-1	190	9-27-03	0	0	0.00	1	1	0	3	0	0	0	0	5	0	.000	.000	.000	55.6	0.0	9
Nieblas, Angel	R-R	5-8	170	9-4-05	0	0	0.00	1	0	0	1	1	0	0	0	0	0	.250	.250	.500	0.0	0.0	4
Niekro, J.J.	R-R	6-0	185	1-28-98	0	0	5.68	3	1	0	6	7	4	4	0	2	8	.292	.346	.333	30.8	7.7	26
Paez, Styven	R-R	5-11	170	10-29-04	0	1	5.40	5	0	0	7	6	4	4	0	3	5	.231	.310	.346	17.2	10.3	29
Patino, Marco	R-R	6-0	175	11-17-04	1	3	3.10	13	0	0	29	25	15	10	2	20	12	.245	.374	.382	9.8	16.3	123
Pina, Rudit	R-R	6-3	170	3-20-06	0	6	7.08	11	8	0	34	38	35	27	4	30	25	.290	.442	.466	14.5	17.4	172
Pirela, Yorvi	R-R	6-0	160	1-3-05	2	3	5.17	14	6	0	38	49	29	22	1	9	22	.312	.357	.439	12.7	5.2	173
Salinas, Royber	R-R	6-3	205	4-10-01	0	0	0.00	2	2	0	3	0	0	0	0	1	1	.000	.111	.000	11.1	11.1	9
Sanchez, Juan	R-R	6-2	180	5-21-03	0	0	7.20	5	0	1	5	6	5	4	0	6	6	.286	.429	.429	21.4	21.4	28
Schanaman, Shay	R-R	6-0	195	8-12-99	0	0	0.00	2	0	0	3	0	0	0	0	7	0	.000	.000	.000	77.8	0.0	9
Shafer, Jacob	R-R	6-8	240	4-30-02	0	1	3.38	4	4	0	11	9	4	4	0	5	12	.231	.311	.359	26.7	11.1	45
Sifontes, Lewis	L-L	5-9	155	2-7-06	1	2	3.29	4	2	0	14	10	7	5	0	11	14	.200	.355	.260	22.2	17.5	63
Taveras, Jhonly	R-R	6-1	180	12-16-04	1	4	7.29	12	4	0	21	26	23	17	0	18	18	.299	.436	.345	16.4	16.4	110
Willingham, Amos	R-R	6-4	217	8-21-98	0	0	6.75	2	0	0	3	2	2	2	1	1	4	.200	.273	.500	36.4	9.1	11
Zapata, Daury	R-R	6-1	170	11-8-02	2	1	4.79	13	1	1	21	15	11	0	22	27	.277	.440	.373	24.8	20.2	109

Fielding
C: Dos Passos 27, Martinez 23, Parababire 8, Tolve 5, Shockley 3, Orellana 2. **1B:** Monteverde 28, Benitez 27, Parababire 5, Niazoa 2, Orellana 1. **2B:** Baez 39, Nieblas 9, Mateo 8, Devers 4, Hartman 3, Waddell 2, Campos 1. **3B:** Mateo 23, Nieblas 21, Benitez 16, Alvarez 2, Campos 2, Batten 1. **SS:** Perdomo 46, Mateo 11, Gil 1. **LF:** Estevez 19, Garcia 12, Gonzalez 12, Martinez 9, Niazoa 3, Hartman 2, McIntyre 2. **CF:** McIntyre 34, Garcia 15, Guanipa 5, Kern 5, Gonzalez 3. **RF:** Estevez 22, Garcia 15, Gonzalez 12, Kern 7, Monteverde 4, McIntyre 2, Acuna 1.

DSL BRAVES
DOMINICAN SUMMER LEAGUE

ROOKIE

Batting	B-T	Ht.	Wt.	DOB	AVG	OBP	SLG	G	PA	AB	R	H	2B	3B	HR	RBI	BB	HBP	SH	SF	SO	SB	CS	BB%	SO%
Betancourt, Yoelvis	R-R	5-10	180	5-16-08	.260	.393	.344	28	122	96	18	25	5	0	1	19	15	8	0	3	12	0	1	12.3	9.8
Campos, Manuel	S-R	5-11	150	11-7-07	.291	.396	.380	47	218	179	41	52	6	2	2	26	20	1	4	3	31	13	5	9.2	14.2
Carmona, Angel	R-R	6-2	170	4-20-07	.253	.374	.453	20	91	75	17	19	5	2	2	10	13	2	0	1	19	4	1	14.3	20.9
Cesa, Gabriel	R-R	5-10	166	9-5-06	.299	.410	.423	31	118	97	13	29	3	3	1	18	16	3	0	1	23	4	4	13.6	19.5
Elejandro, Juan	S-R	5-8	160	2-8-08	.248	.369	.301	36	141	113	14	28	4	1	0	21	18	6	0	4	26	5	1	12.8	18.4
Espinal, Juan	R-R	6-2	185	9-26-06	.225	.416	.430	47	190	142	41	32	5	3	6	25	39	8	0	1	63	21	3	20.5	33.2
Fernandez, Malvin	S-R	5-9	155	8-23-08	.195	.340	.230	36	141	113	17	22	4	0	0	11	23	0	2	2	27	5	2	16.3	19.1
Garcia, Yassel	S-R	5-11	185	12-6-07	.202	.404	.282	38	166	124	25	25	5	1	0	16	38	4	0	0	30	9	7	22.9	18.1
Hernandez, Hojans	R-R	5-11	175	3-7-06	.195	.337	.312	27	95	77	16	15	6	0	1	6	15	2	0	1	25	6	1	15.8	26.3

ATLANTA BRAVES

	B-T	Ht.	Wt.	DOB	AVG	OBP	SLG	G	AB	R	H	2B	3B	HR	RBI	BB	SO	HBP	SH	SF	SB	CS	OPS
Manzanillo, Arlenn	S-R	5-9	165	9-7-07	.159	.319	.221	33	141	113	16	18	4	0	1	14	25	2	0	1	28	2	1	17.7	19.9
Martinez, Michael	R-R	6-2	175	1-24-07	.316	.435	.649	16	69	57	16	18	8	1	3	13	9	3	0	0	12	4	1	13.0	17.4
Ramirez, Elisandro	R-R	5-11	175	11-26-07	.235	.381	.282	25	105	85	11	20	2	1	0	4	15	5	0	0	25	6	2	14.3	23.8
Reyno, Elias	R-R	6-1	165	4-17-08	.178	.397	.271	42	184	129	19	23	9	0	1	21	38	12	0	5	46	13	5	20.7	25.0
Rodriguez, Johan	L-R	6-0	161	4-9-08	.225	.309	.271	37	149	129	15	29	3	0	1	22	15	2	0	3	15	3	0	10.1	10.1
Tornes, Diego	B-R	6-2	178	7-3-08	.279	.395	.402	32	147	122	20	34	5	5	0	13	23	1	0	1	32	24	4	15.6	21.8

Pitching	B-T	Ht.	Wt.	DOB	W	L	ERA	G	GS	SV	IP	Hits	Runs	ER	HR	BB	SO	AVG	OBP	SLG	SO%	BB%	BF
Angeles, Gensi	R-R	6-1	185	12-10-07	2	2	3.57	10	4	0	35	24	18	14	4	10	24	.188	.245	.320	17.3	7.2	139
Areinamo, Diego	R-R	6-3	180	3-7-08	2	0	2.70	8	0	0	13	7	11	4	0	8	8	.149	.298	.255	14.0	14.0	57
Cesa, Gabriel	R-R	5-10	166	9-5-06	0	0	0.00	1	0	0	0	0	0	0	0	1	0	.000	.500	.000	0.0	50.0	2
Duarte, Fernando	R-R	6-6	180	3-12-07	1	1	8.31	6	1	0	17	18	17	16	0	14	8	.290	.432	.355	9.9	17.3	81
Duarte, Victor	L-L	6-0	180	1-27-08	0	1	27.00	3	0	0	2	3	5	5	0	4	3	.333	.538	.444	23.1	30.8	13
Gonzalez, Anferni	R-R	6-4	195	1-25-06	2	1	4.88	9	6	0	31	26	19	17	2	20	25	.224	.361	.310	17.4	13.9	144
Hernandez, Hojans	R-R	5-11	175	3-7-06	0	1	0.00	1	0	0	1	1	0	0	1	0	.500	.667	.500	0.0	33.3	3
Hidalgo, Edwarlys	L-L	6-0	170	6-24-06	1	2	5.50	9	5	0	36	31	27	22	5	17	30	.240	.338	.395	19.5	11.0	154
Hidalgo, Melvin	R-R	6-1	205	8-21-05	0	2	4.20	7	1	1	15	12	8	7	1	9	15	.218	.353	.273	22.1	13.2	68
Labastida, Jacksel	R-R	5-11	178	6-6-08	1	1	3.55	8	0	0	13	8	12	5	1	13	11	.167	.385	.250	16.9	20.0	65
Lasorsa, Rafael	R-L	6-1	163	5-27-07	2	0	3.77	6	0	0	14	9	7	6	0	11	7	.180	.339	.220	11.3	17.7	62
Marine, Yansel	L-L	6-2	160	6-11-05	1	2	4.15	10	0	2	26	26	14	12	0	9	19	.255	.319	.314	16.7	7.9	114
Martinez, Yangel	R-R	6-1	160	9-1-07	0	1	9.00	4	0	0	4	4	5	4	0	6	5	.286	.476	.357	23.8	28.6	21
Matos, Dayner	R-R	6-2	199	4-16-04	2	1	3.60	8	6	0	30	23	14	12	0	8	38	.211	.281	.321	31.1	6.6	122
Meza, Ernesto	R-R	6-1	154	7-14-07	1	-1	3.75	10	1	1	24	21	18	10	1	22	13	.236	.391	.371	11.3	19.1	115
Narciso, Robinson	R-R	6-0	170	1-25-05	0	0	9.00	1	0	0	1	2	1	1	0	0	0	.500	.500	.500	0.0	0.0	4
Nunez, Jorge	R-R	6-2	174	8-30-07	0	1	2.57	9	1	1	21	17	6	6	0	12	19	.227	.348	.280	21.3	13.5	89
Pinero, Yander	R-R	6-3	165	6-8-07	2	0	3.57	11	0	3	23	20	12	9	1	15	18	.241	.388	.301	17.3	14.4	104
Pol, Marcos	R-R	6-2	170	7-2-05	1	0	1.10	6	0	1	16	8	3	2	0	8	15	.136	.261	.254	21.7	11.6	69
Prevosti, Lionel	R-R	6-4	188	3-30-07	1	5	10.64	8	5	0	22	23	29	26	4	24	15	.267	.431	.442	12.9	20.7	116
Reyes, Raudy	R-R	6-4	210	8-22-08	0	2	3.67	9	0	9	27	20	12	11	0	29	35	.215	.408	.269	28.0	23.2	125
Rodriguez, Cesar	R-R	6-0	170	2-4-05	2	0	8.68	5	0	0	9	12	12	9	0	6	9	.308	.426	.410	9.1	12.8	47
Sifontes, Lewis	L-L	5-9	155	2-7-06	0	0	5.40	2	0	0	7	3	4	4	2	1	5	.130	.200	.478	20.0	4.0	25
Tovar, Wuilinyer	R-R	6-2	185	12-19-07	1	4	6.83	9	8	1	29	29	25	22	2	18	23	.261	.379	.351	17.4	13.6	132
Valdez, Luisberth	L-L	6-0	165	9-15-07	0	3	4.91	9	6	0	29	26	19	16	1	22	34	.241	.371	.315	25.6	16.5	133

Fielding

C: Manzanillo 26, Betancourt 25, Rodriguez 4, Hernandez 2. **1B:** Rodriguez 32, Hernandez 24. **2B:** Elejandro 29, Campos 15, Fernandez 10. **3B:** Garcia 32, Fernandez 16, Elejandro 6. **SS:** Campos 28, Carmona 17, Fernandez 9. **LF:** Reyno 20, Cesa 15, Ramirez 11, Martinez 7, Espinal 1. **CF:** Tornes 23, Espinal 11, Reyno 10, Cesa 5, Ramirez 1. **RF:** Espinal 27, Ramirez 10, Reyno 8, Cesa 7, Martinez 2.

Baltimore Orioles

SEASON SYNOPSIS: Baltimore finished last in the American League East for the fifth time in the last eight full seasons dating to 2017. This one was the most surprising, as the Orioles followed consecutive playoff seasons with a brutal start and the third-worst ERA in the American League.

HIGH POINT: Acquired at the 2024 trade deadline from the Marlins in a deal that cost them 2025 all-star Kyle Stowers, lefthander Trevor Rogers made the trade look better. In 18 starts, he went 9-3, 1.81 with a 5.5 bWAR, posting the best ERA in Orioles history (since the 1954 move from St. Louis). He made 15 consecutive starts allowing two or fewer runs until yielding six to the Yankees on the season's final weekend.

LOW POINT: Rogers opened the season in the minors; the rotation without him was a disaster, from injured righties Kyle Bradish (returned in August) and Grayson Rodriguez (missed the whole season) to free-agent signees Charlie Morton (7-8, 5.42) and Tomoyuki Sugano (10-10, 4.64, league-worst 33 HR allowed) to trade pickup Zach Eflin (6-5, 5.93) to emergency signee Kyle Gibson (0-3, 16.78 in just four starts). Gibson's final start on May 17—the day after manager Brandon Hyde was fired after a 15-28 start—immediately doused any hopes of a turnaround, giving up six hits and six runs while getting two outs in the first inning of a 10-6 loss to the Nationals. It was the fifth loss of a season-long eight-game losing streak.

NOTABLE ROOKIES: Sugano, 35, was in his first year coming over from Japan and at least was durable if middling. Coby Mayo got extended second-half run at first base and hit 11 home runs in a .217/.288/.388 debut over 263 at-bats. OF/3B Jeremiah Jackson, a minor league free-agent pickup, finished a strong season with a .276/.328/.447 line in 170 big league at-bats. Org success story Brandon Young, a 2020 nondrafted free agent, struggled in a rotation spot (1-7, 6.24).

KEY TRANSACTIONS: GM Mike Elias' offseason acquisitions mostly missed; Sugano and OF Ramon Laureano worked out fine, but OFs Dylan Carlson (.614 OPS) and Tyler O'Neill (.684 OPS) didn't hit enough, and Morton was a disaster. The O's sold at the deadline, trading away reliever Brian Baker (Rays), Laureano and 1B/DH Ryan O'Hearn (Padres) and Morton (Tigers). The biggest move may have come in August, when the Orioles signed C/1B Samuel Basallo—still rookie-eligible for 2026—to an eight-year contract extension guaranteeing him at least $67 million.

OPENING DAY PAYROLL: $94,520,400 (27th)

PLAYERS OF THE YEAR

MAJOR LEAGUE
Trevor Rogers
LHP
9-3, 1.81 ERA
103 SO in 109.2 IP
.108 AVG, 0.90 WHIP

MINOR LEAGUE
Samuel Basallo
C/1B
(AAA)
.270/.377/.589
23 HR in 76 G

ORGANIZATION LEADERS

Batting — * Qualifiers

MAJORS
* AVG	Gunnar Henderson	.274
* OPS	Gunnar Henderson	.787
HR	Gunnar Henderson	17
HR	Jordan Westburg	17
HR	Jackson Holliday	17
RBI	Gunnar Henderson	68

MINORS
* AVG	Nate George, Aberdeen/Delmarva/FCL Orioles	.337
* OBP	Dylan Beavers, Norfolk	.420
* SLG	Jeremiah Jackson, Norfolk/Chesapeake	.537
* OPS	Dylan Beavers, Norfolk	.934
R	Dylan Beavers, Norfolk	78
H	Vimael Machin, Norfolk	130
TB	Vimael Machin, Norfolk	216
2B	Jeremiah Jackson, Norfolk/Chesapeake	31
3B	Nate George, Aberdeen/Delmarva/FCL Orioles	9
HR	Samuel Basallo, Norfolk	23
RBI	Vimael Machin, Norfolk	79
BB	Jud Fabian, Norfolk/Aberdeen	75
SO	Vance Honeycutt, Aberdeen	178
SB	Austin Overn, Chesapeake/Aberdeen	64

Pitching — # Qualifiers

MAJORS
W	Dean Kremer	11
ERA	Dean Kremer	4.19
SO	Dean Kremer	142
SV	Felix Bautista	19

MINORS
W	Thaddeus Ward, Norfolk	9
L	Chase Allsup, Aberdeen/Delmarva	13
# ERA	Nestor German, Norfolk/Chesapeake/Aberdeen	3.93
G	Keagan Gillies, Norfolk/Chesapeake	42
GS	Cameron Weston, Norfolk	26
SV	Keagan Gillies, Norfolk/Chesapeake	9
IP	Cameron Weston, Norfolk	135
BB	Thaddeus Ward, Norfolk	94
SO	Trey Gibson, Norfolk/Chesapeake/Aberdeen	166
# AVG	Nestor German, Norfolk/Chesapeake/Aberdeen	.220

2025 PERFORMANCE

General Manager: Mike Elias. **Farm Director:** Anthony Villa. **Scouting Director:** Matt Blood.

Class	Team	League	W	L	PCT	Finish	Manager
Majors	Baltimore Orioles	American	75	87	.463	12 (15)	Brandon Hyde
Triple-A	Norfolk Tides	International	63	84	.429	15 (20)	Tim Federowicz
Double-A	Chesapeake Baysox	Eastern	59	77	.434	9 (12)	Roberto Mercado
High-A	Aberdeen IronBirds	South Atlantic	57	72	.442	9 (12)	Ryan Goll
Low-A	Delmarva Shorebirds	Carolina	51	79	.392	12 (12)	Collin Woody
Rookie	FCL Orioles	Florida Complex	35	24	.593	5 (15)	Christian Frias
Rookie	DSL Orioles Black	Dominican	21	32	.396	44 (52)	Elvis Morel
Rookie	DSL Orioles Orange	Dominican	20	34	.370	45 (52)	Chris Madera
Overall 2025 Minor League Record			306	402	.432	30th (30)	

ORGANIZATION STATISTICS

BALTIMORE ORIOLES
AMERICAN LEAGUE

Batting	B-T	Ht.	Wt.	DOB	AVG	OBP	SLG	G	PA	AB	R	H	2B	3B	HR	RBI	BB	HBP	SH	SF	SO	SB	CS	BB%	SO%
Adams, Jordyn	R-R	6-2	181	10-18-99	.000	.000	.000	10	5	5	1	0	0	0	0	0	0	0	0	0	2	0	0	0.0	40.0
Allen, Greg	S-R	6-0	185	3-15-93	.000	.000	.000	7	14	14	1	0	0	0	0	0	0	0	0	0	5	0	1	0.0	35.7
Banuelos, David	R-R	6-0	205	10-1-96	.000	.500	.000	1	2	1	0	0	0	0	0	0	1	0	0	1	0	0	0	0.0	50.0
Basallo, Samuel	L-R	6-3	180	8-13-04	.165	.229	.330	31	118	109	10	18	6	0	4	15	6	3	0	0	30	0	0	5.1	25.4
Beavers, Dylan	L-R	6-4	206	8-11-01	.227	.375	.400	35	137	110	16	25	5	1	4	14	26	0	1	0	36	2	2	19.0	26.3
Brujan, Vidal	S-R	5-10	180	2-9-98	1.000	1.000	1.000	1	1	1	0	1	0	0	0	0	0	0	0	0	0	0	0	0.0	0.0
Carlson, Dylan	S-L	6-2	205	10-23-98	.203	.278	.336	83	241	217	17	44	9	1	6	20	21	2	0	1	54	3	3	8.7	22.4
Cowser, Colton	L-R	6-2	220	3-20-00	.196	.269	.385	92	360	327	36	64	14	0	16	40	27	6	0	0	128	14	0	7.5	35.6
Handley, Maverick	R-R	5-10	210	3-10-98	.073	.133	.073	16	47	41	2	3	0	0	0	3	2	1	2	1	18	0	0	4.3	38.3
Henderson, Gunnar	L-R	6-3	220	6-29-01	.274	.349	.438	154	651	577	85	158	34	5	17	68	62	7	0	5	137	30	5	9.5	21.0
Holliday, Jackson	L-R	6-0	185	12-4-03	.242	.314	.375	149	649	586	70	142	21	3	17	55	56	6	0	1	140	17	11	8.6	21.6
Hummel, Cooper	S-R	5-10	198	11-28-94	.000	.000	.000	1	1	1	0	0	0	0	0	0	0	0	0	0	1	0	0	0.0	100.0
Jackson, Alex	R-R	5-11	238	12-25-95	.220	.290	.473	37	100	91	17	20	8	0	5	8	5	4	0	0	37	0	0	5.0	37.0
Jackson, Jeremiah	R-R	6-0	165	3-26-00	.276	.328	.447	48	183	170	20	47	10	2	5	21	11	2	0	0	50	0	2	6.0	27.3
Johnson, Daniel	L-L	5-9	200	7-11-95	.208	.269	.250	17	26	24	8	5	1	0	0	2	0	0	0	0	5	1	1	7.7	19.2
Kjerstad, Heston	L-R	6-3	205	2-12-99	.192	.240	.327	54	167	156	16	30	5	2	4	19	6	4	0	1	45	1	0	3.6	26.9
Laureano, Ramon	R-R	5-11	203	7-15-94	.290	.355	.529	82	290	259	45	75	17	0	15	46	22	6	0	3	72	4	3	7.6	24.8
Machin, Vimael	L-R	5-11	185	9-25-93	.091	.167	.364	4	12	11	1	1	0	0	1	1	0	0	0	2	0	0	0	8.3	16.7
Mateo, Jorge	R-R	6-1	200	6-23-95	.177	.217	.266	43	83	79	9	14	4	0	1	3	4	0	0	0	30	15	2	4.8	36.1
Mayo, Coby	R-R	6-5	230	12-10-01	.217	.299	.388	85	294	263	30	57	12	0	11	28	27	4	0	0	84	3	0	9.2	28.6
Mountcastle, Ryan	R-R	6-4	220	2-18-97	.250	.286	.367	89	357	332	34	83	18	0	7	35	15	4	0	6	98	3	0	4.2	27.5
Mullins, Cedric	L-L	5-9	175	10-1-94	.229	.305	.433	91	355	314	42	72	19	0	15	49	34	2	1	4	85	14	4	9.6	23.9
Noda, Ryan	L-L	6-3	217	3-30-96	.154	.214	.154	7	14	13	0	2	0	0	0	1	1	0	0	0	6	1	0	7.1	42.9
O'Hearn, Ryan	L-L	6-3	225	7-26-93	.283	.374	.463	94	361	311	45	88	15	1	13	43	42	5	0	3	63	3	1	11.6	17.5
O'Neill, Tyler	R-R	5-11	200	6-22-95	.199	.292	.392	54	209	181	22	36	6	1	9	26	22	3	0	3	51	4	0	10.5	24.4
Rivera, Emmanuel	R-R	6-2	225	6-29-96	.250	.291	.283	43	127	120	5	30	4	0	0	13	6	1	0	0	24	1	0	4.7	18.9
Rogers, Trevor	L-L	6-5	217	11-13-97	.000	.000	.000	18	2	2	0	0	0	0	0	0	0	0	0	0	2	0	0	0.0	100.0
Rutschman, Adley	S-R	6-2	230	2-6-98	.220	.307	.366	90	365	322	37	71	16	2	9	29	40	1	0	2	57	0	0	11.0	15.6
Sanchez, Gary	R-R	6-2	230	12-2-92	.231	.297	.418	30	101	91	13	21	2	0	5	24	4	5	0	1	27	0	0	4.0	26.7
Stallings, Jacob	R-R	6-5	225	12-22-89	.114	.139	.143	14	36	35	1	4	1	0	0	3	1	0	0	0	9	0	0	2.8	25.0
Tromp, Chadwick	R-R	5-8	221	3-21-95	.188	.188	.438	6	16	16	2	3	1	0	1	1	0	0	0	0	4	0	0	0.0	25.0
Urias, Ramon	R-R	5-10	185	6-3-94	.248	.300	.388	77	290	258	27	64	12	0	8	34	21	2	0	9	60	2	0	7.2	20.7
Vavra, Terrin	L-R	6-0	185	5-12-97	.000	.000	.000	1	1	1	0	0	0	0	0	0	0	0	0	0	0	0	0	0.0	0.0
Vazquez, Luis	R-R	6-0	165	10-10-99	.160	.208	.240	36	53	50	6	8	1	0	1	3	3	0	0	0	14	2	0	5.7	26.4
Westburg, Jordan	R-R	6-2	210	2-18-99	.265	.313	.457	85	352	328	59	87	10	1	17	41	17	6	0	1	80	1	2	4.8	22.7

Pitching	B-T	Ht.	Wt.	DOB	W	L	ERA	G	GS	SV	IP	Hits	Runs	ER	HR	BB	SO	AVG	OBP	SLG	SO%	BB%	BF
Akin, Keegan	L-L	6-0	240	4-1-95	5	4	3.41	64	3	8	63	54	28	24	10	33	59	.233	.328	.401	22.0	12.3	268
Baker, Bryan	R-R	6-6	235	12-2-94	3	2	3.52	42	0	2	38	33	17	15	8	9	49	.232	.278	.451	32.5	6.0	151
Bautista, Felix	R-R	6-8	285	6-20-95	1	1	2.60	35	0	19	35	16	10	10	3	23	50	.134	.275	.244	35.2	16.2	142
Blewett, Scott	R-R	6-6	245	4-10-96	1	0	6.17	13	1	0	23	25	17	16	4	8	17	.269	.320	.452	16.5	7.8	103
Bowman, Matt	R-R	6-0	185	5-31-91	0	1	6.20	20	0	0	25	31	18	17	4	6	18	.292	.342	.500	15.8	5.3	114
Bradish, Kyle	R-R	6-3	215	9-12-96	1	1	2.53	6	6	0	32	23	9	9	3	10	47	.200	.270	.296	37.3	7.9	126
Cano, Yennier	R-R	6-4	245	3-9-94	3	7	5.12	65	0	2	58	62	36	33	7	24	53	.284	.360	.422	21.1	9.6	251
Castillo, Jose	L-L	6-6	252	1-10-96	0	0	2.45	5	0	0	7	6	3	2	0	1	3	.214	.290	.321	22.6	9.7	31
Contreras, Roansy	R-R	6-0	175	11-7-99	0	0	0.00	1	0	0	4	3	0	0	0	1	2	.200	.294	.267	11.8	5.9	17
Dominguez, Seranthony	R-R	6-1	225	11-25-94	2	3	3.24	43	0	2	42	32	19	15	4	24	54	.212	.320	.318	30.9	13.7	175
Dubin, Shawn	R-R	6-1	171	9-6-95	0	0	3.38	7	0	0	8	3	3	3	0	2	7	.120	.280	.240	20.6	8.8	34
Eflin, Zach	R-R	6-6	220	4-8-94	6	5	5.93	14	14	0	71	88	48	47	18	13	50	.304	.336	.557	16.2	4.2	309
Enns, Dietrich	L-L	6-1	210	5-16-91	2	2	3.14	17	1	2	29	27	13	10	4	11	34	.243	.311	.378	27.6	8.9	123
Espada, Jose	R-R	6-0	170	2-22-97	0	0	0.00	1	0	0	3	1	0	0	0	4	1	.111	.111	.111	44.4	0.0	9
Garcia, Rico	R-R	5-9	201	1-10-94	0	2	2.84	20	1	0	19	21	6	6	5	6	20	.276	.329	.421	24.4	7.3	82
Gibson, Kyle	R-R	6-6	200	10-23-87	0	3	16.78	4	4	0	6	12	29	23	7	7	10	.453	.493	.938	13.9	9.6	73

BALTIMORE ORIOLES

Batting	B-T	Ht.	Wt.	DOB	AVG	OBP	SLG	G	PA	AB	R	H	2B	3B	HR	RBI	BB	HBP	SH	SF	SO	SB	CS	BB%	SO%
Hiraldo, Yaramil	R-R	6-1	180	12-31-95	0	0	4.58	18	0	0	20	17	3	10	4	9	21	.230	.313	.432	25.0	10.7	84		
Jackson, Alex	R-R	5-11	238	12-25-95	0	0	27.00	1	0	0	1	3	3	3	0	2	0	.600	.625	1.000	0.0	25.0	8		
Kittredge, Andrew	R-R	6-1	230	3-17-90	2	2	3.45	31	0	0	31	26	13	12	4	8	32	.222	.270	.385	25.4	6.3	126		
Kremer, Dean	R-R	6-2	210	1-7-96	11	10	4.19	31	29	0	172	163	83	80	22	45	142	.248	.297	.407	20.1	6.4	708		
Martin, Corbin	R-R	6-2	225	12-28-95	1	0	6.00	17	0	2	18	22	15	12	4	9	23	.289	.379	.539	25.8	10.1	89		
Mateo, Jorge	R-R	6-1	200	6-23-95	0	0	45.00	1	0	0	1	5	5	5	1	2	0	.625	.727	1.000	0.0	18.2	11		
McDermott, Chayce	L-R	6-3	197	8-22-98	0	1	15.58	4	1	0	9	12	15	15	3	12	9	.333	.500	.639	17.6	23.5	51		
Morton, Charlie	R-R	6-5	215	11-12-83	7	8	5.42	23	17	0	101	110	63	61	16	48	101	.276	.362	.450	21.8	10.3	464		
Perez, Cionel	R-L	6-0	175	4-21-96	0	0	8.31	19	0	0	22	28	22	20	3	18	21	.322	.444	.494	19.1	16.4	110		
Poteet, Cody	R-R	6-1	190	7-30-94	0	0	16.88	1	0	0	3	6	5	5	0	2	1	.429	.500	.714	6.3	12.5	16		
Povich, Cade	L-L	6-3	185	4-12-00	3	8	5.21	22	20	0	112	125	70	65	17	43	118	.285	.347	.465	24.2	8.8	488		
Ragsdale, Carson	R-R	6-8	225	5-25-98	0	0	14.40	2	0	0	5	10	8	8	1	1	4	.417	.440	.708	16.0	4.0	25		
Rivera, Emmanuel	R-R	6-2	225	6-29-96	0	0	72.00	1	0	0	1	8	8	8	1	2	0	.727	.769	1.364	0.0	15.4	13		
Rodriguez, Elvin	R-R	6-3	160	3-31-98	0	0	18.00	1	0	0	1	3	2	2	2	0	1	.500	.500	1.500	16.7	0.0	6		
Rogers, Trevor	L-L	6-5	217	11-13-97	9	3	1.81	18	18	0	110	70	23	22	6	29	103	.180	.240	.263	24.3	6.9	423		
Sanchez, Gary	R-R	6-2	230	12-2-92	0	0	36.00	1	0	0	1	2	4	4	1	1	0	.400	.571	1.200	0.0	14.3	7		
Selby, Colin	R-R	6-2	220	10-4-97	0	2	3.21	11	0	0	14	16	5	5	2	4	12	.276	.300	.431	23.3	3.3	60		
Soto, Gregory	L-L	6-1	234	2-11-95	0	2	3.96	45	0	1	36	29	17	16	2	18	44	.216	.327	.321	27.5	11.3	160		
Strowd, Kade	R-R	6-2	200	9-17-97	0	1	1.71	25	0	0	26	16	6	5	1	13	24	.178	.286	.222	22.9	12.4	105		
Suarez, Albert	R-R	6-3	235	10-8-89	2	0	2.31	5	1	0	12	9	4	3	0	2	10	.225	.273	.325	22.7	4.5	44		
Sugano, Tomoyuki	R-R	6-1	198	10-11-89	10	10	4.64	30	30	0	157	173	85	81	33	36	106	.276	.321	.478	15.7	5.3	675		
Vazquez, Luis	R-R	6-0	165	10-10-99	0	0	0.00	4	0	0	4	3	0	0	0	1	0	.231	.286	.231	0.0	7.1	14		
Wells, Tyler	R-R	6-8	260	8-26-94	2	1	2.91	4	4	0	22	17	7	7	4	2	18	.213	.232	.425	22.0	2.4	82		
Wolfram, Grant	L-L	6-6	235	12-12-96	3	1	5.40	21	0	0	27	35	20	16	2	15	31	.302	.383	.422	23.3	11.3	133		
Young, Brandon	R-R	6-6	210	8-19-98	1	7	6.24	12	12	0	58	67	42	40	12	22	47	.291	.350	.522	18.4	8.6	256		

Fielding

Catcher	PCT	G	PO	A	E	DP	PB
Basallo	.989	22	169	9	2	0	1
Handley	.993	16	147	1	1	0	0
Jackson	.992	35	244	13	2	5	2
Rutschman	.996	73	518	27	2	3	1
Sanchez	.978	22	176	3	4	0	1
Stallings	.991	13	101	4	1	0	2
Tromp	.966	6	28	0	1	0	1

First Base	PCT	G	PO	A	E	DP
Basallo	1.000	2	16	0	0	2
Mayo	.998	70	486	30	1	49
Mountcastle	1.000	56	361	37	0	37
O'Hearn	.991	48	282	32	3	21
Rivera	1.000	8	44	3	0	3
Urias	1.000	3	11	0	0	0
Vazquez	1.000	1	3	0	0	0

Second Base	PCT	G	PO	A	E	DP
Holliday	.981	139	190	331	10	72

	PCT	G	PO	A	E	DP
Jackson	1.000	1	0	1	0	0
Mateo	.913	6	8	13	2	3
Urias	1.000	1	1	4	0	0
Vavra	.000	1	0	0	0	0
Vazquez	1.000	3	6	7	0	2
Westburg	1.000	17	17	36	0	9

Third Base	PCT	G	PO	A	E	DP
Jackson	.875	13	7	14	3	1
Machin	1.000	4	3	6	0	1
Mateo	.000	2	0	0	0	0
Mayo	.800	3	1	7	2	1
Rivera	.964	30	11	43	2	2
Urias	.983	68	43	127	3	18
Vazquez	.933	12	4	10	1	0
Westburg	.975	52	36	81	3	6

Shortstop	PCT	G	PO	A	E	DP
Henderson	.986	145	206	371	8	76
Holliday	1.000	8	3	11	0	0

	PCT	G	PO	A	E	DP
Mateo	.906	11	12	17	3	3
Vazquez	.957	11	8	14	1	5

Outfield	PCT	G	PO	A	E	DP
Adams	1.000	9	6	0	0	0
Allen	1.000	8	12	0	0	0
Beavers	.952	41	59	1	3	0
Brujan	.000	1	0	0	0	0
Carlson	1.000	84	138	3	0	0
Cowser	.991	93	206	4	2	1
Hummel	.000	1	0	0	0	0
Jackson	.985	34	62	3	1	0
Johnson	1.000	17	19	0	0	0
Kjerstad	1.000	53	70	4	0	0
Laureano	.965	80	131	7	5	0
Mateo	.963	11	26	0	1	0
Mullins	.986	88	218	0	3	0
Noda	1.000	5	7	1	0	0
O'Hearn	1.000	20	26	0	0	0
O'Neill	.977	39	80	5	2	2

NORFOLK TIDES
INTERNATIONAL LEAGUE — TRIPLE-A

Batting	B-T	Ht.	Wt.	DOB	AVG	OBP	SLG	G	PA	AB	R	H	2B	3B	HR	RBI	BB	HBP	SH	SF	SO	SB	CS	BB%	SO%
Adams, Jordyn	R-R	6-2	181	10-18-99	.213	.291	.379	89	310	272	41	58	7	4	10	44	29	2	3	3	94	14	5	9.4	30.3
Ardoin, Silas	R-R	6-0	215	9-19-00	.258	.361	.430	34	108	93	12	24	4	0	4	11	15	0	0	0	31	0	0	13.9	28.7
Banuelos, David	R-R	6-0	205	10-7-96	.107	.206	.214	21	63	56	4	6	3	0	1	2	7	0	0	0	25	0	0	11.1	33.3
Barrero, Jose	R-R	6-2	211	4-5-98	.190	.261	.344	53	218	195	22	37	6	0	8	27	15	5	0	3	68	9	3	6.9	31.2
Basallo, Samuel	L-R	6-3	180	8-13-04	.270	.377	.589	76	321	270	49	73	17	0	23	67	44	4	0	3	76	0	0	13.7	23.7
Beavers, Dylan	L-R	6-4	206	8-11-01	.304	.420	.515	94	418	342	78	104	14	2	18	51	68	3	1	4	76	23	5	16.3	18.2
Bowens, TT	R-R	6-4	235	5-27-98	.250	.318	.485	79	296	268	41	67	13	1	16	50	23	4	0	1	91	0	0	7.8	30.7
Bradfield, Enrique	L-L	6-1	170	12-2-01	.179	.226	.286	15	62	56	9	10	1	1	1	5	4	0	0	2	19	6	1	6.5	30.6
Cameron, Daz	R-R	6-2	185	1-15-97	.222	.333	.278	5	21	18	1	4	1	0	0	3	2	1	0	0	6	0	0	9.5	28.6
Carlson, Dylan	S-L	6-2	205	10-23-98	.294	.421	.451	28	126	102	26	30	4	0	4	17	23	0	0	1	25	4	0	18.3	19.8
Cowser, Colton	L-R	6-3	220	3-20-00	.545	.615	.909	3	13	11	2	6	4	0	0	3	2	0	0	0	2	1	0	15.4	15.4
Fabian, Jud	R-L	6-1	195	9-27-00	.183	.322	.349	109	431	350	56	64	11	1	15	39	72	2	3	4	136	8	1	16.7	31.6
Gordon, Nick	L-R	6-0	160	10-24-95	.308	.357	.385	4	14	13	4	4	1	0	0	0	1	0	0	0	4	1	1	7.1	28.6
Handley, Maverick	R-R	5-10	210	3-10-98	.258	.373	.367	38	154	128	17	33	7	2	1	10	23	1	1	1	32	3	1	14.9	20.8
Haskin, Hudson	R-R	6-0	200	12-31-98	.196	.288	.275	24	60	51	8	10	1	0	1	6	5	2	1	1	16	0	2	8.3	26.7
Henderson, Gunnar	L-R	6-3	220	6-29-01	.263	.300	.579	5	20	19	2	5	0	0	2	7	1	0	0	0	4	0	0	5.0	20.0
Jackson, Jeremiah	R-R	6-0	165	3-26-00	.377	.420	.673	40	171	162	29	61	15	0	11	22	6	1	0	1	20	9	4	3.5	11.7
Johnson, Daniel	L-L	6-0	200	7-11-95	.158	.238	.211	5	21	19	2	3	1	0	0	3	1	1	0	0	6	0	0	4.8	28.6
Kjerstad, Heston	L-R	6-3	205	2-12-99	.149	.225	.248	27	112	101	7	15	2	1	2	6	9	0	0	0	30	0	1	8.9	26.8
Laureano, Ramon	R-R	5-11	203	7-15-94	.375	.375	.875	2	8	8	3	3	1	0	1	1	0	0	0	0	2	0	0	0.0	25.0
Machin, Vimael	L-R	5-11	185	9-25-93	.286	.347	.476	124	505	454	60	130	28	2	18	79	44	1	0	5	90	15	4	8.7	17.8
Mateo, Jorge	R-R	6-1	200	6-23-95	.318	.362	.432	12	47	44	2	14	2	0	1	4	3	0	0	0	7	2	0	6.4	14.9

BALTIMORE ORIOLES

Batting	B-T	Ht.	Wt.	DOB	AVG	OBP	SLG	G	AB	H	2B	3B	HR	RBI	BB	SO	SB	CS	R	HBP	SF	BB%	SO%
Mayo, Coby	R-R	6-5	230	12-10-01	.226	.318	.452	45	195	168	24	38	10	2	8	28	23	1	0	3	53	1	1	11.8	27.2
Mountcastle, Ryan	R-R	6-4	220	2-18-97	.387	.486	.806	9	37	31	8	12	4	0	3	10	5	1	0	0	5	0	0	13.5	13.5
Noda, Ryan	L-L	6-3	217	3-30-96	.152	.491	.333	16	55	33	11	5	0	0	2	4	18	4	0	0	19	2	0	32.7	34.5
O'Neill, Tyler	R-R	5-11	200	6-22-95	.370	.433	.481	8	30	27	5	10	0	0	1	2	3	0	0	0	5	0	0	10.0	16.7
Pavolony, Connor	R-R	6-1	195	10-25-99	.162	.225	.189	12	40	37	5	6	1	0	0	3	2	1	0	0	12	0	0	5.0	30.0
Peguero, Fernando	S-R	5-9	145	12-27-04	.162	.253	.243	30	83	74	8	12	3	0	1	10	9	0	0	0	21	4	0	10.8	25.3
Reetz, Jakson	R-R	6-0	205	1-3-96	.180	.346	.246	22	78	61	8	11	4	0	0	5	13	3	0	1	22	2	1	16.7	28.2
Rivera, Emmanuel	R-R	6-2	225	6-29-96	.297	.362	.356	58	246	222	20	66	8	1	1	31	19	4	0	1	50	3	0	7.7	20.3
Romero, Noelberth	R-R	6-0	183	12-5-01	.100	.100	.100	4	10	10	0	1	0	0	0	0	0	0	0	0	2	0	0	0.0	20.0
Rutschman, Adley	S-R	6-2	230	2-6-98	.231	.382	.423	8	34	26	3	6	2	0	1	2	7	0	0	1	6	0	0	20.6	17.6
Sanchez, Gary	R-R	6-2	230	12-2-92	.367	.456	.755	15	57	49	11	18	1	0	6	13	5	3	0	0	11	0	0	8.8	19.3
Soto, Livan	L-R	5-10	160	6-22-00	.195	.302	.259	96	366	313	42	61	5	0	5	30	44	5	2	2	80	3	1	12.0	21.9
Stallings, Jacob	R-R	6-5	225	12-22-89	.400	.500	.400	3	12	10	2	4	0	0	0	2	2	0	0	0	3	0	0	16.7	25.0
Trimble, Reed	S-R	6-0	175	10-6-00	.259	.319	.435	30	119	108	21	28	4	0	5	12	9	1	0	1	32	8	0	7.6	26.9
Tromp, Chadwick	R-R	5-8	221	3-21-95	.250	.330	.370	28	103	92	11	23	2	0	3	12	11	0	0	0	23	0	0	10.7	22.3
Vavra, Terrin	L-L	6-0	185	5-12-97	.257	.348	.340	86	298	253	34	65	13	1	2	25	34	2	8	1	58	7	1	11.4	19.5
Vazquez, Luis	R-R	6-0	165	10-10-99	.271	.343	.413	43	174	155	19	42	5	1	5	23	13	4	2	0	37	4	2	7.5	21.3
Westburg, Jordan	R-R	6-2	210	2-18-99	.333	.395	.744	11	43	39	8	13	4	0	4	9	3	1	0	0	10	0	0	7.0	23.3
Young, Carter	S-R	6-0	180	1-24-01	.333	.391	.429	8	23	21	4	7	2	0	0	3	2	0	0	0	4	0	0	8.7	17.4

Pitching	B-T	Ht.	Wt.	DOB	W	L	ERA	G	GS	SV	IP	H	R	ER	HR	BB	SO	AVG	OBP	SLG	SO%	BB%	BF
Akin, Keegan	L-L	6-0	240	4-1-95	0	0	4.50	2	0	0	2	1	2	1	0	0	1	.125	.125	.125	12.5	0.0	8
Alcantara, Raul	L-L	6-0	167	1-22-01	0	3	8.37	12	5	0	24	33	25	22	1	23	26	.333	.468	.404	20.6	18.3	126
Armbruester, Justin	R-R	6-4	235	10-21-98	1	0	0.00	3	0	0	6	5	2	0	0	3	7	.217	.333	.217	25.9	11.1	27
Blewett, Scott	R-R	6-6	245	4-10-96	0	1	8.53	7	2	0	6	13	6	6	1	3	.464	.452	.679	9.7	3.2	31
Bowman, Matt	R-R	6-0	185	5-31-91	1	2	4.10	22	0	1	26	26	14	12	5	6	24	.252	.291	.437	21.8	5.5	110
Bradish, Kyle	R-R	6-3	215	9-12-96	1	0	6.06	4	4	0	16	20	13	11	2	7	19	.294	.364	.441	24.7	9.1	77
Brnovich, Kyle	L-R	6-2	190	10-20-97	2	4	6.34	15	14	0	61	65	45	43	8	34	67	.270	.375	.448	23.7	12.0	283
Caldon, Michael	R-R	6-3	225	10-14-02	0	0	3.38	3	2	0	8	5	3	3	1	4	.172	.400	.276	10.0	27.5	40
Cano, Yennier	R-R	6-4	245	3-9-94	0	0	4.50	2	0	0	2	1	1	0	0	2	.250	.250	.375	25.0	0.0	8
Coleman, Dylan	R-R	6-5	230	9-16-96	1	0	8.10	5	0	0	7	7	6	0	6	.269	.412	.385	17.6	17.6	34
Contreras, Roansy	R-R	6-0	175	11-7-99	7	3	3.73	28	14	1	92	86	43	38	13	33	70	.242	.309	.419	17.8	8.4	393
Espada, Jose	R-R	6-0	170	2-22-97	2	2	5.94	16	0	3	17	8	14	11	3	11	25	.143	.279	.321	36.8	16.2	68
Foster, Cameron	R-R	6-5	200	3-17-99	0	0	3.38	10	1	0	16	14	11	6	1	8	23	.233	.334	.333	32.9	11.4	70
German, Nestor	R-R	6-3	225	2-26-02	0	0	7.04	7	2	0	8	9	7	6	3	4	10	.281	.361	.594	27.8	11.1	36
Gibson, Kyle	R-R	6-6	200	10-23-87	0	1	5.14	2	2	0	7	9	4	4	0	0	8	.310	.344	.379	25.0	0.0	32
Gibson, Trey	R-R	6-3	180	5-18-02	1	4	7.98	7	7	0	29	41	29	26	5	12	31	.333	.399	.561	22.3	8.6	139
Gillies, Keagan	R-R	6-8	255	1-27-98	0	1	4.84	16	0	1	22	29	15	12	3	9	17	.337	.400	.500	17.3	9.2	98
Gonzalez, Luis	L-L	6-2	170	1-17-92	1	0	5.79	4	0	0	5	6	3	3	2	4	4	.316	.435	.632	17.4	17.4	23
Heid, Dylan	R-R	6-0	180	5-18-98	0	0	5.87	7	0	0	8	7	5	5	1	8	10	.259	.432	.481	26.3	21.1	38
Hiraldo, Yaramil	R-R	6-1	180	12-31-95	1	0	4.17	25	1	1	37	31	17	17	4	12	55	.223	.283	.374	35.9	7.8	153
Johnson, Preston	R-R	6-4	250	3-11-00	0	1	14.73	7	1	0	11	10	18	18	3	15	11	.250	.446	.550	19.6	26.8	56
Kittredge, Andrew	R-R	6-1	230	3-17-90	0	0	0.00	5	0	0	5	4	0	0	0	2	4	.222	.300	.222	19.0	9.5	21
Long, Ryan	R-R	6-0	240	10-19-99	0	0	3.00	2	0	0	3	4	3	1	1	2	0	.333	.400	.667	0.0	13.3	15
Martin, Corbin	R-R	6-2	225	12-28-95	3	3	5.82	34	1	1	39	37	25	25	5	23	38	.259	.357	.427	22.5	13.6	169
Martinez, Rodolfo	R-R	6-2	200	4-4-94	2	1	4.96	16	0	3	16	17	12	9	1	15	21	.254	.386	.328	25.0	17.9	84
McDermott, Chayce	L-R	6-3	197	8-22-98	2	7	6.21	25	10	1	58	59	41	40	5	42	60	.274	.402	.405	22.7	15.9	264
Nittoli, Vinny	R-R	6-1	210	11-11-90	0	0	6.35	10	0	0	11	11	8	8	3	4	9	.256	.320	.488	18.0	8.0	50
Nunez, Anthony	S-R	6-1	190	7-10-01	1	4	3.45	16	4	16	7	9	6	2	7	21	.135	.258	.250	32.3	10.8	65
Pavolony, Connor	R-R	6-1	195	10-25-99	0	0	0.00	1	0	0	0	0	0	0	0	0	0	.000	.000	.000	0.0	0.0	1
Pennington, Walter	L-L	6-2	205	4-14-98	0	1	54.00	1	0	0	0	4	2	0	4	0	.000	1.000	.000	0.0	80.0	5
Perez, Cionel	R-L	6-0	175	4-21-96	1	2	6.85	21	0	0	22	30	17	17	1	19	23	.323	.442	.398	20.4	16.8	113
Pham, Alex	R-R	5-11	165	10-10-99	0	0	2.45	2	0	0	4	3	1	1	0	1	5	.231	.286	.308	35.7	7.1	14
Poteet, Cody	R-R	6-1	190	7-30-94	0	1	9.00	6	0	0	12	10	10	2	4	14	.286	.348	.452	30.4	8.7	46
Povich, Cade	L-L	6-3	185	4-12-00	0	2	4.67	4	4	0	17	19	13	9	1	4	18	.279	.307	.397	23.7	5.3	76
Ragsdale, Carson	R-R	6-8	225	5-25-98	2	2	3.47	7	5	0	23	19	9	9	2	8	18	.224	.298	.306	19.1	8.5	94
Reetz, Jakson	R-R	6-0	205	1-3-96	0	0	18.00	1	0	0	1	2	2	2	0	1	0	.400	.500	.800	0.0	16.7	6
Richmond, Nick	R-R	6-4	195	1-16-97	1	0	10.54	12	0	0	14	21	20	16	7	13	13	.350	.462	.533	16.7	16.7	78
Rodriguez, Elvin	R-R	6-3	160	3-31-98	2	0	5.06	9	0	0	11	16	6	6	4	3	6	.286	.333	.595	13.0	6.5	46
Rogers, Trevor	L-L	6-5	217	11-13-97	0	3	5.46	7	7	0	30	38	20	18	3	8	26	.304	.346	.432	19.5	6.0	133
Roth, Houston	R-R	6-3	220	3-9-98	5	2	3.32	28	0	3	41	32	19	15	5	18	37	.215	.306	.356	21.6	10.5	171
Selby, Colin	R-R	6-1	195	12-4-97	2	0	2.45	25	0	2	26	21	7	7	2	13	35	.216	.306	.330	31.5	11.7	111
Stoudt, Levi	R-R	6-1	195	12-4-97	1	4	6.93	18	0	0	25	27	21	19	3	14	17	.281	.369	.448	15.3	12.6	111
Strowd, Kade	L-L	6-2	200	9-17-97	3	2	4.15	29	4	0	78	84	35	36	3	21	16	2	15	41	.243	.322	.324	26.8	9.8	153
Suarez, Albert	R-R	6-3	235	10-8-89	1	0	0.84	4	2	0	11	4	1	1	0	5	5	.118	.231	.176	12.8	12.8	39
Tavera, Carlos	R-R	6-1	195	10-6-98	0	1	2.40	11	0	0	15	13	4	4	1	5	19	.241	.343	.352	23.9	13.4	67
Tyler, Kyle	R-R	6-0	185	12-27-96	0	0	2.25	2	0	0	4	6	2	1	0	3	3	.316	.409	.368	13.6	13.6	22
Van Loon, Peter	R-R	6-5	210	2-18-99	0	3	10.45	10	0	0	16	16	12	12	5	8	13	.356	.463	.689	20.4	14.8	54
Vavra, Terrin	L-R	6-0	185	5-12-97	0	0	0.00	1	0	0	0	0	0	0	0	0	.000	.000	.000	0.0	0.3	3
Walker, Josh	L-L	6-6	225	12-1-94	0	0	2.70	6	0	0	7	3	3	2	1	1	7	.125	.160	.250	28.0	4.0	25
Ward, Thaddeus	R-R	6-3	204	1-16-97	9	6	5.34	32	23	0	120	125	77	71	11	94	131	.271	.404	.403	22.7	16.3	576
Webb, Nathan	R-R	6-3	185	8-20-97	0	1	4.33	16	0	0	27	28	15	13	1	23	18	.220	.380	.288	15.0	19.2	120
Wells, Levi	R-R	6-2	216	9-21-01	1	0	4.79	5	5	0	21	17	11	11	3	13	16	.233	.371	.397	17.8	14.4	90
Wells, Tyler	R-R	6-8	260	8-26-94	1	2	2.70	5	5	0	23	22	7	7	3	6	23	.256	.309	.372	24.5	6.4	94
Weston, Cameron	R-R	6-2	215	8-27-00	5	9	4.59	29	26	0	135	130	76	69	16	71	133	.254	.356	.405	22.0	11.7	605

BALTIMORE ORIOLES

Wolfram, Grant	L-L	6-6	235	12-12-96	1	4	3.38	26	0	0	29	27	12	11	0	9	33	.239	.306	.301	26.6	7.3	124
Yates, Evan	R-R	6-1	180	9-17-02	0	0	18.00	1	0	0	1	3	2	2	0	2	1	.500	.625	.667	12.5	25.0	8
Young, Brandon	R-R	6-6	210	8-19-98	2	1	2.63	5	5	0	27	19	10	8	3	4	27	.190	.221	.320	26.0	3.8	104

Fielding

Catcher	PCT	G	PO	A	E	DP	PB
Ardoin	.974	23	142	9	4	0	0
Banuelos	.992	14	112	5	1	1	1
Basallo	.983	33	282	11	5	1	1
Handley	.986	30	267	13	4	2	3
Pavolony	.965	8	81	2	3	0	1
Reetz	.990	10	97	2	1	1	0
Rutschman	1.000	6	39	4	0	0	1
Sanchez	.985	8	65	2	1	0	0
Stallings	1.000	2	15	0	0	0	0
Tromp	.980	22	183	15	4	2	5

First Base	PCT	G	PO	A	E	DP
Ardoin	.970	6	31	1	1	3
Banuelos	1.000	6	20	1	0	2
Basallo	1.000	20	147	8	0	10
Bowens	.981	38	232	28	5	29
Machin	1.000	20	103	5	0	12
Mayo	1.000	22	138	13	0	15
Mountcastle	1.000	6	38	4	0	4
Noda	.968	11	55	5	2	7
Pavolony	1.000	1	9	0	0	1
Reetz	1.000	6	40	3	0	7
Rivera	.991	16	108	8	1	20
Tromp	.966	4	26	2	1	3
Vavra	1.000	3	12	3	0	4

Second Base	PCT	G	PO	A	E	DP
Ardoin	1.000	1	0	2	0	0
Banuelos	1.000	2	1	3	0	0
Barrero	1.000	2	3	6	0	3
Gordon	1.000	3	4	7	0	3

	PCT	G	PO	A	E	DP
Jackson	1.000	8	17	19	0	7
Machin	.986	43	53	93	2	15
Peguero	.970	15	11	21	1	4
Romero	1.000	1	0	3	0	1
Soto	.993	34	66	76	1	24
Vavra	.993	38	61	75	1	18
Vazquez	.965	11	23	32	2	8
Westburg	1.000	2	3	4	0	1
Young	.909	3	5	15	2	4

Third Base	PCT	G	PO	A	E	DP
Barrero	.929	6	2	11	1	3
Jackson	.875	3	3	4	1	0
Machin	.926	41	33	54	7	6
Mateo	.000	1	0	0	0	0
Mayo	.806	19	6	23	7	1
Peguero	.917	5	4	7	1	0
Rivera	.965	36	18	37	2	4
Romero	.800	3	2	2	1	0
Soto	.000	1	0	0	0	0
Vavra	.974	24	16	22	1	6
Vazquez	.786	7	2	9	3	1
Westburg	1.000	6	3	8	0	0
Young	1.000	2	1	1	0	0

Shortstop	PCT	G	PO	A	E	DP
Barrero	.934	39	47	95	10	24
Gordon	.000	1	0	0	1	0
Henderson	.824	4	7	7	3	1
Jackson	.932	24	39	57	7	14
Machin	.000	1	0	0	0	0
Mateo	1.000	4	4	12	0	1

	PCT	G	PO	A	E	DP
Peguero	.000	1	0	0	0	0
Soto	.980	54	78	117	4	37
Vavra	.900	5	2	7	1	0
Vazquez	.989	23	33	55	1	13
Young	.750	1	1	2	1	1

Outfield	PCT	G	PO	A	E	DP
Adams	.971	82	163	2	5	0
Barrero	1.000	4	9	0	0	0
Beavers	.959	90	137	2	6	1
Bowens	.975	27	39	0	1	0
Bradfield	.967	15	28	1	1	0
Cameron	1.000	4	5	1	0	0
Carlson	.950	22	56	1	3	0
Cowser	1.000	3	7	0	0	0
Fabian	.996	107	213	10	1	4
Gordon	.000	1	0	0	0	0
Haskin	.969	23	31	0	1	0
Jackson	1.000	3	9	0	0	0
Johnson	1.000	3	6	0	0	0
Kjerstad	.976	21	39	1	1	0
Laureano	1.000	2	4	0	0	0
Machin	1.000	15	25	3	0	0
Mateo	.929	5	12	1	1	0
Noda	1.000	3	1	0	0	0
O'Neill	1.000	6	4	1	0	0
Peguero	1.000	9	13	0	0	0
Reetz	.800	1	3	1	1	0
Trimble	.983	25	57	1	1	1
Vavra	1.000	6	14	0	0	0
Vazquez	1.000	1	3	0	0	0

CHESAPEAKE BAYSOX — DOUBLE-A
EASTERN LEAGUE

Batting	B-T	Ht.	Wt.	DOB	AVG	OBP	SLG	G	PA	AB	R	H	2B	3B	HR	RBI	BB	HBP	SH	SF	SO	SB	CS	BB%	SO%
Adams, Jordyn	R-R	6-2	181	10-18-99	.200	.200	.200	1	5	5	1	1	0	0	0	1	0	0	0	0	2	0	0	0.0	40.0
Anderson, Ethan	S-R	6-2	205	9-21-03	.215	.338	.277	20	80	65	9	14	1	0	1	3	12	1	0	2	13	0	0	15.0	16.3
Ardoin, Silas	R-R	6-0	215	9-19-00	.197	.340	.322	66	264	208	22	41	12	1	4	29	45	3	2	6	74	4	0	17.0	28.0
Banuelos, David	R-R	6-0	205	10-1-96	.250	.294	.250	4	17	16	2	4	0	0	0	0	1	0	0	0	6	0	0	5.9	35.3
Bencosme, Frederick	L-R	6-0	160	12-25-02	.192	.266	.318	56	227	198	21	38	7	0	6	19	20	1	5	3	37	3	2	8.8	16.3
Bowens, TT	R-R	6-4	235	5-27-98	.059	.273	.059	5	22	17	1	1	0	0	0	1	5	0	0	0	0	0	0	22.7	36.4
Bradfield, Enrique	L-L	6-1	170	12-2-01	.269	.393	.386	50	208	171	32	46	12	1	2	14	32	3	2	0	37	26	3	15.4	17.8
Butterworth, Brandon	R-R	5-11	168	8-29-02	.215	.322	.355	34	143	121	16	26	9	1	2	14	16	4	0	2	21	8	2	11.2	14.7
Estrada, Aron	S-R	5-8	142	1-13-05	.300	.355	.500	27	110	100	11	30	3	1	5	13	9	0	0	1	17	4	0	8.2	15.5
Guevara, Luis	S-R	5-8	167	2-6-06	.000	.000	.000	2	5	5	0	0	0	0	0	0	0	0	0	0	3	0	0	0.0	60.0
Haskin, Hudson	R-R	6-0	200	12-31-98	.211	.318	.316	25	89	76	7	16	3	1	1	14	10	2	1	0	22	4	1	11.2	24.7
Hodo, Douglas	R-R	6-0	185	9-25-00	.201	.316	.334	112	435	368	47	74	19	0	10	32	55	8	1	3	127	29	10	12.6	29.2
Jackson, Jeremiah	R-R	6-0	165	3-26-00	.254	.291	.412	45	189	177	18	45	16	0	4	19	9	1	0	2	31	2	3	4.8	16.4
Josenberger, Tavian	S-R	6-0	185	10-23-01	.192	.336	.315	67	257	203	31	39	6	2	5	21	43	2	6	2	64	21	7	16.7	24.9
O'Ferrall, Griff	R-R	6-1	185	2-2-03	.250	.357	.361	10	42	36	4	9	2	1	0	0	6	0	0	0	6	2	1	14.3	14.3
O'Neill, Tyler	R-R	5-11	200	6-22-95	.222	.300	.389	6	20	18	1	4	0	0	1	2	2	0	0	0	7	0	0	10.0	35.0
Overn, Austin	L-R	6-0	175	5-10-03	.266	.326	.427	30	136	124	23	33	5	0	5	13	9	2	1	0	34	21	1	6.6	25.0
Perez, Jose	L-R	5-10	150	5-15-05	.179	.200	.214	10	32	28	2	5	1	0	0	0	2	1	0	2	16	0	0	3.1	50.0
Retzbach, Adam	R-R	6-4	220	11-13-00	.221	.324	.379	117	446	380	33	84	19	1	13	57	45	14	4	3	141	3	1	10.1	31.6
Romero, Noelberth	R-R	6-0	183	5-25-03	.254	.291	.291	45	189	177	18	45	16	0	1	2	8	5	2	3	1	40	4	0	3.8	30.6
Servideo, Anthony	L-R	5-10	175	3-11-99	.156	.264	.226	95	350	301	26	47	12	3	1	22	43	1	5	0	107	9	5	12.3	30.6
Sosa, Thomas	L-L	6-1	160	1-18-05	.158	.220	.342	11	41	38	2	6	1	0	2	6	2	1	0	0	11	0	0	4.9	26.8
Trimble, Reed	S-R	6-0	180	6-6-00	.257	.352	.503	53	217	187	34	48	8	4	10	30	22	6	1	1	47	13	0	10.1	21.7
Urman, Cole	R-R	6-1	195	7-28-01	.244	.320	.356	15	50	45	6	11	5	0	0	4	5	0	0	0	14	0	0	10.0	28.0
Valdez, Luis	S-R	5-11	165	1-22-00	.181	.211	.244	57	138	127	15	23	2	3	0	6	4	1	5	1	48	14	2	2.9	34.8
Vasquez, Jalen	L-R	6-0	175	1-18-02	.154	.240	.234	55	198	175	17	27	6	1	2	12	19	1	2	1	57	4	2	9.6	28.8
Vavra, Terrin	L-R	6-0	185	5-12-97	.250	.400	.250	1	5	4	0	1	0	0	0	0	1	0	0	0	0	0	0	20.0	0.0
Velasquez, Alfredo	R-R	5-11	153	9-30-04	.259	.286	.272	24	84	81	10	21	1	0	0	4	3	0	0	0	12	1	0	3.6	14.3
Wagner, Max	R-R	6-0	215	8-19-01	.218	.301	.339	87	347	307	52	67	18	2	5	27	36	1	2	1	106	7	7	10.4	30.5
Willems, Creed	L-R	6-0	225	6-4-03	.253	.338	.441	105	434	379	41	96	21	1	16	59	38	12	2	3	83	1	2	8.8	19.1
Young, Carter	S-R	6-0	180	1-24-01	.163	.230	.211	61	232	209	15	34	4	0	2	19	16	3	2	2	81	1	0	6.9	34.9

BALTIMORE ORIOLES

Pitching	B-T	Ht.	Wt.	DOB	W	L	ERA	G	GS	SV	IP	Hits	Runs	ER	HR	BB	SO	AVG	OBP	SLG	SO%	BB%	BF
Achen, Cohen	R-R	6-2	210	7-31-01	0	0	1.08	2	1	0	8	4	1	1	0	4	6	.154	.303	.192	18.2	12.1	33
Alcantara, Raul	L-L	6-0	167	1-22-01	0	1	5.94	10	0	0	17	14	15	11	0	13	15	.222	.367	.286	18.8	16.3	80
Ashman, Micah	L-L	6-7	200	8-22-02	0	1	4.80	13	0	2	15	11	9	8	0	4	23	.200	.250	.236	38.3	6.7	60
Barnhart, Zane	R-R	5-10	190	5-30-02	0	1	5.40	3	0	0	3	4	3	2	1	2	4	.308	.400	.615	25.0	12.5	16
Baumler, Carter	R-R	6-2	195	1-31-02	0	0	0.00	6	0	0	8	3	0	0	0	2	6	.115	.179	.115	21.4	7.1	28
Bradish, Kyle	R-R	6-3	215	9-12-96	0	0	0.00	1	1	0	4	1	0	0	0	0	2	.091	.182	.167	0.0	12	
Bragg, Braxton	R-R	6-2	207	10-28-00	2	2	2.32	9	8	0	43	36	19	11	3	12	59	.225	.286	.338	33.7	6.9	175
Bright, Trace	R-R	6-4	199	10-26-00	3	8	4.74	23	15	1	87	67	52	46	4	58	82	.215	.340	.324	21.8	15.4	377
Cheney, Wyatt	R-R	6-0	185	1-10-01	0	0	10.80	3	0	0	5	8	6	6	2	2	4	.400	.455	.750	18.2	9.1	22
Coleman, Dylan	R-R	6-5	230	9-16-96	1	0	2.25	6	0	0	8	6	3	2	0	8	8	.222	.400	.259	22.9	22.9	35
Cooper, Riley	L-L	6-2	264	10-19-01	0	0	4.91	5	0	0	7	6	6	4	1	2	4	.194	.286	.323	11.4	5.7	35
Correa, Eccel	R-R	6-0	170	2-1-03	0	0	0.00	1	1	0	5	4	2	0	0	0	2	.211	.286	.263	4.8	9.5	21
De Leon, Luis	L-L	6-3	168	4-14-03	1	0	1.69	3	3	0	16	13	5	3	0	7	24	.217	.294	.283	35.3	10.3	68
De Los Santos, Juan	R-R	6-3	250	5-25-02	0	1	7.11	8	0	0	6	10	5	5	1	7	6	.385	.515	.538	18.2	21.2	33
Eflin, Zach	R-R	6-6	220	4-8-94	0	1	4.50	1	1	0	4	5	2	2	1	1	2	.294	.333	.529	11.1	5.6	18
Forret, Michael	L-R	6-3	190	4-6-04	1	0	1.88	3	3	0	14	9	4	3	0	4	15	.180	.241	.260	27.3	7.3	55
Fruit, Zach	R-R	6-4	203	4-12-00	1	5	7.01	12	11	0	44	47	38	34	5	30	40	.272	.381	.445	19.0	14.2	211
German, Nestor	R-R	6-3	225	2-26-02	6	6	3.76	18	17	0	91	68	44	38	8	32	96	.207	.279	.354	26.0	8.7	369
Gibson, Trey	R-R	6-5	230	5-18-02	3	2	1.55	10	10	0	52	29	11	9	1	18	68	.157	.245	.222	32.5	8.6	209
Gillies, Keagan	R-R	6-8	255	1-27-98	4	1	1.15	26	0	8	31	14	5	4	2	4	34	.128	.159	.183	30.1	3.5	113
Heid, Dylan	R-R	6-1	180	5-18-98	0	0	2.61	7	0	1	10	7	3	3	1	7	9	.200	.326	.314	20.9	16.3	43
Herberholz, Christian	R-R	5-11	195	10-5-00	0	0	0.00	2	0	0	4	1	0	0	0	1	3	.067	.125	.133	18.8	6.3	16
Hiraldo, Yaramil	R-R	6-1	180	12-31-95	0	0	0.00	2	0	0	3	3	0	0	0	0	3	.273	.273	.273	27.3	0.0	11
Johnson, Preston	R-R	6-4	250	3-11-00	4	4	3.58	19	1	0	38	29	17	15	3	20	45	.209	.313	.331	27.6	12.3	163
Lloyd, Daniel	R-R	6-3	232	8-8-00	7	5	3.70	38	0	1	56	41	26	23	5	28	47	.205	.304	.320	20.2	12.0	233
Long, Ryan	R-R	6-6	240	10-19-99	5	5	4.04	26	16	0	91	91	46	41	11	35	65	.256	.323	.423	16.2	8.7	401
Martinez, Robinson	R-R	6-1	190	3-20-98	0	0	4.86	13	0	0	17	15	10	9	1	19	18	.259	.450	.414	22.0	23.2	82
McDermott, Chayce	L-R	6-3	197	8-22-98	0	1	5.40	1	1	0	2	1	1	1	1	3	3	.167	.444	.667	33.3	33.3	9
Money, Blake	R-R	6-7	240	11-14-01	4	5	4.21	15	9	1	68	59	33	32	9	25	87	.230	.303	.402	30.3	8.7	287
Neighbors, Tyson	R-R	6-1	220	10-9-02	2	0	0.59	12	0	0	15	7	1	1	0	5	19	.140	.241	.160	32.8	8.6	58
Nunez, Anthony	S-R	6-1	190	7-10-01	0	0	0.00	1	0	0	1	0	0	0	0	1	0	.000	.200	.000	0.0	0.0	5
Nunez, Juan	R-R	5-11	190	12-7-00	0	1	7.07	8	3	0	14	13	12	11	2	12	26	.255	.379	.490	39.4	18.2	66
Ogando, Gerald	R-R	6-2	180	7-28-00	1	2	3.58	36	0	5	50	37	27	20	2	23	59	.202	.321	.279	27.1	10.6	218
Pennington, Walter	L-L	6-2	205	4-14-98	0	1	2.60	14	0	0	17	18	5	5	0	7	21	.273	.347	.318	28.0	9.3	75
Pham, Alex	R-R	5-11	165	10-10-99	2	3	4.17	14	5	1	41	38	21	19	5	14	51	.241	.306	.411	29.3	8.0	174
Portes, Edgar	R-R	6-2	165	10-2-02	1	0	8.68	7	0	0	9	13	9	9	2	9	12	.325	.449	.575	24.5	18.4	49
Reilly, Patrick	R-R	6-3	208	10-7-01	0	1	1.86	3	3	0	10	6	2	2	0	4	8	.182	.270	.182	21.6	10.8	37
Retzbach, Adam	R-R	6-4	220	11-13-00	0	1	18.00	1	0	0	1	3	2	2	0	0	0	.500	.571	.500	0.0	0.0	7
Richmond, Nick	R-R	6-4	195	4-2-98	1	0	0.00	1	0	0	1	1	0	0	0	0	0	.250	.250	.250	0.0	0.0	4
Rivera, Yaqui	R-R	6-2	150	7-19-03	1	3	3.97	27	0	3	34	30	21	15	3	25	47	.234	.372	.367	29.9	15.9	157
Rogers, Trevor	L-L	6-5	217	11-13-97	0	0	6.00	1	1	0	3	4	2	2	1	1	3	.333	.385	.583	23.1	7.7	13
Romero, Noelberth	R-R	6-0	183	12-5-01	0	0	0.00	1	0	0	1	1	0	0	0	1	0	.250	.333	.250	0.0	16.7	6
Roth, Houston	R-R	6-3	220	3-9-98	1	0	1.64	8	0	0	11	5	2	2	0	7	17	.139	.295	.194	38.6	15.9	44
Rustad, Carter	R-R	6-4	194	4-23-01	0	3	3.32	15	0	1	19	16	10	7	1	7	21	.211	.277	.289	25.3	8.4	83
Servideo, Anthony	L-R	5-10	175	3-11-99	0	0	0.00	1	0	0	2	2	0	0	0	0	0	.250	.250	.250	0.0	0.0	8
Suarez, Albert	R-R	6-3	235	10-8-89	0	0	18.00	1	1	0	2	5	4	4	1	0	0	.500	.500	1.000	0.0	8.3	12
Van Loon, Peter	R-R	6-5	210	2-18-99	3	4	3.38	26	1	1	43	33	17	16	1	16	49	.214	.299	.279	27.2	8.9	180
Vespi, Ben	R-R	6-3	190	5-28-01	0	0	9.00	1	0	0	2	1	1	0	0	1	.500	.500	.750	5.0	0.0	4	
Virbitsky, Kyle	R-R	6-7	235	10-8-98	2	0	1.88	9	0	0	14	10	5	3	1	6	13	.189	.271	.283	22.0	10.2	59
Watts-Brown, Juaron	R-R	6-3	190	2-23-02	1	3	3.82	7	7	0	35	28	20	15	10	12	43	.159	.232	.429	31.2	8.7	138
Webb, Nathan	R-R	6-2	215	8-20-97	1	1	5.29	12	0	1	17	16	11	10	2	11	17	.254	.351	.413	21.5	13.9	79
Wells, Levi	R-R	6-2	216	9-21-01	1	6	3.12	20	16	2	75	70	35	26	4	26	80	.238	.306	.327	24.5	8.0	327
Wells, Tyler	R-R	6-8	260	8-26-94	0	0	0.00	1	1	0	2	0	0	0	0	0	1	.000	.000	.000	16.7	0.0	6

Fielding

Catcher	PCT	G	PO	A	E	DP	PB
Anderson	.990	9	93	5	1	0	2
Ardoin	.985	33	296	23	5	1	1
Banuelos	1.000	2	22	0	0	0	0
Retzbach	.985	38	370	22	6	2	3
Urman	.957	3	21	1	1	0	0
Willems	.990	53	476	35	5	2	4

First Base	PCT	G	PO	A	E	DP
Anderson	.985	10	61	3	1	4
Ardoin	.967	22	112	7	4	8
Banuelos	1.000	1	7	0	0	1
Bowens	1.000	2	4	1	0	0
Retzbach	.988	57	363	37	5	28
Romero	1.000	6	23	2	0	2
Servideo	.977	7	41	2	1	3
Urman	.933	10	54	2	4	5
Wagner	1.000	1	3	0	0	0
Willems	.995	29	188	14	1	18

Second Base	PCT	G	PO	A	E	DP
Bencosme	.925	29	47	52	8	11
Butterworth	.969	8	12	19	1	6
Estrada	.968	18	27	34	2	8
Guevara	1.000	2	4	4	0	1
Jackson	1.000	4	4	4	0	1
Josenberger	.947	8	13	23	2	2
O'Ferrall	1.000	3	5	9	0	0
Perez	1.000	1	0	1	0	0
Romero	1.000	2	1	7	0	1
Servideo	1.000	10	10	23	0	4
Vasquez	.958	17	20	26	2	3
Vavra	1.000	1	1	2	0	0
Velasquez	.974	8	15	22	1	3
Wagner	.988	22	35	49	1	11
Young	.975	11	18	21	1	4

Third Base	PCT	G	PO	A	E	DP
Jackson	.947	10	6	12	1	0
Perez	.786	7	4	7	3	1
Romero	.941	7	8	8	1	0
Servideo	.925	37	28	46	6	1
Vasquez	.930	12	17	23	3	2
Velasquez	1.000	2	1	4	0	0
Wagner	.956	48	42	66	5	2
Young	.929	19	11	28	3	4

Shortstop	PCT	G	PO	A	E	DP
Bencosme	.967	24	26	62	3	9
Butterworth	.970	17	28	36	2	4
Jackson	.920	26	48	56	9	16
O'Ferrall	.957	6	11	11	1	3
Servideo	.954	16	23	39	3	8
Vasquez	.887	14	18	37	7	10
Velasquez	.889	8	12	20	4	5
Young	1.000	27	31	40	0	5

Outfield	PCT	G	PO	A	E	DP
Adams	1.000	1	3	0	0	0
Bowens	1.000	3	2	0	0	0
Bradfield	1.000	46	102	1	0	0
Butterworth	1.000	6	13	0	0	0
Estrada	1.000	6	11	0	0	0
Haskin	.963	23	50	2	2	0
Hodo	.981	111	207	3	4	1
Josenberger	1.000	52	97	5	0	0
O'Neill	1.000	3	9	0	0	0
Overn	1.000	27	60	1	0	0
Romero	.976	24	38	2	1	0
Servideo	.967	20	26	3	1	0
Sosa	.955	10	21	0	1	0
Trimble	.971	45	97	3	3	1
Urman	.000	1	0	0	0	0
Valdez	.957	47	65	2	3	0
Vasquez	.750	10	9	0	3	0
Velasquez	1.000	5	10	1	0	1

ABERDEEN IRONBIRDS — HIGH-A
SOUTH ATLANTIC LEAGUE

Batting	B-T	Ht.	Wt.	DOB	AVG	OBP	SLG	G	PA	AB	R	H	2B	3B	HR	RBI	BB	HBP	SH	SF	SO	SB	CS	BB%	SO%
Amparo, Edwin	S-R	6-0	165	10-14-04	.226	.305	.434	16	59	53	8	12	3	1	2	9	5	1	0	0	15	10	4	8.5	25.4
Anderson, Ethan	S-R	6-2	205	9-21-03	.257	.338	.355	70	283	245	26	63	13	1	3	42	31	1	0	4	51	15	3	11.0	18.0
Arias, Leandro	S-R	6-1	155	2-5-05	.219	.315	.273	78	299	256	29	56	8	0	2	27	32	5	3	2	50	4	5	10.7	16.7
Banuelos, David	R-R	6-0	205	10-1-96	.000	.100	.000	3	10	9	0	0	0	0	0	0	1	0	0	0	4	0	0	10.0	40.0
Bradfield, Enrique	L-L	6-1	170	12-2-01	.179	.258	.250	8	31	28	7	5	2	0	0	3	0	0	0	0	10	4	0	9.7	32.3
Bucce, Yasmil	S-R	5-11	168	8-13-04	.159	.309	.159	15	55	44	2	7	0	0	0	5	9	1	0	1	20	0	0	16.4	36.4
Cowser, Colton	L-R	6-2	220	3-20-00	.222	.364	.556	3	11	9	3	2	0	0	1	1	2	0	0	0	4	0	0	18.2	36.4
Cuevas, Elis	S-R	5-11	150	11-8-04	.196	.313	.278	29	117	97	18	19	3	1	1	14	15	2	1	1	33	16	2	12.8	28.2
Cunningham, Jake	R-R	6-4	205	7-3-02	.206	.295	.303	76	271	238	30	49	12	1	3	26	29	2	0	2	90	24	6	10.7	33.2
De Los Santos, Anderson	R-R	5-11	185	1-11-04	.230	.360	.361	103	381	313	35	72	15	4	6	44	55	9	3	1	83	19	5	14.4	21.8
Estrada, Aron	S-R	5-8	142	1-13-05	.284	.369	.429	81	333	289	41	82	13	7	5	40	35	6	0	3	58	30	6	10.5	17.4
Fabian, Jud	R-L	6-1	195	9-27-00	.273	.429	.200	7	21	15	3	4	1	0	0	2	5	1	0	0	3	0	0	21.4	21.4
Figueroa, Victor	L-R	6-5	240	12-31-03	.182	.337	.247	25	99	77	8	14	3	1	0	5	19	0	0	2	29	2	2	19.2	29.3
George, Nate	R-R	6-0	200	6-4-06	.291	.380	.392	21	92	79	15	23	5	0	1	7	11	0	1	0	19	12	6	12.0	20.7
Haskin, Hudson	R-R	6-0	200	12-31-98	.111	.158	.167	5	19	18	2	2	1	0	0	1	1	0	0	0	9	0	0	5.3	47.4
Hernandez, Maikol	R-R	6-3	175	10-4-03	.221	.278	.314	27	99	86	4	19	5	0	1	12	8	0	2	3	28	4	0	8.1	28.3
Honeycutt, Vance	R-R	6-3	190	5-17-03	.171	.284	.275	101	436	374	48	64	12	6	5	24	56	3	2	0	178	32	7	12.8	40.8
Josenberger, Tavian	S-R	6-0	185	10-23-01	.154	.294	.231	4	17	13	2	2	1	0	0	1	3	0	0	1	6	1	0	17.6	35.3
Mejia, Jose	R-R	5-11	175	9-29-05	.200	.429	.200	2	7	5	1	1	0	0	0	1	1	1	0	0	3	2	0	14.3	42.9
Mordan, Aneudis	R-R	6-1	175	6-10-04	.199	.280	.293	65	221	191	21	38	9	0	3	21	20	2	7	1	56	1	2	9.0	25.3
O'Ferrall, Griff	R-R	6-1	185	2-2-03	.226	.318	.299	111	474	411	57	93	14	2	4	38	53	4	3	3	71	42	7	11.2	15.0
O'Neill, Tyler	R-R	5-11	200	6-22-95	.333	.333	.333	1	3	3	0	1	0	0	0	0	0	0	0	0	2	0	0	0.0	66.7
Overn, Austin	R-R	6-0	175	5-10-03	.242	.367	.386	84	341	277	51	67	8	4	8	30	53	4	3	4	96	43	7	15.5	28.2
Peguero, Fernando	S-R	5-9	145	12-27-04	.100	.167	.100	3	12	10	0	1	0	0	0	1	1	0	0	1	5	0	0	8.3	41.7
Perez, Jose	L-R	5-10	150	5-15-05	.000	.167	.000	2	6	5	2	0	0	0	0	0	1	0	0	0	3	0	0	16.7	50.0
Sosa, Thomas	L-L	6-1	160	1-18-05	.222	.309	.407	47	191	167	24	37	9	2	6	31	18	4	0	2	46	3	2	9.4	24.1
Stafford, Ryan	R-R	5-10	200	1-15-03	.178	.306	.248	96	332	270	29	48	15	2	0	26	41	11	5	5	82	22	4	12.3	24.7
Tejada, Angel	R-R	5-10	160	1-30-04	.169	.231	.218	51	135	124	16	21	3	0	1	10	9	1	0	0	32	13	4	6.7	23.7
Trimble, Reed	S-R	6-0	205	3-21-95	.154	.267	.538	4	15	13	3	2	1	0	1	2	1	0	0	1	3	0	0	6.7	20.0
Tromp, Chadwick	R-R	5-8	221	3-21-95	.154	.267	.154	3	15	13	1	2	0	0	0	0	2	0	0	0	3	0	0	13.3	20.0
Tuft, Colin	R-R	6-2	195	1-24-03	.232	.348	.339	17	66	56	5	13	1	1	1	6	9	1	0	0	15	7	1	13.6	22.7
Urman, Cole	R-R	6-1	195	7-28-01	.170	.204	.213	18	50	47	4	8	0	1	0	1	2	0	1	0	24	0	0	4.0	48.0
Valdez, Luis	S-R	5-11	165	1-22-00	.250	.250	.333	3	12	12	1	3	1	0	0	5	0	0	0	0	4	1	1	0.0	33.3
Vasquez, Jalen	L-R	6-0	175	1-18-02	.253	.367	.361	30	98	83	15	21	4	1	1	10	15	0	0	0	26	4	5	15.3	26.5
Velasquez, Alfredo	R-R	5-11	153	9-30-04	.151	.167	.189	16	55	53	7	8	2	0	0	2	1	0	0	1	8	2	0	1.8	14.5
Young, Carter	S-R	6-0	180	1-24-01	.194	.306	.194	9	36	31	3	6	0	1	1	4	5	0	0	0	11	1	1	13.9	38.9

Pitching	B-T	Ht.	Wt.	DOB	W	L	ERA	G	GS	SV	IP	Hits	Runs	ER	HR	BB	SO	AVG	OBP	SLG	SO%	BB%	BF
Achen, Cohen	R-R	6-2	210	7-31-01	5	8	3.70	17	9	0	58	53	32	24	3	23	48	.240	.315	.317	19.0	9.1	253
Allsup, Chase	R-R	6-1	220	4-21-03	1	1	2.08	2	2	0	9	4	2	2	0	7	6	.154	.353	.192	17.1	20.0	35
Aracena, Wellington	R-R	6-3	180	12-27-04	1	1	2.35	5	5	0	23	10	8	6	0	15	24	.130	.277	.156	25.5	16.0	94
Barnhart, Zane	R-R	5-10	190	5-30-02	3	6	3.72	36	0	4	48	36	23	20	2	20	54	.211	.306	.269	27.1	10.1	199
Bateman, Boston	R-L	6-8	240	9-20-05	0	0	5.56	3	0	0	11	12	7	7	1	11	13	.279	.429	.372	23.2	19.6	56
Baumler, Carter	R-R	6-2	195	1-31-02	2	0	2.45	20	0	2	29	19	8	8	0	13	38	.184	.282	.214	32.5	11.1	117
Beck, Jared	L-L	7-0	225	7-1-00	0	1	12.00	8	0	0	6	7	8	8	1	11	6	.292	.541	.417	16.2	29.7	37
Bradish, Kyle	R-R	6-2	215	9-12-96	0	0	4.50	1	1	0	2	1	1	1	0	1	4	.222	.300	.333	40.0	10.0	10
Bragg, Braxton	R-R	6-2	207	10-28-00	2	0	0.00	3	3	0	16	6	1	0	0	5	18	.109	.183	.127	30.0	8.3	60
Cabarcas, Ryan	L-L	5-10	170	4-24-01	1	1	2.70	12	0	2	17	20	7	5	0	6	24	.294	.347	.294	31.2	7.8	77
Caldon, Michael	R-R	6-3	225	10-14-02	0	1	3.65	3	0	1	12	14	6	5	0	2	13	.275	.296	.373	23.6	3.6	55
Cartaya, Yeiber	R-R	6-5	165	1-20-03	1	1	4.50	5	5	0	20	11	11	10	1	15	21	.159	.341	.261	23.6	16.9	89
Cheney, Wyatt	R-R	6-0	185	1-10-01	0	2	2.51	24	0	4	32	20	12	9	3	23	43	.179	.319	.313	31.2	16.7	138
Cooper, Riley	L-L	6-2	264	10-19-01	0	5	5.68	19	2	1	32	42	23	20	5	11	32	.311	.365	.489	21.5	7.4	149
Correa, Eccel	R-R	6-0	170	2-1-03	0	2	2.30	7	4	0	27	17	9	7	1	6	14	.192	.324	.283	13.0	5.6	108
Cravey, Jacob	R-R	6-6	215	9-28-01	0	1	0.77	10	2	1	23	11	4	2	1	14	25	.139	.269	.190	26.9	15.1	93
Crowder, Jack	R-R	6-4	220	7-25-02	0	0	3.22	6	1	3	22	18	8	8	1	8	23	.187	.262	.307	27.1	9.4	85
De Leon, Luis	L-L	6-3	168	11-4-04	4	3	3.58	13	11	0	60	46	29	24	0	26	69	.207	.304	.252	26.7	10.1	258
De Los Santos, Juan	R-R	6-3	250	5-25-02	1	1	3.79	17	0	1	19	12	9	8	0	12	21	.171	.310	.229	25.0	14.3	84
Eflin, Zach	R-R	6-6	220	4-8-94	0	0	0.00	1	1	0	4	2	0	0	0	2	4	.154	.267	.154	26.7	13.3	15
Federman, Daniel	L-R	6-1	205	9-18-98	0	0	4.00	4	0	0	9	8	4	4	1	4	4	.133	.235	.233	23.5	5.9	17
Forret, Michael	R-R	6-4	186	4-6-04	1	2	1.51	16	15	0	60	31	13	10	3	17	76	.152	.223	.201	33.5	7.5	227
Freeberger, Dominic	R-R	6-0	205	4-5-00	4	2	5.24	26	0	2	34	28	23	20	4	7	40	.220	.359	.362	25.5	17.2	157
Fruit, Zach	R-R	6-4	203	4-12-00	0	0	1.13	2	2	0	8	4	1	1	1	2	12	.143	.200	.250	40.0	3.3	30
German, Nestor	R-R	6-3	225	2-26-02	0	1	3.60	6	6	0	25	11	11	10	2	10	37	.242	.314	.358	35.2	9.5	105

Player	B-T	Ht	Wt	DOB	G	GS	ERA	W	L	SV	IP	H	R	ER	HR	BB	SO	AVG	OBP	SLG	BABIP	GB%	BB%
Gibson, Kyle	R-R	6-6	200	10-23-87	1	0	1.80	1	1	0	5	1	2	1	1	2	5	.059	.158	.235	26.3	10.5	19
Gibson, Trey	R-R	6-5	230	5-18-02	1	2	5.12	9	8	0	39	32	27	22	7	14	67	.216	.295	.426	40.4	8.4	166
Glassey, Joe	R-R	6-3	215	7-17-01	0	0	0.00	1	0	0	1	0	0	0	0	1	2	.250	.400	.250	40.0	20.0	5
Gongora, Sebastian	L-L	6-5	215	9-1-01	2	2	5.28	13	12	0	46	48	30	27	3	22	52	.267	.350	.383	25.6	10.8	203
Herberholz, Christian	R-R	5-11	195	10-5-00	5	4	3.00	24	0	1	36	32	16	12	3	12	36	.239	.300	.328	23.8	7.9	151
Hiraldo, Yaramil	R-R	6-1	180	12-31-95	1	0	1.50	3	0	0	6	4	1	1	0	1	6	.190	.227	.286	27.3	4.5	22
Kirby, Devin	R-R	5-10	220	8-10-99	0	0	13.50	6	0	0	5	6	10	7	0	5	6	.300	.533	.400	20.0	16.7	30
Kittredge, Andrew	R-R	6-1	230	3-17-90	0	0	9.00	1	0	0	1	2	1	1	0	0	2	.400	.400	.600	40.0	0.0	5
Marsh, Chandler	R-R	6-4	235	9-6-02	0	0	1.80	9	0	0	10	6	2	2	0	3	11	.167	.250	.222	27.5	7.5	40
Martinez, Robinson	R-R	6-0	190	3-20-98	1	0	4.50	5	0	0	6	4	3	3	0	3	7	.190	.320	.238	28.0	12.0	25
Martinez, Rodolfo	R-R	6-2	200	4-4-94	0	3	4.63	9	0	0	12	11	7	6	0	9	10	.268	.407	.366	18.2	16.4	55
Mejia, Jose	R-R	5-11	175	9-29-05	0	0	0.00	1	0	0	1	0	0	0	0	0	0	.000	.000	.000	0.0	0.0	2
Mendez, Alejandro	R-R	6-5	254	2-28-01	1	1	6.86	22	0	1	21	15	19	16	1	27	28	.203	.430	.311	26.2	25.2	107
Money, Blake	R-R	6-7	240	11-14-01	2	3	3.57	11	9	0	53	48	26	21	7	18	65	.230	.300	.373	29.1	8.1	223
Nierman, Hayden	S-R	6-2	170	1-27-00	0	0	7.88	8	0	1	8	12	8	7	1	6	4	.353	.450	.500	10.0	15.0	40
Pennington, Walter	L-L	6-2	205	4-14-98	0	1	6.75	3	1	0	4	1	3	3	0	2	6	.071	.188	.071	37.5	12.5	16
Pham, Alex	R-R	5-11	165	10-10-99	0	0	0.00	1	1	0	3	1	0	0	0	0	1	2	.091	.167	.091	16.7	8.3	12
Povich, Cade	L-L	6-3	185	4-12-00	0	0	0.00	1	1	0	3	0	0	0	0	0	3	.000	.000	.000	33.3	0.0	9
Richmond, Nick	R-R	6-4	195	4-2-98	0	0	4.91	3	0	0	4	4	2	2	1	1	6	.286	.333	.714	37.5	6.3	16
Rodriguez, Aneuris	R-R	6-3	185	6-14-04	0	0	0.00	1	0	0	2	1	0	0	0	1	2	.143	.250	.143	25.0	12.5	8
Rojas, Juan	L-L	6-0	165	1-31-04	4	8	4.43	23	14	0	85	95	46	42	6	41	70	.279	.361	.374	17.9	10.5	390
Rustad, Carter	R-R	6-4	194	4-23-01	1	0	4.15	11	1	1	22	18	13	10	1	7	19	.220	.297	.280	20.9	7.7	91
Sharkey, Teddy	R-R	5-11	215	8-1-01	1	1	3.68	5	0	0	5	3	3	1	6	10	.192	.333	.308	30.3	18.2	33
Sharp, Reese	R-R	6-3	220	8-7-00	0	0	3.86	6	0	0	7	8	4	3	1	3	6	.286	.344	.500	18.8	9.4	32
Smith, Tanner	R-R	6-6	245	8-5-02	0	0	0.00	4	0	1	5	3	0	0	0	0	11	.167	.167	.167	57.9	0.0	19
Stoudt, Levi	R-R	6-1	195	12-4-97	0	0	1.93	3	0	0	5	3	1	1	1	0	4	.188	.188	.375	25.0	0.0	16
Tejada, Angel	R-R	5-10	160	1-30-04	1	1	5.40	7	0	1	5	5	8	3	3	3	4	.238	.393	.667	14.3	10.7	28
Turzenski, Trent	R-R	6-6	240	5-11-01	2	1	3.66	14	0	1	20	15	9	8	1	9	23	.217	.321	.304	28.0	11.0	82
Van Loon, Peter	R-R	6-5	210	2-18-99	0	0	0.00	1	0	0	1	0	0	0	0	1	1	.000	.250	.000	25.0	25.0	4
Vespi, Ben	R-R	6-3	190	5-28-01	3	1	1.54	8	0	0	12	13	3	2	1	3	11	.283	.327	.413	22.0	6.0	50
Virbitsky, Kyle	R-R	6-7	235	10-8-98	2	1	3.86	6	0	0	9	9	4	4	1	4	8	.257	.317	.400	19.5	9.8	41
Weatherly, Ty	L-R	6-6	200	9-19-00	1	3	8.31	15	7	0	43	57	46	40	4	26	46	.328	.430	.500	22.1	12.5	208
Yates, Evan	R-R	6-1	180	9-17-02	2	1	2.70	5	0	0	20	18	7	6	1	9	19	.240	.329	.333	22.4	10.6	85
Young, Brandon	R-R	6-6	210	8-19-98	0	0	3.00	2	2	0	6	7	2	2	0	3	9	.292	.357	.333	32.1	10.7	28

Fielding

Catcher	PCT	G	PO	A	E	DP	PB
Anderson	.983	40	388	21	7	1	2
Banuelos	1.000	3	31	2	0	0	0
Bucce	.952	6	55	4	3	0	1
Mordan	.985	19	128	7	2	1	3
Stafford	.980	50	462	29	10	1	10
Tromp	1.000	2	24	2	0	0	1
Tuft	.982	10	98	13	2	0	6
Urman	.962	9	47	3	2	0	0

First Base	PCT	G	PO	A	E	DP
Anderson	.978	14	80	10	2	6
Bucce	1.000	5	30	0	0	1
Cuevas	1.000	4	24	2	0	1
Cunningham	.909	1	10	0	1	0
De Los Santos	.979	28	178	8	4	15
Figueroa	.994	20	153	9	1	11
Mordan	.950	40	220	8	12	17
Stafford	1.000	19	118	10	0	8
Tejada	1.000	5	34	2	0	3
Tuft	1.000	2	11	1	0	0
Urman	1.000	6	47	1	0	3

Second Base	PCT	G	PO	A	E	DP
Amparo	1.000	6	6	14	0	1
Arias	.935	13	16	27	3	3
Estrada	.951	44	45	91	7	11
Hernandez	.947	4	7	11	1	1

Third Base	PCT	G	PO	A	E	DP
Amparo	.857	7	3	9	2	3
Arias	.868	20	9	24	5	0
Cuevas	1.000	1	0	0	1	0
De Los Santos	.890	75	53	93	18	8
Estrada	.857	4	2	4	1	1
Hernandez	1.000	3	2	4	0	0
Tejada	.895	9	4	13	2	0
Vasquez	.968	17	13	17	1	1
Velasquez	.800	2	1	3	1	0
Young	1.000	3	5	5	0	1

Shortstop	PCT	G	PO	A	E	DP
Amparo	1.000	1	1	1	0	0
Arias	.939	32	29	64	6	9
Estrada	.893	8	12	13	3	2
Hernandez	.981	17	15	37	1	7
O'Ferrall	.974	66	90	139	6	24
Velasquez	1.000	5	5	17	0	1

	PCT	G	PO	A	E	DP
Josenberger	.900	2	3	6	1	1
O'Ferrall	.986	37	49	92	2	18
Peguero	1.000	2	1	6	0	1
Perez	1.000	1	0	4	0	0
Stafford	.880	12	22	22	6	5
Tejada	.929	9	12	14	2	1
Vasquez	1.000	1	0	1	0	0
Velasquez	1.000	6	9	16	0	3
Young	.900	3	4	5	1	0

Outfield	PCT	G	PO	A	E	DP
Anderson	.875	2	6	1	1	0
Bradfield	.909	6	9	1	1	0
Cowser	1.000	2	2	0	0	0
Cuevas	1.000	25	38	0	0	0
Cunningham	1.000	58	106	1	0	0
Estrada	.968	23	30	0	1	0
Fabian	1.000	3	4	0	0	0
Figueroa	1.000	3	3	0	0	0
George	.969	17	31	0	1	0
Haskin	1.000	3	6	0	0	0
Honeycutt	.960	90	179	11	8	4
Josenberger	1.000	2	5	0	0	0
Mejia	1.000	1	2	0	0	0
Overn	.983	84	162	9	3	2
Peguero	1.000	1	1	1	0	0
Perez	1.000	1	0	1	0	0
Sosa	.919	40	66	2	6	0
Stafford	.920	16	23	0	2	0
Tejada	.935	21	40	3	3	1
Trimble	1.000	3	5	2	0	0
Tuft	1.000	2	4	0	0	0
Valdez	.800	3	4	0	1	0
Vasquez	1.000	4	4	0	0	0
Velasquez	1.000	2	2	0	0	0

DELMARVA SHOREBIRDS
CAROLINA LEAGUE

LOW-A

Batting	B-T	Ht.	Wt.	DOB	AVG	OBP	SLG	G	PA	AB	R	H	2B	3B	HR	RBI	BB	HBP	SH	SF	SO	SB	CS	BB%	SO%
Almeyda, Luis	B-R	6-2	180	4-17-06	.238	.314	.348	53	204	181	16	43	9	1	3	24	18	3	0	2	52	14	9	8.8	25.5
Aloy, Wehiwa	R-R	6-2	195	2-4-04	.288	.356	.500	20	90	80	14	23	9	1	2	14	8	1	0	1	25	6	2	8.9	27.8
Amparo, Edwin	S-R	6-0	165	10-14-04	.195	.321	.300	60	239	200	21	39	6	3	3	17	34	3	2	0	70	23	8	14.2	29.3
Amparo, Felix	R-R	5-10	205	2-27-06	.182	.250	.273	4	12	11	1	2	1	0	0	1	1	0	0	0	2	0	1	8.3	16.7
Austin, RJ	R-R	5-11	189	12-18-03	.263	.364	.316	18	68	57	7	15	3	0	0	4	7	2	2	0	9	1	10.3	14.7
Bencosme, Frederick	L-R	6-0	160	12-25-02	.091	.214	.091	4	14	11	2	1	0	0	0	1	1	0	1	4	1	0	7.1	28.6
Bodine, Caden	S-R	5-10	190	12-2-03	.326	.408	.349	11	49	43	6	14	1	0	0	4	5	1	0	0	8	0	0	10.2	16.3

BALTIMORE ORIOLES

Batting	B-T	Ht.	Wt.	DOB	AVG	OBP	SLG	G	AB	R	H	2B	3B	HR	RBI	BB	SO	SB	CS	HBP	SO%	BB%
Bucce, Yasmil	S-R	5-11	168	8-13-04	.255	.401	.413	81	339	271	43	69	13	3	8	50	62	5	0	1	82	2	1	18.3	24.2
Campos, Edrei	L-R	6-1	165	5-8-05	.159	.248	.222	41	144	126	7	20	2	0	2	9	13	2	3	0	48	2	5	9.0	33.3
Cuevas, Elis	S-R	5-11	150	11-8-04	.229	.340	.307	50	210	179	27	41	5	0	3	20	24	6	1	0	39	19	3	11.4	18.6
George, Nate	R-R	6-0	200	6-4-06	.337	.410	.491	43	186	163	31	55	8	7	1	21	18	2	3	0	29	25	13	9.7	15.6
Guerrero, Kevin	R-R	6-3	165	4-17-04	.236	.321	.314	72	276	242	27	57	11	1	2	29	30	1	2	1	81	6	9	10.9	29.3
Guevara, Luis	S-R	5-8	167	2-6-06	.243	.382	.314	24	91	70	13	17	1	2	0	9	13	4	1	2	18	6	2	14.3	19.8
Haskin, Hudson	R-R	6-0	200	12-31-98	.000	.300	.000	3	10	7	0	0	0	0	0	0	2	1	0	0	4	0	0	20.0	40.0
Hernandez, Maikol	R-R	6-3	175	10-4-03	.173	.312	.243	70	268	214	20	37	7	1	2	20	41	4	5	4	76	5	3	15.3	28.4
Hightower, Cobb	R-R	6-0	180	3-20-05	.250	.337	.321	24	97	84	9	21	3	0	1	7	10	1	2	0	21	7	2	10.3	21.6
Irish, Ike	L-R	6-2	190	11-26-03	.230	.296	.297	20	81	74	9	17	2	0	1	12	6	1	0	0	19	3	0	7.4	23.5
Liranzo, Joshua	R-R	6-3	180	8-25-06	.181	.304	.264	54	214	182	25	33	8	2	1	13	27	5	0	0	65	13	3	12.6	30.4
Martinez, Stiven	R-R	6-4	198	8-8-07	.125	.263	.188	25	95	80	5	10	3	1	0	2	13	2	0	0	46	3	2	13.7	48.4
Mejia, Adriander	R-R	6-0	165	8-29-06	.000	.250	.000	2	8	6	1	0	0	0	0	0	2	0	0	0	1	0	0	25.0	12.5
Nolaya, Andres	R-R	6-1	185	3-27-05	.204	.307	.269	65	196	167	16	34	6	1	1	15	17	8	4	0	50	16	2	8.7	25.5
Ondina, Steven	S-R	5-8	156	3-30-02	.189	.318	.189	14	45	37	2	7	0	0	0	1	7	0	1	0	13	1	1	15.6	28.9
Peguero, Fernando	S-R	5-9	145	12-27-04	.221	.319	.263	63	251	213	26	47	4	1	1	18	27	5	3	3	58	27	3	10.8	23.1
Ramos, Raylin	R-R	6-1	180	12-1-04	.258	.326	.348	96	396	353	45	91	12	4	4	50	30	6	5	1	100	15	7	7.6	25.3
Rodriguez, Miguel	R-R	5-11	160	12-29-05	.206	.357	.265	10	42	34	5	7	2	0	0	5	6	2	0	0	4	0	1	14.3	9.5
Sanchez, Jordan	L-L	6-1	176	10-9-05	.267	.267	.667	4	15	15	2	4	0	0	2	4	0	0	0	0	5	0	0	0.0	33.3
Smith, Brayden	L-R	6-0	190	12-15-03	.200	.343	.327	16	68	55	7	11	2	1	1	9	12	0	1	0	18	3	1	17.6	26.5
Sosa, Thomas	L-L	6-1	160	1-18-05	.237	.326	.316	10	43	38	3	9	1	0	0	5	4	1	0	0	12	1	2	9.3	27.9
Soto, Livan	L-R	5-10	160	6-22-00	.143	.400	.143	9	10	7	3	1	0	0	0	1	2	1	0	0	2	0	0	20.0	20.0
Tavera, Braylin	R-R	6-2	175	2-19-05	.226	.339	.336	108	443	372	51	84	14	3	7	44	58	8	1	4	135	18	9	13.1	30.5
Tess, Andrew	R-R	6-0	186	8-18-04	.233	.395	.300	11	39	30	2	7	2	0	0	1	6	2	1	0	14	1	1	15.4	35.9
Tromp, Chadwick	R-R	5-8	221	3-21-95	.222	.200	.333	3	10	9	2	1	0	0	0	1	0	0	0	1	2	0	0	0.0	20.0
Tuft, Colin	R-R	6-2	195	1-24-03	.207	.369	.280	56	207	164	26	34	5	2	1	13	37	5	1	0	58	19	7	17.9	28.0
Urman, Cole	R-R	6-1	195	7-28-01	.230	.331	.336	33	131	113	12	26	4	1	2	12	17	0	1	0	44	0	2	13.0	33.6
Velasquez, Alfredo	S-R	5-11	153	9-30-04	.275	.311	.351	191	180	23	45	2	3	1	9	6	1	2	1	17	5	1	7.6	8.9
Yeaman, Colin	R-R	6-2	200	4-15-04	.185	.366	.204	17	72	54	6	10	1	0	0	2	10	6	1	1	17	2	1	13.9	23.6

Pitching	B-T	Ht.	Wt.	DOB	W	L	ERA	G	GS	SV	IP	Hits	Runs	ER	HR	BB	SO	AVG	OBP	SLG	SO%	BB%	BF
Achen, Cohen	R-R	6-2	210	7-31-01	2	0	3.21	3	0	0	14	8	5	5	1	6	14	.170	.259	.319	25.9	11.1	54
Allsup, Chase	R-R	6-1	220	4-21-03	2	12	5.64	23	21	0	91	82	68	57	3	65	96	.239	.368	.350	22.8	15.4	421
Aracena, Wellington	R-R	6-3	180	12-27-04	0	0	0.00	1	1	0	5	1	0	0	0	1	6	.063	.118	.063	35.3	5.9	17
Bateman, Boston	R-L	6-8	240	9-20-05	0	0	2.45	2	2	0	7	11	2	2	0	2	6	.379	.455	.414	18.2	6.1	33
Bautista, Bryan	R-R	6-3	175	2-8-04	3	3	8.22	19	0	2	23	28	26	21	0	20	29	.253	.414	.330	25.0	17.2	116
Beck, Jared	L-L	7-0	225	7-4-02	1	2	1.56	15	0	1	17	10	7	3	2	18	23	.172	.359	.293	29.1	22.8	79
Beltran, Luis	R-R	6-4	175	4-6-04	0	1	5.16	20	0	1	23	14	13	13	0	22	38	.177	.374	.241	35.5	20.6	107
Beriguete, Randy	R-R	6-4	221	11-2-02	0	1	10.13	2	1	0	3	2	3	3	0	4	1	.222	.462	.667	7.7	30.8	13
Biller, Denton	R-R	6-4	215	12-8-04	0	0	0.00	2	0	0	6	2	0	0	0	4	4	.100	.250	.100	16.7	16.7	24
Cabarcas, Ryan	L-L	5-10	170	4-24-01	1	0	5.59	6	0	0	10	15	7	6	0	6	9	.385	.447	.410	19.1	12.8	47
Caldon, Michael	R-R	6-3	225	10-14-02	2	2	2.31	18	9	1	62	47	22	16	2	28	70	.205	.303	.262	26.5	10.6	264
Cartaya, Yeiber	R-R	6-5	165	1-20-03	3	4	3.56	19	11	0	78	50	40	31	2	50	96	.177	.324	.241	27.7	14.4	347
Correa, Eccel	R-R	6-0	170	2-1-05	1	3	3.31	8	3	0	33	33	20	12	1	14	35	.254	.329	.338	24.0	9.6	146
Cravey, Jacob	R-R	6-6	215	9-28-01	5	4	3.67	15	8	0	69	59	30	28	7	27	55	.231	.314	.396	19.1	9.4	288
Crowder, Jack	R-R	6-4	220	7-25-02	1	5	6.32	14	3	1	53	58	38	37	3	19	60	.282	.346	.388	25.5	8.1	235
Cruz, Deivy	L-L	5-11	154	2-13-04	3	1	3.57	29	0	2	35	6	17	14	1	31	40	.206	.375	.246	23.8	18.5	168
De Leon, Luis	L-L	6-3	168	10-14-03	0	0	4.09	4	0	0	11	6	6	5	0	8	4	.158	.306	.211	28.6	16.3	49
Delgado, Adrian	R-R	6-3	182	5-12-05	3	2	5.63	29	0	0	32	22	32	20	2	37	37	.191	.390	.296	23.3	23.3	159
Diederich, Sayer	L-L	6-1	190	10-10-00	1	2	3.29	10	1	0	27	23	12	10	1	7	39	.225	.279	.275	35.1	6.3	111
Dorsey, Carson	L-L	6-2	165	2-24-03	2	2	4.04	11	10	0	42	32	24	19	1	17	58	.206	.281	.271	33.1	9.7	175
Downer, Brandon	R-R	6-5	225	5-10-03	2	1	3.24	5	4	0	25	20	10	9	0	6	18	.217	.270	.250	18.0	6.0	100
Fabian, Andy	L-L	6-4	210	1-1-03	2	0	1.19	13	0	2	23	12	4	3	0	15	36	.156	.293	.169	38.7	16.1	93
Glassey, Joe	R-R	6-3	215	7-17-01	2	1	2.22	15	0	1	24	17	7	6	3	0	32	.191	.207	.348	34.8	0.0	92
Gongora, Sebastian	L-L	6-5	215	9-1-01	0	2	4.43	9	8	0	22	14	12	11	1	14	34	.173	.302	.259	35.4	14.6	96
Gonzalez, Javier	R-R	6-0	150	9-22-05	0	0	1.23	2	0	2	7	3	1	1	0	5	8	.115	.258	.192	25.8	16.1	31
Heid, Dylan	R-R	6-1	180	5-18-98	0	0	0.00	2	0	0	2	2	0	0	0	1	1	.222	.300	.222	10.0	10.0	10
Herberholz, Christian	R-R	5-11	195	10-5-01	1	1	6.14	5	0	0	7	7	5	5	0	3	8	.241	.313	.241	25.0	9.4	32
Heredia, Adrian	R-R	6-1	185	11-16-04	0	3	8.79	4	3	0	14	18	16	14	1	6	14	.300	.377	.417	20.0	8.6	70
Kirby, Devin	R-R	5-10	220	8-10-99	0	0	3.18	4	0	0	6	5	3	2	0	6	2	.278	.480	.278	8.0	24.0	25
Kniebbe, Todd	R-R	6-5	220	12-6-03	1	0	2.70	4	0	0	7	5	2	2	1	1	11	.200	.231	.480	42.3	3.8	26
Leandro, Alberto	R-R	6-3	171	4-24-02	2	1	6.00	21	0	3	30	24	24	20	2	15	26	.229	.317	.305	21.1	12.2	123
Leiner, Kenny	S-R	6-3	225	7-7-01	1	4	4.87	32	0	1	41	33	26	22	0	36	46	.226	.389	.247	24.2	18.9	190
Lord, Kiefer	R-R	6-3	195	6-22-02	0	0	3.52	3	0	0	8	6	3	3	0	7	12	.222	.400	.259	34.3	20.0	35
Mejia, Esteban	R-R	6-3	170	4-7-02	4	2	4.63	3	0	12	8	7	6	4	0	6	14	.195	.320	.244	27.5	11.8	51
Menard, Chipper	L-L	5-11	175	12-27-01	0	3	6.04	16	6	0	28	27	20	19	3	18	39	.252	.367	.402	30.2	14.0	129
Mesa, Miguel	R-R	6-2	188	2-5-03	0	0	9.00	1	0	0	1	1	1	1	0	1	1	.250	.400	.250	20.0	20.0	5
Morfe, Keeler	R-R	5-8	161	6-9-06	0	3	9.39	9	8	0	15	19	18	16	0	24	12	.190	.442	.224	14.0	27.9	86
Nolaya, Andres	R-R	6-1	185	3-27-05	0	0	3.60	3	0	0	5	4	2	2	0	4	3	.235	.364	.353	13.6	18.2	22
Palmer, Twine	R-R	6-5	200	8-31-04	0	2	9.15	5	5	0	20	22	22	20	2	11	20	.305	.406	.488	20.4	11.2	98
Rustad, Carter	R-R	6-4	194	4-23-01	0	0	1.46	7	0	1	12	6	5	2	0	9	16	.136	.296	.182	29.6	16.7	54
Salazar, Grabiel	R-R	6-0	165	2-19-01	0	1	6.35	4	0	0	6	5	7	1	2	3	.286	.333	.667	12.5	8.3	24
Sharp, Reese	R-R	6-3	220	8-7-00	0	0	0.93	5	0	0	10	7	1	1	0	6	9	.206	.325	.206	22.5	15.0	40
Smith, Tanner	R-R	6-6	245	8-5-02	0	2	6.00	4	0	0	6	7	4	4	0	7	7	.240	.345	.280	24.1	13.8	29
Stretch, Jacob	S-R	6-0	190	12-27-02	2	1	3.29	8	0	1	14	6	5	1	6	16	.286	.351	.367	28.1	10.5	57

Player	B-T	Ht	Wt	DOB			AVG																
Tavera, Carlos	R-R	6-1	195	10-6-98	0	0	9.45	6	1	0	7	12	7	7	0	4	7	.414	.486	.586	20.0	11.4	35
Turzenski, Trent	R-R	6-6	240	5-11-01	0	0	1.54	9	0	2	12	7	4	2	0	6	19	.175	.292	.225	39.6	12.5	48
Urman, Cole	R-R	6-1	195	7-28-01	0	0	0.00	1	0	0	2	0	0	0	0	0	0	.000	.000	.000	0.0	0.0	6
Vespi, Ben	R-R	6-3	190	5-28-01	3	2	3.02	22	2	1	51	51	18	17	2	18	68	.258	.326	.328	31.2	8.3	218
Yates, Evan	R-R	6-1	180	9-17-02	4	6	4.52	19	13	1	72	61	41	36	2	30	87	.222	.309	.302	28.0	9.6	311

Fielding

Catcher	PCT	G	PO	A	E	DP	PB
Bodine	.981	9	98	7	2	0	3
Bucce	.975	38	319	31	9	0	13
Irish	1.000	7	59	3	0	1	0
Nolaya	.976	40	347	24	9	6	10
Rodriguez	.968	6	57	4	2	0	1
Tess	.955	7	56	8	3	1	3
Tromp	1.000	2	18	1	0	0	0
Tuft	.984	22	235	15	4	3	6
Urman	.978	13	116	18	3	2	1

First Base	PCT	G	PO	A	E	DP
Almeyda	.963	6	48	4	2	4
Amparo	1.000	2	10	0	0	1
Austin	.966	5	26	2	1	0
Bucce	.983	32	222	12	4	14
Cuevas	.976	16	117	5	3	13
Guerrero	.949	11	70	5	4	2
Hernandez	1.000	1	3	0	0	0
Irish	.975	7	37	2	1	1
Liranzo	.950	5	35	3	2	2
Nolaya	.958	11	60	8	3	2
Ondina	1.000	2	12	1	0	3
Rodriguez	.955	4	20	1	1	3
Tess	1.000	4	20	0	0	1
Tuft	.991	16	105	8	1	13
Urman	.975	15	110	6	3	9
Yeaman	1.000	1	11	0	0	1

Second Base	PCT	G	PO	A	E	DP
Almeyda	.000	1	0	0	0	0
Amparo	.940	26	31	47	5	9
Amparo	1.000	3	3	9	0	2

Third Base	PCT	G	PO	A	E	DP
Austin	.957	7	11	11	1	2
Bencosme	1.000	2	2	4	0	0
Campos	.938	13	19	26	3	7
Guevara	.949	9	10	27	2	3
Hernandez	.973	8	17	19	1	3
Hightower	1.000	11	11	25	0	2
Ondina	.900	2	3	6	1	1
Peguero	.951	32	45	72	6	18
Smith	.958	7	6	17	1	3
Soto	.800	2	1	3	1	0
Velasquez	.953	16	29	32	3	4

Third Base	PCT	G	PO	A	E	DP
Almeyda	.840	25	16	47	12	2
Aloy	.875	3	4	3	1	0
Amparo	.958	10	8	15	1	0
Campos	.968	10	13	17	1	1
Guevara	.857	9	5	7	2	1
Hernandez	.938	23	16	45	4	3
Liranzo	.855	22	14	33	8	4
Nolaya	1.000	2	1	0	0	0
Ondina	.000	1	0	0	0	0
Peguero	.903	9	4	24	3	4
Velasquez	1.000	12	14	15	0	4
Yeaman	1.000	9	7	22	0	1

Shortstop	PCT	G	PO	A	E	DP
Almeyda	.978	14	15	29	1	3
Aloy	.977	11	16	26	1	3
Amparo	.905	7	11	8	2	3
Bencosme	1.000	1	3	2	0	1
Campos	.921	11	17	18	3	6
Guevara	1.000	2	2	7	0	2

Outfield	PCT	G	PO	A	E	DP
Almeyda	1.000	3	3	0	0	0
Amparo	.667	3	2	0	1	0
Amparo	1.000	1	1	0	0	0
Austin	1.000	5	10	0	0	0
Campos	1.000	4	4	0	0	0
Cuevas	.983	29	57	1	1	0
George	.961	40	70	4	3	0
Guerrero	.966	50	80	4	3	1
Guevara	.500	2	1	0	1	0
Haskin	1.000	1	1	0	0	0
Irish	.889	5	8	0	1	0
Liranzo	1.000	3	4	2	0	0
Martinez	.971	19	32	1	1	0
Nolaya	1.000	4	3	0	0	0
Ondina	.833	8	7	3	2	0
Peguero	1.000	17	26	1	0	0
Ramos	.986	82	131	6	2	2
Sanchez	1.000	3	4	0	0	0
Smith	1.000	8	14	2	0	0
Sosa	.923	7	11	1	1	0
Tavera	.942	102	169	9	11	3
Tuft	1.000	9	9	0	0	0
Velasquez	.909	12	19	1	2	0

FCL ORIOLES
FLORIDA COMPLEX LEAGUE — ROOKIE

Batting	B-T	Ht.	Wt.	DOB	AVG	OBP	SLG	G	PA	AB	R	H	2B	3B	HR	RBI	BB	HBP	SH	SF	SO	SB	CS	BB%	SO%
Almeyda, Luis	R-R	6-2	180	4-17-06	.246	.352	.377	20	71	61	10	15	6	1	0	18	8	2	0	0	14	6	1	11.3	19.7
Amparo, Edwin	S-R	6-0	165	10-14-04	.211	.318	.263	10	44	38	2	8	2	0	0	4	6	0	0	0	16	3	2	13.6	36.4
Amparo, Felix	R-R	5-10	180	2-27-06	.260	.364	.337	41	122	104	25	27	3	1	1	20	17	0	1	0	15	10	2	13.9	12.3
Aybar, Junior	L-R	6-0	145	7-14-06	.294	.400	.365	29	101	85	19	25	4	1	0	11	15	0	1	0	23	5	6	14.9	22.8
Bradfield, Enrique	L-L	6-1	170	12-2-01	.333	.455	.333	3	11	9	1	3	0	0	0	0	2	0	0	0	0	0	0	18.2	0.0
Cuevas, Elis	S-R	5-11	150	11-8-04	.333	.400	.444	3	10	9	2	3	1	0	0	0	1	0	0	0	2	0	0	10.0	20.0
Garcia, Elvin	S-R	6-2	165	1-18-07	.234	.365	.330	31	115	94	12	22	4	1	1	13	17	3	0	1	42	1	2	14.8	36.5
Garcia, Juan	R-R	5-11	165	9-2-06	.250	.500	.250	4	6	4	1	1	0	0	0	1	2	0	0	0	2	0	0	33.3	33.3
George, Nate	R-R	6-0	200	6-8-06	.383	.451	.556	23	92	81	20	31	1	2	3	14	9	1	1	0	14	13	6	9.8	15.2
Guevara, Luis	S-R	5-8	167	2-6-06	.300	.500	.500	4	10	6	3	3	0	1	0	3	3	0	1	0	2	2	1	28.6	14.3
Josenberger, Tavian	S-R	6-1	185	10-23-01	.500	.571	1.500	2	7	6	3	3	0	0	2	2	1	0	0	0	1	0	1	14.3	14.3
Layton, DJ	S-R	6-1	185	7-21-06	.183	.366	.231	40	135	104	28	19	5	0	0	5	25	5	1	0	37	10	1	18.5	27.4
Liranzo, Joshua	R-R	6-3	180	5-16-04	.292	.452	.417	24	94	72	21	21	2	1	1	10	18	3	1	0	19	3	5	19.1	20.2
Martinez, Steven	R-R	6-4	198	8-8-07	.217	.368	.362	49	191	152	29	33	7	3	3	20	33	4	1	5	54	2	4	17.3	28.3
Mejia, Adrianner	R-R	6-0	165	8-29-06	.268	.388	.351	35	122	97	17	26	5	0	1	15	17	4	1	3	27	3	0	13.9	22.1
Mejia, Jose	R-R	5-11	175	9-29-05	.274	.418	.411	47	158	124	22	34	9	1	2	23	26	6	0	2	16	6	5	16.5	10.1
Ortega, Juan	R-R	5-8	177	4-10-06	.264	.397	.436	41	136	110	22	29	3	2	4	19	21	4	0	1	30	11	4	15.4	22.1
Perez, Jose	L-R	5-10	150	5-15-05	.250	.455	.403	24	99	72	23	18	8	0	1	13	24	3	0	0	24	6	3	24.2	24.2
Romero, Noelberth	R-R	6-0	183	12-5-01	.167	.250	.167	3	8	6	0	1	0	0	0	3	1	0	0	1	3	0	0	12.5	37.5
Sanchez, Jordan	L-L	6-1	176	10-9-05	.293	.421	.529	54	195	157	36	46	3	5	5	45	31	5	2	0	57	3	2	15.9	29.2
Tess, Andrew	R-R	6-0	186	8-18-06	.256	.457	.368	54	188	133	33	34	5	2	2	27	34	7	0	3	39	17	4	18.1	20.7
Trimble, Reed	S-R	6-0	180	6-6-00	.333	.462	.667	3	13	9	3	3	0	0	1	5	3	0	0	1	3	0	0	23.1	23.1
Tuft, Colin	R-R	6-2	195	1-24-03	.250	.400	.375	4	12	8	1	2	1	0	0	1	4	0	0	0	0	0	0	33.3	0.0
Urbina, Omar	R-R	6-1	175	9-1-05	.262	.345	.377	26	74	61	14	16	2	1	1	5	10	0	0	2	15	0	0	13.5	20.3
Whitaker, Braylon	L-L	5-10	160	3-2-06	.154	.267	.154	8	15	13	0	2	0	0	0	5	2	0	0	0	3	2	0	13.3	20.0

Pitching	B-T	Ht.	Wt.	DOB	W	L	ERA	G	GS	SV	IP	Hits	Runs	ER	HR	BB	SO	AVG	OBP	SLG	SO%	BB%	BF
Akin, Keegan	L-L	6-0	240	4-1-95	0	0	0.00	1	1	0	1	0	0	0	0	2	.250	.250	.250	50.0	0.0	4
Baumler, Carter	R-R	6-2	195	1-31-02	0	0	3.38	2	0	0	3	1	1	0	0	2	.300	.462	.500	15.4	23.1	13
Bautista, Bryan	R-R	6-3	175	2-8-04	1	0	1.59	4	0	0	6	3	1	1	0	3	9	.143	.240	.238	36.0	12.0	25
Beltran, Luis	R-R	6-4	175	4-6-04	2	0	0.93	6	0	0	10	5	1	1	0	4	17	.147	.237	.206	44.7	10.5	38

BALTIMORE ORIOLES

Name	B-T	Ht	Wt	DOB			ERA										AVG	OBP	SLG			
Beriguete, Randy	R-R	6-4	221	11-2-02	1	1	3.52	6	0	0	8	6	4	3	0	7	7	.222	.421	.222	18.4	18.4	38
Bolivar, Angel	R-R	6-1	175	10-1-05	2	0	5.40	10	1	0	18	17	17	11	1	12	8	.246	.384	.391	9.3	14.0	86
Brnovich, Kyle	L-R	6-2	190	10-20-97	0	0	2.45	1	1	0	4	3	2	1	0	0	7	.214	.214	.286	50.0	0.0	14
Cabarcas, Ryan	L-L	5-10	170	4-24-01	0	0	2.84	5	0	1	6	7	2	2	0	5	9	.269	.387	.346	29.0	16.1	31
Castillo, Luis	R-R	6-3	212	3-10-95	0	0	3.38	2	2	0	3	4	1	1	0	0	5	.364	.364	.545	45.5	0.0	11
Diederich, Sayer	L-L	6-1	190	10-10-00	1	0	2.84	2	1	0	6	6	2	2	1	2	4	.250	.308	.375	15.4	7.7	26
Dorsey, Carson	L-L	6-2	165	2-25-03	0	0	4.50	1	1	0	2	2	1	1	0	3	0	.333	.556	.333	0.0	33.3	9
Downer, Brandon	R-R	6-5	225	5-10-03	0	0	4.32	5	3	1	17	14	11	8	2	7	17	.209	.293	.313	22.7	9.3	75
Eflin, Zach	R-R	6-6	220	4-8-94	0	0	0.00	1	1	0	4	3	5	0	0	1	5	.176	.211	.235	26.3	5.3	19
Fabian, Andy	L-L	6-4	210	1-1-03	0	1	2.12	13	1	2	17	11	4	4	0	12	26	.175	.307	.190	34.7	16.0	75
Glassey, Joe	R-R	6-3	215	7-17-01	0	0	0.00	1	0	0	2	1	0	0	0	1	3	.167	.286	.167	42.9	14.3	7
Gonzalez, Javier	R-R	6-0	150	9-22-05	2	3	6.82	11	4	1	32	34	26	24	2	14	33	.266	.345	.391	22.8	9.7	145
Heredia, Adrian	R-R	6-1	185	11-16-04	3	1	2.53	9	5	0	32	28	14	9	0	11	36	.233	.303	.292	27.1	8.3	133
Hernandez, Jakob	L-L	6-4	260	5-19-96	1	0	0.00	1	0	0	1	1	0	0	0	1	2	.250	.400	.250	40.0	20.0	5
Leandro, Alberto	R-R	6-0	171	4-24-02	3	0	2.45	4	0	0	7	8	4	2	0	4	5	.296	.375	.333	15.6	12.5	32
Magallanes, Fermin	R-R	6-7	170	2-17-02	2	0	0.00	9	0	2	9	2	0	0	0	10	10	.074	.324	.074	27.0	27.0	37
Mejia, Esteban	R-R	6-3	175	3-7-07	1	2	2.45	11	1	0	40	28	18	11	0	25	53	.190	.324	.238	30.1	14.2	176
Mejia, Jose	R-R	5-11	175	9-29-05	1	0	10.13	2	0	0	3	4	3	3	1	0	2	.333	.333	.583	16.7	0.0	12
Mora, Jeyderson	R-R	6-0	145	3-13-05	1	2	3.38	13	0	0	16	11	14	6	0	21	19	.180	.400	.213	22.4	24.7	85
Morao, Francisco	L-L	6-0	178	11-15-05	3	2	3.38	9	6	1	35	27	16	13	1	19	42	.209	.313	.287	27.8	12.6	151
Morfe, Keeler	R-R	5-8	161	6-9-06	0	0	2.84	3	2	0	6	4	3	2	0	8	12	.174	.406	.174	37.5	25.0	32
Naut, Harlin	R-R	6-2	161	4-26-05	3	2	2.30	11	2	0	31	20	13	8	2	11	24	.175	.269	.325	18.5	8.5	130
Palacios, Jesus	R-R	6-2	167	3-7-05	2	3	6.50	11	7	0	36	28	33	26	2	29	52	.215	.393	.338	30.1	16.8	173
Pham, Alex	R-R	5-11	165	10-10-99	0	0	18.00	1	0	0	1	1	2	2	0	1	2	.250	.400	.500	40.0	20.0	5
Rasquin, Juan	S-R	6-3	165	12-24-05	0	2	7.80	12	0	1	15	17	17	13	1	18	13	.293	.494	.345	16.0	22.2	81
Rodriguez, Aneuris	R-R	6-3	185	6-14-04	3	1	4.50	12	0	2	14	13	11	7	1	19	17	.224	.430	.310	21.5	24.1	79
Sanchez, Brayner	R-R	6-4	189	6-2-01	1	0	0.00	1	0	0	1	0	0	0	0	0	0	.000	.000	.000	0.0	0.0	4
Sharp, Reese	R-R	6-3	220	8-7-00	0	0	0.00	2	1	0	3	2	1	0	0	3	1	.167	.231	.167	23.1	7.7	13
Stretch, Jacob	S-R	6-0	190	12-27-02	1	0	0.00	3	0	0	6	1	0	0	0	5	9	.056	.261	.056	39.1	21.7	23
Tavera, Carlos	R-R	6-1	195	10-6-98	0	0	4.50	1	1	0	2	1	1	1	0	2	2	.167	.375	.500	25.0	25.0	8
Urbina, Omar	R-R	6-1	175	9-9-05	0	0	4.50	2	0	0	2	2	1	1	0	1	2	.250	.250	.625	12.5	0.0	8
Velasco, Kevin	R-R	6-11	155	1-11-06	1	3	3.75	11	8	0	36	38	21	15	3	12	34	.268	.333	.394	21.8	7.7	156
Virbitsky, Kyle	R-R	6-7	235	10-8-98	0	0	0.00	1	0	0	2	2	1	0	0	2	.333	.333	.500	33.3	0.0	6

Fielding

C: Tess 28, Ortega 24, Urbina 8, Garcia 2, Tuft 2. **1B:** Tess 19, Ortega 14, Urbina 14, E. Garcia 6, Liranzo 6, Almeyda 3, Cuevas 1, J. Garcia 1, Layton 1, Romero 1. **2B:** Layton 17, Mejia 16, F. Amparo 12, Garcia 7, Almeyda 4, Perez 3, E. Amparo 1, Guevara 1, Josenberger 1. **3B:** Mejia 17, Garcia 9, Liranzo 9, Perez 9, Almeyda 7, Amparo 6, Layton 4, Romero 2. **SS:** Layton 16, Perez 12, Garcia 9, Liranzo 7, Almeyda 6, E. Amparo 5, F. Amparo 5, Guevara 2. **LF:** Aybar 16, Amparo 12, Sanchez 11, Mejia 7, Martinez 5, Tess 5, Whitaker 4, George 2, Urbina 2, Garcia 1, Guevara 1. **CF:** Martinez 17, George 14, Sanchez 14, Aybar 10, Whitaker 3, Amparo 2, Bradfield 2, Trimble 1. **RF:** Sanchez 26, Martinez 16, George 7, Amparo 3, Aybar 3, Mejia 3, Tess 3, Cuevas 2, Whitaker 2, Trimble 1.

DSL ORIOLES BLACK
DOMINICAN SUMMER LEAGUE

Batting	B-T	Ht.	Wt.	DOB	AVG	OBP	SLG	G	PA	AB	R	H	2B	3B	HR	RBI	BB	HBP	SH	SF	SO	SB	CS	BB%	SO%
Brea, Anthwan	R-R	6-0	168	1-22-07	.129	.203	.210	23	70	62	8	8	0	1	1	5	6	0	1	1	24	2	1	8.6	34.3
Chirinos, Frainner	R-R	6-3	164	2-1-07	.210	.300	.258	26	71	62	9	13	3	0	0	2	3	5	1	0	22	7	1	4.2	31.0
Chirinos, Ricardo	R-R	6-0	180	2-7-08	.162	.333	.265	22	87	68	9	11	4	0	1	8	13	5	0	1	9	1	0	14.9	10.3
Flores, Jose	R-R	5-11	165	11-3-07	.157	.256	.200	24	84	70	7	11	3	0	0	9	9	1	2	2	27	1	0	10.7	32.1
Gomez, Saul	R-R	6-0	178	7-27-07	.333	.333	.333	1	3	3	0	1	0	0	0	0	0	0	0	0	2	0	0	0.0	66.7
Mieses, Starlin	R-R	6-0	175	3-14-08	.280	.464	.424	45	171	125	28	35	6	3	2	18	38	5	3	0	39	13	5	22.2	22.8
Pena, Jose	R-R	6-2	150	8-16-08	.240	.356	.341	51	206	167	28	40	11	0	2	23	30	3	1	5	42	14	6	14.6	20.4
Ramirez, Breiny	L-L	6-4	180	5-19-06	.056	.143	.056	10	21	18	3	1	0	0	0	1	2	0	0	1	8	1	0	9.5	38.1
Rincon, Alexander	L-L	6-2	175	9-16-06	.277	.356	.326	52	210	184	27	51	5	2	0	23	21	2	2	1	26	7	0	10.0	12.4
Saez, Victor	R-R	5-9	162	2-17-08	.179	.273	.179	15	45	39	4	7	0	0	0	3	5	0	1	0	9	1	0	11.1	20.0
Sanchez, Emilio	L-R	6-1	160	4-13-07	.214	.369	.260	53	220	173	33	37	4	2	0	6	40	3	3	1	62	20	5	18.2	28.2
Sanchez, Lisandro	R-R	6-0	198	9-2-07	.317	.395	.467	49	191	167	29	53	10	6	1	26	22	0	1	1	54	10	7	11.5	28.3
Terrero, Ronald	R-R	6-0	190	9-7-07	.257	.409	.284	30	93	74	15	19	2	0	0	4	17	2	0	0	22	5	2	18.3	23.7
Valdez, Argenis	R-R	6-3	160	1-15-07	.241	.343	.355	45	169	141	18	34	9	2	1	21	23	3	2	2	28	9	2	11.8	16.6
Valenzuela, Cleudis	L-R	5-10	160	11-9-06	.262	.364	.383	42	130	107	19	28	6	2	1	20	18	1	1	3	17	5	4	13.8	13.1
Vasquez, Manuel	R-R	5-11	183	3-21-08	.183	.355	.200	24	78	60	7	11	1	0	0	9	15	1	0	1	19	4	1	19.2	24.4

Pitching	B-T	Ht.	Wt.	DOB	W	L	ERA	G	GS	SV	IP	Hits	Runs	ER	HR	BB	SO	AVG	OBP	SLG	SO%	BB%	BF
Andujar, Luis	R-R	6-2	160	8-16-05	0	0	3.18	6	0	0	11	11	5	4	0	10	7	.256	.396	.326	13.2	18.9	53
Arias, Alberto	L-L	6-2	198	12-21-07	1	0	0.00	1	0	0	3	0	0	0	0	3	.000	.000	.000	33.3	0.0	9
Arias, Asael	R-R	6-2	172	9-13-05	0	1	4.87	14	0	1	20	9	20	11	0	20	20	.122	.333	.135	20.2	20.2	99
Benitez, Edgar	R-R	6-0	165	9-9-04	0	1	4.32	7	1	0	17	14	9	8	1	8	12	.226	.314	.306	16.9	11.3	71
Confidente, Roynel	R-R	6-2	170	4-28-08	3	2	9.33	15	0	1	18	24	27	19	1	22	17	.293	.463	.476	15.5	20.0	110
Cruz, Naykel	L-L	6-0	185	9-29-99	3	2	4.58	11	0	2	19	13	10	0	5	28	.244	.289	.308	33.7	6.0	83
De Jesus, Angel	R-R	6-2	158	10-19-05	3	2	9.00	15	0	1	20	18	23	20	2	16	16	.231	.384	.397	16.0	16.0	100
Espinoza, Luis	R-R	6-2	194	12-11-06	1	3	2.33	10	10	0	39	29	16	10	0	15	30	.200	.287	.234	18.3	9.1	164
Javier, Robinson	R-R	6-2	170	10-8-05	0	3	7.00	15	0	3	18	23	18	14	2	12	17	.303	.407	.461	18.7	13.2	91
Luna, Esteban	R-R	5-11	190	9-28-06	1	4	5.27	11	10	0	43	44	33	25	3	22	41	.257	.352	.380	20.6	11.1	199
Marmolejos, Jainer	R-R	6-0	165		0	1	5.73	10	0	0	33	30	31	21	1	21	30	.229	.374	.336	18.3	14.0	164
Medina, David	R-R	6-1	180	3-15-07	2	1	6.06	9	0	0	16	19	15	11	1	5	21	.279	.347	.412	28.0	6.7	75
Medina, Junior	R-R	6-2	180	5-31-07	2	0	3.38	12	0	2	19	18	9	7	2	11	13	.240	.352	.360	14.3	12.1	91

	B-T	Ht.	Wt.	DOB			AVG			G	PA	AB	R	H	2B	3B	HR	RBI	BB	HBP	SH	SF	SO	SB	CS	BB%	SO%
Moscoso, Elias	R-R	5-11	162	3-27-05	0	0	8.71			8	0	0	10	12	11	10	1	4	13	.279	.360	.442	26.0	8.0	50		
Pena, Emmanuel	R-R	6-0	145	12-6-07	0	5	7.99			11	11	0	33	36	35	29	1	33	27	.286	.433	.405	16.3	19.9	166		
Perez, Waner	R-R	5-11	178	12-10-05	0	2	5.79			10	0	1	19	23	19	12	0	14	9	.319	.440	.347	9.9	15.4	91		
Santos, Victor	L-L	6-0	153	4-19-07	0	2	6.21			10	10	0	33	30	28	23	0	32	36	.240	.407	.320	22.0	19.5	164		
Sosa, Laurens	R-R	6-2	185	11-15-07	0	0	0.00			1	0	0	3	0	0	0	0	0	3	.000	.111	.000	33.3	0.0	9		
Sosa, Raymond	R-R	6-4	185	5-3-06	3	2	6.35			15	0	2	23	20	17	16	1	19	21	.247	.392	.383	20.6	18.6	102		
Terrero, Ronald	R-R	6-0	190	9-7-07	0	0	0.00			1	0	0	0	0	0	0	0	0	0	.000	.000	.000	0.0	0.0	1		
Valencio, Darling	L-L	6-3	172	4-24-08	2	1	3.14			11	0	0	14	10	9	5	0	16	12	.196	.408	.216	16.9	22.5	71		
Valenzuela, Cleudis	L-R	5-10	160	11-9-06	0	0	8.10			3	0	0	3	5	3	3	0	1	2	.357	.438	.571	12.5	6.3	16		

Fielding
C: Flores 18, Vasquez 17, Chirinos 11, Saez 10. **1B:** Valenzuela 14, Valdez 13, R. Chirinos 11, Saez 5, Terrero 5, Vasquez 4, F. Chirinos 4, Flores 4, Gomez 1. **2B:** Valenzuela 26, Terrero 25, Sanchez 7, Pena 3. **3B:** Chirinos 21, Sanchez 18, Pena 16, Valenzuela 2. **SS:** Pena 30, Sanchez 27. **LF:** Valdez 20, Brea 15, Rincon 7, Sanchez 6, Mieses 5, Ramirez 5. **CF:** Rincon 36, Sanchez 19, Mieses 1. **RF:** Mieses 30, Sanchez 16, Valdez 7, Ramirez 2, Brea 1.

DSL ORIOLES ORANGE
DOMINICAN SUMMER LEAGUE

Batting	B-T	Ht.	Wt.	DOB	AVG	OBP	SLG	G	PA	AB	R	H	2B	3B	HR	RBI	BB	HBP	SH	SF	SO	SB	CS	BB%	SO%
Acosta, Yeison	S-R	5-11	190	9-22-07	.179	.350	.236	39	138	106	12	19	2	2	0	16	23	6	1	2	28	2	1	16.7	20.3
Astudillo, Christian	R-R	6-0	188	6-13-07	.236	.374	.338	44	182	148	28	35	9	0	2	27	26	7	0	1	25	0	0	14.3	13.7
Aybar, Junior	L-R	6-0	145	7-14-06	.250	.500	.250	4	6	4	1	1	0	0	0	1	2	0	0	0	1	0	0	33.3	16.7
Baro, Meykel	R-R	6-1	172	8-14-08	.190	.368	.324	33	137	105	24	20	1	2	3	21	25	5	1	1	45	12	1	18.2	32.8
Campusano, Hector	S-R	5-10	160	4-24-07	.305	.492	.344	44	187	131	33	40	3	1	0	30	49	1	4	2	27	19	3	26.2	14.4
Chirinos, Frainner	R-R	6-3	164	2-1-07	.200	.385	.200	4	14	10	4	2	0	0	0	0	2	3	0	1	3	1	1	21.4	21.4
Chirinos, Ricardo	R-R	6-0	180	2-7-08	.212	.341	.333	14	41	33	6	7	1	0	1	6	5	2	0	1	6	0	0	12.2	14.6
Cohen, Abraham	L-L	6-1	175	6-15-06	.254	.389	.356	20	72	59	9	15	6	0	0	9	12	1	0	0	16	2	0	16.7	22.2
Cordero, Fabian	L-L	5-10	176	3-6-08	.235	.339	.324	39	121	102	16	24	6	0	1	16	17	0	0	2	31	3	1	14.0	25.6
Corniel, Enmanuel	L-R	6-1	160	2-16-07	.057	.250	.086	19	45	35	5	2	1	0	0	2	9	0	1	0	13	0	0	20.0	28.9
De La Cruz, Wilfri	B-R	6-2	170	9-15-07	.235	.509	.352	13	55	34	8	8	2	1	0	8	20	0	0	1	12	6	2	36.4	21.8
Drullard, Jorge	L-R	5-10	154	10-4-07	.229	.383	.354	22	60	48	11	11	3	0	1	4	11	1	0	0	16	7	1	18.3	26.7
Garcia, Angel	R-R	6-2	195	11-13-06	.289	.403	.414	43	154	128	13	37	9	2	1	16	12	13	0	1	28	4	1	7.8	18.2
Garcia, Juan	R-R	5-11	165	9-2-06	.063	.286	.063	7	21	16	2	1	0	0	0	0	5	0	0	0	6	0	1	23.8	28.6
Gomez, Johanse	L-L	6-2	175	11-1-07	.137	.343	.221	45	176	131	14	18	7	2	0	18	37	5	1	2	52	4	3	21.0	29.5
Guillen, Frandy	R-R	6-0	188	10-10-07	.190	.268	.210	36	113	100	11	19	2	0	0	6	11	0	1	1	19	1	0	9.7	16.8
Herrera, Rayner	L-R	6-1	160	9-1-07	.184	.335	.336	40	156	125	19	23	3	2	4	25	25	4	1	1	45	12	4	16.0	28.8
Nuel, Jemone	S-R	6-0	150	1-3-07	.261	.433	.398	53	235	176	49	46	9	3	3	15	51	4	2	2	48	45	8	21.7	20.4
Perez, Jose	L-R	5-10	150	5-15-05	.200	.273	.300	7	11	10	3	2	1	0	0	0	1	0	0	0	2	0	0	9.1	18.2
Ramirez, Breiny	L-L	6-4	180	5-19-06	.261	.333	.348	10	27	23	7	6	2	0	0	2	2	1	0	1	4	0	1	7.4	14.8
Saez, Victor	R-R	5-9	162	2-17-08	.243	.404	.351	13	47	37	7	9	1	0	1	5	9	1	0	0	13	1	0	19.1	27.7

Pitching	B-T	Ht.	Wt.	DOB	W	L	ERA	G	GS	SV	IP	Hits	Runs	ER	HR	BB	SO	AVG	OBP	SLG	SO%	BB%	BF
Aybar, Junior	L-R	6-0	145	7-14-06	0	0	0.00	1	0	0	0	0	0	0	0	0	0	.000	.000	.000	0.0	0.0	1
Casado, Salvador	R-R	6-3	198	3-16-06	0	3	3.60	11	10	0	40	31	25	16	0	28	36	.205	.342	.212	19.3	15.0	187
Chirinos, Ricardo	R-R	6-0	180	2-7-08	0	0	0.00	1	0	0	1	0	0	0	0	1	1	.250	.400	.750	20.0	20.0	5
De Los Santos, David	R-R	6-1	179	10-6-05	1	3	4.97	10	9	0	38	31	29	21	2	26	29	.218	.358	.331	16.4	14.7	177
Diaz, Alexander	R-R	6-0	180	1-14-08	1	3	7.47	11	11	0	37	41	35	31	2	19	30	.281	.380	.384	17.4	11.0	172
Herrera, Ronal	R-R	6-2	180	3-10-03	1	2	4.15	5	0	1	9	5	4	4	0	1	10	.172	.194	.345	32.3	3.2	31
Marte, Edwin	R-R	6-1	160	5-7-07	0	4	5.09	11	9	0	35	34	27	20	1	24	42	.256	.387	.376	25.6	14.6	164
Ozoria, Julio	R-R	6-1	192	11-30-05	2	0	3.38	10	0	0	11	9	4	4	0	11	17	.225	.392	.275	32.7	21.2	52
Perdomo, Luis	R-R	6-0	176	1-27-07	2	0	3.86	11	1	0	21	16	10	9	1	8	21	.205	.287	.231	24.1	9.2	87
Perez, Jose	L-R	5-10	150	5-15-05	0	0	0.00	1	0	0	2	0	0	0	0	1	0	.400	.500	.400	0.0	16.7	6
Reyes, Anderson	R-R	6-2	200	4-7-08	0	0	6.75	5	0	0	7	11	6	5	0	8	7	.393	.528	.464	19.4	22.2	36
Rodriguez, Deimer	R-R	6-4	180	6-23-08	1	1	14.04	15	0	0	17	28	29	26	1	18	12	.384	.530	.562	12.0	18.0	100
Rubi, Reykelly	L-L	6-0	185	10-5-05	2	4	9.00	18	2	3	23	22	25	23	1	21	23	.253	.421	.356	20.2	18.4	114
Sandoval, Joismer	R-R	6-2	170	4-29-05	0	1	21.21	6	0	0	5	9	12	11	1	10	6	.409	.588	.545	17.6	29.4	34
Sierra, Luis	R-R	6-2	190	11-20-05	0	2	9.95	11	0	0	13	9	17	14	0	20	8	.209	.500	.326	10.7	26.7	75
Sosa, Ezequiel	R-R	6-0	180	4-8-05	1	1	15.70	15	0	0	14	13	31	25	0	28	11	.245	.538	.358	12.4	31.5	89
Sosa, Laurens	R-R	6-2	185	11-15-07	0	1	5.75	6	1	0	19	17	19	13	1	25	12	.221	.450	.299	10.8	22.5	111
Suero, Rafael	R-R	6-2	180	5-7-06	1	1	6.68	17	1	0	32	37	30	24	1	23	27	.301	.409	.455	17.5	14.9	154
Teran, Samuel	S-R	6-2	168	8-24-08	0	0	14.73	7	0	0	7	16	12	12	2	7	6	.457	.558	.714	13.6	15.9	44
Valenzuela, Esmerlyn	S-R	6-0	170	1-2-03	2	3	8.61	18	0	1	23	30	30	22	3	24	30	.319	.449	.479	23.8	19.0	126
Virla, Carlos	R-R	6-0	174	1-24-07	0	1	4.63	7	0	1	12	6	8	6	3	9	14	.162	.347	.459	28.6	18.4	49
Vizcaino, Santhony	R-R	6-5	160	10-18-03	3	2	5.64	13	0	0	22	19	17	14	0	11	14	.319	.411	.440	13.0	10.2	108
Zapata, Kelvin	L-L	6-1	155	5-30-08	0	3	4.62	11	11	0	39	29	26	20	0	39	48	.216	.407	.276	27.1	22.0	177

Fielding
C: Acosta 22, Astudillo 20, Saez 8, Chirinos 6, Garcia 3. **1B:** Acosta 15, Astudillo 15, Guillen 6, Campusano 5, Chirinos 5, Saez 5, Drullard 4, Perez 3, Garcia 2, Aybar 1. **2B:** Campusano 33, Drullard 14, Nuel 6, Baro 4, Chirinos 4, Guillen 1. **3B:** Guillen 29, Nuel 16, Baro 8, De La Cruz 8, Aybar 2, Perez 1. **SS:** Nuel 33, Baro 17, De La Cruz 8, Drullard 1. **LF:** Cordero 32, Herrera 9, Garcia 6, Gomez 5, Ramirez 5, Campusano 3, Cohen 2, Corniel 2. **CF:** Herrera 22, Gomez 18, Corniel 15, Cohen 10, Cordero 2. **RF:** Garcia 29, Gomez 18, Herrera 4, Cohen 2, Cordero 2, Corniel 2, Ramirez 2, Campusano 1

Boston Red Sox

SEASON SYNOPSIS: A season filled with drama brought an acrimonious end to Rafael Devers' Boston tenure, with an in-season trade to the Giants, as well as the highs and lows of a roster surprisingly dependent on rookies. A late injury to the best of them, Roman Anthony, sapped the lineup as Boston earned its first playoff spot since 2021 but lost in three games to the Yankees.

HIGH POINT: Boston traded Devers on June 15 and lost eight of its next 14 games before catching fire, reeling off a season-best 10-game win streak going into the all-star break. Anthony hit safely in all nine games he started in the streak, which included four double-digit scoring outbursts. It also included a three-hit Garrett Crochet 1-0 shutout of the Rays on July 12. He struck out nine en route to leading the majors with 255 while going 18-5, 2.59.

LOW POINT: Boston won the season series with the Yankees 9-4, going 5-2 at Yankee Stadium, but was without Anthony due to an oblique injury for the wild-card series. The Sox won the opener behind Crochet and Aroldis Chapman but scored just six runs in the series overall, losing 4-3 and then 4-0 when Yankees rookie and Massachusetts native Cam Schlittler dominated them for eight innings with 12 strikeouts.

NOTABLE ROOKIES: Top prospect Anthony lived up to his hype, striking out a lot (27.7%) but hitting .292/.396/.463 with eight homers in 303 plate appearances. Kristian Campbell, the 2024 Minor League Player of the Year, signed an eight-year, $60 million contract extension but spent the second half at Triple-A Worcester after a .223/.289/.371 start in the big leagues. While IF Marcelo Mayer (.674 OPS) had his moments before right wrist surgery sidelined him in late July, C Carlos Narvaez (.241/.306/.419, 15 HR) provided production behind the plate. RHPs Hunter Dobbins (4.13) and Richard Fitts (5.00) combined for 21 starts.

KEY TRANSACTIONS: The Sox traded prospects for key pieces in the offseason, getting Narvaez from the Yankees for prospect RHP Elmer Rodriguez-Cruz, while acquiring Crochet from the White Sox for four prospects, including Chase Meidroth, Braden Montgomery and Kyle Teel. When Boston signed Alex Bregman as a free agent, club president Craig Breslow told Devers he would move to DH, but after 1B Triston Casas was lost for the season with an April knee injury, the Sox tried but failed to convince Devers to move to first base, causing a rift that prompted Devers' trade to San Francisco.

OPENING DAY PAYROLL: $193,629,093 (12th)

PLAYERS OF THE YEAR

MAJOR LEAGUE
Garrett Crochet
LHP
18-5, 2.59 ERA
AL-leading 255 SO
and 205.1 IP

MINOR LEAGUE
Payton Tolle
LHP
(A +,AA,AAA)
3.04 ERA, 133 SO and
23 BB in 91.2 IP

ORGANIZATION LEADERS

Batting		*Qualifiers
MAJORS		
* AVG	Trevor Story	.263
* OPS	Jarren Duran	.774
HR	Trevor Story	25
RBI	Trevor Story	96
MINORS		
* AVG	Blaze Jordan, Worcester/Portland	.308
* OBP	Nick Sogard, Worcester	.393
* SLG	Blaze Jordan, Worcester/Portland	.495
* OPS	Blaze Jordan, Worcester/Portland	.872
R	Jhostynxon Garcia, Worcester/Portland	79
H	Franklin Arias, Portland/Greenville/Salem	133
TB	Jhostynxon Garcia, Worcester/Portland	204
2B	Mikey Romero, Worcester/Portland	33
3B	Starlyn Nunez, Salem	8
HR	Jhostynxon Garcia, Worcester/Portland	21
RBI	Mikey Romero, Worcester/Portland	76
BB	Nelson Taylor, Greenville	81
SO	Nathan Hickey, Worcester	141
SB	Ahbram Liendo, Portland	42

Pitching		#Qualifiers
MAJORS		
W	Garrett Crochet	18
# ERA	Garrett Crochet	2.59
SO	Garrett Crochet	255
SV	Aroldis Chapman	32
MINORS		
W	Connelly Early, Worcester/Portland	10
L	Jose De Leon, Worcester	9
# ERA	Tyler Uberstine, Worcester/Portland	3.58
G	Alex Hoppe, Worcester/Portland	44
GS	Hayden Mullins, Portland/Greenville	21
GS	Tyler Uberstine, Worcester/Portland	21
SV	Isaac Stebens, Greenville	9
SV	Isaiah Campbell, Worcester	9
IP	Tyler Uberstine, Worcester/Portland	121
BB	Adam Bates, Salem	59
SO	Tyler Uberstine, Worcester/Portland	137
# AVG	Blake Aita, Greenville/Salem	.215

2025 PERFORMANCE

General Manager: Craig Breslow. **Farm Director:** Brian Abraham. **Scouting Director:** Devin Pearson.

Class	Team	League	W	L	PCT	Finish	Manager
Majors	Boston Red Sox	American	89	73	.549	4 (15)	Alex Cora
Triple-A	Worcester Red Sox	International	76	73	.510	10 (20)	Chad Tracy
Double-A	Portland Sea Dogs	Eastern	64	71	.474	8 (12)	Chad Epperson
High-A	Greenville Drive	South Atlantic	66	66	.500	5 (12)	Liam Carroll
Low-A	Salem Red Sox	Carolina	56	74	.431	11 (12)	Ozzie Chavez
Rookie	FCL Red Sox	Florida Complex	25	34	.424	12 (15)	Chase Illig
Rookie	DSL Red Sox Blue	Dominican	32	22	.593	13 (52)	Amaury Garcia
Rookie	DSL Red Sox Red	Dominican	25	30	.455	31 (52)	Sandy Madera
Overall 2025 Minor League Record			**344**	**370**	**.482**	**19th (30)**	

ORGANIZATION STATISTICS

BOSTON RED SOX
AMERICAN LEAGUE

Batting	B-T	Ht.	Wt.	DOB	AVG	OBP	SLG	G	PA	AB	R	H	2B	3B	HR	RBI	BB	HBP	SH	SF	SO	SB	CS	BB%	SO%
Abreu, Wilyer	L-L	5-10	217	6-24-99	.247	.317	.469	115	417	373	53	92	17	0	22	69	40	0	1	3	101	6	3	9.6	24.2
Anthony, Roman	L-R	6-2	200	5-13-04	.292	.396	.463	71	303	257	48	75	18	1	8	32	40	5	0	1	84	4	1	13.2	27.7
Bregman, Alex	R-R	6-0	192	3-30-94	.273	.360	.462	114	495	433	64	118	28	0	18	62	51	9	0	2	70	1	1	10.3	14.1
Campbell, Kristian	R-R	6-3	191	6-28-02	.223	.319	.345	67	263	229	24	51	10	0	6	21	29	4	0	1	72	2	1	11.0	27.4
Casas, Triston	L-R	6-4	252	1-15-00	.182	.277	.303	29	112	99	5	18	3	0	3	11	11	2	0	0	27	0	0	9.8	24.1
Devers, Rafael	L-R	6-0	240	10-24-96	.272	.401	.504	73	334	272	47	74	18	0	15	58	56	4	0	2	76	1	1	16.8	22.8
Duran, Jarren	L-R	6-2	212	9-5-96	.256	.332	.442	157	696	620	86	159	41	13	16	84	60	12	1	3	169	24	6	8.6	24.3
Eaton, Nate	R-R	5-11	185	12-22-96	.296	.348	.383	41	90	81	16	24	4	0	1	4	6	1	1	1	19	9	2	6.7	21.1
Garcia, Jhostynxon	R-R	5-11	163	12-11-02	.143	.333	.286	5	9	7	0	1	0	0	0	2	0	0	0	0	5	0	0	22.2	55.6
Gonzalez, Romy	R-R	6-1	215	9-6-96	.305	.343	.483	96	341	315	47	96	23	3	9	53	18	3	0	5	81	6	5	5.3	23.8
Hamilton, David	L-R	5-10	175	9-29-97	.198	.257	.333	91	194	177	27	35	4	1	6	19	13	1	3	0	47	22	6	6.7	24.2
Lowe, Nathaniel	L-R	6-4	220	7-7-95	.280	.370	.420	34	119	100	14	28	6	1	2	16	15	1	0	3	29	0	0	12.6	24.4
Mayer, Marcelo	L-R	6-2	188	12-12-02	.228	.272	.402	44	136	127	20	29	3	1	6	18	8	0	0	1	41	0	2	5.9	30.1
Narvaez, Carlos	R-R	5-11	190	11-26-98	.241	.306	.419	118	446	403	51	97	27	0	15	50	38	1	2	2	111	1	1	8.5	24.9
Rafaela, Ceddanne	R-R	5-9	152	9-18-00	.249	.295	.414	156	587	546	84	136	34	4	16	63	28	8	3	2	117	20	5	4.8	19.9
Refsnyder, Rob	R-R	6-0	205	3-26-91	.269	.354	.484	70	209	182	29	49	12	0	9	30	24	1	0	2	54	3	0	11.5	25.8
Sabol, Blake	L-R	6-4	225	1-7-98	.125	.167	.188	8	18	16	2	2	1	0	0	1	1	0	0	1	7	0	0	5.6	38.9
Sanchez, Ali	R-R	6-1	200	1-20-97	.000	.000	.000	4	2	2	0	0	0	0	0	0	0	0	0	0	1	0	0	0.0	50.0
Sogard, Nick	S-R	6-1	180	9-9-97	.260	.317	.344	30	104	96	13	25	8	0	0	9	5	3	0	0	24	2	1	4.8	23.1
Story, Trevor	R-R	6-2	213	11-15-92	.263	.308	.433	157	654	612	91	161	29	0	25	96	33	7	1	1	176	31	5	5.0	26.9
Toro, Abraham	S-R	6-0	223	12-20-96	.239	.289	.371	77	284	259	33	62	13	0	7	27	14	6	0	5	42	2	1	4.9	14.8
Wong, Connor	R-R	6-1	181	5-19-96	.190	.262	.238	63	188	168	16	32	8	0	0	7	16	1	1	2	42	2	1	8.5	22.3
Yoshida, Masataka	L-R	5-8	176	7-15-93	.266	.307	.388	55	205	188	16	50	11	0	4	26	10	3	0	4	24	3	0	4.9	11.7

Pitching	B-T	Ht.	Wt.	DOB	W	L	ERA	G	GS	SV	IP	Hits	Runs	ER	HR	BB	SO	AVG	OBP	SLG	SO%	BB%	BF
Alcala, Jorge	R-R	6-3	205	7-28-95	0	0	3.31	19	0	0	16	19	11	6	4	8	18	.288	.355	.530	23.7	10.5	76
Bello, Brayan	R-R	6-1	170	5-17-99	11	9	3.35	29	28	0	167	147	71	62	16	59	124	.237	.314	.355	17.7	8.4	700
Bernardino, Brennan	L-L	6-4	180	1-15-92	4	3	3.14	55	3	1	52	39	23	18	1	26	43	.205	.306	.263	19.2	11.6	224
Buehler, Walker	R-R	6-2	185	7-28-94	7	7	5.45	23	22	0	112	120	72	68	22	55	84	.272	.363	.460	16.5	10.8	508
Burdi, Nick	R-R	6-3	225	1-19-93	0	0	0.00	4	0	0	5	5	0	0	0	2	5	.263	.333	.316	23.8	9.5	21
Campbell, Isaiah	R-R	6-4	230	8-15-97	0	0	7.04	6	0	0	8	13	6	6	1	1	3	.394	.429	.545	8.6	2.9	35
Chapman, Aroldis	L-L	6-4	218	2-28-88	5	3	1.17	67	0	32	61	28	9	8	3	15	85	.132	.189	.198	37.3	6.6	228
Criswell, Cooper	R-R	6-6	200	7-24-96	1	0	3.57	7	1	1	18	23	10	7	3	5	9	.311	.350	.459	11.3	6.3	80
Crochet, Garrett	L-L	6-6	230	6-21-99	18	5	2.59	32	32	0	205	165	62	59	24	46	255	.217	.264	.353	31.3	5.7	814
De Leon, Jose	R-R	6-0	220	8-7-92	1	0	4.05	1	1	0	7	8	3	3	1	3	8	.320	.393	.440	28.6	10.7	28
Dobbins, Hunter	R-R	6-2	185	8-30-99	4	1	4.13	13	11	0	61	61	30	28	6	17	45	.257	.313	.401	17.6	6.6	256
Early, Connelly	L-L	6-3	195	4-3-02	1	2	2.33	4	4	0	19	17	6	5	0	4	29	.230	.278	.243	36.7	5.1	79
Eaton, Nate	R-R	5-11	185	12-22-96	0	0	0.00	1	0	0	1	2	0	0	0	0	0	.500	.500	.750	0.0	0.0	4
Fitts, Richard	R-R	6-3	215	12-17-99	2	4	5.00	11	10	0	45	49	27	25	11	16	40	.251	.323	.456	20.5	8.2	195
Fulmer, Michael	R-R	6-3	224	3-15-93	0	0	10.13	1	0	0	3	4	3	3	1	2	3	.364	.462	.818	15.4	15.4	13
Giolito, Lucas	R-R	6-6	245	7-14-94	10	4	3.41	26	26	0	145	131	62	55	17	56	121	.239	.309	.377	19.7	9.1	613
Guerrero, Luis	R-R	6-0	215	8-5-00	0	1	4.15	13	0	0	17	9	8	8	0	14	10	.158	.319	.211	13.9	19.4	72
Harrison, Kyle	R-L	6-2	200	8-12-01	0	0	3.00	3	2	0	12	14	4	4	0	5	13	.280	.357	.340	23.2	8.9	56
Hendriks, Liam	R-R	6-0	235	2-10-89	0	2	6.59	14	0	0	14	12	11	10	3	6	12	.293	.385	.463	20.3	11.9	59
Hicks, Jordan	R-R	6-2	220	9-6-96	1	2	8.20	21	0	2	19	25	20	17	3	12	15	.321	.436	.513	15.5	12.4	97
Houck, Tanner	R-R	6-5	230	6-29-96	0	3	8.04	9	9	0	44	57	41	39	10	17	32	.318	.389	.531	15.8	8.4	203
Kelly, Zack	R-R	6-3	205	3-3-95	1	3	4.58	28	0	0	35	35	21	18	3	12	35	.261	.333	.396	23.0	7.9	152
Matz, Steven	R-L	6-2	201	5-29-91	0	0	2.08	21	0	1	22	17	6	5	4	2	12	.218	.247	.449	14.6	2.4	82
May, Dustin	R-R	6-6	180	9-6-97	1	4	5.40	6	5	0	28	35	18	17	5	13	26	.307	.391	.474	19.9	9.8	133
Moran, Jovani	L-L	6-1	167	4-24-97	0	0	6.75	2	0	0	4	5	3	3	0	3	5	.294	.400	.412	25.0	15.0	20
Murphy, Chris	L-L	6-1	175	6-5-98	3	0	3.12	23	0	0	35	21	12	12	4	20	30	.172	.311	.287	20.3	13.5	148
Newcomb, Sean	L-L	6-5	255	6-12-93	0	0	3.95	12	5	0	41	59	24	18	3	17	41	.327	.394	.423	21.6	8.9	190
Slaten, Justin	R-R	6-4	222	9-15-97	2	4	4.24	36	0	3	34	27	19	16	3	10	25	.214	.270	.310	18.2	7.3	137
Stock, Robert	L-R	6-1	260	11-21-89	0	0	10.13	2	0	0	3	4	3	3	1	4	1	.364	.533	.636	6.7	26.7	15

Tolle, Payton	L-L	6-6	250	11-1-02	0	1	6.06	7	3	0	16	18	12	11	5	8	19	.277	.351	.538	25.7 10.8 74
Toro, Abraham	S-R	6-0	223	12-20-96	0	0	18.00	1	0	0	1	4	2	2	0	1	0	.667	.625	1.000	0.0 12.5 8
Weissert, Greg	R-R	6-2	235	2-4-95	6	6	2.82	72	0	4	67	57	27	21	6	21	57	.227	.292	.355	20.5 7.6 278
Whitlock, Garrett	R-R	6-5	225	6-11-96	7	3	2.25	62	0	1	72	54	21	18	2	24	91	.206	.283	.260	31.1 8.2 293
Wilson, Justin	L-L	6-2	205	8-18-87	4	1	3.35	61	0	0	48	48	22	18	3	20	57	.262	.340	.366	27.5 9.7 207
Winckowski, Josh	R-R	6-4	202	6-28-98	0	1	3.86	6	0	0	12	11	7	5	0	5	9	.250	.327	.295	17.3 9.6 52

Fielding

Catcher	PCT	G	PO	A	E	DP	PB
Narvaez	.991	112	932	58	9	1	9
Sabol	.964	7	48	5	2	0	1
Sanchez	1.000	4	0	1	0	0	0
Wong	.988	61	408	16	5	2	2

First Base	PCT	G	PO	A	E	DP
Casas	.991	28	213	16	2	26
Gonzalez	.989	58	320	29	4	32
Lowe	1.000	31	193	13	0	16
Sogard	.989	12	83	4	1	9
Toro	.994	68	447	30	3	41
Wong	1.000	1	1	0	0	0

Second Base	PCT	G	PO	A	E	DP
Campbell	.968	59	88	127	7	26
Gonzalez	.978	42	43	91	3	15
Hamilton	.973	68	68	147	6	29
Mayer	1.000	8	10	19	0	3
Rafaela	.958	24	35	34	3	9
Sogard	1.000	8	12	11	0	3

Third Base	PCT	G	PO	A	E	DP
Bregman	.969	113	74	206	9	24
Eaton	1.000	12	3	15	0	2
Gonzalez	.000	2	0	0	1	0
Hamilton	.000	1	0	0	0	0
Mayer	.985	39	17	50	1	4
Sogard	1.000	9	3	7	0	1
Toro	.902	16	6	31	4	3

Shortstop	PCT	G	PO	A	E	DP
Hamilton	.972	12	10	25	1	4
Mayer	.500	2	0	1	1	0
Sogard	.000	2	0	0	0	0
Story	.970	156	219	397	19	89

Outfield	PCT	G	PO	A	E	DP
Abreu	.978	104	215	7	5	3
Anthony	.989	55	91	2	1	0
Campbell	1.000	9	13	0	0	0
Duran	.977	169	289	10	7	0
Eaton	1.000	25	26	1	0	1
Garcia	1.000	4	3	0	0	0
Rafaela	.985	141	319	8	5	0
Refsnyder	.984	45	61	2	1	0
Sogard	1.000	3	3	0	0	0
Yoshida	1.000	6	5	0	0	0

WORCESTER RED SOX — TRIPLE-A
INTERNATIONAL LEAGUE

Batting	B-T	Ht.	Wt.	DOB	AVG	OBP	SLG	G	PA	AB	R	H	2B	3B	HR	RBI	BB	HBP	SH	SF	SO	SB	CS	BB%	SO%
Abreu, Wilyer	L-L	5-10	217	6-24-99	.167	.286	.167	2	7	6	1	1	0	0	0	1	1	0	0	0	2	0	0	14.3	28.6
Anthony, Roman	L-R	6-2	200	5-13-04	.288	.423	.491	58	265	212	45	61	9	2	10	29	51	0	0	2	56	3	3	19.2	21.1
Binelas, Alex	L-R	6-1	225	5-26-00	.257	.366	.457	13	41	35	9	9	1	0	2	6	4	2	0	0	17	1	1	9.8	41.5
Campbell, Kristian	R-R	6-3	191	6-28-02	.273	.382	.417	73	319	271	46	74	11	2	8	38	38	10	0	0	84	4	0	11.9	26.3
Eaton, Nate	R-R	5-11	185	12-22-96	.290	.373	.483	94	400	348	64	101	25	3	12	55	37	11	0	4	88	15	6	9.3	22.0
Ferguson, Max	L-R	6-0	180	8-23-99	.279	.343	.459	19	68	61	7	17	5	0	2	9	6	0	1	0	17	3	0	8.8	25.0
Garcia, Jhostynxon	R-R	5-11	163	12-11-02	.271	.334	.498	81	351	317	60	86	12	3	18	58	27	4	1	2	102	3	0	7.7	29.1
Gonzalez, Romy	R-R	6-1	215	9-6-96	.000	.125	.000	2	8	7	1	0	0	0	0	0	1	0	0	0	0	0	0	12.5	0.0
Grandal, Yasmani	S-R	6-2	225	11-8-88	.256	.372	.397	23	94	78	8	20	5	0	2	16	13	2	0	1	15	0	0	13.8	16.0
Grissom, Vaughn	R-R	6-2	210	1-5-01	.270	.342	.441	96	418	370	69	100	24	0	13	48	37	6	0	5	73	9	2	8.9	17.5
Hamilton, David	L-R	5-10	175	9-29-97	.282	.356	.538	9	45	39	9	11	2	1	2	4	5	0	0	1	6	6	0	11.1	13.3
Hernandez, Ronaldo	R-R	6-1	230	11-11-97	.067	.125	.067	4	16	15	0	1	0	0	0	1	1	0	0	0	3	0	0	6.3	18.8
Hickey, Nathan	L-R	5-11	210	11-23-99	.234	.325	.408	128	514	448	45	105	23	2	17	75	59	3	0	4	141	2	0	11.5	27.4
Jordan, Blaze	R-R	6-2	220	12-19-02	.263	.341	.480	44	182	171	29	51	11	1	6	25	11	0	0	0	19	0	1	6.0	10.4
Kolozsvary, Mark	R-R	5-7	185	9-4-95	.455	.500	.727	7	24	22	3	10	3	0	1	8	2	0	0	0	3	0	0	8.3	12.5
Lira, Enderso	R-R	6-1	185	10-11-03	.333	.500	.333	2	4	3	1	1	0	0	0	0	1	0	0	0	2	0	0	25.0	50.0
Mayer, Marcelo	L-R	6-3	188	12-12-02	.271	.347	.471	43	193	170	31	46	5	1	9	43	20	1	0	2	38	2	0	10.4	19.7
McDonough, Tyler	S-R	5-8	180	4-2-99	.254	.328	.369	79	299	268	32	68	12	2	5	27	26	4	0	1	73	6	5	8.7	24.4
Noda, Ryan	L-L	6-3	217	3-30-96	.378	.519	.703	13	54	37	9	14	3	0	3	13	12	2	0	3	12	2	0	22.2	22.2
Romero, Mikey	L-R	5-11	175	1-12-04	.232	.276	.469	45	192	177	21	41	15	0	9	36	11	1	0	3	58	1	1	5.7	30.2
Rosier, Corey	L-R	5-10	180	9-7-99	.249	.366	.361	85	296	249	36	62	13	0	5	30	42	4	1	0	56	16	8	14.2	18.9
Sabol, Blake	L-R	6-4	225	1-7-98	.167	.281	.299	43	167	144	15	24	8	1	3	17	21	2	0	0	51	7	0	12.6	30.5
Sikes, Phillip	R-R	6-2	190	4-27-99	.200	.292	.335	59	195	170	22	34	5	0	6	20	16	7	0	2	69	4	2	8.2	35.4
Simas, Karson	R-R	5-11	175	6-2-02	.333	.406	.426	19	69	61	10	20	3	0	1	9	8	0	0	0	19	4	1	11.6	27.5
Sogard, Nick	S-R	6-1	180	9-9-97	.276	.393	.385	91	409	340	64	94	22	0	5	28	64	2	2	1	73	16	4	15.6	17.8
Thompson, Trayce	R-R	6-3	225	3-15-91	.226	.312	.405	94	388	341	48	77	20	1	13	44	42	2	0	3	128	11	1	10.8	33.0
Toro, Abraham	S-R	6-0	223	12-20-96	.272	.366	.473	51	216	184	31	50	9	2	8	27	27	2	0	3	56	3	0	12.5	25.9
Tromp, Chadwick	R-R	5-8	221	11-21-94	.135	.167	.183	28	104	96	6	13	3	0	0	8	6	0	0	2	29	2	0	5.8	27.9
Wong, Connor	R-R	6-1	181	5-19-96	.364	.429	.727	3	14	11	2	4	1	0	1	3	2	0	0	1	2	0	0	14.3	14.3
Yoshida, Masataka	L-R	5-8	176	7-15-93	.200	.333	.200	2	6	5	1	1	0	0	0	0	1	0	0	0	1	0	0	16.7	16.7
Zavala, Seby	R-R	5-11	205	8-28-93	.165	.274	.340	67	250	212	28	35	11	1	8	25	32	1	2	3	94	2	0	12.8	37.6

Pitching	B-T	Ht.	Wt.	DOB	W	L	ERA	G	GS	SV	IP	Hits	Runs	ER	HR	BB	SO	AVG	OBP	SLG	SO%	BB%	BF
Adames, Jose	R-R	6-2	165	1-17-93	3	2	6.69	30	0	2	35	33	30	26	7	22	39	.243	.368	.419	23.9	13.5	163
Adams, Austin	R-R	6-3	220	5-5-91	1	2	9.13	24	1	0	24	33	24	24	7	21	34	.320	.445	.466	26.6	16.4	128
Anderson, Jack	R-R	6-3	197	11-23-99	0	3	11.12	3	3	0	11	19	14	14	5	4	11	.365	.411	.712	19.6	7.1	56
Bello, Brayan	R-R	6-1	170	5-17-99	0	2	6.52	3	3	0	10	12	8	7	0	3	14	.300	.341	.375	31.8	6.8	44
Bernardino, Brennan	L-L	6-4	180	1-15-92	0	1	2.25	4	0	0	4	3	1	1	0	4	8	.200	.400	.267	40.0	20.0	20
Brand, Jonathan	R-R	5-9	200	2-20-00	0	0	0.00	1	0	0	1	0	0	0	0	4	0	4	0	1.000	1.000	2.000	0.0	80.0	5
Burdi, Nick	R-R	6-3	225	1-19-93	4	0	2.83	31	0	5	35	28	11	11	1	16	45	.214	.307	.282	30.0	10.7	150
Campbell, Isaiah	R-R	6-4	230	8-15-97	7	7	3.90	43	0	9	58	47	30	25	5	21	47	.290	.359	.416	18.1	8.1	260
Cellucci, Brendan	L-L	6-4	211	6-30-98	2	1	7.90	17	0	1	27	34	26	24	2	23	33	.306	.435	.468	23.9	16.7	138
Coffey, Isaac	R-R	6-1	205	6-21-00	1	2	6.10	37	0	0	25	27	20	17	8	5	18	.270	.342	.486	15.3	4.2	118
Criswell, Cooper	R-R	6-6	200	7-24-96	4	2	3.70	16	14	0	66	60	32	27	6	28	68	.247	.333	.370	24.5	10.1	277
De Leon, Jose	R-R	6-0	220	8-7-92	0	9	6.93	22	13	0	75	94	59	58	16	52	89	.261	.388	.485	24.6	14.4	362

BOSTON RED SOX

Pitcher	B-T	Ht.	Wt.	DOB	W	L	ERA	G	GS	CG	SV	IP	H	R	ER	BB	SO	AVG	OBP	SLG	BB/9	SO/9	BF
Dobbins, Hunter	R-R	6-2	185	8-30-99	1	0	6.39	3	1	0	13	11	9	9	4	6	7	.234	.321	.489	13.2	11.3	53
Drohan, Shane	L-L	6-3	195	1-7-99	5	1	2.27	12	11	0	48	32	13	12	4	16	67	.185	.258	.289	35.3	8.4	190
Early, Connelly	L-L	6-3	195	4-3-02	3	1	2.83	6	6	0	29	19	14	9	2	11	36	.184	.261	.301	30.8	9.4	117
Fitts, Richard	R-R	6-3	215	12-17-99	2	1	4.00	6	6	0	27	26	13	12	2	11	25	.260	.339	.350	21.6	9.5	116
Fulmer, Michael	R-R	6-3	224	3-15-93	0	2	3.09	3	2	0	12	7	6	4	1	6	18	.171	.292	.293	37.5	12.5	48
Giolito, Lucas	R-R	6-6	245	7-14-94	0	1	3.48	3	3	0	10	7	4	4	0	10	9	.200	.370	.343	19.6	21.7	46
Guerrero, Luis	R-R	6-0	215	8-5-00	2	1	4.39	21	0	1	27	17	14	13	5	17	23	.175	.302	.340	19.8	14.7	116
Harris, Hobie	R-R	6-3	212	6-23-93	1	3	4.15	31	0	5	39	39	22	18	7	21	43	.262	.347	.430	24.7	12.1	174
Harrison, Kyle	R-L	6-2	200	8-12-01	4	2	3.75	12	12	0	50	53	22	21	5	27	50	.266	.354	.392	21.8	11.8	229
Hendriks, Liam	R-R	6-0	235	2-10-89	0	0	0.00	2	2	0	2	1	0	0	0	1	4	.143	.250	.143	50.0	12.5	8
Hicks, Jordan	R-R	6-2	220	9-6-96	0	0	10.80	2	1	0	2	4	2	2	1	2	2	.444	.545	.778	18.2	18.2	11
Hoppe, Alex	R-R	6-1	200	12-17-98	0	2	4.76	37	0	5	45	45	26	24	4	24	56	.254	.345	.373	27.6	11.8	203
Houck, Tanner	R-R	6-5	230	6-29-96	0	3	8.44	4	3	0	11	15	10	10	2	6	11	.319	.418	.468	20.0	10.9	55
Jackson, Gabriel	R-R	6-2	180	9-7-01	0	0	0.00	1	0	0	3	1	0	0	0	1	2	.100	.182	.100	18.2	9.1	11
Kelly, Zack	R-R	6-3	205	3-3-95	1	1	6.15	21	1	3	26	23	18	18	3	20	30	.232	.369	.394	24.6	16.4	122
Mata, Bryan	R-R	6-3	238	5-3-99	3	3	5.08	42	0	2	67	73	44	38	6	39	93	.268	.373	.375	29.1	12.2	320
Mills, Wyatt	R-R	6-4	214	1-25-95	4	2	3.12	32	7	1	52	37	20	18	8	30	49	.200	.329	.346	21.7	13.3	226
Moran, Jovani	L-L	6-1	167	4-24-97	1	2	3.58	20	1	0	28	33	16	11	2	5	40	.292	.322	.407	33.9	4.2	118
Murphy, Chris	L-L	6-1	175	6-5-98	1	0	3.38	13	2	0	21	18	8	8	1	13	22	.237	.363	.355	24.2	14.3	91
Olds, Wyatt	R-R	6-0	183	8-5-99	3	2	5.91	34	0	1	53	37	38	35	9	39	59	.198	.356	.354	25.0	16.5	236
Penrod, Zach	L-L	6-2	210	6-16-97	0	1	5.68	6	2	0	6	7	4	4	1	6	7	.292	.452	.542	21.9	18.8	32
Perales, Luis	R-R	6-1	160	4-14-03	0	0	13.50	2	0	0	1	0	2	2	0	2	4	.000	.333	.000	66.7	33.3	6
Priester, Quinn	R-R	6-3	210	9-15-00	0	1	4.50	1	1	0	4	6	2	2	0	0	6	.333	.333	.389	31.6	0.0	19
Sandlin, David	R-R	6-4	215	2-21-01	4	2	7.61	15	1	0	24	35	22	20	3	13	21	.337	.420	.510	17.6	10.9	119
Sikes, Phillip	R-R	6-2	190	4-27-99	0	0	10.13	4	0	0	3	3	3	3	1	1	0	.300	.333	.600	0.0	8.3	12
Slaten, Justin	R-R	6-4	222	9-15-97	1	0	0.00	3	0	0	3	0	0	0	0	1	5	.091	.167	.091	41.7	8.3	12
Song, Noah	R-R	6-4	202	5-28-97	0	0	15.43	3	0	0	5	9	8	8	2	4	6	.391	.481	.826	22.2	14.8	27
Stock, Robert	L-R	6-1	260	11-21-89	5	4	3.92	19	15	0	85	77	43	37	5	36	96	.242	.336	.327	26.2	9.8	367
Tolle, Payton	L-L	6-6	250	11-1-02	1	1	3.60	3	3	0	15	11	7	6	2	2	17	.193	.220	.316	28.8	3.4	59
Uberstine, Tyler	R-R	6-1	200	6-19-96	4	4	3.56	19	15	0	91	84	40	36	16	37	102	.245	.326	.431	26.2	9.5	390
Van Belle, Brian	R-R	6-3	185	9-3-96	5	1	2.29	12	8	0	51	47	14	13	7	7	41	.240	.273	.378	20.0	3.4	205
Webb, Jacob	L-R	6-5	246	3-23-99	1	0	6.35	9	0	0	11	12	8	8	1	7	10	.267	.358	.400	18.9	13.2	53
Winckowski, Josh	R-R	6-4	202	6-28-98	0	1	2.21	5	3	0	20	20	7	5	3	2	18	.256	.275	.410	22.5	2.5	80

Fielding

Catcher	PCT	G	PO	A	E	DP	PB
Grandal	.990	20	181	10	2	3	0
Hernandez	.971	3	32	1	1	0	0
Hickey	1.000	4	35	0	0	0	0
Kolozsvary	1.000	6	33	1	0	0	1
Sabol	.989	29	262	12	3	1	7
Tromp	.988	25	244	8	3	2	1
Wong	1.000	3	33	2	0	0	1
Zavala	.989	64	605	31	7	3	4

First Base	PCT	G	PO	A	E	DP
Binelas	.952	4	19	1	1	1
Campbell	.981	32	198	10	4	14
Garcia	1.000	1	6	0	0	3
Gonzalez	1.000	1	4	0	0	0
Grissom	.977	12	78	6	2	12
Hickey	.998	72	461	30	1	55
Jordan	.991	14	100	7	1	11
Noda	1.000	5	37	4	0	5
Sogard	.970	6	30	2	1	2
Toro	.961	10	73	1	3	6

Second Base	PCT	G	PO	A	E	DP
Campbell	.949	11	18	19	2	6
Eaton	1.000	1	3	4	0	1
Ferguson	.953	14	13	28	2	6
Grissom	.973	49	67	110	5	29
Hamilton	.967	5	8	21	1	3
Mayer	.933	10	20	22	3	5
McDonough	.963	17	25	54	3	16
Romero	.945	19	31	38	4	7
Simas	1.000	8	18	21	0	7
Sogard	1.000	16	24	43	0	13
Toro	.917	3	3	8	1	1

Third Base	PCT	G	PO	A	E	DP
Binelas	1.000	1	0	1	0	0
Eaton	.905	32	26	50	8	11
Grissom	.923	13	6	18	2	2
Jordan	1.000	27	19	33	0	4
Mayer	1.000	4	3	4	0	1
Romero	.959	27	16	31	2	1
Sogard	.964	22	13	41	2	3
Toro	.957	29	17	28	2	2

Shortstop	PCT	G	PO	A	E	DP
Eaton	.935	10	14	29	3	8
Ferguson	.800	1	3	1	1	
Grissom	1.000	25	17	48	0	12
Hamilton	1.000	4	3	17	0	2
Mayer	.981	29	41	61	2	15
McDonough	.943	34	54	78	8	18
Simas	.667	3	1	1	1	1
Sogard	.961	47	50	96	6	28

Outfield	PCT	G	PO	A	E	DP
Abreu	1.000	1	2	0	0	0
Anthony	1.000	44	89	0	0	0
Binelas	.000	1	0	0	0	0
Campbell	.966	22	28	0	1	0
Eaton	.991	54	106	5	1	1
Ferguson	1.000	4	5	0	0	0
Garcia	.975	73	155	2	4	1
McDonough	.953	30	38	3	2	1
Noda	1.000	5	7	0	0	0
Rosier	1.000	81	135	3	0	2
Sikes	.989	56	88	2	1	0
Simas	1.000	7	15	0	0	0
Sogard	1.000	5	6	0	0	0
Thompson	1.000	88	134	5	0	1
Yoshida	1.000	1	3	0	0	0

PORTLAND SEA DOGS — *DOUBLE-A*
EASTERN LEAGUE

Batting	B-T	Ht.	Wt.	DOB	AVG	OBP	SLG	G	PA	AB	R	H	2B	3B	HR	RBI	BB	HBP	SH	SF	SO	SB	CS	BB%	SO%
Alcantara, Marvin	R-R	5-10	157	11-2-04	.226	.289	.298	87	357	319	31	72	15	1	2	32	31	0	0	7	58	4	2	8.7	16.2
Arias, Franklin	R-R	5-11	170	11-19-05	.261	.250	.435	10	48	46	4	12	2	0	2	8	0	0	0	2	6	1	1	0.0	12.5
Bleis, Miguel	R-R	6-0	170	3-1-04	.209	.263	.291	30	118	110	10	23	6	0	1	10	6	2	0	0	31	7	2	5.1	26.3
Brannon, Brooks	R-R	5-11	210	5-4-04	.224	.302	.385	38	159	143	20	32	8	0	5	16	15	1	0	0	54	1	0	9.4	34.0
Castro, Allan	S-R	6-0	170	5-24-03	.268	.353	.400	92	388	340	43	91	20	2	7	37	44	2	0	2	79	15	3	11.3	20.4
Chacon, Juan	R-R	6-1	171	12-4-02	.229	.311	.298	51	151	131	17	30	7	1	0	11	14	2	1	1	41	3	3	9.3	27.2
De Leon, Fraymi	S-R	5-10	170	9-28-04	.133	.200	.133	4	15	15	1	2	1	0	0	1	0	0	0	0	6	0	0	0.0	40.0
Ehrhard, Drew	R-R	5-11	185	1-16-99	.235	.300	.325	61	223	200	20	47	7	1	3	20	16	3	3	1	44	4	2	7.2	19.7
Ehrhard, Zach	R-R	5-11	190	1-21-03	.227	.305	.412	58	237	211	29	48	13	1	8	23	20	4	1	1	49	16	3	8.4	20.7
Ferguson, Max	L-R	6-0	180	8-23-99	.191	.320	.286	99	392	325	45	62	8	1	7	33	59	3	4	1	85	31	7	15.1	21.7

BOSTON RED SOX

Batting

Player	B-T	Ht.	Wt.	DOB	AVG	OBP	SLG	G	AB	R	H	2B	3B	HR	RBI	BB	SO	SB	CS	SLG%	OBP%	BB%	BF
Garcia, Jhostynxon	R-R	5-11	163	12-11-02	.256	.355	.393	33	138	117	19	30	5	1	3	17	18	1	0	2	29	4	1	13.0	21.0
Hernandez, Ronaldo	R-R	6-1	230	11-11-97	.198	.263	.308	26	101	91	9	18	4	0	2	8	8	0	0	23	0	1	7.9	22.8
Jordan, Blaze	R-R	6-2	220	12-19-02	.320	.415	.513	44	176	150	30	48	11	0	6	37	22	3	0	1	19	3	0	12.5	10.8
Kolozsvary, Mark	R-R	5-7	185	9-4-95	.192	.289	.425	23	83	73	8	14	5	0	4	9	9	1	0	0	25	1	0	10.8	30.1
Liendo, Ahbram	S-R	5-8	170	2-1-04	.239	.323	.308	120	463	406	56	97	12	2	4	32	48	4	1	4	112	42	7	10.4	24.2
Lira, Enderso	R-R	6-1	185	10-11-03	.100	.250	.400	4	12	10	1	1	0	0	1	2	2	0	0	0	2	0	0	16.7	16.7
Miller, Tyler	L-R	6-2	193	12-17-99	.201	.265	.355	82	311	279	31	56	11	4	8	34	24	2	1	5	75	2	1	7.7	24.1
Montero, Juan	R-R	5-11	180	6-10-02	.000	.000	.000	2	6	6	0	0	0	0	0	0	0	0	0	0	3	0	0	0.0	50.0
Ravelo, Luis	S-R	6-1	187	11-5-03	.162	.222	.222	31	108	99	9	16	3	0	1	10	8	0	0	1	40	0	0	7.4	37.0
Riemer, Justin	S-R	6-0	170	2-6-02	.222	.391	.278	6	24	18	5	4	1	0	0	2	5	0	1	0	5	0	1	20.8	20.8
Romero, Mikey	L-R	5-11	175	1-12-04	.254	.315	.440	66	297	268	40	68	18	4	8	40	23	2	2	2	74	4	2	7.7	24.9
Rosario, Ronald	R-R	6-0	175	1-1-03	.201	.278	.321	98	402	358	32	72	10	0	11	56	33	6	2	3	95	5	3	8.2	23.6
Rose, Caden	R-R	5-11	175	10-7-01	.287	.284	.286	86	290	243	34	39	6	3	6	14	30	14	1	2	119	11	4	10.3	41.0
Rosier, Corey	L-R	5-10	180	9-7-99	.263	.323	.474	16	65	57	8	15	6	0	2	16	6	0	0	2	15	2	0	9.2	23.1
Simas, Karson	R-R	5-11	175	6-2-01	.217	.282	.303	66	242	221	30	48	8	1	3	20	18	2	1	0	64	12	2	7.4	26.4
Tibbs, James	L-L	6-0	205	10-1-02	.207	.319	.267	30	138	116	16	24	2	1	1	7	19	1	0	2	39	2	1	13.8	28.3
Yoshida, Masataka	L-L	5-8	176	7-15-93	.333	.364	.333	3	11	9	1	3	0	0	0	3	0	0	0	0	1	0	0	9.1	9.1

Pitching

Pitcher	B-T	Ht.	Wt.	DOB	W	L	ERA	G	GS	SV	IP	Hits	Runs	ER	HR	BB	SO	AVG	OBP	SLG	SO%	BB%	BF
Adams, Cooper	L-R	6-3	205	6-14-00	2	0	0.69	10	0	1	26	15	4	2	1	3	25	.165	.208	.253	25.5	3.1	98
Anderson, Jack	R-R	6-3	197	11-23-99	2	5	3.58	23	4	3	75	70	36	30	7	18	90	.244	.288	.401	29.2	5.8	308
Bello, Brayan	R-R	6-1	170	5-17-99	0	0	8.31	1	1	0	4	6	4	4	1	1	7	.353	.421	.529	35.0	5.0	20
Bolden, Caleb	R-R	6-2	190	12-19-98	3	6	5.74	18	10	1	58	63	41	37	3	26	60	.278	.360	.396	22.6	9.8	265
Brand, Jonathan	R-R	5-9	200	2-20-00	1	3	3.48	20	0	2	31	30	17	12	3	12	41	.265	.323	.407	30.4	8.9	135
Bryant, Zach	R-R	6-1	210	6-5-98	1	3	6.14	32	0	3	48	47	40	33	6	21	50	.250	.335	.378	23.3	9.8	215
Cellucci, Brendan	L-L	6-4	211	6-30-98	0	0	0.00	1	0	0	2	1	0	0	0	0	2	.125	.125	.125	25.0	0.0	8
Coffey, Isaac	R-R	6-1	205	6-21-00	0	1	3.00	4	3	0	9	5	3	3	0	4	12	.161	.278	.226	33.3	11.1	36
Cruz, Yovanny	R-R	6-0	180	8-23-99	2	4	3.03	34	0	6	59	34	24	20	5	44	72	.171	.333	.271	28.2	17.3	255
Dean, Noah	L-L	6-2	185	3-10-01	0	0	0.00	1	0	0	3	1	0	0	0	1	1	.125	.222	.250	11.1	11.1	9
Dobbins, Hunter	R-R	6-2	185	8-30-99	0	0	1.80	1	1	0	5	2	1	1	0	0	8	.118	.118	.176	47.1	0.0	17
Early, Connelly	L-L	6-3	195	4-3-02	7	2	2.51	15	12	0	72	52	24	20	3	29	96	.202	.296	.314	32.3	9.8	297
Ehrhard, Drew	R-R	5-11	185	1-16-99	0	0	2.25	4	0	0	4	3	1	1	0	0	0	.188	.188	.313	0.0	0.0	16
Fitts, Richard	R-R	6-3	215	12-17-99	0	0	0.00	1	1	0	3	1	0	0	0	0	2	.364	.364	.364	18.2	0.0	11
Giolito, Lucas	R-R	6-6	245	7-14-94	0	1	7.71	2	2	0	7	11	6	6	1	3	6	.344	.400	.563	22.9	8.6	35
Guerrero, Luis	R-R	6-0	215	8-5-00	0	1	11.57	3	0	0	1	3	0	0	0	6	2	.125	.500	.125	14.3	42.9	14
Hendriks, Liam	R-R	6-0	235	2-10-89	0	0	0.00	1	0	0	1	0	0	0	0	1	1	.000	.050	.000	25.0	25.0	4
Holobetz, John	R-R	6-3	190	7-31-02	1	2	2.39	6	5	0	38	27	10	10	1	5	27	.205	.232	.273	19.6	3.6	138
Hoppe, Alex	R-R	6-1	200	12-17-98	1	1	3.94	7	0	1	16	14	8	7	1	10	17	.246	.357	.333	23.3	13.7	73
Houck, Tanner	R-R	6-5	230	6-29-96	1	0	0.00	1	1	0	5	3	0	0	0	0	4	.158	.158	.158	21.1	0.0	19
Jackson, Gabriel	R-R	6-2	180	9-6-01	1	1	4.97	15	1	1	29	34	16	16	2	17	15	.291	.390	.393	11.0	12.5	136
Juan, Jorge	R-R	6-8	300	3-6-99	1	5	4.78	22	0	0	32	28	21	17	4	33	35	.252	.432	.405	22.4	21.2	156
Kirwin, Danny	R-R	6-2	205	10-12-99	0	0	3.60	1	0	0	5	4	2	2	0	0	2	.211	.211	.316	10.5	0.0	19
Monegro, Yordanny	R-R	6-4	180	10-14-02	2	1	2.67	9	8	0	34	32	12	10	3	8	49	.250	.299	.336	35.8	5.8	137
Mullins, Hayden	L-L	6-4	194	9-14-00	7	2	2.44	18	18	0	85	51	26	23	6	48	96	.175	.299	.285	27.7	13.8	347
Murphy, Chris	L-L	6-1	175	6-5-98	0	0	2.25	3	1	0	4	4	1	1	0	1	2	.286	.333	.357	13.3	6.7	15
Olds, Wyatt	R-R	6-0	183	8-5-99	4	2	2.50	8	0	0	18	18	13	5	2	11	18	.257	.388	.357	20.9	12.8	86
Perales, Luis	R-R	6-1	160	4-14-02	0	0	0.00	1	1	0	1	0	0	0	0	0	1	.000	.000	.000	0.0	33.3	3
Rivera, Eduardo	L-L	6-7	237	6-13-03	1	5	3.40	10	9	0	42	34	20	16	2	30	40	.214	.346	.289	20.8	15.6	192
Rogers, Dalton	R-L	5-11	172	1-18-01	4	5	3.52	18	15	0	84	70	34	33	3	47	101	.228	.331	.313	28.0	13.0	361
Sandlin, David	R-R	6-4	215	2-21-01	5	4	3.61	17	13	0	82	70	33	33	7	27	86	.227	.290	.343	25.4	8.0	338
Sansone, Michael	R-R	5-9	195	11-10-99	0	0	0.00	1	0	0	3	1	0	0	0	0	1	.100	.100	.100	20.0	0.0	10
Sena, Reidis	R-R	5-10	160	4-7-01	5	2	3.46	25	2	6	42	27	18	16	1	30	49	.186	.326	.241	27.4	16.8	179
Smith, Adam	R-R	6-2	180	5-9-00	0	1	0.00	1	0	0	2	1	1	0	0	1	3	.125	.222	.125	33.3	11.1	9
Song, Noah	R-R	6-4	200	5-28-97	3	1	4.19	23	0	1	43	44	21	20	2	22	44	.273	.364	.385	23.3	11.6	189
Tolle, Payton	L-L	6-6	250	11-1-02	1	1	1.67	6	5	1	27	13	8	5	2	7	37	.144	.212	.244	37.4	7.1	99
Troye, Christopher	R-R	6-4	225	2-8-99	3	2	7.20	20	2	0	30	26	27	24	3	31	34	.248	.424	.371	23.6	21.5	144
Uberstine, Tyler	R-R	6-1	200	6-1-99	0	1	3.64	6	6	0	30	27	16	12	4	35	.241	.283	.321	29.2	3.3	120
Webb, Jacob	R-R	6-5	246	3-23-93	2	1	3.26	10	0	0	19	20	7	7	2	6	24	.263	.356	.382	27.6	10.3	87
Wehunt, Blake	R-R	6-6	240	11-9-00	2	8	5.68	17	16	0	63	64	45	40	8	29	76	.263	.346	.449	27.0	10.3	281
Wu-Yelland, Jeremy	L-L	6-2	210	6-24-99	2	0	3.18	10	0	2	34	23	12	12	4	11	51	.193	.292	.328	37.0	8.0	138

Fielding

Catcher	PCT	G	PO	A	E	DP	PB
Brannon	.982	17	145	15	3	0	1
Ehrhard	1.000	1	3	0	0	0	0
Hernandez	.979	14	130	7	3	2	0
Kolozsvary	.980	21	186	14	3	1	1
Lira	.952	4	39	1	2	1	1
Montero	.950	2	16	3	1	0	0
Rosario	.993	80	797	54	6	7	10

First Base	PCT	G	PO	A	E	DP
Brannon	1.000	10	73	4	0	10
Ehrhard	.995	22	171	10	1	18
Ferguson	.982	8	50	4	1	2

Second Base	PCT	G	PO	A	E	DP
Alcantara	.971	15	23	44	2	13
De Leon	.833	2	4	1	1	0
Ferguson	.994	41	64	105	1	31
Liendo	.966	19	30	56	3	11
Ravelo	.959	16	23	24	2	3
Riemer	1.000	1	0	2	0	1
Romero	1.000	9	19	12	0	4

Jordan	1.000	28	187	13	0	21
Miller	.996	64	431	22	2	33
Simas	1.000	3	27	1	0	4
Tibbs	1.000	6	29	2	0	5

| | | | | | | |

Rose	1.000	2	3	4	0	2
Simas	.983	33	42	74	2	15

Third Base	PCT	G	PO	A	E	DP
De Leon	.500	2	0	2	2	0
Ferguson	.833	3	2	3	1	0
Jordan	1.000	14	4	18	0	0
Liendo	.945	78	54	153	12	19
Miller	1.000	2	0	2	0	0
Ravelo	.906	13	7	22	3	2
Riemer	.833	2	0	5	1	0
Romero	.950	20	7	31	2	3
Simas	.933	5	4	10	1	1

Shortstop	PCT	G	PO	A	E	DP
Alcantara	.964	71	89	150	9	30
Arias	.977	10	8	35	1	11
Ferguson	.944	5	9	8	1	2
Liendo	.972	23	19	50	2	7
Romero	.925	20	29	33	5	9
Simas	.885	7	10	13	3	2

Outfield	PCT	G	PO	A	E	DP
Bleis	.973	28	66	5	2	0
Castro	.979	79	174	10	4	3
Chacon	.941	45	63	1	4	1
Ehrhard	1.000	51	96	2	0	0
Ferguson	.976	37	78	5	2	2
Garcia	.982	32	53	3	1	0
Liendo	1.000	1	1	0	0	0
Miller	1.000	5	2	0	0	0
Riemer	.875	3	7	0	1	0
Rose	1.000	81	138	7	0	2
Rosier	1.000	15	26	2	0	1
Simas	.962	18	22	3	1	1
Tibbs	.947	22	34	2	2	0
Yoshida	1.000	1	1	0	0	0

GREENVILLE DRIVE
SOUTH ATLANTIC LEAGUE

HIGH-A

BOSTON RED SOX

Batting	B-T	Ht.	Wt.	DOB	AVG	OBP	SLG	G	PA	AB	R	H	2B	3B	HR	RBI	BB	HBP	SH	SF	SO	SB	CS	BB%	SO%
Alcantara, Marvin	R-R	5-10	157	11-2-04	.271	.344	.331	32	131	118	17	32	4	0	1	15	11	2	0	0	17	4	3	8.4	13.0
Anderson, Antonio	S-R	6-3	205	6-28-05	.212	.279	.290	67	258	231	27	49	10	1	2	26	19	4	0	4	89	0	0	7.4	34.5
Arias, Franklin	R-R	5-11	170	11-19-05	.265	.329	.380	87	392	355	43	94	21	1	6	49	32	3	0	2	35	7	7	8.2	8.9
Bleis, Miguel	R-R	6-0	170	3-1-04	.226	.314	.422	77	325	287	48	65	15	1	13	41	35	2	0	1	75	20	4	10.8	23.1
Brannon, Brooks	R-R	5-11	210	5-4-04	.270	.313	.398	55	224	211	32	57	8	2	5	31	12	1	0	0	63	3	1	5.4	28.1
Chacon, Juan	R-R	6-1	171	12-4-02	.143	.250	.143	2	8	7	1	1	0	0	0	2	1	0	0	0	5	0	0	12.5	62.5
De Leon, Fraymi	S-R	5-10	155	9-28-04	.157	.263	.216	34	118	102	15	16	6	0	0	9	10	5	0	1	33	5	3	8.5	28.0
Diaz, Kelvin	R-R	5-11	148	3-17-03	.063	.167	.094	12	36	32	1	2	1	0	0	2	4	0	0	0	15	1	0	11.1	41.7
Ehrhard, Zach	R-R	5-11	190	1-21-03	.342	.471	.459	31	140	111	24	38	10	0	1	22	26	2	0	1	27	7	0	18.6	19.3
Encarnacion, Freili	R-R	6-1	181	1-26-05	.195	.267	.332	69	266	241	31	47	7	1	8	26	14	10	0	1	73	6	0	5.3	27.4
Feliz, Albert	R-R	6-2	200	4-13-02	.178	.239	.319	63	201	185	13	33	5	0	7	24	14	1	0	1	85	0	0	7.0	42.3
Garcia, Johanfran	R-R	5-10	196	12-8-04	.249	.327	.428	46	196	173	27	43	4	0	9	28	18	3	0	2	60	1	0	9.2	30.6
Godbout, Henry	R-R	6-1	185	11-6-03	.341	.473	.477	13	55	44	6	15	6	0	0	5	9	2	0	0	6	1	1	16.4	10.9
Gonzales, Justin	R-R	6-4	210	12-31-06	.186	.265	.186	11	49	43	5	8	0	0	0	4	4	1	0	1	11	1	3	8.2	22.4
Johnson, Kolby	R-L	5-6	165	9-8-99	.180	.275	.180	19	69	61	5	11	0	0	0	3	7	1	0	0	16	2	1	10.1	23.2
Lugo, Andy	R-R	5-11	160	3-15-04	.265	.327	.430	44	171	151	16	40	11	1	4	20	14	2	0	4	40	4	1	8.2	23.4
Martin, Max	R-R	6-0	180	9-29-03	.325	.426	.400	11	47	40	5	13	3	0	0	9	6	1	0	0	14	0	2	12.8	29.8
Montero, Juan	R-R	5-11	180	6-10-02	.203	.330	.230	24	88	74	9	15	2	0	0	8	13	1	0	0	25	0	0	14.8	28.4
Musett, Andruw	R-R	5-10	198	11-21-05	.197	.275	.279	19	69	61	3	12	2	0	1	5	7	0	0	1	22	0	0	10.1	31.9
Riemer, Justin	S-R	6-0	170	2-6-02	.232	.423	.275	76	279	207	33	48	6	0	1	16	64	6	0	2	55	9	2	22.9	19.7
Rodriguez, Yophery	L-L	6-1	185	12-5-05	.214	.312	.331	101	433	378	44	81	17	6	5	48	52	2	0	1	81	10	6	12.0	18.7
Simas, Karson	R-R	5-11	175	6-2-01	.400	.500	.400	2	6	5	0	2	0	0	0	1	0	1	0	0	2	1	0	0.0	33.3
Taylor, Nelson	L-L	6-1	180	1-22-03	.216	.355	.349	108	473	384	62	83	24	3	7	41	81	4	0	4	133	29	12	17.1	28.1
Turner, Will	L-L	6-1	190	9-07-00	.287	.344	.266	43	163	124	15	20	4	0	3	14	36	0	0	3	36	4	1	22.1	22.1
White, Hudson	R-R	6-1	200	8-9-02	.188	.269	.283	70	271	240	25	45	7	2	4	25	23	5	0	3	68	1	0	8.5	25.1
White, Mason	L-R	5-9	171	9-21-03	.239	.338	.299	18	77	67	11	16	4	0	0	4	10	0	0	0	17	1	1	13.0	22.1
Zanetello, Nazzan	R-R	6-2	190	5-25-05	.173	.309	.275	82	356	295	52	51	12	4	10	36	52	6	0	3	132	17	3	14.6	37.1

Pitching	B-T	Ht.	Wt.	DOB	W	L	ERA	G	GS	SV	IP	Hits	Runs	ER	HR	BB	SO	AVG	OBP	SLG	SO%	BB%	BF
Adams, Cooper	L-R	6-3	205	6-14-00	2	3	3.95	21	1	2	43	42	26	19	2	20	55	.256	.335	.384	29.3	10.6	188
Aita, Blake	R-R	6-4	215	6-11-03	3	4	3.78	13	10	0	64	45	32	27	9	21	54	.194	.264	.358	20.9	8.1	258
Allmer, Jay	R-R	6-6	215	6-27-02	1	0	4.50	1	0	0	2	1	1	1	0	3	2	.200	.556	.200	22.2	33.3	9
Brand, Jonathan	R-R	5-9	200	2-24-05	3	0	0.89	12	0	3	20	11	3	2	1	4	18	.151	.192	.192	23.1	5.1	78
Carlson, Max	R-R	6-1	190	9-13-01	3	1	4.08	11	2	0	35	39	21	16	4	6	49	.271	.298	.438	32.5	4.0	151
Clarke, Brandon	L-L	6-4	225	4-10-03	0	3	5.08	11	11	0	28	15	20	16	0	25	43	.150	.370	.180	31.2	18.1	138
Cohen, Luis	R-R	6-0	172	5-6-03	1	2	5.32	7	3	0	24	24	14	14	5	7	18	.264	.324	.495	17.8	6.9	101
Dean, Noah	L-L	6-2	185	3-10-01	2	6	5.68	22	15	1	63	51	49	40	9	48	81	.219	.382	.361	27.4	16.2	296
Drohan, Shane	L-L	6-3	195	1-7-99	0	1	8.53	3	3	0	6	8	6	6	1	5	10	.320	.438	.520	30.3	15.2	33
Ehrlicher, Austin	L-R	6-5	185	6-2-03	1	0	0.96	6	4	0	19	9	3	2	0	14	20	.148	.325	.180	26.0	18.2	77
Feliz, Albert	R-R	6-2	200	4-13-02	0	3	20.25	6	0	0	7	6	18	15	3	14	3	.300	.581	.850	7.0	32.6	43
Fogell, Zach	L-L	5-11	190	7-23-00	2	0	3.78	8	0	0	17	13	11	7	2	9	18	.210	.338	.339	24.3	12.2	74
Futrell, Devin	L-L	6-5	200	9-20-02	2	1	1.09	5	5	0	25	20	6	3	0	4	12	.213	.253	.234	12.1	4.0	99
Garcia, Darvin	R-R	6-3	170	4-25-99	1	4	10.65	21	0	1	36	39	46	43	2	38	36	.271	.449	.375	18.3	19.3	197
Guerrero, Luis	R-R	6-0	215	8-5-00	0	0	0.00	2	0	0	2	0	0	0	0	1	3	.000	.300	.000	30.0	20.0	10
Holobetz, John	R-R	6-3	190	7-31-02	4	2	3.43	12	11	0	63	69	29	24	8	10	62	.276	.305	.432	23.7	3.8	262
Ingrassia, Joseph	L-L	6-1	170	7-24-02	0	2	3.18	4	0	0	17	10	7	6	3	4	21	.175	.242	.404	33.9	6.5	62
Kelly, Zack	R-R	6-3	205	3-3-95	0	0	0.00	2	1	0	2	0	0	0	0	2	0	.000	.143	.000	28.6	0.0	7
Kirwin, Danny	R-R	6-2	205	10-12-99	6	5	5.18	27	4	2	66	59	39	38	6	23	62	.244	.339	.364	21.8	8.1	284
Labriola, P.J.	L-L	6-7	220	11-13-00	0	0	13.50	1	0	0	1	1	1	1	0	1	0	.333	.500	.333	0.0	25.0	4
McShane, Matt	R-R	6-4	220	11-17-02	2	0	3.54	14	0	2	28	24	13	11	1	7	36	.224	.274	.318	30.3	5.9	119
Medina, Manuel	L-L	5-10	140	3-25-02	3	1	3.58	13	2	1	38	33	16	15	2	12	38	.237	.310	.302	24.5	7.7	155
Moran, Jovani	L-L	6-1	167	4-24-97	0	2	5.79	4	2	0	5	4	3	3	0	3	11	.222	.391	.333	47.8	13.0	23
Mullins, Hayden	L-L	6-0	194	9-14-00	1	0	1.06	4	3	0	17	11	2	2	1	3	27	.186	.238	.288	42.9	4.8	63
Murphy, Chris	L-L	6-1	190	6-5-98	0	0	0.00	2	2	0	2	1	0	0	0	0	6	.143	.125	.125	50.0	20.0	10
Paez, Jedixson	R-R	6-1	170	1-17-04	0	0	2.79	7	7	0	19	18	6	6	4	3	23	.228	.265	.418	27.7	3.6	83
Rivera, Eduardo	L-L	6-7	237	6-13-03	3	1	1.61	10	6	0	45	21	10	8	2	16	68	.138	.234	.197	39.5	9.3	172
Rivera, Erik	R-R	6-2	200	1-4-01	2	1	7.33	21	1	2	47	41	40	38	5	36	60	.237	.384	.347	27.8	16.7	216
Rogers, Dalton	R-L	5-11	172	1-18-01	2	1	1.31	5	1	0	21	15	6	3	0	8	28	.187	.173	.277	32.6	11.6	86
Sansone, Michael	L-L	5-9	195	11-10-99	3	5	3.84	16	7	0	66	66	31	28	8	13	50	.259	.298	.404	18.2	4.7	275
Smith, Adam	R-R	6-2	180	5-9-00	7	3	3.44	31	3	3	73	52	29	28	5	29	72	.198	.285	.319	24.2	9.7	298
Song, Noah	R-R	6-4	200	5-28-97	0	0	0.00	1	1	0	1	0	0	0	0	1	1	.167	.286	.167	14.3	14.3	7
Sprague, Shea	R-L	6-3	185	1-3-03	2	4	3.67	12	6	0	54	46	23	22	3	19	43	.240	.327	.333	19.7	8.7	218

Stebens, Isaac	L-R	6-0	194	12-5-01	6	0	2.15	38	0	9	50	35	14	12	3	29	59	.198	.335	.299	27.4	13.5	215
Tolle, Payton	L-L	6-6	250	11-1-02	1	3	3.62	11	10	0	50	44	20	20	6	14	79	.234	.291	.378	38.3	6.8	206
Tygart, Brady	R-R	6-2	205	1-12-03	0	1	2.25	1	1	0	4	2	1	1	0	5	.143	.143	.357	35.7	0.0	14
Valera, Juan	R-R	6-3	205	5-18-06	1	2	5.45	10	10	0	38	43	25	23	6	10	46	.281	.329	.444	27.5	6.0	167
Vogatsky, Joe	R-R	6-0	215	12-27-01	0	1	2.92	7	0	1	12	13	4	4	1	3	14	.260	.309	.360	25.5	5.5	55
Webb, Jacob	L-R	6-5	246	3-23-99	1	0	0.93	6	0	1	10	6	1	1	0	5	12	.176	.282	.235	30.8	12.8	39
Wu-Yelland, Jeremy	L-L	6-2	210	6-24-99	1	1	3.09	7	0	2	12	10	4	4	0	5	20	.222	.314	.311	39.2	9.8	51

Fielding

Catcher	PCT	G	PO	A	E	DP	PB
Brannon	.988	32	314	24	4	1	4
Garcia	.991	35	297	27	3	2	4
Montero	1.000	3	37	1	0	0	0
Musett	.992	15	111	8	1	1	2
White	.989	49	512	33	6	3	6

First Base	PCT	G	PO	A	E	DP
Anderson	.974	22	141	7	4	9
Brannon	.964	7	48	5	2	5
Encarnacion	.988	30	232	13	3	23
Feliz	.984	53	358	18	6	17
Lugo	.979	21	126	11	3	5
Montero	1.000	5	19	0	0	2
White	1.000	1	1	0	0	0

Second Base	PCT	G	PO	A	E	DP
Alcantara	.945	15	20	32	3	5
Arias	1.000	4	7	8	0	1
De Leon	.976	21	29	52	2	6
Encarnacion	1.000	3	2	10	0	1
Godbout	1.000	6	5	8	0	1

	PCT	G	PO	A	E	DP
Martin	.967	6	10	19	1	4
Riemer	.980	36	41	58	2	14
White	1.000	7	15	19	0	5
Zanetello	.979	37	53	85	3	12

Third Base	PCT	G	PO	A	E	DP
Alcantara	1.000	9	4	12	0	0
Anderson	.900	45	28	62	10	4
De Leon	.950	8	5	14	1	1
Encarnacion	.920	38	29	51	7	3
Lugo	.976	16	15	25	1	2
Montero	.000	1	0	0	1	0
Riemer	.923	19	15	33	4	2
Simas	.000	1	0	0	0	0

Shortstop	PCT	G	PO	A	E	DP
Alcantara	.957	8	8	14	1	2
Arias	.982	75	99	168	5	32
De Leon	1.000	1	2	1	0	0
Godbout	1.000	3	2	4	0	0
Martin	.000	1	0	0	0	0
Riemer	1.000	2	1	3	0	1

	PCT	G	PO	A	E	DP
White	.913	8	9	12	2	2
Zanetello	.923	35	47	73	10	9

Outfield	PCT	G	PO	A	E	DP
Bleis	.985	71	130	5	2	0
Chacon	1.000	2	3	0	0	0
De Leon	.800	4	8	0	2	0
Diaz	1.000	8	13	0	0	0
Ehrhard	1.000	27	41	2	0	0
Gonzales	1.000	11	21	0	0	0
Johnson	1.000	18	32	2	0	0
Lugo	1.000	4	5	0	0	0
Martin	1.000	4	11	0	0	0
Montero	1.000	3	4	0	0	0
Riemer	1.000	16	19	0	0	0
Rodriguez	.982	92	149	13	3	1
Simas	1.000	1	2	0	0	0
Taylor	.958	100	196	9	9	1
Turner	.971	38	64	2	2	0
Zanetello	.857	3	5	1	1	0

SALEM RED SOX — LOW-A
CAROLINA LEAGUE

Batting	B-T	Ht.	Wt.	DOB	AVG	OBP	SLG	G	PA	AB	R	H	2B	3B	HR	RBI	BB	HBP	SH	SF	SO	SB	CS	BB%	SO%
Anderson, Antonio	S-R	6-3	205	6-28-05	.345	.436	.488	22	101	84	18	29	6	0	2	17	15	0	0	2	22	1	2	14.9	21.8
Arias, Franklin	R-R	5-11	170	11-19-05	.346	.407	.397	19	86	78	15	27	4	0	0	9	6	2	0	0	12	4	1	7.0	14.0
Asencio, Yosander	S-R	5-11	160	11-14-04	.185	.333	.321	61	225	184	30	34	6	2	5	15	41	0	0	0	91	5	2	18.2	40.4
Ayubi, Karim	R-R	6-2	165	12-8-03	.230	.315	.311	50	181	161	22	37	9	2	0	10	16	4	0	0	64	2	3	8.8	35.4
Azocar, Eddy	R-R	6-2	168	2-24-07	.202	.273	.314	71	287	258	34	52	9	1	6	26	21	5	1	2	67	11	2	7.3	23.3
Berry, Caleb	R-R	5-9	180	9-5-05	.375	.423	.375	7	26	24	3	9	0	0	0	2	2	0	0	0	3	0	0	7.7	38.5
Cespedes, Yoeilin	R-R	5-9	181	9-8-05	.227	.292	.376	110	477	428	56	97	24	5	10	54	41	1	0	6	101	11	6	8.6	21.2
De Leon, Fraymi	S-R	5-10	155	9-28-04	.217	.260	.268	50	174	157	22	34	3	1	1	17	11	0	1	5	46	11	5	6.3	26.4
Diaz, Kelvin	R-R	5-11	148	3-17-03	.176	.250	.324	36	121	108	17	19	4	0	4	16	10	1	0	1	32	9	4	8.3	26.4
Encarnacion, Freili	R-R	6-1	181	5-26-05	.303	.363	.566	45	193	175	34	53	14	1	10	32	11	6	0	1	39	5	3	5.7	20.2
Fermin, Anderson	S-R	5-11	174	9-2-06	.040	.286	.040	8	35	25	4	1	0	0	0	1	8	1	0	1	12	3	0	22.9	34.3
Gonzales, Justin	R-R	6-2	210	12-31-06	.298	.381	.423	81	357	312	45	93	23	2	4	27	35	8	0	2	52	11	7	9.8	14.6
Jimenez, Frederik	R-R	6-0	178	11-15-04	.196	.307	.292	98	368	312	37	61	9	0	7	31	44	8	0	4	106	12	6	12.0	28.8
King, Skylar	L-L	6-1	175	11-21-03	.258	.359	.382	25	103	89	15	23	2	3	1	9	7	7	0	0	12	7	2	6.8	17.5
Linarez, Yohander	S-R	5-11	160	3-19-05	.221	.262	.293	43	149	140	13	31	3	2	1	15	7	1	0	1	41	2	2	4.7	27.5
Martin, Max	R-R	6-0	180	9-29-03	.224	.345	.347	14	58	49	8	11	3	0	1	5	8	1	0	0	20	4	2	13.8	34.5
Musett, Andruw	R-R	5-10	198	11-21-05	.257	.340	.356	75	321	284	39	73	10	6	6	35	34	2	0	1	71	1	0	10.6	23.4
Nunez, Starlyn	S-R	6-0	155	10-10-05	.249	.306	.407	110	444	405	54	101	24	8	8	52	27	8	0	4	91	21	6	6.1	20.5
Ortiz, D'Angelo	R-R	6-1	190	7-4-04	.261	.340	.284	28	100	88	9	23	2	0	0	10	11	0	0	1	22	2	0	11.0	22.0
Rodriguez, Gerardo	R-R	5-10	172	3-2-05	.277	.372	.500	22	86	74	9	22	4	1	3	11	9	1	0	2	13	1	0	10.5	15.1
Salazar, Kleyver	R-R	6-1	187	5-1-06	.215	.327	.276	99	404	344	34	74	9	0	4	36	56	2	0	2	82	4	3	13.9	20.3
Viloria, Diego	R-R	5-10	165	2-23-03	.200	.200	.200	8	5	5	0	1	0	0	0	0	0	0	0	0	1	0	0	0.0	20.0
White, Mason	L-R	5-9	171	9-21-03	.235	.278	.265	8	36	34	1	8	1	0	0	1	2	0	0	0	9	2	0	5.6	25.0
Winnay, Jack	R-R	6-3	210	6-5-03	.321	.393	.434	15	61	53	10	17	3	1	1	11	6	1	0	1	6	0	0	9.8	9.8
Yuten, Natanael	L-L	6-2	143	10-9-04	.270	.333	.391	99	369	330	42	89	21	5	3	39	28	6	0	5	94	10	6	7.6	25.5

Pitching	B-T	Ht.	Wt.	DOB	W	L	ERA	G	GS	SV	IP	Hits	Runs	ER	HR	BB	SO	AVG	OBP	SLG	SO%	BB%	BF
Aita, Blake	R-R	6-4	215	6-11-03	2	3	4.24	10	9	0	51	46	26	24	4	9	45	.240	.279	.354	22.0	4.4	205
Allmer, Jay	R-R	6-6	215	6-27-02	5	1	2.79	28	0	4	52	30	19	16	1	30	28	.178	.317	.219	13.6	14.6	206
Bates, Adam	R-R	6-1	165	8-8-05	3	4	5.04	22	6	0	80	68	56	45	7	59	65	.226	.358	.349	17.5	15.9	372
Bello, Jose	R-R	6-1	164	5-29-05	1	1	3.09	7	4	0	23	12	8	0	15	17	.247	.352	.258	15.7	13.9	108
Bickerstaff, Calvin	R-R	6-5	205	1-22-02	3	2	4.36	22	0	3	43	41	26	21	1	15	49	.247	.317	.325	25.8	7.9	190
Bouchard, Alex	R-R	6-3	210	8-11-03	0	2	3.63	6	2	0	17	15	7	7	0	18	10	.238	.398	.317	12.0	21.7	83
Brooks, Steven	R-R	6-6	185	9-20-02	3	6	5.29	16	16	0	63	50	38	37	5	42	62	.219	.347	.346	22.4	15.2	277
Clarke, Brandon	L-L	6-4	225	4-10-03	0	0	0.93	3	3	0	10	2	1	1	0	2	17	.061	.139	.091	47.2	5.6	36
Cohen, Luis	R-R	6-0	172	5-26-03	4	2	3.88	16	11	0	67	60	33	29	4	26	50	.235	.321	.339	17.3	9.0	289
Cruz, Nathanael	R-R	6-2	175	2-4-03	1	2	5.08	20	0	3	28	29	18	16	2	19	31	.269	.385	.407	23.1	14.2	134
De La Cruz, Nicolas	L-L	6-4	252	11-18-05	2	3	4.63	32	0	3	47	47	31	24	1	34	44	.263	.382	.346	19.9	15.4	221
De Leon, Fraymi	S-R	5-10	155	9-28-04	0	0	0.00	1	0	0	0	0	0	0	0	1	0	.000	.500	.000	0.0	50.0	2
Ehrlicher, Austin	L-R	6-5	185	6-2-03	3	3	3.22	15	8	0	45	30	17	16	0	25	53	.195	.310	.253	28.8	13.6	184

	B-T	Ht.	Wt.	DOB	W	L	ERA	G	GS	SV	IP	Hits	Runs	ER	HR	BB	SO	AVG	OBP	SLG	SO%	BB%	BF
Fajardo, Yhoiker	R-R	6-3	181	10-3-06	1	3	2.98	13	13	0	51	43	21	17	0	20	59	.229	.302	.309	27.8	9.4	212
Futrell, Devin	L-L	6-5	200	9-20-02	1	4	2.37	12	12	0	38	33	15	10	2	10	28	.234	.288	.355	18.3	6.5	153
Galle, Patrick	R-R	6-2	190	4-5-04	0	0	5.06	3	0	0	5	4	5	3	1	7	3	.200	.407	.350	11.1	25.9	27
Gartrell, Joey	R-R	6-4	215	7-9-03	3	4	6.81	14	5	0	36	32	29	27	2	31	34	.241	.407	.323	19.7	17.9	173
Hansen, Ben	R-R	6-6	210	3-12-02	1	7	6.23	18	15	0	61	78	49	42	4	28	47	.322	.403	.417	16.9	10.1	278
Judice, Nicholas	R-R	6-8	212	4-8-01	0	0	24.30	6	0	0	3	5	11	9	1	16	4	.333	.706	.600	11.8	47.1	34
Kilander, Griffin	R-R	6-5	205	6-30-03	6	5	4.34	20	6	1	64	50	33	31	3	38	58	.216	.336	.328	20.9	13.7	277
Labriola, P.J.	L-L	6-7	220	11-13-00	0	0	3.51	17	0	4	26	24	11	10	0	15	30	.250	.371	.323	25.6	12.8	117
Linarez, Yohander	S-R	5-11	160	3-19-05	0	0	0.00	1	0	0	0	0	0	0	0	1	0	.000	.000	.000	100.0	0	1
McShane, Matt	R-R	6-4	220	11-17-02	3	0	0.63	7	0	0	14	10	2	1	0	4	20	.185	.241	.204	34.5	6.9	58
Medina, Manuel	L-L	5-10	140	3-25-02	1	3	4.95	10	0	1	20	17	16	11	1	8	31	.224	.314	.329	35.6	9.2	87
O'Donnell, Trennor	R-R	6-7	240	6-6-01	1	3	4.70	7	2	0	23	25	15	12	1	13	24	.275	.362	.385	22.6	12.3	106
Polanco, Eybersson	R-R	6-0	170	9-3-03	4	5	5.23	36	0	5	62	62	45	36	2	31	71	.248	.334	.360	24.6	10.7	289
Rodriguez, Wuilliams	R-R	6-2	199	11-3-05	1	0	6.00	9	0	1	12	18	9	8	2	7	8	.340	.429	.491	12.7	11.1	63
Sansone, Michael	R-L	5-9	195	11-10-99	1	2	2.75	10	0	2	20	17	6	6	3	1	22	.233	.240	.342	29.3	1.3	75
Song, Noah	R-R	6-4	200	5-28-97	0	0	0.00	3	2	0	4	0	0	0	0	6	0	.000	.000	.000	50.0	0	12
Sprague, Shea	R-L	6-3	185	1-3-03	2	2	4.01	10	3	0	43	40	22	19	0	16	48	.250	.326	.306	26.4	8.8	182
Travieso, Jesus	R-R	5-11	140	3-22-07	2	0	3.51	7	6	0	26	31	16	10	2	11	38	.287	.350	.407	31.7	9.2	120
Tygart, Brady	R-R	6-2	205	1-12-03	1	2	3.52	5	4	0	15	13	7	6	0	7	22	.228	.348	.263	31.9	10.1	69
Viloria, Diego	R-R	5-10	165	2-23-03	0	1	9.64	5	0	1	5	6	8	5	0	7	2	.333	.571	.389	7.1	25.0	28
Vogatsky, Joe	R-R	6-0	215	12-27-01	1	4	4.87	30	0	1	57	55	35	31	7	32	65	.253	.357	.415	25.5	12.5	255

Fielding

Catcher	PCT	G	PO	A	E	DP	PB
Berry	1.000	4	26	2	0	0	2
Musett	.971	49	370	30	12	2	6
Rodriguez	.973	13	125	18	4	1	4
Salazar	.981	62	564	54	12	1	13
Viloria	.955	2	21	0	1	0	0

First Base	PCT	G	PO	A	E	DP
Anderson	1.000	1	6	1	0	1
Ayubi	.985	8	63	1	1	3
Encarnacion	.974	18	141	6	4	11
Jimenez	.981	89	620	49	13	54
Ortiz	1.000	17	102	6	0	6
Rodriguez	.950	3	18	1	1	3
Salazar	1.000	1	8	1	0	0

Second Base	PCT	G	PO	A	E	DP
Arias	1.000	1	3	4	0	2
Cespedes	.963	92	165	230	15	34
De Leon	.940	11	17	30	3	6
Encarnacion	.889	5	5	11	2	1
Linarez	1.000	4	5	10	0	1
Martin	1.000	2	2	5	0	0
Nunez	.924	17	20	41	5	8
Ortiz	1.000	1	0	1	0	0
White	1.000	1	0	1	0	0

Third Base	PCT	G	PO	A	E	DP
Anderson	.952	17	10	30	2	2
De Leon	.974	17	15	23	1	3
Encarnacion	.930	18	13	27	3	3
Linarez	.929	35	33	45	6	1
Nunez	.875	21	7	21	4	0
Ortiz	.813	10	3	10	3	1
Winnay	.893	14	13	12	3	2

Shortstop	PCT	G	PO	A	E	DP
Arias	.986	16	26	43	1	8
Cespedes	.900	6	7	11	2	4
De Leon	.938	21	35	55	6	11
Linarez	.900	4	5	4	1	0
Martin	.897	9	7	19	3	1
Nunez	.926	69	115	159	22	35
White	1.000	7	8	18	0	2

Outfield	PCT	G	PO	A	E	DP
Asencio	.964	60	103	5	4	0
Ayubi	.986	41	64	4	1	1
Azocar	.978	63	128	6	3	2
Diaz	.945	33	83	3	5	2
Fermin	.900	8	9	0	1	0
Gonzales	.969	65	121	2	4	0
Jimenez	.900	11	9	0	1	0
King	.981	24	50	3	1	2
Yuten	.953	92	141	2	7	0

FCL RED SOX — ROOKIE
FLORIDA COMPLEX LEAGUE

Batting	B-T	Ht.	Wt.	DOB	AVG	OBP	SLG	G	PA	AB	R	H	2B	3B	HR	RBI	BB	HBP	SH	SF	SO	SB	CS	BB%	SO%
Azocar, Enddy	R-R	6-2	168	2-24-07	.385	.448	.558	14	58	52	6	20	7	1	0	5	6	0	0	0	11	4	1	10.3	19.0
Baker, Tavano	L-L	5-11	160	10-13-06	.179	.359	.359	33	117	92	17	20	6	2	1	12	21	3	0	0	27	14	0	17.9	23.1
Barry, Justin	R-R	5-11	159	8-9-06	.220	.286	.402	26	91	82	16	18	6	0	3	16	7	1	0	1	31	7	0	7.7	34.1
Brito, Edwin	R-R	5-11	195	11-23-06	.141	.252	.212	32	115	99	8	14	7	0	0	12	10	5	0	1	38	2	2	8.7	33.0
Cason, Conrad	R-R	6-1	190	8-7-06	.250	.250	.250	2	4	4	0	1	0	0	0	0	1	0	0	0	0	0	0	0.0	50.0
Cruz, Yan	L-L	6-1	180	10-31-06	.155	.335	.248	43	164	129	14	20	4	1	2	12	34	1	0	0	79	1	4	20.7	48.2
Fermin, Anderson	S-R	5-11	174	9-2-06	.283	.454	.377	48	185	138	32	39	7	3	0	14	42	3	0	2	35	25	6	22.7	18.9
Fernandez, Ilan	R-R	6-0	180	10-30-06	.234	.331	.315	38	130	111	21	26	4	1	1	9	15	2	0	2	27	13	2	11.5	20.8
Garcia, Johanfran	R-R	5-10	196	5-18-04	.316	.433	.632	12	42	38	10	12	3	0	3	13	1	1	0	2	8	0	0	2.4	19.0
Gonzales, Justin	R-R	6-4	210	12-31-06	.000	.000	.000	1	4	4	0	0	0	0	0	0	0	0	0	0	2	0	0	0.0	50.0
Linarez, Yohander	S-R	5-11	160	3-19-05	.333	.429	.472	14	42	36	7	12	2	0	1	9	6	0	0	0	4	4	2	14.3	9.5
Lugo, Jesus	R-R	6-0	170	10-25-06	.200	.333	.300	7	24	20	2	4	0	0	0	4	4	0	0	0	5	2	0	16.7	20.8
Mambel, Alexander	R-R	6-0	191	8-4-06	.250	.358	.477	17	53	44	7	11	4	0	2	9	4	4	0	1	15	0	1	7.5	28.3
Marin, Liosward	L-R	5-10	158	5-15-06	.250	.280	.417	11	25	24	3	6	4	0	0	2	1	0	0	0	6	0	0	4.0	24.0
Noria, Franyer	R-R	5-10	135	9-24-04	.173	.323	.231	23	65	52	9	9	3	0	0	4	9	3	0	1	5	5	1	13.8	7.7
Ortiz, D'Angelo	R-R	6-1	190	7-4-06	.273	.384	.305	51	185	154	22	42	3	1	0	18	27	2	0	2	34	12	2	14.6	18.4
Peguero, Jhoan	R-R	6-2	166	9-5-05	.197	.296	.296	32	81	71	14	14	1	0	2	7	8	2	0	0	30	14	1	9.9	37.0
Pinto, Avinson	S-R	5-11	150	5-29-07	.235	.324	.340	43	179	153	29	36	5	4	1	15	21	1	0	4	37	21	6	11.7	20.7
Rodriguez, Gerardo	R-R	5-10	177	12-8-05	.279	.329	.383	47	170	154	17	43	16	0	0	32	10	3	0	3	23	7	0	5.9	13.5
Rodriguez, Jorge	R-R	5-10	147	2-24-06	.191	.312	.213	28	92	78	11	17	0	1	0	3	17	8	1	0	17	8	5	8.7	18.5
Teran, Efren	S-R	5-10	163	11-4-06	.205	.320	.217	28	97	83	11	17	1	0	0	6	13	1	0	0	13	2	3	13.4	13.4
Turner, Will	L-L	6-1	190	9-18-02	.130	.432	.261	9	37	23	9	3	0	0	1	6	13	0	0	1	8	1	1	35.1	21.6
Viloria, Diego	R-R	5-10	165	2-23-03	.273	.273	.273	3	12	11	2	2	1	0	0	1	1	0	0	0	2	0	0	8.3	16.7
Zavala, Seby	R-R	5-11	205	8-28-93	.154	.250	.231	5	16	13	1	2	1	0	0	2	1	0	0	1	0	0	0	12.5	6.34

Pitching	B-T	Ht.	Wt.	DOB	W	L	ERA	G	GS	SV	IP	Hits	Runs	ER	HR	BB	SO	AVG	OBP	SLG	SO%	BB%	BF
Bello, Jose	R-R	6-1	164	5-29-05	2	0	3.14	5	1	0	14	10	6	5	0	6	16	.208	.286	.333	28.6	10.7	56
Bickerstaff, Calvin	R-R	6-5	205	1-22-02	1	0	4.05	3	1	0	7	5	4	3	0	4	3	.208	.345	.333	10.3	13.8	29
Bido, Merlin	R-R	6-0	174	2-27-06	2	2	4.83	11	5	1	32	22	18	17	0	28	31	.216	.397	.304	22.6	20.4	137

Batting	B-T	Ht.	Wt.	DOB			AVG	OBP	SLG	G	PA	AB	R	H	2B	3B	HR	RBI	BB	HBP	SH	SF	SO	SB	CS	BB%	SO%
Bouchard, Alex	R-R	6-3	210	8-11-03	0	0	10.13			4	3	0	5	7	8	6	0	8	7	.350	.548	.400	22.6	25.8	31		
Cason, Conrad	R-R	6-1	190	8-7-06	0	0	0.00			1	1	0	2	0	0	0	0	1	5	.000	.143	.000	71.4	14.3	7		
Chirino, Yoelvin	R-R	6-0	161	5-13-05	4	2	6.48			12	7	0	33	21	25	24	4	35	45	.196	.404	.355	30.8	24.0	146		
De La Cruz, Nicolas	L-L	6-4	252	11-18-05	0	0	6.23			2	0	0	4	3	3	3	0	4	4	.214	.421	.286	21.1	21.1	19		
Frias, Madison	R-R	6-2	205	4-1-05	1	7	6.30			11	3	0	30	35	25	21	0	19	22	.310	.416	.389	16.1	13.9	137		
Galvan, Gilbel	R-R	5-10	167	9-20-06	1	2	7.31			12	0	2	16	17	14	13	3	9	18	.274	.418	.468	22.5	11.3	80		
Gartrell, Joey	R-R	6-4	215	7-9-03	0	0	1.80			3	2	0	5	3	1	1	0	1	8	.158	.200	.263	40.0	5.0	20		
Henriquez, Juan	R-R	6-0	172	6-29-06	1	3	4.21			15	1	1	26	28	13	12	0	19	20	.283	.395	.354	16.8	16.0	119		
Labriola, P.J.	L-L	6-7	220	11-13-00	1	0	6.14			4	0	0	7	8	5	5	0	1	4	.267	.313	.400	12.5	3.1	32		
Moran, Jovani	L-L	6-1	167	4-24-97	0	0	3.00			2	2	0	3	1	1	1	0	2	6	.100	.250	.200	50.0	16.7	12		
Noria, Franyer	R-R	5-10	135	9-24-04	0	0	0.00			1	0	0	1	1	0	0	0	0	0	.250	.250	.500	0.0	0.0	4		
Payano, Roberto	R-R	6-0	187	11-5-05	1	0	3.65			16	0	3	25	18	15	10	2	17	25	.212	.369	.341	22.5	15.3	111		
Penrod, Zach	L-L	6-2	210	6-16-97	0	0	0.00			1	1	0	1	0	0	0	0	1	2	.000	.250	.000	50.0	25.0	4		
Prado, Abis	L-L	6-3	190	10-17-06	0	3	43.20			6	0	0	3	5	20	16	1	21	3	.385	.763	.615	7.9	55.3	38		
Reyes, Dalvinson	R-R	6-5	200	11-19-06	0	4	14.33			10	9	0	16	21	27	26	3	20	12	.328	.511	.533	13.0	21.7	92		
Rodriguez, Wuilliams	R-R	6-2	199	11-3-05	5	2	4.10			17	1	1	42	35	25	19	3	14	30	.220	.303	.346	16.9	7.9	178		
Ruiz, Yermain	R-R	5-11	160	11-27-05	3	1	2.79			12	5	1	42	38	19	13	0	15	45	.242	.313	.331	25.3	8.4	178		
Sanchez, Denison	R-R	6-1	164	8-30-05	1	2	6.25			11	1	0	32	22	22	22	4	30	42	.196	.401	.375	27.6	19.7	152		
Song, Noah	R-R	6-4	200	5-28-97	0	0	0.00			1	1	0	2	0	0	0	0	1	4	.000	.143	.000	57.1	14.3	7		
Travieso, Jesus	R-R	5-11	140	3-22-07	1	3	2.77			12	10	1	39	26	14	12	1	25	52	.194	.325	.269	31.9	15.3	163		
Veraza, Yoandys	R-R	5-11	174	9-2-06	0	1	11.40			11	0	1	15	17	19	19	1	20	10	.304	.512	.446	12.0	24.1	83		
Viloria, Diego	R-R	5-10	165	2-23-03	0	1	27.00			1	0	0	0	2	2	1	0	1	0	.500	.600	.500	0.0	20.0	5		
Wilson, Tejahari	R-R	6-1	186	12-6-06	1	0	6.00			13	0	1	21	12	14	14	2	21	21	.169	.404	.310	21.2	21.2	99		

Fielding
C: G. Rodriguez 31, J. Rodriguez 17, Garcia 9, Mambel 5, Zavala 4, Marin 3, Viloria 2. **1B:** Ortiz 39, Mambel 12, Rodriguez 7, Marin 2, Brito 1. **2B:** Noria 19, Fernandez 17, Teran 11, Pinto 7, Barry 5. **3B:** Fernandez 19, Linarez 14, Barry 13, Ortiz 13, Noria 2, Teran 2. **SS:** Pinto 35, Teran 16, Barry 7, Fernandez 2. **LF:** Brito 21, Baker 13, Fermin 11, Peguero 6, Cruz 4, Lugo 4, Azocar 1. **CF:** Fermin 25, Azocar 11, Baker 10, Peguero 9, Turner 6, Brito 1, Gonzales 1. **RF:** Cruz 29, Peguero 11, Baker 8, Fermin 8, Brito 3, Lugo 2, Azocar 1, Turner 1.

DSL RED SOX BLUE ROOKIE
DOMINICAN SUMMER LEAGUE

Batting	B-T	Ht.	Wt.	DOB	AVG	OBP	SLG	G	PA	AB	R	H	2B	3B	HR	RBI	BB	HBP	SH	SF	SO	SB	CS	BB%	SO%
Alfonzo, Eliezer	S-R	5-11	165	10-4-07	.203	.349	.225	44	172	138	35	28	1	1	0	20	31	1	0	2	43	25	2	18.0	25.0
Alvarado, Christopher	R-R	5-10	162	6-14-07	.281	.423	.430	40	149	114	18	32	10	2	1	23	27	4	0	4	25	13	2	18.1	16.8
Andujar, Louis	R-R	6-0	185	9-25-07	.280	.450	.524	29	111	82	24	23	5	0	5	19	22	5	0	2	20	8	4	19.8	18.0
Asencio, Vladimir	R-R	5-10	165	12-13-06	.228	.253	.253	25	83	79	9	18	2	0	0	10	2	1	0	1	18	2	1	2.4	21.7
Brito, Josue	R-R	6-0	175	4-12-07	.284	.497	.606	43	157	109	31	31	8	0	9	30	41	6	0	1	32	13	2	26.1	20.4
Darville, Edwin	L-R	5-9	163	10-12-06	.352	.469	.533	32	130	105	32	37	5	4	2	18	24	0	0	1	28	14	1	18.5	21.5
De La Cruz, Steven	L-R	6-1	160	2-15-08	.242	.412	.308	36	119	91	20	22	2	2	0	16	25	2	0	1	31	6	2	21.0	26.1
Figuereo, Enmanuel	R-R	6-0	165	2-28-08	.213	.356	.250	36	135	108	15	23	4	0	0	17	23	2	0	2	26	6	6	17.0	14.8
Hidalgo, Diomar	R-R	6-0	163	5-24-07	.269	.447	.346	34	103	78	25	21	9	0	1	7	22	3	0	0	18	13	4	21.4	17.5
Ogando, Jostin	R-R	6-3	215	12-6-07	.282	.433	.427	42	134	103	15	29	4	2	5	24	25	5	0	2	26	1	0	17.9	19.4
Ramos, Hector	R-R	6-1	168	9-19-07	.254	.384	.443	36	151	122	31	31	7	2	4	25	23	4	0	2	32	15	2	15.2	21.2
Rivas, Harold	R-R	6-2	177	5-10-08	.258	.393	.384	46	196	159	41	41	6	4	2	20	35	1	5	3	35	18	8	17.9	17.9
Ruiz, Yoiber	R-R	5-7	171	11-11-05	.171	.370	.257	17	46	35	10	6	0	0	1	8	11	0	0	0	2	4	0	23.9	4.3
Soto, Dorian	B-R	6-2	180	2-14-08	.222	.300	.333	3	10	9	0	2	1	0	0	0	1	0	0	0	2	0	0	10.0	20.0
Suarez, Lester	R-R	6-0	189	8-14-08	.176	.299	.216	25	87	74	7	13	0	0	1	7	7	6	0	0	19	0	0	8.0	21.8
Tovar, Maikol	L-L	6-0	157	1-9-08	.241	.381	.278	28	97	79	16	19	3	0	0	14	16	2	0	0	19	4	6	16.5	19.6
Zambrano, Andruw	R-R	6-0	186	4-8-06	.247	.404	.403	29	99	77	18	19	5	2	1	10	17	4	0	1	19	0	0	17.2	19.2

Pitching	B-T	Ht.	Wt.	DOB	W	L	ERA	G	GS	SV	IP	Hits	Runs	ER	HR	BB	SO	AVG	OBP	SLG	SO%	BB%	BF
Almanza, Jainer	R-R	6-4	205	9-30-07	3	2	9.90	14	1	0	30	23	35	33	1	34	19	.209	.421	.273	12.5	22.4	152
Alvarado, Christopher	R-R	5-10	162	6-14-07	1	0	0.00	1	0	0	1	1	0	0	0	1	0	.200	.400	.200	0.0	20.0	5
Berroa, Wascar	R-R	6-6	237	10-23-05	1	0	0.61	10	0	0	15	7	2	1	0	6	16	.140	.259	.180	27.6	10.3	58
Bonaci, Yander	L-L	5-11	162	10-25-06	4	1	2.54	12	2	0	39	40	18	11	3	15	44	.253	.318	.348	25.4	8.7	173
Brito, Josue	R-R	6-0	175	4-12-07	0	0	0.00	5	0	1	4	3	0	0	0	2	3	.214	.389	.214	16.7	11.1	18
Cabrera, Luis	R-R	6-2	180	5-13-06	2	0	0.90	7	0	1	10	5	1	1	0	6	8	.161	.316	.161	21.1	15.8	38
Calderon, Rony	L-L	5-10	188	6-17-08	2	1	2.00	4	1	0	9	4	4	2	0	3	10	.125	.222	.188	27.8	8.3	36
Castillo, Ranci	R-R	5-11	192	7-17-06	3	1	5.24	15	0	2	22	26	22	13	1	13	24	.284	.385	.420	23.1	12.5	104
Darville, Edwin	L-R	5-9	163	10-12-06	1	0	0.00	1	0	0	1	0	0	0	0	0	1	.000	.000	.000	25.0	0.0	4
De La Rosa, Yomar	R-R	6-1	175	2-23-05	5	0	2.84	13	0	0	38	31	15	12	3	7	30	.217	.252	.301	19.9	4.6	151
Delzine, Sadbiel	R-R	6-5	198	1-9-08	0	0	4.82	3	3	0	9	11	5	5	0	1	9	.297	.333	.405	23.1	2.6	39
Duran, Juanyerlin	R-R	6-0	165	2-25-08	1	3	4.42	10	10	0	37	32	22	18	0	18	37	.230	.335	.252	22.6	11.0	164
Ettien, Erickson	R-R	6-0	140	12-16-06	0	0	6.75	5	0	0	8	8	6	6	2	5	6	.207	.324	.448	17.6	14.7	34
Falcon, Carlos	R-R	5-10	188	4-4-08	0	0	11.57	2	0	0	2	3	3	3	1	2	0	.333	.455	.667	0.0	16.7	12
Griman, Allan	R-R	6-5	217	10-2-06	0	0	0.00	1	0	0	1	0	0	0	0	1	0	.000	.333	.000	33.3	33.3	3
Heredia, Alexander	R-R	6-1	165	6-14-07	1	0	8.53	6	0	0	6	5	6	6	1	4	1	.250	.414	.500	17.2	13.8	29
Lopez, Angel	R-R	6-1	180	5-13-08	1	1	6.89	9	3	0	16	16	12	12	0	14	15	.271	.421	.339	19.7	18.4	76
Manjarres, Michael	L-L	6-3	205	3-10-06	1	0	15.12	8	0	0	6	5	14	14	2	20	11	.200	.510	.300	21.6	39.2	51
Martinez, Jesus	R-R	6-1	145	2-9-08	1	2	16.63	7	1	0	11	16	20	19	1	17	8	.364	.556	.523	12.7	27.0	63
Medina, Juan	R-R	5-11	190	10-28-06	1	4	8.23	14	9	0	35	42	38	32	4	24	27	.296	.430	.401	15.0	13.3	180
Morillo, Dariel	R-R	5-11	204	8-4-06	1	2	4.60	13	8	0	29	35	16	15	0	27	27	.231	.397	.250	19.0	19.0	142
Muzziotti, Cesar	R-R	6-1	182	10-23-06	0	0	9.00	1	0	0	1	0	0	0	0	0	2	.250	.400	.750	40.0	0.0	5

Ogando, Justin	R-R	6-3	215	12-6-07	0	0	0.00	1	0	0	1	0	0	0	0	1	1	.000	.250	.000	25.0 25.0 4
Richar, Dani	L-L	5-11	160	10-24-05	0	3	6.08	9	9	0	27	32	19	18	0	19	25	.308	.426	.404	19.4 14.7 129
Vaamonde, Oscar	R-R	6-1	175	9-24-07	2	2	3.73	11	7	0	31	19	15	13	1	20	30	.174	.324	.229	22.1 14.7 136
Valdez, Yariel	R-R	5-2	160	6-21-08	1	0	9.25	16	0	0	24	28	26	25	1	28	15	.298	.477	.426	11.5 21.5 130

Fielding
C: Suarez 23, Zambrano 23, Ruiz 15. **1B:** Ogando 35, Brito 24, Zambrano 5, Alvarado 1, Hidalgo 1. **2B:** Alfonzo 25, Darville 18, Alvarado 8, Hidalgo 1, Brito 1, Ramos 1. **3B:** Alvarado 28, Andujar 21, Hidalgo 7, Alfonzo 2, Darville 1. **SS:** Ramos 28, Alfonzo 14, Hidalgo 14, Soto 3. **LF:** Asencio 19, De La Cruz 16, Brito 13, Tovar 9, Figuereo 3, Ogando 3, Darville 1. **CF:** Rivas 42, De La Cruz 7, Asencio 4, Tovar 4, Figuereo 2. **RF:** Figuereo 28, Tovar 13, De La Cruz 12, Brito 7, Ogando 2, Hidalgo 1

DSL RED SOX RED — ROOKIE
DOMINICAN SUMMER LEAGUE

Batting	B-T	Ht.	Wt.	DOB	AVG	OBP	SLG	G	PA	AB	R	H	2B	3B	HR	RBI	BB	HBP	SH	SF	SO	SB	CS	BB%	SO%
Alzi, Alexander	R-R	5-11	185	10-27-06	.245	.337	.327	45	169	147	22	36	9	0	1	21	14	7	0	1	56	0	0	8.3	33.1
Antunez, Gustavo	R-R	6-2	169	10-31-07	.258	.378	.340	33	119	97	18	25	8	0	0	12	18	2	0	2	24	5	2	15.1	20.2
Aular, Luis	L-R	5-10	165	11-20-07	.164	.345	.194	29	87	67	8	11	2	0	0	7	15	4	0	1	33	0	1	17.2	37.9
Bravo, Jhorman	L-R	6-1	176	6-4-08	.241	.328	.336	34	134	116	21	28	1	2	2	14	16	0	0	2	9	12	4	11.9	6.7
Martinez, Geomaikel	R-R	5-10	165	11-17-07	.254	.336	.340	45	153	134	18	34	7	2	0	17	14	4	0	1	28	7	2	9.2	18.3
Montesino, Rafi	R-R	5-10	170	5-31-07	.108	.233	.108	21	43	37	6	4	0	0	0	0	5	1	0	0	9	0	0	11.6	20.9
Morillo, Kevin	R-R	5-9	165	10-7-06	.262	.354	.405	16	48	42	8	11	3	0	1	8	5	1	0	0	7	0	0	10.4	14.6
Osta, Jhonny	L-R	6-0	163	9-3-07	.196	.302	.286	35	129	112	16	22	4	0	2	17	13	4	0	0	30	3	1	10.1	23.3
Primera, Franklin	R-R	6-0	179	6-16-07	.333	.465	.430	45	172	135	33	45	10	0	1	27	25	10	0	2	15	2	0	14.5	8.7
Rivera, Miguel	R-R	5-11	170	2-2-07	.233	.411	.326	19	56	43	5	10	1	0	1	7	12	1	0	0	2	0	0	21.4	3.6
Simmons, Kenyon	R-R	6-1	150	4-13-08	.206	.333	.302	25	79	63	9	13	3	0	1	9	8	5	1	2	18	6	2	10.1	22.8
Sirvania, Givian	R-R	5-8	150	8-2-07	.243	.369	.351	50	179	148	22	36	5	4	1	20	23	7	0	1	35	16	1	12.8	19.6
Soto, Dorian	B-R	6-2	180	2-14-08	.312	.366	.433	44	176	157	27	49	9	2	2	18	15	0	1	3	26	1	4	8.5	14.8
Ulacio, Krishan	R-R	6-1	181	1-18-08	.206	.320	.333	26	76	63	5	13	2	0	2	12	10	1	0	1	21	0	2	13.2	27.6
Valdez, Adrian	R-R	6-0	204	11-28-07	.307	.282	.28	101	85	15	17	7	0	1	7	13	3	0	0	30	1	0	12.9	29.7	
Welch, Miguel	L-R	5-11	158	12-2-07	.302	.417	.446	45	168	139	22	42	13	2	1	18	26	2	0	1	20	16	5	15.5	11.9

Pitching	B-T	Ht.	Wt.	DOB	W	L	ERA	G	GS	SV	IP	Hits	Runs	ER	HR	BB	SO	AVG	OBP	SLG	SO%	BB%	BF
Belisario, Felix	R-R	5-11	155	9-11-06	1	3	6.49	16	1	1	26	23	19	19	4	21	28	.230	.376	.430	22.4	16.8	125
Castillo, Ranci	R-R	5-11	192	7-17-06	0	0	2.08	2	0	0	4	3	1	1	0	2	3	.200	.333	.200	16.7	11.1	18
Cordero, Christopher	R-R	5-11	180	7-22-08	0	1	1.79	11	9	0	40	24	12	8	1	25	33	.171	.322	.221	19.3	14.6	171
Cruz, Breylin	R-R	6-2	210	2-28-01	2	1	5.76	15	0	1	30	29	24	19	2	21	23	.259	.381	.384	16.4	15.0	140
Ettien, Erickson	R-R	6-0	140	12-16-06	1	1	6.35	6	0	0	6	6	7	4	0	5	1	.286	.448	.333	3.2	16.1	31
Fernandez, Jomar	R-R	5-11	180	1-22-05	0	0	7.71	2	0	0	2	2	3	2	0	3	3	.200	.467	.300	20.0	20.0	15
Fis, Isael	R-R	5-11	145	2-4-07	1	3	11.77	9	1	0	13	15	18	17	1	16	12	.294	.493	.373	16.2	21.6	74
Gamboa, Jakson	R-R	6-3	186	2-14-07	0	0	1.08	8	0	0	17	10	5	2	0	7	13	.179	.299	.214	19.4	10.4	67
Golindano, Jose	L-L	5-11	170	3-16-06	1	4	9.36	16	0	2	25	22	29	26	3	31	34	.234	.447	.394	25.8	23.5	132
Gonzalez, Yohandry	R-R	5-11	165	3-25-05	2	4	6.92	10	4	1	26	30	22	20	1	15	21	.294	.393	.343	17.2	12.3	122
Griman, Allan	R-R	6-5	217	10-2-06	2	0	2.57	15	0	1	28	13	10	8	1	24	26	.140	.336	.237	21.3	19.7	122
Ladera, Angelo	R-R	6-0	168	10-12-06	5	1	2.20	12	3	0	33	18	8	8	1	15	36	.164	.268	.236	27.9	11.6	129
Lopez, Angel	R-R	6-1	180	5-13-08	1	0	0.00	1	0	0	2	0	0	0	0	4	0	.000	.000	.000	66.7	0.0	6
Martinez, Jesus	R-R	6-1	145	2-29-08	0	0	5.87	4	0	0	8	2	6	5	1	9	1	.083	.353	.208	2.9	26.5	34
Montero, Williams	R-R	6-0	160	1-15-08	1	4	3.30	11	11	0	44	37	20	16	0	16	37	.233	.314	.270	19.9	8.6	186
Montesino, Rafi	R-R	5-10	170	5-31-07	0	0	67.50	3	0	0	1	2	5	5	0	4	1	.333	.600	.333	10.0	40.0	10
Moreno, Robert	R-R	6-1	200	3-12-06	2	2	6.60	9	3	0	15	14	13	11	0	14	15	.250	.394	.304	21.1	19.7	71
Ortiz, Berny	R-R	6-2	167	8-7-05	1	2	4.69	11	9	0	40	30	25	21	1	22	36	.203	.322	.270	20.0	12.2	180
Perez, Leosmar	R-R	6-2	169	1-26-07	2	0	7.09	11	3	0	27	29	22	21	1	27	18	.282	.436	.379	13.5	20.3	133
Septimo, Eddison	R-R	5-10	170	4-5-07	2	1	5.23	14	1	1	21	16	12	12	2	18	18	.232	.426	.377	18.9	18.9	95
Sirvania, Givian	R-R	5-8	150	8-2-07	0	0	0.00	2	0	0	2	0	0	0	0	4	1	.000	.444	.000	11.1	44.4	9
Zink, Charlie	R-R	6-4	180	1-5-06	1	3	27.00	7	2	0	7	6	23	20	0	19	6	.240	.630	.240	11.1	35.2	54

Fielding
C: Primera 39, Morillo 15, Rivera 7. **1B:** Alzi 39, Rivera 12, Valdez 3, Ulacio 2, Montesino 1. **2B:** Welch 21, Aular 16, Bravo 10, Sirvania 10, Simmons 2, Soto 2. **3B:** Simmons 22, Sirvania 15, Aular 12, Bravo 6, Soto 6. **SS:** Soto 32, Bravo 16, Sirvania 12, Welch 3, Simmons 1. **LF:** Valdez 16, Antunez 14, Osta 14, Ulacio 6, Montesino 4, Sirvania 4, Martinez 3. **CF:** Welch 21, Martinez 20, Montesino 9, Sirvania 9, Ulacio 2. **RF:** Martinez 19, Antunez 15, Osta 14, Ulacio 9, Sirvania 2, Montesino 1

Chicago Cubs

SEASON SYNOPSIS: The rebuild is over. The Cubs traded for Kyle Tucker and went for it, and it paid off. They won 92 games, the most since 2018, and won a wild-card series against the Padres, their first postseason wins since 2017. However, they couldn't keep pace with the Brewers, winning the season series 7-6 but finishing second to them in the NL Central and losing Game Five of a tight Division Series to Milwaukee to end their season.

HIGH POINT: The Cubs were at their best in May and early June, winning six consecutive series (two vs. the Reds) during a 14-4 stretch in which they scored 6.2 runs per game. Center fielder Pete Crow-Armstrong had two six-RBI games in that stretch, Tucker had six multi-hit games and Seiya Suzuki hit safely in 13 of the first 14 games with three homers. PCA and Ian Happ homered in a 7-1 win June 5 against the Nationals to cap the stretch.

LOW POINT: The Division Series started poorly, with the Brewers winning convincingly twice in Milwaukee before the Cubs held serve with two victories at Wrigley Field. Game Five featured a Suzuki solo homer to tie the game, but Chicago got just four hits and ran out of pitching with rookie Cade Horton shelved by a late-season fractured rib. The second-half offensive woes continued in the postseason–the Cubs had a .720 OPS in the second half after a .771 mark in the first half.

NOTABLE ROOKIES: The Cubs' rookies were impact players, starting with Horton (11-4, 2.67, 118 IP), the 2022 first-round pick who was trending toward being Chicago's No. 1 playoff starter before his injury. 3B Matt Shaw (.226/.295/.394), the 2023 first-rounder, boosted the offense in the second half (.839 OPS).

KEY TRANSACTIONS: Tucker arrived in an offseason deal that cost Chicago its 2024 first-rounder, Cam Smith, and its big 2024 trade-deadline pickup, Isaac Paredes. He replaced Cody Bellinger, salary-dumped to the Yankees for non-factor RHP Cody Poteet. Several free-agent signees bore fruit, such as LHP Matthew Boyd, the team's top starter (14-8, 3.21); RHP Brad Keller (4-2, 2.07 as a full-time reliever); and C Carson Kelly (.761 OPS, 17 HR). However, in-season trade pickups such as UT Willi Castro and RHPs Andrew Kittredge and Michael Soroka were lower wattage. Only Kittredge qualified as a success, and the Cubs struck out in a thin starting-pitcher trade market.

OPENING DAY PAYROLL: $213,020,500 (9th)

PLAYERS OF THE YEAR

MAJOR LEAGUE
Pete Crow-Armstrong
OF
.247/.287/.481
31 HR, 35 SB, 37 2B
All-star, Gold Glove

MINOR LEAGUE
Jonathon Long
1B
(AAA)
.305/.404/.479
20 HR, 91 RBIs, 79 BB

ORGANIZATION LEADERS

Batting		*Qualifiers
MAJORS		
* AVG	Nico Hoerner	.297
* OPS	Michael Busch	.866
HR	Michael Busch	34
RBI	Seiya Suzuki	103
MINORS		
* AVG	Moises Ballesteros, Iowa	.316
* OBP	Jonathon Long, Iowa	.404
* SLG	Carlos Perez, Iowa	.572
* OPS	Carlos Perez, Iowa	.944
R	Jonathon Long, Iowa	86
H	Jonathon Long, Iowa	157
TB	Jonathon Long, Iowa	246
2B	Carlos Perez, Iowa	32
3B	Ronny Cruz, ACL Cubs	6
3B	Alexey Lumpuy, Myrtle Beach	6
3B	Derik Alcantara, Myrtle Beach/ACL Cubs	6
HR	Carlos Perez, Iowa	27
RBI	Jonathon Long, Iowa	91
BB	BJ Murray, Knoxville	83
SO	Jaylen Palmer, Iowa/Knoxville	154
SO	Alexey Lumpuy, Myrtle Beach	154
SB	Cristian Hernandez, South Bend	52

Pitching		#Qualifiers
MAJORS		
W	Matthew Boyd	14
# ERA	Matthew Boyd	3.21
SO	Matthew Boyd	154
SV	Daniel Palencia	22
MINORS		
W	Will Sanders, Iowa/Knoxville	10
L	Brooks Caple, South Bend/Myrtle Beach	9
L	Antonio Santos, Iowa/Knoxville	9
# ERA	Connor Noland, Iowa	4.07
G	Mitchell Tyranski, Knoxville	47
G	Riley Martin, Iowa	47
GS	Chris Kachmar, Iowa/Knoxville	24
SV	A.J. Puckett, Knoxville	15
IP	Connor Noland, Iowa	133
BB	Chris Kachmar, Iowa/Knoxville	58
SO	Will Sanders, Iowa/Knoxville	123
# AVG	Chris Kachmar, Iowa/Knoxville	.243

2025 PERFORMANCE

President: Jed Hoyer. **Farm Director:** Jason Kanzler. **Scouting Director:** Dan Kantrovitz.

Class	Team	League	W	L	PCT	Finish	Manager
Majors	Chicago Cubs	National	92	70	.568	4 (15)	Craig Counsell
Triple-A	Iowa Cubs	International	74	75	.497	11 (20)	Marty Pevey
Double-A	Knoxville Smokies	Southern	69	67	.507	5 (8)	Lance Rymel
High-A	South Bend Cubs	Midwest	56	75	.427	10 (12)	Nick Lovullo
Low-A	Myrtle Beach Pelicans	Carolina	68	60	.531	3 (12)	Yovanny Cuevas
Rookie	ACL Cubs	Arizona Complex	19	41	.317	14 (15)	Corey Ray
Rookie	DSL Cubs Blue	Dominican	25	31	.446	33 (52)	Enrique Wilson
Rookie	DSL Cubs Red	Dominican	15	41	.268	50 (52)	Carlos Ramirez
Overall 2025 Minor League Record			326	390	.455	28th (30)	

ORGANIZATION STATISTICS

CHICAGO CUBS
NATIONAL LEAGUE

Batting	B-T	Ht.	Wt.	DOB	AVG	OBP	SLG	G	PA	AB	R	H	2B	3B	HR	RBI	BB	HBP	SH	SF	SO	SB	CS	BB%	SO%
Alcantara, Kevin	R-R	6-6	188	7-12-02	.364	.417	.364	10	12	11	2	4	0	0	0	1	1	0	0	0	4	1	0	8.3	33.3
Amaya, Miguel	R-R	6-0	230	3-9-99	.281	.314	.500	28	103	96	14	27	9	0	4	25	4	1	1	1	22	0	0	3.9	21.4
Ballesteros, Moises	L-R	5-7	195	11-8-03	.298	.394	.474	20	66	57	12	17	2	1	2	11	9	0	0	0	12	0	0	13.6	18.2
Berti, Jon	R-R	5-10	190	1-22-90	.210	.262	.230	53	107	100	12	21	2	0	0	2	5	2	0	0	22	11	3	4.7	20.6
Brujan, Vidal	S-R	5-10	180	2-9-98	.222	.234	.289	36	47	45	6	10	3	0	0	3	1	0	0	1	12	2	1	2.1	25.5
Busch, Michael	L-R	6-1	210	11-9-97	.261	.343	.523	155	592	524	78	137	25	5	34	90	56	10	0	2	139	4	0	9.5	23.5
Caissie, Owen	L-R	6-3	190	7-8-02	.192	.222	.346	12	27	26	4	5	1	0	1	4	1	0	0	0	11	0	0	3.7	40.7
Castro, Willi	S-R	6-1	206	4-24-97	.170	.245	.240	34	110	100	10	17	2	1	6	8	2	0	0	0	27	1	1	7.3	24.5
Crow-Armstrong, Pete	L-L	5-11	184	3-25-02	.247	.287	.481	157	647	591	91	146	37	4	31	95	29	9	6	12	155	35	8	4.5	24.0
Happ, Ian	S-R	6-0	205	8-12-94	.243	.342	.420	150	663	569	87	138	32	0	23	79	87	2	0	5	151	6	3	13.1	22.8
Hoerner, Nico	R-R	6-1	200	5-13-97	.297	.345	.394	156	649	599	89	178	29	4	7	61	39	7	0	4	49	29	6	6.0	7.6
Kelly, Carson	R-R	6-2	212	7-14-94	.249	.333	.428	111	421	369	48	92	13	1	17	50	45	3	0	4	80	2	0	10.7	19.0
Lopez, Nicky	L-R	5-11	180	3-13-95	.056	.227	.056	14	22	18	2	1	0	0	0	1	4	0	0	0	3	0	0	18.2	13.6
McGuire, Reese	L-R	6-0	218	3-2-95	.226	.245	.444	45	140	133	17	30	2	0	9	24	4	0	1	2	27	0	0	2.9	19.3
Rea, Colin	R-R	6-5	218	7-1-90	.000	.000	.000	32	1	1	0	0	0	0	0	0	0	0	0	0	1	0	0	0.0	100.0
Santana, Carlos	S-R	5-11	215	4-8-86	.105	.105	.158	8	19	19	0	2	1	0	0	2	0	0	0	0	5	0	0	0.0	26.3
Shaw, Matt	R-R	5-11	185	11-6-01	.226	.295	.394	126	437	393	57	89	21	3	13	44	38	2	0	4	94	17	5	8.7	21.5
Suzuki, Seiya	R-R	5-11	182	8-18-94	.245	.326	.478	151	651	571	75	140	31	3	32	103	71	1	0	8	164	5	2	10.9	25.2
Swanson, Dansby	R-R	6-1	190	2-11-94	.244	.300	.417	159	645	590	84	144	24	3	24	77	47	2	1	5	168	20	3	7.3	26.0
Tucker, Kyle	L-R	6-4	199	1-17-97	.266	.377	.464	136	597	500	91	133	25	4	22	73	87	4	1	3	88	25	3	14.6	14.7
Turner, Justin	R-R	5-11	202	11-23-84	.219	.288	.314	80	191	169	14	37	7	0	3	18	17	1	0	4	37	2	0	8.9	19.4
Workman, Gage	S-R	6-4	202	10-24-99	.214	.267	.286	9	15	14	0	3	1	0	0	2	1	0	0	0	6	1	0	6.7	40.0

Pitching	B-T	Ht.	Wt.	DOB	W	L	ERA	G	GS	SV	IP	Hits	Runs	ER	HR	BB	SO	AVG	OBP	SLG	SO%	BB%	BF
Assad, Javier	R-R	6-1	200	7-30-97	4	1	3.65	8	7	0	37	33	15	15	3	12	23	.243	.320	.382	15.0	7.8	153
Berti, Jon	R-R	5-10	190	1-22-90	0	0	7.36	4	0	0	4	4	3	3	0	4	0	.267	.421	.400	0.0	21.1	19
Boyd, Matthew	L-L	6-3	223	2-2-91	14	8	3.21	31	31	0	180	154	69	64	19	42	154	.235	.288	.369	21.4	5.8	718
Brasier, Ryan	R-R	6-0	227	8-26-87	0	1	4.50	28	1	0	26	27	13	13	2	5	20	.276	.305	.408	19.0	4.8	105
Brown, Ben	R-R	6-6	210	9-9-99	5	8	5.92	25	15	1	106	121	73	70	18	32	121	.279	.333	.467	25.6	6.8	472
Cabrera, Genesis	L-L	6-2	180	10-10-96	0	0	8.68	9	0	0	9	10	9	9	4	3	8	.278	.333	.639	20.5	7.7	39
Civale, Aaron	R-R	6-2	215	6-12-95	1	0	2.08	5	0	1	13	7	3	3	0	0	14	.149	.200	.362	28.0	0.0	50
Cosgrove, Tom	L-L	6-2	190	6-14-96	0	0	2.25	2	0	0	4	3	1	1	0	1	3	.200	.250	.200	18.8	6.3	16
Flexen, Chris	R-R	6-3	219	7-1-94	5	1	3.09	21	1	1	44	38	18	15	7	12	22	.232	.281	.372	12.4	6.7	178
Fulmer, Michael	R-R	6-3	224	3-15-93	0	0	0.00	2	0	0	3	2	0	0	0	1	2	.200	.200	.200	10.0	10.0	10
Hodge, Porter	R-R	6-4	230	2-21-01	2	2	6.27	36	0	2	33	34	24	23	9	18	40	.268	.354	.543	27.2	12.2	147
Hollowell, Gavin	R-R	6-7	215	11-4-97	0	0	4.82	7	0	0	9	5	5	5	1	7	10	.250	.372	.361	23.3	16.3	43
Horton, Cade	R-R	6-1	211	8-20-01	11	4	2.67	23	22	0	118	81	36	35	10	33	97	.219	.282	.333	20.4	6.9	476
Imanaga, Shota	L-L	5-8	176	9-1-93	9	8	3.73	25	25	0	145	117	62	60	31	26	117	.218	.254	.432	20.6	4.6	567
Keller, Brad	R-R	6-5	255	7-27-95	4	2	2.07	68	1	3	70	45	18	16	4	22	75	.182	.265	.247	27.2	8.0	276
Kittredge, Andrew	R-R	6-1	230	3-17-90	2	1	3.32	23	0	5	22	15	9	8	3	3	32	.195	.222	.351	39.0	3.7	82
Kriske, Brooks	R-R	6-3	190	2-3-94	0	0	0.00	4	0	0	6	2	0	0	0	5	4	.105	.158	.158	16.7	20.8	24
Little, Luke	L-L	6-8	220	8-30-00	0	0	3.38	2	0	0	3	1	2	1	0	6	4	.125	.500	.125	26.7	40.0	15
McGuire, Reese	L-R	6-0	218	3-2-95	0	0	9.00	1	0	0	2	1	1	1	1	0	.400	.500	1.000	0.0	16.7	6
Merryweather, Julian	R-R	6-4	215	10-14-91	0	1	5.79	21	0	0	19	23	13	12	2	11	15	.303	.389	.474	17.0	12.5	88
Morgan, Eli	R-R	5-10	190	5-13-96	0	1	12.27	7	0	0	7	12	10	10	3	4	.375	.429	.813	11.4	8.6	35
Palencia, Daniel	R-R	5-11	160	2-5-00	1	6	2.91	54	0	22	53	44	19	17	5	16	61	.224	.288	.362	28.4	7.4	215
Pearson, Nate	R-R	6-6	255	8-20-96	1	0	9.20	11	0	0	15	22	15	15	2	10	7	.361	.440	.525	9.3	13.3	75
Pomeranz, Drew	R-L	6-5	246	11-22-88	2	2	2.17	57	4	1	50	38	14	12	5	15	57	.210	.287	.304	28.1	7.4	203
Pressly, Ryan	R-R	6-2	206	12-15-88	2	3	4.35	44	0	5	41	46	24	20	6	17	28	.288	.363	.450	15.4	9.3	182
Rea, Colin	R-R	6-5	218	7-1-90	11	7	3.95	32	27	1	159	155	73	70	20	44	127	.258	.312	.413	19.2	6.6	662
Roberts, Ethan	R-R	5-10	180	7-4-97	1	0	6.00	10	0	0	9	10	6	6	3	2	6	.286	.333	.629	15.4	5.1	39
Rogers, Taylor	L-L	6-3	190	12-17-90	1	0	5.09	17	0	0	18	18	10	10	4	4	19	.261	.307	.522	25.3	5.3	75

CHICAGO CUBS

Player	B-T	Ht	Wt	DOB	W	L	ERA	G	GS	SV	IP	Hits	Runs	ER	HR	BB	SO	AVG	OBP	SLG	SO%	BB%	BF
Soroka, Michael	R-R	6-5	225	8-4-97	0	0	1.08	6	1	0	8	4	5	1	1	5	8	.133	.278	.233	22.2	13.9	36
Steele, Justin	L-L	6-2	205	7-11-95	3	1	4.76	4	4	0	23	21	12	12	5	5	21	.247	.293	.471	22.8	5.4	92
Taillon, Jameson	R-R	6-5	230	11-18-91	11	7	3.68	23	23	0	130	110	54	53	24	27	98	.225	.265	.427	18.9	5.2	519
Thielbar, Caleb	R-L	6-0	205	1-31-87	3	4	2.64	67	0	1	58	38	17	17	5	13	56	.186	.232	.314	25.5	5.9	220
Wicks, Jordan	L-L	6-3	220	9-1-99	0	1	6.28	8	0	1	14	24	12	10	2	1	13	.369	.379	.554	19.4	1.5	673

Fielding

Catcher	PCT	G	PO	A	E	DP	PB
Amaya	.995	27	205	11	1	0	0
Ballesteros	1.000	1	6	0	0	0	0
Kelly	.998	105	777	23	2	6	4
McGuire	.997	43	314	11	1	1	0

First Base	PCT	G	PO	A	E	DP
Ballesteros	.000	2	0	0	0	0
Busch	.996	151	998	84	4	91
Santana	1.000	6	15	5	0	2
Turner	.995	39	174	17	1	15

Second Base	PCT	G	PO	A	E	DP
Berti	.960	13	8	16	1	7
Brujan	1.000	3	0	4	0	0
Castro	1.000	6	6	12	0	3

Third Base	PCT	G	PO	A	E	DP
Berti	.960	28	16	32	2	4
Brujan	.824	11	2	12	3	0
Castro	1.000	10	6	11	0	1
Lopez	1.000	12	4	9	0	1
Shaw	.977	124	80	214	7	18
Turner	1.000	14	3	4	0	0
Workman	.778	7	3	4	2	1

Shortstop	PCT	G	PO	A	E	DP
Brujan	1.000	2	1	1	0	1
Hoerner	1.000	8	6	9	0	1
Hoerner	.993	153	241	367	4	75
Lopez	.000	1	0	0	0	0
Shaw	1.000	4	1	0	0	0
Lopez	1.000	2	1	1	0	1
Swanson	.981	159	221	354	11	73
Workman	1.000	2	0	1	0	0

Outfield	PCT	G	PO	A	E	DP
Alcantara	1.000	7	7	1	0	1
Berti	.000	1	0	0	0	0
Brujan	1.000	10	5	0	0	0
Caissie	1.000	8	14	0	0	0
Castro	1.000	20	33	1	0	1
Crow-Armstrong	.995	156	427	5	2	2
Happ	.997	146	300	5	1	0
Suzuki	.968	48	91	1	3	1
Tucker	.989	115	253	5	3	0

IOWA CUBS — TRIPLE-A
INTERNATIONAL LEAGUE

Batting	B-T	Ht.	Wt.	DOB	AVG	OBP	SLG	G	PA	AB	R	H	2B	3B	HR	RBI	BB	HBP	SH	SF	SO	SB	CS	BB%	SO%
Alcantara, Kevin	R-R	6-6	188	7-12-02	.266	.349	.470	102	430	379	55	101	26	0	17	69	48	1	0	2	128	10	4	11.2	29.8
Allen, Greg	S-R	6-0	185	3-15-93	.270	.355	.440	61	231	200	31	54	14	1	6	32	15	12	2	1	52	11	3	6.5	22.5
Amaya, Miguel	R-R	6-0	230	3-9-99	.195	.244	.195	13	45	41	2	8	0	0	0	5	3	0	0	1	7	0	0	6.7	15.6
Ballesteros, Moises	L-R	5-7	195	11-8-03	.316	.385	.473	114	509	446	62	141	29	1	13	76	49	6	0	8	67	5	2	9.6	13.2
Brujan, Vidal	S-L	5-10	180	2-9-98	.308	.308	.385	3	13	13	0	4	1	0	0	0	0	0	0	0	4	1	0	0.0	30.8
Caissie, Owen	L-R	6-3	190	7-8-02	.286	.386	.551	99	433	370	74	106	28	2	22	55	57	4	0	2	121	5	4	13.2	27.9
Cantrelle, Hayden	S-R	5-11	175	11-25-98	.234	.339	.332	78	278	235	37	55	9	1	4	28	33	5	4	1	91	19	4	11.9	32.7
Chavers, Parker	L-R	5-9	185	7-25-98	.176	.307	.235	30	101	85	11	15	3	1	0	9	16	0	0	0	28	3	1	15.8	27.7
Cosgrove, Tom	L-L	6-2	190	6-14-96	.000	.000	.000	40	1	1	0	0	0	0	0	0	0	0	0	0	1	0	0	0.0	100.0
Cowles, Benjamin	R-R	6-0	180	2-15-00	.238	.304	.382	113	462	421	55	100	28	3	9	44	33	7	1	0	132	16	6	7.1	28.6
Franklin, Christian	R-R	5-8	195	11-30-99	.265	.393	.427	86	390	321	61	85	20	4	8	41	63	5	1	0	80	11	5	16.2	20.5
Hamilton, Billy	S-R	6-0	160	9-9-90	.000	.000	.000	6	0	2	0	0	0	0	0	0	0	0	0	0	3	2	0		
Hill, Darius	L-L	5-11	190	8-17-97	.212	.307	.323	32	114	99	15	21	6	1	1	9	12	2	0	1	25	1	0	10.5	21.9
Howard, Ed	R-R	6-1	185	1-28-02	.250	.333	.375	4	9	8	1	2	1	0	0	2	1	0	0	0	4	0	0	11.1	44.4
Knight, Cameron	L-R	6-1	200	1-2-96	.212	.268	.379	25	71	66	7	14	5	0	2	10	2	3	0	0	21	1	1	2.8	29.6
Long, Jonathon	R-R	5-11	210	1-20-02	.305	.404	.479	140	607	514	86	157	23	3	20	91	79	9	0	4	116	2	0	13.0	19.1
Lopez, Nicky	L-R	5-11	180	3-13-95	.270	.402	.350	29	127	100	13	27	6	1	0	7	21	3	0	3	17	2	2	16.5	13.4
Machado, Dixon	R-R	6-1	190	2-22-92	.221	.345	.301	84	331	272	36	60	10	0	4	34	50	3	3	3	59	4	2	15.1	17.8
McGuire, Reese	L-R	6-0	218	3-2-95	.280	.360	.467	22	86	75	11	21	5	0	3	19	10	0	0	1	12	0	0	11.6	14.0
Morel, Rafael	R-R	6-0	170	11-22-01	.121	.216	.152	11	37	33	2	4	1	0	0	4	4	0	0	0	15	1	0	10.8	40.5
Opitz, Casey	S-R	5-9	200	7-30-98	.000	.000	.000	1	1	1	0	0	0	0	0	0	0	0	0	0	1	0	0	0.0	100.0
Palmer, Jaylen	R-R	6-3	208	7-31-00	.000	.000	.000	1	4	4	0	0	0	0	0	0	0	0	0	0	1	0	0	0.0	25.0
Perez, Carlos	R-R	5-10	210	10-27-90	.286	.372	.572	111	465	402	75	115	32	1	27	87	51	7	0	5	77	1	1	11.0	16.6
Sanders, Will	L-R	6-6	230	3-30-02	.000	.000	.000	17	2	2	0	0	0	0	0	0	0	0	0	0	2	0	0	0.0	100.0
Shaw, Matt	R-R	5-11	185	11-6-01	.286	.409	.560	24	110	91	22	26	5	1	6	14	17	2	0	0	11	5	0	15.5	10.0
Strumpf, Chase	R-R	6-0	170	3-8-98	.221	.355	.405	99	392	321	52	71	16	2	13	49	63	5	0	3	120	10	0	16.1	30.6
Triantos, James	R-R	6-1	195	1-29-03	.258	.315	.369	102	444	407	65	105	20	2	7	43	31	4	0	2	67	28	10	7.0	15.1
Wall, Forrest	L-R	6-0	195	11-20-95	.245	.367	.429	22	60	49	13	12	3	0	2	13	10	0	0	1	15	8	3	16.7	25.0

Pitching	B-T	Ht.	Wt.	DOB	W	L	ERA	G	GS	SV	IP	Hits	Runs	ER	HR	BB	SO	AVG	OBP	SLG	SO%	BB%	BF
Assad, Javier	R-R	6-1	200	7-30-97	0	0	2.93	4	4	0	15	15	6	5	0	7	15	.254	.328	.271	22.4	10.4	67
Birdsell, Brandon	R-R	6-2	240	3-23-00	1	1	3.38	4	4	0	19	16	11	7	4	8	18	.229	.313	.457	22.5	10.0	80
Brasier, Ryan	R-R	6-0	227	8-26-87	0	1	5.19	10	0	0	9	10	5	5	1	5	7	.303	.395	.455	18.4	13.2	38
Brown, Ben	R-R	6-6	210	9-9-99	1	0	0.82	3	2	0	11	5	1	1	1	2	8	.132	.175	.211	20.0	5.0	40
Chavers, Parker	L-R	5-9	185	7-25-98	0	0	0.00	1	0	0	0	0	0	0	0	1	0	.000	.500	.000	0.0	50.0	2
Clenney, Nolan	L-R	6-2	200	6-16-96	0	0	0.00	1	0	0	2	0	0	0	0	1	3	.250	.333	.250	33.3	11.1	9
Cosgrove, Tom	L-L	6-2	190	6-14-96	4	4	4.30	40	0	0	46	43	22	22	4	25	55	.243	.340	.373	26.7	12.1	206
Flexen, Chris	R-R	6-3	219	7-1-94	3	0	1.16	5	5	0	23	19	4	3	0	8	21	.224	.298	.271	22.3	8.5	94
Fulmer, Michael	R-R	6-3	224	3-15-93	1	0	2.96	15	2	1	24	19	9	8	3	11	32	.218	.310	.368	32.0	11.0	100
Gomber, Austin	L-L	6-5	220	11-23-93	2	0	0.47	4	3	0	19	12	1	1	0	2	19	.179	.203	.209	27.5	2.9	69
Hill, Darius	L-L	5-11	190	8-17-97	0	0	0.00	1	0	0	1	0	0	0	0	2	0	.000	.500	.000	0.0	33.3	6
Hodge, Porter	R-R	6-4	220	2-21-01	1	3	6.61	15	0	0	16	14	15	12	1	15	26	.230	.382	.344	33.8	19.5	77
Hollowell, Gavin	R-R	6-7	215	11-4-97	2	4	6.96	30	0	4	32	37	30	25	6	21	47	.285	.401	.508	29.7	13.3	158
Horton, Cade	R-R	6-1	211	8-20-01	2	1	1.24	6	6	0	29	12	4	4	2	13	33	.129	.241	.204	30.6	12.0	108
Hughes, Brandon	S-L	6-2	215	12-16-95	1	2	5.11	25	5	6.33	21	0	2	7	13	29	.311	.400	.585	22.8	10.2	127
Imanaga, Shota	L-L	5-8	176	9-1-93	0	0	0.00	1	1	0	4	2	0	0	0	0	8	.133	.235	.200	47.1	11.8	17
Kachmar, Chris	R-R	6-3	180	9-3-96	2	3	7.04	9	0	0	38	34	30	30	7	29	47	.239	.367	.437	26.4	16.3	178
Kilian, Caleb	R-R	6-4	190	6-2-97	1	1	7.11	9	1	0	13	15	11	10	3	8	13	.294	.387	.510	20.6	12.7	63

Batting	B-T	Ht.	Wt.	DOB																	
Kriske, Brooks	R-R	6-3	190	2-3-94	3	0	3.13	23	0	0	32	24	14	11	4	10	52	.200	.273	.367	39.4	7.6	132
Little, Luke	L-L	6-8	220	8-30-00	2	1	2.87	43	2	2	60	36	22	19	3	34	75	.174	.315	.266	29.8	13.5	252
Maeda, Kenta	R-R	6-1	185	4-11-88	3	4	5.97	12	12	0	57	54	39	38	8	25	45	.245	.329	.432	18.1	10.0	249
Martin, Riley	L-L	6-1	215	3-19-98	6	2	2.69	47	1	4	64	41	21	19	4	35	80	.186	.300	.286	30.7	13.4	261
Miller, Tyson	R-R	6-5	220	7-29-95	1	2	6.27	31	0	1	37	38	27	26	3	34	36	.266	.412	.420	19.7	18.6	183
Morgan, Eli	R-R	5-10	190	5-13-96	2	0	5.06	9	0	0	11	12	7	6	0	9	11	.279	.404	.326	21.2	17.3	52
Neely, Jack	R-R	6-8	225	6-5-00	0	2	6.23	28	0	5	30	20	21	21	4	27	39	.190	.383	.371	27.5	19.0	142
Noland, Connor	R-R	6-2	215	7-20-99	9	6	4.07	27	22	0	133	133	69	60	13	55	115	.259	.333	.411	19.9	9.5	579
Palencia, Daniel	R-R	5-11	160	2-5-00	0	1	1.93	6	0	1	5	6	1	1	0	2	9	.316	.381	.368	42.9	9.5	21
Pearson, Nate	R-R	6-6	255	8-20-96	3	2	2.22	38	1	7	45	27	17	11	1	24	57	.175	.295	.234	30.6	12.9	186
Pop, Zach	R-R	6-4	220	9-20-96	1	0	5.59	9	0	0	10	12	6	6	0	3	14	.286	.326	.310	30.4	6.5	46
Powell, Walker	R-R	6-8	210	6-11-96	0	0	0.00	1	1	0	6	3	0	0	0	5	5	.143	.143	.190	23.8	0.0	21
Reynolds, Cole	L-L	6-5	225	5-30-02	0	0	0.00	1	0	0	3	1	0	0	0	2	4	.091	.231	.091	30.8	15.4	13
Richards, Trevor	R-R	6-2	205	5-15-93	0	2	7.27	7	1	0	9	7	8	7	0	7	12	.212	.350	.394	29.3	17.1	41
Roberts, Ethan	R-R	5-10	180	7-4-97	2	4	2.16	36	1	3	42	35	18	10	2	20	54	.223	.320	.350	29.8	11.0	181
Romero, Tommy	R-R	6-2	222	7-8-97	0	3	8.54	11	6	1	39	44	37	37	8	24	29	.297	.401	.527	16.1	13.3	180
Ross, Joe	R-R	6-4	232	5-21-93	0	0	2.57	5	1	0	7	4	2	2	0	2	3	.160	.222	.240	11.1	7.4	27
Sanders, Will	L-R	6-6	230	3-30-02	7	4	6.38	17	14	0	79	87	64	56	14	33	79	.278	.360	.524	22.2	9.3	356
Santos, Antonio	R-R	6-3	223	10-6-96	0	4	9.35	5	4	0	17	24	21	18	5	15	22	.316	.441	.618	23.7	16.1	93
Scalzo, Frankie	R-R	6-3	185	11-25-99	1	2	14.09	10	3	0	15	28	26	24	6	13	17	.394	.506	.817	19.5	14.9	87
Solomon, Peter	R-R	6-4	211	8-16-96	0	2	7.50	6	6	0	18	25	19	15	3	11	22	.329	.409	.500	25.0	12.5	88
Soroka, Michael	R-R	6-5	225	8-4-97	1	0	3.86	1	0	0	2	1	1	1	1	0	3	.125	.125	.500	37.5	0.0	8
Taillon, Jameson	R-R	6-5	230	11-18-91	0	1	5.94	4	4	0	17	18	11	11	4	6	13	.324	.515	.588	23.0	4.1	74
Thompson, Keegan	R-R	6-1	210	3-13-95	6	2	4.50	33	5	0	64	65	33	32	7	25	83	.265	.350	.433	29.5	8.9	281
Turnbull, Spencer	R-R	6-3	210	9-18-92	0	3	9.49	6	6	0	25	40	27	26	4	13	24	.367	.437	.560	19.0	10.3	126
Watkins, Chase	L-L	6-4	215	10-4-99	0	0	6.75	1	0	0	1	1	1	1	0	3	3	.000	.500	.000	37.5	37.5	8
Wicks, Jordan	L-L	6-3	220	9-1-99	3	4	3.55	20	16	2	71	66	30	28	4	23	77	.247	.307	.378	26.1	7.8	295
Wiggins, Jaxon	R-R	6-6	225	10-3-01	0	2	4.66	3	3	0	10	9	5	5	2	6	14	.243	.364	.405	31.8	13.6	44
Woodford, Jake	R-R	6-4	215	10-28-96	1	1	4.57	4	3	0	22	24	11	11	3	3	20	.279	.311	.500	22.2	3.3	90

Fielding

Catcher	PCT	G	PO	A	E	DP	PB
Amaya	1.000	10	65	2	0	1	1
Ballesteros	.986	71	679	27	10	5	7
Knight	.971	11	61	6	2	0	3
McGuire	1.000	13	128	5	0	1	1
Opitz	.000	1	0	0	0	0	0
Perez	.995	53	523	39	3	2	6

First Base	PCT	G	PO	A	E	DP
Ballesteros	1.000	3	13	1	0	2
Knight	1.000	3	12	0	0	0
Long	.994	115	777	69	5	69
Lopez	1.000	1	6	0	0	0
Perez	.988	16	78	6	1	9
Strumpf	.979	18	127	10	3	11

Second Base	PCT	G	PO	A	E	DP
Cantrelle	.982	30	45	64	2	13
Cowles	1.000	18	27	34	0	7
Howard	1.000	2	2	2	0	0

	PCT	G	PO	A	E	DP
Lopez	1.000	5	8	12	0	1
Machado	.967	11	25	34	2	13
Strumpf	.974	26	30	46	2	10
Triantos	.964	64	89	125	8	27

Third Base	PCT	G	PO	A	E	DP
Cantrelle	1.000	17	1	22	0	3
Cowles	.971	15	8	25	1	2
Long	1.000	9	3	5	0	0
Lopez	1.000	4	1	4	0	0
Machado	.950	37	35	60	5	6
Shaw	.964	23	9	45	2	3
Strumpf	.890	51	26	71	12	8

Shortstop	PCT	G	PO	A	E	DP
Brujan	1.000	1	2	3	0	2
Cantrelle	.957	15	23	43	3	12
Cowles	.981	81	100	165	5	37
Howard	.667	2	0	2	1	0
Lopez	1.000	20	21	51	0	10

	PCT	G	PO	A	E	DP
Machado	.971	36	47	86	4	12
Outfield	PCT	G	PO	A	E	DP
Alcantara	.970	96	191	6	6	1
Allen	1.000	54	84	3	0	2
Brujan	1.000	2	1	0	0	0
Caissie	.973	85	136	7	4	2
Cantrelle	.968	16	27	3	1	0
Chavers	.981	28	49	2	1	0
Franklin	.994	81	170	5	1	2
Hill	.979	26	45	1	1	0
Long	1.000	6	10	0	0	0
Lopez	1.000	1	3	0	0	0
Morel	1.000	11	14	1	0	0
Palmer	1.000	1	4	0	0	0
Perez	1.000	3	5	0	0	0
Sanders	.000	1	0	0	0	0
Triantos	.974	37	73	1	2	1
Wall	.917	20	21	1	2	1

KNOXVILLE SMOKIES
SOUTHERN LEAGUE — DOUBLE-A

Batting	B-T	Ht.	Wt.	DOB	AVG	OBP	SLG	G	PA	AB	R	H	2B	3B	HR	RBI	BB	HBP	SH	SF	SO	SB	CS	BB%	SO%
Aliendo, Pablo	R-R	6-0	170	5-29-01	.204	.269	.354	96	390	353	40	72	14	0	13	49	24	9	0	4	136	0	3	6.2	34.9
Bateman, Brett	L-L	5-10	190	3-19-02	.261	.376	.307	94	396	329	42	86	9	0	2	33	61	1	2	3	82	19	6	15.4	20.7
Cantrelle, Hayden	S-R	5-11	175	11-25-98	.239	.402	.359	30	118	92	13	22	5	3	0	10	24	1	1	0	35	11	1	20.3	29.7
Chavers, Parker	L-R	5-9	185	7-25-98	.231	.347	.322	71	248	208	32	48	12	2	1	21	36	2	0	2	48	13	4	14.5	19.4
Garcia, Reivaj	S-R	5-9	175	8-12-01	.270	.326	.328	67	266	241	28	65	10	2	0	19	19	2	2	2	45	5	2	7.1	16.9
Garriola, Andy	R-R	6-3	235	12-15-99	.182	.250	.336	42	152	137	17	25	7	1	4	21	12	1	0	2	30	1	0	7.9	19.7
Hearn, Ethan	L-R	5-10	200	8-31-00	.190	.255	.302	89	333	305	30	58	8	1	8	31	24	3	0	1	99	5	0	7.2	29.7
Hill, Darius	L-L	5-11	190	8-17-97	.184	.253	.299	23	95	87	7	16	4	0	2	6	7	1	0	0	24	0	0	7.4	25.3
Howard, Ed	R-R	6-1	185	1-28-02	.104	.218	.125	15	56	48	4	5	1	0	0	2	7	0	1	0	27	2	1	12.5	48.2
Joyce, Corey	R-R	6-0	190	8-28-98	.272	.393	.487	92	389	323	48	88	16	1	12	33	56	8	0	0	81	15	2	14.4	20.8
McGeary, Haydn	R-R	6-4	235	10-9-99	.231	.344	.231	24	93	78	7	18	0	0	0	8	14	0	0	1	31	1	0	15.1	33.3
Murray, BJ	S-R	5-10	205	1-5-00	.242	.363	.418	125	537	443	62	107	18	0	20	89	82	5	0	6	103	20	8	15.5	19.2
Nwogu, Jordan	R-R	6-1	230	3-10-99	.280	.353	.348	99	368	325	50	91	9	2	3	40	26	13	0	4	92	23	7	7.1	25.0
Opitz, Casey	S-R	5-9	205	7-22-98	.202	.297	.295	60	213	183	21	37	5	0	4	25	23	3	1	3	63	2	0	10.8	29.6
Palmer, Jaylen	R-R	6-3	208	7-31-00	.239	.341	.332	117	437	376	57	90	17	1	8	35	53	6	0	2	153	25	9	12.1	35.0
Ramirez, Pedro	S-R	5-8	165	4-1-04	.280	.346	.386	129	563	500	70	140	21	4	8	73	46	9	0	8	85	28	10	8.2	15.1
Ramon, Eriandys	S-R	6-3	170	1-7-03	.130	.130	.261	6	23	23	3	3	0	0	1	2	0	0	0	0	5	1	0	0.0	21.7
Rojas, Jefferson	R-R	5-10	150	4-25-05	.164	.279	.205	39	172	146	17	24	6	0	0	15	20	4	0	2	34	5	0	11.6	19.8

CHICAGO CUBS

Batting (cont.)	B-T	Ht.	Wt.	DOB	AVG	OBP	SLG	G	PA	AB	R	H	2B	3B	HR	RBI	BB	HBP	SH	SF	SO	SB	CS	BB%	SO%
Stevens, Felix	R-R	6-4	225	7-30-99	.239	.318	.354	37	129	113	15	27	5	1	2	13	12	2	0	2	39	2	0	9.3	30.2
Trice, Carter	R-R	6-0	200	8-23-02	.104	.267	.188	20	60	48	4	5	1	0	1	4	10	1	0	1	20	1	1	16.7	33.3

Pitching	B-T	Ht.	Wt.	DOB	W	L	ERA	G	GS	SV	IP	Hits	Runs	ER	HR	BB	SO	AVG	OBP	SLG	SO%	BB%	BF
Almonte, Yency	R-R	6-5	223	6-4-94	0	0	2.53	8	0	0	11	10	3	3	1	7	8	.278	.409	.389	18.2	15.9	44
Armstrong, Sam	R-R	6-2	245	9-26-00	2	7	4.62	19	18	0	90	82	49	46	10	31	72	.250	.325	.378	19.3	8.3	373
Brentz, Jake	L-L	6-1	205	9-14-94	0	1	18.00	7	0	0	6	5	13	12	0	14	6	.208	.500	.292	15.8	36.8	38
Clarke, Chris	R-R	6-7	215	5-13-98	0	0	0.69	4	2	0	13	6	1	1	0	2	13	.133	.170	.178	27.7	4.3	47
Clenney, Nolan	L-R	6-2	200	6-16-96	1	1	4.08	10	0	0	18	13	10	8	1	13	8	.213	.364	.344	10.3	16.7	78
Dean, Nick	R-R	6-3	180	12-26-00	1	4	6.19	8	8	0	32	34	23	22	4	10	36	.270	.321	.421	26.3	7.3	137
Deppermann, Brad	R-R	6-0	195	6-15-96	4	2	2.76	41	0	5	46	41	16	14	0	11	42	.238	.277	.297	22.3	5.9	188
Gallagher, Ryan	L-R	6-3	195	1-19-03	0	0	1.59	2	2	0	11	5	2	2	1	4	11	.132	.233	.263	25.6	9.3	43
Hull, Nick	R-R	6-0	205	8-21-99	2	2	3.61	35	2	0	57	53	27	23	7	26	56	.247	.333	.405	22.7	10.5	247
Jensen, Wil	R-R	6-4	180	9-2-97	0	0	1.74	8	0	1	10	10	2	2	0	4	14	.256	.341	.308	31.8	9.1	44
Kachmar, Chris	R-R	6-3	180	9-3-96	3	5	4.28	15	15	0	74	67	36	35	8	29	73	.245	.320	.414	23.5	9.3	311
Kipp, Grant	R-R	6-6	220	11-11-99	6	7	4.22	26	23	0	109	86	55	51	10	57	110	.222	.347	.348	23.5	12.2	469
Kwiatkowski, Robert	R-R	6-1	190	6-8-97	2	2	4.12	15	0	0	20	28	14	9	1	12	19	.341	.427	.476	19.6	12.4	97
Leeper, Ben	R-R	6-0	195	6-15-97	0	0	2.16	8	0	0	8	5	2	2	0	4	10	.167	.265	.267	29.4	11.8	34
Leigh, Zac	R-R	6-0	170	11-14-97	4	2	4.11	43	0	0	50	33	29	23	3	39	47	.191	.353	.301	21.2	17.6	222
Netz, Dawson	R-R	6-1	190	8-3-00	0	0	6.00	2	0	0	3	3	2	2	0	1	3	.250	.308	.417	23.1	7.7	13
Opitz, Casey	S-R	5-9	200	7-30-98	0	0	16.88	3	0	0	3	6	5	5	2	0	1	.429	.500	.929	6.3	0.0	16
Oquendo, Johzan	R-R	6-2	180	1-6-01	0	0	13.50	4	0	0	3	4	5	5	0	6	3	.286	.524	.286	14.3	28.6	21
Powell, Walker	R-R	6-8	210	6-11-96	0	1	3.33	6	6	0	27	24	12	10	4	6	17	.233	.277	.437	14.9	5.3	114
Puckett, A.J.	R-R	6-4	200	5-27-95	3	6	3.35	46	0	15	51	49	23	19	2	21	46	.249	.333	.320	20.4	9.3	226
Rodriguez, Erian	R-R	6-3	190	11-23-01	2	1	3.54	4	4	0	20	21	8	8	2	10	15	.288	.369	.425	17.4	11.6	86
Rojas, Yenrri	R-R	6-1	186	11-30-03	0	1	6.75	2	2	0	8	8	6	6	2	5	9	.250	.351	.469	24.3	13.5	37
Romero, Tommy	R-R	6-2	222	7-8-97	3	1	2.00	7	5	0	36	23	8	8	2	12	29	.180	.248	.273	20.6	8.5	141
Rujano, Luis	R-R	6-4	200	4-22-03	0	0	0.00	2	0	0	4	0	0	0	0	1	2	.000	.083	.000	16.7	8.3	12
Sanders, Will	L-R	6-6	230	3-30-02	3	2	2.64	9	9	0	44	38	13	13	1	8	44	.233	.276	.307	25.1	4.6	175
Santana, Tyler	R-R	6-1	205	5-13-98	5	4	4.06	35	1	7	64	67	34	29	4	22	50	.270	.328	.379	18.2	8.0	275
Santos, Antonio	R-R	6-3	223	10-6-96	3	5	2.12	20	15	0	76	44	20	18	1	33	64	.171	.273	.202	21.3	11.0	301
Scalzo, Frankie	R-R	6-3	185	11-25-99	5	3	4.44	20	1	0	24	21	14	12	4	12	22	.236	.344	.437	21.2	11.5	104
Schlaffer, Tyler	R-R	6-1	180	5-24-01	4	2	2.78	9	9	0	45	38	16	14	2	18	42	.233	.314	.325	22.5	9.6	187
Schultz, Connor	R-R	6-4	225	2-12-99	1	1	1.47	3	3	0	18	9	5	3	1	4	18	.148	.224	.262	26.5	5.9	68
Taylor, Evan	L-L	6-4	250	12-26-99	3	1	1.86	11	0	0	19	13	6	4	0	11	25	.186	.293	.214	30.5	13.4	82
Thoresen, Sam	R-R	6-3	210	9-21-00	1	0	1.98	15	0	0	14	6	5	3	0	19	16	.133	.394	.156	24.2	28.8	66
Tyranski, Mitchell	L-L	6-2	215	9-2-97	5	3	2.37	47	0	6	57	29	21	15	0	35	59	.157	.306	.222	25.3	15.0	233
Ueckert, Cayne	R-R	6-3	195	5-28-96	4	1	5.46	28	0	0	30	32	19	18	4	22	35	.281	.420	.465	24.5	15.4	143
Watkins, Chase	L-L	6-4	215	10-4-99	1	1	0.92	12	1	0	29	19	5	3	1	5	25	.179	.221	.255	22.1	4.4	113
Wiggins, Jaxon	R-R	6-6	225	10-3-01	2	0	1.93	10	10	0	42	22	9	9	1	17	52	.152	.239	.193	31.7	10.4	164

Fielding

Catcher	PCT	G	PO	A	E	DP	PB
Aliendo	.984	47	382	41	7	2	9
Hearn	.980	40	322	21	7	1	3
Opitz	.992	51	446	44	4	10	5

First Base	PCT	G	PO	A	E	DP
Aliendo	1.000	24	172	14	0	23
Garcia	.800	1	4	0	1	0
Hearn	.978	35	209	14	5	19
McGeary	.985	10	63	2	1	4
Murray	.995	57	388	5	2	32
Opitz	1.000	4	19	2	0	1
Palmer	.000	1	0	0	0	0
Stevens	1.000	12	66	4	0	6
Trice	.947	2	18	0	1	1

Second Base	PCT	G	PO	A	E	DP
Cantrelle	1.000	9	9	26	0	4
Garcia	.983	34	43	70	2	19
Howard	1.000	3	3	8	0	2
Joyce	.967	35	42	77	4	14
Ramirez	.983	59	78	150	4	32

Third Base	PCT	G	PO	A	E	DP
Garcia	1.000	10	8	12	0	1
Joyce	.000	1	0	0	0	0
Murray	.959	50	49	69	5	12
Palmer	.905	12	8	11	2	2
Ramirez	.974	68	60	88	4	6
Ramon	1.000	1	4	0	0	0
Rojas	1.000	2	1	1	0	0

Shortstop	PCT	G	PO	A	E	DP
Cantrelle	1.000	19	30	36	0	8
Garcia	.988	23	42	40	1	13
Howard	.966	12	12	16	1	5
Joyce	.957	30	36	54	4	15
Palmer	.911	13	24	17	4	4
Ramon	1.000	5	5	7	0	2
Rojas	.952	37	53	104	8	21

Outfield	PCT	G	PO	A	E	DP
Bateman	.981	88	201	8	4	0
Cantrelle	1.000	2	3	1	0	0
Chavers	.970	68	126	3	4	0
Garriola	.949	30	54	2	3	1
Hill	1.000	18	26	1	0	0
Nwogu	.984	89	178	5	3	2
Palmer	.995	91	203	0	1	0
Stevens	1.000	24	44	3	0	0
Trice	1.000	15	31	0	0	0

SOUTH BEND CUBS
MIDWEST LEAGUE — HIGH-A

Batting	B-T	Ht.	Wt.	DOB	AVG	OBP	SLG	G	PA	AB	R	H	2B	3B	HR	RBI	BB	HBP	SH	SF	SO	SB	CS	BB%	SO%
Alvarez, Edgar	L-R	6-4	225	2-19-01	.258	.349	.375	105	438	376	49	97	20	0	8	43	52	4	0	6	94	8	1	11.9	21.5
Armas, Ariel	R-R	6-0	180	11-29-02	.234	.325	.347	92	381	334	28	78	21	1	5	47	38	8	0	1	70	11	4	10.0	18.4
Avitia, David	R-R	5-9	205	9-20-98	.000	.143	.000	3	7	6	0	0	0	0	0	0	1	0	0	0	2	0	0	14.3	28.6
Bowser, Drew	R-R	6-4	226	10-4-01	.204	.326	.270	89	340	285	38	58	9	2	2	30	48	5	0	2	91	18	4	14.1	26.8
Brethowr, Ivan	R-R	6-0	245	2-27-03	.221	.398	.312	83	344	263	48	58	10	1	4	26	57	22	0	2	92	25	2	16.6	26.7
Espinoza, Leonel	R-R	6-0	165	4-7-03	.244	.292	.256	23	89	82	13	20	1	0	0	5	6	0	0	1	12	10	0	6.7	13.5
Garcia, Reivaj	S-R	5-9	175	8-12-01	.230	.280	.270	33	133	122	12	28	5	0	0	9	8	1	1	1	19	8	2	6.0	14.3
Garriola, Andy	R-R	6-3	235	12-15-99	.220	.292	.375	63	260	232	30	51	12	0	8	37	19	6	0	3	63	5	1	7.3	24.2
Hernandez, Alexis	R-R	6-0	155	12-27-04	.262	.404	.381	15	52	42	4	11	2	0	1	6	10	0	0	0	10	1	0	19.2	19.2

Name	B-T	Ht.	Wt.	DOB	AVG	OBP	SLG	G	AB	H	R	RBI	2B	3B	HR	BB	SO	HBP	SH	SF	TB	SB	CS	...	...
Hernandez, Cristian	R-R	6-1	175	12-13-03	.252	.329	.365	115	507	444	54	112	25	2	7	53	53	1	0	6	105	52	9	10.5	20.7
Howard, Ed	R-R	6-1	185	1-28-02	.000	.000	.000	2	9	9	0	0	0	0	0	0	0	0	0	0	4	0	0	0.0	44.4
Kalmer, Brian	R-R	6-2	215	8-17-00	.209	.319	.369	89	360	306	41	64	13	3	10	46	50	1	0	3	91	5	0	13.9	25.3
Morel, Rafael	R-R	6-0	170	11-22-01	.172	.298	.245	103	362	302	48	52	13	0	3	35	50	6	0	4	112	23	2	13.8	30.9
Pabon, Miguel	R-R	5-9	165	8-30-00	.192	.286	.233	59	221	193	20	37	3	1	1	14	24	2	1	1	64	6	0	10.9	29.0
Paciolla, Christopher	R-R	6-0	185	3-16-04	.188	.333	.250	11	39	32	4	6	2	0	0	2	5	2	0	0	8	1	0	12.8	20.5
Poteet, Logan	R-R	6-2	214	11-12-03	.176	.176	.353	5	17	17	1	3	0	0	1	3	0	0	0	0	8	0	0	0.0	47.1
Preciado, Reginald	S-R	6-3	185	5-16-03	.218	.292	.302	85	315	285	26	62	15	0	3	32	22	8	0	0	75	10	4	7.0	23.8
Rojas, Jefferson	R-R	5-10	150	4-25-05	.278	.379	.492	67	299	252	50	70	13	4	11	44	38	5	0	3	47	14	3	12.7	15.7
Sisneros, Cameron	L-L	6-2	230	6-1-01	.213	.342	.329	45	190	155	17	33	6	0	4	23	30	2	0	3	36	8	0	15.8	18.9
Snell, Kade	L-L	6-1	220	7-29-02	.167	.268	.219	27	112	96	12	16	3	1	0	7	14	0	0	2	19	11	2	12.5	17.0
Stevens, Felix	R-R	6-4	225	7-30-99	.188	.364	.438	5	22	16	4	3	1	0	1	2	5	0	0	1	4	1	0	22.7	18.2
Triantos, James	R-R	6-1	195	1-29-03	.273	.306	.394	8	36	33	4	9	4	0	0	4	2	0	0	1	5	3	0	5.6	13.9
Trice, Carter	R-R	6-0	200	8-23-02	.198	.352	.405	73	318	257	53	51	9	1	14	34	55	6	0	0	87	22	6	17.3	27.4
Useche, Miguel	R-R	6-0	200	1-23-01	.091	.222	.091	7	27	22	2	2	0	0	0	2	4	0	0	1	7	2	0	14.8	25.9

Pitching

Name	B-T	Ht.	Wt.	DOB	W	L	ERA	G	GS	SV	IP	Hits	Runs	ER	HR	BB	SO	AVG	OBP	SLG	SO%	BB%	BF
Almonte, Yency	R-R	6-5	223	6-4-94	2	0	1.04	7	0	0	9	4	1	1	1	3	9	.148	.233	.259	30.0	10.0	30
Aschenbeck, Evan	R-L	6-2	220	6-26-01	4	4	2.81	16	13	0	80	79	27	25	5	18	56	.256	.305	.351	16.9	5.4	331
Avitia, David	R-R	5-9	205	9-20-98	0	0	0.00	1	0	0	1	0	0	0	0	0	0	.000	.000	.000	0.0	0.0	3
Birdsell, Brandon	R-R	6-2	240	3-23-00	1	0	3.00	2	2	0	9	7	4	3	1	3	8	.206	.289	.382	21.1	7.9	38
Cabrera, Yovanny	R-R	6-2	180	3-22-01	0	1	5.91	7	0	0	11	9	8	7	0	8	8	.243	.408	.243	16.0	16.0	50
Caple, Brooks	R-R	6-6	230	8-23-02	3	8	5.97	14	14	0	63	75	48	42	6	29	44	.305	.371	.439	15.2	10.0	289
Carraway, Burl	L-L	6-0	173	5-27-99	1	0	16.20	7	0	0	5	3	10	9	0	14	4	.188	.588	.188	11.4	40.0	35
Clenney, Nolan	L-R	6-2	200	6-16-96	0	0	6.00	3	0	0	6	10	5	4	1	1	5	.357	.379	.607	16.7	3.3	30
Dean, Nick	R-R	6-3	180	12-26-00	0	3	4.68	7	7	0	33	35	19	17	3	9	39	.273	.321	.445	28.5	6.6	137
Egbert, Kenten	R-R	6-3	205	7-9-01	7	8	4.26	25	17	1	101	113	53	48	7	25	60	.281	.328	.398	13.8	5.8	434
Franklin, Kohl	R-R	6-4	195	9-9-99	0	1	13.50	1	1	0	2	4	3	3	0	3	1	.500	.667	.500	7.7	23.1	13
Gallagher, Ryan	L-R	6-3	195	1-19-03	4	6	3.72	14	14	0	73	65	34	30	9	16	85	.232	.276	.364	28.6	5.4	297
Gray, Drew	L-L	6-3	190	5-9-03	0	1	15.00	1	1	0	3	5	5	5	1	4	3	.385	.556	.769	16.7	22.2	18
Hambley, Dominic	R-R	6-2	230	4-24-03	0	0	6.52	8	0	0	10	9	8	7	1	9	10	.257	.417	.343	20.8	18.8	48
Hernandez, Angel	L-L	6-2	180	5-6-00	1	1	5.79	6	0	0	9	9	8	6	0	6	9	.222	.404	.278	25.5	19.1	47
Kilian, Caleb	R-R	6-4	180	6-2-97	0	0	9.00	2	0	0	3	3	3	3	1	0	1	.250	.308	.667	7.7	0.0	13
Kirkpatrick, Jackson	L-R	6-7	250	8-15-02	1	0	1.19	18	0	3	23	12	3	3	0	17	29	.158	.312	.184	31.2	18.3	93
Martinez-Gomez, Luis	R-R	6-2	178	5-27-03	1	1	0.52	10	0	0	17	11	5	1	0	4	16	.177	.235	.177	23.2	5.8	69
Moore, Grayson	S-R	6-3	215	7-9-01	0	0	4.40	26	0	5	31	27	17	15	0	21	40	.233	.361	.293	27.8	14.6	144
Moreno, Koen	R-R	6-2	170	8-1-01	1	0	2.25	4	1	0	12	8	3	3	0	8	15	.195	.320	.244	30.0	16.0	50
Morgan, Eli	R-R	5-10	190	5-13-96	0	0	0.00	2	0	0	2	0	0	0	0	1	1	.000	.000	.000	16.7	0.0	6
Mule, Nazier	R-R	6-1	210	10-15-04	0	1	5.73	3	3	0	11	13	7	7	1	11	9	.310	.473	.429	16.4	20.0	55
Nahas, Joe	R-R	6-8	225	6-5-00	1	2	6.27	13	0	0	19	27	15	13	2	4	12	.346	.381	.564	14.1	4.7	85
Neely, Jack	R-R	6-8	225	6-5-00	0	0	3.00	3	0	0	3	3	1	1	1	0	4	.250	.308	.500	30.8	0.0	13
Netz, Dawson	R-R	6-1	190	8-3-00	0	1	3.60	2	2	0	10	14	5	4	2	2	12	.333	.364	.500	27.3	4.5	44
Oquendo, Johzan	R-R	6-2	180	1-6-01	4	1	1.64	24	0	2	33	15	7	6	2	16	43	.135	.265	.234	32.6	12.1	132
Perez, Kenyi	R-R	6-2	165	8-9-01	1	0	5.67	36	0	1	40	31	26	25	1	46	55	.226	.447	.314	27.9	23.4	197
Reilly, Vince	R-R	5-10	160	6-7-01	0	6	4.91	29	0	3	29	35	20	16	1	13	25	.292	.356	.417	18.4	9.6	136
Reyes, Carlo	R-R	6-0	212	7-4-98	0	1	17.18	3	0	0	4	8	7	7	1	3	2	.444	.545	.889	11.1	13.6	22
Reynolds, Cole	L-L	6-5	225	5-30-02	1	3	8.31	8	0	0	13	16	12	12	2	10	10	.302	.449	.491	14.5	14.5	69
Risedorph, Brayden	R-R	6-3	235	7-30-03	1	0	0.00	9	0	2	11	4	0	0	0	9	13	.118	.295	.176	29.5	20.5	44
Rodriguez, Erian	R-R	6-3	190	11-23-03	6	4	2.81	12	12	0	64	52	28	20	2	22	58	.223	.312	.330	21.8	8.3	266
Rojas, Yenrri	R-R	6-1	186	11-30-03	2	3	2.10	6	6	0	34	25	8	8	1	7	30	.210	.260	.286	23.6	5.5	127
Rujano, Luis	R-R	6-4	200	4-22-03	1	3	4.25	31	3	3	49	44	28	23	3	38	57	.242	.373	.335	25.3	16.9	225
Santy, Marino	L-L	5-11	170	3-4-02	1	2	9.00	20	0	0	27	37	32	30	1	32	24	.250	.458	.352	15.7	20.9	153
Schlaffer, Tyler	R-R	6-1	180	5-24-01	3	1	4.10	12	12	0	59	41	29	27	7	28	60	.195	.295	.362	24.8	11.6	242
Schultz, Connor	R-R	6-4	225	2-12-99	2	4	4.06	24	10	1	71	79	34	32	6	17	71	.279	.322	.413	23.1	5.5	307
Spencer, Connor	R-R	6-2	220	11-4-00	0	0	1.93	5	0	0	5	3	2	1	1	3	4	.167	.286	.333	19.0	14.3	21
Taylor, Evan	L-L	6-4	250	12-26-99	3	1	3.27	20	0	1	33	24	20	12	1	17	40	.190	.238	.254	27.0	11.5	148
Thoresen, Sam	R-R	6-3	210	9-21-98	0	2	5.93	11	0	1	14	12	9	9	0	10	23	.240	.371	.320	36.5	15.9	63
Valdez, Kevin	R-R	6-4	185	11-13-01	2	3	4.50	7	7	0	32	37	23	16	2	22	19	.296	.400	.400	12.7	14.7	150
Watkins, Chase	L-L	6-4	215	10-4-99	1	1	3.76	19	1	0	41	39	17	17	3	11	40	.237	.300	.346	23.5	6.5	170
Wiggins, Jaxon	R-R	6-6	225	10-3-01	1	2	1.71	6	5	0	26	13	10	5	1	13	31	.143	.257	.231	29.5	12.4	105

Fielding

Catcher	PCT	G	PO	A	E	DP	PB
Armas	.983	79	694	72	13	10	2
Avitia	1.000	2	12	3	0	0	0
Pabon	.988	49	391	20	5	2	2
Poteet	1.000	3	11	1	0	0	0
Useche	1.000	1	9	1	0	0	0

First Base	PCT	G	PO	A	E	DP
Alvarez	1.000	16	98	9	0	7
Bowser	.984	17	109	14	2	13
Kalmer	.983	67	489	31	9	52
Sisneros	.985	27	187	15	3	15
Stevens	1.000	1	4	1	0	0

	PCT	G	PO	A	E	DP
Trice	.974	6	37	0	1	1

Second Base	PCT	G	PO	A	E	DP
Bowser	.947	17	25	46	4	7
Garcia	.955	17	34	30	3	10
Hernandez	.981	13	25	28	1	14
Hernandez	.981	13	22	30	1	4
Morel	.957	10	19	26	2	4
Pabon	1.000	2	3	6	0	1
Paciolla	1.000	4	6	7	0	3
Preciado	.951	19	32	45	4	11
Rojas	.955	33	43	64	5	13
Triantos	.955	6	7	14	1	2

Third Base	PCT	G	PO	A	E	DP
Alvarez	.861	16	8	23	5	2
Bowser	.940	45	28	81	7	6
Garcia	.970	15	11	21	1	4
Morel	1.000	1	1	0	0	0
Paciolla	1.000	7	5	3	0	2
Preciado	.928	49	36	92	10	9
Rojas	1.000	4	6	7	0	0

Shortstop	PCT	G	PO	A	E	DP
Hernandez	1.000	2	2	5	0	1
Hernandez	.948	95	148	237	21	34
Morel	.974	8	19	18	1	6

Preciado	.750	1	2	1	1	0	Espinoza	.979	19	47	0	1	1	Sisneros	1.000 5 5 0 0 0
Rojas	1.000	25	35	52	0	16	Garriola	.984	53	119	2	2	0	Snell	.939 27 44 2 3 0
							Morel	.970	84	153	6	5	2	Stevens	.857 3 6 0 1 0
Outfield	PCT	G	PO	A	E	DP	Pabon	1.000	2	2	0	0	0	Trice	.982 63 157 3 3 0
Alvarez	.974	66	108	4	3	2	Preciado	.955	15	21	0	1	0		
Brethowr	.970	72	128	2	4	1									

MYRTLE BEACH PELICANS   *LOW-A*
CAROLINA LEAGUE

CHICAGO CUBS

Batting	B-T	Ht.	Wt.	DOB	AVG	OBP	SLG	G	PA	AB	R	H	2B	3B	HR	RBI	BB	HBP	SH	SF	SO	SB	CS	BB%	SO%
Alcantara, Derik	L-R	6-0	160	2-20-05	.192	.333	.282	26	99	78	17	15	2	1	1	12	17	1	0	3	13	4	1	17.2	13.1
Avitia, David	R-R	5-9	205	9-20-98	.238	.304	.286	6	24	21	2	5	1	0	0	5	1	1	1	0	12	0	0	4.2	50.0
Ayers, Owen	S-R	6-2	185	6-7-01	.238	.341	.420	65	273	231	30	55	14	5	6	47	31	7	0	4	63	7	0	11.4	23.1
Carico, Michael	L-R	6-0	190	9-4-02	.227	.433	.409	7	30	22	5	5	1	0	1	7	6	2	0	0	7	0	0	20.0	23.3
Cepeda, Angel	R-R	6-1	170	10-29-05	.249	.339	.375	100	433	381	47	95	14	5	8	49	40	12	0	0	136	27	7	9.2	31.4
Diaz, Jairo	L-R	5-10	180	7-14-04	.314	.479	.400	12	48	35	10	11	3	0	0	1	12	0	0	1	11	2	0	25.0	22.9
Escobar, Jose	L-R	5-10	165	9-13-04	.264	.351	.349	105	461	401	61	106	19	0	5	46	47	9	0	4	96	11	9	10.2	20.8
Espinoza, Leonel	R-R	6-0	165	4-7-03	.270	.331	.370	93	408	370	60	100	15	2	6	54	31	4	0	3	90	21	8	7.6	22.1
Granadillo, Dilan	S-R	5-7	175	5-18-01	.190	.292	.252	47	171	147	14	28	6	0	1	12	19	3	0	2	56	0	0	11.1	32.7
Halbach, Matt	R-R	6-3	215	11-8-03	.244	.349	.379	103	436	369	51	90	23	0	9	67	47	15	0	5	90	2	2	10.8	20.6
Hernandez, Alexis	R-R	6-0	155	12-27-04	.173	.258	.222	23	93	81	11	14	4	0	0	7	7	3	0	2	22	4	2	7.5	23.7
Kepley, Kane	L-L	5-8	180	2-14-04	.299	.481	.433	28	131	97	28	29	1	3	2	15	25	9	0	0	15	16	4	19.1	11.5
Lovich, Eli	L-L	6-4	185	8-2-05	.214	.285	.280	50	200	182	19	39	2	2	2	26	18	0	0	0	68	8	1	9.0	34.0
Lumpuy, Alexey	L-L	6-0	180	2-22-04	.209	.294	.364	102	429	382	62	80	14	6	11	46	34	12	1	0	154	30	9	7.9	35.9
Mathis, Cole	R-R	6-1	195	7-25-03	.215	.336	.402	29	128	107	16	23	9	1	3	14	17	3	0	1	29	0	2	13.3	22.7
Melendez, Yahil	L-R	6-2	175	9-5-05	.219	.357	.296	51	207	169	22	37	5	1	2	21	30	7	0	1	75	7	4	14.5	36.2
Olivo, Christian	R-R	5-9	168	10-29-03	.240	.365	.337	92	348	288	52	69	17	1	3	38	47	11	0	2	64	28	10	13.5	18.4
Paciolla, Christopher	R-R	6-0	185	3-16-04	.179	.276	.269	19	76	67	3	12	6	0	0	4	7	2	0	0	17	3	2	9.2	22.4
Ramon, Eriandys	S-R	6-3	170	1-7-03	.188	.247	.261	45	179	165	18	31	5	2	1	12	10	3	0	0	54	1	2	5.6	30.2
Sass, Sammy	R-R	6-1	195	12-18-00	.091	.091	.091	5	12	11	1	1	0	0	0	0	0	0	0	0	4	0	0	0.0	33.3
Sisneros, Cameron	L-L	6-2	230	6-11-01	.352	.478	.488	38	157	125	18	44	8	0	3	26	23	8	0	1	15	5	2	14.6	9.6
Southisene, Ty	R-R	5-9	157	7-8-05	.244	.387	.276	90	389	315	69	77	6	2	0	36	62	11	0	0	58	41	7	15.9	14.9
Stransky, Justin	R-R	6-1	180	9-10-02	.163	.255	.186	13	51	43	4	7	1	0	0	5	6	0	0	2	12	2	0	11.8	23.5
Suriel, Anderson	L-L	5-11	175	4-11-03	.133	.220	.194	28	109	98	11	13	6	0	0	2	7	4	0	0	31	2	1	6.4	28.4

Pitching	B-T	Ht.	Wt.	DOB	W	L	ERA	G	GS	SV	IP	Hits	Runs	ER	HR	BB	SO	AVG	OBP	SLG	SO%	BB%	BF
Aschenbeck, Evan	R-L	6-2	220	6-26-01	1	0	0.00	3	2	0	14	7	1	0	0	4	16	.146	.212	.167	30.8	7.7	52
Bell, Ethan	R-R	6-1	190	2-14-02	1	4	3.90	26	0	2	32	32	22	14	1	33	49	.252	.402	.394	29.9	20.1	164
Bracho, David	R-R	6-0	160	2-24-05	0	0	1.69	2	0	0	5	6	2	1	0	2	3	.286	.348	.333	13.0	8.7	23
Camacho, Kevin	R-R	5-11	200	2-10-05	0	1	1.76	8	6	1	31	17	7	6	0	14	33	.162	.276	.229	26.8	11.4	123
Caple, Brooks	R-R	6-6	230	8-23-02	3	1	1.80	7	7	0	35	24	9	7	0	14	30	.198	.283	.264	21.6	10.1	139
Clarke, Chris	R-R	6-7	215	5-13-98	1	0	3.00	2	1	0	9	9	3	3	0	1	11	.250	.270	.333	28.9	2.6	38
Coppola, Pierce	L-L	6-8	215	12-17-02	0	0	2.25	3	2	0	8	5	2	2	0	9	14	.179	.395	.214	36.8	23.7	38
Edders, Noah	R-R	6-4	232	6-6-03	0	0	1.80	3	0	0	5	2	1	1	0	2	9	.125	.222	.188	50.0	11.1	18
Flanagan, Ethan	L-L	6-3	205	6-5-02	5	1	1.93	12	12	0	56	43	12	12	1	22	54	.216	.302	.256	23.8	9.7	227
Florentino, Jostin	R-R	6-0	175	12-1-04	4	3	1.96	11	10	0	60	42	16	13	1	20	67	.187	.265	.244	26.9	8.0	249
Frank, Hayden	R-L	6-5	210	12-16-02	2	4	7.23	13	12	0	56	75	48	45	6	25	43	.329	.395	.478	16.7	9.7	257
Frisch, Will	R-R	6-0	222	7-14-00	0	4	5.40	12	12	0	45	38	29	27	3	37	45	.232	.397	.335	21.5	17.7	209
Ginn, Landon	S-R	6-3	200	7-19-01	5	2	5.68	22	0	1	38	38	26	24	2	17	40	.259	.333	.347	23.7	10.1	169
Gonzalez, Yoendris	R-R	5-11	215	11-27-02	5	1	4.38	22	0	0	37	29	20	18	3	16	34	.218	.335	.338	21.0	9.9	162
Gordon, Christian	R-L	6-0	180	1-22-01	0	0	12.00	2	1	0	3	6	5	4	0	1	4	.429	.467	.714	26.7	6.7	15
Hambley, Dominic	R-R	6-2	230	4-24-03	2	0	1.36	21	0	1	33	17	6	5	1	23	38	.157	.324	.185	27.7	16.8	137
Hurley, Charlie	L-R	6-8	218	2-21-02	4	5	5.52	30	0	0	60	62	43	37	0	45	49	.268	.404	.325	16.9	15.5	290
Kirkpatrick, Jackson	L-R	6-7	250	8-15-02	3	0	0.84	15	0	7	21	9	6	2	0	13	36	.125	.256	.125	41.9	15.1	86
Lopez, Ronny	R-R	6-1	185	11-18-02	0	2	6.59	7	6	0	27	24	20	20	1	21	12	.247	.389	.361	9.5	16.7	126
Mangus, Thomas	R-R	6-3	215	6-18-03	4	0	0.82	6	0	0	11	4	1	1	0	8	6	.118	.302	.147	14.0	18.6	43
Martinez-Gomez, Luis	R-R	6-2	178	5-27-03	3	1	1.89	27	0	2	38	32	9	8	1	30	52	.227	.370	.303	31.1	18.0	167
Melendez, Edwardo	R-R	6-0	177	2-16-04	1	0	5.79	6	0	0	14	14	11	9	1	12	12	.255	.382	.436	17.4	17.4	69
Mule, Nazier	R-R	6-1	210	10-15-04	3	7	5.79	15	15	0	56	44	43	36	1	44	60	.229	.390	.281	23.9	17.5	251
Netz, Dawson	R-R	6-1	190	8-3-00	2	0	1.62	5	1	0	17	11	3	3	0	8	18	.190	.299	.224	26.9	11.9	67
Peters, Mathew	R-R	6-4	215	12-28-00	1	2	8.31	19	0	4	22	26	22	20	1	23	20	.313	.473	.470	17.9	20.5	112
Powell, Walker	R-R	6-8	210	6-11-96	1	0	2.00	2	2	0	9	8	2	2	0	3	5	.250	.314	.313	13.9	8.3	36
Reyes, Luis A.	R-R	6-3	220	10-23-03	1	1	11.88	14	0	0	17	19	23	22	0	23	16	.275	.480	.319	16.0	23.0	100
Reynolds, Cole	L-L	6-5	230	5-30-02	3	2	4.15	19	2	1	43	39	23	20	2	27	49	.236	.364	.333	24.6	13.6	199
Risedorph, Brayden	R-R	6-3	235	7-30-03	0	0	0.60	9	0	2	15	6	4	1	0	4	18	.118	.196	.118	32.1	7.1	56
Rojas, Yenrri	R-R	6-1	186	11-30-03	3	2	2.63	11	9	0	48	37	14	14	0	20	34	.213	.296	.230	17.3	10.2	197
Romero, Alfredo	R-R	6-3	175	6-27-03	3	3	2.89	21	13	0	75	55	26	24	2	45	66	.206	.332	.270	20.7	14.1	319
Sierra, Joel	R-R	6-1	190	12-31-01	0	0	2.45	5	0	0	7	3	2	2	1	7	9	.120	.303	.240	27.3	21.2	33
Spears, Brayden	R-R	6-5	200	2-27-01	2	7	3.13	36	0	5	60	53	24	21	3	23	55	.272	.347	.353	21.2	8.9	259
Valdez, Kevin	R-R	6-4	185	11-13-01	2	3	3.49	14	7	0	59	47	26	23	2	34	53	.221	.337	.291	20.7	13.3	256
Vizcaino, Jeral	R-R	6-1	155	1-7-02	0	0	9.00	2	0	1	4	5	2	2	0	2	1	.400	.500	.500	8.3	16.7	12
Wheat, JP	R-R	6-5	185	8-3-02	2	2	4.09	7	5	0	33	21	16	15	1	22	34	.196	.355	.280	24.6	15.9	138
Zarraga, Victor	L-L	5-10	160	12-24-03	1	2	4.58	7	3	0	18	14	10	9	0	12	16	.215	.358	.231	19.8	14.8	81

Fielding

Catcher	PCT	G	PO	A	E	DP	PB
Avitia	.938	4	29	1	2	0	0
Ayers	.981	56	523	59	11	7	12
Carico	.971	7	63	4	2	0	2
Diaz	1.000	10	88	4	0	0	1
Granadillo	.990	47	374	38	4	3	10
Stransky	1.000	7	59	16	0	1	0

First Base	PCT	G	PO	A	E
Avitia	1.000	2	17	3	0
Ayers	1.000	8	63	6	0
Diaz	1.000	1	7	3	0
Halbach	.990	86	621	47	7
Ramon	1.000	1	2	0	0
Sisneros	1.000	36	268	26	0

(Ayers 8 63 6 0 2 — correcting: Ayers 1.000 8 63 6 0 2; Halbach .990 86 621 47 7 63; Sisneros 1.000 36 268 26 0 24)

Second Base	PCT	G	PO	A	E	DP
Cepeda	.964	10	14	39	2	7
Escobar	.943	17	32	34	4	8
Hernandez	1.000	1	2	4	0	0
Melendez	1.000	1	0	4	0	0
Olivo	.980	9	25	25	1	6
Ramon	.960	6	10	14	1	2
Southisene	.977	85	146	235	9	56

Third Base	PCT	G	PO	A	E	DP
Cepeda	.859	28	22	33	9	3
Halbach	.938	16	13	17	2	2
Melendez	.952	18	20	20	2	2
Olivo	.933	36	27	56	6	6
Paciolla	.975	19	18	21	1	1
Ramon	.968	15	7	23	1	4

Shortstop	PCT	G	PO	A	E	DP
Cepeda	.966	61	88	138	8	30
Hernandez	.951	22	33	45	4	6
Melendez	.892	29	35	64	12	18
Olivo	1.000	2	1	1	0	0
Ramon	1.000	19	24	46	0	6

Outfield	PCT	G	PO	A	E	DP
Alcantara	.970	24	31	1	1	0
Escobar	.967	64	84	4	3	1
Espinoza	.971	84	162	6	5	0
Kepley	.981	21	52	1	1	0
Lovich	1.000	38	45	1	0	0
Lumpuy	.956	91	166	9	8	4
Olivo	1.000	44	79	4	0	0
Suriel	.959	24	46	1	2	0

ACL CUBS — ROOKIE
ARIZONA COMPLEX LEAGUE

Batting	B-T	Ht.	Wt.	DOB	AVG	OBP	SLG	G	PA	AB	R	H	2B	3B	HR	RBI	BB	HBP	SH	SF	SO	SB	CS	BB%	SO%
Alcala, Henniel	R-R	5-11	175	6-22-06	.182	.354	.221	27	99	77	6	14	3	0	0	11	12	9	0	1	23	4	2	12.1	23.2
Alcantara, Derik	L-R	6-0	160	2-20-05	.320	.394	.475	36	142	122	16	39	6	5	1	17	16	1	0	3	18	6	4	11.3	12.7
Amaya, Miguel	R-R	6-0	230	3-9-99	.200	.429	.200	3	7	5	1	1	0	0	0	1	1	0	0	0	2	0	0	14.3	28.6
Cruz, Fernando	R-R	5-11	155	11-13-06	.165	.247	.316	24	89	79	8	13	3	0	3	12	7	2	0	1	42	5	1	7.9	47.2
Cruz, Ronny	S-R	6-2	170	8-24-06	.270	.314	.431	48	189	174	20	47	10	6	2	21	10	2	0	2	35	10	7	5.3	18.5
De Leon, Darlyn	L-R	5-8	150	2-11-05	.263	.345	.461	21	87	76	14	20	4	1	3	16	8	2	0	1	20	4	2	9.2	23.0
De Leon, Edgardo	R-R	6-0	170	2-22-07	.276	.353	.500	43	153	134	26	37	5	5	5	15	15	2	0	2	44	5	2	9.8	28.8
Delgado, Joan	R-R	5-11	165	12-7-04	.194	.284	.320	32	116	103	20	20	4	3	1	10	11	2	0	0	43	14	0	9.5	37.1
Diaz, Jairo	L-R	5-10	180	7-14-04	.265	.339	.306	32	112	98	9	26	4	0	0	16	10	2	0	2	24	10	1	8.9	21.4
Espinoza, Ludwing	S-R	5-11	170	12-10-05	.229	.318	.314	49	173	153	25	35	6	2	1	18	18	2	0	0	40	19	6	10.4	23.1
Gutierrez, Albert	R-R	6-1	195	2-15-04	.234	.307	.339	40	140	124	8	29	4	0	3	15	13	1	0	2	34	0	0	9.3	24.3
Hernandez, Alexis	R-R	6-0	155	12-27-04	.262	.331	.377	32	136	122	20	32	7	2	1	13	13	0	0	1	28	12	4	9.6	20.6
Lovich, Eli	L-L	6-4	185	8-2-05	.270	.350	.416	23	100	89	14	24	5	1	2	10	9	2	0	0	20	10	3	9.0	20.0
Lugo, Cesar	L-L	6-0	165	2-6-07	.245	.352	.330	31	125	106	15	26	4	5	1	2	10	9	2	0	15	3	0	31	7	4	12.0	24.8
Melendez, Yahil	L-R	6-2	175	9-5-05	.000	.250	.000	1	4	3	0	0	0	0	0	0	1	0	1	0	0	2	0	0	0.0	50.0
Mena, Ismael	L-L	6-3	185	11-30-02	.157	.254	.275	18	59	51	6	8	3	0	1	6	7	0	0	1	10	2	1	11.9	16.9
Mora, Wilme	R-R	6-5	180	6-28-03	1.000	1.000	.000	16	1	0	0	0	0	0	0	0	0	0	0	0	0	0	0	0.0	100.0
Paciolla, Christopher	R-R	6-0	185	3-16-04	.204	.290	.247	28	107	93	8	19	1	0	1	9	6	6	0	2	32	5	2	5.6	29.9
Reyes, Jan Luis	L-L	5-11	165	10-5-05	.232	.318	.311	45	175	151	20	35	6	3	0	16	20	0	0	2	35	21	2	11.4	20.0
Sanchez, Adan	R-R	6-0	205	5-24-05	.256	.333	.372	14	48	43	5	11	5	0	0	5	2	3	0	0	9	1	2	4.2	18.8
Southisene, Ty	R-R	5-9	157	7-8-05	.333	.500	.333	1	4	3	0	1	0	0	0	0	1	0	0	0	1	0	0	25.0	25.0
Stevens, Felix	R-R	6-4	225	7-30-99	.500	.571	1.250	4	14	12	5	6	0	0	3	5	2	0	0	0	1	0	0	0.0	7.1
Valdez, Dernice	R-R	5-11	150	3-29-06	.135	.200	.189	12	40	37	4	5	2	0	0	2	3	0	0	0	15	2	5	7.5	37.5

Pitching	B-T	Ht.	Wt.	DOB	W	L	ERA	G	GS	SV	IP	Hits	Runs	ER	HR	BB	SO	AVG	OBP	SLG	SO%	BB%	BF
Arroyo, Rowell	R-R	5-11	180	2-15-05	0	0	7.50	6	0	0	6	7	8	5	1	9	7	.292	.471	.542	20.6	26.5	34
Assad, Javier	R-R	6-1	200	7-30-97	0	0	0.00	1	1	0	3	1	0	0	0	6	.100	.100	.200	60.0	0.0	10
Brentz, Jake	L-L	6-1	205	9-14-94	0	0	4.50	2	0	0	2	3	1	1	0	0	2	.375	.500	.375	20.0	0.0	10
Camacho, Kevin	R-R	5-11	200	2-10-05	1	1	5.40	8	2	1	23	9	14	14	1	20	31	.118	.337	.197	30.4	19.6	102
Carraway, Burl	L-L	6-0	173	5-27-99	0	0	0.00	2	0	0	3	7	.182	.357	.182	50.0	21.4	14
Castillo, Eduardo	R-R	6-1	176	9-16-03	1	1	10.29	5	0	0	7	12	10	8	1	8	7	.375	.500	.625	17.1	19.5	41
Clarke, Chris	R-R	6-7	215	5-13-98	0	1	3.00	3	1	0	9	9	5	3	1	1	9	.257	.270	.400	24.3	2.7	37
Cruz, Miguel	L-L	6-4	200	8-3-03	0	0	13.21	16	0	0	16	16	25	23	1	29	15	.262	.505	.361	16.1	31.2	93
Fajardo, Fred	R-R	6-3	194	1-27-05	0	2	5.64	14	0	0	22	31	16	14	2	13	22	.326	.429	.505	19.5	11.5	113
Flanagan, Ethan	L-L	6-3	205	6-5-02	1	1	3.86	2	2	0	7	4	3	3	0	2	10	.167	.231	.250	38.5	7.7	26
Florentino, Jostin	R-R	6-0	175	12-1-04	1	2	3.74	5	4	0	22	20	10	9	2	5	34	.238	.289	.321	37.4	5.5	91
Garcia, Anhuar	R-R	6-1	200	2-28-04	1	3	5.91	7	6	0	32	40	24	21	6	14	35	.303	.367	.492	23.6	9.5	148
Ginn, Landon	S-R	6-3	200	7-19-01	1	0	0.00	6	0	0	7	6	2	0	0	2	7	.222	.267	.296	23.3	6.7	30
Gray, Drew	L-L	6-3	190	5-9-03	0	1	0.00	2	2	0	6	2	1	0	0	4	11	.095	.240	.190	44.0	16.0	25
Henriquez, Jordan	R-R	6-4	245	4-30-04	0	1	9.35	6	0	1	9	14	11	9	1	5	8	.359	.457	.550	17.4	10.9	46
Imanaga, Shota	L-L	5-8	176	9-1-93	0	0	0.00	2	2	0	6	4	0	0	0	0	8	.200	.200	.300	40.0	0.0	20
Lopez, Ronny	R-R	6-1	185	11-18-02	1	5	7.03	9	7	0	32	47	27	25	2	20	30	.343	.427	.482	19.1	12.7	157
Mangus, Thomas	R-R	6-3	215	6-18-03	0	0	8.10	3	0	0	3	4	4	3	0	5	2	.267	.467	.400	33.3	0.0	15
Melendez, Edwardo	R-R	6-0	177	2-16-04	1	5	5.36	12	8	0	47	36	29	28	2	42	51	.222	.389	.321	23.9	19.7	213
Moore, Grayson	S-R	6-3	215	7-9-01	0	0	3.86	3	0	0	2	3	1	1	0	2	3	.333	.500	.444	16.7	16.7	12
Mora, Wilme	R-R	6-5	180	6-28-03	1	2	11.39	16	0	0	21	25	34	27	4	22	18	.291	.467	.488	15.0	18.3	120
Morgan, Eli	R-R	5-10	190	5-13-96	0	0	0.00	1	0	0	1	0	0	0	0	0	2	.000	.000	.000	66.7	0.0	3
Netz, Dawson	R-R	6-1	190	8-3-00	1	3	6.88	9	6	0	34	38	28	26	4	15	33	.288	.364	.424	21.9	9.9	151
Peters, Mathew	R-R	6-4	215	12-28-00	3	0	6.46	11	0	0	15	19	15	11	0	14	19	.288	.408	.305	25.0	18.4	76
Powell, Walker	R-R	6-8	210	6-11-96	0	1	5.40	3	3	0	8	7	5	5	0	2	9	.226	.270	.290	27.3	6.1	33
Reyes, Luis A.	R-R	6-3	220	10-23-03	2	1	4.30	11	0	0	15	9	7	7	1	8	15	.173	.306	.327	24.2	12.9	62
Rivero, Darian	R-R	6-1	185	7-8-05	0	2	5.18	11	6	0	33	34	21	19	2	21	29	.272	.373	.384	12.7	14.0	150
Rodriguez, Erian	R-R	6-3	190	11-23-01	0	1	6.00	2	2	0	6	7	4	4	1	3	3	.318	.400	.545	12.0	12.0	25

	B-T	Ht.	Wt.	DOB			ERA	G	GS	SV	IP	Hits	Runs	ER	HR	BB	SO	AVG	OBP	SLG	SO%	BB%
Rojas, Yenrri	R-R	6-1	186	11-30-03	0	0	3.86	1	1	0	2	0	1	1	0	2	1	.000	.300	.000	10.0	20.0	10
Rosario, Jhon	R-R	5-10	180	9-21-04	1	2	5.40	15	0	0	25	31	21	15	0	12	22	.307	.403	.376	17.3	9.4	127
Sierra, Joel	R-R	6-1	190	12-31-01	0	0	12.27	4	0	0	4	3	7	5	1	9	5	.214	.542	.500	20.8	37.5	24
Turnbull, Spencer	R-R	6-3	210	9-18-92	0	0	2.25	1	1	0	4	1	1	1	0	2	5	.077	.200	.077	33.3	13.3	15
Vasquez, Geovanny	R-R	6-3	190	12-15-03	2	4	9.24	15	2	2	25	19	31	26	4	25	24	.211	.421	.356	18.9	19.7	127
Zarraga, Victor	L-L	5-10	160	12-24-03	1	1	2.88	9	2	0	25	22	14	8	0	18	38	.242	.386	.286	33.0	15.7	115

Fielding

C: Alcala 26, Diaz 26, Sanchez 10, Amaya 2. **1B:** Gutierrez 32, De Leon 24, Diaz 5, Sanchez 2, Stevens 2, Paciolla 1. **2B:** Hernandez 22, Espinoza 17, F. Cruz 9, R. Cruz 7, Paciolla 4, Valdez 1. **3B:** Paciolla 22, De Leon 13, Espinoza 11, Cruz 10, Hernandez 4, Southisene 1, Valdez 1. **SS:** R. Cruz 28, Espinoza 14, F. Cruz 14, Valdez 4, Hernandez 2, Melendez 1. **LF:** Lugo 16, Reyes 15, Lovich 10, Mena 9, Alcantara 8, De Leon 1, Delgado 1. **CF:** De Leon 16, Reyes 14, Delgado 9, Lovich 9, Alcantara 5, Valdez 5, Lugo 3, Mena 1. **RF:** Alcantara 16, Reyes 15, Delgado 12, Lugo 6, D. De Leon 4, Mena 4, Lovich 2, E. De Leon 1, Stevens 1

DSL CUBS BLUE — ROOKIE
DOMINICAN SUMMER LEAGUE

Batting	B-T	Ht.	Wt.	DOB	AVG	OBP	SLG	G	PA	AB	R	H	2B	3B	HR	RBI	BB	HBP	SH	SF	SO	SB	CS	BB%	SO%
Acosta, Julio	R-R	5-10	175	10-8-07	.156	.285	.234	42	151	128	15	20	5	1	1	11	23	0	0	0	53	7	2	15.2	35.1
Campos, Daniel	R-R	5-11	170	12-20-05	.250	.361	.380	31	122	100	14	25	8	1	1	17	13	6	0	3	10	6	2	10.7	8.2
Carrillo, Jose	S-R	5-9	171	1-22-07	.167	.384	.222	24	75	54	12	9	3	0	0	6	13	6	0	0	15	3	2	17.3	20.0
De Leon, Darlyn	L-R	5-8	150	2-11-05	.353	.429	.706	5	21	17	4	6	1	1	1	5	2	1	0	1	4	2	0	9.5	19.0
Espinoza, Ronnyel	S-R	5-11	173	8-11-05	.246	.440	.354	31	91	65	14	16	3	2	0	16	22	2	0	2	18	3	1	24.2	19.8
Figuereo, Breyner	L-L	5-11	171	6-9-08	.192	.287	.272	40	143	125	17	24	3	2	1	15	17	0	0	1	35	5	2	11.9	24.5
Garcia, Victor	L-R	6-0	160	1-17-08	.242	.381	.242	11	42	33	7	8	0	0	0	2	8	0	0	1	6	1	0	19.0	14.3
McPhee, Jahni	L-L	5-11	160	12-21-06	.188	.361	.328	26	83	64	9	12	4	1	1	9	9	9	0	1	32	3	1	10.8	38.6
Monso, Juan	L-R	5-11	160	11-10-06	.178	.355	.318	38	138	107	20	19	7	1	2	20	24	6	0	1	28	10	5	17.4	20.3
Ortiz, Robin	R-R	6-4	200	9-12-06	.209	.348	.336	42	164	134	22	28	5	0	4	21	25	4	0	1	35	10	1	15.2	21.3
Pena, Ezequiel	L-R	6-0	165	9-14-06	.327	.469	.481	30	143	113	27	37	4	1	0	17	28	2	0	0	12	17	2	19.6	8.4
Ramirez, Josias	R-R	6-0	155	7-8-05	.159	.397	.318	42	151	107	26	17	3	1	4	12	40	3	0	1	40	5	2	26.5	26.5
Ramirez, Saul	R-R	6-0	175	1-7-06	.111	.429	.111	9	28	18	4	2	0	0	0	1	9	1	0	0	6	4	1	32.1	21.4
Rosario, Enyel	S-R	6-0	160	4-6-07	.242	.315	.339	37	143	124	20	30	5	1	2	15	14	1	0	4	17	15	6	9.8	11.9
Sanchez, Luis	L-L	5-10	163	1-19-08	.242	.414	.424	32	128	99	18	24	5	5	1	12	21	8	0	0	33	8	5	16.4	25.8
Santos, Luis	L-R	5-7	162	10-22-07	.269	.351	.420	35	134	119	21	32	10	1	2	23	15	0	0	0	22	14	5	11.2	16.4
Tomas, Juan	B-R	6-2	177	11-28-07	.186	.352	.301	36	145	113	19	21	6	2	1	18	30	0	0	2	42	9	4	20.7	29.0

Pitching	B-T	Ht.	Wt.	DOB	W	L	ERA	G	GS	SV	IP	Hits	Runs	ER	HR	BB	SO	AVG	OBP	SLG	SO%	BB%	BF
Alejo, Frailin	R-R	5-11	150	10-8-06	0	0	3.24	5	1	0	8	11	7	3	0	4	7	.289	.372	.395	16.3	9.3	43
Aranguren, Cristopher	R-R	6-3	200	1-26-06	0	3	6.09	12	9	0	34	38	26	23	0	14	23	.286	.364	.414	14.8	9.0	155
Chala, Alberto	R-R	5-10	170	9-20-03	0	0	0.00	1	0	0	2	1	0	0	0	1	2	.200	.333	.200	33.3	16.7	6
Corpas, Jider	R-R	6-2	147	11-21-07	4	4	6.67	13	5	0	28	28	22	21	0	21	17	.264	.394	.349	12.9	15.9	132
De La Cruz, Gabriel	R-R	6-0	150	2-1-07	1	0	12.46	11	0	0	13	15	18	18	1	20	13	.300	.527	.460	17.6	27.0	74
Desis, Frankelly	L-L	6-3	183	11-14-06	3	1	2.49	18	0	1	25	14	14	7	1	24	24	.156	.345	.233	20.5	20.5	117
Dias, Roni	R-R	6-0	170	10-17-06	0	2	10.50	8	0	0	6	4	8	7	0	17	7	.211	.634	.263	17.1	41.5	41
Guzman, Jeremy	L-L	6-4	180	4-27-04	3	1	4.91	19	0	1	29	17	17	16	0	32	46	.162	.373	.200	32.4	22.5	142
Hanania, Yusef	R-R	5-11	172	10-27-05	4	2	8.49	13	0	0	23	35	27	22	2	16	25	.337	.448	.519	20.0	12.8	125
Hernandez, Erick	R-R	6-0	184	3-9-08	0	1	3.52	3	3	0	8	4	3	3	0	4	11	.154	.281	.269	34.4	12.5	32
Mata, Luis	R-R	6-1	167	11-11-05	0	3	6.06	8	7	0	16	14	18	11	0	17	20	.219	.409	.313	22.7	19.3	88
Ramirez, Chaily	R-R	6-3	190	1-20-05	1	1	4.45	15	5	2	32	34	17	16	2	9	39	.268	.317	.449	27.9	6.4	140
Ramos, Ariel	R-R	5-11	160	5-24-06	0	1	1.60	11	11	0	34	20	6	6	0	19	27	.187	.326	.262	20.8	14.6	130
Rangel, Carlos	R-R	5-11	183	9-25-05	1	1	5.79	3	0	0	5	4	4	3	1	4	5	.211	.348	.368	21.7	17.4	23
Rivera, Anderson	R-R	6-6	250	1-23-07	1	0	0.00	1	0	0	2	1	2	0	0	2	2	.167	.375	.167	25.0	25.0	8
Romero, Amilkar	R-R	6-2	208	10-24-07	1	0	8.03	6	4	0	12	4	15	11	1	20	7	.111	.468	.250	11.3	32.3	62
Sanmartin, Angel	L-L	6-0	191	4-20-05	0	1	17.12	12	0	0	14	22	27	26	4	21	13	.367	.540	.617	14.9	24.1	87
Soriano, Fleury	R-R	5-10	170	2-21-05	3	2	7.50	20	0	1	30	31	27	25	5	23	30	.272	.411	.509	20.4	15.6	147
Urena, Jose	R-R	6-1	213	10-25-06	0	5	11.14	17	1	1	27	22	37	33	0	35	26	.234	.459	.319	18.3	24.6	142
Valdez, Julio	R-R	6-2	212	1-14-05	3	1	4.02	20	0	8	31	25	15	14	0	16	27	.216	.341	.259	19.6	11.6	138
Villarroel, Geovanny	R-R	5-11	187	7-7-07	0	2	4.66	11	10	0	37	37	29	19	1	14	35	.255	.347	.366	21.0	8.4	167

Fielding

C: Campos 26, Carrillo 23, Garcia 8. **1B:** J. Ramirez 40, Espinoza 5, Campos 4, S. Ramirez 4, Garcia 3. **2B:** Monso 24, Pena 18, Santos 16, Rosario 2, Espinoza 1. **3B:** Espinoza 20, Rosario 18, Santos 14, Pena 4, Monso 3, Tomas 1. **SS:** Tomas 35, Monso 11, Rosario 10, Espinoza 2, Pena 1. **LF:** Acosta 29, McPhee 11, Ortiz 8, Sanchez 5, Figuereo 4, Ramirez 1. **CF:** Ortiz 28, Sanchez 21, Acosta 3, De Leon 2, Figuereo 2, McPhee 1. **RF:** Figuereo 27, McPhee 13, Sanchez 6, Ortiz 4, Ramirez 4, De Leon 3, Acosta 2

DSL CUBS RED — ROOKIE
DOMINICAN SUMMER LEAGUE

Batting	B-T	Ht.	Wt.	DOB	AVG	OBP	SLG	G	PA	AB	R	H	2B	3B	HR	RBI	BB	HBP	SH	SF	SO	SB	CS	BB%	SO%
Abreu, Luis	S-R	5-9	150	2-26-08	.174	.353	.207	34	119	92	14	16	1	1	0	6	22	4	0	1	28	14	2	18.5	23.5
Betencourt, Freiker	L-L	5-7	172	7-20-08	.250	.394	.386	39	165	132	27	33	7	4	1	14	29	3	0	1	24	9	8	17.6	14.5
Cabada, Juan	L-R	5-10	165	4-30-08	.287	.429	.426	42	170	136	22	39	10	0	3	29	20	14	0	0	31	20	3	11.8	18.2
Cespedes, Ivan	R-R	5-11	190	8-1-05	.292	.357	.504	35	126	113	16	33	3	0	7	21	11	1	0	1	31	4	1	8.7	24.6
De La Cruz, Wilfri	B-R	6-2	170	9-15-07	.267	.443	.419	28	115	86	18	23	9	2	0	10	26	2	0	1	24	9	5	22.6	20.9
Gomez, Elerick	R-R	5-9	155	9-11-07	.253	.350	.425	28	100	87	13	22	5	2	2	4	11	2	0	0	23	8	0	11.0	23.0
Gonzalez, Diego	R-R	5-10	170	4-2-07	.238	.446	.286	30	92	63	10	15	3	0	0	10	15	11	0	3	19	3	0	16.3	20.7

CHICAGO CUBS

Batting

Player	B-T	Ht	Wt	DOB	AVG	OBP	SLG	G	PA	AB	R	H	2B	3B	HR	RBI	BB	HBP	SH	SF	SO	SB	CS	BB%	SO%
Herrera, Alexander	R-R	6-2	159	9-7-07	.136	.333	.160	31	105	81	9	11	2	0	0	7	22	2	0	0	24	3	1	21.0	22.9
Lara, Fernando	L-L	5-10	170	1-11-08	.058	.305	.101	26	95	69	6	4	1	1	0	9	22	3	0	1	41	4	0	23.2	43.2
Leon, Luis	R-R	5-10	134	2-4-08	.248	.336	.413	34	137	121	27	30	8	0	4	16	12	4	0	0	22	12	4	8.8	16.1
Lucena, Jhon	R-R	5-11	159	11-14-07	.179	.258	.241	37	124	112	7	20	7	0	0	5	11	1	0	0	40	4	2	8.9	32.3
Maldonado, Luis	R-R	5-11	143	6-16-08	.189	.294	.263	32	109	95	13	18	1	0	2	4	13	1	0	0	22	2	1	11.9	20.2
McPhee, Jahni	L-L	5-11	160	12-21-06	.095	.310	.143	8	29	21	4	2	1	0	0	2	6	1	0	1	14	4	0	20.7	48.3
Ramirez, Jeury	L-R	6-2	175	10-11-07	.207	.371	.405	37	143	111	20	23	5	4	3	28	28	2	0	2	30	7	1	19.6	21.0
Ramirez, Saul	R-R	6-0	175	1-7-06	.218	.338	.364	36	133	110	16	24	7	0	3	15	18	3	0	2	26	1	1	13.5	19.5
Sanchez, Abraham	R-R	5-10	161	9-27-07	.109	.162	.141	22	68	64	6	7	2	0	0	2	3	1	0	0	22	3	0	4.4	32.4
Vivas, Leonel	R-R	6-2	168	1-22-07	.217	.416	.402	37	125	92	27	20	3	1	4	20	19	13	0	1	25	10	3	15.2	20.0

Pitching

Player	B-T	Ht.	Wt.	DOB	W	L	ERA	G	GS	SV	IP	Hits	Runs	ER	HR	BB	SO	AVG	OBP	SLG	SO%	BB%	BF
Alejo, Frailin	R-R	5-11	150	10-8-06	0	0	0.00	1	0	0	1	0	0	0	0	2	1	.000	.429	.000	14.3	28.6	7
Barrientos, Carlos	L-L	5-10	159	1-18-08	2	2	9.10	15	1	1	29	34	35	29	3	32	36	.306	.470	.468	24.2	21.5	149
Burgos, Salvador	R-R	6-0	180	4-17-06	0	5	8.77	10	10	0	26	32	29	25	0	21	14	.314	.454	.402	10.8	16.2	130
Chala, Alberto	R-R	5-10	170	9-20-03	1	2	10.13	17	0	1	21	30	28	24	1	26	18	.326	.471	.435	14.9	21.5	121
Chirinos, Noel	S-R	6-0	186	2-6-07	2	1	8.15	12	0	0	18	25	16	16	3	17	7	.342	.462	.644	7.5	18.3	93
Feliz, Anthony	R-R	6-2	172	11-10-06	0	5	3.68	12	11	0	37	41	28	15	0	20	22	.279	.376	.381	12.9	11.8	170
Ghisays, Luis	R-R	5-11	188	4-18-06	1	5	4.22	12	12	0	49	41	27	23	4	16	51	.218	.295	.351	24.3	7.6	210
Gonzalez, Angel	L-L	6-0	175	8-14-07	2	2	3.44	16	1	0	34	28	16	13	3	29	28	.224	.380	.320	17.7	18.4	158
Hanania, Yusef	R-R	5-11	172	10-27-05	0	0	9.00	1	0	0	1	3	1	1	0	1	2	.500	.571	.667	28.6	14.3	7
Henriquez, Jordan	R-R	6-4	245	4-30-04	0	2	0.00	5	0	1	9	3	5	0	0	5	13	.094	.256	.156	33.3	12.8	39
Javier, Johansel	R-R	6-1	185	11-3-07	1	1	9.82	8	0	0	7	9	12	8	0	14	3	.290	.551	.387	6.1	28.6	49
Landaez, Bryan	R-R	6-1	175	8-3-04	1	1	3.33	17	0	2	27	15	13	10	0	23	30	.167	.364	.189	24.8	19.0	121
Lopez, Sebastian	L-L	5-7	177	11-5-07	0	3	2.51	9	8	0	29	24	9	8	2	5	22	.229	.270	.352	19.8	4.5	111
Madeira, Emannoel	R-R	6-3	225	8-20-06	1	2	9.90	12	10	0	30	38	35	33	3	29	22	.311	.463	.459	13.8	18.1	160
Morey, Ismael	R-R	6-3	165	8-15-06	1	0	6.35	4	0	0	6	4	7	4	0	6	3	.190	.393	.333	10.7	21.4	28
Ortega, Wilfran	R-R	6-2	175	6-12-07	0	0	3.86	2	0	0	2	3	1	1	0	2	1	.300	.417	.400	8.3	16.7	12
Ramirez, Saul	R-R	6-0	175	1-7-06	0	0	0.00	1	0	0	1	0	0	0	0	0	0	.000	.000	.000	0.0	0.0	3
Rangel, Carlos	R-R	5-11	183	9-25-05	1	2	4.78	16	0	2	26	26	22	14	0	14	35	.250	.352	.298	28.5	11.4	123
Rivera, Anderson	R-R	6-6	250	1-23-07	1	1	9.95	11	0	0	13	10	15	14	0	20	15	.217	.456	.261	22.1	29.4	68
Salaya, Jubrayker	R-R	6-2	165	1-9-07	0	1	4.50	1	0	0	2	2	1	1	0	0	2	.286	.286	.429	28.6	0.0	7
Siri, Saul	R-R	6-2	195	12-20-04	1	2	9.91	11	2	0	26	28	34	29	1	29	29	.262	.427	.374	20.3	20.3	143
Ventura, Darlin	L-L	6-1	158	8-31-07	1	4	11.71	16	1	0	28	32	41	36	1	32	22	.299	.466	.383	14.9	21.6	148
Vivas, Leonel	R-R	6-2	168	1-22-07	0	0	0.00	1	0	0	1	1	0	0	0	1	1	.250	.400	.250	20.0	20.0	5

Fielding

C: Gonzalez 28, Sanchez 21, Cespedes 20. **1B:** S. Ramirez 22, Vivas 17, J. Ramirez 10, Cespedes 8, Gonzalez 3. **2B:** Cabada 18, Maldonado 17, Abreu 13, Herrera 7, Gomez 5. **3B:** Herrera 19, Cabada 15, Gomez 15, Maldonado 4, Vivas 4, Abreu 3. **SS:** De La Cruz 26, Vivas 15, Abreu 12, Herrera 6, Gomez 2, Maldonado 1. **LF:** Lucena 18, J. Ramirez 16, S. Ramirez 11, Leon 7, McPhee 6, Lara 1. **CF:** Betencourt 37, Leon 13, Ramirez 7. **RF:** Lara 22, Lucena 16, Leon 13, J. Ramirez 2, McPhee 2, Betencourt 1, S. Ramirez 1

Chicago White Sox

SEASON SYNOPSIS: Chicago improved significantly, winning 19 more games than its record-setting 41-121 campaign in 2024. The White Sox broke in several rookies who had success but still finished with the second-worst mark in the majors and their third consecutive 100-loss season.

HIGH POINT: The Sox won six straight from Aug. 31-Sept. 5, including a four-game sweep in Minnesota that was the first such sweep of their division rivals since the Twins moved from Washington in 1961. They came from behind in all four, capped by an 11-8 win Sept. 4 with late homers from rookies Kyle Teel and Colson Montgomery. The White Sox then won two of three at Detroit, with the only loss coming against Tarik Skubal.

LOW POINT: No Sox starter pitched enough innings to qualify for the ERA title, taxing the bullpen significantly. Only Dodgers relievers pitched more, by one out, than the Sox 'pen. Chicago's 4.18 reliever ERA was respectable, ranking 18th in MLB, but the team went just 15-36 in one-run games, including five one-run defeats during a 2-10 start.

NOTABLE ROOKIES: Only the Marlins and Athletics got more plate appearances from rookies than the Pale Hose, and no team had more than Chicago's 568 innings pitched by rookies. Leading the way on the mound were a pair of Rule 5 draft RHPs—Shane Smith (7-8, 3.81), who led the team in innings pitched (146 ⅓), and Mike Vasil (5-3, 2.50 in 101 IP). Chicago broke in two rookie catchers, both of whom showed offensive and defensive promise in Edgar Quero, 22 (19% chase rate, .689 OPS) and 23-year-old Kyle Teel (.273/.375/.411). Chase Meidroth (.259/.329/.320) ranked second on the team in walks and shifted from shortstop to second base when former top prospect Colson Montgomery (.239/.311/.529) arrived. His 21 homers in just 71 games was good for second on the team.

KEY TRANSACTIONS: Smith and Vasil are Rule 5 picks who appear to have staying power. Teel and Meidroth arrived from Boston in the offseason when the White Sox traded ace lefty Garrett Crochet. Chicago gave up on 2019 first-rounder Andrew Vaughn, trading him to the Brewers for righty Aaron Civale, only to see Vaughn finally blossom in Milwaukee. On the flip side, Chicago signed Adrian Houser in May when the Rangers released him, and he went 6-2, 2.10 in 11 starts for them before being traded at the deadline to Tampa Bay for three players, including IF Curtis Mead.

OPENING DAY PAYROLL: $82,279,825 (27th)

PLAYERS OF THE YEAR

MAJOR LEAGUE
Shane Smith
RHP
3.81 ERA in 146.1 IP
145 SO, 58 BB
Rule 5 turned all-star

MINOR LEAGUE
Caleb Bonemer
SS
(A,A+)
.281/.401/.473
12 HR, 29 SB, 75 BB

ORGANIZATION LEADERS

Batting		*Qualifiers
MAJORS		
* AVG	Lenyn Sosa	.264
* OPS	Lenyn Sosa	.727
HR	Lenyn Sosa	22
RBI	Lenyn Sosa	75
MINORS		
* AVG	Corey Julks, Charlotte	.300
* OBP	Sam Antonacci, Birmingham/W-S/ACL White Sox	.433
* SLG	Tim Elko, Charlotte	.552
* OPS	Tim Elko, Charlotte	.910
R	Sam Antonacci, Birmingham/W-S/ACL White Sox	78
H	William Bergolla, Birmingham	139
TB	Jeral Perez, Winston-Salem	215
2B	Braden Montgomery, Birmingham/W-S/Kannap.	34
3B	Alec Makarewicz, Birmingham/Winston-Salem	7
HR	Tim Elko, Charlotte	26
RBI	Ryan Galanie, Birmingham/Winston-Salem	94
BB	Rikuu Nishida, Birmingham	75
BB	Caleb Bonemer, Winston-Salem/Kannapolis	75
SO	George Wolkow, Kannapolis	147
SB	Jordan Sprinkle, Birm./W-Salem/Kannapolis	80

Pitching		#Qualifiers
MAJORS		
W	Davis Martin	7
W	Shane Smith	7
ERA	No qualifiers	
SO	Shane Smith	145
SV	Jordan Leasure	7
MINORS		
W	Shane Murphy, Charlotte/Birmingham/W-Salem	10
L	Lucas Gordon, Birmingham/Winston-Salem	11
# ERA	Shane Murphy, Charlotte/Birmingham/W-Salem	1.66
G	Peyton Pallette, Charlotte/Birmingham	52
GS	Tanner McDougal, Birmingham/Winston-Salem	28
SV	Peyton Pallette, Charlotte/Birmingham	11
SV	Zach Franklin, Charlotte/Birmingham	11
SV	Phil Fox, Birmingham/Winston-Salem	11
IP	Shane Murphy, Charlotte/Birmingham/W-Salem	135
BB	Tommy Vail, Charlotte/Birmingham/W-Salem	58
SO	Riley Gowens, Birmingham	151
# AVG	Shane Murphy, Charlotte/Birm//W-Salem	.199

2025 PERFORMANCE

General Manager: Chris Getz. **Farm Director:** Paul Janish. **Scouting Director:** Mike Shirley

Class	Team	League	W	L	PCT	Finish	Manager
Majors	Chicago White Sox	American	60	102	.370	15 (15)	Will Venable
Triple-A	Charlotte Knights	International	65	85	.433	14 (20)	Sergio Santos
Double-A	Birmingham Barons	Southern	81	57	.587	1 (8)	Guillermo Quiroz
High-A	Winston-Salem Dash	South Atlantic	56	74	.431	10 (12)	Pat Leyland
Low-A	Kannapolis Cannon Ballers	Carolina	64	68	.485	10 (12)	Chad Pinder
Rookie	ACL White Sox	Arizona Complex	33	27	.550	5 (15)	Danny Gonzalez
Rookie	DSL White Sox	Dominican	29	26	.527	27 (52)	Anthony Nunez
Overall 2025 Minor League Record			328	337	.493	17th (30)	

ORGANIZATION STATISTICS

CHICAGO WHITE SOX
AMERICAN LEAGUE

Batting	B-T	Ht.	Wt.	DOB	AVG	OBP	SLG	G	PA	AB	R	H	2B	3B	HR	RBI	BB	HBP	SH	SF	SO	SB	CS	BB%	SO%
Alexander, Tyler	R-L	6-2	203	7-14-94	.000	.000	.000	31	1	1	0	0	0	0	0	0	0	0	0	0	0	0	0	0.0	0.0
Amaya, Jacob	R-R	6-0	180	9-3-98	.106	.139	.121	37	73	66	7	7	1	0	0	8	3	0	1	3	16	2	0	4.1	21.9
Baldwin, Brooks	S-R	6-2	175	8-15-00	.240	.290	.407	103	328	300	32	72	15	1	11	38	21	1	4	2	86	5	0	6.4	26.2
Benintendi, Andrew	L-L	5-9	190	7-6-94	.240	.307	.431	116	470	420	57	101	16	2	20	63	40	3	0	6	82	1	0	8.5	17.4
Capra, Vinny	R-R	5-8	180	7-7-96	.190	.205	.238	23	46	42	4	8	2	0	0	2	1	0	2	1	10	1	0	2.2	21.7
Dalbec, Bobby	R-R	6-4	227	6-29-95	.222	.333	.278	7	21	18	2	4	1	0	0	1	3	0	0	0	6	0	0	14.3	28.6
Elko, Tim	R-R	6-4	240	12-27-98	.134	.194	.328	23	72	67	6	9	1	0	4	8	5	0	0	0	30	1	0	6.9	41.7
Fletcher, Dominic	L-L	5-6	185	9-2-97	.219	.265	.469	12	34	32	5	7	5	0	1	2	2	0	0	0	2	1	0	5.9	5.9
Hill, Derek	R-R	6-2	206	12-30-95	.286	.375	.286	4	8	7	0	2	0	0	0	1	0	1	0	0	2	0	0	0.0	25.0
Jankowski, Travis	L-R	6-2	190	6-15-91	.214	.267	.214	7	15	14	1	3	0	0	0	0	0	1	0	0	3	0	0	6.7	20.0
Jones, Greg	S-R	6-2	175	3-7-98	.000	.000	.000	3	2	2	0	0	0	0	0	0	0	0	0	0	2	1	0	0.0	100.0
Julks, Corey	R-R	6-1	185	2-27-96	.231	.417	.6	13	12	2	3	2	0	1	0	0	1	3	0	0	0	5	0	23.1	
Lee, Korey	R-R	6-2	210	7-25-98	.257	.333	.429	26	40	35	10	9	3	0	1	3	4	0	1	0	7	0	0	10.0	17.5
Maton, Nick	L-R	6-2	178	2-18-97	.167	.286	.315	25	63	54	5	9	2	0	2	4	9	0	0	0	19	0	1	14.3	30.2
Mead, Curtis	R-R	6-0	171	10-26-00	.240	.280	.304	41	132	125	12	30	8	0	0	11	3	4	0	0	30	1	0	2.3	22.7
Meidroth, Chase	R-R	5-9	170	7-23-01	.253	.329	.320	122	505	414	54	114	15	0	5	23	45	6	3	1	72	14	4	8.9	14.3
Montgomery, Colson	L-R	6-3	205	2-27-02	.239	.311	.529	71	284	255	43	61	9	1	21	55	25	2	0	1	83	0	0	8.8	29.2
Narvaez, Omar	L-R	5-11	220	2-10-92	.286	.400	.286	4	10	7	1	2	0	0	0	0	3	2	0	0	1	0	0	20.0	10.0
Noda, Ryan	L-L	6-3	217	3-30-96	.088	.295	.176	16	45	34	3	3	0	0	1	1	10	0	1	0	19	0	0	22.2	42.2
Palacios, Josh	L-R	6-1	200	7-30-95	.203	.292	.305	51	145	128	11	26	4	0	3	9	12	4	1	0	36	0	0	8.3	24.8
Quero, Edgar	S-R	5-11	170	4-6-03	.268	.333	.356	111	403	365	31	98	17	0	5	36	32	4	0	2	71	0	1	7.9	17.6
Ramos, Bryan	R-R	6-2	190	3-12-02	.167	.167	.333	4	12	12	1	2	2	0	0	2	0	0	0	0	4	0	0	0.0	33.3
Robert, Luis	R-R	6-2	220	8-3-97	.223	.297	.364	110	431	382	52	85	12	0	14	53	40	2	1	3	112	33	8	9.3	26.0
Robertson, Will	L-L	6-0	215	12-26-97	.133	.159	.150	24	63	60	2	8	1	0	0	8	1	1	0	1	20	0	0	1.6	31.7
Rojas, Josh	L-R	6-1	207	6-30-94	.180	.252	.259	69	211	189	14	34	9	0	2	11	19	0	1	2	48	4	1	9.0	22.7
Slater, Austin	R-R	6-1	204	12-13-92	.236	.299	.423	51	135	123	20	29	6	1	5	11	11	0	1	0	35	1	0	8.1	25.9
Sosa, Lenyn	R-R	6-0	180	1-25-00	.264	.293	.434	140	544	518	57	137	20	1	22	75	18	4	1	3	127	2	1	3.3	23.3
Tauchman, Mike	L-L	6-2	220	12-3-90	.263	.356	.400	93	385	335	44	88	17	1	9	40	45	4	0	1	86	0	0	11.7	22.3
Taylor, Michael A.	R-R	6-4	215	3-26-91	.200	.259	.366	134	325	295	33	59	20	1	9	35	23	1	4	2	110	8	3	7.1	33.8
Teel, Kyle	L-R	6-1	190	2-15-02	.273	.375	.411	78	297	253	38	69	11	0	8	35	37	5	1	1	77	3	1	12.5	25.9
Thaiss, Matt	L-R	6-0	215	5-6-95	.212	.382	.294	35	110	85	11	18	4	0	1	8	23	1	0	1	21	1	1	20.9	19.1
Vargas, Miguel	R-R	6-3	205	11-17-99	.234	.316	.401	138	569	504	80	118	32	2	16	60	56	6	0	3	100	6	0	9.8	17.6
Vaughn, Andrew	R-R	6-0	215	4-3-98	.189	.218	.314	48	193	185	9	35	8	0	5	19	7	0	0	1	43	0	0	3.6	22.3
Workman, Gage	S-R	6-4	202	10-24-99	.000	.000	.000	3	2	2	0	0	0	0	0	0	0	0	0	0	1	0	0	0.0	50.0

Pitching	B-T	Ht.	Wt.	DOB	W	L	ERA	G	GS	SV	IP	Hits	Runs	ER	HR	BB	SO	AVG	OBP	SLG	SO%	BB%	BF
Alexander, Tyler	R-L	6-2	203	7-14-94	2	9	4.26	31	1	0	61	65	31	29	6	18	52	.273	.326	.403	20.1	6.9	259
Altavilla, Dan	R-R	5-11	226	9-8-92	0	1	2.48	28	0	2	29	19	9	8	4	15	21	.190	.319	.360	17.5	12.5	120
Amaya, Jacob	R-R	6-0	180	9-3-98	0	0	0.00	1	0	0	1	0	0	0	0	0	0	.000	.000	.000	0	0	3
Booser, Cam	L-L	6-3	225	5-4-92	2	4	5.52	39	0	1	31	28	22	19	8	19	35	.233	.343	.475	24.5	13.3	143
Burke, Sean	R-R	6-6	230	12-18-99	4	11	4.22	28	22	0	134	131	76	63	23	63	133	.251	.337	.444	22.3	10.6	596
Cannon, Jonathan	R-R	6-6	213	7-19-00	4	10	5.82	22	17	0	104	116	69	67	19	38	86	.278	.344	.494	18.5	8.2	466
Capra, Vinny	R-R	5-8	180	7-7-96	0	0	6.00	3	0	0	3	5	4	2	1	0	1	.333	.333	.600	6.7	0.0	15
Castro, Miguel	R-R	6-7	201	12-24-94	0	0	7.50	6	0	0	6	5	5	5	1	5	4	.227	.393	.455	14.3	17.9	28
Civale, Aaron	R-R	6-2	215	6-12-95	2	7	5.37	13	13	0	67	66	44	40	8	26	55	.253	.323	.421	18.9	8.9	291
Clevinger, Mike	R-R	6-4	215	12-21-90	0	0	7.94	8	0	0	6	5	5	5	0	8	3	.227	.419	.273	9.7	25.8	31
Eisert, Brandon	L-L	6-2	205	1-19-98	3	8	4.39	72	2	70	75	36	34	12	25	74	.276	.344	.496	24.2	8.2	306
Ellard, Fraser	L-L	6-4	295	11-6-97	1	2	4.24	18	3	0	17	8	9	8	1	19	22	.148	.378	.222	29.7	25.7	74
Freeman, Caleb	R-R	6-1	195	2-2-98	0	0	5.40	5	0	0	3	5	2	2	1	1	3	.400	.643	.643	18.8	6.3	16
Gilbert, Tyler	L-L	6-3	223	12-22-93	4	2	3.88	46	5	1	51	40	24	22	5	24	49	.215	.310	.355	22.8	11.2	215
Gomez, Yoendrys	R-R	6-3	175	10-15-99	2	2	4.84	12	9	0	48	45	29	26	9	16	47	.243	.314	.443	22.6	7.7	208
Gonzalez, Wikelman	R-R	6-0	167	3-25-02	1	0	2.66	16	0	0	20	13	9	6	1	12	25	.178	.291	.274	28.7	13.8	87
Houser, Adrian	R-R	6-3	242	2-2-93	6	2	2.10	11	11	0	69	62	19	16	3	22	47	.248	.309	.352	17.1	8.0	275
Hudson, Bryan	L-L	6-8	220	5-8-97	0	0	5.79	4	0	0	5	7	3	3	2	1	6	.350	.381	.750	28.6	4.8	21
Leasure, Jordan	R-R	6-3	215	8-15-98	5	6	3.92	68	1	7	64	49	30	28	12	30	81	.207	.297	.426	30.1	11.2	269

Player	B-T	Ht.	Wt.	DOB	G	AB	R	H	2B	3B	HR	RBI	BB	HBP	SH	SF	SO	SB	CS	SLG	OBP	AVG
Lee, Korey	R-R	6-2	210	7-25-98	0	0	3.00	2	0	0	3	4	1	1	0	2	0	.333	.429	.500	0.0	14.3	14
Martin, Davis	L-R	6-2	200	1-4-97	7	10	4.10	26	25	0	143	136	74	65	20	48	104	.251	.317	.427	17.3	8.0	601
Murfee, Penn	R-R	6-2	195	5-2-94	0	1	7.82	15	0	0	13	19	11	11	3	5	13	.333	.397	.561	20.6	7.9	63
Palisch, Jake	L-L	6-4	215	8-19-98	0	0	18.00	1	0	0	1	3	2	2	0	0	0	.500	.500	.667	0.0	0.0	6
Peguero, Elvis	R-R	6-5	237	3-20-97	0	0	13.50	2	1	0	2	4	3	3	0	2	3	.444	.545	.556	27.3	18.2	11
Perez, Martin	L-L	6-0	200	4-4-91	1	6	3.54	11	10	0	56	40	23	22	6	22	44	.198	.281	.347	19.3	9.6	228
Shuster, Jared	L-L	6-3	210	8-3-98	0	0	8.04	12	2	0	16	27	15	14	0	5	12	.365	.415	.473	14.6	6.1	82
Smith, Shane	R-R	6-4	235	4-4-00	7	8	3.81	29	29	0	146	117	70	62	17	58	145	.216	.305	.363	23.5	9.4	616
Taylor, Grant	R-R	6-3	250	5-20-02	2	4	4.91	36	2	6	37	37	20	20	0	15	54	.268	.335	.304	34.4	9.6	157
Vasil, Mike	L-R	6-5	225	3-19-00	5	3	2.50	47	3	4	101	74	32	28	8	52	82	.204	.318	.312	19.4	12.3	423
White, Owen	R-R	6-3	199	8-9-99	0	0	9.00	3	0	0	7	14	7	7	1	3	6	.438	.486	.594	17.1	8.6	35
Wilson, Bryse	R-R	6-2	267	12-20-97	0	2	6.65	20	5	0	47	67	37	35	11	19	28	.335	.395	.570	12.5	8.5	224
Wilson, Steven	R-R	6-2	221	8-24-94	2	2	3.42	59	0	2	55	50	21	21	7	22	51	.239	.311	.373	21.2	9.1	241

Catcher	PCT	G	PO	A	E	DP	PB
Lee	1.000	16	81	0	0	0	0
Narvaez	.964	4	27	0	1	0	0
Quero	.996	72	545	21	2	2	0
Teel	.990	61	484	23	5	2	8
Thaiss	.974	29	179	11	5	1	2

First Base	PCT	G	PO	A	E	DP
Dalbec	1.000	5	15	1	0	1
Elko	1.000	20	134	8	0	20
Maton	1.000	5	19	5	0	2
Mead	1.000	13	65	3	0	6
Noda	1.000	11	61	9	0	11
Slater	1.000	1	1	0	0	0
Sosa	.992	42	228	16	2	29
Thaiss	.000	1	0	0	0	0
Vargas	.995	63	386	41	2	29
Vaughn	1.000	31	199	13	0	25

Second Base	PCT	G	PO	A	E	DP
Amaya	1.000	1	0	2	0	0
Baldwin	1.000	10	14	13	0	4
Capra	1.000	4	2	3	0	1
Maton	.500	1	0	1	1	0

Third Base	PCT	G	PO	A	E	DP
Baldwin	.923	15	6	18	2	1
Capra	1.000	7	6	5	0	0
Dalbec	1.000	1	0	2	0	0
Mead	.947	22	11	25	2	2
Montgomery	.943	12	10	23	2	3
Ramos	1.000	4	3	5	0	2
Rojas	.946	47	39	49	5	5
Sosa	1.000	3	2	1	0	0
Vargas	.949	79	50	118	9	12
Workman	.667	2	1	1	1	1

Shortstop	PCT	G	PO	A	E	DP
Amaya	.989	35	34	52	1	11
Baldwin	1.000	10	4	14	0	4
Capra	1.000	10	6	26	0	5
Dalbec	1.000	3	2	0	0	0
Meidroth	.963	76	95	136	9	31
Montgomery	.982	60	93	123	4	32
Workman	1.000	1	2	0	0	0

Outfield	PCT	G	PO	A	E	DP
Baldwin	.956	83	126	4	6	2
Benintendi	.979	69	141	1	3	1
Fletcher	1.000	13	17	2	0	0
Hill	1.000	4	6	0	0	0
Jankowski	1.000	7	9	0	0	0
Jones	1.000	1	2	0	0	0
Julks	1.000	5	10	0	0	0
Lee	.667	1	2	0	1	0
Maton	1.000	2	1	0	0	0
Noda	1.000	1	2	0	0	0
Palacios	.968	47	59	1	2	0
Robert	.997	105	289	2	1	0
Robertson	.974	21	37	0	1	0
Rojas	1.000	5	3	0	0	0
Slater	.968	43	59	2	2	0
Tauchman	1.000	73	153	5	0	1
Taylor	.987	132	234	0	3	0
Teel	.000	1	0	0	0	0
Vargas	1.000	1	1	0	0	0

CHARLOTTE KNIGHTS
INTERNATIONAL LEAGUE — TRIPLE-A

Batting	B-T	Ht.	Wt.	DOB	AVG	OBP	SLG	G	PA	AB	R	H	2B	3B	HR	RBI	BB	HBP	SH	SF	SO	SB	CS	BB%	SO%
Amaya, Jacob	R-R	6-0	180	9-3-98	.250	.352	.420	58	219	188	25	47	5	0	9	28	29	1	0	1	64	5	4	13.2	29.2
Baker, Dru	R-R	5-11	205	3-22-00	.256	.318	.368	77	276	250	33	64	9	2	5	17	17	6	2	1	81	16	5	6.2	29.3
Baldwin, Brooks	S-R	6-2	175	8-15-00	.368	.427	.752	29	132	117	29	43	5	2	12	25	12	1	1	1	22	4	4	9.1	16.7
Benintendi, Andrew	L-L	5-9	180	7-6-94	.125	.125	.125	2	8	8	0	1	0	0	0	1	0	0	0	0	1	0	0	0.0	12.5
Camilletti, Mario	L-R	5-9	195	4-19-00	.273	.415	.273	13	41	33	3	9	0	0	0	2	8	0	0	0	6	1	0	19.5	14.6
Capra, Vinny	R-R	5-8	180	7-7-96	.286	.384	.440	24	99	84	15	24	2	1	3	10	12	2	0	1	23	3	0	12.1	23.2
Colas, Oscar	L-L	5-11	209	9-17-98	.116	.224	.209	14	49	43	8	5	4	0	0	6	6	0	0	0	17	2	0	12.2	34.7
Connor, Caden	L-L	6-1	200	8-2-00	.333	.422	.410	13	45	39	6	13	0	0	1	7	5	1	0	0	10	1	2	11.1	22.2
Cowles, Benjamin	R-R	6-0	180	2-15-00	.220	.277	.288	15	65	59	6	13	2	1	0	5	5	0	0	1	20	2	2	7.7	30.8
Dalbec, Bobby	R-R	6-4	227	6-29-95	.326	.354	.696	12	48	46	9	15	3	1	4	13	2	0	0	0	16	1	0	4.2	33.3
DeLoach, Zach	L-R	6-0	205	8-18-98	.236	.326	.414	51	181	157	25	37	11	1	5	22	22	0	0	2	50	4	2	12.2	27.6
Drury, Brandon	R-R	6-2	230	8-21-92	.179	.319	.282	10	47	39	5	7	1	0	1	3	7	1	0	0	10	0	0	14.9	21.3
Eberly, Weston	R-R	6-0	195	1-7-01	.000	.111	.000	3	9	8	0	0	0	0	0	0	1	0	0	0	3	0	0	11.1	33.3
Elko, Tim	R-R	6-4	240	12-27-98	.292	.357	.552	96	414	373	64	109	19	0	26	70	34	5	0	2	123	2	0	8.2	29.7
Fletcher, Dominic	L-L	5-6	185	9-2-97	.260	.317	.453	105	446	404	56	105	19	4	17	68	29	7	1	5	87	7	4	6.5	19.5
Gonzalez, Jacob	L-R	6-2	200	5-30-02	.204	.310	.293	45	171	147	15	30	7	0	2	14	20	3	0	1	34	5	0	11.7	19.9
Gonzalez, Juan	R-R	5-9	195	2-20-01	.286	.375	.429	2	8	7	1	2	1	0	0	2	0	1	0	0	1	0	0	12.5
Gray, Tristan	L-R	6-1	215	3-22-96	.270	.333	.472	72	282	248	40	67	15	4	9	44	24	3	0	7	67	3	1	8.5	23.8
Hackenberg, Adam	R-R	6-1	225	9-8-99	.218	.273	.301	38	143	133	12	29	8	0	1	11	10	0	0	0	37	0	0	7.0	25.9
Hogan, Matt	R-R	6-0	195	1-24-00	.250	.250	.250	3	12	12	0	3	0	0	0	0	0	0	0	0	6	0	0	0.0	50.0
Jankowski, Travis	L-R	6-2	190	6-15-91	.261	.321	.391	5	25	23	6	6	0	0	1	2	2	0	0	0	5	0	0	8.0	20.0
Jones, Greg	S-R	6-2	175	3-7-98	.145	.254	.258	16	71	62	3	9	1	0	2	9	5	4	0	0	30	7	3	7.0	42.3
Julks, Corey	R-R	6-1	185	2-27-96	.300	.374	.477	116	487	436	77	131	30	1	15	58	48	3	0	0	99	18	3	9.9	20.3
Lee, Korey	R-R	6-2	210	7-25-98	.255	.313	.405	55	240	220	34	56	9	0	8	28	17	2	0	1	55	5	0	7.1	22.9
Lipcius, Andre	R-R	6-0	190	5-22-98	.240	.318	.447	106	421	371	56	89	21	1	18	71	37	8	0	5	77	3	2	8.8	18.3
Logan, Drake	R-R	6-2	205	9-5-00	.306	.390	.389	11	41	36	7	11	3	0	0	5	5	0	0	0	13	2	0	12.2	31.7
Maton, Nick	L-R	6-2	178	2-18-97	.346	.346	.346	16	65	52	6	18	2	0	2	8	11	2	0	0	20	0	0	16.9	35.4
Matthews, Jason	R-R	6-0	187	4-9-97	.349	.451	.512	15	52	43	14	15	0	2	1	4	6	2	1	0	17	1	0	11.5	32.7
Mead, Curtis	R-R	6-0	171	10-26-00	.571	.700	.857	2	10	7	2	4	2	0	0	2	3	0	0	0	2	0	0	30.0	20.0
Meidroth, Chase	R-R	5-9	170	7-23-01	.267	.450	.600	9	40	30	11	8	1	0	3	4	8	2	0	0	5	2	0	20.0	12.5
Mitchell, Cal	L-L	6-0	205	3-8-99	.111	.111	.148	10	27	27	0	3	1	0	0	0	0	0	0	0	14	1	1	0.0	51.9
Montgomery, Colson	L-R	6-3	205	2-27-02	.218	.298	.435	55	242	216	27	47	10	2	11	30	19	6	0	1	82	2	1	7.9	33.9
Narvaez, Omar	L-R	5-11	220	2-10-92	.218	.317	.345	15	63	55	6	12	2	0	2	5	6	2	0	0	13	0	0	9.5	20.6

Batting	B-T	Ht	Wt	DOB	AVG	OBP	SLG	G	AB	R	H	2B	3B	HR	RBI	BB	SO	SB	CS	OBP	SLG	SO%	BB%
Noda, Ryan	L-L	6-3	217	3-30-96	.130	.286	.304	7	28	23	6	3	1	0	1	2	5	0	0	10	0	0	17.9	35.7
Palacios, Josh	L-R	6-1	200	7-30-95	.197	.329	.379	21	82	66	7	13	3	0	3	9	11	3	0	2	16	3	3	13.4	19.5
Quero, Edgar	S-R	5-11	170	4-6-03	.333	.444	.412	15	63	51	9	17	1	0	1	4	11	0	0	1	14	0	0	17.5	22.2
Ramos, Bryan	R-R	6-2	190	3-12-02	.216	.309	.396	105	431	371	60	80	17	1	16	51	42	10	1	4	96	13	4	9.7	22.3
Robertson, Will	L-L	6-0	215	12-26-97	.284	.355	.560	27	121	109	19	31	10	1	6	16	12	0	0	0	31	0	1	9.9	25.6
Rojas, Josh	L-R	6-1	207	6-30-94	.083	.154	.167	3	13	12	0	1	1	0	0	1	1	0	0	0	3	0	1	7.7	23.1
Sabol, Blake	L-R	6-4	225	1-7-98	.216	.326	.378	23	86	74	10	16	3	0	3	13	9	3	0	0	25	0	2	10.5	29.1
Santos, Miguel	R-R	5-11	174	3-12-01	.000	.500	.000	1	4	2	0	0	0	0	0	0	2	0	0	0	0	0	0	50.0	0.0
Slater, Austin	R-R	6-1	204	12-13-92	.385	.529	.462	4	17	13	3	5	1	0	0	2	4	0	0	0	3	0	0	23.5	17.6
Sosa, Lenyn	R-R	6-0	180	1-25-00	.100	.100	.200	3	10	10	0	1	1	0	0	0	0	0	0	0	4	0	0	40.0
Tauchman, Mike	L-L	6-2	220	12-3-90	.111	.233	.194	11	43	36	3	4	0	0	1	4	6	0	0	1	13	0	0	14.0	30.2
Teel, Kyle	L-R	6-1	190	2-15-02	.295	.394	.492	50	213	183	34	54	10	1	8	30	30	0	0	0	54	7	1	14.1	25.4
Vaughn, Andrew	R-R	6-0	215	4-3-98	.211	.328	.351	15	67	57	9	12	2	0	2	11	10	0	0	0	10	0	0	14.9	14.9
Workman, Gage	S-R	6-4	202	10-24-99	.250	.500	.250	3	12	8	3	2	0	0	0	1	4	0	0	0	6	2	0	33.3	50.0

CHICAGO WHITE SOX

Pitching	B-T	Ht.	Wt.	DOB	W	L	ERA	G	GS	SV	IP	Hits	Runs	ER	HR	BB	SO	AVG	OBP	SLG	SO%	BB%	BF
Adler, Eric	R-R	6-2	190	10-12-00	0	2	8.71	9	1	0	10	14	11	10	1	9	7	.341	.462	.439	13.2	17.0	53
Altavilla, Dan	R-R	5-11	226	9-8-92	1	1	2.42	24	0	7	26	21	9	7	2	13	21	.226	.339	.355	18.9	11.7	111
Anderson, Justin	L-R	6-3	230	9-28-92	3	4	7.29	31	0	4	33	37	28	27	2	26	35	.291	.436	.386	21.3	15.9	164
Bell, Luke	R-R	6-4	200	8-9-00	2	0	6.23	6	0	0	9	7	6	6	1	6	4	.212	.341	.364	9.8	14.6	41
Booser, Cam	L-L	6-3	225	5-4-92	2	1	7.36	16	0	2	15	23	12	12	5	10	24	.354	.455	.708	31.2	13.0	77
Burke, Sean	R-R	6-6	230	12-18-99	0	3	7.82	3	3	0	13	18	11	11	3	5	15	.333	.390	.574	25.4	8.5	59
Cannon, Jonathan	R-R	6-6	213	7-19-00	1	3	5.40	7	7	0	32	39	22	19	5	14	21	.307	.385	.465	14.6	9.7	144
Clevinger, Mike	R-R	6-4	215	12-21-90	7	3	4.20	22	22	0	101	98	51	47	17	36	93	.257	.322	.471	21.9	8.5	425
Coffey, Adisyn	R-R	6-2	185	1-22-99	2	4	5.22	31	1	1	40	36	26	23	10	26	56	.232	.344	.452	30.3	14.1	185
Davitt, Duncan	R-R	6-3	235	9-23-99	2	3	5.03	9	9	0	48	39	27	27	4	24	45	.222	.329	.352	21.5	11.5	209
DeLoach, Zach	L-R	6-0	205	8-18-98	0	0	0.00	1	0	0	1	0	0	0	0	1	0	.000	.333	.000	0.0	33.3	3
Dunn, Justin	R-R	6-2	209	9-22-95	2	3	7.64	10	7	0	33	40	31	28	4	25	38	.299	.430	.440	23.0	15.2	165
Eisert, Brandon	L-L	6-2	205	1-19-98	0	0	4.50	2	0	0	2	3	1	1	0	1	3	.429	.500	.571	37.5	12.5	8
Ellard, Fraser	L-L	6-4	205	11-6-97	2	1	6.48	23	0	0	25	27	19	18	4	17	34	.270	.392	.470	28.1	14.0	121
Fletcher, Dominic	L-L	5-6	185	9-2-97	0	0	9.00	1	0	1	2	2	1	0	0	1	.500	.400	.750	20.0	0.0	5
Franklin, Zach	R-R	6-1	198	10-27-98	1	1	4.40	13	0	1	14	12	7	7	2	6	19	.235	.310	.412	32.8	10.3	58
Freeman, Caleb	R-R	6-1	195	2-23-98	3	1	4.91	29	0	3	33	30	20	18	6	22	31	.240	.354	.432	21.1	15.0	147
Gilbert, Tyler	L-L	6-3	223	12-22-93	0	0	12.00	6	0	0	6	8	8	8	1	5	7	.308	.419	.615	22.6	16.1	31
Gomez, Yoendrys	R-R	6-3	175	10-15-99	4	3	2.12	14	11	0	47	38	11	11	3	21	64	.217	.312	.326	32.0	10.5	200
Gonzalez, Wikelman	R-R	6-0	167	3-25-02	6	2	5.18	22	0	0	33	22	20	19	2	27	30	.195	.361	.310	20.7	18.6	145
Gray, Tristan	L-R	6-1	215	3-22-96	0	0	0.00	1	0	1	1	0	0	0	1	0	.333	.500	.667	0.0	25.0	4
Hudson, Bryan	L-L	6-8	220	5-8-97	0	0	2.70	5	0	0	7	6	2	2	1	2	6	.250	.308	.375	23.1	7.7	26
Iriarte, Jairo	R-R	6-2	160	12-15-01	2	3	7.24	35	5	1	46	53	43	37	9	37	48	.299	.416	.531	21.6	16.7	222
Karinchak, James	R-R	6-3	215	9-22-95	3	1	2.45	24	0	2	29	20	9	8	3	20	34	.200	.333	.340	28.1	16.5	121
Kela, Keone	R-R	6-1	220	4-16-93	0	2	8.44	10	0	1	16	17	15	15	3	9	23	.266	.356	.453	31.5	12.3	73
Lipcius, Andre	R-R	6-0	190	5-22-98	0	0	10.80	1	0	0	2	4	2	2	0	2	0	.500	.545	.625	0.0	18.2	11
Martin, Davis	L-R	6-2	200	1-4-97	0	0	4.76	2	2	0	6	7	3	3	0	1	5	.318	.375	.409	20.8	4.2	24
McGough, Trey	L-L	6-3	195	3-29-98	0	0	9.00	7	1	0	15	18	15	15	3	15	13	.305	.425	.525	17.5	20.0	75
McKendry, Evan	R-R	6-3	200	2-6-98	5	9	5.15	20	13	0	80	85	56	46	17	18	57	.263	.315	.480	16.3	5.1	350
Murfee, Penn	R-R	6-2	195	5-2-94	2	1	4.09	22	0	0	22	22	12	10	0	18	16	.278	.416	.367	15.7	17.6	102
Murphy, Shane	L-L	6-5	210	1-19-01	0	1	2.45	3	3	0	15	11	4	4	2	7	10	.216	.353	.431	16.9	11.9	59
Pallette, Peyton	R-R	6-1	180	5-9-01	1	2	4.36	36	0	3	43	32	22	21	3	20	54	.204	.308	.369	29.3	10.9	184
Peguero, Elvis	R-R	6-5	237	3-20-97	0	1	9.00	2	0	0	2	1	2	2	1	3	1	.167	.444	.667	11.1	33.3	9
Peoples, Ben	L-R	6-1	175	5-1-01	0	2	5.56	10	0	0	11	9	10	7	1	6	8	.214	.327	.286	16.3	12.2	49
Perez, Martin	L-L	6-0	200	4-4-91	0	0	6.75	1	1	0	3	4	2	2	1	0	3	.333	.333	.667	25.0	0.0	12
Plymell, Chase	R-R	6-4	205	5-29-98	1	1	3.44	31	2	2	52	52	28	20	4	19	33	.269	.333	.399	14.7	8.5	224
Roach, Dalton	R-R	6-2	210	4-8-96	1	1	4.85	10	0	0	13	17	9	7	5	1	10	.304	.310	.607	17.2	1.7	58
Rodriguez, Chris	R-R	6-2	180	7-20-98	1	3	5.71	18	8	0	41	44	30	26	6	24	35	.278	.384	.481	18.5	12.7	189
Schoenle, Garrett	L-L	6-5	185	6-21-98	0	3	6.51	22	0	0	28	35	22	20	5	15	21	.307	.391	.474	15.8	11.3	133
Scholtens, Jesse	R-R	6-4	230	4-6-94	1	1	5.28	8	6	0	29	26	22	17	3	9	25	.234	.290	.378	20.2	7.3	124
Schultz, Noah	L-L	6-9	220	8-5-03	0	2	9.37	5	5	0	16	23	18	17	3	9	18	.359	.429	.578	23.4	11.7	77
Schweitzer, Tyler	L-L	6-0	185	9-19-00	2	7	7.92	15	10	0	50	61	47	44	13	26	39	.298	.373	.566	16.6	11.1	235
Shuster, Jared	L-L	6-3	210	8-3-98	3	0	6.04	16	0	0	22	31	16	15	5	7	21	.326	.377	.558	19.8	6.6	106
Syndergaard, Noah	L-R	6-6	242	8-29-92	0	1	10.13	2	2	0	8	10	9	9	5	1	2	.294	.314	.765	5.7	2.9	35
Tyler, Kyle	R-R	6-0	225	12-27-96	0	2	6.58	12	0	0	26	31	22	19	4	11	23	.277	.341	.464	18.7	8.9	123
Vail, Tommy	R-L	6-0	195	5-18-99	0	0	21.60	5	0	0	3	4	8	8	2	6	3	.333	.550	.833	15.0	30.0	20
Varland, Gus	L-R	6-1	213	11-6-96	0	0	5.06	7	0	0	5	5	3	3	1	5	9	.250	.423	.500	34.6	19.2	26
White, Owen	R-R	6-3	199	8-9-99	0	8	4.44	20	17	0	81	74	43	40	7	43	65	.253	.357	.380	18.8	12.4	346
Wilson, Bryse	R-R	6-2	267	12-20-97	4	3	4.25	18	8	1	49	50	26	23	6	11	41	.270	.315	.432	20.5	5.5	200
Wilson, Steven	R-R	6-3	221	8-24-94	0	0	1.69	5	0	1	5	1	1	1	1	10	.238	.273	.476	45.5	4.5	22

Fielding

Catcher	PCT	G	PO	A	E	DP	PB
Eberly	1.000	3	20	1	0	0	0
Gonzalez	1.000	2	10	0	0	0	0
Hackendy	.994	37	299	22	2	1	0
Lee	.988	45	371	26	5	2	4
Narvaez	.956	6	64	1	3	0	1

	PCT	G	PO	A	E	DP	PB
Quero	.988	9	78	7	1	1	1
Sabol	.988	18	152	7	2	0	2
Teel	.990	33	272	23	3	0	3

First Base	PCT	G	PO	A	E	DP
Colas	1.000	5	34	1	0	4
Connor	1.000	7	50	3	0	2
Dalbec	1.000	2	9	3	0	1
Drury	.889	1	7	1	1	0
Elko	.992	80	548	46	5	62
Gray	1.000	1	8	0	0	1
Lipcius	.997	38	284	20	1	24

CHICAGO WHITE SOX

	PCT	G	PO	A	E	DP
Maton	1.000	1	4	0	0	0
Narvaez	.917	2	11	0	1	1
Noda	.969	5	29	2	1	0
Ramos	1.000	1	8	0	0	2
Sabol	1.000	2	8	0	0	4
Vaughn	.988	10	75	5	1	6

Second Base	PCT	G	PO	A	E	DP
Amaya	1.000	12	23	30	0	8
Baker	1.000	1	1	4	0	1
Baldwin	1.000	8	18	11	0	2
Camilletti	1.000	3	3	5	0	1
Capra	.976	9	18	22	1	4
Cowles	1.000	7	14	16	0	4
Gonzalez	.976	21	32	51	2	11
Gray	.967	27	50	68	4	20
Jones	1.000	6	10	13	0	3
Lipcius	.974	28	55	56	3	13
Maton	.962	13	22	28	2	10
Matthews	.980	9	13	37	1	2
Mead	1.000	2	2	2	0	0
Meidroth	1.000	4	4	17	0	3
Rojas	1.000	1	1	4	0	2
Santos	.833	1	1	4	1	2
Sosa	1.000	1	1	3	0	0

Third Base	PCT	G	PO	A	E	DP
Baldwin	1.000	5	4	6	0	1
Camilletti	1.000	2	1	2	0	0
Cowles	1.000	3	7	2	0	1
Dalbec	.900	6	4	5	1	1
Gonzalez	1.000	8	10	9	0	0
Gray	.975	20	14	25	1	3
Lipcius	.889	11	7	17	3	2
Matthews	1.000	1	0	1	0	0
Montgomery	1.000	4	2	7	0	2
Ramos	.931	93	71	144	16	10
Rojas	.857	1	1	5	1	1
Sosa	1.000	1	1	0	0	0
Workman	1.000	2	0	3	0	0

Shortstop	PCT	G	PO	A	E	DP
Amaya	.953	47	52	112	8	21
Baldwin	.778	2	2	5	2	1
Capra	1.000	13	10	17	0	5
Cowles	.947	4	8	10	1	2
Gonzalez	.962	14	24	27	2	11
Gray	.970	14	29	36	2	10
Jones	1.000	1	1	2	0	0
Maton	1.000	1	0	1	0	0
Matthews	1.000	4	6	8	0	2
Meidroth	1.000	5	6	8	0	2

	PCT	G	PO	A	E	DP
Montgomery	.963	50	60	98	6	23
Rojas	.800	1	1	3	1	1

Outfield	PCT	G	PO	A	E	DP
Baker	1.000	75	140	5	0	2
Baldwin	.971	14	33	0	1	0
Benintendi	1.000	1	1	0	0	0
Camilletti	1.000	8	7	0	0	0
Capra	1.000	4	6	0	0	0
Colas	1.000	10	15	2	0	0
Connor	1.000	6	8	1	0	0
Dalbec	1.000	4	7	0	0	0
DeLoach	1.000	52	89	6	0	2
Fletcher	.987	100	228	7	3	2
Hogan	.667	3	2	0	1	0
Jankowski	1.000	5	12	1	0	0
Jones	1.000	9	25	0	0	1
Julks	.985	106	193	9	3	0
Lipcius	1.000	4	7	0	0	0
Logan	1.000	11	19	0	0	0
Mitchell	.923	10	12	0	1	0
Palacios	.933	17	27	1	2	0
Ramos	1.000	2	3	0	0	0
Robertson	.944	24	33	1	2	0
Slater	1.000	3	2	0	0	0
Tauchman	1.000	8	15	0	0	0

BIRMINGHAM BARONS — DOUBLE-A
SOUTHERN LEAGUE

Batting	B-T	Ht.	Wt.	DOB	AVG	OBP	SLG	G	PA	AB	R	H	2B	3B	HR	RBI	BB	HBP	SH	SF	SO	SB	CS	BB%	SO%
Antonacci, Sam	L-R	6-0	185	2-6-03	.292	.435	.381	49	217	168	27	49	8	2	1	25	28	16	3	2	32	21	2	12.9	14.7
Bergolla, William	L-R	5-11	165	10-20-04	.286	.342	.333	125	551	486	70	139	19	2	0	36	37	5	21	2	26	40	11	6.7	4.7
Burke, Jacob	R-R	6-1	208	2-26-01	.212	.287	.273	61	227	198	18	42	6	0	2	25	17	5	3	3	58	9	5	7.5	25.6
Camilletti, Mario	R-R	5-9	195	4-19-99	.230	.336	.295	82	326	278	30	64	6	3	2	25	43	2	2	1	77	6	0	13.2	23.6
Colas, Oscar	L-L	5-11	209	9-17-98	.200	.262	.291	15	61	55	5	11	2	0	1	6	5	0	0	1	16	1	1	8.2	26.2
Connor, Caden	L-L	6-0	200	8-2-00	.266	.345	.363	95	390	342	39	91	19	1	4	43	43	0	2	3	59	10	1	11.0	15.1
Corona, Jorge	R-R	6-2	190	9-12-00	.125	.344	.292	9	32	24	5	3	1	0	1	1	2	6	0	0	10	0	0	6.3	31.3
Eberly, Weston	R-R	6-0	195	1-7-01	.000	.200	.000	3	10	8	0	0	0	0	0	0	1	1	0	0	7	0	0	10.0	70.0
Galanie, Ryan	R-R	6-2	215	6-20-00	.266	.320	.386	98	409	365	49	97	19	2	7	71	29	5	0	10	63	12	2	7.1	15.4
Gladney, DJ	R-R	6-3	195	7-14-01	.235	.277	.368	100	405	375	44	88	14	3	10	45	21	3	1	5	126	8	6	5.2	31.1
Gonzalez, Jacob	L-R	6-2	200	5-30-02	.244	.305	.369	89	368	328	41	80	19	2	6	47	28	4	1	7	52	12	3	7.6	14.1
Gonzalez, Juan	R-R	5-9	195	2-20-01	.250	.250	.250	1	4	4	0	1	0	0	0	0	0	0	0	0	2	0	0	0.0	50.0
Goosenberg, Shawn	R-R	6-1	195	12-4-99	.188	.230	.275	22	74	69	6	13	4	1	0	2	2	2	0	1	24	3	0	2.7	32.4
Hackenberg, Adam	R-R	6-1	225	9-8-99	.188	.247	.294	25	93	85	7	16	3	0	2	11	6	1	0	1	31	1	0	6.5	33.3
Harris, Calvin	L-R	6-0	205	11-15-01	.253	.317	.312	56	205	186	25	47	5	0	2	17	16	2	0	1	50	3	1	7.8	24.4
Hogan, Matt	R-R	6-0	195	1-24-00	.171	.358	.268	15	55	41	5	7	1	0	1	4	7	5	2	0	14	3	0	12.7	25.5
Makarewicz, Alec	S-R	6-2	217	9-12-00	.241	.313	.414	8	32	29	3	7	1	0	1	3	0	0	0	0	13	0	0	9.4	40.6
Matthews, Jason	R-R	6-0	187	4-9-97	.180	.307	.242	68	254	211	30	38	7	0	2	16	35	4	3	1	59	7	3	13.8	23.2
Montgomery, Braden	S-R	6-2	201	4-26-03	.272	.364	.416	34	143	125	14	34	13	1	1	11	15	3	0	0	41	3	3	10.5	28.7
Narvaez, Omar	L-R	5-11	220	2-10-92	.250	.333	.375	3	9	8	1	2	1	0	0	2	1	0	0	0	1	0	0	11.1	11.1
Nishida, Rikuu	L-R	5-6	150	5-6-01	.273	.403	.308	115	502	403	72	110	8	3	0	31	75	14	8	2	69	40	12	14.9	13.7
Podkul, Nick	R-R	6-1	200	4-11-97	.158	.304	.171	25	92	76	6	12	1	0	0	6	14	2	0	0	32	0	0	15.2	34.8
Smelley, Colby	R-R	5-11	200	11-15-00	.250	.321	.316	23	85	76	5	19	2	0	1	4	7	1	1	0	16	0	0	8.2	18.8
Sprinkle, Jordan	R-R	5-11	180	3-6-01	.308	.357	.308	4	14	13	3	4	0	0	0	2	1	0	0	0	4	3	0	7.1	28.6
Turner, Michael	L-R	6-2	205	8-18-98	.295	.384	.368	31	112	95	8	28	7	0	0	13	15	0	0	2	33	0	0	13.4	29.5
Veras, Wilfred	R-R	6-2	180	11-15-02	.215	.293	.327	111	464	410	40	88	27	4	9	53	43	5	0	6	139	16	8	9.3	30.0

Pitching	B-T	Ht.	Wt.	DOB	W	L	ERA	G	GS	SV	IP	Hits	Runs	ER	HR	BB	SO	AVG	OBP	SLG	SO%	BB%	BF
Adler, Eric	R-R	6-2	190	10-12-00	3	3	4.78	25	0	1	26	28	18	14	1	22	26	.277	.409	.337	20.3	17.2	128
Coffey, Adisyn	R-R	6-2	185	1-22-99	2	1	5.52	12	0	0	15	16	11	9	2	2	19	.286	.310	.482	32.2	3.4	59
Dalquist, Andrew	R-R	6-1	175	11-13-00	6	3	3.20	43	0	1	56	37	21	20	4	40	50	.192	.331	.290	21.2	16.9	236
Davis, Tyler	R-R	6-3	210	10-3-98	2	7	3.17	41	0	3	54	39	23	19	1	27	64	.198	.296	.279	28.2	11.9	227
Fox, Phil	R-R	5-10	170	10-26-02	0	0	0.00	2	0	0	4	2	0	0	0	0	4	.143	.143	.143	28.6	0.0	14
Franklin, Zach	R-R	6-1	198	10-27-98	3	0	1.71	35	0	10	42	23	10	8	2	19	60	.162	.259	.254	36.1	11.4	166
Freeman, Caleb	R-R	6-1	195	2-23-98	0	3	3.06	14	0	2	18	14	9	6	0	14	18	.212	.346	.258	22.0	17.1	82
Gonzalez, Wikelman	R-R	6-0	167	3-25-02	0	2	4.41	4	4	0	16	13	8	8	0	14	21	.217	.390	.350	27.3	18.2	77
Goosenberg, Shawn	R-R	6-1	195	12-5-99	0	0	0.00	1	0	0	1	0	0	0	0	0	0	.000	.500	.000	0.0	0.0	2
Gordon, Lucas	L-L	6-1	193	2-13-02	2	1	2.11	4	4	0	21	15	5	5	0	7	24	.130	.221	.188	31.2	9.1	77
Gowens, Riley	R-R	6-2	220	10-18-99	7	6	3.34	27	27	0	132	108	52	49	12	49	151	.222	.300	.348	27.7	9.0	546
Jacobs, Carson	R-R	6-9	215	8-17-01	1	0	3.00	2	0	0	3	4	1	1	1	3	5	.333	.500	.750	31.3	18.8	16
Kela, Keone	R-R	6-1	220	4-16-93	1	0	0.00	2	0	0	3	1	0	0	0	2	4	.111	.273	.222	36.4	18.2	11
Kelley, Jared	R-R	6-3	230	10-3-01	3	1	3.89	30	0	39	36	20	17	2	22	41	.252	.345	.343	24.3	13.0	169
Luna, Gil	L-L	5-10	173	7-29-99	0	3	9.00	16	0	1	21	13	.225	.492	.375	20.0	32.3	65
McCullough, Connor	R-R	6-1	185	10-5-99	0	2	3.16	8	8	0	31	21	14	11	3	7	28	.188	.248	.286	23.1	5.8	121

Batter	B-T	Ht	Wt	DOB	G	GS	IP	H	R	ER	HR	BB	SO	AVG	OBP	SLG	SO%	BB%	BF
McDougal, Tanner	R-R	6-5	185	4-9-03	3	2	3.23	15	15	0	56	49	20	20	3	17	63	.240	.310	.338	27.8	7.5	227
McLaughlin, Mark	R-R	6-3	205	2-14-01	2	1	4.44	23	0	2	26	22	14	13	2	12	22	.232	.310	.337	19.5	10.6	113
Mikel, Jordan	R-R	6-5	190	3-24-99	2	3	4.11	25	2	1	46	44	22	21	4	14	38	.256	.325	.384	19.8	7.3	192
Murphy, Shane	L-L	6-5	210	1-19-01	9	4	1.38	20	18	0	111	77	20	17	8	15	82	.198	.230	.301	20.1	3.7	408
Palisch, Jake	L-L	6-4	215	8-19-98	8	3	2.14	29	13	0	105	86	35	25	5	26	67	.223	.273	.327	16.1	6.3	416
Pallette, Peyton	R-R	6-1	180	5-9-01	1	1	3.43	16	0	8	21	12	8	8	3	8	32	.164	.247	.301	39.5	9.9	81
Perez, Martin	L-L	6-0	200	4-4-91	0	1	2.25	1	1	0	4	3	1	1	0	3	2	.231	.375	.308	11.8	17.6	17
Plymell, Chase	R-R	6-4	205	5-29-98	0	0	0.00	2	0	0	4	2	0	0	0	0	2	.154	.154	.231	15.4	0.0	13
Roach, Dalton	R-R	6-2	210	4-8-96	3	0	3.26	26	3	2	47	38	17	17	3	20	45	.222	.312	.327	22.5	10.0	200
Roberts, Max	R-L	6-6	190	7-23-97	0	0	6.48	8	0	0	8	9	6	6	3	6	12	.265	.375	.529	30.0	15.0	40
Rosado, Jarold	R-R	6-3	215	7-13-02	2	0	6.61	14	0	1	16	15	12	12	1	16	14	.246	.397	.328	17.9	20.5	78
Schoenle, Garrett	L-L	6-5	185	6-21-98	5	1	1.60	26	0	7	34	22	9	6	2	6	35	.180	.219	.270	27.1	4.7	129
Schultz, Noah	L-L	6-9	220	8-5-03	4	3	3.34	12	12	0	57	54	22	21	3	36	58	.261	.378	.357	23.2	14.4	250
Schweitzer, Tyler	L-L	6-0	185	9-19-00	6	0	1.27	12	0	0	50	32	9	7	0	15	42	.183	.250	.217	21.8	7.8	193
Smith, Hagen	L-L	6-3	215	8-19-03	3	3	3.57	20	20	0	76	42	31	30	5	56	108	.166	.332	.285	33.9	17.6	319
Taylor, Grant	R-R	6-3	220	5-20-02	0	1	1.01	15	6	0	27	12	4	3	0	11	37	.135	.230	.169	36.6	10.9	101
Vail, Tommy	R-L	6-0	195	5-18-99	4	2	3.00	15	5	0	51	41	19	17	3	34	50	.218	.341	.303	22.1	15.0	226

Fielding

Catcher	PCT	G	PO	A	E	DP	PB
Corona	.988	9	77	5	1	0	2
Eberly	1.000	3	24	3	0	0	0
Gonzalez	1.000	1	6	0	0	0	0
Hackenberg	.992	25	242	15	2	2	2
Harris	.988	55	482	25	6	4	3
Narvaez	1.000	3	26	0	0	0	0
Smelley	.986	23	204	12	3	3	4
Turner	1.000	26	200	18	0	4	2

First Base	PCT	G	PO	A	E	DP
Antonacci	1.000	1	1	0	0	0
Colas	1.000	2	12	1	0	1
Connor	.996	32	247	11	1	22
Galanie	.994	86	660	27	4	58
Gladney	.833	1	5	0	1	0
Goosenberg	1.000	3	19	1	0	5
Makarewicz	1.000	1	9	1	0	2

Second Base	PCT	G	PO	A	E	DP
Podkul	.988	11	76	5	1	6
Turner	1.000	4	18	1	0	3
Antonacci	1.000	34	53	92	0	19
Bergolla	1.000	10	17	25	0	8
Camilletti	.968	6	11	19	1	6
Gonzalez	.995	55	78	122	1	34
Matthews	1.000	3	0	8	0	0
Nishida	.954	32	34	70	5	14
Sprinkle	1.000	4	9	7	0	3

Third Base	PCT	G	PO	A	E	DP
Antonacci	1.000	9	5	16	0	0
Camilletti	.940	47	34	76	7	7
Gonzalez	1.000	8	5	18	0	2
Makarewicz	1.000	7	9	3	0	1
Matthews	.974	62	44	108	4	13

Shortstop	PCT	G	PO	A	E	DP
Podkul	.938	8	3	12	1	2
Antonacci	1.000	3	1	4	0	0
Bergolla	.981	113	117	253	7	59
Gonzalez	.976	23	27	56	2	11
Matthews	1.000	4	5	7	0	1

Outfield	PCT	G	PO	A	E	DP
Burke	.992	61	130	1	1	0
Colas	1.000	8	8	0	0	0
Connor	.991	56	104	2	1	0
Gladney	.989	84	179	8	2	3
Goosenberg	1.000	16	24	0	0	0
Hogan	.976	15	37	3	1	2
Montgomery	1.000	29	63	4	0	0
Nishida	.987	79	141	11	2	3
Veras	.993	76	141	6	1	3

WINSTON-SALEM DASH — HIGH-A
SOUTH ATLANTIC LEAGUE

Batting	B-T	Ht.	Wt.	DOB	AVG	OBP	SLG	G	PA	AB	R	H	2B	3B	HR	RBI	BB	HBP	SH	SF	SO	SB	CS	BB%	SO%
Antonacci, Sam	L-R	6-0	185	2-6-03	.279	.425	.412	64	288	226	48	63	10	4	4	29	39	19	3	1	37	27	7	13.5	12.8
Appel, Jackson	B-R	6-0	195	8-31-01	.248	.387	.318	85	326	258	43	64	13	1	1	25	51	10	1	4	53	11	2	15.6	16.3
Bonemer, Caleb	R-R	6-1	195	10-5-05	.278	.409	.611	11	44	36	8	10	4	1	2	6	7	1	0	0	10	2	0	15.9	22.7
Burke, Jacob	R-R	6-1	208	2-26-01	.222	.357	.333	14	56	45	10	10	2	0	1	5	6	4	0	1	3	5	1	10.7	5.4
Burrowes, Ryan	R-R	6-2	170	8-17-04	.254	.338	.386	36	130	114	19	29	7	1	2	14	12	3	0	1	34	16	2	9.2	26.2
Connor, Caden	L-L	6-1	200	8-2-00	.266	.383	.359	18	81	64	10	17	0	0	2	14	12	2	0	3	12	2	0	14.8	14.8
Eberly, Weston	R-R	6-0	195	1-7-01	.154	.308	.250	19	66	52	10	8	2	0	1	5	10	2	1	1	13	2	0	15.2	19.7
Galanie, Ryan	R-R	6-2	215	6-20-00	.315	.356	.565	21	101	92	8	29	7	2	4	23	6	1	0	2	16	2	1	5.9	15.8
Gonzalez, Juan	R-R	5-9	195	2-20-01	.086	.172	.086	21	64	58	4	5	0	0	0	2	4	0	0	1	18	1	0	3.1	28.1
Hernandez, Arxy	R-R	6-2	170	7-29-03	.205	.256	.292	75	309	288	28	59	7	3	4	19	14	6	0	1	84	3	0	4.5	27.2
Hogan, Matt	L-R	6-0	195	1-24-00	.187	.306	.288	29	108	91	13	17	5	3	0	12	14	2	0	1	38	1	0	13.0	35.2
Kath, Wes	L-R	6-3	200	8-3-02	.149	.228	.221	46	171	154	13	23	8	0	1	14	12	4	0	1	69	1	1	7.0	40.4
Lodise, Kyle	R-R	5-11	180	10-17-03	.185	.319	.370	28	113	92	14	17	3	1	4	10	15	4	0	2	21	7	1	13.3	18.6
Logan, Drake	R-R	6-4	205	9-5-00	.258	.327	.364	46	171	151	23	39	0	2	4	23	14	3	0	3	65	21	5	8.2	38.0
Magill, Grant	R-R	6-0	195	11-30-00	.143	.250	.143	2	8	7	3	1	0	0	0	1	1	0	0	0	0	0	0	12.5	0.0
Makarewicz, Alec	S-R	6-2	217	7-6-00	.228	.301	.390	110	438	390	45	89	20	5	11	61	39	4	0	5	116	10	0	8.9	26.5
McCants, T.J.	R-R	6-3	190	6-6-01	.264	.313	.374	29	100	91	13	24	8	1	0	11	6	1	0	1	31	8	4	6.0	31.0
McConnell, Cole	L-L	6-1	210	9-5-00	.217	.331	.366	87	358	304	42	66	12	0	5	28	42	10	0	1	107	5	6	11.7	29.9
Miller-Green, Lyle	R-R	6-4	229	9-4-00	.195	.327	.333	28	104	87	12	17	4	1	2	14	15	2	0	0	32	2	0	14.4	30.8
Montgomery, Braden	S-R	6-2	201	4-26-03	.260	.348	.445	69	290	254	36	66	17	3	8	38	32	3	0	1	70	5	2	11.0	24.1
Perez, Jeral	R-R	6-0	179	11-6-04	.244	.315	.448	125	537	480	65	117	24	4	22	70	44	8	0	5	112	10	3	8.2	20.9
Pineda, Luis	R-R	6-1	193	3-19-02	.276	.286	.382	22	78	76	9	21	2	0	2	12	1	0	0	0	26	1	0	1.3	33.3
Sanchez, Wilber	R-R	5-10	160	2-27-01	.313	.313	.46	144	128	11	19	5	0	2	14	14	2	0	0	36	6	4	9.7	25.0
Santos, Miguel	R-R	5-11	174	3-12-01	.059	.200	.059	6	20	17	1	1	0	0	0	0	2	1	0	0	5	0	0	10.0	25.0
Sprinkle, Jordan	R-R	5-11	180	3-6-01	.172	.284	.264	33	103	87	10	15	3	1	1	9	12	2	1	1	17	12	0	11.7	16.5
Tatum, Terrell	L-L	5-9	167	7-27-99	.188	.305	.268	44	131	112	17	21	6	1	0	6	12	18	1	0	0	46	18	1	13.7	35.1
Turner, Michael	R-R	6-2	215	8-18-98	.167	.167	.333	2	6	6	1	1	1	0	0	1	0	0	0	0	1	0	0	0.0	16.7
Zavala, Samuel	L-L	6-1	175	7-15-04	.254	.360	.372	119	486	409	65	104	17	2	9	51	65	5	2	5	104	18	8	13.4	21.4

Pitching	B-T	Ht.	Wt.	DOB	W	L	ERA	G	GS	SV	IP	Hits	Runs	ER	HR	BB	SO	AVG	OBP	SLG	SO%	BB%	BF
Altermatt, Nick	R-R	6-0	225	9-28-99	2	0	2.35	24	0	1	38	38	16	10	1	5	44	.259	.286	.347	28.4	3.2	155
Arias, Frankeli	L-L	6-0	170	4-5-03	2	7	3.76	26	17	0	89	71	41	37	8	40	69	.220	.306	.331	18.6	10.8	370
Austin, Morris	R-R	6-2	215	3-27-00	5	4	4.33	29	0	2	35	23	20	17	2	21	32	.187	.318	.293	21.1	13.8	152

CHICAGO WHITE SOX

Pitching

Player	B-T	Ht	Wt	DOB	W	L	ERA	G	GS	CG	SV	IP	H	R	ER	HR	BB	SO	AVG	OBA	SLG	K/9	BB/9	BF
Batista, Aldrin	R-R	6-2	185	5-4-03	2	0	5.79	7	2	0	14	13	12	9	0	7	17	.245	.379	.340	25.8	10.6	66
Bell, Luke	R-R	6-4	200	8-9-00	5	1	4.71	32	1	0	50	49	26	26	7	22	40	.257	.332	.440	18.4	10.1	217
Bockenstedt, Jacob	R-R	6-1	190	11-15-99	6	7	4.81	27	18	0	103	95	58	55	8	43	95	.247	.323	.393	21.9	9.9	433
Clark, Jonathan	R-R	6-1	190	6-3-00	2	0	0.61	14	0	0	15	7	2	1	0	11	20	.143	.311	.184	32.3	17.7	62
Coffey, Adisyn	R-R	6-2	185	1-22-99	0	0	0.00	1	0	0	1	0	0	0	0	0	0	.000	.000	.000	0.0	0.0	3
Cumming, Dylan	R-R	6-4	175	5-14-99	3	5	5.34	15	14	0	56	64	35	33	5	14	52	.286	.351	.420	20.7	5.6	251
Eberly, Weston	R-R	6-0	195	1-7-01	0	0	0.00	1	0	0	0	0	0	0	0	0	0	.000	.000	.000	0.0	0.0	1
Fox, Phil	R-R	5-10	170	10-26-02	2	3	3.47	44	0	11	60	46	25	23	5	14	74	.204	.257	.329	30.2	5.7	245
Gonzalez, Juan	R-R	5-9	195	2-20-01	0	0	0.00	1	0	0	1	0	0	0	0	0	0	.750	.750	.750	0.0	0.0	4
Gordon, Lucas	L-L	6-1	193	2-13-02	1	10	3.96	20	20	0	86	74	40	38	10	35	92	.233	.316	.377	25.4	9.7	362
Hartzog, Clete	L-R	6-1	183	6-12-01	1	1	2.93	15	0	1	15	14	5	5	1	4	14	.233	.292	.333	21.5	6.2	65
Jacobs, Carson	R-R	6-9	215	8-17-01	6	5	4.61	42	0	2	55	50	30	28	6	36	80	.248	.364	.366	33.1	14.9	242
Jeffrey, Madison	L-R	6-0	190	3-14-00	1	1	8.59	20	0	0	22	18	22	21	0	34	22	.243	.482	.338	19.3	29.8	114
Kath, Wes	L-R	6-3	200	8-3-02	0	0	0.00	1	0	0	0	0	0	0	0	0	0	.000	.000	.000	0.0	0.0	1
Keener, Seth	R-R	6-1	195	10-4-01	1	6	11.18	16	6	0	33	48	48	41	8	25	36	.331	.441	.566	20.1	14.0	179
Kelley, Jared	R-R	6-3	230	10-3-01	1	0	0.00	8	0	0	9	4	0	0	0	3	12	.138	.242	.207	36.4	9.1	33
Luna, Gil	L-L	5-10	173	7-29-99	0	1	2.16	9	0	1	8	7	4	2	0	8	6	.259	.487	.370	15.0	20.0	40
McAtee, Aric	R-R	6-5	220	5-31-00	1	1	9.45	7	0	0	7	9	7	7	0	5	8	.333	.455	.481	24.2	15.2	33
McCullough, Connor	R-R	6-1	185	10-5-99	0	0	1.50	2	2	0	6	3	2	1	0	1	3	.136	.167	.227	12.5	4.2	24
McDougal, Tanner	R-R	6-5	185	4-9-03	0	3	3.28	13	13	0	58	53	29	21	4	32	73	.242	.343	.342	28.7	12.6	254
McLaughlin, Mark	R-R	6-3	205	2-14-01	1	2	2.78	22	0	6	36	29	14	11	3	9	45	.221	.270	.336	31.7	6.3	142
Murphy, Shane	L-L	6-5	210	1-19-01	1	0	3.60	3	2	0	10	7	4	4	2	3	12	.189	.250	.378	30.0	7.5	40
Oppor, Christian	L-L	6-2	175	7-23-04	2	6	3.31	17	17	0	65	50	29	26	4	35	82	.212	.332	.309	29.3	12.5	280
Peppers, Jake	R-R	6-3	160	12-26-01	3	3	4.91	29	0	0	44	52	27	24	1	30	30	.310	.409	.393	14.8	14.8	203
Peters, Connery	R-R	6-0	240	2-3-00	0	2	5.75	16	0	1	20	16	16	13	2	17	19	.211	.367	.382	19.4	17.3	98
Roberts, Max	R-L	6-6	190	7-23-97	0	0	0.00	4	0	4	5	0	0	0	0	6	.313	.313	.375	37.5	0.0	16
Rosado, Jarold	R-R	6-3	215	7-10-02	1	0	2.25	14	0	0	16	13	9	4	0	11	18	.210	.347	.226	24.0	14.7	75
Scholtens, Jesse	R-R	6-4	230	4-6-94	0	0	5.14	2	2	0	7	9	4	4	0	3	5	.333	.387	.444	16.1	9.7	31
Sprinkle, Jordan	R-R	5-11	180	3-6-01	0	0	9.00	1	0	0	1	1	1	1	0	0	0	.250	.400	.500	0.0	0.0	5
Umberger, Grant	R-L	6-4	225	10-14-01	0	0	2.45	1	0	0	4	4	1	1	0	1	3	.250	.368	.375	15.8	5.3	19
Vail, Tommy	R-L	6-0	195	5-18-99	2	0	4.15	11	4	0	30	19	14	14	3	18	38	.174	.295	.330	29.5	14.0	129
Vannelle, Vince	R-R	5-10	202	12-19-97	1	0	6.30	12	0	1	20	21	14	14	3	4	16	.266	.301	.430	19.3	4.8	83
Veloz, Manuel	R-R	6-2	185	1-28-01	0	2	7.13	9	4	0	24	25	23	19	6	17	18	.275	.402	.549	16.1	15.2	112
Yabbour, Joseph	R-R	6-1	185	7-9-03	0	0	8.27	21	0	1	21	23	20	19	4	30	21	.288	.491	.488	18.1	25.9	116
Young, Jack	R-R	5-10	185	1-25-02	2	2	5.00	17	1	0	27	22	16	15	2	12	24	.214	.308	.301	20.0	10.0	120
Ziehl, Gage	R-R	6-0	212	5-15-03	2	2	4.01	6	0	0	25	28	15	11	0	5	20	.283	.315	.333	18.5	4.6	108

Fielding

Catcher	PCT	G	PO	A	E	DP	PB
Appel	.985	80	718	65	12	4	9
Eberly	1.000	18	153	23	0	0	0
Gonzalez	1.000	19	157	9	0	1	1
Magill	1.000	2	22	1	0	1	0
Pineda	.958	13	107	8	5	1	3
Turner	1.000	2	11	0	0	0	0

First Base	PCT	G	PO	A	E	DP
Antonacci	1.000	3	9	2	0	1
Galanie	1.000	12	80	7	0	6
Gonzalez	.000	1	0	0	0	0
Kath	1.000	18	120	9	0	7
Makarewicz	.998	76	491	35	1	34
Miller-Green	1.000	23	157	4	0	9
Pineda	.968	5	28	2	1	3

Second Base	PCT	G	PO	A	E	DP
Antonacci	.980	29	47	53	2	5
Burrowes	.972	11	14	21	1	2

	PCT	G	PO	A	E	DP
Perez	.975	79	110	167	7	31
Sanchez	1.000	2	0	6	0	0
Santos	1.000	5	2	9	0	1
Sprinkle	1.000	11	13	23	0	4

Third Base	PCT	G	PO	A	E	DP
Antonacci	.970	19	16	16	1	2
Bonemer	1.000	10	6	17	0	2
Burrowes	.920	10	4	19	2	3
Hernandez	.931	47	35	59	7	2
Kath	1.000	17	15	19	0	4
Makarewicz	.945	29	19	33	3	2
Sanchez	1.000	1	1	5	0	0
Santos	.000	1	0	0	0	0
Sprinkle	.750	6	2	1	1	0

Shortstop	PCT	G	PO	A	E	DP
Antonacci	1.000	6	13	7	0	0
Bonemer	.750	1	1	2	1	1
Burrowes	.892	10	10	23	4	7

	PCT	G	PO	A	E	DP
Hernandez	.917	28	39	60	9	11
Lodise	.954	27	25	58	4	5
Perez	.906	25	42	45	9	2
Sanchez	.959	40	53	63	5	16

Outfield	PCT	G	PO	A	E	DP
Burke	.963	13	24	2	1	0
Burrowes	1.000	5	4	0	0	0
Connor	.960	18	22	2	1	0
Galanie	1.000	1	3	0	0	0
Hogan	.987	28	77	0	1	0
Logan	1.000	44	67	1	0	0
McCants	1.000	27	44	0	0	0
McConnell	.954	72	142	2	7	0
Montgomery	.962	45	72	4	3	0
Sprinkle	.966	15	26	2	1	1
Tatum	.971	40	65	2	2	1
Zavala	.996	108	236	7	1	2

KANNAPOLIS CANNON BALLERS — LOW-A
CAROLINA LEAGUE

Batting	B-T	Ht.	Wt.	DOB	AVG	OBP	SLG	G	PA	AB	R	H	2B	3B	HR	RBI	BB	HBP	SH	SF	SO	SB	CS	BB%	SO%
Alsinois, Leandro	R-R	5-10	175	9-6-04	.182	.182	.364	3	11	11	1	2	2	0	0	1	0	0	0	0	3	0	0	0.0	27.3
Archer, Nathan	L-R	6-0	175	3-14-03	.219	.305	.327	98	391	343	40	75	14	4	5	36	43	1	1	3	128	20	9	11.0	32.7
Bonemer, Caleb	R-R	6-1	195	10-5-05	.281	.400	.458	96	432	349	69	98	26	3	10	58	68	7	0	8	91	28	15	15.7	21.1
Brown, Ely	L-L	6-0	190	7-13-04	.317	.417	.347	27	122	101	22	32	3	0	0	16	17	1	1	19	15	0	13.9	15.6
Burrowes, Ryan	R-R	6-2	170	8-11-04	.341	.417	.535	75	299	258	42	66	8	1	4	25	27	9	2	3	76	31	4	9.0	25.4
Corona, Jorge	R-R	6-2	190	9-12-00	.184	.303	.263	25	89	76	5	14	3	0	1	6	9	4	0	0	32	0	0	10.1	36.0
DePino, Anthony	R-R	5-11	218	2-19-03	.223	.359	.320	29	128	103	15	23	4	0	2	18	20	3	0	2	29	11	0	15.6	22.7
Eblin, Bryce	L-R	5-11	165	10-20-01	.211	.333	.211	6	24	19	4	4	0	0	0	1	1	3	0	1	2	1	1	4.2	8.3
Freeman, Kaleb	S-R	5-11	190	11-11-02	.148	.352	.204	17	71	54	8	8	0	0	0	5	17	0	0	0	19	2	1	23.9	26.8
Galvan, Rylan	R-R	6-0	185	6-12-03	.130	.333	.174	8	30	23	5	3	1	0	0	1	6	1	0	0	14	0	1	20.0	46.7
Gil, Adrian	R-R	6-0	193	11-17-05	.141	.272	.205	24	93	78	10	11	5	0	0	4	11	3	0	0	34	4	2	11.8	36.6
Harris, Calvin	L-R	6-0	205	11-15-01	.286	.356	.412	31	135	119	21	34	6	3	1	21	14	0	0	2	30	5	1	10.4	22.2

Batting	B-T	Ht.	Wt.	DOB	AVG	OBP	SLG	G	AB	R	H	2B	3B	HR	RBI	BB	SO	SB	CS	OBP	SLG	BB%	K%
Hernandez, Arxy	R-R	6-2	170	7-29-03	.224	.358	.312	37	151	125	18	28	3	1	2	15	23	3	0	0	33	5	2	15.2	21.9
Hernandez, Ronny	R-R	6-1	200	11-9-04	.251	.344	.336	82	355	307	33	77	12	1	4	34	45	0	0	3	75	4	0	12.7	21.1
Kane, Mikey	R-R	6-3	195	7-11-01	.243	.363	.293	56	216	181	15	44	2	2	1	23	29	5	1	0	26	1	1	13.4	12.0
Magill, Grant	R-R	6-0	195	11-30-00	.239	.325	.266	33	126	109	11	26	3	0	0	13	14	1	0	2	32	0	2	11.1	25.4
McCants, T.J.	L-R	6-3	190	6-6-01	.306	.409	.417	29	127	108	12	33	3	0	3	15	18	1	0	0	32	9	4	14.2	25.2
McLain, Nick	S-L	5-10	185	12-16-02	.261	.414	.304	13	58	46	7	12	2	0	0	9	11	1	0	0	17	4	0	19.0	29.3
Miller-Green, Lyle	R-R	6-6	229	9-4-00	.263	.400	.392	71	301	240	44	63	8	4	5	34	52	5	1	3	86	7	4	17.3	28.6
Mogollon, Javier	R-R	5-8	160	11-1-05	.220	.347	.387	51	224	186	36	41	10	3	5	19	30	6	2	0	56	15	6	13.4	25.0
Montgomery, Braden	S-R	6-2	201	4-26-03	.304	.393	.493	18	84	69	14	21	4	0	3	19	10	2	0	3	19	6	2	11.9	22.6
Nunez, Abraham	L-R	6-2	175	2-17-06	.204	.279	.278	69	273	245	34	50	8	2	2	22	23	3	1	1	60	16	8	8.4	22.0
Prado, Arnold	R-R	6-3	194	11-20-04	.191	.304	.250	21	80	68	11	13	2	1	0	5	10	1	1	0	25	1	1	12.5	31.3
Sanchez, Wilber	R-R	5-10	160	2-21-02	.182	.280	.227	6	25	22	3	4	1	0	0	2	1	2	0	0	8	2	1	4.0	32.0
Santos, Miguel	R-R	5-11	174	3-12-01	.256	.337	.341	69	295	258	25	66	10	3	2	31	25	8	1	3	51	12	4	8.5	17.3
Saucke, Casey	R-R	6-3	198	7-24-03	.050	.136	.050	5	22	20	1	1	0	0	0	0	2	0	0	0	10	1	0	9.1	45.5
Shelton, Colby	L-R	6-0	185	12-6-02	.141	.243	.172	27	115	99	11	14	0	0	1	10	11	3	0	2	25	4	2	9.6	21.7
Smith, Grant	R-R	6-0	190	10-2-00	.167	.231	.194	9	39	36	2	6	1	0	0	4	1	2	0	0	12	1	0	2.6	30.8
Sprinkle, Jordan	R-R	5-11	180	3-6-01	.271	.411	.295	63	269	210	46	57	5	0	0	15	47	4	6	2	48	65	9	17.5	17.8
Taussig, James	L-R	6-6	230	3-30-03	.304	.333	.478	6	24	23	4	7	2	1	0	3	1	0	0	0	3	0	0	4.2	12.5
Wolkow, George	L-R	6-7	225	1-11-06	.223	.317	.362	116	496	426	58	95	16	2	13	69	54	8	1	7	147	33	6	10.9	29.6

Pitching	B-T	Ht.	Wt.	DOB	W	L	ERA	G	GS	SV	IP	Hits	Runs	ER	HR	BB	SO	AVG	OBP	SLG	SO%	BB%	BF
Altermatt, Nick	R-R	6-0	225	9-28-99	0	0	0.00	2	0	1	3	3	0	0	0	0	1	.429	.375	.429	12.5	0.0	8
Austin, Morris	R-R	6-2	215	3-27-00	1	0	3.38	14	0	3	21	18	8	8	0	10	23	.228	.322	.278	25.6	11.1	90
Barrios, Marco	R-R	6-3	195	5-25-06	1	1	3.27	8	0	1	11	6	4	4	2	6	11	.158	.273	.342	25.0	13.6	44
Brizuela, Ricardo	R-R	6-3	198	6-30-03	1	10	4.98	23	23	0	87	86	53	48	10	37	74	.263	.355	.416	19.5	9.7	380
Clark, Jonathan	R-R	6-1	190	6-3-00	1	1	2.40	27	0	5	41	27	16	11	3	19	53	.182	.301	.284	29.9	10.7	177
Curtis, Jake	R-R	5-10	170	3-21-02	3	2	4.34	17	1	1	37	50	19	18	2	8	40	.318	.351	.427	23.8	4.8	168
Davis, Kevin	R-R	6-9	280	5-7-99	4	3	5.01	23	0	2	32	29	19	18	0	24	53	.238	.367	.262	35.3	16.0	150
Eblin, Bryce	L-R	5-11	165	10-20-01	0	0	0.00	1	0	0	1	2	0	0	0	0	1	.400	.400	.600	20.0	0.0	5
George, Pierce	R-R	6-6	215	6-10-03	1	3	6.42	45	0	2	48	36	38	34	0	45	52	.206	.391	.257	22.3	19.3	233
Hammerberg, Ethan	L-R	6-5	250	12-18-00	0	1	9.00	3	0	0	3	3	4	3	0	6	6	.250	.500	.333	33.3	33.3	18
Housley, Connor	L-R	6-4	205	8-18-01	0	0	4.50	4	0	0	6	5	3	3	0	1	5	.227	.261	.318	21.7	4.3	23
Jeffrey, Madison	L-R	6-0	190	3-14-00	1	0	10.13	2	0	0	3	3	3	3	1	3	3	.273	.467	.545	20.0	20.0	15
Kane, Mikey	R-R	6-3	195	7-11-01	0	0	1.69	6	0	0	5	4	1	1	0	3	1	.211	.360	.263	4.0	12.0	25
Keener, Seth	R-R	6-1	195	10-4-01	2	1	5.73	9	9	0	44	45	30	28	6	20	39	.265	.351	.418	20.1	10.3	194
LaCombe, Mathias	R-R	6-3	178	6-12-02	0	0	4.08	7	5	0	18	12	8	8	0	13	23	.197	.351	.213	29.9	16.9	77
McAtee, Aric	R-R	6-5	220	5-31-00	1	1	3.57	10	0	1	18	11	8	7	1	6	20	.175	.257	.286	28.6	8.6	70
Mendez, Jesus	R-R	5-11	180	7-30-04	2	1	6.46	26	0	2	31	30	24	22	3	20	30	.261	.374	.417	21.4	14.3	140
Moore, Mason	R-R	6-4	215	9-29-01	0	0	0.00	1	1	0	5	2	1	0	0	3	6	.125	.263	.125	31.6	15.8	19
Oppor, Christian	L-L	6-2	175	7-23-04	2	2	2.42	5	5	0	22	12	6	6	0	7	34	.160	.256	.240	39.5	8.1	86
Paddack, Liam	L-L	6-4	210	7-23-03	1	4	4.50	13	0	2	44	26	24	22	0	37	55	.174	.365	.195	27.2	18.3	202
Peppers, Jake	R-R	6-3	160	12-26-01	3	1	4.82	12	0	0	19	23	11	10	3	9	30	.299	.372	.481	34.9	10.5	86
Perkins, Carlton	R-R	6-3	185	11-9-02	4	3	5.75	33	0	2	41	34	28	26	3	34	37	.222	.387	.314	19.1	17.5	194
Peters, Connery	R-R	6-6	240	2-3-00	0	0	0.00	1	0	0	2	1	0	0	0	1	3	.143	.250	.143	37.5	12.5	8
Pinto, Nick	L-L	6-0	175	6-22-00	0	1	5.89	5	5	0	18	23	15	12	2	7	18	.307	.376	.493	21.2	8.2	85
Reyes, Luis	R-R	6-2	190	10-13-05	4	9	4.34	23	23	0	87	85	55	42	6	37	88	.251	.332	.358	22.9	9.6	385
Rodriguez, Gabriel	R-R	5-11	180	5-22-02	4	2	4.43	28	4	1	67	61	36	33	5	39	49	.248	.366	.394	16.4	13.0	299
Shepardson, Blake	R-R	6-5	220	7-6-03	0	1	6.84	27	0	0	26	18	24	20	0	39	36	.196	.464	.261	25.7	27.9	140
Sims, Hale	R-R	6-4	290	8-30-99	4	3	3.73	41	0	5	63	64	31	26	4	15	71	.260	.307	.362	26.6	5.6	267
Sinibaldi, Justin	L-L	6-5	220	3-3-02	2	8	3.76	22	22	0	91	78	40	38	6	35	80	.237	.337	.347	21.4	9.4	373
Sophy, Kaleb	L-L	6-3	185	3-3-01	3	4	5.66	16	15	0	56	53	37	35	1	48	35	.266	.411	.327	13.7	18.8	255
Sprinkle, Jordan	R-R	5-11	180	3-6-01	0	0	18.00	1	0	0	1	4	2	2	0	0	0	.571	.571	.714	0.0	0.0	7
Umberger, Grant	R-L	6-4	225	10-14-01	9	2	2.56	24	17	0	102	82	32	29	1	33	113	.223	.289	.283	27.5	8.0	411
Vasquez, Wardquelin	R-R	6-3	194	7-25-01	2	2	4.50	12	0	0	16	15	10	8	2	13	16	.246	.382	.426	21.1	17.1	76
Veloz, Manuel	R-R	6-2	185	1-28-01	4	0	4.15	13	1	0	26	28	12	12	1	10	23	.232	.339	.293	20.0	8.7	115
Yabbour, Joseph	R-R	6-0	175	7-9-03	2	1	3.15	15	0	0	20	9	8	7	1	12	33	.134	.306	.209	38.8	14.1	85
Young, Jack	R-R	5-10	185	1-25-02	1	0	0.35	19	0	3	26	12	2	1	0	16	29	.132	.288	.132	26.1	14.4	111
Ysalla, Fabian	R-R	6-0	161	12-14-04	0	1	5.14	3	1	0	7	6	6	4	1	5	4	.231	.375	.423	12.1	15.2	33

Fielding

Catcher	PCT	G	PO	A	E	DP	PB
Corona	1.000	10	67	8	0	1	1
Freeman	.952	4	37	3	2	0	2
Galvan	.973	7	68	3	2	0	0
Gil	1.000	9	80	3	0	0	4
Harris	.989	17	159	13	2	1	0
Hernandez	.984	64	562	50	10	4	4
Magill	.992	26	224	21	2	0	0

First Base	PCT	G	PO	A	E	DP
Corona	1.000	9	71	6	0	5
DePino	.990	25	177	15	2	14
Gil	1.000	12	72	5	0	5
Kane	.995	26	195	12	1	21
Miller-Green	.996	60	448	24	2	34

Second Base	PCT	G	PO	A	E	DP
Burrowes	.977	36	64	103	4	15
Eblin	1.000	3	5	2	0	1
Freeman	1.000	1	0	1	0	0
Kane	.800	2	3	1	1	0
Mogollon	.971	27	37	62	3	15
Sanchez	1.000	2	1	6	0	0
Santos	.985	33	52	82	2	19
Shelton	.958	6	12	11	1	2
Smith	1.000	5	10	14	0	5
Sprinkle	1.000	21	33	44	0	5

	PCT	G	PO	A	E	DP
Smith	1.000	3	10	2	0	1
Sprinkle	1.000	1	1	0	0	0

Third Base	PCT	G	PO	A	E	DP
Bonemer	.969	24	16	47	2	3
Burrowes	.973	19	10	26	1	3
Hernandez	.987	29	31	44	1	1
Kane	.957	25	14	31	2	2
Sanchez	1.000	1	0	2	0	0
Santos	.857	19	10	26	6	5
Shelton	.833	3	3	7	2	1
Smith	1.000	1	1	0	0	0
Sprinkle	.935	16	9	20	2	0

Shortstop	PCT	G	PO	A	E	DP
Bonemer	.941	67	99	155	16	36
Burrowes	.907	10	21	28	5	6
Eblin	.842	4	6	10	3	1

Mogollon	.931	19	26	41	5	6			
Sanchez	.900	3	3	6	1	1			
Santos	.925	14	11	26	3	3			
Shelton	.974	17	34	41	2	8			
Sprinkle	1.000	1	2	1	0	0			

Outfield	PCT	G	PO	A	E	DP
Alsinois	1.000	3	1	1	0	0
Archer	.974	90	147	4	4	1
Brown	1.000	27	43	3	0	1
Burrowes	1.000	9	7	2	0	1
Freeman	1.000	12	11	0	0	0
McCants	1.000	23	43	2	0	2
McLain	1.000	12	23	2	0	0
Montgomery	1.000	16	31	0	0	0
Nunez	.977	67	167	3	4	1
Prado	1.000	19	33	1	0	0
Sprinkle	1.000	22	45	0	0	0
Taussig	1.000	3	4	0	0	0
Wolkow	.972	100	163	12	5	4

ACL WHITE SOX — ROOKIE
ARIZONA COMPLEX LEAGUE

Batting	B-T	Ht.	Wt.	DOB	AVG	OBP	SLG	G	PA	AB	R	H	2B	3B	HR	RBI	BB	HBP	SH	SF	SO	SB	CS	BB%	SO%
Albertus, Alexander	R-R	6-1	176	10-27-04	.333	.520	.444	8	25	18	4	6	2	0	0	2	6	1	0	0	3	3	0	24.0	12.0
Alcala, Marcelo	R-R	6-0	183	3-23-06	.233	.325	.479	42	168	146	33	34	7	4	7	19	14	6	2	0	63	14	1	8.3	37.5
Alsinois, Leandro	R-R	5-10	175	9-6-04	.223	.320	.362	49	150	130	22	29	6	0	4	13	18	1	0	1	41	10	1	12.0	27.3
Antonacci, Sam	L-R	6-0	185	2-6-03	.500	.571	.750	3	14	12	3	6	3	0	0	3	2	0	0	0	4	0	1	14.3	28.6
Asigen, Albertson	R-R	5-10	175	8-27-01	.306	.447	.477	40	141	111	25	34	7	3	2	13	25	4	0	1	41	13	5	17.7	29.1
Dinesen, Mason	R-R	6-4	180	7-24-98	.232	.259	.329	52	172	164	21	38	13	0	1	15	5	1	2	0	64	13	2	2.9	37.2
Eblin, Bryce	L-R	5-11	165	10-20-01	.529	.636	.706	8	22	17	4	9	0	0	1	4	4	1	0	0	3	0	1	18.2	13.6
Flores, Steven	R-R	5-11	180	12-26-05	.289	.340	.394	53	200	180	28	52	11	1	2	33	16	0	0	4	18	3	2	8.0	9.0
Gil, Adrian	R-R	6-0	193	11-17-05	.246	.364	.448	55	221	183	32	45	10	3	7	41	24	11	0	2	75	18	5	10.9	33.9
Gonzalez, Christian	L-L	5-11	185	9-4-06	.381	.435	.500	12	46	42	7	16	2	0	1	4	4	0	0	0	9	2	4	8.7	19.6
Hernandez, Angelo	R-R	6-1	200	9-11-05	.254	.413	.324	29	92	71	12	18	2	0	1	5	17	3	0	1	26	0	1	18.5	28.3
Hogan, Matt	R-R	6-0	195	1-24-00	.360	.529	.480	9	34	25	5	9	1	1	0	4	8	1	0	0	11	5	3	23.5	32.4
Kath, Wes	L-R	6-3	200	8-3-02	.375	.412	.375	5	17	16	1	6	0	0	0	1	1	0	0	0	4	0	0	5.9	23.5
Logan, Drake	R-R	6-4	205	9-5-00	.319	.407	.511	14	54	47	15	15	5	2	0	2	4	3	0	0	16	4	1	7.4	29.6
Magill, Grant	R-R	6-0	195	11-30-00	.421	.476	.632	9	22	19	3	8	1	0	1	4	2	0	1	0	5	0	1	9.1	22.7
McCants, T.J.	R-R	6-3	190	6-6-01	.292	.333	.417	13	52	48	9	14	2	2	0	7	3	0	1	0	17	4	1	5.8	32.7
Montgomery, Colson	L-R	6-3	205	2-27-02	.176	.263	.176	5	19	17	3	3	0	0	0	2	2	0	0	0	4	2	0	10.5	21.1
Prado, Arnold	R-R	6-3	194	11-20-04	.189	.286	.216	24	84	74	5	14	0	1	0	7	10	0	0	0	28	8	3	11.9	33.3
Profar, Jurdrick	R-R	5-11	170	4-24-07	.189	.280	.301	49	161	143	21	27	5	1	3	18	16	2	0	0	56	5	6	9.9	34.8
Rios, Alvaro	R-R	6-2	175	9-25-06	.125	.300	.250	8	10	8	2	1	0	0	1	1	0	0	0	6	0	0	10.0	60.0
Smith, Grant	R-R	6-0	190	10-2-00	.244	.290	.378	37	138	127	17	31	8	0	3	22	5	4	0	2	39	3	0	3.6	28.3
Tejada, D'Angelo	R-R	6-0	160	11-12-05	.264	.346	.385	56	206	182	27	48	7	3	3	29	20	3	0	0	65	13	8	9.7	31.6
Turner, Michael	L-R	6-2	205	8-18-98	.000	.000	.000	2	3	3	0	0	0	0	0	0	0	0	0	0	1	0	0	0.0	33.3
Willits, Bryce	L-R	6-2	200	8-25-99	.375	.524	.625	7	21	16	2	6	2	1	0	3	5	0	0	0	2	1	0	23.8	9.5

Pitching	B-T	Ht.	Wt.	DOB	W	L	ERA	G	GS	SV	IP	Hits	Runs	ER	HR	BB	SO	AVG	OBP	SLG	SO%	BB%	BF
Altermatt, Nick	R-R	6-0	225	9-28-99	1	0	0.00	2	0	0	3	0	0	0	0	0	7	.000	.000	.000	77.8	0.0	9
Barrios, Marco	R-R	6-3	195	5-25-06	0	2	4.56	19	0	2	24	23	14	12	2	13	27	.250	.355	.370	25.0	12.0	108
Bello, Angel	R-R	6-3	170	7-22-06	0	1	9.00	3	2	0	4	5	5	4	0	2	1	.333	.444	.400	5.3	10.5	19
Chirinos, Jordany	R-R	6-3	196	5-4-06	1	3	5.72	13	12	0	46	43	33	29	3	29	37	.254	.374	.361	18.0	14.1	206
Curtis, Jake	R-R	5-10	170	3-21-02	2	1	2.05	14	0	4	22	18	8	5	2	6	29	.214	.267	.369	32.2	6.7	90
Davis, Kevin	R-R	6-9	280	5-7-99	1	0	3.46	10	0	3	13	11	7	5	0	5	16	.234	.308	.319	30.8	9.6	52
Diaz, Reudis	R-R	6-1	180	2-16-06	1	1	2.28	21	0	1	28	22	10	7	0	8	18	.224	.333	.255	15.7	7.0	115
Dinesen, Mason	R-R	6-4	180	7-24-98	0	0	0.00	1	0	0	1	0	0	0	0	0	1	.000	.000	.000	50.0	0.0	2
Gonzalez, Jeremy	L-L	6-0	168	4-1-05	3	2	4.98	20	3	0	34	34	22	19	0	14	31	.266	.342	.328	20.9	9.5	148
Hammerberg, Ethan	L-R	6-5	250	12-18-00	2	0	6.43	6	0	0	7	9	8	5	1	4	13	.290	.371	.484	37.1	11.4	35
Hernandez, Angelo	R-R	6-1	200	9-11-05	0	0	0.00	1	0	0	1	1	0	0	0	0	0	.333	.333	.333	0.0	0.0	3
Hernandez, Jommy	R-R	6-3	185	4-18-06	3	3	9.43	21	0	1	21	28	24	22	3	24	15	.341	.513	.549	13.0	20.9	115
Housley, Connor	L-R	6-4	205	8-18-01	2	1	2.13	9	0	1	13	13	4	3	1	2	13	.265	.294	.429	25.5	3.9	51
Iriarte, Jairo	R-R	6-2	160	12-15-01	1	0	4.50	2	0	0	2	2	1	1	0	2	.286	.286	.286	25.0	0.0	8
Jeffrey, Madison	L-R	6-0	190	3-14-00	1	2	2.19	10	0	2	12	13	4	3	0	10	13	.289	.421	.333	22.8	17.5	57
LaCombe, Mathias	R-R	6-3	178	6-12-02	0	1	2.52	12	9	0	36	23	12	10	3	11	50	.184	.295	.288	34.0	7.5	147
Lima, Denny	R-R	6-0	170	8-22-04	2	0	5.01	10	9	0	32	29	22	18	5	13	29	.244	.352	.378	20.3	9.1	143
Luna, Gil	L-L	5-10	173	7-29-99	1	0	1.69	10	0	3	16	6	3	3	0	10	23	.120	.290	.160	37.1	16.1	62
Magill, Grant	R-R	6-0	195	11-30-00	0	0	0.00	1	0	0	2	2	0	0	0	1	2	.300	.364	.300	18.2	9.1	11
Martinez, Maximo	R-R	6-2	185	6-21-04	0	1	9.45	6	2	0	7	11	7	7	0	7	8	.355	.487	.484	20.5	17.9	39
McCullough, Connor	R-R	6-1	185	10-5-99	0	2	7.71	3	3	0	5	6	5	4	0	4	7	.300	.348	.350	34.8	8.7	23
Mendez, Jesus	R-R	5-11	180	7-30-04	1	0	0.00	5	0	0	7	5	0	0	0	4	7	.208	.393	.375	25.0	14.3	28
Nolasco, Yohemy	R-R	6-3	160	7-12-03	2	0	14.14	9	0	0	7	17	15	11	0	10	7	.472	.592	.583	14.0	20.0	50
Perez, Joe	R-R	6-2	195	4-12-99	0	0	27.00	3	0	0	2	5	5	5	0	6	2	.333	.615	.500	15.4	46.2	13
Rios, Alvaro	R-R	6-1	170	9-25-06	0	1	0.00	1	0	0	1	2	1	0	0	3	1	.200	.556	.333	0.0	33.3	9
Roberts, Max	R-L	6-6	190	7-23-97	0	0	8.10	3	0	0	3	3	3	3	0	1	6	.231	.286	.308	42.9	7.1	14
Sheehan, Tommy	L-L	6-0	209	6-17-99	0	2	17.47	5	3	0	6	8	13	11	0	10	5	.320	.541	.320	13.5	27.0	37
Smith, Grant	R-R	6-0	190	10-2-00	0	0	0.00	1	0	0	1	0	0	0	0	1	.000	.000	.000	33.3	0.0	3
Syndergaard, Noah	L-R	6-6	242	8-29-92	1	0	2.93	4	4	0	15	14	6	5	0	1	12	.241	.250	.310	20.0	1.7	60
Thomas, Gray	R-R	6-3	212	12-17-02	3	2	4.66	17	0	0	19	10	12	10	1	14	18	.156	.375	.328	20.5	15.9	88
Tyler, Kyle	R-R	6-2	190	10-2-96	0	0	2.45	2	2	0	7	5	2	2	0	1	11	.192	.222	.192	40.7	3.7	27
Valladares, Marcelo	R-R	6-4	187	8-28-04	2	0	6.75	4	0	0	5	4	4	0	3	4	.200	.333	.400	16.7	12.5	24
Vannelle, Vince	R-R	5-10	202	12-19-97	0	0	3.60	4	0	0	5	7	2	2	0	1	4	.350	.381	.500	19.0	4.8	21
Varland, Gus	L-R	6-1	213	11-6-96	0	0	9.00	1	1	0	2	1	2	2	1	2	.500	.600	.750	40.0	20.0	5
Vasquez, Wardquelin	R-R	6-3	194	7-25-01	0	0	3.12	5	0	1	9	3	3	3	1	5	11	.103	.257	.207	31.4	14.3	35
Wright, Garrett	R-R	6-2	220	2-11-02	1	0	4.91	5	0	0	7	6	4	4	1	3	10	.231	.300	.462	33.3	10.0	30
Ysalla, Fabian	R-R	6-0	161	12-14-04	4	0	2.02	12	10	0	49	41	14	11	1	16	40	.232	.297	.299	20.4	8.2	196

Fielding
C: Flores 37, Gil 15, Magill 7, Rios 5, Hernandez 4, Turner 1. **1B:** Gil 37, Dinesen 14, Hernandez 8, Willits 4, Kath 3, Flores 1. **2B:** Profar 33, Smith 16, Tejada 9, Dinesen 4, Eblin 3, Antonacci 1. **3B:** Dinesen 24, Smith 18, Tejada 15, Albertus 8, Eblin 3, Antonacci 1, Gil 1, Kath 1, Profar 1. **SS:** Tejada 32, Dinesen 11, Profar 10, Smith 4, Montgomery 3. **LF:** Asigen 31, Gonzalez 10, Prado 9, Alsinois 5, McCants 4, Hogan 3, Dinesen 2, Alcala 1, Willits 1. **CF:** Alcala 29, Alsinois 15, Logan 9, McCants 9, Gonzalez 1, Hogan 1. **RF:** Alsinois 27, Prado 15, Alcala 9, Asigen 6, Hogan 3, Gonzalez 1, Logan 1

DSL WHITE SOX   ROOKIE
DOMINICAN SUMMER LEAGUE

Batting	B-T	Ht.	Wt.	DOB	AVG	OBP	SLG	G	PA	AB	R	H	2B	3B	HR	RBI	BB	HBP	SH	SF	SO	SB	CS	BB%	SO%
Alcala, Hendry	S-R	6-3	170	1-25-07	.206	.407	.294	36	91	68	17	14	2	2	0	13	19	4	0	0	16	4	3	20.9	17.6
Aponte, Jeremias	L-R	6-1	180	11-30-07	.241	.389	.276	15	36	29	4	7	1	0	0	2	2	5	0	0	9	0	1	5.6	25.0
Castillo, Osniel	R-R	5-11	170	1-18-06	.375	.444	.542	15	54	48	9	18	3	1	1	6	5	1	0	0	9	9	1	9.3	16.7
Cruz, Alejandro	R-R	6-2	165	1-2-07	.228	.396	.378	48	164	127	41	29	7	0	4	15	31	5	0	1	36	18	4	18.9	22.0
Escobar, Alan	L-L	6-0	185	8-3-08	.306	.409	.343	38	129	108	27	33	4	0	0	15	17	2	2	0	20	5	1	13.2	15.5
Escobar, Igor	S-R	5-11	155	8-8-08	.235	.371	.275	28	62	51	11	12	2	0	0	5	9	2	0	0	26	0	0	14.5	41.9
Gonzalez, Christian	L-L	5-11	185	9-4-06	.424	.553	.606	22	86	66	21	28	6	3	0	10	15	4	1	0	10	2	4	17.4	11.6
Herrera, Eduardo	R-R	6-3	212	10-23-06	.235	.379	.397	48	174	136	23	32	7	0	5	33	30	4	0	4	41	2	0	17.2	23.6
Mendez, Jehancarlos	R-R	6-2	180	8-9-07	.221	.354	.298	42	127	104	17	23	5	0	1	13	20	2	0	1	21	5	3	15.7	16.5
Mendoza, Jose	R-R	6-2	210	3-10-08	.333	.410	.407	37	122	108	17	36	5	0	1	22	13	1	0	0	21	1	1	10.7	17.2
Mieses, Frank	R-R	6-1	170	2-9-08	.285	.410	.415	44	161	130	24	37	4	2	3	27	22	7	0	2	39	8	3	13.7	24.2
Natera, Diego	R-R	5-10	190	10-17-07	.156	.415	.267	29	65	45	15	7	2	0	1	5	18	2	0	0	18	5	3	27.7	27.7
Patino, Orlando	R-R	6-2	190	11-4-07	.167	.294	.214	13	51	42	9	7	2	0	0	4	7	1	0	1	15	1	0	13.7	29.4
Paulino, Hector	L-R	6-0	150	6-5-08	.210	.351	.274	24	77	62	12	13	1	0	1	6	10	4	0	1	9	4	1	13.0	11.7
Rodriguez, Erasmi	R-R	5-8	180	5-18-04	.289	.404	.458	29	99	83	10	24	6	1	2	20	11	5	0	0	20	1	0	11.1	20.2
Silva, Jefrank	L-R	6-1	190	9-8-07	.248	.346	.345	37	130	113	15	28	2	0	3	13	14	3	0	0	23	3	5	10.8	17.7
Soto, Yordani	S-R	5-11	160	8-11-08	.274	.423	.363	46	156	124	22	34	6	1	1	27	28	4	0	0	31	21	6	17.9	19.9

Pitching	B-T	Ht.	Wt.	DOB	W	L	ERA	G	GS	SV	IP	Hits	Runs	ER	HR	BB	SO	AVG	OBP	SLG	SO%	BB%	BF
Almanzar, Darlyn	L-L	5-11	150	2-1-07	3	3	8.72	16	0	0	22	24	26	21	1	34	25	.296	.504	.420	20.8	28.3	120
Bolivar, Cesar	R-R	6-1	155	2-8-08	1	0	9.33	16	0	3	18	25	24	19	4	20	15	.301	.448	.554	14.3	19.0	105
Escobar, Igor	S-R	5-11	155	8-8-08	0	0	0.00	5	0	0	5	5	0	0	0	3	0	.238	.333	.238	0.0	12.5	24
Familia, Cesar	R-R	6-3	200	10-16-07	1	1	11.74	8	0	0	8	10	13	10	0	10	5	.323	.522	.419	10.9	21.7	46
Felix, Juan	R-R	6-2	185	7-10-08	0	0	24.30	9	1	1	7	10	20	18	1	16	6	.357	.627	.536	11.8	31.4	51
Fortuna, Oriel	L-L	6-3	180	5-26-06	1	1	9.45	7	0	0	7	8	8	7	1	8	7	.320	.500	.480	19.4	22.2	36
Gomez, Reinder	R-R	6-0	174	5-9-07	5	3	5.19	17	7	2	35	42	21	20	5	11	35	.302	.353	.453	22.9	7.2	153
Hernandez, Gerardo	R-R	6-2	190	10-16-03	1	0	1.86	5	1	0	10	9	3	2	1	3	5	.250	.308	.321	12.8	7.7	39
Martinez, Alexander	R-R	6-5	210	12-30-02	1	0	4.55	15	4	3	30	24	16	15	3	15	46	.218	.323	.364	35.4	11.5	130
Mendez, Jehancarlos	R-R	6-2	180	8-9-07	0	0	0.00	1	0	0	0	0	0	0	0	0	0	.000	.000	.000	0.0	0.0	1
Montero, Fidel	R-R	6-0	178	12-19-03	4	2	4.40	16	1	2	29	29	19	14	0	15	34	.274	.373	.311	26.6	11.7	128
Morao, Jhonny	R-R	6-2	175	10-11-07	1	0	5.79	3	0	0	5	8	5	3	1	5	8	.381	.519	.714	29.6	18.5	27
Munoz, Albert	R-R	6-2	160	7-19-08	2	3	8.17	17	3	0	25	33	25	23	2	27	28	.314	.471	.438	20.3	19.6	138
Nunez, Cesar	L-L	6-1	180	4-16-07	3	1	6.75	13	1	1	15	18	18	11	1	13	23	.300	.456	.467	29.1	16.5	79
Peralta, Andy	L-L	6-0	175	1-6-07	3	2	5.81	14	2	0	26	26	20	17	1	12	21	.263	.373	.343	17.8	10.2	118
Perez, Diego	R-R	6-0	153	7-3-08	1	2	5.12	16	11	0	32	29	21	18	2	22	33	.246	.386	.364	22.8	15.2	145
Pinales, Hansel	R-R	6-4	190	10-18-07	1	2	7.83	15	0	3	23	24	23	20	1	16	22	.273	.396	.386	19.8	14.4	111
Ramirez, Enmanuel	R-R	6-2	170	8-7-08	0	1	15.00	8	1	0	6	7	15	10	0	10	5	.250	.462	.286	12.8	25.6	39
Rodriguez, Erasmi	R-R	5-8	180	5-18-04	0	0	0.00	1	0	0	2	2	0	0	0	1	1	.250	.400	.250	10.0	10.0	10
Rodriguez, Yobal	R-R	6-2	155	2-9-08	0	3	2.97	13	10	0	30	18	21	10	0	13	33	.161	.277	.188	25.4	10.0	130
Rodriguez, Yoneiber	R-R	6-0	172	3-19-07	0	0	4.15	4	0	0	4	4	3	2	0	3	3	.250	.429	.375	14.3	14.3	21
Suarez, Orlando	R-R	6-4	217	12-7-06	1	2	3.60	15	12	0	40	34	17	16	2	20	49	.227	.328	.340	28.2	11.5	174
Valerio, Natanael	R-R	5-11	165	3-6-07	0	0	0.00	1	0	0	1	0	0	0	0	1	0	.500	.667	.500	0.0	33.3	3

Fielding
C: Natera 25, Rodriguez 19, Mendoza 18, Herrera 3. **1B:** Herrera 38, Silva 10, Mendoza 7, Mendez 3, Natera 1. **2B:** Cruz 24, Escobar 18, Silva 10, Mendez 7, Paulino 5, Soto 1. **3B:** Cruz 26, Mendez 10, Silva 14, Soto 2, Escobar 1, Herrera 1. **SS:** Soto 42, Mendez 16, Paulino 1. **LF:** Alcala 28, A. Escobar 20, Paulino 9, Aponte 6, I. Escobar 6, Gonzalez 4, Mieses 3. **CF:** Mieses 33, Castillo 15, Patino 6, Paulino 4, Alcala 1, Gonzalez 1. **RF:** Escobar 16, Gonzalez 15, Aponte 10, Mieses 8, Alcala 7, Patino 6, Castillo 2

Cincinnati Reds

SEASON SYNOPSIS: The Reds lured Terry Francona out of retirement, and he squeezed just enough out of a pitching-heavy club at hitter-friendly Great American Ballpark. Cincinnati stuck around as the Mets faltered, won more than it lost late and earned the final NL wild-card spot, its first playoff trip since 2020 and first in a full season since 2013.

HIGH POINT: The Reds had four different five-game win streaks, including a well-timed Sept. 17-21 streak that included a four-game sweep of the Cubs. Ace Hunter Greene opened the series with his second career shutout, striking out nine in a 1-0 victory, before Andrew Abbott and three relievers shut the Cubs out again 1-0 in the series finale, putting them into a tie with the Mets for the last wild card spot. They split their final six games, but that was good enough to tie the Mets, and the Reds owned the tiebreaker, having won both series against New York.

LOW POINT: Facing the Dodgers in the wild-card series showed the Reds' fight, but also how far they have to go to be a true contender. The Dodgers out-homered them 5-0, three coming off Greene in a three-inning, five-run Game One 8-4 loss. While top prospect Sal Stewart hit a two-run single in the first inning of Game Two, his errant throw at first base opened the door for an LA rally and 10-5 season-ending victory.

NOTABLE ROOKIES: Stewart played just 18 games but tantalized with his power (5 HR, .545 SLG). Two other rookies contributed in the postseason bullpen, and 2024 No. 2 overall draft pick Chase Burns (0-3, 4.57, 67 SO/43 IP) was one of the hardest-throwing starters in the major leagues. He struck out five straight Yankees to open his MLB debut and figures to earn a rotation spot in 2026. Connor Phillips (5-0, 2.28) should earn a bullpen spot again after securing a postseason spot, while Lyon Richardson (0-3, 4.54) was left off.

KEY TRANSACTIONS: Cincinnati had an active offseason, trading former Florida Gators teammates for each other, acquiring RHP Brady Singer from the Royals for 2B Jonathan India. Singer (14-12, 4.03) led the Reds in starts (32), innings (169 ⅔) and strikeouts (163). They dealt minor league OF Mike Sirota for 2B/OF Gavin Lux, whose .350 OBP ranked second on the team, and were active at the trade deadline, adding OF/DH Miguel Andujar (.944 OPS with the Reds), 3B Ke'Bryan Hayes (.656 OPS but good defense) and RHP Zack Littell, who wound up starting Game Two of the Dodgers playoff series.

OPENING DAY PAYROLL: $115,466,833 (22nd)

PLAYERS OF THE YEAR

MAJOR LEAGUE
Andrew Abbott
LHP
2.87 ERA in 166.1 IP
149 SO and 43 BB
1.15 WHIP, all-star

MINOR LEAGUE
Sal Stewart
3B
(AA,AAA)
.309/.383/.524
20 HR, 17 SB, 34 2B

ORGANIZATION LEADERS

Batting		*Qualifiers
MAJORS		
* AVG	Elly De La Cruz	.264
* OPS	Elly De La Cruz	.777
HR	Elly De La Cruz	22
RBI	Elly De La Cruz	86
MINORS		
* AVG	Francisco Urbaez, Louisville	.314
* OBP	Alfredo Duno, Daytona	.430
* SLG	Rece Hinds, Louisville	.563
* OPS	Alfredo Duno, Daytona	.948
R	Hector Rodriguez, Louisville/Chattanooga	92
H	Hector Rodriguez, Louisville/Chattanooga	149
TB	Hector Rodriguez, Louisville/Chattanooga	237
2B	Sal Stewart, Louisville/Chattanooga	34
3B	Sammy Stafura, Daytona	9
HR	Edwin Rios, Louisville	26
RBI	Edwin Rios, Louisville	94
BB	Alfredo Duno, Daytona	95
SO	Edwin Rios, Louisville	180
SB	Kyle Henley, Daytona	57

Pitching		#Qualifiers
MAJORS		
W	Brady Singer	14
# ERA	Andrew Abbott	2.87
SO	Brady Singer	163
SV	Emilio Pagan	32
MINORS		
W	Jose Franco, Louisville/Chattanooga	10
L	Chase Petty, Louisville	13
# ERA	Kevin Abel, Louisville/Chattanooga	4.55
G	Zach Maxwell, Louisville	51
GS	Kevin Abel, Louisville/Chattanooga	26
GS	Chase Petty, Louisville	26
GS	Jose Franco, Louisville/Chattanooga	26
SV	Trevor Kuncl, Chattanooga	20
IP	Kevin Abel, Louisville/Chattanooga	125
BB	Luke Hayden, Dayton	72
SO	Kevin Abel, Louisville/Chattanooga	119
AVG	Kevin Abel, Louisville/Chattanooga	.226

2025 PERFORMANCE

General Manager: Nick Krall. **Farm Director:** Jeremy Farrell. **Scouting Director:** Joe Katuska.

Class	Team	League	W	L	PCT	Finish	Manager
Majors	Cincinnati Reds	National	83	79	.512	6 (15)	Terry Francona
Triple-A	Louisville Bats	International	71	79	.473	12 (20)	Pat Kelly
Double-A	Chattanooga Lookouts	Southern	73	61	.545	3 (8)	Jose Moreno
High-A	Dayton Dragons	Midwest	52	76	.406	11 (12)	Vince Harrison
Low-A	Daytona Tortugas	Florida State	65	66	.496	5 (10)	Willie Harris
Rookie	ACL Reds	Arizona Complex	25	35	.417	13 (15)	Gustavo Molina
Rookie	DSL Reds	Dominican	30	25	.545	21 (52)	Jose Montilla
Rookie	DSL Rojos	Dominican	23	30	.434	36 (52)	Juan Ballara
Overall 2025 Minor League Record			339	372	.477	23rd (30)	

ORGANIZATION STATISTICS

CINCINNATI REDS
NATIONAL LEAGUE

Batting	B-T	Ht.	Wt.	DOB	AVG	OBP	SLG	G	PA	AB	R	H	2B	3B	HR	RBI	BB	HBP	SH	SF	SO	SB	CS	BB%	SO%
Andujar, Miguel	R-R	6-0	211	3-2-95	.359	.400	.544	34	110	103	14	37	7	0	4	17	6	1	0	0	19	0	0	5.5	17.3
Banfield, Will	R-R	6-0	215	11-18-99	.100	.100	.100	7	10	10	0	1	0	0	0	0	0	0	0	0	6	0	0	0.0	60.0
Benson, Will	L-L	6-5	230	6-16-98	.226	.273	.435	90	253	230	31	52	8	2	12	41	16	1	0	6	67	2	2	6.3	26.5
Callihan, Tyler	L-R	6-1	205	6-22-00	.167	.167	.167	4	6	6	0	1	0	0	0	1	0	0	0	0	1	0	0	0.0	16.7
Candelario, Jeimer	S-R	6-2	222	11-24-93	.113	.198	.213	22	91	80	3	9	2	0	2	10	9	0	0	2	29	0	1	9.9	31.9
De La Cruz, Elly	S-R	6-5	200	1-11-02	.264	.336	.440	162	699	629	102	166	31	7	22	86	67	2	0	1	181	37	8	9.6	25.9
Dunn, Blake	R-R	6-0	210	9-5-98	.150	.320	.233	30	75	60	10	9	2	0	1	7	8	7	0	0	25	1	1	10.7	33.3
Encarnacion-Strand, Christian	R-R	6-0	224	12-1-99	.208	.234	.377	36	137	130	13	27	4	0	6	19	3	2	0	2	32	0	2	2.2	23.4
Espinal, Santiago	R-R	5-10	185	11-13-94	.243	.292	.282	114	328	301	25	73	12	0	0	19	16	1	3	2	38	2	1	6.4	11.6
Fraley, Jake	L-L	6-0	206	5-25-95	.232	.332	.387	67	193	168	29	39	8	0	6	23	24	1	0	0	41	4	2	12.4	21.2
Friedl, TJ	L-L	5-10	180	8-14-95	.261	.364	.378	152	685	579	82	151	22	2	14	53	81	16	4	5	115	12	3	11.8	16.8
Hampson, Garrett	R-R	5-11	196	10-10-94	.167	.211	.222	9	19	18	0	3	1	0	0	0	1	0	0	0	6	0	0	5.3	31.6
Hayes, Ke'Bryan	R-R	5-10	205	1-28-97	.234	.315	.342	52	178	158	16	37	4	1	3	13	18	1	0	1	30	2	1	10.1	16.9
Hays, Austin	R-R	5-11	200	7-5-95	.266	.315	.453	103	416	380	60	101	16	5	15	64	29	1	0	6	107	7	0	7.0	25.7
Hinds, Rece	R-R	6-4	215	9-5-00	.116	.136	.279	15	44	43	6	5	1	0	2	3	1	0	0	0	21	0	0	2.3	47.7
Hurtubise, Jacob	L-R	6-0	180	12-11-97	.083	.267	.083	12	15	12	3	1	0	0	0	0	1	2	0	0	6	0	0	6.7	40.0
Joe, Connor	R-R	6-0	205	8-16-92	.213	.286	.279	35	70	61	2	13	4	0	0	4	6	1	0	2	14	2	2	8.6	20.0
Lux, Gavin	L-R	6-2	190	11-23-97	.269	.350	.374	140	503	446	49	120	28	2	5	53	56	0	0	1	114	1	0	11.1	22.7
Marte, Noelvi	R-R	6-0	216	10-16-01	.263	.300	.448	90	360	339	45	89	17	2	14	51	16	3	0	2	85	10	3	4.4	23.6
McLain, Matt	R-R	5-8	180	8-6-99	.220	.300	.343	147	577	510	73	112	18	0	15	50	55	5	3	4	167	18	2	9.5	28.9
Steer, Spencer	R-R	5-11	185	12-7-97	.238	.312	.411	146	568	509	66	121	21	2	21	75	51	5	1	2	129	7	1	9.0	22.7
Stephenson, Tyler	R-R	6-4	225	8-16-96	.231	.316	.421	88	342	299	40	69	18	0	13	50	37	2	0	4	116	0	1	10.8	33.9
Stewart, Sal	R-R	6-3	215	6-27-03	.293	.545	.18	58	55	11	14	1	0	5	8	3	0	0	0	15	0	0	5.2	25.9
Trevino, Jose	R-R	5-10	215	11-28-92	.238	.272	.351	94	302	282	30	67	20	0	4	22	15	0	1	4	39	0	0	5.0	12.9
Wynns, Austin	R-R	6-0	190	12-10-90	.400	.442	.700	18	43	40	6	16	3	0	3	11	3	0	0	0	12	0	0	7.0	27.9

Pitching	B-T	Ht.	Wt.	DOB	W	L	ERA	G	GS	SV	IP	Hits	Runs	ER	HR	BB	SO	AVG	OBP	SLG	SO%	BB%	BF
Abbott, Andrew	L-L	6-0	192	6-1-99	10	7	2.87	29	29	0	166	148	60	53	19	43	149	.235	.285	.374	21.8	6.3	684
Ashcraft, Graham	L-R	6-2	248	2-11-98	8	5	3.99	62	0	0	65	68	37	29	2	25	64	.268	.333	.362	22.5	8.8	284
Barlow, Scott	R-R	6-3	210	12-18-92	6	3	4.21	75	1	1	68	50	35	32	8	45	75	.200	.333	.336	24.8	14.9	303
Burns, Chase	R-R	6-4	195	1-16-03	0	3	4.57	13	8	0	43	41	25	22	5	16	67	.240	.305	.409	35.6	8.5	188
Diaz, Alexis	R-R	6-2	224	9-28-96	0	0	12.00	6	0	0	6	8	8	8	4	5	3	.308	.455	.846	9.1	15.2	33
Gibaut, Ian	R-R	6-3	250	11-19-93	0	1	4.62	25	0	0	25	26	13	13	3	8	15	.260	.312	.410	13.8	7.3	109
Greene, Hunter	R-R	6-5	242	8-6-99	7	4	2.76	19	19	0	108	75	35	33	15	26	132	.192	.246	.368	31.4	6.2	420
LaSorsa, Joe	L-L	6-5	215	4-29-98	0	1	10.80	5	0	0	7	13	9	8	4	2	2	.419	.455	.871	6.1	6.1	33
Littell, Zack	R-R	6-4	220	10-5-95	2	0	4.39	10	10	0	53	46	28	26	10	11	41	.224	.268	.424	18.5	5.0	222
Lodolo, Nick	L-L	6-6	216	2-5-98	9	8	3.33	29	28	0	157	138	60	58	22	31	156	.233	.285	.387	24.3	4.8	642
Martinez, Nick	L-R	6-1	200	8-5-90	11	14	4.45	40	26	0	166	158	86	82	22	42	116	.254	.304	.435	17.0	6.1	683
Maxwell, Zach	R-R	6-6	275	1-26-01	0	0	4.50	8	0	0	10	5	5	5	3	4	13	.256	.326	.590	30.2	9.3	43
Mey, Luis	R-R	6-2	160	4-20-01	2	0	3.43	23	0	0	21	17	8	8	3	17	21	.221	.365	.324	21.9	17.7	96
Miley, Wade	L-L	6-1	220	11-13-86	1	0	6.75	3	2	0	12	15	9	9	3	6	7	.319	.407	.553	12.7	10.9	55
Moll, Sam	L-L	5-9	190	1-3-92	1	0	6.38	23	0	0	18	16	16	13	4	10	22	.229	.325	.471	27.2	12.3	81
Pagan, Emilio	L-R	6-2	208	5-7-91	2	4	2.88	70	0	32	69	41	26	22	10	22	81	.168	.241	.336	30.0	8.1	270
Petty, Chase	R-R	6-1	190	4-4-03	0	3	19.50	3	2	0	6	14	14	13	3	8	7	.452	.519	.839	17.5	20.0	40
Phillips, Connor	R-R	6-2	209	5-4-01	5	0	2.88	21	0	0	25	11	9	8	3	12	32	.133	.255	.277	32.7	12.2	98
Richardson, Lyon	S-R	6-2	207	1-18-00	0	3	4.54	34	0	0	38	37	25	19	2	21	30	.255	.349	.372	17.4	12.2	172
Rogers, Taylor	L-L	6-3	190	12-17-90	2	2	2.45	40	0	0	33	29	15	9	3	19	34	.240	.345	.388	23.3	13.0	146
Sanmartin, Reiver	L-L	6-2	160	4-15-96	0	0	0.00	1	0	0	2	1	0	0	0	1	2	.286	.375	.429	25.0	12.5	8
Santillan, Tony	R-R	6-3	285	4-15-97	1	5	2.44	80	0	7	74	53	23	20	7	29	75	.200	.290	.336	24.9	9.6	301
Singer, Brady	R-R	6-5	215	8-4-96	14	12	4.03	32	32	0	170	150	80	76	19	60	163	.238	.314	.404	22.8	8.4	716
Spiers, Carson	R-R	6-3	205	11-5-97	0	2	6.08	3	2	0	13	13	9	9	3	7	11	.260	.356	.480	18.3	11.7	60
Suter, Brent	L-L	6-4	213	8-29-89	1	2	4.52	48	3	0	68	69	38	34	11	18	53	.257	.307	.424	18.2	6.2	291
Trevino, Jose	R-R	5-10	215	11-28-92	0	0	3.86	2	0	0	2	4	1	1	0	1	1	.400	.417	.600	8.3	8.3	12

	B-T	Ht.	Wt.	DOB	W	L	ERA	G	GS	SV	IP	H	R	ER	HR	BB	SO	AVG	OBP	SLG	SB	CS	BB%	SO%
Wynne, Randy	R-R	6-1	180	3-9-93	0	0	3.00	1	0	1	3	3	1	1	1	1	3	.250	.308	.583	23.1		7.7	13
Zulueta, Yosver	R-R	6-1	190	1-23-98	1	0	6.14	7	0	0	5	5	5	1	4	5	.192	.290	.308	15.6		12.5	32

Fielding

Catcher	PCT	G	PO	A	E	DP	PB
Banfield	.974	7	37	0	1	0	0
Stephenson	.996	69	551	16	2	6	1
Trevino	.995	90	751	30	4	2	3
Wynns	1.000	15	81	3	0	0	1

First Base	PCT	G	PO	A	E	DP
Andujar	1.000	2	6	2	0	0
Candelario	1.000	8	38	4	0	1
Encarnacion-Strand	.989	27	172	14	2	14
Espinal	1.000	3	16	0	0	1
Joe	1.000	5	22	0	0	0
Steer	.998	122	791	75	2	70
Stewart	.988	11	73	6	1	4
Wynns	1.000	1	6	0	0	0

Second Base	PCT	G	PO	A	E	DP
Callihan	1.000	1	0	1	0	0
Espinal	.980	19	23	27	1	2
Hampson	1.000	2	1	1	0	1
Lux	.967	17	26	32	2	8
McLain	.988	138	196	288	6	58

Third Base	PCT	G	PO	A	E	DP
Candelario	.950	12	4	15	1	0
Encarnacion-Strand	.895	9	7	10	2	0
Espinal	.992	75	34	93	1	2
Hampson	1.000	1	0	2	0	1
Hayes	.991	52	34	81	1	4
Lux	.909	6	5	5	1	0
Marte	.936	38	27	46	5	4
Stewart	1.000	6	7	6	0	0

Shortstop	PCT	G	PO	A	E	DP
De La Cruz	.955	158	217	340	26	69
Espinal	1.000	2	1	2	0	0
Hampson	1.000	1	1	1	0	0
McLain	.929	6	4	9	1	1

Outfield	PCT	G	PO	A	E	DP
Andujar	1.000	2	1	0	0	0
Benson	.988	85	155	3	2	1
Callihan	1.000	3	2	0	0	0
Dunn	1.000	32	60	0	0	0
Espinal	.900	16	9	1	0	0
Fraley	.976	62	116	4	3	0
Friedl	.992	149	371	4	3	0
Hampson	1.000	5	6	0	0	0
Hays	.977	61	125	0	3	0
Hinds	1.000	14	28	1	0	1
Hurtubise	1.000	6	6	0	0	0
Joe	.966	29	27	1	1	0
Lux	.973	54	71	2	2	0
Marte	1.000	56	95	3	0	1
Steer	1.000	12	13	1	0	0
Vilade	1.000	1	1	0	0	0

LOUISVILLE BATS — TRIPLE-A
INTERNATIONAL LEAGUE

Batting	B-T	Ht.	Wt.	DOB	AVG	OBP	SLG	G	PA	AB	R	H	2B	3B	HR	RBI	BB	HBP	SH	SF	SO	SB	CS	BB%	SO%
Banfield, Will	R-R	6-0	215	11-18-99	.214	.270	.292	79	270	243	22	52	13	0	2	23	18	3	0	6	69	0	0	6.7	25.6
Benson, Will	L-L	6-5	230	6-16-98	.275	.367	.458	41	178	153	32	42	5	1	7	33	22	1	0	1	49	6	0	12.4	27.5
Brigman, Bryson	R-R	5-11	180	6-19-95	.237	.313	.289	45	151	135	20	32	4	0	1	9	14	1	1	0	27	5	1	9.3	17.9
Callihan, Tyler	L-R	6-1	205	6-22-00	.303	.410	.528	24	106	89	19	27	4	2	4	12	16	0	1	0	29	6	1	15.1	27.4
Candelario, Jeimer	S-R	6-2	222	11-24-93	.211	.318	.333	15	66	57	7	12	4	0	1	10	6	3	0	0	19	0	0	9.1	28.8
Dunn, Blake	R-R	6-0	210	9-8-98	.291	.397	.401	98	422	354	59	103	14	2	7	40	54	9	4	1	102	24	3	12.8	24.2
Encarnacion-Strand, Christian	R-R	6-0	224	12-1-99	.245	.310	.493	62	252	229	33	56	20	2	11	37	17	5	0	1	62	0	0	6.7	24.6
Faltine, Trey	R-R	6-2	198	1-8-01	.185	.228	.352	24	57	54	8	10	5	2	0	2	2	1	0	0	26	0	1	3.5	45.6
Fraley, Jake	L-L	6-0	206	5-25-95	.185	.241	.333	7	29	27	3	5	1	0	1	2	2	0	0	0	4	1	0	6.9	13.8
Hays, Austin	R-R	5-11	200	7-5-95	.222	.200	.556	3	10	9	2	2	0	0	1	2	0	0	0	1	5	1	0	0.0	50.0
Higgins, P.J.	R-R	5-10	195	5-10-93	.240	.300	.345	111	408	371	36	89	16	1	7	42	29	4	1	3	75	0	1	7.1	18.4
Hinds, Rece	R-R	6-4	215	9-5-00	.302	.359	.563	107	436	391	79	118	26	2	24	83	33	5	0	6	113	21	5	7.6	25.9
Hurtubise, Jacob	L-L	6-0	180	12-11-97	.144	.336	.186	34	133	97	21	14	4	0	0	8	22	7	3	2	29	7	0	16.5	21.8
Joe, Connor	R-R	6-0	205	8-16-92	.204	.313	.283	36	131	113	15	23	5	2	0	13	16	2	0	0	26	1	1	12.2	19.8
Johnson, Ivan	S-R	6-0	190	10-11-98	.221	.337	.378	58	202	172	35	38	6	0	7	25	30	0	0	0	59	10	2	14.9	29.2
Jordan, Levi	R-R	5-8	170	9-24-95	.237	.307	.345	122	461	414	53	98	20	2	7	30	36	7	1	3	67	17	2	7.8	14.5
Marte, Noelvi	R-R	6-0	216	10-16-01	.326	.434	.535	12	53	43	8	14	6	0	1	10	8	1	0	1	7	3	1	15.1	13.2
Rios, Edwin	L-R	6-3	220	4-21-94	.246	.337	.468	130	546	472	69	116	23	2	26	94	63	5	0	6	180	1	1	11.5	33.0
Rodriguez, Hector	L-R	5-8	186	3-11-04	.260	.304	.405	53	230	215	34	56	8	1	7	20	12	2	0	1	38	9	2	5.2	16.5
Rogers, Jack	L-L	6-2	205	4-5-99	.200	.308	.357	51	187	168	16	42	9	0	3	30	14	1	2	2	60	0	1	7.5	32.1
Stephenson, Tyler	R-R	6-4	225	8-16-96	.152	.200	.364	10	40	33	6	5	1	0	2	4	6	1	0	0	9	0	0	15.0	22.5
Stewart, Sal	R-R	6-3	215	12-7-03	.315	.394	.629	38	165	143	27	45	15	0	10	36	19	1	0	2	26	4	1	11.5	15.8
Urbaez, Francisco	R-R	5-11	195	10-13-97	.314	.381	.464	97	411	360	58	113	32	5	4	50	38	5	0	6	40	5	4	9.2	9.7
Vilade, Ryan	R-R	6-2	226	2-18-99	.296	.381	.536	65	269	233	42	69	18	1	12	35	26	7	1	2	51	6	1	9.7	19.0
Wendzel, Davis	R-R	5-10	206	5-23-97	.251	.346	.433	94	356	307	50	77	17	0	13	53	37	9	0	3	63	1	0	10.4	17.7
Yang, Eric	R-R	5-11	185	3-26-98	.235	.333	.247	34	99	85	6	20	1	0	0	10	8	5	0	1	29	0	0	8.1	29.3

Pitching	B-T	Ht.	Wt.	DOB	W	L	ERA	G	GS	SV	IP	Hits	Runs	ER	HR	BB	SO	AVG	OBP	SLG	SO%	BB%	BF
Abbott, Andrew	L-L	6-0	192	0	0	3.60	2	2	0	10	10	4	4	3	5	8	.270	.357	.568	18.6	11.6	43
Abel, Kevin	R-R	6-1	195	2-19-99	0	1	6.75	1	0	4	5	3	3	1	5	6	.294	.400	.471	30.0	15.0	20
Abreu, Albert	R-R	6-2	190	9-26-95	0	0	5.79	17	2	1	23	29	15	15	2	16	18	.305	.411	.411	15.9	14.2	113
Antone, Tejay	R-R	6-4	230	12-5-93	0	1	9.53	6	0	0	6	10	6	6	0	3	4	.385	.484	.385	12.9	9.7	31
Barnes, Charlie	L-L	6-2	190	10-1-95	1	3	7.13	6	6	0	24	41	19	19	5	5	27	.366	.393	.607	23.1	4.3	117
Benschoter, Sam	R-R	6-3	215	3-17-98	8	3	4.12	38	5	2	79	82	36	36	11	22	68	.272	.325	.432	20.9	6.7	326
Burns, Chase	R-R	6-4	195	1-16-03	1	0	2.19	2	2	0	12	7	3	3	0	4	14	.171	.239	.220	30.4	8.7	46
Busenitz, Alan	R-R	6-1	180	8-22-90	2	3	6.75	18	0	1	25	29	21	19	9	8	21	.290	.342	.620	18.8	7.1	112
Cardona, Ryan	R-R	6-1	200	5-7-00	0	0	7.20	2	1	0	5	6	4	4	2	2	3	.300	.391	.600	13.0	8.7	23
Diaz, Alexis	R-R	6-2	224	9-28-96	1	2	4.61	14	0	2	14	14	9	7	2	12	16	.255	.400	.418	22.9	17.1	70
Farmer, Buck	L-R	6-4	243	2-20-91	2	0	1.98	25	0	6	27	16	8	6	2	16	25	.168	.298	.257	21.7	13.9	115
Franco, Jose	R-R	6-2	175	11-25-00	3	2	3.51	17	14	0	51	43	27	20	10	28	52	.228	.336	.434	23.5	12.7	221
Gibaut, Ian	R-R	6-3	250	11-19-93	1	0	6.35	6	0	0	6	4	4	0	3	5	.150	.261	.250	21.7	13.0	23
Greene, Hunter	R-R	6-5	242	8-6-99	0	2	7.36	3	3	0	11	10	9	9	4	20	.227	.292	.500	41.7	8.3	48
Jordan, Levi	R-R	5-8	170	9-24-95	0	1	0.00	1	0	0	0	1	0	0	0	0	0	.333	.333	.333	0.0	0.0	3
Komar, Brandon	R-R	6-0	200	5-8-99	0	0	5.89	0	0	18	27	12	12	2	12	35	.351	.429	.481	13.2	13.2	91
Kravetz, Evan	L-L	6-8	240	12-19-96	0	0	5.59	19	0	0	19	24	14	12	5	12	21	.300	.387	.538	22.6	12.9	93
LaSorsa, Joey	L-L	6-5	215	10-7-98	3	2	2.82	45	0	0	45	34	17	14	2	26	41	.206	.321	.345	21.1	13.4	194
Lowder, Rhett	R-R	6-2	200	3-8-02	0	1	13.50	3	3	0	3	6	5	5	2	2	2	.375	.474	.563	15.8	10.5	19
Lyons, Jared	R-R	6-1	190	9-27-00	1	0	4.66	2	2	0	10	7	6	5	3	6	7	.194	.310	.472	16.7	14.3	42

Batting	B-T	Ht.	Wt.	DOB	AVG	OBP	SLG	G	PA	AB	R	H	2B	3B	HR	RBI	BB	HBP	SH	SF	SO	SB	CS	BB%	SO%
Maxwell, Zach	R-R	6-6	275	1-26-01	1	3	4.17	51	0	5	50	42	23	23	6	32	59	.225	.338	.358		26.8	14.5	220	
Mey, Luis	R-R	6-2	160	6-24-01	5	3	2.48	40	0	11	40	27	16	11	0	21	46	.189	.304	.259		27.2	12.4	169	
Miley, Wade	L-L	6-1	220	11-13-86	1	0	5.93	4	4	0	14	19	9	9	0	4	7	.333	.397	.386		11.1	6.3	63	
Moll, Sam	L-L	5-9	190	1-3-92	0	3	5.00	28	0	0	27	26	17	15	2	11	27	.265	.357	.347		23.9	9.7	113	
Parks, Hunter	R-R	6-4	187	4-28-01	0	4	9.72	17	3	0	25	37	31	27	6	22	17	.343	.459	.565		12.5	16.2	136	
Parrish, Drew	L-L	5-11	200	12-8-97	1	3	6.58	9	8	0	26	35	19	19	6	14	15	.330	.398	.594		12.2	11.4	123	
Petty, Chase	R-R	6-1	190	4-4-03	6	13	6.39	26	26	0	113	123	91	80	17	58	102	.271	.356	.460		19.6	11.2	520	
Phillips, Connor	R-R	6-2	209	5-4-01	1	2	2.88	31	0	0	34	18	13	11	3	21	36	.159	.312	.301		25.4	14.8	142	
Plutko, Adam	R-R	6-3	215	10-3-91	8	7	4.74	21	20	0	99	95	54	52	17	30	61	.248	.306	.452		14.6	7.2	419	
Richardson, Lyon	S-R	6-2	207	1-18-00	5	0	4.22	22	0	0	32	31	17	15	3	13	32	.254	.331	.361		23.5	9.6	136	
Rudd, Carson	R-R	6-5	190	9-17-98	1	0	12.00	3	0	0	6	10	9	8	0	4	3	.385	.469	.462		9.1	12.1	33	
Sanmartin, Reiver	L-L	6-2	160	4-15-96	7	2	2.67	46	2	0	67	65	25	20	5	18	55	.255	.311	.361		19.6	6.4	281	
Shaw, Bryan	S-R	6-1	226	11-8-87	0	0	27.00	4	0	0	2	6	8	5	0	4	1	.545	.625	.909		6.3	25.0	16	
Sikkema, T.J.	L-L	6-0	221	7-25-98	2	1	3.47	5	4	0	23	22	11	9	1	8	16	.247	.323	.371		16.2	8.1	99	
Spiers, Carson	R-R	6-3	205	11-11-97	0	1	5.94	4	0	0	17	16	11	11	2	11	11	.246	.380	.462		13.9	13.9	79	
Torres, Lenny	R-R	6-1	190	10-15-00	1	3	6.34	43	0	1	44	43	34	31	8	33	43	.261	.391	.485		21.1	16.2	204	
Valdez, Joel	L-L	6-4	171	4-28-00	0	0	6.00	9	0	0	12	16	9	8	1	5	12	.320	.414	.460		20.7	8.6	58	
Van Belle, Brian	R-R	6-3	185	9-3-96	1	4	4.95	7	7	0	36	43	24	20	2	8	31	.287	.331	.407		19.1	4.9	162	
Wilkerson, Aaron	R-R	6-2	230	5-24-89	4	2	4.17	18	18	0	95	84	45	44	19	17	78	.237	.274	.458		20.7	4.5	377	
Wynne, Randy	R-R	6-1	180	3-9-93	2	5	5.55	16	13	0	60	75	37	37	5	10	32	.309	.337	.588		12.5	3.9	257	
Yang, Eric	R-R	5-11	185	3-26-98	0	0	7.00	8	0	0	9	13	7	7	3	6	0	.333	.422	.641		0.0	13.3	45	
Zulueta, Yosver	R-R	6-1	190	1-23-98	2	2	3.28	44	0	0	60	37	27	22	7	32	78	.175	.296	.297		31.2	12.8	250	

Fielding

Catcher	PCT	G	PO	A	E	DP	PB
Banfield	.996	70	507	27	2	3	1
Higgins	.991	66	405	23	4	0	4
Jordan	.000	1	0	0	0	0	0
Stephenson	1.000	6	38	2	0	0	0
Yang	1.000	29	202	7	0	2	1

First Base	PCT	G	PO	A	E	DP
Banfield	1.000	1	1	0	0	0
Callihan	1.000	2	8	1	0	1
Candelario	1.000	4	28	0	0	0
Encarnacion-Strand	.993	20	135	9	1	11
Higgins	.992	29	218	20	2	35
Joe	.982	9	47	8	1	7
Jordan	.000	1	0	0	0	0
Rios	.993	72	509	48	4	46
Rogers	1.000	12	69	5	0	8
Stewart	.944	2	15	2	1	1
Vilade	1.000	7	56	1	0	2
Wendzel	1.000	5	26	3	0	6
Yang	1.000	1	2	0	0	0

Second Base	PCT	G	PO	A	E	DP

	PCT	G	PO	A	E	DP
Brigman	.949	13	12	25	2	5
Callihan	.957	16	23	43	3	8
Faltine	1.000	6	3	7	0	1
Johnson	1.000	5	6	14	0	0
Jordan	.970	16	24	40	2	7
Stewart	.982	13	21	33	1	7
Urbaez	.957	72	129	163	13	46
Vilade	.989	21	33	59	1	12

Third Base	PCT	G	PO	A	E	DP
Candelario	1.000	7	6	15	0	1
Encarnacion-Strand	.953	33	21	61	4	4
Faltine	1.000	1	1	0	0	0
Higgins	.961	22	11	38	2	4
Jordan	.981	50	31	74	2	9
Marte	.952	10	3	17	1	1
Rios	1.000	1	1	2	0	1
Stewart	.956	23	16	27	2	2
Urbaez	.867	10	5	8	2	1
Vilade	.909	5	3	7	1	0
Wendzel	1.000	2	1	0	0	0

Shortstop	PCT	G	PO	A	E	DP
Brigman	.920	5	7	16	2	4
Faltine	.903	8	13	15	3	5
Jordan	.982	56	84	133	4	38
Marte	.923	2	5	7	1	2
Wendzel	.987	87	105	195	4	35

Outfield	PCT	G	PO	A	E	DP
Benson	.990	40	95	1	1	0
Brigman	1.000	16	27	0	0	0
Callihan	1.000	8	13	0	0	0
Dunn	.995	98	213	4	1	2
Faltine	1.000	6	8	0	0	0
Fraley	.909	5	10	0	1	0
Hays	1.000	2	4	1	0	0
Hinds	.973	100	213	6	6	1
Hurtubise	.985	35	64	1	1	1
Joe	.941	7	16	0	1	0
Johnson	.983	42	57	1	1	0
Jordan	1.000	8	13	0	0	0
Rodriguez	1.000	49	77	4	0	0
Rogers	.972	36	66	4	2	1
Urbaez	1.000	5	9	0	0	0
Vilade	.935	32	57	1	4	1

CHATTANOOGA LOOKOUTS
SOUTHERN LEAGUE — DOUBLE-A

Batting	B-T	Ht.	Wt.	DOB	AVG	OBP	SLG	G	PA	AB	R	H	2B	3B	HR	RBI	BB	HBP	SH	SF	SO	SB	CS	BB%	SO%
Allen, Jay	R-R	6-2	190	11-22-02	.227	.308	.343	118	482	423	54	96	19	3	8	60	43	9	2	5	118	21	10	8.9	24.5
Arroyo, Edwin	S-S	6-0	175	8-25-03	.284	.345	.371	120	521	464	63	132	23	4	3	44	40	7	2	8	88	12	7	7.7	16.9
Ascanio, Johnny	S-R	5-10	150	7-4-03	.122	.213	.146	17	47	41	3	5	1	0	0	2	5	0	0	1	14	0	0	10.6	29.8
Balcazar, Leonardo	R-R	5-10	190	6-17-04	.263	.349	.328	51	217	186	29	49	3	0	3	20	23	3	2	3	24	4	5	10.6	11.1
Burns, Connor	R-R	6-1	185	12-25-01	.275	.227	.26	91	75	6	9	2	0	2	4	16	0	0	0	40	0	0	17.6	44.0
Callahan, Austin	L-R	6-3	215	6-6-01	.199	.264	.260	93	275	246	27	49	9	0	2	21	22	1	2	4	81	6	4	8.0	29.5
Collier, Cam	L-R	6-2	210	11-20-04	.263	.377	.347	74	308	259	39	68	16	0	2	38	45	3	0	1	86	0	1	14.6	27.9
Faltine, Trey	R-R	6-2	198	1-8-01	.105	.227	.105	10	23	19	2	2	0	0	0	2	3	0	1	0	10	2	0	13.0	43.5
Hays, Austin	R-R	5-11	200	7-5-95	.286	.375	.286	2	8	7	1	2	0	0	0	0	1	0	0	0	2	0	0	12.5	25.0
Hendrick, Austin	L-L	6-0	195	6-15-01	.246	.322	.422	93	357	313	39	77	13	0	14	52	32	6	0	6	116	6	3	9.0	32.5
Hunter, Cade	L-R	6-2	200	11-29-00	.219	.322	.324	72	243	210	29	46	10	0	4	17	30	2	1	0	68	2	1	12.3	28.0
Ibarra, Ruben	R-R	6-5	290	4-26-99	.232	.348	.470	104	400	336	49	78	17	0	21	69	47	14	0	3	103	0	0	11.8	25.8
Marte, Noelvi	R-R	6-0	216	10-16-01	.267	.353	.400	4	17	15	3	4	0	1	0	3	1	1	0	0	1	0	0	5.9	5.9
Nelson, Matheu	R-R	5-11	209	1-14-99	.088	.253	.138	29	99	80	5	7	1	0	1	3	16	2	0	1	30	0	0	16.2	30.3
O'Donnell, Peyton	L-R	5-10	190	3-27-02	.236	.327	.335	127	489	424	59	100	13	2	7	56	54	7	10	8	129	20	3	10.7	25.6
Pitelli, Dominic	R-R	5-11	175	1-18-02	.186	.283	.248	100	352	306	39	57	10	3	1	20	39	3	2	2	116	19	4	11.1	33.0
Rodriguez, Hector	L-R	5-8	186	3-11-04	.298	.357	.481	82	345	312	58	93	15	3	12	45	28	2	0	3	48	6	5	8.1	13.9
Rogers, Jack	L-L	6-2	205	4-5-99	.257	.356	.357	42	163	140	13	36	7	2	1	19	22	0	0	1	42	1	2	13.5	25.8
Stewart, Bryan	R-R	6-3	215	12-7-03	.306	.377	.473	80	329	294	51	90	19	0	10	44	27	7	0	1	51	13	2	8.2	15.5
Trautwein, Michael	L-R	6-1	205	9-13-99	.203	.358	.328	23	81	64	9	13	2	0	2	7	13	3	0	1	29	1	1	16.0	35.8
Yerzy, Andy	L-R	6-3	215	7-5-98	.167	.286	.167	2	7	6	0	1	0	0	0	0	1	0	0	0	2	0	0	14.3	28.6

CINCINNATI REDS

Pitching	B-T	Ht.	Wt.	DOB	W	L	ERA	G	GS	SV	IP	Hits	Runs	ER	HR	BB	SO	AVG	OBP	SLG	SO%	BB%	BF
Abel, Kevin	R-R	6-1	195	2-19-99	4	8	4.48	26	25	0	121	99	65	60	11	56	113	.223	.319	.343	22.0	10.9	513
Acuna, Jose	R-R	6-2	175	10-20-02	6	6	3.64	18	18	0	72	58	31	29	8	38	69	.226	.329	.377	22.9	12.6	301
Antone, Tejay	R-R	6-4	230	12-5-93	0	0	30.00	4	0	0	3	7	10	10	1	4	3	.467	.619	.933	14.3	19.0	21
Benoit, Donovan	R-R	6-3	203	1-22-99	3	1	4.50	18	1	0	48	47	28	24	5	23	47	.260	.349	.365	22.5	11.0	209
Burns, Chase	R-R	6-4	195	1-16-03	6	1	1.29	8	8	0	42	26	7	6	3	4	55	.177	.199	.265	36.4	2.6	151
Callahan, Austin	L-R	6-3	215	6-6-01	0	0	0.00	1	0	0	1	0	0	0	0	2	0	.000	.400	.000	0.0	40.0	5
Cannon, Will	R-R	6-1	201	7-8-03	0	0	0.00	2	0	0	2	0	0	0	0	3	.000	.000	.000	50.0	0	6
Cardona, Ryan	R-R	6-1	200	5-7-00	5	7	4.64	24	22	0	107	85	56	55	9	62	68	.223	.340	.369	14.8	13.5	459
Crawford, Brooks	R-R	6-4	215	8-19-96	1	4	8.28	15	0	2	25	27	27	23	4	14	20	.276	.372	.459	17.7	12.4	113
Farr, Thomas	R-R	6-0	203	4-29-99	0	1	3.12	20	0	0	26	25	13	9	3	7	16	.250	.309	.420	14.5	6.4	110
Franco, Jose	R-R	6-2	175	11-25-00	7	2	2.76	14	12	0	59	42	20	18	4	26	66	.194	.296	.301	26.7	10.5	247
Fransen, Arij	R-R	6-3	190	5-20-01	4	4	6.34	30	0	0	55	54	48	39	3	41	49	.254	.383	.371	18.5	15.5	265
Garcia, Julian	L-R	6-3	206	5-13-95	1	1	1.13	3	3	0	16	10	4	2	0	4	21	.192	.271	.250	35.6	6.8	59
Komar, Brandon	R-R	6-0	200	5-8-99	2	5	5.00	21	5	1	63	64	36	35	8	17	56	.262	.320	.422	20.9	6.3	268
Kuncl, Trevor	R-R	6-0	185	2-28-99	4	0	2.34	47	0	20	50	37	13	13	3	17	51	.206	.278	.300	25.6	8.5	199
Lyons, Jared	R-R	6-1	190	9-27-00	5	5	3.62	21	13	0	77	67	34	31	3	26	73	.239	.303	.350	23.1	8.2	316
Miley, Wade	L-L	6-1	220	11-13-86	0	1	5.40	1	1	0	2	1	1	1	1	2	2	.167	.375	.667	25.0	25.0	8
Miller, Simon	R-R	6-2	210	9-8-00	4	4	3.71	44	0	8	51	53	26	21	9	23	64	.264	.341	.473	28.1	10.1	228
Moore, Andrew	L-R	6-5	205	8-11-99	0	0	4.15	6	0	0	9	3	5	4	0	8	12	.103	.333	.172	30.8	20.5	39
Parks, Hunter	R-R	6-4	187	4-28-01	2	0	1.74	13	3	0	31	19	7	6	2	16	38	.183	.331	.250	29.2	12.3	130
Parrish, Drew	L-L	5-11	200	12-8-97	3	2	3.07	20	1	0	44	35	18	15	3	15	42	.211	.289	.313	22.5	8.0	187
Rudd, Carson	R-R	6-5	190	9-17-98	2	0	6.48	19	0	0	33	35	26	24	2	22	21	.273	.368	.414	13.5	14.1	156
Sando, Nick	L-L	6-2	203	5-11-01	1	0	0.00	2	0	0	5	0	0	0	0	2	8	.000	.118	.000	47.1	11.8	17
Sikkema, T.J.	L-L	6-0	221	7-25-98	6	3	4.97	18	11	0	63	56	38	35	6	23	56	.238	.326	.362	20.9	8.6	268
Sikorski, Easton	R-R	6-0	210	1-12-00	1	1	7.78	14	0	0	20	24	17	17	4	11	15	.308	.389	.564	16.7	12.2	90
Torres, Lenny	R-R	6-1	190	10-15-00	0	0	1.80	6	0	1	5	5	2	1	0	4	9	.238	.385	.238	34.6	15.4	26
Valdez, Joel	L-L	6-4	171	4-28-00	2	1	1.38	26	0	0	46	35	10	7	1	20	55	.212	.316	.261	28.8	10.5	191
Willeman, Zach	R-R	6-2	219	3-27-96	4	4	4.34	12	11	0	58	56	30	28	4	23	33	.258	.327	.359	13.4	9.3	246

Fielding

Catcher	PCT	G	PO	A	E	DP	PB
Burns	.991	26	193	20	2	2	0
Hunter	.992	66	481	18	4	4	8
Nelson	.990	26	197	10	2	1	0
Trautwein	.991	22	220	13	2	2	1

First Base	PCT	G	PO	A	E	DP
Callahan	1.000	28	163	15	0	14
Collier	.981	38	295	17	6	17
Hunter	1.000	2	8	1	0	0
Ibarra	.998	73	485	50	1	57
Rogers	.977	6	38	4	1	2
Yerzy	1.000	1	8	0	0	0

Second Base	PCT	G	PO	A	E	DP
Arroyo	1.000	12	6	34	0	7

	PCT	G	PO	A	E	DP
Ascanio	1.000	5	6	9	0	1
Balcazar	.964	38	73	88	6	19
Callahan	1.000	29	44	69	0	16
Faltine	1.000	4	1	7	0	0
Pitelli	.985	54	73	124	3	25
Stewart	1.000	4	3	11	0	1

Third Base	PCT	G	PO	A	E	DP
Ascanio	1.000	3	2	5	0	1
Callahan	.954	31	17	45	3	8
Collier	.956	17	10	33	2	1
Faltine	1.000	2	1	1	0	0
Marte	1.000	2	3	0	0	0
Pitelli	.957	19	13	32	2	2
Stewart	.984	67	39	82	2	10

Shortstop	PCT	G	PO	A	E	DP
Arroyo	.954	99	123	226	17	48
Ascanio	.833	1	2	3	1	1
Balcazar	.946	9	11	24	2	5
Pitelli	.962	27	36	66	4	13

Outfield	PCT	G	PO	A	E	DP
Allen	.992	114	237	4	2	2
Ascanio	1.000	6	5	1	0	0
Faltine	1.000	2	4	0	0	0
Hays	1.000	1	5	0	0	0
Hendrick	.975	74	115	4	3	1
Hunter	1.000	3	3	1	0	1
O'Donnell	.984	123	245	5	4	2
Rodriguez	.973	67	104	3	3	1
Rogers	.979	27	45	1	1	1

DAYTON DRAGONS
MIDWEST LEAGUE
HIGH-A

Batting	B-T	Ht.	Wt.	DOB	AVG	OBP	SLG	G	PA	AB	R	H	2B	3B	HR	RBI	BB	HBP	SH	SF	SO	SB	CS	BB%	SO%
Acosta, Victor	S-R	5-11	170	6-10-04	.225	.339	.280	88	391	325	45	73	11	2	1	29	38	19	7	2	73	13	4	9.7	18.7
Almonte, Ariel	L-L	6-1	170	12-1-03	.193	.262	.322	91	359	326	30	63	17	2	7	31	30	1	0	2	121	3	1	8.4	33.7
Ascanio, Johnny	S-R	5-10	150	7-4-03	.240	.379	.350	73	275	217	32	52	8	2	4	21	42	8	6	2	44	3	3	15.3	16.0
Balcazar, Leonardo	R-R	5-10	190	6-17-04	.262	.333	.413	75	343	305	40	80	17	1	9	37	29	5	1	3	51	4	0	8.5	14.9
Burns, Connor	R-R	6-1	185	12-25-01	.192	.271	.374	58	226	198	27	38	9	0	9	30	18	5	1	4	86	0	0	8.0	38.1
Cabrera, Ricky	R-R	5-11	178	10-31-04	.187	.276	.240	21	89	75	8	14	2	1	0	7	8	2	2	2	25	0	2	9.0	28.1
Collier, Cam	L-R	6-2	210	11-20-04	.293	.370	.415	11	46	41	6	12	2	0	1	4	5	0	0	0	10	0	0	10.9	21.7
Confidan, Yerlin	L-L	6-3	170	12-16-02	.224	.315	.320	112	474	416	50	93	20	4	4	48	51	5	1	1	133	12	6	10.8	28.1
Espinoza, Iverson	R-R	5-10	155	10-6-03	.053	.217	.053	8	25	19	3	1	0	0	0	3	4	0	2	0	5	0	0	16.0	20.0
Faile, John Michael	R-R	6-0	218	5-11-00	.233	.290	.406	91	365	335	38	78	19	0	13	56	24	4	0	2	102	1	1	6.6	27.9
Faltine, Trey	R-R	6-2	198	1-8-01	.214	.298	.286	14	49	42	5	9	3	0	0	6	4	1	0	2	20	3	0	8.2	40.8
Graham, Carter	R-R	6-2	232	9-17-01	.248	.306	.354	57	229	206	29	51	10	0	4	22	13	6	0	4	50	7	1	5.7	21.8
Jorge, Carlos	L-R	5-10	160	9-22-03	.251	.342	.355	110	469	406	66	102	16	4	6	37	52	5	4	2	87	40	7	11.1	18.6
McCrystal, Ryan	L-R	6-2	206	10-4-02	.271	.311	.371	20	74	70	8	19	7	0	0	9	3	1	0	0	17	0	0	4.1	23.0
Moss, Jack	L-R	6-5	215	10-30-01	.237	.329	.418	31	110	92	13	31	4	0	0	13	13	2	0	3	21	0	0	11.8	19.1
Omana, Diego	R-R	5-11	165	1-10-03	.200	.279	.227	35	124	110	8	22	3	0	0	6	12	0	2	0	30	0	0	9.7	24.2
Pineda, Esmith	R-R	5-10	183	11-13-04	.200	.259	.240	8	27	25	3	5	1	0	0	0	1	0	0	0	8	0	0	3.7	29.6
Sanchez, Carlos	R-R	6-0	177	1-12-05	.244	.320	.373	56	228	201	26	49	10	2	4	29	22	1	2	5	54	7	5	9.6	23.7
Serrano, Jose	R-R	6-0	180	10-14-04	.250	.290	.250	9	31	28	1	7	0	0	0	2	1	0	0	0	14	0	0	9.7	45.2
Smith, Myles	L-R	6-1	205	7-9-02	.128	.273	.173	50	163	133	18	17	3	0	1	8	25	2	2	1	45	3	2	15.3	27.6
Stephan, Anthony	L-R	5-11	180	12-16-02	.245	.349	.397	85	342	290	39	71	19	2	7	38	39	9	1	3	72	9	2	11.4	21.1
Stovall, Peyton	L-R	5-11	195	2-4-03	.191	.315	.279	69	298	251	43	48	8	2	3	30	43	3	0	1	53	11	1	14.4	17.8
Tanner, Logan	R-R	6-0	215	11-10-00	.121	.310	.121	12	43	33	5	4	0	0	0	3	9	0	0	1	14	0	0	20.9	32.6
Vargas, Alexander	S-R	5-10	148	10-29-01	.242	.294	.323	18	69	62	8	15	3	0	0	5	5	0	1	1	13	6	1	7.2	18.8
Wendzel, Davis	R-R	5-10	206	5-23-97	.182	.357	.273	4	14	11	1	2	1	0	0	0	3	0	0	0	3	0	0	21.4	21.4

CINCINNATI REDS

Pitching	B-T	Ht.	Wt.	DOB	W	L	ERA	G	GS	SV	IP	Hits	Runs	ER	HR	BB	SO	AVG	OBP	SLG	SO%	BB%	BF
Adcock, Cody	R-R	6-4	210	6-21-02	2	4	4.19	40	0	4	62	52	39	29	10	42	69	.218	.345	.395	24.1	14.7	286
Aguilera, Gabriel	R-R	6-0	165	8-19-00	2	2	5.52	7	4	0	29	31	20	18	0	18	27	.267	.370	.371	20.0	13.3	135
Antone, Tejay	R-R	6-4	230	12-5-93	0	0	1.42	5	0	0	6	6	1	1	1	2	8	.240	.321	.400	28.6	7.1	28
Benoit, Donovan	R-R	6-3	203	1-22-99	0	0	3.00	1	0	0	3	4	1	1	0	4	5	.308	.471	.308	29.4	23.5	17
Braithwaite, Trey	R-R	6-3	220	9-23-97	4	2	4.66	16	0	2	29	31	20	15	2	19	26	.267	.372	.371	19.0	13.9	137
Burns, Chase	R-R	6-4	195	1-16-03	0	2	3.09	3	3	0	12	5	4	4	2	5	20	.125	.222	.300	44.4	11.1	45
Cannon, Will	R-R	6-1	201	7-8-03	1	3	4.30	22	0	1	38	30	20	18	4	26	34	.216	.351	.374	20.2	15.5	168
Edgington, Brian	R-R	6-0	200	9-2-98	2	4	4.21	16	11	1	58	52	31	27	9	26	61	.241	.320	.449	25.0	10.7	244
Farr, Thomas	R-R	6-0	203	4-29-99	0	0	0.00	1	0	0	2	1	0	0	0	1	2	.167	.286	.333	28.6	14.3	7
Harmon, Johnathan	R-R	6-5	195	9-4-00	0	0	1.59	5	5	0	23	18	5	4	1	7	19	.214	.280	.274	20.4	7.5	93
Hayden, Luke	R-R	6-1	210	12-5-02	4	7	4.09	24	24	0	101	82	46	46	8	72	79	.228	.362	.336	17.6	16.0	449
Hubbart, Bryce	L-L	6-1	181	6-28-01	2	0	2.31	8	0	0	12	11	3	3	1	6	9	.250	.346	.341	17.3	11.5	52
Hurney, Jonah	L-L	5-8	180	3-3-00	5	4	5.09	28	0	2	64	74	41	36	5	17	52	.282	.341	.412	18.1	5.9	287
Jessee, Brody	R-R	6-4	217	12-1-00	3	1	7.17	28	1	1	48	53	42	38	9	28	46	.283	.413	.471	19.9	12.1	231
Lorant, Nestor	R-R	6-2	175	5-4-02	2	10	5.79	24	23	0	98	121	73	63	11	40	91	.294	.360	.474	19.7	8.7	462
Lowder, Rhett	R-R	6-2	200	3-8-02	0	1	12.00	1	1	0	3	5	5	4	0	1	5	.333	.412	.333	29.4	5.9	17
Machuca, Irving	R-R	6-2	205	5-1-00	2	4	6.37	23	0	6	30	28	24	21	2	14	45	.246	.341	.377	34.1	10.6	132
Martinez, Juan	R-R	6-1	160	12-30-02	0	0	3.00	1	0	0	3	3	1	1	0	1	2	.231	.333	.231	13.3	6.7	15
Menefee, Joseph	L-L	6-2	220	10-6-99	3	3	3.65	32	0	3	49	37	22	20	7	33	66	.206	.330	.389	30.3	15.1	218
Miley, Wade	L-L	6-1	220	11-13-86	0	2	15.88	3	3	0	6	13	10	10	4	0	8	.433	.452	1.033	25.8	0.0	31
Montero, Jose	R-R	6-2	180	7-14-03	7	5	3.93	23	23	0	103	95	52	45	5	43	87	.244	.328	.357	19.6	9.7	445
Osman, Graham	L-L	6-3	183	1-29-01	4	2	4.98	26	2	0	56	58	35	31	8	40	52	.270	.385	.428	19.6	15.1	265
Phillips, Connor	R-R	6-2	209	5-4-01	0	0	2.45	3	0	0	4	3	1	1	0	2	6	.231	.333	.385	37.5	12.5	16
Romano, Jimmy	R-R	6-1	200	6-11-03	1	4	5.07	29	0	2	50	49	31	28	5	34	39	.261	.376	.420	17.2	15.0	227
Rudd, Carson	R-R	6-5	190	9-17-98	0	0	9.00	4	0	0	5	6	5	5	1	2	4	.300	.391	.550	17.4	8.7	23
Sando, Nick	L-L	6-2	203	5-11-01	3	3	4.06	18	11	0	64	47	31	29	5	30	67	.198	.290	.333	24.9	11.2	269
Serwinowski, Adam	L-L	6-5	190	6-7-04	1	7	4.84	18	17	0	74	60	45	40	9	39	92	.241	.350	.379	27.7	11.7	332
Sikorski, Easton	R-R	6-0	210	1-12-00	2	4	1.87	21	0	5	43	29	14	9	3	16	57	.187	.269	.310	32.6	9.1	175
Simmons, Dylan	R-R	6-3	245	10-5-00	2	2	5.51	34	0	4	51	52	32	31	3	23	37	.268	.347	.387	16.6	10.3	223

Fielding

Catcher	PCT	G	PO	A	E	DP	PB
Burns	.991	58	540	25	5	4	3
Faile	.955	8	57	7	3	1	2
McCrystal	1.000	19	164	7	0	0	3
Omana	.971	35	278	27	9	0	2
Tanner	.984	11	115	6	2	0	1

First Base	PCT	G	PO	A	E	DP
Collier	.977	6	40	2	1	4
Faile	.981	61	440	21	9	46
Graham	1.000	13	82	11	0	8
Moss	.992	16	114	4	1	6
Serrano	1.000	2	15	1	0	0
Stephan	1.000	8	43	0	0	2
Stovall	.995	26	176	17	1	18

Second Base	PCT	G	PO	A	E	DP
Acosta	.988	43	69	91	2	19
Ascanio	.985	37	54	81	2	16
Balcazar	.979	10	23	24	1	5
Cabrera	1.000	1	2	1	0	0

	PCT	G	PO	A	E	DP	PB
Espinoza	1.000	2	3	7	0	2	
Serrano	1.000	1	1	1	0	0	
Stovall	.972	37	65	76	4	19	
Vargas	1.000	2	1	3	0	0	

Third Base	PCT	G	PO	A	E	DP
Acosta	.969	19	7	24	1	5
Ascanio	.974	30	23	52	2	6
Cabrera	.844	18	13	25	7	3
Collier	.929	3	2	11	1	1
Espinoza	.667	2	2	2	2	0
Faltine	1.000	2	1	6	0	2
Graham	.879	37	31	49	11	5
Sanchez	.933	23	21	35	4	2
Serrano	1.000	3	0	3	0	0
Stovall	1.000	0	2	0	0	0
Vargas	.000	1	0	0	0	0

Shortstop	PCT	G	PO	A	E	DP
Acosta	.976	24	26	57	2	13
Ascanio	.833	2	3	2	1	0

	PCT	G	PO	A	E	DP
Balcazar	.955	60	95	136	11	28
Espinoza	1.000	1	0	1	0	0
Faltine	1.000	2	0	6	0	0
Sanchez	.957	26	32	56	4	8
Vargas	.967	15	20	39	2	8
Wendzel	.900	3	6	3	1	1

Outfield	PCT	G	PO	A	E	DP
Almonte	.945	64	100	4	6	0
Ascanio	1.000	3	5	0	0	0
Confidan	.972	108	204	3	6	3
Espinoza	.000	1	0	0	0	0
Faltine	1.000	9	6	0	0	0
Jorge	.992	105	244	6	2	0
Pineda	.875	7	7	0	1	0
Sanchez	1.000	9	22	1	0	0
Smith	1.000	44	65	2	0	0
Stephan	.955	57	100	6	5	2

DAYTONA TORTUGAS
FLORIDA STATE LEAGUE — LOW-A

Batting	B-T	Ht.	Wt.	DOB	AVG	OBP	SLG	G	PA	AB	R	H	2B	3B	HR	RBI	BB	HBP	SH	SF	SO	SB	CS	BB%	SO%
Alcantara, Alfredo	R-R	5-9	165	10-25-05	.267	.438	.476	38	139	105	23	28	4	0	6	20	21	11	2	0	30	3	2	15.1	21.6
Cano, Ichiro	S-R	5-11	175	2-7-05	.215	.338	.246	22	77	65	8	14	2	0	0	6	9	3	0	0	23	1	0	11.7	29.9
Davies, Drew	L-R	6-2	171	12-4-05	.238	.372	.320	49	184	147	23	35	4	0	6	22	33	0	1	3	40	6	3	17.9	21.7
Duno, Alfredo	R-R	6-2	210	1-7-06	.287	.430	.518	113	495	390	78	112	32	2	18	81	95	6	0	4	91	6	6	19.2	18.4
Espinoza, Iverson	R-R	5-10	155	1-6-03	.207	.324	.276	38	110	87	20	18	3	0	1	12	12	4	4	2	27	3	0	10.9	24.5
Faltine, Trey	R-R	6-2	198	1-8-01	.182	.217	.182	6	23	22	2	4	0	0	0	1	1	0	0	0	9	2	0	4.3	39.1
Friend, Jacob	L-R	6-1	185	2-21-03	.191	.424	.348	67	206	141	29	27	5	1	5	18	50	9	3	3	58	6	4	24.3	28.2
Graham, Carter	R-R	6-2	232	9-17-01	.231	.307	.391	44	179	156	19	36	8	1	5	20	16	3	0	4	41	5	1	8.9	22.9
Henley, Kyle	R-R	6-3	180	12-15-04	.267	.328	.325	99	423	378	70	101	15	2	1	33	29	7	4	4	135	57	9	6.9	31.9
Holt, Peyton	R-R	5-10	205	8-6-00	.151	.287	.252	43	144	119	18	18	5	1	1	42	4	0	1	2	5	4	0	12.5	29.2
Lantigua, Arnaldo	R-R	6-2	200	12-19-05	.261	.318	.445	32	129	119	16	31	12	2	16	9	1	0	0	34	1	3	7.0	26.4	
Leonard, Dayne	S-R	6-0	190	5-1-00	.214	.389	.214	7	18	14	2	3	0	0	0	2	4	0	0	0	2	0	0	22.2	11.1
Leones, Juan	L-L	5-10	155	4-2-05	.273	.370	.337	60	186	150	38	31	2	1	2	11	23	7	3	1	69	22	0	12.4	37.1
Lewis, Tyson	L-R	6-2	195	1-10-06	.268	.347	.417	35	144	127	21	34	8	1	3	19	14	2	0	1	51	8	4	9.7	35.4
McCrystal, Ryan	L-R	6-2	206	10-4-02	.295	.359	.432	67	264	234	35	69	14	3	4	48	20	4	5	1	48	1	1	7.6	18.2
Moon, Bernard	R-R	6-0	185	4-15-03	.236	.322	.367	108	451	390	65	92	24	3	7	54	39	13	4	5	90	17	9	8.6	20.0
Neville, Mason	L-L	6-3	200	1-13-04	.247	.333	.442	23	90	77	8	19	8	2	1	9	9	2	0	2	31	2	0	10.0	34.4

Omana, Diego	R-R	5-11	165	1-10-03	.200	.214	.325	13	42	40	5	8	2	0	1	8	0	1	0	1	15	0	0	0.0	35.7
Pineda, Esmith	R-R	5-10	183	11-13-04	.259	.343	.384	102	414	352	47	91	21	1	7	57	38	12	3	9	87	3	2	9.2	21.0
Reyes, Luis	R-R	5-11	193	11-15-03	.204	.266	.293	57	193	167	20	34	7	1	2	23	13	3	5	5	35	2	0	6.7	18.1
Sanchez, Carlos	L-R	6-0	177	1-12-05	.308	.429	.449	60	264	214	36	66	10	4	4	33	45	1	3	1	67	13	9	17.0	25.4
Smith, Myles	L-R	6-1	205	7-9-02	.193	.343	.265	29	102	83	11	16	3	0	1	8	15	4	0	0	15	11	3	14.7	14.7
Stafura, Sammy	R-R	6-0	188	11-15-04	.261	.392	.410	89	403	322	48	84	18	9	4	48	63	10	1	6	97	28	5	15.6	24.1
Torres, Rafhlmil	S-R	5-11	150	9-5-05	.268	.400	.415	17	50	41	6	11	3	0	1	6	7	2	0	0	4	3	3	14.0	8.0
Trautwein, Michael	L-R	6-1	205	9-13-99	.222	.563	.667	4	16	9	5	2	1	0	1	3	7	0	0	0	2	0	0	43.8	12.5
Valdez, Malvin	R-R	6-2	178	10-14-03	.209	.322	.250	78	261	220	34	46	3	0	2	17	33	4	3	1	66	11	5	12.6	25.3
Valencia, Anthuan	R-R	5-8	177	10-14-04	.143	.333	.143	7	18	14	3	2	0	0	0	1	3	1	0	0	5	1	0	16.7	27.8
Vu, Kien	L-L	5-11	170	10-13-03	.273	.371	.532	23	91	77	15	21	8	0	4	18	9	3	2	0	25	7	1	9.9	27.5

Pitching	B-T	Ht.	Wt.	DOB	W	L	ERA	G	GS	SV	IP	Hits	Runs	ER	HR	BB	SO	AVG	OBP	SLG	SO%	BB%	BF
Afthim, Brady	R-R	6-0	180	11-25-02	0	0	3.00	2	0	0	3	3	1	1	0	0	2	.273	.273	.364	18.2	0.0	11
Blanchard, Beau	R-R	6-5	220	2-9-02	2	3	4.47	23	1	2	50	60	37	25	6	14	50	.283	.329	.448	21.9	6.1	228
Brutti, Ben	R-R	6-3	200	5-16-03	1	3	4.41	18	0	2	33	24	21	16	2	23	36	.195	.344	.309	23.8	15.2	151
Cannon, Will	R-R	6-1	201	7-8-03	1	1	1.96	13	0	2	18	9	5	4	2	5	21	.145	.209	.274	31.3	7.5	67
Colon, Edgar	R-R	6-3	180	3-13-06	0	5	5.23	15	12	0	43	44	28	25	5	30	30	.277	.408	.434	15.3	15.3	196
Cruz, Reynardo	R-R	6-2	165	10-24-01	3	2	4.66	14	4	1	46	36	28	24	3	30	44	.214	.359	.315	21.1	14.4	209
Diaz, Victor	R-R	6-4	220	12-2-02	3	2	7.78	27	0	2	39	41	36	34	0	33	46	.268	.405	.366	24.2	17.4	190
Edwards, Jacob	L-L	5-9	190	7-31-00	5	2	3.88	23	0	1	49	47	24	21	2	21	46	.258	.340	.390	22.0	10.0	209
Espinoza, Iverson	R-R	5-10	155	1-6-03	0	0	0.00	2	0	0	1	1	0	0	0	0	0	.333	.333	.667	0.0	0.0	3
Farr, Thomas	R-R	6-0	203	4-29-99	0	0	4.15	4	0	0	13	13	7	6	1	7	5	.283	.389	.413	9.3	13.0	54
Floyd, Ty	R-R	6-2	194	8-28-01	0	1	3.25	8	8	0	28	14	12	10	4	11	31	.147	.257	.295	28.4	10.1	109
Gilbert, Jake	R-R	6-7	220	12-1-96	1	1	6.55	7	0	0	11	10	9	8	1	5	14	.233	.327	.395	28.6	10.2	49
Herrera, Adrian	R-R	6-1	190	8-10-04	5	5	6.06	14	5	0	36	45	28	24	5	25	47	.308	.420	.500	26.7	14.2	176
Hodgdon, Trent	R-R	6-3	205	7-9-03	4	1	4.11	32	0	7	46	37	26	21	1	42	58	.216	.376	.275	26.6	19.3	218
Hollan, Hunter	L-L	6-5	200	3-5-02	1	2	7.84	4	2	1	10	8	9	9	0	13	9	.229	.420	.314	17.6	25.5	51
Holman, Luke	R-R	6-4	190	1-6-03	0	0	1.00	2	2	0	9	2	1	1	0	4	10	.071	.182	.071	30.3	12.1	33
Holt, Peyton	R-R	5-10	205	8-6-00	0	0	0.00	1	0	0	1	0	0	0	0	1	0	.000	.250	.000	0.0	25.0	4
Hubbart, Bryce	L-L	6-1	181	6-28-01	2	0	6.03	14	1	1	34	46	27	23	3	23	43	.319	.414	.458	25.4	13.6	169
Huggins, Kenya	R-R	6-3	215	12-12-02	2	2	3.69	18	15	0	63	44	26	26	3	26	57	.196	.283	.321	22.4	10.2	254
Lin, Sheng-En	L-R	5-11	185	9-1-05	0	1	3.78	5	5	0	17	10	8	7	1	5	21	.159	.232	.254	30.4	7.2	69
Lorduy, David	R-R	6-0	198	10-15-03	2	3	3.88	19	15	0	65	59	31	28	5	24	60	.237	.313	.337	21.6	8.6	278
Machuca, Irving	R-R	6-2	205	5-1-00	1	0	0.00	6	0	1	12	1	1	0	0	6	17	.027	.182	.027	37.8	13.3	45
Martinez, Juan	R-R	6-1	160	12-30-02	2	4	5.74	14	9	1	53	52	36	34	4	32	36	.257	.364	.411	15.1	13.4	239
Morris, Mason	R-R	6-5	230	8-21-03	0	0	9.00	2	2	0	4	3	4	4	1	1	7	.200	.250	.400	43.8	6.3	16
Murray, Zachary	R-R	6-0	170	10-18-01	2	2	5.74	10	4	0	31	40	21	20	3	10	23	.310	.369	.473	16.3	7.1	141
Ortiz, JeanPierre	R-R	6-0	185	2-18-04	7	1	2.86	26	10	0	91	77	36	29	7	33	83	.228	.312	.353	21.7	8.6	382
Payano, Nelfri	R-R	5-10	179	11-9-04	0	1	22.85	3	0	0	4	4	11	11	2	8	8	.235	.519	.647	29.6	29.6	27
Pelio, Mason	R-R	6-3	230	7-15-00	0	2	5.14	3	3	0	7	6	5	4	0	6	6	.250	.387	.333	19.4	19.4	31
Pestka, Drew	R-R	6-5	225	5-18-04	6	2	4.67	31	0	0	54	49	38	28	0	32	64	.238	.354	.316	26.3	13.2	243
Portes, Ovis	R-R	6-4	167	12-3-04	3	2	5.87	23	15	0	61	53	46	40	6	49	67	.228	.373	.375	23.3	17.1	287
Quigley, Stephen	S-R	6-0	175	5-3-00	3	2	4.79	10	0	1	21	23	13	11	0	5	16	.277	.341	.337	17.6	5.5	91
Reyes, Luis	R-R	5-11	193	11-15-03	0	0	0.00	2	0	1	2	1	0	0	0	1	2	.125	.222	.125	22.2	11.1	9
Rosario, Dalvin	R-R	6-1	167	6-15-00	0	1	1.93	4	0	0	5	2	1	1	1	3	7	.133	.278	.400	38.9	16.7	18
Sando, Nick	L-L	6-2	203	5-11-01	3	1	1.99	10	0	0	23	15	7	5	2	10	32	.183	.292	.305	33.3	10.4	96
Scheffler, Dominic	L-L	6-4	196	7-27-04	0	3	20.86	8	0	0	7	14	18	17	0	19	11	.400	.625	.486	19.6	33.9	56
Schoenwetter, Cole	R-R	6-3	190	10-1-04	3	8	5.86	26	18	2	78	66	62	51	9	60	75	.227	.360	.375	20.9	16.8	358
Smith, Tristan	R-L	6-2	200	5-25-03	0	0	13.50	1	0	0	2	2	3	3	0	4	4	.250	.500	.500	33.3	33.3	12
Starks, Gabe	R-R	6-1	230	12-26-01	2	1	3.69	25	0	5	39	30	16	16	1	28	46	.210	.335	.287	26.6	16.2	173
Van Treeck, Logan	L-L	6-5	220	12-26-00	0	1	5.79	2	0	0	5	5	3	3	1	1	7	.263	.300	.526	35.0	5.0	20
Villani, Mike	R-R	6-3	185	1-4-03	1	1	7.46	18	0	1	25	26	24	21	3	19	32	.268	.388	.464	26.4	15.7	121

Fielding

Catcher	PCT	G	PO	A	E	DP	PB
Duno	.988	81	711	57	9	6	13
Friend	.989	25	160	12	2	1	6
Leonard	1.000	4	26	3	0	0	1
McCrystal	.984	18	168	11	3	1	3
Omana	.978	8	85	6	2	1	3
Trautwein	1.000	3	34	2	0	1	1

First Base	PCT	G	PO	A	E	DP
Cano	.955	10	62	1	3	3
Davies	.988	46	301	16	4	23
Friend	1.000	1	1	0	0	0
Graham	1.000	28	145	14	0	12
Holt	1.000	4	10	1	0	0
Leonard	1.000	2	5	3	0	0
McCrystal	1.000	20	113	10	0	13
Omana	1.000	2	2	0	0	0
Reyes	.992	44	236	19	2	21

Second Base	PCT	G	PO	A	E	DP
Alcantara	1.000	5	4	7	0	1
Espinoza	.953	22	28	33	3	10
Faltine	1.000	3	6	6	0	2
Holt	1.000	6	7	8	0	2
Moon	.943	95	147	168	19	38
Reyes	.958	9	12	11	1	2
Stafura	1.000	2	5	5	0	2
Torres	.952	6	8	12	1	3

Third Base	PCT	G	PO	A	E	DP
Alcantara	.902	24	12	43	6	0
Cano	.913	13	5	16	2	3
Espinoza	1.000	13	5	16	0	0
Faltine	1.000	3	5	3	0	0
Graham	.909	19	24	26	5	1
Holt	.899	28	23	48	8	6
Sanchez	.941	45	35	61	6	2
Valencia	1.000	6	3	2	0	0

Shortstop	PCT	G	PO	A	E	DP
Alcantara	.967	10	12	17	1	4
Holt	.938	5	5	10	1	0
Lewis	.936	20	17	27	3	5
Sanchez	.917	10	7	15	2	3
Stafura	.968	83	125	179	10	47
Torres	.870	12	6	34	6	3

Outfield	PCT	G	PO	A	E	DP
Almonte	.964	90	126	9	5	4
Davies	1.000	4	4	0	0	0
Friend	1.000	16	12	0	0	0
Henley	.991	94	228	4	2	1
Holt	1.000	5	6	0	0	0
Lantigua	.950	28	35	3	2	0
Leones	.964	58	104	4	4	1
Moon	1.000	8	4	0	0	0
Neville	.964	19	27	0	1	0
Pineda	.960	90	155	11	7	3
Sanchez	1.000	3	8	0	0	0
Smith	1.000	20	41	1	0	0
Valdez	.988	79	152	7	2	0
Valencia	.000	1	0	0	0	0
Vu	1.000	25	34	2	0	0

ACL REDS — ROOKIE
ARIZONA COMPLEX LEAGUE

CINCINNATI REDS

Batting	B-T	Ht.	Wt.	DOB	AVG	OBP	SLG	G	PA	AB	R	H	2B	3B	HR	RBI	BB	HBP	SH	SF	SO	SB	CS	BB%	SO%
Alcantara, Alfredo	R-R	5-9	165	10-25-05	.315	.444	.443	44	189	149	35	47	13	0	2	27	33	4	0	3	44	7	1	17.5	23.3
Buten, Anielson	R-R	5-9	155	9-22-05	.282	.321	.409	46	163	149	31	42	6	5	1	25	7	3	1	3	48	8	3	4.3	29.4
Candelario, Jeimer	S-R	6-2	222	11-24-93	.500	.625	.833	2	8	6	1	3	2	0	0	3	2	0	0	0	1	0	0	25.0	12.5
Cano, Ichiro	S-R	5-11	175	2-7-05	.285	.437	.400	42	167	130	24	37	5	2	2	22	34	2	0	1	42	3	2	20.4	25.1
Casiano, Yanuel	R-R	6-0	185	2-7-07	.170	.270	.255	31	122	106	12	18	4	1	1	14	12	3	0	1	44	0	0	9.8	36.1
Chevalier, Luis	S-R	5-11	160	1-18-02	.154	.185	.346	8	27	26	4	4	2	0	1	3	1	0	0	0	7	0	0	3.7	25.9
Collier, Cam	L-R	6-2	210	11-20-04	.394	.524	.636	10	42	33	3	13	3	1	1	6	9	0	0	0	8	1	0	21.4	19.0
Davies, Drew	L-R	6-2	171	12-4-05	.257	.405	.406	32	127	101	25	26	5	2	2	16	23	2	1	0	35	2	1	18.1	27.6
Encarnacion-Strand, Christian	R-R	6-0	224	12-1-99	.286	.429	2	7	7	1	2	1	0	0	2	0	0	0	0	3	0	0	0.0	42.9	
Friend, Jacob	R-R	6-1	185	2-21-03	.067	.300	.067	5	20	15	2	1	0	0	0	1	5	0	0	0	6	0	1	25.0	30.0
Gomes, Gabriel	R-R	5-9	170	3-31-04	.216	.268	.270	16	41	37	6	8	0	1	0	5	1	2	0	1	12	0	0	2.4	29.3
Hairston, Jalen	R-R	6-0	180	3-4-04	.214	.285	.304	29	124	112	17	24	4	0	2	7	10	1	0	0	30	7	0	8.1	24.2
Lantigua, Arnaldo	R-R	6-2	200	12-19-05	.268	.345	.519	49	206	183	34	49	14	1	10	40	18	4	0	1	44	1	1	8.7	21.4
Leonard, Dayne	S-R	6-0	190	5-1-00	.395	.489	.553	13	45	38	10	15	4	1	0	7	6	1	0	0	8	0	0	13.3	17.8
Lewis, Tyson	L-R	6-2	195	1-10-06	.340	.396	.532	46	207	188	44	64	8	5	6	35	15	3	0	1	51	19	4	7.2	24.6
Lin, Sheng-En	L-R	5-11	185	9-1-05	.172	.348	.310	36	113	87	14	15	4	1	2	13	24	0	1	1	30	1	2	21.2	26.5
Marte, Noelvi	R-R	6-0	216	10-16-01	.400	.455	.700	3	11	10	1	4	0	0	1	3	1	0	0	0	0	0	0	9.1	0.0
Mora, Angelo	R-R	5-11	150	6-10-05	.143	.213	.143	15	47	42	1	6	0	0	0	7	2	2	0	1	11	0	0	4.3	23.4
Moss, Jack	L-R	6-5	215	10-30-01	.269	.367	.423	8	30	26	5	7	4	0	0	2	4	0	0	0	4	0	0	13.3	13.3
Romero, Yael	L-R	5-11	175	10-15-05	.233	.423	.425	27	98	73	28	17	4	2	2	10	19	5	0	0	22	3	0	19.4	22.4
Serrano, Jose	R-R	6-0	180	10-14-03	.091	.091	.091	4	11	11	2	1	0	0	0	0	0	0	0	0	5	0	0	0.0	45.5
Soriano, Yeycol	L-L	6-0	150	9-3-05	.239	.344	.341	47	164	138	18	33	4	2	2	23	22	1	1	2	52	6	1	13.4	31.7
Stephan, Anthony	L-R	5-11	180	12-16-02	.313	.476	.375	5	21	16	2	5	1	0	0	2	4	1	0	0	3	0	0	19.0	14.3
Torres, Rafhlmil	S-R	5-11	150	9-6-05	.232	.335	.404	41	179	151	33	35	9	4	3	24	18	7	0	3	23	8	4	10.1	12.8
Valencia, Anthuan	R-R	5-8	177	10-14-04	.313	.382	.458	34	111	96	20	30	11	0	1	14	9	3	1	2	27	3	0	8.1	24.3

Pitching	B-T	Ht.	Wt.	DOB	W	L	ERA	G	GS	SV	IP	Hits	Runs	ER	HR	BB	SO	AVG	OBP	SLG	SO%	BB%	BF
Aguilera, Gabriel	R-R	6-0	165	8-19-00	0	0	0.00	1	0	0	2	2	0	0	0	0	3	.250	.250	.250	37.5	0.0	8
Arellano, Joneiker	R-R	5-11	155	2-20-05	0	1	30.38	2	1	0	3	10	11	9	2	2	3	.556	.619	1.111	13.6	9.1	22
Brutti, Ben	R-R	6-3	200	5-16-03	0	0	6.43	4	0	1	7	9	5	5	1	4	11	.333	.459	.667	29.7	10.8	37
Colina, Jesus	R-R	5-11	170	3-21-05	2	1	8.53	15	0	0	19	25	19	18	1	10	27	.338	.409	.473	30.7	11.4	88
Colmenares, Mauricio	R-R	6-0	170	11-4-03	0	1	5.79	11	0	1	19	16	12	12	2	11	19	.232	.337	.406	22.9	13.3	83
Colon, Edgar	R-R	6-3	180	3-13-06	0	0	3.00	1	0	3	2	1	1	0	3	5	.222	.417	.444	41.7	25.0	12
Cruz, Reynardo	R-R	6-2	165	10-24-01	3	1	3.66	6	3	0	20	14	8	8	1	13	23	.192	.314	.301	26.7	15.1	86
Farmer, Buck	L-R	6-4	243	2-20-91	1	0	4.32	6	0	0	8	9	4	4	0	0	7	.273	.265	.394	20.6	0.0	34
Gaitan, Abraham	R-R	6-2	180	2-6-04	4	3	5.06	16	0	2	32	35	25	18	8	9	36	.267	.312	.527	25.5	6.4	141
Gomes, Gabriel	R-R	5-9	170	3-31-04	0	1	0.00	1	0	0	4	2	1	0	0	0	5	1.000	1.000	1.000	0.0	0.0	4
Greene, Hunter	R-R	6-5	242	8-6-99	0	0	0.00	1	1	0	2	0	0	0	0	0	1	.000	.143	.000	57.1	14.3	7
Harmon, Johnathan	R-R	6-5	195	9-4-00	1	0	10.50	3	2	0	6	11	8	7	0	6	6	.423	.545	.577	17.6	17.6	34
Herrera, Adrian	R-R	6-1	190	8-10-04	1	1	4.50	3	2	0	6	5	3	3	0	1	6	.250	.318	.250	27.3	4.5	22
Hollan, Hunter	L-L	6-5	200	3-5-02	0	1	1.93	3	3	0	5	5	6	1	0	4	8	.278	.409	.333	36.4	18.2	22
Lantigua, Lisnerkin	R-R	6-0	181	9-1-04	2	1	4.13	13	0	1	28	23	13	13	2	10	29	.230	.296	.360	25.2	8.7	115
Lin, Sheng-En	L-R	5-11	185	9-1-05	0	1	2.67	10	7	0	30	19	12	9	3	10	42	.260	.321	.321	32.5	8.1	123
Lopez, Christian	L-L	6-2	207	7-6-06	1	1	4.50	7	3	0	26	29	18	13	4	4	23	.282	.327	.485	20.7	3.6	111
Lopez, Josue	R-R	6-2	175	2-6-02	2	0	5.06	11	0	0	11	6	9	6	0	11	15	.167	.404	.278	28.8	21.2	52
Lorduy, David	R-R	6-0	198	10-15-03	0	0	2.25	2	2	0	4	2	1	1	0	2	5	.154	.294	.231	29.4	11.8	17
Lowder, Rhett	R-R	6-2	200	3-8-02	0	1	6.00	1	1	0	3	4	2	2	1	0	5	.308	.308	.692	38.5	0.0	13
Morellis, Luis	R-R	6-2	165	2-7-04	1	4	8.90	10	6	0	29	33	30	29	1	27	27	.287	.432	.391	18.1	18.1	149
Payano, Nelfri	R-R	5-10	179	11-9-04	0	2	16.36	13	0	0	11	17	21	20	0	24	10	.347	.573	.429	13.3	32.0	75
Pelio, Mason	R-R	6-3	230	7-15-00	0	0	0.00	1	1	0	2	0	0	0	0	1	1	.000	.250	.000	12.5	12.5	8
Pena, Ayendy	R-R	6-1	172	3-16-04	0	2	9.49	13	0	0	12	16	16	13	3	15	14	.308	.464	.538	20.3	21.7	69
Perez, Samuel	R-R	6-1	178	8-3-04	2	5	8.26	12	8	0	45	65	42	41	5	10	31	.344	.376	.550	15.0	4.9	206
Pimentel, Luis	R-R	5-11	175	8-11-03	0	1	1.50	3	1	0	12	6	2	2	0	1	12	.143	.182	.190	27.3	2.3	44
Quigley, Stephen	S-R	6-0	175	5-3-00	0	0	0.00	2	0	0	2	0	0	0	0	2	.000	.000	.000	33.3	0.0	6
Rosario, Dalvin	R-R	6-1	167	6-15-00	0	0	27.00	1	1	0	1	2	3	3	0	3	0	.333	.667	.333	0.0	50.0	6
Salgado, Bryan	R-R	5-10	170	1-16-07	0	0	7.36	3	0	1	4	4	3	3	0	2	6	.267	.353	.467	35.3	11.8	17
Scheffler, Dominic	L-L	6-4	196	7-27-04	2	0	6.15	11	0	0	26	29	19	18	1	9	27	.305	.373	.389	24.3	8.1	111
Smith, Tristan	R-L	6-2	200	5-25-03	0	1	10.50	5	2	0	6	9	7	7	0	8	.346	.471	.500	23.5	20.6	34
Solano, Mendry	R-R	6-3	182	10-22-03	1	1	11.08	10	1	13	19	17	16	2	13	15	.358	.500	.660	22.1	19.1	68
Spiers, Carson	R-R	6-3	205	11-11-97	0	0	0.00	1	1	0	2	0	0	0	0	4	.222	.300	.222	40.0	0.0	10
Starks, Gabe	S-R	6-1	230	12-26-01	0	1	13.50	2	0	0	4	5	7	6	3	6	1	.294	.455	.889	18.2	9.1	11
Torres, Stharlin	R-R	6-0	182	6-19-06	0	1	1.88	10	6	0	38	26	9	8	2	7	44	.193	.236	.239	30.6	4.9	144
Villafana, Deivi	R-R	6-4	175	5-25-03	1	3	6.56	12	8	0	47	78	42	34	4	9	42	.364	.385	.523	18.5	4.0	227
Villani, Mike	R-R	6-3	185	1-4-03	0	0	9.00	1	0	0	1	2	1	1	0	1	0	.400	.500	.400	0.0	16.7	6

Fielding
C: Casiano 30, Leonard 13, Mora 11, Gomes 9, Friend 3. **1B:** Cano 23, Romero 23, Collier 7, Davies 6, Moss 3, Encarnacion-Strand 2. **2B:** Alcantara 33, Torres 24, Valencia 3, Serrano 2. **3B:** Hairston 28, Cano 18, Valencia 8, Chevalier 4, Alcantara 3, Marte 2, Serrano 2, Candelario 1, Collier 1. **SS:** Lewis 40, Torres 16, Alcantara 6, Valencia 1. **LF:** Buten 28, Valencia 19, Davies 12, Stephan 4, Moss 3, Chevalier 2, Friend 2, Lantigua 1. **CF:** Soriano 46, Buten 14, Lantigua 7. **RF:** Lantigua 36, Davies 13, Buten 8, Valencia 3, Chevalier 1, Soriano 1.

DSL REDS — ROOKIE
DOMINICAN SUMMER LEAGUE

Batting	B-T	Ht.	Wt.	DOB	AVG	OBP	SLG	G	PA	AB	R	H	2B	3B	HR	RBI	BB	HBP	SH	SF	SO	SB	CS	BB%	SO%
Brown, Juan	R-R	6-3	185	7-5-07	.257	.366	.375	41	161	136	23	35	7	0	3	29	17	7	0	1	49	0	2	10.6	30.4
Calzado, Yojanser	S-R	5-11	158	4-17-07	.292	.429	.358	42	171	137	45	40	3	3	0	14	31	2	1	0	34	41	5	18.1	19.9
Frias, Jealmy	S-R	5-11	155	3-8-08	.186	.286	.326	15	49	43	5	8	1	1	1	9	6	0	0	0	17	1	0	12.2	34.7
Guadamuz, Omar	R-R	5-9	170	10-23-07	.235	.341	.353	12	41	34	4	8	2	1	0	10	5	1	0	1	12	4	1	12.2	29.3
Jimenez, Hansel	R-R	6-1	179	12-5-06	.269	.374	.445	35	147	119	23	32	6	0	5	20	14	9	0	5	38	12	1	9.5	25.9
Joseph, Brayan	S-R	5-10	145	9-22-05	.000	.000	.000	1	3	3	0	0	0	0	0	0	0	0	0	0	1	0	0	0.0	33.3
Legito, Qyshawn	R-R	5-10	181	11-13-05	.270	.365	.351	23	85	74	10	20	6	0	0	13	11	0	0	0	22	0	3	12.9	25.9
Mariano, Naibel	R-R	6-3	182	9-6-06	.289	.329	.459	34	143	135	23	39	7	2	4	26	6	2	0	0	30	9	3	4.2	21.0
Martinez, Jaset	L-L	5-10	170	12-15-06	.298	.460	.471	39	137	104	31	31	9	0	3	25	31	1	0	1	29	1	1	22.6	21.2
Martinus, Shendrion	R-R	5-10	161	12-23-06	.229	.363	.289	28	102	83	16	19	1	2	0	7	14	4	0	1	23	6	1	13.7	22.5
Morillo, Jirvin	S-R	5-11	177	1-10-07	.259	.381	.431	33	139	116	20	30	8	0	4	27	23	0	0	0	25	6	2	16.5	18.0
Nunez, Pablo	L-L	5-10	145	10-23-06	.327	.542	.413	36	157	104	42	34	4	1	1	13	41	9	2	1	6	16	4	26.1	3.8
Pena, Abel	R-R	6-2	198	1-24-08	.214	.290	.250	9	31	28	4	6	1	0	0	2	1	2	0	0	10	0	0	3.2	32.3
Reyes, Rey	L-R	5-8	163	1-7-08	.129	.289	.129	12	38	31	7	4	0	0	0	3	7	0	0	0	10	0	0	18.4	26.3
Richardson, Riangelo	R-R	5-9	159	7-1-07	.135	.270	.176	27	89	74	9	10	3	0	0	6	12	2	0	1	31	2	0	13.5	34.8
Sabino, Jose	L-R	6-0	150	6-18-07	.229	.389	.257	27	90	70	15	16	2	0	0	8	15	4	0	1	10	1	1	16.7	11.1
Sanchez, Adolfo	L-L	6-1	185	9-19-06	.339	.474	.504	36	154	121	36	41	8	3	2	27	24	8	0	1	21	10	4	15.6	13.6
Waterfort, Nayerith	R-R	5-10	154	3-30-06	.299	.432	.460	29	111	87	24	26	6	2	2	16	18	4	0	2	18	3	3	16.2	16.2
Zambrano, Diorland	R-R	5-10	168	11-2-06	.270	.342	.350	44	185	163	26	44	7	0	2	27	17	2	1	2	11	5	3	9.2	5.9

Pitching	B-T	Ht.	Wt.	DOB	W	L	ERA	G	GS	SV	IP	Hits	Runs	ER	HR	BB	SO	AVG	OBP	SLG	SO%	BB%	BF
Aguilera, Dony	R-R	5-11	154	9-18-06	6	0	1.70	14	9	1	58	40	17	11	2	17	52	.194	.262	.272	22.7	7.4	229
Almeida, Jhan	R-R	6-3	185	4-29-05	1	1	2.57	9	6	0	21	21	6	6	1	10	15	.266	.363	.342	16.5	11.0	91
Aquino, Anthony	R-R	6-2	180	4-25-06	0	0	6.00	3	0	0	3	5	2	2	0	3	4	.231	.444	.385	22.2	16.7	18
Avila, Luis	R-R	5-11	145	4-15-07	3	0	1.59	9	0	2	17	9	4	3	0	5	18	.158	.234	.211	27.7	7.7	65
Baldelomar, Guillermo	R-R	6-3	165	2-10-07	2	0	5.23	12	6	0	33	27	21	19	4	20	32	.227	.348	.395	22.5	14.1	142
Camargo, Ramces	R-R	6-3	185	1-25-07	1	1	5.63	9	2	0	24	15	17	15	1	28	25	.181	.386	.289	21.9	24.6	114
Chirino, Luisangel	R-R	5-10	150	6-21-07	1	2	6.23	13	0	0	22	20	21	15	2	22	23	.250	.421	.375	21.5	20.6	107
Cruz, Luis	R-R	6-3	175	8-21-06	1	1	4.00	9	0	0	18	21	13	8	1	15	14	.296	.411	.451	15.6	16.7	90
De La Cruz, Ariel	L-L	6-2	165	4-25-06	3	4	6.90	14	2	2	30	20	28	23	2	34	23	.194	.403	.291	16.5	24.5	139
Diaz, Dennis	R-R	6-3	198	9-10-05	0	1	5.63	5	4	0	16	14	13	10	1	15	17	.226	.380	.371	21.5	19.0	79
Escalona, Ysaias	R-R	6-0	154	9-3-06	3	2	5.26	10	4	0	26	22	20	15	0	17	25	.239	.359	.348	21.4	14.5	117
Garcia, Deivi	R-R	5-11	170	7-10-04	1	1	5.91	6	0	0	11	12	9	7	0	4	6	.286	.367	.357	12.2	8.2	49
Garcia, Malvin	L-L	6-2	165	5-31-06	1	4	3.86	13	0	1	16	13	8	7	1	17	18	.188	.353	.250	21.2	20.0	85
Gonzalez, Irvin	R-R	5-10	150	6-9-06	3	1	5.04	16	0	3	25	25	16	14	1	11	28	.260	.351	.385	24.6	9.6	114
Leon, Rafael	R-R	6-1	175	1-11-06	0	0	3.86	5	4	0	5	4	2	2	0	5	5	.222	.417	.333	20.8	20.8	24
Maiz, Cesar	L-R	6-0	195	5-22-08	0	0	4.09	4	4	0	11	10	6	5	1	4	11	.238	.304	.500	23.9	8.7	46
Marchan, Manuel	R-R	6-3	165	3-28-07	1	2	11.00	3	2	0	9	15	12	11	0	4	14	.366	.404	.488	29.8	8.5	47
Marte, Jefersson	R-R	6-0	170	4-18-08	0	1	3.86	5	0	1	5	6	3	2	0	4	4	.316	.435	.474	16.7	16.7	24
Martinez, Jaset	L-L	5-10	170	12-15-06	0	1	6.75	2	0	0	1	2	2	1	0	0	0	.400	.400	.600	0.0	0.0	6
Merite, Ryjeteri	L-L	6-3	150	12-16-05	1	2	0.81	14	11	0	33	23	8	3	0	15	44	.197	.319	.265	31.9	10.9	138
Nino, Dulger	R-R	6-1	185	12-29-04	0	0	27.00	1	0	0	1	3	3	3	0	1	0	.429	.500	.571	0.0	12.5	8
Prodanovic, Nicola	R-R	6-0	190	4-5-04	0	0	14.49	14	0	1	14	13	26	22	0	33	11	.250	.581	.327	11.8	35.5	93
Redona, Iker	L-L	5-11	170	12-5-07	1	0	0.00	1	0	0	2	1	0	0	0	0	4	.125	.125	.125	50.0	0.0	8
Santana, Jonathan	R-R	6-5	157	3-12-07	1	1	6.85	14	0	1	24	15	21	18	0	31	31	.181	.425	.253	25.8	25.8	120
Talavera, Enmanuel	R-R	6-2	170	10-7-05	0	0	3.60	1	0	0	5	5	2	2	0	1	3	.278	.300	.444	15.0	5.0	20
Yepes, Luis	R-R	6-4	183	3-24-06	0	0	6.23	3	0	0	4	5	5	3	1	3	6	.278	.440	.444	24.0	12.0	25

Fielding
C: Morillo 25, Legito 18, Sabino 14. 1B: Martinez 35, Zambrano 15, Brown 9, Pena 2. 2B: Richardson 18, Waterfort 13, Zambrano 9, Guadamuz 7, Martinus 7, Frias 3, Joseph 1. 3B: Jimenez 16, Martinus 15, Mariano 11, Guadamuz 5, Waterfort 5, Zambrano 4, Richardson 2. SS: Mariano 21, Jimenez 18, Zambrano 15, Richardson 3. LF: Calzado 16, Nunez 14, Brown 11, Reyes 5, Frias 4, Sabino 4, Sanchez 3, Waterfort 2, Martinez 1. CF: Calzado 22, Nunez 17, Sanchez 16, Reyes 2, Brown 1, Frias 1. RF: Brown 19, Sanchez 16, Sabino 7, Calzado 5, Nunez 5, Frias 4, Reyes 4, Waterfort 2, Martinez 1

DSL ROJOS — ROOKIE
DOMINICAN SUMMER LEAGUE

Batting	B-T	Ht.	Wt.	DOB	AVG	OBP	SLG	G	PA	AB	R	H	2B	3B	HR	RBI	BB	HBP	SH	SF	SO	SB	CS	BB%	SO%
Aponte, Liberts	R-R	6-0	160	11-8-07	.247	.368	.461	45	193	154	34	38	6	3	7	36	29	4	0	6	35	9	0	15.0	18.1
Barboza, Angel	R-R	5-9	173	11-29-06	.205	.404	.231	15	52	39	8	8	1	0	0	2	10	3	0	0	4	2	0	19.2	7.7
Caricipe, Juan	S-R	5-11	155	5-21-08	.233	.352	.322	29	108	90	17	21	2	3	0	9	14	3	0	1	27	15	2	13.0	25.0
Chourio, Deinis	R-R	5-9	157	7-2-08	.183	.310	.282	24	84	71	8	13	2	1	1	4	13	0	0	0	33	4	4	15.5	39.3
De La Cruz, Wanderly	L-L	5-10	153	5-25-08	.245	.421	.377	36	140	106	27	26	6	4	0	14	29	4	0	1	25	12	1	20.7	17.9
Feliciano, Sandor	S-R	6-0	165	12-27-07	.278	.373	.383	37	153	133	24	37	10	2	0	14	11	9	0	0	29	13	3	7.2	19.0
Frias, Jealmy	S-R	5-11	155	3-8-08	.138	.282	.215	23	78	65	10	9	1	2	0	6	11	2	0	0	21	6	1	14.1	26.9
Garcia, Isaac	R-R	5-11	163	9-12-07	.275	.365	.399	43	159	138	21	38	10	2	1	24	13	7	0	1	13	5	0	8.2	8.2
Guadamuz, Omar	R-R	5-9	170	10-23-07	.212	.388	.327	19	68	52	8	11	3	0	1	9	11	4	0	0	23	6	1	16.2	33.8
Martinez, Jose	L-R	5-8	150	10-5-07	.328	.469	.344	25	82	64	20	21	1	0	0	6	17	0	1	0	15	7	4	20.7	18.3
Munoz, Diego	R-R	6-0	174	4-29-08	.208	.453	.287	40	150	101	24	21	5	0	1	14	37	10	0	2	23	7	1	24.7	15.3

CINCINNATI REDS

	B-T	Ht.	Wt.	DOB	AVG	OBP	SLG	G	AB	R	H	2B	3B	HR	RBI	BB	SO	SB	CS	OPS	BB%
Ouanyou, Jordan	L-L	6-1	192	10-29-07	.196	.231	.239	15	52	46	4	9	2	0	0	4	3	0	0	3	17	0	0	5.8	32.7
Pena, Abel	R-R	6-2	198	1-24-08	.181	.307	.208	24	88	72	8	13	2	0	0	7	10	4	0	2	21	0	0	11.4	23.9
Reyes, Rey	L-R	5-8	163	1-7-08	.148	.378	.148	11	37	27	3	4	0	0	0	5	9	1	0	0	12	3	1	24.3	32.4
Rosillo, Erndys	L-R	6-0	170	8-4-06	.257	.303	.327	34	122	113	12	29	6	1	0	16	8	0	0	1	19	0	0	6.6	15.6
Salio, Angel	L-R	6-2	170	2-16-08	.331	.402	.507	42	169	148	29	49	9	7	1	23	19	0	0	2	17	14	1	11.2	10.1
Torres, Enry	L-R	5-10	167	3-8-08	.232	.372	.274	31	122	95	14	22	1	0	1	10	22	1	0	3	15	3	1	18.0	12.3

Pitching	B-T	Ht.	Wt.	DOB	W	L	ERA	G	GS	SV	IP	Hits	Runs	ER	HR	BB	SO	AVG	OBP	SLG	SO%	BB%	BF
Alberto, Starlin	R-R	6-1	185	1-1-08	1	5	11.50	15	0	0	18	11	25	23	1	34	27	.183	.485	.267	27.3	34.3	99
Almeida, Jhan	R-R	6-3	185	4-29-05	0	0	5.63	3	3	0	8	9	6	5	0	5	4	.290	.389	.419	11.1	13.9	36
Aquino, Anthony	R-R	6-2	180	4-25-06	0	1	18.69	9	0	0	9	16	25	18	0	17	10	.364	.569	.455	15.4	26.2	65
Barboza, Angel	R-R	5-9	173	11-29-06	0	0	0.00	1	0	0	0	0	0	0	0	0	0	.000	.000	.000	0.0	0.0	1
Burgos, Deivid	R-R	6-2	190	4-19-05	3	1	6.23	13	1	0	26	21	27	18	1	23	16	.216	.398	.268	12.4	17.8	129
Cabeza, Johan	R-R	6-0	155	7-25-06	0	1	3.90	12	11	0	30	31	14	13	0	11	30	.267	.333	.362	23.1	8.5	130
Castillo, Moises	R-R	5-10	172	5-23-05	2	4	3.51	13	10	0	51	40	22	20	2	26	58	.209	.315	.304	26.1	11.7	222
Concepcion, Rayly	R-R	6-0	160	12-4-04	1	0	5.56	8	0	2	11	16	12	7	2	10	10	.348	.467	.630	16.7	16.7	60
Cruz, Luis	R-R	6-3	175	8-21-06	1	0	8.22	6	0	1	8	12	10	7	0	9	4	.343	.478	.457	8.7	19.6	46
Diaz, Dennis	R-R	6-3	198	9-10-05	0	2	7.71	9	6	0	26	28	25	22	2	27	15	.277	.442	.426	10.8	19.4	139
Diaz, Jorge	L-L	6-4	187	7-14-07	5	0	4.79	14	0	0	21	15	11	11	1	16	18	.200	.396	.280	17.6	15.7	102
Gil, Michael	R-R	6-2	170	3-14-05	2	2	6.45	15	0	4	22	23	20	16	1	12	20	.267	.354	.360	20.2	12.1	99
Lugo, Edgar	R-R	6-3	183	10-8-07	0	0	13.50	3	0	0	3	1	4	4	0	4	4	.111	.429	.111	28.6	28.6	14
Marchan, Manuel	R-R	6-3	165	3-28-07	0	5	7.92	10	7	0	25	24	24	22	1	33	24	.273	.476	.386	19.4	26.6	124
Marte, Jefersson	R-R	6-0	170	4-18-08	1	1	11.15	9	0	0	15	14	24	19	2	18	13	.259	.447	.444	16.7	23.1	78
Nino, Dulger	R-R	6-1	185	12-29-04	2	1	4.86	14	0	2	17	11	10	9	1	15	19	.180	.351	.246	24.7	19.5	77
Perez, Anderson	R-R	6-1	170	3-9-06	0	1	0.00	3	0	0	4	2	1	0	0	4	3	.154	.353	.154	17.6	23.5	17
Pinales, Julio	R-R	6-6	168	8-29-06	1	0	1.50	6	0	0	6	1	1	1	1	5	4	.063	.318	.250	18.2	22.7	22
Redona, Iker	L-L	5-11	170	12-5-07	0	1	0.92	12	6	0	29	17	5	3	1	3	38	.167	.198	.216	35.8	2.8	106
Talavera, Enmanuel	R-R	6-2	170	10-7-05	0	1	2.84	5	5	0	19	16	6	6	2	8	23	.235	.316	.382	30.3	10.5	76
Villa, Sergio	R-R	6-2	155	10-20-05	2	2	5.65	12	3	2	29	25	19	18	4	17	28	.229	.336	.404	21.7	13.2	129
Yepes, Luis	R-R	6-4	180	3-24-06	2	2	8.61	10	1	0	23	29	31	22	2	19	17	.319	.453	.473	14.5	16.2	117

Fielding

C: Torres 28, Rosillo 12, Barboza 9, Pena 4. **1B:** Rosillo 21, Pena 19, Ouanyou 15. **2B:** Feliciano 32, Caricipe 16, Guadamuz 6, Frias 1. **3B:** Salio 33, Guadamuz 11, Caricipe 9. **SS:** Aponte 41, Salio 8, Feliciano 4, Caricipe 1. **LF:** Garcia 31, Martinez 9, Munoz 8, Frias 6, Reyes 2. **CF:** De La Cruz 36, Martinez 13, Frias 5, Reyes 3. **RF:** Munoz 30, Garcia 12, Frias 8, Martinez 3, Reyes 3

Cleveland Guardians

SEASON SYNOPSIS: Sporting one of baseball's worst offenses, the Guardians somehow staged one of the greatest comebacks in baseball history to win the AL Central for the third time in four seasons and second straight time under second-year manager Stephen Vogt. After chasing down the Tigers in the Division, though, the Guardians lost a three-game wild-card set at home to Detroit.

HIGH POINT: Cleveland trailed the Tigers by 15½ games in July and by 11 games on Sept. 4, when it fell to 69-70, before the true comeback began. The Guardians won 17 of 19, a span that included five wins against reeling Detroit. The club turned to a six-man rotation, and in that 19-game span, Guards starters posted a 1.35 ERA over 120 innings. One highlight was a doubleheader shutout in Minnesota with Logan Allen (8 IP) and Slade Cecconi (7 IP) giving the bullpen a break; another was a Sept. 23 Gavin Williams outing when he struck out 12 in six innings to outduel Tarik Skubal in a 5-2 victory.

LOW POINT: The offense ranked 28th in the majors in runs scored, and during a 10-game losing streak from June 26-July 6, the Guardians were shut out four times while scoring 15 runs total in the streak.

NOTABLE ROOKIES: Lefties Joey Cantillo (5-3, 3.21) and Parker Messick (3-1, 2.72 in seven starts) served as two key pieces in the club's September turn to a six-man rotation. OF/1B C.J. Kayfus (.220/.292/.415) provided a late offensive jolt.

KEY TRANSACTIONS: Cleveland took two huge roster hits in July as two key pitchers were placed on leave due to separate gambling investigations. Luis Ortiz, acquired in the offseason in a three-team trade that sent Andres Gimenez from Cleveland to Toronto, made his last start June 27 before his investigation sidelined him. Closer Emmanuel Clase was placed on leave after working both ends of a July 26 doubleheader, and neither returned to the mound the rest of the season. In the offseason, Cleveland traded Josh Naylor to Arizona and replaced him at first base with the third Cleveland stint of Carlos Santana. The veteran hit just .225/.316/.333 before being released on Aug. 28. Instead of adding at the deadline like a contender would, the Guards traded their rehabbing one-time Cy Young Award winner, Shane Bieber, to Toronto for prospect RHP Khal Stephen.

OPENING DAY PAYROLL: $100,522,729 (25th)

PLAYERS OF THE YEAR

MAJOR LEAGUE
Jose Ramirez
3B
.283/.360/.503
30 HR, 44 SB, 66 BB
7x all-star; 5 in a row

MINOR LEAGUE
Parker Messick
LHP
(AAA)
3.47 ERA in 98.2 IP
Made MLB debut

ORGANIZATION LEADERS

Batting		*Qualifiers
MAJORS		
* AVG	Jose Ramirez	.283
* OPS	Jose Ramirez	.863
HR	Jose Ramirez	30
RBI	Jose Ramirez	85
MINORS		
* AVG	Johnathan Rodriguez, Columbus	.312
* OBP	Johnathan Rodriguez, Columbus	.397
* SLG	C.J. Kayfus, Columbus/Akron	.539
* OPS	C.J. Kayfus, Columbus/Akron	.930
R	Petey Halpin, Columbus	86
H	Ralphy Velazquez, Akron/Lake County	128
TB	Ralphy Velazquez, Akron/Lake County	240
2B	Jose Devers, Lake County	36
2B	Cooper Ingle, Columbus/Akron	36
3B	Ralphy Velazquez, Akron/Lake County	9
HR	Ralphy Velazquez, Akron/Lake County	22
RBI	Ralphy Velazquez, Akron/Lake County	85
BB	Cooper Ingle, Columbus/Akron	86
SO	Milan Tolentino, Columbus	158
SB	Tommy Hawke, Lake County/Lynchburg	65

Pitching		#Qualifiers
MAJORS		
W	Tanner Bibee	12
W	Gavin Williams	12
# ERA	Gavin Williams	3.06
SO	Gavin Williams	173
SV	Emmanuel Clase	24
MINORS		
W	Yorman Gomez, Akron/Lake County	12
L	Jackson Humphries, Lake County	10
# ERA	Josh Hartle, Akron/Lake County	2.54
G	Parker Mushinski, Columbus	46
GS	Austin Peterson, Columbus/Akron	26
GS	Jackson Humphries, Lake County	26
SV	Jack Jasiak, Akron/Lake County	13
IP	Austin Peterson, Columbus/Akron	146
BB	Jackson Humphries, Lake County	91
SO	Yorman Gomez, Akron/Lake County	139
# AVG	Yorman Gomez, Akron/Lake County	.207

2025 PERFORMANCE

President: Chris Antonetti. **Farm Director:** Stephen Osterer. **Scouting Director:** Ethan Purser.

Class	Team	League	W	L	PCT	Finish	Manager
Majors	Cleveland Guardians	American	88	74	.543	5 (15)	Stephen Vogt
Triple-A	Columbus Clippers	International	64	81	.441	13 (20)	Andy Tracy
Double-A	Akron RubberDucks	Eastern	77	60	.562	3 (12)	Greg DiCenzo
High-A	Lake County Captains	Midwest	74	58	.561	2 (12)	Omir Santos
Low-A	Lynchburg Hillcats	Carolina	70	59	.543	1 (12)	Jordan Smith
Rookie	ACL Guardians	Arizona Complex	31	29	.517	8 (15)	Juan De La Cruz
Rookie	DSL CLE Goryl	Dominican	31	25	.554	17 (52)	Mac Seibert
Rookie	DSL CLE Mendoza	Dominican	19	36	.345	47 (52)	Jonathan Lopez
Overall 2025 Minor League Record			366	348	.513	11th (30)	

ORGANIZATION STATISTICS

CLEVELAND GUARDIANS
AMERICAN LEAGUE

Batting	B-T	Ht.	Wt.	DOB	AVG	OBP	SLG	G	PA	AB	R	H	2B	3B	HR	RBI	BB	HBP	SH	SF	SO	SB	CS	BB%	SO%
Arias, Gabriel	R-R	6-1	217	2-27-00	.220	.274	.363	129	471	432	44	95	25	2	11	54	27	7	1	4	162	8	4	5.7	34.4
Brennan, Will	L-L	6-0	200	2-2-98	.091	.231	.091	6	13	11	0	1	0	0	0	0	1	0	0	0	1	0	1	7.7	7.7
Fry, David	R-R	6-0	215	11-20-95	.171	.229	.363	66	157	146	16	25	4	0	8	23	9	2	0	0	58	1	0	5.7	36.9
Halpin, Petey	L-R	6-0	200	5-26-02	.333	.500	.333	6	8	6	5	2	0	0	0	2	0	0	0	0	2	0	0	25.0	25.0
Hedges, Austin	R-R	6-1	223	8-18-92	.161	.250	.277	70	180	155	13	25	3	0	5	10	18	1	4	2	43	1	2	10.0	23.9
Jones, Nolan	L-R	6-4	195	5-7-98	.211	.296	.304	136	403	355	34	75	14	2	5	34	39	5	1	3	113	8	3	9.7	28.0
Kayfus, C.J.	L-L	6-0	188	10-28-01	.220	.292	.415	44	138	123	16	27	10	1	4	19	11	2	1	1	38	4	0	8.0	27.5
Kwan, Steven	L-L	5-9	170	9-5-97	.272	.330	.374	156	693	625	81	170	29	1	11	56	55	3	3	7	60	21	5	7.9	8.7
Manzardo, Kyle	L-R	6-0	205	7-18-00	.234	.313	.455	142	531	470	47	110	19	2	27	70	48	8	0	5	135	2	0	9.0	25.4
Martinez, Angel	S-R	6-0	200	1-27-02	.224	.269	.359	139	484	446	56	100	23	2	11	45	23	6	5	4	110	8	2	4.8	22.7
Naylor, Bo	L-R	6-0	205	2-21-00	.195	.282	.379	123	414	359	46	70	22	1	14	47	45	1	3	6	99	1	2	10.9	23.9
Noel, Jhonkensy	R-R	6-3	250	7-15-01	.162	.183	.297	69	153	148	19	24	2	0	6	13	4	0	0	1	52	0	0	2.6	34.0
Nunez, Dom	L-R	5-8	212	1-17-95	.286	.286	.286	2	7	7	2	2	0	0	0	0	0	0	0	0	4	0	0	0.0	57.1
Ramirez, Jose	S-R	5-9	190	9-17-92	.283	.360	.503	158	673	593	103	168	34	3	30	85	66	8	0	5	74	44	7	9.8	11.0
Rocchio, Brayan	S-R	5-10	170	1-13-01	.233	.290	.340	115	383	344	34	80	18	2	5	44	22	8	4	5	77	8	4	5.7	20.1
Rodriguez, Johnathan	R-R	6-3	224	11-4-99	.197	.260	.366	31	77	71	6	14	4	1	2	10	6	0	0	0	22	1	0	7.8	28.6
Santana, Carlos	S-R	5-11	215	4-8-86	.225	.316	.333	116	455	396	49	89	10	0	11	52	52	3	0	4	86	7	0	11.4	18.9
Schneemann, Daniel	L-R	6-0	185	1-23-97	.206	.283	.354	131	422	379	48	78	18	1	12	41	38	3	1	1	117	9	3	9.0	27.7
Thomas, Lane	R-R	6-0	198	8-23-95	.160	.246	.272	39	142	125	10	20	2	0	4	11	14	1	0	2	44	4	1	9.9	31.0
Valera, George	L-L	6-0	195	11-13-00	.220	.333	.415	16	48	41	7	9	2	0	2	5	7	0	0	0	13	0	0	14.6	27.1
Wilson, Will	R-R	6-0	184	7-21-98	.202	.267	.244	34	91	78	7	15	4	0	2	9	10	1	2	0	34	2	0	7.7	37.4

Pitching	B-T	Ht.	Wt.	DOB	W	L	ERA	G	GS	SV	IP	Hits	Runs	ER	HR	BB	SO	AVG	OBP	SLG	SO%	BB%	BF
Allard, Kolby	L-L	6-1	195	8-13-97	2	2	2.63	33	2	0	65	64	22	19	5	14	42	.261	.300	.384	15.8	5.3	266
Allen, Logan	R-L	6-0	190	9-5-98	8	11	4.25	30	29	0	157	157	84	74	18	62	122	.262	.334	.403	18.0	9.2	676
Bibee, Tanner	R-R	6-2	205	3-5-99	12	11	4.24	31	31	0	182	170	93	86	27	54	162	.246	.308	.412	21.3	7.1	762
Bolton, Cody	R-R	6-3	230	6-19-98	0	0	13.50	1	0	0	2	4	3	3	0	0	1	.400	.400	.500	10.0	0.0	10
Cantillo, Joey	L-L	6-4	225	12-18-99	5	3	3.21	34	13	1	95	78	39	34	10	42	108	.218	.299	.353	26.9	10.5	401
Cecconi, Slade	R-R	6-4	219	6-24-99	7	7	4.30	23	23	0	132	125	66	63	24	32	109	.247	.294	.451	20.0	5.9	545
Clase, Emmanuel	R-R	6-2	206	3-18-98	5	3	3.23	48	0	24	47	46	20	17	2	12	47	.256	.310	.344	23.4	6.0	201
Enright, Nic	R-R	6-3	205	1-8-97	2	1	2.03	27	0	1	31	24	8	7	3	12	30	.212	.299	.319	23.6	9.4	127
Festa, Matt	R-R	6-1	195	3-11-93	5	4	4.12	63	0	0	55	44	29	25	4	15	56	.221	.288	.322	24.8	6.6	226
Gaddis, Hunter	R-R	6-6	260	4-9-98	2	2	3.11	73	0	3	67	58	24	23	8	21	73	.234	.294	.383	26.6	7.7	274
Hedges, Austin	R-R	6-1	223	8-18-92	0	0	6.00	3	0	0	3	6	2	2	0	1	1	.429	.438	.571	6.3	6.3	16
Hernandez, Carlos	R-R	6-4	245	3-11-97	0	0	3.86	5	0	0	7	4	3	3	0	3	3	.167	.259	.208	11.1	11.1	27
Herrin, Tim	L-L	6-6	230	10-8-96	5	4	4.85	54	0	0	43	37	23	23	5	30	45	.239	.376	.387	23.2	15.5	194
Junis, Jakob	R-R	6-3	220	9-16-92	4	1	2.97	57	0	0	67	64	24	22	5	18	55	.257	.315	.378	20.1	6.6	274
Kent, Zak	R-R	6-3	208	2-24-98	1	0	4.58	12	0	0	18	17	10	9	1	8	16	.254	.342	.328	21.1	10.5	76
Lively, Ben	R-R	6-4	235	3-5-92	2	2	3.22	9	9	0	45	38	16	16	6	15	29	.233	.298	.393	16.3	8.4	178
McKenzie, Triston	R-R	6-5	165	8-2-97	0	0	11.12	4	0	0	6	7	7	7	1	7	4	.318	.467	.545	13.3	23.3	30
Messick, Parker	L-L	6-0	225	10-26-00	3	1	2.72	7	7	0	40	46	12	12	6	6	38	.289	.315	.409	23.0	3.6	165
Nikhazy, Doug	L-L	6-0	210	8-11-99	0	1	13.50	2	1	0	4	5	6	6	0	6	5	.294	.478	.529	21.7	26.1	23
Ortiz, Luis	R-R	6-2	240	1-27-99	4	9	4.36	16	16	0	89	80	44	43	12	42	96	.237	.322	.386	25.1	11.0	382
Sabrowski, Erik	R-L	6-4	235	10-31-97	0	1	1.84	33	0	0	29	14	8	6	2	21	42	.144	.257	.237	34.7	17.4	121
Sewald, Paul	R-R	6-3	219	5-26-90	1	1	4.70	18	0	2	15	14	9	8	3	4	18	.246	.290	.439	29.0	6.5	62
Smith, Cade	R-R	6-5	230	5-9-99	8	5	2.93	76	0	16	74	55	31	24	4	19	104	.201	.261	.328	34.7	6.3	300
Walters, Andrew	R-R	6-4	220	12-8-00	0	0	13.50	2	0	0	1	2	2	2	1	0	2	.333	.333	1.000	33.3	0.0	6
Williams, Gavin	R-R	6-6	250	7-26-99	12	5	3.06	31	31	0	168	130	62	57	23	83	173	.211	.307	.364	24.6	11.8	704
Wilson, Will	R-R	6-0	184	7-21-98	0	0	9.00	1	0	0	2	2	2	2	1	0	0	.250	.250	.750	0.0	0.0	8

Fielding

Catcher	PCT	G	PO	A	E	DP	PB
Hedges	.998	67	471	21	1	3	0
Naylor	.993	119	931	58	7	9	3
Nunez	1.000	2	10	0	0	0	0

First Base	PCT	G	PO	A	E	DP
Kayfus	.980	17	91	6	2	11
Manzardo	.990	56	372	24	4	33
Noel	1.000	9	37	3	0	5
Santana	.997	96	694	49	2	57

Second Base	PCT	G	PO	A	E	DP
Arias	1.000	28	30	44	0	11
Martinez	.953	37	46	56	5	14

Rocchio	.979	50	73	118	4	18	
Schneemann	.991	74	88	136	2	37	
Wilson	.970	17	15	17	1	3	

Third Base	PCT	G	PO	A	E	DP
Arias	.909	8	7	3	1	0
Ramirez	.961	134	82	235	13	21
Santana	.000	1	0	0	0	0
Schneemann	1.000	27	8	22	0	0
Wilson	.949	15	13	24	2	0

Shortstop	PCT	G	PO	A	E	DP
Arias	.966	106	136	239	13	48
Rocchio	.963	72	77	129	8	32

Schneemann	1.000	11	4	13	0	1

Outfield	PCT	G	PO	A	E	DP
Brennan	1.000	5	8	1	0	1
Halpin	1.000	5	2	0	0	0
Jones	.995	149	212	8	1	1
Kayfus	1.000	29	47	0	0	0
Kwan	.976	153	309	13	8	2
Martinez	.979	118	226	4	5	0
Noel	1.000	61	77	4	0	2
Rodriguez	.929	28	39	0	3	0
Schneemann	1.000	44	67	2	0	0
Thomas	.989	40	89	3	1	0
Valera	1.000	5	5	0	0	0

COLUMBUS CLIPPERS — TRIPLE-A
INTERNATIONAL LEAGUE

Batting	B-T	Ht.	Wt.	DOB	AVG	OBP	SLG	G	PA	AB	R	H	2B	3B	HR	RBI	BB	HBP	SH	SF	SO	SB	CS	BB%	SO%
Anchia, Jake	R-R	5-10	210	3-5-97	.215	.268	.338	19	71	65	6	14	0	0	2	10	4	1	0	1	26	0	0	5.6	36.6
Arias, Gabriel	R-R	6-1	217	2-27-00	.308	.438	.538	4	16	13	1	4	0	0	1	1	3	0	0	0	3	0	1	18.8	18.8
Bazzana, Travis	L-R	5-9	170	8-28-02	.225	.420	.438	26	120	89	21	20	3	2	4	14	29	1	1	0	32	2	1	24.2	26.7
Boyd, Justin	R-R	6-0	201	3-30-01	.083	.290	.083	9	32	24	5	2	0	0	0	1	5	2	1	0	10	0	0	15.6	31.3
Brennan, Will	L-L	6-0	200	2-2-98	.304	.340	.419	35	156	148	19	45	8	0	3	18	8	0	0	0	20	2	1	5.1	12.8
Brito, Juan	S-R	5-11	162	9-24-01	.256	.357	.463	24	99	82	15	21	6	1	3	15	13	1	1	2	21	4	2	13.1	21.2
Cairo, Christian	R-R	5-8	170	6-11-01	.237	.338	.331	112	416	354	56	84	21	3	2	28	45	11	2	4	97	33	7	10.8	23.3
Datres, Kyle	R-R	6-0	205	1-5-96	.204	.311	.292	39	135	113	11	23	4	0	2	9	18	1	0	3	36	1	2	13.3	26.7
DeLauter, Chase	L-L	6-4	235	10-8-01	.278	.383	.476	34	149	126	25	35	8	1	5	21	22	0	0	1	23	0	0	14.8	15.4
Dernedde, Kyle	R-R	5-8	183	11-8-00	.000	.000	.000	1	1	1	0	0	0	0	0	0	0	0	0	0	1	0	0	0.0	100.0
Frias, Dayan	S-R	5-9	140	6-25-02	.203	.269	.266	48	176	158	21	32	7	0	1	10	15	0	1	2	41	7	4	8.5	23.3
Fry, David	R-R	6-0	215	11-20-95	.167	.231	.417	3	13	12	1	2	0	0	1	3	1	0	0	0	3	0	0	7.7	23.1
Halpin, Petey	L-R	6-0	200	5-26-02	.249	.321	.414	126	553	493	86	123	29	5	14	44	51	3	0	5	156	15	3	9.2	28.2
Huff, Kody	R-R	5-10	198	12-11-00	.222	.301	.330	101	407	361	31	80	19	1	6	47	37	5	2	2	104	3	3	9.1	25.6
Ingle, Cooper	L-R	5-10	185	2-23-02	.207	.383	.329	28	107	82	13	17	7	0	1	6	21	3	0	1	21	3	0	19.6	14.0
Kayfus, C.J.	L-L	6-0	188	10-28-01	.283	.367	.526	68	289	251	39	71	14	4	13	43	33	2	0	3	79	2	1	11.4	27.3
Lampe, Joe	L-R	5-11	185	12-5-00	.185	.241	.296	8	30	27	1	5	1	1	0	4	2	0	1	0	8	2	1	6.7	26.7
Leon, David	L-R	5-11	156	2-2-04	.200	.333	.200	4	12	10	0	2	0	0	0	0	2	0	0	0	5	0	0	16.7	50.0
Lipscomb, Guy	L-R	6-2	195	3-11-01	.250	.308	.250	6	13	12	2	3	0	0	0	0	1	0	0	0	2	1	0	0.0	15.4
Martinez, Angel	S-R	6-0	200	1-27-02	.344	.324	.531	8	34	32	7	11	6	0	0	8	0	0	0	2	9	1	0	0.0	26.5
Noel, Jhonkensy	R-R	6-3	250	7-15-01	.273	.337	.493	61	252	227	22	62	14	0	12	39	21	2	0	2	67	1	1	8.3	26.6
Nunez, Dom	L-R	5-8	212	11-4-99	.312	.397	.515	87	373	324	48	101	16	1	16	66	43	4	0	2	86	0	2	11.5	23.1
Pries, Micah	L-R	6-3	210	2-27-98	.139	.230	.307	28	114	101	16	14	1	2	4	10	10	2	1	0	27	2	2	8.8	23.7
Rocchio, Brayan	S-R	5-10	170	1-13-01	.252	.353	.484	41	188	159	26	40	12	2	7	30	23	3	1	2	27	7	3	12.2	14.4
Rodriguez, Johnathan	R-R	6-3	224	11-4-99	.312	.397	.515	87	373	324	48	101	16	1	16	66	43	4	0	2	86	0	2	11.5	23.1
Thomas, Lane	R-R	6-0	198	8-23-95	.333	.370	.667	7	27	24	7	8	2	0	2	5	2	0	0	1	6	1	1	7.4	22.2
Tolentino, Milan	L-R	6-1	185	11-17-01	.216	.314	.437	121	460	394	58	85	20	2	21	66	55	4	2	5	158	20	6	12.0	34.3
Valdes, Yordys	S-R	5-10	170	8-16-01	.187	.225	.302	90	337	315	31	59	17	2	5	28	13	3	3	3	108	10	2	3.9	32.0
Valera, George	L-L	6-0	195	11-13-00	.255	.346	.457	28	107	94	11	24	6	2	3	10	13	0	0	0	27	0	0	12.1	25.2
Watson, Kahlil	L-R	5-10	178	4-16-03	.255	.358	.477	43	176	149	23	38	7	1	8	25	22	5	0	0	47	10	2	12.5	26.7
Wilson, Will	R-R	6-0	184	7-21-98	.246	.325	.435	70	292	260	38	64	12	2	11	35	28	3	0	1	65	4	3	9.6	22.3

Pitching	B-T	Ht.	Wt.	DOB	W	L	ERA	G	GS	SV	IP	Hits	Runs	ER	HR	BB	SO	AVG	OBP	SLG	SO%	BB%	BF
Aleman, Franco	R-R	6-6	235	6-26-00	2	5	7.85	37	0	5	37	41	33	32	4	24	57	.281	.385	.425	32.6	13.7	175
Allard, Kolby	L-L	6-1	195	8-13-97	0	0	4.86	4	4	0	17	16	9	9	5	5	13	.250	.300	.453	18.6	7.1	70
Bolton, Cody	R-R	6-3	230	6-19-98	1	1	4.50	4	0	0	4	4	2	2	0	0	5	.250	.250	.313	31.3	0.0	16
Burns, Tanner	R-R	6-0	210	12-28-98	3	1	5.86	24	0	0	35	36	26	23	4	19	28	.267	.353	.393	17.7	12.0	158
Cantillo, Joey	L-L	6-4	225	12-18-99	0	1	5.06	6	6	0	21	18	12	12	1	3	8	.272	.325	.388	30.3	9.0	89
Carver, Ross	R-R	6-2	205	8-27-99	0	0	15.00	4	0	0	6	12	10	10	5	4	10	.400	.486	1.000	28.6	11.4	35
Cecconi, Slade	R-R	6-4	219	6-24-99	0	2	4.85	3	3	0	13	12	7	7	0	2	10	.255	.275	.298	19.6	3.9	51
Davenport, Aaron	R-R	6-0	185	7-25-00	4	7	5.23	20	16	0	93	92	55	54	11	55	77	.262	.374	.447	18.5	13.2	417
Denholm, Trenton	R-R	6-2	210	3-27-00	0	1	8.10	1	1	0	3	3	3	3	0	1	2	.231	.267	.385	20.0	6.7	15
Dion, Will	L-L	5-10	180	4-17-00	4	8	4.09	31	13	1	99	109	53	45	9	37	96	.279	.338	.427	22.1	8.5	434
Enright, Nic	R-R	6-3	205	1-8-97	0	0	1.38	13	0	1	13	7	4	2	0	7	12	.163	.280	.186	24.0	14.0	50
Espino, Daniel	R-R	6-2	205	1-5-01	0	0	40.50	1	1	0	0	3	3	3	0	1	0	.600	.600	.600	0.0	0.0	5
Frias, Luis	R-R	6-3	245	5-23-98	2	0	3.00	30	0	4	36	38	17	12	1	19	75	.273	.373	.374	21.7	11.8	161
Hanner, Bradley	R-R	6-4	210	2-10-99	4	4	4.74	42	0	2	49	45	28	26	13	25	62	.249	.360	.497	29.0	11.7	214
Hernandez, Carlos	R-R	6-4	245	3-11-97	0	0	4.70	7	0	1	8	6	4	4	1	2	9	.207	.258	.345	29.0	6.5	31
Herrin, Tim	L-L	6-6	230	10-8-96	0	0	3.38	8	0	1	8	10	3	3	1	2	9	.323	.364	.452	27.3	6.1	33
Hickman, Mason	R-R	6-8	228	12-23-98	1	2	9.28	12	1	0	21	34	23	22	3	19	22	.304	.447	.456	21.2	18.3	104
Jacobs, Zach	R-R	6-1	170	9-9-01	0	0	16.20	1	0	0	2	6	3	3	0	2	2	.286	.500	.286	20.0	20.0	10
Kent, Zak	R-R	6-3	208	12-24-97	2	3	2.84	34	0	2	38	30	12	12	2	21	50	.221	.330	.316	31.4	13.2	159
Krook, Matt	L-L	6-4	225	10-21-94	2	0	3.18	30	0	0	34	18	13	12	2	24	40	.158	.324	.281	28.2	16.9	142
Leftwich, Jack	R-R	6-4	220	9-26-98	2	0	4.50	22	0	0	26	16	14	13	4	18	22	.255	.372	.402	18.2	14.9	121
Leon, David	L-R	5-11	156	2-2-04	0	0	18.00	1	0	0	1	3	2	2	0	0	0	.500	.500	1.167	0.0	0.0	6

Player	B-T	Ht	Wt	DOB	G	GS	IP	H	R	ER	HR	BB	SO	AVG	OBP	SLG	K/9	BB/9	SO
Mace, Tommy	R-R	6-6	230	11-11-98	1	0	4.05	9	0	0	13	11	6	6	2	8	13	.229	.333 .417 22.8 14.0 57
McKenzie, Triston	R-R	6-5	165	8-2-97	0	1	7.71	8	0	0	7	4	7	6	0	17	11	.167	.512 .167 25.6 39.5 43
Means, John	L-L	6-4	230	4-24-93	0	2	7.97	5	5	0	20	20	19	18	7	10	15	.256	.344 .590 16.7 11.1 90
Messick, Parker	L-L	6-0	225	10-26-00	5	6	3.47	20	20	0	99	78	39	38	9	42	119	.216	.304 .346 29.1 10.3 409
Mikolajchak, Nick	R-R	6-2	215	11-21-97	1	2	4.75	26	0	4	30	29	19	16	6	19	25	.250	.353 .466 18.4 14.0 136
Miller, Jake	R-R	6-2	210	7-14-00	0	3	4.96	11	2	0	16	20	13	9	2	11	11	.317	.421 .508 14.5 14.5 76
Misiaszek, Andrew	R-L	6-2	215	8-24-97	1	1	7.31	23	0	2	28	35	24	23	4	18	27	.294	.396 .420 19.4 12.9 139
Mushinski, Parker	L-L	6-0	218	11-22-95	6	5	3.78	46	0	7	50	43	24	21	2	33	66	.230	.347 .305 29.6 14.8 223
Nikhazy, Doug	L-L	6-0	210	8-11-99	5	7	5.02	21	19	1	86	89	52	48	15	43	87	.262	.346 .476 22.5 11.1 387
Peterson, Austin	R-R	6-6	234	9-19-99	4	4	4.27	17	15	0	91	94	44	43	10	30	78	.270	.334 .445 20.2 7.8 386
Rapp, Shawn	R-L	6-2	200	7-3-00	0	0	0.00	1	0	0	1	1	0	0	0	2	2	.333	.600 .333 40.0 40.0 5
Richardson, Alonzo	R-R	5-11	165	10-7-02	0	1	10.80	1	0	0	2	3	2	1	1	1	1	.400	.500 1.200 11.1 11.1 9
Sabrowski, Erik	R-L	6-4	235	10-31-97	0	0	5.14	6	0	1	7	6	5	4	1	5	9	.231	.375 .385 28.1 15.6 32
Sewald, Paul	R-R	6-3	219	5-26-90	0	0	0.00	1	0	0	1	0	0	0	0	0	2	.000	.000 .000 66.7 0.0 3
Spivey, Carter	R-R	6-1	193	10-13-99	0	0	4.26	3	0	0	6	3	3	3	1	3	6	.150	.261 .350 26.1 13.0 23
Stephan, Trevor	R-R	6-5	225	11-25-95	1	2	11.65	19	0	0	17	26	22	22	8	11	16	.351	.444 .757 17.8 12.2 90
Velasquez, Vince	R-R	6-3	212	6-7-92	5	4	3.42	18	18	0	82	71	35	31	8	50	95	.236	.349 .395 26.8 14.1 355
Walters, Andrew	R-R	6-4	220	12-8-00	0	0	1.50	12	0	0	12	5	3	2	0	9	23	.125	.280 .175 46.0 18.0 50
Webb, Ryan	L-L	6-1	202	4-19-99	8	7	4.15	28	21	0	121	100	61	56	12	61	119	.227	.330 .361 22.8 11.7 521

Fielding

Catcher	PCT	G	PO	A	E	DP	PB
Anchia	.990	10	94	5	1	0	0
Huff	.989	79	758	39	9	3	4
Ingle	.987	18	142	6	2	0	1
Leon	1.000	2	16	0	0	0	0
Nunez	.994	38	339	18	2	1	4

First Base	PCT	G	PO	A	E	DP
Brito	1.000	5	30	2	0	3
Datres	.995	29	179	12	1	16
Frias	.995	31	197	17	1	21
Huff	1.000	2	10	0	0	0
Kayfus	.991	36	221	11	2	20
Noel	1.000	26	173	15	0	24
Nunez	1.000	14	93	5	0	9
Pries	1.000	13	95	2	0	12

Second Base	PCT	G	PO	A	E	DP
Bazzana	.989	23	30	56	1	12
Brito	1.000	17	27	40	0	10
Cairo	.991	26	58	51	1	12
Datres	1.000	1	1	1	0	0

Third Base	PCT	G	PO	A	E	DP
Dernedde	1.000	1	2	0	0	0
Frias	.962	7	9	16	1	6
Martinez	1.000	2	5	5	0	2
Rocchio	1.000	4	9	9	0	4
Tolentino	.993	34	64	79	1	25
Valdes	.980	28	35	65	2	13
Wilson	.967	7	13	16	1	2

Third Base	PCT	G	PO	A	E	DP
Cairo	.919	32	24	55	7	11
Datres	.833	3	0	5	1	1
Frias	1.000	6	7	11	0	1
Rocchio	1.000	4	3	9	0	2
Tolentino	.955	32	23	41	3	6
Valdes	.959	18	15	32	2	6
Wilson	.980	54	41	105	3	16

Shortstop	PCT	G	PO	A	E	DP
Arias	1.000	4	6	9	0	2
Cairo	.957	16	19	25	2	4
Frias	1.000	3	4	8	0	1
Rocchio	.925	34	29	70	8	14

	PCT	G	PO	A	E	DP
Tolentino	.993	48	54	97	1	23
Valdes	.979	43	39	101	3	17
Wilson	1.000	2	0	3	0	0

Outfield	PCT	G	PO	A	E	DP
Boyd	1.000	9	12	0	0	0
Brennan	.958	33	67	2	3	0
Cairo	.986	36	68	3	1	2
DeLauter	.981	26	50	3	1	0
Halpin	.997	124	271	19	1	2
Kayfus	.986	34	68	4	5	1	1
Lampe	1.000	8	13	1	0	0
Lipscomb	1.000	4	2	0	0	0
Martinez	1.000	6	8	1	0	0
Noel	1.000	27	45	1	0	0
Pries	1.000	7	13	0	0	0
Rodriguez	.978	77	128	6	3	0
Thomas	1.000	4	7	0	0	0
Valera	.971	19	34	0	1	0
Watson	.985	40	67	0	1	0

AKRON RUBBERDUCKS
EASTERN LEAGUE
DOUBLE-A

Batting	B-T	Ht.	Wt.	DOB	AVG	OBP	SLG	G	PA	AB	R	H	2B	3B	HR	RBI	BB	HBP	SH	SF	SO	SB	CS	BB%	SO%
Advincula, Jonah	L-R	6-1	197	1-6-01	.187	.301	.228	42	148	123	18	23	5	0	0	11	20	1	2	2	24	17	1	13.5	16.2
Antunez, Wuilfredo	L-R	6-0	150	5-16-02	.301	.333	.528	31	133	127	17	37	10	3	4	21	6	1	0	2	26	5	1	4.5	19.5
Barstad, Cameron	L-R	6-1	195	11-29-00	.208	.290	.309	70	269	236	21	49	9	0	5	36	20	9	0	4	82	1	0	7.4	30.5
Bazzana, Travis	L-R	5-9	170	8-28-02	.256	.364	.426	51	228	195	43	50	12	3	5	23	29	4	0	0	55	9	1	12.7	24.1
Boyd, Justin	R-R	6-0	201	3-30-01	.208	.283	.250	15	53	48	4	10	2	0	0	2	4	1	0	0	23	0	0	7.5	43.4
Burgos, Jorge	L-L	5-10	165	12-26-01	.206	.295	.386	98	407	355	44	73	16	3	14	73	43	4	0	5	95	2	1	10.6	23.3
Cozart, Jacob	L-R	6-3	205	1-9-03	.256	.330	.390	21	94	82	13	21	3	1	2	11	8	2	0	2	24	0	0	8.5	25.5
Dernedde, Kyle	R-R	5-8	183	11-8-00	.256	.327	.279	15	49	43	4	11	1	0	0	4	5	0	0	1	16	1	0	10.2	32.7
Fox, Jake	L-R	5-11	185	2-12-03	.197	.321	.310	90	330	274	41	54	10	6	3	34	52	0	0	4	73	12	2	15.8	22.1
Frias, Dayan	S-R	5-9	140	6-25-02	.224	.347	.353	71	292	241	35	54	13	0	6	30	43	4	1	3	81	13	5	14.7	27.7
Fry, David	R-R	6-0	215	11-20-95	.111	.100	.111	3	10	9	0	1	0	0	0	0	2	0	0	1	3	0	0	0.0	30.0
Genao, Angel	S-R	5-9	150	5-19-04	.259	.323	.359	77	341	309	39	80	17	4	2	37	29	1	0	2	54	6	0	8.5	15.8
Ingle, Cooper	L-L	5-10	185	2-23-02	.273	.391	.441	92	403	333	55	91	29	0	9	49	65	1	1	3	70	0	2	16.1	17.4
Kayfus, C.J.	L-L	6-0	188	10-28-01	.364	.475	.591	18	80	66	12	24	4	4	1	11	11	3	0	0	14	2	1	13.8	17.5
Knapczyk, Christian	L-R	5-9	165	12-16-01	.242	.356	.293	25	118	99	13	24	3	1	0	10	17	1	0	1	21	0	2	14.4	17.8
Lampe, Joe	L-R	5-11	185	12-5-00	.234	.322	.397	109	450	393	57	92	24	5	10	59	45	7	3	2	107	17	2	10.0	23.8
Lipscomb, Guy	L-R	6-2	195	3-11-01	.243	.320	.353	94	372	329	47	80	19	1	5	39	36	2	3	2	63	20	6	9.7	16.9
Mooney, Alex	R-R	6-1	195	7-6-02	.200	.294	.288	115	442	375	49	75	19	1	4	37	47	6	6	8	129	25	4	10.6	29.2
Rivas, Kevin	S-R	5-7	128	4-7-03	.000	.000	.000	2	2	2	0	0	0	0	0	0	0	0	0	0	1	0	0	0.0	50.0
Rosario, Alfonsin	R-R	6-2	215	6-21-04	.211	.303	.391	33	145	128	20	27	6	1	5	17	15	2	0	0	48	2	1	10.3	33.1
Thomas, Lane	R-R	6-0	198	8-23-95	.000	.200	.000	3	10	8	0	0	0	0	0	0	2	0	0	0	4	0	0	10.0	40.0
Turcino, Michael	L-R	5-10	185	6-24-99	.116	.271	.174	24	85	69	8	8	2	1	0	4	14	1	0	1	32	0	1	16.5	37.6
Turner, Tyresse	S-R	5-10	170	1-5-00	.193	.315	.252	76	262	218	35	42	8	1	1	9	35	4	5	0	86	21	4	13.4	32.8
Valdes, Yordys	S-R	5-10	170	8-16-01	.000	.000	.000	3	12	11	0	0	0	0	0	0	1	0	0	1	2	0	0	0.0	16.7
Velazquez, Ralphy	L-R	6-2	220	5-28-05	.330	.405	.589	28	126	112	18	37	8	3	5	22	12	2	0	0	19	0	1	9.5	15.1
Watson, Kahlil	L-R	5-10	178	4-16-03	.247	.337	.461	59	253	219	30	54	13	5	8	36	26	5	1	2	72	7	5	10.3	28.5

CLEVELAND GUARDIANS

Pitching	B-T	Ht.	Wt.	DOB	W	L	ERA	G	GS	SV	IP	Hits	Runs	ER	HR	BB	SO	AVG	OBP	SLG	SO%	BB%	BF
Abney, Alaska	R-R	6-1	205	5-5-00	2	1	1.77	14	0	2	20	13	5	4	2	2	18	.181	.224	.278	23.4	2.6	77
Bieber, Shane	R-R	6-3	200	5-31-95	0	0	2.25	1	1	0	4	3	1	1	1	0	7	.231	.286	.462	50.0	0.0	14
Boone, Rodney	L-L	6-1	195	4-9-00	6	4	2.31	18	18	0	78	60	23	20	5	22	72	.211	.272	.316	22.9	7.0	315
Carver, Ross	R-R	6-2	205	8-27-99	3	2	3.40	31	1	2	50	45	20	19	4	29	47	.243	.359	.373	21.0	12.9	224
Davenport, Aaron	R-R	6-0	185	7-25-00	3	0	2.66	8	8	0	41	25	12	12	7	7	40	.170	.223	.333	25.3	4.4	158
DeLucia, Dylan	R-R	6-1	205	8-1-00	5	4	3.19	13	13	0	62	47	24	22	3	23	52	.208	.285	.296	20.6	9.1	253
Denholm, Trenton	R-R	5-11	180	11-29-99	11	7	3.77	26	18	1	127	125	67	53	14	26	109	.253	.294	.408	20.5	4.9	532
Ellerts, Magnus	R-R	6-5	225	3-15-01	2	0	4.71	32	0	5	42	33	23	22	3	34	63	.210	.356	.293	32.5	17.5	194
Gomez, Yorman	R-R	5-11	167	11-10-02	4	2	3.15	10	9	0	46	38	17	16	1	19	56	.215	.295	.277	28.0	9.5	200
Hartle, Josh	L-L	6-4	210	3-24-03	0	1	4.50	2	2	0	10	13	5	5	0	2	7	.325	.372	.375	16.3	4.7	43
Hernandez, Allan	R-R	6-5	205	1-19-01	0	0	0.00	5	0	0	5	3	0	0	0	8	1	.158	.407	.158	3.7	29.6	27
Jachec, Matt	R-R	6-0	205	7-25-01	2	2	2.66	19	0	4	24	25	11	7	1	7	20	.260	.311	.313	19.2	6.7	104
Jacobs, Zach	R-R	6-1	170	9-9-01	3	3	4.16	36	3	4	67	46	32	31	8	42	59	.201	.333	.389	20.9	14.9	282
Jasiak, Jack	R-R	6-1	198	3-6-01	1	1	4.02	9	0	0	16	16	8	7	1	6	17	.254	.314	.365	24.3	8.6	70
Leftwich, Jack	R-R	6-4	220	9-26-98	0	0	1.17	7	0	2	8	6	1	1	0	2	8	.207	.258	.241	25.8	6.5	31
Mace, Tommy	R-R	6-6	230	11-11-98	10	6	3.69	21	20	0	102	71	46	42	7	67	73	.204	.336	.307	17.1	15.7	428
Maltrud, Rorik	R-R	6-4	223	3-21-00	4	3	4.38	19	19	0	64	53	32	31	6	30	68	.226	.320	.329	25.2	11.1	270
Miller, Jake	R-R	6-2	210	7-14-00	6	1	2.17	31	0	2	50	34	16	12	2	11	45	.193	.247	.284	23.2	5.7	194
Morehouse, Zane	R-R	6-4	200	11-16-99	0	7	6.00	42	0	8	48	47	39	32	4	33	53	.261	.386	.361	23.8	14.8	223
Perez, Steven	L-L	6-0	155	4-21-01	2	2	2.20	27	0	2	49	35	12	12	4	16	47	.200	.269	.303	24.2	8.2	194
Peterson, Austin	R-R	6-6	234	9-19-99	4	2	1.47	11	11	0	55	36	14	9	5	10	49	.186	.229	.304	23.9	4.9	205
Rapp, Shawn	R-L	6-2	200	7-3-00	0	3	6.60	24	0	0	30	31	26	22	2	19	23	.267	.397	.422	16.1	13.3	143
Richardson, Yorman	R-R	5-11	165	10-7-02	0	0	3.60	4	0	0	10	13	4	4	0	3	8	.317	.364	.488	18.2	6.8	44
Sabrowski, Erik	R-L	6-4	235	10-31-97	0	0	0.00	1	0	0	1	0	0	0	0	1	2	.000	.500	.000	50.0	25.0	4
Sewald, Paul	R-R	6-3	219	5-26-90	0	0	6.00	3	1	0	3	4	2	2	1	0	3	.333	.333	.667	25.0	0.0	12
Sharpe, Davis	R-R	6-4	215	1-30-00	4	5	4.60	42	4	4	72	66	47	37	6	23	69	.245	.318	.368	22.5	7.5	307
Spivey, Carter	R-R	6-1	193	10-13-99	2	1	4.20	12	4	1	30	29	14	14	5	13	25	.269	.347	.500	18.4	10.4	125
Stanley, Hunter	R-R	5-11	203	11-25-97	0	0	0.00	2	0	0	2	1	0	0	0	2	.143	.143	.143	28.6	0.0	7
Stephan, Trevor	R-R	6-5	225	11-25-95	0	0	1.93	4	0	0	5	4	1	1	0	0	4	.235	.235	.412	23.5	0.0	17
Stephen, Khal	R-R	6-4	215	12-21-02	0	1	6.35	4	4	0	11	17	8	8	0	2	11	.347	.373	.408	21.6	3.9	51
Thornton, Tyler	L-R	6-3	200	7-8-00	2	1	5.00	29	0	0	36	19	21	20	5	27	43	.150	.333	.307	26.1	16.4	165
Tulloch, Adam	L-L	6-2	200	7-1-00	1	1	5.59	18	1	0	29	29	18	18	2	22	22	.257	.388	.398	15.8	15.8	139

Fielding

Catcher	PCT	G	PO	A	E	DP	PB
Barstad	.987	52	424	27	6	3	4
Cozart	.983	19	167	7	3	0	2
Ingle	.990	68	560	21	6	2	3
Rivas	.000	1	0	0	0	0	0

First Base	PCT	G	PO	A	E	DP
Advincula	.966	13	84	2	3	3
Boyd	1.000	1	4	0	0	1
Burgos	.995	86	587	45	3	58
Frias	1.000	1	6	1	0	0
Kayfus	1.000	11	76	5	0	9
Turner	1.000	8	40	4	0	3
Velazquez	.979	23	173	12	4	13

Second Base	PCT	G	PO	A	E	DP
Bazzana	.981	44	59	93	3	23
Dernedde	1.000	8	9	17	0	3

Third Base	PCT	G	PO	A	E	DP
Dernedde	1.000	5	5	3	0	0
Frias	.920	57	41	97	12	9
Knapczyk	1.000	2	2	1	0	0
Mooney	.930	44	37	69	8	7
Turner	.892	34	28	46	9	7

Shortstop	PCT	G	PO	A	E	DP
Dernedde	.909	3	6	4	1	0
Frias	.944	10	16	18	2	3
Genao	.958	72	81	147	10	30

Frias	1.000	2	5	1	0	1
Knapczyk	.971	23	34	67	3	9
Mooney	.971	23	52	49	3	16
Rivas	.000	1	0	0	0	0
Turconi	1.000	24	28	48	0	10
Turner	.948	17	27	28	3	6
Mooney	.928	49	51	90	11	16
Valdes	1.000	3	4	10	0	2

Outfield	PCT	G	PO	A	E	DP
Advincula	1.000	26	46	0	0	0
Antunez	.958	22	46	0	2	0
Boyd	1.000	14	26	1	0	0
Burgos	1.000	7	11	0	0	0
Fox	.996	89	219	3	1	2
Kayfus	1.000	3	7	0	0	0
Lampe	.991	100	202	13	2	2
Lipscomb	.990	88	191	7	2	4
Rosario	.981	26	51	0	1	0
Thomas	1.000	1	2	0	0	0
Turner	1.000	7	13	1	0	0
Velazquez	1.000	2	5	0	0	0
Watson	1.000	47	114	2	0	1

LAKE COUNTY CAPTAINS
MIDWEST LEAGUE — HIGH-A

Batting	B-T	Ht.	Wt.	DOB	AVG	OBP	SLG	G	PA	AB	R	H	2B	3B	HR	RBI	BB	HBP	SH	SF	SO	SB	CS	BB%	SO%
Advincula, Jonah	L-R	6-1	197	1-6-01	.278	.431	.456	55	205	158	29	44	5	4	5	23	39	5	1	2	28	26	8	19.0	13.7
Antunez, Wuilfredo	L-R	6-0	150	5-16-02	.263	.336	.517	70	293	259	46	68	16	4	14	46	27	3	0	3	68	11	1	9.2	23.2
Benjamin, Juan	S-R	5-8	150	4-25-03	.276	.365	.385	88	352	301	50	83	22	1	3	42	41	4	.1	5	64	18	3	11.6	18.2
Cesarini, Ryan	L-R	5-10	205	12-16-02	.292	.373	.469	25	110	96	18	28	6	1	3	15	11	2	0	1	18	7	0	10.0	16.4
Chourio, Jaison	S-R	6-1	162	5-19-05	.235	.380	.284	79	353	285	37	67	6	1	2	24	66	1	0	1	77	9	7	18.7	21.8
Collado, Maick	S-R	5-11	160	12-24-02	.249	.310	.332	84	320	289	31	72	13	1	3	30	26	1	1	3	47	2	1	8.1	14.7
Cozart, Jacob	L-R	6-3	205	1-9-03	.229	.344	.364	72	308	258	35	59	12	1	7	38	41	6	0	3	65	0	0	13.3	21.1
Dernedde, Kyle	R-R	5-8	183	11-8-00	.154	.250	.228	53	188	162	18	25	6	0	2	21	14	8	0	4	62	2	0	7.4	33.0
Devers, Jose	R-R	6-0	140	5-17-03	.240	.293	.415	119	516	475	68	114	36	4	13	67	31	6	0	4	142	12	5	6.0	27.5
Gonzalez, Esteban	R-R	5-8	150	3-19-03	.273	.336	.430	110	447	400	57	109	28	4	9	48	33	8	0	5	97	24	7	7.4	21.7
Hawke, Tommy	L-R	5-6	160	7-7-02	.278	.316	.278	4	19	18	3	5	0	0	0	1	0	0	0	0	4	2	0	5.3	21.1
Howe, Garrett	L-R	5-11	185	7-12-02	.235	.291	.314	15	56	51	5	12	1	0	1	3	4	0	0	1	15	4	1	7.1	26.8
Knapczyk, Christian	L-R	5-9	165	12-16-01	.213	.349	.370	94	424	370	53	96	18	1	7	44	42	10	0	2	79	11	3	9.9	18.6
Mercedes, Jeffrey	S-R	5-8	146	10-2-04	.182	.234	.364	13	47	44	3	8	0	1	2	6	3	0	0	0	6	0	0	6.4	12.8
Mitchell, Nick	L-R	5-9	178	9-3-03	.267	.380	.422	38	166	135	27	36	7	0	5	22	13	25	2	0	4	28	8	1	15.1	16.9
Rivas, Kevin	S-R	5-7	128	4-7-03	.178	.300	.244	30	116	90	15	16	1	0	0	3	15	1	0	1	40	3	54	2	0	12.3	41.5
Rosario, Alfonsin	R-R	6-2	215	6-21-04	.268	.362	.490	82	354	306	49	82	16	2	16	47	37	9	0	2	89	12	1	10.5	25.1
Thompson, Bennett	R-R	5-10	196	12-16-02	.302	.400	.460	17	75	63	8	19	5	1	2	5	10	1	0	1	10	1	13.3	14.7

	B-T	Ht.	Wt.	DOB	AVG	OBP	SLG	G	PA	AB	R	H	2B	3B	HR	RBI	BB	HBP	SH	SF	SO	SB	CS	BB%	SO%
Tincher, Johnny	R-R	5-8	170	8-25-01	.202	.308	.268	59	234	198	18	40	10	0	1	30	27	5	0	4	47	3	1	11.5	20.1
Velazquez, Ralphy	L-R	6-2	220	5-28-05	.245	.323	.469	94	418	371	59	91	20	6	17	63	40	4	0	3	85	1	2	9.6	20.3

Pitching	B-T	Ht.	Wt.	DOB	W	L	ERA	G	GS	SV	IP	Hits	Runs	ER	HR	BB	SO	AVG	OBP	SLG	SO%	BB%	BF
Bieber, Shane	R-R	6-3	200	5-31-95	0	0	3.00	1	1	0	3	2	1	1	0	0	4	.200	.182	.300	36.4	0.0	11
Collado, Maick	S-R	5-11	160	12-24-02	0	0	0.00	1	0	0	1	0	0	0	0	0	0	.000	.000	.000	0.0	0.0	3
DeLucia, Dylan	R-R	6-1	205	8-1-00	2	3	4.08	11	9	1	46	35	24	21	11	19	54	.208	.306	.446	28.0	9.8	193
Driver, Jay	R-R	6-3	195	2-25-02	5	2	4.11	34	0	3	46	36	26	21	2	27	49	.212	.325	.300	23.7	13.0	207
Favors, Caden	R-L	6-3	205	8-29-01	8	9	4.08	25	25	0	108	95	51	49	8	52	113	.233	.320	.339	24.4	11.2	463
Flores, Luis	L-L	6-1	160	10-5-03	1	0	3.00	7	0	0	9	7	3	3	0	9	9	.241	.436	.241	23.1	23.1	39
Garcia, Jogly	R-R	6-1	170	9-8-03	0	0	5.40	3	2	0	8	8	6	5	1	3	9	.258	.324	.387	24.3	8.1	37
Gomez, Yorman	R-R	5-11	167	11-10-02	8	0	2.84	17	6	3	76	55	24	24	3	29	83	.201	.280	.319	27.3	9.5	304
Harlow, Josh	R-R	6-3	215	4-18-01	6	4	4.44	36	0	1	51	46	32	25	5	47	55	.242	.407	.358	22.2	19.0	248
Hartle, Josh	L-L	6-4	210	3-24-03	10	2	2.35	22	22	0	103	72	32	27	2	37	100	.195	.284	.276	24.0	8.9	416
Humphries, Jackson	R-L	6-1	200	7-20-04	1	10	5.12	26	26	0	97	71	69	55	12	91	102	.205	.379	.367	22.6	20.2	451
Jasiak, Jack	R-R	6-1	198	3-6-01	5	4	3.19	31	0	13	54	55	24	19	3	13	60	.258	.312	.324	25.9	5.6	232
Kennedy, Michael	L-L	6-1	205	11-30-04	2	2	3.32	16	9	1	62	60	25	23	5	25	61	.251	.326	.368	22.8	9.3	268
Luna, Jesus	R-R	6-6	165	11-6-00	1	0	5.02	8	0	1	14	13	9	8	0	11	11	.232	.371	.268	15.7	15.7	70
Martinez, Izaak	L-L	5-10	180	9-12-01	4	2	3.29	29	0	0	52	43	25	19	3	19	38	.226	.301	.354	17.3	8.6	220
Martinez, Xavier	R-R	6-1	190	2-6-03	1	1	3.21	9	0	2	14	13	5	5	1	8	16	.250	.350	.327	26.7	13.3	60
Matos, Dwayne	R-R	6-1	155	11-7-00	3	0	6.23	10	0	0	22	20	15	15	3	13	11	.247	.361	.481	11.2	13.3	98
Matson, Sean	S-R	6-2	220	6-2-02	0	1	4.00	8	2	1	27	29	13	12	3	11	26	.276	.356	.400	22.0	9.3	118
Means, John	L-L	6-4	230	4-24-93	0	0	0.00	2	2	0	6	3	0	0	0	1	7	.143	.182	.143	31.8	4.5	22
Naquin, Tyler	R-R	6-1	202	4-24-91	1	0	7.02	14	0	0	17	11	14	13	0	18	12	.190	.372	.276	15.4	23.1	78
Perez, Steven	L-L	6-0	155	4-21-01	1	0	0.90	12	0	2	20	10	2	2	1	4	23	.147	.194	.235	31.9	5.6	72
Richardson, Alonzo	R-R	5-11	165	10-7-02	0	0	5.46	22	0	0	56	55	34	34	10	37	38	.263	.377	.474	15.3	14.9	249
Rivas, Kevin	S-R	5-7	128	4-7-03	0	0	0.00	1	0	0	0	0	0	0	0	0	0	.000	.000	.000	0.0	0.0	1
Schlesinger, Rafe	L-L	6-3	199	1-22-03	1	2	4.50	5	3	1	20	21	10	10	1	9	24	.276	.353	.395	27.9	10.5	86
Scott, Kyle	R-R	6-0	185	4-16-02	4	4	3.00	26	0	3	42	38	21	14	2	21	39	.235	.333	.352	20.6	11.1	189
Tulloch, Adam	L-L	6-2	200	7-1-00	0	0	2.28	14	0	2	28	19	8	7	2	13	33	.196	.291	.309	30.0	11.8	110
Wegielnik, Robert	R-R	6-0	185	9-6-01	4	3	6.40	29	0	6	45	51	38	32	5	34	58	.277	.410	.418	25.6	15.0	227
Whittaker, Conner	R-R	6-0	172	6-30-03	2	0	1.96	5	0	0	18	14	4	4	0	5	10	.219	.286	.297	14.3	7.1	70
Wilkinson, Matthew	R-L	5-11	260	12-10-02	4	9	4.24	25	25	0	104	98	55	49	13	45	117	.249	.327	.396	26.2	10.1	447

Fielding

Catcher	PCT	G	PO	A	E	DP	PB
Cozart	.984	65	577	44	10	2	5
Rivas	1.000	9	66	4	0	0	1
Thompson	.936	13	109	8	8	0	0
Tincher	.991	49	430	22	4	3	1

First Base	PCT	G	PO	A	E	DP
Collado	.993	40	282	18	2	25
Rivas	.989	25	170	7	2	11
Velazquez	.991	72	531	32	5	39

Second Base	PCT	G	PO	A	E	DP
Benjamin	.936	20	13	31	3	2
Dernedde	.959	17	28	42	3	9
Howe	.975	9	14	25	1	8

Third Base	PCT	G	PO	A	E	DP
Benjamin	.950	56	37	76	6	7
Collado	.921	38	28	65	8	4
Dernedde	.921	20	11	24	3	2
Howe	.000	1	0	0	1	0
Knapczyk	1.000	14	4	19	0	0
Mercedes	1.000	5	2	8	0	0

Shortstop	PCT	G	PO	A	E	DP
Dernedde	.939	13	23	23	3	2
Devers	.972	113	166	288	13	49
Knapczyk	.986	76	102	171	4	29
Mercedes	.957	5	8	14	1	3
Rivas	1.000	6	5	15	0	3
Howe	.947	5	3	15	1	1
Knapczyk	1.000	2	2	1	0	0

Outfield	PCT	G	PO	A	E	DP
Advincula	1.000	50	76	1	0	1
Antunez	.972	55	102	2	3	0
Benjamin	1.000	1	1	0	0	0
Cesarini	1.000	20	45	1	0	1
Chourio	.988	67	156	4	2	1
Gonzalez	.974	107	213	9	6	4
Mitchell	.984	32	56	4	1	0
Rosario	.979	69	135	2	3	0
Velazquez	.909	10	10	0	1	0

LYNCHBURG HILLCATS LOW-A
CAROLINA LEAGUE

Batting	B-T	Ht.	Wt.	DOB	AVG	OBP	SLG	G	PA	AB	R	H	2B	3B	HR	RBI	BB	HBP	SH	SF	SO	SB	CS	BB%	SO%
Baptiste, Yanki	S-R	5-11	185	11-18-04	.121	.341	.152	11	44	33	3	4	1	0	0	2	11	0	0	0	20	1	3	25.0	45.5
Caceres, Juneiker	L-L	5-10	168	8-15-07	.250	.331	.345	30	130	116	15	29	8	0	1	7	9	5	0	0	17	2	3	6.9	13.1
Cesarini, Ryan	L-R	5-10	205	12-16-02	.235	.362	.319	78	315	260	37	61	8	4	2	41	44	9	0	2	42	33	7	14.0	13.3
Clark, Logun	R-R	6-2	195	6-4-03	.209	.345	.264	57	223	182	22	38	5	1	1	15	30	9	0	2	71	2	2	13.5	31.8
Curley, Dean	R-R	6-3	195	4-15-04	.242	.286	.273	9	35	33	4	8	1	0	0	2	2	0	0	0	11	1	1	5.7	31.4
Espinola, Christopher	L-L	5-7	165	9-19-03	.168	.306	.242	47	183	149	20	25	6	1	1	19	28	3	0	3	32	9	1	15.3	17.5
Fernandez, Dauri	S-R	5-9	155	3-7-07	.273	.250	.318	7	24	22	3	6	1	0	0	3	0	0	0	2	3	2	0	0.0	12.5
Francisca, Welbyn	S-R	5-8	148	5-17-06	.229	.320	.302	98	428	371	54	85	14	2	3	45	51	1	0	5	73	45	12	11.9	17.1
Gutierrez, Carlos	L-L	5-6	135	6-18-04	.250	.292	.318	15	48	44	8	11	3	0	0	7	3	0	0	1	9	2	2	6.3	18.8
Hawke, Tommy	L-R	5-6	160	7-7-02	.309	.453	.382	63	267	207	65	64	11	2	0	22	53	3	1	2	44	63	5	19.9	16.5
Hill, Curtis	R-R	6-0	190	4-9-04	.347	.459	.510	15	62	49	7	17	3	1	1	7	11	0	1	1	11	7	4	17.7	17.7
Howard, Tyler	R-R	6-1	195	3-26-04	.313	.421	.344	9	38	32	5	10	1	0	0	4	4	2	0	0	7	0	0	10.5	18.4
Howe, Garrett	L-R	5-11	185	7-12-02	.211	.322	.264	81	315	265	36	56	9	1	1	28	41	4	1	4	80	30	10	13.0	25.4
Lopez, Robert	L-R	5-10	150	1-2-04	.198	.308	.253	48	195	167	20	33	8	0	1	22	25	2	0	1	44	2	1	12.8	22.6
Luis, Yerlin	S-R	5-9	155	9-9-05	.109	.269	.145	19	67	55	5	6	2	0	0	7	12	0	0	0	31	7	2	17.9	46.3
Martinez, Anthony	L-R	6-3	245	4-12-04	.214	.267	.321	7	30	28	1	6	0	0	1	5	2	0	0	0	5	0	0	6.7	16.7
Mendez, Alberto	L-R	5-9	146	11-29-04	.247	.335	.329	48	167	146	26	36	5	2	1	17	18	2	0	1	29	3	2	10.8	19.8
Mercedes, Jeffrey	S-R	5-8	146	10-2-04	.239	.318	.340	80	309	268	31	64	14	3	4	33	40	0	6	6	59	7	9	19.4	19.4
Merejo, Luis	R-R	6-2	185	6-28-06	.180	.300	.321	111	457	383	55	69	14	2	12	53	54	14	0	6	147	11	3	11.8	32.2
Mijares, Yaikel	S-R	5-9	145	12-13-05	.184	.316	.234	86	313	261	35	48	8	1	1	22	48	3	0	1	105	17	5	15.3	33.5
Mitchell, Nick	L-R	5-9	178	9-3-03	.255	.367	.305	39	169	141	21	36	3	2	0	20	24	2	0	2	21	21	2	14.2	12.4
Nelson, Riley	L-R	6-3	222	12-21-03	.316	.381	.474	15	65	57	7	18	6	0	1	7	3	5	0	0	12	1	0	4.6	18.5

CLEVELAND GUARDIANS

Batting (cont.)	B-T	Ht.	Wt.	DOB	AVG	OBP	SLG	G	PA	AB	R	H	2B	3B	HR	RBI	BB	HBP	SH	SF	SO	SB	CS	BB%	SO%
Peebles, Cannon	S-R	5-11	198	1-16-04	.276	.344	.379	8	32	29	3	8	1	1	0	1	3	0	0	0	9	4	0	9.4	28.1
Pirela, Jose	L-R	6-3	181	4-9-06	.206	.292	.326	96	360	316	33	65	15	7	3	38	25	15	0	4	118	13	8	6.9	32.8
Schubart, Nolan	L-R	6-5	227	5-10-04	.255	.424	.471	15	66	51	10	13	2	0	3	7	15	0	0	0	24	1	0	22.7	36.4
Silva, Anthony	R-R	6-2	200	7-17-03	.213	.321	.255	14	56	47	6	10	2	0	0	4	7	1	0	1	14	3	1	12.5	25.0
Thompson, Bennett	R-R	5-10	196	12-16-02	.269	.372	.352	73	301	253	40	68	15	0	2	34	38	6	0	4	41	8	5	12.6	13.6
Walton, Aaron	R-R	6-3	219	5-14-04	.238	.324	.397	16	71	63	9	15	5	1	1	9	7	1	0	0	21	6	1	9.9	29.6

Pitching	B-T	Ht.	Wt.	DOB	W	L	ERA	G	GS	SV	IP	Hits	Runs	ER	HR	BB	SO	AVG	OBP	SLG	SO%	BB%	BF
Alcantara, Eudry	R-R	5-11	150	12-27-04	3	4	4.79	30	0	2	36	36	25	19	0	31	28	.273	.419	.379	16.8	18.6	167
Aldeano, Austin	R-R	6-1	180	6-6-04	2	2	6.89	23	0	0	33	29	27	25	10	26	48	.232	.385	.512	30.8	16.7	156
Alfaro, Jervis	R-R	5-11	170	10-24-03	4	5	3.63	20	16	0	89	93	40	36	3	24	72	.261	.308	.360	18.7	6.2	386
Doughty, Braylon	R-R	6-1	196	12-7-05	0	7	3.48	22	22	0	85	84	39	33	4	23	99	.254	.309	.353	27.3	6.4	362
Fernandez, Luke	R-R	6-2	236	3-12-04	0	1	6.55	7	0	0	11	14	9	8	0	7	11	.318	.412	.545	21.6	13.7	51
Flores, Luis	L-L	6-1	160	10-5-03	4	2	4.98	30	0	5	43	33	30	24	2	37	71	.212	.370	.301	35.5	18.5	200
Garcia, Jogly	R-R	6-1	170	9-8-03	2	1	2.05	8	6	0	31	18	12	7	0	14	54	.162	.254	.198	42.9	11.1	126
Hawke, Tommy	L-R	5-6	160	7-7-02	0	0	0.00	1	0	0	1	1	0	0	0	0	0	.333	.333	.333	0.0	0.0	3
Heppner, Sean	R-R	6-2	175	9-14-02	6	3	5.79	33	0	0	42	36	32	27	1	35	35	.226	.406	.308	16.4	16.4	213
Hernandez, Melkis	L-L	6-0	186	1-18-05	6	3	3.64	25	21	0	114	93	50	46	7	51	116	.226	.319	.365	24.6	10.8	472
Luna, Jesus	R-R	6-6	165	11-6-00	0	0	0.00	8	0	0	10	5	0	0	0	5	8	.094	.244	.094	19.5	12.2	41
Martinez, Izaak	L-L	5-10	180	9-12-01	1	0	3.07	7	0	1	15	10	6	5	1	2	20	.192	.218	.346	36.4	3.6	55
Martinez, Xavier	R-R	6-1	190	2-6-03	4	1	2.63	23	0	1	38	32	14	11	0	17	49	.232	.275	.275	30.8	10.7	159
Matson, Sean	S-R	6-2	220	6-2-02	3	2	1.21	20	5	2	60	34	9	8	1	16	70	.161	.230	.213	30.4	7.0	230
McCausland, Will	R-R	6-0	190	10-19-03	1	1	2.70	4	2	0	10	6	3	3	0	4	15	.182	.263	.212	39.5	10.5	38
McGuire, Logan	R-R	6-3	180	9-12-02	8	4	4.43	37	0	7	67	64	39	33	3	11	75	.242	.276	.358	26.8	3.9	280
Mijares, Yaikel	S-R	5-9	145	12-13-05	0	1	0.00	1	0	0	0	1	1	0	0	0	0	1.000	1.000	1.000	0.0	0.0	1
Mobley, Chase	R-R	6-5	205	6-5-06	0	2	15.00	2	2	0	3	5	7	5	0	6	4	.357	.571	.643	19.0	28.6	21
Oakie, Joey	R-R	6-3	200	5-9-06	1	1	2.22	6	6	0	24	17	8	6	3	15	31	.202	.320	.333	30.7	14.9	101
Perez, Angel	R-R	6-2	176	5-22-04	1	1	3.06	11	0	0	18	10	6	6	0	14	18	.179	.352	.232	25.4	19.7	71
Petty, Zane	R-R	6-1	165	12-19-03	1	0	2.89	7	0	2	9	7	5	3	0	9	8	.212	.386	.242	18.2	20.5	44
Prager, Ryan	L-L	6-3	200	10-26-02	0	0	4.15	2	2	0	4	7	3	2	0	3	7	.350	.435	.600	30.4	13.0	23
Rivera, Raudy	R-R	5-10	195	5-3-05	1	0	1.80	7	0	1	15	6	3	3	0	9	17	.130	.276	.152	29.3	15.5	58
Schlesinger, Rafe	L-L	6-3	199	1-22-03	4	6	3.33	20	16	0	84	76	35	31	2	34	88	.241	.322	.314	24.6	9.5	358
Schuelke, Cam	R-R	6-0	190	1-14-02	3	1	4.37	14	0	3	23	22	11	11	2	10	25	.259	.344	.388	25.8	10.3	97
Walty, Cam	R-R	6-0	209	5-14-02	1	2	4.28	16	11	0	48	55	25	23	2	11	38	.282	.316	.400	18.2	5.3	209
Whittaker, Conner	R-R	6-0	172	6-30-03	6	2	2.85	30	1	5	66	59	23	21	3	14	45	.239	.289	.324	16.9	5.3	266
Zapata, Julio	R-R	6-1	184	11-22-02	3	1	3.62	19	0	0	27	39	15	11	1	11	25	.355	.419	.436	20.2	8.9	124
Zibin, Jacob	L-R	6-4	218	1-30-05	5	0	3.62	19	0	0	60	53	33	24	4	31	44	.237	.338	.353	16.7	11.8	263
Zinn, Keegan	R-R	6-3	165	3-30-05	2	0	4.85	9	0	0	13	12	9	7	0	12	12	.240	.400	.260	18.5	18.5	65
Zsak, Donovan	L-L	6-3	185	7-12-03	3	1	7.26	26	0	2	31	46	27	25	3	28	43	.326	.380	.400	28.3	18.4	152

Fielding

Catcher	PCT	G	PO	A	E	DP	PB
Clark	.998	44	386	36	1	3	8
Howard	1.000	8	66	5	0	1	0
Lopez	1.000	11	120	8	0	0	2
Peebles	.988	7	71	9	1	1	2
Thompson	.987	59	564	35	8	6	7

First Base	PCT	G	PO	A	E	DP
Baptiste	.972	9	66	3	2	3
Lopez	.987	33	220	5	3	20
Martinez	1.000	3	18	0	0	2
Mercedes	1.000	3	14	2	0	0
Merejo	.972	71	487	40	15	37
Nelson	.974	10	69	7	2	7
Schubart	1.000	7	39	1	0	4

Second Base	PCT	G	PO	A	E	DP
Fernandez	1.000	1	1	2	0	0
Hawke	.905	5	10	9	2	4
Hill	1.000	3	6	4	0	0

Third Base	PCT	G	PO	A	E	DP
Curley	1.000	2	0	5	0	1
Hill	1.000	11	10	12	0	1
Howe	.882	8	4	11	2	1
Mendez	.917	20	17	38	5	1
Mercedes	.943	39	29	54	5	5
Mijares	.930	49	35	85	9	4
Silva	1.000	2	1	2	0	0

Shortstop	PCT	G	PO	A	E	DP
Curley	.857	7	4	14	3	2

	PCT	G	PO	A	E	DP
Fernandez	.900	5	5	13	2	4
Francisca	.935	86	97	178	19	27
Howe	.965	30	35	76	4	16
Silva	1.000	4	6	5	0	2

Outfield	PCT	G	PO	A	E	DP
Caceres	.962	28	46	5	2	1
Cesarini	.985	67	131	3	2	0
Espinola	1.000	41	53	3	0	0
Gutierrez	.952	12	19	1	1	1
Hawke	.991	53	104	5	1	0
Luis	.971	18	28	5	1	0
Merejo	.956	28	39	4	2	1
Mitchell	.978	38	88	3	2	1
Pirela	.981	89	150	5	3	1
Schubart	1.000	8	11	0	0	0
Walton	1.000	13	38	2	0	0

ACL GUARDIANS — ROOKIE
ARIZONA COMPLEX LEAGUE

Batting	B-T	Ht.	Wt.	DOB	AVG	OBP	SLG	G	PA	AB	R	H	2B	3B	HR	RBI	BB	HBP	SH	SF	SO	SB	CS	BB%	SO%
Abreus, Jhorvic	S-R	5-7	144	10-27-05	.167	.278	.202	31	97	84	13	14	3	0	0	5	12	1	0	0	25	3	0	12.4	25.8
Arias, Robert	L-L	6-1	168	9-13-06	.287	.389	.402	46	198	164	33	47	11	1	2	28	29	1	0	4	22	29	4	14.6	11.1
Bazzana, Travis	L-R	5-9	170	8-28-02	.222	.462	.333	7	26	18	7	4	2	0	0	2	8	0	0	0	4	1	0	30.8	15.4
Bolivar, Mason	L-R	5-10	192	8-18-06	.147	.250	.176	14	41	34	3	5	1	0	0	6	4	1	1	1	14	0	1	9.8	34.1
Brito, Juan	S-R	5-11	162	9-24-01	.190	.346	.333	7	26	21	2	4	0	0	1	2	3	2	0	0	8	0	1	11.5	30.8
Caceres, Juneiker	L-L	5-10	168	8-15-07	.289	.419	.469	40	160	128	25	37	10	2	3	20	27	3	0	2	18	5	2	16.9	11.3
Castillo, Yeiferth	L-L	5-8	155	11-18-06	.297	.369	.430	46	187	165	26	49	7	0	5	27	17	3	0	2	24	2	1	9.1	12.8
Chourio, Jaison	S-R	6-1	162	5-19-05	.261	.370	.304	8	27	23	6	6	1	0	0	2	4	0	0	0	10	1	0	14.8	37.0
Dalmacy, Pedro	S-R	5-11	170	12-17-05	.357	.404	.405	15	52	42	9	15	2	0	0	11	4	2	0	4	11	1	1	7.7	21.2
De La Cruz, Luis	S-R	5-11	166	9-24-06	.265	.362	.349	51	199	166	30	44	7	2	1	38	25	5	0	5	34	20	4	11.6	17.1
DeLauter, Chase	L-R	6-4	235	10-8-01	.182	.357	.455	8	28	22	3	4	0	0	2	3	6	0	0	0	5	1	0	21.4	17.9
Fernandez, Dauri	R-R	5-9	155	3-7-07	.333	.398	.558	43	176	156	33	52	9	4	6	27	16	2	0	2	22	16	4	9.1	12.5
Fry, David	R-R	6-0	215	11-20-95	.000	.200	.000	3	10	8	1	0	0	0	0	0	2	0	0	0	3	0	0	20.0	30.0

Batting	B-T	Ht.	Wt.	DOB	AVG	OBP	SLG	G	PA	AB	R	H	2B	3B	HR	RBI	BB	HBP	SH	SF	SO	SB	CS	BB%	SO%
Genao, Angel	S-R	5-9	150	5-19-04	.308	.438	.654	8	32	26	10	8	0	0	3	5	6	0	0	0	4	0	1	18.8	12.5
Gutierrez, Carlos	L-L	5-6	135	6-18-04	.125	.333	.156	10	42	32	5	4	1	0	0	0	9	1	0	0	10	1	2	21.4	23.8
Herrera, Reiner	L-R	5-11	170	10-20-05	.239	.364	.415	43	173	142	23	34	2	4	5	29	23	6	0	2	33	3	1	13.3	19.1
Izturis, Victor	L-R	5-9	165	3-22-05	.242	.405	.394	16	43	33	6	8	2	0	1	7	8	1	0	0	8	1	0	18.6	18.6
Leon, David	L-R	5-11	156	5-22-04	.161	.381	.258	19	43	31	7	5	0	0	1	3	11	0	1	0	12	1	0	25.6	27.9
Luis, Yerlin	S-R	5-9	155	9-9-05	.220	.394	.440	26	66	50	14	11	1	2	2	11	14	1	0	1	24	3	1	21.2	36.4
Martinez, Jonathan	S-R	5-9	131	8-16-06	.288	.364	.414	41	129	111	22	32	5	3	1	17	13	2	0	3	26	16	3	10.1	20.2
Mitchell, Nick	L-R	5-9	178	9-3-03	.417	.533	.458	8	30	24	6	10	1	0	0	1	5	1	0	0	3	1	2	16.7	10.0
Morillo, Estivel	R-R	6-0	155	7-21-07	.109	.222	.200	18	63	55	6	6	1	2	0	4	6	2	0	0	33	1	0	9.5	52.4
Rodriguez, Gabriel	L-R	6-0	161	5-3-07	.294	.393	.402	28	122	102	21	30	4	2	1	15	15	3	0	2	23	11	2	12.3	18.9
Rodriguez, Johan	R-R	5-11	165	7-28-07	.217	.332	.338	46	187	157	30	34	13	0	2	22	18	10	0	2	39	4	2	9.6	20.9
Silva, Heribert	L-L	5-9	152	3-31-06	.267	.306	.333	28	49	45	8	12	3	0	0	3	2	1	0	1	11	5	0	4.1	22.4
Valera, George	L-L	6-0	195	11-13-00	.421	.460	.702	16	63	57	10	24	4	0	4	14	5	0	0	1	11	0	0	7.9	17.5

Pitching	B-T	Ht.	Wt.	DOB	W	L	ERA	G	GS	SV	IP	Hits	Runs	ER	HR	BB	SO	AVG	OBP	SLG	SO%	BB%	BF
Abney, Alaska	R-R	6-1	205	5-5-00	0	0	0.00	4	0	0	5	3	0	0	0	0	6	.176	.176	.294	35.3	0.0	17
Bieber, Shane	R-R	6-3	200	5-31-95	0	0	0.00	2	2	0	4	2	0	0	0	1	10	.125	.176	.125	58.8	5.9	17
Crisostomo, Yatner	R-R	5-11	155	6-21-03	3	1	1.37	16	0	0	20	16	11	3	0	17	22	.235	.382	.265	24.7	19.1	89
Flores, Miguel	L-L	6-2	185	10-15-04	1	3	5.02	12	8	1	38	35	29	21	4	23	36	.240	.345	.363	20.9	13.4	172
Jachec, Matt	R-R	6-0	205	7-25-01	0	0	3.86	4	0	0	5	2	2	2	0	3	3	.133	.278	.133	16.7	16.7	18
Jimenez, Ezequiel	R-R	6-1	182	6-10-03	2	1	4.74	18	0	0	25	29	17	13	1	19	26	.290	.407	.450	21.1	15.4	123
Kennedy, Michael	L-L	6-1	205	11-30-04	0	0	15.00	2	2	0	3	7	7	5	0	6	4	.500	.619	.571	19.0	28.6	21
Leftwich, Jack	R-R	6-4	220	9-26-98	0	0	0.00	3	1	1	4	0	0	0	0	1	5	.000	.083	.000	41.7	8.3	12
Leon, David	L-R	5-11	156	2-2-04	0	1	5.06	3	0	0	5	7	6	3	0	2	2	.333	.385	.476	7.7	7.7	26
Mariano, Diovel	R-R	6-1	175	2-23-04	3	1	3.77	21	0	3	29	27	15	12	2	18	32	.257	.373	.343	25.4	14.3	126
McKenzie, Triston	R-R	6-5	165	8-2-97	0	2	6.91	8	5	0	14	10	12	11	2	14	20	.200	.385	.460	30.8	21.5	65
Mobley, Chase	R-R	6-5	205	6-5-06	0	3	8.47	8	7	0	17	16	19	16	2	18	25	.242	.425	.348	28.7	20.7	87
Naquin, Tyler	L-R	6-1	202	4-24-91	2	0	5.14	13	0	0	14	8	8	8	0	11	8	.170	.322	.277	13.3	18.3	60
Oakie, Joey	R-R	6-3	200	5-9-06	2	3	7.46	9	0	35	36	30	29	1	23	47	.267	.385	.348	27.6	13.5	170
Osorio, Manuel	L-L	5-10	170	3-24-06	1	3	5.11	11	6	0	37	33	26	21	2	26	38	.228	.354	.290	21.6	14.8	176
Peraza, Santiago	R-R	5-11	135	5-17-05	1	1	7.32	3	0	1	20	18	17	16	0	23	24	.254	.470	.352	24.0	23.0	100
Perez, Angel	R-R	6-2	176	5-22-04	3	0	3.08	18	0	1	26	21	10	9	0	7	46	.214	.262	.337	43.0	6.5	107
Perez, Erigaldi	R-R	6-2	185	1-25-06	1	5	5.02	12	6	0	38	52	33	24	21	3	9	34	.346	.399	.503	20.1	5.3	169
Perez, Joelvis	R-R	6-3	180	12-8-04	1	0	2.67	18	0	3	30	27	10	9	0	16	27	.239	.338	.372	20.3	12.0	133
Ramirez, Jose	R-R	5-11	155	9-3-04	2	1	7.77	19	0	1	24	18	23	21	2	28	35	.202	.405	.326	28.9	23.1	121
Ramos, Renil	R-R	6-2	143	12-1-05	1	0	0.00	2	0	0	2	0	0	0	0	1	3	.000	.125	.000	37.5	12.5	8
Remily, Jacob	R-R	6-6	190	5-8-06	0	1	5.63	4	4	0	8	7	5	2	2	7	3	.303	.361	.636	19.4	5.6	36
Rivera, Raudy	R-R	5-10	195	5-3-05	3	2	3.21	22	0	0	28	16	13	10	0	22	48	.165	.349	.227	38.1	17.5	126
Sabrowski, Erik	R-L	6-4	235	10-31-97	0	0	0.00	2	1	0	1	0	0	0	0	4	1	.000	.500	.000	12.5	50.0	8
Schuelke, Cam	R-R	6-0	190	1-14-02	1	0	1.80	5	0	0	5	3	1	1	0	2	8	.200	.333	.200	44.4	11.1	18
Silva, Heribert	L-L	5-9	152	3-31-06	1	0	6.00	2	0	0	3	7	2	2	0	1	.438	.438	.563	6.3	0.0	16	
Stephan, Trevor	R-R	6-5	225	11-25-95	0	0	9.00	2	2	0	2	3	2	2	0	0	5	.333	.333	.444	55.6	0.0	9
Thornton, Tyler	L-R	6-3	200	7-8-00	1	0	0.00	4	0	0	4	2	0	0	0	3	12	.125	.300	.125	60.0	15.0	20
Torres, Javi	R-R	6-1	210	12-29-04	0	1	54.00	1	0	0	0	2	5	2	0	2	0	.500	.667	.500	0.0	33.3	6
Virguez, Kendeglys	R-R	6-2	160	5-6-04	1	0	5.87	7	0	0	8	7	5	5	0	6	13	.233	.395	.300	34.2	15.8	38
Zapata, Julio	R-R	6-1	184	11-22-02	0	0	2.70	3	0	0	3	4	1	1	0	3	.308	.308	.538	23.1	0.0	13	
Zinn, Keegan	R-R	6-3	165	3-30-05	1	2	7.85	12	7	0	39	39	38	34	2	30	42	.264	.396	.405	22.5	16.0	187

Fielding

C: Herrera 40, Dalmagro 9, Izturis 9, Leon 8. **1B:** De La Cruz 49, Leon 8, Izturis 6, Dalmagro 5, Herrera 1. **2B:** J. Rodriguez 18, Martinez 17, Abreus 16, Fernandez 11, Bazzana 5, Brito 5, G. Rodriguez 4. **3B:** Fernandez 18, Abreus 14, Martinez 11, G. Rodriguez 8, J. Rodriguez 8, De La Cruz 7. **SS:** J. Rodriguez 21, Fernandez 16, G. Rodriguez 16, Martinez 9, Genao 7, Abreus 3. **LF:** Castillo 22, Caceres 12, Gutierrez 9, Luis 7, Arias 6, Silva 6, Bolivar 4, Valera 4. **CF:** Arias 38, Morillo 9, Silva 8, Mitchell 7, Chourio 6, Bolivar 2, Luis 2, Caceres 1, Castillo 1. **RF:** Caceres 23, Castillo 19, Valera 9, Silva 8, Luis 7, DeLauter 6, Morillo 3, Bolivar 1, Brito 1, Chourio 1

DSL CLEVELAND MENDOZA
DOMINICAN SUMMER LEAGUE
ROOKIE

Batting	B-T	Ht.	Wt.	DOB	AVG	OBP	SLG	G	PA	AB	R	H	2B	3B	HR	RBI	BB	HBP	SH	SF	SO	SB	CS	BB%	SO%
Alvarez, Robert	R-R	5-10	160	11-13-07	.155	.244	.173	33	128	110	10	17	2	0	0	12	13	1	1	3	25	0	0	10.2	19.5
Arias, Dariel	L-R	6-0	152	10-7-06	.202	.283	.234	34	106	94	15	19	3	0	0	9	9	2	0	1	16	4	1	8.5	15.1
Arosemena, Pablo	R-R	5-8	154	2-17-06	.208	.380	.236	26	92	72	10	15	2	0	0	8	15	5	0	0	26	2	0	16.3	28.3
Belen, Marcos	R-R	5-10	157	11-9-06	.176	.361	.209	27	120	91	14	16	3	0	0	10	26	1	1	1	24	12	4	21.7	20.0
Blasco, Alejandro	S-R	5-7	154	3-29-07	.259	.475	.447	31	122	85	22	22	8	1	2	21	28	8	0	1	20	8	1	23.0	16.4
Cadiz, Sebastian	L-R	5-11	180	2-1-06	.265	.392	.398	28	102	83	8	22	5	3	0	14	18	0	0	1	18	1	0	17.6	17.6
Caripa, Carlos	L-L	5-10	155	6-29-07	.246	.296	.292	20	72	65	6	16	3	0	0	9	4	1	1	1	11	0	1	5.6	15.3
De Los Santos, Sebastian	S-R	5-10	145	6-16-06	.182	.438	.182	6	16	11	2	2	0	0	0	4	1	0	0	6	0	0	25.0	37.5	
Galan, Luis	R-R	5-9	144	8-14-08	.264	.388	.300	40	170	140	29	37	3	1	0	12	24	5	0	1	35	6	2	14.1	20.6
Garces, Carlos	S-R	5-7	143	9-30-06	.234	.400	.362	46	191	141	29	33	5	5	1	22	28	15	1	6	11	16	2	14.7	5.8
Garcia, Luis	S-R	5-11	169	12-21-07	.304	.308	.46	194	159	22	33	14	1	0	26	33	0	0	2	29	5	3	17.0	14.9
López, Hiverson	R-R	5-10	175	1-19-08	.193	.310	.241	46	197	166	23	32	3	1	1	19	19	10	0	2	45	6	0	9.6	22.8
Morillo, Estivel	R-R	6-0	155	7-21-07	.333	.316	.500	4	19	18	3	6	3	0	0	4	0	0	0	1	3	2	0	0.0	15.8
Riera, Angel	R-R	5-8	145	5-10-08	.229	.340	.394	46	200	176	26	39	7	3	5	27	24	5	0	1	29	18	5	12.0	14.5
Taveras, Romer	L-L	5-7	145	9-11-06	.167	.282	.217	24	71	60	10	10	1	1	0	9	8	2	0	1	20	1	0	11.3	28.2
Vargas, Jefferson	L-R	5-9	148	10-4-07	.211	.363	.258	43	161	128	27	27	4	1	0	11	29	2	1	1	36	5	1	18.0	22.4
Velasquez, Nomar	L-R	5-9	158	5-21-05	.295	.409	.388	43	138	112	32	33	3	0	1	16	19	4	1	2	21	9	1	13.8	15.2

Pitching	B-T	Ht.	Wt.	DOB	W	L	ERA	G	GS	SV	IP	Hits	Runs	ER	HR	BB	SO	AVG	OBP	SLG	SO%	BB%	BF
Cabrera, Luilli	R-R	6-3	187	10-30-05	1	0	6.52	9	0	0	10	12	7	7	0	7	10	.308	.429	.359	20.4	14.3	49

Colina, Handrychson	R-R	6-1	170	1-27-07	1	3	4.86	9	1	0	17	19	14	9	0	8	7	.284	.367	.388	8.8	10.0	80
De Jesus, Victor	R-R	6-1	153	8-12-06	1	2	13.79	15	1	1	16	15	26	24	0	35	11	.263	.567	.298	11.3	36.1	97
Farfan, Yoshtner	L-L	5-8	161	5-31-08	3	2	6.66	17	0	1	26	26	23	19	1	19	22	.289	.435	.444	18.6	16.1	118
Henriquez, Jodainy	L-L	6-2	193	10-3-05	0	0	4.15	4	0	0	4	2	3	2	0	6	3	.143	.409	.214	13.6	27.3	22
Hernandez, Daiher	L-L	5-11	141	3-2-06	0	3	6.75	12	11	0	43	40	35	32	2	33	33	.258	.404	.348	16.7	16.7	198
Lopez, Carlos	L-L	6-0	148	6-12-06	1	0	7.00	15	0	2	18	16	24	14	1	26	19	.232	.461	.333	18.6	25.5	102
Mejia, Algeni	L-L	6-4	183	9-13-04	2	1	5.93	10	0	0	14	17	13	9	0	11	18	.309	.418	.400	26.9	16.4	67
Melgarejo, Oscar	R-R	5-10	169	11-29-05	0	0	5.40	1	1	0	3	3	2	2	0	0	2	.231	.286	.462	14.3	0.0	14
Montana, Antwan	R-R	5-11	196	6-10-08	4	3	5.91	15	0	0	21	17	14	14	0	18	15	.233	.375	.342	15.5	18.6	97
Negrin, Abraham	R-R	5-10	158	4-7-06	4	4	3.72	15	0	0	29	21	13	12	1	14	21	.210	.314	.280	17.8	11.9	118
Padilla, Erick	R-R	5-10	145	11-26-03	0	1	11.65	15	0	2	17	26	28	22	0	17	18	.338	.495	.416	17.5	16.5	103
Rivera, Alejandro	R-R	5-10	154	12-27-06	0	2	1.02	11	11	0	44	28	8	5	0	20	34	.189	.297	.216	19.8	11.6	172
Rossi, Julio	R-R	5-10	160	7-23-08	0	0	4.96	16	0	1	16	12	13	9	1	20	12	.214	.432	.339	14.8	24.7	81
Rossi, Julio J	R-R	5-10	157	4-18-07	1	0	15.63	4	0	0	6	6	12	11	1	8	5	.240	.472	.520	13.9	22.2	36
Ruiz, Harrison	R-R	6-1	192	10-2-03	0	5	8.27	12	12	0	41	56	39	38	0	18	31	.326	.403	.424	15.8	9.2	196
Sanchez, Carlos	R-R	6-3	200	12-4-07	0	0	8.38	13	0	0	19	24	19	18	3	15	20	.296	.418	.481	20.2	15.2	99
Tovar, Erich	R-R	5-11	160	11-11-06	0	0	2.35	6	0	0	8	6	6	2	0	13	6	.214	.476	.250	14.0	30.2	43
Trujillo, Raul	R-R	5-11	205	5-20-07	0	3	7.28	11	9	0	38	37	35	31	1	36	21	.285	.467	.369	11.6	19.9	181
Uribe, Delni	R-R	5-10	155	3-1-07	0	5	4.30	11	10	1	46	37	29	22	0	18	25	.222	.325	.293	12.6	9.1	198
Vasquez, Eriberto	R-R	5-11	175	3-8-04	1	2	5.55	13	0	0	24	26	25	15	0	22	25	.277	.400	.404	20.8	18.3	1205

Fielding

C: Lopez 36, Alvarez 17, Cadiz 9, Arosemena 2. **1B:** Cadiz 21, Arosemena 17, Alvarez 10, Galan 7, López 6, Blasco 3, Velasquez 2. **2B:** Riera 19, Garcia 13, Vargas 11, Garces 7, Galan 6, Blasco 2, Velasquez 1. **3B**: Galan 15, Vargas 15, Garcia 9, Riera 7, Velasquez 6, Garces 4, Blasco 3, De Los Santos 1. **SS:** Garcia 19, Riera 16, Vargas 15, Galan 8. **LF:** Velasquez 19, Blasco 13, Arias 11, Garces 6, Taveras 6, Caripa 4, Cadiz 2, De Los Santos 2, Arosemena 1, Belen 1. **CF:** Belen 24, Garces 23, Taveras 5, Morillo 3, Blasco 2. **RF:** Arias 17, Caripa 12, Taveras 9, Velasquez 8, Blasco 6, Garces 6, Belen 2, De Los Santos 1, Morillo 1

DSL CLEVELAND GORYL — *ROOKIE*

DOMINICAN SUMMER LEAGUE

Batting	B-T	Ht.	Wt.	DOB	AVG	OBP	SLG	G	PA	AB	R	H	2B	3B	HR	RBI	BB	HBP	SH	SF	SO	SB	CS	BB%	SO%
Abreu, Angel	R-R	5-9	152	8-12-08	.308	.423	.372	46	209	172	48	53	4	2	1	24	33	2	1	1	19	13	1	15.8	9.1
Alvarez, Israel	S-R	5-9	136	10-8-07	.221	.337	.266	43	184	154	24	34	5	1	0	19	20	8	0	2	29	2	0	10.9	15.8
Baptista, Gustavo	L-R	5-10	158	2-7-08	.262	.466	.414	46	206	145	50	38	7	3	3	26	46	12	0	3	47	7	0	22.3	22.8
Brito, Heins	S-R	5-8	142	10-14-07	.209	.316	.297	39	177	148	24	31	5	1	2	29	23	2	0	4	34	9	1	13.0	19.2
Cruz, Steven	S-R	5-7	145	12-8-06	.248	.429	.327	39	154	113	25	28	6	0	1	18	36	2	0	3	23	10	2	23.4	14.9
De Los Santos, Sebastian	S-R	5-10	145	6-16-06	.158	.333	.158	7	24	19	3	3	0	0	0	0	5	0	0	0	6	0	0	20.8	25.0
Marcano, Jose	L-R	5-10	155	10-3-05	.261	.343	.337	28	106	92	15	24	5	1	0	19	11	1	1	1	17	1	1	10.4	16.0
Martinez, Randy	S-R	5-9	163	4-17-07	.276	.463	.370	42	177	127	31	35	7	1	1	31	46	1	0	3	41	7	3	26.0	23.2
Rodriguez, Freilyn	L-R	5-8	142	4-19-08	.158	.299	.196	45	195	158	33	25	4	1	0	16	29	4	0	3	48	11	2	14.9	24.6
Romero, Ricardo	L-R	5-5	158	3-1-08	.312	.415	.476	46	205	170	40	53	12	5	2	35	28	4	0	3	21	3	0	13.7	10.2
Rosario, Rodny	S-R	5-10	172	11-21-07	.307	.452	.464	39	177	140	33	43	4	6	2	23	34	3	0	0	34	5	2	19.2	19.2
Taveras, Romer	L-L	5-7	145	9-11-06	.324	.489	.412	14	45	34	7	11	1	1	0	6	11	0	0	0	16	2	0	24.4	35.6
Torrealba, Osmar	L-L	5-9	161	4-2-07	.207	.342	.259	20	73	58	10	12	3	0	0	7	13	0	0	2	6	1	1	17.8	8.2
Torres, Wuinder	R-R	5-10	130	1-28-07	.235	.271	.343	42	181	166	24	39	12	3	0	41	7	3	0	5	20	0	0	3.9	11.0
Ustariz, Santiago	L-R	5-10	165	11-8-06	.239	.380	.330	28	108	88	19	21	3	1	1	18	16	4	0	0	25	0	0	14.8	23.1

Pitching	B-T	Ht.	Wt.	DOB	W	L	ERA	G	GS	SV	IP	Hits	Runs	ER	HR	BB	SO	AVG	OBP	SLG	SO%	BB%	BF
Abreu, Javier	R-R	5-11	150	5-24-06	5	2	5.27	17	0	1	27	38	22	16	0	12	15	.342	.413	.423	11.9	9.5	126
Amaya, Enderson	R-R	5-11	165	3-29-07	3	3	5.53	11	6	0	42	42	28	26	1	17	33	.263	.331	.350	18.3	9.4	180
Ardiles, Wilinyer	R-R	5-11	140	8-14-07	0	1	12.71	4	4	0	6	6	8	8	0	7	2	.273	.448	.409	6.9	24.1	29
Arias, Ronny	R-R	5-10	150	7-24-08	1	1	6.23	14	0	0	17	18	14	12	1	12	12	.269	.405	.433	14.3	14.3	84
Baron, Randy	R-R	6-0	185	1-13-08	2	0	3.16	15	0	0	31	22	13	11	1	13	21	.198	.299	.315	16.4	10.2	128
Castillo, Hector	R-R	6-0	180	5-2-07	5	1	4.11	18	0	2	31	31	15	14	0	20	41	.270	.394	.330	28.9	14.1	142
Dorante, Luis	R-R	6-0	190	11-24-06	2	2	5.34	17	0	5	29	27	18	17	2	14	25	.252	.333	.421	20.3	11.4	123
Feliz, Rey	L-R	6-4	186	2-9-07	0	0	6.39	13	0	0	13	14	9	9	0	15	15	.326	.516	.488	24.2	24.2	62
Garcia, Alexander	R-R	6-0	161	7-27-06	1	2	1.32	11	11	0	48	22	9	7	0	18	48	.135	.237	.178	25.8	9.7	186
Gentile, Daniel	R-R	6-0	155	8-8-08	3	1	2.81	12	11	0	48	37	16	15	1	23	40	.215	.312	.326	20.1	11.6	199
Jimenez, Jhordari	L-R	6-1	181	6-25-08	0	1	13.50	7	0	0	7	8	11	10	1	11	6	.348	.568	.522	15.8	28.9	38
Mejia, Algeni	L-L	6-4	183	9-13-04	1	0	2.61	6	0	1	10	9	3	3	0	8	11	.237	.370	.263	23.9	17.4	46
Meza, Jonaikel	R-R	5-11	154	3-23-07	1	1	3.97	15	0	1	23	22	12	10	0	13	17	.262	.366	.369	16.8	12.9	101
Milan, Abrahan	R-R	5-11	219	1-22-06	0	2	86.40	8	0	0	2	3	16	16	0	25	1	.429	.889	.714	2.8	69.4	36
Perez, Edelvis	R-R	6-3	190	5-2-05	0	2	5.45	12	12	0	38	28	25	23	3	30	43	.203	.351	.326	24.7	17.2	174
Perez, Josh	R-R	6-0	170	1-23-08	1	1	4.45	10	10	0	32	30	20	16	1	18	22	.254	.362	.339	15.5	12.7	142
Rivero, Johander	L-L	5-10	149	6-27-08	2	2	5.89	14	1	0	18	11	15	12	0	20	17	.177	.378	.226	20.5	24.1	83
Rodriguez, Wilfi	R-R	5-9	160	12-20-07	0	1	8.53	5	0	0	6	6	6	6	0	6	3	.273	.469	.364	9.1	18.2	33
Salvador, Rodarni	R-R	6-3	158	4-1-05	1	0	13.50	2	0	0	1	5	2	2	1	3	2	.714	.800	1.143	20.0	30.0	10
Teran, Amilcar	R-R	5-10	180	9-17-07	3	1	6.11	18	1	1	28	24	27	19	3	19	13	.233	.382	.417	9.9	14.5	131
Yan, Juan	R-R	6-0	186	1-27-08	0	1	6.14	6	0	0	7	9	9	5	2	4	6	.281	.395	.594	15.8	10.5	38

Fielding

C: Baptista 30, Torres 25, Ustariz 4. **1B:** Marcano 16, Martinez 15, Torres 12, Baptista 10, Ustariz 3. **2B:** Romero 20, Alvarez 19, Brito 10, Abreu 4, Marcano 3, Rosario 1. **3B:** Rosario 21, Romero 15, Martinez 11, Alvarez 6, Brito 4, Marcano 1. **SS:** Brito 20, Alvarez 15, Rosario 14, Abreu 8, Romero 2. **LF:** Abreu 17, Torrealba 10, Ustariz 9, Cruz 7, Romero 7, Marcano 3, Martinez 3, Taveras 3, De Los Santos 1. **CF:** Rodriguez 45, Abreu 9, Cruz 2, Torrealba 2, Taveras 1. **RF:** Cruz 27, Martinez 11, Taveras 9, Torrealba 8, De Los Santos 5, Ustariz 1

Colorado Rockies

SEASON SYNOPSIS: The Rockies continued to plumb new depths, losing 100 games for the third straight season and the third time in franchise history. They reached a new low in 2025, though, going 43-119, narrowly avoiding the worst record in National League history. Their -424 run differential was the worst since the 1899 Cleveland Spiders, and their starters' ERA of 6.65 was the highest mark since ERA became an official statistic.

HIGH POINT: In an Aug. 1 Coors Field classic, the Rockies gave up nine runs in the first inning and trailed the Pirates 16-10 heading into the eighth before hitting three homers in the last two innings to pull off a stunning 17-16 victory. Rookie outfielder Yanquiel Fernandez hit his first career homer in the eighth, then catcher Hunter Goodman hit one in the ninth before center fielder Brenton Doyle walked it off with a two-run shot.

LOW POINT: No modern team has gotten off to a worse start after 50 games than Colorado, which fell to 8-42 after a four-game home sweep May 19-22 to the Phillies. The Rockies were blown out (losing by five or more runs) 44 times, with a 21-0 loss to the Padres on May 10 and an 18-0 whitewash July 26 at Baltimore. The worst was a home sweep Aug. 4-6 against Toronto, capped by a 20-1 defeat, by a collective score of 45-6, with Toronto recording a three-game-series record 63 hits, and the 39-run differential in a series is the largest since 1901.

NOTABLE ROOKIES: Righthander Chase Dollander, the club's 2023 first-round pick, debuted April 6 with a win against the Athletics but had issues with hard contact all season, with hitters slugging .556 off his fastball. His former Tennessee teammate, closer Seth Halvorsen, led the team with 11 saves but saw his season end in early August due to a right flexor strain. The Rockies broke in more rookies over the season's second half such as Warming Bernabel (.252/.288/.410) and third baseman Kyle Karros, but none shined.

KEY TRANSACTIONS: Colorado's best offseason was March signee Mickey Moniak, the 2016 No. 1 overall pick who wound up second on the team with 24 home runs. The club did sell a bit at the trade deadline, sending third baseman Ryan McMahon and righthander Jake Bird to the Yankees in separate deals for minor leaguers led by lefty Griffin Herring and righty Josh Grosz. GM Bill Schmidt was ousted at season's end.

OPENING DAY PAYROLL: $120,693,976 (21st)

PLAYERS OF THE YEAR

MAJOR LEAGUE
Hunter Goodman
C
.278/.323/.520
31 HR, 28 2B, 91 RBIs
Started 97 G at C

MINOR LEAGUE
Kyle Karros
3B
(Rk,AA,AAA)
.301/.398/.476
6 HR, 23 2B in 75 G

ORGANIZATION LEADERS

Batting		*Qualifiers
MAJORS		
* AVG	Hunter Goodman	.278
* OPS	Hunter Goodman	.843
HR	Hunter Goodman	31
RBI	Hunter Goodman	91
MINORS		
* AVG	Roldy Brito, Fresno/ACL Rockies	.371
* OBP	Roldy Brito, Fresno/ACL Rockies	.444
* SLG	Sam Hilliard, Albuquerque	.565
* OPS	Roldy Brito, Fresno/ACL Rockies	.959
R	Jared Thomas, Hartford/Spokane	92
H	Braylen Wimmer, Hartford/Spokane	148
TB	Braylen Wimmer, Hartford/Spokane	233
2B	Aidan Longwell, Spokane	35
3B	Sam Hilliard, Albuquerque	12
HR	Keston Hiura, Albuquerque	21
RBI	Aidan Longwell, Spokane	80
BB	Jared Thomas, Hartford/Spokane	70
SO	Jared Thomas, Hartford/Spokane	145
SO	Cole Carrigg, Hartford	145
SB	Braiden Ward, Albuquerque/Hartford	57

Pitching		#Qualifiers
MAJORS		
W	Tanner Gordon	6
# ERA	Kyle Freeland	4.98
SO	Kyle Freeland	124
SV	Seth Halvorsen	11
MINORS		
W	Michael Prosecky, Hartford/Spokane	11
L	Jack Mahoney, Hartford	10
# ERA	Everett Catlett, Spokane/Fresno	3.71
G	Welinton Herrera, Hartford/Spokane	52
GS	Michael Prosecky, Hartford/Spokane	27
GS	Konner Eaton, Hartford/Spokane	27
SV	Nathan Blasick, Fresno	19
IP	Konner Eaton, Hartford/Spokane	140
BB	Michael Prosecky, Hartford/Spokane	64
SO	Konner Eaton, Hartford/Spokane	149
# AVG	Michael Prosecky, Hartford/Spokane	.230

2025 PERFORMANCE

General Manager: Bill Schmidt. **Farm Director:** Chris Forbes. **Scouting Director:** Danny Montgomery.

Class	Team	League	W	L	PCT	Finish	Manager
Majors	Colorado Rockies	National	43	119	.265	15 (15)	B. Black/W.Schaeffer
Triple-A	Albuquerque Isotopes	Pacific Coast	62	87	.416	10 (10)	Pedro Lopez
Double-A	Hartford Yard Goats	Eastern	69	68	.504	6 (12)	Bobby Meacham
High-A	Spokane Indians	Northwest	58	74	.439	6 (6)	Robinson Cancel
Low-A	Fresno Grizzlies	California	70	62	.530	2 (8)	Cesar Galvez
Rookie	ACL Rockies	Arizona Complex	37	23	.617	3 (15)	Fred Ocasio
Rookie	DSL Colorado	Dominican	22	33	.400	43 (52)	Eugenio Jose
Rookie	DSL Rockies	Dominican	42	14	.750	1 (52)	Mauricio Gonzalez
Overall 2025 Minor League Record			360	361	.499	14th (30)	

ORGANIZATION STATISTICS

COLORADO ROCKIES
NATIONAL LEAGUE

Batting	B-T	Ht.	Wt.	DOB	AVG	OBP	SLG	G	PA	AB	R	H	2B	3B	HR	RBI	BB	HBP	SH	SF	SO	SB	CS	BB%	SO%
Amador, Adael	S-R	6-0	160	4-11-03	.177	.256	.265	41	128	113	5	20	7	0	1	10	11	1	3	0	27	1	1	8.6	21.1
Arcia, Orlando	R-R	6-0	187	8-4-94	.203	.242	.302	62	182	172	12	35	6	1	3	12	9	0	0	1	39	0	1	4.9	21.4
Beck, Jordan	R-R	6-3	225	4-19-01	.258	.317	.416	148	588	539	62	139	27	5	16	53	43	4	0	1	174	19	8	7.3	29.6
Bernabel, Warming	R-R	6-1	180	6-6-02	.252	.288	.410	40	146	139	15	35	8	1	4	14	7	0	0	0	25	1	1	4.8	17.1
Bouchard, Sean	R-R	6-3	215	5-16-96	.167	.247	.242	32	73	66	7	11	0	1	1	7	7	0	0	0	27	1	1	9.6	37.0
Bryant, Kris	R-R	6-5	230	1-4-92	.154	.195	.205	11	41	39	2	6	2	0	0	1	2	0	0	0	13	0	0	4.9	31.7
Crim, Blaine	R-R	5-10	200	6-17-97	.241	.295	.556	15	61	54	9	13	2	0	5	12	5	0	0	2	22	0	0	8.2	36.1
Doyle, Brenton	R-R	6-2	200	5-14-98	.233	.274	.376	138	538	502	57	117	23	2	15	57	30	0	2	4	138	18	2	5.6	25.7
Estrada, Thairo	R-R	5-10	185	2-22-96	.253	.285	.370	39	165	154	14	39	9	0	3	21	6	2	0	3	26	1	3	3.6	15.8
Farmer, Kyle	R-R	6-0	205	8-17-90	.227	.280	.365	97	300	277	24	63	14	0	8	31	17	4	0	2	66	0	1	5.7	22.0
Fernandez, Yanquiel	L-L	6-2	198	1-1-03	.225	.265	.348	52	147	138	13	31	5	0	4	11	8	0	0	1	44	0	1	5.4	29.9
Freeman, Tyler	R-R	6-0	190	5-21-99	.281	.354	.361	110	428	377	50	106	20	2	2	31	34	11	2	4	51	18	9	7.9	11.9
Fulford, Braxton	R-R	5-10	190	12-9-98	.213	.267	.324	38	120	108	11	23	5	2	1	16	7	2	0	3	36	1	0	5.8	30.0
Goodman, Hunter	R-R	5-11	210	10-8-99	.278	.323	.520	144	579	540	73	150	28	5	31	91	33	4	0	2	152	1	2	5.7	26.3
Hilliard, Sam	L-L	6-5	236	2-21-94	.196	.328	.412	20	61	51	8	10	3	1	2	3	10	0	0	0	23	2	1	16.4	37.7
Hiura, Keston	R-R	5-11	208	8-2-96	.222	.333	.278	8	21	18	3	4	1	0	0	1	3	0	0	0	7	0	0	0.0	33.3
Karros, Kyle	R-R	6-3	220	7-26-02	.226	.308	.277	43	156	137	20	31	4	0	1	9	15	2	0	2	41	0	0	9.6	26.3
Martini, Nick	L-L	5-11	205	6-27-90	.225	.288	.294	43	111	102	9	23	4	0	1	4	9	0	0	0	18	0	0	8.1	16.2
McMahon, Ryan	L-R	6-2	219	12-14-94	.217	.314	.403	100	401	350	42	76	15	1	16	35	49	1	0	1	127	2	1	12.2	31.7
Miller, Owen	R-R	5-11	195	11-15-96	.143	.294	.143	9	17	14	0	2	0	0	0	1	2	1	0	0	4	1	0	11.8	23.5
Moniak, Mickey	L-R	6-2	195	5-13-98	.270	.306	.518	135	461	434	62	117	20	8	24	68	22	2	0	3	110	9	3	4.8	23.9
Nola, Austin	R-R	6-0	197	12-28-89	.184	.225	.211	15	41	38	2	7	1	0	0	1	2	0	1	0	5	0	0	4.9	12.2
Ritter, Ryan	R-R	6-2	200	4-3-00	.296	.337	.620	60	207	187	22	45	9	3	11	38	10	5	4	1	61	3	1	4.8	29.5
Romo, Drew	S-R	5-11	205	8-29-01	.000	.000	.000	3	3	3	0	0	0	0	0	0	0	0	0	0	3	0	0	0.0	100.0
Schunk, Aaron	R-R	6-1	205	7-24-97	.188	.188	.219	16	33	32	1	6	1	0	0	0	0	0	1	0	10	0	0	0.0	30.3
Stallings, Jacob	R-R	6-5	225	12-22-89	.143	.217	.179	29	93	84	4	12	3	0	0	6	5	3	1	0	31	0	0	5.4	33.3
Toglia, Michael	S-L	6-5	226	8-16-98	.190	.258	.353	88	337	306	22	58	15	1	11	32	28	1	0	2	132	3	0	8.3	39.2
Tovar, Ezequiel	R-R	6-0	162	8-1-01	.253	.294	.400	95	390	360	44	91	18	4	9	33	21	1	6	2	98	5	3	5.4	25.1
Trejo, Alan	R-R	6-2	205	5-30-96	.175	.190	.225	14	43	40	3	7	2	0	0	1	1	0	1	1	7	0	0	2.3	16.3
Veen, Zac	L-R	6-3	190	12-12-01	.118	.189	.235	12	37	34	1	4	1	0	1	2	2	1	0	0	14	1	1	5.4	37.8

Pitching	B-T	Ht.	Wt.	DOB	W	L	ERA	G	GS	SV	IP	Hits	Runs	ER	HR	BB	SO	AVG	OBP	SLG	SO%	BB%	BF
Agnos, Zach	R-R	6-0	210	8-15-00	1	3	6.61	30	0	4	31	31	25	23	5	17	19	.261	.350	.487	13.8	12.3	138
Alexander, Scott	L-L	6-2	195	7-10-89	1	1	6.06	19	0	0	16	20	11	11	4	7	6	.313	.389	.609	8.3	9.7	72
Anderson, Nick	R-R	6-4	205	7-5-90	0	0	6.14	12	0	0	15	17	10	10	3	2	10	.288	.311	.508	16.4	3.3	61
Bird, Jake	R-R	6-3	200	12-4-95	4	1	4.73	45	0	0	53	56	30	28	5	23	62	.271	.347	.411	26.3	9.7	236
Blalock, Bradley	R-R	6-2	200	12-25-00	2	6	9.36	14	12	0	59	85	61	61	17	23	27	.350	.405	.597	9.8	8.4	275
Brown, McCade	R-R	6-6	225	8-15-00	0	5	7.36	7	7	0	26	30	21	21	6	17	23	.291	.413	.524	18.3	13.5	126
Chivilli, Angel	R-R	6-2	162	7-28-02	1	5	7.06	43	0	0	59	76	49	46	13	23	43	.309	.382	.516	15.6	8.4	273
Contreras, Roansy	R-R	6-0	175	11-7-99	0	0	8.64	4	0	0	8	9	8	8	3	1	4	.273	.294	.545	11.8	2.9	34
Darnell, Dugan	L-R	6-2	205	6-26-97	1	0	3.86	9	0	0	12	10	5	5	1	7	5	.244	.354	.366	10.4	14.6	48
Dollander, Chase	R-R	6-2	200	10-26-01	2	12	6.52	21	21	0	98	103	76	71	18	49	82	.270	.359	.454	18.6	11.1	441
Farmer, Kyle	R-R	6-0	205	8-17-90	0	0	9.00	1	0	0	1	3	1	1	1	0	0	.600	.600	1.200	0.0	0.0	5
Feltner, Ryan	R-R	6-4	190	9-2-96	2	4	4.75	6	6	0	30	33	17	16	4	12	25	.270	.333	.443	18.5	8.9	135
Freeland, Kyle	L-L	6-4	204	5-14-93	5	17	4.98	31	31	0	163	193	105	90	22	38	124	.294	.335	.461	17.5	5.4	709
Gilbreath, Lucas	L-L	6-1	185	3-5-96	0	0	9.00	1	0	0	1	1	1	1	0	2	0	.250	1.000	.500	0.0	0	4
Gomber, Austin	L-L	6-5	320	11-23-93	0	7	7.49	12	12	0	58	82	51	48	16	17	34	.325	.369	.603	12.5	6.3	272
Gordon, Tanner	L-R	6-5	215	10-26-97	6	8	6.33	15	15	0	75	96	60	53	16	17	62	.304	.344	.532	15.0	5.0	337
Halvorsen, Seth	R-R	6-2	225	2-18-00	1	2	4.99	42	0	11	40	41	26	22	7	21	36	.273	.360	.493	20.8	12.1	173
Herget, Jimmy	R-R	6-3	190	9-9-93	1	2	2.48	59	0	0	83	72	24	23	6	26	81	.233	.303	.346	23.3	7.5	347
Hill, Jaden	R-R	6-4	234	12-22-99	1	1	3.38	28	0	0	29	27	14	11	2	12	31	.243	.326	.378	24.0	9.3	129
Kinley, Tyler	R-R	6-4	220	1-31-91	1	3	5.66	49	0	5	43	52	33	27	5	27	51	.230	.332	.366	23.8	12.6	214
Marquez, German	R-R	6-1	230	2-22-95	3	16	6.70	26	26	0	126	168	106	94	23	48	83	.317	.378	.545	14.0	8.1	591

Batting																						
Mejia, Juan	R-R	6-3	200	7-4-00	2	2	3.96	55	0	1	61	52	34	27	6	25	68	.230	.319	.385	26.1	9.6	261
Molina, Anthony	R-R	6-1	170	1-12-02	1	1	7.27	17	1	0	35	52	30	28	12	6	24	.351	.382	.649	15.0	3.8	160
Nola, Austin	R-R	6-0	197	12-28-89	0	0	72.00	1	0	0	1	8	8	8	2	0	0	.889	.727	2.000	0.0	0.0	11
Palmquist, Carson	L-L	6-3	185	10-17-00	0	4	8.91	9	7	0	34	45	35	34	10	25	27	.321	.420	.614	15.4	14.3	175
Peralta, Luis	L-L	5-11	170	1-6-01	1	3	9.47	22	0	0	19	26	22	20	6	18	16	.325	.455	.588	15.8	17.8	101
Rolison, Ryan	L-L	6-2	213	7-11-97	1	0	7.02	31	1	0	42	55	35	33	11	20	25	.324	.391	.565	13.0	10.4	193
Senzatela, Antonio	R-R	6-1	236	1-21-95	4	15	6.65	30	23	0	130	192	103	96	22	47	73	.347	.402	.547	11.8	7.6	618
Stallings, Jacob	R-R	6-5	225	12-22-89	0	0	4.50	1	0	0	2	2	1	1	0	0	1	.250	.250	.375	12.5	0.0	8
Trejo, Alan	R-R	6-2	205	5-30-96	0	0	0.00	1	0	0	1	0	0	0	0	0	0	.333	.333	.333	0.0	0.0	3
Vodnik, Victor	R-R	6-0	200	10-9-99	4	3	3.02	52	0	10	51	45	19	17	4	26	49	.239	.330	.372	22.8	12.1	215

Fielding

Catcher	PCT	G	PO	A	E	DP	PB
Fulford	.972	32	203	8	6	1	1
Goodman	.987	104	657	39	9	3	7
Nola	1.000	12	64	1	0	0	0
Romo	1.000	1	3	0	0	0	0
Stallings	.980	27	184	12	4	0	1

First Base	PCT	G	PO	A	E	DP
Arcia	1.000	11	59	3	0	8
Bernabel	.989	37	260	20	3	29
Bouchard	1.000	1	9	1	0	0
Crim	1.000	14	87	5	0	9
Farmer	.986	17	122	15	2	14
Hiura	.950	8	36	2	2	4
Nola	1.000	1	5	0	0	0
Toglia	.996	86	717	48	3	80

Second Base	PCT	G	PO	A	E	DP
Amador	.978	41	46	90	3	18
Arcia	.982	21	18	37	1	7
Estrada	.973	39	46	100	4	28
Farmer	1.000	33	35	84	0	27
Freeman	.977	17	18	25	1	5
Miller	1.000	5	7	11	0	2
Ritter	.991	29	49	63	1	19
Schunk	1.000	5	1	9	0	0

Third Base	PCT	G	PO	A	E	DP
Arcia	.929	20	12	27	3	2
Bernabel	1.000	2	0	2	0	0
Farmer	.944	10	8	9	1	0
Freeman	.000	1	0	0	0	0
Karros	.981	42	31	71	2	8
McMahon	.978	100	75	195	6	15
Miller	1.000	2	1	1	0	0
Schunk	1.000	5	0	2	0	0

Shortstop	PCT	G	PO	A	E	DP
Arcia	.948	16	25	30	3	13
Farmer	.975	12	11	28	1	6
Ritter	.962	30	46	80	5	19
Schunk	1.000	9	8	18	0	3
Tovar	.977	95	148	237	9	57
Trejo	.968	13	23	38	2	9

Outfield	PCT	G	PO	A	E	DP
Beck	.989	140	270	12	3	2
Bouchard	.955	19	21	0	1	0
Doyle	.995	131	375	6	2	2
Fernandez	.957	22	41	4	2	1
Freeman	.991	67	105	2	1	0
Hilliard	1.000	17	24	0	0	0
Martini	1.000	17	28	3	0	0
Moniak	.972	125	242	3	7	1
Veen	1.000	10	16	0	0	0

COLORADO ROCKIES

ALBUQUERQUE ISOTOPES
PACIFIC COAST LEAGUE — TRIPLE-A

Batting	B-T	Ht.	Wt.	DOB	AVG	OBP	SLG	G	PA	AB	R	H	2B	3B	HR	RBI	BB	HBP	SH	SF	SO	SB	CS	BB%	SO%
Amador, Adael	S-R	6-0	160	4-11-03	.303	.405	.478	80	371	314	49	95	16	3	11	59	50	5	1	1	47	20	9	13.5	12.7
Beck, Jordan	R-R	6-3	225	4-19-01	.143	.189	.286	8	37	35	4	5	0	1	1	3	2	0	0	0	9	2	0	5.4	24.3
Bernabel, Warming	R-R	6-1	180	6-6-02	.301	.356	.450	75	316	282	46	85	18	0	8	45	23	4	0	6	39	5	1	7.3	12.3
Boone, Trevor	R-R	6-2	210	9-9-97	.210	.258	.479	38	128	119	23	25	4	2	8	26	7	1	0	1	51	2	0	5.5	39.8
Bouchard, Sean	R-R	6-3	215	5-16-96	.234	.373	.406	68	300	244	40	57	11	2	9	32	50	5	0	1	91	10	2	16.7	30.3
Carreras, Julio	R-R	6-1	190	1-12-00	.280	.353	.373	50	173	150	31	42	7	2	1	17	16	2	3	2	38	11	4	9.2	22.0
Clifford, Nolan	L-R	5-10	175	2-4-02	.368	.455	.474	6	23	19	3	7	1	0	1	0	3	3	0	1	5	0	0	13.0	21.7
Cope, Daniel	R-R	6-0	195	6-15-97	.206	.325	.338	23	80	68	11	14	4	1	1	9	9	3	0	0	18	2	1	11.3	26.3
Crim, Blaine	R-R	5-10	200	6-17-97	.273	.360	.424	26	114	99	13	27	6	0	3	14	13	1	0	1	20	1	0	11.4	17.5
Estrada, Thairo	R-R	5-10	185	2-22-96	.304	.333	.348	5	24	23	4	7	1	0	0	1	1	0	0	0	5	0	0	4.2	20.8
Fernandez, Yanquiel	L-L	6-2	198	1-1-03	.284	.347	.502	64	271	243	43	69	14	0	13	39	23	2	0	3	38	0	1	8.5	14.0
Freeman, Tyler	R-R	6-0	190	5-21-99	.167	.375	.250	4	16	12	2	2	1	0	0	0	2	2	0	0	2	0	0	12.5	12.5
Fulford, Braxton	R-R	5-10	190	12-9-98	.354	.433	.714	43	171	147	35	52	10	2	13	37	17	5	0	2	40	3	2	9.9	23.4
Hilliard, Sam	L-L	6-5	236	2-21-94	.288	.367	.565	91	414	361	64	104	25	12	17	66	47	1	0	5	108	15	1	11.4	26.1
Hiura, Keston	R-R	5-11	208	8-2-96	.272	.369	.507	100	445	383	62	104	31	3	21	67	47	13	0	2	123	1	1	10.6	27.6
Karros, Kyle	R-R	6-5	220	7-26-02	.306	.368	.500	16	68	62	9	19	4	1	2	4	5	1	0	0	12	0	0	7.4	17.6
Miller, Owen	R-R	5-11	195	11-15-96	.277	.329	.429	102	441	394	64	109	25	1	11	65	29	7	0	11	71	13	3	6.6	16.1
Nola, Austin	R-R	6-0	197	12-28-89	.347	.411	.474	26	107	95	14	33	7	1	1	19	10	1	0	1	14	0	0	9.3	13.1
Palma, Ronaiker	R-R	5-8	180	1-2-00	.324	.375	.378	22	81	74	10	24	4	0	0	5	6	0	1	0	9	0	0	7.4	12.3
Quezada, Andrew	L-R	6-1	185	6-28-97	.000	.000	.000	27	1	1	0	0	0	0	0	0	0	0	0	0	1	0	0	0.0	100.0
Ritter, Ryan	R-R	6-2	210	4-11-00	.303	.405	.610	55	260	218	45	66	13	3	16	50	34	4	3	1	54	3	2	13.1	20.8
Romo, Drew	S-R	5-11	205	8-29-01	.264	.329	.409	60	244	220	28	58	11	0	7	23	18	4	1	1	63	2	0	7.4	25.8
Schunk, Aaron	R-R	6-1	205	7-24-97	.291	.352	.477	90	363	323	57	94	16	7	10	59	29	4	2	5	66	3	2	8.0	18.2
Thompson, Sterlin	L-R	6-4	200	6-26-01	.296	.392	.519	120	513	439	82	130	28	8	18	66	53	18	0	3	107	12	4	10.3	20.9
Toglia, Michael	S-L	6-5	226	8-16-98	.331	.401	.624	42	177	157	31	52	9	2	11	36	19	0	0	1	46	0	2	10.7	26.0
Torres, Jose	R-R	6-0	171	9-28-99	.239	.299	.436	35	127	117	20	28	4	2	5	13	10	0	0	0	39	1	0	7.9	30.7
Tovar, Ezequiel	R-R	6-0	162	8-1-01	.163	.196	.209	11	46	43	3	7	2	0	0	1	2	0	0	0	10	0	0	4.3	21.7
Veen, Zac	L-R	6-4	190	12-12-01	.289	.354	.468	90	412	370	57	107	23	5	11	59	35	3	2	2	84	15	5	8.5	20.4
Ward, Braiden	L-R	5-10	160	1-18-99	.331	.440	.466	41	163	133	45	44	7	1	1	21	16	10	4	0	23	35	2	9.8	14.1

Pitching	B-T	Ht.	Wt.	DOB	W	L	ERA	G	GS	SV	IP	Hits	Runs	ER	HR	BB	SO	AVG	OBP	SLG	SO%	BB%	BF
Agnos, Zach	R-R	6-0	210	8-15-00	0	0	2.25	10	0	3	12	6	3	3	1	4	14	.146	.222	.244	30.4	8.7	46
Albright, Mason	L-L	6-0	190	11-26-02	3	7	7.80	21	19	0	85	120	79	74	28	35	65	.332	.390	.640	16.0	8.6	405
Anderson, Nick	R-R	6-4	205	7-5-90	1	1	4.73	15	0	4	13	15	8	7	1	7	18	.288	.367	.462	29.5	11.5	61
Baumgartner, Collin	R-R	6-6	250	9-26-98	0	3	2.42	17	0	2	22	18	8	6	2	9	25	.225	.315	.338	27.2	9.8	92
Blalock, Bradley	R-R	6-2	200	12-25-00	1	5	8.60	15	15	0	61	83	60	58	11	35	52	.324	.400	.559	17.5	11.8	297
Brnovich, Kyle	L-R	6-2	190	10-20-97	1	2	11.57	7	4	0	19	26	26	24	7	15	17	.342	.441	.750	17.9	15.8	95
Castillo, Bryan	R-R	6-0	145	5-29-97	0	0	4.50	15	0	0	18	12	9	9	1	10	24	.194	.336	.315	31.6	13.2	76
Castillo, Diego	R-R	6-3	268	1-18-94	3	3	5.06	20	0	2	21	20	13	12	4	13	23	.253	.372	.418	24.2	13.7	95
Chivilli, Angel	R-R	6-2	162	7-28-02	0	1	7.00	10	0	1	9	7	7	0	2	10	.278	.316	.333	26.3	5.3	38

COLORADO ROCKIES

	B-T	Ht.	Wt.	DOB			AVG	OBP	SLG	G	PA	AB	R	H	2B	3B	HR	RBI	BB	HBP	SH	SF	SO	SB	CS	BB%	SO%
Curry, Xzavion	R-R	6-0	195	7-27-98	2	3	7.97	8	8	0	35	45	31	31	8	18	19	.310	.394	.593			11.5	10.9		165	
Darnell, Dugan	L-R	6-2	205	6-26-97	5	2	3.19	35	1	1	54	42	21	19	4	19	63	.216	.287	.376			28.8	8.7		219	
Dollander, Chase	R-R	6-2	200	10-26-01	0	2	7.04	4	4	0	15	19	12	12	1	10	17	.306	.411	.419			23.3	13.7		73	
Feltner, Ryan	R-R	6-4	190	9-2-96	0	3	8.57	6	6	0	21	29	23	20	5	23	13	.349	.491	.614			11.9	21.1		109	
Gilbreath, Lucas	L-L	6-1	185	3-5-96	1	0	7.59	43	0	1	43	48	36	36	9	28	39	.284	.390	.521			19.3	13.9		202	
Gomber, Austin	L-L	6-5	220	11-23-93	0	1	2.25	2	2	0	8	4	3	2	1	5	10	.138	.265	.276			29.4	14.7		34	
Gordon, Tanner	L-R	6-5	215	10-26-97	1	4	5.25	12	12	0	58	78	36	34	9	11	47	.324	.353	.531			18.6	4.3		253	
Green, Mason	L-L	6-1	195	2-5-99	0	0	0.00	3	0	0	5	1	5	0	1	3	2	.059	.238	.235			9.5	14.3		21	
Hardy, Brendan	R-R	6-4	170	12-15-99	0	0	6.75	2	0	0	1	1	1	1	1	4	1	.200	.556	.800			11.1	44.4		9	
Hill, Jaden	R-R	6-4	234	12-22-99	2	1	3.57	14	0	1	18	10	7	7	1	3	28	.159	.209	.270			41.8	4.5		67	
Hughes, Gabriel	R-R	6-4	220	8-22-01	4	3	5.11	14	14	0	62	67	38	35	9	29	48	.277	.359	.475			17.5	10.6		274	
Juarez, Victor	R-R	6-0	173	6-19-03	1	0	4.15	2	0	0	4	9	3	2	0	2	3	.429	.478	.571			13.0	8.7		23	
Justice, Evan	L-L	6-4	205	7-4-98	4	1	7.50	25	1	1	30	31	27	25	6	25	27	.267	.403	.466			18.6	17.2		145	
Kauffmann, Karl	R-R	6-2	200	8-15-97	2	3	5.51	42	2	1	82	90	51	50	11	55	62	.284	.391	.457			16.2	14.4		382	
Kelly, Antoine	L-L	6-5	205	12-5-99	3	5	5.63	34	0	4	38	45	32	24	2	27	61	.287	.409	.389			21.2	14.0		193	
Marquez, German	R-R	6-1	230	2-22-95	0	0	3.68	2	2	0	7	7	3	3	1	1	10	.241	.267	.517			33.3	3.3		30	
McGowan, Bryce	R-R	6-1	205	3-20-00	0	0	18.00	2	0	0	1	4	4	2	0	3	0	.500	.636	.625			0.0	27.3		11	
Mejia, Juan	R-R	6-3	200	7-4-00	1	0	4.73	10	0	0	13	8	8	7	0	6	22	.170	.291	.234			39.3	10.7		56	
Molina, Anthony	R-R	6-1	170	1-12-02	4	5	6.59	15	15	0	70	102	58	51	9	30	51	.336	.395	.523			15.0	8.8		339	
O'Loughlin, Jack	L-L	6-5	223	3-14-00	1	3	6.91	17	10	0	42	51	38	32	7	36	28	.304	.431	.506			13.4	17.2		209	
Palmquist, Carson	L-L	6-3	185	10-17-00	4	5	4.64	26	10	0	78	62	43	40	7	42	94	.219	.334	.371			27.8	12.4		338	
Peralta, Luis	L-L	5-11	170	1-6-01	1	4	9.09	34	0	0	35	46	40	35	6	28	51	.311	.423	.486			28.0	15.4		182	
Quezada, Andrew	L-L	6-1	185	6-28-97	2	9	6.90	27	18	1	91	132	82	70	14	39	55	.347	.410	.561			12.8	9.1		429	
Rolison, Ryan	R-L	6-2	213	7-11-97	3	1	3.34	20	1	1	30	33	13	11	1	9	32	.287	.346	.383			25.2	7.1		127	
Skipper, Carson	L-L	6-2	211	8-12-99	2	0	3.27	12	0	0	22	23	9	8	3	9	22	.271	.340	.435			22.7	9.3		97	
Turner, Matt	L-L	6-4	180	8-4-99	1	2	6.45	31	4	1	45	53	37	32	3	25	42	.294	.398	.394			19.7	11.7		213	
Van Scoyoc, Connor	R-R	6-6	234	11-26-99	8	6	4.19	41	0	0	86	85	48	40	6	29	46	.255	.319	.369			12.5	7.9		368	
Van Sickle, Bryson	L-L	6-0	165	12-31-00	0	0	9.00	2	0	0	3	8	7	3	1	3	2	.421	.500	.684			9.1	13.6		22	
Yan, Jefry	L-L	6-3	185	8-17-96	1	3	7.28	27	1	0	30	33	27	24	4	22	45	.275	.390	.442			30.8	15.1		146	

Fielding

Catcher	PCT	G	PO	A	E	DP	PB
Cope	.986	21	135	4	2	0	2
Fulford	.991	37	299	28	3	3	6
Nola	.987	25	212	9	3	0	1
Palma	.982	17	105	6	2	3	2
Romo	.985	54	442	29	7	2	2

First Base	PCT	G	PO	A	E	DP
Bernabel	.990	26	178	13	2	22
Boone	.938	2	12	3	1	2
Bouchard	1.000	1	9	1	0	0
Crim	.990	12	98	4	1	14
Hiura	.994	75	586	37	4	62
Karros	1.000	2	14	0	0	3
Miller	1.000	5	29	2	0	3
Toglia	.996	28	225	16	1	28

Second Base	PCT	G	PO	A	E	DP
Amador	.979	75	133	189	7	54

	PCT	G	PO	A	E	DP
Carreras	.962	39	64	115	7	22
Clifford	1.000	5	4	9	0	3
Estrada	.947	4	4	14	1	4
Freeman	1.000	2	2	5	0	1
Miller	1.000	12	23	26	0	7
Palma	.667	1	1	1	1	1
Ritter	1.000	4	9	8	0	4
Schunk	.967	8	12	17	1	3
Ward	.970	6	16	16	1	4

Third Base	PCT	G	PO	A	E	DP
Bernabel	.905	39	29	57	9	7
Carreras	.864	5	7	12	3	2
Clifford	.000	1	0	0	0	0
Karros	.975	14	12	27	1	1
Miller	.932	24	17	38	4	9
Ritter	1.000	1	3	2	0	0
Schunk	.942	65	48	115	10	14
Ward	.667	3	0	2	1	0

Shortstop	PCT	G	PO	A	E	DP
Carreras	1.000	1	1	2	0	0
Miller	.967	52	74	130	7	38
Ritter	.981	48	58	149	4	29
Schunk	1.000	11	16	33	0	7
Torres	.919	35	49	98	13	18
Tovar	.947	8	8	10	1	4

Outfield	PCT	G	PO	A	E	DP
Beck	1.000	8	9	1	0	0
Boone	.969	31	59	3	2	0
Bouchard	.968	60	92	0	3	0
Fernandez	.983	53	112	5	2	2
Freeman	1.000	2	3	0	0	0
Hilliard	.977	87	205	3	5	0
Miller	.923	8	12	0	1	0
Thompson	.968	101	172	9	6	4
Veen	.971	80	133	3	4	1
Ward	1.000	27	62	2	0	2

HARTFORD YARD GOATS
EASTERN LEAGUE
DOUBLE-A

Batting	B-T	Ht.	Wt.	DOB	AVG	OBP	SLG	G	PA	AB	R	H	2B	3B	HR	RBI	BB	HBP	SH	SF	SO	SB	CS	BB%	SO%
Betancourt, Bryant	L-R	5-11	170	10-12-03	.234	.314	.363	90	344	303	37	71	9	0	10	42	35	2	0	4	65	3	1	10.2	18.9
Carreras, Julio	R-R	6-1	190	1-12-00	.220	.309	.376	33	126	109	11	24	4	2	3	19	12	2	3	0	38	8	0	9.5	30.2
Carrigg, Cole	S-R	6-3	190	5-8-02	.237	.316	.394	123	537	477	81	113	18	6	15	64	35	11	3	1	145	46	10	8.4	27.0
Condon, Charlie	R-R	6-6	211	4-14-03	.235	.342	.465	55	237	200	27	47	7	3	11	38	25	9	0	3	67	1	0	10.5	28.3
Cordova, Jose	R-R	6-0	180	1-11-00	.243	.356	.366	84	330	276	42	67	14	1	6	27	45	4	1	1	65	5	0	13.6	19.7
Guerrero, Juan	R-R	6-1	160	9-10-01	.259	.322	.103	413	370	36	96	17	0	2	34	32	1	2	8	63	13	6	7.7	15.3
Hill, Glenallen	S-R	5-9	170	9-30-00	.164	.263	.315	55	192	165	16	27	7	3	4	21	18	5	2	2	72	10	0	9.4	37.5
Jorge, Dyan	R-R	6-3	170	3-18-03	.198	.274	.246	120	445	398	40	79	13	0	2	30	38	4	3	2	90	18	9	8.5	20.2
Karros, Kyle	R-R	6-5	220	7-26-02	.294	.399	.462	55	234	197	34	58	17	2	4	21	32	3	0	1	45	7	0	13.7	19.2
Kent, Nic	R-R	6-2	185	4-10-00	.220	.304	.298	104	384	336	38	74	10	2	4	44	33	9	2	3	80	6	1	8.6	20.8
Kokoska, Zach	L-L	6-1	200	10-20-98	.187	.279	.382	77	280	246	40	46	10	1	12	35	27	5	0	2	101	12	3	9.6	36.1
McCabe, Ben	R-R	6-0	185	2-4-00	.105	.246	.158	21	70	57	6	6	3	0	0	2	4	7	0	1	25	0	0	5.7	35.7
Messina, Cole	R-R	6-0	230	5-14-00	.200	.200	.200	3	10	10	0	2	0	0	0	0	0	0	0	0	1	0	0	0.0	10.0
Montgomery, Benny	R-R	6-4	200	9-9-02	.201	.274	.263	86	355	319	34	64	8	0	4	36	31	2	1	2	129	6	5	8.7	36.3
Palma, Ronaiker	R-R	5-8	180	1-2-00	.179	.220	.231	23	82	78	6	14	1	0	1	4	4	0	0	0	12	1	0	4.9	14.6
Riggio, Roc	L-R	5-10	180	6-11-02	.256	.346	.389	26	107	90	13	23	6	0	2	14	14	0	0	3	23	8	4	13.1	21.5
Thomas, Jared	L-L	6-2	175	7-1-03	.245	.347	.374	45	191	163	28	40	10	1	3	15	25	1	1	1	56	6	11	5	13.1	34.6
Torres, Jose	R-R	6-0	171	9-28-99	.244	.310	.421	65	272	242	32	59	13	0	10	42	22	3	1	4	89	8	1	8.1	32.7
Ward, Braiden	L-R	5-10	160	1-18-99	.259	.360	.333	53	205	174	29	45	10	0	1	16	19	5	1	3	38	22	5	9.3	18.5
Wimmer, Braylen	R-R	6-4	200	12-27-00	.284	.346	.389	45	183	162	20	46	8	0	3	16	13	4	1	3	42	11	2	7.1	23.0

COLORADO ROCKIES

Pitching	B-T	Ht.	Wt.	DOB	W	L	ERA	G	GS	SV	IP	Hits	Runs	ER	HR	BB	SO	AVG	OBP	SLG	SO%	BB%	BF
Adams, Blake	R-R	6-2	215	9-11-00	6	7	5.48	30	16	0	90	88	58	55	15	27	86	.254	.309	.484	22.6	7.1	381
Albright, Mason	L-L	6-0	190	11-26-02	3	2	2.51	6	6	0	32	26	10	9	4	8	20	.224	.272	.379	15.9	6.3	126
Barger, Alec	R-R	6-2	201	3-24-98	1	2	5.40	29	0	0	33	27	20	20	7	16	32	.235	.338	.478	23.4	11.7	137
Baumgartner, Collin	L-R	6-6	250	9-26-98	3	2	2.79	32	0	5	39	30	15	12	3	20	48	.213	.309	.362	29.4	12.3	163
Brown, McCade	R-R	6-6	225	8-15-00	4	2	3.14	11	11	0	43	31	16	15	4	15	57	.203	.276	.353	33.5	8.8	170
Castillo, Brayan	R-R	6-0	145	9-11-00	2	2	2.12	26	0	9	34	22	11	8	1	17	40	.179	.282	.236	28.2	12.0	142
Eaton, Konner	R-L	6-3	210	10-30-02	1	1	5.30	4	4	0	19	15	12	11	1	10	24	.227	.350	.318	30.0	12.5	80
Gomber, Austin	L-L	6-5	220	11-23-93	0	0	2.25	1	1	0	4	2	1	1	0	0	3	.143	.143	.214	21.4	0.0	14
Green, Mason	L-L	6-1	195	2-5-99	6	4	4.22	36	8	0	70	61	37	33	4	36	78	.230	.330	.355	25.4	11.7	307
Herrera, Welinton	L-L	6-0	166	4-3-04	4	5	3.50	37	0	7	46	41	22	18	2	19	70	.232	.315	.333	34.3	9.3	204
Hughes, Gabriel	R-R	6-4	220	8-22-01	1	3	3.07	9	9	0	41	27	15	14	4	8	35	.184	.236	.313	22.3	5.1	157
Juarez, Victor	R-R	6-0	173	6-19-03	6	3	3.49	35	1	4	77	64	32	30	9	18	68	.230	.291	.406	22.4	5.9	303
Mahoney, Jack	R-R	6-3	205	8-13-01	3	10	5.93	24	24	0	105	129	71	69	11	46	81	.310	.386	.469	17.1	9.7	473
McGowan, Bryce	R-R	6-1	205	3-20-00	2	2	4.09	46	0	3	55	52	28	25	3	27	55	.255	.352	.373	23.2	11.4	237
Palermo, Davison	R-R	6-4	200	12-16-99	0	1	4.20	11	0	0	15	17	11	7	1	11	8	.283	.403	.417	11.1	15.3	72
Prosecky, Michael	L-L	6-3	200	2-28-01	4	2	4.97	9	9	0	38	36	22	21	3	23	34	.257	.361	.386	20.5	13.9	166
Shawver, Evan	R-L	6-0	175	9-11-99	1	0	5.30	36	0	1	53	64	33	31	7	23	56	.300	.369	.488	23.0	9.5	243
Shields, Ben	R-L	6-4	210	1-23-99	1	0	2.33	5	5	0	19	13	5	5	1	6	24	.191	.267	.294	31.6	7.9	76
Skipper, Carson	L-L	6-2	211	8-12-99	4	1	2.82	32	0	1	45	39	15	14	3	15	46	.234	.306	.347	24.6	8.0	187
Smith, Austin	R-R	6-4	210	6-22-99	2	3	1.69	15	0	4	16	11	6	3	1	6	12	.204	.270	.333	18.8	9.4	64
Staine, Connor	R-R	6-4	200	1-12-01	3	8	4.91	25	25	0	106	105	65	58	15	56	82	.259	.352	.436	17.3	11.8	475
Sullivan, Sean	R-L	6-4	190	7-22-02	9	6	3.14	18	18	0	97	82	35	34	7	24	95	.227	.283	.340	24.2	6.1	392
Torres, Carlos	R-R	6-4	240	5-3-01	2	1	4.39	27	0	1	41	48	21	20	4	14	27	.302	.367	.447	14.9	7.7	181
Turner, Matt	L-L	6-4	180	8-4-99	1	0	3.18	10	0	3	11	9	4	4	0	6	17	.209	.306	.279	34.7	12.2	49
Vodnik, Victor	R-R	6-0	200	10-9-99	0	0	10.80	2	0	0	2	1	2	2	0	1	2	.167	.250	.167	25.0	12.5	8
Weatherly, Sam	L-L	6-4	205	5-28-99	0	1	8.06	39	0	2	48	44	46	43	10	44	66	.239	.396	.484	28.0	18.6	236

Fielding

Catcher	PCT	G	PO	A	E	DP	PB
Betancourt	.986	79	667	55	10	3	7
Cordova	.990	35	274	13	3	3	5
McCabe	1.000	13	123	4	0	2	2
Messina	1.000	1	7	1	0	0	0
Palma	.984	16	116	8	2	1	3

First Base	PCT	G	PO	A	E	DP
Betancourt	1.000	7	30	2	0	2
Condon	.997	48	350	28	1	27
Cordova	.993	35	248	22	2	12
Karros	1.000	6	37	3	0	4
Kent	1.000	16	100	7	0	9
Kokoska	.990	30	186	18	2	19

Second Base	PCT	G	PO	A	E	DP
Carreras	1.000	1	0	2	0	0
Hill	.959	17	21	26	2	4
Jorge	.975	50	84	115	5	18
Kent	.991	34	47	65	1	14
Riggio	1.000	23	32	54	0	15
Torres	1.000	3	4	9	0	2
Wimmer	1.000	11	15	29	0	6

Third Base	PCT	G	PO	A	E	DP
Carreras	.941	24	15	33	3	4
Condon	1.000	3	2	4	0	0
Karros	.984	44	41	85	2	9
Kent	.982	51	43	66	2	5
Torres	1.000	5	2	10	0	3
Wimmer	.925	13	14	23	3	2

Shortstop	PCT	G	PO	A	E	DP
Carreras	.964	9	11	16	1	4
Jorge	.966	69	107	148	9	28
Kent	.917	3	5	6	1	1
Torres	.974	57	59	125	5	22

Outfield	PCT	G	PO	A	E	DP
Carrigg	.979	110	267	18	6	5
Guerrero	.967	91	171	7	6	1
Hill	.972	30	67	2	2	0
Kokoska	1.000	28	38	1	0	0
Montgomery	.989	53	88	1	1	0
Thomas	.979	44	90	3	2	0
Ward	.981	51	101	3	2	1
Wimmer	.957	21	21	1	1	0

SPOKANE INDIANS
NORTHWEST LEAGUE — HIGH-A

Batting	B-T	Ht.	Wt.	DOB	AVG	OBP	SLG	G	PA	AB	R	H	2B	3B	HR	RBI	BB	HBP	SH	SF	SO	SB	CS	BB%	SO%
Andrews, EJ	R-R	6-1	210	9-28-00	.156	.284	.307	62	217	179	22	28	8	2	5	18	27	5	6	0	69	5	2	12.4	31.8
Belyeu, Max	L-R	6-2	195	12-15-03	.150	.244	.300	21	90	80	13	12	0	0	4	9	9	1	0	0	32	3	0	10.0	35.6
Bugarin, Jesus	R-R	5-10	180	12-2-01	.212	.257	.279	67	222	208	21	44	8	0	2	22	11	2	0	1	63	8	0	5.0	28.4
Clifford, Nolan	L-R	5-10	175	2-4-02	.000	.429	.000	3	7	4	0	0	0	0	0	0	3	0	0	0	2	0	1	42.9	28.6
Condon, Charlie	R-R	6-6	211	4-14-03	.312	.431	.420	35	167	138	30	43	6	0	3	17	26	3	0	0	35	0	2	15.6	21.0
Hedges, Jean	R-R	6-1	185	4-19-04	.195	.303	.234	20	89	77	8	15	3	0	0	3	10	2	0	0	17	2	0	11.2	19.1
Hill, Glenallen	S-R	5-9	170	9-30-00	.229	.270	.486	9	37	35	3	8	3	0	2	2	1	1	0	0	11	5	1	2.7	29.7
Hobson, Caleb	R-R	6-1	183	1-24-02	.158	.317	.234	96	349	278	54	44	9	3	2	16	58	7	5	1	141	30	6	16.6	40.4
Hopfe, Tommy	S-R	6-1	195	10-11-02	.236	.322	.321	30	121	106	8	25	3	0	2	6	11	3	0	1	18	4	3	9.1	14.9
Longwell, Aidan	L-L	6-2	205	10-17-01	.274	.345	.465	121	516	452	55	124	35	3	15	80	48	5	2	8	99	5	2	9.3	19.2
McCabe, Ben	R-R	6-0	185	2-4-00	.160	.288	.200	18	59	50	4	8	2	0	0	1	5	4	0	0	23	0	1	8.5	39.0
Messina, Cole	R-R	6-0	230	5-14-03	.259	.358	.382	107	434	374	48	97	23	1	7	42	51	7	0	1	72	14	6	11.8	16.6
Messinger, Skyler	R-R	6-3	220	.11-1-98	.239	.299	.366	116	462	415	40	99	21	1	10	51	27	12	0	8	107	12	8	5.8	23.2
Obertop, Jimmy	R-L	6-2	230	6-12-00	.239	.321	.500	14	53	46	6	11	1	1	3	7	6	0	0	1	16	0	1	11.3	30.2
Ordonez, Jesus	R-R	5-8	180	12-26-99	.145	.211	.229	25	91	83	6	12	4	0	1	7	5	2	1	0	20	2	1	5.5	22.0
Perez, Andy	L-R	6-3	165	6-3-04	.271	.314	.389	115	483	447	56	121	26	3	7	59	24	5	4	2	81	19	4	5.0	16.8
Perez, Jean	R-R	5-10	178	7-20-02	.197	.240	.301	74	271	249	22	49	6	0	6	15	8	7	4	3	63	9	3	3.0	23.2
Perry, Darius	R-R	6-2	200	5-3-01	.076	.129	.212	23	71	66	3	5	0	0	3	4	4	0	1	0	31	0	1	5.6	43.7
Thomas, Jared	L-L	6-2	175	7-1-03	.330	.427	.495	73	342	291	64	96	13	1	11	45	45	5	0	1	79	22	5	13.2	23.1
Tucker, Tevin	R-R	6-0	190	2-10-00	.197	.324	.289	86	288	239	35	47	13	0	3	31	43	1	2	7	63	13	1	14.9	25.0
Wimmer, Braylen	R-R	6-4	200	12-27-00	.302	.376	.503	86	386	338	52	102	22	2	14	53	31	11	3	3	85	26	1	8.0	22.0
Wright, Blake	R-R	5-11	195	2-12-02	.255	.301	.443	56	232	212	25	54	17	1	7	25	10	5	3	2	38	2	0	4.3	16.4

Pitching	B-T	Ht.	Wt.	DOB	W	L	ERA	G	GS	SV	IP	Hits	Runs	ER	HR	BB	SO	AVG	OBP	SLG	SO%	BB%	BF
Becker, Austin	R-R	6-5	215	9-2-99	0	2	3.90	19	0	0	28	28	13	12	4	17	32	.255	.364	.436	24.6	13.1	130
Brown, McCade	R-R	6-6	225	8-15-00	0	0	1.60	9	9	0	34	21	9	6	2	15	48	.178	.287	.237	35.3	11.0	136

COLORADO ROCKIES

Player	B-T	Ht.	Wt.	DOB																		
Catlett, Everett	L-L	6-7	220	7-17-02	2	3	4.14	9	9	0	50	50	24	23	5	21	45	.263	.352	.411	20.5	9.5	220
Coupet, Isaiah	L-L	6-1	190	9-27-02	0	1	4.66	3	0	0	10	8	7	5	1	8	11	.235	.386	.353	25.0	18.2	44
Denton, Cade	R-R	6-3	180	12-28-01	3	5	3.73	42	0	7	51	51	25	21	8	20	63	.264	.348	.430	28.1	8.9	224
Eaton, Konner	R-L	6-3	210	10-30-02	5	8	3.56	23	23	0	121	109	52	48	13	42	125	.238	.316	.378	24.4	8.2	512
Flesland, Stu	R-L	6-5	207	10-1-00	2	3	3.97	30	10	0	95	83	43	42	14	25	83	.237	.301	.411	21.5	6.5	386
Grosz, Josh	R-R	6-4	199	9-5-02	1	6	5.87	7	7	0	38	42	25	25	9	20	41	.278	.374	.536	23.6	11.5	174
Hammer, Bryson	L-L	6-1	186	10-8-01	5	2	4.54	30	0	2	36	33	22	18	2	22	36	.246	.367	.336	21.6	13.2	167
Herrera, Welinton	L-L	6-0	166	4-3-04	1	0	0.49	15	0	10	18	8	1	1	0	6	29	.129	.206	.129	42.6	8.8	68
Herring, Griffin	R-L	6-2	182	5-7-03	1	1	2.40	7	7	0	30	14	9	8	1	13	47	.141	.254	.293	40.5	11.2	116
Hyde, Braxton	R-R	6-3	195	6-6-01	2	4	5.31	32	11	0	83	100	58	49	12	41	68	.308	.377	.526	18.1	10.9	375
Johnson, Lebarron	R-R	6-4	207	6-19-02	0	4	4.89	7	7	0	35	30	20	19	4	26	37	.238	.378	.357	23.4	16.5	158
Madden, Jake	R-R	6-6	185	12-26-01	0	0	0.00	2	0	0	4	2	0	0	0	2	4	.167	.286	.250	28.6	14.3	14
Mann, Hunter	R-R	6-7	225	8-15-01	2	5	6.61	38	0	0	49	46	40	36	6	38	55	.253	.396	.434	23.9	16.5	230
Omlid, Hunter	R-R	6-2	200	5-31-00	8	3	5.34	29	0	0	62	62	41	37	7	31	69	.263	.365	.432	24.2	10.9	285
Pacheco, Alberto	L-L	6-1	176	11-29-02	7	9	6.53	29	21	0	113	134	88	82	16	58	89	.300	.395	.483	17.0	11.1	524
Palermo, Davison	R-R	6-4	200	12-16-99	4	2	3.06	35	0	4	53	40	20	18	7	18	65	.207	.273	.389	30.1	8.3	216
Perdomo, Alan	R-R	6-4	150	8-24-01	3	2	6.48	44	0	0	50	56	38	36	11	28	31	.290	.389	.544	13.4	12.1	231
Prosecky, Michael	L-L	6-3	200	2-28-01	7	5	3.86	18	18	0	89	71	43	38	10	41	93	.218	.321	.383	24.2	10.7	384
Ramires, Felix	L-L	6-4	175	9-26-99	0	0	5.40	14	0	0	15	15	9	9	1	5	16	.259	.313	.414	24.6	7.7	65
Rivera, Francis	R-R	6-4	160	9-14-00	3	2	5.31	35	0	1	39	36	27	21	7	16	38	.238	.331	.444	22.1	9.3	172
Taggart, Luke	R-R	6-3	228	10-10-97	0	2	6.64	19	0	1	20	20	17	15	2	8	22	.256	.333	.397	25.0	9.1	88
Ulloa, Fidel	R-R	6-1	196	1-3-03	2	1	1.06	13	0	5	17	12	4	2	1	5	23	.203	.279	.271	33.8	7.4	68
Vargas, Jordy	R-R	6-3	153	11-6-03	0	4	7.84	10	10	0	21	21	23	18	4	21	28	.253	.418	.470	25.5	19.1	110

Fielding

Catcher	PCT	G	PO	A	E	DP	PB
McCabe	.993	18	133	3	1	0	1
Messina	.986	83	715	67	11	4	12
Obertop	.974	4	37	0	1	0	0
Ordonez	.980	17	139	10	3	1	2
Perry	.995	23	166	15	1	2	2

First Base	PCT	G	PO	A	E	DP
Condon	1.000	23	159	13	0	16
Longwell	.990	95	639	67	7	57
Messinger	1.000	17	91	10	0	10
Obertop	1.000	4	24	0	0	3

Second Base	PCT	G	PO	A	E	DP
Clifford	.800	1	2	2	1	0
Hill	1.000	1	3	1	0	1
Hopfe	1.000	1	1	2	0	1
Perez	.975	51	85	112	5	21

Third Base	PCT	G	PO	A	E	DP
Clifford	.000	1	0	0	0	0
Condon	.500	2	0	2	2	0
Hedges	.979	20	21	25	1	4
Messinger	.931	68	41	93	10	7
Perez	.800	5	2	6	2	1
Perez	1.000	1	0	2	0	0
Tucker	1.000	4	2	2	0	0
Wimmer	.929	16	10	16	2	3
Wright	.902	21	13	24	4	2

Shortstop	PCT	G	PO	A	E	DP
Clifford	1.000	1	0	3	0	0
Perez	.964	113	176	279	17	62

Outfield	PCT	G	PO	A	E	DP
Andrews	.984	62	121	5	2	0
Belyeu	.974	20	34	3	1	2
Bugarin	1.000	56	85	2	0	1
Condon	1.000	8	13	2	0	0
Hill	.952	8	19	1	1	0
Hobson	.990	93	184	6	2	1
Hopfe	1.000	29	58	1	0	0
Longwell	1.000	7	9	1	0	0
Messinger	1.000	10	24	0	0	0
Obertop	1.000	1	1	0	0	0
Perez	1.000	2	2	0	0	0
Thomas	.972	74	135	4	4	0
Tucker	1.000	16	35	0	0	0
Wimmer	.989	41	90	3	1	0

Catcher: Tucker .994 42 59 99 1 21; Wimmer .982 18 21 35 1 4; Wright 1.000 23 37 57 0 15
Third Base: Tucker 1.000 17 22 28 0 4; Wimmer .900 4 3 6 1 1

FRESNO GRIZZLIES — LOW-A
CALIFORNIA LEAGUE

Batting	B-T	Ht.	Wt.	DOB	AVG	OBP	SLG	G	PA	AB	R	H	2B	3B	HR	RBI	BB	HBP	SH	SF	SO	SB	CS	BB%	SO%
Bernard, Derek	L-R	6-0	190	8-9-05	.302	.385	.448	72	290	252	46	76	17	1	6	33	32	3	2	1	70	13	6	11.0	24.1
Brito, Roldy	S-R	5-11	183	4-8-07	.375	.442	.463	33	156	136	26	51	7	1	1	17	14	3	2	1	27	13	7	9.0	17.3
Calaz, Robert	R-R	6-2	202	11-22-05	.259	.338	.399	99	424	371	50	96	16	3	10	55	37	10	0	5	110	7	3	8.7	25.9
Castillo, Juan	R-R	6-1	170	1-16-03	.234	.313	.306	68	250	222	22	52	7	0	3	27	24	2	1	1	54	3	1	9.6	21.6
Clifford, Nolan	L-R	5-10	175	2-4-02	.200	.325	.230	58	198	165	16	33	5	0	0	12	26	5	1	1	44	5	3	13.1	22.2
Cope, Daniel	R-R	6-0	195	6-15-97	.500	.500	.625	2	8	8	0	4	1	0	0	1	0	0	0	0	1	0	0	0.0	12.5
Dalis, Wilder	S-R	6-0	172	7-30-06	.241	.333	.379	31	137	116	17	28	7	0	3	22	16	1	2	2	26	6	3	11.7	19.0
Espinal, Alan	R-R	6-0	209	1-6-02	.183	.255	.271	73	257	229	25	42	8	0	4	26	17	6	2	3	83	7	3	6.6	32.3
Fitzer, Kevin	R-R	6-3	200	10-16-01	.245	.328	.350	113	469	408	53	100	18	5	5	54	40	13	3	5	102	7	4	8.5	21.7
Freitez, Jesus	R-R	5-11	176	12-19-05	.000	.000	.000	4	7	7	0	0	0	0	0	0	0	0	0	0	4	0	0	0.0	57.1
Garcia, Francisco	R-R	6-0	190	11-10-02	.152	.197	.232	41	149	138	14	21	3	1	2	13	7	1	2	1	46	4	1	4.7	30.9
Gray, Clayton	L-R	5-10	185	10-14-01	.133	.133	.133	6	15	15	3	2	0	0	0	0	0	0	0	0	6	1	0	0.0	40.0
Hernandez, Roynier	R-R	5-11	180	12-6-04	.293	.358	.366	75	323	287	39	84	11	5	0	39	29	2	2	3	50	7	5	9.0	15.5
Hidalgo, Kelvin	R-R	6-2	166	3-1-05	.247	.311	.345	116	506	449	65	111	21	4	5	52	37	7	8	5	125	43	6	7.3	24.7
Hinderleider, Jacob	R-R	6-0	205	1-13-01	.297	.317	.379	79	313	281	38	65	15	1	3	25	23	5	0	4	113	12	6	7.3	36.1
Holliday, Ethan	L-R	6-4	210	2-23-07	.239	.357	.380	18	84	71	14	17	4	0	2	6	12	0	0	0	25	0	0	14.3	39.3
Hopfe, Tommy	S-R	6-1	195	10-11-02	.263	.378	.394	58	292	236	38	62	14	1	5	31	30	17	3	5	46	15	4	10.3	15.8
Humphrey, Jacob	R-R	5-10	175	1-30-03	.233	.395	.300	11	39	30	8	7	2	0	1	8	8	0	1	0	8	2	1	20.5	20.5
Klein, Matt	R-R	6-2	190	10-12-03	.227	.393	.318	7	28	22	3	5	0	0	1	3	4	2	0	0	8	0	0	14.3	28.6
Mendez, Luis	L-R	5-11	157	10-30-02	.130	.200	.174	8	25	23	4	3	1	0	0	1	2	0	0	0	10	1	0	8.0	40.0
Obertop, Jimmy	R-R	6-2	230	6-12-00	.301	.396	.434	27	97	83	6	25	3	1	2	21	10	3	0	1	32	3	0	10.3	33.0
Perez, Andy	L-R	6-3	165	8-5-04	.196	.208	.348	11	49	46	7	9	1	0	2	6	1	0	1	1	13	3	0	2.0	26.5
Reyes, Yeiker	R-R	6-0	175	10-17-05	.222	.317	.277	105	381	329	45	73	10	1	2	18	43	4	2	3	97	33	9	11.3	25.5
Tena, Felix	R-R	6-0	196	9-27-03	.169	.241	.219	55	202	178	14	30	4	1	1	17	15	3	3	3	40	6	2	7.4	19.8
Thach, Tanner	L-L	6-3	215	3-11-04	.279	.375	.397	18	80	68	7	19	2	0	2	15	8	1	0	1	19	1	0	10.0	23.8
Wright, Blake	R-R	5-11	195	2-12-02	.297	.370	.370	69	288	246	36	73	7	1	3	33	31	1	4	6	41	10	7	10.8	14.2

COLORADO ROCKIES

Pitching

Pitching	B-T	Ht.	Wt.	DOB	W	L	ERA	G	GS	SV	IP	Hits	Runs	ER	HR	BB	SO	AVG	OBP	SLG	SO%	BB%	BF
Becker, Austin	R-R	6-5	215	9-2-99	0	0	0.00	5	0	0	8	3	0	0	0	5	14	.125	.276	.125	48.3	17.2	29
Blasick, Nathan	L-R	6-3	210	6-26-01	5	3	3.59	43	0	19	53	40	27	21	3	29	66	.209	.327	.309	28.7	12.6	230
Brecht, Brody	R-R	6-4	205	9-27-02	1	4	2.60	16	16	0	55	42	18	16	2	32	87	.210	.325	.290	36.7	13.5	237
Catlett, Everett	L-L	6-7	220	7-17-02	5	5	3.46	21	12	0	83	81	42	32	2	28	89	.256	.320	.332	25.4	8.0	351
Clausen, Seth	R-R	6-0	195	3-8-03	2	0	0.00	5	0	0	7	2	2	0	0	2	11	.091	.200	.091	42.3	7.7	26
Correa, Yanzel	S-R	6-4	210	12-17-04	1	0	13.14	14	0	0	25	40	37	37	4	26	24	.360	.490	.577	16.6	17.9	145
Cox, Jackson	R-R	6-1	185	9-25-03	4	6	3.39	23	23	0	85	70	35	32	12	25	92	.225	.291	.376	27.0	7.3	341
Hammer, Bryson	L-L	6-1	186	10-8-01	2	0	1.42	5	0	0	6	5	1	1	1	3	10	.217	.308	.391	38.5	11.5	26
Hampu, Tyler	R-R	6-0	165	7-14-02	2	1	2.61	43	0	10	48	32	15	14	4	25	56	.186	.307	.320	27.7	12.4	202
Harris, Zach	R-R	6-1	181	10-21-03	1	0	10.80	3	0	0	3	6	4	4	0	2	5	.353	.421	.412	26.3	10.5	19
Herrera, Marcos	R-R	6-2	182	10-11-04	6	7	3.93	21	19	0	101	90	47	44	8	53	102	.242	.345	.331	23.2	12.0	440
Hill, Brady	L-R	6-0	180	11-10-00	6	2	6.11	41	0	1	46	44	39	31	2	37	65	.254	.384	.353	30.1	17.1	216
Jameson, Fisher	R-R	6-5	220	5-5-03	6	4	2.81	39	7	1	99	95	43	31	5	22	93	.249	.290	.330	22.8	5.4	408
Jewett, Luke	R-R	6-4	200	11-16-02	1	2	4.57	33	0	0	43	44	28	22	2	21	34	.254	.345	.347	17.2	10.6	198
Jimenez, Angel	R-R	6-2	190	7-4-03	1	5	4.70	10	10	0	38	43	21	20	2	21	47	.287	.378	.413	27.2	12.1	173
Johnson, Lebarron	R-R	6-4	207	6-19-02	3	2	3.50	9	9	0	44	34	17	17	1	25	44	.213	.319	.294	23.3	13.2	189
Loer, Justin	R-L	6-5	214	2-25-03	6	3	5.49	40	0	2	77	90	61	47	2	49	66	.290	.396	.371	18.0	13.4	366
Luciano, Ismael	R-R	6-0	170	3-4-03	3	2	5.24	19	7	1	57	62	44	33	3	35	42	.274	.380	.372	15.5	12.9	271
Mena, Bryan	R-R	6-2	185	6-14-04	2	8	5.62	29	18	0	107	124	77	67	9	57	97	.291	.388	.423	19.5	11.4	498
Morris, Zack	L-L	6-3	225	2-28-01	4	1	3.57	14	3	2	40	44	23	16	4	13	43	.272	.322	.383	24.3	7.3	177
Olivares, Manuel	R-R	5-11	145	12-4-01	2	1	3.38	7	7	0	29	30	13	11	2	15	27	.263	.351	.342	20.6	11.5	131
Paulino, Wilmis	R-R	6-0	181	1-16-06	0	0	27.00	5	0	1	5	20	16	16	3	4	2	.571	.615	.943	5.0	10.0	40
Ramires, Felix	L-L	6-4	175	9-26-99	2	4	4.29	26	0	1	42	39	25	20	0	25	40	.248	.366	.306	21.5	13.4	186
Sullivan, Sean	R-L	6-4	190	7-22-02	0	0	0.00	.1	1	0	4	3	0	0	0	0	2	.214	.214	.286	14.3	0.0	14
Taggart, Luke	R-R	6-3	228	10-10-97	1	0	0.00	4	0	0	4	2	0	0	0	0	5	.167	.167	.250	41.7	0.0	12
Thelen, Luke	R-R	6-5	210	9-18-02	0	0	12.84	20	0	0	20	28	32	29	1	26	16	.318	.483	.477	13.3	21.7	120
Torres, Carlos	R-R	6-4	240	5-3-01	1	0	2.57	5	0	0	7	8	2	2	1	1	8	.286	.310	.500	26.7	3.3	30
Ulloa, Fidel	R-R	6-1	196	1-3-03	3	2	1.77	26	0	2	36	28	9	7	1	13	46	.222	.298	.294	31.9	9.0	144

Fielding

Catcher	PCT	G	PO	A	E	DP	PB
Castillo	.989	62	505	56	6	6	16
Cope	1.000	1	6	1	0	0	1
Espinal	.994	72	653	61	4	5	10
Freitez	1.000	2	6	0	0	0	0
Klein	1.000	3	27	1	0	1	3
Obertop	1.000	4	24	4	0	0	1

First Base	PCT	G	PO	A	E	DP
Fitzer	.990	51	367	31	4	41
Garcia	.978	20	128	7	3	13
Hinderleider	.991	45	317	28	3	34
Obertop	.987	12	74	2	1	6
Thach	.993	18	139	11	1	13

Second Base	PCT	G	PO	A	E	DP
Brito	.959	11	15	32	2	4
Clifford	1.000	12	18	32	0	5
Dalis	.955	4	10	11	1	7

Hernandez	.959	60	100	133	10	42
Hldalgo	1.000	7	7	16	0	4
Hopfe	.981	35	56	99	3	21
Mendez	1.000	5	8	13	0	1
Wright	.944	4	6	11	1	3

Third Base	PCT	G	PO	A	E	DP
Clifford	1.000	7	6	5	0	0
Dalis	.963	12	6	20	1	2
Fitzer	.813	10	2	11	3	0
Hernandez	1.000	4	3	8	0	1
Hldalgo	.922	40	28	55	7	10
Hinderleider	.958	10	3	20	1	2
Hopfe	1.000	1	1	2	0	0
Mendez	1.000	1	1	4	0	0
Perez	1.000	1	1	2	0	0
Wright	.922	53	29	77	9	10

Shortstop	PCT	G	PO	A	E	DP
Clifford	.929	36	42	89	10	19
Dalis	.940	13	21	26	3	6
Hldalgo	.964	62	88	153	9	34
Holliday	.935	17	14	44	4	8
Perez	.981	11	18	34	1	6

Outfield	PCT	G	PO	A	E	DP
Bernard	.963	71	99	6	4	2
Brito	.979	21	46	0	1	0
Calaz	.940	97	182	5	12	2
Fitzer	.976	49	77	4	2	0
Gray	.750	6	3	0	1	0
Hopfe	.946	29	35	0	2	0
Humphrey	.944	10	17	0	1	0
Reyes	.986	103	210	2	3	1
Tena	.983	44	56	1	1	0
Thach	1.000	1	1	0	0	0

ACL ROCKIES — ROOKIE
ARIZONA COMPLEX LEAGUE

Batting	B-T	Ht.	Wt.	DOB	AVG	OBP	SLG	G	PA	AB	R	H	2B	3B	HR	RBI	BB	HBP	SH	SF	SO	SB	CS	BB%	SO%
Aguilar, Tayler	L-L	5-10	205	8-15-00	.122	.217	.293	17	48	41	3	5	2	1	1	2	3	2	2	0	20	0	1	6.3	41.7
Andujar, Ashly	S-R	6-1	163	7-29-07	.319	.370	.356	53	217	191	32	61	7	0	0	23	15	2	6	3	31	7	2	6.9	14.3
Arias, Cruzmel	R-R	5-11	176	2-20-04	.167	.228	.236	25	79	72	6	12	5	0	0	10	4	2	0	1	22	1	1	5.1	27.8
Bernard, Derek	L-R	6-0	190	8-9-05	.345	.367	.483	9	30	29	4	10	4	0	0	2	1	0	0	0	8	2	0	3.3	26.7
Brito, Roldy	S-R	5-11	183	4-8-07	.368	.445	.555	52	209	182	46	67	13	6	3	21	22	4	0	1	42	22	7	10.5	20.1
Ciriaco, Jeremy	R-R	5-10	163	8-15-06	.266	.331	.329	45	158	143	21	38	9	0	0	14	13	1	1	0	32	4	4	8.2	20.3
Condon, Charlie	R-R	6-6	211	4-14-03	.296	.345	.407	9	29	27	2	8	3	0	0	3	1	1	0	0	10	1	0	3.4	34.5
Cope, Daniel	R-R	6-0	195	6-15-97	.300	.462	.367	10	39	30	3	9	2	0	0	7	7	2	0	0	9	0	0	17.9	23.1
Dalis, Wilder	S-R	6-0	172	7-30-06	.352	.440	.525	56	219	179	37	63	12	5	3	42	29	3	3	5	44	10	3	13.2	20.1
De La Cruz, Alessander	R-R	6-1	208	1-2-06	.269	.368	.408	41	152	130	27	35	6	3	2	18	15	6	0	1	52	1	4	9.9	34.2
Freitez, Jesus	R-R	5-11	176	12-19-05	.322	.396	.411	33	103	90	16	29	6	1	0	6	9	2	2	0	12	3	2	8.7	11.7
Gray, Clayton	L-R	5-10	185	10-14-01	.271	.429	.292	21	63	48	13	13	1	0	0	5	14	0	0	1	14	3	0	22.2	22.2
Hernandez, Roynier	L-R	5-11	180	12-6-04	.368	.409	.474	6	22	19	2	7	0	1	0	7	2	0	0	1	3	0	0	9.1	13.6
Hopfe, Tommy	S-R	6-1	195	10-11-02	.273	.636	3	11	11	2	3	1	0	1	6	6	0	0	0	2	0	0	0.0	18.2
Karros, Kyle	R-R	6-2	220	7-26-02	.400	.538	.600	4	13	10	3	4	2	0	0	3	3	0	0	0	1	0	0	23.1	7.7
Kolokie, Aldalay	R-R	6-0	187	8-29-04	.243	.351	.365	38	135	115	18	28	9	1	1	16	15	4	1	0	24	3	0	11.1	17.8
Ledesma, Bairon	R-R	5-9	180	5-3-05	.216	.318	.257	31	89	74	9	16	3	0	0	8	11	1	1	2	19	1	1	12.4	21.3
McElveny, Daniel	R-R	6-2	220	4-21-03	.242	.400	.379	26	85	66	9	16	1	1	2	12	14	4	0	1	26	1	2	16.5	30.6
Mendez, Luis	L-R	5-11	157	10-30-02	.266	.350	.424	42	162	139	22	37	7	6	1	24	19	0	2	2	22	9	1	11.7	13.6
Nola, Austin	R-R	6-0	197	12-28-89	.125	.222	.250	3	9	8	1	1	1	0	0	1	1	0	0	0	0	0	0	11.1	0.0
Obertop, Jimmy	R-R	6-2	230	6-12-00	.333	.429	.500	2	7	6	1	2	1	0	0	3	1	0	0	0	3	1	0	14.3	42.9

COLORADO ROCKIES

	B-T	Ht.	Wt.	DOB	AVG	OBP	SLG	G	PA	AB	R	H	2B	3B	HR	RBI	BB	HBP	SH	SF	SO	SB	CS	BB%	SO%
Renzullo, Carlos	S-R	5-8	150	9-30-06	.277	.396	.336	41	146	119	29	33	5	1	0	11	22	2	2	1	15	8	3	15.1	10.3
Romo, Drew	S-R	5-11	205	8-29-01	.188	.235	.188	5	17	16	2	3	0	0	0	1	1	0	0	0	1	1	1	5.9	5.9
Veen, Zac	L-R	6-3	190	12-12-01	.286	.545	.286	3	11	7	2	2	0	0	0	1	4	0	0	0	2	0	0	36.4	18.2

Pitching	B-T	Ht.	Wt.	DOB	W	L	ERA	G	GS	SV	IP	Hits	Runs	ER	HR	BB	SO	AVG	OBP	SLG	SO%	BB%	BF
Brecht, Brody	R-R	6-4	205	9-27-02	0	1	1.59	4	4	0	6	6	1	1	0	3	8	.261	.346	.261	30.8	11.5	26
Brito, Biembenido	R-R	6-3	180	2-13-03	1	2	2.97	9	7	0	33	21	14	11	0	18	38	.186	.324	.274	27.3	12.9	139
Camacho, Reiver	R-R	6-2	170	4-1-07	4	2	4.59	10	3	0	33	33	18	17	2	6	33	.258	.294	.383	24.3	4.4	136
Correa, Yanzel	S-R	6-4	210	12-17-04	1	0	6.97	6	0	0	10	10	8	8	1	6	6	.250	.404	.400	11.5	11.5	52
Cubilla, Efrain	R-R	6-1	190	2-18-05	0	1	5.16	14	0	0	23	23	16	13	0	7	19	.267	.333	.453	19.8	7.3	96
Emener, Austin	L-L	6-0	210	6-1-02	1	0	4.50	2	0	0	2	3	1	1	0	0	4	.375	.375	.375	50.0	0.0	8
Feltner, Ryan	R-R	6-4	190	9-2-96	0	0	0.00	1	1	0	2	2	0	0	0	0	2	.286	.286	.286	28.6	0.0	7
Gerth, Sam	R-R	6-3	225	9-29-04	0	0	11.81	5	0	0	5	12	7	7	1	5	7	.444	.531	.593	21.9	15.6	32
Hammer, Bryson	L-L	6-1	186	10-8-01	0	0	0.00	3	0	0	3	5	0	0	0	0	5	.333	.333	.467	33.3	0.0	15
Hardy, Brendan	R-R	6-4	170	12-15-99	2	0	4.85	11	0	0	13	17	9	7	0	9	21	.309	.409	.364	31.8	13.6	66
Hill, Jaden	R-R	6-4	234	12-22-99	0	1	3.00	3	2	0	3	4	3	1	0	1	3	.364	.462	.545	23.1	7.7	13
Hughes, Gabriel	R-R	6-4	220	8-22-01	0	0	0.00	1	1	0	1	0	0	0	0	0	5	.100	.182	.100	45.5	9.1	11
Jewett, Luke	R-R	6-4	200	11-16-02	0	0	9.00	2	0	0	2	3	2	2	1	1	4	.333	.400	.667	40.0	10.0	10
Jimenez, Angel	R-R	6-2	190	7-4-03	0	1	2.82	7	7	0	22	19	10	7	0	4	26	.229	.273	.265	29.5	4.5	88
Lee, David	R-R	6-2	185	3-22-00	0	1	12.96	12	0	0	8	9	12	12	2	9	7	.290	.450	.581	17.1	22.0	41
Luciano, Ismael	R-R	6-3	213	4-4-03	0	0	9.00	4	0	0	6	7	6	6	0	4	6	.417	.500	.583	21.4	14.3	28
Medina, Jhon	L-L	6-0	195	1-9-06	2	3	3.83	12	11	0	45	41	20	19	2	25	41	.256	.364	.363	21.9	13.4	187
Meza, Moises	R-R	6-0	188	8-19-05	0	2	7.00	3	2	0	9	15	12	7	1	4	8	.357	.413	.476	17.4	8.7	46
Morris, Zack	L-L	6-3	225	2-28-01	1	0	1.50	3	0	0	6	4	1	1	0	1	8	.190	.227	.286	36.4	4.5	22
Olivares, Manuel	R-R	5-11	145	12-4-01	4	3	4.31	15	4	1	48	49	28	23	1	17	48	.262	.335	.316	23.0	8.1	209
O'Loughlin, Jack	L-L	6-5	223	3-14-00	0	0	4.50	2	0	0	4	4	3	2	0	0	4	.250	.250	.375	25.0	0.0	16
Ozuna, Sandy	R-R	6-3	177	5-25-06	1	0	1.50	2	1	0	6	5	1	1	0	1	6	.250	.280	.292	24.0	4.0	25
Paulino, Wilmis	R-R	6-0	181	1-16-06	5	1	3.03	22	0	7	30	24	14	10	0	11	32	.220	.317	.294	25.4	8.7	126
Silvestre, Engel	R-R	6-2	230	9-27-05	6	1	2.55	18	0	2	35	25	13	10	1	26	41	.198	.335	.286	26.5	16.8	155
Starling, Gant	R-R	6-0	210	2-8-01	0	1	63.00	2	0	0	1	4	7	7	1	3	0	.800	.818	1.400	0.0	25.0	12
Sullivan, Sean	R-L	6-4	190	7-22-02	0	0	0.00	1	1	0	3	0	0	0	0	0	7	.000	.273	.000	58.3	8.3	12
Taggart, Luke	R-R	6-3	228	10-10-97	2	0	0.00	2	0	0	2	0	0	0	0	0	2	.000	.000	.000	33.3	0.0	6
Tejeda, Luis	R-R	6-2	170	12-13-04	3	0	3.54	16	0	2	20	20	12	8	3	14	17	.274	.418	.507	18.7	15.4	91
Ulloa, Fidel	R-R	6-1	196	1-3-03	1	0	0.00	2	0	0	3	1	0	0	0	0	3	.091	.091	.273	27.3	0.0	11
Van Sickle, Bryson	L-L	6-0	165	12-31-00	2	0	2.92	9	0	0	12	9	4	4	1	1	15	.196	.229	.348	31.3	2.1	48
Vargas, Jordy	R-R	6-3	153	11-6-03	0	1	5.91	4	4	0	11	10	8	7	2	5	17	.233	.340	.419	34.0	10.0	50
Zacarias, Alison	R-R	6-3	200	11-10-05	1	2	3.48	12	12	0	41	38	20	16	0	24	27	.253	.367	.327	14.9	13.3	181

Fielding

C: Freitez 33, Arias 10, Cope 9, McElveny 8, Romo 4, Nola 2, Obertop 1. **1B:** Mendez 34, Arias 12, Aguilar 8, Ledesma 5, Condon 3, Obertop 1. **2B:** Brito 25, Ciriaco 15, Ledesma 14, Renzullo 4, Hernandez 3, Dalis 2, Hopfe 2. **3B:** Dalis 46, Ledesma 13, Karros 3, Renzullo 2, Ciriaco 1. **SS:** Andujar 53, Dalis 9. **LF:** Kolokie 27, Renzullo 21, Gray 11, Condon 3, McElveny 3. **CF:** Ciriaco 24, Brito 20, Renzullo 18, Veen 2, Aguilar 1. **RF:** De La Cruz 32, McElveny 10, Kolokie 9, Bernard 7, Gray 6, Veen 1

DSL COLORADO
DOMINICAN SUMMER LEAGUE
ROOKIE

Batting	B-T	Ht.	Wt.	DOB	AVG	OBP	SLG	G	PA	AB	R	H	2B	3B	HR	RBI	BB	HBP	SH	SF	SO	SB	CS	BB%	SO%
Aguirre, Victor	L-R	6-0	157	11-8-06	.111	.220	.111	12	41	36	4	4	0	0	0	3	5	0	0	0	11	1	0	12.2	26.8
Alvarez, Jjam	R-R	5-11	160	6-3-06	.196	.359	.255	19	65	51	9	10	0	0	1	7	12	1	1	0	14	0	0	18.5	21.5
Arache, Leudy	L-L	6-2	178	2-20-08	.219	.324	.329	43	172	146	26	32	5	4	1	14	21	2	2	1	45	6	1	12.2	26.2
Barroso, Hector	L-R	6-1	165	4-22-08	.183	.327	.232	30	102	82	9	15	2	1	0	5	17	1	1	1	17	3	2	16.7	16.7
Bello, Jesus	R-R	5-7	180	5-21-08	.245	.387	.286	17	62	49	6	12	2	0	0	7	8	4	0	1	5	2	0	12.9	8.1
Cancro, Danny	R-R	5-10	148	4-24-07	.229	.361	.271	15	61	48	5	11	1	2	0	10	9	2	0	2	8	7	1	14.8	13.1
Capellan, Jarol	L-R	5-11	176	5-23-06	.228	.366	.348	33	112	92	14	21	4	2	1	14	16	4	0	0	25	2	1	14.3	21.4
Comenencia, Ishel	L-L	6-1	162	1-8-08	.273	.419	.394	12	43	33	10	9	1	0	1	5	9	0	0	1	12	2	0	20.9	27.9
De Paula, Rosniell	R-R	5-10	163	8-24-08	.185	.328	.241	50	200	162	30	30	7	1	0	13	30	5	2	1	53	6	5	15.0	26.5
Elvira, Abraham	R-R	6-1	184	1-28-08	.100	.100	.200	3	10	10	0	1	1	0	0	1	0	0	0	0	6	0	0	0.0	60.0
Feliz, Wandi	R-R	6-3	202	9-11-07	.185	.293	.304	37	157	135	23	25	3	2	3	16	20	1	0	1	46	6	3	12.7	29.3
Guerra, Jose	S-R	5-11	180	12-18-05	.242	.330	.347	32	115	95	17	23	7	0	1	16	8	6	3	3	21	2	1	7.0	18.3
Herrera, Herlinton	L-R	5-11	150	1-22-07	.230	.384	.341	43	162	126	19	29	8	4	3	18	28	4	3	1	30	10	3	17.3	18.5
Morejon, Luis	R-R	6-2	201	4-22-08	.320	.442	.477	39	157	128	29	41	6	1	4	20	23	5	1	0	19	3	3	14.6	12.1
Mota, Carlos	R-R	6-3	170	7-7-07	.294	.393	.549	15	61	51	6	15	5	1	2	11	6	4	0	0	14	0	3	8.2	23.0
Ortiz, Nicolas	R-R	6-0	173	12-24-06	.205	.345	.250	16	56	44	5	9	0	1	0	4	9	1	1	1	21	1	0	16.1	37.5
Rodriguez, Bryan	R-R	5-11	188	3-13-08	.192	.356	.308	29	102	78	11	15	3	0	2	13	11	10	1	2	14	0	1	10.8	13.7
Suero, Larry	L-R	6-2	183	4-17-08	.212	.371	.353	45	199	156	27	33	8	1	4	17	27	13	2	1	45	8	4	13.6	22.6
Tovar, Anderson	R-R	6-1	205	12-7-06	.186	.294	.233	14	52	43	5	8	2	0	0	3	5	2	1	1	9	0	3	9.6	17.3
Villar, Kamuel	R-R	6-1	189	9-5-07	.277	.358	.386	23	96	83	8	23	5	2	0	11	9	2	1	1	22	2	6	9.4	22.9

Pitching	B-T	Ht.	Wt.	DOB	W	L	ERA	G	GS	SV	IP	Hits	Runs	ER	HR	BB	SO	AVG	OBP	SLG	SO%	BB%	BF
Alburqueque, Cristopher	L-L	6-1	180	8-31-07	0	2	8.53	11	9	0	19	14	19	18	1	27	19	.215	.495	.323	18.8	26.7	101
Arroyo, Diego	L-L	5-11	173	8-10-07	1	2	5.86	11	9	1	43	49	32	28	8	17	49	.295	.374	.512	26.2	9.1	187
Barboza, Julian	R-R	6-2	196	10-16-06	2	2	6.92	9	0	0	13	10	12	10	2	12	9	.213	.383	.362	15.0	20.0	60
Castellan, Victor	L-L	6-0	156	4-28-08	2	1	8.20	12	0	0	19	26	20	17	1	17	19	.342	.454	.447	17.3	17.3	98
Centeno, Luis	R-R	6-2	164	9-13-07	3	1	6.43	9	4	0	20	20	17	15	3	11	25	.259	.344	.398	20.5	9.0	122
Compres, Brailyn	R-R	6-1	200	7-16-05	2	2	3.63	15	0	5	17	9	7	7	1	12	15	.286	.434	.381	17.9	14.3	84
Cruz, Odarlin	R-R	6-7	188	2-18-05	4	6	4.94	21	0	3	67	57	27	15	2	8	35	.295	.357	.438	27.6	6.3	127

	B-T	Ht.	Wt.	DOB	AVG	OBP	SLG	G	PA	AB	R	H	2B	3B	HR	RBI	BB	HBP	SH	SF	SO	SB	CS	BB%	SO%
De La Cruz, Onofer	R-R	6-2	186	11-9-07	0	0			5.40	4	0	0	7	6	4	4	3	4		7	.250	.357	.708	25.0	14.3	28
Espinoza, Jhoan	R-R	6-1	161	11-7-07	0	2			13.50	4	0	0	9	19	14	14	2	4		9	.463	.479	.756	18.8	8.3	48
Fernandez, Brian	R-R	6-2	176	3-20-07	1	2			6.89	12	0	0	16	21	13	12	0	8		9	.333	.434	.429	11.8	10.5	76
Gonzalez, Maximo	R-R	5-11	175	5-5-07	1	2			5.23	13	7	0	41	44	32	24	11	23		25	.272	.375	.549	13.0	12.0	192
Leonardi, Almonte	R-R	6-2	190	3-25-05	1	1			4.55	17	0	0	30	33	19	15	4	14		19	.282	.378	.427	14.1	10.4	135
Martorella, Carlos	R-R	6-2	179	8-2-06	2	1			4.42	15	2	2	37	39	18	18	2	12		31	.283	.346	.399	19.9	7.7	156
Mendoza, Gleiderson	R-R	6-0	181	4-1-08	0	0			4.13	14	3	0	28	28	15	13	1	22		19	.275	.427	.382	14.5	16.8	131
Pena, Edwin	R-R	6-3	207	8-10-07	0	0			4.15	11	0	1	17	14	10	8	1	17		13	.246	.421	.333	17.1	22.4	76
Pena, Eliezer	R-R	6-0	167	10-8-05	0	3			3.66	8	5	0	32	19	14	13	1	16		38	.168	.293	.230	28.6	12.0	133
Ramon, Yadiel	R-R	6-2	180	8-17-07	0	1			16.62	2	2	0	4	7	8	8	2	4		3	.368	.520	.789	12.0	16.0	25
Sanchez, Gregory	R-R	6-4	189	1-12-07	0	0			10.80	2	2	0	3	5	4	4	0	2		2	.357	.438	.500	12.5	12.5	16
Tiburcio, Brian	R-R	6-5	223	4-1-08	0	3			7.94	11	4	1	23	27	24	20	3	15		21	.307	.418	.523	19.1	13.6	110
Ventura, Melky	R-R	6-1	179	11-1-07	2	2			5.35	10	8	0	37	48	29	22	3	16		27	.310	.374	.484	15.8	9.4	171

Fielding

C: Rodriguez 25, Guerra 16, Bello 11, Ortiz 11. **1B:** Guerra 18, Herrera 18, Capellan 16, Alvarez 7, Ortiz 2, Rodriguez 2, Bello 1. **2B:** Herrera 17, De Paula 14, Capellan 7, Villar 7, Alvarez 6, Aguirre 4, Cancro 2. **3B:** Suero 44, Capellan 11, Cancro 2. **SS:** De Paula 31, Villar 14, Aguirre 8, Herrera 3, Alvarez 1, Cancro 1. **LF:** Morejon 38, Tovar 9, Barroso 4, Mota 3, Alvarez 1. **CF:** Arache 24, Feliz 20, Comenencia 8, Barroso 4, Tovar 1. **RF:** Barroso 19, Feliz 14, Mota 2, Tovar 5, Cancro 4, Comenencia 4, Alvarez 1

DSL ROCKIES — ROOKIE
DOMINICAN SUMMER LEAGUE

Batting	B-T	Ht.	Wt.	DOB	AVG	OBP	SLG	G	PA	AB	R	H	2B	3B	HR	RBI	BB	HBP	SH	SF	SO	SB	CS	BB%	SO%
Aguirre, Victor	L-R	6-0	157	11-8-06	.333	.500	.444	4	12	9	3	3	1	0	0	2	3	0	0	0	2	0	0	25.0	16.7
Alvarez, Jjam	R-R	5-11	160	6-3-06	.238	.418	.310	14	55	42	15	10	3	0	0	4	12	1	0	0	6	2	0	21.8	10.9
Arache, Leudy	L-L	6-2	178	2-20-08	.375	.444	.375	3	9	8	2	3	0	0	0	1	1	0	0	0	1	0	0	11.1	11.1
Arguelles, Cristian	L-L	6-0	177	6-30-07	.422	.528	.652	52	236	187	56	79	16	6	5	55	34	11	1	3	25	6	7	14.4	10.6
Bello, Jesus	R-R	5-7	180	5-21-08	.000	.231	.000	5	13	9	1	0	0	0	0	1	2	1	0	1	2	0	0	15.4	15.4
Blanco, Sebastian	R-R	6-1	181	1-9-08	.345	.449	.453	54	248	203	60	70	7	3	3	37	33	7	3	2	34	11	2	13.3	13.7
Comenencia, Ishel	L-L	6-1	162	1-4-08	.176	.341	.221	24	88	68	14	12	1	1	0	8	18	0	0	2	26	2	0	20.5	29.5
De La Cruz, Jose	R-R	5-11	190	3-19-07	.275	.402	.350	24	97	80	20	22	4	1	0	12	12	5	0	0	30	0	0	12.4	30.9
Dihigo, Eriel	R-R	6-2	180	11-10-06	.267	.434	.407	53	226	172	43	46	6	3	4	29	43	9	0	2	31	15	6	19.0	13.7
Elvira, Abraham	R-R	6-1	184	1-28-08	.236	.358	.327	17	67	55	7	13	2	1	0	9	8	3	0	1	17	0	2	11.9	25.4
Feliz, Wandi	R-R	6-3	202	9-11-07	.357	.500	.607	11	38	28	5	10	1	0	2	11	8	1	0	1	6	3	1	21.1	15.8
Garcia, Dariel	S-R	5-10	155	11-28-06	.268	.395	.357	45	190	157	45	42	11	0	1	22	28	5	0	0	43	24	5	14.7	22.6
Lopez, Gabriel	R-R	5-8	169	3-24-06	.214	.365	.345	26	105	84	17	18	6	1	1	10	18	2	1	0	22	1	2	17.1	21.0
Meza, Daniel	L-R	5-11	163	1-28-08	.229	.400	.244	40	170	131	36	30	2	0	0	17	35	0	0	1	44	7	2	20.6	25.9
Morejon, Luis	R-R	6-2	201	4-22-08	.180	.358	.280	16	67	50	9	9	2	0	1	7	14	1	0	2	8	3	1	20.9	11.9
Mota, Carlos	R-R	6-3	170	7-7-07	.248	.344	.286	36	157	133	21	33	5	0	0	17	12	9	0	3	39	5	1	7.6	24.8
Munoz, Omar	S-R	6-0	168	11-6-07	.275	.388	.319	24	85	69	11	19	3	0	0	16	14	0	0	2	12	4	1	16.5	14.1
Suero, Larry	L-R	6-2	183	4-17-08	.143	.333	.286	4	9	7	1	1	0	0	0	0	1	0	0	1	3	1	0	11.1	33.3
Tovar, Anderson	R-R	6-1	205	12-7-06	.188	.361	.333	14	61	48	12	9	1	2	0	8	12	1	0	0	9	3	2	16.4	14.8
Ugarte, Ronny	R-R	6-3	205	12-10-04	.335	.416	.485	54	238	206	36	69	19	0	4	68	28	2	0	2	39	1	1	11.8	16.4
Villar, Kamuel	L-R	6-0	169	9-5-07	.263	.391	.316	5	23	19	4	5	1	0	0	1	4	0	0	0	4	1	0	17.4	17.4

Pitching	B-T	Ht.	Wt.	DOB	W	L	ERA	G	GS	SV	IP	Hits	Runs	ER	HR	BB	SO	AVG	OBP	SLG	SO%	BB%	BF
Armas, Lenixon	R-R	6-0	168	12-9-05	0	0	18.00	1	0	0	1	2	2	2	0	0	0	.500	.600	1.000	0.0	0.0	5
Cabeza, Yeremmy	R-R	6-0	165	12-21-05	0	0	27.00	1	1	0	1	3	7	3	0	2	0	.750	.833	.750	0.0	33.3	6
Cedeno, Keywill	R-R	6-4	204	1-31-05	4	3	2.53	16	0	3	21	18	10	6	1	7	29	.222	.308	.296	31.9	7.7	91
Centeno, Luis	R-R	6-2	164	9-13-07	2	0	0.00	5	1	1	9	6	1	0	0	6	6	.200	.368	.300	15.8	15.8	38
Concepcion, Kevin	R-R	6-2	185	4-11-08	3	1	3.79	11	8	0	38	29	19	16	4	13	31	.206	.280	.340	19.7	8.3	157
Cruz, Odarlin	R-R	6-7	182	2-18-05	0	0	0.00	2	0	1	2	1	0	0	0	3	.143	.143	.143	42.9	0.0	7
De La Cruz, Onofer	R-R	6-2	186	11-9-07	2	0	6.75	4	0	0	4	2	3	3	0	5	4	.143	.368	.143	21.1	26.3	19
Espinoza, Jhoan	R-R	6-1	161	11-7-07	1	0	7.79	7	4	0	17	26	19	15	4	5	10	.338	.407	.571	11.6	5.8	86
Florencio, Ronaldo	R-R	6-0	165	8-13-07	0	0	2.14	10	1	2	21	13	6	5	1	7	22	.176	.247	.284	27.2	8.6	81
Henrique, Josue	R-R	6-3	193	10-3-06	2	1	4.70	17	3	1	31	31	18	16	5	9	40	.252	.306	.431	29.9	6.7	134
Herrera, Andres	R-R	6-4	180	6-10-06	1	2	7.32	13	0	1	20	30	23	16	2	15	14	.353	.457	.576	13.3	14.3	105
Martinez, Kevin	R-R	6-1	183	10-19-07	6	1	2.15	10	10	0	46	43	12	11	5	7	40	.251	.287	.380	22.0	3.8	182
Martorella, Carlos	R-R	6-2	179	8-2-06	0	0	0.00	1	0	0	2	0	0	0	0	0	0	.000	.000	.000	0.0	0.0	6
Mendez, Wander	L-L	6-1	175	3-18-07	1	0	7.94	14	0	0	17	24	17	15	4	11	10	.338	.435	.606	11.8	12.9	85
Mendoza, Gleiderson	R-R	6-0	181	4-1-08	1	0	0.00	1	0	0	4	1	0	0	0	2	2	.091	.231	.091	15.4	15.4	13
Pena, Edwin	R-R	6-0	167	10-8-05	0	0	4.22	3	1	0	11	8	7	5	0	6	16	.205	.354	.205	33.3	12.5	48
Pimentel, Marcos	R-R	6-1	172	9-30-06	4	2	4.83	9	9	0	41	38	25	22	7	11	39	.247	.298	.468	23.2	6.5	168
Pinales, Netali	R-R	6-1	168	5-28-07	2	1	5.57	12	0	0	21	22	13	13	2	11	22	.272	.362	.407	23.4	11.7	94
Pineda, Euri	R-R	6-2	200	8-13-05	3	0	5.87	9	0	0	15	16	10	10	1	7	11	.281	.359	.386	16.9	10.8	65
Pujols, Oscar	R-R	6-2	165	11-15-06	1	0	0.00	8	0	4	13	0	0	0	0	12	.154	.154	.192	46.2	0.0	72
Ramon, Yadiel	R-R	6-2	180	8-17-07	0	2	10.38	10	3	0	13	16	15	15	0	19	8	.265	.500	.367	11.1	26.4	72
Salas, Roberto	R-R	5-11	150	9-12-07	3	1	0.25	9	7	0	37	20	5	1	3	41	.157	.189	.213	31.1	2.3	132
Tejada, Kevin	R-R	6-5	187	5-8-05	2	0	3.16	17	0	0	26	25	11	9	3	12	21	.256	.343	.400	20.0	11.4	105
Torres, Ervin	L-L	6-0	185	11-3-04	1	0	3.38	6	0	0	8	6	3	3	1	6	.207	.233	.345	20.0	3.3	30
Ventura, Antony	R-R	6-2	168	8-5-08	2	0	2.30	10	0	0	27	8	7	1	12	16	.232	.333	.283	14.0	10.5	114
Veras, Eric	L-L	6-0	182	12-18-06	2	0	3.97	5	5	0	23	21	12	10	1	9	15	.241	.320	.356	15.5	9.3	97

Fielding

C: Lopez 24, De La Cruz 23, Elvira 7, Bello 5. **1B:** Ugarte 49, Garcia 5, Alvarez 3, Elvira 1. **2B:** Meza 35, Garcia 13, Villar 4, Aguirre 3, Blanco 2, Lopez 2, Alvarez 1, Munoz 1. **3B:** Dihigo 53, Suero 2, Alvarez 1, Garcia 1, Meza 1. **SS:** Blanco 52, Meza 2, Villar 2, Garcia 1. **LF:** Garcia 13, Morejon 13, Comenencia 12, Feliz 9, Alvarez 5, Tovar 4, Munoz 2. **CF:** Arguelles 51, Garcia 5, Arache 4, Munoz 1. **RF:** Mota 34, Munoz 12, Comenencia 7, Tovar 3, Garcia 1

Detroit Tigers

SEASON SYNOPSIS: After a 31-13 streak down the stretch led to a wild-card spot in 2024, the Tigers continued the hot play in '25 and were the first team to win 30, 40, 50 and 60 games. They squandered a 14-game lead with a 9-22 finish, with Cleveland catching them to win the AL Central, but Detroit beat the Guardians in a three-game wild card series before dropping a dramatic five-game Division Series to the Mariners. Game Five was a 15-inning classic in which Detroit's only runs came on a two-run homer by Kerry Carpenter.

HIGH POINT: Detroit was baseball's best team in the first half with a 59-38 record, placing six players on the American League all-star team as well. One of their four five-game win streaks included a sweep in Cleveland just before the all-star break in which Detroit gave up just three runs in three games. A 7-2 series finale had everything go the Tigers' way, with pinch-runner Zach McKinstry stealing second after the original out call was overturned, a groundball to advance him and McKinstry scoring the tying run in the ninth on a wild pitch. Detroit then scored six in the 10th to finish the sweep.

LOW POINT: After playing roughly .500 ball for July and August, the Tigers went 7-17 in September and could do nothing to stop their slide. An eight-game losing streak including a winless homestand with sweeps by the Guardians and Braves, including blowing a 5-3 lead Sept. 20 to Atlanta while Cleveland swept a doubleheader in Minnesota to draw within a game of first. Detroit won just twice more but held on to a wild-card spot as Houston also struggled late.

NOTABLE ROOKIES: Top prospect Jackson Jobe (4-1, 4.22) made 10 starts before requiring reconstructive elbow surgery. Righty Troy Melton (3-2, 2.76) emerged as a key swingman in his stead, while shortstop Trey Sweeney, who emerged as a starter late in '24, was less successful over a full season (.548 OPS).

KEY TRANSACTIONS: Jack Flaherty, traded in July 2024 to the Dodgers, returned on a two-year deal with an opt-out after the season, but the sequel (8-15, 4.64) wasn't as successful as the original. Jahmai Jones proved a sneaky good signing, providing platoon pop (.287.387/.550, 7 HR in 150 PA) against lefthanders. Trade deadline pickup Kyle Finnegan (3-0, 1.50, 4 SV) thrived while fellow July addition Chris Paddack (14 HR allowed in 47 IP) flopped.

OPENING DAY PAYROLL: $143,193,033 (17th)

PLAYERS OF THE YEAR

MAJOR LEAGUE
Tarik Skubal
LHP
13-6, 2.21 ERA
241 SO in 195.1 IP
2 straight Cy Youngs

MINOR LEAGUE
Kevin McGonigle
SS
(A,A+,AA)
.305/.408/.583
19 HR, 31 2B in 88 G

ORGANIZATION LEADERS

Batting		*Qualifiers
MAJORS		
* AVG	Zach McKinstry	.259
* OPS	Riley Greene	.806
HR	Riley Greene	36
RBI	Riley Greene	111
MINORS		
* AVG	Eduardo Valencia, Toledo/Erie	.311
* OBP	Trei Cruz, Toledo/Erie	.411
* SLG	Kevin McGonigle, Erie/West Michigan/Lakeland	.583
* OPS	Kevin McGonigle, Erie/West Michigan/Lakeland	.991
R	Trei Cruz, Toledo/Erie	95
H	Max Anderson, Toledo/Erie	149
TB	Max Anderson, Toledo/Erie	241
2B	Trei Cruz, Toledo/Erie	33
3B	Hao-Yu Lee, Toledo	8
HR	Eduardo Valencia, Toledo/Erie	24
RBI	Eduardo Valencia, Toledo/Erie	95
BB	Trei Cruz, Toledo/Erie	102
SO	Patrick Lee, West Michigan/Lakeland	132
SB	Seth Stephenson, Erie/West Michigan	49

Pitching		#Qualifiers
MAJORS		
W	Casey Mize	14
# ERA	Tarik Skubal	2.21
SO	Tarik Skubal	241
SV	Will Vest	23
MINORS		
W	Garrett Burhenn, Erie	13
L	Carlos Pena, Toledo/Erie	8
# ERA	Joe Miller, Toledo/West Michigan	2.95
G	Drew Sommers, Toledo/Erie	48
GS	Garrett Burhenn, Erie	24
SV	Moises Rodriguez, West Michigan/Lakeland	10
IP	Garrett Burhenn, Erie	125
BB	Lael Lockhart, Toledo/West Michigan/Lakeland	55
SO	Andrew Sears, Erie/West Michigan	123
AVG	Kenny Serwa, Erie/West Michigan	.225
SO	Konner Eaton, Hartford/Spokane	149
# AVG	Michael Prosecky, Hartford/Spokane	.230

2025 PERFORMANCE

President: Scott Harris. **Farm Director:** Ryan Garko. **Scouting Director:** Mark Conner.

Class	Team	League	W	L	PCT	Finish	Manager
Majors	Detroit Tigers	American	87	75	.537	6 (15)	A.J. Hinch
Triple-A	Toledo Mud Hens	International	84	66	.560	7 (20)	Gabe Alvarez
Double-A	Erie SeaWolves	Eastern	84	54	.609	2 (12)	Andrew Graham
High-A	West Michigan Whitecaps	Midwest	92	39	.702	1 (12)	Tony Cappuccilli
Low-A	Lakeland Flying Tigers	Florida State	75	53	.586	2 (10)	Rene Rivera
Rookie	DSL Tigers 1	Dominican	24	30	.444	35 (52)	Marcos Yepez
Rookie	DSL Tigers 2	Dominican	24	29	.453	32 (52)	Sandy Acevedo
Rookie	FCL Tigers	Florida Complex	37	22	.627	3 (15)	Salvador Paniagua
Overall 2025 Minor League Record			420	293	.589	1st (30)	

ORGANIZATION STATISTICS

DETROIT TIGERS
AMERICAN LEAGUE

Batting	B-T	Ht.	Wt.	DOB	AVG	OBP	SLG	G	PA	AB	R	H	2B	3B	HR	RBI	BB	HBP	SH	SF	SO	SB	CS	BB%	SO%
Baddoo, Akil	L-L	6-1	214	8-16-98	.118	.167	.176	7	18	17	0	2	1	0	0	1	1	0	0	0	5	1	0	5.6	27.8
Baez, Javier	R-R	6-0	190	12-1-92	.257	.282	.398	126	437	417	55	107	17	3	12	57	10	6	0	3	109	5	1	2.3	24.9
Carpenter, Kerry	L-R	6-2	220	9-2-97	.252	.291	.497	130	464	433	66	109	18	5	26	62	18	7	0	2	106	1	1	3.9	22.8
Dingler, Dillon	R-R	6-3	210	9-17-98	.278	.327	.425	126	469	435	54	121	21	2	13	57	23	9	0	1	110	0	0	4.9	23.5
Greene, Riley	L-L	6-3	200	9-28-00	.258	.313	.493	157	655	600	84	155	31	1	36	111	46	4	0	5	201	2	1	7.0	30.7
Hicklen, Brewer	R-R	6-1	220	2-9-96	.667	.750	.667	1	4	3	2	2	0	0	0	0	1	0	0	0	1	1	0	25.0	25.0
Ibanez, Andy	R-R	5-10	205	4-3-93	.239	.301	.352	91	193	176	24	42	8	0	4	21	12	4	0	1	26	4	1	6.2	13.5
Jones, Jahmai	R-R	6-0	210	8-4-97	.287	.387	.550	72	150	129	21	37	11	1	7	23	18	3	0	0	32	2	0	12.0	21.3
Jung, Jace	L-R	6-0	205	10-4-00	.106	.236	.106	21	55	47	8	5	0	0	0	3	7	1	0	0	16	0	0	12.7	29.1
Keith, Colt	L-R	6-2	211	8-14-01	.256	.333	.413	137	468	414	65	106	22	2	13	45	48	2	0	4	102	1	1	10.3	21.8
Kreidler, Ryan	R-R	6-4	208	11-12-97	.105	.190	.105	17	44	38	5	4	0	0	0	0	4	0	2	0	19	2	0	9.1	43.2
Malloy, Justyn-Henry	R-R	6-1	212	2-19-00	.221	.346	.308	52	127	104	15	23	6	0	1	17	20	1	0	2	32	0	0	15.7	25.2
Margot, Manuel	R-R	5-11	180	9-28-94	.316	.300	.316	6	20	19	1	6	0	0	0	3	0	0	1	0	6	0	0	0.0	30.0
McKinstry, Zach	L-R	6-0	180	4-29-95	.259	.333	.438	144	511	452	68	117	23	11	12	49	46	7	1	5	111	19	5	9.0	21.7
Meadows, Parker	L-R	6-5	205	11-2-99	.215	.291	.330	58	213	191	22	41	6	2	4	16	21	0	0	1	56	4	0	9.9	26.3
Nido, Tomas	R-R	6-0	211	4-12-94	.343	.361	.343	11	37	35	4	12	0	0	0	2	0	1	1	0	10	0	0	2.7	27.0
Perez, Wenceel	S-R	5-11	203	10-30-99	.244	.308	.430	100	383	344	47	84	17	4	13	43	31	3	0	5	87	8	3	8.1	22.7
Rogers, Jake	R-R	6-1	201	4-18-95	.187	.277	.333	49	142	123	14	23	5	2	3	19	15	1	1	2	39	0	0	10.6	27.5
Sweeney, Trey	L-R	6-2	200	4-24-00	.196	.258	.291	118	326	296	36	58	6	2	6	32	26	0	0	4	92	3	1	8.0	28.2
Torkelson, Spencer	R-R	6-1	220	8-26-99	.240	.333	.456	155	649	563	82	135	27	1	31	78	72	9	0	5	169	2	1	11.1	26.0
Torres, Gleyber	R-R	6-1	205	12-13-96	.256	.358	.387	145	628	532	79	136	22	0	16	74	85	4	0	7	101	4	1	13.5	16.1
Vierling, Matt	R-R	6-3	205	9-16-96	.239	.310	.307	31	100	88	6	21	3	0	1	11	7	3	0	2	24	2	0	7.0	24.0

Pitching	B-T	Ht.	Wt.	DOB	W	L	ERA	G	GS	SV	IP	Hits	Runs	ER	HR	BB	SO	AVG	OBP	SLG	SO%	BB%	BF
Brebbia, John	L-R	6-1	200	5-30-90	1	0	7.71	19	0	0	19	22	18	16	3	11	20	.286	.391	.494	21.5	11.8	93
Brieske, Beau	R-R	6-3	200	4-4-98	1	3	6.55	22	1	1	22	24	20	16	5	12	16	.273	.353	.489	15.5	11.7	103
Enns, Dietrich	L-L	6-1	210	5-16-91	1	1	5.60	7	2	0	18	23	12	11	2	4	15	.319	.351	.486	19.5	5.2	77
Finnegan, Kyle	R-R	6-2	200	9-4-91	3	0	1.50	16	0	4	18	9	3	3	1	4	23	.153	.203	.254	34.8	6.1	66
Flaherty, Jack	R-R	6-4	225	10-15-95	8	15	4.64	31	31	0	161	147	85	83	23	59	188	.239	.311	.406	27.6	8.7	681
Gage, Matt	L-L	6-3	265	2-11-93	0	0	0.00	6	0	0	6	7	0	0	0	2	3	.304	.360	.348	12.0	8.0	25
Gipson-Long, Sawyer	R-R	6-4	225	12-12-97	0	2	7.18	8	3	0	31	34	26	25	8	6	26	.281	.316	.554	19.5	4.5	133
Guenther, Sean	L-L	5-11	194	12-29-95	0	1	5.23	9	1	0	10	10	7	6	0	5	8	.263	.349	.316	18.6	11.6	43
Hanifee, Brenan	R-R	6-5	215	5-29-98	3	3	3.00	54	0	0	60	65	31	20	3	14	40	.267	.312	.379	15.4	5.4	260
Hartlieb, Geoff	R-R	6-5	240	12-9-93	0	0	9.00	2	0	0	2	3	2	2	1	2	1	.333	.455	.778	9.1	18.2	11
Hernandez, Carlos	R-R	6-4	245	3-11-97	0	0	10.13	11	0	0	11	14	13	12	0	6	13	.311	.385	.356	24.5	11.3	53
Heuer, Codi	R-R	6-5	200	7-3-96	0	0	5.40	2	0	0	3	3	2	2	2	2	4	.214	.313	.643	25.0	12.5	16
Holton, Tyler	L-L	6-2	200	6-13-96	6	5	3.66	70	6	0	79	65	34	32	15	17	64	.226	.266	.408	20.5	5.4	312
Horn, Bailey	L-L	6-2	210	1-15-98	0	1	1.59	10	0	0	11	7	2	2	1	7	10	.256	.360	.349	20.0	14.0	50
Hurter, Brant	L-L	6-6	250	9-6-98	4	3	2.43	43	4	2	63	57	26	17	4	27	68	.242	.345	.326	24.5	9.7	277
Jackson, Luke	R-R	6-2	210	8-24-91	0	0	7.71	3	0	0	5	3	4	4	0	5	4	.188	.381	.188	18.2	22.7	22
Jobe, Jackson	R-R	6-2	190	7-30-02	4	1	4.22	10	10	0	49	46	24	23	7	27	39	.249	.347	.422	17.9	12.4	218
Kahnle, Tommy	R-R	6-1	230	8-7-89	1	5	4.43	66	0	9	63	51	32	31	8	31	50	.217	.311	.370	18.7	11.6	267
Lange, Alex	R-R	6-3	202	10-2-95	0	0	0.00	1	0	0	1	2	0	0	0	1	1	.400	.500	.400	16.7	16.7	6
Lee, Chase	R-R	6-0	170	8-13-98	4	1	4.10	32	0	0	37	32	17	17	7	9	36	.239	.291	.478	24.3	6.1	148
Maeda, Kenta	R-R	6-1	185	4-11-88	0	0	7.88	7	0	0	8	9	8	7	1	6	8	.273	.429	.455	18.6	14.0	43
McKinstry, Zach	L-R	6-0	180	4-29-95	0	0	0.00	1	0	0	1	0	0	0	0	0	0	.000	.000	.000	0.0	0.0	1
Melton, Troy	R-R	6-4	210	12-3-00	3	2	2.76	16	4	0	46	31	15	14	7	15	36	.191	.263	.346	20.0	8.3	180
Mize, Casey	R-R	6-3	212	5-1-97	14	6	3.87	28	28	0	149	153	68	64	21	36	139	.263	.307	.437	22.2	5.7	627
Montero, Keider	R-R	6-1	145	7-6-00	5	3	4.37	20	12	0	91	95	46	44	16	31	72	.268	.330	.445	18.5	8.0	389
Montero, Rafael	R-R	6-0	190	10-17-90	1	1	2.86	20	0	0	22	12	10	7	2	14	19	.164	.299	.274	21.8	16.1	87
Morton, Charlie	R-R	6-5	215	11-12-83	2	3	7.09	9	9	0	39	40	31	31	7	23	47	.260	.374	.500	25.5	12.5	184
Nido, Tomas	R-R	6-0	211	4-12-94	0	0	0.00	1	0	0	2	0	0	0	0	0	0	.000	.167	.000	0.0	0.0	6

Batting	B-T	Ht.	Wt.	DOB																	
Olson, Reese	R-R	6-1	160	7-31-99	4	4	3.15	13	13	0	69	58	24	24	5	25	65	.228	.310	.335	22.8	8.8	285
Owens, Tyler	R-R	5-10	185	1-9-01	0	0	3.00	3	0	0	3	3	1	1	0	3	1	.250	.400	.250	6.7	20.0	15
Paddack, Chris	R-R	6-5	217	1-8-96	2	3	6.32	12	7	1	47	51	33	33	14	10	29	.273	.308	.572	14.6	5.1	198
Rainey, Tanner	R-R	6-2	250	12-25-92	0	0	13.50	2	0	0	2	1	3	3	0	3	2	.143	.400	.286	20.0	30.0	10
Rogers, Jake	R-R	6-1	201	4-18-95	0	0	2.45	4	0	0	4	5	1	1	0	0	0	.357	.375	.429	0.0	0.0	16
Sewald, Paul	R-R	6-3	219	5-26-90	0	0	4.15	4	0	0	4	4	2	2	1	2	2	.250	.316	.500	10.5	10.5	19
Skubal, Tarik	R-L	6-3	240	11-20-96	13	6	2.21	31	31	0	195	141	55	48	18	33	241	.200	.240	.319	32.2	4.4	748
Smith, Dylan	R-R	6-2	180	5-28-00	1	0	1.38	7	0	0	13	6	2	2	0	5	4	.150	.292	.175	8.3	10.4	48
Sommers, Drew	L-L	6-3	250	8-14-00	0	1	18.00	4	0	0	3	7	6	6	1	3	3	.467	.579	.867	15.8	15.8	19
Urquidy, Jose	R-R	6-0	217	5-1-95	0	0	7.71	2	0	0	2	4	2	2	0	3	3	.364	.500	.364	21.4	21.4	14
Vest, Will	R-R	6-0	180	6-6-95	6	5	3.01	64	0	23	69	61	26	23	4	22	75	.236	.297	.328	26.4	7.7	284

Fielding

Catcher	PCT	G	PO	A	E	DP	PB
Dingler	.993	118	1023	39	7	5	0
Nido	.988	10	85	0	1	0	1
Rogers	.988	41	302	15	4	0	1

First Base	PCT	G	PO	A	E	DP
Ibanez	1.000	4	10	2	0	1
Keith	1.000	18	131	6	0	9
Malloy	1.000	1	4	0	0	1
McKinstry	1.000	1	2	1	0	0
Torkelson	.996	145	1054	100	5	109

Second Base	PCT	G	PO	A	E	DP
Baez	1.000	10	6	15	0	3
Ibanez	1.000	11	3	10	0	2
Jones	.000	1	0	0	0	0
Keith	.953	26	27	54	4	9

McKinstry	.913	6	10	11	2	1
Torres	.990	134	197	310	5	75

Third Base	PCT	G	PO	A	E	DP
Baez	.976	23	15	26	1	4
Ibanez	.969	68	24	69	3	7
Jung	.979	19	9	38	1	3
Keith	.972	37	18	52	2	6
McKinstry	.963	85	37	118	6	11
Vierling	.000	3	0	0	0	0

Shortstop	PCT	G	PO	A	E	DP
Baez	.961	62	57	115	7	23
Ibanez	.000	1	0	0	0	0
McKinstry	.969	40	46	79	4	22
Sweeney	.981	112	120	184	6	36

Outfield	PCT	G	PO	A	E	DP
Baddoo	1.000	8	14	1	0	1
Baez	1.000	53	104	2	0	1
Carpenter	.979	79	136	2	3	0
Greene	.993	141	286	2	2	0
Hicklen	1.000	1	3	0	0	0
Ibanez	.000	1	0	0	0	0
Jones	.938	28	15	0	1	0
Kreidler	1.000	17	34	0	0	0
Malloy	1.000	20	24	0	0	0
Margot	.909	6	10	0	1	0
McKinstry	1.000	45	67	2	0	0
Meadows	.992	57	118	1	1	0
Perez	.984	113	179	5	3	0
Vierling	1.000	29	54	1	0	0

TOLEDO MUD HENS
INTERNATIONAL LEAGUE — TRIPLE-A

Batting	B-T	Ht.	Wt.	DOB	AVG	OBP	SLG	G	PA	AB	R	H	2B	3B	HR	RBI	BB	HBP	SH	SF	SO	SB	CS	BB%	SO%
Alfonzo, Eliezer	S-R	5-10	155	9-23-99	.219	.219	.250	8	33	32	4	7	1	0	0	3	0	0	0	0	4	0	0	0.0	12.1
Anderson, Max	R-R	6-0	195	2-28-02	.267	.327	.422	32	147	135	24	36	6	0	5	23	8	4	0	0	28	1	0	5.4	19.0
Baddoo, Akil	L-L	6-1	214	8-16-98	.281	.385	.483	103	457	385	71	108	21	6	15	48	68	0	0	4	112	25	4	14.9	24.5
Bigbie, Justice	R-R	6-2	200	1-24-99	.250	.250	1.000	1	4	4	1	1	0	0	1	1	0	0	0	0	0	0	0	0.0	0.0
Carpenter, Kerry	L-R	6-2	220	9-2-97	.133	.188	.333	4	16	15	1	2	0	0	1	2	1	0	0	0	4	0	0	6.3	25.0
Cruz, Trei	S-R	6-2	204	7-5-98	.284	.423	.458	58	241	190	39	54	11	2	6	31	48	0	0	3	55	8	3	19.9	22.8
Dunn, Jack	R-R	6-1	185	9-5-96	.180	.300	.220	15	60	50	7	9	0	1	0	5	7	2	0	1	19	3	0	11.7	31.7
Gamel, Ben	L-L	5-10	180	5-17-92	.262	.375	.344	17	72	61	6	16	5	0	0	4	10	1	0	0	22	2	1	13.9	30.6
Hensley, David	R-R	6-6	190	3-28-96	.085	.246	.170	15	58	47	4	4	1	0	1	4	9	1	1	0	26	0	0	15.5	44.8
Hicklen, Brewer	R-R	6-1	220	2-9-96	.227	.335	.394	61	254	216	37	49	8	2	8	31	29	7	0	2	77	18	1	11.4	30.3
Ibanez, Andy	R-R	5-10	205	4-3-93	.259	.350	.381	36	160	139	11	36	9	1	2	16	18	2	0	1	30	4	2	11.3	18.8
Jenkins, Andrew	R-R	5-11	217	11-3-00	.333	.333	.333	1	3	3	0	1	0	0	0	0	0	0	0	0	2	0	0	0.0	66.7
Jones, Jahmai	R-R	6-0	210	8-4-97	.276	.392	.482	52	205	170	33	47	9	4	6	29	4	9	1	1	46	8	2	11.7	22.4
Jung, Jace	L-R	6-0	205	10-4-00	.252	.370	.447	110	495	412	69	104	27	1	17	74	78	1	0	4	125	4	4	15.8	25.3
Kreidler, Ryan	R-R	6-4	208	11-12-97	.251	.374	.410	84	343	283	44	71	25	4	4	37	50	7	1	2	93	13	8	14.6	27.1
Lee, Hao-Yu	R-R	5-9	190	2-3-03	.243	.342	.406	126	579	497	81	121	23	8	14	61	65	12	0	5	121	22	5	11.2	20.9
Madris, Bligh	L-R	6-0	208	2-29-96	.232	.320	.384	50	205	177	29	41	10	1	5	37	24	0	0	2	52	3	2	11.7	25.4
Malloy, Justyn-Henry	R-R	6-1	212	2-19-00	.322	.453	.502	72	329	261	49	84	20	0	9	53	57	8	0	3	67	6	1	17.3	20.4
Margot, Manuel	R-R	5-11	180	9-28-94	.211	.299	.266	37	144	128	14	27	2	1	1	16	12	4	0	0	27	0	1	8.3	18.8
Meadows, Parker	L-R	6-5	205	11-2-99	.267	.400	.533	13	55	45	12	12	3	3	1	6	10	0	0	0	18	1	0	18.2	32.7
Mendoza, Carlos	L-R	5-7	165	12-14-99	.327	.351	.558	14	57	52	5	17	4	1	2	10	2	1	0	2	9	7	2	3.5	15.8
Murr, Austin	L-L	6-2	218	1-26-00	.208	.259	.375	11	27	24	3	5	1	0	1	8	2	0	0	1	10	0	0	7.4	37.0
Navigato, Andrew	R-R	5-11	188	5-28-98	.209	.282	.367	100	376	335	46	70	16	2	11	45	28	8	0	5	116	10	6	7.4	30.9
Newman, Kevin	R-R	6-1	195	8-4-93	.296	.377	.370	15	61	54	10	16	4	0	0	7	6	0	0	1	10	0	0	11.5	16.4
Nido, Tomas	R-R	6-0	211	4-12-94	.209	.267	.331	48	189	172	19	36	6	0	5	21	11	3	2	1	46	0	0	5.8	24.3
Perez, Wenceel	S-R	5-11	203	10-30-99	.111	.111	.111	2	9	9	1	1	0	0	0	0	0	0	0	0	2	0	0	0.0	22.2
Rogers, Jake	R-R	6-1	201	4-18-95	.333	.444	.533	4	18	15	5	5	3	0	0	3	0	0	0	0	3	0	0	16.7	16.7
Scott, Stephen	L-R	5-11	207	5-23-97	.138	.219	.224	21	64	58	7	8	0	1	1	6	4	2	0	0	19	2	0	6.3	29.7
Serven, Brian	R-R	6-0	207	5-5-95	.232	.335	.313	62	233	198	28	46	7	0	3	28	28	4	0	3	59	1	0	12.0	25.3
Sweeney, Trey	L-R	6-2	200	4-24-00	.326	.442	.512	12	52	43	9	14	2	0	2	6	7	2	0	0	11	4	1	13.5	21.2
Unroe, Riley	S-R	5-11	180	8-3-95	.278	.397	.409	68	242	198	28	55	12	1	4	34	39	2	0	3	48	12	1	16.1	19.8
Valencia, Eduardo	R-R	6-1	180	1-25-00	.319	.405	.622	50	215	185	35	59	13	2	13	55	27	1	0	2	41	0	0	12.6	19.1
Vierling, Matt	R-R	6-3	205	9-16-96	.200	.333	.167	7	69	60	9	12	1	0	0	1	8	1	0	0	7	0	1	11.6	33.3
Workman, Gage	S-R	6-4	202	10-24-99	.229	.324	.482	86	346	301	56	69	19	6	15	47	40	3	0	2	131	10	2	11.6	37.9

Pitching	B-T	Ht.	Wt.	DOB	W	L	ERA	G	GS	SV	IP	Hits	Runs	ER	HR	BB	SO	AVG	OBP	SLG	SO%	BB%	BF
Adametz, Joe	L-L	6-5	190	12-23-99	0	1	3.86	1	0	0	2	4	2	1	0	2	2	.333	.429	.500	14.3	14.3	14
Balazovic, Jordan	R-R	6-5	215	9-17-98	5	1	3.69	34	7	1	54	58	24	22	7	23	48	.275	.345	.431	20.4	9.8	235
Bergner, Austin	R-R	6-5	205	5-1-97	1	0	9.00	2	1	0	6	7	6	6	2	5	14	.292	.393	.792	17.9	14.3	28
Boyer, Ryan	R-R	6-2	225	5-4-97	0	0	3.60	3	0	0	5	4	2	2	2	4	.211	.286	.526	19.0	9.5	21
Brebbia, John	L-R	6-1	200	5-30-90	0	0	5.40	2	1	0	2	1	1	1	0	1	1	.167	.286	.167	14.3	14.3	7

DETROIT TIGERS

Player	B-T	Ht	Wt	DOB																		
Brieske, Beau	R-R	6-3	200	4-4-98	0	1	9.90	9	0	0	10	13	11	11	4	9	8	.325	.449	.675	16.3	18.4	49
Calvo, Blair	R-R	6-3	195	2-27-96	0	0	0.00	1	0	0	2	1	0	0	0	1	4	.167	.286	.167	57.1	14.3	7
Chafin, Andrew	R-L	6-2	235	6-17-90	2	0	2.13	13	0	1	13	12	4	3	0	4	17	.255	.321	.277	31.5	7.4	54
Cobb, Alex	R-R	6-3	205	10-7-87	1	0	1.80	5	2	0	10	5	2	2	0	10	10	.156	.349	.156	23.3	23.3	43
Cusick, Ryan	R-R	6-6	235	11-12-99	0	0	0.00	1	0	0	1	0	0	0	0	0	1	.000	.250	.000	0.0	25.0	4
Dobnak, Randy	R-R	6-1	230	1-17-95	1	1	3.79	9	8	0	38	37	17	16	2	16	35	.259	.340	.329	21.5	9.8	163
Enns, Dietrich	L-L	6-1	210	5-16-91	2	2	2.89	14	14	0	62	61	26	20	4	15	71	.250	.299	.361	26.7	5.6	266
Fields, Colin	R-R	6-2	200	3-18-00	0	1	32.40	1	0	0	2	5	7	6	0	3	1	.556	.667	.778	7.7	23.1	13
Finnegan, Kyle	R-R	6-2	200	9-4-91	0	0	0.00	1	1	0	1	0	0	0	0	1	1	.000	.333	.000	33.3	33.3	3
Foley, Jason	R-R	6-4	215	11-1-95	0	0	0.00	5	0	0	7	1	0	0	0	0	9	.045	.045	.045	40.9	0.0	22
Gage, Matt	L-L	6-3	265	2-11-93	1	1	1.67	23	1	3	32	27	10	6	2	4	28	.229	.252	.339	22.8	3.3	123
Gipson-Long, Sawyer	R-R	6-4	225	12-12-97	0	1	4.13	9	8	0	33	26	15	15	1	8	35	.215	.273	.306	26.5	6.1	132
Go, Woo Suk	R-R	5-11	198	8-6-98	1	0	4.29	14	1	3	21	19	12	10	3	11	22	.238	.333	.388	23.7	11.8	93
Guenther, Sean	L-L	5-11	194	12-29-95	1	1	3.60	4	0	0	5	3	2	2	0	2	4	.176	.250	.294	20.0	10.0	20
Hanifee, Brenan	R-R	6-5	215	5-29-98	0	0	1.50	6	1	0	6	4	1	1	0	1	7	.190	.227	.238	31.8	4.5	22
Hartlieb, Geoff	R-R	6-5	240	12-9-93	1	0	4.35	6	1	2	10	7	5	5	2	3	14	.184	.238	.395	33.3	7.1	42
Hernandez, Wilkel	R-R	6-3	195	4-13-99	3	7	4.80	34	19	1	114	119	63	61	14	44	96	.270	.340	.439	19.3	8.9	497
Heuer, Codi	R-R	6-5	200	7-3-96	0	1	1.93	9	0	1	9	5	4	2	0	2	9	.167	.242	.167	26.5	5.9	34
Horn, Bailey	L-L	6-2	210	1-15-98	4	2	3.29	30	4	0	41	40	17	15	4	19	51	.252	.331	.384	28.2	10.5	181
Hurter, Brant	L-L	6-6	250	9-6-98	0	1	9.82	3	0	0	4	5	4	4	0	0	2	.294	.294	.353	11.8	0.0	17
Lange, Alex	R-R	6-3	202	10-2-95	2	1	4.63	24	0	0	23	14	12	12	2	14	29	.171	.306	.293	29.6	14.3	98
Lee, Chase	R-R	6-0	170	8-13-98	1	1	6.47	23	0	1	32	30	24	23	4	10	38	.244	.304	.431	28.1	7.4	135
Lockhart, Lael	S-L	6-3	225	12-31-97	5	7	5.34	20	20	0	86	84	54	51	10	48	83	.258	.360	.445	22.0	12.7	378
Manning, Matt	R-R	6-6	195	1-28-98	2	2	6.04	31	4	2	51	45	37	34	7	37	52	.237	.362	.411	22.4	15.9	232
Margevicius, Nick	L-L	6-5	225	6-18-96	5	3	3.89	17	14	0	74	82	33	32	7	18	70	.278	.318	.441	22.0	5.7	318
Mattison, Tyler	R-R	6-4	235	9-9-99	3	3	3.79	20	0	2	19	17	8	8	1	16	26	.239	.370	.338	29.9	18.4	87
Melton, Troy	R-R	6-4	210	12-3-00	0	2	2.72	8	6	0	36	33	13	11	5	9	56	.239	.286	.420	37.8	6.1	148
Michael, Trevin	R-R	6-2	200	9-15-97	1	0	0.87	4	0	0	7	1	1	1	0	5	14	.184	.295	.237	31.8	11.4	44
Miller, Joe	L-L	5-10	195	3-13-00	1	1	3.27	2	2	0	11	9	4	4	2	4	9	.231	.302	.436	20.9	9.3	43
Miller, Ryan	R-R	6-0	180	3-28-96	2	1	4.32	37	0	2	50	39	25	24	8	16	44	.215	.276	.403	22.0	8.0	200
Montero, Keider	R-R	6-1	145	7-6-00	4	4	5.91	10	8	0	43	42	29	28	5	15	43	.261	.330	.441	23.6	8.2	182
Naughton, Tim	R-R	6-3	195	11-14-95	0	0	0.00	1	0	0	2	1	0	0	0	3	1	.167	.444	.333	11.1	33.3	9
Olson, Reese	R-R	6-1	160	7-31-99	0	1	3.48	3	3	0	10	8	4	4	2	1	14	.216	.268	.378	34.1	4.9	41
Owens, Tyler	R-R	5-10	185	1-9-01	1	1	5.40	28	0	0	30	32	22	18	5	21	27	.264	.373	.446	19.0	14.8	142
Pena, Carlos	L-L	5-11	160	9-7-98	0	2	4.00	4	0	1	9	11	4	4	1	2	9	.297	.325	.514	22.5	5.0	40
Petit, RJ	R-R	6-8	300	9-23-99	4	1	2.74	20	1	1	23	19	7	7	2	10	33	.224	.313	.353	34.4	10.4	96
Poulin, PJ	R-L	6-1	195	7-25-96	7	1	3.38	35	3	2	43	38	20	16	4	17	62	.233	.321	.399	33.7	9.2	184
Rainey, Tanner	R-R	6-2	250	12-2-92	1	0	2.66	19	2	1	24	13	8	7	1	14	33	.160	.284	.247	34.7	14.7	95
Seelinger, Matt	R-R	6-3	190	4-19-95	7	2	3.11	36	0	3	46	35	17	16	5	22	55	.208	.297	.321	28.6	11.5	192
Sewald, Paul	R-R	6-3	219	5-26-90	0	0	3.38	3	0	0	3	2	1	1	1	0	0	.273	.500	0.0	0.0	11	
Smeltzer, Devin	L-L	6-3	195	9-7-95	0	1	8.44	3	3	0	11	18	10	10	5	7	3	.383	.442	.426	13.5	9.6	52
Smith, Dylan	R-R	6-2	180	5-28-00	1	0	3.65	12	0	1	12	8	5	5	1	7	22	.190	.300	.286	44.0	14.0	50
Sommers, Drew	L-L	6-3	250	8-14-00	2	1	3.92	33	1	3	39	31	19	17	0	19	48	.217	.331	.280	28.1	11.1	171
Szapucki, Thomas	L-L	6-2	210	6-12-96	0	0	6.75	2	0	0	1	2	2	1	0	1	2	.286	.375	.429	25.0	12.5	8
Unroe, Riley	S-R	5-11	180	8-3-95	2	3	0.84	7	0	0	11	10	9	1	1	2	0	.250	.279	.350	0.0	4.7	43
Urquidy, Jose	R-R	6-0	217	5-1-95	1	0	3.24	7	4	0	17	11	6	6	2	5	14	.183	.246	.300	21.5	7.7	65
Vanasco, Ricky	R-R	6-3	180	10-13-98	3	3	4.81	18	0	1	24	17	13	13	3	17	32	.193	.283	.375	30.2	16.0	106
Watson, Troy	R-R	6-2	180	6-11-97	1	3	3.12	10	10	0	52	48	19	18	7	15	42	.247	.300	.412	19.7	7.0	213
White, Brendan	R-R	5-11	185	11-18-98	1	3	7.24	27	0	0	32	44	32	26	3	17	27	.326	.409	.519	17.0	10.7	159

Fielding

Catcher	PCT	G	PO	A	E	DP	PB
Alfonzo	1.000	7	60	1	0	0	0
Nido	.992	47	448	29	4	1	2
Rogers	1.000	4	34	3	0	0	0
Scott	1.000	20	154	9	0	0	1
Serven	.991	62	545	33	5	4	1
Valencia	1.000	17	139	8	0	0	0

First Base	PCT	G	PO	A	E	DP
Hensley	1.000	7	65	4	0	5
Ibanez	.990	12	89	8	1	10
Jenkins	1.000	1	7	0	0	0
Madris	.991	40	291	28	3	23
Malloy	.996	32	234	8	1	20
Murr	1.000	8	43	1	0	3
Navigato	.995	27	176	6	1	20
Newman	1.000	1	7	1	0	1
Scott	.000	1	0	0	0	0
Unroe	1.000	5	30	2	0	1
Valencia	.995	24	191	3	1	18

Second Base	PCT	G	PO	A	E	DP
Anderson	.973	11	11	25	1	5
Ibanez	1.000	7	12	12	0	6
Jones	1.000	1	0	1	0	0
Jung	.967	46	72	105	6	32
Kreidler	.875	2	3	4	1	2

Third Base	PCT	G	PO	A	E	DP
Anderson	.955	10	17	25	2	3
Hensley	1.000	1	1	8	0	3
Ibanez	.857	5	2	4	1	0
Jung	.945	48	30	73	6	3
Lee	.943	60	40	108	9	14
Mendoza	1.000	6	2	12	0	1
Navigato	.938	9	3	12	1	1
Newman	1.000	1	0	1	0	0
Unroe	1.000	3	2	1	0	0
Vierling	.667	2	1	1	1	0
Workman	.962	9	4	21	1	1

Shortstop	PCT	G	PO	A	E	DP
Cruz	.976	30	35	86	3	11
Dunn	1.000	8	8	15	0	3
Ibanez	1.000	1	1	4	0	1
Kreidler	.961	42	66	107	7	23
Navigato	.925	28	27	47	6	8

	PCT	G	PO	A	E	DP
Newman	.977	10	9	33	1	1
Sweeney	.980	12	13	37	1	7
Unroe	1.000	1	0	3	0	0
Workman	.929	21	29	50	6	7

Outfield	PCT	G	PO	A	E	DP
Baddoo	.990	104	192	7	2	1
Bigbie	1.000	1	3	0	0	0
Carpenter	1.000	2	5	0	0	0
Cruz	1.000	27	38	3	0	0
Dunn	1.000	7	25	0	0	0
Gamel	.962	13	25	0	1	0
Hicklen	.992	57	119	5	1	1
Ibanez	1.000	2	2	1	0	0
Jones	.988	44	79	3	1	1
Kreidler	.989	42	88	3	1	0
Madris	1.000	8	15	0	0	0
Malloy	1.000	31	46	2	0	0
Margot	1.000	21	30	0	0	0
Meadows	1.000	9	12	0	0	0
Mendoza	1.000	1	2	0	0	0
Murr	1.000	2	1	0	0	0
Navigato	.964	19	27	0	1	0
Perez	.000	2	0	0	0	0
Unroe	.984	37	59	3	1	0
Vierling	1.000	6	7	0	0	0
Workman	.980	55	95	3	2	2

ERIE SEAWOLVES — DOUBLE-A
EASTERN LEAGUE — DETROIT TIGERS

Batting	B-T	Ht.	Wt.	DOB	AVG	OBP	SLG	G	PA	AB	R	H	2B	3B	HR	RBI	BB	HBP	SH	SF	SO	SB	CS	BB%	SO%
Alfonzo, Eliezer	S-R	5-10	155	9-23-99	.251	.308	.333	57	217	195	20	49	13	0	1	31	16	1	1	2	28	0	0	7.4	12.9
Anderson, Max	R-R	6-0	195	2-28-02	.306	.358	.499	90	405	369	54	113	25	2	14	65	28	4	0	4	59	2	3	6.9	14.6
Bastidas, Abel	S-R	6-1	165	11-24-03	.059	.059	.059	4	17	17	1	1	0	0	0	0	1	0	0	0	7	0	0	0.0	41.2
Bigbie, Justice	R-R	6-2	200	1-24-99	.283	.358	.414	108	452	399	58	113	16	0	12	66	47	2	0	4	69	1	2	10.4	15.3
Briceno, Josue	L-R	6-4	200	9-23-04	.232	.335	.381	45	198	168	20	39	6	2	5	19	25	2	0	2	47	0	1	12.6	23.7
Campos, Roberto	R-R	6-3	200	6-14-03	.239	.308	.350	101	403	360	46	86	22	3	4	39	36	1	0	3	101	5	1	8.9	25.1
Clark, Max	L-L	6-1	190	12-21-04	.251	.360	.439	43	203	171	36	43	5	3	7	20	29	1	0	2	34	7	0	14.3	16.7
Cruz, Trei	S-R	6-1	204	7-5-98	.275	.402	.454	69	323	262	56	72	22	2	7	35	54	4	0	3	66	9	4	16.7	20.4
Holton, Jake	R-R	6-0	210	3-2-98	.257	.349	.479	109	464	405	70	104	29	2	19	66	54	4	0	1	118	6	1	11.6	25.4
Jarvis, Jim	L-R	5-10	185	11-6-00	.242	.316	.336	77	310	277	37	67	14	3	2	29	26	5	0	2	31	8	5	8.4	10.0
Liranzo, Thayron	S-R	6-3	195	7-5-03	.206	.308	.351	88	394	339	49	70	16	0	11	45	47	4	0	3	125	0	0	11.9	31.7
Malgeri, Ben	R-R	6-1	215	1-12-00	.279	.351	.474	74	285	251	45	70	20	7	5	26	23	7	0	4	52	4	2	8.1	18.2
McGonigle, Kevin	L-R	5-11	185	8-18-04	.254	.369	.550	46	206	169	30	43	10	2	12	41	33	0	0	4	26	7	2	16.0	12.6
Mendoza, Carlos	L-R	5-7	165	12-14-99	.279	.401	.382	83	350	283	59	79	12	1	5	31	51	9	3	4	36	5	4	14.6	10.3
Meyers, Chris	L-R	6-3	210	4-27-99	.270	.353	.460	77	317	278	45	75	15	3	10	47	32	5	0	2	63	1	0	10.1	19.9
Peck, John	R-R	6-0	185	7-18-02	.274	.340	.358	25	106	95	10	26	5	0	1	10	9	1	0	1	21	2	1	8.5	19.8
Serretti, Danny	S-R	6-0	195	5-7-00	.209	.313	.311	62	240	206	25	43	10	1	3	28	30	2	0	2	47	5	1	12.5	19.6
Stephenson, Seth	R-R	5-8	165	1-10-01	.254	.325	.352	21	81	71	11	18	5	1	0	8	6	2	1	1	10	7	1	7.4	12.3
Valencia, Eduardo	R-R	6-1	180	1-25-00	.304	.359	.500	53	218	194	29	59	5	0	4	20	11	0	1	3	40	4	0	4.5	20.6

Pitching	B-T	Ht.	Wt.	DOB	W	L	ERA	G	GS	SV	IP	Hits	Runs	ER	HR	BB	SO	AVG	OBP	SLG	SO%	BB%	BF
Alba, Max	R-R	6-5	215	7-15-99	0	1	6.12	8	8	0	32	39	24	22	5	9	24	.291	.338	.500	16.4	6.2	146
Ashman, Micah	L-L	6-7	200	8-22-02	0	0	0.00	2	0	0	3	2	0	0	0	1	4	.182	.250	.182	33.3	8.3	12
Bergner, Austin	R-R	6-5	210	5-1-97	8	7	3.07	25	14	1	91	75	35	31	7	39	90	.223	.302	.329	23.6	10.2	381
Boyer, Ryan	R-R	6-2	225	5-4-97	0	0	4.17	27	0	2	45	36	22	21	6	13	52	.217	.285	.398	27.7	6.9	188
Burhenn, Garrett	R-R	6-3	215	9-12-99	13	3	4.18	26	24	0	125	115	59	58	15	33	112	.241	.294	.409	21.4	6.3	523
Calvo, Blair	R-R	6-3	195	2-27-96	0	1	8.00	14	0	1	18	18	16	16	4	8	21	.257	.354	.486	25.6	9.8	82
Fields, Colin	R-R	6-2	200	3-18-00	1	0	6.00	1	0	0	3	3	2	2	0	1	5	.250	.308	.333	38.5	7.7	13
Guasch, Richard	R-R	6-4	205	4-10-98	3	4	2.74	28	0	5	46	28	18	14	3	18	57	.168	.258	.257	30.0	9.5	190
Hamm, Jaden	R-R	6-1	190	9-5-02	2	5	4.88	20	20	0	83	79	46	45	11	32	76	.248	.320	.392	21.1	8.9	361
Hebbert, Duque	R-R	5-10	170	10-29-01	1	0	0.96	5	0	0	9	11	1	1	0	3	7	.297	.366	.432	17.1	7.3	41
Kohlhepp, Tanner	R-R	6-3	215	5-27-99	1	0	4.10	20	0	0	26	30	19	12	6	12	34	.275	.358	.477	27.2	9.6	125
Kuhn, Travis	R-R	5-10	195	5-28-99	3	1	2.70	10	1	0	17	15	5	5	2	5	11	.270	.319	.429	15.9	7.2	69
Magno, Andrew	R-L	5-11	190	4-30-98	8	1	2.31	42	1	4	66	44	20	17	2	31	76	.191	.296	.261	27.7	11.3	274
Malgeri, Ben	R-R	6-1	215	1-12-00	0	0	0.00	3	0	0	3	7	4	0	0	2	0	.467	.500	.467	0.0	11.1	18
Marks, Jordan	L-R	6-2	220	4-29-99	1	1	3.72	20	0	0	29	24	12	12	2	13	19	.226	.314	.311	15.6	10.7	122
Mattison, Tyler	R-R	6-4	235	9-5-99	0	0	3.38	9	0	0	11	4	4	4	1	7	9	.121	.275	.212	22.0	17.1	41
Melton, Troy	R-R	6-4	210	12-3-00	2	1	3.23	10	10	0	39	40	17	14	1	11	45	.265	.311	.397	27.4	6.7	164
Merrill, Matt	R-R	6-4	202	6-11-98	2	3	3.48	15	1	1	21	11	9	8	1	17	24	.167	.333	.273	27.9	19.8	86
Michael, Trevin	R-R	6-2	200	9-15-97	1	0	1.69	16	0	3	27	16	6	5	0	9	27	.170	.250	.234	25.5	8.5	106
Miller, Jake	L-L	6-2	185	6-27-01	0	0	2.12	4	4	0	17	14	4	4	1	4	16	.222	.269	.349	23.9	6.0	67
Montalvo, Joseph	S-R	6-2	185	5-4-02	4	2	4.50	11	10	0	44	38	22	22	7	18	34	.229	.303	.416	18.4	9.7	185
Naughton, Bo	R-R	6-3	195	11-14-95	2	2	2.73	20	0	3	33	23	11	10	2	10	42	.193	.254	.277	31.6	7.5	133
Pena, Carlos	L-L	5-11	160	9-7-98	8	6	3.71	24	17	1	102	90	44	42	9	24	87	.234	.283	.384	21.0	5.8	415
Petit, RJ	R-R	6-8	300	9-23-99	6	1	2.28	27	1	2	43	29	13	11	2	12	46	.187	.256	.316	26.7	7.0	172
Sanchez, Yosber	R-R	6-1	170	5-22-01	2	4	5.40	28	0	4	37	40	29	22	3	20	37	.272	.371	.395	21.5	11.6	172
Sears, Andrew	L-L	6-3	200	10-30-02	1	2	5.02	6	6	0	29	32	17	16	3	7	29	.278	.320	.417	23.8	5.7	122
Seelinger, Matt	R-R	6-3	190	4-19-95	1	0	1.86	11	0	1	19	12	4	4	1	3	20	.174	.208	.275	27.8	4.2	72
Serwa, Kenny	R-R	6-3	205	8-3-97	6	6	3.95	17	17	0	82	72	45	36	1	41	50	.231	.331	.298	13.6	11.2	367
Silva, Eric	R-R	6-1	185	10-3-02	2	0	2.25	2	0	0	8	5	3	2	0	2	9	.185	.241	.185	31.0	6.9	29
Smith, Dylan	R-R	6-2	180	5-28-00	1	1	1.80	12	0	2	20	9	4	4	0	7	27	.136	.219	.197	37.0	9.6	73
Sommers, Drew	L-L	6-3	250	8-14-00	2	0	1.48	15	0	1	24	16	5	4	2	2	22	.190	.207	.298	24.7	2.2	89
Watson, Troy	R-R	6-2	180	6-11-97	3	2	2.39	26	4	2	53	34	14	14	3	22	55	.180	.265	.254	26.1	10.4	211

Fielding

Catcher	PCT	G	PO	A	E	DP	PB
Alfonzo	.983	47	385	18	7	2	7
Briceno	.980	27	234	12	5	2	2
Liranzo	.995	45	362	22	2	1	4
Valencia	.986	22	206	5	3	1	8

First Base	PCT	G	PO	A	E	DP
Alfonzo	1.000	1	1	0	0	0
Bigbie	.938	3	14	1	1	0
Briceno	1.000	10	71	0	0	5
Holton	.993	92	677	59	5	51
Meyers	1.000	19	132	6	0	11
Valencia	1.000	16	115	8	0	9

Second Base	PCT	G	PO	A	E	DP
Anderson	.968	78	86	183	9	38
Bastidas	.909	4	2	8	1	0

Third Base	PCT	G	PO	A	E	DP
Anderson	1.000	11	11	23	0	1
Cruz	.982	24	22	34	1	5
Jarvis	.929	10	12	14	2	1
Mendoza	.896	38	26	43	8	0
Peck	.935	8	12	17	2	2
Serretti	.957	47	39	71	5	5

Shortstop	PCT	G	PO	A	E	DP
Cruz	.963	32	31	73	4	11
Jarvis	.969	50	81	104	6	26
McGonigle	.939	39	56	83	9	17

	PCT	G	PO	A	E	DP	PB
Jarvis	.949	17	15	41	3	9	
Mendoza	.990	25	39	58	1	13	
Peck	1.000	7	15	19	0	5	
Serretti	.946	8	9	26	2	1	
Peck	1.000	10	6	23	0	3	
Serretti	.905	7	4	15	2	1	

Outfield	PCT	G	PO	A	E	DP
Bigbie	.994	92	163	2	1	1
Campos	.985	96	188	3	3	2
Clark	.983	37	114	0	2	0
Cruz	1.000	12	20	0	0	0
Malgeri	.994	73	153	3	1	0
Mendoza	1.000	19	35	1	0	0
Meyers	.979	46	93	1	2	1
Stephenson	1.000	22	46	1	0	0
Murr	.983	33	59	0	1	0

WEST MICHIGAN WHITECAPS — HIGH-A
MIDWEST LEAGUE

DETROIT TIGERS

Batting	B-T	Ht.	Wt.	DOB	AVG	OBP	SLG	G	PA	AB	R	H	2B	3B	HR	RBI	BB	HBP	SH	SF	SO	SB	CS	BB%	SO%
Bastidas, Abel	S-R	6-1	165	11-24-03	.300	.333	.413	21	84	80	12	24	4	1	1	15	4	0	0	0	26	0	1	4.8	31.0
Briceno, Josue	L-R	6-4	200	9-23-04	.296	.422	.602	55	244	196	40	58	13	1	15	57	41	4	0	3	40	1	0	16.8	16.4
Brookman, Archer	R-R	5-11	200	1-8-99	.230	.289	.299	60	228	204	29	47	8	0	2	22	15	4	0	5	38	1	0	6.6	16.7
Callahan, Brett	L-R	6-0	195	11-2-01	.259	.316	.473	55	225	201	29	52	8	4	9	44	14	5	0	5	50	6	2	6.2	22.2
Clark, Max	L-L	6-1	190	12-21-04	.285	.430	.427	68	330	260	49	74	12	2	7	47	65	3	0	2	56	12	2	19.7	17.0
Dobbins, Hunter	R-R	6-2	210	9-28-02	.000	.000	.000	1	1	1	0	0	0	0	0	0	0	0	0	0	0	0	0	0.0	0.0
Gil, Samuel	R-R	5-9	165	11-1-04	.077	.455	.077	5	22	13	5	1	0	0	0	2	9	0	0	0	3	1	0	40.9	13.6
Gold, Luke	R-R	6-0	220	10-10-00	.204	.275	.338	63	247	225	30	46	11	2	5	26	14	8	0	0	58	0	0	5.7	23.5
Graham, Peyton	R-R	6-3	185	1-26-01	.283	.366	.423	100	409	357	55	101	23	3	7	49	40	8	1	2	85	20	2	9.8	20.8
Hadeen, Woody	S-R	6-2	185	7-16-02	.234	.348	.312	42	181	154	26	36	4	1	2	18	21	6	0	0	24	15	2	11.6	13.3
Hicklen, Brewer	R-R	6-1	220	2-9-96	.000	.167	.000	2	6	5	0	0	0	0	0	0	1	0	0	0	3	0	0	16.7	50.0
Jenkins, Andrew	R-R	5-11	217	11-3-00	.262	.344	.413	95	398	351	54	92	17	3	10	59	33	12	0	2	93	0	0	8.3	23.4
Lee, Bennett	R-R	6-0	208	4-26-02	.114	.232	.188	64	237	202	20	23	6	0	3	19	29	3	0	3	92	0	0	12.2	38.8
Lee, Patrick	R-R	5-10	180	10-19-99	.205	.346	.295	65	243	200	26	41	4	1	4	24	37	6	0	0	94	27	4	15.2	38.7
Malgeri, Ben	R-R	6-1	215	1-12-00	.421	.500	.789	5	22	19	5	8	1	0	2	5	3	0	0	0	4	1	0	13.6	18.2
McGonigle, Kevin	L-R	5-11	185	8-18-04	.372	.462	.648	36	171	145	37	54	19	0	7	39	23	2	0	1	19	3	5	13.5	11.1
Murr, Austin	L-L	6-1	218	1-26-99	.280	.386	.451	72	309	257	42	72	15	4	7	43	41	6	1	4	62	13	3	13.3	20.1
Pacheco, Izaac	L-R	6-3	225	11-18-02	.258	.388	.499	99	425	341	72	88	25	3	17	68	74	2	0	6	123	0	0	17.4	28.9
Peck, John	R-R	6-0	185	7-18-02	.307	.364	.452	93	412	374	78	115	22	1	10	59	32	3	0	3	104	17	5	7.8	25.2
Penney, Jack	L-R	6-0	185	8-19-02	.262	.382	.373	71	306	252	34	66	11	1	5	44	46	5	0	3	62	6	2	15.0	20.3
Pennington, Garrett	R-R	6-0	215	10-15-00	.321	.383	.478	36	149	134	20	43	15	0	2	16	7	7	0	1	32	0	2	4.7	21.5
Perez, Wenceel	S-R	5-11	203	10-30-99	.500	.600	.750	2	5	4	1	2	1	0	0	0	1	0	0	0	1	0	0	20.0	20.0
Stephenson, Seth	R-R	5-8	165	1-10-01	.286	.371	.420	90	427	371	76	106	16	5	8	49	30	21	4	1	62	42	5	7.0	14.5
Strong, Jackson	L-L	6-1	185	8-26-03	.222	.330	.420	23	94	81	16	18	4	0	4	6	13	0	0	0	32	2	0	13.8	34.0
Turney, Cole	L-L	6-1	215	1-16-99	.364	.391	.591	5	23	22	4	8	5	0	0	2	1	0	0	0	8	0	0	4.3	34.8

Pitching	B-T	Ht.	Wt.	DOB	W	L	ERA	G	GS	SV	IP	Hits	Runs	ER	HR	BB	SO	AVG	OBP	SLG	SO%	BB%	BF
Adametz, Joe	L-L	6-5	190	12-23-99	3	4	4.66	36	0	1	58	49	32	30	7	21	46	.228	.332	.363	18.4	8.4	250
Alba, Max	R-R	6-5	215	7-15-99	2	4	4.00	18	12	0	72	62	35	32	9	20	66	.230	.284	.370	22.3	6.8	296
Ashman, Micah	L-L	6-7	200	8-22-02	4	3	1.60	28	0	4	39	22	12	7	0	8	46	.163	.211	.222	30.9	5.4	149
Balazovic, Jordan	R-R	6-5	215	9-17-98	0	0	4.50	3	1	0	4	3	2	2	1	0	5	.200	.200	.400	33.3	0.0	15
Brieske, Beau	R-R	6-3	200	4-4-98	0	0	0.00	1	1	0	1	0	0	0	0	0	2	.000	.000	.000	66.7	0.0	3
Calvo, Blair	R-R	6-3	195	2-27-96	0	0	10.13	5	0	2	5	8	8	6	1	2	7	.308	.379	.423	24.1	6.9	29
Castillo, Rayner	R-R	6-3	180	6-30-04	5	6	5.29	25	23	0	99	97	62	58	12	46	80	.256	.343	.401	18.5	10.6	432
Cobb, Alex	R-R	6-3	205	10-7-87	0	2	1.69	5	5	0	11	6	4	2	1	5	14	.167	.268	.278	34.1	12.2	41
Elissalt, Lucas	R-R	6-4	190	7-20-04	1	0	2.59	6	6	0	24	19	9	7	0	15	23	.221	.343	.256	21.9	14.3	105
Erbe, Haden	R-R	6-3	225	8-13-98	3	1	3.12	36	0	0	40	28	18	14	3	26	40	.197	.324	.345	23.1	15.0	173
Fields, Colin	R-R	6-2	200	3-18-00	8	2	1.64	32	4	5	66	39	14	12	3	15	80	.169	.240	.242	31.5	5.9	254
Fregio, Dariel	R-R	6-2	208	5-5-00	5	0	2.28	19	0	2	28	17	8	7	2	10	29	.177	.269	.292	26.6	9.2	109
Gipson-Long, Sawyer	R-R	6-4	225	12-12-97	0	0	1.59	2	2	0	6	5	1	1	0	1	5	.250	.286	.250	23.8	4.8	21
Go, Woo Suk	R-R	5-11	198	8-6-98	1	0	6.00	6	0	0	5	5	4	1	5	2	5	.250	.385	.450	18.5	7.4	27
Guenther, Sean	L-L	5-11	194	12-29-95	0	0	9.00	2	1	0	2	4	2	2	0	2	1	.444	.400	.778	20.0	0.0	10
Harvey, Ryan	R-R	6-3	195	2-8-01	1	0	3.00	2	0	0	3	1	1	1	0	2	3	.417	.417	.750	25.0	0.0	12
Hebbert, Duque	R-R	5-10	170	10-29-01	0	0	10.80	3	0	0	5	6	6	6	3	3	6	.316	.409	.947	27.3	13.6	22
Howey, Preston	R-R	5-10	173	6-20-02	6	4	3.19	32	9	4	62	44	22	22	3	27	48	.203	.300	.286	19.4	10.9	248
Jenkins, Andrew	R-R	5-11	217	11-3-00	0	0	—	1	0	0	0	0	0	0	0	0	0	.000	.000	.000	0.0	0.0	1
Jimenez, Marco	R-R	5-11	239	12-6-99	3	1	1.50	39	0	3	60	33	12	10	5	17	59	.162	.230	.265	26.0	7.5	227
Lange, Alex	R-R	6-3	202	10-2-95	0	0	4.50	2	2	0	2	2	1	1	0	0	3	.250	.250	.375	37.5	0.0	8
Lequerica, Carlos	R-R	6-2	195	9-6-00	8	0	2.35	43	0	3	54	38	15	14	3	21	42	.200	.279	.289	19.4	9.7	216
Lockhart, Lael	S-L	6-3	225	12-31-97	1	0	0.00	3	3	0	13	7	0	0	0	5	14	.163	.250	.163	29.2	10.4	48
Marcano, Carlos	R-R	6-2	150	7-8-03	2	1	3.19	9	7	0	37	36	14	13	5	19	24	.263	.358	.423	15.1	11.9	159
Marks, Andrew	L-R	6-2	220	1-11-01	1	0	1.42	11	0	1	13	8	2	2	0	4	19	.182	.250	.182	39.6	8.3	48
Mattison, Tyler	R-R	6-4	235	9-5-99	1	0	7.56	7	0	0	8	9	7	7	2	6	9	.273	.400	.545	22.5	15.0	40
Michael, Trevin	R-R	6-2	200	9-15-97	4	0	3.10	19	0	3	29	19	11	10	4	10	38	.181	.259	.352	32.8	8.6	116
Miller, Joe	L-L	5-10	195	3-13-00	7	3	2.91	24	21	0	105	100	44	34	8	31	92	.248	.309	.391	20.7	7.0	444
Minton, Hayden	R-R	6-4	220	3-14-01	7	2	3.63	16	11	0	69	60	30	28	8	20	70	.232	.300	.367	24.2	6.9	289
Murr, Austin	L-L	6-1	218	1-26-99	0	0	0.00	2	0	0	2	0	0	0	0	0	0	.000	.000	.000	0.0	0.0	4
Pacheco, Freddy	R-R	5-11	203	4-17-98	1	0	3.64	26	0	0	30	18	14	12	4	23	32	.168	.341	.327	23.7	17.0	135
Randall, Josh	R-R	6-4	242	10-15-02	0	0	0.00	1	1	0	5	5	1	0	0	0	6	.250	.250	.300	30.0	0.0	20
Rodriguez, Moises	R-R	6-2	170	3-3-02	3	0	1.35	14	0	2	20	17	5	3	0	2	20	.230	.269	.257	25.6	3.8	78
Sears, Andrew	L-L	6-3	200	10-30-02	7	4	2.95	20	16	0	82	64	31	27	8	29	94	.208	.290	.319	27.2	8.4	345
Serwa, Kenny	R-R	6-3	205	8-3-97	3	1	2.75	10	5	0	36	28	12	11	1	8	34	.212	.278	.265	23.6	5.6	144
Sewald, Paul	R-R	6-3	219	5-26-90	0	0	0.00	2	1	0	2	1	0	0	0	1	4	.143	.250	.143	50.0	12.5	8
Silva, Eric	R-R	6-1	185	10-3-02	0	0	0.00	1	0	0	4	1	0	0	0	0	5	.077	.143	.154	35.7	0.0	14
Smith, Dylan	R-R	6-2	180	5-28-00	2	0	1.42	5	0	0	6	5	1	1	0	2	7	.227	.292	.227	29.2	8.3	24
Stil, Matt	R-R	6-3	190	7-5-00	0	0	4.50	8	0	0	12	5	5	5	1	5	9	.293	.388	.390	18.4	10.2	49
Weins, CJ	R-R	6-3	223	8-15-00	3	1	3.95	35	0	2	41	34	20	18	2	38	44	.231	.395	.333	23.2	20.0	190

Fielding

Catcher	PCT	G	PO	A	E	DP	PB
Briceno	.988	19	156	11	2	0	2
Brookman	.996	55	471	27	2	3	4
Lee, B	.986	63	526	40	8	1	9
Lee, P	1.000	1	1	0	0	0	0

First Base	PCT	G	PO	A	E	DP
Briceno	.989	22	167	9	2	11

Gold	.995	24	183	8	1	17	Graham	.938	12	11	19	2	0
Jenkins	.991	70	506	42	5	54	Jenkins	.000	1	0	0	0	0
Pacheco	.979	6	46	1	1	7	Pacheco	.932	76	64	129	14	12
Pennington	1.000	16	129	8	0	12	Peck	.942	32	31	50	5	7

Second Base	PCT	G	PO	A	E	DP	Shortstop	PCT	G	PO	A	E	DP
Bastidas	.968	8	11	19	1	5	Graham	1.000	8	13	17	0	4
Graham	.979	66	103	181	6	29	Hadeen	.981	26	45	56	2	16
Hadeen	1.000	7	13	11	0	1	McGonigle	.953	29	48	74	6	14
Peck	1.000	12	16	34	0	7	Peck	.952	45	52	107	8	19
Penney	.989	44	52	123	2	24	Penney	.959	24	31	62	4	11

Third Base	PCT	G	PO	A	E	DP	Outfield	PCT	G	PO	A	E	DP
Bastidas	.885	13	7	16	3	1	Callahan	1.000	51	98	4	0	0
Gil	.875	4	1	6	1	1	Clark	.990	53	92	4	1	0

Gold	.972	24	33	2	1	0
Graham	1.000	6	7	0	0	0
Hadeen	1.000	9	23	0	0	0
Hicklen	1.000	1	1	0	0	0
Lee, B	.000	1	0	0	0	0
Lee, P	.970	64	122	7	4	2
Malgeri	.875	4	7	0	1	0
Murr	.983	65	115	1	2	0
Pennington	1.000	12	23	1	0	0
Perez	1.000	1	1	0	0	0
Stephenson	.978	89	172	6	4	1
Strong	1.000	22	48	2	0	1
Turney	.800	3	4	0	1	0

LAKELAND FLYING TIGERS — LOW-A
FLORIDA STATE LEAGUE

Batting	B-T	Ht.	Wt.	DOB	AVG	OBP	SLG	G	PA	AB	R	H	2B	3B	HR	RBI	BB	HBP	SH	SF	SO	SB	CS	BB%	SO%
Ankeney, Beau	R-R	6-3	210	4-2-03	.267	.421	.400	4	20	15	5	4	0	1	0	5	3	1	0	0	6	0	0	15.0	30.0
Baddoo, Akil	L-L	6-1	214	8-16-98	.261	.370	.391	7	27	23	4	6	0	0	1	4	2	2	0	0	5	2	0	7.4	18.5
Bastidas, Abel	S-R	6-1	165	11-24-03	.230	.308	.248	39	130	113	13	26	2	0	0	12	13	1	0	3	33	1	0	10.0	25.4
Campbell, Clayton	R-R	6-1	209	9-11-03	.133	.307	.183	22	76	60	6	8	3	0	0	3	14	1	1	0	19	1	0	18.4	25.0
De La Cruz, Jose	R-R	6-1	216	1-3-02	.157	.255	.225	25	102	89	11	14	3	0	1	8	11	1	0	1	37	1	1	10.8	36.3
Delgado, Enderson	S-R	5-11	184	9-21-04	.167	.279	.235	34	122	102	12	17	1	0	2	15	13	4	0	3	32	0	0	10.7	26.2
Dumesnil, Nick	R-R	6-2	210	3-27-04	.203	.390	.288	16	79	59	12	12	5	0	0	5	17	1	0	0	14	9	2	21.5	17.7
Fana, Nomar	S-R	5-11	175	9-28-02	.124	.219	.204	32	128	113	15	14	3	0	2	11	14	0	0	1	53	4	0	10.9	41.4
Gil, Samuel	R-R	5-9	165	11-1-04	.242	.359	.304	91	362	306	50	74	12	2	1	27	50	6	0	0	49	11	2	13.8	13.5
Goodman, Jack	R-R	6-0	185	10-9-03	.333	.462	.524	11	52	42	12	14	3	1	1	5	9	1	0	0	8	4	1	17.3	15.4
Hadeen, Woody	S-R	6-2	185	7-16-02	.235	.372	.349	64	290	238	44	56	11	2	4	24	35	17	0	0	54	23	4	12.1	18.6
Hernandez, Juan	L-R	6-0	160	3-27-06	.313	.450	.313	5	20	16	1	5	0	0	0	2	3	1	0	0	4	0	0	15.0	20.0
Hrustich, Stephen	R-R	6-1	235	9-8-01	.246	.368	.362	61	258	207	37	51	8	2	4	31	33	11	0	7	52	3	3	12.8	20.2
Hurtado, Ricardo	R-R	5-10	180	5-23-03	.244	.321	.384	86	345	307	42	75	16	0	9	63	29	6	0	1	92	0	0	8.4	26.7
Lee, Patrick	R-R	5-10	180	10-19-99	.253	.376	.363	30	109	91	12	23	7	0	1	11	16	2	0	0	38	12	4	14.7	34.9
MacDonald, Zach	R-R	6-1	195	8-3-03	.169	.309	.266	47	188	154	27	26	3	0	4	18	24	8	0	2	68	16	3	12.8	36.2
Madris, Bligh	L-R	6-0	208	2-29-96	.273	.368	.545	10	38	33	5	9	0	0	3	9	5	0	0	0	5	1	0	13.2	13.2
McGonigle, Kevin	L-R	5-11	185	8-18-04	.235	.350	.353	6	20	17	1	4	2	0	0	0	3	0	0	0	1	0	0	15.0	5.0
Meadows, Parker	L-R	6-5	205	11-2-99	.200	.333	.200	2	6	5	1	1	0	0	0	1	1	0	0	0	2	0	0	16.7	33.3
Meyers, Chris	L-R	6-3	210	4-27-99	.000	.500	.000	2	8	4	2	0	0	0	0	0	4	0	0	0	2	0	0	50.0	25.0
Montilla, Franyerber	S-R	6-0	160	4-15-05	.271	.368	.395	67	299	258	43	70	16	2	4	29	38	2	0	1	74	27	7	12.7	24.7
Penney, Jack	L-R	6-0	185	8-19-02	.121	.326	.121	11	43	33	5	4	0	0	0	1	7	3	0	0	13	0	0	16.3	30.2
Pennington, Garrett	R-R	6-0	215	5-10-00	.282	.353	.493	65	255	227	37	64	16	1	10	43	22	4	0	2	45	8	3	8.6	17.6
Perez, Wenceel	S-R	5-11	203	10-30-99	.200	.286	.800	2	7	5	2	1	0	0	1	3	1	0	0	1	1	0	0	14.3	14.3
Pinto, Jesus	R-R	5-11	180	3-30-07	.277	.327	.319	10	52	47	10	13	2	0	0	5	3	1	0	1	13	3	1	5.8	25.0
Rainer, Bryce	L-R	6-3	185	7-5-05	.288	.383	.448	35	149	125	19	36	5	0	5	22	20	1	0	3	33	9	3	13.4	22.1
Rucker, Carson	R-R	6-2	195	8-18-04	.235	.305	.295	103	429	387	49	91	14	3	1	43	30	10	0	2	104	11	3	7.0	24.2
Santana, Cristian	R-R	5-11	165	11-25-03	.195	.373	.387	98	394	302	56	59	11	1	15	53	76	12	0	4	98	7	1	19.3	24.9
Serven, Brian	R-R	6-0	207	5-5-95	.217	.333	.348	7	27	23	3	5	3	0	0	4	3	1	0	0	11	0	0	11.1	40.7
Smith, David	S-R	5-11	195	2-20-01	.184	.299	.232	42	147	125	13	23	3	0	1	12	19	2	0	1	25	10	2	12.9	17.0
Strong, Jackson	L-L	6-1	185	8-26-03	.277	.382	.438	73	318	267	38	74	16	6	5	42	39	8	0	3	87	18	5	12.3	27.4
Tapia, Sergio	R-R	5-10	160	8-24-02	.230	.282	.385	38	150	135	17	31	6	0	5	24	9	2	0	3	21	0	0	6.0	14.0
Tilien, Junior	R-R	6-1	168	9-9-02	.269	.333	.356	44	181	160	19	43	9	1	1	23	18	1	0	2	34	1	0	9.9	18.8
Vierling, Matt	R-B	6-3	205	9-16-96	.167	.375	.167	2	8	6	0	1	0	0	0	0	3	0	0	0	2	0	0	25.0	25.0
Warwick, Jude	L-R	6-1	170	9-9-05	.247	.279	.284	21	86	81	8	20	3	0	0	11	3	1	0	1	29	6	1	3.5	33.7

Pitching	B-T	Ht.	Wt.	DOB	W	L	ERA	G	GS	SV	IP	Hits	Runs	ER	HR	BB	SO	AVG	OBP	SLG	SO%	BB%	BF
Berrier, Logan	R-R	6-1	175	2-26-01	3	1	4.73	19	0	2	27	30	20	14	1	16	22	.275	.375	.376	17.2	12.5	128
Briceno, Ignacio	L-L	5-11	155	6-4-01	4	5	3.06	32	0	3	50	46	28	17	0	23	43	.245	.327	.293	19.7	10.6	218
Bruss, Thomas	R-R	6-8	280	5-18-99	2	1	2.31	22	0	5	23	11	10	6	1	14	28	.136	.287	.222	27.7	13.9	101
Calvo, Blair	R-R	6-3	195	2-27-96	1	0	1.46	8	0	2	12	6	2	2	1	5	13	.143	.250	.238	27.1	10.4	48
Chalas, Ronny	R-R	5-10	162	8-19-02	3	2	3.13	32	0	6	55	40	21	19	3	28	44	.206	.309	.325	19.1	12.2	230
Diaz, Jatnk	R-R	6-4	215	4-20-04	0	2	7.20	5	3	0	15	8	12	12	1	10	13	.157	.302	.275	20.6	15.9	63
Elissalt, Lucas	R-R	6-4	190	7-20-04	1	1	2.48	16	10	0	65	44	23	18	4	20	77	.183	.255	.278	28.8	7.5	267
Erbe, Haden	R-R	6-3	225	8-13-98	0	0	9.00	1	0	0	1	1	1	1	0	1	2	.250	.400	.500	40.0	20.0	5
Flores, Wilmer	R-R	6-4	225	2-20-01	0	0	2.25	5	2	0	4	2	1	1	0	3	5	.143	.294	.429	29.4	17.6	17
Florido, Antonio	R-R	6-1	175	2-15-01	0	0	4.50	1	0	0	2	1	1	1	0	1	1	.375	.444	.375	11.1	11.1	9
Fregio, Dariel	R-R	6-2	208	5-5-00	0	0	0.00	4	0	1	5	2	0	0	1	6	1	.133	.188	.133	37.5	6.3	16
Garcia, Pedro	R-R	6-1	190	2-27-02	1	0	1.72	8	0	0	16	8	3	3	1	7	5	.122	.218	.224	10.9	9.1	55
Gipson-Long, Sawyer	R-R	6-4	225	12-12-97	0	0	0.00	1	1	0	3	1	0	0	2	.429	.429	.429	28.6	0.0	7
Guenther, Sean	L-L	5-11	194	12-29-95	0	0	9.00	1	0	0	1	2	1	1	0	0	1	.500	.500	.500	25.0	0.0	4
Hall, Owen	R-R	6-3	185	11-14-05	0	0	7.00	4	4	0	9	7	7	7	1	9	9	.241	.410	.379	23.1	23.1	39
Hamm, Jaden	R-R	6-1	190	5-6-02	0	0	1.80	2	2	0	5	1	1	1	0	5	4	.176	.391	.235	17.4	21.7	23
Harvey, Ryan	R-R	6-4	190	2-8-01	1	0	3.00	9	0	0	12	5	4	4	0	9	6	.128	.261	.256	18.8	12.5	48
Hebbert, Duque	R-R	5-10	170	10-29-01	5	2	4.99	25	1	2	49	51	29	27	3	14	38	.274	.324	.441	18.4	6.8	207
Horn, Bailey	L-L	6-2	210	1-15-98	0	0	16.20	2	2	0	1	2	0	0	1	2	.375	.500	.500	20.0	10.0	10

DETROIT TIGERS

Player	B-T	Ht.	Wt.	DOB			AVG											OBP	SLG			SO
Hoskins, Luke	R-R	6-4	180	5-12-03	0	0	0.00	1	0	0	1	1	0	0	0	0	0	.250	.250	.500	0.0	0.0	4
Kohlhepp, Tanner	L-R	6-4	210	5-27-99	0	0	0.00	4	0	0	5	2	0	0	0	0	2	.133	.133	.200	13.3	0.0	15
Kuhn, Travis	R-R	5-10	195	5-20-98	0	0	3.00	2	0	0	3	2	1	1	0	3	4	.182	.357	.273	28.6	21.4	14
Kuiper, Cash	R-R	6-4	200	12-26-04	0	0	5.40	4	2	0	5	2	3	3	0	8	5	.111	.407	.167	18.5	29.6	27
Lee, Zack	L-R	6-4	200	12-5-00	9	5	3.79	22	12	0	93	74	43	39	10	29	60	.216	.294	.367	15.6	7.6	384
Lockhart, Lael	S-L	6-3	225	12-31-97	0	0	0.00	2	0	0	5	3	0	0	0	0	2	7	.188	.278	.250	38.9	11.1	18
Marcano, Carlos	R-R	6-2	150	7-8-03	0	2	6.75	4	3	0	12	15	9	9	2	7	10	.306	.393	.510	17.9	12.5	56
Mattison, Tyler	R-R	6-4	235	9-5-99	0	0	0.00	1	1	0	1	1	0	0	0	0	1	0	.333	.500	.333	0.0	25.0	4
Mendez, Wuilberth	R-R	6-3	150	5-29-04	0	0	13.50	1	1	0	1	2	1	1	0	0	0	.667	.500	1.000	0.0	0.0	4
Miller, Jake	L-L	6-2	185	6-27-01	0	0	0.00	0	2	2	0	3	6	1	0	0	0	5	.375	.375	.375	31.3	0.0	16
Minton, Hayden	L-R	6-4	220	3-14-01	1	0	2.30	7	7	0	31	25	9	8	1	5	33	.219	.264	.316	27.3	4.1	121
Mota, Eliseo	R-R	6-2	185	11-7-02	1	0	5.40	7	0	0	12	13	8	7	0	9	12	.283	.421	.348	21.1	15.8	57
Owens, Tyler	R-R	5-10	185	1-9-01	0	1	108.00	1	1	0	0	4	4	4	0	2	1	.800	.857	.800	14.3	28.6	7
Pennington, Garrett	R-R	6-0	215	10-15-00	0	0	0.00	1	0	0	1	0	0	0	0	1	2	.000	.250	.000	50.0	25.0	4
Petri, Jorger	L-L	5-10	155	11-3-04	4	1	4.33	28	0	0	44	41	24	21	3	25	50	.248	.342	.345	25.8	12.9	194
Pogue, Andrew	R-R	6-4	185	1-18-01	1	0	6.75	5	0	0	5	5	4	4	0	5	5	.238	.407	.238	18.5	18.5	27
Randall, Josh	R-R	6-4	242	10-15-02	5	5	4.18	16	16	0	75	86	41	35	8	15	64	.282	.315	.407	19.6	4.6	327
Reyes, Gabriel	L-L	6-1	170	7-1-03	4	1	2.40	19	16	0	79	53	26	21	4	28	71	.191	.275	.284	22.5	8.9	316
Rodriguez, Moises	R-R	6-2	290	3-3-02	3	1	3.53	32	0	8	43	33	20	17	0	13	43	.212	.294	.256	23.9	7.2	180
Ruzicka, Joe	R-R	6-3	180	12-14-03	0	0	2.57	6	0	0	7	6	2	2	0	4	6	.250	.387	.250	19.4	12.9	31
Salcedo, Kelvis	R-R	6-0	180	1-23-06	0	0	1.54	6	2	0	23	8	4	4	2	6	32	.107	.183	.213	39.0	7.3	82
Sales, R.J.	R-R	6-0	165	7-22-03	4	3	2.71	16	15	0	66	57	22	20	2	17	63	.236	.284	.318	24.1	6.5	261
Sanchez, Yosber	R-R	6-2	190	2-25-01	1	0	2.25	3	0	0	4	1	1	1	0	3	3	.091	.267	.091	20.0	20.0	15
Santana, Cristian	R-R	5-11	165	11-25-03	0	0	0.00	1	0	0	1	2	0	0	0	1	1	.400	.500	.400	16.7	16.7	6
Silva, Eric	R-R	6-1	185	10-3-02	1	3	5.14	6	3	0	28	28	17	16	3	12	14	.264	.339	.387	11.6	9.9	121
Sloan, Ethan	L-L	5-11	190	8-4-02	6	7	3.61	34	0	3	47	38	28	19	4	19	41	.215	.295	.356	20.2	9.4	203
Smith, David	S-R	5-11	195	2-20-01	0	0	18.00	1	0	0	1	2	2	2	1	0	0	.250	.400	1.000	0.0	0.0	5
Smith, Dylan	R-R	6-2	180	5-28-00	0	0	0.00	1	1	0	1	0	0	0	0	1	1	.000	.250	.000	25.0	25.0	4
Stofel, Luke	R-R	6-5	235	11-25-01	7	4	3.05	23	12	0	97	81	45	33	4	42	72	.224	.313	.293	17.3	10.1	415
Szapucki, Thomas	R-L	6-2	210	6-12-96	0	0	0.00	7	0	1	8	4	0	0	0	2	8	.154	.241	.231	27.6	6.9	29
Timmer, Shay	R-R	6-10	280	7-17-02	1	1	12.46	14	0	1	13	23	26	18	4	16	12	.354	.494	.615	14.5	19.3	83
Urquidy, Jose	R-R	6-0	217	5-1-95	0	1	1.80	4	4	0	5	2	1	1	0	0	4	.125	.125	.125	25.0	0.0	16
Vanasco, Ricky	R-R	6-3	180	10-13-98	1	0	4.50	3	1	0	4	1	2	2	0	3	6	.083	.267	.083	40.0	20.0	15
Wetwiska, Cale	R-R	6-2	190	4-11-05	0	0	6.75	2	2	0	4	6	3	3	0	4	4	.375	.476	.500	19.0	19.0	21
Williams, Chris	L-L	6-2	205	3-3-00	2	3	5.13	28	0	2	33	40	25	19	6	20	42	.284	.384	.511	25.6	12.2	164
Wilson, Paul	R-L	6-3	197	12-11-04	0	1	4.26	3	2	0	6	7	5	3	0	6	11	.280	.438	.280	34.4	18.8	32

Fielding

Catcher	PCT	G	PO	A	E	DP	PB
Delgado	.983	27	217	12	4	1	3
Hurtado	.995	68	512	45	3	2	7
Serven	1.000	4	32	3	0	0	0
Tapia	.989	33	265	15	3	3	1

First Base	PCT	G	PO	A	E	DP
Ankeney	1.000	2	17	2	0	3
Campbell	1.000	17	114	4	0	13
Hurtado	1.000	12	83	4	0	8
Madris	1.000	4	23	1	0	2
Meyers	.000	1	0	0	0	0
Pennington	.984	44	305	10	5	33
Santana	.998	57	435	25	1	49
Tilien	1.000	1	0	1	0	0

Second Base	PCT	G	PO	A	E	DP
Bastidas	.983	16	25	33	1	7
Gil	.978	47	74	101	4	27
Hadeen	1.000	16	34	37	0	11
Hernandez	.933	3	3	11	1	2
McGonigle	1.000	1	1	5	0	0
Montilla	.979	30	69	73	3	29

	PCT	G	PO	A	E	DP
Penney	1.000	5	5	13	0	3
Santana	.900	4	2	7	1	0
Tilien	.984	17	32	29	1	5
Warwick	1.000	6	10	16	0	4

Third Base	PCT	G	PO	A	E	DP
Bastidas	.839	11	6	20	5	2
Gil	.855	22	6	41	8	8
Rucker	.889	89	81	151	29	16
Santana	.813	8	4	9	3	1
Tilien	1.000	5	3	8	0	1
Vierling	1.000	2	2	8	0	1

Shortstop	PCT	G	PO	A	E	DP
Bastidas	.900	5	6	12	2	0
Gil	.971	19	17	50	2	6
Goodman	.898	11	20	24	5	6
Hadeen	.946	20	30	58	5	16
Hernandez	.833	1	1	4	1	2
McGonigle	1.000	2	0	4	0	1
Montilla	.950	35	33	81	6	19
Penney	.667	1	1	1	1	1
Rainer	.937	28	35	69	7	11

	PCT	G	PO	A	E	DP
Rucker	.000	1	0	0	0	0
Warwick	.900	15	19	35	6	4

Outfield	PCT	G	PO	A	E	DP
Baddoo	.833	5	10	0	2	0
De La Cruz	.880	23	42	2	6	0
Dumesnil	1.000	12	33	0	0	0
Fana	.945	29	52	0	3	0
Hadeen	1.000	26	69	0	0	0
Hrustich	.991	61	116	0	1	0
Lee	.985	30	64	2	1	2
MacDonald	.990	45	98	1	1	0
Madris	1.000	3	2	1	0	0
Meadows	1.000	1	1	0	0	0
Meyers	.000	1	0	0	0	0
Pennington	1.000	17	26	1	0	0
Perez	.000	1	0	0	0	0
Pinto	.941	8	16	0	1	0
Santana	1.000	7	11	1	0	1
Smith	.984	42	58	3	1	0
Strong	.994	77	169	5	1	3
Tilien	1.000	19	37	2	0	0
Vierling	1.000	1	1	0	0	0

FCL TIGERS
FLORIDA COMPLEX LEAGUE — ROOKIE

Batting	B-T	Ht.	Wt.	DOB	AVG	OBP	SLG	G	PA	AB	R	H	2B	3B	HR	RBI	BB	HBP	SH	SF	SO	SB	CS	BB%	SO%
Callahan, Brett	L-R	6-0	195	11-2-01	.320	.414	.400	7	29	25	5	8	2	0	0	4	3	1	0	0	8	2	1	10.3	27.6
Campbell, Clayton	R-R	6-1	209	9-11-03	.253	.337	.374	30	104	91	13	23	2	0	3	9	7	5	0	1	18	4	0	6.7	17.3
Cerkownyk, Brady	R-R	6-0	190	2-2-03	.219	.305	.315	24	82	73	8	16	1	0	2	15	6	3	0	0	22	1	0	7.3	26.8
De La Cruz, Jose	R-R	6-1	216	1-3-02	.208	.255	.313	13	51	48	8	10	5	0	0	4	2	1	0	0	20	1	0	3.9	39.2
Dickson, Jose	R-R	6-2	158	11-8-06	.209	.304	.311	44	171	148	23	31	4	1	3	21	20	1	0	2	42	9	2	11.7	24.6
Dobbins, Hunter	R-R	6-2	210	9-28-02	.143	.276	.265	19	58	49	5	7	3	0	1	2	7	2	0	0	19	1	0	12.1	32.8
Fana, Nomar	S-R	5-11	175	9-28-02	.234	.395	.340	36	125	94	10	22	2	1	2	15	24	3	1	3	27	7	3	19.2	21.6
Hernandez, Juan	L-R	6-0	160	3-27-06	.265	.352	.301	44	159	136	18	36	5	0	0	13	15	5	0	3	25	9	3	9.4	22.0
Jimenez, Enrique	S-R	5-10	170	11-3-05	.250	.339	.440	48	192	168	27	42	10	2	6	32	23	0	0	1	42	4	1	12.0	21.9

Batting	B-T	Ht.	Wt.	DOB	AVG	OBP	SLG	G	AB	R	H	2B	3B	HR	RBI	BB	HBP	SH	SF	SO	SB	CS	BB%	SO%
MacDonald, Zach	R-R	6-1	195	8-3-03	.250	.423	.400	13	52	40	11	10	2	2	0	1	9	3	0	0	15	6	0	17.3	28.8
Orozco, Maikol	R-R	5-11	175	9-9-05	.226	.356	.377	36	132	106	17	24	6	2	2	19	17	6	0	3	37	2	1	12.9	28.0
Osorio, Javier	R-R	6-0	165	3-29-05	.304	.386	.488	38	146	125	27	38	8	0	5	27	11	7	0	2	34	20	4	7.5	23.3
Penney, Jack	L-R	6-0	185	8-19-02	.000	.000	.000	1	3	3	0	0	0	0	0	0	0	0	0	0	1	0	0	0.0	33.3
Pinto, Jesus	R-R	5-11	180	3-30-07	.205	.275	.349	21	91	83	15	17	3	0	3	11	7	1	0	0	17	6	3	7.7	18.7
Ramirez, Ronald	R-R	5-10	170	10-12-06	.242	.345	.282	42	145	124	26	30	5	0	0	12	17	3	0	1	31	7	5	11.7	21.4
Rondon, Newremberg	R-R	5-11	170	7-10-03	.186	.260	.209	30	96	86	9	16	2	0	0	6	9	0	0	1	19	0	1	9.4	19.8
Rosado, Gabriel	L-R	6-1	180	2-8-06	.261	.393	.348	20	56	46	8	12	1	0	1	7	10	0	0	0	22	3	1	17.9	39.3
Salas, Anibal	S-R	5-11	180	9-30-05	.232	.352	.397	47	182	151	29	35	7	3	4	19	23	6	0	2	49	8	2	12.6	26.9
Smith, David	S-R	5-11	195	2-20-01	.303	.419	.394	11	43	33	7	10	0	0	1	8	7	1	0	2	8	3	0	16.3	18.6
Tilien, Junior	R-R	6-1	168	9-9-02	.216	.275	.405	11	40	37	4	8	4	0	1	8	3	0	0	0	10	0	0	7.5	25.0
Turney, Cole	L-L	6-1	215	1-16-99	.111	.200	.444	3	10	9	1	1	0	0	1	3	1	0	0	0	6	0	0	10.0	60.0
Warwick, Jude	R-R	6-1	170	9-9-05	.262	.414	.379	47	192	145	35	38	8	0	3	20	26	15	1	5	30	22	5	13.5	15.6

Pitching	B-T	Ht.	Wt.	DOB	W	L	ERA	G	GS	SV	IP	Hits	Runs	ER	HR	BB	SO	AVG	OBP	SLG	SO%	BB%	BF
Alewine, Bryce	R-R	6-4	215	11-18-04	2	0	2.08	14	4	3	30	24	13	7	1	14	23	.211	.298	.325	17.6	10.7	131
Berrier, Logan	R-R	6-1	175	2-26-01	1	0	4.32	7	0	1	8	2	4	4	1	2	11	.074	.138	.185	37.9	6.9	29
Calvo, Blair	R-R	6-3	195	2-27-96	0	0	0.00	2	2	0	3	2	0	0	0	0	2	3	.222	.364	.222	27.3	18.2	11
Daniel, Omari	R-R	6-0	185	5-4-04	1	2	4.44	18	0	4	24	18	14	12	1	16	27	.222	.347	.309	26.7	15.8	101
Diaz, Jatnk	R-R	6-4	215	8-19-04	4	2	3.49	12	11	0	49	44	26	19	4	19	44	.240	.322	.350	21.2	9.1	208
Felix, Eddy	R-R	6-2	180	8-23-03	2	1	2.51	8	8	0	32	33	9	9	5	6	42	.275	.307	.467	33.1	4.7	127
Florido, Antonio	R-R	6-1	175	2-15-05	6	2	4.05	19	0	2	27	20	14	12	1	14	36	.202	.301	.273	31.9	12.4	113
Fregio, Dariel	R-R	6-2	208	5-5-00	1	1	1.29	4	0	0	7	3	1	1	0	0	8	.125	.125	.250	33.3	0.0	24
Garcia, Pedro	R-R	6-1	190	2-27-02	3	0	3.49	15	0	3	28	29	12	11	3	10	20	.266	.339	.422	16.5	8.3	121
Guacache, Xiomer	R-R	6-3	195	2-11-04	1	3	3.82	16	0	1	33	26	19	14	2	18	25	.215	.347	.347	17.0	12.2	147
Haase, Aaron	R-R	5-8	193	5-24-00	1	0	0.00	3	1	0	3	2	1	0	0	1	3	.200	.250	.200	23.1	7.7	13
Harvey, Ryan	R-R	6-3	195	2-8-01	0	0	2.08	3	0	0	4	2	1	1	0	1	10	.133	.188	.133	62.5	6.3	16
Mendez, Wuilberth	R-R	6-3	150	5-29-04	3	3	5.21	12	8	0	47	45	30	27	4	14	38	.256	.332	.381	19.4	7.1	196
Mota, Eliseo	R-R	6-2	185	11-7-02	2	1	2.45	18	0	1	33	26	12	9	0	10	21	.220	.317	.263	14.9	7.1	141
Pacheco, Freddy	R-R	5-11	203	4-17-98	0	1	6.23	2	2	0	4	2	3	3	1	2	3	.143	.250	.357	17.6	11.8	17
Price, Dawson	R-R	6-5	215	9-29-04	2	1	6.94	15	0	2	23	27	21	18	3	14	19	.276	.374	.408	16.5	12.2	115
Ramirez, Wanmer	R-R	6-1	190	1-6-04	0	0	0.00	1	0	0	1	0	0	0	0	0	1	1	.000	.250	.000	25.0	25.0	4
Rogers, Johnathan	R-R	6-3	215	9-5-04	0	0	4.38	6	1	0	12	14	6	6	3	7	15	.255	.349	.491	23.4	10.9	64
Salcedo, Kelvis	R-R	6-0	180	1-23-06	4	0	1.99	12	8	0	45	22	12	10	1	19	53	.147	.251	.173	30.8	11.0	172
Schiefelbein, Ethan	L-L	6-2	180	4-11-06	2	0	6.00	3	1	0	9	9	6	6	0	5	9	.273	.359	.364	22.5	12.5	40
Silva, Eric	R-R	6-1	185	10-23-02	0	0	1.80	2	2	0	5	2	2	1	1	1	2	.125	.167	.133	11.1	5.6	18
Szapucki, Thomas	R-L	6-2	210	6-12-96	0	0	0.00	3	2	0	4	2	5	4	2	2	0	0	7	.143	.143	.214	50.0	0.0	14
Tanner, Ali	R-R	6-0	198	6-9-06	0	4	6.35	12	9	0	40	45	34	28	6	19	31	.290	.383	.458	17.2	10.6	180
Timmer, Shay	R-R	6-10	280	7-17-02	2	1	3.18	15	0	3	23	16	11	8	1	11	24	.200	.301	.275	25.8	11.8	93

Fielding

C: Jimenez 26, Rondon 12, Rosado 12, Cerkownyk 10, Dobbins 10, Campbell 1. **1B:** Campbell 28, Rondon 17, Jimenez 15, Cerkownyk 4. **2B:** Warwick 19, Ramirez 18, Osorio 14, Dickson 9, Hernandez 3, Penney 1, Tilien 1. **3B:** Hernandez 29, Osorio 22, Orozco 6, Ramirez 4, Tilien 2, Campbell 1. **SS:** Dickson 31, Warwick 24, Hernandez 6. **LF:** Orozco 22, Ramirez 13, Fana 8, Salas 5, Smith 5, De La Cruz 4, Tilien 4, Dobbins 3, Callahan 1, Turney 1. **CF:** Salas 29, Pinto 18, MacDonald 9, Fana 7, Ramirez 1. **RF:** Fana 19, Salas 15, De La Cruz 7, Ramirez 6, Orozco 5, Callahan 3, Pinto 3, Dobbins 2, Hernandez 1, Smith 1

DSL TIGERS 1
DOMINICAN SUMMER LEAGUE
ROOKIE

Batting	B-T	Ht.	Wt.	DOB	AVG	OBP	SLG	G	PA	AB	R	H	2B	3B	HR	RBI	BB	HBP	SH	SF	SO	SB	CS	BB%	SO%
Batista, Guillermo	S-R	6-1	195	11-23-06	.245	.434	.396	40	143	106	23	26	7	0	3	18	31	5	0	1	25	4	0	21.7	17.5
Berti, Willian	L-L	6-0	160	11-5-05	.271	.412	.438	51	182	144	30	39	8	2	4	27	31	5	0	2	41	3	0	17.0	22.5
Bustamante, Omar	R-R	5-10	180	8-19-05	.169	.257	.231	36	74	65	10	11	2	1	0	5	8	0	0	1	16	0	0	10.8	21.6
De Los Santos, Angel	R-R	6-1	161	3-3-08	.370	.465	.543	29	99	81	20	30	9	1	1	16	11	5	0	2	17	7	2	11.1	17.2
Dorta, Fabian	R-R	5-10	173	9-6-07	.256	.333	.333	16	45	39	5	10	3	0	0	8	5	0	0	1	6	4	1	11.1	13.3
Gonell, Ronny	R-R	5-10	187	1-15-07	.000	.429	.000	7	7	4	1	0	0	0	0	0	3	0	0	0	3	0	0	42.9	42.9
Gudino, Jeiker	R-R	5-9	171	11-15-06	.254	.357	.373	41	70	59	11	15	2	1	1	7	7	3	0	1	13	3	0	10.0	18.6
Hernandez, Kendrick	R-R	6-2	194	9-4-06	.276	.403	.448	31	72	58	10	16	2	1	2	12	10	3	0	1	28	0	0	13.9	38.9
Lao, Armando	R-R	5-10	170	11-25-06	.353	.450	.353	10	20	17	2	6	0	0	0	1	2	1	0	0	2	1	1	10.0	10.0
Luna, Wagnel	R-0	6-0	155	12-14-05	.252	.396	.315	49	142	111	24	28	7	6	0	0	16	26	1	3	1	28	9	5	18.3	19.7
Madero, Steven	L-R	6-2	175	9-24-06	.429	.500	.857	3	10	7	1	3	0	0	1	4	1	0	0	1	0	0	0	10.0	10.0
Mata, Andy	L-R	5-9	165	10-12-07	.190	.320	.286	19	51	42	6	8	4	0	0	4	6	2	1	0	12	5	0	11.8	23.5
Medrano, Abelardo	R-R	6-2	180	1-27-06	.000	.000	.000	16	0	0	1	0	0	0	0	0	0	0	0	0	0	0	0		
Ochoa, Jhonger	R-R	5-11	187	12-7-07	.248	.378	.301	48	164	133	26	33	7	0	0	18	18	11	0	2	39	14	4	11.0	23.8
Perez, Cristian	R-R	5-11	190	8-15-05	.244	.330	.375	50	182	160	33	39	4	1	5	30	14	7	0	1	55	7	0	7.7	30.2
Pinto, Santiago	R-R	5-11	170	2-25-08	.301	.379	.449	45	177	156	23	47	9	4	2	26	15	5	0	1	31	20	7	8.5	17.5
Reyes, Howard	L-R	5-10	185	11-9-07	.158	.347	.342	17	49	38	8	6	1	4	7	4	0	0	0	17	0	3	14.3	34.7
Roso, Angel	L-L	5-8	166	2-13-08	.000	.192	.000	14	26	21	1	0	0	0	0	5	0	0	0	9	0	0	19.2	34.6
Sanchez, Samuel	L-L	5-11	165	8-16-05	.308	.497	.453	44	162	117	31	36	3	1	4	17	33	11	1	0	45	9	5	20.4	27.8
Tamara, Martin	R-R	6-0	185	2-5-04	.229	.395	.281	47	124	96	22	22	5	0	0	13	20	7	0	1	22	4	3	16.1	17.7

Pitching	B-T	Ht.	Wt.	DOB	W	L	ERA	G	GS	SV	IP	Hits	Runs	ER	HR	BB	SO	AVG	OBP	SLG	SO%	BB%	BF
Amarante, Gregory	L-L	5-11	186	3-18-07	0	0	9.00	1	1	0	1	0	1	1	0	3	2	.000	.500	.000	33.3	50.0	6
Anderson, Branell	R-R	6-4	180	5-23-07	0	1	2.79	3	3	0	10	10	5	3	1	3	8	.244	.311	.463	17.8	6.7	45
Arcia, Marco	L-R	6-2	190	4-14-05	0	0	7.50	5	0	0	6	7	6	5	0	4	5	.292	.400	.375	16.7	13.3	30
Balanta, Yorsua	L-L	6-1	155	6-8-06	1	0	5.87	6	0	0	8	11	6	5	0	8	6	.367	.500	.467	15.0	20.0	40
Castillo, Oliver	R-R	5-11	180	1-26-05	1	1	9.53	6	0	1	11	13	16	12	3	6	11	.271	.417	.521	18.3	10.0	60
De Los Santos, Erickson	L-L	6-6	200	3-24-06	3	1	5.56	16	1	0	23	14	16	14	0	29	31	.194	.468	.250	27.9	26.1	111
De Los Santos, Jhoan	R-R	6-2	170	1-19-05	0	0	6.48	6	0	0	8	5	8	6	1	11	9	.172	.409	.310	20.5	25.0	44
Diaz, Anderson	L-L	6-3	190	9-26-07	0	3	6.35	6	6	0	17	17	15	12	4	14	21	.258	.388	.530	26.3	17.5	80
Gonell, Ronny	R-R	5-10	187	1-15-07	0	0	0.00	2	0	0	2	2	0	0	0	0	0	.286	.250	.286	0.0	0.0	8
Grant, Frenny	L-L	6-1	170	10-14-03	3	1	3.38	12	12	0	45	36	19	17	2	25	45	.213	.328	.284	22.4	12.4	201
Guzman, Jose	R-R	5-10	144	8-30-04	3	2	5.00	17	0	5	27	30	17	15	2	5	18	.275	.316	.376	15.4	4.3	117
Luna, Wagnel	R-R	6-0	155	12-14-05	0	0	0.00	1	0	0	1	0	0	0	0	1	0	.000	.000	.000	33.3	0.0	3
Marinez, Alexis	L-L	6-1	170	2-14-06	1	1	8.85	14	1	0	20	12	23	20	2	39	29	.174	.491	.319	25.0	33.6	116
Martinez, Carlos	R-R	6-1	165	12-16-05	1	2	20.65	10	3	0	11	15	27	26	1	19	3	.349	.586	.488	4.3	27.1	70
Medrano, Abelardo	L-R	6-2	180	1-27-06	2	0	11.15	15	0	0	15	14	20	19	4	26	7	.264	.529	.547	8.0	29.9	87
Mejia, Jesus	R-R	6-1	170	8-8-05	1	3	5.88	13	5	0	34	33	24	22	3	16	32	.266	.383	.444	21.5	10.7	149
Molina, Miguel	L-L	6-0	170	10-2-07	0	3	4.28	10	10	0	34	46	21	16	0	12	35	.336	.393	.394	23.3	8.0	150
Ortiz, Andres	R-R	6-6	195	8-17-06	2	5	5.34	14	9	1	30	21	28	18	0	24	22	.193	.355	.257	15.6	17.0	141
Ramos, Albert	R-R	6-3	185	4-7-06	0	1	12.71	3	2	0	6	10	8	8	1	3	8	.370	.433	.593	26.7	10.0	30
Rodriguez, Deibi	R-R	6-0	175	12-9-05	2	3	16.03	8	0	0	11	25	23	19	2	9	10	.455	.537	.673	14.9	13.4	67
Rodriguez, Sheroky	R-R	5-11	170	2-13-08	2	1	8.64	14	0	0	17	19	19	16	1	15	11	.297	.438	.406	13.6	18.5	81
Rossel, Leonardo	R-R	6-0	170	12-17-04	0	0	7.90	11	0	0	14	18	17	12	2	11	13	.321	.441	.518	19.1	16.2	68
Salas, Henderson	R-R	6-2	165	12-31-05	0	1	36.00	1	1	0	1	3	5	4	0	7	2	.500	.769	.500	14.3	50.0	14
Valerio, Elvin	R-R	6-5	225	8-29-02	0	0	0.00	4	0	0	5	4	0	0	0	2	3	.222	.300	.278	15.0	10.0	20
Vasquez, Luis	R-R	6-4	180	12-11-04	2	1	2.95	12	0	1	21	15	10	7	2	11	9	.192	.323	.295	9.7	11.8	93

Fielding

C: Gudino 35, Bustamante 33, Tamara 29, Gonell 3, Lao 3, Reyes 3, Dorta 2. **1B:** Tamara 26, Berti 8, Dorta 8, Hernandez 7, Batista 6, Lao 6, Reyes 6, Bustamante 5, Madero 2. **2B:** Ochoa 32, Batista 13, Luna 6, Mata 6, De Los Santos 4, Gudino 1. **3B:** Luna 30, Batista 21, Hernandez 18, Mata 2. **SS:** De Los Santos 20, Luna 19, Ochoa 16, Mata 9. **LF:** Pinto 23, Sanchez 16, Roso 11, Berti 9, Perez 2, Reyes 2, Medrano 1. **CF:** Perez 31, Pinto 14, Sanchez 12, Mata 2, Luna 1, Roso 1. **RF:** Berti 24, Perez 14, Sanchez 13, Pinto 7

DSL TIGERS 2 — ROOKIE
DOMINICAN SUMMER LEAGUE

Batting	B-T	Ht.	Wt.	DOB	AVG	OBP	SLG	G	PA	AB	R	H	2B	3B	HR	RBI	BB	HBP	SH	SF	SO	SB	CS	BB%	SO%
Aguilera, Luis	L-R	5-11	145	1-5-07	.253	.326	.337	28	95	83	12	21	3	2	0	12	10	0	0	2	10	5	2	10.5	10.5
Bazil, Sterling	S-R	5-10	164	5-13-08	.181	.321	.341	48	168	138	22	25	2	1	6	21	28	1	0	1	44	19	5	16.7	26.2
Benavides, Carlos	R-R	5-10	195	9-10-07	.244	.326	.361	44	135	119	22	29	9	1	1	15	11	4	0	1	30	3	2	8.1	22.2
Bustamante, Omar	R-R	5-10	180	8-19-05	.000	.154	.000	4	14	11	1	0	0	0	0	0	1	1	1	0	4	1	1	7.1	28.6
Gonell, Ronny	R-R	5-10	187	1-15-07	.000	.250	.000	6	4	3	0	0	0	0	0	0	1	0	0	0	2	0	0		50.0
Hoyte, Adrian	L-L	5-7	145	1-9-06	.278	.429	.333	28	70	54	9	15	3	0	0	6	13	2	0	1	11	1	1	18.6	15.7
Lao, Armando	R-R	5-10	170	11-25-06	.250	.350	.250	15	20	16	3	4	0	0	0	3	3	0	0	1	5	0	0	15.0	25.0
Lugo, Edgar	S-R	5-11	160	8-19-04	.326	.380	.400	41	152	135	27	44	7	0	1	19	9	4	1	2	18	8	5	5.9	11.8
Marin, Nelson	R-R	5-11	195	9-29-05	.240	.380	.339	50	150	121	19	29	6	2	2	16	24	4	0	1	29	2	1	16.0	19.3
Mata, Andy	L-R	5-9	165	10-12-07	.267	.330	.453	25	94	86	17	23	5	1	3	10	7	1	0	0	21	5	1	7.4	22.3
Miranda, Nestor	R-R	6-3	225	2-23-06	.259	.370	.474	37	138	116	17	30	3	2	6	24	15	6	0	1	39	3	4	10.9	28.3
Moya, Jonathan	R-R	5-11	203	9-27-06	.219	.409	.415	34	110	94	12	30	9	0	0	12	9	6	0	1	26	2	2	8.2	23.6
Quinonez, Josueth	R-R	6-1	172	2-22-07	.136	.345	.136	9	29	22	5	3	0	0	0	3	4	0	1	2	4	0	0	10.3	13.8
Ramirez, Jose	R-R	6-0	173	3-13-08	.262	.358	.376	45	173	149	28	39	7	2	2	11	15	8	0	1	28	9	2	8.7	16.2
Rodriguez, Angel	R-R	6-0	185	9-10-06	.265	.429	.388	34	63	49	9	13	1	1	1	6	13	1	0	0	19	1	0	20.6	30.2
Rodriguez, Cris	R-R	6-3	203	1-28-08	.308	.340	.564	50	188	172	38	53	12	1	10	39	11	0	0	5	42	10	2	5.9	22.3
Rodriguez, Enny	L-R	5-10	170	2-25-08	.216	.385	.270	29	96	74	16	16	2	1	0	4	20	1	0	1	27	2	0	20.8	28.1
Roso, Angel	L-L	5-8	166	2-13-08	.214	.290	.357	12	31	28	5	6	2	1	0	4	3	0	0	0	5	0	2	9.7	16.1
Sanchez, Heison	L-R	6-0	170	9-6-04	.391	.576	.435	14	33	23	7	9	1	0	0	5	11	0	0	0	2	2	4	30.3	6.1

Pitching	B-T	Ht.	Wt.	DOB	W	L	ERA	G	GS	SV	IP	Hits	Runs	ER	HR	BB	SO	AVG	OBP	SLG	SO%	BB%	BF
Balanta, Yorsua	L-L	6-1	155	6-8-06	0	0	7.71	9	0	1	12	14	17	10	0	9	4	.292	.419	.375	6.5	14.5	62
Castillo, Oliver	R-R	5-11	180	1-26-05	2	1	6.32	13	0	0	16	17	17	11	1	13	10	.283	.429	.367	13.0	16.9	77
Coba, Jhonan	R-R	6-0	150	7-20-06	3	1	5.14	10	9	1	42	43	25	24	2	15	50	.269	.331	.356	28.1	8.4	178
Constanza, Randy	L-L	6-2	175	10-11-06	0	0	7.20	4	0	0	5	8	4	4	0	5	4	.400	.500	.500	15.4	19.2	26
Cruz, Aleiman	R-R	6-2	176	4-3-06	1	0	0.00	2	1	0	2	0	0	0	0	3	0	.000	.000	.000	50.0	0.0	6
De Sala, Francisco	L-L	6-1	180	4-25-07	0	2	6.27	14	1	0	19	19	15	13	0	20	14	.275	.430	.348	15.1	21.5	93
Diaz, Anderson	L-L	6-3	190	9-26-07	0	3	15.43	3	3	0	7	8	12	12	0	11	9	.296	.487	.407	23.1	28.2	39
Gonell, Ronny	R-R	5-10	187	1-15-07	0	0	0.00	1	0	0	0	0	0	0	0	0	0	.667	.667	1.000	0.0	0.0	3
Leon, Leonardo	R-R	6-4	180	9-21-05	0	4	6.00	12	10	1	33	35	29	22	1	26	32	.278	.410	.389	20.5	16.7	156
Martinez, Carlos	R-R	6-1	165	12-16-05	0	1	21.21	4	0	0	5	7	14	11	0	15	1	.333	.595	.429	2.7	35.1	37
Mercedes, Yowander	L-L	6-5	185	5-2-05	0	0	11.12	14	0	1	17	12	22	21	1	23	20	.207	.530	.345	19.8	29.7	101
Montas, Donal	R-R	6-3	190	5-5-02	3	4	7.15	15	0	2	23	31	26	18	0	14	18	.320	.424	.412	15.3	11.9	118
Peguero, Esmerlin	R-R	6-1	180	4-17-05	3	1	3.24	14	0	0	17	10	7	6	1	17	19	.175	.372	.281	24.4	21.8	78
Ramos, Albert	R-R	6-3	185	4-7-06	0	2	5.72	8	8	0	28	27	21	18	3	12	20	.257	.358	.438	16.7	10.0	120
Ramos, Andres	R-R	5-11	203	3-26-05	2	1	4.50	24	0	6	26	27	14	13	0	17	24	.263	.408	.384	19.2	13.6	125
Reyes, Erinson	R-R	6-1	187	11-18-01	0	0	5.40	5	0	0	5	3	4	3	1	6	4	.214	.450	.429	20.0	30.0	20
Reyes, Franyerson	R-R	6-1	185	9-18-06	3	4	5.40	10	10	0	38	49	32	23	4	16	33	.306	.374	.488	18.4	8.9	179

Rodriguez, Carlos	L-L	6-0	170	4-29-06	3	4	3.94	11	11	0	46	47	26	20	4	12	36	.264	.314 .376	18.8	6.3	192
Rodriguez, Deibi	R-R	6-0	175	12-9-05	1	0	4.15	10	0	2	17	21	8	8	2	7	13	.309 .382 .441	16.7	9.0	78
Valdez, Yoan	R-R	6-1	187	8-19-05	2	0	2.37	13	0	1	19	10	7	5	1	4	14	.154 .222 .262	19.4	5.6	72
Vasquez, Luis	R-R	6-4	180	12-11-04	1	0	4.26	7	0	0	6	7	3	3	0	3	2	.292 .357 .417	7.1	10.7	28

Fielding

C: Marin 31, Rodriguez 31, Benavides 28, Lao 7, Bustamante 4, Gonell 4. **1B:** Marin 40, Benavides 23, Rodriguez 10, Lao 6, Bustamante 4, Sanchez 2, Gonell 1. **2B:** Lugo 21, Aguilera 13, E. Rodriguez 9, Bazil 8, Sanchez 8, Mata 2, A. Rodriguez 1. **3B:** Mata 22, Rodriguez 20, Lugo 12, Sanchez 2, Aguilera 1. **SS:** Bazil 41, Aguilera 16, Mata 1. **LF:** Moya 24, Hoyte 23, Lugo 8, Quinonez 5, Roso 3, Ramirez 2, Rodriguez 1. **CF:** Rodriguez 40, Ramirez 16, Quinonez 2, Lugo 1, Roso 1. **RF:** Ramirez 29, Moya 9, Rodriguez 9, Roso 4, Quinonez 3, Hoyte 1, Lugo 1, Mata 1

Houston Astros

SEASON SYNOPSIS: Houston had an active offseason, again losing stars (Alex Bregman and Kyle Tucker) but restocked its roster and led the AL West well into September. But injuries to stars such as Yordan Alvarez, Jeremy Peña and Josh Hader proved too much for even the Astros to overcome. They lost a seven-game division lead and wound up losing a tiebreaker to the Tigers for the final AL wild-card spot, missing the postseason for the first time since 2016.

HIGH POINT: The Astros won five straight series in late June and early July, wrapping with a July 4-6 sweep in Los Angeles, vanquishing the Dodgers in a series that started with an 18-1 romp that included five home runs, two by Jose Altuve. The franchise icon, who started the year in left field but had moved back to second base by this time, homered again in the ninth inning of the finale to back rookie Ryan Gusto in a 5-1 sweep-finisher. That pushed Houston to a season-best 20 games over .500 at 55-35.

LOW POINT: Injuries and attrition had sapped Houston's strength, and by the start of a Sept. 19-21 series in Houston, the Astros and Mariners were tied for first. Seattle swept the series, holding Houston scoreless the first 15 innings behind Bryan Woo and George Kirby, then blitzed Jason Alexander for seven runs in the second inning of the finale, a 7-3 victory. The Astros wound up losing five straight to fall further behind in the season's final week.

NOTABLE ROOKIES: Cam Smith, a 2024 first-round pick, learned to play the outfield in spring training, made the majors and got off to a great start before the league caught up to him. He finished hitting just .236/.312/.358, batting just .158 with eight extra-base hits in the second half. Gusto (7-4, 4.92) and lefty Colton Gordon (6-4, 5.34) were rotation filler while lefty Brandon Walter (3.35 ERA in nine starts) was thriving when he hurt his elbow.

KEY TRANSACTIONS: The Tucker trade, headlined by Smith and 3B Isaac Paredes, and free-agent signing of 1B Christian Walker (team-best 27 HR, .238/.297/.412) highlighted the offseason moves. Houston re-acquired Carlos Correa in July to play third base (absorbing two-thirds of Correa's remaining contract from Minnesota). Houston also traded Gusto and prospects for outfielder Jesus Sanchez (who hit just .199) from the Marlins. The Astros placed 28 players on the injured list.

OPENING DAY PAYROLL: $220,217,813 (7th)

PLAYERS OF THE YEAR

MAJOR LEAGUE
Hunter Brown
RHP
12-9, 2.43 ERA
206 SO, 57 BB in
185.1 IP; all-star

MINOR LEAGUE
Zach Cole
OF
(AA,AAA)
.279/.377/.539
19 HR, 18 SB in 97 G

ORGANIZATION LEADERS

Batting		*Qualifiers
MAJORS		
* AVG	Jeremy Pena	.304
* OPS	Jeremy Pena	.840
HR	Christian Walker	27
RBI	Christian Walker	88
MINORS		
* AVG	Zach Cole, Sugar Land/Corpus Christi	.279
* OBP	Joseph Sullivan, Corpus Christi/Asheville	.395
* SLG	Zach Cole, Sugar Land/Corpus Christi	.539
* OPS	Zach Cole, Sugar Land/Corpus Christi	.917
R	Lucas Spence, Corpus Christi/Asheville/Fayetteville	76
H	Brice Matthews, Sugar Land	109
TB	Shay Whitcomb, Sugar Land	206
2B	Lucas Spence, Corpus Christi/Asheville/Fayetteville	31
2B	Jesus Bastidas, Sugar Land	31
3B	Zach Cole, Sugar Land/Corpus Christi	7
3B	Brice Matthews, Sugar Land	7
HR	Shay Whitcomb, Sugar Land	25
RBI	Zach Cole, Sugar Land/Corpus Christi	65
RBI	Jesus Bastidas, Sugar Land	65
BB	Joseph Sullivan, Corpus Christi/Asheville	88
SO	Drew Vogel, Asheville	156
SB	Esmil Valencia, Fayetteville	50

Pitching		#Qualifiers
MAJORS		
W	Framber Valdez	13
# ERA	Hunter Brown	2.43
SO	Hunter Brown	206
SV	Josh Hader	28
MINORS		
W	Trey Dombroski, Sugar Land/Corpus Christi	9
L	Yeriel Santos, Asheville	11
# ERA	Miguel Ullola, Sugar Land	3.88
G	Jayden Murray, Sugar Land	50
GS	Tyler Ivey, Sugar Land	25
SV	Nick Hernandez, Sugar Land	11
IP	Joey Mancini, Sugar Land/Corpus Christi	123
BB	Miguel Ullola, Sugar Land	78
SO	Miguel Ullola, Sugar Land	131
# AVG	Miguel Ullola, Sugar Land	.186

2025 PERFORMANCE

General Manager: Dana Brown. **Farm Director:** Jacob Buffa. **Scouting Director:** Deric Ladnier.

Class	Team	League	W	L	PCT	Finish	Manager
Majors	Houston Astros	American	87	75	.537	7 (15)	Joe Espada
Triple-A	Sugar Land Space Cowboys	Pacific Coast	73	76	.490	7 (10)	Mickey Storey
Double-A	Corpus Christi Hooks	Texas	48	89	.350	10 (10)	Ricky Rivera
High-A	Asheville Tourists	South Atlantic	52	76	.406	12 (12)	Nate Shaver
Low-A	Fayetteville Woodpeckers	Carolina	69	63	.523	6 (12)	Carlos Lugo
Rookie	FCL Astros	Florida Complex	37	16	.698	1 (15)	Vincent Blue
Rookie	DSL Astros Blue	Dominican	32	23	.582	15 (52)	Johe Acosta
Rookie	DSL Astros Orange	Dominican	29	26	.527	26 (52)	Carlos Canelon
Overall 2025 Minor League Record			340	369	.480	21st (30)	

ORGANIZATION STATISTICS

HOUSTON ASTROS
AMERICAN LEAGUE

Batting	B-T	Ht.	Wt.	DOB	AVG	OBP	SLG	G	PA	AB	R	H	2B	3B	HR	RBI	BB	HBP	SH	SF	SO	SB	CS	BB%	SO%
Altuve, Jose	R-R	5-6	166	5-6-90	.265	.329	.442	155	654	588	80	156	24	1	26	77	55	4	1	6	109	10	6	8.4	16.7
Alvarez, Yordan	L-R	6-5	225	6-27-97	.273	.367	.430	48	199	165	17	45	8	0	6	27	28	0	0	6	33	1	1	14.1	16.6
Caratini, Victor	S-R	5-11	225	8-17-93	.259	.324	.404	114	386	344	35	89	14	0	12	46	23	13	0	6	65	1	0	6.0	16.8
Cole, Zach	L-R	6-2	190	8-4-00	.255	.327	.553	15	52	47	9	12	2	0	4	11	5	0	0	0	20	3	0	9.6	38.5
Corona, Kenedy	R-R	5-10	184	3-21-00	.000	.500	.000	3	4	2	0	0	0	0	0	0	2	0	0	0	1	0	0	50.0	25.0
Correa, Carlos	R-R	6-4	220	9-22-94	.290	.355	.430	51	220	200	23	58	10	0	6	21	19	1	0	0	45	0	0	8.6	20.5
Dezenzo, Zach	R-R	6-4	220	5-11-00	.245	.321	.367	34	109	98	17	24	6	0	2	10	11	0	0	0	37	1	0	10.1	33.9
Diaz, Yainer	R-R	6-0	195	9-21-98	.256	.284	.417	143	567	542	56	139	25	1	20	70	20	2	0	3	95	1	1	3.5	16.8
Dubon, Mauricio	R-R	6-0	173	7-19-94	.241	.289	.355	133	398	369	43	89	21	0	7	33	24	1	3	1	42	3	0	6.1	10.6
Guillorme, Luis	L-R	5-10	190	9-27-94	.150	.190	.150	12	21	20	2	3	0	0	0	0	0	0	0	0	8	0	0	4.8	38.1
Hummel, Cooper	S-R	5-10	198	11-28-94	.172	.301	.276	36	104	87	10	15	0	0	3	7	14	2	1	0	30	1	0	13.5	28.8
Matthews, Brice	R-R	6-0	175	3-16-02	.167	.222	.452	13	47	42	6	7	0	0	4	9	2	1	2	0	20	1	0	4.3	42.6
McCormick, Chas	R-R	6-0	208	4-19-95	.210	.279	.290	66	116	100	13	21	5	0	1	5	9	1	5	1	31	2	3	7.8	26.7
Melton, Jacob	L-L	6-3	208	9-7-00	.157	.234	.186	32	78	70	7	11	0	1	0	7	6	1	0	0	29	7	2	7.7	37.2
Meyers, Jake	R-L	6-0	200	6-18-96	.292	.354	.373	104	381	343	53	100	15	2	3	24	31	3	2	2	67	16	5	8.1	17.6
Paredes, Isaac	R-R	5-11	213	2-18-99	.254	.352	.458	102	438	378	53	96	15	1	20	53	50	8	0	2	76	0	1	11.4	17.4
Pena, Jeremy	R-R	6-0	202	9-22-97	.304	.363	.477	125	543	493	68	150	30	2	17	62	35	12	1	2	93	20	2	6.4	17.1
Rodgers, Brendan	R-R	6-0	204	8-9-96	.191	.266	.278	43	128	115	12	22	4	0	2	11	11	1	0	1	46	0	1	8.6	35.9
Salazar, Cesar	L-R	5-9	185	3-15-96	.231	.375	.231	11	16	13	0	3	0	0	0	1	2	1	0	0	2	0	0	12.5	12.5
Sanchez, Jesus	L-R	6-3	222	10-7-97	.199	.269	.342	48	160	146	21	29	9	0	4	12	13	1	0	0	40	4	1	8.1	25.0
Short, Zack	R-R	5-10	180	5-29-95	.220	.291	.380	22	56	50	9	11	2	0	2	7	4	1	1	0	18	0	1	7.1	32.1
Singleton, Jon	L-L	6-0	256	9-18-91	.111	.111	.111	3	9	9	0	1	0	0	0	0	0	0	0	0	1	0	0	0.0	11.1
Smith, Cam	R-R	6-3	215	2-22-03	.236	.312	.358	134	493	441	55	104	20	3	9	51	43	7	0	2	137	8	1	8.7	27.8
Trammell, Taylor	L-L	6-2	220	9-13-97	.197	.296	.333	52	135	117	15	23	7	0	3	12	17	0	0	1	41	3	2	12.6	30.4
Urias, Ramon	R-R	5-10	185	6-3-94	.223	.267	.372	35	101	94	6	21	5	0	3	10	6	0	1	0	28	1	0	5.9	27.7
Walker, Christian	R-R	6-0	208	3-28-91	.238	.297	.421	154	640	585	72	139	24	1	27	88	40	11	0	4	177	2	1	6.3	27.7
Whitcomb, Shay	R-R	6-1	202	9-28-98	.125	.219	.20	32	32	4	4	0	0	1	1	0	0	0	0	0	10	0	0	0.0	31.3

Pitching	B-T	Ht.	Wt.	DOB	W	L	ERA	G	GS	SV	IP	Hits	Runs	ER	HR	BB	SO	AVG	OBP	SLG	SO%	BB%	BF
Abreu, Bryan	R-R	6-1	225	4-22-97	3	4	2.28	70	0	7	71	51	18	18	4	31	105	.196	.291	.277	35.5	10.5	296
Alexander, Jason	R-R	6-2	227	3-1-93	4	2	3.66	14	13	1	71	68	32	29	12	21	60	.247	.306	.425	19.9	7.0	301
Arrighetti, Spencer	R-R	6-2	186	1-2-00	1	5	5.35	7	7	0	35	30	21	21	6	20	31	.229	.340	.412	19.9	12.8	156
Blanco, Ronel	R-R	6-0	180	8-31-93	3	4	4.10	9	9	0	48	37	22	22	7	20	48	.210	.288	.381	24.1	10.1	199
Blubaugh, A.J.	R-R	6-2	190	7-4-00	3	1	1.69	11	3	0	32	17	11	6	6	11	35	.152	.226	.339	28.2	8.9	124
Brown, Hunter	R-R	6-2	212	8-29-98	12	9	2.43	31	31	0	185	133	55	50	17	57	206	.201	.271	.318	28.3	7.8	729
Contreras, Luis	R-R	6-1	175	4-10-96	0	0	6.75	9	0	0	12	11	9	9	2	8	13	.239	.352	.435	24.1	14.8	54
De Los Santos, Enyel	R-R	6-3	235	12-25-95	3	0	4.03	22	0	0	22	22	10	10	5	6	24	.265	.311	.506	26.4	6.6	91
Dubin, Shawn	R-R	6-1	171	9-6-95	2	0	5.61	23	0	0	26	30	16	16	6	8	21	.294	.351	.520	18.9	7.2	111
France, J.P.	R-R	6-2	216	4-4-95	1	0	2.25	2	0	0	4	2	1	1	0	2	5	.143	.250	.214	31.3	12.5	16
Garcia, Luis	R-R	5-11	244	12-13-96	1	0	3.52	2	2	0	8	3	3	3	2	1	7	.115	.179	.346	25.0	3.6	28
Gordon, Colton	L-L	6-4	225	12-20-98	6	4	5.34	20	14	1	86	103	54	51	21	19	72	.293	.329	.543	19.0	5.0	379
Gusto, Ryan	R-R	6-4	232	3-11-99	7	4	4.92	24	14	0	86	95	50	47	13	28	87	.276	.333	.445	23.0	7.4	379
Hader, Josh	L-L	5-11	180	4-7-94	6	2	2.05	48	0	28	53	29	16	12	8	16	76	.158	.232	.342	36.9	7.8	206
Hernandez, Nick	R-R	6-1	212	12-30-94	0	0	5.06	10	0	0	11	12	6	6	3	8	11	.273	.385	.591	21.2	15.4	52
Hummel, Cooper	S-R	5-10	198	11-28-94	0	0	36.00	1	0	0	1	5	4	4	1	0	0	.625	.667	1.125	0.0	0.0	9
Javier, Cristian	R-R	6-1	213	3-26-97	2	4	4.62	8	8	0	37	32	22	19	3	15	34	.230	.306	.360	21.7	9.6	157
Kimbrel, Craig	R-R	6-0	215	5-28-88	0	1	2.45	13	0	0	11	9	4	3	2	6	16	.225	.326	.375	34.8	13.0	46
King, Bryan	R-L	6-1	184	11-5-96	5	4	2.78	68	0	2	68	60	21	21	10	11	69	.233	.273	.376	25.1	4.0	275
McCormick, Chas	R-L	6-0	208	4-19-95	0	0	0.00	3	0	0	3	3	3	2	2	0	1	.273	.467	.273	6.7	13.3	15
McCullers, Lance	L-R	6-1	202	10-2-93	2	5	6.51	16	13	0	55	61	45	40	10	39	61	.269	.392	.463	22.3	14.2	274
Montero, Rafael	R-R	6-0	190	10-17-90	0	0	4.50	3	0	0	4	3	2	2	0	2	5	.214	.313	.286	31.3	12.5	16
Murray, Jayden	R-R	6-0	190	4-11-97	0	0	1.54	9	1	0	12	10	2	2	0	3	7	.227	.277	.227	17.0	6.4	47
Neris, Hector	R-R	6-2	227	6-14-89	0	1	5.40	12	0	0	13	19	7	8	3	8	15	.283	.382	.565	26.8	14.3	56

	B-T	Ht.	Wt.	DOB			AVG																
Okert, Steven	L-L	6-2	202	7-9-91	3	2	3.01	68	1	1	72	45	25	24	6	19	84	.181	.242	.286	30.4	6.9	276
Ort, Kaleb	R-R	6-4	240	2-5-92	2	2	4.89	49	0	1	46	35	26	25	8	27	49	.213	.323	.396	25.3	13.9	194
Rooney, John	R-L	6-5	215	1-28-97	0	0	6.75	1	0	0	1	1	1	1	1	1	2	.200	.333	.800	33.3	16.7	6
Salazar, Cesar	L-R	5-9	185	3-15-96	0	0	0.00	1	0	0	1	0	0	0	0	0	0	.000	.250	.000	0.0	0.0	4
Scott, Tayler	R-R	6-3	185	6-1-92	1	2	7.36	18	0	0	18	21	16	15	3	14	17	.296	.409	.535	18.9	15.6	90
Sousa, Bennett	L-L	6-3	220	4-6-95	5	1	2.84	44	0	4	51	37	18	16	4	15	59	.204	.263	.331	29.6	7.5	199
Valdez, Framber	R-L	5-11	239	11-19-93	13	11	3.66	31	31	0	192	171	82	78	15	68	187	.238	.308	.358	23.3	8.5	802
VanWey, Logan	R-R	6-2	205	2-14-99	0	0	5.06	9	0	0	11	15	7	6	2	3	7	.333	.388	.489	14.3	6.1	49
Walter, Brandon	L-L	6-2	200	9-8-96	1	3	3.35	9	9	0	54	46	20	20	10	4	52	.225	.251	.422	24.5	1.9	212
Weems, Jordan	L-R	6-4	212	11-7-92	0	1	14.54	4	0	0	4	9	7	7	0	3	0	.450	.522	.550	0.0	13.0	23
Wesneski, Hayden	R-R	6-3	210	12-5-97	1	3	4.50	6	6	0	32	29	16	16	7	6	29	.240	.279	.479	22.1	4.6	131
Whitley, Forrest	R-R	6-7	238	9-15-97	0	0	12.27	5	0	0	7	9	10	10	2	6	8	.281	.410	.594	20.5	15.4	39

Fielding

Catcher	PCT	G	PO	A	E	DP	PB
Caratini	.989	49	434	15	5	2	1
Diaz	.997	113	1064	38	3	3	7
Salazar	.952	8	39	1	2	0	0

First Base	PCT	G	PO	A	E	DP
Caratini	1.000	15	71	5	0	5
Dezenzo	1.000	4	10	0	0	2
Dubon	1.000	4	7	2	0	1
Singleton	1.000	1	3	0	0	1
Walker	.995	152	1100	55	6	89

Second Base	PCT	G	PO	A	E	DP
Altuve	.981	66	92	115	4	22
Dubon	.987	46	66	85	2	26
Guillorme	1.000	7	3	5	0	1
Matthews	.979	13	18	28	1	9

Third Base	PCT	G	PO	A	E	DP
Correa	.974	48	29	83	3	9
Dubon	1.000	24	13	31	0	3
Guillorme	1.000	7	3	11	0	1
Matthews	1.000	1	0	2	0	0
Paredes	.975	89	50	148	5	13
Urias	.944	10	2	15	1	2
Whitcomb	1.000	8	3	4	0	1

Shortstop	PCT	G	PO	A	E	DP
Correa	1.000	5	2	8	0	0
Dubon	.987	33	17	61	1	4
Pena	.979	124	149	274	9	51
Rodgers	.972	41	39	66	3	18
Urias	1.000	25	22	60	0	7
Whitcomb	.938	9	8	7	1	1

Outfield	PCT	G	PO	A	E	DP
Altuve	.984	47	58	2	1	0
Alvarez	.962	15	25	0	1	0
Cole	1.000	17	27	1	0	0
Corona	1.000	2	1	0	0	0
Dezenzo	.979	26	44	2	1	0
Dubon	.958	68	66	2	3	0
Hummel	1.000	28	25	1	0	0
McCormick	1.000	66	78	2	0	0
Melton	1.000	31	46	1	0	1
Meyers	.996	103	227	1	1	0
Sanchez	.933	50	68	2	5	0
Smith	.992	132	250	6	2	0
Trammell	1.000	59	91	1	0	0
Whitcomb	.000	1	0	0	0	0

SUGAR LAND SPACE COWBOYS — TRIPLE-A
PACIFIC COAST LEAGUE

Batting	B-T	Ht.	Wt.	DOB	AVG	OBP	SLG	G	PA	AB	R	H	2B	3B	HR	RBI	BB	HBP	SH	SF	SO	SB	CS	BB%	SO%
Barber, Colin	L-L	5-11	290	12-4-00	.204	.309	.314	62	223	191	20	39	9	3	2	18	27	3	0	2	61	3	1	12.1	27.4
Bastidas, Jesus	R-R	5-8	145	9-14-98	.263	.353	.460	95	418	361	59	95	31	2	12	65	35	17	1	3	98	10	1	8.4	23.4
Caldera, Fernando	R-R	5-11	170	10-10-02	.100	.182	.200	4	11	10	2	1	1	0	0	2	1	1	0	0	7	0	0	9.1	63.6
Castro, Luis	R-R	6-1	187	9-19-95	.279	.358	.484	66	293	258	47	72	16	2	11	50	28	5	0	2	69	3	4	9.6	23.5
Cole, Zach	L-R	6-2	190	8-4-00	.353	.459	.745	15	61	51	9	18	3	1	5	16	10	0	0	0	17	3	1	16.4	27.9
Corona, Kenedy	R-R	5-10	184	3-21-00	.220	.308	.326	121	433	377	50	83	13	3	7	36	46	3	5	2	101	18	5	10.6	23.3
Davidson, Logan	S-R	6-3	185	12-26-97	.207	.290	.390	22	93	82	12	17	6	0	3	11	9	1	0	1	32	0	1	9.7	34.4
Dezenzo, Zach	R-R	6-4	220	5-11-00	.192	.214	.462	7	28	26	4	5	1	0	2	5	0	1	0	1	6	0	0	0	21.4
Diaz, Edwin	R-R	6-1	223	8-25-95	.214	.312	.409	62	247	215	35	46	12	0	10	29	27	4	0	1	61	2	0	10.9	24.7
Guillorme, Luis	L-R	5-10	190	9-27-94	.247	.382	.312	62	263	215	25	53	8	0	0	2	23	46	1	0	0	49	3	1	17.5	18.6
Hamilton, Quincy	L-L	5-10	190	6-12-98	.157	.254	.288	59	226	198	21	31	6	1	6	23	25	1	2	0	60	5	2	11.1	26.5
Hernandez, Alberto	R-R	6-0	169	2-4-04	.000	.000	.000	1	4	4	0	0	0	0	0	0	0	0	0	0	1	0	0	0	25.0
Hudson, Joe	R-R	5-11	210	5-21-91	.114	.215	.257	21	80	70	7	8	1	0	3	10	8	1	1	0	36	0	0	10.0	45.0
Huezo, Anthony	R-R	6-2	170	11-2-05	1.000	1.000	1.000	2	1	1	0	1	0	0	0	0	0	0	0	0	0	0	0	0.0	0.0
Hummel, Cooper	S-R	5-10	198	11-28-94	.292	.333	.708	6	27	24	8	7	0	2	2	7	2	0	0	1	5	0	0	7.4	18.5
Hurtubise, Jacob	L-R	6-0	180	12-11-97	.207	.395	.276	10	40	29	7	6	0	1	0	2	6	3	2	0	6	3	0	15.0	15.0
Johnson, Ryan	R-R	6-0	175	12-27-00	.000	.200	.000	2	5	4	0	0	0	0	0	0	1	0	0	2	0	0	0	20.0	40.0
Lavastida, Bryan	R-R	6-0	200	11-27-98	.250	.378	.363	24	99	80	12	20	4	1	1	7	15	2	0	1	22	5	5	15.2	22.2
Leon, Pedro	R-R	5-8	170	5-28-98	.241	.312	.422	22	94	83	12	20	6	0	3	10	8	1	1	1	21	5	0	8.5	22.3
Matthews, Brice	R-R	6-0	175	3-16-02	.260	.371	.458	112	498	419	70	109	18	7	17	64	70	6	0	3	139	41	11	14.1	27.9
McCormick, Chas	R-R	6-0	208	4-19-95	.175	.270	.10	40	37	4	0	2	4	3	0	0	2	1	3	1	7.5	30.0
Melton, Jacob	L-L	6-3	208	9-7-00	.286	.389	.556	35	150	126	26	36	16	0	6	17	22	0	1	1	30	12	3	14.7	20.0
Meyers, Jake	R-L	6-0	200	6-18-96	.222	.391	.278	6	23	18	3	4	1	0	0	1	5	0	0	0	2	0	0	21.7	8.7
Narvaez, Omar	L-R	5-11	220	2-10-92	.258	.402	.333	27	117	93	12	24	4	0	1	11	20	3	0	1	18	0	0	17.1	15.4
Palma, Miguel	R-R	5-8	170	1-4-02	.173	.232	.327	15	56	52	2	9	5	0	1	0	2	2	0	0	7	0	0	3.6	12.5
Pena, Jeremy	R-R	6-0	202	9-22-97	.167	.375	.667	2	8	6	3	1	0	0	1	1	1	1	0	0	2	0	0	12.5	25.0
Perez, Reylin	S-R	6-2	160	10-5-04	.167	.167	.167	3	12	12	1	2	0	0	0	0	0	0	0	0	4	0	0	0	33.3
Price, Xavier	R-R	6-6	225	11-15-96	.258	.323	.434	111	449	392	53	92	18	3	18	60	45	8	0	4	136	5	1	10.0	30.3
Rodgers, Brendan	R-R	6-0	204	8-9-96	.167	.167	.167	2	6	6	0	1	0	0	0	0	0	0	0	0	5	0	0	0	83.3
Sacco, Tommy	S-R	5-10	195	5-21-99	.220	.318	.282	64	244	209	20	46	5	1	2	21	29	2	2	2	55	7	0	11.9	22.5
Salazar, Cesar	L-R	5-9	185	3-15-96	.213	.353	.353	47	186	150	21	32	6	1	4	28	34	9	2	1	32	2	0	12.9	17.2
Short, Zack	R-R	5-10	180	5-29-95	.200	.341	.364	112	475	385	55	77	18	0	15	46	78	0	5	7	120	5	2	16.4	25.3
Singleton, Jon	L-L	6-0	256	9-18-91	.191	.319	.316	59	248	209	32	40	8	0	6	24	38	1	0	0	66	1	1	15.3	26.6
Trammell, Taylor	L-L	6-2	220	9-13-97	.250	.362	.611	10	47	36	7	9	3	0	3	6	0	2	1	14.9	12.8				
Whitcomb, Shay	R-R	6-0	202	9-28-98	.207	.300	.509	107	469	405	68	108	23	0	26	65	45	2	0	3	120	16	2	11.1	25.6

Pitching	B-T	Ht.	Wt.	DOB	W	L	ERA	G	GS	SV	IP	Hits	Runs	ER	HR	BB	SO	AVG	OBP	SLG	SO%	BB%	BF
Alexander, Jason	R-R	6-2	227	3-1-93	5	0	1.69	8	7	0	43	32	11	8	2	21	36	.209	.318	.307	20.1	11.7	179
Arrighetti, Spencer	R-R	6-2	186	1-2-00	0	1	9.64	1	1	0	5	6	6	5	2	4	5	.300	.440	.650	20.0	16.0	25
Barber, Colin	L-L	5-11	290	12-4-00	0	0	0.00	1	0	0	1	0	0	0	0	0	0	.250	.250	.500	0.0	0.0	4

HOUSTON ASTROS

Player	B-T	Ht	Wt	DOB	W	L	ERA	G	GS	CG	IP	H	R	ER	HR	BB	SO	AVG	OBP	SLG	K/9	BB/9	BF
Bido, Anderson	R-R	6-3	205	5-7-99	0	0	0.00	1	0	0	2	2	0	0	0	1	0	.250	.333	.375	0.0	11.1	9
Blubaugh, A.J.	R-R	6-2	190	7-4-00	5	8	5.27	22	19	2	99	97	64	58	10	58	101	.252	.350	.400	22.3	12.8	452
Bolton, Cody	R-R	6-3	230	6-19-98	0	0	1.98	4	2	0	14	12	3	3	0	8	15	.226	.349	.264	23.8	12.7	63
Bowman, Matt	R-R	6-0	185	5-31-91	2	2	3.48	9	1	0	10	8	5	4	1	3	11	.211	.295	.342	25.0	6.8	44
Brown, Aaron	R-R	6-4	220	3-19-99	3	10	9.46	20	15	0	72	106	78	76	26	38	46	.340	.417	.670	12.8	10.6	359
Castro, Miguel	R-R	6-7	201	12-24-94	3	0	2.29	17	0	5	20	15	6	5	2	8	20	.211	.291	.352	25.3	10.1	79
Contreras, Luis	R-R	6-1	175	4-29-96	2	3	3.88	45	0	7	46	36	21	20	3	28	42	.217	.337	.331	20.9	13.9	201
Dombroski, Trey	R-L	6-5	235	3-13-01	0	2	8.64	2	2	0	8	8	8	8	0	6	6	.258	.400	.355	15.0	15.0	40
Dubin, Shawn	R-R	6-1	171	9-6-95	1	0	1.04	9	0	0	9	4	1	1	0	1	14	.129	.156	.129	43.8	3.1	32
Fleury, Jose	R-R	6-0	185	3-8-02	2	1	6.95	13	9	1	45	48	35	35	11	26	41	.276	.368	.529	20.4	12.9	201
France, J.P.	R-R	6-0	216	4-4-95	2	1	6.38	7	4	0	24	18	18	17	3	20	23	.209	.361	.372	21.1	18.3	109
Gaither, Ray	R-R	6-4	224	3-4-98	1	2	2.73	24	0	1	26	22	11	8	3	14	21	.229	.339	.385	18.6	12.4	113
Garcia, Luis	R-R	5-11	244	12-13-96	0	1	2.60	4	4	0	17	16	5	5	2	4	20	.242	.286	.424	28.6	5.7	70
Gordon, Colton	L-L	6-4	225	12-20-98	4	2	3.38	11	11	0	56	59	22	21	8	16	56	.276	.328	.458	24.0	6.9	233
Guilfoil, Tyler	R-R	6-4	215	1-19-00	0	0	31.50	2	0	0	2	7	7	7	1	5	3	.538	.667	.846	16.7	27.8	18
Guillorme, Luis	L-R	5-10	190	9-27-94	0	0	27.00	1	0	0	1	3	3	3	1	0	1	.500	.500	1.000	16.7	0.0	6
Halligan, Patrick	R-R	6-6	230	10-4-99	0	0	11.57	4	0	0	5	6	6	6	1	5	2	.333	.480	.611	7.7	19.2	26
Hernandez, Nick	R-R	6-1	212	12-30-94	4	5	2.12	46	0	11	47	25	13	11	5	22	63	.156	.263	.306	33.7	11.8	187
Ivey, Tyler	R-R	6-4	195	5-12-96	4	10	5.83	27	25	0	122	134	86	79	18	66	102	.281	.369	.465	18.4	11.9	554
Javier, Cristian	R-R	6-1	213	3-26-97	0	0	4.66	3	3	0	10	7	5	5	0	10	10	.219	.395	.250	23.3	23.3	43
Knorr, Michael	R-R	6-5	245	5-12-00	2	1	6.51	27	1	0	28	32	23	20	5	14	31	.286	.369	.500	23.8	10.8	130
Kouba, Rhett	R-R	6-0	180	9-3-99	4	3	5.06	38	4	1	80	79	47	45	8	46	51	.263	.371	.423	14.4	13.0	354
Leach, Hudson	R-R	6-3	220	6-16-02	0	1	12.71	5	0	0	6	9	8	8	1	4	8	.360	.448	.480	27.6	13.8	29
Mancini, Joey	L-R	6-1	195	10-4-00	0	0	2.00	2	1	0	9	8	2	2	0	4	5	.242	.324	.333	13.2	10.5	38
McCullers, Lance	L-R	6-1	202	10-2-93	1	0	2.45	3	3	0	11	7	3	3	0	4	13	.184	.279	.237	29.5	9.1	44
Murray, Jayden	R-R	6-1	190	4-11-97	1	2	4.64	50	0	3	64	55	34	33	5	30	66	.239	.342	.378	23.8	10.8	277
Ort, Kaleb	R-R	6-4	240	2-5-92	0	0	2.84	7	0	0	6	7	3	2	2	5	5	.269	.406	.500	15.6	15.6	32
Pecko, Ethan	R-R	6-2	195	8-25-02	1	4	3.09	8	7	0	35	34	15	12	2	12	48	.248	.307	.343	31.8	7.9	151
Robertson, Nick	R-R	6-6	265	7-16-98	1	2	4.25	34	0	3	36	25	20	17	3	26	38	.192	.327	.331	24.2	16.6	157
Rodning, Brody	R-L	6-1	185	1-14-96	1	0	30.86	4	0	0	2	6	8	8	1	5	3	.500	.611	.917	16.7	27.8	18
Rooney, John	R-L	6-5	215	1-28-97	1	0	3.18	5	0	0	6	3	3	2	0	1	10	.158	.273	.263	45.5	4.5	22
Santa, Alimber	R-R	5-10	163	5-3-03	0	1	6.92	15	0	0	13	11	10	10	0	16	19	.220	.426	.260	27.9	23.5	68
Scott, Tayler	R-R	6-3	185	6-1-92	1	3	4.66	20	0	3	19	22	12	10	1	10	22	.289	.379	.395	24.7	11.2	89
Short, Zack	R-R	5-10	180	6-1-95	0	0	54.00	1	0	0	1	7	6	6	0	1	0	.778	.727	1.111	0.0	9.1	11
Sousa, Bennett	L-L	6-3	220	4-6-95	0	0	0.00	4	0	0	5	2	0	0	0	5	5	.118	.118	.118	29.4	0.0	17
Tamarez, Misael	R-R	6-1	206	1-16-00	1	1	9.00	30	0	0	41	47	45	41	6	32	32	.285	.413	.473	15.5	15.5	206
Ullola, Miguel	R-R	6-1	205	6-19-02	7	6	3.88	28	23	1	114	75	49	49	7	78	131	.186	.320	.285	26.6	15.9	492
VanWey, Logan	R-R	6-2	205	2-14-99	2	1	4.70	23	0	3	21	21	12	12	3	26	28	.244	.440	.372	23.9	22.2	117
Walter, Brandon	L-L	6-2	200	9-8-96	3	1	2.08	11	7	0	48	29	12	11	3	7	49	.177	.242	.262	27.5	3.9	178
Weems, Jordan	L-R	6-4	212	11-7-92	4	1	4.03	25	0	0	29	27	14	13	2	13	31	.248	.325	.367	24.6	10.3	126
Weiman, Blake	R-L	6-3	210	11-5-95	2	1	7.94	26	0	0	28	33	25	25	6	13	28	.287	.369	.504	21.5	10.0	130
Whitley, Forrest	R-R	6-7	238	9-15-97	3	0	4.76	6	0	0	6	4	3	3	0	4	9	.190	.320	.381	36.0	16.0	25

Fielding

Catcher	PCT	G	PO	A	E	DP	PB
Hudson	1.000	19	157	6	0	0	3
Lavastida	1.000	7	44	1	0	2	3
Narvaez	.983	15	116	2	2	1	0
Palma	.954	9	82	1	4	0	1
Price	.988	63	550	30	7	4	8
Salazar	.994	39	343	15	2	0	4
Sacco	1.000	15	18	25	0		6
Salazar	1.000	1	0	1	0		0
Short	1.000	4	7	9	0		3
Whitcomb	1.000	20	37	35	0		7

First Base	PCT	G	PO	A	E	DP
Castro	.981	43	274	30	6	34
Davidson	1.000	5	39	3	0	6
Diaz	1.000	4	33	2	0	4
Lavastida	1.000	2	7	0	0	0
Narvaez	.957	2	21	1	1	4
Price	1.000	39	275	18	0	23
Singleton	.994	47	294	37	2	23
Whitcomb	.978	12	80	8	2	16

Second Base	PCT	G	PO	A	E	DP
Bastidas	.964	8	13	14	1	4
Diaz	.000	1	0	0	0	0
Guillorme	1.000	14	22	26	0	6
Hernandez	.750	1	2	1	1	1
Johnson	1.000	2	1	4	0	1
Matthews	.991	87	148	182	3	46
Rodgers	1.000	2	4	1	0	1

Third Base	PCT	G	PO	A	E	DP
Bastidas	.928	40	27	76	8	6
Castro	1.000	3	1	3	0	0
Davidson	.857	4	8	4	2	0
Diaz	.966	18	11	17	1	0
Guillorme	.978	35	24	66	2	7
Matthews	.750	1	1	2	1	0
Sacco	1.000	3	2	3	0	0
Short	.980	22	13	37	1	2
Whitcomb	.985	28	19	45	1	3

Shortstop	PCT	G	PO	A	E	DP
Bastidas	.988	24	32	53	1	11
Diaz	.956	38	47	83	6	21
Guillorme	1.000	3	3	8	0	3
Matthews	.900	6	6	12	2	2
Pena	1.000	1	2	1	0	1
Sacco	1.000	2	4	7	0	1
Short	.963	70	80	152	9	32
Whitcomb	.971	7	10	24	1	6

Outfield	PCT	G	PO	A	E	DP
Barber	.990	59	96	1	1	1
Bastidas	1.000	1	3	0	0	0
Caldera	1.000	1	1	0	0	0
Castro	1.000	23	45	0	0	0
Cole	1.000	13	29	1	0	1
Corona	.989	123	274	6	3	1
Davidson	1.000	12	21	0	0	0
Dezenzo	1.000	4	8	0	0	0
Hamilton	.982	60	102	5	2	2
Huezo	.000	2	0	0	0	0
Hummel	.929	6	13	0	1	0
Hurtubise	1.000	9	12	2	0	1
Lavastida	1.000	8	16	0	0	0
Leon	1.000	20	46	2	0	1
Matthews	1.000	9	14	0	0	0
McCormick	1.000	8	20	0	0	0
Melton	1.000	29	69	6	0	0
Meyers	1.000	4	6	0	0	0
Perez	1.000	3	5	1	0	0
Sacco	.988	43	77	3	1	0
Short	1.000	2	1	0	0	0
Trammell	.929	9	13	0	1	0
Whitcomb	.983	34	55	3	1	1

CORPUS CHRISTI HOOKS
TEXAS LEAGUE
DOUBLE-A
HOUSTON ASTROS

Batting	B-T	Ht.	Wt.	DOB	AVG	OBP	SLG	G	PA	AB	R	H	2B	3B	HR	RBI	BB	HBP	SH	SF	SO	SB	CS	BB%	SO%
Alvarez, Yordan	L-R	6-5	225	6-27-97	.467	.529	.733	4	17	15	4	7	4	0	0	4	2	0	0	0	3	1	0	11.8	17.6
Austin, Trevor	R-R	5-10	188	10-3-01	.218	.332	.309	80	322	275	36	60	15	2	2	23	37	10	0	0	73	9	2	11.5	22.7
Baez, Luis	R-R	6-1	205	1-11-04	.246	.309	.335	66	272	248	28	61	12	2	2	27	22	1	0	1	73	7	0	8.1	26.8
Barber, Colin	L-L	5-11	200	12-4-00	.221	.276	.376	39	163	149	15	33	7	2	4	15	10	2	0	2	45	1	1	6.1	27.6
Bush, Will	R-R	6-4	230	3-4-04	.175	.333	.338	24	99	80	8	14	4	0	3	11	14	5	0	0	21	3	0	14.1	21.2
Caldera, Fernando	R-R	5-11	170	10-10-02	.000	.500	.000	1	4	2	1	0	0	0	0	0	1	1	0	0	2	0	0	25.0	50.0
Castro, Luis	R-R	6-1	187	9-19-95	.231	.320	.352	25	103	91	10	21	5	0	2	9	9	3	0	0	31	3	1	8.7	30.1
Cerny, Logan	R-R	6-1	185	9-28-99	.168	.247	.231	48	158	143	13	24	3	0	2	6	12	3	0	0	48	7	2	7.6	30.4
Clarke, Wes	R-R	6-0	228	10-13-99	.228	.399	.447	63	283	215	39	49	9	1	12	32	63	10	0	4	55	1	1	22.3	19.4
Cole, Zach	L-R	6-2	190	8-4-00	.267	.363	.505	82	355	307	54	82	19	6	14	49	42	5	0	1	129	15	6	11.8	36.3
Deming, Austin	R-R	6-0	200	12-21-99	.178	.248	.347	33	129	118	15	21	6	1	4	14	11	0	0	0	55	4	0	8.5	42.6
Diaz, Edwin	R-R	6-1	223	8-25-95	.253	.364	.495	25	107	91	16	23	4	0	6	14	14	2	0	0	25	2	1	13.1	23.4
Encarnacion, Luis	R-R	5-8	170	9-25-02	.164	.232	.250	46	168	152	13	25	4	0	3	16	10	4	0	2	48	2	0	6.0	28.6
Ferreras, Pascanel	R-R	5-10	185	11-25-01	.242	.322	.365	113	454	405	43	98	23	3	7	42	42	6	0	1	111	11	9	9.3	24.4
Garcia, John	R-R	6-0	190	9-25-00	.189	.312	.268	81	319	265	25	50	9	0	4	28	40	9	2	3	91	9	2	12.5	28.5
Gonzalez, Jose	L-L	6-0	215	8-15-00	.167	.219	.200	10	32	30	2	5	1	0	0	4	1	1	0	0	9	1	0	3.1	28.1
Guillemette, Garret	R-R	6-1	210	9-4-01	.242	.312	.412	40	170	153	23	37	8	0	6	26	14	2	0	1	39	0	2	8.2	22.9
Johnson, Ryan	R-R	6-0	175	12-27-00	.250	.296	.413	28	98	92	10	23	9	0	2	12	4	2	0	0	40	1	1	4.1	40.8
Jordan, Rowdey	S-R	5-10	190	1-27-99	.249	.385	.392	50	162	148	18	36	9	0	0	16	10	2	1	1	52	3	1	6.2	32.1
Lavastida, Bryan	R-R	6-0	200	11-27-98	.253	.327	.404	42	163	146	21	37	7	0	5	15	12	4	0	0	33	12	2	7.4	20.2
Martinez, Orlando	L-L	6-0	185	2-17-98	.270	.348	.376	60	269	237	35	64	12	2	3	25	28	1	1	1	46	4	2	10.4	17.1
Palma, Miguel	R-R	5-8	170	1-4-02	.138	.242	.190	18	66	58	2	8	3	0	0	2	8	0	0	0	15	0	0	12.1	22.7
Perez, Reylin	S-R	6-2	160	10-5-04	.184	.304	.237	13	47	38	3	7	2	0	0	1	7	0	1	1	20	1	0	14.9	42.6
Sacco, Tommy	S-R	5-10	195	5-21-99	.154	.205	.204	53	216	201	9	31	5	1	1	16	12	1	1	1	60	7	3	5.6	27.8
Sherwin, Anthony	L-R	5-11	190	6-20-02	.147	.231	.189	30	108	95	4	14	1	0	1	10	11	0	0	2	51	3	0	10.2	47.2
Spence, Lucas	L-L	6-1	190	1-27-03	.235	.370	.405	30	138	111	22	25	8	0	4	17	25	1	0	1	34	6	0	18.1	24.6
Sullivan, Joseph	L-L	6-0	200	7-1-02	.191	.357	.264	31	140	110	17	21	2	0	2	14	23	6	0	1	42	8	1	16.4	30.0
Williams, Jeron	R-R	6-1	180	9-29-00	.250	.312	.342	56	218	196	23	49	10	1	2	19	15	4	0	3	46	17	1	6.9	21.1
Willits, Bryce	L-R	6-2	200	8-25-99	.213	.303	.284	47	175	155	16	33	8	0	1	19	17	1	0	0	36	5	2	10.9	20.6
Wrobleski, Ryan	R-R	6-1	190	2-2-00	.210	.302	.338	48	179	157	21	33	3	1	5	19	17	4	0	1	59	1	5	9.5	33.0

Pitching	B-T	Ht.	Wt.	DOB	W	L	ERA	G	GS	SV	IP	Hits	Runs	ER	HR	BB	SO	AVG	OBP	SLG	SO%	BB%	BF
Arrighetti, Spencer	R-R	6-2	186	1-2-00	0	1	2.84	2	2	0	6	5	3	2	1	1	6	.200	.231	.320	23.1	3.8	26
Austin, Trevor	R-R	5-10	188	10-3-01	0	0	0.00	1	0	0	1	0	0	0	0	0	0	.000	.000	.000	0.0	0.0	2
Bido, Anderson	R-R	6-3	205	5-7-99	1	4	5.02	41	1	1	66	63	46	37	12	36	40	.250	.347	.452	13.4	12.0	299
Brockhouse, Walker	R-R	6-4	197	2-22-99	1	0	3.38	4	0	0	5	2	2	2	0	0	4	5	.125	.300	.125	23.8	19.0	21
Cerny, Logan	R-R	6-1	185	9-28-99	0	0	0.00	1	0	0	1	1	0	0	0	0	1	.250	.250	.500	25.0	0.0	4
Chirinos, Amilcar	R-R	6-3	200	11-7-01	0	5	4.30	27	0	1	29	28	18	14	3	18	27	.255	.364	.391	20.9	14.0	129
Clarke, Wes	R-R	6-0	228	10-13-99	0	0	0.00	1	0	0	1	2	1	0	0	0	0	.333	.333	.333	0.0	0.0	6
David, Ramsey	R-R	6-3	190	2-8-01	0	1	7.27	8	0	0	9	12	7	7	1	3	7	.333	.400	.472	17.5	7.5	40
Dombroski, Trey	R-L	6-5	235	3-13-01	9	5	3.61	26	17	0	112	91	49	45	7	49	116	.221	.304	.331	24.8	10.5	467
Dubin, Shawn	R-R	6-1	171	9-6-95	1	0	9.00	1	0	0	1	2	1	1	0	1	2	.400	.500	.400	33.3	16.7	6
Fleury, Jose	R-R	6-0	185	3-8-02	3	1	1.82	10	10	0	40	26	8	8	2	9	37	.188	.236	.239	25.0	6.1	148
France, J.P.	R-R	6-0	216	4-4-95	0	1	13.50	1	1	0	2	5	3	3	0	1	3	.455	.500	.455	25.0	8.3	12
Garcia, Luis	R-R	5-11	244	12-13-96	0	1	6.75	2	2	0	7	9	6	5	2	3	9	.321	.375	.607	28.1	9.4	32
Guilfoil, Tyler	R-R	6-4	215	1-19-00	4	2	3.88	46	0	4	72	54	34	31	8	48	77	.206	.340	.347	24.0	15.0	321
Halligan, Patrick	R-R	6-6	230	10-4-99	2	3	3.48	35	0	1	52	48	24	20	6	21	62	.246	.330	.385	27.9	9.5	222
Hicks, James	R-R	6-2	190	5-9-01	1	5	5.59	11	10	0	47	57	33	29	7	14	46	.306	.363	.473	22.3	6.8	206
Javier, Cristian	R-R	6-1	213	3-26-97	0	0	3.00	1	1	0	3	2	1	1	0	2	3	.182	.308	.182	23.1	15.4	13
Jordan, Rowdey	S-R	5-10	190	1-27-99	0	0	0.00	1	0	0	1	0	0	0	0	0	0	.250	.250	.250	0.0	0.0	4
Knorr, Michael	R-R	6-5	245	5-12-00	3	2	3.46	19	0	2	26	21	12	10	3	14	35	.214	.316	.347	30.7	12.3	114
Leach, Hudson	R-R	6-3	220	6-16-02	0	0	3.72	9	0	1	10	7	4	4	1	5	14	.206	.341	.294	34.1	12.2	41
Mancini, Joey	L-R	6-1	195	10-4-00	5	9	4.96	25	13	1	114	125	71	63	16	43	79	.276	.349	.442	15.3	8.3	515
Mayer, Bryce	R-R	6-3	210	2-11-02	1	4	5.90	7	4	0	29	30	23	19	3	12	37	.256	.346	.402	27.6	9.0	134
McCullers, Lance	L-R	6-1	202	10-2-93	0	1	2.70	2	2	0	7	7	4	2	1	4	8	.269	.367	.423	26.7	13.3	30
Nezuh, Jackson	R-R	6-1	180	2-11-02	3	9	4.48	18	16	0	72	69	38	36	9	25	71	.248	.332	.392	23.0	8.1	309
Pecko, Ethan	R-R	6-2	195	8-25-02	2	6	4.40	11	10	0	43	37	21	21	4	15	45	.239	.302	.368	26.2	8.7	172
Perez, Railin	R-R	6-3	185	9-2-01	0	2	6.60	13	0	2	15	16	13	11	1	15	13	.281	.455	.404	16.9	19.5	77
Rodning, Brody	R-L	6-1	185	1-14-96	0	2	7.50	20	0	2	24	40	20	20	3	11	26	.357	.416	.518	20.8	8.8	125
Rodriguez, Luis Angel	L-L	6-1	190	9-10-99	1	3	4.57	13	6	0	41	38	23	21	2	25	24	.250	.363	.368	13.2	13.7	182
Sanchez, Wilmy	R-R	5-9	193	12-17-03	2	4	6.05	46	0	7	61	59	49	41	6	51	75	.248	.381	.378	25.8	17.5	291
Santa, Alimber	R-R	5-10	163	5-3-03	3	1	1.26	31	0	2	57	35	11	8	2	23	63	.176	.271	.236	27.5	10.2	226
Santos, Alex	R-R	6-4	208	7-10-02	0	4	4.60	10	7	0	29	21	17	15	3	23	38	.208	.354	.337	29.5	17.8	129
Swanson, Nic	R-R	6-2	180	7-8-99	2	6	5.61	16	12	0	61	64	41	38	9	31	57	.271	.359	.436	20.7	11.3	275
Torres, Alejandro	R-R	6-1	238	4-26-01	3	2	4.82	15	1	1	28	25	17	15	3	16	26	.238	.352	.362	20.8	12.8	125
Tredwell, Alonzo	L-R	6-8	230	5-8-02	2	1	3.18	7	4	0	23	22	8	8	2	12	40	.244	.340	.378	38.5	11.5	104
Urias, Manuel	R-R	6-6	200	3-8-01	3	8	4.79	22	16	0	92	87	55	49	13	38	69	.244	.319	.401	17.3	9.5	399

Fielding

Catcher	PCT	G	PO	A	E	DP	PB
Bush	.987	15	131	17	2	4	2
Garcia	.981	70	618	48	13	2	11
Guillemette	.992	16	117	11	1	1	0
Lavastida	.988	19	158	10	2	0	5
Palma	.972	8	68	2	2	1	0
Wrobleski	.989	12	88	6	1	0	0

First Base	PCT	G	PO	A	E	DP
Austin	1.000	5	12	3	0	0
Baez	.944	3	16	1	1	2
Bush	1.000	8	61	3	0	3
Castro	.977	5	40	2	1	6
Clarke	.995	49	357	16	2	39
Deming	1.000	20	145	7	0	0
Encarnacion	.984	27	179	10	3	14
Garcia	1.000	3	15	0	0	1
Guillemette	.980	10	48	1	1	4
Lavastida	.933	4	25	3	2	4
Palma	.962	4	23	2	1	4
Willits	.938	4	14	1	1	2
Wrobleski	.933	6	37	5	3	2

Second Base	PCT	G	PO	A	E	DP
Austin	.946	24	40	66	6	14
Encarnacion	1.000	2	2	7	0	1

Ferreras	.969	46	80	109	6	20
Johnson	1.000	9	17	27	0	9
Jordan	1.000	20	29	51	0	12
Perez	.962	5	14	11	1	4
Sacco	.980	13	24	24	1	8
Sherwin	1.000	9	6	20	0	1
Williams	.981	14	30	23	1	11

Third Base	PCT	G	PO	A	E	DP
Austin	.912	27	19	43	6	6
Castro	.875	11	9	12	3	3
Deming	.829	15	9	20	6	0
Diaz	1.000	2	2	3	0	1
Ferreras	.889	24	14	34	6	6
Johnson	1.000	3	2	4	0	0
Jordan	1.000	3	4	3	0	1
Perez	1.000	2	2	1	0	0
Sacco	.966	9	9	19	1	3
Sherwin	.962	15	6	19	1	2
Williams	.833	2	0	5	1	0
Willits	.974	33	32	42	2	8

Shortstop	PCT	G	PO	A	E	DP
Austin	1.000	1	1	0	0	0
Diaz	.978	23	33	55	2	8
Ferreras	.959	35	52	65	5	16

Johnson	.892	12	15	18	4	3
Sacco	.920	28	30	74	9	20
Sherwin	.962	6	8	17	1	3
Williams	.924	37	41	80	10	16

Outfield	PCT	G	PO	A	E	DP
Alvarez	1.000	1	1	0	0	0
Austin	1.000	21	30	3	0	1
Baez	.972	56	105	1	3	0
Barber	1.000	34	57	1	0	1
Castro	1.000	13	12	0	0	0
Cerny	.990	49	99	3	1	0
Cole	.988	82	162	5	2	1
Encarnacion	1.000	5	4	0	0	0
Ferreras	1.000	6	14	0	0	0
Gonzalez	.950	11	19	0	1	0
Johnson	1.000	4	9	0	0	0
Jordan	1.000	15	28	1	0	1
Lavastida	1.000	2	2	0	0	0
Martinez	.990	49	102	2	1	1
Perez	1.000	6	17	0	0	0
Sacco	.923	5	11	1	1	0
Spence	.966	27	54	2	2	0
Sullivan	1.000	21	52	0	0	0
Willits	.967	11	29	0	1	0
Wrobleski	1.000	22	37	4	0	1

ASHEVILLE TOURISTS — HIGH-A
SOUTH ATLANTIC LEAGUE

Batting	B-T	Ht.	Wt.	DOB	AVG	OBP	SLG	G	PA	AB	R	H	2B	3B	HR	RBI	BB	HBP	SH	SF	SO	SB	CS	BB%	SO%
Austin, Trevor	R-R	5-10	188	10-3-01	.182	.297	.351	25	91	77	9	14	4	0	3	13	10	3	0	1	21	1	1	11.0	23.1
Blomgren, Jack	R-R	5-10	180	9-27-98	.121	.256	.212	10	39	33	4	4	0	0	1	3	4	2	0	0	7	5	0	10.3	17.9
Brutcher, Drew	L-R	6-5	203	2-12-02	.185	.274	.261	47	179	157	16	29	6	0	2	9	19	1	0	2	48	2	0	10.6	26.8
Bush, Will	L-R	6-4	230	3-4-04	.247	.370	.441	73	297	247	45	61	12	0	12	36	44	5	0	1	84	7	1	14.8	28.3
Caldera, Fernando	R-R	5-11	170	10-10-02	.095	.136	.095	9	22	21	2	2	0	0	0	0	1	0	0	0	8	0	0	4.5	36.4
Carrillo, Oliver	R-R	5-11	210	1-19-02	.169	.311	.229	26	103	83	9	14	2	0	1	8	15	3	0	2	30	1	0	14.6	29.1
Encarnacion, Luis	R-R	5-8	170	9-25-02	.236	.309	.333	22	81	72	5	17	2	1	1	4	8	0	0	1	22	1	0	9.9	27.2
Encarnacion, Yamal	S-R	5-8	150	9-8-03	.252	.344	.374	33	123	107	16	27	5	1	2	7	14	1	1	0	24	12	0	11.4	19.5
Fisher, Cameron	L-R	6-2	210	6-12-01	.188	.310	.290	22	84	69	7	13	2	1	1	5	13	0	0	2	41	5	1	15.5	48.8
Gomez, Kenni	L-R	5-11	145	10-4-05	.232	.274	.349	89	365	341	34	79	18	2	6	48	20	1	0	3	100	22	7	5.5	27.4
Gonzalez, Cristian	R-R	6-3	210	10-22-01	.221	.255	.300	63	259	240	23	53	10	0	3	31	13	0	0	6	63	1	0	5.0	26.3
Gonzalez, Jose	L-L	6-0	215	8-15-00	.182	.294	.205	14	51	44	5	8	1	0	0	2	5	2	0	0	19	1	1	9.8	37.3
Guillemette, Garret	R-R	6-1	210	9-4-01	.243	.341	.438	41	168	144	23	35	7	0	7	21	18	4	0	1	33	3	2	10.7	19.6
Holy, Max	R-R	6-0	185	7-11-02	.171	.333	.244	26	102	82	14	14	3	0	1	6	20	0	0	0	36	10	4	19.6	35.3
Janek, Walker	R-R	6-0	190	9-24-02	.263	.333	.433	92	399	358	58	94	21	2	12	46	30	9	0	2	106	30	2	7.5	26.6
Jaworsky, Chase	L-R	6-1	170	7-31-04	.242	.353	.359	57	236	198	32	48	10	2	3	29	26	9	1	2	51	24	3	11.0	21.6
Lara, Wilton	R-R	5-11	175	1-21-04	.000	.111	.000	5	18	16	0	0	0	0	0	0	1	1	0	0	10	1	0	5.6	55.6
Lytle, Mason	R-R	5-10	180	3-26-01	.242	.292	.242	18	72	66	3	16	0	0	0	4	5	0	0	1	8	5	1	6.9	11.1
Nunez, Alejandro	L-R	5-10	179	9-8-04	.269	.321	.400	94	402	360	44	97	19	2	8	38	26	4	4	6	96	22	9	6.5	23.9
Perez, Reylin	S-R	6-2	160	10-5-04	.171	.209	.195	13	43	41	1	7	1	0	0	2	2	0	0	0	19	2	1	4.7	44.2
Salas, Hector	R-R	5-11	145	3-9-04	.288	.300	.302	21	72	63	9	15	4	0	0	5	6	0	2	1	16	2	0	8.3	22.2
Schiavone, Jason	R-R	6-3	200	3-19-03	.286	.429	.464	8	35	28	6	8	2	0	1	5	5	2	0	0	11	0	0	14.3	31.4
Spence, Lucas	L-L	6-1	190	1-27-03	.239	.337	.410	63	270	234	38	56	18	2	6	34	30	5	0	1	70	10	4	11.1	25.9
Sullivan, Joseph	L-L	6-0	200	7-1-02	.233	.411	.462	75	341	262	51	61	11	2	15	35	65	14	0	0	91	34	8	19.1	26.7
Trujillo, Kedaur	R-R	5-11	188	3-2-04	.286	.375	.286	5	16	14	0	4	0	0	0	2	2	0	0	0	2	0	0	12.5	12.5
Villarroel, Jancel	R-R	5-8	176	1-17-05	.263	.295	.404	15	61	57	8	15	2	0	2	9	3	0	0	1	13	0	0	4.9	21.3
Vogel, Drew	R-R	6-1	195	5-28-02	.180	.274	.309	109	417	362	43	65	12	1	11	38	39	10	1	5	156	24	6	9.4	37.4
Whitaker, Tyler	R-R	6-1	190	8-2-02	.200	.308	.326	107	402	340	41	68	20	4	5	44	47	9	0	6	116	14	4	11.7	34.1

Pitching	B-T	Ht.	Wt.	DOB	W	L	ERA	G	GS	SV	IP	Hits	Runs	ER	HR	BB	SO	AVG	OBP	SLG	SO%	BB%	BF
Aguilar, Luis	R-R	5-11	176	4-4-04	0	0	0.00	1	0	0	1	0	0	0	0	0	0	.000	.000	.000	0.0	0.0	2
Almonte, Dawill	R-R	5-9	168	10-19-01	1	1	9.24	7	0	0	13	21	15	13	1	9	10	.368	.471	.509	14.3	12.9	70
Apker, Garrett	R-R	6-5	195	9-18-99	0	0	7.71	4	0	0	7	8	6	6	1	11	4	.308	.514	.462	10.8	29.7	37
Bello, Juan	R-R	6-1	173	6-25-04	4	4	3.70	17	9	0	66	54	30	27	5	33	66	.220	.338	.343	23.0	11.5	287
Brito, Anderson	R-R	5-10	155	7-7-04	0	1	3.28	12	12	0	49	36	20	18	1	28	65	.202	.321	.264	31.1	13.4	209
Caldera, Fernando	R-R	5-11	170	10-10-02	0	0	34.71	2	0	0	2	7	9	9	2	2	1	.500	.611	1.000	5.6	11.1	18
Chirinos, Amilcar	R-R	6-3	200	10-7-01	1	2	5.56	19	0	4	23	19	14	14	3	10	38	.258	.343	.393	37.3	9.8	102
Cruz, Anthony	R-R	5-11	179	8-19-02	1	0	5.12	5	2	1	19	15	12	11	3	11	20	.217	.325	.391	24.1	13.3	83
David, Ramsey	R-R	6-3	190	2-8-01	1	0	1.40	9	1	0	26	14	4	4	3	14	29	.159	.302	.273	27.4	13.2	106
DeVos, Nolan	R-R	6-0	185	8-11-00	0	0	3.86	3	3	0	5	2	6	2	8	.214	.320	.357	16.0	12.0	50
Diaz, Norbis	R-R	6-0	165	8-10-04	2	0	5.40	5	0	0	6	6	3	0	5	3	.316	.480	.368	12.0	20.0	25
Gillis, Brett	R-R	6-2	215	9-29-99	3	2	2.70	12	6	1	47	39	25	14	4	15	52	.219	.294	.371	26.4	7.6	197

Batting	B-T	Ht.	Wt.	DOB	AVG	OBP	SLG	G	PA	AB	R	H	2B	3B	HR	RBI	BB	HBP	SH	SF	SO	SB	CS	BB%	SO%
Guedez, Jose	R-R	6-0	169	9-27-01	4	7	4.68	20	11	1	83	77	52	43	8	43	74	.246	.351	.393	20.1	11.7	369		
Howard, Dylan	R-R	6-2	195	5-3-03	1	1	2.66	5	5	0	24	17	9	7	2	8	24	.202	.281	.321	25.0	8.3	96		
Langford, Colby	L-L	6-3	195	4-30-02	4	4	3.26	42	0	1	61	36	26	22	3	63	87	.177	.385	.256	31.1	22.5	280		
Leach, Hudson	R-R	6-3	220	6-16-02	1	1	3.98	17	0	3	20	16	10	9	1	10	35	.222	.333	.306	40.2	11.5	87		
Linskey, Matthew	R-R	6-7	245	4-19-02	0	0	3.29	8	0	0	14	7	6	5	1	12	13	.163	.339	.279	23.2	21.4	56		
Mayer, Bryce	R-R	6-3	210	2-11-02	3	2	2.85	9	9	0	41	29	16	13	4	9	45	.192	.238	.305	28.1	5.6	160		
McPherson, Brandon	R-R	6-3	225	3-23-00	1	3	4.37	6	3	0	23	16	12	11	1	13	23	.200	.319	.288	24.5	13.8	94		
Mikulski, Matt	L-L	6-4	205	5-8-99	0	0	5.68	9	0	0	13	13	10	8	0	10	17	.260	.403	.300	27.4	16.1	62		
Pena, Alain	R-R	5-11	155	4-10-03	2	8	8.12	15	10	0	48	37	37	29	4	23	49	.296	.419	.551	16.1	13.0	223		
Perez, Railin	R-R	6-3	185	9-2-01	7	2	3.72	29	0	4	48	41	26	20	1	28	65	.227	.352	.320	29.5	12.7	220		
Pinto, Jean	R-R	5-11	175	1-9-01	2	2	4.61	14	10	3	57	49	29	29	3	26	45	.231	.315	.363	18.7	10.8	241		
Rodriguez, Julio	R-R	6-3	180	2-10-00	1	0	7.39	18	0	0	28	29	28	23	2	14	41	.259	.366	.375	31.3	10.7	131		
Rodriguez, Luis	R-R	6-2	181	12-29-03	0	3	5.73	6	1	1	22	29	16	14	2	17	17	.319	.398	.462	16.5	11.7	103		
Santos, Yeriel	R-R	6-0	165	11-20-03	1	11	8.16	25	15	2	93	106	93	84	15	63	85	.282	.391	.463	18.9	14.0	450		
Serrano, Jose	R-R	6-2	212	2-14-04	0	0	5.40	1	0	0	2	0	1	1	0	1	1	.000	.286	.000	14.3	14.3	7		
Swiney, Nick	R-L	6-3	185	2-12-99	3	4	5.51	24	2	1	49	58	32	30	6	27	45	.296	.383	.439	19.7	11.8	229		
Taylor, Andrew	R-R	6-5	190	9-23-01	2	3	3.39	18	13	0	58	52	26	22	6	30	54	.244	.333	.380	22.0	12.2	246		
Torres, Alejandro	R-R	6-1	238	4-26-01	0	0	9.00	4	0	0	6	7	6	6	1	3	9	.292	.455	.542	27.3	9.1	33		
Tredwell, Alonzo	L-R	6-8	230	5-8-02	1	1	3.68	7	4	1	29	27	16	12	1	12	30	.250	.344	.333	23.4	9.4	128		
True, Derek	R-R	6-2	180	4-25-01	2	9	6.49	16	10	0	60	77	52	43	10	30	62	.306	.378	.500	21.5	10.4	288		
Tucker, Cody	R-R	6-5	210	3-1-99	2	2	4.05	23	0	2	33	37	21	15	2	23	32	.285	.397	.400	20.4	14.6	157		
Urias, Manuel	R-R	6-6	200	3-8-01	1	0	4.50	4	2	0	14	15	9	7	1	3	15	.263	.295	.404	24.6	4.9	61		
Vogel, Drew	R-R	6-1	195	5-28-02	0	0	4.50	2	0	0	2	3	1	1	0	0	1	.333	.333	.556	11.1	0.0	9		
Wohlgemuth, Nate	R-R	5-11	210	5-30-01	1	1	4.91	9	0	0	11	7	9	6	1	7	11	.189	.367	.297	22.4	14.3	49		

Fielding

Catcher	PCT	G	PO	A	E	DP	PB
Bush	.992	36	324	31	3	3	6
Caldera	.941	3	16	0	1	0	0
Guillemette	.995	19	195	10	1	1	0
Janek	.992	63	568	60	5	5	9
Schiavone	1.000	5	27	5	0	0	0
Trujillo	1.000	1	10	2	0	1	0
Villarroel	.981	6	46	6	1	0	2

First Base	PCT	G	PO	A	E	DP
Austin	.957	7	40	5	2	5
Bush	.991	31	199	12	2	18
Caldera	1.000	1	3	1	0	0
Carrillo	.965	12	75	8	3	6
Encarnacion, L	.982	16	102	5	2	5
Fisher	.960	14	90	7	4	3
Guillemette	.980	18	140	7	3	14
Lara	1.000	1	11	0	0	1
Schiavone	1.000	3	11	1	0	2
Trujillo	1.000	4	27	1	0	1
Villarroel	1.000	1	6	2	0	1
Vogel	1.000	12	94	6	0	5
Whitaker	.976	14	73	10	2	11

Second Base	PCT	G	PO	A	E	DP
Austin	1.000	12	12	23	0	5
Blomgren	1.000	3	3	7	0	0
Encarnacion, L	1.000	1	1	0	0	0
Encarnacion, Y	.889	6	7	17	3	3
Holy	.962	5	8	17	1	5
Jaworsky	.966	17	24	33	2	8
Nunez	.970	38	49	79	4	9
Perez	.966	9	13	15	1	4
Salas	.950	9	18	20	2	4
Vogel	.955	28	48	58	5	9
Whitaker	.975	10	14	25	1	6

Third Base	PCT	G	PO	A	E	DP
Austin	1.000	3	2	7	0	0
Blomgren	1.000	3	3	3	0	1
Gonzalez	.938	32	13	47	4	3
Lara	.750	3	1	2	1	0
Nunez	.950	29	19	38	3	5
Perez	.923	4	7	5	1	1
Salas	.933	8	4	10	1	0
Vogel	.940	51	31	79	7	4
Whitaker	1.000	4	4	3	0	0

Shortstop	PCT	G	PO	A	E	DP
Blomgren	.938	4	6	9	1	2
Gonzalez	.948	27	32	60	5	13
Holy	.963	19	28	49	3	9
Jaworsky	.961	40	67	82	6	17
Nunez	.957	26	38	51	4	14
Vogel	.933	16	25	31	4	5

Outfield	PCT	G	PO	A	E	DP
Brutcher	.981	45	101	3	2	2
Carrillo	.989	9	50	1	1	
Encarnacion, Y	.972	25	31	4	1	0
Fisher	1.000	6	9	0	0	0
Gomez	.958	81	149	9	7	0
Gonzalez	.969	14	30	1	1	1
Lytle	.950	15	37	1	2	0
Nunez	1.000	3	4	0	0	0
Salas	1.000	6	7	0	0	0
Schiavone	1.000	1	1	0	0	0
Spence	.984	63	125	2	2	0
Sullivan	.972	47	103	3	3	0
Villarroel	1.000	5	4	0	0	0
Whitaker	.970	80	127	3	4	0

FAYETTEVILLE WOODPECKERS
CAROLINA LEAGUE
LOW-A

Batting	B-T	Ht.	Wt.	DOB	AVG	OBP	SLG	G	PA	AB	R	H	2B	3B	HR	RBI	BB	HBP	SH	SF	SO	SB	CS	BB%	SO%
Brutcher, Drew	L-R	6-5	203	2-12-02	.330	.429	.467	54	233	197	37	65	15	3	2	27	34	1	0	1	52	1	2	14.6	22.3
Call, Chase	R-R	6-2	210	5-18-02	.235	.380	.373	30	129	102	18	24	8	0	2	12	22	3	0	2	27	12	3	17.1	20.9
Carrillo, Oliver	R-R	5-11	210	1-19-02	.243	.380	.419	23	92	74	14	18	4	0	3	17	12	5	0	1	23	2	0	13.0	25.0
Cauro, Carlos	R-R	6-2	184	6-14-05	.231	.375	.615	12	32	26	4	6	1	0	3	8	6	0	0	0	12	0	1	18.8	37.5
Daudet, Zach	R-R	6-3	200	6-10-03	.294	.427	.353	30	131	102	19	30	6	0	0	19	25	1	0	3	20	10	4	19.1	15.3
Fisher, Cameron	L-R	6-2	210	6-12-01	.164	.338	.377	56	205	159	29	26	4	0	10	27	37	6	1	2	74	19	6	18.0	36.1
Flores, Ryan	R-R	6-3	205	9-18-05	.190	.292	.286	19	72	63	5	12	3	0	1	5	9	0	0	0	30	2	0	12.5	41.7
Forrester, Brandon	R-R	5-9	171	11-19-03	.177	.239	.210	17	67	62	7	11	0	1	0	9	4	1	0	0	14	4	3	6.0	20.9
Frey, Ethan	R-R	6-5	220	3-15-04	.330	.434	.470	26	122	100	20	33	5	0	3	17	20	0	0	2	25	9	5	16.4	20.5
Hernandez, Alberto	R-R	6-0	169	2-4-04	.225	.312	.302	84	344	298	54	67	11	3	2	46	36	4	1	5	59	24	7	10.5	17.2
Hernandez, Cesar	L-L	6-0	197	4-22-03	.233	.347	.325	65	274	227	39	53	7	1	9	32	36	6	0	5	56	24	11	13.1	20.4
Holy, Max	R-R	6-0	185	7-11-02	.229	.369	.296	68	280	223	42	51	6	3	1	23	48	4	0	4	83	30	8	17.1	29.6
Huezo, Anthony	L-R	6-2	170	11-2-05	.301	.363	.410	22	91	83	14	25	1	1	2	12	8	0	0	0	24	6	3	8.8	26.4
Johnson, Ryan	R-R	6-0	175	12-27-00	.188	.375	.250	6	16	16	3	6	5	0	2	1	2	0	0	0	4	3	0	10.0	20.0
Jones, Greg	S-R	6-2	175	3-7-98	.500	.500	.500	1	2	2	0	1	0	0	0	1	0	0	0	0	1	0	0	0	50.0
Lara, Wilton	R-R	5-11	175	1-21-04	.294	.333	.529	5	18	17	3	5	1	0	1	5	1	0	0	0	5	0	0	5.6	27.8
Luciano, Waner	R-R	6-1	170	1-13-05	.179	.269	.267	82	309	273	43	49	9	0	5	32	26	8	0	2	63	13	3	8.4	20.4
Monistere, Nick	R-R	6-0	192	1-27-04	.168	.254	.248	26	114	101	10	17	2	0	2	16	9	3	0	1	28	5	1	7.9	24.6
Perez, Reylin	S-R	6-2	160	10-5-04	.162	.214	.248	34	113	105	11	17	6	0	1	3	6	1	1	0	40	4	3	5.3	35.4
Powell, Caden	R-R	6-2	208	10-24-03	.239	.344	.404	78	346	297	54	71	15	2	10	43	43	5	0	1	103	32	6	12.4	29.8
Ramirez, German	R-R	6-0	179	7-28-06	.143	.208	.157	21	77	70	7	10	1	0	0	8	5	1	0	1	28	2	0	6.5	36.4

HOUSTON ASTROS

	B-T	Ht.	Wt.	DOB		AVG	G	AB	R	H	2B	3B	HR	RBI	BB	SO	SB	CS	OBP	SLG
Salas, Hector	L-R	5-11	145	3-19-04		.239	.362	.275	33	134	109	13	26	4	0	0	9	18	3	4	0	33	10	6	13.4	24.6
Schiavone, Jason	R-R	6-3	200	3-19-03	.165	.385	.304	70	265	194	39	32	10	1	5	24	58	12	0	1	98	11	3	21.9	37.0
Sosa, Andrews	R-R	5-10	160	1-7-05	.300	.500	.400	4	14	10	4	3	1	0	0	0	4	0	0	0	3	0	0	28.6	21.4
Spence, Lucas	L-L	6-1	190	1-27-03	.286	.450	.377	23	101	77	16	22	5	1	0	4	18	5	1	0	18	11	1	17.8	17.8
Thomas, Justin	R-R	6-0	189	9-29-03	.204	.371	.306	14	62	49	8	10	3	1	0	8	11	2	0	0	13	3	3	17.7	21.0
Trimble, Justin	L-R	6-4	215	6-21-03	.184	.285	.307	55	209	179	22	33	8	1	4	21	21	5	1	2	89	11	1	10.0	42.6
Trujillo, Kedaur	R-R	5-11	188	3-2-04	.185	.305	.277	56	204	173	27	32	4	0	4	16	28	2	1	0	67	3	3	13.7	32.8
Valencia, Esmil	R-R	5-10	182	10-9-05	.263	.325	.357	83	333	300	42	79	9	2	5	36	22	7	0	3	82	50	13	6.6	24.6
Vasquez, Yosweld	R-R	5-9	176	11-8-04	.241	.351	.345	8	37	29	4	7	3	0	0	6	5	1	0	2	7	4	0	13.5	18.9
Villarroel, Jancel	R-R	5-8	176	1-17-05	.258	.360	.385	85	372	314	45	81	16	3	6	45	42	11	0	5	64	20	7	11.3	17.2
Walker, Kyle	R-R	5-9	185	1-11-03	.234	.371	.286	23	97	77	15	18	4	0	0	9	12	6	0	2	15	8	4	12.4	15.5

Pitching	B-T	Ht.	Wt.	DOB	W	L	ERA	G	GS	SV	IP	Hits	Runs	ER	HR	BB	SO	AVG	OBP	SLG	SO%	BB%	BF
Aguilar, Luis	R-R	5-11	176	4-4-04	1	2	5.30	5	3	0	19	20	14	11	2	6	16	.274	.349	.452	19.3	7.2	83
Almonte, Dawill	R-R	5-9	168	10-19-01	3	3	1.97	26	0	4	46	33	19	10	2	17	33	.202	.292	.252	17.8	9.2	185
Apker, Garrett	R-R	6-5	195	9-18-99	0	0	3.86	2	0	0	2	0	1	1	0	4	3	.000	.400	.000	30.0	40.0	10
Baez, Jhoster	R-R	6-3	205	12-11-04	0	0	11.57	2	0	0	2	3	3	3	0	3	3	.300	.462	.400	23.1	23.1	13
Bolton, Cody	R-R	6-3	230	6-19-98	0	0	6.00	1	1	0	3	6	2	2	1	0	1	.462	.462	.846	7.7	0.0	13
Brown, Cameron	L-R	6-2	165	5-12-98	6	3	2.43	27	0	4	41	29	16	11	1	18	41	.200	.302	.283	24.0	10.5	171
Burleson, Grant	R-R	6-3	205	9-12-02	1	1	1.93	2	0	0	5	1	2	1	0	4	5	.071	.278	.071	27.8	22.2	18
Carrera, Jesus	R-R	5-11	160	11-27-04	0	1	4.50	6	1	3	22	19	11	11	1	8	29	.229	.309	.289	30.9	8.5	94
Carrillo, Oliver	R-R	5-11	210	1-19-02	0	0	0.00	1	0	0	1	0	0	0	0	0	0	.200	.200	.400	0.0	0.0	5
Cauro, Carlos	R-R	6-2	184	6-14-05	0	0	0.00	2	0	0	1	1	0	0	0	0	1	.250	.200	.500	20.0	0.0	5
Cruz, Anthony	R-R	5-11	179	8-19-02	7	3	3.75	20	9	1	84	72	36	35	6	42	84	.231	.340	.337	23.0	11.5	365
David, Ramsey	R-R	6-3	190	2-8-01	3	4	3.86	13	11	0	51	35	24	22	5	34	51	.206	.350	.324	23.5	15.7	217
DeVos, Nolan	R-R	6-0	185	8-11-00	0	0	3.00	1	1	0	3	1	1	1	1	5	1	.111	.200	.444	45.5	9.1	11
Frias, Francisco	R-R	5-11	190	10-15-04	4	6	3.09	32	0	4	58	39	23	20	3	32	60	.188	.317	.300	24.0	12.8	250
Garcia, Luis	R-R	5-11	244	12-13-96	0	0	0.00	1	0	0	2	0	0	0	0	0	2	.000	.000	.000	33.3	0.0	6
Gonzalez, Rafael	R-R	5-11	195	7-18-04	3	7	4.05	16	10	1	60	53	29	27	3	35	57	.248	.369	.346	21.8	13.4	262
Hebert, Curtis	R-R	6-1	175	8-22-03	0	0	0.00	4	0	1	4	1	0	0	0	2	5	.063	.167	.063	27.8	11.1	18
Hertzler, Cole	R-R	6-4	235	6-21-03	0	0	1.13	4	4	0	16	12	3	2	0	6	22	.211	.297	.263	34.4	9.4	64
Howard, Dylan	R-R	6-2	195	5-3-03	2	1	3.45	8	6	2	31	31	12	12	0	9	28	.261	.323	.311	21.4	6.9	131
Landeta, David	R-R	6-3	244	3-28-03	1	2	5.00	6	0	1	18	17	14	10	0	16	14	.254	.384	.299	15.9	18.2	88
Martich, Eurys	R-R	6-3	206	8-20-02	1	0	1.08	6	0	1	17	7	3	2	0	14	28	.135	.324	.135	41.2	20.6	68
Mayer, Bryce	R-R	6-3	210	2-11-02	0	0	4.08	5	3	0	18	17	8	8	1	6	30	.254	.342	.373	39.0	7.8	77
McPherson, Brandon	R-R	6-3	225	3-23-00	2	0	3.54	6	2	2	20	10	8	8	1	10	23	.145	.272	.217	28.4	12.3	81
Mercedes, Abel	R-R	6-1	185	6-29-02	2	0	4.35	30	0	2	41	29	24	20	1	48	66	.203	.426	.252	32.7	23.8	202
Ogando, Joan	R-R	6-1	179	5-23-04	8	4	4.07	25	13	1	95	55	45	43	5	69	113	.170	.345	.266	27.2	16.6	416
Palmer, Twine	R-R	6-5	200	8-31-04	2	0	2.13	13	8	0	42	26	14	10	0	22	44	.172	.286	.192	25.1	12.6	175
Perez, Javier	R-R	6-1	220	12-22-03	1	2	4.85	6	3	0	26	29	15	14	2	3	22	.284	.305	.402	20.8	2.8	106
Pinto, Jean	R-R	5-11	175	1-9-01	0	0	6.00	1	1	0	3	4	3	2	0	2	2	.333	.429	.333	14.3	14.3	14
Ras, Tyler	S-R	6-4	205	11-9-99	1	1	8.44	5	0	0	5	9	7	5	2	0	7	.375	.375	.708	29.2	0.0	24
Rodriguez, Luis	R-R	6-2	181	12-29-03	5	0	2.70	19	12	1	83	66	26	25	8	38	72	.218	.333	.330	20.5	10.8	352
Rodriguez, Raimy	R-R	6-1	185	7-16-05	4	7	4.95	26	20	0	93	65	59	51	8	73	94	.198	.355	.295	22.7	17.6	415
Rosario, Leomar	R-R	6-6	217	6-11-03	2	2	4.71	17	1	1	42	29	25	22	3	33	56	.187	.339	.290	29.0	17.1	193
Smith, Parker	R-R	6-3	215	3-5-03	5	3	3.32	15	12	0	60	58	31	22	0	25	55	.258	.341	.311	21.6	9.8	255
Smith, Ryan	R-R	6-2	195	11-15-02	3	5	3.13	34	0	4	55	52	28	19	5	41	56	.254	.391	.385	21.9	16.0	256
Tredwell, Alonzo	L-R	6-6	230	5-8-02	1	3	3.94	12	8	0	48	36	22	21	6	21	52	.213	.314	.367	26.7	10.8	195
Trimble, Justin	L-R	6-4	215	6-21-03	0	0	0.00	1	0	0	2	0	0	0	0	0	0	.333	.333	.667	0.0	0.0	6
Trujillo, Kedaur	R-R	5-11	188	3-2-04	0	1	2.45	2	0	0	4	1	1	1	0	3	1	.125	.267	.125	6.7	20.0	15
Varela, Jose	R-R	6-1	183	10-29-04	0	2	3.75	4	0	1	12	9	7	5	0	6	12	.209	.294	.256	23.5	11.8	51
Vasquez, Yosweld	R-R	5-9	176	11-8-04	0	0	9.00	1	0	0	1	1	1	1	1	0	0	.250	.250	1.000	0.0	0.0	4
Verdugo, Ryan	R-R	6-2	205	1-26-03	0	2	14.29	3	3	0	6	6	9	1	8	9	.261	.452	.478	29.0	25.8	31

Fielding

Catcher	PCT	G	PO	A	E	DP	PB
Cauro	1.000	3	21	3	0	0	1
Flores	.992	12	117	8	1	0	1
Schiavone	.980	55	476	52	11	5	4
Sosa	.941	3	13	3	1	0	0
Trujillo	.953	13	91	10	5	1	2
Vasquez	.974	7	68	6	2	0	0
Villarroel	.977	48	440	36	11	1	11

First Base	PCT	G	PO	A	E	DP
Carrillo	.986	11	66	5	1	4
Cauro	1.000	3	8	0	0	0
Daudet	.993	21	126	11	1	9
Fisher	.988	14	75	4	1	4
Flores	1.000	6	45	1	0	2
Hernandez, A	.989	10	84	2	1	10
Lara	1.000	3	27	0	0	2
Monistere	.933	2	13	1	1	1
Schiavone	.975	12	68	9	2	7
Trimble	.995	28	171	17	1	17

Second Base	PCT	G	PO	A	E	DP
Daudet	1.000	2	4	2	0	0
Forrester	.947	5	4	14	1	2
Hernandez, A	.958	35	50	86	6	18
Holy	1.000	20	37	49	0	7
Johnson	1.000	1	1	3	0	1
Lara	1.000	1	1	0	0	0
Luciano	.967	16	25	33	2	5
Monistere	1.000	3	6	8	0	4
Perez	1.000	5	7	7	0	1
Powell	.923	9	17	19	3	2
Ramirez	.944	7	14	20	2	5
Salas	.940	14	16	31	3	6
Villarroel	.964	7	15	12	1	6
Walker	.968	15	24	36	2	3

Third Base	PCT	G	PO	A	E	DP
Daudet	.857	5	3	9	2	3
Trujillo	.983	34	213	22	4	19
Forrester	1.000	4	1	1	0	0
Hernandez, A	1.000	3	1	1	0	1
Johnson	1.000	1	2	1	0	0
Luciano	.938	62	47	88	9	15
Monistere	.938	7	6	9	1	1
Perez	.909	4	5	5	1	1
Powell	.846	21	13	20	6	3
Ramirez	.929	6	3	10	1	1
Salas	1.000	5	3	11	0	1
Trimble	.961	25	20	29	2	0

Shortstop	PCT	G	PO	A	E	DP
Daudet	1.000	2	3	5	0	0
Forrester	1.000	6	5	12	0	3
Hernandez, A	1.000	14	11	32	0	5
Holy	.974	44	90	98	5	22
Johnson	1.000	1	1	1	0	1
Jones	1.000	1	1	0	0	0
Monistere	.909	8	7	13	2	2
Perez	.857	5	7	5	2	2

	PCT	G	PO	A	E	DP
Powell	.918	40	53	59	10	11
Ramirez	.917	6	6	5	1	0
Salas	.818	4	2	7	2	1
Walker	1.000	5	5	4	0	0
Call	.973	29	65	8	2	0
Carrillo	1.000	6	5	0	0	0
Fisher	.967	37	56	3	2	1
Frey	1.000	23	42	1	0	0
Hernandez, C	.974	59	72	2	2	1
Hernandez, A	.968	16	29	1	1	0
Huezo	.982	22	51	3	1	1
Luciano	.000	1	0	0	0	0
Perez	.927	21	33	5	3	1
Salas	1.000	6	7	0	0	0
Spence	1.000	22	38	0	0	0
Thomas	1.000	13	28	1	0	0
Valencia	.960	78	163	7	7	4
Villarroel	.943	18	30	3	2	0

Outfield	PCT	G	PO	A	E	DP
Brutcher	.986	43	68	3	1	0

FCL ASTROS ROOKIE
FLORIDA COMPLEX LEAGUE

Batting	B-T	Ht.	Wt.	DOB	AVG	OBP	SLG	G	PA	AB	R	H	2B	3B	HR	RBI	BB	HBP	SH	SF	SO	SB	CS	BB%	SO%
Baez, Luis	R-R	6-1	205	1-11-04	.333	.429	.667	2	7	6	1	2	2	0	0	1	1	0	0	0	1	0	1	14.3	14.3
Blomgren, Jack	R-R	5-10	180	9-27-98	.263	.516	.421	9	31	19	2	5	0	0	1	8	9	2	0	1	5	1	1	29.0	16.1
Caldera, Fernando	R-R	5-11	170	10-10-02	.300	.391	.450	8	23	20	3	6	1	1	0	2	2	1	0	0	7	0	0	8.7	30.4
De Leon, Darwin	R-R	5-9	156	10-31-03	.271	.417	.375	19	62	48	11	13	3	1	0	7	12	0	0	0	10	2	2	19.4	16.1
Deming, Austin	R-R	6-0	200	12-21-99	.143	.400	.143	3	10	7	2	1	0	0	0	0	3	0	0	0	3	0	0	30.0	30.0
Encarnacion, Yamal	S-R	5-8	150	9-8-03	.208	.387	.250	9	31	24	3	5	1	0	0	2	7	0	0	0	7	4	3	22.6	22.6
Flores, Arturo	R-R	6-3	205	9-18-05	.306	.409	.472	13	44	36	9	11	2	2	0	8	7	0	0	1	11	0	0	15.9	25.0
Gonzalez, Jose	L-L	6-0	215	8-15-00	.000	.400	.000	1	5	3	1	0	0	0	0	0	1	1	0	0	1	0	0	20.0	20.0
Hernandez, Alberto	R-R	6-0	169	2-4-04	.250	.250	.500	2	4	4	0	1	1	0	0	0	0	0	0	0	1	0	0	0.0	25.0
Huezo, Anthony	L-R	6-2	170	11-2-05	.231	.371	.485	43	160	130	28	30	9	3	6	26	19	10	0	0	51	12	3	11.9	31.9
Johnson, Ryan	R-R	6-0	175	12-27-00	.000	.333	.000	1	3	1	1	0	0	0	0	0	1	1	0	0	1	0	0	33.3	33.3
Jones, Greg	S-R	6-2	175	3-7-98	.429	.692	.429	4	13	7	4	3	0	0	0	0	2	5	1	0	0	2	5	0	38.5	15.4
Lara, Wilton	R-R	5-11	175	1-21-04	.196	.278	.412	35	116	102	17	20	4	0	6	20	9	3	1	1	43	2	0	7.8	37.1
Leon, Pedro	R-R	5-8	170	5-28-98	.333	.333	1.083	3	12	12	3	4	0	0	3	5	0	0	0	0	5	0	0	0.0	41.7
McCormick, Chas	R-L	6-0	208	4-19-95	.667	.750	1.667	1	4	3	1	2	0	0	1	2	1	0	0	0	0	0	0	25.0	0.0
Ochoa, Nehomar	R-R	6-4	210	7-31-05	.143	.182	.143	6	22	21	2	3	0	0	0	3	1	0	0	0	8	0	0	4.5	36.4
Palma, Miguel	R-R	5-8	170	1-4-02	.158	.385	.316	8	26	19	5	3	0	0	1	4	6	1	0	0	8	0	0	23.1	30.8
Pereira, Sandro	S-R	5-7	147	9-30-05	.214	.408	.286	19	76	56	15	12	2	1	0	14	12	7	0	1	15	7	4	15.8	19.7
Perez, Reylin	S-R	6-2	160	5-25-05	.353	.167		6	17	12	2	1	1	0	0	0	4	1	0	0	8	1	1	23.5	47.1
Powell, Caden	R-R	6-2	208	10-24-03	.083	.400	.083	6	20	12	1	1	0	0	0	1	5	2	0	1	7	0	0	25.0	35.0
Pratt, Karniel	R-R	5-10	170	1-3-05	.283	.452	.326	20	62	46	10	13	2	0	0	6	12	3	0	1	9	11	4	19.4	14.5
Quintana, Roiner	R-R	5-11	157	6-20-05	.273	.392	.364	24	79	66	15	18	4	1	0	9	11	2	0	0	14	3	4	13.9	17.7
Ramirez, German	R-R	6-0	179	7-28-06	.245	.340	.417	48	191	163	26	40	11	4	3	29	20	5	0	3	41	4	2	10.5	21.5
Rives, Luis	S-L	6-2	216	10-14-04	.207	.393	.402	34	117	87	20	18	2	3	8	25	20	3	0	2	33	9	0	21.4	28.2
Salas, Hector	L-R	5-11	145	3-19-04	.284	.454	.405	22	97	74	25	21	4	1	1	10	23	0	0	0	16	3	0	23.7	16.5
Sierra, Juan	R-R	6-1	208	12-8-03	.402	.402	.402	31	122	97	17	28	5	0	2	18	19	2	0	4	26	1	2	15.6	21.3
Sosa, Andrews	R-R	5-10	160	1-7-05	.217	.313	.348	27	80	69	9	15	4	1	1	10	9	1	0	1	27	1	1	11.3	33.8
Trammell, Taylor	L-L	6-2	220	9-13-97	.400	.474	.733	5	19	15	6	6	2	0	1	5	3	0	0	1	4	2	0	15.8	21.1
Travinski, Hayden	R-R	6-3	218	10-17-00	.188	.395	.188	15	43	32	7	6	0	0	0	2	10	1	0	0	2	0	0	23.3	27.9
Vasquez, Yosweld	R-R	5-9	176	11-8-04	.248	.355	.390	36	124	105	22	26	3	0	4	14	12	6	0	1	27	0	0	9.7	21.8
Wagner, Ethan	R-R	6-0	215	8-5-05	.229	.333	.374	41	153	131	25	30	5	1	4	21	19	2	0	1	37	2	3	12.4	24.2
Williams, Jeron	R-R	6-1	180	9-29-00	.231	.276	.269	8	29	26	5	6	1	0	0	2	2	0	0	1	1	2	0	6.9	3.4

Pitching	B-T	Ht.	Wt.	DOB	W	L	ERA	G	GS	SV	IP	Hits	Runs	ER	HR	BB	SO	AVG	OBP	SLG	SO%	BB%	BF
Aguilar, Luis	R-R	5-11	176	4-4-04	5	1	2.05	12	4	1	44	29	15	10	5	14	49	.188	.263	.318	28.5	8.1	172
Baez, Jhoster	R-R	6-3	205	12-11-04	2	2	6.67	13	1	1	30	27	22	22	4	21	40	.241	.366	.393	29.9	15.7	134
Beck, Jagger	S-R	6-6	205	11-28-06	1	1	5.40	3	1	0	10	9	7	6	2	6	14	.237	.341	.421	31.8	13.6	44
Brockhouse, Walker	R-R	6-4	197	2-22-99	0	0	0.00	1	0	0	2	2	1	0	0	1	4	.286	.375	.286	50.0	12.5	8
Carrera, Jesus	R-R	5-11	160	11-27-04	2	0	0.98	7	3	0	18	11	2	2	0	3	33	.159	.205	.232	45.2	4.1	73
Diaz, Norbis	R-R	6-0	165	8-10-04	3	1	6.41	13	0	2	27	28	21	19	5	23	32	.264	.409	.434	24.2	17.4	132
Fraide, Juan	R-R	5-11	161	4-18-06	2	1	4.20	5	2	0	15	13	7	7	0	8	12	.250	.344	.308	19.7	13.1	61
France, J.P.	R-R	6-0	216	4-4-95	0	0	0.00	1	1	0	2	0	0	0	1	2	.400	.571	.800	28.6	14.3	7
Gaither, Ray	R-R	6-4	224	3-4-98	0	1	7.71	3	2	0	2	1	3	2	0	1	1	.125	.273	.375	9.1	9.1	11
Garcia, Luis	R-R	5-11	244	12-13-96	0	0	2.25	2	2	0	4	3	1	1	0	0	7	.214	.214	.429	50.0	0.0	14
Gonzalez, Rafael	R-R	5-11	195	7-18-04	0	0	15.00	2	1	0	3	5	5	1	4	2	.182	.471	.545	11.8	23.5	17
Huezo, Anthony	L-R	6-2	170	11-2-05	0	0	0.00	1	0	0	1	0	0	0	0	1	0	.000	.000	.000	0.0	0.0	5
Javier, Cristian	R-R	6-1	213	3-26-97	0	1	13.50	1	1	0	1	3	2	0	3	2	.200	.500	.400	25.0	37.5	8
Landeta, David	R-R	6-2	244	3-28-03	1	0	1.08	10	6	1	25	10	7	3	0	8	31	.136	.232	.148	31.3	8.1	99
Leach, Hudson	R-R	6-3	220	6-16-02	1	0	8.10	3	0	0	3	1	3	3	0	5	6	.100	.400	.100	40.0	33.3	15
Martich, Eurys	R-R	6-3	206	8-20-02	4	3	4.50	12	3	1	36	29	24	18	2	24	37	.215	.342	.304	23.0	14.9	161
McPherson, Brandon	R-R	6-3	225	3-23-00	1	0	0.00	2	1	0	7	2	0	0	0	1	10	.083	.120	.083	40.0	4.0	25
Mikulski, Matt	L-L	6-4	205	5-8-99	0	0	16.88	3	0	0	5	6	5	5	1	5	.385	.579	.769	5.3	26.3	19
Nezuh, Jackson	R-R	6-1	180	2-11-02	0	0	2.08	2	1	0	4	2	2	1	1	3	5	.154	.313	.385	31.3	18.8	16
Pecko, Ethan	R-R	6-2	195	8-25-02	0	0	4.50	1	1	0	2	1	1	1	0	0	2	.250	.250	.250	25.0	0.0	8
Pena, Alain	R-R	5-11	155	4-10-03	1	0	0.00	3	2	0	6	0	0	0	0	4	7	.105	.261	.158	30.4	17.4	23
Perez, Javier	R-R	6-1	220	12-22-03	6	0	1.69	13	5	0	43	34	10	8	3	8	48	.215	.253	.329	28.9	4.8	166
Perez, Reylin	S-R	6-2	160	10-5-04	0	0	13.50	1	0	0	1	1	1	1	0	2	1	.333	.600	.333	20.0	40.0	5
Pichardo, Jank	R-R	6-1	170	8-4-04	0	0	8.10	1	0	0	3	3	3	3	2	3	4	.231	.375	.692	25.0	18.8	16
Pinto, Jean	R-R	5-11	175	1-9-01	0	0	1.04	3	2	0	9	4	1	1	0	2	11	.038	.107	.038	39.3	7.1	28
Quintana, Roiner	R-R	5-11	157	6-20-05	0	0	0.00	2	0	0	2	0	2	0	0	1	1	.000	.143	.000	14.3	14.3	7
Ramos, Porfirio	R-R	5-10	163	12-3-03	1	2	7.63	10	2	0	25	27	15	16	6	13	37	14	.286	.359	.500	21.2	10.6	66
Rodning, Brody	R-L	6-1	185	1-14-96	0	0	13.50	2	0	0	1	2	2	2	0	2	0	.400	.571	.800	0.0	28.6	7

Batting	B-T	Ht.	Wt.	DOB	G	GS	AVG	OBP	SLG	G	PA	AB	R	H	2B	3B	HR	RBI	BB	HBP	SH	SF	SO	SB	CS	BB%	SO%

(Continued from previous page — Houston Astros)

Player	B-T	Ht	Wt	DOB			AVG	OBP	SLG																		
Rosario, Leomar	R-R	6-6	217	6-11-03	0	0	2.57	4	4	0	7	4	4	2	0	7	9	.167	.355	.167	29.0	22.6	31				
Salas, Hector	L-R	5-11	145	3-19-04	1	0	13.50	2	0	0	1	2	2	2	0	2	1	.333	.500	.333	12.5	25.0	8				
Serrano, Jose	R-R	6-2	212	2-14-04	2	1	3.86	10	0	0	12	9	5	5	1	5	14	.196	.275	.261	27.5	9.8	51				
Smith, Parker	R-R	6-3	215	3-5-03	0	0	2.08	3	2	0	9	5	3	2	0	5	8	.172	.314	.207	22.2	13.9	36				
Sosa, Andrews	R-R	5-10	160	1-7-05	0	0	0.00	2	0	1	1	1	0	0	0	1	1	.250	.400	.250	20.0	20.0	5				
Swanson, Nic	R-R	6-2	180	7-8-99	0	0	0.00	2	2	0	5	3	0	0	0	0	7	.167	.167	.167	38.9	0.0	18				
True, Derek	R-R	6-2	180	4-25-01	0	1	10.80	1	1	0	2	2	2	2	1	1	3	.286	.375	.714	37.5	12.5	8				
Varela, Jose	R-R	6-1	183	10-29-04	3	0	2.81	8	2	1	26	14	10	8	1	15	27	.161	.291	.230	26.2	14.6	103				
Vasquez, Yoswald	R-R	5-9	176	11-8-04	0	0	0.00	1	0	0	1	1	1	0	0	1	2	.250	.500	.250	33.3	16.7	6				
Verdugo, Ryan	R-R	6-2	205	1-26-03	0	0	0.00	1	1	0	2	1	0	0	0	0	1	.143	.250	.143	12.5	0.0	8				
Wagner, Ethan	R-R	6-0	215	8-5-05	0	1	27.00	1	0	0	0	2	1	0	3	0	0	.000	.750	.000	0.0	75.0	4				
Wohlgemuth, Nate	R-R	5-11	210	5-30-01	1	0	1.50	8	0	2	12	7	3	2	0	5	20	.171	.320	.220	40.0	10.0	50				

Fielding
C: Vasquez 24, Sosa 14, Flores 6, Travinski 6, Caldera 4, Palma 4. **1B:** Lara 11, Vasquez 10, Sierra 9, Travinski 7, Flores 6, Sosa 6, Caldera 2, De Leon 2, Palma 2, Baez 1, Deming 1, Salas 1. **2B:** De Leon 14, Pereira 10, Quintana 9, Salas 6, Sosa 6, Williams 4, Lara 3, Perez 3, Encarnacion 2, Hernandez 2, Jones 2, Ramirez 2, Blomgren 1. **3B:** Ramirez 17, Lara 15, Salas 8, Blomgren 4, De Leon 3, Pereira 3, Deming 2, Perez 2, Powell 2, Sosa 1. **SS:** Ramirez 28, Salas 8, Blomgren 4, Lara 4, Powell 4, Williams 3, Pereira 2, De Leon 1, Johnson 1, Jones 1, Perez 1. **LF:** Rives 17, Huezo 10, Pratt 9, Wagner 7, Sierra 3, Encarnacion 2, Quintana 2, Baez 1, Gonzalez 1, Leon 1, Ochoa 1, Perez 1, Trammell 1. **CF:** Huezo 23, Wagner 20, Encarnacion 3, Trammell 3, Leon 2, Pratt 2, Quintana 2, Jones 1, McCormick 1, Rives 1. **RF:** Sierra 15, Wagner 10, Quintana 2, Huezo 6, Pratt 5, Rives 5, Ochoa 3, Encarnacion 1, Varela 1

DSL ASTROS BLUE — ROOKIE
DOMINICAN SUMMER LEAGUE

Batting	B-T	Ht.	Wt.	DOB	AVG	OBP	SLG	G	PA	AB	R	H	2B	3B	HR	RBI	BB	HBP	SH	SF	SO	SB	CS	BB%	SO%
Alvarez, Kevin	L-L	6-4	184	1-13-08	.301	.419	.455	47	192	156	31	47	12	3	2	33	23	10	1	2	19	11	5	12.0	9.9
Caldera, Francisco	R-R	6-1	193	3-9-06	.222	.371	.556	9	35	27	8	6	1	1	2	9	7	0	0	1	11	0	1	20.0	31.4
Castellano, Alejandro	R-R	5-8	159	9-24-06	.194	.342	.226	26	76	62	10	12	2	0	0	5	14	0	0	0	19	1	3	18.4	25.0
Colon, Christian	R-R	6-2	170	10-9-07	.194	.306	.194	11	36	31	4	6	0	0	0	1	5	0	0	0	11	2	0	13.9	30.6
De La Cruz, Jose	R-R	6-0	175	10-30-07	.195	.409	.220	37	115	82	16	16	2	0	0	7	25	6	0	2	34	7	6	21.7	29.6
De Leon, Luis	R-R	5-10	210	1-15-07	.262	.338	.446	38	148	130	23	34	12	0	4	30	11	5	0	2	21	5	3	7.4	14.2
Garcia, Ire	R-R	6-0	183	10-8-07	.213	.388	.270	33	116	89	22	19	5	0	0	15	25	1	0	1	13	9	0	21.6	11.2
Gonzalez, Cristopfer	R-R	6-5	167	7-20-05	.169	.325	.250	43	154	124	22	21	2	1	2	24	24	5	0	1	52	4	3	15.6	33.8
Lebron, Ariel	R-R	5-11	148	5-18-05	.299	.436	.425	28	111	87	24	26	8	0	1	11	13	9	1	1	20	16	1	11.7	18.0
Manzueta, Sami	R-R	5-10	165	8-21-08	.224	.405	.392	46	195	143	33	32	9	5	2	24	42	5	0	5	36	7	5	21.5	18.5
Martinez, Santiago	R-R	6-0	170	10-9-07	.270	.452	.303	41	168	122	26	33	4	0	0	14	39	4	0	3	27	17	8	23.2	16.1
Millan, Anthony	R-R	5-11	170	5-13-08	.000	.000	.000	2	5	5	0	0	0	0	0	0	0	0	0	0	4	0	0	0.0	80.0
Morgado, Leandro	R-R	5-10	155	2-16-07	.200	.237	.229	9	38	35	7	7	1	0	0	6	2	0	0	0	8	6	1	5.3	21.1
Mota, Eric	R-R	6-0	174	12-6-07	.223	.345	.309	36	113	94	19	21	3	1	1	11	18	0	0	1	29	10	1	15.9	25.7
Perez, Eduardo	R-R	6-4	214	7-24-06	.176	.263	.353	4	19	17	3	3	0	0	1	2	2	0	0	0	8	0	0	10.5	42.1
Puello, Cliuver	L-R	5-11	162	5-3-07	.200	.320	.224	32	103	85	17	17	2	0	0	5	13	3	0	2	23	5	3	12.6	22.3
Quesada, Luis	R-R	6-2	193	1-18-05	.272	.421	.427	37	133	103	19	28	5	1	3	22	23	5	0	2	27	3	0	17.3	20.3
Quiroz, Alexi	R-R	6-0	205	10-26-06	.208	.424	.292	34	99	72	15	15	3	0	1	6	21	6	0	0	17	3	1	21.2	17.2
Ramirez, Amauri	L-L	6-2	203	1-24-07	.222	.343	.333	46	175	144	23	32	8	1	2	15	21	7	0	3	46	5	6	12.0	26.30

Pitching	B-T	Ht.	Wt.	DOB	W	L	ERA	G	GS	SV	IP	Hits	Runs	ER	HR	BB	SO	AVG	OBP	SLG	SO%	BB%	BF
Amador, Luis	R-R	6-4	185	9-15-07	2	1	4.40	14	4	1	31	25	15	15	1	14	26	.227	.331	.309	20.0	10.8	130
Ardines, Adrian	R-R	6-0	186	10-16-06	5	1	1.91	13	5	2	42	32	12	9	1	7	56	.211	.247	.250	34.4	4.3	163
Castellano, Alejandro	R-R	5-8	159	9-24-06	0	0	13.50	1	0	0	1	2	3	1	0	1	0	.500	.600	.750	0.0	20.0	5
Damian, Omar	R-R	6-2	161	7-5-08	2	1	5.17	13	6	1	38	31	24	22	4	24	48	.226	.363	.328	28.6	14.3	168
Delgado, Antonio	R-R	6-5	195	6-13-07	3	0	1.17	7	1	1	15	8	3	2	0	8	27	.154	.267	.231	45.0	13.3	60
Gantes, Anthony	R-R	6-1	165	11-25-05	1	1	2.00	6	4	0	18	13	4	4	0	7	12	.210	.319	.242	16.7	9.7	72
Gonzalez, Alex	R-R	6-3	225	1-2-06	1	1	5.24	14	7	0	34	28	22	20	1	32	29	.230	.396	.320	18.0	19.9	161
Gonzalez, Rafael	R-R	5-11	173	7-31-05	2	3	8.53	13	0	1	19	17	20	18	0	25	13	.254	.480	.328	12.9	24.8	101
Mendoza, Frankelys	R-R	6-2	190	1-24-07	1	2	6.58	16	0	0	26	29	24	19	2	19	20	.274	.408	.443	15.4	14.6	130
Mieses, Juan	R-R	6-1	200	3-31-06	4	1	3.22	12	3	0	34	18	13	12	0	21	43	.248	.356	.307	26.2	12.8	164
Mota, Eddy	R-R	6-3	210	2-13-04	5	0	2.79	13	3	0	42	33	17	13	1	14	34	.221	.292	.322	20.2	8.3	168
Nunez, Jesus	R-R	6-4	220	9-28-05	0	2	27.00	4	3	0	3	11	12	10	0	5	3	.550	.630	.800	11.1	18.5	27
Obregon, Ismael	R-R	5-11	181	10-27-07	2	4	4.12	13	4	1	39	38	26	18	3	15	41	.247	.324	.351	23.7	8.7	173
Quiroz, Alexi	R-R	6-0	205	10-26-06	0	0	0.00	1	0	0	0	0	0	0	0	0	0	.000	.000	.000	0.0	0.0	1
Ruiz, Adrian	R-R	5-11	196	5-12-07	1	2	7.08	13	3	0	20	18	16	0	19	12	.320	.490	.373	11.5	18.3	104
Salazar, Mario	R-R	6-2	195	1-11-05	0	2	4.11	6	3	0	15	10	8	7	0	15	13	.192	.400	.212	18.3	21.1	71
Santana, Jorman	R-R	6-4	190	11-17-06	0	2	6.82	13	5	1	30	28	24	23	0	24	28	.257	.401	.294	17.4	16.7	138
Santana, Kevin	R-R	6-4	175	1-18-07	0	2	14.54	4	4	0	4	4	7	7	1	7	7	.250	.478	.438	30.4	30.4	23
Sosa, Jesus	R-R	6-1	146	10-26-07	2	0	1.14	16	0	4	24	17	6	3	0	16	19	.205	.353	.253	18.6	15.7	102

Fielding
C: De Leon 23, Garcia 16, Castellano 15, Quiroz 15, Mota 1. **1B:** Garcia 16, Quiroz 11, Castellano 10, De Leon 9, De La Cruz 7, Quesada 6, Gonzalez 4, Mota 3, Caldera 1, Colon 1. **2B:** Manzueta 19, De La Cruz 12, Puello 10, Martinez 9, Mota 9, Colon 1. **3B:** Manzueta 19, De La Cruz 14, Martinez 11, Mota 9, Puello 8. **SS:** Martinez 20, Puello 14, Mota 13, Colon 8, Manzueta 5. **LF:** Gonzalez 16, Ramirez 13, Quesada 12, Lebron 9, Alvarez 7, Morgado 4. **CF:** Alvarez 23, Ramirez 13, Lebron 2, Gonzalez 9, Millan 2. **RF:** Ramirez 20, Gonzalez 13, Quesada 13, Lebron 8, Alvarez 5, Morgado 4

DSL ASTROS ORANGE — ROOKIE
DOMINICAN SUMMER LEAGUE

Batting	B-T	Ht.	Wt.	DOB	AVG	OBP	SLG	G	PA	AB	R	H	2B	3B	HR	RBI	BB	HBP	SH	SF	SO	SB	CS	BB%	SO%
Areinamo, Anderson	R-R	5-9	135	5-4-07	.300	.413	.465	51	208	170	40	51	10	0	6	30	28	6	2	2	34	18	0	13.5	16.3
Brito, Samuel	R-R	5-11	170	2-1-07	.246	.411	.298	21	73	57	18	14	3	0	0	7	13	3	0	0	16	5	0	17.8	21.9
Campos, Diego	R-R	6-1	192	10-30-06	.302	.384	.438	33	112	96	16	29	5	1	2	24	11	3	0	2	23	1	0	9.8	20.5
Castellano, Alejandro	R-R	5-8	159	9-24-06	.263	.440	.368	7	25	19	4	5	2	0	0	2	4	2	0	0	4	1	0	16.0	16.0
Castro, Esteban	R-R	5-10	185	2-20-08	.145	.325	.194	28	80	62	10	9	0	0	1	6	10	7	0	1	26	0	0	12.5	32.5
Colon, Christian	R-R	6-2	170	10-9-07	.167	.239	.200	23	67	60	5	10	2	0	0	5	5	1	0	1	16	0	0	7.5	23.9
De La Cruz, Yensi	L-R	6-2	170	5-31-07	.280	.378	.457	53	217	186	37	52	8	5	5	40	28	2	0	1	39	18	3	12.9	18.0
Flores, Miguel	R-R	6-0	177	6-18-05	.241	.344	.324	39	125	108	16	26	4	1	1	13	13	4	0	0	13	0	0	10.4	10.4
Gonzalez, Emilio	R-R	6-0	186	3-26-08	.209	.414	.279	16	58	43	6	9	3	0	0	7	9	6	0	0	10	2	0	15.5	17.2
Martinez, Pablo	R-R	5-1	165	1-18-08	.266	.398	.339	53	221	177	46	47	6	2	1	22	29	12	0	3	30	21	4	13.1	13.6
Matos, Edwilmin	R-R	6-2	194	1-19-08	.231	.336	.296	34	128	108	18	25	4	0	1	14	14	4	0	2	29	0	0	10.9	22.7
Millan, Anthony	R-R	5-11	170	5-13-08	.290	.420	.435	40	162	131	25	38	5	4	2	26	26	4	0	1	30	13	1	16.0	18.5
Morgado, Leandro	R-R	5-10	155	2-16-07	.165	.255	.198	30	102	91	6	15	1	1	0	7	8	3	0	0	14	6	3	7.8	13.7
Perez, Eduardo	R-R	6-4	214	7-24-06	.167	.262	.250	11	42	36	5	6	0	0	1	5	4	1	0	1	15	0	0	9.5	35.7
Puello, Cliuver	L-R	5-11	162	5-3-07	.143	.250	.143	7	16	14	3	2	0	0	0	1	1	0	0	0	2	1	0	6.3	12.5
Ramos, Freddy	R-R	6-0	175	5-20-08	.215	.311	.228	29	90	79	12	17	1	0	0	8	7	4	0	0	25	7	4	7.8	27.8
Rojas, Juan	L-R	6-1	190	1-19-08	.286	.457	.374	50	199	147	34	42	5	1	2	28	44	5	0	3	37	11	5	22.1	18.6
Romero, Esteban	L-R	6-2	180	12-1-06	.296	.408	.309	28	98	81	12	24	1	0	0	9	15	1	0	1	9	1	0	15.3	9.2
Silverio, Franchely	R-R	6-2	201	11-19-06	.205	.262	.308	11	42	39	5	8	1	0	1	6	2	1	0	0	16	0	0	4.8	38.1

Pitching	B-T	Ht.	Wt.	DOB	W	L	ERA	G	GS	SV	IP	Hits	Runs	ER	HR	BB	SO	AVG	OBP	SLG	SO%	BB%	BF
Balza, Miguel	R-R	6-0	195	5-21-04	2	1	4.64	7	5	0	21	13	12	11	1	10	27	.178	.286	.274	32.1	11.9	84
Borquez, Nick	R-R	6-1	186	7-27-06	0	1	3.60	3	1	0	10	7	4	4	3	3	13	.200	.317	.457	31.0	7.1	42
Cova, Dayerson	R-R	6-1	175	2-27-08	2	3	11.08	10	1	0	13	10	16	16	3	14	11	.213	.431	.404	16.9	21.5	65
De Los Santos, Ronald	R-R	6-1	182	11-16-07	1	0	11.40	13	0	0	15	17	24	19	3	24	12	.283	.494	.500	13.5	27.0	89
Flores, Miguel	R-R	6-0	177	6-18-05	0	0	0.00	1	0	0	1	2	0	0	0	0	0	.500	.400	.500	0.0	0.0	5
Fraide, Juan	R-R	5-11	161	4-18-06	2	0	1.80	4	3	0	15	13	3	3	0	2	13	.250	.291	.308	23.6	3.6	55
Heredia, Ricardo	R-R	6-2	185	2-4-06	0	0	4.09	9	3	0	22	12	15	10	0	19	24	.160	.366	.173	23.8	18.8	101
Jimenez, Victor	R-R	5-10	170	4-19-07	1	1	4.50	6	0	1	14	11	8	7	0	15	8	.229	.418	.271	11.9	22.4	67
Mejias, Cristhopher	R-R	6-0	185	3-9-06	3	3	8.14	12	1	0	21	19	21	19	3	27	14	.257	.457	.473	13.1	25.2	107
Morales, Antonio	R-R	6-1	194	2-15-07	3	1	5.54	11	4	0	37	46	24	23	1	20	12	.303	.353	.401	12.0	7.2	167
Movilio, Miguel	R-R	5-11	185	8-24-06	1	0	7.52	10	4	0	20	15	18	17	3	25	21	.203	.433	.351	20.2	24.0	104
Murrieta, Leonel	R-R	6-0	175	5-9-07	3	2	2.79	12	8	0	48	38	18	15	4	17	28	.220	.301	.318	14.4	8.8	194
Navarro, Cristian	R-R	5-10	155	8-4-07	0	0	6.75	6	1	0	5	2	4	4	0	7	4	.125	.448	.188	13.8	24.1	29
Palacio, Isaac	R-R	6-3	187	5-7-06	0	2	6.83	10	4	0	28	31	21	21	2	24	16	.301	.429	.437	11.9	17.9	134
Payro, Emilio	R-R	5-10	190	1-2-08	0	2	9.00	5	4	0	10	9	10	10	0	9	19	.237	.396	.289	39.6	18.8	48
Peralta, Angel	R-R	6-1	160	10-23-06	3	2	3.74	12	8	1	46	31	20	19	1	21	44	.197	.293	.318	23.8	11.4	185
Reyes, Luis	L-L	5-11	180	8-12-06	3	1	5.35	14	5	0	37	35	26	22	1	33	27	.248	.398	.319	15.3	18.8	176
Rivero, Gabriel	R-R	6-0	186	11-10-04	2	1	3.38	7	2	1	21	18	11	8	0	16	23	.228	.347	.278	23.2	16.2	99
Rodriguez, Jhosue	R-R	6-0	165	10-15-05	4	1	3.60	15	2	2	40	37	25	16	4	16	30	.247	.328	.380	17.1	9.1	175
Rosario, Reidy	R-R	6-1	180	10-23-03	0	3	6.97	15	0	5	21	25	22	16	1	15	17	.316	.440	.430	16.8	14.9	101

Fielding
C: Flores 26, Castro 17, Campos 14, Gonzalez 10, Castellano 4. **1B:** Campos 13, Rojas 11, Castro 10, Flores 9, Brito 8, Romero 6, Gonzalez 4, Castellano 3, Colon 3. **2B:** Martinez 19, Areinamo 18, Rojas 16, Colon 6, Brito 2. **3B:** Rojas 18, Martinez 12, Areinamo 11, Colon 11, Brito 7, Puello 4, Silverio 2. **SS:** Areinamo 23, Martinez 23, Silverio 8, Rojas 7, Colon 4, Puello 2. **LF:** De La Cruz 15, Matos 13, Morgado 13, Millan 9, Romero 9, Ramos 3, Martinez 1. **CF:** Millan 26, De La Cruz 20, Morgado 8, Ramos 2, Romero 2. **RF:** De La Cruz 17, Matos 16, Morgado 9, Ramos 9, Romero 7, Millan 5

Kansas City Royals

SEASON SYNOPSIS: The Royals rode starting pitching and an improved offense to a postseason berth in 2024, but injuries to aces Seth Lugo and, more significantly, Cole Ragans slowed them, and the offensive formula faltered in 2025. Their overall stats, such as a .706 OPS and 159 home runs versus .710 and 170 in 2024, were similar, but the Royals scored 84 fewer runs overall en route to an 82-80, third-place finish.

HIGH POINT: Whenever the '25 Royals needed a boost, the White Sox were there. KC went 10-3 against the White Sox, including a four-game early-May sweep during a season-long seven-game winning streak. The May 6 victory came on a Bobby Witt Jr. walk-off single in the ninth, set up when a Drew Waters popup was misplayed by Sox second baseman Chase Meidroth, hitting him in the head and setting up the winning rally. The Royals walked off the Red Sox 2-1 in 12 innings three days later to get to 24-16.

LOW POINT: A June swoon with an 8-18 record proved too big a hurdle for the Royals to overcome, as the club scored 0 or 1 run nine different times. In a June 24-26 home sweep to the Rays, the Royals scored one lone run before being shut out in the final two games of the sweep. They mustered just 12 hits in three games.

NOTABLE ROOKIES: Lefty Noah Cameron rode one of the game's most effective curveballs to a boffo 9-7, 2.99 season, leading the team's pitchers in bWAR (3.8), with several other rookie arms contributing in the rotation (Ryan Bergert, 1-2, 4.43) and bullpen (Steven Cruz went 3-1, 3.74). But looking for help in the outfield, 2024 first-rounder Jac Caglianone (.157, 7 HR) and John Rave (.196, 4 HR) didn't provide enough thump in the lineup to get the Royals to where they wanted to go.

KEY TRANSACTIONS: The Royals traded rotation stalwart Brady Singer for college teammate Jonathan India from the Reds. India's first year was a struggle (.233/.333/.346). Free-agent signee Carlos Estevez (4-5, 2.45) led the majors with 42 saves. GM JJ Picollo's in-season trades were bold, trading catcher Freddy Fermin to San Diego for Bergert and righty Stephen Kolek (and to make room for top prospect and local product Carter Jensen behind the plate). Outfielder Mike Yastrzemski, a rental acquired from the Giants, provided much-needed pop (.237/.339/.500, 9 HR in 186 PA).

OPENING DAY PAYROLL: $130,001,503 (20th)

PLAYERS OF THE YEAR

MAJOR LEAGUE
Bobby Witt Jr.
SS
.295/.351/.501
23 HR, 38 SB
Led MLB 184 H, 47 2B

MINOR LEAGUE
Carter Jensen
C
(AA,AAA)
.290/.377/.501
20 HR, 20 2B, 60 BB

ORGANIZATION LEADERS

Batting		*Qualifiers
MAJORS		
* AVG	Bobby Witt	.295
* OPS	Bobby Witt	.852
HR	Vinnie Pasquantino	32
RBI	Vinnie Pasquantino	113
MINORS		
* AVG	Harold Castro, Omaha/ACL Royals	.303
* OBP	Carter Jensen, Omaha/NW Arkansas	.377
* SLG	Harold Castro, Omaha/ACL Royals	.531
* OPS	Harold Castro, Omaha/ACL Royals	.884
R	Asbel Gonzalez, Columbia	82
H	Sam Kulasingam, Quad Cities	136
TB	Carson Roccaforte, NW Arkansas/Quad Cities	217
2B	MJ Melendez, Omaha	33
3B	Sam Kulasingam, Quad Cities	8
3B	Brett Squires, NW Arkansas	8
HR	Harold Castro, Omaha/ACL Royals	21
RBI	Carter Jensen, Omaha/NW Arkansas	76
BB	Carson Roccaforte, NW Arkansas/Quad Cities	82
SO	Carson Roccaforte, NW Arkansas/Quad Cities	162
SB	Asbel Gonzalez, Columbia	78

Pitching		#Qualifiers
MAJORS		
W	Michael Wacha	10
# ERA	Michael Wacha	3.86
SO	Michael Lorenzen	127
SV	Carlos Estevez	42
MINORS		
W	A.J. Causey, NW Arkansas/Quad Cities	11
L	Ryan Ramsey, Omaha/NW Arkansas	11
# ERA	Felix Arronde, Quad Cities	2.8
G	Brandon Johnson, Omaha/NW Arkansas	54
GS	Drew Beam, Quad Cities	26
SV	Zachary Cawyer, NW Arkansas/Quad Cities	11
IP	Drew Beam, Quad Cities	131.7
BB	Frank Mozzicato, NW Arkansas/Quad Cities	75
SO	Ryan Ramsey, Omaha/NW Arkansas	114.000
SO	Shane Panzini, Omaha/NW Arkansas/Quad Cities	114
# AVG	Felix Arronde, Quad Cities	.210

2025 PERFORMANCE

General Manager: J.J. Picollo. **Farm Director:** Mitch Maier. **Scouting Director:** Brian Bridges.

Class	Team	League	W	L	PCT	Finish	Manager
Majors	Kansas City Royals	American	82	80	.506	8 (15)	Matt Quatraro
Triple-A	Omaha Storm Chasers	International	62	86	.419	17 (20)	Mike Jirschele
Double-A	NW Arkansas Naturals	Texas	66	72	.478	7 (10)	Brooks Conrad
High-A	Quad Cities River Bandits	Midwest	74	58	.561	3 (12)	Jesus Azuaje
Low-A	Columbia Fireflies	Carolina	64	65	.496	9 (12)	David Noworyta
Rookie	ACL Royals	Arizona Complex	32	28	.533	6 (15)	Larry Sutton
Rookie	DSL Royals Fortuna	Dominican	22	32	.407	41 (52)	Ramon Martinez
Rookie	DSL Royals Ventura	Dominican	35	20	.636	7 (52)	Sergio De Luna
Overall 2025 Minor League Record			**355**	**361**	**.496**	**15th (30)**	

ORGANIZATION STATISTICS

KANSAS CITY ROYALS
AMERICAN LEAGUE

Batting	B-T	Ht.	Wt.	DOB	AVG	OBP	SLG	G	PA	AB	R	H	2B	3B	HR	RBI	BB	HBP	SH	SF	SO	SB	CS	BB%	SO%
Biggio, Cavan	L-R	6-2	200	4-11-95	.174	.296	.246	37	83	69	9	12	2	0	1	4	11	1	2	0	21	1	0	13.3	25.3
Blanco, Dairon	R-R	5-11	170	4-26-93	.167	.167	.333	9	8	6	2	1	1	0	0	1	0	0	2	0	2	3	2	0.0	25.0
Caglianone, Jac	L-L	6-5	217	2-9-03	.157	.237	.295	62	232	210	19	33	6	1	7	18	18	4	0	0	52	1	0	7.8	22.4
Canha, Mark	R-R	6-2	209	2-15-89	.212	.272	.265	46	125	113	9	24	3	0	1	6	7	3	0	2	24	0	1	5.6	19.2
Fermin, Freddy	R-R	5-9	200	5-16-95	.255	.309	.339	67	208	192	17	49	7	0	3	12	13	2	1	0	37	1	2	6.3	17.8
Frazier, Adam	L-R	5-10	180	12-14-91	.283	.320	.402	56	197	184	21	52	10	0	4	23	9	2	0	2	36	1	1	4.6	18.3
Garcia, Maikel	R-R	6-0	145	3-3-00	.286	.351	.449	160	666	595	81	170	39	5	16	74	62	1	3	5	84	23	9	9.3	12.6
Grichuk, Randal	R-R	6-2	216	8-13-91	.206	.267	.299	43	105	97	10	20	3	0	2	5	7	1	0	0	22	0	0	6.7	21.0
India, Jonathan	R-R	6-0	200	12-15-96	.233	.323	.346	136	567	497	63	116	29	0	9	45	54	13	1	2	106	0	4	9.5	18.7
Isbel, Kyle	L-R	5-11	190	3-3-97	.255	.301	.353	135	409	368	42	94	16	4	4	33	23	2	13	3	74	4	5	5.6	18.1
Jensen, Carter	L-R	6-1	210	7-3-03	.300	.391	.550	20	69	60	12	18	6	0	3	13	9	0	0	0	12	0	0	13.0	17.4
Loftin, Nick	R-R	5-11	180	9-25-98	.208	.278	.357	67	188	168	17	35	9	2	4	20	14	3	1	2	27	1	1	7.4	14.4
Maile, Luke	R-R	6-3	225	2-6-91	.244	.346	.356	25	54	45	6	11	2	0	1	6	7	0	2	0	16	1	0	13.0	29.6
Massey, Michael	L-R	6-0	190	3-22-98	.244	.268	.313	77	277	262	20	64	9	0	3	20	9	1	1	4	43	2	1	3.2	15.5
Melendez, MJ	L-R	6-1	190	11-29-98	.083	.154	.167	23	65	60	5	5	2	0	1	1	3	2	0	0	23	0	0	4.6	35.4
Pasquantino, Vinnie	L-L	6-4	245	10-10-97	.264	.323	.475	160	682	621	72	164	33	1	32	113	49	7	0	5	107	1	0	7.2	15.7
Perez, Salvador	R-R	6-3	255	5-10-90	.236	.284	.446	155	641	597	54	141	35	0	30	100	28	12	0	1	125	0	0	4.4	19.5
Rave, John	L-L	5-9	185	12-30-97	.196	.283	.307	72	175	153	18	30	5	0	4	14	18	1	2	1	46	7	2	10.3	26.3
Renfroe, Hunter	R-R	6-1	230	1-28-92	.182	.241	.295	63	135	122	11	25	5	0	1	8	6	0	0	0	21	0	0	7.4	19.4
Tolbert, Tyler	R-R	6-0	160	1-27-98	.280	.321	.380	64	57	50	19	14	2	0	1	6	1	3	1	2	11	21	2	1.8	19.3
Waters, Drew	S-R	6-0	185	12-30-98	.243	.288	.316	71	219	206	21	50	6	3	1	14	11	2	0	0	60	5	3	5.0	27.4
Witt, Bobby	R-R	6-1	200	6-14-00	.295	.351	.501	157	687	623	99	184	47	6	23	88	49	8	0	7	125	38	9	7.1	18.2
Yastrzemski, Mike	L-L	5-10	178	8-23-90	.237	.339	.500	50	186	156	30	37	14	0	9	18	25	1	0	4	42	1	1	13.4	11.8

Pitching	B-T	Ht.	Wt.	DOB	W	L	ERA	G	GS	SV	IP	Hits	Runs	ER	HR	BB	SO	AVG	OBP	SLG	SO%	BB%	BF
Avila, Luinder	R-R	6-3	195	8-21-01	1	1	1.29	13	0	0	14	7	2	2	0	6	16	.143	.232	.204	28.6	10.7	56
Bergert, Ryan	R-R	6-1	210	3-8-00	1	2	4.43	8	8	0	41	37	21	20	4	17	39	.239	.312	.387	22.4	9.8	174
Bowlan, Jonathan	R-R	6-6	240	12-1-96	1	2	3.86	34	1	0	44	37	21	19	6	17	46	.230	.302	.398	25.6	9.4	180
Bubic, Kris	L-L	6-3	225	8-19-97	8	7	2.55	20	20	0	116	98	38	33	6	39	116	.227	.294	.332	24.4	8.2	476
Cameron, Noah	L-L	6-3	220	7-17-99	9	7	2.99	24	24	0	138	109	46	46	18	43	114	.214	.279	.361	20.5	7.7	556
Clarke, Taylor	R-R	6-4	217	5-13-93	1	1	3.25	51	0	1	55	38	20	20	8	9	44	.194	.233	.357	21.4	4.4	206
Cruz, Steven	R-R	6-7	225	6-15-99	3	1	3.57	45	7	0	46	36	20	19	5	18	38	.213	.291	.343	20.1	9.5	189
Erceg, Lucas	L-R	6-2	214	5-1-95	8	4	2.64	61	0	2	61	54	19	18	4	18	48	.238	.305	.339	19.3	7.2	249
Estevez, Carlos	R-R	6-6	277	12-28-92	4	5	2.45	67	0	42	66	48	22	18	5	22	54	.199	.276	.315	20.1	8.2	269
Falter, Bailey	R-L	6-4	175	4-24-97	0	2	11.25	4	2	0	12	20	15	15	2	7	11	.370	.443	.574	18.0	11.5	61
Harvey, Hunter	R-R	6-3	239	12-9-94	1	0	0.00	12	0	0	11	6	0	0	0	11	.158	.179	.158	28.2	2.6	39
Hatch, Thomas	R-R	6-1	195	9-29-94	0	0	18.00	1	0	0	1	2	2	2	1	0	1	.400	.400	1.200	20.0	0.0	5
Hill, Rich	L-L	6-5	221	3-11-80	0	2	5.00	2	2	0	9	9	7	5	2	8	4	.257	.395	.457	9.3	18.6	43
Hoffmann, Andrew	R-R	6-5	210	2-2-00	0	0	3.86	3	0	0	5	7	6	2	1	4	5	.318	.423	.545	19.2	15.4	26
Kolek, Stephen	R-R	6-3	210	4-18-97	1	2	1.91	5	5	0	33	20	9	7	1	5	21	.168	.202	.252	16.8	4.0	125
Long, Sam	L-L	6-1	185	7-8-95	2	3	5.36	39	0	0	40	48	31	24	7	22	33	.291	.381	.467	17.5	11.6	189
Lorenzen, Michael	R-R	6-3	217	1-4-92	7	11	4.64	27	26	0	142	149	76	73	25	39	127	.268	.320	.470	21.0	6.4	606
Lugo, Seth	R-R	6-4	225	11-17-89	8	7	4.15	26	26	0	145	133	70	67	27	55	125	.244	.319	.438	20.5	9.0	611
Lynch, Daniel	L-L	6-6	200	11-17-96	6	2	3.06	57	2	1	68	66	24	23	8	26	45	.260	.341	.402	15.6	9.0	289
Maile, Luke	R-R	6-3	225	2-6-91	0	0	0.00	1	0	0	1	0	0	0	0	1	0	.000	.250	.000	0.0	25.0	4
Ragans, Cole	L-L	6-4	190	12-12-97	3	3	4.67	13	13	0	62	53	33	32	7	20	98	.228	.293	.384	38.1	7.8	257
Richards, Trevor	R-R	6-2	205	5-15-93	0	0	12.00	3	0	0	3	7	4	4	0	2	2	.467	.500	.533	11.1	11.1	18
Schreiber, John	R-R	6-1	210	3-5-94	3	3	3.80	74	0	1	64	57	29	27	10	19	62	.234	.292	.414	23.4	7.2	265
Sisk, Evan	L-L	6-2	209	4-23-97	0	0	1.69	5	0	0	5	1	1	0	5	11	.238	.385	.238	42.3	19.2	26
Stratton, Chris	R-R	6-2	205	8-22-90	0	0	7.94	12	0	0	17	29	17	15	2	8	16	.377	.425	.558	18.4	9.2	87
Wacha, Michael	R-R	6-6	215	7-1-91	10	13	3.86	31	31	0	173	166	74	74	15	45	126	.252	.302	.383	17.6	6.3	716
Zerpa, Angel	L-L	6-0	220	9-27-99	5	2	4.18	69	2	0	65	67	30	30	7	22	58	.271	.333	.425	21.1	8.0	275

Fielding

Catcher	PCT	G	PO	A	E	DP	PB
Fermin	.996	59	437	24	2	1	2
Jensen	1.000	10	66	4	0	0	0
Maile	1.000	23	126	1	0	1	2
Perez	1.000	92	663	30	0	2	2

First Base	PCT	G	PO	A	E	DP
Biggio	1.000	6	35	3	0	3
Caglianone	1.000	10	21	6	0	1
Canha	1.000	3	17	1	0	2
Loftin	1.000	5	17	2	0	1
Pasquantino	.996	126	965	63	4	104
Perez	.996	30	221	17	1	10

Second Base	PCT	G	PO	A	E	DP
Biggio	.875	4	4	3	1	2
Fermin	.000	1	0	0	0	0
Frazier	1.000	26	25	45	0	10
Garcia	1.000	11	14	20	0	4

	PCT	G	PO	A	E	DP
India	.976	76	111	177	7	38
Loftin	1.000	16	15	22	0	5
Massey	.996	60	95	152	1	45
Tolbert	1.000	5	2	4	0	1

Third Base	PCT	G	PO	A	E	DP
Biggio	1.000	3	0	1	0	0
Frazier	1.000	7	6	5	0	2
Garcia	.980	136	105	234	7	24
India	.902	20	8	38	5	4
Loftin	.974	14	13	24	1	4
Tolbert	.667	3	1	1	1	1

Shortstop	PCT	G	PO	A	E	DP
Garcia	.973	17	16	20	1	6
Tolbert	1.000	5	1	2	0	0
Witt	.983	154	186	382	10	74

Outfield	PCT	G	PO	A	E	DP
Biggio	1.000	13	15	0	0	0
Blanco	1.000	6	6	0	0	0
Caglianone	.979	52	92	1	2	0
Canha	1.000	34	34	0	0	0
Frazier	.974	25	36	2	1	1
Garcia	1.000	7	7	0	0	0
Grichuk	.973	38	35	1	1	0
India	.969	21	30	1	1	0
Isbel	.997	135	329	3	1	2
Loftin	1.000	38	34	0	0	0
Massey	.962	14	24	1	1	0
Melendez	1.000	23	24	3	0	1
Rave	.973	81	104	3	3	1
Renfroe	.981	33	51	1	1	0
Tolbert	1.000	46	37	1	0	0
Waters	.976	84	120	1	3	0
Yastrzemski	1.000	56	85	2	0	0

OMAHA STORM CHASERS
INTERNATIONAL LEAGUE
TRIPLE-A

Batting	B-T	Ht.	Wt.	DOB	AVG	OBP	SLG	G	PA	AB	R	H	2B	3B	HR	RBI	BB	HBP	SH	SF	SO	SB	CS	BB%	SO%
Becker, Colton	R-R	6-2	200	4-26-01	.000	.000	.000	1	1	1	0	0	0	0	0	0	0	0	0	0	1	0	0	0.0	100.0
Biggio, Cavan	L-R	6-2	200	4-11-95	.285	.375	.464	41	176	151	26	43	11	2	4	23	20	3	0	2	37	1	1	11.4	21.0
Blanco, Dairon	R-R	5-11	170	4-26-93	.253	.332	.405	77	295	257	49	65	13	1	8	26	24	7	5	1	64	32	3	8.1	21.7
Caglianone, Jac	L-L	6-5	217	2-9-03	.357	.426	.705	28	129	112	26	40	6	0	11	29	12	3	0	2	20	1	0	9.3	15.5
Canha, Mark	R-R	6-2	209	2-15-89	.222	.364	.370	9	33	27	5	6	1	0	1	1	6	0	0	0	9	0	0	18.2	27.3
Castillo, Diego	R-R	5-10	185	10-28-97	.283	.369	.424	54	217	191	34	54	9	0	6	26	26	0	0	0	41	0	3	12.0	18.9
Castro, Harold	L-R	5-10	195	11-30-93	.307	.354	.538	99	403	368	54	113	18	2	21	65	26	2	5	2	78	7	2	6.5	19.4
Dalbec, Bobby	R-R	6-4	227	6-29-95	.252	.336	.512	32	143	127	20	32	9	0	8	25	13	3	0	0	50	1	0	9.1	35.0
Devanney, Cam	R-R	6-1	195	4-13-97	.272	.366	.565	69	288	246	41	67	14	2	18	55	34	4	1	3	70	3	1	11.8	24.3
Diaz, Isan	L-R	5-10	201	5-27-96	.189	.294	.356	39	154	132	16	25	1	0	7	18	19	1	1	1	38	0	0	12.3	24.7
Dickerson, Dustin	R-R	6-1	180	3-28-01	.316	.413	.368	11	46	38	6	12	2	0	0	4	6	1	0	1	5	1	0	13.0	10.9
Gentry, Tyler	R-R	6-0	210	2-1-99	.206	.284	.371	86	332	291	39	60	17	2	9	34	28	6	1	6	89	4	1	8.4	26.8
Gordon, Nick	L-R	6-0	160	10-24-95	.260	.327	.320	16	55	50	5	13	3	0	0	4	5	0	0	0	18	2	1	9.1	32.7
Groshans, Jordan	R-R	6-3	200	11-10-99	.200	.360	.300	8	25	20	4	4	2	0	0	2	4	1	0	0	3	0	0	16.0	12.0
Hayes, Kyle	R-R	6-2	190	10-8-97	.143	.310	.190	9	29	21	3	3	1	0	0	2	4	2	0	2	10	0	0	13.8	34.5
Jensen, Carter	L-L	6-1	210	7-3-03	.288	.404	.647	43	184	153	32	44	11	1	14	39	30	0	1	0	52	3	0	16.3	28.3
Loftin, Nick	R-R	5-11	180	9-25-98	.303	.447	.461	43	197	152	30	46	12	0	4	24	39	3	0	3	24	12	1	19.8	12.2
Maile, Luke	R-R	6-3	225	2-6-91	.280	.416	.354	24	101	82	13	23	3	0	1	12	18	1	0	0	22	2	0	17.8	21.8
Martin, Rudy	L-L	5-8	155	1-31-96	.192	.192	.346	7	26	26	2	5	1	0	1	1	0	0	0	0	4	0	1	0.0	15.4
Massey, Michael	L-R	6-0	190	3-22-98	.258	.321	.433	25	106	97	13	25	5	0	4	16	6	3	0	0	21	0	0	5.7	19.8
Melendez, MJ	L-R	6-1	190	11-29-98	.261	.323	.490	107	480	433	70	113	33	3	20	64	39	3	0	5	135	20	8	8.1	28.1
O'Keefe, Brian	R-R	6-1	210	7-15-93	.158	.236	.274	43	162	146	17	23	5	0	4	10	15	0	1	0	43	2	0	9.3	26.5
Pratto, Nick	L-L	6-1	215	10-6-98	.196	.289	.331	114	423	372	49	73	19	2	9	42	46	3	1	5	125	8	0	10.9	29.6
Rave, John	L-L	5-9	185	12-30-97	.285	.373	.515	60	274	235	57	67	13	4	11	34	32	2	3	2	61	19	1	11.7	22.3
Tolbert, Tyler	R-R	6-0	160	1-27-98	.265	.339	.408	29	115	98	20	26	5	0	3	14	9	3	3	2	30	11	4	7.8	26.1
Tresh, Luca	R-R	5-11	193	1-11-00	.259	.321	.473	72	271	243	24	63	16	3	10	37	21	2	3	2	59	3	0	7.7	21.8
Velazquez, Nelson	R-R	6-0	190	12-26-98	.202	.298	.377	33	131	114	11	23	1	0	6	14	16	0	0	1	33	4	1	12.2	25.2
Waters, Drew	S-R	6-0	185	12-30-98	.236	.309	.404	54	231	208	34	49	10	2	7	29	21	1	0	0	67	7	1	9.1	29.0
Wiemer, Joey	R-R	6-4	220	2-11-99	.182	.291	.312	72	296	253	32	46	6	0	9	38	34	6	0	3	79	12	1	11.5	26.7
Wilson, Peyton	S-R	5-8	180	11-1-99	.223	.309	.309	84	319	278	26	62	13	1	3	31	34	2	2	3	85	12	2	10.7	26.6

Pitching	B-T	Ht.	Wt.	DOB	W	L	ERA	G	GS	SV	IP	Hits	Runs	ER	HR	BB	SO	AVG	OBP	SLG	SO%	BB%	BF
Ackenhausen, Nate	L-L	6-2	230	9-23-01	0	0	3.00	5	2	0	9	8	3	3	1	7	11	.229	.372	.400	25.6	16.3	43
Avila, Luinder	R-R	6-3	195	8-21-01	2	3	5.23	14	9	0	53	48	32	31	7	23	61	.236	.320	.379	26.4	10.0	231
Bosacker, Ethan	R-R	6-2	210	2-20-01	0	2	4.91	10	4	0	26	31	16	14	2	10	14	.298	.373	.462	11.9	8.5	118
Bowlan, Jonathan	R-R	6-6	240	12-1-96	3	0	2.25	24	0	5	36	23	9	9	1	11	45	.178	.254	.240	31.7	7.7	142
Brady, Ryan	R-R	6-1	185	3-23-99	1	1	6.23	8	0	0	13	18	9	9	0	8	11	.367	.443	.429	18.0	13.1	61
Cameron, Noah	L-L	6-3	220	7-17-99	2	1	3.31	7	7	0	33	24	13	12	4	13	38	.207	.295	.336	28.6	9.8	133
Castillo, Diego	R-R	5-10	185	10-28-97	0	0	13.50	1	0	0	1	0	1	1	0	1	0	.000	.000	.000	0.0	66.7	6
Cerantola, Eric	R-R	6-5	220	7-23-99	2	2	4.04	38	1	1	49	40	24	22	4	24	63	.223	.315	.374	26.9	11.3	213
Champlain, Chandler	R-R	6-4	220	7-23-99	4	9	7.84	29	25	0	119	160	113	104	20	51	100	.317	.387	.514	17.7	9.0	565
Clarke, Taylor	R-R	6-4	217	5-13-93	0	1	4.40	10	0	0	14	10	7	7	1	5	9	.226	.288	.302	15.3	8.5	59
Cox, Luke	L-L	6-4	235	3-28-97	2	1	3.55	11	0	0	13	11	6	5	1	8	18	.224	.309	.424	32.7	10.9	55
Cruz, Steven	R-R	6-7	225	6-15-99	0	1	2.45	7	0	1	7	6	5	2	0	10	.222	.300	.407	33.3	6.7	30
Dunn, Justin	R-R	6-2	209	9-22-95	0	4	10.34	6	4	0	16	26	18	18	4	16	17	.343	.465	.612	19.8	18.6	86
Erceg, Lucas	L-R	6-2	214	5-1-95	0	0	0.00	1	0	0	1	0	0	0	0	0	0	.000	.000	.000	0.0	0.0	3
Falter, Bailey	L-L	6-4	195	4-24-97	0	0	0.00	2	2	0	2	1	0	0	0	1	6	.125	.364	.125	36.4	27.3	11
Fernandez, Junior	R-R	6-3	215	3-2-97	2	5	4.93	31	0	2	38	33	25	21	2	26	53	.234	.356	.355	30.3	14.9	175
Fulmer, Michael	R-R	6-3	224	3-15-93	0	1	5.89	10	0	1	15	10	7	2	7	18	.278	.350	.486	22.5	8.8	80

KANSAS CITY ROYALS

Player	B-T	Ht.	Wt.	DOB	G	GS	ERA															
Gant, John	R-R	6-4	200	8-6-92	5	5	6.00	19	19	0	81	93	57	54	12	45	69	.286	.373	.477	18.4	12.0	375
Guerrero, Tyson	L-L	6-1	188	2-16-99	1	2	5.91	3	3	0	11	11	11	7	1	4	16	.256	.347	.442	32.7	8.2	49
Hartlieb, Geoff	R-R	6-5	240	12-9-93	0	1	9.00	7	0	0	8	14	8	8	0	4	10	.424	.474	.545	26.3	10.5	38
Hatch, Thomas	R-R	6-1	195	9-29-94	5	6	4.22	18	18	0	92	93	43	43	9	28	78	.262	.322	.406	20.1	7.2	388
Heasley, Jonathan	R-R	6-3	225	1-27-97	0	0	13.50	4	0	0	4	9	6	6	1	0	2	.429	.409	.905	9.1	0.0	22
Hendrix, Ryan	R-R	6-3	215	12-16-94	5	3	7.71	30	0	0	37	40	35	32	4	29	52	.267	.415	.400	27.5	15.3	189
Hill, Rich	L-L	6-5	221	3-11-80	4	4	5.36	9	9	0	42	43	28	25	9	25	48	.264	.372	.485	25.0	13.0	192
Hoffmann, Andrew	R-R	6-5	210	2-2-00	3	3	2.25	32	0	2	40	35	16	10	2	10	55	.230	.274	.309	33.3	6.1	165
Johnson, Brandon	R-R	6-0	195	6-12-99	4	2	6.75	37	2	1	49	57	38	37	15	24	46	.288	.377	.576	20.2	10.5	228
Keuchel, Dallas	L-L	6-2	205	1-1-88	2	1	3.53	7	7	0	36	38	18	14	3	12	30	.264	.321	.375	19.2	7.7	156
Kolek, Stephen	R-R	6-3	210	4-18-97	1	3	6.63	5	5	0	19	30	15	14	2	10	20	.357	.438	.488	20.8	10.4	96
Krehbiel, Joey	R-R	6-3	250	12-20-92	1	1	4.09	20	0	3	22	23	11	10	1	9	17	.261	.327	.375	17.2	9.1	99
Kudrna, Ben	R-R	6-3	175	1-30-03	0	1	14.29	4	3	0	11	14	18	18	3	17	10	.326	.508	.605	15.9	27.0	63
Long, Sam	L-L	6-1	185	7-8-95	0	2	10.00	11	0	0	9	12	12	10	2	10	11	.300	.440	.525	22.0	20.0	50
Lynch, Daniel	L-L	6-6	200	11-17-96	0	0	0.00	1	0	0	2	1	0	0	0	0	3	.143	.143	.286	42.9	0.0	7
Martinez, Chazz	L-L	6-3	210	1-6-00	1	1	5.64	22	0	0	30	29	20	19	2	17	32	.250	.353	.388	23.0	12.2	139
Murdock, Noah	R-R	6-8	205	8-20-98	0	2	6.00	16	0	0	21	22	19	14	2	13	20	.265	.371	.386	20.2	13.1	99
Nogosek, Stephen	R-R	6-2	205	1-11-95	3	3	4.87	41	5	2	57	57	31	31	8	25	60	.258	.343	.430	23.9	10.0	251
Noriega, Cruz	R-R	6-1	175	10-1-97	0	1	12.00	12	1	0	18	29	24	24	4	16	20	.354	.460	.610	20.0	16.0	100
Panzini, Shane	R-R	6-3	220	10-30-01	2	1	4.76	5	5	0	23	25	20	12	7	15	13	.269	.367	.548	11.9	13.8	109
Pratto, Nick	L-L	6-1	215	10-6-98	0	0	0.00	1	0	0	1	0	0	0	0	0	0	.333	.333	.333	0.0	0.0	3
Ragans, Cole	L-L	6-4	190	12-12-97	0	1	1.35	2	2	0	7	3	1	1	1	2	14	.130	.200	.261	56.0	8.0	25
Ramsey, Ryan	R-L	6-0	195	11-8-01	0	1	7.88	2	2	0	8	10	7	7	1	7	6	.333	.452	.469	14.3	16.7	42
Richards, Trevor	R-R	6-2	205	5-15-93	0	0	1.69	10	0	2	11	14	2	2	1	5	11	.318	.388	.455	22.4	10.2	49
Robertson, Nick	R-R	6-6	265	7-16-98	1	0	4.41	9	0	1	16	13	8	8	3	4	14	.213	.273	.377	21.2	6.1	66
Sears, Ben	R-R	6-5	208	6-15-00	1	1	3.21	9	0	0	14	16	6	5	2	6	15	.276	.354	.466	23.1	9.2	65
Simonelli, Anthony	R-R	6-2	200	12-23-98	1	2	5.40	10	3	0	15	11	11	9	2	13	18	.200	.353	.382	26.1	18.8	69
Sisk, Evan	L-L	6-2	209	4-23-97	0	2	3.77	31	0	4	29	37	14	12	4	9	36	.296	.348	.456	26.7	6.7	135
Turnbull, Spencer	R-R	6-3	210	9-18-92	0	2	6.38	4	3	0	18	17	13	13	1	12	17	.250	.373	.353	20.5	14.5	83
Wallace, Jacob	R-R	6-1	190	8-13-98	3	1	4.46	26	1	0	42	34	24	21	5	17	45	.224	.297	.362	26.2	9.9	172
Way, Beck	R-R	6-4	200	8-6-99	1	1	6.87	23	0	0	38	42	29	29	7	26	24	.292	.419	.493	13.4	14.5	179
Williams, Henry	R-R	6-5	200	9-18-01	0	2	10.13	2	2	0	8	9	9	9	1	8	6	.281	.442	.406	14.0	18.6	43
Wright, Kyle	R-R	6-4	215	10-2-95	0	0	6.23	4	4	0	13	19	9	9	2	9	14	.255	.361	.392	23.0	14.8	61

Fielding

Catcher	PCT	G	PO	A	E	DP	PB
Hayes	.969	9	60	3	2	0	1
Jensen	.978	33	250	14	6	1	4
Maile	1.000	20	165	15	0	1	2
O'Keefe	.981	32	302	16	6	2	4
Tresh	.998	61	537	32	1	2	6

First Base	PCT	G	PO	A	E	DP
Biggio	.974	10	70	6	2	8
Caglianone	.982	7	53	3	1	2
Canha	1.000	1	7	1	0	2
Castro	1.000	18	129	12	0	11
Groshans	1.000	2	16	0	0	0
Loftin	1.000	3	23	2	0	3
O'Keefe	1.000	1	1	0	0	0
Pratto	.991	110	853	60	8	74

Second Base	PCT	G	PO	A	E	DP
Becker	.000	1	0	0	0	0
Biggio	.914	11	8	24	3	5
Castillo	1.000	9	15	18	0	6
Castro	.988	18	23	60	1	13
Devanney	1.000	4	6	7	0	4

	PCT	G	PO	A	E	DP
Diaz	1.000	1	1	3	0	0
Dickerson	1.000	1	1	1	0	0
Gordon	.956	14	12	31	2	8
Loftin	1.000	5	5	11	0	2
Massey	1.000	8	12	20	0	5
Tolbert	1.000	11	11	22	0	6
Wilson	.981	71	84	180	5	32

Third Base	PCT	G	PO	A	E	DP
Biggio	.912	15	7	24	3	5
Castillo	.945	27	20	49	4	4
Castro	.955	31	21	43	3	4
Dalbec	.943	31	25	58	5	6
Devanney	1.000	3	2	9	0	1
Diaz	1.000	4	4	8	0	1
Groshans	.833	5	1	4	1	0
Loftin	.946	32	15	55	4	5
Tolbert	.900	5	1	8	1	0

Shortstop	PCT	G	PO	A	E	DP
Castillo	1.000	18	18	41	0	8
Castro	.981	29	37	67	2	13
Devanney	.969	59	66	152	7	25

	PCT	G	PO	A	E	DP
Diaz	.982	35	40	70	2	19
Dickerson	.947	11	16	20	2	7
Tolbert	1.000	2	3	6	0	2

Outfield	PCT	G	PO	A	E	DP
Biggio	1.000	3	10	0	0	0
Blanco	.987	45	76	2	1	0
Caglianone	.957	18	22	0	1	0
Canha	1.000	4	2	0	0	0
Devanney	1.000	2	4	0	0	0
Gentry	.991	74	109	2	1	0
Loftin	.600	3	3	0	2	0
Martin	1.000	6	10	0	0	0
Massey	.958	14	23	0	1	0
Melendez	.976	95	151	9	4	3
Pratto	1.000	1	2	0	0	0
Rave	.982	56	107	0	2	0
Tolbert	1.000	13	26	1	0	0
Velazquez	.929	10	12	1	1	0
Waters	.984	53	121	2	2	2
Wiemer	.994	65	169	3	1	1
Wilson	.857	5	6	0	1	0

NORTHWEST ARKANSAS NATURALS
DOUBLE-A
TEXAS LEAGUE

Batting	B-T	Ht.	Wt.	DOB	AVG	OBP	SLG	G	PA	AB	R	H	2B	3B	HR	RBI	BB	HBP	SH	SF	SO	SB	CS	BB%	SO%
Becker, Colton	R-R	6-2	200	4-26-01	.386	.464	.471	21	84	70	16	27	4	1	0	10	11	1	0	2	12	15	3	13.1	14.3
Caglianone, Jac	L-L	6-5	217	2-9-03	.322	.394	.553	38	175	152	32	49	8	0	9	43	19	1	0	3	37	2	1	10.9	21.1
Canha, Mark	R-R	6-2	209	2-15-89	.273	.333	.545	3	12	11	1	3	0	0	1	5	0	1	0	0	0	0	0	0.0	0.0
Cross, Gavin	L-L	6-1	210	2-13-01	.241	.291	.413	114	507	465	75	112	23	3	17	64	33	2	1	6	134	23	5	6.5	26.4
Diaz, Isan	L-R	5-10	201	5-27-96	.316	.429	.561	16	70	57	8	18	0	0	4	12	11	1	0	1	8	2	2	15.7	11.4
Dickerson, Dustin	R-R	6-1	180	3-28-01	.210	.334	.281	100	406	338	43	71	7	1	5	21	60	4	2	2	98	20	8	14.8	24.1
Emshoff, Kale	R-R	6-2	228	5-2-98	.167	.375	.167	2	8	6	1	1	0	0	0	1	2	0	0	0	4	0	0	25.0	50.0
Groshans, Jordan	R-R	6-2	200	11-10-99	.291	.360	.368	59	250	223	24	65	6	1	3	34	22	3	0	2	35	0	1	8.8	14.0
Guzman, Diego	R-R	5-11	200	9-12-03	.091	.091	.091	3	11	11	0	1	0	0	0	0	0	0	0	0	9	0	0	0.0	81.8
Hayes, Kyle	R-R	6-2	190	10-8-97	.165	.331	.229	36	138	109	15	18	4	0	1	6	19	8	2	0	45	1	0	13.8	32.6

KANSAS CITY ROYALS

	B-T	Ht.	Wt.	DOB	AVG	OBP	SLG	G	AB	R	H	2B	3B	HR	RBI	BB	SO	SB	CS	OBP	SLG	BB%	PA
Hernandez, Diego	L-L	6-0	150	11-21-00	.220	.248	.312	30	115	109	11	24	3	2	1	11	4	0	2	0	34	2	3	3.5	29.6
Hernandez, Omar	R-R	5-11	170	12-10-01	.243	.273	.279	41	155	140	16	34	5	0	0	7	4	3	3	3	27	4	2	2.6	17.4
Jensen, Carter	L-R	6-1	210	7-3-03	.292	.360	.420	68	308	274	40	80	9	4	6	37	30	1	0	3	70	7	1	9.7	22.7
Johnson, Justin	R-R	5-11	185	4-3-00	.232	.305	.368	82	323	285	33	66	15	0	8	31	29	3	1	4	74	7	1	9.0	22.9
Martin, Rudy	L-L	5-8	155	1-31-96	.280	.371	.412	66	286	243	41	68	11	3	5	31	34	2	6	1	60	39	5	11.9	21.0
Massey, Michael	L-R	6-0	190	3-22-98	.071	.071	.071	3	14	14	0	1	0	0	0	0	0	0	0	0	4	0	0	0.0	28.6
Nivens, Spencer	L-R	5-11	185	11-16-01	.250	.348	.346	125	515	436	52	109	20	2	6	57	70	0	0	9	109	14	3	13.6	21.2
Pineda, Jack	L-R	5-7	170	8-10-99	.235	.306	.312	59	248	221	28	52	11	0	2	17	16	7	3	1	52	5	1	6.5	21.0
Roccaforte, Carson	R-L	6-1	195	3-29-02	.290	.387	.475	45	212	183	32	53	15	2	5	29	27	2	0	0	61	10	5	12.7	28.8
Rodriguez, Julio E.	R-R	5-11	245	6-11-97	.250	.317	.359	25	101	92	7	23	7	0	1	16	6	3	0	0	21	0	0	5.9	20.8
Ruta, Sam	L-R	6-2	200	10-22-01	.218	.317	.367	73	291	248	29	54	15	2	6	44	35	3	0	4	108	0	1	12.0	37.1
Salon, Dionmy	R-R	5-11	215	11-18-01	.125	.125	.125	2	8	8	0	1	0	0	0	0	0	0	0	0	4	0	0	0.0	50.0
Scott, Connor	L-L	6-3	208	10-8-99	.333	.367	.407	8	30	27	7	9	2	0	0	0	6	2	0	0	1	3	0	6.7	10.0
Squires, Brett	L-R	6-2	210	2-26-00	.248	.327	.411	116	496	443	51	110	26	8	10	56	48	4	0	1	134	18	4	9.7	27.0
Vaz, Javier	L-R	5-9	151	9-22-00	.256	.360	.326	103	468	387	70	99	16	1	3	31	54	11	11	4	43	25	3	11.5	9.2
Vazquez, Daniel	R-R	6-1	150	12-15-03	.190	.190	.190	5	21	21	0	4	0	0	0	2	0	0	0	0	6	0	1	0.0	28.6
Wilson, Peyton	S-R	5-8	180	11-1-99	.392	.505	.689	19	91	74	19	29	8	4	2	19	13	4	0	0	17	8	2	14.3	18.7

Pitching	B-T	Ht.	Wt.	DOB	W	L	ERA	G	GS	SV	IP	Hits	Runs	ER	HR	BB	SO	AVG	OBP	SLG	SO%	BB%	BF
Ackenhausen, Nate	L-L	6-2	230	9-23-01	1	0	3.15	18	0	0	20	21	9	7	3	10	19	.269	.360	.462	21.3	11.2	89
Bosacker, Ethan	R-R	6-2	210	2-20-01	6	4	3.78	18	11	0	83	63	37	35	11	32	50	.208	.290	.383	14.7	9.4	341
Brady, Ryan	R-R	6-1	185	3-23-99	0	0	6.35	4	0	0	6	8	4	4	3	2	9	.320	.393	.680	32.1	7.1	28
Causey, A.J.	R-R	6-3	210	11-19-02	3	3	1.91	21	0	4	33	23	8	7	0	7	31	.198	.256	.259	24.4	5.5	127
Cawyer, Zachary	R-R	6-3	210	12-2-02	0	0	9.00	2	0	0	2	1	2	2	0	4	1	.167	.455	.167	9.1	36.4	11
Chamberlain, Christian	L-L	5-10	173	7-20-99	3	3	2.93	42	0	3	43	27	19	14	0	36	50	.180	.357	.200	25.5	18.4	196
Colleran, Dennis	R-R	6-3	225	8-20-03	0	0	0.00	1	0	0	1	0	0	0	0	1	0	.000	.333	.000	0.0	33.3	3
Dickerson, Dustin	R-R	6-1	180	3-28-01	0	0	0.00	1	0	0	0	0	0	0	0	0	1	.000	.500	.000	0.0	50.0	2
Garabitos, Natanael	R-R	6-0	185	8-4-00	3	1	5.85	16	0	1	20	21	15	13	2	22	17	.280	.450	.373	16.8	21.8	101
Harvey, Hunter	R-R	6-3	239	12-9-94	0	0	0.00	2	0	0	2	0	0	0	0	0	4	.250	.250	.250	50.0	0.0	8
Heasley, Jonathan	R-R	6-3	225	1-27-97	1	0	4.26	8	0	0	13	14	6	6	3	2	9	.292	.327	.521	17.3	3.8	52
Hendrix, Ryan	R-R	6-3	215	12-16-94	0	1	9.00	4	0	0	4	3	4	4	1	3	8	.214	.389	.429	44.4	16.7	18
Johnson, Brandon	R-R	6-0	195	6-12-99	0	1	0.79	17	0	7	23	5	4	2	0	7	27	.069	.150	.069	33.8	8.8	80
Kudrna, Ben	R-R	6-3	175	1-30-03	2	7	4.21	20	19	0	94	88	50	44	7	33	96	.244	.310	.394	24.0	8.3	400
Lorenzen, Michael	R-R	6-3	217	1-4-92	1	0	7.27	2	2	0	9	11	7	7	2	6	9	.324	.439	.529	22.0	14.6	41
Lynch, Daniel	L-L	6-6	200	11-17-96	0	0	27.00	1	0	0	1	2	2	2	0	1	1	.333	.500	.667	25.0	25.0	4
Martinez, Chazz	R-R	6-3	210	1-6-01	0	2	1.85	31	0	3	44	34	9	9	1	11	45	.210	.239	.309	25.0	6.1	180
Monke, Caden	L-L	6-3	170	9-2-99	3	7	7.41	43	0	3	51	57	45	42	6	46	60	.279	.418	.397	23.4	18.0	256
Mozzicato, Frank	L-L	6-3	175	6-19-03	2	5	7.46	17	13	0	57	58	47	47	10	53	48	.278	.423	.512	17.6	19.4	273
Noriega, Cruz	L-L	6-3	175	10-1-97	1	2	8.14	15	0	1	21	25	20	19	4	9	21	.298	.372	.476	22.3	9.6	94
Owen, Hunter	R-L	6-3	261	1-30-02	5	5	3.80	22	19	1	95	86	49	40	10	40	107	.237	.321	.366	25.9	9.7	413
Panzini, Shane	R-R	6-3	220	10-30-01	5	0	3.16	13	10	0	57	52	21	20	7	21	65	.240	.307	.415	27.0	8.7	241
Patteson, Hunter	L-L	6-4	190	4-4-00	4	0	4.41	11	8	1	49	47	24	24	10	16	44	.250	.316	.436	21.3	7.7	207
Paulino, Anderson	R-R	6-2	200	9-12-98	1	0	12.96	6	0	0	8	17	12	12	2	4	9	.405	.457	.714	19.6	8.7	46
Ragans, Cole	L-L	6-4	190	12-12-97	0	0	9.82	1	1	0	4	7	5	4	1	1	6	.412	.444	.647	33.3	5.6	18
Ramsey, Ryan	R-L	6-0	195	1-18-01	6	10	5.54	25	18	1	106	110	75	65	11	49	108	.267	.352	.417	22.9	10.4	472
Rayo, Oscar	L-L	6-1	180	1-13-02	2	4	3.70	35	3	1	88	77	37	36	7	35	67	.240	.322	.355	18.4	9.6	364
Regalado, Nicholas	R-R	6-2	215	5-15-02	3	0	7.32	14	0	0	20	26	16	16	4	12	21	.313	.412	.590	21.6	12.4	97
Sears, Ben	R-R	6-5	208	6-15-00	2	2	4.66	32	0	5	48	50	29	25	8	18	40	.260	.336	.411	18.6	8.4	215
Veliz, Mauricio	R-R	6-2	220	7-17-02	0	1	2.45	5	0	1	7	3	2	2	1	6	4	.125	.323	.250	12.9	19.4	31
Way, Beck	R-R	6-2	208	8-6-99	3	5	4.95	23	0	1	36	35	21	20	3	16	31	.248	.344	.355	19.0	9.8	163
Williams, Henry	R-R	6-5	200	9-18-01	5	6	4.24	21	19	1	108	112	62	51	11	36	100	.270	.335	.419	21.6	7.8	462
Willis, Marlin	L-L	6-4	190	6-5-98	2	1	8.68	13	0	0	19	21	19	18	2	17	20	.280	.426	.453	21.1	17.9	95
Wright, Kyle	R-R	6-4	215	10-2-95	0	0	4.50	4	4	0	10	9	6	5	1	5	7	.231	.348	.385	15.2	10.9	46
Zobac, Steven	R-R	6-3	185	10-14-00	0	3	7.68	11	11	0	36	55	33	31	8	14	37	.357	.411	.591	21.1	8.0	175

Fielding

Catcher	PCT	G	PO	A	E	DP	PB
Hayes	.997	36	276	17	1	1	1
Hernandez	.986	38	329	26	5	5	5
Jensen	.991	44	415	34	4	4	3
Rodriguez	.983	19	161	11	3	1	3
Salon	.952	2	18	2	1	0	0

First Base	PCT	G	PO	A	E	DP
Cagliaone	.991	29	206	17	2	12
Emshoff	1.000	1	4	0	0	0
Groshans	1.000	2	18	0	0	4
Ruta	.988	23	155	13	2	13
Squires	.988	85	631	43	8	48

Second Base	PCT	G	PO	A	E	DP
Becker	.947	4	4	14	1	3
Diaz	.929	4	5	8	1	2
Dickerson	1.000	2	6	6	0	2
Groshans	1.000	1	1	1	0	0

	PCT	G	PO	A	E	DP
Johnson	.990	47	90	113	2	25
Pineda	1.000	3	6	9	0	1
Vaz	.989	63	108	153	3	31
Wilson	.978	15	18	27	1	2

Third Base	PCT	G	PO	A	E	DP
Becker	.857	6	7	5	2	0
Diaz	1.000	2	1	2	0	0
Groshans	.957	49	30	82	5	11
Guzman	1.000	1	0	1	0	0
Johnson	.984	27	16	46	1	6
Pineda	.968	12	2	28	1	2
Ruta	.953	42	27	74	5	7
Wilson	1.000	1	0	1	0	0

Shortstop	PCT	G	PO	A	E	DP
Becker	.872	8	16	18	5	5
Diaz	.960	7	8	16	1	5

	PCT	G	PO	A	E	DP
Dickerson	.967	98	112	214	11	31
Groshans	1.000	1	1	3	0	0
Guzman	1.000	1	1	0	0	0
Pineda	.932	23	32	50	6	10
Vazquez	1.000	3	3	5	0	0

Outfield	PCT	G	PO	A	E	DP
Cagliaone	1.000	7	17	0	0	0
Canha	1.000	3	3	0	0	0
Cross	.981	96	197	9	4	1
Hernandez	.975	30	76	3	2	0
Martin	.970	63	153	6	5	1
Massey	1.000	2	4	0	0	0
Nivens	.977	115	210	6	5	3
Roccaforte	1.000	41	121	1	0	1
Scott	1.000	8	11	1	0	0
Squires	.919	19	33	1	3	0
Vaz	.970	34	60	4	2	2
Wilson	.833	2	5	0	1	0

QUAD CITIES RIVER BANDITS — HIGH-A
MIDWEST LEAGUE

Batting	B-T	Ht.	Wt.	DOB	AVG	OBP	SLG	G	PA	AB	R	H	2B	3B	HR	RBI	BB	HBP	SH	SF	SO	SB	CS	BB%	SO%
Becker, Colton	R-R	6-2	200	4-26-01	.108	.250	.135	14	46	37	7	4	1	0	0	1	7	0	2	0	10	7	2	15.2	21.7
Brito, Chris	R-R	6-2	215	9-28-99	.262	.367	.377	55	219	183	21	48	9	0	4	26	31	1	1	3	51	5	1	14.2	23.3
Brown, Canyon	R-R	6-2	190	8-7-03	.225	.309	.297	70	259	222	33	50	10	0	2	21	23	6	3	5	60	8	3	8.9	23.2
Charles, Austin	R-R	6-4	215	11-13-03	.205	.264	.298	59	232	205	24	42	9	2	2	20	19	0	1	7	60	11	5	8.2	25.9
Ensley, Hunter	R-R	6-1	200	8-9-01	.163	.229	.163	15	48	43	2	7	0	0	0	8	4	0	0	1	16	1	0	8.3	33.3
Figueroa, Derlin	L-R	6-0	163	9-7-03	.197	.277	.255	52	213	188	22	37	5	0	2	16	21	1	0	3	62	13	2	9.9	29.1
Frederick, Carter	R-R	6-4	235	7-2-02	.223	.316	.342	101	405	354	55	79	25	4	3	43	43	6	0	2	132	16	3	10.6	32.6
Gonzalez, Bryan	R-R	6-0	220	9-18-01	.235	.288	.356	77	314	289	30	68	18	4	3	34	20	2	2	1	94	14	5	6.4	29.9
Guzman, Diego	R-R	5-11	200	9-12-03	.199	.268	.252	52	175	151	17	30	6	1	0	15	14	1	7	2	58	8	4	8.0	33.1
Hernandez, Omar	R-R	5-11	170	12-10-01	.203	.242	.271	34	127	118	9	24	6	1	0	16	5	1	2	0	27	6	1	3.9	21.3
Kulasingam, Sam	S-R	6-2	190	7-10-01	.291	.375	.393	123	547	468	77	136	26	8	2	57	63	3	7	5	86	22	10	11.5	15.7
Mitchell, Blake	R-R	6-1	192	8-3-04	.207	.372	.296	49	216	169	23	35	7	1	2	12	45	0	1	1	71	9	4	20.8	32.9
Moss, Michael Callan	R-R	6-3	230	8-31-03	.270	.372	.418	92	393	330	50	89	22	3	7	70	53	4	0	6	87	14	5	13.5	22.1
Roccaforte, Carson	L-L	6-1	195	3-29-02	.237	.364	.466	82	339	279	49	66	15	5	13	45	55	2	1	2	101	33	7	16.2	29.8
Sailors, Nolan	L-R	6-0	190	7-4-03	.283	.412	.368	32	133	106	18	30	5	2	0	10	20	4	2	1	28	17	4	15.0	21.1
Salon, Dionmy	R-R	5-11	215	11-18-01	.333	.364	.556	3	12	9	1	3	2	0	0	6	1	0	1	1	2	0	0	8.3	16.7
Torres, Erick	R-R	5-10	160	12-20-04	.233	.298	.301	106	446	399	41	93	17	2	2	35	31	7	7	2	71	13	9	7.0	15.9
Vazquez, Daniel	R-R	6-1	150	12-15-03	.260	.336	.349	105	463	404	55	105	23	5	1	42	48	1	3	6	93	26	7	10.4	20.1
Werner, Trevor	R-R	6-3	225	9-3-00	.201	.280	.339	83	341	298	40	60	14	3	7	39	33	2	2	6	111	16	6	9.7	32.6

Pitching	B-T	Ht.	Wt.	DOB	W	L	ERA	G	GS	SV	IP	Hits	Runs	ER	HR	BB	SO	AVG	OBP	SLG	SO%	BB%	BF
Ackenhausen, Nate	L-L	6-2	230	9-23-01	1	1	4.73	8	0	0	13	8	10	7	2	8	18	.163	.293	.306	30.5	13.6	59
Alberini, Hunter	R-R	6-2	210	12-20-01	0	0	4.50	4	0	1	6	5	3	3	0	2	9	.238	.304	.333	37.5	8.3	24
Arronde, Felix	R-R	6-3	185	4-25-03	5	7	2.80	26	24	0	129	97	45	40	9	42	101	.210	.280	.343	19.5	8.1	517
Avila, Luinder	R-R	6-3	195	8-21-01	0	0	3.00	3	3	0	6	4	2	2	0	3	10	.200	.304	.250	43.5	13.0	23
Beam, Drew	R-R	6-4	208	2-14-03	7	10	3.83	26	26	0	132	127	72	56	8	30	110	.256	.304	.386	20.5	5.6	536
Causey, A.J.	R-R	6-3	210	11-19-02	8	2	1.56	27	0	5	40	25	8	7	0	11	44	.176	.244	.239	28.2	7.1	156
Cawyer, Zachary	R-R	6-3	210	12-2-02	4	2	3.21	39	0	11	56	55	30	20	4	21	77	.251	.314	.361	31.7	8.6	243
Colleran, Dennis	R-R	6-3	225	8-20-03	5	0	1.83	21	0	0	34	14	8	7	3	14	33	.126	.258	.216	25.0	10.6	132
Davis, Tyler	L-L	6-2	210	2-2-02	4	2	3.98	26	1	0	43	39	22	19	2	24	43	.247	.348	.335	22.9	12.8	188
Hansell, Josh	R-R	6-6	215	2-7-02	0	1	2.81	8	8	0	32	30	10	10	2	18	28	.254	.362	.347	20.3	13.0	138
Langevin, Louis-Philippe	L-R	6-1	185	7-4-03	3	2	7.20	14	0	0	15	12	14	12	0	17	25	.211	.416	.298	32.5	22.1	77
Martin, Logan	R-R	6-1	180	7-17-01	8	4	3.45	22	22	0	91	74	38	35	5	36	78	.223	.308	.328	20.6	9.5	378
Martin, Max	R-R	6-5	190	12-8-03	1	0	0.00	4	0	0	7	4	0	0	0	1	6	.167	.231	.167	23.1	3.8	26
Martinez, Juan	R-R	5-11	195	4-6-01	0	2	2.08	36	1	4	52	34	20	12	3	20	47	.183	.268	.274	22.4	9.5	210
Miller, Mason	L-L	6-2	200	3-30-02	1	1	0.91	11	10	0	40	27	6	4	2	17	43	.194	.291	.266	27.2	10.8	158
Molsky, Tommy	R-R	6-1	160	2-6-03	3	2	3.03	40	0	1	62	49	25	21	1	29	74	.221	.328	.288	28.0	11.0	264
Monke, Caden	L-L	6-3	170	9-2-99	0	0	0.00	3	0	0	3	2	0	0	0	1	3	.167	.231	.333	23.1	7.7	13
Morones, Andrew	R-R	6-0	200	12-19-00	2	5	4.76	26	1	2	40	36	27	21	1	21	48	.245	.343	.361	27.7	12.1	173
Mozzicato, Frank	L-L	6-3	175	6-19-03	1	0	1.24	7	7	0	36	15	6	5	2	22	37	.124	.255	.207	25.3	15.1	146
Panzini, Shane	R-R	6-3	220	10-30-01	1	2	2.76	8	2	1	29	25	11	9	0	11	36	.229	.306	.294	29.8	9.1	121
Patteson, Hunter	L-L	6-4	190	4-4-00	5	1	1.99	13	13	0	72	52	19	16	3	23	63	.196	.272	.287	22.0	8.0	287
Regalado, Nicholas	R-R	6-2	215	5-15-02	2	1	3.71	20	0	3	34	20	16	14	3	22	25	.175	.333	.298	17.4	15.3	144
Reyes, Emmanuel	R-R	6-0	180	5-16-04	0	3	4.88	7	6	0	31	37	19	17	3	14	24	.291	.366	.457	16.6	9.7	145
Rios, Jesus	R-R	6-1	190	12-27-01	7	4	3.60	35	0	2	55	58	30	22	4	19	44	.272	.344	.427	18.2	7.9	242
Ronan, Cory	L-L	6-2	195	6-14-02	0	0	0.00	2	0	0	3	0	0	0	0	5	0	.000	.500	.000	55.6	0.0	9
Veliz, Mauricio	R-R	6-2	220	7-17-02	3	3	6.63	26	1	1	58	63	49	43	6	30	48	.269	.366	.419	17.4	10.9	276
Widener, Jacob	R-L	6-7	235	6-15-01	1	3	8.44	19	0	0	21	22	22	20	0	18	30	.259	.439	.306	26.3	15.8	114
Willis, Marlin	L-L	6-4	190	6-5-98	2	0	1.35	9	0	0	13	6	3	2	0	4	8	.136	.220	.182	16.0	8.0	50

Fielding

Catcher	PCT	G	PO	A	E	DP	PB
Brito	1.000	1	4	0	0	0	0
Brown	.977	65	551	56	14	2	9
Hernandez	.978	34	283	23	7	1	2
Mitchell	1.000	30	279	19	0	3	3
Salon	.935	3	28	1	2	0	0

First Base	PCT	G	PO	A	E	DP
Brito	1.000	27	190	17	0	11
Figueroa	1.000	12	88	4	0	5
Gonzalez	1.000	7	50	5	0	6
Moss	.978	70	498	46	12	46
Werner	1.000	16	117	9	0	10

Second Base	PCT	G	PO	A	E	DP
Becker	1.000	2	4	3	0	0
Guzman	.959	13	21	26	2	0
Kulasingam	.984	119	225	269	8	63

Third Base	PCT	G	PO	A	E	DP
Becker	1.000	4	2	5	0	0
Charles	.949	39	35	59	5	4
Figueroa	.924	37	31	79	9	10
Guzman	.951	29	32	46	4	8
Werner	.923	26	22	38	5	6

Shortstop	PCT	G	PO	A	E	DP
Becker	.938	7	8	7	1	3
Charles	.961	19	32	42	3	12
Guzman	1.000	10	8	21	0	4
Vazquez	.931	99	90	209	22	39

Outfield	PCT	G	PO	A	E	DP
Ensley	1.000	15	23	1	0	0
Frederick	.984	95	179	6	3	1
Gonzalez	.971	39	66	2	2	1
Kulasingam	1.000	3	4	0	0	0
Roccaforte	.990	81	199	5	2	2
Sailors	1.000	31	72	1	0	0
Torres	.976	103	195	6	5	0
Werner	1.000	35	68	3	0	1

COLUMBIA FIREFLIES LOW-A
CAROLINA LEAGUE

Batting	B-T	Ht.	Wt.	DOB	AVG	OBP	SLG	G	PA	AB	R	H	2B	3B	HR	RBI	BB	HBP	SH	SF	SO	SB	CS	BB%	SO%
Acosta, Angel	L-R	5-9	160	3-2-03	.246	.303	.295	74	275	244	27	60	9	0	1	25	20	2	4	5	34	12	5	7.3	12.4
Allende, Giullianno	L-L	6-0	165	9-4-03	.183	.280	.239	29	83	71	17	13	2	1	0	2	8	2	1	1	24	7	2	9.6	28.9
Becker, Colton	R-R	6-2	200	4-26-01	.231	.343	.277	61	238	195	26	45	6	0	1	15	31	3	8	1	37	38	5	13.0	15.5
Cabrera, Roni	R-R	6-1	175	7-31-05	.092	.216	.171	26	89	76	13	7	1	1	1	8	9	3	1	0	34	7	3	10.1	38.2
Cerice, Jose	R-R	6-2	192	5-12-05	.302	.349	.371	34	126	116	18	35	5	0	1	15	3	6	0	1	15	3	0	2.4	11.9
Figueroa, Derlin	L-R	6-0	163	9-7-03	.268	.353	.394	63	269	231	38	62	11	3	4	31	30	2	2	3	40	11	2	11.2	14.9
Gonzalez, Asbel	R-R	6-2	170	1-2-06	.239	.365	.289	115	505	415	82	99	12	3	1	21	54	29	6	1	86	78	26	10.7	17.0
Hernandez, Jorge	L-R	6-0	180	12-20-05	.218	.321	.276	45	186	156	21	34	4	1	1	16	11	14	2	3	46	4	4	5.9	24.7
Kemp, Tyriq	L-R	5-7	156	11-15-02	.193	.338	.298	16	72	57	10	11	2	2	0	11	11	2	1	1	14	5	3	15.3	19.4
Lucas, Aldrin	R-R	5-10	165	2-7-03	.103	.278	.172	12	36	29	2	3	0	1	0	1	7	0	0	0	8	0	0	19.4	22.2
McNair, Brennon	R-R	5-10	185	9-15-02	.196	.290	.348	100	368	322	41	63	16	3	9	37	36	7	2	1	106	12	3	9.8	28.8
Novas, Josi	R-R	6-4	180	2-12-05	.151	.221	.283	82	308	279	20	42	10	0	9	35	20	6	1	2	121	7	3	6.5	39.3
Nowak, Luke	L-L	6-0	186	12-25-02	.446	.554	.585	19	83	65	15	29	9	0	0	12	15	2	0	1	10	6	3	18.1	12.0
Ramirez, Ramon	R-R	6-0	180	6-15-05	.244	.339	.442	70	307	258	48	63	12	3	11	56	36	5	0	8	65	6	2	11.7	21.2
Ramos, Henry	L-L	6-1	175	9-20-04	.220	.322	.293	73	277	232	27	51	8	3	1	18	34	2	7	2	60	18	9	12.3	21.7
Rasmussen, Connor	L-R	5-9	180	3-1-04	.171	.293	.229	10	41	35	4	6	2	0	0	4	6	0	0	0	7	0	0	14.6	17.1
Ricardo, Yandel	S-R	6-1	180	10-6-06	.212	.279	.268	50	200	179	24	38	6	2	0	14	13	4	3	1	41	14	3	6.5	20.5
Rushford, Milo	L-L	6-0	185	2-12-04	.200	.331	.283	77	289	230	25	46	7	3	2	23	43	6	2	8	85	7	4	14.9	29.4
Russell, Stone	R-R	6-1	195	6-17-04	.222	.333	.321	115	458	383	39	85	14	6	4	53	60	7	1	6	84	4	6	13.1	18.3
Salon, Dionmy	R-R	5-11	215	11-18-01	.218	.307	.257	39	117	101	9	22	1	0	1	9	9	4	3	0	21	3	0	7.7	17.9
Silva, Gabriel	R-R	5-9	218	12-10-03	.206	.289	.412	26	77	68	8	14	2	0	4	9	5	3	1	0	30	0	0	6.5	39.0
Um, Hyungchan	R-R	6-1	190	4-24-04	.225	.337	.324	66	262	222	22	50	13	0	3	22	32	6	1	1	54	4	1	12.2	20.6
Vanek, JC	L-L	6-3	205	9-10-04	.250	.388	.300	13	49	40	3	10	2	0	0	3	9	0	0	0	17	3	1	18.4	34.7

Pitching	B-T	Ht.	Wt.	DOB	W	L	ERA	G	GS	SV	IP	Hits	Runs	ER	HR	BB	SO	AVG	OBP	SLG	SO%	BB%	BF
Albus, Dash	L-L	5-11	185	7-24-02	9	2	3.54	40	2	6	61	59	25	24	4	23	59	.257	.336	.391	22.7	8.8	260
Chourio, Kendry	R-R	6-0	160	10-1-07	1	3	5.16	6	6	0	23	20	16	13	2	4	24	.227	.292	.420	25.0	4.2	96
Colleran, Dennis	R-R	6-3	225	8-20-03	4	0	4.06	22	0	3	31	22	20	14	1	19	39	.198	.313	.279	29.8	14.5	131
Conte, Nick	R-R	5-10	200	4-25-02	0	1	5.84	36	0	2	45	47	33	29	2	39	59	.266	.401	.350	26.6	17.6	222
Davis, Tyler	L-L	6-2	210	2-2-02	0	0	0.00	0	0	0	5	3	0	0	0	0	5	.167	.167	.222	27.8	0.0	18
DeGroat, Kyle	L-R	6-1	195	1-30-06	0	0	0.00	1	1	0	3	0	0	0	0	1	3	.000	.091	.000	27.3	9.1	11
Dudley, Bryson	R-R	6-3	210	2-17-04	2	0	1.35	9	0	2	13	8	3	2	0	4	22	.170	.235	.213	43.1	7.8	51
Edge, Kamden	R-R	6-1	195	9-23-04	1	0	1.88	9	0	0	14	6	3	3	0	11	17	.128	.317	.213	28.3	18.3	60
Gutierrez, Jose	R-R	6-1	155	5-24-03	2	4	5.77	11	9	0	39	48	27	25	0	20	32	.298	.392	.366	17.2	10.8	186
Hansell, Josh	R-R	6-6	215	2-7-02	1	1	4.73	8	8	0	32	41	25	17	1	14	37	.313	.389	.420	24.7	9.3	150
Jones, Tanner	R-R	6-2	195	6-21-03	2	3	4.02	9	7	0	40	42	22	18	3	18	30	.269	.315	.417	20.0	5.9	170
Leal, Henson	R-R	6-1	176	9-19-03	6	4	3.69	41	1	3	68	59	38	28	4	21	74	.223	.298	.366	25.0	7.1	296
Marte, Yunior	R-R	6-5	210	9-8-03	3	5	2.74	19	19	0	82	61	29	25	4	20	79	.205	.256	.303	24.7	6.3	320
Mendieta, Augusto	R-R	5-11	190	8-19-04	3	3	3.58	20	0	5	38	37	20	15	0	11	47	.255	.310	.297	29.4	6.9	160
Michel, Ismael	R-R	6-3	175	2-14-02	0	0	12.96	8	0	0	8	12	12	12	2	9	11	.324	.447	.568	23.4	19.1	47
Miller, Mason	L-L	6-2	200	3-30-02	5	2	3.63	21	1	1	45	40	23	18	1	15	57	.234	.332	.322	28.9	7.6	197
Nova, Fraynel	R-R	6-0	190	5-22-02	2	3	3.77	42	0	2	62	53	30	26	4	29	78	.228	.320	.345	19.0	10.4	269
Novas, Elvis	R-R	6-0	205	9-2-02	1	1	5.23	27	0	2	43	49	28	25	2	13	48	.285	.353	.395	25.0	6.8	192
Perez, Yeri	R-R	6-3	180	10-16-04	4	4	5.34	25	0	0	57	64	43	34	2	53	64	.222	.404	.304	23.4	19.3	274
Presinal, Yimi	R-R	5-11	175	9-18-04	2	1	5.95	15	0	1	20	21	15	15	1	11	28	.263	.355	.375	30.1	11.8	93
Reyes, Emmanuel	R-R	6-0	180	5-16-04	1	2	3.72	8	6	0	29	24	13	12	2	8	20	.216	.273	.378	16.5	6.6	121
Rodriguez, Darwin	L-L	6-1	175	7-24-03	0	2	4.30	4	4	0	15	15	7	7	1	5	13	.268	.359	.375	20.3	7.8	64
Rosario, Julio	R-R	6-2	205	7-12-02	2	7	4.35	30	0	5	50	40	30	24	7	24	51	.212	.312	.360	23.4	11.0	218
Salon, Dionmy	R-R	5-11	215	11-18-01	0	0	0.00	2	0	0	1	0	0	0	0	0	2	.000	.000	.000	66.7	0.0	3
Shields, David	S-L	6-2	210	9-9-06	3	1	2.01	18	18	0	72	58	22	16	3	15	81	.218	.262	.286	28.3	5.2	286
Silva, Gabriel	R-R	5-9	218	12-10-03	0	0	0.00	2	0	0	2	0	0	0	0	2	3	.000	.375	.000	37.5	25.0	8
Sosa, Yenfri	L-L	6-0	170	12-29-03	2	1	2.79	12	0	2	19	10	8	6	2	13	26	.154	.304	.250	29.1	16.5	79
Wolters, Blake	R-R	6-4	215	10-25-04	2	2	3.99	12	12	0	47	34	25	21	3	40	40	.209	.372	.325	19.3	19.3	207
Woods, Jordan	L-L	6-3	183	11-13-03	4	5	4.12	20	9	1	63	58	31	29	4	34	63	.250	.348	.371	23.3	12.6	270
Wyatt, Hiro	R-R	6-1	185	8-25-04	2	7	4.78	21	20	0	79	86	45	42	8	29	78	.284	.366	.426	22.3	8.3	349

Fielding

Catcher	PCT	G	PO	A	E	DP	PB
Lucas	1.000	3	12	0	0	0	0
Ramirez	.981	39	337	31	7	4	3
Salon	.988	36	312	18	4	1	2
Silva	.993	16	126	7	1	2	2
Um	.982	44	397	31	8	0	0

First Base	PCT	G	PO	A	E	DP
Cerice	1.000	14	102	6	0	8
Figueroa	1.000	33	245	16	0	19
Lucas	.988	8	77	3	1	3
Russell	.994	42	437	23	3	31
Silva	.913	4	19	2	2	3
Vanek	.986	10	68	0	1	7

Second Base	PCT	G	PO	A	E	DP
Acosta	.951	59	84	131	11	28
Becker	1.000	11	18	19	0	4
Hernandez	.925	28	39	60	8	12
Kemp	1.000	11	10	34	0	4
Rasmussen	.971	9	15	19	1	6
Russell	.984	17	22	41	1	6

Third Base	PCT	G	PO	A	E	DP
Acosta	.000	1	0	0	0	0
Becker	.926	16	15	35	4	4
Cerice	.941	18	12	20	2	3
Figueroa	.903	24	18	38	6	4
Hernandez	.900	13	7	20	3	1
Novas	.928	33	18	46	5	4
Rasmussen	1.000	1	0	2	0	0
Russell	.953	29	18	43	3	2

Shortstop	PCT	G	PO	A	E	DP
Acosta	.882	6	7	8	2	1
Becker	.962	31	47	55	4	10
Kemp	1.000	6	10	12	0	2
Novas	.915	44	56	84	13	16
Ricardo	.943	46	56	108	10	18

Outfield	PCT	G	PO	A	E	DP
Allende	1.000	24	35	0	0	0
Becker	1.000	1	1	0	0	0
Cabrera	.917	23	41	3	4	2
Gonzalez	.989	113	257	5	3	3
McNair	.986	87	139	4	2	1
Nowak	1.000	17	19	0	0	0
Ramos	.939	73	104	4	7	1
Rushford	.990	58	98	0	1	0
Vanek	1.000	2	3	0	0	0

ACL ROYALS   ROOKIE
ARIZONA COMPLEX LEAGUE

Batting	B-T	Ht.	Wt.	DOB	AVG	OBP	SLG	G	PA	AB	R	H	2B	3B	HR	RBI	BB	HBP	SH	SF	SO	SB	CS	BB%	SO%
Barber, Noah	R-R	6-3	180	5-3-05	.182	.261	.304	48	165	148	23	27	9	3	1	20	12	4	0	1	73	7	2	7.3	44.2
Cabrera, Roni	R-R	6-1	175	7-31-05	.307	.391	.518	39	156	137	30	42	9	1	6	20	15	4	0	0	42	11	3	9.6	26.9
Castro, Harold	L-R	5-10	195	11-30-93	.000	.286	.000	2	7	5	0	0	0	0	0	0	0	2	0	0	1	0	0	0.0	0.0
Cerice, Jose	R-R	6-2	192	5-12-05	.354	.404	.525	28	109	99	18	35	9	1	2	16	3	6	0	1	12	3	0	2.8	11.0
Charles, Austin	R-R	6-4	215	11-13-03	.200	.200	.267	4	15	15	0	3	1	0	0	0	0	0	0	0	5	0	0	0.0	33.3
Chevalier, Luis	S-R	5-11	160	1-18-02	.321	.424	.536	11	33	28	3	9	4	1	0	4	3	2	0	0	6	0	0	9.1	18.2
Garcia, Darison	S-R	5-11	165	5-14-07	.243	.389	.308	49	216	169	33	41	9	1	0	12	40	1	4	1	47	18	4	18.5	21.8
German, Manuel	R-R	6-1	220	4-29-05	.247	.295	.422	44	166	154	22	38	6	3	5	27	7	4	0	1	48	1	2	4.2	28.9
Gonzalez, Ricson	R-R	6-0	170	6-16-05	.221	.337	.286	31	93	77	10	17	3	1	0	5	12	2	1	1	22	0	1	12.9	23.7
Hernandez, Diego	L-L	6-0	150	11-21-00	.391	.391	.739	6	23	23	5	9	0	1	2	5	0	0	0	0	4	2	0	0.0	17.4
Hernandez, Jorge	L-R	6-0	180	12-20-05	.292	.452	.292	16	63	48	9	14	0	0	0	5	7	7	1	0	14	2	1	11.1	22.2
Lopez, Daniel	L-L	6-2	165	9-14-05	.238	.292	.394	52	212	193	33	46	10	4	4	21	15	0	3	1	39	13	0	7.1	18.4
Lopez, John	R-R	5-8	165	10-6-05	.200	.273	.250	7	22	20	2	4	1	0	0	1	2	0	0	0	5	0	0	9.1	22.7
Lucas, Aldrin	R-R	5-10	165	2-7-03	.372	.451	.442	15	51	43	8	16	0	0	1	5	7	0	0	1	8	0	0	13.7	15.7
Medina, Raimel	R-R	5-11	165	11-15-04	.242	.316	.329	29	113	95	11	23	5	1	0	18	11	4	2	1	21	4	4	9.7	18.6
Mitchell, Blake	L-R	6-1	192	8-3-04	.286	.487	.464	11	39	28	5	8	2	0	1	7	8	3	0	0	10	3	1	20.5	25.6
Ramirez, Angel	R-R	6-2	190	3-28-05	.182	.286	.182	4	14	11	1	2	0	0	0	2	2	0	0	1	4	2	0	14.3	28.6
Ramirez, Ramon	R-R	6-0	180	6-15-05	.304	.292	.478	7	24	23	3	7	1	0	1	5	0	0	0	1	3	1	0	0.0	12.5
Ramos, Henry	L-L	6-1	175	9-20-04	.250	.357	.361	10	42	36	9	9	2	1	0	4	6	0	0	0	11	4	0	14.3	26.2
Ricardo, Yandel	S-R	6-1	180	10-6-06	.342	.438	.533	33	145	120	26	41	7	5	2	21	18	4	1	2	35	17	5	12.4	24.1
Sosa, Ivan	R-R	6-2	180	9-9-04	.240	.276	.400	31	107	100	15	24	4	3	2	17	4	1	1	0	36	3	1	3.7	33.6
Ugarte, Jhonayker	R-R	6-2	180	3-12-07	.216	.338	.284	51	214	176	27	38	4	1	2	28	31	3	1	3	66	5	3	14.5	30.8
Um, Hyungchan	R-R	6-1	190	4-24-04	.276	.300	.345	8	31	29	4	8	2	0	0	4	1	0	0	0	0	1	0	3.2	12.9
Vazquez, Daniel	R-R	6-2	150	12-15-03	.318	.400	.545	6	25	22	6	7	2	0	1	6	3	0	0	0	7	1	0	12.0	28.0
Werner, Trevor	R-R	6-3	225	9-9-01	.290	.407	.565	7	27	23	3	7	1	1	1	4	4	0	0	0	6	2	1	14.8	22.2
Zue, Jhosmmel	R-R	5-11	146	2-5-04	.283	.392	.414	37	123	99	19	28	3	2	2	17	18	1	3	2	36	0	0	14.6	29.3

Pitching	B-T	Ht.	Wt.	DOB	W	L	ERA	G	GS	SV	IP	Hits	Runs	ER	HR	BB	SO	AVG	OBP	SLG	SO%	BB%	BF
Basora, Andy	R-R	6-3	155	4-13-05	1	0	4.05	14	0	1	33	47	17	15	0	6	26	.338	.361	.432	17.7	4.1	147
Baules, Jezler	R-R	6-0	186	8-24-05	0	1	7.23	10	7	0	24	29	24	19	3	13	25	.315	.404	.500	21.6	11.2	116
Belen, Adrian	R-R	6-1	180	12-30-04	4	1	3.69	14	0	0	32	23	15	13	5	14	40	.198	.306	.362	29.9	10.4	134
Benitez, Sthiven	R-R	6-3	180	2-10-05	4	3	9.00	13	0	0	20	27	27	20	4	20	25	.321	.463	.548	23.1	18.5	108
Chourio, Kendry	R-R	6-0	160	10-1-07	0	0	2.45	3	3	0	11	12	3	3	0	0	17	.261	.292	.261	35.4	0.0	48
DeGroat, Kyle	L-R	6-1	195	1-30-06	1	1	4.11	12	11	0	46	52	26	21	4	16	41	.283	.335	.413	20.2	7.9	203
Dunn, Justin	R-R	6-2	209	9-22-95	0	3	20.25	3	3	0	5	9	12	12	1	4	2	.375	.500	.625	6.7	13.3	30
Espinoza, Weskendry	R-R	6-1	185	3-18-02	2	1	4.86	13	0	6	17	14	10	9	2	8	13	.233	.361	.367	18.1	11.1	72
Gutierrez, Jose	R-R	6-1	155	5-24-03	3	0	0.99	9	4	0	27	16	4	3	2	10	30	.178	.267	.278	29.7	9.9	101
Harvey, Hunter	R-R	6-3	239	12-9-94	0	0	0.00	1	1	0	1	0	0	0	0	1	1	.250	.250	.250	25.0	0.0	4
Herbold, Brandon	R-R	6-6	180	8-10-04	1	0	2.63	11	0	0	14	9	5	4	0	10	21	.180	.311	.240	34.4	16.4	61
Herrera, Jorge	R-R	6-0	160	5-15-03	2	1	3.30	14	1	2	30	28	11	11	3	6	29	.243	.281	.365	24.0	5.0	121
Hill, Rich	L-L	6-5	221	3-11-80	0	0	4.50	2	2	0	8	7	4	4	2	0	13	.226	.226	.484	41.9	0.0	31
Jorge, Marwys	R-R	6-4	175	2-15-06	2	2	6.95	13	7	0	34	34	34	26	2	27	36	.262	.411	.369	21.4	16.1	168
Langevin, Louis-Philippe	L-R	6-1	185	7-4-03	0	2	2.84	4	2	0	6	3	2	2	0	5	6	.167	.385	.167	22.2	18.5	27
Long, Sam	L-L	6-1	185	7-8-95	1	0	9.00	1	0	0	1	2	1	1	1	0	1	.400	.400	1.000	20.0	0.0	5
Marceaux, Landon	R-R	6-0	199	10-8-99	0	0	14.73	2	2	0	4	10	6	6	0	2	5	.476	.522	.571	21.7	8.7	23
McDonagh, Ryan	R-R	6-5	190	4-14-06	0	0	0.00	1	1	0	3	1	0	0	0	1	5	.111	.200	.111	50.0	10.0	10
Mendieta, Augusto	R-R	5-11	190	8-19-04	0	0	0.00	5	0	1	6	5	2	0	0	2	10	.217	.308	.217	38.5	7.7	26
Morones, Andrew	R-R	6-0	200	12-19-00	1	1	12.46	3	0	0	4	10	7	6	0	1	10	.435	.440	.609	40.0	4.0	25
Oliveira, Jesus	R-R	6-0	160	12-31-04	0	2	7.40	12	0	0	21	25	18	17	5	11	16	.301	.396	.566	16.7	11.5	96
Presinal, Yimi	R-R	5-11	175	9-18-04	0	0	0.00	4	0	1	7	1	0	0	0	0	12	.048	.048	.048	57.1	0.0	21
Reyes, Emmanuel	R-R	6-0	180	5-16-04	1	1	3.00	3	0	0	9	6	3	3	1	2	8	.200	.242	.333	23.5	5.9	34
Reyes, Jhon	R-R	6-1	165	5-30-04	2	0	2.36	16	0	3	27	20	12	7	1	4	28	.204	.252	.296	26.2	3.7	107
Rodriguez, Darwin	L-L	6-1	175	7-24-03	0	3	3.32	12	10	0	41	32	18	15	5	6	50	.209	.262	.353	30.5	3.7	164
Rodriguez, David	L-L	5-11	152	9-27-03	2	0	4.38	4	0	0	12	14	6	6	2	3	15	.275	.327	.490	27.3	5.5	55
Salgado, Edinson	L-L	6-0	150	1-6-05	1	3	11.42	11	1	0	17	24	25	22	3	21	13	.343	.500	.543	13.4	21.6	97
Shields, David	S-L	6-2	210	9-9-06	0	1	9.00	1	0	0	4	4	4	4	1	0	5	.267	.313	.467	31.3	0.0	16
Sosa, Yenfri	L-L	6-0	170	12-29-03	3	1	5.21	10	0	0	19	19	11	11	1	6	26	.253	.309	.360	32.1	7.4	81
Valdez, Luis	R-R	6-0	170	10-25-04	0	0	0.00	1	0	0	1	1	0	0	0	1	1	.500	.500	.500	25.0	25.0	4
Van Den Brink, Gijs	L-L	6-6	200	7-7-05	0	0	0.00	1	1	0	2	1	0	0	0	1	0	.167	.286	.167	0.0	14.3	7
Widener, Jacob	R-L	6-7	235	6-15-01	1	0	0.00	3	0	0	4	1	0	0	0	8	.000	.200	.000	53.3	6.7	15
Willis, Marlin	L-L	6-4	190	6-5-98	0	0	1.42	4	0	0	6	5	1	1	0	2	13	.227	.280	.227	52.0	8.0	25
Zobac, Steven	L-R	6-3	185	10-14-00	0	1	5.40	4	3	0	8	9	5	5	2	2	8	.290	.333	.581	22.2	5.6	36

Fielding
C: Gonzalez 29, Zue 27, Mitchell 10, Ramirez 5, Um 5. **1B:** German 37, Cerice 12, Lucas 12, Sosa 3. **2B:** Garcia 46, Hernandez 6, Sosa 6, Lopez 3, Vazquez 1. **3B:** Ugarte 22, Cerice 13, Chevalier 10, Hernandez 9, Sosa 9, Werner 4, Charles 3, Castro 1. **SS:** Ricardo 29, Ugarte 25, Garcia 3, Vazquez 3, Chevalier 2, Charles 1, Sosa 1. **LF:** Barber 28, Medina 25, Ramirez 4, Lopez 2, Cabrera 1, Hernandez 1. **CF:** Lopez 34, Barber 17, Ramos 8, Hernandez 5, Cabrera 2. **RF:** Cabrera 35, Lopez 13, Sosa 12, Medina 3, Ramos 1, Werner 1.

DSL ROYALS VENTURA   ROOKIE
DOMINICAN SUMMER LEAGUE

Batting	B-T	Ht.	Wt.	DOB	AVG	OBP	SLG	G	PA	AB	R	H	2B	3B	HR	RBI	BB	HBP	SH	SF	SO	SB	CS	BB%	SO%
Angulo, Alan	R-R	5-11	165	10-30-07	.240	.325	.315	46	168	146	24	35	4	0	0	32	16	3	2	1	13	5	2	9.5	7.7
Chacon, Robinson	L-R	5-11	165	4-21-07	.264	.404	.292	27	90	72	16	19	2	0	0	5	17	0	1	0	18	2	2	18.9	20.0
Cruz, Darvin	L-L	5-11	165	11-10-05	.282	.404	.365	27	105	85	22	24	3	2	0	10	15	3	1	1	17	6	1	14.3	16.2
Cruz, Yohandy	R-R	6-0	157	5-26-07	.000	.375	.000	6	9	5	1	0	0	0	0	1	2	1	1	0	2	1	0	22.2	11.1
De La Cruz, Angelmis	L-R	5-10	160	4-26-06	.000	.000	.000	1	1	1	1	0	0	0	0	0	0	0	0	0	0	0	0	0.0	0.0
Fermin, Joshua	R-R	6-3	175	7-28-08	.220	.319	.341	15	49	41	7	9	2	0	1	8	3	3	2	0	17	4	3	6.1	34.7
Garcia, Anderson	R-R	6-0	195	9-14-06	.160	.371	.200	11	37	25	3	4	1	0	0	4	9	0	2	1	10	1	1	24.3	27.0
Garcia, Juan	R-R	5-8	158	3-3-08	.258	.343	.258	12	35	31	5	8	0	0	0	5	3	1	0	0	6	1	0	8.6	17.1
Guerrero, Alejandro	R-R	6-1	156	9-4-07	.160	.236	.200	16	56	50	5	8	0	1	0	5	4	1	1	0	25	3	0	7.1	44.6
King, Luis Ramon	R-R	6-1	160	12-4-07	.238	.304	.238	7	23	21	3	5	0	0	0	2	2	0	0	0	6	1	2	8.7	26.1
King, Luis Steven	R-R	6-1	166	12-4-07	.250	.250	.250	1	4	4	1	1	0	0	0	0	0	0	0	0	2	1	1	0.0	50.0
Liriano, Daniel	R-R	6-1	176	3-14-07	.158	.352	.184	16	55	38	11	6	1	0	0	9	7	6	1	3	15	2	0	12.7	27.3
Longo, Anthony	R-R	6-0	158	2-9-07	.167	.333	.194	12	45	36	3	6	1	0	0	1	8	1	0	0	8	4	0	17.8	17.8
Luciano, Sandy	S-R	6-0	193	1-9-07	.220	.333	.253	29	108	91	13	20	3	0	0	11	16	0	1	0	14	1	1	14.8	13.0
Marchan, Moises	R-R	6-1	160	11-16-07	.296	.369	.388	31	113	98	14	29	5	2	0	11	9	3	2	1	20	6	1	8.0	17.7
Martinez, Emmanuel	L-R	5-10	176	12-25-07	.207	.333	.207	10	37	29	5	6	0	0	0	6	5	1	1	1	1	1	0	13.5	2.7
Medina, Ramcell	R-R	6-1	155	11-13-07	.260	.398	.404	44	186	146	32	38	7	4	2	25	31	5	0	4	26	7	2	16.7	14.0
Mejia, Omar	R-R	6-2	160	9-20-06	.232	.317	.326	45	163	138	25	32	4	0	3	23	14	5	2	4	40	7	2	8.6	24.5
Montilla, Jose	R-R	5-10	160	1-22-08	.233	.366	.411	27	94	73	16	17	7	0	2	13	11	6	0	3	22	0	1	11.7	23.4
Morales, Jesus	R-R	6-0	165	8-2-07	.226	.306	.323	11	36	31	3	7	3	0	0	6	4	0	0	1	9	0	1	11.1	25.0
Mota, Edgar	R-R	6-1	170	12-14-05	.333	.333	.333	1	3	3	0	1	0	0	0	0	0	0	0	0	0	0	0	0.0	0.0
Ortega, Jesus	R-R	5-10	160	6-24-08	.111	.283	.139	16	47	36	4	4	1	0	0	3	8	1	1	1	4	0	2	17.0	8.5
Paulino, Jose	L-L	5-11	165	10-23-05	.224	.396	.346	39	140	107	28	24	3	2	2	15	27	4	1	1	38	11	5	19.3	27.1
Ramirez, Angel	R-R	6-2	190	3-28-05	.308	.427	.415	21	82	65	16	20	4	0	1	8	12	3	0	2	11	5	1	14.6	13.4
Reyes, Omar	L-R	5-11	170	3-3-05	.329	.475	.400	47	182	140	32	46	5	1	1	25	38	2	1	1	25	1	1	20.9	13.7
Rivero, Marwin	R-R	5-11	160	10-21-06	.250	.333	.250	2	9	8	1	2	0	0	0	2	1	0	0	0	1	0	0	11.1	11.1
Rivero, Roy	L-R	5-11	155	2-1-08	.250	.371	.393	9	35	28	6	7	2	1	0	6	6	0	0	1	6	3	2	17.1	17.1
Roque, Pedro	R-R	5-10	160	12-21-05	.310	.394	.379	9	34	29	9	9	2	0	0	6	3	1	1	0	4	3	0	8.8	11.8
Ruiz, Tony	R-R	6-3	170	12-8-05	.000	.000	.000	1	4	4	0	0	0	0	0	0	0	0	0	0	2	0	0	0.0	50.0

Pitching	B-T	Ht.	Wt.	DOB	W	L	ERA	G	GS	SV	IP	Hits	Runs	ER	HR	BB	SO	AVG	OBP	SLG	SO%	BB%	BF
Amezquita, Moises	L-L	5-10	160	7-27-04	5	1	2.63	12	0	3	27	18	11	8	1	16	29	.191	.327	.266	25.7	14.2	113
Beras, Carlos	R-R	5-11	180	1-5-05	1	0	13.50	4	0	0	5	5	7	7	0	6	5	.333	.542	.467	20.8	25.0	24
Campusano, Alving	R-R	6-2	150	4-9-07	0	0	6.75	2	0	0	4	4	5	3	0	6	2	.286	.524	.286	9.5	28.6	21
Carmona, Samuel	R-R	6-0	160	12-23-04	2	1	8.03	7	0	0	12	13	14	11	1	11	9	.277	.424	.404	15.3	18.6	59
Castillo, Keisther	R-R	6-2	180	9-24-07	0	1	5.02	5	5	0	14	12	10	8	1	9	12	.250	.379	.333	20.3	15.3	59
Chourio, Kendry	R-R	6-0	160	10-1-07	1	0	2.04	5	4	0	18	12	5	4	0	1	22	.185	.209	.215	32.8	1.5	67
Colon, Manuel	R-R	6-1	148	12-24-06	5	0	1.26	11	0	1	29	18	4	4	0	7	35	.171	.250	.219	29.9	6.0	117
Contreras, Freddy	S-R	5-11	178	8-10-08	1	1	3.30	10	9	0	30	22	15	11	0	13	37	.202	.304	.266	29.6	10.4	125
Cruz, Jose	R-R	6-4	200	4-29-05	0	1	32.40	1	0	0	2	5	6	6	0	2	2	.500	.583	.700	16.7	16.7	12
De La Rosa, Carlos	R-R	6-4	175	6-6-05	0	1	10.80	4	4	0	3	4	4	4	0	7	2	.231	.545	.385	31.8	31.8	22
Del Rosario, Oliver	R-L	6-1	170	12-11-04	0	0	5.40	2	0	0	3	4	2	2	0	4	3	.333	.500	.333	18.8	25.0	16
Figueroa, Diego	R-R	5-11	175	9-8-05	2	1	6.32	6	2	1	16	23	13	11	1	2	9	.354	.380	.585	12.7	2.8	71
Garcia, Jesus	R-R	6-3	198	12-21-07	0	0	0.00	1	0	1	0	0	0	0	0	0	1	.000	.000	.000	100.0	0.0	1
Gonzalez, Carlos	R-R	6-1	150	2-14-06	3	2	4.78	12	1	2	26	35	18	14	3	6	18	.340	.382	.476	15.9	5.3	113
Gutierrez, Julio	R-R	6-1	175	3-5-05	0	0	0.00	1	0	0	1	1	0	0	0	1	1	.500	.750	.500	25.0	25.0	4
Jhonni, Jordin	R-R	6-1	160	6-19-05	1	2	3.86	8	0	1	12	12	8	5	0	7	10	.261	.358	.348	18.5	13.0	54
Jimenez, Nomar	L-L	6-2	172	1-4-07	0	0	5.40	2	0	0	2	2	1	1	0	3	0	.333	.556	.500	0.0	33.3	9
Montilla, Ricardo	R-R	6-1	160	1-21-07	0	0	0.00	1	0	0	1	1	0	0	0	0	0	.333	.333	.333	0.0	0.0	3
Penaloza, Kenyer	S-R	5-11	172	8-3-08	5	3	5.91	11	0	0	21	27	16	14	0	9	19	.310	.390	.391	18.8	8.9	101
Ramos, Reynell	R-R	5-11	140	10-7-06	4	1	3.26	11	5	0	30	30	13	11	0	8	30	.259	.315	.328	23.4	6.3	128
Regalado, Hancer	R-R	6-0	160	8-21-07	0	0	0.00	1	0	0	2	0	0	0	0	1	2	.000	.250	.000	25.0	12.5	8
Rivera, Juan	R-R	6-1	162	3-4-07	0	1	3.34	10	0	0	32	26	14	12	0	14	12	.213	.314	.254	8.6	10.0	140
Robles, Melvin	L-L	5-11	150	2-7-08	0	0	4.50	1	0	0	2	0	5	3	1	0	0	3	.455	.455	.455	25.0	0.0	12
Rodriguez, David	L-L	5-11	152	9-27-03	0	0	0.64	4	4	0	14	11	1	1	0	2	17	.216	.273	.314	30.9	3.6	55
Rodriguez, Oswal	R-R	6-1	175	4-17-05	3	1	3.86	13	0	1	26	25	14	11	3	11	19	.266	.349	.426	17.9	10.4	106
Rojas, Javier	R-R	6-2	177	3-23-08	1	1	8.10	4	0	0	7	4	6	6	1	4	6	.154	.258	.346	19.4	12.9	31
Romero, Jordi	R-R	6-2	185	7-5-02	0	0	12.40	7	0	1	10	10	13	10	0	9	13	.256	.408	.308	26.5	18.4	49
Samudio, Denis	R-R	5-11	190	2-6-05	0	0	1.72	11	9	0	37	25	11	7	2	10	44	.198	.273	.286	30.6	6.9	144
Santo, Rafi	R-R	5-11	156	4-18-07	0	0	7.36	2	0	0	4	4	3	3	2	2	6	.286	.375	.786	31.3	12.5	16
Suarez, Junior	L-L	6-1	195	6-24-05	1	0	5.06	2	0	0	5	4	3	3	1	4	6	.294	.429	.588	28.6	19.0	21
Taveras, Neftali	R-R	6-1	175	7-18-04	0	1	4.43	9	0	2	20	21	14	10	3	11	8	.269	.367	.462	8.8	12.1	91
Toribio, Alberto	R-R	5-11	165	7-24-06	0	1	2.66	8	1	0	20	13	6	6	0	10	17	.203	.329	.266	21.5	12.7	79

Fielding

C: Marchan 29, Montilla 10, Morales 9, Longo 7, Martinez 5. **1B:** Reyes 48, Mejia 14, Morales 2. **2B:** Angulo 33, Liriano 10, Garcia 7, Roque 7, Ortega 5, Cruz 2, Rivero 1. **3B:** Mejia 36, Ortega 13, A. Garcia 10, J. Garcia 8, Angulo 1, Cruz 1. **SS:** Medina 43, Angulo 9, Rivero 3, Cruz 1, King 1. **LF:** Chacon 16, Paulino 14, Ramirez 13, Fermin 12, Cruz 3, King 3, Guerrero 1, Luciano 1. **CF:** Paulino 24, Cruz 23, Ramirez 7, King 3, Fermin 1. **RF:** Luciano 28, Guerrero 15, Chacon 9, Fermin 3, D. Cruz 1, King 1, Paulino 1, Y. Cruz 1

DSL ROYALS FORTUNA   ROOKIE
DOMINICAN SUMMER LEAGUE

Batting	B-T	Ht.	Wt.	DOB	AVG	OBP	SLG	G	PA	AB	R	H	2B	3B	HR	RBI	BB	HBP	SH	SF	SO	SB	CS	BB%	SO%
Calcano, Warren	S-R	6-1	154	10-17-07	.346	.514	.538	9	35	26	7	9	2	0	1	2	8	1	0	0	10	7	1	22.9	28.6
Chacon, Robinson	L-R	5-11	165	4-21-07	.167	.367	.278	15	50	36	6	6	2	1	0	5	12	0	1	1	10	1	0	24.0	20.0
Cruz, Darvin	L-L	5-11	165	11-10-05	.245	.397	.283	17	68	53	6	13	2	0	0	8	13	1	0	1	7	0	1	19.1	10.3
Cruz, Yohandy	R-R	6-0	157	5-26-07	.263	.440	.342	15	51	38	8	10	3	0	0	4	12	0	1	0	16	7	1	23.5	31.4
De La Cruz, Angelmis	L-R	5-10	160	4-26-06	.083	.302	.083	21	63	48	7	4	0	0	0	2	14	1	0	0	26	6	1	22.2	41.3
Fermin, Joshua	R-R	6-3	175	7-28-08	.192	.300	.308	15	60	52	12	10	4	1	0	4	5	3	0	0	14	1	1	8.3	23.3
Garcia, Anderson	R-R	6-0	195	9-14-06	.273	.391	.364	25	92	77	12	21	4	0	1	7	14	1	0	0	33	3	1	15.2	35.9
Garcia, Juan	R-R	5-8	158	3-3-08	.208	.417	.226	22	72	53	9	11	1	0	0	10	15	4	0	0	18	2	2	20.8	25.0
German, Lewis	R-R	6-4	207	3-13-08	.200	.295	.335	47	177	155	25	31	7	1	4	21	16	5	0	0	54	16	1	9.0	30.5
Guerrero, Alejandro	R-R	6-1	156	9-4-07	.203	.396	.291	31	106	79	17	16	4	0	1	6	20	6	0	1	27	7	2	18.9	25.5
King, Luis Ramon	R-R	6-1	160	12-4-07	.192	.323	.385	8	31	26	4	5	2	0	1	7	1	4	0	0	12	0	0	3.2	38.7
King, Luis Steven	R-R	6-1	166	12-4-07	.288	.441	.415	42	154	118	26	34	12	0	1	18	24	9	0	1	23	12	5	15.6	14.9
Liriano, Daniel	R-R	6-1	176	3-14-07	.184	.295	.211	12	44	38	6	7	1	0	0	2	5	1	0	0	9	3	0	11.4	20.5
Longo, Anthony	R-R	6-0	158	2-9-07	.341	.400	.341	13	45	41	5	14	0	0	0	5	3	1	0	0	3	1	2	6.7	6.7
Luciano, Sandy	S-R	6-0	193	1-9-07	.290	.343	.339	17	67	62	9	18	3	0	0	10	5	0	0	0	4	1	1	7.5	6.0
Martinez, Emmanuel	L-R	5-10	176	12-25-07	.200	.317	.229	14	41	35	3	7	1	0	0	4	6	0	0	0	11	1	0	14.6	26.8
Mata, Richer	L-R	6-2	154	3-18-08	.137	.303	.189	34	119	95	13	13	2	0	1	7	22	1	0	1	37	4	3	18.5	31.1
Montilla, Jose	R-R	5-10	160	1-22-08	.167	.231	.250	3	13	12	1	2	1	0	0	0	1	0	0	0	4	0	1	0.0	30.8
Morales, Jesus	R-R	6-0	165	8-2-07	.182	.378	.200	19	74	55	5	10	1	0	0	5	16	2	0	1	7	2	0	21.6	9.5
Mota, Edgar	R-R	6-1	170	12-14-05	.167	.188	.167	22	65	60	4	10	0	0	0	11	2	0	1	2	10	1	0	3.1	15.4
Ortega, Jesus	R-R	5-10	160	6-24-08	.163	.308	.174	29	104	86	15	14	1	0	0	6	17	1	0	0	18	5	3	16.3	17.3
Rivero, Marwin	R-R	5-11	160	10-21-06	.143	.333	.190	8	27	21	4	3	1	0	0	5	4	2	0	0	7	5	1	14.8	25.9
Rivero, Roy	L-R	5-11	155	2-1-08	.245	.364	.300	33	133	110	21	27	4	1	0	12	21	0	1	1	9	5	6	15.8	6.8
Roque, Pedro	R-R	5-10	160	12-21-05	.222	.222	.444	3	9	9	0	2	0	1	0	0	0	0	0	0	1	0	0	0.0	11.1
Ruiz, Tony	R-R	6-3	170	12-8-05	.221	.298	.402	38	142	122	15	27	6	2	4	27	11	4	1	4	41	4	2	7.7	28.9

Pitching	B-T	Ht.	Wt.	DOB	W	L	ERA	G	GS	SV	IP	Hits	Runs	ER	HR	BB	SO	AVG	OBP	SLG	SO%	BB%	BF
Beras, Carlos	R-R	5-11	180	1-5-05	0	2	6.39	9	0	0	13	14	10	9	1	11	9	.280	.455	.480	13.4	16.4	67
Betemit, Wilson	R-R	6-1	170	7-27-08	0	4	6.23	13	8	0	26	32	23	18	2	18	17	.305	.408	.457	13.1	13.8	130
Campusano, Alving	R-R	6-2	150	4-9-07	0	2	3.20	9	2	0	20	14	11	7	1	19	17	.200	.400	.257	17.7	19.8	96
Carmona, Samuel	R-R	6-0	160	12-23-04	0	0	1.50	4	2	1	12	7	6	2	0	5	3	.163	.275	.209	5.9	9.8	51
Castillo, Keisther	R-R	6-2	180	9-24-07	0	2	3.57	6	6	0	18	13	10	7	3	6	18	.203	.297	.375	24.0	8.0	75
Cepeda, Enyer	R-R	5-9	148	10-27-06	3	1	6.23	7	0	0	9	11	7	6	2	11	3	.344	.511	.688	6.7	24.4	45
Cruz, Jose	R-R	6-4	200	4-29-05	0	1	3.86	7	7	0	21	14	10	9	1	6	19	.184	.287	.342	21.8	6.9	87
De La Rosa, Carlos	R-R	6-4	175	6-16-05	0	0	2.25	3	0	3	4	2	1	1	0	6	5	.143	.400	.214	25.0	30.0	20
Del Rosario, Oliver	R-L	6-1	170	12-11-04	0	1	4.96	11	0	3	16	9	9	9	0	13	18	.167	.366	.259	25.4	18.3	71
Done, Argenis	R-R	6-3	160	8-17-07	0	2	6.35	11	3	0	23	28	17	16	0	20	16	.261	.430	.352	14.0	17.5	114
Figueroa, Diego	R-R	5-11	175		0	0	0.00	1	0	0	2	0	0	0	0	1	0	.000	.000	.000	16.7	0.0	6
Garcia, Angel	S-R	6-1	170	8-25-08	1	1	10.31	11	0	0	18	21	24	21	0	24	11	.309	.500	.368	11.5	25.0	96
Garcia, Jesus	R-R	6-3	198	12-21-07	0	2	21.13	6	0	0	8	19	18	18	1	8	8	.487	.569	.641	15.7	15.7	51
Gutierrez, Julio	R-R	6-1	175	3-5-05	0	1	1.15	6	5	0	16	12	4	2	0	8	14	.214	.323	.268	21.5	12.3	65
Jhonni, Jordin	R-R	6-1	160	6-19-05	0	1	4.91	4	3	0	11	15	6	6	1	3	3	.349	.412	.488	3.9	7.8	51
Jimenez, Nomar	L-L	6-2	172	1-3-07	2	1	4.15	7	0	0	13	11	6	6	1	15	11	.260	.435	.360	15.9	21.7	69
Lara, Alfredo	L-L	6-2	180	12-21-06	0	0	9.39	6	0	0	8	13	11	8	0	7	4	.382	.500	.441	8.9	15.6	45
Luces, Carlos	R-R	5-11	160	5-22-07	4	2	5.82	13	0	1	22	22	20	14	1	18	21	.272	.419	.370	19.6	16.8	107
Mejia, Jose	L-L	6-1	170	12-9-06	1	4	5.86	12	6	0	28	22	22	18	0	23	33	.222	.398	.242	25.8	18.0	128
Montilla, Ricardo	R-R	6-1	160	1-21-07	4	2	4.61	10	2	1	27	27	16	14	1	15	19	.265	.355	.353	15.7	12.4	121
Mota, Edgar	R-R	6-1	170	12-14-05	1	0	0.00	2	0	0	2	0	0	0	0	1	0	.000	.286	.000	0.0	28.6	7
Olmos, Juan	R-R	6-2	175	11-22-04	0	1	7.88	12	0	1	16	18	16	14	1	19	12	.290	.463	.468	14.6	23.2	82
Regalado, Hancer	R-R	6-0	160	8-21-07	0	0	0.00	2	0	0	5	2	0	0	0	3	6	.118	.286	.118	28.6	14.3	21
Robles, Melvin	L-L	5-11	150	2-7-08	2	0	4.32	10	5	0	25	23	15	12	0	7	26	.250	.324	.326	25.2	6.8	103
Rojas, Javier	R-R	6-2	177	3-23-08	0	1	8.38	6	0	0	10	9	10	9	0	8	7	.243	.383	.405	14.9	17.0	47
Rojas, Marvin	R-R	6-3	185	4-10-04	0	1	0.00	1	0	0	4	0	4	0	2	0	.000	1.000	.000	0.0	50.0	4
Santo, Rafi	R-R	5-11	156	4-18-07	1	0	2.79	5	0	1	10	11	4	3	0	6	7	.297	.395	.405	16.3	14.0	43
Suarez, Junior	L-L	6-1	195	6-24-05	1	0	4.50	2	0	0	4	3	3	2	0	4	4	.231	.412	.385	23.5	23.5	17
Taveras, Neftali	R-R	6-1	175	7-18-04	1	0	7.04	4	0	1	8	7	6	6	0	3	5	.233	.324	.467	14.7	8.8	34
Toribio, Alberto	R-R	5-11	165	7-24-06	0	2	3.72	3	2	0	10	7	6	4	0	7	11	.206	.364	.235	25.0	15.9	44
Tovar, Geremy	L-L	6-2	176	4-25-08	0	0	9.58	10	0	0	10	9	11	11	0	16	13	.243	.463	.351	23.6	29.1	55

Fielding

C: Morales 18, Martinez 12, Mata 12, Longo 8, Mota 5, Montilla 2. **1B:** Ruiz 31, Mata 17, Mota 7. **2B:** Garcia 22, Rivero 18, Cruz 10, Ortega 3, De La Cruz 2, Liriano 2, Roque 1. **3B:** Garcia 24, King 18, Ortega 10, Cruz 3, De La Cruz 1. **SS:** King 19, Ortega 19, Rivero 11, Calcano 5, Roque 2, Cruz 1, Liriano 1. **LF:** De La Cruz 15, Chacon 12, Cruz 12, Fermin 10, Liriano 4, German 1, Guerrero 1, King 1. **CF:** German 42, King 7, Cruz 6, Fermin 2, Guerrero 1. **RF:** Guerrero 29, Luciano 16, Fermin 4, German 3, Chacon 2, Liriano 2

Los Angeles Angels

SEASON SYNOPSIS: Ranking 28th in the majors in team ERA and 25th in runs scored, the Angels endured their franchise-record 10th consecutive losing season, finishing 72-90, dropping 28 of their last 41 to finish in last place in the AL West. The losses and health challenges ended the two-year tenure of manager Ron Washington and, counting interim manager Ray Montgomery, the Angels have already had five managers since Mike Scioscia departed after 2018—the last time they won 80 games.

HIGH POINT: The club was 36-38 under Washington and fairly frisky, including an eight-game win streak in May that included a sweep at Dodger Stadium. The Angels swept the six-game season series in the Freeway Series. They hit 17 homers during the win streak en route to finishing fourth overall in the majors with 226, led by outfielders Jo Adell (37) and Taylor Ward (36), first-round picks in 2018 and 2015.

LOW POINT: Six position players pitched for the Angels, who used 35 actual pitchers as well. Their 4.91 starter ERA and 4.86 bullpen ERA both ranked last in the AL. As the team sagged under that weight, franchise icon Mike Trout slumped while stuck on 398 career home runs, with 126 homerless plate appearances. Trout had his worst full season, hitting just .232/.359/.439, but he played 130 games for the first time since 2019, hit No. 400 on a 485-foot tank Sept. 20 in Colorado, and hit four homers in the season's final four games.

NOTABLE ROOKIES: After graduating first-round picks Zach Neto (2022) and Nolan Schanuel (2023) quickly and with some success, 2024 first-rounder Christian Moore (.198/.284/.370 with poor fielding metrics) struggled to hold down a regular role. Undrafted free agent Bryce Teodosio (.553 OPS in 150 plate appearances) provided defensive value in center field, but the club's farm system provided little positive value to the big league club.

KEY TRANSACTIONS: Veteran free agents Kyle Hendricks and Yusei Kikuchi performed basically as expected, making 64 starts between them, with Kikuchi earning an all-star nod. Another free agent pitcher, 37-year-old Kenley Jansen, had a strong season as a closer (5-4, 2.59, 29 SV). The Angels' outfield depth led them to release Mickey Moniak in March, though he latched on in Colorado and hit 24 homers.

OPENING DAY PAYROLL: $190,508,096 (13th)

PLAYERS OF THE YEAR

MAJOR LEAGUE
Zach Neto
SS
.257/.319/.474
26 HR, 26 SB, 29 2B
2.75 assists/9 led SS

MINOR LEAGUE
Raudi Rodriguez
OF
(A)
.281/.372/.470
14 HR, 38 SB, 63 BB

ORGANIZATION LEADERS

Batting		*Qualifiers
MAJORS		
* AVG	Nolan Schanuel	.264
* OPS	Mike Trout	.797
HR	Jo Adell	37
RBI	Taylor Ward	103
MINORS		
* AVG	Carter Kieboom, Salt Lake	.319
* OBP	Rio Foster, Tri-City	.407
* SLG	Chad Stevens, Salt Lake	.480
* OPS	Chad Stevens, Salt Lake	.855
R	Raudi Rodriguez, Inland Empire	90
H	Nelson Rada, Salt Lake/Rocket City	143
TB	Raudi Rodriguez, Inland Empire	226
2B	Ben Gobbel, Salt Lake/Rocket City/Tri-City	30
2B	Denzer Guzman, Salt Lake/Rocket City	30
3B	Raudi Rodriguez, Inland Empire	14
HR	Niko Kavadas, Salt Lake	28
RBI	Niko Kavadas, Salt Lake	84
BB	Ryan Nicholson, Rocket City/Tri-City	76
SO	Cole Fontenelle, Rocket City/Tri-City	172
SB	Nelson Rada, Salt Lake/Rocket City	54

Pitching		#Qualifiers
MAJORS		
W	Tyler Anderson	10
# ERA	Tyler Anderson	3.81
SO	Tyler Anderson	142
SV	Carlos Estevez	29
MINORS		
W	Dakota Hudson, Salt Lake	8
W	Brett Kerry, Salt Lake/ACL Angels	8
W	Samuel Aldegheri, Salt Lake/Rocket City	8
L	George Klassen, Salt Lake/Rocket City	12
# ERA	Samuel Aldegheri, Salt Lake/Rocket City	3.78
G	Jared Southard, Salt Lake/Rocket City	49
G	Sammy Natera, Salt Lake/Rocket City	49
GS	Walbert Urena, Salt Lake/Rocket City	28
SV	Ben Thompson, Inland Empire	11
IP	Chris Clark, Rocket City/Tri-City/Inland Empire	144.7
BB	Francis Texido, Tri-City/Inland Empire	92
SO	Chris Clark, Rocket City/Tri-City/Inland Empire	153
# AVG	Chris Cortez, Tri-City	.224

2025 PERFORMANCE

General Manager: Perry Minasian. **Farm Director:** Joey Prebynski. **Scouting Director:** Tim McIlvaine.

Class	Team	League	W	L	PCT	Finish	Manager
Majors	Los Angeles Angels	American	72	90	.444	13 (15)	Ron Washington
Triple-A	Salt Lake Bees	Pacific Coast	65	84	.436	8 (10)	Keith Johnson
Double-A	Rocket City Trash Pandas	Southern	45	92	.328	8 (8)	Andy Schatzley
High-A	Tri-City Dust Devils	Northwest	61	70	.466	3 (6)	Dann Bilardello
Low-A	Inland Empire 66ers	California	60	72	.455	6 (8)	Dave Stapleton
Rookie	ACL Angels	Arizona Complex	38	22	.633	2 (15)	Hainley Statia
Rookie	DSL Angels	Dominican	34	22	.607	10 (52)	Hector De La Cruz
Overall 2025 Minor League Record			303	362	.456	27th (30)	

ORGANIZATION STATISTICS

LOS ANGELES ANGELS
AMERICAN LEAGUE

Batting	B-T	Ht.	Wt.	DOB	AVG	OBP	SLG	G	PA	AB	R	H	2B	3B	HR	RBI	BB	HBP	SH	SF	SO	SB	CS	BB%	SO%
Adell, Jo	R-R	6-3	215	4-8-99	.236	.293	.485	152	573	526	63	124	18	1	37	98	33	10	0	1	151	5	1	5.8	26.4
Anderson, Tim	R-R	6-1	185	6-23-93	.205	.258	.241	31	90	83	8	17	3	0	0	3	3	3	1	0	29	1	1	3.3	32.2
Campero, Gustavo	S-R	5-8	183	9-20-97	.172	.273	.345	28	66	58	9	10	1	0	3	8	5	3	0	0	14	4	1	7.6	21.2
d'Arnaud, Travis	R-R	6-2	210	2-10-89	.197	.255	.343	69	231	213	16	42	13	0	6	21	13	4	0	1	74	0	0	5.6	32.0
Davidson, Logan	S-R	6-3	185	12-26-97	.182	.182	.364	10	23	22	2	4	1	0	1	2	0	0	1	0	10	0	0	0.0	43.5
Davis, J.D.	R-R	6-3	218	4-27-93	.111	.111	.111	5	9	9	0	1	0	0	0	0	0	0	0	0	3	0	0	0.0	33.3
Guzman, Denzer	R-R	6-1	180	10-04-04	.190	.209	.357	13	43	42	4	8	1	0	2	3	1	0	0	0	22	0	0	2.3	51.2
Kavadas, Niko	L-R	5-11	235	10-27-98	.100	.217	.100	10	23	20	0	2	0	0	0	0	3	0	0	0	10	0	0	13.0	43.5
Kieboom, Carter	R-R	6-2	211	9-3-97	.250	.250	.250	3	8	8	0	2	0	0	0	1	0	0	0	0	1	0	0	0.0	12.5
Kingery, Scott	R-R	5-10	180	4-29-94	.148	.207	.185	19	29	27	3	4	1	0	0	0	2	0	0	0	11	1	1	6.9	37.9
Lopez, Nicky	L-R	5-11	180	3-13-95	.000	.000	.000	5	6	6	0	0	0	0	0	0	0	0	0	0	1	0	0	0.0	16.7
Lugo, Matthew	R-R	6-1	187	5-9-01	.232	.243	.464	31	70	69	9	16	2	1	4	9	0	1	0	0	24	0	0	0.0	34.3
Moncada, Yoan	S-R	6-2	225	5-27-95	.234	.336	.448	84	289	248	39	58	13	2	12	35	32	7	0	2	75	0	0	11.1	26.0
Moore, Christian	R-R	6-1	210	10-21-02	.198	.284	.370	53	184	162	20	32	5	1	7	16	19	1	1	1	62	3	0	10.3	33.7
Neto, Zach	R-R	6-0	185	1-31-01	.257	.319	.474	128	554	502	82	129	29	1	26	62	33	14	2	3	149	26	9	6.0	26.9
Newman, Kevin	R-R	6-1	195	8-4-93	.202	.209	.272	57	116	114	13	23	2	0	2	11	1	0	1	0	23	1	0	0.9	19.8
O'Hoppe, Logan	R-R	6-2	185	2-9-00	.213	.258	.371	119	451	423	35	90	8	1	19	43	24	2	1	1	139	2	1	5.3	30.8
Paris, Kyren	R-R	6-0	180	11-11-01	.190	.266	.381	44	140	126	20	24	4	1	6	11	10	3	0	0	59	7	1	7.1	42.1
Peraza, Oswald	R-R	6-0	200	6-15-00	.186	.245	.267	35	95	86	6	16	1	0	2	7	6	1	0	1	33	6	0	6.3	34.7
Rengifo, Luis	S-R	5-10	195	2-26-97	.238	.287	.335	147	541	501	55	119	16	3	9	43	33	3	1	3	104	10	7	6.1	19.2
Rivero, Sebastian	R-R	6-1	210	11-16-98	.182	.206	.242	11	34	33	4	6	2	0	0	2	1	0	0	0	9	1	0	2.9	26.5
Schanuel, Nolan	L-R	6-3	195	2-14-02	.264	.353	.389	132	564	488	64	129	23	1	12	53	59	10	3	4	71	5	1	10.5	12.6
Soler, Jorge	R-R	6-4	235	2-25-92	.215	.293	.387	82	315	279	31	60	12	0	12	34	28	4	0	3	94	0	0	8.9	29.8
Stevens, Chad	R-R	6-3	215	2-3-99	.154	.154	.154	5	14	13	1	2	0	0	0	0	0	1	0	0	7	0	1	0.0	50.0
Taylor, Chris	R-R	6-1	196	8-29-90	.178	.278	.321	30	90	78	11	14	5	0	2	10	5	6	0	1	29	2	1	5.6	32.2
Teodosio, Bryce	R-L	6-3	220	6-18-99	.203	.248	.304	50	150	138	12	28	7	2	1	7	5	4	1	2	47	7	1	3.3	31.3
Trout, Mike	R-R	6-2	235	8-7-91	.232	.359	.439	130	556	456	73	106	14	1	26	64	87	6	0	6	178	2	0	15.6	32.0
Wade, LaMonte	L-L	6-1	205	1-1-94	.169	.260	.215	30	73	65	7	11	3	0	0	3	8	2	0	0	23	1	0	8.2	31.5
Ward, Taylor	R-R	6-1	200	12-14-93	.228	.317	.475	157	663	579	86	132	31	2	36	103	75	3	0	6	175	4	1	11.3	26.4

Pitching	B-T	Ht.	Wt.	DOB	W	L	ERA	G	GS	SV	IP	Hits	Runs	ER	HR	BB	SO	AVG	OBP	SLG	SO%	BB%	BF
Aldegheri, Samuel	L-L	6-1	180	9-19-01	0	2	7.90	4	2	0	14	20	14	12	3	10	12	.345	.466	.569	16.4	13.7	73
Anderson, Ian	R-R	6-3	170	5-2-98	0	1	11.57	7	0	0	9	17	13	12	2	7	8	.386	.471	.568	15.7	13.7	51
Anderson, Shaun	R-R	6-6	228	10-29-94	1	0	10.32	7	0	0	11	20	13	13	6	3	11	.377	.411	.736	19.6	5.4	56
Anderson, Tyler	L-L	6-2	220	12-30-89	2	8	4.56	26	26	0	136	135	73	69	28	57	104	.253	.326	.477	17.4	9.5	599
Bachman, Sam	R-R	6-1	235	9-30-99	2	3	6.20	23	0	0	20	22	15	14	1	10	18	.268	.355	.354	19.1	10.6	94
Brogdon, Connor	R-R	6-6	205	1-29-95	3	2	5.55	43	0	0	47	45	31	29	11	18	49	.253	.318	.500	24.6	9.0	199
Burke, Brock	L-L	6-4	210	8-4-96	7	1	3.36	69	1	0	62	58	24	23	8	18	52	.254	.311	.417	20.2	7.0	257
Chafin, Andrew	R-L	6-2	235	6-17-90	0	0	1.98	16	0	0	14	9	3	3	1	7	18	.191	.291	.255	32.7	12.7	55
Dana, Caden	R-R	6-4	215	12-17-03	0	4	6.40	7	5	0	32	30	24	23	9	18	33	.256	.350	.513	23.4	12.8	141
Darrell-Hicks, Michael	R-R	6-5	220	11-13-97	1	0	9.39	6	0	0	8	10	8	8	1	4	6	.323	.395	.452	15.8	10.5	38
Davidson, Logan	S-R	6-3	185	12-26-97	0	0	0.00	1	0	0	1	0	0	0	0	0	1	.000	.000	.000	33.3	0.0	3
Detmers, Reid	L-L	6-2	210	7-8-99	5	3	3.96	61	0	3	64	58	29	28	6	25	80	.244	.320	.357	30.1	9.4	266
Eder, Jake	L-L	6-4	215	10-9-98	0	1	4.91	8	0	0	18	15	10	10	3	9	15	.224	.325	.403	19.2	11.5	78
Edwards, Carl	R-R	6-3	165	9-3-91	0	0	9.00	2	0	0	3	4	3	3	1	1	2	.364	.385	.636	15.4	7.7	13
Farris, Mitch	L-L	6-2	187	2-14-01	1	3	6.66	5	5	0	24	24	19	18	4	11	24	.261	.336	.489	22.4	10.3	107
Fermin, Jose	R-R	6-3	248	11-28-01	3	2	4.46	40	0	2	54	35	25	21	17	8	23	.197	.322	.409	25.7	15.1	152
Fulmer, Carson	R-R	6-0	210	12-13-93	0	0	5.83	13	0	0	29	25	19	19	5	11	26	.270	.336	.495	21.8	9.2	120
Garcia, Luis	R-R	6-2	240	1-30-87	0	2	2.00	20	0	2	18	16	5	4	0	8	17	.250	.324	.313	23.0	10.8	74
Hendricks, Kyle	R-R	6-3	190	12-7-89	8	10	4.76	31	31	0	165	167	92	87	25	43	114	.262	.311	.447	16.4	6.2	695
Jansen, Kenley	R-R	6-5	265	9-30-87	5	4	2.59	62	0	29	59	37	18	17	8	19	57	.175	.245	.321	24.4	8.1	234
Johnson, Ryan	R-R	6-6	212	9-8-01	1	1	7.36	14	0	1	15	24	15	12	4	5	16	.364	.403	.561	22.2	6.9	72
Joyce, Ben	R-R	6-5	225	9-17-00	1	0	6.23	5	0	0	4	5	4	3	1	1	2	.263	.300	.579	5.0	5.0	20
Kavadas, Niko	L-R	5-11	235	10-27-98	0	0	0.00	1	0	0	2	0	0	0	0	1	1	.375	.444	.375	11.1	11.1	9

LOS ANGELES ANGELS

Pitching (continued)

Player	B-T	Ht	Wt	DOB	W L	ERA	G	GS	CG SV	IP	H	R	ER	HR	BB	SO	AVG	OBP	SLG	G/F	BB/9	IP
Kikuchi, Yusei	L-L	6-0	210	6-17-91	7 11	3.99	33	33	0	178	180	87	79	24	74	174	.261	.333	.419	22.5	9.6	772
Kingery, Scott	R-R	5-10	180	4-29-94	0 0	36.00	1	0	0	2	12	8	8	2	0	1	.667	1.056	5.6	0.0	18
Kochanowicz, Jack	L-R	6-7	228	12-22-00	3 11	6.81	23	23	0	111	136	89	84	21	58	72	.309	.393	.489	14.1	11.3	512
Lopez, Nicky	L-R	5-11	180	3-13-95	0 0	0.00	1	0	0	0	0	0	0	0	0	1	0	.000	.500	.000	0.0	50.0	2
McDaniels, Garrett	L-L	6-2	180	12-15-99	0 0	5.91	10	0	0	11	13	8	7	2	8	6	.317	.440	.512	12.0	16.0	50
Mederos, Victor	R-R	6-2	227	6-8-01	0 2	7.41	5	3	0	17	18	14	14	4	12	14	.277	.407	.585	17.3	14.8	81
Neris, Hector	R-R	6-2	227	6-14-89	3 0	5.14	20	0	0	14	11	9	8	2	7	19	.216	.322	.412	31.7	11.7	60
Newman, Kevin	R-R	6-1	195	8-4-93	0 0	6.75	2	0	0	4	4	3	3	2	0	0	.250	.250	.750	0.0	0.0	16
Peralta, Sammy	L-L	6-2	205	5-10-98	0 1	7.59	5	0	0	11	14	12	9	0	6	8	.318	.385	.409	15.4	11.5	52
Peraza, Oswald	R-R	6-0	200	6-15-00	0 0	30.86	2	0	0	2	9	8	8	1	0	0	.600	.625	.867	0.0	0.0	16
Quijada, Jose	L-L	5-11	215	11-9-95	0 0	0.00	2	0	0	1	1	0	0	0	2	3	.167	.375	.167	37.5	25.0	8
Silseth, Chase	R-R	6-0	217	5-18-00	0 1	1.64	10	0	0	11	10	2	2	1	6	13	.244	.347	.366	26.5	12.2	49
Soriano, Jose	R-R	6-3	220	10-20-98	10 11	4.26	31	31	0	169	158	89	80	12	78	152	.249	.335	.353	21.0	10.8	724
Stephenson, Robert	R-R	6-3	205	2-24-93	2 0	2.70	12	0	0	10	7	4	3	1	3	10	.189	.268	.378	23.8	7.1	42
Strickland, Hunter	R-R	6-3	225	9-24-88	1 2	3.27	19	0	1	22	17	9	8	2	10	14	.213	.297	.363	15.4	11.0	91
Toussaint, Touki	R-R	6-3	215	6-20-96	0 0	9.00	1	0	0	2	4	2	2	0	1	3	.400	.455	.500	27.3	9.1	11
Urena, Jose	R-R	6-2	208	9-12-91	0 0	3.79	6	1	0	19	17	9	8	2	10	14	.230	.329	.419	16.5	11.8	85
Zeferjahn, Ryan	R-R	6-5	209	2-28-98	6 5	4.74	62	1	2	57	49	31	30	12	35	73	.227	.344	.431	28.4	13.6	257

Fielding

Catcher

Catcher	PCT	G	PO	A	E	DP	PB
d'Arnaud	.996	58	452	18	2	5	1
O'Hoppe	.994	99	757	28	5	3	5
Rivero	.989	11	86	5	1	0	0
Wallach	1.000	1	4	0	0	0	0
Newman	.950	8	7	12	1	3	
Paris	1.000	19	23	60	0	16	
Rengifo	.988	74	82	167	3	44	
Stevens	1.000	3	6	10	0	2	
Taylor	1.000	8	11	16	0	9	
Lopez	.500	1	0	1	1	0	
Neto	.979	125	175	329	11	86	
Newman	.984	14	21	41	1	7	
Peraza	1.000	5	3	10	0	1	
Rengifo	.000	1	0	0	0	0	

First Base

First Base	PCT	G	PO	A	E	DP
Davidson	.963	8	49	3	2	4
Davis	1.000	4	16	1	0	1
Kavadas	1.000	10	56	4	0	7
Kieboom	.933	3	14	0	1	0
Newman	1.000	2	9	3	0	1
Peraza	.963	17	97	7	4	12
Schanuel	.994	131	994	60	6	120
Wade	1.000	4	38	2	0	4

Third Base

Third Base	PCT	G	PO	A	E	DP
Davis	1.000	1	1	2	0	0
Lopez	1.000	2	0	5	0	1
Moncada	.946	76	52	107	9	12
Newman	.915	32	20	23	4	4
Peraza	1.000	15	12	15	0	2
Rengifo	.949	76	47	120	9	15
Stevens	1.000	2	1	1	0	0
Taylor	1.000	3	1	1	0	0

Outfield

Outfield	PCT	G	PO	A	E	DP
Adell	.980	158	333	4	7	1
Campero	.977	26	40	2	1	0
Kingery	1.000	5	3	0	0	0
Lopez	.000	1	0	0	0	0
Lugo	.933	28	27	1	2	0
Paris	1.000	24	54	1	0	0
Rengifo	1.000	10	6	1	0	0
Soler	1.000	40	55	1	0	0
Taylor	1.000	22	33	1	0	1
Teodosio	.993	50	140	0	1	0
Trout	1.000	22	46	2	0	0
Wade	1.000	22	33	2	0	0
Ward	.987	153	303	4	4	1

Second Base

Second Base	PCT	G	PO	A	E	DP
Anderson	.969	16	23	40	2	14
Kingery	1.000	7	5	21	0	3
Moore	.983	53	62	109	3	23

Shortstop

Shortstop	PCT	G	PO	A	E	DP
Anderson	.960	15	20	28	2	9
Guzman	.952	13	16	24	2	5
Kingery	.800	3	2	2	1	1

SALT LAKE BEES — TRIPLE-A
PACIFIC COAST LEAGUE

Batting

Player	B-T	Ht	Wt	DOB	AVG	OBP	SLG	G	PA	AB	R	H	2B	3B	HR	RBI	BB	HBP	SH	SF	SO	SB	CS	BB%	SO%
Biggio, Cavan	L-R	6-2	200	4-11-95	.242	.375	.303	31	120	99	21	24	3	0	1	12	16	5	0	0	37	3	2	13.3	30.8
Campero, Gustavo	S-R	5-8	183	9-7-97	.322	.399	.476	36	164	143	20	46	10	3	2	18	16	3	1	1	20	11	1	9.8	12.2
Daly, Mitchell	R-R	6-1	185	5-16-01	.217	.290	.313	24	94	83	13	18	3	1	1	13	7	2	1	1	29	2	0	7.4	30.9
Davis, J.D.	R-R	6-3	218	4-27-93	.294	.371	.524	50	213	187	36	55	11	1	10	38	21	3	0	2	56	6	1	9.9	26.3
Drury, Brandon	R-R	6-2	230	8-21-92	.233	.338	.346	36	154	133	19	31	7	1	2	13	18	3	0	0	32	0	1	11.7	20.8
Emmerson, Myles	R-R	5-11	185	5-15-98	1.000	1.000	2.000	1	1	1	0	1	0	0	0	0	0	0	0	0	0	0	0	0.0	0.0
Flint, Tucker	L-L	6-2	215	4-5-01	.224	.324	.418	104	395	340	63	76	17	2	15	59	47	4	3	1	151	16	1	11.9	38.2
Gamel, Ben	L-L	5-10	180	5-17-92	.282	.417	.612	32	127	103	19	29	8	1	8	15	22	2	0	0	29	0	1	17.3	22.8
Gobbel, Ben	R-R	6-1	190	1-31-01	.286	.397	.592	13	58	49	16	14	3	0	4	8	7	2	0	0	13	1	2	12.1	22.4
Guzman, Denzer	R-R	6-1	180	2-8-04	.262	.366	.454	36	153	130	26	34	7	0	6	21	21	1	0	1	45	6	0	13.7	29.4
Holland, Korey	R-R	5-10	170	1-1-00	.232	.263	.331	44	161	151	15	35	6	0	3	20	7	0	1	2	60	7	0	4.3	37.3
Humphreys, Zach	R-R	5-10	195	10-7-98	.205	.308	.327	63	227	196	21	44	14	0	2	35	22	3	3	3	48	7	0	9.7	21.1
Kavadas, Niko	L-L	5-11	235	10-27-98	.235	.362	.479	116	527	434	76	102	16	3	28	84	75	14	0	4	163	1	1	14.2	30.9
Kieboom, Carter	R-R	6-2	211	9-3-97	.319	.368	.449	93	402	370	48	118	17	2	9	57	30	0	0	2	76	11	1	7.5	18.9
Kingery, Scott	R-R	5-10	180	4-29-94	.228	.284	.402	59	243	224	29	51	10	4	7	28	16	2	0	1	61	2	0	6.6	25.1
Lugo, Matthew	R-R	6-1	187	5-9-01	.220	.320	.443	102	462	424	63	111	28	5	13	60	32	4	2	0	136	11	7	6.9	29.4
Mershon, David	S-R	5-8	160	5-24-03	.122	.232	.163	14	57	49	2	6	2	0	0	0	7	0	1	0	19	1	2	12.3	33.3
Moore, Christian	R-R	6-1	210	10-21-02	.292	.370	.483	30	138	120	22	35	4	2	5	26	14	2	0	2	40	4	1	10.1	29.0
Neto, Zach	R-R	6-0	185	1-31-01	.286	.397	.592	13	58	49	16	14	3	0	4	8	7	2	0	0	13	1	2	12.1	22.4
Noda, Ryan	L-L	6-3	217	3-30-96	.148	.364	.238	38	154	115	18	17	2	0	4	8	31	8	0	0	53	2	1	20.1	34.4
Paris, Kyren	R-R	6-0	180	11-11-01	.225	.360	.468	32	137	111	24	25	3	3	6	16	20	4	1	1	37	11	1	14.6	27.0
Rada, Nelson	L-L	5-10	160	8-24-05	.323	.433	.416	42	201	161	33	52	6	3	1	17	30	2	7	1	35	20	6	14.9	17.4
Ramirez, Alexander	R-R	6-3	210	11-16-98	.250	.250	.250	5	17	16	3	3	1	0	0	1	0	0	0	1	10	0	1	5.9	58.8
Rivero, Sebastian	R-R	6-1	210	11-16-98	.264	.309	.429	66	254	231	31	61	9	1	9	45	14	2	2	4	45	2	1	5.5	17.7
Robinson, Chuckie	R-R	6-0	215	12-14-94	.272	.315	.388	27	112	103	11	28	5	2	1	18	5	2	1	1	29	0	0	4.5	25.9
Sanchez, Yolmer	S-R	5-8	210	6-29-92	.246	.397	.329	120	492	414	61	102	16	3	4	36	67	5	4	2	114	9	3	13.6	23.2
Schanuel, Nolan	L-R	6-3	195	2-14-02	.500	.500	.625	2	8	8	3	4	1	0	0	0	0	0	0	0	3	0	0	0.0	37.5
Stevens, Chad	R-R	6-3	215	2-3-99	.290	.375	.480	126	528	458	82	133	23	5	18	78	58	7	0	5	117	20	3	11.0	22.2
Taylor, Chris	R-R	6-1	190	8-29-90	.211	.211	.211	5	20	19	3	4	0	0	0	1	0	0	0	1	6	0	0	0.0	30.0
Teodosio, Bryce	R-L	6-3	220	6-18-99	.321	.368	.491	16	58	53	6	17	3	3	0	5	3	1	1	0	10	7	1	5.2	17.2
Wallach, Chad	R-R	6-2	246	11-4-91	.250	.308	.447	39	145	132	18	33	8	6	1	6	25	9	2	2	0	34	0	1	6.2	23.4

LOS ANGELES ANGELS

Pitching	B-T	Ht.	Wt.	DOB	W	L	ERA	G	GS	SV	IP	Hits	Runs	ER	HR	BB	SO	AVG	OBP	SLG	SO%	BB%	BF
Aldegheri, Samuel	L-L	6-1	180	9-19-01	0	0	5.40	1	1	0	5	5	3	3	1	2	3	.250	.375	.500	12.5	8.3	24
Anderson, Shaun	R-R	6-6	228	10-29-94	5	8	6.02	24	23	0	117	146	85	78	15	39	88	.311	.363	.479	16.7	7.4	527
Bachman, Sam	R-R	6-1	235	9-30-99	1	1	0.71	24	0	5	25	19	3	2	0	16	24	.207	.330	.207	21.8	14.5	110
Briceno, Endrys	R-R	6-5	175	2-7-92	2	1	12.46	28	0	0	39	53	57	54	12	36	36	.321	.450	.594	17.1	17.1	210
Brogdon, Connor	R-R	6-6	205	1-29-95	1	2	9.82	17	1	1	22	38	25	24	7	11	30	.369	.444	.641	25.4	9.3	118
Choban, Brady	R-R	6-5	240	9-16-00	1	1	2.38	9	0	0	11	8	3	3	0	4	8	.222	.326	.333	18.6	9.3	43
Crouse, Hans	L-R	6-4	180	9-15-98	0	0	0.00	2	0	1	1	0	0	0	0	0	1	.000	.000	.000	33.3	0.0	3
Dana, Caden	R-R	6-4	215	12-17-03	6	9	5.93	18	18	0	82	84	60	54	14	46	85	.265	.360	.461	23.0	12.4	370
Darrell-Hicks, Michael	R-R	6-5	220	11-13-97	0	2	8.87	17	0	1	22	33	22	22	6	8	23	.340	.389	.598	21.3	7.4	108
Dashwood, Jack	L-L	6-6	240	11-17-97	2	6	7.33	48	2	1	54	77	49	44	10	24	56	.333	.394	.554	21.4	9.2	262
Eder, Jake	L-L	6-4	215	10-9-98	2	7	6.11	13	13	0	63	77	43	43	13	16	52	.297	.343	.506	18.5	5.7	281
Edwards, Carl	R-R	6-3	165	9-3-91	0	0	1.54	7	1	2	12	14	6	2	1	3	13	.292	.346	.417	25.0	5.8	52
Erla, Mason	R-R	6-4	200	8-19-97	1	3	7.48	10	1	0	22	31	21	18	5	13	16	.333	.421	.548	15.0	12.1	107
Farmer, Buck	L-R	6-4	243	2-20-91	1	2	9.00	12	0	2	12	16	13	12	1	7	11	.333	.421	.521	18.6	11.9	59
Felipe, Angel	R-R	6-5	190	8-30-97	0	0	8.89	27	2	0	26	32	26	26	2	35	38	.291	.469	.427	25.9	23.8	147
Fermin, Jose	R-R	6-3	248	11-28-01	1	0	1.74	10	0	2	10	9	2	2	1	5	15	.220	.304	.317	32.6	10.9	46
Fulmer, Carson	R-R	6-0	210	12-13-93	1	0	1.54	9	0	0	12	13	3	2	0	6	12	.283	.358	.348	22.6	11.3	53
Gaston, Sandy	R-R	6-3	200	12-16-01	0	1	13.50	2	0	0	4	6	6	6	2	5	3	.375	.545	.813	13.0	21.7	23
Gonzalez, Victor	L-L	6-0	180	11-16-95	2	0	4.12	35	0	5	39	32	19	18	3	33	35	.224	.380	.329	18.8	17.7	186
Harding, Houston	L-L	6-1	230	5-22-98	0	0	18.00	1	0	0	2	3	4	4	0	4	1	.333	.538	.333	7.7	30.8	13
Holmes, Bridger	R-R	6-4	218	8-27-02	0	0	0.00	1	0	0	2	1	1	0	0	4	2	.125	.417	.125	16.7	33.3	12
Hudson, Dakota	R-R	6-5	215	9-15-94	8	7	6.68	28	24	0	136	193	112	101	22	51	89	.335	.394	.533	13.8	7.9	643
Humphreys, Zach	R-R	5-10	195	10-9-97	0	0	0.00	2	0	0	2	1	0	0	0	0	1	.167	.167	.167	16.7	0.0	6
Hurtado, Joel	R-R	6-2	180	2-6-01	0	0	3.60	1	1	0	5	3	2	2	0	1	3	.176	.222	.235	15.8	5.3	19
Kerry, Brett	R-R	6-0	213	4-12-99	8	9	7.75	21	19	0	108	134	94	93	27	40	81	.306	.366	.610	16.6	8.2	489
Klassen, George	R-R	6-2	170	1-26-02	0	0	3.00	1	1	0	6	6	2	2	0	1	8	.261	.292	.261	33.3	4.2	24
Kochanowicz, Jack	L-R	6-7	228	12-22-00	0	2	5.95	4	4	0	20	18	15	13	3	16	16	.234	.385	.403	16.7	16.7	96
McDaniels, Garrett	L-L	6-2	180	12-15-99	0	0	12.00	2	0	0	3	3	4	4	0	3	4	.250	.400	.333	26.7	20.0	15
Mederos, Victor	R-R	6-2	227	6-8-01	7	5	3.39	16	16	0	88	83	34	33	6	34	71	.247	.333	.354	18.6	8.9	382
Murphy, Luke	R-R	6-5	190	11-5-99	0	.2	12.24	23	1	0	29	51	40	39	7	19	30	.375	.456	.588	19.0	12.0	158
Natera, Sammy	L-L	6-4	225	11-6-99	0	0	3.86	8	0	0	9	5	9	4	2	11	17	.147	.348	.382	37.0	23.9	46
Neris, Hector	R-R	6-2	227	6-14-89	0	1	4.50	4	0	2	4	3	2	2	1	1	8	.200	.250	.400	50.0	6.3	16
Peralta, Sammy	L-L	6-2	205	5-10-98	6	2	4.33	24	7	0	71	66	39	34	9	14	70	.250	.290	.432	24.1	4.8	291
Petersen, Michael	R-R	6-7	195	5-16-94	0	0	13.50	1	0	0	1	4	2	2	0	0	2	.500	.500	.500	25.0	0.0	8
Phillips, Dylan	L-L	6-0	220	6-16-99	0	1	5.73	5	0	0	11	14	7	7	3	1	13	.304	.319	.609	27.7	2.1	47
Quijada, Jose	L-L	5-11	215	11-9-95	1	2	1.98	13	0	2	14	10	4	3	2	8	18	.196	.305	.314	29.5	13.1	61
Rivero, Sebastian	R-R	6-1	195	11-16-98	0	0	5.40	2	0	0	2	1	1	1	1	0	0	.167	.286	.667	0.0	0.0	7
Sanchez, Yolmer	S-R	5-8	210	6-29-92	0	1	33.75	2	0	0	1	7	5	5	0	1	0	.636	.667	.818	0.0	8.3	12
Silseth, Chase	R-R	6-0	217	5-18-00	3	2	3.23	18	7	3	39	27	16	14	1	24	43	.196	.323	.268	25.6	14.3	168
Southard, Jared	R-R	6-2	220	10-4-00	1	0	4.23	27	0	2	38	36	20	18	5	14	42	.250	.331	.417	25.8	8.6	163
Stephenson, Robert	R-R	6-3	205	2-24-93	0	0	5.40	5	0	0	5	4	3	3	2	1	7	.222	.263	.556	36.8	5.3	19
Strickland, Hunter	R-R	6-3	225	9-24-88	0	1	3.00	3	0	0	3	3	1	1	1	1	2	.250	.308	.583	15.4	7.7	13
Toussaint, Touki	R-R	6-3	215	6-20-96	3	3	7.34	24	4	2	69	78	61	56	11	52	72	.293	.410	.466	21.9	15.8	329
Urena, Walbert	R-R	6-0	170	1-25-04	0	0	3.18	1	1	0	6	4	2	2	0	3	10	.190	.292	.238	41.7	12.5	24
Vasquez, Andrew	L-L	6-6	235	9-14-93	0	0	6.23	10	0	0	13	18	10	9	3	5	10	.321	.377	.643	16.1	8.1	62
Yovan, Kenyon	R-R	6-2	221	12-28-97	2	3	5.08	32	2	1	39	47	23	22	2	20	41	.299	.381	.420	22.5	11.0	182

Fielding

Catcher	PCT	G	PO	A	E	DP	PB
Campero	1.000	1	1	0	0	0	0
Emmerson	1.000	1	0	0	0	0	0
Humphreys	.987	39	285	18	4	3	1
Rivero	.990	56	486	20	5	3	5
Robinson	.996	27	222	19	1	5	0
Wallach	.989	32	248	13	3	1	1

First Base	PCT	G	PO	A	E	DP
Biggio	1.000	7	48	6	0	3
Davis	1.000	14	92	10	0	8
Drury	.991	15	110	6	1	7
Flint	.939	3	29	2	2	1
Humphreys	1.000	6	44	0	0	4
Kavadas	.989	68	503	35	6	53
Kieboom	.988	32	227	12	3	30
Noda	1.000	10	67	3	0	7
Schanuel	1.000	2	14	0	0	3
Stevens	.889	1	8	0	1	1
Wallach	1.000	2	7	0	0	1

Second Base	PCT	G	PO	A	E	DP
Biggio	1.000	10	16	15	0	5
Daly	1.000	3	4	9	0	3
Humphreys	1.000	5	8	12	0	2
Kieboom	.929	13	18	34	4	8

	PCT	G	PO	A	E	DP
Kingery	1.000	9	10	17	0	3
Mershon	1.000	1	2	1	0	0
Moore	.984	28	44	82	2	23
Paris	.957	11	13	32	2	5
Sanchez	.979	59	93	145	5	38
Stevens	.976	20	35	47	2	14

Third Base	PCT	G	PO	A	E	DP
Biggio	1.000	4	2	7	0	1
Daly	.977	21	15	27	1	3
Davis	.962	24	13	38	2	5
Drury	.963	11	7	19	1	6
Gobbel	1.000	3	2	6	0	1
Guzman	.983	23	15	42	1	2
Kavadas	.900	5	1	8	1	1
Kieboom	.951	13	13	26	2	3
Kingery	1.000	8	5	15	0	2
Mershon	.900	3	0	9	1	1
Sanchez	.943	15	6	27	2	3
Stevens	.935	27	16	42	4	6
Taylor	1.000	1	2	1	0	0

Shortstop	PCT	G	PO	A	E	DP
Guzman	.962	13	18	33	2	9
Kingery	.940	23	26	68	6	12
Mershon	.927	9	15	23	3	8

	PCT	G	PO	A	E	DP
Neto	.971	8	14	20	1	7
Sanchez	.974	32	49	98	4	12
Stevens	.960	71	83	154	10	31
Taylor	1.000	1	1	3	0	1

Outfield	PCT	G	PO	A	E	DP
Biggio	1.000	8	15	0	0	0
Campero	.983	34	56	1	1	0
Flint	.981	93	156	3	3	0
Gamel	1.000	19	35	1	0	0
Holland	1.000	43	70	2	0	0
Kavadas	.979	28	44	3	1	0
Kingery	.981	16	51	0	1	0
Lugo	.995	100	198	2	1	1
Noda	.973	22	36	0	1	0
Paris	.980	20	45	3	1	1
Rada	.972	42	97	8	3	2
Ramirez	.923	4	12	0	1	0
Sanchez	.969	13	31	0	1	0
Stevens	.944	9	17	0	1	0
Taylor	1.000	2	5	0	0	0
Teodosio	1.000	16	37	0	0	0

ROCKET CITY TRASH PANDAS — DOUBLE-A
SOUTHERN LEAGUE / LOS ANGELES ANGELS

Batting	B-T	Ht.	Wt.	DOB	AVG	OBP	SLG	G	PA	AB	R	H	2B	3B	HR	RBI	BB	HBP	SH	SF	SO	SB	CS	BB%	SO%
Blankenhorn, Travis	L-R	6-0	238	8-3-96	.188	.288	.353	62	251	218	18	41	10	1	8	23	27	4	1	1	69	0	0	10.8	27.5
Brown, Sam	L-L	6-2	218	9-12-01	.244	.350	.358	92	363	307	36	75	12	4	5	40	46	6	0	4	64	2	1	12.7	17.6
Calabrese, David	L-R	5-11	160	9-26-02	.201	.277	.285	77	268	239	25	48	5	0	5	11	22	3	4	0	63	11	3	8.2	23.5
Colas, Oscar	L-L	5-11	209	9-17-98	.221	.289	.409	78	311	281	27	62	5	3	14	46	27	1	0	2	74	2	0	8.7	23.8
Coutney, Matt	L-R	6-1	230	7-8-99	.180	.260	.315	30	100	89	3	16	7	1	1	7	9	1	0	1	26	0	0	9.0	26.0
Crouch, Josh	R-R	6-0	200	12-7-98	.218	.315	.411	65	232	202	27	44	12	0	9	30	24	5	0	1	71	0	2	10.3	30.6
Daly, Mitchell	R-R	6-1	185	5-16-01	.143	.239	.175	21	72	63	4	9	2	0	0	2	7	1	1	0	26	1	0	9.7	36.1
DiChiara, Sonny	R-R	6-1	263	7-29-99	.130	.273	.280	32	121	100	5	13	3	0	4	11	17	3	0	1	37	0	0	14.0	30.6
Edwards, Evan	L-L	5-11	200	6-21-97	.153	.248	.225	36	129	111	5	17	2	0	2	11	12	3	0	3	41	1	0	9.3	31.8
Emmerson, Myles	R-R	5-11	185	5-15-98	.208	.293	.332	83	302	265	26	55	13	1	6	21	29	4	2	2	76	2	2	9.6	25.2
Flint, Tucker	L-L	6-2	215	4-5-01	.106	.259	.255	16	58	47	7	5	1	0	2	7	9	1	0	1	13	1	0	15.5	22.4
Fontenelle, Cole	S-R	6-3	205	3-11-02	.147	.261	.245	48	188	163	17	24	2	1	4	14	15	10	0	0	99	6	3	8.0	52.7
Gobbel, Ben	R-R	6-1	190	11-2-99	.246	.315	.397	70	280	252	31	62	14	0	8	31	20	6	1	1	62	7	1	7.1	22.1
Groshans, Jaxx	R-R	6-0	200	7-20-98	.125	.171	.125	10	35	32	1	4	0	0	0	3	2	0	0	1	15	0	0	5.7	42.9
Guzman, Denzer	R-R	6-1	180	2-8-04	.242	.334	.415	93	386	335	39	81	23	1	11	53	41	7	0	3	92	8	3	10.6	23.8
Holland, Korey	R-R	5-10	170	1-1-00	.194	.269	.326	42	160	144	10	28	7	0	4	8	15	0	0	1	50	3	2	9.4	31.3
Ketchup, Caleb	R-R	5-10	160	1-4-02	.136	.208	.178	38	130	118	14	16	0	1	1	3	11	0	0	1	45	9	2	8.5	34.6
McCroskey, Mac	R-R	6-1	180	12-31-99	.162	.241	.215	96	301	265	26	43	7	2	1	14	26	2	6	2	89	10	5	8.6	29.6
Mershon, David	R-R	5-8	160	5-24-03	.156	.307	.204	69	276	225	29	35	6	1	1	12	48	1	2	0	70	22	2	17.4	25.4
Moore, Christian	R-R	6-1	210	10-21-02	.234	.342	.323	34	146	124	15	29	4	2	1	14	21	0	0	1	40	5	3	14.4	27.4
Nicholson, Ryan	L-L	6-4	220	8-29-00	.187	.289	.333	34	143	123	14	23	3	0	5	14	18	0	1	1	41	0	0	12.6	28.7
Rada, Nelson	L-L	5-10	160	8-24-05	.277	.380	.332	93	388	328	48	91	13	1	1	22	45	10	4	1	82	34	12	11.6	21.1
Redfield, Joe	L-R	6-2	200	10-18-01	.206	.304	.258	35	116	97	8	20	3	1	0	9	11	3	4	1	29	4	2	9.5	25.0
Vera, Arol	S-R	6-2	213	9-12-02	.167	.217	.250	30	95	84	10	14	4	0	1	4	3	3	3	2	27	0	0	3.2	28.4
Villahermosa, Yeremi	S-R	5-9	150	10-16-02	.000	.250	.000	1	4	3	0	0	0	0	0	0	1	0	0	0	2	0	0	25.0	50.0

Pitching	B-T	Ht.	Wt.	DOB	W	L	ERA	G	GS	SV	IP	Hits	Runs	ER	HR	BB	SO	AVG	OBP	SLG	SO%	BB%	BF
Aldegheri, Samuel	L-L	6-1	180	9-19-01	8	8	3.72	23	23	0	128	116	58	53	12	58	110	.240	.330	.357	19.9	10.5	554
Block, A.J.	L-L	6-5	218	4-16-98	0	2	5.06	12	1	0	21	19	13	12	1	17	26	.238	.396	.313	25.7	16.8	101
Briceno, Endrys	R-R	6-5	175	2-7-92	0	0	2.25	2	0	0	4	2	1	1	0	4	3	.167	.375	.167	18.8	25.0	16
Caceres, Kelvin	R-R	6-1	205	1-26-00	0	4	5.50	30	0	0	36	49	30	22	2	27	42	.343	.453	.455	23.5	15.1	179
Choban, Brady	R-R	6-5	240	9-30-02	2	5	2.64	39	0	4	44	44	15	13	3	11	37	.256	.308	.320	19.8	5.9	187
Clark, Chris	R-R	6-4	195	8-14-01	0	0	2.25	1	1	0	4	1	1	1	0	2	6	.267	.333	.333	33.3	11.1	18
Costeiu, Ryan	R-R	6-0	200	11-28-00	0	1	6.43	5	1	0	14	16	11	10	3	11	15	.286	.403	.607	22.4	16.4	67
Cruz, Jesus	R-R	6-1	230	4-15-95	0	1	4.15	11	5	0	26	31	14	12	1	14	23	.290	.371	.374	15.5	11.3	124
Emmerson, Myles	R-R	5-11	185	5-15-98	0	1	0.00	4	0	0	4	4	2	0	0	0	0	.267	.333	.267	0.0	0.0	17
Espinosa, Carlos	R-R	6-2	188	8-8-01	0	1	27.00	2	0	0	1	3	4	3	1	2	2	.500	.625	1.000	22.2	22.2	9
Farris, Mitch	L-L	6-2	187	2-14-01	3	8	4.27	23	22	0	116	115	64	55	10	55	142	.261	.345	.375	28.0	10.8	507
Fermin, Jose	R-R	6-3	248	11-28-01	3	0	1.13	6	0	0	8	3	1	1	0	5	11	.115	.143	.115	53.6	3.6	28
Gieg, Max	R-R	6-5	230	6-8-01	0	1	13.50	8	1	0	8	15	15	12	1	3	4	.405	.558	.514	7.7	25.0	52
Harding, Houston	L-L	6-1	230	5-22-98	0	0	3.57	7	0	0	18	20	10	7	1	6	18	.278	.329	.347	22.8	7.6	79
Holloway, Jordan	R-R	6-6	226	6-13-96	0	1	3.86	20	0	0	21	18	11	9	1	17	23	.234	.368	.286	24.2	17.9	95
Hurtado, Joel	R-R	6-2	180	2-6-01	5	6	2.70	18	18	0	87	81	29	26	6	27	56	.246	.306	.356	15.5	7.5	362
Jones, Nick	L-L	6-6	224	1-22-99	1	3	5.77	36	3	0	53	60	40	34	7	26	57	.282	.366	.455	23.2	10.6	246
Key, Keythel	R-R	6-3	180	10-10-03	0	1	135.00	1	0	0	0	2	5	5	0	3	1	.667	.833	.667	16.7	50.0	6
Klassen, George	R-R	6-2	170	1-26-02	4	12	5.35	24	24	0	103	106	68	61	8	46	126	.264	.386	.383	27.4	10.0	460
Marcheco, Jorge	R-R	6-1	185	8-6-02	0	1	3.52	2	2	0	8	7	3	3	1	1	7	.241	.290	.414	22.6	3.2	31
Minacci, Camden	R-R	6-3	210	1-14-02	1	5	4.60	47	0	4	61	68	38	31	3	26	59	.286	.356	.366	21.9	9.6	270
Murphy, Luke	R-R	6-5	190	11-5-99	0	2	4.32	14	1	0	17	17	8	8	2	4	20	.258	.310	.424	28.2	5.6	71
Natera, Sammy	L-L	6-4	225	10-4-99	4	1	2.64	41	0	8	48	30	19	14	3	31	68	.183	.312	.280	33.7	15.3	202
Osmond, Bryce	R-R	6-3	183	9-5-00	0	4	7.16	6	3	0	16	17	13	13	4	10	11	.279	.384	.590	15.1	13.7	73
Phansalkar, Roman	R-R	6-1	195	6-2-98	0	0	6.08	12	0	0	13	9	9	9	2	13	11	.191	.406	.340	17.2	20.3	64
Phillips, Dylan	L-L	6-0	220	6-5-98	0	0	2.84	10	2	0	19	22	6	6	0	7	20	.289	.365	.355	23.5	8.2	85
Poppen, Sean	R-R	6-3	210	3-15-94	3	4	5.52	21	1	0	29	34	19	18	3	18	35	.296	.407	.391	25.0	12.9	140
Quijada, Jose	L-L	5-11	215	11-9-95	2	1	2.73	27	0	26	21	16	7	6	2	9	39	.223	.305	.383	37.1	8.6	105
Ryan, Sam	R-R	6-3	205	9-22-98	1	4	4.83	25	2	0	41	44	26	22	2	21	41	.280	.364	.350	21.8	11.2	188
Smith, Jake	R-R	6-4	189	10-4-99	0	1	2.35	10	0	0	15	7	5	4	0	16	11	.143	.353	.245	16.2	23.5	68
Southard, Jared	R-R	6-2	220	10-4-00	2	2	2.93	22	0	5	28	20	11	9	3	8	28	.204	.269	.357	25.7	7.3	109
Urena, Walbert	R-R	6-0	170	1-25-04	6	9	4.39	27	27	0	135	115	73	66	8	70	115	.231	.332	.330	19.8	12.1	580
Yovan, Kenyon	R-R	6-2	221	12-28-97	0	2	3.00	10	0	1	12	15	5	4	0	4	13	.300	.357	.380	23.2	7.1	56

Fielding

Catcher	PCT	G	PO	A	E	DP	PB
Crouch	.995	60	514	44	3	5	5
Emmerson	.984	79	681	60	12	8	9
Edwards	.974	12	70	6	2	7	
Gobbel	.969	11	57	6	2	8	
Nicholson	1.000	20	161	9	0	22	
Mershon	.971	20	29	38	2	10	
Moore	.983	32	40	73	2	8	
Vera	.989	19	32	57	1	14	

First Base	PCT	G	PO	A	E	DP
Brown	.996	73	490	35	2	36
Colas	1.000	1	8	0	0	2
Coutney	.991	16	108	3	1	10
DiChiara	.978	13	83	7	2	8

Second Base	PCT	G	PO	A	E	DP
Daly	.975	10	16	23	1	3
Gobbel	.964	9	6	21	1	4
Ketchup	1.000	1	0	2	0	0
McCroskey	.962	53	102	128	9	35

Third Base	PCT	G	PO	A	E	DP
Coutney	.000	1	0	0	0	0
Daly	1.000	10	6	13	0	0
Fontenelle	.940	44	36	74	7	7
Gobbel	.899	47	27	71	11	6

	PCT	G	PO	A	E	DP
Guzman	.927	20	11	27	3	1
McCroskey	.944	10	4	13	1	1
Mershon	1.000	3	2	3	0	2
Vera	1.000	10	7	10	0	0
Shortstop	**PCT**	**G**	**PO**	**A**	**E**	**DP**
Guzman	.955	75	98	154	12	30
McCroskey	.960	27	40	80	5	17
Mershon	.945	36	50	87	8	21
Vera	1.000	1	1	4	0	2
Outfield	**PCT**	**G**	**PO**	**A**	**E**	**DP**
Blankenhorn	.976	48	79	3	2	0
Brown	.750	8	6	0	2	0
Calabrese	1.000	73	151	1	0	0
Colas	.967	62	111	7	4	1
Edwards	1.000	2	5	0	0	0
Flint	1.000	16	23	0	0	0
Holland	.984	42	62	0	1	0
Ketchup	.955	35	61	3	3	1
McCroskey	1.000	1	4	0	0	0
Mershon	.963	10	26	0	1	0
Rada	.980	92	188	7	4	1
Redfield	1.000	33	50	1	0	0

TRI-CITY DUST DEVILS — HIGH-A
NORTHWEST LEAGUE / LOS ANGELES ANGELS

Batting	B-T	Ht.	Wt.	DOB	AVG	OBP	SLG	G	PA	AB	R	H	2B	3B	HR	RBI	BB	HBP	SH	SF	SO	SB	CS	BB%	SO%
Burns, Peter	L-R	5-10	195	10-14-99	.235	.386	.294	39	127	102	13	24	3	0	1	10	23	2	0	0	22	1	2	18.1	17.3
Calabrese, David	L-R	5-11	160	9-26-02	.215	.287	.413	33	137	121	16	26	7	1	5	15	13	0	1	2	28	3	3	9.5	20.4
Coutney, Matt	L-R	6-1	230	7-8-99	.261	.368	.482	75	297	253	36	66	14	0	14	39	37	6	1	0	77	3	1	12.5	25.9
Daly, Mitchell	R-R	6-1	185	5-16-01	.141	.208	.254	21	79	71	9	10	2	0	2	6	6	0	2	0	30	0	0	7.6	38.0
De Jesus, Randy	R-R	6-4	210	2-13-05	.185	.280	.340	118	483	421	42	78	11	0	18	55	49	8	1	4	164	3	2	10.1	34.0
Flores, Juan	R-R	5-10	180	2-13-06	.207	.283	.341	89	342	305	38	63	11	0	10	40	18	15	3	1	94	0	1	5.3	27.5
Flores, Randy	L-R	5-9	180	9-18-00	.000	.167	.000	4	6	5	0	0	0	0	0	0	1	0	0	0	4	1	0	16.7	66.7
Fontenelle, Cole	S-R	6-3	205	3-11-02	.217	.313	.343	58	240	207	26	45	7	2	5	24	24	6	0	3	73	10	6	10.0	30.4
Foster, Rio	R-R	6-3	205	6-18-03	.267	.407	.439	93	378	303	54	81	18	2	10	40	60	13	0	2	96	8	1	15.9	25.4
Gamel, Ben	L-L	5-10	180	5-17-92	.357	.400	.857	3	15	14	5	5	1	0	2	7	1	0	0	0	7	0	0	6.7	46.7
Gobbel, Ben	R-R	6-1	190	11-2-99	.284	.352	.505	55	211	190	30	54	15	0	9	30	14	6	1	0	45	4	2	6.6	21.3
Jackson, Isaiah	L-R	6-3	205	5-16-04	.219	.324	.344	10	37	32	6	7	1	0	1	4	4	1	0	0	13	0	0	10.8	35.1
Ketchup, Caleb	R-R	5-10	160	1-4-02	.143	.400	.357	8	20	14	6	2	0	0	1	4	6	0	0	0	6	3	0	30.0	30.0
Laverde, Dario	R-R	6-2	190	2-26-05	.154	.175	.179	12	40	39	1	6	1	0	0	1	1	0	0	0	12	0	0	2.5	30.0
Nicholson, Ryan	L-L	6-4	220	8-29-00	.264	.381	.448	94	400	330	50	87	17	1	14	53	58	7	1	4	94	1	1	14.5	23.5
Ortiz, Capri	R-R	6-0	150	4-1-05	.229	.305	.322	97	399	354	49	81	12	3	5	33	32	7	5	1	81	27	6	8.0	20.3
Paris, Kyren	R-R	6-0	180	11-11-01	.200	.333	.400	2	6	5	0	1	0	0	0	0	1	0	0	0	1	0	1	0.0	16.7
Pendleton, Caleb	R-R	6-2	185	4-5-02	.174	.191	.304	16	47	46	4	8	0	0	2	6	1	0	0	0	20	0	0	2.1	42.6
Placencia, Adrian	S-R	5-11	173	6-2-03	.212	.339	.383	120	501	410	69	87	14	4	16	61	73	9	2	7	151	6	4	14.6	30.1
Ramirez, Alexander	R-R	6-2	229	8-29-02	.192	.255	.338	42	141	130	17	25	4	0	5	16	11	0	0	0	73	3	2	7.8	51.8
Ramirez, Lucas	R-R	6-3	198	1-16-06	.172	.257	.207	11	35	29	3	5	1	0	0	2	3	1	0	2	14	0	1	8.6	40.0
Redfield, Joe	L-R	6-2	200	10-18-01	.230	.302	.379	24	98	87	11	20	5	1	2	7	7	2	2	0	22	3	2	7.1	24.5
Rios, Alberto	R-R	6-0	203	3-19-02	.097	.211	.113	24	73	62	3	6	1	0	0	5	8	1	2	0	16	0	0	11.0	21.9
Scull, Anthony	L-L	6-0	165	1-26-04	.260	.321	.396	106	465	419	55	109	18	0	13	47	29	11	1	5	107	5	7	6.2	23.0
Summerhill, Colin	R-R	6-3	205	8-4-01	.224	.327	.365	25	98	85	9	19	6	0	2	9	13	0	0	0	22	0	1	13.3	22.4
Vera, Arol	S-R	6-2	213	9-12-02	.230	.330	.375	62	230	200	20	46	10	2	5	20	27	3	0	0	47	2	0	11.7	20.4

Pitching	B-T	Ht.	Wt.	DOB	W	L	ERA	G	GS	SV	IP	Hits	Runs	ER	HR	BB	SO	AVG	OBP	SLG	SO%	BB%	BF
Block, A.J.	L-L	6-5	218	4-16-98	0	3	1.82	21	0	10	30	25	11	6	2	10	39	.223	.282	.304	31.5	8.1	124
Britt, Logan	R-R	6-5	222	7-16-00	4	1	6.38	19	1	0	37	41	26	26	8	23	38	.275	.374	.497	21.7	13.1	175
Burns, Peter	L-R	5-10	195	10-14-99	0	0	13.50	2	0	0	1	5	2	2	0	3	0	.556	.667	.889	0.0	25.0	12
Clark, Chris	R-R	6-4	195	8-14-01	1	2	2.87	7	5	0	38	34	15	12	3	11	39	.238	.304	.343	24.7	7.0	158
Cortez, Chris	R-R	6-1	205	10-6-02	3	8	4.28	26	26	0	114	94	64	54	5	84	114	.224	.359	.302	22.2	16.4	513
Costeiu, Ryan	R-R	6-0	200	11-28-00	7	7	5.07	21	19	0	105	102	62	59	12	44	113	.258	.334	.429	24.8	9.7	455
Espinosa, Carlos	R-R	6-2	188	8-8-01	2	3	5.04	34	5	2	61	58	37	34	7	27	81	.245	.327	.405	29.9	10.0	271
Garcia, Leonard	L-L	6-2	165	8-11-03	5	3	4.28	32	0	1	48	39	26	23	8	22	65	.218	.314	.431	31.3	10.6	208
Gaston, Sandy	R-R	6-3	200	12-16-01	5	1	4.32	38	0	1	67	58	34	32	4	42	86	.236	.352	.346	29.4	14.3	293
Gieg, Max	R-R	6-5	230	6-8-01	2	4	4.87	28	2	2	44	33	25	24	3	37	64	.201	.370	.311	30.2	17.5	212
Gomez, Yendy	R-R	6-2	170	12-19-03	0	2	10.57	5	0	0	8	14	10	9	0	4	5	.389	.439	.417	11.9	9.5	42
Gordon, Austin	R-R	6-4	185	6-14-03	4	5	5.44	21	21	0	84	88	54	51	12	27	95	.260	.324	.478	25.3	7.2	375
Holmes, Bridger	R-R	6-4	218	8-27-02	1	0	10.34	13	0	0	16	15	19	18	3	11	22	.259	.438	.448	27.5	13.8	80
Johnson, Ryan	S-R	6-6	212	8-5-02	4	3	1.88	12	12	0	57	41	13	12	3	10	65	.196	.233	.287	29.7	4.6	219
Key, Keythel	R-R	6-3	180	10-10-03	5	8	5.13	27	17	0	100	98	65	57	13	52	112	.259	.375	.430	24.2	13.2	462
Marcheso, Jorge	R-R	6-1	185	8-6-02	5	6	4.44	25	10	0	77	66	38	38	13	22	77	.230	.293	.439	24.2	6.9	318
Mederos, Victor	R-R	6-2	227	6-8-01	0	2	3.52	3	3	0	15	17	6	6	1	3	14	.288	.348	.458	21.2	4.5	66
Oschell, Fran	R-R	6-7	230	10-18-02	0	0	9.00	1	0	0	1	0	1	1	0	3	.250	.250	1.000	75.0	0.0	4
Pendleton, Caleb	R-R	6-2	185	4-5-02	1	0	13.50	1	0	0	2	3	4	3	0	2	0	.429	.600	.714	0.0	20.0	10
Phansalkar, Roman	R-R	6-1	195	6-2-98	0	0	1.02	12	0	1	18	14	2	2	0	5	21	.219	.311	.344	28.4	6.8	74
Phillips, Dylan	L-L	6-0	220	6-16-99	2	3	3.35	31	0	8	43	35	18	16	5	18	37	.226	.313	.374	20.6	10.0	180
Roche, Kyle	R-R	6-0	190	9-14-01	2	1	5.68	8	0	0	13	16	9	8	1	11	14	.308	.439	.462	21.2	16.7	66
Ryan, Sam	R-R	6-3	205	9-22-98	2	2	3.34	19	0	2	30	31	15	11	2	12	35	.311	.373	.437	26.1	9.0	134
Semmel, Montana	R-R	6-4	225	1-1-02	1	0	4.66	6	0	0	10	7	6	5	0	9	13	.200	.404	.286	27.7	19.1	47
Smith, Angelo	R-R	6-1	185	4-23-04	1	1	6.00	5	0	0	6	6	5	4	2	1	6	.250	.280	.542	24.0	4.0	25
Smith, Jake	R-R	6-4	189	10-4-99	3	3	4.50	29	0	5	42	31	22	21	5	32	49	.209	.365	.326	26.2	17.1	187
Texido, Francis	L-L	6-2	180	4-1-05	1	0	4.05	7	0	4	13	14	6	6	1	6	11	.269	.345	.385	19.0	10.3	58
Tookoian, Sam	L-R	6-5	230	5-25-03	0	0	0.00	7	0	3	12	6	0	0	0	3	14	.077	.172	.077	48.3	10.3	29
Vargas, Yeferson	R-R	6-0	177	8-4-04	1	2	6.26	10	10	0	42	44	30	29	2	23	38	.277	.373	.434	20.3	12.3	187
Victor, Najer	R-R	6-2	180	11-28-01	0	1	4.35	16	0	4	21	16	12	10	2	10	33	.200	.289	.338	36.7	11.1	90

Fielding

Catcher	PCT	G	PO	A	E	DP	PB
Burns	.997	38	322	19	1	2	3
Flores	.988	86	870	38	11	5	9
Rios	.992	15	120	7	1	0	1

First Base	PCT	G	PO	A	E	DP
Coutney	.976	17	115	7	3	11
Gobbel	1.000	5	26	1	0	4
Nicholson	.995	78	557	37	3	43
Pendleton	1.000	11	70	5	0	6
Summerhill	.988	23	154	13	2	9

Second Base	PCT	G	PO	A	E
Daly	1.000	4	3	8	0
Gobbel	1.000	3	2	9	0
Ketchup	.933	4	5	9	1
Ortiz	.955	11	21	21	2

	PCT	G	PO	A	E	DP
Placencia	.982	111	143	288	8	53
Vera	1.000	5	10	11	0	3

Third Base	PCT	G	PO	A	E	DP
Coutney	.958	15	6	17	1	2
Daly	.944	8	5	12	1	1
Fontenelle	.972	55	32	72	3	6
Gobbel	.970	42	22	43	2	7
Ketchup	.500	2	1	0	1	0
Laverde	.000	1	0	0	0	0
Pendleton	1.000	1	0	2	0	1
Vera	.941	20	10	22	2	1

Shortstop	PCT	G	PO	A	E	DP
Daly	1.000	9	12	21	0	3
Fontenelle	1.000	1	1	1	0	0
Ortiz	.946	86	114	167	16	32

	PCT	G	PO	A	E	DP
Vera	.978	41	39	94	3	17

Outfield	PCT	G	PO	A	E	DP
Calabrese	1.000	32	54	1	0	1
De Jesus	.985	112	184	7	3	0
Flores	1.000	2	8	0	0	0
Foster	.993	86	135	6	1	1
Gamel	1.000	2	3	0	0	0
Jackson	1.000	10	24	0	0	0
Ketchup	1.000	1	3	0	0	0
Paris	1.000	1	1	0	0	0
Ramirez, A	.970	34	63	1	2	0
Ramirez, L	1.000	10	22	1	0	1
Redfield	1.000	20	37	1	0	1
Rios	1.000	1	1	0	0	0
Scull	.990	100	191	3	2	0

INLAND EMPIRE 66ERS — LOW-A
CALIFORNIA LEAGUE

Batting	B-T	Ht.	Wt.	DOB	AVG	OBP	SLG	G	PA	AB	R	H	2B	3B	HR	RBI	BB	HBP	SH	SF	SO	SB	CS	BB%	SO%
Alfonso, Edgar	S-R	5-9	175	3-27-04	.333	.500	.333	8	16	12	1	4	0	0	0	0	3	1	0	0	2	0	1	18.8	12.5
Alford, Slate	R-R	6-2	215	8-23-02	.289	.435	.433	28	125	97	22	28	6	1	2	19	21	5	1	1	31	0	0	16.8	24.8
Alvarez, Hayden	R-R	6-3	190	3-19-07	.355	.459	.435	20	76	62	12	22	5	0	0	18	10	2	2	0	8	9	4	13.2	10.5
Bartolero, Caleb	R-R	5-11	175	11-4-99	.269	.363	.468	41	183	156	32	42	9	2	6	27	17	7	0	2	37	3	2	9.3	20.2
Blakely, Werner	L-R	6-3	185	2-21-02	.086	.250	.114	12	44	35	3	3	1	0	0	3	7	1	0	1	16	1	1	15.9	36.4
Bruggeman, Kevin	R-R	5-9	186	7-25-01	.225	.381	.365	90	349	271	47	61	12	7	4	38	60	10	5	3	63	11	3	17.2	18.1
Castillo, Kevyn	L-L	5-10	170	6-12-05	.285	.395	.399	41	192	158	20	45	4	4	2	19	28	2	2	2	39	6	3	14.6	20.3
Coll, Harold	R-R	5-11	200	7-31-01	.276	.369	.422	116	493	424	70	117	27	4	9	62	63	3	0	4	120	29	4	12.6	24.3
Coutney, Matt	L-R	6-1	230	7-8-99	.229	.317	.343	9	41	35	4	8	4	0	0	7	4	1	0	1	9	0	0	9.8	22.0
Daly, Mitchell	R-R	6-1	185	5-16-01	.193	.329	.246	19	71	57	4	11	3	0	0	5	12	0	1	1	18	1	1	16.9	25.4
Espinal, Edwardo	R-R	6-1	182	11-19-05	.212	.289	.265	52	194	170	20	36	9	0	0	13	15	4	2	1	57	4	0	7.7	29.4
Ketchup, Caleb	R-R	5-10	160	1-4-02	.279	.394	.401	42	175	147	33	41	7	1	3	13	26	2	0	0	51	1	2	14.9	29.1
Laverde, Dario	L-R	5-10	160	2-26-05	.222	.301	.305	86	374	334	38	74	12	2	4	39	30	8	1	0	79	0	0	8.0	21.1
Linares, Jonathan	S-R	6-0	200	4-2-05	.198	.295	.340	36	122	106	14	21	2	2	3	13	12	3	0	1	36	1	0	9.8	29.5
Macias, Johan	S-R	5-9	150	1-6-03	.270	.345	.356	112	475	407	71	110	17	6	2	52	40	9	14	5	67	16	3	8.4	14.1
Moncada, Yoan	S-R	6-2	225	5-27-95	.000	.500	.000	2	10	5	0	0	0	0	0	0	4	1	0	0	2	0	0	40.0	20.0
Moore, Christian	R-R	6-1	210	10-21-02	.455	.625	.909	4	16	11	3	5	2	0	1	2	5	0	0	0	2	1	0	31.3	12.5
Munroe, Jake	R-R	6-2	230	9-14-03	.244	.352	.333	12	56	45	10	11	2	1	0	10	7	1	2	1	10	4	0	12.5	17.9
Quintero, Marlon	S-R	5-9	175	11-27-06	.258	.265	.290	18	70	62	8	16	2	0	0	12	2	0	2	4	9	3	0	2.9	12.9
Rios, Alberto	R-R	6-0	203	3-19-02	.207	.299	.326	39	158	135	17	28	3	2	3	18	16	2	4	1	40	2	0	10.1	25.3
Rivero, Eliezer	R-R	6-0	180	3-29-05	.200	.250	.200	6	16	15	2	3	0	0	0	2	1	0	0	0	6	0	0	6.3	37.5
Rodriguez, Luis	R-R	6-1	176	12-2-07	.000	.400	.000	3	6	3	0	0	0	0	0	0	2	0	1	0	3	0	0	33.3	50.0
Rodriguez, Nick	L-R	5-10	185	10-29-02	.281	.396	.371	27	108	89	19	25	3	1	1	13	17	0	2	0	15	8	0	15.7	13.9
Rodriguez, Raudi	R-R	6-0	190	7-7-03	.281	.372	.470	125	560	481	90	135	21	14	8	83	63	10	1	5	130	38	6	11.3	23.2
Ruiz, Jorge	L-L	5-10	164	6-30-04	.285	.357	.364	121	550	478	78	136	23	6	1	50	47	9	12	4	92	22	9	8.5	16.7
Summerhill, Colin	R-R	6-3	205	8-4-01	.215	.322	.324	83	337	284	38	61	19	0	4	31	43	4	2	4	83	3	1	12.8	24.6
Wimmer, John	R-R	6-1	170	3-21-05	.224	.303	.340	87	359	321	35	72	18	5	3	28	30	6	2	0	130	8	2	8.4	36.2

Pitching	B-T	Ht.	Wt.	DOB	W	L	ERA	G	GS	SV	IP	Hits	Runs	ER	HR	BB	SO	AVG	OBP	SLG	SO%	BB%	BF
Bachman, Sam	R-R	6-1	235	9-30-99	0	0	0.00	2	0	0	2	1	1	0	0	1	3	.143	.250	.143	37.5	12.5	8
Baro, Sadiel	L-L	6-2	177	11-10-04	4	3	10.47	28	1	0	33	49	41	38	4	21	35	.345	.435	.556	20.8	12.5	168
Bruggeman, Kevin	R-R	5-9	186	7-25-01	0	0	6.75	2	0	0	3	1	1	1	0	0	0	.500	.429	.500	0.0	0.0	7
Clark, Chris	R-R	6-4	195	8-14-01	3	8	5.50	20	20	0	103	105	69	63	12	34	108	.260	.331	.408	23.8	7.5	454
Davis, Alton	L-L	6-5	190	12-18-03	1	0	2.25	7	0	0	8	5	5	2	0	8	10	.172	.368	.207	26.3	21.1	38
De La Cruz, Rolando	R-R	6-0	234	1-30-01	0	1	8.87	21	0	0	23	27	24	23	2	23	25	.293	.460	.467	20.2	18.5	124
Dufault, Brandon	R-R	6-5	204	10-19-98	5	5	4.53	16	14	0	60	62	38	30	3	41	47	.270	.389	.365	16.7	14.5	282
Encarnacion, Nixon	R-R	6-2	178	12-30-04	0	1	6.38	22	2	0	37	38	26	26	5	39	45	.273	.436	.446	24.7	21.4	182
Felipe, Angel	R-R	6-5	190	8-30-97	0	1	7.71	6	0	0	5	6	4	4	0	7	4	.286	.483	.381	13.8	24.1	29
Garcia, Leonard	L-L	6-2	165	8-11-03	0	1	1.59	9	0	1	11	7	3	2	0	8	19	.179	.347	.231	38.8	16.3	49
Garcia, Victor	R-R	6-1	194	3-28-04	4	5	3.39	40	0	2	66	61	35	25	3	24	76	.239	.315	.333	26.0	8.2	292
Gervase, Will	L-L	6-9	220	5-2-02	1	3	10.69	19	0	0	16	14	22	19	0	35	18	.246	.547	.281	18.8	36.5	96
Gonzalez, Victor	L-L	6-0	180	11-16-95	0	0	0.00	2	0	0	2	0	0	0	0	1	0	.000	.143	.000	0.0	12.5	8
Gregory-Alford, Trey	R-R	6-5	225	5-4-06	1	0	1.42	6	6	0	25	16	5	4	0	13	20	.180	.295	.202	19.0	12.4	105
Hewlett, Jim	L-L	6-1	190	10-4-01	2	0	6.53	17	0	0	21	25	19	15	1	9	28	.294	.371	.400	28.6	9.2	98
Holmes, Bridger	R-R	6-4	218	8-27-02	0	1	3.42	22	0	6	26	18	11	10	1	15	39	.200	.363	.267	34.5	13.3	113
Jordan, Dylan	R-R	6-3	205	10-15-05	2	0	0.94	7	7	0	29	19	6	3	0	9	30	.198	.275	.219	27.5	8.3	109
Kent, Barrett	R-R	6-4	200	9-29-04	1	0	1.98	6	6	0	27	14	6	6	1	16	22	.231	.333	.279	18.3	13.3	120
Lara, Davidxon	R-R	5-10	165	7-31-06	0	1	21.00	2	0	0	3	10	9	7	1	3	3	.526	.524	.684	14.3	4.8	21
Lockhart, Fulton	R-R	6-4	183	12-30-03	0	2	9.15	17	0	0	21	19	25	21	2	30	36	.232	.449	.305	30.5	25.4	118
Macias, Johan	S-R	5-9	150	1-6-03	0	0	81.00	2	0	0	1	5	6	6	0	1	1	.714	.750	1.286	12.5	12.5	8
Olejnik, Peyton	R-R	6-9	242	6-4-02	6	7	4.20	25	25	0	129	122	65	60	7	63	130	.249	.343	.362	23.1	11.2	562
Oschell, Fran	R-R	6-7	230	10-18-02	0	1	12.34	17	0	0	12	18	17	16	1	26	18	.186	.532	.302	23.4	33.8	77
Redner, Zachary	L-R	6-1	200	12-6-04	4	1	4.50	30	1	1	50	62	27	25	1	14	48	.302	.350	.400	21.4	6.3	224

Player	B-T	Ht	Wt	DOB	W	L	ERA	G	GS	SV	IP	Hits	Runs	ER	HR	BB	SO	AVG	OBP	SLG	SO%	BB%	BF
Reyes, Yokelvin	L-L	6-1	195	3-29-04	1	0	1.32	7	0	0	14	10	2	2	0	9	14	.217	.368	.217	24.6	15.8	57
Roche, Kyle	R-R	6-0	190	9-14-01	3	0	4.11	29	0	2	50	56	29	23	4	24	46	.287	.366	.431	20.5	10.7	224
Sanchez, Andre	R-R	5-10	140	2-5-03	0	6	8.28	20	10	0	54	71	58	50	7	45	42	.313	.429	.489	14.9	16.0	282
Soto, Ubaldo	R-R	6-2	185	7-12-06	3	0	1.46	6	4	1	25	12	4	4	2	11	30	.146	.263	.220	31.6	11.6	95
Stephenson, Robert	R-R	6-3	205	2-24-93	1	0	3.00	3	0	0	3	2	1	1	1	0	2	.182	.182	.455	18.2	0.0	11
Texido, Francis	L-L	6-2	180	4-1-05	2	7	6.30	21	19	0	90	80	71	63	6	86	81	.243	.406	.368	18.8	19.9	432
Thompson, Ben	R-R	6-0	215	1-17-02	4	2	1.91	44	0	11	61	31	19	13	1	43	100	.149	.302	.216	39.1	16.8	256
Vargas, Yeferson	R-R	6-0	177	8-4-04	6	5	4.46	16	16	0	69	69	39	34	5	38	62	.259	.362	.383	19.9	12.2	312
Vergara, Brayan	R-R	6-0	145	12-21-05	0	0	4.91	1	1	0	4	5	3	2	0	2	1	.294	.368	.353	5.3	10.5	19
Victor, Najer	R-R	6-2	180	11-28-01	1	5	5.40	19	0	0	20	18	18	12	3	16	32	.234	.381	.429	33.0	16.5	97
Warwick, Jaren	R-R	6-2	175	10-10-01	5	6	5.53	42	0	1	57	57	43	35	1	33	71	.249	.353	.314	26.4	12.3	269

Fielding

Catcher	PCT	G	PO	A	E	DP	PB
Bruggeman	1.000	13	116	5	0	4	1
Laverde	.983	46	429	40	8	5	19
Linares	.984	21	170	19	3	3	4
Quintero	.995	18	160	24	1	2	3
Rios	.986	39	382	29	6	2	10

First Base	PCT	G	PO	A	E	DP
Bartolero	.976	12	75	6	2	6
Bruggeman	.979	37	254	23	6	24
Coutney	.984	8	59	4	1	5
Daly	1.000	1	9	2	0	0
Rivero	1.000	6	24	3	0	2
Summerhill	.993	73	508	26	4	44

Second Base	PCT	G	PO	A	E	DP
Alfonso	1.000	2	1	3	0	0
Bruggeman	.963	10	9	17	1	4

	PCT	G	PO	A	E	DP
Coll	.967	24	35	54	3	8
Daly	1.000	1	0	1	0	0
Ketchup	.800	2	3	1	1	0
Macias	.990	67	121	163	3	38
Moore	1.000	3	2	11	0	2
Rodriguez	.978	23	34	55	2	10
Wimmer	.955	7	9	12	1	1

Third Base	PCT	G	PO	A	E	DP
Alfonso	1.000	2	1	2	0	0
Alford	.857	12	7	11	3	0
Bartolero	.922	21	13	34	4	3
Coll	.923	72	49	107	13	17
Daly	1.000	17	4	33	0	2
Macias	.800	1	2	2	1	0
Moncada	.667	1	0	2	1	1
Munroe	.917	9	6	16	2	0
Rodriguez	.000	1	0	0	0	0

Shortstop	PCT	G	PO	A	E	DP
Coll	.944	10	14	20	2	5
Macias	.955	43	54	96	7	13
Rodriguez	1.000	2	2	4	0	0
Rodriguez	1.000	1	1	4	0	0
Wimmer	.889	80	101	148	31	27

Outfield	PCT	G	PO	A	E	DP
Alfonso	1.000	2	5	0	0	0
Alvarez	.947	19	35	1	2	0
Blakely	1.000	11	15	1	0	0
Bruggeman	1.000	18	31	0	0	0
Castillo	.944	39	64	3	4	1
Espinal	.960	50	116	3	5	1
Ketchup	1.000	38	77	3	0	2
Rodriguez	.963	117	230	7	9	1
Ruiz	.995	121	201	9	1	1

ACL ANGELS — ROOKIE
ARIZONA COMPLEX LEAGUE

Batting	B-T	Ht.	Wt.	DOB	AVG	OBP	SLG	G	PA	AB	R	H	2B	3B	HR	RBI	BB	HBP	SH	SF	SO	SB	CS	BB%	SO%
Alfonso, Edgar	S-R	5-9	175	3-27-04	.302	.366	.444	20	72	63	13	19	5	2	0	12	5	2	1	1	13	2	1	6.9	18.1
Alvarez, Hayden	R-R	6-3	190	3-19-07	.335	.427	.429	55	221	182	38	61	5	3	2	26	31	1	2	4	41	24	5	14.0	18.6
Blakely, Werner	L-R	6-3	185	2-21-02	.125	.300	.125	5	10	8	1	1	0	0	0	0	2	0	0	0	3	0	0	20.0	30.0
Blankenhorn, Travis	L-R	6-0	238	8-3-96	.125	.300	.313	6	20	16	4	2	0	0	0	1	4	3	1	0	0	3	0	15.0	15.0
Campero, Gustavo	S-R	5-8	183	9-20-97	.000	.273	.000	3	11	7	1	0	0	0	0	1	1	2	0	1	3	0	0	9.1	27.3
Caraballo, Bailan	R-R	6-6	205	3-6-06	.204	.313	.278	26	64	54	14	11	0	1	2	12	8	1	0	1	33	1	0	12.5	51.6
Dishmey, Samil	L-R	6-2	175	12-22-05	.232	.324	.305	34	108	95	12	22	1	0	2	17	10	3	0	0	28	3	1	9.3	25.9
Drury, Brandon	R-R	6-2	230	8-21-92	.150	.370	.250	7	27	20	2	3	2	0	0	1	7	0	0	0	5	0	0	25.9	18.5
Duarte, Athanael	R-R	5-10	165	11-11-04	.245	.352	.388	55	231	196	35	48	14	4	2	25	28	5	1	1	56	2	4	12.1	24.2
Flores, Angel	L-R	5-9	180	9-18-00	.240	.367	.480	13	30	25	8	6	4	1	0	3	5	0	0	0	5	0	0	16.7	16.7
Hopson, Kaden	L-R	6-2	200	8-16-00	.241	.477	.310	13	45	29	11	7	2	0	0	8	9	5	1	1	6	0	1	20.0	13.3
Kingery, Scott	R-R	5-10	180	4-29-94	.438	.526	.750	5	19	16	4	7	3	1	0	1	3	0	0	0	4	0	0	15.8	21.1
Lugo, Joswa	R-R	6-3	187	1-24-07	.271	.375	.372	35	152	129	19	35	7	0	2	23	19	3	0	1	40	4	1	12.5	26.3
Marquez, Anyelo	R-R	6-0	166	12-12-05	.230	.311	.364	47	191	165	28	38	6	4	2	26	18	3	1	4	53	4	0	9.4	27.7
Martinez, Bryan	L-R	6-2	170	12-26-05	.259	.311	.407	41	149	135	23	35	5	3	3	18	7	4	1	2	52	3	3	4.7	34.9
Mershon, David	S-R	5-8	160	5-24-03	.500	.533	.714	8	30	28	4	14	4	1	0	9	2	0	0	0	4	0	0	6.7	13.3
Moncada, Yoan	S-R	6-2	225	5-27-95	.444	.615	.778	3	13	9	3	4	0	0	0	1	2	4	0	0	2	0	0	30.8	15.4
Morrobel, Felix	R-R	6-0	175	9-24-05	.218	.364	.322	27	111	87	28	19	1	1	2	17	17	3	4	0	22	8	2	15.3	19.8
Patino, Oswaldo	L-R	5-10	200	7-3-06	.150	.227	.175	20	46	40	6	6	1	0	0	4	4	0	2	0	10	1	0	8.7	21.7
Quintero, Marlon	R-R	5-9	175	11-27-06	.311	.347	.385	45	176	161	20	50	9	0	1	27	7	3	3	2	32	4	0	4.0	18.2
Ramirez, Lucas	L-R	6-3	198	1-16-06	.282	.374	.454	49	191	163	33	46	7	6	3	28	23	2	1	2	39	6	0	12.0	20.4
Rivero, Eliezer	R-R	6-0	180	3-29-05	.314	.409	.373	36	138	118	22	37	7	0	0	16	9	10	1	0	36	4	2	6.5	26.1
Rodriguez, Luis	R-R	6-1	176	12-22-04	.295	.375	.328	25	76	61	13	18	2	0	0	17	7	2	4	2	13	2	0	9.2	17.1
Rodriguez, Victor	R-R	5-10	185	1-24-06	.310	.324	.300	87	74	14	15	1	1	2	15	9	3	0	1	25	1	1	10.3	28.7
Taylor, Chris	R-R	6-1	196	8-29-90	.667	.778	.833	2	9	6	1	4	1	0	0	2	2	1	0	0	0	0	0	22.2	22.2
Teodosio, Bryce	R-L	6-3	220	6-18-99	.343	.410	.543	9	39	35	8	12	2	1	1	7	2	2	0	0	8	3	1	5.1	20.5
Villahermosa, Yeremi	S-R	5-9	150	10-16-02	.115	.294	.115	11	35	26	3	3	0	0	0	1	6	1	1	1	10	1	1	17.1	28.6

Pitching	B-T	Ht.	Wt.	DOB	W	L	ERA	G	GS	SV	IP	Hits	Runs	ER	HR	BB	SO	AVG	OBP	SLG	SO%	BB%	BF
Acosta, Adrian	R-R	6-1	170	5-20-05	1	0	3.24	5	0	1	8	9	5	3	0	4	4	.257	.327	.286	10.0	10.0	40
Cova, Andres	L-L	6-2	165	10-21-04	1	0	6.75	4	0	0	8	7	6	6	1	4	11	.226	.314	.581	31.4	11.4	35
De La Cruz, Rolando	R-R	6-0	234	1-30-01	0	0	0.00	2	0	0	1	2	0	0	0	1	1	.333	.429	.333	14.3	14.3	7
De La Rosa, Dioris	R-R	6-4	200	10-26-06	1	2	5.58	12	8	0	31	32	24	19	1	27	31	.274	.416	.350	20.7	18.0	150
Dufault, Brandon	R-R	6-5	204	10-19-98	2	0	6.97	6	0	0	10	12	10	8	0	16	10	.279	.475	.279	16.9	27.1	59
Fermin, Jose	R-R	6-3	248	11-28-01	0	0	10.80	2	1	0	2	2	2	2	0	1	4	.286	.444	.286	44.4	11.1	9
Gervase, Will	L-L	6-9	220	5-2-02	1	0	3.38	5	0	0	5	3	3	2	0	5	4	.176	.375	.176	16.7	20.8	24
Gomez, Yendy	R-R	6-2	170	12-9-03	4	2	2.59	20	2	3	31	23	13	9	1	7	32	.204	.268	.310	25.8	5.6	124
Gregory-Alford, Trey	R-R	6-5	225	5-4-06	4	4	3.54	12	10	0	53	53	34	21	2	20	48	.266	.341	.352	21.4	8.9	224
Hechavarria, Jan	R-R	6-2	190	1-10-04	2	3	3.33	19	0	5	24	17	11	9	0	15	21	.218	.361	.269	21.4	15.3	98
Holloway, Jordan	R-R	6-6	230	6-13-96	0	0	0.00	1	0	0	1	0	0	0	0	1	2	.250	.400	.500	40.0	20.0	5

Batting	B-T	Ht.	Wt.	DOB			AVG	OBP	SLG	G	PA	AB	R	H	2B	3B	HR	RBI	BB	HBP	SH	SF	SO	SB	CS	BB%	SO%
Jordan, Dylan	R-R	6-3	205	10-15-05	2	1	3.21	12	12	0	48	44	26	17	3	21	55	.239	.322	.332	26.3	10.0	209				
Kent, Barrett	R-R	6-4	200	9-29-04	0	0	2.25	4	3	0	8	8	3	2	0	5	9	.286	.394	.357	27.3	15.2	33				
Kerry, Brett	R-R	6-0	213	4-12-99	0	1	5.63	4	4	0	8	7	5	5	0	6	9	.233	.361	.333	25.0	16.7	36				
Lara, Davidxon	R-R	5-10	165	7-31-06	4	1	4.30	13	0	0	29	36	16	14	1	10	26	.303	.359	.437	19.7	7.6	132				
Lockhart, Fulton	R-R	6-4	183	12-30-03	0	0	8.53	6	0	0	6	9	6	6	0	9	9	.333	.500	.370	25.0	25.0	36				
McDaniels, Garrett	L-L	6-2	180	12-15-99	0	0	2.08	3	1	0	4	3	2	1	0	3	7	.200	.368	.333	35.0	15.0	20				
Mendez, Haminton	R-R	6-1	177	6-5-04	3	1	5.12	19	0	0	32	37	20	18	0	19	23	.294	.392	.357	15.4	12.8	149				
Osmond, Bryce	R-R	6-3	183	9-5-00	0	0	2.45	3	3	0	4	3	4	1	0	1	10	.214	.313	.286	62.5	6.3	16				
Pendleton, Caleb	R-R	6-2	185	4-5-02	0	0	9.00	3	0	0	3	7	5	3	1	2	1	.438	.500	.750	5.3	10.5	19				
Phansalkar, Roman	R-R	6-1	195	6-2-98	0	0	1.42	5	0	0	6	5	3	1	0	1	10	.208	.296	.333	30.0	3.7	27				
Poppen, Sean	R-R	6-3	210	3-15-94	0	0	0.00	1	0	0	1	0	1	0	0	1	3	.000	.200	.000	60.0	20.0	5				
Redner, Zachary	R-R	6-1	200	12-6-04	0	0	27.00	1	0	0	1	2	3	3	1	1	0	.500	.500	1.250	0.0	16.7	6				
Reyes, Yokelvin	L-L	6-1	195	3-29-04	3	1	2.40	11	6	1	41	39	17	11	2	13	35	.247	.305	.348	20.1	7.5	174				
Seig, Hayden	R-R	6-5	227	9-10-98	1	0	6.23	3	0	0	4	5	3	3	1	1	7	.263	.300	.579	35.0	5.0	20				
Semmel, Montana	R-R	6-4	225	1-1-02	0	1	7.94	4	1	0	6	6	5	5	0	3	5	.261	.370	.348	18.5	11.1	27				
Sifontes, Enderjer	R-R	6-0	135	11-19-02	0	1	9.00	5	0	0	5	7	6	5	2	4	7	.333	.423	.714	26.9	15.4	26				
Silseth, Chase	R-R	6-0	217	5-18-00	0	1	5.14	5	1	0	7	9	4	4	0	1	12	.300	.323	.400	38.7	3.2	31				
Soto, Ubaldo	R-R	6-2	185	7-12-06	3	1	5.14	12	6	0	49	39	30	28	5	24	53	.215	.325	.343	24.9	11.3	213				
Vasquez, Andrew	L-L	6-6	235	9-14-93	1	0	0.00	2	0	0	2	0	0	0	1	0	6	.000	.125	.000	75.0	12.5	8				
Vega, Marco	R-R	6-2	165	10-25-04	3	1	5.59	14	0	0	19	19	12	3	11	16	.257	.360	.419	18.6	12.8	86					
Vergara, Brayan	R-R	6-0	145	12-21-05	2	2	2.47	12	4	1	51	56	20	14	3	11	37	.301	.335	.452	18.2	5.4	203				
Yovan, Kenyon	R-R	6-2	221	12-28-97	0	0	0.00	2	0	1	3	0	0	0	0	2	3	.000	.200	.000	27.3	18.2	11				

Fielding
C: Quintero 44, Rivero 10, Villahermosa 7, Hopson 4. **1B:** Duarte 35, Rivero 26, Rodriguez 7, Drury 2, Blakely 1. **2B:** Marquez 39, Morrobel 14, Kingery 4, Alfonso 3, Mershon 3, Patino 3, Rodriguez 3, Duarte 1. **3B:** Duarte 24, V. Rodriguez 18, Patino 17, Alfonso 5, Marquez 5, L. Rodriguez 2, Moncada 2, Drury 1. **SS:** Lugo 28, L. Rodriguez 18, Alfonso 8, Morrobel 8, Mershon 2, Kingery 1, Marquez 1, V. Rodriguez 1. **LF:** Martinez 33, Dishmey 17, Ramirez 6, Blankenhorn 5, Caraballo 4, Alfonso 3, Flores 2, Alvarez 1, Teodosio 1, Villahermosa 1. **CF:** Alvarez 54, Caraballo 4, Blakely 3, Martinez 3, Dishmey 2, Flores 2, Teodosio 2. **RF:** Ramirez 37, Caraballo 12, Dishmey 11, Teodosio 5, Campero 2, Flores 2, Villahermosa 2, Alfonso 1, Blakely 1, Taylor 1

DSL ANGELS — ROOKIE
DOMINICAN SUMMER LEAGUE

Batting	B-T	Ht.	Wt.	DOB	AVG	OBP	SLG	G	PA	AB	R	H	2B	3B	HR	RBI	BB	HBP	SH	SF	SO	SB	CS	BB%	SO%
Betances, Yelinson	R-R	6-1	190	11-13-07	.209	.339	.308	45	114	91	13	19	1	2	18	15	4	2	2	24	9	4	13.2	21.1
Bruno, Luis	S-R	6-1	180	7-2-08	.125	.125	.375	2	8	8	1	1	0	1	0	1	0	0	0	3	0	0	0.0	37.5
Cabrera, Yojancel	L-R	6-2	186	6-25-08	.339	.445	.472	52	219	180	40	61	14	2	2	29	30	6	1	2	37	10	8	13.7	16.9
Camacho, Jose	R-R	6-0	187	1-24-07	.155	.280	.214	35	100	84	10	13	2	0	1	4	13	2	0	1	22	1	1	13.0	22.0
Castillo, Byron	R-R	6-0	197	10-7-05	.312	.391	.496	46	161	141	35	44	7	2	5	24	13	6	0	1	42	9	3	8.1	26.1
Davalillo, Gabriel	R-R	5-11	210	11-6-07	.302	.408	.518	41	169	139	28	42	7	1	7	31	23	4	0	3	21	3	0	13.6	12.4
De La Paz, Greylin	R-R	6-1	170	5-10-07	.302	.437	.420	53	215	169	40	51	11	3	1	20	39	4	0	3	36	9	7	18.1	16.7
De Paula, Yilver	B-R	5-11	180	5-16-08	.387	.525	.484	10	40	31	10	12	0	0	1	7	7	2	0	0	6	3	17.5	15.0	
De Pena, Wilberson	R-R	6-2	185	11-10-06	.227	.306	.493	32	85	75	22	17	6	1	4	20	7	2	0	1	18	5	1	8.2	21.2
Demey, Josue	R-R	5-10	165	12-6-06	.245	.423	.358	24	71	53	12	13	3	0	1	8	15	2	0	1	8	1	1	21.1	11.3
Menendez, Liordanys	R-R	6-0	175	1-31-08	.254	.382	.349	43	153	126	24	32	6	3	0	11	21	5	1	0	19	11	1	13.7	12.4
Paredes, Cesar	R-R	6-1	178	5-6-08	.229	.401	.284	36	142	109	26	25	6	0	0	12	27	5	0	1	30	22	3	19.0	21.1
Rondon, Diego	L-R	5-11	161	9-14-07	.228	.397	.263	26	73	57	9	13	0	1	0	8	13	3	0	0	11	1	1	17.8	15.1
Santa Cruz de Oviedo, Anthony	L-L	6-3	180	3-15-07	.297	.395	.429	52	210	175	34	52	14	3	1	42	29	2	0	4	34	3	2	13.8	16.2
Santana, Jose	R-R	6-1	190	4-25-08	.103	.347	.103	41	121	87	13	9	0	0	0	8	29	4	0	1	29	3	5	24.0	24.0
Suriel, Junior	R-R	6-0	160	8-23-08	.289	.348	.413	40	133	121	24	35	8	2	1	23	8	3	1	0	13	7	0	6.0	9.8
Tiberi, Humberto	R-R	6-2	200	12-22-06	.207	.277	.310	19	65	58	9	12	0	0	2	9	4	2	0	1	18	1	2	6.2	27.7

Pitching	B-T	Ht.	Wt.	DOB	W	L	ERA	G	GS	SV	IP	Hits	Runs	ER	HR	BB	SO	AVG	OBP	SLG	SO%	BB%	BF
Almonte, Jhon	R-R	6-3	185	11-16-06	2	4	5.70	11	11	0	47	52	34	30	1	26	36	.292	.396	.360	16.9	12.2	213
Anzola, Rolando	R-R	6-2	170	5-31-05	2	2	4.70	19	0	7	31	23	21	16	0	27	34	.204	.384	.248	23.3	18.5	146
Berroteran, Wilner	R-R	6-3	192	10-19-07	1	0	1.64	5	5	0	22	13	4	4	0	8	23	.183	.301	.211	27.1	9.4	85
Betances, Jhostin	R-R	6-3	147	3-1-07	1	3	4.32	11	10	0	42	33	22	20	2	26	41	.224	.373	.320	22.0	14.0	186
Cabrera, Miguel	R-R	6-5	195	11-13-07	1	0	9.64	12	0	1	14	13	16	15	4	20	6	.245	.481	.528	7.8	26.0	77
Caseres, Sebastian	L-L	5-11	148	3-2-08	0	3	2.67	17	1	3	34	21	10	10	0	7	40	.178	.228	.212	31.3	5.5	128
Colina, Daniel	R-R	6-1	194	11-16-06	2	0	4.11	17	0	2	31	30	14	14	3	14	14	.259	.360	.422	10.3	10.3	136
Gallardo, Fabian	R-R	6-3	180	1-24-06	4	3	4.75	11	10	0	53	53	37	28	1	25	37	.255	.354	.356	15.2	10.3	243
Hernandez, Freddy	L-L	6-1	190	1-4-08	2	2	3.89	11	11	0	44	47	27	19	2	23	43	.263	.345	.318	21.2	11.3	203
Jordan, Juan	R-R	6-1	200	9-7-07	6	2	4.78	19	4	0	32	32	19	17	1	18	41	.248	.349	.380	27.5	12.1	149
Leon, Kauriel	R-R	6-3	185	8-12-06	0	0	12.51	12	0	0	14	15	21	19	2	18	16	.278	.474	.463	21.1	23.7	76
Liendo, Miguel	R-R	6-1	188	12-5-07	4	1	7.04	16	0	1	23	27	20	18	2	18	26	.281	.388	.458	22.4	15.5	116
Montilla, Christopher	R-R	6-2	170	2-8-07	0	1	16.88	10	0	0	8	11	16	15	0	18	8	.333	.593	.455	14.8	33.3	54
Morel, Albert	R-R	6-4	179	9-25-07	0	2	3.07	8	6	0	15	7	13	5	0	8	10	.283	.403	.317	13.9	11.1	72
Reyes, Starling	R-R	6-1	185	11-16-06	3	0	9.50	14	0	0	18	19	22	19	3	18	16	.268	.415	.408	17.0	19.1	94
Soto, Fabian	R-R	6-2	170	9-21-05	0	1	18.00	2	2	0	2	3	4	4	0	4	.375	.615	.750	30.8	30.8	13	
Tirado, Leudy	L-L	5-10	160	9-27-05	3	1	4.50	14	0	0	22	20	15	11	1	25	24	.253	.460	.342	21.1	21.9	114

Fielding
C: Demey 23, Tiberi 18, Davalillo 16, Rondon 9. **1B:** Santa Cruz de Oviedo 36, Camacho 25. **2B:** Menendez 36, Paredes 12, Santana 9, De Paula 3. **3B:** De La Paz 52, Camacho 4, Menendez 4, Santana 1. **SS:** Santana 27, Paredes 23, De Paula 9, Bruno 2. **LF:** De Pena 22, Suriel 17, Betances 14, Santa Cruz de Oviedo 9, Castillo 3. **CF:** Castillo 24, Betances 21, Suriel 18, De Pena 1. **RF:** Cabrera 46, Castillo 14, Betances 6, De Pena 4, Suriel 2

Los Angeles Dodgers

SEASON SYNOPSIS: After entering the season with lofty expectations following the addition of free agents Blake Snell, Tanner Scott and Japanese phenom Roki Sasaki, the Dodgers won "just" 93 games. But they hit their stride in September to win the NL West for the fourth straight season, powered through the NL playoffs with only one loss, then fought an epic World Series battle with Toronto, winning Games Six and Seven on the road to become MLB's first repeat World Series champion since the 1998-2000 Yankees.

HIGH POINT: Injuries, patient recovery timelines and underwhelming performances by depth starters strained the Dodgers' rotation all season. They leaned heavily on Yoshinobu Yamamoto, who responded with a 12-8, 2.49 season, ranking second in the NL in ERA. He had a postseason for the ages, completing consecutive starts in the NLCS against Milwaukee and in Game Two of the World Series in Toronto. He then won Game Six with six strong innings and pitched the next night to win Game Seven with 2⅔ scoreless. Trailing 4-3 in the ninth, the Dodgers tied the game on Miguel Rojas' solo blast off Jeff Hoffman, and Will Smith provided the winning run in the 11th.

LOW POINT: A 10-14 July trimmed the NL West lead, and the Padres caught LA twice, including with consecutive victories Aug. 22-23 in Petco Park in which the Dodgers scored only one run. Yamamoto, who tossed six strong innings in the series finale, was the stopper, supported by two Freddie Freeman homers and a three-run, eighth-inning homer by rookie catcher Dalton Rushing in an 8-2 win. The Dodgers never trailed in the division race again.

NOTABLE ROOKIES: Sasaki had dominated Japan's NPB when healthy but struggled out of the gate with the Dodgers. He returned from injury as a reliever with a rebuilt delivery in late September and in the postseason. LHPs Jack Dreyer (3-2, 2.95, 4 SV) and Justin Wrobleski (5-5, 4.32) pitched some key postseason innings. Rushing (.582 OPS) struggled. UT Hyeseong Kim (.280/.314/.385) was a versatile speedster.

KEY TRANSACTIONS: Snell (5-year, $182 million) pitched well when healthy, including in the postseason, while Scott (4-year, $72 million) and Kirby Yates (1-year, $13 million) were bullpen duds. OF Michael Conforto (1-year, $17M) hit just .199. OF Alex Call (85 PA) was the Dodgers' top trade-deadline pickup.

OPENING DAY PAYROLL: $321,287,291 (2nd)

PLAYERS OF THE YEAR

MAJOR LEAGUE
Shohei Ohtani
DH/RHP
.282/.392/.622
55 HR, 146 R, 102 RBIs
2.87 ERA, 62 SO in 47 IP

MINOR LEAGUE
Eduardo Quintero
OF
(A,A+)
.293/.415/.508
19 HR, 47 SB, 88 BB

ORGANIZATION LEADERS

Batting		*Qualifiers
MAJORS		
* AVG	Freddie Freeman	.295
* OPS	Shohei Ohtani	1.014
HR	Shohei Ohtani	55
RBI	Shohei Ohtani	102
MINORS		
* AVG	Emil Morales, Rancho Cuca./ACL Dodgers	.314
* OBP	Ching-Hsien Ko, Rancho Cuca./ACL Dodgers	.437
* SLG	Ryan Ward, Okla. City	.557
* OPS	Ryan Ward, Okla. City	.937
R	Ryan Ward, Okla. City	113
H	Ryan Ward, Okla. City	164
TB	Ryan Ward, Okla. City	315
2B	Ryan Ward, Okla. City	31
3B	Kendall George, Great Lakes	7
3B	Eduardo Quintero, Great Lakes/Rancho Cuca.	7
HR	Ryan Ward, Okla. City	36
RBI	Ryan Ward, Okla. City	122
BB	Austin Gauthier, Okla. City	93
SO	Chris Newell, Tulsa	168
SB	Kendall George, Great Lakes	100

Pitching		#Qualifiers
MAJORS		
W	Yoshinobu Yamamoto	12
# ERA	Yoshinobu Yamamoto	2.49
SO	Yoshinobu Yamamoto	201
SV	Tanner Scott	23
MINORS		
W	Jackson Ferris, Tulsa	10
L	Brooks Auger, Great Lakes	8
# ERA	Patrick Copen, Tulsa/Great Lakes	3.59
G	Logan Boyer, Okla. City	50
GS	Patrick Copen, Tulsa/Great Lakes	27
SV	Jack Little, Okla. City	13
IP	Chris Campos, Tulsa	127
BB	Patrick Copen, Tulsa/Great Lakes	84
SO	Patrick Copen, Tulsa/Great Lakes	152
# AVG	Patrick Copen, Tulsa/Great Lakes	.200

2025 PERFORMANCE

President: Andrew Friedman. **Farm Director:** Will Rhymes. **Scouting Director:** Zach Fitzpatrick.

Class	Team	League	W	L	PCT	Finish	Manager
Majors	Los Angeles Dodgers	National	93	69	.574	3 (15)	Dave Roberts
Triple-A	Oklahoma City Comets	Pacific Coast	84	66	.560	2 (10)	Travis Barbary
Double-A	Tulsa Drillers	Texas	66	72	.478	8 (10)	Scott Hennessey
High-A	Great Lakes Loons	Midwest	72	58	.554	4 (12)	Jair Fernandez
Low-A	Rancho Cucamonga Quakes	California	70	62	.530	3 (8)	John Shoemaker
Rookie	ACL Dodgers	Arizona Complex	29	31	.483	11 (15)	Juan Apodaca
Rookie	DSL LAD Bautista	Dominican	17	37	.315	49 (52)	Dunior Zerpa
Rookie	DSL LAD Mega	Dominican	25	30	.455	30 (52)	Leury Bonilla
Overall 2025 Minor League Record			363	356	.505	13th (30)	

ORGANIZATION STATISTICS

LOS ANGELES DODGERS
NATIONAL LEAGUE

Batting	B-T	Ht.	Wt.	DOB	AVG	OBP	SLG	G	PA	AB	R	H	2B	3B	HR	RBI	BB	HBP	SH	SF	SO	SB	CS	BB%	SO%
Barnes, Austin	R-R	5-10	187	12-28-89	.214	.233	.286	13	44	42	4	9	3	0	0	2	1	0	1	0	14	0	0	2.3	31.8
Betts, Mookie	R-R	5-9	180	10-7-92	.258	.326	.406	150	663	589	95	152	23	2	20	82	61	3	0	10	68	8	2	9.2	10.3
Call, Alex	R-R	5-11	189	9-27-94	.247	.333	.384	38	85	73	13	18	4	0	2	5	10	0	1	1	19	1	0	11.8	22.4
Conforto, Michael	L-R	6-1	215	3-1-93	.199	.305	.333	138	486	418	54	83	20	0	12	36	56	9	0	3	121	1	0	11.5	24.9
Dean, Justin	R-R	5-8	185	12-6-96	.000	.000	.000	18	2	2	0	0	0	0	0	0	0	0	0	0	1	1	0	0.0	50.0
Edman, Tommy	S-R	5-10	180	5-9-95	.225	.274	.382	97	377	346	49	78	13	1	13	49	19	6	1	5	61	3	1	5.0	16.2
Feduccia, Hunter	L-R	6-0	215	6-5-97	.000	.333	.000	2	3	2	0	0	0	0	0	0	1	0	0	0	1	0	0	33.3	33.3
Freeland, Alex	S-R	6-2	200	8-24-01	.190	.292	.310	29	97	84	10	16	2	1	2	6	11	1	1	0	35	1	0	11.3	36.1
Freeman, Freddie	L-R	6-5	220	9-12-89	.295	.367	.502	147	627	556	81	164	39	2	24	90	60	6	0	5	128	6	2	9.6	20.4
Hernandez, Enrique	R-R	5-11	190	8-24-91	.203	.255	.366	93	256	232	30	47	8	0	10	35	18	0	1	5	68	0	0	7.0	26.6
Hernandez, Teoscar	R-R	6-2	215	10-15-92	.247	.284	.454	134	546	511	65	126	29	1	25	89	26	3	0	5	134	5	2	4.8	24.5
Kennedy, Buddy	R-R	5-9	190	10-5-98	.059	.111	.059	7	18	17	1	1	0	0	0	1	0	0	0	0	5	0	0	0.0	27.8
Kim, Hyeseong	L-R	5-9	165	1-27-99	.280	.314	.385	71	170	161	19	45	6	1	3	17	7	1	1	0	52	13	1	4.1	30.6
Muncy, Max	L-R	6-0	215	8-25-90	.243	.376	.470	100	388	313	48	76	10	2	19	67	64	6	0	5	83	4	0	16.5	21.4
Ohtani, Shohei	L-R	6-4	210	7-5-94	.282	.392	.622	158	727	611	146	172	25	9	55	102	109	3	0	2	187	20	6	15.0	25.7
Outman, James	L-R	6-3	215	5-14-97	.103	.205	.282	22	44	39	8	4	1	0	2	4	4	1	0	0	16	0	0	9.1	40.9
Pages, Andy	R-R	6-1	212	12-8-00	.272	.313	.461	156	624	581	74	158	27	1	27	86	29	8	0	6	135	14	7	4.6	21.6
Robinson, Chuckie	R-R	6-0	215	12-14-94	.000	.000	.000	1	2	1	1	0	0	0	0	0	0	0	1	0	0	0	0	0.0	0.0
Rojas, Miguel	R-R	6-0	188	2-24-89	.262	.318	.397	114	317	290	35	76	18	0	7	27	24	0	3	0	46	5	0	7.6	14.5
Rortvedt, Ben	L-R	5-9	191	9-25-97	.224	.309	.327	18	58	49	7	11	2	0	1	4	4	2	3	0	9	0	0	6.9	15.5
Rosario, Eddie	L-R	6-1	180	9-28-91	.250	.250	.250	2	4	4	0	1	0	0	0	0	0	0	0	0	0	0	0	0.0	0.0
Ruiz, Esteury	R-R	6-0	169	2-15-99	.191	.333	.19	23	21	2	4	0	0	1	2	2	0	0	8	4	0	8.7	34.8
Rushing, Dalton	L-R	6-1	220	2-21-01	.204	.258	.324	53	155	142	15	29	5	0	4	24	10	1	0	2	58	0	0	6.5	37.4
Smith, Will	R-R	5-10	195	3-28-95	.296	.404	.497	110	436	362	64	107	20	1	17	61	64	5	0	5	89	2	3	14.7	20.4
Taylor, Chris	R-R	6-1	196	8-29-90	.200	.200	.257	28	35	35	4	7	2	0	0	2	0	0	0	0	13	0	1	0.0	37.1

Pitching	B-T	Ht.	Wt.	DOB	W	L	ERA	G	GS	SV	IP	Hits	Runs	ER	HR	BB	SO	AVG	OBP	SLG	SO%	BB%	BF
Banda, Anthony	L-L	6-2	221	8-10-93	5	1	3.18	71	1	0	65	45	23	23	8	34	61	.197	.302	.354	22.8	12.7	268
Casparius, Ben	R-R	6-2	215	2-11-99	7	5	4.64	46	3	2	78	78	41	40	8	21	71	.254	.307	.410	21.3	6.3	333
Davis, Noah	R-R	6-2	195	4-22-97	0	1	19.50	5	0	0	6	10	14	13	3	5	8	.385	.543	.731	22.9	14.3	35
Diaz, Alexis	R-R	6-2	224	9-28-96	1	0	5.00	9	0	0	9	7	5	5	2	2	9	.206	.289	.471	23.7	5.3	38
Dreyer, Jack	L-R	6-2	205	2-27-99	3	2	2.95	67	5	4	76	56	26	25	4	24	74	.203	.263	.312	24.1	7.8	307
Fernandez, Julian	R-R	6-6	230	12-5-95	0	0	9.00	1	0	0	2	2	2	2	1	1	2	.250	.333	.625	11.1	11.1	9
Feyereisen, J.P.	R-R	6-2	215	2-7-93	0	1	13.50	2	0	0	2	8	4	3	1	1	2	.615	.643	.923	14.3	7.1	14
Garcia, Luis	R-R	6-2	240	1-30-87	2	0	5.27	28	0	0	27	34	17	16	1	16	24	.312	.400	.468	19.0	12.7	126
Gervase, Paul	R-R	6-10	230	5-23-00	0	0	4.50	1	0	0	2	2	1	1	0	1	2	.250	.333	.250	22.2	11.1	9
Glasnow, Tyler	L-R	6-8	225	8-23-93	4	3	3.19	18	18	0	90	56	33	32	10	43	106	.177	.279	.310	29.0	11.7	366
Gomez, Yoendrys	R-R	6-3	175	10-15-99	0	0	14.54	3	0	1	4	10	7	7	2	2	6	.435	.480	.739	24.0	8.0	25
Gonsolin, Tony	R-R	6-3	205	5-14-94	3	2	5.00	7	7	0	36	33	21	20	9	18	38	.224	.346	.467	24.2	11.5	157
Heaney, Andrew	L-L	6-2	200	6-5-91	0	0	13.50	1	0	0	2	4	3	3	1	1	2	.400	.455	.800	18.2	9.1	11
Henriquez, Edgardo	R-R	6-4	300	6-24-02	2	1	2.37	22	0	1	19	17	5	5	2	5	18	.236	.282	.361	23.1	6.4	78
Hernandez, Enrique	R-R	5-11	190	8-24-91	0	0	15.19	5	0	0	5	11	9	9	1	8	1	.393	.514	.571	2.7	21.6	37
Kershaw, Clayton	L-L	6-4	225	3-19-88	11	2	3.36	23	22	0	113	102	46	42	8	35	84	.243	.302	.362	18.1	7.6	463
Klein, Will	R-R	6-5	230	11-28-99	1	1	2.35	14	0	0	15	14	6	4	0	10	21	.246	.371	.316	30.0	14.3	70
Knack, Landon	R-R	6-4	240	7-15-97	3	2	4.89	16	7	1	42	40	25	23	10	19	42	.247	.330	.488	22.7	10.3	185
Kopech, Michael	R-R	6-3	210	4-30-96	0	0	2.45	14	0	0	11	6	3	3	0	13	12	.150	.350	.150	22.6	24.5	53
Little, Jack	R-R	6-4	190	1-10-98	0	0	6.00	2	0	0	3	4	2	2	0	1	2	.333	.429	.500	14.3	7.1	14
Loutos, Ryan	R-R	6-5	215	1-29-99	0	0	15.00	2	0	0	4	5	5	1	2	0	.308	.438	.615	12.5	12.5	16
May, Dustin	R-R	6-6	180	9-6-97	6	7	4.85	19	18	0	104	97	60	56	16	43	97	.245	.330	.439	21.5	9.5	451
Miller, Bobby	L-R	6-5	220	4-5-99	0	0	12.60	2	1	0	5	11	7	7	2	2	7	.440	.500	.760	25.0	7.1	28
Ohtani, Shohei	L-R	6-4	210	7-5-94	1	1	2.87	14	14	0	47	40	15	15	3	9	62	.227	.261	.313	33.0	4.8	188
Phillips, Evan	R-R	6-2	215	9-11-94	0	0	0.00	7	0	1	6	4	0	0	0	2	6	.200	.273	.200	27.3	9.1	22

Player	B-T	Ht.	Wt.	DOB																		
Rojas, Miguel	R-R	6-0	188	2-24-89	0	0	12.60	4	0	0	5	11	7	7	3	2	0	.440	.500	.920	0.0	7.1	28
Sasaki, Roki	R-R	6-2	187	11-3-01	1	1	4.46	10	8	0	36	30	18	18	6	22	28	.221	.342	.404	17.4	13.7	161
Sauer, Matt	R-R	6-4	195	1-21-99	2	1	6.37	10	1	1	30	35	23	21	6	8	24	.299	.349	.521	18.6	6.2	129
Scott, Tanner	R-L	6-0	235	7-22-94	1	4	4.74	61	0	23	57	54	33	30	11	18	60	.254	.321	.460	25.2	7.6	238
Sheehan, Emmet	R-R	6-5	220	11-15-99	6	3	2.82	15	12	0	73	49	29	23	7	22	89	.185	.251	.317	30.6	7.6	291
Snell, Blake	L-L	6-4	225	12-4-92	5	4	2.35	11	11	0	61	51	21	16	3	26	72	.230	.307	.315	28.3	10.2	254
Stewart, Brock	L-R	6-3	220	10-3-91	0	1	4.91	4	0	0	4	6	2	2	0	2	3	.353	.450	.412	15.0	10.0	20
Stratton, Chris	R-R	6-2	205	8-22-90	0	0	6.75	3	0	0	4	3	3	3	2	2	6	.200	.294	.667	35.3	11.8	17
Treinen, Blake	R-R	6-5	225	6-30-88	2	7	5.40	32	0	2	27	30	18	16	4	19	36	.280	.395	.439	27.9	14.7	129
Trivino, Lou	R-R	6-5	235	10-1-91	2	1	3.76	26	2	0	26	29	12	11	2	8	18	.293	.360	.414	15.7	7.0	115
Urena, Jose	R-R	6-2	208	9-12-91	0	0	3.00	2	0	0	3	4	1	1	0	1	2	.333	.385	.500	15.4	7.7	13
Vesia, Alex	L-L	6-1	209	4-11-96	4	2	3.02	68	0	5	60	37	21	20	9	22	80	.181	.272	.348	33.8	9.3	237
Wrobleski, Justin	L-L	6-1	194	7-14-00	5	5	4.32	24	2	2	67	65	34	32	6	17	76	.255	.306	.380	27.1	6.1	280
Yamamoto, Yoshinobu	R-R	5-10	176	8-17-98	12	8	2.49	30	30	0	174	113	53	48	14	59	201	.183	.257	.283	29.4	8.6	684
Yates, Kirby	L-R	5-10	205	3-25-87	4	3	5.23	50	0	3	41	38	26	24	9	17	52	.239	.315	.516	29.2	9.6	178

Fielding

Catcher	PCT	G	PO	A	E	DP	PB
Barnes	1.000	12	119	1	0	0	0
Robinson	1.000	1	9	0	0	0	0
Rortvedt	1.000	18	177	7	0	1	0
Rushing	.997	41	349	15	1	2	2
Smith	.996	101	873	37	4	7	2

First Base	PCT	G	PO	A	E	DP
Barnes	1.000	1	2	0	0	0
Feduccia	1.000	1	3	1	0	0
Freeman	.997	146	1008	91	3	75
Hernandez, E	1.000	28	150	10	0	13
Rojas	1.000	1	3	0	0	0
Rushing	1.000	8	23	2	0	1

Second Base	PCT	G	PO	A	E	DP
Edman	.996	66	81	144	1	25

	PCT	G	PO	A	E	DP
Freeland	1.000	15	12	23	0	5
Hernandez, E	.977	18	11	31	1	6
Kim	.976	45	46	74	3	12
Rojas	.989	68	66	116	2	22
Taylor	1.000	4	2	4	0	0

Third Base	PCT	G	PO	A	E	DP
Edman	.973	13	11	25	1	2
Freeland	.958	17	7	39	2	1
Hernandez, E	.947	27	13	41	3	5
Kennedy	1.000	7	3	8	0	0
Muncy	.951	97	58	154	11	13
Rojas	.980	23	15	33	1	5

Shortstop	PCT	G	PO	A	E	DP
Betts	.985	148	160	315	7	51
Kim	1.000	11	9	8	0	3

	PCT	G	PO	A	E	DP
Rojas	.981	22	19	33	1	4

Outfield	PCT	G	PO	A	E	DP
Betts	1.000	1	1	0	0	0
Call	1.000	39	44	0	0	0
Conforto	.980	132	193	5	4	1
Dean	1.000	17	7	0	0	0
Edman	1.000	25	45	2	0	0
Hernandez, E	.962	31	25	0	1	0
Hernandez, T	.992	133	255	6	2	2
Kim	1.000	17	25	1	0	0
Outman	1.000	22	22	0	0	0
Pages	.971	199	354	10	11	5
Ruiz	.923	17	12	0	1	0
Taylor	1.000	24	21	1	0	0

OKLAHOMA CITY COMETS
PACIFIC COAST LEAGUE — TRIPLE-A

Batting	B-T	Ht.	Wt.	DOB	AVG	OBP	SLG	G	PA	AB	R	H	2B	3B	HR	RBI	BB	HBP	SH	SF	SO	SB	CS	BB%	SO%
Alexander, CJ	L-R	6-3	215	7-17-96	.269	.332	.457	52	229	208	32	56	16	4	5	30	20	0	0	1	67	3	1	8.7	29.3
Avila, Carlos	R-R	5-11	180	12-4-03	.000	.000	.000	3	7	7	0	0	0	0	0	0	0	0	0	0	2	0	0	0.0	28.6
Baker, Luken	R-R	6-4	280	3-10-97	.273	.382	.521	33	144	121	18	33	6	0	8	22	22	0	0	1	33	0	0	15.3	22.9
Berroa, Steward	S-R	5-9	178	6-5-95	.224	.433	.27	7	119	97	23	32	7	0	1	11	17	1	1	3	22	11	3	14.3	18.5
Biddison, Nick	L-L	5-10	190	7-30-00	.333	.333	.333	1	3	3	0	1	0	0	0	0	0	0	0	0	1	0	0	0.0	33.3
Chavis, Michael	R-R	5-10	190	8-11-95	.291	.350	.547	63	283	258	45	75	21	3	13	45	24	0	0	1	66	2	2	8.5	23.3
Dean, Justin	R-R	5-8	185	12-6-96	.289	.378	.431	90	347	304	60	88	13	6	6	33	39	4	0	0	82	27	9	11.2	23.6
Edman, Tommy	S-R	5-10	180	5-9-95	.286	.412	.286	5	17	14	1	4	0	0	0	3	3	0	0	0	2	0	0	17.6	11.8
Feduccia, Hunter	L-R	6-0	215	6-5-97	.290	.399	.467	79	333	276	55	80	14	4	9	52	52	1	0	4	71	2	0	15.6	21.3
Freeland, Alex	S-R	6-2	200	8-24-01	.263	.384	.451	106	508	415	77	109	30	0	16	82	83	3	0	7	111	18	6	16.3	21.9
Gauthier, Austin	R-R	6-0	188	5-7-99	.259	.404	.354	118	478	378	69	98	20	2	4	45	93	2	0	5	92	5	1	19.5	19.2
Hainline, Elijah	R-R	5-10	185	12-20-02	.273	.429	.364	5	14	11	1	3	1	0	0	2	3	0	0	0	2	0	0	21.4	14.3
Hernandez, Enrique	R-R	5-11	190	8-24-91	.357	.438	.500	5	16	14	1	5	2	0	0	3	2	0	0	0	3	1	0	12.5	18.8
Hoese, Kody	R-R	6-4	200	7-13-97	.264	.357	.411	99	403	348	51	92	25	1	8	51	50	2	0	3	78	1	0	12.4	19.4
Kim, Hyeseong	L-R	5-9	165	1-27-99	.268	.337	.456	37	169	149	27	40	9	2	5	22	13	3	1	1	42	14	1	7.7	24.9
Miller, Noah	S-R	5-11	190	11-12-02	.238	.269	.344	59	242	227	31	54	12	0	4	35	11	0	0	4	44	1	0	4.5	18.2
Muncy, Max	L-R	6-0	215	8-25-90	.318	.400	.500	8	25	22	4	7	1	0	1	3	3	0	0	0	9	0	0	12.0	36.0
Okey, Chris	R-R	5-11	200	7-30-94	.228	.280	.336	42	161	149	16	34	5	1	3	23	9	2	0	1	40	0	5	5.6	24.8
Outman, James	L-R	6-3	215	5-14-97	.289	.378	.502	70	333	284	61	82	20	3	20	74	39	5	0	5	101	14	3	11.7	30.3
Ramos, Jose	R-R	6-1	200	1-1-01	.295	.359	.557	44	167	149	29	44	9	3	8	27	15	1	0	2	51	2	1	9.0	30.5
Robinson, Chuckie	R-R	6-0	215	12-14-94	.254	.337	.348	51	205	181	32	46	5	0	4	30	20	3	0	1	50	1	0	9.8	24.4
Rodriguez, Frank	R-R	5-11	197	9-28-01	.143	.250	.143	2	8	7	1	1	0	0	0	0	1	0	0	0	3	0	0	12.5	37.5
Rortvedt, Ben	L-R	5-9	191	9-25-97	.228	.281	.386	17	64	57	7	13	3	0	2	6	3	2	0	2	16	0	0	4.7	25.0
Rosario, Eddie	L-R	6-1	180	9-28-91	.339	.406	.542	14	69	59	11	20	6	0	2	12	8	0	0	2	16	3	1	11.6	23.2
Ruiz, Esteury	R-R	6-0	169	2-15-99	.303	.411	.514	104	485	403	94	122	25	6	16	60	63	12	3	1	87	62	11	13.0	17.9
Rushing, Dalton	L-R	6-1	220	2-21-01	.314	.436	.517	35	149	118	26	37	7	1	5	19	26	2	0	3	32	1	0	17.4	21.5
Senzel, Nick	R-R	6-1	218	6-29-95	.252	.341	.408	96	411	353	51	89	15	2	12	62	45	6	0	7	76	7	1	10.9	18.5
Ward, Ryan	L-R	5-9	200	2-23-98	.290	.380	.557	143	652	566	113	164	31	6	36	122	83	1	0	2	122	16	6	12.7	18.7

Pitching	B-T	Ht.	Wt.	DOB	W	L	ERA	G	GS	SV	IP	Hits	Runs	ER	HR	BB	SO	AVG	OBP	SLG	SO%	BB%	BF
Boyer, Logan	R-R	6-3	215	1-24-98	5	5	5.00	50	0	1	54	61	31	30	5	39	51	.293	.406	.404	20.3	15.5	251
Carlson, Sam	R-R	6-4	195	12-3-98	4	2	4.22	45	0	4	60	56	36	28	4	36	78	.251	.369	.377	28.6	13.2	273
Casparius, Ben	R-R	6-2	215	2-11-99	2	0	3.38	5	0	0	5	4	2	2	1	0	7	.200	.200	.450	35.0	0.0	20
Davis, Noah	R-R	6-2	195	4-22-97	3	0	3.94	21	2	1	32	24	16	14	2	15	38	.207	.316	.319	27.5	10.9	138
Diaz, Alexis	R-R	6-2	224	9-28-96	0	1	8.10	10	0	1	10	7	9	9	1	6	8	.200	.391	.457	21.7	17.4	46
Duran, Carlos	R-R	6-7	230	7-30-01	0	0	2.08	1	1	0	4	3	1	1	0	4	8	.200	.368	.267	42.1	21.1	19
Fernandez, Julian	R-R	6-6	290	12-5-95	3	0	3.05	35	4	4	41	37	14	14	4	15	49	.240	.304	.377	28.7	8.8	171

LOS ANGELES DODGERS

Player	B-T	Ht	Wt	DOB	W	L	ERA	G	GS	SV	IP	H	R	ER	BB	SO	AVG	OBP	SLG	K/9	BB/9	BF
Feyereisen, J.P.	R-R	6-2	215	2-7-93	0	0	9.64	4	0	0	5	10	5	5	1	1	1	.435	.440	.652	3.8	3.8	26
Frasso, Nick	R-R	6-5	200	10-18-98	6	1	5.49	43	7	1	77	80	47	47	10	42	68	.274	.366	.435	19.7	12.1	346
Funkhouser, Kyle	R-R	6-3	229	3-16-94	2	5	6.03	17	12	0	63	74	45	42	8	36	56	.295	.390	.458	18.9	12.1	297
Gamboa, Alec	S-L	6-1	205	1-17-97	0	2	4.19	8	2	0	19	14	10	9	0	12	12	.206	.329	.250	14.5	14.5	83
Gervase, Paul	R-R	6-10	230	5-23-00	2	1	4.74	15	0	1	19	14	10	10	3	15	16	.212	.357	.394	19.0	17.9	84
Glasnow, Tyler	L-R	6-8	225	8-23-93	0	0	8.31	3	3	0	9	13	8	8	1	5	12	.351	.442	.486	27.9	11.6	43
Gonsolin, Tony	R-R	6-3	205	5-14-94	1	1	3.21	4	4	0	14	12	6	5	2	6	16	.235	.328	.373	27.6	10.3	58
Harris, Ben	L-L	6-1	195	2-22-00	1	0	4.75	28	2	0	30	21	16	16	2	33	36	.202	.411	.327	24.5	22.4	147
Heaney, Andrew	L-L	6-2	200	6-5-91	0	0	0.90	4	4	0	10	5	1	1	0	2	13	.156	.200	.219	37.1	5.7	35
Henriquez, Edgardo	R-R	6-4	200	6-24-02	1	1	6.85	22	2	0	24	30	19	18	3	14	36	.303	.402	.475	30.8	12.0	117
Hernandez, Jose	L-L	5-10	205	12-31-97	0	4	4.94	21	0	0	27	22	16	15	3	18	34	.214	.328	.340	27.9	14.8	122
Hurt, Kyle	R-R	6-3	240	5-30-98	1	0	1.93	7	0	0	9	10	2	2	0	5	10	.270	.357	.270	23.8	11.9	42
Jacques, Joe	L-L	6-4	210	3-11-95	1	1	6.04	18	0	3	22	28	18	15	1	8	24	.298	.377	.426	22.6	7.5	106
Jarvis, Justin	R-R	6-2	183	2-20-00	3	2	6.38	13	10	0	55	56	39	39	4	34	38	.267	.373	.371	15.2	13.6	250
Kershaw, Clayton	L-L	6-4	225	3-19-88	0	0	3.75	3	3	0	12	8	5	5	3	3	8	.205	.279	.436	18.6	7.0	43
Klein, Will	R-R	6-5	230	11-28-99	1	3	5.16	20	0	1	23	18	15	13	2	17	44	.214	.353	.333	42.7	16.5	103
Knack, Landon	L-R	6-2	220	7-15-97	6	6	6.66	21	18	0	103	105	80	76	15	55	94	.265	.352	.452	20.5	12.0	458
Knowles, Antonio	R-R	6-1	190	1-15-00	1	0	9.00	4	0	0	4	8	4	4	1	3	5	.471	.524	.882	23.8	14.3	21
Kopech, Michael	R-R	6-3	210	4-30-96	1	1	13.89	16	1	0	12	14	18	18	2	20	15	.298	.507	.468	21.7	29.0	69
Kopp, Ronan	L-L	6-7	250	7-29-02	1	1	4.56	21	0	1	26	23	14	13	1	20	41	.242	.374	.368	35.7	17.4	115
Linan, Sean	R-R	6-0	185	11-7-04	0	1	9.82	2	2	0	7	8	8	8	1	7	12	.286	.447	.464	31.6	18.4	38
Little, Jack	L-R	6-4	190	1-10-98	5	4	4.64	36	0	13	43	39	25	22	4	19	39	.242	.326	.366	21.1	10.3	185
Loutos, Ryan	R-R	6-5	215	1-29-99	0	0	1.69	7	0	1	11	5	2	2	0	4	9	.139	.225	.194	22.5	10.0	40
McDaniels, Garrett	L-L	6-2	180	12-15-99	3	1	3.30	25	3	0	30	25	12	11	2	17	30	.234	.346	.336	28.3	13.4	127
Miller, Bobby	L-R	6-5	220	4-5-99	3	6	5.66	35	14	1	91	80	59	57	11	61	83	.233	.350	.369	20.3	14.9	409
Nastrini, Nick	R-R	6-3	215	2-18-00	0	2	54.00	3	0	0	1	0	6	6	0	7	0	.000	.700	.000	0.0	70.0	10
Ortiz, Robinson	L-L	6-0	180	1-4-00	1	0	2.76	15	1	0	16	11	5	5	1	9	14	.190	.299	.293	20.6	13.2	68
Penrod, Zach	L-L	6-2	210	6-16-97	2	0	8.65	19	3	0	26	33	26	25	2	30	23	.308	.465	.421	16.1	21.0	143
Phillips, Evan	R-R	6-2	215	9-11-94	0	0	6.35	6	1	1	6	9	6	4	0	1	9	.375	.385	.458	34.6	3.8	26
Ridings, Stephen	R-R	6-8	220	9-14-95	0	0	0.00	1	0	0	3	5	5	0	3	0	0	1.000	1.000	1.333	0.0	50.0	6
Rodriguez, Jose	S-R	6-6	200	7-18-01	8	2	4.71	37	1	4	42	33	23	22	7	27	64	.213	.339	.426	33.7	14.2	190
Romero, Christian	R-R	6-3	195	12-11-02	1	1	4.91	9	9	0	40	34	23	22	5	15	34	.228	.314	.383	20.1	8.9	169
Sasaki, Roki	R-R	6-2	187	11-3-01	0	2	6.10	7	5	0	21	20	15	14	2	13	19	.263	.372	.368	20.0	13.7	95
Sauer, Matt	R-R	6-4	195	1-21-99	5	5	5.86	18	17	1	83	100	56	54	14	28	79	.299	.363	.500	21.2	7.5	372
Scott, Tanner	R-L	6-0	235	7-22-94	0	0	0.00	1	0	0	1	0	0	0	0	1	2	.000	.250	.000	50.0	25.0	4
Sheehan, Emmet	R-R	6-5	220	11-15-99	1	1	4.58	5	5	0	18	16	9	9	3	2	31	.232	.274	.377	42.5	2.7	73
Snell, Blake	L-L	6-4	225	12-4-92	0	1	1.04	2	2	0	9	4	1	1	0	5	13	.143	.273	.179	39.4	15.2	33
Stewart, Brock	L-R	6-3	220	10-3-91	0	0	0.00	3	0	0	3	4	0	0	2	3	.250	.400	.333	20.0	13.3	15
Sublette, Ryan	R-R	6-2	190	10-1-98	8	3	5.06	39	1	0	53	60	31	30	5	39	56	.283	.407	.420	21.6	15.1	259
Treinen, Blake	R-R	6-5	225	6-30-88	0	0	0.00	6	1	0	6	1	0	0	1	9	.000	.050	.000	45.0	5.0	20
Trivino, Lou	R-R	6-5	235	10-1-91	0	0	0.00	1	0	0	1	0	0	0	0	1	2	.000	.250	.000	50.0	25.0	4
Vesia, Alex	L-L	6-1	209	4-11-96	0	0	0.00	2	0	0	2	0	0	0	0	0	3	.000	.000	.000	50.0	0.0	6
Wrobleski, Justin	L-L	6-1	194	7-14-00	2	1	4.18	11	10	0	52	48	26	24	7	23	47	.247	.327	.402	21.1	10.3	223
Yates, Kirby	L-R	5-10	205	3-25-87	0	0	0.00	1	0	0	1	0	0	0	0	0	1	.000	.250	.000	25.0	25.0	4

Fielding

Catcher	PCT	G	PO	A	E	DP	PB
Avila	1.000	3	25	0	0	0	1
Feduccia	.996	52	475	16	2	1	5
Okey	.990	23	199	8	2	1	4
Robinson	.986	42	398	25	6	0	5
Rodriguez	.966	2	27	1	1	0	0
Rortvedt	.986	15	134	6	2	2	2
Rushing	.989	18	172	12	2	3	1

First Base	PCT	G	PO	A	E	DP
Alexander	.987	29	204	26	3	25
Baker	1.000	26	169	13	0	20
Chavis	.982	31	211	12	4	24
Feduccia	.000	2	0	0	0	0
Hoese	.991	19	107	7	1	13
Okey	.981	7	48	5	1	6
Robinson	1.000	1	1	0	0	0
Rushing	.985	9	57	8	1	6
Ward	.997	40	267	31	1	26

Second Base	PCT	G	PO	A	E	DP
Chavis	1.000	18	20	38	0	7
Freeland	1.000	2	2	4	0	3
Gauthier	.977	111	156	264	10	66
Hoese	.943	12	21	29	3	8
Kim	.978	10	17	27	1	3
Senzel	.941	4	5	11	1	2

Third Base	PCT	G	PO	A	E	DP
Alexander	1.000	3	1	7	0	0
Chavis	1.000	7	5	4	0	1
Freeland	.924	35	34	51	7	8
Gauthier	1.000	1	0	2	0	0
Hernandez	1.000	1	1	0	0	0
Herrera	1.000	1	0	7	1	3
Hoese	.962	58	31	70	4	11
Muncy	.818	6	1	8	2	1
Senzel	.972	48	35	69	3	10

Shortstop	PCT	G	PO	A	E	DP
Freeland	.973	69	88	165	7	39
Hainline	1.000	5	6	10	0	2
Hoese	1.000	4	1	5	0	0
Kim	.934	14	21	36	4	8
Miller	.995	58	76	140	1	36
Senzel	.818	5	3	6	2	1

Outfield	PCT	G	PO	A	E	DP
Alexander	1.000	15	17	0	0	0
Berroa	1.000	26	48	3	0	0
Chavis	1.000	1	1	0	0	0
Dean	.972	89	203	3	6	1
Edman	1.000	2	3	0	0	0
Hernandez	1.000	2	1	0	0	0
Kim	1.000	13	26	0	0	0
Outman	1.000	67	145	5	0	1
Ramos	.988	42	78	5	1	2
Rosario	1.000	12	19	2	0	1
Ruiz	.989	103	180	3	2	0
Rushing	1.000	2	5	0	0	0
Senzel	1.000	28	30	1	0	0
Ward	.979	78	138	3	3	0

TULSA DRILLERS
TEXAS LEAGUE — DOUBLE-A

Batting	B-T	Ht.	Wt.	DOB	AVG	OBP	SLG	G	PA	AB	R	H	2B	3B	HR	RBI	BB	HBP	SH	SF	SO	SB	CS	BB%	SO%
Alleyne, Chris	S-R	5-10	190	11-13-98	.143	.182	.143	12	44	42	2	6	0	0	0	4	1	0	0	1	11	3	0	2.3	25.0
Avila, Carlos	R-R	5-11	180	12-4-03	.333	.250	.333	1	4	3	0	1	0	0	0	1	0	0	0	1	0	0	0	0.0	0.0
Biddison, Nick	R-R	5-10	190	7-30-00	.273	.333	.485	10	36	33	6	9	1	0	2	3	2	1	0	0	13	3	1	5.6	36.1

LOS ANGELES DODGERS

Batting

Player	B-T	Ht	Wt	DOB	AVG	OBP	SLG	G	AB	R	H	2B	3B	HR	RBI	BB	HBP	SH	SF	SO	SB	CS		
Bracho, Aaron	S-R	5-9	193	4-24-01	.194	.257	.343	35	148	134	15	26	5	0	5	16	11	1	0	2	35	3	2	7.4 23.6
De Paula, Josue	L-L	6-3	185	5-24-05	.000	.053	.000	4	19	18	0	0	0	0	0	0	1	0	0	0	5	0	0	5.3 26.3
Ehrhard, Zach	R-R	5-11	190	1-21-03	.282	.391	.466	34	161	131	32	37	7	1	5	20	21	5	0	4	21	14	1	13.0 13.0
Fernandez, Yeiner	R-R	5-9	170	9-19-02	.251	.331	.303	100	442	390	47	98	14	0	2	37	39	9	0	3	49	2	2	8.8 11.1
Guerrero, Eduardo	R-R	6-2	165	5-9-05	.200	.308	.200	14	53	45	5	9	0	0	0	3	7	0	1	0	13	0	1	13.2 24.5
Hope, Zyhir	L-L	6-0	193	1-19-05	.316	.350	.421	6	20	19	2	6	2	0	0	5	1	0	0	0	4	1	0	5.0 20.0
Keith, Damon	R-R	6-3	195	5-28-00	.226	.296	.386	89	362	319	41	72	12	3	11	44	33	2	0	8	111	9	5	9.1 30.7
Lockwood-Powell, Griffin	R-R	6-2	195	2-23-98	.226	.350	.326	81	334	279	35	63	11	1	5	26	53	1	0	1	67	0	0	15.9 20.1
McLain, Sean	R-R	5-11	170	3-22-01	.201	.307	.282	116	439	379	51	76	12	2	5	37	48	10	1	0	95	10	5	10.9 21.6
Miller, Noah	S-R	5-11	190	11-12-02	.291	.336	.369	27	111	103	12	30	3	1	1	11	6	1	0	0	24	0	0	5.4 21.6
Myers, Kole	L-R	6-1	185	12-28-00	.283	.393	.379	76	321	272	54	77	7	2	5	29	41	8	0	0	71	25	9	12.8 22.1
Nevin, Kyle	R-R	6-4	200	8-22-01	.271	.335	.387	48	203	181	27	49	7	1	4	31	19	0	0	3	47	0	0	9.4 23.2
Newell, Chris	L-L	6-3	200	4-23-01	.241	.346	.428	127	549	465	66	112	23	2	20	80	75	3	0	6	168	24	0	13.7 30.6
Pagan, Ezequiel	L-R	5-9	163	7-8-00	.249	.296	.391	77	306	281	28	70	14	4	6	38	15	5	1	3	53	5	6	4.9 17.3
Quiroz, Nelson	S-R	5-8	194	11-5-01	.295	.364	.364	25	99	88	9	26	2	2	0	14	10	0	0	1	6	0	0	10.1 6.1
Ramos, Jose	R-R	6-1	200	1-1-01	.221	.303	.385	58	244	213	28	54	5	0	10	32	24	3	0	4	78	2	7	9.8 32.0
Rhodes, John	R-R	6-0	200	8-15-00	.196	.307	.288	108	430	368	45	72	11	1	7	40	54	6	0	2	111	9	3	12.6 25.8
Rodriguez, Frank	R-R	5-11	197	9-28-01	.188	.250	.208	17	53	48	4	9	1	0	0	2	4	0	1	0	10	0	0	7.5 18.9
Senzel, Nick	R-R	6-1	218	6-29-95	.250	.357	.417	3	11	12	1	3	2	0	0	4	2	0	0	0	2	1	0	14.3 14.3
Simmons, Kendall	R-R	6-0	180	4-11-00	.218	.283	.336	31	120	110	11	24	5	1	2	15	8	2	0	0	35	0	1	6.7 29.2
Tibbs, James	L-L	6-0	205	10-1-02	.269	.407	.493	36	168	134	25	36	5	2	7	32	29	3	1	1	36	5	1	17.3 21.4
Young, Taylor	R-R	5-9	170	8-6-98	.233	.348	.288	133	575	486	79	113	21	0	2	41	80	7	0	2	91	44	9	13.9 15.8

Pitching

Pitching	B-T	Ht.	Wt.	DOB	W	L	ERA	G	GS	SV	IP	Hits	Runs	ER	HR	BB	SO	AVG	OBP	SLG	SO%	BB%	BF
Bautista, Kelvin	L-L	5-11	155	7-7-99	5	2	6.65	41	0	1	47	51	38	35	5	44	42	.283	.438	.417	18.0	18.9	233
Benitez, Jorge	L-L	6-2	155	6-2-99	2	2	4.30	37	0	1	46	29	26	22	2	34	41	.188	.373	.273	19.8	16.4	207
Biddison, Nick	R-R	5-10	190	7-30-00	0	0	0.00	1	0	0	1	0	0	0	0	0	0	.000	.000	.000	0.0	0.0	3
Cabrera, Jeisson	R-R	6-2	170	9-5-98	4	1	3.71	36	0	2	44	30	19	18	2	32	54	.192	.335	.276	28.3	16.8	191
Campos, Chris	R-R	5-10	170	8-13-00	8	6	4.19	26	23	1	127	120	66	59	16	32	111	.246	.297	.387	21.0	6.0	529
Copen, Patrick	R-R	6-6	220	2-15-02	1	6	4.52	17	17	0	70	63	43	35	1	52	75	.241	.375	.287	23.1	16.0	324
Crowell, Wyatt	L-L	6-0	170	10-13-01	1	1	2.75	5	3	1	20	12	7	6	1	12	21	.167	.302	.236	24.4	14.0	86
Day, Cam	R-R	6-2	195	7-23-02	0	0	6.00	2	0	0	3	1	2	2	0	2	4	.125	.333	.125	33.3	16.7	12
Ferris, Jackson	L-L	6-4	195	1-15-04	10	7	3.86	26	24	0	126	118	59	54	9	66	135	.246	.347	.355	24.2	11.8	557
Fox, Luke	L-L	6-2	200	1-4-02	1	2	2.70	9	9	0	43	30	15	13	3	22	46	.199	.313	.265	25.6	12.2	180
Geronimo, Domingo	R-R	5-11	150	10-7-04	0	0	0.00	1	0	0	1	0	1	1	0	3	0	1.000	1.000	1.000	0.0	75.0	4
Gutierrez, Roque	R-R	5-9	177	9-7-02	2	2	5.56	14	11	0	55	67	38	34	9	23	52	.298	.365	.462	20.8	9.2	250
Heubeck, Peter	R-R	6-3	170	7-22-02	2	5	4.34	16	16	0	66	47	35	32	6	34	77	.198	.306	.312	27.7	12.2	278
Hobbs, Carson	R-R	6-1	197	2-27-02	4	2	1.59	17	0	3	23	12	5	4	1	8	27	.148	.225	.210	30.3	9.0	89
Karros, Jared	R-R	6-7	195	11-16-00	1	5	6.54	12	12	0	52	76	42	38	5	28	38	.342	.401	.626	15.3	8.8	249
Kershaw, Clayton	L-L	6-4	225	3-19-88	0	0	3.00	1	1	0	3	4	1	1	0	1	4	.286	.333	.429	26.7	6.7	15
Kiest, Tanner	R-R	6-3	200	9-16-94	0	0	10.66	11	0	1	13	23	15	15	4	8	14	.390	.478	.678	20.3	11.6	69
Knowles, Antonio	R-R	6-1	190	1-15-00	6	1	3.05	36	0	11	44	31	17	15	3	14	51	.191	.263	.296	28.5	7.8	179
Kopp, Ronan	L-L	6-7	250	7-29-02	1	3	2.53	28	0	1	32	23	11	9	0	22	50	.202	.333	.228	36.2	15.9	138
Meador, Jacob	R-R	6-0	183	10-26-00	1	7	8.28	27	10	0	50	62	53	46	8	49	46	.310	.451	.495	18.2	19.4	253
Neeck, Brandon	R-L	6-1	190	10-19-99	4	6	5.40	39	4	1	47	54	34	28	8	35	45	.264	.384	.421	20.7	16.1	217
Ortiz, Robinson	L-L	6-0	180	1-4-00	3	0	1.69	15	0	1	21	11	4	4	0	9	30	.151	.247	.178	34.9	10.5	86
Ramirez, Kelvin	R-R	6-4	187	6-10-01	2	2	4.13	44	0	0	48	33	25	22	1	45	55	.192	.365	.285	24.7	20.2	223
Reinoso, Livan	R-R	6-1	185	8-27-98	0	2	4.39	29	0	0	41	27	25	20	4	39	36	.185	.363	.308	18.9	20.5	190
Rodriguez, Jose	S-R	6-6	200	7-18-01	1	0	8.25	8	1	0	12	14	11	11	1	8	20	.298	.393	.447	35.7	14.3	56
Rosario, Jerming	R-R	6-1	175	5-8-02	1	7	4.67	46	6	1	79	74	49	41	6	51	87	.245	.359	.348	24.3	14.2	358
Serwinowski, Adam	L-L	6-5	190	6-7-04	0	0	9.00	1	1	0	3	6	5	3	0	2	4	.400	.471	.600	23.5	11.8	17
Suarez, Christian	L-L	5-11	160	11-25-00	4	3	3.38	42	0	2	64	48	28	24	3	49	65	.211	.349	.259	23.2	17.5	280
Wepf, Lucas	L-R	6-5	192	12-23-99	2	0	2.79	23	0	1	29	19	9	9	0	16	36	.196	.325	.278	30.5	13.6	118

Fielding

Catcher

	PCT	G	PO	A	E	DP	PB
Avila	1.000	1	11	1	0	0	2
Fernandez	.978	42	362	34	9	4	9
Lockwood-Powell	.992	71	616	32	5	3	6
Quiroz	.983	16	164	10	3	2	4
Rodriguez	.972	16	125	13	4	0	6

First Base

	PCT	G	PO	A	E	DP
Biddison	.857	1	5	1	1	0
Bracho	1.000	11	88	4	0	9
Lockwood-Powell	1.000	5	42	3	0	3
McLain	1.000	2	12	1	0	1
Nevin	.991	16	109	6	1	6
Rhodes	.984	91	653	29	11	65
Simmons	.969	8	60	3	2	8
Tibbs	.979	6	41	5	1	5

Second Base

	PCT	G	PO	A	E	DP
Alleyne	.938	4	10	5	1	1

(Second Base continued)

	PCT	G	PO	A	E	DP
Bracho	.750	3	3	3	2	2
Fernandez	.958	37	63	95	7	25
Guerrero	.975	12	16	23	1	8
McLain	1.000	1	2	1	0	1
Simmons	1.000	5	9	11	0	4
Young	.993	79	100	181	2	34

Third Base

	PCT	G	PO	A	E	DP
Biddison	1.000	7	10	9	0	2
Bracho	.857	19	9	21	5	1
Fernandez	.889	21	20	28	6	4
McLain	.962	17	19	31	2	4
Nevin	.913	28	24	39	6	6
Senzel	1.000	3	0	6	0	1
Simmons	.778	10	7	7	4	0
Young	.954	36	21	62	4	7

Shortstop

	PCT	G	PO	A	E	DP
Guerrero	1.000	2	3	3	0	0

(Shortstop continued)

	PCT	G	PO	A	E	DP
McLain	.971	95	127	236	11	41
Miller	.959	25	41	52	4	13
Young	1.000	18	18	33	0	10

Outfield

	PCT	G	PO	A	E	DP
Alleyne	.923	6	12	0	1	0
De Paula	.000	1	0	0	0	0
Ehrhard	.986	28	69	1	1	1
Hope	.857	4	6	0	1	0
Keith	.957	49	90	0	4	0
Myers	1.000	73	143	2	0	0
Nevin	1.000	2	7	0	0	0
Newell	.984	112	241	4	4	0
Pagan	.943	70	93	6	6	1
Ramos	.966	50	80	4	3	0
Rhodes	1.000	3	2	0	0	0
Tibbs	1.000	25	51	4	0	2

GREAT LAKES LOONS — HIGH-A
MIDWEST LEAGUE / LOS ANGELES DODGERS

Batting	B-T	Ht.	Wt.	DOB	AVG	OBP	SLG	G	PA	AB	R	H	2B	3B	HR	RBI	BB	HBP	SH	SF	SO	SB	CS	BB%	SO%
Biddison, Nick	R-R	5-10	190	7-30-00	.067	.286	.067	5	22	15	2	1	0	0	0	1	4	1	1	1	6	0	0	18.2	27.3
Cueto, Gio	R-R	5-10	190	7-24-03	.167	.286	.167	8	28	24	3	4	0	0	0	0	3	1	0	0	5	0	0	10.7	17.9
De Paula, Josue	L-L	6-3	185	5-24-05	.263	.406	.421	98	426	342	65	90	16	1	12	44	81	2	0	1	86	32	8	19.0	20.2
Decker, Cameron	S-R	6-1	205	9-22-03	.149	.275	.291	44	180	148	15	22	6	0	5	23	22	5	0	3	54	3	1	12.2	30.0
Diaz, Angel	R-R	5-11	180	2-4-04	.000	.250	.000	2	8	6	0	0	0	0	0	0	2	0	0	0	1	0	0	25.0	12.5
Diaz, Wilman	R-R	6-2	182	11-15-03	.203	.304	.322	52	169	143	22	29	6	1	3	15	20	2	1	3	46	6	3	11.8	27.2
Gelof, Jake	R-R	6-1	195	2-25-02	.224	.318	.454	88	362	313	52	70	24	0	16	63	44	1	0	4	96	11	7	12.2	26.5
George, Kendall	L-L	5-10	170	10-29-04	.295	.409	.370	111	514	424	93	125	9	7	3	34	84	1	1	4	78	100	24	16.3	15.2
Guerrero, Eduardo	S-R	6-2	165	5-9-05	.143	.182	.238	6	22	21	1	3	0	1	0	3	1	0	0	0	4	0	0	4.5	18.2
Gutierrez, Roque	R-R	5-9	177	9-7-02	.000	.000	.000	11	1	1	0	0	0	0	0	0	0	0	0	0	1	0	0	0.0	100.0
Hainline, Elijah	R-R	5-10	185	12-20-02	.273	.394	.417	40	171	139	28	38	6	1	4	26	26	3	1	2	36	7	3	15.2	21.1
Hope, Zyhir	R-R	6-0	193	1-19-05	.264	.377	.428	121	524	439	67	116	27	3	13	75	78	3	0	3	139	26	6	14.9	26.5
Martinus, Mairoshendrick	R-R	6-3	161	2-3-05	.273	.385	.364	7	26	22	1	6	0	1	0	3	4	0	0	0	5	1	2	15.4	19.2
Munoz, Samuel	L-R	6-3	190	9-22-04	.183	.300	.250	20	70	60	5	11	1	0	1	5	10	0	0	0	14	0	0	14.3	20.0
Myers, Kole	L-R	6-1	185	12-28-00	.214	.461	.314	24	102	70	16	15	3	2	0	10	30	2	0	0	20	9	1	29.4	19.6
Nevin, Kyle	R-R	6-4	200	8-22-01	.270	.395	.508	17	76	63	8	17	4	1	3	17	11	2	0	0	13	1	1	14.5	17.1
Nicklaus, Jackson	R-R	6-0	182	9-26-02	.164	.262	.288	24	84	73	10	12	6	0	1	10	10	0	0	1	38	0	0	11.9	45.2
Quintero, Eduardo	R-R	6-0	175	9-16-05	.259	.384	.440	32	146	116	28	30	4	1	5	16	23	3	0	4	35	12	2	15.8	24.0
Quiroz, Nelson	S-R	5-8	194	11-5-01	.367	.421	.510	30	107	98	13	36	11	0	1	11	8	1	0	0	12	0	0	7.5	11.2
Rodriguez, Frank	R-R	5-11	197	9-28-01	.234	.336	.379	38	144	124	19	29	7	1	3	16	17	2	0	1	30	1	1	11.8	20.8
Rojas, Carlos	R-R	6-0	165	7-25-02	.215	.285	.273	65	238	209	17	45	6	0	2	31	20	2	3	4	31	0	0	8.4	13.0
Shaw, Evan	L-L	6-4	205	2-2-01	.000	.000	.000	40	1	1	0	0	0	0	0	0	0	0	0	0	1	0	0	0.0	100.0
Shelton, Easton	R-R	6-5	225	9-17-05	.214	.267	.500	4	15	14	3	3	1	0	1	1	1	0	0	0	4	0	0	6.7	26.7
Sirota, Mike	R-R	6-2	180	6-16-03	.316	.458	.556	35	155	117	22	37	8	1	6	30	33	1	0	4	34	4	1	21.3	21.9
Thompson, Jordan	R-R	6-0	175	1-9-02	.210	.286	.311	100	402	357	42	75	15	0	7	34	32	8	0	5	109	10	8	8.0	27.1
Vetrano, Joe	L-L	6-3	220	5-10-02	.223	.314	.360	104	414	364	47	81	18	4	8	50	46	3	0	1	111	21	5	11.1	26.8
Wagner, Logan	S-R	6-1	200	3-9-04	.216	.345	.380	122	533	440	82	95	23	2	15	76	78	11	0	4	140	18	3	14.6	26.3

Pitching	B-T	Ht.	Wt.	DOB	W	L	ERA	G	GS	SV	IP	Hits	Runs	ER	HR	BB	SO	AVG	OBP	SLG	SO%	BB%	BF
Auger, Brooks	R-R	6-5	215	10-20-01	3	8	5.12	22	17	2	91	94	59	52	8	41	61	.272	.354	.405	15.3	10.3	398
Brown, Ryan	R-R	6-2	205	10-9-02	0	1	12.79	7	0	0	6	9	9	9	1	10	13	.321	.500	.500	34.2	26.3	38
Bruns, Maddux	L-L	6-2	205	8-21-01	2	3	5.47	13	13	0	49	46	38	30	2	37	53	.246	.398	.353	22.2	15.5	239
Caba, Myles	R-R	6-1	208	8-21-01	1	2	2.49	17	0	1	22	18	10	6	0	3	24	.222	.264	.284	27.6	3.4	87
Copen, Patrick	R-R	6-6	220	2-15-02	3	1	2.25	10	10	0	48	22	12	12	1	32	77	.135	.295	.172	38.5	16.0	200
Crowell, Wyatt	L-L	6-0	170	10-13-01	3	6	3.23	19	15	0	78	46	30	28	6	57	93	.171	.332	.260	27.7	17.0	336
Cruz, Nicolas	R-R	5-11	160	4-23-04	1	0	2.89	14	0	0	19	12	6	6	1	5	15	.190	.286	.271	21.7	7.2	69
Day, Cam	S-R	6-2	195	7-25-02	5	6	4.17	33	4	6	73	64	38	34	3	38	80	.236	.335	.347	25.2	12.0	317
Diaz, Wilman	R-R	6-2	182	11-15-03	0	0	0.00	2	0	0	2	2	0	0	0	1	1	.250	.333	.250	11.1	11.1	9
Foeller, Aidan	R-R	6-3	220	3-26-02	0	1	8.68	4	2	0	9	8	10	9	0	15	12	.242	.490	.364	23.1	28.8	52
Fox, Luke	L-L	6-2	200	1-4-02	3	3	2.96	13	12	0	55	45	24	18	4	31	64	.218	.340	.266	26.3	12.8	243
Gonzalez, Jorge	R-R	6-5	203	8-30-02	0	0	6.98	19	0	1	19	19	15	15	0	25	21	.260	.466	.329	20.4	24.3	103
Gonzalez, Joseilyn	R-R	5-11	160	4-8-02	5	2	2.80	40	1	4	52	41	14	14	1	38	38	.208	.374	.286	19.2	19.2	198
Gutierrez, Roque	R-R	5-9	177	9-7-02	5	0	3.46	11	1	1	39	28	15	15	5	19	51	.201	.297	.360	32.3	12.0	158
Hobbs, Carson	R-R	6-1	197	2-27-02	5	1	2.37	25	0	8	30	14	8	8	2	13	36	.144	.241	.237	32.1	11.6	112
Ibarra, Joel	R-R	6-0	176	7-10-02	3	1	5.47	28	0	5	17	15	11	11	0	26	18	.195	.418	.230	23.0	21.3	122
Linan, Sean	R-R	6-0	185	10-7-04	1	1	2.65	10	7	1	37	27	15	11	3	14	39	.194	.276	.238	25.0	9.0	156
Luna, Jesus	R-R	6-0	165	11-6-00	1	0	5.14	7	0	0	7	4	4	4	1	11	5	.174	.441	.348	14.7	32.4	34
Makarewich, Alex	R-R	6-0	185	1-17-02	2	3	4.35	32	0	1	31	18	19	15	0	41	48	.170	.414	.198	31.6	27.0	152
Martin, Payton	R-R	6-0	170	5-19-04	6	4	5.08	18	16	0	67	66	39	38	10	25	65	.252	.318	.435	22.4	8.6	290
Ortiz, Robinson	L-L	6-0	180	1-4-00	1	2	3.74	18	0	3	22	22	12	9	3	15	28	.268	.380	.427	28.0	15.0	100
Patick, Sterling	L-L	6-1	155	6-9-05	0	0	3.86	2	2	0	7	8	3	3	0	2	8	.276	.323	.483	25.8	6.5	31
Reinoso, Livan	R-R	6-1	185	8-27-98	1	0	3.38	9	0	1	13	9	8	5	0	9	14	.180	.317	.240	14.8	6.1	
Romero, Christian	R-R	6-3	195	12-11-02	4	3	5.03	16	6	0	63	60	36	35	6	21	49	.247	.321	.387	17.9	7.7	274
Ruebeck, Christian	R-R	6-0	185	9-3-00	2	3	6.81	36	0	2	36	35	31	27	3	20	54	.257	.408	.419	17.1	11.7	175
Ruen, Noah	R-R	6-4	190	3-21-03	1	0	9.88	14	0	0	14	15	17	15	3	19	14	.278	.481	.537	17.9	24.4	78
Serwinowski, Adam	L-L	6-5	190	6-7-04	4	0	1.83	6	6	0	34	23	7	7	3	14	44	.185	.289	.274	31.0	9.9	142
Shaw, Evan	L-L	6-4	205	2-2-01	2	2	2.22	39	0	2	53	30	16	13	0	26	49	.169	.289	.169	23.1	12.3	212
Swan, Eriq	R-R	6-6	240	10-31-01	4	3	4.43	16	14	0	69	49	36	34	5	46	77	.198	.332	.328	25.8	15.4	298
Tabeling, Logan	L-R	6-0	205	8-21-01	3	1	5.48	5	3	0	21	22	14	13	0	19	25	.272	.416	.346	24.5	18.6	152
Yean, Reynaldo	R-R	6-3	190	1-4-04	1	1	6.69	40	0	2	36	19	28	27	0	46	45	.157	.427	.215	25.1	25.7	179
Zazueta, Christian	R-R	6-3	163	10-7-04	0	0	0.00	1	1	0	0	0	0	0	1	.000	.250	.000	25.0	0.0	4		

Fielding

Catcher	PCT	G	PO	A	E	DP	PB
Cueto	.987	8	71	3	1	1	2
Diaz	1.000	2	18	0	0	0	0
Quiroz	.996	26	259	18	1	0	3
Rodriguez	.985	37	364	25	6	1	6
Rojas	.993	63	548	39	4	4	2

First Base	PCT	G	PO	A	E	DP
Decker	.994	20	154	6	1	16
Diaz	1.000	8	44	1	0	3

	PCT	G	PO	A	E	DP
Nevin	.979	5	44	2	1	3
Nicklaus	1.000	12	68	4	0	7
Shelton	.889	1	8	0	1	1
Vetrano	.992	88	606	34	5	49

Second Base	PCT	G	PO	A	E	DP
Biddison	.800	1	0	4	1	0
Diaz	.941	20	27	37	4	2
Gelof	1.000	28	41	62	0	13
Guerrero	1.000	3	3	6	0	0

	PCT	G	PO	A	E	DP
Hainline	1.000	9	15	22	0	5
Martinus	1.000	2	7	7	0	3
Nicklaus	1.000	5	6	10	0	3
Thompson	.981	15	20	32	1	6
Wagner	.974	53	66	123	5	22

Third Base	PCT	G	PO	A	E	DP
Biddison	1.000	4	2	5	0	2
Decker	1.000	2	1	1	0	0
Diaz	.929	8	5	8	1	1

	PCT	G	PO	A	E	
Gelof	.976	53	40	84	3	5
Martinus	.750	1	2	1	1	1
Nevin	1.000	8	1	12	0	0
Nicklaus	.000	1	0	0	0	0
Wagner	.954	57	48	98	7	13

Shortstop	PCT	G	PO	A	E	DP
Diaz	.963	7	9	17	1	5
Guerrero	1.000	3	1	4	0	0
Hainline	.973	31	41	69	3	15

	PCT	G	PO	A	E	DP
Martinus	.895	4	10	7	2	1
Thompson	.943	84	99	167	16	26
Wagner	.857	2	3	3	1	2

Outfield	PCT	G	PO	A	E	DP
De Paula	.972	75	103	2	3	0
Decker	.971	20	32	1	1	1
Diaz	1.000	6	5	0	0	0
George	.962	93	173	3	7	0
Hope	.985	99	182	12	3	5

	PCT	G	PO	A	E	DP
Munoz	.966	20	25	3	1	0
Myers	1.000	22	59	3	0	0
Nevin	1.000	3	2	0	0	0
Nicklaus	1.000	2	3	0	0	0
Quintero	.986	31	66	3	1	1
Shelton	.750	2	3	0	1	0
Sirota	.979	30	45	2	1	1
Thompson	1.000	2	5	1	0	0

RANCHO CUCAMONGA QUAKES — LOW-A
CALIFORNIA LEAGUE
LOS ANGELES DODGERS

Batting	B-T	Ht.	Wt.	DOB	AVG	OBP	SLG	G	PA	AB	R	H	2B	3B	HR	RBI	BB	HBP	SH	SF	SO	SB	CS	BB%	SO%
Avila, Carlos	R-R	5-11	180	12-4-03	.444	.524	.500	5	21	18	1	8	1	0	0	3	3	0	0	0	4	0	0	14.3	19.0
Cueto, Gio	R-R	5-10	190	7-24-03	.273	.413	.352	28	110	88	15	24	4	0	1	7	17	4	1	0	31	2	0	15.5	28.2
Davalan, Charles	L-R	5-8	170	12-16-03	.500	.541	.735	8	37	34	7	17	3	1	1	10	3	0	0	0	5	3	0	8.1	13.5
Decker, Cameron	S-R	6-1	205	9-22-03	.250	.360	.300	6	25	20	2	5	1	0	0	2	3	1	0	1	5	0	1	12.0	20.0
Diaz, Angel	R-R	5-11	180	2-4-04	.233	.313	.364	39	147	129	19	30	5	0	4	20	15	1	0	2	41	0	0	10.2	27.9
Elkins, Jaron	R-R	6-1	193	11-4-04	.264	.350	.414	109	515	447	81	118	30	5	9	72	45	17	0	6	153	63	6	8.7	29.7
Guerrero, Eduardo	R-R	6-2	165	5-9-05	.222	.381	.311	83	330	257	58	57	8	3	3	40	63	5	2	3	51	8	5	19.1	15.5
Hainline, Elijah	R-R	5-10	185	12-20-02	.298	.430	.421	66	291	235	47	70	15	1	4	29	47	8	0	1	69	20	5	16.2	23.7
Harlan, Chase	R-R	6-3	205	7-9-06	.240	.358	.356	26	123	104	12	25	3	0	3	20	18	1	0	0	32	2	1	14.6	26.0
Hernandez, Jose	R-R	6-1	145	4-30-03	.700	.727	1.100	1	3	1	0	3	7	1	0	1	5	1	0	0	0	2	0	1	9.1	18.2
Hernandez, Teoscar	R-R	6-2	215	10-15-92	.000	.667	.000	1	3	1	1	0	0	0	0	0	2	0	0	0	1	0	0	66.7	33.3
Ko, Ching-Hsien	L-R	6-3	215	8-11-06	.219	.355	.281	32	138	114	18	25	3	2	0	4	23	1	0	0	32	1	0	16.7	23.2
Lasso, Roger	S-R	6-0	180	2-27-04	.232	.315	.280	33	144	125	15	29	6	0	0	13	12	4	0	2	36	0	0	8.3	25.0
Lindsey, Kellon	R-R	6-2	175	9-21-05	.280	.394	.390	28	142	118	29	33	7	0	2	19	22	1	0	1	45	10	2	15.5	31.7
Martinus, Mairoshendrick	R-R	6-3	161	2-3-05	.244	.315	.351	90	394	348	54	85	17	1	6	63	35	4	0	7	106	19	4	8.9	26.9
Meza, Jose	R-R	6-1	160	4-22-03	.222	.360	.336	117	531	428	67	95	17	4	8	66	80	16	0	7	125	30	10	15.1	23.5
Morales, Emil	R-R	6-3	191	9-20-06	.339	.420	.548	30	143	124	21	42	11	0	5	27	17	1	0	1	33	5	0	11.9	23.1
Munoz, Samuel	R-R	6-3	190	9-22-04	.248	.355	.411	96	451	375	70	93	16	6	11	65	63	4	0	9	100	18	6	14.0	22.2
Nicklaus, Jackson	L-R	6-0	182	9-26-02	.176	.333	.288	54	210	170	30	30	3	2	4	16	38	2	0	0	79	1	0	18.1	37.6
Ortega, Raynerd	R-R	6-1	154	7-8-05	.195	.263	.368	23	95	87	10	17	1	1	4	13	6	2	0	0	36	0	0	6.3	37.9
Osorio, Oswaldo	L-R	6-1	171	4-12-05	.138	.318	.233	48	201	159	30	22	0	0	5	24	36	6	0	0	69	4	4	17.9	34.3
Perez, Nicolas	R-R	6-0	175	9-20-04	.280	.380	.401	61	251	207	39	58	12	2	3	43	35	2	1	6	55	35	6	13.9	21.9
Quintero, Eduardo	R-R	6-0	175	9-16-05	.306	.426	.533	81	395	317	73	97	18	6	14	53	65	6	0	6	88	35	11	16.5	22.3
Rodrigues, Victor	R-R	6-3	203	9-23-04	.288	.446	.342	76	312	240	60	69	8	1	1	36	62	8	0	2	40	10	2	19.9	12.8
Sirota, Mike	R-R	6-2	180	6-16-03	.354	.443	.687	24	115	99	26	35	8	2	7	24	15	1	0	0	25	1	1	13.0	21.7
Vargas, Joendry	R-R	6-4	175	11-8-05	.221	.285	.361	29	137	122	14	27	3	1	4	22	11	1	0	3	41	17	2	8.0	29.9
Vidourek, Landyn	L-R	6-2	185	11-6-03	.313	.378	.463	16	74	67	5	21	5	1	1	6	7	0	0	0	25	3	0	9.5	33.8

Pitching	B-T	Ht.	Wt.	DOB	W	L	ERA	G	GS	SV	IP	Hits	Runs	ER	HR	BB	SO	AVG	OBP	SLG	SO%	BB%	BF
Abad, Dailoui	R-R	6-0	168	5-2-02	0	0	0.00	2	0	0	2	2	0	0	0	1	1	.250	.333	.250	11.1	11.1	9
Ayon, Isaac	R-R	6-4	235	6-14-02	1	0	1.98	5	3	0	14	13	4	3	0	6	14	.255	.333	.314	24.6	10.5	57
Becerra, Octavio	L-L	6-3	209	2-3-01	1	0	4.32	8	0	0	8	4	4	4	1	10	10	.138	.375	.241	25.0	25.0	40
Brown, Ryan	R-R	6-2	205	10-9-02	2	4	4.75	30	0	0	42	21	26	22	1	37	79	.143	.314	.211	42.7	20.0	185
Caba, Myles	L-L	6-1	208	8-21-01	4	1	3.62	23	0	3	32	20	22	13	1	21	45	.177	.307	.248	32.8	15.3	137
Cabrera, Felix	L-L	6-3	170	4-8-02	1	5	10.71	16	0	0	19	28	33	23	0	20	16	.315	.434	.438	14.2	17.7	113
Cabrera, Jose	R-R	6-4	195	11-14-04	0	1	10.29	11	0	0	14	19	16	16	2	11	17	.339	.457	.589	24.3	15.7	70
Carias, Luis	R-R	6-4	170	9-30-04	0	1	0.96	2	2	0	9	6	1	1	1	2	7	.176	.222	.324	19.4	5.6	36
Chambers, Justin	L-L	6-2	212	8-14-05	3	0	2.70	12	0	0	20	13	7	6	0	9	24	.181	.280	.250	29.3	11.0	82
Chastain, Davis	R-R	5-11	163	6-23-04	1	1	2.45	6	0	0	7	6	2	2	0	1	9	.222	.241	.333	31.0	3.4	29
Corcho, Marco	R-R	6-0	200	5-2-05	4	4	8.24	35	0	1	44	64	41	40	3	35	38	.354	.472	.525	16.5	15.2	231
Cruz, Nicolas	R-R	5-11	160	4-23-04	3	2	3.98	23	2	0	43	41	19	19	1	11	48	.252	.309	.313	26.5	6.1	181
Figueredo, Dilan	R-R	6-0	174	3-28-03	1	3	3.93	26	0	3	37	37	25	16	1	20	28	.264	.365	.343	16.7	11.9	168
Foeller, Aidan	R-R	6-3	220	3-26-02	4	3	4.23	22	20	0	89	72	52	42	8	59	127	.220	.353	.348	31.6	14.7	402
Garcia, Luis	R-R	6-2	240	1-30-07	0	0	0.00	1	1	0	1	0	0	0	0	1	0	.250	.250	.250	25.0	0.0	4
Geronimo, Domingo	R-R	5-11	150	10-7-04	8	0	6.06	26	0	0	49	48	35	33	6	22	47	.255	.329	.441	21.9	10.2	215
Godwin, Connor	R-R	6-4	207	3-26-02	3	5	7.21	36	0	4	44	46	37	35	2	38	50	.267	.430	.360	22.3	17.0	224
Herder, Lucas	R-R	6-2	170	11-2-04	4	7	8.14	24	4	1	63	88	67	57	6	27	43	.321	.396	.460	13.7	8.6	314
Jang, Hyun-Seok	R-R	6-2	185	3-14-04	0	2	4.65	13	13	0	41	23	21	21	4	32	54	.165	.333	.317	30.9	18.3	175
Jimenez, Jhonny	R-R	6-5	180	11-9-03	3	1	2.38	28	1	4	42	33	17	11	2	23	39	.212	.319	.308	21.2	12.5	184
Leon, Edgar	R-R	6-3	170	12-29-04	0	0	18.00	1	0	0	1	0	2	2	1	7	1	.000	.429	.800	28.6	14.3	7
Linan, Sean	R-R	6-0	185	11-7-04	2	1	1.21	6	5	0	30	15	4	4	1	10	50	.147	.222	.245	44.2	8.8	113
Makarewich, Alex	R-R	6-0	185	1-17-02	3	0	0.00	9	0	1	13	4	1	0	0	8	27	.095	.255	.095	51.9	15.4	52
Maynard, William	L-R	6-3	190	6-19-03	0	2	15.43	6	0	0	5	7	10	8	1	11	2	.368	.613	.526	6.5	35.5	31
Morse, Cody	L-L	6-6	190	4-25-03	0	2	4.33	40	1	2	52	49	36	25	3	27	57	.239	.349	.376	23.7	11.2	241
Nieves, Marlon	R-R	6-0	175	6-10-05	1	0	2.21	8	8	0	37	16	9	9	1	19	37	.157	.280	.231	25.5	13.1	145
Oduber, Shawndrick	R-R	6-0	170	12-16-04	4	2	6.23	29	0	0	48	52	36	33	8	22	50	.267	.356	.451	22.3	9.8	224
Patick, Sterling	L-L	6-1	155	6-9-05	2	1	4.01	23	19	0	85	78	46	38	5	37	100	.240	.325	.360	27.0	10.0	371
Sanchez, Samuel	R-R	5-11	150	11-2-03	1	1	5.31	11	7	0	39	48	26	23	7	10	28	.300	.339	.519	16.2	5.8	173
Smith, Brady	R-R	6-2	170	1-27-05	0	0	1.69	4	4	0	11	3	3	2	0	8	14	.088	.262	.147	33.3	19.0	42
Snell, Blake	L-L	6-4	225	12-4-92	0	0	0.00	1	1	0	2	1	0	0	0	4	.125	.125	.125	50.0	0.0	8
Tabeling, Logan	L-R	6-0	205	8-21-01	5	3	3.61	22	12	0	67	53	34	27	1	39	88	.216	.339	.294	29.5	13.1	298

Tate, Dylan	R-R	5-11	194	5-9-04	0	1	8.10	2	0	0	3	8	5	3	0	4	2	.500	.600	.563	10.0	20.0	20
Tillero, Jesus	R-R	6-0	190	5-2-06	1	0	3.09	8	4	0	23	19	8	8	2	13	21	.216	.317	.307	20.8	12.9	101
Vilchez, Michael	R-R	6-3	180	6-3-04	1	2	6.09	30	0	1	44	38	37	30	4	26	46	.233	.358	.411	22.8	12.9	202
Wright, Jakob	L-L	6-0	170	5-30-03	0	1	3.20	9	9	0	20	19	11	7	0	8	24	.247	.344	.286	26.7	8.9	90
Zazueta, Christian	R-R	6-3	163	10-7-04	7	2	2.44	16	16	0	66	53	19	18	7	16	80	.215	.275	.352	29.7	5.9	269

Fielding

Catcher	PCT	G	PO	A	E	DP	PB
Avila	.969	3	28	3	1	0	0
Cueto	.961	27	284	12	12	1	4
Diaz	.978	38	341	22	8	4	12
Rodrigues	.987	70	707	38	10	5	16

First Base	PCT	G	PO	A	E	DP
Diaz	1.000	1	6	0	0	1
Guerrero	1.000	4	24	2	0	1
Lasso	.992	19	120	6	1	13
Meza	.980	68	460	21	10	40
Nicklaus	.983	37	283	10	5	23
Osorio	1.000	2	13	0	0	0
Rodrigues	1.000	6	38	1	0	1

Second Base	PCT	G	PO	A	E	DP
Guerrero	.983	21	17	42	1	8
Hainline	.991	32	37	75	1	15
Martinus	1.000	3	5	7	0	1
Morales	1.000	2	3	5	0	1

	PCT	G	PO	A	E	DP
Ortega	.933	9	9	19	2	2
Osorio	.873	14	16	32	7	4
Perez	.943	56	101	149	15	28

Third Base	PCT	G	PO	A	E	DP
Cueto	.000	1	0	0	1	0
Guerrero	.909	32	25	45	7	3
Hainline	.909	12	6	14	2	1
Harlan	.879	22	13	38	7	6
Martinus	.927	33	24	52	6	10
Nicklaus	.750	7	1	8	3	1
Ortega	.778	9	0	14	4	1
Osorio	.895	16	8	26	4	.6
Vargas	.875	6	4	10	2	0

Shortstop	PCT	G	PO	A	E	DP
Guerrero	.939	22	29	33	4	9
Hainline	.953	22	30	52	4	10
Hernandez, J	.750	1	1	2	1	0
Lindsey	.960	22	25	47	3	8

	PCT	G	PO	A	E	DP
Martinus	.975	19	25	54	2	9
Morales	.930	26	38	68	8	14
Vargas	.931	20	24	30	4	7

Outfield	PCT	G	PO	A	E	DP
Davalan	1.000	7	20	2	0	1
Decker	1.000	4	12	0	0	0
Elkins	.959	101	172	14	8	1
Hernandez, T	1.000	1	2	0	0	0
Hernandez, J	.750	2	3	0	1	0
Ko	.980	27	48	1	1	1
Martinus	.988	36	77	5	1	0
Meza	.917	36	50	5	5	0
Munoz	.986	83	137	0	2	0
Nicklaus	.667	4	2	0	1	0
Quintero	.986	72	142	3	2	1
Sirota	1.000	20	30	0	0	0
Vidourek	.929	11	12	1	1	0

ACL DODGERS — ROOKIE
ARIZONA COMPLEX LEAGUE

Batting	B-T	Ht.	Wt.	DOB	AVG	OBP	SLG	G	PA	AB	R	H	2B	3B	HR	RBI	BB	HBP	SH	SF	SO	SB	CS	BB%	SO%
Avila, Carlos	R-R	5-11	180	12-4-03	.282	.408	.333	19	49	39	7	11	2	0	0	6	7	2	0	1	10	0	0	14.3	20.4
Biddison, Nick	R-R	5-10	190	7-30-00	.000	.250	.000	1	4	3	0	0	0	0	0	0	1	0	0	0	0	0	0	25.0	0.0
Bolivar, Moises	R-R	6-0	175	7-8-07	.210	.279	.249	49	201	181	20	38	4	0	1	15	16	2	0	2	59	2	0	8.0	29.4
Decker, Cameron	S-R	6-1	205	9-22-03	.158	.250	.289	11	44	38	4	6	2	0	1	6	4	1	0	1	15	0	0	9.1	34.1
Diaz, Angel	R-R	5-11	180	2-4-04	.268	.434	.390	14	53	41	9	11	2	0	0	9	9	3	0	0	13	0	0	17.0	24.5
Espinoza, Francisco	R-R	6-1	206	3-16-07	.350	.443	.467	35	140	120	21	42	5	3	1	15	19	1	0	0	17	0	1	13.6	12.1
Gelof, Jake	R-R	6-1	195	2-25-02	.353	.478	.824	6	23	17	6	6	5	0	1	5	5	0	0	1	6	0	2	21.7	26.1
Gonzalez, Bryan	R-R	5-10	160	7-15-05	.178	.256	.220	35	133	118	10	21	2	0	1	11	9	4	0	2	28	1	1	6.8	21.1
Harlan, Chase	R-R	6-3	205	7-9-06	.288	.356	.500	42	177	156	31	45	13	1	6	38	18	0	0	3	35	1	1	10.2	19.8
Herrera, Javier	S-R	5-10	160	2-9-05	.343	.433	.422	36	120	102	19	35	6	1	0	19	15	2	0	1	21	6	4	12.5	17.5
Ko, Ching-Hsien	L-R	6-3	215	8-11-06	.367	.487	.539	53	226	180	43	66	15	2	4	30	39	5	0	2	40	5	3	17.3	17.7
Lasso, Roger	S-R	6-0	180	2-27-04	.263	.333	.368	17	63	57	5	15	3	0	1	9	3	3	0	0	14	0	0	4.8	22.2
Lindsey, Kellon	R-R	6-2	175	9-21-05	.235	.263	.471	4	19	17	3	4	1	0	1	3	1	0	0	1	6	1	0	5.3	31.6
Lorenzo, Abel	L-R	6-0	160	8-4-05	.181	.245	.283	40	139	127	16	23	4	0	3	11	10	1	0	1	47	5	1	7.2	33.8
Medina, Elias	R-R	5-10	171	11-9-05	.348	.426	.565	14	54	46	10	16	6	2	0	8	6	0	0	1	12	6	1	11.1	22.2
Miller, Noah	S-R	5-11	190	11-12-02	.333	.452	.500	8	31	24	6	8	2	1	0	5	6	0	0	1	0	0	0	19.4	3.2
Morales, Emil	R-R	6-3	191	9-22-06	.300	.383	.498	59	269	233	55	70	13	3	9	43	31	2	0	3	76	6	3	11.5	28.3
Nevin, Kyle	R-R	6-4	200	8-22-01	.304	.370	.435	7	27	23	1	7	3	0	0	8	2	1	0	1	7	0	0	7.4	25.9
Ortega, Raynerd	R-R	6-1	154	7-8-05	.278	.350	.500	31	123	108	22	30	10	1	4	21	7	6	0	2	36	3	1	5.7	29.3
Osorio, Oswaldo	L-R	6-1	171	4-12-05	.375	.412	.469	8	34	32	7	12	3	0	0	3	1	1	0	0	12	0	0	2.9	35.3
Shelton, Easton	R-R	6-5	225	9-17-05	.234	.292	.444	37	137	124	16	29	8	0	6	15	8	3	0	2	56	0	1	5.8	40.9
Simmons, Kendall	R-R	6-0	180	4-11-00	.214	.281	.429	8	32	28	3	6	0	0	2	5	3	0	0	1	7	0	0	9.4	25.0
Tunink, Brendan	L-L	6-0	185	10-2-05	.300	.417	.550	39	168	140	35	42	10	5	5	17	27	1	0	0	51	9	2	16.1	30.4
Vargas, Joendry	R-R	6-4	175	11-8-05	.273	.273	.545	3	11	11	3	3	0	0	1	2	0	0	0	0	4	0	0	0.0	36.4

Pitching	B-T	Ht.	Wt.	DOB	W	L	ERA	G	GS	SV	IP	Hits	Runs	ER	HR	BB	SO	AVG	OBP	SLG	SO%	BB%	BF
Abad, Dailoui	R-R	6-0	168	5-2-02	0	0	0.00	4	0	0	4	2	0	0	0	2	2	.143	.294	.143	11.8	11.8	17
Avila, Carlos	R-R	5-11	180	12-4-03	0	0	18.00	1	0	0	1	2	2	2	0	2	0	.500	.714	.750	0.0	28.6	7
Ayon, Isaac	R-R	6-4	235	6-14-02	0	3	5.00	12	12	0	27	26	19	15	4	12	27	.260	.351	.440	23.5	10.4	115
Bartolozzi, Javier	R-R	6-4	193	4-14-05	3	0	4.56	13	0	0	26	27	14	13	2	6	28	.257	.310	.410	24.8	5.3	113
Bonilla, Peter	L-L	6-3	195	12-16-04	0	2	4.50	17	0	0	22	20	12	11	2	21	27	.238	.402	.369	25.2	19.6	107
Bruns, Maddux	L-L	6-2	205	6-20-02	0	2	18.47	3	3	0	6	16	14	13	0	6	9	.500	.579	.625	23.7	15.8	38
Cabrera, Jose	R-R	6-4	195	11-14-04	3	0	2.21	19	0	5	20	17	6	5	1	8	27	.227	.306	.280	31.8	9.4	85
Carias, Luis	R-R	6-4	190	9-30-04	0	4	7.39	12	6	0	35	48	33	29	5	17	37	.331	.431	.531	21.9	10.1	169
Chambers, Justin	L-L	6-2	212	8-14-05	0	1	3.60	9	1	1	15	8	10	6	1	7	30	.154	.338	.231	44.1	16.2	68
Figueredo, Dilan	R-R	6-0	174	3-28-03	0	0	0.00	2	0	0	2	0	0	0	0	2	.000	.111	.000	22.2	0	9
Fischer, Tim	R-R	6-3	195	9-8-04	0	0	6.00	15	0	0	18	16	17	12	2	22	14	.239	.424	.403	15.1	23.7	93
Geronimo, Domingo	R-R	5-11	150	10-7-04	0	0	5.68	3	0	0	6	5	4	4	0	4	6	.217	.321	.391	21.4	14.3	28
Herrera, Wuillians	R-R	6-4	183	3-12-04	0	1	6.60	16	0	0	15	15	13	11	0	10	23	.273	.406	.418	32.9	14.3	70
Jimenez, Jhonny	R-R	6-5	180	11-9-03	0	1	4.76	5	0	3	6	4	4	5	3	0	3	6	.190	.292	.333	24.0	12.0	25
Kershaw, Clayton	L-L	6-4	225	3-19-88	1	0	0.00	1	1	0	6	0	0	0	0	0	9	.000	.000	.000	22.2	5.6	18
Leon, Edgar	R-R	6-3	170	12-29-04	5	1	4.76	15	0	0	28	12	16	12	2	31	40	.124	.341	.237	31.0	24.0	129
Liborius, Jecsua	R-R	6-1	190	5-28-05	1	0	9.95	14	0	0	12	16	16	14	0	17	13	.367	.554	.429	17.6	23.0	74
Martin, Payton	R-R	6-3	170	5-19-04	1	0	0.64	3	3	0	14	3	1	1	0	0	17	.260	.255	.300	33.3	0.0	51

Player	B-T	Ht.	Wt.	DOB	W	L	ERA	G	GS	SV	IP	Hits	Runs	ER	HR	BB	SO	AVG	OBP	SLG	SO%	BB%	BF
Maynard, William	L-R	6-3	190	6-19-03	1	0	0.90	8	0	1	10	7	1	1	0	4	9	.184	.279	.237	20.9	9.3	43
McDaniels, Garrett	L-L	6-2	180	12-15-99	0	0	0.00	1	1	0	1	1	0	0	0	0	1	.250	.250	.250	25.0	0.0	4
Montero, Ricardo	R-R	6-6	237	2-17-04	2	1	10.69	19	0	1	16	15	24	19	1	22	16	.238	.473	.381	17.6	24.2	91
Morales, Accimias	R-R	6-5	190	9-13-04	2	0	4.32	12	1	0	25	23	15	12	2	11	22	.242	.351	.379	19.1	9.6	115
Nieves, Marlon	R-R	6-3	170	6-10-05	4	0	3.23	12	8	0	47	31	18	17	1	25	57	.181	.309	.240	27.8	12.2	205
Oduber, Shawndrick	R-R	6-0	170	12-16-04	0	0	0.00	1	0	0	2	0	0	0	0	0	0	.000	.143	.000	0.0	0.0	7
Oliveira, Christian	R-R	6-4	205	4-8-06	4	1	11.48	14	1	0	27	34	36	34	5	29	25	.306	.469	.514	17.0	19.7	147
Romero, Luciano	R-R	6-2	190	1-8-05	0	0	4.32	15	0	0	17	19	9	8	1	16	13	.288	.424	.439	15.3	18.8	85
Sheehan, Emmet	R-R	6-5	220	11-15-99	0	0	0.00	1	1	0	2	0	0	0	0	0	5	.000	.000	.000	83.3	0.0	6
Simarra, Yoryi	R-R	6-1	174	11-18-04	0	0	11.74	8	0	0	8	6	12	10	1	17	12	.231	.545	.462	27.3	38.6	44
Smith, Brady	R-R	6-2	170	1-27-05	0	3	10.45	6	5	0	10	8	13	12	2	10	15	.211	.367	.421	30.6	20.4	49
Snell, Blake	L-L	6-4	225	12-4-92	0	1	3.00	1	1	0	3	3	1	1	0	0	7	.250	.250	.417	58.3	0.0	12
Tillero, Jesus	R-R	6-0	190	5-2-06	1	3	5.58	11	8	0	31	34	27	19	6	11	31	.274	.340	.484	21.8	7.7	142
Treinen, Blake	R-R	6-5	225	6-30-88	0	0	9.00	1	0	0	1	1	1	1	0	1	0	.250	.250	1.000	25.0	0.0	4
Vasquez, Jose	R-R	6-4	200	12-12-04	1	5	13.79	15	8	0	31	38	51	47	7	34	38	.304	.486	.512	22.0	19.7	173
Villani, Mike	R-R	6-3	185	1-4-03	0	0	0.00	2	0	1	2	0	0	0	0	0	5	.000	.000	.000	83.3	0.0	6

Fielding
C: Gonzalez 27, Espinoza 24, Diaz 9, Avila 3. **1B:** Shelton 16, Bolivar 11, Lasso 11, Espinoza 10, Avila 4, Decker 4, Harlan 4, Diaz 3, Osorio 2, Biddison 1, Lorenzo 1. **2B:** Ortega 26, Bolivar 11, Herrera 8, Gonzalez 7, Simmons 5, Osorio 4, Gelof 3, Medina 2. **3B:** Harlan 31, Bolivar 17, Shelton 5, Herrera 4, Morales 3, Nevin 3, Vargas 3, Gelof 1, Gonzalez 1, Simmons 1. **SS:** Morales 48, Miller 6, Herrera 4, Ortega 3, Bolivar 1, Medina 1. **LF:** Ko 18, Lorenzo 15, Herrera 12, Shelton 7, Tunink 5, Decker 4, Avila 3, Nevin 3, Medina 2, Lasso 1. **CF:** Tunink 29, Ko 23, Lorenzo 6, Herrera 4, Medina 1. **RF:** Lorenzo 21, Bolivar 11, Medina 10, Shelton 9, Herrera 6, Avila 4, Ko 3, Decker 1, Lasso 1, Tunink 1.

DSL DODGERS BAUTISTA ROOKIE
DOMINICAN SUMMER LEAGUE

Batting	B-T	Ht.	Wt.	DOB	AVG	OBP	SLG	G	PA	AB	R	H	2B	3B	HR	RBI	BB	HBP	SH	SF	SO	SB	CS	BB%	SO%
Ajoti, Allen	R-R	6-1	205	11-8-05	.192	.283	.414	32	114	99	16	19	4	0	6	27	9	4	0	1	31	4	0	7.9	27.2
Aparicio, Ezequiel	R-R	5-9	180	2-24-08	.235	.426	.333	26	68	51	10	12	2	0	1	5	10	7	0	0	12	2	1	14.7	17.6
Arvelo, Hendry	L-R	6-0	160	12-3-06	.268	.413	.307	44	160	127	35	34	3	1	0	11	29	3	0	1	24	12	3	18.1	15.0
Diaz, Degerson	R-R	5-10	150	1-31-08	.000	.273	.000	3	11	8	1	0	0	0	0	0	2	1	0	0	1	0	0	18.2	18.2
Familia, Railin	R-R	6-0	186	9-15-04	.067	.263	.067	6	19	15	0	1	0	0	0	0	3	1	0	0	6	2	0	15.8	31.6
Gll, Jhon	R-R	5-9	160	12-15-07	.311	.433	.410	41	150	122	28	38	7	1	1	27	24	3	0	1	20	14	0	16.0	13.3
Guaylupo, Vicente	R-R	6-1	180	5-6-06	.208	.367	.250	10	30	24	3	5	1	0	0	5	5	1	0	0	2	1	16.7	33.3
Laya, Yojackson	R-R	5-9	154	11-12-06	.211	.348	.237	40	139	114	16	24	1	0	0	11	19	5	1	0	20	6	13.7	14.4
Macero, Juan	R-R	5-9	165	11-27-07	.279	.385	.345	51	202	165	33	46	8	0	1	21	25	6	2	4	21	10	4	12.4	10.4
Mielcarek, Daniel	S-R	6-3	185	12-19-05	.231	.407	.444	39	140	108	33	25	6	1	5	20	30	2	0	0	40	12	3	21.4	28.6
Padilla, Leider	R-R	6-0	176	11-25-06	.236	.377	.346	46	159	127	20	30	5	0	3	30	25	5	0	2	43	9	0	15.7	27.0
Pena, Heudy	L-R	6-0	156	3-9-07	.098	.239	.152	33	111	92	18	9	2	0	1	5	16	1	0	2	38	6	1	14.4	34.2
Quezada, Yunior	L-R	6-1	160	10-31-05	.193	.277	.283	45	166	145	19	28	6	2	1	28	14	4	0	3	39	3	4	8.4	23.5
Rosa, Euri	R-R	5-10	165	7-4-07	.274	.380	.440	28	100	84	20	23	2	0	4	17	13	2	0	1	16	5	1	13.0	16.0
Sanchez, Edwin	R-R	5-10	180	8-2-04	.234	.486	.438	54	210	137	33	32	10	0	6	28	61	9	0	3	37	12	4	29.0	17.6
Theran, Jhosman	R-R	6-2	200	10-3-07	.191	.372	.340	43	123	94	18	18	5	0	3	13	26	1	2	0	32	12	6	21.1	26.0
Tovar, Luis	R-R	5-11	210	10-6-07	.286	.310	.286	7	29	28	3	8	0	0	0	0	1	0	0	0	5	2	0	3.4	17.2

Pitching	B-T	Ht.	Wt.	DOB	W	L	ERA	G	GS	SV	IP	Hits	Runs	ER	HR	BB	SO	AVG	OBP	SLG	SO%	BB%	BF
Almonte, Aneudy	L-L	6-1	160	8-31-07	0	3	6.17	9	4	0	23	24	20	16	2	17	31	.255	.368	.394	27.2	14.9	114
Aquino, Derik	R-R	6-5	180	4-18-07	0	2	12.68	18	0	1	22	27	39	31	2	26	28	.290	.464	.430	22.2	20.6	126
Burgos, David	L-L	5-11	178	2-7-06	1	0	7.83	13	0	0	23	22	25	20	0	26	23	.253	.442	.345	19.2	21.7	120
Camacho, Roman	R-R	6-0	194	11-23-04	0	0	27.00	1	0	0	1	3	4	4	0	2	3	.429	.600	.571	30.0	20.0	10
Cruz, Joel	R-R	6-3	182	6-16-04	0	4	3.91	13	11	0	46	48	33	20	3	15	46	.271	.338	.407	23.2	7.6	198
De La Rosa, Emmanuel	R-R	6-1	190	2-1-03	1	0	4.26	3	0	1	6	7	5	3	0	3	14	.259	.333	.296	46.7	10.0	30
De Los Santos, Joldelanio	R-R	6-0	175	9-21-03	2	3	0.98	15	0	1	18	14	9	2	0	9	23	.200	.300	.243	28.8	11.3	80
De Los Santos, Weslin	R-R	6-0	155	4-27-06	2	1	6.28	18	0	0	29	35	27	20	4	23	30	.297	.430	.432	20.1	15.4	149
Dominguez, Alexis	R-R	6-5	183	11-3-05	1	1	17.36	10	0	0	9	11	22	18	1	16	7	.306	.533	.500	11.7	26.7	60
Feliz, Albert	R-R	6-4	175	12-14-05	1	2	13.78	14	0	0	16	14	27	25	1	32	23	.230	.529	.377	22.1	30.8	104
Gamez, Luis	R-R	6-0	176	8-30-06	4	1	2.16	10	2	0	25	20	7	6	0	7	26	.220	.284	.297	25.0	6.7	104
Gonzalez, Oliver	R-R	6-4	200	10-26-06	0	0	2.83	11	0	0	35	16	14	11	2	25	38	.140	.313	.219	26.4	17.4	144
Luna, Andres	R-R	6-0	160	10-12-07	1	0	1.13	4	0	0	8	3	3	1	0	4	7	.111	.294	.111	20.6	11.8	34
Marte, Josehp	R-R	6-2	190	3-13-05	0	3	11.66	9	6	0	15	19	21	19	1	19	17	.283	.477	.400	19.8	22.1	86
Meneses, Gustavo	R-R	6-2	200	8-24-05	1	5	7.04	15	0	0	23	22	24	18	0	21	17	.268	.422	.341	15.3	18.9	111
Ramirez, Michael	L-L	6-0	160	4-21-05	0	3	5.45	13	10	0	35	15	26	21	1	44	58	.129	.392	.190	34.9	26.5	166
Reyes, Yobany	R-R	6-2	195	10-18-04	0	0	10.50	4	0	0	6	11	7	7	0	3	8	.393	.452	.429	25.8	9.7	31
Romero, Shai	R-R	6-5	235	8-22-07	1	4	14.04	15	6	0	17	23	34	26	0	32	11	.329	.557	.443	10.4	30.2	106
Rosas, Johnson	R-R	6-6	192	5-31-07	0	1	1.65	7	1	1	16	10	4	3	1	9	18	.182	.333	.236	27.5	17.4	69
Savinon, Samuel	R-R	6-2	230	11-28-06	0	1	10.80	5	2	0	5	3	7	6	0	7	7	.188	.519	.250	25.9	25.9	27
Tinkam, Logan	R-R	6-3	170	3-30-07	1	1	5.19	12	1	0	16	14	10	9	2	16	21	.239	.418	.403	23.1	17.6	91
Villegas, Jose	R-R	6-7	260	11-8-06	1	2	6.45	13	0	1	22	22	21	16	1	19	17	.278	.435	.316	15.6	17.4	109

Fielding
C: Rosa 22, Gll 17, Ajoti 12, Aparicio 9, Familia 1. **1B:** Sanchez 37, Aparicio 16, Rosa 6, Familia 4, Ajoti 2, Quezada 2. **2B:** Pena 24, Macero 16, Gll 13, Arvelo 10, Laya 1, Mielcarek 1. **3B:** Macero 23, Arvelo 15, Laya 7, Tovar 6, Mielcarek 3, Pena 2. **SS:** Laya 31, Macero 12, Mielcarek 11, Arvelo 5. **LF:** Padilla 25, Theran 15, Arvelo 11, Ajoti 9, Quezada 7, Guaylupo 1, Sanchez 1. **CF:** Quezada 36, Theran 22, Gll 2, Sanchez 2, Diaz 1, Padilla 1. **RF:** Padilla 24, Sanchez 20, Guaylupo 9, Theran 8, Quezada 3, Familia 1.

DSL DODGERS MEGA — ROOKIE
DOMINICAN SUMMER LEAGUE

Batting	B-T	Ht.	Wt.	DOB	AVG	OBP	SLG	G	PA	AB	R	H	2B	3B	HR	RBI	BB	HBP	SH	SF	SO	SB	CS	BB%	SO%
Acacio, Moises	R-R	5-11	155	1-24-08	.241	.366	.325	29	101	83	21	20	7	0	0	16	15	2	0	1	14	7	0	14.9	13.9
Acosta, Agustin	L-R	6-2	173	9-7-04	.327	.473	.564	38	131	101	29	33	9	3	3	25	18	11	0	1	29	14	2	13.7	22.1
Bautista, Devlyn	R-R	6-2	180	12-4-06	.148	.297	.148	29	74	61	8	9	0	0	0	7	12	1	0	0	38	3	0	16.2	51.4
Familia, Railin	R-R	6-0	186	9-15-04	.226	.337	.333	30	101	84	15	19	6	0	1	15	11	4	0	2	21	3	1	10.9	20.8
Gonzalez, Harold	R-R	5-10	175	8-29-06	.257	.412	.353	47	177	136	30	35	5	1	2	26	37	1	0	3	28	11	2	20.9	15.8
Gonzalez, Jose	L-R	6-2	180	1-29-05	.240	.446	.472	45	177	125	40	30	8	3	5	24	43	6	0	3	41	15	2	24.3	23.2
Luna, Luis	R-R	6-0	170	6-9-08	.202	.353	.223	32	116	94	18	19	2	0	0	7	17	5	0	0	26	9	5	14.7	22.4
Mariano, Reyli	S-R	5-7	140	11-7-06	.336	.466	.580	42	165	131	32	44	10	5	4	33	32	0	2	0	26	15	5	19.4	15.8
Orellana, Erny	R-R	6-0	183	3-3-07	.254	.388	.423	43	160	130	32	33	10	0	4	24	24	5	0	1	34	6	2	15.0	21.3
Peguero, Rafy	R-R	6-0	190	9-26-06	.241	.362	.422	36	138	116	24	28	9	0	4	30	19	3	0	0	35	2	0	13.8	25.4
Ramirez, Raynier	R-R	5-10	185	12-13-04	.205	.311	.307	28	106	88	11	18	6	0	1	13	11	4	0	3	25	5	3	10.4	23.6
Rangel, Moises	R-R	5-10	190	5-23-08	.209	.354	.299	27	82	67	8	14	0	0	2	6	13	2	0	0	10	1	0	15.9	28.0
Rivas, Jose	R-R	5-11	170	3-27-08	.282	.415	.329	30	106	85	13	24	4	0	0	13	18	2	0	1	13	7	1	17.0	12.3
Rojas, Eduardo	S-R	5-11	163	2-14-07	.278	.450	.348	38	151	115	23	32	5	0	1	12	31	5	0	0	15	9	4	20.5	9.9
Urena, Antoni	S-R	6-1	160	11-30-06	.237	.369	.304	38	169	135	27	32	4	1	1	20	28	2	1	3	19	8	2	16.6	11.2
Villaflor, Jesus	L-L	6-2	187	1-18-08	.286	.451	.386	27	91	70	12	20	4	0	1	9	14	7	0	0	27	4	0	15.4	29.7

Pitching	B-T	Ht.	Wt.	DOB	W	L	ERA	G	GS	SV	IP	Hits	Runs	ER	HR	BB	SO	AVG	OBP	SLG	SO%	BB%	BF
Acosta, Agustin	L-R	6-2	173	9-7-04	0	0	0.00	1	0	0	0	0	0	0	0	2	0	.000	.750	.000	0.0	50.0	4
Almonte, Aneudy	L-L	6-1	160	8-31-07	0	1	3.68	4	4	0	15	12	7	6	0	8	15	.235	.361	.353	24.2	12.9	62
Burgos, David	L-L	5-11	178	2-7-06	0	0	3.60	2	0	0	5	2	2	2	0	3	4	.125	.333	.125	19.0	14.3	21
Camacho, Roman	R-R	6-0	194	11-23-04	4	1	7.67	18	0	1	27	21	26	23	0	25	24	.221	.403	.305	18.5	19.2	130
Cruz, Angel	R-R	6-1	210	10-12-04	3	1	3.79	18	4	2	36	23	15	15	0	26	43	.189	.351	.254	27.7	16.8	155
De La Cruz, Yuliangel	R-R	6-3	158	1-24-05	3	1	6.15	18	0	0	26	17	22	18	0	26	28	.175	.380	.247	21.7	20.2	129
De La Rosa, Enmanuel	R-R	6-1	190	2-1-03	0	0	4.50	1	0	0	2	2	1	1	0	0	0	.250	.250	.375	0.0	0.0	8
Dominguez, Alexis	R-R	6-5	183	11-3-05	0	0	9.00	2	0	0	1	0	2	1	0	3	0	.000	.500	.000	0.0	50.0	6
Ferrera, Gregg	R-R	6-5	175	3-21-06	0	3	6.43	12	7	0	28	30	23	20	2	26	27	.273	.420	.455	19.6	18.8	138
Florian, Jeremy	R-R	6-4	185	5-4-05	0	1	30.00	5	0	0	3	1	10	10	0	13	5	.111	.640	.111	12.0	52.0	25
Lara, Bryan	R-R	6-0	180	5-15-08	0	3	12.15	3	3	0	7	12	12	9	2	3	6	.364	.462	.667	15.4	7.7	39
Lopez, Jose	R-R	6-0	185	11-13-05	1	1	10.80	12	0	2	13	13	18	16	0	20	14	.265	.507	.367	18.9	27.0	74
Luna, Andres	R-R	6-0	160	10-12-07	3	0	5.65	10	0	0	14	12	11	9	0	19	12	.235	.453	.275	16.0	25.3	75
Maria, Randy	R-R	6-2	190	7-1-04	0	1	5.79	10	1	1	19	21	16	12	0	17	16	.296	.433	.352	17.8	18.9	90
Meneses, Gustavo	R-R	6-2	200	8-24-05	0	1	36.00	1	0	0	1	3	4	4	0	4	0	.600	.778	.600	0.0	44.4	9
Morel, Franderly	L-L	6-2	160	9-12-03	3	0	3.55	18	0	0	33	33	22	13	2	13	39	.246	.331	.343	25.7	8.6	152
Pacheco, Jose	R-R	5-11	150	10-21-04	2	1	3.67	16	0	2	27	24	12	11	4	12	12	.247	.342	.412	10.3	10.3	116
Perez, Axel	R-R	6-4	158	8-13-05	1	1	5.48	10	9	0	23	19	16	14	2	13	32	.226	.363	.381	31.1	12.6	103
Ramirez, Carlos	R-R	6-2	215	7-18-08	0	1	12.00	7	6	0	15	12	20	20	0	23	11	.222	.475	.389	13.8	28.8	80
Reyes, Alexis	R-R	6-3	190	3-5-07	2	2	8.65	14	0	1	26	38	36	25	1	20	21	.328	.432	.509	15.1	14.4	139
Rivero, Alexander	R-R	6-0	165	1-11-06	1	0	11.48	11	0	0	13	10	21	17	0	25	9	.213	.538	.255	11.1	30.9	81
Salazar, Williams	L-L	6-2	175	2-15-05	0	3	2.39	10	10	0	38	28	16	10	2	16	31	.212	.302	.303	20.7	10.7	150
Sanchez, Cesar	R-R	6-3	190	6-16-06	0	2	8.53	2	2	0	6	10	7	6	1	3	4	.345	.424	.517	12.1	9.1	33
Taveras, Jose	R-R	6-1	182	10-2-05	2	3	5.24	12	4	0	34	31	23	20	4	13	18	.240	.336	.395	12.1	8.7	149
Thon, Joseph Deng	R-R	6-6	185	8-5-07	0	3	31.91	8	1	0	4	1	13	13	0	22	5	.091	.697	.091	15.2	66.7	33
Torres, Adrian	L-L	6-3	180	1-23-08	0	0	7.71	5	4	0	9	6	10	8	0	15	9	.188	.460	.219	18.0	30.0	50
Villegas, Jose	R-R	6-7	260	11-8-06	0	0	0.00	1	0	0	2	0	0	0	0	1	1	.000	.222	.000	11.1	11.1	9

Fielding

C: Rojas 31, Rivas 21, Rangel 8, Familia 5. **1B:** Rangel 18, Familia 17, J. Gonzalez 17, H. Gonzalez 8, Rivas 8. **2B:** Mariano 21, Luna 13, Gonzalez 10, Urena 10, Acacio 3, Ramirez 3. **3B:** Gonzalez 28, Ramirez 23, Familia 4, Luna 4, Mariano 4. **SS:** Urena 24, Mariano 16, Luna 11, Acacio 6. **LF:** Peguero 22, Bautista 17, Orellana 15, Villaflor 6, Familia 4, Acosta 1, Gonzalez 1. **CF:** Acosta 27, Villaflor 16, Gonzalez 12, Orellana 8, Bautista 1. **RF:** Orellana 22, Gonzalez 15, Acosta 10, Peguero 10, Villaflor 6, Bautista 5, Familia 3.

Miami Marlins

SEASON SYNOPSIS: In their second season under president of baseball operations Peter Bendix, the Marlins improved by 17 victories over the 2024 season, staying in the wild-card race up until the season's final week. They found new key position players such as all-star outfielder Kyle Stowers (.288/.368/.544, 25 HR), and they did so while having the second-youngest roster in the sport (average age: 26.1).

HIGH POINT: Miami won its last series before the all-star break, then won five straight series coming out of the break, culminating in a sweep of the Yankees to open August and reach the .500 mark at 55-55. The series opener was a 13-12 barnburner in which the Marlins rallied from deficits of 6-0, 9-4 and 12-10 against the remade Yankees pen, scoring three in the bottom of the ninth off David Bednar. Eury Perez outdueled Cam Schlitter in a 2-0 win the next day, and the Marlins completed the sweep in front of a sellout crowd behind Edward Cabrera and a homer by Stowers.

LOW POINT: The Braves had a down year but still dominated the Marlins, who went just 4-9 against Atlanta and might have earned a wild card with a better showing. They lost four of five in Atlanta, including a doubleheader sweep, from Aug. 7-10. And the Braves won two of three in Miami later in August, scoring nine in the ninth on Aug. 26 to win 11-2, then blasting five homers the next day in a 12-1 rout.

NOTABLE ROOKIES: Seven rookies got more than 180 at-bats for the Marlins, from 1B Eric Wagaman (.250/.296/.378), who led all rookies with 140 games played; to C/DH Agustin Ramirez (.231/.287/.413), who ranked second among rookies with 21 homers; to solid role players in utilityman Javier Sanoja (.243/.287/.396), who played every position but catcher and right field, and 3B/OF Graham Pauley (.224/.311/.366); to Jakob Marsee (.292/.363/.478, 14 SB), the best prospect and hitter of the group of youngsters.

KEY TRANSACTIONS: The Marlins held onto 2022 Cy Young Award winner Sandy Alcantara, who struggled badly before going 7-3, 3.33 in the second half. They made a shrewd Rule 5 pick in C/1B Liam Hicks (.247/.346/.346, 6 HR). Two of their key relievers, righties Ronny Henriquez (7-1, 2.22, 98 SO/73 IP) and Tyler Phillips (2-1, 2.78, 78 IP/52 SO), were a January waiver claim and March cash trade. Miami traded away outfielder Jesus Sanchez (Houston) and catcher Nick Fortes (Rays) at the July deadline.

OPENING DAY PAYROLL: $67,412,619 (30th)

PLAYERS OF THE YEAR

MAJOR LEAGUE

Kyle Stowers
OF
.288/.368/.544
25 HR, 21 2B, 73 RBIs
in 117 G; all-star

MINOR LEAGUE

Robby Snelling
LHP
(AA, AAA)
2.51 ERA in 136 IP
166 SO, 39 BB

ORGANIZATION LEADERS

Batting *Qualifiers

MAJORS

*	AVG	Xavier Edwards	.283
*	OPS	Agustin Ramirez	.701
	HR	Kyle Stowers	25
	RBI	Otto Lopez	77

MINORS

*	AVG	Kemp Alderman, Jacksonville/Pensacola	.285
*	OBP	Michael Snyder, Pensacola/Beloit	.386
*	SLG	Kemp Alderman, Jacksonville/Pensacola	.482
*	OPS	Kemp Alderman, Jacksonville/Pensacola	.819
	R	Johnny Olmstead, Jacksonville/Pensacola	74
	H	Kemp Alderman, Jacksonville/Pensacola	139
	TB	Kemp Alderman, Jacksonville/Pensacola	235
	2B	Jacob Berry, Jacksonville	28
	3B	Dillon Head, Beloit/Jupiter	9
	HR	Kemp Alderman, Jacksonville/Pensacola	22
	RBI	Kemp Alderman, Jacksonville/Pensacola	70
	BB	Michael Snyder, Pensacola/Beloit	75
	SO	Andres Valor, Jacksonville	134
	SO	Carter Johnson, Jupiter	134
	SB	Colby Shade, Pensacola/Beloit	53

Pitching #Qualifiers

MAJORS

	W	Sandy Alcantara	11
#	ERA	Sandy Alcantara	5.36
	SO	Edward Cabrera	150
	SV	Calvin Faucher	15

MINORS

	W	Christian Roa, Jacksonville	10
	W	Josh White, Jacksonville/Pensacola	10
	L	Dax Fulton, Jacksonville/Pensacola	11
#	ERA	Robby Snelling, Jacksonville/Pensacola	2.51
	G	Christian Roa, Jacksonville	50
	GS	Robby Snelling, Jacksonville/Pensacola	25
	SV	Josh Ekness, Jacksonville/Pensacola	10
	IP	Robby Snelling, Jacksonville/Pensacola	136
	BB	Orlando Ortiz-Mayr, Pensacola	61
	SO	Robby Snelling, Jacksonville/Pensacola	166
#	AVG	Robby Snelling, Jacksonville/Pensacola	.222

2025 PERFORMANCE

General Manager: Peter Bendix. **Farm Director:** Rachel Balkovec. **Scouting Director:** Frankie Piliere.

Class	Team	League	W	L	PCT	Finish	Manager
Majors	Miami Marlins	National	79	83	.488	10 (15)	Clayton McCullough
Triple-A	Jacksonville Jumbo Shrimp	International	89	61	.593	1 (20)	David Carpenter
Double-A	Pensacola Blue Wahoos	Southern	69	69	.500	6 (8)	Nelson Prada
High-A	Beloit Sky Carp	Midwest	68	63	.519	6 (12)	Angel Espada
Low-A	Jupiter Hammerheads	Florida State	59	72	.450	9 (10)	Nick Weisheipl
Rookie	FCL Marlins	Florida Complex	19	35	.352	14 (15)	Gabe Ortiz
Rookie	DSL Marlins	Dominican	34	22	.607	12 (52)	Carlos Mota
Rookie	DSL Miami	Dominican	37	19	.661	4 (52)	Oscar Escobar
Overall 2025 Minor League Record			375	341	.524	7th (30)	

ORGANIZATION STATISTICS

MIAMI MARLINS
NATIONAL LEAGUE

Batting	B-T	Ht.	Wt.	DOB	AVG	OBP	SLG	G	PA	AB	R	H	2B	3B	HR	RBI	BB	HBP	SH	SF	SO	SB	CS	BB%	SO%
Acosta, Max	R-R	6-1	187	10-29-02	.204	.295	.389	19	61	54	7	11	1	0	3	5	6	1	0	0	17	1	2	9.8	27.9
Brantly, Rob	L-R	6-0	190	7-14-89	.429	.429	.429	3	7	7	0	3	0	0	0	1	0	0	0	0	1	0	0	0.0	14.3
Bride, Jonah	R-R	5-10	200	12-27-95	.100	.200	.100	12	45	40	3	4	0	0	0	2	5	0	0	0	15	0	0	11.1	33.3
Conine, Griffin	L-R	6-1	210	7-11-97	.253	.314	.418	24	86	79	13	20	7	0	2	8	7	0	0	0	25	0	1	8.1	29.1
Edwards, Xavier	S-R	5-10	175	8-9-99	.283	.343	.353	139	619	561	75	159	20	5	3	43	49	3	3	3	88	27	7	7.9	14.2
Fortes, Nick	R-R	5-11	198	11-11-96	.240	.288	.349	59	141	129	11	31	6	1	2	10	7	2	2	1	22	0	0	5.0	15.6
Hernandez, Heriberto	R-R	5-11	195	12-16-99	.266	.347	.438	87	294	256	40	68	12	1	10	45	31	3	0	4	77	1	1	10.5	26.2
Hicks, Liam	L-R	5-11	185	6-2-99	.247	.346	.346	119	390	332	37	82	13	1	6	45	43	9	3	3	56	2	0	11.0	14.4
Hill, Derek	R-R	6-2	206	12-30-95	.213	.275	.331	53	141	127	19	27	6	0	3	10	9	2	3	0	46	7	0	6.4	32.6
Johnston, Troy	L-L	6-0	205	6-22-97	.277	.331	.420	44	121	112	12	31	2	1	4	13	8	1	0	0	26	2	2	6.6	21.5
Lopez, Otto	R-R	5-10	185	10-1-98	.246	.305	.368	143	594	544	66	134	21	0	15	77	44	3	0	3	82	15	6	7.4	13.8
Marsee, Jakob	L-L	6-0	180	6-28-01	.292	.363	.478	55	234	209	28	61	18	3	5	33	22	2	0	1	48	14	6	9.4	20.5
Mervis, Matt	L-R	6-2	225	4-16-98	.175	.254	.383	42	134	120	15	21	4	0	7	14	11	2	0	1	50	0	0	8.2	37.3
Mesa, Victor	L-L	6-0	195	9-8-01	.188	.297	.344	16	38	32	7	6	2	0	1	6	5	0	1	0	5	0	0	13.2	13.2
Myers, Dane	R-R	6-0	205	3-8-96	.235	.291	.326	106	333	307	29	72	10	0	6	31	23	2	0	1	77	18	5	6.9	23.1
Navarreto, Brian	R-R	6-2	233	12-29-94	.286	.267	.643	8	15	14	3	4	2	0	2	1	5	0	0	0	3	0	0	0.0	20.0
Norby, Connor	R-R	5-9	180	6-8-00	.251	.300	.389	88	337	311	42	78	17	1	8	34	18	5	0	3	90	8	2	5.3	26.7
Pauley, Graham	L-R	6-1	200	9-24-00	.224	.311	.366	62	184	161	18	36	9	1	4	11	21	0	1	1	36	2	0	11.4	19.6
Ramirez, Agustin	R-R	6-0	210	9-10-01	.231	.287	.413	136	585	537	72	124	33	1	21	67	36	8	0	4	113	16	3	6.2	19.3
Sanchez, Jesus	L-R	6-3	222	10-7-97	.220	.420	.86	337	305	40	78	12	4	10	36	29	1	0	2	70	9	2	8.6	20.8
Sanoja, Javier	R-R	5-7	150	9-3-02	.243	.287	.396	120	342	313	40	76	22	4	6	38	19	2	4	4	41	6	5	5.6	12.0
Simon, Ronny	S-R	5-7	150	4-17-00	.234	.327	.277	19	56	47	6	11	2	0	0	5	7	0	1	1	7	0	0	12.5	12.5
Stowers, Kyle	L-L	6-3	215	1-2-98	.288	.368	.544	117	457	399	61	115	21	3	25	73	48	5	1	4	125	5	1	10.5	27.4
Wagaman, Eric	R-R	6-4	210	8-14-97	.250	.296	.378	140	514	476	56	119	28	3	9	53	32	1	0	5	100	4	1	6.2	19.5
Wiemer, Joey	R-R	6-4	220	2-11-99	.236	.279	.436	27	61	55	7	13	2	0	3	12	2	0	2	0	23	0	0	3.3	37.7
Winkler, Jack	R-R	6-2	185	11-4-98	.250	.250	.375	14	16	16	2	4	2	0	0	0	0	0	0	0	4	1	0	0.0	25.0

Pitching	B-T	Ht.	Wt.	DOB	W	L	ERA	G	GS	SV	IP	Hits	Runs	ER	HR	BB	SO	AVG	OBP	SLG	SO%	BB%	BF
Alcantara, Sandy	R-R	6-5	200	9-7-95	11	12	5.36	31	31	0	175	165	107	104	22	57	142	.247	.310	.404	19.1	7.7	745
Arias, Luarbert	R-R	6-2	176	12-12-00	0	0	11.32	7	0	0	10	17	13	13	2	5	10	.362	.436	.617	18.2	9.1	55
Bachar, Lake	R-R	6-2	219	6-3-95	8	2	3.93	53	1	3	71	55	34	31	10	30	75	.213	.298	.388	25.3	10.1	296
Bellozo, Valente	R-R	5-10	170	1-4-00	1	4	4.65	32	6	0	81	85	44	42	15	23	54	.269	.324	.465	15.5	6.6	348
Bender, Anthony	R-R	6-4	205	2-3-95	3	5	2.16	51	0	4	50	32	13	12	3	21	42	.177	.270	.276	20.6	10.3	204
Cabrera, Edward	R-R	6-5	217	4-13-98	8	7	3.53	26	26	0	138	121	60	54	17	48	150	.233	.309	.378	25.8	8.3	581
Curry, Xzavion	R-R	6-0	195	7-27-98	0	1	6.00	3	0	0	3	4	4	2	0	3	1	.308	.438	.308	6.3	18.8	16
Faucher, Calvin	R-R	6-1	190	9-22-95	4	4	3.28	67	0	15	66	53	27	22	8	24	59	.236	.314	.369	23.1	9.4	255
Gibson, Cade	L-L	6-2	195	2-18-98	4	5	2.63	44	1	0	55	44	18	16	3	21	43	.219	.310	.318	18.7	9.1	230
Gillispie, Connor	R-R	5-11	185	11-10-97	0	3	8.65	6	6	0	26	32	26	25	6	11	23	.294	.358	.560	18.7	8.9	123
Gusto, Ryan	R-R	6-4	232	3-11-99	0	3	9.77	3	3	0	16	19	17	17	4	8	10	.302	.392	.556	13.5	10.8	74
Henriquez, Ronny	R-R	5-10	155	6-20-00	7	1	2.22	69	0	7	73	53	23	18	8	27	98	.199	.278	.333	32.3	8.9	303
Junk, Janson	R-R	6-2	202	1-15-96	6	4	4.17	21	16	1	110	112	54	51	8	13	77	.266	.289	.397	17.2	2.9	447
Martinez, Seth	R-R	6-2	200	8-29-94	0	0	5.40	6	0	0	7	4	4	2	3	4	.182	.259	.500	14.8	11.1	27
Mazur, Joey	R-R	6-2	200	4-20-01	6	4	6.30	33	21	0	116	129	86	81	14	47	79	.276	.354	.464	13.7	8.6	139
Meyer, Max	L-R	6-0	196	3-12-99	3	5	4.73	12	12	0	65	72	39	34	12	20	68	.276	.330	.460	23.9	7.0	285
Monteverde, Patrick	R-L	6-2	200	9-24-97	0	0	9.82	1	0	0	4	9	4	4	0	1	4	.474	.500	.579	20.0	5.0	20
Perez, Eury	R-R	6-8	220	4-15-03	7	6	4.25	20	20	0	95	68	47	45	12	32	105	.195	.268	.358	27.3	8.3	385
Petersen, Michael	R-R	6-7	195	5-16-94	0	1	3.97	11	0	0	11	11	8	5	2	5	12	.244	.320	.488	23.5	9.8	51
Phillips, Tyler	R-R	6-5	225	10-27-97	2	1	2.78	54	1	4	78	65	26	24	8	24	52	.226	.291	.352	16.6	7.7	313
Pina, Robinson	R-R	6-5	225	11-26-98	0	0	9.00	1	0	0	1	1	1	1	0	0	.250	.250	1.000	0.0	0.0	4
Quantrill, Cal	R-R	6-3	195	2-10-95	4	10	5.50	24	24	0	110	122	69	67	17	30	82	.281	.334	.486	17.4	6.4	470
Roa, Christian	R-R	6-4	220	4-2-99	0	0	0.00	2	0	0	3	1	0	0	0	3	3	.111	.333	.222	25.0	25.0	12
Sanoja, Javier	R-R	5-7	150	9-3-02	0	0	16.39	8	0	0	9	24	17	17	4	5	1	.490	.537	.796	1.9	9.3	54
Simpson, Josh	L-L	6-2	190	8-19-97	4	2	7.34	31	0	0	31	34	28	25	5	22	36	.272	.393	.448	23.8	14.6	151

	B-T	Ht.	Wt.	DOB	AVG	OBP	SLG	G	PA	AB	R	H	2B	3B	HR	RBI	BB	HBP	SH	SF	SO	SB	CS	BB%	SO%
Soriano, George	R-R	6-2	210	3-24-99	2	0	8.35	24	0	1	37	46	36	34	10	19	36	.307	.390	.567	20.8	11.0	173		
Tarnok, Freddy	R-R	6-3	185	11-24-98	1	0	2.45	5	0	1	7	1	2	2	1	4	10	.043	.214	.174	35.7	14.3	28		
Tinoco, Jesus	R-R	6-4	258	4-30-95	2	1	5.12	20	0	4	19	17	12	11	1	8	10	.239	.316	.366	12.5	10.0	80		
Veneziano, Anthony	L-L	6-5	205	9-1-97	0	0	4.71	24	1	0	21	25	11	11	4	10	20	.291	.364	.523	20.0	10.0	100		
Weathers, Ryan	R-L	6-1	230	12-17-99	2	2	3.99	8	8	0	38	37	20	17	7	12	37	.245	.303	.430	22.3	7.2	166		
Zuber, Tyler	R-R	5-11	195	6-16-95	0	1	11.70	9	0	0	10	14	13	13	3	6	11	.318	.400	.636	22.0	12.0	50		

Fielding

Catcher	PCT	G	PO	A	E	DP	PB
Brantly	1.000	3	16	3	0	1	0
Fortes	.988	54	308	13	4	1	3
Hicks	.995	62	381	19	2	1	3
Navarreto	1.000	8	38	2	0	0	0
Ramirez	.983	73	566	19	10	3	19

First Base	PCT	G	PO	A	E	DP
Bride	1.000	4	33	4	0	4
Hicks	.995	28	171	13	1	14
Johnston	1.000	16	97	8	0	8
Mervis	.994	29	165	11	1	11
Pauley	1.000	5	28	2	0	1
Sanoja	.000	1	0	0	0	0
Wagaman	.988	117	757	50	10	60
Winkler	1.000	3	5	0	0	1

Second Base	PCT	G	PO	A	E	DP
Acosta	.895	6	9	8	2	2

Edwards	.989	96	108	248	4	39
Lopez	.986	32	40	97	2	11
Pauley	1.000	7	2	9	0	1
Sanoja	1.000	34	42	61	0	15
Simon	.857	9	12	12	4	2
Winkler	.900	5	4	5	1	2

Third Base	PCT	G	PO	A	E	DP
Acosta	1.000	11	5	10	0	1
Bride	1.000	2	3	4	0	0
Norby	.954	82	42	123	8	12
Pauley	.985	52	40	90	2	6
Sanoja	.972	41	17	53	2	7
Wagaman	1.000	3	1	0	0	0
Winkler	1.000	2	1	0	0	0

Shortstop	PCT	G	PO	A	E	DP
Acosta	1.000	6	7	10	0	4
Edwards	.960	41	51	92	6	24

Lopez	.975	111	159	225	10	44
Sanoja	.970	10	11	21	1	2
Simon	.000	1	0	0	0	0
Winkler	.750	3	2	1	1	1

Outfield	PCT	G	PO	A	E	DP
Conine	1.000	25	36	1	0	0
Hernandez	.964	51	81	0	3	0
Hill	1.000	50	95	4	0	0
Johnston	.964	24	27	0	1	0
Marsee	.993	63	140	1	1	0
Mesa	1.000	16	25	0	0	0
Myers	.987	110	216	7	3	1
Sanchez	.988	88	157	1	2	0
Sanoja	1.000	49	55	3	0	0
Simon	1.000	6	5	0	0	0
Stowers	.996	129	219	6	1	0
Wagaman	1.000	22	31	0	0	0
Wiemer	1.000	23	38	1	0	0

MIAMI MARLINS

JACKSONVILLE JUMBO SHRIMP   *TRIPLE-A*
INTERNATIONAL LEAGUE

Batting	B-T	Ht.	Wt.	DOB	AVG	OBP	SLG	G	PA	AB	R	H	2B	3B	HR	RBI	BB	HBP	SH	SF	SO	SB	CS	BB%	SO%
Acosta, Max	R-R	6-1	187	10-29-02	.224	.314	.366	115	465	410	56	92	13	3	13	50	50	4	0	1	123	33	9	10.8	26.5
Alderman, Kemp	R-R	6-3	265	8-20-02	.303	.341	.671	20	82	76	13	23	7	0	7	17	5	0	0	1	22	2	1	6.1	26.8
Almora, Albert	R-R	6-2	190	4-16-94	.240	.289	.315	44	159	146	20	35	8	0	1	15	9	2	0	2	33	4	2	5.7	20.8
Berry, Jacob	S-R	6-0	212	5-5-01	.261	.348	.394	123	469	406	57	106	28	1	8	54	49	8	1	5	87	27	8	10.4	18.6
Bramwell, Spencer	R-R	5-11	220	1-10-99	.500	.500	.625	6	8	8	2	4	1	0	0	1	0	0	0	0	2	0	0	0.0	25.0
Brantly, Rob	L-R	6-0	190	7-14-89	.359	.390	.590	12	41	39	5	14	6	0	1	7	2	0	0	0	8	0	0	4.9	19.5
Bullard, Tony	R-R	6-4	212	2-17-00	.000	.167	.000	3	12	9	1	0	0	0	0	1	1	1	0	1	4	1	0	8.3	33.3
Coley, Mark	R-R	6-2	193	11-22-00	.214	.421	.429	7	19	14	2	3	0	0	1	2	3	2	0	0	5	1	1	15.8	26.3
Conine, Griffin	L-R	6-1	210	7-11-97	.292	.514	.583	9	35	24	7	7	1	0	2	9	11	0	0	0	9	0	0	31.4	25.7
De Los Santos, Deyvison	R-R	5-11	185	6-21-03	.241	.311	.363	106	444	399	54	96	11	1	12	54	36	6	0	3	99	16	6	8.1	22.3
Edwards, Xavier	S-R	5-10	175	8-9-99	.143	.250	.143	2	8	7	0	1	0	0	0	1	1	0	0	0	1	0	0	12.5	0.0
Etzel, Matthew	L-R	6-2	211	4-30-02	.275	.367	.363	31	121	102	13	28	3	0	2	13	16	0	0	2	29	9	2	13.2	24.0
Fortes, Nick	R-R	5-11	198	11-11-96	.000	.143	.000	2	7	6	0	0	0	0	0	0	1	0	0	0	2	0	0	14.3	28.6
Gleed, Dub	R-R	6-1	195	9-1-02	.000	.333	.000	1	3	2	0	0	0	0	0	0	1	0	0	0	1	0	0	33.3	0.0
Hernandez, Heriberto	R-R	5-11	195	12-16-99	.220	.319	.454	41	163	141	21	31	4	1	9	21	19	2	0	1	57	6	2	11.7	35.0
Hill, Derek	R-R	6-2	206	12-30-95	.171	.277	.220	12	47	41	3	7	2	0	0	2	5	1	0	0	14	3	1	10.6	29.8
Hostetler, Bennett	R-R	6-0	195	9-23-97	.179	.325	.221	36	120	95	9	17	4	0	0	9	15	7	0	3	39	9	1	12.5	32.5
Johnston, Troy	L-L	6-0	205	6-22-97	.252	.333	.439	84	354	314	49	79	15	4	12	39	28	11	0	1	68	31	5	7.9	19.2
Lopez, Otto	R-R	5-10	185	10-1-98	.250	.250	.500	1	4	4	2	1	1	0	0	1	0	0	0	0	1	0	1	0.0	25.0
Mack, Joe	L-R	6-1	210	12-27-02	.250	.320	.459	99	412	364	58	91	18	2	18	53	35	6	0	7	115	8	3	8.5	27.9
Marsee, Jakob	L-L	6-0	180	6-28-01	.246	.379	.438	98	429	345	56	85	14	5	14	37	68	7	7	2	81	47	13	15.9	18.9
Martorella, Nathan	L-L	6-1	224	2-18-01	.198	.303	.328	39	152	131	15	26	3	1	4	14	17	3	0	1	33	5	0	11.2	21.7
Mervis, Matt	L-R	6-2	225	4-16-98	.250	.310	.614	35	145	132	27	33	5	2	13	30	11	0	1	1	39	4	0	7.6	26.9
Mesa, Victor	L-L	6-0	195	9-8-01	.301	.368	.510	42	171	153	19	46	9	1	7	30	17	0	0	1	28	4	1	9.9	16.4
Morissette, Cody	L-R	6-0	175	1-16-00	.290	.446	.333	18	63	56	6	12	5	1	2	8	6	0	0	1	20	5	0	9.5	31.7
Myers, Dane	R-R	6-0	205	3-8-96	.167	.333	.167	4	15	12	3	2	0	0	0	1	3	0	0	0	4	0	0	20.0	26.7
Navarreto, Brian	R-R	6-2	233	12-29-94	.229	.301	.392	47	176	153	22	35	5	1	6	27	16	2	0	5	39	3	0	9.1	22.2
Norby, Connor	R-R	5-9	180	6-28-00	.343	.400	.629	11	40	35	6	12	1	0	3	8	4	0	0	1	8	0	0	10.0	20.0
Olmstead, Johnny	R-R	6-2	185	7-10-00	.198	.298	.306	34	132	111	15	22	5	2	1	12	16	1	1	3	31	9	4	12.1	23.5
Pauley, Graham	L-R	6-1	200	9-24-00	.263	.342	.511	37	155	137	19	36	10	0	8	21	14	3	0	1	18	5	0	9.0	11.6
Pintar, Andrew	R-R	6-2	190	3-23-01	.269	.338	.384	84	332	297	38	80	18	2	4	32	27	5	0	2	98	23	4	8.1	29.5
Ramirez, Agustin	R-R	6-0	210	9-10-01	.254	.313	.479	19	80	71	13	18	7	0	3	12	7	0	0	2	19	5	0	8.8	23.8
Richardson, Grant	L-L	6-0	210	7-13-99	.333	.333	.333	2	3	3	1	1	0	0	0	0	0	0	0	0	1	0	0	0.0	33.3
Rosario, Dalvy	R-R	6-0	185	7-22-00	.143	.222	.286	19	64	56	6	8	0	1	2	5	6	0	1	1	19	0	0	9.4	29.7
Sanchez, Jesus	L-R	6-3	225	10-7-97	.300	.364	.400	3	11	10	2	3	1	0	0	0	1	0	0	0	3	1	0	9.1	27.3
Sasaki, Shane	R-R	5-11	195	7-1-00	.221	.308	.250	23	80	68	11	15	2	0	0	10	7	2	2	1	14	6	1	8.8	17.5
Serna, Jared	R-R	5-6	168	6-1-02	.235	.366	.294	10	41	34	7	8	2	0	0	2	7	0	0	0	6	5	0	17.1	14.6
Simon, Ronny	S-R	5-7	150	4-17-00	.354	.441	.521	15	60	48	8	17	1	2	1	9	9	0	1	2	10	4	1	15.0	16.7
Spohn, Harrison	R-R	6-1	185	12-9-01	.155	.285	.175	39	123	103	7	16	2	0	0	10	18	1	0	1	54	2	3	14.6	43.9
Stowers, Kyle	L-L	6-3	215	1-2-98	.000	.250	.000	1	4	3	0	0	0	0	0	0	1	0	0	0	0	0	0	25.0	0.0
Wiemer, Joey	R-R	6-4	220	2-11-99	.364	.488	.697	10	41	33	6	12	5	0	2	10	7	1	0	0	8	1	1	17.1	19.5
Winkler, Jack	R-R	6-2	185	11-4-98	.225	.299	.333	76	281	249	34	56	9	0	6	26	26	2	0	4	79	25	0	9.3	28.1

MIAMI MARLINS

Pitching	B-T	Ht.	Wt.	DOB	W	L	ERA	G	GS	SV	IP	Hits	Runs	ER	HR	BB	SO	AVG	OBP	SLG	SO%	BB%	BF
Arias, Luarbert	R-R	6-2	176	12-12-00	2	1	5.40	18	1	0	23	23	18	14	2	18	10	.271	.394	.471	9.1	16.4	110
Bachar, Lake	R-R	6-2	219	6-3-95	0	0	3.00	3	0	1	3	2	1	1	0	1	6	.200	.273	.300	54.5	9.1	11
Belgrave, Nigel	R-R	6-4	195	5-12-02	0	0	0.00	5	1	1	5	1	1	0	0	1	7	.067	.176	.067	41.2	5.9	17
Bellozo, Valente	R-R	5-10	170	1-4-00	1	0	1.40	5	4	0	19	16	3	3	0	7	19	.229	.308	.300	24.4	9.0	78
Bramwell, Spencer	R-R	5-11	220	1-10-99	0	1	4.50	1	0	0	2	1	2	1	0	3	0	.143	.455	.143	0.0	27.3	11
Cabrera, Edward	R-R	6-5	217	4-13-98	0	0	2.57	2	2	0	7	9	3	2	1	0	10	.310	.310	.517	34.5	0.0	29
Cronin, Declan	R-R	6-4	225	9-24-97	1	0	4.87	21	2	0	20	18	12	11	2	14	20	.240	.367	.387	22.2	15.6	90
Curry, Xzavion	R-R	6-0	195	7-27-98	1	1	8.04	10	3	0	16	17	15	14	6	13	8	.274	.400	.597	10.7	17.3	75
de Geus, Brett	R-R	6-2	190	11-4-97	0	0	13.50	1	0	0	1	5	4	2	0	0	1	.556	.556	.556	11.1	0.0	9
Ekness, Josh	R-R	6-4	225	2-7-02	0	0	60.75	3	0	0	1	6	9	9	3	5	2	.600	.750	1.200	12.5	31.3	16
Fulton, Dax	L-L	6-7	235	10-16-01	0	1	5.51	4	4	0	16	23	12	10	0	10	19	.329	.410	.386	22.9	12.0	83
Genao, Manuel	R-R	6-1	150	11-11-05	0	0	10.80	1	0	0	2	2	2	2	0	3	2	.333	.583	.333	16.7	25.0	12
Gibson, Cade	L-L	6-2	195	2-18-98	1	1	2.70	9	0	1	20	15	7	6	1	1	7	.25	.200	.277	.280	30.1	8.4	83
Gillispie, Connor	R-R	5-11	185	11-10-97	3	0	4.28	8	7	0	34	22	19	16	7	16	22	.186	.290	.415	15.7	11.4	140
Go, Woo Suk	R-R	5-11	198	8-6-98	0	0	1.59	5	0	0	6	6	1	1	1	1	5	.273	.304	.455	21.7	4.3	23
Gusto, Ryan	R-R	6-2	232	3-11-99	1	0	10.38	2	2	0	4	10	6	5	0	2	2	.455	.480	.545	8.0	8.0	25
Junk, Janson	R-R	6-2	202	1-15-96	5	3	2.68	10	9	0	50	41	16	15	2	7	48	.220	.246	.296	24.6	3.6	195
Kempner, William	R-R	6-0	222	6-18-01	3	0	2.65	13	0	1	17	8	5	5	2	15	25	.138	.342	.241	32.9	19.7	76
King, Justin	L-L	6-1	215	12-19-97	0	0	5.79	4	0	0	5	5	7	3	1	4	8	.250	.375	.550	33.3	16.7	24
Laskey, Adam	R-L	6-3	205	3-9-98	4	4	4.68	16	9	0	33	31	18	17	7	19	25	.254	.368	.492	17.1	13.0	146
Martin, Colby	R-R	5-11	195	4-2-01	0	0	0.00	2	0	0	2	1	1	0	0	1	1	.167	.286	.167	14.3	14.3	7
Martinez, Seth	R-R	6-2	200	8-29-94	3	2	3.71	41	1	8	44	37	22	18	3	18	54	.224	.312	.331	28.9	9.6	187
Mazur, Adam	R-R	6-2	180	4-20-01	6	7	4.36	22	19	0	107	109	58	52	21	30	100	.267	.319	.465	22.2	6.7	450
McCambley, Zach	L-R	6-2	210	5-4-99	1	3	3.32	36	0	1	41	33	17	15	2	15	52	.224	.311	.313	30.8	8.9	169
McSweeney, Morgan	R-R	6-4	210	9-21-97	3	3	2.21	13	12	0	61	45	16	15	3	23	42	.205	.283	.288	17.1	9.3	246
Monteverde, Patrick	R-L	6-2	200	9-24-97	5	1	4.66	25	15	0	95	91	49	49	19	32	85	.253	.312	.464	21.4	8.1	397
Nastrini, Nick	R-R	6-3	215	2-18-00	0	0	9.00	1	1	0	2	2	2	2	0	4	1	.000	.538	.000	7.7	30.8	13
Palacios, Luis	L-L	6-2	160	7-1-00	0	3	6.59	6	2	0	14	20	10	10	1	11	6	.333	.437	.433	8.5	15.5	71
Perez, Eury	R-R	6-8	220	4-15-03	1	1	2.13	3	3	0	13	7	4	3	1	7	15	.156	.264	.267	28.3	13.2	53
Petersen, Michael	R-R	6-7	195	5-16-94	0	1	6.00	12	1	1	12	11	8	8	3	5	19	.239	.327	.522	36.5	9.6	52
Pilar, Anderson	R-R	6-2	208	4-29-98	5	1	4.26	37	2	4	44	40	24	21	2	13	50	.234	.309	.359	25.9	6.7	193
Pina, Robinson	R-R	6-5	225	11-26-98	4	3	3.47	13	11	0	57	53	26	22	4	15	54	.243	.309	.376	22.2	6.2	243
Pushard, Matt	R-R	6-4	245	10-27-97	4	5	3.61	49	1	4	62	49	27	25	3	23	73	.214	.290	.297	28.5	9.0	256
Ramsey, Lane	R-R	6-9	245	7-1-96	0	0	6.00	4	0	1	3	3	2	2	0	1	3	.273	.333	.364	25.0	8.3	12
Roa, Christian	R-R	6-4	220	4-2-99	10	2	2.83	50	2	0	60	38	20	19	6	28	64	.180	.290	.303	26.1	11.4	245
Roberts, Austin	R-R	6-0	205	7-27-98	2	1	4.67	24	1	1	35	34	20	18	5	18	35	.256	.342	.414	22.9	11.8	153
Rooney, John	R-L	6-5	215	7-28-97	2	1	2.45	38	0	4	33	19	9	9	2	23	45	.174	.295	.248	32.4	16.5	139
Simpson, Josh	L-L	6-2	190	8-19-97	3	1	3.41	29	2	3	34	19	13	13	1	16	29	.164	.267	.224	21.3	11.8	136
Snelling, Robby	R-L	6-3	210	12-19-03	6	2	1.27	11	11	0	64	46	11	9	4	17	81	.203	.260	.313	32.9	6.9	246
Soriano, George	R-R	6-3	210	3-24-99	4	1	2.32	29	1	2	43	27	15	11	3	15	49	.178	.265	.283	28.8	8.8	170
Stanavich, Dale	L-L	5-11	175	6-23-99	2	1	5.46	25	1	1	28	30	21	17	6	31	26	.286	.454	.486	18.4	22.0	141
Tarnok, Freddy	R-R	6-3	185	11-24-98	4	2	3.28	29	10	4	69	46	26	25	7	31	73	.189	.281	.324	26.3	11.2	278
Tineo, Riskiel	R-R	6-2	180	2-23-00	0	1	5.14	4	1	0	7	12	7	4	1	4	7	.364	.432	.545	18.9	10.8	37
Veneziani, Anthony	L-L	6-5	205	9-1-97	0	0	5.84	12	1	0	12	12	8	8	2	9	12	.267	.382	.422	21.8	16.4	55
Weathers, Ryan	R-L	6-1	230	12-17-99	1	1	2.40	4	0	15	3	4	1	1	7	16	.232	.317	.304	25.4	11.1	63
White, Josh	R-R	6-1	205	11-24-00	4	1	2.29	27	2	4	39	27	11	10	2	11	57	.193	.247	.286	37.0	7.1	154
White, Thomas	L-L	6-5	210	9-29-04	0	0	3.86	2	2	0	9	3	5	4	0	10	7	.111	.359	.148	42.5	25.0	40
Williams, Alex	L-R	6-3	220	10-22-99	0	0	11.57	1	1	0	5	7	6	6	2	2	2	.350	.417	.650	8.3	8.3	24
Zuber, Tyler	R-R	5-11	195	6-16-95	1	0	3.60	7	0	0	10	7	4	4	2	4	12	.206	.325	.382	30.0	10.0	40

Fielding

Catcher	PCT	G	PO	A	E	DP	PB
Bramwell	1.000	2	8	0	0	0	0
Brantly	1.000	6	47	1	0	0	0
Fortes	1.000	1	12	0	0	0	1
Hostetler	1.000	17	117	7	0	0	3
Mack	.987	75	695	43	10	9	7
Navarreto	.990	41	362	22	4	1	2
Ramirez	.993	14	135	9	1	1	7

First Base	PCT	G	PO	A	E	DP
Berry	1.000	4	30	0	0	2
Brantly	1.000	1	2	1	0	0
De Los Santos	.989	65	422	46	5	39
Johnston	.987	33	223	13	3	22
Martorella	.989	25	159	17	2	20
Mervis	.990	27	191	17	2	22
Pauley	1.000	1	8	1	0	0

Second Base	PCT	G	PO	A	E	DP
Acosta	1.000	5	6	12	0	1
Berry	.969	58	96	120	7	43
Edwards	1.000	1	2	3	0	0
Gleed	1.000	1	3	3	0	2
Hostetler	1.000	2	2	4	0	1
Lopez	1.000	1	0	3	0	1
Morissette	.967	15	20	39	2	8

	PCT	G	PO	A	E	DP	PB
Olmstead	.971	18	22	45	2	8	
Pauley	1.000	3	4	5	0	2	
Serna	.895	5	7	10	2	1	
Simon	.919	11	14	20	3	2	
Spohn	.963	23	30	49	3	14	
Winkler	.957	12	17	28	2	5	

Third Base	PCT	G	PO	A	E	DP
Berry	.886	20	12	27	5	1
Bullard	.500	1	0	1	1	0
De Los Santos	.932	28	23	32	4	3
Hostetler	1.000	11	16	10	0	2
Morissette	1.000	1	1	0	0	0
Norby	.909	9	1	9	1	0
Olmstead	1.000	2	2	2	0	1
Pauley	.959	31	29	65	4	8
Simon	.900	3	6	3	1	0
Spohn	.909	3	5	5	1	1
Winkler	.953	51	33	110	7	13

Shortstop	PCT	G	PO	A	E	DP
Acosta	.962	110	142	234	15	52
Olmstead	.918	14	16	29	4	6
Serna	.962	5	14	11	1	2
Spohn	1.000	13	16	22	0	4
Winkler	.963	11	16	10	1	3

Outfield	PCT	G	PO	A	E	DP
Alderman	1.000	18	23	1	0	0
Almora	.977	40	83	1	2	1
Berry	1.000	37	55	2	0	1
Bullard	.667	1	2	0	1	0
Coley	.900	7	9	0	1	0
Conine	1.000	6	5	0	0	0
Etzel	1.000	30	47	0	0	0
Hernandez	.976	23	41	0	1	0
Hill	1.000	4	9	0	0	0
Hostetler	1.000	3	1	0	0	0
Johnston	.970	32	62	2	2	0
Marsee	.983	99	228	4	4	0
Mesa	1.000	37	67	5	0	1
Morissette	.000	1	0	0	0	0
Myers	1.000	3	5	0	0	0
Pintar	.973	83	142	0	4	0
Richardson	1.000	2	1	0	0	0
Rosario	1.000	19	36	1	0	0
Sanchez	1.000	1	1	0	0	0
Sasaki	1.000	22	41	0	0	0
Wiemer	.941	10	14	2	1	0
Winkler	.000	1	0	0	0	0

PENSACOLA BLUE WAHOOS
SOUTHERN LEAGUE

DOUBLE-A

Batting	B-T	Ht.	Wt.	DOB	AVG	OBP	SLG	G	PA	AB	R	H	2B	3B	HR	RBI	BB	HBP	SH	SF	SO	SB	CS	BB%	SO%
Alderman, Kemp	R-R	6-3	265	8-20-02	.282	.337	.447	110	454	412	56	116	13	5	15	53	34	3	0	5	102	20	9	7.5	22.5
Beshears, Jay	R-R	6-4	215	5-6-02	.289	.308	.421	9	39	38	2	11	2	0	1	5	0	1	0	0	8	0	0	0.0	20.5
Boyd, Emaarion	R-R	5-11	177	8-22-03	.267	.353	.383	19	68	60	8	16	4	0	1	3	6	2	0	0	16	8	5	8.8	23.5
Bramwell, Spencer	R-R	5-11	220	1-10-99	.163	.221	.296	45	145	135	10	22	3	0	5	10	10	0	0	0	57	3	3	6.9	39.3
Bullard, Tony	R-R	6-4	212	2-17-00	.234	.291	.437	44	172	158	20	37	9	1	7	24	12	1	0	1	41	4	0	7.0	23.8
Cappe, Yiddi	R-R	6-3	175	9-17-02	.158	.190	.158	6	21	19	1	3	0	0	0	2	1	0	0	1	4	1	0	4.8	19.0
Caskenette, Connor	R-R	6-0	215	6-14-02	.244	.333	.289	14	52	45	7	11	2	0	0	4	4	2	0	0	13	1	1	7.7	25.0
Clayton, Cam	R-R	6-1	185	7-6-02	.250	.214	.417	4	14	12	0	3	2	0	0	3	0	0	0	2	1	0	0	0.0	7.1
Coley, Mark	R-R	6-2	193	11-22-00	.253	.329	.369	72	280	249	32	63	12	1	5	31	23	6	0	2	86	18	6	8.2	30.7
Etzel, Matthew	L-R	6-2	211	4-30-02	.273	.333	.636	3	12	11	1	3	0	2	0	2	1	0	0	0	2	1	0	8.3	16.7
Gleed, Dub	R-R	6-1	195	9-1-02	.276	.360	.391	26	102	87	9	24	7	0	1	7	11	1	1	1	20	1	3	10.8	19.6
Green, Payton	R-R	6-3	190	1-17-03	.237	.330	.344	27	107	93	11	22	4	0	2	8	11	2	0	0	24	3	1	10.3	22.4
Hernandez, Jesus	R-R	5-9	150	2-20-04	.250	.250	.250	1	4	4	0	1	0	0	0	0	0	0	0	0	1	0	0	0.0	25.0
Ignoffo, Ryan	R-R	5-10	215	7-21-00	.322	.376	.478	34	125	115	25	37	7	1	3	20	9	1	0	0	17	5	2	7.2	13.6
Mack, Joe	L-R	6-1	210	12-27-02	.318	.464	.614	13	56	44	12	14	4	0	3	5	10	2	0	0	12	1	0	17.9	21.4
Martorella, Nathan	L-L	6-1	224	2-18-01	.203	.305	.338	94	394	340	39	69	16	0	10	48	48	3	0	3	75	6	3	12.2	19.0
Miller, Gage	R-R	6-0	200	3-1-03	.226	.314	.339	17	70	62	10	14	1	0	2	5	7	1	0	0	12	1	2	10.0	17.1
Morissette, Cody	L-R	6-0	175	1-16-00	.232	.318	.338	67	269	228	34	53	9	0	5	29	32	0	2	7	58	14	4	11.9	21.6
Olmstead, Johnny	R-R	6-2	185	7-10-00	.227	.290	.381	93	373	339	59	77	15	2	11	35	27	4	1	2	62	16	5	7.2	16.6
Praytor, Sam	R-R	5-9	205	4-4-99	.209	.320	.302	43	152	129	8	27	4	1	2	12	18	3	2	0	30	7	2	11.8	19.7
Rataczak, Eric	L-R	6-3	215	1-19-01	.217	.277	.283	18	65	60	4	13	4	0	0	6	5	0	0	0	22	2	1	7.7	33.8
Richardson, Grant	L-L	6-0	210	7-13-99	.237	.288	.454	28	104	97	18	23	7	0	6	20	7	0	0	0	43	5	2	6.7	41.3
Rios, Nestor	R-R	5-9	175	1-4-05	.500	.667	.500	1	3	2	0	1	0	0	0	0	1	0	0	0	0	0	0	33.3	0.0
Rosario, Dalvy	R-R	6-0	185	7-22-00	.192	.258	.292	39	134	120	15	23	3	0	3	12	11	0	2	1	43	6	2	8.2	32.1
Sasaki, Shane	R-R	5-11	165	7-1-00	.227	.313	.309	73	270	233	23	53	12	2	1	20	30	0	5	2	70	24	2	11.1	25.9
Serna, Jared	R-R	5-6	168	6-1-02	.223	.305	.277	101	437	386	51	86	8	2	3	28	42	5	1	3	69	15	10	9.6	15.8
Shade, Colby	R-R	6-1	205	8-18-01	.170	.362	.208	20	70	53	5	9	2	0	0	3	11	5	1	0	20	5	2	15.7	28.6
Snyder, Michael	R-R	6-4	205	9-16-00	.255	.371	.325	54	237	200	22	51	8	0	2	22	34	3	0	0	46	10	1	14.3	19.4
Spohn, Harrison	R-R	6-1	185	12-3-98	.235	.297	.294	12	37	34	5	8	0	1	0	6	3	0	0	0	13	0	1	8.1	35.1
Thompson, Jake	L-R	6-0	207	3-3-98	.225	.343	.320	54	216	178	14	40	12	1	1	17	32	2	0	4	50	3	2	14.8	23.1
Trimble, Fenwick	R-R	6-3	200	8-29-02	.237	.355	.395	54	229	190	23	45	12	0	6	27	27	7	1	2	43	16	3	12.7	18.8
Zamora, Joshua	R-R	5-10	190	5-18-99	.213	.297	.328	86	341	296	36	63	10	0	8	29	33	4	3	4	58	4	1	9.7	17.0

Pitching	B-T	Ht.	Wt.	DOB	W	L	ERA	G	GS	SV	IP	Hits	Runs	ER	HR	BB	SO	AVG	OBP	SLG	SO%	BB%	BF
Arias, Luarbert	R-R	6-2	176	12-12-00	0	0	7.11	5	1	0	6	8	5	5	0	4	6	.308	.419	.308	19.4	12.9	31
Belgrave, Nigel	R-R	6-4	195	5-12-02	5	2	2.71	36	0	5	63	42	22	19	3	28	85	.186	.290	.265	32.7	10.8	260
Bergin, Jesse	R-R	6-4	205	10-8-99	2	4	2.51	35	0	5	43	25	18	12	4	17	41	.168	.256	.268	23.7	9.8	173
Bierman, Gabe	R-R	6-2	200	9-3-99	1	2	4.58	14	0	0	20	22	11	10	2	12	18	.289	.385	.395	19.8	13.2	91
Brooks, Jake	R-R	6-4	202	7-8-01	2	2	4.58	7	7	0	39	39	21	20	3	9	32	.264	.306	.385	19.8	5.6	162
Buxton, Ike	R-R	6-3	208	7-18-00	0	2	9.00	8	5	0	20	20	20	20	1	22	10	.270	.455	.338	9.9	21.8	101
Centala, Chase	R-R	6-1	175	3-18-02	0	0	0.00	2	0	0	3	1	0	0	0	0	0	.111	.111	.111	0.0	0.0	9
DeVito, Ricky	S-R	6-3	195	8-21-98	1	0	4.23	19	0	0	28	16	15	13	0	26	31	.176	.402	.198	24.0	20.2	129
Ekness, Josh	R-R	6-4	225	2-7-02	4	1	2.73	43	0	10	53	40	25	16	0	21	66	.205	.312	.226	28.6	9.1	231
Fitterer, Evan	R-R	6-3	192	6-26-00	7	6	3.42	33	10	1	95	79	42	36	4	42	94	.230	.322	.314	23.6	10.6	398
Fulton, Dax	L-L	6-7	235	10-16-01	5	10	5.36	19	18	0	87	86	59	52	5	49	96	.253	.354	.362	24.0	12.3	400
Johnson, M.D.	R-R	6-5	200	7-7-97	0	0	3.00	2	0	0	3	2	1	1	1	3	3	.200	.385	.500	23.1	23.1	13
Kempner, William	R-R	6-0	222	6-18-01	3	1	1.13	16	0	0	24	11	4	3	0	15	31	.139	.292	.215	32.3	15.6	96
King, Justin	L-L	6-1	215	12-19-97	0	2	3.18	27	0	0	28	24	16	10	1	26	33	.233	.398	.291	24.6	19.4	134
Laskey, Adam	R-L	6-3	205	3-9-98	2	5	3.76	11	10	0	53	55	26	22	1	13	50	.272	.321	.361	22.8	5.9	219
Martin, Colby	R-R	5-11	195	4-2-01	1	1	2.57	10	0	0	14	11	5	4	0	7	19	.216	.310	.255	32.8	12.1	58
McCambley, Zach	L-R	6-2	220	5-4-99	0	0	2.11	11	0	0	21	13	5	5	1	7	31	.176	.247	.270	37.8	8.5	82
Meachem, Xavier	R-R	5-11	210	9-6-02	0	1	13.50	2	0	0	1	4	2	2	0	1	3	.444	.500	.444	30.0	10.0	10
Milbrandt, Karson	R-R	6-2	190	4-21-04	1	0	1.69	2	2	0	11	8	2	2	1	4	10	.200	.289	.200	22.2	8.9	45
Miller, Jacob	R-R	6-2	180	8-10-03	3	7	4.59	23	22	0	118	109	71	60	6	56	110	.244	.333	.339	21.4	10.9	514
Ortiz-Mayr, Orlando	R-R	6-3	195	12-6-97	6	6	3.82	24	20	0	97	74	42	41	9	61	90	.210	.337	.310	21.2	14.4	425
Palacios, Luis	L-L	6-2	160	7-1-00	4	3	2.83	27	7	1	70	56	29	22	5	27	58	.220	.303	.311	20.0	9.3	290
Polanco, Natanael	R-R	6-1	170	4-24-03	0	0	0.00	1	0	0	3	2	0	0	0	2	0	.200	.200	.200	0.0	20.0	10
Ramsey, Lane	R-R	6-9	245	7-16-96	0	1	3.07	10	0	1	15	9	6	5	1	3	21	.184	.226	.306	38.9	5.6	54
Roberts, Austin	R-R	6-0	205	7-27-98	2	0	0.00	4	0	1	6	4	3	0	0	4	9	.190	.296	.238	33.3	14.8	27
Schomberg, Will	R-R	5-10	170	1-30-01	1	1	1.71	4	3	0	21	15	5	4	1	4	26	.208	.250	.264	32.5	5.0	80
Sellinger, Jack	R-L	6-2	200	11-20-99	0	0	2.16	5	0	0	8	4	3	2	0	4	11	.138	.265	.138	32.4	11.8	34
Snelling, Robby	R-L	6-3	210	12-19-03	3	5	3.61	14	14	0	72	66	32	29	6	22	85	.238	.299	.347	28.2	7.3	301
Stanavich, Dale	L-L	5-11	175	6-23-99	2	1	1.29	19	0	6	28	13	6	4	2	15	41	.135	.272	.198	35.3	12.9	116
Stevens, Tristan	R-R	6-2	200	12-8-97	0	0	7.71	4	0	0	5	4	4	4	2	1	2	.267	.300	.667	25.0	5.0	20
Tineo, Riskiel	R-R	6-3	190	2-27-03	0	0	0.00	2	0	0	3	2	0	0	0	2	3	.200	.385	.300	23.1	15.4	13
White, Josh	R-R	6-1	205	11-24-00	6	0	1.27	18	0	0	12	5	4	0	12	50	.126	.231	.168	46.3	11.1	108
White, Thomas	L-L	6-5	210	9-29-04	2	1	1.59	10	10	0	45	30	9	8	2	24	75	.183	.298	.244	39.3	12.6	191
Williams, Alex	L-R	6-3	220	10-22-99	5	4	4.43	19	9	1	67	74	39	33	3	25	63	.270	.341	.361	20.6	8.2	306

MIAMI MARLINS

Fielding

Catcher	PCT	G	PO	A	E	DP	PB
Bramwell	.986	44	389	29	6	2	4
Caskenette	.970	14	122	9	4	0	1
Ignoffo	.997	33	269	40	1	1	4
Mack	.992	10	107	10	1	1	2
Praytor	.991	43	396	29	4	3	5
Rios	1.000	1	6	1	0	0	0

First Base	PCT	G	PO	A	E	DP
Beshears	1.000	3	24	3	0	0
Bramwell	1.000	1	1	0	0	0
Bullard	.994	19	147	6	1	7
Gleed	.992	15	118	6	1	11
Martorella	.994	80	631	47	4	49
Snyder	1.000	10	55	4	0	4
Thompson	1.000	5	34	0	0	3
Zamora	1.000	13	70	10	0	9

Second Base	PCT	G	PO	A	E	DP
Beshears	.800	1	1	3	1	1
Cappe	1.000	4	1	9	0	2
Green	.970	10	7	25	1	2

	PCT	G	PO	A	E	DP
Miller	1.000	12	14	30	0	5
Morissette	.978	48	63	111	4	20
Olmstead	.954	34	39	86	6	16
Rosario	.000	1	0	0	0	0
Serna	1.000	21	31	43	0	13
Spohn	1.000	5	3	12	0	2
Zamora	.941	4	6	10	1	5

Third Base	PCT	G	PO	A	E	DP
Beshears	1.000	2	2	3	0	0
Bullard	.795	16	11	24	9	1
Cappe	1.000	1	1	1	0	0
Gleed	.909	9	8	12	2	0
Green	1.000	5	3	4	0	0
Hernandez	.000	1	0	0	1	0
Miller	1.000	5	6	6	0	1
Morissette	.950	9	8	11	1	2
Olmstead	.969	11	9	22	1	1
Rosario	.000	1	0	0	0	0
Snyder	.983	24	12	46	1	2
Spohn	1.000	5	0	7	0	1
Zamora	.953	55	39	104	7	11

Shortstop	PCT	G	PO	A	E	DP
Clayton	1.000	4	5	7	0	1
Green	1.000	12	6	30	0	7
Olmstead	.971	44	65	100	5	26
Serna	.962	77	97	179	11	30
Spohn	1.000	3	2	8	0	1

Outfield	PCT	G	PO	A	E	DP
Alderman	.951	91	133	2	7	0
Boyd	.962	14	25	0	1	0
Coley	.969	63	124	1	4	0
Etzel	1.000	2	4	2	0	0
Martorella	.000	1	0	0	0	0
Rataczak	.950	13	19	0	1	0
Richardson	.971	25	32	1	1	0
Rosario	.985	34	61	3	1	0
Sasaki	.984	66	119	2	2	0
Shade	1.000	18	36	1	0	0
Snyder	1.000	16	21	1	0	0
Thompson	1.000	33	38	2	0	0
Trimble	.990	49	93	4	1	0

BELOIT SKY CARP — HIGH-A
MIDWEST LEAGUE

Batting	B-T	Ht.	Wt.	DOB	AVG	OBP	SLG	G	PA	AB	R	H	2B	3B	HR	RBI	BB	HBP	SH	SF	SO	SB	CS	BB%	SO%
Arquette, Aiva	R-R	6-4	200	10-17-03	.242	.350	.323	27	117	99	11	24	5	0	1	10	17	0	0	1	27	7	2	14.5	23.1
Beshears, Jay	R-R	6-4	215	5-6-02	.201	.328	.355	49	204	169	25	34	8	3	4	18	30	3	0	2	50	4	2	14.7	24.5
Boyd, Emaarion	R-R	5-11	177	8-22-03	.235	.333	.317	82	289	243	37	57	10	2	2	27	28	11	1	6	52	43	12	9.7	18.0
Cannarella, Cam	L-R	6-0	170	9-6-03	.284	.337	.375	22	95	88	11	25	6	1	0	6	7	0	0	0	18	1	3	7.4	18.9
Cappe, Yiddi	R-R	6-3	175	9-7-02	.278	.330	.377	53	233	212	33	59	9	0	4	26	18	0	0	3	48	28	7	7.7	20.6
Caskenette, Connor	R-R	6-0	215	6-14-02	.240	.378	.305	48	193	154	16	37	8	1	0	20	33	3	0	3	37	11	3	17.1	19.2
Compton, Brandon	L-L	6-1	210	10-27-03	.217	.354	.359	27	113	92	9	20	3	2	2	17	19	1	0	1	37	8	1	16.8	32.7
Forrester, Garret	R-R	6-3	208	11-11-01	.241	.386	.310	66	272	216	31	52	7	1	2	27	44	9	0	3	65	12	1	16.2	23.9
Green, Payton	R-R	6-3	190	1-17-03	.278	.345	.427	65	275	241	30	67	14	2	6	33	24	4	0	6	63	6	6	8.7	22.9
Head, Dillon	L-L	5-11	180	10-11-04	.333	.500	.333	1	4	3	0	1	0	0	0	0	1	0	0	0	1	1	0	25.0	25.0
Hernandez, Jesus	R-R	5-9	150	2-20-04	.215	.342	.319	41	162	135	17	29	8	0	2	16	21	5	0	0	40	11	4	13.0	24.7
Ignoffo, Ryan	R-R	5-10	215	7-10-01	.225	.294	.431	40	180	160	23	36	13	1	6	39	16	1	0	3	27	8	1	8.9	15.0
Jaworsky, Chase	L-R	6-1	170	7-31-04	.154	.340	.231	13	50	39	6	6	0	1	0	2	8	3	0	0	13	7	1	16.0	26.0
Jenkins-Cowart, Jacob	L-R	6-6	216	12-24-02	.183	.269	.269	60	223	197	21	36	12	1	1	10	21	3	0	2	55	20	9	9.4	24.7
Lara, Wilfredo	R-R	5-10	180	4-28-04	.182	.277	.307	66	268	231	25	42	10	5	3	27	30	2	1	4	60	15	7	11.2	22.4
Lewis, Ian	S-R	5-11	177	2-4-03	.314	.362	.410	27	116	105	10	33	8	1	0	9	8	1	0	2	17	19	3	6.9	14.7
McDowell, Micah	L-R	6-2	175	1-27-01	.216	.344	.314	33	122	102	8	22	4	3	0	12	19	1	0	0	28	2	2	15.6	23.0
Miller, Gage	R-R	6-0	200	3-1-03	.207	.329	.308	85	356	299	36	62	14	2	4	26	48	7	0	2	53	20	4	13.5	14.9
Rataczak, Eric	L-R	6-3	215	1-19-01	.229	.361	.368	63	250	201	28	46	6	2	6	34	41	3	0	4	68	8	3	16.4	27.2
Rios, Nestor	R-R	5-9	175	1-4-05	.105	.182	.105	6	23	19	1	2	0	0	0	1	2	0	1	1	9	0	0	8.7	39.1
Schrier, Cody	R-R	6-1	201	3-3-03	.145	.254	.291	18	63	55	5	8	2	0	2	6	6	2	0	0	18	2	1	9.5	28.6
Shade, Colby	R-R	6-1	205	8-18-01	.246	.386	.342	71	295	240	47	59	12	4	1	19	44	11	0	0	71	48	5	14.9	24.1
Snyder, Michael	R-R	6-4	205	9-16-00	.248	.391	.403	52	211	161	26	40	11	0	4	37	41	4	0	5	43	17	1	19.4	20.4
Trimble, Fenwick	R-R	6-3	200	8-29-02	.284	.407	.422	29	123	102	16	29	7	2	1	14	20	1	0	0	23	15	1	16.3	18.7
Vargas, Echedry	R-R	5-11	170	2-27-05	.201	.255	.322	82	323	298	38	60	11	2	7	29	17	5	1	2	80	8	2	5.3	24.8
Vradenburg, Brock	L-R	6-7	230	5-20-00	.172	.290	.279	66	252	215	29	37	11	3	2	22	36	0	0	1	60	12	0	14.3	23.8
Weber, Wilson	R-R	6-0	200	5-16-02	.172	.264	.234	17	72	64	6	11	1	0	1	6	4	0	0	0	31	1	0	5.6	43.1

Pitching	B-T	Ht.	Wt.	DOB	W	L	ERA	G	GS	SV	IP	Hits	Runs	ER	HR	BB	SO	AVG	OBP	SLG	SO%	BB%	BF
Bergin, Jesse	R-R	6-4	205	10-8-99	1	0	2.00	5	0	2	9	7	2	2	0	4	16	.219	.316	.281	42.1	10.5	38
Bierman, Gabe	R-R	6-2	200	9-3-99	2	1	2.63	23	0	4	41	38	19	12	1	27	44	.239	.370	.321	22.7	13.9	194
Boyd, Emaarion	R-R	5-11	177	8-22-03	0	0	0.00	1	0	0	1	1	0	0	0	0	0	.333	.333	.333	0.0	0.0	3
Brink, Nick	R-R	6-2	210	9-27-01	8	4	2.94	17	16	0	89	84	34	29	4	32	55	.250	.315	.339	14.8	8.6	371
Brooks, Jake	R-R	6-4	202	7-8-01	6	6	4.21	16	16	0	77	82	39	36	3	15	65	.279	.329	.371	20.1	4.6	323
Buxton, Ike	R-R	6-3	208	7-18-00	3	2	2.10	8	2	0	26	19	8	6	1	15	28	.204	.333	.269	24.6	13.2	114
Centala, Chase	R-R	6-1	175	10-21-00	6	8	4.68	28	8	0	40	51	25	21	15	3	11	29	.234	.308	.388	18.1	6.9	160
Cuthbertson, Hayden	L-L	6-2	200	1-19-04	1	0	0.00	4	0	0	5	1	0	0	0	2	6	.067	.222	.067	33.3	11.1	18
Dishmey, Eliazar	R-R	6-1	175	10-25-04	2	0	2.19	5	5	0	25	16	6	6	1	6	32	.184	.237	.253	34.4	6.5	93
Fosher, Peyton	R-R	6-1	200	4-30-03	1	0	0.00	4	0	0	8	1	0	0	0	3	6	.040	.172	.080	20.7	10.3	29
Go, Woo Suk	R-R	5-11	198	8-6-98	0	0	6.75	2	0	0	3	3	2	2	0	2	2	.333	.455	.444	18.2	18.2	11
Jones, Holt	R-R	6-8	235	5-8-99	7	3	4.75	34	0	1	47	47	36	25	2	42	62	.261	.423	.350	26.3	17.8	236
Kempner, William	R-R	6-0	222	6-18-01	1	2	3.04	19	0	6	27	19	11	9	0	10	39	.196	.291	.289	35.1	9.0	111
Lashutka, Luke	R-R	6-2	195	5-24-02	1	3	2.67	10	9	0	30	23	10	9	3	9	32	.204	.288	.336	25.6	7.2	125
Laws, Carson	R-R	6-1	186	3-31-03	2	0	5.87	7	0	1	8	5	5	5	1	6	9	.179	.324	.321	26.5	17.6	34
Maldonado, Nick	R-R	6-1	207	6-12-00	1	1	4.91	13	0	2	22	18	14	12	6	8	18	.220	.286	.341	19.8	8.8	91
Martin, Colby	R-R	5-11	195	4-2-01	1	2	2.45	11	0	4	11	7	3	3	0	3	7	.184	.304	.237	37.0	15.2	46

Batting	B-T	Ht.	Wt.	DOB			AVG	OBP	SLG	G	PA	AB	R	H	2B	3B	HR	RBI	BB	HBP	SH	SF	SO	SB	CS	BB%	SO%
Meachem, Xavier	R-R	5-11	210	9-6-02	1	2	2.63	34	0	0	48	33	15	14	1	29	36	.204	.332	.241	18.2	14.6	198				
Mendoza, Brayan	L-L	6-0	155	1-19-04	6	5	5.18	22	4	1	80	81	54	46	5	42	73	.259	.356	.361	20.0	11.5	365				
Meyer, Noble	R-R	6-5	185	1-10-05	1	7	4.41	19	19	0	65	53	36	32	4	38	72	.218	.338	.333	24.3	12.8	296				
Milbrandt, Karson	R-R	6-2	190	4-21-04	2	5	3.26	19	19	0	77	59	31	28	3	43	101	.208	.321	.292	30.1	12.8	336				
Miller, Gage	R-R	6-0	200	3-1-03	0	0	9.00	1	0	0	1	1	1	1	0	0	0	.250	.400	.250	0.0	0.0	5				
Olson, Emmett	L-L	6-4	230	5-15-02	0	2	4.15	9	8	0	35	38	22	16	4	11	32	.286	.351	.481	21.2	7.3	151				
Reynoso, Juan	R-R	6-0	165	4-4-04	1	0	4.32	7	0	0	8	8	5	4	0	4	6	.258	.361	.323	16.7	11.1	36				
Sanchez, Franklin	R-R	6-6	183	9-12-00	0	0	9.35	9	0	1	9	7	9	9	1	12	12	.226	.467	.355	26.7	26.7	45				
Schomberg, Will	R-R	5-10	170	1-30-01	3	6	3.65	20	10	1	69	51	32	28	6	34	86	.206	.320	.320	29.3	11.6	294				
Schrier, Cody	R-R	6-1	201	3-3-03	0	0	0.00	1	0	0	1	2	0	0	0	0	0	.400	.400	.400	0.0	0.0	5				
Sellinger, Jack	R-L	6-2	200	11-20-99	4	2	2.31	35	0	1	58	35	19	15	1	36	78	.175	.309	.225	32.0	14.8	244				
Shunck, RJ	R-L	6-7	235	12-31-03	0	0	0.00	4	0	0	4	0	0	0	0	2	4	.000	.250	.000	25.0	12.5	16				
Storm, Justin	L-L	6-2	232	9-12-01	2	2	3.21	43	0	9	62	43	26	22	3	41	54	.195	.328	.314	20.2	15.4	267				
Volini, Joey	L-L	6-4	265	12-24-02	0	0	1.23	4	1	0	7	6	1	1	0	1	11	.214	.241	.286	37.9	3.4	29				
White, Brandon	R-R	6-8	230	11-26-99	7	4	4.06	23	12	1	93	87	44	42	6	26	73	.244	.302	.351	18.8	6.7	389				
White, Thomas	L-L	6-5	210	9-29-04	2	2	2.83	9	9	0	35	22	11	11	0	17	53	.176	.283	.216	36.6	11.7	145				
Williams, Alex	L-R	6-3	220	10-22-99	2	0	3.93	6	1	0	18	15	12	8	2	8	14	.214	.304	.357	17.7	10.1	79				

Fielding

Catcher	PCT	G	PO	A	E	DP	PB
Caskenette	.986	42	392	17	6	0	3
Forrester	.986	41	382	31	6	5	2
Ignoffo	.989	28	245	19	3	1	10
Rios	1.000	6	47	9	0	1	0
Weber	.984	15	123	4	2	1	2

First Base	PCT	G	PO	A	E	DP
Beshears	.989	15	85	5	1	6
Forrester	1.000	14	107	7	0	16
Jenkins-Cowart	1.000	1	7	0	0	0
Schrier	1.000	13	104	3	0	15
Snyder	.987	20	150	7	2	15
Vargas	.963	9	74	5	3	5
Vradenburg	.994	63	448	21	3	41

Second Base	PCT	G	PO	A	E	DP
Beshears	.920	7	13	10	2	2
Cappe	.965	26	55	55	4	16
Green	1.000	5	10	7	0	2

Third Base	PCT	G	PO	A	E	DP
Beshears	.929	16	5	34	3	5
Forrester	.905	7	5	14	2	2
Green	1.000	7	3	10	0	1
Lara	.977	14	13	29	1	3
Lewis	1.000	6	5	8	0	1
Miller	.942	36	21	60	5	6
Snyder	.917	4	3	8	1	1
Vargas	.921	45	29	76	9	6

Shortstop	PCT	G	PO	A	E	DP
Arquette	.962	25	34	68	4	18
Green	.981	49	50	106	3	25
Hernandez	1.000	9	12	27	0	6

	PCT	G	PO	A	E	DP
Hernandez	1.000	19	30	36	0	8
Jaworsky	.941	10	23	25	3	10
Lara	.982	13	24	32	1	9
Miller	.981	46	91	120	4	33
Vargas	.976	8	21	19	1	6

	PCT	G	PO	A	E	DP
Jaworsky	.889	2	3	5	1	1
Lara	.907	35	31	66	10	11
Vargas	.965	17	20	35	2	3

Outfield	PCT	G	PO	A	E	DP
Boyd	.978	77	134	2	3	1
Cannarella	.980	21	48	0	1	0
Compton	.974	26	37	1	1	0
Head	1.000	1	2	1	0	0
Hernandez	1.000	12	14	1	0	1
Jenkins-Cowart	.983	54	113	2	2	0
Lara	1.000	1	4	0	0	0
Lewis	.969	13	28	3	1	1
McDowell	1.000	29	46	2	0	0
Rataczak	.976	46	80	2	2	2
Shade	.986	70	140	6	2	0
Snyder	.974	25	34	3	1	1
Trimble	.974	30	37	1	1	0

JUPITER HAMMERHEADS
FLORIDA STATE LEAGUE
LOW-A

Batting	B-T	Ht.	Wt.	DOB	AVG	OBP	SLG	G	PA	AB	R	H	2B	3B	HR	RBI	BB	HBP	SH	SF	SO	SB	CS	BB%	SO%
Arroyo, Chris	L-L	6-2	215	9-17-04	.221	.316	.353	20	79	68	11	15	2	2	1	7	8	2	0	1	16	6	0	10.1	20.3
Barreras, Emilio	L-R	6-0	160	9-12-03	.172	.304	.207	19	69	58	9	10	2	0	0	6	9	2	0	0	18	1	1	13.0	26.1
Brown, Jessada	R-R	5-11	200	2-7-03	.156	.216	.281	11	37	32	5	5	1	0	1	5	2	1	0	2	14	2	0	5.4	37.8
Caba, Starlyn	S-R	5-10	160	12-6-05	.222	.335	.278	51	231	194	28	43	6	1	1	21	34	0	1	2	34	14	6	14.7	14.7
Chirinos, Nixon	R-R	6-0	190	10-25-05	.000	.556	.000	2	9	4	3	0	0	0	0	0	5	0	0	0	3	0	0	55.6	33.3
Clayton, Cam	R-R	6-1	185	7-6-02	.242	.356	.390	67	267	223	35	54	13	4	4	32	36	5	0	3	48	5	2	13.5	18.0
Cruz, John	L-L	6-3	171	8-29-05	.122	.185	.204	14	54	49	5	6	1	1	0	1	9	3	1	0	1	11	1	1	5.6	20.4
De Los Santos, Deyvison	R-R	5-11	185	6-21-03	.333	.500	.333	2	8	6	2	2	0	0	0	0	2	0	0	0	1	0	0	25.0	12.5
Etzel, Matthew	L-R	6-2	211	4-30-02	.400	.500	.400	2	6	5	2	2	0	0	0	0	1	0	0	0	0	0	0	16.7	0.0
Faurot, Drew	L-L	6-3	185	10-9-03	.341	.392	.477	22	97	88	9	30	6	3	0	15	8	0	0	1	19	5	1	8.2	19.6
Gleed, Dub	R-R	6-1	195	9-1-02	.238	.384	.307	32	126	101	13	24	4	0	1	13	19	5	0	0	22	0	0	15.1	19.0
Head, Dillon	L-L	5-11	180	10-11-04	.223	.334	.318	96	425	359	60	80	4	9	4	39	58	3	2	2	81	36	9	13.6	19.1
Henriquez, Julio	R-R	5-11	190	11-4-04	.154	.262	.192	30	122	104	13	16	4	0	0	6	9	7	0	2	34	9	2	7.4	27.9
Hernandez, Jesus	R-R	5-9	150	2-20-04	.247	.343	.432	44	168	146	24	36	10	4	3	25	19	3	0	0	42	10	0	11.3	25.0
Hogue, Josh	L-R	6-2	185	1-1-04	.300	.364	.300	3	11	10	1	3	0	0	0	1	1	0	0	0	1	0	0	9.1	9.1
Jenkins-Cowart, Jacob	L-R	6-6	216	12-24-02	.247	.346	.404	24	104	89	14	22	6	1	2	16	13	1	0	1	25	6	2	12.5	24.0
Johnson, Carter	L-R	6-2	180	2-22-06	.177	.275	.261	106	465	406	42	72	17	4	3	43	47	9	0	3	134	11	3	10.1	28.8
Lara, Wilfredo	R-R	5-10	180	4-28-04	.200	.316	.267	4	19	15	3	3	1	0	0	2	2	1	0	1	2	1	1	10.5	10.5
Lewis, Ian	S-R	5-11	177	2-4-03	.252	.353	.448	46	167	143	31	36	6	2	6	22	20	3	0	1	29	13	5	12.0	17.4
Martinez, Yeral	L-R	6-3	220	10-30-02	.182	.241	.260	20	83	77	7	14	3	0	1	14	4	2	0	0	32	2	0	4.8	38.6
McCutcheon, Jake	L-R	6-0	195	11-6-03	.000	.167	.000	3	12	10	1	0	0	0	0	0	2	0	0	0	4	0	0	16.7	33.3
McDowell, Micah	R-R	6-2	175	1-27-01	.255	.388	.418	17	68	55	10	14	1	1	2	10	10	2	0	0	17	3	1	14.7	25.0
Mesa, Victor	L-L	6-0	195	9-8-01	.222	.282	.250	10	39	36	1	8	1	0	0	3	2	1	0	0	4	0	0	5.1	10.3
Morissette, Cody	L-R	6-0	175	1-16-00	.111	.385	.222	3	13	9	2	1	1	0	0	2	4	5	0	0	2	0	0	30.8	15.4
Morlando, P.J.	L-R	6-3	190	5-16-05	.226	.361	.353	52	233	190	33	43	7	1	5	30	29	0	2	6	62	6	1	15.5	26.6
Ortega, Victor	R-R	6-1	200	1-19-04	.241	.367	.316	67	256	212	26	51	11	1	1	27	37	6	0	1	51	4	0	14.5	19.9
Praytor, Sam	R-R	5-9	205	4-4-99	.222	.300	.222	3	10	9	0	2	0	0	0	0	1	0	0	0	1	0	0	10.0	10.0
Ramirez, Abrahan	L-R	5-9	150	10-8-03	.215	.325	.291	91	403	328	40	78	19	1	0	46	68	4	0	3	86	14	5	16.9	21.3
Salas, Andrew	B-R	6-2	180	3-4-08	.186	.319	.245	104	453	371	56	69	9	2	3	21	72	2	5	3	110	39	10	15.9	24.3
Sanchez, Carlos	S-R	5-9	175	9-20-04	.260	.358	.356	57	204	177	27	46	7	2	2	22	27	0	0	0	50	1	1	13.2	24.5
Schrier, Cody	R-R	6-1	201	3-3-03	.237	.295	.335	47	190	173	25	41	2	3	3	28	13	2	0	2	42	18	2	6.8	22.1

	B-T	Ht.	Wt.	DOB				AVG													OBP	SLG	SO%	BB%
Valencia, Esmil	R-R	5-10	182	10-9-05	.327	.367	.510	24	109	98	13	32	5	2	3	21	8	0	0	3	17	14	6	7.3	15.6
Valor, Andres	R-R	6-3	180	11-8-05	.231	.335	.372	108	462	390	65	90	22	3	9	55	51	14	0	7	134	45	10	11.0	29.0
Williams, Max	L-L	6-2	190	8-18-04	.269	.359	.284	19	78	67	6	18	1	0	0	7	9	1	0	1	11	5	1	11.5	14.1

Pitching	B-T	Ht.	Wt.	DOB	W	L	ERA	G	GS	SV	IP	Hits	Runs	ER	HR	BB	SO	AVG	OBP	SLG	SO%	BB%	BF
Barreras, Emilio	L-R	6-0	160	9-12-03	0	0	0.00	1	0	0	1	0	0	0	0	0	0	.000	.000	.000	0.0	0.0	2
Benitez, Keyner	L-L	6-1	165	5-23-06	1	1	3.89	11	10	0	37	41	16	16	1	24	33	.289	.400	.359	19.3	14.0	171
Brink, Nick	R-R	6-2	210	9-27-01	0	0	3.28	6	6	0	25	23	11	9	2	9	31	.240	.306	.344	28.7	8.3	108
Cardenas, Xavier	R-R	6-6	205	6-12-03	0	0	2.16	6	0	1	8	4	2	2	0	6	11	.154	.303	.154	33.3	18.2	33
Carpio, Samuel	R-R	6-2	200	5-6-03	5	3	5.16	34	0	2	52	44	39	30	4	54	75	.230	.405	.340	29.8	21.4	252
Castillo, Walin	R-R	6-3	175	1-2-05	4	5	6.27	22	13	0	85	99	65	59	9	45	66	.295	.383	.443	16.9	11.5	390
Centala, Chase	R-R	6-1	175	3-18-02	4	1	3.38	19	1	1	29	26	14	11	3	13	32	.245	.339	.368	25.4	10.3	126
Clemente, Jake	R-R	6-4	205	11-10-03	0	0	0.00	5	0	0	8	4	0	0	0	3	9	.160	.250	.160	32.1	10.7	28
Cronin, Declan	R-R	6-4	225	9-24-97	0	0	3.00	2	1	0	3	2	1	1	1	1	3	.200	.273	.500	27.3	9.1	11
Cuevas, Melvin	R-R	6-1	160	10-1-04	0	0	13.50	5	0	0	6	9	9	9	2	9	9	.261	.469	.565	28.1	28.1	32
De La Cruz, Juan	R-R	6-3	180	3-4-05	0	1	14.85	4	1	0	7	7	14	11	1	15	6	.292	.595	.500	14.0	34.9	43
De La Cruz, Luis	R-R	6-0	182	8-4-02	0	3	10.65	11	2	0	24	34	34	28	2	22	19	.324	.463	.419	14.0	16.2	136
Dishmey, Eliazar	R-R	6-1	175	10-25-04	3	5	3.13	17	15	0	75	48	27	26	2	42	76	.191	.335	.247	24.4	13.5	311
Espinoza, Eiver	R-R	6-6	168	1-11-04	0	0	3.52	7	0	0	8	2	3	3	1	7	11	.083	.313	.208	34.4	21.9	32
Faherty, Jake	R-R	6-3	190	6-11-03	2	1	7.36	29	0	5	29	16	25	24	1	37	43	.167	.453	.240	28.9	24.8	149
Fernandez, Jose	R-R	6-1	155	10-16-03	0	0	11.57	3	0	0	2	2	3	3	1	5	1	.250	.538	.625	7.7	38.5	13
Fosher, Peyton	R-R	6-0	215	4-30-03	1	0	0.00	2	0	0	4	1	0	0	0	8	1	.071	.071	.143	57.1	0.0	14
Genao, Manuel	R-R	6-1	150	11-11-05	0	0	5.17	6	0	1	16	19	11	9	1	6	11	.292	.387	.446	14.7	8.0	75
Gerardo, Jose	R-R	6-0	179	6-12-05	0	0	0.00	1	0	0	2	0	0	0	0	2	0	.000	.444	.000	22.2	0.0	9
Go, Woo Suk	R-R	5-11	198	8-6-98	0	1	7.20	4	0	0	5	7	4	4	0	5	4	.350	.462	.450	15.4	19.2	26
Henriquez, Wilfredo	R-R	6-2	180	2-11-03	0	0	2.00	8	0	0	9	4	3	2	1	9	6	.129	.325	.226	15.0	22.5	40
Hernandez, Jeckferxon	R-R	6-3	185	9-18-02	3	1	5.03	16	0	0	20	18	16	11	2	22	22	.247	.429	.356	21.8	21.8	101
Hernandez, Leandro	R-R	6-1	170	1-27-02	0	1	4.50	3	2	0	8	8	5	4	1	5	3	.308	.382	.577	8.8	14.7	34
Lashutka, Luke	R-R	6-2	195	5-24-02	7	2	1.79	16	3	1	40	22	9	8	1	11	40	.162	.227	.235	26.7	7.3	150
Laws, Carson	R-R	6-1	186	3-31-03	0	0	0.00	2	0	0	3	1	0	0	0	6	1	.111	.111	.111	66.7	0.0	9
Maldonado, Nick	R-R	6-1	207	6-12-00	0	2	7.84	9	0	3	10	14	10	9	1	3	18	.311	.360	.489	36.0	6.0	50
Martinez, Liomar	R-R	6-2	165	6-25-05	5	5	3.30	22	20	0	101	72	45	37	9	41	119	.197	.292	.317	28.1	9.7	424
May, Aiden	R-R	6-2	188	4-22-01	1	1	3.05	6	5	0	21	12	10	7	2	14	20	.164	.307	.260	22.5	15.7	89
Mendez, Julio	L-L	5-11	180	1-7-05	5	7	3.83	22	20	0	92	72	44	39	5	43	95	.213	.314	.290	24.2	10.9	393
Mercedes, Jorge	R-R	6-3	185	7-1-00	0	0	27.00	2	0	0	2	3	5	5	0	5	1	.429	.667	.571	8.3	41.7	12
Milbrandt, Karson	R-R	6-2	200	4-21-04	0	0	0.00	1	1	0	2	0	0	0	0	2	2	.000	.250	.000	25.0	12.5	8
Payne, Nate	L-L	6-3	200	8-19-05	0	1	3.24	6	0	0	17	6	6	6	1	14	18	.120	.323	.180	27.7	21.5	65
Perez, Eury	R-R	6-8	220	4-15-03	0	0	1.80	5	5	0	10	9	3	2	1	3	12	.231	.286	.385	28.6	7.1	42
Perez, Michael	R-R	6-3	160	9-5-02	1	5	5.32	21	5	1	64	57	51	38	4	42	83	.244	.378	.333	27.7	14.0	300
Pickell, Cannon	R-R	6-2	230	10-3-02	1	0	8.31	8	0	1	9	6	8	8	0	16	11	.207	.500	.310	23.9	34.8	46
Polanco, Natanael	R-R	6-1	170	4-24-03	3	4	7.03	17	0	2	32	25	30	25	1	34	28	.223	.413	.295	18.7	22.7	150
Ramirez, Luis	R-R	6-3	175	2-19-02	0	2	6.86	18	0	1	21	20	18	16	5	18	22	.253	.410	.494	21.8	17.8	101
Renner, Chase	R-R	6-4	229	8-3-03	2	1	2.57	6	0	0	7	3	2	2	0	8	6	.095	.429	.095	17.1	22.9	35
Reyes, Jean	R-R	5-11	165	8-16-02	0	1	14.40	4	0	0	5	5	8	8	0	14	5	.263	.576	.316	15.2	42.4	33
Reynoso, Juan	R-R	6-0	165	4-4-04	5	2	3.17	36	0	4	48	54	18	17	2	22	57	.284	.361	.395	26.4	10.2	216
Rodriguez, Darwin	R-R	6-1	180	11-10-04	0	0	7.36	4	0	0	4	1	3	3	0	6	4	.100	.500	.100	22.2	33.3	18
Salas, Braulio	R-R	6-2	175	11-5-05	0	2	5.40	11	0	0	22	33	18	13	1	14	13	.351	.438	.447	11.4	12.3	114
Sanchez, Franklin	R-R	6-6	183	9-12-00	0	2	1.32	10	0	0	14	4	5	2	0	11	23	.095	.310	.167	39.7	19.0	58
Serrata, Elian	R-R	6-0	160	1-27-02	0	0	28.69	6	0	0	5	9	17	17	0	11	6	.375	.643	.583	14.3	26.2	42
Shepardson, Grant	R-R	6-1	195	10-4-05	2	2	5.93	6	0	0	14	10	13	9	0	15	12	.204	.435	.224	17.4	21.7	69
Shunck, RJ	R-L	6-7	235	12-31-03	0	0	7.71	2	0	0	2	1	2	2	1	3	5	.125	.364	.500	45.5	27.3	11
Tineo, Dameivi	L-L	6-3	170	8-1-03	2	5	3.88	13	13	0	56	49	33	24	5	30	64	.236	.350	.370	25.9	12.1	247
Tineo, Riskiel	R-R	6-3	190	2-27-03	1	4	6.81	24	0	0	36	43	41	27	8	19	36	.293	.394	.558	20.3	10.7	177
Vaupel, Kevin	R-L	6-1	210	8-3-01	1	1	3.71	30	1	1	53	55	31	22	5	23	62	.258	.346	.376	25.4	9.4	244
Volini, Joey	L-L	6-4	265	12-24-02	0	0	0.00	2	0	0	3	1	0	0	0	4	1	.100	.100	.100	40.0	0.0	10
Weathers, Ryan	R-L	6-1	230	12-17-99	0	0	0.00	1	1	0	3	0	0	0	0	6	0	.000	.000	.000	66.7	0.0	9
Williamson, Jadon	R-R	6-5	215	9-1-02	0	0	27.00	2	0	0	3	4	4	0	3	4	.429	.636	.714	36.4	27.3	11
Wilson, Kaiden	L-L	6-2	190	5-20-04	0	0	13.50	1	0	0	1	0	4	1	.000	.667	.000	16.7	66.7	6

Fielding

Catcher	PCT	G	PO	A	E	DP	PB
Brown	.969	11	86	7	3	0	2
Chirinos	1.000	2	17	1	0	0	0
Gleed	.857	1	6	0	1	0	1
Ortega	.990	67	633	70	7	7	11
Praytor	.958	3	23	0	1	0	1
Sanchez	.983	57	505	57	10	8	8

First Base	PCT	G	PO	A	E	DP
Arroyo	.972	19	129	10	4	13
Clayton	.971	26	191	7	6	19
De Los Santos	1.000	1	6	0	0	0
Gleed	1.000	10	83	3	0	6
Henriquez	.974	28	180	4	5	19
Martinez	1.000	16	124	7	0	11
Schrier	.993	33	263	9	2	20

Second Base	PCT	G	PO	A	E	DP
Barreras	.944	5	9	8	1	3
Caba	1.000	12	24	24	0	6
Clayton	1.000	6	16	11	0	3
Faurot	.973	10	20	16	1	4
Hernandez	1.000	2	3	3	0	1
Johnson	.962	33	69	82	6	25
Lewis	1.000	10	18	20	0	5
Morissette	1.000	1	3	1	4	0	1
Ramirez	.983	29	50	56	2	18
Salas	.938	16	29	31	4	7
Schrier	.977	10	20	23	1	7

Third Base	PCT	G	PO	A	E	DP
Barreras	.969	12	4	27	1	3
Clayton	.911	11	12	29	4	2

	PCT	G	PO	A	E	DP
Faurot	.944	5	4	13	1	2
Gleed	.906	12	11	18	3	5
Hernandez	.878	31	14	51	9	9
Lewis	.879	9	4	25	4	2
Morissette	1.000	2	4	0	0	0
Ramirez	.878	46	32	90	17	5
Salas	1.000	5	4	7	0	2

Shortstop	PCT	G	PO	A	E	DP
Barreras	.500	1	1	1	2	0
Caba	.938	39	54	83	9	18
Clayton	.935	14	13	30	3	8
Faurot	.500	1	0	1	1	0
Johnson	.933	59	61	135	14	22
Lara	1.000	4	4	11	0	1
Salas	.939	18	23	39	4	7

Outfield	PCT	G	PO	A	E	DP
Cruz	.929	13	25	1	2	0
Etzel	.000	2	0	0	0	0
Head	.984	91	180	9	3	1
Hernandez	1.000	2	4	0	0	0

Hogue	1.000	3	3	1	0	0
Jenkins-Cowart	.974	15	37	1	1	0
Lewis	.950	17	15	4	1	1
Martinez	.000	1	0	0	1	0
McCutcheon	1.000	3	4	1	0	0
McDowell	1.000	16	29	3	0	0

Mesa	.944	9	17	0	1	0
Morlando	.987	43	72	5	1	1
Salas	.965	59	102	7	4	2
Valencia	.933	23	42	0	3	0
Valor	.963	99	148	7	6	3
Williams	1.000	12	15	1	0	0

FCL MARLINS   *ROOKIE*
FLORIDA COMPLEX LEAGUE

Batting	B-T	Ht.	Wt.	DOB	AVG	OBP	SLG	G	PA	AB	R	H	2B	3B	HR	RBI	BB	HBP	SH	SF	SO	SB	CS	BB%	SO%
Almonte, Jeremy	R-R	6-0	170	10-12-05	.279	.333	.360	25	96	86	12	24	1	0	2	12	4	4	0	2	14	4	3	4.2	14.6
Brown, Jessada	R-R	5-11	200	2-7-03	.174	.310	.217	21	84	69	13	12	0	0	1	7	11	3	0	1	26	5	1	13.1	31.0
Cappe, Yiddi	R-R	6-3	175	9-17-02	.500	.545	1.200	3	11	10	3	5	1	0	2	4	1	0	0	0	0	0	0	9.1	0.0
Chirinos, Nixon	R-R	6-0	190	10-25-05	.250	.347	.375	33	121	104	12	26	7	0	2	8	13	3	0	1	38	6	2	10.7	31.4
Clayton, Cam	R-R	6-1	185	7-6-02	.133	.263	.267	4	19	15	2	2	2	0	0	3	3	0	0	1	4	0	2	15.8	21.1
Cruz, John	L-L	6-3	171	8-29-05	.211	.358	.284	35	134	109	10	23	5	0	1	12	24	1	0	0	21	14	1	17.9	15.7
De La Cruz, Jancory	L-L	6-2	180	2-17-06	.208	.333	.315	39	156	130	19	27	3	1	3	15	24	1	0	1	49	4	3	15.4	31.4
Dean, Breyias	R-R	6-2	175	9-1-05	.220	.292	.382	38	137	123	13	27	6	1	4	21	10	3	0	1	42	2	2	7.3	30.7
Gerardo, Jose	R-R	6-0	179	6-12-05	.000	.000	.000	14	4	4	0	0	0	0	0	0	0	0	0	0	4	0	0	0.0	100.0
Gleed, Dub	R-R	6-1	195	9-1-02	.250	.478	.375	12	46	32	7	8	4	0	0	6	12	2	0	0	4	2	0	26.1	8.7
Gonzalez, Danny	R-R	6-0	160	11-26-04	.257	.328	.352	33	116	105	13	27	4	0	2	8	8	3	0	0	27	3	2	6.9	23.3
Henriquez, Julio	R-R	5-11	190	11-4-04	.429	.600	.786	5	20	14	7	6	2	0	1	3	5	1	0	0	2	2	0	25.0	10.0
Lara, Wilfredo	R-R	5-10	180	4-28-04	.286	.375	.429	2	8	7	1	2	1	0	0	1	1	0	0	0	1	0	0	12.5	12.5
Leon, Luis	R-R	6-2	160	7-21-06	.110	.261	.164	24	88	73	9	8	4	0	0	2	13	2	0	0	41	10	2	14.8	46.6
Lopez, Fabian	S-R	6-0	165	9-18-05	.216	.291	.306	44	151	134	12	29	7	1	1	19	12	3	0	2	56	6	1	7.9	37.1
Martinez, Yeral	L-R	6-3	220	10-30-02	.203	.344	.329	26	96	79	9	16	1	0	3	13	15	2	0	0	29	5	2	15.6	30.2
Monserrate, Jose	R-R	6-0	176	9-20-04	.223	.363	.288	44	171	139	20	31	7	1	0	10	28	3	0	1	41	22	1	16.4	24.0
Morissette, Cody	L-R	6-0	175	1-16-00	.000	.143	.000	2	7	6	2	0	0	0	0	0	1	0	0	0	2	2	0	14.3	28.6
Morlando, P.J.	L-R	6-3	190	5-16-05	.067	.462	.067	6	26	15	5	1	0	0	0	0	10	1	0	0	9	2	0	38.5	34.6
Neymour, Cherif	S-R	5-11	150	3-4-05	.143	.277	.157	28	83	70	9	10	1	0	0	4	12	1	0	0	28	8	2	14.5	33.7
Sanchez, Carlos	S-R	5-9	175	9-20-04	.200	.385	.300	3	13	10	3	2	1	0	0	1	3	0	0	0	4	0	0	23.1	30.8
Schrier, Cody	R-R	6-1	201	3-3-03	.381	.536	.619	6	28	21	7	8	2	0	1	5	7	0	0	0	3	0	0	25.0	14.3
Solano, Yoffry	S-R	5-10	155	11-4-04	.279	.384	.375	39	159	136	25	38	4	3	1	13	18	5	0	0	26	8	2	11.3	16.4
Tailor, Joseph	L-R	5-11	175	6-14-06	.133	.261	.153	32	115	98	10	13	2	0	0	11	12	5	0	0	29	8	4	10.4	25.2
Trimble, Fenwick	R-R	6-3	200	8-29-02	.250	.250	.250	1	4	4	0	1	0	0	0	0	0	0	0	0	1	0	0	0.0	25.0

Pitching	B-T	Ht.	Wt.	DOB	W	L	ERA	G	GS	SV	IP	Hits	Runs	ER	HR	BB	SO	AVG	OBP	SLG	SO%	BB%	BF
Arias, Josue	L-L	6-2	165	5-5-05	0	3	8.78	13	0	0	13	10	19	13	0	23	10	.217	.493	.239	13.7	31.5	73
Benitez, Keyner	L-L	6-1	165	5-23-06	1	0	1.59	4	3	0	17	9	4	3	0	7	18	.155	.265	.190	26.5	10.3	68
Cabral, Jhon	R-R	6-1	172	8-9-05	0	2	6.08	15	0	0	13	10	14	9	0	17	17	.204	.435	.224	24.6	24.6	69
Cesar, Luis	L-L	6-3	183	2-24-04	3	2	4.85	10	0	0	26	22	21	14	0	24	27	.222	.403	.263	20.9	18.6	129
Cuevas, Melvin	L-L	6-2	160	10-1-04	1	1	6.10	11	0	0	10	10	7	7	2	11	11	.286	.458	.486	22.9	22.9	48
De La Cruz, Juan	R-R	6-3	180	3-4-05	1	2	2.70	9	6	0	23	7	8	7	0	15	37	.093	.258	.133	39.8	16.1	93
De La Cruz, Luis	R-R	6-0	182	8-4-02	0	1	5.40	5	0	0	12	8	8	7	0	8	15	.200	.373	.250	29.4	15.7	51
Faherty, Jake	R-R	6-3	190	6-11-03	0	0	0.00	2	0	0	2	1	0	0	0	1	2	.143	.250	.143	25.0	12.5	8
Fernandez, Jose	R-R	6-1	155	10-16-03	1	3	6.41	15	0	1	27	27	25	19	3	14	28	.260	.355	.413	22.4	11.2	125
Genao, Manuel	R-R	6-2	150	11-11-05	2	1	3.52	10	7	1	38	36	17	15	3	12	40	.242	.315	.369	24.0	7.2	167
Gerardo, Jose	R-R	6-0	179	6-12-05	2	0	7.53	13	0	0	14	9	14	12	0	19	24	.173	.443	.212	30.4	24.1	79
Go, Woo Suk	R-R	5-11	198	8-6-98	0	0	0.00	1	1	0	2	0	0	0	0	1	3	.000	.125	.000	37.5	12.5	8
Henriquez, Wilfredo	R-R	6-2	180	2-11-03	0	2	6.75	8	0	0	9	15	10	7	0	4	8	.341	.408	.409	16.3	8.2	49
Hernandez, Jeckferxon	R-R	6-3	185	9-18-02	0	0	0.00	4	0	1	6	4	3	0	0	7	6	.211	.423	.211	23.1	26.9	26
Hernandez, Leandro	R-R	6-1	170	1-27-02	1	1	5.00	5	1	0	9	7	9	5	2	6	8	.219	.375	.438	20.0	15.0	40
May, Aiden	R-R	6-2	188	4-22-03	0	0	1.35	4	4	0	7	2	2	1	1	2	10	.091	.200	.227	40.0	8.0	25
Mercedes, Jorge	R-R	6-3	185	7-1-00	0	0	16.88	6	1	0	5	6	12	10	1	9	6	.286	.545	.619	18.2	27.3	33
Payne, Luis	L-L	6-3	200	8-19-05	2	5	3.18	11	11	0	40	26	15	14	1	23	55	.197	.335	.267	33.7	14.1	163
Polanco, Natanael	R-R	6-1	170	4-24-03	0	1	3.18	5	1	0	11	7	5	4	2	7	16	.184	.311	.421	34.8	15.2	46
Ramirez, Luis	R-R	6-3	175	2-19-02	0	0	0.00	3	0	1	3	1	0	0	0	1	6	.111	.308	.333	46.2	7.7	13
Reyes, Jean	R-R	5-11	165	8-16-02	0	0	40.50	1	0	0	1	3	3	0	2	2	.333	.714	.667	28.6	28.6	7
Romero, Luifer	L-L	6-2	160	12-9-04	1	1	6.05	12	1	0	19	21	14	13	1	12	25	.280	.433	.413	25.8	12.4	97
Salas, Braulio	R-R	6-2	175	11-5-04	0	0	1.42	3	0	0	6	4	1	1	0	4	8	.182	.308	.227	30.8	15.4	26
Serrano, Jhoniel	R-R	6-2	178	10-17-03	0	2	9.39	12	7	0	23	15	27	24	0	31	33	.195	.472	.221	26.6	25.0	124
Serrata, Elian	R-R	6-0	160	1-27-02	1	1	7.79	16	0	3	17	13	17	15	2	22	19	.213	.443	.344	21.3	24.7	89
Shepardson, Grant	R-R	6-1	195	10-4-05	2	3	3.67	11	10	0	42	36	20	17	3	18	47	.238	.347	.318	26.4	10.1	178
Shim, Jun-Seok	R-R	6-4	215	4-9-04	0	3	10.80	13	0	1	15	19	19	16	1	23	16	.196	.513	.283	20.5	29.5	78
Tineo, Dameivi	L-L	6-3	170	8-1-03	1	0	3.27	4	1	0	11	6	4	4	0	2	7	.15	.286	.400	.405	30.0	14.0	50

Fielding

C: Chirinos 26, Almonte 19, Brown 8, Sanchez 2. **1B:** Martinez 19, Dean 15, Gonzalez 8, Henriquez 5, Chirinos 4, Schrier 4, Tailor 2. **2B:** Solano 35, Tailor 15, Neymour 4, Cappe 1, Lara 1, Lopez 1, Morissette 1. **3B:** Dean 18, Neymour 14, Gleed 11, Tailor 8, Martinez 2, Cappe 1, Clayton 1, Lopez 1, Morissette 1, Schrier 1. **SS:** Lopez 41, Neymour 9, Clayton 3, Schrier 2, Tailor 2, Cappe 1, Lara 1. **LF:** De La Cruz 22, Gonzalez 16, Brown 11, Monserrate 6, Leon 1, Morlando 1. **CF:** Leon 23, Monserrate 22, Cruz 5, Morlando 5, Neymour 2, Trimble 1. **RF:** Cruz 24, Monserrate 12, Gonzalez 9, De La Cruz 7, Martinez 2, Morlando 1

DSL MARLINS — ROOKIE
DOMINICAN SUMMER LEAGUE

Batting	B-T	Ht.	Wt.	DOB	AVG	OBP	SLG	G	PA	AB	R	H	2B	3B	HR	RBI	BB	HBP	SH	SF	SO	SB	CS	BB%	SO%
Abreu, Anthony	L-R	6-1	180	1-8-08	.201	.364	.403	43	176	139	35	28	4	3	6	23	30	6	0	1	67	6	3	17.0	38.1
Abreu, Jesus	R-R	6-2	190	9-15-05	.171	.337	.329	23	89	70	11	12	3	1	2	13	14	4	0	1	27	1	0	15.7	30.3
Bello, Adrian	S-R	5-11	165	5-19-06	.275	.427	.442	43	178	138	28	38	5	3	4	32	36	2	0	2	34	8	3	20.2	19.1
Cova, Luis	R-R	6-1	160	2-1-07	.299	.422	.537	50	218	177	49	53	11	2	9	35	34	5	0	2	40	35	6	15.6	18.3
Encarnacion, Diwarys	R-R	6-2	170	10-16-05	.291	.398	.484	52	216	182	40	53	11	0	8	44	27	6	0	1	30	25	5	12.5	13.9
Estevez, Samuel	R-R	6-0	184	3-26-07	.125	.276	.250	8	29	24	4	3	0	0	1	7	5	0	0	0	8	2	1	17.2	27.6
Felicia, Jayden	S-R	6-0	150	3-14-06	.242	.427	.331	46	164	124	27	30	6	1	1	15	39	1	0	0	37	12	3	23.8	22.6
Garcia, Cesar	L-R	5-9	164	9-21-07	.187	.378	.333	29	98	75	15	14	1	2	2	15	20	3	0	0	29	3	3	20.4	29.6
Heredia, Osvaldo	L-R	6-2	170	3-7-06	.143	.462	.143	3	13	7	1	1	0	0	0	1	3	2	0	1	4	0	1	23.1	30.8
Herrera, Steven	R-R	6-0	160	2-21-08	.268	.411	.472	46	180	142	40	38	11	0	6	26	32	4	0	2	54	17	5	17.8	30.0
Mosquera, Deivis	R-R	6-2	178	11-5-04	.254	.391	.323	44	161	130	20	33	4	1	1	21	21	9	0	1	37	9	3	13.0	23.0
Naveo, Rendy	S-R	6-1	155	11-7-07	.184	.380	.211	14	50	38	8	7	1	0	0	3	9	3	0	0	8	3	2	18.0	16.0
Perez, Robert	R-R	6-2	165	4-27-04	.266	.359	.523	41	153	128	32	34	10	1	7	30	18	3	0	4	48	15	5	11.8	31.4
Rivera, Jose	S-R	6-0	145	11-17-04	.232	.323	.268	22	66	56	12	13	2	0	0	5	8	0	1	1	14	8	4	12.1	21.2
Shirley, David	R-R	6-1	195	2-15-08	.286	.389	.468	21	90	77	14	22	3	1	3	16	11	2	0	0	14	1	2	12.5	15.6
Tolentino, Almen	L-R	6-1	160	1-12-07	.301	.446	.532	47	204	156	41	47	10	4	6	25	34	10	0	4	34	20	11	16.7	16.7

Pitching	B-T	Ht.	Wt.	DOB	W	L	ERA	G	GS	SV	IP	Hits	Runs	ER	HR	BB	SO	AVG	OBP	SLG	SO%	BB%	BF
Canelon, Edelson	R-R	6-4	165	10-28-07	1	0	3.68	4	0	0	7	4	4	3	1	3	12	.160	.250	.320	42.9	10.7	28
De La Cruz, Alejandro	R-R	6-0	190	2-5-07	1	2	14.04	8	0	0	8	9	17	13	1	14	7	.273	.509	.394	13.2	26.4	53
Gutierrez, Eric	L-R	6-5	170	11-23-05	2	2	9.00	13	0	1	17	15	22	17	3	23	22	.238	.456	.413	24.4	25.6	90
Hernandez, Abraham	L-L	6-2	170	3-22-07	0	1	9.00	1	1	0	1	1	3	1	0	2	1	.250	.500	.250	16.7	33.3	6
Jimenez, Richard	R-R	6-0	150	5-16-05	1	0	6.00	7	0	0	12	11	9	8	1	8	10	.244	.382	.400	18.2	14.5	55
Linares, Santiago	R-R	6-1	187	12-8-07	2	1	4.50	11	7	0	32	26	17	16	4	17	26	.220	.338	.373	18.7	12.2	139
Marrero, Adriano	R-R	6-3	184	9-18-07	0	1	3.82	10	10	0	33	32	21	14	1	12	35	.260	.368	.358	24.3	8.3	144
Melo, Bayant	R-R	6-5	165	12-31-04	1	4	5.26	11	4	0	26	20	23	15	0	35	34	.220	.467	.275	25.0	25.7	136
Mendez, Gerinton	R-R	6-2	180	9-4-06	2	0	2.61	11	7	0	38	24	15	11	2	15	37	.179	.290	.261	23.9	9.7	155
Miller, Janero	S-L	6-2	195	1-10-06	3	1	3.49	11	3	0	28	21	15	11	2	19	43	.202	.328	.327	33.6	14.8	128
Moreta, Franklyn	R-R	6-0	160	1-11-04	3	1	3.27	12	5	0	33	27	17	12	1	19	49	.225	.356	.300	33.6	13.0	146
Nakamura, Raisei	L-R	6-3	172	5-6-03	3	3	4.82	12	0	1	19	12	13	10	1	12	17	.194	.376	.258	19.8	14.0	86
Ortiz, Albert	R-R	5-11	146	8-7-06	3	1	3.48	12	1	1	34	21	19	13	2	17	46	.183	.329	.278	32.9	12.1	140
Paulino, Jose	R-R	6-3	175	10-15-06	0	3	4.70	12	12	0	38	31	24	20	0	20	56	.217	.329	.273	32.9	11.8	170
Polanco, Albert	R-R	6-2	174	6-30-05	6	0	4.54	12	0	0	36	30	21	18	0	15	56	.225	.316	.360	36.1	9.7	155
Porfirio, Luis	L-L	6-0	155	11-7-05	0	0	4.18	11	4	0	24	12	12	11	0	22	27	.145	.339	.205	24.8	20.2	109
Prince, Isaac	R-R	6-1	175	9-20-07	1	0	2.45	2	0	0	4	3	4	1	1	1	4	.200	.250	.467	25.0	6.3	16
Rosario, Angel	L-L	6-3	190	3-21-03	2	0	4.82	11	0	0	19	16	11	10	0	16	30	.239	.409	.313	34.1	18.2	88
Sanchez, Ramon	R-R	6-3	160	11-14-01	2	0	3.94	11	0	3	16	11	10	7	0	12	22	.204	.362	.259	31.0	16.9	71
Torrealba, Jonfreider	R-R	6-0	175	5-15-07	2	0	2.45	8	1	1	11	5	5	3	0	14	9	.147	.392	.147	17.6	27.5	51
Uzcategui, Jonas	L-L	6-0	155	10-30-04	0	1	12.86	6	1	0	7	6	11	10	0	10	10	.240	.512	.440	24.4	24.4	41

Fielding
C: Bello 25, Tolentino 22, Abreu 13. **1B:** Felicia 37, Bello 9, J. Abreu 6, A. Abreu 4, Encarnacion 4, Herrera 1. **2B:** Herrera 28, Naveo 14, Garcia 8, Rivera 7, Felicia 4, Abreu 2. **3B:** Abreu 18, Encarnacion 13, Garcia 10, Rivera 10, Herrera 7, Felicia 3. **SS:** Encarnacion 33, Abreu 17, Herrera 10, Rivera 4. **LF:** Perez 33, Garcia 8, Shirley 8, Estevez 5, Mosquera 4, Encarnacion 3. **CF:** Cova 48, Perez 3, Estevez 3, Encarnacion 2, Heredia 2, Mosquera 1. **RF:** Mosquera 39, Shirley 12, Perez 4, Encarnacion 2, Cova 1, Garcia 1, Heredia 1

DSL MIAMI — ROOKIE
DOMINICAN SUMMER LEAGUE

Batting	B-T	Ht.	Wt.	DOB	AVG	OBP	SLG	G	PA	AB	R	H	2B	3B	HR	RBI	BB	HBP	SH	SF	SO	SB	CS	BB%	SO%
Alva, Juan	R-L	6-1	183	3-10-06	.323	.438	.429	47	201	161	32	52	12	1	1	41	27	9	0	4	30	19	4	13.4	14.9
Arana, Luis	S-R	5-10	154	3-19-08	.297	.419	.476	52	227	185	47	55	10	4	5	35	30	10	0	2	18	28	9	13.2	7.9
Castillo, Rafael	S-R	5-11	160	4-7-06	.234	.333	.404	25	57	47	11	11	3	1	1	18	7	1	0	2	11	2	1	12.3	19.3
Castro, Jose	R-R	6-3	180	10-31-06	.264	.399	.585	52	238	193	46	51	14	0	16	51	34	10	0	1	62	8	7	14.3	26.1
Estevez, Samuel	R-R	6-0	184	3-26-07	.250	.419	.417	15	31	24	2	6	2	1	0	4	5	2	0	0	8	3	1	16.1	32.3
Garcia, Cesar	L-R	5-9	164	9-21-07	.000	.143	.000	3	7	6	0	0	0	0	0	1	1	0	0	0	4	0	0	14.3	57.1
Heredia, Osvaldo	L-R	6-2	170	3-7-06	.136	.410	.197	32	100	66	24	9	2	1	0	13	28	4	0	2	28	10	4	28.0	28.0
Machado, Johan	S-R	6-1	140	11-7-07	.273	.397	.366	54	237	194	48	53	10	4	0	19	36	5	0	2	36	25	9	15.2	15.2
Martinez, Yordani	R-R	5-7	170	1-15-07	.250	.408	.395	51	196	152	37	38	8	4	2	29	36	6	0	2	37	31	6	18.4	18.9
Morales, Moises	L-R	6-0	172	5-2-08	.239	.412	.364	31	119	88	23	21	4	2	1	23	25	5	0	3	26	1	3	19.3	21.8
Mosquera, Deivis	R-R	6-2	178	11-5-04	.000	.000	.000	1	2	2	0	0	0	0	0	0	0	0	0	0	1	0	0	0.0	50.0
Padilla, Wanderlin	R-R	5-10	155	2-17-08	.185	.400	.204	24	75	54	16	10	1	0	0	9	17	3	0	1	9	3	3	22.7	12.0
Perez, Jesus	R-R	5-11	174	3-12-08	.245	.362	.336	45	174	143	31	35	1	0	4	20	25	5	0	2	28	14	4	13.2	16.1
Presbot, Sandy	S-R	5-7	160	10-20-07	.274	.396	.397	54	222	179	43	49	6	5	2	32	32	7	0	4	48	28	12	14.4	21.6
Requena, Alexander	R-R	6-0	175	10-5-05	.310	.417	.521	21	84	71	21	22	6	0	3	11	7	6	0	0	11	5	2	8.3	15.5
Robledo, Kevin	R-R	5-11	176	9-15-06	.260	.395	.328	41	167	131	28	34	6	0	0	1	22	28	4	0	4	33	11	2	16.8	19.8

Pitching	B-T	Ht.	Wt.	DOB	W	L	ERA	G	GS	SV	IP	Hits	Runs	ER	HR	BB	SO	AVG	OBP	SLG	SO%	BB%	BF
Arellan, Derek	R-R	6-2	175	2-19-06	2	1	7.31	12	0	1	16	19	15	13	1	18	19	.302	.482	.381	22.4	21.2	85
Arredondo, Ricardo	R-R	6-0	163	10-16-06	0	0	5.40	2	0	0	2	1	1	1	0	2	0	.167	.375	.167	0.0	25.0	8
Cedeno, Keyner	L-L	6-0	180	9-13-07	2	1	3.09	13	1	1	32	26	17	11	2	18	44	.213	.340	.279	29.9	12.2	147
Cueto, Derek	R-R	5-10	167	10-24-05	4	1	3.79	12	0	0	38	27	21	16	3	19	35	.209	.329	.333	22.6	12.3	155
De La Rosa, Fernando	R-R	6-1	155	11-22-05	1	1	5.40	8	0	1	12	10	8	7	0	10	11	.227	.382	.273	20.0	18.2	55

Player	B-T	Ht	Wt	DOB	W	L	ERA	G	GS	SV	IP	H	R	ER	BB	SO	AVG	OBP	SLG			
Defrank, Kevin	R-R	6-5	202	8-11-08	0	1	3.19	10	10	0	31	30	15	11	1	10	34	.250	.348	.333	24.1	7.1	141
Encarnacion, Kifraidy	L-L	6-4	187	10-26-05	0	2	39.00	5	2	0	3	3	14	13	0	16	6	.250	.690	.417	20.7	55.2	29
Francisco, Estarlin	R-R	6-3	155	10-15-06	2	0	8.44	7	0	0	11	9	12	10	1	14	8	.231	.455	.410	14.5	25.5	55
Godoy, Diego	L-L	6-0	165	11-29-04	5	1	2.75	11	6	0	36	26	11	11	2	7	49	.198	.255	.282	34.8	5.0	141
Gomez, Luis	R-R	5-11	168	2-23-05	1	2	2.50	10	0	3	18	12	7	5	0	8	25	.179	.263	.239	32.9	10.5	76
Jimenez, Elvin	R-R	6-2	210	3-19-05	4	3	3.98	14	1	0	20	9	14	9	0	27	35	.141	.439	.219	35.4	27.3	99
Medina, Ian	L-L	6-0	195	7-7-04	4	1	3.19	16	0	5	31	22	14	11	2	13	37	.206	.289	.299	30.3	10.7	122
Montero, Pedro	R-R	6-1	144	7-11-07	0	1	3.00	11	11	0	36	27	12	12	2	14	44	.214	.317	.341	30.1	9.6	146
Morillo, Elier	L-L	5-11	160	10-6-05	2	1	3.23	11	8	1	31	22	12	11	0	16	54	.206	.356	.280	40.9	12.1	132
Mosquera, Eiver	R-R	6-2	175	9-10-06	1	0	2.45	9	6	0	29	23	12	8	4	8	33	.205	.276	.330	26.8	6.5	123
Pena, Adrian	R-R	6-7	194	5-2-08	0	1	3.12	5	4	0	9	2	4	3	0	13	9	.080	.410	.080	23.1	33.3	39
Rodriguez, Maikel	R-R	6-1	180	8-25-06	5	0	2.86	11	0	0	35	26	16	11	2	7	38	.198	.271	.336	26.2	4.8	145
Rodriguez, Victor	R-R	6-1	185	10-24-06	1	0	4.76	6	2	1	17	16	14	9	0	7	17	.235	.342	.294	21.5	8.9	79
Rosario, Jonathan	L-L	6-2	165	1-3-07	3	0	5.57	16	0	21	19	19	13	2	18	25	.238	.402	.338	24.5	17.6	102
Rueda, Cristian	R-R	6-1	180	1-5-05	0	0	9.00	5	0	0	6	8	8	6	0	10	5	.320	.514	.520	14.3	28.6	35
Salas, Braulio	R-R	6-2	175	11-5-04	0	0	1.69	3	0	0	11	8	2	2	0	7	10	.229	.357	.371	23.8	16.7	53
Santana, Yohanfer	R-R	6-7	200	10-13-05	0	2	4.66	5	5	0	10	8	7	5	0	6	8	.242	.381	.364	18.6	14.0	43

Fielding

C: Morales 25, Robledo 24, Requena 12. **1B:** Alva 45, Castillo 7, Padilla 7, Robledo 4. **2B:** Martinez 38, Padilla 15, Castillo 8, Machado 2, Alva 1. **3B:** Arana 24, Machado 23, Martinez 8, Garcia 2, Padilla 2, Castillo 1. **SS:** Machado 30, Arana 27, Padilla 2. **LF:** Perez 33, Heredia 10, Estevez 7, Castro 6, Castillo 5, Garcia 1, Presbot 1. **CF:** Presbot 44, Heredia 9, Castro 4, Estevez 1, Mosquera 1. **RF:** Castro 38, Heredia 9, Presbot 9, Estevez 4, Castillo 3, Perez 1

Milwaukee Brewers

SEASON SYNOPSIS: Which will Brewers fans remember most? The franchise-record 97 victories and fourth NL Central division title in five seasons, led by a dynamic, multi-faceted offense and pitching staff with enviable depth, variety and power? Or the bookends to the season, when the $300 million Yankees (36 runs in three games) and Dodgers (15-4 aggregate score) swept the Brewers in record-setting fashion?

HIGH POINT: Having trailed the Cubs by 6 ½ games in May, the Brew Crew passed them at the end of July, taking two of three in Milwaukee. That set the stage for a franchise-record 14-game August win streak, part of a 52-17 stretch. The last two wins included coming back from an 8-1 deficit to beat the Reds 10-8, and Andruw Monasterio's three-run homer to cap a 6-5 improbable victory. The Crew hit 27 home runs in the 14-game streak.

LOW POINT: After edging the Cubs in a five-game Division Series, the Brewers met the Dodgers for the NLCS and were humbled. They scored a single run in each game of the four-game sweep, batting .118 for the series, the lowest batting average ever for a team in a playoff series of at least three games.

NOTABLE ROOKIES: RHP Jacob Misiorowski took the league by storm, no-hitting St. Louis for five innings in his June 12 debut and being named to the all-star team after just five electric starts, throwing up to 103 mph with a curve that reached 90 and a mid-90s slider. While he had growing pains (5-3, 4.36), he recovered to post a 1.50 ERA in 12 postseason innings with 16 strikeouts. RHP Chad Patrick (3-8, 3.53) proved a productive, versatile arm in the rotation or bullpen. 3B Caleb Durbin (.721 OPS), a 5-foot-7 Division III alumnus, and OF Isaac Collins (.779 OPS), a 5-8 former minor league Rule 5 draft pick, were solid regulars on both sides of the ball.

KEY TRANSACTIONS: Durbin arrived in the offseason trade of former closer Devin Williams to the Yankees. LHP Jose Quintana, signed in March as a free agent, and RHP Quinn Priester, acquired from Boston in an April trade, provided quality innings in the rotation. Improved rotation depth allowed the Brewers to deal Aaron Civale to the White Sox in June for Andrew Vaughn. The Brewers moved his stance closer to the plate, and the No. 3 overall pick in the 2019 draft blossomed, hitting .308/.375/.493 in 64 games.

OPENING DAY PAYROLL: $115,136,227 (23rd)

PLAYERS OF THE YEAR

MAJOR LEAGUE
Freddy Peralta
RHP
17-6, 2.70 ERA
204 SO, 66 BB,
1.08 WHIP in 176.2 IP

MINOR LEAGUE
Jesus Made
SS
(A, A+, AA)
.285/.379/.413
6 HR, 47 SB, 67 BB

ORGANIZATION LEADERS

Batting		*Qualifiers
MAJORS		
* AVG	Sal Frelick	.288
* OPS	Christian Yelich	.795
HR	Christian Yelich	29
RBI	Christian Yelich	103
MINORS		
* AVG	Jadher Areinamo, Wisconsin	.297
* OBP	Blake Burke, Biloxi/Wisconsin	.379
* SLG	Jadher Areinamo, Wisconsin	.463
* OPS	Blake Burke, Biloxi/Wisconsin	.832
R	Jesus Made, Biloxi/Wisconsin/Carolina	81
H	Blake Burke, Biloxi/Wisconsin	143
TB	Blake Burke, Biloxi/Wisconsin	222
2B	Luis Lara, Biloxi	32
3B	Juan Martinez, DSL Brewers 2	7
3B	Jonathan Rangel, DSL Brewers 2	7
HR	Eric Bitonti, Carolina	19
RBI	Blake Burke, Biloxi/Wisconsin	82
BB	Luis Lara, Biloxi	86
SO	Eric Bitonti, Carolina	169
SB	Jared Oliva, Nashville	57

Pitching		#Qualifiers
MAJORS		
W	Freddy Peralta	17
# ERA	Freddy Peralta	2.70
SO	Freddy Peralta	204
SV	Trevor Megill	30
MINORS		
W	Zach Peek, Biloxi/Wisconsin	11
L	Sam Garcia, Wisconsin/Carolina	11
# ERA	Melvin Hernandez, Carolina	2
G	Will Childers, Nashville/Biloxi	54
GS	Alexander Cornielle, Nashville/Biloxi	29
SV	Justin Yeager, Nashville/Biloxi	10
IP	Bruce Zimmermann, Nashville	138
BB	Ryan Birchard, Wisconsin	73
SO	Alexander Cornielle, Nashville/Biloxi	135
# AVG	Melvin Hernandez, Carolina	.217

2025 PERFORMANCE

General Manager: Matt Arnold. **Farm Director:** Tom Flanagan. **Scouting Director:** Tod Johnson.

Class	Team	League	W	L	PCT	Finish	Manager
Majors	Milwaukee Brewers	National	97	65	.599	1 (15)	Pat Murphy
Triple-A	Nashville Sounds	International	85	63	.574	5 (20)	Rick Sweet
Double-A	Biloxi Shuckers	Southern	74	64	.536	4 (8)	Joe Ayrault
High-A	Wisconsin Timber Rattlers	Midwest	56	74	.431	8 (12)	Victor Estevez
Low-A	Carolina Mudcats	Carolina	68	60	.531	2 (12)	Nick Stanley
Rookie	ACL Brewers	Arizona Complex	30	30	.500	10 (15)	Rafael Neda
Rookie	DSL Brewers 1	Dominican	29	25	.537	22 (52)	Victor Rey
Rookie	DSL Brewers 2	Dominican	27	29	.482	28 (52)	Natanael Mejia
Overall 2025 Minor League Record			369	345	.517	8th (30)	

ORGANIZATION STATISTICS

MILWAUKEE BREWERS
NATIONAL LEAGUE

Batting	B-T	Ht.	Wt.	DOB	AVG	OBP	SLG	G	PA	AB	R	H	2B	3B	HR	RBI	BB	HBP	SH	SO	SB	CS	BB%	SO%
Avans, Drew	L-L	5-9	195	6-13-96	.000	.000	.000	1	3	2	0	0	0	0	0	1	0	0	0	1	0	0	0.0	33.3
Bauers, Jake	L-L	5-11	195	10-6-95	.235	.353	.399	86	218	183	28	43	9	0	7	28	32	2	0	1	59	8	1	14.7	27.1
Berroa, Steward	S-R	5-9	178	6-5-99	.000	.167	.000	2	6	5	0	0	0	0	0	0	1	0	0	0	2	1	0	16.7	33.3
Black, Tyler	L-R	5-10	190	7-26-00	.250	.538	.375	5	13	8	1	2	1	0	0	1	5	0	0	0	1	0	1	38.5	7.7
Cameron, Daz	R-R	6-2	185	1-15-97	.195	.214	.293	21	42	41	7	8	1	0	1	3	1	0	0	0	13	1	0	2.4	31.0
Capra, Vinny	R-R	5-8	180	7-7-96	.074	.121	.130	24	59	54	6	4	0	0	1	4	2	1	1	1	15	1	0	3.4	25.4
Chourio, Jackson	R-R	5-11	165	3-11-04	.270	.308	.463	131	589	549	88	148	35	4	21	78	30	3	1	6	121	21	7	5.1	20.5
Collins, Isaac	S-R	5-7	185	7-22-97	.263	.368	.411	130	441	372	56	98	22	3	9	54	57	6	3	3	93	16	7	12.9	21.1
Contreras, William	R-R	5-11	216	12-24-97	.260	.355	.399	150	659	566	89	147	28	0	17	76	84	3	0	6	120	6	4	12.7	18.2
Dunn, Oliver	L-R	5-10	185	9-2-97	.167	.205	.222	14	41	36	4	6	2	0	0	6	2	0	0	2	11	1	0	4.9	26.8
Durbin, Caleb	R-R	5-6	175	2-22-00	.256	.334	.387	136	506	445	60	114	25	0	11	53	30	24	3	4	50	18	6	5.9	9.9
Frelick, Sal	L-R	5-10	182	4-19-00	.288	.351	.405	142	594	528	76	152	20	3	12	63	47	7	3	5	80	19	6	7.9	13.5
Haase, Eric	R-R	5-10	210	12-18-92	.229	.289	.357	30	77	70	11	16	3	0	2	9	4	2	1	0	31	0	0	5.2	40.3
Hoskins, Rhys	R-R	6-4	245	3-17-93	.237	.332	.416	90	328	279	30	66	12	1	12	43	38	5	0	6	91	2	1	11.6	27.7
Jansen, Danny	R-R	6-2	215	4-15-95	.254	.346	.433	25	78	67	10	17	3	0	3	7	9	1	0	1	18	0	0	11.5	23.1
Lockridge, Brandon	R-R	5-11	185	3-14-97	.261	.308	.370	20	53	46	8	12	3	1	0	6	4	0	1	2	12	2	0	7.5	22.6
Mitchell, Garrett	L-R	6-3	224	9-4-98	.206	.286	.294	25	78	68	9	14	4	1	0	3	7	1	1	1	25	3	0	9.0	32.1
Monasterio, Andruw	R-R	5-11	186	5-30-97	.270	.319	.437	68	135	126	19	34	9	0	4	16	7	2	0	0	32	2	1	5.2	23.7
Ortiz, Joey	R-R	5-9	190	7-14-98	.230	.276	.317	149	506	470	62	108	18	1	7	45	27	3	6	0	74	14	3	5.3	14.6
Perkins, Blake	S-R	5-11	197	9-10-96	.226	.298	.348	54	171	155	25	35	6	2	3	19	15	1	0	0	47	7	2	8.8	27.5
Seigler, Anthony	S-S	5-9	200	6-20-99	.194	.292	.210	34	73	62	6	12	1	0	0	5	8	1	1	1	16	2	0	11.0	21.9
Turang, Brice	L-R	6-0	176	11-21-99	.288	.359	.435	156	659	584	97	168	28	2	18	81	66	2	2	5	150	24	8	10.0	22.8
Vaughn, Andrew	R-R	6-0	215	4-3-98	.308	.375	.493	64	254	221	26	68	14	0	9	46	24	3	1	5	37	0	0	9.4	14.6
Yelich, Christian	L-R	6-3	207	12-5-91	.264	.343	.452	150	644	573	88	151	21	0	29	103	64	6	0	1	167	16	6	9.9	25.9

Pitching	B-T	Ht.	Wt.	DOB	W	L	ERA	G	GS	SV	IP	Hits	Runs	ER	HR	BB	SO	AVG	OBP	SLG	SO%	BB%	BF
Alexander, Tyler	R-L	6-2	203	7-14-94	3	5	6.19	21	4	1	36	42	31	25	3	12	30	.284	.340	.412	18.3	7.3	164
Anderson, Grant	R-R	6-0	180	6-21-97	2	6	3.23	66	0	0	70	59	35	25	8	29	74	.223	.303	.352	24.7	9.7	299
Ashby, Aaron	R-L	6-1	188	5-24-98	5	2	2.16	43	1	3	67	54	16	16	3	24	76	.227	.307	.311	28.1	8.9	270
Bauers, Jake	L-L	5-11	195	10-6-95	0	0	3.60	5	0	0	5	8	4	2	0	3	1	.348	.448	.435	3.4	10.3	29
Civale, Aaron	R-R	6-2	215	6-12-95	1	2	4.91	5	5	0	22	23	12	12	5	7	19	.274	.344	.512	20.2	7.4	94
Cortes, Nestor	R-L	5-11	210	12-10-94	1	1	9.00	2	2	0	8	7	8	8	5	7	8	.226	.368	.742	21.1	18.4	38
Fedde, Erick	R-R	6-4	203	2-25-93	0	1	3.38	7	0	0	16	11	7	6	2	7	7	.186	.273	.322	10.6	10.6	66
Gasser, Robert	L-L	6-0	192	5-31-99	0	2	3.18	2	2	0	6	5	6	2	1	4	5	.217	.379	.391	17.2	13.8	29
Hall, DL	L-L	6-2	210	9-19-98	1	0	3.49	20	3	0	39	24	15	15	2	17	27	.174	.265	.275	17.4	11.0	155
Henderson, Logan	R-R	5-11	194	3-2-02	3	0	1.78	5	5	0	25	17	5	5	3	8	33	.187	.253	.297	33.3	8.1	99
Hudson, Bryan	L-L	6-8	220	5-8-97	0	1	4.35	12	0	0	10	8	7	5	0	12	13	.205	.415	.256	24.1	22.2	54
Koenig, Jared	R-L	6-5	235	11-14-89	7	3	2.86	72	0	2	66	57	21	21	6	20	68	.237	.305	.365	25.4	7.5	268
McGee, Easton	R-R	6-6	205	12-26-97	0	0	5.52	9	0	0	15	15	9	9	1	5	13	.268	.323	.393	21.0	8.1	62
Mears, Nick	R-R	6-2	200	10-7-96	5	3	3.49	63	0	1	57	42	25	22	7	13	46	.213	.255	.371	20.8	5.9	221
Megill, Trevor	L-R	6-8	250	12-5-93	6	3	2.49	50	0	30	47	36	16	13	3	17	60	.209	.276	.386	31.3	8.9	192
Miller, Shelby	R-R	6-3	225	10-10-90	1	0	5.59	11	0	0	10	9	6	6	2	4	14	.237	.326	.447	32.6	9.3	43
Misiorowski, Jacob	R-R	6-7	190	4-3-02	5	3	4.36	15	14	0	66	51	34	32	8	31	87	.213	.311	.360	31.9	11.4	273
Myers, Tobias	R-R	6-1	217	8-5-98	1	2	3.55	22	6	0	51	54	21	20	5	15	38	.269	.323	.398	17.3	6.8	220
Patrick, Chad	R-R	6-1	205	8-14-98	3	8	3.53	27	23	0	120	113	49	47	13	40	127	.248	.313	.387	25.2	8.0	503
Payamps, Joel	R-R	6-2	217	4-7-94	0	1	7.23	28	0	1	24	29	19	19	3	9	22	.309	.370	.585	20.4	8.3	108
Peguero, Elvis	R-R	6-5	237	3-20-97	0	0	4.91	6	0	0	7	8	6	4	1	4	5	.258	.361	.387	13.9	11.1	36
Peralta, Freddy	R-R	6-0	196	6-4-96	17	6	2.70	33	33	0	177	124	54	53	21	66	204	.193	.277	.337	28.2	9.1	723
Priester, Quinn	R-R	6-3	210	9-15-00	13	3	3.32	29	24	0	157	145	62	58	18	50	132	.245	.309	.400	20.2	7.7	653
Quintana, Jose	R-L	6-1	220	1-24-89	11	7	3.96	24	24	0	132	120	65	58	18	50	89	.241	.315	.382	16.0	9.0	556
Rodriguez, Carlos F.	R-R	6-0	206	11-27-01	1	0	6.52	4	0	0	10	13	7	7	1	9	11	.317	.440	.512	22.0	18.0	50
Rodriguez, Elvin	R-R	6-3	160	3-31-98	0	2	8.68	6	2	0	19	23	18	18	7	7	17	.303	.369	.645	20.2	8.3	84

MILWAUKEE BREWERS

	B-T	Ht.	Wt.	DOB																
Seigler, Anthony	S-S	5-9	200	6-20-99	0	0	0.00	1	0	0	1	1	0	0	0	0	0	.250	.250	.250	0.0	0.0	4
Thomas, Connor	L-L	5-11	173	5-29-98	0	0	20.25	2	0	0	5	12	12	12	3	2	5	.462	.484	.885	16.1	6.5	31
Uribe, Abner	R-R	6-3	225	6-20-00	3	2	1.67	75	0	7	75	51	18	14	4	27	90	.194	.284	.255	30.2	9.1	298
Woodruff, Brandon	L-R	6-4	244	2-10-93	7	2	3.20	12	12	0	65	45	26	23	9	14	83	.188	.242	.331	32.3	5.4	257
Yoho, Craig	R-R	6-3	205	10-23-99	0	0	7.27	8	0	0	9	8	7	7	1	9	7	.276	.450	.414	17.1	22.0	41
Zastryzny, Rob	R-L	6-3	205	3-26-92	2	1	2.45	26	1	0	22	16	7	6	3	10	20	.203	.293	.342	21.5	10.8	93
Zimmermann, Bruce	L-L	6-1	220	2-9-95	0	1	7.50	1	1	0	6	7	6	5	2	2	1	.269	.321	.500	3.6	7.1	28

Fielding

Catcher	PCT	G	PO	A	E	DP	PB
Contreras	.995	128	1149	43	6	6	6
Haase	.994	28	166	5	1	1	1
Jansen	1.000	21	168	7	0	1	0
Seigler	.000	1	0	0	0	0	1

First Base	PCT	G	PO	A	E	DP
Bauers	.994	40	163	14	1	24
Black	.909	2	10	0	1	2
Contreras	.000	1	0	0	0	0
Dunn	1.000	2	2	0	0	0
Frelick	.000	1	0	0	0	0
Hoskins	.991	82	538	35	5	48
Monasterio	1.000	15	13	2	0	3
Seigler	1.000	1	2	0	0	0
Vaughn	.991	64	403	26	4	35

Second Base	PCT	G	PO	A	E	DP
Capra	1.000	2	0	3	0	1
Collins	1.000	1	1	1	0	1
Durbin	.947	10	8	10	1	5
Monasterio	1.000	10	8	20	0	4
Turang	.985	153	255	343	9	83

Third Base	PCT	G	PO	A	E	DP
Capra	.964	17	5	22	1	0
Collins	1.000	2	1	0	0	0
Dunn	.889	13	4	12	2	1
Durbin	.979	131	84	201	6	17
Frelick	1.000	1	2	0	0	0
Monasterio	1.000	8	5	7	0	1
Seigler	.947	25	13	23	2	4

Shortstop	PCT	G	PO	A	E	DP
Capra	1.000	2	3	7	0	4
Durbin	1.000	3	0	3	0	1

	PCT	G	PO	A	E	DP
Monasterio	.986	37	26	44	1	12
Ortiz	.982	149	166	325	9	67
Turang	.500	3	0	1	1	1

Outfield	PCT	G	PO	A	E	DP
Avans	1.000	1	2	0	0	0
Bauers	.946	26	34	1	2	0
Berroa	1.000	2	2	1	0	0
Black	.000	2	0	0	0	0
Cameron	1.000	17	17	0	0	0
Chourio	.993	149	285	5	2	0
Collins	.972	116	172	2	5	0
Contreras	.000	1	0	0	0	0
Frelick	.990	148	294	10	3	2
Lockridge	1.000	20	31	2	0	0
Mitchell	1.000	25	68	1	0	1
Monasterio	.000	2	0	0	0	0
Perkins	.991	52	113	1	1	0
Yelich	.977	19	41	1	1	0

NASHVILLE SOUNDS
INTERNATIONAL LEAGUE — TRIPLE-A

Batting	B-T	Ht.	Wt.	DOB	AVG	OBP	SLG	G	PA	AB	R	H	2B	3B	HR	RBI	BB	HBP	SH	SF	SO	SB	CS	BB%	SO%
Alfaro, Jorge	R-R	6-3	230	6-11-93	.244	.285	.430	82	326	307	49	75	10	1	15	49	11	7	0	1	119	12	0	3.4	36.5
Avans, Drew	L-L	5-9	195	6-13-96	.251	.329	.367	52	222	199	31	50	11	0	4	24	20	3	0	0	54	24	3	9.0	24.3
Bauers, Jake	L-L	5-11	195	10-6-95	.211	.318	.737	5	22	19	4	4	1	0	3	5	3	0	0	0	8	0	0	13.6	36.4
Berroa, Steward	S-R	5-9	178	6-5-99	.195	.330	.268	26	105	82	14	16	3	0	1	7	18	0	2	3	33	11	3	17.1	31.4
Black, Tyler	L-R	5-10	190	7-26-00	.243	.369	.360	61	268	222	33	54	10	2	4	34	43	2	0	1	71	22	3	16.0	26.5
Cameron, Daz	R-R	6-2	185	1-15-97	.287	.381	.599	60	278	237	49	68	14	3	18	54	32	6	0	3	62	18	6	11.5	22.3
Chourio, Jackson	R-R	5-11	165	3-11-04	.035	.143	.105	5	21	19	1	1	1	0	0	2	0	0	0	0	8	0	0	9.5	38.1
Clarke, Wes	R-R	6-0	228	10-13-99	.216	.352	.358	46	182	148	18	32	3	0	6	16	32	0	0	2	55	2	0	17.6	30.2
Dalbec, Bobby	R-R	6-4	227	6-29-95	.266	.356	.498	61	264	229	36	61	15	1	12	44	30	3	0	2	89	3	0	11.4	33.7
Delgado, Raynel	L-R	6-1	200	4-4-00	.281	.363	.378	125	474	413	58	116	19	3	5	53	48	7	3	3	95	40	8	10.1	20.0
Dunn, Oliver	L-R	5-10	185	9-2-97	.208	.315	.338	110	465	400	53	83	18	5	8	43	54	9	1	0	146	25	5	11.6	31.4
Durbin, Caleb	R-R	5-6	175	2-22-00	.278	.316	.481	58	54	12	15	5	0	2	3	3	0	1	0	5	3	2	5.2	8.6
Haase, Eric	R-R	5-10	210	12-18-92	.203	.312	.313	19	77	64	6	13	4	0	1	15	11	0	0	2	20	0	0	14.3	26.0
Hall, Adam	R-R	5-10	165	5-22-99	.222	.300	.313	43	160	144	14	32	4	3	1	11	8	8	0	0	56	12	0	5.0	35.0
Herron, Jimmy	R-L	6-0	195	7-27-96	.219	.297	.287	78	270	237	33	52	5	1	3	23	23	5	1	4	59	18	0	8.5	21.9
Hoskins, Rhys	R-R	6-4	245	3-17-93	.275	.371	.471	14	62	51	8	14	4	0	2	6	9	0	0	2	11	0	0	14.5	21.0
Kahle, Nick	R-R	5-8	210	2-28-98	.250	.307	.397	25	77	68	9	17	4	0	2	14	5	1	2	1	20	0	0	6.5	26.0
Lockridge, Brandon	R-R	5-11	185	3-14-97	.351	.413	.404	13	63	57	12	20	3	0	0	7	6	0	0	0	11	4	0	9.5	17.5
Martinez, Ernesto	L-L	6-5	250	6-20-99	.255	.357	.388	80	311	263	40	67	13	2	6	40	39	5	0	4	81	1	3	12.5	26.0
Mitchell, Garrett	L-R	6-3	224	9-4-98	.556	.636	.556	3	11	9	5	5	0	0	0	1	2	0	0	0	1	0	0	18.2	9.1
Monasterio, Andruw	R-R	5-11	186	5-30-97	.250	.346	.411	30	130	112	18	28	6	0	4	11	16	1	0	1	31	8	3	12.3	23.8
Murray, Ethan	R-R	5-10	201	5-13-00	.198	.272	.248	29	114	101	13	20	2	0	1	12	10	1	0	2	32	4	1	8.8	28.1
Oliva, Jared	R-R	6-1	200	11-27-95	.252	.335	.413	95	398	349	63	88	15	4	11	44	35	9	1	1	82	57	6	8.8	20.6
Perkins, Blake	S-R	5-11	197	9-10-96	.192	.382	.346	8	34	26	6	5	1	0	1	2	8	0	0	0	13	2	1	23.5	38.2
Quero, Jefferson	R-R	5-11	215	5-25-02	.336	.412	.58	250	216	32	55	14	1	6	44	25	4	0	5	35	2	0	10.0	14.0
Rosario, Eddie	L-R	6-1	180	9-28-91	.290	.373	.449	20	83	69	13	20	5	2	2	11	11	0	0	3	17	6	1	13.3	20.5
Seigler, Anthony	S-S	5-9	200	6-20-99	.285	.414	.478	72	307	249	51	71	16	4	8	39	52	4	0	2	59	23	4	16.9	19.2
Spain, Garrett	L-R	5-10	178	9-21-00	.162	.256	.216	11	43	37	4	6	2	0	0	2	11	6	1	0	15	3	0	9.3	34.9
Urias, Luis	R-R	5-10	202	6-3-97	.260	.351	.380	13	57	50	6	13	3	1	1	6	6	1	0	0	6	1	0	10.5	10.5
Vaughn, Andrew	R-R	6-0	215	4-3-98	.259	.338	.500	16	65	58	8	15	3	1	3	16	7	0	0	0	13	0	0	10.8	20.0
Zamora, Freddy	R-R	5-10	190	11-1-98	.257	.353	.348	104	396	339	49	87	19	0	7	46	50	2	2	3	70	13	7	12.6	17.7

Pitching	B-T	Ht.	Wt.	DOB	W	L	ERA	G	GS	SV	IP	Hits	Runs	ER	HR	BB	SO	AVG	OBP	SLG	SO%	BB%	BF
Anderson, Grant	R-R	6-0	180	6-21-97	0	0	13.50	2	0	0	2	2	3	3	1	1	1	.250	.333	.625	11.1	11.1	9
Ashby, Aaron	R-L	6-1	188	5-24-98	0	0	1.50	4	0	0	6	3	1	1	0	5	4	.150	.320	.200	16.0	20.0	25
Childers, Will	L-R	6-4	210	11-14-00	2	1	4.50	24	0	2	26	19	15	13	4	18	21	.204	.333	.376	18.4	15.8	114
Civale, Aaron	R-R	6-2	215	6-12-95	1	0	0.00	2	2	0	9	3	0	0	0	2	5	.107	.167	.107	16.7	6.7	30
Cornielle, Alexander	R-R	6-2	180	8-22-01	0	1	3.21	3	0	14	7	5	4	10	19	.212	.359	.442	29.7	15.6	64
Cortes, Nestor	R-L	5-11	210	12-10-94	1	1	1.29	3	3	0	14	7	3	2	1	3	16	.140	.204	.240	29.6	5.6	54
Crow, Coleman	R-R	6-0	175	12-30-00	0	1	7.71	2	2	0	7	9	6	6	1	4	12	.321	.394	.500	36.4	12.1	33
Davidson, Tucker	L-L	6-2	215	3-25-96	2	0	4.68	6	6	0	25	28	14	13	1	7	25	.277	.330	.347	22.9	6.4	109
Fitzpatrick, Brian	S-L	6-7	230	6-1-00	1	1	6.87	13	0	0	18	14	14	0	14	18	.212	.357	.227	21.2	16.5	85

MILWAUKEE BREWERS

	B-T	Ht.	Wt.	DOB	G	GS	ERA	W	L	SV	IP	H	R	ER	HR	BB	SO	AVG	BB/9	SO/9	BF
Fowler, Michael	R-R	6-3	185	7-23-02	0	0	18.00	1	0	0	1	2	2	2	0	3	0	.400	.625	.800	0.0	37.5	8
Garcia, Deivi	R-R	5-9	163	5-19-99	3	2	5.45	10	6	0	33	40	24	20	2	17	27	.296	.387	.400	17.4	11.0	155
Gasser, Robert	L-L	6-0	192	5-31-99	3	2	2.25	10	6	0	32	25	9	8	1	10	36	.214	.279	.282	27.7	7.7	130
Hall, DL	L-L	6-2	210	9-19-98	1	0	0.00	2	1	0	6	3	0	0	0	4	7	.143	.280	.143	28.0	16.0	25
Henderson, Logan	R-R	5-11	194	3-2-02	10	4	3.59	16	15	0	78	62	32	31	9	24	87	.218	.283	.352	27.9	7.7	312
Holub, Blake	R-R	6-6	230	10-23-98	3	2	3.70	39	0	3	41	33	21	17	1	31	53	.217	.351	.296	28.6	16.8	185
Hudson, Bryan	L-L	6-8	220	5-8-97	2	1	6.84	25	0	2	25	27	20	19	2	12	25	.276	.351	.378	22.3	10.7	112
Jay, Tyler	L-L	6-1	185	4-19-94	2	1	3.33	28	0	2	27	18	11	10	1	14	21	.188	.310	.250	18.6	12.4	113
Kahle, Nick	R-R	5-8	210	2-28-98	0	1	15.00	3	0	0	3	4	5	5	2	1	0	.308	.400	.769	0.0	6.7	15
Kuehner, Tate	L-L	6-1	195	2-7-01	0	1	5.59	2	2	0	10	12	6	6	3	4	5	.316	.381	.658	11.9	9.5	42
Liranzo, Jesus	R-R	6-2	225	3-7-95	3	4	3.39	48	0	6	58	48	34	22	6	23	64	.222	.310	.366	25.8	9.3	248
Maciejewski, Josh	R-L	6-3	175	8-14-95	3	5	5.66	25	6	0	48	54	32	30	3	20	40	.286	.354	.392	18.9	9.4	212
McGee, Easton	R-R	6-6	205	12-24-97	5	0	3.59	32	1	1	48	34	21	19	3	19	53	.190	.274	.296	26.4	9.5	201
McKendry, Evan	R-R	6-3	200	2-6-98	0	1	6.43	4	1	0	7	10	5	5	0	1	4	.345	.394	.379	12.1	3.0	33
McWilliams, Sam	R-R	6-7	230	9-4-95	0	2	5.66	18	0	0	21	24	16	13	3	17	31	.282	.400	.494	29.5	16.2	105
Mears, Nick	R-R	6-2	200	10-7-96	0	0	0.00	3	0	0	4	2	0	0	0	1	1	.154	.214	.231	7.1	7.1	14
Merryweather, Julian	R-R	6-4	215	10-14-91	0	0	7.36	11	0	1	11	13	9	9	4	3	16	.283	.327	.609	32.7	6.1	49
Middendorf, Ryan	L-R	6-6	220	12-22-97	3	1	7.50	14	0	0	12	18	12	10	0	7	8	.360	.450	.440	13.3	11.7	60
Miller, Shelby	R-R	6-3	225	10-10-90	0	0	0.00	1	0	0	1	0	0	0	0	3	0	.000	.000	.000	100.0	0.0	3
Misiorowski, Jacob	R-R	6-7	190	4-3-02	4	2	2.13	13	12	0	63	38	16	15	4	31	80	.175	.280	.240	31.6	12.3	253
Myers, Tobias	R-R	6-1	217	8-5-98	2	5	3.77	12	12	0	60	61	28	25	5	17	55	.266	.323	.389	21.9	6.8	251
Nittoli, Vinny	R-R	6-1	210	11-11-90	0	1	3.86	27	1	0	28	32	14	12	3	11	37	.276	.344	.414	28.9	8.6	128
Patrick, Chad	R-R	6-1	205	8-14-98	2	4	4.04	8	8	0	42	37	22	19	8	17	45	.233	.314	.454	25.0	9.4	180
Payamps, Joel	R-R	6-2	217	4-7-94	1	1	4.73	27	0	6	27	24	17	14	2	6	30	.235	.273	.353	27.3	5.5	110
Peguero, Elvis	R-R	6-5	237	3-20-97	3	2	3.55	27	0	4	25	22	14	10	4	15	25	.227	.336	.402	21.6	12.9	116
Peterson, Nate	L-L	5-10	180	2-15-00	0	0	0.00	3	0	1	6	3	1	0	0	2	5	.158	.238	.158	23.8	9.5	21
Rodriguez, Carlos F.	R-R	6-0	206	11-27-01	3	4	3.82	17	15	1	78	67	35	33	8	38	82	.226	.321	.385	24.1	11.2	340
Rodriguez, Elvin	R-R	6-3	160	3-31-98	2	0	4.25	16	2	0	30	31	14	14	7	6	25	.272	.309	.518	20.3	4.9	123
Stallings, Garrett	R-R	6-2	200	8-8-97	5	3	3.99	30	15	0	99	97	45	44	9	22	72	.257	.294	.403	17.7	5.4	406
Wolfram, Grant	L-L	6-6	235	12-12-96	0	0	6.00	2	0	0	3	1	2	2	0	4	3	.111	.429	.222	21.4	28.6	14
Woodruff, Brandon	L-R	6-4	244	2-10-93	1	1	3.55	7	7	0	25	23	10	10	2	8	23	.242	.302	.347	21.7	7.5	106
Yeager, Justin	L-R	6-4	215	1-20-98	1	0	0.84	18	0	0	21	9	4	2	0	14	17	.130	.274	.159	20.2	16.7	84
Yoho, Craig	R-R	6-3	205	10-23-99	6	1	0.94	43	0	8	48	26	7	5	0	20	60	.157	.262	.223	31.4	10.5	191
Zastryzny, Rob	R-L	6-3	205	3-26-92	0	0	9.00	9	1	0	7	9	7	7	2	4	7	.321	.412	.643	20.6	11.8	34
Zimmermann, Bruce	L-L	6-1	220	2-9-95	10	7	4.11	28	21	2	138	140	69	63	17	30	109	.259	.296	.411	18.8	5.2	579

Fielding

Catcher	PCT	G	PO	A	E	DP	PB
Alfaro	.996	58	490	27	2	0	2
Haase	.979	16	134	5	3	1	2
Kahle	.984	22	184	6	3	1	0
Quero	.993	34	282	12	2	2	1
Seigler	.995	24	201	6	1	1	3

First Base	PCT	G	PO	A	E	DP
Bauers	1.000	3	23	2	0	2
Black	.980	19	139	7	3	10
Clarke	.984	26	178	8	3	18
Dalbec	1.000	11	70	3	0	5
Delgado	1.000	9	62	3	0	4
Hoskins	.975	10	72	5	2	6
Martinez	.983	65	407	43	8	41
Murray	1.000	2	13	2	0	0
Vaughn	1.000	10	57	7	0	1

Second Base	PCT	G	PO	A	E	DP
Delgado	.978	74	126	192	7	24
Dunn	.957	11	17	27	2	7

	PCT	G	PO	A	E	DP
Durbin	1.000	2	6	4	0	0
Monasterio	1.000	4	9	12	0	5
Murray	.986	18	30	42	1	9
Seigler	.992	30	56	73	1	16
Urias	1.000	5	2	15	0	0
Zamora	1.000	6	13	12	0	3

Third Base	PCT	G	PO	A	E	DP
Dalbec	.980	19	18	31	1	3
Delgado	.962	23	15	35	2	1
Dunn	.954	69	45	101	7	7
Durbin	.900	8	1	17	2	2
Monasterio	.944	4	5	12	1	0
Murray	1.000	3	0	5	0	0
Seigler	.947	14	8	28	2	2
Urias	.905	6	6	13	2	0
Zamora	.889	6	2	6	1	1

Shortstop	PCT	G	PO	A	E	DP
Delgado	.969	10	11	20	1	3
Dunn	.986	20	25	44	1	3

	PCT	G	PO	A	E	DP
Monasterio	.933	21	39	44	6	15
Murray	.966	6	14	14	1	3
Zamora	.973	92	124	199	9	34

Outfield	PCT	G	PO	A	E	DP
Avans	1.000	55	101	3	0	0
Bauers	1.000	2	0	0	0	0
Berroa	1.000	26	63	1	0	0
Black	1.000	35	60	1	0	0
Cameron	.991	53	109	2	1	0
Chourio	1.000	4	12	0	0	0
Dalbec	1.000	31	57	1	0	0
Delgado	1.000	1	1	0	0	0
Hall	.966	43	85	1	3	0
Herron	.971	75	130	3	4	0
Lockridge	1.000	13	31	1	0	1
Mitchell	.889	3	8	0	1	0
Oliva	1.000	92	188	3	0	0
Perkins	1.000	6	17	0	0	0
Rosario	.966	19	26	2	1	0
Spain	.952	10	19	1	1	0

BILOXI SHUCKERS
SOUTHERN LEAGUE
DOUBLE-A

Batting	B-T	Ht.	Wt.	DOB	AVG	OBP	SLG	G	PA	AB	R	H	2B	3B	HR	RBI	BB	HBP	SH	SF	SO	SB	CS	BB%	SO%
Adams, Luke	R-R	6-4	210	4-24-04	.232	.409	.450	64	278	211	50	49	13	0	11	38	43	21	0	1	60	10	3	15.5	21.6
Boeve, Mike	L-R	6-3	200	5-5-02	.233	.329	.336	68	301	262	35	61	8	2	5	28	34	4	0	1	68	8	0	11.3	22.6
Brown, Eric	R-R	5-10	190	12-19-00	.157	.225	.235	28	111	102	9	16	5	0	1	17	9	0	0	0	26	2	2	8.1	23.4
Burke, Blake	L-L	6-3	240	6-11-03	.300	.377	.579	37	159	140	21	42	6	0	11	34	16	2	0	1	41	3	1	10.1	25.8
Garcia, Eduardo	R-R	6-1	160	7-10-02	.212	.297	.265	33	128	113	12	24	6	0	0	9	14	0	0	1	38	5	3	10.9	29.7
Hall, Adam	R-R	5-11	165	5-22-99	.245	.350	.294	32	123	102	15	25	5	0	0	10	13	4	0	1	30	13	1	10.6	24.4
Lara, Luis	S-R	5-7	155	11-17-04	.257	.369	.343	136	612	513	79	132	32	3	2	40	86	8	0	5	99	44	7	14.1	16.2
Made, Jesus	S-R	6-1	187	5-8-07	.261	.292	.348	5	24	23	6	6	0	1	0	3	1	0	0	0	8	2	0	4.2	33.3
Martinez, Eric	R-R	6-0	175	4-6-04	.167	.286	.333	5	14	12	3	2	0	0	0	1	1	0	0	0	5	0	0	7.1	35.7
Miller, Darrien	L-R	5-10	186	3-10-01	.192	.381	.329	81	316	240	40	46	10	1	7	37	57	17	1	1	77	4	0	18.0	24.4
Murray, Ethan	R-R	5-10	201	5-13-00	.257	.385	.438	64	258	210	46	54	12	1	8	30	39	6	1	2	58	12	0	15.1	22.5
Perez, Hedbert	L-L	5-10	160	4-4-03	.250	.357	.250	4	14	12	1	3	0	0	0	1	2	0	0	0	5	1	0	14.3	35.7

MILWAUKEE BREWERS

Batting	B-T	Ht.	Wt.	DOB	AVG	OBP	SLG	G	PA	AB	R	H	2B	3B	HR	RBI	BB	HBP	SH	SF	SO	SB	CS	BB%	SO%
Pratt, Cooper	R-R	6-4	195	8-18-04	.238	.343	.348	120	527	437	71	104	22	1	8	62	67	8	2	10	80	31	5	12.7	15.2
Restituyo, Bladimir	R-R	5-10	151	7-2-01	.198	.227	.287	101	351	324	36	64	10	2	5	19	10	4	8	5	74	18	8	2.8	21.1
Rodriguez, Ramon	R-R	6-0	210	10-30-98	.359	.457	.484	21	81	64	8	23	2	0	2	19	9	5	0	3	4	0	0	11.1	4.9
Spain, Garrett	L-R	5-10	178	9-21-00	.207	.282	.377	120	486	430	58	89	17	4	16	67	39	9	0	8	131	6	7	8.0	27.0
Torres, Victor	R-R	6-0	180	7-29-00	.000	.231	.000	4	13	10	1	0	0	0	0	0	3	0	0	0	1	0	0	23.1	7.7
Vargas, Jheremy	R-R	5-10	160	5-10-03	.220	.287	.234	88	321	291	26	64	4	0	0	31	26	2	0	2	65	10	6	8.1	20.2
Warren, Zavier	S-R	5-10	215	1-8-99	.228	.314	.371	117	478	412	48	94	14	6	11	67	53	3	0	9	113	11	2	11.1	23.6
Wilken, Brock	R-R	6-4	225	6-17-02	.226	.387	.489	79	344	270	46	61	17	0	18	46	69	3	0	2	93	2	0	20.1	27.0
Wood, Matthew	L-R	5-10	190	3-2-01	.271	.371	.415	59	245	207	28	56	12	0	6	31	30	5	0	3	33	8	1	12.2	13.5

Pitching	B-T	Ht.	Wt.	DOB	W	L	ERA	G	GS	SV	IP	Hits	Runs	ER	HR	BB	SO	AVG	OBP	SLG	SO%	BB%	BF
Alcantara, Raul	L-L	6-0	167	1-22-01	2	2	6.55	10	0	0	11	8	9	8	1	7	9	.205	.392	.308	17.0	13.2	53
Bowman, Kaleb	R-R	6-1	195	5-22-97	2	1	2.76	38	0	6	46	32	15	14	5	19	37	.203	.300	.342	20.2	10.4	183
Broca, Jesus	L-L	5-8	174	10-16-03	1	2	4.22	5	0	0	11	7	6	5	0	5	14	.184	.273	.237	31.8	11.4	44
Bryant, Tyler	R-R	6-4	203	1-23-99	2	2	4.95	31	0	2	36	30	21	20	4	20	49	.234	.335	.391	31.2	12.7	157
Childers, Will	L-R	6-4	210	11-14-00	3	1	2.33	30	0	7	39	21	10	10	3	17	47	.157	.250	.254	30.9	11.2	152
Cornielle, Alexander	R-R	6-2	180	8-22-01	5	8	3.88	26	26	0	123	105	58	53	11	61	116	.230	.332	.349	21.8	11.5	531
Costello, Chase	R-R	6-4	215	4-13-00	0	0	5.28	13	0	1	15	21	9	9	0	10	12	.350	.458	.533	16.2	13.5	74
Crow, Coleman	R-R	6-0	175	12-30-00	4	0	2.51	10	10	0	43	31	12	12	2	8	52	.199	.251	.301	31.1	4.8	167
Cruz, Stiven	R-R	6-2	165	11-14-01	2	0	4.91	14	0	0	22	22	15	12	1	5	19	.247	.292	.326	19.8	5.2	96
DeBerry, Jaron	R-R	6-3	168	8-28-02	2	1	3.62	7	7	0	37	32	17	15	4	10	34	.229	.289	.357	22.1	6.5	154
Fitzpatrick, Brian	S-L	6-7	230	6-1-00	4	3	1.82	23	0	2	35	25	10	7	3	10	38	.207	.265	.322	28.6	7.5	133
Hardin, Tyson	R-R	6-2	185	11-19-01	2	2	3.29	10	10	0	38	39	14	14	3	8	34	.267	.308	.404	21.8	5.1	156
Hunt, K.C.	L-R	6-3	200	7-14-00	7	9	4.45	26	26	0	121	111	63	60	15	43	122	.241	.305	.375	23.8	8.4	513
Kuehner, Tate	L-L	6-1	195	2-7-01	7	5	2.50	21	21	0	101	80	38	28	6	53	112	.224	.336	.305	26.5	12.6	422
Letson, Bishop	R-R	6-4	170	9-15-04	0	0	9.00	1	1	0	4	3	4	4	1	3	6	.214	.353	.429	35.3	17.6	17
MacGregor, Travis	R-R	6-2	215	10-15-97	0	3	3.48	11	0	3	10	15	6	4	2	2	11	.349	.391	.535	22.9	4.2	48
Maciejewski, Josh	R-L	6-3	175	8-14-95	2	0	4.50	10	0	0	22	18	11	11	2	10	26	.220	.301	.317	28.0	10.8	93
Manfredi, Mark	R-R	6-5	210	1-28-00	3	2	3.30	44	0	1	60	38	23	22	2	38	76	.184	.327	.222	29.8	14.9	255
Mendoza, Abdiel	R-R	5-10	160	9-19-98	5	3	4.09	33	6	1	81	84	40	37	7	28	78	.267	.329	.375	22.4	8.0	348
Merkel, Nick	R-R	6-7	255	7-3-98	1	1	3.28	18	0	1	25	23	9	9	1	12	29	.242	.333	.326	26.9	11.1	108
Middendorf, Ryan	L-R	6-6	220	12-22-97	0	2	7.48	20	0	1	22	28	22	18	2	17	19	.308	.435	.473	16.5	14.8	115
Peek, Zach	R-R	6-3	190	5-6-98	7	2	3.97	26	0	1	45	43	22	20	5	22	45	.251	.337	.374	22.8	11.2	197
Peterson, Nate	L-L	5-10	180	2-15-00	6	6	4.33	28	8	0	69	76	34	33	5	32	54	.286	.359	.417	17.7	10.5	305
Roberts, Austin	R-R	6-0	205	7-27-98	2	0	4.76	12	0	1	17	19	10	9	0	4	17	.275	.324	.319	22.7	5.3	75
Rodriguez, Manuel	R-R	6-2	175	8-8-05	0	0	3.00	1	1	0	6	4	2	2	1	0	4	.174	.208	.348	16.7	0.0	24
Root, Bayden	R-R	6-3	235	10-27-98	0	0	9.00	4	0	0	6	9	6	6	1	3	4	.391	.429	.652	13.8	10.3	29
Warren, Zavier	S-R	5-10	215	1-8-99	0	0	0.00	1	0	0	0	0	0	0	0	0	0	.000	.000	.000	0.0	0.0	1
Wichrowski, Brett	L-R	6-2	177	8-15-02	3	6	3.44	22	22	0	99	93	51	38	5	44	72	.249	.340	.332	16.7	10.2	432
Woessner, Tyler	R-R	6-4	230	10-26-99	0	0	7.20	5	0	0	5	4	4	4	1	3	6	.222	.364	.389	27.3	13.6	22
Yeager, Justin	R-R	6-4	215	1-20-98	2	3	2.75	31	0	10	36	26	12	11	2	11	33	.203	.268	.281	23.2	7.7	142

Fielding

Catcher	PCT	G	PO	A	E	DP	PB
Martinez	1.000	3	24	2	0	0	1
Miller	.984	68	582	31	10	3	3
Rodriguez	.977	14	123	7	3	1	0
Torres	1.000	4	25	3	0	0	1
Wood	.998	53	449	34	1	4	4

First Base	PCT	G	PO	A	E	DP
Adams	.984	39	283	26	5	25
Boeve	1.000	20	163	13	0	16
Burke	.984	32	223	18	4	22
Martinez	1.000	2	4	0	0	0
Miller	1.000	3	12	2	0	0
Warren	.997	45	327	34	1	28

Second Base	PCT	G	PO	A	E	DP
Brown	.985	18	21	44	1	9
Garcia	.933	4	3	11	1	1
Hall	.786	4	5	6	3	3
Made	1.000	1	2	1	0	1
Murray	.959	23	29	42	3	6
Vargas	.988	70	79	164	3	34
Warren	.980	23	39	60	2	10

Third Base	PCT	G	PO	A	E	DP
Adams	.897	21	10	25	4	4
Garcia	1.000	14	9	19	0	2
Murray	1.000	22	13	34	0	3
Vargas	1.000	5	6	9	0	2
Warren	.911	23	15	26	4	2
Wilken	.933	58	37	75	8	12

Shortstop	PCT	G	PO	A	E	DP
Brown	1.000	2	5	6	0	1
Garcia	1.000	11	15	22	0	4
Made	1.000	4	3	10	0	1
Murray	.984	14	19	43	1	7
Pratt	.969	103	138	239	12	49
Vargas	1.000	5	5	13	0	3

Outfield	PCT	G	PO	A	E	DP
Brown	1.000	7	14	0	0	0
Garcia	1.000	6	14	0	0	0
Hall	.982	27	53	3	1	1
Lara	.994	126	309	10	2	0
Murray	1.000	5	7	0	0	0
Restituyo	1.000	99	169	4	0	1
Spain	.987	116	218	13	3	4
Vargas	.875	9	5	2	1	0
Warren	1.000	24	35	1	0	0

WISCONSIN TIMBER RATTLERS   *HIGH-A*
MIDWEST LEAGUE

Batting	B-T	Ht.	Wt.	DOB	AVG	OBP	SLG	G	PA	AB	R	H	2B	3B	HR	RBI	BB	HBP	SH	SF	SO	SB	CS	BB%	SO%
Adamczewski, Josh	L-R	6-0	190	5-10-05	.196	.292	.250	16	65	56	7	11	3	0	0	6	8	0	1	11	3	0	12.3	16.9
Adams, Luke	R-R	6-4	210	4-24-04	.217	.472	.304	8	37	23	8	5	2	0	0	4	9	3	0	1	4	0	0	24.3	10.8
Alastre, Luiyin	S-R	5-10	160	9-27-05	.223	.290	.255	85	303	274	22	61	7	1	0	25	23	4	0	2	61	10	5	7.6	20.1
Areinamo, Jadher	R-R	5-8	160	11-28-03	.297	.355	.463	94	415	367	51	109	24	2	11	51	34	4	0	9	48	15	8	8.2	11.6
Baez, Juan	R-R	5-9	178	6-27-05	.201	.287	.224	110	442	389	37	78	7	1	0	29	46	3	0	4	48	6	2	10.4	10.9
Berroa, Steward	S-R	5-9	178	6-5-99	.143	.379	.286	8	29	21	3	3	1	1	0	3	6	2	0	0	6	3	0	20.7	20.7
Burke, Blake	L-L	6-3	240	6-11-03	.289	.380	.403	95	408	350	43	101	21	2	5	48	49	5	0	4	94	12	4	12.0	23.0
Castillo, Luis	L-L	6-0	175	10-11-03	.096	.246	.202	29	114	94	6	9	2	1	2	11	19	0	0	1	37	0	0	16.7	32.5
Diaz, Blayberg	R-R	5-11	190	1-31-03	.228	.290	.293	53	200	184	14	42	12	0	0	12	11	5	0	0	46	1	2	5.5	23.0
Dinges, Marco	R-R	6-0	190	9-5-03	.273	.371	.483	51	205	172	29	47	4	1	10	35	28	1	0	4	47	1	1	13.7	22.9

MILWAUKEE BREWERS

	B-T	Ht.	Wt.	DOB	AVG	OBP	SLG	G	AB	R	H	2B	3B	HR	RBI	BB	SO	SB	CS	HBP	SH	SF	SO%	BB%
Fischer, Andrew	L-R	6-1	200	5-25-04	.311	.402	.446	19	87	74	8	23	5	1	1	10	11	1	0	1	22	8	2	12.6	25.3
Garcia, David	S-R	5-10	201	2-6-00	.105	.227	.105	7	22	19	3	2	0	0	0	0	2	1	0	0	9	0	0	9.1	40.9
Garcia, Eduardo	R-R	6-1	160	7-10-02	.252	.341	.435	96	411	361	61	91	23	2	13	47	41	8	0	1	107	36	4	10.0	26.0
Garcia, Yhoswar	R-R	5-9	150	9-13-01	.204	.267	.280	86	302	275	30	56	12	3	1	29	24	0	2	1	47	48	13	7.9	15.6
Guilarte, Daniel	R-R	5-11	160	10-29-03	.157	.247	.193	102	345	300	34	47	6	1	1	22	36	2	1	6	120	15	11	10.4	34.8
Hall, Tayden	L-R	6-4	215	1-12-03	.157	.336	.261	88	336	261	36	41	9	3	4	21	67	5	0	3	79	8	1	19.9	23.5
Made, Jesus	S-R	6-1	187	5-8-07	.343	.415	.500	27	123	108	20	37	7	2	2	12	13	1	0	1	22	5	4	10.6	17.9
Martinez, Eric	R-R	6-0	175	4-6-04	.000	.000	.000	4	7	7	0	0	0	0	0	0	0	0	0	0	4	0	0	0.0	57.1
Nava, Andrick	S-R	5-10	175	10-6-01	.219	.296	.266	19	71	64	5	14	3	0	0	8	7	0	0	0	13	2	0	9.9	18.3
Nicasia, Kaylan	S-R	5-11	176	4-10-02	.156	.307	.303	75	257	211	28	33	9	2	6	19	41	5	0	0	98	11	2	16.0	38.1
Pena, Luis	R-R	5-11	185	11-13-06	.168	.220	.297	25	109	101	10	17	4	0	3	12	6	1	0	1	27	3	0	5.5	24.8
Perez, Hedbert	L-L	5-10	160	4-4-03	.209	.330	.411	84	345	292	39	61	11	3	14	43	51	2	0	0	90	7	3	14.8	26.1
Rodriguez, Yophery	L-L	6-1	185	12-5-05	.417	.462	.667	3	13	12	3	5	1	1	0	0	1	0	0	0	3	0	0	7.7	23.1
Torres, Victor	R-R	6-0	180	7-29-00	.000	.000	.000	5	13	13	0	0	0	0	0	0	0	0	0	0	1	0	0	0.0	7.7
Vargas, Jheremy	R-R	5-10	160	5-10-03	.194	.242	.226	11	33	31	3	6	1	0	0	2	2	0	0	0	6	3	1	6.1	18.2
Wood, Matthew	L-R	5-10	190	3-2-01	.222	.374	.300	30	116	90	13	20	4	0	1	12	20	3	0	2	18	2	1	17.2	15.5

Pitching	B-T	Ht.	Wt.	DOB	W	L	ERA	G	GS	SV	IP	Hits	Runs	ER	HR	BB	SO	AVG	OBP	SLG	SO%	BB%	BF
Alastre, Luiyin	S-R	5-10	160	9-27-05	0	0	16.88	3	0	0	3	5	5	5	0	3	2	.417	.500	.417	12.5	18.8	16
Aquino, Patricio	R-R	6-0	175	5-1-03	5	3	4.16	33	2	3	67	74	37	31	2	27	57	.284	.373	.406	18.8	8.9	303
Birchard, Ryan	L-R	6-0	207	7-12-03	4	8	3.91	25	22	0	104	71	48	45	5	73	121	.191	.330	.259	26.8	16.2	451
Broca, Jesus	L-L	6-4	174	10-16-03	6	1	2.95	30	0	5	61	54	25	20	3	34	47	.247	.354	.329	17.8	12.9	264
Corniel, Daniel	R-R	6-0	177	7-7-04	0	1	0.00	3	0	3	3	1	1	0	0	4	.250	.250	.417	33.3	0.0	12
Cortes, Nestor	R-L	5-11	210	12-10-94	0	0	0.00	1	1	0	4	3	0	0	0	0	2	.200	.200	.200	13.3	0.0	15
Cruz, Stiven	R-R	6-2	165	11-14-01	1	2	4.12	21	1	2	44	45	26	20	4	26	44	.271	.359	.440	22.2	13.1	198
DeBerry, Jaron	R-R	6-3	168	8-28-02	2	4	5.43	12	9	0	55	60	33	33	7	20	55	.280	.343	.435	23.0	8.4	239
Figueroa, Jeferson	R-R	6-0	180	8-22-00	3	3	5.53	26	0	1	42	34	30	26	7	42	32	.222	.392	.425	16.1	21.1	199
Fitzpatrick, Brian	S-L	6-7	230	6-1-00	0	0	3.86	2	0	0	5	4	3	2	0	2	6	.222	.300	.333	30.0	10.0	20
Flores, Anthony	L-L	5-11	165	10-21-04	3	6	3.86	32	11	1	91	87	45	39	9	48	92	.254	.356	.399	22.8	11.9	404
Garcia, Sam	L-L	6-4	218	5-22-02	1	10	5.56	15	13	0	66	67	51	41	13	29	63	.261	.334	.482	21.4	9.8	295
Gasser, Robert	L-L	6-0	192	5-31-99	0	1	3.60	3	3	0	5	3	2	2	0	1	5	.200	.235	.267	29.4	5.9	17
Gillis, Tanner	R-R	6-3	220	8-10-00	2	3	3.22	14	14	0	64	55	27	23	2	14	41	.230	.272	.326	16.1	5.5	255
Guilarte, Daniel	R-R	5-11	160	10-29-03	0	0	0.00	1	0	0	1	0	0	0	0	2	0	.500	.750	.500	0.0	50.0	4
Hardin, Tyson	R-R	6-2	185	11-19-01	4	3	2.34	11	11	0	58	57	19	15	0	9	62	.258	.293	.344	26.7	3.9	232
Langhorne, Miles	R-R	6-4	210	4-30-03	1	0	8.36	12	0	1	14	17	13	13	1	14	15	.309	.465	.418	21.1	19.7	71
Letson, Bishop	R-R	6-4	170	9-15-04	2	2	1.69	10	8	0	37	28	10	7	1	9	43	.214	.270	.260	30.3	6.3	142
Maldonado, Aidan	R-R	6-0	170	5-27-00	0	1	1.86	7	0	0	10	6	3	2	0	3	11	.167	.268	.250	26.8	7.3	41
Nova, Jose	R-R	6-5	185	4-2-02	0	0	18.00	2	0	0	1	2	2	2	0	1	0	.333	.500	.333	0.0	16.7	6
Peek, Zach	R-R	6-3	190	5-6-98	4	1	3.00	17	0	2	24	19	9	8	0	9	30	.209	.294	.297	29.4	8.8	102
Quintana, Jose	R-L	6-1	220	1-24-89	0	0	6.75	1	1	0	4	6	3	3	1	1	3	.353	.389	.353	16.7	5.6	18
Rodriguez, Manuel	R-R	6-2	175	8-8-05	3	5	3.01	18	18	0	84	68	29	28	12	15	84	.220	.257	.405	25.6	4.6	328
Rodriguez, Yerlin	R-R	6-2	172	3-22-02	5	3	5.30	43	0	3	56	39	43	33	4	60	83	.197	.402	.308	30.9	22.3	269
Root, Bayden	R-R	6-3	235	10-27-98	2	3	3.91	29	0	1	48	38	23	21	3	17	43	.221	.314	.312	21.6	8.5	199
Rund, Aaron	R-R	6-5	225	6-16-99	2	4	5.09	36	0	5	46	41	31	26	1	26	44	.237	.351	.318	21.2	12.5	208
Sanchez, Dikember	R-R	5-11	160	2-20-04	0	3	16.20	11	0	0	12	15	23	21	3	23	10	.319	.542	.574	13.9	31.9	72
Seppings, Jack	R-R	6-1	190	7-3-02	2	1	3.82	20	0	1	35	36	17	15	2	25	25	.283	.389	.386	15.9	15.9	157
Shears, Tanner	R-R	6-3	205	6-20-99	0	0	20.25	5	0	0	4	2	10	9	0	12	5	.154	.533	.154	16.7	40.0	30
Smith, Travis	R-R	6-4	185	11-9-02	1	2	4.10	6	6	0	26	14	13	12	0	9	16	.255	.327	.309	14.7	8.3	109
Torres, Victor	R-R	6-0	180	7-29-00	0	0	18.00	1	0	0	1	4	3	2	0	0	.667	.571	.667	0.0	0.0	7
Welch, Chandler	R-R	6-0	170	5-6-01	3	0	5.85	7	7	0	32	41	22	21	1	20	17	.331	.427	.468	11.3	13.3	150
Woessner, Tyler	R-R	6-4	230	10-26-99	1	1	6.23	3	0	0	4	5	3	0	4	12	.237	.281	.288	18.8	6.3	64
Woodruff, Brandon	L-R	6-4	244	2-10-93	2	1	1.62	3	3	0	17	14	5	3	0	4	12	.237	.281	.288	18.8	6.3	64

Fielding

Catcher	PCT	G	PO	A	E	DP	PB
Diaz	.978	48	362	42	9	1	15
Dinges	.970	31	266	23	9	2	8
Garcia	.970	7	62	2	2	0	0
Martinez	.900	3	9	0	1	0	0
Nava	.972	19	170	5	5	1	2
Torres	.946	4	33	2	2	0	0
Wood	.991	24	208	20	2	3	1

First Base	PCT	G	PO	A	E
Adams	.981	7	43	8	1	3
Baez	1.000	2	11	0	0	0
Burke	.992	79	589	34	5	72
Diaz	.976	5	37	3	1	6
Guilarte	1.000	1	1	0	0	0
Hall	.993	38	287	11	2	27
Martinez	.000	1	0	0	0	0

Second Base	PCT	G	PO	A	E	DP
Adamczewski	1.000	5	9	11	0	2
Alastre	.952	9	7	13	1	2
Areinamo	1.000	2	49	50	0	18
Baez	.992	31	50	71	1	26
Garcia	.000	1	0	0	0	0
Guilarte	.966	44	92	105	7	29
Made	.931	9	12	15	2	2
Pena	.980	12	23	27	1	8

Third Base	PCT	G	PO	A	E	DP
Alastre	1.000	1	2	1	0	0
Areinamo	.975	18	13	26	1	4
Baez	.936	74	62	144	14	22
Fischer	1.000	15	14	26	0	6
Guilarte	.970	24	23	42	2	5

Shortstop	PCT	G	PO	A	E	DP
Areinamo	.963	50	66	142	8	24
Garcia	.967	47	61	117	6	28
Guilarte	.941	9	13	19	2	3
Made	.932	16	25	44	5	9
Pena	.971	13	12	22	1	3

Outfield	PCT	G	PO	A	E	DP
Adamczewski	1.000	4	8	0	0	0
Alastre	.984	82	117	8	2	1
Berroa	1.000	6	10	0	0	0
Castillo	.976	30	38	3	1	0
Garcia	.986	85	137	3	2	0
Garcia	.976	51	17	3	1	1
Guilarte	.960	21	47	1	2	0
Hall	1.000	18	23	0	0	0
Nicasia	.963	78	126	3	5	1
Perez	.956	42	83	3	4	2
Rodriguez	1.000	3	1	0	0	0
Vargas	1.000	10	13	2	0	0

CAROLINA MUDCATS   LOW-A
CAROLINA LEAGUE

MILWAUKEE BREWERS

Batting	B-T	Ht.	Wt.	DOB	AVG	OBP	SLG	G	PA	AB	R	H	2B	3B	HR	RBI	BB	HBP	SH	SF	SO	SB	CS	BB%	SO%
Adamczewski, Josh	L-R	6-0	190	5-10-05	.359	.459	.569	46	206	167	36	60	12	4	5	38	29	5	0	4	37	4	0	14.1	18.0
Alastre, Luiyin	S-R	5-10	160	9-27-05	.311	.391	.508	17	69	61	13	19	3	3	1	13	6	2	0	0	8	1	2	8.7	11.6
Anderson, Jose	R-R	6-0	183	11-28-06	.193	.270	.340	84	341	306	29	59	15	3	8	29	27	6	0	2	101	7	4	7.9	29.6
Bitonti, Eric	L-R	6-4	205	11-17-05	.238	.341	.421	118	505	428	58	102	21	0	19	77	66	4	0	7	169	17	10	13.1	33.5
Di Turi, Filippo	S-R	5-11	165	11-9-05	.212	.322	.336	116	479	405	53	86	14	3	10	55	67	1	0	6	126	6	8	14.0	26.3
Diaz, Blayberg	R-R	5-11	190	1-31-03	.310	.370	.333	12	46	42	11	13	1	0	0	7	4	0	0	0	3	0	1	8.7	6.5
Dinges, Marco	R-R	6-0	190	9-5-03	.353	.500	.576	26	112	85	13	30	8	1	3	27	21	5	0	1	14	4	0	18.8	12.5
Ebel, Brady	L-R	6-3	195	7-25-07	.241	.333	.259	16	66	58	6	14	1	0	0	4	6	2	0	0	17	0	1	9.1	25.8
Encarnacion, Handelfry	L-L	5-11	172	6-8-07	.155	.237	.214	28	114	103	8	16	4	1	0	11	10	1	0	0	22	0	1	8.8	19.3
Garcia, Kevin	R-R	6-0	177	7-20-07	.300	.352	.340	14	54	50	5	15	2	0	0	5	3	1	0	0	10	0	0	5.6	18.5
Holguin, Gery	R-R	6-0	160	8-3-05	.158	.289	.203	54	211	177	19	28	6	1	0	13	31	2	0	1	74	5	1	14.7	35.1
Ibarguen, Pedro	R-R	5-10	180	7-2-06	.268	.397	.321	17	68	56	6	15	0	0	1	8	11	1	0	0	16	6	1	16.2	23.5
Lameda, Luis	S-R	5-10	160	1-17-06	.211	.362	.259	78	287	228	30	48	9	1	0	25	55	1	0	3	51	7	3	19.2	17.8
Made, Jesus	S-R	6-1	187	5-8-07	.267	.373	.388	83	378	322	55	86	21	3	4	46	53	2	0	1	78	40	9	14.0	20.6
Martinez, Eric	R-R	6-0	175	4-6-04	.355	.382	.677	9	34	31	5	11	2	1	2	7	0	2	0	1	10	0	0	0.0	29.4
Nadal, Demetrio	R-R	5-7	125	7-3-04	.206	.357	.250	40	171	136	22	28	3	0	1	16	27	6	0	2	37	11	3	15.8	21.6
Nicasia, Kaylan	S-R	5-11	176	4-10-02	.167	.286	.500	3	14	12	2	2	1	0	1	2	2	0	0	0	7	0	0	14.3	50.0
Ordonez, Edgardo	L-R	5-11	155	9-24-03	.141	.325	.219	25	83	64	8	9	2	0	1	8	17	1	0	1	26	0	0	20.5	31.3
Ortuno, Juan	R-R	5-8	165	4-26-07	.200	.385	.200	4	13	10	0	2	0	0	0	0	2	1	0	0	3	2	0	15.4	23.1
Payne, Braylon	L-L	6-2	186	8-14-06	.240	.354	.382	77	342	288	55	69	9	4	8	30	52	0	0	2	103	31	10	15.2	30.1
Pena, Luis	R-R	5-11	185	11-13-06	.308	.375	.469	71	309	273	59	84	14	6	6	52	28	4	0	4	41	41	7	9.1	13.3
Ragsdale, Josiah	L-L	6-0	185	12-21-03	.300	.437	.314	21	92	70	15	21	1	0	0	6	16	1	0	0	15	9	3	17.4	16.3
Rodriguez, Tyler	R-R	5-10	165	2-8-06	.217	.388	.266	91	343	263	38	57	7	0	2	30	59	17	0	4	54	22	8	17.2	15.7
Walling, Reece	L-R	6-5	202	9-22-03	.140	.332	.209	70	277	215	34	30	5	2	2	9	59	3	0	0	98	0	1	21.3	35.4
Walther, Yannic	R-R	6-0	185	4-12-04	.200	.318	.270	65	236	200	22	40	11	0	1	14	33	2	0	1	69	0	2	14.0	29.2

Pitching	B-T	Ht.	Wt.	DOB	W	L	ERA	G	GS	SV	IP	Hits	Runs	ER	HR	BB	SO	AVG	OBP	SLG	SO%	BB%	BF
Broca, Jesus	L-L	5-8	174	10-16-03	0	0	9.45	4	0	0	7	8	7	7	1	3	11	.286	.375	.429	33.3	9.1	33
Carra, Carlos	R-R	5-11	181	11-19-06	1	1	2.45	2	0	0	11	11	3	3	0	1	11	.262	.279	.405	25.6	2.3	43
DeBerry, Jaron	R-R	6-3	168	8-28-02	0	0	1.04	3	3	0	9	8	1	1	0	1	13	.250	.294	.281	38.2	2.9	34
DeCarlo, Nick	R-R	6-5	205	9-25-01	0	0	2.25	3	0	0	4	2	1	1	0	6	6	.143	.429	.143	28.6	28.6	21
Dorchies, Ethan	R-R	6-5	215	10-22-06	0	3	3.27	13	8	2	55	36	22	20	4	27	57	.183	.289	.294	25.0	11.8	228
Dubanewicz, Jayden	R-R	6-3	160	3-23-06	5	4	2.30	14	7	0	59	53	26	15	4	11	41	.242	.288	.374	17.2	4.6	239
Flores, Jesus	S-R	6-2	180	3-16-05	2	1	3.03	16	0	2	39	46	17	13	2	15	40	.311	.380	.405	24.1	9.0	166
Fowler, Michael	R-R	6-3	185	7-23-02	0	1	1.08	9	0	1	8	5	2	1	0	3	11	.172	.250	.207	34.4	9.4	32
Garcia, Sam	L-L	6-4	218	5-22-02	5	1	2.08	10	2	1	35	24	8	8	2	19	44	.197	.308	.311	30.8	13.3	143
Gillis, Tanner	R-R	6-3	220	8-10-00	1	1	1.32	7	0	1	27	29	8	4	0	8	28	.274	.325	.321	24.6	7.0	114
Hernandez, Melvin	R-R	5-11	139	7-3-06	10	5	2.00	24	17	0	122	98	32	27	3	22	97	.217	.270	.303	19.9	4.5	487
Hodges, Garrett	R-R	6-3	220	6-26-03	3	2	3.67	32	0	7	42	27	20	17	1	35	54	.188	.364	.222	29.2	18.9	185
Holobetz, John	R-R	6-3	190	7-31-02	3	0	3.00	5	3	0	24	16	10	8	1	5	31	.180	.229	.225	31.3	5.1	99
Hostetler, Jack	R-R	6-2	210	8-2-03	1	1	5.52	5	5	0	15	17	10	9	0	5	14	.298	.369	.368	21.5	7.7	65
Johnson, Bjorn	L-L	6-2	185	1-11-05	9	4	4.33	30	0	3	73	67	41	35	2	38	75	.251	.344	.371	24.3	12.3	309
Lameda, Luis	S-R	5-10	160	11-17-06	0	0	6.35	4	0	0	6	7	4	4	1	3	2	.318	.407	.455	7.4	11.1	27
Langhorne, Miles	R-R	6-4	210	4-30-03	2	0	3.33	15	0	3	24	15	15	9	3	11	28	.176	.301	.306	26.9	10.6	104
Meccage, Bryce	R-R	6-4	210	3-21-06	1	4	4.35	19	19	0	70	61	36	34	4	26	69	.238	.316	.391	23.6	8.9	292
Meneses, Jose	R-R	6-1	150	3-9-05	0	0	21.60	2	0	0	2	1	4	4	0	6	1	.167	.615	.167	7.7	46.2	13
Mercado, Enderson	L-L	5-11	177	3-23-07	0	3	4.10	7	5	1	26	28	14	12	3	9	22	.277	.342	.475	19.1	7.8	115
Mercedes, Miqueas	R-R	6-3	200	7-7-06	0	0	13.83	5	2	0	14	18	22	11	4	14	17	.295	.456	.377	21.5	17.7	79
Nova, Jose	R-R	6-5	185	4-2-02	2	3	4.76	18	0	5	23	20	17	12	1	16	29	.233	.358	.302	26.9	14.8	108
Quezada, Joshua	R-R	6-2	185	5-4-04	1	1	2.45	4	1	0	11	8	3	3	1	5	13	.211	.311	.263	28.9	11.1	45
Renz, Tyler	R-R	6-4	180	11-24-06	0	1	2.33	5	3	0	19	12	10	5	1	10	21	.174	.275	.232	26.3	12.5	80
Reyes, Anfernny	L-L	6-3	170	2-23-04	4	3	4.43	35	0	5	45	40	28	22	2	40	53	.237	.393	.325	24.8	18.7	214
Rivera, Bryan	R-R	6-3	170	5-28-05	3	3	5.82	25	3	0	73	65	55	47	8	49	84	.236	.387	.384	24.8	14.5	339
Sanchez, Dikember	R-R	5-11	160	2-20-04	2	0	6.60	13	0	1	15	16	12	11	3	18	13	.281	.391	.474	10.8	11.6	69
Seppings, Jack	R-R	6-1	190	7-3-02	1	1	3.46	17	0	4	26	29	12	10	1	14	31	.290	.388	.380	26.7	12.1	116
Smith, Travis	R-R	6-4	185	11-9-02	4	6	3.20	19	19	0	76	71	33	27	1	20	57	.251	.308	.319	18.3	6.4	311
Timmerman, Josh	R-R	6-4	195	8-4-02	1	0	11.81	5	0	0	5	4	8	7	2	11	8	.222	.531	.667	25.0	34.4	32
Tobias, Griffin	R-R	6-0	185	7-20-05	1	1	4.50	7	1	0	22	29	11	11	0	8	20	.312	.366	.441	19.6	7.8	102
Torres, Wande	L-L	6-3	190	1-31-05	1	10	4.81	23	23	0	86	84	51	46	3	36	85	.267	.354	.371	22.7	9.6	374
Vire, Caden	L-L	6-6	170	9-9-03	0	0	19.64	5	0	0	4	2	8	8	1	10	7	.167	.560	.417	28.0	40.0	25
Welch, Chandler	R-R	6-0	170	3-5-03	0	2	5.91	5	5	0	21	22	16	14	5	17	22	.272	.394	.506	22.0	17.0	100

Fielding

Catcher	PCT	G	PO	A	E	DP	PB
Diaz	.970	10	92	6	3	0	0
Dinges	.981	16	140	14	3	1	0
Garcia	.967	12	108	10	4	0	4
Martinez	.933	8	82	2	6	0	1
Ordonez	.981	23	179	25	4	1	8
Walther	.990	63	545	49	6	5	2

First Base	PCT	G	PO	A	E	DP
Bitonti	.989	107	781	50	9	67
Diaz	1.000	1	3	0	0	1
Holguin	.975	11	74	5	2	8
Walling	.989	12	84	2	1	6

Second Base	PCT	G	PO	A	E	DP
Adamczewski	.957	36	59	73	6	12

Di Turi	.943	27	49	67	7	21
Holguin	.000	1	0	0	0	0
Lameda	.961	43	80	91	7	26
Made	1.000	8	13	19	0	4
Nadal	1.000	2	5	4	0	2
Ortuno	1.000	1	0	3	0	0
Pena	1.000	16	16	38	0	5

Third Base	PCT	G	PO	A	E	DP
Alastre	.857	5	1	5	1	0
Bitonti	1.000	1	1	0	0	0
Di Turi	.963	54	42	89	5	5
Holguin	.956	31	18	47	3	4
Lameda	.818	15	8	19	6	3
Made	.846	8	12	10	4	3
Nadal	.778	4	4	3	2	1
Ortuno	.600	3	1	2	2	0
Pena	.920	11	7	16	2	1

Shortstop	PCT	G	PO	A	E	DP
Di Turi	.959	30	38	79	5	10
Ebel	.967	12	23	35	2	10
Lameda	.500	1	0	1	1	
Made	.963	55	70	139	8	22
Pena	.915	32	35	73	10	13

Outfield	PCT	G	PO	A	E	DP
Alastre	.941	10	13	3	1	0
Anderson	.949	78	137	11	8	5
Encarnacion	.939	22	27	4	2	1
Holguin	.875	2	7	0	1	0
Ibarguen	1.000	14	21	2	0	0
Lameda	.963	16	26	0	1	0
Nadal	.922	30	44	3	4	0
Nicasia	1.000	4	6	1	0	0
Payne	.973	66	138	8	4	2
Ragsdale	1.000	19	31	2	0	0
Rodriguez	.987	85	145	8	2	0
Walling	.978	50	85	5	2	2

ACL BREWERS
ARIZONA COMPLEX LEAGUE — ROOKIE

Batting	B-T	Ht.	Wt.	DOB	AVG	OBP	SLG	G	PA	AB	R	H	2B	3B	HR	RBI	BB	HBP	SH	SF	SO	SB	CS	BB%	SO%
Adamczewski, Josh	L-R	6-0	190	5-10-05	.333	.432	.500	9	37	30	12	10	3	1	0	2	6	0	0	1	5	0	1	16.2	13.5
Anderson, Jose	R-R	6-0	183	11-28-06	.333	.467	.750	10	45	36	16	12	2	2	3	13	8	1	0	0	9	3	0	17.8	20.0
Berroa, Steward	S-R	5-9	178	6-5-99	.000	.000	.000	1	3	3	0	0	0	0	0	0	0	0	0	0	0	0	0	0.0	0.0
Black, Tyler	L-R	5-10	190	7-26-00	.387	.513	.613	10	39	31	7	12	2	1	1	5	8	0	0	0	3	0	1	20.5	7.7
Boeve, Mike	L-R	6-3	200	5-5-02	1.000	1.000	1.000	1	3	2	1	2	0	0	0	1	1	0	0	0	0	0	0	33.3	0.0
Castillo, Luis	L-L	6-0	175	10-11-03	.235	.278	.294	5	18	17	2	4	1	0	0	1	1	0	0	0	3	0	0	5.6	16.7
Corobo, Luis	R-R	5-11	183	5-2-07	.246	.363	.303	38	146	122	18	30	7	0	0	22	20	3	0	1	37	1	0	13.7	25.3
Encarnacion, Handelfry	L-L	5-11	172	6-8-07	.289	.369	.463	48	214	190	40	55	18	0	5	37	19	5	0	0	33	6	5	8.9	15.4
Ereu, Kevin	R-R	5-10	165	5-24-06	.148	.320	.211	47	181	142	23	21	2	2	1	15	26	11	0	2	62	5	4	14.4	34.3
Fielder, Jadyn	R-R	6-1	210	8-17-04	.268	.426	.444	48	183	142	30	38	6	5	3	26	30	10	0	1	41	8	4	16.4	22.4
Flores, Roderick	R-R	5-9	167	8-24-06	.235	.386	.341	43	171	132	17	31	6	0	0	8	21	31	4	0	4	36	3	0	18.1	21.1
Garcia, Kevin	R-R	6-0	177	7-20-07	.246	.345	.397	40	142	121	24	29	4	0	5	22	10	10	0	1	50	1	1	7.0	35.2
Holguin, Gery	R-R	6-0	160	8-3-05	.347	.418	.694	15	55	49	15	17	3	1	4	14	6	0	0	0	14	0	0	10.9	25.5
Ibarguen, Pedro	R-R	5-10	180	7-2-06	.303	.415	.461	28	106	89	18	27	4	2	2	16	16	1	0	0	15	12	4	15.1	14.2
Mitchell, Garrett	L-R	6-3	224	9-4-98	.000	.000	.000	1	2	2	0	0	0	0	0	0	0	0	0	0	2	0	0	0.0	100.0
Montero, Frederi	R-R	6-2	188	1-12-07	.265	.371	.316	55	232	196	28	52	10	0	0	32	32	2	0	2	47	5	3	13.8	20.3
Nadal, Demetrio	R-R	5-7	125	7-3-04	.247	.351	.423	29	114	97	18	24	4	2	3	18	13	3	0	1	20	6	4	11.4	17.5
Ortuno, Juan	R-R	5-8	165	4-26-07	.250	.467	.422	20	92	64	21	16	2	0	2	13	21	6	0	1	15	3	3	22.8	16.3
Paulino, Engel	R-R	5-9	162	12-2-06	.247	.384	.495	49	178	146	29	36	9	4	1	28	29	1	0	2	62	19	2	16.3	34.8
Perkins, Blake	S-R	5-11	197	9-10-96	.389	.500	.389	7	22	18	4	7	0	0	0	2	4	0	0	0	4	1	1	18.2	18.2
Quero, Jeferson	R-R	5-11	215	10-8-02	.371	.500	.886	11	44	35	10	13	3	0	5	13	7	2	0	0	5	0	0	15.9	11.4
Quintana, Jorge	S-R	6-2	183	4-5-07	.246	.349	.403	50	229	201	30	53	13	3	3	23	24	3	0	1	50	19	4	10.5	21.8
Rojas, Freider	S-R	5-8	155	10-23-05	.200	.308	.267	17	52	45	9	9	1	1	0	4	7	0	0	0	16	0	0	13.5	30.8

Pitching	B-T	Ht.	Wt.	DOB	W	L	ERA	G	GS	SV	IP	Hits	Runs	ER	HR	BB	SO	AVG	OBP	SLG	SO%	BB%	BF
Aparicio, Argenis	S-R	6-0	180	9-23-05	1	1	7.53	15	0	3	29	37	25	24	3	13	20	.311	.382	.529	14.7	9.6	136
Ashby, Aaron	R-L	6-1	188	5-24-98	0	1	20.25	1	1	0	1	3	3	3	0	2	1	.429	.556	.571	11.1	22.2	9
Bravo, Ayendy	R-R	5-10	180	1-24-07	2	2	5.74	7	0	1	16	24	14	10	1	5	13	.343	.410	.471	16.5	6.3	79
Carra, Carlos	R-R	5-11	181	11-19-06	1	2	4.79	12	4	0	41	40	24	22	2	11	44	.248	.313	.410	24.2	6.0	182
Colmenarez, Gabriel	R-R	6-1	155	3-28-06	1	0	4.91	3	0	0	11	9	6	6	2	6	5	.268	.367	.463	10.2	12.2	49
DeCarlo, Nick	R-R	6-5	205	9-25-01	0	0	40.50	1	0	0	1	2	3	3	1	1	2	.500	.600	1.250	40.0	20.0	5
Dorchies, Ethan	R-R	6-5	215	10-22-06	0	0	1.67	6	3	2	27	15	9	5	0	8	32	.158	.229	.200	30.5	7.6	105
Dubanewicz, Jayden	R-R	6-3	160	3-23-06	3	0	2.66	5	4	0	24	20	11	7	0	8	23	.217	.280	.304	23.0	8.0	100
Espinal, Cesar	R-R	6-2	165	8-25-05	2	2	7.20	14	0	2	15	23	13	12	2	10	12	.338	.430	.529	15.2	12.7	79
Flores, Roderick	R-R	5-9	167	8-24-06	0	0	0.00	1	0	0	1	0	0	0	0	0	0	.250	.250	.250	0.0	0.0	4
Gasser, Robert	L-L	6-0	192	5-31-99	0	0	0.00	1	1	0	1	0	0	0	0	0	0	.000	.333	.333	0.0	0	3
Gonzalez, Aldrin	R-R	6-1	180	4-6-06	1	0	18.41	6	0	0	7	14	18	15	1	8	7	.378	.540	.568	14.0	16.0	50
Hall, DL	L-L	6-2	210	9-19-98	0	0	0.00	2	2	0	5	1	0	0	0	2	8	.063	.167	.063	44.4	11.1	18
King, Wenderlyn	R-R	5-9	165	8-24-05	2	1	4.26	9	0	2	25	27	15	12	4	9	27	.265	.336	.471	23.7	7.9	114
Meneses, Jose	L-L	6-1	150	3-9-05	1	1	7.54	16	0	1	23	19	20	19	2	23	31	.226	.400	.345	28.2	20.9	110
Mercado, Enderson	L-L	5-11	177	3-23-07	0	2	5.05	12	11	1	46	44	30	26	5	19	55	.251	.333	.411	27.1	9.4	203
Mercedes, Miqueas	R-R	6-3	200	7-7-06	1	4	4.11	12	11	0	46	48	31	21	2	20	45	.268	.345	.391	22.1	9.8	204
Merkel, Nick	R-R	6-7	255	7-3-98	0	0	0.00	2	0	0	2	0	0	0	0	1	0	.000	.000	.000	16.7	0.0	6
Mora, Daurys	R-R	5-10	180	1-20-04	1	1	2.08	11	0	2	13	8	11	3	0	10	15	.167	.355	.229	24.2	16.1	62
Nova, Jose	R-R	6-5	185	4-2-02	2	1	4.91	7	0	1	9	6	5	4	0	4	8	.222	.313	.296	25.0	12.5	32
Quezada, Joshua	R-R	6-2	185	6-8-05	1	1	8.15	14	2	1	35	42	34	32	3	11	38	.288	.360	.418	23.2	6.7	164
Renz, Tyler	R-R	6-4	180	11-24-06	3	3	3.50	12	9	0	54	50	22	21	4	15	46	.238	.295	.367	20.3	6.6	227
Robinson, Hayden	R-R	6-0	180	7-12-05	0	3	8.76	7	7	0	12	17	12	12	1	15	10	.261	.452	.348	15.9	23.8	63
Rodriguez, Carlos F.	R-R	6-0	206	11-21-01	0	0	4.26	2	2	0	6	5	3	3	1	0	4	.346	.346	.500	15.4	0.0	26
Shears, Tanner	R-R	6-3	205	6-20-99	1	0	9.00	2	0	0	3	5	1	3	0	5	5	.100	.308	.100	38.5	15.4	13
Thomas, Connor	L-L	5-11	173	5-29-98	0	0	18.00	1	0	0	1	3	2	2	0	1	0	.500	.571	.500	0.0	14.3	7
Tobias, Griffin	R-R	6-0	185	7-20-05	1	3	5.15	9	2	1	37	44	27	21	4	1	29	.293	.308	.447	18.5	0.6	157
Vallecillo, Alexander	R-R	6-0	150	7-1-02	0	1	108.00	1	1	0	0	2	4	4	1	2	0	.667	.800	2.000	0.0	40.0	5
Yanez, Ismael	R-R	6-0	180	11-9-05	2	1	9.00	9	0	1	9	11	9	9	1	9	1	.305	.500	.455	18.8	22.9	48

Fielding

C: Garcia 26, Corobo 25, Rojas 10, Quero 8. **1B:** Montero 22, Ereu 14, Holguin 11, Flores 10, Black 4, Garcia 2. **2B:** Nadal 14, Fielder 12, Flores 12, Ortuno 10, Ereu 8, Adamczewski 7. **3B:** Montero 32, Ereu 13, Quintana 6, Flores 4, Holguin 3, Ortuno 3, Nadal 2. **SS:** Quintana 40, Ereu 12, Ortuno 7, Nadal 2. **LF:** Fielder 29, Flores 11, Nadal 10, Paulino 8, Black 3, Ibarguen 3. **CF:** Encarnacion 27, Paulino 22, Anderson 8, Ibarguen 5, Perkins 5, Mitchell 1. **RF:** Paulino 19, Encarnacion 17, Ibarguen 17, Flores 6, Castillo 4, Anderson 1, Nadal 1, Perkins 1.

DSL BREWERS 1 — ROOKIE
DOMINICAN SUMMER LEAGUE

MILWAUKEE BREWERS

Batting	B-T	Ht.	Wt.	DOB	AVG	OBP	SLG	G	PA	AB	R	H	2B	3B	HR	RBI	BB	HBP	SH	SF	SO	SB	CS	BB%	SO%
Antunez, Brailyn	R-R	6-0	187	11-30-07	.215	.353	.282	55	241	195	39	42	10	0	1	25	30	13	0	3	41	21	6	12.4	17.0
De La Rosa, Sharlisson	R-R	5-10	190	11-15-07	.236	.345	.375	22	84	72	12	17	6	2	0	12	5	7	0	0	13	2	0	6.0	15.5
Done, Carlos	R-R	5-10	182	1-3-07	.252	.379	.409	46	198	159	29	40	8	1	5	28	26	9	0	4	39	17	5	13.1	19.7
Gonzalez, Angel	L-R	5-10	171	1-18-07	.252	.414	.402	35	140	107	25	27	9	2	1	12	21	10	0	2	23	13	6	15.0	16.4
Gutierrez, Joan	L-R	5-11	165	10-7-05	.226	.431	.264	41	144	106	28	24	4	0	0	13	33	5	0	0	25	12	4	22.9	17.4
Lafond, Frandy	R-R	6-1	180	1-27-07	.209	.375	.331	47	176	139	36	29	7	2	2	25	33	4	0	0	46	13	2	18.8	26.1
Lista, Jefer	R-R	6-2	184	5-28-08	.229	.395	.263	55	233	179	32	41	4	1	0	30	38	13	0	3	37	9	4	16.3	15.9
Lugo, Yoneiker	R-R	5-8	155	4-27-07	.313	.398	.414	30	123	99	14	31	7	0	1	24	17	1	0	6	15	1	0	13.8	12.2
Payano, Gerlyn	L-L	6-1	192	6-2-08	.176	.300	.176	6	20	17	6	3	0	0	0	1	2	1	0	0	6	2	0	10.0	30.0
Polanco, Moises	R-R	5-10	150	5-30-07	.286	.437	.416	49	199	154	37	44	12	1	2	38	41	2	0	2	31	11	3	20.6	15.6
Rijo, Leonard	R-R	5-7	140	11-23-07	.214	.365	.253	54	230	182	41	39	1	3	0	21	35	10	0	3	35	21	3	15.2	15.2
Saez, Jhoanjel	R-R	5-9	150	4-13-07	.202	.347	.298	33	118	94	15	19	4	1	1	16	21	1	0	2	27	11	4	17.8	22.9
Seijas, Kegnnalex	R-R	5-8	150	11-5-05	.292	.438	.438	22	64	48	12	14	5	0	1	4	19	12	2	0	2	2	0	18.8	12.5
Tarazona, Johanderson	S-R	5-9	174	6-2-08	.262	.435	.415	21	85	65	13	17	5	1	1	9	14	6	0	0	23	5	1	16.5	27.1

Pitching	B-T	Ht.	Wt.	DOB	W	L	ERA	G	GS	SV	IP	Hits	Runs	ER	HR	BB	SO	AVG	OBP	SLG	SO%	BB%	BF
Aguirrez, Brailin	R-R	6-1	175	2-18-08	0	1	12.00	5	3	0	9	11	12	12	0	8	4	.314	.510	.343	7.8	15.7	51
Barreras, Fausto	R-R	6-0	175	11-22-07	0	0	0.00	1	0	0	1	0	0	0	0	1	0	.000	.333	.000	0.0	33.3	3
Bravo, Ayendy	R-R	5-10	180	1-24-07	1	0	0.00	1	1	0	5	3	1	0	0	0	7	.167	.167	.222	38.9	0.0	18
Downs, Lonell	R-R	5-9	184	4-7-07	2	2	5.87	11	7	0	38	34	27	25	0	26	37	.233	.371	.308	20.6	14.4	180
Duran, Steven	R-R	6-1	175	7-24-08	3	2	2.77	9	5	0	26	12	9	8	0	16	22	.136	.330	.193	19.1	13.9	115
Galindo, Carlos	R-R	6-1	184	9-3-07	4	1	4.08	11	5	0	46	46	25	21	2	12	28	.261	.316	.369	14.5	6.2	193
Gonzalez, Lukas	R-R	6-0	140	11-23-06	2	0	3.72	5	2	1	19	17	8	8	1	10	18	.233	.352	.342	20.5	11.4	88
Lugo, Justin	R-R	6-3	200	11-26-05	1	3	4.50	17	0	1	22	20	16	11	1	17	29	.253	.417	.329	28.2	16.5	103
Manrique, Merwin	R-R	5-10	176	7-13-07	1	0	16.20	9	0	0	8	11	15	15	2	17	9	.314	.579	.514	15.5	29.3	58
Martinez, Santiago	L-L	5-11	160	7-25-08	0	2	18.00	3	3	0	3	2	8	6	0	6	0	.167	.444	.167	0.0	33.3	18
Mayorquin, Diustin	R-R	5-11	190	10-28-07	2	1	2.45	11	5	2	48	44	17	13	0	7	49	.246	.288	.346	25.7	3.7	191
Mendez, Lenin	R-R	6-3	193	9-22-04	3	3	8.37	17	0	2	24	29	24	22	2	21	17	.312	.454	.495	14.2	17.5	120
Moreno, Manuel	R-R	6-1	170	10-23-06	2	1	4.50	11	7	0	42	32	22	21	1	19	32	.204	.302	.325	17.9	10.6	179
Ospino, Jhosep	R-R	6-0	142	9-6-04	3	1	2.93	17	0	2	28	25	15	9	1	14	33	.248	.358	.317	26.8	11.4	123
Ramirez, Johandry	R-R	6-1	160	8-22-07	0	0	5.56	7	0	0	11	12	8	7	0	7	10	.279	.404	.326	19.2	13.5	52
Regalado, Bryan	R-R	6-3	185	4-24-07	0	1	20.25	2	2	0	1	5	3	3	0	3	1	.556	.667	.778	8.3	25.0	12
Rodriguez, Jean	R-R	6-2	170	6-1-07	2	1	6.92	13	2	1	26	18	22	20	2	31	20	.217	.462	.398	15.0	23.3	133
Toledo, Josue	R-R	5-11	182	5-19-06	2	2	4.91	11	4	2	40	42	29	22	3	27	46	.273	.406	.403	23.8	14.0	193
Velasquez, Luis	R-R	6-0	155	10-24-07	1	5	6.18	11	4	0	39	31	33	27	3	37	25	.226	.403	.380	13.7	20.3	182
Zapata, Johan	R-R	5-11	160	11-10-05	0	1	10.80	9	0	1	12	18	16	14	1	8	11	.333	.471	.444	16.2	11.8	68

Fielding

C: Lugo 30, Tarazona 21, Seijas 7. **1B:** Lista 29, Seijas 11, De La Rosa 9, Gutierrez 8, Gonzalez 6, Tarazona 1. **2B:** Polanco 21, Saez 21, Rijo 9, Gutierrez 6. **3B:** Gutierrez 29, Polanco 18, Saez 11, De La Rosa 1. **SS:** Rijo 45, Polanco 11. **LF:** Gonzalez 19, Done 17, Lafond 13, Lista 8, Gutierrez 2, Payano 1. **CF:** Antunez 44, Lafond 12, Gonzalez 3. **RF:** Done 23, Lafond 19, Lista 8, Gonzalez 7, Payano 3.

DSL BREWERS 2 — ROOKIE
DOMINICAN SUMMER LEAGUE

Batting	B-T	Ht.	Wt.	DOB	AVG	OBP	SLG	G	PA	AB	R	H	2B	3B	HR	RBI	BB	HBP	SH	SF	SO	SB	CS	BB%	SO%
Acosta, Cristopher	R-R	5-11	175	1-28-08	.172	.349	.243	50	218	169	34	29	3	3	1	17	43	4	0	2	45	16	6	19.7	20.6
Barrios, Nicolas	L-L	5-9	161	4-25-08	.209	.327	.349	31	104	86	13	18	5	2	1	13	11	5	0	2	22	8	3	10.6	21.2
Chavez, Isais	R-R	5-11	193	5-16-08	.232	.359	.424	39	153	125	24	29	6	0	6	22	19	7	0	2	38	9	1	12.4	24.8
Donato, Romano	R-R	5-10	167	8-5-08	.176	.341	.245	41	129	102	21	18	4	0	1	6	22	4	0	1	22	10	4	17.1	17.1
Fenelon, Kenny	R-R	6-0	184	9-30-07	.206	.356	.347	50	219	170	26	35	5	2	5	25	33	10	0	6	52	18	10	15.1	23.7
Frias, Alexander	L-R	6-2	177	3-10-08	.316	.411	.400	27	112	95	22	30	5	0	1	17	14	2	0	1	21	7	3	12.5	18.8
Martinez, Juan	S-R	5-11	170	4-18-07	.321	.445	.532	47	191	156	38	50	13	7	2	24	30	5	0	0	22	24	1	15.7	11.5
Montilla, Cristian	L-R	5-10	152	4-23-08	.276	.353	.345	45	167	145	23	40	8	1	0	24	17	2	0	3	25	8	7	10.2	15.0
Moses, Matthew	R-R	5-11	183	9-24-07	.214	.296	.405	38	144	126	19	27	12	0	4	28	14	1	0	1	34	5	3	9.7	16.7
Paulino, Roniel	R-R	5-10	182	10-30-07	.190	.333	.310	18	51	42	12	8	2	0	1	9	9	0	0	0	5	2	1	17.6	9.8
Pena, Joandrew	R-R	6-3	172	12-14-06	.214	.450	.286	6	20	14	0	3	1	0	0	4	6	0	0	0	7	0	1	30.0	35.0
Rangel, Jonathan	L-R	5-9	176	2-23-07	.288	.434	.500	41	159	118	29	34	5	7	2	25	31	4	0	6	28	5	0	19.5	17.6
Rivero, Eryks	R-R	6-1	186	10-13-07	.182	.375	.273	42	160	121	20	22	1	2	3	1	14	33	5	0	1	49	2	1	20.6	30.6
Sosa, Francis	R-R	5-11	190	10-26-07	.153	.307	.360	38	141	111	15	17	5	0	6	15	19	7	0	3	52	6	6	13.5	36.9
Tovar, Pedro	L-L	6-1	160	6-23-06	.238	.443	.381	20	61	42	13	10	4	1	0	11	17	0	0	2	18	5	0	27.9	29.5

Pitching	B-T	Ht.	Wt.	DOB	W	L	ERA	G	GS	SV	IP	Hits	Runs	ER	HR	BB	SO	AVG	OBP	SLG	SO%	BB%	BF
Arias, Jose	R-R	6-1	163	3-20-07	2	6	5.77	11	8	0	39	34	25	25	3	26	28	.234	.369	.379	15.6	14.4	180
Cabrera, Wandy	R-R	6-2	170	6-6-06	1	1	9.14	12	0	22	80	25	22	0	22	19	.238	.420	.321	17.0	19.6	112	
Canales, Carlos	R-R	6-1	160	1-10-06	3	0	2.16	11	0	1	25	20	8	6	0	10	19	.225	.307	.360	18.6	9.8	102
Colmenarez, Gabriel	R-R	6-1	155	3-28-06	1	1	2.14	5	5	0	21	13	10	5	0	6	23	.167	.233	.231	26.7	7.0	86
Garcia, Daniel	L-L	6-0	170	3-30-08	0	1	7.50	7	5	0	18	12	7	5	0	8	13	.190	.316	.254	17.1	10.5	76
Garcia, Derlin	R-R	6-1	160	11-3-06	3	1	1.86	7	2	0	19	12	5	4	0	6	22	.182	.267	.227	29.3	8.0	75
Garcia, Gustavo	R-R	6-1	195	9-19-07	3	2	3.63	11	7	0	45	32	21	18	1	18	32	.201	.291	.277	17.5	9.8	183
Gonzalez, Aldrin	R-R	6-1	180	4-6-06	0	1	4.76	2	2	0	6	3	7	3	0	6	2	8	.150	.292	.150	33.3	8.3	24
Jimenez, Linbel	R-R	6-5	198	10-26-04	1	0	5.09	13	0	0	18	10	12	10	0	20	21	.161	.402	.226	24.1	23.0	87
Lin, Chang Tzu-Chun	R-R	6-0	165	10-6-05	0	0	4.50	2	2	0	2	2	1	1	0	0	2	.143	.250	.143	0.0	12.5	8

Parra, Alejandro	R-R	6-3	195	11-28-05	0	1	18.00	2	2	0	2	3	4	4	0	3	3	.333	.500	.556	25.0	25.0	12
Pena, Joan	L-L	5-11	205	9-21-07	4	2	3.25	10	6	0	44	40	23	16	1	15	42	.248	.335	.329	22.6	8.1	186
Peralta, Christopher	R-R	5-11	165	5-16-07	0	3	5.84	11	6	0	37	32	31	24	4	24	39	.234	.361	.453	23.1	14.2	169
Reyes, Fabian	R-R	6-4	175	10-5-04	3	1	7.94	15	0	1	17	13	17	15	1	15	24	.210	.375	.290	29.6	18.5	81
Saldana, Ruben	R-R	5-10	153	2-1-06	2	2	5.17	14	2	2	31	38	22	18	3	23	31	.314	.428	.438	20.3	15.0	153
Sanchez, Saul	R-R	5-11	175	8-8-06	2	3	5.96	17	0	1	23	29	16	15	2	5	22	.322	.364	.478	22.0	5.0	100
Sarmiento, Raymond	R-R	6-1	163	2-2-08	1	2	4.50	11	5	1	42	37	23	21	2	11	37	.227	.298	.374	20.3	6.0	182
Toledo, Josue	R-R	5-11	182	5-19-06	0	0	0.00	1	0	0	4	1	0	0	0	0	3	.083	.083	.083	25.0	0.0	12
Vargas, Albert	R-R	6-2	185	5-18-06	1	2	6.75	15	0	2	17	25	13	13	1	5	12	.333	.375	.520	15.0	6.3	80
Velasquez, Enrique	R-R	6-2	180	4-5-08	0	1	9.19	9	2	0	16	12	18	16	1	18	3	.218	.442	.327	3.8	23.1	78

Fielding

C: Chavez 33, Rangel 14, Paulino 13. **1B:** Moses 32, Rangel 20, Paulino 4, Pena 4. **2B:** Martinez 24, Donato 19, Montilla 14. **3B:** Martinez 23, Montilla 16, Donato 15, Moses 5. **SS:** Acosta 42, Montilla 14, Donato 1, Fenelon 1. **LF:** Barrios 28, Sosa 13, Frias 10, Rivero 5, Tovar 1. **CF:** Fenelon 45, Sosa 11, Acosta 1. **RF:** Rivero 26, Tovar 15, Frias 13, Sosa 4.

Minnesota Twins

SEASON SYNOPSIS: The malaise that started in a 2024 collapse deepened in 2025. En route to missing the playoffs for the fourth time in five seasons, Minnesota blew up its roster, trading 11 players—10 on the 26-man active roster—in the last days of July. The result was a 70-92 finish, the most losses for the club since 2016, and the firing of manager Rocco Baldelli after season's end.

HIGH POINT: After a 13-20 start, the Twins won 13 in a row and kept winning, including the first three games (by a score of 26-8) of a four-game set in Sacramento against the Athletics to peak at 34-27. They were healthy too—oft-injured stars Byron Buxton, Carlos Correa and Royce Lewis all played for the series in Sacramento.

LOW POINT: Pablo Lopez threw six innings in a 7-0 shutout of the A's on May 17 but went on the IL before his next start with a lat strain, and the Twins were never the same. Their last gasp was snuffed July 23 in Dodger Stadium. An out away from closing out a winning road series, Griffin Jax couldn't hold the one-run lead, then criticized Baldelli after the game for having him intentionally walk Shohei Ohtani. The Twins fell to 48-52, the front office started exploring the seller's market and the season felt lost.

NOTABLE ROOKIES: Luke Keaschall debuted ahead of schedule on April 18, set a club record with five stolen bases in his first five games and hit safely in six straight before being hit by a pitch and breaking his right forearm April 25. He returned in August after the deadline and batted .302/.382/.445 with 14 steals in 182 at-bats before an injury to his left thumb ended his season a week early.

KEY TRANSACTIONS: The Pohlad family announced in October 2024 that the club was for sale, but in August they announced they were keeping the club while taking on two minority investors. That came less than two weeks after the trade deadline fire sale that included trading Correa—the biggest free-agent contract in franchise history—back to Houston for a non-prospect, with the Astros taking on two-thirds of the $96 million Correa is owed through 2028. The deals gutted the bullpen as Minnesota dealt five top five relievers—Jhoan Duran (Philadelphia), Jax (Tampa Bay), Louis Varland (Toronto), Brock Stewart (LA Dodgers) and Danny Coulombe (Texas), with the best returning assets including righties Mick Abel and Taj Bradley and minor league catcher Eduardo Tait.

OPENING DAY PAYROLL: $142,762,022 (18th)

PLAYERS OF THE YEAR

MAJOR LEAGUE
Byron Buxton
OF
.264/.327/.551
Career-high 35 HR,
129 H, 83 RBIs, 41 BB

MINOR LEAGUE
Walker Jenkins
OF
(Rk,A,AA,AAA)
.286/.399/.451
10 HR, 17 2B in 84 G

ORGANIZATION LEADERS

Batting		*Qualifiers
MAJORS		
* AVG	Byron Buxton	.264
* OPS	Byron Buxton	.878
HR	Byron Buxton	35
RBI	Byron Buxton	83
MINORS		
* AVG	Gabriel Gonzalez, St. Paul/Wichita/Cedar Rapids	.329
* OBP	Walker Jenkins, St. Paul/Wichita/Ft. Myers	.399
* SLG	Gabriel Gonzalez, St. Paul/Wichita/Cedar Rapids	.513
* OPS	Gabriel Gonzalez, St. Paul/Wichita/Cedar Rapids	.909
R	Kala'i Rosario, Wichita	92
H	Gabriel Gonzalez, St. Paul/Wichita/Cedar Rapids	159
TB	Gabriel Gonzalez, St. Paul/Wichita/Cedar Rapids	248
2B	Gabriel Gonzalez, St. Paul/Wichita/Cedar Rapids	38
3B	Jhomnardo Reyes, DSL Twins	9
HR	Kyler Fedko, St. Paul/Wichita	28
RBI	Kala'i Rosario, Wichita	83
BB	Kyler Fedko, St. Paul/Wichita	79
SO	Kala'i Rosario, Wichita	159
SB	Kyle DeBarge, Cedar Rapids	66

Pitching		#Qualifiers
MAJORS		
W	Pablo Lopez	15
# ERA	Bailey Ober	3.98
SO	Pablo Lopez	198
SV	Jhoan Duran	23
MINORS		
W	Randy Dobnak, St. Paul	12
L	Aaron Rozek, St. Paul/Wichita	10
L	Darren Bowen, Cedar Rapids	10
# ERA	Andrew Morris, Cedar Rapids/Wichita/St. Paul	2.37
G	Kyle Bischoff, Cedar Rapids/St. Paul/Wichita	45
GS	Caleb Boushley, St. Paul	26
SV	Nolan Santos, Cedar Rapids/Fort Myers	11
IP	Caleb Boushley, St. Paul	134
BB	Randy Dobnak, St. Paul	63
SO	Randy Dobnak, St. Paul	134
# AVG	Andrew Morris, Cedar Rapids/Wichita/St. Paul	.221

2025 PERFORMANCE

General Manager: Derek Falvey. **Farm Director:** Drew MacPhail. **Scouting Director:** Sean Johnson.

Class	Team	League	W	L	PCT	Finish	Manager
Majors	Minnesota Twins	American	70	92	.432	14 (15)	Rocco Baldelli
Triple-A	St. Paul Saints	International	62	86	.419	18 (20)	Toby Gardenhire
Double-A	Wichita Wind Surge	Texas	76	62	.551	2 (10)	Brian Dinkelman
High-A	Cedar Rapids Kernels	Midwest	72	60	.545	5 (12)	Brian Meyer
Low-A	Fort Myers Mighty Mussels	Florida State	52	73	.416	10 (10)	Seth Feldman
Rookie	FCL Twins	Florida Complex	39	20	.661	2 (15)	Nico Giarratano
Rookie	DSL Twins	Dominican	24	32	.429	39 (52)	Rafael Martinez
Overall 2025 Minor League Record			325	333	.494	16th (30)	

ORGANIZATION STATISTICS

MINNESOTA TWINS
AMERICAN LEAGUE

Batting	B-T	Ht.	Wt.	DOB	AVG	OBP	SLG	G	PA	AB	R	H	2B	3B	HR	RBI	BB	HBP	SH	SF	SO	SB	CS	BB%	SO%
Bader, Harrison	R-R	6-0	210	6-3-94	.258	.339	.439	96	307	271	31	70	13	0	12	38	27	7	0	2	81	10	4	8.8	26.4
Bride, Jonah	R-R	5-10	200	12-27-95	.208	.275	.236	33	80	72	4	15	2	0	0	3	6	1	0	1	24	0	0	7.5	30.0
Buxton, Byron	R-R	6-2	190	12-18-93	.264	.327	.551	126	542	488	97	129	21	7	35	83	41	7	0	6	148	24	0	7.6	27.3
Castro, Willi	S-R	6-1	206	4-24-97	.245	.335	.407	86	344	302	48	74	15	2	10	27	32	9	1	0	84	9	3	9.3	24.4
Clemens, Kody	L-R	6-1	200	5-15-96	.216	.284	.442	112	379	342	46	74	12	4	19	52	28	5	2	2	93	5	1	7.4	24.5
Correa, Carlos	R-R	6-4	220	9-22-94	.267	.319	.386	93	364	337	40	90	19	0	7	31	26	0	0	1	68	0	0	7.1	18.7
Fitzgerald, Ryan	L-R	6-0	185	6-17-94	.196	.302	.457	24	53	46	10	9	0	0	4	9	7	0	0	0	8	1	0	13.2	15.1
France, Ty	R-R	5-11	215	7-13-94	.251	.320	.357	101	387	350	41	88	19	0	6	44	19	17	0	1	63	1	0	4.9	16.3
Gasper, Mickey	S-R	5-9	205	10-11-95	.158	.257	.232	45	110	95	15	15	1	0	2	11	10	3	1	1	20	2	0	9.1	18.2
Jeffers, Ryan	R-R	6-4	235	6-3-97	.266	.356	.397	119	464	406	47	108	26	0	9	47	50	7	0	1	91	1	1	10.8	19.6
Julien, Edouard	L-R	6-0	195	4-30-99	.220	.309	.324	64	208	182	13	40	10	0	3	12	22	2	1	1	61	0	3	10.6	29.3
Keaschall, Luke	R-R	6-1	190	8-15-02	.302	.382	.445	49	207	182	25	55	14	0	4	28	19	5	0	1	29	14	3	9.2	14.0
Keirsey, DaShawn	L-L	6-0	195	5-13-97	.107	.138	.179	74	88	84	11	9	0	0	2	6	2	1	1	0	33	10	3	2.3	37.5
Larnach, Trevor	L-R	6-4	223	2-26-97	.250	.323	.404	142	567	503	62	126	24	1	17	60	53	4	0	6	122	4	4	9.3	21.5
Lee, Brooks	S-R	5-11	205	2-14-01	.236	.285	.370	139	527	487	50	115	15	1	16	64	31	4	0	5	92	3	1	5.9	17.5
Lewis, Royce	R-R	6-2	200	6-5-99	.237	.283	.388	106	403	376	36	89	18	0	13	52	25	0	0	2	80	12	2	6.2	19.9
Martin, Austin	R-R	6-0	185	3-23-99	.282	.374	.365	50	181	156	22	44	8	1	1	7	22	1	2	0	31	11	4	12.2	17.1
McCusker, Carson	R-R	6-8	250	5-22-98	.172	.200	.172	16	30	29	0	5	0	0	0	1	1	0	0	0	16	0	1	3.3	53.3
Miranda, Jose	R-R	6-2	210	6-29-98	.167	.167	.250	12	36	36	2	6	0	0	1	5	0	0	0	0	13	0	0	0.0	36.1
Outman, James	L-R	6-3	215	5-14-97	.221	.337	.337	104	95	11	14	4	1	4	7	8	1	0	0	45	1	0	7.7	43.3
Pereda, Jhonny	R-R	6-1	202	4-18-96	.345	.387	.483	11	32	29	1	10	4	0	0	2	2	1	0	0	0	0	0	6.3	25.0
Roden, Alan	L-R	5-11	215	12-22-99	.158	.200	.263	12	40	38	5	6	1	0	1	1	0	2	0	0	13	1	0	0.0	32.5
Vazquez, Christian	R-R	5-9	205	8-21-90	.189	.271	.274	65	214	190	14	36	7	0	3	14	18	4	0	2	35	1	1	8.4	16.4
Wallner, Matt	L-R	6-4	220	12-12-97	.202	.311	.464	104	392	336	47	68	16	3	22	40	46	8	0	2	114	4	3	11.7	29.1

Pitching	B-T	Ht.	Wt.	DOB	W	L	ERA	G	GS	SV	IP	Hits	Runs	ER	HR	BB	SO	AVG	OBP	SLG	SO%	BB%	BF
Abel, Mick	R-R	6-5	190	8-18-01	1	2	8.36	4	2	0	14	18	14	13	1	7	18	.305	.379	.373	27.3	10.6	66
Adams, Travis	R-R	6-1	197	1-19-00	1	4	7.49	18	2	0	34	39	29	28	6	17	31	.295	.376	.515	19.6	10.8	158
Alcala, Jorge	R-R	6-3	205	7-28-95	0	2	8.88	22	0	0	24	29	25	24	5	15	28	.302	.395	.531	24.6	13.2	114
Blewett, Scott	R-R	6-6	245	4-10-96	0	0	1.93	2	0	0	5	4	1	1	0	0	5	.222	.263	.333	26.3	0.0	19
Bradley, Taj	R-R	6-2	190	3-20-01	0	2	6.61	6	6	0	31	32	23	23	6	12	32	.267	.331	.500	23.9	9.0	134
Bride, Jonah	R-R	5-10	200	12-27-95	0	0	15.00	1	0	0	6	14	10	10	1	3	2	.452	.514	.613	5.4	8.1	37
Cabrera, Genesis	L-L	6-2	180	10-10-96	0	1	7.98	16	0	1	15	17	14	13	5	11	13	.298	.414	.561	18.6	15.7	70
Castro, Willi	S-R	6-1	206	4-24-97	0	0	0.00	1	0	0	1	1	0	0	0	0	0	.250	.250	.250	0.0	0.0	4
Clemens, Kody	L-R	6-1	200	5-15-96	0	0	18.00	1	0	0	1	3	2	2	2	0	0	.500	.500	1.500	0.0	0.0	6
Coulombe, Danny	L-L	5-10	190	10-26-89	1	0	1.16	40	1	2	31	21	4	4	0	9	31	.188	.246	.214	25.4	7.4	122
Davis, Noah	R-R	6-2	195	4-22-97	0	1	16.20	4	0	0	5	12	10	9	4	1	7	.462	.533	.962	23.3	3.3	30
Dobnak, Randy	R-R	6-1	230	1-17-95	0	0	1.69	1	0	0	5	2	1	1	2	1	1	.118	.211	.294	5.3	10.5	19
Duran, Jhoan	R-R	6-5	230	1-8-98	6	4	2.01	49	0	16	49	40	13	11	1	18	53	.219	.296	.257	25.7	8.7	206
Festa, David	R-R	6-6	185	3-8-00	3	4	5.40	11	10	0	53	49	35	32	10	19	53	.240	.316	.422	23.1	8.3	229
Fitzgerald, Ryan	L-R	6-0	185	6-17-94	0	0	0.00	2	0	0	2	2	0	0	0	0	0	.250	.250	.250	0.0	0.0	8
Funderburk, Kody	L-L	6-4	230	11-27-96	4	1	3.51	39	0	1	41	44	17	16	2	18	40	.275	.355	.369	21.9	9.8	183
Hatch, Thomas	R-R	6-1	195	9-29-94	2	1	5.45	11	1	0	33	38	21	20	6	17	21	.292	.374	.477	14.3	11.6	147
Jax, Griffin	R-R	6-2	195	11-22-94	1	5	4.50	50	0	0	46	46	24	23	4	13	72	.251	.305	.377	36.4	6.6	198
Kriske, Brooks	R-R	6-3	190	2-3-94	0	1	11.25	12	0	0	12	18	15	15	1	10	14	.340	.458	.547	21.9	15.6	64
Laweryson, Cody	R-R	6-4	205	5-10-98	0	1	1.17	5	0	0	8	4	2	1	0	0	7	.167	.160	.167	26.9	0.0	26
Lopez, Pablo	R-R	6-4	225	3-7-96	5	4	2.74	14	14	0	76	64	28	23	6	20	73	.225	.282	.340	23.4	6.4	312
Matthews, Zebby	R-R	6-5	225	5-22-00	5	6	5.56	16	16	0	79	94	50	49	12	24	88	.291	.335	.449	24.9	6.8	354
McCaughan, Darren	R-R	6-1	200	3-18-96	0	0	1.69	3	0	0	5	5	1	1	0	1	6	.227	.261	.273	26.1	4.3	23
Misiewicz, Anthony	R-L	6-1	196	11-1-94	0	0	9.64	5	0	0	5	5	5	2	4	5	.263	.391	.579	21.7	17.4	23
Ober, Bailey	R-R	6-9	260	7-12-95	4	8	5.10	27	27	0	146	159	84	83	30	31	120	.275	.314	.494	19.2	5.0	624
Ohl, Pierson	R-R	6-1	180	9-10-99	0	3	5.10	14	3	0	30	38	22	17	5	7	22	.302	.335	.500	20.3	5.3	133
Paddack, Chris	R-R	6-5	217	1-8-96	3	9	4.95	21	21	0	111	115	65	61	17	27	83	.266	.309	.444	17.6	5.7	472
Ramirez, Erasmo	R-R	6-0	220	5-2-90	0	1	2.45	9	0	1	11	10	3	3	2	2	5	.256	.286	.436	11.9	4.8	42

Player	B-T	Ht.	Wt.	DOB	G	GS	SV	IP	Hits	Runs	ER	HR	BB	SO	AVG	OBP	SLG	SO%	BB%	BF
Ryan, Joe	R-R	6-2	205	6-5-96	13	10		3.42	31	30	0	171	138	69	65	26	39	194	.218	.275	.392	28.2	5.7	689
Sands, Cole	R-R	6-3	215	7-17-97	4	6		4.50	69	3	3	72	65	41	36	7	19	64	.242	.297	.390	21.4	6.4	299
Stewart, Brock	L-R	6-3	220	10-3-91	2	1		2.38	39	0	0	34	26	9	9	3	11	41	.210	.290	.323	29.5	7.9	139
Tonkin, Michael	R-R	6-7	220	11-19-89	2	1		4.88	21	0	0	24	20	13	13	3	8	19	.225	.320	.382	18.4	7.8	103
Topa, Justin	R-R	6-4	200	3-7-91	1	5		3.90	54	1	4	60	68	32	26	2	18	49	.281	.338	.376	18.3	6.7	268
Urena, Jose	R-R	6-2	208	9-12-91	0	1		4.58	4	3	0	18	17	9	9	1	8	10	.258	.351	.379	12.8	10.3	78
Varland, Louie	L-R	6-1	205	12-9-97	3	3		2.02	51	0	0	49	41	14	11	3	13	47	.230	.289	.337	23.9	6.6	197
Wentz, Joey	L-L	6-5	220	10-6-97	0	0		15.75	6	0	0	8	17	14	14	3	9	6	.436	.531	.744	12.2	18.4	49
Woods Richardson, Simeon	R-R	6-3	210	9-27-00	7	4		4.04	23	22	0	111	96	53	50	17	46	107	.230	.308	.395	22.7	9.8	471

Fielding

Catcher	PCT	G	PO	A	E	DP	PB
Gasper	.983	19	110	5	2	0	0
Jeffers	.993	88	678	32	5	3	4
Pereda	.957	11	84	4	4	0	0
Vazquez	.998	64	542	20	1	3	1

First Base	PCT	G	PO	A	E	DP
Bride	1.000	5	17	4	0	2
Clemens	1.000	58	294	27	0	31
Fitzgerald	1.000	1	2	1	0	0
France	.999	101	634	58	1	89
Gasper	1.000	7	20	2	0	3
Julien	.986	26	129	10	2	12

Second Base	PCT	G	PO	A	E	DP
Bride	1.000	3	0	2	0	0
Castro	1.000	42	40	38	0	9
Clemens	.986	50	54	86	2	10
Fitzgerald	1.000	9	4	8	0	1

	PCT	G	PO	A	E	DP
France	1.000	1	1	0	0	0
Gasper	.857	2	4	2	1	0
Julien	.976	25	27	56	2	11
Keaschall	.965	41	71	96	6	25
Lee	.963	37	36	67	4	11
Martin	.900	4	4	5	1	1

Third Base	PCT	G	PO	A	E	DP
Bride	1.000	21	18	18	0	1
Castro	.769	13	3	7	3	0
Fitzgerald	.750	4	1	2	1	0
Lee	1.000	43	32	37	0	3
Lewis	.966	99	68	131	7	14
Miranda	.950	12	7	12	1	1

Shortstop	PCT	G	PO	A	E	DP
Castro	.800	5	3	1	1	0
Correa	.970	92	118	176	9	30

	PCT	G	PO	A	E	DP
Fitzgerald	1.000	9	9	15	0	7
Julien	.000	1	0	0	0	0
Lee	.974	77	83	140	6	26

Outfield	PCT	G	PO	A	E	DP
Bader	.995	108	205	5	1	2
Buxton	.993	118	284	2	2	0
Castro	.977	6	69	83	1	2
Clemens	1.000	22	24	2	0	0
Gasper	1.000	1	2	0	0	0
Keirsey	1.000	65	54	1	0	0
Larnach	1.000	63	118	1	0	0
Martin	1.000	48	82	2	0	0
McCusker	1.000	12	10	0	0	0
Outman	.985	42	65	0	1	0
Roden	1.000	15	25	0	0	0
Wallner	.980	85	144	3	3	0

ST. PAUL SAINTS — TRIPLE-A
INTERNATIONAL LEAGUE

Batting	B-T	Ht.	Wt.	DOB	AVG	OBP	SLG	G	PA	AB	R	H	2B	3B	HR	RBI	BB	HBP	SH	SF	SO	SB	CS	BB%	SO%
Alvarez, Armando	R-R	6-0	195	7-14-94	.226	.307	.365	38	153	137	19	31	7	0	4	22	14	2	0	0	44	0	0	9.2	28.8
Bischoff, Kyle	R-R	6-2	210	7-29-99	.000	.000	.000	28	1	1	0	0	0	0	0	0	0	0	0	0	1	0	0	0.0	100.0
Bosiokovic, Jacob	R-R	6-5	240	12-21-93	.000	.000	.000	19	1	0	0	0	0	0	0	0	1	0	0	0	1	0	0	0.0	100.0
Bride, Jonah	R-R	5-10	200	12-27-95	.281	.423	.453	43	175	139	28	39	9	0	5	24	33	2	0	1	33	1	1	18.9	18.9
Camargo, Jair	R-R	5-10	230	7-1-99	.212	.258	.319	31	120	113	11	24	6	0	2	13	7	0	0	0	46	1	0	5.8	38.3
Cardenas, Noah	R-R	5-11	195	9-10-99	.234	.364	.458	39	129	107	16	25	3	0	7	16	20	2	0	0	26	0	0	15.5	20.2
Cartaya, Diego	R-R	6-3	219	9-7-01	.085	.217	.136	20	69	59	4	5	0	0	1	1	9	1	0	0	40	0	0	13.0	58.0
Eeles, Payton	L-R	5-7	180	11-16-99	.253	.379	.321	86	378	308	51	78	7	1	4	32	47	18	1	4	65	21	7	12.4	17.2
Fedko, Kyler	R-R	6-1	195	9-21-99	.268	.353	.476	42	187	164	29	44	10	0	8	24	21	1	0	1	41	12	2	11.2	21.9
Fitzgerald, Ryan	R-R	6-0	185	6-17-94	.271	.367	.469	59	245	213	30	59	16	2	7	31	28	3	0	1	58	5	4	11.4	23.7
Ford, Mike	L-R	6-0	225	7-4-92	.239	.351	.436	49	191	163	24	39	8	0	8	27	27	1	0	0	47	0	2	14.1	24.6
Gasper, Mickey	S-R	5-9	205	10-11-95	.285	.385	.531	47	208	179	32	51	14	0	10	26	25	4	0	0	38	2	0	12.0	18.3
Gonzalez, Gabriel	R-R	5-10	165	1-14-04	.358	.504	.504	34	148	133	14	42	7	0	6	23	9	2	0	4	28	2	2	6.1	18.9
Holland, Will	R-R	5-9	181	4-18-98	.197	.296	.341	76	261	223	37	44	8	0	8	32	26	7	1	4	76	11	3	10.0	29.1
Houghton, Maddux	R-R	5-11	190	2-23-99	.200	.200	.800	3	5	5	2	1	0	0	1	1	0	0	0	0	3	0	0	0.0	60.0
Jenkins, Walker	L-R	6-3	205	2-19-05	.242	.324	.396	23	102	91	13	22	6	1	2	8	9	2	0	0	26	4	0	8.8	25.5
Julien, Edouard	L-R	6-1	195	4-30-99	.276	.415	.464	70	299	239	33	66	8	2	11	34	53	5	0	2	82	5	1	17.7	27.4
Keaschall, Luke	R-R	6-1	190	8-15-02	.263	.373	.337	28	118	95	16	25	2	1	1	9	17	2	0	4	17	11	2	14.4	14.4
Keirsey, DaShawn	L-L	6-0	195	5-13-97	.250	.335	.436	36	161	140	23	35	11	3	3	23	17	2	0	2	36	7	0	10.6	22.4
Lee, Brooks	S-R	5-11	205	11-14-00	.364	.300	3	11	10	0	3	0	0	0	0	1	0	0	0	2	0	0	9.1	18.2
Lewis, Royce	R-R	6-2	200	6-5-99	.129	.152	.161	9	33	31	3	4	1	0	0	1	1	0	0	1	8	0	0	3.0	24.2
MacLeod, Christian	L-L	6-4	227	4-12-00	.000	.000	.000	12	1	1	0	0	0	0	0	0	0	0	0	0	1	0	0	0.0	100.0
Martin, Austin	R-R	6-0	185	3-23-99	.319	.431	.398	32	137	113	13	36	6	0	1	14	21	2	0	1	17	2	2	15.3	12.4
McCusker, Carson	R-R	6-8	250	5-22-98	.246	.316	.479	106	438	390	57	96	25	0	22	70	36	5	0	3	148	5	2	8.2	33.8
Miranda, Jose	R-R	6-2	210	6-29-98	.195	.272	.296	90	371	334	31	65	13	0	7	28	30	6	0	1	57	1	0	8.1	15.4
Morales, Jeferson	R-R	5-8	170	5-13-99	.249	.349	.402	74	269	229	37	57	11	3	6	26	29	8	0	3	49	4	1	10.8	18.2
Outman, James	L-R	6-3	215	5-14-97	.235	.316	.490	12	57	51	9	12	1	1	3	10	6	0	0	0	19	3	0	10.5	33.3
Pereda, Jhonny	R-R	6-1	202	4-18-96	.294	.448	.500	20	87	68	13	20	6	1	2	10	18	1	0	0	17	0	0	20.7	19.5
Prato, Anthony	R-R	5-9	186	5-11-98	.259	.396	.360	82	284	228	38	59	9	1	4	20	37	16	1	2	48	16	3	13.0	16.9
Rodriguez, Emmanuel	L-L	5-10	210	2-28-03	.258	.429	.423	52	212	163	35	42	7	1	9	27	45	4	0	0	67	9	3	21.2	31.6
Sabato, Aaron	R-R	6-2	230	6-4-99	.245	.288	.453	65	264	245	28	60	7	1	14	41	15	1	0	3	83	0	0	5.7	31.4
Schobel, Tanner	R-R	5-9	170	6-4-01	.220	.311	.341	30	103	91	7	20	5	0	2	9	10	2	0	0	33	0	1	9.7	32.0
Severino, Yunior	S-R	6-0	189	10-3-99	.196	.344	.324	33	125	102	14	20	7	0	2	10	19	2	0	0	44	1	0	18.4	35.2
Shuffield, Dalton	R-R	5-5	170	3-31-99	.150	.190	.150	11	21	20	1	3	1	0	0	0	0	0	0	0	7	0	0	4.8	33.3
Vazquez, Christian	R-R	5-9	205	8-21-90	.133	.278	.333	4	18	15	3	2	0	0	0	1	4	3	0	0	0	0	0	16.7	5.6
Wallner, Matt	L-R	6-4	220	12-12-97	.320	.370	.960	4	6	27	25	8	8	1	0	8	6	5	13	2	0	0	6	0	0	7.4	22.2
Whorff, Jarret	R-R	6-3	195	10-2-98	.000	.000	.000	27	1	1	0	0	0	0	0	0	0	0	0	0	0	0	0	0.0	0.0
Winkel, Pat	L-R	6-0	200	1-27-00	.217	.278	.386	47	180	166	14	36	7	0	7	25	13	1	0	0	59	0	0	7.2	32.8

Pitching	B-T	Ht.	Wt.	DOB	W	L	ERA	G	GS	SV	IP	Hits	Runs	ER	HR	BB	SO	AVG	OBP	SLG	SO%	BB%	BF
Abel, Mick	R-R	6-5	190	8-18-01	0	0	1.85	5	5	0	24	15	7	5	1	8	33	.179	.247	.250	35.5	8.6	93
Adams, Travis	R-R	6-1	197	1-19-00	4	4	3.93	23	5	3	69	64	32	30	5	23	64	.245	.310	.368	22.0	7.9	291

MINNESOTA TWINS

Player	B-T	HT	WT	DOB	W	L	ERA	G	GS	CG	SV	IP	H	R	ER	BB	SO	AVG	OBP	SLG	K/9	BB/9	BF
Baker, Trent	R-R	6-3	243	12-28-98	2	3	4.96	24	4	3	45	54	28	25	10	20	48	.292	.362	.530	23.1	9.6	208
Beede, Tyler	R-R	6-2	216	5-23-93	1	0	8.00	7	1	1	9	12	8	8	3	9	7	.324	.457	.649	15.2	19.6	46
Bischoff, Kyle	R-R	6-2	210	7-29-99	4	2	6.03	28	0	1	34	30	28	23	1	28	37	.231	.384	.315	22.6	17.1	164
Blewett, Scott	R-R	6-6	245	4-10-96	0	1	11.57	2	0	0	2	3	3	3	0	2	3	.300	.417	.500	25.0	16.7	12
Bosiokovic, Jacob	R-R	6-5	240	12-21-93	0	3	7.66	19	0	0	22	20	19	19	5	19	26	.235	.394	.447	23.9	17.4	109
Bradley, Taj	R-R	6-2	190	3-20-01	0	0	7.53	3	3	0	14	21	12	12	4	2	18	.339	.369	.605	27.7	3.1	65
Cabrera, Genesis	L-L	6-2	180	10-10-96	0	0	9.00	1	0	0	1	2	1	1	1	0	1	.400	.400	1.000	20.0	0.0	5
Coulombe, Danny	L-L	5-10	190	10-26-89	0	0	0.00	1	0	0	1	0	0	0	0	0	0	.000	.000	.000	0.0	0.0	3
Davis, Noah	R-R	6-2	195	4-22-97	1	0	3.78	14	0	2	17	11	7	7	3	9	16	.186	.314	.390	22.9	12.9	70
Dobnak, Randy	R-R	6-1	230	1-17-95	1	7	7.12	17	10	0	61	69	51	48	11	35	42	.291	.387	.485	14.7	12.3	285
Feigl, Brady	R-L	6-4	195	12-27-90	2	1	5.93	12	0	2	14	15	11	9	2	5	16	.263	.323	.456	25.8	8.1	62
Festa, David	R-R	6-6	185	3-8-00	2	1	2.59	7	7	0	31	24	10	9	2	7	39	.211	.256	.316	32.0	5.7	122
Funderburk, Kody	L-L	6-4	230	11-27-96	3	0	1.78	19	0	2	25	18	6	5	2	9	25	.200	.291	.311	24.0	8.7	104
Gillispie, Connor	R-R	5-11	185	11-10-97	1	1	14.49	4	3	0	14	22	22	22	6	9	6	.379	.471	.810	8.6	12.9	70
Jensen, Ryan	R-R	6-0	190	11-23-97	2	4	6.59	21	1	0	29	27	24	21	4	26	39	.257	.403	.438	28.3	18.8	138
Klein, John	R-R	6-5	225	4-22-01	0	5	6.66	7	4	0	26	26	20	19	1	13	33	.260	.359	.350	28.2	11.1	117
Kriske, Brooks	R-R	6-3	190	2-3-94	0	0	6.00	3	0	0	3	5	2	2	0	1	3	.385	.429	.462	21.4	7.1	14
Laweryson, Cody	L-R	6-4	205	5-10-98	2	1	2.84	17	0	0	25	22	9	8	2	10	25	.229	.308	.344	23.4	9.3	107
Lewis, Cory	R-R	6-5	220	10-9-00	4	6	7.27	24	11	0	73	83	62	59	13	68	87	.283	.418	.485	23.8	18.6	366
Lopez, Pablo	L-R	6-4	225	3-7-96	0	2	2.81	4	4	0	16	17	5	5	2	2	18	.279	.313	.475	27.7	3.1	65
Lovelady, Richard	L-L	6-0	185	7-7-95	0	1	1.31	19	0	6	21	15	6	3	2	7	22	.200	.265	.333	26.5	8.4	83
MacLeod, Christian	L-L	6-4	227	4-12-00	4	2	7.20	12	2	0	35	42	31	28	7	26	41	.294	.405	.524	23.6	14.9	174
Matthews, Zebby	R-R	6-5	225	6-27-00	1	4	1.72	8	8	0	37	31	9	7	1	9	47	.225	.250	.304	31.8	6.1	148
McCaughan, Darren	R-R	6-1	200	3-18-96	5	8	5.10	26	12	0	97	112	61	55	20	33	96	.289	.354	.510	22.2	7.6	433
Misiewicz, Anthony	R-L	6-1	196	11-1-94	2	2	3.82	28	0	8	33	23	17	14	5	11	30	.204	.272	.381	23.8	8.7	126
Morris, Andrew	R-R	6-0	195	9-1-01	4	6	4.09	21	19	0	95	98	49	43	11	28	89	.272	.328	.428	22.4	7.0	398
Nowlin, Jaylen	L-L	6-1	180	1-29-01	0	0	10.80	2	0	0	2	4	2	2	2	2	3	.400	.500	1.000	25.0	16.7	12
Ober, Bailey	R-R	6-9	260	7-12-95	0	0	1.00	2	2	0	9	6	1	1	1	1	9	.188	.212	.250	27.3	3.0	33
Ohl, Pierson	R-R	6-1	180	9-10-99	0	2	3.29	9	4	1	27	25	11	10	3	6	30	.231	.278	.361	26.1	5.2	115
Paredes, Mike	R-R	5-11	185	7-27-00	0	0	0.00	1	0	0	2	0	0	0	0	1	0	.000	.000	.000	0.0	16.7	6
Percival, Cole	R-R	6-5	220	2-26-99	0	1	24.00	3	0	0	3	8	8	8	0	5	2	.500	.636	.688	9.1	22.7	22
Prato, Anthony	R-R	5-9	186	5-11-98	0	0	31.50	3	0	0	2	8	7	7	3	1	0	.571	.600	1.286	0.0	6.7	15
Prielipp, Connor	L-L	6-2	210	1-10-01	1	3	5.14	5	4	0	21	20	12	12	2	13	25	.253	.355	.392	26.9	14.0	93
Ramirez, Erasmo	R-R	6-0	220	5-2-90	1	1	4.67	12	0	0	17	21	10	9	1	5	17	.292	.338	.431	21.8	6.4	78
Raya, Marco	R-R	6-1	170	8-7-02	2	8	6.02	30	20	0	99	103	72	66	16	57	102	.269	.371	.462	22.6	12.6	451
Rojas, Kendry	L-L	6-2	190	11-26-02	1	2	5.67	8	8	0	27	37	25	20	3	23	28	.314	.438	.483	19.3	15.9	145
Rozek, Aaron	L-L	6-2	225	8-20-95	1	0	6.90	13	2	0	30	42	23	23	6	17	23	.341	.427	.561	16.1	11.9	143
Speas, Alex	R-R	6-3	225	3-4-98	2	1	11.12	5	0	1	17	27	22	21	1	20	20	.365	.495	.486	20.4	20.4	98
Stankiewicz, John	R-R	6-4	230	9-8-98	1	1	2.35	5	1	0	8	4	2	2	0	5	12	.160	.300	.160	40.0	16.7	30
Tonkin, Michael	R-R	6-7	220	11-19-89	2	0	4.82	18	0	0	28	27	16	15	7	7	34	.252	.322	.505	28.1	5.8	121
Urena, Jose	R-R	6-2	208	9-12-91	0	1	4.05	6	4	0	13	13	6	6	1	10	13	.271	.417	.417	21.7	16.7	60
Whorff, Jarret	R-R	6-3	195	10-2-98	3	3	7.54	27	0	1	45	55	41	38	7	21	49	.294	.371	.471	22.9	9.8	214
Woods Richardson, Simeon	R-R	6-3	210	9-27-00	2	0	4.43	5	4	0	22	21	12	11	4	6	27	.236	.292	.438	28.1	6.3	96
Yanez, Gabriel	L-L	6-3	168	7-22-99	0	0	7.20	2	0	0	5	2	4	4	0	4	8	.125	.300	.125	40.0	20.0	20
Ynoa, Huascar	R-R	6-2	220	5-28-98	0	1	10.38	5	0	0	4	4	8	7	1	0	.222	.462	.389	3.8	26.9	26	

Fielding

Catcher	PCT	G	PO	A	E	DP	PB
Camargo	.989	21	161	22	2	1	1
Cardenas	.991	37	303	16	3	7	
Cartaya	.984	20	180	8	3	2	1
Gasper	.994	17	158	8	1	0	1
Pereda	.994	15	156	5	1	1	1
Vazquez	1.000	2	8	0	0	0	0
Winkel	.997	42	374	17	1	6	2

First Base	PCT	G	PO	A	E	DP
Bride	1.000	12	91	7	0	10
Camargo	1.000	1	5	0	0	0
Fedko	1.000	7	35	4	0	4
Ford	.989	41	257	21	3	22
Gasper	1.000	6	35	2	0	4
Julien	1.000	9	57	5	0	4
Miranda	1.000	18	113	9	0	10
Sabato	.995	55	378	12	2	45
Severino	.962	8	47	4	2	4
Winkel	1.000	1	3	0	0	0

Second Base	PCT	G	PO	A	E	DP
Alvarez	1.000	5	4	7	0	0
Bride	1.000	11	16	15	0	4
Eeles	.951	26	42	55	5	12
Fitzgerald	1.000	2	6	8	0	3
Gasper	1.000	8	9	19	0	2
Julien	.981	53	84	124	4	31
Keaschall	1.000	12	27	27	0	8

Third Base	PCT	G	PO	A	E	DP
Alvarez	.941	25	16	32	3	5
Bride	.925	19	13	24	3	6
Camargo	.000	2	0	0	0	0
Holland	1.000	7	2	12	0	2
Lee	.000	1	0	0	0	0
Lewis	1.000	6	3	9	0	0
Miranda	.966	69	41	101	5	15
Morales	1.000	2	1	2	0	0
Prato	.800	6	1	3	1	0
Schobel	1.000	14	7	15	0	0
Severino	.895	10	5	12	2	2
Shuffield	1.000	1	0	1	0	0

Shortstop	PCT	G	PO	A	E	DP
Alvarez	.750	2	0	3	1	0
Eeles	.933	41	32	79	8	12
Fitzgerald	.979	58	59	127	4	20
Holland	.956	39	53	77	6	16
Lee	1.000	1	3	3	0	1
Prato	.000	1	0	0	0	0
Schobel	.959	12	16	31	2	7

Lee	1.000	1	0	1	0	0
Martin	1.000	5	10	8	0	3
Morales	1.000	5	3	8	0	0
Prato	.977	27	33	53	2	14
Schobel	.960	6	8	16	1	3
Severino	1.000	3	2	4	0	2
Shuffield	.000	1	0	0	0	0

Outfield	PCT	G	PO	A	E	DP
Alvarez	1.000	6	9	1	0	1
Cardenas	.000	1	0	0	0	0
Eeles	1.000	19	27	1	0	0
Fedko	.957	31	65	1	3	0
Gasper	1.000	3	4	0	0	0
Gonzalez	.944	27	49	2	3	0
Holland	1.000	28	47	2	0	1
Houghton	1.000	3	3	0	0	0
Jenkins	1.000	22	38	0	0	0
Keirsey	1.000	32	74	0	0	0
MacLeod	1.000	1	1	0	0	0
Martin	1.000	24	62	2	0	0
McCusker	.994	89	160	2	1	1
Morales	.988	61	78	7	1	2
Outman	1.000	9	19	0	0	0
Prato	.988	47	83	0	1	0
Rodriguez	.965	47	107	4	4	0
Severino	1.000	8	15	1	0	0
Shuffield	.900	9	9	0	1	0
Wallner	1.000	4	4	0	0	0

WICHITA WIND SURGE
TEXAS LEAGUE

DOUBLE-A

MINNESOTA TWINS

Batting	B-T	Ht.	Wt.	DOB	AVG	OBP	SLG	G	PA	AB	R	H	2B	3B	HR	RBI	BB	HBP	SH	SF	SO	SB	CS	BB%	SO%
Baez, Nate	R-R	5-11	191	5-17-01	.237	.297	.400	51	212	190	22	45	8	4	5	31	13	5	0	4	35	2	0	6.1	16.5
Cardenas, Noah	R-R	5-11	195	9-10-99	.257	.409	.416	30	127	101	21	26	7	0	3	17	22	4	0	0	25	0	1	17.3	19.7
Cerda, Allan	R-R	6-3	203	11-24-99	.125	.200	.313	10	35	32	3	4	1	1	1	5	3	0	0	0	15	0	0	8.6	42.9
Cespedes, Rubel	L-R	6-0	210	8-29-00	.244	.314	.394	93	398	360	41	88	21	3	9	53	35	2	0	1	67	1	1	8.8	16.8
Cossetti, Andrew	R-R	5-10	215	1-31-00	.226	.346	.432	84	350	287	48	65	15	1	14	51	52	11	0	0	97	3	1	14.9	27.7
Culpepper, Kaelen	R-R	6-0	185	12-29-02	.285	.367	.460	59	270	239	39	68	7	1	11	30	24	7	0	0	50	10	2	8.9	18.5
Dearden, Tyler	L-R	6-2	185	7-6-98	.277	.351	.378	36	134	119	10	33	4	1	2	16	12	2	0	1	24	2	0	9.0	17.9
Fedko, Kyler	R-R	6-1	195	9-21-99	.253	.375	.494	88	379	312	62	79	15	0	20	58	58	5	0	4	79	26	6	15.3	20.8
Genth, Harry	R-R	5-8	165	9-3-02	.152	.243	.364	10	37	33	7	5	1	0	2	5	3	1	0	0	12	4	0	8.1	32.4
Gonzalez, Gabriel	R-R	5-10	165	1-4-04	.344	.429	.509	55	246	212	39	73	19	2	4	15	26	6	0	1	30	5	1	10.6	12.2
Hess, Kyle	L-R	6-0	210	5-20-99	.059	.111	.118	6	18	17	1	1	1	0	0	0	1	0	0	0	6	0	0	5.6	33.3
Houghton, Maddux	R-R	5-11	190	2-23-99	.284	.338	.446	21	80	74	11	21	6	0	2	8	6	0	0	0	21	6	0	7.5	26.3
Jenkins, Walker	L-R	6-3	205	2-19-05	.309	.426	.487	52	235	191	38	59	11	1	7	24	34	7	0	3	44	11	3	14.5	18.7
Mendez, Hendry	L-L	6-2	175	11-7-03	.324	.461	.450	33	142	111	24	36	3	1	3	16	27	2	1	1	21	4	3	19.0	14.8
Olivar, Ricardo	R-R	5-10	176	8-10-01	.264	.356	.412	93	407	352	56	93	13	0	13	59	49	3	0	3	74	13	3	12.0	18.2
Ortega, Jorel	R-R	6-0	194	1-22-01	.218	.313	.354	74	263	229	30	50	7	0	8	28	30	2	1	1	67	9	1	11.4	25.5
Rosario, Kala'i	R-R	6-0	205	7-2-02	.256	.358	.487	130	579	497	92	127	30	5	25	83	73	7	0	2	159	32	7	12.6	27.5
Ross, Ben	R-R	6-0	180	6-6-01	.219	.308	.363	120	490	424	60	93	17	1	14	60	55	3	0	8	111	18	5	11.2	22.7
Rucker, Jake	R-R	6-0	195	9-14-99	.236	.317	.356	85	322	284	36	67	9	2	7	36	31	4	0	3	43	8	4	9.6	13.4
Sabato, Aaron	R-R	6-2	230	6-4-99	.305	.399	.574	39	163	141	21	43	11	0	9	26	20	2	0	0	42	1	0	12.3	25.8
Salas, Jose	S-R	6-0	191	4-26-03	.210	.275	.352	48	179	162	21	34	8	0	5	22	13	2	1	1	49	10	1	7.3	27.4
Schobel, Tanner	R-R	5-9	170	6-4-01	.292	.372	.465	49	234	202	39	59	12	1	7	29	25	3	0	4	33	7	1	10.7	14.1
Shuffield, Dalton	R-R	5-10	170	3-31-99	.429	.500	.714	2	8	7	2	3	2	0	0	1	0	0	0	0	1	0	0	12.5	25.0

Pitching	B-T	Ht.	Wt.	DOB	W	L	ERA	G	GS	SV	IP	Hits	Runs	ER	HR	BB	SO	AVG	OBP	SLG	SO%	BB%	BF
Andrews, Tanner	R-R	6-3	220	11-15-95	1	3	3.78	14	0	2	17	21	8	7	0	3	18	.300	.338	.386	24.0	4.0	75
Armstrong, Sam	R-R	6-2	245	9-26-00	3	2	4.91	8	8	0	40	41	22	22	3	9	32	.258	.312	.340	18.4	5.2	174
Baker, Trent	R-R	6-3	243	12-28-98	2	2	2.86	11	11	0	50	40	19	16	2	12	51	.211	.268	.289	24.9	5.9	205
Bischoff, Kyle	R-R	6-2	210	7-29-00	0	0	6.75	5	0	1	4	4	3	3	0	2	4	.250	.368	.375	21.1	15.8	19
Bowen, Darren	R-R	6-0	180	2-3-01	3	7	5.14	27	16	0	84	83	53	48	17	38	58	.256	.344	.444	15.5	10.2	373
Bragg, Kade	R-L	6-1	190	7-2-01	4	0	3.22	15	0	3	22	14	8	8	3	9	21	.179	.264	.321	24.1	10.3	87
Castro, Ricky	R-R	6-1	200	8-5-99	3	4	5.48	28	15	2	95	99	60	58	14	31	93	.263	.319	.446	22.5	7.5	414
Cesar, Joel	R-R	5-11	191	1-26-96	3	1	7.15	26	0	3	34	39	30	27	4	13	25	.281	.346	.446	15.9	8.3	157
Chaney, Chase	R-R	6-1	199	12-16-99	0	0	4.63	3	2	0	12	16	7	6	1	3	5	.333	.358	.438	9.4	5.7	53
Culpepper, C.J.	R-R	6-3	193	11-2-01	2	2	2.65	15	15	0	54	45	20	16	4	30	45	.227	.333	.313	19.5	13.0	231
Gallagher, Ryan	L-R	6-3	195	11-19-03	4	1	5.50	8	8	0	38	47	28	23	7	10	37	.301	.343	.500	21.9	5.9	169
Hidalgo, Alejandro	R-R	6-1	160	5-22-03	0	5	9.55	7	7	0	22	29	25	23	6	13	21	.315	.402	.565	19.6	12.1	107
Hoopes, Hunter	R-R	6-1	195	3-4-00	1	0	7.07	12	0	1	14	8	11	11	1	9	12	.160	.311	.220	19.7	14.8	61
Klein, John	R-R	6-5	225	4-22-02	7	5	3.12	24	11	0	87	70	42	28	6	24	95	.225	.294	.331	27.4	6.9	347
Laweryson, Cody	L-R	6-4	205	5-10-98	0	3	2.89	17	0	6	19	20	9	6	0	4	20	.282	.329	.324	26.3	5.3	76
MacLeod, Christian	L-L	6-4	227	4-12-00	0	3	2.63	13	13	0	48	42	17	14	0	19	45	.236	.312	.287	22.2	9.4	203
Macuare, Angel	R-R	6-2	250	3-3-00	2	0	5.82	13	0	0	22	24	15	14	4	8	17	.286	.358	.500	17.7	8.3	96
Martinez, Michael	R-R	6-1	185	7-11-99	3	2	2.50	30	0	0	40	25	13	11	2	26	59	.180	.322	.281	22.7	15.1	172
Nowlin, Jaylen	L-L	6-1	180	1-29-01	5	0	4.96	39	0	1	53	41	30	29	5	40	59	.216	.362	.326	25.0	16.9	236
Ohl, Pierson	R-R	6-1	180	9-10-99	4	1	2.08	13	2	1	39	31	10	9	2	4	46	.209	.230	.291	30.3	2.6	152
Paredes, Mike	R-R	5-11	185	7-27-00	11	0	2.43	37	2	7	104	79	32	28	8	28	91	.207	.270	.296	21.7	6.7	420
Percival, Cole	R-R	6-5	220	2-26-99	2	2	3.00	14	0	3	18	15	8	6	1	5	19	.224	.274	.299	25.7	6.8	74
Prielipp, Connor	L-L	6-2	210	1-10-01	0	6	3.65	19	19	0	62	74	36	25	5	18	73	.307	.367	.419	27.0	6.7	270
Rozek, Aaron	L-L	6-2	225	8-20-95	3	1	3.53	19	9	1	79	80	35	31	9	19	79	.267	.316	.400	24.1	5.8	328
Stankiewicz, John	R-R	6-4	230	9-8-98	3	5	4.84	39	0	4	48	43	29	26	4	26	43	.240	.363	.374	20.5	12.4	210
Stull, Eston	R-R	6-2	195	1-20-99	0	0	0.00	1	0	0	1	2	0	0	0	1	2	.333	.429	.333	28.6	14.3	7
Whitaker, Logan	R-R	6-6	225	5-25-00	1	0	1.65	11	0	0	16	16	4	3	0	8	16	.250	.333	.297	22.2	11.1	72
Whorff, Jarret	R-R	6-3	195	10-2-98	3	2	2.28	15	0	0	28	20	9	7	3	6	33	.200	.241	.340	30.3	5.5	109
Wosinski, Jacob	R-R	6-8	320	3-9-99	6	1	4.54	26	0	2	36	35	19	18	2	20	24	.261	.363	.373	15.3	12.7	157
Yanez, Gabriel	L-L	6-3	168	7-22-99	1	0	2.29	10	0	0	20	21	6	5	0	1	14	.276	.278	.329	17.7	1.3	79

Fielding

Catcher	PCT	G	PO	A	E	DP	PB
Baez	.984	29	222	24	4	0	2
Cardenas	.991	23	199	15	2	2	2
Cossetti	.975	51	406	28	11	3	6
Olivar	.991	38	333	14	3	2	3

First Base	PCT	G	PO	A	E	DP
Baez	.994	21	150	6	1	16
Cardenas	1.000	2	10	0	0	0
Cespedes	.992	15	121	4	1	10
Cossetti	1.000	14	81	4	0	3
Fedko	.988	13	79	5	1	7
Ortega	.992	19	121	6	1	14
Rucker	1.000	7	54	4	0	7
Sabato	.996	34	237	13	1	25

Second Base	PCT	G	PO	A	E	DP
Culpepper	1.000	5	6	11	0	3
Genth	.933	9	19	23	3	3
Ortega	.992	31	46	80	1	20
Rucker	.970	71	120	171	9	34
Salas	.980	14	23	26	1	4
Schobel	.973	8	14	22	1	4
Shuffield	1.000	1	4	1	0	0

Third Base	PCT	G	PO	A	E	DP
Cespedes	.910	70	49	93	14	5
Culpepper	1.000	4	3	9	0	0
Ortega	.833	10	7	8	3	0

Salas	.966	17	112	2	4	7
Ross	.983	26	19	38	1	7
Rucker	.813	6	2	11	3	1
Salas	1.000	3	4	3	0	0
Schobel	.923	19	16	20	3	2

Shortstop	PCT	G	PO	A	E	DP
Culpepper	.962	49	66	109	7	26
Ortega	1.000	2	5	8	0	2
Ross	.965	65	91	156	9	30
Salas	.933	5	3	11	1	1
Schobel	.971	19	21	47	2	4

Outfield	PCT	G	PO	A	E	DP
Cerda	.950	10	18	1	1	1
Dearden	.982	30	56	0	1	0

Fedko	.975	65	154	2	4	1	Jenkins	.993	41	135	3 1 2
Gonzalez	.989	44	87	1	1	0	Mendez	1.000	24	37	1 0 0
Hess	.923	5	12	0	1	0	Olivar	.979	26	46	1 1 0
Houghton	1.000	21	58	0	0	0	Ortega	1.000	10	12	1 0 1

Rosario	.987	114	219	4	3	1
Ross	.975	28	75	3	2	0
Salas	1.000	6	12	1	0	0
Shuffield	1.000	1	1	0	0	0

CEDAR RAPIDS KERNELS
MIDWEST LEAGUE
HIGH-A

Batting	B-T	Ht.	Wt.	DOB	AVG	OBP	SLG	G	PA	AB	R	H	2B	3B	HR	RBI	BB	HBP	SH	SF	SO	SB	CS	BB%	SO%
Amick, Billy	R-R	6-0	210	11-4-02	.310	.418	.455	54	244	200	37	62	15	1	4	31	29	11	0	4	63	1	2	11.9	25.8
Baez, Nate	R-R	5-11	191	5-17-01	.331	.457	.453	45	184	148	34	49	9	0	3	23	32	3	0	1	30	1	0	17.4	16.3
Carr, Peyton	R-R	6-2	205	3-26-02	.125	.222	.250	3	9	8	0	1	1	0	0	0	1	0	0	1	0	0	0	11.1	0.0
Connell, Justin	R-R	5-11	185	3-11-99	.231	.375	.431	24	80	65	10	15	5	1	2	10	12	3	0	0	12	4	0	15.0	15.0
Culpepper, Kaelen	R-R	6-0	185	12-29-02	.293	.385	.479	54	247	215	38	63	9	2	9	34	26	6	0	0	40	15	2	10.5	16.2
De Andrade, Danny	R-R	5-11	173	4-10-04	.229	.317	.387	121	495	437	55	100	26	8	9	58	43	14	0	1	115	15	6	8.7	23.2
DeBarge, Kyle	R-R	5-9	170	7-15-03	.237	.347	.362	121	543	459	77	109	23	5	8	65	70	9	0	4	121	66	8	12.9	22.3
Diaw, Khadim	R-R	6-1	215	8-23-03	.294	.446	.420	39	157	119	24	35	4	1	3	20	19	6	0	3	27	4	1	12.1	17.2
Doncon, Rayne	R-R	6-2	176	9-22-03	.146	.245	.271	29	110	96	7	14	1	1	3	9	13	0	0	1	32	0	0	11.8	29.1
Eeles, Payton	L-R	5-7	180	11-16-99	.364	.462	.455	3	13	11	5	4	1	0	0	1	2	0	0	0	3	4	0	15.4	23.1
Ferrer, Jaime	R-R	6-1	222	12-27-02	.216	.296	.339	101	373	319	34	69	20	2	5	36	23	16	1	7	84	1	1	6.2	22.5
Gonzalez, Gabriel	R-R	5-10	165	1-4-04	.319	.378	.529	34	156	138	22	44	12	1	5	28	13	2	0	3	22	1	0	8.3	14.1
Hernandez, Luis	R-R	6-1	190	6-17-02	.250	.250	.250	5	8	8	1	2	0	0	0	0	0	0	0	0	4	0	0	0.0	50.0
Hess, Kyle	L-R	6-0	210	5-20-99	.231	.373	.363	69	226	182	30	42	9	3	3	22	36	6	0	1	59	4	3	15.9	26.1
Houghton, Maddux	R-R	5-11	190	2-23-99	.265	.351	.429	34	111	98	17	26	3	2	3	16	12	1	0	0	31	8	1	10.8	27.9
Houston, Marek	R-R	6-3	180	4-14-04	.152	.220	.239	12	51	46	4	7	1	0	1	2	3	1	1	0	7	1	1	5.9	15.7
Kendle, Caden	R-R	5-11	195	3-13-02	.236	.323	.382	97	371	322	52	76	19	2	8	39	33	11	0	5	69	14	4	8.9	18.6
Lugo, Andy	R-R	5-11	160	3-15-04	.309	.374	.515	28	109	97	18	30	7	2	3	11	10	0	0	0	16	9	0	9.2	17.4
Maitan, Kevin	S-R	6-2	190	2-12-00	.208	.279	.312	23	86	77	10	16	6	1	0	8	6	2	0	1	30	0	0	7.0	34.9
Napleton, Luke	R-R	6-1	205	1-5-02	.111	.250	.194	14	44	36	5	4	0	0	1	5	6	1	0	1	19	0	0	13.6	43.2
Ruiz, Poncho	R-R	6-2	210	2-22-03	.229	.348	.320	57	210	175	28	40	13	0	1	19	30	3	0	2	41	0	1	14.3	19.5
Salas, Jose	S-R	6-0	191	4-26-03	.244	.358	.533	16	55	45	10	11	2	1	3	11	5	3	2	0	14	4	1	9.1	25.5
Tait, Eduardo	L-R	6-0	175	8-27-06	.250	.286	.408	30	126	120	11	30	10	0	3	14	6	0	0	0	34	0	0	4.8	27.0
Thomason, Jay	L-R	6-1	200	4-11-02	.167	.235	.333	20	68	60	7	10	2	1	2	9	5	1	0	2	22	3	0	7.4	32.4
Urbina, Misael	R-R	5-10	190	4-26-02	.247	.357	.404	75	268	223	33	55	15	4	4	35	37	3	2	3	45	2	2	13.8	16.8
Valladares, Jefferson	R-R	6-0	190	5-30-02	.258	.347	.409	22	75	66	6	17	4	0	2	4	6	3	0	0	18	0	0	8.0	24.0
Winokur, Brandon	R-R	6-5	210	12-16-04	.226	.304	.388	122	529	474	65	107	20	3	17	68	44	10	0	1	131	26	4	8.3	24.8

Pitching	B-T	Ht.	Wt.	DOB	W	L	ERA	G	GS	SV	IP	Hits	Runs	ER	HR	BB	SO	AVG	OBP	SLG	SO%	BB%	BF
Bengard, Spencer	R-R	6-4	220	4-19-02	5	2	3.93	17	1	1	50	38	27	22	4	18	54	.202	.281	.309	25.6	8.5	211
Bohorquez, Adrian	R-R	6-1	190	3-3-05	1	1	3.52	5	4	0	23	19	10	9	1	6	28	.224	.306	.329	28.6	6.1	98
Bonilla, Julio	R-R	6-3	180	11-15-00	0	0	4.50	5	0	0	6	2	3	3	0	6	9	.105	.346	.211	34.6	23.1	26
Bragg, Kade	R-L	6-1	190	7-2-01	3	2	2.73	18	0	1	33	19	12	10	2	18	43	.170	.289	.250	31.9	13.3	135
Chaney, Chase	R-R	6-1	199	12-16-99	7	4	3.68	23	19	1	108	111	48	44	9	27	86	.268	.321	.377	19.1	6.0	451
Dunn, Ross	R-L	6-3	225	2-20-02	0	1	5.40	1	1	0	3	3	2	2	0	2	1	.250	.357	.333	7.1	14.3	14
Gabbert, Matt	L-R	6-4	200	6-28-02	1	2	3.66	9	1	1	32	27	16	13	3	2	27	.220	.230	.333	21.4	1.6	126
Gomez, Ruddy	R-R	6-2	215	1-9-00	1	2	0.00	11	0	5	16	8	2	0	0	3	22	.151	.171	.211	38.6	5.3	57
Hall, Tanner	R-R	6-1	186	3-18-02	3	4	5.53	18	16	0	72	79	48	44	6	45	46	.276	.398	.392	13.1	12.8	351
Hamilton, Xander	L-R	6-3	216	7-7-01	0	0	4.26	3	0	0	6	6	3	3	0	2	4	.286	.333	.381	16.7	8.3	24
Hess, Kyle	L-R	6-0	210	5-20-99	0	0	0.00	1	0	0	1	2	0	0	0	1	0	.400	.400	.400	0.0	0.0	5
Hidalgo, Alejandro	R-R	6-1	160	5-2-03	0	3	5.43	17	17	0	63	57	42	38	9	33	78	.228	.333	.417	27.9	11.8	280
Hill, Dasan	R-L	6-5	165	12-25-05	0	2	5.40	3	3	0	10	9	6	6	0	7	15	.243	.356	.378	33.3	15.6	45
Hoopes, Hunter	R-R	6-1	195	3-4-00	4	1	1.56	14	0	1	17	6	3	3	2	5	20	.103	.200	.207	30.8	7.7	65
Horn, Garrett	L-L	6-2	196	3-23-03	0	2	3.78	5	5	0	17	13	9	7	0	14	21	.232	.370	.321	28.8	19.2	73
Kisting, Jacob	R-R	6-5	220	4-9-03	2	4	3.63	16	5	0	40	25	16	16	2	15	36	.180	.258	.273	23.2	9.7	155
Langenberg, Ty	R-R	6-2	190	12-8-01	5	6	4.87	22	21	0	105	107	62	57	4	47	98	.263	.346	.371	21.1	10.1	465
Lee, Jeremy	R-R	5-11	203	9-7-01	4	4	7.88	19	6	0	46	62	48	40	5	23	33	.321	.391	.482	14.6	10.2	226
Mendez, Juan	R-R	6-4	240	10-18-98	0	0	15.43	6	0	1	7	10	12	12	0	7	4	.345	.500	.552	10.0	17.5	40
Mercedes, Juan	R-R	5-10	181	1-7-02	0	0	9.26	9	0	0	12	16	13	12	1	9	7	.333	.452	.458	14.5	19.4	62
Mikulski, Matt	L-L	6-4	205	5-8-99	0	1	8.44	6	0	0	5	2	6	5	0	13	7	.125	.531	.188	21.2	39.4	33
Noble, Jay	R-R	6-2	200	4-6-02	0	1	3.86	6	0	0	7	7	4	3	1	1	5	.259	.310	.444	17.2	3.4	29
Olivares, Jose	R-R	6-1	199	1-18-03	6	6	4.38	22	21	0	90	66	47	44	4	57	107	.202	.322	.288	27.6	14.7	388
Oxford, Brennen	R-L	6-2	205	11-11-99	2	1	8.31	9	0	1	9	10	8	8	0	8	9	.286	.419	.286	20.5	18.2	44
Pasqualotto, Paulshawn	R-R	6-2	200	6-14-01	4	0	3.51	36	0	10	51	53	22	20	2	18	39	.275	.333	.352	18.1	8.3	216
Percival, Cole	R-R	6-5	220	2-26-99	1	0	2.70	9	0	0	13	3	4	4	0	6	16	.250	.308	.267	10.0	10.0	60
Perez, Samuel	L-L	5-11	205	11-29-99	4	0	2.05	28	0	3	44	38	14	10	0	18	35	.232	.306	.317	19.1	9.8	183
Peschl, Cole	R-R	6-1	215	11-26-02	4	1	3.40	9	9	0	42	19	16	3	10	30	.254	.308	.367	16.5	5.5	182
Reyes, Wilker	L-L	6-0	170	2-25-02	2	2	5.66	25	0	0	41	41	30	26	4	23	44	.247	.347	.392	22.8	11.9	193
Romero, Ivran	R-R	6-0	200	11-19-01	1	0	1.93	8	0	0	10	9	9	8	1	7	9	.250	.356	.417	19.6	15.2	46
Soto, Charlee	S-R	6-5	210	8-31-05	0	1	1.38	3	3	0	13	9	2	2	0	4	19	.196	.288	.283	28.3	7.5	53
Stull, Eston	R-R	6-2	195	1-20-99	1	1	3.04	18	0	1	27	12	9	9	1	9	23	.229	.306	.302	8.2	11.0	
Trabachek, Nick	R-R	5-11	205	11-8-99	1	1	3.81	20	0	1	28	24	12	12	1	13	28	.235	.284	.392	22.6	10.5	124
Whitaker, Logan	R-R	6-6	225	5-25-00	3	0	2.45	14	0	0	22	20	7	6	1	2	17	.244	.271	.366	20.0	2.4	85
Wosinski, Jacob	R-R	6-8	220	3-9-99	2	2	3.20	17	0	5	26	16	9	1	3	25	.220	.247	.319	25.8	3.1	97
Yanez, Gabriel	L-L	6-3	168	7-22-99	4	2	5.35	25	0	2	35	35	24	21	2	13	34	.261	.324	.388	23.0	8.8	148

MINNESOTA TWINS

Fielding

Catcher	PCT	G	PO	A	E	DP	PB
Baez	.983	16	112	5	2	0	2
Diaw	.987	25	212	17	3	3	3
Ferrer	.966	26	209	17	8	2	0
Hernandez	.962	4	23	2	1	0	1
Napleton	.942	9	46	3	3	0	0
Ruiz	.976	45	339	25	9	3	2
Tait	.981	16	148	10	3	0	1
Valladares	1.000	2	12	0	0	0	0

First Base	PCT	G	PO	A	E	DP
Amick	.979	26	187	4	4	16
Baez	1.000	22	186	9	0	16
Carr	1.000	1	8	0	0	0
Doncon	1.000	5	30	4	0	2
Ferrer	.985	36	239	20	4	17
Lugo	.943	5	33	0	2	3
Maitan	.993	18	133	6	1	12
Ruiz	1.000	4	14	3	0	2
Salas	1.000	2	14	0	0	1
Thomason	1.000	5	22	2	0	0
Valladares	.984	17	116	6	2	13

Second Base	PCT	G	PO	A	E	DP
Culpepper	1.000	1	4	4	0	2
De Andrade	.980	47	83	116	4	28
DeBarge	.979	73	125	158	6	31
Doncon	.800	3	2	6	2	0
Eeles	1.000	1	1	3	0	0
Lugo	1.000	5	13	11	0	2
Salas	.900	5	8	10	2	3
Thomason	1.000	3	5	7	0	0

Third Base	PCT	G	PO	A	E	DP
Amick	.894	21	15	27	5	5
Carr	.750	2	1	2	1	0
De Andrade	.974	56	41	106	4	11
Doncon	.893	15	6	19	3	3
Hess	.000	1	0	0	0	0
Lugo	.939	10	7	24	2	2
Maitan	1.000	2	2	2	0	0
Salas	.667	2	0	2	1	0
Valladares	.000	1	0	0	0	0
Winokur	.897	30	17	44	7	5

Shortstop	PCT	G	PO	A	E	DP
Culpepper	.965	46	48	116	6	18
De Andrade	.875	1	1	9	1	2
DeBarge	1.000	24	30	70	0	16
Houston	.946	12	11	24	2	6
Winokur	.952	46	56	101	8	12

Outfield	PCT	G	PO	A	E	DP
Connell	.973	22	36	0	1	0
DeBarge	1.000	21	48	0	0	0
Diaw	.935	10	28	1	2	0
Eeles	.000	1	0	0	0	0
Ferrer	.964	32	53	0	2	0
Gonzalez	.956	26	41	2	2	0
Hess	.978	53	89	1	2	1
Houghton	1.000	34	87	0	0	0
Kendle	.979	97	179	4	4	1
Salas	1.000	7	5	0	0	0
Thomason	.923	8	12	0	1	0
Urbina	1.000	69	111	5	0	1
Valladares	.500	1	1	0	1	0
Winokur	.981	48	98	4	2	1

FORT MYERS MIGHTY MUSSELS — LOW-A
FLORIDA STATE LEAGUE

Batting	B-T	Ht.	Wt.	DOB	AVG	OBP	SLG	G	PA	AB	R	H	2B	3B	HR	RBI	BB	HBP	SH	SF	SO	SB	CS	BB%	SO%
Acuna, Bryan	R-R	6-0	176	8-11-05	.236	.341	.246	57	223	191	19	45	2	0	0	17	29	2	0	1	66	10	5	13.0	29.6
Agbayani, Bruin	L-R	6-2	185	3-26-07	.250	.478	.250	5	23	16	4	4	0	0	0	0	7	0	0	0	3	3	0	30.4	13.0
Amick, Billy	R-R	6-0	210	11-4-02	.267	.313	.400	4	16	15	2	4	2	0	0	0	1	0	0	0	6	0	0	6.3	37.5
Bass, Jayson	L-R	5-11	165	4-29-06	.125	.125	.125	8	24	24	2	3	0	0	0	0	0	0	0	0	9	1	0	0.0	37.5
Beltre, Eduardo	R-R	5-11	175	10-10-06	.151	.269	.247	26	108	93	9	14	3	0	2	8	14	1	0	0	28	6	2	13.0	25.9
Briceno, Miguel	R-R	5-9	155	7-6-03	.208	.281	.286	59	192	168	11	35	7	0	2	21	18	1	0	5	33	10	2	9.4	17.2
Carr, Peyton	R-R	6-2	204	3-26-02	.226	.332	.322	84	304	261	35	59	9	2	4	28	35	7	0	1	63	1	1	11.5	20.7
Chourio, Byron	S-R	6-2	171	5-20-05	.193	.340	.234	57	241	197	28	38	3	1	1	8	41	3	0	0	50	11	5	17.0	20.7
Daniels, Ryan	L-R	6-0	191	8-13-03	.000	.000	.000	2	9	9	0	0	0	0	0	0	0	0	0	0	4	0	0	0.0	44.4
Daugherty, Ian	R-R	6-2	204	10-7-02	.222	.364	.481	9	33	27	7	6	1	0	2	7	5	1	0	0	8	0	0	15.2	24.2
Del Rosario, Angel	R-R	6-0	160	1-11-03	.234	.311	.324	69	214	188	32	44	3	4	2	20	17	4	4	0	51	32	8	7.9	23.8
Diaw, Khadim	R-R	6-1	215	8-23-03	.333	.500	.778	3	12	9	1	3	1	0	1	4	1	2	0	0	3	0	0	8.3	25.0
Doncon, Rayne	R-R	6-2	176	9-22-03	.254	.333	.356	15	66	59	8	15	3	0	1	5	7	0	0	0	11	2	0	10.6	16.7
Eeles, Payton	L-R	5-7	180	11-19-96	.303	.378	.394	10	37	33	5	10	1	1	0	1	4	0	0	0	5	2	1	10.8	13.5
Genth, Harry	R-R	5-8	165	9-3-02	.053	.217	.053	7	23	19	1	1	0	0	0	1	3	1	0	0	11	1	1	13.0	47.8
Hernandez, Luis	R-R	6-1	190	6-17-02	.444	.615	.444	4	13	9	0	4	0	0	0	1	3	1	0	0	3	0	1	23.1	23.1
Herrera, Yilber	S-R	5-11	145	11-5-05	.227	.412	.423	10	34	26	5	6	2	0	1	3	8	0	0	0	10	3	0	23.5	29.4
Holland, Will	R-R	5-9	181	4-18-98	.500	.500	.750	1	4	4	1	2	1	0	0	1	0	0	0	0	0	0	0	0.0	0.0
Houghton, Maddux	R-R	5-11	190	2-23-99	.269	.376	.471	39	141	119	32	32	4	1	6	20	16	5	0	1	38	12	1	11.3	27.0
Houston, Marek	R-R	6-3	180	4-14-04	.370	.424	.444	12	59	54	10	20	4	0	0	9	5	0	0	0	13	6	0	8.5	22.0
Jenkins, Walker	L-R	6-3	205	2-19-05	.280	.419	.400	8	31	25	4	7	0	0	1	2	5	1	0	0	6	2	0	16.1	19.4
Jimenez, Enrique	S-R	5-10	170	11-3-05	.269	.431	.551	23	102	78	15	21	2	1	6	18	23	0	0	1	24	1	0	22.5	23.5
Lee, Brooks	S-R	5-11	205	2-14-01	.000	.000	.000	1	3	3	0	0	0	0	0	0	0	0	0	0	2	0	0	0.0	66.7
Maitan, Kevin	R-R	6-2	190	2-12-00	.300	.417	.300	3	12	10	3	3	0	0	0	0	2	0	0	0	3	0	0	16.7	25.0
Martinez, Yohander	R-R	5-10	175	1-8-02	.196	.319	.273	63	233	194	20	38	7	1	2	23	30	6	1	2	48	3	4	12.9	20.6
McCombs, Jacob	L-R	6-2	200	7-7-04	.250	.323	.250	8	31	28	2	7	0	0	0	3	3	0	0	0	4	5	0	0.0	12.9
McNeely, Caleb	R-R	6-1	180	12-16-99	.197	.316	.299	43	177	147	21	29	3	0	4	21	26	1	0	3	43	14	1	14.7	24.3
Mercedes, Yasser	R-R	6-2	175	11-6-04	.186	'.296	.307	94	419	355	48	66	13	0	10	42	55	3	0	6	105	34	1	13.1	25.1
Napleton, Luke	R-R	6-2	205	1-5-02	.250	.340	.325	12	50	40	3	10	0	0	1	8	6	1	0	3	11	1	0	12.0	22.0
O'Saben, Blaze	R-R	5-10	195	7-13-00	.225	.323	.296	43	164	142	16	32	7	0	1	14	18	7	0	1	24	16	2	8.5	14.6
Pena, Dameury	R-R	5-10	170	10-5-05	.241	.317	.316	96	417	370	50	89	10	0	6	43	35	8	0	4	37	28	5	8.4	8.9
Pena, Daniel	R-R	5-11	205	3-9-05	.199	.302	.265	55	212	181	24	36	6	0	2	27	23	5	0	3	28	0	0	10.8	13.2
Pena, Isaac	S-R	5-10	160	12-27-03	.118	.250	.118	5	20	17	4	2	0	0	0	0	3	0	0	0	8	0	0	15.0	40.0
Pena, Ricardo	R-R	6-0	180	5-30-05	.150	.146	.200	12	41	40	3	6	2	0	0	1	0	0	1	0	17	0	0	0.0	41.5
Robinson, Shai	R-R	6-0	180	5-30-05	.294	.077	.077	4	17	13	1	1	0	0	0	4	0	0	0	0	6	0	0	23.5	35.3
Rodriguez, Emmanuel	L-L	5-10	210	2-28-03	.321	.472	.357	8	36	28	4	9	1	0	0	3	8	0	0	0	12	1	0	22.2	33.3
Rodriguez, Jose	R-R	6-2	196	6-10-05	.149	.264	.321	60	250	215	24	32	9	2	8	29	32	2	0	1	80	1	0	12.8	32.0
Roman, Javier	R-R	6-0	155	3-26-03	.045	.276	.045	7	29	22	1	1	0	0	0	3	7	0	0	0	6	0	0	24.1	41.4
Ruiz, Poncho	R-R	6-2	210	2-23-02	.296	.424	.389	31	132	108	13	32	6	0	0	9	24	0	0	0	27	1	0	18.2	20.5
Sabato, Aaron	R-R	6-2	230	6-4-99	.118	.273	.118	5	22	17	0	2	0	0	0	1	3	1	0	1	4	0	0	13.6	18.2
Salas, Jose	S-R	6-0	191	4-26-03	.444	.476	.778	7	22	18	5	8	3	0	1	7	0	2	0	1	5	3	0	9.1	22.7
Schobel, Tanner	R-R	5-10	175	6-4-01	.111	.467	.222	3	15	9	2	1	0	0	0	1	6	0	0	0	4	0	0	40.0	26.7
Smith, JP	R-R	6-2	240	10-31-04	.237	.297	.344	24	101	93	10	22	2	1	2	14	7	1	0	0	25	1	0	6.9	24.8
Sprock, Ryan	R-R	5-10	205	9-27-04	.257	.395	.386	23	86	70	13	18	1	1	2	11	14	2	0	0	19	2	0	16.3	22.1
Thomason, Ty	L-R	6-1	200	4-11-02	.298	.466	.579	39	161	121	28	36	8	1	8	34	34	5	0	1	38	19	1	21.1	23.6
Valladares, Jefferson	R-R	6-0	190	5-30-02	.173	.255	.315	53	192	168	16	29	9	0	5	26	11	9	0	4	49	4	1	5.7	25.5
Young, Quentin	R-R	6-6	225	3-2-07	.118	.227	.118	5	20	17	2	2	0	0	0	3	2	1	0	0	9	1	0	9.1	40.9

Pitching	B-T	Ht.	Wt.	DOB	W	L	ERA	G	GS	SV	IP	Hits	Runs	ER	HR	BB	SO	AVG	OBP	SLG	SO%	BB%	BF
Armbruester, Will	R-R	6-6	235	12-15-00	1	1	2.25	8	0	0	12	6	5	3	0	4	10	.143	.213	.190	20.8	8.3	48
Bass, Jayson	L-R	5-11	165	4-29-06	0	0	0.00	1	0	0	1	0	0	0	0	0	1	.000	.000	.000	33.3	0.0	3
Becerra, Christian	S-R	6-1	170	6-2-03	3	2	2.90	13	8	0	50	40	18	16	1	16	30	.222	.284	.289	14.9	7.9	202
Bengard, Spencer	R-R	6-4	220	4-19-02	0	0	4.50	1	1	0	2	1	1	1	0	0	4	.143	.143	.286	57.1	0.0	7
Bohorquez, Adrian	R-R	6-1	190	3-3-05	2	3	4.66	14	10	0	48	34	28	25	6	25	57	.192	.324	.333	26.6	11.7	214
Bonilla, Julio	R-R	6-3	180	11-15-00	1	0	3.60	8	0	1	10	10	4	4	1	4	12	.250	.318	.350	27.3	9.1	44
Bortka, Josh	R-R	6-5	225	7-12-99	1	2	14.59	12	0	0	12	18	23	20	1	18	17	.327	.513	.382	21.8	23.1	78
Bragg, Kade	R-L	6-1	190	7-2-01	0	1	3.00	9	0	1	12	5	4	4	1	4	18	.279	.360	.419	36.0	8.0	50
Briceno, Miguel	R-R	5-9	155	7-6-03	0	0	18.00	1	0	0	1	3	2	2	0	1	1	.500	.571	.500	14.3	14.3	7
Carpenter, Michael	R-L	6-1	195	7-28-04	1	6	4.70	18	17	0	54	61	34	28	4	23	58	.279	.344	.397	23.8	9.4	244
Carr, Peyton	R-R	6-2	205	3-26-02	0	0	7.71	3	0	0	2	6	2	2	0	0	1	.545	.500	.636	8.3	0.0	12
Culpepper, C.J.	R-R	6-3	193	11-2-01	0	0	0.00	1	1	0	3	1	0	0	0	0	4	.100	.182	.100	36.4	9.1	11
Doktorczyk, Jason	R-R	6-6	230	4-3-03	3	6	5.00	21	12	0	86	88	59	48	11	29	88	.257	.338	.429	22.5	7.4	391
Feigl, Brady	R-L	6-4	195	12-27-90	0	0	4.50	2	0	0	2	1	1	1	1	1	1	.143	.250	.571	12.5	12.5	8
Francisco, Brent	R-R	6-7	250	6-11-01	1	0	0.71	7	0	0	13	10	2	1	0	2	19	.204	.250	.204	36.5	3.8	52
Gabbert, Matt	L-R	6-4	200	6-28-02	0	1	2.21	10	1	0	20	16	5	5	1	1	16	.216	.227	.297	21.1	1.3	76
Garcia, Joel	R-R	5-10	165	7-3-04	0	4	16.68	4	4	0	11	24	21	21	3	7	9	.429	.515	.804	13.2	10.3	68
Gomez, Ruddy	R-R	6-2	215	1-9-00	0	1	3.15	14	0	6	20	18	8	7	2	5	23	.240	.296	.373	28.4	6.2	81
Hall, Jakob	R-R	6-2	195	8-14-02	3	1	6.83	28	3	0	54	62	44	41	5	22	45	.286	.360	.459	18.2	8.9	247
Hilker, Michael	R-R	6-1	190	8-24-04	1	0	0.00	1	0	0	2	0	0	0	0	0	3	.000	.000	.000	50.0	0.0	6
Hill, Dasan	R-L	6-5	165	12-25-05	0	2	2.77	16	16	0	52	35	20	16	2	33	68	.190	.321	.250	30.6	14.9	222
Hoopes, Hunter	R-R	6-1	195	3-4-00	2	3	2.14	16	0	0	21	11	8	5	1	9	32	.155	.282	.225	37.6	10.6	85
Houghton, Maddux	R-R	5-11	190	2-23-99	0	0	10.13	2	0	0	3	3	3	3	1	1	0	.273	.385	.545	0.0	7.7	13
Jones, Eli	R-R	6-1	200	6-17-03	2	10	5.13	23	18	0	100	102	65	57	2	40	84	.261	.342	.340	18.8	8.9	447
Jones, Kyle	L-R	6-1	200	2-7-00	0	0	0.00	2	0	0	2	2	3	0	0	3	2	.200	.385	.200	15.4	23.1	13
Jones, Merit	R-R	6-3	190	7-26-03	0	0	0.00	1	0	1	2	1	0	0	0	0	1	.143	.143	.143	14.3	0.0	7
Kirby, Devin	R-R	5-10	220	8-10-99	2	1	6.45	15	0	1	22	24	19	16	2	16	26	.286	.439	.429	24.1	14.8	108
Kisting, Jacob	R-R	6-5	220	4-9-03	3	1	3.97	14	0	2	34	32	17	15	1	8	41	.237	.290	.311	28.3	5.5	145
Kolhosser, Xavier	R-R	6-5	194	7-2-03	0	1	7.88	4	1	0	8	9	7	7	2	4	13	.281	.361	.656	36.1	11.1	36
MacLeod, Christian	L-L	6-4	227	4-12-00	0	0	0.00	2	2	0	4	0	0	0	0	2	8	.000	.143	.000	57.1	14.3	14
Narvaez, Anthony	R-R	6-1	175	7-30-03	1	2	4.50	7	0	1	10	9	6	5	1	7	7	.265	.386	.412	15.9	15.9	44
Ohl, Pierson	R-R	6-1	180	9-10-99	1	0	0.00	2	0	0	5	2	0	0	0	1	10	.125	.176	.125	58.8	5.9	17
Oxford, Brennen	R-L	6-2	205	11-11-99	3	1	2.63	19	0	1	27	21	12	8	2	12	33	.214	.307	.327	28.9	10.5	114
Peschl, Cole	R-R	6-1	215	11-26-02	1	1	1.03	6	2	1	26	22	5	3	0	9	37	.218	.288	.307	33.3	8.1	111
Questad, Dylan	R-R	6-1	200	11-2-04	4	7	6.87	25	11	1	75	64	65	57	9	62	83	.230	.375	.385	23.7	17.7	350
Rocha, Liam	R-R	6-3	200	5-8-02	1	1	11.37	7	0	0	8	9	8	8	1	10	8	.286	.487	.464	20.5	25.6	39
Rochard, Sam	R-R	6-1	200	7-23-00	0	2	4.05	6	1	2	13	16	12	6	1	7	19	.286	.365	.429	30.2	11.1	63
Romero, Ivran	R-R	6-0	200	11-19-01	4	1	2.60	28	0	4	45	37	23	13	2	16	50	.220	.306	.286	25.8	8.2	194
Ross, Michael	L-R	6-2	205	7-4-02	4	6	3.18	20	16	0	82	72	34	29	8	29	76	.233	.307	.362	22.0	8.4	346
Sechrist, Zander	R-L	6-2	192	5-4-02	4	5	3.00	36	0	2	69	62	28	23	2	20	58	.236	.297	.327	19.9	6.9	291
Stasiowski, Tyler	R-R	6-0	185	8-13-01	2	1	6.70	35	0	1	47	61	40	35	5	22	45	.314	.385	.495	20.3	9.9	222
Stevens, Jonathan	R-R	6-1	215	6-24-04	1	0	6.92	14	0	1	13	17	14	10	2	12	20	.315	.433	.481	29.9	17.9	67
Stewart, Brock	L-R	6-3	220	10-3-91	0	0	0.00	2	0	0	2	0	0	0	0	0	5	.000	.000	.000	83.3	0.0	6
Tonkin, Michael	R-R	6-7	220	11-19-89	0	0	0.00	1	0	0	2	1	0	0	0	0	3	.250	.250	.250	37.5	0.0	8
Valladares, Jefferson	R-R	6-0	190	5-30-02	0	0	0.00	1	0	0	1	3	2	0	0	0	0	.500	.429	.667	0.0	0.0	7

Fielding

Catcher	PCT	G	PO	A	E	DP	PB
Daugherty	.958	7	61	8	3	0	0
Diaw	1.000	1	6	0	0	0	0
Hernandez	1.000	4	30	1	0	0	0
Jimenez	1.000	15	119	9	0	1	2
Napleton	1.000	4	46	3	0	0	1
Pena	.978	29	246	27	17	6	1	11
Pena	.929	7	43	9	4	1	0
Roman	1.000	3	20	1	0	0	0
Ruiz	.984	22	229	20	4	0	9
Sprock	.938	3	15	0	1	0	0
Valladares	.984	38	339	23	6	1	7

First Base	PCT	G	PO	A	E	DP
Amick	1.000	1	5	1	0	1
Carr	.994	51	323	12	2	19
Doncon	1.000	4	25	1	0	1
Jimenez	.939	6	44	3	4	3
Maitan	1.000	2	19	1	0	1
Martinez	.974	19	141	6	4	8
Napleton	1.000	4	32	1	0	1
Pena	1.000	3	12	1	0	1
Roman	1.000	4	32	2	0	2
Ruiz	1.000	3	10	0	0	1
Sabato	1.000	3	22	1	0	0
Smith	.975	19	148	5	4	9
Thomason	1.000	9	41	7	0	6

Second Base	PCT	G	PO	A	E	DP
Acuna	.955	8	9	12	1	2
Agbayani	1.000	3	2	6	0	0
Briceno	.921	13	13	22	3	2
Del Rosario	1.000	3	5	6	0	1
Eeles	1.000	3	5	6	0	1
Genth	.818	2	3	6	2	1
Herrera	.950	5	8	11	1	2
Martinez	.965	18	23	32	2	4
Pena	.944	72	105	130	14	13
Robinson	1.000	2	5	8	0	2
Schobel	.000	1	0	0	1	0
Thomason	.967	7	14	15	1	1

Third Base	PCT	G	PO	A	E	DP
Acuna	.884	17	12	26	5	2
Amick	1.000	2	2	1	0	0
Briceno	.808	12	9	12	5	2
Carr	.902	21	10	27	4	6
Doncon	1.000	7	2	7	0	0
Genth	1.000	3	2	4	0	0
Herrera	.000	2	0	0	0	0
Maitan	.500	1	0	1	1	0
Martinez	.868	25	21	25	7	4
McNeely	.875	18	12	23	5	2

	PCT	G	PO	A	E	DP
Valladares	.952	5	19	1	1	1
Pena	1.000	4	8	1	0	2
Schobel	1.000	1	0	2	0	0
Sprock	.810	9	4	13	4	1
Thomason	.923	15	6	30	3	4
Valladares	.000	1	0	0	1	0
Young	.800	2	0	4	1	0

Shortstop	PCT	G	PO	A	E	DP
Acuna	.977	25	39	47	2	7
Agbayani	1.000	2	2	4	0	0
Briceno	.852	10	12	11	4	1
Del Rosario	.929	59	68	129	15	19
Doncon	.889	3	6	2	1	1
Eeles	.900	3	2	7	1	0
Herrera	.900	6	12	2	3	
Holland	1.000	1	1	1	0	0
Houston	.957	11	16	28	2	4
Lee	1.000	1	1	1	0	0
McNeely	.974	12	13	24	1	3
Robinson	1.000	1	1	3	0	1
Salas	1.000	4	4	1	0	1
Young	.889	3	1	7	1	0

Outfield	PCT	G	PO	A	E	DP
Acuna	1.000	5	6	1	0	0
Bass	.889	5	8	0	1	0
Beltre	.911	30	50	1	5	1

Briceno	.914	24	32	0	3	0	Houghton	1.000	37	78	1	0	1	Robinson	1.000	1	2	0	0	0
Chourio	.986	52	66	2	1	0	Jenkins	.900	4	8	1	1	0	Rodriguez	1.000	46	56	2	0	0
Daniels	1.000	2	5	0	0	0	McCombs	1.000	6	8	1	0	0	Rodriguez	1.000	7	16	0	0	0
Del Rosario	1.000	4	3	0	0	0	McNeely	1.000	14	33	3	0	1	Salas	1.000	3	6	0	0	0
Diaw	1.000	1	1	1	0	0	Mercedes	.956	91	207	8	10	2	Sprock	1.000	5	8	0	0	0
Eeles	1.000	2	4	0	0	0	O'Saben	1.000	45	102	5	0	0	Thomason	.889	5	8	0	1	0
Genth	1.000	2	3	0	0	0	Pena	.966	15	28	0	1	0	Valladares	1.000	7	13	0	0	0

FCL TWINS — ROOKIE
FLORIDA COMPLEX LEAGUE

Batting	B-T	Ht.	Wt.	DOB	AVG	OBP	SLG	G	PA	AB	R	H	2B	3B	HR	RBI	BB	HBP	SH	SF	SO	SB	CS	BB%	SO%
Acuna, Bryan	R-R	6-0	176	8-11-05	.254	.420	.365	21	81	63	19	16	4	0	1	8	15	3	0	0	14	2	1	18.5	17.3
Amick, Billy	R-R	6-0	210	11-4-02	.333	.667	.333	1	6	3	3	1	0	0	0	0	3	0	0	0	1	0	0	50.0	16.7
Bass, Jayson	L-R	5-11	165	4-29-06	.314	.419	.490	20	62	51	6	16	4	1	1	12	9	1	0	1	15	6	1	14.5	24.2
Beltre, Eduardo	R-R	5-11	175	10-10-06	.206	.313	.370	52	195	165	33	34	10	1	5	32	21	6	0	3	46	19	3	10.8	23.6
Castro, Ariel	L-L	6-2	178	2-17-06	.104	.256	.260	41	117	96	10	10	2	2	3	14	13	7	0	1	43	3	2	11.1	36.8
Chourio, Byron	S-R	6-2	171	5-20-05	.222	.222	.333	2	9	9	0	2	1	0	0	1	0	0	0	0	0	0	1	0.0	0.0
De Los Santos, Daiber	R-R	6-1	160	10-6-06	.167	.296	.333	48	186	156	29	26	10	2	4	17	21	8	0	1	89	15	7	11.3	47.8
Dominguez, Ramiro	R-R	5-9	163	3-26-07	.248	.366	.414	49	172	145	26	36	15	0	3	24	20	7	0	0	18	16	2	11.6	10.5
Doncon, Rayne	R-R	6-2	176	9-22-03	.111	.385	.222	4	13	9	1	1	1	0	0	1	4	0	0	0	6	0	0	30.8	46.2
Escalante, Rafael	R-R	5-10	160	9-13-01	.308	.500	.538	6	18	13	4	4	0	0	1	4	5	0	0	0	4	0	0	27.8	22.2
Fragoza, Luis	R-R	6-1	160	10-26-06	.177	.349	.297	49	169	138	25	30	8	0	3	16	17	12	0	2	40	14	3	10.1	23.7
Hernandez, Merphy	L-L	5-11	150	12-12-06	.163	.333	.256	16	54	43	8	7	2	1	0	5	8	3	0	0	13	8	5	14.8	24.1
Hernandez, Yandro	R-R	5-11	175	5-13-05	.207	.368	.337	37	117	92	16	19	6	2	2	16	21	3	0	1	29	7	3	17.9	24.8
Herrera, Yilber	S-R	5-11	145	1-15-05	.128	.381	.231	39	113	78	15	10	2	0	2	9	30	3	0	2	28	7	6	26.5	24.8
Jenkins, Walker	L-R	6-3	205	2-19-05	.000	.667	.000	1	3	1	1	0	0	0	0	0	2	0	0	0	0	1	0	66.7	0.0
Leal, Victor	R-R	5-11	174	9-29-06	.161	.345	.161	30	84	62	7	10	0	0	0	8	17	2	0	3	12	1	2	20.2	14.3
Martin, Austin	R-R	6-0	185	3-23-99	.182	.308	.182	3	13	11	0	2	0	0	0	2	2	0	0	0	2	1	0	15.4	15.4
Mercedes, Yasser	R-R	5-11	175	11-16-04	.471	.571	.824	5	21	17	4	8	3	0	1	6	2	2	0	0	4	2	2	9.5	19.0
Nunez, Irvin	R-R	5-10	160	2-21-06	.233	.408	.310	43	152	116	25	27	4	1	1	14	29	6	0	1	33	3	0	19.1	21.7
Paez, Ricardo	L-L	5-10	165	4-14-07	.242	.398	.295	39	124	95	20	23	3	1	0	10	19	7	1	2	30	13	3	15.3	24.2
Pena, Isaac	S-R	5-10	160	12-27-03	.208	.385	.229	22	65	48	9	10	1	0	0	6	14	1	0	2	11	5	2	21.5	16.9
Pena, Ricardo	R-R	5-8	180	5-30-05	.222	.548	.389	10	31	18	5	4	0	0	1	2	11	2	0	0	9	0	0	35.5	29.0
Rodriguez, Emmanuel	L-L	5-10	210	2-28-03	.294	.368	.353	5	19	17	4	5	1	0	0	1	2	0	0	0	6	0	0	10.5	31.6
Roman, Javier	R-R	6-0	155	3-26-03	.214	.313	.464	10	32	28	5	6	1	0	2	4	4	0	0	0	14	0	0	12.5	43.8
Silva, Carlos	R-R	5-10	168	3-1-06	.162	.358	.297	16	54	37	4	6	2	0	0	2	10	1	8	10	3	1	3	11	0	0	18.5	20.4
Thomason, Jay	L-R	6-1	200	4-11-02	.083	.389	.167	5	18	12	2	1	1	0	0	2	6	0	0	0	6	6	1	33.3	33.3

Pitching	B-T	Ht.	Wt.	DOB	W	L	ERA	G	GS	SV	IP	Hits	Runs	ER	HR	BB	SO	AVG	OBP	SLG	SO%	BB%	BF
Armbruester, Will	R-R	6-6	235	12-15-00	2	0	2.61	15	0	1	31	32	11	9	1	2	28	.267	.276	.358	22.8	1.6	123
Becerra, Christian	S-R	6-1	170	6-2-03	0	0	2.25	2	1	0	4	5	2	1	0	0	5	.294	.294	.294	29.4	0.0	17
Bonilla, Julio	R-R	6-3	180	11-15-06	1	0	7.11	6	0	0	6	7	5	5	1	3	8	.280	.367	.520	26.7	10.0	30
Chivilli, Hendry	R-R	6-3	165	9-14-05	2	0	2.51	7	5	0	14	8	4	4	0	10	15	.160	.300	.180	25.0	16.7	60
Conrad, Teague	R-R	6-4	185	6-17-01	2	0	3.70	7	2	0	24	26	12	10	1	9	14	.277	.346	.372	13.5	8.7	104
Cordero, Miguel	R-R	6-1	170	8-15-06	1	1	4.43	9	1	1	22	16	15	11	1	2	8	.211	.200	.297	22.8	8.7	92
Cota, Juan	R-R	6-1	170	6-2-05	3	0	6.08	9	4	0	24	30	17	16	4	7	25	.306	.358	.531	23.4	6.5	107
Culpepper, C.J.	R-R	6-3	193	11-2-01	0	0	0.00	1	1	0	2	2	0	0	0	0	4	.286	.375	.286	50.0	0.0	8
Francisco, Brent	R-R	6-7	250	6-11-01	3	1	2.08	12	0	4	17	14	5	4	0	2	24	.215	.239	.292	35.8	3.0	67
Gabbert, Matt	L-R	6-4	200	6-28-02	0	0	3.86	5	4	1	14	13	6	6	0	2	12	.250	.273	.327	21.8	3.6	55
Garcia, Joel	R-R	5-10	165	7-3-04	2	4	3.35	11	11	0	43	40	19	16	1	12	51	.247	.305	.333	28.8	6.8	177
Gomez, Ruddy	R-R	6-2	215	1-9-00	1	0	0.96	5	0	0	9	6	1	1	0	2	12	.194	.265	.194	35.3	5.9	34
Hamilton, Xander	L-R	6-3	216	7-1-07	0	0	0.00	7	0	1	10	2	0	0	0	2	11	.061	.114	.061	31.4	5.7	35
Huffman, Andrew	R-R	6-2	225	8-20-99	5	1	1.17	11	0	0	15	14	6	2	2	10	19	.230	.347	.377	26.4	13.9	72
Kolhosser, Xavier	R-R	6-5	194	7-2-03	2	1	2.55	10	3	0	18	11	8	5	0	5	10	.175	.307	.270	25.3	13.3	75
Machuca, Eider	R-R	6-2	190	8-11-04	2	0	3.38	6	0	0	8	5	3	3	0	3	6	.185	.258	.185	19.4	9.7	31
Marcano, Rafael	L-L	6-1	200	4-16-00	0	0	27.00	1	0	0	0	2	2	1	0	1	0	.667	.750	.667	25.0	25.0	4
Mueller, Mitch	R-R	6-4	235	9-13-01	1	0	1.59	5	0	1	11	11	2	2	0	2	14	.262	.326	.310	30.4	4.3	46
Narvaez, Anthony	R-R	6-1	175	7-30-03	0	0	0.00	5	0	1	7	3	0	0	0	1	7	.136	.174	.136	30.4	4.3	23
Pulido, Sebastian	R-R	6-2	200	3-8-01	0	0	5.79	6	0	1	9	10	6	6	1	5	11	.286	.386	.429	25.0	11.4	44
Ramirez, Erasmo	R-R	6-0	220	5-2-90	0	0	4.50	3	1	0	4	3	2	2	0	1	3	.214	.267	.214	18.8	6.3	16
Ramos, Anderson	R-R	6-1	182	4-24-06	3	3	3.81	17	0	6	28	15	17	12	1	17	38	.153	.292	.214	31.1	13.9	122
Rocha, Liam	R-R	6-3	200	5-8-02	0	0	0.00	5	0	1	5	1	0	0	0	2	9	.067	.176	.067	52.9	11.8	17
Rochard, Sam	R-R	6-1	200	7-25-03	1	0	1.00	4	3	0	9	8	1	1	0	1	13	.235	.278	.235	36.1	2.8	36
Rodriguez, Melvin	R-R	6-2	195	2-27-06	1	2	3.53	11	9	0	43	32	17	17	1	22	32	.209	.328	.294	17.5	12.0	183
Rojas, Santiago	R-R	6-0	165	4-8-07	1	0	0.00	2	0	0	2	0	0	0	0	1	1	.000	.143	.000	14.3	14.3	7
Rondon, Leonardo	R-R	5-10	176	5-17-07	1	3	5.70	11	3	1	24	18	18	15	4	19	23	.205	.357	.398	20.5	17.0	112
Roque, Yoel	R-R	6-2	175	1-21-07	0	3	16.97	10	0	0	12	16	32	22	1	17	13	.314	.507	.392	18.3	23.9	71
Ventura, Aiberson	R-R	6-4	176	11-23-05	1	0	5.59	15	0	2	19	24	15	12	1	7	13	.308	.371	.474	14.4	7.8	90

Fielding

C: Nunez 28, Leal 18, Pena 6, Silva 6, Roman 4, Escalante 2. **1B:** Bass 16, Fragoza 15, Nunez 9, Hernandez 8, Leal 7, Escalante 4, Roman 4, Doncon 2. **2B:** Dominguez 39, Herrera 11, Acuna 7, Pena 3, Thomason 2, Martin 1. **3B:** Herrera 16, Pena 15, Acuna 12, Fragoza 8, Dominguez 5, Thomason 4, Doncon 1. **SS:** De Los Santos 45, Herrera 8, Dominguez 6, Acuna 2. **LF:** Fragoza 18, Paez 16, Castro 13, Y. Hernandez 11, Bass 2, Herrera 2, Chourio 1, M. Hernandez 1, Thomason 1. **CF:** Beltre 23, Castro 14, Hernandez 12, Paez 10, Rodriguez 4, Fragoza 2, Mercedes 2, Chourio 2, Jenkins 1, Martin 1. **RF:** Castro 15, Y. Hernandez 15, Fragoza 9, Paez 9, Beltre 8, M. Hernandez 3, Bass 2, Herrera 1, Mercedes 1

DSL TWINS ROOKIE
DOMINICAN SUMMER LEAGUE

Batting	B-T	Ht.	Wt.	DOB	AVG	OBP	SLG	G	PA	AB	R	H	2B	3B	HR	RBI	BB	HBP	SH	SF	SO	SB	CS	BB%	SO%
Almanzar, Darwin	S-R	5-10	179	10-23-07	.252	.347	.497	44	176	151	32	38	17	1	6	41	20	3	0	2	28	6	2	11.4	15.9
Barrios, Jose	S-R	5-9	152	1-21-08	.254	.352	.361	37	143	122	29	31	3	2	2	19	16	3	1	1	24	10	5	11.2	16.8
Bonifacio, Cristian	L-L	6-1	199	2-23-08	.161	.295	.280	33	112	93	12	15	5	0	2	19	17	1	0	1	47	3	3	15.2	42.0
Cardona, Gerardo	R-R	5-11	192	5-22-07	.192	.397	.231	27	73	52	12	10	2	0	0	9	18	1	0	2	15	1	0	24.7	20.5
Castillo, Haritzon	S-R	5-10	175	3-23-08	.283	.395	.428	39	167	138	32	39	8	3	2	31	24	3	0	2	22	12	3	14.4	13.2
Castillo, Pablo	R-R	6-0	189	4-30-08	.315	.474	.411	28	95	73	13	23	4	0	1	15	14	8	0	0	22	2	4	14.7	23.2
Diaz, Dencer	R-R	6-2	170	7-24-08	.247	.356	.303	31	104	89	20	22	2	0	1	10	15	0	0	0	17	4	2	14.4	16.3
Duran, Yovanny	S-R	5-11	173	11-3-07	.296	.452	.382	46	197	152	41	45	7	3	0	20	39	5	0	1	30	31	7	19.8	15.2
Leon, Santiago	R-R	5-11	169	6-25-08	.223	.391	.313	47	215	166	52	37	8	2	1	24	39	8	0	2	39	11	7	18.1	18.1
Perez, Joyner	R-R	5-11	215	6-19-08	.313	.457	.494	25	105	83	15	26	6	0	3	26	18	4	0	0	17	2	1	17.1	16.2
Reyes, Jhomnardo	L-L	6-3	186	10-6-07	.291	.386	.469	50	207	175	33	51	10	9	1	33	24	5	0	3	59	10	7	11.6	28.5
Salazar, Aaron	R-R	5-10	172	3-28-08	.192	.380	.269	39	137	104	21	20	8	0	0	18	26	6	0	1	39	7	2	19.0	28.5
Serrano, Teilon	L-R	5-11	200	5-22-08	.258	.386	.426	41	189	155	47	40	7	2	5	21	28	5	0	1	48	21	5	14.8	25.4
Taveras, Carlos	L-R	6-0	185	5-31-08	.246	.389	.439	18	72	57	15	14	3	1	2	13	13	1	0	1	15	2	1	18.1	20.8
Val, Jamesson	S-R	6-1	163	12-13-05	.232	.403	.389	44	129	95	28	22	2	2	3	22	27	3	0	4	24	21	2	20.9	18.6

Pitching	B-T	Ht.	Wt.	DOB	W	L	ERA	G	GS	SV	IP	Hits	Runs	ER	HR	BB	SO	AVG	OBP	SLG	SO%	BB%	BF
Cafe, Nestor	R-R	6-4	185	11-6-05	1	1	9.30	17	0	0	20	13	24	21	0	31	20	.183	.439	.254	18.7	29.0	107
Campusano, Agustin	R-R	6-2	190	11-13-07	0	1	4.80	12	0	1	30	30	18	16	3	17	25	.265	.363	.354	18.5	12.6	135
Cardona, Gerardo	R-R	5-11	192	5-22-07	0	1	20.25	2	0	0	3	5	7	6	2	3	0	.385	.500	.846	0.0	18.8	16
Carranza, Aaron	R-R	6-2	165	7-11-05	1	1	10.70	12	0	0	18	15	22	21	1	21	18	.234	.443	.344	20.2	23.6	89
Castellanos, Santiago	R-R	5-10	150	7-17-08	1	2	7.79	9	8	0	29	23	12	9	0	9	36	.215	.306	.252	29.8	7.4	121
Castillo, Angel	R-R	6-2	215	10-24-06	0	0	20.25	2	2	0	1	1	3	3	0	4	2	.200	.556	.400	22.2	44.4	9
Ceballos, Brandy	R-R	5-11	176	6-9-07	2	0	10.26	15	0	0	17	21	30	19	2	26	15	.323	.495	.538	15.2	26.3	99
Compres, Manuel	R-R	6-4	226	7-9-05	0	0	54.00	1	0	0	1	1	4	4	0	2	0	.333	.667	.333	0.0	33.3	6
Figaro, Juan	R-R	61-2	166	10-13-06	0	1	5.19	9	2	0	9	5	6	5	0	14	6	.185	.500	.259	13.6	31.8	44
Gomez, Jesus	R-R	6-1	170	1-30-06	1	2	5.52	14	2	1	29	30	23	18	1	18	30	.259	.371	.353	21.4	12.9	140
Infante, Jensi	R-R	6-3	167	9-30-06	2	0	3.47	16	2	1	23	17	12	9	1	17	17	.213	.365	.325	16.3	16.3	104
Jose, Yordi	L-L	6-2	180	10-30-06	1	0	2.08	7	0	1	9	7	2	2	1	5	11	.226	.333	.323	30.6	13.9	36
Lucena, Eliezer	R-R	5-11	165	12-17-07	3	0	3.35	11	1	0	38	38	16	14	0	19	31	.264	.369	.313	18.3	11.2	169
Marin, Rainer	R-R	6-0	168	7-15-05	2	3	6.21	11	6	0	29	29	24	20	1	27	27	.279	.438	.404	19.7	19.7	137
Mirabal, Marlon	L-L	5-10	184	7-6-06	2	2	9.11	15	0	0	28	49	34	28	4	18	25	.392	.459	.568	17.0	12.2	147
Montano, Omar	R-R	6-0	160	2-10-06	0	6	10.80	12	12	0	32	48	46	38	0	19	32	.353	.455	.412	19.3	11.4	166
Pacheco, Rey	R-R	5-9	189	1-6-07	5	2	3.00	16	3	1	33	32	16	11	0	7	31	.256	.299	.352	22.6	5.1	137
Pina, Greidi	R-R	6-4	180	12-17-06	0	1	5.87	7	0	0	8	6	8	5	3	7	5	.194	.390	.548	12.2	17.1	41
Quinones, Juan	L-L	6-2	170	10-15-07	2	2	9.12	14	2	0	25	36	29	25	2	20	26	.346	.450	.490	20.2	15.5	129
Rosal, Diego	R-R	6-1	202	7-24-06	0	2	11.37	6	1	0	13	16	17	16	2	8	10	.314	.410	.510	16.4	13.1	61
Surumuy, Jeicol	R-R	6-3	180	1-9-06	2	1	6.48	12	8	0	33	30	26	24	2	21	33	.244	.381	.366	21.3	13.5	155
Urena, Eli	R-R	6-3	192	4-27-06	0	3	10.54	10	4	0	14	26	20	16	0	27	13	.333	.480	.156	17.3	36.0	75
Val, Jamesson	S-R	6-1	163	12-13-05	0	0	16.20	2	0	0	2	5	3	3	0	0	1	.556	.500	.667	10.0	0.0	10
Villoria, Geremy	R-R	6-2	175	8-14-08	0	0	2.25	3	3	0	8	9	6	2	0	3	5	.273	.351	.333	13.5	8.1	37

Fielding

C: Cardona 24, Salazar 23, Castillo 20. **1B:** Val 23, Salazar 15, Diaz 13, Castillo 9, Perez 6, Cardona 1. **2B:** Barrios 19, Castillo 15, Leon 14, Almanzar 8, Val 2, Diaz 1. **3B:** Almanzar 27, Val 10, Diaz 7, Barrios 6, Castillo 5, Leon 4. **SS:** Leon 29, Castillo 21, Barrios 8. **LF:** Bonifacio 24, Perez 15, Reyes 10, Duran 7, Serrano 4, Taveras 2. **CF:** Duran 22, Serrano 19, Reyes 9, Taveras 7. **RF:** Reyes 21, Duran 17, Serrano 9, Taveras 6, Bonifacio 2, Val 2, Perez 1

New York Mets

SEASON SYNOPSIS: Stakes were high after signing Juan Soto to baseball's biggest contract ever in the offseason, and the Mets held a playoff spot for 174 of the 186 days of the season. But as SNY play-by-play broadcaster Gary Cohen put it, the Mets staged an agonizing, slow-motion collapse after a strong start, barely finishing above .500 and missing out on a playoff spot, losing a tiebreaker to the Reds.

HIGH POINT: The Mets got off to a 45-24 start after holding on to beat the Nationals 4-3 on June 12 behind 5 ⅔ scoreless innings from righthander Kodai Senga. Jeff McNeil contributed a key three-run homer (his seventh home run) and had a .911 OPS at game's end. But Senga went down with a pulled hamstring that game while covering first base, and he posted a 5.90 ERA in 39 ⅔ innings the rest of the season. McNeil slumped badly late as well, including a .514 OPS in September.

LOW POINT: The Mets just had to beat the Marlins on the season's final day to edge the Reds for the final wild-card spot but sustained their eighth shutout of the season in a crushing 4-0 defeat. Lefty Sean Manaea, the team's pitching hero in 2024, only lasted 1 ⅔ innings in the finale and posted a 5.64 ERA over 60 ⅔ innings on the season. After the finale, Manaea called his season "a complete failure." New York used 17 starting pitchers over the course of the season.

NOTABLE ROOKIES: Their best starter was rookie righthander Nolan McLean (5-1, 2.06), who struck out 57 in 48 innings over eight starts. Rookies comprised half the Mets' rotation in September, with Brandon Sproat and Minor League Pitcher of the Year Jonah Tong combining for nine starts joining McLean. Longtime prospect Ronny Mauricio (.663 OPS) flashed power potential.

KEY TRANSACTIONS: Free-agent signee Clay Holmes, transitioning from reliever to starter, was a success, going 12-8, 3.53 in 165 ⅔ innings. But fellow free-agent Frankie Montas (6.28 ERA) started hurt, pitched poorly and required Tommy John surgery in August, embodying some of the Mets' rotation struggles. Club president David Stearns focused on buoying the bullpen at the July trade deadline, and submariner Tyler Rogers (2.30 ERA in 27 IP) performed well. But relievers Gregory Soto (1-3, 4.50) and Ryan Helsley (0-3, 7.20) couldn't be trusted with leads in September. Cedric Mullins, added to plug a hole in center field, failed (.182/.284/.281).

OPENING DAY PAYROLL: $323,099,999 (1st)

PLAYERS OF THE YEAR

MAJOR LEAGUE
Juan Soto
OF
.263/.396/.525
43 HR, 38 SB, 120 R
105 RBIs, 127 BB

MINOR LEAGUE
Jonah Tong
RHP
(AA,AAA)
Led minors with
179 SO and 1.43 ERA

ORGANIZATION LEADERS

Batting		*Qualifiers
MAJORS		
* AVG	Pete Alonso	.272
* OPS	Juan Soto	.921
HR	Juan Soto	43
RBI	Pete Alonso	126
MINORS		
* AVG	A.J. Ewing, Binghamton/Brooklyn/St. Lucie	.315
* OBP	A.J. Ewing, Binghamton/Brooklyn/St. Lucie	.401
* SLG	Jacob Reimer, Binghamton/Brooklyn	.491
* OPS	Jacob Reimer, Binghamton/Brooklyn	.870
R	Jett Williams, Syracuse/Binghamton	91
H	A.J. Ewing, Binghamton/Brooklyn/St. Lucie	153
TB	Ryan Clifford, Syracuse/Binghamton	226
TB	Jett Williams, Syracuse/Binghamton	226
2B	Joey Meneses, Syracuse	35
3B	A.J. Ewing, Binghamton/Brooklyn/St. Lucie	10
HR	Ryan Clifford, Syracuse/Binghamton	29
RBI	Ryan Clifford, Syracuse/Binghamton	93
BB	Ryan Clifford, Syracuse/Binghamton	85
SO	Colin Houck, Brooklyn/St. Lucie	155
SB	A.J. Ewing	70

Pitching		#Qualifiers
MAJORS		
W	Clay Holmes	12
# ERA	Clay Holmes	3.53
SO	David Peterson	150
SV	Edwin Diaz	28
MINORS		
W	Jack Wenninger, Binghamton	12
L	Brandon Waddell, Syracuse/Binghamton	9
L	William Watson, Binghamton/Brooklyn/St. Lucie	9
# ERA	Jonah Tong, Syracuse/Binghamton	1.43
G	Dylan Ross, Syracuse/Binghamton/Brooklyn	49
GS	Jack Wenninger, Binghamton	26
SV	Hoss Brewer, Brooklyn/St. Lucie	9
SV	Carlos Guzman, Syracuse/Binghamton	9
IP	Jack Wenninger, Binghamton	136
# BB	Noah Hall, Brooklyn	63
SO	Jonah Tong, Syracuse/Binghamton	179
AVG	Jonah Tong, Syracuse/Binghamton	.148

2025 PERFORMANCE

President: David Stearns. **Farm Director:** Andy Green. **Scouting Director:** Kris Gross.

Class	Team	League	W	L	PCT	Finish	Manager
Majors	New York Mets	National	83	79	.512	7 (15)	Carlos Mendoza
Triple-A	Syracuse Mets	International	77	73	.513	9 (20)	Dick Scott
Double-A	Binghamton Rumble Ponies	Eastern	90	46	.662	1 (12)	Reid Brignac
High-A	Brooklyn Cyclones	South Atlantic	72	59	.550	3 (12)	Gilbert Gomez
Low-A	St. Lucie Mets	Florida State	77	53	.592	1 (10)	Luis Rivera
Rookie	FCL Mets	Florida Complex	25	28	.472	9 (15)	Lino Diaz
Rookie	DSL Mets Blue	Dominican	19	37	.339	48 (52)	Felix Fermin
Rookie	DSL Mets Orange	Dominican	31	25	.554	18 (52)	J.C. Rodriguez
Overall 2025 Minor League Record			391	321	.549	5th (30)	

ORGANIZATION STATISTICS

NEW YORK METS
NATIONAL LEAGUE

Batting	B-T	Ht.	Wt.	DOB	AVG	OBP	SLG	G	PA	AB	R	H	2B	3B	HR	RBI	BB	HBP	SH	SF	SO	SB	CS	BB%	SO%
Acuna, Luisangel	R-R	5-8	181	3-12-02	.234	.293	.274	95	193	175	30	41	7	0	0	8	13	2	2	1	37	16	1	6.7	19.2
Alonso, Pete	R-R	6-3	245	12-7-94	.272	.347	.524	162	709	624	87	170	41	1	38	126	61	15	0	9	162	1	2	8.6	22.8
Alvarez, Francisco	R-R	5-10	233	11-19-01	.256	.339	.447	76	277	246	32	63	12	1	11	32	27	4	0	0	73	0	0	9.7	26.4
Azocar, Jose	R-R	5-11	181	5-11-96	.278	.350	.278	12	20	18	5	5	0	0	0	1	2	0	0	0	1	1	0	10.0	5.0
Baty, Brett	L-R	6-3	210	11-13-99	.254	.313	.435	130	432	393	53	100	13	2	18	50	33	2	0	3	108	8	0	7.6	25.0
Jankowski, Travis	L-R	6-2	190	6-15-91	.000	.000	.000	5	1	0	1	0	0	0	0	0	0	0	0	0	0	0	0	0.0	0.0
Lindor, Francisco	S-R	5-11	190	11-14-93	.267	.346	.466	160	732	644	117	172	35	0	31	86	65	16	0	7	131	31	6	8.9	17.9
Marte, Starling	R-R	6-1	195	10-9-88	.270	.335	.410	98	329	293	37	79	14	0	9	34	22	9	1	4	68	7	2	6.7	20.7
Mauricio, Ronny	S-R	6-3	166	4-4-01	.226	.293	.369	61	184	168	19	38	6	0	6	10	15	1	0	0	54	4	0	8.2	29.3
McNeil, Jeff	L-R	6-1	195	4-8-92	.243	.335	.411	122	462	399	42	97	21	5	12	54	49	8	2	4	55	3	0	10.6	11.9
Mullins, Cedric	L-L	5-9	175	10-1-94	.182	.284	.281	42	143	121	16	22	4	1	2	10	16	2	2	2	35	8	0	11.2	24.5
Nimmo, Brandon	L-R	6-3	206	3-27-93	.262	.324	.436	155	652	587	81	154	27	0	25	92	50	7	1	7	141	13	1	7.7	21.6
Senger, Hayden	R-R	6-1	210	4-3-97	.181	.221	.194	33	78	72	8	13	1	0	0	4	3	1	1	2	22	0	0	3.8	28.2
Siri, Jose	R-R	6-2	175	7-22-95	.063	.167	.125	16	36	32	7	2	2	0	0	1	4	0	0	0	17	2	0	11.1	47.2
Soto, Juan	L-L	6-2	224	10-25-98	.263	.396	.525	160	715	577	120	152	20	1	43	105	127	3	1	6	137	38	4	17.8	19.2
Taylor, Tyrone	R-R	6-1	218	1-22-94	.223	.279	.319	113	341	310	34	69	18	3	2	27	16	9	3	2	76	12	2	4.7	22.3
Torrens, Luis	R-R	6-0	217	5-2-96	.226	.284	.345	93	283	261	20	59	14	1	5	29	19	2	1	0	56	1	0	6.7	19.8
Vientos, Mark	R-R	6-4	185	12-11-99	.233	.289	.413	121	463	424	44	99	21	2	17	61	30	5	0	4	115	1	0	6.5	24.8
Winker, Jesse	L-L	6-2	230	8-17-93	.229	.309	.400	26	81	70	8	16	5	2	1	10	9	0	0	2	21	1	0	11.1	25.9
Young, Jared	L-R	6-0	185	7-9-95	.186	.234	.488	23	47	43	5	8	1	0	4	6	2	1	0	1	16	0	0	4.3	34.0

Pitching	B-T	Ht.	Wt.	DOB	W	L	ERA	G	GS	SV	IP	Hits	Runs	ER	HR	BB	SO	AVG	OBP	SLG	SO%	BB%	BF
Adcock, Ty	R-R	6-0	213	2-7-97	0	0	3.00	3	0	0	3	2	1	1	1	2	5	.182	.308	.455	35.7	14.3	14
Blackburn, Paul	R-R	6-1	196	12-4-93	0	3	6.85	7	4	1	24	31	19	18	3	8	18	.316	.364	.520	16.4	7.3	110
Brazoban, Huascar	R-R	6-3	155	10-15-89	5	2	3.57	52	3	2	63	51	29	25	6	27	57	.227	.315	.347	21.8	10.3	262
Butto, Jose	R-R	6-1	202	3-19-98	3	2	3.64	34	0	1	47	43	21	19	2	22	41	.251	.337	.368	20.7	11.1	198
Cabrera, Genesis	L-L	6-2	180	10-10-96	0	0	3.52	6	0	0	8	7	3	3	1	3	7	.241	.313	.379	21.9	9.4	32
Carrillo, Alex	R-R	6-2	220	6-6-97	0	1	13.50	3	0	0	5	6	7	7	4	2	4	.316	.409	1.000	18.2	9.1	22
Castillo, Jose	L-L	6-6	252	1-10-96	1	1	2.35	16	0	0	15	21	6	4	0	6	19	.333	.419	.413	25.7	8.1	74
Devenski, Chris	R-R	6-3	211	11-13-90	0	0	2.16	13	1	0	17	10	4	4	1	5	14	.179	.262	.304	21.5	7.7	65
Diaz, Edwin	R-R	6-3	165	3-22-94	6	3	1.63	62	0	28	66	37	14	12	4	21	98	.164	.258	.244	38.0	8.1	258
Garcia, Rico	R-R	5-9	201	1-10-94	0	0	2.13	8	0	0	13	7	3	3	1	2	16	.159	.191	.273	34.0	4.3	47
Garrett, Reed	R-R	6-2	195	1-2-93	3	6	3.90	58	1	3	55	47	27	24	5	26	64	.223	.311	.351	26.9	10.9	238
Garza, Justin	R-R	5-10	170	3-20-94	0	0	5.40	5	0	0	7	8	4	4	1	1	3	.296	.321	.481	10.7	3.6	28
Hagenman, Justin	R-R	6-3	205	10-7-96	0	1	4.56	9	1	1	24	24	13	12	4	2	23	.250	.273	.427	23.2	2.0	99
Hamel, Dominic	R-R	6-2	206	3-2-99	0	0	0.00	1	0	0	1	3	0	0	0	0	0	.600	.667	.600	0.0	0.0	6
Helsley, Ryan	R-R	6-2	230	7-18-94	0	3	7.20	22	0	0	20	25	20	16	4	11	22	.301	.379	.554	23.2	11.6	95
Herget, Kevin	L-R	5-10	185	4-3-91	0	0	3.00	6	0	0	12	11	5	4	0	3	6	.239	.280	.326	12.0	6.0	50
Holmes, Clay	R-R	6-5	245	3-27-93	12	8	3.53	33	31	0	166	150	74	65	14	66	129	.241	.324	.352	18.2	9.3	708
Jankowski, Travis	L-R	6-2	190	6-15-91	0	0	18.00	1	0	0	1	2	2	2	0	1	0	.667	.667	.667	0.0	16.7	6
Kranick, Max	R-R	6-3	220	7-21-97	3	2	3.65	24	0	0	37	34	15	15	5	5	25	.239	.264	.380	16.9	3.4	148
Lovelady, Richard	L-L	6-0	185	7-7-95	0	0	6.30	8	0	0	10	10	8	7	1	5	8	.333	.538	.500	20.0	8.9	45
Manaea, Sean	R-L	6-5	245	2-1-92	2	4	5.64	15	12	0	61	62	38	38	13	12	75	.257	.310	.473	28.5	4.6	263
McLean, Nolan	R-R	6-4	214	7-24-01	5	1	2.06	8	8	0	48	34	13	11	4	16	57	.200	.277	.294	30.3	8.5	188
Megill, Tylor	R-R	6-7	230	7-28-95	5	5	3.95	14	14	0	68	60	37	30	6	33	89	.230	.329	.345	29.2	10.8	305
Minter, A.J.	L-L	6-0	215	9-2-93	0	0	1.64	13	0	0	11	6	2	2	0	5	14	.154	.250	.179	31.8	11.4	44
Montas, Frankie	R-R	6-2	255	3-21-93	3	2	6.28	9	7	0	39	48	29	27	8	14	32	.298	.356	.534	18.0	7.9	178
Nunez, Dedniel	R-R	6-2	180	6-5-96	0	0	4.66	10	0	0	6	5	5	1	6	11	.293	.343	26.8	14.6	41
Peterson, David	L-L	6-6	240	9-3-95	9	6	4.22	30	30	0	169	166	84	79	11	65	150	.258	.330	.370	20.7	9.0	723
Pintaro, Jonathan	R-R	6-2	235	11-7-97	0	0	27.00	1	0	0	1	2	2	0	2	1	.500	.667	.500	16.7	33.3	6
Poche, Colin	L-L	6-3	225	1-17-94	0	0	27.00	1	0	0	1	2	2	2	0	2	1	.500	.667	.750	16.7	33.3	6
Pop, Zach	R-R	6-4	220	9-20-96	0	0	20.25	1	0	0	1	5	3	3	0	0	.556	.556	1.000	0.0	0.0	9
Raley, Brooks	L-L	6-3	200	6-29-88	3	1	2.45	30	0	0	26	14	7	7	0	6	25	.154	.222	.209	25.3	6.1	99
Rogers, Tyler	R-R	6-3	181	12-17-90	0	3	2.30	28	0	0	27	27	9	7	1	3	10	.260	.287	.317	9.5	2.7	111

Senga, Kodai	L-R	6-1	202	1-30-93	7	6	3.02	22	22	0	113	94	44	38	12	55	109	.224	.317	.395	22.6	11.4	482
Soto, Gregory	L-L	6-1	234	2-11-95	1	3	4.50	25	0	0	24	33	16	12	2	6	26	.308	.378	.374	21.8	5.0	119
Sproat, Brandon	R-R	6-3	210	9-17-00	0	2	4.79	4	4	0	21	18	11	11	0	7	17	.243	.321	.351	20.2	8.3	84
Stanek, Ryne	R-R	6-4	226	7-26-91	4	6	5.30	65	0	3	56	56	39	33	7	32	58	.253	.345	.403	22.7	12.5	255
Tidwell, Blade	R-R	6-4	207	6-8-01	1	1	9.00	4	2	0	15	23	15	15	4	10	10	.348	.436	.561	12.8	12.8	78
Tong, Jonah	R-R	6-1	180	6-19-03	2	3	7.71	5	5	0	19	24	20	16	3	9	22	.312	.379	.494	25.3	10.3	87
Torrens, Luis	R-R	6-0	217	5-2-96	0	0	54.00	2	0	0	1	5	4	4	2	1	0	.714	.750	2.000	0.0	12.5	8
Urena, Jose	R-R	6-2	208	9-12-91	0	0	15.00	1	0	1	3	7	5	5	2	1	3	.438	.471	.875	17.6	5.9	17
Waddell, Brandon	L-L	6-3	180	6-8-94	0	0	3.45	11	1	0	31	29	12	12	4	11	22	.240	.306	.438	16.4	8.2	134
Warren, Austin	R-R	6-0	170	2-5-96	1	0	0.96	5	0	0	9	5	1	1	1	4	9	.167	.265	.267	26.5	11.8	34
Young, Danny	L-L	6-3	200	5-27-94	0	0	4.32	10	0	0	8	9	5	4	0	3	13	.281	.361	.281	35.1	8.1	37
Young, Jared	L-R	6-0	185	7-9-95	0	0	0.00	1	0	0	0	1	0	0	0	1	0	.500	.667	.500	0.0	33.3	3
Zuber, Tyler	R-R	5-11	195	6-16-95	0	0	9.00	1	0	0	2	3	2	2	0	3	.375	.333	.500	33.3	0.0	9	

Fielding

Catcher	PCT	G	PO	A	E	DP	PB
Alvarez	.988	74	557	28	7	2	7
Senger	.991	31	205	11	2	3	1
Torrens	.993	86	651	37	5	4	5

First Base	PCT	G	PO	A	E	DP
Alonso	.992	160	1178	124	10	100
McNeil	.000	2	0	0	0	0
Torrens	1.000	1	2	0	0	1
Vientos	1.000	3	19	1	0	2
Young	1.000	1	1	0	0	0

Second Base	PCT	G	PO	A	E	DP
Acuna	.990	81	70	120	2	26

Third Base	PCT	G	PO	A	E	DP
Acuna	1.000	6	1	2	0	0
Baty	.968	87	48	136	6	15
Mauricio	.971	42	30	70	3	5
Vientos	.950	72	39	112	8	12

Shortstop	PCT	G	PO	A	E	DP
Acuna	1.000	7	5	10	0	5
Lindor	.979	158	217	377	13	73
Mauricio	1.000	5	2	4	0	0

	PCT	G	PO	A	E	DP
Baty	.989	57	83	96	2	25
Mauricio	.920	7	10	13	2	4
McNeil	.983	79	109	183	5	33

Outfield	PCT	G	PO	A	E	DP
Acuna	1.000	2	1	0	0	0
Azocar	1.000	9	10	0	0	0
Jankowski	.000	2	0	0	0	0
Marte	1.000	2	6	1	0	1
McNeil	.987	51	73	1	1	1
Mullins	1.000	42	93	2	0	0
Nimmo	.996	155	258	5	1	2
Siri	1.000	14	17	0	0	0
Soto	.996	157	249	8	1	1
Taylor	.992	114	245	8	2	2
Winker	1.000	2	1	1	0	1
Young	1.000	1	1	0	0	0

SYRACUSE METS — TRIPLE-A
INTERNATIONAL LEAGUE

Batting	B-T	Ht.	Wt.	DOB	AVG	OBP	SLG	G	PA	AB	R	H	2B	3B	HR	RBI	BB	HBP	SH	SF	SO	SB	CS	BB%	SO%
Acuna, Luisangel	R-R	5-8	181	3-12-02	.303	.347	.385	28	122	109	16	33	7	1	0	10	9	0	1	3	19	8	2	7.4	15.6
Alvarez, Francisco	R-R	5-10	233	11-19-01	.258	.355	.688	26	107	93	19	24	4	0	12	28	11	3	0	0	33	0	0	10.3	30.8
Azocar, Jose	R-R	5-11	181	5-11-96	.241	.314	.352	71	291	261	41	63	13	2	4	28	24	4	1	1	59	17	6	8.2	20.3
Baty, Brett	L-R	6-3	210	11-13-99	.300	.364	.500	3	11	10	2	3	2	0	0	3	1	0	0	0	3	0	0	9.1	27.3
Benge, Carson	L-R	6-1	184	1-20-03	.178	.272	.311	24	103	90	12	16	1	1	3	13	9	3	0	1	19	3	0	8.7	18.4
Castillo, Diego	R-R	5-10	185	10-28-97	.217	.262	.413	46	42	1	7	1	0	1	5	3	0	0	1	10	0	0	6.5	21.7
Celestino, Gilberto	R-L	6-0	170	2-13-99	.272	.362	.382	111	426	372	66	101	12	1	9	40	51	2	0	0	93	13	2	12.0	21.8
Clifford, Ryan	L-L	6-3	200	7-20-03	.219	.359	.395	34	142	114	15	25	5	0	5	18	22	4	0	2	35	3	2	15.5	24.6
De Los Santos, Luis	R-R	6-1	160	6-9-98	.242	.287	.340	105	382	356	51	86	11	0	8	42	18	5	1	1	95	3	1	4.7	24.9
De Los Santos, Omar	R-R	6-1	172	8-8-99	.303	.303	.636	14	33	33	5	10	0	1	3	8	0	0	0	0	14	2	2	0.0	42.4
Gilbert, Drew	L-L	5-9	195	9-27-00	.243	.347	.430	82	361	305	45	74	17	2	12	47	41	10	0	4	60	4	3	11.4	16.6
Goodrum, Niko	S-R	6-3	215	2-28-92	.229	.391	.400	12	46	35	6	8	3	0	1	3	8	2	0	1	12	2	2	17.4	26.1
Hernandez, Yonny	S-R	5-9	140	4-4-98	.325	.404	.404	97	361	314	48	102	16	3	1	33	35	7	5	0	35	8	3	9.7	9.7
Jankowski, Travis	L-R	6-2	190	6-15-91	.200	.263	.286	8	38	35	7	7	0	0	1	5	3	0	0	0	7	2	0	7.9	18.4
Jordan, Rowdey	S-R	5-10	190	1-27-99	.250	.250	.250	4	8	8	1	2	0	0	0	1	0	0	0	0	3	0	0	0.0	37.5
Mauricio, Ronny	S-R	6-3	166	4-4-01	.515	.564	.818	9	39	33	10	17	1	0	3	8	5	0	0	1	5	4	1	12.8	12.8
McKinney, Billy	L-L	6-1	205	8-23-94	.184	.285	.307	33	130	114	10	21	3	1	3	9	16	0	0	0	34	0	1	12.3	26.2
McNeil, Jeff	L-R	6-1	195	4-8-92	.250	.333	.250	2	9	8	1	2	0	0	0	1	1	0	0	0	0	0	0	11.1	0.0
Meneses, Joey	R-R	6-3	240	5-6-92	.265	.322	.447	110	419	385	37	102	35	1	11	55	29	4	0	1	62	2	0	6.9	14.8
O'Neill, Matt	R-R	5-10	205	4-20-97	.203	.277	.305	21	65	59	6	12	3	0	1	6	6	0	0	0	20	0	0	9.2	30.8
Ortega, Rafael	L-L	5-11	180	5-15-91	.237	.250	.447	12	40	38	7	9	2	0	2	11	1	0	0	1	7	1	0	2.5	17.5
Parada, Kevin	R-R	5-11	197	8-3-01	.196	.281	.286	16	64	56	8	11	2	0	1	7	7	0	0	1	13	2	1	10.9	20.3
Reetz, Jakson	R-R	6-0	205	1-3-96	.197	.287	.470	43	150	132	21	26	3	0	11	26	12	5	0	1	38	1	1	8.0	25.3
Reyes, Pablo	R-R	5-8	175	9-5-93	.289	.385	.484	44	189	159	25	46	11	1	6	25	22	4	2	2	29	4	2	11.6	15.3
Ritter, Luke	R-R	5-11	187	2-15-97	.225	.331	.366	115	438	377	63	85	16	2	11	40	51	9	0	1	138	2	1	11.6	31.5
Sanchez, Ali	R-R	6-1	200	1-20-97	.182	.167	.273	3	12	11	1	2	1	0	0	4	0	0	0	1	3	0	0	0.0	25.0
Senger, Hayden	R-R	6-1	210	4-3-97	.218	.268	.339	46	182	165	24	36	3	1	5	17	10	2	2	2	44	2	1	5.5	24.2
Singleton, Jon	L-L	6-0	256	9-18-91	.213	.353	.448	55	224	183	37	39	7	0	12	42	39	1	0	1	60	1	0	17.4	26.8
Siri, Jose	R-R	6-2	175	7-22-95	.200	.200	.400	5	20	20	3	4	1	0	1	4	0	0	0	0	10	0	0	0.0	50.0
Swaggerty, Travis	L-L	5-10	200	8-19-97	.316	.440	.368	10	25	19	3	6	1	0	0	5	4	1	0	1	7	0	0	16.0	28.0
Taylor, Tyrone	R-R	6-1	218	1-22-94	.222	.222	.222	2	9	9	1	2	0	0	0	2	0	0	0	0	1	0	0	0.0	11.1
Torrens, Luis	R-R	6-0	217	5-2-96	.000	.000	.000	1	4	4	0	0	0	0	0	0	0	0	0	0	2	0	0	0.0	50.0
Vega, Onix	R-R	5-9	200	9-7-98	.000	.125	.000	3	8	7	0	0	0	0	0	1	1	0	0	0	2	0	0	12.5	25.0
Vientos, Mark	R-R	6-4	185	12-11-99	.269	.261	.500	6	26	23	4	4	2	0	3	5	0	0	0	0	3	0	0	11.5	11.5
Villar, David	R-R	6-1	215	1-27-97	.196	.322	.346	43	183	154	17	30	5	0	6	18	27	2	0	1	45	1	0	14.8	24.6
Walton, Donovan	L-R	5-9	190	5-25-94	.222	.315	.377	73	295	257	42	57	7	0	11	37	30	6	0	2	39	1	1	10.2	13.2
Williams, Chris	R-R	5-11	225	11-23-96	.170	.304	.319	21	57	47	7	8	4	0	1	8	9	0	0	0	18	0	0	15.8	31.6
Williams, Jett	R-R	5-6	175	11-3-03	.285	.433	.475	34	151	134	21	28	5	2	7	15	14	1	0	2	35	2	2	9.3	23.2
Winker, Jesse	L-L	6-2	230	8-17-93	.143	.333	.571	2	9	7	1	1	0	0	1	2	2	0	0	0	0	0	0	22.2	11.1
Young, Jared	L-R	6-0	185	7-9-95	.300	.396	.560	75	321	273	51	82	14	3	17	50	41	4	0	3	57	8	2	12.8	17.8

NEW YORK METS

Pitching	B-T	Ht.	Wt.	DOB	W	L	ERA	G	GS	SV	IP	Hits	Runs	ER	HR	BB	SO	AVG	OBP	SLG	SO%	BB%	BF
Adcock, Ty	R-R	6-0	213	2-7-97	1	3	4.66	31	1	3	37	25	23	19	7	14	35	.197	.267	.394	23.8	9.5	147
Blackburn, Paul	R-R	6-1	196	12-4-93	5	1	2.55	8	8	0	42	33	13	12	2	12	34	.217	.281	.316	20.4	7.2	167
Brazoban, Huascar	R-R	6-3	155	10-15-89	1	0	5.93	10	0	0	14	16	9	9	2	3	15	.286	.344	.429	24.6	4.9	61
Butto, Jose	R-R	6-1	202	3-19-98	0	0	0.00	2	1	0	2	2	0	0	0	0	2	.250	.250	.250	25.0	0.0	8
Cabrera, Genesis	L-L	6-2	180	10-10-96	1	0	7.88	7	0	2	8	4	7	7	1	5	12	.143	.294	.250	35.3	14.7	34
Carrillo, Alex	R-R	6-2	220	6-6-97	3	0	4.03	20	0	2	22	14	10	10	2	18	34	.184	.347	.289	35.8	18.9	95
Castillo, Jose	L-L	6-6	252	1-10-96	1	0	1.69	10	0	0	11	8	2	2	0	6	16	.211	.333	.237	35.6	13.3	45
Cornielly, Joshua	R-R	6-2	175	1-15-01	0	0	0.00	1	0	0	2	0	0	0	0	1	2	.250	.333	.500	22.2	11.1	9
Cosper, Colton	L-L	6-1	190	9-8-02	0	0	0.00	2	0	0	3	1	0	0	0	0	2	.100	.100	.200	20.0	0.0	10
De La Cruz, Felipe	L-L	6-0	160	5-26-01	1	2	7.30	15	2	1	25	24	21	20	5	17	32	.250	.379	.448	27.6	14.7	116
Devenski, Chris	R-R	6-3	211	11-13-90	0	3	3.35	35	1	4	38	39	18	14	7	8	32	.273	.307	.448	20.8	5.2	154
Fernandez, Junior	R-R	6-3	215	3-2-97	1	0	0.00	4	0	0	5	3	0	0	0	1	4	.176	.250	.176	22.2	5.6	18
Foster, Cameron	R-R	6-5	230	3-17-99	1	1	17.18	2	1	0	4	7	7	7	1	3	5	.412	.500	.647	25.0	15.0	20
Garcia, Rico	R-R	5-9	201	1-10-94	0	1	4.45	24	2	1	30	27	18	15	7	20	37	.237	.351	.465	27.4	14.8	135
Garza, Justin	R-R	5-10	170	3-20-94	3	1	7.86	22	1	1	26	29	23	23	4	11	20	.271	.345	.477	16.8	9.2	119
Geber, Jordan	R-R	6-3	205	7-31-99	0	0	8.03	7	1	1	12	14	11	11	4	10	11	.280	.393	.540	18.0	16.4	61
Gose, Anthony	L-L	6-0	200	8-10-90	2	1	4.30	21	0	1	23	21	14	11	5	14	25	.241	.353	.460	24.5	13.7	102
Guzman, Carlos	R-R	6-1	210	5-16-98	0	0	4.26	5	0	1	6	7	4	3	1	5	7	.269	.387	.385	22.6	16.1	31
Hagenman, Justin	R-R	6-3	205	10-7-96	2	4	5.58	21	13	0	69	76	48	43	13	13	73	.274	.305	.495	24.7	4.4	295
Hamel, Dominic	R-R	6-2	206	3-2-99	4	6	5.32	31	11	1	68	68	42	40	12	22	75	.258	.330	.424	25.2	7.4	298
Hartwig, Grant	R-R	6-5	235	12-18-97	2	3	3.42	21	0	2	24	27	22	9	5	10	33	.270	.348	.450	29.2	8.8	113
Hawkins, Dakota	R-R	6-0	208	3-20-01	1	1	1.50	3	0	0	6	5	2	1	1	0	7	.217	.217	.391	30.4	0.0	23
Herget, Kevin	L-R	5-10	185	4-3-91	2	0	2.81	23	3	2	32	28	12	10	7	8	35	.237	.286	.475	27.8	6.3	126
Hernandez, Yonny	S-R	5-9	140	5-4-98	0	0	9.00	1	0	0	1	1	1	1	0	3	1	.250	.571	.250	14.3	42.9	7
Herrera, Eduardo	S-R	5-9	179	1-5-00	0	0	3.00	1	0	0	3	2	1	1	0	2	1	.250	.400	.250	10.0	20.0	10
Juarez, Daniel	L-L	5-11	155	9-28-00	0	0	2.25	2	0	0	4	2	1	1	0	2	3	.143	.294	.143	17.6	11.8	17
Kranick, Max	R-R	6-3	220	7-21-97	0	0	7.71	2	0	0	2	4	2	2	1	0	5	.364	.364	.636	45.5	0.0	11
LaSorsa, Joe	L-L	6-5	215	4-29-98	0	0	0.00	4	0	0	4	1	0	0	0	1	3	.077	.143	.077	21.4	7.1	14
Lovelady, Richard	L-L	6-0	185	7-7-95	0	0	2.08	16	1	2	17	12	4	4	2	6	18	.200	.304	.333	26.1	8.7	69
Manaea, Sean	R-L	6-5	245	2-1-92	0	0	4.00	2	1	0	9	6	4	4	1	1	12	.182	.206	.273	35.3	2.9	34
McLean, Nolan	R-R	6-4	214	7-24-01	5	4	2.78	16	13	0	87	58	31	27	8	38	97	.185	.285	.291	27.0	10.6	359
Megill, Tylor	R-R	6-7	230	7-28-95	1	1	6.60	4	4	0	15	15	11	11	2	9	16	.254	.371	.390	22.9	12.9	70
Merryweather, Julian	R-R	6-4	215	10-14-91	1	0	4.50	12	0	2	12	7	6	6	1	9	15	.163	.308	.279	28.8	17.3	52
Montas, Frankie	R-R	6-2	255	3-21-93	0	3	13.19	4	4	0	14	26	21	21	8	6	8	.388	.447	.896	10.5	7.9	76
Moreno, Luis	R-R	5-8	170	5-29-99	2	1	6.58	10	1	0	26	27	20	19	3	18	26	.267	.380	.396	21.5	14.9	121
Nunez, Dedniel	R-R	6-2	180	6-5-96	1	1	3.79	19	2	0	19	22	9	8	2	11	21	.282	.371	.410	23.6	12.4	89
Orellana, Douglas	R-R	6-1	196	5-1-02	2	1	5.30	16	1	1	19	21	11	11	1	17	17	.300	.438	.400	19.1	19.1	89
Ortega, Oliver	R-R	6-0	165	10-2-96	0	0	3.86	5	0	1	7	3	3	3	1	3	4	.130	.231	.261	15.4	11.5	26
Pintaro, Jonathan	R-R	6-2	235	11-7-97	2	3	5.22	17	5	1	40	37	26	23	5	29	46	.250	.379	.419	25.0	15.8	184
Poche, Colin	L-L	6-3	225	1-17-94	0	1	4.82	17	1	1	19	15	11	10	3	14	16	.224	.338	.433	19.8	17.3	81
Raley, Brooks	L-L	6-3	200	6-29-88	1	0	0.00	3	0	3	3	0	0	0	0	1	3	.250	.400	.250	20.0	6.7	15
Reid-Foley, Sean	R-R	6-3	230	8-30-95	1	2	8.36	15	0	0	14	20	13	13	4	14	24	.323	.447	.548	31.6	18.4	76
Rios, Yacksel	R-R	6-3	215	6-27-93	0	0	18.00	2	0	0	2	3	4	4	1	1	2	.375	.444	.750	20.0	10.0	10
Ritter, Luke	R-R	5-11	187	2-15-97	0	0	4.50	5	0	0	6	5	3	3	1	2	0	.333	.400	.519	0.0	6.7	30
Ross, Dylan	R-R	6-5	251	9-1-00	0	0	1.69	28	0	3	32	11	7	6	1	22	39	.107	.268	.175	30.7	17.3	127
Senga, Kodai	L-R	6-1	202	1-30-93	1	1	4.66	2	2	0	10	9	5	5	0	2	12	.308	.306	.308	30.8	5.1	39
Shook, TJ	R-R	6-4	217	5-29-98	0	0	3.00	3	2	1	5	2	2	1	5	5	.227	.370	.364	18.5	18.5	27
Sproat, Brandon	R-R	6-3	210	9-17-00	8	6	4.24	26	25	0	121	97	62	57	9	53	113	.218	.315	.330	22.1	10.4	512
Suarez, Joander	R-R	6-3	223	2-27-00	1	2	9.28	3	3	0	11	15	14	11	2	4	9	.319	.385	.489	17.3	7.7	52
Suero, Wander	R-R	6-4	216	9-15-91	0	0	0.00	2	0	1	2	1	0	0	0	0	5	.143	.250	.143	62.5	0.0	8
Tidwell, Blade	R-R	6-4	207	6-8-01	6	4	4.10	17	14	0	79	70	37	36	8	32	87	.233	.314	.360	25.7	9.5	338
Tong, Jonah	R-R	6-1	180	6-19-03	2	0	0.00	2	2	0	12	8	0	0	0	3	17	.190	.244	.238	37.8	6.7	45
Urena, Jose	R-R	6-2	208	9-12-91	0	1	2.89	3	3	0	9	9	3	3	0	4	8	.250	.341	.278	19.5	9.8	41
Vega, Alfred	R-R	6-1	169	1-19-01	0	1	6.75	1	0	0	1	1	1	1	0	1	1	.167	.375	.167	12.5	12.5	8
Waddell, Brandon	L-L	6-3	180	6-3-94	3	9	5.02	19	15	0	75	84	48	42	12	25	63	.282	.350	.456	19.0	7.6	331
Walton, Donovan	L-R	5-9	190	5-25-94	0	0	36.00	1	0	0	1	6	4	4	1	0	0	.667	.667	1.222	0.0	0.0	9
Warren, Austin	R-R	6-0	170	2-5-96	8	4	4.97	34	4	1	51	53	29	28	9	19	58	.268	.342	.460	25.9	8.5	224
Williams, Chris	R-R	5-11	225	11-23-96	0	0	13.50	1	0	0	2	4	3	3	1	1	0	.400	.455	.700	0.0	9.1	11
Zuber, Tyler	R-R	5-11	195	6-16-95	1	1	6.11	24	2	1	28	32	20	19	3	15	27	.283	.366	.442	20.6	11.5	131

Fielding

Catcher	PCT	G	PO	A	E	DP	PB
Alvarez	.984	18	164	16	3	2	5
O'Neill	.990	21	193	7	2	0	3
Parada	.989	9	90	3	1	0	1
Reetz	.995	43	353	15	2	3	1
Sanchez	1.000	3	29	1	0	1	0
Senger	.988	46	404	24	5	2	4
Torrens	1.000	1	9	1	0	0	0
Vega	1.000	3	13	1	0	0	0
Williams	1.000	15	107	4	0	0	1

First Base	PCT	G	PO	A	E	DP
Clifford	1.000	13	90	1	0	13
Meneses	.993	65	402	41	3	37
Ritter	1.000	14	74	5	0	5
Singleton	.975	15	71	7	2	9
Villar	.987	30	196	34	3	15
Young	1.000	26	182	10	0	18

Second Base	PCT	G	PO	A	E	DP
Acuna	1.000	7	14	15	0	5
Baty	1.000	2	1	5	0	1
Castillo	.950	5	8	11	1	2
De Los Santos	.959	17	16	31	2	4
Goodrum	1.000	5	4	7	0	2
Hernandez	.993	35	59	87	1	21
Mauricio	1.000	4	10	11	0	3
McNeil	.800	1	1	3	1	0
Reyes	1.000	10	9	20	0	3
Ritter	1.000	30	42	76	0	16
Walton	1.000	29	56	60	0	16
Williams	.974	12	15	23	1	6
Young	.000	1	0	0	0	0

Third Base	PCT	G	PO	A	E	DP
Acuna	1.000	1	0	4	0	0
Baty	1.000	1	2	1	0	0
Castillo	1.000	5	5	5	0	1
De Los Santos	.909	72	38	112	15	14

	PCT	G	PO	A	E	DP
Goodrum	1.000	2	1	2	0	1
Hernandez	1.000	5	3	9	0	0
Mauricio	1.000	4	4	8	0	1
Meneses	.000	1	0	0	0	0
Reyes	.952	8	6	14	1	2
Ritter	.926	33	19	44	5	4
Vientos	1.000	4	2	3	0	0
Villar	.960	10	9	15	1	1
Walton	1.000	7	10	11	0	1
Young	.857	5	3	3	1	0
Shortstop	**PCT**	**G**	**PO**	**A**	**E**	**DP**
Acuna	.973	13	17	19	1	2
Castillo	.000	1	0	0	1	0
De Los Santos	.982	17	23	31	1	3

	PCT	G	PO	A	E	DP
Goodrum	.941	5	4	12	1	3
Hernandez	.963	56	68	113	7	17
Reyes	.939	21	21	56	5	13
Ritter	1.000	1	1	0	0	0
Walton	.973	22	34	38	2	11
Williams	.975	16	10	29	1	10
Outfield	**PCT**	**G**	**PO**	**A**	**E**	**DP**
Acuna	1.000	6	17	0	0	0
Azocar	.977	69	122	4	3	2
Benge	.980	27	48	0	1	0
Celestino	.990	107	184	7	2	1
Clifford	.976	21	40	1	1	0
De Los Santos	1.000	13	18	0	0	0
Gilbert	.983	79	172	3	3	1

	PCT	G	PO	A	E	DP
Jankowski	1.000	8	15	0	0	0
Jordan	.750	3	3	0	1	0
McKinney	.976	28	40	0	1	0
McNeil	1.000	1	1	0	0	0
Meneses	.667	2	2	0	1	0
Ortega	1.000	13	16	1	0	0
Ritter	.980	32	47	1	1	0
Siri	1.000	4	8	0	0	0
Swaggerty	1.000	5	11	0	0	0
Taylor	1.000	2	5	0	0	0
Walton	1.000	13	17	0	0	0
Williams	1.000	8	6	0	0	0
Young	.985	36	65	2	1	0

BINGHAMTON RUMBLE PONIES — DOUBLE-A
EASTERN LEAGUE

Batting	B-T	Ht.	Wt.	DOB	AVG	OBP	SLG	G	PA	AB	R	H	2B	3B	HR	RBI	BB	HBP	SH	SF	SO	SB	CS	BB%	SO%
Alvarez, Francisco	R-R	5-10	233	11-19-01	.273	.333	.409	5	24	22	3	6	0	0	1	3	1	1	0	0	4	0	0	4.2	16.7
Aular, Jose	R-R	5-11	175	1-2-04	.000	.000	.000	2	8	8	0	0	0	0	0	0	0	0	0	0	4	0	0	0.0	50.0
Benge, Carson	L-R	6-1	184	1-20-03	.317	.407	.571	32	145	126	28	40	6	1	8	23	18	1	0	0	23	4	2	12.4	15.9
Clifford, Ryan	L-L	6-3	200	7-20-03	.243	.355	.493	105	437	367	56	89	18	1	24	75	63	3	0	4	113	4	2	14.4	25.9
De Los Santos, Jeffrey	L-R	5-11	154	5-30-03	.244	.279	.317	13	44	41	5	10	3	0	0	2	2	0	1	0	15	2	1	4.5	34.1
De Los Santos, Omar	R-R	6-1	172	8-8-99	.212	.256	.364	42	126	118	18	25	2	2	4	11	5	2	1	0	52	17	3	4.0	41.3
Ewing, A.J.	L-R	6-0	160	8-10-04	.339	.371	.430	28	132	121	20	41	7	2	0	9	7	1	0	3	29	12	2	5.3	22.0
Hernandez, Yonny	S-R	5-9	140	5-4-98	.173	.218	.173	17	56	52	4	9	0	0	0	5	3	0	1	0	4	2	2	5.4	7.1
Jordan, Rowdey	S-R	5-10	190	1-27-99	.111	.200	.444	3	10	9	2	1	0	0	1	3	1	0	0	0	3	0	0	10.0	30.0
Lorusso, Nick	R-R	6-2	212	9-11-00	.241	.312	.368	112	446	394	42	95	29	0	7	56	41	3	0	8	108	8	3	9.2	24.2
Lugo, William	R-R	6-2	215	1-2-02	.205	.283	.292	113	427	380	38	78	15	0	6	38	39	4	0	4	113	5	1	9.1	26.5
Mauricio, Ronny	S-R	6-3	166	4-4-01	.118	.167	.235	5	18	17	1	2	2	0	0	2	1	0	0	0	7	0	0	5.6	38.9
McNeil, Jeff	L-R	6-1	195	4-8-92	.667	.667	1.444	2	9	9	4	6	1	0	1	2	2	0	0	0	0	0	0	22.2	0.0
Morabito, Nick	R-R	5-11	185	5-7-03	.273	.348	.385	118	492	436	63	119	27	2	6	59	47	5	0	3	115	49	11	9.6	23.4
O'Neill, Matt	R-R	5-10	205	8-20-97	.250	.373	.369	31	102	84	12	21	4	0	2	8	16	1	0	1	26	2	1	15.7	25.5
Parada, Kevin	R-R	5-11	197	8-3-01	.254	.326	.429	92	360	315	38	80	23	1	10	50	33	4	1	7	100	4	0	9.2	27.8
Ramirez, Alex	R-R	6-3	170	1-13-03	.222	.304	.298	54	191	171	23	38	7	0	2	14	19	1	0	0	50	22	6	9.9	26.2
Reimer, Jacob	R-R	6-2	205	2-22-04	.279	.374	.479	61	254	215	36	60	14	1	9	38	26	9	0	4	60	4	1	10.2	23.6
Schwartz, JT	L-R	6-4	215	12-17-99	.205	.308	.332	84	335	283	33	58	19	1	5	35	39	6	1	6	57	0	2	11.6	17.0
Smith, D'Andre	R-R	5-8	180	5-10-01	.279	.334	.411	87	353	326	39	91	14	4	7	41	18	9	0	0	69	24	3	5.1	19.5
Suero, Christopher	R-R	5-10	205	1-27-04	.221	.374	.324	41	174	136	25	30	5	0	3	17	29	6	0	3	53	10	1	16.7	30.5
Swaggerty, Travis	L-L	5-10	200	8-19-97	.176	.263	.250	24	76	68	7	12	5	0	0	3	8	0	0	0	24	2	1	10.5	31.6
Vega, Onix	R-R	5-9	200	9-1-01	.000	.000	.000	2	4	4	0	0	0	0	0	0	0	0	0	0	2	0	0	0.0	50.0
Williams, Jett	R-R	5-6	175	11-3-03	.281	.390	.477	96	421	352	70	99	29	5	10	37	62	3	1	3	96	32	7	14.7	22.8
Winker, Jesse	L-L	6-2	230	8-17-93	.333	.500	.833	2	8	6	2	2	0	0	1	4	2	0	0	0	1	0	0	25.0	12.5
Young, Wyatt	L-R	5-6	160	12-5-99	.244	.365	.292	99	333	271	43	66	8	1	1	24	54	0	4	4	66	10	3	16.2	19.8

Pitching	B-T	Ht.	Wt.	DOB	W	L	ERA	G	GS	SV	IP	Hits	Runs	ER	HR	BB	SO	AVG	OBP	SLG	SO%	BB%	BF
Blackburn, Paul	R-R	6-1	196	12-4-93	0	1	6.23	1	1	0	4	1	5	3	1	3	7	.067	.222	.267	38.9	16.7	18
Carrillo, Alex	R-R	6-2	220	6-6-97	2	1	4.19	15	0	0	19	15	9	9	1	8	30	.205	.293	.315	36.6	9.8	82
Cornielly, Joshua	R-R	6-2	175	1-15-01	5	3	4.08	36	1	4	53	50	25	24	4	19	62	.242	.309	.367	26.8	8.2	231
Cota, Irving	R-R	5-9	165	2-14-04	1	0	0.00	1	0	0	5	1	0	0	0	0	5	.063	.063	.063	31.3	0.0	16
De La Cruz, Felipe	L-L	6-0	160	5-26-01	3	1	3.63	18	4	1	40	32	18	16	5	15	58	.213	.287	.367	34.7	9.0	167
Foster, Cameron	R-R	6-5	230	3-17-99	4	1	1.01	19	0	2	27	17	3	3	0	5	34	.179	.200	.232	34.0	5.0	100
Garcia, Saul	R-R	6-0	180	6-11-03	1	0	1.32	9	0	0	14	8	2	2	1	6	17	.167	.259	.271	31.5	11.1	54
Garrett, Reed	R-R	6-2	195	1-2-93	0	0	0.00	1	0	1	1	0	0	0	0	0	2	.250	.250	.250	50.0	0.0	4
Geber, Jordan	R-R	6-3	205	7-31-99	1	0	1.17	13	5	0	23	23	6	3	0	7	21	.264	.316	.287	21.6	7.2	97
Girton, Brendan	R-R	6-2	220	11-10-01	0	1	6.75	4	4	0	11	10	11	8	0	6	10	.244	.380	.244	19.6	11.8	51
Gordon, R.J.	R-R	6-0	195	10-21-01	6	1	3.69	11	10	0	61	53	33	25	7	15	71	.231	.275	.389	28.7	6.1	247
Guzman, Carlos	R-R	6-1	210	5-16-98	4	5	2.95	35	0	8	43	24	17	14	4	14	49	.163	.247	.265	29.0	8.3	169
Hawkins, Dakota	R-R	6-0	208	3-20-00	0	0	6.75	1	0	1	2	2	1	1	1	1	.333	.429	1.000	12.5	12.5	8
Herrera, Eduardo	S-R	5-9	179	1-5-00	0	0	0.00	1	0	0	1	0	0	0	0	3	.125	.125	.250	37.5	0.0	8
Juarez, Daniel	L-L	5-11	155	9-28-01	0	3	7.43	20	0	1	27	33	26	22	7	12	27	.289	.372	.571	20.9	9.3	129
Lambert, Ryan	R-R	6-3	222	9-2-02	2	1	1.71	39	0	6	42	28	9	8	1	26	64	.190	.322	.252	36.2	14.7	177
Manaea, Sean	R-L	6-5	245	2-1-92	0	0	6.00	1	1	0	3	6	3	2	0	1	3	.400	.438	.533	18.8	6.3	16
McLean, Nolan	R-R	6-4	214	7-24-01	3	2	1.37	5	5	0	26	20	5	4	0	12	30	.213	.315	.266	27.8	11.1	108
McLoughlin, Trey	R-R	6-2	210	2-15-98	2	0	4.09	18	0	0	22	17	12	10	1	12	25	.218	.333	.333	26.9	12.9	93
Megill, Tylor	R-R	6-7	230	7-28-95	0	0	0.00	2	2	0	5	4	0	0	0	1	13	.200	.238	.200	61.9	4.8	21
Metoyer, Brian	R-R	6-3	173	11-13-96	1	1	2.35	19	0	1	23	16	7	6	0	13	54	.200	.333	.213	35.1	13.4	97
Moreno, Luis	R-R	5-8	170	5-29-99	8	2	4.80	30	6	0	54	50	29	29	3	21	51	.248	.333	.371	22.0	9.1	232
Nunez, Anthony	R-R	6-1	190	7-10-01	1	0	2.10	22	0	4	26	12	6	6	1	12	36	.067	.260	.171	36.7	12.2	98
Orellana, Douglas	R-R	6-1	196	5-1-02	2	0	1.64	25	0	4	33	18	6	6	1	13	46	.158	.242	.211	35.7	10.1	129
Parsons, Hunter	R-R	6-2	215	6-24-97	3	1	4.91	22	0	0	29	19	19	16	7	19	40	.179	.315	.434	31.5	15.0	127
Pintaro, Jonathan	R-R	6-2	220	1-14-99	0	2	3.40	11	11	0	42	32	17	16	4	15	57	.212	.290	.345	33.3	8.8	171
Raley, Brooks	L-L	6-3	200	6-29-88	0	0	0.00	2	0	0	3	1	0	0	0	0	4	.125	.222	.125	44.4	0.0	9
Ross, Dylan	R-R	6-5	251	9-1-00	0	0	4.35	11	0	4	10	8	5	3	3	18	.244	.289	.488	40.0	6.7	45

	B-T	Ht.	Wt.	DOB																		
Santucci, Jonathan	L-L	6-2	205	12-28-02	4	0	2.52	10	10	0	50	33	22	14	2	18	63	.189	.265	.274	32.0	9.1	197
Senga, Kodai	L-R	6-1	202	1-30-93	0	0	7.36	1	1	0	4	6	4	3	1	2	4	.375	.421	.563	19.0	9.5	21
Shook, TJ	R-R	6-4	217	5-29-98	6	2	2.34	33	0	7	50	43	18	13	4	12	56	.231	.286	.376	27.5	5.9	204
Simon, Ben	R-R	5-11	197	3-22-02	1	1	1.06	11	0	0	17	12	3	2	0	5	20	.194	.275	.210	28.6	7.1	70
Suarez, Joander	R-R	6-3	223	2-27-00	5	2	3.05	20	15	2	83	66	30	28	8	13	84	.214	.248	.331	25.9	4.0	324
Thornton, Zach	L-L	6-3	170	1-17-02	3	2	2.60	10	10	0	52	36	16	15	4	9	53	.197	.233	.339	27.0	4.6	196
Tong, Jonah	R-R	6-1	180	6-19-03	8	5	1.59	20	20	0	102	50	20	18	2	44	162	.143	.242	.191	40.8	11.1	397
Waddell, Brandon	L-L	6-3	180	6-3-94	0	0	0.00	1	1	0	3	0	0	0	0	0	6	.000	.000	.000	75.0	0.0	8
Watson, William	R-R	6-1	170	11-7-02	2	2	3.44	4	2	0	18	13	8	7	2	9	22	.200	.297	.354	29.7	12.2	74
Wenninger, Jack	L-R	6-4	210	3-14-02	12	6	2.92	26	26	0	136	114	53	44	13	42	147	.225	.286	.364	26.4	7.6	556

Fielding

Catcher	PCT	G	PO	A	E	DP	PB
Alvarez	1.000	4	34	4	0	0	4
Aular	.882	2	14	1	2	0	0
O'Neill	.986	31	335	19	5	1	3
Parada	.994	74	764	34	5	9	7
Suero	.980	27	267	21	6	1	3
Vega	1.000	2	25	1	0	1	1

First Base	PCT	G	PO	A	E	DP
Clifford	.980	57	322	23	7	24
Lorusso	.993	39	256	21	2	32
Reimer	.970	4	31	1	1	0
Schwartz	.994	40	289	26	2	26
Suero	1.000	4	25	2	0	3

Second Base	PCT	G	PO	A	E	DP
De Los Santos, J	1.000	6	11	11	0	4
Ewing	.903	8	17	11	3	4

	PCT	G	PO	A	E	DP
Hernandez	.980	16	19	30	1	5
Lugo	.944	22	29	38	4	10
Mauricio	1.000	1	1	1	0	0
McNeil	1.000	2	2	4	0	0
Smith	1.000	4	4	8	0	2
Williams	.984	16	25	35	1	9
Young	.991	69	82	143	2	32

Third Base	PCT	G	PO	A	E	DP
Hernandez	1.000	1	1	2	0	0
Lorusso	.935	56	19	82	7	4
Lugo	.976	25	13	28	1	6
Mauricio	1.000	2	0	4	0	1
Reimer	.894	47	29	81	13	10
Schwartz	.909	4	7	3	1	0
Young	.882	9	6	9	2	1

Shortstop	PCT	G	PO	A	E	DP

	PCT	G	PO	A	E	DP
Lugo	.965	66	65	154	8	34
Williams	.932	54	47	91	10	23
Young	.986	19	26	42	1	11

Outfield	PCT	G	PO	A	E	DP
Benge	.971	33	64	3	2	1
Clifford	1.000	32	55	2	0	0
De Los Santos, O	.909	7	10	0	1	0
De Los Santos, Y	.925	37	33	4	3	1
Ewing	.969	20	30	1	1	0
Jordan	1.000	3	3	0	0	0
Morabito	.995	107	177	8	1	2
Ramirez	.942	52	77	4	5	1
Schwartz	1.000	14	24	0	0	0
Smith	.967	77	140	8	5	6
Suero	1.000	6	7	0	0	0
Swaggerty	1.000	18	23	0	0	0
Williams	.931	19	24	3	2	0

BROOKLYN CYCLONES — HIGH-A
SOUTH ATLANTIC LEAGUE

Batting	B-T	Ht.	Wt.	DOB	AVG	OBP	SLG	G	PA	AB	R	H	2B	3B	HR	RBI	BB	HBP	SH	SF	SO	SB	CS	BB%	SO%
Baez, Jesus	R-R	5-9	180	2-26-05	.244	.337	.406	70	294	254	43	62	11	0	10	42	33	4	0	3	49	7	2	11.2	16.7
Baro, Boston	L-R	6-1	175	8-23-04	.224	.282	.321	103	433	393	43	88	16	5	4	38	31	3	0	6	88	28	2	7.2	20.3
Bay, John	R-R	6-1	211	5-16-01	.103	.333	.207	10	39	29	5	3	0	0	1	4	7	3	0	0	12	2	1	17.9	30.8
Benge, Carson	L-R	6-1	184	1-20-03	.302	.417	.480	60	271	225	47	68	18	5	4	37	41	4	0	1	50	15	2	15.1	18.5
Collins, Corey	L-R	6-3	220	10-10-01	.183	.299	.267	41	157	131	12	24	1	2	2	15	17	6	0	3	51	4	2	10.8	32.5
Cuevas, Yohairo	L-L	6-3	172	9-16-03	.206	.289	.271	30	121	107	12	22	5	1	0	12	10	3	0	1	31	10	1	8.3	25.6
De Los Santos, Jefrey	L-R	5-11	154	5-30-03	.194	.289	.335	55	195	170	24	33	4	4	4	19	21	2	1	1	58	6	2	10.8	29.7
Ewing, A.J.	L-R	6-0	160	8-10-04	.288	.387	.388	78	351	299	52	86	16	4	2	26	46	4	0	2	66	44	7	13.1	18.8
Henriquez, Yonatan	S-R	5-10	185	10-12-04	.250	.344	.357	7	32	28	2	7	1	1	0	2	4	0	0	0	8	2	0	12.5	25.0
Hernandez, Ronald	S-R	5-11	155	10-23-03	.224	.318	.335	101	393	340	47	76	14	3	6	52	42	7	0	4	86	23	5	10.7	21.9
Houck, Colin	R-R	6-2	190	9-30-04	.198	.269	.289	54	212	187	22	37	7	2	2	15	19	1	0	5	78	3	1	9.0	36.8
Mercado, Estarling	L-R	6-0	195	3-6-03	.254	.345	.381	38	145	126	17	32	5	1	3	20	17	1	0	1	26	4	1	11.7	20.7
Mosquera, Diego	L-R	5-9	156	3-14-04	.217	.323	.253	63	231	198	17	43	7	0	0	16	24	7	2	0	47	6	4	10.4	20.3
Ortega, Rafael	L-R	5-11	180	5-15-91	.083	.120	.125	6	25	24	0	2	1	0	0	2	1	0	0	0	7	1	1	4.0	28.0
Perozo, Vincent	L-R	6-0	170	3-6-03	.167	.265	.200	20	68	60	7	10	2	0	0	4	5	3	0	0	19	2	2	7.4	27.9
Reimer, Jacob	R-R	6-2	205	2-22-04	.284	.384	.502	61	268	229	52	65	18	4	8	39	32	6	0	1	52	11	2	11.9	19.4
Roselli, Nick	L-R	5-10	200	3-31-03	.136	.223	.232	36	139	125	11	17	7	1	1	18	12	2	0	0	41	1	2	8.6	29.5
Rudick, Matt	L-L	5-6	170	7-2-98	.167	.333	.333	3	15	12	2	2	0	1	0	1	3	0	0	0	5	0	0	20.0	33.3
Schreffler, Troy	R-R	5-11	190	10-27-00	.215	.276	.329	52	163	149	20	32	2	3	1	19	12	1	0	1	56	7	1	7.4	34.4
Serrano, Eli	L-L	6-5	193	5-1-03	.222	.332	.358	88	383	324	51	72	21	1	7	46	50	5	0	4	77	9	3	13.1	20.1
Smith, D'Andre	R-R	5-8	180	5-10-01	.302	.415	.465	14	53	43	9	13	4	0	1	6	9	0	0	1	7	7	0	17.0	13.2
Suero, Christopher	R-R	5-10	205	1-24-04	.240	.382	.455	74	301	242	53	58	11	1	13	51	41	16	0	2	86	5	7	13.6	28.6
Vargas, Marco	L-R	6-0	170	5-14-05	.239	.328	.296	95	408	355	45	85	9	4	1	42	48	1	0	4	82	38	7	11.8	20.1
Vega, Onix	R-R	5-9	200	9-7-98	.214	.282	.343	23	78	70	8	15	4	1	1	6	7	0	0	1	14	0	1	9.0	17.9
Villavicencio, Kevin	R-R	5-9	172	11-24-03	.455	.500	.545	4	13	11	0	5	1	0	0	1	1	0	0	0	3	0	1	7.7	23.1
Willhoite, Trace	R-R	6-2	195	11-17-00	.186	.292	.339	19	72	59	5	11	3	0	2	7	4	6	0	3	29	2	2	5.6	40.3
Winker, Jesse	L-L	6-2	230	8-17-93	1.000	1.000	2.000	1	3	1	0	1	0	0	0	1	1	1	0	0	0	0	0	33.3	0.0

Pitching	B-T	Ht.	Wt.	DOB	W	L	ERA	G	GS	SV	IP	Hits	Runs	ER	HR	BB	SO	AVG	OBP	SLG	SO%	BB%	BF
Allan, Matt	R-R	6-3	225	4-17-01	0	1	3.60	4	2	0	5	4	5	2	0	5	6	.200	.370	.350	22.2	18.5	27
Ammons, Ryan	L-L	6-0	200	4-17-01	7	2	2.92	33	0	1	37	17	14	12	1	27	53	.136	.308	.184	33.5	17.1	158
Ankeney, Eli	L-L	6-0	200	1-10-01	0	0	4.50	3	0	0	4	3	2	2	0	1	6	.214	.267	.214	37.5	6.3	16
Arnaud, Juan	R-R	6-2	164	6-22-03	0	2	8.59	6	0	0	9	9	7	0	6	11	.300	.462	.367	28.2	15.4	39
Austin, Channing	R-R	6-3	200	12-21-01	0	0	6.00	1	1	0	3	1	2	2	0	2	3	.273	.333	.333	27.3	18.2	11
Banks, Brett	L-R	6-3	210	10-3-01	2	1	2.49	23	2	2	25	18	10	7	1	11	26	.200	.291	.300	25.2	10.7	103
Beck, Jace	R-R	6-9	200	6-14-00	4	3	5.80	42	0	1	45	33	29	29	3	30	68	.202	.335	.331	34.0	15.0	200
Blackburn, Paul	R-R	6-1	196	12-4-93	0	0	5.40	2	2	0	5	6	3	3	2	2	7	.316	.381	.684	33.3	9.5	21
Blum, Josh	R-R	6-1	195	5-1-03	0	0	2.36	15	0	2	27	25	8	7	0	9	19	.243	.310	.320	16.8	8.0	113
Brewer, Hoss	L-R	6-4	205	2-20-01	1	0	3.10	22	1	3	29	25	19	10	5	7	24	.268	.314	.366	19.7	5.7	122
Cota, Irving	R-R	5-9	165	2-14-04	1	0	5.00	2	1	0	9	7	5	5	1	4	8	.206	.289	.353	21.1	10.5	38

NEW YORK METS

Batting	B-T	Ht.	Wt.	DOB	G	GS	ERA	W	L	SV	IP	H	R	ER	HR	BB	SO	AVG	OBP	SLG	K/9	BB/9
Diaz, Joel	R-R	6-2	208	2-26-04	5	5	3.80	25	18	0	107	106	48	45	9	25	98	.255	.299	.385	21.9	5.6	448
Dohm, Nate	R-R	6-4	220	1-9-03	1	2	2.62	11	10	0	34	28	15	10	4	13	43	.217	.297	.395	29.7	9.0	145
Elissalt, Frank	S-R	6-2	210	3-25-02	1	1	3.18	2	0	0	6	5	2	2	1	0	8	.250	.286	.500	38.1	0.0	21
Garcia, Saul	R-R	6-0	180	6-11-03	4	2	1.85	30	0	6	34	21	10	7	2	22	59	.175	.320	.267	39.9	14.9	148
Girton, Brendan	R-R	6-2	220	11-10-01	3	3	2.59	21	17	0	76	51	32	22	3	34	91	.190	.289	.294	29.1	10.9	313
Gomez, Cristofer	R-R	6-4	222	5-13-03	0	2	5.82	9	0	0	17	10	12	11	1	14	26	.164	.333	.311	33.3	17.9	78
Gomez, Franklin	L-L	6-0	145	7-6-05	0	2	4.70	6	6	0	23	31	18	12	1	11	26	.330	.422	.447	23.4	9.9	111
Gomez, Raimon	R-R	6-2	175	9-6-01	3	5	6.95	21	0	2	22	16	20	17	3	15	28	.198	.350	.309	27.2	14.6	103
Gordon, R.J.	R-R	6-0	195	10-21-01	5	2	3.06	15	11	0	68	60	29	23	8	31	76	.233	.322	.372	26.0	10.6	292
Guevara, Jose	R-R	6-1	178	4-20-05	1	1	16.20	2	1	0	3	5	6	6	1	4	5	.357	.474	.643	26.3	21.1	19
Hall, Noah	R-R	6-0	195	3-30-01	5	7	2.72	25	21	1	113	80	40	34	6	63	115	.200	.317	.287	24.2	13.3	475
Hawkins, Dakota	R-R	6-0	208	3-20-00	2	2	2.44	24	3	1	44	29	14	12	3	15	50	.180	.250	.304	28.2	8.5	177
Herrera, Eduardo	S-R	5-9	179	1-5-05	1	1	2.30	28	0	1	31	16	13	8	0	28	31	.157	.376	.206	21.7	19.6	143
Hodges, Hunter	R-R	6-3	225	10-3-02	1	1	3.86	8	0	1	14	9	6	6	0	13	18	.184	.375	.265	28.1	20.3	64
Lambert, Ryan	R-R	6-3	222	9-2-02	0	0	1.13	7	0	1	8	3	1	1	0	1	17	.111	.143	.185	60.7	3.6	28
Lawson, Justin	R-R	6-3	198	12-1-00	0	0	5.73	8	0	1	11	8	8	7	0	3	10	.205	.250	.333	22.7	6.8	44
Louis, Gregori	L-L	6-3	161	10-28-02	0	2	4.91	10	0	0	11	12	7	6	3	6	12	.286	.415	.548	22.6	11.3	53
Manaea, Sean	R-L	6-5	245	2-1-92	0	1	9.45	3	3	0	7	11	8	7	1	3	8	.355	.447	.452	21.1	7.9	38
Marsh, Chandler	R-R	6-4	235	9-6-02	3	1	3.45	25	0	2	31	17	12	12	1	16	38	.153	.275	.198	28.8	12.1	132
Metoyer, Brian	R-R	6-3	173	11-13-96	0	0	0.93	14	0	2	19	7	3	2	0	10	25	.119	.278	.136	34.7	13.9	72
Montas, Frankie	R-R	6-2	255	3-21-93	0	0	8.31	2	2	0	4	4	4	4	0	4	4	.250	.381	.438	19.0	19.0	21
Nunez, Anthony	S-R	6-1	190	7-10-01	1	1	0.63	10	0	1	14	3	2	1	0	5	24	.068	.157	.091	46.2	9.6	52
Ovalles, Layonel	R-R	6-3	216	6-16-03	1	0	5.68	5	0	0	6	4	4	4	0	9	5	.200	.419	.300	16.1	29.0	31
Ross, Dylan	R-R	6-5	251	9-1-00	2	0	1.54	10	0	0	12	8	4	2	0	8	23	.182	.308	.205	44.2	15.4	52
Santucci, Jonathan	L-L	6-2	205	12-28-02	5	4	3.46	15	13	0	68	62	29	26	7	23	75	.240	.307	.376	26.4	8.1	284
Simon, Ben	R-R	5-11	197	3-22-02	4	0	3.86	27	0	2	37	32	18	16	4	13	40	.234	.314	.358	25.6	8.3	156
Thornton, Zach	L-L	6-3	170	11-17-02	3	0	0.44	4	4	0	21	12	5	1	1	2	25	.162	.205	.216	32.1	2.6	78
Troesser, Austin	R-R	6-3	189	3-29-02	2	1	4.80	12	0	0	15	13	9	8	0	7	18	.236	.318	.291	27.3	10.6	66
Vega, Alfred	R-R	6-1	169	1-19-01	3	1	3.24	10	0	0	17	13	8	6	0	7	18	.236	.328	.291	25.7	10.0	70
Watson, William	R-R	6-1	170	11-7-02	1	3	1.70	14	13	0	64	45	14	12	3	28	77	.199	.301	.257	29.7	10.8	259

Fielding

Catcher	PCT	G	PO	A	E	DP	PB
Hernandez	.989	67	669	33	8	4	22
Perozo	.962	13	124	4	5	0	3
Suero	.990	46	484	29	5	3	8
Vega	.974	8	70	5	2	0	3

First Base	PCT	G	PO	A	E	DP
Collins	.995	30	199	13	1	14
Cuevas	1.000	3	13	1	0	1
Hernandez	.983	27	163	14	3	20
Mercado	.975	33	179	16	5	13
Reimer	1.000	12	66	12	0	7
Suero	1.000	12	68	8	0	5
Vega	.970	7	26	6	1	4
Willhoite	1.000	12	85	9	0	7

Second Base	PCT	G	PO	A	E	DP
Baez	1.000	12	26	20	0	6
Baro	.986	18	29	40	1	8
De Los Santos	1.000	10	18	18	0	5
Ewing	1.000	9	12	21	0	2

Third Base	PCT	G	PO	A	E	DP
Baez	.895	21	16	18	4	4
Baro	.863	32	20	43	10	6
De Los Santos	.786	7	4	7	3	1
Henriquez	1.000	1	0	2	0	0
Houck	.952	29	9	31	2	7
Mosquera	.958	10	12	11	1	1
Reimer	.965	37	17	66	3	4
Roselli	.000	1	0	1	0	0
Willhoite	.000	1	0	0	0	0

Shortstop	PCT	G	PO	A	E	DP
Baez	.935	27	31	56	6	8
Baro	.936	42	56	76	9	11
Henriquez	1.000	2	5	5	0	1

	PCT	G	PO	A	E	DP
Houck	.833	6	6	9	3	0
Mosquera	.971	10	16	17	1	3
Roselli	.984	18	26	34	1	7
Smith	.867	5	3	10	2	0
Vargas	.994	44	76	90	1	25

	PCT	G	PO	A	E	DP
Houck	.943	17	28	38	4	8
Vargas	.943	41	47	102	9	16
Villavicencio	1.000	4	5	7	0	1

Outfield	PCT	G	PO	A	E	DP
Bay	.833	11	10	0	2	0
Benge	.991	55	109	6	1	0
Cuevas	.983	26	55	4	1	0
De Los Santos	.958	30	44	2	2	1
Ewing	.972	66	135	2	4	1
Henriquez	1.000	5	5	1	0	0
Mercado	1.000	1	1	0	0	0
Mosquera	.986	41	69	3	1	1
Ortega	1.000	4	5	0	0	0
Perozo	.857	5	6	0	1	0
Roselli	.824	15	14	0	3	0
Schreffler	.975	44	77	2	2	0
Serrano	.971	80	158	10	5	0
Smith	1.000	8	10	0	0	0
Suero	1.000	15	23	3	0	1

ST. LUCIE METS — LOW-A
FLORIDA STATE LEAGUE

Batting	B-T	Ht.	Wt.	DOB	AVG	OBP	SLG	G	PA	AB	R	H	2B	3B	HR	RBI	BB	HBP	SH	SF	SO	SB	CS	BB%	SO%
Alvarez, Francisco	R-R	5-10	233	11-19-01	.100	.250	.100	3	12	10	1	1	0	0	0	0	2	0	0	0	3	0	0	16.7	25.0
Baez, Jesus	R-R	5-9	180	2-26-05	.217	.308	.217	6	26	23	3	5	0	0	0	3	0	0	0	3	0	1	11.5	11.5
Bay, John	R-R	6-1	211	5-16-01	.333	.464	.593	17	69	54	18	18	3	1	3	19	9	5	0	1	21	4	1	13.0	30.4
Biller, Sam	L-L	5-10	180	7-7-02	.235	.381	.294	6	21	17	6	4	1	0	0	3	1	0	0	9	5	0	14.3	42.9
Collins, Corey	L-R	6-3	220	10-10-01	.153	.406	.292	26	106	72	12	11	4	0	2	9	28	4	0	2	23	1	0	26.4	21.7
Cuevas, Yohairo	L-L	6-3	172	9-16-03	.278	.440	.369	63	257	198	41	55	12	0	2	11	50	8	0	1	50	11	2	19.5	19.5
Ewing, A.J.	L-R	6-0	160	8-10-04	.400	.506	.615	18	81	65	15	26	3	4	1	20	15	0	0	1	10	14	2	18.5	12.3
Fanas, Willy	S-R	6-1	190	1-23-04	.188	.286	.227	46	147	128	12	24	2	0	1	12	13	5	0	1	53	7	3	8.8	36.1
Gilbert, Drew	L-L	5-9	195	9-27-00	.375	.444	.708	6	27	24	4	9	2	0	2	6	3	0	0	0	3	0	0	11.1	11.1
Gutierrez, Daiverson	R-R	5-11	206	9-11-05	.242	.362	.309	91	395	327	54	79	10	0	4	41	53	11	0	4	58	6	4	13.4	14.7
Guzman, Randy	R-R	6-4	215	4-19-05	.333	.381	.604	26	105	96	15	32	13	2	3	24	6	2	0	1	21	2	3	5.7	20.0
Henriquez, Yonatan	S-R	5-10	185	10-12-04	.264	.354	.395	104	405	349	59	92	18	2	8	50	51	0	1	4	72	33	8	12.6	17.8
Houck, Colin	R-R	6-2	190	9-30-04	.252	.351	.461	62	268	230	43	58	14	5	8	38	33	3	0	2	77	11	2	12.3	28.7
Jimenez, Antonio	R-R	5-11	190	3-8-05	.274	.354	.464	26	110	95	12	26	5	1	4	12	10	2	1	0	2	15	8	3	10.9	13.6
Juan, Simon	R-R	5-11	195	7-13-05	.222	.290	.340	98	376	338	44	75	13	3	7	50	29	5	0	4	111	17	4	7.7	29.5
Mauricio, Ronny	S-R	6-3	166	4-4-01	.133	.188	.133	5	16	15	2	2	0	0	0	1	1	0	0	0	5	2	0	6.3	31.3
McNeil, Jeff	L-R	6-1	195	4-8-92	.273	.429	.273	4	14	11	3	3	0	0	0	0	3	0	0	0	2	0	0	21.4	14.3

NEW YORK METS

	B-T	Ht.	Wt.	DOB	AVG	OBP	SLG	G	AB	R	H	2B	3B	HR	RBI	BB	SO	SB	CS	OPS	BB%	PA
Meggers, Chase	L-R	6-0	195	1-6-03	.276	.382	.328	19	68	58	9	16	3	0	0	6	7	3	0	0	19	5	0	10.3	27.9
Ortega, Rafael	L-R	5-11	180	5-15-91	.429	.519	.810	6	27	21	8	9	5	0	1	5	5	0	0	1	3	2	0	18.5	11.1
Perozo, Vincent	L-R	6-0	170	3-6-03	.259	.376	.378	58	222	185	30	48	9	2	3	26	25	10	0	1	42	3	4	11.3	18.9
Robertson, Sam	R-R	6-1	180	7-17-04	.172	.294	.172	20	68	58	8	10	0	0	0	8	9	1	0	0	27	9	1	13.2	39.7
Rodriguez, Jeremy	L-R	6-0	170	7-4-06	.202	.304	.236	112	492	420	56	85	7	2	1	40	60	4	2	6	94	34	13	12.2	19.1
Roselli, Nick	L-R	5-10	200	3-31-03	.233	.327	.394	52	208	180	29	42	8	0	7	31	21	4	3	0	55	6	0	10.1	26.4
Salgado, AJ	R-R	6-3	215	9-16-01	.264	.353	.375	23	85	72	14	19	5	0	1	12	10	1	0	2	19	6	1	11.8	22.4
Schwartz, JT	L-R	6-4	215	12-17-99	.143	.250	.143	3	8	7	0	1	0	0	0	1	0	1	0	0	4	0	1	0.0	50.0
Siri, Jose	R-R	6-2	175	7-22-95	.500	.625	.667	3	8	6	2	3	1	0	0	3	1	1	0	0	0	0	0	12.5	0.0
Snyder, Trey	R-R	6-1	197	9-21-05	.220	.336	.288	115	512	431	58	95	12	1	5	48	72	5	0	4	96	41	8	14.1	18.8
Vargas, Marco	L-R	6-0	170	5-14-05	.409	.527	.545	13	55	44	14	18	3	0	1	5	10	1	0	0	7	2	1	18.2	12.7
Villavicencio, Kevin	R-R	5-9	172	11-24-03	.219	.295	.309	83	318	278	40	61	12	2	3	34	27	5	3	5	46	19	9	8.5	14.5
Voit, Mitch	R-R	6-0	190	9-30-04	.235	.343	.294	22	99	85	18	20	2	0	1	8	13	1	0	0	24	20	1	13.1	24.2
Willhoite, Trace	R-R	6-2	195	11-17-00	.265	.382	.470	85	346	287	59	76	13	2	14	66	47	9	0	3	76	14	0	13.6	22.0
Winker, Jesse	L-L	6-2	230	8-17-93	.000	.000	.000	2	5	5	0	0	0	0	0	0	0	0	0	0	4	0	0	0.0	80.0
Young, Jared	L-R	6-0	185	7-9-95	.364	.533	.727	4	15	11	3	4	1	0	1	2	4	0	0	0	0	0	0	26.7	0.0

Pitching	B-T	Ht.	Wt.	DOB	W	L	ERA	G	GS	SV	IP	Hits	Runs	ER	HR	BB	SO	AVG	OBP	SLG	SO%	BB%	BF
Allan, Matt	R-R	6-3	225	4-17-01	0	2	3.60	7	7	0	15	11	6	6	1	11	17	.204	.377	.370	24.6	15.9	69
Alvarez, Luis	R-R	6-5	185	5-5-03	4	3	5.40	16	0	0	23	15	19	14	2	15	30	.170	.324	.284	27.5	13.8	109
Ankeney, Eli	L-L	6-0	200	1-10-01	1	0	7.27	9	0	0	9	7	7	7	1	6	14	.206	.317	.324	34.1	14.6	41
Aracena, Wellington	R-R	6-3	180	12-27-04	1	1	2.38	17	8	0	64	38	23	17	0	35	84	.166	.275	.210	31.7	13.2	265
Arnaud, Juan	R-R	6-2	164	6-22-03	6	2	2.45	29	0	3	40	31	18	11	1	18	45	.214	.320	.297	26.3	10.5	171
Austin, Channing	R-R	6-3	200	12-21-01	2	4	4.31	20	11	2	71	67	40	34	2	43	66	.249	.367	.327	20.3	13.2	325
Banks, Brett	L-R	6-3	210	10-3-01	2	0	0.87	8	0	1	10	6	1	1	0	4	9	.182	.263	.182	23.7	10.5	38
Blum, Josh	R-R	6-1	195	5-1-03	5	0	4.31	20	0	3	31	28	16	15	5	13	32	.235	.313	.387	23.7	9.6	135
Brewer, Hoss	L-R	6-4	205	2-20-01	2	0	1.00	18	0	6	27	21	5	3	0	7	34	.216	.274	.278	32.1	6.6	106
Carreno, Nicolas	L-L	5-10	155	6-9-06	1	1	1.50	2	1	0	6	6	4	1	0	0	7	.273	.346	.318	25.0	0.0	28
Chirinos, Jose	R-R	6-3	170	10-16-04	5	2	3.20	15	10	0	56	40	24	20	1	30	51	.195	.324	.239	20.6	12.1	247
Cosper, Colton	L-L	6-1	190	9-8-02	0	1	6.23	3	0	1	9	10	7	6	1	2	4	.286	.324	.486	10.5	5.3	38
Cota, Irving	R-R	5-9	165	2-14-04	5	6	4.36	22	11	0	85	86	46	41	5	19	72	.265	.311	.404	20.5	5.4	352
De Leon, Jorge	R-R	6-5	180	11-24-02	0	0	6.27	21	0	0	19	10	15	13	1	24	27	.154	.409	.262	29.0	25.8	93
Dohm, Nate	R-R	6-4	220	1-9-03	2	3	3.18	7	7	0	28	28	13	10	1	10	34	.255	.314	.318	27.9	8.2	122
Dominguez, Robert	R-R	6-5	195	11-30-01	0	1	9.00	1	0	0	1	1	1	1	0	3	0	.250	.625	.250	0.0	37.5	8
Elissalt, Frank	S-R	6-2	210	3-25-02	3	4	3.02	18	7	0	51	30	19	17	4	21	57	.172	.268	.299	28.4	10.4	201
Escalante, Estarlin	R-R	6-4	235	8-22-03	3	0	7.56	18	0	0	25	25	27	21	5	22	23	.253	.413	.465	18.3	17.5	126
Gomez, Cristofer	R-R	6-4	222	5-13-03	7	1	3.76	22	1	0	41	35	20	17	2	17	23	.236	.352	.338	35.2	13.1	176
Gomez, Franklin	L-L	6-0	145	7-6-05	3	1	1.85	14	7	0	49	30	12	10	1	23	42	.178	.282	.231	21.4	11.7	196
Gomez, Raimon	R-R	6-2	175	9-6-01	2	0	0.69	6	3	0	13	6	6	1	0	10	20	.136	.291	.159	36.4	18.2	55
Guevara, Jose	R-R	6-1	195	4-20-05	0	1	7.58	6	4	1	19	13	19	16	4	14	15	.188	.341	.391	17.4	16.3	86
Hampson, Jace	L-R	6-1	175	8-4-05	0	1	6.75	1	1	0	4	2	3	3	0	3	2	.143	.294	.143	11.8	17.6	17
Hodges, Hunter	R-R	6-3	225	10-3-02	1	1	2.37	29	0	4	38	25	11	10	1	28	55	.180	.327	.230	32.2	16.4	171
Hurtado, Daviel	L-L	6-1	166	1-26-01	0	2	2.70	13	7	0	47	45	19	14	3	19	50	.246	.320	.339	24.6	9.4	203
Jenkins, Bryce	R-R	5-11	175	4-3-01	1	0	5.79	8	0	0	9	8	6	6	0	13	11	.235	.438	.294	22.9	27.1	48
Jimenez, Jonathan	R-R	6-2	182	3-21-04	0	0	3.00	7	6	0	24	22	10	8	1	11	20	.237	.321	.323	18.7	10.3	107
Lanthier, Ethan	R-R	6-5	230	6-10-03	0	2	4.61	5	5	0	14	11	7	7	1	10	13	.208	.328	.321	20.3	15.6	64
Lara, Joel	R-R	6-2	210	1-11-07	3	1	3.45	6	0	0	16	9	9	6	1	14	17	.164	.338	.255	23.9	19.7	71
Lopez, Wilson	R-R	6-1	216	7-15-02	0	1	7.45	10	0	2	10	11	9	8	1	11	9	.306	.479	.444	18.8	22.9	48
Louis, Gregori	L-L	6-3	161	10-28-02	1	0	4.97	9	0	1	13	16	8	7	2	6	21	.314	.390	.451	35.0	10.0	60
Mack, Zack	R-R	6-5	240	10-8-02	0	0	0.00	2	0	0	1	0	0	0	0	1	0	.000	.167	.000	0.0	16.7	6
Marsh, Chandler	R-R	6-4	235	9-6-02	1	0	0.00	8	0	1	11	2	0	0	0	1	14	.063	.088	.063	41.2	2.9	34
McLoughlin, Trey	R-R	6-2	210	6-11-99	0	0	0.00	1	1	0	1	0	0	0	0	1	.000	.000	.000	33.3	0	3
McLoughlin, Tyler	R-R	6-3	222	7-1-02	0	0	7.71	2	1	0	2	1	2	2	0	2	4	.125	.364	.125	36.4	18.2	11
Mercedes, Ernesto	R-R	6-2	180	10-14-03	4	2	3.38	23	4	2	43	27	21	16	5	37	54	.174	.347	.297	27.1	18.6	199
Mijares, Elwis	R-R	6-0	180	12-29-05	0	0	0.00	2	0	0	4	2	0	0	0	7	.154	.154	.154	53.8	0.0	13
Moreta, Edgar	R-R	6-4	192	9-5-03	4	3	4.10	12	9	0	48	44	28	22	6	13	52	.233	.300	.402	25.0	6.3	208
Ortega, Oliver	R-R	6-0	165	10-2-96	0	1	2.35	8	3	0	8	4	4	2	0	3	12	.148	.250	.148	36.4	9.1	33
Ovalles, Layonel	R-R	6-3	216	6-16-03	2	0	1.50	16	0	1	24	12	4	4	1	14	26	.148	.296	.210	23.2	14.1	99
Pauley, Truman	R-R	6-2	200	12-26-03	0	0	2.08	3	3	0	4	0	1	1	0	4	3	.000	.235	.000	17.6	23.5	17
Raley, Brooks	L-L	6-3	200	6-29-88	0	0	0.00	3	1	0	3	0	0	0	0	0	6	.250	.250	.250	50.0	0	12
Rios, Yacksel	R-R	6-3	215	6-27-93	0	0	0.00	1	0	0	2	2	2	0	0	2	1	.000	1.000	1.000	0.0	33.3	3
Rodriguez, Christian	R-R	6-0	160	10-12-04	3	0	5.06	14	1	1	21	22	13	12	0	20	18	.282	.420	.359	18.0	20.0	100
Sako, Yuhi	R-R	5-10	183	8-7-99	0	1	5.79	7	0	2	9	9	7	6	1	4	15	.243	.317	.351	36.6	9.8	41
Scarborough, Joe	L-R	6-2	205	4-18-04	0	0	27.00	1	0	0	1	2	2	3	0	3	0	.500	.667	.500	0.0	50.0	6
Stratton, Garrett	R-R	6-2	175	8-1-03	0	0	0.00	1	0	0	1	0	0	0	0	0	4	.400	.400	.400	0.0	0.0	5
Tebrake, Dylan	R-R	6-3	225	7-13-99	0	0	0.00	3	0	0	4	2	0	0	0	3	4	.154	.313	.231	25.0	18.8	16
Troesser, Austin	R-R	6-3	189	3-29-02	0	0	0.00	1	0	0	2	1	0	0	0	2	1	.333	.600	.333	20.0	40.0	5
Vega, Alfred	R-R	6-1	169	1-19-01	1	0	2.81	11	0	2	16	6	5	5	0	11	20	.113	.277	.151	30.3	16.7	66
Victorino, Omar	R-R	6-2	170	6-9-05	2	0	4.15	7	3	0	26	16	14	12	1	21	17	.176	.353	.231	14.7	18.1	116
Watson, William	R-R	6-1	170	11-7-02	0	4	3.66	10	8	1	39	30	17	16	3	21	43	.211	.313	.317	25.9	12.7	166
Willhoite, Trace	R-R	6-2	195	11-17-00	0	0	0.00	1	0	0	1	0	0	0	0	0	1	.000	.500	.667	.500	0.0	33.3	3
Witt, Tanner	R-R	6-5	215	7-11-02	0	0	0.00	2	0	2	1	0	0	0	0	0	1	3	.125	.222	.125	33.3	11.1	9
Wooster, Caden	R-R	6-8	255	9-5-04	0	0	0.00	1	0	0	1	0	0	0	0	1	0	.000	.333	.000	0.0	33.3	3

Fielding

Catcher	PCT	G	PO	A	E	DP	PB
Alvarez	.964	3	26	1	1	1	1
Gutierrez	.973	86	821	39	24	6	17
Meggers	.972	12	97	7	3	0	0
Perozo	.990	33	279	20	3	4	8

First Base	PCT	G	PO	A	E	DP
Collins	1.000	3	10	4	0	1
Cuevas	.983	18	112	7	2	5
Guzman	.987	14	72	5	1	11
Meggers	.983	7	54	4	1	3
Perozo	.994	26	164	13	1	9
Salgado	.969	8	57	5	2	6
Schwartz	1.000	2	9	2	0	1
Willhoite	.991	64	406	24	4	40

Second Base	PCT	G	PO	A	E	DP
Baez	1.000	1	1	4	0	1
Ewing	1.000	2	7	9	0	3
Henriquez	.000	1	0	0	0	0
Houck	1.000	6	5	10	0	2
Mauricio	1.000	1	2	1	0	1
McNeil	1.000	3	6	4	0	1
Robertson	.909	2	5	5	1	3
Rodriguez	.964	26	31	49	3	7
Roselli	.989	25	42	49	1	11

Snyder	.957	45	52	102	7	18	
Vargas	.962	5	8	17	1	4	
Villavicencio	1.000	12	20	21	0	4	
Voit	.977	12	20	22	1	8	

Third Base	PCT	G	PO	A	E	DP
Baez	1.000	3	2	5	0	1
Henriquez	.895	7	3	14	2	1
Houck	.932	27	16	53	5	6
Jimenez	.900	5	1	8	1	0
Mauricio	.000	1	0	0	0	0
Robertson	1.000	5	2	8	0	0
Rodriguez	.957	24	20	25	2	2
Schwartz	1.000	1	1	2	0	0
Snyder	.892	34	23	43	8	3
Villavicencio	.979	34	26	66	2	8
Voit	.667	1	1	1	1	0

Shortstop	PCT	G	PO	A	E	DP
Baez	.778	2	3	4	2	1
Henriquez	.923	4	5	7	1	0
Houck	.901	24	22	42	7	6
Jimenez	.943	17	20	46	4	7
Mauricio	1.000	2	3	3	0	0
Robertson	1.000	2	2	3	0	0
Rodriguez	.915	57	74	99	16	14

Snyder	.859	19	20	35	9	8
Vargas	1.000	4	5	9	0	1
Villavicencio	1.000	2	2	4	0	2
Voit	1.000	5	13	15	0	5

Outfield	PCT	G	PO	A	E	DP
Bay	.977	14	40	2	1	1
Biller	1.000	6	10	1	0	1
Cuevas	.983	35	56	2	1	1
Ewing	.964	17	53	1	2	0
Fanas	.984	44	54	6	1	1
Gilbert	.900	5	9	0	1	0
Guzman	1.000	10	7	0	0	0
Henriquez	.950	92	204	7	11	2
Juan	.964	96	153	7	6	3
McNeil	1.000	1	1	0	0	0
Ortega	1.000	5	7	0	0	0
Robertson	1.000	9	17	0	0	0
Roselli	.974	23	36	1	1	1
Salgado	.958	15	22	1	1	0
Siri	1.000	1	1	0	0	0
Snyder	1.000	7	13	0	0	0
Villavicencio	.982	36	54	1	1	0
Young	1.000	4	2	0	0	0

FCL METS — ROOKIE
FLORIDA COMPLEX LEAGUE

Batting	B-T	Ht.	Wt.	DOB	AVG	OBP	SLG	G	PA	AB	R	H	2B	3B	HR	RBI	BB	HBP	SH	SF	SO	SB	CS	BB%	SO%
Adderley, Bohan	R-R	6-3	180	11-10-06	.175	.296	.263	49	189	160	19	28	3	1	3	15	25	3	0	1	59	21	6	13.2	31.2
Aular, Jose	R-R	5-11	175	1-2-04	.182	.362	.182	19	58	44	9	8	0	0	0	4	10	3	0	1	13	0	0	17.2	22.4
Collins, Corey	L-R	6-3	220	10-10-01	.000	.286	.000	2	7	5	1	0	0	0	0	0	2	0	0	0	3	0	0	28.6	42.9
De Oleo, Branny	R-R	6-1	156	5-15-05	.194	.291	.290	44	141	124	18	24	5	2	1	13	16	1	0	0	26	16	2	11.3	18.4
German, Haniel	R-R	6-2	185	12-5-05	.192	.297	.248	47	145	125	16	24	7	0	0	11	16	3	0	1	51	1	1	11.0	35.2
Gomez, Vladi	L-R	5-11	150	9-22-05	.221	.338	.221	46	152	122	28	21	1	1	1	8	26	2	1	3	33	19	3	17.1	21.7
Guzman, Randy	R-R	6-4	215	4-19-05	.282	.371	.474	49	178	156	18	44	9	0	7	33	15	7	0	0	33	0	3	8.4	18.5
Lantigua, Edward	R-R	6-3	174	11-13-06	.288	.433	.399	49	194	153	23	44	6	1	3	27	33	7	0	1	29	13	10	17.0	14.9
Ortega, Rafael	L-R	5-11	180	5-15-91	.125	.364	.125	3	11	8	2	1	0	0	0	3	0	0	0	4	0	0	27.3	36.4
Rosa, Jeffry	R-R	6-1	190	9-11-04	.180	.279	.328	45	147	128	19	23	7	0	4	10	18	0	1	0	43	0	1	6.8	29.3
Sarmiento, Dangelo	R-R	6-0	160	1-4-05	.165	.306	.243	45	124	103	16	17	1	2	1	6	19	2	0	0	40	5	2	15.3	32.3
Silva, Daniel	S-R	6-2	200	1-12-05	.188	.391	.333	29	92	69	10	13	4	0	2	9	21	2	0	0	24	0	0	22.8	26.1
Toledo, Francisco	R-R	5-9	160	4-25-03	.221	.338	.265	25	80	68	15	15	3	0	0	3	12	0	0	0	13	0	1	15.0	16.3
Zayas, Julio	R-R	5-11	190	2-16-06	.284	.400	.369	48	173	141	14	40	9	0	1	18	22	6	0	1	24	0	0	12.7	13.9
Zitella, Jacob	R-R	5-11	195	2-24-05	.100	.167	.100	5	12	10	0	1	0	0	0	1	1	0	0	1	4	0	0	8.3	33.3

Pitching	B-T	Ht.	Wt.	DOB	W	L	ERA	G	GS	SV	IP	Hits	Runs	ER	HR	BB	SO	AVG	OBP	SLG	SO%	BB%	BF
Albino, Eris	R-R	6-6	223	1-24-04	0	1	12.86	3	1	0	7	11	10	10	2	5	3	.355	.432	.742	8.1	13.5	37
Alvarez, Luis	R-R	6-5	185	5-5-03	0	0	0.00	2	0	0	4	1	1	0	0	2	6	.091	.231	.091	46.2	15.4	13
Anton, Jesus	R-R	6-3	175	2-17-06	0	0	21.60	4	0	0	2	4	4	4	0	10	2	.000	.706	.000	11.8	58.8	17
Banks, Brett	L-R	6-3	210	10-3-01	0	0	13.50	1	0	0	0	1	1	0	3	1	.000	.600	.000	20.0	60.0	5
Blackburn, Paul	R-R	6-1	196	12-4-93	0	1	2.45	1	1	0	4	3	1	1	0	2	8	.231	.333	.231	53.3	13.3	15
Butto, Jose	R-R	6-1	202	3-19-98	0	0	0.00	1	1	0	1	1	0	0	0	0	1	.333	.333	.333	33.3	0.0	3
Carreno, Nicolas	L-L	5-10	155	6-9-06	0	3	6.85	12	3	0	22	20	22	17	0	19	25	.227	.355	.250	22.7	17.3	110
Chirinos, Jose	R-R	6-3	170	10-16-04	0	1	2.35	4	3	0	15	11	5	4	0	6	22	.200	.279	.255	36.1	9.8	61
Crespo, Anthony	R-R	6-0	197	5-4-05	0	0	3.72	6	1	0	10	10	6	4	2	8	11	.263	.375	.421	22.9	16.7	48
Cuevas, Candido	R-R	6-1	202	4-24-04	0	0	20.25	2	1	0	1	3	3	3	0	4	1	.429	.667	.429	8.3	33.3	12
Escalante, Estarlin	R-R	6-4	235	8-22-03	0	0	0.00	1	0	0	2	1	0	0	0	1	2	.125	.222	.125	22.2	11.1	9
Guevara, Jose	R-R	6-1	178	4-20-05	1	4	5.50	11	7	1	34	28	23	21	2	11	48	.215	.285	.354	33.1	7.6	145
Hampson, Jace	R-R	6-1	175	8-4-05	3	3	2.37	11	8	0	38	38	15	10	1	7	35	.268	.300	.345	23.0	4.6	152
Hurtado, Daviel	L-L	6-1	166	1-26-05	1	0	0.47	5	5	0	19	8	1	1	0	5	25	.125	.188	.172	36.2	7.2	69
Jenkins, Bryce	R-R	5-11	175	4-3-01	0	1	6.75	3	1	0	9	7	7	7	0	3	2	.000	.364	.000	18.2	27.3	11
Jimenez, Jonathan	R-R	6-2	210	6-22-03	1	5	3.79	12	7	0	36	30	20	15	2	11	34	.226	.313	.301	22.4	7.2	152
Lara, Joel	R-R	6-2	210	1-11-07	2	1	3.93	11	1	0	18	18	17	8	1	19	25	.243	.398	.324	26.9	20.4	93
Lopez, Wilson	R-R	6-1	216	7-15-02	0	0	1.93	11	0	0	9	3	2	2	0	8	8	.094	.310	.188	19.0	19.0	42
Louis, Gregori	L-L	6-3	161	10-28-02	0	2	8.10	6	0	0	7	5	7	6	0	7	5	.208	.375	.250	15.2	21.2	33
Mejias, Miguel	R-R	6-1	150	11-2-04	0	0	4.15	4	0	0	4	4	4	2	0	6	3	.235	.480	.294	12.0	24.0	25
Mercedes, Ernesto	R-R	6-2	180	10-14-03	0	0	0.00	1	1	0	1	0	0	0	0	2	2	.000	.429	.000	25.0	25.0	8
Mijares, Elwis	R-R	6-0	180	12-29-05	5	0	2.84	10	0	0	13	7	4	4	2	7	11	.163	.294	.233	21.6	13.7	51
Ovalles, Layonel	R-R	6-3	216	6-13-05	1	0	1.29	6	0	1	7	5	3	1	0	1	7	.200	.269	.200	26.9	3.8	26
Paulino, Deivy	R-R	6-2	205	6-15-05	2	0	6.75	9	0	0	19	22	22	14	0	13	14	.286	.411	.364	14.7	13.7	95
Rios, Yacksel	R-R	6-3	215	6-27-93	0	0	0.00	1	1	0	1	0	0	0	0	1	.000	.250	.000	25.0	0.0	4
Rodriguez, Christian	R-R	6-0	160	10-12-04	0	0	3.26	14	0	2	19	15	9	7	0	11	23	.214	.333	.243	27.4	13.1	84

	B-T	Ht.	Wt.	DOB																			
Rodriguez, Jorge	R-R	6-3	180	12-18-01	0	1	3.18	4	1	0	6	4	4	2	1	1	5	.182	.217	.409	21.7	4.3	23
Rodriguez, Luis	L-L	6-3	190	12-3-02	0	0	0.00	1	0	1	1	1	0	0	0	1	1	.333	.500	.667	25.0	25.0	4
Sako, Yuhi	R-R	5-10	183	8-7-99	1	0	2.77	10	1	0	13	12	4	4	3	0	17	.240	.255	.440	33.3	0.0	51
Valle, John	R-R	6-3	196	11-24-04	1	2	11.77	13	0	1	13	10	18	17	0	17	20	.204	.443	.327	28.2	23.9	71
Verdu, Jermayne	R-R	6-0	150	7-27-06	0	1	3.31	8	0	0	16	13	8	6	1	10	14	.213	.342	.311	19.2	13.7	73
Victorino, Omar	R-R	6-2	170	6-9-05	2	2	3.86	12	8	0	40	35	20	17	3	19	35	.238	.349	.327	20.3	11.0	172

Fielding

C: Zayas 30, Toledo 16, Aular 7, Silva 1. **1B:** Guzman 25, Silva 18, Aular 11, Zitella 4. **2B:** Gomez 28, Sarmiento 18, De Oleo 7, Adderley 2. **3B:** De Oleo 19, Sarmiento 17, Adderley 12, Guzman 4, Gomez 2, Zitella 1. **SS:** Adderley 35, De Oleo 18, Gomez 3. **LF:** German 21, Rosa 21, Guzman 11, Lantigua 2, Ortega 1. **CF:** Lantigua 43, Gomez 11, German 1, Ortega 1. **RF:** German 25, Rosa 17, Guzman 8, Lantigua 5, Ortega 1.

DSL METS BLUE   *ROOKIE*
DOMINICAN SUMMER LEAGUE

Batting	B-T	Ht.	Wt.	DOB	AVG	OBP	SLG	G	PA	AB	R	H	2B	3B	HR	RBI	BB	HBP	SH	SF	SO	SB	CS	BB%	SO%
Acosta, Alex	R-R	6-1	187	11-24-05	.254	.338	.336	40	139	122	20	31	5	1	1	15	13	3	0	1	32	12	1	9.4	23.0
Acosta, Cesar	L-R	6-2	180	7-29-08	.206	.317	.343	33	120	102	15	21	6	1	2	15	15	2	0	1	34	1	2	12.5	28.3
Amparo, Yunior	R-R	6-0	170	9-18-06	.429	.524	.694	20	63	49	18	21	2	1	3	11	10	2	0	2	6	7	1	15.9	9.5
Blanco, Aiberson	S-R	5-11	157	2-12-08	.235	.409	.353	7	22	17	3	4	2	0	0	1	5	0	0	0	9	2	0	22.7	40.9
Cuello, Jhonael	L-L	6-0	167	11-7-07	.255	.340	.362	31	106	94	19	24	4	0	2	10	12	0	0	0	13	7	1	11.3	12.3
De Aza, Diover	S-R	6-1	160	8-15-07	.229	.240	.375	13	50	48	4	11	3	0	1	7	0	0	1	1	14	1	0	2.0	28.0
Eneas, Alexander	R-R	6-0	180	9-12-07	.100	.217	.100	9	23	20	2	2	0	0	0	2	3	0	0	0	7	1	1	13.0	30.4
Francis, Hector	L-L	6-1	160	10-11-07	.194	.306	.355	12	36	31	5	6	2	0	1	1	4	1	0	0	17	3	1	11.1	47.2
Garcia, Keiver	S-R	5-10	145	8-6-06	.227	.330	.273	30	103	88	22	20	4	0	0	8	11	3	0	1	19	9	1	10.7	18.4
Griman, Jesus	R-R	6-1	170	3-13-08	.250	.400	.250	1	5	4	0	1	0	0	0	0	1	0	0	0	1	0	0	0.0	20.0
Guerrero, Vladi	L-L	6-2	220	9-21-06	.233	.333	.337	31	99	86	16	20	2	2	1	10	13	0	0	0	30	3	0	13.1	30.3
Hernandez, Julian	R-R	6-0	180	9-24-05	.286	.545	.286	3	11	7	2	2	0	0	0	1	4	0	0	0	2	0	0	36.4	18.2
Matos, Alvaro	L-R	5-11	180	6-20-06	.212	.333	.364	11	39	33	4	7	3	1	0	4	5	1	0	0	9	4	0	12.8	23.1
Mella, Leandy	S-R	5-10	170	2-4-07	.296	.364	.417	35	129	115	17	34	5	3	1	15	10	3	0	1	44	5	4	7.8	34.1
Padilla, Jose	L-R	6-1	159	6-4-08	.111	.226	.296	9	31	27	3	3	0	1	1	4	4	0	0	0	16	0	0	3.2	51.6
Pinango, Fidel	R-R	6-1	176	7-13-07	.190	.261	.286	9	23	21	2	4	0	0	0	2	1	1	0	0	6	3	0	4.3	26.1
Ramirez, Justin	L-L	6-3	190	2-9-05	.283	.389	.443	34	126	106	18	30	6	1	3	20	15	4	0	1	23	9	5	11.9	18.3
Rivas, Yensi	S-R	6-0	170	10-6-06	.261	.378	.312	44	164	138	27	36	4	0	1	10	21	5	0	0	33	23	8	12.8	20.1
Rodriguez, Georwill	L-R	5-9	155	3-11-08	.273	.414	.273	10	29	22	5	6	0	0	0	4	6	0	0	1	3	7	2	20.7	10.3
Rodriguez, Yovanny	R-R	6-0	175	11-7-06	.345	.459	.504	38	148	119	24	41	11	1	2	24	22	5	0	2	34	2	0	14.9	23.0
Sanchez, Jonnhan	L-L	6-0	160	5-4-07	.259	.373	.370	20	67	54	7	14	1	1	1	9	10	1	0	2	7	6	2	14.9	10.4
Semprun, Yorber	L-R	6-0	165	9-14-07	.339	.411	.455	33	129	112	22	38	6	2	1	19	13	2	0	2	16	12	1	10.1	12.4
Silva, Adrian	S-R	5-11	168	2-6-08	.000	.333	.000	1	3	2	0	0	0	0	0	0	1	0	0	0	2	0	0	33.3	66.7
Terrero, Marcos	L-R	5-11	155	11-11-05	.258	.429	.333	30	91	66	10	17	3	1	0	12	20	2	0	3	19	3	0	22.0	20.9
Ubiera, Giomar	R-R	6-2	170	11-27-07	.212	.434	.327	42	159	113	23	24	7	2	2	15	38	7	0	1	38	14	8	23.9	23.9

Pitching	B-T	Ht.	Wt.	DOB	W	L	ERA	G	GS	SV	IP	Hits	Runs	ER	HR	BB	SO	AVG	OBP	SLG	SO%	BB%	BF
Acosta, Greison	L-L	6-2	185	12-15-07	1	2	8.87	18	1	1	22	25	27	22	0	22	22	.298	.453	.452	18.8	18.8	117
Albino, Eris	R-R	6-6	223	1-24-04	0	0	3.00	5	4	0	12	10	8	4	0	7	11	.227	.333	.250	20.4	13.0	54
Batista, Aurelvys	R-R	6-0	180	5-31-06	0	1	1.04	5	1	0	9	4	2	1	0	6	7	.138	.306	.138	19.4	16.7	36
Brito, Jean	R-R	6-3	180	3-28-06	1	4	2.36	10	5	0	34	21	14	9	1	9	16	.175	.275	.258	19.1	11.3	141
Cadiz, Yoralbert	R-R	6-1	171	10-24-04	1	1	13.50	5	1	0	7	8	13	11	0	13	10	.308	.591	.462	22.7	29.5	44
Gomez, Jose	L-L	6-1	160	9-9-06	0	1	9.00	3	0	0	4	3	5	4	0	5	3	.231	.444	.231	16.7	27.8	18
Lantigua, Sebastian	R-R	6-2	174	10-22-05	0	0	0.00	1	0	0	1	0	0	0	0	2	1	0	0	1.000	1.000	0.0	66.7	3
Lugo, Wilmer	L-L	6-0	190	3-5-06	1	3	9.00	9	0	0	11	16	16	11	0	8	3	.306	.574	.333	13.1	31.1	61
Martinez, Yoelvis	R-R	6-2	188	6-21-06	3	1	4.66	14	0	1	29	31	22	15	1	26	23	.267	.392	.414	15.5	17.6	148
Medina, Pablo	L-L	6-6	192	10-12-06	0	0	4.15	2	0	0	4	4	3	2	1	9	2	.235	.316	.412	47.4	5.3	19
Meza, Abner	R-R	6-0	175	5-6-07	2	1	1.67	8	6	0	27	22	8	5	1	8	20	.212	.281	.240	17.5	7.0	114
Montas, Jahzeel	R-R	6-2	176	1-6-05	0	0	3.38	4	0	0	5	4	4	2	1	4	6	.190	.346	.333	23.1	15.4	26
Montero, Angel	L-L	6-2	190	2-2-08	2	3	4.73	13	6	0	27	20	17	14	1	27	28	.217	.410	.293	23.0	22.1	122
Montero, Luis	R-R	6-3	172	9-9-06	0	0	4.50	3	0	0	4	3	2	2	0	4	6	.214	.421	.214	21.1	21.1	19
Morelli, Matteo	L-L	5-10	175	2-27-06	0	0	8.76	5	1	0	12	16	15	12	0	14	11	.314	.500	.412	15.5	19.7	71
Osoria, Jhony	R-R	6-2	182	1-9-07	0	2	5.00	6	0	0	9	8	6	5	1	3	6	.229	.289	.429	15.8	7.9	38
Ozuna, Anderson	R-R	6-0	153	4-20-07	0	0	2.35	4	0	1	8	6	3	2	1	4	4	.231	.333	.385	12.9	12.9	31
Perez, Darling	R-R	6-3	165	3-13-07	1	2	4.50	10	0	0	32	35	22	16	3	19	26	.280	.376	.384	17.4	12.8	149
Portel, Danny	L-L	6-4	224	8-5-04	2	1	12.46	13	0	0	17	24	24	18	0	12	12	.258	.467	.379	12.9	19.4	93
Reyes, Rayner	R-R	5-11	200	10-20-05	0	1	6.50	12	0	1	18	21	14	13	0	16	16	.304	.461	.377	18.0	18.0	89
Reynoso, Anthony	L-L	5-9	160	1-20-07	3	2	3.68	16	0	0	29	21	13	12	0	14	18	.198	.333	.311	13.8	10.8	130
Rochin, Christopher	R-R	6-2	200	9-18-06	0	1	3.10	9	3	1	20	19	15	7	8	20	.238	.311	.363	22.0	8.8	91
Rodriguez, Leyvi	R-R	6-1	195	5-17-06	2	1	11.74	13	4	0	23	34	39	30	1	28	23	.351	.526	.454	17.3	21.1	133
Sanchez, Yobanny	R-R	6-2	191	12-17-06	0	0	5.63	3	3	0	8	5	5	0	4	6	.267	.361	.367	16.7	11.1	36
Sotillo, Luis	L-L	6-3	176	6-15-05	0	2	10.13	4	3	0	8	11	11	12	0	12	10	.268	.385	.415	23.1	15.4	52
Vasquez, Maykol	R-R	6-1	160	10-29-07	0	0	21.21	6	0	0	5	12	12	11	0	14	3	.118	.559	.235	8.8	41.2	34
Vielma, Jose	R-R	6-1	176	3-29-07	0	3	6.53	9	8	0	21	19	17	15	0	8	20	.294	.375	.376	20.8	8.3	96

Fielding

C: Acosta 24, Rodriguez 24, Terrero 9, Griman 1, Hernandez 1, Silva 1. **1B:** Guerrero 15, Amparo 13, Terrero 10, Matos 7, De Aza 5, Rivas 4, A. Acosta 3, Sanchez 3, C. Acosta 2. **2B:** Garcia 10, Rodriguez 10, Semprun 10, Ubiera 9, Eneas 8, Rivas 8, Padilla 4, Terrero 3, De Aza 2, Amparo 1, Pinango 1. **3B:** Rivas 25, Semprun 10, Ubiera 7, Garcia 4, Padilla 4, Pinango 4, Amparo 3, De Aza 3, Matos 1. **SS:** Ubiera 27, Semprun 13, Garcia 11, De Aza 7, Padilla 3, Amparo 1. **LF:** Mella 19, Acosta 11, Ramirez 8, Guerrero 5, Sanchez 3, Cuello 3, Francis 3, Garcia 3, Amparo 3, Blanco 1. **CF:** Cuello 23, Ramirez 14, Acosta 8, Blanco 4, Mella 4, Garcia 3, Amparo 2, Francis 1, Pinango 1, Sanchez 1. **RF:** Acosta 17, Sanchez 9, Francis 8, Mella 8, Ramirez 6, Cuello 4, Pinango 3, Amparo 1, Blanco 1.

DSL METS ORANGE
DOMINICAN SUMMER LEAGUE
ROOKIE

NEW YORK METS

Batting	B-T	Ht.	Wt.	DOB	AVG	OBP	SLG	G	PA	AB	R	H	2B	3B	HR	RBI	BB	HBP	SH	SF	SO	SB	CS	BB%	SO%
Amparo, Yunior	R-R	6-0	170	9-18-06	.250	.373	.359	30	110	92	18	23	7	0	1	6	16	2	0	0	18	9	4	14.5	16.4
Baptist, Anthony	L-L	5-11	155	10-17-05	.143	.368	.143	5	19	14	2	2	0	0	0	4	5	0	0	0	4	1	1	26.3	21.1
Blanco, Aiberson	S-R	5-11	157	2-12-08	.189	.333	.270	18	45	37	5	7	0	0	1	2	7	1	0	0	11	0	3	15.6	24.4
Cuello, Jhonael	L-L	6-0	167	11-7-07	.000	.100	.000	3	10	9	0	0	0	0	0	0	0	1	0	0	3	0	0	0.0	30.0
De Aza, Diover	S-R	6-1	160	8-15-07	.276	.333	.408	27	87	76	15	21	1	0	3	9	8	0	0	3	22	6	2	9.2	25.3
Francis, Hector	L-L	6-1	160	10-11-07	.107	.194	.107	13	31	28	2	3	0	0	0	1	3	0	0	0	12	0	0	9.7	38.7
Garcia, Roni	L-R	5-9	180	3-5-08	.200	.371	.327	24	70	55	9	11	2	1	1	8	9	6	0	0	22	4	1	12.9	31.4
Griman, Jesus	R-R	6-1	170	3-13-08	.000	.000	.000	1	1	1	0	0	0	0	0	0	0	0	0	0	1	0	0	0.0	100.0
Hernandez, Julian	R-R	6-0	180	9-24-05	.000	.500	.000	2	4	1	0	0	0	0	0	1	2	0	0	1	0	0	0	50.0	0.0
Herrera, Roybert	L-R	6-2	175	6-30-07	.285	.371	.488	39	143	123	22	35	3	2	6	17	15	3	0	2	30	6	1	10.5	21.0
Larez, Cristopher	R-R	6-1	190	1-10-06	.188	.361	.313	20	61	48	9	9	3	0	1	8	10	3	0	0	18	3	2	16.4	29.5
Matos, Alvaro	L-R	5-11	180	6-20-06	.200	.347	.300	18	49	40	12	8	0	2	0	4	4	5	0	0	11	3	0	8.2	22.4
Mindiola, Yeider	R-R	6-0	200	7-28-06	.250	.387	.411	42	142	112	14	28	4	1	4	25	24	3	0	3	24	10	3	16.9	16.9
Miranda, Adolfo	R-R	6-2	190	10-4-06	.290	.353	.473	51	187	169	30	49	14	1	5	29	10	7	0	1	32	11	2	5.3	17.1
Padilla, Jose	L-R	6-1	159	6-24-08	.145	.284	.255	22	67	55	8	8	4	1	0	5	9	2	0	1	17	1	0	13.4	25.4
Pena, Elian	L-R	5-10	180	10-19-07	.292	.421	.528	55	223	178	47	52	13	1	9	33	36	5	0	2	36	21	4	16.1	16.1
Pinango, Fidel	R-R	6-1	176	7-13-07	.204	.291	.306	21	55	49	5	10	1	2	0	2	6	0	0	0	10	7	2	10.9	18.2
Ramirez, Justin	L-L	6-3	190	2-9-05	.349	.472	.651	15	53	43	8	15	1	3	2	9	10	0	0	0	10	2	2	18.9	18.9
Reyes, Josmir	L-R	6-0	180	9-21-06	.300	.426	.480	50	190	150	28	45	11	2	4	28	34	2	0	4	15	5	2	17.9	7.9
Rincon, Heriberto	R-R	6-1	160	2-16-06	.314	.383	.438	53	206	185	42	58	11	3	2	27	19	2	0	0	30	34	6	9.2	14.6
Rodriguez, Georwil	L-R	5-9	155	3-11-08	.128	.404	.128	18	57	39	7	5	0	0	0	4	15	3	0	0	6	5	3	26.3	10.5
Rodriguez, Yovanny	R-R	6-0	175	11-7-06	.235	.350	.412	5	20	17	2	4	3	0	0	2	3	0	0	0	5	1	0	15.0	25.0
Semprun, Yorber	R-R	6-0	165	9-14-07	.160	.276	.200	8	29	25	6	4	1	0	0	1	4	0	0	0	7	3	0	13.8	24.1
Silva, Adrian	S-R	5-11	168	2-6-08	.000	.000	.000	2	3	3	0	0	0	0	0	0	0	0	0	0	3	0	0	0.0	100.0
Terrero, Marcos	L-R	5-11	155	11-11-05	.000	.000	.000	1	4	4	0	0	0	0	0	0	0	0	0	0	1	0	0	0.0	25.0

Pitching	B-T	Ht.	Wt.	DOB	W	L	ERA	G	GS	SV	IP	Hits	Runs	ER	HR	BB	SO	AVG	OBP	SLG	SO%	BB%	BF
Batista, Aurelvys	R-R	6-0	180	5-31-06	0	0	27.00	1	0	0	0	1	1	1	0	2	0	.000	.667	.000	0.0	66.7	3
Brito, Jean	R-R	6-3	180	3-28-06	0	1	4.50	3	2	0	10	10	6	5	1	5	9	.250	.333	.350	20.0	11.1	45
Cadiz, Yoralbert	R-R	6-1	171	10-24-04	2	0	2.49	13	0	2	22	15	7	6	0	12	15	.200	.355	.307	16.1	12.9	93
Calvo, Osiris	L-L	6-4	195	5-6-04	5	1	2.51	11	9	0	43	33	15	12	2	9	45	.206	.256	.281	26.2	5.2	172
Carrillo, Alvaro	R-R	6-4	175	4-5-05	3	1	4.96	14	4	0	33	21	20	18	1	36	33	.186	.399	.265	21.6	23.5	153
Cornelia, Jamdrick	L-L	6-0	140	11-17-05	3	0	2.76	18	1	4	33	27	15	10	3	16	31	.216	.310	.312	21.8	11.3	142
Diaz, Franyel	R-R	6-7	208	12-18-04	1	1	4.13	14	3	0	33	22	18	15	0	28	38	.190	.377	.241	25.0	18.4	152
Gomez, Jose	L-L	6-1	160	9-9-06	0	0	0.00	1	0	1	1	0	0	0	0	2	1	.000	.400	.000	20.0	40.0	5
Gonzalez, Julio	R-R	6-2	205	11-10-06	3	1	2.55	12	4	0	35	22	10	10	0	11	30	.176	.252	.232	21.6	7.9	139
Hernandez, Henderson	R-R	6-2	182	12-19-06	1	2	5.01	9	5	0	23	24	16	13	2	7	19	.270	.365	.393	18.1	6.7	105
Lantigua, Sebastian	R-R	6-2	174	10-22-05	0	0	27.00	1	0	0	1	1	2	2	0	1	0	.333	.667	.333	0.0	16.7	6
Lopez, Jose	R-R	6-1	180	5-22-04	1	1	5.75	10	8	0	20	19	18	13	0	15	17	.250	.379	.316	17.9	15.8	95
Martinez, Yoelvis	R-R	6-2	188	6-21-06	0	0	13.50	1	0	0	3	3	5	4	0	3	3	.273	.429	.364	21.4	21.4	14
Medina, Pablo	L-L	6-6	192	10-12-06	3	3	5.09	14	0	2	23	30	17	13	0	9	27	.250	.382	.388	26.0	8.7	104
Meza, Abner	R-R	6-0	175	5-6-07	2	2	5.40	4	2	0	12	12	7	7	0	2	12	.261	.306	.370	24.5	4.1	49
Montas, Jahzeel	R-R	6-2	176	1-6-05	0	0	18.00	1	0	0	1	1	2	2	0	2	1	.333	.625	.333	12.5	25.0	8
Montero, Luis	L-L	6-3	172	9-9-06	2	0	6.48	6	0	0	8	8	9	6	0	9	4	.242	.409	.242	9.1	20.5	44
Morelli, Matteo	L-L	5-10	175	2-27-06	0	0	13.50	1	1	0	1	0	3	2	0	5	1	.000	.600	.000	10.0	50.0	10
Osoria, Jhony	R-R	6-2	182	1-9-07	0	0	0.00	1	0	0	2	1	0	0	0	1	3	.125	.222	.125	33.3	11.1	9
Ozuna, Anderson	R-R	6-0	153	4-20-07	1	2	3.26	14	0	3	19	18	13	7	1	8	19	.231	.315	.333	21.3	9.0	89
Perez, Darling	R-R	6-3	165	3-13-07	0	0	3.18	2	2	0	6	3	3	2	0	2	6	.150	.227	.150	27.3	9.1	22
Pinango, Fidel	R-R	6-1	176	7-13-07	0	0	0.00	1	0	1	0	0	0	0	0	2	1	.000	.500	.000	25.0	50.0	4
Reynoso, Anthony	L-L	5-9	160	1-20-07	0	1	12.27	4	0	0	4	6	5	0	9	5	.000	.526	.000	25.0	45.0	20
Rochin, Christopher	R-R	6-2	200	9-18-06	0	3	6.52	4	3	0	10	14	11	7	0	4	7	.326	.375	.465	14.6	8.3	48
Sanchez, Yobanny	R-R	6-2	191	12-12-07	0	3	6.35	8	4	0	17	23	21	12	2	13	13	.299	.415	.455	13.8	13.8	94
Sotillo, Luis	L-L	6-3	176	6-15-05	0	0	5.14	8	0	21	13	15	12	1	20	10	.169	.354	.273	10.1	20.2	99
Victora, Deivy	R-R	6-4	209	8-15-05	4	3	4.08	17	0	0	35	28	20	16	3	19	36	.217	.344	.333	23.2	12.3	155

Fielding

C: Mindiola 30, Reyes 24, Hernandez 2, Rodriguez 2. **1B:** Matos 15, Herrera 14, Reyes 11, De Aza 6, Pinango 6, Miranda 3, Amparo 2, Mindiola 2, Terrero 1. **2B:** Garcia 12, Rodriguez 11, Pena 9, De Aza 7, Padilla 7, Semprun 6, Amparo 5, Larez 4, Pinango 1. **3B:** Herrera 13, Padilla 12, De Aza 10, Larez 9, Rodriguez 8, Amparo 7, Pinango 3, Semprun 1. **SS:** Pena 43, Amparo 6, Larez 3, Padilla 3, De Aza 2, Semprun 1. **LF:** Miranda 12, Garcia 11, Rincon 10, Ramirez 7, Blanco 6, Francis 6, Pinango 6, Cuello 2, Herrera 2, Amparo 1. **CF:** Rincon 34, Blanco 8, Amparo 7, Miranda 7, Ramirez 3, Baptist 2, Cuello 1, Francis 1. **RF:** Miranda 24, Rincon 9, Francis 8, Ramirez 5, Amparo 4, Baptist 4, Blanco 4, Pinango 4.

New York Yankees

SEASON SYNOPSIS: The Yankees reshaped and reloaded the roster after losing Juan Soto to the Mets in free agency and Gerrit Cole to Tommy John surgery. They got a modern Triple Crown season from Player of the Year Aaron Judge (.331/.457/.688, 53 HR) and posted an identical 94-68 record from their 2024 pennant-winning season. But the Blue Jays proved to be their kryptonite, winning the season series to earn the AL East title on a tiebreaker, then beating the Yanks in a convincing four-game Division Series.

HIGH POINT: New York was at its best against a soft September schedule, storming back after being five games back in the division after 150 games. The Yankees won 11 of their last 12 against the Twins, Orioles and White Sox—all sub-.500 teams—while scoring 75 runs in that stretch. They stayed hot in a wild-card series at Yankee Stadium against rival Boston, losing the first game but winning the next two. Rookie righthander Cam Schlittler won the series with eight scoreless frames while striking out 12 in a 4-0 clincher. It was a record for strikeouts by a Yankees pitcher in his playoff debut.

LOW POINT: Toronto won the season series 8-5, including winning six of seven at Rogers Centre, and the Blue Jays continued that mastery in the Division Series. They outscored the Yanks 23-8 in the first two games in Toronto, outhomering them 8-1. The Yankees fought back behind homers by Judge and Jazz Chisholm Jr. to win Game Three, but a game performance by Schlittler (6 ⅓ IP) wasn't enough in a Game Four loss. Eight Jays pitchers held them to six hits.

NOTABLE ROOKIES: The Yankees leaned heavily on Schlittler (4-3, 2.96 in 73 IP) in the postseason, and fellow rookie RHP Will Warren (9-8, 4.44) made 33 starts in the regular season and ranked third on the team in innings (162 ⅓). Jasson Dominguez earned most of the starts in left field (.257/.331/.388, 10 HR) and ranked second on the team with 23 stolen bases but got only one postseason at-bat.

KEY TRANSACTIONS: New York traded fringy pitcher Cody Poteet for Cody Bellinger and signed veteran 1B Paul Goldschmidt. The Yankees acquired David Bednar, Jose Caballero, Ryan McMahon, Jake Bird, Austin Slater and Camilo Doval, in-season after the team added Devin Williams and Fernando Cruz in the off-season.

OPENING DAY PAYROLL: $293,488,972 (3rd)

PLAYERS OF THE YEAR

MAJOR LEAGUE
Aaron Judge
OF
.331/.457/.688
53 HR, 30 2B, 137 R,
114 RBIs, 124 BB

MINOR LEAGUE
Elmer Rodriguez
RHP
(A+,AA,AAA)
2.58 ERA in 150 IP
176 SO, 1.07 WHIP

ORGANIZATION LEADERS

Batting		*Qualifiers
MAJORS		
* AVG	Aaron Judge	.331
* OPS	Aaron Judge	1.144
HR	Aaron Judge	53
RBI	Aaron Judge	114
MINORS		
* AVG	Marshall Toole, Tampa	.305
* OBP	Marshall Toole, Tampa	.406
* SLG	Jose Rojas, Scranton/WB	.599
* OPS	Jose Rojas, Scranton/WB	.978
R	George Lombard Jr., Somerset/Hudson Valley	90
H	T.J. Rumfield, Somerset/Hudson Valley	142
TB	Jose Rojas, Scranton/WB	267
2B	Jose Rojas, Scranton/WB	35
3B	Marshall Toole, Tampa	13
HR	Jose Rojas, Scranton/WB	32
RBI	Jose Rojas, Scranton/WB	105
BB	George Lombard Jr., Somerset/Hudson Valley	87
SO	George Lombard Jr., Somerset/Hudson Valley	146
SB	Brendan Jones, Somerset/Hudson Valley	51

Pitching		#Qualifiers
MAJORS		
W	Max Fried	19
# ERA	Max Fried	2.86
SO	Carlos Rodon	203
SV	Devin Williams	18
MINORS		
W	Brendan Beck, Scranton/WB/Somerset	13
L	Erick Leal, Scranton/WB	10
# ERA	Elmer Rodriguez, Scr./WB/Somer./H.Valley	2.58
G	Harrison Cohen, Scranton/WB/Somerset	49
GS	Erick Leal, Scranton/WB	26
GS	Elmer Rodriguez, Scr./WB/Somer./H.Valley	26
SV	Tony Rossi, Hudson Valley/Tampa	10
IP	Elmer Rodriguez, Scr./WB/Somer./H.Valley	150
BB	Greysen Carter, Tampa/FCL Yankees	67
SO	Elmer Rodriguez, Scr./WB/Somer./H.Valley	176
# AVG	Carlos Lagrange, Somerset/Hudson Valley	.191

2025 PERFORMANCE

General Manager: Brian Cashman. **Farm Director:** Kevin Reese. **Scouting Director:** Damon Oppenheimer.

Class	Team	League	W	L	PCT	Finish	Manager
Majors	New York Yankees	American	94	68	.580	1 (15)	Aaron Boone
Triple-A	Scranton/W-B RailRiders	International	87	60	.592	2 (20)	Shelley Duncan
Double-A	Somerset Patriots	Eastern	73	65	.529	4 (12)	Raul Dominguez
High-A	Hudson Valley Renegades	South Atlantic	79	50	.612	2 (12)	James Cooper
Low-A	Tampa Tarpons	Florida State	63	63	.500	4 (10)	Aaron Bossi
Rookie	FCL Yankees	Florida Complex	28	30	.483	8 (15)	Ryan Chipka
Rookie	DSL NYY Bombers	Dominican	31	25	.554	19 (52)	Chase Gerbrick
Rookie	DSL NYY Yankees	Dominican	24	32	.429	38 (52)	Carlos Vidal
Overall 2025 Minor League Record			385	325	.542	6th (30)	

ORGANIZATION STATISTICS

NEW YORK YANKEES
AMERICAN LEAGUE

Batting	B-T	Ht.	Wt.	DOB	AVG	OBP	SLG	G	PA	AB	R	H	2B	3B	HR	RBI	BB	HBP	SH	SF	SO	SB	CS	BB%	SO%
Bellinger, Cody	L-L	6-4	203	7-13-95	.272	.334	.480	152	656	588	89	160	25	5	29	98	57	2	0	9	90	13	2	8.7	13.7
Caballero, Jose	R-R	5-9	185	8-30-96	.266	.372	.456	40	95	79	15	21	6	0	3	9	14	0	1	1	18	15	3	14.7	18.9
Cabrera, Oswaldo	S-R	5-11	200	3-1-99	.243	.322	.308	34	122	107	17	26	4	0	1	11	11	2	1	1	25	1	0	9.0	20.5
Chisholm, Jazz	L-R	5-11	184	2-1-98	.242	.332	.481	130	531	462	75	112	15	1	31	80	58	6	1	4	148	31	8	10.9	27.9
Dominguez, Jasson	S-R	5-9	190	2-7-03	.257	.331	.388	123	429	381	58	98	18	1	10	47	41	3	0	4	115	23	5	9.6	26.8
Escarra, J.C.	L-R	6-3	205	4-24-95	.202	.296	.333	40	98	84	5	17	5	0	2	11	11	1	0	2	14	1	0	11.2	14.3
Goldschmidt, Paul	R-R	6-3	220	9-10-87	.274	.328	.403	146	534	489	76	134	31	1	10	45	36	4	0	2	100	5	1	6.7	18.7
Grisham, Trent	L-L	5-11	224	11-1-96	.235	.348	.464	143	581	494	87	116	9	1	34	74	82	4	0	1	137	3	2	14.1	23.6
Judge, Aaron	R-R	6-7	282	4-26-92	.331	.457	.688	152	679	541	137	179	30	2	53	114	124	7	0	7	160	12	5	18.3	23.6
LeMahieu, DJ	R-R	6-4	220	7-13-88	.266	.338	.336	45	142	128	13	34	3	0	2	12	14	0	0	0	35	0	0	9.9	24.6
McMahon, Ryan	L-R	6-2	219	12-14-94	.208	.308	.333	54	185	159	20	33	8	0	4	18	21	3	0	2	62	1	0	11.4	33.5
Peraza, Oswaldo	R-R	6-0	200	6-15-00	.152	.212	.241	71	170	158	18	24	5	0	3	13	11	1	0	0	47	3	0	6.5	27.6
Reyes, Pablo	R-R	5-8	175	9-5-93	.194	.242	.226	25	34	31	4	6	1	0	0	2	2	0	1	0	10	1	0	5.9	29.4
Rice, Ben	L-R	6-1	205	2-22-99	.255	.337	.499	138	530	467	74	119	28	4	26	65	50	9	0	2	100	3	2	9.4	18.9
Rosario, Amed	R-R	6-2	190	11-20-95	.303	.303	.485	16	33	33	1	10	3	0	1	5	0	0	0	0	9	0	0	0.0	27.3
Slater, Austin	R-R	6-1	204	12-13-92	.120	.120	.120	14	25	25	2	3	0	0	0	2	0	0	0	0	16	0	0	0.0	64.0
Stanton, Giancarlo	R-R	6-6	245	11-8-89	.266	.338	.594	77	281	249	36	68	8	0	24	66	29	1	0	1	96	0	0	10.3	34.2
Vivas, Jorbit	L-R	5-10	171	3-9-01	.161	.266	.250	29	66	56	6	9	2	0	1	5	5	3	0	0	13	0	0	7.6	19.7
Volpe, Anthony	R-R	5-9	180	4-28-01	.212	.272	.391	153	596	539	65	114	32	4	19	72	43	4	3	7	150	18	8	7.2	25.2
Wells, Austin	L-R	6-0	220	7-12-99	.219	.275	.436	126	448	401	51	88	22	1	21	71	30	5	0	11	118	5	1	6.7	26.3

Pitching	B-T	Ht.	Wt.	DOB	W	L	ERA	G	GS	SV	IP	Hits	Runs	ER	HR	BB	SO	AVG	OBP	SLG	SO%	BB%	BF
Bednar, David	L-R	6-1	250	10-10-94	4	0	2.19	22	0	10	25	14	6	6	2	9	35	.159	.237	.273	36.1	9.3	97
Beeter, Clayton	R-R	6-2	220	10-9-98	0	1	14.73	2	0	0	4	5	6	6	2	4	3	.333	.474	.800	5.0	20.0	20
Bird, Jake	R-R	6-3	200	12-4-95	0	1	27.00	0	0	0	2	4	7	6	2	2	4	.400	.500	1.000	33.3	16.7	12
Blackburn, Paul	R-R	6-1	196	12-4-93	0	0	5.28	8	0	0	15	16	10	9	3	4	16	.262	.308	.475	24.6	6.2	65
Brubaker, JT	R-R	6-3	185	11-17-93	0	0	3.38	12	0	0	16	10	6	6	0	9	10	.189	.317	.264	15.9	14.3	63
Carrasco, Carlos	R-R	6-4	224	3-21-87	2	2	5.91	8	6	0	32	39	21	21	7	10	25	.298	.345	.527	17.6	7.0	142
Cruz, Fernando	R-R	6-2	237	3-28-90	3	4	3.56	49	0	2	48	33	21	19	5	24	72	.192	.300	.320	36.0	12.0	200
De Los Santos, Yerry	R-R	6-2	215	12-12-97	0	1	3.28	25	0	0	36	37	15	13	1	17	28	.266	.348	.331	17.5	10.6	160
Doval, Camilo	R-R	6-2	185	7-4-97	0	1	4.82	22	0	1	19	19	14	10	2	11	22	.253	.356	.387	25.3	12.6	87
Effross, Scott	R-R	6-2	202	12-28-93	0	0	8.44	11	0	0	11	16	10	10	1	3	6	.333	.373	.583	11.8	5.9	51
Fried, Max	L-L	6-4	190	1-18-94	19	5	2.86	32	32	0	195	164	73	62	14	51	189	.223	.281	.334	23.6	6.4	801
Garcia, Rico	R-R	5-9	201	1-10-94	0	0	10.13	1	0	0	3	3	3	3	1	2	2	.273	.385	.636	15.4	15.4	13
Gil, Luis	R-R	6-2	185	6-3-98	4	1	3.32	11	11	0	57	47	23	21	5	33	41	.226	.332	.365	16.8	13.5	244
Gomez, Yoendrys	R-R	6-3	175	10-15-99	1	1	2.70	6	0	0	10	5	4	3	1	9	5	.143	.318	.229	11.4	20.5	44
Hamilton, Ian	R-R	6-1	200	6-16-95	2	1	4.28	36	1	0	40	28	20	19	5	22	42	.201	.313	.253	13.3	14.0	166
Hartlieb, Geoff	R-R	6-5	240	12-9-93	0	0	40.50	2	0	0	1	5	6	6	1	4	4	.556	.692	1.000	30.8	30.8	13
Headrick, Brent	L-L	6-6	235	12-17-97	0	0	3.13	17	0	0	23	17	8	8	4	7	30	.202	.272	.405	32.6	7.6	92
Hill, Tim	R-L	6-4	200	2-10-90	4	4	3.09	70	0	0	67	58	27	23	8	16	37	.231	.276	.363	13.8	5.9	269
Leiter, Mark	R-R	6-0	210	3-13-91	6	7	4.84	59	0	2	48	57	31	26	5	17	54	.293	.388	.448	24.7	7.8	219
Loaisiga, Jonathan	R-R	5-11	165	11-2-94	0	1	4.25	30	0	1	30	34	15	14	7	10	25	.281	.351	.521	18.5	7.4	135
Matzek, Tyler	L-L	6-3	230	10-19-90	0	0	4.26	7	0	0	6	11	3	3	0	5	7	.379	.457	.517	20.0	14.3	35
Uttavino, Adam	S-R	6-5	246	11-25-85	0	0	0.00	3	0	0	2	0	0	0	0	4	3	.000	.444	.000	33.3	44.4	9
Reyes, Pablo	R-R	5-8	175	9-5-93	0	0	27.00	1	0	0	1	5	3	3	1	0	0	.625	.625	1.250	0.0	0.0	8
Rodon, Carlos	L-L	6-2	255	12-10-92	18	9	3.09	33	33	0	195	132	74	67	22	73	203	.188	.272	.321	25.7	9.3	789
Sandridge, Jayvien	L-L	6-5	220	2-11-99	0	0	27.00	1	0	0	1	2	2	1	2	2	2	.333	.667	1.333	33.3	33.3	6
Schlittler, Cam	R-R	6-6	230	2-5-01	4	3	2.96	14	14	0	73	58	24	24	8	31	84	.217	.309	.337	27.6	10.2	304
Schmidt, Clarke	R-R	6-1	200	2-20-96	4	4	3.32	14	14	0	79	56	29	29	9	30	73	.199	.276	.351	23.1	9.5	316
Slater, Austin	R-R	6-1	204	12-13-92	0	0	0.00	1	0	0	1	0	0	0	0	0	0	.333	.333	.333	0.0	0.0	3
Stroman, Marcus	R-R	5-7	180	5-1-91	3	2	6.23	9	9	0	39	44	27	27	6	16	26	.282	.354	.468	14.9	9.1	175
Warren, Will	R-R	6-2	175	6-16-99	8	4.44	33	33	0	162	158	90	80	22	65	171	.250	.320	.418	24.1	9.1	711

	B-T	Ht	Wt	DOB			AVG			G		AB	R	H			HR	RBI	BB				
Weaver, Luke	R-R	6-2	183	8-21-93	4	4	3.62	64	0	8	65	46	28	26	10	20	72	.195	.258	.364	27.5	7.6	262
Williams, Devin	R-R	6-2	192	9-21-94	4	6	4.79	67	0	18	62	45	37	33	5	25	90	.197	.287	.320	34.7	9.7	259
Winans, Allan	R-R	6-2	165	8-10-95	0	1	8.68	3	1	0	9	13	11	9	2	3	6	.333	.391	.590	13.0	6.5	46
Yarbrough, Ryan	R-L	6-5	205	12-31-91	3	1	4.36	19	8	1	64	58	31	31	13	19	55	.240	.299	.438	20.8	7.2	264

Fielding

Catcher	PCT	G	PO	A	E	DP	PB
Escarra	.987	30	229	2	3	0	0
Rice	.991	36	227	4	2	0	5
Wells	.997	122	1001	36	3	5	5

First Base	PCT	G	PO	A	E	DP
Bellinger	1.000	7	29	2	0	5
Cabrera	1.000	2	2	0	0	0
Escarra	1.000	6	9	0	0	0
Goldschmidt	.995	139	840	84	5	73
Rice	.991	50	318	21	3	21

Second Base	PCT	G	PO	A	E	DP
Caballero	.938	6	9	6	1	2
Chisholm	.970	100	146	239	12	41
LeMahieu	1.000	45	59	84	0	18
Peraza	.975	17	19	20	1	6

	PCT	G	PO	A	E	DP
Reyes	1.000	6	4	8	0	1
Rosario	1.000	1	1	2	0	0
Vivas	1.000	15	24	17	0	6

Third Base	PCT	G	PO	A	E	DP
Caballero	.889	10	4	4	1	0
Cabrera	.933	33	22	48	5	6
Chisholm	.920	29	18	51	6	5
Escarra	.000	2	0	0	0	0
McMahon	.971	54	33	102	4	8
Peraza	.971	49	19	82	3	2
Reyes	.714	5	1	4	2	0
Rosario	1.000	9	2	11	0	1
Vivas	1.000	14	8	15	0	2

Shortstop	PCT	G	PO	A	E	DP
Caballero	.980	12	18	32	1	9

	PCT	G	PO	A	E	DP
Peraza	.950	8	6	13	1	1
Volpe	.963	153	171	326	19	60

Outfield	PCT	G	PO	A	E	DP
Bellinger	.990	178	302	6	3	1
Caballero	.923	15	12	0	1	0
Cabrera	.000	2	0	0	0	0
Dominguez	.989	100	181	2	2	0
Goldschmidt	.000	1	0	0	0	0
Grisham	.993	140	267	5	2	1
Judge	.995	95	201	1	1	0
Reyes	1.000	9	6	0	0	0
Rosario	1.000	5	2	1	0	0
Slater	1.000	13	15	0	0	0
Stanton	.963	20	26	0	1	0

SCRANTON/WILKES-BARRE RAILRIDERS — TRIPLE-A
INTERNATIONAL LEAGUE

Batting	B-T	Ht.	Wt.	DOB	AVG	OBP	SLG	G	PA	AB	R	H	2B	3B	HR	RBI	BB	HBP	SH	SF	SO	SB	CS	BB%	SO%
Alexander, CJ	L-R	6-3	215	7-17-96	.196	.302	.196	13	53	46	3	9	0	0	0	3	7	0	0	0	16	2	1	13.2	30.2
Brantly, Rob	L-R	6-0	190	7-14-89	.250	.250	.250	2	4	4	0	1	0	0	0	0	0	0	0	0	0	0	0	0.0	0.0
Burt, Max	R-R	6-1	185	8-28-96	.250	.357	.417	4	14	12	2	3	0	1	0	1	2	0	0	0	4	0	0	14.3	28.6
Candelario, Jeimer	S-R	6-2	222	11-24-93	.203	.289	.357	61	256	227	30	46	14	0	7	31	25	3	0	1	75	0	1	9.8	29.3
Davis, Brennen	R-R	6-0	210	11-2-99	.248	.324	.576	36	142	125	19	31	5	0	12	30	11	4	0	2	44	1	0	7.7	31.0
De La Cruz, Bryan	R-R	6-2	175	12-16-96	.271	.340	.456	91	368	329	46	89	14	1	15	48	32	4	0	3	89	8	1	8.7	24.2
Duran, Edinson	R-R	5-6	180	7-22-02	.308	.308	.385	7	14	13	3	4	1	0	0	0	0	1	0	0	0	0	0	28.6
Ellis, Duke	L-L	6-1	180	1-16-98	.322	.371	.468	68	192	171	31	55	14	1	3	22	14	0	5	1	49	36	7	7.3	25.5
Escarra, J.C.	L-R	6-3	205	4-24-95	.300	.391	.400	30	133	110	16	33	3	1	2	20	18	1	0	4	23	2	1	13.5	17.3
Flores, Rafael	R-R	6-4	220	11-7-00	.211	.388	.289	10	49	38	3	8	0	0	1	4	11	0	0	0	13	0	0	22.4	26.5
Gatewood, Henry	R-R	6-5	190	9-25-95	.174	.274	.349	35	125	109	14	19	4	0	5	17	12	3	1	0	43	3	2	9.6	34.4
Hernandez, Ronaldo	R-R	6-1	230	11-11-97	.221	.287	.351	25	88	77	7	17	4	0	2	13	8	0	0	2	19	1	0	9.1	21.6
Hummel, Cooper	S-R	5-10	198	11-28-94	.258	.415	.290	10	41	31	6	8	1	0	0	2	9	0	0	1	8	1	1	22.0	19.5
Jackson, Alex	R-R	5-11	238	12-25-95	.226	.308	.463	44	185	164	31	37	7	1	10	34	19	1	0	1	53	1	1	10.3	28.6
Jones, Spencer	L-L	6-6	225	5-14-01	.274	.342	.555	67	298	263	60	72	15	1	19	48	26	4	0	5	109	19	4	8.7	36.6
LeMahieu, DJ	R-R	6-4	220	7-13-88	.455	.500	.455	3	12	11	1	5	0	0	0	1	1	0	0	0	1	0	1	8.3	8.3
Lopez, Nicky	L-R	5-11	180	3-13-95	.263	.338	.333	17	65	57	9	15	2	1	0	6	7	0	0	1	11	4	0	10.8	16.9
Martinez, Omar	L-R	5-10	192	7-5-01	.200	.307	.280	23	88	75	10	15	1	1	1	9	11	0	1	0	37	0	0	12.5	42.0
Munguia, Ismael	L-L	5-10	158	10-19-98	.246	.313	.342	91	315	281	42	69	11	2	4	31	22	7	2	3	25	23	7	7.0	7.9
Pereira, Everson	R-R	5-11	191	4-10-01	.254	.357	.507	70	314	268	68	68	9	1	19	52	38	6	0	2	90	9	1	12.1	28.7
Richardson, Grant	L-L	6-0	210	7-13-99	.275	.362	.525	15	48	40	8	11	4	0	2	8	6	0	1	1	18	0	1	12.5	37.5
Rodriguez, Jesus	R-R	5-9	182	4-23-02	.317	.409	.430	78	362	309	54	98	14	3	5	41	46	4	0	3	55	16	8	12.7	15.2
Rojas, Jose	L-R	6-2	200	2-24-93	.287	.379	.599	124	517	446	77	128	35	4	32	105	65	3	0	3	108	5	2	12.6	20.9
Rumfield, T.J.	L-R	6-4	225	5-17-00	.285	.378	.447	138	587	499	85	142	31	1	16	87	70	10	0	8	108	5	2	11.9	18.4
Shewmake, Braden	L-R	6-3	190	11-19-97	.244	.318	.362	85	315	279	41	68	13	4	4	29	30	2	1	3	52	15	2	9.5	16.5
Slater, Austin	R-R	6-1	204	12-13-92	.214	.389	.214	5	18	14	3	3	0	0	0	0	4	0	0	0	4	0	0	22.2	22.2
Smith, Dominic	L-L	6-0	224	6-15-95	.255	.333	.448	45	189	165	26	42	6	1	8	28	20	1	0	3	30	4	0	10.6	15.9
Velazquez, Andrew	R-R	5-9	170	7-14-94	.242	.304	.345	106	368	330	49	80	19	0	5	41	28	2	6	2	93	25	4	7.6	25.3
Vivas, Jorbit	L-R	5-10	171	3-9-01	.270	.389	.364	100	459	374	59	101	21	1	4	43	64	11	1	4	45	12	9	13.9	9.8

Pitching	B-T	Ht.	Wt.	DOB	W	L	ERA	G	GS	SV	IP	Hits	Runs	ER	HR	BB	SO	AVG	OBP	SLG	SO%	BB%	BF
Anderson, Ryan	L-L	6-6	205	9-9-98	1	0	13.50	2	0	0	2	4	3	3	0	2	4	.364	.500	.545	28.6	14.3	14
Barclay, Edgar	L-L	5-10	200	5-25-98	0	0	0.00	1	1	0	3	1	0	0	0	1	0	.111	.273	.111	0.0	9.1	11
Beck, Brendan	R-R	6-2	205	10-6-98	8	3	4.44	15	15	0	77	65	39	38	12	24	71	.229	.293	.451	22.8	7.7	312
Beeter, Clayton	R-R	6-2	220	10-9-98	1	0	3.10	18	0	2	20	17	8	7	0	16	33	.227	.370	.280	35.1	17.0	94
Bird, Jake	R-R	6-3	200	12-4-95	1	2	6.32	15	0	1	16	8	15	11	1	12	23	.154	.366	.231	31.5	16.7	72
Boyle, Sean	R-R	6-1	205	10-29-96	9	9	4.61	28	23	1	135	124	76	69	16	51	120	.241	.320	.385	20.5	8.7	585
Brewer, Colten	R-R	6-4	222	10-29-92	1	1	3.94	22	0	5	30	19	13	13	3	15	32	.188	.305	.366	27.1	12.7	118
Brubaker, JT	R-R	6-3	185	11-17-93	1	0	4.63	3	3	0	12	7	6	6	2	6	11	.171	.292	.317	22.9	12.5	48
Carrasco, Carlos	R-R	6-4	224	3-21-87	4	2	3.27	11	10	0	52	47	22	19	4	14	38	.240	.292	.352	17.8	6.6	213
Castro, Kervin	R-R	6-0	185	2-7-99	5	1	1.53	35	0	4	47	27	12	8	1	22	52	.164	.270	.200	27.4	11.6	190
Cohen, Harrison	R-R	6-0	190	5-28-99	0	2	1.57	29	1	3	29	14	5	5	0	17	29	.146	.284	.177	25.0	14.7	116
Cruz, Fernando	R-R	6-2	237	3-28-90	0	0	27.00	2	0	0	1	4	4	4	1	1	.500	.556	.875	11.1	11.1	9
De Los Santos, Yerry	R-R	6-2	215	12-12-97	1	1	1.62	17	0	1	17	16	4	3	2	5	18	.246	.300	.369	25.7	7.1	70
Dees, Kevin	R-R	6-8	250	3-5-99	2	1	2.76	17	0	0	16	13	7	5	0	14	19	.220	.373	.271	25.3	18.7	75
DeSclafani, Anthony	R-R	6-2	195	4-18-90	1	1	4.50	5	5	0	20	24	11	10	1	9	20	.300	.371	.425	22.2	10.0	90
Duran, Edinson	R-R	5-6	180	7-22-02	0	0	13.50	2	0	1	3	3	2	0	3	1	.429	.600	.571	10.0	30.0	10
Effross, Scott	R-R	6-2	202	12-28-93	2	4	6.37	28	0	3	30	38	26	21	1	10	23	.304	.355	.392	16.5	7.2	139

NEW YORK YANKEES

Name	B-T	Ht.	Wt.	DOB			AVG	G	GS	ERA	IP	H	R	ER	HR	BB	SO	AVG	BB/9	SO/9
Gil, Luis	R-R	6-2	185	6-3-98	0	0	7.04	2	2	0	8	7	6	6	2	4	11	.241	.343	.483	31.4	11.4	35
Hamilton, Ian	R-R	6-1	200	6-16-95	1	0	6.00	19	0	0	18	23	12	12	1	12	20	.307	.398	.440	22.7	13.6	88
Hartlieb, Geoff	R-R	6-5	240	12-9-93	3	2	3.34	24	0	2	35	35	16	13	2	10	38	.267	.322	.359	26.2	6.9	145
Headrick, Brent	L-L	6-6	235	12-17-97	2	1	2.63	20	0	0	24	25	8	7	2	7	24	.278	.337	.367	24.5	7.1	98
Hummel, Cooper	S-R	5-10	198	11-28-94	1	0	0.00	1	0	0	0	0	0	0	0	0	1	.000	.667	.000	0.0	33.3	3
Kuhnel, Joel	R-R	6-5	290	2-19-95	1	1	3.45	24	2	5	31	29	18	12	1	7	29	.246	.291	.322	22.7	5.5	128
Leal, Erick	R-R	6-3	180	3-17-95	8	10	5.61	28	26	0	127	115	89	79	28	58	133	.239	.331	.469	23.9	10.4	557
Leibrandt, Brandon	L-L	6-4	190	12-13-92	1	0	2.85	10	9	1	41	32	13	13	6	14	37	.215	.282	.389	22.7	8.6	163
Loaisiga, Jonathan	R-R	5-11	165	11-2-94	0	0	0.00	4	0	0	5	2	0	0	0	3	.125	.176	.125	17.6	5.9	17
Maeda, Kenta	R-R	6-1	185	4-11-88	3	3	4.64	8	8	0	43	39	24	22	5	14	38	.247	.314	.411	21.5	7.9	177
Matzek, Tyler	L-L	6-3	230	10-19-90	0	0	1.93	4	0	0	5	4	1	1	0	2	5	.235	.350	.353	25.0	10.0	20
Messinger, Zach	R-R	6-6	225	10-4-99	4	3	5.27	28	7	3	67	70	41	39	7	38	65	.262	.360	.442	21.1	12.3	308
Moore, McKinley	R-R	6-6	225	8-24-98	0	0	6.23	8	0	0	9	6	6	6	1	9	6	.200	.375	.333	15.0	22.5	40
Munguia, Ismael	L-L	5-10	158	10-19-98	0	1	18.00	2	0	0	2	7	4	4	0	0	0	.583	.538	.667	0.0	0.0	13
Olsen, Jon	R-R	6-2	190	5-13-97	0	0	27.00	1	0	0	1	3	3	3	0	1	1	.500	.571	1.000	14.3	14.3	7
Pacheco, Luis	R-R	6-2	185	4-22-99	0	0	0.00	1	0	0	1	0	0	0	0	0	0	.000	1.000	.000	0.0	40.0	5
Pestana, Leonardo	R-R	6-4	198	7-30-98	2	3	6.49	33	1	0	43	36	32	31	10	34	49	.225	.377	.444	24.6	17.1	199
Reyzelman, Eric	R-R	6-2	188	6-27-01	1	2	4.29	34	0	1	42	26	20	20	5	42	45	.182	.372	.315	23.9	22.3	188
Richardson, Grant	L-L	6-0	210	7-13-99	0	0	0.00	1	0	0	0	0	0	0	0	0	0	.000	.000	.000	0.0	0.0	1
Rodriguez, Wilking	R-R	6-1	180	3-2-90	2	1	3.20	27	0	0	25	17	10	9	2	22	36	.200	.367	.365	33.0	20.2	109
Rodriguez, Elmer	L-R	6-3	160	8-18-03	0	1	7.20	1	1	0	5	8	4	4	0	0	3	.381	.409	.524	13.6	0.0	22
Rojas, Jose	L-R	6-0	200	2-24-93	0	0	54.00	1	0	0	1	6	4	4	0	0	0	.750	.750	.875	0.0	0.0	8
Sandridge, Jayvien	L-L	6-5	220	2-11-99	3	1	4.55	34	0	3	32	29	17	16	3	17	47	.242	.348	.375	33.1	12.0	142
Schlittler, Cam	R-R	6-6	210	2-5-01	2	1	3.80	5	5	0	24	20	11	10	3	9	35	.227	.306	.364	35.7	9.2	98
Stuart, Baron	R-R	6-4	209	7-24-99	0	0	4.91	12	0	1	15	13	8	8	1	12	5	.236	.373	.345	7.5	17.9	67
Vinyard, Mason	R-R	6-2	210	6-22-99	0	0	16.20	1	0	0	2	2	3	3	2	2	1	.286	.444	1.143	11.1	22.2	9
Winans, Allan	R-R	6-2	165	8-10-95	12	1	1.63	21	18	1	99	75	21	18	4	27	105	.206	.270	.297	26.4	6.8	397
Woodford, Jake	R-R	6-4	215	10-28-96	2	2	4.54	10	7	0	40	45	23	20	6	17	39	.285	.361	.462	21.5	9.4	181
Yarbrough, Ryan	R-L	6-5	205	12-31-91	0	1	4.09	3	3	0	11	9	5	5	1	1	12	.225	.238	.350	28.6	2.4	42
Zastryzny, Rob	R-L	6-3	205	3-26-92	0	0	4.50	13	0	0	12	16	8	6	2	0	12	.314	.314	.451	23.5	0.0	51

Fielding

Catcher	PCT	G	PO	A	E	DP	PB
Brantly	1.000	2	7	0	0	0	0
Duran	.846	3	20	2	4	0	0
Escarra	.985	22	185	10	3	1	3
Flores	.972	10	101	2	3	1	0
Hernandez	.982	14	102	6	2	0	1
Jackson	.982	37	313	15	6	1	4
Martinez	.990	23	190	9	2	1	1
Rodriguez	.983	42	385	29	7	2	7

First Base	PCT	G	PO	A	E	DP
Alexander	1.000	3	14	0	0	3
Candelario	.974	3	35	3	1	4
Gatewood	1.000	1	4	0	0	0
Hernandez	.889	1	7	1	1	0
Rojas	1.000	10	56	2	0	7
Rumfield	.991	126	939	73	9	81
Smith	1.000	9	58	11	0	6

Second Base	PCT	G	PO	A	E	DP
Burt	1.000	4	10	13	0	4
Gatewood	.986	18	28	44	1	11
LeMahieu	1.000	2	3	6	0	0
Lopez	.975	11	21	18	1	5
Rojas	.969	17	27	36	2	8
Shewmake	.939	9	13	18	2	7
Velazquez	1.000	26	35	63	0	10
Vivas	.983	68	126	159	5	40

Third Base	PCT	G	PO	A	E	DP
Alexander	.905	9	3	16	2	0
Candelario	.968	53	37	83	4	6
Gatewood	.963	11	6	20	1	4
LeMahieu	1.000	1	1	2	0	0
Rodriguez	.873	19	13	35	7	4
Rojas	.818	17	9	18	6	3
Shewmake	1.000	5	3	10	0	1
Velazquez	.875	8	4	3	1	1
Vivas	.924	33	13	60	6	5

Shortstop	PCT	G	PO	A	E	DP
Gatewood	.969	7	12	19	1	4
Lopez	1.000	6	6	20	0	4
Shewmake	.981	70	86	173	5	27
Velazquez	.976	71	93	187	7	34

Outfield	PCT	G	PO	A	E	DP
Alexander	1.000	5	6	0	0	0
Davis	.963	24	24	2	1	0
De La Cruz	.979	88	131	6	3	1
Ellis	.983	62	116	1	2	1
Hummel	1.000	5	2	0	0	0
Jones	.993	67	140	0	1	0
Munguia	.987	86	148	2	2	1
Pereira	.974	60	109	4	3	0
Richardson	.950	14	19	0	1	0
Rojas	1.000	37	55	2	0	1
Slater	1.000	4	4	0	0	0
Smith	1.000	27	33	1	0	0
Velazquez	.000	1	0	0	0	0

SOMERSET PATRIOTS
EASTERN LEAGUE
DOUBLE-A

Batting	B-T	Ht.	Wt.	DOB	AVG	OBP	SLG	G	PA	AB	R	H	2B	3B	HR	RBI	BB	HBP	SH	SF	SO	SB	CS	BB%	SO%
Avina, Jace	R-R	5-11	180	6-6-03	.224	.314	.341	46	194	170	18	38	11	0	3	14	19	4	0	1	50	2	2	9.8	25.8
Burt, Max	R-R	6-1	185	8-28-96	.221	.292	.289	64	215	190	25	42	13	0	0	22	13	7	3	2	56	11	1	6.0	26.0
Castillo, Jackson	L-L	6-0	195	5-2-03	.210	.301	.321	23	93	81	11	17	3	0	2	8	10	1	0	1	21	1	0	10.8	22.6
Chisholm, Jazz	L-R	5-11	184	2-1-98	.333	.400	.444	3	10	9	2	3	1	0	0	0	1	0	0	0	1	0	0	10.0	10.0
Colmenares, Jose	R-R	5-11	173	4-3-02	.100	.174	.150	9	23	20	1	2	1	0	0	1	1	1	0	0	9	0	0	4.3	39.1
Davis, Brennen	R-R	6-0	210	11-2-99	.231	.429	.462	8	35	26	7	6	0	0	2	5	8	1	0	0	9	1	0	22.9	25.7
Eden, Cam	R-R	6-0	205	3-31-98	.176	.247	.270	26	81	74	7	13	2	1	1	2	6	1	0	0	31	6	3	7.4	38.3
Familia, Christopher	L-L	5-11	170	6-10-00	.158	.273	.368	6	22	19	3	3	2	1	0	2	3	0	0	0	8	0	0	13.6	36.4
Flores, Rafael	R-R	6-4	220	11-7-00	.287	.346	.496	87	370	335	48	96	23	1	15	56	30	2	0	3	94	6	0	8.1	25.4
Frick, Tomas	R-R	6-0	200	10-11-00	.245	.321	.347	16	56	49	3	12	2	0	1	6	4	0	0	1	10	0	0	10.7	17.9
Gabrielson, Cole	R-R	6-0	185	7-5-00	.188	.306	.314	77	272	229	43	9	1	6	30	37	3	0	2	96	14	3	13.6	35.3
Gatewood, Henry	R-R	6-5	190	9-25-95	.233	.313	.395	38	145	129	18	30	13	1	2	12	14	0	0	46	2	1	9.7	31.7
Gomez, Antonio	R-R	6-2	210	11-13-01	.140	.225	.168	35	121	107	6	15	3	0	0	7	12	0	1	1	41	2	0	9.9	33.9
Hardman, Tyler	R-R	6-2	204	1-27-99	.228	.294	.458	115	453	413	57	94	25	5	20	65	38	1	0	1	143	12	3	8.4	31.6
Hernandez, Diomedes	R-R	5-11	165	2-6-05	.156	.219	.156	10	34	32	1	5	2	0	0	2	0	0	0	0	15	0	0	0.0	47.1
Jasso, Dylan	R-R	6-3	196	11-30-02	.257	.326	.400	127	537	478	62	123	17	6	13	76	42	10	0	7	130	1	2	7.8	24.2
Jones, Brendan	L-L	5-10	175	4-24-02	.250	.365	.415	80	340	284	54	71	14	6	7	46	52	1	0	3	71	28	5	15.3	20.9
LeMahieu, DJ	R-R	6-4	220	7-13-88	.438	.500	.688	6	18	16	5	7	1	0	1	3	2	0	0	0	3	0	0	11.1	16.7

NEW YORK YANKEES

Batting

Player	B-T	Ht	Wt	DOB	AVG	OBP	SLG	G	AB	R	H	2B	3B	HR	RBI	BB	SO	HBP	SH	SF	SB	CS	XBH%	K%
Lombard, George	R-R	6-3	190	6-2-05	.215	.337	.358	108	469	391	68	84	24	4	8	36	64	10	0	4	124	24	6	13.6	26.4
Martin, Garrett	R-R	6-4	216	6-28-00	.222	.292	.389	102	408	360	50	80	14	2	14	48	28	10	0	6	97	20	4	6.9	23.8
Martinez, Omar	L-R	5-10	192	7-5-01	.212	.281	.376	24	96	85	11	18	5	0	3	10	9	0	0	2	26	0	0	9.4	27.1
Morales, Coby	L-R	6-3	225	12-5-01	.211	.260	.244	26	96	90	7	19	3	0	0	2	6	0	0	0	31	2	0	6.3	32.3
Palencia, Manuel	R-R	5-11	175	9-5-02	.230	.253	.284	21	80	74	7	17	4	0	0	7	3	0	1	2	18	1	0	3.8	22.5
Pastore, Duncan	R-R	6-3	175	5-27-00	.196	.263	.235	20	57	51	3	10	2	0	0	3	3	2	0	1	12	0	0	5.3	21.1
Richardson, Grant	L-L	6-0	210	7-13-99	.137	.228	.235	17	58	51	4	7	2	0	1	4	6	0	1	0	24	1	0	10.3	41.4
Riggio, Roc	L-R	5-9	180	6-11-02	.261	.335	.542	40	170	153	25	40	10	0	11	28	13	4	0	0	37	7	3	7.6	21.8
Rodriguez, Jesus	R-R	5-9	182	4-23-02	.107	.167	.107	7	30	28	1	3	0	0	0	2	2	0	0	0	6	1	1	6.7	20.0
Stanton, Giancarlo	R-R	6-6	245	11-8-89	.273	.333	.364	3	12	11	0	3	1	0	0	4	1	0	0	0	3	0	0	8.3	25.0
Vargas, Alexander	S-R	5-10	148	10-29-01	.227	.299	.333	42	147	132	13	30	7	2	1	13	12	2	0	1	33	10	4	8.2	22.4
Wegner, Jared	R-R	6-0	220	7-25-99	.168	.262	.242	47	172	149	18	25	5	0	2	14	15	5	0	3	61	4	2	8.7	35.5

Pitching

Player	B-T	Ht.	Wt.	DOB	W	L	ERA	G	GS	SV	IP	Hits	Runs	ER	HR	BB	SO	AVG	OBP	SLG	SO%	BB%	BF
Anderson, Ryan	L-L	6-6	205	9-9-98	3	1	4.14	33	0	2	41	34	20	19	3	18	34	.222	.309	.353	19.3	10.2	176
Arias, Michael	R-R	6-0	155	11-15-01	3	0	2.57	17	0	1	21	19	9	6	2	15	29	.235	.354	.370	30.2	15.6	96
Austin, Kelly	R-R	6-0	195	12-17-00	3	2	2.95	43	0	7	43	35	17	14	2	28	37	.215	.326	.313	19.2	14.5	193
Ayers, Cole	R-R	6-3	185	8-17-99	1	1	5.29	28	1	1	32	35	19	19	3	22	29	.271	.377	.411	18.7	14.2	155
Barclay, Edgar	L-L	5-10	200	5-25-98	1	0	3.77	4	3	0	14	10	6	6	1	8	16	.200	.333	.340	26.2	13.1	61
Beck, Brendan	R-R	6-2	205	10-6-98	5	2	1.82	11	9	0	54	38	12	11	2	12	52	.193	.238	.279	24.8	5.7	210
Beeter, Clayton	R-R	6-2	220	10-9-98	0	1	13.50	2	0	0	2	1	3	3	0	3	2	.167	.400	.167	20.0	30.0	10
Brian, Will	L-L	5-11	220	4-25-99	2	1	2.48	29	1	2	36	30	13	10	1	18	38	.222	.318	.289	24.5	11.6	155
Brubaker, JT	R-R	6-3	185	11-17-93	0	0	1.35	2	2	0	7	2	2	1	0	3	3	.095	.208	.095	12.5	12.5	24
Carr, Kyle	L-L	6-1	175	5-6-02	0	1	8.56	3	3	0	14	14	13	13	2	8	13	.275	.373	.490	22.0	13.6	59
Cohen, Harrison	R-R	6-0	190	5-26-99	1	2	2.01	20	0	2	22	12	6	5	1	13	30	.158	.290	.224	32.3	14.0	93
Coleman, Carson	R-R	6-2	190	4-7-98	0	0	2.57	7	0	2	7	5	3	2	0	1	5	.200	.222	.280	18.5	3.7	27
Cruz, Fernando	R-R	6-2	237	3-28-90	0	0	3.86	2	0	0	2	2	1	1	0	1	5	.222	.300	.556	50.0	10.0	10
De Los Santos, Yerry	R-R	6-2	215	12-12-97	0	0	18.00	1	0	0	1	3	2	2	1	0	2	.500	.500	1.000	33.3	0.0	6
Dees, Bailey	R-R	6-8	250	2-5-99	5	4	4.21	17	9	0	62	50	30	29	7	31	71	.222	.327	.347	26.9	11.7	264
Diaz, Indigo	R-R	6-5	250	10-14-98	8	3	2.58	42	0	6	52	36	18	15	2	22	46	.191	.274	.261	21.4	10.2	215
Effross, Scott	R-R	6-2	202	12-28-93	1	0	5.40	3	0	0	3	6	2	2	0	1	4	.375	.412	.500	23.5	5.9	17
Gil, Luis	R-R	6-2	185	6-3-98	0	0	4.05	2	2	0	7	4	3	3	2	3	13	.167	.259	.458	48.1	11.1	27
Gilbert, Geoffrey	L-L	6-0	215	5-3-01	0	0	2.16	6	0	0	8	7	2	2	0	5	12	.233	.343	.267	34.3	14.3	35
Greene, Zach	R-R	6-1	215	8-29-96	0	1	0.00	2	0	0	2	1	0	0	0	1	2	.167	.286	.167	28.6	14.3	7
Hernandez, Diomedes	R-R	5-11	165	2-6-05	0	0	0.00	1	0	0	2	0	0	0	0	1	1	.000	.286	.000	14.3	14.3	7
Hess, Ben	R-R	6-5	215	9-19-01	3	3	2.70	7	7	0	37	22	11	11	1	13	45	.172	.250	.203	31.3	9.0	144
Keane, Sebastian	R-R	6-3	187	11-2-00	0	0	4.50	1	0	0	2	1	1	1	1	0	1	.143	.333	.571	0.0	11.1	9
Lagrange, Carlos	R-R	6-7	195	5-25-03	7	6	3.22	16	15	0	78	51	31	28	4	50	104	.185	.320	.268	31.0	14.9	335
Leiter, Mark	R-R	6-0	210	3-13-91	0	0	0.00	1	0	0	1	0	0	0	0	1	0	.000	.000	.000	0.0	25.0	4
Merda, Hayden	R-R	6-4	202	3-21-00	3	1	4.38	22	0	1	25	16	13	12	3	19	21	.182	.339	.364	19.3	17.4	109
Messinger, Zach	R-R	6-6	225	10-4-99	0	1	8.53	5	0	0	6	9	7	6	2	2	6	.321	.367	.571	20.0	6.7	30
Morrill, Hueston	R-R	6-0	168	11-27-99	0	0	4.15	3	0	0	4	3	2	2	1	5	4	.188	.381	.563	19.0	23.8	21
Olsen, Jon	R-R	6-2	190	11-10-99	0	0	4.50	2	1	0	4	4	2	2	1	6	1	.250	.294	.313	35.3	5.9	17
Pacheco, Luis	R-R	6-2	185	4-22-99	3	1	5.82	35	0	0	39	40	28	25	5	16	37	.265	.335	.457	21.6	9.4	171
Pastore, Duncan	R-R	6-3	175	5-27-00	0	0	0.00	1	0	0	1	0	0	0	0	1	0	.500	.667	.500	0.0	33.3	3
Percival, Cole	R-R	6-5	220	2-26-99	0	1	12.60	5	0	0	5	9	7	7	1	5	7	.391	.500	.522	24.1	17.2	29
Rodriguez-Cruz, Elmer	L-R	6-3	160	8-18-03	5	3	2.64	11	11	0	61	44	21	18	2	20	74	.198	.263	.279	30.3	8.2	244
Schlittler, Cam	R-R	6-6	210	2-5-01	4	5	2.38	10	9	0	53	47	19	14	1	17	64	.242	.303	.314	30.2	8.0	212
Schmidt, Clarke	R-R	6-1	200	2-20-96	0	0	0.00	2	2	0	7	4	0	0	0	1	11	.154	.185	.231	40.7	3.7	27
Sellers, Trent	R-R	6-1	200	10-30-99	2	5	3.92	22	22	0	96	80	45	42	10	50	111	.225	.328	.379	26.9	12.1	412
Selvidge, Brock	R-L	6-3	205	8-28-02	2	6	4.92	16	15	0	75	69	43	41	6	38	61	.251	.339	.378	18.9	11.8	323
Shields, Ben	R-L	6-4	210	1-23-99	1	2	3.42	5	5	0	24	19	9	9	1	10	26	.232	.305	.317	27.1	10.4	96
Stroman, Marcus	R-R	5-7	180	5-1-91	0	1	6.97	3	3	0	10	13	9	8	0	5	9	.317	.391	.439	19.6	10.9	46
Stuart, Baron	R-R	6-4	209	7-24-99	1	2	4.20	21	6	1	45	28	25	21	3	28	45	.177	.311	.285	23.6	14.7	191
Ventura, Jordany	R-R	6-0	162	7-6-00	3	1	5.66	17	0	1	21	16	17	13	1	19	23	.211	.374	.316	23.2	19.2	99
Vinyard, Mason	R-R	6-2	210	6-22-99	3	3	4.05	40	1	2	47	33	21	21	4	26	53	.202	.321	.331	26.9	13.2	197
Vrieling, Trystan	R-R	6-4	200	6-10-00	1	2	4.50	12	10	0	46	52	26	23	6	18	42	.286	.361	.462	20.5	8.8	205
Watson, Danny	R-R	6-7	235	10-6-00	1	4	4.74	43	0	5	57	61	31	30	6	8	57	.275	.312	.419	24.3	3.4	235
White, Colby	R-R	6-0	190	7-4-98	1	0	12.79	4	0	0	6	11	9	9	1	7	5	.355	.487	.516	12.8	17.9	39
Ziehl, Gage	R-R	6-0	212	5-15-03	0	0	9.00	1	1	0	5	4	9	4	4	1	0	.429	.429	.571	19.0	0.0	21

Fielding

Catcher

	PCT	G	PO	A	E	DP	PB
Flores	.990	60	556	33	6	2	4
Frick	.993	16	137	7	1	1	4
Gomez	.995	18	180	10	1	0	1
Hernandez	1.000	7	60	3	0	0	2
Martinez	.975	13	107	8	3	0	2
Palencia	.995	21	209	8	1	0	1
Rodriguez	1.000	3	31	3	0	0	1

First Base

	PCT	G	PO	A	E	DP
Flores	.988	12	78	6	1	7
Hardman	.995	101	689	49	4	61
Hernandez	.909	2	19	1	2	2

Second Base

	PCT	G	PO	A	E	DP
Burt	1.000	23	24	53	0	9
Colmenares	.963	9	16	10	1	3
Gatewood	.969	17	21	41	2	10
Jasso	.969	18	20	42	2	5
LeMahieu	1.000	6	6	7	0	0
Lombard	.973	9	15	21	1	6
Pastore	.942	18	13	31	3	5
Riggio	.974	38	62	88	4	29
Vargas	.900	10	10	17	3	2

	PCT	G	PO	A	E
Jasso	.991	15	96	12	1
Morales	.973	10	70	1	2
Pastore	1.000	1	2	0	0

Third Base

	PCT	G	PO	A	E	DP
Burt	.960	20	15	33	2	1
Chisholm	1.000	2	1	0	0	0
Gatewood	1.000	10	4	15	0	1
Hardman	1.000	3	0	4	0	0
Jasso	.955	83	46	123	8	16
Lombard	.963	10	8	18	1	1
Rodriguez	1.000	4	1	5	0	0
Vargas	1.000	14	8	21	0	0

Shortstop

	PCT	G	PO	A	E
Burt	.970	18	24	41	2	6
Gatewood	.930	14	13	27	3	3

Lombard	.983	89	135	217	6	44			
Vargas	.983	17	21	36	1	6			

Outfield	PCT	G	PO	A	E	DP
Avina	.988	41	80	2	1	1
Castillo	1.000	20	36	1	0	0

Davis	1.000	7	16	0	0	0
Eden	1.000	22	51	3	0	0
Familia	1.000	6	5	0	0	0
Gabrielson	.984	66	120	2	2	1
Hardman	1.000	1	1	0	0	0
Jones	.985	70	124	4	2	1

Martin	.984	90	182	5	3	2
Morales	.875	4	7	0	1	0
Richardson	1.000	15	39	2	0	0
Wegner	.975	41	76	2	2	0

HUDSON VALLEY RENEGADES — HIGH-A
SOUTH ATLANTIC LEAGUE

Batting	B-T	Ht.	Wt.	DOB	AVG	OBP	SLG	G	PA	AB	R	H	2B	3B	HR	RBI	BB	HBP	SH	SF	SO	SB	CS	BB%	SO%
Avina, Jace	R-R	5-11	180	6-6-03	.295	.412	.506	52	221	176	37	52	13	0	8	31	30	9	0	6	54	3	1	13.6	24.4
Burnett, Robbie	L-R	5-10	185	12-1-02	.176	.310	.265	13	42	34	7	6	0	0	1	3	6	1	0	1	14	1	0	14.3	33.3
Castillo, Jackson	L-L	6-0	195	5-2-03	.242	.337	.336	91	406	351	49	85	16	1	5	47	48	4	0	3	81	21	1	11.8	20.0
Cobb, Owen	R-R	6-2	193	6-24-01	.111	.200	.111	9	20	18	3	2	0	0	0	0	1	1	0	0	6	2	0	5.0	30.0
Colmenares, Jose	R-R	5-11	173	4-3-02	.222	.322	.376	76	308	266	36	59	17	3	6	33	35	5	1	1	76	12	5	11.4	24.7
Cristino, John	R-R	6-2	225	12-8-99	.167	.233	.258	21	74	66	11	11	3	0	1	4	3	3	0	1	37	1	0	4.1	50.0
De Los Santos, Joe	R-R	5-10	195	6-26-01	.067	.176	.133	9	34	30	1	2	0	1	0	1	3	1	0	0	12	2	0	8.8	35.3
Durango, Luis	L-L	5-10	135	4-8-03	.258	.351	.268	40	112	97	15	25	1	0	0	9	9	5	1	0	22	17	7	8.0	19.6
Ellis, Duke	L-L	6-1	180	1-16-98	.353	.476	.706	5	21	17	4	6	0	0	2	3	3	1	0	0	4	1	0	14.3	19.0
Escanio, Brenny	S-R	5-9	145	12-16-02	.206	.331	.285	68	256	214	33	44	6	1	3	19	39	1	1	0	72	10	7	15.2	28.1
Frick, Tomas	R-R	6-0	200	10-1-00	.227	.344	.383	44	157	128	22	29	8	0	4	19	16	9	0	4	38	2	0	10.2	24.2
Gomez, Antonio	R-R	6-2	210	11-13-01	.316	.350	.632	6	20	19	2	6	0	0	2	6	1	0	0	0	7	0	0	5.0	35.0
Hall, Anthony	L-L	6-1	200	2-9-01	.222	.300	.306	48	162	144	21	32	7	1	1	13	16	0	0	0	50	6	1	9.9	30.9
Harber, Parks	R-R	6-3	225	9-25-01	.326	.395	.489	34	152	135	20	44	11	1	3	27	16	0	1	5	31	2	1	10.5	23.0
Jackson, Core	R-R	6-0	185	10-11-03	.183	.287	.280	25	108	93	12	17	7	1	0	5	11	3	0	1	31	1	1	10.2	28.7
Jones, Brendan	L-L	5-10	175	4-24-02	.236	.349	.362	44	209	174	35	41	6	2	4	23	30	2	0	3	38	23	4	14.4	18.2
Kent, Kaeden	L-R	6-2	200	8-29-03	.186	.217	.265	25	106	102	8	19	6	2	0	2	17	3	1	0	0	19	0	1	2.8	17.9
Lewis, Dillon	R-R	6-3	205	6-12-03	.228	.320	.426	76	332	289	39	66	12	3	13	50	36	4	0	2	69	1	1	10.8	20.8
Lombard, George	R-R	6-3	190	6-2-05	.329	.495	.488	24	111	82	22	27	8	1	1	13	23	5	0	1	22	11	2	20.7	19.8
Martinez, Omar	L-R	5-10	192	7-5-01	.231	.337	.377	57	249	212	28	49	7	0	8	36	32	3	0	2	76	1	2	12.9	30.5
Matheus, Juan	S-R	5-10	155	4-29-04	.287	.381	.398	28	126	108	10	31	9	0	1	13	16	1	0	1	22	5	3	12.7	17.5
McGinnis, Connor	R-R	6-1	185	12-9-02	.196	.297	.250	17	64	56	6	11	1	1	0	6	8	0	0	0	17	0	0	12.5	26.6
Morales, Coby	L-R	6-3	225	12-5-01	.251	.332	.385	90	382	338	45	85	18	3	7	47	37	5	0	2	92	15	3	9.7	24.1
Moylan, Josh	L-R	6-4	216	7-3-02	.221	.343	.348	114	452	376	46	83	21	3	7	50	64	8	0	4	134	9	2	14.2	29.6
Palencia, Manuel	R-R	5-11	175	5-9-02	.250	.286	.300	16	63	60	11	15	3	0	0	8	3	0	0	0	12	0	1	4.8	19.0
Pastore, Duncan	R-R	6-3	195	5-27-00	.256	.360	.326	16	50	43	6	11	3	0	0	5	7	0	0	0	12	1	2	14.0	24.0
Riggio, Roc	L-R	5-9	180	6-11-02	.264	.436	.597	20	94	72	20	19	4	1	6	15	20	2	0	0	22	2	4	21.3	23.4
Romero, Kiko	R-R	5-11	185	9-18-00	.204	.333	.333	20	66	54	6	11	1	0	2	6	7	4	0	1	16	2	0	10.6	24.2
Troyer, Camden	L-L	6-0	195	8-3-02	.253	.356	.320	22	87	75	12	19	2	0	1	8	12	0	0	0	13	1	1	13.8	14.9
Urena, Engelth	R-R	5-11	196	8-17-04	.158	.278	.197	22	90	76	8	12	3	0	0	4	12	1	0	1	17	0	1	13.3	18.9
Vargas, Alexander	S-R	5-10	148	10-29-01	.225	.285	.379	47	186	169	20	38	4	2	6	22	13	2	0	2	23	10	1	7.0	12.4
Vivas, Edison	R-R	6-0	184	6-3-06	.000	.000	.000	1	1	1	0	0	0	0	0	0	0	0	0	0	0	0	0	0.0	0.0
Wilson, Tyler	S-R	6-2	210	7-10-02	.277	.333	.319	14	52	47	3	13	2	0	0	4	4	0	0	0	9	0	1	7.7	17.3

Pitching	B-T	Ht.	Wt.	DOB	W	L	ERA	G	GS	SV	IP	Hits	Runs	ER	HR	BB	SO	AVG	OBP	SLG	SO%	BB%	BF
Arias, Michael	R-R	6-0	155	11-15-01	0	0	3.00	2	0	0	3	1	2	1	0	1	3	.091	.286	.273	21.4	7.1	14
Ayers, Cole	R-R	6-3	185	8-17-99	0	0	0.00	4	0	2	6	0	0	0	0	1	5	.000	.050	.000	25.0	5.0	20
Brian, Will	L-L	5-11	220	4-25-99	1	0	0.00	4	0	1	7	4	0	0	0	1	12	.160	.192	.200	46.2	3.8	26
Brubaker, JT	R-R	6-3	185	11-17-93	0	0	0.00	1	1	0	3	1	0	0	0	0	3	.111	.200	.111	30.0	0.0	10
Carr, Kyle	L-L	6-1	175	5-6-02	8	6	1.96	22	22	0	119	81	35	26	6	47	104	.190	.276	.255	21.7	9.8	479
Cebert, Jack	R-R	6-3	190	4-1-02	0	0	2.84	5	0	0	6	4	2	2	1	11	.167	.200	.417	44.0	4.0	25
Cobb, Owen	R-R	6-2	193	6-24-01	0	0	0.00	1	0	0	0	0	0	0	0	0	0	.000	.000	.000	0.0	0.0	1
Coleman, Carson	R-R	6-2	190	4-7-98	0	0	0.00	4	0	0	4	1	0	0	0	1	3	.083	.154	.083	23.1	7.7	13
Cousins, Jake	R-R	6-4	193	7-14-94	0	0	7.71	2	0	0	2	4	2	2	0	0	4	.400	.400	.400	36.4	0.0	11
Cunningham, Bryce	R-R	6-5	234	12-8-02	5	3	2.82	12	11	0	54	42	20	17	4	19	55	.213	.292	.325	25.0	8.6	220
Decker, Brandon	R-R	6-3	175	7-10-02	2	4	4.26	6	6	0	32	25	16	15	1	16	39	.208	.317	.317	27.9	11.4	140
Dees, Bailey	R-R	6-8	250	2-5-99	1	0	0.00	1	1	0	7	0	0	0	0	5	.045	.087	.091	39.1	0.0	23
Gabonia, Ocean	R-R	6-1	175	7-31-01	5	2	3.27	31	0	1	41	34	20	15	0	15	42	.217	.311	.344	23.9	8.5	176
Gilbert, Geoffrey	L-L	6-3	215	5-3-01	3	0	2.55	25	1	2	35	23	11	10	2	17	51	.180	.289	.266	34.2	11.4	149
Grosz, Josh	R-R	6-4	199	9-5-02	4	8	4.14	16	15	0	87	66	46	40	5	35	94	.211	.292	.342	26.0	9.7	361
Herring, Griffin	R-L	6-2	182	5-7-03	2	2	2.22	8	8	0	45	32	13	11	1	20	44	.201	.291	.289	23.9	10.9	184
Hess, Ben	R-R	6-5	210	6-5-02	4	3	3.51	15	15	0	67	43	30	26	2	33	94	.179	.288	.288	33.9	11.9	277
Kean, Chris	R-R	6-5	210	6-12-02	6	2	3.48	33	0	0	41	35	18	16	4	16	37	.227	.298	.383	21.5	9.3	172
Keane, Sebastian	R-R	6-3	183	11-2-00	7	0	3.38	26	1	1	37	27	18	14	3	20	38	.200	.313	.304	23.8	12.5	160
Keating, Matt	R-R	6-3	215	12-8-00	3	1	2.57	34	1	2	49	34	17	14	1	26	58	.195	.324	.284	27.9	12.5	208
Kirtner, Brady	R-R	5-11	170	11-21-01	0	0	3.60	5	0	1	5	5	2	2	0	1	5	.263	.300	.368	25.0	5.0	20
Lagrange, Carlos	R-R	6-7	195	5-25-03	4	2	4.10	8	8	0	42	31	20	19	4	12	64	.203	.268	.359	38.1	7.1	168
Landry, Andrew	R-R	6-1	175	2-20-02	3	4	3.95	8	8	0	43	39	19	19	2	25	39	.197	.322	.303	21.2	13.6	184
Merda, Hayden	R-R	6-4	202	3-21-01	0	1	3.68	12	1	1	29	22	14	12	3	13	43	.210	.311	.324	34.7	10.5	124
Morrill, Hueston	R-R	6-0	168	11-27-99	4	1	0.42	33	0	4	43	15	3	2	1	12	38	.110	.182	.147	25.5	8.1	149
Rivas, Xavier	L-L	6-3	220	7-11-02	3	1	1.23	5	5	0	29	9	4	4	1	14	44	.095	.230	.147	38.9	12.4	113
Rodriguez-Cruz, Elmer	L-R	6-3	160	8-18-03	6	4	2.26	15	14	0	84	52	27	21	1	37	99	.174	.268	.234	29.0	10.9	341
Rossi, Tony	R-R	6-3	230	7-7-99	0	2	2.63	35	0	9	38	27	15	11	0	26	52	.126	.317	.134	31.5	15.8	165
Sandridge, Jayvien	L-L	6-5	220	2-11-99	0	1	11.57	2	0	0	2	3	4	2	0	5	3	.250	.250	.417	25.0	0.0	12
Shields, Ben	R-L	6-4	210	1-23-96	0	0	0.00	2	2	0	7	1	0	0	0	4	7	.130	.310	.217	24.1	13.8	29

Batting	B-T	Ht.	Wt.	DOB																			
Smith, Cade	L-R	6-1	190	4-9-02	2	1	2.76	8	8	0	33	20	10	10	2	16	35	.172	.271	.250	26.3	12.0	133
Ventura, Jordany	R-R	6-0	162	7-6-00	0	0	1.32	13	0	0	14	6	4	2	0	16	18	.125	.382	.146	26.5	23.5	68
Warrecker, Bryce	L-R	6-8	225	9-13-01	2	1	2.05	40	1	5	57	35	13	13	1	13	61	.176	.228	.261	28.2	6.0	216
Yulie, Tyrone	R-R	6-4	180	8-4-01	1	3	5.50	36	0	0	38	32	24	23	5	24	43	.227	.345	.376	25.6	14.3	168
Ziehl, Gage	R-R	6-0	212	5-15-03	1	0	2.25	1	0	0	4	3	1	1	0	0	3	.231	.214	.231	21.4	0.0	14

Fielding

Catcher	PCT	G	PO	A	E	DP	PB
Cristino	.989	20	175	8	2	0	1
Frick	.989	38	343	16	4	2	4
Gomez	.957	3	21	1	1	0	3
Martinez	.981	38	394	25	8	4	9
Palencia	.980	15	141	8	3	2	1
Urena	.990	18	189	12	2	0	5

First Base	PCT	G	PO	A	E	DP
Harber	1.000	6	43	3	0	2
Morales	.995	52	374	33	2	27
Moylan	.993	59	407	38	3	35
Pastore	1.000	3	12	2	0	1
Romero	1.000	12	73	5	0	2
Wilson	1.000	3	17	0	0	2

Second Base	PCT	G	PO	A	E	DP
Cobb	.933	6	6	8	1	1
Colmenares	.964	57	88	126	8	19
Escanio	1.000	20	21	45	0	10

Third Base	PCT	G	PO	A	E	DP
Colmenares	.913	12	7	14	2	0
Escanio	.920	12	10	13	2	0
Harber	.960	20	17	31	2	5
Kent	1.000	3	0	4	0	0
Lombard	1.000	1	0	3	0	0
Matheus	.967	25	19	39	2	0
Moylan	.899	47	25	73	11	2
Vargas	.957	11	4	18	1	1

Shortstop	PCT	G	PO	A	E	DP
Colmenares	.968	6	14	16	1	5
Escanio	.944	37	26	75	6	9

	PCT	G	PO	A	E	DP	PB
Jackson	1.000	9	17	21	0	4	
Lombard	1.000	1	0	4	0	0	
McGinnis	.978	14	16	29	1	6	
Pastore	.967	10	9	20	1	2	
Riggio	1.000	14	18	28	0	2	
Vargas	1.000	1	2	2	0	1	

	PCT	G	PO	A	E	DP
Jackson	.962	12	21	29	2	6
Kent	.980	18	14	36	1	5
Lombard	.986	22	27	41	1	8
Vargas	.948	35	35	75	6	17

Outfield	PCT	G	PO	A	E	DP
Avina	.974	42	72	4	2	1
Burnett	.967	13	28	1	1	0
Castillo	1.000	87	128	4	0	2
De Los Santos	1.000	5	7	0	0	0
Durango	.963	34	51	1	2	1
Ellis	.909	5	10	0	1	0
Hall	1.000	46	64	0	0	0
Jones	1.000	42	87	1	0	1
Lewis	.972	64	133	5	4	1
Morales	1.000	25	48	1	0	0
Moylan	1.000	1	2	0	0	0
Romero	1.000	3	3	0	0	0
Troyer	1.000	20	33	0	0	0
Wilson	1.000	11	25	0	0	0

NEW YORK YANKEES

TAMPA TARPONS
FLORIDA STATE LEAGUE
LOW-A

Batting	B-T	Ht.	Wt.	DOB	AVG	OBP	SLG	G	PA	AB	R	H	2B	3B	HR	RBI	BB	HBP	SH	SF	SO	SB	CS	BB%	SO%
Arias, Roderick	S-R	6-0	178	9-9-04	.208	.325	.315	103	465	394	61	82	19	1	7	53	65	4	0	1	134	34	10	14.0	28.8
Bonomolo, Richard	R-R	5-11	195	10-30-03	.167	.296	.233	18	71	60	12	10	4	0	0	4	9	2	0	0	18	5	0	12.7	25.4
Cobb, Owen	R-R	6-2	193	6-24-01	.310	.363	.488	40	148	129	22	40	8	3	2	22	12	1	0	4	30	12	3	8.1	20.3
Eden, Cam	R-R	6-1	205	3-31-98	.313	.389	.438	5	18	16	2	5	0	1	0	1	2	0	0	0	2	1	0	11.1	11.1
Genther, Eric	L-R	6-3	200	6-16-02	.256	.448	.419	17	58	43	10	11	4	0	1	3	10	5	0	0	7	2	0	17.2	12.1
Gomez, Santiago	R-R	5-11	160	4-5-04	.170	.310	.255	15	58	47	5	8	1	0	1	7	7	3	0	1	16	9	1	12.1	27.6
Gonzalez, Josue	R-R	5-9	170	10-30-03	.171	.306	.287	78	265	216	35	37	9	2	4	20	37	7	0	5	60	14	2	14.0	22.6
Green, Austin	S-R	6-0	195	5-20-02	.184	.292	.291	49	185	158	26	29	3	1	4	30	20	5	0	2	39	8	0	10.8	21.1
Harber, Parks	L-R	6-3	225	9-25-01	.304	.422	.551	20	83	69	12	21	4	2	3	13	12	2	0	0	22	4	1	14.5	26.5
Kilby, Dax	L-R	6-2	190	11-17-06	.353	.457	.441	18	81	68	19	24	2	2	0	9	13	0	0	0	11	16	1	16.0	13.6
Lewis, Dillon	R-R	6-3	205	6-12-03	.250	.323	.477	46	195	176	33	44	9	2	9	29	18	1	0	0	55	13	1	9.2	28.2
Lovich, Jackson	R-R	6-4	192	11-18-03	.636	.692	1.000	6	26	22	9	14	4	2	0	9	4	0	0	0	3	0	0	15.4	11.5
Martin-Grudzielanek, Bryce	R-R	6-3	185	6-5-03	.247	.294	.416	24	85	77	15	19	2	4	1	18	6	0	0	2	16	6	1	7.1	18.8
Matheus, Juan	S-R	5-10	155	4-29-04	.271	.360	.369	95	394	336	51	91	23	2	2	43	48	3	0	7	74	35	8	12.2	18.8
Montero, Hans	R-R	5-9	160	12-25-03	.269	.357	.431	89	334	290	43	78	13	2	10	53	36	5	1	2	112	25	8	10.8	33.5
Montero, Willy	R-R	6-4	202	8-4-04	.271	.324	.329	45	185	170	14	46	5	1	1	27	14	0	0	1	42	2	3	7.6	22.7
Pastore, Duncan	R-R	6-3	175	5-27-00	.143	.143	.286	3	7	7	1	1	0	0	1	0	0	0	0	0	1	0	0	0.0	14.3
Perez, Edgleen	R-R	5-10	155	5-25-06	.209	.369	.235	84	382	302	41	63	8	0	0	26	69	9	0	2	74	5	1	18.1	19.4
Rivera, Ediel	R-R	6-1	185	9-23-05	.164	.303	.200	18	66	55	11	9	2	0	0	7	5	6	0	0	20	6	1	7.6	30.3
Rodriguez, Wilson	L-L	6-1	186	9-10-04	.237	.342	.392	30	117	97	13	23	5	2	2	8	15	2	0	3	23	3	2	12.8	19.7
Sanchez, Brian	L-R	5-9	170	7-4-04	.281	.373	.438	63	286	242	39	68	16	5	4	36	36	2	0	4	67	24	4	12.6	23.4
Tejeda, Emanuel	R-R	5-11	158	12-25-04	.242	.389	.342	35	149	120	25	29	1	0	3	20	26	3	0	0	20	13	1	17.4	13.4
Toole, Marshall	L-R	5-11	185	3-17-03	.305	.406	.479	96	372	315	66	96	14	13	5	48	52	3	0	2	73	44	6	14.0	19.6
Urena, Engelth	R-R	5-11	196	8-17-04	.207	.328	.329	91	400	334	54	69	14	0	9	42	53	9	0	4	77	8	3	13.3	19.3
West, Kyle	L-R	6-4	215	9-10-02	.246	.375	.306	11	40	36	7	9	2	0	0	3	3	1	0	0	14	1	0	7.5	35.0
Wilson, Tyler	S-R	6-2	210	7-10-02	.283	.375	.372	77	314	269	41	76	9	0	5	38	41	0	0	2	68	15	8	13.1	21.7

Pitching	B-T	Ht.	Wt.	DOB	W	L	ERA	G	GS	SV	IP	Hits	Runs	ER	HR	BB	SO	AVG	OBP	SLG	SO%	BB%	BF
Arias, Michael	R-R	6-0	155	11-15-01	0	0	6.75	2	1	0	3	2	2	2	0	1	1	.250	.300	.250	10.0	10.0	10
Austin, Cade	R-R	6-3	230	9-28-01	5	1	3.08	37	1	2	53	46	25	18	5	24	57	.235	.323	.352	25.1	10.6	227
Bauman, Tanner	L-L	6-5	225	5-7-02	4	7	7.91	25	7	0	60	63	59	53	3	55	60	.276	.421	.389	19.8	18.2	303
Beeter, Clayton	R-R	6-2	220	10-9-98	0	0	0.00	1	0	0	1	0	0	0	0	4	.000	.000	.000	100.0	0.0	4
Boudreau, Tyler	S-R	6-0	170	12-23-02	0	0	1.80	4	1	0	5	3	1	1	0	3	9	.176	.300	.235	45.0	15.0	20
Bustamante, Alex	R-R	6-3	195	6-22-00	0	0	4.76	6	0	1	5	2	3	3	0	7	6	.100	.333	.100	22.2	25.9	27
Carter, Greysen	R-R	6-4	241	12-15-02	1	3	6.75	7	7	0	24	20	20	18	1	27	25	.177	.403	.283	20.2	21.8	124
Coleman, Carson	R-R	6-2	190	4-7-98	0	0	0.00	3	1	0	3	0	0	0	0	4	.000	.000	.000	40.0	0.0	10
Decker, Brandon	R-R	6-3	195	7-10-02	1	4	3.23	19	11	0	53	50	27	19	2	26	53	.243	.345	.306	22.2	10.9	239
Facundo, Allen	L-R	6-0	171	9-3-02	1	1	2.14	8	8	0	34	22	10	8	0	14	35	.195	.303	.239	26.5	10.6	132
Flatt, Danny	R-R	6-0	190	6-6-04	1	2	4.33	7	7	0	27	17	17	13	2	17	21	.255	.359	.377	16.3	13.2	129
Fristoe, Jackson	R-R	6-4	210	3-6-01	7	2	4.30	32	0	2	59	46	29	28	9	32	46	.216	.323	.390	18.3	12.7	251
Gomez, Antonio	R-R	6-2	210	11-13-01	0	1	20.25	4	0	0	3	6	6	6	2	4	.429	.500	.500	25.0	12.5	16
Gonzalez, Josue	R-R	5-9	170	10-30-03	0	0	18.00	1	0	0	1	0	2	2	0	0	.750	.600/1.000		0.0	0.0	5
Hermann, Sean	R-R	6-0	160	6-13-03	2	1	3.17	37	0	33	45	30	21	0	33	45	.211	.335	.258	17.4	12.8	258
Herrera, Franyer	L-L	6-2	165	5-3-05	2	0	0.00	5	0	0	5	3	0	0	0	5	12	.143	.250	.143	29.3	12.2	41

NEW YORK YANKEES

Player	B-T	Ht.	Wt.	DOB				AVG																		
Herring, Griffin	R-L	6-2	182	5-7-03	4	1	1.21	8	8	0	45	24	7	6	2	16	58	.155	.236	.232	33.3	9.2	174			
Hughes, Gus	R-R	6-0	195	5-1-02	4	3	3.80	35	0	1	45	38	26	19	4	20	42	.229	.332	.349	21.4	10.2	196			
Kirtner, Brady	R-R	5-11	170	11-21-01	4	2	2.59	30	0	3	42	27	13	12	2	20	47	.180	.287	.260	26.7	11.4	176			
Lalane, Henry	L-L	6-7	211	5-18-04	0	0	1.65	6	6	0	16	10	3	3	1	13	20	.182	.370	.273	27.4	17.8	73			
Landry, Andrew	R-R	6-1	175	2-20-02	4	4	4.59	15	14	0	69	77	44	35	5	27	66	.280	.359	.393	21.1	8.6	313			
Lange, Justin	R-R	6-4	220	9-11-01	1	1	7.94	6	0	0	6	9	5	5	2	3	4	.360	.467	.680	13.3	10.0	30			
Loaisiga, Jonathan	R-R	5-11	165	11-2-94	0	0	2.70	3	1	0	3	2	1	1	0	0	7	.167	.167	.250	58.3	0.0	12			
Marquez, Edinzo	R-R	6-2	208	12-16-04	1	2	8.57	5	4	0	21	27	23	20	0	13	7	.307	.404	.375	6.7	12.5	104			
Martina, Sunayro	R-R	6-3	165	10-9-03	1	0	7.88	5	3	0	16	23	17	14	1	17	13	.338	.489	.456	14.8	19.3	88			
Matzek, Tyler	L-L	6-3	230	10-19-90	0	0	9.00	1	0	0	1	2	1	1	0	0	2	.400	.400	.400	40.0	0.0	5			
Mendoza, Jordarlin	R-R	6-0	175	11-14-03	0	0	6.75	9	0	0	11	8	8	8	1	10	10	.211	.415	.316	18.9	18.9	53			
Montero, Hans	R-R	5-9	160	12-25-03	0	1	13.50	2	0	0	2	4	4	3	1	0	0	.444	.500	.889	0.0	0.0	12			
Pastore, Duncan	R-R	6-3	175	5-27-00	0	0	0.00	1	0	0	0	0	0	0	0	0	0	.000	.000	.000	0.0	0.0	1			
Rivas, Xavier	L-L	6-3	220	7-11-02	2	3	5.80	10	10	0	40	37	29	26	5	27	47	.237	.353	.397	25.1	14.4	187			
Rodriguez, Jose	R-R	5-11	160	1-6-04	4	1	5.14	6	5	0	28	24	17	16	3	19	28	.238	.363	.386	22.6	15.3	124			
Rossi, Tony	R-R	6-3	230	7-7-99	0	0	0.00	5	0	1	8	2	0	0	0	12	.083	.120	.083	48.0	0.0	25				
Salomon, Mariano	R-R	6-3	185	8-5-02	1	5	5.35	11	4	0	35	35	22	21	5	11	31	.254	.316	.406	20.3	7.2	153			
Sanchez, Juan	L-R	5-11	190	3-21-03	0	0	0.00	2	0	0	1	0	0	0	0	1	0	.000	.333	.000	0.0	16.7	6			
Sandridge, Jayvien	L-L	6-5	220	2-11-99	0	0	0.00	2	0	0	3	1	0	0	0	2	4	.111	.273	.111	36.4	18.2	11			
Selvidge, Brock	R-L	6-3	205	8-28-02	0	1	3.60	2	2	0	5	2	7	2	0	5	5	.100	.280	.100	20.0	20.0	25			
Serna, Luis	R-R	5-11	162	7-20-04	0	2	5.14	4	4	0	7	4	4	4	0	7	10	.167	.355	.208	32.3	22.6	31			
Shields, Ben	R-L	6-4	210	1-23-99	0	0	3.86	1	1	0	2	4	2	1	0	5	.364	.364	.455	45.5	0.0	11				
Smith, Cade	L-R	6-1	190	4-9-02	0	0	3.38	1	1	0	3	3	1	1	0	0	3	.273	.273	.273	27.3	0.0	11			
Sokol, Jack	R-R	6-3	202	12-17-01	5	3	3.60	32	0	1	45	46	27	18	3	22	40	.258	.342	.326	19.7	10.8	203			
Stevens, Kevin	R-R	6-2	225	1-26-98	0	0	0.00	1	0	0	1	1	0	0	0	1	0	.333	.500	.333	0.0	25.0	4			
Tiedemann, Josh	R-R	6-2	190	6-9-04	0	1	7.27	4	0	0	9	7	7	7	2	10	7	.219	.395	.438	16.3	23.3	43			
Veach, Chris	R-R	6-0	195	11-21-01	2	4	2.53	43	0	7	57	46	26	16	5	29	75	.219	.313	.348	30.5	11.8	246			
Vrieling, Trystan	R-R	6-4	200	10-2-00	0	0	4.50	1	1	0	4	4	2	2	0	1	5	.267	.313	.333	31.3	6.3	16			
Zaffiro, Cole	R-R	6-2	190	5-15-02	0	1	4.42	23	0	0	39	33	22	19	8	28	36	.232	.370	.444	20.6	16.0	175			
Ziehl, Gage	R-R	6-0	212	5-15-03	4	4	4.00	14	14	0	74	76	41	33	6	14	63	.262	.308	.379	20.2	4.5	312			

Fielding

Catcher	PCT	G	PO	A	E	DP	PB
Gonzalez	.977	18	113	12	3	0	2
Perez	.973	47	399	35	12	1	7
Rivera	.980	18	135	10	3	0	8
Urena	.987	50	422	26	6	0	9

First Base	PCT	G	PO	A	E	DP
Gonzalez	.984	57	352	22	6	36
Harber	1.000	8	55	5	0	8
Lovich	1.000	6	31	4	0	2
Montero	.968	34	228	15	8	19
West	1.000	10	70	3	0	6
Wilson	.983	21	157	20	3	13

Second Base	PCT	G	PO	A	E	DP
Cobb	.988	22	31	54	1	11
Gomez	1.000	15	26	31	0	8

Third Base	PCT	G	PO	A	E	DP
Arias	.897	14	10	16	3	1
Cobb	.906	12	6	23	3	1
Harber	.919	13	11	23	3	3
Martin-Grudzielanek	.968	15	5	25	1	1
Matheus	.926	63	40	135	14	15
Montero	.909	13	6	24	3	2
Tejeda	.700	3	2	5	3	1

Shortstop	PCT	G	PO	A	E	DP
Arias	.932	82	106	197	22	37

	PCT	G	PO	A	E	DP
Green	.933	35	80	73	11	16
Martin-Grudzielanek	1.000	6	14	12	0	1
Matheus	.958	7	12	11	1	1
Montero	.951	22	35	42	4	13
Tejeda	.964	27	35	71	4	13

Outfield	PCT	G	PO	A	E	DP
Bonomolo	1.000	10	27	0	0	0
Cobb	.818	7	2	7	2	0
Eden	1.000	5	8	2	0	0
Genther	.933	16	27	1	2	0
Green	1.000	13	20	0	0	0
Kilby	.979	14	14	33	1	8
Lewis	.976	44	76	6	2	1
Martin-Grudzielanek	1.000	2	1	0	0	0
Matheus	.964	27	36	72	4	14
Montero	.967	22	27	2	1	0
Montero	1.000	40	42	74	5	0
Rodriguez	.984	29	59	2	1	1
Sanchez	.983	61	115	4	2	1
Toole	.995	97	186	4	1	1
Wilson	.959	54	91	3	4	1

FCL YANKEES — ROOKIE
FLORIDA COMPLEX LEAGUE

Batting	B-T	Ht.	Wt.	DOB	AVG	OBP	SLG	G	PA	AB	R	H	2B	3B	HR	RBI	BB	HBP	SH	SF	SO	SB	CS	BB%	SO%
Arias, Isael	R-R	6-0	178	8-11-05	.182	.259	.240	56	217	192	26	35	6	1	1	20	19	2	1	3	45	26	2	8.8	20.7
Contreras, Johan	R-R	6-1	218	3-10-05	.182	.250	.273	25	72	66	7	12	3	0	1	7	4	2	0	0	31	0	0	5.6	43.1
Cristino, John	R-R	6-2	225	12-4-99	.333	.400	.538	32	105	93	20	31	5	1	4	17	7	4	0	1	25	6	0	6.7	23.8
Davis, Brennen	R-R	6-0	210	11-2-99	.474	.524	1.053	6	21	19	4	9	2	0	3	4	1	1	0	0	4	1	0	4.8	19.0
De Los Santos, Joe	R-R	5-10	195	6-26-01	.000	.333	.000	1	3	2	0	0	0	0	0	0	1	0	0	0	1	0	0	33.3	33.3
Durango, Luis	L-L	5-10	135	4-8-03	.125	.176	.125	5	18	16	2	2	0	0	0	1	1	0	0	0	5	0	1	5.6	27.8
Eden, Juan	R-R	6-1	205	3-31-98	.273	.324	.394	10	37	33	4	9	4	0	0	10	3	0	0	1	4	3	0	8.1	10.8
Ellis, Duke	L-L	6-1	180	1-16-98	.067	.222	.133	5	18	15	2	1	1	0	0	1	3	0	0	0	6	3	0	16.7	33.3
Escudero, Luis	S-R	5-8	165	2-9-06	.212	.333	.314	52	189	156	31	33	3	2	3	20	30	0	0	3	28	13	5	15.9	14.8
Gomez, Santiago	R-R	5-11	160	9-4-05	.254	.374	.325	40	140	114	22	29	2	0	2	15	10	13	0	2	31	20	4	7.1	22.1
Jackson, JoJo	S-L	6-2	215	10-6-02	.071	.133	.071	6	15	14	1	1	0	0	0	0	1	0	0	0	4	1	0	6.7	26.7
Lara, Gabriel	L-L	5-9	165	11-27-05	.277	.312	.406	35	109	101	17	28	5	1	2	15	5	1	0	2	26	4	5	4.6	23.9
Mayea, Brando	R-R	6-1	175	5-27-05	.212	.289	.500	20	84	74	19	22	4	1	3	9	6	3	0	0	19	4	3	7.1	22.6
Montero, Willy	R-R	6-4	202	8-4-04	.212	.235	.212	10	34	33	2	7	0	0	0	1	1	0	0	0	6	1	0	2.9	17.6
Palencia, Manuel	R-R	5-11	175	9-5-02	.312	.380	.422	29	121	109	15	34	7	1	1	14	10	2	0	0	17	1	0	8.3	14.0
Peralta, Dexters	S-R	6-1	170	7-1-05	.221	.423	.221	42	162	140	18	22	3	0	2	8	18	1	0	3	50	10	3	11.1	30.9
Puello, Luis	R-R	5-11	162	1-22-06	.227	.290	.361	39	131	119	24	27	3	1	7	19	7	4	0	1	46	4	0	5.3	35.1
Riggio, Roc	L-R	5-9	180	6-11-02	.333	.333	.833	2	6	6	2	2	0	0	1	2	0	0	0	0	1	0	0	0.0	16.7
Rivera, Ediel	R-R	6-1	185	9-23-05	.233	.346	.346	48	185	153	27	35	10	1	2	16	17	12	0	3	49	12	4	9.2	26.5
Rodriguez, Wilson	L-L	6-1	186	9-10-04	.263	.359	.375	26	93	80	10	21	3	0	2	13	10	2	0	1	12	8	2	10.8	15.1
Tejeda, Enmanuel	R-R	5-11	158	12-25-04	.296	.406	.407	9	32	27	3	8	3	0	0	1	4	1	0	0	7	2	2	12.5	21.9
Terrero, Gabriel	S-R	5-6	169	9-26-05	.277	.333	.436	36	111	101	19	28	5	1	3	21	8	1	0	1	26	9	1	7.2	23.4
Verde, Kevin	R-R	5-9	160	12-12-05	.191	.233	.272	45	146	136	14	26	5	0	2	21	7	1	0	2	25	6	0	4.8	17.1

NEW YORK YANKEES

Pitching	B-T	Ht.	Wt.	DOB	W	L	ERA	G	GS	SV	IP	Hits	Runs	ER	HR	BB	SO	AVG	OBP	SLG	SO%	BB%	BF
Alcantara, Stanly	R-R	6-6	187	4-12-04	1	3	8.89	17	0	0	27	29	35	27	1	20	21	.264	.425	.373	14.4	13.7	146
Arias, Michael	R-R	6-0	155	11-15-01	0	0	0.00	2	2	0	3	1	0	0	0	0	3	.091	.231	.091	23.1	0.0	13
Carter, Greysen	S-R	6-4	241	12-15-02	2	3	4.40	8	6	0	31	21	21	15	0	40	24	.198	.416	.283	16.1	26.8	149
Coleman, Carson	R-R	6-2	190	4-7-98	0	0	3.00	3	1	0	3	2	1	1	0	0	3	.167	.231	.167	23.1	0.0	13
Contreras, Johan	R-R	6-1	218	3-10-05	0	1	30.38	3	0	0	3	9	10	9	3	2	1	.529	.600	1.059	5.0	10.0	20
Cristino, John	R-R	6-2	225	12-8-99	0	0	0.00	1	0	0	1	3	0	0	2	0	1.000	.750	1.000	0.0	50.0	4
Effross, Scott	R-R	6-2	202	12-28-93	0	0	0.00	1	1	0	1	1	0	0	0	0	1	.250	.250	.500	25.0	0.0	4
Escudero, Luis	S-R	5-8	165	2-9-06	0	0	27.00	1	0	0	0	2	1	1	0	1	1	.667	.800	.667	20.0	20.0	5
Etheridge, J.T.	R-R	6-6	225	1-30-02	1	0	2.31	3	1	0	12	8	4	3	0	8	22	.186	.327	.209	42.3	15.4	52
Facundo, Allen	L-L	6-0	171	9-3-02	0	0	0.00	2	1	0	5	2	0	0	0	3	10	.111	.238	.167	47.6	14.3	21
Gomez, Santiago	R-R	5-11	160	4-5-04	3	0	0.00	4	0	0	2	2	0	0	0	2	3	.222	.417	.333	25.0	16.7	12
Gonzalez, Omar	R-R	6-4	175	7-25-05	1	3	3.86	11	10	0	47	26	20	20	5	31	44	.160	.305	.307	22.3	15.7	197
Herrera, Franyer	L-L	6-0	165	5-3-05	1	1	2.33	17	1	1	27	20	11	7	1	9	28	.208	.294	.292	25.7	8.3	109
Lalane, Henry	L-L	6-7	211	5-18-04	0	0	6.00	1	1	0	3	1	2	2	1	1	2	.100	.182	.400	18.2	9.1	11
Lange, Justin	R-R	6-4	220	9-11-01	1	0	2.08	3	1	0	4	0	3	1	0	3	6	.000	.176	.000	35.3	17.6	17
Ledesma, Jose	L-L	6-0	170	4-10-03	1	2	6.53	16	0	1	21	22	20	15	1	15	19	.268	.381	.354	19.6	15.5	97
Marquez, Edinzo	R-R	6-2	208	12-16-04	2	2	2.19	11	10	0	53	42	18	13	4	20	41	.210	.282	.340	18.6	9.1	220
Martina, Sunayro	R-R	6-3	165	10-9-03	3	3	5.01	13	1	0	32	29	20	18	3	23	37	.242	.387	.392	24.5	15.2	151
Martinez, Jose	R-R	6-1	204	1-7-05	1	0	3.20	13	1	0	20	19	7	7	2	4	23	.253	.291	.400	29.1	5.1	79
Mendoza, Jordarlin	R-R	6-0	175	11-14-03	0	0	5.79	3	2	0	5	7	4	3	0	4	3	.350	.519	.500	11.1	14.8	27
Nolan, Chance	R-R	6-3	209	9-7-99	1	1	1.50	16	0	0	18	13	6	3	0	13	12	.217	.356	.250	16.2	17.6	74
Paulino, Alexis	R-R	6-0	175	5-5-03	2	2	4.12	16	0	3	20	18	15	9	2	12	24	.237	.394	.461	24.5	12.2	98
Rivas, Xavier	L-L	6-3	220	7-11-02	1	0	1.15	4	3	0	16	4	2	2	0	9	22	.078	.230	.118	36.1	14.8	61
Rodriguez, Jose	R-R	5-11	160	1-6-04	1	5	2.25	11	8	0	44	26	16	11	0	27	45	.173	.308	.220	24.2	14.5	186
Rodriguez, Pedro	L-L	5-10	145	8-11-02	1	0	5.23	8	0	2	10	6	7	6	1	5	11	.167	.295	.278	25.0	11.4	44
Rosario, Hansel	R-R	6-4	174	8-5-02	2	1	7.91	13	0	0	19	13	19	17	2	31	25	.188	.462	.290	24.0	29.8	104
Ruiz, Yarison	R-R	6-4	216	3-26-00	0	1	3.86	3	0	0	2	1	1	1	0	7	7	.125	.563	.125	43.8	43.8	16
Salomon, Mariano	R-R	6-3	185	8-5-02	3	2	2.30	9	2	0	31	16	8	8	5	7	39	.154	.226	.327	33.9	6.1	115
Selvidge, Brock	L-L	6-3	205	8-28-02	0	0	0.00	1	1	0	3	2	0	0	1	2	.273	.333	.273	16.7	8.3	12
Shields, Ben	R-L	6-4	210	1-23-99	0	0	6.75	1	1	0	3	4	2	2	0	4	4	.333	.333	.417	33.3	0.0	12
Smith, Cade	L-R	6-1	190	4-9-02	0	0	0.00	2	2	0	4	1	0	0	0	2	4	.071	.235	.071	23.5	11.8	17
Stevens, Kevin	R-R	6-2	225	1-26-98	0	0	0.00	1	1	0	1	0	0	0	0	0	3	.000	.000	.000	100.0	0.0	3
Terrero, Gabriel	S-R	5-6	169	9-26-05	0	0	27.00	1	0	0	0	1	1	1	1	0	0	.500	.500	2.000	0.0	0.0	2
Tiedemann, Josh	R-R	6-2	190	6-9-04	0	0	11.25	6	0	0	8	11	12	10	2	5	15	.297	.381	.486	35.7	11.9	42
Vrieling, Trystan	R-R	6-4	200	10-2-00	0	0	2.45	1	1	0	4	3	1	1	0	1	7	.214	.267	.214	46.7	6.7	15

Fielding

C: Rivera 33, Palencia 17, Cristino 7, Puello 3. 1B: Cristino 24, Contreras 19, Palencia 11, Gomez 4, Puello 4, Terrero 1. 2B: Escudero 33, Terrero 24, Gomez 4, Riggio 2, Peralta 1, Tejeda 1. 3B: Verde 24, Escudero 17, Gomez 17, Tejeda 6. SS: Peralta 39, Verde 18, Gomez 4. LF: Lara 18, Rodriguez 17, Arias 13, Gomez 12, Mayea 5, Durango 4, Jackson 2, Verde 2, Eden 1, Ellis 1, Puello 1, Terrero 1. CF: Arias 38, Mayea 12, Eden 6, Montero 4, Lara 3, Rodriguez 1. RF: Puello 19, Lara 14, Rodriguez 11, Arias 10, Contreras 6, Davis 5, Jackson 3, Gomez 3, Montero 3, De Los Santos 1, Durango 1, Verde 1.

DSL NYY BOMBERS — ROOKIE
DOMINICAN SUMMER LEAGUE

Batting	B-T	Ht.	Wt.	DOB	AVG	OBP	SLG	G	PA	AB	R	H	2B	3B	HR	RBI	BB	HBP	SH	SF	SO	SB	CS	BB%	SO%
Carrera, David	R-R	6-3	180	9-7-06	.266	.419	.336	44	167	128	33	34	3	0	2	16	34	2	0	3	37	14	6	20.4	22.2
Castillo, Ruben	L-L	5-9	168	1-4-08	.220	.338	.366	50	225	191	33	42	9	5	3	19	25	9	0	0	55	20	12	11.1	24.4
Castro, Jose	R-R	6-2	176	10-4-05	.243	.384	.449	35	138	107	32	26	4	0	6	24	21	6	0	4	29	20	4	15.2	21.0
Charles, Eddinson	R-R	6-4	182	1-9-08	.167	.242	.267	20	66	60	8	10	3	0	1	7	3	3	0	0	44	2	0	4.5	66.7
Ciriaco, Alfred	L-R	5-11	156	10-5-06	.214	.353	.214	5	17	14	2	3	0	0	0	1	2	1	0	0	5	1	0	11.8	29.4
Done, Leni	R-R	6-2	184	6-5-07	.277	.414	.454	46	175	141	39	39	8	1	5	27	20	13	0	0	32	16	4	11.4	18.3
Feliz, Adrian	R-R	6-1	180	8-2-08	.231	.250	.256	14	40	39	8	9	1	0	0	4	1	0	0	0	8	3	2	2.5	20.0
Guerrero, Jesus	R-R	5-10	180	5-21-07	.250	.375	.300	11	24	20	4	5	1	0	0	3	3	1	0	0	5	0	0	12.5	20.8
Jimenez, Edgar	R-R	5-10	165	11-3-06	.269	.345	.385	12	29	26	5	7	3	0	1	8	3	0	0	0	7	2	0	10.3	24.1
Marinez, Stiven	L-R	5-10	175	8-20-07	.275	.424	.375	47	205	160	37	44	7	3	1	17	41	0	0	2	46	22	6	20.0	22.4
Martinez, Browm	R-R	5-10	161	11-26-06	.404	.507	.632	18	69	57	21	23	4	0	3	16	6	6	0	0	8	13	1	8.7	11.6
Meran, Richard	R-R	6-0	165	6-25-06	.300	.481	.538	30	108	80	20	24	6	2	3	20	22	6	0	0	23	2	5	20.4	21.3
Peralta, Jose	R-R	6-1	185	10-10-07	.000	.000	.000	1	3	3	0	0	0	0	0	0	0	0	0	0	1	0	0	0.0	33.3
Pineda, Queni	R-R	5-10	190	5-29-07	.270	.459	.381	20	85	63	22	17	4	0	1	9	19	3	0	0	12	5	0	22.4	14.1
Reyes, Cristofer	R-R	5-10	154	8-23-07	.245	.339	.329	42	165	143	30	35	7	1	1	13	19	2	0	1	48	26	6	11.5	29.1
Rodriguez, Alessandro	R-R	6-2	190	8-10-08	.133	.133	.133	9	15	15	1	2	0	0	0	1	0	0	0	0	3	0	0	0.0	20.0
Rondon, Carlos	R-R	6-0	190	2-16-06	.281	.453	.484	27	86	64	11	18	4	0	3	20	18	3	0	1	10	2	0	20.9	34.9
Torres, Juan	R-R	5-10	162	9-27-07	.359	.406	.516	27	170	153	32	55	10	1	4	43	6	8	0	3	20	12	8	3.5	11.8
Veldhuisen, Remy	L-R	6-2	190	2-11-05	.301	.459	.398	42	146	113	16	34	6	1	1	24	27	6	0	0	34	5	1	18.5	23.3
Ventura, Axel	R-R	6-1	165	3-10-06	.200	.478	.467	6	23	15	7	3	2	0	4	8	0	0	0	0	5	4	0	34.8	21.7
Villarroel, Carlos	R-R	6-1	188	6-4-07	.228	.348	.421	17	70	57	10	13	2	0	3	9	9	2	1	1	22	5	2	12.9	31.4

Pitching	B-T	Ht.	Wt.	DOB	W	L	ERA	G	GS	SV	IP	Hits	Runs	ER	HR	BB	SO	AVG	OBP	SLG	SO%	BB%	BF
Abreu, Ranciel	R-R	6-4	197	4-9-07	0	0	0.00	2	2	0	3	4	0	0	6	2	.231	.474	.231	10.5	31.6	19
Acosta, Cesar	R-R	5-11	163	6-30-06	1	5	8.33	12	8	0	31	24	33	29	3	35	37	.222	.453	.370	23.3	22.0	159
Almonte, Alexander	R-R	6-4	205	9-14-06	4	2	3.29	11	10	0	52	46	27	19	3	21	48	.229	.316	.318	21.0	9.2	229
Angomas, Randy	R-R	6-1	198	5-26-08	1	3	6.63	12	12	0	38	37	39	28	1	31	40	.247	.412	.307	20.6	16.0	194
Avila, Andre	L-L	6-0	165	8-16-05	1	1	4.50	6	0	0	20	15	11	10	0	15	22	.221	.384	.353	25.3	17.2	87
Burgos, Luis	R-R	6-2	186	9-6-05	3	4	2.44	11	8	0	52	37	20	14	2	23	48	.204	.305	.287	22.7	10.9	211

Player	B-T	Ht.	Wt.	DOB			AVG	OBP	SLG	G	PA	AB	R	H	2B	3B	HR	RBI	BB	HBP	SH	SF	SO	SB	CS	BB%	SO%
Caceres, Lenin	R-R	6-2	190	7-12-02	0	0	18.00		1	0	0	1		1	2	2	0	1	1	.250	.400	.500	20.0	20.0	5		
Carrillo, Diego	R-R	6-1	177	6-30-07	4	0	4.08	16	0	0	35	30	18	16	5	18	33	.227	.329	.409	21.7	11.8	152				
Centeno, Kevin	L-L	6-2	189	2-8-06	3	1	4.59	18	1	2	33	25	20	17	2	23	53	.208	.373	.308	34.6	15.0	153				
Feliz, Adrian	R-R	6-1	180	8-2-08	0	1	135.00	1	0	0	0	3	6	5	0	2	0	1.000	.857	1.667	0.0	28.6	7				
Gomez, Chaury	R-R	6-1	166	11-6-06	1	0	7.15	13	0	2	11	12	10	9	0	16	15	.286	.524	.357	23.8	25.4	63				
Gonzalez, Alexis	R-R	6-0	172	9-8-07	3	1	4.64	18	0	1	21	16	14	11	2	21	18	.222	.408	.389	17.8	20.8	101				
Guerrero, Jesus	R-R	5-10	180	5-21-07	0	0	0.00	2	0	0	2	3	0	0	0	1	3	.300	.364	.300	27.3	9.1	11				
Hampshire, Carlos	R-R	5-9	181	10-11-04	3	2	5.46	8	4	0	28	21	19	17	0	19	32	.212	.360	.293	25.6	15.2	125				
Jimenez, Edgar	R-R	5-10	165	11-3-06	0	0	0.00	1	0	0	1	0	0	0	1	0	0	.500	.750	.500	0.0	25.0	4				
Manzano, Marco	L-L	6-3	176	8-24-03	0	0	0.00	2	0	0	1	1	0	0	0	0	1	.250	.250	.250	25.0	0.0	4				
Penuelas, Fredy	L-L	5-11	190	5-22-07	0	0	0.00	1	0	0	3	1	0	0	0	1	5	.125	.222	.250	55.6	11.1	9				
Silvestre, Josue	R-R	6-7	198	7-13-04	2	0	24.65	13	0	0	8	9	28	21	1	22	16	.243	.554	.486	24.6	33.8	65				
Tavera, Junior	L-L	6-0	184	5-23-07	2	1	6.94	12	11	0	36	43	33	28	2	28	38	.293	.420	.415	21.0	15.5	181				
Tejada, Ronald	L-L	6-3	160	1-11-07	2	3	7.09	19	0	1	27	23	31	21	2	25	41	.225	.385	.382	31.5	19.2	130				
Vargas, Jose	R-R	6-0	150	2-29-08	1	0	3.86	2	0	0	2	2	1	1	1	2	1	.222	.364	.556	9.1	18.2	11				
Vasquez, Christopher	R-R	5-11	168	9-12-06	1	1	9.00	13	0	0	23	27	26	23	1	21	22	.297	.421	.473	19.3	18.4	114				
Veldhuisen, Remy	L-R	6-2	190	2-11-05	0	0	6.75	2	0	0	1	2	1	1	0	2	0	.333	.500	.333	0.0	25.0	8				

Fielding
C: Rondon 25, Pineda 15, Villarroel 13, Jimenez 4, Rodriguez 4, Guerrero 2. **1B:** Veldhuisen 37, Done 7, Guerrero 7, Jimenez 5, Peralta 1, Rodriguez 1, Rondon 1, Villarroel 1. **2B:** Torres 26, Reyes 23, Feliz 8, Ciriaco 4, Jimenez 1. **3B:** Done 36, Torres 17, Feliz 5, Ciriaco 2. **SS:** Marinez 41, Reyes 13, Done 4. **LF:** Carrera 21, Castro 14, Meran 11, Martinez 6, Charles 5, Ventura 2, Veldhuisen 1. **CF:** Castillo 45, Martinez 6, Castro 5. **RF:** Carrera 15, Charles 14, Castro 12, Meran 12, Ventura 3, Veldhuisen 2, Martinez 1.

DSL NYY YANKEES   ROOKIE
DOMINICAN SUMMER LEAGUE

Batting	B-T	Ht.	Wt.	DOB	AVG	OBP	SLG	G	PA	AB	R	H	2B	3B	HR	RBI	BB	HBP	SH	SF	SO	SB	CS	BB%	SO%
Adames, Eliezer	R-R	5-10	171	9-16-07	.116	.309	.163	20	55	43	9	5	0	1	0	3	11	1	0	0	26	1	1	20.0	47.3
Bello, Carlos	R-R	5-11	190	12-19-07	.217	.359	.354	46	198	161	34	35	8	1	4	31	28	8	0	1	49	14	3	14.1	24.7
Capellan, Justin	R-R	5-10	180	7-18-06	.255	.382	.443	45	186	149	33	38	10	0	6	37	26	7	0	4	34	16	4	14.0	18.3
Castillo, Isaias	R-R	5-11	190	6-15-08	.247	.362	.382	27	105	89	14	22	5	2	1	17	16	0	0	0	31	14	2	15.2	29.5
Cedeno, Mani	L-R	5-10	188	8-14-08	.183	.371	.305	49	213	164	41	30	5	3	3	19	43	6	0	0	76	21	2	20.2	35.7
Ciriaco, Alfred	L-R	5-11	156	10-5-06	.286	.394	.304	19	66	56	6	16	1	0	0	8	4	6	0	0	8	10	3	6.1	12.1
De Pena, Wilberson	R-R	6-2	185	11-10-06	.143	.351	.321	10	37	28	5	4	0	1	1	4	9	0	0	0	9	4	3	24.3	24.3
Feliz, Adrian	R-R	6-1	180	8-2-08	.100	.357	.100	9	28	20	4	2	0	0	0	2	6	2	0	0	7	2	2	21.4	25.0
Flores, Diego	R-R	5-11	160	3-10-07	.246	.323	.323	21	65	57	7	14	5	0	0	7	6	1	0	1	14	3	2	9.2	21.5
Guerrero, Jesus	R-R	5-10	180	5-21-07	.208	.457	.292	11	35	24	5	5	2	0	0	4	8	3	0	0	6	1	0	22.9	17.1
Jimenez, Edgar	R-R	5-10	165	11-3-06	.196	.274	.250	17	62	56	5	11	3	0	0	7	6	0	0	0	18	4	2	9.7	29.0
Lavagnino, Jose	L-R	5-9	205	6-21-07	.241	.373	.389	23	67	54	13	13	2	0	2	12	12	0	0	1	12	1	1	17.9	17.9
Matic, Richard	R-R	6-0	200	7-26-07	.336	.487	.566	46	191	143	41	48	12	3	5	30	40	5	0	3	43	11	6	20.9	22.5
Matos, Alfiery	R-R	5-10	165	9-10-07	.159	.329	.159	26	82	63	9	10	0	0	0	2	15	2	0	2	27	10	3	18.3	32.9
Montero, Estivenzon	R-R	6-1	189	10-9-06	.285	.384	.506	46	185	158	23	45	7	2	8	30	24	2	0	1	53	9	5	13.0	28.6
Orozco, Emmanuel	S-R	5-10	153	7-27-08	.075	.302	.150	19	53	40	8	3	1	0	0	3	11	2	0	0	14	8	2	20.8	26.4
Ventura, Angel	R-R	6-1	185	3-10-06	.284	.398	.358	29	113	95	17	27	5	1	0	9	16	2	0	0	36	17	3	14.2	31.9
Villarroel, Carlos	R-R	6-1	188	6-4-07	.244	.366	.462	23	93	78	17	19	2	0	5	15	13	2	0	0	23	2	2	14.0	24.7
Vilorio, Francisco	R-R	6-4	212	10-31-06	.279	.387	.366	49	217	183	39	51	10	3	0	19	30	3	0	1	54	8	5	13.8	24.9

Pitching	B-T	Ht.	Wt.	DOB	W	L	ERA	G	GS	SV	IP	Hits	Runs	ER	HR	BB	SO	AVG	OBP	SLG	SO%	BB%	BF
Adames, Eliezer	R-R	5-10	171	9-16-07	0	0	0.00	1	0	0	0	0	0	0	0	0	0	.000	.000	.000	0.0	0.0	1
Arias, Rafael	R-R	6-2	190	11-5-03	5	0	4.05	20	0	3	40	42	24	18	0	16	53	.266	.337	.373	29.8	9.0	178
Colina, Jhosneyker	R-R	5-11	150	3-27-08	1	3	4.85	11	10	0	43	45	30	23	3	20	30	.262	.343	.360	15.1	10.1	199
Cruz, Manuel	R-R	6-2	178	2-18-06	0	5	8.60	12	12	0	38	48	38	36	3	25	30	.312	.422	.487	16.2	13.5	185
De La Rosa, Carlos	L-L	6-1	180	11-30-07	0	1	5.32	7	7	0	22	27	15	13	1	5	36	.281	.320	.385	35.0	4.9	103
Guerrero, Jesus	R-R	5-10	180	5-21-07	0	0	0.00	1	0	0	1	0	0	0	0	0	0	.000	.000	.000	0.0	0.0	3
Hampshire, Carlos	R-R	5-9	181	10-11-04	0	1	7.88	3	2	0	8	6	7	7	0	14	9	.200	.478	.200	19.6	30.4	46
Ilarraza, Luis	R-R	6-1	155	7-30-06	0	1	11.05	15	0	1	15	15	22	18	3	20	11	.278	.468	.500	13.9	25.3	79
Lavagnino, Jose	L-R	5-9	205	6-21-07	0	0	0.00	1	0	0	2	0	0	0	0	0	0	.667	.667	.667	0.0	0.0	3
Manzano, Marco	L-L	6-3	176	8-24-03	3	1	4.26	15	0	1	25	25	18	12	2	23	36	.250	.387	.350	28.8	14.8	125
Mena, Anthony	R-R	6-2	173	10-12-04	4	1	3.15	12	2	0	46	43	30	16	5	16	57	.242	.311	.360	29.1	8.2	196
Moreno, Hector	R-R	6-6	196	12-26-07	0	4	16.43	10	9	0	15	16	31	28	0	29	19	.276	.527	.345	20.9	31.9	91
Orozco, Emmanuel	S-R	5-10	153	7-27-08	0	0	0.00	1	0	0	1	0	0	0	0	0	0	.500	.750	.500	25.0	0.0	4
Penuelas, Fredy	L-L	5-11	190	5-22-07	1	3	11.64	15	0	0	19	27	28	25	1	20	16	.346	.477	.487	15.0	18.7	107
Rodriguez, Luis	L-L	5-10	139	5-26-05	3	2	4.99	19	0	3	40	38	24	22	2	15	41	.260	.327	.363	24.4	8.9	168
Sanchez, Enixon	R-R	6-0	150	7-7-07	1	4	5.04	12	11	0	45	49	33	25	3	33	48	.278	.403	.409	22.2	15.3	216
Vargas, Emanuel	R-R	6-1	178	10-10-05	2	3	7.45	12	3	1	39	45	37	32	4	44	44	.281	.421	.413	22.9	15.1	192
Vargas, Jose	R-R	6-0	150	2-29-08	0	0	3.65	12	0	1	12	7	5	5	1	3	8	.167	.300	.286	16.0	6.0	50
Villarreal, Varis	R-R	5-11	157	7-1-05	4	3	6.06	16	0	0	33	48	29	22	3	9	37	.340	.382	.496	24.3	5.9	152

Fielding
C: Capellan 31, Villarroel 10, Flores 9, Jimenez 6, Lavagnino 5, Guerrero 1. **1B:** Lavagnino 19, Flores 12, Jimenez 10, Guerrero 9, Villarroel 9, Adames 4, Ciriaco 4. **2B:** Bello 36, Orozco 7, Ciriaco 6, Feliz 3, Jimenez 3, Adames 2. **3B:** Matic 42, Ciriaco 6, Feliz 6, Orozco 4. **SS:** Cedeno 45, Bello 7, Orozco 5, Ciriaco 3. **LF:** Montero 17, Castillo 12, Ventura 12, Matos 7, Adames 5, De Pena 5. **CF:** Vilorio 41, Ventura 10, Castillo 6, Adames 1. **RF:** Montero 21, Matos 15, Adames 7, Ventura 7, Castillo 3, De Pena 3.

Philadelphia Phillies

SEASON SYNOPSIS: For the seventh straight full season, the Phillies won more games than the previous year, a 96-66 season in which they repeated as NL East champs. Yet the team with the best home record in the game dropped both playoff games at Citizens Bank Park and endured an excruciating four-game, walk-off exit in the Division Series round to the Dodgers.

HIGH POINT: Philadelphia had an eight-game winning streak in May and a four-game sweep of the Mets in September that salted away the division. But in August, just after the Mets had pulled within four games with a sweep of their own, the Phillies needed a boost, and no one was better at boosting the 2025 club than DH Kyle Schwarber. His four-homer, nine-RBI effort in a 19-4 shellacking of the Braves on Aug. 28 set the club's vibes back to positive after the Mets sweep. Schwarber went on to lead the NL with 56 homers and 132 RBIs in a .240/.365/.563 season.

LOW POINT: The Phils blew an early three-run lead in Game One of the Division Series and were shut down by Blake Snell in Game Two. After pummelling the Dodgers in Game Three in L.A., Philadelphia couldn't expand a 1-0 lead in Game Four, heading to extra innings. With the bases full and two outs in the bottom of the 11th, Orion Kerkering induced a weak comebacker from Andy Pages, only to muff it, panic, pick up the ball and throw it wildly, errantly, home, producing a sad, walk-off defeat.

NOTABLE ROOKIES: A nondrafted free-agent signing in 2022 out of Division II Point Loma Nazarene, Otto Kemp (.709 OPS, 8 HR) provided pop, especially against lefthanders, and played four positions. Signed as a minor league free agent prior to 2024, RHP Max Lazar (1-1, 4.79 in 41 ⅓ IP) provided a depth arm.

KEY TRANSACTIONS: Club president Dave Dombrowski added to a deep rotation in the offseason by trading two prospects for lefty Jesus Luzardo (15-7, 3.92) from the Marlins. Free agent addition Max Kepler (.691 OPS) struggled in his first season since leaving the Twins, but Dombrowski went back to the Twins well at the trade deadline, adding closer Jhoan Duran for prospects Mick Abel and Eduardo Tait, then veteran OF Harrison Bader a day later in a separate deal. Ace Zack Wheeler (10-5, 2.71 in 24 starts) went on the IL Aug. 17 and had surgery the next day to remove a blood clot in his right shoulder region, ending his season.

OPENING DAY PAYROLL: $284,210,820 (4th)

PLAYERS OF THE YEAR

MAJOR LEAGUE
Cristopher Sanchez
LHP
13-5, 2.50 ERA
212 SO in 202 IP
44 BB, 12 HR in 32 GS

MINOR LEAGUE
Justin Crawford
OF
(AAA)
.334/.411/.452
46 SB, 147 H in 112 G

ORGANIZATION LEADERS

Batting		*Qualifiers
MAJORS		
* AVG	Trea Turner	.304
* OPS	Kyle Schwarber	.928
HR	Kyle Schwarber	56
RBI	Kyle Schwarber	132
MINORS		
* AVG	Justin Crawford, Lehigh Valley	.334
* OBP	Justin Crawford, Lehigh Valley	.411
* SLG	Felix Reyes, Lehigh Valley/Reading	.562
* OPS	Felix Reyes, Lehigh Valley/Reading	.923
R	Justin Crawford, Lehigh Valley	88
H	Justin Crawford, Lehigh Valley	147
TB	Felix Reyes, Lehigh Valley/Reading	219
2B	Felix Reyes, Lehigh Valley/Reading	34
3B	Dante Nori, Reading/Jersey Shore/Clearwater	12
HR	Rodolfo Castro, Lehigh Valley	19
RBI	Rodolfo Castro, Lehigh Valley	82
BB	Aidan Miller, Lehigh Valley/Reading	82
SO	Cade Fergus, Lehigh Valley/Reading	143
SB	Aidan Miller, Lehigh Valley/Reading	59

Pitching		#Qualifiers
MAJORS		
W	Jesus Luzardo	15
# ERA	Cristopher Sanchez	2.50
SO	Jesus Luzardo	216
SV	Jhoan Duran	16
MINORS		
W	Ryan Dromboski, Jersey Shore/Clearwater	9
L	Mitch Neunborn, Lehigh Valley/Reading	10
L	Casey Steward, Jersey Shore	10
# ERA	Jean Cabrera, Reading	3.81
G	Tommy McCollum, L. Valley/Reading/Jersey Shore	47
GS	Andrew Painter, Lehigh Valley/Clearwater	26
GS	Jean Cabrera, Reading	26
SV	Saul Teran, Reading/Jersey Shore/Clearwater	15
IP	Jean Cabrera, Reading	137
BB	Jean Cabrera, Reading	61
SO	Alan Rangel, Lehigh Valley	131
# AVG	Jean Cabrera, Reading	.214

2025 PERFORMANCE

President: Dave Dombrowski. **Farm Director:** Luke Murton. **Scouting Director:** Brian Barber.

Class	Team	League	W	L	PCT	Finish	Manager
Majors	Philadelphia Phillies	National	96	66	.593	2 (15)	Rob Thomson
Triple-A	Lehigh Valley IronPigs	International	87	61	.588	3 (20)	Anthony Contreras
Double-A	Reading Fightin Phils	Eastern	55	81	.404	12 (12)	Al Pedrique
High-A	Jersey Shore BlueClaws	South Atlantic	62	65	.488	7 (12)	Greg Brodzinski
Low-A	Clearwater Threshers	Florida State	68	60	.531	3 (10)	Marty Malloy
Rookie	FCL Phillies	Florida Complex	16	42	.276	15 (15)	Shawn Williams
Rookie	DSL Phillies Red	Dominican	25	31	.446	34 (52)	Felix Castillo
Rookie	DSL Phillies White	Dominican	13	42	.236	52 (52)	Waner Santana
Overall 2025 Minor League Record			326	382	.460	25th (30)	

ORGANIZATION STATISTICS

PHILADELPHIA PHILLIES
NATIONAL LEAGUE

Batting	B-T	Ht.	Wt.	DOB	AVG	OBP	SLG	G	PA	AB	R	H	2B	3B	HR	RBI	BB	HBP	SH	SF	SO	SB	CS	BB%	SO%
Bader, Harrison	R-R	6-0	210	6-3-94	.305	.361	.463	50	194	177	30	54	11	1	5	16	12	4	0	1	55	1	3	6.2	28.4
Bohm, Alec	R-R	6-5	218	8-3-96	.287	.331	.409	120	504	464	53	133	18	3	11	59	29	5	0	6	82	2	0	5.8	16.3
Castellanos, Nick	R-R	6-4	203	3-4-92	.250	.294	.400	147	589	547	72	137	27	2	17	72	32	4	0	6	133	4	0	5.4	22.6
Clemens, Kody	L-R	6-1	200	5-15-96	.000	.143	.000	7	7	6	0	0	0	0	0	0	1	0	0	0	0	0	0	14.3	0.0
Harper, Bryce	L-R	6-3	210	10-16-92	.261	.357	.487	132	580	501	72	131	32	0	27	75	70	6	0	3	121	12	2	12.1	20.9
Kemp, Otto	R-R	5-11	185	9-9-99	.234	.298	.411	62	218	197	26	46	11	0	8	28	12	7	0	2	67	2	2	5.5	30.7
Kennedy, Buddy	R-R	5-9	190	10-5-98	.000	.125	.000	4	8	7	0	0	0	0	0	0	1	0	0	0	2	0	0	12.5	25.0
Kepler, Max	L-L	6-4	225	2-10-93	.216	.300	.391	127	474	417	58	90	19	0	18	52	48	4	1	4	93	3	0	10.1	19.6
Marchan, Rafael	S-R	5-9	170	2-25-99	.210	.282	.305	42	118	105	9	22	4	0	2	13	10	1	1	1	17	0	0	8.5	14.4
Marsh, Brandon	L-R	6-4	215	12-18-97	.280	.342	.443	133	425	379	59	106	25	2	11	43	38	0	3	4	110	7	1	8.9	25.9
Realmuto, J.T.	R-R	6-1	212	3-18-91	.257	.315	.384	134	550	502	57	129	26	1	12	52	35	9	0	3	129	8	2	6.4	23.5
Rojas, Johan	R-R	5-11	165	8-14-00	.224	.289	.280	71	172	152	23	34	3	2	1	18	13	0	4	3	40	12	2	7.6	23.3
Schwarber, Kyle	L-R	6-0	229	3-5-93	.240	.365	.563	162	724	604	111	145	23	2	56	132	108	11	0	1	197	10	2	14.9	27.2
Sosa, Edmundo	R-R	6-0	210	3-6-96	.276	.307	.469	89	261	243	30	67	12	1	11	39	10	2	3	2	56	1	1	3.8	21.5
Stevenson, Cal	L-L	5-9	175	9-12-96	.250	.250	.250	5	8	8	0	2	0	0	0	1	0	0	0	0	2	0	0	0.0	25.0
Stott, Bryson	L-R	6-3	200	10-6-97	.257	.328	.391	147	560	499	66	128	22	3	13	66	54	1	2	4	91	24	5	9.6	16.3
Stubbs, Garrett	L-L	5-10	170	5-26-93	.000	.000	.000	5	1	1	2	0	0	0	0	0	0	0	0	0	0	0	0	0.0	0.0
Turner, Trea	R-R	6-2	185	6-30-93	.304	.355	.457	141	639	589	94	179	31	7	15	69	43	5	0	2	107	36	7	6.7	16.7
Walton, Donovan	L-R	5-9	190	5-26-94	.125	.125	.125	2	9	8	1	1	0	0	0	1	0	0	1	0	1	0	0	0.0	11.1
Wilson, Weston	R-R	6-3	215	9-11-94	.198	.282	.369	54	125	111	15	22	4	0	5	17	12	1	1	0	34	2	3	9.6	27.2

Pitching	B-T	Ht.	Wt.	DOB	W	L	ERA	G	GS	SV	IP	Hits	Runs	ER	HR	BB	SO	AVG	OBP	SLG	SO%	BB%	BF
Abel, Mick	R-R	6-5	190	8-18-01	2	2	5.04	6	6	0	25	25	14	14	7	9	21	.255	.324	.520	19.4	8.3	108
Alvarado, Jose	L-L	6-2	245	5-21-95	4	2	3.81	28	0	7	26	27	12	11	4	7	32	.262	.313	.398	28.1	6.1	114
Banks, Tanner	R-L	6-1	210	10-24-91	6	2	3.07	69	1	1	67	56	24	23	9	12	61	.224	.261	.372	22.8	4.5	267
Buehler, Walker	R-R	6-2	185	7-28-94	3	0	0.66	3	2	0	14	10	1	1	0	6	8	.204	.316	.224	14.0	10.5	57
de Geus, Brett	R-R	6-2	190	11-4-97	0	0	4.50	1	0	0	2	1	1	1	0	3	0	.143	.400	.143	0.0	30.0	10
Duran, Jhoan	R-R	6-5	230	1-8-98	1	2	2.18	23	0	16	21	18	6	5	2	1	27	.225	.235	.350	33.3	1.2	81
Hernandez, Carlos	R-R	6-4	245	3-11-97	1	0	5.26	25	0	0	26	32	16	15	4	13	23	.302	.385	.462	18.7	10.6	123
Hoffman, Nolan	R-R	6-4	190	8-9-97	0	0	27.00	1	0	0	1	3	3	3	0	1	2	.500	.571	.833	28.6	14.3	7
Johnson, Seth	R-R	6-1	205	9-19-98	1	1	4.26	10	0	0	13	11	8	6	3	4	17	.220	.278	.460	31.5	7.4	54
Kerkering, Orion	R-R	6-2	204	4-4-01	8	4	3.30	69	0	4	60	55	28	22	6	27	65	.238	.323	.364	24.4	10.2	266
Lazar, Max	R-R	6-1	200	6-3-99	1	0	4.79	36	0	1	41	41	23	22	7	12	26	.261	.312	.452	15.3	7.1	170
Luzardo, Jesus	L-L	6-0	218	9-30-97	15	7	3.92	32	32	0	184	167	85	80	16	57	216	.240	.299	.356	28.5	7.5	758
Mayza, Tim	L-L	6-3	215	1-15-92	0	0	4.91	8	0	0	7	8	4	4	1	4	7	.276	.382	.379	20.6	11.8	34
Mercado, Michael	R-R	6-4	160	4-15-99	0	0	15.00	3	0	0	3	7	5	5	1	4	4	.467	.550	.667	20.0	20.0	2
Nola, Aaron	R-R	6-2	200	6-4-93	5	10	6.01	17	17	0	94	99	65	63	18	28	97	.267	.325	.480	24.0	6.9	404
Rangel, Alan	R-R	6-2	170	8-21-97	0	0	2.45	5	0	1	11	10	3	3	1	6	8	.250	.348	.400	17.4	13.0	46
Robert, Daniel	R-R	6-4	210	8-30-94	0	0	4.15	15	0	0	13	11	7	6	2	10	15	.224	.356	.408	25.4	16.9	59
Robertson, David	R-R	5-11	195	4-9-85	2	0	4.08	20	0	2	18	18	9	8	4	8	22	.257	.333	.486	28.2	10.3	78
Romano, Jordan	R-R	6-5	210	4-21-93	2	4	8.23	49	0	8	43	45	40	39	10	17	47	.276	.348	.515	25.1	9.1	187
Ross, Joe	R-R	6-4	232	5-21-93	2	1	5.12	37	1	0	51	57	30	29	8	18	39	.282	.344	.495	17.1	7.9	228
Ruiz, Jose	R-R	6-1	245	10-21-94	1	0	8.16	16	0	0	14	16	13	13	6	11	12	.350	.397	.617	17.6	8.8	68
Sanchez, Cristopher	L-L	6-1	165	12-12-96	13	5	2.50	32	32	0	202	171	58	56	12	44	212	.227	.275	.321	26.3	5.5	807
Strahm, Matt	R-L	6-2	190	11-12-91	2	3	2.74	66	0	6	62	47	22	19	5	20	70	.208	.273	.341	27.3	7.8	256
Suarez, Ranger	L-L	6-1	207	8-26-95	12	8	3.20	26	26	0	157	154	57	56	14	38	151	.256	.305	.374	23.2	5.8	651
Trivino, Lou	R-R	6-5	235	10-1-91	0	1	2.00	10	0	0	9	6	3	2	0	5	8	.194	.316	.226	21.1	13.2	38
Walker, Taijuan	R-R	6-4	235	8-13-92	5	8	4.08	34	21	1	124	132	62	56	21	42	86	.270	.331	.444	16.0	7.8	538
Wheeler, Zack	L-R	6-4	195	5-30-90	10	5	2.71	24	24	0	150	107	48	45	19	33	195	.197	.253	.349	33.3	5.6	585
Wilson, Weston	R-R	6-3	215	9-11-94	0	0	0.00	2	0	0	3	3	0	0	0	0	0	.250	.250	.250	0.0	0.0	12

Fielding

Catcher	PCT	G	PO	A	E	DP	PB
Marchan	.993	42	269	14	2	1	2
Realmuto	.995	132	1216	37	6	10	2
Stubbs	1.000	2	8	0	0	0	0

First Base	PCT	G	PO	A	E	DP
Bohm	1.000	13	92	7	0	6
Harper	.998	130	933	71	2	72
Kemp	.993	17	132	9	1	10
Kennedy	1.000	2	12	0	0	2
Wilson	.964	9	23	4	1	1

Second Base	PCT	G	PO	A	E	DP
Clemens	1.000	1	0	1	0	0
Kemp	.800	2	1	3	1	1

	PCT	G	PO	A	E	DP
Sosa	.991	33	55	59	1	12
Stott	.994	135	220	296	3	59
Walton	1.000	2	3	3	0	1
Wilson	1.000	11	10	24	0	3

Third Base	PCT	G	PO	A	E	DP
Bohm	.981	108	58	207	5	17
Kemp	.922	31	21	38	5	1
Kennedy	1.000	1	0	1	0	0
Sosa	.974	33	22	53	2	2
Wilson	.000	1	0	0	0	0

Shortstop	PCT	G	PO	A	E	DP
Sosa	.977	19	19	24	1	5
Stott	.980	13	17	32	1	5

	PCT	G	PO	A	E	DP
Turner	.984	139	159	341	8	55

Outfield	PCT	G	PO	A	E	DP
Bader	.973	48	105	2	3	1
Castellanos	1.000	143	243	4	0	2
Clemens	.000	1	0	0	0	0
Kemp	1.000	11	13	1	0	0
Kepler	.995	139	208	2	1	0
Marsh	.984	148	234	6	4	1
Rojas	.983	65	111	3	2	1
Schwarber	.941	8	16	0	1	0
Sosa	1.000	3	6	0	0	0
Stevenson	1.000	5	1	0	0	0
Wilson	1.000	27	31	0	0	0

LEHIGH VALLEY IRONPIGS
INTERNATIONAL LEAGUE — TRIPLE-A

Batting	B-T	Ht.	Wt.	DOB	AVG	OBP	SLG	G	PA	AB	R	H	2B	3B	HR	RBI	BB	HBP	SH	SF	SO	SB	CS	BB%	SO%
Anthony, Keaton	R-R	6-4	211	6-24-01	.313	.374	.433	33	148	134	14	42	10	0	2	10	12	1	0	0	33	0	0	8.1	22.3
Arroyo, Christian	R-R	6-1	210	5-30-95	.314	.384	.485	45	190	169	25	53	14	0	5	37	16	4	0	1	37	1	0	8.4	19.5
Bohm, Alec	R-R	6-5	218	8-3-96	.143	.182	.381	5	22	21	2	3	0	1	1	2	1	0	0	0	2	0	0	4.5	9.1
Breaux, Josh	R-R	6-1	220	10-7-97	.226	.318	.330	37	132	115	16	26	4	1	2	12	14	2	0	1	35	0	0	10.6	26.5
Brito, Erick	R-R	5-8	134	5-25-02	.250	.341	.313	49	168	144	19	36	7	1	0	18	17	3	4	0	36	7	3	10.1	21.4
Castro, Rodolfo	S-R	6-0	205	5-21-99	.235	.324	.421	133	525	456	72	107	26	1	19	82	54	9	0	6	119	18	8	10.3	22.7
Crawford, Justin	L-R	6-1	175	1-13-04	.334	.411	.452	112	506	440	88	147	23	4	7	47	58	1	5	2	91	46	11	11.5	18.0
Dunn, Nick	L-R	5-8	185	1-29-97	.265	.324	.382	10	38	34	5	9	1	0	1	3	3	0	1	0	6	0	0	7.9	15.8
Fergus, Cade	R-R	6-2	195	8-22-00	.333	.371	.788	10	36	33	9	11	0	0	5	13	2	0	1	0	15	3	1	5.6	41.7
Henry, Payton	R-R	6-0	229	6-24-97	.404	.323	.415	65	269	241	35	60	7	0	11	47	20	7	0	1	70	1	0	7.4	26.0
Hicklen, Brewer	R-R	6-1	220	2-9-96	.218	.293	.437	32	133	119	22	26	2	0	8	25	11	2	0	1	42	7	1	8.3	31.6
Kemp, Otto	R-R	5-11	185	9-9-99	.310	.417	.570	74	343	284	64	88	24	1	16	67	36	19	0	4	84	13	2	10.5	24.5
Kennedy, Buddy	R-R	5-9	190	10-5-98	.283	.388	.447	61	268	226	35	64	11	1	8	40	31	9	0	2	43	1	3	11.6	15.3
Kroon, Matt	R-R	6-0	195	12-5-96	.232	.362	.321	19	69	56	7	13	2	0	1	9	11	1	0	1	15	7	1	15.9	21.7
Lantigua, Rafael	R-R	5-7	153	4-28-98	.230	.356	.330	125	495	400	82	92	15	2	7	56	77	5	6	7	73	17	7	15.6	14.7
Marsh, Brandon	L-R	6-4	215	12-18-97	.300	.400	.450	6	25	20	3	6	0	0	1	4	4	0	0	1	8	2	0	16.0	32.0
McIntosh, Paul	R-R	6-1	220	11-20-97	.133	.300	.333	10	40	30	3	4	0	0	1	4	6	2	0	2	8	0	0	15.0	20.0
Mercado, Oscar	R-R	6-2	197	12-16-94	.249	.369	.373	115	477	389	65	97	13	1	11	65	69	8	5	6	68	40	10	14.5	14.3
Miller, Aidan	R-R	6-2	210	6-9-04	.333	.514	.519	8	37	27	8	9	2	0	1	1	9	1	0	0	7	7	1	24.3	18.9
Moore, Robert	S-R	5-9	170	3-31-02	.222	.344	.407	8	32	27	5	6	2	0	1	4	3	2	0	0	1	1	0	9.4	3.1
Reyes, Felix	R-R	6-3	195	3-26-01	.261	.320	.391	6	26	23	2	6	0	0	1	2	2	0	0	0	5	0	0	7.7	19.2
Rincones, Gabriel	L-R	6-3	225	3-3-01	.240	.370	.430	119	506	412	81	99	22	1	18	73	80	8	0	6	114	21	5	15.8	22.5
Rojas, Johan	R-R	5-11	165	8-14-00	.279	.338	.361	35	161	147	18	41	7	1	1	13	13	0	1	0	32	8	2	8.1	19.9
Stevenson, Cal	L-L	5-9	175	9-12-96	.237	.346	.278	48	66	11	6	38	59	1	4	4	78	22	4	17.1	22.5
Stubbs, Garrett	L-R	5-10	170	5-26-93	.265	.352	.402	71	309	264	45	70	12	0	8	50	31	6	3	3	62	5	2	10.0	20.1
Taylor, Carson	S-R	6-2	205	6-2-99	.714	.750	1.429	3	8	7	2	5	2	0	1	2	1	0	0	0	2	0	0	12.5	25.0
Verdugo, Luis	R-R	6-0	160	10-12-00	.180	.234	.260	31	109	100	14	18	2	0	2	9	7	0	2	0	36	0	0	6.4	32.1
Walton, Donovan	L-R	5-9	190	5-25-94	.339	.413	.424	50	209	177	27	60	9	0	2	27	25	1	1	5	28	3	3	12.0	13.4
Wilson, Weston	R-R	6-3	215	9-11-94	.250	.366	.404	25	123	104	21	26	5	1	3	12	18	1	0	0	26	4	3	14.6	21.1

Pitching	B-T	Ht.	Wt.	DOB	W	L	ERA	G	GS	SV	IP	Hits	Runs	ER	HR	BB	SO	AVG	OBP	SLG	SO%	BB%	BF
Abel, Mick	R-R	6-5	190	8-18-01	7	2	2.31	13	13	0	74	54	21	19	5	32	81	.200	.289	.304	26.6	10.5	305
Alvarado, Jose	L-L	6-2	245	5-21-95	0	0	0.00	5	0	0	5	4	0	0	0	4	4	.235	.381	.235	19.0	19.0	21
Aoyagi, Koyo	R-R	5-11	175	12-11-93	0	1	7.45	19	2	0	19	21	19	16	2	23	16	.269	.457	.385	15.1	21.7	106
Bechtold, Andrew	R-R	6-1	185	4-18-96	0	0	18.00	5	0	0	4	8	8	8	2	3	5	.444	.500	.833	22.7	13.6	22
Bickford, Phil	R-R	6-4	200	7-10-95	3	0	4.91	19	0	0	18	15	10	10	0	11	17	.221	.338	.294	21.3	13.8	80
Brito, Erick	R-R	5-8	134	5-25-02	0	0	5.40	2	0	0	2	5	1	1	0	0	0	.556	.556	.556	0.0	0.0	9
Buehler, Walker	R-R	6-2	185	7-28-94	0	0	3.00	1	1	0	3	5	2	1	1	3	5	.333	.444	.667	27.8	16.7	18
Castro, Rodolfo	S-R	6-0	205	5-21-99	0	0	18.00	1	0	0	1	1	2	2	0	3	0	.500	.667	.500	0.0	50.0	6
Crismatt, Nabil	R-R	6-1	220	12-25-94	5	6	4.04	19	19	0	100	99	49	45	15	25	68	.253	.303	.448	16.2	6.0	419
Crowe, Wil	R-R	6-2	245	9-9-94	0	2	11.57	2	2	0	7	12	12	9	1	10	5	.375	.524	.688	11.9	23.8	42
Cuas, Jose	R-R	6-3	195	6-28-94	1	0	13.50	7	0	0	5	8	8	2	5	4	.333	.484	.625	12.9	16.1	31
Cusick, Ryan	R-R	6-6	235	11-12-99	2	0	7.90	19	4	0	27	34	25	24	6	13	35	.301	.383	.549	27.3	10.2	128
de Geus, Brett	R-R	6-2	190	11-4-97	3	1	5.35	29	0	3	37	47	26	22	3	17	24	.315	.399	.430	13.7	11.4	175
Dunn, Nick	L-R	5-8	185	1-29-97	0	0	18.00	1	0	0	1	3	2	2	1	0	0	.600	.600	1.600	0.0	0.0	5
Garnett, Tristan	L-L	6-6	240	3-29-98	0	0	9.00	1	0	0	1	1	1	1	0	2	1	.250	.500	.250	16.7	33.3	6
Harper, Daniel	R-R	6-4	225	9-12-99	2	1	2.10	57	0	15	60	35	18	14	5	9	13	.313	.387	.677	17.3	12.0	75
Hoffman, Nolan	R-R	6-4	190	8-9-97	5	0	3.60	27	0	3	40	29	13	9	12	2	15	.35	.261	.366	.378	26.1	11.2	134
Johnson, Seth	R-R	6-1	205	9-19-98	5	5	4.75	39	4	1	61	58	35	34	2	35	67	.253	.351	.362	24.7	12.9	271
Kuhnel, Joel	R-R	6-5	250	2-19-95	3	1	3.62	26	0	2	32	35	15	13	4	4	27	.280	.305	.432	20.6	3.1	131
Lantigua, Rafael	R-R	5-7	153	4-28-98	0	0	27.00	1	0	0	1	2	3	3	1	1	0	.500	.500	2.000	0.0	25.0	4
Lazar, Max	R-R	6-1	200	6-3-99	3	2	3.38	18	0	5	21	15	12	8	3	7	23	.192	.256	.372	26.4	8.0	87
McCollum, Tommy	R-R	6-5	260	6-8-00	0	0	6.75	3	0	0	5	5	5	2	0	2	1	.417	.467	.500	6.7	13.3	15
McGarry, Griff	R-R	6-2	190	6-8-99	1	0	1.80	1	1	0	5	1	1	1	1	2	8	.063	.211	.250	42.1	10.5	19

PHILADELPHIA PHILLIES

Batting	B-T	Ht.	Wt.	DOB	AVG	OBP	SLG	G	PA	AB	R	H	2B	3B	HR	RBI	BB	HBP	SH	SF	SO	SB	CS	BB%	SO%
McMillon, John	L-R	6-3	230	1-27-98	0	0	14.29	7	0	0	6	8	10	9	0	10	10	.320	.514	.360	28.6	28.6	35		
Medina, Adonis	R-R	6-1	187	12-18-96	0	3	3.41	10	7	0	32	33	16	12	3	25	29	.268	.395	.407	19.1	16.4	152		
Mercado, Michael	R-R	6-4	160	4-15-99	6	1	4.59	42	0	3	49	51	26	25	6	29	53	.273	.379	.449	23.6	12.9	225		
Mosser, Gabe	R-R	6-4	185	6-8-96	4	5	5.29	17	17	0	83	88	50	49	19	36	77	.271	.351	.508	20.9	9.8	368		
Neunborn, Mitch	R-R	6-0	190	6-27-97	0	5	8.80	8	8	0	31	39	30	30	8	23	19	.312	.414	.592	12.4	15.0	153		
Nola, Aaron	R-R	6-2	200	6-4-93	0	1	2.19	3	3	0	12	11	3	3	0	3	17	.229	.275	.313	33.3	5.9	51		
Padilla, Nicholas	R-R	6-2	220	12-24-96	4	4	5.10	34	2	0	42	36	31	24	4	29	41	.226	.344	.333	21.6	15.3	190		
Painter, Andrew	R-R	6-7	215	4-10-03	5	6	5.40	22	22	0	107	119	67	64	18	46	111	.281	.348	.493	23.4	9.7	475		
Rangel, Alan	R-R	6-2	170	8-21-97	5	5	4.55	25	25	0	125	122	67	63	29	40	131	.251	.308	.499	24.7	7.5	530		
Robert, Daniel	L-R	6-4	210	8-30-94	1	0	3.38	18	0	4	19	17	8	7	1	5	19	.227	.293	.320	23.2	6.1	82		
Robertson, David	R-R	5-11	195	4-9-85	0	1	10.13	6	0	0	5	11	6	6	1	1	6	.423	.444	.654	22.2	3.7	27		
Ross, Joe	R-R	6-4	232	5-21-93	0	0	0.00	2	0	0	2	1	0	0	0	1	4	.143	.250	.143	50.0	12.5	8		
Ruiz, Jose	R-R	6-1	245	10-71-94	0	0	0.00	2	0	0	2	0	0	0	0	0	1	.000	.000	.000	16.7	0.0	6		
Schulfer, Austin	R-R	6-2	175	12-22-95	2	0	5.57	21	2	0	21	14	13	2	12	15	.263	.358	.413	15.8	12.6	95		
Sims, Lucas	R-R	6-2	213	5-10-94	4	1	5.56	34	0	1	34	23	21	21	4	29	36	.197	.391	.359	23.1	18.6	156		
Suarez, Ranger	L-L	6-1	217	8-26-95	1	0	0.93	2	2	0	10	6	1	1	0	4	13	.182	.270	.273	34.2	10.5	38		
Sweet, Devin	S-R	5-11	183	9-6-96	3	1	5.08	46	2	2	51	47	37	29	8	27	49	.241	.332	.462	21.2	11.7	231		
Trivino, Lou	R-R	6-5	235	10-1-91	0	0	0.00	6	0	0	7	5	0	0	0	3	7	.208	.296	.208	25.9	11.1	27		
Tyler, Kyle	R-R	6-0	185	12-27-96	5	3	4.31	12	12	0	63	67	33	30	8	21	43	.270	.335	.435	15.6	7.6	276		
Vespi, Nick	L-L	6-3	235	10-10-95	0	0	7.85	20	0	1	18	22	17	16	3	15	13	.310	.437	.507	14.8	17.0	88		
Waguespack, Jacob	R-R	6-6	235	11-5-93	1	0	5.40	10	0	0	13	9	8	8	2	7	13	.191	.286	.319	23.2	12.5	56		
Walker, Josh	L-L	6-6	225	12-1-94	2	1	4.50	23	0	0	26	25	14	13	4	12	22	.260	.351	.406	19.8	10.8	111		
Walling, Andrew	L-L	6-2	220	10-29-99	1	1	3.60	5	0	0	5	3	2	2	1	4	7	.167	.348	.333	30.4	17.4	23		
Zuniga, Guillermo	R-R	6-5	230	10-10-98	3	1	5.14	38	0	3	42	36	24	24	3	20	43	.231	.341	.353	23.5	10.9	183		

Fielding

Catcher	PCT	G	PO	A	E	DP	PB
Breaux	1.000	18	122	8	0	1	0
Henry	.993	62	513	17	4	1	5
McIntosh	.974	4	37	0	1	0	0
Stubbs	.993	69	572	33	4	1	3

First Base	PCT	G	PO	A	E	DP
Anthony	.996	31	254	20	1	31
Arroyo	.995	31	201	14	1	19
Breaux	.950	8	53	4	3	8
Kemp	.990	18	87	8	1	8
Kennedy	.993	33	250	19	2	24
Taylor	1.000	3	18	1	0	1
Verdugo	1.000	24	138	16	0	19
Wilson	1.000	8	61	7	0	8

Second Base	PCT	G	PO	A	E	DP
Arroyo	1.000	9	18	20	0	6
Brito	1.000	4	7	13	0	4
Dunn	1.000	7	14	19	0	4
Kemp	.971	11	9	25	1	3
Kennedy	1.000	3	6	7	0	1

Third Base	PCT	G	PO	A	E	DP
Arroyo	1.000	2	2	2	0	1
Bohm	1.000	3	2	2	0	0
Brito	.962	22	12	38	2	6
Castro	.944	15	13	21	2	3
Dunn	1.000	2	2	2	0	0
Kemp	.914	43	27	47	7	5
Kennedy	.978	15	12	33	1	2
Kroon	.000	1	0	0	1	0
Lantigua	1.000	34	28	45	0	5
Moore	.667	4	1	3	2	0
Verdugo	.846	6	4	7	2	0
Walton	1.000	4	3	5	0	0
Wilson	.917	3	1	10	1	0

Shortstop	PCT	G	PO	A	E	DP
Brito	.981	14	19	34	1	7

	PCT	G	PO	A	E	DP
Castro	.955	111	159	264	20	65
Lantigua	.938	6	5	10	1	0
Miller	1.000	7	7	14	0	3
Verdugo	1.000	1	0	2	0	0
Walton	.961	11	16	33	2	10

Outfield	PCT	G	PO	A	E	DP
Castro	1.000	6	11	0	0	0
Crawford	.985	106	194	6	3	1
Fergus	1.000	7	12	0	0	0
Hicklen	1.000	22	48	1	0	1
Kemp	.947	9	18	0	1	0
Kroon	.962	14	24	1	1	0
Lantigua	1.000	4	7	0	0	0
Marsh	1.000	5	8	0	0	0
Mercado	.981	85	150	5	3	1
Reyes	1.000	3	7	0	0	0
Rincones	.982	78	160	5	3	0
Rojas	1.000	35	90	2	0	1
Stevenson	1.000	84	170	6	0	1
Wilson	1.000	11	15	1	0	0

READING FIGHTIN PHILS — DOUBLE-A
EASTERN LEAGUE

Batting	B-T	Ht.	Wt.	DOB	AVG	OBP	SLG	G	PA	AB	R	H	2B	3B	HR	RBI	BB	HBP	SH	SF	SO	SB	CS	BB%	SO%
Albrecht, Lou	R-R	6-0	210	11-7-01	.000	.250	.000	4	8	6	1	0	0	0	0	0	2	0	0	0	4	0	0	25.0	50.0
Anthony, Keaton	R-R	6-4	211	6-24-01	.330	.380	.522	49	200	182	23	60	21	1	4	29	14	2	0	2	40	0	0	7.0	20.0
Arnold, Zach	R-R	6-2	205	6-13-01	.148	.138	.185	7	29	27	1	4	1	0	0	5	0	0	0	2	12	0	0	0.0	41.4
Beer, Seth	L-R	6-0	225	9-18-96	.190	.283	.314	30	120	105	15	20	4	0	3	10	11	3	0	1	27	0	0	9.2	22.5
Bender, Colton	R-R	5-9	195	1-13-99	.000	.000	.000	1	3	3	0	0	0	0	0	0	0	0	0	0	1	0	0	0.0	33.3
Binelas, Alex	L-R	6-1	225	5-26-00	.265	.372	.425	68	269	226	34	60	10	1	8	37	39	1	0	3	73	1	0	14.5	27.1
Breaux, Josh	R-R	6-1	220	10-7-97	.209	.277	.372	14	47	43	5	9	2	1	1	3	2	2	0	0	14	0	0	4.3	29.8
Brito, Erick	R-R	5-8	134	5-25-02	.243	.297	.320	30	112	103	10	25	5	0	1	11	7	1	1	0	27	5	1	6.3	24.1
Caicuto, Luis	R-R	5-10	160	3-5-03	.000	.000	.000	1	3	3	0	0	0	0	0	0	0	0	0	0	1	0	0	0.0	33.3
Campbell, Dylan	R-R	5-11	205	7-2-02	.209	.295	.347	64	271	239	33	50	12	0	7	25	29	1	0	2	52	18	7	10.7	19.2
DeMartini, Carson	L-R	6-0	185	12-27-02	.202	.291	.288	66	292	257	37	52	10	3	2	22	28	5	0	2	75	27	7	9.6	25.7
Dissin, Jordan	R-R	6-3	185	5-29-02	.235	.297	.235	10	37	34	6	8	0	0	0	3	0	0	0	0	15	0	1	8.1	48.6
Dunn, Nick	L-R	5-8	185	1-29-97	.225	.333	.404	43	177	151	21	34	6	0	7	25	23	2	0	1	12	2	1	13.0	6.8
Escobar, Aroon	R-R	5-11	180	1-1-05	.182	.250	.273	5	24	22	2	4	0	0	1	0	1	2	0	0	0	0	0	8.3	25.0
Farquhar, Trent	L-R	5-8	180	3-12-01	.197	.333	.283	37	153	127	15	25	5	0	2	11	25	1	0	0	25	11	2	16.3	16.3
Fergus, Cade	R-R	6-2	195	8-22-00	.148	.266	.314	86	280	236	32	35	7	1	10	26	31	8	2	3	128	11	4	11.1	45.7
Hettiger, Kehden	R-R	6-2	195	2-6-00	.182	.308	.318	7	26	22	4	4	0	0	1	4	4	0	0	0	6	1	0	15.4	23.1
Lee Sang, Marcus	L-L	5-11	200	1-2-01	.182	.308	.182	4	13	11	1	2	0	0	0	0	2	0	0	0	2	1	0	15.4	15.4
McIntosh, Paul	R-R	6-2	220	11-20-97	.267	.345	.447	58	232	206	21	55	13	0	8	35	23	2	0	1	40	2	0	9.9	17.2
Mendez, Hendry	L-L	6-1	175	11-8-03	.274	.334	.434	85	349	297	44	86	15	3	11	42	36	9	0	7	44	6	1	11.5	12.6
Miller, Aidan	R-R	6-2	210	6-9-04	.259	.382	.427	108	489	405	74	105	25	2	13	41	73	9	0	2	116	52	14	14.9	23.7
Moore, Robert	S-R	5-9	170	3-31-02	.199	.284	.320	81	321	281	36	56	17	1	5	31	32	2	4	2	79	4	3	10.0	24.6
Nava, Andrick	S-R	5-10	175	10-6-01	.176	.278	.221	24	79	68	4	12	3	0	0	7	10	0	0	1	16	0	0	12.7	20.3

PHILADELPHIA PHILLIES

Batting (cont.)	B-T	Ht.	Wt.	DOB	AVG	OBP	SLG	G	PA	AB	R	H	2B	3B	HR	RBI	BB	HBP	SH	SF	SO	SB	CS	BB%	SO%
Nori, Dante	L-L	5-10	190	10-7-04	.190	.227	.286	5	22	21	1	4	0	1	0	0	1	0	0	0	2	2	1	4.5	9.1
Pineda, Leandro	L-L	6-1	165	6-4-02	.211	.320	.364	105	394	332	46	70	22	1	9	37	47	9	0	6	90	7	0	11.9	22.8
Prado, Elio	R-R	6-0	160	11-29-01	.200	.278	.275	23	90	80	9	16	3	0	1	8	8	1	0	1	32	2	2	8.9	35.6
Reyes, Felix	R-R	6-3	195	3-26-01	.335	.365	.572	95	395	367	62	123	34	4	15	65	18	3	0	7	61	13	2	4.6	15.4
Ricketts, Caleb	L-R	6-3	225	5-10-00	.256	.303	.399	58	238	223	26	57	14	0	6	27	14	1	0	0	44	0	1	5.9	18.5
Roberts, Cole	R-R	5-9	165	10-9-00	.231	.286	.231	6	14	13	2	3	0	0	0	1	0	0	0	0	4	0	0	7.1	28.6
Rodriguez, Jose	R-R	5-11	175	5-13-01	.303	.343	.384	26	108	99	11	30	5	0	1	16	6	1	0	2	13	5	3	5.6	12.0
Verdugo, Luis	R-R	6-0	160	10-12-00	.177	.272	.293	46	170	147	13	26	8	0	3	19	18	2	1	2	47	1	3	10.6	27.6
Ware, Bryson	R-R	6-2	193	12-28-00	.280	.322	.476	21	87	82	13	23	5	1	3	10	5	0	0	0	27	2	0	5.7	31.0

Pitching	B-T	Ht.	Wt.	DOB	W	L	ERA	G	GS	SV	IP	Hits	Runs	ER	HR	BB	SO	AVG	OBP	SLG	SO%	BB%	BF
Alvarez, Nelson L.	R-R	6-4	220	6-11-98	2	4	5.19	28	0	4	35	35	25	20	5	14	36	.263	.342	.429	22.8	8.9	158
Aoyagi, Koyo	R-R	5-11	175	12-11-93	1	2	6.91	4	4	0	14	10	11	11	4	15	12	.217	.424	.522	18.2	22.7	66
Baker, Andrew	R-R	6-1	190	3-24-00	1	1	5.95	16	0	1	20	25	15	13	2	9	27	.305	.374	.476	29.7	9.9	91
Barbosa, Gabriel	R-R	6-0	183	1-22-02	0	2	5.70	13	0	1	24	28	16	15	2	6	18	.311	.354	.478	18.0	6.0	100
Bechtold, Andrew	R-R	6-1	185	4-18-96	0	3	4.26	36	0	3	38	37	21	18	4	20	53	.242	.329	.405	30.6	11.6	173
Beckel, Brandon	R-R	6-4	225	10-20-01	0	0	18.00	1	0	0	2	5	4	4	0	3	1	.455	.571	.636	7.1	21.4	14
Cabrera, Jean	R-R	6-0	145	10-20-01	9	6	3.81	26	26	0	137	107	62	58	11	61	127	.214	.308	.334	22.2	10.6	573
Castellano, Eiberson	R-R	6-3	160	5-9-01	4	2	5.14	20	1	0	35	37	23	20	4	14	39	.270	.352	.394	24.2	8.7	161
Chace, Moises	R-R	6-1	213	6-9-03	0	0	3.24	6	6	0	17	15	6	6	3	12	19	.242	.360	.419	25.3	16.0	75
Crowe, Wil	R-R	6-2	245	9-9-94	3	3	7.00	11	9	0	36	41	30	28	5	15	27	.283	.350	.497	16.4	9.1	165
Dallas, Jack	R-R	5-11	200	12-18-98	1	1	3.47	31	3	0	49	46	25	19	4	14	49	.240	.297	.354	23.3	6.7	210
Estanista, Jaydenn	R-R	6-3	180	10-3-01	1	1	6.14	19	0	2	22	17	17	15	2	17	24	.221	.365	.351	24.7	17.5	97
Fausnaught, Braeden	L-L	6-3	235	7-29-99	2	6	4.61	12	10	0	53	63	35	27	9	17	52	.292	.349	.509	21.8	7.1	239
Fergus, Cade	R-R	6-2	195	8-22-00	0	0	0.00	1	0	0	0	0	0	0	0	1	0	.000	.500	.000	0.0	50.0	2
Garnett, Tristan	L-L	6-6	240	3-29-98	1	1	2.16	20	0	1	25	22	8	6	1	12	37	.232	.315	.368	33.9	11.0	109
Harper, Daniel	R-R	6-4	225	6-1-99	0	0	0.00	6	0	0	8	3	0	0	0	2	9	.120	.185	.160	33.3	7.4	27
Hejka, Josh	R-R	6-1	175	3-20-97	0	0	3.52	6	0	1	8	6	3	3	0	5	5	.214	.371	.286	14.3	14.3	35
Jimenez, Estibenzon	R-R	6-1	172	1-25-02	3	4	4.63	13	13	0	70	70	38	36	11	19	60	.263	.313	.417	20.3	6.4	295
King, Charles	R-R	6-5	215	1-6-98	8	6	4.38	25	23	0	123	138	65	60	18	37	105	.283	.335	.455	19.6	6.9	535
Kuhn, Travis	R-R	5-10	195	5-20-98	4	4	6.00	26	0	0	33	34	26	22	6	19	28	.258	.380	.417	17.7	12.0	158
Manning, Matt	R-R	6-6	195	1-28-98	0	1	10.80	2	2	0	5	3	6	6	0	7	8	.176	.440	.294	32.0	28.0	25
Mayer, Gunner	R-R	6-6	190	7-27-00	3	3	5.19	39	0	1	52	50	40	30	6	34	66	.248	.371	.406	26.5	13.7	249
McCollum, Tommy	R-R	6-5	260	6-8-99	0	3	3.20	37	0	9	45	38	21	16	3	11	48	.225	.274	.314	25.8	5.9	186
McFarlane, Alex	R-R	6-3	215	6-9-01	2	0	6.35	4	0	0	6	7	4	4	0	3	8	.318	.400	.455	32.0	12.0	25
McGarry, Griff	R-R	6-2	200	4-8-99	1	4	3.25	17	17	0	72	44	33	26	4	45	103	.175	.307	.274	33.9	14.8	304
McMillon, John	L-R	6-3	230	1-27-98	0	3	5.05	32	0	1	36	27	24	20	7	22	42	.203	.321	.414	26.3	13.8	160
Moore, Wesley	L-L	6-2	200	9-5-99	1	1	7.04	8	0	1	8	11	12	6	1	6	9	.344	.436	.594	23.1	15.4	39
Mosser, Gabe	R-R	6-4	185	6-8-96	2	4	5.01	8	8	0	41	39	28	23	6	13	50	.236	.292	.406	28.1	7.3	178
Neunborn, Mitch	R-R	6-0	190	6-27-97	3	5	5.12	24	7	0	58	54	34	33	11	14	62	.242	.289	.466	25.8	5.8	240
Russo, Luke	L-R	6-4	199	2-21-01	0	1	5.14	3	0	0	14	13	10	8	2	8	12	.236	.344	.382	18.8	12.5	64
Schultz, Andrew	R-R	6-4	225	7-31-97	0	1	6.14	14	0	0	15	20	14	10	2	10	18	.303	.410	.439	23.1	12.8	78
Teran, Saul	R-R	6-1	165	3-20-02	0	0	2.08	3	0	0	4	4	1	1	0	0	2	.235	.235	.412	11.8	0.0	17
Tortosa, Cristhian	L-L	6-4	170	10-30-98	0	0	6.75	2	0	0	3	4	2	2	0	1	4	.364	.385	.545	30.8	7.7	13
Tucker, Braydon	L-R	6-3	205	7-19-99	1	1	3.98	4	4	0	20	19	9	9	0	12	14	.264	.372	.319	16.1	13.8	87
Walling, Andrew	L-L	6-2	220	10-29-99	3	5	4.10	37	0	6	42	32	25	19	1	18	45	.203	.291	.285	24.9	9.9	181

Fielding

Catcher	PCT	G	PO	A	E	DP	PB
Albrecht	1.000	2	9	0	0	0	2
Breaux	1.000	12	91	2	0	0	0
Caicuto	.875	1	7	0	1	0	0
Dissin	1.000	10	83	12	0	1	1
Hettiger	1.000	7	78	8	0	2	3
McIntosh	.988	38	305	20	4	2	5
Nava	.976	21	157	8	4	1	3
Ricketts	.985	52	494	25	8	2	7

First Base	PCT	G	PO	A	E	DP
Anthony	.991	43	332	16	3	19
Arnold	.978	6	39	5	1	5
Beer	.974	16	103	8	3	10
Binelas	.994	48	289	25	2	27
Pineda	.974	7	35	3	1	2
Reyes	1.000	18	129	6	0	11
Ware	.857	1	6	0	1	1

Second Base	PCT	G	PO	A	E	DP
Brito	1.000	10	12	29	0	8
Dunn	.982	35	38	72	2	16
Escobar	.867	4	5	8	2	1
Farquhar	.976	32	49	75	3	14
Moore	.950	33	33	63	5	12
Roberts	.955	5	7	14	1	1
Rodriguez	.988	18	35	44	1	13
Verdugo	.929	5	2	11	1	0

Third Base	PCT	G	PO	A	E	DP
Binelas	.963	15	11	15	1	0
Brito	.941	8	5	11	1	0
DeMartini	.917	52	45	65	10	5
Farquhar	1.000	2	1	1	0	0
Moore	.900	25	5	31	4	3
Reyes	.909	4	2	8	1	1
Verdugo	.950	32	29	66	5	7
Ware	1.000	5	1	6	0	0

Shortstop	PCT	G	PO	A	E	DP
Brito	1.000	10	15	21	0	4
DeMartini	.872	11	16	18	5	4
Farquhar	1.000	1	1	1	0	0
Miller	.940	96	121	190	20	43
Moore	.971	12	10	23	1	1
Rodriguez	1.000	1	1	2	0	1
Verdugo	1.000	7	8	14	0	4

Outfield	PCT	G	PO	A	E	DP
Campbell	.994	63	172	8	1	1
Fergus	.974	82	149	3	4	1
Lee Sang	1.000	2	1	0	0	0
Mendez	.981	78	149	4	3	0
Moore	1.000	6	14	0	0	0
Nori	.929	5	13	0	1	0
Pineda	.965	89	158	7	6	2
Prado	.960	23	48	0	2	0
Reyes	.969	57	91	4	3	0
Rodriguez	1.000	3	8	0	0	0
Ware	1.000	16	35	0	0	0

JERSEY SHORE BLUECLAWS — HIGH-A
SOUTH ATLANTIC LEAGUE

Batting	B-T	Ht.	Wt.	DOB	AVG	OBP	SLG	G	PA	AB	R	H	2B	3B	HR	RBI	BB	HBP	SH	SF	SO	SB	CS	BB%	SO%
Arnold, Zach	R-R	6-2	205	6-13-01	.202	.272	.329	83	305	277	33	56	8	0	9	29	20	7	0	1	81	6	1	6.6	26.6
Bennett, Pierce	R-R	6-1	195	6-28-01	.196	.282	.277	69	255	224	23	44	5	2	3	24	25	3	0	3	37	2	3	9.8	14.5
Biddison, Nick	R-R	5-10	190	7-30-00	.210	.338	.306	19	75	62	13	13	3	0	1	6	7	5	0	0	19	7	1	9.3	25.3
Caicuto, Luis	R-R	5-10	160	3-5-03	.299	.372	.338	27	89	77	11	23	3	0	0	8	5	4	1	0	16	1	0	5.6	18.0

PHILADELPHIA PHILLIES

Batting

Player	B-T	Ht.	Wt.	DOB	AVG	OBP	SLG	G	AB	R	H	2B	3B	HR	RBI	BB	SO	SB	CS	OBP2	SLG2	BB%	SO%
Campbell, Dylan	R-R	5-11	205	7-2-02	.221	.302	.390	58	243	213	30	47	11	2	7	35	22	4	1	3	58	15	4	9.1	23.9
Colmenares, Jose	R-R	5-11	173	4-3-02	.207	.254	.379	17	63	58	6	12	2	1	2	10	3	1	0	1	16	5	3	4.8	25.4
Davis, Luke	S-R	6-0	190	1-9-03	.143	.364	.204	37	132	98	14	14	0	0	2	7	33	1	0	0	27	0	0	25.0	20.5
DeMartini, Carson	L-R	6-0	185	12-27-02	.284	.402	.474	53	229	190	34	54	10	1	8	30	31	7	0	1	64	18	5	13.5	27.9
Dissin, Jordan	R-R	6-3	185	5-29-02	.170	.303	.211	48	178	147	13	25	6	0	0	13	27	2	0	2	55	2	1	15.2	30.9
Dragoo, Joel	R-R	6-1	210	1-8-03	.169	.274	.253	28	96	83	6	14	5	1	0	7	11	1	1	0	25	2	1	11.5	30.8
Escobar, Aroon	R-R	5-11	180	1-1-05	.256	.348	.369	46	198	168	28	43	1	3	4	19	22	4	0	4	41	14	2	11.1	20.7
Farquhar, Trent	L-R	5-8	180	3-12-01	.229	.359	.281	29	119	96	16	22	5	0	0	10	19	1	2	1	18	7	3	16.0	15.1
Gonzalez, Diego	R-R	5-11	160	6-7-03	.222	.241	.333	10	30	27	4	6	0	0	1	8	1	0	1	1	6	0	0	3.3	20.0
Henry, Payton	R-R	6-0	229	6-24-97	.000	.333	.000	1	3	2	0	0	0	0	0	0	1	0	0	0	0	0	0	33.3	0.0
Heredia, Raylin	R-R	6-0	174	11-10-03	.285	.343	.467	50	184	165	24	47	7	1	7	41	12	3	0	1	46	5	1	6.5	25.0
Hettiger, Kehden	R-R	6-2	195	5-25-04	.232	.330	.389	85	355	306	35	71	20	2	8	50	44	2	0	3	104	1	1	12.4	29.3
Kroon, Matt	R-R	6-0	195	12-5-96	.185	.241	.370	7	29	27	2	5	2	0	1	1	1	0	0	0	11	2	1	3.4	37.9
Lopez, Eduardo	S-R	5-11	187	5-8-02	.169	.250	.331	34	144	130	17	22	4	1	5	20	13	1	0	0	40	3	1	9.0	27.8
McIntosh, Paul	R-R	6-1	220	11-20-97	.455	.455	.636	3	11	11	1	5	2	0	0	3	0	0	0	0	1	0	0	0.0	9.1
Nori, Dante	L-L	5-10	190	10-7-04	.279	.396	.326	11	53	43	8	12	2	0	0	4	8	1	0	1	8	13	2	15.1	15.1
Owusu-Asiedu, Avery	R-R	6-4	230	6-16-03	.247	.350	.368	49	207	174	34	43	9	3	2	21	28	1	1	3	50	17	3	13.5	24.2
Pouaka-Grego, Nikau	R-R	5-9	175	9-4-04	.154	.353	.154	5	17	13	4	2	0	0	0	1	4	0	0	0	3	0	0	23.5	17.6
Prado, Elio	R-R	6-0	160	11-29-01	.222	.294	.304	43	156	135	16	30	5	0	2	20	12	3	3	3	39	3	1	7.7	25.0
Ricketts, Caleb	L-R	6-3	225	5-10-00	.333	.313	.333	4	16	15	0	5	0	0	0	2	0	0	0	1	1	0	0	0.0	6.3
Rincon, Bryan	R-R	5-10	185	2-8-04	.181	.304	.298	84	359	299	58	54	13	2	6	31	50	4	4	2	103	40	5	13.9	28.7
Roberts, Cole	R-R	5-9	165	10-9-00	.143	.259	.143	25	83	70	5	10	0	0	0	6	11	0	2	0	16	2	0	13.3	19.3
Rodriguez, Jose	R-R	5-11	175	5-13-01	.333	.385	.333	4	13	12	1	4	0	0	0	1	0	0	0	0	3	0	0	7.7	23.1
Saltiban, Devin	R-R	5-10	180	2-14-05	.190	.269	.308	66	295	263	36	50	10	3	5	22	21	8	0	2	92	19	5	7.1	31.2
Shojinaga, Kodey	R-R	5-10	195	2-22-03	.239	.397	.283	15	58	46	9	11	2	0	0	2	10	2	0	0	8	0	0	17.2	13.8
Spikerman, John	S-R	6-0	177	4-2-03	.217	.362	.277	24	106	83	6	18	3	1	0	7	18	2	1	2	30	15	0	17.0	28.3
Tait, Eduardo	L-R	6-0	175	8-27-06	.296	.286	.407	7	28	27	2	8	3	0	0	6	0	0	1	1	0	0	0	0.0	3.6
Viars, Jordan	L-L	6-2	215	7-18-03	.138	.190	.202	31	100	94	9	13	1	1	2	5	5	1	0	0	38	1	0	5.0	38.0
Vradenburg, Brock	L-L	6-7	230	3-20-02	.205	.390	.318	15	59	44	8	9	2	0	1	4	14	0	0	1	18	1	0	23.7	30.5
Ware, Bryson	R-R	6-2	193	12-28-00	.229	.326	.379	72	281	240	44	55	12	0	8	28	29	7	1	3	83	5	2	10.3	29.5

Pitching

Player	B-T	Ht.	Wt.	DOB	W	L	ERA	G	GS	SV	IP	Hits	Runs	ER	HR	BB	SO	AVG	OBP	SLG	SO%	BB%	BF
Armenta, Erubiel	L-L	6-3	189	3-11-00	0	0	3.38	21	0	0	21	16	12	8	0	17	26	.205	.360	.231	26.0	17.0	100
Arnold, Zach	R-R	6-2	205	6-13-01	0	0	0.00	1	0	0	1	2	0	0	0	0	0	.500	.500	.500	0.0	0.0	4
Avila, Luis	R-R	6-1	170	5-26-03	1	2	9.26	11	0	0	12	13	13	12	2	10	9	.277	.435	.404	14.5	16.1	62
Baker, Andrew	R-R	6-1	190	3-24-00	1	1	4.24	27	0	6	34	33	17	16	3	13	43	.254	.319	.377	29.9	9.0	144
Barbosa, Gabriel	R-R	6-0	183	1-22-02	3	0	1.16	4	4	0	23	15	6	3	0	6	18	.174	.228	.221	19.6	6.5	92
Beckel, Brandon	R-R	6-4	225	10-20-01	3	3	3.20	27	7	0	76	62	35	27	7	27	70	.220	.290	.351	22.2	8.5	316
Brown, Cam	R-R	6-3	225	10-5-01	0	0	40.50	1	0	0	1	1	3	3	0	5	1	.333	.750	.333	12.5	62.5	8
Calderon, Augusto	R-R	6-0	190	10-6-00	3	0	12.60	16	0	0	15	28	23	21	1	9	19	.400	.489	.571	21.6	10.2	88
Castellano, Eiberson	R-R	6-3	160	5-9-01	0	1	40.50	1	1	0	1	4	6	6	0	3	0	.500	.636	.500	0.0	27.3	11
Chenault, Ethan	R-R	6-5	200	3-28-01	3	2	5.95	19	0	0	20	21	14	13	1	9	19	.276	.371	.408	21.3	10.1	89
Combs, Aaron	R-R	6-3	190	12-28-01	0	0	6.40	10	9	0	32	38	25	23	7	15	37	.292	.387	.538	24.5	9.9	151
Dromboski, Ryan	R-R	6-2	220	6-1-03	2	1	2.81	5	4	0	26	22	8	8	1	5	23	.232	.288	.305	22.1	4.8	104
Dutton, Reese	R-R	6-3	195	5-15-01	2	5	4.13	18	10	0	65	65	35	30	1	29	45	.264	.356	.354	15.8	10.2	284
Eddington, Jacob	R-R	6-2	185	4-26-01	3	1	4.66	19	0	0	29	27	17	15	1	22	31	.250	.378	.343	22.5	15.9	138
Estanista, Jaydenn	R-R	6-3	180	10-3-01	1	1	3.57	21	0	4	23	17	9	9	2	13	23	.213	.330	.375	24.2	13.7	95
Gabrysh, Luke	R-R	6-3	200	4-16-03	2	0	4.24	4	3	0	17	16	9	8	1	7	10	.250	.319	.328	13.9	9.7	72
Garrett, Drew	R-R	6-6	205	6-20-00	0	0	5.49	20	0	0	20	14	13	12	3	26	26	.200	.426	.386	25.7	25.7	101
Graves, Mavis	L-L	6-6	205	11-20-03	6	7	4.41	21	21	0	82	74	51	40	6	51	103	.239	.362	.390	27.7	13.7	372
Hayes, Titan	R-R	6-2	220	11-12-01	0	2	5.23	10	0	0	10	5	8	6	1	5	14	.135	.273	.216	31.8	11.4	44
Hejka, Josh	R-R	6-1	175	3-20-97	1	1	7.29	21	0	0	21	26	17	17	3	9	20	.299	.361	.540	20.6	9.3	97
Hernandez, Maxwel	R-R	6-2	190	5-14-03	0	0	0.00	1	0	0	1	0	0	0	0	1	0	.000	.000	.000	100.0	0	3
Highfill, Sam	R-R	6-3	203	11-30-00	2	1	3.77	6	6	0	31	28	14	13	0	9	17	.246	.312	.360	13.6	7.2	125
Jimenez, Estibenzon	R-R	6-1	172	1-25-02	5	2	5.09	14	6	0	53	52	31	30	9	15	56	.251	.308	.425	24.6	6.6	228
McCollum, Tommy	R-R	6-5	260	6-8-99	1	0	1.13	7	0	3	8	3	1	1	0	3	10	.120	.267	.200	33.3	10.0	30
McFarlane, Alex	R-R	6-3	215	6-9-01	2	9	4.72	24	18	0	74	60	42	39	4	40	74	.221	.327	.313	23.1	12.5	321
Moore, Wesley	L-L	6-2	200	9-5-99	1	4	5.04	25	1	0	30	28	18	17	1	19	27	.241	.360	.319	19.4	13.7	139
Ottenbreit, Micah	R-R	6-4	190	5-7-03	0	1	4.81	6	6	0	24	27	16	13	1	4	20	.290	.353	.398	19.0	3.8	105
Pena, Jose	R-R	6-3	200	7-8-03	0	0	2.87	14	0	0	16	15	7	5	1	6	18	.263	.333	.368	27.3	9.1	66
Ritchie, Erik	L-R	6-1	201	6-22-03	1	0	0.00	4	0	0	5	1	0	0	0	2	8	.063	.167	.125	44.4	11.1	18
Russo, Luke	L-R	6-4	199	2-21-01	1	0	2.28	7	0	0	24	16	7	6	2	8	32	.182	.250	.273	33.3	8.3	96
Steward, Casey	R-R	6-5	260	8-2-01	3	10	5.93	25	19	1	88	95	63	58	9	44	80	.274	.362	.427	19.7	10.8	407
Teran, Saul	R-R	6-1	165	3-20-02	3	0	1.38	22	0	11	26	16	5	4	0	13	23	.184	.290	.241	23.0	13.0	100
Thompson, Paxton	R-R	6-1	205	5-10-01	3	1	5.59	27	0	3	37	44	27	23	3	15	30	.293	.361	.447	18.1	9.0	166
Tortosa, Cristhian	L-L	6-4	170	10-30-98	4	3	3.93	27	0	0	34	23	19	15	3	21	53	.187	.320	.285	36.1	14.3	147
Tucker, Braydon	L-R	6-3	205	7-19-99	4	3	3.19	19	12	0	85	69	33	30	5	21	61	.223	.277	.313	18.2	6.3	336
Walling, Andrew	L-R	6-2	220	10-29-99	0	0	0.00	1	0	0	1	0	0	0	0	2	2	.400	.400	.400	40.0	0	5
Warunek, Kevin	L-L	6-4	201	11-19-02	1	0	5.87	7	0	1	8	7	5	5	0	6	9	.333	.421	.400	23.7	15.8	38
Wilkinson, Danny	L-L	6-0	206	10-19-00	0	0	4.50	2	0	0	2	3	1	1	0	1	5	.375	.444	.500	55.6	11.1	9
Wilson, A.J.	L-L	6-2	210	12-17-00	0	0	3.86	4	0	0	5	4	2	2	0	1	4	.250	.316	.375	21.1	5.3	199

Fielding

Catcher	PCT	G	PO	A	E	DP	PB
Caicuto	.975	16	110	5	3	0	4
Davis	.978	17	125	7	3	1	5
Dissin	.983	34	266	26	5	2	3
Henry	1.000	1	6	0	0	0	0
Hettiger	.990	52	452	29	5	5	3
McIntosh	.929	2	13	0	1	0	0
Ricketts	1.000	3	19	1	0	1	1
Shojinaga	.975	7	73	6	2	1	1
Tait	1.000	4	33	0	0	0	0

First Base	PCT	G	PO	A	E	DP
Arnold	.962	28	161	15	7	9
Caicuto	1.000	4	18	0	0	0
Davis	.953	9	59	2	3	10
Dissin	1.000	4	24	3	0	3

	PCT	G	PO	A	E	DP
Hettiger	.969	26	170	17	6	21
Lopez	1.000	7	39	2	0	4
Shojinaga	1.000	9	49	8	0	5
Vradenburg	.975	14	113	6	3	7
Ware	.983	17	107	6	2	10

Second Base	PCT	G	PO	A	E	DP
Arnold	.971	10	14	20	1	4
Biddison	1.000	2	4	2	0	0
Campbell	.955	11	14	28	2	4
Escobar	.981	42	55	102	3	23
Farquhar	.923	4	4	8	1	2
Gonzalez	.000	1	0	0	0	0
Pouaka-Grego	1.000	4	2	14	0	2
Roberts	.975	24	34	44	2	5
Saltiban	.962	20	30	46	3	7
Ware	.963	15	20	32	2	10

Third Base	PCT	G	PO	A	E	DP
Arnold	.949	39	28	47	4	4
Biddison	.933	18	14	28	3	2
DeMartini	.919	37	24	44	6	3
Farquhar	.977	22	20	22	1	3
Gonzalez	1.000	1	1	1	0	1
Pouaka-Grego	.000	1	0	0	0	0
Ware	.850	12	10	7	3	0

Shortstop	PCT	G	PO	A	E	DP
Colmenares	1.000	17	34	35	0	11
DeMartini	.957	14	18	26	2	3
Farquhar	1.000	3	0	6	0	2
Gonzalez	.964	8	10	17	1	2
Rincon	.975	80	124	154	7	36
Roberts	1.000	2	0	3	0	2
Rodriguez	1.000	3	5	4	0	1
Ware	1.000	5	6	10	0	1

Outfield	PCT	G	PO	A	E	DP
Bennett	.993	65	133	3	1	2
Campbell	.991	47	108	5	1	3
Dragoo	.970	20	31	1	1	1
Heredia	.921	42	67	3	6	1
Kroon	1.000	6	10	0	0	0
Lopez	.935	22	29	0	2	0
Nori	1.000	10	20	0	0	0
Owusu-Asiedu	.981	42	105	1	2	0
Prado	.978	40	87	0	2	0
Saltiban	.974	35	74	1	2	0
Spikerman	.950	20	35	3	2	0
Viars	1.000	27	31	2	0	1
Ware	1.000	20	32	1	0	0

CLEARWATER THRESHERS LOW-A
FLORIDA STATE LEAGUE

Batting	B-T	Ht.	Wt.	DOB	AVG	OBP	SLG	G	PA	AB	R	H	2B	3B	HR	RBI	BB	HBP	SH	SF	SO	SB	CS	BB%	SO%
Arroyo, Christian	R-R	6-1	210	5-30-95	.176	.176	.176	5	17	17	0	3	0	0	0	2	0	0	0	0	3	0	0	0.0	17.6
Barker, Jack	L-L	6-0	200	6-23-05	.138	.324	.138	9	37	29	4	4	0	0	0	7	1	0	0	0	11	1	1	18.9	29.7
Beltran, Nolan	R-R	6-0	160	1-24-05	.183	.264	.261	35	131	115	6	21	4	1	1	12	13	0	2	1	18	0	0	9.9	13.7
Burkholder, Griffin	R-R	6-2	195	8-30-05	.203	.309	.406	19	81	69	11	14	6	1	2	5	7	4	0	1	25	0	0	8.6	30.9
Caicuto, Luis	R-R	5-10	160	3-5-03	.167	.167	.167	9	6	6	0	1	0	0	0	0	0	0	0	0	3	0	0	0.0	50.0
Cardoza, Victor	R-R	5-11	181	1-19-06	.250	.400	.250	1	5	4	0	1	0	0	0	0	1	0	0	0	2	0	0	20.0	40.0
Davis, Luke	S-R	6-0	190	1-9-03	.195	.381	.280	30	113	82	11	16	4	0	1	17	25	2	0	4	23	0	0	22.1	20.4
Dawson, Logan	L-R	6-3	190	6-15-06	.333	.500	.333	1	4	3	0	1	0	0	0	1	0	0	0	0	2	0	0	25.0	50.0
Day, Brady	L-R	5-11	185	8-6-02	.261	.346	.348	65	270	230	35	60	10	2	2	25	32	1	1	6	36	9	4	11.9	13.3
Dragoo, Joel	R-R	6-1	210	1-8-03	.177	.294	.226	47	194	164	15	29	8	0	0	12	27	1	0	2	57	2	0	13.9	29.4
Escalona, Yhoan	R-R	6-2	185	11-4-05	.143	.143	.143	2	7	7	1	1	0	0	0	0	0	0	0	0	1	0	0	0.0	14.3
Escobar, Aroon	R-R	5-11	180	1-1-05	.285	.377	.452	69	316	270	52	77	12	0	11	42	32	10	0	4	51	10	3	10.1	16.1
Farquhar, Trent	L-R	5-8	180	3-12-01	.241	.389	.276	9	36	29	8	7	1	0	0	3	6	1	0	0	1	0	0	16.7	2.8
Ferrara, Matthew	L-R	6-0	183	6-4-07	.130	.266	.204	15	64	54	6	7	1	0	1	3	5	5	0	0	23	1	0	7.8	35.9
Ferrebus, Alirio	R-R	6-2	174	9-12-05	.219	.272	.275	44	174	160	22	35	6	0	1	25	6	6	0	1	28	2	0	3.4	16.1
Gonzalez, Diego	R-R	5-11	160	6-7-03	.170	.286	.191	45	168	141	16	24	0	0	1	11	20	4	0	3	41	1	1	11.9	24.4
Hettiger, Kehden	S-R	6-2	195	5-25-04	.080	.250	.120	8	32	25	4	2	1	0	0	1	6	0	0	1	10	0	0	18.8	31.3
Hogart, Jonathan	R-R	6-1	205	5-1-02	.284	.439	.444	24	107	81	19	23	2	1	3	10	17	7	0	2	28	1	1	15.9	26.2
Humphreys, Nathan	R-R	6-2	202	8-16-02	.233	.337	.360	24	102	86	10	20	5	0	2	14	14	0	1	1	33	4	1	13.7	32.4
Jimenez, Manolfi	L-L	6-0	190	11-14-04	.235	.323	.272	25	94	81	11	19	3	0	0	6	8	3	1	1	20	2	2	8.5	21.3
Mathison, Carter	L-L	6-0	190	7-13-04	.200	.313	.338	70	269	225	29	45	8	1	7	32	32	7	0	4	94	9	1	11.9	34.9
Mujica, Cesar	R-R	6-2	198	3-30-07	.000	.000	.000	1	3	3	0	0	0	0	0	0	0	0	0	0	2	0	0	0.0	66.7
Nori, Dante	L-L	5-10	190	10-7-04	.262	.363	.381	109	502	423	63	111	16	11	4	43	66	4	3	6	75	37	7	13.1	14.9
Owusu-Asiedu, Avery	R-R	6-4	230	6-16-03	.268	.382	.402	58	218	179	37	48	7	1	5	23	30	5	1	3	52	16	2	13.8	23.9
Pettorini, Tyler	L-R	5-11	170	11-9-02	.241	.326	.291	24	92	79	10	19	2	1	0	9	9	2	0	2	16	3	3	9.8	17.4
Phelps, Robert	R-R	5-10	170	1-30-04	.231	.415	.282	12	53	39	8	9	2	0	0	7	12	1	0	1	8	5	1	22.6	15.1
Pouaka-Grego, Nikau	L-R	5-9	175	9-13-04	.186	.308	.256	32	106	86	11	16	3	0	1	12	14	2	2	2	22	0	0	13.2	20.8
Ricketts, Caleb	L-R	6-3	225	5-10-00	.538	.538	1.231	3	13	13	6	7	3	0	2	5	0	0	0	0	2	0	0	0.0	15.4
Roberts, Cole	R-R	5-9	165	10-9-00	.150	.190	.150	7	21	20	3	3	0	0	0	0	1	0	0	0	1	0	0	4.8	4.8
Rodriguez, Jose	R-R	5-11	175	5-13-01	.273	.273	.318	11	44	44	4	12	0	1	0	2	0	0	0	0	7	1	1	0.0	15.9
Rosario, Guillermo	R-R	6-2	190	4-22-05	.115	.188	.149	27	96	87	3	10	0	0	1	7	8	0	0	1	38	0	0	8.3	39.6
Saltiban, Devin	R-R	5-10	180	2-14-05	.600	.600	1.200	1	5	5	2	3	0	0	1	3	0	0	0	0	0	0	0	0.0	0.0
Shojinaga, Kodey	R-R	5-10	195	2-22-03	.229	.340	.296	70	283	240	30	55	11	1	1	33	39	2	0	1	46	1	1	13.8	16.3
Spikerman, John	S-R	6-0	177	4-2-03	.138	.330	.376	28	130	100	25	17	4	1	5	11	30	1	3	0	37	12	0	9.6	32.2
Tait, Eduardo	L-R	6-0	175	8-27-06	.251	.322	.436	75	332	291	41	73	19	1	11	51	30	4	0	7	64	0	0	9.0	19.3
Tello, Raider	R-R	6-0	205	2-25-01	.277	.347	.398	101	398	354	42	98	19	0	8	55	32	7	2	2	93	1	0	8.0	23.4
Thomas, Jared	L-R	6-0	190	12-3-00	.500	.500	.500	2	4	2	0	1	0	0	0	0	0	0	0	0	0	0	0	0.0	50.0
Vierling, Will	L-R	6-1	220	8-23-03	.191	.321	.298	14	56	47	6	9	2	0	1	6	7	2	0	0	13	0	0	12.5	23.2
Villavicencio, Juan	L-R	5-10	155	11-24-04	.146	.298	.207	26	104	82	13	12	2	0	1	0	17	2	0	3	30	9	0	16.3	28.8
Walton, TayShaun	R-R	6-3	225	1-29-06	.296	.256	.342	34	142	125	20	25	3	2	0	12	15	2	0	0	48	10	5	10.6	33.8
Wilson, Weston	R-R	6-3	215	9-11-94	.100	.357	.100	4	14	10	4	1	0	0	0	1	4	0	0	0	3	1	0	28.6	21.4

Pitching	B-T	Ht.	Wt.	DOB	W	L	ERA	G	GS	SV	IP	Hits	Runs	ER	HR	BB	SO	AVG	OBP	SLG	SO%	BB%	BF
Amarante, Juan	L-L	5-10	177	4-14-04	1	3	4.45	13	12	0	55	52	30	27	5	23	49	.248	.333	.357	20.4	9.6	240
Armenta, Erubiel	L-L	6-3	189	3-11-00	2	0	9.00	4	0	0	4	4	4	4	0	4	11	.077	.294	.154	64.7	23.5	17
Avila, Luis	R-R	6-1	170	5-26-03	4	0	3.60	24	0	4	40	22	16	16	2	26	47	.163	.310	.244	27.8	15.4	169
Barbosa, Gabriel	R-R	6-0	183	1-22-02	1	1	3.83	16	4	0	40	43	19	17	4	17	33	.274	.346	.414	18.4	9.5	179
Batka, Keegan	R-R	6-1	205	5-1-02	0	0	0.00	2	0	0	2	0	0	0	0	0	2	.250	.250	.250	25.0	0.0	8
Brown, Cam	R-R	6-3	225	10-15-01	0	1	81.00	1	0	0	0	1	3	3	0	2	1	.500	.750	.500	25.0	50.0	4
Combs, Aaron	R-R	6-3	190	12-28-01	0	0	0.00	1	0	0	1	0	0	0	0	2	0	.000	.400	.400	0.0	40.0	5
Craig, Gabe	R-R	6-5	190	7-3-01	0	0	0.00	3	0	0	5	3	0	0	0	1	5	.000	.100	.000	50.0	10.0	10
Degges, Bryan	R-R	5-11	180	9-9-02	3	2	3.89	22	18	0	81	75	40	35	9	50	72	.253	.362	.400	20.3	14.1	354
Dromboski, Ryan	R-R	6-2	220	6-1-03	7	5	2.63	17	9	0	55	45	17	16	3	19	53	.230	.303	.342	24.2	8.7	219
Dutton, Reese	R-R	6-2	195	5-15-01	1	1	3.86	11	4	0	40	29	16	17	3	11	39	.245	.319	.408	23.5	6.6	166
Eddington, Jacob	R-R	6-2	185	4-26-01	3	1	5.20	13	0	2	28	24	18	16	3	17	25	.231	.344	.385	20.5	13.9	122

PHILADELPHIA PHILLIES

Batting	B-T	Ht.	Wt.	DOB			AVG															OBP	SLG
Gabrysh, Luke	R-R	6-3	200	4-16-03	5	4	3.08	17	16	0	61	50	21	21	5	25	49	.231	.313	.324	19.9	10.2	246
Gair, Marty	R-R	6-6	230	7-17-03	0	0	4.33	24	0	0	27	20	15	13	2	34	40	.215	.426	.312	31.0	26.4	129
Garria, Josbel	R-R	6-0	165	3-30-04	1	0	9.72	4	0	0	8	15	9	9	1	3	4	.385	.429	.641	9.5	7.1	42
Garnett, Tristan	L-L	6-6	240	3-29-98	0	0	0.00	4	0	1	5	4	0	0	0	1	6	.200	.238	.200	28.6	4.8	21
Gilley, Cole	R-R	6-0	238	7-22-01	0	0	0.00	1	0	0	2	0	0	0	0	1	3	.000	.143	.000	42.9	14.3	7
Gonzalez, Luis	R-R	6-0	170	7-15-05	0	1	6.43	2	2	0	7	8	7	5	0	4	5	.286	.394	.357	14.7	11.8	34
Gonzalez, Orlando	R-R	6-1	220	11-22-02	3	3	4.29	23	2	5	42	45	23	20	2	17	40	.269	.341	.389	21.6	9.2	185
Harper, Daniel	R-R	6-4	225	6-1-99	0	0	2.08	4	0	0	4	3	1	1	0	2	6	.188	.278	.250	33.3	11.1	18
Havard, Peyton	R-R	6-0	215	1-30-02	0	0	0.00	1	0	0	1	0	0	0	0	2	2	.000	.400	.000	40.0	40.0	5
Hayes, Titan	R-R	6-2	220	11-12-01	1	4	4.58	30	0	6	35	36	25	18	2	25	52	.265	.388	.397	31.1	15.0	167
Hernandez, Maxwell	R-R	6-2	190	5-14-03	0	1	11.37	3	0	0	6	11	9	8	3	2	6	.367	.429	.733	17.1	5.7	35
Highfill, Sam	R-R	6-3	203	11-30-00	3	7	4.80	18	16	0	75	81	46	40	13	24	74	.270	.321	.463	22.6	7.3	327
Hill, Camron	L-L	6-6	220	6-15-03	0	1	5.40	5	4	0	15	14	9	9	0	18	18	.246	.449	.316	22.8	22.8	79
Liranzo, Angel	L-L	6-1	172	8-5-06	0	1	4.66	5	4	0	19	20	14	10	3	10	13	.256	.356	.423	14.4	11.1	90
Marquez, Ramon	R-R	6-2	182	9-19-05	2	0	4.24	4	4	0	17	16	8	8	0	5	22	.258	.329	.371	31.4	7.1	70
McGarry, Griff	R-R	6-2	190	6-8-99	0	1	6.75	3	3	0	7	8	5	5	0	2	13	.308	.400	.346	43.3	6.7	30
Morgan, Marcus	L-R	6-2	200	12-27-02	1	1	10.13	8	4	0	13	15	17	15	0	24	12	.300	.538	.400	15.0	30.0	80
Painter, Andrew	R-R	6-7	215	4-10-03	0	2	3.97	4	4	0	11	10	5	5	2	1	12	.227	.244	.432	26.7	2.2	45
Pena, Jose	R-R	6-3	200	7-8-03	4	1	0.71	20	0	5	25	11	5	2	1	7	23	.129	.196	.165	25.0	7.6	92
Peralta, Adilson	R-R	6-4	175	6-17-03	4	1	3.68	28	1	2	51	38	26	21	3	29	48	.203	.309	.316	21.8	13.2	220
Pulido, Danyony	R-R	6-1	165	10-19-02	5	1	1.17	22	0	5	31	12	8	4	0	19	35	.122	.279	.122	28.7	15.6	122
Ritchie, Erik	L-L	6-1	201	6-22-03	3	1	8.07	21	0	1	29	35	27	26	4	25	31	.302	.424	.457	21.5	17.4	144
Rosario, Raymon	L-L	6-2	198	6-6-05	0	0	8.59	5	0	0	7	9	7	7	0	3	6	.300	.417	.367	16.7	8.3	36
Segura, Enrique	R-R	6-3	175	12-19-04	1	2	3.18	4	3	0	17	12	8	6	0	8	19	.190	.307	.222	25.0	10.5	76
Suarez, Ranger	L-L	6-1	217	8-26-95	0	0	1.29	2	2	0	7	4	1	1	0	1	11	.167	.200	.250	44.0	4.0	25
Teran, Saul	R-R	6-1	165	3-20-02	2	1	1.00	15	0	4	18	13	2	2	0	3	31	.203	.250	.297	44.9	4.3	69
Trop, Eli	R-R	6-4	225	5-4-02	0	2	6.46	23	0	0	31	24	22	22	5	31	31	.216	.421	.396	20.4	20.4	152
Tukis, Zack	R-R	6-5	180	9-10-02	5	3	7.82	28	6	0	51	52	48	44	3	52	53	.263	.422	.384	20.5	20.2	258
Velasquez, Giuseppe	R-R	6-1	170	4-30-03	1	4	6.42	8	7	0	34	35	25	24	5	15	21	.267	.349	.466	14.1	10.1	149
Warunek, Kevin	L-L	6-4	201	11-19-02	1	0	2.91	19	0	1	34	25	13	11	4	11	44	.198	.266	.325	31.7	7.9	139
Wilkinson, Danny	L-L	6-0	206	10-19-00	0	1	1.46	9	0	0	12	6	2	2	1	8	17	.143	.275	.238	33.3	15.7	51
Wilson, A.J.	R-R	6-2	210	12-17-00	3	1	6.23	23	0	0	35	20	26	24	4	25	45	.169	.329	.305	30.0	16.7	150
Wood, Gage	R-R	6-0	210	12-15-03	0	1	4.50	1	1	0	2	1	1	1	0	2	5	.143	.333	.143	55.6	22.2	9
Yousuf, Zuher	L-L	5-10	174	5-24-06	2	1	2.04	5	2	0	18	15	4	4	2	11	22	.221	.338	.338	27.5	13.8	80

Fielding

Catcher	PCT	G	PO	A	E	DP	PB
Caicuto	.920	2	21	2	2	0	1
Davis	1.000	8	60	7	0	0	0
Escalona	1.000	2	14	0	0	0	0
Ferrebus	.994	19	165	12	1	0	2
Hettiger	1.000	2	26	0	0	1	1
Mujica	1.000	1	8	0	0	0	0
Ricketts	1.000	2	10	0	0	2	15
Rosario	.968	11	89	3	3	0	4
Shojinaga	.985	36	300	23	5	2	14
Tait	.988	39	362	36	5	2	7
Thomas	1.000	2	16	0	0	1	0
Vierling	.991	11	99	11	1	0	3

First Base	PCT	G	PO	A	E	DP
Arroyo	1.000	3	16	1	0	1
Davis	.974	19	108	6	3	9
Ferrebus	.984	18	119	7	2	10
Hettiger	1.000	4	22	0	0	4
Rosario	.984	17	111	9	2	10
Shojinaga	.991	31	214	19	2	15
Tello	.997	44	278	21	1	21

Second Base	PCT	G	PO	A	E	DP
Arroyo	1.000	1	2	1	0	0

Day	1.000	2	4	1	0	1
Escobar	.958	61	114	134	11	28
Farquhar	1.000	7	8	8	0	3
Ferrara	.940	15	18	29	3	3
Gonzalez	.875	1	5	2	1	3
Pettorini	.971	12	12	22	1	4
Phelps	1.000	3	9	4	0	0
Pouaka-Grego	.956	19	31	34	3	10
Roberts	1.000	5	10	7	0	0
Tello	.914	9	19	13	3	4

Third Base	PCT	G	PO	A	E	DP
Arroyo	1.000	1	0	1	0	0
Davis	.000	1	0	0	0	0
Day	.967	62	53	121	6	14
Escobar	.833	3	2	3	1	0
Farquhar	.000	1	0	0	0	0
Gonzalez	.926	11	6	19	2	1
Pettorini	.897	12	9	17	3	2
Pouaka-Grego	.944	10	3	14	1	0
Tello	1.000	34	20	49	0	2
Wilson	1.000	1	0	2	0	0

Shortstop	PCT	G	PO	A	E	DP
Beltran	.942	35	51	79	8	13

Dawson	1.000	1	2	2	0	0
Gonzalez	.945	32	35	85	7	14
Phelps	.947	9	9	27	2	4
Pouaka-Grego	.714	3	2	3	2	0
Roberts	1.000	2	1	8	0	0
Rodriguez	.917	11	8	25	3	4
Tello	.979	14	17	30	1	7
Villavicencio	.968	23	31	60	3	10

Outfield	PCT	G	PO	A	E	DP
Barker	1.000	7	11	0	0	0
Burkholder	.974	19	36	2	1	1
Cardoza	1.000	1	2	0	0	0
Dragoo	.971	40	63	3	2	1
Hogart	1.000	20	38	3	0	0
Humphreys	1.000	20	51	1	0	0
Jimenez	1.000	22	26	1	0	0
Mathison	.983	69	114	5	2	2
Nori	.995	87	193	3	1	0
Owusu-Asiedu	.971	54	95	4	3	0
Saltiban	1.000	1	2	0	0	0
Spikerman	1.000	20	45	5	0	2
Tello	1.000	2	1	0	0	0
Walton	.984	29	59	2	1	0
Wilson	1.000	3	7	0	0	0

FCL PHILLIES — ROOKIE
FLORIDA COMPLEX LEAGUE

Batting	B-T	Ht.	Wt.	DOB	AVG	OBP	SLG	G	PA	AB	R	H	2B	3B	HR	RBI	BB	HBP	SH	SF	SO	SB	CS	BB%	SO%
Albrecht, Lou	R-R	6-0	210	11-7-01	.100	.182	.100	5	11	10	0	1	0	0	0	1	1	0	0	0	2	0	0	9.1	18.2
Beltran, Nolan	L-R	6-0	160	1-24-05	.250	.400	.250	4	10	8	1	2	0	0	0	0	1	0	0	0	2	0	0	10.0	20.0
Burkholder, Griffin	R-R	6-2	195	8-30-05	.190	.266	.362	15	64	58	5	11	4	0	2	8	5	1	0	0	17	1	0	7.8	26.6
Calderon, Jaeden	R-R	6-1	208	9-17-05	.235	.366	.324	12	41	34	4	8	3	0	0	1	7	0	0	0	9	3	0	17.1	22.0
Cardoza, Victor	R-R	5-11	181	1-19-06	.222	.287	.342	46	174	158	18	35	8	1	3	15	13	2	0	1	55	6	2	7.5	31.6
Davis, Luke	S-R	6-0	190	7-1-04	.476	.533	.476	12	42	30	5	8	2	0	2	2	12	0	0	0	7	0	0	28.6	16.7
De Leon, Meylin	R-R	5-11	170	4-21-07	.116	.200	.170	40	125	112	9	13	3	0	1	7	10	2	0	1	29	1	0	8.0	23.2
Dipre, Isaias	R-R	5-11	159	6-7-03	.252	.336	.412	46	137	119	15	30	5	3	0	2	13	12	4	0	2	27	3	0	8.8	19.7
Escalona, Yhoan	R-R	6-2	185	11-4-05	.143	.294	.214	4	17	14	2	2	1	0	0	0	3	0	0	0	4	0	0	17.6	23.5
Familia, Jose	R-R	6-2	163	8-16-07	.164	.238	.192	46	160	146	8	24	4	0	0	12	2	0	0	0	61	3	1	7.5	38.1
Farquhar, Trent	L-R	5-8	180	3-12-01	.111	.111	.111	3	9	9	1	1	0	0	0	0	0	0	0	0	1	0	0	0.0	0.0
Ferrebus, Alirio	R-R	6-2	174	9-12-05	.267	.368	.478	25	106	90	15	24	5	1	4	18	11	4	0	1	17	0	1	10.4	16.0

Batting	B-T	Ht.	Wt.	DOB	AVG	OBP	SLG	G	PA	AB	R	H	2B	3B	HR	RBI	BB	HBP	SH	SF	SO	SB	CS	BB%	SO%
Garcia, Adrian	S-R	6-2	170	11-27-06	.262	.329	.369	44	143	130	13	34	6	4	0	8	10	3	0	0	28	3	2	7.0	19.6
Heredia, Raylin	R-R	6-0	174	11-10-03	.343	.351	.486	10	37	35	5	12	2	0	1	4	1	0	0	1	6	2	0	2.7	16.2
Jimenez, Manolfi	L-L	6-0	190	11-14-04	.306	.339	.529	46	171	157	27	48	13	5	4	20	6	4	0	4	26	3	4	3.5	15.2
Julio, Jorge	R-R	6-1	182	8-4-06	.253	.297	.301	26	91	83	4	21	4	0	0	10	6	0	0	2	18	2	0	6.6	19.8
Loreto, Francisco	R-R	6-0	178	6-21-07	.237	.332	.396	47	193	169	28	40	10	1	5	16	19	5	0	0	46	2	0	9.8	23.8
Mata, Angel	R-R	6-1	175	1-4-05	.204	.292	.296	44	162	142	15	29	10	0	1	20	15	3	1	1	33	0	0	9.3	20.4
Mathison, Carter	L-L	6-1	190	1-26-03	.182	.438	.273	4	16	11	4	2	1	0	0	0	3	2	0	0	5	2	0	18.8	31.3
Mujica, Cesar	R-R	6-2	198	3-30-07	.176	.279	.220	31	104	91	6	16	4	0	0	5	11	2	0	0	28	0	2	10.6	26.9
Perez, Rickardo	L-R	5-10	172	12-4-03	.234	.275	.313	19	69	64	4	15	3	1	0	8	4	0	0	1	12	0	1	5.8	17.4
Pouaka-Grego, Nikau	L-R	5-9	175	9-13-04	.333	.500	.333	1	4	3	1	1	0	0	0	0	1	0	0	0	2	0	0	25.0	50.0
Rosario, Guillermo	R-R	6-2	190	4-22-05	.180	.333	.260	19	63	50	5	9	1	0	1	7	10	2	0	1	11	2	0	15.9	17.5
Saltiban, Devin	R-R	5-10	180	2-14-05	.054	.146	.162	10	41	37	4	2	1	0	1	1	2	2	0	0	10	0	4	4.9	24.4
Spikerman, John	S-R	6-0	177	4-2-03	.192	.417	.231	10	36	26	8	5	1	0	0	1	9	1	0	0	10	3	0	25.0	27.8
Villavicencio, Juan	L-R	5-10	155	11-24-04	.286	.318	.524	7	22	21	2	6	2	0	1	3	1	0	0	0	7	2	1	4.5	31.8
Walton, TayShaun	R-R	6-3	225	1-29-05	.306	.381	.389	11	42	36	7	11	1	1	0	5	0	1	0	0	15	5	0	11.9	35.7

Pitching	B-T	Ht.	Wt.	DOB	W	L	ERA	G	GS	SV	IP	Hits	Runs	ER	HR	BB	SO	AVG	OBP	SLG	SO%	BB%	BF
Amarante, Juan	L-L	5-10	177	4-14-04	1	3	4.09	5	5	0	22	19	12	10	0	8	25	.229	.305	.289	26.3	8.4	95
Arias, Eligio	R-R	6-7	230	3-26-03	1	2	4.94	15	0	1	24	18	15	13	2	14	26	.212	.368	.341	24.5	13.2	106
Brown, Cam	R-R	6-3	225	10-15-01	0	1	14.21	6	0	0	6	9	10	10	0	11	6	.346	.561	.385	14.6	26.8	41
Cusick, Ryan	R-R	6-6	235	11-12-99	0	0	0.00	1	1	0	1	0	0	0	0	1	1	.000	.500	.000	25.0	25.0	4
De La Cruz, Alexis	R-R	6-6	205	9-20-04	1	4	7.61	16	0	0	24	22	27	20	2	16	25	.242	.381	.352	22.1	14.2	113
De Los Santos, Alexander	R-R	6-1	160	8-23-06	0	1	5.79	2	1	0	5	4	4	3	1	4	7	.222	.391	.444	30.4	17.4	23
Garcia, Josbel	R-R	6-0	165	3-30-04	0	1	5.64	16	0	3	22	25	18	14	3	6	19	.291	.347	.488	19.4	6.1	98
Gonzalez, Luis	R-R	6-0	170	7-15-05	2	3	3.04	12	7	0	47	44	21	16	2	13	33	.237	.297	.328	16.3	6.4	202
Gonzalez, Orlando	R-R	6-1	220	11-22-02	0	1	3.86	5	0	0	7	12	6	3	0	2	7	.387	.424	.452	21.2	6.1	33
Heredia, Joel	R-R	6-6	190	1-15-04	2	1	4.32	14	0	0	17	14	11	8	0	15	12	.237	.403	.305	15.6	19.5	77
Hernandez, Maxwell	R-R	6-2	190	5-14-03	2	2	4.31	13	1	0	31	38	19	15	3	11	25	.304	.364	.472	17.9	7.9	140
Hill, Camron	L-L	6-6	220	6-15-03	0	1	1.35	3	3	0	7	5	2	1	0	5	9	.200	.333	.240	30.0	16.7	30
Liranzo, Angel	L-L	6-1	172	8-5-06	0	5	3.60	12	10	0	55	59	29	22	6	18	46	.274	.330	.400	19.2	7.5	240
Marquez, Ramon	R-R	6-2	182	9-19-05	1	3	4.50	10	8	0	38	36	20	19	4	12	50	.245	.333	.381	29.8	7.1	168
Pacheco, Brad	R-R	6-0	175	6-9-05	2	6	6.15	12	12	0	45	46	38	31	4	14	46	.261	.325	.392	23.2	7.1	198
Peralta, Adilson	R-R	6-4	215	6-17-03	0	0	0.00	1	0	0	1	0	0	0	0	1	1	.250	.250	.250	25.0	0.0	4
Pulido, Danyony	R-R	6-1	165	10-19-02	1	0	0.90	6	2	1	10	7	1	1	0	2	14	.189	.268	.189	34.1	4.9	41
Ramos, Fernando	R-R	6-0	164	1-25-03	0	2	2.54	14	0	0	28	25	12	8	0	8	25	.245	.319	.333	21.6	6.9	116
Reyes, Pedro	R-R	6-3	175	11-26-02	0	3	7.82	12	2	2	25	35	30	22	1	14	19	.318	.412	.409	14.5	10.7	131
Ritchie, Erik	L-L	6-1	201	6-2-02	0	0	1.80	3	0	0	5	2	3	1	0	4	4	.105	.250	.105	16.7	16.7	24
Rosario, Raymon	L-L	6-2	198	6-6-05	1	2	7.54	13	1	0	23	29	26	19	0	15	21	.319	.418	.385	19.1	13.6	110
Velasquez, Giussepe	R-R	6-1	170	4-30-03	0	2	0.54	5	2	0	17	6	2	1	0	2	20	.150	.177	.167	32.3	3.2	62
Wilkinson, Danny	L-L	6-0	206	10-19-00	0	1	0.00	1	0	0	2	1	0	0	0	2	2	.400	.400	.600	40.0	0.0	5
Yousuf, Zuher	L-L	5-10	175	5-24-06	0	1	1.89	4	3	0	19	12	4	4	1	5	15	.174	.237	.290	19.7	6.6	76

Fielding

C: Mata 25, Ferrebus 15, Mujica 12, Rosario 7, Albrecht 3, Davis 1, Escalona 1. **1B:** Perez 15, Rosario 12, Mata 10, Calderon 9, Mujica 9, Davis 6, Ferrebus 5. **2B:** Garcia 40, De Leon 16, Familia 3, Saltiban 3, Farquhar 2, Loreto 2, Pouaka-Grego 1. **3B:** Loreto 44, De Leon 12, Escalona 4, Beltran 1, Garcia 1. **SS:** Familia 45, De Leon 11, Villavicencio 7, Beltran 2, Farquhar 1. **LF:** Dipre 32, Jimenez 10, Julio 9, Walton 9, Heredia 4, Calderon 3, Cardoza 1, De Leon 1, Garcia 1. **CF:** Cardoza 33, Jimenez 14, Spikerman 7, Saltiban 5, Burkholder 3, Mathison 3, Dipre 1. **RF:** Jimenez 19, Julio 14, Burkholder 12, Cardoza 11, Heredia 5, Dipre 3, Mathison 1, Spikerman 1

DSL PHILLIES RED — ROOKIE
DOMINICAN SUMMER LEAGUE

Batting	B-T	Ht.	Wt.	DOB	AVG	OBP	SLG	G	PA	AB	R	H	2B	3B	HR	RBI	BB	HBP	SH	SF	SO	SB	CS	BB%	SO%
Alcantara, Jonathan	L-R	5-11	135	2-24-08	.192	.272	.247	19	81	73	16	14	1	0	1	4	6	2	0	0	18	4	2	7.4	22.2
Araujo, Anderson	R-R	5-11	177	4-8-08	.289	.377	.528	45	183	159	35	46	11	3	7	29	19	4	0	1	37	11	5	10.4	20.2
Arias, Jalvin	R-R	6-2	230	10-1-06	.210	.328	.248	34	125	105	12	22	2	1	0	7	18	1	0	1	34	7	5	14.4	27.2
Castillo, Winifer	R-R	6-3	182	11-15-06	.207	.309	.329	29	94	82	11	17	4	3	0	13	9	3	0	0	46	5	3	9.6	48.9
Cespede, Roiner	R-R	6-0	161	10-23-07	.250	.455	.250	3	11	8	1	2	0	0	0	0	3	0	0	0	3	2	0	27.3	27.3
Cijntje, Nathanael	R-R	5-9	166	1-16-07	.237	.379	.281	40	143	114	17	27	5	0	0	11	22	4	3	0	26	10	7	15.4	18.2
Cruz, Rey	S-R	5-9	156	2-3-08	.600	.750	1.000	3	8	5	2	3	0	1	0	3	2	1	0	0	2	0	0	25.0	25.0
Fuentes, Yadimir	R-R	6-2	202	1-10-07	.153	.317	.214	34	123	98	11	15	4	1	0	10	21	3	0	1	30	0	0	17.1	24.4
Guillen, Eduardo	L-L	5-11	182	3-12-08	.237	.358	.403	44	165	139	17	33	7	5	2	13	18	8	0	0	51	15	4	10.9	30.9
Izaguirre, Nieves	R-R	5-9	160	1-9-08	.235	.391	.294	22	87	68	14	16	2	1	0	6	15	3	0	1	24	7	2	17.2	27.6
Marrero, Elias	L-R	6-1	181	9-4-07	.175	.294	.190	40	160	137	15	24	3	0	0	8	18	5	0	0	55	2	1	11.3	34.4
Morla, Domingo	R-R	6-1	200	1-25-08	.184	.246	.313	46	179	163	22	30	9	0	4	29	14	0	0	2	56	2	1	7.8	31.3
Navas, Anderson	R-R	6-2	175	2-16-07	.256	.289	.390	43	173	164	25	42	10	3	2	21	6	2	0	1	41	7	2	3.5	23.7
Nieto, Michael	R-R	5-9	165	3-22-08	.260	.163	.163	13	50	43	3	6	1	0	0	3	5	2	0	0	10	2	1	10.0	20.0
Oropeza, Rafael	R-R	6-2	170	4-7-08	.000	.000	.000	1	3	3	0	0	0	0	0	0	0	0	0	0	2	0	0	0.0	66.7
Prado, Santiago	L-R	6-0	160	10-18-06	.239	.333	.291	41	139	117	14	28	6	0	0	15	14	4	1	3	33	5	6	10.1	23.7
Quinonez, Josueth	R-R	6-1	172	2-22-07	.287	.397	.380	32	131	108	20	31	5	0	2	16	12	9	0	2	9	5	1	9.2	6.9
Salcedo, Samuel	R-R	5-9	167	12-19-07	.128	.272	.151	31	104	86	10	11	2	0	0	5	14	3	1	0	16	2	1	13.5	15.4

Pitching	B-T	Ht.	Wt.	DOB	W	L	ERA	G	GS	SV	IP	Hits	Runs	ER	HR	BB	SO	AVG	OBP	SLG	SO%	BB%	BF
Duarte, Juan	R-R	6-1	185	9-28-04	1	2	4.50	17	0	3	28	22	15	14	3	18	28	.216	.347	.373	22.6	14.5	124
Duran, Carlos	L-L	5-11	181	5-16-08	0	5	10.62	10	8	0	31	32	24	0	22	16	.352	.488	.420	13.2	18.2	121
Garcia, Enyel	R-R	6-4	190	7-3-07	0	0	5.79	7	0	0	19	21	13	12	0	8	14	.284	.322	.392	15.7	9.0	89
Gonzalez, Deiry	R-R	6-1	172	4-8-08	2	0	1.13	10	10	0	40	30	10	5	0	8	34	.213	.265	.241	22.5	5.3	151
Guerra, Yordanis	L-L	6-3	210	9-19-06	1	3	3.03	12	3	0	33	26	14	11	2	16	35	.218	.340	.294	24.8	11.3	141
Hernandez, Alvaro	R-R	6-1	157	7-5-08	0	1	18.00	2	0	0	2	6	4	0	4	1	.250	.462	.250	7.1	28.6	14

Batting	B-T	Ht.	Wt.	DOB	G	AB	R	H	2B	3B	HR	RBI	BB	HBP	SH	SF	SO	SB	CS	BB%	SO%
Hiraldo, Anthony	R-R	6-1	160	3-21-07	0	1	7.82	7	0	1	13	14	15	11	0	12	11	.275	.422	.412	17.2	18.8	64
Jean, Enderson	R-R	6-3	175	9-21-04	4	1	5.63	15	0	1	24	19	15	15	3	19	28	.216	.360	.364	25.2	17.1	111
Lauriano, Mairol	R-R	6-4	190	1-29-06	2	1	4.43	14	1	0	22	18	15	11	2	13	22	.214	.327	.381	21.8	12.9	101
Lopez, Gerardo	R-R	5-11	183	7-30-05	1	3	3.54	7	7	0	28	29	15	11	1	5	26	.261	.299	.351	22.0	4.2	118
Magdariaga, Yordy	R-R	6-0	175	1-3-03	0	1	8.31	5	0	1	9	11	9	8	0	6	9	.297	.400	.405	20.0	13.3	45
Mitre, Jorge	R-R	6-2	179	6-12-06	0	0	4.28	14	1	3	27	25	14	13	2	12	26	.250	.339	.400	22.4	10.3	116
Montiel, Jesus	R-R	6-4	195	9-24-06	1	5	6.23	11	11	0	39	47	29	27	3	14	46	.297	.364	.430	26.1	8.0	176
Montilla, Aneury	L-L	6-3	190	7-11-06	1	3	6.43	13	10	0	35	47	34	25	2	17	39	.322	.405	.438	23.2	10.1	168
Mota, Rainy	R-R	6-1	170	1-26-06	5	0	7.16	15	0	0	28	32	25	22	1	19	26	.299	.420	.421	19.8	14.5	131
Ramirez, Henry	R-R	6-1	160	8-20-05	2	2	2.59	14	0	3	24	23	12	7	0	10	25	.245	.318	.319	23.4	9.3	107
Sanchez, Markos	R-R	5-7	154	7-7-06	1	0	2.45	5	0	0	15	18	6	4	1	3	15	.305	.349	.458	23.8	4.8	63
Utrera, Josias	R-R	6-2	170	12-6-06	0	0	1.69	3	0	0	5	3	3	1	0	4	2	.167	.304	.167	8.7	17.4	23
Vargas, Hanfermin	R-R	6-3	158	8-12-04	2	0	7.18	15	0	0	26	24	27	21	3	20	26	.242	.398	.404	20.2	15.5	129
Villoria, Geremy	R-R	6-2	175	8-14-08	0	1	4.50	5	5	0	14	11	8	7	0	4	19	.212	.281	.365	33.3	7.0	57
Yrish, Rene	R-R	6-1	165	11-20-06	0	1	17.05	6	0	0	6	6	12	12	1	15	3	.273	.579	.545	7.7	38.5	39

Fielding
C: Araujo 24, Navas 20, Fuentes 11, Cruz 1, Prado 1. **1B:** Navas 20, Araujo 18, Fuentes 16, Prado 2, Guillen 1, Morla 1. **2B:** Prado 24, Salcedo 20, Marrero 12, Nieto 3, Cespede 1, Morla 1. **3B:** Morla 43, Prado 9, Nieto 2, Salcedo 2, Cespede 1, Izaguirre 1. **SS:** Izaguirre 21, Alcantara 16, Salcedo 9, Nieto 7, Marrero 4, Oropeza 1, Prado 1. **LF:** Guillen 27, Cijntje 16, Arias 15, Castillo 8, Quinonez 1. **CF:** Cijntje 19, Quinonez 17, Guillen 14, Castillo 7, Arias 1. **RF:** Arias 14, Quinonez 14, Guillen 12, Castillo 9, Cijntje 5, Prado 3, Nieto 1

DSL PHILLIES WHITE   ROOKIE
DOMINICAN SUMMER LEAGUE

Batting	B-T	Ht.	Wt.	DOB	AVG	OBP	SLG	G	PA	AB	R	H	2B	3B	HR	RBI	BB	HBP	SH	SF	SO	SB	CS	BB%	SO%
Adames, Elian	R-R	6-2	190	9-15-07	.265	.324	.341	49	188	170	20	45	7	3	0	22	14	2	0	2	52	7	4	7.4	27.7
Azocar, Gabriel	R-R	6-2	187	11-11-07	.192	.278	.240	39	145	125	12	24	1	1	1	13	13	3	0	3	32	1	2	9.0	22.1
Carpio, Leonardo	R-R	6-3	206	10-1-07	.139	.254	.191	37	134	115	11	16	6	0	0	1	11	7	0	1	60	0	0	8.2	44.8
Casanova, Maylerson	S-R	5-11	165	11-13-06	.267	.331	.382	41	145	131	18	35	6	3	1	14	9	4	0	1	41	12	2	6.2	28.3
Castillo, Winifer	R-R	6-3	182	11-15-06	.286	.333	.357	4	15	14	2	4	1	0	0	2	1	0	0	0	7	1	0	6.7	46.7
Cespede, Roiner	R-R	6-0	161	10-23-07	.237	.343	.237	33	108	93	14	22	0	0	0	11	14	1	0	0	19	2	2	13.0	17.6
Cruceta, Dayber	L-L	6-1	147	3-6-08	.291	.438	.373	42	169	134	25	39	6	1	1	17	30	5	0	0	32	12	5	17.8	18.9
Cruz, Rey	S-R	5-9	156	2-3-08	.257	.371	.257	32	124	105	14	27	0	0	0	9	13	6	0	0	27	5	3	10.5	21.8
Espinosa, Romeli	R-R	6-4	169	6-5-08	.282	.363	.430	41	168	149	28	42	6	5	2	12	10	9	0	0	34	12	4	6.0	20.2
Fernandez, Maykol	R-R	6-2	193	12-04-07	.204	.426	.327	20	68	49	10	10	1	1	1	5	13	6	0	0	20	2	2	19.1	29.4
Flores, Gabriel	R-R	5-9	170	3-3-08	.181	.305	.257	35	128	105	10	19	3	1	1	9	11	9	0	3	24	7	5	8.6	18.8
Hernandez, Luis	L-R	6-0	194	9-29-07	.102	.260	.120	38	131	108	12	11	2	0	0	4	19	4	0	0	44	0	0	14.5	33.6
Nieto, Michael	R-R	5-9	145	3-22-07	.314	.368	.457	12	39	35	3	11	3	1	0	5	2	1	1	0	9	5	0	5.1	23.1
Oropeza, Rafael	R-R	6-2	170	4-7-08	.215	.333	.280	37	126	107	15	23	7	0	0	7	16	3	0	0	29	7	0	12.7	23.0
Rodriguez, Esterling	L-R	5-11	140	9-8-05	.214	.421	.500	5	19	14	3	3	2	1	0	2	4	1	0	0	4	0	1	21.1	21.1
Ruiz, Ibrahim	R-R	5-11	170	11-6-06	.200	.237	.288	36	131	125	8	25	4	2	1	13	3	3	0	0	32	6	2	2.3	24.4
Salcedo, Samuel	R-R	5-9	167	12-19-07	.163	.260	.256	14	51	43	5	7	1	0	1	5	4	1	0	1	12	1	2	9.8	23.5

Pitching	B-T	Ht.	Wt.	DOB	W	L	ERA	G	GS	SV	IP	Hits	Runs	ER	HR	BB	SO	AVG	OBP	SLG	SO%	BB%	BF
Arias, Yael	R-R	6-5	176	8-16-04	1	0	9.24	8	0	0	13	15	13	13	1	13	15	.300	.446	.500	23.1	20.0	65
De La Cruz, Gustavo	R-R	6-3	190	6-6-06	0	2	7.94	11	3	0	17	15	20	15	0	31	16	.234	.505	.313	16.2	31.3	99
De La Cruz, Jose	R-R	5-11	165	9-11-04	1	1	4.58	9	0	1	18	14	18	9	0	13	20	.200	.329	.271	23.5	15.3	85
De La Cruz, Joshue	R-R	6-2	193	10-17-05	1	2	2.40	9	8	0	30	24	13	8	1	12	22	.220	.320	.294	17.2	9.4	128
Espinosa, Cristhian	R-R	6-3	155	12-30-02	2	4	3.24	17	0	2	25	18	10	9	1	6	17	.196	.255	.272	16.7	5.9	102
Guzman, Jorge	L-L	6-1	170	3-17-07	1	1	3.03	11	7	0	36	26	17	12	2	16	32	.203	.309	.305	21.3	10.7	150
Magdariaga, Yordy	R-R	6-0	175	1-3-03	0	0	6.61	9	1	0	16	24	15	12	0	8	16	.329	.388	.466	18.8	9.4	85
Marquez, Diego	R-R	6-1	210	6-10-06	1	2	4.50	7	0	0	10	13	9	5	0	2	8	.333	.378	.538	17.8	4.4	45
Martinez, Gabriel	R-R	6-1	176	7-18-06	1	0	2.08	6	0	0	9	6	2	2	0	5	5	.200	.306	.233	13.9	13.9	36
Medina, Albertt	R-R	6-1	162	6-3-08	1	3	2.49	14	0	1	25	19	11	7	1	9	20	.211	.294	.356	19.4	8.7	103
Moreno, Jesus	R-R	6-0	172	1-27-08	0	0	0.00	2	0	0	2	0	0	0	0	4	2	.000	.400	.000	20.0	40.0	10
Parra, Juan	L-L	6-2	179	3-21-08	0	0	13.50	6	0	0	7	7	10	10	0	14	2	.269	.537	.308	4.9	34.1	41
Peralta, Pedro	R-R	5-11	185	7-27-06	0	6	4.96	12	12	0	45	34	29	25	1	34	37	.215	.366	.310	18.3	16.8	202
Polanco, Julio	R-R	6-3	195	9-11-06	0	4	7.76	16	0	1	27	39	31	23	1	15	26	.342	.445	.439	18.8	10.9	138
Quintero, Luis	R-R	6-0	208	2-3-07	1	3	5.28	9	8	0	29	39	26	17	2	16	18	.317	.394	.455	12.7	11.3	142
Reyes, Darling	R-R	6-1	175	10-29-04	2	1	13.50	15	0	0	24	54	44	36	1	15	23	.425	.500	.591	15.5	10.1	148
Robles, Eduardo	R-R	5-9	176	6-27-06	0	6	6.35	11	10	0	40	47	36	28	2	19	45	.285	.362	.430	23.9	10.1	188
Sipion, Marco	R-R	6-4	205	6-16-07	0	1	9.19	11	0	0	16	16	18	16	0	19	12	.276	.470	.345	14.5	22.9	83
Utrera, Josias	R-R	6-2	170	12-6-06	0	0	27.00	6	0	0	4	7	13	12	0	13	4	.389	.703	.556	10.8	35.1	37
Yousuf, Zuher	L-L	5-10	174	5-24-06	1	0	0.73	3	3	0	12	8	1	1	0	3	18	.186	.239	.233	39.1	6.5	46
Yrish, Rene	R-R	6-1	165	11-20-06	0	2	21.32	6	0	0	6	7	15	15	0	12	5	.304	.564	.304	12.8	30.8	39
Zambrano, Reyner	L-L	6-3	180	5-27-07	1	3	8.06	13	3	0	22	27	23	20	1	27	22	.300	.467	.389	18.3	22.5	120

Fielding
C: Azocar 24, Cruz 13, Flores 11, Hernandez 10. **1B:** Hernandez 26, Flores 13, Azocar 10, Cruz 4, Cespede 2, Fernandez 2. **2B:** Casanova 20, Cespede 14, Salcedo 10, Oropeza 9, Nieto 4. **3B:** Fernandez 16, Cespede 15, Oropeza 12, Nieto 6, Espinosa 5, Casanova 4, Salcedo 3. **SS:** Espinosa 36, Oropeza 15, Casanova 3, Cespede 1, Nieto 1, Salcedo 1. **LF:** Carpio 27, Ruiz 22, Adames 2, Casanova 2, Castillo 2, Cespede 1, Cruceta 1. **CF:** Cruceta 25, Adames 21, Casanova 9, Castillo 1, Ruiz 1. **RF:** Adames 26, Cruceta 15, Carpio 7, Ruiz 7, Casanova 2, Castillo 1

Pittsburgh Pirates

SEASON SYNOPSIS: The story remained the same in Pittsburgh, which hasn't finished above fourth place since 2017. The team never contended in 2025 despite a Cy Young Award season from Paul Skenes in his sophomore season and the fourth-best team ERA in baseball, due to the game's worst offense. No one scored fewer runs than the Pirates, who tallied 583 and were shut out a big league-high 16 times.

HIGH POINT: Every Paul Skenes start is a high point for the sport of baseball. He started the All-Star Game for the second consecutive year (both his MLB seasons) and held opponents scoreless in nine of his final 15 starts to help the Pirates record a league-best 19 shutouts. Since ERA became an official statistic in 1913, he's the only pitcher to strike out at least 200 batters with an ERA below 2.00 without a winning record. Six of his 10 wins came at home, including six scoreless Sept. 4 to beat the Dodgers, as the Pirates went 44-37 at PNC Park.

LOW POINT: The Buccos had just shut out the Cardinals in three straight home wins when they went to their house of horrors—the road. They went just 27-54 on the road, and July 4-12, they lost eight straight, all on the road, starting with a sweep in Seattle where they failed to score for the entire series. Center fielder Oneil Cruz, as toolsy as any player in the game, went 0-for-10 in the series en route to a .200/.298/.378 season, ranking last among MLB qualified hitters in batting average.

NOTABLE ROOKIES: A lineup desperate for production got little from rookies, but several young arms looked like keepers. Righties Braxton Ashcraft and Mike Burrows, both homegrown products who have come back from UCL reconstruction surgery, showed flashes in bulk-inning roles and surpassed 100 innings for the first time (including their minor league time). Righty Bubba Chandler regularly hit 100 mph in his 31-inning debut, while Pitt Panthers alum Isaac Mattson (3-3, 2.45) emerged as a dependable reliever.

KEY TRANSACTIONS: The Pirates' biggest offseason move involved adding Spencer Horwitz from the Blue Jays in a three-team trade that cost them starter Luis Ortiz plus minor league lefties Josh Hartle and Michael Kennedy. Offseason right wrist surgery slowed Horwitz early but he led the team in the slash categories, hitting .273/.353/.434 with 11 homers in 411 plate appearances. Sellers at the July deadline, Pittsburgh shed spare parts (Bailey Falter) and recent mainstays in third baseman Ke'Bryan Hayes (Reds) and David Bednar (Yankees).

OPENING DAY PAYROLL: $87,645,246 (26th)

PLAYERS OF THE YEAR

MAJOR LEAGUE
Paul Skenes
RHP
1.97 ERA in 187.2 IP
216 SO, 42 BB
2x all-star in 2 seasons

MINOR LEAGUE
Konnor Griffin
SS
(A, A+, AA)
.333/.415/.527
21 HR, 65 SB, 117 R

ORGANIZATION LEADERS

Batting		*Qualifiers
MAJORS		
* AVG	Bryan Reynolds	.245
* OPS	Bryan Reynolds	.720
HR	Oneil Cruz	20
RBI	Bryan Reynolds	73
MINORS		
* AVG	Konnor Griffin, Altoona/Greensboro/Bradenton	.333
* OBP	Konnor Griffin, Altoona/Greensboro/Bradenton	.415
* SLG	Edward Florentino, Bradenton/FCL Pirates	.548
* OPS	Edward Florentino, Bradenton/FCL Pirates	.948
R	Konnor Griffin, Altoona/Greensboro/Bradenton	117
H	Konnor Griffin, Altoona/Greensboro/Bradenton	161
TB	Konnor Griffin, Altoona/Greensboro/Bradenton	255
2B	Yordany De Los Santos, Greensboro/Bradenton	27
3B	Ji Hwan Bae, Indianapolis	7
HR	Esmerlyn Valdez, Altoona/Greensboro	26
RBI	Konnor Griffin, Altoona/Greensboro/Bradenton	94
BB	Keiner Delgado, Greensboro	73
SO	Yordany De Los Santos, Greensboro/Bradenton	140
SB	Konnor Griffin, Altoona/Greensboro/Bradenton	65

Pitching		#Qualifiers
MAJORS		
W	Paul Skenes	10
# ERA	Paul Skenes	1.97
SO	Paul Skenes	216
SV	David Bednar	17
MINORS		
W	Victor Cabreja, Greensboro/Bradenton	9
W	Drake Fellows, Indianapolis	9
L	Po-Yu Chen, Indianapolis/Altoona	11
# ERA	Connor Wietgrefe, Altoona/Greensboro/Brad.	3.10
G	Eddy Yean, Indianapolis	50
G	Ryan Harbin, Indianapolis/Altoona/Greensboro	50
GS	Wilber Dotel, Altoona	27
SV	Cam Sanders, Indianapolis/Altoona	14
IP	Wilber Dotel, Altoona	126
BB	Po-Yu Chen, Indianapolis/Altoona	54
SO	Wilber Dotel, Altoona	131
# AVG	Connor Wietgrefe, Altoona/Greensboro/Brad.	.216

2025 PERFORMANCE

General Manager: Ben Cherington. **Farm Director:** Michael Chernow. **Scouting Director:** Justin Horowitz.

Class	Team	League	W	L	PCT	Finish	Manager
Majors	Pittsburgh Pirates	National	71	91	.438	13 (15)	Derek Shelton
Triple-A	Indianapolis Indians	International	87	62	.584	4 (20)	Chris Truby
Double-A	Altoona Curve	Eastern	69	68	.504	5 (12)	Andy Fox
High-A	Greensboro Grasshoppers	South Atlantic	88	43	.672	1 (12)	Blake Butler
Low-A	Bradenton Marauders	Florida State	60	69	.465	8 (10)	Jim Horner
Rookie	FCL Pirates	Florida Complex	27	32	.458	10 (15)	Jose Mendez
Rookie	DSL Pirates Black	Dominican	34	20	.630	8 (52)	Joel Fuentes
Rookie	DSL Pirates Gold	Dominican	31	25	.554	20 (52)	Jose Mosquera
Overall 2025 Minor League Record			396	319	.554	3rd (30)	

ORGANIZATION STATISTICS

PITTSBURGH PIRATES
NATIONAL LEAGUE

Batting	B-T	Ht.	Wt.	DOB	AVG	OBP	SLG	G	PA	AB	R	H	2B	3B	HR	RBI	BB	HBP	SH	SF	SO	SB	CS	BB%	SO%
Bae, Ji Hwan	L-R	6-1	185	7-26-99	.050	.240	.050	13	25	20	4	1	0	0	0	0	5	0	0	0	9	4	1	20.0	36.0
Bart, Joey	R-R	6-2	238	12-15-96	.249	.355	.340	93	332	285	21	71	12	1	4	30	40	7	0	0	93	1	1	12.0	28.0
Canario, Alexander	R-R	5-11	165	5-7-00	.218	.274	.338	87	234	216	25	47	6	1	6	20	17	0	0	1	80	3	1	7.3	34.2
Cheng, Tsung-Che	L-R	5-7	154	7-26-01	.000	.000	.000	3	7	7	0	0	0	0	0	0	0	0	0	0	3	0	1	0.0	42.9
Cook, Billy	R-R	6-1	200	1-7-99	.333	.333	.333	3	6	6	1	2	0	0	0	0	0	0	0	0	1	0	0	0.0	16.7
Cruz, Oneil	L-R	6-7	220	10-4-98	.200	.298	.378	135	544	471	62	94	18	3	20	61	64	4	0	5	174	38	5	11.8	32.0
Davis, Henry	R-R	6-0	220	9-21-99	.167	.234	.278	87	283	252	25	42	7	0	7	22	18	5	3	3	76	2	1	6.4	26.9
Devanney, Cam	R-R	6-1	195	4-13-97	.139	.184	.167	14	38	36	1	5	1	0	0	1	2	0	0	0	21	0	1	5.3	55.3
Flores, Rafael	R-R	6-4	220	11-7-00	.200	.294	.333	7	17	15	0	3	2	0	0	0	2	0	0	0	7	0	0	11.8	41.2
Frazier, Adam	L-R	5-10	180	12-14-91	.255	.318	.336	78	262	235	22	60	10	0	3	21	17	6	1	3	45	7	5	6.5	17.2
Gonzales, Nick	R-R	5-9	195	5-27-99	.260	.299	.362	96	408	381	39	99	18	3	5	30	21	2	0	4	73	0	2	5.1	17.9
Gorski, Matt	R-R	6-2	198	12-22-97	.195	.214	.390	15	42	41	2	8	0	1	2	4	1	0	0	0	16	0	1	2.4	38.1
Hayes, Ke'Bryan	R-R	5-10	205	1-28-97	.236	.279	.290	100	392	369	34	87	10	2	2	36	18	4	1	0	81	10	2	4.6	20.7
Horwitz, Spencer	L-R	5-10	190	11-14-97	.272	.353	.434	108	411	364	55	99	26	0	11	51	44	2	0	1	73	0	1	10.7	17.8
Kiner-Falefa, Isiah	R-R	5-11	190	3-23-95	.264	.300	.332	119	428	401	40	106	20	2	1	35	17	4	5	1	69	15	4	4.0	16.1
McCutchen, Andrew	R-R	5-11	195	10-10-86	.239	.333	.367	135	551	477	51	114	22	0	13	57	62	2	0	3	118	1	1	12.2	21.4
Peguero, Liover	R-R	6-0	210	12-31-00	.200	.273	.363	33	88	80	9	16	1	0	4	8	6	2	0	0	25	4	0	6.8	28.4
Pham, Tommy	R-R	6-1	223	3-8-88	.245	.330	.370	120	449	392	44	96	17	1	10	52	50	2	0	5	94	5	3	11.1	20.9
Reynolds, Bryan	S-R	6-3	205	1-27-95	.245	.318	.402	154	654	587	68	144	38	3	16	73	57	7	0	3	173	3	2	8.7	26.5
Rodriguez, Endy	S-R	5-10	170	5-26-00	.173	.246	.250	18	57	52	5	9	4	0	0	2	5	0	0	0	14	0	1	8.8	24.6
Simon, Ronny	S-R	5-7	150	4-17-00	.233	.250	.267	8	32	30	4	7	1	0	0	0	2	1	0	0	1	8	1	0	3.1	25.0
Solak, Nick	R-R	5-9	185	1-11-95	.091	.091	.091	4	11	11	0	1	0	0	0	0	0	0	0	0	2	0	0	0.0	18.2
Sullivan, Brett	L-R	6-1	195	2-22-94	.333	.167	.333	9	6	1	1	0	0	0	0	2	1	1	0	1	3	0	0	11.1	33.3
Suwinski, Jack	L-L	6-2	215	7-29-98	.147	.281	.253	59	178	150	15	22	7	0	3	10	24	4	0	0	57	7	1	13.5	32.0
Triolo, Jared	R-R	6-3	212	2-8-98	.227	.311	.356	107	376	331	41	75	18	2	7	24	39	2	3	1	76	13	2	10.4	20.2
Valdez, Enmanuel	L-R	5-8	191	12-28-98	.209	.294	.363	31	102	91	7	19	4	2	2	12	11	0	0	0	16	0	0	10.8	15.7
Yorke, Nick	R-R	5-11	200	4-2-02	.232	.264	.319	22	72	69	7	16	3	0	1	8	3	0	0	0	15	1	0	4.2	20.8

Pitching	B-T	Ht.	Wt.	DOB	W	L	ERA	G	GS	SV	IP	Hits	Runs	ER	HR	BB	SO	AVG	OBP	SLG	SO%	BB%	BF
Ashcraft, Braxton	L-R	6-5	195	10-5-99	4	4	2.71	26	8	0	70	63	22	21	3	24	71	.239	.306	.341	24.3	8.2	292
Barco, Hunter	L-L	6-4	210	12-15-00	1	0	0.00	2	0	0	3	3	0	0	0	3	3	.250	.250	.333	25.0	0.0	12
Bednar, David	L-R	6-1	250	10-10-94	2	5	2.37	42	0	17	38	32	12	10	2	10	51	.225	.279	.324	33.1	6.5	154
Borucki, Ryan	L-L	6-4	210	3-31-94	1	3	5.28	35	0	0	31	26	20	18	4	12	27	.236	.312	.418	21.4	9.5	126
Burrows, Mike	R-R	6-2	195	11-8-99	2	4	3.94	23	19	0	96	88	43	42	13	31	97	.243	.308	.392	24.1	7.7	402
Cabrera, Genesis	L-L	6-2	180	10-10-96	0	0	4.91	9	0	0	11	12	6	6	2	1	7	.279	.304	.558	15.2	2.2	46
Chandler, Bubba	R-R	6-2	200	9-14-02	4	1	4.02	7	4	1	31	25	14	14	2	4	31	.214	.258	.333	25.0	3.2	124
Darrell-Hicks, Michael	R-R	6-5	220	11-13-97	0	0	0.00	1	0	0	2	0	0	0	0	0	2	.000	.000	.000	40.0	0.0	5
Falter, Bailey	R-L	6-4	175	4-24-97	7	5	3.73	22	22	0	113	95	53	47	17	39	70	.232	.297	.415	15.3	8.5	457
Ferguson, Caleb	R-L	6-3	226	7-2-96	2	2	3.74	45	0	0	43	33	18	18	1	14	34	.214	.297	.286	19.3	8.0	176
Harrington, Thomas	R-R	6-2	185	7-12-01	0	1	15.58	3	1	1	9	18	15	15	3	7	7	.429	.500	.762	14.0	14.0	50
Heaney, Andrew	L-L	6-2	200	6-5-91	5	10	5.39	26	23	0	120	125	74	72	24	39	84	.267	.332	.495	16.0	7.4	525
Holderman, Colin	R-R	6-7	240	10-8-95	0	2	7.01	24	0	1	26	34	21	20	4	16	18	.327	.419	.510	14.4	12.8	125
Keller, Mitch	R-R	6-2	220	4-4-96	6	15	4.19	32	32	0	176	171	91	82	21	51	150	.249	.310	.405	20.0	6.8	749
Lawrence, Justin	R-R	6-2	213	11-25-94	1	0	0.51	17	0	0	18	9	1	1	0	8	23	.153	.275	.220	33.3	11.6	69
Mattson, Isaac	R-R	6-2	205	7-14-95	3	3	2.45	44	0	0	48	35	14	13	4	19	45	.203	.286	.314	22.7	9.6	198
Mayza, Tim	L-L	6-2	215	1-15-92	0	0	2.89	7	0	0	9	9	3	3	1	1	8	.243	.275	.432	20.0	2.5	40
Mlodzinski, Carmen	R-R	6-2	225	2-19-99	5	8	3.55	34	12	0	99	102	42	39	8	27	89	.265	.320	.390	21.2	6.4	419
Moreta, Dauri	R-R	6-2	185	4-15-96	1	1	3.24	18	0	0	17	16	8	6	2	7	19	.267	.338	.400	27.9	10.3	68
Nicolas, Kyle	R-R	6-4	223	2-22-99	1	2	4.74	31	0	0	38	34	21	20	3	18	34	.233	.323	.356	20.4	10.8	167
Oviedo, Johan	R-R	6-5	245	3-2-98	2	1	3.57	9	9	0	40	26	17	16	6	23	42	.182	.306	.336	24.7	13.5	170
Rainey, Tanner	R-R	6-2	250	12-25-92	0	1	10.57	11	0	0	8	7	9	9	0	9	6	.250	.389	.286	24.3	16.2	37
Ramirez, Yohan	R-R	6-4	212	5-6-95	3	3	5.40	24	0	0	33	35	25	20	4	16	45	.246	.342	.396	29.0	10.3	155
Sanders, Cam	R-R	6-2	175	12-9-96	0	0	8.10	6	0	0	7	9	6	6	2	5	4	.310	.412	.552	11.8	14.7	34

Player	B-T	Ht	Wt	DOB			AVG	OBP	SLG	G	PA	AB	R	H	2B	3B	HR	RBI	BB	HBP	SH	SF	SO	SB	CS	BB%	SO%
Santana, Dennis	R-R	6-2	190	4-12-96	4	5	2.18	70	0	16	70	44	18	17	5	17	60	.179	.237	.297	22.2			6.3	270		
Shugart, Chase	L-R	5-10	198	10-24-96	4	3	3.40	35	0	0	45	33	18	17	6	17	31	.206	.282	.388	17.1			9.4	181		
Sisk, Evan	L-L	6-2	209	4-23-97	1	1	4.38	14	0	0	12	11	6	6	1	5	14	.244	.340	.333	25.9			9.3	54		
Skenes, Paul	R-R	6-6	235	5-29-02	10	10	1.97	32	32	0	188	136	45	41	11	42	216	.199	.251	.307	29.5			5.7	733		
Stratton, Hunter	R-R	6-4	225	11-17-96	0	0	23.63	3	0	0	3	10	7	7	1	2	1	.588	.619	.824	4.8			9.5	21		
Triolo, Jared	R-R	6-3	212	2-8-98	0	0	0.00	1	0	0	1	3	2	0	1	1	0	.429	.500	1.000	0.0			12.5	8		
Wentz, Joey	L-L	6-5	220	10-6-97	2	1	4.15	19	0	0	26	25	14	12	2	11	22	.245	.322	.373	19.1			9.6	115		

Fielding

Catcher	PCT	G	PO	A	E	DP	PB
Bart	.995	83	583	21	3	5	5
Davis	.996	83	682	27	3	4	2
Flores	1.000	1	9	1	0	0	0
Rodriguez	.964	9	51	2	2	0	0
Sullivan	1.000	3	23	1	0	1	0

First Base	PCT	G	PO	A	E	DP
Cook	1.000	1	4	0	0	0
Flores	1.000	6	19	4	0	4
Gorski	.988	12	83	2	1	10
Horwitz	.994	102	659	53	4	49
Peguero	1.000	9	45	3	0	6
Rodriguez	.974	11	71	5	2	9
Solak	1.000	4	14	1	0	2
Triolo	1.000	24	111	6	0	6
Valdez	1.000	26	170	15	0	18
Yorke	1.000	6	22	5	0	2

Second Base	PCT	G	PO	A	E	DP
Cheng	1.000	1	3	2	0	0
Frazier	.995	53	79	122	1	27
Gonzales	.974	85	127	177	8	38
Horwitz	.000	1	0	0	0	0
Peguero	1.000	5	5	12	0	2
Solak	.000	1	0	0	0	0
Triolo	1.000	11	21	30	0	11
Valdez	.889	6	4	4	1	3
Yorke	1.000	14	22	41	0	8

Third Base	PCT	G	PO	A	E	DP
Devanney	.920	14	9	14	2	1
Hayes	.986	100	66	210	4	22
Kiner-Falefa	.968	25	15	45	2	4
Triolo	.972	32	24	46	2	6
Yorke	1.000	1	1	0	0	0

Shortstop	PCT	G	PO	A	E	DP
Cheng	1.000	2	2	4	0	0
Gonzales	.964	13	6	21	1	3
Kiner-Falefa	.982	94	122	207	6	33
Peguero	1.000	16	17	25	0	4
Triolo	.967	47	68	109	6	28

Outfield	PCT	G	PO	A	E	DP
Bae	1.000	9	11	0	0	0
Canario	.987	84	143	4	2	2
Cook	1.000	3	3	0	0	0
Cruz	.966	125	302	6	11	2
Frazier	.969	18	31	0	1	0
Gorski	1.000	4	4	0	0	0
McCutchen	1.000	7	11	0	0	0
Pham	.981	122	204	6	4	0
Reynolds	.992	117	244	4	2	0
Simon	.875	7	7	0	1	0
Solak	1.000	1	3	0	0	0
Suwinski	.991	60	107	1	1	0
Valdez	.000	1	0	0	0	0
Yorke	1.000	4	5	0	0	0

INDIANAPOLIS INDIANS
INTERNATIONAL LEAGUE
TRIPLE-A

Batting	B-T	Ht.	Wt.	DOB	AVG	OBP	SLG	G	PA	AB	R	H	2B	3B	HR	RBI	BB	HBP	SH	SF	SO	SB	CS	BB%	SO%
Bae, Ji Hwan	L-R	6-1	185	7-26-99	.292	.380	.424	67	305	264	55	77	18	7	1	21	34	5	0	2	61	23	4	11.1	20.0
Bart, Joey	R-R	6-2	238	12-15-96	.231	.444	.231	5	18	13	1	3	0	0	0	2	4	1	0	0	6	0	0	22.2	33.3
Bowen, Jase	R-R	6-0	190	9-2-00	.294	.386	.484	36	145	126	20	37	9	3	3	17	19	0	0	0	36	7	3	13.1	24.8
Castillo, Jesus	S-S	5-10	144	7-12-03	.154	.214	.154	4	14	13	0	2	0	0	0	0	1	0	0	0	1	0	0	7.1	7.1
Cheng, Tsung-Che	L-R	5-7	154	7-26-01	.209	.307	.271	107	397	340	36	71	12	3	1	36	47	3	3	4	99	18	7	11.8	24.9
Cook, Billy	R-R	6-1	200	1-7-99	.248	.323	.384	94	375	331	45	82	17	2	8	46	34	4	3	3	102	13	2	9.1	27.2
Davis, Henry	R-R	6-0	220	9-21-99	.286	.355	.393	8	31	28	5	8	3	0	0	2	3	0	0	0	4	2	0	9.7	12.9
Devanney, Cam	R-R	6-1	195	4-13-97	.256	.327	.361	34	147	133	11	34	6	1	2	11	10	4	0	0	37	2	2	6.8	25.2
Flores, Rafael	R-R	6-4	220	11-7-00	.281	.363	.459	36	157	135	17	38	4	1	6	28	15	0	4	0	41	0	0	9.6	26.1
Fraizer, Matt	L-R	6-3	220	1-12-98	.305	.361	.452	62	220	197	29	60	18	1	3	20	19	0	1	3	44	14	2	8.6	20.0
Gonzales, Nick	R-R	5-9	195	5-27-99	.194	.211	.250	9	38	36	3	7	0	1	0	1	1	0	0	1	11	0	0	0	28.9
Gorski, Matt	R-R	6-2	198	12-22-97	.278	.318	.519	22	88	79	14	22	7	0	4	15	6	0	0	3	23	2	0	6.8	26.1
Gutierrez, Abraham	R-R	6-0	214	10-31-99	.250	.333	.295	28	99	88	9	22	1	0	1	5	8	3	0	0	21	0	1	8.1	21.2
Hall, Darick	L-R	6-4	232	7-25-95	.211	.307	.300	55	205	180	18	38	4	0	4	23	22	3	0	0	58	0	1	10.7	28.3
Horwitz, Spencer	L-R	5-10	190	11-14-97	.323	.333	.484	8	33	31	5	10	2	0	1	2	1	0	0	1	7	0	0	3.0	21.2
Jarvis, Mike	R-R	5-10	180	5-12-98	.181	.241	.278	25	79	72	14	13	4	0	1	4	5	1	0	1	24	8	1	6.3	30.4
Johnson, Bryce	S-R	6-1	195	10-07-95	.080	.179	.120	10	28	25	1	2	1	0	0	1	3	0	0	0	9	1	0	10.7	32.1
Kreidler, Ryan	R-R	6-4	208	11-12-97	.163	.293	.265	15	58	49	2	8	2	0	1	8	1	0	0	0	16	5	1	13.8	27.6
Nunez, Malcom	R-R	6-0	205	3-9-01	.283	.335	.428	45	173	152	16	43	16	0	2	22	13	2	0	6	26	0	0	7.5	15.0
Peguero, Liover	R-R	6-0	210	12-31-00	.247	.313	.375	75	303	267	39	66	14	1	6	40	27	1	3	5	59	8	3	8.9	19.5
Prato, Anthony	R-R	5-9	186	5-11-98	.156	.372	.156	13	43	32	3	5	0	0	0	2	7	4	0	0	9	5	0	16.3	20.9
Rodriguez, Endy	S-R	5-9	170	5-26-00	.154	.241	.385	8	29	26	4	4	0	0	2	4	3	0	0	0	5	0	0	10.3	17.2
Ross, Shawn	R-R	6-0	185	9-30-99	.183	.288	.303	33	125	109	13	20	4	0	3	16	14	2	0	0	54	0	1	11.2	43.2
Siani, Sammy	L-L	5-10	195	12-4-00	.261	.337	.424	25	100	87	13	23	4	0	4	12	11	0	0	1	21	3	3	10.6	20.2
Simon, Ronny	S-R	5-7	150	4-17-00	.284	.381	.436	54	248	211	35	60	9	1	7	30	33	1	1	2	41	24	6	13.3	16.5
Solak, Nick	R-R	5-9	185	1-11-95	.332	.411	.492	111	482	419	76	139	23	1	14	73	48	11	0	4	66	10	3	10.0	13.7
Stewart, DJ	L-R	6-0	210	11-30-93	.125	.245	.257	45	159	136	15	17	3	0	5	20	20	2	0	1	48	1	1	12.6	30.2
Sullivan, Brett	L-R	6-1	195	2-22-94	.265	.328	.365	65	253	232	28	47	9	4	4	29	19	1	0	1	38	6	1	7.5	15.0
Suwinski, Jack	L-L	6-2	215	7-29-98	.283	.389	.565	56	230	191	45	54	10	1	14	51	31	4	1	3	69	6	0	13.5	30.0
Triolo, Jared	R-R	6-3	212	2-8-98	.239	.397	.413	15	58	46	12	11	2	0	2	4	12	0	0	0	9	3	0	20.7	15.5
Velazquez, Nelson	R-R	6-0	190	12-26-98	.249	.329	.554	18	79	74	13	21	5	0	5	17	5	0	0	0	16	1	0	6.3	20.3
Williams, Alika	R-R	6-1	180	3-12-99	.268	.329	.393	103	391	351	50	94	11	3	9	42	27	7	2	4	70	5	4	6.9	17.9
Wilson, Eli	R-R	6-0	190	7-6-98	.294	.314	.441	11	35	34	3	10	2	0	1	7	1	0	0	0	10	0	0	2.9	28.6
Yorke, Nick	R-R	5-11	200	4-2-02	.287	.348	.406	103	440	401	55	115	21	3	7	59	36	2	0	1	97	17	6	8.2	22.0

Pitching	B-T	Ht.	Wt.	DOB	W	L	ERA	G	GS	SV	IP	Hits	Runs	ER	HR	BB	SO	AVG	OBP	SLG	SO%	BB%	BF
Ashcraft, Braxton	R-R	6-5	195	10-5-99	3	3	5.03	10	0	4	48	53	29	27	5	19	56	.277	.359	.414	25.6	8.7	219
Barco, Hunter	L-L	6-4	210	12-15-00	3	1	3.79	21	17	0	74	59	35	5	42	82	.215	.334	.328	25.4	13.0	323
Bayless, Jarod	R-R	6-4	225	12-29-96	0	1	3.91	9	4	0	23	23	10	10	3	6	17	.253	.337	.396	16.3	5.8	104
Bednar, David	R-R	6-1	250	10-10-94	0	0	0.00	5	0	0	5	1	0	0	0	0	7	.063	.063	.063	43.8	0.0	16
Bidois, Brandan	R-R	6-2	158	6-21-01	1	0	0.00	9	0	2	13	5	1	0	0	6	15	.026	.159	.026	34.1	13.6	44
Borucki, Ryan	L-L	6-4	210	3-31-94	0	0	1.42	6	0	0	6	2	1	0	4	9	.095	.269	.095	34.6	15.4	26

PITTSBURGH PIRATES

Player	B-T	HT	WT	DOB			AVG	AB	R	H	2B	3B	HR	RBI	BB	SO	SB	OBP	SLG			
Burrows, Beau	R-R	6-2	210	9-18-96	1	2	6.20	16	1	3	20	17	16	14	6	9	19	.218	.299	.526	21.8	10.3	87
Burrows, Mike	R-R	6-2	195	11-8-99	2	1	2.51	.8	7	0	32	23	10	9	6	11	41	.195	.264	.381	31.5	8.5	130
Chandler, Bubba	S-R	6-2	200	9-14-02	5	6	4.05	24	24	0	100	95	46	45	8	53	121	.250	.349	.374	27.4	12.0	442
Chen, Po-Yu	L-R	6-2	187	10-2-01	2	0	0.66	3	3	0	14	13	1	1	0	6	10	.255	.345	.294	17.2	10.3	58
Darrell-Hicks, Michael	R-R	6-5	220	11-13-97	2	0	7.88	15	0	0	16	24	15	14	2	10	19	.353	.451	.544	23.2	12.2	82
Del Bonta-Smith, Fineas	R-R	6-0	190	2-2-97	0	0	16.20	3	0	0	3	9	6	6	0	2	4	.500	.524	.833	19.0	9.5	21
Dombkowski, Nick	R-L	6-2	210	8-9-98	3	6	5.68	26	12	0	71	76	47	45	14	29	63	.275	.350	.467	20.3	9.4	310
Fellows, Drake	L-R	6-5	216	3-6-98	9	6	4.41	33	19	0	112	110	58	55	11	46	94	.258	.335	.398	19.5	9.5	483
Fulmer, Carson	R-R	6-0	210	12-13-93	1	3	4.64	13	6	0	43	44	22	22	5	16	38	.267	.330	.430	20.5	8.6	185
Hall, Darick	L-R	6-4	232	7-25-95	0	0	9.00	1	0	0	1	1	1	1	0	0	0	.250	.250	1.000	0.0	0.0	4
Harbin, Ryan	R-R	6-4	195	8-6-01	1	1	11.48	14	1	2	13	20	19	17	0	16	15	.351	.493	.404	20.3	21.6	74
Harrington, Thomas	R-R	6-2	185	7-12-01	7	9	5.34	21	20	0	96	93	59	57	20	33	90	.251	.319	.480	21.7	8.0	415
Holderman, Colin	R-R	6-7	240	10-8-95	1	1	5.40	17	1	1	18	21	12	11	3	7	21	.288	.354	.493	25.6	8.5	82
Jarvis, Mike	R-R	5-10	180	5-12-98	0	0	0.00	1	0	0	1	1	0	0	0	0	0	.200	.200	.200	0.0	0.0	5
Labaut, Randy	L-L	6-2	205	10-1-96	4	1	5.06	22	2	0	37	32	21	21	6	20	41	.232	.327	.435	25.8	12.6	159
Lawrence, Justin	R-R	6-3	213	11-25-94	0	0	11.81	6	0	0	5	4	7	7	0	6	9	.211	.444	.211	33.3	22.2	27
Linarez, Valentin	R-R	6-5	226	2-14-00	1	0	1.93	3	0	0	5	3	1	1	1	1	5	.200	.294	.400	29.4	5.9	17
Little, Jack	L-R	6-4	190	1-10-98	2	1	2.79	14	0	0	19	17	7	6	1	3	14	.230	.256	.324	17.9	3.8	78
Mattson, Isaac	R-R	6-2	205	7-14-95	2	0	2.57	19	0	4	21	14	8	6	1	6	25	.182	.238	.273	29.8	7.1	84
Mayza, Tim	L-L	6-3	215	1-15-92	0	0	3.00	2	0	0	3	3	1	1	0	0	4	.250	.250	.333	33.3	0.0	12
Mlodzinski, Carmen	R-R	6-2	225	2-19-99	2	0	1.15	3	3	0	16	11	2	2	0	7	16	.196	.286	.250	25.0	10.9	64
Moreta, Dauri	R-R	6-2	185	4-15-96	4	0	2.43	35	0	1	37	24	14	10	2	21	57	.186	.307	.302	37.0	13.6	154
Nicolas, Kyle	R-R	6-4	223	2-22-99	2	2	3.79	30	1	5	36	35	15	15	1	20	50	.248	.342	.312	31.1	12.4	161
Oviedo, Johan	R-R	6-5	245	3-2-98	0	0	2.63	3	3	0	14	8	5	4	3	3	20	.170	.220	.404	40.0	6.0	50
Prato, Anthony	R-R	5-9	186	5-11-98	0	0	0.00	2	0	0	2	3	0	0	0	0	0	.429	.429	.571	0.0	0.0	7
Rainey, Tanner	R-R	6-2	250	12-25-92	0	0	3.18	17	0	3	17	12	6	6	0	9	21	.194	.297	.242	28.4	12.2	74
Ramirez, Yohan	R-R	6-4	212	5-6-95	2	1	3.19	27	0	7	31	27	15	11	2	12	41	.233	.343	.353	29.3	8.6	140
Ramos, Wilkin	R-R	6-5	165	10-31-00	1	2	6.60	12	1	0	15	14	13	11	1	5	15	.237	.318	.339	22.7	7.6	66
Ross, Shawn	R-R	6-0	185	9-30-99	0	0	0.00	2	0	0	1	1	0	0	0	0	0	.200	.333	.200	0.0	0.0	6
Ryan, Ryder	R-R	6-2	205	5-11-95	8	1	4.73	42	3	0	72	58	41	38	4	38	61	.222	.330	.326	19.7	12.3	309
Sanders, Cam	R-R	6-2	175	12-9-96	2	2	2.30	23	0	5	27	14	8	7	2	13	36	.152	.269	.277	33.3	12.0	108
Shugart, Chase	L-R	5-10	198	10-24-96	1	0	1.74	12	1	1	21	12	4	4	0	6	20	.164	.228	.247	25.3	7.6	79
Sisk, Evan	L-L	6-2	209	4-23-97	0	0	6.48	7	0	1	8	9	6	6	0	6	6	.290	.405	.290	16.2	16.2	37
Smith, Burch	R-R	6-4	225	4-12-90	2	0	7.08	19	0	0	20	22	18	16	4	12	26	.262	.357	.512	26.5	12.2	98
Stratton, Hunter	R-R	6-2	225	11-17-96	1	1	3.65	21	0	1	25	23	10	10	1	8	24	.250	.307	.348	23.8	7.9	101
Sullivan, Sean	R-R	6-1	180	10-2-00	2	4	4.57	17	5	1	41	37	21	21	6	18	41	.237	.318	.410	23.2	10.2	177
Townsend, Blake	L-L	6-4	220	4-5-01	1	0	0.00	1	0	0	2	2	0	0	0	1	.286	.375	.286	12.5	0.0	8	
Williams, Alika	R-R	6-1	180	3-12-99	0	0	36.00	1	0	0	1	3	4	4	1	0	0	.500	.571	1.000	0.0	0.0	7
Yean, Eddy	R-R	6-1	180	6-25-01	8	5	3.06	50	4	7	71	68	27	24	5	45	54	.266	.380	.371	17.5	14.6	309

Fielding

Catcher	PCT	G	PO	A	E	DP	PB
Bart	1.000	3	25	2	0	0	0
Davis	1.000	7	82	2	0	1	0
Flores	.985	21	194	9	3	0	1
Gutierrez	.991	23	213	10	2	1	2
Rodriguez	1.000	5	47	2	0	0	0
Ross	.995	25	194	8	1	0	3
Sullivan	.995	60	534	27	3	3	7
Wilson	.985	8	62	2	1	0	0

First Base	PCT	G	PO	A	E	DP
Bowen	1.000	4	41	1	0	4
Castillo	1.000	2	18	1	0	0
Cook	.977	21	121	7	3	12
Flores	.985	7	59	5	1	7
Gorski	1.000	4	32	2	0	2
Gutierrez	1.000	3	22	3	0	1
Hall	.996	37	211	21	1	22
Horwitz	1.000	5	31	5	0	2
Nunez	.990	13	87	13	1	10
Peguero	1.000	5	38	0	0	1
Rodriguez	1.000	2	8	1	0	2
Ross	1.000	1	8	0	0	0
Solak	.997	40	279	15	1	32
Stewart	1.000	5	28	0	0	4
Triolo	.917	2	10	1	1	2
Yorke	1.000	5	41	1	0	4

Second Base	PCT	G	PO	A	E	DP
Castillo	1.000	1	1	6	0	0
Cheng	.984	14	26	37	1	6
Devanney	1.000	5	7	10	0	2
Gonzales	1.000	4	5	10	0	2
Jarvis	1.000	11	17	28	0	4
Peguero	1.000	9	11	20	0	3
Prato	.970	8	12	20	1	3
Solak	.983	19	26	33	1	8
Williams	1.000	28	39	56	0	18
Yorke	.991	57	87	127	2	36

Third Base	PCT	G	PO	A	E	DP
Castillo	1.000	1	1	0	0	0
Cheng	.934	26	18	39	4	5
Devanney	.920	14	5	18	2	2
Jarvis	.923	5	3	9	1	1
Kreidler	1.000	4	2	9	0	1
Nunez	.915	25	14	40	5	5
Peguero	.942	23	17	32	3	3
Ross	1.000	1	1	2	0	0
Triolo	1.000	8	7	9	0	0
Williams	.958	50	26	65	4	5
Wilson	1.000	2	1	1	0	0

Shortstop	PCT	G	PO	A	E	DP
Cheng	.973	70	84	136	6	27
Devanney	1.000	14	18	35	0	11
Gonzales	1.000	4	1	7	0	0
Kreidler	.950	5	9	10	1	2
Peguero	.929	30	37	55	7	12
Triolo	1.000	5	7	14	0	4
Williams	.978	25	28	59	2	15

Outfield	PCT	G	PO	A	E	DP
Bae	1.000	62	136	4	0	1
Bowen	1.000	35	51	0	0	0
Cook	.980	66	141	6	3	1
Fraizer	.991	57	109	2	1	0
Gorski	.972	17	31	4	1	2
Jarvis	.938	9	15	0	1	0
Johnson	1.000	11	13	0	0	0
Kreidler	1.000	7	18	0	0	0
Peguero	1.000	8	17	0	0	0
Siani	.956	23	41	2	2	1
Simon	.974	43	73	3	2	0
Solak	.961	27	47	2	2	0
Stewart	1.000	15	23	0	0	0
Suwinski	.983	52	114	0	2	0
Triolo	1.000	1	2	1	0	1
Velazquez	1.000	16	29	0	0	0
Yorke	.979	29	45	2	1	1

ALTOONA CURVE
EASTERN LEAGUE
DOUBLE-A — PITTSBURGH PIRATES

Batting	B-T	Ht.	Wt.	DOB	AVG	OBP	SLG	G	PA	AB	R	H	2B	3B	HR	RBI	BB	HBP	SH	SF	SO	SB	CS	BB%	SO%
Alfonzo, Omar	L-R	6-1	180	8-3-03	.218	.302	.335	49	193	170	15	37	9	1	3	22	19	2	1	1	58	0	0	9.8	30.1
Berg, Derek	R-R	6-3	200	9-21-01	.321	.457	.393	9	35	28	5	9	2	0	0	2	6	1	0	0	10	0	0	17.1	28.6
Bowen, Jase	R-R	6-0	190	9-2-00	.257	.328	.417	52	196	175	22	45	11	1	5	17	17	2	1	1	63	13	2	8.7	32.1
Brannigan, Jack	R-R	6-0	190	3-11-01	.225	.329	.358	59	237	204	29	46	8	2	5	30	25	7	0	1	62	9	0	10.5	26.2
Cimillo, Nick	R-R	6-2	215	2-23-00	.239	.319	.474	112	455	401	50	96	26	4	20	71	44	5	1	4	97	5	2	9.7	21.3
Cruz, Oneil	L-R	6-7	220	10-4-98	.167	.375	.500	2	8	6	2	1	0	1	0	3	2	0	0	0	2	1	0	25.0	25.0
Dixon, Brenden	R-R	5-11	205	11-20-00	.176	.286	.264	67	215	182	23	32	5	1	3	12	27	2	1	2	63	9	2	12.6	29.3
Escotto, Maikol	R-R	5-10	180	6-4-02	.135	.211	.198	40	142	126	17	17	2	0	2	10	9	4	0	3	29	3	2	6.3	20.4
Gonzalez, Tres	L-L	5-11	185	10-4-00	.246	.351	.303	76	270	228	19	56	10	0	1	19	32	6	2	2	49	0	3	11.9	18.1
Gourson, Duce	R-R	6-1	190	9-20-02	.284	.372	.431	56	226	197	27	56	12	1	5	20	23	5	0	1	61	10	1	10.2	27.0
Griffin, Konnor	R-R	6-4	215	4-24-06	.337	.418	.542	21	98	83	20	28	2	0	5	22	7	6	0	2	23	6	2	7.1	23.5
Head, Hudson	L-L	6-0	180	4-8-01	.116	.183	.174	33	93	86	8	10	0	1	1	4	6	1	0	0	32	1	1	6.5	34.4
Hendrie, Wyatt	R-R	5-10	200	2-8-99	.179	.350	.283	40	140	106	18	19	2	0	3	13	24	5	3	2	30	3	1	17.1	21.4
Hilson, P.J.	R-R	5-10	175	8-25-00	.273	.338	.333	22	74	66	9	18	2	1	0	6	7	0	0	1	14	0	2	9.5	18.9
Horwitz, Spencer	L-R	5-10	190	11-14-97	.125	.222	.188	5	18	16	2	2	1	0	0	0	2	0	0	0	2	0	0	11.1	11.1
Jarvis, Mike	R-R	5-10	180	5-12-98	.202	.259	.273	65	204	183	25	37	5	1	2	25	12	3	3	3	50	17	4	5.9	24.5
Jebb, Mitch	L-R	6-1	185	5-13-02	.265	.350	.317	122	513	445	55	118	11	6	0	34	59	1	4	4	56	33	5	11.5	10.9
Johnson, Termarr	L-R	5-8	175	6-11-04	.272	.363	.382	119	503	434	67	118	15	3	9	35	59	4	4	2	93	20	12	11.7	18.5
McKeithan, Aaron	R-R	6-1	220	12-13-99	.299	.272	.41	139	114	11	20	2	0	3	12	18	3	2	2	21	0	1	12.9	15.1
Pichardo, Kervin	R-R	6-0	180	10-15-01	.201	.288	.332	92	361	313	33	63	13	2	8	41	35	5	3	5	97	5	3	9.7	26.9
Rivas, Javier	R-R	6-6	165	9-1-02	.209	.239	.355	31	118	110	11	23	7	0	3	14	3	2	1	2	26	0	0	2.5	22.0
Ross, Shawn	R-R	6-0	185	9-30-99	.163	.281	.286	35	114	98	10	16	6	0	2	12	15	1	0	0	48	0	0	13.2	42.1
Siani, Sammy	L-L	5-10	195	12-14-00	.192	.289	.289	76	305	266	33	51	9	4	3	29	36	1	1	1	66	16	3	11.8	21.6
Valdez, Esmerlyn	R-R	6-2	181	1-27-04	.260	.363	.409	51	215	181	29	47	7	1	6	29	25	6	0	3	53	1	2	11.6	24.7
Vargas, Imanol	L-R	6-3	215	6-29-98	.204	.331	.265	36	121	98	8	20	3	0	1	12	20	0	0	3	34	0	0	16.5	28.1

Pitching	B-T	Ht.	Wt.	DOB	W	L	ERA	G	GS	SV	IP	Hits	Runs	ER	HR	BB	SO	AVG	OBP	SLG	SO%	BB%	BF
Barco, Hunter	L-L	6-4	210	12-15-00	1	0	0.00	6	6	0	26	11	0	0	0	7	34	.131	.223	.155	36.2	7.4	94
Bayless, Jarod	R-R	6-4	225	12-29-96	0	5	5.28	11	8	0	29	27	22	17	4	7	25	.241	.306	.429	20.2	5.6	124
Bidois, Brandan	R-R	6-2	158	6-21-01	4	0	1.08	14	0	0	25	10	6	3	0	8	26	.120	.198	.145	28.0	8.6	93
Burrows, Beau	R-R	6-2	210	9-18-96	1	1	0.44	15	0	5	21	7	1	1	0	5	21	.106	.192	.167	28.4	6.8	74
Carey, Jack	R-R	6-0	205	9-9-00	0	1	3.86	9	0	0	2	2	2	1	0	1	1	.333	.500	.333	11.1	11.1	9
Chapman, Emmanuel	R-R	6-6	255	9-23-98	7	2	3.72	32	5	0	73	56	34	30	2	41	72	.212	.333	.318	22.5	12.8	320
Chen, Po-Yu	L-R	6-2	187	10-2-01	4	11	5.73	26	23	0	99	105	66	63	11	48	87	.267	.362	.425	19.2	10.6	453
Curtis, Khristian	R-R	6-5	210	5-9-02	0	0	1.00	1	0	0	2	0	0	0	0	5	0	.000	.000	.000	50.0	0	6
Del Bonta-Smith, Fineas	R-R	6-0	190	2-2-97	2	1	5.47	15	1	0	26	36	18	16	3	11	18	.327	.388	.491	14.9	9.1	121
Diamond, Derek	R-R	6-2	200	1-4-01	1	3	14.79	9	1	0	14	31	23	23	2	10	12	.449	.519	.768	14.6	12.2	82
Dixon, Brenden	R-R	5-11	205	11-20-00	0	0	27.00	1	0	0	1	1	1	1	0	0	0	.500	.500	2.000	0.0	0.0	2
Dombkowski, Nick	R-L	6-2	210	8-9-98	0	0	2.45	5	0	1	11	8	3	3	1	4	10	.200	.273	.325	22.7	9.1	44
Dotel, Wilber	R-R	6-3	178	9-25-02	7	9	4.15	27	27	0	126	111	62	58	14	43	131	.234	.307	.403	24.5	8.0	535
Ercolani, Alessandro	R-R	6-2	185	4-20-04	1	8	4.04	25	21	0	100	84	48	45	12	39	68	.220	.305	.408	15.7	9.0	434
Flowers, J.C.	R-R	6-3	195	5-19-98	0	1	8.66	9	1	0	18	29	17	17	3	10	18	.292	.378	.514	22.0	12.2	82
Gonzalez, Tres	L-L	5-11	185	10-4-00	0	0	2.70	4	0	0	3	3	1	1	0	1	1	.231	.286	.385	7.1	7.1	14
Harbin, Ryan	R-R	6-4	195	8-6-01	1	3	3.66	14	0	1	20	17	10	8	2	7	31	.227	.293	.387	37.8	8.5	82
Head, Hudson	L-L	6-0	180	4-8-01	0	0	0.00	2	0	0	1	1	0	0	0	1	0	.333	.500	.333	0.0	25.0	4
Hendrie, Wyatt	R-R	5-10	200	2-8-99	0	0	0.00	1	0	0	1	0	0	0	0	0	0	.000	.000	.000	0.0	0.0	3
Jarvis, Mike	R-R	5-10	180	5-12-98	0	0	0.00	2	0	0	1	1	0	0	0	0	1	.200	.333	.200	0.0	16.7	6
Kelly, Antwone	R-R	5-10	183	9-1-03	2	2	3.00	11	11	0	48	40	17	16	2	16	46	.226	.296	.328	23.5	8.2	196
Linarez, Valentin	R-R	6-5	226	2-14-00	5	2	3.16	37	1	1	57	39	21	20	4	27	57	.192	.298	.300	23.9	11.3	238
Loeschorn, Joshua	L-R	6-3	215	3-10-00	0	0	0.00	1	0	0	2	4	4	0	0	2	0	.571	.667	.571	0.0	18.2	11
McMillan, Garrett	L-R	6-4	230	2-10-01	1	1	4.26	4	4	0	19	19	9	9	1	4	15	.271	.303	.400	19.7	5.3	76
Meis, Justin	R-R	6-2	160	11-23-99	4	4	2.89	42	0	7	62	49	21	20	5	21	67	.213	.276	.330	26.1	8.2	257
Melendez, Cristofer	R-R	6-3	226	9-16-97	0	0	12.27	4	0	0	4	5	5	5	0	6	5	.333	.522	.467	21.7	26.1	23
Nielson, Cy	R-L	6-3	210	2-25-01	3	2	5.40	38	2	0	55	62	37	33	5	31	67	.287	.390	.431	25.8	11.9	260
Oviedo, Johan	R-R	6-5	245	3-2-98	1	0	2.16	2	2	0	8	7	2	2	0	0	8	.226	.250	.387	25.0	0.0	32
Perachi, Dominic	L-L	6-4	195	2-27-01	3	1	4.89	8	7	0	35	32	22	19	2	15	22	.241	.331	.361	14.3	9.7	154
Ramos, Wilkin	R-R	6-5	165	10-31-00	3	2	1.45	35	0	7	50	28	10	8	1	19	53	.161	.251	.224	27.0	9.7	196
Samaniego, Tyler	R-L	6-4	205	1-30-99	1	1	3.08	20	0	3	26	18	10	9	1	6	30	.189	.250	.274	28.3	5.7	106
Sanders, Cam	R-R	6-2	175	12-9-96	2	0	1.90	18	0	9	24	12	7	5	1	13	26	.154	.287	.256	27.4	13.7	95
Solomeno, Anthony	L-L	6-5	220	12-2-02	1	0	0.90	2	2	0	10	2	1	1	0	4	7	.067	.194	.133	19.4	11.1	36
Sullivan, Sean	R-R	6-1	180	10-2-00	1	1	1.15	7	2	0	16	7	4	2	1	4	14	.135	.196	.192	24.6	7.0	57
Tomkins, Landon	R-R	6-3	200	6-23-00	2	0	2.84	10	0	0	13	20	4	4	0	6	10	.370	.443	.463	16.1	9.7	62
Townsend, Blake	L-L	6-4	220	4-5-01	5	4	2.05	22	12	0	66	53	19	15	4	18	52	.222	.276	.318	19.8	6.9	262
Walsh, Mike	R-R	6-2	195	1-17-01	1	0	3.38	11	0	1	19	17	7	7	0	4	16	.239	.299	.338	20.5	5.1	78
Wietgrefe, Connor	L-R	6-2	200	6-6-02	0	0	1.80	1	1	0	5	2	1	1	0	0	4	.118	.118	.294	23.5	0.0	17
Woods, Jaden	L-L	6-2	205	2-1-02	5	5	5.81	44	0	0	62	68	49	40	5	34	68	.273	.376	.406	22.7	11.4	299

Fielding

Catcher	PCT	G	PO	A	E	DP	PB
Alfonzo	.989	43	329	28	4	2	2
Berg	1.000	8	39	5	0	0	1
Hendrie	.996	27	231	13	1	1	5
McKeithan	.991	39	314	24	3	3	0
Ross	.996	30	231	9	1	0	2

First Base	PCT	G	PO	A	E	DP
Alfonzo	.986	9	68	1	1	5
Bowen	1.000	1	5	0	0	0
Cimillo	.985	70	490	27	8	35
Dixon	.995	36	182	11	1	14
Gourson	1.000	20	130	9	0	13
Horwitz	.952	4	17	3	1	1
Jarvis	1.000	4	6	0	0	0
Valdez	1.000	2	13	0	0	1
Vargas	1.000	9	51	4	0	8

Second Base	PCT	G	PO	A	E	DP
Brannigan	.000	1	0	0	0	0

	PCT	G	PO	A	E	DP
Escotto	1.000	1	2	1	0	0
Gourson	1.000	4	5	7	0	1
Jarvis	.968	10	15	15	1	5
Jebb	.965	26	30	52	3	8
Johnson	.959	101	120	229	15	45
Pichardo	1.000	1	2	2	0	1

Third Base	PCT	G	PO	A	E	DP
Brannigan	1.000	14	7	24	0	2
Dixon	.949	24	16	21	2	0
Gourson	.899	31	15	56	8	3
Jarvis	1.000	11	6	16	0	0
Pichardo	.941	48	29	67	6	5
Rivas	1.000	15	8	24	0	1
Ross	1.000	3	4	2	0	0

Shortstop	PCT	G	PO	A	E	DP
Brannigan	.977	42	55	71	3	20
Escotto	.962	23	37	63	4	13
Griffin	1.000	18	26	45	0	12
Jarvis	.975	11	10	29	1	5
Pichardo	.952	33	31	69	5	5
Rivas	1.000	14	11	23	0	2
Ross	.000	1	0	0	0	0

Outfield	PCT	G	PO	A	E	DP
Bowen	.990	48	101	0	1	0
Cruz	1.000	1	2	0	0	0
Escotto	.974	16	35	3	1	2
Gonzalez	.982	69	111	0	2	0
Griffin	1.000	2	7	1	0	1
Head	.967	29	58	0	2	0
Hendrie	.833	9	13	2	3	0
Hilson	.966	24	55	1	2	0
Jarvis	.984	33	57	3	1	2
Jebb	.982	85	218	2	4	2
Siani	.979	74	179	5	4	0
Valdez	.989	43	83	3	1	1
Vargas	1.000	20	34	1	0	0

GREENSBORO GRASSHOPPERS — HIGH-A
SOUTH ATLANTIC LEAGUE

Batting	B-T	Ht.	Wt.	DOB	AVG	OBP	SLG	G	PA	AB	R	H	2B	3B	HR	RBI	BB	HBP	SH	SF	SO	SB	CS	BB%	SO%
Alfonzo, Omar	L-R	6-1	180	8-3-03	.261	.389	.440	67	284	234	41	61	9	0	11	34	44	5	1	0	79	2	0	15.5	27.8
Berg, Derek	R-R	6-3	200	9-21-01	.250	.352	.398	27	106	88	15	22	5	1	2	18	13	2	1	2	38	2	3	12.3	35.8
Bowen, Jase	R-R	6-0	190	9-2-00	.500	.556	1.125	2	9	8	3	4	2	0	1	3	1	0	0	0	2	0	1	11.1	22.2
Brethowr, Ivan	R-R	6-6	245	2-27-03	.234	.417	.375	21	84	64	15	15	1	1	2	8	14	6	0	0	21	5	2	16.7	25.0
Carmichael, Easton	R-R	6-1	189	11-3-03	.120	.185	.180	14	54	50	3	6	0	1	1	2	2	2	0	0	11	1	0	3.7	20.4
Castillo, Jesus	S-S	5-10	144	7-12-03	.241	.326	.287	106	397	348	47	84	10	0	2	28	36	9	1	3	89	13	12	9.1	22.4
De Los Santos, Yordany	R-R	6-1	170	2-17-05	.000	.000	.000	2	3	3	0	0	0	0	0	0	0	0	0	0	3	0	0	0.0	100.0
Delgado, Keiner	S-R	5-7	145	11-7-04	.243	.370	.389	120	514	424	74	103	18	1	14	59	73	13	3	1	112	24	2	14.2	21.8
Dumitru, Titus	R-R	6-2	220	5-17-03	.245	.335	.415	43	182	159	20	39	7	1	6	19	18	4	0	1	47	5	4	9.9	25.8
Escotto, Maikol	R-R	5-10	180	6-4-02	.319	.370	.525	38	156	141	32	45	9	1	6	20	10	2	1	1	34	18	4	6.4	21.8
Gonzalez, Tres	L-L	5-11	185	10-4-00	.286	.400	.286	6	25	21	4	6	0	0	0	3	4	0	0	0	7	2	0	16.0	28.0
Gourson, Duce	L-R	6-1	190	9-20-02	.261	.368	.449	39	166	138	29	36	9	1	5	18	17	7	3	1	28	21	2	10.2	16.9
Griffin, Konnor	R-R	6-4	215	4-24-06	.325	.432	.510	51	234	194	48	63	11	2	7	36	28	10	0	2	46	33	7	12.0	19.7
Harrison, Kalae	L-R	5-11	188	6-5-02	.173	.212	.296	30	104	98	15	17	3	0	3	9	5	0	0	1	25	6	0	4.8	24.0
Hilson, P.J.	R-R	5-10	175	8-25-04	.259	.317	.465	60	207	185	31	48	5	0	11	35	11	6	1	3	53	10	3	5.3	25.6
Jones, Jared	R-R	6-4	235	8-1-03	.160	.276	.420	15	58	50	8	8	1	0	4	8	6	2	0	0	26	0	0	10.3	44.8
King, Matt	R-R	6-1	195	8-25-02	.190	.190	.333	6	21	21	2	4	3	0	0	1	0	0	0	0	2	1	0	0.0	9.5
Miknis, Justin	L-R	6-0	195	9-6-00	.188	.286	.250	17	58	48	2	9	0	0	1	7	7	0	2	1	19	0	1	12.1	32.8
Moss, Michael Callan	R-R	6-3	230	8-31-03	.339	.422	.571	30	128	112	17	38	8	0	6	19	12	4	0	0	29	3	1	9.4	22.7
Planchart, Geovanny	R-R	6-1	176	9-17-01	.193	.307	.293	56	179	150	21	29	6	0	3	18	23	3	0	3	34	0	0	12.8	19.0
Plaz, Axiel	R-R	5-11	165	8-12-05	.086	.214	.200	11	42	35	5	3	1	0	1	6	5	1	0	1	5	0	0	11.9	14.3
Polanco, Shalin	L-L	6-0	168	2-6-04	.209	.292	.389	93	350	306	39	64	8	4	13	37	35	2	4	3	88	9	7	10.0	25.1
Rivas, Javier	R-R	6-6	165	9-1-02	.266	.320	.460	94	389	354	53	94	13	1	18	72	19	11	1	4	92	4	1	4.9	23.7
Stafura, Sammy	R-R	6-0	188	11-15-04	.160	.257	.255	26	110	94	11	15	3	0	2	12	10	3	1	2	26	4	1	9.1	23.6
Taylor, Will	R-R	6-0	175	1-10-03	.231	.351	.410	64	280	234	44	54	10	1	10	43	33	11	1	1	76	15	7	11.8	27.1
Terrero, Enmanuel	L-L	5-9	160	9-14-02	.206	.270	.343	36	118	102	15	21	2	0	4	17	8	2	3	3	39	8	1	6.8	33.1
Valdez, Esmerlyn	R-R	6-2	181	1-27-04	.303	.385	.592	72	314	277	46	84	18	1	20	57	31	6	0	0	77	2	0	9.9	24.5
White, Lonnie	R-R	6-3	212	12-31-02	.220	.329	.394	82	329	282	52	62	11	1	12	39	36	10	1	0	118	23	5	10.9	35.9

Pitching	B-T	Ht.	Wt.	DOB	W	L	ERA	G	GS	SV	IP	Hits	Runs	ER	HR	BB	SO	AVG	OBP	SLG	SO%	BB%	BF
Bayless, Jarod	R-R	6-4	225	12-29-96	3	0	2.52	17	0	2	25	19	10	7	4	3	35	.209	.258	.407	36.1	3.1	97
Bidois, Brandan	R-R	6-2	158	6-21-01	2	0	0.86	16	0	5	21	11	5	2	0	13	27	.151	.276	.178	31.0	14.9	87
Bosnic, Julian	L-L	6-3	218	12-28-99	6	2	3.51	42	1	0	51	39	21	20	4	38	58	.215	.360	.315	26.0	17.0	223
Burrows, Beau	R-R	6-2	210	9-18-96	0	0	0.00	3	0	1	4	2	0	0	0	2	6	.125	.222	.125	33.3	11.1	18
Cabreja, Victor	L-L	6-3	180	1-10-02	0	1	7.00	3	1	0	9	12	7	7	2	4	6	.316	.395	.474	13.6	9.1	44
Carey, Jack	R-R	6-0	205	9-20-99	5	0	3.62	41	0	4	55	43	24	22	4	22	65	.211	.293	.333	28.3	9.6	230
Castillo, Carlos	R-R	6-1	165	2-4-06	0	0	0.00	1	0	0	1	0	0	0	0	0	2	.000	.000	.000	50.0	0.0	4
Chang, Hung-Leng	R-R	6-3	159	10-7-01	5	7	4.82	25	24	0	106	110	63	57	14	26	97	.261	.331	.428	21.4	5.7	454
Curtis, Khristian	R-R	6-5	210	5-9-02	8	5	3.98	26	26	0	109	91	59	48	12	46	116	.222	.308	.369	24.8	9.8	468
De La Rosa, Franck	R-R	6-8	200	6-9-00	1	0	4.32	6	0	2	8	6	4	4	1	7	11	.200	.351	.300	29.7	18.9	37
Deese, Jaycob	R-R	6-1	195	5-30-00	7	3	3.72	33	0	0	39	41	20	16	1	12	30	.275	.335	.356	18.0	7.2	167
Diamond, Derek	R-R	6-2	200	1-4-01	1	0	0.00	2	0	0	3	1	0	0	0	7	.100	.100	.100	70.0	0.0	10
Dombkowski, Nick	R-L	6-2	210	8-9-98	0	0	0.00	2	0	0	2	0	0	0	0	0	2	.250	.250	.250	25.0	0.0	8
Furtado, Hunter	R-L	6-3	160	2-18-02	4	0	6.00	10	0	0	12	9	8	8	0	11	14	.237	.385	.289	26.9	21.2	52
Garces, Jose	R-R	6-2	160	8-6-00	0	0	0.00	1	0	0	1	0	0	0	0	1	0	.500	.600	.500	0.0	20.0	5
Harbin, Ryan	R-R	6-4	195	8-6-01	2	2	2.37	22	0	4	30	18	9	8	3	25	46	.173	.336	.231	34.8	17.4	132
Jimenez, Carlos	R-R	6-2	140	7-14-02	3	3	3.98	34	1	0	40	39	22	18	6	24	55	.192	.353	.377	29.7	18.2	192
Kelly, Antwone	R-R	5-10	183	9-1-03	1	1	3.03	14	14	0	59	61	29	20	4	17	70	.192	.252	.286	30.4	7.4	230

Batting	B-T	Ht.	Wt.	DOB		AVG	OBP	SLG	G	PA	AB	R	H	2B	3B	HR	RBI	BB	HBP	SH	SF	SO	SB	CS	BB%	SO%
Labaut, Randy	L-L	6-2	205	10-1-96	1	0	0.00		1	0	0	2	0	0	0	0	0	3	.000	.000	.000	50.0	0.0	6		
Lobo, Inmer	L-L	6-1	193	2-12-04	0	1	2.74	20	0	1	23	17	8	7	1	8	21	.198	.263	.314	22.1	8.4	95			
Loeschorn, Joshua	L-R	6-3	215	3-10-00	1	0	2.66	19	0	3	20	11	6	6	1	3	17	.155	.189	.225	23.0	4.1	74			
Massey, J.P.	R-R	6-5	205	4-1-00	4	1	6.80	34	0	0	46	42	36	35	6	32	44	.239	.367	.369	20.1	14.6	219			
McMillan, Garrett	L-R	6-4	230	2-10-01	3	0	1.55	6	6	0	29	20	5	5	3	3	29	.196	.226	.314	27.4	2.8	106			
Oliver, Connor	L-L	6-2	170	5-26-01	6	2	4.68	22	6	0	50	40	30	26	9	36	54	.216	.345	.411	24.1	16.1	224			
Perachi, Dominic	L-L	6-4	195	2-27-01	0	0	0.00	2	2	0	8	3	0	0	0	2	6	.115	.179	.154	21.4	7.1	28			
Reed, Carlson	L-R	6-4	200	11-27-02	2	4	4.14	16	16	0	63	42	33	29	6	50	61	.194	.344	.309	22.2	18.2	275			
Samaniego, Tyler	R-L	6-4	205	1-30-99	1	0	3.86	6	0	0	7	3	3	3	0	3	6	.130	.214	.174	21.4	10.7	28			
Shirk, Jake	R-R	6-2	200	6-5-02	2	0	3.18	18	0	0	23	17	8	8	0	6	17	.215	.279	.253	19.5	6.9	87			
Stumbo, Peyton	R-R	6-1	200	6-28-02	1	3	4.17	12	10	0	41	35	21	19	3	19	35	.232	.324	.351	20.2	11.0	173			
Sullivan, Sean	R-R	6-1	180	10-2-00	1	0	2.25	2	0	0	4	3	1	1	1	1	3	.231	.286	.538	20.0	6.7	15			
Tomkins, Landon	R-R	6-3	200	6-23-00	6	3	2.47	39	0	6	47	30	15	13	1	19	47	.184	.295	.239	24.6	9.9	191			
Torres, Alexis	R-R	6-0	153	3-16-03	0	0	1.00	6	0	0	9	4	1	1	0	3	13	.129	.250	.129	36.1	8.3	36			
Townsend, Blake	L-L	6-4	220	4-5-01	2	0	1.14	11	0	1	24	18	3	3	3	5	28	.205	.278	.330	28.6	5.1	98			
Walsh, Mike	R-R	6-2	195	1-17-01	4	1	2.76	38	0	7	49	41	15	15	2	11	51	.223	.278	.288	25.8	5.6	198			
Wietgrefe, Connor	L-L	6-2	200	6-6-02	6	4	3.17	24	24	0	108	88	38	38	11	25	93	.223	.269	.349	21.7	5.8	428			

Fielding

Catcher	PCT	G	PO	A	E	DP	PB
Alfonzo	.985	48	446	23	7	2	6
Berg	.983	23	213	19	4	2	1
Carmichael	.985	14	123	12	2	1	0
Miknis	1.000	4	32	2	0	1	0
Planchart	.994	41	313	24	2	2	4
Plaz	1.000	9	73	5	0	0	1

First Base	PCT	G	PO	A	E	DP
Alfonzo	.991	16	99	12	1	9
Berg	1.000	4	24	1	0	0
Castillo	.992	35	223	16	2	18
Escotto	1.000	11	58	7	0	5
Gourson	1.000	2	9	0	0	0
Jones	.988	10	77	3	1	9
Miknis	1.000	10	70	10	0	8
Moss	.965	22	154	12	6	10
Planchart	.975	15	110	8	3	5
Valdez	.991	14	107	8	1	7

Second Base	PCT	G	PO	A	E	DP
Castillo	.987	20	30	45	1	10

	PCT	G	PO	A	E	DP
De Los Santos	.800	1	1	3	1	0
Delgado	.966	61	92	167	9	26
Escotto	.950	9	15	23	2	4
Gourson	.962	20	31	44	3	12
Harrison	.939	13	14	32	3	3
King	1.000	2	1	3	0	0
Stafura	.971	9	17	17	1	3

Third Base	PCT	G	PO	A	E	DP
Castillo	.952	27	17	42	3	6
De Los Santos	.000	1	0	0	0	0
Delgado	.957	40	30	58	4	5
Escotto	1.000	8	7	8	0	0
Gourson	.941	9	6	10	1	1
Harrison	.957	12	9	13	1	2
King	.800	2	2	2	1	1
Rivas	.956	35	26	61	4	1

Shortstop	PCT	G	PO	A	E	DP
Castillo	.907	15	16	23	4	4
Delgado	.952	10	23	17	2	6
Escotto	.857	2	3	3	1	2

	PCT	G	PO	A	E	DP
Griffin	.966	39	51	90	5	18
Harrison	1.000	3	6	8	0	2
King	1.000	2	1	8	0	0
Rivas	.975	47	65	93	4	16
Stafura	1.000	17	27	33	0	6

Outfield	PCT	G	PO	A	E	DP
Bowen	1.000	2	3	0	0	0
Brethowr	.950	15	19	0	1	0
Castillo	1.000	13	19	0	0	0
Dumitru	1.000	31	57	1	0	1
Escotto	1.000	1	1	0	0	0
Gonzalez	1.000	5	7	0	0	0
Griffin	1.000	5	14	0	0	0
Hilson	.989	55	87	4	1	1
Polanco	.980	86	145	1	3	0
Taylor	.984	58	119	1	2	0
Terrero	1.000	29	54	0	0	0
Valdez	.977	42	84	1	2	1
White	.991	71	110	3	1	1

BRADENTON MARAUDERS
FLORIDA STATE LEAGUE
LOW-A

Batting	B-T	Ht.	Wt.	DOB	AVG	OBP	SLG	G	PA	AB	R	H	2B	3B	HR	RBI	BB	HBP	SH	SF	SO	SB	CS	BB%	SO%
Aguiar, Roinny	S-R	5-7	160	4-1-05	.000	.000	.000	1	3	3	0	0	0	0	0	0	0	0	0	0	1	0	0	0.0	33.3
Berg, Derek	R-R	6-3	200	9-21-01	.205	.342	.355	52	202	166	24	34	4	3	5	17	30	5	0	1	68	8	2	14.9	33.7
Bishop, Braylon	L-L	6-2	193	4-23-03	.195	.306	.288	80	316	267	40	52	12	2	3	31	37	7	2	3	98	24	6	11.7	31.0
Blanco, Tony	R-R	6-6	243	5-14-05	.264	.368	.491	28	125	106	10	28	3	0	7	21	18	0	0	1	42	0	0	14.4	33.6
Bowen, Dave	R-R	6-0	190	9-2-00	.143	.250	.143	4	16	14	2	2	0	0	0	0	2	0	0	0	4	0	0	12.5	25.0
Caro, Carlos	R-R	5-11	160	11-4-04	.149	.245	.177	46	161	141	16	21	2	1	0	12	14	4	2	0	51	4	2	8.7	31.7
Cheng, Tsung-Che	L-R	5-7	154	7-26-01	.125	.222	.125	3	9	8	0	1	0	0	0	0	1	0	0	0	2	2	1	11.1	22.2
De Los Santos, Yordany	R-R	6-1	170	2-17-05	.249	.311	.388	116	512	461	62	115	27	2	11	54	40	4	1	6	137	51	14	7.8	26.8
Farrow, Ian	R-R	6-1	210	7-26-02	.224	.301	.404	51	183	161	20	36	9	1	6	30	18	1	0	3	61	0	1	9.8	33.3
Florentino, Edward	L-R	6-4	200	11-11-06	.262	.380	.503	54	238	195	37	51	17	0	10	36	33	6	1	3	56	29	5	13.9	23.5
Griffin, Konnor	R-R	6-4	215	4-24-06	.338	.396	.536	50	231	207	49	70	10	2	9	36	15	6	1	2	53	26	4	6.5	22.9
Gutierrez, Abrahan	R-R	6-0	214	10-31-99	.143	.200	.143	4	15	14	2	2	0	0	0	1	1	0	0	0	4	0	0	6.7	26.7
Guzman, Adonys	R-R	5-10	215	12-4-03	.400	.400	1.000	1	5	5	2	2	0	0	1	2	0	0	0	0	0	0	0	0.0	0.0
Hall, Darick	L-R	6-4	232	7-25-95	.077	.294	.154	4	17	13	1	1	1	0	0	1	4	0	0	0	4	0	0	23.5	23.5
Iredale, Brent	R-R	6-1	190	7-12-03	.214	.405	.375	18	74	56	10	12	3	0	2	9	14	4	0	0	19	5	0	18.9	25.7
Janik, Camden	R-R	5-10	195	7-16-02	.266	.383	.323	39	150	124	14	33	5	1	0	7	21	3	1	1	25	2	1	14.0	16.7
King, Matt	R-R	6-1	195	8-25-02	.083	.353	.083	5	18	12	3	1	0	0	0	0	3	2	1	0	2	0	0	16.7	11.1
Lege, Ethan	L-R	6-0	210	3-12-01	.221	.331	.284	63	243	204	35	45	7	0	2	20	26	9	0	3	50	10	1	10.7	20.6
Maguire, Solomon	L-R	5-10	168	3-4-03	.408	.200	.048	17	50	42	6	2	1	0	0	8	8	0	0	0	19	1	1	15.7	37.3
Mendez, Joel	R-R	6-1	180	1-28-03	.215	.305	.326	57	210	181	21	39	8	3	2	22	22	3	0	4	76	2	0	10.5	36.2
Nunez, Malcom	R-R	6-0	205	3-9-01	.100	.182	.200	3	11	10	2	1	0	0	0	1	1	0	0	0	2	0	0	9.1	18.2
Palmer, Dylan	R-R	5-9	170	10-5-03	.400	.538	.400	3	13	10	3	4	0	0	0	2	3	0	0	0	1	3	1	23.1	7.7
Patrick, Andrew	R-R	6-4	195	1-19-03	.137	.274	.176	21	62	51	4	7	2	0	0	8	8	2	0	1	24	2	0	12.9	38.7
Perez, Edgleen	R-R	5-10	155	5-25-06	.182	.361	.218	19	72	55	5	10	2	0	0	4	15	1	0	1	10	0	0	20.8	13.9
Plaz, Axiel	R-R	5-11	165	8-12-05	.262	.348	.450	55	233	202	27	53	11	0	9	40	21	7	0	3	47	1	0	9.0	20.2
Ramirez, Richard	R-R	6-0	160	7-3-05	.264	.384	.428	45	173	152	21	42	8	0	5	20	19	2	0	0	46	2	0	11.0	26.6
Reeder, Canon	R-R	6-0	188	4-23-03	.375	.444	.625	3	9	8	2	3	2	0	0	2	1	0	0	0	2	0	0	11.1	22.2
Rodriguez, Eddy	R-R	6-0	181	11-5-03	.189	.298	.343	94	366	312	34	59	14	2	10	31	45	4	2	2	107	9	3	12.3	29.2
Rynders, Eddie	L-R	6-2	195	10-31-05	.200	.273	.300	5	11	10	1	2	1	0	0	1	0	0	0	0	3	0	0	0.0	27.3

PITTSBURGH PIRATES

	B-T	Ht.	Wt.	DOB																		
Sanford, Wyatt	L-R	6-1	175	11-24-05	.238	.342	.378	44	194	164	29	39	7	2	4	19	19	7	3	0	39	21	7	9.8	20.1
Scherrer, Luke	R-R	6-2	210	12-13-04	.164	.270	.164	18	63	55	8	9	0	0	0	4	7	1	0	0	19	1	1	11.1	30.2
Severino, Jhonny	R-R	6-1	185	11-8-04	.215	.277	.359	113	468	423	44	91	24	2	11	49	32	6	3	4	118	10	8	6.8	25.2
Siani, Sammy	L-L	5-10	195	12-14-00	.111	.273	.111	3	11	9	1	1	0	0	0	0	2	0	0	0	1	0	0	18.2	9.1
Stafura, Sammy	R-R	6-0	188	11-15-04	.250	.294	.438	4	17	16	1	4	1	1	0	0	1	0	0	0	6	0	0	5.9	35.3
Suero, Estuar	S-R	6-5	180	8-29-05	.179	.378	.250	9	37	28	3	5	2	0	0	2	9	0	0	0	11	3	1	24.3	29.7
Tate, Josh	R-R	5-11	178	9-1-03	.238	.286	.333	18	70	63	9	15	2	2	0	5	4	1	0	2	13	2	1	5.7	18.6
Taylor, Will	R-R	6-0	175	1-10-03	.333	.424	.569	29	118	102	24	34	10	1	4	19	16	0	0	0	30	8	6	13.6	25.4
Toledo, Jeral	S-R	5-10	135	1-22-03	.215	.321	.289	45	145	121	10	26	3	0	2	7	17	2	5	0	33	2	3	11.7	22.8

Pitching	B-T	Ht.	Wt.	DOB	W	L	ERA	G	GS	SV	IP	Hits	Runs	ER	HR	BB	SO	AVG	OBP	SLG	SO%	BB%	BF
Adams, Gavin	R-R	6-3	170	2-8-03	0	0	0.00	1	0	0	1	0	0	0	0	1	1	.000	.400	.000	20.0	20.0	5
Ager, Matt	R-R	6-5	210	5-21-03	2	6	4.86	22	19	0	76	78	52	41	7	47	50	.261	.375	.415	14.0	13.2	357
Anker, Jack	R-R	6-2	185	4-8-04	0	1	0.00	1	0	0	1	0	0	0	0	0	1	.000	.000	.000	33.3	0.0	3
Aquino, Cesar	R-R	6-1	201	2-27-05	0	1	6.75	5	0	0	13	13	10	10	1	3	6	.245	.286	.396	10.7	5.4	56
Bidois, Brandan	R-R	6-2	158	6-21-01	1	0	0.00	1	0	0	2	0	0	0	0	0	1	.000	.000	.000	16.7	0.0	6
Borucki, Ryan	L-L	6-4	210	3-31-94	0	0	0.00	1	1	0	1	0	0	0	0	0	1	.000	.000	.000	33.3	0.0	3
Burrows, Beau	R-R	6-2	210	9-18-96	1	0	2.45	3	0	0	4	1	1	1	1	1	3	.091	.167	.364	23.1	7.7	13
Cabreja, Victor	L-L	6-3	180	1-10-02	9	1	2.48	21	14	0	91	71	28	25	4	26	45	.218	.280	.344	12.6	7.3	357
Castillo, Carlos	R-R	6-1	165	2-4-06	4	4	3.84	23	20	0	94	86	49	40	4	33	74	.251	.330	.351	19.1	8.5	387
Clode, Jesus	R-R	6-2	180	8-28-01	1	1	4.84	22	0	1	22	19	15	12	5	7	20	.226	.287	.464	21.3	7.4	94
Cotto, Magdiel	L-L	6-3	225	6-24-02	1	0	3.65	11	0	0	12	12	7	5	0	12	11	.245	.400	.265	16.9	18.5	65
De La Rosa, Franck	R-R	6-8	200	6-9-00	1	0	0.00	1	0	0	2	1	0	0	0	2	2	.167	.375	.167	25.0	25.0	8
Diamond, Derek	R-R	6-2	200	1-4-01	0	1	7.71	2	0	0	2	4	3	2	0	0	1	.333	.333	.417	8.3	0.0	12
Francia, Dariel	R-R	6-2	165	7-23-06	1	0	5.00	4	1	0	9	12	6	5	0	10	8	.333	.479	.417	16.7	20.8	48
Furtado, Hunter	R-L	6-3	160	2-18-02	0	0	2.77	9	0	1	13	8	4	4	1	4	17	.174	.240	.326	34.0	8.0	50
Garces, Jose	R-R	6-2	149	6-9-04	2	5	3.44	40	0	3	50	34	29	19	3	27	42	.200	.340	.276	19.7	12.7	213
Holderman, Colin	R-R	6-7	240	10-8-95	0	1	9.00	1	0	0	1	1	1	1	1	0	3	.250	.250	1.000	75.0	0.0	4
Janik, Camden	R-R	5-10	195	7-16-02	0	0	0.00	1	0	0	1	1	0	0	0	0	0	.250	.250	.250	0.0	0.0	4
Kellington, Owen	R-R	6-3	193	2-5-03	2	1	3.46	9	5	0	26	19	10	10	4	10	30	.196	.278	.361	27.8	9.3	108
Kennedy, Tyler	R-R	6-2	223	6-7-02	0	0	29.70	5	0	0	3	3	11	11	1	8	3	.273	.571	.727	14.3	38.1	21
Keshock, Cameron	R-R	6-6	220	10-29-03	1	0	1.86	7	0	0	10	9	2	2	0	3	11	.243	.317	.270	26.8	7.3	41
Labaut, Randy	L-L	6-2	205	10-1-96	0	0	0.00	1	1	0	0	0	0	0	0	0	0	.000	.000	.000	0.0	0.0	3
Lawrence, Justin	R-R	6-3	213	11-25-94	1	0	0.00	2	0	0	2	0	0	0	0	1	4	.000	.250	.000	50.0	12.5	8
Lobo, Inmer	L-L	6-1	193	2-12-04	2	0	1.71	13	0	1	32	22	6	6	0	10	35	.191	.260	.226	27.1	7.8	129
Loeschorn, Joshua	L-R	6-3	215	3-10-00	0	0	0.00	2	0	0	3	0	0	0	0	2	0	.000	.000	.000	22.2	0.0	9
Malone, Brennan	R-R	6-4	205	9-8-00	1	0	4.45	25	0	0	28	27	15	14	3	21	26	.255	.404	.406	19.1	15.4	136
Martinez, Jeter	R-R	6-4	180	2-16-06	0	1	30.86	2	1	0	2	7	8	8	0	4	6	.500	.632	.714	31.6	21.1	19
Matoma, David	R-R	6-0	154	2-2-06	0	2	4.25	32	0	0	42	42	22	20	3	24	37	.273	.372	.383	20.6	13.3	180
Mayza, Tim	L-L	6-3	215	1-15-92	0	0	0.00	2	1	0	2	2	0	0	0	2	2	.286	.286	.429	28.6	0.0	7
Mendez, Greiber	R-R	6-0	150	4-3-04	6	4	3.50	35	3	3	75	58	29	29	4	40	65	.220	.332	.322	20.8	12.8	313
Moreta, Dauri	R-R	6-2	185	4-15-96	0	0	0.00	2	1	0	2	2	0	0	0	0	1	.286	.286	.429	14.3	0.0	7
Mueth, Zander	R-R	6-6	205	6-22-05	0	4	7.36	10	10	0	22	22	23	18	1	25	28	.259	.448	.388	24.1	21.6	116
Navarro, Reinold	L-L	6-0	178	10-21-06	0	1	15.63	6	4	0	6	3	11	11	0	20	14	.136	.568	.182	31.8	45.5	44
Noble, Jack	R-R	6-2	200	4-2-00	0	3	6.23	7	0	0	9	10	7	6	1	4	6	.313	.375	.469	15.0	10.0	40
Oliver, Connor	L-L	6-1	170	5-26-01	0	0	0.00	1	0	0	1	1	0	0	0	0	5	.143	.143	.143	71.4	0.0	7
Oviedo, Adolfo	R-R	6-1	165	11-17-04	2	3	5.53	28	0	3	54	63	35	33	8	10	44	.292	.332	.468	18.7	4.3	235
Oviedo, Johan	R-R	6-5	245	3-2-98	0	1	2.70	2	2	0	3	2	1	1	0	4	7	.167	.375	.167	43.8	25.0	16
Perachi, Dominic	L-L	6-4	195	2-27-01	0	0	0.00	1	0	0	3	0	0	0	0	1	4	.000	.111	.000	44.4	11.1	9
Quintana, Yulian	R-R	6-3	185	7-15-00	2	2	3.96	8	3	0	25	25	13	11	4	18	30	.255	.378	.449	25.0	15.0	120
Reed, Carlson	L-R	6-4	200	11-27-02	0	0	0.00	1	0	0	3	1	1	0	0	1	2	.100	.250	.100	16.7	8.3	12
Rosa, Pitterson	R-R	6-2	178	11-30-04	0	1	9.00	1	0	0	2	4	2	2	0	1	3	.400	.455	.400	27.3	9.1	11
Samaniego, Tyler	R-L	6-4	205	1-30-99	1	1	13.50	2	0	0	3	6	4	4	1	1	3	.500	.538	.917	23.1	7.7	13
Shirk, Jake	R-R	6-2	200	6-5-02	4	3	4.67	23	0	6	35	41	23	18	1	9	34	.301	.356	.382	22.8	6.0	149
Shugart, Chase	L-R	5-10	198	10-24-96	0	1	9.00	1	1	0	1	1	5	1	0	1	1	.250	.400	.500	20.0	20.0	5
Smith, Burch	R-R	6-4	225	4-12-90	0	0	0.00	1	0	0	1	0	0	0	0	0	2	.000	.250	.000	50.0	25.0	4
Solometo, Anthony	L-L	6-5	290	12-2-02	0	0	27.00	1	1	0	1	2	3	3	0	1	1	.400	.500	.400	16.7	16.7	6
Sterling, Levi	R-R	6-5	202	9-2-06	0	0	0.00	1	0	0	2	2	0	0	0	2	4	.222	.417	.333	33.3	16.7	12
Stumbo, Peyton	R-R	6-1	200	6-28-02	0	3	4.41	13	11	0	49	53	26	24	4	8	46	.273	.311	.418	22.0	3.8	209
Sullivan, Sean	R-R	6-1	180	10-2-00	0	0	6.75	4	0	0	7	7	5	5	2	5	6	.269	.406	.500	18.8	15.6	32
Takacs, Noah	L-R	6-3	195	4-9-02	2	3	3.60	41	0	9	50	42	25	20	6	34	45	.228	.364	.391	19.7	14.8	229
Tejada, Clevari	R-R	6-1	204	9-23-04	4	7	4.99	26	23	0	92	81	53	51	4	40	74	.237	.330	.371	18.8	10.2	394
Tejada, Joaquin	R-R	5-11	160	7-16-03	1	0	9.00	3	0	0	3	2	3	3	0	8	2	.200	.579	.200	10.5	42.1	19
Toledo, Jeral	S-R	5-10	135	1-22-03	0	0	6.75	2	0	0	1	2	1	1	1	1	4	.400	.667	.400	0.0	44.4	9
Torres, Alexis	R-R	6-0	153	5-16-03	3	2	3.75	20	0	0	36	34	18	15	3	19	35	.262	.368	.400	22.4	12.2	156
Uribe, Isaias	L-L	6-3	172	8-13-02	0	2	4.26	9	0	0	13	11	7	6	0	8	13	.234	.345	.340	22.4	13.8	58
Valdez, Jonawel	R-R	6-1	185	3-19-04	5	4	3.60	29	3	1	70	56	33	28	4	28	49	.218	.301	.335	16.8	9.6	292
Wietgrefe, Connor	L-L	6-2	200	6-6-02	0	0	3.00	1	1	0	3	1	1	1	0	4	1	.100	.100	.400	40.0	0.0	10
Zeigler, Draven	R-R	6-4	220	6-15-01	0	0	5.40	7	0	0	10	9	8	6	0	7	7	.237	.383	.342	14.9	14.9	47

Fielding

Catcher	PCT	G	PO	A	E	DP	PB
Berg	.988	28	232	22	3	3	0
Gutierrez	1.000	3	21	0	0	0	0
Guzman	.900	1	8	1	1	0	1
Perez	.994	19	147	10	1	0	0
Plaz	.974	41	306	28	9	0	7
Ramirez	.996	33	220	20	1	2	3
Scherrer	.966	10	79	7	3	0	3

First Base	PCT	G	PO	A	E	DP
Berg	.989	22	164	11	2	21
Blanco	1.000	3	24	1	0	1
Florentino	.977	6	40	2	1	7
Hall	1.000	3	21	1	0	3
Lege	.992	32	222	15	2	26
Plaz	1.000	13	99	10	0	11
Ramirez	.978	13	82	8	2	11
Rodriguez	.979	32	221	12	5	22
Scherrer	.970	8	63	1	2	5
Toledo	.982	9	52	4	1	10

Second Base	PCT	G	PO	A	E	DP
Aguiar	1.000	1	3	5	0	1
Caro	.982	27	45	67	2	18
Cheng	1.000	1	1	1	0	0
De Los Santos	.960	26	55	65	5	22

King	.900	2	5	4	1	0
Lege	1.000	1	3	4	0	1
Palmer	1.000	2	5	0	0	0
Sanford	.988	19	35	47	1	16
Severino	.964	25	48	58	4	20
Stafura	1.000	2	3	3	0	2
Toledo	.966	28	52	62	4	20

Third Base	PCT	G	PO	A	E	DP
Caro	.909	6	2	8	1	2
De Los Santos	.898	17	14	30	5	4
Iredale	.938	10	3	27	2	0
Lege	.962	20	21	30	2	3
Nunez	1.000	2	3	2	0	2
Rynders	1.000	3	1	4	0	1
Sanford	.000	1	0	0	0	0
Scherrer	.500	1	1	0	1	0
Severino	.934	76	71	140	15	14
Toledo	.000	1	0	0	1	0

Shortstop	PCT	G	PO	A	E	DP
Caro	1.000	5	6	14	0	5
Cheng	1.000	2	3	3	0	1
De Los Santos	.967	65	100	166	9	38
Griffin	.985	32	40	93	2	20
King	1.000	3	2	6	0	0

Palmer	1.000	1	0	1	0	0
Sanford	1.000	21	26	52	0	15
Severino	1.000	2	0	8	0	0
Stafura	1.000	2	1	3	0	0

Outfield	PCT	G	PO	A	E	DP
Bishop	.971	83	162	4	5	2
Bowen	1.000	2	5	1	0	0
Caro	1.000	7	7	1	0	0
Farrow	.974	47	73	3	2	0
Florentino	.991	40	110	3	1	1
Griffin	1.000	8	18	0	0	0
Iredale	1.000	3	7	0	0	0
Janik	1.000	24	42	0	0	0
Maguire	1.000	17	33	0	0	0
Mendez	.943	49	65	1	4	0
Patrick	1.000	19	38	2	0	0
Reeder	1.000	3	4	0	0	0
Rodriguez	.979	55	90	4	2	1
Severino	1.000	4	7	0	0	0
Siani	1.000	2	5	0	0	0
Suero	.923	9	12	0	1	0
Tate	1.000	18	37	2	0	1
Taylor	.981	26	50	1	1	0
Toledo	.500	2	1	0	1	0

FCL PIRATES — ROOKIE
FLORIDA COMPLEX LEAGUE

Batting	B-T	Ht.	Wt.	DOB	AVG	OBP	SLG	G	PA	AB	R	H	2B	3B	HR	RBI	BB	HBP	SH	SF	SO	SB	CS	BB%	SO%
Aguiar, Roinny	S-R	5-7	160	4-1-05	.179	.385	.179	23	54	39	9	7	0	0	0	4	13	0	2	0	9	4	1	24.1	16.7
Blanco, Tony	R-R	6-6	243	5-14-05	.167	.167	.667	2	6	6	1	1	0	0	1	2	0	0	0	0	4	0	0	0.0	66.7
Brazoban, Bralyn	L-L	6-1	180	9-1-06	.205	.289	.333	13	45	39	4	8	1	2	0	5	4	1	0	1	10	2	0	8.9	22.2
Calixte, Carl	S-S	6-1	166	11-9-06	.154	.273	.246	27	77	65	8	10	2	2	0	6	10	1	0	1	32	1	3	13.0	41.6
Caro, Carlos	R-R	5-11	160	11-4-04	.228	.383	.293	31	116	92	18	21	6	0	0	10	20	3	1	0	23	13	3	17.2	19.8
Escudero, Samuel	R-R	5-9	155	2-27-04	.167	.288	.233	25	73	60	4	10	1	0	1	10	10	1	0	2	15	0	0	13.7	20.5
Farrow, Ian	R-R	6-1	210	7-26-02	.172	.333	.310	9	36	29	6	5	1	0	1	6	6	1	0	0	12	0	0	16.7	33.3
Florentino, Edward	L-R	6-4	200	11-11-06	.347	.442	.642	29	113	95	23	33	6	2	6	23	16	1	0	1	22	6	1	14.2	19.5
Gonzalez, Tres	L-L	5-11	185	10-4-00	.000	.000	.000	1	3	3	0	0	0	0	0	0	0	0	0	0	0	0	0	0.0	0.0
Herrera, Kendrick	R-R	6-0	170	1-11-04	.234	.353	.291	52	208	175	26	41	5	1	1	18	28	4	1	0	42	5	1	13.5	20.2
Jauregui, Cristian	S-R	5-11	180	2-9-06	.214	.364	.296	39	121	98	15	21	4	2	0	9	18	5	0	0	25	10	1	14.9	20.7
Mola, Raymond	R-R	6-2	190	12-1-05	.258	.324	.355	12	37	31	5	8	0	0	1	5	3	1	0	2	9	3	0	8.1	24.3
Nunez, Malcom	R-R	6-0	205	3-9-011	.000	1.000	1.333	1	3	3	3	1	0	0	1	0	0	0	0	0	0	0	0	0.0	0.0
Ojeda, Michell	L-R	6-0	158	1-23-07	.185	.279	.306	32	122	108	18	20	2	1	3	13	12	2	0	0	34	4	3	9.8	27.9
Oviedo, Eduardo	R-R	6-1	169	9-2-04	.222	.296	.238	20	71	63	11	14	1	0	0	9	6	1	0	1	22	5	1	8.5	31.0
Patrick, Andrew	R-R	6-4	195	1-19-03	.139	.267	.167	12	45	36	5	5	1	0	0	3	7	0	0	2	17	3	0	15.6	37.8
Ramirez, Richard	R-R	6-0	160	7-3-05	.276	.357	.429	29	115	98	12	27	2	0	4	17	13	0	1	3	36	0	0	11.3	31.3
Rivero, Jonathan	R-R	6-0	191	12-15-05	.180	.314	.250	42	156	128	15	23	4	1	1	11	23	3	0	2	43	2	1	14.7	27.6
Rynders, Eddie	L-R	6-2	195	10-31-05	.208	.333	.274	51	201	168	31	35	4	2	1	24	30	2	0	1	50	7	1	14.9	24.9
Sanford, Wyatt	L-R	6-1	175	11-24-05	.259	.487	.370	20	79	54	19	14	1	1	1	6	15	9	1	0	15	13	1	19.0	19.0
Scherrer, Luke	R-R	6-2	210	12-13-04	.194	.359	.250	26	92	72	8	14	1	0	1	4	12	7	0	1	15	7	2	13.0	16.3
Siani, Sammy	L-L	5-10	195	12-14-00	.333	.333	.667	1	3	3	0	1	0	0	0	0	0	0	0	0	0	0	0	0.0	0.0
Suero, Estuar	S-R	6-5	180	8-29-05	.208	.331	.368	40	151	125	23	26	7	2	3	16	24	0	0	2	57	8	2	15.9	37.7
Tirado, Carlos	L-R	6-1	187	3-13-05	.189	.268	.338	25	82	74	14	14	5	0	2	10	7	1	0	0	21	0	0	8.5	25.6

Pitching	B-T	Ht.	Wt.	DOB	W	L	ERA	G	GS	SV	IP	Hits	Runs	ER	HR	BB	SO	AVG	OBP	SLG	SO%	BB%	BF
Adams, Gavin	R-R	6-3	170	2-8-03	2	0	2.45	12	6	0	15	8	6	4	0	23	20	.160	.447	.180	26.0	29.9	77
Aguiar, Roinny	S-R	5-7	160	4-1-05	0	0	0.00	1	0	0	0	0	0	0	0	0	0	.000	.000	.000	0.0	0.0	1
Aquino, Cesar	R-R	6-1	201	2-27-05	4	1	3.18	16	1	3	34	31	16	12	2	5	28	.248	.293	.328	20.9	3.7	134
Camacho, Angel	L-L	5-11	150	1-13-04	2	2	3.33	17	1	1	27	24	10	10	1	17	30	.255	.365	.457	26.1	14.8	115
Caro, Carlos	R-R	5-11	160	11-4-04	0	0	0.00	1	0	0	0	0	0	0	0	0	0	.000	.000	.000	0.0	0.0	1
Cotto, Magdiel	L-L	6-3	225	6-24-02	0	1	13.50	5	0	0	5	11	8	8	0	6	2	.478	.567	.478	6.7	20.0	30
De La Paz, Yoldin	L-L	6-0	165	5-10-02	0	1	6.23	5	0	1	4	5	3	3	0	4	3	.263	.391	.474	13.0	17.4	23
Escudero, Samuel	R-R	5-9	155	2-27-04	0	0	0.00	1	0	0	0	0	0	0	0	0	0	.000	.000	.000	0.0	0.0	1
Francia, Dariel	R-R	6-2	165	7-23-06	4	2	4.30	11	0	0	23	18	17	11	1	16	32	.209	.340	.256	30.2	15.1	106
Gallo, Ronaldo	R-R	6-6	176	6-20-01	0	0	27.00	1	0	0	1	1	3	3	0	1	0	.500	.500	1.500	0.0	50.0	2
Grounds, Jackson	R-R	6-1	190	7-13-04	0	1	22.09	5	0	0	4	8	10	9	0	7	5	.444	.600	.500	20.0	28.0	25
Jimenez, Ronaldys	L-L	5-11	165	11-29-05	2	1	4.18	15	2	0	28	20	18	13	0	30	41	.196	.415	.245	28.9	21.1	142
Kellington, Owen	L-R	6-3	193	2-5-03	0	0	2.70	3	1	0	7	4	2	2	0	2	2	.364	.417	.455	8.3	8.3	24
Kennedy, Tyler	R-R	6-3	223	6-7-02	0	2	10.13	15	2	0	19	16	24	21	1	24	15	.239	.490	.418	14.7	23.5	102
Loeschorn, Joshua	R-R	6-3	215	3-10-00	0	0	7.36	4	0	0	4	5	5	4	0	6	4	.444	.600	.444	26.3	0.0	19
Martinez, Dioris	R-R	6-2	185	6-20-06	0	1	7.56	10	6	0	25	19	24	21	2	29	27	.213	.433	.360	21.3	22.8	127
Mateo, Carlos	R-R	6-2	185	10-25-05	2	3	15.98	16	2	0	16	18	33	29	0	36	22	.286	.568	.333	19.8	32.4	111

Batting	B-T	Ht.	Wt.	DOB	AVG	OBP	SLG	G	PA	AB	R	H	2B	3B	HR	RBI	BB	HBP	SH	SF	SO	SB	CS	BB%	SO%
Mueth, Zander	R-R	6-6	205	6-22-05	0	0	2.25	2	2	0	4	3	2	1	0	4	6	.200	.368	.200	31.6	21.1	19		
Navarro, Reinold	L-L	6-0	178	10-21-06	0	1	2.81	9	8	0	26	7	9	8	0	20	47	.088	.295	.100	44.8	19.0	105		
Noble, Jack	R-R	6-2	200	4-2-00	0	0	18.00	1	0	0	1	2	2	2	2	0	2	.400	.400	1.600	40.0	0.0	5		
Oviedo, Johan	R-R	6-5	245	3-2-98	0	1	27.00	1	1	0	1	3	2	2	0	0	1	.600	.667	.600	16.7	0.0	6		
Perachi, Dominic	L-L	6-4	195	2-27-01	0	0	0.00	2	2	0	5	1	1	0	0	3	7	.071	.235	.071	41.2	17.6	17		
Pichardo, Bladimir	R-R	6-3	193	10-24-05	1	4	6.07	19	1	4	30	27	22	20	5	18	24	.243	.361	.432	17.9	13.4	134		
Quintana, Yulian	R-R	6-3	185	7-15-00	4	1	1.63	15	0	0	28	24	6	5	0	14	20	.235	.331	.294	16.8	11.8	119		
Ramirez, Irwin	R-R	6-3	175	1-10-07	1	4	4.41	11	8	0	33	30	17	16	0	25	22	.254	.389	.305	15.3	17.4	144		
Reed, Carlson	L-R	6-4	200	11-27-02	0	0	5.40	2	2	0	5	5	3	3	0	2	2	.294	.368	.353	10.0	10.0	20		
Regalado, Jose	L-L	6-0	189	6-15-02	0	1	4.76	15	1	0	23	24	16	12	0	23	27	.279	.441	.372	24.1	20.5	112		
Rosa, Pitterson	R-R	6-2	178	11-30-04	1	1	7.67	17	2	1	27	29	30	23	3	27	25	.271	.440	.495	17.6	19.0	142		
Samaniego, Tyler	R-L	6-4	205	1-30-99	0	1	3.86	2	1	0	2	2	3	1	1	1	5	.222	.300	.556	45.5	9.1	11		
Silvera, Andres	R-R	6-0	188	7-20-04	0	1	1.80	4	1	0	5	5	1	1	0	3	7	.263	.364	.316	31.8	13.6	22		
Sterling, Levi	R-R	6-5	202	9-2-06	3	2	6.54	11	9	0	32	35	23	23	2	21	30	.282	.393	.452	20.0	14.0	150		
Tejada, Joaquin	R-R	5-11	160	7-16-03	1	0	10.80	8	0	0	10	11	12	12	0	13	7	.268	.474	.317	12.3	22.8	57		
Torres, Alexis	R-R	6-0	153	3-16-03	0	0	3.38	1	0	0	3	1	1	1	1	1	5	.111	.200	.444	50.0	10.0	10		

Fielding
C: Rivero 31, Ramirez 21, Escudero 7, Ojeda 1, Scherrer 1. **1B:** Tirado 16, Scherrer 15, Mola 8, Ramirez 8, Florentino 6, Rivero 6, Escudero 3. **2B:** Ojeda 20, Aguiar 15, Herrera 12, Caro 10, Sanford 8. **3B:** Rynders 49, Herrera 9, Aguiar 1, Nunez 1. **SS:** Herrera 30, Caro 13, Sanford 13, Ojeda 6. **LF:** Jauregui 22, Suero 15, Calixte 9, Oviedo 5, Florentino 3, Brazoban 2, Caro 1, Gonzalez 1, Mola 1, Tirado 1. **CF:** Florentino 15, Suero 14, Oviedo 13, Brazoban 9, Calixte 8, Siani 1. **RF:** Jauregui 11, Calixte 10, Patrick 9, Caro 7, Suero 7, Farrow 5, Scherrer 5, Florentino 4, Tirado 3, Brazoban 2, Mola 2, Oviedo 2

DSL PIRATES BLACK   ROOKIE
DOMINICAN SUMMER LEAGUE

Batting	B-T	Ht.	Wt.	DOB	AVG	OBP	SLG	G	PA	AB	R	H	2B	3B	HR	RBI	BB	HBP	SH	SF	SO	SB	CS	BB%	SO%
Acevedo, Javier	L-R	5-10	145	2-27-07	.338	.495	.450	30	105	80	19	27	2	2	1	14	24	1	0	0	15	7	3	22.9	14.3
Crespo, Yadier	R-R	5-11	175	2-8-08	.211	.367	.316	14	51	38	6	8	2	1	0	9	7	3	2	1	14	1	2	13.7	27.5
Cruz, Luis	L-R	6-1	155	6-9-08	.240	.400	.310	39	131	100	19	24	3	2	0	18	23	5	1	2	19	6	5	17.6	14.5
De Los Santos, Johan	L-R	5-11	165	7-24-08	.353	.451	.460	44	174	139	43	49	9	3	0	27	27	2	1	5	13	34	6	15.5	7.5
Familia, Victor	R-R	5-11	196	2-12-07	.247	.395	.330	33	106	81	21	20	8	2	0	8	17	7	0	1	36	1	3	16.0	34.0
Feliz, Adbiel	S-R	6-0	175	2-23-07	.225	.371	.271	38	164	129	31	29	2	2	0	13	29	1	5	0	12	17	1	17.7	7.3
Lee, Hyun Seung	L-R	6-0	170	2-14-08	.241	.423	.353	45	176	133	32	32	7	1	2	22	38	4	1	0	32	17	4	21.6	18.2
Marquez, Victor	R-R	6-0	170	6-20-08	.222	.391	.343	35	134	99	29	22	3	0	3	22	28	2	1	4	30	14	0	20.9	22.4
Mola, Raymond	R-R	6-2	190	12-1-05	.311	.492	.533	16	63	45	14	14	1	0	3	11	14	3	0	1	12	12	1	22.2	19.0
Ovalle, Fredderick	R-R	5-10	156	6-27-07	.000	.333	.000	4	6	4	2	0	0	0	0	0	2	0	0	0	1	0	0	33.3	16.7
Payero, Limanol	R-R	6-4	176	11-20-07	.168	.380	.274	38	129	95	23	16	2	0	0	8	29	4	0	1	43	5	2	22.5	33.3
Pimentel, Antonio	L-R	5-10	161	10-2-05	.385	.492	.606	34	128	104	26	40	10	5	1	34	22	1	0	1	13	18	2	17.2	10.2
Ramirez, Hanley	R-R	6-0	170	6-24-07	.188	.323	.200	27	99	80	11	15	1	0	0	12	15	0	2	2	28	7	1	15.2	28.3
Rodriguez, Miguel	R-R	5-10	152	4-7-06	.224	.376	.299	22	87	67	17	15	2	1	0	7	15	2	1	5	6	1	7	17.4	5.8
Santana, Yoander	L-R	6-0	180	12-13-07	.286	.371	.452	39	143	126	16	36	5	5	2	21	13	4	0	0	34	5	4	9.1	23.8
Sequera, Joseph	R-R	6-0	185	12-12-05	.200	.333	.200	2	6	5	1	1	0	0	0	0	1	0	0	0	2	0	0	16.7	33.3
Walker, Edgar	R-R	6-0	180	10-18-07	.301	.388	.404	45	171	146	27	44	8	2	1	34	20	2	1	2	32	15	5	11.7	18.7
Williams, Phillando	S-R	5-9	162	9-30-06	.235	.360	.294	25	87	68	16	16	2	1	0	10	10	5	1	3	19	8	1	11.5	21.8

Pitching	B-T	Ht.	Wt.	DOB	W	L	ERA	G	GS	SV	IP	Hits	Runs	ER	HR	BB	SO	AVG	OBP	SLG	SO%	BB%	BF
Aponte, Welin	R-R	6-2	170	10-12-06	1	2	6.10	9	0	0	10	8	10	7	0	13	11	.216	.431	.243	21.6	25.5	51
Blanco, Hader	L-L	5-11	150	2-14-05	1	1	3.95	13	0	2	27	17	12	12	1	20	22	.195	.366	.276	19.3	17.5	114
De La Cruz, Mauricio	R-R	6-3	180	11-4-05	0	0	0.00	1	0	0	1	2	2	0	0	0	0	.286	.250	.286	0.0	0.0	8
Fermin, Eydan	R-R	6-1	186	12-13-07	0	0	16.88	3	1	0	3	2	5	5	0	5	2	.250	.563	.375	12.5	31.3	16
Figuera, Fernando	R-R	6-1	170	5-2-06	1	0	12.89	13	0	1	15	24	24	21	1	20	13	.358	.537	.582	13.7	21.1	95
Florentino, Dariel	R-R	6-5	175	11-4-05	1	1	6.50	13	9	0	36	42	31	26	3	25	38	.280	.400	.420	21.0	13.8	181
Francisco, Justino	R-R	6-2	178	4-4-07	0	0	0.00	3	2	0	4	5	0	0	0	2	2	.333	.444	.467	11.1	11.1	18
Herrera, Angel	R-R	6-1	168	7-18-07	1	0	1.56	7	5	0	17	8	4	3	0	15	15	.143	.324	.143	21.1	21.1	71
Linares, Janderson	L-L	6-2	175	10-18-05	4	1	5.61	14	0	1	26	23	16	16	5	20	35	.242	.407	.337	28.5	16.3	123
Martinez, Randol	R-R	6-1	168	5-31-07	1	2	12.38	10	0	0	16	23	25	22	2	16	23	.343	.471	.507	18.6	18.6	86
Muniz, Juan	R-R	6-1	194	1-21-08	3	1	2.22	12	1	2	24	19	12	6	1	18	20	.209	.339	.297	18.3	16.5	109
Ordonez, Dermis	R-R	6-2	170	9-5-04	0	1	3.38	4	0	0	5	2	4	2	0	9	9	.111	.414	.111	31.0	31.0	29
Reyes, Leudy	R-R	6-1	174	9-11-07	1	1	8.14	14	1	3	21	16	20	19	1	25	26	.216	.439	.351	24.1	23.1	108
Reyes, Maickol	R-R	6-2	196	4-25-08	2	0	6.05	12	1	3	19	25	19	13	0	15	10	.301	.414	.386	10.1	15.2	99
Rosado, Angel	R-R	5-11	191	8-15-05	3	1	4.74	14	0	0	19	16	14	10	0	16	29	.229	.367	.314	32.2	17.8	90
Salcedo, Yeraldo	L-L	6-2	190	3-22-07	4	0	1.99	13	3	0	32	20	12	7	0	13	36	.177	.277	.248	27.7	10.0	130
Santos, Hamlet	R-R	6-4	182	2-25-08	0	4	10.13	12	6	0	19	12	24	21	1	38	12	.190	.519	.270	11.3	35.8	106
Smith, Robinson	R-R	6-4	163	11-22-07	2	1	8.87	9	0	0	23	24	23	23	4	12	28	.270	.365	.517	26.9	11.5	104
Soriano, Angel	L-L	6-1	188	2-9-07	0	1	1.59	4	4	0	11	7	3	2	0	6	11	.184	.333	.237	22.9	12.5	48
Tapia, Jesus	R-R	6-1	173	4-10-07	4	0	3.04	12	0	1	24	19	8	8	1	12	16	.224	.320	.282	16.0	12.0	100
Torres, Yhosneiber	R-L	5-10	159	4-18-08	1	2	6.53	11	9	0	30	38	26	22	2	10	34	.314	.375	.488	24.6	7.2	138
Valdez, Stainer	R-R	6-2	190	8-1-06	1	0	2.87	12	1	3	16	11	5	5	1	7	10	.182	.274	.236	16.1	11.3	62
Vega, Albert	R-R	6-4	193	6-11-06	3	1	4.35	14	0	0	21	14	12	10	1	14	18	.272	.381	.358	18.6	14.4	97

Fielding
C: Marquez 24, Familia 15, Acevedo 14, Crespo 8, Sequera 1. **1B:** Santana 15, Acevedo 13, Familia 12, Marquez 10, Mola 10, Crespo 1, Pimentel 1, Sequera 1. **2B:** De Los Santos 22, Feliz 18, Pimentel 10, Cruz 8, Ovalle 1, Santana 1. **3B:** Lee 25, Santana 21, Pimentel 10, Ovalle 2. **SS:** De Los Santos 20, Feliz 18, Lee 15, Pimentel 2. **LF:** Cruz 24, Williams 12, Pimentel 11, Walker 7, Payero 4, Mola 3, Ramirez 2. **CF:** Payero 17, Ramirez 10, Walker 16, Williams 10, De Los Santos 1. **RF:** Walker 22, Payero 16, Ramirez 10, Williams 5, Cruz 3, Mola 2

DSL PIRATES GOLD — ROOKIE
DOMINICAN SUMMER LEAGUE

PITTSBURGH PIRATES

Batting	B-T	Ht.	Wt.	DOB	AVG	OBP	SLG	G	PA	AB	R	H	2B	3B	HR	RBI	BB	HBP	SH	SF	SO	SB	CS	BB%	SO%
Acevedo, Javier	L-R	5-10	145	2-27-07	.000	.000	.000	3	6	6	0	0	0	0	0	0	0	0	0	0	2	0	0	0.0	33.3
Allen, Iverson	R-R	6-0	160	8-18-07	.236	.438	.355	41	154	110	18	26	2	4	1	18	29	12	1	2	36	18	0	18.8	23.4
Aquino, Angel	R-R	6-5	207	6-18-05	.150	.246	.200	35	114	100	12	15	5	0	0	12	9	4	0	1	37	7	1	7.9	32.5
Brazoban, Bralyn	L-L	6-1	180	9-1-06	.231	.292	.277	20	73	65	10	15	3	0	0	7	3	3	1	1	16	3	0	4.1	21.9
Familia, Victor	R-R	5-11	196	2-12-07	.250	.250	.500	1	4	4	1	1	1	0	0	0	0	0	0	0	2	0	0	0.0	50.0
Gimenez, Yosmar	L-R	6-2	150	5-2-06	.217	.333	.217	8	30	23	4	5	0	0	0	2	4	0	3	0	4	0	0	13.3	13.3
Kim, Jayden	R-R	5-11	150	8-2-06	.175	.367	.227	44	131	97	14	17	3	1	0	19	28	2	3	1	30	4	2	21.4	22.9
Lizardo, Jesus	S-R	5-11	170	11-4-06	.222	.356	.259	35	136	108	18	24	2	1	0	12	24	0	1	3	20	2	0	17.6	14.7
Mesta, Frankeli	S-R	6-1	175	5-29-07	.250	.381	.321	51	196	156	24	39	5	3	0	17	33	2	2	3	38	5	4	16.8	19.4
Morel, Darell	L-R	6-4	180	9-15-07	.287	.425	.414	50	202	157	45	45	9	4	1	25	37	3	2	3	45	26	7	18.3	22.3
Muhoozi, Armstrong	R-R	5-11	180	7-13-07	.246	.350	.339	36	142	118	26	29	6	1	1	16	15	5	2	2	28	24	4	10.6	19.7
Ovalle, Fredderick	R-R	5-10	160	6-27-07	.293	.425	.422	45	182	147	31	43	14	1	1	22	33	1	1	0	24	26	5	18.1	13.2
Perez, Angel	R-R	5-10	160	9-12-05	.191	.352	.300	39	142	110	21	21	6	0	2	25	17	12	0	3	44	1	0	12.0	31.0
Ramirez, Hanley	R-R	6-0	170	6-24-07	.292	.346	.292	8	26	24	4	7	0	0	0	2	2	0	0	0	9	1	1	7.7	34.6
Rodriguez, Gabriel	R-R	6-1	172	9-26-07	.232	.417	.354	29	108	82	20	19	4	0	2	10	21	5	0	0	45	12	1	19.4	41.7
Rodriguez, Miguel	R-R	5-10	152	4-7-06	.250	.300	.250	3	10	8	0	2	0	0	0	1	0	1	0	1	1	0	0	10.0	10.0
Sequera, Jose	R-R	5-11	170	8-15-06	.000	.000	.000	4	6	6	0	0	0	0	0	0	0	0	0	0	3	0	0	0.0	50.0
Sequera, Joseph	R-R	6-0	185	12-12-05	.221	.413	.324	25	92	68	11	15	4	0	1	15	19	4	0	1	15	6	1	20.7	16.3
Tromp, Deshandro	R-R	6-0	170	9-20-06	.177	.361	.355	28	83	62	12	11	2	3	1	5	15	4	0	2	25	10	0	18.1	30.1
Villafane, Andres	L-L	5-11	175	3-17-06	.276	.373	.319	41	137	116	17	32	5	0	0	9	13	5	2	0	19	16	5	9.5	13.9
Williams, Phillando	S-R	5-9	162	9-30-06	.219	.359	.219	12	40	32	7	7	0	0	0	5	4	3	1	0	8	4	0	10.0	20.0

Pitching	B-T	Ht.	Wt.	DOB	W	L	ERA	G	GS	SV	IP	Hits	Runs	ER	HR	BB	SO	AVG	OBP	SLG	SO%	BB%	BF
Almonte, Keuri	L-L	6-2	190	10-16-05	0	0	2.60	6	6	0	17	8	7	5	2	15	32	.140	.338	.281	43.2	20.3	74
Aray, Adrian	R-R	6-2	175	9-15-06	2	3	3.43	12	8	0	39	23	16	15	1	22	35	.167	.293	.210	21.3	13.4	164
De La Cruz, Mauricio	R-R	6-3	180	11-4-05	0	1	4.50	12	0	2	22	21	13	11	0	16	14	.269	.378	.308	14.3	16.3	98
Estelie, Claudio	R-R	6-5	197	6-1-04	2	0	3.60	5	1	0	15	10	8	6	0	5	12	.185	.267	.296	20.0	8.3	60
Fermin, Eydan	R-R	6-1	186	12-13-07	0	0	0.00	3	0	0	6	3	0	0	0	3	4	.167	.318	.333	18.2	13.6	22
Gaetano, Yonleg	R-R	6-2	185	8-12-05	2	2	0.93	13	3	5	29	17	6	3	0	9	39	.168	.248	.178	34.2	7.9	114
Gonzalez, Tony	L-L	6-2	194	5-9-04	0	0	5.40	11	0	3	15	14	10	9	0	15	15	.259	.438	.333	20.3	20.3	74
Hernandez, Yoslaniel	L-L	6-3	170	8-7-07	0	0	0.00	4	4	0	6	1	0	0	0	4	6	.063	.250	.063	30.0	20.0	20
Jaquez, Wifrailyn	R-R	6-1	170	10-5-06	1	3	5.18	12	11	0	40	37	26	23	2	22	41	.252	.348	.354	22.9	12.3	179
Lorenzo, Carlos	R-R	6-3	240	8-25-06	0	1	30.86	8	0	0	5	7	16	16	0	21	3	.368	.683	.474	5.1	51.2	41
Martinez, Yeison	R-R	6-0	143	8-6-07	0	1	3.97	7	6	0	23	17	11	10	0	7	21	.202	.287	.274	22.3	7.4	94
Miguel, Dariel	L-L	6-2	180	9-11-06	4	1	3.00	13	0	1	18	15	7	6	0	16	18	.238	.415	.254	21.7	19.3	83
Mueses, Raimi	R-R	6-0	170	12-22-06	7	0	1.78	9	0	0	25	13	6	5	0	11	11	.160	.286	.198	11.2	11.2	98
Ordonez, Dermis	R-R	6-1	170	9-5-04	0	1	6.75	3	0	0	3	6	2	2	0	4	.462	.611	.615	22.2	22.2	18
Polanco, Brandison	R-R	6-2	170	8-1-02	2	2	4.50	12	0	1	16	17	10	8	2	5	14	.274	.333	.403	20.3	7.2	69
Portuondo, Roilan	R-R	6-3	266	5-10-99	4	3	4.30	16	0	3	29	29	16	14	2	15	33	.259	.356	.348	25.0	11.4	132
Quintana, Marlon	R-R	6-2	192	6-16-06	0	2	4.32	9	8	0	25	27	14	12	0	8	17	.273	.342	.323	15.3	7.2	111
Roa, Darwin	R-R	5-10	188	4-5-07	1	0	2.79	8	0	0	10	7	5	3	0	13	10	.212	.471	.273	19.6	25.5	51
Rodriguez, Luis	R-R	5-10	185	8-23-04	2	3	7.85	15	0	0	18	20	19	16	1	17	21	.278	.422	.417	23.3	18.9	90
Rondon, Alejandro	R-R	5-11	160	3-21-07	0	0	2.82	7	0	2	22	17	10	7	0	8	13	.224	.322	.289	14.9	9.2	87
Rondon, Jose	R-R	6-5	241	3-24-05	3	0	4.50	11	2	1	24	22	17	12	2	14	19	.253	.374	.379	17.6	13.0	108
Sequera, Jose	R-R	5-11	170	8-15-06	0	0	54.00	1	0	0	0	0	2	2	0	3	1	1.000	.800	.000	20.0	60.0	5
Trejo, Victor	R-R	6-0	175	5-11-06	1	2	1.65	18	0	5	33	24	9	6	0	13	28	.209	.303	.252	21.1	9.8	133

Fielding
C: Lizardo 29, Perez 17, Joseph Sequera 14, Jose Sequera 3, Acevedo 1. **1B:** Perez 24, Aquino 17, Tromp 14, Gimenez 6, Sequera 3, Acevedo 2, Familia 1. **2B:** Ovalle 24, Kim 21, Tromp 8, Mesta 7, Gimenez 1. **3B:** Mesta 27, Ovalle 16, Kim 7, Lizardo 5, Tromp 5, Gimenez 1. **SS:** Morel 40, Kim 16, Mesta 2, Ovalle 1. **LF:** Allen 24, Villafane 15, Williams 7, Muhoozi 6, Ramirez 3, Aquino 2, Brazoban 2, Rodriguez 1. **CF:** Muhoozi 27, Rodriguez 18, Brazoban 9, Williams 4, Ovalle 1, Ramirez 1, Villafane 1. **RF:** Villafane 23, Aquino 18, Allen 11, Brazoban 5, Rodriguez 3, Ramirez 3, Williams 2

St. Louis Cardinals

SEASON SYNOPSIS: The Cardinals continued to slide from relevance after an inactive offseason marked more by what they didn't do—trade Nolan Arenado—than what they did. Their 78-84 finish ended club president John Mozeliak's 18-year run atop baseball operations as he handed off the reins to former Red Sox and Rays executive Chaim Bloom. Fans voted with their feet, with attendance plummeting by 628,000 from 2024 to its lowest mark ever at Busch Stadium III, which opened in 2006.

HIGH POINT: St. Louis was streaky, especially early in the season, and ended June by winning 10 of 14, capped by a sweep in Cleveland that included a pair of shutouts. Ace Sonny Gray tossed a complete-game one-hitter with 11 strikeouts in the opener, while lefthander Matthew Liberatore—who had his best season at age 25—tossed six scoreless in the finale. The victory left them 47-38, just 2½ games behind the Cubs in the NL Central.

LOW POINT: In a year when 83 wins was enough for a NL wild-card spot, St. Louis was still at .500 after a Sept. 7 win against the Giants, but a road trip to Seattle and Milwaukee ended their playoff hopes. The Mariners swept them in three close games, striking out 37 Cardinals, and the finale was an excruciating 4-2, 13-inning loss when the Redbirds went 2-for-22 with runners in scoring position. When they blew a 6-1 lead in Milwaukee to lose 9-8 on Sept. 13, they fell to 10th in the NL.

NOTABLE ROOKIES: Righty Michael McGreevy, a 2021 first-round pick, went 8-4, 4.42 with a 14.5 strikeout percentage, ranking in the third percentile in MLB. Sinkerballer Matt Svanson shined in relief (4-0, 1.94, 68 SO in 60 IP). Versatile infielder Thomas Saggese (.258/.299/.338) and rags-to-riches reserve catcher Yohel Pozo (.231/.262/.375) had their moments, with Pozo reveling in his role after having been homeless in 2020-2021, living out of his car to help pay for medical expenses after his young son suffered a stroke.

KEY TRANSACTIONS: Reliever Phil Maton was St. Louis' only MLB free-agent signing in the offseason, and when the team slid in July, Mozeliak decided to sell, trading closer Ryan Helsley to the Mets while moving Maton to the Rangers. Starter Erick Fedde, acquired to bolster the rotation in 2024, turned back into a pumpkin in '25 and was traded to the Braves in July.

OPENING DAY PAYROLL: $141,455,581 (19th)

PLAYERS OF THE YEAR

MAJOR LEAGUE
Willson Contreras
1B
.257/.344/.447
20 HR, 31 2B,
80 RBIs, 70 R in 135 G

MINOR LEAGUE
JJ Wetherholt
SS
(AA, AAA)
.306/.421/.510
17 HR, 23 SB, 72 BB

ORGANIZATION LEADERS

Batting		*Qualifiers
MAJORS		
* AVG	Alec Burleson	.290
* OPS	Alec Burleson	.801
HR	Willson Contreras	20
RBI	Willson Contreras	80
MINORS		
* AVG	Nathan Church, Memphis/Spring./Palm Beach	.329
* OBP	Bryan Torres, Memphis	.441
* SLG	Rainiel Rodriguez, Peoria/P. Beach/FCL Cardinals	.555
* OPS	Rainiel Rodriguez, Peoria/P. Beach/FCL Cardinals	.954
R	JJ Wetherholt, Memphis/Springfield	82
H	Cesar Prieto, Memphis	138
TB	Joshua Baez, Springfield/Peoria	209
2B	Cesar Prieto, Memphis	35
3B	Jonathan Mejia, Palm Beach	6
HR	Joshua Baez, Springfield/Peoria	20
HR	Rainiel Rodriguez, Peoria/P. Beach/FCL Cardinals	20
RBI	Josh Kross, Peoria/Palm Beach	81
BB	JJ Wetherholt, Memphis/Springfield	72
SO	Chase Davis, Springfield	146
SB	Joshua Baez, Springfield/Peoria	54

Pitching		#Qualifiers
MAJORS		
W	Sonny Gray	14
# ERA	Sonny Gray	4.28
SO	Sonny Gray	201
SV	Ryan Helsley	21
MINORS		
W	Curtis Taylor, Memphis	10
W	Nick Raquet, Memphis/Springfield	10
L	Gerardo Salas, Peoria	13
# ERA	Ixan Henderson, Springfield	2.59
G	Oddanier Mosqueda, Memphis	55
GS	Max Rajcic, Memphis/Springfield	27
SV	Luis Gastelum, Springfield	10
IP	Curtis Taylor, Memphis	137
IP	Pete Hansen, Springfield	137
BB	Braden Davis, Peoria/Palm Beach	75
# SO	Braden Davis, Peoria/Palm Beach	153
AVG	Ixan Henderson, Springfield	.210

2025 PERFORMANCE

General Manager: John Mozeliak. **Farm Director:** Larry Day. **Scouting Director:** Randy Flores.

Class	Team	League	W	L	PCT	Finish	Manager
Majors	St. Louis Cardinals	National	78	84	.481	11 (15)	Oliver Marmol
Triple-A	Memphis Redbirds	International	80	68	.541	8 (20)	Ben Johnson
Double-A	Springfield Cardinals	Texas	88	50	.638	1 (10)	Patrick Anderson
High-A	Peoria Chiefs	Midwest	51	79	.392	12 (12)	Roberto Espinoza
Low-A	Palm Beach Cardinals	Florida State	63	67	.485	6 (10)	Gary Kendall
Rookie	FCL Cardinals	Florida Complex	24	31	.436	11 (15)	Willi Martin
Rookie	DSL Cardinals	Dominican	30	26	.536	24 (52)	Fray Peniche
Overall 2025 Minor League Record			336	321	.511	12th (30)	

ORGANIZATION STATISTICS

ST. LOUIS CARDINALS
NATIONAL LEAGUE

Batting	B-T	Ht.	Wt.	DOB	AVG	OBP	SLG	G	PA	AB	R	H	2B	3B	HR	RBI	BB	HBP	SH	SF	SO	SB	CS	BB%	SO%
Arenado, Nolan	R-R	6-2	215	4-16-91	.237	.289	.377	107	436	401	48	95	18	1	12	52	28	3	0	4	49	3	0	6.4	11.2
Baker, Luken	R-R	6-4	280	3-10-97	.235	.366	.324	19	41	34	3	8	3	0	0	2	7	0	0	0	10	0	0	17.1	24.4
Barrero, Jose	R-R	6-2	211	4-5-98	.138	.194	.276	22	31	29	4	4	1	0	1	3	1	1	0	0	9	0	0	3.2	29.0
Burleson, Alec	L-L	6-2	212	11-25-98	.290	.343	.459	139	546	497	54	144	26	2	18	69	39	3	1	4	79	5	1	7.1	14.5
Church, Nathan	L-L	5-10	180	7-12-00	.179	.254	.250	27	65	56	9	10	1	0	1	8	3	3	2	1	18	1	0	4.6	27.7
Contreras, Willson	R-R	6-1	225	5-13-92	.257	.344	.447	135	563	490	70	126	31	1	20	80	44	23	1	4	142	5	1	7.8	25.2
Crooks, Jimmy	L-R	6-1	210	7-19-01	.133	.152	.244	15	46	45	3	6	0	1	1	1	0	1	0	0	17	0	0	0.0	37.0
Donovan, Brendan	L-R	6-1	195	1-16-97	.287	.353	.422	118	515	460	64	132	32	0	10	50	42	7	2	4	67	3	3	8.2	13.0
Fermin, Jose	R-R	5-9	200	3-29-99	.283	.377	.417	30	70	60	5	17	5	0	1	9	8	1	1	0	10	2	2	11.4	14.3
Gorman, Nolan	L-R	6-1	210	5-10-00	.205	.296	.370	111	402	351	48	72	14	1	14	46	47	0	0	4	136	1	1	11.7	33.8
Hampson, Garrett	R-R	5-11	196	10-10-94	.103	.133	.138	35	31	29	9	3	1	0	0	1	1	0	1	0	13	1	0	3.2	41.9
Herrera, Ivan	R-R	5-11	220	6-1-00	.284	.373	.464	107	452	388	54	110	13	0	19	66	43	15	0	4	84	8	2	9.5	18.6
Nootbaar, Lars	L-R	6-3	210	9-8-97	.234	.325	.361	135	583	509	68	119	24	1	13	48	64	6	1	3	119	4	5	11.0	20.4
Pages, Pedro	R-R	6-1	234	9-17-98	.230	.272	.363	112	389	361	38	83	15	0	11	45	19	3	3	3	107	0	0	4.9	27.5
Pozo, Yohel	R-R	5-10	201	6-14-97	.232	.375	.67	168	160	16	37	8	0	5	19	7	0	0	1	22	0	0	4.2	13.1
Prieto, Cesar	L-R	5-9	175	5-10-99	.167	.167	.167	3	6	6	0	1	0	0	0	0	0	0	0	0	5	0	0	0.0	83.3
Saggese, Thomas	R-R	5-11	175	4-10-02	.258	.299	.342	82	295	275	25	71	17	0	2	25	16	1	1	2	83	3	0	5.4	28.1
Scott, Victor	L-L	5-10	190	2-12-01	.216	.305	.296	138	463	398	54	86	15	1	5	37	42	10	10	3	111	34	4	9.1	24.0
Siani, Michael	L-L	6-1	188	7-16-99	.235	.235	.19	17	4	4	0	0	0	0	2	0	0	0	7	0	0	10.5	36.8		
Vilade, Ryan	R-R	6-2	226	2-18-99	.077	.200	.077	7	15	13	1	1	0	0	0	0	2	0	0	0	5	0	0	13.3	33.3
Walker, Jordan	R-R	6-6	245	5-22-02	.215	.278	.306	111	396	363	40	78	13	1	6	41	29	3	0	1	126	10	3	7.3	31.8
Winn, Masyn	R-R	5-11	180	3-21-02	.253	.310	.363	129	537	491	72	124	27	0	9	51	34	8	2	2	102	9	5	6.3	19.0

Pitching	B-T	Ht.	Wt.	DOB	W	L	ERA	G	GS	SV	IP	Hits	Runs	ER	HR	BB	SO	AVG	OBP	SLG	SO%	BB%	BF
Alcala, Jorge	R-R	6-3	205	7-28-95	0	0	5.02	15	0	0	14	18	8	8	4	7	15	.305	.379	.610	22.4	10.4	67
Burleson, Alec	L-L	6-2	212	11-25-98	0	0	0.00	1	0	0	1	1	0	0	0	0	0	.333	.500	.333	0.0	0.0	4
Fedde, Erick	R-R	6-4	203	2-25-93	3	10	5.22	20	20	0	102	106	62	59	14	47	63	.270	.350	.439	14.1	10.5	446
Fernandez, Ryan	R-R	6-0	170	6-11-98	0	4	7.71	32	0	1	30	36	30	26	6	16	34	.293	.379	.520	24.3	11.4	140
Graceffo, Gordon	R-R	6-4	210	3-17-00	3	1	6.28	26	0	1	43	50	33	30	2	13	40	.286	.337	.457	20.7	6.7	193
Granillo, Andre	R-R	6-4	245	5-12-00	1	0	4.71	14	0	1	21	22	11	11	3	7	18	.278	.333	.481	19.8	7.7	91
Gray, Sonny	R-R	5-10	195	11-7-89	14	8	4.28	32	32	0	181	185	93	86	25	38	201	.262	.302	.424	26.7	5.0	753
Hampson, Garrett	R-R	5-11	196	10-10-94	0	0	0.00	1	0	0	1	0	0	0	0	0	0	.000	.000	.000	0.0	0.0	3
Helsley, Ryan	R-R	6-2	230	7-18-94	3	1	3.00	36	0	21	36	36	12	12	4	14	41	.259	.327	.367	26.1	8.9	157
King, John	L-L	6-2	215	9-14-94	2	1	4.66	51	0	0	48	65	30	25	8	14	28	.316	.357	.466	12.6	6.3	222
Leahy, Kyle	S-R	6-5	200	6-4-97	4	2	3.07	62	1	1	88	80	32	30	5	28	80	.244	.319	.379	22.0	7.7	363
Liberatore, Matthew	L-L	6-4	200	11-6-99	8	12	4.21	29	29	0	152	158	79	71	19	40	122	.266	.313	.423	18.8	6.2	648
Maton, Phil	R-R	6-2	206	3-25-93	1	3	2.35	40	0	2	38	28	12	10	1	15	48	.206	.306	.287	30.4	9.5	158
Matz, Steven	R-L	6-2	215	5-29-91	5	2	3.44	32	2	1	55	56	25	21	4	9	47	.260	.292	.377	20.7	4.0	227
McGreevy, Michael	L-R	6-4	215	7-8-00	8	4	4.42	17	16	0	96	100	50	47	12	20	58	.268	.309	.426	14.5	5.0	400
Mikolas, Miles	R-R	6-4	230	8-23-88	8	11	4.84	31	31	0	156	169	87	84	29	37	100	.272	.313	.492	14.9	5.5	669
Munoz, Roddery	R-R	6-2	210	4-14-00	0	0	8.18	9	0	0	11	9	10	10	4	9	14	.225	.360	.575	27.5	17.6	51
O'Brien, Riley	R-R	6-4	180	2-6-95	3	1	2.06	42	0	6	48	33	11	11	2	22	45	.196	.313	.274	22.6	11.1	199
Pallante, Andre	R-R	6-0	203	9-18-98	6	15	5.31	31	31	0	163	173	109	96	21	62	111	.270	.337	.431	15.5	8.7	715
Raquet, Nick	R-L	6-0	215	12-12-95	0	0	0.00	2	0	0	2	0	0	0	0	1	0	.000	.143	.000	14.3	14.3	7
Romero, JoJo	L-L	5-11	200	9-9-96	4	6	2.07	65	0	8	61	47	21	14	2	29	55	.217	.311	.286	21.6	11.4	255
Roycroft, Chris	R-R	6-8	230	6-21-97	1	3	7.84	20	0	0	21	26	21	18	2	12	15	.306	.390	.518	14.9	11.9	101
Svanson, Matt	R-R	6-5	235	1-31-99	4	0	1.94	39	0	0	60	33	14	13	3	20	68	.160	.244	.248	29.1	8.5	234
Veneziano, Anthony	L-L	6-5	205	9-1-97	0	0	4.50	2	0	0	4	3	2	2	0	1	5	.200	.294	.267	29.4	5.9	17

Fielding

Catcher	PCT	G	PO	A	E	DP	PB
Crooks	1.000	14	97	4	0	0	2
Herrera	.989	14	85	6	1	0	1
Pages	.994	110	769	49	5	6	8

	PCT	G	PO	A	E	DP	
Pozo	.982	46	268	12	5	0	4
First Base	PCT	G	PO	A	E	DP	
Baker	1.000	2	6	0	0	0	

	PCT	G	PO	A	E	DP	
Burleson	.990	50	354	25	4	27	
Contreras	.991	120	960	84	9	78	
Gorman	1.000	7	37	5	0	4	
Pages	1.000	2	3	0	0	1	

	PCT	G	PO	A	E	DP
Pozo	1.000	6	13	0	0	2
Second Base	**PCT**	**G**	**PO**	**A**	**E**	**DP**
Barrero	1.000	6	1	1	0	0
Donovan	.990	100	136	266	4	46
Fermin	1.000	15	20	27	0	5
Gorman	.990	28	33	68	1	9
Hampson	1.000	1	1	2	0	1
Pages	1.000	1	0	2	0	0
Prieto	.500	2	0	1	1	0
Saggese	.973	35	52	91	4	24
Third Base	**PCT**	**G**	**PO**	**A**	**E**	**DP**
Arenado	.982	102	71	207	5	24

	PCT	G	PO	A	E	DP
Barrero	.500	1	0	1	1	0
Fermin	1.000	5	0	4	0	0
Gorman	.951	54	31	86	6	11
Hampson	1.000	1	1	0	0	0
Saggese	.939	18	4	27	2	0
Shortstop	**PCT**	**G**	**PO**	**A**	**E**	**DP**
Barrero	.900	5	7	11	2	2
Donovan	1.000	6	8	16	0	3
Hampson	.000	4	0	0	0	0
Saggese	.988	33	24	58	1	7
Winn	.994	129	163	335	3	64

Outfield	**PCT**	**G**	**PO**	**A**	**E**	**DP**
Barrero	1.000	8	13	0	0	0
Burleson	.992	75	122	2	1	1
Church	.983	30	55	2	1	0
Donovan	1.000	18	33	2	0	1
Fermin	1.000	5	4	0	0	0
Hampson	1.000	29	20	0	0	0
Herrera	1.000	4	9	0	0	0
Nootbaar	.996	142	223	3	1	0
Scott	.983	147	333	4	6	3
Siani	1.000	17	15	0	0	0
Vilade	1.000	6	7	0	0	0
Walker	.981	108	204	5	4	2

MEMPHIS REDBIRDS — TRIPLE-A
INTERNATIONAL LEAGUE

Batting	B-T	Ht.	Wt.	DOB	AVG	OBP	SLG	G	PA	AB	R	H	2B	3B	HR	RBI	BB	HBP	SH	SF	SO	SB	CS	BB%	SO%
Antico, Mike	L-R	5-10	200	2-16-98	.279	.366	.420	104	381	326	53	91	21	2	7	57	42	6	1	6	94	21	4	11.0	24.7
Baker, Luken	R-R	6-4	280	3-10-97	.196	.309	.397	62	265	224	29	44	15	0	10	34	36	2	0	3	71	0	0	13.6	26.8
Barrero, Jose	R-R	6-2	211	4-5-98	.299	.396	.517	23	101	87	15	26	5	1	4	13	14	0	0	0	27	5	1	13.9	26.7
Church, Nathan	L-L	5-10	180	7-12-00	.335	.400	.521	53	242	215	43	72	11	4	7	30	24	0	1	1	25	9	4	9.9	10.3
Collins, Gavin	R-R	5-10	205	7-17-95	.221	.299	.297	76	299	263	32	58	10	2	2	29	28	3	1	4	32	4	1	9.4	10.7
Crooks, Jimmy	L-R	6-1	210	7-19-01	.274	.337	.441	98	430	390	61	107	21	1	14	79	36	2	0	2	114	0	0	8.4	26.5
Fermin, Jose	R-R	5-9	200	3-29-99	.300	.428	.485	65	293	237	47	71	23	0	7	40	45	9	1	1	25	20	5	15.4	8.5
Helman, Michael	R-R	5-11	195	5-23-96	.185	.260	.292	18	73	65	12	12	4	0	1	5	6	1	0	1	16	1	0	8.2	21.9
Herrera, Ivan	R-R	5-11	220	6-1-00	.433	.433	.600	8	30	30	6	13	2	0	1	5	0	0	0	0	8	2	0	0.0	26.7
Jordan, Blaze	R-R	6-2	220	12-19-02	.198	.242	.366	41	186	172	21	34	6	1	7	37	10	1	0	3	22	2	0	5.4	11.8
Koperniak, Matt	L-R	6-0	200	2-8-98	.246	.317	.382	121	536	479	71	118	19	2	14	65	48	4	0	5	103	9	3	9.0	19.2
Linarez, Carlos	R-R	6-0	170	10-24-01	.200	.273	.800	3	11	10	2	2	0	0	2	3	1	0	0	0	5	0	0	9.1	45.5
Lloyd, Matt	L-R	6-1	205	3-17-96	.272	.364	.434	78	317	272	39	74	18	1	8	50	41	0	1	3	77	7	3	12.9	24.3
Mendlinger, Noah	L-R	5-9	180	4-6-00	.289	.402	.446	24	102	83	15	24	6	2	1	10	11	6	0	2	8	2	2	10.8	7.8
Moore, Brody	R-R	5-11	183	7-20-00	.239	.305	.315	60	221	197	28	47	7	1	2	27	17	3	1	3	49	6	0	7.7	22.2
Pozo, Yohel	R-R	5-10	201	6-14-97	.333	.333	.762	5	21	21	7	7	3	0	2	6	0	0	0	0	2	1	0	0.0	9.5
Prieto, Cesar	L-R	5-9	175	5-10-99	.300	.363	.452	121	515	460	79	138	35	4	9	71	39	9	3	4	70	12	14	7.6	13.6
Saggese, Thomas	R-R	5-11	175	4-10-02	.317	.402	.445	42	189	164	34	52	6	0	5	24	23	1	0	1	45	5	4	12.2	23.8
Siani, Michael	L-L	6-1	188	7-16-99	.209	.307	.329	101	430	368	64	77	12	4	8	41	50	4	3	5	106	28	5	11.6	24.7
Stauss, Wade	L-R	6-2	225	4-4-99	.000	.000	.000	1	4	4	0	0	0	0	0	0	0	0	0	0	4	0	0	0.0	100.0
Torres, Bryan	L-R	5-11	165	7-2-97	.328	.441	.464	104	414	332	58	109	16	1	9	51	70	1	6	5	57	26	6	16.9	13.8
Vilade, Ryan	R-R	6-2	226	2-18-99	.280	.375	.476	48	192	164	33	46	11	3	5	31	24	2	0	2	38	5	1	12.5	19.8
Walker, Jordan	R-R	6-6	245	5-22-02	.250	.294	.250	4	17	16	2	4	0	0	0	5	1	0	0	0	6	0	0	5.9	35.3
Wetherholt, JJ	L-R	5-10	190	9-10-02	.314	.416	.562	47	221	185	43	58	14	1	10	25	28	6	0	2	33	9	1	12.7	14.9
Winn, Masyn	R-R	5-11	180	3-21-02	.300	.727	3	7	3	3	13	1	2	2	2	2	0	0	0	0	5	0	0	15.4	38.5
Yerzy, Andy	L-R	6-3	215	7-5-98	.203	.289	.330	51	204	182	20	37	5	0	6	17	20	2	0	0	67	1	1	9.8	32.8

Pitching	B-T	Ht.	Wt.	DOB	W	L	ERA	G	GS	SV	IP	Hits	Runs	ER	HR	BB	SO	AVG	OBP	SLG	SO%	BB%	BF
Anderson, Nick	R-R	6-4	205	7-5-90	0	1	6.20	17	0	0	20	21	14	14	3	8	20	.256	.323	.402	21.5	8.6	93
Bedell, Ian	R-R	6-2	214	9-5-99	0	5	7.96	16	14	0	52	65	46	46	14	24	51	.300	.374	.553	20.7	9.8	246
Berrios, Osvaldo	R-R	6-2	200	11-29-99	0	1	9.20	12	0	0	15	23	16	15	5	9	14	.354	.427	.646	18.7	12.0	75
Cornwell, Alex	L-L	6-0	202	5-9-99	4	6	5.92	35	12	1	93	110	66	61	9	45	71	.295	.375	.426	16.7	10.6	424
Fernandez, Ryan	R-R	6-0	170	6-11-98	4	1	3.12	29	0	2	35	23	12	12	1	20	49	.185	.299	.250	33.3	13.6	147
Gomez, Michael	R-R	6-3	210	8-15-96	2	2	6.88	23	2	0	34	33	30	26	5	23	30	.254	.395	.438	18.5	14.2	162
Graceffo, Gordon	R-R	6-4	210	3-17-00	2	4	3.77	24	2	2	45	45	23	19	5	13	45	.259	.312	.397	23.7	6.8	190
Granillo, Andre	R-R	6-4	245	5-12-00	5	0	1.29	29	0	2	42	21	6	6	2	14	58	.144	.224	.212	36.0	8.7	161
Hales, Skylar	R-R	6-4	220	10-24-01	5	0	5.40	16	0	0	20	17	13	12	3	9	18	.230	.326	.405	20.0	10.0	90
Kaminsky, Rob	R-L	6-0	195	9-2-94	1	0	0.00	1	0	0	1	0	0	0	0	1	1	.000	.250	.000	25.0	25.0	4
King, John	L-L	6-2	215	9-14-94	0	1	3.38	3	0	0	3	4	3	1	0	1	2	.333	.385	.333	15.4	7.7	13
Loutos, Ryan	R-R	6-5	215	1-29-99	0	0	3.38	8	0	2	8	7	3	3	1	2	6	.219	.257	.375	17.1	5.7	35
Mathews, Quinn	L-L	6-4	192	10-4-00	4	7	3.93	22	22	0	94	76	44	41	6	74	107	.224	.364	.316	25.4	17.5	422
McGreevy, Michael	R-R	6-4	215	7-8-00	8	3	3.72	15	15	0	75	78	33	31	7	15	78	.271	.311	.403	25.5	4.9	306
Mills, Zane	R-R	6-4	220	7-4-00	0	0	2.45	2	1	0	4	2	1	1	0	2	4	.154	.313	.231	25.0	12.5	16
Moore, Brody	R-R	5-11	183	7-20-00	1	0	0.00	1	0	0	2	0	0	0	0	0	0	.182	.182	.182	0.0	0.0	11
Moreno, Gerson	R-R	6-0	218	9-10-95	1	0	1.23	14	0	0	15	4	2	2	0	11	15	.087	.300	.087	25.0	18.3	60
Mosqueda, Oddanier	L-L	5-10	155	5-6-99	5	5	4.52	55	0	2	66	51	36	33	7	31	68	.215	.321	.388	24.3	11.1	280
Munoz, Roddery	R-R	6-2	210	4-14-00	4	3	3.28	38	0	3	58	46	22	21	4	30	76	.218	.318	.313	30.8	12.1	247
O'Brien, Riley	R-R	6-4	180	2-6-95	1	0	2.79	19	0	3	19	16	7	6	1	5	25	.239	.297	.284	37.2	9.3	86
Plesac, Zach	R-R	6-3	220	1-21-95	1	8	7.67	15	14	0	59	69	54	50	13	31	47	.296	.373	.541	17.5	11.6	268
Rajcic, Max	R-R	6-0	210	8-3-01	0	4	6.40	11	10	0	45	58	32	32	10	27	28	.314	.409	.557	12.7	12.2	221
Ralston, Jack	R-R	6-4	237	4-13-97	1	1	5.50	14	0	0	18	16	11	11	2	16	22	.286	.409	.429	25.0	18.2	88
Raquet, Nick	R-L	6-0	215	12-12-95	2	3	5.19	14	0	5	17	19	11	10	4	6	22	.242	.324	.470	29.3	8.0	75
Robberse, Sem	R-R	6-1	185	10-12-01	1	1	7.36	4	4	0	15	22	14	12	2	8	19	.343	.421	.493	24.7	10.4	77
Roby, Tekoah	R-R	6-3	185	9-18-01	3	2	4.02	6	6	0	31	33	17	14	4	8	30	.266	.311	.468	22.6	6.0	133
Rom, Drew	L-L	6-2	175	12-15-99	0	4	5.65	4	4	0	19	27	14	12	2	6	11	.380	.455	.590	18.6	10.2	59
Roycroft, Chris	R-R	6-8	230	6-21-97	3	2	4.82	35	0	5	47	50	29	25	6	24	47	.276	.356	.376	22.4	11.4	210
Shreve, Ryan	R-R	6-6	215	6-23-98	2	0	6.75	10	1	0	25	17	16	7	11	6	.301	.384	.651	14.0	11.0	100

	B-T	Ht.	Wt.	DOB			ERA	G			IP		R	ER		BB	SO	AVG	OBP	SLG	SO%	BB%	BF
Svanson, Matt	R-R	6-5	235	1-31-99	1	0	3.32	15	0	1	22	26	9	8	1	9	22	.295	.367	.409	22.4	9.2	98
Taveras, Leonardo	R-R	6-5	190	9-7-98	2	1	6.65	13	3	0	22	15	16	16	2	21	20	.190	.373	.316	19.6	20.6	102
Taylor, Curtis	R-R	6-6	235	7-25-95	10	4	3.21	31	24	1	137	112	55	49	14	51	118	.226	.305	.374	21.0	9.1	561
Veneziano, Anthony	L-L	6-5	205	9-1-97	1	0	4.38	10	0	0	12	14	6	6	1	11	6	.298	.433	.362	10.0	18.3	60
Weiss, Zack	R-R	6-3	210	6-16-92	3	2	5.43	43	0	2	66	65	44	40	17	36	77	.262	.355	.528	26.7	12.5	288
Wilkerson, Aaron	R-R	6-2	230	5-24-89	3	1	3.43	11	11	0	58	51	22	22	8	13	40	.238	.284	.444	17.3	5.6	231

Fielding

Catcher	PCT	G	PO	A	E	DP	PB
Collins	.988	29	229	14	3	1	1
Crooks	.989	77	655	52	8	7	12
Herrera	1.000	3	21	0	0	0	0
Linarez	1.000	1	7	0	0	0	0
Pozo	1.000	2	18	2	0	1	0
Stauss	1.000	1	10	2	0	1	0
Yerzy	.995	39	345	17	2	1	5

First Base	PCT	G	PO	A	E	DP
Baker	.992	52	373	19	3	36
Collins	.968	13	89	2	3	10
Jordan	1.000	24	177	9	0	17
Lloyd	.991	41	306	29	3	37
Moore	1.000	2	15	2	0	1
Pozo	1.000	1	6	0	0	0
Vilade	1.000	12	64	7	0	5
Yerzy	1.000	9	53	0	0	7

Second Base	PCT	G	PO	A	E	DP
Fermin	1.000	31	48	71	0	16
Helman	1.000	3	3	6	0	2
Lloyd	1.000	1	3	3	0	0
Mendlinger	1.000	15	18	36	0	6
Moore	.980	17	22	28	1	5
Prieto	.967	30	44	74	4	16
Saggese	1.000	2	3	7	0	2
Torres	.973	45	63	117	5	25
Vilade	.957	5	11	11	1	3
Wetherholt	1.000	3	3	8	0	1

Third Base	PCT	G	PO	A	E	DP
Barrero	1.000	5	3	6	0	0
Collins	.908	26	11	48	6	3
Fermin	.927	19	14	37	4	1
Jordan	.923	8	3	9	1	0
Mendlinger	.950	5	5	14	1	3
Moore	.921	17	8	27	3	7
Prieto	.979	44	30	63	2	10
Saggese	1.000	8	3	12	0	0
Torres	.000	1	0	0	0	0
Vilade	.957	10	10	12	1	1
Wetherholt	.949	12	5	32	2	6

Shortstop	PCT	G	PO	A	E	DP
Barrero	.982	16	19	36	1	7
Fermin	.882	5	5	10	2	1
Helman	1.000	4	4	8	0	2
Mendlinger	1.000	2	1	4	0	1
Moore	.954	23	30	53	4	12
Prieto	.973	43	71	108	5	25
Saggese	.991	32	42	68	1	13
Wetherholt	.962	25	45	55	4	15
Winn	.875	2	1	6	1	0

Outfield	PCT	G	PO	A	E	DP
Antico	.982	92	160	2	3	2
Barrero	1.000	4	12	0	0	0
Church	.981	48	98	3	2	0
Fermin	1.000	10	2	0	0	0
Helman	.950	10	16	3	1	0
Koperniak	.984	111	186	4	3	2
Lloyd	.941	8	15	1	1	1
Mendlinger	1.000	2	1	1	0	0
Siani	.988	94	239	10	3	2
Torres	.982	54	103	4	2	0
Vilade	.946	17	32	3	2	1
Walker	1.000	2	6	0	0	0

SPRINGFIELD CARDINALS
TEXAS LEAGUE — DOUBLE-A

Batting	B-T	Ht.	Wt.	DOB	AVG	OBP	SLG	G	PA	AB	R	H	2B	3B	HR	RBI	BB	HBP	SH	SF	SO	SB	CS	BB%	SO%
Adkison, Chase	R-R	6-0	205	6-5-00	.000	.200	.000	1	5	4	0	0	0	0	0	0	1	0	0	0	1	0	0	20.0	20.0
Arenado, Nolan	R-R	6-2	215	4-16-91	.077	.143	.077	4	14	13	2	1	0	0	0	0	1	0	0	0	3	0	0	7.1	21.4
Baez, Joshua	R-R	6-3	220	6-28-03	.271	.374	.509	79	331	273	46	74	15	1	16	55	41	8	0	7	67	34	7	12.4	20.2
Bernal, Leonardo	S-R	6-0	200	2-13-04	.247	.332	.394	107	455	396	58	98	19	0	13	70	49	3	2	4	77	13	3	10.8	16.9
Buchberger, Jacob	R-R	6-0	215	10-1-97	.300	.417	.500	6	24	20	4	6	1	0	1	8	4	0	0	0	5	1	0	16.7	20.8
Church, Nathan	L-L	5-10	180	7-12-00	.336	.380	.563	29	129	119	21	40	7	1	6	19	8	1	0	1	10	6	6	6.2	7.8
Davis, Chase	L-L	6-1	216	12-5-01	.242	.358	.353	113	494	414	61	100	16	0	10	48	67	10	0	3	146	9	2	13.6	29.6
Donovan, Brendan	L-R	6-1	195	1-16-97	.000	.429	.000	2	7	4	1	0	0	0	0	0	3	0	0	0	1	0	0	42.9	14.3
Gazdar, Jon Jon	R-R	5-11	180	3-3-02	.233	.298	.279	11	47	43	5	10	2	0	0	3	3	1	0	0	8	0	0	6.4	17.0
Gorman, Nolan	L-R	6-1	210	5-10-00	.231	.231	.538	3	13	13	1	3	1	0	1	2	0	0	0	0	4	0	0	0.0	30.8
Harris, Dakota	S-R	6-0	197	2-19-02	.264	.316	.372	117	477	435	67	115	17	0	10	49	26	9	3	4	82	23	6	5.5	17.2
Levenson, Zach	R-R	6-2	210	3-6-02	.275	.350	.484	26	103	91	11	25	7	0	4	19	10	1	0	1	22	2	1	9.7	21.4
Linarez, Carlos	R-R	6-0	170	10-24-01	.244	.304	.348	40	149	135	19	33	3	1	3	17	12	0	1	1	60	0	2	8.1	40.3
Madron, Bryce	L-L	5-8	175	7-1-01	.000	.167	.000	5	18	15	2	0	0	0	0	0	3	0	0	0	6	0	0	16.7	33.3
Mendlinger, Noah	L-R	5-9	180	8-9-00	.279	.398	.330	86	361	297	51	83	13	2	1	29	46	14	1	2	34	10	4	12.7	9.4
Mendoza, Ramon	R-R	5-11	174	8-31-00	.275	.390	.452	105	404	334	59	92	13	2	14	62	60	5	1	4	80	3	4	14.9	19.8
Moore, Brody	R-R	5-11	183	7-20-00	.244	.291	.306	46	173	160	25	39	4	0	2	22	10	1	1	1	30	6	0	5.8	17.3
Moquete, Darlin	R-R	5-8	175	9-19-99	.245	.315	.356	78	290	261	37	64	9	1	6	36	22	5	1	1	66	18	7	7.6	22.8
Nootbaar, Lars	L-R	6-3	210	9-8-97	.286	.286	.286	3	14	14	1	4	0	0	0	1	0	0	0	0	4	0	0	0.0	28.6
Paige, Trey	L-R	6-0	215	11-9-00	.235	.336	.380	59	234	200	35	47	6	4	5	19	30	1	2	1	61	6	2	12.8	26.1
Rivas, Jeremy	R-R	6-0	172	3-4-03	.204	.298	.319	116	487	427	57	87	17	1	10	50	48	10	0	1	135	21	8	9.9	27.7
Scott, Victor	L-L	5-10	190	2-12-01	.125	.300	.125	3	10	8	1	1	0	0	0	0	1	1	0	0	1	1	1	10.0	10.0
Stauss, Wade	L-R	6-2	225	4-4-99	.036	.206	.036	11	34	28	0	1	0	0	0	0	6	0	0	0	13	0	0	17.6	38.2
Tarlow, Graysen	R-R	5-11	190	7-7-01	.278	.412	.296	17	69	54	6	15	1	0	0	6	13	0	1	1	15	0	1	18.8	21.7
Uguoeto, Miguel	R-R	5-11	185	9-3-02	.254	.276	.339	50	199	189	22	48	8	1	2	22	6	1	0	3	25	9	5	3.0	12.6
Walker, Jordan	R-R	6-6	245	5-22-02	.158	.256	.395	10	43	38	5	6	3	0	2	4	5	0	0	0	12	0	1	11.6	27.9
Wetherholt, JJ	L-R	5-10	190	9-10-02	.300	.425	.466	62	275	223	39	67	14	1	7	34	44	6	0	2	40	14	2	16.0	14.5
Yeager, R.J.	R-R	6-2	200	10-2-98	.210	.282	.317	77	309	271	42	57	11	0	6	32	23	7	1	7	54	4	3	7.4	17.5

Pitching	B-T	Ht.	Wt.	DOB	W	L	ERA	G	GS	SV	IP	Hits	Runs	ER	HR	BB	SO	AVG	OBP	SLG	SO%	BB%	BF
Berrios, Osvaldo	R-R	6-2	200	11-29-99	4	3	3.74	28	4	4	43	35	22	18	6	15	48	.212	.279	.388	26.2	8.2	183
Bradt, Tyler	R-R	5-11	196	2-11-01	1	1	2.50	11	2	0	18	11	7	5	1	11	19	.177	.311	.274	25.3	14.7	75
Burns, Mason	R-R	6-3	215	4-4-02	0	0	12.00	2	0	0	3	4	4	4	2	4	.308	.400	.615	26.7	13.3	15
Clemente, Randel	R-R	6-3	173	11-17-01	0	0	6.43	12	0	0	14	8	10	10	1	18	19	.163	.406	.286	27.5	26.1	69
Doyle, Liam	R-L	6-2	220	6-3-04	0	0	0.00	1	1	0	2	0	0	0	0	3	3	.000	.250	.250	37.5	0.0	8
Gastelum, Luis	R-R	6-2	168	9-27-01	3	5	4.02	46	0	10	63	52	29	28	3	17	92	.218	.285	.311	35.4	6.5	260
Hansen, Pete	R-L	6-2	205	7-28-00	8	5	3.93	26	26	0	137	137	71	60	12	37	123	.256	.302	.379	21.0	6.3	583
Harney, Sean	L-R	6-0	190	7-10-98	1	1	4.24	22	1	5	28	16	16	2	20	31	.222	.336	.341	20.8	13.4	149
Hayes, Hunter	R-R	6-1	185	8-5-00	0	1	2.20	9	0	0	16	14	4	4	6	18	.237	.324	.288	25.7	8.6	70

ST. LOUIS CARDINALS

Hence, Tink	R-R	6-1	185	8-6-02	0	0	4.22	3	3	0	11	6	5	5	1	6	14	.167	.286	.278	33.3 14.3 42
Henderson, Ixan	L-L	6-2	180	1-29-02	9	7	2.59	25	25	0	132	99	41	38	5	51	134	.210	.291	.294	25.2 9.6 532
Heredia, Nathanael	L-L	6-3	190	9-10-00	0	1	3.54	25	0	1	28	18	13	11	3	29	29	.186	.388	.229	22.5 22.5 129
King, John	L-L	6-2	215	9-14-94	0	0	9.00	1	0	0	1	1	1	1	0	2	.250	.250	1.000	50.0	0.0 4
Lin, Chen-Wei	R-R	6-7	188	11-22-01	0	0	9.31	4	4	0	10	9	10	10	2	9	20	.237	.383	.474	41.7 18.8 48
Love, Austin	R-R	6-3	232	12-6-99	6	1	2.41	41	0	2	56	33	16	15	3	26	63	.168	.274	.230	27.3 11.3 231
Marrero, Andrew	R-R	5-10	196	5-8-00	5	0	5.19	24	0	1	35	37	21	20	5	32	47	.276	.420	.470	27.8 18.9 169
Mautz, Brycen	L-L	6-3	190	7-17-01	8	3	2.98	25	25	0	115	94	39	38	13	33	134	.219	.282	.343	28.6 7.1 468
Mills, Zane	R-R	6-4	220	7-4-00	5	5	4.91	29	1	1	51	48	32	28	5	21	54	.247	.326	.387	24.3 9.5 222
Nunez, Edwin	R-R	6-3	185	11-5-01	3	0	10.54	22	0	0	27	26	34	32	3	35	33	.260	.469	.420	23.1 24.5 143
Rajcic, Max	R-R	6-0	210	8-3-01	3	3	4.07	16	16	0	73	73	41	33	5	27	72	.253	.329	.370	22.4 8.4 322
Ralston, Jack	R-R	6-6	231	8-13-97	3	3	2.75	24	0	3	39	32	14	12	4	27	50	.229	.351	.350	29.6 16.0 169
Raquet, Nick	R-L	6-0	215	12-12-95	8	1	0.77	25	0	5	35	29	6	3	0	6	38	.223	.271	.238	26.8 4.2 142
Rincon, Hancel	R-R	6-2	160	4-28-02	3	3	3.61	9	8	0	47	47	20	19	4	13	59	.257	.303	.383	29.8 6.6 198
Roby, Tekoah	R-R	6-1	185	9-18-01	4	2	2.49	10	10	0	47	34	14	13	4	11	57	.200	.253	.306	31.1 6.0 183
Shreve, Ryan	R-R	6-6	215	6-23-98	0	1	11.81	3	0	0	5	11	9	7	1	4	2	.393	.469	.643	6.3 12.5 32
Taveras, Leonardo	R-R	6-5	190	9-7-98	3	1	5.47	15	1	0	25	27	16	15	2	15	30	.278	.387	.402	25.2 12.6 119
Thompson, Brandt	R-R	5-9	180	7-4-02	1	0	1.00	2	2	0	9	6	2	1	0	3	5	.207	.281	.241	15.6 9.4 32
Velez, Ricardo	R-R	6-1	180	8-21-98	5	1	1.99	30	1	2	59	41	18	13	3	26	53	.195	.302	.286	21.8 10.7 243
Watson, Michael	L-L	6-2	190	6-18-02	2	1	1.11	17	0	3	24	12	4	3	0	10	29	.154	.272	.244	30.5 10.5 95
Winquest, Cade	R-R	6-2	205	4-30-00	3	1	3.19	8	8	0	42	42	16	15	3	12	42	.263	.318	.344	23.9 6.8 176

Fielding

Catcher	PCT	G	PO	A	E	DP	PB
Bernal	.989	87	839	41	10	5	13
Linarez	.980	32	271	19	6	1	2
Stauss	.985	8	63	1	1	0	2
Tarlow	.988	15	155	5	2	1	0

First Base	PCT	G	PO	A	E	DP
Adkison	1.000	1	7	0	0	0
Harris	.985	22	129	5	2	12
Linarez	1.000	4	29	3	0	3
Paige	.994	43	301	18	2	34
Yeager	1.000	69	487	28	0	44

Second Base	PCT	G	PO	A	E	DP
Donovan	1.000	2	2	4	0	0
Gazdar	.964	9	10	17	1	5
Gorman	1.000	2	2	2	0	0
Harris	.975	31	47	69	3	12
Mendlinger	.976	21	39	44	2	15
Mendoza	.958	5	6	17	1	0

Third Base	PCT	G	PO	A	E	DP
Arenado	1.000	2	1	1	0	0
Harris	.935	52	16	85	7	12
Mendlinger	1.000	2	2	1	0	0
Mendoza	.938	81	48	102	10	12
Moore	1.000	2	1	2	0	0
Paige	1.000	1	0	3	0	0
Yeager	1.000	1	3	1	0	1

Shortstop	PCT	G	PO	A	E	DP
Gazdar	1.000	2	2	4	0	0
Harris	.875	3	3	4	1	0
Moore	.962	18	29	46	3	7
Rivas	.969	81	94	190	9	35
Wetherholt	.957	36	43	89	6	21

	PCT	G	PO	A	E	DP
Moore	1.000	24	44	46	0	11
Rivas	.968	33	51	69	4	16
Wetherholt	1.000	17	27	46	0	7

Outfield	PCT	G	PO	A	E	DP
Baez	.975	73	150	6	4	2
Buchberger	1.000	6	8	0	0	0
Church	.986	28	68	1	1	0
Davis	.996	109	231	7	1	3
Harris	1.000	5	4	0	0	0
Levenson	1.000	22	34	0	0	0
Madron	1.000	5	6	0	0	0
Mendlinger	.982	58	108	3	2	1
Mendoza	.000	2	0	0	0	0
Moquete	.974	57	69	5	2	1
Nootbaar	1.000	2	8	0	0	0
Scott	1.000	3	8	0	0	0
Ugueto	.984	50	121	0	2	0
Walker	.917	5	10	1	1	0

PEORIA CHIEFS
MIDWEST LEAGUE
HIGH-A

Batting	B-T	Ht.	Wt.	DOB	AVG	OBP	SLG	G	PA	AB	R	H	2B	3B	HR	RBI	BB	HBP	SH	SF	SO	SB	CS	BB%	SO%
Adkison, Chase	R-R	6-0	205	6-5-00	.298	.452	.394	33	124	94	17	28	6	0	1	15	23	5	0	2	15	1	0	18.5	12.1
Baez, Jesus	R-R	5-9	180	2-26-05	.243	.303	.378	27	122	111	14	27	3	0	4	15	10	0	0	1	28	2	2	8.2	23.0
Baez, Joshua	R-R	6-3	220	6-28-03	.317	.404	.483	38	168	145	32	46	8	2	4	24	18	3	0	0	36	20	2	10.7	21.4
Campos, Ryan	L-R	5-9	180	10-16-02	.235	.356	.340	95	421	353	54	83	22	3	3	47	64	3	0	1	74	15	3	15.2	17.6
Cho, Won-Bin	L-L	6-1	200	8-20-03	.236	.346	.342	90	368	313	44	74	15	0	6	47	50	3	1	1	87	25	4	13.6	23.6
Cordoba, Jose	R-R	5-11	165	1-13-03	.263	.323	.351	14	62	57	7	15	5	0	0	5	3	2	0	0	11	5	0	4.8	17.7
Curialle, Michael	R-R	6-1	199	6-16-01	.226	.320	.335	64	241	212	35	48	7	2	4	26	18	11	0	0	64	5	1	7.5	26.6
Encarnacion, Anyelo	R-R	5-11	164	1-2-04	.219	.270	.307	33	122	114	8	25	4	0	2	13	7	1	0	0	37	5	1	5.7	30.3
Gazdar, Jon Jon	R-R	5-11	180	3-3-02	.287	.378	.531	89	416	359	51	103	13	1	30	34	20	0	2	40	20	5	8.2	9.6
Hernandez, Sammy	R-R	5-9	185	6-1-04	.100	.217	.250	6	23	20	2	2	0	0	0	1	3	0	0	0	3	0	2	13.0	13.0
Honeyman, Travis	R-R	6-2	190	10-2-01	.268	.390	.322	53	228	183	35	49	5	1	1	20	27	13	0	5	43	3	0	11.8	18.9
Jobert, Brayden	L-R	6-1	215	11-14-00	.210	.326	.346	88	350	295	38	62	12	2	8	36	44	8	0	3	86	8	6	12.6	24.6
Kross, Josh	S-R	6-2	200	2-2-03	.211	.288	.385	58	243	213	25	45	9	2	8	44	22	3	0	5	65	0	1	9.1	26.7
Levenson, Zach	R-R	6-2	210	3-6-02	.236	.373	.377	82	346	284	48	67	12	2	8	38	56	6	0	0	63	7	6	16.2	18.2
Madron, Bryce	L-L	5-8	175	7-1-01	.212	.366	.303	12	41	33	9	7	3	0	0	0	7	1	0	0	14	1	0	17.1	34.1
Martin, Christian	L-R	5-10	170	1-16-03	.167	.300	.167	7	30	24	2	4	0	0	0	2	4	1	0	1	8	1	1	13.3	26.7
Ortiz, Deniel	R-R	6-1	228	8-24-04	.336	.438	.500	30	130	110	15	37	9	0	3	15	18	2	0	0	29	8	6	13.8	22.3
Paige, Trey	L-R	6-0	215	11-9-00	.242	.317	.355	35	139	124	19	30	6	1	2	21	13	1	0	1	42	2	1	9.4	30.2
Petrutz, Ian	L-L	6-0	205	8-26-02	.247	.354	.351	87	371	316	35	78	16	1	5	45	40	11	1	49	3	10	10.8	13.2	
Richardson, Tre	R-R	6-0	180	2-14-01	.230	.330	.295	82	345	303	42	73	18	0	3	30	33	8	0	1	60	16	9	9.6	17.4
Rodriguez, Rainiel	R-R	5-10	197	1-4-07	.294	.294	.353	4	17	17	2	5	1	0	0	4	0	0	0	0	2	0	0	0.0	11.8
Salazar, Johnfrank	R-R	6-1	159	8-5-03	.225	.273	.270	32	121	111	12	25	5	0	0	13	6	2	0	2	17	6	0	5.0	14.0
Sojka, Andrew	R-R	6-1	200	5-16-01	.164	.238	.260	20	81	73	13	12	4	0	1	4	7	0	1	0	19	1	2	8.6	23.5
Tarlow, Graysen	R-R	5-11	190	7-7-01	.304	.396	.357	37	139	115	15	35	3	0	1	23	18	5	0	1	23	1	3	8.6	21.6
Ugueto, Miguel	R-R	5-11	185	9-3-02	.278	.350	.333	4	20	18	3	5	1	0	0	2	0	2	0	0	2	0	1	0.0	10.0
Villarroel, Miguel	R-R	6-0	165	12-23-01	.254	.307	.331	66	272	248	40	63	9	2	2	25	19	1	1	2	66	22	4	7.0	24.3

ST. LOUIS CARDINALS

Pitching

Pitching	B-T	Ht.	Wt.	DOB	W	L	ERA	G	GS	SV	IP	Hits	Runs	ER	HR	BB	SO	AVG	OBP	SLG	SO%	BB%	BF
Adkison, Chase	R-R	6-0	205	6-5-00	0	0	0.00	1	0	0	1	1	0	0	0	0	0	.250	.250	.250	0.0	0.0	4
Arias, Benjamin	R-R	6-5	195	11-5-01	2	1	3.67	33	0	2	56	43	28	23	3	24	43	.213	.315	.322	17.7	9.9	243
Bradt, Tyler	R-R	5-11	196	2-11-01	1	4	3.18	26	1	1	45	32	27	16	3	36	49	.198	.353	.302	23.9	17.6	205
Burns, Mason	R-R	6-3	215	4-4-02	2	1	2.33	17	0	4	27	17	10	7	1	10	32	.179	.255	.274	29.6	9.3	108
Carpenter, D.J.	R-R	6-8	242	2-8-00	3	2	5.35	36	0	2	37	39	25	22	2	30	41	.273	.401	.364	23.0	16.9	178
Clemente, Randel	R-R	6-3	173	11-17-01	0	0	1.86	7	0	0	10	3	2	2	0	4	12	.094	.216	.156	32.4	10.8	37
Davila, Jose	R-R	6-3	177	11-9-02	3	6	6.06	24	22	0	98	108	68	66	11	50	88	.281	.380	.464	19.4	11.0	453
Davis, Braden	L-L	5-11	180	4-9-03	3	2	2.21	8	8	0	37	15	11	9	0	23	50	.123	.277	.180	33.6	15.4	149
Dohm, Nate	R-R	6-4	220	1-9-03	0	2	5.11	5	5	0	12	11	7	7	2	9	13	.239	.375	.413	23.2	16.1	56
Elissalt, Frank	S-R	6-2	210	3-25-02	0	2	5.59	4	3	0	10	7	6	6	0	8	6	.206	.357	.235	14.3	19.0	42
Findlay, Jack	L-L	6-3	200	8-18-02	0	1	1.93	5	0	0	9	6	3	2	0	3	11	.194	.257	.290	31.4	8.6	35
Franklin, Tanner	R-R	6-5	225	5-25-04	0	0	2.25	2	2	0	4	3	1	1	0	4	5	.214	.450	.286	25.0	20.0	20
Gonzalez, Angel	R-R	6-2	175	8-26-02	1	4	6.37	25	0	2	35	22	28	25	1	47	41	.186	.429	.280	23.3	26.7	176
Hayes, Hunter	R-R	6-2	185	8-5-00	2	3	5.66	27	0	2	48	50	31	30	5	25	49	.263	.356	.411	22.3	11.4	220
Hence, Tink	R-R	6-2	185	8-6-02	0	1	4.91	1	1	0	4	2	2	2	0	3	1	.182	.333	.182	6.7	20.0	15
Holiday, Aaron	R-R	6-3	205	5-28-00	1	0	7.71	4	0	0	7	6	7	6	1	5	8	.214	.333	.321	24.2	15.2	33
Jacobson, Tanner	R-R	6-1	190	1-24-00	6	5	3.20	31	0	2	51	39	18	18	2	37	61	.214	.347	.297	27.7	16.8	220
King, Joseph	R-R	6-1	194	2-23-01	0	0	4.82	7	0	1	9	11	5	5	2	8	15	.289	.404	.579	31.9	17.0	47
Lin, Chen-Wei	R-R	6-7	188	11-22-01	0	2	4.89	12	12	0	39	27	25	21	1	29	46	.196	.337	.283	27.2	17.2	169
Molina, Mason	R-L	6-2	215	7-8-03	2	1	2.08	5	5	0	22	15	6	5	2	15	27	.192	.323	.231	29.0	16.1	93
Paniagua, Inohan	R-R	6-1	148	2-6-00	0	0	16.20	1	0	0	2	3	3	3	0	5	0	.429	.667	.714	0.0	41.7	12
Picone, Domenic	R-R	5-9	185	10-16-00	0	3	4.58	10	0	0	18	17	9	9	1	11	13	.254	.370	.343	16.0	13.6	81
Ramirez, Jawilme	R-R	6-2	170	11-28-01	5	3	3.02	39	0	2	60	50	28	20	5	31	53	.228	.336	.356	20.4	11.9	260
Rincon, Hancel	R-R	6-2	160	4-28-02	1	2	4.22	10	9	0	49	41	23	23	4	17	49	.224	.298	.393	23.9	8.3	205
Rodriguez, Dionys	L-R	6-0	188	9-3-00	2	5	8.74	23	1	0	35	44	40	34	2	22	19	.301	.408	.425	10.9	12.6	174
Saladin, Darlin	R-R	5-11	150	12-28-02	3	5	4.85	26	13	2	95	87	54	51	8	47	81	.245	.337	.392	19.8	11.5	409
Salas, Gerado	R-R	6-0	189	2-14-03	4	13	8.10	25	19	0	97	125	91	87	15	39	90	.322	.391	.562	20.3	8.8	444
Salazar, Johnfrank	R-R	6-1	159	8-5-03	0	1	16.20	1	0	0	2	3	5	3	0	0	0	.600	.375	.800	0.0	0.0	8
Savacool, Jason	R-R	6-1	210	5-21-02	3	2	4.66	12	10	0	46	49	26	24	4	26	47	.277	.375	.418	22.6	12.5	208
Showalter, Zack	R-R	6-2	195	1-23-04	1	0	4.50	13	1	1	18	9	9	9	0	21	23	.148	.372	.197	26.7	24.4	86
Tarlow, Graysen	R-R	5-11	190	7-7-01	0	0	0.00	1	0	0	1	0	0	0	0	1	0	.500	.667	1.000	0.0	33.3	3
Thompson, Brandt	R-R	5-9	180	7-4-02	0	1	4.20	4	3	0	15	10	7	7	1	4	23	.196	.271	.294	39.0	6.8	59
Velez, Ricardo	R-R	6-1	180	8-21-98	2	0	0.00	3	0	0	6	5	1	0	0	3	2	.238	.333	.238	8.3	12.5	24
Watson, Michael	L-L	6-2	190	6-18-02	2	1	3.41	22	0	3	34	20	15	13	4	22	37	.164	.311	.336	25.0	14.9	148
Winquest, Cade	R-R	6-2	205	4-30-00	2	6	4.52	17	15	0	64	63	38	32	4	27	68	.259	.342	.370	23.9	9.5	284
Wood, Zeke	R-R	6-4	210	3-2-00	0	0	7.20	4	0	0	5	8	4	4	1	3	6	.348	.423	.652	23.1	11.5	26
Worley, Christian	R-R	6-1	170	6-14-02	0	0	6.48	4	0	0	8	12	6	6	0	7	4	.333	.455	.389	9.1	15.9	44

Fielding

Catcher	PCT	G	PO	A	E	DP	PB
Adkison	1.000	8	74	3	0	1	0
Campos	.992	73	667	37	6	5	4
Hernandez	1.000	3	26	0	0	0	0
Kross	.994	17	152	7	1	1	1
Rodriguez	.955	2	16	5	1	0	0
Tarlow	.972	28	229	15	7	0	1

First Base	PCT	G	PO	A	E	DP
Adkison	.982	10	53	1	1	2
Curialle	.979	14	91	3	2	7
Hernandez	1.000	3	13	0	0	1
Jobert	.996	30	210	18	1	22
Kross	.996	35	233	3	1	22
Ortiz	.966	16	105	9	4	8
Paige	.989	10	81	5	1	8
Salazar	.983	14	113	5	2	12

Second Base	PCT	G	PO	A	E	DP
Baez	1.000	4	6	12	0	1

	PCT	G	PO	A	E	DP	PB
Curialle	.917	5	7	4	1	1	
Encarnacion	1.000	3	10	4	0	2	
Gazdar	1.000	24	32	59	0	11	
Martin	.800	2	2	2	1	0	
Paige	1.000	1	0	1	0	0	
Richardson	.978	75	160	150	7	51	
Salazar	.960	6	12	12	1	2	
Villarroel	.981	11	25	28	1	5	

Third Base	PCT	G	PO	A	E	DP
Baez	.700	4	4	3	3	0
Curialle	.897	39	21	84	12	8
Encarnacion	.889	7	6	10	2	1
Gazdar	.964	23	25	29	2	5
Jobert	.941	14	14	18	2	1
Martin	1.000	3	2	2	0	1
Ortiz	1.000	14	12	20	0	2
Paige	.944	21	20	48	4	4
Salazar	.909	5	3	7	1	0
Sojka	1.000	3	4	7	0	2

	PCT	G	PO	A	E	DP
Villarroel	1.000	1	0	1	0	0
Shortstop	**PCT**	**G**	**PO**	**A**	**E**	**DP**
Baez	.977	14	18	25	1	4
Encarnacion	.934	23	24	33	4	7
Gazdar	.975	38	33	86	3	22
Richardson	1.000	5	4	12	0	1
Villarroel	.946	53	45	147	11	27

Outfield	PCT	G	PO	A	E	DP
Baez	1.000	33	66	4	0	0
Cho	.966	86	167	4	6	2
Cordoba	1.000	13	35	1	0	0
Honeyman	.987	45	75	1	1	0
Jobert	.985	38	59	6	1	1
Levenson	.994	76	161	2	1	0
Madron	1.000	13	21	1	0	1
Petrutz	.978	79	128	5	3	1
Sojka	1.000	16	22	2	0	1
Ugueto	1.000	4	10	1	0	0

PALM BEACH CARDINALS
FLORIDA STATE LEAGUE — LOW-A

Batting	B-T	Ht.	Wt.	DOB	AVG	OBP	SLG	G	PA	AB	R	H	2B	3B	HR	RBI	BB	HBP	SH	SF	SO	SB	CS	BB%	SO%
Birge, Alex	L-R	6-0	195	8-23-02	.167	.444	.167	2	9	6	1	1	0	0	0	1	2	1	0	0	3	0	0	22.2	33.3
Caraballo, Heriberto	R-R	5-8	191	2-18-05	.148	.254	.197	20	71	61	8	9	0	0	1	4	8	1	0	1	19	1	0	11.3	26.8
Cho, Won-Bin	L-L	6-1	200	8-20-03	.313	.353	.500	4	17	16	5	5	0	0	1	6	1	0	0	0	7	1	0	5.9	41.2
Church, Nathan	L-L	5-10	180	7-12-00	.154	.214	.231	4	14	13	3	2	1	0	0	1	1	0	0	0	2	0	1	7.1	14.3
Cordoba, Jose	R-R	5-11	165	1-3-03	.274	.381	.411	37	147	124	24	34	10	2	1	18	19	3	0	1	19	7	4	12.9	12.9
Dattalo, Michael	R-R	6-0	200	1-22-04	.259	.338	.328	15	65	58	7	15	4	0	0	5	4	3	0	0	11	0	0	6.2	16.9
Encarnacion, Anyelo	R-R	5-11	164	1-20-04	.210	.351	.333	75	297	243	33	51	9	3	5	33	49	4	1	0	91	15	4	16.5	30.6
Flores, Jalin	R-R	6-2	185	7-31-03	.223	.295	.319	24	105	94	11	21	3	0	2	15	10	0	1	0	34	1	0	9.5	32.4
Gurevitch, Jack	L-R	6-0	215	3-9-04	.181	.303	.253	22	99	83	10	15	1	1	1	4	13	2	0	1	33	5	1	13.1	33.3
Haskins, Trevor	R-R	5-11	175	3-16-03	.172	.172	.310	7	29	29	2	5	1	0	1	3	0	0	0	0	8	0	0	0.0	27.6

ST. LOUIS CARDINALS

BATTING	B-T	Ht.	Wt.	DOB	AVG	OBP	SLG	G	AB	R	H	2B	3B	HR	RBI	BB	SO	SB	CS	OPS
Heath, Chase	R-R	5-10	185	7-14-03	.267	.431	.489	16	58	45	14	12	1	0	3	7	12	1	0	0	12	2	0	20.7	20.7
Hernandez, Maikel	S-R	6-0	163	2-20-03	.103	.205	.205	14	45	39	4	4	1	0	1	7	5	0	1	0	11	0	0	11.1	24.4
Hernandez, Sammy	R-R	5-9	185	6-1-04	.235	.362	.294	89	360	293	40	69	11	0	2	49	46	14	3	3	67	12	1	12.8	18.6
Honeyman, Travis	R-R	6-2	190	10-2-01	.321	.446	.443	29	130	106	19	34	5	1	2	8	20	4	0	0	19	7	1	15.4	14.6
Kross, Josh	S-R	6-2	200	2-2-03	.244	.311	.488	42	183	164	27	40	10	3	8	37	10	7	0	2	48	1	0	5.5	26.2
Lloyd, Matt	L-R	6-1	205	3-17-96	.250	.455	.438	5	22	16	3	4	0	0	0	1	4	6	0	0	3	1	0	27.3	13.6
Madron, Bryce	L-L	5-8	175	7-1-01	.172	.381	.224	36	156	116	18	20	3	0	1	8	36	3	1	0	36	3	8	23.1	23.1
Martin, Christian	L-R	5-10	170	1-16-03	.260	.349	.344	77	337	288	40	75	16	1	2	30	38	4	1	5	56	20	6	11.3	16.6
McGee, Cade	R-R	6-1	195	1-12-03	.214	.334	.362	78	335	276	44	59	14	0	9	50	46	7	0	6	76	22	5	13.7	22.7
Mejia, Jonathan	S-R	5-11	185	4-12-05	.183	.303	.308	74	324	273	43	50	4	6	6	30	46	2	1	2	106	18	4	14.2	32.7
Miura, Matthew	R-R	5-11	185	9-23-03	.197	.330	.250	21	91	76	14	15	1	0	1	9	15	0	0	0	13	7	3	16.5	14.3
Nickens, Cameron	R-R	6-3	193	7-11-03	.179	.238	.179	10	42	39	2	7	0	0	0	3	3	0	0	0	14	0	1	7.1	33.3
Ortiz, Deniel	R-R	6-1	228	8-24-04	.285	.406	.446	77	320	260	46	74	10	1	10	36	49	7	0	4	88	31	3	15.3	27.5
Pena, Yordalin	R-R	6-3	177	9-17-04	.228	.299	.361	103	412	368	54	84	21	5	6	39	35	4	0	5	108	20	10	8.5	26.2
Pino, Luis	R-R	5-10	175	2-7-04	.200	.327	.336	98	413	345	43	69	16	2	9	42	54	12	0	2	129	7	2	13.1	31.2
Rodriguez, Rainiel	R-R	5-10	197	1-4-07	.249	.498	.460	271	225	34	56	15	1	13	43	38	7	0	1	48	3	4	14.0	17.7
Salazar, Johnfrank	R-R	6-1	159	8-5-03	.265	.384	.349	27	99	83	7	22	4	0	1	12	14	2	0	0	13	6	2	14.1	13.1
Suarez, Jose	R-R	6-2	200	8-9-04	.248	.325	.324	88	366	327	51	81	12	2	3	29	30	8	0	1	99	17	6	8.2	27.0
Taveras, Bracewell	S-R	6-0	182	6-5-06	.000	.100	.000	3	10	9	1	0	0	0	0	0	1	0	0	0	4	0	0	10.0	40.0
Ugueto, Miguel	R-R	5-11	185	9-3-02	.240	.269	.320	6	26	25	3	6	2	0	0	3	1	0	0	0	6	2	0	3.8	23.1
Weingartner, Ryan	R-R	5-11	180	7-5-04	.145	.326	.174	21	90	69	7	10	0	1	0	6	18	1	1	1	26	5	4	20.0	28.9

Pitching	B-T	Ht.	Wt.	DOB	W	L	ERA	G	GS	SV	IP	Hits	Runs	ER	HR	BB	SO	AVG	OBP	SLG	SO%	BB%	BF
Batista, Yadiel	L-L	6-3	170	4-17-04	1	2	6.18	7	0	0	28	33	20	19	2	14	21	.306	.386	.417	16.4	10.9	128
Bedell, Ian	R-R	6-2	214	9-5-99	0	1	7.94	2	2	0	6	4	5	5	1	3	8	.190	.292	.429	33.3	12.5	24
Breckheimer, Alex	R-R	6-5	270	9-12-03	0	0	9.00	4	0	0	4	5	5	4	0	4	6	.333	.450	.467	30.0	20.0	20
Brodersen, Sam	R-R	6-1	190	5-17-02	2	5	5.91	36	0	2	46	43	38	30	4	39	59	.247	.388	.368	27.6	18.2	214
Burns, Mason	R-R	6-3	215	4-4-02	2	0	3.49	21	0	3	28	20	13	11	3	19	43	.202	.333	.333	35.0	15.4	123
Clemente, Randel	R-R	6-3	173	11-17-01	3	2	3.99	20	0	4	29	21	15	13	2	18	45	.196	.317	.290	35.7	14.3	126
Cuello, Antoni	R-R	6-5	186	11-7-02	0	0	0.00	1	0	0	3	3	0	0	0	1	2	.300	.364	.300	18.2	9.1	11
Cuenca, Angel	R-R	6-1	160	7-10-01	1	1	6.75	22	0	1	36	37	32	27	3	31	33	.270	.418	.416	18.6	17.5	177
Davis, Braden	L-L	5-11	180	4-9-01	3	2	3.18	17	14	0	74	43	28	26	4	52	103	.173	.320	.277	33.9	17.1	304
Day, Ernie	R-R	6-4	230	10-24-01	0	2	7.20	17	0	0	15	14	13	12	0	20	16	.255	.462	.327	20.3	25.3	79
Doyle, Liam	R-L	6-2	220	6-3-04	0	0	5.40	1	1	0	2	1	1	1	1	2	3	.200	.429	.800	42.9	28.6	7
Dutkanych, Andrew	R-R	6-3	220	7-31-03	0	0	2.51	6	6	0	14	9	4	4	2	10	21	.184	.322	.347	35.6	16.9	59
Fabian, Samuel	R-R	6-4	177	5-21-03	1	1	9.72	6	0	0	9	9	10	9	0	12	7	.281	.457	.344	15.2	26.1	46
Findlay, Jack	L-L	6-3	200	8-18-02	2	4	5.44	28	0	1	51	48	38	31	2	38	56	.246	.374	.354	23.4	15.9	239
Franklin, Tanner	R-R	6-5	225	5-25-04	0	0	0.00	1	1	0	2	1	0	0	0	1	4	.143	.250	.143	50.0	12.5	8
Galvez, Jovi	R-R	6-2	223	7-5-04	0	1	12.00	6	0	1	6	9	9	8	0	7	6	.375	.529	.458	17.6	20.6	34
Harrison, Charles	R-R	6-1	191	12-23-01	2	2	4.31	21	0	3	31	27	16	15	2	26	36	.229	.366	.381	24.7	17.8	146
Hence, Tink	R-R	6-1	185	8-6-02	0	0	0.00	3	3	0	6	4	0	0	0	3	8	.200	.333	.200	33.3	12.5	24
Hernandez, Maikel	S-R	6-0	163	2-20-03	0	0	0.00	1	0	0	1	0	0	0	0	0	0	.000	.000	.000	0.0	0.0	1
Herrera, Yordy	L-L	6-2	150	12-2-04	8	1	5.65	33	0	0	57	50	44	36	4	41	68	.233	.375	.330	25.3	15.2	269
Holiday, Aaron	R-R	6-3	205	5-28-00	1	0	2.08	8	0	0	13	7	4	3	1	8	16	.152	.286	.239	28.1	14.0	57
King, Joseph	R-R	6-1	194	2-23-01	2	0	1.69	4	0	0	5	1	1	1	0	5	8	.059	.059	.235	47.1	0.0	17
Kublick, Hunter	R-R	6-4	200	7-1-03	3	0	5.19	11	0	0	17	25	10	10	1	9	13	.373	.455	.507	16.7	11.5	78
Lin, Chen-Wei	R-R	6-7	188	11-22-01	0	0	0.00	1	1	0	2	0	0	0	0	0	1	.000	.167	.000	66.7	16.7	6
Lopez, Bruno	R-R	6-4	220	4-18-02	0	0	1.50	4	0	1	6	2	1	1	1	0	10	.100	.100	.500	50.0	0.0	20
Mack, Bernard	R-R	6-2	160	10-24-05	2	1	2.63	4	2	0	14	8	4	4	1	14	17	.178	.393	.289	27.9	23.0	61
Mathews, Quinn	L-L	6-4	192	10-4-00	0	0	0.00	1	1	0	3	2	0	0	0	0	4	.182	.182	.182	36.4	0.0	11
Menes, Ruben	R-R	6-3	185	4-17-02	0	2	14.63	3	3	0	8	13	16	13	2	6	6	.333	.426	.590	12.8	12.8	47
Nunez, Edwin	R-R	6-3	195	11-5-01	0	0	1.93	5	0	0	5	6	1	1	0	2	3	.316	.435	.368	13.0	8.7	23
Odle, Jacob	R-R	6-5	215	11-30-03	0	5	6.28	13	13	0	43	39	30	30	1	35	54	.252	.395	.361	27.7	17.9	195
Olsen, Bobby	R-R	6-0	210	8-31-01	2	0	3.00	5	0	0	15	10	5	5	0	3	16	.182	.224	.218	27.6	5.2	58
Picone, Domenic	R-R	5-9	185	10-16-00	2	0	2.53	5	0	1	11	4	3	3	0	4	12	.114	.200	.114	30.0	10.0	40
Ramirez, Keiverson	R-R	6-1	170	4-5-06	2	0	2.45	3	1	0	11	10	3	3	0	6	4	.238	.333	.333	8.3	12.5	48
Reyes, Alan	R-R	5-9	176	10-25-03	2	0	2.49	13	0	0	22	23	9	6	2	7	26	.271	.333	.376	28.0	7.5	93
Rom, Drew	L-L	6-2	215	12-15-99	0	1	1.00	3	3	0	9	3	1	1	0	3	12	.182	.182	.273	39.4	0.0	33
Savacool, Jason	R-R	6-1	210	5-21-02	4	2	1.61	11	10	0	56	37	14	10	2	16	46	.189	.254	.260	21.5	7.5	214
Sequera, Leonel	R-R	6-0	190	8-6-05	5	10	4.33	24	24	0	108	107	55	52	4	41	99	.258	.340	.341	20.9	8.7	473
Showalter, Zack	R-R	6-2	195	1-23-04	2	1	2.70	7	0	0	10	4	3	3	0	3	11	.133	.395	.133	14.0	25.6	43
Sparks, Nolan	R-R	5-10	185	8-12-02	4	6	4.85	18	12	1	72	61	44	39	7	46	78	.227	.346	.364	24.1	14.2	323
Steinbaugh, Conor	R-R	6-0	205	5-22-99	0	2	5.40	11	0	1	13	11	8	8	1	6	10	.220	.381	.400	15.0	15.6	64
Thompson, Brandt	R-R	5-9	180	7-4-02	2	6	3.84	16	15	0	80	71	34	34	15	17	64	.232	.272	.425	19.8	5.2	324
Van Dyke, Tyler	R-R	6-2	225	8-4-03	0	0	2.57	5	5	0	14	11	4	4	1	3	12	.212	.255	.288	21.8	5.5	55
Vargas, Giovanni	R-R	6-1	179	3-3-06	0	0	45.00	1	0	0	1	5	6	5	0	7	5	1	.571	.700	1.000	10.0	20.0	17
Watson, Michael	L-L	6-2	190	6-18-02	0	1	8.59	4	0	1	7	8	7	7	0	4	10	.240	.367	.360	33.3	13.3	30
Watts, Anthony	R-R	6-4	175	3-8-04	0	1	13.50	3	0	0	5	3	8	7	2	6	3	.273	.357	.818	21.4	7.1	14
Wood, Zeke	R-R	6-4	210	3-2-00	0	0	9.45	8	0	5	7	8	7	7	1	4	7	.286	.375	.536	21.9	12.5	32
Worley, Christian	R-R	6-1	170	6-14-02	1	1	3.89	29	0	1	39	32	18	17	1	30	42	.232	.401	.312	22.6	16.1	186
Ynfante, Nelfy	R-R	6-3	168	2-1-05	5	6	4.60	24	13	2	90	98	50	46	8	44	83	.277	.357	.418	20.3	10.8	409

Fielding

Catcher	PCT	G	PO	A	E	DP	PB
Birge	1.000	1	7	2	0	0	0
Caraballo	.986	8	62	6	1	1	2
Heath	.992	11	116	7	1	1	2

	PCT	G	PO	A	E	DP	PB
Hernandez, S	.989	50	495	42	6	2	3
Kross	.988	17	159	12	2	0	4
Rodriguez	.986	43	395	28	6	3	4

First Base	PCT	G	PO	A	E	DP
Caraballo	1.000	8	58	3	0	6
Dattalo	1.000	3	22	1	0	2
Gurevitch	1.000	20	154	9	0	12

	PCT	G	PO	A	E	DP
Hernandez, M	.983	10	59	0	1	4
Hernandez, S	.984	29	173	8	3	17
Kross	.994	20	161	11	1	17
Lloyd	1.000	2	18	3	0	1
McGee	1.000	1	3	0	0	0
Ortiz	.974	31	211	18	6	17
Salazar	.986	11	68	2	1	2

Second Base	PCT	G	PO	A	E	DP
Encarnacion	1.000	3	4	5	0	0
Haskins	1.000	4	6	17	0	2
Martin	.954	55	103	147	12	32
McGee	.986	20	33	37	1	4
Mejia	.942	34	49	65	7	12
Salazar	.920	8	9	14	2	4
Taveras	1.000	2	1	3	0	1
Weingartner	.946	9	11	24	2	5

Third Base	PCT	G	PO	A	E	DP
Dattalo	.920	11	6	17	2	0
Encarnacion	.947	9	6	12	1	1
Flores	.958	12	9	14	1	0
Lloyd	1.000	1	1	2	0	0
Martin	1.000	4	0	13	0	0
McGee	.970	51	32	66	3	7
Ortiz	.932	38	39	70	8	7
Salazar	1.000	9	5	14	0	1
Taveras	1.000	1	1	2	0	0

Shortstop	PCT	G	PO	A	E	DP
Encarnacion	.946	63	88	157	14	33
Flores	.906	10	10	19	3	6
Haskins	.875	3	3	4	1	1
Martin	.962	4	14	11	1	2
McGee	.964	8	13	14	1	2
Mejia	.892	32	30	53	10	12
Weingartner	.978	12	17	28	1	3

Outfield	PCT	G	PO	A	E	DP
Cho	1.000	3	4	0	0	0
Church	1.000	3	5	1	0	0
Cordoba	.982	35	52	3	1	0
Honeyman	1.000	27	54	2	0	1
Lloyd	1.000	1	3	0	0	0
Madron	.955	25	42	0	2	0
Martin	.923	6	12	0	1	0
Miura	1.000	21	47	2	0	0
Nickens	1.000	9	22	0	0	0
Pena	.977	100	166	6	4	1
Pino	.960	90	134	10	6	1
Suarez	1.000	71	132	5	0	0
Ugueto	1.000	5	8	0	0	0

FCL CARDINALS — ROOKIE
FLORIDA COMPLEX LEAGUE

Batting	B-T	Ht.	Wt.	DOB	AVG	OBP	SLG	G	PA	AB	R	H	2B	3B	HR	RBI	BB	HBP	SH	SF	SO	SB	CS	BB%	SO%
Almonte, Hancel	R-R	6-1	193	12-6-05	.145	.185	.248	42	145	124	10	18	5	0	0	14	14	4	0	3	63	6	0	9.7	43.4
Arthur, Andru	L-L	6-1	176	11-1-05	.179	.385	.239	41	156	117	21	21	4	0	1	9	30	9	0	0	48	13	3	19.2	30.8
Asprilla, Paulo	R-R	5-8	177	4-28-06	.196	.295	.215	34	123	107	10	21	2	0	0	14	14	1	0	0	22	1	1	11.4	17.9
Batista, Arfeni	R-R	6-0	161	9-4-04	.222	.300	.222	3	10	9	0	2	0	0	0	1	0	0	0	0	4	1	0	10.0	40.0
Cabrera, Romtres	R-R	6-0	182	9-13-03	.184	.349	.245	19	63	49	8	9	3	0	0	10	11	2	0	1	19	9	0	17.5	30.2
Caraballo, Heriberto	R-R	5-8	191	2-18-05	.256	.420	.333	14	50	39	8	10	3	0	0	5	8	3	0	0	9	3	1	16.0	18.0
Cordoba, Jose	R-R	5-11	165	1-3-03	.050	.095	.050	6	21	20	3	1	0	0	0	1	1	0	0	0	6	0	0	4.8	28.6
Guerrero, Yancel	R-R	6-1	169	4-06-04	.219	.337	.308	48	176	146	23	32	7	0	2	19	17	10	1	2	49	26	6	9.7	27.8
Junco, Yoerny	S-R	5-9	165	11-8-04	.222	.347	.303	33	118	99	14	22	6	1	0	14	18	1	0	0	28	7	4	15.3	23.7
Loaiza, Alejandro	R-R	5-11	163	12-23-03	.265	.342	.441	14	38	34	4	9	3	0	1	6	4	0	0	0	10	0	0	10.5	26.3
Lopez, Chris	R-R	5-9	175	6-28-05	.233	.343	.367	13	35	30	3	7	1	0	1	4	5	0	0	0	9	0	0	14.3	25.7
Martin, Christian	L-R	5-10	170	1-16-03	.214	.500	.286	6	22	14	3	3	1	0	0	0	4	0	0	0	3	1	0	18.2	13.6
Padilla, Yairo	S-R	6-0	170	6-28-07	.283	.396	.367	38	148	120	21	34	4	3	0	18	18	5	4	1	21	24	4	12.2	14.2
Ramos, Yaisel	R-R	6-4	185	2-20-03	.145	.267	.237	32	90	76	7	11	2	1	1	5	12	1	0	1	31	2	2	13.3	34.4
Rodriguez, Rainiel	R-R	5-10	197	1-4-07	.373	.513	.831	20	80	59	23	22	6	0	7	16	16	3	0	2	15	1	1	20.0	18.8
Rojas, Daniel	R-R	5-8	151	11-16-05	.214	.275	.270	40	139	126	14	27	1	0	2	10	10	1	0	1	34	14	5	7.2	24.5
Salazar, Johnfrank	R-R	6-1	159	8-5-03	.176	.263	.412	10	38	34	7	6	2	0	2	10	3	1	0	0	7	6	0	7.9	18.4
Taveras, Bracewell	R-R	6-0	182	6-5-06	.316	.318	.316	51	195	177	24	45	8	0	1	18	14	3	0	1	46	13	0	7.2	23.6
Velasquez, Facundo	S-R	6-2	179	1-16-06	.184	.351	.257	49	191	152	30	28	7	2	0	9	37	2	0	0	73	12	6	19.4	38.2

Pitching	B-T	Ht.	Wt.	DOB	W	L	ERA	G	GS	SV	IP	Hits	Runs	ER	HR	BB	SO	AVG	OBP	SLG	SO%	BB%	BF
Batista, Yadiel	L-L	6-3	170	4-17-04	4	2	3.06	12	5	2	47	41	17	16	4	9	42	.236	.280	.368	22.5	4.8	187
Bedell, Ian	R-R	6-2	214	9-5-99	0	0	0.00	1	1	0	2	1	0	0	0	0	2	.167	.167	.167	33.3	0.0	6
Bolivar, Andrew	R-R	6-1	170	10-20-05	2	3	8.19	11	4	0	30	34	31	27	2	31	28	.286	.437	.403	18.5	20.5	151
Cuello, Antoni	R-R	6-5	186	11-7-02	2	2	5.59	15	0	1	19	16	12	12	1	11	26	.229	.345	.457	30.6	12.9	85
Dutkanych, Andrew	R-R	6-3	220	7-31-03	0	1	10.80	3	3	0	3	6	4	4	0	1	4	.353	.389	.412	22.2	5.6	18
Fabian, Samuel	R-R	6-4	177	5-21-03	1	3	6.11	11	1	0	28	29	23	19	1	18	28	.257	.372	.363	20.4	13.1	137
Galvez, Jovi	R-R	6-2	223	7-5-04	1	1	8.53	15	0	1	19	21	22	18	0	25	18	.292	.500	.333	17.0	23.6	106
Harrison, Charles	R-R	6-1	191	12-23-01	0	0	0.00	3	0	0	3	1	0	0	0	0	4	.091	.167	.091	33.3	0.0	12
Hence, Tink	R-R	6-1	185	8-6-02	0	0	0.00	1	1	0	1	1	0	0	0	1	1	.250	.400	.250	20.0	20.0	5
Holiday, Aaron	R-R	6-3	205	5-28-00	1	0	3.38	2	0	0	3	5	2	1	0	1	3	.455	.462	.636	23.1	7.7	13
Kaminsky, Rob	R-L	6-0	195	9-2-94	0	0	0.00	2	1	0	3	2	0	0	0	6	.167	.167	.167	50.0	0.0	12
Kublick, Hunter	R-R	6-4	200	7-1-03	1	1	5.00	6	5	0	9	8	7	5	1	5	12	.222	.333	.361	28.6	11.9	42
Loaiza, Alejandro	R-R	5-11	163	12-23-03	1	0	6.00	3	0	1	3	2	2	2	0	2	2	.182	.182	.182	14.3	14.3	14
Lopez, Bruno	R-R	6-4	220	4-18-02	1	0	5.87	17	0	1	15	10	12	10	0	21	31	.179	.439	.232	37.8	25.6	82
Lopez, Chris	R-R	5-9	175	6-28-05	0	0	0.00	1	0	0	0	0	0	0	0	0	0	.000	.000	.000	0.0	0.0	1
Mack, Bernard	L-L	6-3	160	10-24-05	0	2	5.70	12	7	0	36	27	25	23	1	35	49	.206	.379	.298	28.8	20.6	170
Mathews, Quinn	L-L	6-4	192	10-4-00	0	0	0.00	1	1	0	2	1	0	0	0	0	4	.143	.143	.143	57.1	0.0	7
Menes, Ruben	R-R	6-3	185	4-17-02	2	3	3.72	10	6	0	29	30	16	12	1	9	30	.259	.333	.362	23.3	7.0	129
Moran, Jefferson	R-R	6-1	155	6-4-04	0	1	2.45	6	4	0	15	11	7	4	0	13	23	.216	.358	.235	33.8	19.1	68
Nunez, Edwin	R-R	6-3	185	11-5-01	3	2	10.54	11	0	0	14	9	19	16	2	16	10	.184	.387	.245	17.9	23.9	67
Odle, Jacob	R-R	6-5	215	11-30-03	0	1	4.15	4	4	0	9	4	5	4	0	2	15	.118	.167	.235	41.7	5.6	36
Oliver, Ronny	R-R	6-2	155	1-1-04	0	2	4.11	11	6	2	31	20	18	14	1	15	40	.183	.313	.294	30.3	11.4	132
Paulino, Brailyn	R-R	6-0	185	4-4-04	0	2	6.00	4	0	1	6	7	6	4	1	7	5	.304	.467	.435	16.7	23.3	30
Ramirez, Keiverson	R-R	6-1	170	4-5-06	1	2	3.86	10	5	0	30	34	14	13	3	12	25	.286	.378	.413	18.0	8.6	139
Reyes, Alan	R-R	5-9	176	10-25-03	2	1	0.70	14	1	2	26	15	6	2	0	9	26	.155	.255	.206	23.6	8.2	110
Severino, Juan	R-R	6-0	165	6-6-04	0	1	3.27	8	0	1	11	10	5	4	0	3	15	.244	.304	.390	32.6	6.5	46
Showalter, Zack	R-R	6-2	195	1-23-04	0	0	0.00	2	0	0	5	2	0	0	0	1	3	.222	.300	.222	30.0	10.0	10
Vargas, Giovanni	R-R	6-1	179	3-3-06	2	1	3.32	10	1	0	19	17	9	7	1	5	11	.243	.312	.329	14.3	6.5	77

Fielding
C: Asprilla 24, Rodriguez 14, Caraballo 9, Salazar 6, Lopez 5. **1B:** Almonte 28, Guerrero 11, Loaiza 10, Caraballo 4, Salazar 3. **2B:** Taveras 28, Guerrero 10, Junco 10, Rojas 6, Martin 3. **3B:** Taveras 21, Junco 19, Guerrero 9, Rojas 5, Batista 3. **SS:** Padilla 35, Guerrero 15, Rojas 7. **LF:** Velasquez 15, Rojas 12, Arthur 11, Cabrera 8, Almonte 7, Guerrero 2, Martin 1, Ramos 1. **CF:** Velasquez 19, Arthur 18, Ramos 18, Cordoba 3, Cabrera 1, Rojas 1. **RF:** Velasquez 14, Rojas 12, Ramos 10, Cabrera 8, Arthur 6, Almonte 4, Guerrero 3, Cordoba 1

DSL CARDINALS — ROOKIE
DOMINICAN SUMMER LEAGUE

Batting	B-T	Ht.	Wt.	DOB	AVG	OBP	SLG	G	PA	AB	R	H	2B	3B	HR	RBI	BB	HBP	SH	SF	SO	SB	CS	BB%	SO%
Amoroso, Brayan	R-R	6-2	198	7-7-07	.228	.356	.276	38	149	123	17	28	3	0	1	17	21	4	0	1	30	1	1	14.1	20.1
Cabrera, Hector	R-R	6-3	160	12-9-07	.098	.230	.118	15	61	51	8	5	1	0	0	7	5	4	0	1	21	0	0	8.2	34.4
Cabrera, Juan Pablo	R-R	5-11	185	11-11-06	.247	.385	.400	27	104	85	13	21	5	1	2	14	15	4	0	0	17	2	0	14.4	16.3
Chaparro, Jhonny	L-R	6-0	176	1-15-07	.200	.365	.246	20	85	65	8	13	1	1	0	13	15	3	0	2	8	1	1	17.6	9.4
Cordero, Michael	R-R	6-1	170	8-24-08	.212	.359	.356	32	128	104	21	22	6	0	3	16	21	3	0	0	41	1	0	16.4	32.0
Dos Santos, Sebastian	S-R	6-0	140	1-29-08	.313	.452	.570	38	166	128	44	40	13	4	4	26	30	5	0	3	29	13	4	18.1	17.5
Guribe, Edward	R-R	6-1	195	11-16-06	.248	.346	.436	36	159	133	22	33	10	0	5	24	15	7	0	4	27	0	0	9.4	17.0
Hernandez, Miguel	R-R	6-0	145	6-2-08	.281	.408	.444	36	169	135	30	38	5	1	5	34	25	6	0	3	35	15	4	14.8	20.7
Hunter, Kenly	R-R	6-0	156	5-9-08	.314	.442	.400	37	173	140	41	44	6	3	0	15	24	8	0	0	20	25	2	13.9	11.6
Lebron, Cristofer	R-R	6-2	170	3-20-07	.277	.402	.428	47	194	159	36	44	12	0	4	35	29	5	0	1	39	12	6	14.9	20.1
Lucena, Yaxson	L-R	6-0	190	7-23-07	.299	.442	.469	42	190	147	35	44	10	3	3	32	30	10	0	3	20	4	3	15.8	10.5
Perez, Jesus	R-R	5-11	165	10-4-07	.241	.302	.379	26	96	87	17	21	7	1	1	13	8	0	0	1	25	6	0	8.3	26.0
Portolatin, Yeferson	S-R	5-10	170	11-29-07	.226	.483	.374	40	174	115	43	26	9	1	2	21	51	7	0	1	31	23	4	29.3	17.8
Rujano, Juan	R-R	6-3	185	12-14-07	.279	.405	.418	35	148	122	25	34	8	0	3	23	19	7	0	0	34	2	1	12.8	23.0
Saez, Christian	L-R	6-2	185	2-20-07	.225	.319	.375	11	47	40	7	9	1	1	1	8	6	0	0	1	18	0	0	12.8	38.3
Strop, Royel	L-L	6-1	178	6-4-08	.226	.345	.355	24	110	93	19	21	7	1	1	11	14	3	0	0	34	2	1	12.7	30.9
Takahashi, Lucas	L-L	5-10	170	7-18-08	.103	.438	.103	12	48	29	6	3	0	0	0	2	17	1	0	1	10	2	1	35.4	20.8

Pitching	B-T	Ht.	Wt.	DOB	W	L	ERA	G	GS	SV	IP	Hits	Runs	ER	HR	BB	SO	AVG	OBP	SLG	SO%	BB%	BF
Baez, Jarol	R-R	6-1	200	10-21-05	2	0	5.16	14	2	1	23	17	15	13	0	29	28	.210	.412	.259	24.6	25.4	114
Cabrera, Jan	R-R	6-3	196	2-14-05	3	1	3.93	9	9	0	37	37	19	16	1	10	32	.262	.323	.348	20.6	6.5	155
Cana, Hendrick	L-L	6-0	181	12-20-07	2	0	2.43	11	4	0	37	28	11	10	3	20	37	.207	.321	.333	23.3	12.6	159
Chinchilla, Gabriel	R-R	6-3	163	10-20-06	3	2	4.84	12	10	0	48	56	27	26	1	21	50	.290	.361	.399	23.1	9.7	216
Correa, Michael	R-R	6-3	168	8-6-05	0	1	0.00	3	0	0	3	1	1	0	0	2	3	.111	.273	.111	27.3	18.2	11
Cruz, Xavier	R-R	6-3	153	9-4-05	0	2	4.32	9	8	0	25	18	15	12	0	19	30	.205	.351	.216	27.0	17.1	111
Fernandez, Ricardo	R-R	6-4	181	8-10-08	0	1	8.10	14	0	0	13	15	18	12	2	18	20	.306	.507	.510	28.2	25.4	71
Franco, Branneli	R-R	6-3	187	2-5-07	0	0	3.31	10	2	0	16	12	8	6	0	5	16	.200	.314	.267	22.9	7.1	70
Garcia, Jesus	S-R	5-11	141	1-25-06	2	1	2.78	14	0	2	23	15	7	7	2	7	30	.181	.269	.265	32.3	7.5	93
Garcia, Juan	R-R	6-2	187	5-30-08	4	2	3.40	12	10	0	48	48	19	18	0	4	38	.264	.279	.396	19.8	2.1	192
Gomez, Daniel	R-R	6-1	184	1-6-08	1	5	5.11	12	6	0	44	53	27	25	4	13	43	.296	.344	.413	22.1	6.7	195
Lopez, Reiner	R-R	6-8	196	4-11-06	3	3	4.85	13	0	1	26	25	19	14	0	11	22	.245	.319	.324	19.5	9.7	113
Martinez, Guanchi	R-R	6-0	185	8-17-06	0	1	6.00	2	0	0	3	2	2	2	1	4	1	.222	.533	.556	6.7	26.7	15
Olivero, Pedro	R-R	6-2	165	5-24-07	1	0	9.58	14	0	0	21	33	24	22	0	10	12	.379	.461	.517	11.8	9.8	102
Paulino, Brailyn	R-R	6-0	185	4-26-06	0	0	7.00	6	0	0	9	8	8	7	0	5	9	.229	.364	.371	20.5	11.4	44
Peralta, Kriscol	R-R	6-6	221	12-15-07	0	0	6.08	11	0	0	13	16	9	9	5	13	8	.302	.387	.528	21.0	8.1	62
Reyes, Briam	R-R	5-11	180	8-14-07	5	1	5.31	13	0	1	20	24	12	12	4	5	20	.296	.341	.543	22.7	5.7	88
Rodriguez, Beiker	L-R	5-11	165	3-7-07	3	1	10.13	13	0	0	16	29	23	18	2	14	17	.403	.500	.556	19.3	15.9	88
Rodriguez, Ryan	R-R	6-0	168	8-31-07	1	4	14.09	14	0	0	15	23	30	24	1	26	13	.343	.542	.522	13.3	26.5	98
Zulueta, Earle	R-R	6-4	180	12-20-06	0	1	3.29	6	5	0	14	9	6	5	1	5	11	.188	.264	.271	20.8	9.4	53

Fielding
C: J. Cabrera 21, Rujano 15, Chaparro 13, H. Cabrera 9. **1B:** Amoroso 24, Cordero 14, Saez 9, Chaparro 6, Cabrera 5. **2B:** Portolatin 30, Dos Santos 15, Lebron 12. **3B:** Guribe 31, Cordero 18, Portolatin 7, Perez 1. **SS:** Hernandez 31, Dos Santos 24, Portolatin 2. **LF:** Perez 24, Lebron 14, Takahashi 10, Lucena 9, Strop 2. **CF:** Hunter 29, Strop 15, Lebron 13, Takahashi 2. **RF:** Lucena 27, Amoroso 13, Lebron 8, Hunter 7, Strop 2

San Diego Padres

SEASON SYNOPSIS: The Padres went 90-72, marking the first time in franchise history (dating to 1969) that they've won 90 or more games in consecutive seasons. They had baseball's best bullpen (3.06 ERA), but a sputtering offense left San Diego three games behind the Dodgers in the NL West and came up short in a three-game Wild Card Series loss to the Cubs.

HIGH POINT: The Padres went 52-29 at home, tied for the third-best home record in MLB, helping them draw a franchise-record 3.4 million fans, continuing what has been steady growth. They won seven straight at home to open the season, and they won five in a row at Petco in late August, against division rivals San Francisco and Los Angeles, to take a one-game lead in the division. Trade pickup Nestor Cortes' start and win Aug. 23, in front of 46,236, was the last day they held first place.

LOW POINT: San Diego's 152 homers were its fewest in a full season in a decade, and the offense wasn't good enough for them to earn a home postseason series. They hit .189 over three games at Wrigley Field and scored just five runs.

NOTABLE ROOKIES: Righty Ryan Bergert broke into the rotation as a solid depth piece before being traded to the Royals. Lefty Kyle Hart, signed out of the KBO, provided a versatile if homer-prone swingman (3-3, 5.86) and made the playoff roster. David Morgan, an NDFA signed in 2022 out of NAIA Hope International (Calif.), earned a role in the talented, deep bullpen (1-3, 2.66, 47 IP/50 SO).

KEY TRANSACTIONS: GM A.J. Preller was as active as ever. In the offseason he trimmed payroll and dumpster dived for free agents such as Gavin Sheets (.252/.317/.429, 19 HR), who was nontendered by the White Sox. He worked out better than C Martin Maldonado, IF Jose Iglesias or OF Jason Heyward, none of whom posted an OPS above .600. True to form, though, Preller used trades for fortify the roster for the home stretch, trading top prospect Leo De Vries, RHP Braden Nett and other prospects to the A's for JP Sears and 104 mph-throwing reliever Mason Miller (0.77 ERA, 45 SO in 23 IP), who was electric in the postseason, striking out all eight batters he faced. Preller traded Bergert and RHP Stephen Kolek to Kansas City for a new primary catcher, Freddy Fermin, and added OF Ramon Laureano and 1B/DH Ryan O'Hearn from Baltimore to fortify the offense. Laureano missed the postseason due to a broken bone in his right hand, a key blow to the lineup.

OPENING DAY PAYROLL: $208,909,333 (9th)

PLAYERS OF THE YEAR

MAJOR LEAGUE
Nick Pivetta
RHP
13-5, 2.87 ERA
190 SO, 50 BB in career-high 181.2 IP

MINOR LEAGUE
Miguel Mendez
RHP
(A,A+,AA)
3.22 ERA in 95 IP, 118 SO, .209 AVG

ORGANIZATION LEADERS

Batting		*Qualifiers
MAJORS		
* AVG	Luis Arraez	.292
* OPS	Fernando Tatis	.814
HR	Manny Machado	27
RBI	Manny Machado	95
MINORS		
* AVG	Luis Campusano, El Paso	.336
* OBP	Luis Campusano, El Paso	.441
* SLG	Luis Campusano, El Paso	.595
* OPS	Luis Campusano, El Paso	1.036
R	Yonathan Perlaza, El Paso	106
H	Yonathan Perlaza, El Paso	166
TB	Yonathan Perlaza, El Paso	276
2B	Yonathan Perlaza, El Paso	49
3B	Clay Dungan, El Paso	8
HR	Luis Campusano, El Paso	25
RBI	Yonathan Perlaza, El Paso	113
BB	Ryan Jackson, San Antonio/Fort Wayne/L. Elsinore	91
SO	Rosman Verdugo, Fort Wayne	158
SB	Kai Roberts, Fort Wayne/ACL Padres	35

Pitching		# Qualifiers
MAJORS		
W	Nick Pivetta	13
W	Adrian Morejon	13
# ERA	Nick Pivetta	2.87
SO	Dylan Cease	215
SV	Robert Suarez	40
MINORS		
W	Enmanuel Pinales, San Antonio/Fort Wayne	10
L	Jared Kollar, El Paso/San Antonio	13
# ERA	Luis Gutierrez, El Paso/S. Ant./Ft. Wayne/L. Elsin.	3.31
G	Raul Brito, El Paso	48
GS	Jackson Wolf, El Paso/San Antonio	27
SV	Manuel Castro, El Paso/San Antonio	11
IP	Jackson Wolf, El Paso/San Antonio	129
BB	Jagger Haynes, San Antonio	62
SO	Jackson Wolf, El Paso/San Antonio	134
AVG	Luis Gutierrez, El Paso/S. Ant./Ft. Wayne/L. Elsin.	.228

2025 PERFORMANCE

General Manager: A.J. Preller. **Farm Director:** Ryley Westman. **Scouting Director:** Chris Kemp.

Class	Team	League	W	L	PCT	Finish	Manager
Majors	San Diego Padres	National	90	72	.556	5 (15)	Mike Shildt
Triple-A	El Paso Chihuahuas	Pacific Coast	81	68	.544	4 (10)	Pete Zamora
Double-A	San Antonio Missions	Texas	65	72	.474	9 (10)	Luke Montz
High-A	Fort Wayne TinCaps	Midwest	56	75	.427	9 (12)	Lukas Ray
Low-A	Lake Elsinore Storm	California	56	76	.424	8 (8)	Brian Burres
Rookie	ACL Padres	Arizona Complex	14	46	.233	15 (15)	Jhonaldo Pozo
Rookie	DSL Padres Brown	Dominican	20	35	.364	46 (52)	Diego Cedeno
Rookie	DSL Padres Gold	Dominican	39	17	.696	2 (52)	Brallan Perez
Overall 2025 Minor League Record			331	389	.460	26th (30)	

ORGANIZATION STATISTICS

SAN DIEGO PADRES
NATIONAL LEAGUE

Batting	B-T	Ht.	Wt.	DOB	AVG	OBP	SLG	G	PA	AB	R	H	2B	3B	HR	RBI	BB	HBP	SH	SF	SO	SB	CS	BB%	SO%
Arraez, Luis	L-R	5-10	175	4-9-97	.292	.327	.392	154	675	620	66	181	30	4	8	61	34	2	12	7	21	11	4	5.0	3.1
Bogaerts, Xander	R-R	6-2	218	10-1-92	.263	.328	.391	136	552	491	63	129	30	0	11	53	48	4	1	8	94	20	2	8.7	17.0
Brooks, Trenton	L-L	5-10	195	7-3-95	.146	.186	.268	25	43	41	5	6	2	0	1	2	2	0	0	0	13	0	0	4.7	30.2
Campusano, Luis	R-R	5-11	232	9-29-98	.000	.000	.000	10	27	21	0	0	0	0	0	0	6	0	0	0	11	0	0	22.2	40.7
Cronenworth, Jake	L-R	6-0	187	1-21-94	.246	.367	.377	135	515	419	61	103	20	1	11	59	69	15	4	7	107	3	3	13.4	20.8
Diaz, Elias	R-R	6-1	223	11-17-90	.204	.270	.337	106	283	255	34	52	7	0	9	29	21	2	5	0	74	0	0	7.4	26.1
Fermin, Freddy	R-R	5-9	200	5-16-95	.244	.278	.339	42	139	127	15	31	6	0	2	14	6	0	6	0	28	0	0	4.3	20.1
Gonzalez, Oscar	R-R	6-4	240	1-10-98	.220	.246	.237	21	61	59	2	13	1	0	0	4	2	0	0	0	13	0	1	3.3	21.3
Gurriel, Yuli	R-R	6-0	215	6-9-84	.111	.200	.139	16	40	36	2	4	1	0	0	3	4	0	0	0	8	0	0	10.0	20.0
Heyward, Jason	L-L	6-5	240	8-9-89	.176	.223	.271	34	95	85	9	15	2	0	2	12	6	0	3	2	0	0	1	6.3	21.1
Iglesias, Jose	R-R	5-11	195	1-5-90	.229	.298	.294	112	343	306	29	70	11	0	3	36	24	7	4	2	56	5	1	7.0	16.3
Joe, Connor	R-R	6-0	205	8-16-92	.000	.100	.000	7	10	9	0	0	0	0	0	0	1	0	0	0	6	0	0	10.0	60.0
Johnson, Bryce	S-R	6-1	195	10-27-95	.342	.383	.434	55	84	76	9	26	4	0	1	8	3	2	3	0	19	4	1	3.6	22.6
Laureano, Ramon	R-R	5-11	203	7-15-94	.269	.323	.489	50	198	182	27	49	9	2	9	30	13	2	0	1	47	3	1	6.6	23.7
Lockridge, Brandon	R-R	5-11	185	3-14-97	.216	.258	.261	47	95	88	9	19	4	0	0	5	4	1	2	0	24	8	1	4.2	25.3
Machado, Manny	R-R	6-3	218	7-6-92	.275	.335	.460	159	678	615	91	169	33	0	27	95	55	3	0	5	131	14	3	8.1	19.3
Maldonado, Martin	R-R	6-0	230	8-16-86	.204	.245	.327	64	161	147	11	30	6	0	4	12	8	0	6	0	57	0	0	5.0	35.4
McCoy, Mason	R-R	5-11	185	3-31-95	.136	.269	.182	18	26	22	5	3	1	0	0	1	3	1	0	0	7	2	0	11.5	26.9
Merrill, Jackson	L-R	6-3	195	4-19-03	.264	.317	.457	115	483	440	59	116	25	6	16	67	33	4	1	5	108	1	2	6.8	22.4
O'Hearn, Ryan	L-L	6-3	220	7-26-93	.276	.350	.387	50	183	163	22	45	6	0	4	20	16	3	0	1	46	0	0	8.7	25.1
Ornelas, Tirso	L-R	6-2	200	3-11-00	.071	.188	.071	7	16	14	0	1	0	0	0	0	1	2	0	0	2	0	0	12.5	12.5
Sheets, Gavin	L-R	6-5	230	4-23-96	.252	.317	.429	145	545	492	57	124	28	1	19	71	44	5	0	4	107	2	1	8.1	19.6
Tatis, Fernando	R-R	6-3	217	1-2-99	.268	.368	.446	155	691	594	111	159	27	2	25	71	89	6	0	2	129	32	7	12.9	18.7
Wade, Tyler	L-R	6-1	188	11-23-94	.206	.309	.252	60	127	107	13	22	1	2	0	9	15	1	4	0	31	1	2	11.8	24.4
Wagner, Will	L-R	5-11	210	7-29-98	.133	.235	.133	15	17	15	2	2	0	0	0	0	2	0	0	0	2	0	0	11.8	11.8

Pitching	B-T	Ht.	Wt.	DOB	W	L	ERA	G	GS	SV	IP	Hits	Runs	ER	HR	BB	SO	AVG	OBP	SLG	SO%	BB%	BF
Adam, Jason	R-R	6-3	229	8-4-91	8	4	1.93	65	0	0	65	50	18	14	4	25	70	.210	.291	.282	25.9	9.3	270
Bergert, Ryan	R-R	6-1	210	3-8-00	1	0	2.78	11	7	0	36	24	11	11	4	18	34	.186	.291	.310	22.8	12.1	149
Cease, Dylan	R-R	6-2	195	12-28-95	8	12	4.55	32	32	0	168	152	91	85	21	71	215	.239	.318	.399	29.8	9.8	722
Cortes, Nestor	R-L	5-11	210	12-10-94	1	3	5.47	6	6	0	26	29	16	16	8	13	21	.282	.370	.544	17.6	10.9	119
Cruz, Omar	L-L	6-0	210	1-26-99	0	0	4.91	2	0	0	4	4	2	2	0	3	5	.267	.389	.333	27.8	16.7	18
Darvish, Yu	R-R	6-5	220	8-16-86	5	5	5.38	15	15	0	72	66	44	43	14	19	68	.245	.310	.465	23.0	6.4	296
Estrada, Jeremiah	S-R	6-1	185	11-1-98	4	5	3.45	77	0	3	73	58	34	28	12	27	108	.216	.291	.390	35.5	8.9	304
Gillaspie, Logan	R-R	6-2	215	4-17-97	0	0	2.57	3	0	0	7	7	2	2	1	4	4	.269	.387	.385	12.9	12.9	31
Hart, Kyle	L-L	6-5	200	11-23-92	3	3	5.86	20	6	0	43	38	28	28	9	13	37	.233	.296	.448	20.7	7.3	179
Hoeing, Bryan	R-R	6-6	210	10-9-96	1	0	3.38	7	0	0	8	9	3	3	0	3	5	.281	.333	.406	13.9	8.3	36
Jacob, Alek	R-R	6-3	190	6-16-98	1	0	5.13	29	0	0	33	36	20	19	6	14	23	.275	.366	.466	15.0	9.2	153
King, Michael	R-R	6-3	210	5-25-95	5	3	3.44	15	15	0	73	62	31	28	12	26	76	.224	.299	.397	24.7	8.4	308
Kolek, Stephen	R-R	6-3	210	4-18-97	4	5	4.18	14	14	0	80	78	40	37	8	26	56	.262	.330	.376	16.7	7.7	336
Marinaccio, Ron	R-R	6-2	205	7-1-95	0	0	0.84	7	0	0	11	6	1	1	0	4	12	.162	.238	.162	28.6	9.5	42
Matsui, Yuki	L-L	5-8	165	10-30-95	3	1	3.98	61	0	1	63	53	29	28	10	33	61	.227	.321	.416	22.4	12.1	272
Miller, Mason	R-R	6-5	200	8-24-98	0	0	0.77	22	0	2	23	7	2	2	1	10	45	.096	.205	.137	54.2	12.0	83
Morejon, Adrian	L-L	5-11	224	2-27-99	13	6	2.08	75	0	3	74	49	23	17	2	17	70	.186	.233	.358	24.5	5.9	286
Morgan, David	R-R	6-0	185	10-26-99	1	2	2.66	41	2	0	47	35	14	14	4	23	50	.208	.311	.327	25.9	11.9	193
Nunez, Eduarnil	R-R	6-2	170	6-7-99	0	0	3.86	4	0	0	5	4	2	2	1	4	2	.250	.429	.625	9.5	19.0	21
Peralta, Wandy	L-L	6-0	210	7-27-91	6	1	3.14	71	1	0	72	66	29	25	5	23	56	.234	.310	.354	20.1	9.6	313
Pivetta, Nick	R-R	6-5	214	2-14-93	13	5	2.87	31	31	0	182	129	63	58	22	50	190	.195	.253	.330	26.4	6.9	721
Reynolds, Sean	L-R	6-8	250	4-19-98	0	1	5.33	19	1	0	27	20	16	16	4	17	25	.206	.342	.371	21.4	14.5	117
Rodriguez, Bradgley	R-R	6-1	160	11-16-03	1	0	1.17	7	0	0	8	4	1	1	0	3	9	.160	.323	.200	29.0	9.7	31
Sears, JP	R-L	5-11	180	2-19-96	2	2	5.47	5	5	0	25	31	16	15	7	2	20	.306	.358	.580	18.0	6.3	111
Suarez, Robert	R-R	6-2	210	3-1-91	4	6	2.97	70	0	40	70	47	24	23	6	16	75	.189	.243	.293	27.9	5.9	269
Vasquez, Randy	R-R	6-0	165	11-3-98	6	7	3.84	28	26	0	134	125	59	57	16	52	78	.247	.323	.383	13.7	9.1	570

Wade, Tyler	L-R	6-1	188	11-23-94	0	0	9.00	1	0	0	1	2	1	1	0	1	0	.400	.500	.600	0.0	16.7	6
Waldron, Matt	R-R	6-2	185	9-26-96	0	1	7.71	1	1	0	5	6	4	4	1	6	3	.316	.480	.474	12.0	24.0	25

Fielding

Catcher	PCT	G	PO	A	E	DP	PB
Diaz	.989	105	676	21	8	2	2
Fermin	.993	42	386	18	3	1	4
Maldonado	.995	64	409	12	2	2	8

First Base	PCT	G	PO	A	E	DP
Arraez	.999	117	737	62	1	76
Cronenworth	1.000	13	76	3	0	9
Gurriel	1.000	4	22	1	0	2
Joe	1.000	1	4	0	0	1
O'Hearn	.989	27	170	7	2	12
Sheets	.988	13	74	9	1	8

Second Base	PCT	G	PO	A	E	DP
Arraez	1.000	14	12	14	0	4
Cronenworth	.975	118	166	221	10	57
Iglesias	.993	40	68	83	1	22

	PCT	G	PO	A	E	DP
McCoy	1.000	2	3	5	0	0
Wade	1.000	8	11	7	0	1
Wagner	1.000	4	1	4	0	1

Third Base	PCT	G	PO	A	E	DP
Iglesias	.957	24	13	32	2	5
Machado	.956	145	117	230	16	34
Wade	1.000	4	0	2	0	0
Wagner	.000	1	0	0	0	0

Shortstop	PCT	G	PO	A	E	DP
Bogaerts	.980	125	147	255	8	55
Cronenworth	1.000	13	8	23	0	2
Iglesias	.975	32	22	57	2	8
McCoy	.958	12	5	18	1	2
Wade	1.000	2	1	2	0	1

Outfield	PCT	G	PO	A	E	DP
Brooks	1.000	2	3	0	0	0
Gonzalez	.963	19	25	1	1	0
Heyward	1.000	36	48	0	0	0
Iglesias	1.000	1	2	0	0	0
Joe	1.000	2	2	0	0	0
Johnson	1.000	54	59	0	0	0
Laureano	.989	58	85	4	1	1
Lockridge	.969	44	61	1	2	0
Merrill	.997	114	284	9	1	1
O'Hearn	1.000	3	5	0	0	0
Ornelas	1.000	6	9	0	0	0
Sheets	.990	64	94	3	1	0
Tatis	.992	153	351	5	3	3
Wade	1.000	39	66	2	0	0

EL PASO CHIHUAHUAS

PACIFIC COAST LEAGUE

TRIPLE-A

SAN DIEGO PADRES

Batting	B-T	Ht.	Wt.	DOB	AVG	OBP	SLG	G	PA	AB	R	H	2B	3B	HR	RBI	BB	HBP	SH	SF	SO	SB	CS	BB%	SO%
Acuna, Francisco	R-R	5-7	150	1-12-00	.364	.452	.667	12	42	33	11	12	2	1	2	9	4	3	0	2	4	0	0	9.5	9.5
Brooks, Trenton	L-L	5-10	195	7-3-95	.275	.388	.491	90	399	324	59	89	23	1	15	68	64	1	2	8	63	3	0	16.0	15.8
Brosseau, Mike	R-R	5-11	203	3-15-94	.222	.308	.358	86	344	302	38	67	14	0	9	39	33	6	0	3	68	6	1	9.6	19.8
Campusano, Luis	R-R	5-11	232	9-29-98	.336	.441	.595	105	475	393	83	132	25	1	25	95	72	4	0	3	82	2	0	15.2	17.3
Castanon, Marcos	R-R	6-0	195	3-23-99	.300	.386	.550	16	70	60	14	18	4	1	3	18	7	2	0	1	19	0	0	10.0	27.1
Cronenworth, Jake	L-R	6-0	187	1-21-94	.500	.750	1.250	2	8	4	5	2	0	0	1	2	4	0	0	0	2	0	0	50.0	25.0
Dungan, Clay	L-R	5-11	190	6-2-96	.273	.368	.448	140	625	527	105	144	34	8	14	80	73	10	8	7	142	30	7	11.7	22.7
Duran, Rodolfo	R-R	5-8	181	2-19-98	.288	.344	.503	86	352	316	63	91	16	2	16	73	27	1	6	2	68	3	1	7.7	19.3
Gomez, Moises	R-R	5-11	200	8-27-98	.000	.000	.000	1	4	4	0	0	0	0	0	0	0	0	0	0	3	0	0	0.0	75.0
Gonzalez, Oscar	R-R	6-4	240	1-10-98	.333	.368	.704	12	57	54	13	18	3	1	5	16	3	0	0	0	14	1	1	5.3	24.6
Heyward, Jason	L-L	6-5	240	8-9-89	.095	.174	.143	5	23	21	2	2	1	0	0	1	1	1	0	0	8	0	0	4.3	34.8
Joe, Connor	R-R	6-0	205	8-16-92	.267	.405	.350	16	74	60	16	16	5	0	0	4	13	1	0	0	10	4	2	17.6	13.5
Johnson, Bryce	S-R	6-1	195	10-27-95	.303	.407	.458	42	172	142	28	43	11	1	3	22	22	3	5	0	40	10	2	12.8	23.3
Locastro, Tim	R-R	6-1	200	7-14-92	.270	.367	.433	104	414	344	69	93	21	4	9	52	36	19	10	4	67	32	5	8.7	16.2
Lockridge, Brandon	R-R	5-11	185	3-14-97	.291	.408	.468	21	99	79	19	23	4	2	2	6	15	2	1	2	17	7	0	15.2	17.2
Mathey, Jack	R-R	5-10	165	7-28-03	.250	.400	.250	3	5	4	0	1	0	0	0	0	2	0	0	0	1	0	0	20.0	20.0
McCoy, Mason	R-R	5-11	185	3-31-95	.272	.354	.450	90	386	331	62	90	22	2	11	59	43	2	5	5	99	17	7	11.1	25.6
Mondou, Nate	L-R	5-7	205	3-4-94	.000	.400	.422	130	552	467	69	144	27	4	6	74	65	9	7	4	79	8	6	11.8	14.3
Ornelas, Tirso	L-R	6-2	200	3-11-00	.289	.384	.456	82	371	318	63	92	21	0	16	57	46	4	1	2	64	7	2	12.4	17.3
Perlaza, Yonathan	S-R	5-9	170	11-10-98	.307	.391	.510	138	624	541	106	166	49	2	19	113	74	4	0	5	125	15	7	11.9	20.0
Reyes, Ripken	S-R	5-7	185	4-1-97	.273	.382	.373	42	139	110	21	30	7	2	0	19	15	5	8	1	13	0	0	10.8	9.4
Roberts, Cody	R-R	6-1	195	6-16-96	.223	.313	.321	39	133	112	20	25	5	0	2	11	16	0	2	3	46	2	0	12.0	34.6
Rosario, Eguy	R-R	5-7	150	8-25-99	.194	.264	.245	29	110	98	10	19	2	0	1	9	10	0	2	0	26	5	2	9.1	23.6
Sullivan, Brett	L-R	6-1	195	2-22-94	.231	.262	.308	10	42	39	4	9	1	1	0	9	2	0	0	1	10	0	0	4.8	23.8
Turbi, Emil	S-R	5-8	150	11-26-04	.500	.500	.500	2	6	4	0	1	0	0	0	0	2	0	0	0	1	0	0	33.3	16.7
Wade, Tyler	L-R	6-1	188	11-23-94	.279	.372	.356	23	121	104	18	29	5	0	1	12	15	1	0	1	26	10	2	12.4	21.5
Wagner, Will	L-R	5-11	210	7-29-98	.270	.333	.405	17	81	74	10	20	2	1	2	17	7	0	0	0	8	1	1	8.6	9.9
Wall, Forrest	L-R	6-0	195	11-20-95	.298	.384	.429	69	279	238	51	71	15	2	4	39	29	6	3	3	61	21	1	10.4	21.9

Pitching	B-T	Ht.	Wt.	DOB	W	L	ERA	G	GS	SV	IP	Hits	Runs	ER	HR	BB	SO	AVG	OBP	SLG	SO%	BB%	BF
Bellatti, Andrew	R-R	6-1	190	8-5-91	0	0	11.57	1	0	0	2	5	3	3	0	0	5	.476	.571	.619	17.9	17.9	28
Benjamin, Wes	R-L	6-2	210	7-26-93	4	8	6.42	28	22	1	108	131	94	77	16	49	88	.302	.376	.495	17.6	9.8	500
Bergert, Ryan	R-R	6-1	200	3-8-00	0	2	4.03	11	11	0	45	49	21	20	7	18	44	.283	.359	.474	22.6	9.2	195
Blanchard, Jason	R-L	6-0	185	6-25-97	3	3	6.70	32	1	0	43	44	35	32	5	24	44	.275	.397	.438	22.6	12.3	195
Brito, Raul	R-R	6-1	180	5-23-97	6	4	6.11	48	0	2	63	72	44	40	10	35	82	.288	.382	.508	27.6	11.8	297
Castro, Manuel	R-R	5-8	180	5-11-02	4	1	3.66	24	0	1	32	22	17	13	2	23	30	.198	.328	.342	21.7	16.7	138
Chirino, Harold	R-R	6-2	173	1-12-98	0	2	5.91	40	0	3	46	53	33	30	2	29	42	.286	.402	.395	18.7	12.9	225
Cienfuegos, Miguel	L-L	6-4	195	2-10-97	1	3	5.30	24	6	1	53	55	34	31	5	25	40	.268	.349	.356	17.2	10.8	232
Cosgrove, Tom	L-L	6-2	190	6-14-96	1	0	7.36	4	0	0	4	4	3	3	0	4	2	.286	.474	.429	10.5	21.1	19
Cruz, Omar	L-L	6-0	210	1-26-99	5	5	4.75	31	1	0	83	76	52	44	9	55	88	.241	.358	.371	23.2	14.5	379
Darvish, Yu	R-R	6-5	220	8-16-86	0	1	4.50	1	1	0	4	2	2	2	1	1	4	.154	.214	.231	28.6	7.1	14
Davis, Austin	L-L	6-4	235	2-3-93	0	1	11.91	11	1	1	11	15	15	15	1	10	12	.313	.459	.458	19.7	16.4	61
Edmondson, Clay	R-R	6-2	185	6-24-03	0	0	0.00	1	0	0	1	0	0	0	0	1	1	.000	.333	.000	16.7	16.7	6
Espada, Daison	R-R	6-0	170	2-22-97	2	0	4.80	12	0	0	15	14	9	8	3	11	21	.241	.362	.448	30.0	15.7	70
Gillaspie, Logan	R-R	6-2	215	4-17-97	1	3	7.08	18	13	0	55	72	43	43	9	21	45	.316	.377	.526	17.7	8.3	254
Gutierrez, Luis	L-L	6-0	175	7-31-03	0	0	5.40	1	1	0	5	6	4	3	1	0	6	.300	.333	.450	28.6	0	21
Hart, Kyle	L-L	6-5	200	11-23-92	4	4	4.10	20	10	0	64	63	35	29	6	34	52	.262	.356	.406	18.5	12.1	281
Higginbotham, Jake	L-L	6-0	175	11-19-96	2	2	8.88	16	0	2	24	39	24	24	3	16	24	.348	.435	.580	18.3	12.2	131
Hoeing, Bryan	R-R	6-6	210	10-19-96	1	0	4.70	14	0	0	15	21	8	8	1	6	16	.313	.378	.478	21.6	8.1	74
Jacob, Alek	L-R	6-3	190	6-16-98	4	2	5.27	26	0	2	27	23	18	16	4	17	39	.228	.347	.396	32.0	13.9	122

SAN DIEGO PADRES

Player	B-T	Ht	Wt	DOB																				
Jones, Stephen	R-R	6-4	195	7-30-97	0	0	6.14	6	1	1	7	12	5	5	0	4	6	.364	.432	.394	16.2	10.8	37	
King, Michael	R-R	6-3	210	5-25-95	0	0	16.20	1	1	0	3	4	6	6	2	1	5	.286	.375	.786	31.3	6.3	16	
Knehr, Reiss	L-R	6-2	205	11-3-96	2	2	2.70	18	0	8	17	9	6	5	2	7	24	.158	.262	.298	36.9	10.8	65	
Kolek, Stephen	R-R	6-3	210	4-18-97	1	0	6.00	6	6	0	27	38	19	18	4	5	21	.325	.360	.564	5.6	4.0	125	
Kollar, Jared	R-R	6-0	195	7-24-98	2	5	8.81	13	9	0	47	72	50	46	13	28	21	.362	.431	.638	9.1	12.1	232	
Kopps, Kevin	R-R	6-0	200	3-2-97	3	2	5.30	25	1	0	36	35	26	21	5	23	32	.250	.371	.400	19.2	13.8	167	
Krob, Austin	L-L	6-3	205	9-20-99	0	1	5.74	20	6	1	47	48	34	30	4	35	42	.261	.385	.397	18.6	15.5	226	
Lizarraga, Victor	R-R	6-3	180	11-30-03	1	0	1.80	2	2	0	10	8	3	2	0	6	5	.229	.372	.314	11.6	14.0	43	
Loewen, Carter	R-R	6-4	240	9-28-98	0	0	0.00	2	0	0	2	0	0	0	0	1	3	.000	.125	.000	37.5	12.5	8	
Marinaccio, Ron	R-R	6-2	205	7-1-95	6	0	5.05	41	0	6	46	48	28	26	7	21	51	.258	.343	.430	24.1	9.9	212	
Miralles, Maikel	R-R	5-11	160	10-22-04	0	0	54.00	1	0	0	1	4	4	4	1	2	1	.667	.750	1.167	12.5	25.0	8	
Moore, Andrew	L-R	6-5	205	8-11-99	0	1	13.50	2	0	0	2	3	3	3	0	2	2	.375	.500	.625	20.0	20.0	10	
Morgan, David	R-R	6-0	185	10-26-99	0	2	12.71	7	0	0	6	8	8	8	2	1	11	.320	.357	.600	39.3	3.6	28	
Nunez, Eduarnil	R-R	6-2	170	6-7-99	2	0	0.00	11	0	5	12	2	0	0	0	6	18	.054	.186	.054	41.9	14.0	43	
Pena, Francis	R-R	6-1	170	1-25-01	4	4	4.99	43	0	0	52	50	33	29	4	34	47	.255	.366	.383	19.8	14.3	237	
Reynolds, Sean	L-R	6-8	250	4-19-98	2	1	2.86	27	0	6	28	16	9	9	2	22	22	.170	.333	.266	18.3	18.3	120	
Roberts, Cody	R-R	6-1	195	6-16-96	0	0	7.71	2	0	0	2	3	2	2	1	2	1	.300	.417	.600	8.3	16.7	12	
Rodriguez, Bradley	R-R	6-1	160	11-16-03	2	0	3.14	15	0	0	14	9	5	5	0	11	7	.188	.339	.292	11.5	18.0	61	
Routzahn, Ethan	R-R	6-4	225	3-19-98	3	1	3.75	22	0	0	24	29	16	10	3	14	19	.293	.385	.485	16.1	11.9	118	
Sears, JP	R-L	5-11	192	2-19-96	1	0	3.29	4	4	0	14	12	5	5	3	6	16	.226	.305	.434	27.1	10.2	59	
Tamarez, Misael	R-R	6-1	206	1-16-00	1	1	9.00	7	0	0	14	24	15	14	4	12	12	.375	.412	.641	17.6	2.9	68	
Vasquez, Randy	R-R	6-0	165	11-3-98	0	1	5.63	2	2	0	8	7	5	5	1	5	6	.226	.324	.387	16.2	13.5	37	
Waldron, Matt	R-R	6-2	185	9-26-96	7	4	6.67	18	18	0	82	102	63	61	11	26	76	.309	.362	.506	20.7	7.1	368	
Wendelken, J.B.	R-R	6-1	242	3-24-93	0	0	0.00	2	0	1	2	0	0	0	1	1	5	.000	.600	.750	20.0	0.0	5	
Wolf, Jackson	L-L	6-7	205	4-22-99	7	3	5.47	22	22	0	104	119	76	63	12	44	103	.286	.359	.464	21.6	9.2	477	

Fielding

Catcher	PCT	G	PO	A	E	DP	PB
Campusano	.986	52	453	25	7	2	3
Duran	.983	69	530	38	10	2	8
Roberts	.976	32	239	8	6	0	7
Sullivan	.973	4	34	2	1	0	0

First Base	PCT	G	PO	A	E	DP
Brooks	.992	45	344	38	3	44
Brosseau	.984	8	57	5	1	2
Campusano	.988	14	74	7	1	11
Castanon	1.000	2	12	1	0	0
Duran	1.000	2	8	0	0	1
Joe	.971	5	33	1	1	4
Locastro	.993	37	260	13	2	17
Mondou	.988	43	315	25	4	32
Ornelas	1.000	1	1	0	0	0
Roberts	1.000	3	19	0	0	5
Wagner	1.000	2	15	1	0	1

Second Base	PCT	G	PO	A	E	DP
Brosseau	1.000	1	0	2	0	1
Cronenworth	1.000	1	3	2	0	0
Dungan	1.000	50	101	126	0	42

	PCT	G	PO	A	E	DP
McCoy	1.000	6	4	16	0	3
Mondou	.970	73	133	195	10	49
Reyes	.974	14	15	22	1	3
Rosario	1.000	9	13	23	0	8
Turbi	1.000	2	0	4	0	0
Wade	.971	7	11	22	1	3
Wagner	1.000	4	6	10	0	2

Third Base	PCT	G	PO	A	E	DP
Brosseau	.946	72	44	131	10	13
Castanon	1.000	14	7	21	0	2
Dungan	.964	14	7	20	1	1
Duran	.714	4	0	5	2	0
McCoy	1.000	9	5	11	0	0
Mondou	.875	12	1	20	3	1
Reyes	.957	15	14	30	2	8
Rosario	1.000	2	2	2	0	0
Sullivan	.833	2	2	3	1	1
Wade	.938	5	3	12	1	2
Wagner	.933	11	4	10	1	4

Shortstop	PCT	G	PO	A	E	DP
Acuna	.971	12	14	20	1	2

	PCT	G	PO	A	E	DP
Dungan	.968	43	43	108	5	21
McCoy	.957	76	99	209	14	42
Reyes	.966	9	12	16	1	6
Rosario	.906	13	21	27	5	9
Wade	.941	5	4	12	1	4

Outfield	PCT	G	PO	A	E	DP
Brooks	.960	28	46	2	2	0
Dungan	.976	38	81	2	2	0
Gomez	1.000	1	2	0	0	0
Gonzalez	1.000	9	14	0	0	0
Heyward	1.000	1	2	0	0	0
Joe	1.000	11	18	0	0	0
Johnson	1.000	39	85	1	0	0
Locastro	1.000	53	102	6	0	0
Lockridge	.979	21	47	0	1	0
Ornelas	1.000	75	149	2	0	0
Perlaza	.970	110	187	7	6	1
Reyes	1.000	5	8	0	0	0
Rosario	.667	4	2	0	1	0
Sullivan	1.000	3	6	0	0	0
Wade	1.000	7	18	0	0	0
Wall	.993	66	132	2	1	0

SAN ANTONIO MISSIONS — DOUBLE-A
TEXAS LEAGUE

Batting	B-T	Ht.	Wt.	DOB	AVG	OBP	SLG	G	PA	AB	R	H	2B	3B	HR	RBI	BB	HBP	SH	SF	SO	SB	CS	BB%	SO%
Acuna, Francisco	R-R	5-7	150	1-12-00	.251	.350	.356	109	477	407	59	102	17	1	8	42	54	10	2	3	106	23	7	11.3	22.2
Campbell, Jacob	R-R	6-0	200	5-21-00	.257	.350	.257	12	40	35	1	9	0	0	0	4	3	2	0	0	15	1	0	5.0	37.5
Castanon, Marcos	R-R	6-0	195	3-23-99	.269	.332	.426	106	431	390	47	105	23	1	12	57	33	5	0	3	94	4	4	7.7	21.8
Cedeno, Nerwilian	S-R	5-11	175	3-16-02	.200	.273	.312	36	140	125	14	25	8	0	2	14	12	1	1	1	38	4	1	8.6	27.1
Dues, Damon	L-R	6-0	180	6-21-98	.259	.434	.414	22	76	58	11	15	2	2	1	7	18	0	0	0	14	6	0	23.7	18.4
Fabian, Albert	L-L	6-0	215	12-21-01	.249	.330	.379	48	200	177	20	44	8	0	5	20	19	3	0	1	37	2	4	9.5	18.5
Gomez, Moises	R-R	5-11	200	8-27-98	.231	.304	.363	110	444	394	40	91	27	2	7	46	38	6	0	6	128	9	1	8.6	28.8
Hoffman, Wyatt	R-R	5-9	170	3-16-99	.158	.254	.186	73	207	177	18	28	5	0	0	7	19	4	6	1	73	8	2	9.2	35.3
Jackson, Ryan	R-R	5-10	180	11-27-01	.194	.270	.224	19	74	67	6	13	2	0	0	3	7	0	0	0	18	4	1	9.5	24.3
Karpathios, Braedon	L-L	6-1	186	6-19-03	.225	.295	.425	21	88	80	10	18	3	2	3	10	8	0	0	0	28	0	1	9.1	31.8
Kopack, Addison	R-R	6-2	215	8-6-01	.300	.462	.450	9	26	20	4	6	3	0	0	6	0	0	0	0	9	1	0	23.1	34.6
Linares, Oswaldo	R-R	5-11	150	4-28-03	.200	.294	.267	15	52	45	2	9	3	0	0	5	4	2	1	0	13	1	1	7.7	25.0
Mathey, Jack	R-R	5-10	165	7-28-01	.000	.500	.000	2	4	2	0	0	0	0	0	0	2	0	0	0	1	0	0	50.0	25.0
Mears, Joshua	R-R	6-3	230	2-21-01	.167	.256	.306	47	164	144	16	24	3	1	5	13	12	6	0	2	55	5	4	7.3	33.5
Merrill, Jackson	L-R	6-3	195	4-19-03	.333	.500	.333	2	8	6	2	2	0	0	0	2	1	0	0	0	2	0	0	12.5	25.0
Murphy, Kai	L-L	5-8	173	8-26-00	.219	.322	.262	101	379	324	34	71	9	1	1	21	43	8	0	4	69	8	7	11.3	18.2
Ortiz, Devin	R-R	6-2	215	2-7-99	.242	.325	.317	126	532	467	60	113	15	1	16	40	52	6	6	1	97	19	4	9.8	18.2
Reyes, Ripken	S-R	5-7	185	4-1-97	.207	.344	.324	58	223	179	22	37	7	4	2	22	30	8	5	1	24	3	0	13.5	10.8
Roberts, Cody	R-R	6-1	195	6-16-96	.304	.347	.413	12	49	46	6	14	0	1	1	9	0	0	0	3	14	1	0	6.1	28.6
Robertson, Tyler	R-R	6-4	200	3-10-00	.083	.211	.100	20	73	60	3	5	1	0	0	3	8	2	1	2	25	0	0	11.0	34.2
Rosario, Eguy	R-R	5-8	180	8-25-99	.238	.304	.524	5	23	21	4	5	0	0	2	4	2	0	0	0	9	1	0	8.7	39.1

Player	B-T	Ht.	Wt.	DOB																	
Salas, Ethan	L-R	6-2	185	6-1-06	.188	.325	.219	10	41	32	5	6	1	0	0	5	6	1	1	1	5	2	0	14.6	12.2
Sanabria, Romeo	L-R	6-2	200	5-2-02	.257	.309	.376	119	499	452	54	116	18	0	12	56	38	0	1	8	107	4	1	7.6	21.4
Sargent, Christopher	R-R	5-11	185	7-11-00	.121	.167	.242	9	37	33	3	4	1	0	1	4	1	0	1	11	1	0	2.7	29.7
Snider, Jake	L-R	6-1	190	5-19-98	.333	.478	.333	7	23	18	4	6	0	0	0	1	3	2	0	0	3	3	1	13.0	13.0
Valentine, Chase	R-R	5-11	160	4-22-02	.167	.167	.167	2	6	6	0	1	0	0	0	0	0	0	0	0	1	0	0	0.0	16.7
Valenzuela, Brandon	S-R	6-0	225	10-2-00	.229	.313	.387	87	374	328	42	75	14	1	12	46	40	2	0	4	83	6	2	10.7	22.2
Vilar, Anthony	R-R	5-10	190	4-1-99	.209	.316	.317	100	382	325	38	68	11	3	6	32	49	3	1	3	101	12	4	12.8	26.4
Wilson, Eli	R-R	6-0	190	7-6-98	.182	.250	.318	7	25	22	2	4	0	0	1	4	1	1	1	0	7	0	0	4.0	28.0

Pitching	B-T	Ht.	Wt.	DOB	W	L	ERA	G	GS	SV	IP	Hits	Runs	ER	HR	BB	SO	AVG	OBP	SLG	SO%	BB%	BF
Baez, Henry	R-R	6-3	175	10-12-02	4	2	1.96	20	20	0	97	66	26	21	2	31	89	.195	.277	.254	23.4	8.1	381
Castro, Manuel	R-R	5-8	180	5-11-02	3	2	4.39	23	0	10	27	20	16	13	2	13	43	.208	.313	.323	38.4	11.6	112
Cienfuegos, Miguel	L-L	6-4	195	2-10-97	2	0	1.13	6	0	0	16	12	4	2	0	2	17	.211	.246	.263	27.4	3.2	62
Espada, Jose	R-R	6-0	170	2-22-97	1	1	2.42	17	0	3	22	12	7	6	1	8	37	.154	.233	.244	43.0	9.3	86
Geraldo, Jose	R-R	6-3	200	1-30-99	4	2	3.75	38	0	0	48	45	25	20	4	33	50	.245	.375	.380	22.2	14.7	225
Gustin, Harry	S-L	6-0	160	5-6-02	0	1	0.00	8	1	2	13	8	1	0	0	6	10	.186	.286	.256	20.4	12.2	49
Gutierrez, Luis	L-L	6-0	175	7-31-03	1	0	0.00	1	1	0	5	2	0	0	0	2	4	.125	.222	.125	22.2	11.1	18
Hawkins, Garrett	R-R	6-5	230	2-10-00	1	0	1.69	13	0	2	16	11	3	3	0	10	20	.196	.318	.268	30.3	15.2	66
Haynes, Jagger	L-L	6-3	170	9-20-02	3	4	4.11	26	25	0	103	83	55	47	12	62	101	.223	.344	.398	22.8	14.0	443
Higginbotham, Jake	L-L	6-0	190	1-11-96	5	3	2.21	31	0	0	41	31	11	10	1	13	55	.204	.267	.289	33.3	7.9	165
Hoeing, Bryan	R-R	6-6	210	10-19-96	1	0	0.00	2	0	0	2	1	0	0	0	0	3	.143	.143	.429	42.9	0.0	7
Hoffman, Wyatt	R-R	5-9	170	3-16-99	0	0	10.38	4	0	0	4	7	5	5	1	0	0	.368	.381	.579	0.0	0.0	21
Jones, Stephen	R-R	6-4	195	7-30-97	3	3	3.64	40	0	1	54	54	24	22	6	15	49	.269	.326	.428	22.1	6.8	222
Kollar, Jared	R-R	6-4	195	7-24-98	3	8	5.35	18	7	0	66	76	43	39	5	19	50	.297	.345	.422	17.7	6.7	282
Kopps, Kevin	R-R	6-0	200	3-2-97	1	1	4.21	20	0	1	26	23	13	12	2	13	20	.245	.357	.372	17.9	11.6	112
Krob, Austin	L-L	6-3	205	9-20-99	0	0	7.04	6	0	0	8	7	6	6	1	6	0	.259	.400	.481	0.0	17.1	35
Lizarraga, Victor	R-R	6-3	180	11-30-03	4	10	6.21	25	23	0	91	97	69	63	10	54	87	.271	.368	.441	20.8	12.9	419
Loewen, Carter	R-R	6-4	240	9-28-98	0	0	2.38	18	0	0	23	10	6	6	2	7	20	.137	.222	.247	24.7	8.6	81
Mallitz, Josh	R-R	6-3	195	10-20-01	0	0	0.00	4	0	0	6	2	0	0	0	1	2	.095	.174	.143	8.7	4.3	23
Mendez, Miguel	R-R	6-2	165	7-1-02	0	4	8.06	6	6	0	22	22	22	20	4	17	30	.259	.402	.482	28.0	15.9	107
Moore, Andrew	L-R	6-5	205	8-11-99	3	3	4.95	31	0	1	36	27	20	20	2	33	54	.201	.374	.261	31.4	19.2	172
Moreno, Johan	R-R	6-1	180	3-26-03	0	1	7.36	2	0	0	4	4	3	3	1	1	4	.286	.333	.500	26.7	6.7	15
Morgan, David	R-R	6-0	185	10-26-99	0	0	3.12	7	0	0	9	9	3	3	1	19	19	.257	.316	.543	50.0	2.6	38
Neighbors, Tyson	R-R	6-1	220	10-9-02	2	0	2.57	14	0	1	21	10	7	6	3	10	25	.143	.259	.300	30.9	12.3	81
Nett, Braden	R-R	6-3	185	6-18-02	5	4	3.39	17	17	0	74	71	33	28	5	34	86	.247	.330	.378	26.3	10.4	327
Nunez, Eduarniel	R-R	6-2	170	6-7-99	2	1	3.57	18	0	2	23	17	11	9	1	11	38	.210	.312	.284	40.9	11.8	93
Och, Ryan	R-L	6-0	205	7-18-98	1	3	3.46	45	0	2	55	43	26	21	2	29	55	.218	.323	.325	24.0	12.7	229
Paplham, Cole	R-R	6-3	215	3-19-00	0	0	17.05	6	0	0	6	7	12	12	1	6	5	.292	.457	.417	14.3	17.1	35
Patino, Luis	R-R	6-1	192	10-26-99	1	2	2.95	5	5	0	18	15	7	6	1	8	19	.214	.295	.300	24.4	10.3	78
Pinales, Enmanuel	R-R	6-2	185	4-16-01	7	6	5.32	20	15	1	88	92	54	52	10	41	81	.268	.354	.423	20.8	10.5	389
Rodriguez, Bradley	R-R	6-1	160	11-16-03	4	0	3.22	18	0	5	22	15	9	8	1	5	31	.181	.236	.253	34.8	5.6	89
Routzahn, Ethan	R-R	6-4	225	3-19-98	1	4	5.19	24	0	4	26	22	19	15	4	11	21	.227	.304	.423	18.6	9.7	113
Sanchez, Fernando	L-L	6-0	198	9-13-00	0	1	6.55	7	0	0	11	9	9	8	0	6	16	.214	.313	.262	33.3	12.5	48
Tamarez, Misael	R-R	6-1	206	1-16-00	0	0	0.87	6	0	0	10	5	1	1	0	2	9	.143	.189	.143	23.7	5.3	38
Waldron, Matt	R-R	6-2	185	9-26-96	0	0	4.26	2	2	0	6	8	3	3	1	3	6	.320	.414	.440	20.7	10.3	29
Wendelken, J.B.	R-R	6-0	242	3-24-93	1	1	7.41	10	0	0	17	18	15	14	1	11	19	.281	.395	.375	25.0	14.5	76
Whiting, Sam	R-R	6-3	220	12-15-00	0	1	6.65	8	2	0	23	29	17	17	2	11	23	.302	.385	.490	21.1	10.1	109
Wolf, Jackson	L-L	6-7	205	4-22-99	2	1	3.24	6	5	0	25	17	9	9	3	3	31	.185	.211	.304	32.6	3.2	95
Yost, Eric	R-R	6-1	190	10-15-02	1	4	5.79	8	8	0	37	42	28	24	2	27	26	.292	.405	.417	14.9	15.5	174

Fielding

Catcher	PCT	G	PO	A	E	DP	PB
Kopack	.000	1	0	0	0	0	0
Linares	1.000	14	110	11	0	1	1
Mathey	1.000	1	11	0	0	0	0
Roberts	1.000	6	54	3	0	0	1
Salas	1.000	8	94	4	0	0	2
Sargent	1.000	8	60	11	0	1	2
Valenzuela	.991	64	593	50	6	5	3
Vilar	.994	36	313	14	2	2	13
Wilson	.938	5	27	3	2	1	0

First Base	PCT	G	PO	A	E	DP
Castanon	.952	4	20	0	1	2
Gomez	1.000	1	1	0	0	0
Hoffman	1.000	2	22	0	0	2
Ortiz	.992	19	115	16	1	11
Roberts	1.000	1	13	1	0	2
Sanabria	.993	111	795	70	6	83
Valenzuela	.957	5	21	1	1	2

Second Base	PCT	G	PO	A	E	DP
Acuna	1.000	2	4	6	0	0
Castanon	1.000	43	53	95	0	18
Cedeno	.000	1	0	0	0	0
Hoffman	.981	15	31	21	1	7
Jackson	1.000	12	22	26	0	8
Reyes	1.000	22	39	43	0	14
Rosario	.929	2	4	9	1	3
Vilar	.974	55	81	106	5	37

Third Base	PCT	G	PO	A	E	DP
Acuna	1.000	1	0	1	0	0
Castanon	.942	24	11	38	3	8
Hoffman	.917	8	7	4	1	0
Jackson	1.000	2	1	7	0	0
Ortiz	.930	105	61	191	19	22
Reyes	1.000	4	2	5	0	0
Rosario	1.000	1	2	1	0	0

Shortstop	PCT	G	PO	A	E	DP
Acuna	.970	102	113	239	11	52
Hoffman	.967	8	15	14	1	6
Jackson	.920	6	9	14	2	3
Ortiz	1.000	2	1	3	0	0
Reyes	1.000	17	21	37	0	14
Rosario	1.000	2	2	9	0	1
Valentine	1.000	1	0	2	0	0
Vilar	1.000	8	9	12	0	2

Outfield	PCT	G	PO	A	E	DP
Campbell	1.000	12	13	2	0	1
Cedeno	.988	36	78	3	1	1
Dues	.976	19	39	1	1	0
Fabian	1.000	26	52	2	0	1
Gomez	.972	102	168	6	5	0
Hoffman	.985	37	65	1	1	0
Karpathios	.977	21	41	1	1	0
Mears	.984	45	60	0	1	0
Merrill	1.000	1	1	0	0	0
Murphy	.972	101	203	4	6	1
Reyes	1.000	17	26	3	0	1
Roberts	1.000	2	3	0	0	0
Robertson	.971	21	34	0	1	0
Snider	1.000	4	11	2	0	1

FORT WAYNE TINCAPS — HIGH-A
MIDWEST LEAGUE

SAN DIEGO PADRES

Batting	B-T	Ht.	Wt.	DOB	AVG	OBP	SLG	G	PA	AB	R	H	2B	3B	HR	RBI	BB	HBP	SH	SF	SO	SB	CS	BB%	SO%
Barnett, Sean	R-R	6-2	200	6-22-03	.191	.314	.283	67	207	173	19	33	5	1	3	19	23	9	0	2	72	2	1	11.1	34.8
Butterworth, Brandon	R-R	5-11	168	8-29-02	.267	.327	.455	89	377	341	61	91	17	7	11	46	26	6	0	3	78	13	2	6.9	20.7
Campbell, Jacob	R-R	6-0	200	5-21-00	.219	.273	.331	49	173	160	21	35	7	1	3	22	10	2	1	0	44	3	1	5.8	25.4
Cantwell, Luke	L-R	6-0	200	1-14-03	.250	.318	.400	5	22	20	2	5	0	0	1	1	1	0	0	2	0	0	4.5	9.1
Cedeno, Nerwilian	S-R	5-11	175	3-16-02	.273	.313	.347	32	131	121	23	33	6	0	1	18	7	1	0	2	22	5	2	5.3	16.8
Costello, Jack	R-R	6-1	195	5-17-01	.220	.298	.342	110	439	395	44	87	18	0	10	46	26	18	0	0	76	10	1	5.9	17.3
De Vries, Leodalis	S-R	6-2	183	10-11-06	.245	.357	.410	82	368	310	46	76	19	4	8	46	52	3	1	2	72	8	7	14.1	19.6
Duarte, Victor	R-R	5-11	170	2-23-01	.167	.194	.200	19	65	60	7	10	2	0	0	3	2	0	0	0	19	2	0	3.1	29.2
Durfee, Brendan	L-R	6-4	221	7-31-01	.220	.309	.329	90	376	328	35	72	16	1	6	31	35	9	0	3	98	0	0	9.3	26.1
Evans, Zach	R-R	6-4	210	7-16-02	.194	.240	.214	27	105	98	8	19	2	0	0	10	5	1	1	0	34	1	0	4.8	32.4
Hollow, Kaden	L-R	6-1	210	3-17-01	.246	.333	.368	18	68	57	6	14	2	1	1	8	8	0	2	1	13	1	0	11.8	19.1
Jackson, Ryan	R-R	5-10	180	11-27-01	.234	.357	.287	48	208	171	17	40	4	1	1	22	29	5	1	2	32	0	3	13.9	15.4
Karpathios, Braedon	L-L	6-1	186	6-19-03	.254	.370	.410	103	433	366	53	93	19	1	12	55	65	2	0	0	118	9	4	15.0	27.3
King, Lamar	R-R	6-3	215	12-7-03	.233	.289	.300	24	97	90	4	21	6	0	0	7	6	1	0	0	25	3	0	6.2	25.8
Kopack, Addison	R-R	6-2	215	6-8-01	.189	.292	.264	19	66	53	5	10	2	1	0	5	8	1	1	3	19	1	2	12.1	28.8
Linares, Oswaldo	R-R	5-11	150	4-28-03	.202	.301	.298	37	135	114	15	23	6	1	1	15	13	4	1	2	37	1	0	9.6	27.4
Long, Ethan	R-R	6-3	215	5-10-01	.184	.278	.270	49	187	163	15	30	2	0	4	13	20	2	0	2	59	0	0	10.7	31.6
Roberts, Kai	L-R	6-4	200	3-15-01	.211	.335	.271	83	342	280	39	59	3	1	4	22	47	7	5	3	97	30	7	13.7	28.4
Rosario, Eguy	R-R	5-7	150	8-25-99	.145	.242	.327	14	62	55	5	8	4	0	2	7	7	0	0	0	25	3	1	11.3	40.3
Sanabria, Jose	R-R	5-10	150	10-30-02	.170	.252	.220	31	112	100	6	17	2	0	1	9	11	0	0	1	37	2	0	9.8	33.0
Snider, Jake	L-R	6-1	190	5-19-98	.243	.364	.336	37	130	107	14	26	6	2	0	14	19	2	1	1	33	6	2	14.6	25.4
Valentine, Chase	R-R	5-11	160	4-22-02	.125	.267	.167	20	61	48	4	6	2	0	0	5	9	1	1	2	22	2	1	14.8	36.1
Vastine, Jonathan	L-R	5-11	176	10-17-02	.235	.329	.309	22	79	68	7	16	2	0	1	7	10	0	0	1	25	3	0	12.7	31.6
Verdugo, Rosman	R-R	6-0	180	2-2-05	.205	.339	.354	117	490	404	59	83	15	3	13	43	72	11	0	3	158	6	3	14.7	32.2
Wells, Kasen	L-R	5-8	180	8-8-03	.239	.318	.291	31	132	117	10	28	5	0	0	8	14	0	0	1	24	2	5	10.6	18.2

Pitching	B-T	Ht.	Wt.	DOB	W	L	ERA	G	GS	SV	IP	Hits	Runs	ER	HR	BB	SO	AVG	OBP	SLG	SO%	BB%	BF
Barnett, Sean	R-R	6-2	200	6-22-03	0	1	21.09	14	0	0	11	22	27	25	1	16	8	.415	.573	.585	10.4	20.8	77
Candiotti, Clark	R-R	6-5	220	9-2-00	1	7	5.77	17	17	0	48	49	37	31	4	31	65	.265	.378	.422	28.9	13.8	225
Duarte, Victor	R-R	5-11	170	2-23-01	0	0	36.00	1	0	0	1	4	4	4	1	2	0	.667	.667	1.167	0.0	22.2	9
Galindo, Ruben	R-R	6-1	175	1-24-01	1	2	7.03	20	0	1	24	25	23	19	1	19	29	.258	.361	.424	24.2	15.8	120
German, Luis	R-R	6-2	160	10-14-01	0	1	5.77	37	0	1	44	44	32	28	4	38	45	.260	.419	.444	20.7	17.5	217
Gustin, Harry	S-L	6-0	160	5-6-02	4	2	2.36	21	1	3	50	35	13	13	3	20	60	.197	.281	.320	29.9	10.0	201
Gutierrez, Luis	L-L	6-0	175	7-31-03	2	3	3.74	13	13	0	65	67	35	27	4	22	59	.263	.334	.384	20.7	7.7	285
Hawkins, Garrett	R-R	6-5	230	2-10-00	8	1	1.43	32	0	8	44	17	7	7	1	13	60	.116	.198	.150	37.0	8.0	162
Huizi, Eiker	R-R	6-0	155	9-24-00	2	4	6.27	28	0	1	37	40	26	26	3	21	38	.272	.376	.395	22.0	12.1	173
Koenig, Ian	L-R	6-2	225	4-10-01	5	8	5.40	21	21	0	103	106	67	62	17	34	71	.268	.342	.476	16.0	7.7	444
Lowe, Isaiah	R-R	6-1	220	5-12-02	3	12	5.69	22	22	0	92	110	67	58	8	51	70	.296	.387	.431	16.2	11.8	433
Mallitz, Josh	R-R	6-3	195	10-20-01	3	1	4.09	23	0	1	44	41	21	20	4	12	51	.243	.288	.373	27.7	6.5	184
Mendez, Miguel	R-R	6-2	165	7-1-02	7	3	1.32	12	12	0	61	38	11	9	3	24	70	.180	.286	.275	28.6	9.8	245
Miralles, Maikel	R-R	5-11	160	10-22-04	1	1	2.13	2	2	0	13	3	3	0	1	11	.255	.289	.294	20.8	1.9	53
Moreno, Johan	R-R	6-1	180	3-26-03	0	0	9.00	5	0	0	7	8	7	7	2	5	12	.296	.382	.519	35.3	14.7	34
Morgan, Tyler	R-R	6-0	200	11-4-00	2	0	3.51	13	0	0	26	16	11	10	3	9	29	.184	.276	.356	29.3	9.1	99
Neighbors, Tyson	R-R	6-1	220	10-9-02	1	0	1.19	18	0	5	23	13	3	3	1	8	39	.171	.276	.250	43.8	9.0	89
Papham, Cole	R-R	6-3	215	3-19-00	0	2	4.73	11	0	1	13	14	8	7	1	12	13	.255	.397	.382	19.1	17.6	68
Pinales, Enmanuel	R-R	6-2	185	4-16-01	3	0	1.40	5	5	0	26	16	4	4	1	7	27	.184	.253	.276	28.4	7.4	95
Rascon, Bodi	L-L	6-5	205	2-3-01	0	2	6.70	22	0	0	43	52	37	32	3	37	32	.295	.414	.381	14.9	17.2	215
Reyes, Jose Luis	R-R	6-3	190	8-20-02	1	3	5.54	9	9	0	39	53	31	24	4	17	31	.325	.390	.497	17.0	9.3	182
Ruiz, Xavier	R-R	6-1	180	11-19-02	1	0	6.17	11	0	0	12	13	8	8	0	12	11	.277	.417	.383	18.0	19.7	61
Salazar, Braian	L-L	6-2	165	6-12-05	0	0	9.00	3	0	0	4	4	4	0	6	6	.250	.478	.375	26.1	26.1	23
Sanchez, Fernando	L-L	6-0	198	9-13-00	4	3	2.14	29	0	1	63	45	20	15	2	26	52	.204	.296	.290	20.6	10.3	253
Tamarez, Misael	R-R	6-1	200	1-16-00	0	1	1.23	6	0	1	7	4	2	1	0	4	10	.154	.185	.192	48.1	0.0	27
Varmette, Will	R-R	6-2	195	2-28-03	2	6	7.50	10	6	0	36	47	32	30	7	20	35	.326	.426	.569	20.7	11.8	169
Whiting, Sam	R-R	6-3	220	12-15-00	0	4	5.45	13	6	0	40	35	25	24	3	27	29	.238	.362	.381	16.4	15.3	177
Widger, C.J.	L-L	6-2	205	5-25-99	0	2	7.20	9	0	0	10	12	8	8	0	9	12	.293	.420	.488	24.0	18.0	50
Wissman, Nick	R-R	6-1	195	9-18-00	1	1	4.64	37	0	2	52	62	27	27	3	18	39	.291	.353	.413	16.5	7.6	236
Yost, Eric	R-R	6-1	190	10-15-02	4	7	2.89	17	17	0	87	72	34	28	4	33	87	.222	.309	.302	23.6	8.9	369

Fielding

Catcher	PCT	G	PO	A	E	DP	PB
Duarte	.987	17	140	11	2	2	1
Durfee	.992	59	446	34	4	2	6
King	.990	11	94	7	1	1	4
Kopack	.975	12	114	3	3	1	3
Linares	.994	36	328	13	2	0	4

First Base	PCT	G	PO	A	E	DP
Cantwell	1.000	4	28	3	0	3
Costello	.995	56	389	38	2	35
Duarte	1.000	1	2	1	0	0

Second Base	PCT	G	PO	A	E	DP
Butterworth	.970	62	111	145	8	38
Campbell	1.000	1	1	1	0	0
Cedeno	.933	5	12	16	2	3
Evans	.973	17	28	45	2	9

	PCT	G	PO	A	E	DP
Jackson	.833	1	4	1	1	1
Sanabria	1.000	6	4	8	0	0
Valentine	.950	4	7	12	1	3
Verdugo	.973	37	57	85	4	21

Third Base	PCT	G	PO	A	E	DP
Costello	1.000	2	2	1	0	0
Evans	.889	9	5	11	2	2
Jackson	.978	27	30	59	2	7
Long	1.000	2	3	2	0	0
Rosario	.909	6	4	6	1	0

	PCT	G	PO	A	E	DP
Sanabria	.979	24	9	37	1	4
Valentine	1.000	1	0	1	0	0
Verdugo	.950	62	43	91	7	15
Shortstop	**PCT**	**G**	**PO**	**A**	**E**	**DP**
Butterworth	.943	22	35	47	5	9
De Vries	.932	72	85	174	19	36
Jackson	1.000	11	13	26	0	5
Rosario	.950	6	8	11	1	3
Sanabria	1.000	1	0	2	0	0
Vastine	.988	22	33	47	1	8
Outfield	**PCT**	**G**	**PO**	**A**	**E**	**DP**
Butterworth	1.000	5	9	1	0	0
Campbell	1.000	48	87	3	0	1
Cedeno	.964	24	53	1	2	0
Costello	.983	49	57	1	1	0
Hollow	1.000	10	17	1	0	1
Jackson	1.000	8	14	2	0	1
Karpathios	.957	99	185	14	9	1
Roberts	.989	78	184	2	2	0
Snider	1.000	34	61	1	0	1
Valentine	1.000	12	15	1	0	0
Wells	.986	31	66	2	1	0

LAKE ELSINORE STORM — LOW-A
CALIFORNIA LEAGUE

Batting	B-T	Ht.	Wt.	DOB	AVG	OBP	SLG	G	PA	AB	R	H	2B	3B	HR	RBI	BB	HBP	SH	SF	SO	SB	CS	BB%	SO%
Barnett, Sean	R-R	6-2	200	6-22-03	.289	.396	.511	11	53	45	10	13	4	0	2	10	7	1	0	0	18	1	0	13.2	34.0
Bilecki, George	L-L	6-2	205	9-26-03	.128	.226	.170	18	53	47	2	6	2	0	0	2	6	0	0	0	17	1	1	11.3	32.1
Choi, B.Y.	L-R	6-3	203	4-30-02	.249	.345	.312	64	236	205	27	51	11	1	0	30	29	1	0	0	63	6	2	12.3	26.7
Coffman, Spence	R-R	6-1	170	1-7-04	.188	.235	.188	6	17	16	2	3	0	0	0	2	1	0	0	0	5	1	0	5.9	29.4
Cross, Kerrington	R-R	6-0	200	4-15-02	.190	.433	.214	14	61	42	10	8	1	0	0	3	14	4	1	0	15	1	1	23.0	24.6
DeCriscio, Justin	R-R	5-10	160	3-24-03	.190	.292	.286	13	49	42	5	8	1	0	1	5	5	1	1	0	6	2	0	10.2	12.2
Duarte, Victor	R-R	5-11	170	2-23-01	.206	.254	.270	17	67	63	5	13	4	0	0	5	4	0	0	0	13	1	0	6.0	19.4
Evans, Zach	R-R	6-4	210	7-16-02	.296	.367	.377	96	430	379	50	112	20	1	3	62	42	4	0	5	67	14	3	9.8	15.6
Figueroa, Victor	L-R	6-5	240	12-31-03	.262	.375	.456	53	232	195	28	51	17	0	7	30	34	2	0	1	47	3	1	14.7	20.3
Fountain, Kale	R-R	6-4	215	8-14-05	.195	.311	.260	34	148	123	16	24	2	0	2	16	17	5	0	3	34	9	1	11.5	23.0
Frye, Bradley	R-R	6-2	185	7-8-02	.159	.245	.182	14	50	44	3	7	1	0	0	2	3	2	1	0	15	3	0	6.0	30.0
Grego, Dylan	S-R	6-1	195	3-16-04	.246	.326	.369	32	138	122	18	30	4	1	3	13	14	1	0	1	32	2	1	10.1	23.2
Harvey, Ty	R-R	6-2	215	7-28-06	.174	.367	.174	7	30	23	3	4	0	0	0	1	7	0	0	0	12	0	0	23.3	40.0
Hightower, Cobb	R-R	6-0	180	3-20-05	.239	.363	.314	40	190	159	30	38	7	1	1	21	28	3	0	0	31	7	0	14.7	16.3
Hollow, Kaden	L-R	6-1	210	3-17-01	.264	.387	.345	70	294	235	35	62	13	0	2	40	48	3	2	6	48	1	2	16.3	16.3
Jackson, Ryan	R-R	5-10	180	11-27-01	.298	.442	.418	62	286	225	39	67	14	2	3	33	55	4	1	1	49	15	1	19.2	17.1
King, Lamar	R-R	6-3	215	12-7-03	.286	.370	.408	81	359	311	50	89	24	1	4	37	38	6	0	4	68	18	3	10.6	18.9
Madonna, Truitt	R-R	6-3	215	3-14-07	.185	.267	.278	14	60	54	4	10	3	1	0	5	6	0	0	0	20	0	0	10.0	38.3
McCoy, Alex	R-R	6-6	258	2-10-02	.318	.394	.513	53	226	195	45	62	12	4	6	33	20	7	0	4	53	14	2	8.8	23.5
Montesino, Daniel	L-L	6-0	180	2-12-04	.083	.083	.167	3	12	12	0	1	1	0	0	0	0	0	0	0	8	0	0	0.0	66.7
Ocopio, Yoiber	R-R	5-10	175	8-24-04	.214	.320	.286	14	50	42	4	9	3	0	0	8	5	2	0	1	15	0	0	10.0	30.0
Quintana, Jorge	S-R	6-2	183	4-5-07	.193	.317	.265	25	101	83	12	16	3	0	1	5	15	1	0	2	34	7	4	14.9	33.7
Rodriguez, Carlos	S-R	5-10	155	5-12-03	.276	.404	.454	46	189	152	25	42	11	2	4	26	31	3	1	2	36	2	1	16.4	19.0
Rojas, Yendry	R-R	6-0	185	1-27-05	.208	.293	.255	73	266	231	29	48	11	0	0	21	29	1	0	5	56	12	5	10.9	21.1
Tears, Kavares	L-L	6-0	205	8-25-02	.227	.320	.385	107	475	410	49	93	22	2	13	65	58	1	0	6	138	6	5	12.2	29.1
Thibodeaux, Cardell	L-L	5-8	175	12-18-03	.108	.216	.138	21	74	65	3	7	2	0	0	4	9	0	0	0	17	0	1	12.2	23.0
Tovar, Yimy	R-R	6-0	160	4-7-06	.409	.435	.545	8	23	22	1	9	3	0	0	2	1	0	0	0	3	1	2	4.3	13.0
Turbi, Emil	S-R	5-8	150	11-26-04	.143	.143	.143	2	7	7	1	1	0	0	0	0	0	0	0	0	4	0	0	0.0	57.1
Valentine, Chase	R-R	5-11	160	4-22-02	.214	.288	.289	58	209	187	31	40	11	0	1	13	17	3	1	1	57	11	7	8.1	27.3
Vincent, Colton	R-R	6-1	182	1-25-00	.179	.260	.201	50	150	134	13	24	3	0	0	11	11	4	0	1	28	1	0	7.3	18.7
Wells, Kasen	L-R	5-8	180	8-8-03	.275	.381	.368	49	227	193	45	53	8	2	2	20	28	5	1	0	40	28	1	12.3	17.6
Wideman, Ryan	R-R	6-5	204	11-4-03	.229	.330	.271	26	112	96	13	22	2	1	0	12	12	3	0	1	32	11	1	10.7	28.6
Wilson, Ryan	R-R	6-1	195	1-12-02	.226	.358	.306	89	350	288	39	65	15	1	2	29	47	13	1	1	54	6	5	13.4	15.4

Pitching	B-T	Ht.	Wt.	DOB	W	L	ERA	G	GS	SV	IP	Hits	Runs	ER	HR	BB	SO	AVG	OBP	SLG	SO%	BB%	BF
Balzer, Bryan	L-R	6-1	190	10-27-04	1	6	7.92	16	13	0	50	61	45	44	3	28	49	.310	.429	.421	20.3	11.6	241
Bateman, Boston	R-L	6-8	240	9-20-05	5	5	4.08	15	15	0	68	65	34	31	1	25	75	.249	.321	.326	25.8	8.6	291
Chacon, Javier	L-L	5-11	190	12-24-02	0	0	2.70	3	0	0	7	6	2	2	0	6	4	.250	.400	.333	13.3	20.0	30
Chourio, Winyer	R-R	6-2	180	11-4-03	0	0	6.30	9	2	0	20	25	17	14	0	11	17	.309	.400	.407	17.9	11.6	95
Conrad, Adam	R-R	6-3	205	4-8-03	7	1	3.48	37	0	5	62	50	29	24	1	54	61	.219	.379	.289	21.0	18.6	291
Cruz, Humberto	R-R	6-1	190	12-18-06	0	3	6.97	6	6	0	21	20	16	16	5	9	20	.253	.352	.494	21.7	9.8	92
Dalena, Jaxon	L-R	6-3	215	3-28-02	0	0	1.80	3	2	0	5	4	1	1	0	4	9	.222	.364	.333	40.9	18.2	22
Domingo, Vicarte	R-R	5-10	195	11-18-02	1	2	3.86	37	0	4	63	44	29	27	2	34	86	.193	.302	.294	32.0	12.6	269
Edmondson, Clay	R-R	6-2	185	6-24-03	0	0	4.76	6	0	0	11	11	6	6	0	6	10	.262	.340	.357	20.8	8.3	48
Gil, Igor	L-L	5-11	170	3-23-01	3	2	3.86	32	0	3	51	39	29	22	1	43	62	.214	.380	.291	26.2	18.1	237
Gutierrez, Luis	L-L	6-0	175	7-31-03	2	3	2.88	10	6	0	50	32	20	16	3	20	46	.180	.269	.281	22.7	9.9	203
Jose, Bernard	R-R	5-11	160	3-3-03	2	4	3.95	40	0	5	66	59	35	29	5	32	75	.236	.334	.340	25.7	11.0	292
Jurecka, Landry	R-R	6-2	195	1-21-03	1	1	6.75	6	0	0	9	11	9	7	0	3	7	.282	.326	.410	16.3	7.0	43
Kemp, Kannon	R-R	6-6	225	9-3-04	3	5	5.87	13	7	0	54	64	38	35	3	24	48	.298	.378	.433	19.3	9.6	249
Koger, Will	L-R	6-2	195	11-10-02	0	1	5.40	2	0	0	3	1	3	2	0	1	3	.143	.333	.143	23.1	7.7	13
Lopez, Jesus	R-R	5-11	175	3-14-06	0	0	8.53	3	0	0	6	7	6	6	1	7	5	.292	.452	.500	16.1	22.6	31
Lugo, Alejandro	R-R	6-0	165	8-20-02	0	0	3.72	4	0	1	10	6	4	4	0	5	7	.194	.316	.290	18.4	13.2	38
Mayfield, Kash	L-L	6-4	200	2-8-05	1	5	2.97	19	19	0	61	46	26	20	2	28	88	.207	.301	.293	34.1	10.9	258
Mendez, Miguel	R-R	6-2	165	7-1-02	1	0	3.97	3	3	0	11	11	5	5	0	4	18	.256	.340	.360	36.0	8.0	50
Miralles, Maikel	R-R	5-11	160	10-22-04	2	4	5.17	16	11	1	56	55	33	32	4	28	48	.267	.363	.388	20.0	13.3	240
Moreno, Johan	R-R	6-1	180	3-26-03	3	6	4.48	30	2	1	68	62	43	34	4	34	83	.238	.340	.345	27.1	11.1	306
Musgrove, Tucker	R-R	6-2	175	2-1-02	2	0	5.40	14	7	0	20	15	12	12	2	10	26	.205	.310	.342	30.6	11.8	85
Nohos, Cameron	R-R	6-8	235	6-29-05	3	5	3.10	8	4	0	29	13	10	10	1	12	40	.455	.500	.500	13.6	9.1	22
Olmedo, Kleiber	R-R	6-1	155	8-23-04	5	7	6.49	32	8	0	78	82	59	56	7	37	86	.265	.341	.429	24.3	10.5	354
Parra, Abraham	R-R	6-2	170	12-29-05	4	4	5.29	18	11	0	82	81	56	48	7	35	74	.254	.342	.389	20.3	9.6	365
Pascual, Yovannki	L-L	5-11	185	8-4-02	0	2	15.95	8	0	0	7	13	16	13	1	15	10	.351	.547	.541	18.9	28.3	53
Patino, Luis	R-R	6-1	192	10-26-99	0	0	2.00	4	4	0	9	7	4	2	1	5	8	.219	.342	.344	21.1	13.2	38
Rascon, Bodi	L-L	6-5	205	2-3-01	2	2	8.64	4	0	0	8	10	9	8	1	8	8	.294	.429	.412	18.6	18.6	43
Reed, Ryan	L-L	6-3	232	12-12-03	0	0	0.00	2	0	0	3	3	0	0	0	1	1	.300	.364	.300	8.3	8.3	12

Batting	B-T	Ht.	Wt.	DOB			AVG	OBP	SLG	G	PA	AB	R	H	2B	3B	HR	RBI	BB	HBP	SH	SF	SO	SB	CS	BB%	SO%
Reyes, Jimmy	R-R	5-10	170	11-15-05	2	1	10.50	5	0	0	6	9	9	7	2	4	4	.321	.424	.679	11.8	11.8	34				
Ruiz, Xavier	R-R	6-1	180	11-19-02	1	2	5.29	13	0	1	17	12	12	10	1	16	17	.194	.383	.323	20.5	19.3	83				
Salazar, Braian	L-L	6-2	165	6-12-05	2	1	5.23	31	2	1	52	49	36	30	0	39	74	.244	.386	.348	29.6	15.6	250				
Salinas, Ruben	R-L	6-0	154	1-13-03	0	3	12.15	9	0	0	13	20	19	18	2	8	14	.345	.443	.569	19.7	11.3	71				
Schoolcraft, Kruz	L-L	6-8	229	4-18-07	0	0	10.80	1	1	0	2	1	2	2	0	3	4	.167	.444	.333	44.4	33.3	9				
Smith, Tanner	R-R	6-6	245	8-5-02	1	1	1.80	9	0	0	15	11	5	3	0	8	19	.208	.323	.226	30.2	12.7	63				
Swilling, Carson	R-R	5-11	196	1-9-02	2	0	3.29	9	0	0	14	15	9	5	1	3	19	.254	.302	.322	30.2	4.8	63				
Valdez, Miguel	R-R	6-0	170	8-1-03	0	0	27.00	3	0	0	2	4	6	6	0	8	3	.444	.700	.444	15.0	40.0	20				
Valenzuela, Jordan	R-R	6-2	190	5-20-05	0	0	4.61	10	0	0	14	9	11	7	0	21	18	.188	.437	.250	25.4	29.6	71				
Varmette, Will	R-R	6-2	195	2-28-03	3	4	5.86	13	9	2	43	30	31	28	2	21	36	.196	.296	.281	20.1	11.7	179				
Walker, Charlie	R-R	6-2	205	9-23-03	0	0	18.00	1	0	0	1	3	2	2	0	1	0	.500	.571	.500	0.0	14.3	7				
Whiting, Sam	R-R	6-3	220	12-15-00	0	0	0.00	1	1	0	4	1	0	0	0	0	2	.077	.077	.077	15.4	0.0	13				
Zabala, Mario	R-R	6-2	195	5-8-02	0	0	6.52	6	0	0	10	16	7	7	0	5	10	.400	.447	.500	21.3	10.6	47				

Fielding

Catcher	PCT	G	PO	A	E	DP	PB
Duarte	.957	16	144	10	7	0	2
Harvey	.947	4	30	6	2	0	1
King	.986	50	463	24	7	2	10
Madonna	1.000	7	76	7	0	0	2
Ocopio	.981	11	94	7	2	1	8
Rodriguez	.959	27	249	11	11	1	7
Vincent	.983	23	213	17	4	2	4

First Base	PCT	G	PO	A	E	DP
Choi	.991	15	106	3	1	15
Cross	1.000	1	12	1	0	0
Evans	1.000	2	15	1	0	1
Figueroa	.974	33	249	17	7	19
Fountain	.979	26	214	15	5	22
Hollow	.991	15	109	4	1	10
King	.977	30	213	4	5	23
Madonna	.938	2	15	0	1	2
Ocopio	1.000	1	5	0	0	2
Rodriguez	1.000	7	56	10	0	0
Tears	1.000	3	20	1	0	1
Vincent	1.000	1	2	0	0	0

Second Base	PCT	G	PO	A	E	DP
Choi	.975	20	28	50	2	16
DeCriscio	.875	3	3	4	1	1

Evans	1.000	8	9	18	0	2
Frye	1.000	2	1	1	0	1
Grego	.976	21	30	53	2	8
Jackson	.973	10	17	19	1	4
Rojas	.965	69	113	163	10	39
Tovar	1.000	4	9	6	0	2
Valentine	1.000	5	8	12	0	3

Third Base	PCT	G	PO	A	E	DP
Choi	.941	9	6	10	1	2
Cross	.938	13	6	24	2	4
DeCriscio	.947	9	4	14	1	0
Evans	.950	87	59	150	11	16
Fountain	1.000	4	0	3	0	0
Frye	1.000	9	2	11	0	0
Grego	1.000	2	1	5	0	1
Jackson	1.000	2	0	3	0	0
Quintana	.000	1	0	0	0	0
Valentine	1.000	5	4	12	0	1

Shortstop	PCT	G	PO	A	E	DP
Choi	1.000	2	2	2	0	0
Evans	.000	1	0	0	0	0
Frye	1.000	3	3	7	0	1
Grego	.970	9	7	25	1	7
Hightower	.972	39	48	91	4	20

Jackson	.965	50	73	145	8	22
Quintana	.940	23	26	53	5	7
Rojas	.000	1	0	0	0	0
Tovar	.857	3	1	5	1	3
Turbi	1.000	1	0	3	0	1
Valentine	1.000	10	11	30	0	5

Outfield	PCT	G	PO	A	E	DP
Bilecki	.957	13	22	0	1	0
Choi	.909	19	19	1	2	0
Coffman	1.000	5	6	1	0	0
Figueroa	.950	13	18	1	1	1
Hollow	.944	53	84	0	5	0
McCoy	.909	45	48	2	5	0
Montesino	1.000	3	1	1	0	0
Rodriguez	1.000	1	0	1	0	0
Tears	.915	30	42	1	4	0
Thibodeaux	.939	23	31	0	2	0
Turbi	.000	1	0	0	0	0
Valentine	.930	39	63	3	5	2
Vincent	.920	22	21	2	2	2
Wells	.955	49	106	0	5	0
Wideman	.984	26	59	4	1	0
Wilson	.982	88	154	9	3	1

ACL PADRES — ROOKIE
ARIZONA COMPLEX LEAGUE

Batting	B-T	Ht.	Wt.	DOB	AVG	OBP	SLG	G	PA	AB	R	H	2B	3B	HR	RBI	BB	HBP	SH	SF	SO	SB	CS	BB%	SO%
Arias, Jesmaylin	L-L	5-11	175	4-20-07	.178	.276	.290	51	196	169	13	30	8	1	3	20	21	3	0	3	62	3	1	10.7	31.6
Castro, Jesus	R-R	5-10	158	7-7-04	.286	.385	.375	24	65	56	6	16	5	0	0	11	7	2	0	0	18	0	0	10.8	27.7
Cronenworth, Jake	L-R	6-0	187	1-21-94	.333	.333	.333	1	3	3	0	1	0	0	0	0	0	0	0	0	1	0	0	0.0	33.3
Davila, Manuel	R-R	6-0	140	8-8-07	.000	.000	.000	13	1	1	0	0	0	0	0	0	0	0	0	0	1	0	0	0.0	100.0
De Leon, Luis	S-R	5-8	155	1-8-06	.293	.419	.359	54	243	198	42	58	3	2	2	24	38	5	2	0	56	19	3	15.6	23.0
Fabian, Albert	L-L	6-0	215	12-21-01	.288	.351	.462	14	57	52	9	15	3	0	2	10	4	1	0	0	11	1	0	7.0	19.3
Figueroa, Victor	L-R	6-5	240	12-31-03	.605	.659	1.263	11	44	38	11	23	4	3	5	17	6	0	0	0	7	2	0	13.6	15.9
Fountain, Kale	R-R	6-4	215	8-14-05	.262	.386	.364	31	132	107	24	28	6	1	1	18	18	5	0	2	31	12	0	13.6	23.5
Grant, Donte	L-R	6-0	175	8-29-04	.240	.378	.355	56	252	200	38	48	10	5	1	26	28	19	1	4	61	17	4	11.1	24.2
Guzman, Walfrent	R-R	5-11	185	10-4-05	.167	.222	.167	6	19	18	1	3	1	0	0	2	0	0	1	0	10	0	0	0.0	52.6
Hacen, Kevin	R-R	6-2	160	1-30-06	.190	.288	.241	42	160	137	13	26	5	1	0	13	15	5	0	3	37	3	0	9.4	23.1
Hernandez, Alcides	L-R	5-8	160	4-27-05	.190	.300	.190	13	50	42	4	8	0	0	0	4	7	0	0	1	10	1	2	14.0	20.0
Javier, Ismael	S-R	5-8	160	8-27-05	.197	.322	.222	43	144	117	21	23	3	3	0	10	20	3	1	3	29	4	2	13.9	20.1
Marquez, Gustavo	R-R	6-0	190	12-28-04	.227	.345	.270	47	171	141	23	32	6	0	0	15	18	8	3	1	45	6	2	10.5	26.3
Mathey, Jack	R-R	5-10	165	7-28-03	.160	.400	.200	10	35	25	6	4	1	0	0	0	9	1	0	0	10	0	0	25.7	28.6
McCoy, Alex	R-R	6-6	258	2-10-02	.278	.381	.611	5	21	18	4	5	2	0	1	7	3	0	0	0	7	0	1	0.0	33.3
Ocopio, Yoiber	R-R	5-10	175	2-04-04	.223	.346	.338	46	182	148	23	33	5	0	4	26	24	6	0	4	45	4	2	13.2	24.7
Roberts, Kai	L-R	6-4	200	3-15-01	.533	.667	.933	7	22	15	8	8	3	0	1	2	6	0	1	0	5	0	0	27.3	22.7
Rodriguez, Carlos	S-R	5-10	155	5-12-03	.357	.471	.393	9	34	28	1	10	1	0	0	3	6	0	0	0	5	1	0	17.6	14.7
Rosario, Eguy	R-R	5-7	150	8-25-99	.222	.286	.267	12	49	45	5	10	2	0	0	4	4	0	0	0	14	1	0	8.2	28.6
Sanabria, Jose	R-R	5-10	150	10-30-02	.300	.385	.438	23	91	80	13	24	5	3	0	15	10	1	0	0	17	3	3	11.0	18.7
Tovar, Yimy	R-R	6-0	160	4-7-06	.301	.356	.384	38	163	146	24	44	6	0	2	22	13	1	0	3	34	4	2	8.0	20.9
Turbi, Emil	S-R	5-8	150	11-26-03	.336	.305	.35	120	15	10	37	3	1	0	9	10	3	1	1	47	2	2	8.3	39.2
Wells, Kasen	L-R	5-8	180	8-8-03	.421	.476	.579	5	21	19	7	8	1	1	0	5	2	0	0	0	3	2	0	9.5	14.3

Pitching	B-T	Ht.	Wt.	DOB	W	L	ERA	G	GS	SV	IP	Hits	Runs	ER	HR	BB	SO	AVG	OBP	SLG	SO%	BB%	BF
Batista, Erick	R-R	6-0	155	9-7-05	0	2	8.15	12	3	1	18	24	19	16	0	22	20	.338	.510	.408	20.2	22.2	99
Burgos, Roberto	R-R	6-2	185	10-6-03	1	0	4.87	14	0	0	20	12	16	11	2	29	24	.164	.421	.288	22.4	27.1	107
Burkett, Langston	L-R	6-6	220	4-2-05	0	3	9.14	9	5	0	23	33	29	22	1	11	16	.363	.450	.538	14.5	10.0	110
Castro, Jesus	R-R	5-10	158	7-7-04	0	1	9.82	5	0	0	4	7	5	4	1	1	0	.412	.444	.647	0.0	5.6	18

Player	B-T	Ht	Wt	DOB			AVG	G	AB	R	H	2B	3B	HR	RBI	BB	HBP	SH	SF	SO	SB	CS	OBP	SLG
Chourio, Winyer	R-R	6-2	180	11-4-03	3	6	.637	12	3	0	35	44	33	25	5	16	38	.308	.396	.538	22.4	9.4	170	
Cruz, Humberto	R-R	6-1	190	12-18-06	0	4	8.31	8	8	0	17	21	16	16	3	8	15	.304	.380	.551	19.0	10.1	79	
Davila, Manuel	R-R	6-0	140	8-8-07	0	5	9.61	13	0	0	20	27	27	21	4	11	13	.321	.404	.548	13.1	11.1	99	
Galindo, Ruben	R-R	6-1	175	1-24-01	0	1	9.00	5	2	0	5	9	5	5	0	4	6	.409	.536	.591	21.4	14.3	28	
Gil, Igor	L-L	5-11	170	3-23-01	0	0	0.00	2	0	0	7	4	1	0	0	0	8	.160	.160	.200	32.0	0.0	25	
Gillaspie, Logan	R-R	6-2	215	4-17-97	0	0	0.00	1	0	0	2	3	0	0	0	0	1	.429	.429	.429	14.3	0.0	7	
Herrera, Joseph	L-L	5-8	145	11-10-05	0	0	6.75	4	0	0	5	9	4	4	0	4	5	.360	.467	.440	16.7	13.3	30	
Hoeing, Bryan	R-R	6-6	210	10-19-96	0	0	33.75	2	2	0	1	6	6	5	1	0	2	.545	.545	1.000	18.2	0.0	11	
Huizi, Eiker	R-R	6-0	155	9-24-00	0	0	2.25	3	3	0	4	2	1	1	0	1	5	.154	.200	.154	33.3	6.7	15	
Javier, Ismael	S-R	5-8	160	8-27-05	0	0	3.86	3	0	0	2	4	1	1	1	1	0	.400	.500	.700	0.0	8.3	12	
Kemp, Kannon	R-R	6-6	225	9-3-04	0	2	4.88	5	3	0	24	22	13	13	1	8	16	.244	.317	.356	15.8	7.9	101	
Lais, Dane	R-R	6-4	205	6-18-05	0	0	3.86	3	1	0	5	3	2	2	2	2	.167	.286	.333	9.5	9.5	21		
Lopez, Jesus	R-R	5-11	175	3-14-06	0	2	17.36	7	4	0	9	14	18	18	3	10	12	.326	.473	.628	21.8	18.2	55	
Lugo, Alejandro	R-R	6-0	165	8-20-02	1	0	7.13	14	1	0	18	16	14	14	2	12	21	.235	.373	.426	25.0	14.5	83	
Mallitz, Josh	R-R	6-3	195	10-20-01	0	0	4.50	3	3	0	4	3	2	2	1	0	4	.200	.200	.467	26.7	0.0	15	
Maracara, Luis	R-R	6-0	175	8-19-07	2	4	9.19	12	4	0	32	35	36	33	2	30	41	.276	.417	.394	25.2	18.4	163	
Mejia, Rordy	R-R	6-0	180	4-28-05	1	1	8.44	3	0	0	5	7	6	5	0	4	7	.333	.440	.381	28.0	16.0	25	
Mendez, Darlin	R-R	6-1	210	7-19-04	0	2	17.05	12	0	0	13	19	28	24	6	16	15	.339	.513	.732	19.2	20.5	78	
Miralles, Maikel	R-R	5-11	160	10-22-04	0	0	0.00	1	1	0	2	0	0	0	0	0	0	2	.000	.000	.000	33.3	0.0	6
Moreno, Adan	R-R	6-1	185	9-8-04	0	2	6.46	8	6	0	15	18	12	11	2	7	14	.290	.371	.516	20.0	10.0	70	
Ortega, Jose	R-R	6-3	160	6-11-05	0	0	10.38	4	0	0	4	7	5	5	0	2	3	.389	.522	.500	13.0	8.7	23	
Paplham, Cole	R-R	6-3	215	3-19-00	0	0	1.93	4	3	0	5	1	1	1	0	3	3	.077	.278	.154	16.7	16.7	18	
Parra, Abraham	R-R	6-2	170	12-29-05	1	0	3.00	2	0	0	6	4	2	2	0	6	.182	.257	.225	25.0	0.0	24		
Pascual, Yovannki	L-L	5-11	185	8-4-02	1	2	7.91	17	1	1	19	30	19	17	1	9	22	.357	.426	.500	23.4	9.6	94	
Polanco, Dariel	R-R	5-11	150	9-28-05	2	1	5.79	15	1	1	37	54	26	24	1	7	28	.340	.366	.497	16.3	4.1	172	
Reyes, Elvis	R-R	6-2	180	4-28-03	0	0	7.83	15	1	1	23	24	24	20	1	30	21	.276	.447	.448	17.1	24.4	123	
Reyes, Jimmy	R-R	5-10	170	11-15-05	0	1	9.55	14	0	0	22	31	23	23	2	15	20	.360	.453	.663	18.9	14.2	106	
Ruiz, Xavier	R-R	6-1	180	11-19-02	0	1	4.91	6	0	1	7	10	5	4	0	2	11	.357	.400	.393	36.7	6.7	30	
Salinas, Ruben	R-L	6-0	154	1-13-03	0	0	9.64	12	0	0	19	33	20	20	2	11	22	.375	.450	.580	22.0	11.0	100	
Smith, Tanner	R-R	6-6	245	8-5-02	0	2	5.73	8	2	0	11	16	13	7	0	6	15	.308	.379	.423	25.9	10.3	58	
Swilling, Carson	R-R	5-11	196	1-9-02	0	0	18.00	1	0	0	1	3	2	2	0	0	2	.500	.500	.833	33.3	0.0	6	
Valdez, Miguel	R-R	6-0	170	8-1-03	1	2	6.32	14	0	3	16	20	13	11	1	14	17	.317	.436	.476	21.3	17.5	80	
Valenzuela, Jordan	R-R	6-2	190	5-20-05	1	1	10.02	17	0	0	21	28	24	23	0	14	20	.308	.413	.396	18.3	12.8	109	
Waldron, Matt	R-R	6-2	185	9-26-96	0	0	5.40	1	1	0	2	2	1	1	0	1	3	.286	.375	.429	37.5	12.5	8	
Wendelken, J.B.	R-R	6-1	242	3-24-93	0	0	8.44	4	2	0	5	9	5	5	0	1	5	.429	.458	.476	20.8	4.2	24	

Fielding

C: Ocopio 31, Castro 12, Mathey 9, Rodriguez 6, Hernandez 4, Guzman 2. **1B:** Hacen 22, Figueroa 11, Fountain 11, Ocopio 11, Fabian 7, Guzman 3, Castro 2, Rodriguez 1. **2B:** De Leon 50, Javier 9, Cronenworth 1, Turbi 1. **3B:** Javier 29, Hacen 22, Turbi 13, Rosario 3. **SS:** Tovar 30, Sanabria 21, Turbi 11, Hacen 1. **LF:** Marquez 31, Turbi 10, Rosario 8, Grant 6, De Leon 3, McCoy 3, Arias 2, Fabian 2, Sanabria 1. **CF:** Grant 41, Arias 7, Marquez 5, Roberts 5, Wells 5. **RF:** Arias 42, Marquez 12, Grant 10

DSL PADRES BROWN — ROOKIE
DOMINICAN SUMMER LEAGUE

Batting

Player	B-T	Ht.	Wt.	DOB	AVG	OBP	SLG	G	PA	AB	R	H	2B	3B	HR	RBI	BB	HBP	SH	SF	SO	SB	CS	BB%	SO%
Alfonzo, Dayquer	R-R	6-1	190	8-2-07	.244	.357	.329	30	98	82	9	20	4	0	1	17	13	2	0	1	19	2	3	13.3	19.4
Bastidas, Abraham	R-R	6-0	175	11-17-06	.333	.440	.412	37	125	102	17	34	8	0	0	16	13	8	0	2	20	2	1	10.4	16.0
Benavides, Cristian	R-R	6-0	175	10-8-07	.188	.305	.347	42	118	101	14	19	5	1	3	12	13	4	0	0	36	2	1	11.0	30.5
Bericoto, Jose	R-R	6-0	160	4-23-07	.215	.353	.273	45	151	121	23	26	2	1	1	15	25	2	1	2	37	8	2	16.6	24.5
Castillo, Darian	S-R	5-7	150	9-12-06	.325	.476	.388	31	103	80	18	26	3	1	0	11	18	5	0	0	14	6	5	17.5	13.6
Enriche, Alberto	R-R	5-8	165	12-20-07	.125	.333	.375	8	21	16	5	2	1	0	1	2	5	0	0	0	10	0	0	23.8	47.6
Garza, Andres	L-R	5-11	165	6-12-07	.205	.369	.265	46	150	117	13	24	2	1	1	16	24	7	1	1	42	0	1	16.0	28.0
Guerrero, Tom	R-R	6-0	170	1-5-06	.158	.331	.237	43	145	114	16	18	9	0	0	13	27	3	0	1	32	1	2	18.6	22.1
Hernandez, Kaden	R-R	6-1	165	10-17-07	.130	.268	.159	32	82	69	7	9	2	0	0	6	10	3	0	0	15	0	0	12.2	18.3
Hernandez, Yonaiker	R-R	6-0	155	4-8-08	.254	.311	.287	38	132	122	11	31	4	0	0	18	6	4	0	0	21	3	1	4.5	15.9
Martinez, Juan	R-R	6-3	175	2-1-07	.087	.210	.146	40	120	103	11	9	3	1	1	7	11	5	1	0	35	0	0	9.2	29.2
Mejia, Angel	S-R	5-8	155	7-16-08	.203	.373	.254	32	75	59	8	12	1	1	0	2	14	2	0	0	19	3	2	18.7	25.3
Morla, Yorvin	S-R	5-10	150	12-24-05	.000	.600	.000	2	5	2	1	0	0	0	0	0	2	1	0	0	2	0	1	40.0	40.0
Pena, Sebastian	L-L	6-1	180	10-3-07	.219	.291	.307	40	151	137	22	30	8	2	0	9	14	0	0	0	31	4	5	9.3	20.5
Primera, Eliander	L-R	5-10	160	2-10-08	.000	.286	.000	5	7	5	2	0	0	0	0	0	2	0	0	0	1	1	0	28.6	14.3
Rios, Endy	R-R	6-0	155	2-15-07	.260	.357	.340	40	116	100	16	26	4	2	0	10	12	3	1	0	21	5	3	10.3	18.1
Saguita, Frederick	L-R	5-10	165	12-19-07	.102	.200	.122	23	56	49	2	5	1	0	0	4	4	5	1	1	0	28	1	0	8.9	50.0
Teran, Gabriel	R-R	5-8	160	11-17-07	.308	.438	.308	5	17	13	1	4	0	0	0	3	3	1	0	0	2	1	1	17.6	11.8
Verdugo, Jose	R-R	5-9	160	9-26-07	.455	.556	.455	5	18	11	4	5	0	0	0	6	5	0	0	2	1	0	0	27.8	5.6
Winklaar, Clay	R-R	5-8	195	9-13-06	.167	.329	.250	26	76	60	12	10	4	0	0	5	11	4	0	2	18	3	1	14.5	36.8

Pitching

Player	B-T	Ht.	Wt.	DOB	W	L	ERA	G	GS	SV	IP	Hits	Runs	ER	HR	BB	SO	AVG	OBP	SLG	SO%	BB%	BF
Alvarez, Carlos	L-L	6-4	195	11-14-07	0	0	0.00	1	0	0	4	1	1	0	0	5	0	.083	.250	.083	25.0	18.8	16
Aquino, Gensy	L-L	5-10	165	9-20-07	1	1	9.17	11	0	0	18	14	21	18	0	20	15	.222	.416	.238	16.9	22.5	89
Beltre, Yoesmerli	R-R	6-4	180	5-31-06	1	0	2.45	3	0	2	4	3	1	0	0	3	.200	.368	.267	15.8	15.8	19	
Burciaga, Daniel	R-R	5-10	160	6-3-08	2	2	4.55	11	5	1	30	31	21	15	2	16	20	.279	.381	.396	14.9	11.9	134
Cruz, Randoll	R-R	6-7	220	1-10-07	2	3	11.74	17	0	3	15	20	26	20	6	19	.303	.525	.409	19.2	28.3	99	
Dilone, Ariel	L-R	6-0	170	9-14-07	0	0	10.45	12	2	1	21	22	26	24	0	26	16	.282	.477	.346	14.4	23.4	111
Eluscat, Marco	L-L	6-1	145	7-5-06	1	3	5.85	10	10	0	40	42	28	26	3	21	48	.275	.379	.392	26.2	11.5	183
Figueroa, Josias	R-R	6-1	175	1-4-07	2	3	3.31	9	8	0	35	30	17	13	1	20	31	.231	.355	.323	20.0	12.9	155

	B-T	Ht.	Wt.	DOB	AVG	OBP	SLG	G	PA	AB	R	H	2B	3B	HR	RBI	BB	HBP	SH	SF	SO	SB	CS	BB%	SO%
Franco, Oliver	R-R	6-8	210	9-16-06	0	2	5.66	6	5	0	21	21	19	13	0	12	26	.273	.396	.312	26.8		12.4		97
Guzman, Jeuris	R-R	6-4	210	8-27-05	1	0	5.68	16	0	2	19	18	14	12	0	24	11	.254	.436	.282	10.9		23.8		101
Marte, Kelvin	R-R	5-11	170	6-26-07	1	5	4.83	10	9	0	32	31	24	17	0	17	16	.265	.375	.325	11.1		11.8		144
Matos, Wilkins	R-R	6-6	166	1-12-07	1	0	13.03	9	0	0	10	12	16	14	2	12	5	.300	.482	.500	8.9		21.4		56
Montijo, Jose	R-R	6-0	170	9-14-07	2	1	10.64	6	2	0	11	18	14	13	1	5	12	.375	.426	.500	22.2		9.3		54
Navarro, Cristian	R-R	6-2	181	5-31-07	1	4	8.89	14	2	0	26	41	28	26	3	12	25	.353	.415	.569	19.2		9.2		130
Nunez, Dalvi	R-R	5-8	200	11-25-06	0	0	4.05	4	4	0	13	9	7	6	1	9	15	.188	.350	.271	25.0		15.0		60
Paca, Wilfred	R-R	5-11	155	12-5-05	2	6	5.79	14	7	0	37	37	28	24	3	25	23	.266	.404	.410	12.9		14.0		178
Perez, Albert	R-R	6-0	180	12-11-07	1	0	0.00	3	0	0	6	3	0	0	0	0	7	.143	.143	.143	33.3		0.0		21
Pilar, Victor	L-L	6-0	175	3-21-08	1	1	5.06	16	0	0	32	23	26	18	0	38	23	.219	.455	.238	14.9		24.7		154
Romero, Guillermo	L-L	6-0	160	5-7-05	0	1	7.20	5	0	0	5	7	4	4	0	2	4	.389	.520	.444	16.0		8.0		25
Sanchez, Angel	R-R	5-9	168	4-20-06	0	3	6.39	6	0	0	13	9	9	9	0	6	11	.231	.382	.333	20.0		10.9		55

Fielding
C: Garza 29, Mejia 27, Alfonzo 6, Enriche 4. **1B:** Martinez 25, Alfonzo 16, Garza 13, Bastidas 3, Mejia 3, Hernandez 2, Rios 1. **2B:** Bastidas 9, Castillo 16, K. Hernandez 12, Guerrero 6, Rios 6, Y. Hernandez 6, Morla 1, Verdugo 1. **3B:** Y. Hernandez 28, Rios 14, Bastidas 9, Martinez 5, Garza 2, K. Hernandez 1. **SS:** Guerrero 35, Hernandez 12, Rios 6, Verdugo 4, Bastidas 3. **LF:** Winklaar 19, Bericoto 14, Pena 10, Benavides 6, Rios 4, Saguita 3, Alfonzo 1, Castillo 1, Martinez 1, Morla 1, Primera 1. **CF:** Pena 27, Bericoto 14, Benavides 9, Rios 3, Saguita 3, Winklaar 3, Castillo 2, Primera 2. **RF:** Benavides 23, Bericoto 13, Saguita 8, Alfonzo 5, Castillo 5, Martinez 4, Winklaar 4, Rios 3, Pena 2, Hernandez 1, Primera 1

DSL PADRES GOLD   ROOKIE
DOMINICAN SUMMER LEAGUE

Batting	B-T	Ht.	Wt.	DOB	AVG	OBP	SLG	G	PA	AB	R	H	2B	3B	HR	RBI	BB	HBP	SH	SF	SO	SB	CS	BB%	SO%
Alcala, Antonio	R-R	5-5	180	12-2-05	.167	.300	.167	9	10	6	1	1	0	0	0	2	2	0	0	2	1	0	0	20.0	10.0
Alcantara, Fabian	R-R	6-0	170	12-12-05	.275	.387	.560	35	111	91	22	25	5	0	7	28	17	1	0	2	31	6	2	15.3	27.9
Alfonzo, Dayquer	R-R	6-1	190	8-2-07	.195	.358	.195	17	53	41	8	8	0	0	0	2	7	4	0	1	14	1	1	13.2	26.4
Bastidas, Abraham	R-R	6-0	175	11-17-06	.190	.526	.333	11	38	21	8	4	3	0	0	6	12	4	0	1	5	3	2	31.6	13.2
Benavides, Cristian	R-R	6-0	175	10-8-07	.125	.364	.125	4	11	8	1	1	0	0	0	1	3	0	0	0	2	0	0	27.3	18.2
Castillo, Darian	S-R	5-7	150	9-12-06	.167	.306	.200	16	36	30	6	5	1	0	0	3	4	2	0	0	8	2	0	11.1	22.2
Contreras, Santiago	R-R	6-2	155	8-16-05	.299	.443	.423	39	124	97	24	29	5	2	1	8	18	7	2	0	29	16	2	14.5	23.4
Coronil, Deivid	B-R	6-3	162	10-4-07	.186	.327	.214	45	174	140	23	26	2	1	0	12	21	9	3	1	47	8	0	12.1	27.0
De La Cruz, Jhoan	S-R	5-9	165	11-16-07	.259	.477	.360	51	198	139	37	36	5	3	1	21	46	12	1	0	45	11	4	23.2	22.7
Downer, Jhojan	R-R	5-10	170	6-9-07	.194	.347	.254	44	168	134	25	26	6	1	0	18	29	3	1	1	40	9	4	17.3	23.8
Enriche, Alberto	R-R	5-8	165	12-20-07	.000	.000	.000	1	1	1	0	0	0	0	0	0	0	0	0	0	1	0	0	0.0	100.0
Garcia, Alexander	L-R	6-0	170	5-06-05	.154	.321	.200	32	84	65	13	10	1	1	0	9	17	0	0	2	21	4	0	20.2	25.0
Guerrero, Tom	R-R	6-0	170	1-5-06	.091	.231	.091	3	13	11	1	1	0	0	0	0	2	0	0	0	4	0	0	15.4	30.8
Hernandez, Jason	R-R	5-11	160	1-11-06	.154	.313	.154	5	16	13	1	2	0	0	0	1	3	0	0	0	5	1	0	18.8	31.3
Martinez, Eddson	L-L	5-5	145	8-21-07	.304	.462	.382	38	136	102	16	31	6	1	0	18	25	5	4	0	19	5	5	18.4	14.0
Morla, Yorvin	S-R	5-10	150	12-24-05	.226	.419	.302	29	75	53	15	12	2	1	0	10	17	2	1	2	8	5	3	22.7	10.7
Pena, Sebastian	L-L	6-1	180	10-3-07	.182	.250	.182	5	12	11	2	2	0	0	0	1	1	0	0	0	2	0	0	8.3	16.7
Ponce, Isaac	R-R	6-2	192	11-1-06	.266	.390	.429	46	187	154	28	41	7	0	6	36	23	9	0	1	30	4	0	12.3	16.0
Tamburini, Kevin	R-R	6-1	150	4-26-06	.225	.281	.292	39	135	120	14	27	6	1	0	18	7	4	0	4	30	5	2	5.2	22.2
Tejeda, Eduarlin	S-R	5-9	150	2-24-05	.301	.446	.392	51	190	143	39	43	7	3	0	25	37	3	4	3	30	5	0	19.5	15.8
Valdez, Moises	R-R	5-8	165	11-28-05	.309	.410	.422	56	243	204	47	63	10	5	1	21	28	7	3	0	37	26	5	11.5	15.2
Verdugo, Jose	R-R	5-9	160	9-26-07	.321	.416	.512	25	102	84	19	27	8	1	2	25	14	1	1	2	16	7	1	13.7	15.7

Pitching	B-T	Ht.	Wt.	DOB	W	L	ERA	G	GS	SV	IP	Hits	Runs	ER	HR	BB	SO	AVG	OBP	SLG	SO%	BB%	BF
Alvarez, Carlos	L-L	6-4	195	11-14-07	0	2	11.84	11	11	0	19	17	30	25	1	28	19	.233	.462	.356	'17.9	'26.4	106
Alvarez, Miguel	R-R	5-11	165	10-8-04	5	0	2.88	15	1	2	34	32	13	11	0	13	25	.244	.320	.282	17.0	8.8	147
Belliard, Raymel	R-R	6-1	155	12-9-05	2	3	2.45	17	2	1	29	19	12	8	0	19	35	.177	.297	.238	20.0	10.9	175
Beltre, Yoesmerli	R-R	6-4	180	5-31-06	1	0	1.50	16	0	0	18	16	5	3	0	7	23	.209	.280	.254	30.7	9.3	75
Blanco, Jose	R-R	6-2	185	6-20-04	2	1	3.22	15	0	1	22	18	9	8	2	11	25	.217	.330	.289	25.8	11.3	97
Burciaga, Daniel	R-R	5-10	160	6-3-08	0	1	11.57	2	0	0	2	5	3	3	0	0	1	.545	.500	.545	8.3	0.0	12
Castro, Aaron	L-R	5-8	134	5-20-06	3	0	2.91	11	8	0	43	30	19	14	1	10	46	.194	.265	.258	27.1	5.9	170
Eluscat, Marco	L-L	6-1	145	7-5-06	1	0	3.86	2	1	0	7	3	3	3	1	3	10	.136	.240	.318	40.0	12.0	25
Figuereo, Josias	R-R	6-1	175	1-4-07	0	0	9.00	3	1	0	4	7	5	4	1	4	5	.368	.478	.579	21.7	17.4	23
Hernandez, Edinson	R-R	6-2	175	6-9-06	1	0	0.00	1	0	0	1	0	0	0	1	3	.250	.400	.250	60.0	20.0	5
Hernandez, Edwyn	L-L	6-0	180	7-28-07	4	0	2.75	18	0	2	36	32	13	11	1	25	27	.252	.380	.307	17.0	15.7	159
Herrera, Joseph	L-L	5-8	165	11-6-06	1	1	5.02	4	3	0	14	14	8	8	1	7	13	.259	.355	.370	20.6	11.1	63
Mejia, Rordy	R-R	6-0	180	4-28-05	0	2	6.92	4	3	0	13	18	10	10	0	3	15	.305	.339	.390	24.2	4.8	62
Minaya, Johan	R-R	6-1	165	10-22-04	7	1	4.13	16	0	1	33	34	18	15	1	23	35	.202	.336	.269	16.1	143	
Montijo, Jose	R-R	6-0	170	9-14-07	1	2	9.00	7	0	0	11	13	11	11	2	12	7	.317	.474	.585	12.3	21.1	57
Nunez, Dalvi	R-R	5-8	200	11-25-06	1	0	6.00	8	7	0	24	16	17	16	0	15	25	.195	.353	.244	24.5	14.7	102
Ortega, Jose	R-R	6-3	160	6-11-05	1	1	1.54	8	0	2	12	6	3	2	0	5	14	.190	.292	.214	29.2	10.4	48
Palmeros, Jeronimo	L-L	6-3	170	12-11-07	2	1	2.88	11	10	0	41	40	15	13	2	10	48	.261	.311	.314	28.6	6.0	168
Perez, Albert	R-R	6-0	180	12-11-07	1	0	3.86	2	0	0	2	1	1	1	0	1	0	.143	.333	.143	0.0	11.1	9
Romero, Guillermo	L-L	6-0	160	5-7-05	0	0	5.14	7	0	0	7	6	5	4	0	5	5	.231	.375	.308	15.6	15.6	32
Sanchez, Angel	R-R	5-9	168	4-20-06	1	0	5.52	11	0	1	15	17	11	9	0	15	12	.288	.488	.373	14.3	17.9	84
Vasquez, Florangel	R-R	6-0	195	3-3-06	5	1	3.79	21	0	0	36	29	15	15	1	13	46	.242	.333	.358	32.6	9.2	141
Villabona, Jefferson	R-R	5-11	176	11-1-00	1	0	1.96	19	0	8	23	14	7	5	0	5	25	.169	.250	.200	31.9	8.3	72
Sanchez, Angel	R-R	5-9	168	4-20-06	1	0	2.57	14	0	2	21	10	7	6	1	12	17	.215	.337	.342	17.17	12.12	99
Valenzuela, Jordan	R-R	6-2	192	5-20-05	1	1	12.46	8	0	0	13	14	20	18	0	21	12	.269	.493	.288	16.00	28.00	75

Fielding
C: Downer 32, Ponce 25, Alcala 2, Alfonzo 1. **1B:** Tamburini 18, Ponce 15, Garcia 11, Downer 9, Bastidas 7, Alfonzo 3, Tejeda 2, Martinez 1. **2B:** Morla 20, De La Cruz 18, Tejeda 16, Verdugo 10, Castillo 6, Alcala 1, Guerrero 1. **3B:** Coronil 27, Tejeda 17, Tamburini 14, De La Cruz 4, Morla 4, Bastidas 1, Contreras 1, Guerrero 1. **SS:** De La Cruz 31, Coronil 14, Verdugo 3, Tejeda 2, Guerrero 1, Morla 1. **LF:** Contreras 28, Tejeda 17, Martinez 7, Pena 3, Alfonzo 2, Garcia 2, Hernandez 2, Alcantara 1, Benavides 1, Castillo 1, Morla 1. **CF:** Valdez 50, Martinez 8, Contreras 4, Alcantara 3, Alfonzo 1, Castillo 1. **RF:** Alcantara 29, Garcia 10, Martinez 9, Castillo 6, Contreras 6, Tejeda 2, Alfonzo 4, Benavides 3, Hernandez 2, Pena 2

San Francisco Giants

SEASON SYNOPSIS: In the first season under president of baseball operations Buster Posey, the Giants made big changes to the roster before and during the season, but in the end the results were all too similar. San Francisco hasn't won more than 81 or lost more than 83 in each of the last four seasons, with the second 81-81 season in the last four costing manager Bob Melvin his job after just two seasons.

HIGH POINT: San Francisco played well in April and most of May, and a seven-game win streak left them 40-28, a half-game out of first place, on June 11. The streak included a sweep of preseason-favorite Atlanta, with consecutive walk-offs capped when Matt Chapman's two-run homer walked the Braves off in the finale. The streak ended in dramatic fashion as well as the Giants blew a 7-2 lead in Colorado, losing 8-7.

LOW POINT: After winning the first game of a home series with the Dodgers on July 11, pulling within five games of first place in the NL West, the Giants collapsed. They lost 12 of their last 14 in July, including 10 of 12 coming out of the all-star break with home sweeps to the Mets and Pirates. They scored 1 or 0 runs in six of the 12 losses, and they lost 15 out of 16 home games in a stretch that lasted into mid-August.

NOTABLE ROOKIES: Injuries to the Giants' rotation opened opportunities for Taiwanese righty Kai-Wei Teng (2-4, 6.37), lefty Carson Whisenhunt (2-1, 5.01) and eventually Trevor McDonald, a 2019 11th-round pick who showed promise by beating the Dodgers and Rockies in his two starts. Christian Koss, 27, showed some athleticism while hitting .264/.309/.368. Outfielder Drew Gilbert provided a brief spark after being acquired from the Mets but still hit .190.

KEY TRANSACTIONS: Willy Adames signed a seven-year, $182 million deal in the offseason, and while he got off to a slow start, he finished strong and became the first Giant to hit 30 homers in a season since Barry Bonds in 2004. Posey boldly pounced when the Red Sox were at loggerheads with Rafael Devers, trading lefty Kyle Harrison and righty Jordan Hicks for Devers' big bat and about $250 million on his 10-year, $313.5 million contract. But Devers didn't spark the Giants enough to avoid the team from deciding to sell veterans at the deadline, as Posey traded away key relievers Camilo Doval (Yankees) and Tyler Rogers (Mets).

OPENING DAY PAYROLL: $173,019,524 (14th)

PLAYERS OF THE YEAR

MAJOR LEAGUE
Logan Webb
RHP
15-11, 3.22 ERA,
Career-high 224 SO in
MLB-leading 207 IP

MINOR LEAGUE
Bryce Eldridge
1B
(Rk,AA,AAA)
.260/.333/.510
25 HR, 21 2B, 84 RBIs

ORGANIZATION LEADERS

Batting		*Qualifiers
MAJORS		
* AVG	Jung Hoo Lee	.266
* OPS	Matt Chapman	.770
HR	Willy Adames	30
RBI	Willy Adames	87
MINORS		
* AVG	Dakota Jordan, San Jose	.311
* OBP	Drew Cavanaugh, Sac./Richmond/Eugene/SJ	.396
* SLG	Bryce Eldridge, Sac./Richmond/ACL Giants	.510
* OPS	Dakota Jordan, San Jose	.875
R	Scott Bandura, Richmond/Eugene	91
H	Lisbel Diaz, San Jose	139
TB	Charlie Szykowny, Eugene	234
2B	Lisbel Diaz, San Jose	32
3B	Jonah Cox, Eugene	10
HR	Bryce Eldridge, Sacramento/Richmond/ACL Giants	25
RBI	Charlie Szykowny, Eugene	85
BB	Marco Luciano, Sacramento	85
SO	Marco Luciano, Sacramento	170
SB	Jonah Cox, Eugene	58

Pitching		#Qualifiers
MAJORS		
W	Logan Webb	15
# ERA	Logan Webb	3.22
SO	Logan Webb	224
SV	Ryan Walker	17
MINORS		
W	Four tied	9
L	Manuel Mercedes, Richmond/Eugene	13
# ERA	John Bertrand, Sacramento/Richmond	2.82
G	Miguel Diaz, Sacramento	50
GS	Seth Lonsway, Sacramento/Richmond	28
SV	Tyler Myrick, Sacramento/Richmond	10
SV	Ben Peterson, Eugene/San Jose	10
IP	John Bertrand, Sacramento/Richmond	144
BB	Seth Lonsway, Sacramento/Richmond	67
SO	Trevor McDonald, Sacramento	144
# AVG	Josh Bostick, Eugene	.218

2025 PERFORMANCE

President: Buster Posey. **Farm Director:** Kyle Haines. **Scouting Director:** Michael Holmes.

Class	Team	League	W	L	PCT	Finish	Manager
Majors	San Francisco Giants	National	81	81	.500	8 (15)	Bob Melvin
Triple-A	Sacramento River Cats	Pacific Coast	77	73	.513	6 (10)	Dave Brundage
Double-A	Richmond Flying Squirrels	Eastern	56	79	.415	10 (12)	Dennis Pelfrey
High-A	Eugene Emeralds	Northwest	81	51	.614	1 (6)	Jeremiah Knackstedt
Low-A	San Jose Giants	California	81	51	.614	1 (8)	Ydwin Villegas
Rookie	ACL Giants	Arizona Complex	42	18	.700	1 (15)	Jacob Heyward
Rookie	DSL Giants Black	Dominican	33	23	.589	14 (52)	Juan Ciriaco
Rookie	DSL Giants Orange	Dominican	35	19	.648	5 (52)	Drew Martinez
Overall 2025 Minor League Record			405	314	.563	2nd (30)	

ORGANIZATION STATISTICS

SAN FRANCISCO GIANTS
NATIONAL LEAGUE

Batting	B-T	Ht.	Wt.	DOB	AVG	OBP	SLG	G	PA	AB	R	H	2B	3B	HR	RBI	BB	HBP	SH	SF	SO	SB	CS	BB%	SO%
Adames, Willy	R-R	6-1	214	9-2-95	.225	.318	.421	160	686	591	94	133	22	2	30	87	80	5	0	9	179	12	4	11.7	26.1
Alcantara, Sergio	S-R	6-4	151	7-10-96	.000	.000	.000	1	4	4	0	0	0	0	0	0	0	0	0	0	2	0	0	0.0	50.0
Bailey, Patrick	S-R	6-0	210	5-29-99	.222	.277	.325	135	452	409	47	91	18	3	6	55	30	3	4	6	133	1	0	6.6	29.4
Chapman, Matt	R-R	6-0	215	4-28-93	.231	.340	.430	128	535	454	76	105	23	2	21	61	71	6	0	4	126	9	4	13.3	23.6
Devers, Rafael	L-R	6-0	240	10-24-96	.236	.347	.460	90	395	335	52	79	15	0	20	51	56	2	0	2	116	0	0	14.2	29.4
Eldridge, Bryce	L-R	6-7	219	10-20-04	.107	.297	.179	10	37	28	1	3	2	0	0	4	7	1	0	1	13	0	0	18.9	35.1
Encarnacion, Jerar	R-R	6-4	250	10-22-97	.200	.214	.364	19	56	55	5	11	3	0	2	7	1	0	0	0	15	1	0	1.8	26.8
Fitzgerald, Tyler	R-R	6-3	205	9-15-97	.217	.278	.327	72	243	217	19	47	10	1	4	14	17	2	6	1	70	9	4	7.0	28.8
Flores, Wilmer	R-R	6-2	213	8-6-91	.241	.307	.379	125	463	419	44	101	10	0	16	71	34	7	0	3	88	1	0	7.3	19.0
Gilbert, Drew	L-L	5-9	195	9-27-00	.190	.248	.350	39	109	100	12	19	5	1	3	13	7	1	0	1	20	1	1	6.4	18.3
Huff, Sam	R-R	6-4	240	1-14-98	.208	.259	.340	20	58	53	5	11	1	0	2	4	4	0	0	1	25	0	0	6.9	43.1
Johnson, Daniel	L-L	5-9	200	7-11-95	.172	.226	.345	14	31	29	5	5	2	0	1	1	2	0	0	0	8	1	0	6.5	25.8
Knizner, Andrew	R-R	6-1	225	2-3-95	.221	.299	.299	33	88	77	12	17	1	1	1	5	7	2	1	1	10	0	0	8.0	11.4
Koss, Christian	R-R	6-1	182	1-27-98	.264	.309	.368	76	191	174	25	46	9	0	3	23	9	3	3	2	45	4	1	4.7	23.6
Lee, Jung Hoo	L-R	6-0	171	8-20-98	.266	.327	.407	150	617	560	73	149	31	12	8	55	47	6	0	4	71	10	3	7.6	11.5
Matos, Luis	R-R	5-11	160	1-28-02	.221	.266	.424	57	184	172	26	38	9	1	8	22	11	0	0	1	27	4	0	6.0	14.7
McCray, Grant	L-R	6-2	200	12-7-00	.091	.160	.182	22	26	22	3	2	1	0	0	2	2	0	1	1	11	0	0	7.7	42.3
Porter, Logan	R-R	6-0	200	7-12-95	.143	.333	.143	5	9	7	2	1	0	0	0	1	1	1	0	0	2	0	0	11.1	22.2
Ramos, Heliot	R-R	6-1	188	9-7-99	.256	.328	.400	157	695	620	85	159	24	1	21	69	52	17	0	6	158	6	4	7.5	22.7
Schmitt, Casey	R-R	6-2	215	3-1-99	.237	.305	.401	95	348	312	34	74	15	0	12	40	27	5	1	3	83	0	0	7.8	23.9
Smith, Dominic	L-L	6-0	224	6-15-95	.284	.333	.417	63	225	204	26	58	10	0	5	33	15	2	0	4	42	2	0	6.7	18.7
Villar, David	R-R	6-1	215	1-27-97	.200	.360	.250	9	25	20	4	4	1	0	0	1	4	1	0	0	5	0	0	16.0	20.0
Wade, LaMonte	L-L	6-1	205	1-1-94	.167	.275	.271	50	169	144	12	24	8	2	1	15	21	1	2	1	35	0	0	12.4	20.7
Wisely, Brett	L-R	5-10	180	1-8-99	.269	.354	.354	22	54	48	5	10	4	0	1	10	4	0	2	0	10	1	1	7.4	18.5
Yastrzemski, Mike	L-L	5-10	178	8-23-90	.231	.330	.355	97	372	321	38	74	14	1	8	28	47	1	2	1	86	6	2	12.6	23.1

Pitching	B-T	Ht.	Wt.	DOB	W	L	ERA	G	GS	SV	IP	Hits	Runs	ER	HR	BB	SO	AVG	OBP	SLG	SO%	BB%	BF
Alexander, Scott	L-L	6-2	195	7-10-89	0	0	6.75	2	0	0	1	3	1	1	1	2	2	.429	.556	1.143	22.2	22.2	9
Beck, Tristan	R-R	6-4	165	6-24-96	1	0	4.61	31	1	2	57	47	29	29	7	16	41	.223	.280	.379	17.7	6.9	232
Birdsong, Hayden	R-R	6-4	215	8-30-01	4	4	4.80	21	10	0	66	61	42	35	10	37	68	.242	.347	.425	22.8	12.4	298
Bivens, Spencer	R-R	6-5	205	6-28-94	4	3	4.00	54	0	3	81	83	42	36	6	25	61	.269	.331	.408	17.8	7.3	343
Black, Mason	R-R	6-3	230	12-10-99	0	0	6.75	1	0	0	4	5	5	3	2	0	5	.263	.263	.737	26.3	0.0	19
Brubaker, JT	R-R	6-3	185	11-17-93	0	0	4.26	5	1	0	13	13	6	6	0	3	12	.260	.302	.320	22.2	5.6	54
Butto, Jose	R-R	6-2	202	6-19-98	2	1	4.50	21	0	0	20	19	10	10	2	10	17	.268	.353	.437	19.8	11.6	86
Doval, Camilo	R-R	6-2	185	7-4-97	4	2	3.09	47	0	15	47	32	20	16	2	24	50	.196	.305	.264	26.2	12.6	191
Gage, Matt	L-L	6-3	265	2-11-93	0	1	3.91	27	2	0	25	28	11	11	0	10	24	.283	.360	.343	21.4	8.9	112
Harrison, Kyle	R-L	6-2	200	8-12-01	1	1	4.56	8	4	0	24	21	12	12	4	9	25	.231	.300	.440	25.0	9.0	100
Hicks, Jordan	R-R	6-2	220	9-6-96	1	5	6.47	13	9	0	49	55	36	35	3	20	43	.288	.366	.414	19.8	9.2	217
Hjelle, Sean	R-R	6-11	228	5-7-97	1	1	7.80	12	1	0	15	21	13	13	2	9	11	.339	.417	.532	15.1	12.3	73
Koss, Christian	R-R	6-1	182	1-27-98	0	0	0.00	4	0	0	4	0	0	0	0	0	0	.250	.250	.250	0.0	0.0	16
Lucchesi, Joey	L-L	6-5	225	6-6-93	0	1	3.76	38	0	0	38	35	17	16	4	12	31	.245	.301	.383	18.8	7.3	165
McDonald, Trevor	R-R	6-2	200	2-26-01	1	0	1.80	3	2	0	15	13	6	3	1	2	14	.228	.254	.298	23.3	3.3	60
Miller, Erik	L-L	6-5	240	2-13-98	4	1	1.50	36	0	0	30	24	5	5	0	20	22	.238	.373	.287	17.2	15.6	128
Peguero, Joel	R-R	5-11	160	5-7-95	3	1	2.42	17	0	0	22	15	7	6	2	8	17	.197	.271	.316	19.8	9.3	86
Porter, Logan	R-R	6-0	200	7-12-95	0	0	9.00	1	0	0	1	2	1	1	0	0	0	.400	.400	1.000	0.0	0.0	5
Ray, Robbie	L-L	6-2	225	10-1-91	11	8	3.65	32	32	0	182	148	81	74	22	73	186	.221	.298	.383	24.6	9.7	755
Rodriguez, Randy	R-R	6-0	166	9-5-99	3	5	1.78	50	0	4	51	34	12	10	4	11	67	.187	.247	.286	33.8	5.6	198
Rogers, Tyler	R-R	6-3	181	12-17-90	4	3	1.80	53	0	0	50	39	11	10	3	5	38	.213	.229	.300	20.2	2.1	188
Roupp, Landen	R-R	6-2	205	9-10-98	7	7	3.80	22	22	0	107	113	55	45	11	45	102	.268	.340	.400	21.4	9.5	476
Seymour, Carson	R-R	6-6	260	12-16-98	1	3	4.75	16	3	0	36	37	21	19	9	13	26	.262	.329	.489	16.7	8.3	156
Teng, Kai-Wei	R-R	6-4	260	12-1-98	2	4	6.37	8	7	0	30	29	24	21	2	17	39	.254	.381	.351	28.1	12.2	139
Trivino, Lou	R-R	6-5	235	10-1-91	1	0	5.84	14	0	0	12	11	8	8	4	5	11	.229	.315	.479	20.4	9.3	54

	B-T	Ht.	Wt.	DOB																		
Verlander, Justin	R-R	6-5	235	2-20-83	4	11	3.85	29	29	0	152	155	74	65	16	52	137	.261	.323	.413	20.7	7.9	662
Walker, Ryan	R-R	6-2	200	11-26-95	5	7	4.11	68	0	17	61	60	32	28	4	18	60	.254	.326	.373	22.6	6.8	266
Webb, Logan	R-R	6-1	220	11-18-96	15	11	3.22	34	34	0	207	210	82	74	14	46	224	.264	.308	.386	26.2	5.4	856
Whisenhunt, Carson	L-L	6-3	209	10-20-00	2	1	5.01	5	5	0	23	22	14	13	6	12	16	.250	.353	.511	15.7	11.8	102
Winn, Keaton	R-R	6-4	238	2-20-98	0	0	4.50	7	0	0	10	12	5	5	1	2	9	.300	.333	.475	21.4	4.8	42
Yastrzemski, Mike	L-L	5-10	178	8-23-90	0	0	18.00	1	0	0	1	2	2	2	0	1	0	.400	.571	.600	0.0	14.3	7

Fielding

Catcher	PCT	G	PO	A	E	DP	PB
Bailey	.994	132	1013	57	7	9	8
Huff	1.000	20	135	7	0	0	1
Knizner	.986	32	198	9	3	1	0
Porter	1.000	4	20	0	0	1	0

First Base	PCT	G	PO	A	E	DP
Devers	.991	28	208	24	2	19
Eldridge	1.000	4	35	2	0	4
Encarnacion	.875	1	6	1	1	0
Flores	1.000	30	181	13	0	17
Schmitt	.992	18	106	13	1	12
Smith	.998	53	390	38	1	40
Villar	1.000	8	60	3	0	4
Wade	.989	45	325	28	4	26

Second Base	PCT	G	PO	A	E	DP
Fitzgerald	.985	69	104	166	4	35
Koss	.983	46	56	118	3	19
Schmitt	.981	53	84	125	4	30
Wisely	.982	16	18	38	1	7

Third Base	PCT	G	PO	A	E	DP
Alcantara	.500	1	0	1	1	0
Chapman	.961	127	93	224	13	30
Devers	1.000	1	0	3	0	1
Flores	1.000	2	0	1	0	0
Koss	.905	13	5	14	2	3
Schmitt	.917	26	18	37	5	2
Villar	.000	1	0	0	0	0
Wisely	.857	4	1	5	1	0

Shortstop	PCT	G	PO	A	E	DP
Adames	.974	158	200	398	16	76
Alcantara	.000	1	0	0	0	0
Koss	.909	7	7	13	2	4
Schmitt	1.000	1	1	1	0	0
Wisely	1.000	1	1	0	0	0

Outfield	PCT	G	PO	A	E	DP
Encarnacion	1.000	16	28	1	0	0
Fitzgerald	1.000	3	7	0	0	0
Gilbert	1.000	38	67	2	0	0
Johnson	1.000	10	18	0	0	0
Lee	.991	147	315	7	3	2
Matos	.953	51	82	0	4	0
McCray	.857	23	11	1	2	1
Ramos	.970	154	284	5	9	1
Smith	.000	1	0	0	0	0
Yastrzemski	.994	94	147	9	1	0

SACRAMENTO RIVER CATS — TRIPLE-A
PACIFIC COAST LEAGUE

Batting	B-T	Ht.	Wt.	DOB	AVG	OBP	SLG	G	PA	AB	R	H	2B	3B	HR	RBI	BB	HBP	SH	SF	SO	SB	CS	BB%	SO%
Alcantara, Sergio	S-R	6-4	151	7-10-96	.206	.319	.252	68	256	218	28	45	10	0	0	14	35	1	2	0	56	2	2	13.7	21.9
Auerbach, Brett	R-R	5-9	185	8-27-98	.223	.358	.364	41	148	121	21	27	5	0	4	14	25	1	0	1	38	2	1	16.9	25.7
Barnes, Austin	R-R	5-10	187	12-28-89	.212	.297	.212	10	37	33	7	7	0	0	0	2	4	0	0	0	6	0	0	10.8	16.2
Basabe, Osleivis	R-R	5-11	188	9-13-00	.249	.309	.412	125	477	430	62	107	24	2	14	56	33	6	4	3	84	7	1	6.9	17.6
Bericoto, Victor	R-R	6-1	155	12-3-01	.196	.196	.283	11	46	46	1	9	1	0	1	4	0	0	0	0	9	0	1	0.0	19.6
Bishop, Hunter	L-R	6-5	210	6-25-98	.252	.316	.406	96	356	318	46	80	16	6	7	48	27	5	2	4	106	11	4	7.6	29.8
Cavanaugh, Drew	S-R	6-0	190	1-27-02	.184	.245	.265	14	53	49	4	9	1	0	1	3	4	0	0	0	15	0	0	7.5	28.3
Chapman, Matt	R-R	6-0	215	4-28-93	.000	.250	.000	1	4	3	1	0	0	0	0	0	1	0	0	0	1	0	0	25.0	25.0
Croes, Dayson	L-R	5-11	205	10-8-99	.349	.417	.465	14	48	43	8	15	3	1	0	1	2	3	0	0	5	0	0	4.2	10.4
Eldridge, Bryce	L-R	6-7	219	10-20-04	.249	.322	.514	66	286	253	31	63	13	0	18	63	28	1	0	4	88	1	0	9.8	30.8
Ellis, Drew	R-R	6-3	205	12-1-95	.222	.333	.437	52	186	158	23	35	4	0	10	26	23	4	0	1	48	0	0	12.4	25.8
Encarnacion, Jerar	R-R	6-4	250	11-13-97	.378	.464	.784	24	98	84	11	23	4	0	4	16	11	3	0	0	27	2	1	11.2	27.6
Fitzgerald, Tyler	R-R	6-3	205	9-15-97	.246	.321	.379	54	237	211	34	52	10	0	6	27	17	7	0	2	62	2	0	7.2	26.2
Gavello, Thomas	L-R	5-10	180	6-6-01	.262	.347	.488	51	197	168	29	44	9	1	9	38	18	6	1	4	64	2	1	9.1	32.5
Gilbert, Drew	L-L	5-9	195	9-27-00	.500	.650	.857	5	20	14	3	7	1	2	0	2	6	0	0	0	3	2	0	30.0	15.0
Gonzalez, Fernando	L-R	5-10	199	12-2-01	.250	.250	.250	1	4	4	1	1	0	0	0	0	0	0	0	0	0	0	0	0.0	0.0
Hill, Turner	L-L	5-10	180	4-4-99	.333	.333	.667	1	3	3	1	1	1	0	0	0	0	0	0	0	0	0	0	0.0	0.0
Huff, Sam	R-R	6-4	240	1-14-98	.189	.282	.333	27	103	90	10	17	5	1	2	7	12	0	0	1	36	0	0	11.7	35.0
Johnson, Daniel	L-L	5-9	200	7-11-95	.278	.322	.519	48	199	187	30	52	12	3	9	32	11	1	0	0	32	7	1	5.5	16.1
Knizner, Andrew	R-R	6-1	225	2-3-95	.367	.500	.567	8	38	30	6	11	6	0	0	10	6	2	0	0	7	0	0	15.8	18.4
Koss, Christian	R-R	6-1	182	1-27-98	.296	.296	.481	6	27	27	3	8	2	0	1	5	0	0	0	0	6	0	1	0.0	22.2
Lamb, Jake	L-R	6-3	215	10-9-90	.240	.352	.353	45	176	150	22	36	11	0	2	20	21	5	0	0	44	0	0	11.9	25.0
Luciano, Marco	R-R	6-1	178	9-10-01	.214	.335	.413	125	555	462	76	99	21	1	23	66	85	2	0	6	170	10	3	15.3	30.6
Mann, Devin	R-R	6-2	180	2-11-97	.252	.382	.356	48	199	163	27	41	11	0	2	23	28	7	0	1	36	1	0	14.1	18.1
Matos, Luis	R-R	5-11	160	1-28-02	.293	.327	.510	36	159	147	25	43	11	0	7	29	8	1	0	3	20	6	0	5.0	12.6
McCray, Grant	L-R	6-2	200	12-3-00	.239	.417	.110	510	444	73	111	19	5	15	71	55	1	3	7	138	27	3	10.8	27.1
Meckler, Wade	L-R	5-10	178	4-21-00	.287	.390	.387	87	401	338	45	97	21	2	1	32	57	2	1	3	72	11	3	14.2	18.0
Morgan, Zach	R-R	6-0	180	3-30-00	.268	.348	.390	14	48	41	5	11	2	0	1	3	4	1	2	0	9	0	0	8.3	18.8
Porter, Logan	R-R	6-0	200	7-12-95	.212	.346	.316	73	286	231	39	49	6	0	6	29	47	2	3	3	69	2	0	16.4	24.1
Ramos, Jose	R-R	5-11	143	10-25-02	.167	.167	.167	2	6	6	0	1	0	0	0	0	0	0	0	0	3	0	0	0.0	50.0
Rodriguez, Jesus	R-R	5-9	182	4-23-02	.322	.399	.401	39	173	152	21	49	6	0	2	16	18	2	0	1	17	4	0	10.4	9.8
Schmitt, Casey	R-R	6-2	215	3-1-99	.154	.353	.154	5	17	13	3	2	0	0	0	4	0	0	0	0	2	0	0	23.5	11.8
Stassi, Max	R-R	5-10	200	3-15-91	.265	.405	.382	20	84	68	8	18	5	0	1	18	13	3	0	0	18	1	0	15.5	21.4
Villar, David	R-R	6-1	215	1-27-97	.368	.439	.439	15	66	57	8	21	1	0	1	7	8	0	0	1	13	0	0	12.1	19.7
Wisely, Brett	L-R	5-10	180	5-8-99	.253	.332	.387	80	342	300	45	76	17	1	7	42	33	4	2	3	66	12	0	9.6	19.3

Pitching	B-T	Ht.	Wt.	DOB	W	L	ERA	G	GS	SV	IP	Hits	Runs	ER	HR	BB	SO	AVG	OBP	SLG	SO%	BB%	BF
Alexander, Scott	L-L	6-2	195	7-10-89	0	0	13.50	7	0	0	5	12	8	8	1	2	3	.414	.452	.552	9.7	6.5	31
Beck, Tristan	R-R	6-4	165	6-24-96	3	0	2.59	19	0	2	31	21	11	9	0	14	38	.194	.298	.250	30.2	11.1	126
Bednar, Will	R-R	6-2	230	6-13-00	0	1	27.00	2	0	0	2	6	6	6	5	0	1	.600	.667	.900	0.0	8.3	12
Bertrand, John	L-R	6-3	205	2-8-98	2	0	2.25	2	1	0	12	12	3	3	0	1	10	.273	.289	.318	22.2	2.2	45
Birdsong, Hayden	R-R	6-4	215	8-30-01	1	3	6.23	10	10	0	39	42	29	27	9	30	47	.264	.392	.509	24.1	15.4	195
Black, Mason	R-R	6-3	230	12-10-99	3	10	5.81	30	24	0	119	114	83	77	17	62	114	.250	.347	.447	21.5	11.7	531
Brubaker, JT	R-R	6-3	185	11-17-93	1	0	1.64	3	2	0	11	6	2	2	1	5	7	.162	.262	.270	16.3	11.6	43
Burgos, Raymond	L-L	6-5	170	11-29-98	1	2	8.22	17	0	0	23	37	26	21	4	8	23	.370	.438	.550	20.4	7.1	113

SAN FRANCISCO GIANTS

Batting	B-T	Ht.	Wt.	DOB	AVG	OBP	SLG	G	PA	AB	R	H	2B	3B	HR	RBI	BB	HBP	SH	SF	SO	SB	CS	BB%	SO%
Diaz, Miguel	R-R	6-0	224	11-28-94	5	1	3.45	50	0	9	57	41	24	22	4	32	55	.203	.321	.302	23.1	13.4	238		
Ellis, Drew	R-R	6-3	205	12-1-95	0	0	13.50	4	0	0	4	8	6	6	2	0	0	.400	.429	.800	0.0	0.0	21		
Gage, Matt	L-L	6-3	265	2-11-93	2	0	0.00	5	0	0	5	2	1	0	0	2	4	.118	.211	.176	21.1	10.5	19		
Garza, Justin	R-R	5-10	170	3-20-94	1	2	6.11	19	0	6	18	20	12	12	4	6	20	.286	.338	.514	26.0	7.8	77		
Harris, Trent	R-R	6-2	200	1-22-99	3	1	5.44	30	0	0	41	43	25	25	5	15	40	.269	.331	.450	22.7	8.5	176		
Harrison, Kyle	R-L	6-2	200	8-12-01	1	0	3.46	6	6	0	26	26	13	10	2	8	38	.252	.316	.350	33.3	7.0	114		
Hjelle, Sean	R-R	6-11	228	5-7-97	6	1	3.06	38	0	0	68	62	26	23	2	16	70	.240	.295	.357	24.6	5.6	285		
Jimenez, Antonio	L-L	5-11	145	5-6-01	2	2	3.55	29	3	1	46	35	19	18	4	35	56	.216	.362	.321	27.9	17.4	201		
Lonsway, Seth	L-L	6-2	210	10-7-98	2	4	4.29	9	9	0	42	43	23	20	2	25	38	.281	.386	.405	20.5	13.5	185		
Lucchesi, Joey	L-L	6-5	225	6-6-93	2	1	3.23	20	0	0	31	22	11	11	4	8	31	.206	.271	.355	26.1	6.7	119		
McDonald, Trevor	R-R	6-2	200	2-26-01	9	9	5.31	29	24	0	142	144	98	84	22	62	144	.264	.352	.457	22.9	9.9	629		
Mercedes, Juan	R-R	6-2	190	4-3-00	2	5	9.35	17	6	0	52	64	56	54	17	32	49	.299	.388	.621	19.6	12.8	250		
Miller, Erik	L-L	6-5	240	2-13-98	1	1	6.00	4	0	0	3	5	4	2	0	2	5	.333	.412	.533	29.4	11.8	17		
Myrick, Tyler	R-R	6-0	205	6-25-98	0	0	6.14	7	0	0	15	15	10	10	2	10	9	.273	.379	.509	13.6	15.2	66		
Olivarez, Helcris	L-L	6-2	192	8-8-00	0	0	4.00	26	0	1	27	13	15	15	0	32	39	.153	.431	.165	29.8	24.4	131		
Peguero, Joel	R-R	5-11	160	5-7-97	2	2	5.10	35	0	0	42	45	26	24	4	23	46	.271	.366	.440	24.1	12.0	191		
Pferrer, Cameron	R-R	5-11	182	12-18-98	0	0	0.00	1	0	0	0	0	0	0	1	0	.000	.500	.000	0.0	50.0	2			
Porter, Logan	R-R	6-0	200	7-12-95	0	0	9.00	1	0	0	2	4	2	2	0	0	0	.444	.444	.556	0.0	0.0	9		
Ragsdale, Carson	R-R	6-8	225	5-25-98	5	5	5.37	18	14	1	65	61	45	39	16	38	58	.245	.348	.502	19.9	13.0	292		
Roupp, Landen	R-R	6-2	205	9-10-98	0	0	6.00	1	1	0	3	3	2	2	0	0	4	.250	.250	.500	33.3	0.0	12		
Roxby, Braxton	R-R	6-3	215	3-12-99	2	2	5.91	23	0	0	32	29	25	21	6	18	42	.244	.352	.454	29.6	12.7	142		
Seymour, Carson	R-R	6-6	260	12-16-98	4	8	3.86	16	15	0	77	64	35	33	7	39	90	.225	.333	.365	26.9	11.6	335		
Small, Ethan	L-L	6-2	200	2-14-97	0	0	7.11	7	0	0	6	5	5	5	2	5	6	.208	.345	.500	20.7	17.2	29		
Teng, Kai-Wei	R-R	6-4	260	12-1-98	3	2	3.63	26	4	2	57	42	25	23	3	22	89	.197	.288	.291	37.1	9.2	240		
Tidwell, Blade	R-R	6-4	207	6-8-01	0	0	1.50	4	3	0	18	9	4	3	0	5	24	.145	.209	.258	35.3	7.4	68		
Vogel, Tyler	R-R	6-0	175	11-16-00	0	0	18.00	2	0	0	2	5	4	4	0	3	2	.455	.571	.636	14.3	21.4	14		
Waites, Cole	R-R	6-3	180	6-10-98	0	0	0.00	4	0	4	0	0	0	2	3	.308	.400	.385	20.0	13.3	15				
Watson, Ryan	R-R	6-5	225	11-15-97	4	3	4.26	46	0	9	51	58	28	24	5	16	64	.278	.330	.440	28.1	7.0	228		
Whisenhunt, Carson	L-L	6-3	209	10-20-00	9	5	4.43	21	21	0	108	112	55	53	13	35	95	.273	.327	.443	20.9	7.7	454		
Winn, Keaton	R-R	6-4	238	2-20-98	1	1	8.49	14	3	0	23	34	24	22	4	8	22	.337	.393	.525	19.5	7.1	113		
Zwack, Nick	L-L	6-3	230	8-1-98	0	2	9.00	4	4	0	14	21	14	14	7	11	8	.344	.452	.754	11.0	15.1	73		

Fielding

Catcher	PCT	G	PO	A	E	DP	PB
Auerbach	1.000	2	17	0	0	0	0
Barnes	.991	10	105	4	1	0	0
Cavanaugh	.986	14	135	8	2	0	1
Gonzalez	1.000	1	9	0	0	0	1
Huff	1.000	22	186	10	0	0	4
Knizner	1.000	7	68	2	0	0	0
Morgan	.991	13	101	13	1	2	0
Porter	.990	53	489	24	5	3	6
Rodriguez	.973	15	133	11	4	1	3
Stassi	1.000	18	167	5	0	0	2

First Base	PCT	G	PO	A	E	DP
Bericoto	.982	6	50	4	1	7
Eldridge	.992	66	502	26	4	65
Ellis	.978	24	168	11	4	22
Encarnacion	.950	3	16	3	1	3
Fitzgerald	1.000	1	5	0	0	0
Lamb	.987	30	198	29	3	25
Luciano	1.000	1	7	1	0	0
Mann	1.000	16	86	3	0	11
Porter	.939	7	43	3	3	4
Schmitt	.929	3	12	1	1	0
Villar	1.000	5	37	4	0	2

Second Base	PCT	G	PO	A	E	DP
Alcantara	1.000	4	6	8	0	3
Auerbach	1.000	3	7	1	0	0
Basabe	.983	45	59	112	3	33
Croes	.976	10	17	23	1	9
Fitzgerald	.983	32	47	70	2	24
Gavello	.976	11	16	24	1	7
Koss	1.000	1	6	5	0	3
Meckler	.909	8	12	18	3	5
Ramos	1.000	2	2	2	0	0
Schmitt	1.000	2	1	3	0	0
Wisely	1.000	45	65	117	0	29

Third Base	PCT	G	PO	A	E	DP
Alcantara	1.000	6	1	11	0	0
Auerbach	.900	21	6	39	5	6
Basabe	.984	20	14	48	1	7
Chapman	1.000	1	0	2	0	0
Croes	1.000	4	4	8	0	0
Ellis	.963	23	16	36	2	6
Gavello	.922	34	22	84	9	5
Koss	.667	1	1	1	1	0
Lamb	1.000	1	4	0	0	0
Mann	.938	36	21	40	4	7

	PCT	G	PO	A	E	DP
Morgan	.000	1	0	0	0	0
Villar	.909	7	4	6	1	0
Wisely	.923	5	5	7	1	1

Shortstop	PCT	G	PO	A	E	DP
Alcantara	.973	57	84	129	6	32
Basabe	.961	58	82	141	9	43
Fitzgerald	1.000	8	7	22	0	5
Koss	1.000	2	1	8	0	2
Wisely	.955	29	38	69	5	19

Outfield	PCT	G	PO	A	E	DP
Auerbach	1.000	12	13	0	0	0
Bericoto	1.000	4	5	1	0	0
Bishop	.984	59	119	1	2	0
Encarnacion	.962	14	24	1	1	0
Fitzgerald	.970	13	30	2	1	0
Gavello	1.000	5	4	0	0	0
Gilbert	1.000	5	7	0	0	0
Hill	.000	1	0	0	0	0
Johnson	.970	39	64	1	2	0
Luciano	.967	107	171	5	6	1
Matos	.918	30	55	1	5	0
McCray	.982	108	213	6	4	0
Meckler	.958	67	111	2	5	0

RICHMOND FLYING SQUIRRELS
EASTERN LEAGUE
DOUBLE-A

Batting	B-T	Ht.	Wt.	DOB	AVG	OBP	SLG	G	PA	AB	R	H	2B	3B	HR	RBI	BB	HBP	SH	SF	SO	SB	CS	BB%	SO%
Arteaga, Aeverson	R-R	6-1	170	3-16-03	.189	.239	.269	134	474	435	32	82	15	1	6	39	29	1	3	4	124	5	1	6.1	26.2
Bandura, Scott	L-L	6-4	190	8-2-01	.199	.303	.323	45	186	161	26	32	9	1	3	20	23	1	1	0	57	11	0	12.4	30.6
Bericoto, Victor	R-R	6-1	155	12-3-01	.267	.351	.433	93	393	344	43	92	15	3	12	49	43	3	0	3	92	2	1	10.9	23.4
Brown, Vaun	R-R	6-0	215	6-23-98	.247	.347	.282	32	99	85	9	21	3	0	0	3	11	2	1	0	24	13	3	11.1	24.2
Cavanaugh, Drew	S-R	6-0	190	1-27-02	.186	.375	.302	14	56	43	5	8	2	0	1	4	8	5	0	0	15	1	0	14.3	26.8
Ceballos, Sabin	R-R	6-3	225	8-17-02	.232	.332	.338	108	420	358	36	83	20	0	6	47	47	8	4	3	73	4	3	11.2	17.4
Croes, Dayson	L-R	5-11	205	10-8-99	.307	.354	.400	20	83	75	9	23	2	1	1	12	5	1	1	1	15	0	0	6.0	18.1
Davidson, Bo	L-R	6-2	265	7-5-02	.234	.312	.401	42	187	167	23	39	2	1	8	14	19	0	1	0	45	7	3	10.2	24.1
Eldridge, Bryce	L-R	6-7	219	10-20-04	.280	.350	.512	34	140	125	14	35	8	0	7	20	13	1	0	1	39	0	1	9.3	27.9
Ellis, Drew	R-R	6-3	205	12-1-95	.137	.279	.235	16	61	51	5	7	2	0	1	3	10	0	0	0	17	0	0	16.4	27.9
Furman, Nate	L-R	5-8	180	7-23-01	.387	.486	.484	9	39	31	4	12	1	1	0	5	6	0	2	0	8	0	0	15.4	20.5
Gavello, Thomas	L-R	5-10	180	6-6-01	.261	.320	.432	31	99	88	13	23	6	0	3	15	6	2	2	1	29	3	0	6.1	29.3

SAN FRANCISCO GIANTS

Batting	B-T	Ht.	Wt.	DOB	AVG	OBP	SLG	G	PA	AB	R	H	2B	3B	HR	RBI	BB	HBP	SH	SF	SO	SB	CS	BB%	SO%
Higgins, Matt	L-R	6-1	215	7-2-99	.224	.333	.265	17	60	49	3	11	2	0	0	1	8	0	0	0	6	1	0	13.3	10.0
Hill, Turner	L-L	5-10	180	4-4-99	.256	.356	.357	80	314	266	40	68	11	5	2	26	36	7	2	3	32	18	6	11.5	10.2
Howell, Carter	R-R	6-0	200	2-7-99	.221	.304	.335	109	439	385	41	85	17	3	7	32	36	12	1	4	95	8	4	8.2	21.6
Mann, Devin	R-R	6-2	180	2-11-97	.150	.239	.283	16	68	60	6	9	2	0	2	5	6	1	0	0	20	0	0	8.8	29.4
Mitchell, Cal	L-L	6-0	205	3-8-99	.169	.244	.268	40	156	142	14	24	5	0	3	7	14	0	0	0	46	1	4	9.0	29.5
Morgan, Zach	R-R	6-0	180	3-30-00	.200	.291	.284	31	112	95	7	19	2	0	2	13	11	2	1	2	14	2	0	9.8	12.5
Nolasco, Rodolfo	R-R	5-11	175	9-23-01	.038	.188	.077	11	32	26	1	1	1	0	0	1	4	1	0	1	13	0	0	12.5	40.6
Perez, Onil	R-R	6-1	187	9-10-02	.189	.290	.245	18	62	53	6	10	3	0	0	8	8	0	0	1	3	2	0	12.9	4.8
Pomares, Jairo	L-R	6-0	185	8-4-00	.209	.268	.352	76	299	273	29	57	10	1	9	34	22	1	1	2	80	9	4	7.4	26.8
Sugastey, Adrian	R-R	6-1	210	10-23-02	.231	.284	.343	92	355	324	35	75	10	1	8	37	24	1	3	3	39	4	3	6.8	11.0
Velasquez, Diego	S-R	6-1	150	10-1-03	.256	.362	.315	128	566	473	60	121	20	1	2	32	70	10	10	3	81	19	6	12.4	14.3
Wishkoski, Justin	R-R	6-3	195	1-19-01	.229	.328	.337	87	289	249	40	57	10	1	5	27	25	12	1	1	62	16	2	8.7	21.5

Pitching	B-T	Ht.	Wt.	DOB	W	L	ERA	G	GS	SV	IP	Hits	Runs	ER	HR	BB	SO	AVG	OBP	SLG	SO%	BB%	BF
Bednar, Will	R-R	6-2	230	6-13-00	2	2	4.97	36	0	1	51	45	29	28	2	38	84	.239	.379	.340	35.7	16.2	235
Bertrand, John	L-L	6-3	205	2-8-98	6	10	2.87	25	25	0	132	122	47	42	11	51	91	.249	.325	.376	16.6	9.3	549
Burgos, Raymond	L-L	6-5	170	11-29-98	0	0	2.89	9	0	1	9	11	4	3	0	4	11	.282	.349	.436	25.6	9.3	43
Choate, Jack	L-L	6-6	249	4-18-01	4	6	3.51	29	24	0	103	94	47	40	12	51	123	.247	.347	.392	27.6	11.5	445
Cotter, Cameron	R-R	6-3	220	12-17-98	1	0	5.88	27	0	0	34	47	22	22	2	10	30	.329	.377	.483	19.4	6.5	155
Cumming, Dylan	R-R	6-4	175	5-14-99	2	2	4.05	14	0	0	20	18	9	9	1	11	23	.247	.353	.370	27.1	12.9	85
Dabovich, R.J.	R-R	6-3	208	1-11-99	0	0	0.00	3	0	0	3	1	0	0	0	4	5	.111	.385	.222	38.5	30.8	13
Franco, Sadrac	R-R	6-0	155	6-4-00	0	0	54.00	1	0	0	1	5	4	4	0	0	0	.833	1.333	0.0	0.0	6
Garcia, Nick	L-R	6-4	215	4-20-99	2	2	8.04	14	0	1	16	15	14	14	3	11	15	.250	.370	.500	20.5	15.1	73
Gates, Evan	R-R	6-0	210	1-13-98	3	2	3.23	41	1	5	70	60	28	25	7	31	80	.238	.321	.369	27.8	10.8	288
Harris, Trent	R-R	6-2	200	1-22-99	1	1	1.69	13	0	2	16	11	3	3	1	4	25	.183	.234	.300	39.1	6.3	64
Hecht, Dylan	R-R	6-1	195	3-29-94	1	0	5.21	18	0	0	19	14	11	11	3	22	21	.203	.404	.348	22.3	23.4	94
Hillier, Cole	R-R	6-2	205	12-7-00	2	0	0.00	4	0	0	6	0	0	0	0	3	6	.182	.243	.182	16.2	8.1	37
Johnson, Marques	R-R	6-2	210	7-4-00	1	2	2.90	24	0	2	31	28	11	10	0	16	45	.246	.341	.272	33.3	11.9	135
Lonsway, Seth	L-L	6-2	205	4-14-99	3	8	5.32	19	19	0	92	89	38	36	7	42	84	.264	.360	.362	21.3	10.7	394
Mercedes, Manuel	R-R	6-4	190	9-21-02	5	13	7.29	26	16	0	84	101	74	68	10	46	54	.297	.390	.476	13.6	11.6	398
Morreale, Nick	R-R	6-5	220	7-27-97	0	0	7.71	8	0	0	14	17	13	12	0	8	10	.288	.377	.441	14.5	11.6	69
Murphy, Ryan	R-R	6-1	190	10-8-99	0	0	3.86	4	3	0	14	17	6	6	2	5	8	.309	.387	.473	12.9	8.1	62
Myrick, Tyler	R-R	6-0	205	6-25-98	1	5	4.47	35	0	10	44	49	25	22	8	12	31	.283	.337	.462	16.4	6.3	189
Olivarez, Helcris	L-L	6-2	192	8-8-00	0	0	2.70	8	0	0	10	4	3	3	0	11	7	.129	.386	.161	15.9	25.0	44
Pferrer, Cameron	R-R	5-11	182	12-18-98	0	1	8.44	6	0	0	5	8	7	5	2	9	3	.348	.531	.652	9.4	28.1	32
Rademacher, Shane	R-R	6-3	215	1-30-01	2	1	7.28	10	5	0	30	35	24	24	10	16	12	.302	.388	.612	9.0	11.9	134
Roxby, Braxton	R-R	6-3	215	3-12-99	3	3	1.20	22	0	3	30	15	8	4	0	9	40	.144	.239	.183	33.6	7.6	119
Sinacola, Nick	L-R	6-2	205	10-29-99	4	2	3.30	21	3	1	57	53	21	21	1	27	47	.251	.331	.332	19.4	11.2	242
Stryffeler, Michael	R-R	6-2	210	5-22-96	1	2	4.13	25	0	0	33	31	19	15	3	25	36	.250	.373	.388	24.0	16.7	150
Villers, Ian	R-R	6-6	245	9-1-00	2	1	5.09	23	0	0	35	38	22	20	4	16	26	.270	.348	.447	16.4	10.1	159
Vogel, Tyler	R-R	6-0	175	11-16-00	1	1	1.13	13	0	6	16	14	8	2	1	3	18	.219	.254	.344	26.9	4.5	67
Vrieling, Trystan	R-R	6-4	200	10-2-00	1	1	5.14	7	7	0	28	27	17	16	3	10	29	.264	.336	.415	23.8	8.2	122
Whitman, Joe	L-L	6-3	185	9-17-01	5	11	5.29	26	26	0	117	129	72	69	10	47	124	.285	.354	.422	24.2	9.2	513
Wright, Chris	L-L	6-1	205	10-14-98	3	0	2.65	14	0	0	17	10	5	5	1	12	17	.179	.333	.250	24.6	17.4	69
Zwack, Nick	L-L	6-3	230	8-1-98	0	3	2.53	7	7	0	32	28	9	9	1	9	32	.248	.318	.336	24.8	7.0	129

Fielding

Catcher	PCT	G	PO	A	E	DP	PB
Cavanaugh	1.000	14	116	13	0	1	0
Morgan	.989	20	167	16	2	3	0
Perez	.970	15	119	10	4	1	3
Sugastey	.994	89	746	76	5	8	4

First Base	PCT	G	PO	A	E	DP
Bericoto	.991	44	303	21	3	34
Ceballos	1.000	8	43	2	0	4
Eldridge	.974	24	178	13	5	18
Ellis	1.000	4	22	2	0	3
Higgins	.960	4	23	1	1	1
Mann	.984	8	58	3	1	8
Morgan	1.000	6	50	10	0	6
Perez	1.000	1	6	0	0	1
Wishkoski	.997	42	306	26	1	37

Second Base	PCT	G	PO	A	E	DP
Croes	1.000	4	2	8	0	1
Furman	.846	3	5	6	2	2
Gavello	.909	2	5	5	1	0
Mann	1.000	1	2	0	0	1
Velasquez	.988	123	225	281	6	95
Wishkoski	.895	5	7	10	2	2

Third Base	PCT	G	PO	A	E	DP
Ceballos	.948	90	62	157	12	26
Croes	1.000	13	15	14	0	3
Ellis	1.000	5	1	6	0	1
Gavello	.875	3	2	5	1	1
Mann	.857	2	2	4	1	0
Morgan	1.000	2	0	3	0	0
Wishkoski	.923	26	9	27	3	2

Shortstop	PCT	G	PO	A	E	DP
Arteaga	.980	132	181	321	10	81
Gavello	1.000	3	5	10	0	2
Velasquez	1.000	1	1	2	0	0
Wishkoski	1.000	3	3	1	0	0

Outfield	PCT	G	PO	A	E	DP
Bandura	1.000	38	75	0	0	0
Bericoto	.981	34	46	5	1	2
Brown	.956	28	42	1	2	0
Davidson	.987	31	72	2	1	0
Gavello	.963	19	25	1	1	1
Higgins	1.000	8	14	1	0	1
Hill	.994	69	167	5	1	1
Howell	.980	91	188	4	4	2
Mitchell	.986	37	72	1	1	0
Nolasco	.889	9	8	0	1	0
Pomares	.986	55	72	1	1	0
Wishkoski	.929	5	13	0	1	0

EUGENE EMERALDS
NORTHWEST LEAGUE — HIGH-A

Batting	B-T	Ht.	Wt.	DOB	AVG	OBP	SLG	G	PA	AB	R	H	2B	3B	HR	RBI	BB	HBP	SH	SF	SO	SB	CS	BB%	SO%
Ahuna, Maui	L-R	6-1	170	3-11-02	.311	.404	.467	11	52	45	11	14	7	0	0	5	7	0	0	0	14	1	0	13.5	26.9
Bandura, Scott	L-R	6-4	190	8-2-01	.307	.399	.439	81	373	319	65	98	15	3	7	45	44	7	0	3	90	30	2	11.8	24.1
Bravo, Damian	R-R	6-2	195	9-8-03	.276	.337	.322	24	98	87	10	24	4	0	0	17	5	4	0	2	18	1	2	5.1	18.4
Brown, Vaun	R-R	6-0	215	6-23-98	.182	.231	.182	3	13	11	1	2	0	0	0	1	0	0	1	5	1	1	7.7	38.5
Cavanaugh, Drew	S-R	6-0	190	1-27-02	.298	.407	.496	35	162	131	27	39	6	1	6	33	22	5	0	4	46	4	2	13.6	28.4

SAN FRANCISCO GIANTS

Batting

Player	B-T	Ht.	Wt.	DOB	AVG	OBP	SLG	G	AB	R	H	2B	3B	HR	RBI	BB	SO	SB	CS	OBP	SLG	SO%	BB%
Christian, Jakob	R-R	6-5	225	9-17-02	.304	.380	.570	23	92	79	18	24	9	0	4	14	8	3	0	2	32	3	0	8.7	34.8
Cox, Jonah	R-R	6-3	190	8-4-01	.257	.333	.398	126	597	525	89	135	24	10	10	68	54	7	9	2	134	58	11	9.0	22.4
Croes, Dayson	L-R	5-11	205	10-8-99	.283	.381	.416	47	204	173	25	49	18	1	1	27	24	4	2	1	30	2	1	11.8	14.7
Darby, Zander	L-R	6-3	197	11-26-00	.123	.228	.261	21	69	57	10	7	3	0	1	4	9	2	0	1	29	1	0	13.0	42.0
Davidson, Bo	R-R	6-2	205	7-5-02	.309	.412	.507	72	335	282	53	87	14	6	10	56	49	2	0	2	74	12	3	14.6	22.1
Foster, Cole	S-R	6-1	193	10-8-01	.150	.264	.260	54	201	173	20	26	4	0	5	13	21	6	0	1	65	2	3	10.4	32.3
Furman, Nate	L-R	5-8	180	7-23-01	.364	.490	.649	21	96	77	22	28	4	0	6	15	15	4	0	0	7	3	0	15.6	7.3
Gavello, Thomas	L-R	5-10	180	6-6-01	.204	.295	.370	16	62	54	8	11	3	0	2	8	3	4	1	0	20	3	0	4.8	32.3
Harber, Parks	R-R	6-3	225	9-25-01	.333	.454	.644	25	108	87	20	29	6	0	7	24	16	4	0	1	22	0	0	14.8	20.4
McDaniel, Quinn	R-R	5-11	180	9-27-02	.227	.333	.355	108	428	366	60	83	14	3	9	46	52	7	1	2	123	14	4	12.1	28.7
Payton, Jack	R-R	5-11	200	8-7-01	.252	.351	.437	73	282	238	41	60	13	2	9	42	34	5	0	5	72	4	1	12.1	25.5
Perez, Onil	R-R	6-1	187	9-10-02	.271	.401	.361	43	177	144	22	39	5	1	2	20	29	3	0	1	22	7	4	16.4	12.4
Ramos, Jose	R-R	5-11	143	10-25-02	.260	.396	.329	27	91	73	19	19	2	0	1	5	14	3	0	1	24	6	3	15.4	26.4
Reckley, Ryan	S-R	5-10	160	9-6-04	.000	.000	.000	1	1	1	0	0	0	0	0	0	0	0	0	0	1	0	0	0.0	100.0
Shliger, Luke	L-R	5-9	180	5-10-01	.263	.380	.366	58	230	186	19	49	7	0	4	44	34	1	5	53	11	3	14.8	23.0
Sio, Jean Carlos	L-R	6-0	167	4-3-04	.279	.385	.423	28	122	104	23	29	6	0	3	17	10	8	0	0	22	3	2	8.2	18.0
Szykowny, Charlie	L-R	6-4	210	6-30-00	.276	.339	.478	124	549	490	74	135	28	4	21	85	29	22	0	8	102	5	5	5.3	18.6
Tibbs, James	L-L	6-0	205	10-1-02	.246	.379	.478	57	256	207	41	51	10	1	12	32	42	4	0	3	45	3	1	16.4	17.6
Williamson, Guillermo	L-L	6-1	200	3-16-04	.218	.361	.359	27	97	78	8	17	2	0	3	17	18	0	0	1	26	0	0	18.6	26.8
Wishkoski, Justin	R-R	6-3	195	1-19-01	.160	.192	.200	6	26	25	1	4	1	0	0	2	1	0	0	0	7	1	0	0.0	26.9
Zielinski, Zane	R-R	6-3	175	7-28-01	.240	.338	.303	118	483	412	63	99	10	2	4	44	49	14	3	4	123	32	9	10.1	25.5

Pitching

Pitching	B-T	Ht.	Wt.	DOB	W	L	ERA	G	GS	SV	IP	Hits	Runs	ER	HR	BB	SO	AVG	OBP	SLG	SO%	BB%	BF
Blair, Daniel	R-R	6-3	205	4-8-99	0	1	7.71	6	0	0	7	9	6	6	0	10	5	.310	.487	.414	12.8	25.6	39
Bostick, Josh	R-R	6-4	200	10-20-01	9	6	3.71	24	23	0	119	97	54	49	21	39	139	.218	.293	.402	28.2	7.9	493
Carmouche, Dylan	S-L	6-2	225	8-22-01	7	0	2.84	13	13	0	70	61	23	22	7	19	63	.239	.299	.357	22.6	6.8	279
Dunaway, Matt	R-R	6-0	225	4-29-99	2	0	1.84	8	1	0	15	12	3	3	1	2	9	.226	.250	.321	16.1	3.6	56
Farone, Greg	L-L	6-6	245	5-3-02	4	2	4.25	11	11	0	55	48	27	26	8	17	48	.233	.295	.417	21.1	7.5	227
Flores, Junior	R-R	6-1	170	2-13-02	0	0	0.00	1	0	0	2	1	0	0	0	1	3	.000	.143	.000	42.9	14.3	7
Franco, Sadrac	R-R	6-0	155	6-4-00	0	1	1.74	14	0	0	21	13	4	4	1	9	20	.188	.278	.246	25.3	11.4	79
Hecht, Dylan	R-R	6-1	195	3-29-94	0	1	1.98	13	0	1	14	9	3	3	1	3	10	.188	.183	.292	30.0	16.7	60
Herold, Nicolas	L-R	6-6	215	10-5-98	0	3	8.79	15	0	3	14	16	16	14	2	8	21	.281	.397	.439	30.9	11.8	68
Johnson, Marques	R-R	6-2	210	7-4-00	1	1	2.08	17	0	3	26	14	6	6	1	14	33	.163	.277	.221	32.7	13.9	101
Kane, Tom	L-L	6-1	195	10-31-01	0	1	11.12	6	0	0	5	8	7	6	2	7	7	.227	.414	.318	24.1	20.7	29
Lansville, Cale	R-R	6-1	205	1-6-03	0	1	9.00	5	5	0	18	28	18	18	3	11	14	.350	.435	.538	15.1	11.8	93
McDaniel, Charlie	L-L	6-3	195	7-4-01	1	0	5.77	7	7	0	34	29	25	22	6	9	32	.223	.284	.431	22.7	6.4	141
Mejias, Ubert	R-R	6-3	205	3-24-01	0	0	0.00	1	0	0	1	0	0	0	0	1	0	.250	.250	.250	0.0	0	4
Mercedes, Manuel	R-R	6-4	190	9-21-02	0	0	0.00	6	0	0	7	2	0	0	0	3	8	.087	.192	.130	30.8	11.5	26
Palencia, Brayan	R-R	5-11	142	1-14-03	5	2	4.34	30	5	1	58	53	30	28	8	14	41	.243	.298	.450	17.3	5.9	237
Perdomo, Cesar	L-L	6-0	170	2-9-02	8	6	3.96	26	26	0	127	120	61	56	13	38	118	.247	.304	.397	21.9	7.1	538
Peterson, Ben	R-R	6-5	215	8-18-01	3	1	4.33	22	0	3	27	29	17	13	3	12	27	.269	.380	.407	20.8	9.2	130
Pferrer, Cameron	R-R	5-11	182	12-18-98	0	0	2.20	23	0	6	29	13	8	7	4	10	27	.138	.234	.298	25.2	9.3	107
Pleasants, Elijah	R-R	6-4	193	5-4-00	1	1	13.14	12	0	0	12	12	19	18	6	13	12	.255	.519	.319	15.6	29.7	129
Rademacher, Shane	R-R	6-3	215	1-30-01	6	5	2.60	18	16	0	97	80	33	28	13	15	71	.219	.249	.381	18.5	3.9	384
Ramos, Jose	R-R	5-11	143	10-25-02	0	0	54.00	1	0	0	1	3	4	4	0	2	0	.750	.750	.750	0.0	25.0	8
Simon, Liam	R-R	6-4	220	10-16-00	3	4	10.80	29	0	0	27	22	35	32	1	38	28	.220	.430	.320	20.0	27.1	140
Smith, Darien	R-R	6-3	205	12-1-99	2	0	2.59	7	1	2	24	19	8	7	2	5	26	.213	.260	.326	26.8	5.2	97
Strickland, Austin	R-R	6-2	210	5-31-02	8	2	4.45	36	1	5	61	45	32	30	6	30	65	.207	.323	.336	25.4	11.7	256
Switalski, Tyler	L-L	6-4	220	6-18-03	2	0	1.17	6	4	0	23	9	3	3	0	7	17	.117	.190	.156	20.2	8.3	84
Tucker, Cody	R-R	6-5	210	3-1-99	1	0	13.50	5	1	0	7	10	10	10	3	7	8	.333	.474	.633	21.1	18.4	38
Vanderhei, Ryan	R-R	6-6	185	6-1-01	3	5	4.33	35	0	2	54	51	32	26	5	32	46	.251	.358	.399	18.9	13.2	243
Villers, Ian	R-R	6-6	245	9-1-01	0	0	1.88	15	0	0	24	21	6	5	1	8	25	.239	.318	.253	8.1	99
Vinicio, Esmerlin	L-L	6-2	141	1-31-03	2	2	6.14	29	5	1	48	53	34	33	3	42	55	.282	.422	.383	23.1	17.6	238
Vogel, Tyler	R-R	6-0	175	11-16-00	6	1	2.83	25	0	3	41	38	20	13	3	21	47	.242	.341	.408	25.8	11.5	182
Widger, C.J.	L-L	6-6	220	5-25-99	1	1	7.82	24	0	1	25	20	22	22	5	19	29	.222	.372	.414	24.0	15.7	121
Wolf, Josh	R-R	6-3	170	9-1-00	5	3	4.74	29	9	1	57	46	32	30	5	57	67	.217	.394	.340	24.0	20.4	279
Zwack, Nick	L-L	6-3	230	8-1-98	0	1	6.89	4	4	0	16	17	12	12	5	5	12	.283	.343	.600	17.6	7.4	68

Fielding

Catcher	PCT	G	PO	A	E	DP	PB
Cavanaugh	.986	32	276	12	4	2	3
Payton	.971	7	63	4	2	0	2
Perez	.978	41	389	18	9	3	17
Shliger	.992	53	417	54	4	4	4

First Base	PCT	G	PO	A	E	DP
Darby	1.000	2	9	0	0	0
Payton	1.000	18	124	7	0	15
Szykowny	.994	97	741	48	5	53
Williamson	.984	17	114	6	2	9
Wishkoski	1.000	1	4	0	0	0

Second Base	PCT	G	PO	A	E	DP
Croes	1.000	13	19	27	0	5
Darby	.875	2	3	4	1	0
Foster	1.000	2	2	3	0	1
Furman	.923	15	14	22	3	2
Gavello	1.000	2	7	3	14	0	2
McDaniel	.984	74	85	164	4	31
Ramos	1.000	2	7	10	14	0	3

Reckley	1.000	1	1	0	0	0
Sio	.974	12	16	21	1	5
Zielinski	1.000	9	20	24	0	4

Third Base	PCT	G	PO	A	E	DP
Croes	.889	23	19	37	7	3
Darby	.923	9	6	6	1	0
Foster	.960	33	22	50	3	5
Gavello	1.000	7	11	11	0	1
Harber	.972	16	6	29	1	2
Ramos	1.000	6	8	9	0	1
Sio	1.000	1	0	4	0	0
Szykowny	.972	27	17	53	2	7
Wishkoski	1.000	5	3	4	0	1
Zielinski	.972	14	12	23	1	1

Shortstop	PCT	G	PO	A	E	DP
Ahuna	.952	11	16	24	2	5
Foster	.964	15	21	32	2	9
Ramos	.941	4	7	9	1	1

Outfield	PCT	G	PO	A	E	DP
Bandura	.992	71	119	3	1	0
Bravo	.983	24	55	2	1	0
Brown	1.000	2	5	0	0	0
Christian	.978	23	44	1	1	0
Cox	.990	119	294	10	3	3
Davidson	.966	61	142	2	5	1
Harber	1.000	8	16	1	0	0
McDaniel	.968	23	30	0	1	0
Payton	1.000	27	42	2	0	1
Ramos	1.000	7	14	0	0	0
Tibbs	1.000	47	82	5	0	1

SAN JOSE GIANTS
CALIFORNIA LEAGUE
LOW-A

Batting	B-T	Ht.	Wt.	DOB	AVG	OBP	SLG	G	PA	AB	R	H	2B	3B	HR	RBI	BB	HBP	SH	SF	SO	SB	CS	BB%	SO%
Ahuna, Maui	L-R	6-1	170	3-11-02	.266	.375	.427	37	168	143	30	38	10	2	3	21	19	6	0	0	42	9	2	11.3	25.0
Arias, Rayner	R-R	6-2	185	4-29-06	.040	.133	.040	7	30	25	1	1	0	0	0	2	2	1	0	2	9	1	0	6.7	30.0
Astudillo, Jose	R-R	5-10	150	2-27-04	.314	.359	.400	19	78	70	7	22	6	0	0	11	5	1	0	2	10	5	1	6.4	12.8
Cartaya, Diego	R-R	6-3	219	9-7-01	.235	.278	.471	4	18	17	3	4	1	0	1	5	0	1	0	0	3	0	0	0.0	16.7
Cavanaugh, Drew	S-R	6-0	190	1-27-02	.293	.450	.556	28	131	99	29	29	6	1	6	25	27	3	0	2	34	2	0	20.6	26.0
Christian, Jakob	R-R	6-5	225	9-17-02	.272	.355	.460	70	318	272	56	74	19	1	10	60	32	7	0	7	90	12	2	10.1	28.3
Cohen, Trevor	L-L	6-1	180	10-29-03	.327	.438	.402	28	130	107	23	35	3	1	1	15	20	2	0	1	15	8	2	15.4	11.5
Darby, Zander	L-R	6-3	197	11-26-00	.291	.403	.459	58	244	196	39	57	14	2	5	50	37	4	1	6	45	10	1	15.2	18.4
Diaz, Lisbel	R-R	6-2	201	7-19-05	.269	.320	.405	122	561	516	79	139	32	4	10	72	33	7	1	4	105	26	6	5.9	18.7
Diaz, Nomar	R-R	6-1	180	4-15-04	.143	.308	.310	14	52	42	7	6	1	0	2	3	10	0	0	0	14	0	0	19.2	26.9
Francisco, Javier	R-R	6-1	162	11-11-02	.000	.111	.000	2	9	8	0	0	0	0	0	0	1	0	0	0	1	0	0	11.1	11.1
Furman, Nate	L-R	5-8	180	7-23-01	.417	.533	.750	5	15	12	5	5	1	0	1	2	3	0	0	0	2	0	0	20.0	13.3
Gonzalez, Fernando	R-R	5-10	199	12-2-01	.229	.351	.375	26	114	96	20	22	5	0	3	8	14	4	0	0	22	0	0	12.3	19.3
Gutierrez, Carlos	L-R	5-10	174	8-22-04	.351	.445	.452	60	293	248	60	87	11	4	2	30	37	5	3	0	40	26	3	12.6	13.7
Hipwell, Robert	L-R	6-2	215	3-6-03	.201	.374	.450	102	429	349	59	84	28	6	11	66	67	9	1	3	134	3	2	15.6	31.2
Huff, Sam	R-R	6-4	240	1-14-98	.250	.400	.250	5	20	16	1	4	0	0	0	1	4	0	0	0	4	0	0	20.0	20.0
Jenkins, Jeremiah	L-L	6-4	238	5-5-03	.230	.332	.364	50	217	187	26	43	9	2	4	38	24	5	0	1	38	0	0	11.1	17.5
Jordan, Dakota	R-R	6-0	215	5-9-03	.311	.397	.497	88	416	370	71	115	15	6	14	82	37	5	0	4	95	27	4	8.9	22.8
Kilen, Gavin	L-R	5-11	185	3-28-04	.205	.279	.282	10	43	39	5	8	1	1	0	5	3	1	0	0	5	0	0	7.0	11.6
Level, Jhonny	S-R	5-10	154	3-29-07	.236	.333	.339	31	147	127	30	30	2	1	3	12	17	2	0	1	30	4	2	11.6	20.4
Maldonado, Cam	R-R	6-3	195	11-8-03	.237	.352	.339	17	71	59	6	14	6	0	0	10	11	0	0	1	18	5	0	15.5	25.4
Martin, Walker	L-R	6-2	188	2-20-04	.234	.353	.384	108	482	406	67	95	19	3	12	70	69	6	0	1	137	13	4	14.3	28.4
Meola, Lorenzo	R-R	5-11	172	12-17-03	.273	.314	.470	16	70	66	7	18	4	0	3	7	4	0	0	0	17	3	1	5.7	24.3
Ortiz, Jose	R-R	5-10	160	2-13-05	.308	.438	.455	15	66	52	16	16	3	0	4	7	5	2	0	2	12	0	0	10.6	18.2
Perez, Juan	R-R	6-1	182	9-2-04	.194	.299	.219	57	237	201	20	39	5	0	0	21	27	4	3	2	72	3	0	11.4	30.4
Ramos, Jose	R-R	5-11	143	10-25-02	.206	.346	.346	37	130	107	23	22	4	1	3	12	22	1	0	0	29	14	0	16.9	22.3
Rayo, Elian	R-R	6-0	202	3-4-03	.218	.287	.310	40	165	142	20	31	7	0	2	20	14	2	1	6	41	0	1	8.5	24.8
Reckley, Ryan	S-R	5-10	160	9-6-04	.171	.276	.212	43	170	146	19	25	2	2	0	10	22	0	0	2	48	4	1	12.9	28.2
Reynoso, Dario	R-R	5-10	180	3-22-05	.128	.281	.191	15	57	47	7	6	3	0	0	2	10	0	0	0	22	2	0	17.5	38.6
Rogers, Daniel	L-R	6-3	215	12-7-01	.278	.391	.333	16	65	54	8	15	3	0	0	9	8	2	1	0	17	0	0	12.3	26.2
Sio, Jean Carlos	L-R	6-0	167	4-3-04	.311	.398	.422	90	385	334	67	104	16	3	5	58	46	3	1	1	46	15	5	11.9	11.9

Pitching	B-T	Ht.	Wt.	DOB	W	L	ERA	G	GS	SV	IP	Hits	Runs	ER	HR	BB	SO	AVG	OBP	SLG	SO%	BB%	BF
Bresnahan, Jacob	L-L	6-3	175	6-27-05	9	3	2.61	22	22	0	93	67	32	27	2	43	124	.201	.290	.279	32.5	11.3	381
Carter, Dylan	R-R	6-2	210	8-6-01	1	0	6.75	2	0	0	3	2	3	2	0	4	1	.286	.500	.429	7.7	30.8	13
Cayama, Argenis	R-R	6-1	180	9-15-06	1	0	8.16	3	0	0	14	24	13	13	2	10	7	.387	.466	.532	9.6	13.7	73
Dabovich, R.J.	R-R	6-3	208	1-11-99	0	0	0.00	3	0	0	3	0	0	0	0	1	6	.000	.100	.000	60.0	10.0	10
De La Torre, Luis	L-L	6-0	188	9-6-03	2	2	1.77	8	8	0	36	22	8	7	0	11	47	.173	.250	.213	33.6	7.9	140
Dryden, Hunter	R-R	5-11	168	6-10-02	5	3	2.90	21	21	0	93	74	35	30	3	41	103	.216	.313	.312	26.0	0.4	396
Estrada, Ricardo	L-L	6-0	170	6-25-02	3	1	2.63	14	0	3	38	31	12	11	2	20	30	.226	.327	.292	18.5	12.3	162
Estrella, Mauricio	R-R	6-2	180	4-15-04	0	1	9.00	2	0	0	4	6	4	4	0	1	1	.400	.444	.467	5.6	5.6	18
Farone, Greg	L-L	6-6	245	5-3-02	2	1	3.73	12	12	0	51	46	24	21	3	23	73	.240	.330	.408	33.0	10.4	221
Flores, Junior	R-R	6-1	170	2-13-02	0	0	4.15	6	0	0	9	5	4	4	0	9	7	.167	.359	.200	17.9	23.1	39
George, Drake	R-R	6-1	184	9-30-01	2	1	3.20	13	12	0	56	48	24	20	1	15	62	.223	.276	.279	26.7	6.5	232
Gray, Evan	R-R	6-4	205	4-10-01	7	4	4.53	37	0	4	48	45	30	24	1	29	59	.246	.373	.301	26.1	12.8	226
Herold, Nicolas	L-R	6-6	215	10-5-98	1	0	0.00	3	0	0	4	0	0	0	0	9	0	.000	.000	.000	69.2	0.0	13
Hillier, Cole	R-R	6-2	205	12-7-00	4	5	2.78	31	0	4	58	53	26	18	2	33	64	.242	.344	.324	24.5	12.6	261
Lansville, Cale	R-R	6-1	205	1-6-03	1	2	5.31	6	0	2	20	23	14	12	1	9	17	.303	.391	.447	18.9	10.0	90
Maldonado, Gerelmi	R-R	6-2	170	12-21-03	0	4	3.97	23	20	0	59	49	34	26	2	44	69	.225	.394	.294	25.4	16.2	272
Marte, Yunior	R-R	6-5	210	9-8-03	0	0	3.60	5	3	0	20	16	8	8	0	9	17	.219	.313	.274	20.5	10.8	83
Martinez, Keyner	R-R	6-1	165	8-16-04	2	1	2.86	6	3	0	22	21	9	7	2	11	30	.250	.333	.357	31.3	11.5	96
Mazza, Niko	L-R	5-10	175	2-20-02	4	3	2.22	21	21	0	93	68	34	23	3	52	90	.208	.323	.275	23.0	13.3	392
McDaniel, Charlie	L-L	6-3	195	7-4-01	7	6	2.59	16	5	1	66	66	27	19	2	16	63	.263	.304	.355	23.2	5.9	272
Mejias, Ubert	R-R	6-3	230	3-24-01	4	1	5.26	26	0	0	65	73	51	38	5	18	52	.278	.323	.399	17.9	6.2	291
Murphy, Ryan	R-R	6-1	190	10-8-99	0	1	10.13	4	0	0	5	8	6	6	0	4	5	.348	.429	.391	17.9	14.3	28
Olsen, Mat	R-R	5-11	185	7-4-00	0	0	12.00	3	0	3	5	4	4	4	0	3	1	.385	.500	.385	6.3	18.8	16
Perez, Jose T	R-R	6-2	180	8-9-03	0	0	15.43	2	0	0	2	4	4	4	2	3	5	.364	.533	.909	33.3	20.0	15
Peterson, Ben	R-R	6-5	215	8-18-01	1	1	4.18	18	0	7	24	19	12	11	2	6	25	.209	.280	.297	25.0	6.0	100
Pferrer, Cameron	R-R	5-11	182	12-18-98	1	1	7.50	6	0	1	6	11	6	5	0	3	9	.393	.452	.536	29.0	9.7	31
Pineda, Melvin	R-R	5-11	170	5-4-04	0	2	10.80	9	0	1	16	25	14	14	3	14	13	.283	.452	.565	21.0	22.6	62
Pleasants, Elijah	R-R	6-4	193	5-4-00	1	0	14.21	6	0	1	6	6	10	0	15	4	.300	.583	.450	11.1	41.7	36	
Slater, Ryan	R-R	6-3	175	5-23-02	6	2	2.54	33	0	2	71	55	22	20	2	22	70	.213	.282	.271	24.4	7.7	287
Smith, Darien	R-R	6-5	205	12-1-99	6	5	1.55	13	2	0	46	35	16	8	2	16	42	.200	.278	.278	21.6	8.2	194
Switalski, Tyler	L-L	6-4	220	6-18-03	6	2	4.89	18	0	0	74	66	48	40	3	33	65	.238	.323	.339	20.1	10.2	323
Vasquez, Fernando	R-R	5-11	180	12-2-01	0	0	4.66	9	0	0	10	7	5	5	0	11	9	.206	.400	.206	19.6	23.9	46
Vernon, Cade	S-R	6-3	210	1-17-02	4	1	1.60	36	0	7	56	35	14	10	3	15	43	.176	.251	.251	19.5	6.8	220
Winn, Keaton	R-R	6-4	238	2-20-98	1	0	0.00	2	0	0	2	1	0	0	0	0	3	.143	.143	.286	42.9	0.0	7
Wright, Chris	L-L	6-1	205	10-14-98	0	2	20.25	4	0	0	3	4	6	6	2	4	3	.364	.533	.909	20.0	26.7	15

Fielding

Catcher	PCT	G	PO	A	E	DP	PB
Cartaya	1.000	4	43	3	0	1	1
Cavanaugh	.986	20	191	13	3	2	2
Diaz, N	1.000	13	104	5	0	0	3
Gonzalez	.995	22	211	9	1	1	1
Huff	.975	4	38	1	1	0	0
Perez	.988	57	518	42	7	4	10
Rogers	.966	13	126	14	5	2	4

First Base	PCT	G	PO	A	E	DP
Christian	.985	40	317	9	5	26
Darby	.969	7	54	8	2	4
Francisco	1.000	1	8	0	0	1
Hipwell	.981	54	390	22	8	26
Jenkins	.993	35	248	27	2	20

Second Base	PCT	G	PO	A	E	DP
Ahuna	.938	3	3	12	1	0
Astudillo	1.000	3	5	8	0	1
Darby	1.000	24	36	51	0	9
Francisco	1.000	1	1	1	0	0
Furman	1.000	4	1	5	0	1

	PCT	G	PO	A	E	DP
Kilen	1.000	3	2	9	0	2
Level	1.000	5	9	8	0	1
Meola	.977	11	18	24	1	6
Ramos	.974	18	34	40	2	10
Rayo	1.000	1	0	1	0	0
Reckley	.938	16	26	49	5	10
Reynoso	.875	7	8	20	4	6
Sio	.976	44	91	114	5	20

Third Base	PCT	G	PO	A	E	DP
Darby	.955	7	8	13	1	2
Hipwell	.909	30	18	52	7	4
Martin	.905	50	23	82	11	10
Ramos	1.000	1	2	2	0	0
Rayo	.913	32	13	60	7	3
Reynoso	.882	7	3	12	2	0
Sio	1.000	10	8	14	0	0

Shortstop	PCT	G	PO	A	E	DP
Ahuna	.944	31	29	89	7	11
Kilen	1.000	6	5	11	0	2
Level	.973	25	33	40	2	10

	PCT	G	PO	A	E	DP
Martin	.921	41	49	91	12	16
Meola	.913	4	11	10	2	2
Ramos	.955	15	23	40	3	5
Sio	.933	16	20	36	4	5

Outfield	PCT	G	PO	A	E	DP
Arias	.929	7	13	0	1	0
Astudillo	.900	13	18	0	2	0
Christian	.907	28	38	1	4	0
Cohen	1.000	25	59	0	0	0
Darby	.000	1	0	0	0	0
Diaz, L	.971	122	225	12	7	5
Diaz, N	.000	1	0	0	0	0
Gutierrez	.988	55	82	3	1	1
Jordan	.984	84	184	3	3	0
Maldonado	.938	16	28	2	2	1
Ortiz	1.000	13	22	5	0	0
Ramos	1.000	4	7	0	0	0
Reckley	.939	28	44	2	3	2
Sio	1.000	18	18	2	0	0

ACL GIANTS — ROOKIE
ARIZONA COMPLEX LEAGUE

Batting	B-T	Ht.	Wt.	DOB	AVG	OBP	SLG	G	PA	AB	R	H	2B	3B	HR	RBI	BB	HBP	SH	SF	SO	SB	CS	BB%	SO%
Ahuna, Maui	L-R	6-1	170	3-11-02	.239	.321	.522	15	54	46	8	11	5	1	2	10	5	1	1	1	18	2	0	9.3	33.3
Alexander, Jesus	L-R	6-2	185	9-4-05	.248	.336	.294	32	125	109	19	27	5	0	0	14	15	0	0	1	25	1	0	12.0	20.0
Arias, Rayner	R-R	6-2	185	4-29-06	.242	.333	.366	47	178	153	27	37	6	2	3	18	15	7	0	2	46	4	2	8.4	25.8
Astudillo, Jose	R-R	5-10	150	2-27-04	.393	.449	.492	18	69	61	13	24	4	1	0	8	6	1	0	1	4	3	2	8.7	5.8
Barnes, Austin	R-R	5-10	187	12-28-89	.167	.444	.167	3	9	6	0	1	0	0	0	0	2	1	0	0	1	0	0	22.2	11.1
Bericotto, Victor	R-R	6-1	155	12-31-01	.478	.480	1.000	6	25	23	6	11	4	1	2	12	1	0	0	1	5	1	0	4.0	20.0
Brown, Vaun	R-R	6-0	215	6-23-98	.333	.400	.444	3	10	9	3	3	1	0	0	3	1	0	0	0	1	0	0	10.0	10.0
Camacho, Santiago	S-R	5-11	176	1-27-07	.234	.295	.426	41	156	141	19	33	10	1	5	28	10	3	0	2	25	0	0	6.4	16.0
Croes, Dayson	L-R	5-10	180	8-0-99	.308	.400	.462	9	30	26	2	8	1	0	1	1	4	0	0	0	5	0	1	13.3	16.7
Diaz, Nomar	R-R	6-1	180	4-15-04	.250	.357	.250	3	14	12	3	3	0	0	0	2	1	1	0	0	3	0	0	7.1	21.4
Eldridge, Bryce	L-R	6-7	219	10-20-04	.333	.429	.333	2	7	6	1	2	0	0	0	1	1	0	0	0	0	0	0	14.3	0
Encarnacion, Jerar	R-R	6-4	250	10-22-97	.667	.714	.667	2	7	6	1	4	0	0	0	0	0	1	0	0	1	0	0	0.0	14.3
Foster, Cole	S-R	6-1	193	10-6-01	.167	.167	.250	3	12	12	1	2	1	0	0	1	0	0	0	0	3	0	0	0.0	25.0
Francisco, Javier	R-R	6-1	162	11-11-02	.204	.278	.306	15	54	49	4	10	2	0	1	8	3	2	0	0	16	0	0	5.6	29.6
Furman, Nate	L-R	5-8	180	7-23-01	.000	.500	.000	1	4	2	0	0	0	0	0	0	2	0	0	0	1	0	1	50.0	25.0
Guzman, Angel	L-L	5-11	170	11-15-05	.221	.365	.360	47	167	136	19	30	5	4	2	22	29	2	0	0	44	3	1	17.4	26.3
Hill, Turner	L-L	5-10	180	4-4-99	.412	.500	.647	6	22	17	5	7	4	0	0	4	0	1	2	2	0	0	0	18.2	9.1
Huff, Sam	R-R	6-4	240	1-14-98	.333	.417	.556	4	12	9	1	3	2	0	0	2	1	1	0	0	4	0	0	8.3	33.3
Jenkins, Jeremiah	L-L	6-4	238	5-5-03	.370	.470	.685	16	66	54	16	20	4	2	3	21	10	1	0	1	9	0	0	15.2	13.6
Koss, Christian	R-R	6-1	182	1-27-98	.667	.667	.667	1	3	3	2	2	0	0	0	0	0	0	0	0	0	0	0	0.0	0.0
Level, Jhonny	S-R	5-10	154	3-29-07	.288	.375	.493	58	261	219	50	63	10	4	9	38	33	2	0	7	40	17	5	12.6	15.3
Meckler, Wade	L-R	5-10	178	4-21-00	.333	.400	.333	3	10	9	3	3	0	0	0	0	4	1	0	0	2	0	0	10.0	20.0
Ortiz, Jose	R-R	5-10	160	2-13-05	.231	.259	.269	8	28	26	1	6	1	0	0	5	1	0	1	1	2	0	0	3.6	39.3
Peralta, Ramon	R-R	5-11	165	10-2-03	.261	.372	.442	51	199	165	29	43	9	3	5	33	26	5	0	3	60	6	2	13.1	30.2
Polanco, Andy	R-R	6-4	195	4-29-05	.264	.346	.336	47	163	140	32	37	5	1	1	16	17	2	1	3	43	22	3	10.4	26.4
Ramirez, Jorge	R-R	5-11	155	3-7-06	.091	.091	.091	8	22	22	5	2	0	0	0	0	0	0	0	0	11	0	0	0.0	50.0
Reckley, Ryan	S-R	5-10	160	6-4-06	.306	.479	.472	14	48	36	8	11	1	1	1	5	12	0	0	0	11	3	0	25.0	22.9
Reynoso, Dario	R-R	5-10	180	3-22-05	.298	.442	.556	54	227	178	59	53	12	2	10	45	40	7	1	1	72	18	5	17.6	31.7
Tejada, Oliver	R-R	5-11	180	12-9-06	.258	.371	.389	57	230	190	35	49	16	3	1	24	21	15	1	3	48	7	1	9.1	20.9

Pitching	B-T	Ht.	Wt.	DOB	W	L	ERA	G	GS	SV	IP	Hits	Runs	ER	HR	BB	SO	AVG	OBP	SLG	SO%	BB%	BF
Bello, Jose	R-R	6-1	164	5-29-05	1	0	2.00	8	0	2	18	10	5	4	0	3	28	.156	.194	.203	41.8	4.5	67
Caraballo, Jan	R-R	6-6	181	10-20-03	0	0	4.30	12	0	2	15	20	10	7	1	4	17	.323	.364	.484	25.8	6.1	66
Carmouche, Dylan	S-L	6-6	225	8-22-01	0	1	6.75	6	2	1	11	11	8	2	4	12	.262	.313	.500	24.5	8.2	49
Cayama, Argenis	R-R	6-1	180	9-15-06	1	1	2.25	12	12	0	48	33	15	12	0	18	55	.191	.279	.243	27.8	9.1	198
Chires, Samir	R-R	6-0	160	7-03-01	1	1	6.23	16	0	3	17	19	13	12	2	14	27	.284	.417	.433	31.4	16.3	86
Dabovich, R.J.	R-R	6-3	208	1-11-99	0	0	7.36	4	0	0	4	2	3	3	0	3	8	.167	.313	.167	50.0	18.8	16
De La Torre, Luis	L-L	6-0	188	9-6-03	2	1	3.72	10	7	0	39	28	17	16	2	16	62	.200	.286	.307	38.3	9.9	162
Estrella, Ricardo	L-L	6-0	170	6-25-02	2	1	1.53	8	3	1	35	21	13	6	2	7	44	.160	.209	.261	31.7	5.0	139
Estrella, Mauricio	R-R	6-2	165	9-18-02	4	3	5.00	14	5	0	54	57	30	30	5	16	51	.324	.370	.455	20.7	6.5	246
Franco, Marlon	R-R	6-2	165	9-18-02	4	3	5.00	14	5	0	54	57	30	30	5	16	51	.324	.370	.455	20.7	6.5	246
Fuentes, Alexander	R-R	6-7	242	1-13-05	3	1	2.62	12	5	0	35	19	10	0	17	39	.265	.357	.318	25.2	11.0	155
Hernandez, Alix	R-R	6-2	160	7-16-04	4	0	2.51	12	0	0	14	7	5	4	1	6	24	.143	.250	.245	42.9	10.7	56
Martinez, Keyner	R-R	6-1	165	8-16-04	1	1	1.90	15	8	2	47	42	13	10	1	10	67	.240	.289	.314	35.6	5.3	188
Olsen, Mat	R-R	5-11	185	7-8-00	1	0	3.18	4	0	0	6	5	2	2	0	0	6	.250	.238	.450	28.6	0.0	21

Batting	B-T	Ht.	Wt.	DOB	AVG	OBP	SLG	G	PA	AB	R	H	2B	3B	HR	RBI	BB	HBP	SH	SF	SO	SB	CS	BB%	SO%
Perez, Jose T	R-R	6-2	180	8-9-03	4	1	4.57	7	3	0	22	19	12	11	2	13	23	.224	.327	.353	23.2	13.1	99		
Pineda, Melvin	R-R	5-11	170	5-4-04	3	0	1.93	9	4	0	14	6	4	3	1	6	25	.133	.264	.200	47.2	11.3	53		
Rengel, Jose	L-L	6-0	168	9-8-05	7	1	7.62	13	0	0	26	35	27	22	0	12	28	.313	.383	.393	21.9	9.4	128		
Rodriguez, Johan	R-R	6-0	170	11-12-02	2	1	2.61	17	0	1	21	17	11	6	0	21	27	.230	.402	.297	27.8	21.6	97		
Simon, Liam	R-R	6-4	220	10-16-00	0	0	0.00	1	0	0	1	0	0	0	0	0	3	.000	.000	.000	100.0	0.0	3		
Vasquez, Fernando	R-R	5-11	180	12-2-01	0	0	2.31	8	0	1	12	6	4	3	0	6	19	.146	.300	.195	38.0	12.0	50		
Waites, Cole	R-R	6-3	180	6-10-98	0	0	0.00	1	0	0	1	1	0	0	0	0	0	.333	.333	.333	0.0	0.3	3		
Winn, Keaton	R-R	6-4	238	2-20-98	0	0	9.00	2	1	0	2	4	2	2	0	1	1	.444	.500	.556	10.0	10.0	10		
Wright, Chris	L-L	6-1	205	10-14-98	1	1	9.00	6	2	1	6	6	8	6	0	4	11	.231	.333	.346	36.7	13.3	30		
Yang, Nien-Shi	L-R	6-2	198	8-10-06	0	0	5.40	4	2	0	5	5	3	3	0	2	8	.263	.333	.316	36.4	9.1	22		
Zwack, Nick	L-L	6-3	230	8-1-98	0	0	0.00	6	6	0	12	6	0	0	0	1	16	.150	.171	.150	39.0	2.4	41		

Fielding

C: Camacho 38, Alexander 11, Ramirez 8, Diaz 3, Huff 3, Barnes 2. **1B:** Guzman 32, Alexander 14, Jenkins 11, Francisco 6, Bericoto 2, Eldridge 2. **2B:** Reynoso 25, Peralta 18, Reckley 9, Croes 4, Astudillo 3, Level 2, Ahuna 1, Foster 1, Koss 1. **3B:** Peralta 28, Reynoso 19, Francisco 7, Croes 5, Alexander 1, Foster 1, Reckley 1. **SS:** Level 53, Reynoso 7, Ahuna 2. **LF:** Arias 26, Tejada 11, Astudillo 9, Guzman 9, Hill 6, Brown 1, Polanco 1, Reckley 1. **CF:** Polanco 46, Tejada 6, Astudillo 5, Meckler 3, Ortiz 3, Arias 2, Brown 1. **RF:** Tejada 37, Arias 17, Ortiz 5, Bericoto 3, Brown 1, Encarnacion 1, Guzman 1

DSL GIANTS BLACK
DOMINICAN SUMMER LEAGUE
ROOKIE

Batting	B-T	Ht.	Wt.	DOB	AVG	OBP	SLG	G	PA	AB	R	H	2B	3B	HR	RBI	BB	HBP	SH	SF	SO	SB	CS	BB%	SO%
Alambarrio, Diego	R-R	5-9	179	3-12-08	.316	.458	.368	8	24	19	7	6	1	0	0	2	3	2	0	0	3	1	0	12.5	12.5
Benitez, Yoxander	R-R	6-2	165	11-1-06	.233	.343	.291	30	102	86	16	20	3	1	0	9	12	3	0	1	11	15	1	11.8	10.8
Blanco, Miguel	R-R	6-0	155	10-26-05	.186	.288	.195	39	132	113	12	21	1	0	0	9	16	1	0	2	22	8	3	12.1	16.7
Camacaro, Keiberg	R-R	5-11	158	8-24-06	.169	.373	.247	33	118	89	18	15	2	1	1	7	24	5	0	0	29	7	3	20.3	24.6
Crespo, Ricardo	L-L	5-10	168	9-26-06	.250	.424	.276	30	102	76	19	19	2	0	0	6	17	6	3	0	13	4	2	16.7	12.7
Dos Santos, Vinicius	R-R	6-2	195	6-5-07	.198	.324	.244	30	102	86	10	17	4	0	0	10	11	5	0	0	25	2	2	10.8	24.5
Duran, Alessandro	S-R	5-10	170	7-2-05	.207	.349	.293	29	106	82	16	17	4	0	1	15	18	2	0	4	26	0	0	17.0	24.5
Estevez, Evan	R-R	6-3	165	8-14-07	.263	.381	.436	51	215	179	31	47	13	3	4	38	31	4	0	1	60	12	4	14.4	27.9
Frias, Luis	R-R	5-11	155	8-7-04	.288	.337	.388	46	178	160	28	46	7	3	1	21	12	2	0	4	41	13	3	6.7	23.0
Gonzalez, Josuar	B-R	6-0	167	10-16-07	.288	.404	.455	52	228	191	52	55	10	5	4	24	37	0	0	0	36	33	5	16.2	15.8
Jimenez, Albert	R-R	6-1	174	10-28-06	.242	.350	.383	36	140	120	14	29	5	0	4	11	20	0	0	0	20	0	0	14.3	14.3
Martinez, Carlos	S-R	5-11	160	9-4-07	.238	.273	.476	6	22	21	4	5	2	0	1	3	0	1	0	0	4	0	0	0.0	18.2
Oviedo, Yeison	R-R	5-10	160	16-11-07	.183	.310	.233	22	71	60	12	11	3	0	0	4	9	0	0	2	12	1	0	12.7	16.9
Riera, Dennys	R-R	5-9	165	2-17-05	.200	.306	.292	38	144	120	14	24	5	3	0	9	8	12	0	4	30	3	1	5.6	20.8
Rivas, Yosneiker	L-R	5-10	161	10-6-05	.315	.412	.462	40	172	143	29	45	9	3	2	26	19	6	2	2	29	6	3	11.0	16.9
Sanchez, Yohendry	R-R	6-0	207	11-9-06	.275	.359	.394	42	170	142	18	39	10	2	1	30	18	4	0	6	23	0	0	10.6	13.5
Tandron, Anthony	R-R	6-3	175	11-8-05	.000	.000	.000	1	4	4	0	0	0	0	0	0	0	0	0	0	2	0	0	0.0	50.0

Pitching	B-T	Ht.	Wt.	DOB	W	L	ERA	G	GS	SV	IP	Hits	Runs	ER	HR	BB	SO	AVG	OBP	SLG	SO%	BB%	BF
Bracho, Lender	R-R	6-0	150	2-24-05	3	2	4.05	24	0	6	27	29	16	12	1	17	29	.271	.381	.336	22.8	13.4	127
Custodio, Luis	L-L	6-2	184	7-8-04	2	1	7.94	12	0	0	11	13	12	10	1	20	4	.317	.547	.537	6.2	30.8	65
De La Rosa, Carlos	L-L	6-1	180	11-30-07	0	0	3.48	3	2	0	10	10	4	4	0	5	15	.256	.341	.385	34.1	11.4	44
De La Rosa, Jose	R-R	6-0	174	9-3-07	2	3	2.77	16	0	1	26	26	11	8	2	7	21	.263	.308	.384	19.4	6.5	108
Duran, Rainiel	R-R	6-5	195	5-24-04	0	1	4.15	5	2	0	4	2	2	2	0	3	5	.154	.353	.154	29.4	17.6	17
Fernandez, Dilan	R-R	5-11	168	4-6-05	2	1	3.24	11	10	0	42	35	18	15	2	13	32	.230	.293	.388	18.9	7.7	169
Gonzalez, Mario	R-R	6-0	182	1-23-07	1	4	6.10	15	8	0	31	30	26	21	1	21	26	.254	.390	.356	17.7	14.3	147
Heredia, Delvis	L-R	5-11	190	10-27-04	1	0	11.37	0	0	1	13	18	16	16	3	12	9	.316	.466	.526	12.3	16.4	73
Jones, Jeremiah	R-R	6-2	192	8-19-07	2	2	6.85	15	2	1	24	26	18	18	4	16	19	.289	.385	.533	17.4	14.7	109
Laroche, Alberto	R-R	5-11	171	12-1-05	1	3	2.11	10	10	0	38	30	14	9	0	6	34	.213	.270	.262	22.2	3.9	153
Leon, Jhon	R-R	6-3	180	2-4-04	0	0	9.00	16	0	0	19	18	19	19	0	21	16	.273	.446	.318	17.4	22.8	92
Lopez, Jesus	R-R	6-2	170	3-3-05	0	0	4.22	4	4	0	11	7	6	5	0	10	13	.189	.423	.270	25.0	19.2	52
Mejias, Frainer	R-R	6-1	170	1-10-06	5	1	4.01	17	1	0	34	24	19	15	1	17	30	.200	.314	.308	21.4	12.1	140
Narvaez, Brayan	R-R	6-0	175	10-2-05	0	4	2.49	11	11	0	47	33	15	13	1	12	40	.194	.258	.276	21.5	6.5	186
Perez, Alfonso	R-R	6-2	175	8-14-05	2	2	3.42	14	0	0	24	21	10	9	1	8	28	.241	.338	.283	28.3	8.1	99
Perez, Josue	R-R	6-3	226	10-25-06	0	0	21.60	5	0	0	3	2	9	8	0	11	6	.154	.571	.231	21.4	39.3	28
Riera, Dennys	R-R	5-9	165	2-17-05	0	0	9.00	1	0	0	1	3	2	1	0	0	0	.600	.600	.800	0.0	0.0	5
Rodriguez, Leandro	L-L	6-0	171	2-26-06	4	3	2.41	16	6	0	41	19	16	11	1	19	46	.138	.283	.181	27.7	11.4	166
Toro, Carlos	R-R	6-2	175	5-21-07	7	0	2.15	17	0	2	29	16	7	7	0	15	29	.195	.167	.316	.208	16.2	12.8	117
Vasquez, Fernando	R-R	5-11	180	12-2-01	0	0	0.00	5	0	1	8	5	0	0	0	2	8	.192	.250	.192	28.6	7.1	28

Fielding

C: Sanchez 38, Alambarrio 8, Duran 7, Martinez 6. **1B:** Duran 20, Estevez 18, Riera 11, Jimenez 9, Tandron 1. **2B:** Rivas 34, Oviedo 20, Benitez 4, Riera 2. **3B:** Camacaro 26, Riera 20, Jimenez 9, Rivas 6, Oviedo 3. **SS:** Gonzalez 46, Camacaro 6, Riera 6. **LF:** Dos Santos 20, Benitez 17, Estevez 11, Crespo 9. **CF:** Frias 37, Blanco 23, Crespo 2. **RF:** Blanco 19, Crespo 17, Estevez 17, Dos Santos 5, Frias 5, Benitez 1

DSL GIANTS ORANGE — ROOKIE
DOMINICAN SUMMER LEAGUE

Batting	B-T	Ht.	Wt.	DOB	AVG	OBP	SLG	G	PA	AB	R	H	2B	3B	HR	RBI	BB	HBP	SH	SF	SO	SB	CS	BB%	SO%
Alambarrio, Diego	R-R	5-9	179	3-12-08	.000	.000	.000	1	1	1	0	0	0	0	0	0	0	0	0	0	0	0	0	0.0	0.0
Astudillo, Jose	R-R	5-10	150	2-27-04	.413	.491	.522	13	53	46	14	19	2	0	1	8	4	3	0	0	5	2	4	7.5	9.4
Barreto, Yulian	R-R	5-10	175	9-20-07	.322	.449	.394	53	227	180	43	58	6	2	1	29	36	8	0	3	33	9	4	15.9	14.5
Camacaro, Alexander	R-R	5-9	150	9-17-07	.133	.328	.156	17	58	45	6	6	1	0	0	6	12	1	0	0	14	0	1	20.7	24.1
Caraballo, Miguel	S-R	6-0	190	8-26-08	.264	.432	.442	41	169	129	34	34	4	2	5	22	28	11	0	1	38	8	2	16.6	22.5
Colorado, Juan	R-R	6-0	165	9-18-06	.183	.317	.252	36	139	115	17	21	5	0	1	20	19	4	0	1	46	12	4	13.7	33.1
Concepcion, Carlos	R-R	6-1	189	1-6-06	.282	.372	.497	48	196	163	33	46	9	4	6	38	21	6	0	6	53	1	0	10.7	27.0
Espinoza, Rainer	R-R	6-1	183	8-18-08	.198	.417	.344	37	132	96	25	19	3	1	3	24	31	5	0	0	31	5	0	23.5	23.5
Macares, Djean	L-L	5-10	175	5-1-08	.214	.354	.286	50	200	154	31	33	3	4	0	24	29	8	1	7	26	7	4	14.5	13.0
Marquez, Anthony	R-R	5-11	155	9-23-06	.276	.423	.362	51	221	174	42	48	12	0	1	24	41	4	1	1	31	13	4	18.6	14.0
Martinez, Carlos	S-R	5-11	160	9-4-07	.114	.256	.171	21	86	70	9	8	1	0	1	6	10	4	0	2	9	1	2	11.6	10.5
Moya, Jeyson	R-R	6-1	165	10-28-06	.133	.355	.133	17	62	45	9	6	0	0	0	6	16	0	0	1	17	1	0	25.8	27.4
Pena, Fernando	R-R	5-11	175	3-28-07	.276	.409	.368	24	93	76	11	21	4	0	1	13	11	6	0	0	16	1	0	11.8	17.2
Ramirez, Jorge	R-R	5-11	155	3-7-06	.222	.462	.222	4	13	9	1	2	0	0	0	2	2	2	0	0	2	0	0	15.4	15.4
Sarduy, Boris	L-R	6-1	155	2-3-07	.167	.380	.194	17	50	36	5	6	1	0	0	7	12	1	0	1	21	0	1	24.0	42.0
Vasquez, Brandon	L-L	5-10	165	12-6-06	.241	.344	.301	28	96	83	11	20	5	0	0	12	12	1	0	0	14	4	2	12.5	14.6
Villegas, Diego	L-L	5-10	170	3-23-04	.231	.459	.269	19	74	52	10	12	2	0	0	5	18	4	0	0	13	0	0	24.3	17.6
Willias, Franco	R-R	6-0	184	4-6-05	.281	.388	.412	38	134	114	22	32	4	1	3	26	12	8	0	0	22	11	1	9.0	16.4

Pitching	B-T	Ht.	Wt.	DOB	W	L	ERA	G	GS	SV	IP	Hits	Runs	ER	HR	BB	SO	AVG	OBP	SLG	SO%	BB%	BF
Cabello, Brayan	R-R	6-0	155	12-6-03	5	0	3.81	16	0	1	28	29	14	12	2	8	18	.269	.331	.398	15.3	6.8	118
Calcurian, Omar	R-R	5-11	168	5-25-05	7	0	2.73	16	0	1	33	22	12	10	4	14	17	.196	.313	.348	13.0	10.7	131
Castro, Kendry	R-R	6-2	160	1-11-07	2	2	4.28	17	5	2	34	31	20	16	0	18	20	.248	.347	.272	13.6	12.2	147
Colmenares, Simon	R-R	6-1	160	7-1-06	0	0	6.00	4	2	0	3	4	2	2	0	2	5	.286	.375	.429	31.3	12.5	16
De Leon, Randry	R-R	6-4	201	7-21-05	3	0	3.66	17	6	3	32	18	14	13	0	28	46	.162	.340	.243	32.6	19.9	141
Del Rosario, Winkel	L-L	6-3	180	10-7-06	1	0	6.00	3	0	0	3	2	2	2	0	3	3	.200	.385	.300	23.1	23.1	13
Dos Santos, Hector	L-L	6-3	185	9-27-05	2	0	4.97	12	0	0	13	10	8	7	1	10	11	.227	.393	.318	19.6	17.9	56
Gonzalez, Jose	R-R	6-1	176	2-21-06	0	1	2.40	12	12	0	41	35	16	11	0	15	30	.226	.307	.265	16.9	8.5	177
Gonzalez, Jose	R-R	6-1	180	6-15-02	3	1	5.12	19	0	6	32	20	19	18	2	21	22	.189	.331	.302	16.4	15.7	134
Hernandez, Luis	R-R	6-1	211	10-4-05	0	1	3.80	13	6	0	24	17	11	10	1	21	23	.210	.387	.309	21.7	19.8	106
Loina, Ebduar	R-R	5-11	168	10-27-06	0	0	11.57	3	0	0	2	1	3	3	0	4	1	.143	.571	.429	7.1	28.6	14
Meza, Jose	R-R	5-11	180	4-24-06	3	0	4.55	16	0	1	30	30	15	15	2	15	27	.256	.338	.410	-20.3	11.3	133
Paulino, Iverson	L-R	6-6	212	12-18-06	1	6	5.05	13	12	0	41	32	28	23	4	24	35	.212	.335	.358	19.2	13.2	182
Perez, Jose T	R-R	6-2	180	8-9-03	0	0	0.00	1	1	0	3	2	0	0	0	6	.200	.200	.300	60.0	0.0	10
Reynoso, Edwin	L-L	6-2	160	11-30-06	0	0	4.85	10	0	0	13	7	7	7	2	18	10	.175	.426	.350	16.4	29.5	61
Trevizo, Jose	R-R	5-10	150	6-11-08	4	2	4.02	15	0	0	31	35	17	14	2	11	24	.280	.353	.424	17.3	7.9	139
Utrera, Abraham	R-R	6-0	168	9-1-04	2	2	4.50	17	1	0	24	27	18	12	3	18	21	.293	.421	.467	18.3	15.7	115
Vasquez, Brandon	L-L	5-10	165	12-6-06	0	1	13.50	1	0	0	1	1	2	1	0	1	0	.500	.600	.500	0.0	20.0	5
Villarreal, Elkyns	R-R	6-0	160	11-18-06	2	3	4.97	16	9	0	38	30	28	21	1	32	39	.219	.399	.299	21.7	17.8	180

Fielding

C: Caraballo 23, Martinez 21, Pena 7, Ramirez 4, Alambarrio 1. **1B:** Willias 23, Pena 14, Villegas 13, Astudillo 4, Concepcion 1, Sarduy 1. **2B:** Barreto 40, Camacaro 11, Sarduy 2, Willias 8, Astudillo 1. **3B:** Colorado 36, Moya 17, Willias 2, Astudillo 1, Barreto 1. **SS:** Marquez 45, Barreto 6, Camacaro 5, Sarduy 1. **LF:** Espinoza 26, Vasquez 17, Sarduy 12, Willias 5, Villegas 4, Astudillo 1. **CF:** Macares 46, Espinoza 14. **RF:** Concepcion 45, Vasquez 9, Espinoza 4, Camacaro 1

Seattle Mariners

SEASON SYNOPSIS: In a year when Ichiro was inducted into the Hall of Fame, Seattle finally broke through, winning the AL West for the first time since Ichiro's rookie 2001 season. After winning a tough five-game Division Series, the Mariners won the first two of the ALCS but limped through the rest of the series offensively and lost a seven-game thriller to the Blue Jays.

HIGH POINT: It was Cal Raleigh's season of highlights, starting with a six-year, $105 million contract extension prior to the season. He hit 38 homers by the all-star break, won the Home Run Derby in Atlanta with his father Todd throwing BP (and younger brother Todd Jr. catching) and set the single-season record for homers by a catcher with Nos. 48 and 49 in an Aug. 24 game against the A's. Exactly one month later, he hit his final two of the regular season against the Rockies, finishing with 60, breaking Ken Griffey Jr.'s old Mariners record and Mickey Mantle's mark for most homers by a switch-hitter. He added five postseason homers, his last being the final run Seattle scored in Game Seven in the ALCS.

LOW POINT: George Springer's three-run homer off Eduard Bazardo in the seventh inning of Game Seven will sting for a while. The Mariners missed a key cog when righty Bryan Woo (15-7, 2.94) pulled a pectoral muscle during his Sept. 19 start. He returned to pitch twice in relief in the ALCS, leaving Game Seven in favor of Bazardo after yielding two baserunners in the seventh.

NOTABLE ROOKIES: 3B Ben Williamson provided solid defense but not enough offense (.604 OPS in 277 AB), while top prospect 2B Cole Young (.607 OPS) provided a walk-off winner in his May 31 debut and another July 19 to beat the Astros, but neither was a postseason factor. RHP Carlos Vargas (5-5, 3.97) made 70 appearances and made the postseason roster, while RHP Logan Evans (6-5, 4.32), who got extended rotation time, did not.

KEY TRANSACTIONS: Inactive much of the offseason, Seattle acquired Arizona's corner infielders before the trade deadline, trading for 1B Josh Naylor (.831 OPS, 19 SB, 9 HR in 54 G) on July 25. Six days later, the Mariners went for a return engagement with 3B Eugenio Suarez (49 HR overall, 13 with the Mariners). Both were key figures in the Mariners' postseason run with Naylor providing solid defense and baserunning. Suarez's grand slam broke a tie to win Game Five of the ALCS.

OPENING DAY PAYROLL: $146,793,414 (16th)

PLAYERS OF THE YEAR

MAJOR LEAGUE
Cal Raleigh
C
.247/.359/.589
MLB-best and catcher record 60 HR

MINOR LEAGUE
Lazaro Montes
OF
(A+,AA)
.241/.354/.504
32 HR, 89 RBIs, 83 BB

ORGANIZATION LEADERS

Batting		*Qualifiers
MAJORS		
* AVG	Julio Rodriguez	.267
* OPS	Cal Raleigh	.948
HR	Cal Raleigh	60
RBI	Cal Raleigh	125
MINORS		
* AVG	Rhylan Thomas, Tacoma	.325
* OBP	Harry Ford, Tacoma	.408
* SLG	Tyler Locklear, Tacoma	.542
* OPS	Tyler Locklear, Tacoma	.942
R	Samad Taylor, Tacoma	124
H	Rhylan Thomas, Tacoma	178
TB	Samad Taylor, Tacoma	257
2B	Carter Dorighi, Everett/Modesto	30
3B	Samad Taylor, Tacoma	7
3B	Lazaro Montes, Arkansas/Everett	7
HR	Lazaro Montes, Arkansas/Everett	32
RBI	Lazaro Montes, Arkansas/Everett	89
BB	Lazaro Montes, Arkansas/Everett	83
SO	Lazaro Montes, Arkansas/Everett	169
SB	Samad Taylor, Tacoma	44
SB	Bill Knight, Arkansas	44
SB	Victor Labrada, Tacoma/Arkansas	44
Pitching		#Qualifiers
MAJORS		
W	Bryan Woo	15
# ERA	Bryan Woo	2.94
SO	Bryan Woo	198
SV	Andres Munoz	38
MINORS		
W	Jhonathan Diaz, Tacoma	11
L	Evan Truitt, Everett	8
# ERA	Adam Seminaris, Arkansas	3.02
G	Hagen Danner, Tacoma	54
GS	Jhonathan Diaz, Tacoma	26
SV	Jimmy Kingsbury, Arkansas	10
IP	Jhonathan Diaz, Tacoma	139
BB	Jurrangelo Cijntje, Arkansas/Everett	51
BB	Blas Castano, Tacoma	51
SO	Jurrangelo Cijntje, Arkansas/Everett	120
# AVG	Adam Seminaris, Arkansas	.243

2025 PERFORMANCE

General Manager: Jerry Dipoto. **Farm Director:** Justin Toole. **Scouting Director:** Scott Hunter.

Class	Team	League	W	L	PCT	Finish	Manager
Majors	Seattle Mariners	American	90	72	.556	3 (15)	Dan Wilson
Triple-A	Tacoma Rainiers	Pacific Coast	86	64	.573	1 (10)	John Russell
Double-A	Arkansas Travelers	Texas	69	69	.500	5 (10)	Ryan Scott
High-A	Everett AquaSox	Northwest	60	72	.455	5 (6)	Zach Vincej
Low-A	Modesto Nuts	California	69	63	.523	4 (8)	Luis Caballero
Rookie	ACL Mariners	Arizona Complex	31	29	.517	9 (15)	Rico Reyes
Rookie	DSL Mariners	Dominican	30	26	.536	25 (52)	Luis Matias
Overall 2025 Minor League Record			345	323	.516	9th (30)	

ORGANIZATION STATISTICS

SEATTLE MARINERS
AMERICAN LEAGUE

Batting	B-T	Ht.	Wt.	DOB	AVG	OBP	SLG	G	PA	AB	R	H	2B	3B	HR	RBI	BB	HBP	SH	SF	SO	SB	CS	BB%	SO%
Arozarena, Randy	R-R	5-11	185	2-28-95	.238	.334	.426	160	709	613	95	146	32	1	27	76	64	27	0	5	191	31	6	9.0	26.9
Bliss, Ryan	R-R	5-6	165	12-13-99	.200	.282	.314	11	39	35	1	7	1	0	1	3	4	0	0	0	11	2	2	10.3	28.2
Canzone, Dominic	L-R	5-11	190	8-16-97	.300	.358	.481	82	269	243	30	73	11	0	11	32	20	3	0	2	59	3	1	7.4	21.9
Crawford, J.P.	L-R	6-2	202	1-11-95	.265	.352	.370	157	654	570	69	151	24	0	12	58	74	3	6	1	122	8	1	11.3	18.7
Ford, Harry	R-R	5-10	200	2-21-03	.167	.250	.167	8	8	6	1	1	0	0	0	0	1	0	1	0	3	0	0	0.0	37.5
Garver, Mitch	R-R	6-1	220	1-15-91	.209	.297	.343	87	290	254	29	53	5	1	9	30	30	3	0	3	80	3	0	10.3	27.6
Mastrobuoni, Miles	L-R	5-11	185	10-31-95	.250	.324	.296	76	175	152	20	38	4	0	1	12	17	0	5	1	29	6	3	9.7	16.6
Moore, Dylan	R-R	6-0	205	8-2-92	.193	.263	.359	88	213	192	29	37	5	0	9	19	19	0	0	2	76	12	4	8.9	35.7
Naylor, Josh	L-L	5-11	250	6-22-97	.299	.341	.490	54	210	194	32	58	10	0	9	33	11	2	0	1	34	19	0	5.2	16.2
Polanco, Jorge	S-R	5-11	208	7-5-93	.265	.326	.495	138	524	471	64	125	30	0	26	78	42	3	5	3	82	6	3	8.0	15.6
Raleigh, Cal	S-R	6-3	235	11-26-96	.247	.359	.589	159	705	596	110	147	24	0	60	125	97	9	0	3	188	14	4	13.8	26.7
Raley, Luke	L-R	6-4	235	9-19-94	.202	.319	.311	73	219	183	23	37	8	0	4	19	19	13	3	1	64	2	1	8.7	29.2
Rivas, Leo	S-R	5-10	150	10-10-97	.244	.387	.333	48	111	90	19	22	2	0	2	9	20	1	0	0	24	6	0	18.0	21.6
Robles, Victor	R-R	6-0	194	5-19-97	.245	.281	.330	32	114	106	12	26	4	1	1	9	3	0	2	0	26	6	2	2.6	22.8
Rodriguez, Julio	R-R	6-3	228	12-29-00	.267	.324	.474	160	710	652	106	174	31	4	32	95	44	12	0	2	152	30	6	6.2	21.4
Solano, Donovan	R-R	5-8	210	12-17-87	.252	.295	.344	69	176	163	10	41	4	1	3	21	8	3	0	2	38	0	0	4.5	21.6
Suarez, Eugenio	R-R	5-11	213	7-18-91	.189	.255	.428	53	220	201	27	38	9	0	13	31	17	1	0	1	79	3	1	7.7	35.9
Taveras, Leody	S-R	6-2	195	9-8-98	.174	.198	.272	28	98	92	6	16	3	0	2	9	3	0	2	1	27	3	2	3.1	27.6
Taylor, Samad	R-R	5-8	160	7-11-98	.125	.125	.125	4	9	8	1	1	0	0	0	0	0	0	1	0	1	0	0	0.0	11.1
Tellez, Rowdy	L-L	6-4	255	3-16-95	.208	.249	.434	62	185	173	20	36	6	0	11	27	8	2	0	2	49	1	0	4.3	26.5
Thomas, Rhylan	L-L	5-10	170	4-15-00	.125	.200	.250	3	10	8	2	1	1	0	0	0	2	1	0	0	1	0	0	10.0	0.0
Williamson, Ben	R-R	6-0	190	11-5-00	.253	.294	.310	85	295	277	36	70	13	0	1	21	15	1	2	0	64	5	1	5.1	21.7
Young, Cole	L-R	6-0	180	7-29-03	.211	.302	.305	77	257	223	24	47	7	1	4	24	28	2	2	2	47	1	0	10.9	18.3

Pitching	B-T	Ht.	Wt.	DOB	W	L	ERA	G	GS	SV	IP	Hits	Runs	ER	HR	BB	SO	AVG	OBP	SLG	SO%	BB%	BF
Bazardo, Eduard	R-R	6-0	190	9-17-95	5	0	2.52	73	0	0	79	53	23	22	9	27	82	.189	.262	.311	26.2	8.6	313
Brash, Matt	R-R	6-1	173	5-12-98	1	3	2.47	53	0	4	47	41	15	13	4	18	58	.236	.313	.339	29.1	9.0	199
Burgos, Juan	R-R	6-0	155	12-22-99	0	0	4.05	4	0	0	7	7	3	3	0	2	8	.259	.333	.370	26.7	6.7	30
Castano, Blas	R-R	5-10	162	9-8-98	0	0	9.00	1	0	0	3	4	3	3	1	2	1	.308	.438	.692	6.3	12.5	16
Castillo, Jose	L-L	6-6	252	1-10-96	1	0	0.00	3	0	0	3	3	1	0	0	2	1	.273	.385	.273	7.7	15.4	13
Castillo, Luis	R-R	6-3	212	3-10-95	0	0	7.71	2	2	0	7	12	7	6	0	7	5	.364	.475	.455	12.2	17.1	41
Castillo, Luis	R-R	6-2	200	12-12-92	11	8	3.54	32	32	0	181	168	76	71	23	46	162	.244	.297	.402	21.7	6.2	745
Diaz, Jhonatan	L-L	6-0	170	9-16-96	0	0	0.00	1	0	0	1	1	0	0	0	1	0	.200	.200	.200	0.0	0	5
Evans, Logan	R-R	6-4	215	6-5-01	6	5	4.32	16	15	0	81	82	45	39	13	31	59	.262	.335	.447	16.9	8.9	350
Ferguson, Caleb	R-L	6-3	226	7-2-96	3	2	3.27	25	0	0	22	21	9	8	1	8	17	.256	.326	.329	18.1	8.5	94
Garcia, Brandyn	L-L	6-4	225	5-27-00	0	0	4.50	2	0	0	2	4	2	1	1	3	1	.500	.636	.625	9.1	27.3	11
Gilbert, Logan	R-R	6-6	225	5-5-97	6	6	3.44	25	25	0	131	104	53	50	20	31	173	.211	.266	.377	32.3	5.8	535
Hahn, Jesse	R-R	6-5	205	7-30-89	0	1	5.40	3	0	0	5	6	4	3	1	5	3	.333	.500	.500	12.0	20.0	25
Hancock, Emerson	R-R	6-4	213	5-31-99	4	5	4.90	22	16	0	90	93	51	49	15	31	64	.269	.336	.445	16.6	8.1	385
Jackson, Luke	R-R	6-2	210	8-24-91	0	0	2.38	10	0	0	11	6	3	3	0	6	4	.171	.310	.162	22.2	8.9	45
Kirby, George	R-R	6-4	215	2-4-98	10	8	4.21	23	23	0	126	121	60	59	15	29	137	.252	.300	.392	26.1	5.5	524
Kowar, Jackson	R-R	6-5	200	10-4-96	2	0	4.24	15	0	0	17	14	8	8	4	7	15	.222	.310	.444	21.1	9.9	71
Lao, Sauryn	R-R	6-2	182	8-14-99	0	0	8.10	2	0	0	3	6	4	3	1	4	.375	.412	.688	23.5	5.9	17
Lawrence, Casey	R-R	6-0	180	10-28-87	1	2	3.00	5	0	0	15	20	12	5	2	1	6	.317	.323	.492	9.2	1.5	65
Legumina, Casey	R-R	6-2	195	6-19-97	4	6	5.62	48	1	0	50	47	36	31	7	25	55	.247	.339	.405	25.1	11.4	219
Mastrobuoni, Miles	L-R	5-11	185	10-31-95	0	0	0.00	1	0	0	1	0	0	0	0	2	0	.250	.500	.250	0.0	33.3	6
Miller, Bryce	R-R	6-2	180	8-23-98	4	6	5.68	18	18	0	90	93	57	57	17	34	74	.267	.333	.483	18.9	8.7	392
Munoz, Andres	R-R	6-2	222	1-16-99	3	3	1.73	64	0	38	62	36	18	12	2	28	83	.167	.271	.222	32.7	11.0	254
Pop, Zach	R-R	6-4	220	9-20-96	0	0	13.50	4	0	0	5	10	9	8	3	2	3	.370	.433	.815	10.0	6.7	30
Rivas, Leo	S-R	5-10	150	10-10-97	0	0	0.00	1	0	0	1	0	0	0	0	1	0	.600	.667	.600	0.0	16.7	6
Santos, Gregory	R-R	6-2	190	8-28-99	1	1	5.14	8	0	0	7	8	4	4	0	2	6	.296	.457	.407	0.0	22.2	36
Saucedo, Tayler	L-L	6-4	205	6-18-93	0	0	7.43	10	0	0	13	19	12	11	2	6	12	.322	.394	.475	18.2	9.1	66
Snider, Collin	R-R	6-4	195	10-10-95	2	1	5.47	24	0	0	26	32	16	3	6	24	.299	.342	.533	20.2	5.0	119

	B-T	Ht.	Wt.	DOB	W	L	ERA	G	GS	SV	IP	H	R	ER	BB	SO	2B	3B	HR	RBI	BB	HBP	SH	SF	SO	SB	CS	BB%	SO%

	B-T	Ht.	Wt.	DOB			ERA				IP																			

Speier, Gabe — L-L 5-11 200 4-12-95 4 3 2.61 76 0 0 62 43 19 18 5 11 82 .192 .243 .326 33.7 4.5 243
Taylor, Troy — R-R 6-0 195 9-9-01 0 0 12.15 8 0 0 7 14 9 9 2 3 2 .467 .500 .700 5.4 8.1 37
Thornton, Trent — R-R 6-0 190 9-30-93 2 0 4.68 33 0 0 42 41 23 22 6 14 32 .258 .330 .403 17.8 7.8 180
Vargas, Carlos — R-R 6-4 210 10-13-99 5 5 3.97 70 0 1 77 81 39 34 10 23 54 .273 .337 .421 16.3 6.9 331
Woo, Bryan — R-R 6-2 205 1-30-00 15 7 2.94 30 30 0 187 137 64 61 26 36 198 .200 .243 .353 27.1 4.9 731

Fielding

Catcher	PCT	G	PO	A	E	DP	PB
Ford	1.000	4	11	1	0	0	0
Garver	.992	43	375	10	3	0	1
Raleigh	.996	121	1060	42	4	3	0

First Base	PCT	G	PO	A	E	DP
Mastrobuoni	1.000	1	6	0	0	0
Moore	.964	16	25	2	1	0
Naylor	.997	53	357	36	1	28
Raley	.989	31	166	19	2	12
Solano	1.000	66	331	28	0	30
Suarez	.800	2	4	0	1	0
Tellez	.992	59	327	34	3	40

Second Base	PCT	G	PO	A	E	DP
Bliss	1.000	11	15	33	0	5
Mastrobuoni	.970	15	9	23	1	3
Moore	.976	28	27	56	2	10
Polanco	1.000	38	48	86	0	22
Rivas	.989	34	32	55	1	14
Young	.984	73	94	155	4	28

Third Base	PCT	G	PO	A	E	DP
Mastrobuoni	1.000	27	12	27	0	1
Moore	.926	16	5	20	2	4
Polanco	1.000	5	5	5	0	1
Rivas	1.000	2	0	2	0	0
Solano	.000	2	0	0	0	0
Suarez	.966	53	32	80	4	8
Williamson	.985	85	62	137	3	9

Shortstop	PCT	G	PO	A	E	DP
Crawford	.977	157	193	367	13	80
Moore	1.000	6	10	13	0	4
Rivas	1.000	7	4	6	0	2
Young	1.000	1	0	3	0	0

Outfield	PCT	G	PO	A	E	DP
Arozarena	.984	158	297	5	5	1
Canzone	.991	70	111	4	1	1
Mastrobuoni	1.000	25	28	0	0	0
Moore	.970	30	31	1	1	0
Raley	.980	44	48	1	1	0
Rivas	1.000	2	3	0	0	0
Robles	1.000	32	55	1	0	1
Rodriguez	.991	159	431	6	4	2
Taveras	.966	27	55	1	2	0
Taylor	1.000	3	6	0	0	0
Thomas	1.000	3	8	0	0	0

TACOMA RAINIERS
PACIFIC COAST LEAGUE — TRIPLE-A

Batting	B-T	Ht.	Wt.	DOB	AVG	OBP	SLG	G	PA	AB	R	H	2B	3B	HR	RBI	BB	HBP	SH	SF	SO	SB	CS	BB%	SO%
Bliss, Ryan	R-R	5-6	165	12-13-99	.385	.500	.615	6	18	13	0	5	3	0	0	7	4	0	0	1	5	2	3	22.2	27.8
Canzone, Dominic	L-R	5-11	190	8-16-97	.296	.360	.564	45	197	179	35	53	9	0	13	36	18	0	0	0	42	3	2	9.1	21.3
Davis, Colin	R-R	6-0	190	2-8-99	.233	.337	.368	27	90	76	12	17	2	0	3	8	11	2	1	0	19	5	0	12.2	21.1
Dunn, Nick	L-R	5-8	185	1-29-97	.184	.250	.255	29	108	98	14	18	2	1	1	11	9	0	0	1	10	1	0	8.3	9.3
Emerson, Colt	L-R	6-0	185	7-20-05	.364	.444	.727	6	27	22	5	8	2	0	2	9	3	1	0	1	6	1	1	11.1	22.2
Ford, Harry	R-R	5-10	200	2-21-03	.283	.408	.460	97	458	374	68	106	18	0	16	74	74	7	0	3	88	7	4	16.2	19.2
Hunt, Blake	R-R	6-3	215	11-10-98	.272	.368	.452	68	280	239	30	65	15	1	8	35	35	3	0	3	62	1	0	12.5	22.1
Hurtubise, Jacob	L-R	6-0	180	12-11-97	.167	.353	.167	12	34	24	8	4	0	0	0	3	5	3	0	2	3	3	0	14.7	8.8
Labrada, Victor	L-L	5-9	165	1-16-00	.265	.397	.376	61	236	189	40	50	12	3	1	25	37	6	1	2	42	14	2	15.7	17.8
Locklear, Tyler	R-R	6-1	210	11-24-00	.316	.401	.542	98	434	373	70	118	25	1	19	82	47	9	0	5	95	18	6	10.8	21.9
Lopez, Jack	R-R	5-10	160	12-16-92	.232	.275	.347	108	396	357	56	83	14	0	9	52	20	3	11	5	111	13	0	5.1	28.0
Marlowe, Cade	L-R	6-1	210	6-24-97	.316	.401	.474	46	182	152	24	48	12	0	4	22	23	2	0	5	43	12	3	12.6	23.6
Mastrobuoni, Miles	L-R	5-11	185	11-26-95	.415	.417	.417	31	142	115	22	34	11	0	1	18	25	0	0	2	18	9	2	17.6	12.7
McClaughry, Nik	R-R	5-9	159	9-14-99	.500	.500	.500	1	2	2	0	1	0	0	0	0	0	0	0	0	1	0	0	0.0	50.0
Nottingham, Jacob	R-R	6-2	220	4-3-95	.193	.277	.298	17	65	57	7	11	6	0	0	7	4	3	0	1	25	0	0	6.2	38.5
Otosaka, Tomo	L-R	5-11	182	1-6-94	.261	.261	.261	9	23	23	3	6	0	0	0	2	0	0	0	0	5	1	1	0.0	21.7
Packard, Spencer	L-R	5-10	210	10-12-97	.278	.391	.413	116	494	414	61	115	24	1	10	75	64	14	0	2	65	1	0	13.0	13.2
Raley, Luke	L-R	6-4	235	9-19-94	.314	.368	.600	9	38	35	7	11	9	2	1	0	0	1	0	0	12	0	0	5.3	31.6
Rivas, Leo	S-R	5-10	150	10-10-97	.318	.471	.507	66	299	223	63	71	8	2	10	46	62	5	6	3	59	24	3	20.7	19.7
Robles, Victor	R-R	6-0	194	5-19-97	.310	.375	.517	8	32	29	4	9	3	0	1	9	3	0	0	0	9	2	1	0.0	28.1
Shenton, Austin	L-R	6-0	205	1-22-98	.217	.324	.413	83	352	300	50	65	17	0	14	50	45	4	0	3	92	0	0	12.8	26.1
Taveras, Leody	S-R	6-2	195	9-8-98	.280	.358	.446	81	372	325	62	91	15	3	11	69	41	1	0	5	57	27	1	11.0	15.3
Taylor, Samad	R-R	5-8	160	7-11-98	.296	.378	.461	137	657	558	124	165	27	7	17	86	73	4	17	5	123	44	10	11.1	18.7
Thomas, Rhylan	L-L	5-10	170	4-15-00	.325	.380	.411	134	618	547	178	24	1	7	78	46	6	11	7	32	35	8	7.4	5.2	
Williamson, Ben	R-R	6-0	190	11-5-00	.314	.392	.462	52	240	210	35	66	12	2	5	46	25	3	0	2	32	10	1	10.4	13.3
Young, Cole	L-R	6-0	180	7-29-03	.277	.392	.461	54	245	206	39	57	13	5	5	26	31	8	0	0	28	4	2	12.7	11.4

Pitching	B-T	Ht.	Wt.	DOB	W	L	ERA	G	GS	SV	IP	Hits	Runs	ER	HR	BB	SO	AVG	OBP	SLG	SO%	BB%	BF
Anderson, Nick	R-R	6-4	205	7-5-90	1	0	3.18	6	0	0	6	2	2	2	1	4	10	.105	.261	.263	43.5	17.4	23
Bard, Daniel	R-R	6-4	215	6-25-85	1	0	3.18	6	0	0	6	6	2	2	0	1	9	.261	.292	.304	37.5	4.2	24
Bolton, Cody	R-R	6-3	230	6-19-98	0	0	9.00	2	0	1	2	3	2	2	0	1	1	.333	.462	.333	7.7	23.1	13
Brash, Matt	R-R	6-1	173	5-12-98	0	0	8.44	6	0	0	5	9	6	5	1	2	5	.360	.407	.560	17.9	7.1	28
Burgos, Juan	R-R	6-0	155	12-22-99	1	0	3.00	4	0	3	4	1	1	2	0	2	.333	.429	.417	14.3	14.3	14	
Castano, Blas	R-R	5-10	162	9-8-98	8	6	5.19	29	24	0	127	125	76	73	14	51	97	.263	.348	.423	17.8	9.3	546
Castillo, Luis	R-R	6-3	212	3-10-95	0	1	5.02	4	4	0	14	11	8	8	1	5	12	.208	.288	.340	20.3	8.5	59
Cronin, Matt	L-L	6-2	210	9-20-97	2	0	0.69	10	0	0	13	7	1	1	0	6	10	.159	.255	.205	19.6	11.8	51
Danner, Hagen	R-R	6-1	215	9-30-98	6	4	5.59	54	0	0	56	64	36	35	9	21	54	.296	.371	.426	21.4	8.3	252
Diaz, Jhonathan	L-L	6-0	170	9-13-96	11	6	4.15	27	26	0	139	159	68	64	18	24	116	.289	.325	.444	19.8	4.1	586
Evans, Logan	R-R	6-4	215	6-5-01	1	3	5.32	11	11	0	44	51	26	26	3	13	45	.287	.344	.421	23.1	6.7	195
File, Dylan	R-R	6-1	205	6-4-96	0	0	3.60	1	0	1	0	5	6	5	2	2	0	0	.273	.409	0.0	0.0	22	
Fleming, Josh	L-L	6-2	220	5-18-96	5	5	4.91	47	3	1	84	100	53	46	9	29	44	.294	.353	.482	11.5	7.6	381
Fleming, William	R-R	6-6	220	3-6-99	3	2	6.31	18	5	0	41	59	35	29	5	10	37	.324	.365	.511	19.3	5.2	192
Fraze, Nick	R-R	6-3	180	10-24-97	0	1	6.46	6	0	0	15	22	11	11	4	13	23	.280	.385	.505	21.1	11.9	109
Fujinami, Shintaro	R-R	6-6	180	4-12-94	2	1	5.79	21	0	0	19	11	13	12	0	26	24	.172	.426	.203	25.3	27.4	95
Fulmer, Michael	R-R	6-3	224	3-15-93	0	0	0.75	12	0	1	12	7	2	1	1	6	18	.163	.250	.233	36.7	10.2	49
Garcia, Brandyn	L-L	6-4	225	5-27-00	1	0	2.16	8	0	0	8	9	3	2	0	5	9	.273	.368	.303	23.1	12.8	39

SEATTLE MARINERS

Player	B-T	Ht	Wt	DOB			AVG															
Gilbert, Logan	R-R	6-6	215	5-5-97	0	0	2.79	3	3	0	10	8	3	3	0	4	11	.222	.326	.306	25.6	9.3	43
Gonzalez, Domingo	R-R	6-0	185	9-27-99	1	0	5.02	11	0	0	14	12	8	8	3	6	9	.231	.310	.462	15.5	10.3	58
Gott, Trevor	R-R	5-11	185	8-26-92	2	3	8.20	22	0	0	19	27	19	17	5	8	16	.346	.411	.641	17.4	8.7	92
Hahn, Jesse	R-R	6-5	205	7-30-89	0	2	5.85	35	0	9	32	38	24	21	3	16	34	.292	.371	.431	22.4	10.5	152
Hancock, Emerson	R-R	6-4	213	5-31-99	1	2	5.24	11	9	0	45	54	27	26	5	15	56	.298	.363	.497	27.7	7.4	202
Jackson, Luke	R-R	6-2	210	8-24-91	0	0	7.71	3	0	0	2	5	2	2	0	0	4	.417	.417	.500	33.3	0.0	12
Jacques, Joe	L-L	6-4	210	3-11-95	2	0	6.00	29	1	0	30	36	23	20	4	15	37	.305	.390	.483	26.4	10.7	140
Kirby, George	R-R	6-4	215	2-4-98	0	0	7.20	3	3	0	10	15	8	8	3	2	13	.349	.378	.628	28.9	4.4	45
Kitchen, Austin	L-L	6-0	200	2-11-97	3	3	3.36	48	1	1	70	69	29	26	5	20	53	.259	.318	.395	18.1	6.8	293
Klein, Will	R-R	6-5	230	11-28-99	2	0	7.17	22	0	3	21	23	17	17	2	19	32	.277	.423	.422	30.5	18.1	105
Kowar, Jackson	R-R	6-5	200	10-4-96	1	0	2.57	16	0	2	14	9	7	4	0	10	15	.173	.328	.250	23.4	15.6	64
Lao, Sauryn	R-R	6-2	182	8-14-99	2	4	3.13	22	19	1	69	61	26	24	5	19	73	.237	.300	.346	25.9	6.7	282
Lawrence, Casey	R-R	6-0	180	10-28-87	9	3	5.31	20	19	0	100	113	64	59	16	19	54	.283	.314	.475	12.6	4.4	430
Legumina, Casey	R-R	6-2	195	6-19-97	3	0	0.87	10	0	1	10	9	2	1	0	5	13	.231	.333	.256	28.9	11.1	45
Lopez, Jack	R-R	5-10	160	12-16-92	0	0	9.00	1	0	0	1	2	1	1	0	2	.400	.400	1.000	40.0	0.0	5
Mariot, Michael	R-R	6-0	190	10-20-88	4	4	5.74	23	8	0	69	93	47	44	11	25	52	.325	.383	.549	16.1	7.7	323
Medina, Adonis	R-R	6-1	187	12-18-96	3	2	5.03	27	0	0	34	37	24	19	1	18	26	.276	.386	.403	16.5	11.4	158
Miller, Bryce	R-R	6-2	180	8-23-98	1	0	4.05	3	3	0	13	7	6	6	4	3	15	.149	.200	.426	30.0	6.0	50
Nottingham, Jacob	R-R	6-2	220	4-3-95	0	0	27.00	1	0	0	1	1	2	2	0	2	0	.500	.667	.500	0.0	33.3	6
Pomeranz, Drew	R-L	6-5	246	11-22-88	0	1	4.66	9	0	2	10	6	6	5	0	6	14	.176	.333	.206	32.6	14.0	43
Pop, Zach	R-R	6-4	220	9-20-96	2	1	3.52	9	0	1	8	5	5	3	0	4	6	.192	.344	.192	17.1	11.4	35
Santos, Gregory	R-R	6-2	190	8-28-99	0	0	5.40	6	0	0	5	4	3	3	0	9	5	.235	.500	.235	19.2	34.6	26
Saucedo, Tayler	L-L	6-4	205	6-18-93	3	0	2.75	22	0	1	20	16	6	6	3	10	24	.216	.326	.378	27.9	11.6	86
Shaw, Bryan	S-R	6-1	226	11-8-87	0	2	3.29	15	0	1	14	12	8	5	0	14	11	.226	.406	.283	15.9	20.3	69
Snider, Collin	R-R	6-4	195	10-10-95	0	1	8.06	25	0	1	26	38	25	23	10	4	21	.345	.385	.691	17.9	3.4	117
Taylor, Troy	R-R	6-0	195	9-9-01	3	4	6.85	50	0	7	45	46	37	34	7	29	54	.266	.379	.439	26.0	13.9	208
Tellache, Nico	L-L	6-0	205	1-14-98	0	3	9.78	5	4	0	19	33	22	21	5	9	23	.363	.426	.571	22.8	8.9	101
Thornton, Trent	R-R	6-0	190	9-30-93	1	0	3.38	2	0	0	3	2	1	1	1	0	3	.200	.200	.600	30.0	0.0	10
Zuniga, Guillermo	R-R	6-5	230	10-10-98	1	0	6.23	4	0	0	4	4	3	3	0	4	3	.267	.400	.267	15.0	20.0	20

Fielding

Catcher	PCT	G	PO	A	E	DP	PB
Ford	.984	81	657	30	11	2	0
Hunt	.986	60	471	21	7	1	2
Nottingham	.990	9	95	5	1	1	1

First Base	PCT	G	PO	A	E	DP
Locklear	.994	88	740	54	5	83
Mastrobuoni	.992	13	94	24	1	10
Nottingham	1.000	1	11	0	0	1
Packard	.996	31	215	13	1	25
Raley	1.000	3	23	2	0	2
Shenton	.987	21	146	10	2	14

Second Base	PCT	G	PO	A	E	DP
Bliss	.933	4	8	6	1	3
Dunn	.973	18	23	50	2	12
Lopez	1.000	3	6	5	0	1
Mastrobuoni	1.000	2	2	4	0	0
McClaughry	1.000	1	1	2	0	1

Third Base	PCT	G	PO	A	E	DP
Dunn	.909	6	2	8	1	0
Lopez	.940	58	41	100	9	12
Mastrobuoni	1.000	2	2	4	0	0
Shenton	.894	42	28	82	13	5
Taylor	.000	2	0	0	0	0
Williamson	.970	50	33	131	5	11

Shortstop	PCT	G	PO	A	E	DP
Emerson	1.000	6	8	13	0	2
Lopez	.953	42	38	103	7	27
Mastrobuoni	.977	9	13	29	1	7
Rivas	.987	64	102	196	4	47
Taylor	.667	1	1	1	1	0

	PCT	G	PO	A	E	DP
Rivas	.875	2	6	1	1	1
Taylor	.978	101	182	270	10	73
Williamson	.833	1	2	3	1	1
Young	.992	26	42	75	1	18
Young	.953	29	37	85	6	17

Outfield	PCT	G	PO	A	E	DP
Canzone	.986	40	70	0	1	0
Davis	1.000	27	46	0	0	0
Hurtubise	1.000	11	16	1	0	0
Labrada	1.000	55	73	5	0	0
Lopez	1.000	6	6	0	0	0
Marlowe	.911	25	41	0	4	0
Mastrobuoni	1.000	4	10	0	0	0
Otosaka	1.000	8	6	0	0	0
Packard	.960	55	70	2	3	1
Raley	1.000	4	7	0	0	0
Robles	1.000	5	4	0	0	0
Taveras	.983	71	169	3	3	0
Taylor	.988	38	78	2	1	0
Thomas	.993	135	268	5	2	1

ARKANSAS TRAVELERS — DOUBLE-A
TEXAS LEAGUE

Batting	B-T	Ht.	Wt.	DOB	AVG	OBP	SLG	G	PA	AB	R	H	2B	3B	HR	RBI	BB	HBP	SH	SF	SO	SB	CS	BB%	SO%
Bliss, Ryan	R-R	5-6	165	12-13-99	.385	.500	.615	6	18	13	0	5	3	0	0	7	4	0	0	1	5	2	3	22.2	27.8
Canzone, Dominic	L-R	5-11	190	8-06-97	.296	.360	.564	45	197	179	35	53	9	0	13	36	18	0	0	0	43	3	2	9.1	21.3
Davis, Colin	R-R	6-0	190	2-8-99	.224	.337	.368	27	90	76	12	17	2	0	3	8	11	2	1	0	19	5	0	12.2	21.1
Dunn, Nick	L-R	5-8	185	1-29-97	.184	.250	.255	29	108	98	14	18	2	1	1	11	9	0	0	1	10	1	0	8.3	9.3
Emerson, Colt	L-L	5-11	185	7-20-05	.364	.444	.727	6	27	22	5	8	2	0	2	9	3	1	0	1	6	1	1	11.1	22.2
Ford, Harry	R-R	5-10	200	2-21-03	.283	.408	.460	97	458	374	68	106	18	0	16	74	74	7	0	3	88	7	4	16.2	19.2
Hunt, Blake	R-R	6-3	215	11-10-98	.272	.368	.452	68	280	239	30	65	15	2	8	35	35	3	0	3	62	1	0	12.5	22.1
Hurtubise, Jacob	L-R	6-0	180	12-11-97	.167	.353	.167	12	34	24	8	4	0	0	0	3	5	3	0	2	3	0	0	14.7	8.8
Labrada, Victor	L-L	5-9	165	11-06-00	.265	.397	.376	61	236	189	40	50	12	3	1	25	37	6	1	2	42	14	2	15.7	17.8
Locklear, Tyler	R-R	6-1	210	11-24-00	.316	.401	.542	98	434	373	70	118	25	1	19	82	47	9	0	5	95	18	6	10.8	21.9
Lopez, Jack	R-R	5-10	160	12-16-92	.232	.275	.347	108	396	357	56	83	14	0	9	52	20	3	11	5	111	13	0	5.1	28.0
Marlowe, Cade	L-R	6-1	210	6-4-97	.316	.401	.474	46	182	152	24	48	12	0	4	22	23	2	0	5	43	12	3	12.6	23.6
Mastrobuoni, Miles	L-R	5-11	185	10-31-95	.296	.415	.417	31	142	115	22	34	11	0	1	18	25	0	0	2	9	2	1	17.6	12.7
McClaughry, Nik	R-R	5-9	159	9-14-99	.500	.500	.500	1	2	2	0	1	0	0	0	0	0	0	0	0	1	0	0	0.0	50.0
Nottingham, Jacob	R-R	6-2	220	4-3-95	.193	.277	.298	17	65	57	7	11	6	0	0	7	4	3	0	1	25	0	0	6.2	38.5
Otosaka, Tomo	R-R	5-11	177	6-24-96	.261	.261	.261	9	23	23	3	6	0	0	0	2	0	0	0	0	5	1	1	0.0	21.7
Packard, Spencer	L-L	5-10	210	10-12-97	.278	.391	.413	116	494	414	61	115	24	1	10	75	64	14	0	2	65	1	0	13.0	13.2
Raley, Luke	L-R	6-4	235	9-19-94	.314	.368	.600	9	38	35	7	11	1	0	3	9	2	1	0	0	12	0	0	5.3	31.6
Rivas, Leo	S-R	5-10	150	10-10-97	.318	.431	.507	46	207	171	35	62	11	4	0	36	29	4	0	3	57	13	4	14.0	27.5
Robles, Victor	R-R	6-0	194	5-19-97	.310	.375	.517	8	32	29	4	9	3	0	1	6	0	0	0	3	9	2	1	0.0	28.1
Shenton, Austin	L-R	6-0	205	1-22-98	.217	.324	.413	83	352	300	50	65	17	0	14	50	45	4	0	3	92	0	0	12.8	26.1

Batting (cont.)	B-T	Ht.	Wt.	DOB	AVG	OBP	SLG	G	PA	AB	R	H	2B	3B	HR	RBI	BB	HBP	SH	SF	SO	SB	CS	BB%	SO%
Taveras, Leody	S-R	6-2	195	9-8-98	.280	.358	.446	81	372	325	62	91	15	3	11	69	41	1	0	5	57	27	1	11.0	15.3
Taylor, Samad	R-R	5-8	160	7-11-98	.296	.378	.461	137	657	558	124	165	27	7	17	86	73	4	17	5	123	44	10	11.1	18.7
Thomas, Rhylan	L-L	5-10	170	4-15-00	.325	.380	.411	134	618	547	105	178	24	1	7	78	46	6	11	7	32	35	8	7.4	5.2
Williamson, Ben	R-R	6-0	190	11-5-00	.314	.392	.462	52	240	210	35	66	12	2	5	46	25	3	0	2	32	10	1	10.4	13.3
Young, Cole	L-R	6-0	180	7-29-03	.277	.392	.461	54	245	206	39	57	13	5	5	26	31	8	0	0	28	4	2	12.7	11.4

Pitching	B-T	Ht.	Wt.	DOB	W	L	ERA	G	GS	SV	IP	Hits	Runs	ER	HR	BB	SO	AVG	OBP	SLG	SO%	BB%	BF
Alford, Peyton	L-L	6-0	190	8-15-97	4	3	4.18	43	0	1	56	44	31	26	6	26	67	.216	.306	.348	28.3	11.0	237
Beilenson, Charlie	R-R	6-0	215	12-10-99	2	3	4.08	24	0	4	29	36	17	13	4	4	27	.300	.328	.492	21.4	3.2	126
Burgos, Juan	R-R	6-0	155	12-22-99	2	1	0.64	21	0	3	28	10	4	2	1	7	29	.106	.167	.202	27.6	6.7	105
Calderon, Yorlin	R-R	6-3	155	8-17-01	3	2	6.39	15	0	0	25	25	19	18	7	10	21	.263	.351	.547	18.8	8.9	112
Cijntje, Jurrangelo	S-S	5-11	170	5-31-03	1	0	2.67	7	7	0	34	27	11	10	1	16	37	.218	.324	.282	25.5	11.0	145
Cleveland, Tyler	L-R	6-3	185	9-9-99	3	1	0.89	18	0	0	20	11	4	2	0	8	13	.159	.266	.188	16.5	10.1	79
Cronin, Matt	L-L	6-2	210	9-20-97	0	0	1.13	5	0	0	8	5	2	1	1	5	11	.167	.286	.300	31.4	14.3	35
Davila, Nick	R-R	6-3	202	11-21-98	1	4	3.55	39	0	4	51	47	26	20	2	22	40	.247	.323	.316	18.3	10.1	218
File, Dylan	R-R	6-1	205	6-4-96	8	4	4.74	27	23	0	125	129	67	66	9	35	98	.262	.317	.371	18.2	6.5	539
Fleming, William	R-R	6-6	220	3-6-99	0	0	2.08	3	0	0	4	4	1	1	0	3	4	.235	.350	.353	20.0	15.0	20
Floyd, Taylor	R-R	6-1	185	12-8-97	5	7	4.53	45	0	3	58	63	38	29	8	19	68	.267	.336	.445	25.9	7.2	263
Fraze, Nick	R-R	6-3	180	10-24-97	0	4	7.55	13	7	0	31	37	28	26	3	15	22	.303	.386	.434	15.0	10.2	147
Garcia, Brandyn	L-L	6-4	225	5-27-00	4	4	3.96	24	0	5	25	20	14	11	3	12	33	.215	.321	.333	30.0	10.9	110
Hill, Garrett	R-R	6-0	185	1-16-96	1	3	4.04	10	10	0	42	32	23	19	1	34	37	.211	.368	.257	19.0	17.4	195
Hobbs, Michael	R-R	6-3	215	7-10-99	1	2	2.47	45	0	4	51	40	17	14	2	40	60	.220	.371	.280	26.2	17.5	229
Hunter, Leon	R-R	6-3	253	3-17-97	1	0	5.40	26	0	1	27	28	16	16	2	17	34	.272	.377	.388	27.9	13.9	122
Joyce, Jimmy	R-R	6-2	210	1-13-99	2	0	0.00	6	0	0	9	3	0	0	0	4	7	.100	.206	.167	20.6	11.8	34
Kingsbury, Jimmy	R-R	6-1	187	2-13-99	5	3	2.93	44	2	10	71	51	33	23	4	18	60	.198	.264	.271	21.1	6.3	285
Morales, Michael	R-R	6-2	205	8-13-02	4	7	4.60	22	22	0	102	105	57	52	5	37	70	.271	.343	.371	16.1	8.5	435
Perez, Marcelo	R-R	5-10	180	11-16-99	2	4	4.31	11	11	0	56	52	27	27	7	18	28	.244	.309	.380	11.9	7.6	236
Raeth, Stefan	L-R	6-1	180	8-31-00	1	0	5.50	12	2	0	18	18	11	11	2	6	18	.265	.333	.456	23.1	7.7	78
Ramirez, Ben	L-R	6-2	200	12-2-98	0	0	0.00	1	0	0	1	0	0	0	0	1	0	.000	.500	.000	0.0	50.0	2
Raposo, Nick	R-R	5-10	200	6-3-98	0	0	9.00	1	0	0	1	2	1	1	1	0	0	.400	.400	1.000	0.0	0.0	5
Ruffcorn, Jason	R-R	6-2	215	7-27-98	7	1	3.02	47	0	1	66	55	26	22	4	29	70	.224	.310	.347	25.1	10.4	279
Seminaris, Adam	R-L	6-0	191	10-19-98	7	7	3.02	24	22	0	125	116	47	42	2	36	105	.243	.301	.303	20.2	6.9	519
VanScoter, Reid	L-L	6-0	190	11-25-98	4	6	5.38	21	21	0	87	110	55	52	11	34	72	.306	.367	.468	18.2	8.6	396
Wirchansky, Dan	L-L	6-1	200	7-2-97	1	3	4.52	24	11	0	68	61	38	34	8	34	47	.242	.336	.409	16.1	11.6	292

Fielding

Catcher	PCT	G	PO	A	E	DP	PB
Batista	.982	14	102	6	2	0	3
Charping	.985	36	247	13	4	1	5
Raposo	.996	78	653	48	3	5	5
Rodriguez	.990	12	92	3	1	1	1

First Base	PCT	G	PO	A	E	DP
Cali	.981	8	51	2	1	4
Fitz-Gerald	.997	80	635	46	2	58
Ramirez	1.000	1	1	1	0	0
Windish	.989	54	415	29	5	34

Second Base	PCT	G	PO	A	E	DP
Arroyo	.995	47	81	132	1	32

	PCT	G	PO	A	E	DP
Cali	.972	8	14	21	1	3
Fajardo	1.000	1	3	2	0	0
Oyama	.889	1	2	6	1	1
Rambusch	.976	54	91	152	6	36
Rodden	1.000	12	19	25	0	7
Sanchez	.955	10	12	30	2	3
Windish	.935	11	14	15	2	2

Third Base	PCT	G	PO	A	E	DP
Cali	.941	79	52	125	11	10
Hood	.969	25	22	40	2	6
Rambusch	1.000	.2	1	0	0	0
Ramirez	.918	32	18	60	7	4
Rodden	1.000	6	4	8	0	2

Shortstop	PCT	G	PO	A	E	DP
Emerson	.971	30	48	88	4	22
Hood	.961	76	112	182	12	30
Rodden	.955	15	14	49	3	12
Sanchez	.968	22	18	42	2	6

Outfield	PCT	G	PO	A	E	DP
Fajardo	.972	36	70	0	2	0
Hood	1.000	4	3	0	0	0
Knight	.985	123	329	6	5	3
Labrada	.980	56	96	1	2	0
Montes	.989	55	83	4	1	1
Rambusch	1.000	43	89	2	0	0
Sundstrom	.986	100	205	8	3	2

EVERETT AQUASOX
NORTHWEST LEAGUE — HIGH-A

Batting	B-T	Ht.	Wt.	DOB	AVG	OBP	SLG	G	PA	AB	R	H	2B	3B	HR	RBI	BB	HBP	SH	SF	SO	SB	CS	BB%	SO%
Arroyo, Michael	R-R	5-8	160	11-3-04	.269	.422	.512	65	306	242	41	65	14	0	15	39	39	25	0	0	65	3	2	12.7	21.2
Batista, Freuddy	R-R	6-0	182	12-12-99	.303	.411	.585	53	224	188	27	57	15	1	12	38	23	12	0	1	40	0	0	10.3	17.9
Caron, Josh	R-R	6-0	215	8-3-03	.197	.269	.331	79	331	299	39	59	9	2	9	26	25	5	0	2	96	11	2	7.6	29.0
Celesten, Felnin	S-R	6-1	175	9-15-05	.158	.313	.289	11	48	38	6	6	0	1	1	4	9	0	0	1	15	1	1	18.8	31.3
Davis, Colin	R-R	6-0	190	2-8-99	.160	.270	.273	18	63	55	8	9	3	0	1	2	7	1	0	0	20	1	0	11.1	31.7
Donofrio, Anthony	L-R	6-3	195	6-28-00	.230	.333	.375	87	330	283	45	65	23	0	6	34	40	5	0	2	97	10	0	12.1	29.4
Dorighi, Carter	L-R	6-0	190	6-11-03	.262	.312	.369	36	154	141	11	37	9	3	0	12	10	1	0	2	38	5	0	6.5	24.7
Eike, Brandon	L-R	6-0	220	10-1-01	.208	.272	.368	95	387	351	34	73	23	0	11	38	26	6	0	3	121	1	0	6.7	31.3
Ellis, Matthew	L-R	6-4	240	1-19-00	.208	.343	.19	78	70	5	16	5	0	1	5	6	2	0	0	25	0	0	7.7	32.1
Emerson, Colt	L-R	6-0	185	7-20-05	.281	.388	.453	90	412	342	58	96	16	5	11	51	54	10	0	6	68	6	4	13.1	16.5
Farmelo, Jonny	L-R	6-2	205	9-9-04	.230	.318	.460	29	129	113	18	26	6	1	6	16	14	1	0	1	38	2	1	10.9	29.5
Jones, Carson	L-L	6-2	205	5-4-00	.265	.326	.440	64	245	213	31	34	9	0	6	22	26	5	0	1	87	17	0	10.6	35.5
Marlowe, Cade	L-R	6-1	210	6-24-97	.429	.556	.429	2	9	7	2	3	0	0	0	1	2	0	0	0	2	1	0	22.2	22.2
Miller, Andrew	R-R	6-2	230	9-2-97	.100	.308	.400	12	39	30	8	3	0	0	3	4	7	2	0	0	16	0	0	17.9	41.0
Montes, Lazaro	L-R	6-3	210	10-22-04	.268	.387	.572	67	301	250	43	67	12	5	18	50	48	1	0	1	83	3	1	15.9	27.6
Pagliarini, Charlie	R-R	6-2	210	12-20-00	.160	.229	.451	116	349	419	68	94	21	0	42	121	48	21	6	23	62	75	6	0	1	133	2	2	15.0	26.5
Peete, Tai	L-R	6-2	193	8-11-05	.217	.288	.404	125	529	475	58	103	24	4	19	63	46	3	1	4	162	25	11	8.7	30.6
Perez, Milkar	S-R	5-11	200	10-16-01	.215	.321	.301	78	299	256	21	55	14	1	2	16	38	3	0	2	64	1	0	12.7	21.4
Sanchez, Axel	R-R	5-10	170	12-10-02	.108	.292	.270	13	48	37	4	4	3	0	1	8	2	0	1	5	0	1	16.7	31.3
Suisbel, Luis	S-R	6-1	190	5-23-03	.211	.308	.412	113	491	427	62	90	15	1	23	68	48	13	0	3	135	8	1	9.8	27.5
Washington, Curtis	R-R	6-2	180	5-22-00	.148	.266	.213	40	144	122	16	18	6	1	0	7	18	2	1	1	38	10	2	12.5	26.4

SEATTLE MARINERS

Pitching	B-T	Ht.	Wt.	DOB	W	L	ERA	G	GS	SV	IP	Hits	Runs	ER	HR	BB	SO	AVG	OBP	SLG	SO%	BB%	BF
Beilenson, Charlie	R-R	6-0	215	12-10-99	2	1	3.97	20	0	3	34	28	17	15	6	8	48	.224	.272	.408	35.3	5.9	136
Cijntje, Jurrangelo	S-S	5-11	170	5-31-03	4	7	4.58	19	16	0	75	54	39	38	14	35	83	.201	.318	.392	26.4	11.1	314
Cleveland, Tyler	L-R	6-3	185	9-9-99	0	0	0.86	23	0	2	31	11	5	3	0	9	37	.107	.214	.107	31.6	7.7	117
Cranton, Hunter	R-R	6-3	215	10-24-00	2	0	1.13	8	0	3	8	4	1	1	0	3	11	.154	.233	.154	36.7	10.0	30
Dale, Elijah	S-R	5-11	175	1-7-01	1	2	5.52	24	0	1	31	19	19	19	5	24	33	.179	.370	.387	23.9	17.4	138
Davis, Colin	R-R	6-0	190	2-8-99	0	0	32.40	1	0	0	2	4	6	6	2	0	0	.444	.545	1.222	0.0	0.0	11
Denner, Jacob	L-L	6-0	195	8-14-00	0	1	4.34	9	0	0	19	21	12	9	3	3	15	.296	.333	.521	19.7	3.9	76
Dollard, Taylor	R-R	6-3	195	2-17-99	3	3	3.90	13	12	0	55	59	29	24	11	13	37	.267	.328	.493	15.4	5.4	241
Fleming, William	R-R	6-6	220	3-6-99	0	2	8.79	7	4	0	14	29	22	14	2	7	12	.392	.444	.514	14.8	8.6	81
Garabitos, Natanael	R-R	6-0	185	8-4-00	1	1	9.88	15	0	2	14	17	16	15	2	12	12	.304	.458	.536	16.7	16.7	72
Geraldo, Jose	R-R	5-10	185	12-3-99	0	2	5.66	15	0	1	21	16	20	13	6	9	22	.203	.289	.443	24.4	10.0	90
Hawks, Ryan	R-R	6-2	235	11-24-00	10	6	3.79	22	21	0	116	113	53	49	13	34	86	.259	.314	.413	18.1	7.2	475
Hernandez, Ben	R-R	6-2	205	7-1-01	4	2	3.46	37	0	0	55	46	31	21	2	29	49	.229	.354	.303	20.1	11.9	244
Hintz, Casey	R-R	5-10	161	11-4-03	0	1	9.00	2	0	0	2	1	2	2	1	1	1	.143	.250	.571	12.5	12.5	8
Izzi, Ashton	R-R	6-3	165	11-18-03	2	4	5.51	12	12	0	47	53	33	29	8	21	54	.275	.355	.435	24.9	9.7	217
Jackson, Jordan	R-R	6-6	204	10-14-98	1	0	6.86	31	0	0	42	53	36	32	7	22	35	.305	.390	.511	17.5	11.0	200
Kelly, Lucas	R-R	6-3	220	7-26-03	0	0	7.50	5	0	0	6	4	5	5	2	5	6	.182	.333	.500	22.2	18.5	27
Lemos, Pedro Da Costa	R-R	6-0	179	5-22-03	1	1	3.00	10	0	0	18	16	7	6	1	6	18	.225	.286	.338	23.4	7.8	77
Little, Christian	R-R	6-4	210	7-5-03	0	1	3.00	2	2	0	9	6	3	3	0	5	5	.207	.333	.345	13.9	13.9	36
McGraw, Teddy	R-R	6-2	210	10-30-01	0	3	3.26	9	8	0	19	24	7	7	1	4	24	.304	.337	.405	28.9	4.8	83
Moore, Brock	R-R	6-6	230	5-17-00	1	2	9.64	25	0	0	19	18	23	20	2	28	26	.254	.476	.380	24.8	26.7	105
Payero, Nick	R-R	6-2	200	6-21-00	5	7	4.61	23	16	0	107	105	58	55	18	48	99	.258	.339	.455	21.5	10.4	460
Peavyhouse, Shaddon	R-R	6-3	205	8-18-98	2	4	6.17	28	3	0	54	54	38	37	10	28	40	.260	.359	.471	16.3	11.4	245
Perez, Marcelo	R-R	5-10	180	11-16-99	4	2	2.04	8	8	0	35	28	8	8	3	5	34	.222	.261	.317	25.4	3.7	134
Perez, Milkar	S-R	5-11	200	10-16-01	0	0	11.57	4	0	0	5	12	6	6	2	0	1	.480	.480	.760	4.0	0.0	25
Raeth, Stefan	L-R	6-1	180	8-31-00	4	2	2.06	31	0	5	39	24	11	9	6	7	44	.176	.233	.346	29.7	4.7	148
Saathoff, Allan	R-R	6-1	230	9-18-99	1	1	7.76	23	0	0	29	31	28	25	5	24	26	.279	.411	.505	18.4	17.0	141
Schapira, Calvin	R-L	6-5	230	10-7-99	1	1	1.69	11	0	0	11	8	2	2	0	3	11	.200	.256	.250	25.6	7.0	43
Sloan, Ryan	R-R	6-5	220	1-29-06	0	2	5.56	3	3	0	11	14	8	7	3	0	13	.298	.306	.553	26.5	0.0	49
Sosa, Gabriel	R-R	6-2	182	4-17-01	2	1	2.90	42	0	9	40	25	14	13	4	27	50	.176	.320	.317	29.1	15.7	172
Tellache, Nico	L-L	6-2	205	1-14-98	4	4	5.60	18	8	0	63	76	44	39	4	16	54	.302	.348	.405	19.4	5.8	278
Truitt, Evan	R-R	6-0	187	5-2-03	5	8	4.58	22	19	0	98	100	54	50	16	46	72	.267	.363	.473	16.6	10.6	433
Wainscott, Jesse	R-R	6-1	200	6-15-00	0	1	9.13	17	0	0	24	27	24	24	4	26	19	.287	.449	.500	15.0	20.5	127
Washington, Curtis	R-R	6-2	180	5-22-00	0	0	0.00	1	0	0	0	0	0	0	0	2	0	.000	.667	.000	0.0	66.7	3
Zerpa, Jose	R-R	6-2	180	10-19-04	0	0	5.68	4	0	0	6	4	4	4	0	2	3	.182	.250	.227	12.5	8.3	24

Fielding

Catcher	PCT	G	PO	A	E	DP	PB
Batista	1.000	35	269	23	0	3	5
Caron	.993	76	632	49	5	4	11
Ellis	1.000	17	129	7	0	0	3
Miller	.982	6	51	3	1	0	5

First Base	PCT	G	PO	A	E	DP
Batista	.857	1	5	1	1	1
Dorighi	1.000	9	73	8	0	3
Eike	.988	42	319	23	4	32
Miller	1.000	3	5	2	0	0
Pagliarini	1.000	16	117	7	0	16
Perez	.986	62	472	38	7	60
Suisbel	.976	4	40	0	1	5

Second Base	PCT	G	PO	A	E	DP
Arroyo	.965	48	92	130	8	36
Dorighi	.982	12	18	37	1	7
Pagliarini	.987	70	114	200	4	44
Sanchez	1.000	3	4	10	0	3

Third Base	PCT	G	PO	A	E	DP
Dorighi	1.000	1	0	1	0	0
Eike	.935	42	22	65	6	6
Emerson	1.000	2	1	4	0	1
Suisbel	.975	89	55	177	6	20

Shortstop	PCT	G	PO	A	E	DP
Celesten	.956	11	13	30	2	7
Dorighi	.931	15	23	31	4	7

Emerson	.977	87	153	221	9	49
Sanchez	.943	10	15	18	2	7
Suisbel	.979	11	16	31	1	8

Outfield	PCT	G	PO	A	E	DP
Davis	1.000	10	19	0	0	0
Donofrio	1.000	84	141	11	0	1
Farmelo	.940	22	46	1	3	0
Jones	.991	56	109	2	1	1
Marlowe	1.000	2	6	0	0	0
Miller	1.000	1	3	0	0	0
Montes	.981	60	94	10	2	1
Pagliarini	1.000	9	14	0	0	0
Peete	.985	120	261	7	4	1
Washington	.940	40	74	5	5	0

MODESTO NUTS
CALIFORNIA LEAGUE
LOW-A

Batting	B-T	Ht.	Wt.	DOB	AVG	OBP	SLG	G	PA	AB	R	H	2B	3B	HR	RBI	BB	HBP	SH	SF	SO	SB	CS	BB%	SO%
Aguilar, Starlin	L-R	5-11	170	1-26-04	.169	.230	.243	43	148	136	14	23	7	0	1	11	9	2	0	1	55	0	0	6.1	37.2
Becker, Nick	R-R	6-4	190	12-4-06	.208	.321	.208	6	28	24	5	5	0	0	0	2	4	0	0	0	9	2	0	14.3	32.1
Caguana, Jose	R-R	5-10	175	4-5-02	.230	.313	.377	68	288	252	36	58	13	0	8	47	29	3	0	4	68	8	1	10.1	23.6
Celesten, Felnin	S-R	6-1	175	9-5-05	.285	.349	.384	93	424	383	52	109	19	2	5	55	37	2	0	2	96	20	8	8.7	22.6
Cova, Ricardo	R-R	5-9	145	5-24-04	.273	.321	.398	85	377	344	59	94	23	1	6	58	19	8	0	6	75	26	5	5.0	19.9
Crenshaw, Dustin	L-R	6-2	190	11-12-01	.176	.300	.200	26	101	85	12	15	2	0	0	7	15	0	1	0	20	2	1	14.9	19.8
Davis, Dalton	R-R	6-0	195	10-17-00	.391	.464	.565	6	28	23	3	9	1	0	1	5	4	0	0	1	4	1	1	14.3	14.3
Dickerson, Korbyn	R-R	6-1	190	10-30-03	.429	.556	.571	2	9	7	2	3	1	0	0	1	1	0	0	0	2	0	0	11.1	22.2
Dorighi, Carter	L-R	6-0	190	6-11-03	.299	.382	.368	85	348	304	59	91	21	0	0	47	34	8	0	2	68	19	4	9.8	19.5
Dykstra, Connor	R-R	6-1	230	3-16-01	.205	.361	.319	59	232	185	34	38	11	2	2	13	22	23	0	0	64	3	0	9.5	27.6
Ellis, Matthew	L-R	6-4	240	8-1-00	.238	.393	.421	60	260	202	42	48	11	1	8	37	49	4	0	2	54	3	1	18.8	20.8
Feliz, George	R-R	5-10	160	9-21-02	.237	.287	.329	49	165	152	20	36	4	2	2	21	9	2	1	1	61	3	0	5.5	37.0
Jimenez, Carlos	L-L	5-10	170	2-14-03	.258	.358	.419	105	489	418	75	108	17	4	14	63	60	7	0	4	116	30	13	12.3	23.7
Moncada, Gabe	L-L	6-2	175	7-28-01	.259	.278	.278	57	228	209	16	57	1	0	0	11	2	11	0	0	2	68	0	1	7.5	29.8
Picollo, Ryan	R-R	6-5	225	4-25-02	.205	.266	.360	78	304	278	45	57	11	4	8	44	22	2	0	2	124	3	1	7.2	40.8
Quintas, Cesar	R-R	6-1	175	3-25-03	.245	.361	.384	75	352	294	47	72	20	3	5	48	29	26	0	3	78	12	4	8.2	22.2
St. Laurent, Austin	R-R	6-1	188	7-13-02	.257	.361	.327	123	521	443	73	114	17	1	4	55	70	4	0	4	97	18	7	13.4	18.6
Stevenson, Luke	L-R	6-1	200	7-22-04	.280	.460	.400	22	100	75	16	21	4	1	1	14	23	2	0	0	19	1	0	23.0	19.0

Batting	B-T	Ht.	Wt.	DOB	AVG	OBP	SLG	G	PA	AB	R	H	2B	3B	HR	RBI	BB	SO	AVG	OBP	SLG	SO%	BB%	BF
Taurek, Aiden	R-R	5-11	170	10-21-03	.336	.395	.418	27	124	110	24	37	9	0	0	10	12	0	0	2	16	7	1	9.7	12.9
Ventura, Dervy	S-R	5-10	165	1-20-04	.276	.383	.363	108	440	366	67	101	21	1	3	45	65	1	3	4	96	41	7	14.8	21.8
Washington, Curtis	R-R	6-2	180	5-22-00	.308	.373	.460	55	220	198	42	61	15	3	3	24	17	4	0	1	47	22	2	7.7	21.4

Pitching	B-T	Ht.	Wt.	DOB	W	L	ERA	G	GS	SV	IP	Hits	Runs	ER	HR	BB	SO	AVG	OBP	SLG	SO%	BB%	BF
Bello, Yensy	R-R	5-10	180	12-2-02	1	2	5.57	34	0	0	52	53	36	32	2	31	46	.262	.369	.381	18.9	12.7	244
Boehm, Gage	R-R	6-5	255	11-21-01	1	2	6.75	19	0	2	20	17	23	15	0	36	20	.224	.473	.263	17.5	31.6	114
Butler, Aiden	R-R	6-6	193	9-25-03	1	5	5.37	13	13	0	59	65	42	35	10	15	40	.280	.322	.470	15.6	5.8	257
Carson, Andrew	R-R	6-2	188	6-2-00	2	3	3.63	24	0	4	22	17	11	9	0	21	19	.215	.364	.278	17.6	19.4	108
Diaz, Gleiner	R-R	6-0	170	9-20-03	6	0	4.50	13	0	1	18	18	10	9	0	4	17	.257	.325	.314	22.1	5.2	77
Dorighi, Carter	L-R	6-0	190	6-11-03	0	0	4.50	1	0	0	2	3	1	1	1	0	0	.333	.333	.778	0.0	0.0	9
Dykstra, Connor	R-R	6-1	230	3-16-01	0	0	0.00	1	0	0	0	0	0	0	0	0	0	.000	.000	.000	0.0	0.0	1
Easterly, Reid	L-L	6-0	200	1-23-02	0	0	1.93	3	0	0	5	5	1	1	0	1	3	.294	.316	.294	15.8	5.3	19
Fajardo, German	R-R	5-11	165	1-29-01	1	0	0.00	2	0	0	3	1	0	0	0	1	4	.091	.167	.091	33.3	8.3	12
Ford, Walter	R-R	6-3	198	12-28-04	5	5	4.67	23	23	0	125	130	74	65	11	30	95	.267	.309	.428	17.9	5.6	531
Geraldo, Jose	R-R	5-10	185	12-3-99	3	2	3.21	24	0	6	28	26	12	10	0	9	33	.234	.320	.288	25.8	7.0	128
Hintz, Casey	R-R	5-10	161	11-4-03	0	0	6.00	5	0	2	6	8	4	4	0	5	8	.296	.406	.296	25.0	15.6	32
Lemos, Pedro Da Costa	R-R	6-0	179	5-22-03	4	2	3.86	25	0	1	49	43	24	21	5	20	56	.235	.324	.377	26.3	9.4	213
Little, Christian	R-R	6-4	210	7-5-03	1	4	4.09	15	15	0	62	49	31	28	4	27	68	.220	.311	.332	26.5	10.5	257
Long, Trevor	R-R	6-1	198	5-22-01	0	0	40.50	1	0	0	1	4	3	3	0	1	1	.667	.714	.833	14.3	14.3	7
Lora, Aneury	R-R	6-2	155	3-30-04	4	4	5.20	36	1	1	81	86	54	47	3	27	76	.267	.331	.366	21.2	7.5	359
Lumpkin, Reese	R-R	6-5	200	11-8-01	2	0	5.40	8	0	0	8	9	7	5	0	7	10	.265	.405	.265	23.8	16.7	42
Lunsford-Shenkman, Wyatt	R-R	6-2	236	6-9-03	1	1	8.53	7	0	0	6	6	8	6	0	8	7	.250	.452	.292	21.2	24.2	33
Lyon, Isaac	R-R	6-3	205	1-26-04	0	2	7.30	4	0	0	12	16	10	10	4	3	15	.308	.345	.577	27.3	5.5	55
Martinez, Jeter	R-R	6-4	280	2-16-06	2	6	6.18	16	16	0	63	63	50	43	1	38	60	.264	.371	.356	20.9	13.2	287
Melenge, Harold	L-L	5-10	170	11-5-02	6	7	5.00	22	20	0	95	119	62	53	2	36	53	.307	.373	.379	11.9	8.1	444
Munoz, Jean	R-R	6-1	155	9-17-02	1	2	4.61	37	0	4	41	37	23	21	1	35	44	.239	.393	.297	22.2	17.7	198
Ouderkirk, Daniel	R-R	6-9	255	3-16-00	0	0	0.00	2	0	0	2	2	0	0	0	0	2	.286	.375	.429	25.0	0.0	8
Ovando, Anyelo	R-R	6-5	222	12-25-00	4	3	7.23	27	0	1	37	46	31	30	2	24	38	.305	.408	.430	20.7	13.0	184
Perez, Roberto	R-R	5-9	145	1-27-04	0	0	54.00	1	0	0	1	3	6	6	1	4	1	.500	.700	1.000	10.0	40.0	10
Quintana, Adrian	R-R	6-0	175	11-20-02	7	4	4.41	36	0	0	49	47	27	24	5	23	43	.250	.340	.367	19.9	10.6	216
Romero, Jose	R-R	6-1	160	7-26-04	0	0	6.00	2	0	0	6	4	4	4	0	6	5	.190	.393	.238	17.9	21.4	28
Sanchez, Justin	L-L	6-0	183	10-11-03	4	1	4.99	25	0	0	49	44	28	27	2	34	51	.238	.373	.351	22.7	15.1	225
Sanchez, Steven	R-R	6-0	160	8-19-03	3	0	3.72	7	0	0	19	16	8	8	2	6	19	.213	.272	.387	23.5	7.4	81
Schapira, Calvin	R-L	6-5	230	10-7-99	2	1	2.33	16	0	3	19	16	11	5	0	13	21	.222	.349	.278	23.9	14.8	88
Shaw, Colton	R-R	6-2	205	6-26-03	0	0	3.72	3	0	0	11	4	4	0	0	8	.297	.282	.324	20.5	0.0	39
Shen, Chia-Shi	R-R	6-3	185	12-3-03	1	4	6.53	9	9	0	41	49	35	30	6	10	34	.290	.360	.509	18.1	5.3	188
Sloan, Ryan	R-R	6-5	220	1-29-06	2	2	3.44	18	18	0	71	66	32	27	2	15	77	.249	.293	.351	27.1	5.3	284
Tiberia, Matt	R-R	6-3	192	6-12-02	3	0	2.27	10	0	0	44	29	11	11	0	18	40	.191	.282	.243	22.5	10.1	178
Wainscott, Jesse	R-R	6-1	200	6-15-00	1	1	6.75	6	0	0	7	8	6	5	0	8	7	.286	.444	.393	19.4	22.2	36
Washington, Curtis	R-R	6-2	180	5-22-00	0	0	0.00	2	0	0	1	2	0	0	0	3	0	.333	.556	.333	0.0	33.3	9
Zerpa, Jose	R-R	6-2	180	10-19-04	1	0	3.35	27	0	2	48	50	20	18	2	9	39	.267	.299	.369	19.7	4.5	198

Fielding

Catcher	PCT	G	PO	A	E	DP	PB
Caguana	.979	19	137	4	3	1	5
Dykstra	.982	56	466	38	9	1	9
Ellis	.990	46	380	34	4	2	2
Stevenson	.981	13	91	10	2	1	7

First Base	PCT	G	PO	A	E	DP
Caguana	.997	39	308	16	1	22
Davis	1.000	3	19	1	0	1
Dorighi	.990	26	178	13	2	9
Ellis	.857	2	6	0	1	1
Moncada	.986	48	341	16	5	21
Quintas	.995	30	188	15	1	19

Second Base	PCT	G	PO	A	E	DP
Cova	1.000	3	3	7	0	0
Crenshaw	.933	4	6	8	1	2

	PCT	G	PO	A	E	DP
Dorighi	.969	9	15	16	1	3
St. Laurent	.991	28	42	70	1	12
Ventura	.975	94	153	233	10	36

Third Base	PCT	G	PO	A	E	DP
Aguilar	.917	16	12	21	3	2
Cova	.922	19	19	28	4	1
Crenshaw	.913	18	14	28	4	3
Dorighi	.947	44	31	76	6	6
St. Laurent	.937	42	25	79	7	4

Shortstop	PCT	G	PO	A	E	DP
Becker	.967	6	10	19	1	3
Celesten	.910	78	90	184	27	33
St. Laurent	.942	42	39	107	9	16
Ventura	.853	10	9	20	5	4

Outfield	PCT	G	PO	A	E	DP
Aguilar	.667	8	4	0	2	0
Cova	1.000	59	117	6	0	0
Crenshaw	.889	4	7	1	1	1
Davis	1.000	2	1	0	0	0
Dickerson	1.000	2	6	0	0	0
Dorighi	1.000	1	1	0	0	0
Feliz	.960	49	96	1	4	0
Jimenez	.951	92	205	7	11	0
Moncada	1.000	5	10	0	0	0
Picollo	.970	70	126	4	4	0
Quintas	.981	57	100	5	2	2
St. Laurent	.000	1	0	0	0	0
Taurek	1.000	24	51	1	0	0
Ventura	1.000	3	3	0	0	0
Washington	.971	54	129	3	4	0

ACL MARINERS
ARIZONA COMPLEX LEAGUE
ROOKIE

Batting	B-T	Ht.	Wt.	DOB	AVG	OBP	SLG	G	PA	AB	R	H	2B	3B	HR	RBI	BB	HBP	SH	SF	SO	SB	CS	BB%	SO%
Alcantara, Kelvin	L-L	6-0	165	9-15-05	.258	.362	.394	55	235	198	29	51	13	1	4	29	27	7	0	3	45	3	0	11.5	19.1
Caguana, Jose	R-R	5-10	175	4-5-02	.059	.304	.059	6	23	17	5	1	0	0	0	2	6	0	0	0	8	0	0	26.1	34.8
Crenshaw, Dustin	L-R	6-2	190	11-12-01	.327	.412	.480	55	228	196	40	64	9	3	5	23	29	1	0	2	33	8	4	12.7	14.5
Cruz, Juan	R-R	5-11	140	4-30-04	.188	.284	.304	30	81	69	14	13	2	0	2	16	8	2	0	2	20	4	1	9.9	24.7
Davis, Dalton	R-R	6-0	195	10-17-00	.438	.531	.500	30	128	113	22	42	10	2	1	15	9	5	0	1	12	7	1	7.0	9.4
De Andrade, Sebastian	R-R	5-9	165	5-11-06	.260	.376	.325	44	186	154	26	40	7	0	1	22	27	3	0	2	43	0	1	14.5	23.1
Feliz, George	R-R	5-10	160	9-21-02	.270	.373	.533	36	161	137	28	37	7	4	7	23	21	2	0	1	33	1	0	13.0	20.5
Gonzalez, Carlos	R-R	5-11	170	11-20-03	.190	.340	.353	37	147	116	20	22	4	0	5	18	27	1	0	3	41	1	1	18.4	27.9
Gonzalez, Martin	R-R	5-10	165	9-28-04	.201	.326	.320	55	219	179	25	36	9	2	2	25	30	5	1	4	66	5	2	13.7	30.1
Marlowe, Cade	L-R	6-1	210	6-24-97	.308	.438	.462	4	16	13	2	4	2	0	0	3	3	0	0	0	5	1	1	18.8	31.3

SEATTLE MARINERS

	B-T	Ht.	Wt.	DOB	AVG	OBP	SLG	G	PA	AB	R	H	2B	3B	HR	RBI	BB	HBP	SH	SF	SO	SB	CS	BB%	SO%
McClaughry, Nik	R-R	5-9	159	9-14-99	.208	.312	.254	52	202	173	26	36	5	0	1	18	17	10	0	2	40	5	2	8.4	19.8
Mendez, Bryant	R-R	5-7	165	9-15-03	.254	.377	.354	44	159	130	26	33	6	2	1	25	24	3	0	2	40	12	1	15.1	25.2
Oyama, Jo	L-R	5-7	170	11-3-00	.625	.600	.750	2	10	8	2	5	1	0	0	2	1	0	0	1	0	0	0	10.0	0.0
Ponce, Eduardo	R-R	5-9	172	9-2-06	.216	.335	.302	45	194	162	27	35	3	1	3	23	27	3	0	2	29	1	0	13.9	14.9
Rodden, Brock	S-R	5-9	170	5-25-00	.273	.467	.273	4	15	11	1	3	0	0	0	1	3	1	0	0	4	2	1	20.0	26.7
Rose, Nathan	R-R	6-1	178	2-11-01	.236	.361	.423	40	147	123	21	29	8	0	5	18	16	8	0	0	38	0	1	10.9	25.9
Salcedo, Andruw	S-R	5-11	175	9-29-02	.138	.293	.188	29	101	80	7	11	4	0	0	5	17	1	2	1	30	1	0	16.8	29.7

Pitching	B-T	Ht.	Wt.	DOB	W	L	ERA	G	GS	SV	IP	Hits	Runs	ER	HR	BB	SO	AVG	OBP	SLG	SO%	BB%	BF
Bard, Daniel	R-R	6-4	215	6-25-85	0	0	18.00	1	1	0	1	2	2	2	0	0	0	.500	.600	.750	0.0	0.0	5
Butler, Aiden	R-R	6-6	193	9-25-03	1	0	9.53	3	0	0	6	7	6	6	0	1	12	.280	.308	.480	46.2	3.8	26
Carson, Andrew	R-R	6-2	188	6-2-00	0	0	4.50	2	0	0	2	1	1	1	0	0	0	.200	.167	.400	0.0	0.0	8
Cazarez, Juan	R-R	5-11	172	9-5-05	3	3	4.91	12	8	0	40	39	23	22	3	17	35	.258	.333	.384	20.5	9.9	171
Cranton, Hunter	R-R	6-3	215	10-24-00	0	0	0.00	2	0	0	2	1	0	0	0	0	3	.143	.143	.143	42.9	0.0	7
Denner, Jacob	L-L	6-0	195	8-14-00	2	0	3.21	16	0	3	28	31	14	10	0	9	31	.287	.339	.352	26.1	7.6	119
Diaz, Gleiner	R-R	6-0	170	9-20-03	0	3	9.43	16	0	3	21	29	23	22	4	8	25	.315	.382	.500	24.3	7.8	103
Dollard, Taylor	R-R	6-3	195	2-17-99	0	1	7.07	6	6	0	14	22	11	11	0	4	17	.355	.403	.484	25.0	5.9	68
Fajardo, German	R-R	5-11	165	1-29-01	0	0	0.00	3	0	0	4	1	0	0	0	2	3	.077	.200	.154	20.0	13.3	15
Gott, Trevor	R-R	5-11	185	8-26-92	1	0	0.00	2	0	0	2	1	1	0	0	0	3	.143	.143	.143	42.9	0.0	7
Guevara, Anderson	R-R	5-10	170	11-4-04	2	0	7.56	14	0	2	17	16	14	14	0	19	25	.258	.447	.403	29.4	22.4	85
Hunter, Leon	R-R	6-3	253	3-17-97	1	0	1.50	5	1	0	6	4	1	1	0	3	10	.190	.280	.238	40.0	12.0	25
Kowar, Jackson	R-R	6-5	200	10-4-96	0	0	4.50	2	2	0	2	2	2	1	0	0	1	.222	.222	.333	11.1	0.0	9
Manning, Noah	R-R	6-1	175	4-30-02	0	2	5.03	16	0	0	20	16	12	11	1	13	17	.232	.375	.319	19.3	14.8	88
McGraw, Teddy	R-R	6-2	210	10-30-01	0	0	3.00	5	4	0	9	8	3	3	0	4	9	.258	.343	.258	24.3	10.8	37
Meza, Kendal	R-R	6-0	160	12-13-05	2	1	7.65	13	4	0	20	17	18	17	3	25	24	.230	.443	.405	22.6	23.6	106
Pazos, Francisco	R-R	5-9	200	11-16-05	3	2	4.18	12	10	0	52	52	25	24	4	15	60	.257	.327	.386	26.9	6.7	223
Perez, Roberto	R-R	5-9	145	1-27-04	1	0	1.42	17	0	2	25	11	5	4	0	8	35	.139	.231	.177	35.9	8.7	92
Pop, Zach	R-R	6-4	220	9-20-96	0	0	0.00	2	0	2	1	2	0	0	0	1	3	.167	.250	.333	33.3	11.1	9
Ramirez, Ruben	R-R	6-2	204	2-6-05	2	1	3.12	13	0	2	17	16	8	6	0	9	21	.239	.342	.299	26.6	11.4	79
Rodriguez, Wuilliams	R-R	6-4	195	2-20-04	1	1	1.17	15	0	1	23	20	5	3	1	9	30	.230	.302	.322	30.9	9.3	97
Romero, Jose	R-R	6-1	160	7-26-04	4	5	4.09	12	9	0	51	62	29	23	4	15	43	.304	.363	.426	18.9	6.6	227
Sanchez, Steven	R-R	6-0	160	8-19-03	1	1	2.79	15	1	0	29	31	12	9	0	6	30	.272	.306	.342	24.2	4.8	124
Shen, Chia-Shi	R-R	6-3	185	12-3-03	2	1	1.93	7	3	0	28	19	7	6	0	4	34	.186	.224	.255	31.8	3.7	107
Talavera, Roiber	R-R	6-0	160	3-31-04	4	2	5.60	14	2	0	27	28	22	17	3	20	20	.267	.406	.400	14.8	14.8	135
Wilson, Dylan	R-R	6-0	160	12-1-05	1	6	5.47	12	9	0	51	50	32	31	4	24	40	.265	.366	.407	17.7	10.6	226
Zerpa, Jose	R-R	6-2	180	10-19-04	0	0	0.00	3	0	1	4	1	0	0	0	4	4	.091	.333	.182	26.7	26.7	15

Fielding

C: Ponce 21, De Andrade 20, Salcedo 9, Gonzalez 8, Caguana 2. **1B:** C. Gonzalez 28, Davis 12, Salcedo 12, M. Gonzalez 9, Caguana 3, Ponce 1. **2B:** Rose 39, Mendez 15, McClaughry 4, Crenshaw 2, Gonzalez 1, Oyama 1, Rodden 1. **3B:** Gonzalez 47, McClaughry 12, Crenshaw 5. **SS:** McClaughry 39, Crenshaw 12, Mendez 10, Rodden 3, Oyama 1. **LF:** Crenshaw 37, Mendez 14, Davis 9, Cruz 6. **CF:** Feliz 36, Cruz 19, Davis 6, Marlowe 3. **RF:** Alcantara 52, Davis 4, Mendez 4, Crenshaw 2, Cruz 2.

DSL MARINERS — ROOKIE
DOMINICAN SUMMER LEAGUE

Batting	B-T	Ht.	Wt.	DOB	AVG	OBP	SLG	G	PA	AB	R	H	2B	3B	HR	RBI	BB	HBP	SH	SF	SO	SB	CS	BB%	SO%
Almeida, Manuel	S-R	5-11	187	10-5-07	.280	.343	.473	44	169	150	22	42	5	0	8	25	16	0	0	3	46	0	3	9.5	27.2
Baez, Manuel	R-R	5-9	192	5-22-05	.161	.381	.226	19	42	31	4	5	2	0	0	2	8	3	0	0	13	0	0	19.0	31.0
Bautista, Yorger	L-L	6-1	176	9-19-07	.223	.326	.404	53	225	193	38	43	8	3	7	25	21	9	0	1	67	10	0	9.3	29.8
Castillo, Deuri	L-R	5-10	170	6-18-04	.231	.420	.308	42	138	104	21	24	1	2	1	8	29	5	0	0	26	17	6	21.0	18.8
Contreras, Diego	S-R	6-1	185	10-17-07	.324	.454	.410	38	132	105	20	34	5	2	0	15	22	3	2	0	12	8	4	16.7	9.1
De Cesare, Manuel	R-R	6-4	185	5-8-07	.219	.294	.328	42	143	128	15	28	5	0	3	22	11	0	0	1	31	2	0	7.7	21.7
Francis, Joshua	S-R	5-11	155	11-20-06	.272	.359	.368	46	156	136	21	37	4	3	1	12	15	4	0	1	20	10	0	9.6	12.8
Guanchez, Gabriel	R-R	6-2	196	3-14-07	.227	.320	.460	44	172	150	23	34	11	0	8	25	18	3	0	1	46	0	0	10.5	26.7
Joseph, Dawel	R-R	5-10	157	5-15-07	.186	.370	.286	52	211	161	26	30	7	0	3	18	40	8	0	2	64	20	5	19.0	30.3
Martínez, Kendry	L-R	5-10	157	10-2-07	.157	.308	.167	37	133	108	12	17	1	0	0	10	21	3	0	1	37	1	3	15.8	27.8
Nunez, Zeus	R-R	6-1	185	11-20-06	.208	.295	.264	18	61	53	8	11	0	0	1	5	7	0	0	1	29	0	0	11.5	47.5
Perez, Elias	S-R	5-10	160	9-17-07	.245	.372	.301	50	196	163	30	40	4	1	1	20	30	3	0	0	39	5	3	15.3	19.9
Rodriguez, Maikol	S-R	6-1	168	3-21-07	.145	.344	.275	30	91	69	10	10	5	2	0	4	18	3	1	0	22	4	1	19.8	31.9
Romero, Leandro	R-R	6-1	170	11-8-06	.304	.367	.557	42	180	158	32	48	11	1	9	35	16	2	0	4	35	6	3	8.9	19.4

Pitching	B-T	Ht.	Wt.	DOB	W	L	ERA	G	GS	SV	IP	Hits	Runs	ER	HR	BB	SO	AVG	OBP	SLG	SO%	BB%	BF
Alcantara, Henry	R-R	6-0	170	11-23-07	5	0	1.57	18	1	2	34	21	10	6	1	15	37	.174	.292	.231	25.7	10.4	144
Aray, Cristian	R-R	5-10	155	4-5-07	3	1	1.87	11	11	0	43	29	10	9	1	22	34	.191	.291	.276	19.4	12.6	175
Benitez, Kleiver	L-R	6-0	159	8-11-08	1	0	2.87	13	0	1	16	8	7	5	0	12	12	.154	.333	.173	17.6	17.6	68
Carpinteiro, Alan	R-R	6-0	163	12-1-06	1	2	2.17	11	5	0	37	26	12	9	1	16	33	.193	.287	.244	21.0	10.2	157
Chicuate, Angel	R-R	5-9	176	8-16-06	0	0	3.86	3	0	0	2	2	1	1	0	4	0	.222	.222	.333	44.4	0.0	9
Farias, Cesar	R-R	5-11	145	8-16-07	1	2	8.53	7	4	0	13	13	15	12	1	6	20	.265	.472	.388	27.8	22.2	72
Infante, Wisler	R-R	5-10	155	12-8-07	2	6	7.50	11	5	0	36	46	34	30	2	11	31	.315	.368	.445	18.9	6.7	164
Jaspe, Carlos	R-R	6-1	155	6-5-07	0	0	11.12	7	0	0	6	9	7	7	0	9	4	.333	.514	.333	10.8	24.3	37
Jimenez, Anderson	R-R	6-0	160	5-17-08	1	1	4.15	11	6	0	30	27	15	14	3	14	22	.228	.245	.383	17.3	20.7	16.3	135
Lanza, Erick	R-R	6-2	169	9-1-06	2	3	4.13	14	5	0	24	28	18	11	1	16	17	.295	.393	.368	15.2	14.3	112
Meyer, Danery	R-R	6-4	202	9-8-06	1	1	5.40	14	0	1	8	9	5	5	0	12	9	.290	.488	.323	20.9	27.9	43
Munoz, Randal	R-R	6-2	174	3-14-08	0	2	5.49	9	6	0	20	16	14	12	0	25	17	.154	.398	.200	18.1	26.6	94
Orbe, Eliezer	L-L	6-0	165	11-7-05	0	0	6.97	9	0	0	10	11	8	8	2	12	8	.268	.444	.488	14.8	22.2	54

Pina, Ismanuel	R-R	6-2	175	9-11-05	1	3	5.12	15	0	2	19	13	15	11	1	16	16	.191	.345 .309	18.2	18.2	88
Pino, Kevin	R-R	6-2	185	12-5-06	1	0	4.80	10	0	1	15	16	9	8	1	5	13	.271	.348 .407	19.7	7.6	66
Platas, Osvaldo	R-R	6-2	190	3-28-07	1	1	7.88	10	0	0	16	16	14	14	0	11	18	.258	.385 .339	23.1	14.1	78
Quiroz, Christopher	R-R	6-1	160	12-12-07	3	1	3.03	10	5	0	30	18	17	10	0	22	25	.170	.343 .208	18.7	16.4	134
Ramirez, Jheifer	R-R	6-0	155	6-21-07	0	1	9.82	12	0	1	11	10	12	12	0	14	9	.263	.482 .368	16.1	25.0	56
Ramos, Darwin	R-R	6-2	161	3-15-07	0	0	7.56	9	0	0	8	9	7	7	0	7	8	.250	.372 .361	18.6	16.3	43
Rodriguez, Maximo	R-R	5-9	181	12-23-05	5	1	2.16	19	0	7	33	18	12	8	1	8	35	.149	.206 .215	26.7	6.1	131
Sato, Mathias	L-R	5-11	163	1-28-07	2	1	6.14	12	8	0	37	30	27	25	3	27	39	.222	.367 .356	23.4	16.2	167

Fielding
C: Almeida 28, Guanchez 25, Baez 6. **1B:** De Cesare 33, Castillo 24, Nunez 7, Francis 4, Baez 3. **2B:** Martínez 23, Contreras 19, Francis 15, Romero 7, Castillo 1. **3B:** Joseph 36, Contreras 11, Romero 7, Francis 4, Nunez 3. **SS:** Romero 30, Joseph 16, Martínez 11, Francis 2. **LF:** Castillo 21, Francis 19, Rodriguez 12, Contreras 7, Perez 7, De Cesare 1. **CF:** Bautista 52, Perez 6, Castillo 1. **RF:** Perez 37, Rodriguez 18, Francis 3, Castillo 2, De Cesare 2, Contreras 1.

Tampa Bay Rays

SEASON SYNOPSIS: Different venue, similar season for Tampa Bay, which missed the playoffs for the second straight season. The Rays had to play the entire season at the Yankees' spring-training home, Steinbrenner Field, after Hurricane Milton shredded the roof at Tropicana Field in October 2024. The Rays got 45 homers from second-year third baseman Junior Caminero but still went 77-85, their worst record since manager Kevin Cash's second season in 2016.

HIGH POINT: Three Rays pitchers made 30 or more starts for the first time since 2016, including Drew Rasmussen (10-5, 2.75, 1.02 WHIP in 150 IP), who was recovering from his third significant elbow surgery. Ten of his 31 starts were scoreless, he had a 23-inning scoreless streak, and he shut down host Kansas City for five innings June 25 in a 3-0 win as the Rays swept the series. They gave up one run in three games and climbed to 46-35, a season-high 11 games over .500.

LOW POINT: The club went just 7-18 in July, winning only one series. A 7-4 loss to the Yankees on July 31 was a killer as Jonathan Aranda fractured his wrist in a collision with Giancarlo Stanton. The all-star first baseman was slashing .314/.394/.478 at the time and homered in each of his first two games upon his return … which didn't happen until Sept. 26.

NOTABLE ROOKIES: Speedy outfielders Jake Mangum (.296/.330/.368) and 24-year-old Chandler Simpson (.295/.326/.345) made plenty of contact while combining for 71 stolen bases in 89 attempts. They also combined for just three home runs (all by Mangum, 29). Lefty Ian Seymour (4-3, 3.67) broke in as a reliever but got stretched out in September and struck out 38 in his final 34 innings.

KEY TRANSACTIONS: The club was sold for $1.7 billion to a group led by Florida businessman Patrick Zalupski and new chief executive officer Ken Babby, ending the 20-year run of previous owner Stu Sternberg. Tampa traded two lefthanders in the offseason, Jeffrey Springs and Jacob Lopez, for a package of players from the Athletics that included righty Joe Boyle, who averaged 98.5 mph on his fastball but had his struggles (1-4, 4.67). A two-year, $29 million contract for veteran shortstop Ha-Seong Kim didn't work out; the Rays released him in August. Tampa was active at the deadline, getting Adrian Houser from the White Sox and trading Taj Bradley to the Twins for righty Griffin Jax, whom it intends to make a starter in 2026.

OPENING DAY PAYROLL: $79,216,312 (28th)

PLAYERS OF THE YEAR

MAJOR LEAGUE
Junior Caminero
3B
.264/.311/.535
45 HR, 110 RBIs
93 R, 28 2B

MINOR LEAGUE
Brody Hopkins
RHP
(AA)
2.72 ERA in 116 IP,
141 SO, .204 AVG

ORGANIZATION LEADERS

Batting		*Qualifiers
MAJORS		
* AVG	Yandy Diaz	.300
* OPS	Yandy Diaz	.848
HR	Junior Caminero	45
RBI	Junior Caminero	110
MINORS		
* AVG	Homer Bush, Montgomery	.301
* OBP	Tatem Levins, Montgomery	.405
* SLG	Bobby Seymour, Durham	.553
* OPS	Bobby Seymour, Durham	.881
R	Narciso Polanco, Charleston	84
H	Homer Bush, Montgomery	142
TB	Bobby Seymour, Durham	223
2B	Tanner Murray, Durham	29
2B	Jamie Westbrook, Durham	29
3B	Homer Bush, Montgomery	8
HR	Bobby Seymour, Durham	30
RBI	Bobby Seymour, Durham	87
BB	Nathan Flewelling, Bowling Green/Charleston	94
SO	Carson Williams, Durham	154
SB	Homer Bush, Montgomery	57

Pitching		#Qualifiers
MAJORS		
W	Ryan Pepiot	11
# ERA	Ryan Pepiot	3.86
SO	Shane Baz	176
SV	Pete Fairbanks	27
MINORS		
W	T.J. Nichols, Montgomery/Bowling Green	14
L	Marcus Johnson, Bowling Green	10
# ERA	Brody Hopkins, Montgomery	2.72
G	Derrick Edington, Montgomery/Bowling Green	49
GS	Logan Workman, Durham	28
SV	Derrick Edington, Montgomery/Bowling Green	13
IP	Logan Workman, Durham	152
BB	Brody Hopkins, Montgomery	60
SO	T.J. Nichols, Montgomery/Bowling Green	156
# AVG	Brody Hopkins, Montgomery	.204

2025 PERFORMANCE

General Manager: Erik Neander. **Farm Director:** Blake Butera. **Scouting Director:** Chuck Ricci.

Class	Team	League	W	L	PCT	Finish	Manager
Majors	Tampa Bay Rays	American	77	85	.475	10 (15)	Kevin Cash
Triple-A	Durham Bulls	International	85	64	.570	6 (20)	Morgan Ensberg
Double-A	Montgomery Biscuits	Southern	78	60	.565	2 (8)	Kevin Boles
High-A	Bowling Green Hot Rods	South Atlantic	69	61	.531	4 (12)	Rafael Valenzuela
Low-A	Charleston RiverDogs	Carolina	68	62	.523	4 (12)	Sean Smedley
Rookie	FCL Rays	Florida Complex	29	29	.500	7 (15)	Hector Gimenez
Rookie	DSL Rays	Dominican	32	24	.571	16 (52)	Albert Lantigua
Rookie	DSL Tampa Bay	Dominican	34	21	.618	9 (52)	Henry Lugo
Overall 2025 Minor League Record			395	321	.552	4th (30)	

ORGANIZATION STATISTICS

TAMPA BAY RAYS
AMERICAN LEAGUE

Batting	B-T	Ht.	Wt.	DOB	AVG	OBP	SLG	G	PA	AB	R	H	2B	3B	HR	RBI	BB	HBP	SH	SF	SO	SB	CS	BB%	SO%
Aranda, Jonathan	L-R	6-0	210	5-23-98	.316	.393	.489	106	422	370	56	117	22	0	14	59	41	8	0	3	107	0	2	9.7	25.4
Caballero, Jose	R-R	5-9	185	8-30-96	.226	.327	.311	86	275	235	37	53	12	1	2	27	33	3	3	1	80	34	8	12.0	29.1
Caminero, Junior	R-R	6-1	157	7-5-03	.264	.311	.535	154	653	602	93	159	28	0	45	110	41	3	0	7	125	7	1	6.3	19.1
DeLuca, Jonny	R-R	6-0	200	7-10-98	.333	.356	.456	20	59	57	5	19	1	3	0	4	2	0	0	0	13	6	0	3.4	22.0
Diaz, Yandy	R-R	6-2	215	8-8-91	.300	.366	.482	150	651	583	79	175	29	1	25	83	57	6	0	5	92	3	1	8.8	14.1
Feduccia, Hunter	L-R	6-0	215	6-5-97	.151	.265	.209	36	102	86	5	13	5	0	0	8	14	0	0	2	28	1	0	13.7	27.5
Fortes, Nick	R-R	5-11	198	11-11-96	.213	.307	.348	38	101	89	8	19	3	0	3	11	7	5	0	0	25	1	0	6.9	24.8
Gray, Tristan	L-R	6-1	215	3-22-96	.231	.282	.410	30	86	78	9	18	5	0	3	9	6	0	1	1	19	0	0	7.0	22.1
Jankowski, Travis	L-R	6-2	190	6-15-91	.258	.294	.323	14	34	31	6	8	2	0	0	2	2	0	0	1	9	2	0	5.9	26.5
Jansen, Danny	R-R	6-2	215	4-15-95	.204	.314	.389	73	259	221	28	45	8	0	11	29	33	3	1	1	68	0	0	12.7	26.3
Kim, Ha-Seong	R-R	5-9	168	10-17-95	.214	.290	.321	24	93	84	5	18	3	0	2	2	5	8	1	0	23	6	1	8.6	24.7
Lowe, Brandon	L-R	5-10	185	7-6-94	.256	.307	.477	134	553	507	79	130	19	0	31	83	38	2	0	6	149	3	2	6.9	26.9
Lowe, Josh	L-R	6-4	205	2-2-98	.220	.283	.366	108	435	396	56	87	21	2	11	40	33	3	1	2	109	18	4	7.6	25.1
Mangum, Jake	S-L	6-2	179	3-8-96	.296	.330	.368	118	428	405	37	120	18	1	3	40	19	2	1	1	64	27	6	4.4	15.0
Mead, Curtis	R-R	6-0	171	10-26-00	.226	.318	.339	49	132	115	14	26	2	1	3	8	12	4	0	1	33	4	1	9.1	25.0
Misner, Kameron	L-L	6-4	218	1-8-98	.213	.273	.345	71	217	197	27	42	9	1	5	22	16	1	1	2	69	8	1	7.4	31.8
Montes, Coco	R-R	6-1	200	10-7-96	.200	.200	.200	5	10	10	0	2	0	0	0	1	0	0	0	0	3	0	0	0.0	30.0
Morel, Christopher	R-R	5-11	145	6-24-99	.219	.289	.396	105	305	278	37	61	16	0	11	33	25	2	0	0	109	7	2	8.2	35.7
Palacios, Richie	L-R	5-10	180	5-16-97	.333	.396	.452	17	48	42	10	14	2	0	1	3	5	0	0	1	9	4	0	10.4	18.8
Pereira, Everson	R-R	5-11	191	4-10-01	.138	.219	.246	23	73	65	7	9	1	0	2	8	7	0	0	1	28	2	0	9.6	38.4
Peters, Tristan	L-R	5-11	180	2-29-00	.000	.000	.000	4	12	12	0	0	0	0	0	0	0	0	0	0	7	0	0	0.0	58.3
Rortvedt, Ben	L-R	5-9	191	9-25-97	.095	.186	.111	26	70	63	2	6	1	0	0	6	7	0	0	0	14	0	0	10.0	20.0
Seymour, Bobby	L-R	6-4	250	10-7-98	.205	.253	.282	26	83	78	9	16	1	1	1	5	4	1	0	0	32	1	0	4.8	38.6
Simpson, Chandler	L-R	6-2	170	11-18-00	.295	.326	.345	109	441	414	53	122	15	3	0	26	20	0	3	2	43	44	12	4.5	9.8
Thaiss, Matt	L-R	6-0	215	5-6-95	.225	.304	.282	25	80	71	5	16	2	0	1	6	8	2	1	0	25	0	0	7.5	31.3
Walls, Taylor	S-R	5-10	185	7-10-96	.220	.280	.319	101	317	282	36	62	14	1	4	38	26	0	3	6	70	14	6	8.2	22.1
Williams, Carson	R-R	6-1	180	6-25-03	.172	.219	.354	32	106	99	11	17	3	0	5	12	6	0	1	0	44	2	1	5.7	41.5

Pitching	B-T	Ht.	Wt.	DOB	W	L	ERA	G	GS	SV	IP	Hits	Runs	ER	HR	BB	SO	AVG	OBP	SLG	SO%	BB%	BF
Acton, Garrett	L-R	6-2	215	6-15-98	0	0	0.00	1	0	0	1	0	0	0	0	2	0	.000	.400	.000	0.0	40.0	5
Baker, Bryan	R-R	6-6	235	12-2-94	1	2	4.75	31	0	1	30	26	16	16	5	8	34	.230	.279	.416	27.6	6.5	123
Baz, Shane	R-R	6-2	190	6-17-99	10	12	4.87	31	31	0	166	158	91	90	26	64	176	.250	.325	.433	24.8	9.0	711
Bigge, Hunter	R-R	6-1	205	6-12-98	0	0	2.40	13	0	0	15	11	4	4	4	5	12	.204	.283	.444	20.0	8.3	60
Boyle, Joe	R-R	6-7	240	8-14-99	1	4	4.67	13	9	0	52	43	33	27	6	28	58	.221	.327	.374	25.7	12.4	226
Bradley, Taj	R-R	6-2	190	3-20-01	6	6	4.61	21	21	0	111	99	65	57	13	44	95	.236	.312	.375	20.2	9.3	471
Caballero, Jose	R-R	5-9	185	8-30-96	0	0	54.00	1	0	0	1	5	6	6	2	1	0	.625	.667	1.750	0.0	11.1	9
Cleavinger, Garrett	R-L	6-1	220	4-23-94	2	6	2.35	67	0	2	61	40	17	16	9	18	82	.184	.267	.341	33.7	7.4	243
Englert, Mason	S-R	6-4	206	11-1-99	1	1	3.83	29	0	0	45	33	20	19	4	11	44	.251	.299	.345	23.8	5.9	185
Fairbanks, Pete	R-R	6-6	225	12-16-93	4	5	2.83	61	0	27	60	45	22	19	7	18	59	.201	.263	.348	24.2	7.4	244
Gerber, Joey	R-R	6-4	212	5-3-97	0	0	2.08	2	0	0	4	3	1	1	0	4	.200	.200	.400	26.7	0.0	15
Gervase, Paul	R-R	6-10	230	5-23-00	0	0	4.26	5	0	0	6	6	3	3	5	6	.240	.367	.480	20.0	16.7	30
Houser, Adrian	R-R	6-3	242	2-2-93	2	3	4.79	10	10	0	56	60	30	30	7	16	45	.276	.343	.424	18.5	6.6	243
Jax, Griffin	R-R	6-2	195	11-22-94	0	2	3.60	23	2	0	20	18	9	8	3	8	27	.243	.313	.405	31.8	9.4	85
Kelly, Kevin	R-R	6-2	200	11-28-97	2	5	5.90	41	0	0	40	45	29	26	11	9	35	.281	.316	.556	20.5	5.3	171
Littell, Zack	R-R	6-4	220	10-5-95	8	8	3.58	22	22	0	133	128	53	53	26	21	89	.252	.287	.454	16.6	3.9	537
Montgomery, Mason	L-L	6-2	195	6-17-00	1	3	5.67	57	0	1	46	49	32	29	6	27	63	.277	.372	.435	30.1	12.9	209
Orze, Eric	R-R	6-4	195	8-21-97	1	1	3.02	33	0	3	42	38	16	14	4	19	40	.244	.337	.378	22.5	10.7	178
Pepiot, Ryan	R-R	6-3	215	8-21-97	11	12	3.86	31	31	0	168	134	77	72	26	61	167	.221	.297	.404	24.6	9.0	679
Rasmussen, Drew	R-R	6-1	211	7-27-95	10	5	2.76	31	31	0	150	116	47	46	18	37	127	.214	.271	.340	21.7	6.3	585
Rock, Joe	L-L	6-6	200	7-29-00	0	0	2.35	3	0	0	8	7	2	2	1	2	11	.226	.314	.323	31.4	5.7	35
Rodriguez, Manuel	R-R	5-11	210	8-6-96	1	2	2.08	31	0	0	30	26	9	7	2	6	25	.232	.275	.313	20.7	5.0	121
Scholtens, Jesse	R-R	6-4	230	4-6-94	0	1	5.40	2	0	0	8	9	7	5	1	3	12	.265	.316	.353	31.6	7.9	38
Seabold, Connor	R-R	6-2	190	1-24-96	0	0	1.35	3	0	0	7	1	1	0	3	5	.280	.345	.280	17.2	10.3	29

	B-T	Ht.	Wt.	DOB																
Seymour, Ian	L-L	6-0	210	12-13-98	4	3	3.63	19	5	0	57	48	33	23	5	19	64	.221	.290	.327	26.4	7.9	242
Sulser, Cole	R-R	6-1	190	3-12-90	2	1	1.99	18	0	0	23	20	5	5	1	7	22	.241	.300	.301	24.4	7.8	90
Uceta, Edwin	R-R	6-0	155	1-9-98	10	3	3.79	70	0	1	76	62	33	32	11	27	103	.220	.303	.390	32.1	8.4	321
Van Belle, Brian	R-R	6-3	185	9-3-96	1	0	5.40	4	0	0	8	13	5	5	2	0	6	.361	.361	.556	16.7	0.0	36
Whitley, Forrest	R-R	6-7	238	9-15-97	0	0	15.43	5	0	0	5	10	10	8	1	2	4	.417	.444	.750	14.8	7.4	27
Wilcox, Cole	R-R	6-5	232	7-14-99	0	0	27.00	1	0	0	1	4	7	3	0	3	1	.444	.583	.556	8.3	25.0	12

Fielding

Catcher	PCT	G	PO	A	E	DP	PB
Feduccia	1.000	34	258	5	0	0	0
Fortes	.989	37	268	14	3	2	2
Jansen	.990	72	565	23	6	1	1
Rortvedt	.994	26	154	10	1	2	1
Thaiss	1.000	24	192	5	0	0	0

First Base	PCT	G	PO	A	E	DP
Aranda	.993	93	677	52	5	80
Caminero	1.000	1	4	0	0	0
Diaz	1.000	37	248	13	0	24
Gray	.917	5	11	0	1	0
Lowe	1.000	3	20	1	0	4
Mead	1.000	19	94	6	0	11
Palacios	.909	3	9	1	1	0
Seymour	.994	25	156	16	1	19
Thaiss	1.000	1	1	0	0	0

Second Base	PCT	G	PO	A	E	DP
Caballero	.923	17	17	31	4	6
Gray	.973	12	17	19	1	5
Kim	1.000	5	12	15	0	7
Lowe	.984	121	183	302	8	86
Mead	.977	17	13	29	1	4
Montes	1.000	2	2	4	0	1
Morel	.000	1	0	0	0	0
Palacios	.950	5	10	9	1	2
Walls	1.000	5	7	10	0	0

Third Base	PCT	G	PO	A	E	DP
Caballero	1.000	27	8	17	0	3
Caminero	.945	148	82	225	18	27
Gray	.800	5	1	3	1	0
Mead	1.000	7	4	10	0	4
Montes	1.000	2	0	2	0	0
Walls	.000	1	0	0	0	0

Shortstop	PCT	G	PO	A	E	DP
Caballero	.974	31	34	77	3	20
Gray	1.000	9	12	15	0	6
Kim	1.000	19	19	39	0	5
Walls	.986	94	125	234	5	56
Williams	.955	32	30	76	5	13

Outfield	PCT	G	PO	A	E	DP
Caballero	1.000	35	45	2	0	1
DeLuca	1.000	19	40	1	0	0
Jankowski	1.000	14	13	0	0	0
Lowe	.995	103	186	3	1	2
Mangum	1.000	136	225	6	0	0
Misner	.980	71	145	2	3	1
Montes	1.000	1	1	0	0	0
Morel	.972	70	101	2	3	0
Palacios	1.000	7	6	0	0	0
Pereira	1.000	22	33	1	0	0
Peters	1.000	4	9	0	0	0
Simpson	.995	112	196	5	1	0

DURHAM BULLS
INTERNATIONAL LEAGUE — TRIPLE-A

Batting	B-T	Ht.	Wt.	DOB	AVG	OBP	SLG	G	PA	AB	R	H	2B	3B	HR	RBI	BB	HBP	SH	SF	SO	SB	CS	BB%	SO%
Baker, Dru	R-R	5-11	205	3-22-00	.245	.344	.302	17	61	53	10	13	0	0	1	3	8	0	0	0	11	1	3	13.1	18.0
Barrera, Tres	R-R	6-0	215	9-15-94	.238	.297	.413	41	156	143	17	34	4	0	7	26	9	3	1	0	42	0	0	5.8	26.9
Battles, Jalen	R-R	6-1	210	12-20-99	.240	.328	.260	18	59	50	7	12	1	0	0	2	7	0	1	1	13	2	2	11.9	22.0
DeLuca, Jonny	R-R	6-0	200	7-10-98	.120	.214	.140	14	56	50	8	6	1	0	0	1	5	1	0	0	11	0	0	8.9	19.6
Hummel, Cooper	S-R	5-10	198	11-28-94	.312	.471	.731	28	121	93	24	29	2	2	11	26	24	4	0	0	30	1	2	19.8	24.8
Jankowski, Travis	L-R	6-2	190	6-15-91	.286	.583	.429	4	12	7	0	2	1	0	0	0	5	0	0	0	2	1	41.7	0.0	
Jimenez, Eloy	R-R	6-4	240	11-27-96	.278	.335	.397	40	167	151	14	42	9	0	3	29	13	1	0	2	29	1	0	7.8	17.4
Jones, Brock	L-L	5-11	197	3-28-01	.151	.195	.397	27	77	73	12	11	3	0	5	13	4	0	0	0	42	5	1	5.2	54.5
Keegan, Dominic	R-R	6-0	210	8-1-00	.241	.306	.429	69	297	266	34	64	16	2	10	36	24	3	0	4	91	0	0	8.1	30.6
Kim, Ha-Seong	R-R	5-9	168	10-17-95	.208	.352	.250	21	97	72	11	15	3	0	0	6	15	2	0	2	10	6	0	16.5	11.0
Lowe, Josh	L-R	6-1	205	2-2-98	.235	.364	.412	5	22	17	3	4	0	0	1	2	4	0	0	1	6	1	0	18.2	27.3
Mangum, Jake	S-L	6-1	179	3-8-96	.444	.545	.500	5	22	18	2	8	1	0	0	3	4	0	0	0	3	0	0	18.2	13.6
Mead, Curtis	R-R	6-0	171	10-26-00	.264	.339	.472	14	59	53	10	14	2	0	3	7	4	2	0	0	15	0	0	6.8	25.4
Misner, Kameron	L-L	6-4	218	1-8-98	.210	.333	.442	38	165	138	25	29	8	0	8	18	25	1	0	1	43	9	2	15.2	26.1
Montes, Coco	R-R	6-1	200	10-7-96	.229	.287	.333	107	415	375	44	82	19	0	8	38	32	5	0	3	123	7	2	7.7	29.6
Morgan, Tre'	L-L	6-2	191	7-16-02	.274	.398	.412	92	402	328	53	90	15	3	8	45	64	4	0	4	77	8	4	15.9	19.2
Murray, Tanner	R-R	6-1	190	9-3-99	.241	.299	.400	137	572	522	67	126	29	0	18	58	39	6	1	4	138	5	4	6.8	24.1
Palacios, Richie	L-R	5-10	180	5-16-97	.158	.220	.263	20	82	76	7	12	2	0	2	3	6	0	0	0	20	3	1	7.3	24.4
Pereira, Everson	R-R	5-11	191	4-10-01	.276	.382	.517	8	34	29	3	8	1	0	2	5	5	0	0	0	11	0	1	14.7	29.4
Peters, Tristan	L-L	5-11	180	2-29-00	.266	.355	.429	136	555	482	73	128	28	3	15	76	65	4	0	4	102	11	7	11.7	18.4
Piper, Kenny	R-R	5-9	190	7-12-98	.191	.297	.376	49	185	157	28	30	5	0	8	24	20	5	0	3	56	9	0	10.8	30.3
Rortvedt, Ben	L-R	5-9	191	9-26-97	.183	.315	.283	19	73	60	9	11	3	0	1	5	11	1	0	1	27	0	1	15.1	37.0
Seymour, Bobby	R-R	6-4	250	10-7-98	.263	.327	.553	105	443	403	70	106	21	3	30	87	38	1	0	1	114	1	0	8.6	25.7
Simpson, Chandler	L-R	6-2	170	11-18-00	.333	.370	.396	33	156	144	24	48	3	3	0	14	9	0	2	1	15	19	3	5.8	9.6
Spikes, Ryan	R-R	5-8	185	3-13-03	.364	.364	.364	3	11	11	2	4	0	0	0	2	0	0	0	0	0	0	0	0.0	18.2
Stevenson, Andrew	L-L	5-11	191	6-1-94	.294	.366	.467	58	202	180	19	53	14	1	5	22	10	1	0	1	45	18	6	9.9	22.3
Stovall, Hunter	R-R	5-6	170	9-5-96	.267	.343	.349	30	100	86	16	23	4	0	1	4	10	1	1	2	22	7	0	10.0	22.0
Thaiss, Matt	L-R	6-0	215	5-6-95	.200	.323	.309	16	65	55	3	11	3	0	1	7	8	9	1	0	0	13	0	0	13.8	20.0
Westbrook, Jamie	R-R	5-7	193	6-18-95	.266	.350	.401	116	430	372	47	99	29	0	7	49	48	8	1	5	70	2	0	10.0	16.3
Williams, Carson	R-R	6-1	180	6-25-03	.213	.318	.447	111	457	389	72	83	12	5	23	55	56	4	1	1	154	22	6	12.4	34.1

Pitching	B-T	Ht.	Wt.	DOB	W	L	ERA	G	GS	SV	IP	Hits	Runs	ER	HR	BB	SO	AVG	OBP	SLG	SO%	BB%	BF
Acton, Garrett	L-R	6-2	215	6-15-98	5	1	3.68	45	4	3	59	39	24	24	7	27	71	.188	.280	.337	30.1	11.4	236
Boushley, Caleb	R-R	6-3	190	10-1-93	0	0	5.19	3	0	0	9	8	5	5	1	4	6	.235	.316	.382	15.8	10.5	38
Boyle, Joe	R-R	6-7	240	8-14-99	4	1	1.88	18	17	0	86	46	21	18	7	41	114	.154	.266	.258	32.9	11.8	346
Bradley, Taj	R-R	6-2	190	3-20-01	1	0	0.00	1	1	0	7	0	0	0	0	2	3	.000	.083	.000	12.5	8.3	24
Cuevas, Jonny	R-R	6-3	200	11-20-00	2	1	4.97	5	0	0	13	14	8	7	4	4	8	.292	.340	.583	15.1	7.5	53
Cummings, Ty	R-R	6-2	205	11-1-01	1	0	2.57	3	1	0	7	7	2	2	2	3	6	.259	.355	.481	19.4	9.7	31
Curet, Yoniel	R-R	6-2	190	11-3-02	1	3	6.03	8	7	0	31	34	24	21	2	26	25	.298	.430	.404	23.5	17.4	149
Davitt, Duncan	R-R	6-3	235	9-23-99	0	2	6.30	4	4	0	20	25	14	14	5	6	24	.305	.352	.537	27.3	6.8	88
Englert, Mason	S-R	6-4	206	11-1-99	1	0	1.23	14	1	2	22	20	7	3	1	5	26	.235	.286	.341	28.6	5.5	91
Faedo, Alex	R-R	6-5	225	11-12-95	0	0	5.68	5	0	0	6	4	4	4	1	6	6	.182	.379	.455	20.7	20.7	29

	B-T	Ht.	Wt.	DOB	W	L	ERA	G	GS	SV	IP	H	R	ER	HR	BB	SO	AVG	BB/9	SO/9
Flynn, Michael	R-R	6-4	185	8-7-96	1	1	4.41	19	0	1	16	14	8	8	3	12	10	.233	.370 .383 13.5 16.2 74	
Gainey, Garrett	L-L	6-1	200	6-22-00	1	0	0.00	2	1	0	6	3	0	0	0	0	5	.143	.182 .143 22.7 0.0 22	
Garcia, Roel	R-R	6-4	245	11-21-98	0	0	3.00	1	0	0	3	2	1	1	1	1	2	.182	.250 .545 16.7 8.3 12	
Gerber, Joey	R-R	6-4	212	5-3-97	0	2	6.23	34	9	2	43	48	31	30	9	15	54	.279	.347 .506 28.0 7.8 193	
Gervase, Paul	R-R	6-10	230	5-23-00	2	3	3.12	28	1	4	40	27	14	14	6	12	63	.186	.263 .324 39.1 7.5 161	
Gibson, Kyle	R-R	6-6	200	10-23-87	1	0	0.52	4	4	0	17	12	1	1	0	6	22	.203	.277 .220 33.8 9.2 65	
Hernandez, Jonathan	R-R	6-3	190	7-6-96	1	0	2.25	12	1	0	12	9	3	3	1	6	13	.205	.327 .273 25.0 11.5 52	
Hunley, Sean	R-R	6-4	220	7-5-99	2	2	6.46	15	0	1	31	36	26	22	5	18	21	.298	.394 .512 14.8 12.7 142	
Kelly, Kevin	R-R	6-2	200	11-28-97	1	1	1.64	11	0	0	11	12	2	2	0	1	15	.273	.304 .295 32.6 2.2 46	
Krehbiel, Joey	R-R	6-3	250	12-20-92	4	1	6.11	25	0	1	35	47	28	24	4	10	34	.307	.352 .438 20.6 6.1 165	
Lindsey, Andrew	R-R	6-3	216	11-15-99	0	1	13.50	1	0	0	1	2	1	1	0	0	.667	.750 .667 0.0 25.0 4		
Martin, Trevor	R-R	6-5	238	12-15-00	0	1	6.75	3	0	0	4	6	3	3	1	1	7	.353	.389 .588 38.9 5.6 18	
McClanahan, Shane	L-L	6-1	200	4-28-97	0	0	15.43	2	2	0	2	7	4	4	2	1	4	.500	.533 1.143 26.7 6.7 15	
Menendez, Antonio	R-R	6-4	215	3-11-99	1	1	8.31	20	0	1	22	24	20	20	3	11	24	.282	.384 .494 24.2 11.1 99	
Montgomery, Mason	L-L	6-2	195	6-17-00	1	0	2.00	9	0	2	9	6	2	2	0	1	15	.188	.235 .250 44.1 2.9 34	
Orze, Eric	R-R	6-4	195	8-21-97	4	0	2.20	24	0	2	29	19	7	7	4	10	37	.192	.270 .343 32.7 8.8 113	
Peoples, Ben	L-R	6-1	175	5-1-01	2	2	2.65	35	0	0	37	25	13	11	3	20	39	.189	.303 .288 25.2 12.9 155	
Reifert, Evan	R-R	6-2	190	5-14-99	2	2	2.48	31	0	5	29	19	12	8	3	18	51	.181	.307 .295 39.8 14.1 128	
Rock, Joe	L-L	6-6	200	7-29-00	3	7	5.21	32	15	0	97	102	65	56	16	39	88	.275	.344 .450 21.1 9.3 418	
Rodriguez, Manuel	R-R	5-11	210	8-6-96	0	0	6.75	2	0	0	1	2	1	1	0	0	1	.400	.400 .400 20.0 0.0 5	
Scholtens, Jesse	R-R	6-4	230	4-6-94	1	1	4.13	7	7	0	33	29	15	15	5	9	43	.230	.279 .413 31.6 6.6 136	
Seabold, Connor	R-R	6-2	190	1-24-96	8	4	6.49	16	16	0	61	64	44	44	14	26	57	.274	.361 .509 21.0 9.6 272	
Seymour, Ian	L-L	6-0	210	12-13-98	9	3	2.62	16	15	0	86	78	29	25	10	20	104	.236	.289 .373 29.2 5.6 356	
Shreve, Ryan	R-R	6-6	215	6-23-98	0	1	5.87	5	0	0	8	11	6	5	0	3	7	.333	.389 .394 18.9 8.1 37	
Strzelecki, Peter	R-R	6-2	216	10-24-94	0	0	4.50	2	0	0	2	1	1	1	1	1	3	.143	.250 .571 37.5 12.5 8	
Suarez, Santiago	R-R	6-2	175	1-11-05	0	1	4.09	2	2	0	11	9	5	5	3	2	9	.225	.256 .525 20.9 4.7 43	
Sulser, Cole	R-R	6-1	190	3-12-90	3	0	1.30	30	0	2	35	23	7	5	2	5	34	.187	.223 .268 26.2 3.8 130	
Van Belle, Brian	R-R	6-3	185	9-3-96	3	0	2.04	3	3	0	18	10	4	4	1	2	16	.161	.188 .242 25.0 3.1 64	
Vernon, Austin	R-R	6-8	265	2-8-99	2	1	3.72	14	3	0	19	9	10	8	2	14	17	.143	.308 .238 21.5 17.7 79	
Villaman, Chris	L-L	6-2	217	3-16-01	0	0	0.00	1	0	0	2	3	0	0	0	1	.333	.400 .444 10.0 10.0 10		
Waguespack, Jacob	R-R	6-6	235	11-5-93	1	0	0.46	15	0	0	20	10	2	1	0	4	18	.149	.197 .194 25.4 5.6 71	
Wantz, Andrew	R-R	6-4	235	10-13-95	1	0	0.00	7	0	1	7	3	0	0	0	5	9	.136	.296 .136 32.1 17.9 28	
Whitley, Forrest	R-R	6-7	238	9-15-97	5	4	2.60	13	12	0	55	36	16	16	5	19	66	.188	.269 .318 30.4 8.8 217	
Whitley, Kodi	R-R	6-3	220	2-21-95	1	3	5.31	15	0	2	20	17	12	12	4	3	25	.227	.250 .480 31.3 3.8 80	
Wilcox, Cole	R-R	6-5	232	7-14-99	2	5	3.71	34	1	2	51	46	24	21	9	24	57	.234	.320 .442 25.6 10.8 223	
Workman, Logan	R-R	6-4	235	12-6-98	9	7	4.02	29	28	0	152	138	70	68	27	45	152	.244	.298 .434 24.4 7.2 623	

Fielding

Catcher	PCT	G	PO	A	E	DP	PB
Barrera	.994	33	307	14	2	0	2
Keegan	.996	52	513	23	2	3	3
Piper	.995	42	401	23	2	3	1
Rortvedt	.993	12	134	8	1	4	0
Thaiss	.967	10	85	4	3	0	0

First Base	PCT	G	PO	A	E	DP
Barrera	1.000	1	6	0	0	0
Hummel	.971	7	32	2	1	2
Jimenez	1.000	2	13	1	0	4
Morgan	1.000	60	412	29	0	36
Seymour	.991	81	501	37	5	52

Second Base	PCT	G	PO	A	E	DP
Baker	1.000	1	0	5	0	0
Battles	1.000	1	1	2	0	0
Kim	1.000	5	11	13	0	5
Mead	1.000	6	6	5	0	0
Montes	.976	26	37	43	2	8

	PCT	G	PO	A	E	DP	PB
Murray	.981	26	30	73	2	13	
Palacios	1.000	5	3	13	0	3	
Stovall	1.000	4	3	3	0	1	
Westbrook	.983	84	116	168	5	41	

Third Base	PCT	G	PO	A	E	DP
Battles	.943	15	10	23	2	2
Mead	1.000	7	6	6	0	2
Montes	.931	34	24	43	5	6
Murray	.961	42	38	61	4	10
Spikes	1.000	3	1	1	0	0
Stovall	.976	21	12	28	1	3
Westbrook	.911	24	14	27	4	5
Williams	.857	6	5	7	2	2

Shortstop	PCT	G	PO	A	E	DP
Kim	.962	9	11	14	1	2
Montes	1.000	5	7	6	0	1
Murray	.969	32	34	61	3	12
Williams	.968	105	137	231	12	53

Outfield	PCT	G	PO	A	E	DP
Baker	.964	15	27	0	1	0
DeLuca	1.000	13	27	0	0	0
Hummel	1.000	10	17	1	0	0
Jankowski	.667	3	2	0	1	0
Jimenez	1.000	25	46	0	0	0
Jones	.957	24	44	1	2	1
Lowe	.875	4	7	0	1	0
Mangum	1.000	5	9	0	0	0
Misner	.987	39	72	4	1	1
Montes	1.000	40	57	3	0	0
Morgan	1.000	15	30	0	0	0
Murray	.986	40	68	1	1	0
Palacios	1.000	14	21	0	0	0
Pereira	1.000	8	17	1	0	1
Peters	.993	139	287	3	2	1
Simpson	1.000	33	72	3	0	2
Stevenson	1.000	54	79	3	0	0
Stovall	1.000	6	9	1	0	0

MONTGOMERY BISCUITS
SOUTHERN LEAGUE
DOUBLE-A

Batting	B-T	Ht.	Wt.	DOB	AVG	OBP	SLG	G	PA	AB	R	H	2B	3B	HR	RBI	BB	HBP	SH	SF	SO	SB	CS	BB%	SO%
Areinamo, Jadher	R-R	5-8	160	11-28-03	.255	.316	.397	37	159	141	18	36	8	0	4	19	12	2	0	3	19	6	0	7.5	11.9
Barrera, Tres	R-R	6-0	215	9-15-94	.163	.301	.207	29	113	92	8	15	1	0	1	7	17	2	0	2	24	1	0	15.0	21.2
Barrios, Gregory	R-R	6-0	180	4-8-04	.241	.292	.277	79	297	274	36	66	7	0	1	27	18	2	2	1	42	28	7	6.1	14.1
Battles, Jalen	R-R	6-1	210	12-20-99	.127	.184	.197	21	76	71	8	9	2	0	1	1	2	3	0	0	27	2	0	2.6	35.5
Bush, Homer	R-R	6-3	200	10-13-01	.301	.375	.360	121	546	472	69	142	12	8	0	45	48	11	8	5	98	57	12	8.8	17.9
Etzel, Matthew	L-R	6-2	211	4-30-02	.230	.347	.347	56	239	196	47	45	8	0	5	34	41	0	0	2	62	17	7	17.2	25.9
Genoves, Ricardo	R-R	6-2	190	5-14-99	.195	.256	.280	26	90	82	9	16	1	0	2	7	6	1	0	1	30	0	0	6.7	33.3
Isaac, Xavier	L-L	6-3	240	12-17-03	.201	.366	.446	41	175	139	21	28	5	1	9	22	34	2	0	0	52	1	2	19.4	29.7
James, Kamren	R-R	6-2	205	5-24-01	.196	.347	.248	41	147	121	10	30	1	0	1	7	14	1	2	0	47	2	1	9.0	30.3
Jones, Brock	L-L	5-11	197	3-28-01	.189	.373	.378	69	247	185	32	35	7	2	8	33	49	7	3	3	85	19	6	19.8	34.4
Kinney, Cooper	L-R	6-1	200	1-27-03	.242	.299	.386	91	501	458	54	111	21	3	13	62	36	3	0	4	125	0	1	7.2	25.0
Ledbetter, Colton	L-R	6-2	205	11-15-01	.265	.337	.378	123	535	465	67	123	24	4	7	49	51	6	1	12	128	37	11	9.5	23.9

TAMPA BAY RAYS

Batting	B-T	Ht.	Wt.	DOB	AVG	OBP	SLG	G	AB	R	H	2B	3B	HR	RBI	BB	HBP	SH	SF	SO	SB	CS	BB%	SO%
Levins, Tatem	L-R	6-0	206	5-29-99	.244	.405	.383	100	396	308	50	75	20	1	7	54	77	8	1	2	100	2	0	19.4	25.3
Myers, Noah	L-R	6-1	190	11-11-99	.197	.329	.328	26	75	61	10	12	2	0	2	4	12	0	2	0	20	5	0	16.0	26.7
Palacios, Richie	L-R	5-10	180	5-16-97	.286	.375	.286	2	8	7	1	2	0	0	0	1	1	0	0	0	3	0	0	12.5	37.5
Piper, Kenny	R-R	5-9	190	7-12-98	.176	.295	.275	17	61	51	6	9	2	0	1	6	8	1	0	1	15	1	0	13.1	24.6
Simpson, Will	R-R	6-4	225	8-28-01	.217	.289	.350	118	479	428	46	93	21	0	12	49	42	3	1	5	109	8	3	8.8	22.8
Spikes, Ryan	R-R	5-8	185	3-13-03	.189	.259	.321	18	58	53	4	10	0	2	1	6	4	1	0	0	16	4	1	6.9	27.6
Stovall, Hunter	R-R	5-6	170	9-5-96	.211	.272	.319	62	235	213	20	45	3	1	6	28	17	2	0	3	40	3	2	7.2	17.0
Taylor, Brayden	L-R	6-1	180	5-22-02	.173	.289	.286	108	437	370	47	64	14	2	8	43	61	1	1	4	121	17	3	14.0	27.7
Vasquez, Willy	R-R	6-2	191	9-6-01	.256	.297	.359	44	165	156	14	40	6	2	2	15	7	2	0	0	32	6	3	4.2	19.4

Pitching	B-T	Ht.	Wt.	DOB	W	L	ERA	G	GS	SV	IP	Hits	Runs	ER	HR	BB	SO	AVG	OBP	SLG	SO%	BB%	BF
Askew, Keyshawn	L-L	6-4	310	1-5-00	4	0	6.29	29	0	1	34	21	28	24	0	35	29	.171	.381	.203	17.3	20.8	168
Baumeister, Jackson	R-R	6-4	226	7-10-02	2	4	4.62	15	15	0	62	53	37	32	6	25	51	.230	.312	.361	19.5	9.6	261
Cook, Alex	R-R	6-2	220	3-29-01	1	1	2.30	13	0	4	16	10	4	4	1	3	18	.179	.220	.286	30.5	5.1	59
Cuevas, Jonny	R-R	6-3	200	11-20-00	3	2	3.44	30	2	2	52	43	22	20	1	25	36	.243	.325	.305	17.0	11.8	212
Cummings, Ty	R-R	6-2	205	11-1-01	7	4	3.34	26	19	0	116	114	54	43	14	37	86	.256	.316	.390	17.5	7.5	491
Curet, Yoniel	R-R	6-2	190	11-3-02	1	0	1.45	5	5	0	19	12	3	3	0	5	19	.185	.274	.215	26.0	6.8	73
Davitt, Duncan	R-R	6-3	235	9-23-99	5	3	3.55	15	15	0	84	75	34	33	10	15	81	.240	.279	.371	24.3	4.5	333
Edington, Derrick	R-R	6-8	210	7-22-99	2	3	3.45	35	0	9	44	34	18	17	2	20	46	.219	.304	.297	25.3	11.0	182
Fondtain, T.J.	L-L	6-4	210	2-22-01	0	0	0.00	1	0	0	1	1	0	0	0	1	1	.250	.500	.250	16.7	16.7	6
Gainey, Garrett	L-L	6-1	200	6-22-00	1	0	3.12	4	1	0	9	8	4	3	0	4	9	.267	.353	.333	26.5	11.8	34
Garcia, Roel	R-R	6-4	245	11-21-98	2	0	3.45	16	0	0	29	20	12	11	2	8	28	.194	.246	.291	24.6	7.0	114
Genoves, Ricardo	R-R	6-2	190	5-14-99	0	0	0.00	1	0	0	1	1	1	0	0	1	0	.333	.500	.333	0.0	16.7	6
Goss, JJ	R-R	6-3	185	12-25-00	4	3	3.38	33	0	11	40	29	16	15	1	12	31	.203	.275	.259	19.4	7.5	160
Hammer, Dan	R-R	6-2	210	9-10-97	2	4	6.57	31	1	0	38	52	30	28	3	29	40	.325	.433	.425	20.4	14.8	196
Hartman, Jack	R-R	6-3	205	7-13-98	0	4	2.14	34	0	4	46	28	14	11	3	22	40	.177	.275	.266	21.7	12.0	184
Hopkins, Brody	R-R	6-4	200	1-18-02	5	7	2.72	25	25	0	116	85	48	35	7	60	141	.204	.316	.288	28.7	12.2	492
Hunley, Sean	R-R	6-4	220	7-5-99	1	1	3.00	12	0	1	21	20	9	7	2	5	15	.253	.310	.342	17.2	5.7	87
James, Kamren	R-R	6-2	205	5-25-00	0	0	18.00	1	0	0	1	2	2	2	0	1	0	.333	.500	.333	0.0	16.7	6
Johnson, Bryce	R-R	6-0	190	9-25-01	7	6	2.61	26	20	0	110	66	36	32	5	38	149	.174	.261	.272	34.7	8.8	430
Lancaster, Jackson	L-L	6-1	195	3-22-99	3	1	2.76	17	0	2	29	22	11	9	3	11	25	.220	.301	.350	21.7	9.6	115
Martin, Trevor	L-L	6-5	238	12-15-00	5	1	2.92	35	0	3	49	42	17	16	5	18	48	.231	.303	.357	23.6	8.9	203
Menendez, Antonio	R-R	6-2	215	3-11-99	3	1	1.99	15	0	2	23	16	7	5	0	11	18	.205	.233	.231	19.1	11.7	94
Nichols, T.J.	R-R	6-4	215	8-24-02	4	0	0.97	6	6	0	37	22	4	4	1	9	37	.182	.235	.256	28.0	6.8	132
Shreve, Ryan	R-R	6-6	215	6-23-98	4	3	5.84	12	0	0	25	27	19	16	1	12	15	.290	.361	.430	13.6	10.9	110
Snyder, Jack	R-R	6-2	205	8-4-98	1	0	7.88	11	0	0	16	14	14	3	10	10	.309	.397	.515	12.8	12.8	78
Stovall, Hunter	R-R	5-6	170	9-5-96	1	0	0.00	1	0	0	1	0	0	0	0	0	0	.000	.000	.000	0.0	0.0	3
Vernon, Austin	R-R	6-8	265	2-8-99	2	0	2.48	18	0	1	29	19	8	8	2	13	39	.173	.267	.250	32.5	10.8	120
Watters, Jacob	R-R	6-4	230	3-3-01	1	4	4.87	6	6	0	20	21	13	11	4	10	23	.256	.344	.463	24.7	10.8	93
Whitley, Kodi	R-R	6-3	220	2-21-95	0	0	0.00	2	0	0	3	3	1	0	0	0	5	.231	.231	.231	38.5	0.0	13
Wilcox, Cole	R-R	6-5	232	7-14-99	0	0	3.68	5	0	1	7	5	3	3	1	2	6	.200	.286	.400	21.4	10.7	28
Wild, Owen	R-R	6-2	230	7-30-02	7	8	4.71	23	23	0	105	106	56	55	16	39	96	.262	.329	.408	21.5	8.7	446
Zarraga, Alfredo	R-R	5-11	158	11-16-00	0	0	1.59	3	0	2	6	5	1	1	1	2	10	.238	.304	.429	43.5	8.7	23

Fielding

Catcher	PCT	G	PO	A	E	DP	PB
Barrera	.988	19	150	8	2	1	0
Genoves	.993	18	133	13	1	0	5
James	1.000	4	34	1	0	0	2
Levins	.991	88	738	52	7	4	8
Piper	1.000	13	119	13	0	0	0

First Base	PCT	G	PO	A	E	DP
Barrera	1.000	8	53	1	0	6
Etzel	1.000	1	1	0	0	0
Genoves	.981	7	45	6	1	5
James	1.000	12	86	3	0	1
Kinney	.990	14	97	3	1	14
Simpson	.992	97	685	55	6	60

Second Base	PCT	G	PO	A	E	DP
Barreat	.923	3	2	10	1	2
Battles	.995	58	79	118	1	27

Third Base	PCT	G	PO	A	E	DP
Battles	1.000	6	4	11	0	2
James	.960	9	5	19	1	0
Kinney	.931	28	19	35	4	2
Spikes	1.000	4	0	4	0	0
Stovall	.974	14	11	26	1	3
Taylor	.973	74	69	110	5	9
Vasquez	.944	6	5	12	1	0

Shortstop	PCT	G	PO	A	E	DP
Areinamo	1.000	7	16	13	0	3
Barrios	.964	73	86	182	10	44
Battles	.857	4	3	3	1	1

Outfield	PCT	G	PO	A	E	DP
Murray	.983	54	94	141	4	27
Taylor	1.000	13	19	25	0	4
Turner	1.000	1	4	1	0	1
Vasquez	.907	10	19	20	4	5
Stovall	.977	35	50	79	3	14
Taylor	.917	5	2	9	1	1
Vasquez	.981	17	20	32	1	4
Bush	.987	116	299	2	4	0
Etzel	.989	53	89	0	1	0
James	1.000	20	32	2	0	1
Jones	1.000	65	142	4	0	1
Ledbetter	.982	105	209	6	4	0
Myers	1.000	23	41	2	0	1
Palacios	1.000	2	2	0	0	0
Simpson	1.000	7	10	0	0	0
Spikes	1.000	10	17	3	0	0
Stovall	1.000	2	3	0	0	0
Vasquez	.971	19	32	1	1	0

BOWLING GREEN HOT RODS
SOUTH ATLANTIC LEAGUE — HIGH-A

Batting	B-T	Ht.	Wt.	DOB	AVG	OBP	SLG	G	PA	AB	R	H	2B	3B	HR	RBI	BB	HBP	SH	SF	SO	SB	CS	BB%	SO%
Broecker, Bryan	R-R	6-2	200	1-26-02	.209	.364	.286	63	229	182	27	38	8	0	2	13	43	2	1	1	59	1	0	18.8	25.8
Cermak, Ryan	R-R	6-0	205	7-1-01	.225	.310	.416	26	100	89	10	20	6	1	3	11	9	2	0	0	30	7	2	9.0	30.0
Colmenarez, Carlos	L-R	5-9	170	11-15-03	.208	.339	.320	76	280	231	34	48	6	1	6	29	38	8	2	0	94	3	3	13.6	33.6
Diaz, Jhon	L-L	5-7	160	10-1-02	.187	.260	.328	98	369	332	40	62	9	4	10	40	31	3	0	3	89	13	3	8.4	24.1
Flewelling, Nathan	L-R	6-1	185	11-11-06	.250	.409	.438	5	22	16	2	4	1	1	0	3	5	0	0	1	6	0	1	22.7	27.3
Haas, Hunter	R-R	6-0	180	4-7-02	.162	.269	.247	83	303	259	27	42	10	0	4	21	33	6	1	3	92	6	3	10.9	30.4
Herron, Tyler	R-R	6-1	190	6-20-03	.053	.182	.158	6	22	19	2	1	0	1	0	0	2	1	0	0	5	0	0	9.1	22.7

Batting	B-T	Ht.	Wt.	DOB	AVG	OBP	SLG	G	PA	AB	R	H	2B	3B	HR	RBI	BB	HBP	SH	SF	SO	SB	CS	BB%	SO%
Horvath, Mac	R-R	6-1	195	7-22-01	.233	.333	.395	105	453	382	77	89	14	0	16	66	60	2	0	9	95	41	7	13.2	21.0
Martinez, Raudelis	L-R	6-0	180	5-30-02	.239	.339	.317	74	290	243	20	58	7	0	4	38	36	2	7	2	40	2	1	12.4	13.8
Mateo, Angel	R-R	6-2	190	2-13-05	.241	.337	.354	22	92	79	5	19	6	0	1	9	7	5	0	1	14	1	0	7.6	15.2
Myers, Noah	L-R	6-1	190	11-11-99	.247	.395	.361	85	363	288	56	71	11	2	6	43	68	4	1	2	97	31	1	18.7	26.7
Perez, Jose	R-R	5-9	170	3-12-04	.182	.333	.182	4	15	11	1	2	0	0	0	2	2	1	0	1	5	0	1	13.3	33.3
Pitre, Emilien	L-R	5-11	160	10-4-02	.268	.356	.393	118	524	448	61	120	23	3	9	63	61	5	0	9	107	14	6	11.6	20.4
Robertson, Blake	L-R	6-5	200	5-19-01	.202	.337	.289	85	335	277	35	56	12	0	4	28	53	4	0	1	86	2	0	15.8	25.7
Santa Maria, Tony	R-R	5-11	195	4-6-02	.274	.333	.468	17	69	62	7	17	6	0	2	12	3	3	0	1	20	3	1	4.3	29.0
Santana, Adrian	S-R	5-11	155	7-18-05	.263	.324	.326	89	409	365	64	96	13	2	2	43	35	1	1	7	49	47	8	8.6	12.0
Smith, Aidan	R-R	6-3	190	7-23-04	.237	.331	.388	102	459	397	77	94	14	2	14	59	53	5	0	4	143	41	6	11.5	31.2
Spikes, Ryan	R-R	5-8	185	3-13-03	.259	.303	.461	64	251	232	36	60	9	1	12	40	11	5	0	3	67	11	6	4.4	26.7
Vellojin, Daniel	L-R	5-11	160	3-15-00	.193	.304	.311	75	300	254	30	49	10	1	6	32	36	6	1	3	78	4	1	12.0	26.0

Pitching	B-T	Ht.	Wt.	DOB	W	L	ERA	G	GS	SV	IP	Hits	Runs	ER	HR	BB	SO	AVG	OBP	SLG	SO%	BB%	BF
Alberto, Alexander	R-R	6-8	290	11-2-01	2	2	2.83	31	0	3	35	30	12	11	1	17	45	.224	.329	.299	29.0	11.0	155
Beal, Noah	L-R	6-4	205	11-30-01	1	3	5.11	17	0	1	25	26	18	14	3	5	21	.274	.324	.421	19.6	4.7	107
Boucher, Adam	R-R	6-5	235	10-29-01	3	2	4.05	37	0	4	40	32	20	18	2	31	42	.225	.368	.331	23.9	17.6	176
Chavez, Seth	R-R	6-2	200	10-4-99	1	2	3.56	22	0	1	30	21	14	12	3	11	27	.191	.272	.336	21.6	8.8	125
Citelli, Cade	R-R	6-3	195	8-10-01	1	0	4.50	12	0	0	14	11	9	7	2	7	19	.220	.333	.360	31.7	11.7	60
Dowd, Drew	L-L	6-1	190	1-3-02	4	4	2.60	38	2	5	55	39	17	16	3	17	71	.196	.268	.286	32.3	7.7	220
Edington, Derrick	R-R	6-8	210	7-22-99	1	1	2.40	14	0	4	15	13	6	4	0	2	17	.228	.279	.263	27.4	3.2	62
Edwards, Garrett	R-R	6-5	195	1-3-02	5	5	2.78	22	22	0	107	80	38	33	8	27	102	.206	.267	.306	24.0	6.4	425
Fondtain, T.J.	L-L	6-4	210	2-22-01	0	2	7.71	11	0	0	14	17	12	12	5	5	20	.279	.343	.525	29.9	7.5	67
Fowler, Dalton	L-L	6-7	200	1-7-00	1	0	11.57	8	0	0	9	11	12	12	0	14	.297	.480	.405	28.0	22.0	50
Gainey, Garrett	L-L	6-1	200	6-22-00	4	4	3.29	21	10	0	63	49	24	23	4	13	57	.213	.265	.339	22.9	5.2	249
Galan, Andres	R-R	6-2	170	7-4-03	0	0	1.59	1	1	0	6	4	1	1	0	4	4	.211	.375	.263	16.7	16.7	24
Gill Hill, Gary	R-R	6-2	160	9-20-04	7	8	3.82	25	25	0	137	129	63	58	17	30	107	.247	.303	.397	18.8	5.3	569
Harrison, Trevor	R-R	6-4	225	8-8-05	1	1	3.33	5	5	0	24	23	15	9	2	13	25	.258	.362	.360	23.8	12.4	105
Johnson, Marcus	R-R	6-6	200	12-11-00	7	10	5.11	25	25	0	138	160	69	69	28	16	138	.292	.314	.484	24.2	2.8	570
Lancaster, Jackson	L-L	6-1	195	3-22-01	2	0	3.09	13	0	0	23	13	8	8	1	8	26	.160	.250	.210	28.3	8.7	92
Lesko, Dylan	R-R	6-2	195	9-7-03	0	0	23.63	4	0	0	3	8	8	7	1	6	3	.615	.762	.846	14.3	28.6	21
Murphy, Chandler	L-R	6-3	203	12-18-00	0	1	8.10	2	1	0	7	9	6	6	0	2	6	.333	.419	.407	19.4	6.5	31
Nichols, T.J.	R-R	6-5	189	6-24-02	10	3	3.63	19	18	0	97	84	43	39	20	21	119	.233	.289	.438	30.4	5.4	392
Rosario, Gerlin	R-R	6-3	211	2-15-02	2	0	2.27	30	0	2	48	35	17	12	2	18	43	.194	.282	.289	21.3	8.9	202
Rumbol, Jonalbert	R-R	5-9	170	11-11-98	1	1	4.24	17	0	1	23	21	12	11	4	12	17	.250	.376	.393	16.8	11.9	101
Snelsire, Hayden	L-L	6-1	213	1-16-01	4	2	2.97	22	10	1	79	56	26	26	6	17	72	.198	.243	.314	23.6	5.6	305
Snyder, Jack	R-R	6-2	205	8-4-98	0	3	5.66	18	0	0	21	19	15	13	4	12	20	.241	.340	.443	21.1	12.6	95
Suarez, Santiago	R-R	6-2	175	1-11-05	0	4	2.88	10	10	0	41	35	24	13	4	6	45	.223	.251	.357	26.9	3.6	167
Urbina, Jose	R-R	6-3	180	11-2-05	0	0	4.50	1	1	0	4	4	2	2	0	5	.250	.250	.688	31.3	0.0	16
Villaman, Chris	L-L	6-2	217	3-16-01	7	0	6.00	22	0	1	33	38	24	22	6	11	31	.286	.345	.519	20.9	7.4	148
Wantz, Andrew	R-R	6-4	235	10-13-95	0	0	1.50	5	0	0	6	4	1	1	0	3	6	.200	.304	.250	26.1	13.0	23
William, Junior	R-R	6-4	187	3-6-00	5	3	4.89	28	1	1	37	37	28	19	4	15	42	.264	.348	.393	26.4	9.4	159

Fielding

Catcher	PCT	G	PO	A	E	DP	PB
Broecker	.995	40	350	24	2	3	4
Flewelling	1.000	3	36	2	0	0	0
Herron	1.000	4	36	0	0	0	0
Martinez	.977	28	267	29	7	5	5
Vellojin	.977	56	471	43	12	3	4

First Base	PCT	G	PO	A	E	DP
Broecker	.980	7	46	4	1	2
Haas	.992	21	122	7	1	11
Martinez	.986	31	201	11	3	20
Robertson	.996	71	514	21	2	47
Vellojin	1.000	5	37	2	0	1

Second Base	PCT	G	PO	A	E	DP
Haas	.977	14	18	24	1	4

	PCT	G	PO	A	E	DP	PB
Horvath	.957	26	46	65	5	10	
Pitre	.977	85	141	195	8	47	
Santa Maria	.964	5	8	19	1	3	
Santana	1.000	4	6	6	0	1	

Third Base	PCT	G	PO	A	E	DP
Colmenarez	.925	44	20	66	7	2
Haas	.918	41	22	56	7	5
Horvath	.863	19	15	29	7	2
Santa Maria	.867	5	2	11	2	0
Spikes	.941	23	20	28	3	0

Shortstop	PCT	G	PO	A	E	DP
Colmenarez	.976	24	21	62	2	11
Pitre	.925	26	25	49	6	10
Santana	.966	82	127	210	12	52

	PCT	G	PO	A	E	DP
Spikes	1.000	1	3	1	0	0

Outfield	PCT	G	PO	A	E	DP
Cermak	1.000	21	58	0	0	0
Colmenarez	1.000	6	7	1	0	0
Diaz	.946	86	152	6	9	1
Haas	1.000	3	1	0	0	0
Horvath	.984	58	124	0	2	0
Mateo	1.000	10	16	0	0	0
Myers	.993	74	146	2	1	0
Perez	.875	4	7	0	1	0
Robertson	1.000	10	10	0	0	0
Santa Maria	.889	6	8	0	1	0
Smith	.991	94	225	8	2	1
Spikes	1.000	32	51	3	0	0

CHARLESTON RIVERDOGS
CAROLINA LEAGUE — LOW-A

Batting	B-T	Ht.	Wt.	DOB	AVG	OBP	SLG	G	PA	AB	R	H	2B	3B	HR	RBI	BB	HBP	SH	SF	SO	SB	CS	BB%	SO%
Aybar, Nicandro	S-R	6-1	170	9-8-04	.105	.150	.158	6	20	19	0	2	1	0	0	0	1	0	0	0	4	0	0	5.0	20.0
Contreras, Jose	R-R	6-2	205	11-30-04	.224	.283	.245	15	54	49	5	11	1	0	0	1	4	0	1	0	17	1	0	7.4	31.5
Cotes, Felix	S-R	5-11	176	8-13-05	.233	.395	.267	11	39	30	4	7	1	0	0	5	10	1	0	0	6	0	0	20.5	15.4
Datil, Derek	L-L	6-2	160	11-9-05	.200	.317	.200	11	41	35	8	7	0	0	0	1	6	0	0	0	8	0	0	14.6	19.5
Donay, Brody	R-R	6-5	215	9-4-01	.308	.353	.9	39	39	34	4	7	2	0	1	5	4	1	0	0	9	1	0	10.3	23.1
Flewelling, Nathan	L-R	6-1	185	11-11-06	.229	.393	.336	102	439	336	46	77	16	1	6	49	89	6	3	2	121	9	2	20.3	27.6
Garcia, Yirer	R-R	5-11	165	9-18-05	.246	.349	.257	58	220	183	14	45	2	0	0	21	28	3	2	4	43	3	1	12.7	19.5
Gillen, Theo	L-R	6-2	195	9-12-05	.267	.433	.387	73	324	243	62	65	12	1	5	18	64	10	3	4	75	36	3	19.8	23.1
Gonzalez, JD	L-R	6-1	165	10-3-05	.173	.221	.224	27	104	98	3	17	1	0	0	12	6	0	0	0	27	0	0	5.8	26.0
Gonzalez, Ricardo	S-R	5-11	165	7-6-04	.224	.328	.262	103	431	366	43	82	10	2	6	40	54	4	4	3	81	23	7	12.5	18.8
Guerrero, Brailer	L-R	6-1	215	6-25-06	.251	.341	.403	50	220	191	22	48	7	2	6	32	22	2	0	5	64	9	1	11.4	29.1

TAMPA BAY RAYS

	B-T	Ht.	Wt.	DOB																		
Guillen, Xavier	S-R	5-10	167	9-2-04	.192	.263	.192	19	58	52	5	10	0	0	0	1	4	1	1	0	23	3	1	6.9	39.7
Herron, Tyler	R-R	6-1	190	6-20-03	.000	.500	.000	1	4	2	1	0	0	0	0	0	1	1	0	0	0	0	0	25.0	0.0
Hujsak, Connor	R-R	6-2	200	1-25-02	.234	.296	.381	99	426	381	57	89	20	6	8	53	33	4	0	8	123	28	2	7.7	28.9
Lines, Jack	L-R	6-0	170	11-8-05	.167	.345	.256	28	118	90	14	15	5	0	1	7	15	10	2	1	36	4	1	12.7	30.5
Marget, Brady	L-R	6-5	195	9-15-02	.231	.375	.308	7	32	26	3	6	2	0	0	0	5	1	0	0	7	0	0	15.6	21.9
Martinez, Larry	R-R	5-11	170	8-6-05	.248	.299	.280	85	332	307	31	76	10	0	0	27	16	7	0	1	49	4	0	4.8	14.8
Mateo, Angel	R-R	6-2	190	2-13-05	.282	.343	.383	92	388	347	50	98	15	1	6	66	28	7	0	6	71	16	7	7.2	18.3
McCoy, Ryan	L-R	6-5	225	6-6-02	.215	.329	.323	18	76	65	10	14	5	1	0	7	7	4	0	0	29	2	1	9.2	38.2
Monzon, Jose	L-R	6-0	160	11-17-05	.209	.305	.255	93	349	302	30	63	11	0	1	33	43	0	1	3	78	8	7	12.3	22.3
Palma, Alberth	R-R	6-0	170	2-2-06	.225	.287	.250	21	87	80	6	18	2	0	0	6	6	1	0	0	12	1	0	6.9	13.8
Perez, Jose	R-R	5-9	170	3-12-04	.175	.335	.229	61	208	166	19	29	4	1	1	16	35	5	2	0	30	2	0	16.8	14.4
Polanco, Narciso	L-R	5-10	161	10-28-04	.228	.346	.320	120	524	435	84	99	16	6	4	43	73	9	1	6	82	35	15	13.9	15.6
Poole, Tom	R-R	6-1	206	10-7-02	.200	.326	.357	20	86	70	10	14	2	0	3	12	10	4	0	2	32	0	1	11.6	37.2
Quinn-Irons, James	R-R	6-5	230	6-28-03	.259	.375	.259	8	32	27	2	7	0	0	0	2	4	1	0	0	10	2	2	12.5	31.3
Shin, Wooyeoul	R-R	6-0	215	12-30-01	.229	.347	.343	49	200	166	28	38	8	1	3	19	26	5	1	2	34	10	2	13.0	17.0
Summerhill, Brendan	L-R	6-2	191	11-13-03	.333	.429	.444	10	42	36	8	12	2	1	0	5	6	0	0	5	5	1	1	14.3	11.9

Pitching	B-T	Ht.	Wt.	DOB	W	L	ERA	G	GS	SV	IP	Hits	Runs	ER	HR	BB	SO	AVG	OBP	SLG	SO%	BB%	BF
Alberto, Alexander	R-R	6-8	190	11-2-01	0	0	1.98	11	0	3	14	6	4	3	0	4	19	.130	.259	.174	35.2	7.4	54
Andrade, Ryan	R-R	6-2	175	3-17-03	11	5	2.87	23	23	0	119	100	46	38	5	47	90	.228	.308	.310	18.3	9.6	491
Auer, Mason	R-R	6-1	210	3-1-01	0	2	12.71	6	1	1	6	9	9	8	0	10	4	.360	.528	.400	11.1	27.8	36
Bercovich, Jadon	R-R	6-2	210	4-3-02	0	0	2.91	17	0	3	22	19	9	7	0	6	30	.232	.300	.317	33.3	6.7	90
Campos, Alexander	R-R	6-1	190	4-14-03	1	0	3.46	5	2	0	13	12	5	5	1	3	5	.240	.291	.340	9.1	5.5	55
Chavez, Seth	R-R	6-2	200	10-4-99	0	0	0.00	1	0	0	1	0	0	0	0	1	0	.000	.250	.000	0.0	25.0	4
Citelli, Cade	R-R	6-3	195	8-10-01	0	2	3.68	27	0	3	37	24	19	15	3	20	43	.189	.302	.315	28.7	13.3	150
Contreras, Jose	R-R	6-1	200	5-5-05	0	0	0.00	1	0	0	0	0	0	0	0	0	0	.500	.500	.500	0.0	0.0	2
Corbett, Kaleb	R-R	6-5	215	2-26-01	3	2	5.23	29	0	2	41	41	26	24	2	20	45	.253	.342	.321	24.3	10.8	185
Fowler, Dalton	L-L	6-7	230	1-7-00	0	0	3.55	11	0	2	13	7	6	5	1	5	17	.149	.231	.255	32.7	9.6	52
Gainey, Garrett	L-L	6-1	200	6-22-00	1	1	6.30	7	0	0	10	8	7	7	2	4	10	.211	.286	.395	23.8	9.5	42
Galan, Andres	R-R	6-2	170	7-4-03	5	4	3.31	15	13	0	82	70	33	30	5	26	63	.230	.288	.338	18.9	7.8	333
Garcia, Engert	R-R	5-11	190	4-30-00	2	0	6.23	19	0	1	26	18	21	18	1	29	22	.202	.416	.315	17.5	23.0	126
Harrison, Trevor	R-R	6-4	225	8-8-05	7	2	2.61	17	17	0	83	63	26	24	1	36	75	.211	.299	.275	22.4	10.7	335
Hartlaub, Jacob	R-R	6-4	188	9-4-02	1	0	3.60	6	0	1	10	10	4	4	1	0	7	.278	.256	.417	17.9	0.0	39
Hilario, Danny	R-R	6-0	185	9-17-04	2	1	2.00	8	0	0	18	11	5	4	0	5	9	.180	.239	.262	13.4	7.5	67
Keisel, Janzen	R-R	6-4	208	2-24-03	2	4	7.22	15	8	1	39	32	34	31	2	33	30	.222	.395	.326	16.2	17.8	185
Kmatz, Jacob	R-R	6-4	215	9-28-02	4	9	5.56	23	19	0	110	132	70	68	12	35	80	.306	.354	.458	16.9	7.4	473
Lesko, Dylan	R-R	6-2	195	9-7-03	0	1	12.19	11	0	1	10	11	15	14	1	21	7	.297	.533	.432	11.7	35.0	60
Lindsey, Andrew	R-R	6-3	216	11-15-99	0	2	7.04	6	6	0	15	25	14	12	1	7	12	.379	.446	.500	16.2	9.5	74
McCleve, Zac	R-R	6-4	215	8-1-00	0	0	0.00	2	0	0	3	2	0	0	0	2	4	.167	.286	.167	28.6	14.3	14
Nichols, Mason	R-R	6-5	205	4-23-03	1	0	0.00	7	0	1	9	2	0	0	0	3	9	.067	.152	.133	27.3	6.1	33
Niman, Dominic	L-L	6-3	220	8-25-00	4	2	1.60	14	1	1	39	30	12	7	3	12	39	.205	.266	.301	24.7	7.6	158
Palma, Moises	R-R	6-4	195	9-1-04	0	0	11.42	7	0	1	9	12	12	11	1	6	6	.308	.413	.462	13.0	13.0	46
Parish, Trendan	R-R	6-0	175	2-14-02	0	0	12.71	4	0	0	6	7	9	8	1	4	7	.304	.429	.435	25.0	14.3	28
Perez, Jose	R-R	5-9	170	3-12-04	0	0	16.88	3	0	0	3	4	6	5	0	2	2	.333	.429	.583	13.3	13.3	15
Pilon, Jeremy	L-L	6-0	185	9-11-05	0	1	9.00	1	1	0	3	4	3	3	1	1	4	.308	.357	.692	28.6	7.1	14
Pooser, Trey	R-R	6-3	200	7-30-01	1	3	3.54	6	5	0	28	31	15	11	3	4	28	.274	.303	.381	22.7	3.4	119
Rodriguez, Andy	R-R	6-1	182	7-28-02	4	4	4.61	39	0	5	53	62	33	27	1	11	38	.298	.338	.375	16.7	4.8	228
Rojas, Cesar	R-R	6-3	162	5-12-02	0	0	27.00	3	0	0	2	7	7	7	0	5	2	.200	.579	.300	10.5	26.3	19
Rumbol, Jonalbert	R-R	5-9	170	11-11-98	1	2	1.72	12	0	0	16	10	4	3	0	5	12	.175	.238	.211	19.0	7.9	63
Russell, Jonathan	R-R	6-1	180	3-14-05	4	0	2.17	25	0	6	37	32	13	9	0	11	46	.235	.298	.301	30.5	7.3	151
Schiefer, Ryan	R-R	6-3	180	8-20-03	0	1	9.45	7	1	0	7	6	7	7	0	7	10	.286	.553	.381	10.3	25.6	39
Shaffer, Bryce	L-L	6-2	195	8-3-01	2	1	3.29	27	0	2	41	45	21	15	0	13	43	.281	.337	.300	24.4	7.4	176
Stevenson, Owen	R-R	6-4	205	9-1-02	1	0	4.63	6	0	0	12	14	6	6	0	5	4	.311	.380	.400	8.0	10.0	50
Urbina, Jose	R-R	6-3	180	11-2-05	7	2	2.05	19	19	0	92	68	29	21	7	30	96	.207	.281	.319	26.4	8.2	364
Voelker, Jayden	L-R	6-4	215	2-13-03	4	8	5.50	18	14	0	69	69	44	42	9	30	54	.261	.338	.439	18.1	10.0	299
William, Junior	R-R	6-4	187	3-6-00	0	0	0.00	4	0	1	4	0	0	0	0	3	4	.000	.188	.000	25.0	18.8	16

Fielding

Catcher	PCT	G	PO	A	E	DP	PB
Donay	1.000	4	36	1	0	0	3
Flewelling	.991	75	577	59	6	5	6
Garcia	.980	30	228	16	5	1	6
Gonzalez	.989	20	164	16	2	1	5
Martinez	1.000	3	17	1	0	0	0

First Base	PCT	G	PO	A	E	DP
Contreras	1.000	2	17	2	0	3
Donay	.933	4	27	1	2	2
Garcia	.971	10	65	3	2	8
Herron	1.000	1	7	0	0	0
Hujsak	.989	11	81	6	1	7
Marget	1.000	7	46	5	0	2
Martinez	.986	65	468	37	7	53
McCoy	1.000	5	38	0	0	4
Poole	.980	6	46	3	1	1
Shin	1.000	22	177	6	0	12

Second Base	PCT	G	PO	A	E	DP
Cotes	.947	8	15	21	2	0

	PCT	G	PO	A	E	DP
Gonzalez	.975	9	16	23	1	9
Lines	.923	21	34	38	6	5
Monzon	.975	18	39	38	2	9
Palma	.979	9	19	28	1	11
Perez	1.000	8	12	12	0	3
Polanco	.967	58	94	168	9	33

Third Base	PCT	G	PO	A	E	DP
Garcia	1.000	1	0	2	0	0
Gonzalez	.889	3	0	8	1	2
Martinez	.000	1	0	0	0	0
Monzon	.971	63	54	82	4	9
Palma	1.000	1	0	4	0	0
Perez	.818	23	20	25	10	3
Polanco	.956	41	32	76	5	6

Shortstop	PCT	G	PO	A	E	DP
Gonzalez	.962	90	149	227	15	56
Lines	.917	4	7	15	2	2
Monzon	.907	8	14	25	4	3
Palma	.911	11	16	35	5	6

	PCT	G	PO	A	E	DP
Polanco	.969	17	25	38	2	10

Outfield	PCT	G	PO	A	E	DP
Aybar	.842	6	16	0	3	0
Contreras	1.000	11	19	1	0	0
Datil	1.000	11	15	0	0	0
Gillen	.975	68	151	5	4	1
Guerrero	.896	38	58	2	7	1
Guillen	1.000	15	34	2	0	0
Hujsak	.982	80	153	9	3	1
Martinez	.000	1	0	0	0	0
Mateo	.968	87	171	8	6	0
McCoy	.935	13	28	1	2	0
Perez	.977	25	41	2	1	0
Poole	.947	13	18	0	1	0
Quinn-Irons	1.000	7	16	0	0	0
Shin	1.000	23	38	0	0	0
Summerhill	.957	6	22	0	1	0

FCL RAYS
FLORIDA COMPLEX LEAGUE — ROOKIE
TAMPA BAY RAYS

Batting	B-T	Ht.	Wt.	DOB	AVG	OBP	SLG	G	PA	AB	R	H	2B	3B	HR	RBI	BB	HBP	SH	SF	SO	SB	CS	BB%	SO%
Ariza, Luis	R-R	5-11	155	5-8-04	.173	.338	.212	21	65	52	6	9	2	0	0	5	8	5	0	0	16	0	0	12.3	24.6
Aybar, Nicandro	S-R	6-1	170	9-8-04	.323	.404	.364	35	114	99	15	32	2	1	0	12	13	1	0	1	11	6	1	11.4	9.6
Baker, Dru	R-R	5-11	205	3-22-00	.067	.300	.067	6	20	15	2	1	0	0	0	0	5	0	0	0	7	0	0	25.0	35.0
Barrios, Gregory	R-R	6-0	180	4-8-04	.276	.400	.345	11	35	29	9	8	2	0	0	4	3	3	0	0	1	8	0	8.6	2.9
Cermak, Ryan	R-R	6-0	205	6-2-01	.474	.545	1.211	5	22	19	10	9	5	0	3	8	2	1	0	0	1	1	0	9.1	4.5
Colmenarez, Carlos	L-R	5-9	170	11-15-03	.320	.370	.480	6	27	25	6	8	1	0	1	3	1	1	0	0	8	0	0	3.7	29.6
Contreras, Jose	R-R	6-1	200	5-5-05	.286	.359	.457	11	39	35	5	10	3	0	1	4	2	2	0	0	9	2	1	5.1	23.1
Cotes, Felix	S-R	5-11	176	8-13-05	.255	.391	.293	49	200	157	19	40	4	1	0	21	32	5	3	3	29	14	8	16.0	14.5
Datil, Derek	L-L	6-2	160	11-9-05	.273	.404	.348	50	203	161	32	44	7	1	1	20	33	3	5	1	33	11	1	16.3	16.3
DeLuca, Jonny	R-R	6-0	200	7-10-98	.182	.357	.182	4	14	11	1	2	0	0	0	1	3	0	0	0	2	0	0	21.4	14.3
Garcia, Yirer	R-R	5-11	165	9-18-05	.478	.618	.522	11	35	23	3	11	1	0	0	9	8	2	1	1	2	3	1	22.9	5.7
Genoves, Ricardo	R-R	6-2	190	5-14-99	.333	.333	.333	1	3	3	1	1	0	0	0	0	0	0	0	0	0	0	0	0.0	0.0
Guerrero, Brailer	L-R	6-1	215	6-25-06	.000	.000	.000	1	2	2	0	0	0	0	0	0	0	0	0	0	1	0	0	0.0	50.0
Guillen, Xavier	S-R	5-10	167	9-2-04	.286	.436	.405	22	55	42	10	12	1	2	0	5	11	1	0	1	13	5	1	20.0	23.6
Herron, Tyler	R-R	6-1	190	6-20-03	.181	.330	.194	24	88	72	6	13	1	0	0	6	10	6	0	0	19	0	3	11.4	21.6
Jimenez, Eloy	R-R	6-4	240	11-27-96	.095	.296	.095	8	27	21	3	2	0	0	0	1	6	0	0	0	3	0	0	22.2	11.1
Keegan, Dominic	R-R	6-0	210	8-1-00	.292	.469	.625	8	32	24	7	7	2	0	2	4	8	0	0	0	6	0	1	25.0	18.8
Lara, Erick	L-R	6-2	165	6-10-06	.183	.340	.268	32	106	82	14	15	3	2	0	11	21	0	0	3	35	2	2	19.8	33.0
Lines, Jack	L-R	6-0	170	11-8-05	.333	.524	.400	6	21	15	3	5	1	0	0	0	5	1	0	0	6	3	1	23.8	28.6
Lowe, Josh	L-R	6-4	205	2-2-98	.333	.600	1.333	1	5	3	2	1	0	0	1	2	2	0	0	0	1	0	0	40.0	20.0
Mangum, Jake	S-L	6-1	179	3-8-96	.333	.333	.333	1	3	3	1	1	0	0	0	1	0	0	0	0	0	0	0	0.0	0.0
Martinez, Alfonzo	R-R	6-0	180	11-28-05	.237	.286	.295	45	189	173	27	41	5	1	1	26	10	3	0	3	37	7	6	5.3	19.6
Palacios, Richie	L-R	5-10	180	5-16-97	.143	.250	.286	2	8	7	0	1	1	0	0	0	1	0	0	0	1	0	0	12.5	12.5
Palma, Alberth	R-R	6-0	170	2-2-06	.318	.462	.388	44	171	129	27	41	1	4	0	24	33	4	2	3	17	15	9	19.3	9.9
Peguero, Juanfel	S-R	5-11	142	12-31-04	.274	.392	.306	23	75	62	9	17	2	0	0	10	10	2	1	0	9	0	1	13.3	12.0
Pineda, Leonardo	R-R	5-11	185	4-21-07	.183	.319	.221	38	161	131	19	24	5	0	0	11	22	5	1	2	47	5	3	13.7	29.2
Rodriguez, Alfredo	R-R	5-11	187	9-9-05	.213	.294	.361	24	68	61	9	13	3	0	2	12	7	0	0	0	17	0	1	10.3	25.0
Santa Maria, Tony	S-R	5-11	195	4-6-02	.333	.333	.667	2	3	3	0	1	1	0	0	0	0	0	0	0	0	0	0	0.0	0.0
Tapia, Roosbert	R-R	6-2	177	6-23-05	.270	.298	.330	35	121	115	12	31	5	1	0	10	4	1	0	1	21	3	0	3.3	17.4
Tovar, Jose	R-R	5-10	168	11-23-05	.167	.306	.250	39	146	120	21	20	6	2	0	12	24	0	2	0	34	2	1	16.4	23.3
Trinidad, Wilian	L-R	5-8	165	10-6-05	.204	.259	.241	19	59	54	5	11	2	0	0	6	4	0	1	0	17	2	0	6.8	28.8

Pitching	B-T	Ht.	Wt.	DOB	W	L	ERA	G	GS	SV	IP	Hits	Runs	ER	HR	BB	SO	AVG	OBP	SLG	SO%	BB%	BF
Bercovich, Jadon	R-R	6-2	210	4-3-02	1	0	0.00	3	1	0	4	0	0	0	0	5	6	.000	.294	.000	35.3	29.4	17
Bitsko, Nick	R-R	6-4	225	6-16-02	0	0	12.60	6	3	0	5	3	11	7	0	13	4	.188	.576	.188	12.1	39.4	33
Cabrera, Baldemix	R-R	6-2	191	3-28-03	3	3	4.11	12	3	0	35	25	20	16	5	30	25	.205	.355	.402	16.1	19.4	155
Campos, Alexander	R-R	6-1	190	4-14-03	3	1	2.73	16	0	1	30	31	14	9	3	6	29	.263	.297	.449	22.7	4.7	128
Canizalez, Joel	R-R	6-1	185	9-22-02	1	2	6.85	16	0	1	22	25	23	17	0	21	17	.281	.434	.393	14.9	18.4	114
Chavez, Seth	R-R	6-2	200	10-4-99	0	0	0.00	2	0	0	3	1	0	0	0	2	1	.111	.273	.111	9.1	18.2	11
Clemente, Jharold	R-R	5-10	200	8-5-02	0	1	4.54	12	6	1	38	37	28	19	5	17	25	.247	.341	.387	14.5	9.8	173
Cook, Alex	R-R	6-2	220	3-29-01	1	0	3.86	4	0	0	5	4	5	2	0	5	10	.211	.375	.263	41.7	20.8	24
Curet, Yoniel	R-R	6-2	190	11-3-02	1	0	0.00	3	2	0	5	2	0	0	0	0	8	.111	.238	.111	38.1	0.0	21
De Jesus, Cesar	L-L	6-1	140	9-28-03	3	2	4.13	16	0	0	28	19	17	13	0	23	24	.202	.361	.213	20.2	19.3	119
Faedo, Alex	R-R	6-5	225	11-12-95	0	0	0.00	1	1	0	2	2	0	0	0	0	2	.250	.250	.250	0.0	0.0	8
Flynn, Michael	R-R	6-4	185	8-7-96	0	1	1.59	5	1	0	6	2	4	1	1	2	5	.095	.167	.286	20.8	8.3	24
Fowler, Dalton	L-L	6-7	200	1-7-00	0	0	0.00	5	0	0	7	4	2	0	0	0	10	.154	.154	.154	38.5	0.0	26
Galan, Andres	R-R	6-2	170	7-4-03	1	0	0.75	3	2	0	12	11	1	1	0	4	10	.250	.313	.295	20.8	8.3	48
Garcia, Engert	R-R	5-11	190	4-30-00	0	0	1.29	2	1	0	7	5	1	1	0	2	6	.208	.269	.208	23.1	7.7	26
Gerber, Joey	R-R	6-4	212	5-3-97	0	0	0.00	1	1	0	1	1	0	0	0	0	1	.250	.250	.250	25.0	0.0	4
Hilario, Danny	R-R	6-0	185	9-17-04	5	3	2.52	14	0	0	25	15	10	7	2	6	32	.165	.214	.253	32.7	6.1	98
Keisel, Janzen	R-R	6-4	208	2-24-03	0	1	2.51	5	2	0	14	13	8	4	0	13	14	.236	.400	.273	19.7	18.3	71
Kelly, Kevin	R-R	6-2	200	11-28-97	0	0	9.00	1	1	0	1	1	1	1	0	0	3	.250	.400	.250	60.0	0.0	5
Knowles, Nate	R-R	6-0	185	9-21-03	1	1	5.25	7	4	0	12	9	8	7	0	6	10	.196	.315	.261	18.5	11.1	54
Lesko, Dylan	R-R	6-2	195	9-7-03	0	0	0.00	3	1	0	5	1	2	0	0	6	8	.063	.318	.063	36.4	27.3	22
Lindsey, Andrew	R-R	6-3	216	11-15-99	0	0	5.14	4	0	4	7	8	4	4	0	3	10	.296	.367	.333	33.3	10.0	30
McClanahan, Shane	L-L	6-1	200	4-28-97	0	0	0.00	1	1	0	1	0	0	0	0	1	0	.000	.250	.000	25.0	25.0	4
Medina, Roberto	L-L	6-1	170	1-19-05	2	1	2.92	17	0	1	25	19	15	8	0	14	24	.207	.303	.217	22.0	12.8	109
Palma, Moises	R-R	6-4	195	9-1-04	0	0	1.37	15	0	6	20	10	3	3	0	6	15	.145	.244	.159	19.2	7.7	78
Pilon, Jeremy	L-L	6-0	185	9-11-05	1	2	3.91	7	7	0	25	20	15	11	0	18	25	.227	.378	.307	22.3	16.1	112
Pooser, Trey	R-R	6-4	200	7-30-01	1	1	5.40	6	0	0	12	13	8	7	0	4	6	.260	.327	.300	10.9	7.3	55
Reifert, Evan	R-R	6-4	190	5-14-99	0	2	20.25	2	2	0	1	4	4	3	0	2	3	.500	.583	.625	25.0	16.7	12
Rojas, Cesar	S-R	6-3	162	5-12-02	0	1	0.63	10	2	1	14	1	1	1	0	8	18	.024	.192	.024	34.6	15.4	52
Russell, Jonathan	R-R	6-1	180	3-14-05	0	0	6.00	3	0	0	3	3	2	2	0	0	2	.273	.273	.273	18.2	0.0	11
Schiefer, Ryan	R-R	6-3	180	8-20-03	3	2	4.32	12	0	0	17	19	12	8	1	11	22	.284	.407	.358	27.2	13.6	81
Teus, Yereny	L-L	5-10	157	8-1-03	1	3	5.08	16	0	6	34	28	20	19	1	22	42	.220	.338	.307	27.8	14.6	151
Toscano, Miguel	R-R	6-3	170	5-12-06	1	2	3.83	11	7	1	40	36	20	17	1	28	35	.237	.364	.316	19.0	15.2	184
Whitley, Kodi	R-R	6-3	220	2-21-95	0	0	1.69	4	0	0	5	5	2	1	1	1	8	.227	.261	.364	34.8	4.3	23

Fielding

C: Tovar 29, Rodriguez 14, Herron 12, Ariza 6, Garcia 6, Keegan 4. **1B:** Tapia 24, Herron 10, Ariza 8, Garcia 6, Contreras 5, Tovar 4, Rodriguez 3, Jimenez 2, Genoves 1, Lara 1. **2B:** Cotes 43, Lara 4, Trinidad 4, Lines 3, Palma 3, Peguero 3, Colmenarez 1, Santa Maria 1. **3B:** Lara 16, Trinidad 13, Peguero 9, Aybar 8, Cotes 6, Palma 6, Colmenarez 3, Tapia 3, Ariza 1. **SS:** Palma 35, Peguero 11, Barrios 10, Lara 10. **LF:** Guillen 14, Aybar 13, Pineda 9, Martinez 8, Datil 5, Tapia 3, Baker 2, Cermak 2, Colmenarez 2, Contreras 2, Jimenez 2, Palacios 1. **CF:** Datil 27, Martinez 13, Pineda 13, DeLuca 9, Aybar 1, Palacios 1. **RF:** Martinez 18, Datil 15, Pineda 13, Aybar 7, Cermak 3, Guillen 3, Baker 2, Tapia 2, Contreras 1, Jimenez 1

DSL RAYS — ROOKIE
DOMINICAN SUMMER LEAGUE

Batting	B-T	Ht.	Wt.	DOB	AVG	OBP	SLG	G	PA	AB	R	H	2B	3B	HR	RBI	BB	HBP	SH	SF	SO	SB	CS	BB%	SO%
Batista, Domingo	L-R	6-1	170	2-8-07	.200	.319	.238	25	94	80	11	16	1	1	0	13	14	0	0	0	23	1	1	14.9	24.5
Cedeno, Emmanuel	S-R	5-9	160	9-25-07	.304	.466	.361	47	212	158	35	48	4	1	1	23	48	1	4	1	12	14	5	22.6	5.7
Coret, Maykel	R-R	6-4	187	9-24-07	.273	.394	.370	41	188	154	37	42	7	1	2	21	24	8	0	2	42	15	4	12.8	22.3
Del Rosario, Ismael	L-R	6-1	185	1-19-07	.156	.255	.200	14	52	45	5	7	2	0	0	1	4	2	1	0	17	1	1	7.7	32.7
Figueredo, Bladimir	R-R	6-2	180	5-22-08	.267	.369	.337	29	103	86	13	23	3	0	1	9	13	2	0	2	23	2	2	12.6	22.3
Figueroa, Santiago	R-R	5-8	177	8-31-08	.276	.424	.355	29	99	76	17	21	6	0	0	11	13	8	0	2	5	6	1	13.1	5.1
Garces, Eliomar	R-R	5-8	159	11-9-07	.257	.385	.361	43	181	144	26	37	5	2	2	25	29	3	2	3	22	10	5	16.0	12.2
Medina, Raymer	S-R	5-11	177	10-31-07	.194	.317	.281	40	164	139	23	27	8	2	0	18	23	2	0	0	45	6	1	14.0	27.4
Mendoza, Santiago	R-R	5-7	184	9-2-07	.259	.426	.324	37	142	108	31	28	4	0	1	12	30	2	1	1	25	8	1	21.1	17.6
Palacios, Brainerh	R-R	5-11	160	5-30-08	.222	.335	.259	45	191	158	16	35	4	0	0	23	26	3	0	4	36	7	4	13.6	18.8
Rubio, Kadil	R-R	6-2	165	12-11-07	.184	.327	.200	42	155	125	21	23	2	0	0	13	13	14	2	1	26	6	1	8.4	16.8
Salazar, Carlos	R-R	5-10	165	1-28-08	.214	.384	.268	26	74	56	10	12	3	0	0	12	13	3	1	1	14	0	3	17.6	18.9
Solano, Warel	R-R	6-5	165	9-19-07	.319	.391	.418	48	207	182	29	58	13	1	1	37	19	4	0	2	34	3	4	9.2	16.4
Torres, Emile	R-R	6-3	175	1-2-08	.126	.238	.205	38	147	127	13	16	4	0	2	13	16	3	0	1	49	6	3	10.9	33.3
Torres, Ivan	R-R	5-11	220	1-23-08	.294	.459	.373	33	135	102	19	30	8	0	0	10	20	12	0	1	12	4	2	14.8	8.9

Pitching	B-T	Ht.	Wt.	DOB	W	L	ERA	G	GS	SV	IP	Hits	Runs	ER	HR	BB	SO	AVG	OBP	SLG	SO%	BB%	BF
Alcala, Damian	R-R	6-1	164	6-10-05	0	0	40.50	1	0	0	1	2	3	3	0	3	0	.500	.714	.500	0.0	42.9	7
Arredondo, Omar	R-R	6-3	188	10-22-05	3	1	6.43	14	0	0	21	24	19	15	2	13	10	.296	.412	.457	10.2	13.3	98
Cabral, Ismael	R-R	6-1	194	12-19-03	1	3	4.79	12	8	0	47	48	31	25	3	27	37	.262	.378	.383	17.1	12.4	217
Castro, Daniel	R-R	6-2	194	6-19-08	3	0	2.03	10	0	0	13	10	4	3	0	12	10	.233	.433	.302	16.7	20.0	60
Ciriaco, Jhendry	R-R	6-2	186	8-23-05	3	1	3.86	8	1	0	21	14	11	9	2	13	14	.187	.347	.293	14.7	13.7	95
Cruz, Ransel	R-R	6-2	144	9-17-05	0	1	6.75	2	2	0	5	6	4	4	0	9	6	.286	.500	.286	20.0	30.0	30
Dishmey, Brandol	R-R	6-3	220	11-21-04	0	0	18.00	9	1	0	6	2	12	12	2	11	5	.111	.529	.444	14.7	32.4	34
Florian, Frailin	L-L	6-6	222	8-5-04	0	1	18.00	1	1	0	1	3	2	2	0	0	2	.500	.500	1.000	33.3	0.0	6
Infante, Jordi	R-R	6-3	193	10-10-04	4	2	3.19	17	0	2	37	24	16	13	1	22	35	.194	.336	.250	22.6	14.2	155
Lopez, Alexander	R-R	6-0	172	12-13-05	0	1	12.96	7	0	0	8	9	13	12	0	10	9	.281	.477	.313	20.0	22.2	45
Martinez, Ezequiel	R-R	6-2	190	10-21-06	0	1	3.09	9	1	0	12	12	6	4	0	5	13	.267	.346	.378	24.5	9.4	53
Mesa, Yolvin	R-R	6-1	160	9-5-05	5	2	3.86	19	0	8	28	26	14	12	1	17	36	.245	.347	.330	29.0	13.7	124
Moris, Yohangel	S-R	6-0	160	11-22-05	0	0	5.40	6	1	0	7	5	5	4	0	9	3	.238	.467	.238	10.0	30.0	30
Paez, Gabriel	L-L	6-3	183	7-4-06	1	3	7.15	12	5	0	23	21	20	18	0	29	24	.263	.473	.300	21.2	25.7	113
Palacios, Diego	R-R	6-0	174	9-22-05	0	3	5.56	3	3	0	11	13	12	7	0	5	15	.271	.344	.438	28.3	9.4	53
Pena, Rubender	R-R	5-10	183	8-18-04	1	0	2.35	10	9	0	46	28	14	12	1	25	41	.179	.301	.237	22.0	13.4	186
Perez, Sebastian	R-R	6-4	170	9-30-06	0	1	15.43	3	3	0	2	4	4	4	1	4	3	.400	.600	1.100	20.0	26.7	15
Radney, Chariel	L-L	6-0	189	3-27-05	1	0	6.94	7	0	0	12	15	14	9	1	12	7	.326	.459	.457	11.5	19.7	61
Ramos, Efrailin	R-R	5-11	165	12-13-05	1	0	2.58	12	7	0	52	37	16	15	1	15	54	.196	.262	.280	26.1	7.2	207
Rojas, Cesar	R-R	6-3	162	5-12-02	1	0	0.00	2	1	0	4	1	0	0	0	0	5	.083	.154	.083	38.5	0.0	13
Savinon, Starlin	L-L	6-0	182	10-30-04	1	2	3.38	9	9	0	35	24	16	13	1	15	40	.200	.289	.308	29.6	11.1	135
Sierra, Ralph	R-R	6-1	218	6-11-08	4	1	2.12	16	0	2	30	24	14	7	2	17	31	.229	.346	.314	24.4	13.4	127
Silgado, Yeison	R-R	5-11	160	10-28-04	1	0	4.26	10	0	0	25	24	14	12	2	16	18	.261	.387	.413	16.2	14.4	111
Soriano, Diego	R-R	6-4	200	11-2-04	1	0	2.77	8	3	0	13	8	5	4	0	11	9	.200	.358	.200	17.0	20.8	53
Tamayo, Jean	R-R	6-0	169	1-25-07	1	0	3.48	6	1	0	10	12	4	4	0	2	11	.286	.333	.333	24.4	4.4	45
Valdez, Francis	R-R	6-1	200	3-14-05	1	1	9.00	8	0	0	8	4	9	8	1	10	11	.154	.439	.346	26.8	24.4	41

Fielding

C: Palacios 30, Torres 16, Mendoza 8, Figueroa 6, Figueredo 4. **1B:** Mendoza 26, Figueroa 14, Torres 8, Figueredo 7, Batista 2, Palacios 2. **2B:** Cedeno 32, Salazar 13, Garces 12, Solano 4, Figueroa 1, Medina 1. **3B:** Solano 36, Cedeno 9, Medina 7, Salazar 4. **SS:** Garces 30, Medina 28, Cedeno 5. **LF:** Rubio 19, Figueredo 14, Del Rosario 10, Batista 6, Salazar 6, Torres 4, Figueroa 2. **CF:** Coret 34, Torres 20, Batista 3. **RF:** Rubio 23, Batista 14, Torres 14, Del Rosario 4, Coret 3, Figueredo 2, Salazar 2, Figueroa 1

DSL TAMPA BAY — ROOKIE
DOMINICAN SUMMER LEAGUE

Batting	B-T	Ht.	Wt.	DOB	AVG	OBP	SLG	G	PA	AB	R	H	2B	3B	HR	RBI	BB	HBP	SH	SF	SO	SB	CS	BB%	SO%
Antunez, Andreimi	R-R	5-10	143	11-5-06	.369	.447	.517	49	209	176	38	65	9	7	1	43	16	11	3	3	29	13	5	7.7	13.9
Batista, Domingo	L-R	6-1	170	2-8-07	.050	.269	.050	26	29	20	4	1	0	0	0	1	5	1	0	0	6	2	0	19.2	23.1
Bautista, Israfell	S-R	6-2	155	10-13-06	.278	.412	.324	47	218	176	61	49	4	2	0	16	38	2	2	0	35	45	5	17.4	16.1
Brachi, Angel	R-R	5-10	165	1-5-07	.337	.453	.408	51	228	184	49	62	9	2	0	21	26	14	3	1	18	17	5	11.4	7.9
Chauran, Kleiver	S-R	5-11	165	11-23-05	.289	.484	.388	49	215	152	39	44	9	0	2	41	52	7	2	2	33	32	5	24.2	15.3
De Sousa, Carlos	R-R	6-1	166	2-24-06	.167	.271	.242	36	141	120	17	20	1	1	2	16	16	2	1	2	34	7	1	11.3	24.1
Galan, Emiliano	R-R	6-1	205	11-11-06	.270	.449	.378	15	49	37	9	10	4	0	0	1	10	2	0	0	10	1	0	20.4	20.4
Gonzalez, Deinys	R-R	5-9	178	1-24-07	.271	.407	.451	46	183	144	24	39	5	3	5	34	24	11	3	1	29	0	1	13.1	15.8
Lugo, Erick	R-R	6-0	165	9-15-06	.329	.343	.329	30	100	85	18	22	6	0	0	10	10	2	1	2	10	0	0	10.0	10.0
Matias, Carlos	R-R	6-2	195	11-10-06	.240	.356	.301	47	182	146	25	35	6	0	1	27	20	9	2	5	26	20	6	11.0	14.3
Pardo, Samuel	R-R	5-11	185	6-16-08	.114	.244	.114	13	41	35	3	4	0	0	0	1	4	2	0	0	2	0	0	9.8	24.4
Pinero, Aaron	R-R	5-9	180	5-15-07	.262	.402	.383	42	179	141	27	37	11	0	2	25	24	11	0	3	30	13	1	13.4	16.8
Santana, John	L-R	6-3	176	9-24-05	.205	.320	.345	50	206	171	26	35	8	0	5	40	26	5	0	4	41	7	5	12.6	19.9
Torres, Andres	L-R	5-11	145	5-1-07	.271	.427	.326	49	192	144	28	39	8	0	0	28	34	9	0	5	24	8	5	17.7	12.5

Pitching	B-T	Ht.	Wt.	DOB	W	L	ERA	G	GS	SV	IP	Hits	Runs	ER	HR	BB	SO	AVG	OBP	SLG	SO%	BB%	BF
Alcala, Damian	R-R	6-1	164	6-10-05	1	3	8.57	15	0	1	21	22	21	20	1	17	13	.289	.429	.368	13.1	17.2	99
Alvarez, Anderson	R-R	5-11	161	2-23-08	1	1	3.23	10	10	0	39	31	15	14	2	15	25	.218	.292	.317	15.5	9.3	161
Aranguren, Jhonny	R-R	6-1	184	10-24-06	2	1	5.91	13	1	1	21	18	14	14	1	24	20	.225	.415	.313	18.9	22.6	106
Arias, John	L-L	6-2	187	5-18-05	1	1	10.43	10	0	0	15	17	22	17	2	11	14	.274	.405	.468	17.7	13.9	79
Carrera, Alonso	R-R	5-9	180	11-22-04	4	3	4.73	18	0	6	32	29	20	17	1	18	30	.250	.362	.328	21.0	12.6	143
Castro, Diego	R-R	6-0	190	10-4-06	2	3	4.99	12	7	0	40	38	23	22	4	19	28	.257	.353	.378	16.4	11.1	171
Chessman, Frank	R-R	5-11	170	5-8-07	2	1	6.93	14	4	0	25	25	20	19	2	30	22	.275	.460	.385	17.7	24.2	124
Ciriaco, Jhendry	R-R	6-2	186	8-23-05	0	1	9.53	3	0	0	6	4	7	6	0	5	2	.200	.393	.250	7.1	17.9	28
Dishmey, Brandol	R-R	6-3	220	11-21-04	1	0	0.00	1	0	0	2	0	0	0	0	0	2	.000	.000	.000	33.3	0.0	6
Florian, Frailin	L-L	6-6	222	8-5-04	1	0	6.23	11	0	0	13	13	10	9	0	17	20	.255	.435	.275	29.0	24.6	69
Gamez, Alvaro	L-L	6-3	175	2-19-05	2	0	9.28	15	0	1	21	17	25	22	3	22	25	.205	.416	.373	22.1	19.5	113
Lopez, Xavier	R-R	6-2	160	5-30-05	3	0	2.06	10	10	0	39	21	11	9	3	13	37	.154	.237	.243	24.3	8.6	152
Menendez, Yosniel	R-R	6-4	230	5-2-07	1	3	5.92	11	11	0	38	36	26	25	0	18	26	.265	.366	.346	15.8	10.9	165
Menes, Jose	R-R	6-1	180	12-11-03	4	1	5.53	12	9	0	42	46	29	26	1	21	28	.288	.382	.381	15.0	11.2	187
Moreno, Moises	R-R	6-2	169	11-1-05	1	0	3.90	17	0	1	28	25	13	12	0	17	15	.253	.364	.333	12.5	14.2	120
Paredes, Israel	R-R	6-2	180	12-19-06	2	1	2.63	8	0	0	14	13	5	4	0	9	12	.245	.375	.321	18.8	14.1	64
Pateti, Samuel	R-R	6-1	186	10-2-06	1	0	4.85	10	1	1	13	14	9	7	0	12	10	.286	.455	.367	15.2	18.2	66
Pena, Rubender	R-R	5-10	183	8-18-04	0	0	10.38	1	1	0	4	5	5	5	0	1	4	.278	.316	.333	21.1	5.3	19
Perez, Yonaiker	R-R	6-1	195	12-8-06	0	1	7.11	5	0	0	6	9	5	5	0	4	10	.333	.455	.444	30.3	12.1	33
Pina, Sebastian	R-R	6-1	180	6-30-08	2	0	2.60	12	0	0	17	14	7	5	2	4	12	.226	.269	.403	17.6	5.9	68
Savinon, Starlin	L-L	6-0	182	10-30-04	1	0	1.35	4	0	1	7	6	4	1	0	4	6	.261	.370	.348	22.2	14.8	27
Tamayo, Jean	R-R	6-0	169	1-25-07	1	1	15.19	4	0	0	5	11	9	9	1	2	4	.440	.500	.720	13.8	6.9	29
Vegas, Isaac	R-R	5-11	204	5-4-06	1	0	3.68	14	2	0	22	18	11	9	3	12	21	.217	.330	.361	21.6	12.4	97

Fielding

C: Gonzalez 28, De Sousa 20, Torres 11, Lugo 2. **1B:** Torres 37, De Sousa 16, Gonzalez 3, Batista 2, Lugo 1. **2B:** Brachi 21, Chauran 21, Pinero 9, Pardo 7, Bautista 1. **3B:** Pinero 25, Chauran 21, Brachi 12. **SS:** Antunez 41, Brachi 16, Chauran 1. **LF:** Matias 37, Lugo 13, Galan 9, Batista 2, Pardo 1, Santana 1. **CF:** Bautista 45, Santana 15, Matias 1. **RF:** Santana 32, Lugo 12, Matias 9, Pardo 4, Galan 3, Batista 2, Torres 1

Texas Rangers

SEASON SYNOPSIS: Texas finally got a healthy, full season of Jacob deGrom (12-8, 2.97), and not coincidentally, the Rangers led the majors with a 3.47 ERA. But Globe Life Field continued to play as an extreme pitcher's park, helping the Rangers rank 22nd in runs, and the club underperformed its run differential (+79), finishing at .500, crumbling after a late hot stretch. Manager Bruce Bochy, who led the team to the 2023 World Series title, and the Rangers mutually cut the cord after the season.

HIGH POINT: The Rangers went 8-1 on a nine-game homestand coming out of the all-star break and were healthy, with their full lineup and rotation at Bochy's disposal. They gave up just 17 runs to the Tigers, A's and Braves, the lone loss coming in a 2-1 defeat when Tarik Skubal started for Detroit.

LOW POINT: Texas just couldn't score consistently, whether the roster was healthy or not. It came to a head in August, when it lost 11 of 14, dropping series to the Phillies and Diamondbacks at home, then to Toronto and Kansas City on the road. The Arizona series was particularly galling, as the Rangers couldn't expand leads against Arizona's decimated bullpen, and trade deadline pickup Phil Maton yielded four runs in the ninth in a 6-4 series-swinging finale.

NOTABLE ROOKIES: The Rangers' Vanderbilt first-round duo of Jack Leiter (2021) and Kumar Rocker (2022) combined for 43 starts, with Leiter (10-10, 3.86) making 29 of them and holding down a spot all year for the first time. Rocker (4-4, 5.79), coming off 2023 UCL surgery, finished the year in Triple-A rehabbing a shoulder impingement issue. Rookies Alejandro Osuna (.313 OBP), Cody Freeman and Michael Helman—dubbed "The Little Rascals" by color TV analyst David Murphy—spurred a September hot streak with key hits and energetic play that got the Rangers to a season-best nine games over .500, but Texas lost 11 of its last 13.

KEY TRANSACTIONS: Offseason efforts to bolster the offense, such as trading for Jake Burger (.236/.269/.419, 16 HR) or signing DH Joc Pederson (.181/.285/.328, 9 HR), didn't work out, though free-agent catcher Kyle Higashioka did (11 HR in 303 AB). Injuries to Nathan Eovaldi and Tyler Mahle forced the Rangers to lean heavily on lefty Patrick Corbin (7-11, 4.40), signed in mid-March for just $1.1 million. Texas added at the deadline, trading for relievers Maton and Danny Coulombe and starter Merrill Kelly (3-3, 4.23 with Texas).

OPENING DAY PAYROLL: $220,541,332 (6th)

PLAYERS OF THE YEAR

MAJOR LEAGUE
Nathan Eovaldi, RHP
11-3, 1.73 ERA
129 SO in 130 IP,
21 BB, 0.85 WHIP

MINOR LEAGUE
Cody Freeman, 3B
(AAA)
.336/.382/.549
Won MiLB batting title

ORGANIZATION LEADERS

Batting		*Qualifiers
MAJORS		
* AVG	Josh Jung	.251
* OPS	Wyatt Langford	.775
HR	Wyatt Langford	22
RBI	Adolis Garcia	75
MINORS		
* AVG	Cody Freeman, Round Rock	.336
* OBP	Antonis Macias, Hub City/Hickory	.394
* SLG	Cody Freeman, Round Rock	.549
* OPS	Cody Freeman, Round Rock	.932
R	Abimelec Ortiz, Round Rock/Frisco	85
H	Cody Freeman, Round Rock	129
TB	Abimelec Ortiz, Round Rock/Frisco	229
2B	Justin Foscue, Round Rock/ACL Rangers	28
3B	Yolfran Castillo, Hickory/ACL Rangers	8
HR	Abimelec Ortiz, Round Rock/Frisco	25
RBI	Abimelec Ortiz, Round Rock/Frisco	89
BB	Antonis Macias, Hub City/Hickory	77
SO	Aaron Zavala, Round Rock/Frisco	158
SB	Anthony Gutierrez, Hub City	48

Pitching		#Qualifiers
MAJORS		
W	Jacob deGrom	12
# ERA	Jacob deGrom	2.97
SO	Jacob deGrom	185
SV	Shawn Armstrong	9
SV	Luke Jackson	9
SV	Robert Garcia	9
MINORS		
W	Trey Supak, Round Rock/Frisco	10
L	Two tied	9
# ERA	Jose Gonzalez, Frisco/Hub City	2.97
G	Robby Ahlstrom, Round Rock/Frisco	53
GS	Trey Supak, Round Rock/Frisco	26
SV	Robby Ahlstrom, Round Rock/Frisco	8
SV	Gavin Collyer, Round Rock/Frisco	8
IP	Trey Supak, Round Rock/Frisco	129
BB	D.J. McCarty, Hub City	52
SO	Trey Supak, Round Rock/Frisco	131
# AVG	Trey Supak, Round Rock/Frisco	.236

2025 PERFORMANCE

General Manager: Chris Young. **Farm Director:** Josh Bonifay. **Scouting Director:** Kip Fagg.

Class	Team	League	W	L	PCT	Finish	Manager
Majors	Texas Rangers	American	81	81	.500	9 (15)	Bruce Bochy
Triple-A	Round Rock Express	Pacific Coast	77	73	.513	5 (10)	Doug Davis
Double-A	Frisco RoughRiders	Texas	73	63	.537	3 (10)	Carlos Cardoza
High-A	Hub City Spartanburgers	South Atlantic	65	66	.496	6 (12)	Chad Comer
Low-A	Hickory Crawdads	Carolina	68	62	.523	5 (12)	Carlos Maldonado
Rookie	ACL Rangers	Arizona Complex	33	27	.550	4 (15)	Nick Janssen
Rookie	DSL Rangers Blue	Dominican Summer	15	41	.268	51 (52)	Ruben Sosa
Rookie	DSL Rangers Red	Dominican Summer	37	17	.685	3 (52)	Esteban Cordoza
Overall 2025 Minor League Record			368	349	.513	10th (30)	

ORGANIZATION STATISTICS

TEXAS RANGERS
AMERICAN LEAGUE

Batting	B-T	Ht.	Wt.	DOB	AVG	OBP	SLG	G	PA	AB	R	H	2B	3B	HR	RBI	BB	HBP	SH	SF	SO	SB	CS	BB%	SO%
Ahmed, Nick	R-R	6-2	201	3-15-90	.000	.100	.000	5	10	9	1	0	0	0	0	0	1	0	0	0	3	1	0	10.0	30.0
Barnhart, Tucker	L-R	5-11	192	1-7-91	.231	.333	.231	8	15	13	0	3	0	0	0	0	1	1	0	0	4	0	0	6.7	26.7
Burger, Jake	R-R	6-2	230	4-10-96	.236	.269	.419	103	376	356	43	84	15	1	16	53	12	5	0	3	93	1	1	3.2	24.7
Carter, Evan	L-R	6-2	190	8-29-02	.247	.336	.392	63	204	194	31	48	9	2	5	25	19	7	0	0	41	14	2	8.6	18.6
Crim, Blaine	R-R	5-10	200	6-17-97	.000	.154	.000	5	13	11	1	0	0	0	0	0	1	0	0	0	6	0	0	7.7	46.2
Duran, Ezequiel	R-R	5-11	185	5-22-99	.224	.266	.293	90	219	205	16	46	14	0	0	14	8	4	1	1	55	11	2	3.7	25.1
Foscue, Justin	R-R	5-11	205	3-2-99	.111	.111	.222	4	9	9	1	1	0	0	0	2	0	0	0	0	3	0	0	0.0	33.3
Freeman, Cody	R-R	5-8	180	1-5-01	.228	.258	.342	36	121	114	13	26	4	0	3	15	5	0	1	1	18	1	1	4.1	15.7
Garcia, Adolis	R-R	6-1	205	3-2-93	.227	.271	.394	135	547	507	58	115	28	0	19	75	28	5	0	7	135	13	4	5.1	24.7
Haggerty, Sam	S-R	5-11	175	5-26-94	.253	.328	.370	64	182	162	31	41	7	3	2	13	16	2	1	0	37	12	4	8.8	20.3
Harris, Dustin	L-R	6-3	185	7-8-99	.200	.256	.350	19	43	40	5	8	3	0	1	2	3	0	0	0	13	1	1	7.0	30.2
Heim, Jonah	S-R	6-4	220	6-27-95	.213	.271	.332	124	433	395	38	84	14	0	11	43	32	1	1	4	88	3	0	7.4	20.3
Helman, Michael	R-R	5-11	195	5-23-96	.232	.290	.455	38	110	99	18	23	5	1	5	20	7	1	3	0	21	4	0	6.4	19.1
Higashioka, Kyle	R-R	6-1	202	4-20-90	.241	.291	.403	94	327	303	33	73	14	1	11	47	20	2	0	2	72	3	1	6.1	22.0
Jung, Josh	R-R	6-2	214	2-12-98	.251	.294	.390	131	511	482	53	121	23	1	14	61	27	2	0	0	129	4	1	5.3	25.2
Langford, Wyatt	R-R	6-2	225	11-15-01	.241	.344	.431	134	573	489	73	118	25	1	22	62	74	5	0	5	151	22	6	12.9	26.4
Leiter, Jack	R-R	6-1	205	4-21-00	.000	.000	.000	30	1	1	0	0	0	0	0	0	0	0	0	0	1	0	0	0.0	100.0
McKinney, Billy	L-L	5-11	205	8-23-94	.200	.238	.250	6	21	20	4	4	1	0	0	1	1	0	0	0	1	0	0	4.8	4.8
Moore, Dylan	R-R	6-0	205	8-2-92	.259	.300	.481	18	30	27	6	7	0	0	2	6	1	0	1	1	6	2	1	3.3	20.0
Ornelas, Jonathan	R-R	6-0	196	5-26-00	.000	.167	.000	4	6	5	0	0	0	0	0	0	1	0	0	0	3	0	0	16.7	50.0
Osuna, Alejandro	L-L	6-0	185	10-4-02	.313	.278	.63	176	151	12	32	4	0	2	15	21	-	2	0	2	34	5	4	11.9	19.3
Pederson, Joc	L-L	6-1	220	4-21-92	.181	.285	.328	96	306	265	28	48	10	1	9	26	34	5	0	1	65	2	0	11.1	21.2
Pillar, Kevin	R-R	6-0	200	1-4-89	.209	.209	.256	20	43	43	6	9	2	0	0	0	0	0	0	0	8	3	0	0.0	18.6
Seager, Corey	L-R	6-4	215	4-27-94	.271	.373	.487	102	445	380	61	103	19	0	21	50	58	5	0	2	87	3	0	13.0	19.6
Semien, Marcus	R-R	6-0	195	9-17-90	.230	.305	.364	127	534	470	62	108	16	1	15	62	50	5	0	9	93	11	1	9.4	17.4
Smith, Josh H.	L-R	5-10	172	8-7-97	.251	.335	.366	144	563	495	70	124	23	2	10	35	55	8	3	1	100	12	3	9.8	17.8
Solano, Donovan	R-R	5-8	210	12-17-87	.000	.000	.000	2	3	3	0	0	0	0	0	0	0	0	0	0	2	0	0	0.0	66.7
Taveras, Leody	S-R	6-2	195	9-8-98	.241	.259	.342	30	82	79	7	19	3	1	1	8	2	0	1	0	23	6	1	2.4	28.0
Tellez, Rowdy	L-L	6-4	270	3-16-95	.259	.315	.457	50	127	116	14	30	5	0	6	22	9	1	1	0	31	0	0	7.1	26.8

Pitching	B-T	Ht.	Wt.	DOB	W	L	ERA	G	GS	SV	IP	Hits	Runs	ER	HR	BB	SO	AVG	OBP	SLG	SO%	BB%	BF
Armstrong, Shawn	R-R	6-2	225	9-11-90	4	3	2.31	71	2	9	74	40	21	19	5	20	74	.157	.232	.264	26.1	7.0	284
Barnhart, Tucker	L-R	5-11	192	1-7-91	0	0	13.50	1	0	0	2	5	3	3	0	0	0	.500	.545	.600	0.0	0.0	11
Boushley, Caleb	R-R	6-3	190	10-1-93	0	0	6.02	25	1	1	43	54	33	29	5	14	41	.305	.363	.458	21.2	7.3	193
Church, Marc	R-R	6-3	189	3-30-01	0	0	3.86	5	0	0	5	4	2	2	0	6	5	.250	.435	.375	21.7	26.1	23
Corbin, Patrick	L-L	6-4	226	7-19-89	7	11	4.40	31	30	0	155	161	79	76	21	51	131	.267	.326	.430	19.8	7.7	663
Corniell, Jose	R-R	6-3	165	6-22-03	0	1	16.20	1	0	0	2	3	4	3	1	1	1	.375	.444	.875	11.1	11.1	9
Coulombe, Danny	L-L	5-10	190	10-26-89	1	1	5.25	15	0	0	12	11	7	7	3	9	12	.250	.377	.477	22.2	16.7	54
Curvelo, Luis	R-R	6-1	170	10-21-00	1	1	5.68	17	0	0	19	17	13	12	3	10	20	.236	.321	.444	23.8	11.9	84
deGrom, Jacob	L-R	6-4	169-88	12	8	2.97	30	30	0	173	122	57	57	26	37	185	.196	.242	.354	27.7	5.5	669
Dunning, Dane	R-R	6-4	225	12-20-94	0	0	3.38	5	0	2	11	9	4	4	2	5	10	.231	.326	.462	21.7	10.9	46
Duran, Ezequiel	R-R	5-11	185	5-22-99	0	0	0.00	4	0	0	3	1	0	0	0	0	0	.091	.091	.091	0.0	0.0	11
Edwards, Carl	R-R	6-3	165	9-3-91	0	0	0.00	2	0	0	3	0	0	0	0	2	4	.000	.182	.000	36.4	18.2	11
Eovaldi, Nathan	R-R	6-2	217	2-13-90	11	3	1.73	22	22	0	130	90	28	25	10	21	129	.194	.239	.307	26.0	4.2	496
Garabito, Gerson	R-R	6-0	160	8-19-95	0	0	9.00	3	0	0	8	15	12	8	1	8	.395	.439	.526	19.5	2.4	41
Garcia, Robert	R-L	6-4	225	6-14-96	4	8	2.95	71	0	9	64	58	26	21	8	22	68	.240	.305	.372	25.3	8.2	269
Gray, Jon	R-R	6-4	225	11-5-91	1	1	7.71	6	0	0	14	15	12	12	5	6	12	.263	.333	.579	19.0	9.5	63
Heuer, Codi	R-R	6-5	200	7-3-96	0	0	6.75	1	0	0	1	1	1	1	0	1	1	.200	.200	.200	20.0	0.0	5
Jackson, Luke	R-R	6-2	210	8-24-91	2	5	4.11	39	0	9	35	32	20	16	4	19	24	.248	.351	.357	15.8	12.5	152
Kelly, Merrill	R-R	6-2	202	10-14-88	3	3	4.23	10	10	0	55	59	26	26	9	10	46	.267	.300	.439	19.7	4.3	234
Latz, Jake	R-L	6-2	185	4-8-96	2	0	2.84	33	8	1	86	69	28	27	7	37	76	.223	.305	.355	21.8	10.6	348
Leiter, Jack	R-R	6-1	205	4-21-00	10	10	3.86	29	29	0	152	127	69	65	18	67	148	.222	.309	.361	22.9	10.4	646
Mahle, Tyler	R-R	6-3	210	9-29-94	6	4	2.18	16	16	0	87	66	21	21	5	29	66	.218	.283	.310	19.1	8.4	346

TEXAS RANGERS

Martin, Chris	R-R	6-8	225	6-2-86	2	6	2.98	49	0	2	42	43	18	14	6	8	43	.262	.299	.390	24.7	4.6	174
Maton, Phil	R-R	6-2	206	3-25-93	3	2	3.52	23	0	3	23	14	9	9	2	8	33	.179	.270	.308	36.7	8.9	90
Milner, Hoby	L-L	6-3	184	1-13-91	3	4	3.84	73	0	0	70	68	35	30	5	21	58	.256	.312	.380	19.8	7.2	293
Rocker, Kumar	R-R	6-5	245	11-22-99	4	5	5.74	14	14	0	64	71	42	41	11	23	56	.277	.343	.477	19.5	8.0	287
Tellez, Rowdy	L-L	6-4	270	3-16-95	0	0	13.50	1	0	0	2	5	3	3	1	0	0	.500	.545	.800	0.0	0.0	11
Webb, Jacob	R-R	6-2	210	8-15-93	5	4	3.00	55	0	1	66	49	24	22	10	19	58	.202	.264	.358	21.7	7.1	267
Winn, Cole	R-R	6-2	190	11-25-99	0	1	1.51	33	0	0	42	23	8	7	3	17	35	.167	.275	.297	21.6	10.5	162

Fielding

Catcher	PCT	G	PO	A	E	DP	PB
Barnhart	1.000	7	37	0	0	0	0
Heim	.996	96	766	28	3	4	4
Higashioka	.995	71	585	16	3	2	4

First Base	PCT	G	PO	A	E	DP
Burger	.993	91	609	79	5	50
Crim	1.000	3	20	4	0	3
Duran	1.000	25	116	14	0	14
Foscue	1.000	3	10	2	0	2
Moore	1.000	2	6	0	0	1
Pederson	1.000	4	17	2	0	2
Smith	.995	27	166	25	1	26
Tellez	1.000	38	200	13	0	16

Second Base	PCT	G	PO	A	E	DP
Duran	1.000	17	15	21	0	5
Freeman	.972	24	35	34	2	9
Haggerty	1.000	5	1	3	0	1

	PCT	G	PO	A	E	DP
Moore	1.000	11	3	9	0	1
Ornelas	1.000	1	0	2	0	0
Semien	.996	127	183	308	2	67
Smith	1.000	4	2	7	0	2
Solano	1.000	2	1	2	0	0

Third Base	PCT	G	PO	A	E	DP
Duran	.913	11	5	16	2	1
Freeman	1.000	6	3	3	0	0
Jung	.978	126	86	221	7	18
Smith	.985	32	22	43	1	6

Shortstop	PCT	G	PO	A	E	DP
Ahmed	1.000	5	7	10	0	4
Duran	.984	30	25	35	1	5
Helman	1.000	1	1	0	0	0
Ornelas	1.000	3	1	7	0	1
Seager	.988	97	119	217	4	54
Smith	.974	60	48	99	4	18

Outfield	PCT	G	PO	A	E	DP
Carter	1.000	60	123	2	0	0
Duran	1.000	11	14	1	0	0
Freeman	1.000	9	9	0	0	0
Garcia	.993	128	268	6	2	1
Haggerty	1.000	43	62	0	0	0
Harris	.971	16	34	0	1	0
Helman	1.000	35	89	1	0	1
Langford	.994	149	302	4	2	0
McKinney	1.000	5	11	0	0	0
Moore	1.000	2	2	0	0	0
Osuna	1.000	58	88	2	0	0
Pederson	1.000	1	1	0	0	0
Pillar	1.000	17	20	1	0	0
Smith	1.000	17	29	1	0	0
Taveras	.967	30	57	2	2	0

ROUND ROCK EXPRESS — TRIPLE-A
PACIFIC COAST LEAGUE

Batting	B-T	Ht.	Wt.	DOB	AVG	OBP	SLG	G	PA	AB	R	H	2B	3B	HR	RBI	BB	HBP	SH	SF	SO	SB	CS	BB%	SO%
Barnhart, Tucker	L-R	5-11	192	1-7-91	.214	.339	.330	31	125	103	15	22	6	0	2	13	17	3	1	1	24	0	1	13.6	19.2
Biggers, Jax	L-R	5-8	175	4-7-97	.087	.160	.087	8	26	23	0	2	0	0	0	0	1	2	0	1	8	0	0	7.7	30.8
Burger, Jake	R-R	6-2	230	4-10-96	.444	.500	.806	9	40	36	9	16	4	0	3	12	4	0	0	0	2	0	0	10.0	5.0
Carter, Evan	L-R	6-2	190	8-29-02	.207	.314	.379	24	102	87	13	18	2	2	3	10	14	0	0	1	26	6	2	13.7	25.5
Chavez, Frainyer	S-R	5-8	170	5-24-99	.257	.409	.543	11	44	35	9	9	1	0	3	9	8	1	0	0	7	1	1	18.2	15.9
Crim, Blaine	R-R	5-10	200	6-17-97	.284	.373	.515	83	378	328	54	93	20	1	18	71	43	5	0	2	70	3	3	11.4	18.5
De Goti, Alex	R-R	6-0	192	8-19-94	.229	.330	.301	91	335	279	35	64	15	0	3	33	41	4	4	6	74	3	3	12.2	22.1
Duran, Ezequiel	R-R	5-11	185	5-22-99	.345	.390	.673	16	59	55	13	19	6	0	4	4	4	0	0	0	13	5	0	6.8	22.0
Emshoff, Kale	R-R	6-2	228	5-2-98	.182	.182	.182	5	11	11	1	2	0	0	0	0	0	0	0	0	5	0	0	0.0	45.5
Foscue, Justin	R-R	5-11	205	3-2-99	.261	.341	.474	103	453	399	65	104	28	0	19	68	45	5	1	3	63	7	0	9.9	13.9
Freeman, Cody	R-R	5-8	180	1-5-01	.336	.382	.549	97	426	384	75	129	25	0	19	71	32	1	2	7	37	8	5	7.5	8.7
Haggerty, Sam	S-R	5-11	175	5-26-94	.302	.371	.384	23	98	86	14	26	2	1	1	12	9	1	1	1	21	7	0	9.2	21.4
Harris, Dustin	L-R	6-3	185	7-8-99	.285	.369	.435	91	425	372	70	106	19	2	11	41	44	6	2	1	74	33	4	10.4	17.4
Hauver, Trevor	L-R	5-11	205	11-20-98	.275	.391	.446	104	440	363	64	100	20	3	12	66	67	5	0	5	106	3	1	15.2	24.1
Helman, Michael	R-R	6-1	195	5-23-96	.245	.304	.440	53	238	216	41	53	16	1	8	32	15	4	1	2	45	11	3	6.3	18.9
Higashioka, Kyle	R-R	6-1	202	4-20-90	.250	.250	.500	2	8	8	1	2	0	0	0	0	0	0	0	0	4	0	0	0.0	50.0
Johnson, Cooper	R-R	6-1	209	4-25-98	.209	.318	.319	82	322	273	31	57	10	1	6	32	42	3	1	3	88	4	0	13.0	27.3
Jung, Josh	R-R	6-2	214	2-12-98	.225	.410	.336	8	40	39	4	8	2	0	2	4	1	0	0	0	8	0	1	2.5	20.0
Marrero, Elih	S-R	5-7	185	6-21-97	.000	.250	.000	2	8	6	1	0	0	0	0	0	2	0	0	0	2	0	0	25.0	25.0
Martin, Richie	R-R	5-11	190	12-22-94	.258	.348	.369	79	303	260	50	67	6	7	3	30	23	13	3	0	63	25	4	7.6	20.8
McKinney, Billy	L-L	5-11	205	8-23-94	.336	.357	.455	65	255	224	33	60	11	2	9	39	28	3	0	0	58	6	2	11.0	22.7
Mitchell, Tucker	R-R	6-1	210	2-10-01	.050	.091	.050	8	22	20	0	1	0	0	0	1	1	0	0	1	9	0	0	4.5	40.9
Moore, Dylan	R-R	6-0	205	8-2-92	.250	.250	.500	1	4	4	1	1	1	0	0	0	0	0	0	0	1	1	0	0.0	25.0
Narvaez, Omar	L-R	5-11	220	2-10-92	.271	.383	.375	30	115	96	12	26	4	0	2	17	17	1	0	1	19	0	0	14.8	16.5
Ornelas, Jonathan	R-R	6-0	196	5-26-00	.204	.339	.235	30	121	98	9	20	3	0	0	7	18	3	0	2	29	3	0	14.9	24.0
Ortiz, Abimelec	L-L	6-0	230	2-22-02	.283	.388	.565	41	165	138	32	39	6	3	9	33	21	4	0	2	36	1	1	12.7	21.8
Osuna, Alejandro	L-L	6-0	185	10-10-02	.292	.493	.417	15	67	48	10	14	6	0	0	7	16	3	0	0	4	3	23.9	14.9
Piotto, Konner	L-R	5-9	195	1-1-98	.221	.263	.345	36	114	95	10	21	1	0	1	12	16	2	1	2	33	2	1	14.0	28.9
Rodriguez, Keyber	R-R	5-10	178	10-24-00	.294	.400	.412	5	20	17	3	5	2	0	0	1	2	1	0	0	6	1	0	10.0	30.0
Smith, Marcus	L-L	5-11	185	9-11-00	.283	.421	.617	19	76	60	15	17	4	2	4	10	15	0	0	1	26	4	0	19.7	34.2
Solano, Donovan	R-R	5-8	210	12-17-87	.212	.308	.303	10	39	33	1	7	1	0	2	5	0	0	1	10	0	0	12.8	25.6
Strahm, Kellen	R-R	6-0	200	8-12-97	.347	.344	.408	108	429	363	50	88	13	0	8	40	59	1	2	4	91	32	5	13.8	21.2
Tellez, Rowdy	L-L	6-4	270	3-16-95	.333	.375	.800	4	16	15	3	5	1	0	2	4	1	0	0	0	6	3	37.5
Trejo, Alan	R-R	6-2	205	5-30-96	.261	.323	.466	93	381	341	58	89	26	1	14	63	30	3	3	4	90	2	1	7.9	23.6
Wallach, Chad	R-R	6-2	246	11-4-91	.245	.333	.408	28	114	98	15	24	4	0	4	18	13	1	0	2	31	0	0	11.4	27.2
Zavala, Aaron	L-R	6-0	193	6-24-00	.214	.318	.375	16	67	56	8	12	3	0	2	13	9	1	0	1	19	2	2	13.4	28.4

Pitching	B-T	Ht.	Wt.	DOB	W	L	ERA	G	GS	SV	IP	Hits	Runs	ER	HR	BB	SO	AVG	OBP	SLG	SO%	BB%	BF
Abbott, Cory	R-R	6-2	217	9-20-95	3	4	6.48	20	7	0	76	86	59	55	11	38	91	.289	.368	.470	26.2	11.0	347
Acker, Dane	R-R	6-2	189	4-1-99	4	1	5.40	30	1	0	50	59	34	30	5	26	49	.298	.381	.439	21.5	11.4	228
Ahlstrom, Robby	L-L	6-3	195	6-19-99	2	4	3.59	47	0	4	53	45	32	21	4	34	51	.238	.349	.381	22.1	14.7	231
Anderson, Aidan	R-R	6-1	195	6-21-97	5	2	4.84	26	0	1	35	30	22	19	5	24	20	.229	.368	.389	12.1	14.5	165
Anderson, Ben	R-R	6-4	200	5-2-98	1	4	8.16	9	7	0	32	46	34	29	4	17	16	.323	.401	.500	10.5	11.1	153

TEXAS RANGERS

Player	B-T	Ht	Wt	DOB	W	L	ERA	G	SV	IP	H	BB	SO	HR	BB9	SO9	AVG	OBP	SLG			
Barlow, Joe	R-R	6-2	210	9-28-95	5	3	4.57	50	0	2	65	72	35	33	11	26	73	.283	.348	.480	25.7	9.2	284
Blach, Ty	R-L	6-1	215	10-20-90	3	0	3.88	11	11	0	51	61	29	22	5	13	40	.298	.342	.439	17.9	5.8	224
Boushley, Caleb	R-R	6-3	190	10-1-93	2	1	1.08	8	5	0	25	20	4	3	1	9	18	.222	.290	.311	18.0	9.0	100
Buchanan, David	R-R	6-3	200	5-11-89	0	1	5.28	6	6	0	29	38	21	17	5	12	19	.317	.383	.525	14.2	9.0	134
Carrillo, Gerardo	R-R	6-1	170	9-13-98	0	0	7.71	2	0	0	2	4	2	2	0	0	3	.364	.417	.364	25.0	0.0	12
Chargois, JT	S-R	6-3	200	12-3-90	0	1	19.29	5	0	0	5	11	14	10	5	3	7	.478	.536	1.174	24.1	10.3	29
Church, Marc	R-R	6-3	189	3-30-01	0	0	11.57	6	0	0	5	10	6	6	1	9	4	.435	.594	.739	12.5	28.1	32
Collyer, Gavin	R-R	6-1	165	5-12-01	1	1	5.63	14	0	0	16	16	10	10	1	15	21	.258	.400	.355	26.3	18.8	80
Corniell, Jose	R-R	6-3	165	6-22-03	1	1	3.65	3	3	0	12	11	5	5	0	6	14	.234	.333	.340	25.9	11.1	54
Curvelo, Luis	R-R	6-1	170	10-21-00	3	3	3.76	36	0	2	41	34	19	17	4	19	41	.218	.322	.340	22.8	10.6	180
Drake, Kohl	L-L	6-5	220	7-17-00	1	1	5.19	4	3	0	17	20	11	10	2	6	17	.294	.351	.441	23.0	8.1	74
Dugger, Robert	R-R	6-0	198	7-3-95	1	4	14.40	10	4	0	25	41	40	40	9	24	21	.380	.489	.713	15.4	17.6	136
Dunning, Dane	R-R	6-4	225	12-20-94	2	1	4.47	12	11	0	46	41	24	23	6	18	49	.234	.317	.423	24.4	9.0	201
Edwards, Carl	R-R	6-3	165	9-3-91	2	1	5.31	8	7	0	39	44	25	23	6	13	44	.286	.343	.461	26.0	7.7	169
Festa, Matt	R-R	6-1	195	3-11-93	2	0	0.00	9	0	1	15	10	0	0	0	7	20	.185	.290	.204	32.3	11.3	62
Garabito, Gerson	R-R	6-0	160	8-19-95	0	7	8.53	10	10	0	32	39	31	30	8	18	28	.307	.399	.583	18.9	12.2	148
Garcia, Ryan	R-R	6-0	180	1-24-98	2	4	7.64	27	6	0	55	59	48	47	15	41	57	.276	.392	.528	21.8	15.7	261
Gray, Jon	R-R	6-4	225	11-5-91	0	0	3.18	2	2	0	6	4	2	2	1	2	6	.200	.261	.450	26.1	8.7	23
Gray, Peyton	R-R	6-4	235	6-2-95	5	6	3.84	38	2	1	61	67	29	26	8	23	68	.283	.350	.443	25.8	8.7	264
Hales, Skylar	R-R	6-4	220	10-24-01	0	1	15.95	7	0	0	9	13	13	4	6	8	.321*	.457	.821	21.1	15.8	38	
Heuer, Codi	R-R	6-5	200	7-3-96	3	2	3.43	35	0	4	39	36	18	15	4	15	53	.242	.321	.369	31.4	8.9	169
Hoffman, Nolan	R-R	6-4	190	8-9-97	2	0	5.91	22	3	0	35	30	23	23	4	21	46	.234	.369	.398	28.9	13.2	159
Houser, Adrian	R-R	6-3	242	2-2-93	2	2	5.03	9	8	0	39	30	22	22	4	15	37	.214	.311	.343	22.8	9.3	162
Kimbrel, Craig	R-R	6-0	215	5-28-88	0	1	3.86	24	0	5	21	12	10	9	4	12	28	.158	.293	.316	30.4	13.0	92
Krauth, Nick	R-R	6-3	170	9-6-99	0	0	7.71	5	0	0	7	11	6	6	1	3	6	.367	.424	.567	17.6	8.8	34
Latz, Jake	R-L	6-2	185	4-8-96	0	2	1.84	9	1	0	15	10	5	3	1	11	22	.179	.313	.286	32.8	16.4	67
Leiter, Jack	R-R	6-1	205	4-21-00	0	0	0.00	1	1	0	5	1	0	0	0	1	4	.071	.133	.071	26.7	6.7	15
Mahle, Tyler	R-R	6-3	210	9-29-94	0	0	6.14	3	3	0	8	8	5	5	1	2	10	.276	.323	.448	32.3	6.5	31
Murphy, Patrick	R-R	6-5	211	6-10-95	1	2	3.18	14	2	0	23	23	9	8	0	10	16	.271	.340	.318	16.5	10.3	97
Piotto, Konner	L-R	5-9	195	1-1-98	0	0	18.00	2	0	0	1	3	2	2	1	2	0	.500	.625	1.167	0.0	25.0	8
Plassmeyer, Michael	L-L	6-2	197	11-5-96	9	4	4.43	28	16	0	106	102	58	52	17	34	99	.252	.318	.415	21.9	7.5	452
Quantrill, Cal	L-R	6-2	195	2-10-95	1	0	1.64	2	2	0	11	8	4	2	1	1	14	.195	.214	.390	33.3	2.4	42
Robert, Daniel	L-R	6-4	210	8-30-94	0	0	1.54	10	0	2	12	11	4	2	0	4	17	.244	.300	.289	34.0	8.0	50
Rocker, Kumar	R-R	6-5	245	11-22-99	1	0	3.94	4	4	0	16	14	7	7	2	3	15	.237	.266	.424	23.1	4.6	65
Ruiz, Jose	R-R	6-1	245	10-21-94	1	0	2.31	20	0	7	23	19	6	6	1	6	24	.229	.283	.277	25.8	6.5	93
Sanders, Josh	R-R	6-3	180	10-22-01	0	0	0.00	1	0	0	1	1	0	0	0	0	1	.250	.400	.500	0.0	20.0	5
Santos, Winston	R-R	6-0	160	4-15-02	0	0	2.45	1	1	0	4	3	1	1	0	2	4	.231	.333	.308	26.7	13.3	15
Sborz, Josh	R-R	6-3	215	12-17-93	1	2	5.79	10	1	0	9	15	7	6	2	6	9	.375	.447	.600	19.1	12.8	47
Serrano, Florencio	R-R	6-1	205	2-23-00	0	1	5.06	6	0	0	11	14	10	6	3	5	8	.298	.365	.553	15.4	9.6	52
Stephan, Josh	R-R	6-3	185	11-1-01	1	0	2.35	2	1	0	8	8	2	2	1	3	6	.267	.371	.400	17.1	8.6	35
Strickland, Hunter	R-R	6-3	225	9-24-88	1	2	8.22	12	0	0	15	20	14	14	3	9	15	.323	.408	.581	21.1	12.7	71
Supak, Trey	R-R	6-5	268	5-31-96	4	2	3.55	12	12	0	58	51	25	23	6	18	55	.231	.293	.371	22.6	7.4	243
Teodo, Emiliano	R-R	6-1	165	2-14-01	2	1	9.00	14	0	0	18	19	19	18	4	17	23	.260	.407	.479	25.3	18.7	91
Trejo, Alan	R-R	6-2	205	5-30-96	0	0	18.00	1	0	0	1	3	2	2	0	1	0	.500	.571	.833	0.0	14.3	7
Webb, Jacob	R-R	6-2	210	8-15-93	0	0	2.70	3	0	0	3	3	1	1	0	1	4	.231	.333	.231	26.7	6.7	15
Winn, Cole	R-R	6-2	190	11-25-99	3	1	0.59	17	0	0	31	17	5	2	1	14	25	.165	.265	.194	21.2	11.9	118

Fielding

Catcher	PCT	G	PO	A	E	DP	PB
Barnhart	.993	28	273	15	2	1	1
Emshoff	1.000	1	1	0	0	0	0
Higashioka	1.000	1	5	0	0	0	0
Johnson	.990	70	562	38	6	4	2
Marrero	1.000	2	11	1	0	0	1
Mitchell	.955	4	21	0	1	0	0
Narvaez	.985	19	185	6	3	0	1
Piotto	1.000	21	148	4	0	0	6
Wallach	.994	16	143	10	1	1	4

First Base	PCT	G	PO	A	E	DP
Burger	1.000	6	37	4	0	4
Crim	.994	68	480	39	3	59
Foscue	.994	47	300	35	2	35
Freeman	1.000	1	7	0	0	0
Harris	1.000	1	1	1	0	0
McKinney	.959	7	45	2	2	7
Ortiz	.982	23	149	15	3	10
Piotto	1.000	2	9	2	0	1
Solano	1.000	1	1	0	0	0
Tellez	1.000	2	13	2	0	1
Trejo	.000	1	0	0	0	0
Wallach	1.000	4	19	1	0	4

Second Base	PCT	G	PO	A	E	DP
Biggers	1.000	1	1	1	0	0
Chavez	1.000	5	7	13	0	3
De Goti	.986	57	100	108	3	30
Foscue	.967	51	78	128	7	34
Freeman	.987	15	39	37	1	9
Haggerty	1.000	4	7	14	0	5
Helman	1.000	4	3	8	0	1
Moore	1.000	1	1	3	0	0
Ornelas	.960	6	6	18	1	5
Rodriguez	1.000	1	0	1	0	0
Trejo	.988	16	36	48	1	13

Third Base	PCT	G	PO	A	E	DP
Chavez	.944	6	6	11	1	0
De Goti	.929	11	7	19	2	2
Duran	.889	4	1	7	1	1
Freeman	.942	63	62	116	11	20
Jung	1.000	7	2	8	0	2
Martin	.878	21	13	30	6	5
Ornelas	1.000	4	3	6	0	0
Rodriguez	1.000	3	2	5	0	0
Solano	1.000	8	2	9	0	0
Trejo	.971	30	16	52	2	6

Shortstop	PCT	G	PO	A	E	DP
Biggers	1.000	4	6	4	0	0
Duran	1.000	10	14	15	0	6
Freeman	.972	11	6	29	1	6
Haggerty	1.000	1	2	3	0	0
Helman	.971	23	21	45	2	11
Martin	.984	55	69	114	3	19
Ornelas	.971	17	17	49	2	9
Rodriguez	1.000	1	0	2	0	0
Trejo	.955	37	38	89	6	24

Outfield	PCT	G	PO	A	E	DP
Biggers	1.000	3	6	2	0	0
Carter	.978	22	42	2	1	1
De Goti	1.000	24	29	3	0	0
Freeman	1.000	4	9	0	0	0
Haggerty	1.000	16	30	0	0	0
Harris	.980	91	197	0	4	0
Hauver	.974	79	108	4	3	1
Helman	1.000	26	66	1	0	1
McKinney	.987	50	75	2	1	0
Ornelas	.857	2	6	0	1	0
Ortiz	.964	15	27	0	1	0
Osuna	1.000	15	31	0	0	0
Smith	.926	18	24	1	2	0
Strahm	.982	106	212	4	4	2
Zavala	.966	15	28	0	1	0

FRISCO ROUGHRIDERS
TEXAS LEAGUE
DOUBLE-A

Batting	B-T	Ht.	Wt.	DOB	AVG	OBP	SLG	G	PA	AB	R	H	2B	3B	HR	RBI	BB	HBP	SH	SF	SO	SB	CS	BB%	SO%
Antonini, Aaron	L-R	6-0	200	7-27-98	.308	.357	.385	4	14	13	2	4	1	0	0	3	1	0	0	0	1	0	0	7.1	7.1
Biggers, Jax	L-R	5-8	175	4-7-97	.229	.381	.284	67	253	201	37	46	6	1	1	23	50	0	1	1	56	11	3	19.8	22.1
Brock, Julian	R-R	6-3	220	6-3-01	.321	.400	.446	17	65	56	7	18	4	0	1	10	7	1	0	1	16	3	2	10.8	24.6
Burger, Jake	R-R	6-2	230	4-10-96	.182	.250	.273	3	12	11	0	2	1	0	0	0	1	0	0	0	1	0	0	8.3	8.3
Carter, Evan	L-R	6-2	190	8-29-02	.000	.600	.000	2	5	2	0	0	0	0	0	0	2	1	0	0	0	0	0	40.0	0.0
Cauley, Cameron	R-R	5-10	170	2-6-03	.253	.325	.448	113	490	435	74	110	26	7	15	51	47	2	1	5	121	28	7	9.6	24.7
Chavez, Frainyer	S-R	5-8	170	5-24-99	.254	.345	.333	98	395	342	51	87	12	0	5	32	46	3	1	3	86	6	9	11.6	21.8
Emshoff, Kale	R-R	6-2	228	5-2-98	.100	.182	.100	3	11	10	0	1	0	0	0	0	1	0	0	0	4	0	0	9.1	36.4
Haggerty, Sam	S-R	5-11	175	5-26-94	.000	.000	.000	1	4	4	0	0	0	0	0	0	0	0	0	0	1	0	0	0.0	25.0
Hardy, Theo	S-R	6-1	185	11-27-01	.222	.282	.278	14	39	36	3	8	2	0	0	6	3	0	0	0	8	1	1	7.7	20.5
Hatcher, Josh	L-L	6-2	200	9-3-98	.234	.261	.345	90	376	359	35	84	11	1	9	51	13	1	0	3	106	10	5	3.5	28.2
Johnson, Cooper	R-R	6-1	209	4-25-98	.267	.380	.500	18	71	60	9	16	5	0	3	8	10	1	0	0	24	0	0	14.1	33.8
Jones, Keith	L-L	6-2	210	4-29-02	.244	.333	.381	52	201	176	21	43	9	3	3	26	23	1	0	1	51	8	2	11.4	25.4
Jung, Josh	R-R	6-2	214	2-12-98	.400	.500	.400	2	6	5	0	2	0	0	0	2	1	0	0	0	0	0	0	16.7	0.0
Langford, Wyatt	R-R	6-1	225	11-15-01	.333	.455	1.000	3	11	9	3	3	0	0	2	2	2	0	0	0	1	0	0	18.2	9.1
Marrero, Elih	S-R	5-7	185	6-21-97	.233	.270	.300	18	63	60	7	14	4	0	0	7	3	0	0	0	18	1	2	4.8	28.6
Mendez, Wady	L-L	6-0	155	10-14-04	.000	.000	.000	6	2	2	2	0	0	0	0	0	0	0	0	0	1	0	0	0.0	50.0
Mieses, Luis	L-L	6-3	180	5-31-00	.234	.290	.388	109	428	394	45	92	15	2	14	54	31	1	0	2	85	1	2	7.2	19.9
Mitchell, Tucker	R-R	6-1	210	2-10-01	.218	.241	.261	53	170	165	7	36	4	0	1	15	2	3	0	0	49	3	0	1.2	28.8
Moller, Ian	R-R	6-0	190	10-26-02	.207	.306	.295	77	289	251	27	52	10	0	4	29	35	1	1	1	87	2	2	12.1	30.1
Ortiz, Abimelec	L-L	6-0	220	2-22-02	.247	.343	.444	89	391	340	53	84	19	0	16	56	44	6	0	1	87	3	1	11.3	22.3
Osuna, Alejandro	L-L	6-0	185	10-10-02	.267	.351	.377	37	169	146	28	39	6	2	2	16	13	7	1	2	25	10	2	7.7	14.8
Pederson, Joc	L-L	6-1	220	4-21-92	.333	.429	.333	2	7	6	1	2	0	0	0	0	1	0	0	0	2	0	0	14.3	28.6
Pillar, Kevin	R-R	6-0	200	1-4-89	.100	.100	.100	3	10	10	1	1	0	0	0	0	0	0	0	0	1	0	0	0.0	10.0
Rodriguez, Keyber	R-R	5-10	178	10-24-00	.251	.310	.316	116	481	434	47	109	18	2	2	42	37	3	1	6	91	14	5	7.7	18.9
Smith, Marcus	L-L	5-11	185	9-11-00	.140	.230	.252	53	162	143	16	20	2	1	4	16	16	1	1	1	71	3	0	9.9	43.8
Sulbaran, Juan	R-R	5-11	165	10-1-051.000	1.000	1.000	1	1	1	0	1	0	0	0	0	0	0	0	0	0	0	0	0.0	0.0
Walcott, Sebastian	R-R	6-4	190	3-14-06	.255	.355	.386	124	552	474	71	121	19	2	13	59	70	5	0	3	108	32	10	12.7	19.6
Zavala, Aaron	L-R	6-0	193	6-24-00	.246	.359	.420	108	471	395	71	97	17	5	14	55	66	6	0	4	139	8	4	14.0	29.5

Pitching	B-T	Ht.	Wt.	DOB	W	L	ERA	G	GS	SV	IP	Hits	Runs	ER	HR	BB	SO	AVG	OBP	SLG	SO%	BB%	BF
Ahlstrom, Robby	L-L	6-3	195	6-19-99	0	0	1.17	6	0	4	8	5	1	1	0	2	11	.185	.241	.222	37.9	6.9	29
Anderson, Aidan	R-R	6-1	195	6-21-97	1	0	0.00	8	0	0	5	5	0	0	0	1	8	.192	.222	.269	29.6	3.7	27
Anderson, Ben	R-R	6-4	200	5-2-98	4	5	4.65	17	15	0	79	86	43	41	7	29	54	.277	.338	.431	15.6	8.4	346
Bormie, Wilian	R-R	6-3	175	2-23-03	1	0	2.31	12	0	1	12	12	3	3	0	8	14	.267	.377	.311	26.4	15.1	53
Bratt, Mitch	L-L	6-1	190	7-6-03	3	3	3.18	18	17	0	91	91	33	32	13	16	106	.259	.299	.442	28.5	4.3	372
Carrillo, Gerardo	R-R	6-1	170	9-13-98	2	3	3.69	40	0	7	46	38	22	19	2	19	53	.218	.308	.310	26.8	9.6	198
Chavez, Frainyer	S-R	5-8	170	5-24-99	0	0	0.00	2	0	0	2	3	1	0	0	0	0	.300	.300	.300	0.0	0.0	10
Collyer, Gavin	R-R	6-1	165	5-12-01	4	5	3.97	37	0	8	45	35	23	20	3	31	65	.207	.338	.325	31.3	14.9	208
Corniell, Jose	R-R	6-3	165	6-22-03	0	0	0.45	6	6	0	20	5	2	1	0	1	20	.078	.106	.109	30.3	1.5	66
Coulombe, Danny	L-L	5-10	190	10-26-89	0	0	0.00	2	0	0	2	2	0	0	0	0	2	.250	.333	.250	22.2	0.0	9
Danielson, Joey	R-R	6-3	235	1-11-01	1	1	6.14	15	0	0	15	15	12	10	2	14	19	.273	.420	.382	27.1	20.0	70
Davalillo, David	R-R	6-1	175	9-21-02	2	3	2.73	12	11	0	56	40	17	17	4	17	58	.196	.270	.319	25.7	7.5	220
Drake, Kohl	L-L	6-5	220	7-17-00	4	3	2.44	12	12	0	55	32	17	15	5	22	70	.164	.256	.313	31.8	10.0	220
Gonzalez, Jose	R-R	6-3	200	8-5-01	2	2	3.41	5	5	0	29	27	13	11	0	6	24	.241	.301	.330	19.5	4.9	123
Gray, Peyton	R-R	6-4	235	6-2-95	3	0	2.25	7	0	0	12	5	3	3	0	4	21	.128	.209	.205	48.8	9.3	43
Hales, Skylar	R-R	6-4	220	10-24-01	1	4	5.26	27	0	5	26	21	16	15	3	8	32	.223	.305	.351	30.2	7.5	106
Ireland, Thomas	L-L	6-1	170	6-27-02	1	0	3.86	3	0	1	7	6	3	3	0	3	3	.240	.321	.360	10.7	10.7	28
Jennings, Steven	R-R	6-2	175	11-13-98	1	0	5.68	5	0	0	6	7	5	4	2	5	6	.280	.375	.560	18.8	15.6	32
Kelley, Jackson	R-R	6-0	185	4-26-00	2	1	2.40	20	0	0	30	22	9	8	1	17	26	.206	.344	.280	19.8	13.0	131
Kindreich, Larson	L-L	6-4	210	6-21-99	5	4	4.56	35	0	2	51	52	26	26	8	22	61	.263	.338	.485	27.4	9.9	223
Krauth, Nick	R-R	6-3	170	9-6-99	2	0	4.50	10	0	1	26	34	16	13	4	9	20	.318	.393	.495	16.3	7.3	123
Lara, Janser	R-R	6-0	170	8-10-96	1	0	3.32	11	0	1	19	15	9	7	1	5	23	.214	.286	.329	29.5	6.4	78
Lobus, Peyton	R-R	6-2	180	9-7-00	7	3	3.48	45	3	0	67	51	31	26	5	27	82	.208	.305	.322	28.9	9.5	284
Loomis, Eric	R-R	6-0	195	3-27-02	0	0	7.04	7	0	2	8	7	6	6	1	6	15	.250	.436	.357	38.5	15.4	39
Lopez, Leandro	R-R	6-1	200	6-17-02	1	0	2.78	9	8	0	36	25	11	11	3	15	43	.197	.282	.331	30.3	10.6	142
MacGregor, Travis	R-R	6-4	215	10-15-97	0	3	5.31	36	0	2	41	34	26	24	1	26	44	.231	.367	.320	24.2	14.3	182
Magdaleno, Bryan	L-L	6-1	202	2-22-01	2	0	6.31	36	0	2	36	32	31	25	0	44	45	.239	.441	.306	24.2	23.7	186
Martin, Chris	R-R	6-8	225	6-2-86	0	0	0.00	1	0	0	1	0	0	0	0	0	1	.000	.000	.000	33.3	0.0	3
Missaki, Daniel	R-R	6-0	170	4-9-96	0	5	4.38	30	8	2	74	73	41	36	7	30	83	.255	.341	.392	25.0	9.0	332
Mollerus, Josh	R-R	6-3	215	10-6-99	1	2	7.27	7	0	0	9	11	7	7	3	5	7	.297	.381	.568	16.7	11.9	42
Rocker, Kumar	R-R	6-5	245	11-22-99	0	0	0.00	1	1	0	3	2	0	0	0	0	6	.200	.200	.300	30.0	0.0	10
Sanders, Josh	R-R	6-3	180	10-22-01	0	0	2.70	3	0	0	3	2	1	1	0	1	1	.167	.167	.417	8.3	0.0	12
Santos, Winston	R-R	6-0	160	4-15-02	0	1	7.90	5	5	0	14	19	13	12	2	5	22	.328	.381	.431	34.9	7.9	63
Sborz, Josh	R-R	6-3	215	12-17-93	0	0	3.38	2	0	0	3	1	1	1	0	2	3	.111	.273	.111	27.3	18.2	11
Serrano, Florencio	R-R	6-1	205	2-23-00	2	2	5.40	10	3	0	25	17	14	15	5	15	25	.269	.310	.419	15.0	5.0	100
Stephan, Josh	R-R	6-3	185	11-1-01	6	7	4.85	23	21	0	104	112	60	56	15	28	85	.271	.326	.435	18.8	6.2	452
Supak, Trey	R-R	6-5	268	5-31-96	6	3	4.09	14	14	0	70	63	33	32	2	15	76	.240	.299	.332	26.3	5.2	289

Teodo, Emiliano	R-R	6-1	165	2-14-01	1	1	5.59	11	0	0	10	6	7	6	0	12	10	.171	.396	.257	20.8	25.0	48
Trentadue, Josh	L-L	6-2	185	1-25-02	0	1	5.24	7	7	0	22	23	13	13	3	16	23	.264	.393	.425	21.5	15.0	107
Weems, Avery	R-L	6-2	205	6-6-97	4	1	6.63	34	0	3	38	48	32	28	7	13	44	.300	.356	.494	25.3	7.5	174

Fielding

Catcher	PCT	G	PO	A	E	DP	PB
Antonini	1.000	3	24	0	0	0	0
Brock	.993	13	133	7	1	1	0
Emshoff	.917	1	11	0	1	0	0
Johnson	.994	17	160	14	1	0	2
Marrero	.978	9	87	3	2	0	1
Mitchell	.986	30	270	13	4	1	2
Moller	.998	70	635	30	1	5	4

First Base	PCT	G	PO	A	E	DP
Brock	1.000	1	5	0	0	0
Burger	1.000	1	7	2	0	0
Chavez	.997	48	293	44	1	32
Hatcher	1.000	26	163	17	0	18
Mieses	.963	5	25	1	1	2
Mitchell	1.000	13	71	4	0	8
Ortiz	.992	50	338	27	3	30
Pederson	1.000	1	4	0	0	0

Second Base	PCT	G	PO	A	E	DP
Biggers	.987	63	89	137	3	30
Cauley	.990	25	44	53	1	14
Chavez	.984	31	44	83	2	15
Hardy	.957	13	19	26	2	6
Rodriguez	1.000	13	34	31	0	7

Third Base	PCT	G	PO	A	E	DP
Biggers	.909	2	0	10	1	0
Chavez	.955	21	8	34	2	4
Hardy	1.000	2	2	3	0	0
Jung	1.000	1	1	1	0	0
Rodriguez	.970	98	66	128	6	10
Walcott	.957	17	16	29	2	5

Shortstop	PCT	G	PO	A	E	DP
Cauley	.969	48	61	96	5	18
Rodriguez	1.000	5	6	15	0	4
Walcott	.924	88	114	177	24	42

Outfield	PCT	G	PO	A	E	DP
Biggers	1.000	5	5	0	0	0
Cauley	.978	43	87	3	2	1
Hatcher	1.000	62	116	2	0	1
Jones	.984	40	63	0	1	0
Langford	1.000	2	3	0	0	0
Marrero	.000	2	0	0	0	0
Mendez	1.000	3	3	0	0	0
Mieses	.991	75	106	5	1	0
Ortiz	1.000	20	35	1	0	0
Osuna	1.000	36	97	0	0	0
Pillar	1.000	1	1	0	0	0
Smith	.992	54	120	2	1	1
Zavala	.973	101	177	4	5	1

HUB CITY SPARTANBURGERS — HIGH-A
SOUTH ATLANTIC LEAGUE

Batting	B-T	Ht.	Wt.	DOB	AVG	OBP	SLG	G	PA	AB	R	H	2B	3B	HR	RBI	BB	HBP	SH	SF	SO	SB	CS	BB%	SO%
Brock, Julian	R-R	6-3	220	6-3-01	.208	.278	.290	62	245	221	29	46	12	0	2	24	18	4	0	2	66	10	5	7.3	26.9
Cook, Casey	L-R	6-0	195	10-2-02	.205	.302	.294	119	493	425	57	87	16	2	6	50	52	9	3	4	106	29	12	10.5	21.5
Cueva, Danyer	L-R	6-1	160	5-27-04	.248	.287	.327	34	123	113	15	28	6	0	1	9	6	1	2	1	25	5	0	4.9	20.3
Disla, Arturo	L-R	6-2	240	10-8-00	.223	.292	.352	99	411	372	34	83	21	0	9	36	33	4	0	2	95	7	1	8.0	23.1
Dreiling, Dylan	L-L	5-11	197	4-17-03	.226	.319	.381	110	483	420	50	95	21	4	12	62	58	1	0	4	101	15	5	12.0	20.9
Figuereo, Gleider	L-R	6-0	165	6-27-04	.201	.287	.353	113	464	408	44	82	8	0	18	62	44	7	0	5	132	6	3	9.5	28.4
Gutierrez, Anthony	R-R	6-3	180	11-25-04	.258	.333	.320	89	381	337	53	87	15	0	2	28	31	8	3	2	79	48	9	8.1	20.7
Hanson, Luke	R-R	6-2	185	8-26-03	.364	.440	.409	8	25	22	3	8	1	0	0	4	2	1	0	0	8	1	1	8.0	32.0
Hardy, Theo	S-R	6-1	185	11-27-01	.192	.349	.232	42	127	99	21	19	2	1	0	13	21	4	1	2	33	6	2	16.5	26.0
Hartl, Ben	R-R	5-11	200	1-7-03	.375	.521	.429	18	73	56	11	21	3	0	0	11	9	8	0	0	17	1	1	12.3	23.3
Jones, Keith	L-L	6-2	210	4-29-02	.270	.406	.451	68	294	237	33	64	13	0	10	35	51	4	1	1	79	15	5	17.3	26.9
Kling, Paxton	R-R	6-2	210	5-26-04	.244	.320	.311	11	50	45	6	11	3	0	0	2	4	1	0	0	10	1	1	8.0	20.0
Macias, Antonis	S-L	5-11	185	2-1-05	.288	.362	.385	16	59	52	8	15	2	0	1	7	6	0	1	0	13	1	1	10.2	22.0
Marquez, Luis	R-R	5-10	150	8-31-05	.333	.368	.413	20	68	63	6	21	5	0	0	7	4	0	0	1	18	0	0	5.9	26.5
Martin, Max	L-R	6-1	205	5-5-05	.256	.385	.488	14	52	43	9	11	2	1	2	3	7	2	0	0	14	2	0	13.5	26.9
Mejia, Esteban	R-R	5-11	165	11-3-04	.235	.323	.383	69	287	243	39	57	13	0	10	38	25	1	0	0	99	4	1	8.7	34.5
Mendez, Wady	L-L	6-0	155	10-14-04	.154	.343	.173	23	67	52	10	8	1	0	0	2	14	1	0	0	16	5	1	20.9	23.9
Moore, Malcolm	L-R	6-2	210	7-31-03	.198	.293	.271	57	242	207	25	41	9	0	2	22	20	10	0	5	47	4	1	8.3	19.4
Morrobel, Yeison	L-L	6-2	170	7-26-04	.248	.295	.328	77	298	270	22	46	9	1	6	24	25	3	0	0	59	4	1	8.4	19.8
Perich, Rafe	S-R	6-3	225	5-22-02	.202	.322	.274	38	146	124	14	25	3	0	2	14	21	1	0	0	30	2	0	14.4	20.5
Pollard, Chandler	R-R	6-2	173	5-3-04	.000	.000	.000	1	3	3	0	0	0	0	0	0	0	0	0	0	1	0	0	0.0	33.3
Scott, Quincy	R-R	6-4	215	1-15-03	.231	.328	.321	78	273	234	29	54	9	0	4	23	32	3	2	2	79	15	3	11.7	28.9
Smith, Marcus	L-L	5-11	185	9-11-00	.158	.304	.289	16	46	38	7	6	0	1	1	4	8	0	0	0	15	2	0	17.4	32.6
Stark, Cal	R-R	6-1	204	7-27-02	.180	.270	.246	41	144	122	15	22	2	0	2	12	11	5	3	3	57	2	3	7.6	39.6
Sulbaran, Juan	R-R	5-11	165	10-1-05	.000	.000	.000	1	4	4	0	0	0	0	0	0	0	0	0	0	1	0	0	25.0
Taylor, John	L-R	6-0	200	4-26-01	.256	.336	.352	58	223	199	25	51	11	1	2	20	20	4	0	0	46	7	3	9.0	20.6
Vargas, Jhocsuanth	R-R	5-11	170	8-31-06	.143	.143	.143	2	7	7	1	1	0	0	0	1	0	0	0	0	2	0	0	0.0	28.6

Pitching	B-T	Ht.	Wt.	DOB	W	L	ERA	G	GS	SV	IP	Hits	Runs	ER	HR	BB	SO	AVG	OBP	SLG	SO%	BB%	BF
Agreda, Ismael	R-R	6-0	150	10-8-03	1	0	0.00	1	0	0	3	3	1	0	0	1	2	.250	.308	.250	15.4	7.7	13
Bonzagni, Paul	R-R	6-3	195	4-1-02	0	1	4.82	3	2	0	9	11	6	5	1	5	15	.282	.378	.359	33.3	11.1	45
Bormie, Wilian	R-R	6-3	175	2-23-03	3	6	3.12	33	0	6	52	39	21	18	3	29	76	.209	.329	.289	34.2	13.1	222
Church, Marc	R-R	6-3	189	3-30-01	0	1	18.00	1	0	0	1	3	2	2	0	0	3	.500	.500	.500	50.0	0.0	6
Clark, Seth	R-L	6-3	220	11-18-99	2	4	6.25	28	0	3	32	29	31	22	1	27	35	.238	.380	.232	23.0	17.8	152
Curry, Aidan	R-R	6-5	185	7-5-02	3	2	4.01	17	13	1	58	52	28	26	5	41	77	.232	.353	.397	28.9	15.4	266
Curtis, Kolton	S-R	6-4	170	5-5-04	3	3	5.18	19	16	0	66	50	43	38	4	44	75	.211	.346	.321	25.9	15.2	290
Danielson, Joey	R-R	6-3	235	1-11-01	3	3	3.70	34	0	4	41	46	19	17	4	15	48	.275	.339	.467	26.1	8.2	184
Davalillo, David	R-R	6-1	175	9-21-02	4	1	2.12	11	11	0	51	31	13	12	2	11	68	.170	.231	.253	34.0	5.5	200
Felix, Mailon	R-R	6-4	205	11-29-99	3	3	4.13	37	0	2	48	43	29	22	2	35	42	.251	.405	.333	19.0	15.8	221
Fowler, Brooks	R-R	6-3	205	1-29-03	2	1	2.21	5	2	0	20	5	5	5	1	12	16	.174	.296	.246	19.5	14.6	82
Gamez, Jesus	R-R	6-0	190	3-4-03	0	1	1.80	12	0	2	15	5	3	3	0	16	24	.064	.297	.085	37.5	25.0	64
Gonzalez, Jose	R-R	6-3	200	6-14-99	4	7	2.83	18	17	0	86	80	33	27	7	18	90	.244	.295	.366	25.4	5.1	355
Hardy, Theo	S-R	6-1	185	11-27-01	0	0	0.00	1	0	0	1	0	0	0	0	0	0	.333	.333	.333	0.0	0.0	3
Ireland, Thomas	L-L	6-1	170	6-27-02	0	0	4.50	6	0	0	14	13	9	7	0	5	9	.260	.339	.380	15.8	8.8	57
Kindreich, Larson	L-L	6-4	210	6-21-99	3	0	0.00	7	0	2	12	2	1	0	0	7	17	.054	.222	.054	37.8	15.6	45
Loomis, Ben	R-R	6-1	195	3-27-02	3	0	1.80	25	0	4	35	13	7	7	0	16	55	.116	.261	.152	40.1	11.7	137
Lopez, Leandro	R-R	6-1	200	6-17-02	2	4	2.19	14	14	0	66	46	21	16	4	26	73	.199	.279	.294	28.2	10.0	259
MacLean, Dylan	R-L	6-4	190	7-12-02	4	1	3.34	16	15	0	73	53	30	27	9	15	65	.200	.243	.366	22.8	5.3	285

TEXAS RANGERS

Batting	B-T	Ht.	Wt.	DOB	G	AVG	OBP	SLG	G	PA	AB	R	H	2B	3B	HR	RBI	BB	HBP	SH	SF	SO	SB	CS	BB%	SO%
Matter, Case	R-R	6-2	180	1-16-02	0	1	15.00	6	0	0	6	6	10	10	1	7	10	.250	.438	.375	31.3	21.9	32			
McCarty, D.J.	R-R	6-2	145	9-9-02	2	6	4.83	23	17	0	88	93	53	47	4	52	98	.276	.397	.344	23.9	12.7	410			
Molina, Mason	R-L	6-2	215	7-8-03	1	2	2.63	7	6	0	27	18	9	8	0	12	30	.191	.291	.245	27.3	10.9	110			
Mollerus, Josh	R-R	6-3	215	10-6-99	6	2	2.57	21	0	1	35	21	14	10	3	11	31	.178	.242	.263	23.3	8.3	133			
Pence, Dalton	L-L	6-2	205	8-28-02	1	3	1.55	14	11	0	46	32	12	8	0	16	51	.192	.259	.234	27.6	8.6	185			
Porter, Brock	R-R	6-4	208	6-3-03	0	0	0.00	1	0	0	1	0	0	0	0	2	2	.000	.500	.000	50.0	50.0	4			
Rodriguez, Adrian	R-R	6-5	192	5-18-01	1	1	2.11	16	0	1	21	9	5	5	0	16	39	.129	.303	.157	43.8	18.0	89			
Sanders, Josh	R-R	6-3	180	10-22-01	2	2	3.71	14	0	0	27	25	12	11	2	9	18	.250	.322	.350	15.7	7.8	115			
Scarborough, Caden	R-R	6-5	180	4-1-05	0	0	0.00	3	3	0	13	6	0	0	0	2	19	.133	.204	.133	38.8	4.1	49			
Serrano, Florencio	R-R	6-1	205	2-23-00	0	0	0.00	1	0	0	3	2	0	0	0	0	2	.182	.182	.182	18.2	0.0	11			
Simeon, Victor	R-R	6-2	160	12-4-00	4	0	4.43	36	0	5	45	31	24	22	1	44	66	.196	.385	.285	31.7	21.2	208			
Susac, Anthony	R-R	6-3	212	7-31-02	3	5	5.11	37	0	1	44	42	28	25	4	38	44	.253	.392	.398	21.1	18.2	209			
Trentadue, Josh	L-L	6-2	185	1-25-02	1	2	1.15	15	9	1	55	28	11	7	2	18	71	.148	.232	.249	33.6	8.5	211			
Villavicencio, Adonis	R-R	6-2	200	12-22-00	4	3	6.33	37	0	3	48	56	40	34	3	35	49	.292	.429	.406	20.5	14.6	239			
Wynyard, Kai-Noa	R-R	6-0	176	6-22-02	0	1	5.91	8	0	0	11	7	8	7	0	10	7	.200	.370	.314	15.2	21.7	46			

Fielding

Catcher	PCT	G	PO	A	E	DP	PB
Brock	.989	57	601	39	7	3	11
Hartl	.989	14	166	14	2	0	1
Moore	.992	38	346	20	3	1	6
Stark	.986	21	207	12	3	2	2
Vargas	.952	2	19	1	1	0	0

First Base	PCT	G	PO	A	E	DP
Disla	.988	80	540	56	7	63
Gutierrez	1.000	4	28	0	0	3
Macias	.949	7	36	1	2	6
Mejia	1.000	4	22	2	0	2
Perich	.992	18	115	7	1	11
Scott	.982	17	105	7	2	5
Stark	1.000	10	54	5	0	6

Second Base	PCT	G	PO	A	E	DP
Cook	.966	95	120	190	11	35

Third Base	PCT	G	PO	A	E	DP
Cueva	1.000	2	3	1	0	0
Figueroa	.962	107	74	152	9	20
Mejia	.889	7	7	9	2	1
Perich	.951	15	12	27	2	3
Taylor	1.000	2	0	1	0	0

Shortstop	PCT	G	PO	A	E	DP
Cook	.963	18	22	30	2	11
Cueva	.948	24	33	58	5	7
Hanson	1.000	7	7	14	0	2
Hardy	.936	31	39	63	7	23
Marquez	.926	8	10	15	2	2

Cueva	.955	7	19	23	2	9
Hardy	.971	6	11	23	1	5
Marquez	.952	11	17	23	2	7
Mejia	1.000	3	6	6	0	4
Taylor	.978	11	18	27	1	9

	PCT	G	PO	A	E	DP
Mejia	.952	6	9	11	1	2
Pollard	1.000	1	1	2	0	0
Taylor	.960	40	48	73	5	12

Outfield	PCT	G	PO	A	E	DP
Cook	1.000	4	0	2	0	0
Disla	.000	1	0	0	0	0
Dreiling	.970	104	188	3	6	0
Gutierrez	.952	33	73	7	4	3
Jones	.955	56	81	3	4	0
Kling	1.000	11	23	2	0	0
Macias	1.000	11	19	0	0	0
Martin	.964	14	27	0	1	0
Mendez	.956	21	42	1	2	0
Morrobel	1.000	77	103	4	0	0
Scott	.983	62	113	6	2	4
Smith	.923	14	24	0	2	0
Stark	1.000	5	5	1	0	0
Taylor	1.000	2	2	1	0	0

HICKORY CRAWDADS — LOW-A
CAROLINA LEAGUE

Batting	B-T	Ht.	Wt.	DOB	AVG	OBP	SLG	G	PA	AB	R	H	2B	3B	HR	RBI	BB	HBP	SH	SF	SO	SB	CS	BB%	SO%
Alvarez, Erick	R-R	5-10	150	2-1-05	.222	.325	.278	39	152	126	22	28	7	0	0	12	21	0	1	4	30	4	1	13.8	19.7
Arredondo, Angel	R-R	5-8	160	10-25-06	.045	.087	.045	6	23	22	1	1	0	0	0	1	1	0	0	0	15	1	0	4.3	47.8
Barroso, Beycker	R-R	5-10	160	1-24-03	.194	.333	.245	49	198	155	21	30	8	0	0	14	17	17	5	3	35	8	3	8.6	17.7
Cabrera, Yeremi	L-L	5-11	155	7-2-05	.256	.364	.366	102	451	383	66	98	12	3	8	52	52	14	1	1	86	43	4	11.5	19.1
Castillo, Yolfran	R-R	6-3	165	2-8-07	.255	.325	.321	28	120	106	8	27	5	1	0	10	10	2	0	2	17	11	0	8.3	14.2
Collins, Jack	R-R	6-0	180	5-12-03	.179	.281	.250	9	32	28	5	5	2	0	0	1	3	1	0	0	5	0	1	9.4	15.6
De Jesus, Jose	S-L	6-1	170	1-8-05	.067	.125	.067	9	32	30	3	2	0	0	0	4	2	0	0	0	4	2	0	6.3	12.5
Fien, Gavin	R-R	6-3	200	3-8-07	.220	.267	.341	10	45	41	4	9	3	1	0	7	3	0	0	1	11	1	0	6.7	24.4
Fitz-Gerald, Devin	S-R	5-10	185	8-17-05	.250	.442	.281	10	43	32	8	8	1	0	0	1	11	0	0	0	9	3	1	25.6	20.9
Flames, Daniel	S-R	5-11	160	10-27-06	.304	.385	.391	7	26	23	7	7	2	0	0	1	3	0	0	0	3	1	0	11.5	11.5
Guerrero, Pablo	R-R	6-2	200	7-31-06	.208	.303	.318	95	396	346	43	72	17	0	7	34	45	3	0	2	99	0	0	11.4	25.0
Hanson, Luke	R-R	6-2	185	8-26-03	.119	.269	.119	16	52	42	4	5	0	0	0	0	2	8	1	0	16	5	1	15.4	30.8
Hartl, Ben	R-R	5-11	200	1-4-04	.211	.352	.272	62	264	213	31	45	8	1	1	27	24	24	0	3	59	5	2	9.1	22.3
Kling, Paxton	L-L	6-2	210	5-28-03	.368	.395	.605	10	43	38	6	14	4	1	1	5	3	0	0	2	9	1	0	7.0	20.9
Lemos, Kleimer	S-R	6-1	175	6-3-05	.190	.190	.429	5	21	21	3	4	3	1	0	1	0	0	0	0	7	1	0	0.0	33.3
Lopez, Jesus	L-R	6-1	180	5-24-05	.128	.253	.218	22	91	78	10	10	4	0	1	6	12	1	0	0	23	1	1	13.2	25.3
Macias, Antonis	S-L	5-11	185	2-1-05	.266	.398	.333	92	401	312	48	83	14	2	1	40	71	5	2	11	67	4	3	17.7	16.7
Marquez, Luis	R-R	5-10	150	8-31-05	.229	.322	.309	53	199	175	22	40	6	1	2	18	17	7	0	0	42	5	4	8.5	21.1
Martin, Max	L-R	6-1	205	5-5-05	.259	.343	.440	102	458	402	72	104	25	6	12	64	45	8	0	3	101	13	0	9.8	22.1
Mejia, Esteban	R-R	5-11	165	11-4-04	.268	.362	.373	66	254	220	27	59	7	2	4	37	31	2	0	1	43	11	7	12.2	16.9
Mendez, Wady	L-L	6-0	155	10-14-04	.234	.320	.387	33	128	111	13	26	4	2	3	17	14	1	0	2	32	6	2	10.9	25.0
Morel, Braylin	R-R	6-2	180	1-19-06	.233	.278	.356	24	97	90	11	21	3	1	2	11	5	1	0	1	26	0	1	5.2	26.8
Osorio, Hector	L-L	6-0	150	4-6-05	.251	.393	.339	90	358	283	39	71	5	4	4	43	55	14	2	4	43	11	6	15.4	12.0
Owens, Josh	R-R	6-3	185	1-8-07	.083	.083	.125	8	24	24	3	2	1	0	0	0	0	0	0	0	11	0	0	0.0	45.8
Perich, Rafe	S-R	6-3	225	5-22-02	.249	.361	.364	58	252	209	34	52	10	1	4	39	36	3	0	4	52	5	0	14.3	20.6
Pollard, Chandler	R-R	6-2	173	5-3-04	.261	.352	.319	53	236	207	39	54	7	1	4	18	16	13	0	0	53	28	7	6.8	22.5
Santana, Paulino	R-R	6-2	180	11-17-06	.299	.333	.387	17	67	60	6	13	3	0	2	9	0	4	0	0	29	3	4	6.0	43.3
Springer, Josh	R-R	6-2	195	6-12-06	.220	.239	.268	14	46	41	5	9	2	0	0	5	2	0	0	3	11	1	1	4.3	2.2
Sulbaran, Juan	R-R	5-11	165	10-1-05	.262	.299	.410	19	67	61	6	16	4	1	1	6	1	3	0	2	15	0	1	1.5	22.4
Torres, Marcos	L-L	6-3	163	9-30-04	.248	.343	.376	80	304	258	39	64	9	3	6	38	37	2	2	3	74	22	3	12.2	24.3
Tovar, Deward	L-L	5-11	180	4-4-06	.310	.310	.345	7	29	29	3	9	1	0	0	1	0	0	0	0	13	0	1	0.0	44.8
Vargas, Jhocsuanth	R-R	5-10	177	8-31-06	.000	.143	.000	2	8	6	1	0	0	0	0	0	0	1	0	1	0	2	0	12.5	25.0

TEXAS RANGERS

Pitching	B-T	Ht.	Wt.	DOB	W	L	ERA	G	GS	SV	IP	Hits	Runs	ER	HR	BB	SO	AVG	OBP	SLG	SO%	BB%	BF
Agreda, Ismael	R-R	6-0	150	10-8-03	3	5	2.72	23	19	1	83	47	32	25	4	44	95	.163	.276	.235	28.2	13.1	337
Anazco, Angel	L-L	6-3	195	11-17-01	0	1	11.70	7	1	0	10	13	16	13	0	13	12	.302	.483	.349	20.7	22.4	58
Barroso, Beycker	R-R	5-10	160	1-24-03	0	0	0.00	1	0	1	0	0	0	0	0	1	0	.000	.667	.000	0.0	33.3	3
Cherry, Grant	R-R	6-3	210	3-24-03	4	2	5.76	23	0	1	45	52	30	29	3	31	45	.299	.412	.385	21.2	14.6	212
Deakins, Aidan	L-L	6-3	185	3-6-04	0	0	4.74	6	3	0	19	19	10	10	1	9	19	.268	.373	.380	22.9	10.8	83
Easley, J'Briell	R-R	6-3	225	10-12-01	3	2	3.55	11	8	0	38	33	16	15	4	10	37	.228	.278	.331	23.4	6.3	158
Fowler, Brooks	R-R	6-3	205	1-29-03	1	0	3.00	8	7	0	33	34	11	11	0	9	32	.276	.326	.325	23.5	6.6	136
Gamez, Jesus	R-R	6-0	190	3-4-03	2	1	0.95	15	0	4	19	8	5	2	0	11	29	.129	.289	.145	37.7	14.3	77
Hagaman, David	R-R	6-4	185	4-16-03	0	1	3.52	5	5	0	15	10	9	6	0	6	16	.182	.258	.218	25.8	9.7	62
Horn, Garrett	L-L	6-2	196	3-23-03	0	2	2.95	6	6	0	18	15	7	6	1	3	21	.224	.268	.299	29.6	4.2	71
Ireland, Thomas	L-L	6-1	170	6-27-02	7	2	2.69	18	2	1	60	52	27	18	1	16	59	.234	.294	.311	23.7	6.4	249
Jekielek, Jake	R-R	6-0	195	9-4-02	7	2	5.15	34	0	0	44	38	31	25	1	31	45	.228	.372	.329	21.4	14.8	210
Lafalaise, Jesus	R-R	6-1	175	2-4-05	2	2	5.66	6	3	0	21	10	13	13	0	16	13	.152	.329	.197	15.3	18.8	85
Larsen, Kyle	R-R	6-2	240	6-14-03	0	1	3.48	12	0	1	21	17	10	8	3	12	30	.215	.319	.392	33.0	13.2	91
Lockhart, Nick	R-R	6-6	204	2-12-01	0	0	0.00	1	0	0	1	1	0	0	0	0	1	.200	.200	.200	20.0	0.0	5
Loomis, Eric	R-R	6-0	195	3-27-02	0	0	2.89	7	0	1	9	10	3	3	1	3	14	.270	.341	.459	31.8	6.8	44
Lopez, Enyel	L-L	6-4	180	9-9-05	0	0	0.00	1	0	0	1	1	0	0	0	0	2	.250	.400	.250	40.0	0.0	5
Martinez, Frank	R-R	6-2	165	4-30-02	0	1	4.63	8	0	3	12	11	7	6	1	4	11	.256	.313	.372	22.9	8.3	48
Mejia, Aneudis	R-R	5-11	165	12-13-03	4	5	6.16	22	9	0	61	58	50	42	2	43	67	.248	.367	.363	23.3	14.9	288
Mejia, Esteban	R-R	5-11	165	11-3-04	0	0	0.00	1	0	0	1	0	0	0	0	0	0	.000	.000	.000	0.0	0.0	3
Molina, Mason	R-L	6-2	215	7-8-03	2	3	3.86	11	11	0	47	37	21	20	6	16	62	.215	.297	.372	32.3	8.3	192
Mota, Alberto	R-R	5-11	170	2-17-03	0	0	2.20	12	0	0	16	9	7	4	0	18	20	.161	.368	.179	26.0	23.4	77
Nivar, Jormy	R-R	6-3	170	5-7-03	1	3	2.55	6	0	1	18	11	5	5	1	5	11	.180	.271	.295	15.3	6.9	72
Owens, Josh	L-R	6-3	185	1-8-07	0	0	0.00	2	2	0	4	1	1	0	0	3	6	.083	.267	.167	40.0	20.0	15
Pence, Dalton	L-L	6-2	205	8-28-02	3	1	4.25	17	7	0	36	25	17	17	5	11	52	.195	.262	.359	36.6	7.7	142
Perry, Kamdyn	R-R	6-4	200	8-9-05	2	6	5.92	13	12	0	52	52	35	34	6	24	43	.265	.360	.398	18.9	10.5	228
Porter, Brock	R-R	6-4	208	6-3-03	5	1	3.06	41	0	2	68	44	24	23	8	38	77	.184	.324	.310	26.6	13.1	290
Privette, William	R-R	6-6	200	2-1-02	3	3	4.00	37	1	5	45	31	27	20	0	30	59	.193	.328	.286	30.1	15.3	196
Proksch, Owen	L-L	6-3	225	12-25-03	2	1	3.09	7	0	0	12	11	6	4	1	4	17	.262	.367	.357	34.0	8.0	50
Reyes, Maicol	R-R	6-2	210	3-4-05	0	1	21.60	3	0	0	2	5	4	4	2	6	1	.500	.688	1.100	6.3	37.5	16
Rodriguez, Adrian	R-R	6-5	192	5-18-01	1	0	6.52	7	0	1	10	12	7	7	0	5	17	.293	.370	.415	37.0	10.9	46
Rodriguez, Geury	L-L	6-0	155	10-20-04	1	1	6.43	4	0	0	7	6	5	5	1	6	11	.222	.382	.333	32.4	17.6	34
Sanders, Josh	R-R	6-3	180	10-22-01	1	1	3.18	2	0	0	6	4	3	2	0	1	4	.190	.261	.190	17.4	4.3	23
Savage, Luke	R-R	6-1	200	8-10-01	0	1	1.49	26	0	6	36	26	6	6	1	15	33	.215	.317	.306	22.9	10.4	144
Scarborough, Caden	R-R	6-5	180	4-1-05	2	5	2.88	19	18	0	75	50	26	24	7	19	95	.189	.254	.287	32.3	6.5	294
Segura, Enrique	R-R	6-3	175	12-19-04	2	4	5.02	16	13	0	66	56	38	37	6	23	63	.230	.324	.325	22.3	8.2	282
Siary, Evan	R-R	6-2	195	10-18-03	0	0	7.50	4	3	0	6	8	5	5	1	2	6	.320	.370	.560	22.2	7.4	27
Trausch, Michael	L-L	6-2	190	2-13-04	3	1	3.05	29	0	1	41	30	15	14	1	29	50	.204	.343	.245	27.9	16.2	179
Valverde, Michael	L-L	6-2	211	12-7-02	1	0	8.10	9	0	1	10	6	10	9	0	13	17	.162	.380	.270	34.0	26.0	50
Villar, Willy	R-R	6-4	215	8-18-98	0	1	18.69	5	0	0	4	9	9	9	0	7	4	.409	.552	.545	13.8	24.1	29
Wynyard, Kai-Noa	R-R	6-0	176	6-22-02	6	2	3.51	21	0	1	49	44	24	19	5	22	45	.237	.325	.355	21.2	10.4	212

Fielding

Catcher	PCT	G	PO	A	E	DP	PB
Barroso	.984	19	169	17	3	1	7
Collins	.988	9	73	7	1	0	1
Hartl	.980	60	592	50	13	3	8
Lopez	.981	15	146	7	3	0	0
Springer	.990	12	94	4	1	0	0
Sulbaran	.983	19	161	16	3	2	2
Vargas	1.000	1	11	1	0	0	1

First Base	PCT	G	PO	A	E	DP
Alvarez	1.000	8	42	0	0	4
Barroso	1.000	10	83	6	0	7
Guerrero	.992	80	574	36	5	45
Hartl	1.000	1	1	0	0	0
Lemos	.960	5	46	2	2	4
Macias	.984	9	56	4	1	1
Marquez	1.000	1	9	0	0	0
Martin	1.000	2	14	1	0	0
Torres	.993	18	127	14	1	7

Second Base	PCT	G	PO	A	E	DP
Alvarez	.818	3	2	7	2	1

Third Base	PCT	G	PO	A	E	DP
Arredondo	1.000	3	4	6	0	0
Barroso	1.000	18	13	19	0	0
Castillo	.963	10	9	17	1	3
Flames	1.000	3	1	5	0	1
Hanson	1.000	10	7	17	0	0
Marquez	.857	4	1	5	1	1
Mejia	.911	34	25	47	7	5
Perich	.908	54	26	82	11	4

Shortstop	PCT	G	PO	A	E	DP
Arredondo	1.000	1	3	2	0	0
Castillo	.952	18	35	44	4	16
Fien	.818	4	5	4	2	0

	PCT	G	PO	A	E	DP
Fitz-Gerald	1.000	10	9	20	0	2
Flames	1.000	1	1	4	0	0
Hanson	1.000	6	8	16	0	4
Marquez	.933	24	39	45	6	10
Mejia	.957	19	29	38	3	7
Owens	1.000	1	3	2	0	1
Perich	1.000	1	2	3	0	1
Pollard	.900	47	45	90	15	15

Outfield	PCT	G	PO	A	E	DP
Alvarez	1.000	17	27	0	0	0
Cabrera	.982	98	211	8	4	0
De Jesus	1.000	8	12	1	0	0
Kling	1.000	8	18	0	0	0
Martin	.971	71	97	2	3	1
Mendez	.931	21	27	0	2	0
Morel	.941	14	12	4	1	0
Osorio	.987	82	147	6	2	1
Pollard	.875	2	7	0	1	0
Santana	1.000	17	31	2	0	0
Torres	1.000	51	87	2	0	0
Tovar	1.000	7	9	0	0	0

ACL RANGERS — ROOKIE
ARIZONA COMPLEX LEAGUE

Batting	B-T	Ht.	Wt.	DOB	AVG	OBP	SLG	G	PA	AB	R	H	2B	3B	HR	RBI	BB	HBP	SH	SF	SO	SB	CS	BB%	SO%
Arredondo, Angel	R-R	5-8	190	10-25-06	.310	.440	.373	40	160	126	29	39	6	1	0	19	25	6	1	2	24	4	2	15.6	15.0
Baquera, Sebastian	R-R	5-7	176	1-11-07	.159	.250	.175	26	75	63	5	10	1	0	0	6	3	5	3	1	21	0	1	4.0	28.0
Batista, Andry	R-R	6-4	170	3-26-07	.200	.325	.292	29	78	65	15	13	3	0	1	4	11	1	1	0	23	1	1	14.1	29.5
Biggers, Jax	L-R	5-8	175	4-7-97	.214	.313	.286	4	16	14	1	3	1	0	0	0	0	2	0	0	5	0	0	0.0	31.3
Castillo, Yolfran	R-R	6-3	165	2-8-07	.260	.310	.366	60	258	235	41	61	8	7	1	31	16	3	0	4	52	18	2	6.2	20.2
Fitz-Gerald, Devin	S-R	5-10	185	8-17-05	.318	.423	.542	31	130	107	25	34	6	0	6	19	17	4	0	2	15	5	1	13.1	11.5
Flames, Daniel	S-R	5-11	160	10-27-06	.133	.188	.133	6	16	15	1	2	0	0	0	0	0	1	0	0	3	0	0	0.0	18.8
Foscue, Justin	R-R	5-11	205	3-2-99	.000	.111	.000	3	9	8	1	0	0	0	0	0	1	0	0	0	1	0	0	11.1	11.1
Guzman, Michael	R-R	6-1	165	1-31-06	.179	.360	.256	19	50	39	8	7	3	0	0	3	11	0	0	0	14	1	0	22.0	28.0
Hauver, Trevor	L-R	5-11	205	11-20-98	.188	.278	.250	5	18	16	0	3	1	0	0	0	2	0	0	0	4	0	1	11.1	22.2
Lemos, Kleimer	S-R	6-1	175	6-3-05	.264	.305	.428	55	220	201	30	53	13	1	6	46	10	4	0	5	58	3	3	4.5	26.4
Lopez, Jesus	L-R	6-1	180	5-24-05	.095	.323	.095	8	31	21	4	2	0	0	0	3	8	0	0	2	4	0	1	25.8	12.9
Marquez, Luis	R-R	5-10	150	8-31-05	.077	.077	.308	4	13	13	1	1	0	0	1	1	0	0	0	0	6	0	0	0.0	0.0
Martha, Curley	R-R	5-11	165	9-19-06	.000	.250	.000	4	13	9	1	0	0	0	0	1	2	1	1	0	3	0	1	15.4	23.1
Moore, Malcolm	L-R	6-2	210	7-31-03	.143	.381	.357	5	21	14	2	2	0	0	1	5	6	0	0	1	4	1	0	28.6	19.0
Morel, Braylin	R-R	6-2	180	1-19-06	.268	.302	.423	37	149	142	18	38	11	1	3	17	5	2	0	0	40	3	0	3.4	26.8
Morrobel, Yeison	L-L	6-2	170	12-8-03	.250	.400	.250	1	5	4	1	1	0	0	0	1	1	0	0	0	0	0	0	20.0	0.0
Pinder, Rashawn	L-R	5-8	145	6-4-07	.254	.329	.373	53	209	185	27	47	6	5	2	19	16	5	1	1	59	7	5	7.7	28.2
Sanchez, Javier	R-R	5-11	160	8-17-07	.237	.356	.316	35	135	114	15	27	3	0	2	12	15	6	0	0	22	0	0	11.1	16.3
Santana, Paulino	R-R	6-2	180	11-17-06	.265	.339	.412	56	239	211	38	56	10	3	5	28	21	4	0	3	65	8	4	8.8	27.2
Springer, Josh	R-R	6-2	195	6-12-06	.284	.364	.388	34	133	116	15	33	9	0	1	16	11	4	1	1	9	3	1	8.3	6.8
Tovar, Deward	L-L	5-11	180	4-4-06	.313	.434	.536	33	136	112	20	35	6	2	5	19	23	1	0	0	40	2	1	16.9	29.4
Vargas, Jhocsuanth	R-R	5-11	170	8-31-06	.333	.429	.333	2	7	6	2	2	0	0	0	0	1	0	0	0	1	0	0	14.3	
Wong, Williams	L-R	5-10	180	10-12-05	.214	.314	.291	33	120	103	10	22	2	0	2	14	15	0	2	0	33	2	1	12.5	27.5

Pitching	B-T	Ht.	Wt.	DOB	W	L	ERA	G	GS	SV	IP	Hits	Runs	ER	HR	BB	SO	AVG	OBP	SLG	SO%	BB%	BF
Acker, Dane	R-R	6-2	189	4-1-99	1	0	3.00	2	1	0	3	2	1	1	0	0	7	.182	.182	.455	63.6	0.0	11
Anazco, Angel	L-L	6-3	195	11-17-01	1	0	12.00	11	0	0	9	12	12	12	0	10	14	.316	.480	.421	28.0	20.0	50
Anderson, Aidan	R-R	6-1	195	6-21-97	0	0	0.00	2	1	0	3	0	0	0	0	1	5	.000	.111	.000	55.6	11.1	9
Arias, Jordy	R-R	5-11	185	8-4-05	0	0	10.57	6	0	1	8	6	9	9	1	11	6	.240	.474	.400	15.8	28.9	38
Arias, Yeimison	R-R	6-1	165	1-9-05	2	0	4.15	8	0	0	9	6	7	4	0	8	10	.188	.381	.344	23.8	19.0	42
Blach, Ty	R-L	6-1	215	10-20-90	0	0	0.00	1	1	0	5	3	0	0	0	0	8	.176	.176	.176	47.1	0.0	17
Cherry, Grant	R-R	6-3	210	3-24-01	0	0	4.50	2	0	0	4	4	2	2	1	3	5	.267	.389	.600	27.8	16.7	18
Chiquillo, Alejandro	R-R	6-1	180	12-6-02	1	2	6.75	9	4	1	29	38	23	22	3	12	37	.317	.385	.500	27.2	8.8	136
Church, Marc	R-R	6-3	189	3-30-01	0	0	0.00	1	0	0	2	0	0	0	0	3	0	.000	.000	.000	50.0	0.0	6
Corniell, Jose	R-R	6-3	165	6-22-03	0	0	3.18	4	4	0	6	7	3	2	1	2	7	.304	.346	.522	26.9	7.7	26
Curry, Aidan	R-R	6-5	185	7-5-02	2	1	3.42	5	4	0	26	19	10	10	5	3	39	.192	.223	.374	37.9	2.9	103
Deakins, Aidan	L-L	6-3	185	3-6-04	3	1	4.03	10	7	0	38	37	18	17	5	8	47	.253	.319	.390	29.2	5.0	161
Delgado, Jesus	L-L	5-10	176	9-15-03	1	3	5.23	14	0	0	31	33	23	18	2	16	29	.277	.371	.454	20.7	11.4	140
Fowler, Brooks	R-R	6-3	205	1-29-03	0	1	4.50	3	3	0	6	8	3	3	1	4	8	.333	.429	.458	27.6	13.8	29
Gamez, Jesus	R-R	6-0	190	3-4-03	1	0	0.00	3	0	1	4	0	0	0	0	2	8	.000	.188	.000	50.0	12.5	16
Garcia, Jaiker	R-R	6-4	175	12-23-04	3	3	4.66	18	0	2	19	20	11	10	3	14	26	.282	.400	.535	29.5	15.9	88
Gray, Jon	R-R	6-4	225	11-5-91	0	0	3.00	1	1	0	3	6	1	1	0	0	2	.462	.462	.462	15.4	0.0	13
Hagaman, David	R-R	6-4	185	4-16-03	0	0	1.29	3	3	0	7	5	1	1	0	0	12	.200	.200	.240	48.0	0.0	25
Horn, Garrett	L-L	6-2	196	3-23-03	0	1	2.84	3	3	0	6	2	2	2	1	3	13	.095	.240	.238	52.0	12.0	25
Kelley, Jackson	R-R	6-0	185	4-26-00	0	0	0.00	3	1	0	4	1	0	0	0	6	.071	.071	.143	42.9	0.0	14	
Lafalaise, Jesus	R-R	6-1	175	2-4-05	3	1	3.82	14	2	0	31	29	15	13	0	9	36	.240	.308	.331	27.1	6.8	133
Larsen, Kyle	R-R	6-2	240	6-14-03	1	0	5.11	8	0	0	12	12	10	7	1	5	14	.245	.321	.408	24.6	8.8	57
Lopez, Enyel	L-L	6-4	180	9-9-05	0	2	5.88	11	6	0	26	28	19	17	0	26	32	.280	.442	.370	24.8	20.2	129
Martinez, Frank	R-R	6-2	165	4-30-02	2	0	4.45	17	0	0	30	28	19	15	0	14	34	.248	.341	.398	25.8	10.6	132
Morales, Moises	R-R	6-1	175	2-15-04	2	3	3.51	14	4	0	41	36	19	16	1	17	41	.235	.337	.359	22.9	9.5	179
Murphy, Patrick	R-R	6-5	211	6-10-95	0	0	0.00	1	1	0	1	0	0	0	0	1	.250	.250	.250	25.0	0.0	4	
Nivar, Jormy	R-R	6-3	170	5-7-03	2	3	6.91	12	8	0	42	53	36	32	9	16	39	.353	.377	.480	19.9	8.2	196
Nunez, German	R-R	6-3	155	5-24-02	1	2	4.82	7	3	1	19	20	10	10	1	7	26	.286	.350	.343	32.5	8.8	80
Perry, Kamdyn	R-R	6-4	200	8-9-05	0	0	9.00	1	1	0	2	6	4	2	0	0	.545	.500	.545	0.0	0.0	13	
Reyes, Maicol	R-R	6-2	210	3-4-05	2	3	2.73	21	0	3	30	22	10	9	0	12	39	.198	.326	.261	29.5	9.1	132
Rodriguez, Adrian	R-R	6-5	192	5-18-01	2	0	4.66	7	0	0	10	7	5	5	1	9	13	.219	.390	.406	31.7	22.0	41
Rodriguez, Geury	L-L	6-0	155	10-20-04	1	0	3.32	11	0	2	19	12	7	7	2	11	26	.185	.321	.354	33.3	14.1	78
Sanders, Josh	R-R	6-3	180	10-22-01	0	0	0.00	1	0	3	2	0	0	0	4	.200	.273	.200	36.4	0.0	11		
Segura, Enrique	R-R	6-3	175	12-19-04	0	1	4.32	2	2	0	8	8	4	4	0	1	13	.250	.314	.344	37.1	2.9	35
Teodo, Emiliano	R-R	6-1	165	2-14-01	0	0	0.00	1	1	0	6	4	2	0	0	0	5	.222	.300	.222	50.0	0.0	18
Valverde, Michael	L-L	6-2	211	12-7-02	0	0	5.68	7	0	0	6	3	4	0	10	7	.136	.441	.136	20.6	29.4	34	
Villar, Willy	R-R	6-4	215	8-18-98	1	0	11.25	4	0	0	4	7	5	5	1	2	4	.389	.476	.722	19.0	9.5	21

Fielding

C: Springer 32, Baquera 25, Lopez 3, Moore 3, Sanchez 2, Vargas 1. **1B:** Lemos 42, Sanchez 17, Tovar 4, Foscue 1. **2B:** Wong 30, Arredondo 12, Fitz-Gerald 10, Flames 5, Guzman 3, Marquez 3, Martha 3, Foscue 2, Biggers 1. **3B:** Arredondo 27, Castillo 13, Fitz-Gerald 13, Guzman 10, Biggers 1, Wong 1. **SS:** Castillo 48, Fitz-Gerald 9, Arredondo 2, Biggers 1, Martha 1. **LF:** Santana 34, Pinder 16, Tovar 5, Hauver 5, Morel 2, Biggers 1. **CF:** Pinder 37, Santana 21, Batista 6, Morel 1. **RF:** Tovar 22, Batista 17, Morel 15, Lemos 7, Santana 3, Guzman 2, Hauver 1, Morrobel 1, Pinder 1

DSL RANGERS BLUE — ROOKIE
DOMINICAN SUMMER LEAGUE

Batting	B-T	Ht.	Wt.	DOB	AVG	OBP	SLG	G	PA	AB	R	H	2B	3B	HR	RBI	BB	HBP	SH	SF	SO	SB	CS	BB%	SO%
Alarcon, Rosnel	R-R	6-2	200	1-30-08	.288	.431	.378	47	195	156	29	45	11	0	1	25	22	17	0	0	26	11	4	11.3	13.3
Arias, Joaquin	L-L	6-1	160	10-4-06	.310	.412	.416	33	140	113	22	35	8	2	0	15	19	2	4	2	23	3	3	13.6	16.4
Castillo, Wesly	L-R	6-0	175	2-13-08	.317	.400	.397	31	145	126	20	40	8	1	0	29	13	5	0	1	18	10	0	9.0	12.4
Genao, Jhostin	L-R	6-2	160	1-6-08	.270	.364	.361	36	144	122	26	33	3	1	2	19	16	3	1	2	24	12	2	11.1	16.7
Leen, Klendy	R-R	5-11	190	6-12-07	.093	.220	.116	22	50	43	1	4	1	0	0	3	7	0	0	0	18	0	0	14.0	36.0
Martinez, Emil	R-R	6-1	165	12-20-07	.207	.302	.268	44	189	164	22	34	4	0	2	13	20	3	0	2	40	5	6	10.6	21.2
Neely, Dave	L-R	5-10	165	6-18-07	.230	.414	.264	36	116	87	22	20	3	0	0	15	26	2	0	1	43	12	6	22.4	37.1
Ortiz, David	L-L	6-0	210	8-19-07	.124	.361	.168	39	155	113	19	14	5	0	0	7	39	3	0	0	46	0	0	25.2	29.7
Pereira, Raul	R-R	6-0	160	6-2-08	.310	.402	.407	29	132	113	23	35	7	2	0	24	14	4	0	1	25	1	2	10.6	18.9
Pinder, Jaylin	L-R	5-10	190	5-24-08	.277	.431	.375	33	145	112	30	31	6	1	1	9	21	10	1	1	36	11	7	14.5	24.8
Rodriguez, Alex	L-R	5-11	185	11-26-07	.311	.401	.383	47	213	180	20	56	10	0	1	30	25	4	1	3	27	1	1	11.7	12.7
Santa, Fraimy	R-R	6-0	180	9-5-07	.249	.355	.349	49	200	169	28	42	9	1	2	25	25	4	0	2	51	3	2	12.5	25.5
Santos, Steven	R-R	5-11	200	7-6-07	.207	.258	.276	16	62	58	6	12	2	1	0	5	4	0	0	0	19	1	0	6.5	30.6
Tiamo, Ruben	R-R	6-0	180	6-28-08	.190	.301	.190	25	73	63	11	12	0	0	0	4	7	3	0	0	24	3	0	9.6	32.9
Torres, Carlos	R-R	5-10	200	1-3-08	.299	.365	.388	38	167	147	22	44	9	2	0	23	14	3	0	3	17	0	0	8.4	10.2
Valdes, Abel	L-R	5-10	170	7-24-06	.217	.451	.253	31	122	83	16	18	1	1	0	10	30	7	0	2	24	0	0	24.6	19.7

Pitching	B-T	Ht.	Wt.	DOB	W	L	ERA	G	GS	SV	IP	Hits	Runs	ER	HR	BB	SO	AVG	OBP	SLG	SO%	BB%	BF
Beles, Daniel	R-R	6-3	190	6-17-06	0	3	14.46	6	0	0	9	15	16	15	3	14	9	.366	.526	.659	15.8	24.6	57
Cordero, Albert	R-R	5-11	165	8-15-05	1	1	6.93	9	4	0	25	33	26	19	3	20	28	.314	.426	.476	21.7	15.5	129
Dolsi, Frederik	R-R	6-3	172	7-24-07	1	5	5.12	10	9	0	39	32	28	22	1	29	43	.235	.394	.324	24.4	16.5	176
Encarnacion, Jefferson	R-R	6-1	190	4-8-05	0	0	22.74	6	0	0	6	18	20	16	0	6	7	.500	.604	.722	14.6	12.5	48
Figuereo, Enmanuel	R-R	6-0	160	7-23-08	1	3	10.18	10	4	0	20	22	35	23	3	25	17	.278	.491	.468	14.9	21.9	114
Fukuda, Masahiro	R-R	5-9	172	7-11-01	1	4	6.37	8	2	1	30	33	24	21	1	11	27	.277	.331	.429	20.3	8.3	133
Garcia, Luis	L-L	6-4	220	2-18-04	2	2	5.53	14	0	0	28	19	22	17	1	30	59	.183	.368	.250	43.4	22.1	136
Gomez, Angel	R-R	6-2	175	7-7-06	1	1	10.08	16	0	0	28	42	36	31	5	26	19	.347	.468	.612	12.3	16.8	155
Gomez, Manuel	R-R	6-4	175	11-12-03	0	0	0.00	2	0	0	3	1	1	0	0	2	3	.091	.286	.091	21.4	14.3	14
Gonzalez, Nestor	R-R	6-1	175	9-19-07	0	2	10.24	7	5	0	19	28	25	22	2	20	19	.346	.485	.519	18.4	19.4	103
Gonzalez, Yeferson	R-R	6-0	165	1-11-07	1	4	10.88	10	3	1	24	20	32	29	1	36	26	.220	.463	.374	19.1	26.5	136
Jimenez, Danny	L-L	5-11	170	2-22-06	0	2	11.37	6	3	0	13	10	16	16	0	23	14	.250	.531	.325	21.9	35.9	64
Lanzoa, Diego	R-R	5-11	155	9-15-07	1	2	3.21	11	7	0	34	31	19	12	6	15	49	.242	.331	.445	33.6	10.3	146
Leen, Klendy	R-R	5-11	190	6-12-07	0	0	9.00	7	0	0	8	15	13	8	3	5	6	.366	.458	.683	12.5	10.4	48
Liriano, Edgar	R-R	6-2	165	4-12-07	0	0	38.57	2	0	0	2	6	10	10	0	4	2	.545	.632	.818	10.5	21.1	19
Lopez, Jesus	R-R	6-1	170	7-10-07	0	0	0.00	2	0	0	2	1	0	0	0	1	2	.143	.250	.143	25.0	12.5	8
Martinez, Emmanuel	L-L	6-1	170	8-28-03	0	0	2.53	4	0	0	11	5	3	3	1	7	19	.147	.356	.265	42.2	15.6	45
Medina, Ruben	R-R	6-1	175	7-8-05	1	3	6.59	11	5	0	41	48	38	30	5	18	37	.289	.372	.458	19.3	9.4	192
Morban, Brian	L-L	6-1	200	12-8-04	0	0	8.68	7	0	0	9	11	9	9	1	9	11	.278	.491	.389	20.8	17.0	53
Neely, Dave	L-R	5-10	165	6-18-07	0	0	9.00	1	0	0	1	2	1	1	0	1	0	.400	.500	.600	0.0	16.7	6
Pena, Dariel	R-R	6-3	205	10-5-05	0	1	45.00	2	1	0	1	2	5	5	0	4	1	.500	.750	1.250	12.5	50.0	8
Ramos, Daniel	R-R	6-2	180	8-15-06	1	0	3.97	13	0	0	23	24	15	10	4	8	18	.264	.337	.462	17.8	7.9	101
Romero, Oscar	R-R	6-1	175	4-14-06	0	1	6.55	4	4	0	11	17	16	8	1	14	8	.362	.508	.468	13.1	23.0	61
Roquez, Yadiel	R-R	6-0	185	2-26-07	3	0	2.93	15	2	0	31	23	13	10	2	18	45	.205	.326	.313	34.1	13.6	132
Sanchez, Maykel	R-R	6-0	165	1-24-06	0	2	12.08	10	0	1	13	20	20	17	3	20	13	.370	.553	.574	16.9	26.0	77
Santos, Aneudy	R-R	6-1	195	4-19-06	0	5	8.10	12	7	0	37	44	42	33	2	35	36	.299	.447	.463	18.9	18.4	190
Santos, Steven	R-R	5-11	200	7-6-07	0	0	0.00	1	0	0	2	0	0	0	0	0	0	.000	.000	.000	0.0	0.0	4
Ulloa, Noel	R-R	6-3	190	6-4-03	0	0	9.00	1	0	0	2	2	2	2	0	2	1	.286	.500	.429	10.0	10.0	10
Yean, Ariel	R-R	6-2	165	9-14-05	0	0	20.77	4	0	0	4	8	11	10	3	7	4	.381	.552	.905	13.8	24.1	29

Fielding
C: Torres 28, Valdes 27, Leen 7, Santos 1. **1B:** Ortiz 36, Santos 11, Rodriguez 6, Leen 3, Santa 3. **2B:** Pinder 30, Neely 12, Martinez 11, Pereira 4, Genao 2. **3B:** Santa 44, Martinez 6, Genao 4, Neely 4, Pereira 1, Rodriguez 1. **SS:** Pereira 23, Martinez 18, Neely 17, Genao 2, Santa 1. **LF:** Pinder 27, Rodriguez 27, Genao 3, Alarcon 2, Castillo 2, Tiamo 2, Neely 1. **CF:** Alarcon 29, Genao 26, Arias 3, Tiamo 2. **RF:** Castillo 24, Tiamo 19, Alarcon 10, Rodriguez 7, Arias 1

DSL RANGERS RED — ROOKIE
DOMINICAN SUMMER LEAGUE

Batting	B-T	Ht.	Wt.	DOB	AVG	OBP	SLG	G	PA	AB	R	H	2B	3B	HR	RBI	BB	HBP	SH	SF	SO	SB	CS	BB%	SO%
Almao, Santiago	S-R	5-7	160	1-23-08	.309	.434	.441	46	189	152	46	47	10	2	2	18	33	2	0	2	27	14	2	17.5	14.3
Argudin, Marco	L-L	5-10	170	12-5-05	.397	.497	.587	32	149	121	32	48	9	4	2	28	21	5	0	2	12	15	3	14.1	8.1
Arias, Joaquin	L-L	6-1	160	10-4-06	.400	.571	.400	3	7	5	4	2	0	0	0	0	2	0	0	0	1	1	0	28.6	14.3
Castillo, Wesly	L-R	6-0	175	2-13-08	.000	.200	.000	2	5	4	2	0	0	0	0	0	1	0	0	0	1	1	0	20.0	20.0
Celesten, Yeisy	L-R	5-11	260	6-28-05	.277	.417	.473	37	144	112	25	31	7	0	5	18	27	2	0	3	29	7	2	18.8	20.1
Diaz, Jord David	R-R	5-10	170	11-18-07	.258	.302	.290	41	148	124	31	32	2	1	0	13	9	1	1	1	28	13	2	8.8	18.9
Genao, Jhostin	L-R	6-2	160	1-6-08	.333	.400	.333	2	10	9	2	3	0	0	0	1	1	0	0	0	1	0	0	10.0	10.0
Guerrero, Oliver	L-R	6-3	200	1-4-08	.245	.379	.409	45	195	159	37	39	1	2	7	32	30	5	0	1	43	4	0	15.4	22.1
Kim, Seong-Jun	R-R	6-2	185	5-1-07	.167	.231	.333	3	13	12	1	2	0	0	1	0	1	0	0	0	3	0	0	7.7	23.1
Marcano, Jose	R-R	5-10	160	10-25-06	.270	.389	.389	38	149	126	29	34	6	0	3	32	19	2	0	2	15	4	4	12.8	10.1
Montero, Neurelin	R-R	5-10	170	5-26-06	.316	.435	.474	19	46	38	8	12	3	0	1	9	7	1	0	0	11	0	1	13.0	26.1
Perez, Francisco	R-R	6-0	188	10-21-06	.279	.359	.505	30	132	111	28	31	4	0	7	26	11	5	1	4	19	3	1	8.3	14.4
Pinder, Jaylin	L-R	5-10	160	5-24-08	.080	.343	.080	9	36	25	5	2	0	0	0	2	10	0	1	0	9	5	0	27.8	25.0
Ramirez, Manni	R-R	6-5	190	4-25-07	.275	.377	.507	38	167	142	29	39	10	1	7	24	20	4	0	1	42	5	3	12.0	25.1

TEXAS RANGERS

Player	B-T	Ht.	Wt.	DOB	AVG	OBP	SLG	G	AB	R	H	2B	3B	HR	RBI	BB	SO	SB	CS	OBP2	SLG2
Rodriguez, Daniel	R-R	6-1	165	3-12-08	.228	.429	.289	43	207	149	39	34	5	2	0	19	50	4	2	2	41 12 3 24.2 19.8
Rodriguez, Elorky	L-R	5-10	175	12-26-07	.337	.473	.506	46	226	178	46	60	10	1	6	48	39	8	0	1	38 9 8 17.3 16.8
Simon, Jhon	R-R	5-11	210	1-1-08	.315	.419	.427	23	105	89	9	28	7	0	1	17	14	2	0	0	18 0 0 13.3 17.1
Tiamo, Ruben	R-R	6-0	180	6-28-08	.333	.429	.500	6	14	12	3	4	2	0	0	4	2	0	0	0	2 0 0 14.3 14.3
Torres, Carlos	R-R	5-10	200	1-3-08	.000	.000	.000	2	10	10	0	0	0	0	0	0	0	0	0	0	1 0 0 0.0 10.0
Volquez, Fabelin	R-R	6-0	165	12-12-07	.234	.333	.406	18	78	64	13	15	5	0	2	8	9	2	0	3	17 1 1 11.5 21.8
Zayas, Saivel	R-R	6-0	180	11-18-07	.236	.324	.330	45	210	182	29	43	9	1	2	35	19	6	0	3	49 14 5 9.0 23.3

Pitching	B-T	Ht.	Wt.	DOB	W	L	ERA	G	GS	SV	IP	Hits	Runs	ER	HR	BB	SO	AVG	OBP	SLG	SO%	BB%	BF
Armas, Keiber	R-R	6-1	170	3-24-03	5	0	4.15	21	0	1	30	34	28	14	1	10	42	.266	.347	.352	29.2	6.9	144
Astudillo, Anthony	R-R	6-0	165	7-11-05	5	2	2.93	11	11	0	46	45	22	15	2	13	62	.262	.319	.378	32.8	6.9	189
Beles, Daniel	R-R	6-3	190	6-17-06	1	0	11.40	9	1	0	15	25	23	19	3	16	14	.391	.529	.625	16.1	18.4	87
Belisario, Pedro	L-L	6-1	160	12-20-03	0	0	8.82	6	5	0	16	16	20	16	1	15	18	.258	.455	.371	20.5	17.0	88
Celesten, Yeisy	L-R	5-11	160	6-28-05	1	1	37.80	2	0	0	2	6	8	7	2	2	1	.600	.692	1.300	7.1	14.3	14
De Jesus, Yunier	R-R	6-5	170	11-28-05	0	1	3.24	11	0	1	17	10	13	6	1	15	20	.167	.383	.267	24.7	18.5	81
Encarnacion, Jefferson	R-R	6-1	190	4-8-05	3	0	2.31	13	0	2	23	19	6	6	1	12	24	.232	.357	.329	24.5	12.2	98
Fukuda, Masahiro	R-R	5-9	172	7-11-01	0	0	0.00	1	0	1	3	1	0	0	0	0	5	.100	.100	.100	50.0	0.0	10
Garcia, Luis	L-L	6-4	220	2-18-04	1	0	0.00	2	0	0	3	0	1	0	0	4	7	.000	.308	.000	53.8	30.8	13
Gomez, Angel	R-R	6-2	175	7-7-06	0	0	9.00	1	0	0	2	4	2	2	0	1	2	.444	.500	.444	16.7	8.3	12
Gonzalez, Yeferson	R-R	6-0	165	1-11-07	0	1	5.87	2	2	0	8	8	5	5	0	8	6	.286	.432	.321	16.2	21.6	37
Hernandez, Christopher	R-R	6-0	160	4-8-06	3	1	4.67	11	3	3	35	30	23	18	2	27	50	.240	.374	.352	32.3	17.4	155
Kim, Seong-Jun	R-R	6-2	185	5-1-07	0	0	0.00	1	1	0	1	0	0	0	0	0	2	.000	.000	.000	0.0	0.0	3
Lanzosa, Diego	R-R	5-11	165	5-21-06	1	0	2.08	1	0	0	4	2	1	1	1	2	2	.143	.250	.357	12.5	12.5	16
Lopez, Gilberto	R-R	6-1	175	3-30-04	2	0	3.12	11	8	0	49	39	18	17	3	15	56	.211	.291	.319	27.2	7.3	206
Lopez, Jesus	R-R	6-1	170	7-10-07	0	0	1.80	5	1	0	10	8	2	2	0	2	10	.229	.270	.429	27.0	5.4	37
Martinez, Emmanuel	L-L	6-1	170	8-28-03	2	2	5.61	13	0	0	26	25	30	16	1	36	29	.253	.479	.323	20.3	25.2	143
Montero, Neurelin	R-R	5-10	170	5-26-06	0	0	19.29	2	0	0	2	5	5	5	2	1	0	.417	.500	1.083	0.0	7.1	14
Morban, Brian	L-L	6-1	200	12-8-04	1	0	6.14	7	0	2	7	8	5	5	1	7	12	.308	.486	.538	34.3	20.0	35
Neira, Miguel	L-L	5-10	175	9-7-04	0	1	1.98	6	2	1	14	6	4	3	0	5	20	.128	.212	.170	38.5	9.6	52
Peralta, Eddy	R-R	6-2	165	1-27-03	4	4	6.68	11	0	1	32	34	28	24	0	19	35	.286	.462	.370	22.0	11.9	159
Ramos, Daniel	R-R	6-2	180	8-15-06	0	0	0.00	1	0	0	2	1	1	0	0	0	4	.111	.273	.111	36.4	0.0	11
Rivera, Bernardo	R-R	6-0	165	3-17-05	3	0	3.92	11	8	0	49	54	34	24	17	2	24	50	.230	.348	.338	28.1	13.5	178
Roquez, Yadiel	R-R	6-0	185	2-26-07	0	0	4.50	2	0	0	4	5	5	2	0	5	3	.313	.476	.438	14.3	23.8	21
Rubio, Johander	R-R	6-1	185	7-6-06	1	2	3.96	11	11	0	39	29	22	17	1	23	42	.212	.335	.292	25.6	14.0	164
Ulloa, Noel	R-R	6-3	190	6-4-03	2	1	2.55	12	1	2	25	23	15	7	2	7	36	.235	.290	.337	33.6	6.5	107
Villar, Willy	R-R	6-4	215	8-18-98	2	1	2.04	10	0	2	18	10	5	4	0	10	29	.167	.306	.217	40.3	13.9	72

Fielding
C: Marcano 23, Perez 22, Montero 17, Torres 2. **1B:** Celesten 19, Marcano 16, Diaz 11, Guerrero 9, Perez 5. **2B:** Almao 23, E. Rodriguez 15, Diaz 7, Pinder 6, Celesten 4, D. Rodriguez 2. **3B:** Celesten 14, Rodriguez 12, Almao 10, Diaz 10, Simon 10, Volquez 7. **SS:** Rodriguez 29, Almao 16, Volquez 8, Kim 2. **LF:** Diaz 11, Guerrero 11, Argudin 10, Simon 7, Zayas 7, Ramirez 5, Tiamo 4, Arias 3, Pinder 3, Castillo 2. **CF:** Argudin 18, Rodriguez 17, Zayas 16, Ramirez 4, Genao 2. **RF:** Ramirez 24, Zayas 18, Guerrero 10, Argudin 4, Tiamo 2

Toronto Blue Jays

SEASON SYNOPSIS: Toronto went from worst to first in the AL East, winning 94 games to claim the AL's top seed. The Blue Jays blitzed the Yankees and rallied from a 3-2 deficit to beat Seattle and claim their first pennant since 1993. Leading the World Series 3-2, they couldn't finish off the Dodgers, including losing a 4-3 ninth-inning lead and dropping the series finale in 11 innings.

HIGH POINT: The Jays went 8-5 against the Yankees in the regular season, giving them the tiebreaker that led to the top seed and home field against the Yankees in the Division Series. They pummeled Yankee lefties Max Fried and Carlos Rodon en route to 23 runs in the first two games of the series, winning it in four. After dropping the first two ALCS games to the Mariners, the Blue Jays won seven of their next 10 games, winning the ALCS and taking a 3-2 lead back to Toronto.

LOW POINT: The Jays had a halting start and scored just two runs en route to a three-game sweep in Tampa as the Rays outscored them 19-2. Toronto fell to 25-27 on May 25, seven games back of the Yankees, and were eight games back when Texas shut them out two days later. But by July 3, after a four-game sweep of New York, the Jays took over the division lead, which they never relinquished. The Jays' offense, fourth in the majors in runs, came up just short in the last two World Series games, stranding 22 runners—14 left on base in Game Seven.

NOTABLE ROOKIES: Relievers Braydon Fisher (7-0, 2.70) and Mason Fluharty (5-2, 4.44) were key contributors, but 2024 first-rounder Trey Yesavage saved his best for last. He moved through four minor league levels before making three big league starts in September. Unleashed in October, he went 3-1, 3.58 as a playoff starter, including a Series-record (by a rookie) 12 strikeouts in a Game Five defeat of the Dodgers. He remains rookie-eligible for 2026.

KEY TRANSACTIONS: Free agent signee Anthony Santander (5-year, $92.5 million deal) had an injury-riddled season after hitting 44 homers in '24 for Baltimore. Reliever Jeff Hoffman (3-year, $33 million) saved 33 games in a 9-7, 4.37 season; he threw well in the postseason but blew the save in the ninth inning of Game Seven. Trade deadline acquisitions Shane Bieber (4-2, 3.57) and heavily used reliever Louis Varland (1-0, 4.94) proved vital, pitching a record 15 games in the postseason.

OPENING DAY PAYROLL: $239,642,532 (5th)

PLAYERS OF THE YEAR

MAJOR LEAGUE
George Springer
OF
.309/.399/.560
32 HR, 27 2B, 69 BB,
106 R, 84 RBIs

MINOR LEAGUE
Trey Yesavage
RHP
(A,A+,AA,AAA)
3.12 ERA in 98 IP
160 SO, .158 AVG

ORGANIZATION LEADERS

Batting		*Qualifiers
MAJORS		
* AVG	Bo Bichette	.311
* OPS	George Springer	.959
HR	George Springer	32
RBI	Bo Bichette	94
MINORS		
* AVG	Jackson Hornung, New Hampshire/Vancouver	.287
* OBP	Michael Stefanic, Buffalo	.403
* SLG	RJ Schreck, Buffalo/NH/Dunedin/FCL Blue Jays	.459
* OPS	RJ Schreck, Buffalo/NH./Dunedin/FCL Blue Jays	.854
R	Arjun Nimmala, Vancouver	70
H	Yohendrick Pinango, Buffalo/New Hampshire	117
TB	Yohendrick Pinango, Buffalo/New Hampshire	195
2B	Yohendrick Pinango, Buffalo/New Hampshire	29
2B	Arjun Nimmala, Vancouver	29
3B	Victor Arias, New Hampshire/Vancouver	7
HR	Sean Keys, Vancouver	19
RBI	Sean Keys, Vancouver	72
BB	Sean Keys, Vancouver	86
SO	Josh Rivera, Buffalo/New Hampshire	148
SB	Dasan Brown	36

Pitching		#Qualifiers
MAJORS		
W	Chris Bassitt	11
# ERA	Kevin Gausman	3.59
SO	Kevin Gausman	189
SV	Jeff Hoffman	33
MINORS		
W	Grant Rogers, New Hampshire/Vancouver	11
L	Colby Holcombe, Vancouver/Dunedin	11
# ERA	Fernando Perez, New Hampshire/Vancouver	3.04
G	Ryan Jennings, Buffalo/New Hampshire	45
GS	Grant Rogers, New Hampshire/Vancouver	28
SV	Dillon Tate, Buffalo	7
SV	Conor Larkin, New Hampshire	7
SV	Yondrei Rojas, New Hampshire/Vancouver	7
IP	Grant Rogers, New Hampshire/Vancouver	150
BB	Gage Stanifer, New Hampshire/Vanc./Dunedin	58
BB	Devereaux Harrison, Buffalo/New Hampshire	58
SO	Gage Stanifer, New Hampshire/Vanc./Dunedin	161
# AVG	Fernando Perez, New Hampshire/Vancouver	.242

2025 PERFORMANCE

Head Of Baseball Operations: Mark Shapiro. **Farm Director:** Joe Sclafani. **Scouting Director:** Marc Tramuta.

Class	Team	League	W	L	PCT	Finish	Manager
Majors	Toronto Blue Jays	American	94	68	.580	1 (15)	John Schneider
Triple-A	Buffalo Bisons	International	61	85	.418	19 (20)	Casey Candaele
Double-A	New Hampshire Fisher Cats	Eastern	56	81	.409	11 (12)	Cesar Martin
High-A	Vancouver Canadians	Northwest	75	57	.568	2 (6)	Jose Mayorga
Low-A	Dunedin Blue Jays	Florida State	60	66	.476	7 (10)	Gil Kim
Rookie	FCL Blue Jays	Florida Complex	36	23	.610	4 (15)	John Tamargo
Rookie	DSL Blue Jays	Dominican	22	33	.400	42 (52)	Daniel Canellas
Rookie	DSL Blue Jays 2	Dominican	30	26	.536	23 (52)	Ashley Ponce
Overall 2025 Minor League Record			340	371	.478	22nd (30)	

ORGANIZATION STATISTICS

TORONTO BLUE JAYS
AMERICAN LEAGUE

Batting	B-T	Ht.	Wt.	DOB	AVG	OBP	SLG	G	PA	AB	R	H	2B	3B	HR	RBI	BB	HBP	SH	SF	SO	SB	CS	BB%	SO%
Barger, Addison	L-R	6-0	210	11-12-99	.243	.301	.454	135	502	460	61	112	32	1	21	74	36	3	0	2	121	4	1	7.2	24.1
Bichette, Bo	R-R	6-0	190	3-5-98	.311	.357	.483	139	628	582	78	181	44	1	18	94	40	3	0	3	91	4	3	6.4	14.5
Clase, Jonatan	S-R	5-9	150	5-23-02	.210	.288	.300	34	112	100	10	21	3	0	2	9	10	1	0	0	28	3	1	8.9	25.0
Clement, Ernie	R-R	6-0	170	3-22-96	.277	.313	.398	157	588	545	83	151	35	2	9	50	27	4	7	5	61	6	5	4.6	10.4
France, Ty	R-R	5-11	215	7-13-94	.277	.320	.372	37	103	94	9	26	6	0	1	8	3	4	0	2	20	0	0	2.9	19.4
Gimenez, Andres	L-R	5-11	161	9-4-98	.210	.285	.313	101	369	329	39	69	11	1	7	35	25	11	1	3	66	12	2	6.8	17.9
Guerrero Jr., Vladimir	R-R	6-2	245	3-16-99	.292	.381	.467	156	680	589	96	172	34	0	23	84	81	6	0	4	94	6	3	11.9	13.8
Heineman, Tyler	S-R	5-10	190	6-19-91	.289	.361	.416	64	174	149	25	43	8	1	3	20	12	6	5	2	31	2	0	6.9	17.8
Jimenez, Leo	R-R	5-10	215	5-17-01	.069	.129	.172	18	32	29	2	2	0	0	1	1	2	0	1	0	8	0	0	6.3	25.0
Kennedy, Buddy	R-R	5-9	190	10-5-98	.200	.333	.400	2	6	5	1	1	0	0	0	1	0	0	0	0	1	0	0	16.7	16.7
Kiner-Falefa, Isiah	R-R	5-11	190	3-23-95	.233	.258	.367	19	31	30	5	7	1	0	1	5	0	1	0	0	0	0	0	25.8	
Kirk, Alejandro	R-R	5-8	245	11-6-98	.282	.348	.421	130	506	451	45	127	18	0	15	76	48	1	0	6	59	1	0	9.5	11.7
Loperfido, Joey	L-R	6-3	220	5-11-99	.333	.379	.500	41	104	96	12	32	4	0	4	14	4	3	1	0	27	1	2	3.8	26.0
Lukes, Nathan	L-R	5-11	180	7-12-94	.255	.323	.407	135	438	388	55	99	19	2	12	65	38	2	7	3	62	2	4	8.7	13.7
Robertson, Will	L-L	6-0	215	12-26-97	.100	.250	.100	3	12	10	0	1	0	0	0	1	1	1	0	0	7	0	0	8.3	58.3
Roden, Alan	L-R	5-11	215	12-22-99	.204	.283	.306	43	113	98	12	20	5	1	1	8	8	4	0	3	24	0	1	7.1	21.2
Sanchez, Ali	R-R	6-1	200	1-20-97	.238	.238	.333	8	21	21	2	5	2	0	0	0	0	0	0	0	5	0	0	0.0	23.8
Santander, Anthony	S-R	6-2	230	10-19-94	.175	.271	.294	54	221	194	16	34	5	0	6	18	25	1	0	1	61	0	0	11.3	27.6
Schneider, Davis	R-R	5-9	190	1-26-99	.234	.361	.436	82	227	188	33	44	5	0	11	31	36	2	0	1	60	3	1	15.9	26.4
Springer, George	R-R	6-3	220	9-19-89	.309	.399	.560	140	586	498	106	154	27	1	32	84	69	8	0	4	111	18	1	11.8	18.9
Stefanic, Michael	R-R	5-8	180	2-24-96	.182	.280	.182	9	25	22	1	4	0	0	0	0	3	0	0	0	3	0	0	12.0	12.0
Straw, Myles	R-R	5-10	178	10-17-94	.262	.313	.367	137	299	267	51	70	14	1	4	32	19	1	11	1	50	12	1	6.4	16.7
Varsho, Daulton	L-R	5-10	207	7-2-96	.238	.284	.548	71	271	248	43	59	13	2	20	55	17	1	0	5	77	2	0	6.3	28.4
Wagner, Will	L-R	5-11	210	7-29-98	.237	.336	.298	40	132	114	13	27	7	0	0	7	15	2	1	0	26	1	0	11.4	19.7

Pitching	B-T	Ht.	Wt.	DOB	W	L	ERA	G	GS	SV	IP	Hits	Runs	ER	HR	BB	SO	AVG	OBP	SLG	SO%	BB%	BF
Barnes, Jacob	R-R	6-2	231	4-14-90	0	1	9.00	6	0	0	8	10	9	8	1	3	5	.323	.361	.452	13.9	8.3	36
Bassitt, Chris	R-R	6-5	217	2-22-89	11	9	3.96	32	31	0	170	174	80	75	22	52	166	.261	.325	.415	22.6	7.1	736
Berrios, Jose	R-R	6-0	205	5-27-94	9	5	4.17	31	30	0	166	160	86	77	26	56	138	.253	.320	.430	19.8	8.0	698
Bieber, Shane	R-R	6-3	200	5-31-95	4	2	3.57	7	7	0	40	34	16	16	8	7	37	.225	.264	.417	23.3	4.4	159
Borucki, Ryan	L-L	6-4	210	3-31-94	0	0	0.00	4	0	0	4	3	0	0	0	4	5	.200	.368	.200	26.3	21.1	19
Bruihl, Justin	L-L	6-2	215	6-26-97	0	0	5.27	15	0	0	14	19	10	8	2	7	18	.333	.415	.474	27.7	10.8	65
Burr, Ryan	R-R	6-4	225	12-31-94	1	0	0.00	2	0	0	2	1	0	0	0	0	1	.143	.250	.143	37.5	12.5	8
Dominguez, Seranthony	R-R	6-1	225	11-25-94	2	1	3.00	24	0	0	21	12	11	7	1	12	25	.169	.302	.268	29.1	14.0	86
Estrada, Lazaro	R-R	5-10	180	4-24-99	0	0	8.59	2	0	0	7	10	7	7	2	1	10	.323	.382	.581	28.6	2.9	35
Fisher, Braydon	R-R	6-4	180	7-26-00	7	0	2.70	52	1	0	50	32	15	15	4	19	62	.181	.269	.282	30.7	9.4	202
Fluharty, Mason	L-L	6-2	213	8-13-01	5	2	4.44	55	0	1	53	36	28	26	6	24	56	.193	.290	.332	26.0	11.2	215
Francis, Bowden	R-R	6-5	220	4-22-96	2	8	6.05	14	14	0	64	71	46	43	19	27	54	.283	.361	.538	18.8	9.4	288
Garcia, Yimi	R-R	6-1	230	8-18-90	1	2	3.86	22	0	3	21	13	10	9	2	12	25	.171	.292	.263	27.8	13.3	90
Gausman, Kevin	L-R	6-2	205	1-6-91	10	11	3.59	32	32	0	193	155	79	77	21	50	189	.216	.269	.358	24.4	6.5	775
Green, Chad	R-R	6-3	215	5-24-91	3	2	5.56	45	0	1	44	51	28	27	14	13	35	.291	.347	.566	18.4	6.8	190
Heineman, Tyler	S-R	5-10	190	6-19-91	0	0	32.40	3	0	0	3	15	12	12	1	0	0	.625	.630	.833	0.0	0.0	27
Hoffman, Jeff	R-R	6-5	235	1-8-93	9	7	4.37	71	0	33	68	54	34	33	15	27	84	.213	.298	.447	29.3	9.4	287
Kiner-Falefa, Isiah	R-R	5-11	190	3-23-95	0	0	0.00	1	0	0	1	0	0	0	0	0	0	.000	.000	.000	0.0	0.0	2
Lauer, Eric	R-L	6-3	209	6-3-95	9	2	3.18	28	15	0	105	90	39	37	15	26	102	.227	.278	.407	23.9	6.1	426
Lawrence, Casey	R-R	6-0	180	10-28-87	0	0	10.13	1	0	0	3	6	3	3	0	0	1	.429	.467	.500	6.7	0.0	15
Little, Brendon	L-L	6-2	195	5-31-96	4	2	3.03	79	0	1	68	48	28	23	2	45	91	.196	.323	.273	30.8	15.3	295
Lovelady, Richard	L-L	6-0	185	7-7-95	0	1	21.60	2	0	0	2	4	4	2	0	3	.333	.583	.667	25.0	16.7	12
Lucas, Easton	L-L	6-4	180	9-23-96	3	3	6.66	6	5	0	24	29	18	18	5	12	23	.272	.343	.478	21.3	11.1	108
Nance, Tommy	R-R	6-6	235	3-19-91	2	0	1.99	30	0	0	32	25	11	7	0	7	32	.214	.262	.231	25.4	5.6	126
Pina, Robinson	R-R	6-5	225	11-26-98	0	0	6.75	1	0	0	4	5	3	3	1	0	1	.444	.500	.556	10.0	10.0	10
Rodriguez, Yariel	R-R	6-0	165	3-10-97	3	2	3.08	66	1	2	73	50	26	25	8	34	66	.196	.304	.325	22.1	11.4	298
Sanchez, Ali	R-R	6-1	200	1-20-97	0	0	18.00	1	0	0	1	3	2	2	0	0	1	.600	.500	1.000	16.7	0.0	6

Player	B-T	Ht	Wt	DOB	W	L	ERA	G	GS	CG	SV	IP	H	R	ER	BB	SO	AVG	OBP	SLG	K/9	BB/9
Sandlin, Nick	R-R	5-11	175	1-10-97	0	2	2.20	19	0	1	16	11	7	4	2	8	16	.186	.304	.322	23.2	11.6	69
Scherzer, Max	R-R	6-3	208	7-27-84	5	5	5.19	17	17	0	85	87	49	49	19	23	82	.262	.313	.497	22.9	6.4	358
Schultz, Paxton	L-R	6-3	205	1-5-98	0	0	4.38	13	2	0	25	27	16	12	4	8	28	.276	.327	.490	25.5	7.3	110
Swanson, Erik	R-R	6-3	225	9-4-93	1	0	15.19	6	0	0	5	8	9	9	2	5	3	.364	.467	.773	10.0	16.7	30
Tate, Dillon	R-R	6-2	190	5-1-94	0	0	4.26	6	0	0	6	8	3	3	1	6	8	.296	.441	.444	23.5	17.6	34
Turnbull, Spencer	R-R	6-3	210	9-18-92	1	1	7.11	3	1	0	6	12	5	5	1	4	4	.414	.485	.621	12.1	12.1	33
Urena, Jose	R-R	6-2	208	9-12-91	0	0	3.65	6	2	0	12	12	5	5	3	3	5	.245	.288	.449	9.6	5.8	52
Varland, Louie	L-R	6-1	205	12-9-97	1	0	4.94	23	1	0	24	24	13	13	3	9	28	.273	.333	.477	28.3	9.1	99
Walker, Josh	L-L	6-6	225	12-1-94	0	0	7.20	3	0	0	5	8	4	4	0	2	8	.364	.440	.500	32.0	8.0	25
Yesavage, Trey	R-R	6-4	225	7-28-03	1	0	3.21	3	3	0	14	13	5	5	0	7	16	.236	.323	.273	25.8	11.3	62

Fielding

Catcher	PCT	G	PO	A	E	DP	PB
Heineman	.983	61	441	30	8	2	0
Kirk	.991	118	968	35	9	4	4
Sanchez	1.000	7	51	0	0	0	0

First Base	PCT	G	PO	A	E	DP
Clement	.982	15	50	4	1	5
France	.986	23	121	16	2	8
Guerrero	.991	133	897	69	9	87
Sanchez	1.000	1	3	0	0	0
Santander	.000	1	0	0	0	0
Wagner	1.000	12	57	3	0	5

Second Base	PCT	G	PO	A	E	DP
Clement	.980	60	75	126	4	30
Gimenez	.994	87	137	193	2	41
Jimenez	1.000	15	13	22	0	4
Kennedy	.000	1	0	0	0	0
Kiner-Falefa	1.000	13	3	8	0	1

	PCT	G	PO	A	E	DP
Schneider	1.000	24	17	28	0	4
Stefanic	1.000	9	10	13	0	3
Straw	1.000	1	0	1	0	0
Wagner	1.000	1	0	1	0	0

Third Base	PCT	G	PO	A	E	DP
Barger	.966	91	55	114	6	10
Clement	.979	89	61	129	4	14
Kennedy	1.000	1	1	0	0	0
Kiner-Falefa	.929	7	3	10	1	1
Schneider	.000	1	0	0	0	0
Wagner	.947	24	14	22	2	2

Shortstop	PCT	G	PO	A	E	DP
Clement	.980	60	75	126	4	30
Gimenez	.994	87	137	193	2	41
Jimenez	1.000	15	13	22	0	4
Kennedy	.000	1	0	0	0	0
Kiner-Falefa	1.000	13	3	8	0	1

	PCT	G	PO	A	E	DP
Schneider	1.000	24	17	28	0	4
Stefanic	1.000	9	10	13	0	3
Straw	1.000	1	0	1	0	0
Wagner	1.000	1	0	1	0	0

Outfield	PCT	G	PO	A	E	DP
Barger	.970	57	88	9	3	3
Clase	1.000	36	59	1	0	0
Loperfido	1.000	41	58	1	0	0
Lukes	.991	159	218	9	2	4
Robertson	1.000	4	8	0	0	0
Roden	.986	43	68	3	1	1
Santander	1.000	24	46	0	0	0
Schneider	.977	59	85	1	2	0
Springer	.988	67	81	1	1	0
Straw	.995	142	181	5	1	2
Varsho	.993	68	146	1	1	0

BUFFALO BISONS
INTERNATIONAL LEAGUE — TRIPLE-A

Batting	B-T	Ht.	Wt.	DOB	AVG	OBP	SLG	G	PA	AB	R	H	2B	3B	HR	RBI	BB	HBP	SH	SF	SO	SB	CS	BB%	SO%
Barger, Addison	L-R	6-0	210	11-12-99	.211	.311	.421	12	45	38	6	8	2	0	2	7	5	1	0	1	13	0	0	11.1	28.9
Berroa, Steward	S-R	5-9	178	6-5-99	.195	.267	.234	24	86	77	15	15	3	0	0	4	8	0	0	1	24	9	3	9.3	27.9
Bethancourt, Christian	R-R	6-3	205	9-2-91	.173	.219	.332	58	214	196	19	34	10	0	7	21	11	1	4	2	56	2	1	5.1	26.2
Brooks, Robert	R-R	5-7	215	11-21-98	.200	.273	.200	3	11	10	1	2	0	0	0	2	1	0	0	0	2	0	0	9.1	18.2
Brown, Dasan	R-R	5-11	185	9-25-01	.154	.267	.462	15	15	13	4	2	1	0	1	1	2	0	0	0	2	5	2	13.3	13.3
Brown, Devonte	R-R	5-9	207	10-15-99	.238	.273	.429	9	22	21	1	5	1	0	1	2	1	0	0	0	7	1	0	4.5	31.8
Clarke, Phil	L-R	5-11	190	3-24-98	.281	.385	.363	48	175	146	21	41	6	0	2	15	25	1	0	2	20	1	0	14.3	11.4
Clase, Jonatan	S-R	5-9	150	5-23-02	.255	.335	.403	87	352	310	41	79	25	0	7	21	35	3	3	1	90	30	4	9.9	25.6
Gimenez, Andres	S-R	5-9	161	9-4-98	.389	.421	.389	5	19	18	3	7	0	0	0	1	0	1	0	0	5	1	0	0.0	26.3
Heineman, Tyler	S-R	5-10	190	6-19-91	.500	.714	.750	2	7	4	1	2	1	0	0	1	2	1	0	0	0	1	0	28.6	0.0
Jimenez, Eloy	R-R	6-4	240	11-27-96	.167	.286	.222	6	21	18	0	3	1	0	0	0	3	0	0	0	5	0	0	14.3	23.8
Jimenez, Leo	R-R	5-10	215	5-17-01	.304	.437	.375	19	71	56	12	17	3	0	0	4	11	3	0	1	13	0	1	15.5	18.3
Kasevich, Josh	R-R	6-1	200	1-17-01	.173	.272	.184	29	114	98	6	17	1	0	0	6	13	1	0	2	20	0	2	11.4	17.5
Kennedy, Buddy	R-R	5-9	190	10-5-98	.275	.353	.333	27	116	102	15	28	6	0	0	9	12	1	0	1	14	1	0	10.3	12.1
Kirk, Alejandro	R-R	5-8	245	11-6-98	.333	.333	.333	1	3	3	0	1	0	0	0	0	0	0	0	0	0	0	0	0.0	0.0
Loperfido, Joey	L-R	6-3	220	5-11-99	.264	.341	.401	91	373	329	46	87	22	1	7	44	29	10	4	1	80	11	1	7.8	21.4
Lukes, Nathan	L-R	5-11	180	7-12-94	.571	.571	1.000	2	7	7	2	4	0	0	0	1	0	0	0	0	1	0	0	0.0	14.3
Martinez, Orelvis	R-R	5-11	200	11-19-01	.176	.288	.348	99	394	336	38	59	17	1	13	32	47	7	0	3	112	2	1	11.9	28.4
McCarty, Ryan	R-R	5-9	182	4-22-99	.240	.321	.440	10	28	25	4	6	0	1	1	1	2	1	0	0	8	0	0	7.1	28.6
Nunez, Rainer	R-R	6-2	180	1-20-02	.252	.323	.374	81	300	270	32	68	12	0	7	30	24	5	0	1	72	2	1	8.0	24.0
Palmegiani, Damiano	R-R	6-0	195	1-24-00	.159	.299	.232	52	167	138	9	22	7	0	1	15	18	10	0	1	47	0	1	10.8	28.1
Pinango, Yohendrick	L-L	5-11	170	5-7-02	.235	.335	.379	84	341	293	39	69	19	1	7	47	43	2	0	2	65	1	0	12.6	19.1
Pinto, Rene	R-R	5-10	195	11-2-96	.214	.214	.393	8	28	28	2	6	2	0	1	5	0	0	0	0	11	0	0	0.0	39.3
Rivera, Josh	R-R	6-2	215	10-10-00	.226	.332	.330	110	394	336	44	76	15	1	6	30	53	1	2	2	124	1	1	13.5	31.5
Robertson, Will	L-L	6-0	215	12-26-97	.292	.403	.578	62	233	192	39	56	11	1	14	44	36	2	0	3	57	1	2	15.5	24.5
Roden, Alan	L-R	5-11	215	12-22-99	.331	.423	.496	32	142	121	25	40	9	1	3	18	16	4	0	1	13	4	1	11.3	9.2
Sanchez, Ali	R-R	6-1	200	1-20-97	.279	.347	.419	54	199	179	24	50	7	0	6	28	18	1	0	1	47	0	0	9.0	23.6
Santander, Anthony	S-R	6-2	230	10-19-94	.219	.342	.469	40	38	32	4	7	2	0	2	5	6	0	0	0	6	0	0	15.8	15.8
Schneider, Davis	R-R	5-9	190	1-26-99	.226	.350	.391	38	160	133	17	30	6	2	4	18	24	2	0	1	46	3	1	15.0	28.8
Schreck, RJ	L-R	6-1	210	7-12-00	.242	.351	.435	58	234	183	32	45	7	1	9	33	38	8	2	0	49	2	0	16.2	20.9
Springer, George	R-R	6-3	220	9-19-89	.400	.500	1.200	2	6	5	3	2	1	0	1	1	1	0	0	0	0	0	0	16.7	0.0
Stefanic, Michael	R-R	5-8	180	2-24-96	.287	.403	.383	106	442	363	48	104	17	0	6	51	59	15	0	5	44	6	6	13.3	10.0
Tirotta, Michael	R-R	6-3	195	8-21-98	.268	.359	.417	116	463	403	61	108	20	2	12	60	53	5	0	2	137	13	3	11.4	29.6
Turconi, Michael	L-R	5-10	185	6-24-99	.130	.250	.174	12	28	23	4	3	1	0	0	3	4	0	0	1	8	0	0	14.3	28.6
Valenzuela, Brandon	S-R	6-0	225	10-2-00	.207	.295	.370	26	105	92	9	19	6	0	3	12	10	0	1	2	32	0	0	11.4	30.5
Varsho, Daulton	L-R	5-10	207	7-2-96	.133	.182	.233	8	33	30	2	4	0	0	1	5	1	0	1	0	8	0	0	3.0	24.2
Wagner, Will	L-R	5-11	210	7-29-98	.268	.342	.451	18	79	71	13	19	4	0	3	13	8	0	0	0	12	1	0	10.1	15.2

TORONTO BLUE JAYS

Pitching	B-T	Ht.	Wt.	DOB	W	L	ERA	G	GS	SV	IP	Hits	Runs	ER	HR	BB	SO	AVG	OBP	SLG	SO%	BB%	BF
Barnes, Jacob	R-R	6-2	231	4-14-90	2	1	6.84	22	0	1	25	35	24	19	5	12	20	.337	.395	.529	16.8	10.1	119
Bash, Andrew	R-R	6-0	190	8-1-96	6	2	2.57	40	5	2	84	73	33	24	4	36	72	.228	.316	.325	19.7	9.9	365
Bieber, Shane	R-R	6-3	200	5-31-95	1	1	2.04	3	3	0	18	15	4	4	2	2	16	.238	.262	.381	24.6	3.1	65
Bloss, Jake	R-R	6-3	205	6-23-01	0	5	6.46	6	6	0	24	33	25	17	3	13	24	.330	.400	.490	20.9	11.3	115
Borucki, Ryan	L-L	6-4	210	3-31-94	1	0	0.00	1	0	0	2	1	0	0	0	1	0	.200	.429	.200	0.0	14.3	7
Boyer, Ryan	R-R	6-2	225	5-4-97	0	0	20.25	1	0	0	1	2	3	3	1	1	2	.333	.429	1.000	28.6	14.3	7
Bruihl, Justin	L-L	6-2	215	6-26-97	3	4	3.43	39	0	3	42	32	18	16	3	16	49	.205	.287	.295	27.8	9.1	176
Burnette, Jimmy	L-L	6-2	205	10-19-98	3	1	11.45	12	0	0	11	13	17	14	1	19	16	.289	.543	.378	22.9	27.1	70
Burr, Ryan	R-R	6-4	220	5-28-94	1	0	3.52	7	0	0	8	4	3	3	1	5	11	.154	.290	.269	35.5	16.1	31
Estrada, Lazaro	R-R	5-10	180	4-24-99	4	7	5.73	26	20	0	97	109	69	62	17	32	99	.278	.336	.508	23.1	7.5	429
Fisher, Braydon	R-R	6-4	180	7-26-00	1	0	1.62	14	0	2	17	12	5	3	0	5	22	.197	.254	.230	32.8	7.5	67
Fluharty, Mason	L-L	6-2	215	8-13-01	0	0	3.27	11	0	0	11	11	4	4	0	7	15	.256	.365	.439	28.8	13.5	52
Garcia, Yimi	R-R	6-1	230	8-18-90	0	0	0.00	1	0	0	1	0	0	0	0	1	1	.333	.500	.333	25.0	25.0	4
Garrett, Amir	R-L	6-5	239	5-3-92	0	0	5.06	5	0	1	5	3	3	3	0	4	6	.176	.318	.294	27.3	18.2	22
Gowdy, Kevin	R-R	6-4	205	11-16-97	3	2	5.25	33	0	1	36	45	31	21	5	20	32	.308	.401	.479	18.6	11.6	172
Gregory, Hunter	R-R	6-3	215	11-16-98	0	1	14.29	11	1	0	11	15	19	18	3	16	12	.333	.492	.578	18.8	25.0	64
Harrison, Devereaux	R-R	6-0	190	11-8-00	0	1	6.30	6	0	0	10	14	9	7	0	9	7	.326	.442	.442	13.5	17.3	52
Hernandez, Elieser	R-R	6-1	214	5-3-95	0	3	7.91	4	4	0	19	17	18	17	1	7	15	.236	.296	.417	18.5	8.6	81
Jennings, Ryan	R-R	6-0	190	6-23-99	1	3	4.25	34	0	0	36	39	20	17	6	29	54	.275	.410	.486	30.2	16.2	179
Juenger, Hayden	R-R	6-0	180	8-9-00	4	0	5.00	31	2	3	36	36	24	20	4	23	34	.261	.364	.413	21.0	14.2	162
Kloffenstein, Adam	R-R	6-5	243	8-25-00	2	8	6.26	19	16	1	82	88	63	57	20	44	90	.272	.368	.515	23.9	11.7	377
Lauer, Eric	R-L	6-3	209	6-3-95	1	3	4.50	5	5	0	24	24	12	12	2	6	21	.253	.304	.411	20.6	5.9	102
Lucas, Easton	L-L	6-4	180	9-23-96	2	3	3.78	17	13	0	64	58	27	27	8	28	68	.241	.326	.390	24.9	10.3	273
Macko, Adam	L-L	6-0	170	12-30-00	3	8	5.06	18	10	0	64	61	37	36	6	36	65	.253	.353	.402	22.6	12.5	287
Manoah, Alek	R-R	6-6	285	1-9-98	1	1	2.97	7	7	0	33	27	19	11	6	18	30	.218	.331	.411	20.4	12.2	147
Mantiply, Joe	R-L	6-4	219	3-1-91	2	1	3.45	14	0	0	16	19	8	6	1	0	19	.297	.297	.406	29.7	0.0	64
Milacki, Bobby	R-R	6-2	210	11-6-96	2	2	4.40	20	3	0	43	44	23	21	5	17	24	.268	.355	.433	12.8	9.1	187
Nance, Tommy	R-R	6-6	235	3-19-91	0	4	4.60	27	0	4	31	31	20	16	2	7	42	.256	.308	.364	31.3	5.2	134
Nunez, Rainer	R-R	6-2	180	12-4-00	0	0	18.00	1	0	0	1	3	2	2	0	1	0	.600	.667	.600	0.0	16.7	6
Overton, Connor	L-R	6-0	205	7-24-93	0	0	15.26	3	0	0	8	15	13	13	3	4	6	.395	.439	.579	9.8	7.3	41
Pardinho, Eric	R-R	5-10	155	1-5-01	1	2	3.50	15	0	0	18	20	7	7	0	12	24	.290	.395	.348	29.6	14.8	81
Pina, Robinson	R-R	6-5	225	11-26-98	0	0	4.32	4	2	0	8	4	4	4	2	4	8	.286	.375	.536	25.0	12.5	32
Robertson, Will	L-L	6-0	215		0	0	6.75	2	0	0	1	1	1	1	1	1	0	.200	.333	.800	0.0	16.7	6
Rojas, Kendry	L-L	6-2	190	11-26-02	0	1	10.80	1	1	0	5	10	6	6	2	1	6	.435	.480	.739	24.0	8.0	25
Sandlin, Nick	R-R	5-11	175	1-10-97	0	0	33.75	3	0	0	1	6	5	5	2	2	1	.600	.667	1.600	8.3	16.7	12
Scherzer, Max	R-R	6-3	208	7-27-84	0	0	2.08	2	2	0	9	5	2	2	1	2	12	.167	.235	.333	35.5	5.9	34
Schultz, Paxton	L-R	6-3	205	3-31-97	5	4	3.31	25	1	1	49	37	19	18	5	17	46	.211	.278	.354	23.6	8.7	195
Swanson, Erik	R-R	6-3	225	9-4-93	0	1	9.00	4	0	0	4	4	4	4	0	1	3	.250	.294	.313	17.6	5.9	17
Tate, Dillon	R-R	6-2	190	5-1-94	4	0	2.06	36	0	7	39	29	9	9	2	20	38	.203	.309	.294	22.8	12.0	167
Tolhurst, Anders	R-R	6-4	190	9-13-99	4	5	4.67	16	14	0	71	65	40	37	12	31	60	.241	.323	.433	19.6	10.1	306
Turnbull, Spencer	R-R	6-3	210	9-18-92	0	2	9.95	2	2	0	6	11	7	7	0	5	4	.333	.455	.333	11.8	14.7	34
Van Eyk, CJ	R-R	6-1	198	9-15-98	4	6	4.94	20	17	1	89	96	63	49	15	40	73	.270	.348	.444	18.1	9.9	403
Walker, Josh	L-L	6-6	235	12-1-94	0	1	6.30	11	0	0	13	8	7	7	2	16	19	.195	.392	.568	31.4	13.7	51
Wallace, Trenton	L-L	6-1	200	3-31-99	0	2	4.18	25	8	1	52	44	26	24	6	36	65	.233	.357	.381	28.1	15.6	231
Yesavage, Trey	R-R	6-4	225	7-28-03	0	0	3.63	6	4	0	17	9	8	7	0	11	26	.150	.278	.217	36.1	15.3	72

Fielding

Catcher	PCT	G	PO	A	E	DP	PB
Bethancourt	.983	51	414	36	8	3	5
Brooks	1.000	2	17	2	0	0	0
Clarke	.972	24	166	10	5	1	3
Heineman	1.000	1	7	1	0	0	0
Kirk	1.000	1	7	1	0	0	0
Pinto	1.000	8	90	3	0	1	0
Sanchez	.993	47	389	29	3	2	1
Valenzuela	.985	21	182	16	3	0	3

First Base	PCT	G	PO	A	E	DP
Clarke	.964	8	53	1	2	4
Jimenez	1.000	3	13	0	0	1
Kennedy	.962	7	47	4	2	4
Loperfido	1.000	9	56	2	0	6
Nunez	.987	67	476	51	7	35
Palmegiani	1.000	24	149	15	0	9
Stefanic	1.000	2	4	1	0	0
Tirotta	.985	36	187	14	3	17
Valenzuela	1.000	2	7	1	0	1
Wagner	1.000	7	33	3	0	2

Second Base	PCT	G	PO	A	E	DP
Gimenez	.875	5	5	2	1	0
Jimenez	1.000	6	10	11	0	1
Kennedy	.972	9	9	26	1	4
Loperfido	.000	1	0	0	0	0

	PCT	G	PO	A	E	DP
Martinez	.981	79	121	183	6	29
McCarty	1.000	2	1	6	0	1
Rivera	.941	5	6	10	1	4
Schneider	1.000	10	16	20	0	7
Stefanic	.980	34	37	63	2	11
Tirotta	1.000	1	0	1	0	0
Turconi	.958	6	11	12	1	4

Third Base	PCT	G	PO	A	E	DP
Barger	.909	6	3	7	1	1
Kasevich	.905	11	7	12	2	2
Kennedy	.950	9	6	13	1	0
Martinez	1.000	7	0	14	0	0
McCarty	1.000	2	3	4	0	1
Palmegiani	.784	15	11	18	8	3
Rivera	1.000	8	4	14	0	0
Schneider	1.000	9	1	5	0	0
Stefanic	.967	41	32	57	3	6
Tirotta	.918	43	26	63	8	4
Wagner	1.000	5	8	11	0	2

Shortstop	PCT	G	PO	A	E	DP
Barger	.667	2	1	5	3	1
Jimenez	.913	7	7	14	2	1
Kasevich	.983	17	20	37	1	4
McCarty	1.000	2	2	5	0	2
Rivera	.961	97	114	205	13	33

	PCT	G	PO	A	E	DP
Stefanic	.953	27	28	54	4	12
Tirotta	1.000	2	0	1	0	0
Turconi	.875	5	5	9	2	1

Outfield	PCT	G	PO	A	E	DP
Barger	.962	18	23	2	1	1
Barger	1.000	4	6	2	0	0
Berroa	.947	21	35	1	2	1
Das. Brown	1.000	10	12	1	0	0
Dav. Brown	.909	8	10	0	1	0
Clase	.968	80	151	1	5	0
Jimenez	1.000	2	3	0	0	0
Kennedy	.750	2	1	2	1	0
Loperfido	1.000	72	154	2	0	1
Lukes	.000	1	0	0	0	0
McCarty	1.000	3	5	0	0	0
Palmegiani	1.000	2	4	1	0	0
Pinango	.979	76	134	4	3	0
Robertson	.989	49	89	2	1	0
Roden	.961	28	47	2	2	1
Santander	1.000	2	2	0	0	0
Schneider	.943	20	33	0	2	0
Schreck	.972	54	102	1	3	0
Tirotta	.905	36	54	3	6	1
Varsho	1.000	6	11	0	0	0

NEW HAMPSHIRE FISHER CATS   DOUBLE-A
EASTERN LEAGUE

Batting	B-T	Ht.	Wt.	DOB	AVG	OBP	SLG	G	PA	AB	R	H	2B	3B	HR	RBI	BB	HBP	SH	SF	SO	SB	CS	BB%	SO%
Arias, Victor	L-L	5-11	150	8-24-03	.226	.293	.331	36	150	133	20	30	4	2	2	11	14	0	0	3	38	6	1	9.3	25.3
Bohrofen, Jace	L-R	6-2	205	10-19-01	.204	.311	.377	83	335	289	36	59	16	2	10	34	42	3	0	0	114	11	2	12.5	34.0
Brooks, Robert	R-R	5-7	215	11-21-98	.129	.214	.224	46	131	116	4	15	5	0	2	9	11	2	0	2	46	0	1	8.4	35.1
Brown, Dasan	R-R	5-11	185	9-25-01	.175	.286	.249	86	276	229	34	40	6	1	3	14	32	4	3	1	84	31	2	11.6	30.4
Brown, Devonte	R-R	5-9	207	10-15-99	.190	.326	.335	65	218	179	27	34	8	0	6	22	34	3	0	2	63	9	0	15.6	28.9
De Jesus, Alex	R-R	6-1	170	3-22-02	.188	.262	.266	61	214	192	16	36	6	3	1	13	20	0	0	2	66	3	0	9.3	30.8
De Los Santos, Raimundo	S-R	5-10	147	2-27-05	.200	.333	.200	2	6	5	0	1	0	0	0	0	1	0	0	0	2	0	0	16.7	33.3
Deschamps, Nicolas	L-R	5-11	180	8-25-02	.094	.171	.125	13	35	32	3	3	1	0	0	3	0	0	0	0	12	0	0	8.6	34.3
Doughty, Cade	R-R	6-1	195	3-26-01	.237	.279	.322	104	373	342	28	81	17	0	4	33	20	2	4	5	83	4	2	5.4	22.3
Freethy, J.R.	S-R	5-11	185	12-23-02	.200	.333	.500	4	12	10	1	2	0	0	1	3	2	0	0	0	4	0	0	16.7	33.3
Gilliland, Hayden	L-R	5-11	175	10-29-01	.200	.429	.400	2	7	5	1	1	1	0	0	0	1	1	0	0	4	0	0	14.3	57.1
Harry, Jay	R-R	6-0	195	7-18-02	.153	.255	.226	44	141	124	14	19	3	0	2	9	15	2	0	0	33	4	0	10.6	23.4
Hornung, Jackson	R-R	6-2	215	2-6-01	.269	.341	.446	52	214	186	30	50	11	2	6	23	21	1	0	3	73	4	0	9.8	34.1
Martinez, Gabriel	R-R	5-9	170	7-24-02	.250	.312	.348	73	248	224	20	56	14	1	2	21	19	2	0	2	48	4	0	7.7	19.4
McAdoo, Charles	R-R	6-2	210	3-6-02	.247	.318	.413	121	494	445	62	110	24	1	16	45	45	2	1	1	137	34	6	9.1	27.7
McCarty, Ryan	R-R	5-9	182	4-22-99	.224	.326	.319	102	377	326	36	73	17	1	4	26	41	9	0	1	92	9	5	10.9	24.4
Palmegiani, Damiano	R-R	6-0	195	1-24-00	.200	.294	.300	8	34	30	4	6	1	1	0	2	4	0	0	0	11	0	0	11.8	32.4
Paulino, Eddinson	L-R	5-10	155	7-2-02	.198	.264	.362	97	360	329	36	65	11	2	13	39	25	5	0	1	98	6	3	6.9	27.2
Pinango, Yohendrick	L-L	5-11	170	5-7-02	.298	.406	.522	47	192	161	18	48	10	1	8	23	27	3	0	1	42	5	0	14.1	21.9
Rivera, Josh	R-R	6-2	215	10-10-00	.163	.217	.256	13	46	43	2	7	1	0	1	5	3	0	0	0	24	1	0	6.5	52.2
Schreck, RJ	L-R	6-1	210	7-12-00	.266	.396	.518	41	169	139	27	37	6	3	9	20	26	4	0	0	40	5	1	15.4	23.7
Sharp, Jacob	R-R	5-10	190	9-15-01	.161	.271	.206	68	209	180	16	29	5	0	1	10	17	10	2	0	58	1	0	8.1	27.8
Stone, Alex	R-R	6-5	235	11-3-01	.180	.226	.250	33	107	100	9	18	1	0	2	11	5	1	1	0	23	0	0	4.7	21.5
Ward, Je'Von	L-R	6-2	190	10-25-99	.230	.303	.393	51	198	178	26	41	9	1	6	30	19	0	0	1	60	3	0	9.6	30.3
Williams, Peyton	L-L	6-5	255	9-14-00	.217	.280	.353	88	329	300	31	65	12	1	9	39	26	1	0	2	105	0	0	7.9	31.9

Pitching	B-T	Ht.	Wt.	DOB	W	L	ERA	G	GS	SV	IP	Hits	Runs	ER	HR	BB	SO	AVG	OBP	SLG	SO%	BB%	BF
Amalfi, Alex	R-R	6-1	185	2-18-01	6	8	4.41	34	11	4	88	70	45	43	4	47	100	.217	.323	.313	26.6	12.5	376
Boyer, Ryan	R-R	6-2	225	5-4-97	0	0	8.22	6	0	0	8	9	7	7	3	2	6	.300	.353	.667	17.6	5.9	34
Burnette, Jimmy	L-L	6-2	205	10-19-98	0	0	1.04	8	0	1	9	3	1	1	0	4	12	.107	.219	.143	37.5	12.5	32
Dominguez, Michael	R-R	5-10	175	8-17-00	1	2	5.22	23	6	0	50	46	32	29	9	29	61	.237	.349	.459	26.6	12.7	229
Gallagher, Pat	R-R	6-0	196	6-30-00	2	3	2.75	18	0	0	36	33	11	11	2	11	38	.237	.298	.317	25.2	7.3	151
Garkow, Nate	R-R	5-11	190	9-4-97	3	0	1.22	29	0	1	37	12	5	5	1	17	54	.098	.214	.172	38.6	12.1	140
Gregory, Hunter	R-R	6-3	215	11-16-98	2	2	2.84	33	0	4	44	39	19	14	7	18	48	.235	.321	.398	25.1	9.4	191
Harrison, Devereaux	R-R	6-0	190	11-8-00	6	8	3.68	28	14	0	88	70	38	36	8	49	93	.219	.324	.339	24.7	13.0	377
Jennings, Ryan	R-R	6-0	190	6-23-99	3	1	2.86	11	0	0	22	16	7	7	2	14	28	.200	.337	.313	28.6	14.3	98
Kelly, Justin	R-R	6-1	195	12-2-98	1	3	7.01	22	0	0	26	37	27	20	4	13	21	.327	.397	.504	16.4	10.2	128
Larkin, Conor	R-R	6-1	205	3-17-99	5	4	4.14	39	0	7	50	40	25	23	2	25	50	.222	.338	.317	23.7	11.8	211
Lavallee, Johnathan	R-R	6-4	240	8-11-99	1	2	6.19	28	0	2	32	30	29	22	3	25	38	.246	.372	.410	25.2	16.6	151
Manoah, Alek	R-R	6-6	285	1-9-98	0	0	6.00	1	1	0	3	5	2	2	0	3	2	.357	.500	.500	11.1	16.7	18
Milacki, Bobby	R-R	6-2	210	11-6-96	0	3	3.18	12	4	0	28	32	13	10	4	10	25	.276	.333	.440	19.8	7.9	126
Miranda, Kevin	R-R	5-10	178	11-14-98	0	0	9.45	4	0	0	7	9	7	7	3	2	3	.300	.333	.667	9.1	6.1	33
Perez, Fernando	R-R	6-3	170	2-12-04	0	3	3.00	6	6	0	27	26	13	9	1	9	21	.243	.302	.299	17.9	7.7	117
Peterson, Kai	L-L	6-1	190	8-14-02	0	0	4.70	9	0	0	8	9	4	4	1	7	13	.300	.450	.467	32.5	17.5	40
Rogers, Grant	R-R	6-2	230	5-22-01	8	9	4.07	20	20	0	111	118	61	50	9	20	76	.269	.331	.390	16.0	4.2	475
Rojas, Kendry	L-L	6-2	190	11-26-02	0	2	3.86	4	4	0	19	18	9	8	2	2	30	.247	.267	.384	40.0	2.7	75
Rojas, Yondrei	R-R	5-10	180	11-22-02	1	0	0.64	11	0	3	14	5	1	1	0	5	11	.111	.216	.156	21.6	9.8	51
Sanchez, Rafael	R-R	6-1	215	8-22-99	2	8	5.54	25	19	2	91	108	63	56	7	31	71	.292	.346	.441	17.3	7.6	410
Simon, Johan	L-L	6-1	166	7-1-01	1	1	2.38	6	0	0	11	9	3	3	1	5	16	.205	.286	.364	32.7	10.2	49
Stanifer, Gage	R-R	6-3	201	11-18-03	0	1	6.75	2	2	0	8	5	6	6	2	9	8	.192	.400	.423	22.9	25.7	35
Stephen, Khal	R-R	6-4	215	12-21-02	0	0	9.00	1	1	0	4	5	5	4	2	1	2	.313	.353	.750	11.1	5.6	18
Thurman, Grayson	R-R	6-3	205	12-27-01	1	1	4.62	23	0	2	25	19	13	13	3	12	20	.230	.331	.330	18.9	11.3	106
Tolhurst, Anders	R-R	6-4	190	9-13-99	0	0	4.50	2	2	0	10	9	6	5	0	3	11	.237	.286	.263	26.2	7.1	42
Urbaez, Geison	R-R	6-1	180	7-5-00	2	3	3.18	29	4	0	57	53	32	20	5	35	42	.247	.359	.372	16.1	13.4	261
Van Eyk, CJ	R-R	6-1	198	9-15-98	2	4	4.42	7	7	0	37	30	24	18	5	11	36	.224	.298	.396	23.8	7.3	151
Watson, Ryan	R-R	6-4	207	4-9-99	5	8	4.79	19	17	0	98	105	66	52	14	29	67	.277	.330	.467	16.1	7.0	415
Watts-Brown, Juaron	R-R	6-3	190	2-23-02	2	2	3.48	11	11	0	52	38	23	20	4	26	53	.201	.309	.344	24.0	11.8	221
Yeager, Chay	S-R	5-11	180	9-11-02	1	2	4.50	17	1	1	20	21	12	10	4	7	21	.269	.329	.526	24.7	8.2	85
Yesavage, Trey	R-R	6-4	225	7-28-03	1	1	4.50	8	7	0	30	21	15	15	3	11	46	.198	.267	.387	38.0	9.1	121

Fielding

Catcher	PCT	G	PO	A	E	DP	PB
Brooks	.988	43	305	22	4	1	7
Deschamps	.973	10	68	3	2	0	0
Gilliland	1.000	2	16	1	0	0	0
Sharp	.984	68	481	26	8	2	11
Stone	.989	31	256	21	3	0	3

First Base	PCT	G	PO	A	E	DP
De Jesus	.991	18	98	9	1	5
Hornung	.982	27	204	15	4	14
McAdoo	.978	13	87	4	2	6
McCarty	.983	11	54	3	1	4
Palmegiani	1.000	3	20	1	0	2
Williams	.995	74	509	36	3	50

Second Base	PCT	G	PO	A	E	DP
Brown	.000	1	0	0	0	0
De Los Santos	1.000	1	1	1	0	1
Doughty	.988	20	29	52	1	13
Harry	1.000	2	4	5	0	1
McAdoo	1.000	1	0	1	0	0
McCarty	.978	53	72	103	4	20
Paulino	.975	71	79	157	6	32

Rivera	1.000	1	1	3	0	0

Third Base	PCT	G	PO	A	E	DP
De Jesus	.879	22	9	42	7	4
Doughty	.943	17	12	21	2	2
McAdoo	.925	96	52	132	15	12
McCarty	.933	10	3	11	1	1

Shortstop	PCT	G	PO	A	E	DP
De Jesus	.977	16	11	31	1	4
Doughty	.954	65	84	142	11	29

Harry	.966	39	49	91	5	17
Paulino	.826	14	11	27	8	4
Rivera	.977	12	7	35	1	3

Outfield	PCT	G	PO	A	E	DP
Arias	.957	26	65	1	3	0
Bohrofen	.984	66	122	4	2	2
Dav. Brown	.983	62	114	2	2	0
Das. Brown	.977	79	168	5	4	0
De Los Santos	1.000	2	2	0	0	0

Freethy	1.000	4	7	0	0	0
Harry	1.000	2	7	0	0	0
Hornung	1.000	12	26	3	0	0
Martinez	.987	65	152	0	2	0
McCarty	.950	20	36	2	2	0
Palmegiani	1.000	4	5	0	0	0
Pinango	.913	31	41	1	4	1
Schreck	.982	28	54	2	1	1
Ward	.952	43	59	1	3	0

VANCOUVER CANADIANS — HIGH-A
NORTHWEST LEAGUE

Batting	B-T	Ht.	Wt.	DOB	AVG	OBP	SLG	G	PA	AB	R	H	2B	3B	HR	RBI	BB	HBP	SH	SF	SO	SB	CS	BB%	SO%
Arias, Victor	L-L	5-11	150	8-24-03	.294	.381	.437	66	318	279	49	82	15	5	5	36	36	3	0	0	64	12	4	11.3	20.1
Arnold, Bryce	R-R	5-10	175	7-24-01	.188	.316	.325	25	98	80	15	15	5	0	2	13	12	4	0	2	28	0	0	12.2	28.6
Coffey, Cutter	R-R	6-1	190	5-21-04	.273	.359	.427	99	440	384	68	105	26	0	11	62	47	6	0	3	100	10	3	10.7	22.7
Cunningham, Carter	L-R	6-4	210	11-6-00	.220	.346	.414	102	419	345	64	76	15	2	16	59	67	2	0	5	136	11	4	16.0	32.5
Deschamps, Nicolas	L-R	5-11	180	8-25-02	.196	.348	.286	20	70	56	5	11	3	1	0	3	7	6	1	0	28	0	0	10.0	40.0
Duran, Edward	R-R	5-11	170	5-29-04	.230	.329	.336	34	140	122	15	28	4	0	3	12	16	2	0	0	36	1	0	11.4	18.6
Freethy, J.R.	S-R	5-11	185	12-23-02	.253	.383	.364	25	120	99	18	25	8	0	1	10	18	3	0	0	23	2	0	15.0	19.2
Gilliland, Hayden	L-R	5-11	175	10-29-01	.206	.325	.338	23	83	68	11	14	3	0	2	15	13	0	0	2	28	0	0	15.7	33.7
Goodwin, Nick	R-R	6-0	190	9-6-01	.244	.366	.403	96	385	320	51	78	13	1	12	47	52	10	2	1	69	10	3	13.5	17.9
Harry, Jay	L-R	6-0	195	7-18-02	.228	.302	.327	56	225	202	24	46	9	1	3	22	21	1	0	1	42	5	3	9.3	18.7
Hernandez, Alexis	R-R	6-0	170	10-5-02	.293	.358	.467	26	106	92	19	27	5	1	3	14	10	1	0	3	18	4	1	9.4	17.0
Hornung, Jackson	R-R	6-2	215	2-6-01	.308	.396	.459	44	189	159	33	49	9	3	3	24	23	2	0	3	51	5	0	12.2	27.0
Keys, Sean	L-R	6-2	225	5-26-03	.217	.365	.408	119	529	424	67	92	22	1	19	72	86	15	0	4	117	8	1	16.3	22.1
Lojewski, Jacob	R-R	5-10	180	11-16-01	.136	.136	.182	5	22	22	2	3	1	0	0	0	0	0	0	0	4	0	0	0.0	18.2
Martinez, Gabriel	R-R	5-9	170	7-24-02	.236	.354	.309	15	65	55	10	13	4	0	0	1	7	3	0	0	16	1	0	10.8	24.6
Micheletti, Eddie	L-R	6-1	200	12-29-01	.228	.375	.418	106	464	368	53	84	24	2	14	70	78	12	0	6	70	3	0	16.8	15.1
Nimmala, Arjun	R-R	6-1	170	10-16-05	.224	.313	.381	120	543	473	70	106	29	3	13	61	55	9	0	6	116	17	3	10.1	21.4
Orf, Brennan	L-R	6-3	225	9-6-01	.186	.385	.254	18	78	59	9	11	2	1	0	12	17	2	0	0	20	2	0	21.8	25.6
Parker, Aaron	R-R	5-9	200	1-17-03	.233	.301	.386	63	276	249	32	58	12	1	8	36	21	4	0	2	54	5	0	7.6	19.6
Pinto, Adrian	R-R	5-6	156	9-22-02	.284	.376	.608	19	85	74	18	21	3	0	7	9	8	3	0	0	14	3	1	9.4	16.5
Powell, Peyton	L-R	6-1	195	9-2-00	.203	.338	.219	20	78	64	10	13	1	0	0	2	13	0	1	0	20	1	0	16.7	25.6
Scannell, Matt	L-L	6-0	200	8-31-01	.171	.209	.244	11	43	41	3	7	0	0	1	6	2	0	0	0	16	0	1	4.7	37.2
Shaw, Sam	L-R	5-10	175	2-26-05	.111	.143	.148	7	28	27	2	3	1	0	0	1	1	0	0	0	9	0	0	3.6	32.1
Stone, Alex	R-R	6-5	235	11-3-01	.185	.270	.259	15	63	54	2	10	4	0	0	10	4	3	0	2	11	0	0	6.3	17.5
Toman, Tucker	S-R	5-11	190	11-12-03	.302	.415	.349	12	53	43	7	13	2	0	0	7	6	3	0	1	12	0	0	11.3	22.6
Ward, Je'Von	L-R	6-2	190	10-25-99	.215	.437	.362	56	229	163	43	35	6	3	4	33	64	1	0	1	49	5	3	27.9	21.4
Wetzel, Jacob	L-L	5-9	215	3-26-00	.154	.313	.256	12	48	39	5	6	3	0	0	0	7	0	0	0	11	1	0	18.8	22.9

Pitching	B-T	Ht.	Wt.	DOB	W	L	ERA	G	GS	SV	IP	Hits	Runs	ER	HR	BB	SO	AVG	OBP	SLG	SO%	BB%	BF
Batista, Edinson	R-R	6-2	210	5-19-02	6	8	5.15	27	8	0	58	59	37	33	3	36	52	.261	.382	.394	19.1	13.2	272
Bonds, Bo	R-R	5-11	200	1-10-01	2	1	3.34	28	1	4	35	23	13	13	3	13	35	.183	.261	.302	24.6	9.2	142
Carter, Irv	R-R	6-4	210	10-9-02	6	4	5.67	27	0	1	60	70	42	38	12	20	62	.285	.349	.500	22.7	7.3	273
Cates, Austin	L-R	6-1	200	5-20-03	3	0	1.95	5	5	0	28	16	6	6	1	6	37	.167	.214	.250	35.9	5.8	103
Coleman, Javen	L-L	6-2	173	12-3-01	1	0	1.40	18	0	3	26	15	4	4	0	6	40	.163	.222	.207	40.4	6.1	99
Gallagher, Pat	R-R	6-0	196	6-30-00	3	0	1.13	20	1	0	40	22	11	5	0	17	46	.158	.248	.194	29.3	10.8	157
Garcia, Brett	R-R	6-1	205	8-18-99	1	1	1.74	6	0	0	10	9	4	2	2	6	11	.250	.349	.444	25.6	14.0	43
Garkow, Nate	R-R	5-11	190	9-4-97	1	0	7.56	10	0	2	17	17	14	14	2	14	32	.258	.390	.455	39.0	17.1	82
Gilliland, Hayden	L-R	5-11	175	10-29-01	0	0	0.00	1	0	0	1	1	0	0	0	0	0	.250	.250	.250	0.0	0.0	4
Hechavarria, Silvano	R-R	6-4	200	3-18-03	3	0	3.22	4	4	0	22	19	8	8	1	8	19	.229	.293	.337	20.7	8.7	92
Holcombe, Colby	R-R	6-7	225	12-12-02	1	2	9.00	9	0	0	10	10	10	10	1	12	14	.278	.481	.472	26.4	22.6	53
LaRue, Nate	R-R	6-3	217	7-27-01	0	1	5.40	3	0	0	5	5	3	3	1	1	5	.263	.333	.474	23.8	4.8	21
Marozas, Austin	R-R	6-8	230	12-13-98	0	0	4.91	3	0	0	7	5	4	4	0	4	6	.310	.417	.379	11.1	16.7	36
Martin, Colby	R-R	5-11	190	4-2-01	0	0	0.00	1	0	0	1	0	0	0	0	0	1	.000	.000	.000	33.3	0.0	3
McElvain, Chris	R-R	6-0	205	9-15-00	0	4	4.09	16	10	0	62	73	35	28	5	21	51	.293	.350	.402	18.5	7.6	276
Miranda, Kevin	R-R	5-10	178	11-14-98	3	4	7.57	9	6	0	27	33	24	23	5	11	23	.300	.381	.500	18.3	8.7	126
Munson, Aaron	L-R	5-10	180	3-15-02	3	2	2.81	30	0	3	48	40	17	15	0	18	40	.229	.292	.276	19.5	8.8	205
O'Halloran, Connor	R-L	6-2	190	9-1-02	0	1	2.70	2	2	0	7	5	2	2	0	2	7	.208	.208	.208	25.9	7.4	27
Ortiz, Julio	R-R	6-3	165	12-30-00	3	1	7.71	28	0	0	40	34	37	34	3	47	69	.221	.412	.338	33.8	23.0	204
Perez, Fernando	R-R	6-3	170	2-12-04	6	4	3.05	20	20	0	94	87	37	32	6	19	84	.242	.283	.331	21.8	4.9	386
Peterson, Kai	L-L	6-1	190	8-14-02	3	1	2.74	29	0	1	43	30	17	13	3	22	48	.201	.335	.302	26.5	12.2	181
Powell, Peyton	L-R	6-1	195	9-2-00	1	0	3.00	1	0	0	3	2	1	1	0	0	0	.250	.222	.750	0.0	0.0	9
Rogers, Grant	R-R	6-7	230	5-22-01	3	1	1.82	8	8	0	40	32	11	8	1	18	39	.215	.310	.268	22.8	10.5	171
Rojas, Yondrei	R-R	5-10	180	11-22-02	0	1	1.90	19	0	4	24	17	5	5	1	6	36	.195	.245	.264	38.3	6.4	94
Sanchez, J.J.	L-L	5-11	185	9-8-99	0	5	3.28	35	0	3	47	41	26	17	5	32	46	.229	.362	.346	21.1	14.7	218
Simon, Johan	L-L	6-1	166	7-1-01	1	0	3.26	7	0	1	19	16	8	7	1	8	18	.216	.293	.284	22.0	9.8	82
Stanifer, Gage	R-R	6-3	201	11-18-03	4	5	3.20	18	14	2	76	56	29	27	2	37	115	.204	.303	.270	36.5	11.7	315
Stephen, Khal	R-R	6-4	215	12-21-02	6	1	1.89	9	9	0	48	31	9	8	2	10	49	.182	.224	.238	26.6	5.4	184
Todd, Jonathan	R-R	6-4	225	8-21-01	5	2	4.76	32	0	1	45	42	25	24	8	20	59	.241	.327	.443	29.6	10.1	199
Vasquez, Juanmi	L-L	5-11	140	12-1-03	0	0	6.30	5	0	0	10	9	7	7	1	7	15	.231	.348	.359	32.6	15.2	46
Watts-Brown, Juaron	R-R	6-3	190	2-23-02	0	3	3.62	8	8	0	37	36	15	15	2	12	62	.232	.299	.362	39.7	7.7	156

Wentworth, Jackson	R-R	6-1	195	8-8-02	5	5	4.35	26	26	0	124	120	62	60	13	47	116	.252	.320 .392 21.7 8.8 534
Yeager, Chay	S-R	5-11	180	9-11-02	4	2	1.77	25	0	4	36	15	8	7	1	13	43	.126	.222 .176 31.9 9.6 135
Yesavage, Trey	R-R	6-4	225	7-28-03	1	0	1.56	4	4	0	17	5	3	3	2	11	33	.086	.232 .207 47.8 15.9 69

Fielding

Catcher	PCT	G	PO	A	E	DP	PB
Deschamps	.988	19	146	16	2	0	0
Duran	.986	32	325	16	5	1	5
Gilliland	.993	16	135	16	1	1	3
Lojewski	1.000	1	9	3	0	1	0
Parker	.989	51	509	36	6	1	6
Powell	1.000	3	22	4	0	0	0
Stone	1.000	15	145	9	0	1	5

First Base	PCT	G	PO	A	E	DP
Cunningham	.988	70	468	24	6	22
Hornung	.994	20	153	5	1	7
Keys	.990	30	192	6	2	13
Orf	.962	12	95	5	4	6
Powell	.982	6	51	5	1	3

Second Base	PCT	G	PO	A	E	DP
Arnold	1.000	3	7	6	0	2
Coffey	.962	33	39	87	5	11
Freethy	1.000	9	12	21	0	3
Goodwin	.973	68	91	129	6	20
Harry	1.000	9	6	16	0	1
Pinto	.966	16	18	39	2	7

Third Base	PCT	G	PO	A	E	DP
Coffey	.965	47	31	51	3	4
Goodwin	.875	5	2	5	1	1
Keys	.959	73	53	110	7	10
Lojewski	1.000	1	1	3	0	0
Toman	.947	10	7	11	1	1

Shortstop	PCT	G	PO	A	E	DP
Coffey	.941	5	6	10	1	3
Goodwin	.980	16	17	33	1	2
Harry	1.000	17	26	30	0	3
Nimmala	.957	98	123	189	14	28

Outfield	PCT	G	PO	A	E	DP
Arias	.993	56	133	3	1	2
Arnold	.939	22	41	5	3	0
Cunningham	.979	28	46	0	1	0
Freethy	.850	13	17	0	3	0
Harry	.984	32	59	2	1	1
Hernandez	1.000	25	45	0	0	0
Hornung	1.000	16	26	1	0	0
Martinez	1.000	15	26	1	0	1
Micheletti	.975	96	189	8	5	1
Orf	1.000	5	9	0	0	0
Pinto	1.000	4	4	0	0	0
Powell	1.000	10	18	0	0	0
Scannell	1.000	11	27	0	0	0
Shaw	1.000	7	15	0	0	0
Ward	.991	54	102	3	1	0
Wetzel	.944	12	17	0	1	0

DUNEDIN BLUE JAYS
FLORIDA STATE LEAGUE — LOW-A

Batting	B-T	Ht.	Wt.	DOB	AVG	OBP	SLG	G	PA	AB	R	H	2B	3B	HR	RBI	BB	HBP	SH	SF	SO	SB	CS	BB%	SO%
Aponte, Yhoangel	R-R	5-10	190	2-12-04	.209	.271	.362	70	281	254	29	53	13	1	8	39	19	4	0	3	85	4	4	6.8	30.2
Arnold, Bryce	R-R	5-10	175	7-24-01	.256	.377	.461	55	220	180	39	46	8	1	9	31	26	11	0	3	51	10	0	11.8	23.2
Barry, Braden	R-R	6-4	190	2-6-02	.294	.400	.373	32	120	102	16	30	8	0	0	8	13	5	0	0	31	8	3	10.8	25.8
Beckles, David	R-R	6-3	215	4-23-04	.215	.311	.323	19	74	65	10	14	4	0	1	4	9	0	0	0	21	0	0	12.2	28.4
Beltre, Manuel	R-R	5-10	155	6-09-01	.237	.320	.335	106	431	376	57	89	20	1	5	40	44	5	0	6	76	26	7	10.2	17.6
Bohrofen, Jace	L-R	6-2	205	10-19-01	.333	.500	.833	2	8	6	2	2	0	0	1	2	2	0	0	0	3	0	0	25.0	37.5
Brown, Devonte	R-R	5-9	207	10-15-99	.320	.393	.560	6	28	25	3	8	3	0	1	9	2	1	0	0	7	0	0	7.1	25.0
Casey, Luke	R-R	6-2	195	4-17-03	.281	.439	.531	23	82	64	14	18	3	2	3	14	10	8	0	0	19	4	1	12.2	23.2
Chirinos, Kendry	R-R	5-11	170	10-6-04	.255	.359	.370	95	382	322	41	82	13	3	6	43	49	6	0	5	97	0	1	12.8	25.4
Clarke, Phil	L-R	5-11	190	3-24-98	.269	.345	.423	6	29	26	4	7	1	0	1	5	3	0	0	0	2	0	0	10.3	6.9
Cresswell, Will	R-R	6-0	210	8-18-03	.200	.259	.240	7	27	25	0	5	1	0	0	5	1	1	0	0	9	0	0	3.7	33.3
De Jesus, Alex	R-R	6-1	170	3-22-02	.185	.371	.222	9	35	27	1	5	1	0	0	0	6	2	0	0	11	1	1	17.1	31.4
Doughty, Cade	R-R	6-1	195	3-26-01	.080	.258	.080	7	31	25	4	2	0	0	0	2	6	0	0	0	6	4	0	19.4	19.4
Duran, Edward	R-R	5-11	170	5-29-04	.296	.378	.439	66	291	253	40	75	11	5	5	35	26	9	0	3	62	6	4	8.9	21.3
Freethy, J.R.	S-R	5-11	185	10-22-02	.252	.404	.377	46	193	151	35	38	6	2	3	17	35	5	0	2	41	4	3	18.1	21.2
Gilliland, Hayden	R-R	5-11	175	10-29-01	.188	.308	.313	12	39	32	2	6	3	0	1	4	6	1	0	0	10	0	0	15.4	25.6
Gimenez, Andres	L-R	5-11	161	9-4-98	.167	.267	.250	4	15	12	0	2	1	0	0	3	2	0	0	1	1	0	0	13.3	6.7
Hernandez, Alexis	R-R	6-0	170	10-5-02	.244	.360	.401	53	204	172	24	42	12	0	5	22	26	5	1	0	47	10	3	12.7	23.0
Jimenez, Leo	R-R	5-10	215	5-17-01	.250	.308	.333	6	26	24	3	6	2	0	0	2	2	0	0	0	5	0	0	7.7	19.2
Joseph, Jean	R-R	5-11	160	2-4-05	.245	.322	.364	85	323	286	33	70	19	0	5	30	19	15	0	3	60	5	5	5.9	18.6
Kasevich, Josh	R-R	6-1	200	1-17-01	.375	.444	.417	7	27	24	2	9	1	0	0	3	3	0	0	0	3	0	0	11.1	11.1
Latta, Maddox	R-R	5-11	193	1-21-03	.267	.340	.333	24	100	90	14	24	4	1	0	14	9	1	0	0	25	9	2	9.0	25.0
Licourt, Yorman	S-R	6-2	192	2-6-04	.171	.244	.244	13	45	41	5	7	0	0	1	4	4	0	0	0	22	0	0	8.9	48.9
Lojewski, Jacob	R-R	5-10	180	11-16-01	.190	.264	.291	25	87	79	9	15	5	0	1	10	6	2	0	0	14	1	1	6.9	16.1
Minoso, Maykel	R-R	5-8	170	7-3-05	.000	.000	.000	4	14	13	0	0	0	0	0	1	0	0	0	1	0	0	0	0.0	7.1
Munoz, Yeuni	R-R	6-1	190	10-4-03	.265	.357	.520	27	112	98	20	26	7	0	6	27	12	2	0	0	33	1	1	10.7	29.5
Palmegiani, Damiano	R-R	6-0	195	1-24-00	.000	.400	.000	4	15	8	3	0	0	0	0	1	4	2	0	1	4	0	0	26.7	26.7
Powell, Peyton	L-R	6-1	195	9-2-00	.241	.362	.299	53	210	174	24	42	5	1	0	15	33	1	0	2	55	0	4	15.7	26.2
Ramon, Dariel	R-R	5-7	160	5-4-04	.229	.288	.313	15	52	48	7	11	4	0	0	3	4	0	0	0	14	4	1	7.7	26.9
Rodriguez, Lizandro	S-R	5-11	180	11-16-02	.223	.342	.340	36	111	94	14	21	4	2	1	5	16	1	0	0	23	7	4	14.4	20.7
Rudd, Jaden	L-L	5-10	185	8-16-02	.267	.389	.400	6	18	15	3	4	2	0	0	9	3	0	0	0	6	1	1	16.7	33.3
Scannell, Matt	L-L	6-0	200	8-31-01	.269	.367	.577	10	30	26	4	7	2	0	2	5	3	1	0	0	11	1	1	10.0	36.7
Schreck, RJ	L-R	6-1	210	7-12-00	.182	.438	.273	4	16	11	1	2	1	0	0	4	4	1	0	0	1	0	0	25.0	12.5
Shaw, Sam	L-R	5-10	175	2-26-05	.253	.383	.418	62	274	225	42	57	10	3	7	27	45	3	0	1	54	9	0	16.4	19.7
Smith, Austin	L-L	5-10	184	4-11-03	.259	.394	.395	23	99	81	14	21	5	0	2	7	12	6	0	0	12	7	3	12.1	12.1
Snow, Chris	R-R	5-10	180	3-08-04	.308	.301	.26	104	93	10	22	6	0	0	8	6	4	0	1	9	2	1	5.8	8.7
Tibbitts, Brock	R-R	6-4	210	10-4-02	.210	.330	.342	42	176	143	23	30	9	2	2	25	22	6	0	5	52	5	0	12.5	29.5
Toman, Tucker	S-R	5-11	190	11-12-03	.260	.345	.375	89	371	323	49	84	17	1	6	52	36	8	0	4	92	5	0	9.7	24.8
Varsho, Daulton	L-R	5-10	207	7-2-96	.286	.286	.714	5	14	14	3	4	0	0	2	5	0	0	0	0	4	0	0	0.0	28.6
Wagner, Will	L-R	5-11	210	7-29-98	.000	.000	.000	1	3	3	0	0	0	0	0	0	0	0	0	0	1	0	0	0.0	33.3
West, Jaxson	L-R	6-0	200	8-8-03	.160	.311	.200	16	61	50	5	8	2	0	0	3	11	0	0	0	7	0	2	18.0	11.5

Pitching	B-T	Ht.	Wt.	DOB	W	L	ERA	G	GS	SV	IP	Hits	Runs	ER	HR	BB	SO	AVG	OBP	SLG	SO%	BB%	BF
Alcalde, Eliander	R-R	5-9	171	8-9-03	0	3	3.86	13	1	2	30	26	13	13	2	15	29	.230	.333	.319	22.0	11.4	132
Batista, Edinson	R-R	6-2	210	5-19-02	0	0	12.27	3	0	0	4	7	5	5	0	4	7	.438	.545	.625	31.8	18.2	22
Bautista, Gilberto	R-R	6-0	165	1-8-05	3	7	4.96	23	8	0	85	96	55	47	15	22	83	.284	.329	.482	22.4	5.9	371
Beltre, Manuel	R-R	5-10	155	6-9-04	0	0	0.00	1	0	0	1	0	0	0	0	0	1	.000	.500	.500	0.0	0.0	2
Burr, Ryan	R-R	6-4	220	5-28-94	0	0	9.00	2	0	0	2	3	2	2	0	1	1	.375	.400	.625	10.0	10.0	10

TORONTO BLUE JAYS

Player	B-T	Ht	Wt	DOB	W	L	ERA	G	GS	SV	IP	H	BB	SO	HBP	AVG	OBP	SLG			
Cates, Austin	L-R	6-1	200	5-20-03	5	3	3.51	20	18	1	82	67	32	32	9	27	76	.226	.288	.358	23.2 8.3 327
Coleman, Javen	L-L	6-2	173	12-3-01	1	1	4.45	20	0	3	28	23	17	14	3	17	45	.223	.333	.359	36.3 13.7 124
Dominguez, Diego	R-R	6-0	178	7-2-04	1	0	3.18	5	0	0	11	13	6	4	1	5	9	.283	.377	.370	17.0 9.4 53
Eshleman, Jack	R-R	6-2	185	10-13-03	4	2	3.32	28	0	4	41	29	18	15	2	22	40	.204	.315	.275	23.4 12.9 171
Flores, Eminen	R-R	5-11	160	2-27-03	5	2	7.78	30	0	1	42	47	39	36	4	33	53	.288	.421	.436	26.2 16.3 202
Flynn, Bennett	R-R	6-1	175	5-29-01	3	4	7.75	22	0	2	34	42	32	29	6	22	41	.316	.418	.519	25.6 13.8 160
Garcia, Yimi	R-R	6-1	230	8-18-90	0	0	0.00	1	1	0	1	1	1	0	0	0	3	.250	.250	.250	75.0 0.0 4
Garrett, Amir	R-L	6-5	239	5-3-92	0	0	0.00	2	0	0	2	0	0	0	0	0	3	.000	.000	.000	42.9 0.0 7
Guerra, Daniel	R-R	6-6	230	3-13-04	4	5	3.40	22	13	2	82	61	34	31	9	39	84	.203	.305	.339	24.2 11.2 347
Hechavarria, Silvano	R-R	6-4	200	3-18-03	1	2	1.90	11	7	0	47	36	12	10	4	11	53	.209	.259	.291	28.5 5.9 186
Holcombe, Colby	R-R	6-7	225	12-12-02	2	9	4.85	16	15	0	65	70	40	35	3	33	56	.282	.362	.387	19.3 11.4 290
Hughes, Grif	L-L	6-4	225	1-24-02	0	0	9.00	5	0	0	12	12	12	12	3	8	8	.261	.382	.500	14.5 14.5 55
Juenger, Hayden	R-R	6-0	180	8-9-00	1	0	0.00	3	0	4	0	0	0	0	0	0	4	.000	.000	.000	33.3 0.0 12
Kelly, Justin	R-R	6-1	195	12-2-98	1	0	1.42	4	0	0	6	7	2	1	0	2	6	.280	.379	.320	20.7 6.9 29
King, Johnny	L-L	6-3	210	7-26-06	1	3	3.35	11	10	0	38	27	16	14	4	30	64	.203	.363	.323	38.1 17.9 168
Kloffenstein, Adam	R-R	6-5	243	8-25-00	0	0	0.00	1	1	0	4	5	3	0	0	1	5	.278	.350	.389	25.0 5.0 20
LaRue, Nate	R-R	6-3	217	7-27-01	3	1	5.28	24	0	0	31	34	21	18	1	14	25	.288	.377	.449	18.1 10.1 138
Manoah, Alek	R-R	6-6	285	1-9-98	0	0	4.50	1	1	0	2	3	1	1	0	0	2	.333	.333	.333	22.2 0.0 9
Mantiply, Joe	R-L	6-4	219	3-1-91	0	0	0.00	1	1	0	1	0	0	0	0	0	1	0.000	.250	.000	25.0 4
Maroudis, Landen	R-R	6-3	195	12-16-04	0	6	7.42	12	12	0	30	26	26	25	1	35	21	.248	.467	.390	13.7 22.9 153
Martin, Colby	R-R	5-11	195	4-2-01	0	1	1.61	20	0	5	22	6	4	4	0	14	29	.082	.230	.096	33.3 16.1 87
McElvain, Chris	R-R	6-0	205	9-15-00	0	2	9.00	3	3	0	11	13	11	11	1	6	14	.295	.392	.455	27.5 11.8 51
Mracna, Christian	R-R	6-3	220	6-9-00	0	1	12.15	9	0	1	7	4	11	9	0	14	6	.174	.462	.217	15.4 35.9 39
Myers, Carson	L-L	6-3	213	6-3-03	3	1	3.18	10	0	0	11	14	4	4	0	9	13	.318	.426	.341	24.1 16.7 54
Olson, Mason	R-L	5-10	165	12-23-01	3	2	3.48	6	2	0	21	18	8	8	0	8	21	.240	.333	.293	24.1 9.2 87
Overton, Connor	L-R	6-0	205	7-24-93	0	0	4.50	1	0	0	2	2	1	1	0	1	2	.286	.375	.429	22.2 11.1 9
Pardinho, Eric	R-R	5-10	155	1-5-01	0	0	8.10	3	0	0	3	8	5	3	1	3	4	.471	.550	.647	19.0 14.3 21
Pengelly, Dayne	L-R	6-3	205	2-18-03	0	0	3.18	4	4	0	11	12	4	4	1	5	15	.273	.347	.364	30.6 10.2 49
Rojas, Kendry	L-L	6-2	190	11-26-02	1	0	0.00	4	3	0	13	5	0	0	0	3	18	.122	.217	.146	39.1 6.5 46
Schueler, Jay	R-R	6-3	195	6-5-01	6	2	4.19	31	0	1	34	27	19	16	3	19	32	.221	.351	.324	21.6 12.8 148
Severino, Lluveres	R-R	6-1	180	8-9-03	0	0	6.91	7	0	1	14	15	12	11	1	10	11	.259	.394	.397	15.5 14.1 71
Simon, Johan	L-L	6-1	166	7-1-01	1	2	3.79	18	0	0	40	42	22	17	1	16	45	.266	.341	.329	24.5 8.7 184
Stanifer, Gage	R-R	6-3	201	11-18-03	4	0	0.69	7	0	2	26	10	3	2	0	12	38	.112	.233	.124	36.9 11.7 103
Stephen, Khal	R-R	6-4	215	12-21-02	3	0	2.06	8	7	1	39	29	10	9	1	7	48	.200	.235	.269	31.4 4.6 153
Swanson, Erik	R-R	6-3	225	9-4-93	0	0	0.00	2	0	0	1	1	0	0	0	0	2	.167	.167	.167	33.3 0.0 6
Thompson, Danny	R-R	6-0	180	8-9-02	0	0	0.66	10	1	3	14	8	1	1	4	15	.170	.250	.255	28.8 7.7 52
Turnbull, Spencer	R-R	6-3	210	9-18-92	0	1	5.56	3	3	0	11	14	8	7	1	4	10	.292	.356	.396	18.5 7.4 54
Vasquez, Juanmi	L-L	5-11	140	12-1-03	1	3	3.89	18	2	0	44	40	22	19	3	11	52	.238	.280	.357	28.4 6.0 183
Wilkerson, Holden	R-R	6-4	205	6-7-03	0	3	7.06	7	6	0	29	40	25	23	4	13	25	.331	.391	.504	18.1 9.4 138
Yesavage, Trey	R-R	6-4	225	7-28-03	3	0	2.43	7	7	0	33	19	13	9	3	8	55	.162	.220	.274	43.3 6.3 127

Fielding

Catcher	PCT	G	PO	A	E	DP	PB
Clarke	1.000	5	62	3	0	1	2
Cresswell	1.000	7	63	4	0	0	0
Duran	.979	55	560	43	13	4	2
Gilliland	.983	8	52	5	1	0	1
Lojewski	.988	19	155	15	2	1	3
Minoso	.974	4	34	4	1	0	0
Powell	.913	4	19	2	2	0	1
Tibbitts	.975	19	151	8	4	1	2
West	.981	12	101	2	2	0	0

First Base	PCT	G	PO	A	E	DP
Beckles	1.000	15	82	9	0	11
Chirinos	.986	65	392	24	6	40
De Jesus	1.000	1	2	1	0	1
Palmegiani	1.000	2	9	1	0	1
Powell	1.000	24	165	7	0	14
Tibbitts	.974	14	67	7	2	4
Toman	.984	9	56	4	1	3

Second Base	PCT	G	PO	A	E	DP
Arnold	1.000	5	7	10	0	0
Beltre	1.000	10	12	18	0	5
Doughty	1.000	2	1	5	0	0
Freethy	.952	28	45	54	5	17
Gimenez	1.000	3	2	8	0	0
Jimenez	1.000	1	1	1	0	0

	PCT	G	PO	A	E	DP
Latta	.978	11	25	20	1	5
Lojewski	1.000	2	4	0	0	0
Ramon	.974	9	16	22	1	7
Rodriguez	1.000	7	9	15	0	4
Shaw	.929	47	85	72	12	16
Snow	1.000	9	15	17	0	2
Toman	1.000	3	4	3	0	3

Third Base	PCT	G	PO	A	E	DP
Beltre	.966	11	7	21	1	0
Chirinos	.950	23	7	31	2	5
De Jesus	.938	5	3	12	1	1
Doughty	1.000	6	6	5	0	1
Latta	1.000	3	3	4	0	1
Lojewski	.750	3	0	3	1	0
Palmegiani	1.000	2	1	4	0	1
Powell	.667	1	1	1	1	0
Rodriguez	.857	10	6	12	3	1
Snow	1.000	4	1	5	0	1
Toman	.973	66	48	98	4	11

Shortstop	PCT	G	PO	A	E	DP
Arnold	.929	11	12	27	3	4
Beltre	.948	77	93	162	14	23
De Jesus	1.000	1	1	1	0	0
Jimenez	1.000	1	3	5	0	0
Kasevich	1.000	5	7	3	0	3

	PCT	G	PO	A	E	DP
Latta	1.000	9	10	18	0	1
Ramon	.875	6	6	8	2	1
Rodriguez	.875	12	14	21	5	7
Snow	1.000	13	16	33	0	6

Outfield	PCT	G	PO	A	E	DP
Aponte	.984	67	120	3	2	0
Arnold	.980	6	47	1	1	0
Barry	.960	29	47	1	2	0
Beltre	1.000	4	7	0	0	0
Bohrofen	1.000	2	5	0	0	0
Brown	1.000	6	14	0	0	0
Freethy	.966	16	26	2	1	0
Hernandez	.987	43	73	1	1	0
Jake	.971	21	32	1	1	1
Joseph	.973	85	200	13	6	2
Licourt	1.000	11	14	1	0	0
Munoz	1.000	25	47	3	0	0
Powell	.960	20	24	0	1	0
Rudd	1.000	5	7	0	0	0
Scannell	.941	8	15	1	1	0
Schreck	1.000	2	3	0	0	0
Shaw	1.000	12	29	2	0	0
Smith	1.000	19	35	1	0	0
Tibbitts	1.000	1	4	0	0	0
Toman	1.000	1	1	0	0	0
Varsho	1.000	4	2	0	0	0

FCL BLUE JAYS — ROOKIE
FLORIDA COMPLEX LEAGUE

Batting	B-T	Ht.	Wt.	DOB	AVG	OBP	SLG	G	PA	AB	R	H	2B	3B	HR	RBI	BB	HBP	SH	SF	SO	SB	CS	BB%	SO%
Arias, Andres	R-R	6-4	180	10-6-06	.167	.290	.295	49	183	156	21	26	3	1	5	21	21	6	0	0	57	9	2	11.5	31.1
Barry, Braden	R-R	6-4	190	2-6-02	.200	.429	.400	3	7	5	2	1	1	0	0	0	2	0	0	0	1	3	0	28.6	14.3
Beckles, David	R-R	6-3	215	4-23-04	.304	.388	.483	57	237	207	36	63	11	1	8	42	24	5	0	1	63	2	1	10.1	26.6
Bonilla, Enmanuel	R-R	6-1	180	1-22-06	.186	.260	.282	55	217	188	25	35	4	1	4	22	17	4	1	6	59	9	4	7.8	27.2
De Jesus, Alex	R-R	6-1	170	3-22-02	.250	.500	.333	4	18	12	3	3	1	0	0	4	5	1	0	0	2	0	0	27.8	11.1
De Los Santos, Raimundo	S-R	5-10	147	2-27-05	.271	.382	.319	50	170	144	26	39	5	1	0	14	26	0	0	0	33	11	5	15.3	19.4
Felix, Edrick	R-R	6-0	198	1-14-02	.241	.297	.362	18	64	58	9	14	2	1	1	6	4	1	0	1	15	5	0	6.3	23.4
Freethy, J.R.	S-R	5-11	185	12-23-02	.167	.375	.233	10	40	30	4	5	0	1	0	3	7	3	0	0	11	1	0	17.5	27.5
Gaxiola, Aldo	R-R	6-2	187	6-10-06	.258	.344	.333	58	225	198	25	51	7	1	2	17	25	1	0	0	40	3	1	11.1	17.8
Hernandez, Alexis	R-R	6-0	170	10-5-02	.231	.231	.231	4	13	13	3	3	0	0	0	1	0	0	0	0	2	3	0	0.0	15.4
Jemison, Andrew	R-R	6-0	195	10-22-00	.242	.411	.374	37	130	99	18	24	5	1	2	16	22	7	1	1	24	1	2	16.9	18.5
Jimenez, Leo	R-R	5-10	215	5-17-01	1.000	1.000	1.000	1	2	1	0	1	0	0	0	0	1	0	0	0	0	0	0	0.0	0.0
Kasevich, Josh	R-R	6-1	200	1-17-01	.357	.526	.357	6	19	14	0	5	0	0	0	3	5	0	0	0	1	0	1	26.3	5.3
Leach, Dylan	S-R	6-2	215	9-13-02	.163	.276	.204	19	58	49	6	8	2	0	0	3	8	0	0	1	15	0	0	13.8	25.9
Licourt, Yorman	R-R	6-2	192	6-24-06	.230	.356	.428	55	225	187	29	43	15	2	6	41	35	2	0	1	67	0	4	15.6	29.8
Meza, Luis	R-R	5-8	150	9-23-04	.186	.280	.209	14	50	43	7	8	1	0	0	5	5	1	0	1	12	0	0	10.0	24.0
Minoso, Maykel	R-R	5-8	170	7-3-05	.162	.305	.200	36	128	105	18	17	4	0	0	7	21	1	0	1	18	0	1	16.4	14.1
Munoz, Yeuni	R-R	6-1	190	10-4-03	.133	.133	.200	5	15	15	0	2	1	0	0	2	0	0	0	0	5	1	0	0.0	33.3
Ramon, Dariel	R-R	5-7	160	3-17-06	.245	.410	.316	50	200	155	39	38	7	2	0	17	35	9	0	1	29	14	2	17.5	14.5
Rosas, Juan	R-R	6-0	180	5-5-06	.169	.272	.211	27	81	71	3	12	3	0	0	3	8	2	0	0	25	0	1	9.9	30.9
Schreck, RJ	L-R	6-1	210	7-12-00	.167	.375	.167	2	8	6	2	1	0	0	0	0	2	0	0	0	0	1	0	25.0	0.0
Tibbitts, Brock	R-R	6-4	210	10-4-02	.308	.357	.385	6	21	13	2	4	1	0	0	1	7	1	0	0	3	0	0	33.3	14.3
Varsho, Daulton	L-R	5-10	207	7-2-96	.000	.000	.000	1	3	3	0	0	0	0	0	0	0	0	0	0	1	0	0	0.0	33.3
Wagner, Will	L-R	5-11	210	7-29-98	.364	.462	.545	4	13	11	0	4	2	0	0	1	0	0	0	0	1	0	0	7.7	0.0

Pitching	B-T	Ht.	Wt.	DOB	W	L	ERA	G	GS	SV	IP	Hits	Runs	ER	HR	BB	SO	AVG	OBP	SLG	SO%	BB%	BF
Alcalde, Eliander	R-R	5-9	171	8-9-03	1	0	9.82	3	0	0	7	11	9	8	1	3	8	.344	.405	.625	21.6	8.1	37
Barriera, Brandon	L-L	6-2	180	3-4-04	0	1	14.29	5	5	0	6	3	9	9	0	8	6	.158	.429	.158	21.4	28.6	28
Burr, Ryan	R-R	6-4	220	5-28-94	0	0	0.00	2	1	0	3	0	0	0	0	5	0	.000	.000	.000	62.5	0.0	8
Colmenares, Samuel	R-R	5-10	187	11-25-04	2	2	4.02	9	3	1	31	27	15	14	2	8	30	.225	.271	.358	23.3	6.2	129
De Los Santos, Raimundo	S-R	5-10	147	2-27-05	1	0	0.00	2	0	0	1	0	0	0	0	0	2	.000	.000	.000	50.0	0	4
Dominguez, Diego	R-R	6-0	178	7-2-04	6	2	2.25	21	0	5	28	20	11	7	0	13	26	.206	.304	.278	22.6	11.3	115
Eshleman, Jack	R-R	6-2	185	10-13-03	1	1	3.68	4	0	0	7	4	4	3	0	3	9	.154	.258	.231	29.0	9.7	31
Garcia, Brett	R-R	6-1	205	8-18-99	2	0	4.24	9	0	0	17	13	9	8	1	9	19	.213	.311	.328	25.7	12.2	74
Garcia, Yimi	R-R	6-1	230	8-18-90	0	0	0.00	1	1	0	1	1	0	0	0	0	3	.250	.250	.250	75.0	0	4
Garrett, Amir	R-L	6-5	239	5-3-92	0	1	16.20	1	0	0	3	6	6	6	2	0	5	.375	.412	.938	29.4	0.0	17
Gonzalez, Eduar	L-L	5-11	155	5-1-06	1	1	3.99	10	1	0	29	31	13	13	2	10	23	.267	.336	.379	17.8	7.8	129
Guthrie, Troy	R-R	6-3	205	11-3-05	3	2	2.28	11	3	0	43	33	13	11	1	7	36	.212	.246	.333	21.6	4.2	167
Hechavarria, Silvano	R-R	6-0	200	3-18-03	1	0	2.12	4	3	0	17	14	6	4	2	4	10	.222	.279	.349	14.7	5.9	68
Hughes, Grif	L-L	6-4	225	1-24-02	0	0	2.84	6	0	0	13	8	6	4	0	6	14	.174	.278	.196	25.9	11.1	54
Juenger, Hayden	R-R	6-0	180	8-9-00	1	0	0.00	1	0	0	1	1	0	0	0	1	2	.250	.400	.250	40.0	20.0	5
King, Johnny	L-L	6-3	210	7-26-06	0	0	1.13	7	5	0	24	17	6	3	0	7	41	.195	.286	.276	41.8	7.1	98
Kloffenstein, Adam	R-R	6-5	243	8-25-00	0	1	0.00	1	1	0	5	5	1	0	0	1	8	.294	.333	.353	44.4	5.6	18
Lucas, Easton	L-L	6-4	180	9-23-96	0	1	1.69	2	0	0	5	1	1	1	0	1	6	.063	.167	.063	33.3	5.6	18
Macko, Adam	L-L	6-0	170	12-30-00	0	1	3.63	5	4	0	17	14	7	7	0	3	26	.219	.271	.281	37.1	4.3	70
Manoah, Alek	R-R	6-6	285	1-9-98	0	0	81.00	1	1	0	0	1	4	3	0	2	1	.500	.800	.500	20.0	40.0	5
Maroudis, Landen	R-R	6-3	195	12-16-04	1	2	4.80	6	5	0	15	10	9	8	0	10	13	.196	.349	.235	20.6	15.9	63
Marozas, Austin	R-R	6-8	230	12-13-98	0	0	0.00	4	1	0	10	5	1	0	0	5	7	.156	.270	.188	18.9	13.5	37
McElvain, Chris	R-R	6-0	205	9-15-00	0	1	0.00	2	2	0	7	3	0	0	0	2	7	.136	.208	.136	29.2	8.3	24
Messina, Carson	R-R	6-1	200	4-15-06	0	0	9.00	1	0	0	2	3	2	2	0	0	2	.333	.333	.444	22.2	0.0	9
Olson, Mason	R-L	5-10	165	12-23-01	2	1	1.72	3	2	0	16	12	3	3	0	4	18	.207	.258	.259	29.0	6.5	62
Omosako, Sann	R-R	6-1	200	12-25-05	3	4	4.09	12	5	1	44	52	25	20	6	4	39	.292	.319	.438	20.7	2.1	188
Overton, Connor	L-R	6-0	205	7-24-93	0	0	1.23	4	0	0	7	7	2	1	0	2	8	.241	.290	.345	25.8	6.5	31
Pardinho, Eric	R-R	5-10	155	1-5-01	0	0	2.70	3	2	0	3	4	1	1	0	2	3	.308	.400	.385	20.0	13.3	15
Quinones, Luis	R-R	6-0	205	7-14-04	0	0	8.10	3	2	0	3	4	3	3	1	2	6	.250	.357	.667	42.9	14.3	14
Rojas, Kendry	L-L	6-2	190	11-26-02	0	0	3.60	2	2	0	5	5	2	2	0	1	8	.263	.333	.316	38.1	9.5	21
Sandlin, Nick	R-R	5-11	175	1-10-97	0	1	3.86	2	1	0	2	2	1	1	0	1	4	.222	.300	.333	40.0	10.0	10
Schultz, Paxton	R-R	6-3	215	7-5-00	0	0	0.00	1	1	0	2	0	0	0	0	0	5	.000	.000	.000	83.3	0.0	6
Severino, Lluveres	R-R	6-1	180	8-9-03	4	2	3.48	19	0	2	31	29	13	12	3	7	24	.250	.315	.362	18.9	5.5	127
Swanson, Erik	R-R	6-3	225	9-4-93	0	0	0.00	1	0	0	2	4	2	1	0	0	2	.667	.667	2.000	0.0	0.0	4
Taggart, Aiden	R-R	6-3	185	10-9-04	1	0	6.17	10	0	0	12	14	9	9	1	8	13	.298	.414	.468	22.4	13.8	58
Torres, Luis	L-L	6-1	165	2-24-05	0	0	0.00	1	1	0	2	0	0	0	0	3	4	.167	.444	.333	44.4	33.3	9
Tucent, Pedro	R-R	6-3	190	10-18-02	2	0	4.05	12	0	0	20	14	11	9	1	15	16	.200	.349	.314	18.6	17.4	86
Urena, Franly	R-R	5-8	160	8-8-04	1	0	6.38	16	0	2	18	17	13	11	1	16	24	.239	.433	.380	26.1	17.4	92
Wallace, Trenton	L-L	6-1	200	3-31-99	0	0	0.00	2	0	0	4	2	0	0	0	1	2	.111	.273	.111	18.2	18.2	11
Wilkerson, Holden	R-R	6-4	205	6-7-03	3	2	5.40	7	2	0	22	27	17	13	2	5	23	.297	.333	.462	23.2	5.1	99

Fielding

C: Minoso 30, Rosas 16, Meza 10, Leach 7, Tibbitts 4. **1B:** Beckles 38, Jemison 12, Gaxiola 4, Rosas 3, Meza 2, Minoso 2, De Jesus 1, Leach 1, Wagner 1. **2B:** Jemison 25, Ramon 21, De Los Santos 8, Felix 8, Freethy 4. **3B:** Gaxiola 52, De Los Santos 3, Felix 3, De Jesus 2, Wagner 2, Beckles 1. **SS:** De Los Santos 31, Ramon 30, Kasevich 4, Jimenez 1. **LF:** Arias 21, Bonilla 13, De Los Santos 11, Licourt 10, Beckles 9, Freethy 4, Munoz 2, Ramon 1. **CF:** Bonilla 40, Arias 18, Barry 2. **RF:** Licourt 41, Arias 13, Bonilla 3, Beckles 2, Hernandez 2, Schreck 2, Munoz 1.

DSL BLUE JAYS — ROOKIE
DOMINICAN SUMMER LEAGUE

TORONTO BLUE JAYS

Batting	B-T	Ht.	Wt.	DOB	AVG	OBP	SLG	G	PA	AB	R	H	2B	3B	HR	RBI	BB	HBP	SH	SF	SO	SB	CS	BB%	SO%
Arrieche, Esmeiquel	R-R	5-7	152	12-21-06	.188	.368	.240	38	125	96	18	18	3	1	0	11	26	2	0	1	26	0	0	20.8	20.8
Bain, J.T.	R-R	6-1	160	7-2-07	.147	.328	.255	39	132	102	18	15	4	2	1	19	23	5	1	1	55	5	2	17.4	41.7
Blanca, Wilmer	R-R	5-11	178	1-17-07	.250	.500	1.000	2	6	4	2	1	0	0	1	1	1	1	0	0	1	0	0	16.7	16.7
Crespo, Yeicer	R-R	5-9	220	11-28-07	.212	.366	.273	33	123	99	12	21	3	0	1	12	21	3	0	0	35	0	2	17.1	28.5
Dominguez, Daniel	R-R	5-11	163	1-22-08	.161	.306	.248	52	180	149	20	24	1	3	2	7	27	4	0	0	43	1	1	15.0	23.9
Flores, Rafael	R-R	5-10	172	3-28-07	.256	.434	.357	44	175	129	32	33	5	1	2	22	25	18	0	3	28	12	2	14.3	16.0
Garcia, Carlos	L-R	5-9	174	3-19-07	.227	.350	.273	25	80	66	9	15	3	0	0	8	12	1	0	1	15	0	0	15.0	18.8
Gonzalez, Fabian	R-R	6-0	175	9-21-07	.255	.314	.319	15	51	47	3	12	3	0	0	6	2	2	0	0	10	0	0	3.9	19.6
Guzman, Angel	S-R	5-11	190	12-7-06	.230	.357	.365	46	182	148	19	34	7	2	3	22	30	1	0	3	26	9	2	16.5	14.3
Núñez, Darwin	R-R	6-0	166	9-22-07	.196	.380	.229	53	201	153	18	30	5	0	0	15	45	1	1	1	31	8	2	22.4	15.4
Pieternella, Keegan	S-R	5-8	169	9-9-07	.000	.077	.000	4	13	12	0	0	0	0	0	0	1	0	0	0	2	0	0	7.7	15.4
Polanco, Cristopher	L-R	5-10	174	1-3-08	.177	.392	.232	53	222	164	34	29	7	1	0	19	52	6	0	0	56	9	5	23.4	25.2
Reyes, Elian	L-R	6-4	185	7-30-08	.219	.370	.266	23	81	64	10	14	3	0	0	6	15	1	0	1	24	1	0	18.5	29.6
Reyes, Endry	R-R	5-10	168	12-13-06	.000	.000	.000	1	3	3	0	0	0	0	0	0	1	0	0	0	1	0	0	0.0	33.3
Rojas, Franklin	R-R	5-10	176	3-20-07	.255	.407	.330	34	140	106	15	27	5	0	1	18	21	9	0	4	21	1	0	15.0	15.0
Soto, Jaurlin	R-R	6-0	170	12-23-06	.216	.370	.309	53	208	162	17	35	9	0	2	26	36	6	0	4	30	1	0	17.3	14.4
Vergara, Nicolas	L-R	6-0	172	12-4-07	.500	.500	.500	1	2	2	0	1	0	0	0	0	0	0	0	0	1	0	0	0.0	50.0

Pitching	B-T	Ht.	Wt.	DOB	W	L	ERA	G	GS	SV	IP	Hits	Runs	ER	HR	BB	SO	AVG	OBP	SLG	SO%	BB%	BF
Andrades, Jose	R-R	6-2	195	7-13-06	0	5	4.84	11	9	0	35	36	25	19	1	15	32	.257	.338	.364	19.9	9.3	161
Barco, Freigher	R-R	6-0	190	1-13-06	2	1	6.49	13	0	0	26	36	22	19	1	11	21	.333	.398	.444	17.1	8.9	123
Barroso, Geremy	R-R	6-0	180	2-14-06	3	2	3.77	17	0	1	29	22	12	12	0	16	25	.216	.331	.284	20.7	13.2	121
Brito, Gabriel	R-R	6-2	190	12-28-07	0	0	24.30	5	0	0	3	6	9	9	0	16	4	.400	.727	.400	12.1	48.5	33
Castro, Gabriel	L-L	6-1	175	11-5-04	1	2	18.00	4	2	0	3	6	8	6	0	8	1	.375	.600	.500	4.0	32.0	25
Cerezo, Cesar	L-L	6-3	199	5-29-08	0	0	3.55	11	0	0	13	6	8	5	1	7	15	.140	.315	.233	27.3	12.7	55
De La Cruz, Michael	R-R	6-2	202	7-28-06	1	2	3.65	12	7	0	37	22	16	15	1	26	42	.176	.331	.288	26.8	16.6	157
Dominguez, Enyer	R-R	6-5	173	6-10-07	0	4	5.00	15	0	4	18	20	14	10	0	16	14	.274	.430	.329	15.1	17.2	93
Duarte, Cristhian	R-R	6-0	180	10-3-07	3	8	6.04	12	12	0	45	43	35	30	4	20	32	.250	.333	.398	15.2	10.1	198
Francisco, Edwin	R-R	5-11	170	11-15-06	0	0	0.00	6	0	0	7	8	0	0	0	3	8	.296	.387	.333	25.8	9.7	31
Gonzalez, Jorge	R-R	6-5	200	4-21-06	0	1	6.17	10	0	0	12	4	9	8	1	21	7	.125	.525	.219	11.9	35.6	59
Martinez, Ire	L-L	6-0	170	2-24-08	0	0	9.00	1	0	0	1	2	1	1	0	1	0	.400	.500	.400	0.0	16.7	6
Pineda, Deiker	R-R	6-1	159	4-15-06	4	4	3.57	12	7	2	40	39	19	16	1	24	25	.264	.327	.372	14.9	8.3	168
Ramirez, Juan	R-R	6-0	170	4-30-06	2	0	1.71	13	0	2	21	12	5	4	0	21	21	.169	.359	.225	22.6	22.6	93
Ramirez, Rodrigo	R-R	6-0	180	1-10-07	1	1	4.15	7	1	0	13	11	7	6	0	8	11	.224	.345	.306	19.0	13.8	58
Rivas, Jhon	S-R	5-9	155	8-26-07	1	0	7.56	12	0	0	17	18	16	14	2	10	16	.269	.367	.478	20.3	12.7	79
Rivero, Angel	R-R	5-11	172	11-28-06	0	2	3.96	11	11	0	36	34	22	16	1	16	42	.250	.348	.360	25.9	9.9	162
Suero, Manuel	R-R	6-0	180	8-31-05	1	0	6.33	12	1	0	27	16	23	19	1	35	19	.174	.421	.217	14.2	26.1	134
Valiente, Alexander	R-R	6-0	190	10-20-02	0	0	16.62	4	3	0	4	2	10	8	0	15	4	.167	.667	.167	13.3	50.0	30
Veras, Edrwin	R-R	6-1	180	4-24-03	3	1	2.37	12	2	0	30	21	17	8	1	12	31	.191	.280	.245	24.8	9.6	125

Fielding

C: Arrieche 21, Rojas 21, Garcia 13, Crespo 5. **1B:** Núñez 47, Garcia 8, Arrieche 5, Rojas 2, Reyes 1. **2B:** Guzman 41, Flores 10, Núñez 5, Soto 3, Polanco 1. **3B:** Soto 49, Flores 5, Guzman 1, Núñez 1. **SS:** Polanco 49, Flores 6, Guzman 2. **LF:** Flores 26, Arrieche 12, Bain 7, Núñez 6, Dominguez 5, Pieternella 3, Gonzalez 2, Reyes 2, Blanca 1. **CF:** Dominguez 37, Bain 15, Gonzalez 3. **RF:** Reyes 21, Bain 15, Gonzalez 10, Dominguez 9, Arrieche 3, Pieternella 1, Vergara 1.

DSL BLUE JAYS 2 — ROOKIE
DOMINICAN SUMMER LEAGUE

Batting	B-T	Ht.	Wt.	DOB	AVG	OBP	SLG	G	PA	AB	R	H	2B	3B	HR	RBI	BB	HBP	SH	SF	SO	SB	CS	BB%	SO%
Arce, Diego	R-R	5-10	225	10-29-07	.160	.395	.217	39	147	106	17	17	3	0	1	5	23	18	0	0	46	0	0	15.6	31.3
Archila, Pascual	L-L	5-10	172	1-23-07	.246	.433	.351	56	232	171	36	42	12	0	2	23	50	8	1	2	52	19	4	21.6	22.4
Bain, J.T.	R-R	6-1	160	7-2-07	.185	.290	.407	10	31	27	5	5	0	0	2	2	2	2	0	0	14	2	0	6.5	45.2
Blanca, Wilmer	R-R	5-11	178	1-17-07	.149	.365	.191	19	63	47	7	7	2	0	0	5	11	5	0	0	10	0	0	17.5	15.9
Blanco, Kennew	R-R	6-3	205	6-21-06	.274	.342	.377	56	237	212	29	58	11	1	3	33	17	6	0	2	27	2	3	7.2	11.4
Campos, Renyel	L-R	5-10	161	6-8-07	.171	.354	.250	31	100	76	14	13	3	0	1	10	17	5	1	1	26	0	3	17.0	26.0
Coronado, Elaineiker	L-R	5-10	160	10-4-07	.346	.504	.383	56	248	188	40	65	5	1	0	21	57	3	0	0	27	5	4	23.0	10.9
Felipe, Luis	R-R	6-3	225	11-27-06	.206	.292	.258	50	178	155	12	32	6	1	0	19	20	0	0	3	42	3	0	11.2	23.6
Pieternella, Keegan	S-R	5-8	169	9-9-07	.231	.400	.256	31	101	78	19	18	2	0	0	8	20	2	1	0	16	0	0	19.8	15.8
Reyes, Endry	R-R	5-10	168	12-13-06	.182	.333	.205	16	55	44	7	8	1	0	0	5	9	1	0	0	19	1	1	16.4	34.5
Sanchez, Juan	R-R	6-3	180	9-27-07	.341	.439	.565	56	253	214	47	73	16	4	8	40	26	12	0	1	44	4	3	10.3	17.4
Soto, Randy	S-R	5-10	176	11-16-06	.196	.362	.256	52	213	168	17	33	8	1	0	27	40	4	0	1	33	2	0	18.8	15.5
Urbina, Nestor	R-R	5-10	168	6-13-07	.272	.345	.437	31	116	103	16	28	10	2	1	20	10	2	0	1	21	2	0	8.6	18.1
Vergara, Nicolas	L-R	6-0	172	12-4-07	.143	.301	.238	29	103	84	11	12	5	0	1	11	14	5	0	0	38	1	2	13.6	36.9

Pitching	B-T	Ht.	Wt.	DOB	W	L	ERA	G	GS	SV	IP	Hits	Runs	ER	HR	BB	SO	AVG	OBP	SLG	SO%	BB%	BF
Andrades, Jose	R-R	6-2	195	7-13-06	0	5	4.84	11	9	0	35	36	25	19	1	15	32	.257	.338	.364	19.9	9.3	161
Barco, Freigher	R-R	6-0	190	1-13-06	2	1	6.49	13	0	0	26	36	22	19	1	11	21	.333	.398	.444	17.1	8.9	123
Barroso, Geremy	R-R	6-0	180	2-14-06	3	2	3.77	17	0	1	29	22	12	12	0	16	25	.216	.331	.284	20.7	13.2	121
Brito, Gabriel	R-R	6-2	190	12-28-07	0	0	24.30	5	0	0	3	6	9	9	0	16	4	.400	.727	.400	12.1	48.5	33
Castro, Gabriel	L-L	6-1	175	11-5-04	1	2	18.00	4	2	0	3	6	8	6	0	8	1	.375	.600	.500	4.0	32.0	25
Cerezo, Cesar	L-L	6-3	199	5-29-08	0	0	3.55	11	0	0	13	6	8	5	1	7	15	.140	.315	.233	27.3	12.7	55
De La Cruz, Michael	R-R	6-2	202	7-28-06	1	2	3.65	12	7	0	37	22	16	15	1	26	42	.176	.331	.288	26.8	16.6	157
Dominguez, Enyer	R-R	6-5	173	6-10-07	0	4	5.00	15	0	4	18	20	14	10	0	16	14	.274	.430	.329	15.1	17.2	93

Player	B-T	Ht	Wt	DOB	W	L	ERA	G	GS	SV	IP	H	R	ER	HR	BB	SO	AVG	OBP	SLG	K/9	BB/9	BF
Duarte, Cristhian	R-R	6-0	180	10-3-07	3	8	6.04	12	12	0	45	43	35	30	4	20	32	.250	.343	.395	16.2	10.1	198
Francisco, Edwin	R-R	5-11	170	11-15-06	0	0	0.00	6	0	0	7	8	0	0	0	3	8	.296	.387	.333	25.8	9.7	31
Gonzalez, Jorge	R-R	6-5	200	4-21-06	0	1	6.17	10	0	0	12	4	9	8	1	21	7	.125	.525	.219	11.9	35.6	59
Martinez, Ire	L-L	6-0	170	2-24-08	0	0	9.00	1	0	0	1	2	1	1	0	1	0	.400	.500	.400	0.0	16.7	6
Pineda, Deiker	R-R	6-1	159	4-15-06	4	4	3.57	12	7	2	40	39	19	16	1	14	25	.264	.327	.372	14.9	8.3	168
Ramirez, Juan	R-R	6-0	170	4-30-06	2	0	1.71	13	0	2	21	12	5	4	0	21	21	.169	.359	.225	22.6	22.6	93
Ramirez, Rodrigo	R-R	6-1	180	1-10-07	1	1	4.15	7	1	0	13	11	7	6	0	8	11	.224	.345	.306	19.0	13.8	58
Rivas, Jhon	S-R	5-9	155	8-26-07	1	0	7.56	12	0	0	17	18	16	14	2	10	16	.269	.367	.478	20.3	12.7	79
Rivero, Angel	R-R	5-11	172	11-28-06	0	2	3.96	11	11	0	36	34	22	16	1	16	42	.250	.348	.360	25.9	9.9	162
Suero, Manuel	R-R	6-0	180	8-31-05	1	0	6.33	12	1	0	27	16	23	19	1	35	19	.174	.421	.217	14.2	26.1	134
Valiente, Alexander	R-R	6-0	190	10-20-02	0	0	16.62	4	3	0	4	2	10	8	0	15	4	.167	.667	.167	13.3	50.0	30
Veras, Edrwin	R-R	6-1	180	4-24-03	3	1	2.37	12	2	0	30	21	17	8	1	12	31	.191	.280	.245	24.8	9.6	125

Fielding

C: Soto 25, Arce 16, Campos 14, Pieternella 9. **1B:** Soto 23, Arce 13, Campos 13, Reyes 12. **2B:** Coronado 33, Blanco 18, Pieternella 5. **3B:** Sanchez 26, Blanco 11, Urbina 10, Coronado 8, Pieternella 1, Reyes 1. **SS:** Blanco 24, Sanchez 21, Coronado 11. **LF:** Felipe 30, Blanca 15, Urbina 9, Bain 6, Campos 5, Pieternella 1, Reyes 1, Vergara 1. **CF:** Archila 56, Pieternella 1, Vergara 1. **RF:** Vergara 25, Felipe 22, Pieternella 10, Bain 5, Blanca 1, Campos 1

Washington Nationals

SEASON SYNOPSIS: After a couple of years of apparent progress, the Nationals' rebuild fizzled. The big league club took an unacceptable step back at 66-96, despite steps forward by individual players, and it cost manager Davey Martinez and GM/club president Mike Rizzo—key pieces of the 2019 World Series championship—their jobs. Rizzo had been with the organization since 2006 and GM since 2009.

HIGH POINT: The Nats' offense showed dynamism it had lacked in recent years in May, spurring a 10-3 spurt to finish the month at 28-30 after a poor start. The hot stretch included seven road wins, with a sweep in Baltimore (including a 4-3, come-from-behind win in the opener), and seven games scoring at least eight runs, capped by an 11-7 win at Arizona. Washington scored a club-record (since the '05 move to DC) 10 runs in the first inning, a frame that included five doubles and in which the Nats left the bases loaded

LOW POINT: The season's tide turned in June, a 7-19 month that included an 11-game losing streak and sank Washington to last place. The stretch included a home series loss to the Rockies, one of the worst teams in MLB history, as German Marquez picked up the last of his three wins on the season, shutting out the Nats June 19 for 5 ⅔ innings (he finished the year 3-16, 6.70). Two weeks later, after a home sweep against the Red Sox, the Lerner family ownership decided to change direction and fired both Rizzo and Martinez, elevating Miguel Cairo to interim manager and Mike DeBartolo as interim GM.

NOTABLE ROOKIES: The best rookie seasons came from 2021 second-rounder Daylen Lile (.299/.347/.499, 11 3B) and RHP Brad Lord (5-10, 4.34), an 18th-round pick in 2022. The Nats will need more in the future from pedigreed rookies such as OF Dylan Crews (.208/.280/.352), 3B Brady House (.234/.252/.322) and 2019 first-rounder RHP Jackson Rutledge (4-2, 5.77). The news was better for 2020 first-rounder Cade Cavalli (3-1, 4.25 in 10 starts), who looked on the mend from several injury-plagued seasons.

KEY TRANSACTIONS: Paul Toboni, previously scouting director and later assistant GM of the Red Sox, was hired as president of baseball operations after the season, replacing Mike DeBartolo, who had replaced Rizzo as interim GM just a week before the draft. It was DeBartolo, not Rizzo, who pulled the trigger with the No. 1 overall pick, taking Oklahoma prep shortstop Eli Willits as the third 1/1 pick in Nats history, joining Stephen Strasburg and Bryce Harper.

OPENING DAY PAYROLL: $107,653,761 (24th)

PLAYERS OF THE YEAR

MAJOR LEAGUE
James Wood
OF
.256/.350/.475
31 HR, 38 2B, 15 SB,
87 R, 94 RBIs, 85 BB

MINOR LEAGUE
Alex Clemmey
LHP
(A+/AA)
3.47 ERA in 116.1 IP,
136 SO, .208 AVG

ORGANIZATION LEADERS

Batting		*Qualifiers
MAJORS		
* AVG	CJ Abrams	.257
* OPS	James Wood	.825
HR	James Wood	31
RBI	James Wood	94
MINORS		
* AVG	Phillip Glasser, Rochester/Harrisburg	.302
* OBP	Phillip Glasser, Rochester/Harrisburg	.389
* SLG	Nick Schnell, Rochester/Harrisburg	.478
* OPS	Nick Schnell, Rochester/Harrisburg	.799
R	Yohandy Morales, Rochester/Harrisburg	85
H	Phillip Glasser, Rochester/Harrisburg	143
TB	Nick Schnell, Rochester/Harrisburg	242
2B	Yohandy Morales, Rochester/Harrisburg	31
3B	Nick Schnell, Rochester/Harrisburg	11
HR	Nick Schnell, Rochester/Harrisburg	23
RBI	Nick Schnell, Rochester/Harrisburg	84
BB	Joe Naranjo, Harrisburg	61
SO	Nick Schnell, Rochester/Harrisburg	175
SB	Nasim Nunez, Rochester	36

Pitching		#Qualifiers
MAJORS		
W	Jake Irvin	9
W	Mitchell Parker	9
# ERA	Mitchell Parker	5.68
SO	MacKenzie Gore	185
SV	Kyle Finnegan	20
MINORS		
W	Merrick Baldo, Fredericksburg	8
L	Jackson Kent, Harrisburg/Wilmington	10
# ERA	Riley Cornelio, Rochester/Harrisburg/Wilmington	3.28
G	Garrett Davila, Rochester/Harrisburg	57
GS	Riley Cornelio, Rochester/Harrisburg/Wilmington	26
SV	Junior Santos, Harrisburg	12
IP	Travis Sthele, Wilmington	139
BB	Alexander Clemmey, Harrisburg/Wilmington	73
SO	Alexander Clemmey, Harrisburg/Wilmington	136
# AVG	Riley Cornelio, Rochester/Harrisburg/Wilmington	.205

2025 PERFORMANCE

General Manager: Mike Rizzo/Mike DeBartolo. **Farm Director:** Eddie Longosz. **Scouting Director:** Danny Haas.

Class	Team	League	W	L	PCT	Finish	Manager
Majors	Washington Nationals	National	66	96	.407	14 (15)	Dave Martinez
Triple-A	Rochester Red Wings	International	59	88	.401	20 (20)	Matthew LeCroy
Double-A	Harrisburg Senators	Eastern	68	70	.493	7 (12)	Delino DeShields
High-A	Wilmington Blue Rocks	South Atlantic	54	76	.415	11 (12)	Jake Lowery
Low-A	Fredericksburg Nationals	Carolina	65	64	.504	8 (12)	Billy McMillon
Rookie	FCL Nationals	Florida Complex	30	25	.545	6 (15)	Carmelo Jaime
Rookie	DSL Nationals	Dominican	27	29	.482	29 (52)	Sandy Martinez
Overall 2025 Minor League Record			303	352	.463	24th (30)	

ORGANIZATION STATISTICS

WASHINGTON NATIONALS
NATIONAL LEAGUE

Batting	B-T	Ht.	Wt.	DOB	AVG	OBP	SLG	G	PA	AB	R	H	2B	3B	HR	RBI	BB	HBP	SH	SF	SO	SB	CS	BB%	SO%
Abrams, CJ	L-R	6-2	191	10-3-00	.257	.315	.433	144	635	580	92	149	35	5	19	60	37	14	1	3	125	31	3	5.8	19.7
Adams, Riley	R-R	6-4	260	6-26-96	.186	.252	.308	83	286	263	29	49	8	0	8	24	18	5	0	0	110	1	0	6.3	38.5
Alfaro, Jorge	R-R	6-3	230	6-11-93	.256	.256	.308	14	39	39	3	10	2	0	0	3	0	0	0	0	14	1	0	0.0	35.9
Bell, Josh	S-R	6-4	261	8-14-92	.237	.325	.417	140	533	468	54	111	16	1	22	63	57	5	0	3	88	0	3	10.7	16.5
Call, Alex	R-R	5-11	189	9-27-94	.274	.371	.386	72	237	197	30	54	9	2	3	26	26	6	5	3	36	1	1	11.0	15.2
Chaparro, Andres	R-R	6-0	200	5-4-99	.182	.247	.258	34	73	66	4	12	2	0	1	5	5	1	0	1	22	0	0	6.8	30.1
Crews, Dylan	R-R	6-0	203	2-26-02	.208	.280	.352	85	322	293	43	61	8	2	10	27	24	5	0	0	76	17	5	7.5	23.6
DeJong, Paul	R-R	6-0	205	8-2-93	.228	.269	.373	57	208	193	18	44	10	0	6	23	11	1	0	3	70	4	0	5.3	33.7
Garcia, Luis	L-R	6-2	220	5-16-00	.252	.289	.412	139	526	488	67	123	28	1	16	66	27	2	0	9	84	14	5	5.1	16.0
Hassell, Robert	L-L	6-1	195	8-15-01	.223	.257	.315	70	206	197	22	44	9	0	3	18	8	1	0	0	62	4	0	3.9	30.1
House, Brady	R-R	6-4	215	6-4-03	.234	.252	.322	73	274	261	26	61	11	0	4	29	8	0	0	5	78	5	3	2.9	28.5
Lile, Daylen	L-R	5-11	195	11-30-02	.299	.347	.498	91	351	321	51	96	15	11	9	41	21	4	1	3	56	8	6	6.0	16.0
Lipscomb, Trey	R-R	6-2	200	6-14-00	.500	.500	.500	3	4	4	1	2	0	0	0	0	0	0	0	0	1	0	0	0.0	25.0
Lowe, Nathaniel	L-R	6-4	220	7-7-95	.216	.292	.373	119	490	440	50	95	17	2	16	68	47	1	0	2	130	1	0	9.6	26.5
Millas, Drew	S-R	6-0	198	1-15-98	.306	.358	.449	18	55	49	6	15	5	1	0	7	4	0	1	0	7	2	0	7.3	12.7
Nunez, Nasim	S-R	5-9	168	8-18-00	.232	.297	.402	39	92	82	13	19	2	0	4	13	8	0	1	1	20	9	1	8.7	21.7
Ogasawara, Shinnosuke	L-L	5-11	205	10-8-97	.000	.000	.000	23	1	1	0	0	0	0	0	0	0	0	0	0	1	0	0	0.0	100.0
Rosario, Amed	R-R	6-2	190	11-20-95	.270	.310	.426	47	158	148	19	40	8	0	5	18	7	2	0	1	22	1	0	4.4	13.9
Ruiz, Keibert	S-R	6-0	227	7-20-98	.247	.277	.318	68	267	255	19	63	12	0	2	25	8	3	0	1	26	0	2	3.0	9.7
Stubbs, C.J.	R-R	6-3	207	11-6-94	.000	.000	.000	1	3	3	0	0	0	0	0	0	0	0	0	0	0	0	0	0.0	0.0
Tena, Jose	L-R	5-11	195	3-20-01	.243	.314	.355	50	169	152	19	37	13	2	0	16	15	1	0	1	37	3	1	8.9	21.9
Wood, James	L-R	6-6	240	9-17-02	.256	.350	.475	157	689	598	87	153	38	0	31	94	85	3	0	3	221	15	7	12.3	32.1
Young, Jacob	R-R	5-11	180	7-27-99	.231	.296	.287	120	364	324	34	75	10	1	2	31	27	3	9	1	65	15	11	7.4	17.9

Pitching	B-T	Ht.	Wt.	DOB	W	L	ERA	G	GS	SV	IP	Hits	Runs	ER	HR	BB	SO	AVG	OBP	SLG	SO%	BB%	BF
Alvarez, Andrew	L-L	6-3	215	6-13-99	1	1	2.31	5	5	0	23	16	8	6	1	10	20	.184	.276	.241	20.4	10.2	98
Beeter, Clayton	R-R	6-2	220	10-9-98	0	2	2.49	24	0	1	22	8	6	6	1	14	32	.116	.262	.159	38.1	16.7	84
Brzykcy, Zach	R-R	6-2	232	7-12-99	0	1	9.00	26	0	0	23	28	23	23	6	12	24	.292	.382	.531	21.8	10.9	110
Cavalli, Cade	R-R	6-4	232	8-14-98	3	1	4.25	10	10	0	49	57	28	23	7	15	40	.289	.350	.447	18.3	6.8	219
Chafin, Andrew	R-L	6-2	235	6-17-90	1	1	2.70	26	0	0	20	20	8	6	1	12	18	.267	.368	.320	20.5	13.6	88
Fernandez, Julian	R-R	6-6	230	12-5-95	1	0	3.00	3	0	0	3	1	1	1	1	1	4	.100	.182	.400	36.4	9.1	11
Ferrer, Jose A.	L-L	6-1	229	3-3-00	4	4	4.48	72	0	11	76	81	41	38	5	16	71	.276	.326	.381	21.9	4.9	324
Finnegan, Kyle	R-R	6-2	200	9-4-91	1	4	4.38	40	0	20	39	36	21	19	3	14	32	.248	.315	.386	19.6	8.6	163
Garcia, Luis	R-R	6-2	240	1-30-87	0	0	0.90	10	0	0	10	5	1	1	1	2	7	.167	.219	.300	21.2	6.1	33
Gore, MacKenzie	L-L	6-2	192	2-24-99	5	15	4.17	30	30	0	160	152	75	74	20	64	185	.252	.326	.402	27.2	9.4	680
Henry, Cole	R-R	6-4	215	7-15-99	1	2	4.27	57	0	2	53	43	27	25	7	32	52	.219	.358	.367	21.6	13.3	241
Irvin, Jake	R-R	6-6	227	2-18-97	9	13	5.70	33	33	0	180	195	120	114	38	62	124	.272	.334	.492	15.8	7.9	787
Lao, Sauryn	R-R	6-2	182	8-14-99	1	0	3.52	6	0	0	8	8	3	3	1	1	5	.267	.313	.433	15.6	3.1	32
Lara, Andry	R-R	6-4	180	1-6-03	0	0	8.79	9	0	0	14	27	15	14	2	8	10	.403	.468	.567	12.8	10.3	78
Lopez, Jorge	R-R	6-3	200	2-10-93	6	0	6.57	26	0	1	25	25	18	18	1	7	17	.266	.330	.362	16.0	6.6	106
Lord, Brad	R-R	6-3	210	2-14-00	5	10	4.34	48	19	0	131	126	65	63	17	43	108	.255	.317	.415	19.8	7.9	546
Loutos, Ryan	R-R	6-5	215	1-29-99	1	0	12.00	10	0	0	9	16	16	12	3	6	6	.364	.442	.614	11.5	11.5	52
Ogasawara, Shinnosuke	L-L	5-11	205	10-8-97	1	1	6.98	23	2	0	39	43	30	30	9	17	30	.289	.364	.523	17.3	9.8	173
Parker, Mitchell	L-L	6-4	224	9-27-99	9	16	5.68	33	30	1	165	178	116	104	25	58	103	.273	.359	.430	14.2	8.0	725
Pilkington, Konnor	L-L	6-3	240	9-12-97	2	0	4.45	32	0	0	28	22	16	14	7	17	34	.216	.333	.471	27.6	13.8	123
Poche, Colin	L-L	6-3	225	1-17-94	1	2	11.42	13	0	0	9	10	12	11	1	12	10	.313	.478	.563	21.7	26.1	46
Poulin, PJ	R-L	6-1	195	7-25-96	2	1	3.65	28	0	1	25	23	10	10	2	13	27	.247	.365	.333	24.5	11.8	110
Ribalta, Orlando	R-R	6-7	245	3-5-98	0	0	7.03	22	0	0	24	28	19	19	6	17	25	.277	.383	.505	20.8	14.2	120
Rosario, Amed	R-R	6-2	190	11-20-95	0	0	36.00	1	0	0	1	5	4	4	1	2	0	.625	.700	1.000	0.0	20.0	10
Rutledge, Jackson	R-R	6-8	251	4-1-99	4	2	5.77	63	0	0	73	87	49	47	16	24	65	.297	.359	.515	19.7	7.3	330
Salazar, Eduardo	R-R	6-2	177	5-21-97	0	1	8.38	30	0	0	29	47	29	27	7	16	23	.359	.430	.611	15.3	10.7	150
Sims, Lucas	R-R	6-2	213	5-10-94	1	0	13.86	18	0	0	12	14	19	19	2	14	13	.275	.486	.490	18.1	19.4	72
Soroka, Michael	R-R	6-5	225	8-4-97	3	8	4.87	16	16	0	81	68	44	44	11	24	87	.224	.309	.388	25.4	7.0	343

	B-T	Ht.	Wt.	DOB																		
Thompson, Mason	R-R	6-6	244	2-20-98	1	1	11.81	14	0	0	11	16	16	14	1	12	11	.333	.467	.542	18.3	20.0	60
Williams, Trevor	R-R	6-3	231	4-25-92	3	10	6.21	17	17	0	83	106	59	57	11	21	65	.310	.347	.477	17.4	5.6	373

Fielding

Catcher	PCT	G	PO	A	E	DP	PB
Adams	.993	80	542	28	4	2	3
Alfaro	1.000	14	85	2	0	0	2
Millas	.966	16	109	6	4	1	0
Ruiz	.995	66	529	31	3	5	2
Stubbs	1.000	1	10	1	0	0	0

First Base	PCT	G	PO	A	E	DP
Adams	1.000	1	1	0	0	0
Bell	.988	33	245	12	3	26
Chaparro	1.000	30	121	12	0	10
DeJong	1.000	1	9	0	0	1
Garcia	1.000	2	16	0	0	1
Lipscomb	1.000	1	2	0	0	0
Lowe	.992	115	815	60	7	82

Second Base	PCT	G	PO	A	E	DP
DeJong	.974	13	8	29	1	7
Garcia	.987	129	226	314	7	76
Nunez	1.000	13	17	27	0	6
Rosario	.966	16	26	31	2	9
Tena	.947	5	9	9	1	0

Third Base	PCT	G	PO	A	E	DP
DeJong	.970	33	16	48	2	13
House	.961	72	36	137	7	10
Lipscomb	1.000	1	0	1	0	0
Rosario	.911	24	13	28	4	1
Tena	.948	46	23	69	5	7

Shortstop	PCT	G	PO	A	E	DP
Abrams	.962	142	205	352	22	72
DeJong	1.000	10	6	21	0	3
Lipscomb	1.000	1	1	0	0	0
Nunez	1.000	19	25	33	0	7
Rosario	.000	1	0	0	0	0

Outfield	PCT	G	PO	A	E	DP
Call	1.000	65	118	3	0	0
Crews	.964	87	186	4	7	1
Hassell	.993	68	131	2	1	1
Lile	.994	76	151	2	1	0
Nunez	1.000	2	4	0	0	0
Rosario	1.000	1	1	0	0	0
Wood	.987	123	231	5	3	0
Young	1.000	112	278	4	0	0

ROCHESTER RED WINGS — TRIPLE-A
INTERNATIONAL LEAGUE

Batting	B-T	Ht.	Wt.	DOB	AVG	OBP	SLG	G	PA	AB	R	H	2B	3B	HR	RBI	BB	HBP	SH	SF	SO	SB	CS	BB%	SO%
Arruda, J.T.	S-R	5-10	180	10-20-97	.250	.333	.369	69	199	176	28	44	4	1	5	19	21	1	1	0	43	13	0	10.6	21.6
Baker, Darren	S-R	5-10	180	2-11-99	.256	.343	.318	107	393	340	50	87	14	2	1	25	44	2	5	2	70	26	6	11.2	17.8
Chaparro, Andres	R-R	6-0	200	5-4-99	.275	.384	.577	48	216	182	31	50	13	0	14	45	32	1	0	1	50	1	0	14.8	23.1
Cluff, Jackson	L-R	5-11	181	12-3-96	.242	.349	.422	103	383	322	62	78	14	4	12	40	51	4	2	4	110	23	4	13.3	28.7
Cordero, Franchy	L-R	6-3	225	9-2-94	.213	.289	.333	44	166	150	11	32	6	0	4	17	15	1	0	0	43	0	0	9.0	25.9
Crews, Dylan	R-R	6-0	203	2-26-02	.244	.311	.415	13	45	41	5	10	1	0	2	7	1	3	0	0	7	1	0	2.2	15.6
De La Cruz, Carlos	R-R	6-8	210	10-6-99	.200	.333	.300	3	12	10	0	2	1	0	0	2	1	1	0	0	4	0	0	8.3	33.3
Franklin, Christian	R-R	5-8	195	10-30-99	.290	.382	.427	31	145	124	16	36	3	1	4	23	17	2	1	1	30	8	4	11.7	20.7
Garrett, Stone	R-R	6-2	224	11-22-95	.087	.176	.130	15	51	46	1	4	2	0	0	2	5	0	0	0	22	1	0	9.8	43.1
Glasser, Phillip	L-R	6-0	200	12-3-99	.391	.481	.522	12	54	46	8	18	1	1	1	8	8	0	0	0	7	2	0	14.8	13.0
Hassell, Robert	L-L	6-1	195	8-15-01	.310	.383	.456	76	330	294	45	91	13	0	10	49	35	0	1	0	57	16	3	10.6	17.3
House, Brady	R-R	6-4	215	6-4-03	.304	.353	.519	65	283	260	42	79	15	1	13	41	20	1	0	2	75	0	1	7.1	26.5
Knizner, Andrew	R-R	6-1	225	2-3-95	.382	.516	.500	23	91	68	10	26	5	0	1	11	13	8	0	2	11	0	1	14.3	12.1
Lile, Daylen	L-R	5-11	195	11-30-02	.337	.407	.500	26	119	104	18	35	7	2	2	15	11	2	0	1	20	6	2	9.2	16.8
Lindsly, Brady	L-R	6-1	221	3-8-98	.138	.265	.207	24	69	58	5	8	1	0	1	6	9	1	1	0	22	0	0	13.0	31.9
Lipscomb, Trey	R-R	6-2	200	6-14-00	.249	.305	.392	122	489	449	53	112	29	1	11	65	35	2	1	2	95	12	6	7.2	19.4
Mejia, Francisco	S-R	5-8	188	10-27-95	.215	.258	.362	42	159	149	23	32	4	0	6	19	9	0	0	1	32	2	0	5.7	20.1
Millas, Drew	S-R	6-0	198	1-15-98	.247	.306	.374	52	209	190	27	47	6	3	4	25	17	0	0	2	25	8	1	8.1	12.0
Morales, Yohandy	R-R	6-4	209	10-9-01	.249	.330	.401	95	433	382	66	95	21	2	11	49	46	2	0	3	131	5	0	10.6	30.3
Nunez, Nasim	S-R	5-9	168	8-18-00	.254	.339	.313	63	232	201	37	51	6	0	2	29	25	2	2	2	58	36	6	10.8	25.0
Pena, Viandel	S-R	5-7	148	11-22-00	.100	.250	.100	4	12	10	1	1	0	0	0	0	2	0	0	0	4	0	0	16.7	33.3
Pinckney, Andrew	R-R	6-3	205	7-10-00	.269	.348	.431	125	509	450	77	121	9	2	20	66	44	12	1	2	148	34	5	8.6	29.1
Schnell, Nick	L-R	6-3	180	3-27-00	.244	.322	.490	92	402	357	56	87	15	5	21	68	37	5	1	2	136	12	3	9.2	33.8
Stubbs, C.J.	R-R	6-3	207	11-12-96	.209	.336	.462	33	110	91	19	19	3	1	6	14	11	7	0	1	35	2	1	10.0	31.8
Tena, Jose	L-R	5-11	195	3-20-01	.287	.377	.431	52	240	209	27	60	13	1	5	24	30	0	1	0	59	21	5	12.5	24.6
Witt, Paul	R-R	5-10	170	10-29-97	.294	.368	.529	8	19	17	4	5	1	0	1	2	2	0	0	0	3	0	0	10.5	15.8
Yepez, Juan	R-R	6-1	200	2-19-98	.222	.289	.316	62	235	212	23	47	8	0	4	24	21	0	0	2	29	0	0	8.9	12.3

Pitching	B-T	Ht.	Wt.	DOB	W	L	ERA	G	GS	SV	IP	Hits	Runs	ER	HR	BB	SO	AVG	OBP	SLG	SO%	BB%	BF
Acosta, Daison	R-R	6-2	160	8-24-98	1	0	4.71	19	0	0	21	20	13	11	2	15	24	.250	.376	.375	23.8	14.9	101
Adon, Joan	R-R	6-2	245	8-12-98	2	2	5.70	34	2	0	43	41	30	27	6	31	46	.252	.389	.448	22.5	15.2	204
Alston, Garvin	R-L	6-4	175	3-12-97	0	0	7.36	7	0	0	11	18	9	9	1	7	7	.367	.458	.490	11.9	15.3	59
Alvarez, Andrew	L-L	6-3	215	6-13-99	3	7	4.10	25	25	0	123	114	74	56	13	52	114	.246	.326	.412	21.5	9.8	530
Arruda, J.T.	S-R	5-10	180	10-20-97	0	0	0.00	5	0	0	4	4	0	0	0	2	0	.250	.333	.438	0.0	11.1	18
Beeter, Clayton	R-R	6-2	220	10-9-98	0	0	6.75	3	0	0	4	2	3	3	0	4	7	.154	.353	.231	41.2	23.5	17
Bollenbacher, Matthew	R-R	6-1	203	11-9-99	0	0	9.82	2	0	0	4	2	4	4	1	6	0	.167	.500	.417	0.0	30.0	20
Brzykcy, Zach	R-R	6-2	232	7-12-99	0	2	9.39	23	0	1	23	33	26	24	4	21	26	.340	.458	.536	22.0	17.8	118
Cavalli, Cade	R-R	6-4	232	8-14-98	3	7	6.09	15	15	0	65	74	45	44	8	27	72	.294	.378	.448	25.1	9.4	287
Choi, Hyun-il	R-R	6-2	205	2-27-00	0	3	15.12	4	3	0	8	16	14	14	3	5	6	.421	.532	.763	12.8	10.6	47
Cluff, Jackson	L-R	5-11	181	12-3-96	0	0	9.00	5	0	0	5	12	5	5	1	3	1	.480	.517	.760	3.4	10.3	29
Conley, Bryce	R-R	6-3	200	8-22-94	2	4	6.11	15	14	0	74	77	50	50	17	26	69	.266	.325	.505	21.8	8.2	317
Cornelio, Riley	R-R	6-3	195	6-4-00	1	3	5.35	8	8	0	35	35	22	21	6	7	40	.237	.287	.437	25.5	8.7	149
Cuevas, Michael	R-R	6-2	165	6-29-01	0	1	6.10	9	0	0	14	17	11	11	3	9	13	.326	.473	.512	23.6	20.0	55
Davila, Garrett	L-L	6-2	180	1-17-97	1	1	3.78	18	0	0	17	11	9	7	2	11	22	.183	.324	.350	29.7	14.9	74
Dunshee, Parker	R-R	6-0	215	2-12-95	2	5	5.12	33	0	0	39	43	25	22	5	22	33	.295	.391	.514	18.9	12.6	175
Eder, Jake	L-L	6-4	215	10-9-98	0	2	12.60	2	2	0	5	9	7	7	4	9	7	.391	.464	.870	32.1	14.3	28
Fernandez, Julian	R-R	6-6	230	12-5-95	1	2	7.82	12	0	1	13	21	12	11	4	3	18	.344	.375	.574	28.1	4.7	64
Gray, Josiah	R-R	6-1	210	12-21-97	0	0	0.00	1	1	0	3	0	0	0	0	3	2	.000	.273	.000	18.2	27.3	11
Grissom, Marquis	R-R	6-2	202	7-19-01	2	2	5.73	27	0	2	33	31	22	21	7	19	32	.250	.354	.484	21.8	12.9	147
Helvey, Clay	R-R	6-3	195	2-14-97	0	1	9.53	21	0	0	23	31	30	24	6	27	23	.303	.450	.576	17.6	20.6	131
Henry, Cole	R-R	6-4	215	7-15-99	0	0	0.00	2	0	0	2	1	0	0	0	3	4	.143	.400	.143	40.0	30.0	10

Player	B-T	Ht	Wt	DOB	G	GS		AVG	OBP	SLG	G	PA	AB	R	H	2B	3B	HR	RBI	BB	HBP	SH	SF	SO	SB	CS	BB%	SO%
Lao, Sauryn	R-R	6-2	182	8-14-99	0	0		1.59	3	0	0	6	5	1	1	1	2	2	.250	.318	.500	9.1	9.1	22
Lara, Andry	R-R	6-4	180	1-6-03	1	6		8.92	17	6	0	36	50	40	36	4	22	26	.323	.400	.465	14.4	12.2	181
Law, Derek	R-R	6-3	225	9-14-90	0	1		13.50	2	1	0	2	4	3	3	1	1	1	.400	.455	.800	9.1	9.1	11
Loutos, Ryan	R-R	6-5	215	1-29-99	4	1		4.32	23	0	3	25	24	14	12	4	13	27	.250	.339	.385	24.8	11.9	109
Luckham, Kyle	R-R	6-2	205	10-1-99	0	2		5.46	7	6	0	31	39	19	19	1	9	23	.310	.360	.460	16.4	6.4	140
Mejia, Erick	S-R	5-11	195	11-9-94	0	0		10.80	11	0	0	10	10	12	12	1	9	13	.250	.400	.375	26.0	18.0	50
Ogasawara, Shinnosuke	L-L	5-11	205	10-8-97	2	1		3.60	5	5	0	25	28	11	10	1	8	19	.280	.330	.410	17.4	7.3	109
Peterson, Todd	R-R	6-5	230	1-22-98	0	1		21.00	7	0	0	6	15	15	14	1	8	7	.484	.590	.839	17.1	19.5	41
Pilkington, Konnor	L-L	6-3	240	9-12-97	4	3		2.59	36	3	2	42	23	19	12	2	27	50	.158	.298	.219	28.1	15.2	178
Powell, Holden	R-R	6-0	190	9-9-99	4	1		4.54	31	0	0	36	35	21	18	1	34	32	.269	.433	.362	18.6	19.8	172
Ribalta, Orlando	R-R	6-7	245	3-5-98	0	0		2.57	7	0	0	7	7	2	2	1	2	6	.292	.370	.417	22.2	7.4	27
Romero, Carlos	R-R	6-6	179	7-15-99	2	3		6.09	38	0	1	44	47	35	30	6	28	41	.272	.385	.451	15.5	13.3	210
Rutledge, Jackson	R-R	6-8	251	4-1-99	1	0		0.00	2	0	0	3	1	0	0	0	1	4	.111	.200	.111	40.0	10.0	10
Saenz, Dustin	L-L	5-11	197	6-2-99	0	0		0.00	1	0	0	3	2	0	0	0	1	0	.200	.273	.300	0.0	9.1	11
Salazar, Eduardo	R-R	6-2	177	5-5-98	1	3		5.05	34	0	5	36	35	26	20	4	22	32	.252	.347	.374	19.2	13.2	167
Sampson, Adrian	R-R	6-2	210	10-7-91	5	5		4.41	16	16	0	84	79	44	41	11	30	45	.246	.318	.405	12.6	8.4	358
Schoff, Tyler	R-R	6-4	220	12-6-98	0	1		6.43	5	0	0	7	6	5	5	2	3	9	.222	.300	.444	29.0	9.7	31
Schultz, Thomas	R-R	6-6	243	8-3-99	0	0		32.40	1	0	0	2	5	6	6	1	2	1	.500	.583	1.000	8.3	16.7	12
Shuman, Seth	R-R	6-1	195	12-1-97	4	5		6.60	31	14	0	91	110	72	67	21	21	81	.299	.342	.533	20.3	5.3	400
Sinclair, Jack	R-R	6-4	170	5-3-99	3	2		5.95	35	2	0	42	46	30	28	4	26	43	.282	.390	.436	21.9	13.3	196
Solesky, Chase	R-R	6-3	201	9-26-97	6	5		5.17	24	23	0	110	119	65	63	16	45	96	.275	.346	.469	19.7	9.2	487
Soroka, Michael	R-R	6-5	225	8-4-97	0	0		1.80	1	1	0	5	4	1	1	1	3	11	.211	.318	.368	50.0	13.6	22
Thompson, Mason	R-R	6-6	244	2-20-98	0	1		5.59	10	0	0	10	11	6	6	1	6	10	.289	.391	.447	21.7	13.0	46
Weigel, Patrick	R-R	6-6	240	7-8-94	4	5		8.29	31	0	3	34	38	35	31	10	16	46	.286	.368	.594	29.5	10.3	156
Witt, Paul	R-R	5-11	170	10-29-97	0	0		27.00	1	0	0	2	9	6	6	2	0	0	.643	.600	1.286	0.0	0.0	15

Fielding

Catcher	PCT	G	PO	A	E	DP	PB
Knizner	.988	17	155	7	2	1	1
Lindsly	.969	22	154	4	5	1	3
Mejia	.986	42	338	16	5	1	6
Millas	.986	45	323	17	5	2	4
Stubbs	.993	31	251	23	2	0	3

First Base	PCT	G	PO	A	E	DP
Chaparro	.994	25	160	10	1	15
Cluff	1.000	1	1	0	0	0
Cordero	1.000	2	9	1	0	1
Lindsly	1.000	1	1	0	0	0
Lipscomb	.988	16	76	8	1	14
Morales	.992	73	544	44	5	66
Stubbs	.000	2	0	0	0	0
Witt	1.000	1	5	0	0	0
Yepez	.989	37	244	24	3	21

Second Base	PCT	G	PO	A	E	DP
Arruda	.981	34	40	62	2	22
Baker	.976	53	85	117	5	28

	PCT	G	PO	A	E	DP
Cluff	.985	17	23	43	1	11
Lipscomb	.971	29	38	64	3	12
Nunez	1.000	2	6	5	0	2
Pena	1.000	2	2	2	0	0
Tena	1.000	23	34	68	0	12
Witt	1.000	4	3	7	0	1

Third Base	PCT	G	PO	A	E	DP
Arruda	.923	5	6	6	1	1
Chaparro	.000	1	0	0	0	0
Cluff	1.000	9	9	12	0	2
House	.938	61	41	81	8	4
Lipscomb	.960	44	27	69	4	8
Morales	.893	17	11	14	3	3
Tena	.865	18	7	38	7	2
Witt	.000	1	0	0	0	0

Shortstop	PCT	G	PO	A	E	DP
Arruda	.953	20	21	40	3	5
Cluff	.968	73	107	162	9	49
Lipscomb	.000	2	0	0	0	0

	PCT	G	PO	A	E	DP
Nunez	.959	58	76	155	10	32
Pena	.833	2	2	3	1	1

Outfield	PCT	G	PO	A	E	DP
Arruda	1.000	2	1	0	0	0
Baker	.978	45	88	2	2	0
Cordero	1.000	14	9	2	0	0
Crews	.952	9	19	1	1	0
De La Cruz	1.000	3	5	0	0	0
Franklin	.964	31	52	1	2	0
Garrett	1.000	15	29	3	0	1
Glasser	1.000	11	22	0	0	0
Hassell	.994	69	163	1	1	1
Lile	.953	24	40	1	2	0
Lipscomb	.963	29	51	1	2	0
Nunez	1.000	1	1	0	0	0
Pinckney	.979	124	271	7	6	1
Schnell	.982	85	157	5	3	2
Yepez	1.000	4	5	1	0	0

HARRISBURG SENATORS — DOUBLE-A
EASTERN LEAGUE

Batting	B-T	Ht.	Wt.	DOB	AVG	OBP	SLG	G	PA	AB	R	H	2B	3B	HR	RBI	BB	HBP	SH	SF	SO	SB	CS	BB%	SO%
Abrams, CJ	L-R	6-2	191	10-3-00	.000	.286	.000	2	7	4	0	0	0	0	0	0	2	0	0	1	0	0	0	28.6	14.3
Arruda, J.T.	S-R	5-10	180	10-20-97	.265	.306	.500	10	36	34	4	9	2	0	2	3	1	0	0	1	11	2	0	2.8	30.6
Boissiere, Branden	L-L	6-1	205	3-23-00	.291	.369	.450	51	214	189	25	55	14	2	4	27	21	3	0	1	49	0	0	9.8	22.9
Brown, Sam	L-L	6-2	218	9-12-01	.307	.384	.472	35	146	127	15	39	8	2	3	17	15	2	0	2	25	1	0	10.3	17.1
De La Cruz, Carlos	R-R	6-8	210	10-6-99	.221	.285	.389	114	470	429	46	95	19	7	13	55	35	4	0	2	155	12	4	7.4	33.0
De La Rosa, Jeremy	L-L	6-0	215	1-16-02	.190	.282	.333	19	71	63	7	12	4	1	1	5	7	1	0	0	18	3	0	9.9	25.4
DeJong, Paul	R-R	6-1	205	8-2-93	.275	.348	.375	12	46	40	4	11	1	0	1	6	4	1	0	1	12	1	1	8.7	26.1
DeShields, Delino	R-R	5-7	190	8-16-92	.262	.372	.320	37	127	103	19	27	4	1	0	6	16	2	0	6	35	3	1	12.6	27.6
Farmer, Caleb	R-R	6-2	205	9-8-99	.188	.235	.250	5	18	16	1	3	1	0	0	1	1	0	1	0	2	0	0	5.6	11.1
Glasser, Phillip	L-R	6-0	200	12-3-99	.293	.379	.391	112	490	427	63	125	18	3	6	41	52	8	2	1	55	30	11	10.6	11.2
King, Seaver	R-R	6-0	190	4-25-03	.233	.287	.313	80	357	326	37	76	13	2	7	32	23	3	2	3	74	18	3	6.4	20.7
Lawson, Cortland	R-R	6-2	200	5-12-00	.208	.268	.257	32	114	101	5	21	2	0	1	9	7	2	2	2	30	1	2	6.1	26.3
Lile, Daylen	L-R	5-11	195	11-30-02	.319	.340	.505	21	94	91	17	29	5	3	2	14	3	0	0	0	13	6	1	3.2	13.8
Lomavita, Caleb	R-R	5-11	200	11-18-02	.273	.351	.485	9	37	33	3	9	1	0	2	3	4	0	0	0	9	0	1	10.8	24.3
Mack, Charles	L-R	5-9	190	11-12-99	.000	.000	.000	1	1	1	0	0	0	0	0	0	0	0	0	0	1	0	0	0.0	100.0
Made, Kevin	R-R	5-9	160	9-10-02	.217	.286	.275	89	348	309	32	67	6	0	4	38	27	5	2	5	54	9	2	7.8	15.5
McKenzie, Jared	L-L	6-0	205	10-17-00	.204	.275	.275	100	374	321	30	66	13	1	8	50	27	1	1	0	38	2	0	4.6	34.9
Morales, Yohandy	R-R	6-4	209	10-9-01	.315	.366	.520	33	142	127	19	40	10	2	4	22	11	1	0	3	33	2	2	7.7	23.2
Naranjo, Joe	L-L	5-10	205	5-11-01	.227	.344	.299	103	418	348	45	79	14	1	3	35	61	2	4	4	98	2	0	14.6	23.4
Pena, Viandel	S-R	5-7	148	11-22-00	.201	.262	.371	53	173	159	22	32	5	2	6	26	13	0	1	0	46	6	2	7.5	26.6
Romero, Maxwell	R-R	6-1	218	4-29-01	.196	.266	.322	86	316	276	22	54	14	0	7	45	24	5	4	7	112	1	3	7.6	35.4
Ruiz, Keibert	S-R	6-0	227	7-20-98	.000	.273	.000	3	11	8	2	0	0	0	0	0	3	0	0	0	6	0	0	27.3	54.5

WASHINGTON NATIONALS

	B-T	Ht.	Wt.	DOB			AVG														
Schnell, Nick	L-R	6-1	180	3-27-00	.289	.319	.450	37	160	149	26	43	6	6	2	16	8	0	0	3	39	6	1	5.0	24.4
Stehly, Murphy	R-R	5-10	205	9-27-98	.328	.417	.529	35	140	119	26	39	9	0	5	18	15	4	1	1	25	4	0	10.7	17.9
Stubbs, C.J.	R-R	6-3	207	11-12-96	.142	.263	.216	42	156	134	20	19	4	0	2	10	19	3	0	0	62	2	1	12.2	39.7
Suggs, Matt	R-R	5-9	195	5-31-00	.174	.235	.283	15	51	46	4	8	2	0	1	4	4	0	0	1	17	0	0	7.8	33.3
Thomas, Johnathon	R-R	5-7	175	3-1-00	.229	.287	.307	71	249	218	36	50	9	1	2	21	13	5	7	1	47	23	4	5.2	18.9
Wallace, Cayden	R-R	5-10	205	8-7-01	.242	.310	.376	121	481	426	49	103	21	3	10	55	40	6	1	8	113	16	2	8.3	23.5
Williams, Donta'	L-L	5-10	185	6-30-99	.125	.218	.229	16	55	48	5	6	2	0	1	4	4	2	0	1	12	1	0	7.3	21.8
Witt, Paul	R-R	5-11	170	10-29-97	.139	.279	.194	12	44	36	4	5	2	0	0	1	5	2	1	0	5	0	0	11.4	11.4
Young, Jacob	R-R	5-11	180	7-27-99	.273	.385	.364	3	13	11	2	3	0	0	0	0	1	1	0	0	1	1	0	7.7	7.7

Pitching

	B-T	Ht.	Wt.	DOB	W	L	ERA	G	GS	SV	IP	Hits	Runs	ER	HR	BB	SO	AVG	OBP	SLG	SO%	BB%	BF
Acosta, Daison	R-R	6-2	160	8-24-98	4	1	0.90	26	0	5	30	16	5	3	1	12	46	.157	.246	.216	40.4	10.5	114
Amaral, Austin	R-R	6-0	200	12-4-01	2	2	2.40	10	0	0	15	9	5	4	1	7	9	.170	.290	.321	14.3	11.1	63
Armstrong, Ivan	R-R	6-5	247	7-27-00	1	3	7.64	17	0	0	18	22	17	15	5	12	14	.301	.414	.589	16.1	13.8	87
Bennett, Jake	L-L	6-6	234	12-2-00	1	2	2.56	10	9	0	46	40	14	13	2	11	33	.234	.284	.322	17.9	6.0	184
Boissiere, Branden	L-L	6-1	205	3-23-00	0	0	27.00	1	0	0	1	4	3	3	2	1	0	.667	.714	1.667	0.0	14.3	7
Cavalli, Cade	R-R	6-4	232	8-14-98	1	0	0.00	1	1	0	5	2	0	0	0	1	4	.118	.167	.118	22.2	5.6	18
Choi, Hyun-il	R-R	6-2	215	5-27-00	7	5	4.08	26	17	0	108	92	55	49	20	29	82	.227	.291	.412	18.3	6.5	447
Clemmey, Alexander	L-L	6-6	205	7-18-05	0	1	6.44	6	6	0	29	32	22	21	8	13	23	.278	.354	.513	17.6	9.9	131
Conley, Bryce	R-R	6-3	200	8-22-94	2	4	3.20	8	8	0	45	33	19	16	5	17	38	.202	.288	.374	20.5	9.2	185
Cornelio, Riley	R-R	6-3	195	6-6-00	4	2	2.31	12	11	0	66	39	18	17	3	26	58	.172	.258	.269	22.6	10.1	257
Cuevas, Michael	R-R	6-2	165	6-29-01	2	1	2.10	24	0	8	26	17	11	6	0	12	22	.183	.303	.204	20.0	10.9	110
Davila, Garrett	L-L	6-2	180	1-17-97	6	3	2.72	39	0	1	40	20	13	12	1	15	38	.149	.243	.201	24.7	9.7	154
Eder, Jake	L-L	6-4	215	10-9-98	0	0	0.00	1	1	0	2	1	0	0	0	0	1	.143	.250	.143	12.5	0.0	8
Gomez, Miguel	R-R	6-3	170	9-10-01	2	1	4.71	17	5	0	29	30	15	15	3	16	27	.270	.362	.423	21.3	12.6	127
Gray, Josiah	R-R	6-1	210	12-21-97	0	0	0.00	1	1	0	2	4	0	0	0	0	2	.500	.500	.500	25.0	0.0	8
Grissom, Marquis	R-R	6-2	202	7-19-01	0	0	1.86	9	0	5	10	8	2	2	1	5	8	.250	.351	.406	21.1	13.2	38
Huff, Chance	R-R	6-4	220	4-19-00	5	3	3.54	35	5	0	56	49	25	22	4	29	47	.238	.343	.330	19.4	12.0	242
Kent, Jackson	L-L	6-3	218	2-10-03	2	3	5.59	6	6	0	29	26	19	18	4	13	35	.241	.322	.417	28.7	10.7	122
Knowles, Lucas	L-L	6-2	185	3-14-98	2	0	3.68	6	0	0	7	6	3	3	1	2	5	.231	.310	.346	17.2	6.9	29
Lara, Andry	R-R	6-4	180	1-6-03	0	2	10.80	2	2	0	8	14	10	10	1	5	5	.389	.452	.694	11.9	11.9	42
Law, Derek	R-R	6-3	225	9-14-90	0	0	10.13	2	2	0	3	6	4	3	1	1	1	.333	.385	.583	7.7	7.7	13
Luckham, Kyle	R-R	6-2	205	10-1-99	4	7	3.67	20	19	0	103	102	49	42	8	35	70	.259	.326	.368	15.9	7.9	441
Mejia, Erick	S-R	5-11	195	11-9-94	0	0	2.33	24	0	0	27	16	12	7	1	21	28	.176	.327	.242	24.8	18.6	113
Peterson, Todd	R-R	6-5	230	1-22-98	1	1	3.43	16	0	0	21	18	9	8	2	13	15	.231	.358	.333	15.8	13.7	95
Powell, Holden	R-R	6-0	190	9-9-99	1	1	3.10	19	0	1	20	8	7	7	1	12	23	.125	.278	.234	28.8	15.0	80
Ribalta, Orlando	R-R	6-7	245	3-5-98	0	0	0.00	2	0	0	2	0	0	0	0	2	1	.000	.286	.000	14.3	28.6	7
Saenz, Dustin	L-L	5-11	197	6-2-99	6	7	4.50	38	9	0	84	95	55	42	9	21	52	.286	.332	.443	14.2	5.8	365
Sampson, Adrian	R-R	6-2	210	10-7-91	0	0	2.31	2	2	0	12	8	3	3	0	6	11	.211	.318	.237	25.0	13.6	44
Santos, Junior	R-R	6-7	244	8-16-01	6	5	2.03	54	0	12	62	41	19	14	4	39	49	.196	.316	.306	19.1	15.2	257
Schoff, Tyler	R-R	6-4	220	12-6-98	2	0	4.15	4	0	0	4	6	2	2	0	5	7	.333	.478	.611	30.4	21.7	23
Schultz, Thomas	R-R	6-6	243	8-3-99	1	0	3.22	32	5	0	50	31	22	18	6	25	47	.178	.276	.328	22.7	12.1	207
Shuman, Seth	R-R	6-1	195	12-1-97	0	1	4.11	3	3	0	15	18	7	7	2	0	13	.290	.313	.419	20.3	0.0	64
Sinclair, Jack	R-R	6-4	170	5-3-99	0	2	5.14	18	0	0	21	23	12	12	2	17	18	.274	.408	.440	17.5	16.5	103
Soroka, Michael	R-R	6-5	225	8-4-97	0	1	5.14	2	2	0	5	6	4	4	2	2	7	.222	.276	.519	24.1	6.9	29
Stuart, Tyler	R-R	6-9	250	10-8-99	1	2	6.05	5	4	0	19	24	13	13	3	12	17	.320	.409	.547	19.3	13.6	88
Susana, Jarlin	R-R	6-6	235	3-23-04	1	2	3.61	11	11	0	47	34	20	19	3	32	79	.204	.345	.293	38.0	15.4	208
Sykora, Travis	R-R	6-6	220	4-28-04	0	1	7.71	2	2	0	5	4	4	4	0	9	.211	.400	.211	36.0	24.0	25
Thompson, Mason	R-R	6-6	244	2-20-98	0	1	9.53	4	1	0	6	7	6	6	2	6	4	.333	.481	.429	25.9	14.8	27
Tolman, Erik	L-L	6-2	193	6-3-99	0	2	5.97	7	6	0	29	22	19	19	5	20	25	.214	.346	.388	19.1	15.3	131
Vasquez, Samuel	R-R	6-3	170	9-20-99	3	1	3.26	25	0	1	30	22	13	11	2	16	23	.208	.315	.292	18.3	12.7	126
Young, Luke	R-R	6-2	170	10-31-03	1	3	4.31	45	0	0	54	55	28	26	8	23	44	.274	.363	.463	18.4	9.6	239

Fielding

Catcher	PCT	G	PO	A	E	DP	PB
Farmer	1.000	5	28	3	0	0	0
Lomavita	1.000	8	58	6	0	0	1
Romero	.989	83	618	32	7	5	2
Ruiz	1.000	2	15	0	0	0	0
Stubbs	.993	31	247	21	2	3	7
Suggs	.990	14	92	9	1	1	2

First Base	PCT	G	PO	A	E	DP
Boissiere	.993	34	271	22	2	27
Brown	1.000	7	47	4	0	7
Morales	1.000	9	83	7	0	7
Naranjo	.987	75	526	61	8	57
Stehly	1.000	9	43	7	0	2
Stubbs	1.000	1	1	0	0	0
Witt	1.000	5	38	2	0	6

Second Base	PCT	G	PO	A	E	DP
Arruda	1.000	5	19	19	0	7
DeJong	1.000	2	1	6	0	0
Glasser	1.000	11	13	21	0	6

	PCT	G	PO	A	E	DP	PB
Lawson	1.000	6	7	11	0	1	
Made	.973	63	120	164	8	54	
Pena	.972	36	48	89	4	13	
Stehly	1.000	3	4	3	0	0	
Wallace	.947	17	23	31	3	5	

Third Base	PCT	G	PO	A	E	DP
Arruda	1.000	2	3	7	0	2
DeJong	1.000	5	2	5	0	0
Made	.000	1	0	0	0	0
Morales	.939	21	14	32	3	4
Pena	.917	8	6	16	2	1
Stehly	.972	12	9	26	1	1
Wallace	.972	93	78	161	7	18
Witt	1.000	1	1	0	0	0

Shortstop	PCT	G	PO	A	E	DP
Abrams	.889	2	0	8	1	2
Arruda	.900	3	5	4	1	1
DeJong	1.000	9	13	0	1	
King	.953	78	123	178	15	51

	PCT	G	PO	A	E	DP
Lawson	.942	26	29	69	6	14
Made	.971	26	43	58	3	14
Pena	.950	5	8	11	1	1

Outfield	PCT	G	PO	A	E	DP
Brown	1.000	14	19	2	0	1
De La Cruz	.969	100	184	2	6	1
De La Rosa	1.000	15	16	2	0	0
DeShields	1.000	35	90	1	0	1
Glasser	.993	83	143	8	1	3
Lile	.967	20	28	1	1	0
McKenzie	.986	29	67	2	1	1
Naranjo	.973	18	35	1	1	0
Schnell	.978	33	90	1	2	1
Thomas	.994	74	163	8	1	0
Williams	1.000	16	25	0	0	0
Young	1.000	3	6	0	0	0

WILMINGTON BLUE ROCKS   HIGH-A
SOUTH ATLANTIC LEAGUE

Batting	B-T	Ht.	Wt.	DOB	AVG	OBP	SLG	G	PA	AB	R	H	2B	3B	HR	RBI	BB	HBP	SH	SF	SO	SB	CS	BB%	SO%
Banks, Teo	R-R	6-2	190	7-10-03	.123	.210	.156	55	141	122	13	15	1	0	1	9	11	3	2	2	32	4	0	7.8	22.7
Boissiere, Branden	L-L	6-1	205	3-23-00	.257	.319	.409	74	301	269	28	69	16	2	7	41	23	4	0	5	80	1	1	7.6	26.6
Brown, Marcus	L-R	6-0	187	9-14-01	.224	.302	.307	94	345	303	33	68	12	2	3	16	28	7	4	3	67	13	3	8.1	19.4
Colmenares, Jose	R-R	5-10	165	8-23-02	.214	.371	.214	10	35	28	0	6	0	0	0	0	7	0	0	0	6	0	0	20.0	17.1
Cox, Brenner	L-R	6-3	195	5-11-04	.132	.205	.184	44	168	152	12	20	8	0	0	8	13	1	2	0	71	4	2	7.7	42.3
Cruz, Armando	R-R	5-10	160	1-16-04	.177	.222	.233	94	333	305	23	54	8	3	1	21	17	1	9	1	75	5	3	5.1	22.5
De La Rosa, Jeremy	L-L	6-0	215	1-16-02	.198	.278	.257	32	115	101	4	20	3	0	1	11	12	0	0	2	32	3	5	10.4	27.8
Dugas, Gavin	R-R	5-10	204	5-19-00	.181	.304	.272	92	332	276	27	50	10	0	5	30	38	13	0	5	88	4	4	11.4	26.5
Farmer, Caleb	R-R	6-2	205	9-8-99	.107	.193	.253	26	83	75	9	8	1	2	2	8	5	3	0	0	25	0	0	6.0	30.1
Green, Elijah	R-R	6-3	225	12-4-03	.171	.271	.260	35	140	123	12	21	2	0	3	7	16	1	0	0	64	7	1	11.4	45.7
Henseler, Wyatt	R-R	6-1	215	8-6-01	.098	.140	.195	11	43	41	2	4	1	0	1	1	0	2	0	0	20	0	0	4.6	46.5
King, Seaver	R-R	6-0	190	4-25-03	.263	.307	.380	45	194	179	28	47	6	3	3	17	9	3	2	1	42	12	1	4.6	21.6
Lawson, Cortland	R-R	6-2	200	5-12-00	.239	.320	.311	59	250	222	24	53	10	0	2	19	17	0	0	1	60	5	2	10.8	24.0
Lomavita, Caleb	R-R	5-11	200	11-18-02	.275	.339	.364	99	409	363	32	100	16	2	4	44	19	19	0	6	83	7	0	4.6	20.3
McKenzie, Jared	L-L	6-0	180	5-16-01	.201	.242	.314	55	208	194	25	39	6	2	4	11	9	2	1	2	59	7	2	4.3	28.4
Nunez, Elijah	L-L	5-10	180	12-6-01	.299	.415	.393	36	142	117	21	35	9	1	0	10	21	3	0	1	32	14	1	14.8	22.5
Petersen, Sam	R-R	6-0	195	1-20-03	.297	.398	.490	44	172	145	31	43	6	2	6	21	20	5	1	1	31	18	0	11.6	18.0
Pimentel, Brandon	L-L	6-3	210	6-16-00	.194	.256	.261	54	195	180	14	35	7	1	1	16	7	8	0	0	42	3	0	3.6	21.5
Quintana, Roismar	R-R	6-1	175	2-6-03	.100	.182	.100	6	22	20	1	2	0	0	0	1	2	0	0	0	6	0	0	9.1	27.3
Rombach, Nate	R-R	6-4	222	11-26-00	.121	.203	.190	22	64	58	3	7	1	0	1	2	6	0	0	0	22	0	0	9.4	34.4
Ross, Jackson	R-R	6-2	210	4-5-00	.158	.278	.248	52	195	165	19	26	8	2	1	11	26	2	1	1	53	4	1	13.3	27.2
Stehly, Murphy	R-R	5-10	205	9-27-98	.182	.386	.394	13	44	33	4	6	1	0	2	4	8	3	0	0	12	0	1	18.2	27.3
Suggs, Matt	R-R	5-9	195	5-31-00	.203	.330	.278	28	94	79	13	16	6	0	0	6	14	1	0	0	25	2	0	14.9	26.6
Thomas, Johnathon	R-R	5-7	175	3-1-00	.230	.302	.322	32	99	87	8	20	4	2	0	6	7	2	2	0	18	9	2	7.1	18.2
White, T.J.	S-R	6-2	210	7-23-03	.231	.308	.337	106	427	377	30	87	15	2	7	41	40	4	0	4	114	6	1	9.4	26.7
Williams, Donta'	L-L	5-10	185	6-30-99	.200	.282	.243	22	79	70	3	14	3	0	0	2	8	0	0	0	25	0	2	10.1	31.6
Yepez, Juan	R-R	6-1	200	2-19-98	.214	.306	.571	13	49	42	7	9	4	0	4	10	4	0	0	1	6	0	0	10.2	12.2

Pitching	B-T	Ht.	Wt.	DOB	W	L	ERA	G	GS	SV	IP	Hits	Runs	ER	HR	BB	SO	AVG	OBP	SLG	SO%	BB%	BF
Aldonis, Pablo	L-L	6-1	160	3-21-02	2	0	2.05	10	1	0	22	13	5	5	0	3	22	.171	.198	.263	27.2	3.7	81
Amaral, Austin	R-R	6-0	200	12-4-01	1	2	1.96	23	0	8	41	30	11	9	0	12	33	.207	.269	.283	20.6	7.5	160
Arguelles, Anthony	R-R	5-10	195	8-16-00	5	3	3.34	38	0	2	57	38	24	21	2	32	59	.193	.308	.264	25.0	13.6	236
Arias, Wander	R-R	6-4	230	11-3-99	4	4	6.90	33	4	0	59	63	51	45	10	36	50	.276	.398	.504	17.9	12.9	279
Bennett, Jake	L-L	6-6	234	12-2-00	1	2	1.90	7	7	0	24	17	5	5	1	8	24	.205	.275	.301	26.4	8.8	91
Bloebaum, Adam	L-L	6-6	225	5-3-01	1	1	1.23	6	0	0	7	4	3	1	1	3	9	.143	.226	.286	29.0	9.7	31
Bollenbacher, Matthew	R-R	6-3	203	11-9-99	0	0	3.52	11	0	1	15	12	6	6	2	3	8	.211	.246	.351	13.1	4.9	61
Brzykcy, Zach	R-R	6-2	232	7-12-99	0	0	0.00	1	0	0	1	0	0	0	0	0	1	.000	.000	.000	33.3	0.0	3
Caceres, Bryan	R-R	6-1	170	2-19-00	3	4	6.20	28	3	0	49	52	40	34	3	39	46	.274	.417	.384	19.0	16.1	242
Clemmey, Alexander	L-L	6-6	205	7-18-05	7	4	2.47	19	19	0	87	56	30	24	4	60	113	.182	.324	.244	30.0	15.9	377
Cornelio, Riley	R-R	6-3	195	6-6-00	1	2	3.03	7	7	0	33	25	15	11	2	16	39	.208	.304	.300	28.3	11.6	138
Cranz, Robert	R-R	6-3	200	5-28-03	0	1	1.80	5	0	2	5	1	2	1	1	1	4	.063	.118	.250	23.5	5.9	17
Davis, Marc	R-R	6-3	195	11-11-99	1	0	10.07	14	0	0	20	20	23	22	3	25	13	.270	.462	.500	12.5	24.0	104
Dugas, Gavin	R-R	5-10	204	5-19-00	0	0	0.00	1	0	0	0	0	0	0	0	0	0	.000	.000	.000	0.0	0.0	1
Garcia, Davian	R-R	6-1	188	10-10-03	1	4	5.54	7	6	0	26	31	17	16	4	15	22	.292	.405	.443	17.5	11.9	126
Glavine, Peyton	R-L	5-11	180	3-23-99	2	0	3.64	27	2	0	42	38	18	17	3	24	29	.257	.358	.372	16.4	13.6	177
Gomez, Miguel	R-R	6-3	170	9-10-01	1	0	0.84	8	0	5	11	4	2	1	0	6	12	.118	.250	.147	30.0	15.0	40
Gray, Josiah	R-R	6-1	210	12-21-97	0	0	0.00	1	1	0	1	0	0	0	0	2	1	.000	.429	.000	14.3	28.6	7
Hall, Bubba	R-R	6-1	212	4-10-00	1	0	3.00	5	0	0	6	6	4	2	1	2	5	.240	.296	.440	18.5	7.4	27
Huff, Chance	R-R	6-4	220	4-19-00	0	2	5.73	8	0	0	11	15	7	7	0	4	9	.333	.380	.467	17.6	7.8	51
Jimenez, Yeuris	R-R	6-3	218	3-23-01	3	2	7.16	35	0	0	44	38	43	35	3	49	53	.248	.415	.369	24.3	22.5	218
Kent, Jackson	L-L	6-3	218	2-10-03	5	7	4.31	18	18	0	94	86	48	45	10	25	97	.244	.302	.378	25.1	6.5	387
Knowles, Lucas	L-L	6-2	185	3-14-98	0	1	9.00	5	0	0	6	6	7	6	1	4	5	.250	.345	.542	17.2	13.8	29
Lara, Andry	R-R	6-4	180	1-6-03	0	1	0.79	3	2	0	11	10	2	1	0	4	10	.233	.298	.233	21.3	8.5	47
Linan, Sean	R-R	6-0	185	11-7-04	0	1	9.00	1	1	0	3	4	3	3	0	2	5	.333	.429	.333	35.7	14.3	14
Meckley, Xander	R-R	6-2	235	7-12-03	0	3	5.94	4	3	0	17	22	13	11	1	10	19	.314	.415	.457	23.2	12.2	82
Montero, Euri	R-R	6-4	170	3-28-02	0	3	6.10	7	0	0	10	13	12	7	0	6	7	.302	.404	.326	13.5	11.5	52
Ogasawara, Shinnosuke	L-L	5-11	205	10-8-97	0	0	5.14	2	2	0	7	6	4	4	1	2	10	.231	.276	.423	34.5	6.9	29
Otanez, Johan	R-R	6-1	168	2-19-02	0	0	1.69	6	0	0	5	3	1	1	0	9	6	.176	.481	.176	22.2	33.3	27
Randall, Josh	R-R	6-4	242	10-15-02	0	4	6.44	6	6	0	29	37	24	21	2	5	26	.301	.328	.480	19.5	3.8	133
Schultz, Thomas	R-R	6-6	243	8-3-99	1	1	2.65	13	0	2	17	9	7	5	1	5	21	.153	.219	.339	32.8	7.8	64
Simpson, Jared	L-L	6-4	205	6-24-00	1	5	6.23	41	0	0	52	35	44	36	2	57	64	.196	.395	.307	25.8	23.0	248
Sthele, Travis	R-R	6-0	198	9-21-01	7	7	4.22	23	22	0	139	130	70	65	10	24	82	.246	.280	.371	14.6	4.3	561
Stuart, Tyler	R-R	6-9	250	10-8-99	1	0	0.00	2	2	0	9	5	0	0	0	1	9	.156	.182	.188	27.3	3.0	33
Susana, Jarlin	R-R	6-6	235	3-23-04	0	2	3.00	3	3	0	9	6	3	3	0	2	16	.172	.222	.206	44.4	5.6	36
Swan, Eriq	R-R	6-6	240	10-31-01	0	3	4.37	5	5	0	23	19	12	11	2	17	25	.235	.380	.383	25.0	17.0	100
Sykora, Travis	R-R	6-6	220	4-28-04	3	0	1.21	6	6	0	30	12	4	4	0	8	47	.124	.198	.165	44.3	7.5	106
Tejeda, Yoel	S-R	6-7	210	7-8-03	0	2	9.72	2	2	0	8	9	9	9	2	6	5	.273	.375	.545	12.5	15.0	40
Tepper, Mikey	L-R	6-0	210	6-2-02	0	2	10.57	2	2	0	9	11	11	9	2	4	7	.306	.447	.697	18.4	10.5	38
Tolman, Erik	L-L	6-2	193	6-3-99	2	1	2.91	20	6	1	56	34	18	18	2	27	55	.183	.295	.253	25.2	12.4	218
Vasquez, Samuel	R-R	6-3	170	9-20-99	1	1	3.04	21	0	4	27	10	9	0	13	26	.265	.356	.353	22.0	11.0	118
Young, Luke	R-R	6-3	170	10-31-01	0	0	13.50	2	0	0	2	2	3	3	1	2	1	.286	.444	.714	11.1	22.2	9

Fielding

Catcher	PCT	G	PO	A	E	DP	PB
Colmenares	.969	10	90	3	3	0	0
Farmer	.994	24	151	6	1	0	1
Lomavita	.971	73	655	40	21	4	7
Rombach	1.000	8	42	0	0	0	0
Suggs	.995	26	196	21	1	1	3

First Base	PCT	G	PO	A	E	DP
Boissiere	.998	60	412	32	1	43
Pimentel	1.000	37	224	16	0	26
Quintana	.929	4	24	2	2	2
Rombach	1.000	14	73	12	0	9
Ross	1.000	15	100	3	0	6
Yepez	1.000	9	48	1	0	3

Second Base	PCT	G	PO	A	E	DP
Brown	.993	40	53	95	1	26
Cruz	.962	73	95	157	10	30
Dugas	.980	11	20	28	1	9
Lawson	.975	11	18	21	1	9

Third Base	PCT	G	PO	A	E	DP
Brown	.944	32	19	48	4	4
Cruz	.000	1	0	0	0	0
Dugas	.907	56	47	51	10	4
Henseler	.906	11	8	21	3	2
Ross	.886	20	17	22	5	4
Stehly	.964	13	13	14	1	2

Shortstop	PCT	G	PO	A	E	DP
Brown	.957	20	17	49	3	9

	PCT	G	PO	A	E	DP
Cruz	.919	18	30	38	6	10
King	.953	44	66	98	8	24
Lawson	.969	48	75	113	6	27

Outfield	PCT	G	PO	A	E	DP
Banks	.971	57	97	4	3	0
Cox	.950	43	74	2	4	0
De La Rosa	.949	27	37	0	2	0
Dugas	1.000	4	7	0	0	0
Green	1.000	35	87	0	0	0
McKenzie	.990	51	94	2	1	0
Nunez	.986	39	73	0	1	0
Petersen	.991	42	108	5	1	0
Ross	1.000	10	16	0	0	0
Thomas	.981	28	52	0	1	0
White	.987	76	146	3	2	0
Williams	1.000	19	33	0	0	0

FREDERICKSBURG NATIONALS
CAROLINA LEAGUE
LOW-A

Batting	B-T	Ht.	Wt.	DOB	AVG	OBP	SLG	G	PA	AB	R	H	2B	3B	HR	RBI	BB	HBP	SH	SF	SO	SB	CS	BB%	SO%
Barbieri, Francesco	L-R	6-1	180	4-14-00	.192	.344	.308	26	98	78	11	15	3	0	0	9	17	1	2	0	37	12	0	17.3	37.8
Bazzell, Kevin	R-R	6-1	205	3-29-03	.239	.340	.267	84	335	285	42	68	8	0	0	25	34	12	0	4	32	8	1	10.1	9.6
Colmenares, Jose	R-R	5-10	165	8-23-02	.000	.333	.000	2	6	4	0	0	0	0	0	0	2	0	0	0	1	0	0	33.3	16.7
Cooper, Everett	R-R	6-1	184	7-31-03	.140	.262	.280	21	62	50	7	7	2	1	1	7	8	1	0	2	10	4	0	12.9	16.1
Cox, Brenner	L-R	6-3	195	5-11-04	.196	.315	.413	28	111	92	12	18	6	1	4	17	16	1	0	2	36	4	0	14.4	32.4
Diaz, Kelvin	R-R	6-2	143	10-3-02	.181	.310	.277	35	102	83	15	15	3	1	1	3	15	1	2	1	33	8	3	14.7	32.4
Diaz-Morales, Randal	R-R	6-0	205	5-20-03	.319	.436	.319	28	112	94	18	30	0	0	0	3	16	0	0	0	12	6	2	12.5	9.4
Dickerson, Luke	R-R	5-11	197	8-9-05	.204	.309	.319	83	333	285	34	58	14	2	5	31	41	4	0	3	84	21	5	12.3	25.2
Fagnant, Christian	L-R	5-10	195	6-20-01	.167	.167	.167	9	12	12	1	2	0	0	0	0	0	0	0	0	4	0	0	0.0	33.3
Feliz, Angel	R-R	6-3	185	11-16-06	.230	.307	.370	31	116	100	16	23	3	1	3	15	12	0	2	2	27	5	0	10.3	23.3
Gallardo, Moises	R-R	6-0	160	4-23-03	.165	.200	.198	25	95	91	10	15	0	0	1	4	4	0	0	0	35	3	1	4.2	36.8
Green, Elijah	R-R	6-3	225	12-4-03	.233	.301	.359	26	113	103	17	24	6	2	1	13	9	1	0	0	39	5	0	8.0	34.5
Henseler, Wyatt	R-R	6-1	215	8-6-01	.351	.478	.486	11	46	37	5	13	2	0	1	3	5	4	0	0	10	0	0	10.9	21.7
Hollifield, Nick	R-R	5-11	190	7-20-03	.242	.370	.258	18	81	66	12	16	1	0	0	10	14	0	0	1	14	0	0	17.3	17.3
Made, Kevin	R-R	5-9	160	9-10-02	.474	.524	.579	5	21	19	3	9	2	0	0	5	2	0	0	0	4	0	0	9.5	19.0
Mota, Jorgelys	R-R	6-3	170	6-3-05	.270	.341	.409	81	328	296	34	80	17	3	6	42	26	6	0	0	101	25	7	7.9	30.8
Nunez, Elijah	L-L	5-10	180	12-6-01	.212	.359	.271	38	145	118	17	25	2	1	1	13	25	2	0	0	37	9	4	17.2	25.5
Ochoa Leyva, Nathaniel	R-R	6-4	215	10-15-03	.170	.254	.239	55	209	188	19	32	5	1	2	22	19	2	0	0	75	7	1	9.1	35.9
Peoples, Nick	S-R	6-5	205	7-24-04	.201	.295	.328	104	386	338	45	68	18	2	7	36	41	5	0	2	150	15	5	10.6	38.9
Petersen, Sam	R-R	6-0	195	1-20-03	.250	.250	.375	2	8	8	2	2	1	0	0	0	0	0	0	0	2	1	0	0.0	25.0
Petry, Ethan	R-R	6-4	230	6-17-04	.287	.386	.414	24	101	87	11	25	3	1	2	10	13	1	0	0	25	1	0	12.9	24.8
Quintana, Roismar	R-R	6-1	175	2-6-03	.233	.269	.300	58	228	210	19	49	11	0	1	20	10	2	1	5	45	2	0	4.4	19.7
Ramirez, Enmanuel	R-R	6-1	170	11-5-03	.174	.192	.261	9	26	23	1	4	0	1	0	5	1	0	0	2	5	0	1	3.8	19.2
Ramirez, Rafael	L-R	6-0	159	7-22-05	.125	.222	.250	9	18	16	5	2	0	1	0	1	2	0	0	5	0	0	11.1	27.8
Rombach, Nate	R-R	6-4	222	11-26-00	.228	.300	.335	58	233	206	22	47	11	3	2	21	22	1	0	4	46	2	1	9.4	19.7
Ross, Jackson	R-R	6-2	210	4-5-03	.289	.349	.526	32	129	114	19	33	9	0	6	17	12	0	0	3	36	2	0	9.3	27.9
Tavares, Carlos	L-L	6-2	190	9-17-05	.153	.233	.221	55	180	163	11	25	6	1	1	12	16	1	0	0	61	1	0	8.9	33.3
Vaquero, Cristhian	S-R	6-3	180	9-13-04	.256	.342	.396	101	445	379	54	97	13	8	8	47	46	8	1	8	110	27	5	10.3	24.7
Walsh, Jacob	L-L	6-4	225	3-11-03	.128	.258	.192	22	93	78	7	10	2	0	1	3	13	1	0	1	29	3	0	14.0	31.2
Willits, Eli	S-R	6-1	180	12-9-07	.300	.397	.360	15	58	50	7	15	1	0	0	5	7	1	0	0	12	0	2	12.1	20.7

Pitching	B-T	Ht.	Wt.	DOB	W	L	ERA	G	GS	SV	IP	Hits	Runs	ER	HR	BB	SO	AVG	OBP	SLG	SO%	BB%	BF
Acosta, Daison	R-R	6-2	160	8-24-98	0	0	0.00	1	0	0	1	0	0	0	0	0	2	.000	.000	.000	66.7	0	3
Adon, Joan	R-R	6-2	245	8-12-98	0	0	0.00	1	0	0	0	4	4	0	0	0	0	.000	1.000	.000	0	100.0	4
Aldonis, Pablo	L-L	6-1	160	3-21-02	2	0	0.35	15	0	2	26	14	1	1	0	6	33	.159	.227	.182	34.0	6.2	97
Amaral, Austin	R-R	6-0	200	12-4-01	1	1	4.05	10	0	1	13	9	6	6	2	2	17	.188	.235	.354	32.7	3.8	52
Baldo, Merrick	R-R	6-1	200	7-17-00	8	2	3.33	46	0	5	54	48	23	20	5	24	57	.239	.325	.328	24.8	10.4	230
Beeker, Merritt	R-L	6-2	187	11-12-01	3	2	1.85	38	1	0	63	43	18	13	2	28	78	.192	.287	.272	30.2	10.9	258
Bennett, Jake	L-L	6-6	234	12-2-00	0	1	1.50	2	2	0	6	5	1	1	0	0	7	.227	.227	.273	31.8	0.0	22
Biven, Tucker	R-R	6-1	200	2-21-04	0	0	2.25	4	0	1	4	4	1	1	0	3	6	.250	.368	.313	31.6	15.8	19
Bloebaum, Adam	L-L	6-6	225	5-3-01	0	2	0.46	16	0	3	20	8	1	1	0	5	26	.123	.186	.154	37.1	7.1	70
Bollenbacher, Matthew	R-R	6-1	203	11-9-99	1	1	3.15	27	0	0	34	28	13	12	1	14	25	.226	.308	.355	17.2	9.7	145
Bruni, Gavin	L-L	6-3	225	10-12-02	3	1	3.80	17	0	0	24	18	13	10	1	23	35	.220	.383	.354	32.7	21.5	107
Brzykcy, Zach	R-R	6-2	232	7-12-99	0	0	0.00	2	0	0	2	1	0	0	0	0	4	.143	.143	.286	57.1	0.0	7
Cavalli, Cade	R-R	6-4	232	8-14-98	0	0	0.00	1	0	0	1	1	0	0	0	1	0	.077	.200	.077	0.0	13.3	15
Cranz, Robert	R-R	6-3	200	5-28-03	1	2	2.05	26	0	9	31	13	11	7	2	16	41	.127	.246	.216	34.7	13.6	118
Dowdell, Kevin	L-L	6-1	210	12-3-99	1	0	6.12	37	0	0	43	40	34	29	5	41	44	.258	.428	.394	21.1	19.6	209
Farias, Victor	R-R	6-2	150	7-17-02	1	2	5.19	10	1	0	13	9	6	6	2	2	10	.237	.447	.271	9.4	18.8	85
Fischer, Carson	R-R	6-5	225	10-18-02	0	0	0.00	2	0	0	2	1	0	0	0	0	1	.000	.000	.000	50.0	0.0	6
Garcia, Davian	R-R	6-1	188	10-10-03	4	2	2.70	15	14	0	70	45	24	21	5	43	65	.188	.315	.288	22.7	15.0	286
Johnson, Luke	R-R	6-1	195	4-15-02	1	3	5.67	8	8	0	33	41	23	21	8	24	31	.311	.364	.470	16.8	5.6	143
Kane, Will	L-L	6-1	195	10-31-01	1	0	9.90	8	0	0	10	10	13	11	0	14	10	.263	.472	.316	18.9	26.4	53
Luis, Andy	L-R	6-0	150	1-14-03	0	0	2.89	9	0	0	9	6	3	3	0	6	7	.176	.364	.176	15.9	22.7	44
Maddox, Riley	R-R	6-1	205	10-3-02	0	0	3.60	2	1	0	5	3	2	2	1	0	7	.176	.176	.353	41.2	0.0	17

	B-T	Ht.	Wt.	DOB			AVG															
Meckley, Xander	R-R	6-2	235	7-12-03	6	6	3.78	19	19	0	86	83	46	36	3	39	70	.259	.340	.336	18.9	10.5	371
Mejia, Erick	S-R	5-11	195	11-9-94	1	0	4.50	10	0	2	12	8	6	6	2	4	17	.170	.235	.383	33.3	7.8	51
Minckler, Ryan	R-R	6-2	185	10-1-02	4	6	4.74	39	0	0	49	32	31	26	2	52	56	.189	.387	.284	24.3	22.6	230
Montero, Euri	R-R	6-4	170	3-28-02	2	1	3.00	12	0	2	18	16	8	6	1	2	10	.242	.278	.318	13.9	2.8	72
Moore, Ben	L-L	6-4	215	3-24-04	0	0	0.00	1	0	0	2	0	0	0	0	1	3	.000	.143	.000	42.9	14.3	7
Olson, Bryant	L-L	6-4	190	12-19-02	0	0	4.35	10	0	0	10	4	5	5	0	16	14	.121	.426	.121	25.9	29.6	54
Otanez, Johan	R-R	6-1	168	2-19-02	5	1	2.67	25	0	4	34	26	15	10	3	15	39	.206	.289	.317	27.5	10.6	142
Polanco, Bryan	R-R	6-2	190	9-12-01	7	8	3.71	24	23	0	112	96	52	46	14	44	88	.226	.317	.382	18.2	9.1	483
Puk, Owen	R-R	6-4	209	10-27-02	1	1	5.68	5	0	0	6	7	4	4	1	5	6	.280	.400	.480	20.0	16.7	30
Roman, Angel	L-L	5-11	162	9-24-03	2	8	7.79	28	12	0	80	105	76	69	7	33	51	.322	.397	.463	13.6	8.8	374
Romero, Brayan	R-R	6-1	180	1-6-02	2	6	5.40	14	14	0	60	61	41	36	2	49	37	.275	.415	.347	13.1	17.3	283
Sales, R.J.	R-R	6-0	165	7-22-03	2	3	3.18	6	6	0	28	29	12	10	2	11	37	.264	.339	.345	29.8	8.9	124
Solesky, Chase	R-R	6-3	201	9-26-97	0	0	0.00	1	1	0	3	1	0	0	0	0	1	.100	.100	.100	0.0	0.0	10
Sullivan, Liam	L-L	6-6	255	5-16-02	1	2	3.23	7	7	0	31	27	11	11	5	7	36	.241	.289	.429	29.8	5.8	121
Sykora, Travis	R-R	6-6	220	4-28-04	0	0	0.00	2	2	0	6	1	0	0	0	2	9	.056	.190	.056	42.9	9.5	21
Tejeda, Yoel	S-R	6-7	210	7-8-03	4	3	3.43	16	16	0	79	71	33	30	4	21	74	.243	.298	.349	22.9	6.5	323
Tolman, Erik	L-L	6-2	193	6-3-99	1	0	1.59	6	1	0	11	10	3	2	0	7	16	.256	.388	.333	32.0	14.0	50

Fielding

Catcher	PCT	G	PO	A	E	DP	PB
Bazzell	.989	76	613	81	8	5	9
Colmenares	1.000	2	11	1	0	1	0
Hollifield	1.000	14	125	7	0	1	3
Rombach	.982	39	337	35	7	2	3

First Base	PCT	G	PO	A	E	DP
Diaz-Morales	1.000	11	61	6	0	5
Petry	1.000	4	22	2	0	2
Quintana	.984	36	222	25	4	19
Ross	.983	15	103	10	2	9
Tavares	.981	49	285	25	6	23
Walsh	.989	22	173	6	2	20

Second Base	PCT	G	PO	A	E	DP
Cooper	.950	15	26	31	3	5
Diaz	.889	7	11	13	3	1
Diaz-Morales	.969	45	84	103	6	25
Dickerson	.957	22	35	55	4	11

	PCT	G	PO	A	E	DP
Feliz	.980	11	24	24	1	7
Made	.900	2	5	4	1	1
Ochoa Leyva	.000	1	0	0	0	0
Ramirez, R	1.000	1	1	2	0	1
Ross	.800	1	0	4	1	0

Third Base	PCT	G	PO	A	E	DP
Diaz	.963	26	12	40	2	4
Diaz-Morales	.902	21	13	42	6	5
Henseler	.929	11	9	17	2	3
Mota	.914	72	60	88	14	6
Ochoa Leyva	.000	1	0	0	0	0
Ramirez, R	.000	2	0	0	0	0
Ross	1.000	8	9	12	0	2

Shortstop	PCT	G	PO	A	E	DP
Diaz-Morales	.938	26	42	48	6	8
Dickerson	.944	55	77	110	11	21
Feliz	.973	18	22	51	2	13

	PCT	G	PO	A	E	DP
Made	.750	3	3	3	2	0
Willits	.984	14	27	35	1	9

Outfield	PCT	G	PO	A	E	DP
Barbieri	.976	26	39	1	1	0
Cooper	.000	2	0	0	0	0
Cox	.981	27	52	1	1	0
Diaz-Morales	1.000	12	22	2	0	0
Gallardo	1.000	19	41	0	0	0
Green	.982	23	52	4	1	1
Nunez	.972	38	69	0	2	0
Ochoa Leyva	1.000	38	55	0	0	1
Peoples	.954	102	164	2	8	1
Petersen	1.000	2	2	1	0	1
Petry	1.000	11	13	0	0	0
Ramirez, E	1.000	4	3	0	0	0
Ramirez, R	.000	1	0	0	0	0
Tavares	1.000	3	5	1	0	0
Vaquero	.984	99	237	11	4	4

FCL NATIONALS
FLORIDA COMPLEX LEAGUE
ROOKIE

Batting	B-T	Ht.	Wt.	DOB	AVG	OBP	SLG	G	PA	AB	R	H	2B	3B	HR	RBI	BB	HBP	SH	SF	SO	SB	CS	BB%	SO%
Acevedo, Andy	L-L	6-1	170	11-26-05	.188	.378	.212	40	115	85	14	16	2	0	0	12	19	7	4	0	37	9	6	16.5	32.2
Arias, Luis	R-R	6-0	165	7-19-05	.293	.371	.388	34	132	116	19	34	5	0	2	12	13	2	0	1	28	4	0	9.8	21.2
Baca, Tyler	S-L	5-9	180	5-22-00	.261	.370	.261	11	27	23	7	6	0	0	0	5	4	0	0	0	7	1	0	14.8	25.9
Banks, Teo	R-R	6-2	190	7-10-03	.200	.273	.300	10	33	30	4	6	1	1	0	1	2	1	0	0	8	1	1	6.1	24.2
Barbieri, Francesco	L-R	6-1	180	4-14-00	.400	.591	.400	16	23	15	6	6	0	0	0	1	7	0	1	0	2	1	3	30.4	8.7
Batista, Carlos	R-R	6-1	170	11-3-05	.140	.272	.163	35	105	86	12	12	2	0	0	3	11	5	2	1	39	2	1	10.5	37.1
Cabrera, Manuel	R-R	5-10	155	2-16-06	.220	.322	.270	37	115	100	9	22	2	0	1	13	11	4	0	0	41	2	0	9.6	35.7
Chaparro, Andres	R-R	6-0	200	5-4-99	.267	.353	.533	5	17	15	1	4	1	0	1	3	2	0	0	0	5	0	0	11.8	29.4
Colmenares, Jose	R-R	5-10	165	8-23-02	.222	.417	.222	5	12	9	2	2	0	0	0	1	2	1	0	0	1	0	0	16.7	8.3
Cooper, Everett	L-R	6-1	184	7-31-03	.267	.313	.333	6	16	15	2	4	1	0	0	1	1	0	0	0	3	0	1	6.3	18.8
De La Rosa, Jeremy	L-L	6-0	215	1-16-02	.333	.333	.833	3	6	6	1	2	0	0	1	2	0	0	0	0	2	0	0	0.0	33.3
Diaz, Kelvin	R-R	6-2	143	10-3-02	.190	.346	.238	9	26	21	3	4	1	0	0	1	5	0	0	0	11	2	0	19.2	42.3
Dickerson, Luke	R-R	5-11	197	8-9-05	.273	.385	.409	6	26	22	5	6	0	0	1	0	4	0	0	0	4	1	1	15.4	15.4
Feliz, Angel	R-R	6-3	185	11-16-06	.264	.366	.358	53	228	193	37	51	7	4	1	28	30	2	1	2	44	10	7	13.2	19.3
Green, Elijah	R-R	6-3	225	12-19-03	.231	.436	.609	20	78	64	16	20	4	0	5	8	14	0	0	0	24	6	0	17.9	30.8
Jones, Sir Jamison	R-R	6-3	220	5-19-06	.233	.379	.383	40	153	120	16	28	6	0	4	25	26	4	0	3	38	2	0	17.0	24.8
Marcano, Agustin	R-R	6-0	160	6-28-06	.154	.303	.154	14	35	26	3	4	0	0	0	2	5	1	1	1	10	0	0	14.3	28.6
Maricuto, Jermaine	L-R	5-10	155	10-7-05	.000	.000	.000	2	3	3	0	0	0	0	0	0	0	0	0	0	0	0	0	0.0	0.0
Petersen, Sam	R-R	6-0	195	1-20-03	.387	.524	.516	11	42	31	11	12	1	0	1	7	6	4	0	1	9	4	1	14.3	21.4
Ramirez, Enmanuel	R-R	6-1	170	11-5-03	.283	.406	.434	16	64	53	8	15	3	1	1	10	10	1	0	0	8	4	1	15.6	12.5
Ramirez, Rafael	L-R	6-0	159	7-22-05	.211	.483	.263	10	29	19	7	4	1	0	0	0	9	1	0	0	9	1	3	31.0	27.6
Rojas, Eyeksson	R-R	5-10	160	9-5-05	.252	.328	.328	41	151	131	20	33	2	1	2	25	13	4	1	2	25	4	1	8.6	16.6
Rosario, Helder	R-R	6-1	165	1-26-05	.143	.368	.143	14	39	28	5	4	0	0	0	3	9	1	1	0	16	1	0	23.1	41.0
Soto, Elian	L-L	6-1	182	1-10-06	.139	.307	.264	49	179	144	25	20	6	0	4	19	30	5	0	0	59	2	2	16.8	33.0
Tavarez, Feldi	R-R	6-0	160	1-30-03	.238	.209	.372	11	50	43	7	10	3	0	1	7	9	3	0	0	39	4	3	7.4	32.0
Tejeda, Dashyll	R-R	6-0	170	3-16-06	.268	.376	.323	41	153	127	17	34	2	1	1	20	18	4	4	0	26	4	1	17.6	17.0
Williams, Donta'	L-L	5-10	185	6-30-99	.250	.348	.400	7	23	20	3	5	1	1	0	2	2	1	0	0	5	1	1	8.7	21.7

Pitching	B-T	Ht.	Wt.	DOB	W	L	ERA	G	GS	SV	IP	Hits	Runs	ER	HR	BB	SO	AVG	OBP	SLG	SO%	BB%	BF
Agostini, Gabriel	L-L	6-0	160	7-24-04	1	1	3.09	7	3	0	12	9	6	4	0	12	8	.209	.368	.233	14.0	21.1	57
Aldonis, Pablo	L-L	6-1	160	3-21-02	2	1	5.14	6	0	1	7	6	4	4	0	1	9	.222	.310	.310	31.0	3.4	29
Colon, Leodarlyn	R-R	6-4	190	12-1-04	2	0	4.60	14	0	2	16	13	12	8	1	11	18	.213	.342	.311	24.7	15.1	73
Farias, Victor	R-R	6-2	150	7-17-02	0	2	4.86	13	5	1	37	33	26	20	3	28	46	.250	.394	.379	27.1	16.5	170
Feliz, Jose	R-R	6-1	170	10-9-05	2	1	2.20	14	13	0	61	57	20	15	2	12	51	.246	.289	.328	20.6	4.8	248

WASHINGTON NATIONALS

Batting	B-T	Ht.	Wt.	DOB			AVG	OBP	SLG	G	PA	AB	R	H	2B	3B	HR	RBI	BB	HBP	SH	SF	SO	SB	CS	BB%	SO%
Johnson, Luke	R-R	6-1	195	4-15-02	4	1	1.23	14	2	0	37	26	8	5	0	14	36	.206	.299	.270	25.0	9.7	144				
Kane, Tom	L-L	6-1	195	10-31-01	6	4	2.92	18	0	3	25	15	11	8	0	16	34	.170	.311	.193	32.1	15.1	106				
Luis, Andy	L-R	6-0	150	1-14-03	1	1	4.80	14	0	1	15	16	10	8	1	11	11	.276	.408	.466	15.5	15.5	71				
Lunar, Darrel	R-R	6-3	150	2-7-06	1	4	4.93	14	10	0	46	49	28	25	3	24	47	.283	.377	.405	23.0	11.8	204				
Martina, Clarence	R-R	6-2	195	12-16-04	2	1	9.72	9	0	0	8	10	10	9	1	6	6	.303	.439	.455	14.6	14.6	41				
Montero, Euri	R-R	6-4	170	3-28-02	0	0	3.68	11	0	0	15	22	6	6	1	6	6	.379	.439	.448	9.1	9.1	66				
Ogasawara, Shinnosuke	L-L	5-11	205	10-8-97	0	0	0.00	1	1	0	2	1	0	0	0	0	2	.167	.286	.167	28.6	0.0	7				
Olson, Bryant	L-L	6-4	190	12-19-02	2	0	3.72	17	0	0	19	11	8	8	2	19	33	.167	.356	.288	37.9	21.8	87				
Otanez, Johan	R-R	6-1	168	2-19-02	0	1	3.86	3	0	0	2	1	3	1	0	3	2	.125	.333	.250	16.7	25.0	12				
Perez, Doimil	R-R	6-3	170	11-3-03	1	1	3.00	15	0	1	18	6	9	6	2	16	14	.109	.301	.218	19.2	21.9	73				
Portorreal, Leuris	R-R	6-3	160	8-13-05	0	2	5.13	11	6	1	40	49	28	23	5	12	31	.290	.344	.467	16.9	6.6	183				
Ramirez, Reilin	R-R	6-2	180	5-19-04	2	0	10.24	10	0	0	10	16	12	11	4	8	7	.372	.481	.767	13.5	15.4	52				
Romero, Brayan	R-R	6-1	180	1-6-02	2	1	2.93	5	2	0	15	13	5	5	0	9	15	.228	.353	.316	22.1	13.2	68				
Sampson, Adrian	R-R	6-2	210	10-7-91	1	0	0.00	1	1	0	5	3	0	0	0	0	9	.176	.176	.235	52.9	0.0	17				
Sanchez, Bryan	R-R	6-1	175	8-12-02	1	3	9.39	13	0	0	15	19	19	16	4	9	24	.297	.387	.625	32.0	12.0	75				
Stuart, Tyler	R-R	6-9	250	10-8-99	0	0	4.91	3	3	0	7	7	5	4	0	6	10	.241	.371	.345	28.6	17.1	35				
Sullivan, Liam	L-L	6-6	255	5-16-02	0	1	1.35	8	7	0	20	8	4	3	0	13	28	.129	.299	.226	35.9	16.7	78				
Sykora, Travis	R-R	6-6	220	4-28-04	0	0	1.80	2	2	0	5	1	1	1	0	1	14	.063	.118	.063	82.4	5.9	17				
Thompson, Mason	R-R	6-6	244	2-20-98	0	0	0.00	1	0	0	1	2	0	0	0	0	2	.400	.400	.600	40.0	0.0	5				

Fielding
C: Tavarez 28, Jones 25, Marcano 6, Colmenares 5, Rosario 4. **1B:** Soto 39, Cabrera 18, Chaparro 5, Maricuto 1. **2B:** Rojas 38, Ramirez 10, Cabrera 4, Diaz 3, Dickerson 3, Feliz 2, Cooper 1. **3B:** Arias 34, Cabrera 16, Cooper 5, Diaz 3, Rojas 3. **SS:** Feliz 51, Diaz 3, Dickerson 2. **LF:** Batista 18, Acevedo 13, Banks 9, Baca 8, Tejeda 7, Soto 5, Ramirez 4, Barbieri 3, Williams 2, Petersen 1. **CF:** Acevedo 22, Green 17, Petersen 10, Tejeda 9, Williams 5, Barbieri 4, Banks 1, Batista 1. **RF:** Tejeda 25, Batista 14, Ramirez 9, Barbieri 6, Acevedo 3, De La Rosa 3, Soto 3

DSL NATIONALS — ROOKIE
DOMINICAN SUMMER LEAGUE

Batting	B-T	Ht.	Wt.	DOB	AVG	OBP	SLG	G	PA	AB	R	H	2B	3B	HR	RBI	BB	HBP	SH	SF	SO	SB	CS	BB%	SO%
Araujo, Andry	R-R	5-11	165	12-25-07	.192	.344	.192	17	32	26	4	5	0	0	0	1	3	3	0	0	7	1	1	9.4	21.9
Bello, Rony	R-R	5-10	150	10-18-07	.202	.324	.292	40	105	89	15	18	4	2	0	10	14	2	0	0	16	8	0	13.3	15.2
Castillo, Junior	S-R	6-1	190	9-11-07	.216	.396	.297	31	98	74	10	16	3	0	1	7	20	2	2	0	33	4	0	20.4	33.7
Cortesia, Brayan	R-R	6-1	165	11-14-07	.317	.440	.358	39	150	120	26	38	3	1	0	12	25	3	0	2	25	22	13	16.7	16.7
De La Cruz, Nauris	L-L	6-0	160	9-4-07	.294	.448	.450	39	143	109	18	32	9	1	2	20	30	2	0	2	17	15	5	21.0	11.9
Figueroa, Edgardo	R-R	5-10	177	9-10-07	.212	.279	.333	34	111	99	10	21	3	0	3	8	5	5	0	2	39	4	2	4.5	35.1
Garces, Jonierbis	R-R	6-5	176	12-22-07	.202	.339	.287	43	118	94	15	19	3	1	1	11	17	4	0	3	27	23	5	14.4	22.9
Garcia, Rodrigo	R-R	6-0	173	4-13-07	.222	.417	.222	17	24	18	2	4	0	0	0	1	4	2	0	0	8	0	0	16.7	33.3
German, Marconi	S-R	5-10	170	9-9-07	.283	.479	.513	53	213	152	37	43	9	1	8	30	43	16	0	2	42	33	6	20.2	19.7
Hernandez, Daniel	L-R	6-0	165	2-16-08	.225	.277	.275	45	148	138	19	31	7	0	0	11	8	2	0	0	16	3	2	5.4	10.8
Hurtado, Victor	L-L	6-3	175	5-24-07	.236	.359	.314	46	168	140	18	33	3	1	2	14	19	8	1	0	26	3	1	11.3	13.7
Liriano, Hector	L-R	6-2	180	5-17-06	.185	.308	.277	24	78	65	9	12	3	0	1	7	9	3	0	1	27	2	2	11.5	34.6
Marmolejos, Eddy	R-R	6-0	175	2-17-07	.250	.370	.300	33	110	100	13	25	9	0	1	12	7	1	0	2	24	4	1	6.4	21.8
Obispo, Juan	R-R	6-0	180	5-9-06	.283	.336	.384	34	108	99	17	28	6	2	0	19	7	1	1	0	21	15	8	6.5	19.4
Requena, Angel	R-R	6-1	160	6-8-07	.252	.343	.303	44	140	119	17	30	6	0	0	13	9	9	0	3	21	24	4	6.4	15.0
Tusen, Adrian	S-R	6-1	140	10-8-07	.100	.265	.100	27	50	40	9	4	0	0	0	8	11	0	1	0	15	5	2	16.0	30.0
Vargas, Esnaider	R-R	6-2	162	11-17-07	.223	.279	.309	34	104	94	12	21	5	2	0	7	6	0	0	4	22	3	1	5.8	23.1

Pitching	B-T	Ht.	Wt.	DOB	W	L	ERA	G	GS	SV	IP	Hits	Runs	ER	HR	BB	SO	AVG	OBP	SLG	SO%	BB%	BF
Carela, Enmanuel	R-R	5-11	160	3-10-07	0	1	2.08	12	4	0	30	22	16	7	2	14	25	.202	.289	.330	19.5	10.9	128
Carrasco, Jesus	R-R	6-3	152	6-6-06	0	2	7.99	10	5	0	24	38	26	21	1	10	9	.362	.430	.514	7.4	8.3	121
Chivilli, Julio	R-R	6-3	190	7-15-08	0	0	18.00	5	0	0	5	10	16	10	1	9	6	.400	.583	.520	16.7	25.0	36
Colina, Greider	R-R	6-2	180	4-24-05	0	0	12.86	8	0	0	7	9	11	10	1	6	7	.290	.405	.516	18.9	16.2	37
De La Cruz, Marlon	R-R	6-2	155	11-3-05	1	6	4.50	12	12	0	50	50	36	25	2	30	52	.256	.374	.390	22.1	12.8	235
Gimenez, Greyson	R-R	6-0	152	9-21-04	2	0	1.42	12	2	0	25	23	6	4	0	10	16	.240	.311	.281	15.1	9.4	106
Lopez, Juan	R-R	6-2	190	1-26-05	5	0	2.70	15	0	1	33	28	16	10	4	20	51	.219	.333	.359	32.7	12.8	156
Manzueta, Anyel	R-R	6-7	185	10-15-06	1	1	9.00	12	0	0	17	21	20	17	1	13	11	.339	.476	.516	13.4	15.9	82
Martinez, Jousuet	L-L	6-0	175	12-11-07	0	0	5.91	8	0	0	11	8	11	7	0	14	8	.211	.446	.289	14.3	25.0	56
Mejia, Hernan	L-L	6-2	170	9-7-07	0	3	12.00	6	3	0	12	15	19	16	0	15	10	.319	.500	.382	14.5	21.7	69
Pena, Angel	R-R	6-0	190	9-30-04	0	1	7.50	12	0	1	18	25	16	15	3	8	10	.347	.430	.514	9.3	11.6	86
Reyes, Juan	L-L	6-2	180	3-24-05	5	2	2.40	12	12	0	60	45	19	16	2	13	52	.209	.258	.312	22.6	5.7	230
Robles, Jean	R-R	6-1	170	10-20-06	3	6	5.31	12	11	0	42	34	30	25	3	26	45	.217	.356	.363	23.6	13.6	191
Ruiz, Manuel	R-R	5-11	165	3-24-06	3	2	5.55	17	0	7	24	25	18	15	2	19	20	.272	.417	.424	17.1	16.2	117
Salas, Jhondel	R-R	5-11	159	11-13-07	2	0	3.45	11	0	1	16	14	9	6	2	7	20	.233	.343	.383	28.6	10.0	70
Sanchez, Jose	R-R	6-3	180	2-6-06	3	2	7.64	13	0	1	18	21	17	15	5	9	17	.273	.356	.545	19.5	10.3	87
Sarit, Ranger	R-R	6-3	190	12-4-05	0	1	9.31	7	0	1	10	10	12	10	0	11	10	.270	.442	.405	19.2	21.2	52
Torrelles, Yaiker	R-R	5-11	187	2-20-07	2	2	4.38	9	7	0	25	24	13	12	12	24	.258	.346	.333	22.4	11.2	107

Fielding
C: Figueroa 30, Hernandez 22, Garcia 15, Castillo 7. **1B:** Requena 35, Castillo 22, Liriano 9. **2B:** German 30, Bello 26, Tusen 6, Cortesia 5, Marmolejos 3. **3B:** Marmolejos 31, Bello 16, Requena 11, Tusen 10. **SS:** Cortesia 32, German 27, Tusen 10. **LF:** Hurtado 36, Araujo 11, Obispo 9, De La Cruz 6, Vargas 4, Garces 1, Liriano 1. **CF:** De La Cruz 27, Garces 17, Obispo 9. **RF:** Vargas 25, Garces 17, Obispo 12, De La Cruz 6, Araujo 3, Requena 2.

MINOR LEAGUES

Changes Keep Coming To Minor Leagues

BY JOSH NORRIS

In 2021, after the sport had emerged from the pandemic, things were very different. Major League Baseball absorbed Minor League Baseball, in furtherance of commissioner Rob Manfred's One Baseball agenda.

The biggest resulting change was the realignment and reduction of the minor leagues. Forty teams were slashed from affiliated ball, and the Rookie and short-season levels were eliminated. The draft was reduced as well, going from 40 rounds to 20.

An upgrade in facility standards sealed the fate of many of the teams who lost their affiliation, and it's about to shake up the minor league map once more. The number of teams will stay the same come springtime, but plenty of clubs took their final bow in 2025 before packing up and hitting the road for the next chapter.

The biggest changes will come out west, where the California League will undergo an extreme makeover. The Modesto Nuts, formerly Seattle's Low-A team, will drop from affiliated ball. In their place, the league adds the Ontario Tower Buzzers, which will begin their life as the Dodgers' representative in the league.

The Angels' team will move to Rancho Cucamonga from Inland Empire, which in turn will welcome Mariners minor leaguers for the 2026 season.

But that's not all.

A year after Down East was excised from the Carolina League, the Carolina Mudcats ended their time in affiliated ball. The Mudcats, one of the frequent last stops in the previous era of the Affiliation Shuffle, won't be going far. The team is sticking in North Carolina and moving roughly 25 miles east to Wilson, where it will become the Wilson Warbirds.

Moving up the coast to Maryland, the Orioles bid farewell to one affiliate and will welcome one back into the nest. The Aberdeen IronBirds, who had been with the Orioles both in the New York-Penn and South Atlantic Leagues will make way for the return of the Frederick Keys, which had been in the MLB Draft League since 2021.

That's all for 2026, but more changes are on the horizon.

In the Northwest League, the Eugene Emeralds,

The Carolina Mudcats' final season included top prospects like Jesús Made.

who share PK Park with the Oregon Ducks, lost their bid to build a new stadium in Lane County and instead will move in the forthcoming years. In early November, the city of Medford, which is about 170 miles south of Eugene, approved a measure that would include the construction of a ballpark among a mixed-use district.

Nothing is final and there is no certain timeline for the change, but things are in motion to spread the NWL's footprint even wider.

The 2025 season also saw the final days of Hillsboro Ballpark, which had been the home of the Hops since the team's inception in 2013.

The team isn't going much farther than the average foul ball. The city approved construction of a new, modernized ballpark, which will be open in time for the 2026 season, just a few hundred feet from home plate in their old digs.

Similarly, the Richmond Flying Squirrels ended their time at The Diamond and prepped for a move to shiny new Carmax Stadium in 2026. Thus ends a yearslong saga of whether The Diamond—which opened in 1985—would get a facelift or the team would get a new ballpark with all the current amenities.

The Asheville Tourists' longtime home of McCormick Field was slated to get a $38.5

million refresh as well, and the Chattanooga Lookouts closed up shop at AT&T Field in 2025 before heading to Erlanger Park for the franchise's next chapter.

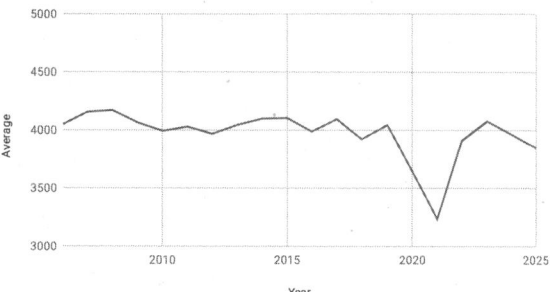

MiLB Average Yearly Attendance

Attendance Tops 30 Million

That's the future. Now, let's take a look back. Before we get to the games on the field, a few words on the state of attendance in the minor leagues.

Thanks to a furious finish, MiLB once again drew more than 30 million fans in announced attendance. But numbers were still down in 2025.

Combined, the 120 MiLB teams drew a total of 30,360,682 fans in 2025, representing a drop of 2.9 percent from last year. In 2025, MiLB drew 3,847 fans per game on average, compared to 3,962 in 2024.

Part of the late surge came courtesy of good, old-fashioned nostalgia. The teams whose ballparks were on the way out—like Carolina and Aberdeen—saw spikes from fans who wanted one more chance to take in a game before the old stadiums went by the wayside.

In their final 10 games at Five County Stadium before next year's move to Wilson, the Mudcats averaged 3,585 fans per game. They had averaged 2,083 fans over their first 48 games. The result was a net gain of 438 fans per game compared to 2024.

Similarly, on July 31, Richmond was on pace to equal last year's numbers, but they ended up averaging 173 more fans per game than last year after welcoming 7,334 fans per game over the final 18 home dates.

Other clubs had even bigger late-season surges. Nine of the Wisconsin Timber Rattlers' 10 largest crowds came from Aug. 1 onward. The St. Paul Saints' five largest crowds all came after July.

The biggest gainers overall were a pair of teams that moved to new cities. The High-A Hub City Spartanburgers drew 2,297 more fans per game than the Down East Wood Ducks did in 2024. The Double-A Columbus Clingstones drew 1,483 more fans per game than the Mississippi Braves did last year.

Some of the biggest declines came from teams facing unusual circumstances. For example, Triple-A Sacramento is normally one of the biggest draws in minor league baseball. They shared their facility with the Athletics' MLB team, however, and attendance was down 1,498 fans per game.

The Tampa Tarpons, meanwhile, were moved out of Steinbrenner Field to a backfield because the Rays were taking over as temporary tenants after Tropicana Field was rendered unplayable by the damage left in the wake of Hurricane Milton. The result was 645 fewer fans per game for the Tarpons.

A Bucs Breakout

On the field, the season was marked by the ascent of a teenage Pirates prospect into the sport's top talent. Konnor Griffin, Pittsburgh's first-rounder from 2024, hit his way from Low-A to Double-A with nary a hiccup.

The Mississippi prep product removed an arm bar that led evaluators to question whether he could get his hit tool to anywhere near the same level as his other four standout tools. The answer was quick, loud and affirmative. By season's end, he'd put forth the kind of remarkable stat line rarely seen in the minor leagues.

Over the last 20 minor league seasons, Griffin was the only player to produce a season with a .300 average, 20 or more home runs, 60 or more stolen bases and 100 or more runs. He also became just the fifth teenager—and the only American one—since 1963 to hit 20 or more home runs and steal 40 or more bases.

The other four? Jackson Chourio, Andruw Jones, Ronald Acuña Jr. and Alex Escobar.

On the hill, a trio of Mets arms ruled the day.

Righthander Jonah Tong took home BA's Minor League Pitcher of the Year thanks to a season that saw him finish with MiLB bests in ERA (1.43) and strikeouts (179). Those numbers earned him his first big league callup and a place in the Mets' rotation down the stretch.

Alongside Tong in Queens were two more of New York's vaunted pitching prospects. Nolan McLean, a former two-way prospect at Oklahoma State, spent 2025 exclusively on the mound and emerged as one of the best prospects in the sport. He struck out 127 in 113.2 innings across the upper levels before reaching the Mets and punching the tickets of 57 more big league hitters.

The final member of the new-look Mets was righthander Brandon Sproat, who debuted on Sept. 7 and made four starts before season's end. Sproat, Tong and McLean should be key pieces of the big league rotation in 2026 and beyond.

On the flip side, the Tigers ruled the minor leagues in batter's boxes all across the Midwest and Eastern leagues thanks to four of the sport's most fearsome hitters, including one who used the 2025 season as a tinderbox for his prospect stock.

The group was led by infielder Kevin McGonigle, whose only weakness to this point seems to be durability. He has been limited to fewer than 100 games in each of the last two regular seasons, but the results when he's been on the field have been spectacular.

The lefthanded Pennsylvanian swatted 19 home runs in a year split between High-A West Michigan and Double-A Erie. The former club took home the Midwest League title while the latter made it to the Eastern League finals before falling to the Mets' affiliate in Binghamton.

McGonigle wasn't alone in the middle of Detroit's minor league renaissance. He was backed by fellow Top 100 prospects Max Clark and Josue Briceño, the latter of whom entered the year as the reigning Arizona Fall League MVP. The group also got a boost from infielder Max Anderson, who bopped 31 doubles and 19 home runs in a year split between the upper levels.

The Tigers took home titles at both Class A levels, including a sweep of Daytona to capture the Florida State League crown.

The sport's top two prospects entering the season—Dodgers righthander Roki Sasaki and Red Sox outfielder Roman Anthony—each made their mark in a different way.

Although Sasaki struggled with underperformance and injuries for the bulk of the year, he returned late in the season as a fire-breathing reliever who earned the team's closer role down the stretch and into the playoffs. He helped Los Angeles lock down the late innings en route to the Dodgers' second straight World Series victory.

Anthony debuted on June 9 and was one of the best rookies in the sport until an injury sidelined him for the season after 71 games. Still, he produced 3.1 bWAR in that time and finished third behind the Athletics' dynamic duo of Nick Kurtz and Jacob Wilson for the American League's Rookie of the Year award.

At the lowest levels of the minor leagues, it was hard to top the prospect power produced by the youngest Giants talents. In Arizona, shortstop Jhonny Level used a .288/.375/.493 line to hit his way to the No. 1 spot on BA's Arizona Complex League top prospects. He was one of four San Francisco prospects on the list, joining righthanders Keyner Martinez, Argenis Cayama and Luis De La Torre.

All four graduated to Low-A after the ACL season included and helped San Jose take home the California League championship.

A level lower, 2025 international signee Josuar

ORGANIZATION STANDINGS

Cumulative minor league records for all 30 organizations, with annual winning percentages back to 2021. This is the combined record for all MiLB teams from Triple-A to the rookie levels.

Rk	MLB Org	W	L	PCT	2024	2023	2022	2021
1	Tigers	420	293	.589	.555	.522	.522	.480
2	Giants	405	314	.563	.527	.514	.503	.529
3	Pirates	396	319	.554	.497	.529	.517	.537
4	Rays	395	321	.552	.529	.543	.576	.623
5	Mets	391	321	.549	.465	.468	.485	.457
6	Yankees	385	325	.542	.525	.539	.548	.595
7	Marlins	375	341	.524	.517	.485	.501	.505
8	Brewers	369	345	.517	.549	.525	.516	.497
9	Mariners	345	323	.516	.517	.544	.493	.571
10	Rangers	368	349	.513	.535	.513	.522	.534
11	Guardians	366	348	.513	.553	.475	.528	.521
12	Cardinals	336	321	.511	.522	.478	.487	.398
13	Dodgers	363	356	.505	.517	.582	.545	.533
14	Rockies	360	361	.499	.522	.522	.549	.546
15	Royals	355	361	.496	.513	.472	.426	.509
16	Twins	325	333	.494	.486	.515	.532	.507
17	White Sox	328	337	.493	.474	.434	.441	.404
18	Athletics	328	339	.492	.466	.451	.426	.436
19	Red Sox	344	370	.482	.547	.502	.529	.588
20	D-backs	348	375	.481	.501	.490	.469	.443
21	Astros	340	369	.480	.459	.470	.457	.484
22	Blue Jays	340	371	.478	.458	.494	.479	.525
23	Reds	339	372	.477	.480	.495	.463	.505
24	Nationals	303	352	.463	.494	.438	.486	.415
25	Phillies	326	382	.460	.486	.553	.483	.484
26	Padres	331	389	.460	.439	.487	.522	.462
27	Angels	303	362	.456	.467	.482	.523	.463
28	Cubs	326	390	.455	.486	.494	.499	.453
29	Braves	289	364	.443	.433	.466	.502	.513
30	Orioles	306	402	.432	.469	.503	.463	.463

POSTSEASON RESULTS

League (Level)	Champion	Runner-Up
International (AAA)	Jacksonville (MIA)	Scranton/W-B (NYY)
Pacific Coast (AAA)	Las Vegas (ATH)	Tacoma (SEA)
Eastern (AA)	Binghamton (NYM)	Erie (DET)
Southern (AA)	Birmingham (CWS)*	Montgomery (TB)
Texas (AA)	Springfield (STL)	Midland (OAK)
Midwest (A+)	West Michigan (DET)	Cedar Rapids (MIN)
Northwest (A+)	Everett (SEA)	Eugene (SFG)
South Atlantic (A+)	Brooklyn (NYM)	Hub City (TEX)
California (A)	San Jose (SFG)	Inland Empire (LAA)
Carolina (A)	Lynchburg (CLE)	Columbia (KCR)
Florida State (A)	Lakeland (DET)	Daytona (CIN)
Arizona Complex (R)	Angels (LAA)	Giants (SFG)
Florida Complex (R)	Blue Jays (TOR)	Twins (MIN)
Dominican Summer (R)	Padres Gold (SDP)	Athletics (ATH)

* Repeat champion from 2024

Griffin Dominated Three Levels

BY GEOFF PONTES

PLAYER OF THE YEAR

When Konnor Griffin began his professional career this April, it didn't start on a high note.

In his first eight professional at-bats, Griffin struck out six times. It would be the last time that happened, however, as the 19-year-old shortstop and Pirates 2024 first-round draft pick didn't record another two-game stretch with six strikeouts all season.

"There were some swing adjustments that I had to make," Griffin told Baseball America.

Adjust he did.

After getting over the rough start, Griffin hit .333/.415/.527 with 21 home runs, 65 stolen bases and 117 runs en route to a historically successful debut season in which he climbed three levels and ascended to become Baseball America's No. 1 overall prospect.

Konnor Griffin

Now, Griffin has also been named BA's Minor League Player of the Year for 2025.

Griffin achieved the honor thanks in part to offensive dominance not seen in years. Over the last 20 minor league seasons, he is the only player to produce a season with a .300 average, 20 or more home runs, 60 or more stolen bases and 100 or more runs.

And while the offensive numbers speak for themselves, what set Griffin apart from his top prospect peers in 2025 was the versatility he showed in the field. Drafted ninth overall as a shortstop with plus defense, Griffin also stood out defensively in center field—rare value at two premium defensive positions.

Such was the season for Griffin, who spent 2025 as one of the youngest players on every professional ball field he stepped on while also always being the most talented.

"It's been a crazy year and a long journey," Griffin said. "I really didn't know what to expect. I've learned a lot about myself and just try and get better every day."

After hitting .338/.396/.536 over 50 games with Low-A Bradenton—a line 56% better than his Florida State League peers—Griffin's numbers got better in High-A. Over 51 games with Greensboro, he hit .325/.432/.510 for a line 70% better than South Atlantic League competition. This trend continued over the final month of the season upon promotion to Double-A Altoona, where Griffin slashed .337/.418/.542 over 21 games to finish with a line that was 75% better than the average Eastern League hitter.

Griffin helped lead Altoona into the playoffs, pushing a talented Erie team to a deciding game three as he he went 6-for-10 with three walks.

The results had people taking notice even before the season began. Still only 18 at the time and without an official professional game on his ledger, Griffin was the talk of minor league spring training in Florida, and his performances on the back fields left scouts plenty impressed, both with his tools but also his maturity.

Griffin's hit tool quality is backed not only by his .333 batting average and 21.7% strikeout rate but by advanced metrics, as well. His 16.5% in-zone whiff rate this season is quite a bit lower than the minor league average, and he displays a good balance of patience and aggression within his plate approach.

At just 19 years old, Griffin heads into the offseason as the No. 1 prospect in baseball and Minor League Player of the Year.

And after his breakout 2025 campaign, he joins Paul Skenes in carrying the fortunes of a Pirates fanbase desperate for reasons to be hopeful after a woeful 30 years. ■

LAST 10 WINNERS

2014: Kris Bryant, Iowa (Cubs)
2015: Blake Snell, Charlotte/Montgomery/Durham (Rays)
2016: Yoan Moncada, Salem/Portland (Red Sox)
2017: Ronald Acuña Jr., Florida/Mississippi/Gwinnett (Braves)
2018: Vladimir Guerrero Jr., New Hampshire/Buffalo (Blue Jays)
2019: Gavin Lux, SS, Tulsa/Oklahoma City (Dodgers)
2021: Bobby Witt Jr., SS, NW Arkansas/Omaha (Royals)
2022: Gunnar Henderson, SS, Bowie/Norfolk (Orioles)
2023: Jackson Holliday, SS, Del./Aber./Bowie/Norfolk (Orioles)
2024: Kristian Campbell, OF/2B, Salem/Port./Worcest. (Red Sox)

Full list: search "Baseball America awards"

Josuar Gonzalez was the standout of the Dominican Summer League season, giving San Francisco another top prospect to dream on.

Gonzalez made waves as the easy choice for the No. 1 prospect in the Dominican Summer League. The 17-year-old Gonzalez quickly lived up to his reputation as a sublime defender who should one day help the Giants return to regular playoff contention.

On the other coast, Orioles righthander Esteban Mejia used electric stuff to pitch his way to the top spot on BA's ranking of the Florida Complex League's best prospects. A year after making a name for himself in the DSL, Mejia overpowered hitters in southwest Florida with a fastball that peaked at 102 mph and a slider and changeup that garnered plenty of silly swings.

By season's end he'd reached Low-A, where he learned he'd have to polish his command a bit more to get his stuff to play to its full potential.

Tragedy Strikes In The FCL

The FCL season was also interrupted by tragedy. On June 15, Orioles minor leaguer Luis Guevara was killed in a head-on collision between two vessels in Lido Key, Fla., which is near Baltimore's spring training home in Sarasota. According to local media, officials with Florida Fish and Wildlife. Two people were on each watercraft, and all four were taken to the hospital after being rescued by onlookers.

"Luis was a beloved member of our organization, and we are devastated following his tragic passing," Orioles general manager Mike Elias said in a statement. "Our thoughts and prayers are with his family, friends and teammates, and we ask for their continued privacy during this difficult time."

The team's next three games after the incident were postponed.

The 2025 minor league season was marked by endings across the country, from California, to Maryland, to North Carolina, giving way to what should be a 2026 season chock full of new beginnings. ■

Maxson Did The Impossible

BY J.J. COOPER

The staff of the Sacramento River Cats pulled off the seemingly impossible in 2025. They somehow managed to become the temporary home of the major league Athletics, while also hosting a Triple-A team in the same ballpark.

But among many questions of "How Did They Do That?," there's one that seems the most improbable. The A's and River Cats played on the same grass field for the entire 2025 season.

The Sutter Health Park field was never resodded. It survived days in the 40s and 50s in April and high 90s in July and August. It weathered more than 150 home dates and still looked full, lush and green in late September.

The Sacramento turf was the subject of many discussions. The worry was that a natural grass field would wither and die without getting the regenerative breaks that normally occur when a baseball team hits the road.

With a schedule that had the Triple-A River Cats playing at home on the weeks that the big league A's were on the road, and vice versa, the grass would never have time to recover.

Originally, it was planned to bring in artificial turf to handle the extreme wear and tear. But concerns about how players would fare on a surface that held and radiated heat on near triple-digit days led to the decision to stick with natural grass.

And so Major League Baseball and the River Cats staff attacked the problem by being proactive. MLB head groundskeeper Murray Cook advised the RiverCats to use a well-wearing Bermuda hybrid grass. The River Cats laid it over a clay and sand mixture that helped the grass retain moisture and nutrients. A Sacramento homestand in June was moved to Tacoma to give time to re-sod if needed.

And then the staff worked day and night to keep that from ever being needed. Drones with infrared cameras monitored for hot spots in need of extra care to prevent those spots from getting worse. Heating and cooling was piped underneath the turf to keep the grass in tip-top shape.

With a lot of work, the field held up extremely well. And it ended up using less fertilizer than the year before thanks to the adaptations.

It's one example of what was going on all year in West Sacramento. Team president Chip Maxson and the Sacramento River Cats did the difficult or near-impossible all season, which is why Maxson is the 2025 Minor League Executive of the Year.

From day one, the River Cats embraced what could have been viewed as a never-ending marathon. No one had ever before hosted a Triple-A and MLB season in the same ballpark. It meant that Sutter Health Park hosted 151 games in an 182-day stretch.

"When the idea first came up, my first answer was, 'Of course we can do it. It's baseball. This is what we do,'" Maxson said. "I got excited thinking about the opportunity. It's something that has never been done before."

After an all-hands-on-deck April, Maxson and the staff settled into a schedule, and everyone was ordered to take days off. No one ended up going 151-for-151, with most full-time staff ending up working 125 to 135 games. Over one million fans attended A's and River Cats games in Sacramento.

"We are excited to run it back and do it again," Maxson said. "We learned so much. We want to apply that in 2026." ∎

EXECUTIVE OF THE YEAR

LAST 10 WINNERS

2015: Dave Oster, Lake Elsinore (California)
2016: Tom Kayser, president, Texas League
2017: Ryan Keur, Daytona (Florida State)
2018: Bob Murphy, Dayton (Midwest)
2019: Don Logan, Las Vegas (Pacific Coast)
2020: Adam Giardino, broadcaster
2021: K.L. Wombacher, president/GM, Hillsboro (Northwest)
2022: Kristin Call, GM, Myrtle Beach (Carolina)
2023: Rob Zerjac, president/CEO, Wisconsin (Midwest)
2024: Mike Abramson, GM, Hartford (Eastern)

For full list, search "Baseball America awards"

Chip Maxson

Brignac Drove The Ponies Well

BY MATT EDDY

MANAGER OF THE YEAR

Two weeks into the Eastern League season, the Binghamton Rumble Ponies had as many postponements as wins. They had five of each thanks to unforgiving April weather in the Northeast.

The Mets' Double-A affiliate actually started the season in worse shape than that. They went 3-6 before reeling off an eight-game winning streak to set the stage for the most successful season in Binghamton franchise history.

The Rumble Ponies went 90-46, including a 20-3 stretch at one point, and set a franchise record for wins. Binghamton defeated Somerset and Erie in the playoffs to win its first Eastern League championship since 2014.

At the center of Binghamton's success was Reid Brignac, our pick as Minor League Manager of the Year.

The 39-year-old Brignac sensed early in the season that the Rumble Ponies could be destined for big things.

"We were clicking on all cylinders," Brignac said. "The pitching, the hitting and the pre-game preparation were all outstanding. The attention to detail was excellent. The players were ready to play every night.

"They worked on org goals pre-game, but once the game started they were playing for each other."

Binghamton's 2.96 ERA was the second-lowest in the full-season minor leagues. Their pitchers struck out 30% of batters, far and away the highest rate in the minors. They walked 8.7% of batters, the fourth-lowest rate among 120 teams.

Four pitchers who began the season with Binghamton made their MLB debuts with the Mets in 2025: starters Nolan McLean, Jonah Tong and Jonathan Pintaro and reliever Alex Carrillo.

To compensate for the promotions of key pitchers, Binghamton turned to 23-year-old righthander Jack Wenninger, who started both of the Rumble Ponies' clinching games in the EL playoffs, going 2-0 while striking out 20, walking three and allowing four hits in 11 innings.

"He was dominating all year," Brignac said of Wenninger. "He was our most consistent pitcher all season and he got better as the year went on."

A trio of 2024 draft picks—Jonathan Santucci, Will Watson and R.J. Gordon—proved they were up to the challenge in their first full pro seasons by helping Binghamton continue its winning ways in the second half.

Binghamton hitters finished second in the Eastern League in OPS and second in runs, but by the time the playoffs rolled around, outfielder Carson Benge, shortstop Jett Williams and first baseman Ryan Clifford had been promoted to Triple-A.

That's OK. Outfielders AJ Ewing, third baseman Jacob Reimer and catcher Chris Suero arrived and helped keep the lineup running. In all, nine of the Mets' top 10 prospects spent time at Binghamton. But many of them moved on as well, as the team saw plenty of promotions to Triple-A.

"When you have a group of guys seeing how fast other players are moving, it's easy for them to say, '(The coaches) are here to help us and get us to MLB as quickly as possible.'

"We took pride in getting guys promoted, and then helping the next wave not skip a beat at Double-A." ■

LAST 10 WINNERS

2014: Mark Johnson, Low-A Kane County (Cubs)
2015: Tony DeFrancesco, Triple-A Fresno (Astros)
2016: Dave Wallace, Double-A Akron (Indians)
2017: Stubby Clapp, Triple-A Memphis (Cardinals)
2018: Drew Saylor, High-A Rancho Cucamonga (Dodgers)
2019: Corey Ragsdale, High-A Down East (Rangers)
2021: Chris Widger, High-A Quad Cities (Royals)
2022: Gil Velazquez, Triple-A Reno (D-backs)
2023: Brian Dinkelman, High-A Cedar Rapids (Twins)
2024: Zach Vincej, Low-A Modesto (Mariners)

For full list, search "Baseball America awards"

Reid Brignac

CLASSIFICATION ALL-STARS

TRIPLE-A
INTERNATIONAL · PACIFIC COAST

Pos	Player, Team (Organization)	Age	AVG	OBP	SLG	PA	H	2B	3B	HR	RBI	BB	SO	SB
C	Samuel Basallo, Norfolk (Orioles)	20	.270	.377	.589	321	73	17	0	23	67	44	76	0
1B	Jonathon Long, Iowa (Cubs)	23	.305	.404	.479	607	157	23	3	20	91	79	116	2
2B	Jordan Lawlar, Reno (D-backs)	22	.313	.403	.564	300	81	22	5	11	50	36	70	20
3B	Cody Freeman, Round Rock (Rangers)	24	.336	.382	.549	426	129	25	0	19	71	32	37	8
SS	JJ Wetherholt, Memphis (Cardinals)	22	.314	.416	.562	221	58	14	1	10	25	28	33	9
OF	Dylan Beavers, Norfolk (Orioles)	23	.304	.420	.515	418	104	14	2	18	51	68	76	23
OF	Owen Caissie, Iowa (Cubs)	22	.286	.386	.551	433	106	28	2	22	55	57	121	5
OF	Justin Crawford, Lehigh Valley (Phillies)	21	.334	.411	.452	506	147	23	4	7	47	58	91	46
DH	Luis Campusano, El Paso (Padres)	26	.336	.441	.595	475	132	25	1	25	95	72	82	2

Pos	Pitcher, Team (Organization)	Age	W	L	ERA	G	SV	IP	H	BB	SO	HR	K-BB%	WHIP
SP	Mick Abel, Lehigh Valley/St. Paul (Phillies/Twins)	23	7	2	2.20	18	0	98	69	40	114	6	18.6	1.11
SP	Joe Boyle, Durham (Rays)	25	8	4	1.88	18	0	86	46	41	114	7	21.1	1.01
SP	Nolan McLean, Syracuse (Mets)	23	5	4	2.78	16	0	87	58	38	97	8	16.4	1.10
SP	Ian Seymour, Durham (Rays)	26	9	3	2.62	16	0	86	78	20	104	10	23.6	1.14
SP	Robby Snelling, Jacksonville (Marlins)	21	6	2	1.27	11	0	64	46	17	81	4	26.0	0.99
RP	Josh White, Jacksonville (Marlins)	24	4	1	2.29	27	4	39	27	11	57	2	29.9	0.97

DOUBLE-A
EASTERN · SOUTHERN · TEXAS

Pos	Player, Team (Organization)	Age	AVG	OBP	SLG	PA	H	2B	3B	HR	RBI	BB	SO	SB
C	Cooper Ingle, Akron (Guardians)	23	.273	.391	.441	403	91	29	0	9	49	65	70	0
1B	Ryan Clifford, Binghamton (Mets)	21	.243	.355	.493	437	89	18	1	24	75	63	113	4
2B	Jett Williams, Binghamton (Mets)	21	.281	.390	.477	421	99	29	5	10	37	62	96	32
3B	Sal Stewart, Chattanooga (Reds)	21	.306	.377	.473	329	90	19	0	10	44	27	51	13
SS	JJ Wetherholt, Springfield (Cardinals)	22	.300	.425	.466	275	67	14	1	7	34	44	40	14
OF	Kemp Alderman, Pensacola (Marlins)	22	.282	.337	.447	454	116	13	5	15	53	34	102	20
OF	Walker Jenkins, Wichita (Twins)	20	.309	.426	.487	235	59	11	1	7	24	34	44	11
OF	Ryan Waldschmidt, Amarillo (D-backs)	22	.309	.423	.498	300	77	14	3	9	35	45	53	19
DH	Felix Reyes, Reading (Phillies)	24	.335	.365	.572	395	123	34	4	15	65	18	61	13

Pos	Pitcher, Team (Organization)	Age	W	L	ERA	G	SV	IP	H	BB	SO	HR	K-BB%	WHIP
SP	Henry Baez, San Antonio/Midland (Padres/Athletics)	22	5	3	2.39	23	0	109	79	35	100	3	14.9	1.05
SP	Ixan Henderson, Springfield (Cardinals)	23	9	7	2.59	25	0	132	99	51	134	5	15.6	1.14
SP	Ty Johnson, Montgomery (Rays)	23	7	6	2.61	26	0	110	66	38	149	5	25.8	0.94
SP	Shane Murphy, Birmingham (White Sox)	24	9	4	1.38	20	0	111	77	15	82	8	16.4	0.83
SP	Jonah Tong, Binghamton (Mets)	22	8	5	1.59	20	0	102	50	44	162	2	29.7	0.92
RP	Alimber Santa, Corpus Christi (Astros)	22	3	1	1.26	31	2	57	35	23	63	2	17.7	1.02

Jonah Tong dominated multiple levels. He was 8-5, 1.59 at Double-A Binghamton.

CLASSIFICATION ALL-STARS

HIGH-A
MIDWEST · NORTHWEST · SOUTH ATLANTIC

Pos	Player, Team (Organization)	Age	AVG	OBP	SLG	PA	H	2B	3B	HR	RBI	BB	SO	SB
C	Josue Briceño, West Michigan (Tigers)	20	.296	.422	.602	244	58	13	1	15	57	41	40	1
1B	Esmerlyn Valdez, Greensboro (Pirates)	21	.303	.385	.592	314	84	18	1	20	57	31	77	2
2B	Michael Arroyo, Everett (Mariners)	20	.269	.422	.512	306	65	14	0	15	39	39	65	3
3B	Jacob Reimer, Brooklyn (Mets)	21	.284	.384	.502	268	65	18	4	8	39	32	52	11
SS	Konnor Griffin, Greensboro (Pirates)	19	.325	.432	.510	234	63	11	2	7	36	28	46	33
OF	Carson Benge, Brooklyn (Mets)	22	.302	.417	.480	271	68	18	5	4	37	41	50	15
OF	Max Clark, West Michigan (Tigers)	20	.285	.430	.427	330	74	12	2	7	47	65	56	12
OF	Bo Davidson, Eugene (Giants)	22	.309	.412	.507	335	87	14	6	10	56	49	74	12
DH	Kevin McGonigle, West Michigan (Tigers)	20	.372	.462	.648	171	54	19	0	7	39	23	19	3

Pos	Pitcher, Team (Organization)	Age	W	L	ERA	G	SV	IP	H	BB	SO	HR	K-BB%	WHIP
SP	Kyle Carr, Hudson Valley (Yankees)	23	8	6	1.96	22	0	119	81	47	104	6	11.9	1.07
SP	David Davalillo, Hub City (Rangers)	22	4	1	2.12	11	0	51	31	11	68	2	28.5	0.82
SP	Daniel Eagen, Hillsboro (D-backs)	22	7	5	2.49	19	0	98	63	41	132	7	23.5	1.06
SP	Josh Hartle, Lake County (Guardians)	22	10	2	2.35	22	0	103	72	37	100	2	15.1	1.05
SP	Elmer Rodriguez-Cruz, Hudson Valley (Yankees)	21	6	4	2.26	15	0	84	52	37	99	1	18.2	1.06
RP	Garrett Hawkins, Fort Wayne (Padres)	25	8	1	1.43	32	8	44	17	13	60	1	29.0	0.68

LOW-A
CALIFORNIA · CAROLINA · FLORIDA STATE

Pos	Player, Team (Organization)	Age	AVG	OBP	SLG	PA	H	2B	3B	HR	RBI	BB	SO	SB
C	Alfredo Duno, Daytona (Reds)	19	.287	.430	.518	495	112	32	2	18	81	95	91	6
1B	Victor Figueroa, Lake Elsinore (Padres)	21	.262	.375	.456	232	51	17	0	7	30	34	47	3
2B	Luis Peña, Carolina (Brewers)	18	.308	.375	.469	309	84	14	6	6	52	28	41	41
3B	Caleb Bonemer, Kannapolis (White Sox)	19	.281	.400	.458	432	98	26	3	10	58	68	91	27
SS	Konnor Griffin, Bradenton (Pirates)	19	.338	.396	.536	231	70	10	2	9	36	15	53	26
OF	Slade Caldwell, Visalia (D-backs)	19	.294	.460	.454	216	48	13	2	3	20	44	62	13
OF	Theo Gillen, Charleston (Rays)	19	.267	.433	.387	324	65	12	1	5	18	64	75	36
OF	Eduardo Quintero, Rancho Cucamonga (Dodgers)	19	.306	.426	.533	395	97	18	6	14	53	65	88	35
DH	Raudi Rodriguez, Inland Empire (Angels)	21	.281	.372	.470	560	135	21	14	14	83	63	130	38

Pos	Pitcher, Team (Organization)	Age	W	L	ERA	G	SV	IP	H	BB	SO	HR	K-BB%	WHIP
SP	Jacob Bresnahan, San Jose (Giants)	20	9	3	2.61	22	0	93	67	43	124	2	21.3	1.18
SP	Caden Scarborough, Hickory (Rangers)	20	2	5	2.88	19	0	75	50	19	95	7	25.9	0.92
SP	Lucas Elissalt, Lakeland (Tigers)	20	4	1	2.48	16	0	65	44	20	77	4	21.3	0.98
SP	David Shields, Columbia (Royals)	18	3	1	2.01	18	0	72	58	15	81	3	23.1	1.02
SP	Ryan Sloan, Modesto (Mariners)	19	2	3	3.44	18	0	71	66	15	77	2	21.8	1.15
RP	Benny Thompson, Inland Empire (Angels)	23	4	2	1.91	44	11	61	31	43	100	1	22.3	1.21

ROOKIE
ARIZONA COMPLEX · FLORIDA COMPLEX · DOMINICAN SUMMER

Pos	Player, Team (Organization)	Age	AVG	OBP	SLG	PA	H	2B	3B	HR	RBI	BB	SO	SB
C	Rainiel Rodriguez, FCL Cardinals	18	.373	.513	.831	80	22	6	0	7	16	16	15	1
1B	David Beckles, FCL Blue Jays	21	.304	.388	.483	237	63	11	1	8	42	24	63	2
2B	Dauri Fernandez, ACL Guardians	18	.333	.398	.558	176	52	9	4	6	27	16	22	16
3B	Juan Sanchez, DSL Blue Jays	17	.341	.439	.565	253	73	16	4	8	40	26	44	4
SS	Yandel Ricardo, ACL Royals	18	.342	.438	.533	145	41	7	5	2	21	18	35	17
OF	Roldy Brito, ACL Rockies	18	.368	.445	.555	209	67	13	6	3	21	22	42	22
OF	Edward Florentino, FCL Pirates	18	.347	.442	.642	113	33	6	2	6	23	16	22	6
OF	Ching-Hsien Ko, ACL Dodgers	18	.367	.487	.539	226	66	15	2	4	30	39	40	5
DH	Edgar Montero, DSL Athletics	18	.313	.484	.580	244	55	14	3	9	50	60	54	11

Pos	Pitcher, Team (Organization)	Age	W	L	ERA	G	SV	IP	H	BB	SO	HR	K-BB%	WHIP
SP	Argenis Cayama, ACL Giants	18	1	1	2.25	12	0	48	33	18	55	0	18.7	1.06
SP	Keyner Martinez, ACL Giants	20	3	1	1.90	15	2	47	42	10	67	1	30.3	1.10
SP	Esteban Mejia, FCL Orioles	18	1	2	2.45	11	0	40	28	25	53	0	15.9	1.31
SP	Javier Perez, FCL Astros	21	6	0	1.69	13	0	43	34	8	48	3	24.1	0.98
SP	Franco Zabaleta, DSL Athletics	18	4	0	0.51	11	0	53	31	14	44	0	15.2	0.85
RP	Roberto Perez, ACL Mariners	21	1	0	1.42	17	2	25	11	8	33	0	27.2	0.75

MINOR LEAGUE ALL-STARS

Kevin McGonigle hit for average and power at three different levels.

Payton Tolle began the season in High-A and finished it in the majors.

FIRST TEAM

Pos	Player, Organization (Levels)	Age	AVG	OBP	SLG	AB	HR	RBI	BB	SO	SB	wRC+
C	Samuel Basallo, Orioles (AAA)	20	.270	.377	.589	270	23	67	44	76	0	151
1B	Josue Briceño, Tigers (A+,AA)	20	.266	.383	.500	364	20	76	66	87	1	153
2B	JJ Wetherholt, Cardinals (AA,AAA)	22	.306	.421	.510	408	17	59	72	73	23	152
3B	Sal Stewart, Reds (AA,AAA)	21	.309	.383	.524	437	20	80	46	77	17	152
SS	Konnor Griffin, Pirates (A,A+,AA)	19	.333	.415	.527	484	21	94	50	122	65	165
OF	Dylan Beavers, Orioles (AAA)	23	.304	.420	.515	342	18	51	68	76	23	153
OF	Max Clark, Tigers (A+,AA)	20	.271	.403	.432	431	14	67	94	90	19	148
OF	Eduardo Quintero, Dodgers (A,A+)	19	.293	.415	.508	433	19	69	88	123	47	153
DH	Kevin McGonigle, Tigers (A,A+,AA)	20	.305	.408	.583	331	19	80	59	46	10	182

Pos	Pitcher, Organization (Levels)	Age	W	L	ERA	G	IP	HR	BB	SO	WHIP	FIP
SP	Elmer Rodriguez-Cruz, Yankees (A+,AA,AAA)	21	11	8	2.58	27	150	3	57	176	1.07	2.47
SP	Robby Snelling, Marlins (AA,AAA)	21	9	7	2.51	25	136	10	39	166	1.11	2.77
SP	Payton Tolle, Red Sox (A+,AA,AAA)	22	3	5	3.04	20	92	10	23	133	0.99	2.75
SP	Jonah Tong, Mets (AA,AAA)	22	10	5	1.43	22	114	2	47	179	0.92	1.68
SP	Trey Yesavage, Blue Jays (A,A+,AA,AAA)	21	5	1	3.12	25	98	8	41	160	0.97	2.52
RP	Hayden Harris, Braves (AA,AAA)	26	6	0	0.52	43	52	1	19	79	0.75	2.07

SECOND TEAM

Pos	Player, Organization (Levels)	Age	AVG	OBP	SLG	AB	HR	RBI	BB	SO	SB	wRC+
C	Carter Jensen, Royals (AA,AAA)	21	.290	.377	.501	427	20	76	60	122	10	136
1B	Esmerlyn Valdez, Pirates (A+,AA)	21	.286	.376	.520	458	26	86	56	130	3	156
2B	Michael Arroyo, Mariners (A+,AA)	20	.262	.401	.433	450	17	54	69	104	12	139
3B	Jacob Reimer, Mets (A+,AA)	21	.282	.379	.491	444	17	77	58	112	15	157
SS	Caleb Bonemer, White Sox (A,A+)	19	.281	.401	.473	385	12	64	75	101	29	151
OF	Carson Benge, Mets (A+,AA,AAA)	22	.281	.385	.472	441	15	73	68	92	22	150
OF	AJ Ewing, Mets (A,A+,AA)	20	.315	.401	.429	485	3	55	68	105	70	147
OF	Ryan Waldschmidt, D-backs (A+,AA)	22	.289	.419	.473	484	18	78	96	106	29	143
DH	Alfredo Duno, Reds (A)	19	.287	.430	.518	390	18	81	95	91	6	164

Pos	Pitcher, Organization (Levels)	Age	W	L	ERA	G	IP	HR	BB	SO	WHIP	FIP
SP	David Davalillo, Rangers (A+,AA)	22	6	4	2.44	23	107.0	6	28	126	0.93	2.81
SP	Connelly Early, Red Sox (AA,AAA)	23	10	3	2.60	21	100.1	5	40	132	1.11	2.74
SP	Carlos Lagrange, Yankees (A+,AA)	22	11	8	3.53	24	120.0	8	62	168	1.20	3.14
SP	TJ Nichols, Rays (A+,AA)	23	14	3	2.90	25	133.2	21	30	156	1.02	3.90
SP	JR Ritchie, Braves (A+,AA,AAA)	22	8	6	2.64	26	140.0	12	54	140	1.01	3.84
RP	Welinton Herrera, Rockies (A+,AA)	21	5	5	2.64	52	64.2	2	25	99	1.14	2.02

Whitecaps Set Records

TEAM OF THE YEAR

BY EMILY WALDON

When asked to describe the West Michigan Whitecaps' season, manager Tony Cappuccilli admitted he needed a moment.

He grinned.

"It's been incredible," he said. "There isn't really any other way to put it. I mean, we were 53 games over .500 before the (Midwest League) playoffs. It obviously exceeded our expectations.

"You can't expect to have that kind of a season."

After spending more than 20 years in a variety of roles with different organizations, Cappuccilli made his managerial debut with West Michigan in 2024, finishing 68-63 and in a tie for fifth place. That would set the table for a 2025 season to remember for the Tigers' High-A affiliate.

"Coming out of spring training, the Whitecaps' roster was the strongest I have ever seen," West Michigan vice president and GM Jim Jarecki said. "The players came up to West Michigan, not with a chip on their shoulder, but with confidence that was as strong as it could be.

"The Detroit Tigers' player development and drafting and training are as dominant as they have ever been, and the results continue to show."

For the player it was the camaraderie from multiple seasons spent together that set the tone.

"I think everyone truly wanted everyone else on the team to win," outfielder Seth Stephenson said. "Not only did we want everyone to win, but we also wanted to win collectively as a group."

The Whitecaps went 92-39 this year. They never lost more than three games in a row. Their .702 winning percentage was the best in the minor leagues since the Modesto A's had a .706 mark in 1994.

"I felt like this team was really good because I already felt that energy of us showing up every day and doing what we have to do,"

Tony Cappuccilli

middle infielder Jack Penney said. "We never changed our attitude, and I think the results never changed our attitude. As we played more games, we realized that we never really changed what we did.

"That's how special it was."

The Whitecaps plus-294 run differential was the best in the minors since at least 2005.

"I think we just took it game by game," reliever Carlos Lequerica said. "And then once you kind of get deep into it, you're like, 'Whoa, there's kind of something crazy brewing here.' Then before you know it, you're at 92 wins."

Cappuccilli had a new coaching staff in 2025, including pitching coach Nick Green and hitting coach Matt Malott. With most of the West Michigan players having known both Green and Malott, that ability to bond quickly played into the makeup of the Whitecaps' roster.

Throughout the year, the players commented on the ease that comes with being trusted to do your job. From the scouting reports to the personal conversations, the players noticed and are the first to admit that leadership made all the difference.

"I love these guys," Cappuccilli said. "It's truly such a good group of guys and just the way that they maneuvered themselves through the course of this season. This is my 22nd year coaching baseball, and I've never had a group like this." ∎

LAST 10 WINNERS

2014: Double-A Portland Sea Dogs/Eastern (Red Sox)
2015: Double-A Biloxi Shuckers/Southern (Brewers)
2016: Low-A Rome Braves/South Atlantic (Braves)
2017: Double-A Midland RockHounds/Texas (Athletics)
2018: Low-A Bowling Green Hot Rods/Midwest (Rays)
2019: Double-A Amarillo/Texas (Padres)
2021: Triple-A Durham/International (Rays)
2022: Low-A Charleston/Carolina (Rays)
2023: Triple-A Norfolk/International (Orioles)
2024: High-A Lake County Captains (Guardians)

Full list: search "Baseball America awards"

2025 OVERALL MINOR LEAGUE DEPARTMENT LEADERS

Full-season teams only

FULL-SEASON TEAM LEADERS

WINS
West Michigan Whitecaps (Midwest)	92
Binghamton Rumble Ponies (Eastern)	90
Jacksonville Jumbo Shrimp (International)	89
Greensboro Grasshoppers (South Atlantic)	88
Springfield Cardinals (Texas)	88

LOSSES
Rocket City Trash Pandas (Southern)	92
Corpus Christi Hooks (Texas)	89
Rochester Red Wings (International)	88
Albuquerque Isotopes (Pacific Coast)	87
Gwinnett Stripers (International)	87
Reno Aces (Pacific Coast)	87

BATTING AVERAGE
Las Vegas Aviators (Pacific Coast)	.288
Albuquerque Isotopes (Pacific Coast)	.285
El Paso Chihuahuas (Pacific Coast)	.284
Reno Aces (Pacific Coast)	.283
Tacoma Rainiers (Pacific Coast)	.283

RUNS
Las Vegas Aviators (Pacific Coast)	978
El Paso Chihuahuas (Pacific Coast)	959
Tacoma Rainiers (Pacific Coast)	944
Oklahoma City Comets (Pacific Coast)	936
Reno Aces (Pacific Coast)	924

HOME RUNS
Albuquerque Isotopes (Pacific Coast)	199
Charlotte Knights (International)	199
Omaha Storm Chasers (International)	199
Las Vegas Aviators (Pacific Coast)	190
Oklahoma City Comets (Pacific Coast)	188

STOLEN BASES
Beloit Sky Carp (Midwest)	334
Fayetteville Woodpeckers (Carolina)	334
Nashville Sounds (International)	316
Aberdeen IronBirds (South Atlantic)	314
Tampa Tarpons (Florida State)	307

EARNED RUN AVERAGE
Hudson Valley Renegades (South Atlantic)	2.82
Binghamton Rumble Ponies (Eastern)	2.96
Birmingham Barons (Southern)	2.99
West Michigan Whitecaps (Midwest)	3.17
Quad Cities River Bandits (Midwest)	3.29

STRIKEOUTS
Iowa Cubs (International)	1438
Binghamton Rumble Ponies (Eastern)	1435
Durham Bulls (International)	1422
Oklahoma City Comets (Pacific Coast)	1408
Worcester Red Sox (International)	1403

WALKS ALLOWED
Oklahoma City Comets (Pacific Coast)	782
Jupiter Hammerheads (Florida State)	767
Inland Empire 66ers (California)	746
Tulsa Drillers (Texas)	734
Great Lakes Loons (Midwest)	729

INDIVIDUAL BATTING

BATTING AVERAGE*
Minimum 378 PA
Cody Freeman (Round Rock)	.336
Luis Campusano (El Paso)	.336
Justin Crawford (Lehigh Valley)	.334
Konnor Griffin (Altoona, Bradenton, Greensboro)	.333
Nick Solak (Indianapolis)	.332

RUNS
Samad Taylor (Tacoma)	124
Konnor Griffin (Altoona, Bradenton, Greensboro)	117
Ryan Waldschmidt (Amarillo, Hillsboro)	114
Ryan Ward (Okla. City)	113
Yonathan Perlaza (El Paso)	106

HITS
Rhylan Thomas (Tacoma)	178
Yonathan Perlaza (El Paso)	166
Samad Taylor (Tacoma)	165
Ryan Ward (Okla. City)	164
Konnor Griffin (Altoona, Bradenton, Greensboro)	161

TOP HITTING STREAKS
Jorge Barros (Reno)	29
Luis Campusano (El Paso)	25

Ryan Ward

MOST HITS (ONE GAME)
Nayerich Waterfort (DSL-Reds)	6
72 tied	5

TOTAL BASES
Ryan Ward (Okla. City)	315
Yonathan Perlaza (El Paso)	276
Jose Rojas (Scranton/WB)	267
Samad Taylor (Tacoma)	257
Konnor Griffin (Altoona, Bradenton, Greensboro)	255

EXTRA-BASE HITS
Ryan Ward (Okla. City)	73
Jose Rojas (Scranton/WB)	71
Yonathan Perlaza (El Paso)	70
Junior Perez (Las Vegas, Midland)	61
Carlos Perez (Iowa)	60
Kala'i Rosario (Wichita)	60

DOUBLES
Yonathan Perlaza (El Paso)	49
Gabriel Gonzalez (Cedar Rapids, St. Paul, Wichita)	38
Jesus Bastidas (Gwinnett, Sugar Land)	37
Cooper Ingle (Akron, Columbus)	36
Jose Devers (Lake County)	36

TRIPLES
Raudi Rodriguez (Inland Empire)	14
Marshall Toole (Tampa)	13
Dante Nori (Clearwater, Jersey Shore, Reading)	12
Sam Hilliard (Albuquerque)	12
Nick Schnell (Harrisburg, Rochester)	11

HOME RUNS
Ryan Ward (Okla. City)	36
Jose Rojas (Scranton/WB)	32
Lazaro Montes (Arkansas, Everett)	32
Bobby Seymour (Durham)	30
Ryan Clifford (Binghamton, Syracuse)	29

RUNS BATTED IN
Ryan Ward (Okla. City)	122
Yonathan Perlaza (El Paso)	113
Drew Avans (Las Vegas)	24
Andrew Jenkins (West Michigan)	22
Nate Mondou (El Paso)	22

Jose Rojas (Scranton/WB)	105
Blaze Jordan (Memphis, Portland, Worcester)	99
Eduardo Valencia (Erie, Toledo)	95
Luis Campusano (El Paso)	95

MOST RBIs (ONE GAME)
11 tied	8

WALKS
Trei Cruz (Erie, Toledo)	102
Ryan Waldschmidt (Amarillo, Hillsboro)	96
Alfredo Duno (Daytona)	95
Wes Clarke (Corpus Christi, Nashville)	95
Max Clark (Erie, West Michigan)	94
Nathan Flewelling (Bowling Green, Charleston)	94

INTENTIONAL WALKS
Blaine Crim (Albuquerque, Round Rock)	4
Bobby Seymour (Durham)	4
Bryce Eldridge (ACL Giants, Richmond, Sacramento)	4
Chris Newell (Tulsa)	4
Josue Briceno (Erie, West Michigan)	4
Max Anderson (Erie, Toledo)	4
Nathan Martorella (Jacksonville, Pensacola)	4
Nick Solak (Indianapolis)	4

STRIKEOUTS
Edwin Rios (Louisville)	180
Vance Honeycutt (Aberdeen)	178
Nick Schnell (Harrisburg, Rochester)	175
Cole Fontenelle (Rocket City, Tri-City)	172
Marco Luciano (Sacramento)	170

STOLEN BASES
Kendall George (Great Lakes)	100
Jordan Sprinkle (Birmingham, Kannapolis, W-S)	80
Patrick Clohisy (Columbus, Rome)	79
Asbel Gonzalez (Columbia)	78
A.J. Ewing (Binghamton, Brooklyn, St. Lucie)	70

CAUGHT STEALING
Asbel Gonzalez (Columbia)	26
Nate George (Aberdeen, Delmarva, FCL Orioles)	25
Kendall George (Great Lakes)	24
Esmil Valencia (Fayetteville, Jupiter)	19
Nelson Rada (Rocket City, Salt Lake)	18

EDDIE KELLY

ON-BASE PERCENTAGE*
Minimum 378 PA

Bryan Torres (Memphis)	.441
Luis Campusano (El Paso)	.441
Sam Antonacci (ACL White Sox, Birm., W-S)	.433
Alfredo Duno (Daytona)	.430
JJ Wetherholt (Memphis, Springfield)	.421

SLUGGING PERCENTAGE*
Minimum 378 PA

Jose Rojas (Scranton/WB)	.599
Luis Campusano (El Paso)	.595
Kevin McGonigle (Erie, Lakeland, West Michigan)	.583
James Outman (Okla. City, St. Paul)	.576
Carlos Perez (Iowa)	.572

ON-BASE PLUS SLUGGING (OPS)*
Minimum 378 PA

Luis Campusano (El Paso)	1.036
Kevin McGonigle (Erie, Lakeland, West Michigan)	.991
Jose Rojas (Scranton/WB)	.978
Alfredo Duno (Daytona)	.948
James Outman (Okla. City, St. Paul)	.945

HIT BY PITCH

Michael Arroyo (Arkansas, Everett)	36
Sam Antonacci (ACL White Sox, Birm., W-S)	35
Ben Hartl (Hickory, Hub City)	32
T.J. Schofield-Sam (Lansing, Midland)	30
Asbel Gonzalez (Columbia)	29

SACRIFICE BUNTS

William Bergolla (Birmingham)	21
Samad Taylor (Tacoma)	17
Johan Macias (Inland Empire)	14
Ripken Reyes (El Paso, San Antonio)	13
Jorge Ruiz (Inland Empire)	12

SACRIFICE FLIES

Jared Dickey (Lansing, Midland)	13
Angel Ortiz (Hillsboro)	12
Colton Ledbetter (Montgomery)	12
Jadher Areinamo (Montgomery, Wisconsin)	12
Ryan Galanie (Birmingham, Winston-Salem)	12

GROUNDED INTO DOUBLE PLAY

Javier Rivas (Altoona, Greensboro)	22
Marcos Castanon (El Paso, San Antonio)	22
Gabriel Gonzalez (Cedar Rapids, St. Paul, Wichita)	21
Blaze Jordan (Memphis, Portland, Worcester)	20
Jadher Areinamo (Montgomery, Wisconsin)	20

BATTING AVERAGE BY POSITION*

CATCHERS

Luis Campusano (El Paso)	.336
Moises Ballesteros (Iowa)	.316
Carter Jensen (NW Arkansas, Omaha)	.290
Alfredo Duno (Daytona)	.287
Carlos Pérez (Iowa)	.286

FIRST BASEMEN

Nick Solak (Indianapolis)	.332
Tanner English (Reno)	.325
Tyler Locklear (Tacoma)	.316
Eduardo Valencia (Erie, Toledo)	.311
Jonathon Long (Iowa)	.305

SECOND BASEMEN

Bryan Torres (Memphis)	.328
Francisco Urbanez (Louisville)	.314
Nate Mondou (El Paso)	.308
Jansel Luis (Hillsboro)	.304
Jean Carlos Sio (San Jose, Eugene)	.304

THIRD BASEMEN

Cody Freeman (Round Rock)	.336
Sal Stewart (Chatt., Louisville)	.309
LuJames Groover (Amarillo)	.309
Cesar Prieto (Memphis)	.300
Braylen Wimmer (Modesto, Hartford)	.296

SHORTSTOPS

Konnor Griffin (Altoona, Bradent., Greensboro)	.333
JJ Wetherholt (Memphis, Arkansas, Memphis)	.306
Kevin McGonigle (Lakeland, W. Michigan, Erie)	.305
Darell Hernaiz (Las Vegas)	.305
Yonny Hernandez (Binghamton, Syracuse)	.303

OUTFIELDERS

Justin Crawford (Lehigh Valley)	.334
Gabby Gonzalez (C. Rapids, Wichita, St. Paul)	.329
Rhylan Thomas (Tacoma)	.325
A.J. Ewing (St. Lucie, Brooklyn, Bingham.)	.315
Dakota Jordan (San Jose)	.311

INDIVIDUAL PITCHING

EARNED RUN AVERAGE*
Minimum 110 IP

Jonah Tong (Binghamton, Syracuse)	1.43
Shane Murphy (Birmingham, Charlotte, W-S)	1.66
Griffin Herring (Hudson Valley, Spokane, Tampa)	1.89
Melvin Hernandez (Carolina)	2.00
Nolan McLean (Binghamton, Syracuse)	2.45

WORST ERA*

Chandler Champlain (Omaha)	7.84
Brett Kerry (ACL Angels, Salt Lake)	7.60
Jared Kollar (El Paso, San Antonio)	6.79
Dakota Hudson (Salt Lake)	6.68
Landon Knack (Okla. City)	6.66

WINS

T.J. Nichols (Bowling Green, Montgomery)	14
Brendan Beck (Scranton/WB, Somerset)	13
Garrett Burhenn (Erie)	13
Allan Winans (Scranton/WB)	12
Dylan Ray (Amarillo, Reno)	12
Ian Mejia (Columbus, Gwinnett)	12
Jack Wenninger (Binghamton)	12
Yorman Gomez (Akron, Lake County)	12

LOSSES

Josh Grosz (Hudson Valley, Spokane)	14
Chase Allsup (Aberdeen, Delmarva)	13
Chase Petty (Louisville)	13
Gerado Salas (Peoria)	13
Jared Kollar (El Paso, San Antonio)	13
Manuel Mercedes (Eugene, Richmond)	13

GAMES

Garrett Davila (Harrisburg, Rochester)	57
Oddanier Mosqueda (Memphis)	55
Brandon Johnson (NW Arkansas, Omaha)	54
Hagen Danner (Tacoma)	54
Junior Santos (Harrisburg)	54
Will Childers (Biloxi, Nashville)	54

GAMES STARTED

Aaron Wilkerson (Louisville, Memphis)	29
Alexander Cornielle (Biloxi, Nashville)	29
8 tied	28

COMPLETE GAMES

Travis Sthele	3
Juan Reyes	2
Rafael Sanchez	2
72 tied	1

SHUTOUTS

Rafael Sanchez	2
Travis Sthele	2
30 tied	1

GAMES FINISHED

Trevor Kuncl (Chattanooga)	41
Junior Santos (Harrisburg)	38
Mark Adamiak (Lansing, Midland)	37
A.J. Causey (NW Arkansas, Quad Cities)	36
Landon Sims (Amarillo)	36

HOLDS

Luke Jewett (ACL Rockies, Fresno)	14
Andrew Dalquist (Birmingham)	12
Garrett Davila (Harrisburg, Rochester)	12
John Rooney (Jacksonville, Sugar Land)	12
Landon Tomkins (Altoona, Greensboro)	12
Ryan Lambert (Binghamton, Brooklyn)	12
Travis MacGregor (Biloxi, Frisco)	12

SAVES

Mark Adamiak (Lansing, Midland)	21
Trevor Kuncl (Chattanooga)	20
Nathan Blasick (Fresno)	19
Welinton Herrera (Hartford, Spokane)	17
A.J. Puckett (Knoxville)	15
Saul Teran (Clearwater, Jersey Shore, Reading)	15

INNINGS PITCHED

Aaron Wilkerson (Louisville, Memphis)	152.2
Logan Workman (Durham)	152.1
Duncan Davidson (Charlotte, Durham, Montgomery)	152
Grant Rogers (New Hampshire, Vancouver)	150.1
Elmer Rodriguez-Cruz (H. Valley, Scrant./WB, Somer.)	150
Kade Morris (Las Vegas, Midland)	150

WALKS

Thaddeus Ward (Norfolk)	94
Francis Texido (Inland Empire, Tri-City)	92
Jackson Humphries (Lake County)	91
Chris Cortez (Tri-City)	84
Patrick Copen (Great Lakes, Tulsa)	84

STRIKEOUTS

Jonah Tong (Binghamton, Syracuse)	179
Elmer Rodriguez-Cruz (H. Valley, S/WB, Somer.)	176
Carlos Lagrange (Hudson Valley, Somerset)	168
Robby Snelling (Jacksonville, Pensacola)	166
Trey Gibson (Aberdeen, Chesapeake, Norfolk)	166

HITS ALLOWED

Dakota Hudson (Salt Lake)	193
Chandler Champlain (Omaha)	160
Marcus Johnson (Bowling Green)	160
Jhonathan Diaz (Tacoma)	159
Kade Morris (Las Vegas, Midland)	154

HOME RUNS ALLOWED

Mason Albright (Albuquerque, Hartford)	32
Alan Rangel (Lehigh Valley)	29
Erick Leal (Scranton/WB)	28
Marcus Johnson (Bowling Green)	28
Aaron Wilkerson (Louisville, Memphis)	27
Brett Kerry (ACL Angels, Salt Lake)	27
Logan Workman (Durham)	27

STRIKEOUTS PER NINE (STARTERS)*
Minimum 100 IP

Jonah Tong (Binghamton, Syracuse)	14.2
Gage Stanifer (Dunedin, N. Hampshire, Vanc.)	13.2
Carlos Lagrange (Hudson Valley, Somerset)	12.6
Braden Davis (Palm Beach, Peoria)	12.5
Trey Gibson (Aberdeen, Chesapeake, Norfolk)	12.4

STRIKEOUTS PER NINE (RELIEVERS)*
Minimum 50 IP

Ben Thompson (Inland Empire)	14.7
Ryan Lambert (Binghamton, Brooklyn)	14.6
Eric Loomis (Frisco, Hickory, Hub City)	14.5
Nate Garkow (New Hampshire, Vancouver)	14.4
Will Bednar (Richmond, Sacramento)	14.4

OPPONENT AVERAGE (STARTERS)*
Minimum 100 IP

Jonah Tong (Binghamton, Syracuse)	.148
Braden Davis (Palm Beach, Peoria)	.156
Griffin Herring (Hudson Valley, Spokane, Tampa)	.169
Ty Johnson (Montgomery)	.174
JR Ritchie (Columbus, Gwinnett, Rome)	.175

OPPONENT AVERAGE (RELIEVERS)*
Minimum 50 IP

Brandan Bidois (Altoona, Braden., Greensb., Indian.)	.109
Hayden Harris (Columbus, Gwinnett)	.119
Anthony Nunez (Bingh., Brooklyn, Chesap., Norfolk)	.121
Ryan Bourassa (Columbus, Rome)	.128
Tyler Cleveland (Arkansas, Everett)	.128

MOST STRIKEOUTS (ONE GAME)

Drue Hackenberg (Mississippi)	16
Matt Wilkinson (Lynchburg)	15
Brett Kerry (Rocket City)	14
Trevor Martin (Bowling Green)	14
Jean Cabrera (Jersey Shore)	14

WILD PITCHES

Francis Texido (Inland Empire, Tri-City)	30
Yerlin Rodriguez (Wisconsin)	26
Manuel Suero (DSL Blue Jays)	24
Luis A. Reyes (ACL Cubs, Myrtle Beach)	23
Greysen Carter (FCL Yankees, Tampa)	22
Yeri Perez (Columbia)	22

BALKS

Luis Flores (Lake County, Lynchburg)	9
Andy Peralta (DSL White Sox)	8
Brandt Thompson (Palm Beach, Peoria, Springfield)	8
Jake Brooks (Beloit, Pensacola)	8
5 tied	7

HIT BATTERS

Jefferson Jean (Stockton)	21
Eddy Peralta (DSL Rangers Red)	20
Joan Ogando (Fayetteville)	19
Grant Kipp (Knoxville)	18
Bridger Holmes (Inland Empire, Salt Lake, Tri-City)	17
D.J. McCarty (Hub City)	17
Enrique Segura (ACL Rangers, Clearwater, Hickory)	17

GROUNDBALL DOUBLE PLAYS

Seth Lonsway (Richmond, Sacramento)	22
John Bertrand (Richmond, Sacramento)	19
Kade Morris (Las Vegas, Midland)	19
4 tied	18

INTERNATIONAL LEAGUE TRIPLE-A

Awards selected by Major League Baseball

CHAMPION: The Jacksonville Jumbo Shrimp didn't just capture the International League title—they took it all the way to Las Vegas Ballpark for the Triple-A National Championship. Their storybook season reached a perfect ending when Jacob Berry delivered a dramatic, walk-off two-run homer to seal the title.

MOST VALUABLE PLAYER: Dylan Beavers slashed .304/.420/.515 while hitting 18 home runs and driving in 51 RBIs He was promoted to the majors on Aug. 16.

PITCHER OF THE YEAR: Mick Abel had a busy and eventful 2025. He began the year with the Phillies, making his MLB debut on May 18, before being traded to the Twins alongside Eduardo Tait in exchange for Jhoan Duran. Abel started 18 games, posting a 7-2 record with an impressive 2.20 ERA split between the Lehigh Valley IronPigs and the St. Paul Saints.

TOP MLB PROSPECT: Cardinals prospect JJ Wetherholt dominated his first full pro season, cementing himself as one of the top prospects in baseball. The West Virginia alum slashed .314/.416/.562, with a .978 OPS, 10 home runs and 25 RBIs. Wetherholt, the seventh overall pick in 2024, should reach the majors in 2026.

MANAGER OF THE YEAR: Scranton/Wilkes-Barre manager Shelley Duncan guided the RailRiders to an 87-60 record, posting the best mark in the second half of the season. The team lost in the International League championship series.

Beavers

INTERNATIONAL LEAGUE ALL-STARS

Pos	Player	Team	AVG	OPS	HR
C	Samuel Basallo	Norfolk	.270	.966	23
1B	Jonathon Long	Iowa	.305	.883	20
2B	José Fermín	Memphis	.300	.913	7
3B	Otto Kemp	Lehigh Valley	.310	.987	16
SS	Cam Devanney	Indianapolis	.266	.846	20
OF	Dylan Beavers	Norfolk	.304	.935	18
OF	Justin Crawford	Lehigh Valley	.334	.863	7
OF	Owen Caissie	Iowa	.286	.937	22
DH	Rece Hinds	Louisville	.302	.922	24
UTIL	Jose Rojas	Scranton/W-B	.287	.978	32
Pos	Pitcher	Team	G	ERA	SO
SP	Allan Winans	Scranton/W-B	21	1.63	105
SP	Joe Boyle	Durham	18	1.88	114
SP	Mick Abel	Lehigh Val./St. Paul	18	2.20	114
SP	Robby Snelling	Jacksonville	11	1.27	81
RP	Andre Granillo	Memphis	29	1.29	58

OVERALL STANDINGS

East Division	W	L	PCT	GB	Manager	Attendance	Avg	Last Title
Jacksonville Jumbo Shrimp (Marlins)	89	61	.593	—	David Carpenter	369,679	4,929	2025
Scranton/WB (Yankees)	87	60	.592	0.5	Shelley Duncan	261,127	3,577	2016
Lehigh Valley IronPigs (Phillies)	87	61	.588	1	Anthony Contreras	585,167	7,907	Never
Durham Bulls (Rays)	85	64	.570	3.5	Morgan Ensberg	485,017	6,466	2022
Syracuse Mets (Mets)	77	73	.513	12	Dick Scott	342,977	4,573	1976
Worcester Red Sox (Red Sox)	76	73	.510	12.5	Chad Tracy	455,467	6,154	Never
Charlotte Knights (White Sox)	65	85	.433	24	Sergio Santos	425,461	5,672	1999
Norfolk Tides (Orioles)	63	84	.429	24.5	Tim Federowicz	370,537	5,075	2023
Buffalo Bisons (Blue Jays)	61	85	.418	26	Casey Candaele	425,517	5,673	2004
Rochester Red Wings (Nationals)	59	88	.401	28.5	Matthew LeCroy	431,265	5,750	1997
East Division	W	L	PCT	GB	Manager	Attendance	Avg	Last Title
Indianapolis Indians (Pirates)	87	62	.584	—	Chris Truby	570,676	7,711	2000
Nashville Sounds (Brewers)	85	63	.574	1.5	Rick Sweet	500,002	6,756	*2005
Toledo Mud Hens (Tigers)	84	66	.560	3.5	Gabe Alvarez	452,049	6,027	2006
Memphis Redbirds (Cardinals)	80	68	.541	6.5	Ben Johnson	183,980	2,520	*2018
Iowa Cubs (Cubs)	74	75	.497	13	Marty Pevey	408,556	5,447	Never
Louisville Bats (Reds)	71	79	.473	16.5	Pat Kelly	331,629	4,421	2001
Columbus Clippers (Guardians)	64	81	.441	21	Andy Tracy	513,085	7,226	2019
Gwinnett Stripers (Braves)	63	87	.420	24.5	Kanekoa Texeira	191,271	2,550	Never
Omaha Storm Chasers (Royals)	62	86	.419	24.5	Mike Jirschele	273,200	3,742	2024
St. Paul Saints (Twins)	62	86	.419	24.5	Toby Gardenhire	420,428	5,605	Never

* Pacific Coast League title won prior to 2021 minor league realignment

International League divisions do not determine the playoff field. The team with the best first-half record plays the best second-half team in the finals.
Playoffs: Jacksonville defeated Scranton/W-B 2-1. Jacksonville defeated Las Vegas in Triple-A National Championship Game.

INTERNATIONAL LEAGUE | STATISTICS

CLUB BATTING

	AVG	G	AB	R	H	2B	3B	HR	RBI	BB	SO	SB	OBP	SLG
Memphis Redbirds	.267	148	4957	816	1323	270	30	143	757	616	1109	174	.352	.420
Lehigh Valley IronPigs	.265	148	4877	837	1291	233	17	151	777	690	1173	236	.363	.412
Iowa Cubs	.263	149	4956	788	1304	291	24	164	741	667	1273	149	.357	.431
Scranton/W-B RailRiders	.262	147	4867	803	1277	248	25	176	754	606	1226	203	.349	.432
Rochester Red Wings	.259	147	4938	744	1278	216	27	161	695	562	1326	228	.340	.411
Louisville Bats	.257	150	4967	760	1278	276	25	158	713	548	1264	127	.338	.418
Indianapolis Indians	.257	149	4913	709	1264	240	33	121	663	546	1238	184	.337	.393
Charlotte Knights	.253	150	4988	764	1262	243	25	199	718	557	1398	125	.335	.431
Worcester Red Sox	.252	149	4868	753	1229	261	22	169	705	624	1387	122	.343	.419
Toledo Mud Hens	.251	150	4954	796	1243	270	47	155	753	724	1456	165	.353	.418
Norfolk Tides	.250	147	4761	719	1189	211	19	184	678	620	1309	129	.341	.418
Nashville Sounds	.249	148	4828	748	1203	233	31	134	688	623	1379	315	.342	.394
Omaha Storm Chasers	.249	148	4921	759	1225	259	26	199	714	587	1373	167	.334	.433
Durham Bulls	.246	149	4853	714	1196	239	22	178	667	578	1334	140	.332	.415
Syracuse Mets	.245	150	4852	735	1191	217	22	170	681	565	1170	96	.332	.404
St. Paul Saints	.245	148	4793	693	1174	229	18	170	654	654	1374	123	.345	.407
Buffalo Bisons	.243	146	4702	642	1143	246	12	128	596	621	1250	97	.340	.382
Jacksonville Jumbo Shrimp	.243	150	4847	693	1178	226	30	162	653	575	1329	304	.330	.402
Columbus Clippers	.238	145	4739	670	1130	255	32	156	629	590	1397	129	.327	.405
Gwinnett Stripers	.225	150	4736	512	1066	179	19	111	473	501	1161	126	.304	.341

CLUB PITCHING

	ERA	G	CG	SHO	SV	IP	H	R	ER	HR	BB	SO	AVG
Jacksonville Jumbo Shrimp	3.73	150	1	0	44	1304	1098	607	540	140	570	1344	.228
Durham Bulls	3.82	149	1	0	31	1285	1105	596	545	174	490	1422	.231
Nashville Sounds	3.91	148	0	0	39	1286	1145	627	558	123	520	1277	.236
Gwinnett Stripers	4.09	150	2	0	35	1277	1164	654	580	121	535	1289	.242
Toledo Mud Hens	4.17	150	0	0	32	1313	1214	673	609	138	558	1376	.244
Scranton/W-B RailRiders	4.22	147	1	0	38	1273	1131	661	597	138	585	1294	.237
Indianapolis Indians	4.41	149	0	0	44	1288	1179	675	631	136	594	1329	.242
Iowa Cubs	4.63	149	0	0	35	1286	1187	738	662	144	640	1438	.244
Syracuse Mets	4.64	150	0	0	37	1272	1179	729	656	177	574	1330	.244
Worcester Red Sox	4.69	149	0	0	35	1267	1215	728	660	163	648	1403	.249
Memphis Redbirds	4.69	148	1	0	29	1285	1229	734	670	164	618	1268	.252
Columbus Clippers	4.73	145	0	0	32	1255	1191	711	660	176	667	1315	.251
Buffalo Bisons	4.79	146	0	0	28	1241	1236	762	661	157	609	1252	.258
Louisville Bats	4.82	150	2	1	29	1284	1287	761	687	187	571	1133	.260
Lehigh Valley IronPigs	4.96	148	0	0	30	1278	1281	770	705	182	631	1218	.260
Norfolk Tides	5.06	147	1	0	26	1246	1243	784	700	143	675	1253	.260
St. Paul Saints	5.38	148	0	0	31	1255	1308	822	750	145	697	1381	.268
Charlotte Knights	5.43	150	1	1	31	1292	1308	864	780	195	680	1229	.264
Omaha Storm Chasers	5.50	148	1	1	27	1281	1354	861	783	168	647	1304	.269
Rochester Red Wings	5.77	147	0	0	18	1261	1360	899	808	185	656	1191	.275

CLUB FIELDING

	PCT	PO	A	E	DP
Columbus	.985	3764	1178	75	116
Indianapolis	.984	3865	1165	82	114
Louisville	.984	3851	1294	86	128
Durham	.983	3856	1088	83	109
Lehigh Valley	.983	3834	1242	89	124
Toledo	.981	3940	1312	99	109
St. Paul	.981	3765	1180	95	117
Nashville	.981	3857	1208	98	92
Gwinnett	.980	3832	1229	101	119
Memphis	.980	3854	1262	103	125
Iowa	.980	3859	1199	102	108
Omaha	.980	3843	1284	105	116
Syracuse	.979	3815	1192	106	105
Worcester	.979	3801	1169	107	112
Charlotte	.978	3877	1271	114	119
Scranton/W-B	.978	3818	1303	115	113
Rochester	.977	3784	1245	118	124
Jacksonville	.976	3912	1239	126	117
Norfolk	.974	3738	1158	131	130
Buffalo	.974	3723	1215	134	86

INDIVIDUAL BATTING

Batter, Club	AVG	G	AB	R	H	2B	3B	HR	RBI	BB	SO	SB
Justin Crawford, Lehigh Valley	.334	112	440	88	147	23	4	7	47	58	91	46
Nick Solak, Indianapolis	.332	111	419	76	139	23	1	14	73	48	66	10
Bryan Torres, Memphis	.328	104	332	58	109	16	1	9	51	70	57	26
Moises Ballesteros, Iowa	.316	114	446	62	141	29	1	13	76	49	67	5
Francisco Urbaez, Louisville	.314	97	360	58	113	32	5	4	50	38	40	5
Jonathon Long, Iowa	.305	140	514	86	157	23	3	20	91	79	116	2
Dylan Beavers, Norfolk	.304	94	342	78	104	14	2	18	51	68	76	23
Rece Hinds, Louisville	.302	107	397	79	118	26	2	24	83	33	113	21
Corey Julks, Charlotte	.300	116	436	77	131	30	1	15	58	48	99	18
Cesar Prieto, Memphis	.300	121	460	79	138	35	4	9	71	39	70	12
Tim Elko, Charlotte	.292	96	373	64	109	19	0	26	70	34	123	2

INDIVIDUAL PITCHING

Pitcher, Club	W	L	ERA	G	GS	CG	SV	IP	H	R	ER	BB	SO
Curtis Taylor, Memphis	10	4	3.21	31	24	1	1	137	112	55	49	51	118
Aaron Wilkerson, Louisv/Memphis	7	3	3.89	29	29	0	0	153	135	67	66	30	118
Logan Workman, Durham	9	7	4.02	29	28	1	0	152	138	70	68	45	152
Connor Noland, Iowa	9	6	4.07	27	22	0	0	133	133	69	60	55	115
Andrew Alvarez, Rochester	3	7	4.10	25	25	0	0	123	114	74	56	52	114
Bruce Zimmermann, Nashville	10	7	4.11	28	21	0	2	138	140	69	63	30	109
Ryan Webb, Columbus	8	7	4.15	28	21	0	0	121	100	61	56	61	119
Brandon Sproat, Syracuse	8	6	4.24	26	25	0	0	121	97	62	57	53	113
Alan Rangel, Lehigh Valley	5	5	4.55	25	25	0	0	125	122	67	63	40	131
Cameron Weston, Norfolk	5	9	4.59	29	26	0	0	135	130	76	69	71	133

DEPARTMENT LEADERS

BATTING
OBP	Bryan Torres, Memphis	.441
SLG	Jose Rojas, Scranton/WB	.599
OPS	Jose Rojas, Scranton/WB	.978
Runs	Justin Crawford, Lehigh Valley	88
Hits	Jonathon Long, Iowa	157
TB	Jose Rojas, Scranton/WB	267
XBH	Jose Rojas, Scranton/WB	71
2B	Joey Meneses, Syracuse	35
2B	Jose Rojas, Scranton/WB	35
2B	Cesar Prieto, Memphis	35
3B	Hao-Yu Lee, Toledo	8
HR	Jose Rojas, Scranton/WB	32
RBI	Jose Rojas, Scranton/WB	105
SAC	Terrin Vavra, Norfolk	8
BB	Gabriel Rincones, Lehigh Valley	80
HBP	Otto Kemp, Lehigh Valley	19
SO	Edwin Rios, Louisville	180
SB	Jared Oliva, Nashville	57
CS	Cesar Prieto, Memphis	14

FIELDING
C PCT	Eric Yang, Louisville	1
PO	Kody Huff, Columbus	758
A	Jimmy Crooks, Memphis	52
E	Joe Mack, Jacksonville	10
DP	Joe Mack, Jacksonville	9
CS	Jimmy Crooks, Memphis	30
SB	Moises Ballesteros, Iowa	92
PB	Jimmy Crooks, Memphis	12
1B PCT	Jonathon Long, Iowa	.994
PO	T.J. Rumfield, Scranton/WB	939
A	T.J. Rumfield, Scranton/WB	73
E	T.J. Rumfield, Scranton/WB	9
DP	T.J. Rumfield, Scranton/WB	81
2B PCT	No qualifiers	
PO	Francisco Urbaez, Louisville	129
A	Rafael Lantigua, Lehigh Valley	204
E	Francisco Urbaez, Louisville	13
DP	Francisco Urbaez, Louisville	46
3B PCT	No qualifiers	
PO	Bryan Ramos, Charlotte	71
A	Bryan Ramos, Charlotte	144
E	Bryan Ramos, Charlotte	16
DP	Will Wilson, Charlotte	16
SS PCT	Carson Williams, Durham	.968
PO	Rodolfo Castro, Lehigh Valley	159
A	Rodolfo Castro, Lehigh Valley	264
E	Rodolfo Castro, Lehigh Valley	20
DP	Rodolfo Castro, Lehigh Valley	65
OF PCT	Petey Halpin, Columbus	.996
PO	Tristan Peters, Durham	287
A	Petey Halpin, Columbus	19
E	Rece Hinds, Louisville	6
DP	10 tied	2

PITCHING
G	Oddanier Mosqueda, Memphis	55
GS	Logan Workman, Durham	28
GF	Wander Suero, Gwinnett	33
SV	Wander Suero, Gwinnett	12
W	Allan Winans, Scranton/WB	12
L	Chase Petty, Louisville	13
IP	Logan Workman, Durham	152
H	Chandler Champlain, Omaha	160
R	Chandler Champlain, Omaha	113
ER	Chandler Champlain, Omaha	104
SO	Logan Workman, Durham	152
SO/9	Alan Rangel, Lehigh Valley	9.46
BB/9	Bruce Zimmermann, Nashville	1.96
WP	Thaddeus Ward, Norfolk	14
Balks	Owen White, Charlotte	6
HR	Alan Rangel, Lehigh Valley	29
AVG	Brandon Sproat, Syracuse	.218

PACIFIC COAST LEAGUE TRIPLE-A

Awards selected by Major League Baseball

CHAMPION: By the time the championship series rolled around, the Las Vegas Aviators had a much different look. In the first half, stars like Nick Kurtz, Colby Thomas and Denzel Clarke powered the club, but a reshuffled roster rose to the occasion when it mattered most. The Aviators swept the Tacoma Rainiers, outscoring them 14–4 across two games.

MOST VALUABLE PLAYER: It's hard to find a hitter who showcased more power in 2025 than Ryan Ward. Ward has been a consistent performer in recent years, but the 27-year-old slugger found another gear for Triple-A Oklahoma City in 2025, blasting 36 home runs, driving in 122 RBIs and racking up 73 extra-base hits.

PITCHER OF THE YEAR: Giants lefthander Carson Whisenhunt entered the year with one of the most talked-about pitches in the minors—his devastating changeup—and he used it to excellent effect in the PCL. The ECU product finished the Triple-A season with a 9–5 record, a 4.43 ERA and 95 strikeouts over 107.2 innings for the Sacramento River Cats. His breakout stretch came in May, when he fanned 34 batters across 38.2 innings, setting the tone for a strong campaign that earned him an MLB callup on July 28.

TOP MLB PROSPECT: Cal Raleigh wasn't the only catcher generating excitement for the Mariners in 2025. Harry Ford, the Mariners' 2021 first-round pick, delivered a breakout campaign, slashing .283/.408/.868 while setting career highs in home runs (16) and RBIs (74). His stellar performance earned him a September callup, and he made his MLB debut on Sept. 5, capping the year as a little-used member of Seattle's playoff roster.

MANAGER OF THE YEAR: Veteran manager Fran Riordan led Las Vegas to an 83-67 record and the league title.

Whisenhunt

PACIFIC COAST LEAGUE ALL-STARS

Pos	Player	Team	AVG	OPS	HR
C	Luis Campusano	El Paso	.336	1.036	25
1B	Tyler Locklear	Tacoma	.316	.943	19
2B	Adael Amador	Albuquerque	.303	.883	11
3B	Cody Freeman	Round Rock	.336	.931	19
SS	Leo Rivas	Tacoma	.318	.978	10
OF	Yonathan Perlaza	El Paso	.307	.901	19
OF	Carlos Cortes	Las Vegas	.322	1.017	17
OF	Esteury Ruiz	Las Vegas/Okla	.304	.923	16
DH	Ryan Ward	Okla. City	.290	.937	36
UT	Jordan Lawlar	Reno	.313	.910	11

Pos	Pitcher	Team	G	ERA	SO
SP	Jhonathan Díaz	Tacoma	27	4.15	116
SP	Carson Seymour	Sacramento	16	3.86	90
SP	Carson Whisenhunt	Sacramento	21	4.43	95
SP	Victor Mederos	Salt Lake	16	3.39	71
RP	Ben Bowden	Las Vegas	31	1.36	41
RP	Nick Hernandez	Sugar Land	46	4.64	39

OVERALL STANDINGS

East Division	W	L	PCT	GB	Manager	Attendance	Avg	Last Title
Oklahoma City Dodgers (Dodgers)	84	66	.560	—	Travis Barbary	395,026	5,267	2023
El Paso Chihuahuas (Padres)	81	68	.544	2.5	Pete Zamora	472,125	6,380	2016
Round Rock Express (Rangers)	77	73	.513	7	Doug Davis	354,867	4,731	Never
Sugar Land Space Cowboys (Astros)	73	76	.490	10.5	Mickey Storey	270,571	3,607	2024
Albuquerque Isotopes (Rockies)	62	87	.416	21.5	Pedro Lopez	493,850	6,673	1994

West Division	W	L	PCT	GB	Manager	Attendance	Avg	Last Title
Tacoma Rainiers (Mariners)	86	64	.573	—	John Russell	406,727	5,423	2021
Las Vegas Aviators (Athletics)	83	67	.553	3	Fran Riordan	491,881	6,558	2025
Sacramento River Cats (Giants)	77	73	.513	9	Dave Brundage	327,047	4,360	2019
Salt Lake Bees (Angels)	65	84	.436	20.5	Keith Johnson	395,534	5,273	1979
Reno Aces (D-backs)	63	87	.420	23	Jeff Gardner	352,375	4,698	2022

Pacific Coast League divisions do not determine the playoff field. The team with the best first-half record plays the best second-half team in the finals.
Playoffs: Las Vegas defeated Tacoma 2-0. Jacksonville defeated Las Vegas in the Triple-A championship.

PACIFIC COAST LEAGUE | STATISTICS

CLUB BATTING

	AVG	G	AB	R	H	2B	3B	HR	RBI	BB	SO	SB	OBP	SLG
Las Vegas Aviators	.288	150	5268	978	1519	304	34	190	931	702	1275	181	.378	.467
Albuquerque Isotopes	.285	149	5145	895	1465	291	63	199	838	576	1237	154	.364	.482
Reno Aces	.283	150	5304	924	1503	330	45	174	871	651	1291	97	.366	.461
El Paso Chihuahuas	.283	149	5103	959	1446	319	36	160	904	699	1166	184	.375	.454
Tacoma Rainiers	.283	150	5141	944	1455	275	28	160	885	704	1084	236	.375	.441
Oklahoma City Comets	.276	150	5178	936	1429	303	44	188	871	747	1321	194	.369	.460
Round Rock Express	.262	150	5069	824	1326	266	27	172	772	664	1214	172	.352	.427
Salt Lake Bees	.259	149	5067	811	1314	243	46	165	758	617	1510	159	.347	.423
Sacramento River Cats	.250	150	5062	757	1266	259	25	154	724	644	1370	112	.340	.402
Sugar Land Space Cowboys	.231	149	4834	698	1116	243	27	171	657	689	1408	152	.336	.398

CLUB PITCHING

	ERA	G	CG	SHO	SV	IP	H	R	ER	HR	BB	SO	AVG
Sacramento River Cats	4.96	150	0	0	31	1324	1289	804	730	169	634	1393	.255
Round Rock Express	4.98	150	0	0	29	1319	1345	816	730	182	626	1325	.265
Sugar Land Space Cowboys	4.99	149	0	0	38	1293	1215	768	717	154	715	1270	.248
Tacoma Rainiers	5.03	150	1	0	33	1325	1442	811	740	160	515	1197	.277
Las Vegas Aviators	5.18	150	1	1	36	1326	1345	845	763	191	651	1355	.263
Oklahoma City Comets	5.28	150	0	0	39	1330	1288	830	780	144	782	1408	.255
El Paso Chihuahuas	5.69	149	0	0	38	1312	1441	920	829	164	696	1237	.279
Albuquerque Isotopes	5.99	149	2	1	24	1287	1476	956	856	185	674	1168	.288
Salt Lake Bees	6.13	149	0	0	32	1303	1516	959	887	201	638	1210	.290
Reno Aces	6.32	150	0	0	19	1323	1512	1016	929	203	720	1260	.287

CLUB FIELDING

	PCT	PO	A	E	DP
Sugar Land	.982	3879	1207	91	120
Oklahoma City	.981	3990	1262	99	131
Round Rock	.981	3957	1306	104	134
Las Vegas	.981	3977	1359	106	128
Salt Lake	.979	3910	1349	111	134
Tacoma	.979	3974	1497	119	144
Reno Aces	.978	3969	1335	120	151
El Paso	.977	3935	1406	128	134
Sacramento	.975	3972	1345	134	145
Albuquerque	.974	3860	1380	139	149

INDIVIDUAL BATTING

Batter, Club	AVG	G	AB	R	H	2B	3B	HR	RBI	BB	SO	SB
Cody Freeman, Round Rock	.336	97	384	75	129	25	0	19	71	32	37	8
Luis Campusano, El Paso	.336	105	393	83	132	25	1	25	95	72	82	2
Rhylan Thomas, Tacoma	.325	134	547	105	178	24	1	7	78	46	32	35
Tristin English, Reno	.325	93	385	55	125	31	0	14	77	21	62	0
Tyler Locklear, Tacoma	.316	98	373	70	118	25	1	19	82	47	95	18
Nate Mondou, El Paso	.308	130	467	69	144	27	4	6	74	65	79	8
Yonathan Perlaza, El Paso	.307	138	541	106	166	49	2	19	113	74	125	15
Darell Hernaiz, Las Vegas	.305	96	387	67	118	28	3	4	50	46	51	12
Esteury Ruiz, LV/Okla. City	.304	106	411	97	125	25	6	16	61	64	89	63
Sterlin Thompson, Albuquerque	.296	120	439	82	130	28	8	18	66	53	107	12

INDIVIDUAL PITCHING

Pitcher, Club	W	L	ERA	G	GS	CG	SV	IP	H	R	ER	BB	SO
Jhonathan Díaz, Tacoma	11	6	4.15	27	26	0	0	139	159	68	64	24	116
Blas Castaño, Tacoma	8	6	5.19	29	24	0	0	127	125	76	73	51	97
Trevor McDonald, Sacramento	9	9	5.31	29	24	0	0	142	144	98	84	62	144
Tyler Ivey, Sugar Land	4	10	5.83	27	25	0	0	122	134	86	79	66	102
Dakota Hudson, Salt Lake	8	7	6.68	28	24	0	0	136	193	112	101	51	89

DEPARTMENT LEADERS

BATTING
OBP	Luis Campusano, El Paso	.441
SLG	Luis Campusano, El Paso	.595
OPS	Luis Campusano, El Paso	1.036
Runs	Samad Taylor, Tacoma	124
Hits	Rhylan Thomas, Tacoma	178
TB	Ryan Ward, Oklahoma City	315
XBH	Ryan Ward, Oklahoma City	73
2B	Yonathan Perlaza, El Paso	49
3B	Sam Hilliard, Albuquerque	12
HR	Ryan Ward, Oklahoma City	36
RBI	Ryan Ward, Oklahoma City	122
SAC	Samad Taylor, Tacoma	17
BB	Austin Gauthier, Oklahoma City	93
HBP	Tim Locastro, El Paso	19
SO	Marco Luciano, Sacramento	170
SB	Esteury Ruiz, Oklahoma City	62
CS	Esteury Ruiz, Oklahoma City	11
CS	Brice Matthews, Sugar Land	11

FIELDING
C PCT	Daniel Susac, Las Vegas	.990
PO	Daniel Susac, Las Vegas	721
A	Daniel Susac, Las Vegas	40
E	Harry Ford, Tacoma	11
DP	2 tied	5
CS	Daniel Susac, Las Vegas	24
SB	Chuckie Robinson, Oklahoma City	78
PB	Rodolfo Duran, El Paso	8
1B PCT	No qualifiers	
PO	Tyler Locklear, Tacoma	740
A	Tyler Locklear, Tacoma	54
E	Luis Castro, Sugar Land	6
DP	Tyler Locklear, Tacoma	83
2B PCT	Samad Taylor, Tacoma	.978
PO	Samad Taylor, Tacoma	182
A	Samad Taylor, Tacoma	270
E	Nate Mondou, El Paso	10
DP	Samad Taylor, Tacoma	73
3B PCT	No qualifiers	
PO	Cody Freeman, Round Rock	62
A	Mike Brosseau, Round Rock	131
E	Austin Shenton, Tacoma	13
DP	Cody Freeman, Round Rock	20
SS PCT	Sergio Alcantara, Sac./Reno	.967
PO	Darell Hernaiz, Las Vegas	106
A	Darell Hernaiz, Las Vegas	228
E	Mason McCoy, Las Vegas	14
DP	Sergio Alcantara, Sac./Reno	61
OF PCT	Grant McCray, Sacramento	.981
PO	Kenedy Corona, Sugar Land	274
A	A.J. Vukovich, Reno	10
E	Justin Dean, Oklahoma City	6
DP	3 tied	2

PITCHING
G	Hagen Danner, Tacoma	54
GS	Jhonathan Díaz, Tacoma	26
GF	Ryan Watson, Sacramento	33
SV	Jack Little, Oklahoma City	13
W	Jhonathan Díaz, Tacoma	11
W	Jack Cushing, Las Vegas	11
L	Three tied	10
IP	Trevor McDonald, Sacramento	142
H	Dakota Hudson, Salt Lake	193
R	Dakota Hudson, Salt Lake	112
ER	Dakota Hudson, Salt Lake	101
SO	Trevor McDonald, Sacramento	144
SO/9	Trevor McDonald, Sacramento	9.11
BB/9	Jhonathan Díaz, Tacoma	1.56
WP	Bobby Miller, Oklahoma City	13
Balks	Chase Silseth, Salt Lake	5
HR	Mason Albright, Albuquerque	28
AVG	Blas Castano, Tacoma	.263

EASTERN LEAGUE — DOUBLE-A

Awards selected by Major League Baseball

CHAMPION: Binghamton captured its fourth Eastern League championship in franchise history by defeating the Erie SeaWolves in a decisive Game Three of the title series, earning its first crown since 2014.

MOST VALUABLE PLAYER: Felix Reyes was nearly untouchable at the plate this season, asserting his dominance in the Eastern League. The Phillies prospect ed the league in batting by 29 points with a .335 average and topped the circuit in slugging (.572), OPS (.937), wRC+ (160) and doubles (34). Reyes also set career highs with 16 home runs and 13 stolen bases, showcasing his blend of power and speed. He earned a promotion to Triple-A in the final week of the season.

PITCHER OF THE YEAR: Jonah Tong's over-the-top delivery is impossible to overlook, and his results this season were equally striking. The right-hander struck out 162 batters over 102 innings with Binghamton and distinguished himself as the only pitcher in the league with at least 100 innings to post both an ERA under 2.00 (1.59) and a WHIP below 1.00 (0.92). He was promoted to Triple-A and made his way to the majors with the Mets.

TOP MLB PROSPECT: After an injury-plagued 2024, Jett Williams made a resounding statement this season with Binghamton. The dynamic outfielder excelled at the plate, showcasing a potent combination of power and speed with 10 home runs, five triples and 29 doubles, while maintaining an impressive .390 on-base percentage. Williams' impact wasn't limited to hitting—he also swiped 32 bases.

MANAGER OF THE YEAR: In his fourth season with Binghamton, Reid Brignac led a talented team to a 90-46, the second-best record in MiLB in 2025.

Williams

EASTERN LEAGUE ALL-STARS

Pos	Player	Team	AVG	OPS	HR
C	Rafael Flores	Somerset	.287	.842	15
1B	Ryan Clifford	Binghamton	.243	.848	24
2B	Max Anderson	Erie	.306	.857	14
3B	Carlos Mendoza	Erie	.279	.783	5
SS	Aidan Miller	Reading	.259	.809	13
OF	Felix Reyes	Reading	.335	.937	15
OF	Phillip Glasser	Harrisburg	.293	.770	6
OF	Hendry Mendez	Reading	.290	.808	8
DH	Cooper Ingle	Akron	.273	.832	9
UT	Jett Williams	Binghamton	.281	.867	10
Pos	Pitcher	Team	G	ERA	SO
SP	Jonah Tong	Binghamton	20	1.59	162
SP	Jack Wenninger	Binghamton	26	2.92	147
SP	Connelly Early	Portland	15	2.51	96
SP	Joander Suarez	Binghamton	20	3.05	84
RP	Wilkin Ramos	Altoona	35	1.45	53
RP	Douglas Orellana	Binghamton	25	1.64	46

OVERALL STANDINGS

Northeast Division	W	L	PCT	GB	Manager	Attendance	Avg	Last Title
Binghamton (Mets)	90	46	.662	—	Reid Brignac	120,628	1,773	2025
Somerset (Yankees)	73	65	.529	18	Raul Dominguez	348,758	5,054	2022
Hartford (Rockies)	69	68	.504	21.5	Bobby Meacham	389,496	5,644	Never
Portland (Red Sox)	64	71	.474	25.5	Chad Epperson	366,442	5,469	2006
New Hampshire (Blue Jays)	56	81	.409	34.5	Brent Lavallee/Cesar Martin	205,102	3,016	2018
Reading (Phillies)	55	81	.404	35	Al Pedrique	396,455	5,745	2001
Southwest Division	W	L	PCT	GB	Manager	Attendance	Avg	Last Title
Erie (Tigers)	84	54	.609	—	Andrew Graham	196,011	2,840	2024
Akron (Guardians)	77	60	.562	6.5	Greg DiCenzo	280,841	4,070	2021
Altoona (Pirates)	69	68	.504	14.5	Andy Fox	293,487	4,315	2017
Harrisburg (Nationals)	68	70	.493	16	Delino DeShields	258,972	3,753	1999
Chesapeake (Orioles)	59	77	.434	24	Roberto Mercado	202,741	2,938	2015
Richmond (Giants)	56	79	.415	26.5	Dennis Pelfrey	446,679	6,568	Never

Southwest: Erie defeated Altoona 2-1. **Northeast:** Binghamton defeated Somerset 2-0. **Championship Series:** Binghamton defeated Erie 2-1.

EASTERN LEAGUE | STATISTICS

CLUB BATTING

	AVG	G	AB	R	H	2B	3B	HR	RBI	BB	SO	SB	OBP	SLG
Erie SeaWolves	.258	138	4585	711	1183	261	32	130	653	574	1008	70	.345	.414
Binghamton R.Ponies	.249	137	4331	612	1077	238	21	109	559	534	1194	212	.336	.389
Reading Fightin Phils	.239	136	4417	602	1056	245	21	118	551	518	1138	169	.324	.384
Harrisburg Senators	.239	138	4500	572	1075	201	38	86	518	444	1198	151	.313	.358
Akron RubberDucks	.230	138	4427	625	1020	233	43	90	580	588	1235	162	.326	.363
Hartford Yard Goats	.229	137	4373	577	1002	186	21	97	520	473	1256	198	.313	.348
Richmond Flying Squirrels	.228	136	4358	501	994	178	19	88	453	484	1029	125	.313	.338
Somerset Patriots	.228	138	4411	600	1005	228	30	129	559	489	1377	167	.312	.381
Altoona Curve	.228	137	4316	548	983	169	30	90	494	532	1138	154	.320	.343
Portland Sea Dogs	.223	135	4362	549	971	189	23	95	499	479	1193	170	.305	.342
N. Hampshire Fisher Cats	.215	137	4297	501	925	189	20	108	441	473	1360	138	.299	.344
Chesapeake Baysox	.212	137	4323	494	915	196	24	99	454	516	1280	183	.304	.337

CLUB PITCHING

	ERA	G	CG	SHO	SV	IP	H	R	ER	HR	BB	SO	AVG
Binghamton R. Ponies	2.97	137	2	1	44	1163	877	455	384	87	413	1435	.207
Erie SeaWolves	3.57	138	1	0	33	1205	1012	534	478	100	436	1166	.225
Akron RubberDucks	3.63	138	0	0	37	1205	992	553	486	99	508	1129	.224
Chesapeake Baysox	3.66	137	2	2	29	1187	959	577	483	96	542	1280	.219
Portland Sea Dogs	3.67	135	1	1	30	1178	976	552	480	85	551	1324	.226
Harrisburg Senators	3.75	138	2	0	33	1193	1008	564	497	121	538	1043	.231
Altoona Curve	3.85	137	0	0	35	1177	1016	564	503	88	474	1125	.231
Somerset Patriots	3.86	138	1	0	33	1188	986	563	509	89	575	1259	.225
N. Hampshire Fisher Cats	4.20	137	3	2	27	1147	1052	624	536	115	493	1123	.242
Richmond Flying Squirrels	4.21	136	1	0	32	1172	1142	600	548	105	563	1137	.258
Hartford Yard Goats	4.27	137	0	0	40	1180	1083	613	560	120	496	1166	.245
Reading Fightin Phils	4.61	138	0	0	30	1168	1103	693	598	134	515	1219	.247

CLUB FIELDING

	PCT	PO	A	E	DP		PCT	PO	A	E	DP
Hartford	.982	3541	1129	85	87	Altoona	.978	3532	1077	104	86
Somerset	.981	3563	1115	92	87	Akron	.977	3588	1058	110	95
Harrisburg	.981	3579	1241	95	121	Binghamton	.975	3490	1049	115	104
Richmond	.980	3515	1225	95	132	New Hampshire	.973	3442	1108	126	89
Erie	.979	3615	1104	101	84	Reading	.973	3504	1061	129	86
Portland	.978	3535	1138	103	103	Chesapeake	.971	3534	1061	138	77

INDIVIDUAL BATTING

Batter, Club	AVG	G	AB	R	H	2B	3B	HR	RBI	BB	SO	SB
Felix Reyes, Reading	.335	95	367	62	123	34	4	15	65	18	61	13
Max Anderson, Erie	.306	90	369	54	113	25	2	14	65	28	59	2
Phillip Glasser, Harrisburg	.293	112	427	63	125	18	3	6	41	52	55	30
Justice Bigbie, Erie	.283	108	399	58	113	16	0	12	66	47	69	1
Jett Williams, Binghamton	.281	96	352	70	99	29	5	10	37	62	96	32
Cooper Ingle, Akron	.273	92	333	55	91	29	0	9	49	65	70	0
Nick Morabito, Binghamton	.273	118	436	63	119	27	2	6	59	47	115	49
Termarr Johnson, Altoona	.272	119	434	67	118	15	3	9	35	59	93	20
Allan Castro, Portland	.268	92	340	43	91	20	2	7	37	44	79	15
Victor Bericoto, Richmond	.267	93	344	43	92	15	3	12	49	43	92	2

INDIVIDUAL PITCHING

Pitcher, Club	W	L	ERA	G	GS	CG	SV	IP	H	R	ER	BB	SO
John Bertrand, Richmond	6	10	2.87	25	25	0	0	132	122	47	42	51	91
Jack Wenninger, Binghamton	12	6	2.92	26	26	1	0	136	114	53	44	42	147
Trenton Denholm, Akron	11	7	3.77	26	18	0	1	127	125	67	53	26	109
Jean Cabrera, Reading	6	9	3.81	26	26	0	0	137	107	62	58	61	127
Grant Rogers, New Hampshire	8	9	4.07	20	20	0	0	111	118	61	50	20	76
Wilber Dotel, Altoona	7	9	4.15	27	27	0	0	126	111	62	58	43	131
Garrett Burhenn, Erie	13	3	4.18	26	24	0	0	125	115	59	58	33	112
Charles King, Reading	8	6	4.38	25	23	0	0	123	138	65	60	37	105
Joe Whitman, Richmond	5	11	5.29	26	26	1	0	117	129	72	69	47	124

DEPARTMENT LEADERS

BATTING

OBP	Cooper Ingle, Akron	.391
SLG	Felix Reyes, Reading	.572
OPS	Felix Reyes, Reading	.937
Runs	Cole Carrigg, Hartford	81
Hits	Phillip Glasser, Harrisburg	125
TB	Felix Reyes, Reading	210
XBH	Felix Reyes, Reading	53
2B	Felix Reyes, Reading	34
3B	Carlos De La Cruz, Harrisburg	7
3B	Ben Malgeri, Erie	7
HR	Ryan Clifford, Binghamton	24
RBI	Dylan Jasso, Somerset	76
SAC	Diego Velasquez, Richmond	10
BB	Aidan Miller, Reading	73
HBP	Adam Retzbach, Chesapeake	14
HBP	Caden Rose, Portland	14
SO	Carlos De La Cruz, Harrisburg	155
SB	Aidan Miller, Reading	52
CS	Aidan Miller, Reading	143

FIELDING

C PCT	Adrian Sugastey, Richmond	.994
PO	Ronald Rosario, Portland	797
A	Adrian Sugastey, Richmond	76
E	Bryant Betancourt, Hartford	10
DP	Kevin Parada, Binghamton	9
CS	Adrian Sugastey, Richmond	50
SB	Rafael Flores, Somerset	108
PB	Jacob Sharp, New Hampshire	11
1B PCT	Tyler Hardman, Somerset	.995
PO	Tyler Hardman, Somerset	689
A	Joe Naranjo, Harrisburg	61
E	Joe Naranjo, Harrisburg	8
DP	Tyler Hardman, Somerset	61
2B PCT	Diego Velasquez, Richmond	.988
PO	Diego Velasquez, Richmond	225
A	Diego Velasquez, Richmond	281
E	Termarr Johnson, Altoona	15
DP	Diego Velasquez, Richmond	95
3B PCT	Cayden Wallace, Harrisburg	.972
PO	Cayden Wallace, Harrisburg	78
A	Cayden Wallace, Harrisburg	161
E	Charles McAdoo, New Hampshire	15
DP	Sabin Ceballos, Richmond	26
SS PCT	Aeverson Arteaga, Richmond	.980
PO	Aeverson Arteaga, Richmond	181
A	Aeverson Arteaga, Richmond	321
E	Aidan Miller, Reading	20
DP	Aeverson Arteaga, Richmond	81
OF PCT	Cole Carrigg, Hartford	.985
PO	Cole Carrigg, Hartford	267
A	Cole Carrigg, Hartford	18
E	Carlos De La Cruz, Harrisburg	6
DP	2 tied	5

PITCHING

G	Junior Santos, Harrisburg	54
GS	Wilber Dotel, Altoona	27
GF	Junior Santos, Harrisburg	38
SV	Junior Santos, Harrisburg	12
W	Garrett Burhenn, Erie	13
L	Manuel Mercedes, Richmond	13
IP	Jean Cabrera, Reading	137
H	Charles King, Reading	138
R	Manuel Mercedes, Richmond	74
ER	Jack Mahoney, Hartford	69
ER	Joe Whitman, Richmond	69
SO	Jonah Tong, Binghamton	162
SO/9	Jack Wenninger, Binghamton	9.75
BB/9	Grant Rogers, New Hampshire	1.63
WP	Gunner Mayer, Reading	12
WP	Jack Wenninger, Binghamton	12
Balks	Peter Van Loon, Chesapeake	5
HR	Hyun-il Choi, Harrisburg	20
AVG	Jean Cabrera, Reading	.214

SOUTHERN LEAGUE DOUBLE-A

Awards selected by Major League Baseball

Stewart

CHAMPION: In one of the most unconventional minor league championship series in recent memory, the Birmingham Barons rose above the chaos to capture their second consecutive league title. The dramatic series stretched across 19 hours and 40 minutes of real time due to multiple delays.

MOST VALUABLE PLAYER: First/third baseman Sal Stewart's rapid rise through the Reds' minor league system took off in Chattanooga this season, when he quickly established himself as one of the organization's most exciting prospects. Over the course of his time with the Lookouts, Stewart slashed .306/.377/.473, posting an .850 OPS while hitting 10 home runs and driving in 44 RBIs.

PITCHER OF THE YEAR: Righthander Ty Johnson quickly established himself as the league's most dominant starter. The Rays pitcher ranked first among pitchers with at least 100 innings with a 2.33 FIP and a 34.7% strikeout rate, while his 2.61 ERA was second-best. The 6-foot-6 righty recorded more strikeouts than innings pitched in 20 of 26 starts and surrendered more than three runs in just two outings all season.

TOP MLB PROSPECT: Stewart's combination of power, plate discipline and consistent contact at the plate made him a constant threat in the lineup, and his performance in Chattanooga served as a springboard to further success. After showing improved power with the Lookouts, Stewart was promoted to Triple-A on July 18, where he hit .315 with 10 home runs before being called up to the big league club on Sept. 1. He batted cleanup for the Reds in the postseason. He hit five home runs with a .255 batting average with a .838 OPS.

MANAGER OF THE YEAR: In his first season back after undergoing treatment for cancer, long-time Brewers MiLB manager Joe Ayrault led the Biloxi Shuckers to a 74-64 record. Biloxi was the first half South Division champions, although they were knocked out in the division finals by Montgomery.

SOUTHERN LEAGUE ALL-STARS

Pos	Player	Team	AVG	OPS	HR
C	Tatem Levins	Montgomery	.244	.788	7
1B	Luke Adams	Biloxi	.232	.859	11
2B	Pedro Ramirez	Knoxville	.280	.732	8
3B	Sal Stewart	Chattanooga	.306	.850	10
SS	Denzer Guzman	Rocket City	.242	.749	11
OF	Héctor Rodriguez	Chattanooga	.298	.838	12
OF	Kemp Alderman	Pensacola	.282	.784	15
OF	Homer Bush Jr	Montgomery	.301	.735	0
DH	Brock Wilken	Biloxi	.226	.876	18
UT	BJ Murray Jr	Knoxville	.242	.781	20
Pos	Pitcher	Team	G	ERA	SO
SP	Ty Johnson	Montgomery	26	2.61	149
SP	Ian Mejia	Columbus	24	2.62	106
SP	Shane Murphy	Birmingham	20	1.38	82
SP	Brody Hopkins	Montgomery	25	2.72	141

OVERALL STANDINGS

North Division	W	L	PCT	GB	Manager	Attendance	Avg	Last Title
Birmingham (White Sox)	81	57	.587	—	Guillermo Quiroz	225,745	3,271	2025
Chattanooga (Reds)	73	61	.545	6	Jose Moreno	191,309	2,943	2017
Knoxville (Cubs)	69	67	.507	11	Lance Rymel	289,007	4,250	2023
Rocket City (Angels)	45	92	.328	35.5	Andy Schatzley	275,423	3,991	Never
South Division	**W**	**L**	**PCT**	**GB**	**Manager**	**Attendance**	**Avg**	**Last Title**
Montgomery (Rays)	78	60	.565	—	Kevin Boles	159,802	2,315	2007
Biloxi (Brewers)	74	64	.536	4	Joe Ayrault	144,750	2,097	Never
Pensacola (Marlins)	69	69	.500	9	Nelson Prada	270,029	3,913	2022
Columbus (Braves)	58	77	.430	18.5	Cody Gabella	231,433	3,354	Never

North: Birmingham def. Chattanooga 2-1. **South:** Montgomery def. Biloxi 2-0. **Championship Series:** Birmingham def. Montgomery 2-1.

SOUTHERN LEAGUE | STATISTICS

CLUB BATTING

	AVG	G	AB	R	H	2B	3B	HR	RBI	BB	SO	SB	OBP	SLG
Birmingham Barons	.244	138	4457	553	1086	177	26	52	497	494	1054	196	.328	.330
Chattanooga Lookouts	.240	134	4220	578	1014	179	18	93	526	508	1198	113	.329	.357
Knoxville Smokies	.235	136	4358	567	1026	160	18	79	529	557	1232	179	.329	.335
Pensacola Blue Wahoos	.234	138	4430	559	1036	188	19	103	496	502	1118	201	.317	.355
Biloxi Shuckers	.231	138	4385	639	1013	197	21	111	589	620	1109	190	.336	.361
Montgomery Biscuits	.228	138	4362	565	996	165	26	91	519	557	1195	215	.321	.341
Columbus Clingstones	.219	135	4252	477	931	164	16	78	440	478	1197	190	.304	.320
Rocket City Trash Pandas	.203	137	4214	445	854	158	20	94	410	506	1303	127	.297	.317

CLUB PITCHING

	ERA	G	CG	SHO	SV	IP	H	R	ER	HR	BB	SO	AVG
Birmingham Barons	3.00	138	0	0	39	1211	920	452	404	74	544	1237	.212
Montgomery Biscuits	3.49	138	1	0	43	1190	980	527	462	94	484	1152	.226
Pensacola Blue Wahoos	3.50	138	1	0	31	1198	978	553	466	63	565	1308	.222
Knoxville Smokies	3.51	136	0	0	34	1173	953	518	457	79	531	1102	.224
Biloxi Shuckers	3.77	138	0	0	37	1186	1045	553	497	95	505	1175	.237
Columbus Clingstones	3.93	135	2	1	36	1159	978	572	506	109	505	1183	.227
Chattanooga Lookouts	4.07	134	2	1	32	1132	968	572	512	97	510	1065	.231
Rocket City Trash Pandas	4.26	137	3	0	22	1165	1134	637	552	90	578	1184	.256

CLUB FIELDING

	PCT	PO	A	E	DP		PCT	PO	A	E	DP
Birmingham	.985	3634	1163	71	117	Knoxville	.980	3520	1107	93	105
Montgomery	.983	3570	1122	83	94	Pensacola	.979	3594	1234	105	91
Biloxi	.982	3557	1193	85	101	Rocket City	.975	3495	1179	121	107
Chattanooga	.982	3397	1132	84	104	Columbus	.974	3478	1121	124	82

INDIVIDUAL BATTING

Batter, Club	AVG	G	AB	R	H	2B	3B	HR	RBI	BB	SO	SB
Homer Bush, Montgomery	.301	121	472	69	142	12	8	0	45	48	98	57
William Bergolla, Birmingham	.286	125	486	70	139	19	2	0	36	37	26	40
David McCabe, Columbus	.286	105	371	54	106	23	1	10	52	58	89	2
Edwin Arroyo, Chattanooga	.284	120	464	63	132	23	4	3	44	40	88	12
Kemp Alderman, Pensacola	.282	110	412	56	116	13	5	15	53	34	102	20
Pedro Ramirez, Knoxville	.280	129	500	70	140	21	4	8	73	46	85	28
Nelson Rada, Rocket City	.277	93	328	48	91	13	1	1	22	45	82	34
Rikuu Nishida, Birmingham	.273	115	403	72	110	8	3	0	31	75	69	40
Corey Joyce, Knoxville	.272	92	323	48	88	16	1	2	33	56	81	15
Caden Connor, Birmingham	.266	95	342	39	91	19	1	4	43	43	59	10

INDIVIDUAL PITCHING

Pitcher, Club	W	L	ERA	G	GS	CG	SV	IP	H	R	ER	BB	SO
Shane Murphy, Birmingham	9	4	1.38	20	18	0	0	111	77	20	17	15	82
Ty Johnson, Montgomery	7	6	2.61	26	20	0	0	110	66	36	32	38	149
Ian Mejia, Columbus	12	2	2.62	24	17	1	1	127	98	38	37	37	106
Brody Hopkins, Montgomery	5	7	2.72	25	25	1	0	116	85	48	35	60	141
Ty Cummings, Montgomery	7	4	3.34	26	19	0	0	116	114	54	43	37	86
Riley Gowens, Birmingham	7	6	3.34	27	27	0	0	132	108	52	49	49	151
Samuel Aldegheri, Rocket City	8	8	3.72	23	23	0	0	128	116	58	53	58	110
Alexander Cornielle, Biloxi	5	8	3.88	26	26	0	0	123	105	58	53	61	116
Lucas Braun, Columbus	5	5	3.99	24	23	0	0	131	110	64	58	35	134
Mitch Farris, Rocket City	3	8	4.27	23	22	1	0	116	115	64	55	55	142

DEPARTMENT LEADERS

BATTING
OBP	Tatem Levins, Montgomery	.405
SLG	Ruben Ibarra, Chattanooga	.470
OPS	Ruben Ibarra, Chattanooga	.818
Runs	Luis Lara, Biloxi	79
Hits	Homer Bush, Montgomery	142
TB	Pedro Ramirez, Knoxville	193
XBH	BJ Murray, Knoxville	38
XBH	Ruben Ibarra, Chattanooga	38
2B	Luis Lara, Biloxi	32
3B	Homer Bush, Montgomery	8
HR	Ruben Ibarra, Chattanooga	21
RBI	BJ Murray, Knoxville	89
SAC	William Bergolla, Birmingham	21
BB	Luis Lara, Biloxi	86
HBP	Luke Adams, Biloxi	21
SO	Jaylen Palmer, Knoxville	153
SB	Homer Bush, Montgomery	57
CS	Nelson Rada, Rocket City	12
CS	Homer Bush, Montgomery	12
CS	Rikuu Nishida, Birmingham	12

FIELDING
C PCT	Tatem Levins, Montgomery	.991
PO	Tatem Levins, Montgomery	738
A	Myles Emmerson, Rocket City	60
E	Adam Zebrowski, Columbus	21
DP	Casey Opitz, Knoxville	10
CS	Tatem Levins, Montgomery	40
SB	Adam Zebrowski, Columbus	115
PB	Adam Zebrowski, Columbus	11
1B PCT	Drew Compton, Columbus	.994
PO	Drew Compton, Columbus	727
A	Drew Compton, Columbus	59
E	Cam Collier, Chattanooga	6
DP	Will Simpson, Montgomery	60
2B PCT	No qualifiers	
PO	Mac McCroskey, Rocket City	102
A	Jheremy Vargas, Biloxi	164
E	Mac McCroskey, Rocket City	9
DP	Mac McCroskey, Rocket City	35
3B PCT	No qualifiers	
PO	Brayden Taylor, Montgomery	69
A	Brayden Taylor, Montgomery	110
E	Ben Gobbel, Rocket City	11
DP	2 tied	13
SS PCT	William Bergolla, Birmingham	.981
PO	Cal Conley, Columbus	143
A	William Bergolla, Birmingham	253
E	Edwin Arroyo, Chattanooga	17
DP	William Bergolla, Birmingham	59
OF PCT	Luis Lara, Biloxi	.994
PO	Luis Lara, Biloxi	309
A	Garrett Spain, Biloxi	13
E	Kemp Alderman, Pensacola	7
DP	Garrett Spain, Biloxi	4

PITCHING
G	Three tied	47
GS	Walbert Urena, Rocket City	27
GS	Riley Gowens, Birmingham	27
GF	Trevor Kuncl, Chattanooga	41
SV	Trevor Kuncl, Chattanooga	20
W	Ian Mejia, Columbus	12
L	George Klassen, Rocket City	12
IP	Walbert Urena, Rocket City	135
H	Samuel Aldegheri, Rocket City	116
R	Walbert Urena, Rocket City	73
ER	Walbert Urena, Rocket City	66
SO	Riley Gowens, Birmingham	151
SO/9	Ty Johnson, Montgomery	12.15
BB/9	Shane Murphy, Birmingham	1.22
WP	Keyshawn Askew, Montgomery	16
Balks	Ryan Cardona, Chattanooga	7
HR	Lucas Braun, Columbus	19
AVG	Ty Johnson, Montgomery	.174

TEXAS LEAGUE DOUBLE-A

Awards selected by Major League Baseball

CHAMPION: The Springfield Cardinals led the league in ERA (3.55), strikeouts (1,324) and opponents' batting average (.227), showcasing a pitching staff that was both deep and relentless. Their campaign reached its pinnacle in the championship series, winning back-to-back games over the Midland Rockhounds, including a commanding 13-1 victory. Springfield outscored Tulsa and Midland 26-11 in the postseason, capturing four of five playoff games.

MOST VALUABLE PLAYER: Springfield shortstop JJ Wetherholt capped his season with a .300/.425/.466 slash line, leading the Texas League in on-base percentage among qualifying hitters. The versatile infielder was smart on the basepaths, swiping 14 bases in 16 attempts and showcased excellent plate discipline, drawing 28 walks while striking out just 25, before earning a well-deserved promotion to Triple-A.

PITCHER OF THE YEAR: A Fresno State product, Ixan Henderson delivered a dominant season, posting a 2.59 ERA while allowing just five home runs—the second-fewest among qualified pitchers—and a 1.14 WHIP, also second in the league. The Springfield righty struck out 134 batters while issuing just 51 walks over 132 innings.

TOP MLB PROSPECT: Frisco shortstop Sebastian Walcott had a standout season, establishing career bests with 32 stolen bases and 13 home runs while improving his plate discipline. The 6-foot-4 Rangers prospect pairs exceptional arm strength with impressive raw power, solidifying his status as one of the most physically gifted and exciting prospects in the minor leagues.

MANAGER OF THE YEAR: Patrick Anderson, who has been with the Cardinals organization since 2020 and has coached professionally since 2013, guided Springfield to an outstanding 88-50 record. It was the best in the league by a significant 12-game margin.

Walcott

TEXAS LEAGUE ALL-STARS

Pos	Player	Team	AVG	OPS	HR
C	Carter Jensen	NW Arkansas	.292	.780	6
1B	Abimelec Ortiz	Frisco	.247	.787	16
2B	Tommy Troy	Amarillo	.286	.843	12
3B	LuJames Groover	Amarillo	.309	.833	12
SS	JJ Wetherholt	Springfield	.300	.891	7
OF	Victor Labrada	Arkansas	.295	.834	6
OF	Kala'i Rosario	Wichita	.256	.845	25
OF	Joshua Baez	Springfield	.271	.883	16
DH	Kyler Fedko	Wichita	.253	.869	20
UT	Kaelen Culpepper	Wichita	.285	.827	11
Pos	Pitcher	Team	G	ERA	SO
SP	Ixan Henderson	Springfield	25	2.59	134
SP	Mitch Bratt	Frisco/Amarillo	24	3.38	148
SP	Brycen Mautz	Springfield	25	2.98	134
SP	Henry Baez	S. Antonio/Midland	23	2.39	100
RP	Alimber Santa	Corpus Christi	31	1.26	63

OVERALL STANDINGS

North Division	W	L	PCT	GB	Manager	Attendance	Avg	Last Title
Springfield (Cardinals)	88	50	.638	—	Patrick Anderson	241,675	3,502	2025
Wichita (Twins)	76	62	.551	12	Brian Dinkelman	277,722	4,024	Never
Arkansas (Mariners)	69	69	.500	19	Ryan Scott	256,195	3,712	2024
NW Arkansas (Royals)	66	72	.478	22	Brooks Conrad	236,668	3,429	2021
Tulsa (Dodgers)	66	72	.478	22	Scott Hennessey	322,452	4,673	2018
South Division	**W**	**L**	**PCT**	**GB**	**Manager**	**Attendance**	**Avg**	**Last Title**
Frisco (Rangers)	73	63	.537	—	Carlos Cardoza	374,222	5,585	2022
Amarillo (D-backs)	71	67	.514	3	Javier Colina	319,646	4,632	2023
Midland (Athletics)	66	72	.478	8	Gregorio Petit	229,056	3,319	2017
San Antonio (Padres)	65	72	.474	8.5	Luke Montz	268,783	3,895	2013
Corpus Christi (Astros)	48	89	.350	25.5	Ricky Rivera	278,653	4,038	2006

North: Springfield defeated Tulsa 2-0. **South:** Midland defeated Amarillo 2-0. **Championship Series:** Springfield defeated Midland 2-1.

TEXAS LEAGUE | STATISTICS

CLUB BATTING

	AVG	G	AB	R	H	2B	3B	HR	RBI	BB	SO	SB	OBP	SLG
Amarillo Sod Poodles	.264	138	4718	721	1247	244	28	163	668	526	1211	103	.345	.432
Wichita Wind Surge	.256	138	4576	723	1173	227	24	171	673	613	1106	171	.351	.429
NW Arkansas Naturals	.254	138	4647	651	1181	216	34	95	590	549	1209	203	.338	.377
Springfield Cardinals	.249	138	4479	678	1117	187	14	118	600	540	1062	181	.339	.376
Arkansas Travelers	.241	138	4596	628	1106	208	29	93	566	507	1277	248	.325	.359
Midland RockHounds	.241	138	4558	638	1100	211	32	89	594	571	1204	144	.333	.360
Frisco RoughRiders	.240	136	4539	618	1090	190	26	109	563	525	1240	148	.323	.365
Tulsa Drillers	.235	138	4553	625	1071	170	23	99	565	584	1156	169	.328	.348
San Antonio Missions	.229	138	4441	527	1015	181	20	87	475	511	1187	134	.316	.317
Corpus Christi Hooks	.221	137	4483	546	991	212	22	101	500	536	1384	152	.313	.346

CLUB PITCHING

	ERA	G	CG	SHO	SV	IP	H	R	ER	HR	BB	SO	AVG
Springfield Cardinals	3.58	138	0	0	37	1202	1016	535	478	93	522	1324	.227
Midland RockHounds	3.77	138	0	0	28	1208	1095	580	506	91	504	1223	.241
Wichita Wind Surge	3.97	138	0	0	37	1198	1124	608	529	113	440	1137	.246
Arkansas Travelers	3.99	138	0	0	36	1217	1131	613	539	94	489	1078	.245
Frisco RoughRiders	4.09	136	1	0	41	1206	1092	603	548	106	488	1298	.239
San Antonio Missions	4.15	137	0	0	35	1202	1048	622	554	96	565	1255	.235
Corpus Christi Hooks	4.43	137	0	0	23	1191	1112	663	587	130	575	1167	.246
Tulsa Drillers	4.48	138	0	0	28	1209	1079	683	601	109	734	1266	.238
NW Arkansas Naturals	4.69	138	0	0	34	1216	1169	699	634	139	576	1171	.252
Amarillo Sod Poodles	4.99	138	0	0	33	1210	1225	749	671	154	569	1117	.262

CLUB FIELDING

	PCT	PO	A	E	DP		PCT	PO	A	E	DP
Frisco	.982	3619	1101	86	99	Northwest Arkansas	.979	3649	1186	106	93
Midland	.981	3623	1215	96	110	Amarillo	.977	3629	1158	115	113
Springfield	.980	3606	1092	98	103	Wichita	.976	3594	1093	116	102
San Antonio	.979	3605	1216	102	119	Corpus Christi	.972	3574	1123	136	108
Arkansas	.979	3651	1288	106	106	Tulsa	.970	3626	1154	147	107

INDIVIDUAL BATTING

Batter, Club	AVG	G	AB	R	H	2B	3B	HR	RBI	SO	SB
Gino Groover, Amarillo	.309	123	470	73	145	23	0	12	56	63	79	3
Manuel Pena, Amarillo	.288	106	437	68	126	27	3	14	52	24	105	2
Tommy Troy, Amarillo	.286	87	343	56	98	20	2	12	47	49	70	21
Colby Halter, Midland	.280	89	321	54	90	19	6	5	47	50	102	22
Ramon Mendoza, Springfield	.275	105	334	59	92	13	2	14	62	60	80	3
Gavin Conticello, Amarillo	.275	121	444	67	122	27	4	12	67	59	110	4
Jose Fernandez, Amarillo	.272	122	471	68	128	27	4	17	80	32	104	12
Marcos Castanon, San Antonio	.269	106	390	47	105	23	1	12	57	33	94	4
Dakota Harris, Springfield	.264	117	435	67	115	17	0	10	49	26	82	23
Ricardo Olivar, Wichita	.264	93	352	56	93	13	0	13	59	49	74	13

INDIVIDUAL PITCHING

Pitcher, Club	W	L	ERA	G	GS	CG	SV	IP	H	R	ER	BB	SO
Ixan Henderson, Springfield	9	7	2.59	25	25	0	0	132	99	41	38	51	134
Brycen Mautz, Springfield	8	3	2.98	25	25	0	0	115	94	39	38	33	134
Adam Seminaris, Arkansas	7	7	3.02	24	22	0	0	125	116	47	42	36	105
Trey Dombroski, Corpus Christi	9	5	3.61	26	17	0	0	112	91	49	45	49	116
Jackson Ferris, Tulsa	10	7	3.86	26	24	0	0	126	118	59	54	66	135
Pete Hansen, Springfield	8	5	3.93	26	26	0	0	137	137	71	60	37	123
Chen Zhong-Ao Zhuang, Midland	6	11	4.08	28	26	0	0	146	151	79	66	35	145
Chris Campos, Tulsa	8	6	4.19	26	23	0	1	127	120	66	59	72	111
Dylan File, Arkansas	8	4	4.74	27	23	0	0	125	129	67	66	35	98
Jose Cabrera, Amarillo	9	6	4.92	26	26	0	0	135	153	79	74	50	118

DEPARTMENT LEADERS

BATTING
OBP	Gino Groover, Amarillo	.399
SLG	Kyler Fedko, Wichita	.494
OPS	Kyler Fedko, Wichita	.869
Runs	Kala'i Rosario, Wichita	92
Hits	Gino Groover, Amarillo	145
TB	Kala'i Rosario, Wichita	242
XBH	Kala'i Rosario, Wichita	60
2B	Kala'i Rosario, Wichita	30
3B	Brett Squires, NW Arkansas	8
HR	Kala'i Rosario, Wichita	25
RBI	Kala'i Rosario, Wichita	83
SAC	Javier Vaz, NW Arkansas	11
BB	Taylor Young, Tulsa	80
HBP	Noah Mendlinger, Springfield	14
HBP	Bill Knight, Arkansas	14
SO	Chris Newell, Tulsa	168
SB	Taylor Young, Tulsa	44
CS	Bill Knight, Arkansas	10
CS	Caleb Cali, Arkansas	10
CS	Sebastian Walcott, Frisco	10

FIELDING
C PCT	Ian Moller, Frisco	.998
PO	Leonardo Bernal, Springfield	839
A	Brandon Valenzuela, San Antonio	50
E	John Garcia, Corpus Christi	13
DP	4 tied	5
CS	Nick Raposo, Arkansas	31
SB	Griffin Lockwood-Powell, Tulsa	164
PB	Anthony Vilar, San Antonio	13
1B PCT	Romeo Sanabria, San Antonio	.993
PO	Romeo Sanabria, San Antonio	795
A	Romeo Sanabria, San Antonio	70
E	John Rhodes, Tulsa	11
DP	Romeo Sanabria, San Antonio	83
2B PCT	Marcos Castanon, San Antonio	1
PO	Tommy Troy, Amarillo	156
A	Tommy Troy, Amarillo	195
E	Tommy Troy, Amarillo	13
DP	Tommy Troy, Amarillo	43
3B PCT	Keyber Rodriguez, Frisco	.970
PO	Gino Groover, Amarillo	78
A	Devin Ortiz, San Antonio	191
E	Devin Ortiz, San Antonio	19
DP	Devin Ortiz, San Antonio	22
SS PCT	Sean McLain, Tulsa	.971
PO	Jose Fernandez, Amarillo	139
A	Francisco Acuna, San Antonio	239
E	Sebastian Walcott, Frisco	24
DP	Francisco Acuna, San Antonio	52
OF PCT	Bill Knight, Arkansas	.985
PO	Bill Knight, Arkansas	329
A	Gavin Conticello, Amarillo	10
E	Caleb Roberts, Amarillo	6
DP	2 tied	3

PITCHING
G	Colton Johnson, Midland	50
GS	Three tied	26
GF	Landon Sims, Amarillo	36
SV	Landon Sims, Amarillo	12
W	Mike Paredes, Wichita	11
L	Chen Zhong-Ao Zhuang, Midland	11
IP	Chen Zhong-Ao Zhuang, Midland	146
H	Jose Cabrera, Amarillo	153
R	Jose Cabrera, Amarillo	79
R	Chen Zhong-Ao Zhuang, Midland	79
ER	Jose Cabrera, Amarillo	74
SO	Chen Zhong-Ao Zhuang, Midland	145
SO/9	Brycen Mautz, Springfield	10.52
BB/9	Chen Zhong-Ao Zhuang, Midland	2.16
WP	Jaylen Nowlin, Wichita	20
Balks	Ben Anderson, Frisco	7
HR	Chen Zhong-Ao Zhuang, Midland	22
AVG	Ixan Henderson, Springfield	.210

MIDWEST LEAGUE HIGH-A

Awards selected by Major League Baseball

CHAMPION: West Michigan completed a perfect 4-0 postseason with a 3-1 win over Cedar Rapids to claim its first Midwest League title since 2015. The Whitecaps finished 96-35 (.711), winning 19 of their final 23 games, securing their seventh league championship.

MOST VALUABLE PLAYER: On a talent-rich West Michigan roster featuring standouts like Kevin McGonigle, Max Anderson and Josue Briceño, Izaac Pacheco might have been overshadowed—but he emerged as the league's most dominant player. Pacheco paced the circuit in home runs with 17, while also leading in slugging percentage (.499) and OPS (.887). Beyond his power, he enjoyed a career year in several categories, posting personal bests in doubles (25), runs scored (72), RBIs (68) and walks (74).

PITCHER OF THE YEAR: Josh Hartle, acquired by the Guardians in December 2024 as part of the Spencer Horwitz trade with Pittsburgh, made an immediate impact in his first season with his new organization. The Lake County righthander went 10-2 with a 2.35 ERA, 1.05 WHIP and held opponents to a .195 batting average.

TOP MLB PROSPECT: Kevin McGonigle has long been regarded as one of the premier pure hitters in the game, a reputation he reinforced during his stint with West Michigan. The 21-year-old began his season with High-A, where in 36 games he slashed an impressive .372/.462/.648, hitting seven home runs and 19 doubles while driving in 39 runs, scoring 37, drawing 23 walks and stealing three bases. His outstanding performance earned him a promotion to Double-A Erie on July 7, continuing his rapid rise through the minors.

MANAGER OF THE YEAR: Tony Cappuccilli led West Michigan to an 92-39 record, the best record in the minors since 1997.

Pacheco

MIDWEST LEAGUE ALL-STARS

Pos	Player	Team	AVG	OPS	HR
C	Jacob Cozart	Lake County	.229	.708	7
1B	Callan Moss	Quad Cities	.270	.790	7
2B	Jefferson Rojas	South Bend	.278	.871	11
3B	Izaac Pacheco	West Michigan	.258	.887	17
SS	John Peck	West Michigan	.307	.816	10
OF	Max Clark	West Michigan	.285	.857	7
OF	Josue De Paula	Great Lakes	.263	.827	12
OF	Kendall George	Great Lakes	.295	.779	3
DH	Alfonsin Rosario	Lake County	.268	.852	16
UT	Jadher Areinamo	Wisconsin	.297	.818	11
Pos	Pitcher	Team	G	ERA	SO
SP	Josh Hartle	Lake County	22	2.35	100
SP	Miguel Mendez	Fort Wayne	12	1.32	70
SP	Tyson Hardin	Wisconsin	11	2.34	62
SP	Andrew Sears	West Michigan	20	2.95	94
RP	Garrett Hawkins	Fort Wayne	32	1.43	60
RP	Colin Fields	West Michigan	32	1.64	80

OVERALL STANDINGS

East Division	W	L	PCT	GB	Manager	Attendance	Avg	Last Title
West Michigan Whitecaps (Tigers)	92	39	.702	—	Tony Cappuccilli	379,604	5,751	2025
Lake County Captains (Guardians)	74	58	.561	18.5	Omir Santos	166,739	2,526	2024
Great Lakes Loons (Dodgers)	72	58	.554	19.5	Jair Fernandez	198,033	3,000	2016
Lansing Lugnuts (Athletics)	62	70	.470	30.5	Darryl Kennedy	275,713	4,177	2003
Fort Wayne TinCaps (Padres)	56	75	.427	36	Lukas Ray	327,542	4,962	2009
Dayton Dragons (Reds)	52	76	.406	38.5	Vince Harrison	497,980	7,780	Never

West Division	W	L	PCT	GB	Manager	Attendance	Avg	Last Title
Quad Cities River Bandits (Royals)	74	58	.561	—	Jesus Azuaje	156,073	2,329	2021
Cedar Rapids Kernels (Twins)	72	60	.545	2	Brian Meyer	151,222	2,291	2023
Beloit Sky Carp (Marlins)	68	63	.519	5.5	Angel Espada	115,232	1,745	1995
Wisconsin Timber Rattlers (Brewers)	56	74	.431	17	Victor Estevez	236,441	3,582	2012
South Bend Cubs (Cubs)	56	75	.427	17.5	Nick Lovullo	311,839	4,654	2022
Peoria Chiefs (Cardinals)	51	79	.392	22	Roberto Espinoza	137,954	2,122	2002

East: West Michigan def. Lake County 2-0. **West:** Cedar Rapids def. Beloit 2-1. **Championship Series:** West Michigan defeaeted Cedar Rapids 2-0.

MIDWEST LEAGUE | STATISTICS

CLUB BATTING

	AVG	G	AB	R	H	2B	3B	HR	RBI	BB	SO	SB	OBP	SLG
West Michigan Whitecaps	.264	132	4476	765	1181	245	32	128	718	595	1180	170	.361	.419
Lake County Captains	.248	133	4384	629	1086	234	39	110	581	537	1098	154	.337	.394
Peoria Chiefs	.246	131	4279	624	1054	196	19	69	553	546	998	177	.345	.349
Lansing Lugnuts	.244	133	4341	555	1061	206	30	62	495	494	954	128	.333	.349
Cedar Rapids Kernels	.244	133	4275	645	1042	238	41	102	582	526	1107	181	.341	.390
Great Lakes Loons	.238	131	4173	662	995	202	27	109	595	694	1162	268	.351	.378
Quad Cities River Bandits	.237	133	4288	582	1018	220	41	51	522	541	1227	240	.325	.344
Dayton Dragons	.227	129	4251	544	964	199	21	73	473	499	1160	125	.317	.335
Beloit Sky Carp	.226	132	4166	551	940	200	39	63	499	612	1099	338	.333	.338
Fort Wayne TinCaps	.222	132	4231	528	941	174	25	86	485	529	1254	114	.319	.336
South Bend Cubs	.222	132	4199	563	932	187	16	84	509	596	1138	246	.327	.334
Wisconsin Timber Rattlers	.221	131	4178	515	922	179	27	75	463	557	1074	199	.318	.330

CLUB PITCHING

	ERA	G	CG	SHO	SV	IP	H	R	ER	HR	BB	SO	AVG
West Michigan Whitecaps	3.17	132	0	0	33	1168	919	468	412	99	448	1134	.216
Quad Cities River Bandits	3.31	133	0	0	29	1165	946	517	428	64	478	1125	.222
Beloit Sky Carp	3.54	132	0	0	43	1148	949	534	452	57	547	1177	.224
Lake County Captains	3.90	133	0	0	40	1159	992	571	502	97	606	1175	.230
South Bend Cubs	4.15	132	2	1	23	1142	1055	613	526	77	538	1100	.246
Wisconsin Timber Rattlers	4.25	131	2	1	25	1135	1033	621	536	81	586	1087	.245
Great Lakes Loons	4.26	131	0	0	32	1131	890	599	535	72	737	1240	.216
Cedar Rapids Kernels	4.35	133	2	2	35	1139	1038	618	551	70	506	1082	.242
Lansing Lugnuts	4.46	133	2	1	32	1147	1145	654	568	103	467	963	.260
Fort Wayne TinCaps	4.51	132	1	0	26	1138	1091	641	570	89	556	1114	.251
Dayton Dragons	4.62	129	0	0	31	1134	1069	657	582	118	595	1128	.247
Peoria Chiefs	4.80	131	0	0	24	1123	1009	670	599	85	662	1126	.241

CLUB FIELDING

	PCT	PO	A	E	DP		PCT	PO	A	E	DP
West Michigan	.978	3478	1178	103	104	Beloit	.975	3416	1127	117	110
Fort Wayne	.978	3388	1138	102	104	Wisconsin	.975	3381	1174	118	120
Lansing	.977	3416	1152	108	119	Quad Cities	.974	3467	1117	123	91
Lake County	.977	3449	1083	108	83	Dayton	.974	3374	1052	119	90
Great Lakes	.976	3367	1060	108	89	Cedar Rapids	.972	3393	1116	129	98
Peoria	.975	3341	1028	110	94	South Bend	.970	3395	1132	138	101

INDIVIDUAL BATTING

Batter, Club	AVG	G	AB	R	H	2B	3B	HR	RBI	BB	SO	SB
John Peck, West Michigan	.307	93	374	78	115	22	1	10	59	32	104	17
Jadher Areinamo, Wisconsin	.297	94	367	51	109	24	2	11	51	34	48	15
Kendall George, Great Lakes	.295	111	424	93	125	9	7	3	34	84	78	100
Nate Nankil, Lansing	.294	88	316	47	93	19	2	3	44	38	53	7
Josh Kuroda-Grauer, Lansing	.293	80	334	38	98	21	1	0	26	34	37	26
Sam Kulasingam, Quad Cities	.291	123	468	77	136	26	8	2	57	63	86	22
Blake Burke, Wisconsin	.289	95	350	43	101	21	2	5	48	49	94	12
Jon Jon Gazdar, Peoria	.287	89	359	51	103	13	1	1	30	34	40	20
Seth Stephenson, West Michigan	.286	90	371	76	106	16	5	4	49	39	62	42
Peyton Graham, West Michigan	.283	100	357	55	101	23	3	7	49	40	85	20

INDIVIDUAL PITCHING

Pitcher, Club	W	L	ERA	G	GS	CG	SV	IP	H	R	ER	BB	SO
Felix Arronde, Quad Cities	5	7	2.80	26	24	0	0	129	97	45	40	42	101
Joe Miller, West Michigan	7	3	2.91	24	21	0	0	105	100	44	34	31	92
Corey Avant, Lansing	6	6	3.65	29	21	0	0	106	93	46	43	48	91
Chase Chaney, Cedar Rapids	7	4	3.68	23	19	1	1	108	111	48	44	27	86
Drew Beam, Quad Cities	7	10	3.83	26	26	0	0	132	127	72	56	30	110
Caden Favors, Lake County	8	9	4.08	25	25	0	0	108	95	51	49	52	113
Matthew Wilkinson, Lake County	4	9	4.24	25	25	0	0	104	98	53	49	45	117
Steven Echavarria, Lansing	3	7	4.59	26	25	0	0	104	106	57	53	42	88
Grant Judkins, Lansing	8	9	4.73	24	24	1	0	124	123	75	65	42	103
Ty Langenberg, Cedar Rapids	5	6	4.87	22	21	1	0	105	107	62	57	47	98

DEPARTMENT LEADERS

BATTING

OBP	Kendall George, Great Lakes	.409
SLG	Izaac Pacheco, West Michigan	.499
OPS	Izaac Pacheco, West Michigan	.887
Runs	Kendall George, Great Lakes	93
Hits	Sam Kulasingam, Quad Cities	136
TB	Jose Devers, Lake County	197
XBH	Jose Devers, Lake County	53
2B	Jose Devers, Lake County	36
3B	Danny De Andrade, Cedar Rapids	8
3B	Sam Kulasingam, Quad Cities	8
HR	Izaac Pacheco, West Michigan	17
HR	Brandon Winokur, Cedar Rapids	17
HR	Ralphy Velazquez, Lake County	17
RBI	Logan Wagner, Great Lakes	76
SAC	Four tied	7
BB	Kendall George, Great Lakes	84
HBP	T.J. Schofield-Sam, Lansing	30
SO	Rosman Verdugo, Fort Wayne	158
SB	Kendall George, Great Lakes	100
CS	Kendall George, Great Lakes	24

FIELDING

C	PCT	Ryan Campos, Peoria	.992
	PO	Ariel Armas, South Bend	694
	A	Ariel Armas, South Bend	72
	E	Canyon Brown, Quad Cities	14
	DP	Ariel Armas, South Bend	10
	CS	Ariel Armas, South Bend	60
	SB	Ryan Campos, Peoria	134
	PB	Blayberg Diaz, Wisconsin	15
1B	PCT	T.J. Schofield-Sam, Lansing	.994
	PO	T.J. Schofield-Sam, Lansing	668
	A	Michael Callan Moss, Quad Cities	46
	E	Michael Callan Moss, Quad Cities	12
	DP	Blake Burke, Wisconsin	72
2B	PCT	Sam Kulasingam, Quad Cities	.984
	PO	Sam Kulasingam, Quad Cities	225
	A	Casey Yamauchi, Lansing	281
	E	Casey Yamauchi, Lansing	14
	DP	Casey Yamauchi, Lansing	74
3B	PCT	No qualifiers	
	PO	Izaac Pacheco, West Michigan	64
	A	Juan Baez, Wisconsin	144
	E	Izaac Pacheco, West Michigan	14
	DP	Juan Baez, Wisconsin	26
SS	PCT	Jose Devers, Lake County	.972
	PO	Jose Devers, Lake County	166
	A	Jose Devers, Lake County	288
	E	Daniel Vazquez, Quad Cities	22
	DP	Joshua Kuroda-Grauer, Lansing	53
OF	PCT	Carlos Jorge, Dayton	.991
	PO	Carlos Jorge, Dayton	244
	A	Braedon Karpathios, Fort Wayne	14
	E	Braedon Karpathios, Fort Wayne	9
	DP	Zyhir Hope, Great Lakes	3

PITCHING

G	Mark Adamiak, Lansing	44
GS	Jackson Humphries, Lake County	26
GS	Drew Beam, Quad Cities	26
GF	Mark Adamiak, Lansing	37
SV	Mark Adamiak, Lansing	21
W	Josh Hartle, Lake County	10
L	Gerado Salas, Peoria	13
IP	Drew Beam, Quad Cities	132
H	Drew Beam, Quad Cities	127
R	Gerado Salas, Peoria	91
ER	Gerado Salas, Peoria	87
SO	Ryan Birchard, Wisconsin	121
SO/9	Matthew Wilkinson, Lake County	10.13
BB/9	Drew Beam, Quad Cities	2.05
WP	Yerlin Rodriguez, Wisconsin	26
Balks	Two tied	7
HR	Grant Judkins, Lansing	20
AVG	Felix Arronde, Quad Cities	.210

NORTHWEST LEAGUE HIGH-A

Awards selected by Major League Baseball

CHAMPION: The Everett AquaSox won their first league title since 2010. At one point, several of Mariners Top 10 prospects played on the team, and the depth of the system reflected as the team remained consistent throughout the season. They topped Eugene three games to one to win the championship.

MOST VALUABLE PLAYER: Mariners slugger Lazaro Montes made a big impact in High-A this season. In 67 Northwest League games, the 6-foot-5, 210-pound lefthander hit 18 home runs while posting a .572 slugging percentage and a .959 OPS. Montes added 35 extra-base hits and 50 RBIs before earning a promotion to Double-A on June 24.

PITCHER OF THE YEAR: Daniel Eagen made his professional debut this season with Hillsboro—and delivered in a big way. The 6-foot-4, 205-pound right-hander dominated Northwest League hitters, compiling a 2.49 ERA, 1.06 WHIP and .184 opponents' average over 19 starts. His 132 strikeouts in 97.2 innings ranked second in the league, earning a promotion to Double-A on Aug. 19. He was taken by the Diamondbacks in the third round of last year's draft and signed for $650,000.

TOP MLB PROSPECT: After an injury-plagued 2024 season, Mariners prospect Colt Emerson reestablished himself as as prospect, showing himself to be one of the premier contact hitters in the league. Returning to Everett to start the year, he ranked among the top five in batting average (.281), on-base percentage (.388), slugging (.453), OPS (.841) and triples (five) across 90 games. Emerson also set a new personal best with 11 home runs before earning promotions to Double-A on Aug. 14 and then to Triple-A in late September.

MANAGER OF THE YEAR: While the Eugene Emeralds ultimately fell short in the finals, manager Jeremiah Knackstedt was able to lead quite a turnaround. After going 32-34 in the first half, the team was a dominating 49-17 over the second half of the season to finish with the league's best overall record.

Montes

NORTHWEST LEAGUE ALL-STARS

Pos	Player	Team	AVG	OPS	HR
C	Cole Messina	Spokane	.259	.740	7
1B	Charlie Szykowny	Eugene	.276	.817	21
2B	Michael Arroyo	Everett	.269	.934	15
3B	Cutter Coffey	Vancouver	.273	.786	11
SS	Colt Emerson	Everett	.281	.841	11
OF	Lazaro Montes	Everett	.268	.959	18
OF	Jared Thomas	Spokane	.330	.922	11
OF	Bo Davidson	Eugene	.309	.919	10
DH	Ryan Waldschmidt	Hillsboro	.268	.862	9
UT	Braylen Wimmer	Spokane	.302	.879	14
Pos	Pitcher	Team	G	ERA	SO
SP	Daniel Eagen	Hillsboro	19	2.49	132
SP	Gage Stanifer	Vancouver	18	3.20	115
SP	Ryan Johnson	Tri-City	12	1.88	65
SP	Fernando Perez	Vancouver	20	3.05	84
RP	Chay Yeager	Vancouver	25	1.77	43
RP	Tyler Cleveland	Everett	23	0.86	37

OVERALL STANDINGS

Team	W	L	PCT	GB	Manager	Attendance	Avg	Last Penn
Eugene Emeralds (Giants)	81	51	.614	-	Jeremiah Knackstedt	141,195	2,241	2022
Vancouver Canadians (Blue Jays)	75	57	.568	6	Jose Mayorga	277,990	4,344	2023
Tri-City Dust Devils (Angels)	61	70	.466	19.5	Dann Bilardello	116,725	1,796	Never
Hillsboro Hops (D-backs)	60	71	.458	20.5	Mark Reed	174,777	2,648	2019
Everett AquaSox (Mariners)	60	72	.455	21	Zach Vincej	144,111	2,184	2025
Spokane Indians (Rockies)	58	74	.439	23	Robinson Cancel	264,416	4,006	2024

Championship Series: Everett defeated Eugene 3-1.

NORTHWEST LEAGUE | STATISTICS

CLUB BATTING

	AVG	G	AB	R	H	2B	3B	HR	RBI	BB	SO	SB	OBP	SLG
Eugene Emeralds	.262	133	4455	754	1166	217	34	128	689	590	1214	210	.360	.412
Hillsboro Hops	.253	132	4426	637	1118	236	30	70	569	556	1018	133	.340	.367
Spokane Indians	.239	133	4399	580	1053	225	18	108	518	466	1181	203	.323	.372
Vancouver Canadians	.235	133	4391	706	1034	229	25	129	641	694	1160	105	.349	.387
Tri-City Dust Devils	.227	132	4262	577	967	180	16	142	538	526	1329	84	.324	.377
Everett AquaSox	.225	133	4392	609	987	232	29	166	569	570	1373	107	.326	.404

CLUB PITCHING

	ERA	G	CG	SHO	SV	IP	H	R	ER	HR	BB	SO	AVG
Vancouver Canadians	3.69	133	0	0	31	1174	1004	540	481	89	508	1319	.228
Eugene Emeralds	4.27	133	0	0	34	1175	1010	613	558	132	544	1149	.231
Tri-City Dust Devils	4.53	132	1	1	39	1158	1059	637	583	118	578	1312	.242
Spokane Indians	4.56	133	1	0	30	1169	1097	661	593	147	549	1213	.249
Everett AquaSox	4.73	133	0	0	26	1168	1112	690	614	164	516	1087	.251
Hillsboro Hops	4.96	132	0	0	37	1160	1043	722	640	93	707	1195	.241

CLUB FIELDING

	PCT	PO	A	E	DP		PCT	PO	A	E	DP
Tri-City	.983	3447	1053	78	85	Vancouver	.979	3499	994	98	63
Eugene	.982	3499	1101	85	88	Spokane	.978	3481	1121	104	96
Everett	.981	3480	1234	92	126	Hillsboro	.977	3457	1166	107	115

INDIVIDUAL BATTING

Batter, Club	AVG	G	AB	R	H	2B	3B	HR	RBI	BB	SO	SB
Scott Bandura, Eugene	.307	81	319	65	98	15	3	7	45	44	90	30
Jansel Luis, Hillsboro	.304	102	405	60	123	19	7	5	65	27	73	22
Braylen Wimmer, Spokane	.302	86	338	52	102	22	2	14	53	31	85	26
Cristofer Torin, Hillsboro	.287	122	467	78	134	22	3	6	57	66	78	15
Colt Emerson, Everett	.281	90	342	58	96	16	5	11	51	54	68	6
Charlie Szykowny, Eugene	.276	124	490	74	135	28	4	21	85	29	102	5
Aidan Longwell, Spokane	.274	121	452	55	124	35	3	15	80	48	99	5
Cutter Coffey, Vancouver	.273	99	384	68	105	26	0	11	62	47	100	10
Andy Perez, Spokane	.271	115	447	56	121	26	3	7	59	24	81	19
Rio Foster, Tri-City	.267	93	303	54	81	18	2	10	40	60	96	8

INDIVIDUAL PITCHING

Pitcher, Club	W	L	ERA	G	GS	CG	SV	IP	H	R	ER	BB	SO
Konner Eaton, Spokane	5	8	3.56	23	23	0	0	121	109	52	48	42	125
Josh Bostick, Eugene	9	6	3.71	24	23	0	0	119	97	54	49	39	139
Ryan Hawks, Everett	10	6	3.79	22	21	0	0	116	113	53	49	34	86
Cesar Perdomo, Eugene	8	6	3.96	26	26	0	0	127	120	61	56	38	118
Chris Cortez, Tri-City	3	8	4.28	26	26	0	0	114	94	64	54	84	114
Jackson Wentworth, Vancouver	5	5	4.35	26	26	0	0	124	120	62	60	47	116
Nick Payero, Everett	5	7	4.61	23	16	0	0	107	105	58	55	48	99
Ryan Costeiu, Tri-City	7	7	5.07	21	19	0	0	105	102	62	59	44	113
Alberto Pacheco, Spokane	7	9	6.53	29	21	0	0	113	134	88	82	58	89

DEPARTMENT LEADERS

BATTING

OBP	Rio Foster, Tri-City	.407
SLG	Braylen Wimmer, Spokane	.503
OPS	Braylen Wimmer, Spokane	.879
Runs	Jonah Cox, Eugene	89
Hits	Charlie Szykowny, Eugene	135
Hits	Jonah Cox, Eugene	135
TB	Charlie Szykowny, Eugene	234
XBH	Charlie Szykowny, Eugene	53
XBH	Aidan Longwell, Spokane	53
2B	Aidan Longwell, Spokane	35
3B	Jonah Cox, Eugene	10
HR	Luis Suisbel, Everett	23
RBI	Charlie Szykowny, Eugene	85
SAC	Jonah Cox, Eugene	9
BB	Sean Keys, Vancouver	86
HBP	Michael Arroyo, Everett	25
SO	Randy De Jesus, Tri-City	164
SB	Jonah Cox, Eugene	58
CS	Tai Peete, Everett	11
CS	Jonah Cox, Eugene	11

FIELDING

C PCT	Josh Caron, Everett	.993
PO	Juan Flores, Tri-City	870
A	Cole Messina, Spokane	67
E	Juan Flores, Tri-City	11
DP	Juan Flores, Tri-City	5
CS	Cole Messina, Spokane	40
SB	Juan Flores, Tri-City	91
PB	Onil Perez, Eugene	17
1B PCT	Charlie Szykowny, Eugene	.994
PO	Charlie Szykowny, Eugene	741
A	Aidan Longwell, Spokane	67
E	Milkar Perez, Everett	7
DP	Milkar Perez, Everett	60
2B PCT	Adrian Placencia, Tri-City	.982
PO	Adrian Placencia, Tri-City	143
A	Adrian Placencia, Tri-City	288
E	Adrian Placencia, Tri-City	8
DP	Adrian Placencia, Tri-City	53
3B PCT	Luis Suisbel, Everett	.975
PO	Luis Suisbel, Everett	55
A	Luis Suisbel, Everett	177
E	Skyler Messinger, Spokane	10
DP	Luis Suisbel, Everett	20
SS PCT	Zane Zielinski, Eugene	.981
PO	Andy Perez, Spokane	176
A	Andy Perez, Spokane	279
E	Andy Perez, Spokane	17
DP	Andy Perez, Spokane	62
OF PCT	Randy De Jesus, Tri-City	.985
PO	Jonah Cox, Eugene	294
A	Angel Ortiz, Hillsboro	14
E	Curtis Washington, Everett	5
DP	Angel Ortiz, Hillsboro	3

PITCHING

G	Sam Knowlton, Hillsboro	47
GS	Three tied	26
GF	Gabriel Sosa, Everett	34
SV	A.J. Block, Tri-City	10
SV	Welinton Herrera, Spokane	10
W	Ryan Hawks, Everett	10
L	Two tied	9
IP	Cesar Perdomo, Eugene	127
H	Alberto Pacheco, Spokane	134
R	Alberto Pacheco, Spokane	88
ER	Alberto Pacheco, Spokane	82
SO	Josh Bostick, Eugene	139
SO/9	Josh Bostick, Eugene	10.51
BB/9	Ryan Hawks, Everett	2.63
WP	Chris Cortez, Tri-City	17
Balks	Keythel Key, Tri-City	5
HR	Josh Bostick, Eugene	21
AVG	Josh Bostick, Eugene	.218

SOUTH ATLANTIC LEAGUE HIGH-A

Awards selected by Major League Baseball

CHAMPION: After going 46-20 in the first half, the Brooklyn Cyclones struggled to a 26-39 record in the second half. Still, they rallied to go a perfect 4-0 in the playoffs, sweeping the Hub City Spartanburgers in the finals.

MOST VALUABLE PLAYER: After pacing the Florida State League with 22 home runs in 2024, Esmerlyn Valdez carried that power surge into the South Atlantic League. The Pirates prospect hit .303 with a .385 on-base percentage and a .592 slugging percentage. Over 72 games, he tallied 20 home runs and 39 extra-base hits—both ranking second in the league.

PITCHER OF THE YEAR: Yankees lefthander Kyle Carr made the most of his second stint in the South Atlantic League, dominating hitters from start to finish. Over 119 innings, he led the circuit with a 1.96 ERA while limiting opponents to a .190 batting average. He racked up 104 strikeouts, posted a 1.07 WHIP and allowed one run or fewer in 17 of his 22 starts.

TOP MLB PROSPECT: Konnor Griffin, the top prospect in the sport and the standout talent of the South Atlantic League, has quickly lived up to his billing. Selected ninth overall by the Pirates in 2024, Griffin impressed during his 51-game stretch with the Greensboro Grasshoppers. He showcased a potent blend of speed and power, posting a .325/.432/.510 slash line with 20 extra-base hits, 48 runs scored, 36 RBIs and 33 stolen bases. After starting the year in Low-A, he earned a second promotion to Double-A Altoona.

MANAGER OF THE YEAR: In his second season as High-A manager, Blake Butler led Greensboro to a 88-43, the second-best record in the minor leagues.

Valdez

SOUTH ATLANTIC LEAGUE ALL-STARS

Pos	Player	Team	AVG	OPS	HR
C	Chris Suero	Brooklyn	.240	.837	13
1B	Will Bush	Asheville	.247	.811	12
2B	Sam Antonacci	Winston-Salem	.279	.837	4
3B	Jacob Reimer	Brooklyn	.284	.886	8
SS	Konnor Griffin	Greensboro	.325	.942	7
OF	Esmerlyn Valdez	Greensboro	.303	.977	20
OF	Keith Jones II	Hub City	.270	.857	10
OF	Carson Benge	Brooklyn	.302	.897	4
DH	Jeral Perez	Winston-Salem	.244	.763	22
UT	Aron Estrada	Aberdeen	.284	.798	5

Pos	Pitcher	Team	G	ERA	SO
SP	David Davalillo	Hub City	11	2.12	68
SP	Michael Forret	Aberdeen	16	1.51	76
SP	Kyle Carr	Hudson Valley	22	1.96	104
SP	Josh Trentadue	Hub City	15	1.15	71
RP	Hueston Morrill	Hudson Valley	33	0.42	38
RP	Eric Loomis	Hub City	25	1.80	55

OVERALL STANDINGS

North Division	W	L	PCT	GB	Manager	Attendance	Avg	Last Penn
Greensboro Grasshoppers (Pirates)	88	43	.672	—	Blake Butler	254,776	3,919	2011
Hudson Valley Renegades (Yankees)	79	50	.612	8	James Cooper	180,037	2,769	Never
Brooklyn Cyclones (Mets)	72	59	.550	16	Gilbert Gomez	179,016	2,712	Never
Jersey Shore BlueClaws (Phillies)	62	65	.488	24	Greg Brodzinski	222,400	3,530	2010
Aberdeen IronBirds (Orioles)	57	72	.442	30	Ryan Goll	108,174	1,639	Never
Wilmington Blue Rocks (Nationals)	54	76	.415	33.5	Jake Lowery	167,419	2,575	*2019

South Division	W	L	PCT	GB	Manager	Attendance	Avg	Last Penn
Bowling Green Hot Rods (Rays)	69	61	.531	—	Rafael Valenzuela	123,111	1,865	2024
Greenville Drive (Red Sox)	66	66	.500	4	Liam Carroll	307,278	4,586	2023
Hub City (Rangers)	65	66	.496	4.5	Chad Comer	233,762	3,535	Never
Rome Braves (Braves)	58	70	.453	10	Angel Flores	67,027	1,015	2016
Winston-Salem Dash (White Sox)	56	74	.431	13	Pat Leyland	266,352	4,035	*2003
Asheville Tourists (Astros)	52	76	.406	16	Nate Shaver	162,804	2,584	2014

* Carolina League title won prior to 2021 minor league realignment

North: Brooklyn defeated Greensboro 2-0. **South:** Hub City defeated Bowling Green 2-0. **Championship Series:** Brooklyn defeated Hub City 2-0.

SOUTH ATLANTIC LEAGUE | STATISTICS

CLUB BATTING

	AVG	G	AB	R	H	2B	3B	HR	RBI	BB	SO	SB	OBP	SLG
Greensboro Grasshoppers	.245	132	4254	694	1042	172	16	166	629	500	1239	211	.339	.410
Hudson Valley Renegades	.236	130	4160	609	983	196	26	99	558	568	1160	174	.337	.367
Brooklyn Cyclones	.231	132	4230	613	979	189	45	76	547	543	1139	259	.328	.351
Winston-Salem Dash	.230	131	4199	580	965	187	35	93	521	510	1186	194	.325	.357
Bowling Green Hot Rods	.228	131	4200	623	958	167	19	103	564	592	1184	230	.329	.350
Asheville Tourists	.224	129	4148	549	929	192	20	104	485	495	1337	242	.316	.355
Hub City Spartanburgers	.222	132	4268	536	949	177	11	84	485	509	1178	192	.315	.328
Greenville Drive	.222	133	4255	573	945	192	18	83	511	575	1241	138	.322	.334
Rome Emperors	.219	129	4142	449	906	143	18	52	384	452	1148	185	.306	.300
Jersey Shore BlueClaws	.216	128	4029	567	870	161	24	86	489	521	1187	207	.315	.332
Aberdeen IronBirds	.215	130	4052	525	872	166	35	56	450	550	1197	314	.315	.315
Wilmington Blue Rocks	.212	131	4162	428	883	166	26	59	374	399	1197	130	.292	.307

CLUB PITCHING

	ERA	G	CG	SHO	SV	IP	H	R	ER	HR	BB	SO	AVG
Hudson Valley Renegades	2.81	130	1	1	31	1124	745	409	351	51	486	1270	.186
Brooklyn Cyclones	3.30	132	0	0	30	1143	877	507	419	71	537	1333	.211
Greensboro Grasshoppers	3.55	132	0	0	36	1140	896	500	450	100	487	1183	.215
Hub City Spartanburgers	3.57	132	0	0	36	1160	918	544	460	65	601	1335	.217
Rome Emperors	3.71	129	1	0	27	1117	905	516	460	93	477	1100	.221
Aberdeen IronBirds	3.80	130	1	0	28	1125	943	569	475	77	535	1237	.225
Bowling Green Hot Rods	3.81	131	1	0	33	1140	1017	549	482	134	342	1152	.237
Greenville Drive	4.02	133	0	0	31	1141	954	589	509	105	479	1278	.225
Wilmington Blue Rocks	4.25	131	3	2	25	1132	957	614	535	78	577	1105	.230
Winston-Salem Dash	4.42	131	1	0	27	1123	1015	630	552	97	559	1153	.241
Jersey Shore BlueClaws	4.57	128	2	0	29	1089	1008	623	553	82	513	1077	.245
Asheville Tourists	4.84	129	0	0	25	1115	1046	696	600	108	621	1170	.247

CLUB FIELDING

	PCT	PO	A	E	DP		PCT	PO	A	E	DP
Hudson Valley	.979	3345	1023	93	75	Hub City	.973	3457	1044	123	106
Rome	.978	3324	1059	98	91	Wilmington	.972	3368	1032	126	96
Greensboro	.976	3397	1081	109	82	Asheville	.971	3317	1074	130	86
Winston-Salem	.975	3342	999	111	71	Jersey Shore	.971	3241	970	126	90
Bowling Green	.975	3392	1066	116	93	Brooklyn	.971	3401	990	132	83
Greenville	.974	3395	1069	119	74	Aberdeen	.965	3349	1026	161	75

INDIVIDUAL BATTING

Batter, Club	AVG	G	AB	R	H	2B	3B	HR	RBI	BB	SO	SB
A.J. Ewing, Brooklyn	.288	78	299	52	86	16	4	2	26	46	66	44
Caleb Lomavita, Wilmington	.275	99	363	32	100	16	2	4	44	19	83	7
Alejandro Nunez, Asheville	.269	94	360	44	97	19	2	8	38	26	96	22
Emilien Pitre, Bowling Green	.268	118	448	61	120	23	3	9	63	61	107	14
Javier Rivas, Greensboro	.266	94	354	53	94	13	1	18	72	19	92	4
Franklin Arias, Greenville	.265	87	355	43	94	21	1	6	49	32	35	7
Adrian Santana, Bowling Green	.263	89	365	64	96	13	2	2	43	35	49	47
Walker Janek, Asheville	.263	92	358	58	94	21	2	12	46	30	106	30
Anthony Gutierrez, Hub City	.258	89	337	53	87	15	0	2	28	31	79	48
Samuel Zavala, Winston-Salem	.254	119	409	65	104	17	2	9	51	65	104	18

INDIVIDUAL PITCHING

Pitcher, Club	W	L	ERA	G	GS	CG	SV	IP	H	R	ER	BB	SO
Kyle Carr, Hudson Valley	8	6	1.96	22	22	1	0	119	81	35	26	47	104
Noah Hall, Brooklyn	5	7	2.72	25	21	0	1	113	80	40	34	63	115
Garrett Edwards, Bowling Green	5	5	2.78	22	22	0	0	107	80	38	33	27	102
Connor Wietgrefe, Greensboro	6	4	3.17	24	24	0	0	108	88	38	38	25	93
Garrett Baumann, Rome	6	9	3.40	23	23	0	0	114	110	48	43	31	108
Joel Diaz, Brooklyn	5	5	3.80	25	18	0	0	107	106	48	45	25	98
Gary Gill Hill, Bowling Green	7	8	3.82	25	25	0	0	137	129	63	58	30	107
Khristian Curtis, Greensboro	8	5	3.98	26	26	0	0	109	91	59	48	46	116
Travis Sthele, Wilmington	7	7	4.22	23	22	3	0	139	130	70	65	24	82
Marcus Johnson, Bowling Green	7	10	4.50	25	25	1	0	138	160	69	69	16	138

DEPARTMENT LEADERS

BATTING

OBP	Noah Myers, Bowling Green	.395
SLG	Javier Rivas, Greensboro	.460
OPS	Javier Rivas, Greensboro	.780
Runs	Mac Horvath, Bowling Green	77
Runs	Aidan Smith, Bowling Green	77
Hits	Emilien Pitre, Bowling Green	120
TB	Jeral Perez, Winston-Salem	215
XBH	Jeral Perez, Winston-Salem	50
2B	Jeral Perez, Winston-Salem	24
2B	Nelson Taylor, Greenville	24
3B	Aron Estrada, Aberdeen	7
HR	Jeral Perez, Winston-Salem	22
RBI	Javier Rivas, Greensboro	72
SAC	Armando Cruz, Wilmington	9
BB	Nelson Taylor, Greenville	81
HBP	Caleb Lomavita, Wilmington	19
SO	Vance Honeycutt, Aberdeen	178
SB	Patrick Clohisy, Rome	60
CS	Lizandro Espinoza, Rome	13
CS	Patrick Clohisy, Rome	13

FIELDING

C PCT	Ronald Hernandez, Brooklyn	.989
PO	Jackson Appel, Winston-Salem	718
A	Jackson Appel, Winston-Salem	65
E	Caleb Lomavita, Wilmington	21
DP	3 tied	5
CS	Walker Janek, Asheville	46
SB	Jackson Appel, Winston-Salem	136
PB	Ronald Hernandez, Brooklyn	22
1B PCT	No qualifiers	
PO	Arturo Disla, Hub City	540
A	Arturo Disla, Hub City	56
E	Aneudis Mordan, Aberdeen	12
DP	Arturo Disla, Hub City	63
2B PCT	Casey Cook, Hub City	.966
PO	Emilien Pitre, Bowling Green	141
A	Emilien Pitre, Bowling Green	195
E	Casey Cook, Hub City	11
DP	Emilien Pitre, Bowling Green	47
3B PCT	Gleider Figuereo, Hub City	.962
PO	Gleider Figuereo, Hub City	74
A	Gleider Figuereo, Hub City	152
E	Anderson De Los Santos, Aberdeen	18
DP	Gleider Figuereo, Hub City	20
SS PCT	No qualifiers	
PO	Adrian Santana, Bowling Green	127
A	Adrian Santana, Bowling Green	210
E	Lizandro Espinoza, Rome	13
DP	Adrian Santana, Bowling Green	52
OF PCT	No qualifiers	
PO	Samuel Zavala, Winston-Salem	236
A	Yophery Rodriguez, Greenville	13
E	Jhon Diaz, Bowling Green	9
DP	Vance Honeycutt, Aberdeen	4

PITCHING

G	Phil Fox, Winston-Salem	44
GS	Khristian Curtis, Greensboro	26
GF	Isaac Stebens, Greenville	31
SV	Saul Teran, Jersey Shore	11
SV	Phil Fox, Winston-Salem	11
W	T.J. Nichols, Bowling Green	10
L	Adam Maier, Rome	11
L	Yeriel Santos, Asheville	11
IP	Travis Sthele, Wilmington	139
H	Marcus Johnson, Bowling Green	160
R	Yeriel Santos, Asheville	93
ER	Yeriel Santos, Asheville	84
SO	Marcus Johnson, Bowling Green	138
SO/9	Khristian Curtis, Greensboro	9.61
BB/9	Marcus Johnson, Bowling Green	1.04
WP	Yeuris Jimenez, Wilmington	17
Balks	Anderson Brito, Asheville	7
HR	Marcus Johnson, Bowling Green	28
AVG	Kyle Carr, Hudson Valley	.190

CALIFORNIA LEAGUE LOW-A

Awards selected by Major League Baseball

Quintero

CHAMPION: The San Jose Giants proved to be one of the most consistent and talented teams in the California League, a fact perfectly reflected in their dominant championship run, which saw them sweep the Fresno Grizzlies to claim the title. Offensively, Dakota Jordan broke through with a standout season, launching 14 home runs and driving in 82 runs, while Walker Martin enjoyed a strong bounceback campaign, adding 12 homers of his own. The Giants' pitching staff quickly became one of the most formidable in Low-A following the promotions of Luis De La Torre, Argenis Cayama and Keyner Martinez from the Arizona Complex League.

MOST VALUABLE PLAYER: Eduardo Quintero was one of the standout performers in the 2024 Arizona Complex League and carried that success into the California League. He hit .306/.426/.533, adding 14 home runs and 53 RBIs, showcasing his power, plate discipline and ability to make a seamless transition to a higher level of competition. Quintero was promoted to High-A on July 25.

PITCHER OF THE YEAR: Jacob Bresnahan, acquired from the Guardians in the Alex Wood trade, struggled early in Low-A with a 10.98 ERA in 2024. This season, he allowed just two home runs over 93 innings, struck out 124 batters, surrendered just 67 hits and firmly anchored the elite San Jose pitching rotation.

TOP MLB PROSPECT: Quintero's standout season has firmly established him as one of the top prospects in the Dodgers organization, a notable achievement given the depth and talent already present in their lower-level outfield ranks. His performance has clearly propelled him ahead of many highly touted peers.

MANAGER OF THE YEAR: Ydwin Villegas, a former player in the Giants system, led San Jose to a 81-51 record, and the team's first California League title since 2021.

CALIFORNIA LEAGUE ALL-STARS

Pos	Player	Team	AVG	OPS	HR
C	Lamar King Jr	Lake Elsinore	.286	.778	4
1B	Jakob Christian	San Jose	.272	.815	10
2B	Elijah Hainline	R. Cucamonga	.298	.851	4
3B	Harold Coll	Inland Empire	.276	.791	9
SS	Ryan Jackson	Lake Elsinore	.298	.860	3
OF	Eduardo Quintero	R. Cucamonga	.306	.959	14
OF	Dakota Jordan	San Jose	.311	.874	14
OF	Carlos Gutierrez	San Jose	.351	.897	2
DH	Raudi Rodriguez	Inland Empire	.281	.842	14
UT	Jean Carlos Sio	San Jose	.311	.820	5
Pos	Pitcher	Team	G	ERA	SO
SP	Jacob Bresnahan	San Jose	22	2.61	124
SP	Christian Zazueta	Rancho Cucamonga	16	2.44	80
SP	Kash Mayfield	Lake Elsinore	19	2.97	88
SP	Ryan Sloan	Modesto	18	3.44	77
RP	Benny Thompson	Inland Empire	44	1.91	100
RP	Fidel Ulloa	Fresno	26	1.77	46

OVERALL STANDINGS

North Division	W	L	PCT	GB	Manager	Attendance	Avg	Last Title
San Jose Giants (Giants)	81	51	.614	—	Ydwin Villegas	127,819	1,936	2025
Fresno Grizzlies (Rockies)	70	62	.530	11	Cesar Galvez	241,709	3,662	Never
Modesto Nuts (Mariners)	69	63	.523	12	Luis Caballero	83,367	1,244	2024
Stockton Ports (Athletics)	57	75	.432	24	Javier Godard	119,121	1,804	2008
South Division	**W**	**L**	**PCT**	**GB**	**Manager**	**Attendance**	**Avg**	**Last Title**
Rancho Cucamonga Quakes (Dodgers)	70	62	.530	—	John Shoemaker	129,140	1,956	2018
Visalia Rawhide (D-backs)	65	67	.492	5	Dee Garner	120,357	1,823	2019
Inland Empire 66ers (Angels)	60	72	.455	10	Dave Stapleton	132,144	2,002	2013
Lake Elsinore Storm (Padres)	56	76	.424	14	Brian Burres	108,976	1,651	2022

North: San Jose def. Fresno 2-0. **South:** Inland Empire def. Rancho Cucamonga 2-0. **Championship Series:** San Jose defeated Inland Empire 2-0.

CALIFORNIA LEAGUE | STATISTICS

CLUB BATTING

	AVG	G	AB	R	H	2B	3B	HR	RBI	BB	SO	SB	OBP	SLG
San Jose Giants	.261	132	4553	811	1187	236	40	101	731	632	1197	194	.358	.397
R. Cucamonga Quakes	.256	132	4443	807	1139	206	39	101	702	744	1329	289	.371	.388
Modesto Nuts	.254	133	4518	747	1148	239	26	72	632	552	1252	224	.346	.366
Inland Empire 66ers	.253	132	4400	691	1115	211	58	62	577	584	1155	181	.350	.370
Fresno Grizzlies	.246	132	4417	597	1086	184	26	61	529	466	1209	199	.327	.341
Lake Elsinore Storm	.244	132	4447	647	1086	236	20	57	567	641	1138	184	.347	.345
Visalia Rawhide	.235	132	4299	597	1009	181	25	57	499	629	1250	214	.343	.328
Stockton Ports	.225	133	4421	643	995	192	23	72	558	656	1242	130	.335	.328

CLUB PITCHING

	ERA	G	CG	SHO	SV	IP	H	R	ER	HR	BB	SO	AVG
San Jose Giants	3.50	132	0	0	32	1175	1008	560	457	50	548	1228	.231
Visalia Rawhide	4.30	132	0	0	34	1161	1037	657	555	89	652	1136	.239
Fresno Grizzlies	4.38	132	0	0	40	1174	1148	678	571	74	594	1233	.255
R. Cucamonga Quakes	4.64	132	0	0	20	1166	1050	718	601	80	644	1329	.237
Stockton Ports	4.68	133	0	0	22	1172	1141	717	610	91	533	1271	.253
Modesto Nuts	4.76	133	0	0	28	1172	1178	712	620	66	528	1070	.260
Inland Empire 66ers	5.02	132	0	0	25	1157	1116	757	645	73	747	1247	.252
Lake Elsinore Storm	5.05	132	0	0	24	1159	1087	741	651	60	658	1258	.247

CLUB FIELDING

	PCT	PO	A	E	DP		PCT	PO	A	E	DP
Visalia	.971	3484	1280	140	104	Inland Empire	.968	3471	1109	149	96
Fresno	.970	3522	1218	145	120	Stockton	.968	3493	1166	155	108
Modesto	.969	3490	1195	149	80	Lake Elsinore	.967	3478	1204	161	105
San Jose	.969	3524	1197	152	90	Rancho Cucamonga	.961	3497	1075	185	93

INDIVIDUAL BATTING

Batter, Club	AVG	G	AB	R	H	2B	3B	HR	RBI	BB	SO	SB
Jean Carlos Sio, San Jose	.311	90	334	67	104	16	3	5	58	46	46	15
Dakota Jordan, San Jose	.311	88	370	71	115	15	6	14	82	37	95	27
Eduardo Quintero, R. Cucamonga	.306	81	317	73	97	18	6	14	53	65	88	35
Zach Evans, Lake Elsinore	.296	96	379	50	112	20	1	3	62	42	67	14
Lamar King, Lake Elsinore	.286	81	311	50	89	24	1	4	37	38	68	18
Felnin Celesten, Modesto	.285	93	383	52	109	19	2	5	55	37	96	20
Jorge Ruiz, Inland Empire	.285	121	478	78	136	23	6	1	50	47	92	22
Raudi Rodriguez, Inland Empire	.281	125	481	90	135	21	14	14	83	63	130	38
Dervy Ventura, Modesto	.276	108	366	67	101	21	1	3	45	65	96	41
Harold Coll, Inland Empire	.276	116	424	70	117	27	4	9	62	62	120	29

INDIVIDUAL PITCHING

Pitcher, Club	W	L	ERA	G	GS	CG	SV	IP	H	R	ER	BB	SO
Peyton Olejnik, Inland Empire	6	7	4.20	25	25	0	0	129	122	65	60	63	130
Walter Ford, Modesto	5	5	4.67	23	23	0	0	125	130	74	65	30	95
Bryan Mena, Fresno	2	8	5.62	29	18	0	0	107	124	77	67	57	97

DEPARTMENT LEADERS

BATTING

OBP	Eduardo Quintero, R. Cucamonga	.426
SLG	Eduardo Quintero, R. Cucamonga	.533
OPS	Eduardo Quintero, R. Cucamonga	.959
Runs	Raudi Rodriguez, Inland Empire	90
Hits	Lisbel Diaz, San Jose	139
TB	Raudi Rodriguez, Inland Empire	226
XBH	Raudi Rodriguez, Inland Empire	49
2B	Lisbel Diaz, San Jose	32
3B	Raudi Rodriguez, Inland Empire	14
HR	Carlos Jimenez, Modesto	14
HR	Eduardo Quintero, Rancho Cucamonga	14
HR	Dakota Jordan, San Jose	14
HR	Raudi Rodriguez, Inland Empire	14
RBI	Raudi Rodriguez, Inland Empire	83
SAC	Johan Macias, Inland Empire	14
BB	Jose Meza, Rancho Cucamonga	80
HBP	Cesar Quintas, Modesto	26
SO	Jaron Elkins, Rancho Cucamonga	153
SB	Jaron Elkins, Rancho Cucamonga	63
CS	Carlos Jimenez, Modesto	13

FIELDING

C PCT	Alan Espinal, Fresno	.994
PO	Victor Rodrigues, R. Cucamonga	707
A	Alberto Barriga, Visalia	87
E	Alberto Barriga, Visalia	13
DP	Alberto Barriga, Visalia	8
CS	Alberto Barriga, Visalia	37
SB	Dario Laverde, Inland Empire	125
PB	Dario Laverde, Inland Empire	19
1B PCT	No qualifiers	
PO	Colin Summerhill, Inland Empire	508
A	Ruben Santana, Visalia	31
E	Jose Meza, Rancho Cucamonga	10
DP	Colin Summerhill, Inland Empire	44
2B PCT	Dervy Ventura, Modesto	.975
PO	Dervy Ventura, Modesto	153
A	Dervy Ventura, Modesto	233
E	Nicolas Perez, Rancho Cucamonga	15
DP	Roynier Hernandez, Fresno	42
3B PCT	No qualifiers	
PO	Zach Evans, Lake Elsinore	59
A	Yassel Soler, Visalia	161
E	Yassel Soler, Visalia	14
DP	Yassel Soler, Visalia	18
SS PCT	No qualifiers	
PO	John Wimmer, Inland Empire	101
A	Felnin Celesten, Modesto	184
E	John Wimmer, Inland Empire	31
DP	Adrian Rodriguez, Visalia	36
OF PCT	No qualifiers	
PO	Raudi Rodriguez, Inland Empire	230
A	Jaron Elkins, Rancho Cucamonga	14
E	Robert Calaz, Fresno	12
DP	Lisbel Diaz, San Jose	4

PITCHING

G	Ben Thompson, Inland Empire	44
GS	Peyton Olejnik, Inland Empire	25
GF	Nathan Blasick, Fresno	31
SV	Nathan Blasick, Fresno	19
W	Jacob Bresnahan, San Jose	9
L	Jose Dicochea, Stockton	10
L	Erick Reynoso, Visalia	10
IP	Peyton Olejnik, Inland Empire	129
H	Walter Ford, Modesto	130
R	Bryan Mena, Fresno	77
ER	Sam Stuhr, Stockton	70
SO	Peyton Olejnik, Inland Empire	130
SO/9	Peyton Olejnik, Inland Empire	9.09
BB/9	Walter Ford, Modesto	2.15
WP	Francis Texido, Inland Empire	27
Balks	Four tied	4
HR	Jackson Cox, Fresno	12
HR	Chris Clark, Inland Empire	12
AVG	Peyton Olejnik, Inland Empire	.249

CAROLINA LEAGUE LOW-A

Awards selected by Major League Baseball

CHAMPION: Lynchburg edged Columbia 2-1 in the best-of-three championship series. It was the Hillcats' first title since 2017 and their ninth overall.

MOST VALUABLE PLAYER: A 2024 second-round pick, Caleb Bonemer wasted little time making an impact in his pro debut. The 19-year-old infielder showcased an advanced all-around game, topping the Carolina League in on-base percentage (.400), slugging (.458) and OPS (.858) across 117 games. Blending patience, power and speed, Bonemer tallied 58 RBIs, 27 steals and earned a late-season callup to High-A Winston-Salem.

PITCHER OF THE YEAR: Royals lefthander David Shields delivered a dominant season for the Columbia Fireflies, showcasing consistency and command from Opening Day through the playoffs. Over 18 starts, he posted a 2.01 ERA across 72 innings, striking out 81 while issuing only 16 walks. Opponents hit just .218 against him, and he allowed only three home runs all year. The Pittsburgh native finished strong, fanning eight over five innings in Columbia's semifinal opener.

TOP MLB PROSPECT: Carolina shortstop Jesús Made showcased his elite athleticism with a .267/.373/.388 slash line and 40 stolen bases. Considered one of the best prospects in the game, Made was a dominating force at the plate, while showing athleticism in the infield as well. After earning a promotion to High-A Wisconsin, he elevated his game even further, hitting .343 with a .915 OPS over 27 games. Made continues to display poise, polish and upside well beyond his years.

MANAGER OF THE YEAR: Jordan Smith led the Lynchburg Hillcats to a 70-59 record, the best in the Carolina League. They went 4-1 in the playoffs.

Shields

CAROLINA LEAGUE ALL-STARS

Pos	Player	Team	AVG	OPS	HR
C	Yasmil Bucce	Delmarva	.255	.814	8
1B	Eric Bitonti	Carolina	.238	.762	19
2B	Luis Peña	Carolina	.308	.844	6
3B	Jorgelys Mota	Fredericksburg	.270	.750	6
SS	Caleb Bonemer	Kannapolis	.281	.858	10
OF	Tommy Hawke	Lynchburg	.309	.835	0
OF	Theo Gillen	Charleston	.267	.820	5
OF	Justin Gonzales	Salem	.298	.804	4
DH	Maxton Martin	Hickory	.259	.783	12
UT	Jesús Made	Carolina	.267	.761	4
Pos	Pitcher	Team	G	ERA	SO
SP	David Shields	Columbia	18	2.01	81
SP	Jose Urbina	Charleston	19	2.05	96
SP	Jostin Florentino	Myrtle Beach	11	1.96	67
SP	Melvin Hernandez	Carolina	24	2.00	97
RP	Merritt Beeker	Fredericksburg	38	1.85	78
RP	Sean Matson	Lynchburg	20	1.21	70

OVERALL STANDINGS

North Division	W	L	PCT	GB	Manager	Attendance	Avg	Last Title
Lynchburg Hillcats (Guardians)	70	59	.543	—	Jordan Smith	96,831	1,467	2025
Carolina Mudcats (Brewers)	68	60	.531	1.5	Nick Stanley	138,587	2,199	Never
Fayetteville Woodpeckers (Astros)	69	63	.523	2.5	Carlos Lugo	167,508	2,538	Never
Fredericksburg Nationals (Nationals)	65	64	.504	5	Billy McMillon	199,805	3,027	2024
Salem Red Sox (Red Sox)	56	74	.431	14.5	Ozzie Chavez	164,747	2,534	2013
Delmarva Shorebirds (Orioles)	51	79	.392	19.5	Collin Woody	147,547	2,305	*2000
South Division	**W**	**L**	**PCT**	**GB**	**Manager**	**Attendance**	**Avg**	**Last Title**
Myrtle Beach Pelicans (Cubs)	68	60	.531	—	Buddy Bailey/Yovanny Cuevas	219,885	3,490	2016
Charleston RiverDogs (Rays)	68	62	.523	1	Sean Smedley	260,006	4,000	2023
Hickory Crawdads (Rangers)	68	62	.523	1	Carlos Maldonado	114,688	1,764	Never
Augusta GreenJackets (Braves)	67	62	.519	1.5	Wynston Sawyer	246,524	3,851	*2008
Columbia Fireflies (Royals)	64	65	.496	4.5	David Noworyta	224,564	3,454	Never
Kannapolis Cannon Ballers (White Sox)	64	68	.485	6	Chad Pinder	193,704	2,934	*2005

* South Atlantic League title won prior to 2021 minor league realignment

North: Lynchburg def. Fredericksburg 2-0. **South:** Columbia def. Myrtle Beach 2-0. **Championship Series:** Lynchburg defeated Columbia 2-1

CAROLINA LEAGUE | STATISTICS

CLUB BATTING

	AVG	G	AB	R	H	2B	3B	HR	RBI	BB	SO	SB	OBP	SLG
Salem Red Sox	.242	130	4201	572	1018	193	33	77	487	456	1126	142	.323	.359
Kannapolis Cannon Ballers	.238	132	4312	627	1028	166	31	64	533	640	1243	303	.345	.336
Hickory Crawdads	.237	130	4172	608	988	177	34	58	519	550	1028	194	.339	.337
Myrtle Beach Pelicans	.236	128	4185	631	986	182	31	64	552	545	1191	221	.339	.340
Carolina Mudcats	.233	128	4050	602	943	172	33	75	532	684	1188	213	.350	.347
Charleston RiverDogs	.231	130	4136	569	956	155	23	45	484	601	1076	202	.337	.312
Augusta GreenJackets	.230	129	4175	581	960	158	28	57	512	565	1114	242	.332	.322
Fayetteville Woodpeckers	.228	132	4182	639	952	178	22	82	543	635	1286	334	.341	.340
Delmarva Shorebirds	.226	130	4123	513	933	148	38	50	447	574	1249	263	.332	.317
Lynchburg Hillcats	.225	129	4028	574	908	170	30	39	492	598	1105	298	.335	.312
Fredericksburg Nationals	.223	129	4076	529	907	167	36	57	456	505	1208	196	.314	.323
Columbia Fireflies	.222	129	4004	539	888	154	32	54	440	502	1039	249	.322	.317

CLUB PITCHING

	ERA	G	CG	SHO	SV	IP	H	R	ER	HR	BB	SO	AVG
Fayetteville Woodpeckers	3.68	132	0	0	34	1142	884	552	467	69	659	1202	.215
Augusta GreenJackets	3.74	129	2	1	29	1120	905	550	465	68	543	1189	.221
Lynchburg Hillcats	3.75	129	0	0	31	1109	981	546	462	52	510	1176	.236
Myrtle Beach Pelicans	3.80	128	1	1	27	1120	930	550	473	34	666	1110	.228
Fredericksburg Nationals	3.85	129	1	0	30	1098	928	553	470	72	567	1066	.231
Carolina Mudcats	3.91	128	1	0	36	1095	978	566	476	59	512	1115	.240
Hickory Crawdads	4.02	130	0	0	31	1121	906	573	500	73	560	1241	.215
Charleston RiverDogs	4.06	130	0	0	35	1127	1017	590	508	68	474	1003	.241
Columbia Fireflies	4.06	129	0	0	35	1107	999	593	500	63	496	1165	.239
Kannapolis Cannon Ballers	4.29	132	0	0	31	1147	1000	618	547	64	621	1195	.235
Delmarva Shorebirds	4.32	130	0	0	32	1128	935	652	542	45	650	1299	.224
Salem Red Sox	4.35	130	0	0	29	1112	1004	641	538	55	597	1092	.240

CLUB FIELDING

	PCT	PO	A	E	DP		PCT	PO	A	E	DP
Kannapolis	.975	3441	1177	119	93	Charleston	.969	3382	1140	144	108
Myrtle Beach	.972	3360	1148	128	106	Fayetteville	.968	3426	1105	148	88
Hickory	.972	3362	1105	130	76	Carolina	.967	3286	1132	152	99
Augusta	.971	3361	1119	134	92	Fredericksburg	.967	3295	1081	151	92
Lynchburg	.970	3328	1096	137	83	Salem	.964	3337	1103	168	89
Columbia	.970	3322	1042	137	87	Delmarva	.959	3384	1089	192	86

INDIVIDUAL BATTING

Batter, Club	AVG	G	AB	R	H	2B	3B	HR	RBI	BB	SO	SB
Justin Gonzales, Salem	.298	81	312	45	93	23	2	4	27	35	52	11
Angel Mateo, Charleston	.282	92	347	50	98	15	1	6	66	28	71	16
Caleb Bonemer, Kannapolis	.281	96	349	69	98	26	3	10	58	68	91	27
Leonel Espinoza, Myrtle Beach	.270	93	370	60	100	15	2	6	54	31	90	21
Natanael Yuten, Salem	.270	99	330	42	89	21	5	3	39	28	94	10
Jesus Made, Carolina	.267	83	322	55	86	21	3	4	46	53	78	40
Antonis Macias, Hickory	.266	92	312	48	83	14	2	1	40	71	67	4
Jose Escobar, Myrtle Beach	.264	105	401	61	106	19	0	5	46	47	96	11
Isaiah Drake, Augusta	.260	84	319	41	83	6	6	5	47	39	82	35
Max Martin, Hickory	.259	102	402	72	104	25	6	12	64	45	101	13

INDIVIDUAL PITCHING

Pitcher, Club	W	L	ERA	G	GS	CG	SV	IP	H	R	ER	BB	SO
Melvin Hernandez, Carolina	10	5	2.00	24	17	1	0	122	98	32	27	22	97
Ryan Andrade, Charleston	11	5	2.87	23	23	0	0	119	100	46	38	47	90
Melkis Hernandez, Lynchburg	6	3	3.64	25	21	0	0	114	93	50	46	51	116
Bryan Polanco, Fredericksburg	7	8	3.71	24	23	0	0	112	96	52	46	44	88
Jacob Kmatz, Charleston	4	9	5.56	23	19	0	0	110	132	70	68	35	80

DEPARTMENT LEADERS

BATTING

OBP	Caleb Bonemer, Kannapolis	.400
SLG	Caleb Bonemer, Kannapolis	.458
OPS	Caleb Bonemer, Kannapolis	.858
Runs	Narciso Polanco, Charleston	84
Hits	Owen Carey, Augusta	121
TB	Eric Bitonti, Carolina	180
XBH	Max Martin, Hickory	43
2B	Caleb Bonemer, Kannapolis	26
3B	Cristhian Vaquero, Fredericksburg	8
3B	Starlyn Nunez, Salem	8
HR	Eric Bitonti, Carolina	19
RBI	Eric Bitonti, Carolina	77
SAC	Colton Becker, Columbia	8
BB	Nathan Flewelling, Charleston	89
HBP	Asbel Gonzalez, Columbia	29
SO	Eric Bitonti, Carolina	169
SB	Asbel Gonzalez, Columbia	78
CS	Asbel Gonzalez, Columbia	261

FIELDING

C PCT	Nathan Flewelling, Charleston	.991
PO	Kevin Bazzell, Fredericksburg	613
A	Kevin Bazzell, Fredericksburg	81
E	Nicholas Montgomery, Augusta	14
DP	Owen Ayers, Myrtle Beach	7
CS	Kevin Bazzell, Fredericksburg	59
SB	Kleyver Salazar, Salem	152
PB	Yasmil Bucce, Delmarva	13
1B PCT	Eric Bitonti, Carolina	.989
PO	Eric Bitonti, Carolina	781
A	Eric Bitonti, Carolina	50
E	Luis Merejo, Lynchburg	15
DP	Eric Bitonti, Carolina	67
2B PCT	Yoeilin Cespedes, Salem	.963
PO	Yoeilin Cespedes, Salem	165
A	Ty Southisene, Myrtle Beach	235
E	Yoeilin Cespedes, Salem	15
DP	Ty Southisene, Myrtle Beach	56
3B PCT	No qualifiers	
PO	Jorgelys Mota, Fredericksburg	60
A	Filippo Di Turi, Carolina	89
E	Jorgelys Mota, Fredericksburg	14
DP	Waner Luciano, Fayetteville	15
SS PCT	Ricardo Gonzalez, Charleston	.962
PO	Ricardo Gonzalez, Charleston	149
A	Ricardo Gonzalez, Charleston	227
E	Starlyn Nunez, Salem	22
DP	Ricardo Gonzalez, Charleston	56
OF PCT	Asbel Gonzalez, Columbia	.989
PO	Asbel Gonzalez, Columbia	257
A	George Wolkow, Kannapolis	12
E	Braylin Tavera, Delmarva	11
DP	George Wolkow, Kannapolis	4

PITCHING

G	Merrick Baldo, Fredericksburg	46
GS	Four tied	23
GF	Merrick Baldo, Fredericksburg	31
SV	Robert Cranz, Fredericksburg	9
W	Ryan Andrade, Charleston	11
L	Chase Allsup, Delmarva	12
IP	Melvin Hernandez, Carolina	122
H	Jacob Kmatz, Charleston	132
R	Angel Roman, Fredericksburg	76
ER	Angel Roman, Fredericksburg	69
SO	Melkis Hernandez, Lynchburg	116
SO/9	Melkis Hernandez, Lynchburg	9.18
BB/9	Melvin Hernandez, Carolina	1.63
WP	Yeri Perez, Columbia	22
Balks	Leomar Rosario, Fayetteville	7
HR	Bryan Polanco, Fredericksburg	14
AVG	Melvin Hernandez, Carolina	.217

FLORIDA STATE LEAGUE LOW-A

Awards selected by Major League Baseball

CHAMPION: The Lakeland Flying Tigers captured their first Florida State League title since 2012 with a decisive sweep of the Daytona Tortugas. In doing so, Lakeland in 2025 completed a rare FSL sweep, becoming just the third team in league history to win both halves of the regular season and the championship, joining the 1995 Daytona and 2024 Palm Beach clubs. The Flying Tigers finished the regular season with 75 wins and posted a 44-21 home record.

MOST VALUABLE PLAYER: Reds catching prospect Alfredo Duno sizzled as he bounced back from an injury-plagued 2024 season. Duno slashed .287/.430/.518 with a .948 OPS, 18 home runs and 81 RBIs.

PITCHER OF THE YEAR: Lucas Elissalt, a 13th-round pick from Chipola Junior College in 2024, wasted no time making his mark in professional baseball. The righthander dominated in 16 starts for Lakeland, posting a 2.48 ERA and a 0.98 WHIP with 77 strikeouts in 65 innings. He limited hitters to a .183 average. His strong performance earned a late-season promotion to High-A West Michigan, where he continued his dominance with a 2.59 ERA across six starts.

TOP MLB PROSPECT: Duno's bat has never been in question, but injuries have often limited his time on the field. Given a chance to play regularly, he showed the best batting eye in the league. And his power potential is even more impressive than his selectivity. He led the league in most offensive categories including total bases, home runs, on-base percentage and slugging percentage.

MANAGER OF THE YEAR: Former ,ajor league catcher Rene Rivera guided the Lakeland Flying Tigers to a 75-53 record, winning both halves of the season and capturing the Florida State League championship. Rivera capped off the year by managing the Scottsdale Scorpions in the Arizona Fall League.

Duno

FLORIDA STATE LEAGUE ALL-STARS

Pos	Player	Team	AVG	OPS	HR
C	Alfredo Duno	Daytona	.287	.948	18
1B	Trace Willhoite	St. Lucie	.265	.852	14
2B	Aroon Escobar	Clearwater	.285	.829	11
3B	Deniel Ortiz	Palm Beach	.285	.852	10
SS	Sammy Stafura	Daytona/Bradenton	.260	.799	4
OF	Marshall Toole	Tampa	.305	.885	5
OF	Jackson Strong	Lakeland	.277	.820	5
OF	Edward Florentino	Bradenton	.262	.883	10
DH	Rainiel Rodriguez	Palm Beach	.249	.871	13
UT	Carlos Sanchez	Daytona	.308	.878	4
Pos	Pitcher	Team	G	ERA	SO
SP	Lucas Elissalt	Lakeland	16	2.48	77
SP	Jason Savacool	Palm Beach	11	1.61	46
SP	Liomar Martinez	Jupiter	22	3.30	119
SP	Wellington Aracena	St. Lucie	17	2.38	84
RP	Inmer Lobo	Bradenton	13	1.71	35
RP	Chris Veach	Tampa	43	2.53	75

OVERALL STANDINGS

East Division	W	L	PCT	GB	Manager	Attendance	Avg	Last Penn
St. Lucie Mets (Mets)	77	53	.592	—	Luis Rivera	69,133	1,047	2022
Daytona Tortugas (Reds)	65	66	.496	12.5	Willie Harris	108,922	1,650	2011
Palm Beach Cardinals (Cardinals)	63	67	.485	14	Gary Kendall	45,973	707	2024
Jupiter Hammerheads (Marlins)	59	72	.450	18.5	Nick Weisheipl	53,292	807	2023
West Division	**W**	**L**	**PCT**	**GB**	**Manager**	**Attendance**	**Avg**	**Last Penn**
Lakeland Flying Tigers (Tigers)	75	53	.586	—	Rene Rivera	36,788	583	2025
Clearwater Threshers (Phillies)	68	60	.531	7	Marty Malloy	169,193	2,563	2021
Tampa Tarpons (Yankees)	63	63	.500	11	Aaron Bossi	19,475	314	2010
Dunedin Blue Jays (Blue Jays)	60	66	.476	14	Gil Kim	51,910	823	2017
Bradenton Marauders (Pirates)	60	69	.465	15.5	Jim Horner	70,513	1,101	2016
Fort Myers Mighty Mussels (Twins)	52	73	.416	21.5	Seth Feldman	85,126	1,395	2018

East: St. Lucie defeated Daytona 2-1. **West:** Lakeland def. Clearwater 2-0. **Championship Series:** Lakeland defeated Daytona 2-0.

FLORIDA STATE LEAGUE | STATISTICS

CLUB BATTING

	AVG	G	AB	R	H	2B	3B	HR	RBI	BB	SO	SB	OBP	SLG
Tampa Tarpons	.247	126	4048	667	1001	185	44	74	570	613	1078	307	.353	.370
Daytona Tortugas	.247	131	4260	705	1053	222	33	87	611	635	1239	223	.356	.376
St. Lucie Mets	.245	130	4212	692	1030	178	26	79	596	625	1055	282	.351	.355
Dunedin Blue Jays	.244	126	4080	609	994	213	25	85	543	539	1088	134	.345	.371
Lakeland Flying Tigers	.233	128	4175	631	974	182	22	81	570	589	1164	188	.340	.346
Clearwater Threshers	.230	128	4109	578	945	163	25	71	513	555	1067	138	.330	.334
Bradenton Marauders	.228	129	4189	586	956	199	25	103	514	529	1291	227	.325	.361
Palm Beach Cardinals	.227	130	4199	623	954	177	29	90	546	635	1223	220	.339	.347
Jupiter Hammerheads	.225	131	4302	622	966	172	46	56	545	640	1159	276	.333	.325
Fort Myers M. Mussels	.218	125	4050	543	883	140	16	81	475	590	1065	236	.327	.320

CLUB PITCHING

	ERA	G	CG	SHO	SV	IP	H	R	ER	HR	BB	SO	AVG
St. Lucie Mets	3.59	130	0	0	34	1137	881	556	453	60	632	1240	.211
Lakeland Flying Tigers	3.61	128	0	0	36	1122	946	546	450	71	471	1019	.227
Dunedin Blue Jays	4.21	126	0	0	29	1074	962	570	502	88	509	1173	.240
Bradenton Marauders	4.25	129	0	0	27	1127	1013	612	532	82	554	977	.241
Tampa Tarpons	4.27	126	0	0	21	1067	942	624	506	80	577	1063	.235
Clearwater Threshers	4.38	128	0	0	32	1107	971	603	539	94	620	1156	.236
Fort Myers Mighty Mussels	4.51	125	0	0	25	1087	1026	655	545	81	486	1146	.246
Palm Beach Cardinals	4.51	130	0	0	26	1131	989	643	567	80	665	1218	.236
Jupiter Hammerheads	4.76	131	0	0	24	1158	1004	738	613	87	767	1264	.235
Daytona Tortugas	4.82	131	0	0	31	1141	1022	709	611	84	669	1173	.238

CLUB FIELDING

	PCT	PO	A	E	DP		PCT	PO	A	E	DP
Clearwater	.976	3320	1083	110	83	Lakeland	.969	3366	1147	145	118
Bradenton	.974	3382	1201	120	128	Jupiter	.965	3475	1182	168	104
Palm Beach	.974	3392	1107	122	86	St. Lucie	.964	3411	1039	166	89
Dunedin	.972	3222	985	121	83	Tampa	.964	3200	1123	162	92
Daytona	.970	3424	1035	138	91	Fort Myers	.964	3262	991	161	66

INDIVIDUAL BATTING

Batter, Club	AVG	G	AB	R	H	2B	3B	HR	RBI	BB	SO	SB
Marshall Toole, Tampa	.305	96	315	66	96	14	13	5	48	52	73	44
Alfredo Duno, Daytona	.287	113	390	78	112	32	2	18	81	95	91	6
Raider Tello, Clearwater	.277	101	354	42	98	19	0	8	55	32	93	1
Juan Matheus, Tampa	.271	95	336	51	91	23	2	2	43	48	74	35
Kyle Henley, Daytona	.267	99	378	70	101	15	2	1	33	29	135	57
Yonatan Henriquez, St. Lucie	.264	104	349	59	92	18	2	8	50	51	72	33
Dante Nori, Clearwater	.262	109	423	63	111	16	11	4	43	66	75	37
Sammy Stafura, Daytona	.261	89	322	48	84	18	9	4	48	63	97	28
Tucker Toman, Dunedin	.260	89	323	49	84	17	1	6	52	36	92	5
Esmith Pineda, Daytona	.259	102	352	47	91	21	1	7	57	38	87	3

INDIVIDUAL PITCHING

Pitcher, Club	W	L	ERA	G	GS	CG	SV	IP	H	R	ER	BB	SO
Leonel Sequera, Palm Beach	5	10	4.33	24	24	0	0	108	107	55	52	41	99

DEPARTMENT LEADERS

BATTING

OBP	Alfredo Duno, Daytona	.430
SLG	Alfredo Duno, Daytona	.518
OPS	Alfredo Duno, Daytona	.948
Runs	Alfredo Duno, Daytona	78
Hits	Yordany De Los Santos, Bradenton	115
TB	Alfredo Duno, Daytona	202
XBH	Alfredo Duno, Daytona	52
2B	Alfredo Duno, Daytona	32
3B	Marshall Toole, Tampa	13
HR	Alfredo Duno, Daytona	18
RBI	Alfredo Duno, Daytona	81
SAC	Luis Reyes, Daytona	5
BB	Alfredo Duno, Daytona	95
HBP	Woody Hadeen, Lakeland	17
SO	Yordany De Los Santos, Bradenton	137
SB	Kyle Henley, Daytona	57
CS	Yordany De Los Santos, Bradenton	14

FIELDING

C PCT	Ricardo Hurtado, Lakeland	.995
PO	Daiverson Gutierrez, St. Lucie	821
A	Victor Ortega, Jupiter	70
E	Daiverson Gutierrez, St. Lucie	24
DP	Carlos Sanchez, Jupiter	8
CS	Victor Ortega, Jupiter	43
SB	Daiverson Gutierrez, St. Lucie	154
PB	Daiverson Gutierrez, St. Lucie	17
1B PCT	No qualifiers	
PO	Cristian Santana, Lakeland	435
A	Cristian Santana, Lakeland	25
E	Hans Montero, Tampa	8
DP	Cristian Santana, Lakeland	49
2B PCT	Bernard Moon, Daytona	.943
PO	Bernard Moon, Daytona	147
A	Bernard Moon, Daytona	168
E	Bernard Moon, Daytona	19
DP	Bernard Moon, Daytona	38
3B PCT	Carson Rucker, Lakeland	.889
PO	Carson Rucker, Lakeland	81
A	Carson Rucker, Lakeland	151
E	Carson Rucker, Lakeland	29
DP	Carson Rucker, Lakeland	16
SS PCT	No qualifiers	
PO	Sammy Stafura, Daytona	125
A	Roderick Arias, Tampa	197
E	Roderick Arias, Tampa	22
DP	Sammy Stafura, Daytona	47
OF PCT	Kyle Henley, Daytona	.991
PO	Kyle Henley, Daytona	228
A	Jean Joseph, Dunedin	13
E	Yonatan Henriquez, St. Lucie	11
DP	2 tied	3

PITCHING

G	Chris Veach, Tampa	43
GS	Leonel Sequera, Palm Beach	24
GF	Noah Takacs, Bradenton	31
SV	Noah Takacs, Bradenton	9
W	Victor Cabreja, Bradenton	9
W	Zack Lee, Lakeland	9
L	Two tied	10
IP	Leonel Sequera, Palm Beach	108
H	Leonel Sequera, Palm Beach	107
R	Three tied	65
ER	Walin Castillo, Jupiter	59
SO	Liomar Martinez, Jupiter	119
SO/9	Leonel Sequera, Palm Beach	8.25
BB/9	Leonel Sequera, Palm Beach	3.42
WP	Jake Faherty, Jupiter	15
Balks	Brandt Thompson, Palm Beach	6
HR	Gilberto Bautista, Dunedin	15
HR	Brandt Thompson, Palm Beach	15
AVG	Leonel Sequera, Palm Beach	.258

ARIZONA COMPLEX LEAGUE

Awards selected by Major League Baseball

CHAMPION: The Angels captured their first-ever ACL title ever, sweeping the Giants in a best-of-three series. While standout pitching performances from Trey Gregory-Alford and Dylan Jordan highlighted the series, it was Lucas Ramirez, son of Manny Ramirez, who led the offense, hitting .364 in the heart of the lineup. Adding to the offensive firepower, Hayden Alvarez finished the series with an impressive .500 batting average, helping seal a historic championship for the organization.

MOST VALUABLE PLAYER: The Rockies appear to have discovered a diamond in the rough in Roldy Brito, and his performance in the ACL only reinforces that impression. Brito showcased a well-rounded offensive game, slashing .368/.445/.555 with three home runs and driving in 21 RBIs. Beyond his bat, he highlighted his explosive speed, swiping 22 bases and creating havoc on the basepaths. With a combination of contact ability, on-base skills and athleticism.

PITCHER OF THE YEAR: On an ACL Giants team boasting one of the top starting rotations at the rookie level, Keyner Martinez emerged as the standout arm. The righthander dominated with a 1.90 ERA, striking out a league-leading 67 batters while issuing just 11 walks, showcasing advanced command and execution. The 21-year-old showed glimpses of what he could do the year before in his pro debut, but this season, he ascended his way into one of the most intriguing prospects in San Francisco's system.

TOP MLB PROSPECT: It's easy to see why Giants shortstop Jhonny Level was one of the most electrifying teenagers making his stateside debut. One of the Giants' top prospects, Level showcased a complete skill set, hitting .333, blasting nine home runs and swiping 17 bases. He also had the most assists among league shortstops.

MANAGER OF THE YEAR: Jacob Heyward, the brother of MLB vet Jason Heyward, led the Giants to a 42-18 record. The ACL Giants' .700 winning percentage was best in the league.

Brito

ARIZONA COMPLEX LEAGUE ALL-STARS

Pos	Player	Team	AVG	OPS	HR
C	Carlos Virahonda	ACL D-backs	.347	.919	1
1B	Enyervert Perez	ACL D-backs	.283	.844	5
2B	Dario Reynoso	ACL Giants	.298	.998	10
3B	Wilder Dalis	ACL Rockies	.352	.965	3
SS	Tyson Lewis	ACL Reds	.340	.928	6
OF	Ching-Hsien Ko	ACL Dodgers	.367	1.026	4
OF	Roldy Brito	ACL Rockies	.368	1.000	3
OF	Brendan Tunink	ACL Dodgers	.300	.967	5
DH	Dauri Fernandez	ACL Guardians	.333	.956	6

Pos	Player	Team	AVG	OPS	HR
UT	Emil Morales	ACL Dodgers	.300	.881	9

Pos	Pitcher	Team	G	ERA	SO
SP	Argenis Cayama	ACL Giants	12	2.25	55
SP	Darwin Rodriguez	ACL Royals	12	3.32	50
SP	Keyner Martinez	ACL Giants	15	1.90	67
SP	Fabian Ysalla	ACL White Sox	12	2.02	40
RP	Roberto Perez	ACL Mariners	17	1.42	33

OVERALL STANDINGS

East Division	W	L	PCT	GB	Manager
ACL Giants	42	18	.700	—	Jacob Heyward
ACL Rockies	37	23	.617	5	Fred Ocasio
ACL D-backs	31	29	.517	11	Juan Francia
ACL Athletics	25	35	.417	17	Tim Esmay
ACL Cubs	19	41	.317	23	Corey Ray
ACL Central	**W**	**L**	**PCT**	**GB**	
ACL Angels	38	22	.633	—	Hainley Statia
ACL Guardians	31	29	.517	7	Juan De La Cruz
ACL Brewers	30	30	.500	8	Rafael Neda
ACL Dodgers	29	31	.483	9	Juan Apodaca
ACL Reds	25	35	.417	13	Gustavo Molina
ACL West	**W**	**L**	**PCT**	**GB**	
ACL Rangers	33	27	.550	—	Nick Janssen
ACL White Sox	33	27	.550	—	Danny Gonzalez
ACL Royals	32	28	.533	1	Larry Sutton
ACL Mariners	31	29	.517	2	Luis Matias/Rico Reyes
ACL Padres	14	46	.233	19	Jhonaldo Pozo

ARIZONA COMPLEX LEAGUE | STATISTICS

CLUB BATTING

	AVG	G	AB	R	H	2B	3B	HR	RBI	BB	SO	SB	OBP	SLG
ACL Rockies	.287	60	1752	310	502	100	26	14	245	226	414	78	.376	.397
ACL Dodgers	.277	60	1965	352	544	119	19	48	304	247	574	45	.365	.430
ACL Giants	.271	60	1865	376	505	108	26	46	325	260	511	91	.371	.431
ACL Angels	.268	60	1948	368	523	90	26	27	314	248	547	74	.364	.383
ACL Guardians	.263	60	1896	359	499	90	22	40	302	290	437	124	.369	.397
ACL Brewers	.261	60	1910	372	498	102	24	41	317	319	530	90	.381	.404
ACL Royals	.261	60	1921	325	502	94	30	33	274	229	564	98	.352	.393
ACL White Sox	.260	60	1799	301	468	95	22	36	252	213	600	121	.350	.397
ACL Reds	.259	61	1953	374	506	108	29	39	310	281	568	70	.362	.404
ACL D-backs	.258	60	1875	292	483	101	21	28	240	227	563	59	.354	.379
ACL Rangers	.253	60	1939	308	491	89	20	36	264	219	501	57	.341	.375
ACL Padres	.253	61	1934	305	489	85	18	22	268	272	572	90	.360	.350
ACL Athletics	.249	60	1841	311	459	87	19	20	265	307	541	52	.366	.350
ACL Mariners	.246	60	1880	321	462	91	15	37	267	292	487	51	.358	.369
ACL Cubs	.242	60	1855	250	448	83	30	27	217	198	509	137	.325	.362

CLUB PITCHING

	ERA	G	CG	SHO	SV	IP	H	R	ER	HR	BB	SO	AVG
ACL Giants	3.55	60	0	0	15	492	435	248	194	22	202	638	.235
ACL Angels	4.06	60	0	0	11	514	502	289	232	27	251	511	.258
ACL Rockies	4.15	60	0	0	12	451	428	251	208	19	207	470	.252
ACL D-backs	4.17	60	0	0	17	490	446	282	227	35	239	490	.245
ACL Mariners	4.37	60	0	0	14	503	488	277	244	27	220	533	.256
ACL White Sox	4.38	60	0	0	18	473	431	275	230	22	240	483	.246
ACL Rangers	4.60	60	0	0	11	508	485	293	260	39	237	625	.251
ACL Royals	4.76	60	0	0	15	503	500	314	266	50	205	559	.259
ACL Guardians	5.10	60	0	0	11	496	460	345	281	24	338	593	.246
ACL Brewers	5.39	60	0	0	18	499	515	354	299	42	217	490	.262
ACL Cubs	5.93	60	0	0	4	490	488	378	323	37	334	527	.261
ACL Athletics	6.05	60	1	1	7	479	572	371	322	16	236	410	.296
ACL Reds	6.05	61	0	0	7	494	545	378	332	43	236	526	.281
ACL Dodgers	6.06	60	0	0	12	497	469	391	335	47	352	570	.248
ACL Padres	7.61	61	0	0	9	494	615	478	418	44	314	493	.305

CLUB FIELDING

	PCT	PO	A	E	DP
ACL Mariners	.974	1508	554	55	56
ACL Rangers	.971	1525	478	59	44
ACL Reds	.969	1460	473	61	39
ACL White Sox	.969	1418	502	61	58
ACL Rockies	.966	1353	504	66	34
ACL D-backs	.965	1469	540	72	60
ACL Angels	.965	1541	534	76	52
ACL Giants	.963	1476	441	73	33

	PCT	PO	A	E	DP
ACL Athletics	.962	1438	556	79	57
ACL Royals	.962	1509	494	80	32
ACL Cubs	.960	1470	436	79	34
ACL Dodgers	.958	1492	471	85	45
ACL Brewers	.958	1498	496	88	41
ACL Padres	.954	1462	484	93	37
ACL Guardians	.952	1488	428	97	35

INDIVIDUAL BATTING

Batter, Club	AVG	G	AB	R	H	2B	3B	HR	RBI	BB	SO	SB
Roldy Brito, ACL Rockies	.368	51	182	46	67	13	6	3	21	22	42	22
Ching-Hsien Ko, ACL Dodgers	.367	53	180	43	66	15	2	4	30	39	40	5
Wilder Dalis, ACL Rockies	.352	56	179	37	63	12	5	3	42	29	44	10
JD Dix, ACL D-backs	.342	39	152	31	52	12	4	1	19	20	34	9
Tyson Lewis, ACL Reds	.340	46	188	44	64	8	5	6	35	15	51	19
Hayden Alvarez, ACL Angels	.335	55	182	38	61	5	3	2	26	31	41	24
Dauri Fernandez, ACL Guardians	.333	43	156	33	52	9	4	6	27	16	22	16
Dustin Crenshaw, ACL Mariners	.327	55	196	40	64	9	3	5	23	29	33	8
Ashly Andujar, ACL Rockies	.319	53	191	32	61	7	0	0	23	15	31	7
Alfredo Alcantara, ACL Reds	.315	44	149	35	47	13	0	2	27	33	44	7

INDIVIDUAL PITCHING

Pitcher, Club	W	L	ERA	G	GS	CG	SV	IP	H	R	ER	BB	SO
Fabian Ysalla, ACL White Sox	4	0	2.02	12	10	0	0	49.0	41	14	11	16	40
Argenis Cayama, ACL Giants	1	1	2.25	12	12	0	0	48.0	33	15	12	18	55
Brayan Vergara, ACL Angels	2	2	2.47	12	4	0	1	51.0	56	20	14	11	37
Tyler Renz, ACL Brewers	3	3	3.50	12	9	0	0	54.0	50	22	21	15	46
Trey Gregory-Alford, ACL Angels	4	4	3.54	12	10	0	0	53.3	53	24	21	20	48
Drew Conover, ACL Athletics	4	3	4.02	13	9	0	0	53.7	57	25	24	26	41
Jose Romero, ACL Mariners	4	5	4.09	12	9	0	0	50.7	62	29	23	15	43
Francisco Pazos, ACL Mariners	3	2	4.18	12	10	0	0	51.7	52	25	24	15	60
Manuel Olivares, ACL Rockies	4	3	4.31	15	4	0	1	48.0	49	28	23	17	48
Marlon Franco, ACL Giants	4	3	5.00	14	5	0	0	54.0	72	30	30	16	51

DEPARTMENT LEADERS

BATTING
OBP	Ching-Hsien Ko, ACL Dodgers	.487
SLG	Dauri Fernandez, ACL Guardians	.558
OPS	Ching-Hsien Ko, ACL Dodgers	1.026
Runs	Dario Reynoso, ACL Giants	59
Hits	Emil Morales, ACL Dodgers	70
TB	Emil Morales, ACL Dodgers	116
XBH	Arnaldo Lantigua, ACL Reds	25
XBH	Emil Morales, ACL Dodgers	25
2B	Handelfry Encarnacion, ACL Brewers	18
3B	Yolfran Castillo, ACL Rangers	7
HR	Arnaldo Lantigua, ACL Reds	10
HR	Dario Reynoso, ACL Giants	10
RBI	Kleimer Lemos, ACL Rangers	46
SAC	Ashly Andujar, ACL Rockies	6
BB	Dario Reynoso, ACL Giants	40
BB	Darison Garcia, ACL Royals	40
HBP	Donte Grant, ACL Padres	19
SO	Emil Morales, ACL Dodgers	76
SB	Robert Arias, ACL Guardians	29
CS	D'Angelo Tejada, ACL White Sox	8

FIELDING
C	PCT	Stiven Flores, ACL White Sox	.991
	PO	Reiner Herrera, ACL Guardians	397
	A	Marlon Quintero, ACL Angels	59
	E	Reiner Herrera, ACL Guardians	9
	DP	Jesus Freitez, ACL Rockies	5
	CS	Marlon Quintero, ACL Angels	33
	SB	Reiner Herrera, ACL Guardians	90
	PB	Bryan Gonzalez, ACL Dodgers	11
1B	PCT	Luis De La Cruz, ACL Guardians	.987
	PO	Luis De La Cruz, ACL Guardians	293
	A	Kleimer Lemos, ACL Rangers	19
	E	Eliezer Rivero, ACL Angels	6
	DP	Kleimer Lemos, ACL Rangers	31
2B	PCT	Darison Garcia, ACL Royals	.953
	PO	Anyelo Marquez, ACL Angels	85
	A	Luis De Leon, ACL Padres	103
	E	Luis De Leon, ACL Padres	9
	DP	Anyelo Marquez, ACL Angels	25
3B	PCT	Wilder Dalis, ACL Rockies	.927
	PO	Wilder Dalis, ACL Rockies	44
	A	Martin Gonzalez, ACL Mariners	71
	E	Martin Gonzalez, ACL Mariners	12
	DP	Eliesbert Alejos, ACL D-backs	12
SS	PCT	Yolfran Castillo, ACL Rangers	.957
	PO	Ashly Andujar, ACL Rockies	98
	A	Jhonny Level, ACL Giants	112
	E	Jhonny Level, ACL Giants	13
	DP	Nik McClaughry, ACL Mariners	28
OF	PCT	Kevin Alcantara, ACL Mariners	1.000
	PO	Rashawn Pinder, ACL Rangers	112
	A	Leandro Alsinois, ACL White Sox	9
	E	Juneiker Caceres, ACL Guardians	8
	DP	Five tied	2

PITCHING
G	Camilo Hernandez, ACL Athletics	23
GS	Five tied	12
GF	Camilo Hernandez, ACL Athletics	19
SV	Wilmis Paulino, ACL Rockies	7
W	Jose Rengel, ACL Giants	7
L	Dylan Wilson, ACL Mariners	6
L	Winyer Chourio, ACL Padres	6
IP	Manuel Perez, ACL Athletics	56
H	Deivi Villafana, ACL Reds	78
R	Jose Vasquez, ACL Dodgers	51
R	Josiah Romeo, ACL Athletics	51
ER	Jose Vasquez, ACL Dodgers	47
ER	Josiah Romeo, ACL Athletics	47
SO	Keyner Martinez, ACL Giants	67
SO/9	Francisco Pazos, ACL Mariners	10.45
BB/9	Brayan Vergara, ACL Angels	1.94
WP	Josiah Romeo, ACL Athletics	16
Balks	Tyler Naquin, ACL Guardians	5
HR	Jormy Nivar, ACL Rangers	9
AVG	Argenis Cayama, ACL Giants	.191

FLORIDA COMPLEX LEAGUE

Awards selected by Major League Baseball

CHAMPION: While the MLB Blue Jays fell short of capturing the World Series, their FCL affiliate made history by claiming the league crown after sneaking into the postseason via the wild card. It marked the first championship in the Florida Complex League's 61-year history for the Blue Jays organization. David Beckles played a key role all season for the Blue Jays, as he led the circuit with eight home runs along with a .304 average, .871 OPS and 42 RBIs, all of which landed him in the top three.

MOST VALUABLE PLAYER: FCL Orioles outfielder Jordan Sanchez showed glimpses of his dominance in his DSL debut in 2024, but his season was cut short with an injury. There was no slowing him down in 2025. He posted a .293/.421/.529 slash line with five home runs and 45 RBIs.

PITCHER OF THE YEAR: Astros righthander Javier Perez dominated the circuit, racking up a tiny 1.13 ERA while striking out 48 batters against just eight walks before earning a promotion to Low-A in early August. Perez showed a nice blend of command, control and bat-missing stuff.

TOP MLB PROSPECT: Talented prospects are at a premium in the Pirates system, and outfielder Edward Florentino is no exception. He showcased his power early, blasting six home runs in just 29 games before earning a promotion to Low-A Bradenton, where he added 10 more homers. While his stint in the FCL was brief, it left a strong impression, highlighting Florentino's ability to make an immediate impact and his potential to be an impactful middle-of-the-order bat.

MANAGER OF THE YEAR: Christian Frias guided the Orioles to a 35-24 record. More notably, he helped the team navigate a tragic season marked by the sudden death of teammate Luis Guevara in a jet-ski accident, which also left several other players injured.

Florentino

FLORIDA COMPLEX LEAGUE ALL-STARS

Pos	Player	Team	AVG	OPS	HR
C	Andrew Tess	FCL Orioles	.256	.825	2
1B	David Beckles	FCL Blue Jays	.304	.871	8
2B	Jude Warwick	FCL Tigers	.262	.793	3
3B	Javier Osorio	FCL Tigers	.304	.874	5
SS	Alberth Palma	FCL Rays	.318	.850	0
OF	Anderson Fermin	FCL Red Sox	.283	.831	0
OF	Jordan Sanchez	FCL Orioles	.293	.950	5
OF	Manolfi Jimenez	FCL Phillies	.306	.868	4
DH	Edward Lantigua	FCL Mets	.288	.832	3
UT	Randy Guzman	FCL Mets	.282	.845	7

Pos	Pitcher	Team	G	ERA	SO
SP	Javier Perez	FCL Astros	13	1.69	48
SP	Kelvis Salcedo	FCL Tiger	12	1.99	53
SP	Esteban Mejia	FCL Orioles	11	2.45	53
SP	Luis Aguilar	FCL Astros	12	2.05	49
RP	Alan Reyes	FCL Cardinals	14	0.70	26
RP	Danny Hilario	FCL Rays	14	2.52	32

OVERALL STANDINGS

East Division	W	L	PCT	GB	Manager
FCL Astros	37	16	.698	—	Vincent Blue
FCL Nationals	30	25	.545	8	Carmelo Jaime
FCL Mets	25	28	.472	12	Lino DiazL
FCL Cardinals	24	31	.436	14	Willi Martin
FCL Marlins	19	35	.352	18.5	Gabe Ortiz

North Division	W	L	PCT	GB	Manager
FCL Tigers	37	22	.627	—	Salvador Paniagua
FCL Blue Jays	36	23	.610	1	Andy Fermin/John Tamargo
FCL Yankees	28	30	.483	8.5	Ryan Chipka
FCL Phillies	16	42	.276	20.5	Shawn Williams

South Division	W	L	PCT	GB	Manager(s)
FCL Twins	39	20	.661	—	Nico Giarratano
FCL Orioles	35	24	.593	4	Christian Frias
FCL Rays	29	29	.500	9.5	Hector Gimenez
FCL Pirates	27	32	.458	12	Jose Mendez
FCL Red Sox	25	34	.424	14	Chase Illig
FCL Braves	21	37	.362	17.5	Nestor Perez

FLORIDA COMPLEX LEAGUE | STATISTICS

CLUB BATTING

	AVG	G	AB	R	H	2B	3B	HR	RBI	BB	SO	SB	OBP	SLG
FCL Orioles	.263	59	1619	335	425	84	21	28	278	330	458	103	.402	.392
FCL Rays	.246	58	1748	284	430	66	15	12	227	288	403	89	.364	.322
FCL Astros	.241	53	1453	298	350	69	19	37	250	270	441	74	.375	.391
FCL Tigers	.238	59	1820	306	434	80	11	38	258	247	512	115	.345	.357
FCL Red Sox	.237	59	1670	267	395	86	14	20	226	263	460	153	.348	.341
FCL Yankees	.235	58	1799	279	422	78	9	35	235	173	470	134	.316	.346
FCL Nationals	.230	55	1611	274	371	51	9	26	221	263	498	91	.354	.322
FCL Blue Jays	.228	59	1783	278	406	75	12	28	229	280	482	63	.344	.330
FCL Phillies	.222	58	1843	214	410	102	14	28	181	190	486	44	.306	.339
FCL Braves	.217	58	1697	228	369	63	3	14	183	262	403	79	.337	.283
FCL Pirates	.217	59	1664	272	361	66	16	24	218	277	513	91	.340	.319
FCL Marlins	.217	54	1600	224	347	65	7	24	178	248	505	116	.336	.311
FCL Cardinals	.214	55	1532	233	328	65	7	18	174	237	497	139	.336	.301
FCL Mets	.214	53	1416	199	303	55	7	23	158	231	400	74	.340	.311
FCL Twins	.206	59	1522	278	313	80	9	29	222	306	484	127	.361	.327

CLUB PITCHING

	ERA	G	CG	SHO	SV	IP	H	R	ER	HR	BB	SO	AVG
FCL Astros	3.59	53	0	0	14	401	292	196	160	33	209	478	.201
FCL Rays	3.62	58	0	0	12	470	377	261	189	20	279	461	.216
FCL Orioles	3.70	59	0	0	11	436	358	254	179	18	271	494	.219
FCL Blue Jays	3.70	59	0	0	11	484	421	241	199	27	176	505	.233
FCL Tigers	3.72	59	1	0	20	496	414	254	205	39	206	475	.227
FCL Twins	3.77	59	0	0	20	437	374	217	183	21	178	452	.230
FCL Nationals	3.90	55	0	0	10	438	393	235	190	29	237	463	.241
FCL Yankees	3.97	58	2	2	7	483	364	272	213	34	308	512	.207
FCL Mets	4.27	53	0	0	6	386	319	237	183	19	219	417	.222
FCL Phillies	4.52	58	1	1	7	480	473	311	241	29	200	458	.255
FCL Cardinals	4.70	55	0	0	13	416	364	260	217	23	253	464	.233
FCL Braves	4.86	58	1	1	10	450	417	301	243	23	293	383	.248
FCL Marlins	5.10	54	0	0	9	426	331	300	241	24	331	519	.216
FCL Red Sox	5.34	59	0	0	12	445	364	303	264	24	331	461	.229
FCL Pirates	5.61	59	0	0	10	444	403	328	277	21	374	470	.245

CLUB FIELDING

	PCT	PO	A	E	DP		PCT	PO	A	E	DP
FCL Pirates	.967	1332	466	62	59	FCL Rays	.959	1411	469	81	34
FCL Twins	.966	1311	445	62	34	FCL Cardinals	.957	1248	369	73	38
FCL Red Sox	.965	1336	446	64	33	FCL Nationals	.955	1315	443	83	37
FCL Tigers	.964	1487	536	75	50	FCL Mets	.954	1157	406	76	38
FCL Braves	.963	1349	520	71	38	FCL Marlins	.952	1277	413	85	43
FCL Blue Jays	.963	1451	491	75	42	FCL Orioles	.951	1307	428	89	27
FCL Astros	.962	1202	363	62	25	FCL Phillies	.947	1440	461	106	53
FCL Yankees	.960	1448	471	81	41						

INDIVIDUAL BATTING

Batter, Club	AVG	G	AB	R	H	2B	3B	HR	RBI	BB	SO	SB
Alberth Palma, FCL Rays	.318	44	129	27	41	1	4	0	24	33	17	15
Manolfi Jimenez, FCL Phillies	.306	46	157	27	48	13	5	4	20	6	26	3
David Beckles, FCL Blue Jays	.304	57	207	36	63	11	1	8	42	24	63	2
Jordan Sanchez, FCL Orioles	.293	54	157	32	46	16	3	5	45	31	57	3
Edward Lantigua, FCL Mets	.288	49	153	23	44	6	1	3	27	33	29	13
Julio Zayas, FCL Mets	.284	48	141	14	40	9	0	1	18	22	24	0
Anderson Fermin, FCL Red Sox	.283	48	138	32	39	7	3	0	14	42	35	25
Randy Guzman, FCL Mets	.282	49	156	18	44	9	0	7	33	15	33	0
Gerardo Rodriguez, FCL Red Sox	.279	47	154	17	43	16	0	0	32	10	23	7
Juan Mateo, FCL Braves	.277	51	188	22	52	8	0	0	18	21	34	10

INDIVIDUAL PITCHING

Pitcher, Club	W	L	ERA	G	GS	CG	SV	IP	H	R	ER	BB	SO
Edinzo Marquez, FCL Yankees	2	2	2.19	11	10	1	0	53.3	42	18	13	20	41
Jose Feliz, FCL Nationals	2	1	2.20	14	13	0	0	61.3	57	20	15	12	51
Jatnk Diaz, FCL Tigers	4	2	3.49	12	11	1	0	49.0	44	26	19	19	44
Angel Liranzo, FCL Phillies	0	5	3.60	12	10	0	0	55.0	59	29	22	18	46

DEPARTMENT LEADERS

BATTING
OBP	Alberth Palma, FCL Rays	.462
SLG	Manolfi Jimenez, FCL Phillies	.529
OPS	Jordan Sanchez, FCL Orioles	.950
Runs	Dariel Ramon, FCL Rays	39
Hits	David Beckles, FCL Blue Jays	63
TB	David Beckles, FCL Blue Jays	100
XBH	Jordan Sanchez, FCL Orioles	24
2B	Gerardo Rodriguez, FCL Red Sox	16
2B	Jordan Sanchez, FCL Orioles	16
3B	Manolfi Jimenez, FCL Phillies	5
HR	David Beckles, FCL Blue Jays	8
RBI	Jordan Sanchez, FCL Orioles	45
SAC	Derek Datil, FCL Rays	5
BB	Anderson Fermin, FCL Red Sox	42
HBP	Andrew Tess, FCL Orioles	18
SO	Daiber De Los Santos, FCL Twins	89
SB	Dashyll Tejeda, FCL Nationals	29
CS	Edward Lantigua, FCL Mets	10

FIELDING
C	PCT	Maykel Minoso, FCL Blue Jays	.996
	PO	Ediel Rivera, FCL Yankees	287
	A	Gerardo Rodriguez, FCL Red Sox	39
	E	Ediel Rivera, FCL Yankees	11
	DP	2 tied	5
CS		Gerardo Rodriguez, FCL Red Sox	32
SB		Nixon Chirinos, FCL Marlins	72
PB		Ediel Rivera, FCL Yankees	13
1B	PCT	D'Angelo Ortiz, FCL Red Sox	.987
	PO	David Beckles, FCL Blue Jays	245
	A	David Beckles, FCL Blue Jays	19
	E	David Beckles, FCL Blue Jays	7
	DP	David Beckles, FCL Blue Jays	24
2B	PCT	Ramiro Dominguez, FCL Twins	.967
	PO	Adrian Garcia, FCL Phillies	74
	A	Felix Cotes, FCL Rays	98
	E	Eyeksson Rojas, FCL Nationals	9
	DP	Adrian Garcia, FCL Phillies	24
3B	PCT	Eddie Rynders, FCL Pirates	.921
	PO	Eddie Rynders, FCL Pirates	41
	A	Aldo Gaxiola, FCL Blue Jays	81
	E	Francisco Loreto, FCL Phillies	23
	DP	Eddie Rynders, FCL Pirates	7
SS	PCT	Jose Perdomo, FCL Braves	.950
	PO	Daiber De Los Santos, FCL Twins	61
	A	Angel Feliz, FCL Nationals	119
	E	Jose Familia, FCL Phillies	25
	DP	Jose Familia, FCL Phillies	29
OF	PCT	Yorman Licourt, FCL Blue Jays	.978
	PO	Enmanuel Bonilla, FCL Blue Jays	112
	A	Anibal Salas, FCL Tigers	10
	E	Victor Cardoza, FCL Phillies	7
	DP	3 tied	2

PITCHING
G	Diego Dominguez, FCL Blue Jays	21
GS	Jose Feliz, FCL Nationals	13
GF	Diego Dominguez, FCL Blue Jays	20
SV	Moises Palma, FCL Rays	6
SV	Anderson Ramos, FCL Twins	6
W	Three tied	6
L	Madinson Frias, FCL Red Sox	7
IP	Jose Feliz, FCL Nationals	61
H	Angel Liranzo, FCL Phillies	59
R	Brad Pacheco, FCL Phillies	38
ER	Brad Pacheco, FCL Phillies	31
SO	Nate Payne, FCL Marlins	55
SO/9	Jatnk Diaz, FCL Tigers	8.08
BB/9	Jose Feliz, FCL Nationals	1.76
WP	Josue Arias, FCL Marlins	20
Balks	Darrel Lunar, FCL Nationals	5
HR	Three tied	6
AVG	Edinzo Marquez, FCL Yankees	.210

ALL-STAR FUTURES GAME

BY GEOFF PONTES

We singled out the prospects whose tools shined brightest in the 2025 Futures Game, which was won by the National League 4-2.

Best Player: George Lombard, SS, Yankees

Josue De Paula had the best hitting performance and won MVP for his game-winning home run, but Lombard was the best all-around player in the game. He made several heady plays in the field, showing range as well. At the plate, he went 1-for-2 with a double and a walk. Lombard's double was hit 104.4 mph off Trent Harris, while he drew a walk in his first at-bat against Marlins LHP Thomas White.

Best Hitter: Josue De Paula, OF, Dodgers

This year's game only had four extra-base hits and all others paled in comparison to De Paula's big fly. The Dodgers outfield prospect connected on a hanging slider from Noah Schultz, hitting it 108.5 mph and depositing the ball in the right field bleachers.

Best Power: JJ Wetherholt, SS, Cardinals

Wetherholt just missed a homer in the opening at-bat for the NL squad, instead putting it off the center field wall at 105.9 mph. He hit a second ball 102.4 mph on a lineout. Wetherholt was the only player in this year's Futures Game with multiple balls in play above 100 mph.

Best Defensive Play: Slade Caldwell, OF, D-Backs

Caldwell made the defensive play of the game when snagged a falling liner off George Lombard Jr.'s bat in center field in the top of the seventh inning.

Best Fastball: Jonah Tong, RHP, Mets

Tong's fastball sat 95-97 mph on the day, touching 97.4 mph at peak. He averaged between 17-18 inches of induced vertical break with heavy cut. Other pitchers threw a little harder, but no one paired movement and power quite like Tong.

Best Breaking Ball: JR Ritchie, RHP, Braves

Ritchie's sweeper to strike out Red Sox prospect Jhostynxon Garcia to end the first inning stood out as the best of the day. Ritchie ripped the slider at 83.5 mph, generating one inch of vertical drop and 13 inches of horizontal sweep.

Best Changeup: Parker Messick, LHP, Guardians

Carson Whisenhunt's changeup entered the day as the favorite for this superlative, but Messick ultimately took home the honors. He threw six changeups, generating two outs and one called strike. The 84.1 mph called strike to Zyhir Hope was the best of the bunch. ∎

FUTURES GAME BOX SCORE

NATIONAL LEAGUE 4, AMERICAN LEAGUE 2
JULY 12 IN ATLANTA

AL Futures	AB	R	H	RBI	NL Futures	AB	R	H	RBI
Clark, CF	1	0	1	0	Wetherholt, DH-2B	4	0	1	0
Jensen, C	1	0	0	0	Griffin, SS	2	0	1	0
Montgomery, B, LF	3	0	0	1	De Vries, PR-SS	1	0	0	0
Kayfus, 1B	2	0	0	0	Caissie, RF	2	0	1	1
Garcia, Jh, RF	2	0	0	0	Condon, 1B	3	0	0	0
Montes, RF	0	0	0	0	Valdez, Es, 1B	1	0	0	0
Ford, H, C	1	0	0	0	Hope, CF	2	1	1	0
Bradfield, PH-CF	2	0	0	0	Caldwell, CF	1	0	0	0
Briceño, DH	3	1	1	0	Made, 3B	3	1	1	0
Walcott, 3B	1	0	0	1	De Paula, LF	2	1	1	3
White, 3B	1	0	0	0	Benge, LF	1	0	0	0
McGonigle, SS	2	0	0	0	Groover, 3B	2	1	2	0
Culpepper, 2B	1	0	0	0	Stewart, S, 3B	1	0	0	0
Lombard, 2B-SS	2	1	1	0	Mack, C	1	0	0	0
					Tait, C	1	0	0	0
					Duno, C	1	0	0	0
Totals	22	2	3	2	Totals	28	4	8	4

AMERICAN LEAGUE	001	100	0	—	2	3	0
NATIONAL LEAGUE	000	400	0	—	4	8	0

AL: 2B: Lombard Jr. **(1,** Harris). **3B:** Briceño (1, Grissom Jr.). **TB:** Briceño 3; Clark; Lombard Jr. **RBI:** Montgomery, B (1), Walcott (1). **Runners left in scoring position, 2 out:** Kayfus; Garcia, Jh 2. **SF:** Walcott. **GIDP:** Bradfield Jr. **Team RISP:** 1-for-8. **Team LOB:** 4. **SB:** Clark (1, 2nd base off Ritchie/Mack); Lombard Jr. **(1,** 2nd base off White, T/ Mack).

NL: 2B: Wetherholt (1, Messick); Caissie (1, Santa). **HR:** De Paula, Jos (1, 4th inning off Schultz, 2 on, 0 out). **TB:** Caissie 2; De Paula, Jos 4; Griffin; Groover 2; Hope; Made; Wetherholt 2. **RBI:** Caissie (1); De Paula, Jos 3 (3). **2-out RBI:** Caissie. **Runners left in scoring position, 2 out:** Condon 2; Hope. **Team RISP:** 2-for-7. **Team LOB:** 6. **CS:** Griffin (1, 2nd base by Klassen/Ford, H). **DP:** (Wetherholt-De Vries-Valdez, Es).

AL	IP	H	R	ER	BB	SO	NL	IP	H	R	ER	BB	SO
Messick	1	1	0	0	1	1	Ritchie	1	0	0	0	1	2
Cijntje	1	1	0	0	0	2	Tong	1	0	0	0	0	1
Yesavage	0.1	0	0	0	0	1	White, T	1	1	1	1	2	1
Klassen	0.2	1	0	0	1	0	Grissom Jr.	1	1	1	1	1	0
Schultz	0.2	4	4	4	0	0	Harris	1	1	0	0	0	2
Santa	0.1	1	0	0	0	1	Clemmey	0.2	0	0	0	1	0
Mozzicato	1	0	0	0	0	1	Harris, H	0.1	0	0	0	0	0
Hopkins	1	0	0	0	0	0	Whisenhunt	0.2	0	0	0	0	1
Jump	0.2	0	0	0	1	1	Herrera, W	0.1	0	0	0	0	0
Gillies	0.1	0	0	0	0	0							
Totals	7	8	4	4	2	7	Totals	7	3	2	2	4	8

WP: Harris. **HBP:** Griffin (by Santa). **Pitches-strikes:** Messick 16-9; Cijntje 15-11; Yesavage 4-3; Klassen 11-6; Schultz 19-11; Santa 11-7; Mozzicato 10-8; Hopkins 9-8; Jump 4-4; Gillies 5-3; Ritchie 19-11; Tong 19-11; White, T 30-15; Grissom Jr 14-10; Harris 14-10; Clemmey 7-3; Harris, H 5-4; Whisenhunt 6-5; Herrera, W 5-2.

Umpires: HP: Charlie Welling. **1B:** Elliott Melton. **2B:** Bryan Van Vranken. **3B:** Jared Duerson. **T:** 2:09.

MINOR LEAGUE BEST TOOLS

	INTERNATIONAL LEAGUE	PACIFIC COAST LEAGUE	EASTERN LEAGUE	SOUTHERN LEAGUE	TEXAS LEAGUE
Best Batting Prospect	Roman Anthony	Nick Kurtz	Max Anderson	Sal Stewart	JJ Wetherholt
Best Power Prospect	Spencer Jones	Nick Kurtz	Spencer Jones	Brock Wilken	Joshua Baez
Best Strike-Zone Judgment	Roman Anthony	Alex Freeland	Cooper Ingle	Rikuu Nishida	JJ Wetherholt
Best Baserunner	Chandler Simpson	Esteury Ruiz	Aidan Miller	Homer Bush Jr.	Henry Bolte
Fastest Baserunner	Chandler Simpson	Samad Taylor	Enrique Bradfield Jr.	Homer Bush Jr.	Cameron Cauley
Best Pitching Prospect	Bubba Chandler	Jack Perkins	Jonah Tong	Chase Burns	Gage Jump
Best Fastball	Bubba Chandler	Bobby Miller	Jarlin Susana	Grant Taylor	Patrick Copen
Best Breaking Pitch	Cade Cavalli	Carson Seymour	Cam Schlittler	Chase Burns	Brandyn Garcia
Best Changeup	Craig Yoho	Carson Whisenhunt	Connelly Early	Thomas White	Luis Gastelum
Best Control	Michael McGreevy	Jhonathan Diaz	Jonah Tong	Shane Murphy	Mitch Bratt
Best Reliever	Hayden Harris	Eduarniel Nuñez	Welinton Herrera	Josh Ekness	Alimber Santa
Best Defensive C	Hayden Senger	Daniel Susac	Adrian Sugastey	Chandler Seagle	Leonardo Bernal
Best Defensive 1B	Tre' Morgan	Tristin English	Joe Naranjo	Sam Brown	Josh Hatcher
Best Defensive 2B	Rafael Lantigua	Brice Matthews	Max Anderson	Jacob Gonzalez	Tommy Troy
Best Defensive 3B	Jack Winkler	Blaze Alexander	Kyle Karros	Sal Stewart	Keyber Rodriguez
Best Defensive SS	Carson Williams	Darell Hernaiz	Aeverson Arteaga	William Bergolla Jr.	Jose Fernandez
Best Infield Arm	Carson Williams	Blaze Alexander	Aeverson Arteaga	Cooper Pratt	Sebastian Walcott
Best Defensive OF	Petey Halpin	Denzel Clarke	Nick Morabito	Homer Bush Jr.	Chase Davis
Best OF Arm	Billy Cook	Yanquiel Fernandez	Cole Carrigg	Geraldo Quintero	Zach Cole
Most Exciting Player	Roman Anthony	Nick Kurtz	George Lombard Jr.	Sal Stewart	JJ Wetherholt
Best Manager Prospect	Shelley Duncan	Fran Riordan	Reid Brignac	Guillermo Quiroz	Brian Dinkelman

	MIDWEST LEAGUE	NORTHWEST LEAGUE	SOUTH ATLANTIC LEAGUE	CALIFORNIA LEAGUE	CAROLINA LEAGUE	FLORIDA STATE LEAGUE
Best Batting Prospect	Kevin McGonigle	Jared Thomas	Konnor Griffin	Eduardo Quintero	Luis Peña	Konnor Griffin
Best Power Prospect	Josue Briceño	Lazaro Montes	Esmerlyn Valdez	Dakota Jordan	Eric Bitonti	Eduardo Tait
Best Strike-Zone Judgment	Max Clark	Ryan Waldschmidt	Carson Benge	Eduardo Quintero	Antonio Macias	Alfredo Duno
Best Baserunner	Kyle DeBarge	Jonah Cox	Patrick Clohisy	Jaron Elkins	Tommy Hawke	Konnor Griffin
Fastest Baserunner	Kendall George	Jonah Cox	Patrick Clohisy	Jaron Elkins	Asbel Gonzalez	Konnor Griffin
Best Pitching Prospect	Chase Burns	Trey Yesavage	Payton Tolle	Ryan Sloan	Brandon Clarke	Trey Yesavage
Best Fastball	Reynaldo Yean	Jurrangelo Cijntje	Payton Tolle	Gerelmi Maldonado	Brandon Clarke	Trey Yesavage
Best Breaking Pitch	Tyson Neighbors	Daniel Eagen	Trey Gibson	Ryan Sloan	Jose Urbina	Dasan Hill
Best Changeup	Ryan Gallagher	Trey Yesavage	Gary Gill Hill	Sean Paul Liñan	Brock Porter	Chris Veach
Best Control	Tyson Hardin	Shane Rademacher	Travis Sthele	Ryan Sloan	Melvin Hernandez	Josh Randall
Best Reliever	Tyson Neighbors	Welinton Herrera	Hueston Morrill	Nathan Blasick	Robert Cranz	Moises Rodriguez
Best Defensive C	Bennett Lee	Cole Messina	Walker Janek	Alberto Barriga	Jason Schiavone	Edgleen Perez
Best Defensive 1B	Blake Burke	Ben McLaughlin	Branden Boissiere	Colin Summerhill	Eric Bitonti	Garrett Pennington
Best Defensive 2B	Jadher Areinamo	Adrian Placencia	Marco Vargas	Yerald Nin	Luis Peña	Aroon Escobar
Best Defensive 3B	Rosman Verdugo	Kevin Sim	Javier Rivas	Zach Evans	Filippo Di Turi	Colin Houck
Best Defensive SS	Jose Devers	Colt Emerson	Franklin Arias	Maui Ahuna	Franklin Arias	Franyerber Montilla
Best Infield Arm	Eduardo Garcia	Cristofer Torin	Javier Rivas	Maui Ahuna	Freili Encarnacion	Roderick Arias
Best Defensive OF	Max Clark	Druw Jones	Vance Honeycutt	Jakey Josepha	Nate George	Dante Nori
Best OF Arm	Alfonsin Rosario	Lazaro Montes	Vance Honeycutt	Jakey Josepha	Yeremy Cabrera	Yasser Mercedes
Most Exciting Player	Kevin McGonigle	Arjun Nimmala	Konnor Griffin	Dakota Jordan	Nate George	Konnor Griffin
Best Manager Prospect	Nick Lovullo	Zach Vincej	Rafael Valenzuela	John Shoemaker	Ozzie Chavez	Rene Rivera

DOMINICAN SUMMER LEAGUE

Awards selected by Major League Baseball

CHAMPION: The timing couldn't have been better for the DSL Padres Gold to capture the league championship. By the trade deadline, San Diego had unloaded a wave of top prospects in a major fire sale to bolster its big-league roster—making the DSL title a much-needed bright spot for the organization's future. Padres Gold finished 39-17 and beat the A's in a best-of-three series.

MOST VALUABLE PLAYER: Cristian Arguelles, one of the Rockies' top signings from the 2024 international class, delivered video-game numbers in 2025. He dominated at the plate, slashing .422/.528/.652 for a 1.180 OPS, leading the DSL in three of those four categories. Arguelles also showcased his power, blasting five home runs and driving in 55 RBIs, establishing himself as one of the league's premier offensive talents.

PITCHER OF THE YEAR: After a tough rookie campaign in the DSL, Franco Zabaleta bounced back in a big way. The righthander posted a dominant 0.51 ERA with 44 strikeouts and just 14 walks over 52.2 innings, while holding opposing hitters to a mere .176 average.

TOP MLB PROSPECT: Elian Peña, the $5 million Mets signee, was one of the crown jewels of the 2025 international signing period—and he lived up to every bit of the hype. Playing for the DSL Mets Orange, Peña slashed .292/.421/.528 with nine home runs and 33 RBIs, while showing elite baserunning instincts by going 21-for-25 in stolen base attempts. His combination of power, contact and baserunning made him one of the most dynamic performers in the league.

MANAGER OF THE YEAR: While the MLB Rockies wrapped up the season with 43 wins, the DSL Rockies were a powerhouse. Led by Rafael Rosario, the squad tore through the competition with a 42-14 record, posting a league-best .750 winning percentage.

DOMINICAN SUMMER LEAGUE ALL-STARS

Pos	Player	Team	AVG	OPS	HR
C	Almen Tolentino	DSL Marlins	.301	.978	6
1B	Ronny Ugarte	DSL Rockies	.335	.901	4
2B	Juan Torres	NYY Bombers	.359	.922	4
3B	Juan Sanchez	DSL Blue Jays	.341	1.004	8
SS	Edgar Montero	DSL Athletics	.313	1.064	9
OF	Cristian Arguelles	DSL Rockies	.422	1.180	5
OF	José Castro	DSL Miami	.264	.984	16
OF	Luis Cova	DSL Marlins	.299	.959	9
DH	Marconi German	DSL Nationals	.283	.992	8
UT	Elorky Rodriguez	DSL Rangers	.337	.979	6

Pos	Pitcher	Team	G	ERA	SO
SP	Franco Zabaleta	DSL Athletics	11	0.51	44
SP	Dony Aguilera	DSL Reds	14	1.70	52
SP	Adrian Ardines	DSL Astros Blue	13	1.91	91
SP	Deiry Gonzalez	DSL Phillies Red	10	1.13	34
RP	Maximo Rodriguez	DSL Mariners	19	2.16	35
RP	Yonleg Gaetano	DSL Pirates Gold	13	0.93	39

DSL CHAMPIONSHIP: DSL Padres Gold defeated DSL Athletics 2-1 in best-of-3 series.

CENTRAL

Team	W	L	PCT	GB
DSL Pirates Gold	31	25	.554	—
DSL CLE Goryl	31	25	.554	—
DSL Brewers Gold	27	29	.482	4
DSL Cubs Blue	25	31	.446	6
DSL Rojos	23	30	.434	6.5
DSL Orioles Orange	20	34	.370	10

NORTHWEST

Team	W	L	PCT	GB
DSL Padres Gold	39	17	.696	—
DSL Tampa Bay	34	21	.618	4.5
DSL Brewers Blue	29	25	.537	9
DSL LAD Mega	25	30	.455	13.5
DSL Red Sox Red	25	30	.455	13.5
DSL CLE Mendoza	19	36	.345	19.5

SOUTHWEST

Team	W	L	PCT	GB
DSL Giants Orange	35	19	.648	—
DSL Pirates Black	34	20	.630	1
DSL Mariners	30	26	.536	6
DSL White Sox	29	26	.527	6.5
DSL Arizona Black	24	32	.429	12
DSL Blue Jays Blue	22	33	.400	13.5
DSL Cubs Red	15	41	.268	21

SOUTH

Team	W	L	PCT	GB
DSL Arizona Red	34	22	.607	—
DSL Angels	34	22	.607	—
DSL Giants Black	33	23	.589	1
DSL Mets Orange	31	25	.554	3
DSL Blue Jays Red	30	26	.536	4
DSL Nationals	27	29	.482	7
DSL Tigers 1	24	30	.444	9

SOUTHEAST

Team	W	L	PCT	GB
DSL Marlins	34	22	.607	—
DSL NYY Bombers	31	25	.554	3
DSL Cardinals	30	26	.536	4
DSL Phillies Red	25	31	.446	9
DSL Colorado	22	33	.400	11.5
DSL Mets Blue	19	37	.339	15
DSL Rangers Blue	15	41	.268	19

EAST

Team	W	L	PCT	GB
DSL Rockies	42	14	.750	—
DSL Rangers Red	37	17	.685	4
DSL Miami	37	19	.661	5
DSL Tigers 2	24	29	.453	16.5
DSL NYY Yankees	24	32	.429	18
DSL Twins	24	32	.429	18
DSL Phillies White	13	42	.236	28.5

WEST

Team	W	L	PCT	GB
DSL Athletics	35	20	.636	—
DSL Royals Ventura	35	20	.636	—
DSL Astros Blue	32	23	.582	3
DSL Reds	30	25	.545	5
DSL Orioles Black	21	32	.396	13
DSL Padres Brown	20	35	.364	15

NORTH

Team	W	L	PCT	GB
DSL Red Sox Blue	32	22	.593	—
DSL Rays	32	24	.571	1
DSL Astros Orange	29	26	.527	3.5
DSL Braves	22	31	.415	9.5
DSL Royals Fortuna	22	32	.407	10
DSL LAD Bautista	17	37	.315	15

FREITAS AWARDS
Excellence That Starts Off The Field

Triple-A
WORCESTER (INTERNATIONAL)

The Worcester Red Sox—or WooSox—have had a five-year run of success at the gate and on the field as part of Boston's resurgent player development program. And they've won the Triple-A Freitas Award for their success, despite the difficulty of the timing of their move.

"You can see decline after honeymoon, but we're proud to be defying it," said Worcester GM Brooke Cooper, who started with the franchise as an intern in merchandising back in Pawtucket. "We believe we can't just open our park's doors and expect people to just show up. It's core that we show up for them if we want them to show up for us."

To that end, the WooSox Foundation set on four pillars—education, social justice, conquering cancer and diamond sports (such as baseball, softball or kickball). Cooper said they intend to deepen their philanthropic efforts by expanding to a Starting Nine. The new pillars: mental health, veterans, the arts, frontline heroes and pets.

A dog already is one of the team's four official mascots. Steinberg joked that the WooSox "lead the league in mascots," and all have local ties.

Double-A
ROCKET CITY (SOUTHERN)

By the time Rocket City played its first game in the Double-A Southern League, thousands from all over the region had already been to the ballpark. During the pandemic, the team held movie nights on the field, did drive-through light shows around the Christmas holidays and a variety of other community events.

"It was a 52-day homestand," Rocket City GM Garrett Fahrmann said.

So when Opening Day finally arrived, many people who may have never noticed that a new team was coming to town were excited to check out the new baseball park.

Of course, many had already heard of the new team because of the nickname and logo. In the modern era of the minor leagues, it's helpful to find a name and logo that is unique and inspires reactions.

The Trash Pandas—a nickname for racoons—nailed that balance nearly perfectly. Sure, the team heard from some potential fans unhappy with the name. They also saw many more who bought hats, shirts and everything else that had the logo.

Class A
VANCOUVER (NORTHWEST)

It's only natural that a team called the Canadians hosted watch parties for the 2025 World Series.

Considering that the Vancouver Canadians of the High-A Northwest League are the only affiliated minor league team in the entire country, and are affiliated with Canada's lone remaining major league club in Toronto, the watch parties were a chance to feed off the frenzy of attention that the Blue Jays created during their first pennant-winning season since 1993.

Canadians GM Allan Bailey was a child when those Blue Jays won back-to-back World Series in 1992 and '93. He remembers the way it energized his friends and peers about the game.

He recognized what was happening in the Vancouver community, so he and his staff set up watch parties for Games 1 and 3 at the club's Nat Bailey Stadium, in the heart of Canada's eighth-largest city.

There, season ticket holders and their pals got to watch one of their own as Trey Yesavage opened the World Series on the mound for Toronto, one more accomplishment for a club that earned the Class A Freitas Award.

—JOHN MANUEL

LAST 10 WINNERS

TRIPLE-A	DOUBLE-A	CLASS A	SHORT-SEASON
2014: Charlotte (International)	**2014:** Montgomery (Southern)	**2014:** West Michigan (Midwest)	**2010:** Idaho Falls (Pioneer)
2015: Salt Lake (Pacific Coast)	**2015:** Richmond (Eastern)	**2015:** Myrtle Beach (Carolina)	**2011:** Vancouver (Northwest)
2016: Round Rock (Pacific Coast)	**2016:** Pensacola (Southern)	**2016:** San Bernardino (California)	**2012:** Billings (Pioneer)
2017: Fresno (Pacific Coast)	**2017:** Reading (Eastern)	**2017:** Charleston (South Atlantic)	**2013:** State College (NY-Penn)
2018: Oklahoma City (Pacific Coast)	**2018:** Tennessee (Southern)	**2018:** Winston-Salem (Carolina)	**2014:** Brooklyn (NY-Penn)
2019: Nashville (Pacific Coast)	**2019:** Tulsa (Texas)	**2019:** Lexington (South Atlantic)	**2015:** Grand Junction (Pioneer)
2021: Las Vegas (Pacific Coast)	**2021:** Hartford (Eastern)	**2021:** Greensboro (South Atlantic)	**2016:** Pulaski (Appalachian)
2022: St. Paul (International)	**2022:** Portland (Eastern)	**2022:** Wisconsin (Midwest)	**2017:** Hillsboro (Northwest)
2023: Albuquerque (Pacific Coast)	**2023:** Amarillo (Texas)	**2023:** South Bend (Midwest)	**2018:** Spokane (Northwest)
2024: Sacramento (Pacific Coast)	**2024:** Somerset (Eastern)	**2024:** Columbia (Carolina)	**2019:** Hudson Valley (NY-Penn)

ARIZONA FALL LEAGUE

Surprise Rallies To Title

The Surprise Saguaros have made the AFL Championship game for six straight seasons.

BY JESÚS CANO AND J.J. COOPER

Surprise Saguaros manager Jesus Azuaje knew from the moment he met his team in early October that his group was special.

He sensed its resilience even before the season started. Each player had their own journey, their own story and their own reason to maximize their time in the Arizona Fall League.

By mid-November, that notion became true. The Saguaros, playing in their sixth consecutive title game, beat the Javelinas 9-4 in a come-from-behind, seven-inning rally at Salt River Fields in Scottsdale.

"From Day One, they never gave up," said Azuaje, who coaches for the Royals. "All the credit to those guys. They stayed locked in. The guys made adjustments later in the game and we were able to put up some good at-bats and good results."

Down 4-2 in the eighth inning, Brewers prospect Josh Adamczewski stepped to the plate with the bases loaded. Even with the magnitude of the at-bat, the 20-year-old kept his approach the same, and it worked out.

He roped an opposite-field double to tie the game, opening the floodgates. The Saguaros then added five more runs, giving them more than plenty to help win the team's third AFL championship over the past four seasons.

"This group is special," Adamczewski said. "It was an unbelievable fall. These guys are the best, on and off the field. It's a blessing to be around them."

Along with Adamczewski, Brewers teammate Luke Adams had a strong showing, driving in three runs. Guardians prospect Juan Benjamin followed Adamczewski's game-tying hit by giving the Saguaros the two-run lead with a single to right field.

Brewers pitcher Edwin Jimenez delivered a scoreless inning of relief with two strikeouts to earn the win and save, sealing the win for Surprise.

"This is an unbelievable experience for all these guys," Azuaje said. "Every day they're facing elite pitching, and the enviroment is competitive. For these guys to play the Fall League, it's going to benefit so much for them to play down the road."

AFL Standouts

Tigers prospect Kevin McGonigle was named the AFL MVP. He hit .362 with five home runs and 12 extra-base hits, but he had to fight off strong competition from fellow Tigers prospect Max Anderson, who led the league with a .447 average, and Pirates outfielder Esmerlyn Valdez, who led the league with eight home runs.

Astros pitcher James Hicks was an easier pick as the Pitcher of the Year. He did not allow a run in 14 innings. He allowed just six hits and two walks while striking out 19.

The lack of pitching stood out across the league. Teams averaged scoring 6.1 runs per game. While hitters only hit .269, pitchers walked 15% of the batters they faced, leading to plenty of long innings.

ARIZONA FALL LEAGUE STATISTICS

STANDINGS

Team	W	L	PCT	GB
Scottsdale	18	10	.643	-
Surprise	16	10	.615	1
Mesa	14	14	.500	4
Peoria	12	15	.444	5.5
Glendale	11	16	.407	6.5
Salt River	11	17	.393	7

INDIVIDUAL BATTING LEADERS
(Minimum 2 Plate Appearances/League Games)

Player, Team	AVG	G	AB	R	H	HR	RBI
Max Anderson, SCO	.447	14	47	20	21	4	13
Raudi Rodriguez, SRR	.433	18	60	11	26	1	9
Parks Harber, SCO	.383	17	60	11	23	3	15
Owen Ayers, MSS	.379	20	66	17	25	3	16
Sam Antonacci, GDD	.378	19	74	24	28	3	14
Esmerlyn Valdez, SRR	.368	19	57	19	21	8	27
Kevin McGonigle, SCO	.362	19	69	22	25	5	19
Nick Morabito, SCO	.362	17	69	17	25	1	8
Caden Connor, GDD	.359	19	64	15	23	0	10
Seaver King, SCO	.359	18	64	21	23	2	24

INDIVIDUAL PITCHING LEADERS
(Minimum .4 Innings Pitched/League Games)

Player, Team	W	L	ERA	IP	H	BB	SO
James Hicks, SCO	2	0	0.00	14	6	2	19
Darlin Saladin, GDD	1	0	0.82	11	6	7	17
Ryan Hawks, PEJ	0	0	0.82	11	6	1	7
Carlson Reed, SRR	1	0	1.29	14	8	8	12
Jared Simpson, SCO	0	0	1.38	13	10	5	13
Miguelangel Boadas, PEJ	1	0	1.54	12	6	9	8
Cade Smith, MSS	1	0	2.13	13	7	2	14
Trenton Denholm, SUR	1	0	2.13	13	19	6	16
Holt Jones, MSS	1	0	2.19	12	5	7	11
Jimmy Kingsbury, PEJ	1	0	2.45	11	8	2	9

GLENDALE DESERT DOGS

Name	AVG	AB	R	H	2B	3B	HR	RBI	BB	SO	SB
Jose Hernandez	.389	18	4	7	1	0	0	3	2	4	0
Sam Antonacci	.378	74	24	28	3	0	3	14	15	11	11
Braden Montgomery	.366	41	12	15	6	1	1	11	13	12	3
Caden Connor	.359	64	15	23	2	0	0	10	18	9	8
Miguel Ugueto	.350	60	10	21	3	0	1	16	4	13	4
Cutter Coffey	.328	64	13	21	5	0	0	13	11	14	3
Ignacio Alvarez	.324	74	12	24	7	1	1	11	16	13	5
Cade Doughty	.316	19	5	6	2	0	1	3	3	2	2
Patrick Clohisy	.284	81	19	23	3	1	1	11	13	12	22
Jim Jarvis	.259	54	12	14	3	0	2	7	12	9	4
Josh Kasevich	.255	55	10	14	0	0	0	4	17	11	3
Logan Wagner	.218	55	11	12	2	1	2	9	12	17	2
Ryan Galanie	.212	52	5	11	1	0	0	9	9	13	3
Jesus Galiz	.192	26	4	5	1	0	0	0	5	9	0
Travis Honeyman	.182	44	7	8	1	0	2	8	5	12	4
Graysen Tarlow	.161	31	4	5	1	0	0	1	5	7	3
Edward Duran	.156	32	5	5	2	3	0	7	5	7	1
Nicolas Perez	.000	5	1	0	0	0	0	0	3	0	0

Name	W	L	ERA	G	GS	SV	IP	H	BB	SO	AVG
Darlin Saladin	1	0	0.82	5	1	0	11	6	7	17	.154
Alex Makarewich	0	0	2.16	8	0	0	8	6	10	7	.214
Payton Martin	1	1	2.25	3	0	0	4	2	4	1	.182
Hagen Smith	0	0	2.57	5	5	0	14	7	6	21	.143
Jhancarlos Lara	0	1	2.61	11	0	0	10	5	12	16	.152
Tyler Bradt	0	0	4.50	8	0	0	8	7	11	10	.233
Carson Jacobs	0	0	4.50	8	0	0	6	4	11	12	.190
LJ McDonough	0	1	4.50	10	0	0	12	14	5	15	.311
Luke Sinnard	0	0	4.60	5	5	0	16	16	6	20	.276
Justin Chambers	0	2	5.40	8	0	0	8	5	5	10	.161
Randel Clemente	1	1	5.63	8	0	1	8	9	7	11	.281
Jacob Kroeger	1	0	6.14	5	0	0	7	7	6	9	.241
Chen-Wei Lin	3	1	6.57	5	5	0	12	13	8	19	.271
Kelena Sauer	1	0	6.75	4	0	0	4	6	3	6	.353
Kai Peterson	0	0	7.36	8	0	0	7	8	8	8	.276
Tyler Davis	0	0	7.59	9	0	2	11	18	6	18	.375
Hyun-Seok Jang	1	1	9.00	5	4	0	9	11	9	7	.306

Name	W	L	ERA	G	GS	SV	IP	H	BB	SO	AVG
Chay Yeager	0	1	9.00	8	0	0	8	13	7	7	.371
D.J. Carpenter	0	0	9.00	8	0	0	6	7	4	8	.292
Alex Amalfi	1	1	9.95	5	5	0	13	17	13	6	.321
Trent Buchanan	0	1	10.57	9	0	0	8	12	9	7	.353
Jarold Rosado	1	0	12.15	9	0	0	7	4	13	7	.167
Connor McCullough	0	2	12.79	3	0	0	6	6	3	9	.231
Jakob Wright	0	1	14.73	5	2	0	7	14	13	11	.424
Cory Wall	0	2	30.00	4	0	0	3	6	6	2	.400
Yondrei Rojas	0	0	30.86	4	0	0	2	5	2	2	.385

MESA SOLAR SOX

Name	AVG	AB	R	H	2B	3B	HR	RBI	BB	SO	SB
Owen Ayers	.379	66	17	25	5	0	3	16	22	10	1
Ryan Lasko	.357	70	11	25	5	0	0	12	13	19	9
Josh Kuroda-Grauer	.345	58	12	20	6	1	0	8	5	7	7
Coby Morales	.333	27	4	9	2	0	1	7	3	9	2
Starlyn Caba	.297	74	9	22	3	0	2	10	14	19	2
Tommy White	.292	72	22	21	2	0	3	20	9	8	3
Cole Mathis	.280	50	11	14	0	0	2	15	15	16	3
Fenwick Trimble	.265	68	15	18	4	0	2	10	13	14	11
Brayden Taylor	.264	53	9	14	6	1	1	6	12	19	5
Enmanuel Tejeda	.254	67	13	17	4	0	1	15	16	19	13
Max Muncy	.250	32	4	8	1	0	2	2	5	9	0
Ed Howard	.222	54	6	12	2	0	0	5	10	19	4
Aidan Smith	.222	45	11	10	0	2	0	3	11	11	4
Manuel Palencia	.217	46	7	10	1	0	1	7	2	14	1
Logan Poteet	.158	19	1	3	2	0	0	2	1	6	0
P.J. Morlando	.136	59	8	8	0	0	5	9	23	2	
Brailer Guerrero	.077	26	3	2	0	0	1	3	16	2	
Brock Rodden	.342	38	9	13	4	0	1	7	4	9	7

Name	W	L	ERA	G	GS	SV	IP	H	BB	SO	AVG
Will Johnston	1	0	1.86	9	0	1	10	6	4	10	.188
Cade Smith	1	0	2.13	4	2	0	13	7	2	14	.159
Holt Jones	1	0	2.19	8	0	1	12	5	7	11	.135
Aiden May	0	0	2.93	5	5	0	15	9	8	15	.176
Jadon Bercovich	0	0	3.00	6	0	0	6	5	4	5	.227
Hueston Morrill	1	0	3.12	8	0	2	9	10	5	3	.303
Blaze Pontes	0	1	3.72	9	0	0	10	13	4	10	.333
Koen Moreno	0	1	3.86	5	3	0	14	10	7	18	.196
Luis Martinez-Gomez	2	1	3.86	7	1	1	9	6	5	16	.176
Karson Milbrandt	1	1	4.73	5	2	0	13	8	8	23	.170
Jackson Baumeister	0	1	6.00	4	3	0	9	10	9	10	.313
Brady Kirtner	0	1	6.14	7	0	1	7	14	6	6	.389
Darwin Rodriguez	3	0	6.23	7	0	0	9	9	10	6	.257
Andrew Lindsey	2	0	6.75	7	1	0	11	14	6	11	.341
Jack Sellinger	0	0	7.71	7	0	0	7	9	2	12	.310
Mark Adamiak	0	0	9.00	7	0	2	6	7	7	7	.280
Mathew Peters	0	0	9.00	8	0	1	9	9	13	5	.257
Bryce Cunningham	0	4	10.38	5	5	0	13	20	9	8	.345
Adam Stone	0	0	11.81	7	0	0	5	11	3	4	.440
Corey Avant	0	2	12.41	6	3	0	12	21	11	13	.404
Jonathan Russell	1	0	12.86	6	0	0	7	12	3	5	.400
Mason Auer	1	0	13.50	8	0	0	5	11	7	7	.423
Nathan Dettmer	0	0	14.40	6	3	0	15	26	9	13	.406
JP Wheat	0	2	23.63	6	0	0	5	6	16	5	.286

PEORIA JAVELINAS

Name	AVG	AB	R	H	2B	3B	HR	RBI	BB	SO	SB
Brock Rodden	.342	38	9	13	4	0	1	7	4	9	7
Ethan Anderson	.300	70	13	21	7	0	1	14	12	20	2
Hendry Mendez	.300	20	6	6	1	0	1	3	3	2	1
Charlie Pagliarini	.281	64	10	18	3	1	3	9	14	18	6
Leonardo Balcazar	.277	94	13	26	6	0	0	12	9	29	5
Lamar King	.255	51	8	13	2	0	0	0	11	13	3
Jonny Farmelo	.234	77	16	18	4	3	2	16	20	28	12
Enrique Bradfield	.221	77	14	17	5	1	0	9	13	22	17
Cam Collier	.221	77	15	17	5	0	1	14	16	24	1
Alfredo Duno	.213	47	3	10	2	1	0	7	11	16	1
Ryan Jackson	.213	47	9	10	3	1	0	9	15	15	1
Braedon Karpathios	.211	57	8	12	5	0	0	5	11	27	1
Brandon Winokur	.192	73	10	14	3	0	2	12	9	19	2
Thomas Sosa	.178	45	4	8	0	0	1	5	4	15	2
Billy Amick	.033	30	1	1	0	0	0	0	6	20	0

Name	W	L	ERA	G	GS	SV	IP	H	BB	SO	AVG
Stefan Raeth	0	0	0.00	6	0	0	7	3	4	5	.115
Kevin Abel	1	0	0.00	3	0	0	4	2	5	5	.167
Ryan Hawks	0	0	0.82	5	3	0	11	6	1	7	.150
Brandon Downer	1	0	1.00	7	0	1	9	4	3	8	.129
Kannon Kemp	2	0	1.29	6	2	0	7	4	3	6	.154
Miguelangel Boadas	1	0	1.54	4	0	0	12	6	9	8	.158
Carson Montgomery	1	0	1.74	4	4	0	10	11	7	7	.275
Johan Moreno	0	0	2.25	7	0	0	8	4	4	10	.143
Sayer Diederich	0	0	2.35	7	0	1	8	5	4	10	.179
Zander Sechrist	0	0	2.45	7	0	0	7	6	4	6	.240
Jimmy Kingsbury	1	0	2.45	7	0	0	11	8	2	9	.216
Luis De Leon	2	0	2.76	5	5	0	16	10	12	22	.179
Trevor Kuncl	0	0	3.52	7	0	1	8	6	6	15	.207
Tanner Smith	0	2	3.52	7	0	0	8	7	3	13	.233
Carson Dorsey	0	0	3.68	6	2	2	22	18	13	17	.228
Tyler Cleveland	1	0	4.05	6	0	1	7	5	6	12	.200
Rhett Lowder	1	1	5.00	4	4	0	9	9	1	8	.257
Tucker Musgrove	0	0	5.06	6	0	0	5	5	5	8	.263
Johnathan Harmon	1	1	5.27	5	3	0	14	14	10	16	.259
Hunter Parks	0	0	5.40	7	0	0	2	0	4	3	.000
Jakob Hall	0	2	10.13	7	0	0	8	14	1	6	.400
Hunter Hoopes	2	0	10.13	7	0	0	8	9	8	10	.273
Maikel Miralles	0	2	12.15	5	2	0	13	20	10	9	.345
Dylan Questad	0	1	15.19	5	1	0	5	5	13	5	.238
Marcelo Perez	0	3	18.41	5	2	0	7	15	3	9	.429
Luke Hayden	0	1	31.50	4	0	0	2	6	10	1	.600

SALT RIVER RAFTERS

Name	AVG	AB	R	H	2B	3B	HR	RBI	BB	SO	SB
Raudi Rodriguez	.433	60	11	26	6	2	1	9	10	12	5
Esmerlyn Valdez	.368	57	19	21	3	0	8	27	19	12	0
Charlie Condon	.337	83	21	28	1	2	1	13	12	17	0
Jared Thomas	.302	63	9	19	6	1	2	12	3	28	8
Kenny Castillo	.289	38	7	11	2	0	1	5	2	13	0
Stanley Tucker	.278	79	10	22	3	0	0	15	12	21	13
Juan Flores	.273	66	12	18	5	1	1	9	5	20	0
Jack Hurley	.260	50	10	13	3	1	2	12	7	17	4
Tony Blanco	.250	44	5	11	2	0	2	7	8	16	0
David Mershon	.230	61	16	14	1	0	1	8	20	17	12
Johanfran Garcia	.224	67	9	15	5	0	2	10	12	17	0
Braylen Wimmer	.222	54	8	12	1	0	0	7	7	22	4
Jansel Luis	.213	89	12	19	3	0	0	8	12	20	8
Will Taylor	.143	42	8	6	1	0	1	4	10	15	2
Nelson Taylor	.139	36	6	5	0	0	0	2	8	19	7

Name	W	L	ERA	G	GS	SV	IP	H	BB	SO	AVG
Carlson Reed	1	0	1.29	4	2	0	14	8	8	12	.174
Welinton Herrera	0	1	2.00	9	0	1	9	9	8	14	.257
Yordin Chalas	1	0	2.35	8	0	1	8	9	3	9	.290
Lorenzo Encarnacion	0	0	2.45	4	0	1	4	1	3	4	.100
Cade Denton	1	1	3.46	7	0	0	13	7	4	18	.152
Isaac Stebens	1	0	3.86	8	0	0	7	8	6	7	.286
Dominic Perachi	3	1	4.15	5	4	0	17	19	9	20	.284
David Hagaman	0	2	4.50	5	4	0	12	11	7	14	.244
Jack Mahoney	0	1	5.74	5	3	0	16	20	7	10	.328
Drey Jameson	1	0	6.35	6	0	0	6	4	4	4	.200
Brandon Dufault	0	0	6.43	5	3	0	14	7	15	12	.152
Jaden Woods	0	2	6.52	9	0	2	10	16	6	11	.348
Ryan Costeiu	1	1	6.97	5	1	0	10	14	13	9	.326
Joshua Loeschorn	0	1	7.45	8	1	1	10	19	3	6	.404
Derek Diamond	1	0	7.90	9	0	0	14	19	11	9	.365
Joseph Ingrassia	0	0	9.00	5	2	0	10	14	9	13	.311
Kyle Amendt	0	0	9.00	6	0	0	5	6	7	11	.286
Najer Victor	0	1	9.72	8	0	1	8	7	3	13	.226
Luis Perales	0	2	10.32	6	6	0	11	16	11	19	.333
Jay Allmer	1	0	10.80	7	0	0	5	4	9	3	.211
Austin Smith	0	1	10.80	8	0	0	7	11	10	5	.379
Brandon Neely	0	0	10.80	5	1	0	10	16	8	11	.364
Ben Thompson	0	1	13.50	5	0	0	3	2	7	3	.222
Fulton Lockhart	0	1	14.85	7	0	0	7	7	9	3	.304
Ben Shields	0	1	135.00	1	1	0	0	4	1	0	.800

SCOTTSDALE SCORPIONS

Name	AVG	AB	R	H	2B	3B	HR	RBI	BB	SO	SB
Max Anderson	.447	47	20	21	5	0	4	13	18	9	1
Parks Harber	.383	60	11	23	9	0	3	15	14	20	1
Nick Morabito	.362	69	17	25	2	1	1	8	10	15	16
Kevin McGonigle	.362	69	22	25	5	2	5	19	19	12	3
Seaver King	.359	64	21	23	5	1	2	24	11	15	6
Axiel Plaz	.354	48	6	17	0	0	0	7	10	8	0
Sam Petersen	.305	59	13	18	5	0	3	14	7	21	2
Joseph Sullivan	.296	54	13	16	2	1	1	14	13	16	8
Christopher Suero	.283	60	14	17	2	0	5	14	7	18	8
Jack Penney	.278	54	12	15	1	0	1	7	15	20	2
Will Bush	.258	31	9	8	2	0	1	4	13	15	1
Walker Janek	.241	54	6	13	4	0	3	20	4	22	3
Maui Ahuna	.233	43	8	10	2	0	0	5	5	18	2
Ethan Petry	.228	57	12	13	1	0	1	11	13	21	2
Walker Martin	.222	54	6	12	2	1	0	4	6	26	0
D'Andre Smith	.185	27	7	5	3	0	0	1	4	8	6
Jeron Williams	.146	48	8	7	3	0	0	5	6	8	3
John Bay	.100	10	2	1	0	0	0	1	2	5	0

Name	W	L	ERA	G	GS	SV	IP	H	BB	SO	AVG
James Hicks	2	0	0.00	4	2	0	14	6	2	19	.130
Jared Simpson	0	0	1.38	9	0	1	13	10	5	13	.227
Sean Linan	0	0	1.80	2	1	0	5	1	4	6	.063
Juan Sanchez	2	1	2.70	7	0	0	10	7	4	11	.233
Ricardo Estrada	0	0	3.27	6	1	0	11	12	7	11	.267
Austin Troesser	1	0	3.86	4	0	0	5	3	4	4	.176
Anderson Brito	2	0	3.97	4	3	0	11	6	7	22	.154
Hudson Leach	1	0	4.05	7	0	0	7	5	4	13	.217
Spencer Miles	2	0	4.15	5	4	0	9	9	1	12	.250
Ryan Murphy	2	2	4.24	6	5	0	17	16	10	13	.267
Jake Bennett	1	1	4.50	5	4	0	20	20	5	25	.260
Jose T Perez	1	0	5.19	7	0	0	9	10	8	6	.303
Carlos Lequerica	1	1	5.56	8	0	0	11	17	5	8	.354
Pablo Aldonis	0	0	5.56	6	2	0	11	10	5	14	.233
Brett Banks	0	0	6.00	6	0	1	6	6	5	13	.250
Austin Amaral	0	0	6.75	9	0	0	11	10	9	9	.256
Jordan Geber	0	0	6.75	4	0	0	4	4	0	5	.250
Kenny Serwa	2	1	7.24	4	4	0	14	14	10	11	.259
Bryce Jenkins	1	1	7.56	8	0	0	8	6	10	8	.207
Derek True	0	0	8.10	7	1	1	7	13	3	12	.419
Dariel Fregio	1	0	9.00	8	1	0	10	13	5	6	.310
Pedro Garcia	0	1	15.19	4	0	0	5	8	3	3	.333
Nate Wohlgemuth	0	1	24.16	8	0	1	6	15	13	6	.469
Ernesto Mercedes	0	0	30.38	4	0	0	3	9	4	1	.563

SURPRISE SAGUAROS

Name	AVG	AB	R	H	2B	3B	HR	RBI	BB	SO	SB
Sebastian Walcott	.500	4	2	2	1	0	0	0	1	1	0
Wuilfredo Antunez	.500	6	3	3	0	0	2	4	1	2	1
Joe Lampe	.368	38	17	14	1	2	1	5	13	9	10
Luke Adams	.333	51	14	17	3	0	3	10	11	12	4
Daniel Vazquez	.329	79	14	26	5	0	2	21	19	20	11
Dante Nori	.308	39	8	12	2	0	1	7	5	7	2
Dylan Campbell	.304	56	14	17	4	1	4	16	14	17	4
Dylan O'Rae	.302	43	9	13	4	0	0	9	5	15	6
Chandler Pollard	.289	38	11	11	2	0	0	3	10	11	8
Carson Roccaforte	.279	68	9	19	8	0	2	18	13	28	7
Josh Adamczewski	.277	65	14	18	5	0	4	17	15	17	4
Dylan Dreiling	.271	48	7	13	1	2	1	8	7	14	2
Marco Dinges	.250	8	1	2	1	0	0	1	0	3	0
Blake Mitchell	.230	61	20	14	2	0	1	5	20	22	2
Malcolm Moore	.213	61	8	13	4	0	1	8	3	22	0
Juan Benjamin	.152	46	7	7	2	0	1	7	7	14	1
Ben Hartl	.125	24	4	3	2	0	0	4	2	10	0
Alfonsin Rosario	.108	37	5	4	0	0	0	2	6	15	2
Bryan Rincon	.068	44	5	3	0	0	1	6	8	15	4

Name	W	L	ERA	G	GS	SV	IP	H	BB	SO	AVG
Michael Fowler	0	1	0.00	6	0	1	7	4	5	8	.167
Daniel Espino	1	0	0.00	4	4	0	5	4	3	7	.222
Jack Dallas	0	0	1.00	4	1	0	9	5	7	15	.172
Matt Jachec	0	0	1.08	7	0	1	8	6	2	7	.222
Dennis Colleran	0	0	1.17	7	0	0	8	2	3	11	.083
Anthony Flores	0	0	1.86	7	0	0	10	7	10	14	.212

Jesus Broca	1	1	2.00	4	1	0	9	6	5	15	.188
Trenton Denholm	1	0	2.13	5	3	0	13	19	6	16	.345
Edwin Jimenez	0	0	2.16	7	0	1	8	10	3	6	.286
Emiliano Teodo	0	0	2.25	4	0	2	4	0	5	6	.000
Tommy McCollum	2	0	3.00	6	0	0	6	7	5	6	.269
Eiberson Castellano	2	1	3.86	4	4	0	14	10	7	18	.204
Winston Santos	2	1	4.42	5	2	0	18	18	10	19	.254
Jaydenn Estanista	0	0	5.63	8	0	0	8	7	7	10	.241
Zane Morehouse	1	0	6.00	8	0	1	6	3	7	8	.150
Nate Peterson	1	0	6.48	4	0	0	8	8	7	6	.258
Daniel Harper	0	0	6.75	7	0	0	7	8	6	6	.308
Louis-Philippe Langevin	1	0	6.75	6	0	0	7	3	12	11	.130
A.J. Causey	1	1	7.45	9	0	1	10	12	1	13	.300
Joey Danielson	0	0	7.50	7	0	0	6	7	10	10	.269
Jose Corniell	1	2	7.50	5	5	0	18	26	7	19	.333
Rorik Maltrud	1	0	9.64	5	1	0	9	16	2	10	.364
Logan Martin	1	2	9.82	5	5	0	11	16	8	6	.348
Kolton Curtis	0	1	11.74	5	1	0	8	11	9	9	.314
Hunter Owen	0	0	12.46	2	0	0	4	11	1	4	.478

INDEPENDENT LEAGUES

Partner Leagues Now Stretch Across America

BY J.J. COOPER

For many years, independent baseball was a very regional sport. Each league had it's territories, and there was very little overlap.

The Northern League staked out the upper Midwest, stretching into Canada. The Frontier League targeted Midwestern cities left behind by the increased stadium requirements of the 1990s Professional Baseball Agreement.

The Atlantic League and the Northeast/Can-Am League did have some territories that butted up against each other in the Northeast, but the different salary structures and schedules let to the Can-Am League hitting markets that were a bit smaller than the Atlantic Leagues. Often cities that struck out in the Atlantic League moved on to the Can-Am.

And in the South/Texas and out West, there were attempts to gain footholds with leagues like the Western, Golden, Central and Texas-Louisiana, but they had more difficulties sustaining success.

The combining of some Northern and Northeast Leagues into the American Association began to see this approach shift. The Atlantic League then moved to Sugar Land, Texas and eventually multiple cities in North Carolina.

Now in the 2020s, geography seems to play even less of a role than stadiums and markets. The increased stadium requirements of the new MLB Professional Development License, as well as the reduction in affiliated teams had led to an increase in partner leagues, and it has also meant that for the first time in several decades, indy/partner league baseball is spread out across the country.

When the Oakland A's announced their plans to leave town, the Oakland Ballers stepped in as a Pioneer League team, and they won a title in their second season.

When the Rangers left Kinston, N.C. after the 2024 season, the Frontier League snapped up the market. It did the same to the Pearl, Miss. market that saw the Mississippi Braves leave town.

All of a sudden, the Frontier League had teams in the deep South in a league that has multiple Canadian teams. The footprint of the modern Frontier League stretches from the Northeast to Canada to the Great Plains and Chicago to the Deep South.

The Oakland Ballers won the Pioneer League title in their second season

Similarly, the Pioneer League moved from affiliated ball to partner league baseball after the 2020-2021 MLB contraction of the affiliated minor leagues, but now it's moving into California as well. In addition to the Oakland Ballers, the Modesto Glow Riders are set to join the league in 2026, replacing the Modesto Nuts, who were dropped from the California League because of a stadium that failed to meet the upgraded facility requirements.

More of these moves could come in future years. The departing Carolina Mudcats will be replaced by a Coastal Plain League summer college team, but as cities move out of affiliated ball because of stadium requirements, there are leagues who are quite interested, even if it involves lengthy travel.

On the field, the 2025 season saw a level of sustained dominance that is largely unusual in the partner leagues. Quebec has won four straight Frontier League titles, even in a league that now has 18 teams. The Atlantic League saw York repeat as champions, and the American Association has Kane County, another MiLB refugee, as back-to-back champions. ∎

Nelson Goes 30-50 In Atlantic League

When James Nelson was released by the Yankees in 2022, he had to figure out where to go if he wanted to continue his playing career.

But Nelson's path to a partner league was a little clearer than most. His uncle was Rockies 2004 first-round pick Chris Nelson. And like his uncle, James had played at Redan High in Stone Mountain, Ga.

That is the same program that produced Taj Bradley, Domonic Brown and crucially for the purposes of this narrative, brothers Brandon and P.J. Phillips.

When he was left without a team, James Nelson quickly found a spot with the Atlantic League's Lexington Legends, who were managed by P.J. Phillips. After a couple of conversations, Nelson was added to the Legends' roster late in the 2022 season.

In that brief taste of the partner leagues, Nelson was immediately one of the league's best players. He hit .400/.476/.855 with six home runs in just 17 games. On a team that had eight former big leaguers, Nelson matched and exceeded everyone else swing-for-swing.

He was just getting started. Since then, Nelson has been arguably the best player in the partner leagues. There's no debate he's been the best player in each league he's played in. He has MVP awards as proof.

"P.J. took me under his wing," Nelson said.

PLAYER OF THE YEAR

Phillips went to the Frontier League to manage the New Jersey Jackals in 2023. Nelson went with him. Nelson hit .388/.481/.713 that season, posting a 30-30 season in just 91 games. He averaged nearly three total bases per game. His 111 runs scored that season are the all-time Frontier League record. He won the league's MVP award.

James Nelson

The two split up for 2024. Nelson went to the Mexican League and earned a spot on the North Division all-star team for Durango as he hit .297/.425/.459.

But all of that proved to be an appetizer for the 2025 season. Nelson had one of the best seasons in Atlantic League history. He hit .315/.395/.575 with 34 homers and 53 steals in 124 games.

In the first 26 seasons of the Atlantic League, no hitter had ever had a 30-30 season. Only three had had a 20-20 season.

Nelson blew by those marks with ease. By the time he hit his 30th home run, Nelson had already stolen 40 bases. He finished with a 30-50 season and won the Atlantic League MVP award.

For his remarkable season, Nelson is Baseball America's 2025 Independent/Partner Leagues Player of the Year.

"I knew he was going to hit 30 home runs," Phillips said. "There were more games, and he hits better pitching. In a league that throws more strikes, I knew that he'd hit 30 homers. I thought 30-40 was possible.

"For him to steal 53, I didn't expect that." ■

PREVIOUS WINNERS

1996: Darryl Motley, OF, Fargo-Moorhead (Northern)
1997: Mike Meggers, OF, Winnipeg/Duluth (Northern)
1998: Morgan Burkhart, 1B, Richmond (Frontier)
1999: Carmine Cappucio, OF, New Jersey (Northeast)
2000: Anthony Lewis, 1B, Duluth-Superior (Northern)
2001: Mike Warner, OF, Somerset (Atlantic)
2002: Bobby Madritsch, LHP, Winnipeg (Northern)
2003: Jason Shelley, RHP, Rockford (Frontier)
2004: Victor Rodriguez, SS, Somerset (Atlantic)
2005: Eddie Lantigua, 3B, Quebec (Can-Am)
2006: Ian Church, OF, Kalamazoo (Frontier)
2007: Darryl Brinkley, OF, Calgary (Northern)
2008: Patrick Breen, OF, Orange County (Golden)
2009: Greg Porter, OF, Wichita (American Association)
2010: Beau Torbert, OF, Sioux Falls (American Association)
2011: Chris Collabello, 1B, Worcester (Can-Am League)
2012: Blake Gailen, OF, Lancaster (Atlantic)
2013: C.J. Ziegler, 1B, Wichita (American Association)
2014: Balbino Fuenmayor, 1B, Quebec (Can-Am League)
2015: Joe Maloney, OF, Rocland (Can-Am League)
2016: Art Charles, 1B, New Jersey (Can-Am League)
2017: Alonzo Harris, OF, York (Atlantic League)
2018: Jordany Valdespin, INF, Long Island (Atlantic League)
2019: Keon Barnum, 1B, Chicago (American Association)
2021: Adam Brett Walker, OF, Milwaukee (American Association)
2022: Courtney Hawkins, OF, Lexington (Atlantic League)
2023: Bryan Torres, OF, Milwaukee (American Association)
2024: Adam Fogel, OF, Missoula (Pioneer)

INDEPENDENT STATISTICS

AMERICAN ASSOCIATION

After just five years in the league, the Kane County Cougars have settled in nicely. The Cougars went to the playoffs in 2022 and 2023, and now they have become back-to-back league champs. After finishing just under .500 during the regular season, Kane County heated up in the playoffs. In 2024, the Cougars went undefeated in the postseason. This year, they needed to win a deciding winner-takes-all game in all three series, but they made it happen, topping Sioux Falls in the championship series. After the title, manager George Tsamis signed a three-year extension.

East Division	W	L	PCT	GB
Lake Country DockHounds *	55	45	.550	-
Chicago Dogs †	50	49	.505	4.5
Kane County Cougars †	49	51	.490	6
Milwaukee Milkmen †	45	55	.450	10
Cleburne Railroaders	43	57	.430	12
Gary SouthShore RailCats	38	62	.380	17

West Division	W	L	PCT	GB
Sioux City Explorers *	64	36	.640	-
Kansas City Monarchs †	59	41	.590	5
Sioux Falls Canaries †	58	42	.580	6
Fargo-Moorhead RedHawks †	55	45	.550	9
Lincoln Saltdogs	42	58	.420	22
Winnipeg Goldeyes	41	58	.414	22.5

Division Champ. †Wild-Card

PLAYOFFS—Quarterfinals: Chicago defeated Lake Country 2-0; Kane County defeated Milwaukee 2-1; Sioux Falls defeated Sioux City 2-1 and Fargo-Moorhead defeated Kansas City 2-1 in best-of-3 series. **Semifinals:** Sioux Falls defeated Fargo-Moorhead 3-2 and Kane County defeated Chicago 3-2 in best-of-three series. **Finals:** Kane County defeated Sioux Falls 3-2 in best-of-five series.

Attendance: Kane County Cougars 243,426; Chicago Dogs 218,754; Winnipeg Goldeyes 186,541; Lincoln Saltdogs 155,837; Fargo-Moorhead RedHawks 147,661; Gary SouthShore RailCats 147,629; Kansas City Monarchs 101,275; Lake Country DockHounds 86,506; Milwaukee Milkmen 83,501; Cleburne Railroaders 81,778; Sioux Falls Canaries 77,291; Sioux City Explorers 57,534.

All-Star Team: C: Chance Sisco, Chicago. **1B:** Kyle Martin, Cleburne. **2B:** Brantley Bell, Kansas City. **SS:** Jordan Barth, Sioux Falls. **3B:** Calvin Estrada, Sioux Falls. **OF:** Dillon Thomas, Fargo-Moorhead; Josh Rehwaldt, Sioux Falls; Henry George, Sioux City. **DH:** Todd Lott, Kane County. **UTIL:** Robbie Glendinning, Kansas City. **SP:** Jake Dykhoff, Fargo-Moorhead. **RP:** Felix Cepeda, Sioux City. **Player of the Year:** Calvin Estrada, Sioux Falls. **Pitcher of the Year:** Jake Dykhoff, Fargo-Moorhead. **Reliever of the Year:** Felix Cepeda, Sioux City. **Rookie Hitter of the Year:** Henry Kusiak, Chicago. **Rookie Pitcher of the Year:** Luke Hansel, Lake Country. **Manager of the Year:** Steve Montgomery, Sioux City.

BATTING LEADERS

Name	AVG	AB	R	H	HR	RBI	BB	SO	SB
Calvin Estrada, SF	.352	366	71	129	20	88	31	51	20
Todd Lott, KCO	.320	328	41	105	10	58	16	63	0
Jake Rehwaldt, SF	.315	343	74	108	16	61	70	91	11
Elvis Peralta, GAR	.314	389	53	122	3	44	49	80	31
Brantley Bell, KC	.313	297	44	93	11	40	18	51	4
Dillon Thomas, F-M	.312	349	67	109	15	50	59	89	15
Henry Kusiak, CHI	.309	314	50	97	12	47	29	69	7
Chase Estep, MKE	.307	387	66	119	9	54	40	89	20
Fernandez, J, F-M	.307	326	49	100	6	50	34	36	4
Jordan Barth, SF	.303	396	71	120	19	66	20	63	9

PITCHING LEADERS

Player	W	L	ERA	G	IP	H	BB	SO
Jake Dykhoff, F-M	11	4	1.63	27	94	75	12	81
Konor Ash, KCO	10	3	2.76	19	124	87	30	132
Thomas Dorminy, SF	11	1	2.90	20	121	96	32	108
Blake Goldsberry, KC	8	2	2.94	23	86	71	17	84
Kyle Marman, SC	8	3	3.07	19	123	117	35	140
Jared Wetherbee, SC	9	4	3.29	19	107	86	40	125
Julian Garcia, KC	9	2	3.39	19	112	87	32	163
Luke Hansel, LC	9	5	3.48	19	116	103	29	99
Tyler Jandron, F-M	7	4	3.54	17	102	102	26	84

CHICAGO DOGS

PLAYER	AVG	AB	R	H	2B	3B	HR	RBI	SB
Clark, Tripp	.315	54	7	17	1	6	3	13	1
Kusiak, Henry	.309	314	50	97	12	47	29	69	7
Sisco, Chance	.301	342	53	103	17	61	46	70	1
Bell, Brantley	.298	262	40	78	11	38	16	45	13
McGarry, Alex	.297	145	21	43	4	23	16	33	5
Turbo, Johnni	.296	135	17	40	1	10	5	24	1
Maiben, Jacob	.295	132	12	39	2	21	6	9	1
Williams, Jaylyn	.292	24	2	7	1	2	2	5	0
Hopkins, T.J.	.276	261	52	72	11	48	39	69	3
Teter, Jacob	.267	382	60	102	13	55	53	74	0
Coulter, Clint	.261	46	4	12	1	6	7	19	0
Stroup, Dusty	.256	375	52	96	10	51	32	105	10
Reyes, Bryan	.237	38	6	9	0	3	3	12	0
Scolan, Matt	.233	43	5	10	0	5	3	8	2
Nelson, Andy	.231	104	17	24	3	8	12	28	9
Pruitt Jr., Reggie	.226	318	61	72	7	29	39	100	27
Moris, Max	.202	89	12	18	1	7	6	16	1
Rodriguez, Howard	.190	116	18	22	7	23	10	43	7
Schmack, Kyle	.186	113	11	21	4	13	9	48	0
Penzetta, Nick	.182	11	0	2	0	1	1	5	0
Pettigrew, Zion	.130	23	2	3	0	3	11	0	
Novak, Nick	.091	22	0	2	0	0	2	6	0

PLAYER	W	L	ERA	G	SV	IP	H	BB	SO
Marozas, Austin	2	0	0.00	17	1	28	10	9	34
Braithwaite, Trey	1	0	1.93	17	1	23	11	15	27
DeLabio, Jacob	5	2	2.36	43	11	50	35	19	61
Curlis, Connor	4	1	2.42	8	0	45	34	9	56
Lin, Eric	0	1	2.51	22	0	29	22	9	30
Keys, J.C.	2	4	3.19	38	3	42	25	23	49
Lindgren, Jeff	5	2	3.41	11	0	61	52	19	66
Nedrow, Jack	3	4	3.59	12	0	68	59	16	59
Vallone, Michael	2	0	3.96	13	0	25	18	9	18
Miller, Brady	2	2	4.00	9	0	36	30	9	21
Cavaco, Keoni	4	8	4.10	22	0	79	76	27	53
Davidson, Zach	4	2	4.48	39	0	68	54	48	91
Lacey, Steven	2	2	5.59	7	0	29	28	15	23
Baker, John	7	5	5.71	16	0	80	94	20	68
Schaum, Bryce	1	3	5.88	13	0	41	42	22	36
Bell, Brock	2	5	6.04	31	2	57	75	19	57
Ranaudo, Anthony	2	1	6.60	11	0	15	18	5	12
Marshall, Dwayne	1	4	9.00	21	1	43	67	18	35
Kelly, John	1	1	9.31	9	0	10	9	14	4
Scott, Brandon	0	1	12.66	13	0	11	17	6	8

CLEBURNE RAILROADERS

Name	AVG	AB	R	H	HR	RBI	BB	SO	SB
Lujano, Jesus	.318	245	33	78	0	19	18	37	11
Peterson, Dustin	.299	311	62	93	14	54	38	73	0
Martin, Kyle	.279	351	77	98	29	90	45	79	4
Spinn, Zane	.276	29	2	8	0	6	1	7	0
Sosa, Andres	.273	209	30	57	8	34	38	52	1
Altherr, Aaron	.260	361	58	94	20	76	39	114	1
Long, Shed	.258	383	71	99	8	39	56	74	13
Rivas, Steven	.247	267	38	66	11	53	17	88	3
Weiss, Cooper	.243	263	55	64	6	24	48	82	8
Swenson, Sean	.241	29	3	7	1	4	0	8	0
Sparks, Lamar	.233	60	9	14	3	9	6	16	0
Kwitzer, Chris	.225	218	20	49	2	28	9	67	1
Howell, Korry	.217	143	28	31	6	19	18	40	8
Shumpert, Nick	.214	70	6	15	1	1	4	19	4
Sermo, Jose	.184	49	8	9	1	7	11	16	0
Viars, Jordan	.176	51	6	9	0	3	16	24	1
Brocato, Anthony	.174	92	10	16	1	8	13	29	2
Morrow, Jacob	.170	106	8	18	0	9	18	33	0

Name			AVG	AB	R	H	HR	RBI	BB	SO	SB
Gonzalez, Jose			.167	30	2	5	1	4	6	7	0
Groshans, Jaxx			.161	62	2	10	0	2	7	21	0
Rodriguez, Joshua			.154	13	1	2	0	2	0	4	0

Name	W	L	ERA	G	SV	IP	H	BB	SO
Hampton, Ben	0	0	1.46	9	0	12	12	1	10
Wood, Zeke	1	1	2.11	19	3	21	16	9	33
Klobosits, Gabe	0	0	2.84	4	0	13	13	7	14
Scott, Kristian	2	1	2.86	35	5	50	48	25	40
Broadway, Taylor	4	1	3.72	30	0	39	34	15	35
Chalmers, Dakota	2	4	4.19	12	0	62	56	32	79
Mechals, Kade	5	2	4.66	18	1	75	84	31	75
Craft, Derek	7	6	4.67	23	0	96	92	42	63
Rivera, Jerryell	2	2	5.05	22	0	36	34	19	24
McDowell, Theo	0	2	5.24	19	0	22	19	26	25
Shawaryn, Mike	3	1	5.38	19	0	110	118	29	87
Faith, Austin	3	6	5.84	18	0	69	79	32	56
Washington, Mark	3	2	5.85	17	0	20	24	14	24
Wilson, Tyler	2	2	5.96	17	1	23	18	9	28
Krauth, Nick	2	1	6.94	8	0	12	13	9	6
Henley, Blair	2	1	6.99	19	0	103	126	49	117
Lopez, Cristian	2	2	7.27	21	0	43	56	21	36
Dillard, Trey	2	1	13.15	12	0	13	14	24	23

FARGO-MOORHEAD REDHAWKS

Name	AVG	AB	R	H	HR	RBI	BB	SO	SB
Filia, Eric	.412	34	9	14	0	5	12	1	1
Thomas, Dillon	.312	349	67	109	15	50	59	89	15
Fernandez, Juan	.307	326	49	100	6	50	34	36	4
Nelson, Andy	.290	31	5	9	1	3	2	7	3
Sermo, Jose	.286	206	33	59	15	53	32	57	2
Sparks, Lamar	.282	266	42	75	7	34	26	56	15
Maiben, Derek	.277	94	12	26	0	8	4	6	7
Hallquist, Michael	.271	218	37	59	5	25	19	67	19
Byrne, Aidan	.249	265	33	66	0	24	19	55	11
Northcut, Nicholas	.238	160	19	38	4	18	15	37	0
Olund, Alec	.236	275	32	65	5	25	21	53	10
Dadson, Brendon	.227	181	23	41	7	30	36	45	2
Brookshaw, Peter	.218	124	19	27	4	21	27	23	2
Clanin, Hunter	.218	133	19	29	2	9	13	38	12
Planez, Alexfri	.211	123	16	26	2	12	13	23	2
Perez Jr., Robert	.204	152	14	31	1	23	11	41	4
Meza, Eric	.200	25	3	5	2	5	4	4	0
Chiu, Marcus	.193	83	11	16	1	13	4	17	1
Ojeda Jr., Miguel	.186	86	3	16	1	6	2	16	0
Stroh, Ryan	.185	65	6	12	0	5	2	25	0
Ostberg, Erik	.138	58	1	8	1	3	7	15	0
Green, Thomas	.122	41	8	5	0	2	5	13	3

Name	W	L	ERA	G	SV	IP	H	BB	SO
Day, Hunter	0	0	0.90	3	0	10	7	5	10
Alexander, Garrett	1	3	0.92	36	13	39	22	14	50
DuBord, Alex	0	0	1.59	17	12	17	8	6	20
Harm, Parker	3	3	1.61	40	1	50	32	27	71
Jeans, Tyler	1	0	1.62	13	0	17	17	3	19
Dykhoff, Jake	11	4	1.63	27	0	94	75	12	81
Minier, Greg	3	2	2.67	6	0	34	35	10	30
Barringer, Shane	4	1	3.08	8	0	38	37	17	29
Jandron, Tyler	7	4	3.54	17	0	102	102	26	84
Crigger, Kyle	7	5	3.64	18	0	109	99	39	88
Kiser, Kolby	3	5	4.07	19	0	91	91	32	52
Paulino, Naswell	0	2	4.39	32	2	27	19	19	34
Cabral, Angelo	2	3	5.05	15	0	41	44	21	36
Johnston, Kyle	4	2	5.77	37	0	44	43	23	40
Davis, Colten	5	6	5.85	34	3	60	68	28	56
Rodriguez, Orlando	1	6	5.89	16	0	70	80	34	60
Thiels, Brenton	0	0	6.30	9	0	10	9	13	8

GARY SOUTHSHORE RAILCATS

Name	AVG	AB	R	H	HR	RBI	BB	SO	SB
Peralta, Elvis	.314	389	53	122	3	44	49	80	31
Weiss, Cooper	.289	38	6	11	2	7	1	9	2
Machado, Carlos	.288	139	19	40	1	11	5	16	1
Meza, Eric	.273	11	1	3	0	1	0	4	0
Suozzi, Joe	.269	335	43	90	6	46	39	77	10

Name			AVG	AB	R	H	HR	RBI	BB	SO	SB
Gonzalez, Marcos			.265	155	14	41	3	25	13	38	1
Basabe, Olivier			.260	338	34	88	0	29	31	48	4
Valentin, Xavier			.250	52	10	13	2	10	6	15	1
Richards, Jairus			.247	296	48	73	10	37	50	65	52
Noriega, Andres			.242	99	9	24	5	14	9	29	0
Castillo, LG			.242	339	46	82	6	36	15	87	5
Ultsch, Nick			.233	189	18	44	0	13	8	57	7
Hoover, Jake			.228	101	15	23	0	2	6	35	4
Guenther, Jake			.227	203	28	46	5	27	26	28	3
Ordonez, Ernny			.193	119	12	23	0	8	5	42	4
Allgeyer, Jake			.190	100	10	19	1	12	13	19	3
Contreras, Jose			.182	44	8	8	1	6	5	21	3
Radcliff, Baron			.180	150	15	27	7	19	10	59	1
Edwards, Cooper			.161	174	16	28	0	15	18	60	1
Rodriguez, Howard			.063	16	0	1	0	1	1	4	0
Williams, Donivan			.000	11	1	0	0	0	2	5	0

Name	W	L	ERA	G	SV	IP	H	BB	SO
Alexander, Nate	3	7	2.44	41	2	44	41	15	48
Zaragoza, Ernesto	1	1	2.63	5	0	24	17	11	19
Coats, Jacob	1	2	2.89	36	13	37	26	22	38
Evans, Demarcus	2	3	3.48	27	0	34	19	22	27
Martinez, Jonathan	0	3	3.54	23	0	41	35	26	31
Olivero, Deyni	4	6	3.65	17	0	89	101	27	51
Lane, Dawson	5	3	3.73	26	0	63	66	27	65
Long, Peyton	7	8	3.87	20	0	123	137	28	99
Hull, Denson	1	1	4.30	36	0	52	44	28	46
Adams, Spencer	8	8	4.41	20	0	120	130	33	94
Diaz, Andres	4	9	4.89	18	0	103	117	46	79
Cerda, Junior	0	0	5.50	8	1	18	23	14	17
Reed, Cody	1	4	6.21	38	2	33	37	31	31
Acosta, Jaykob	0	2	7.20	26	0	35	46	17	22
Erwin, Chris	1	5	7.90	8	0	35	52	13	32

KANE COUNTY COUGARS

Name	AVG	AB	R	H	HR	RBI	BB	SO	SB
Rutherford, Blake	.333	27	4	9	1	3	2	2	0
Lott, Todd	.320	328	41	105	10	58	16	63	0
Clark, Tripp	.311	61	7	19	2	15	2	11	0
Craig, Trendon	.300	390	65	117	4	31	34	68	22
Spinn, Zane	.291	117	17	34	0	16	17	30	4
Chiu, Marcus	.290	276	58	80	14	57	26	69	7
Upshaw, Armond	.268	336	52	90	5	36	33	81	38
Allen, Josh	.246	313	60	77	7	46	48	65	8
Jackson, Darryl	.241	29	6	7	0	1	1	7	1
Finol, Claudio	.240	321	37	77	4	43	27	57	9
Santos, Oscar	.237	186	23	44	6	36	21	70	2
Cribbs Jr., Galli	.217	120	13	26	0	9	14	40	5
Dalesandro, Nick	.216	236	27	51	1	27	25	56	6
Jones, Thomas	.215	65	6	14	0	9	12	23	2
McGarry, Alex	.202	99	9	20	2	10	12	31	3
Martin Jr., Robby	.198	197	25	39	6	20	16	43	1
Valdez, C.J.	.161	31	4	5	1	5	3	7	0
Armstrong, Andy	.148	54	2	8	0	5	4	7	0
Rijo, Nilo	.148	54	7	8	0	2	9	10	4
Parker, Cade	.107	28	2	3	1	4	1	15	0
Dunhurst, Hayden	.105	19	1	2	0	0	0	7	0

Name	W	L	ERA	G	SV	IP	H	BB	SO
Nissen, Logan	3	0	2.47	44	1	47	39	22	41
Ash, Konnor	10	3	2.76	19	0	124	87	30	132
Gozzo, Jake	2	4	2.86	38	18	44	28	20	50
Veen, Zach	5	1	3.00	25	0	36	22	19	33
Crosby, Casey	3	3	3.07	34	3	41	32	12	55
Mazza, Chris	5	6	3.83	16	0	82	78	23	59
Fox, Jack	3	4	3.83	20	0	101	104	16	68
Sommer, Tommy	1	2	4.18	7	0	32	29	5	32
Timpanelli, Vin	7	8	4.21	25	0	105	95	40	77
Martinson, Jordan	1	2	4.30	40	0	38	27	21	48
Stagliano, Dominic	0	0	4.66	6	0	10	10	5	8
Stevenson, Jake	4	6	5.10	33	2	65	49	43	55
Muir, Westin	4	9	6.72	21	0	82	99	42	54
Kelly, John	1	0	8.71	7	0	10	10	13	7
Gudaitis, Quinn	0	1	10.31	20	0	18	18	21	26

KANSAS CITY MONARCHS

Name	AVG	AB	R	H	HR	RBI	BB	SO	SB
Bell, Brantley	.429	35	4	15	0	2	2	5	1
Gilliam, Isiah	.348	138	33	48	10	33	27	38	7
Pries, Micah	.333	153	34	51	9	34	23	24	10
Bissonette, Josh	.287	321	44	92	2	33	55	58	7
Adolph, Ross	.284	335	54	95	8	30	38	89	18
Nogowski, John	.277	282	37	78	8	49	45	23	6
Bonifacio, Jorge	.259	375	69	97	17	52	50	71	7
Glendinning, Robbie	.256	316	50	81	18	71	53	105	15
Noriega, Andres	.254	71	10	18	1	7	2	13	0
Williams, Jaylyn	.253	288	44	73	3	31	21	40	6
Gonzalez, Alvaro	.243	276	36	67	9	36	41	89	3
Rutherford, Blake	.240	200	26	48	5	30	12	27	5
Leitch, Ryan	.235	179	18	42	6	26	28	78	1
Holt, Peyton	.231	39	10	9	2	5	11	12	3
Ortiz, Jhailyn	.230	87	10	20	3	10	4	22	0
Sandoval, Joshuan	.230	100	9	23	1	12	8	43	0
Fajardo, Yoyner	.211	76	15	16	3	10	5	9	6
McGarry, Alex	.200	45	4	9	3	8	2	9	2
Familia, Christopher	.143	21	2	3	0	3	6	4	0

Name	W	L	ERA	G	SV	IP	H	BB	SO
Moore, Steffon	1	0	1.61	20	1	22	9	14	34
Noriega, Cruz	0	1	2.13	11	0	13	9	6	14
McMahon, Hunter	2	2	2.30	28	13	31	23	11	39
McKay, Tyler	1	1	2.40	15	7	15	11	4	15
Goldsberry, Blake	8	2	2.94	24	1	86	71	17	84
Hakanson, Jeff	5	1	3.35	35	2	51	47	20	60
Garcia, Julian	9	2	3.39	19	0	112	87	32	163
Hendrickson, Josh	10	5	3.61	19	0	105	94	34	116
Goudeau, Ashton	5	5	4.01	18	0	92	89	28	72
Mendez, Leam	2	2	4.21	37	0	47	40	23	50
Gambrell, Grant	4	4	4.50	7	0	28	29	10	23
Martinez, Daniel	5	5	4.60	16	0	72	69	17	89
Goddard, Jackson	2	3	4.83	11	0	54	52	24	67
Brentz, Jake	1	2	5.00	18	1	18	21	12	21
Cerda, Junior	2	1	5.16	19	1	30	37	6	25
Pridgen, Patrick	2	5	5.50	21	0	56	62	34	64
Holden, Connor	0	0	5.59	7	0	10	16	5	12
Bortka, Josh	1	2	10.43	13	1	15	20	14	16

LAKE COUNTRY DOCKHOUNDS

Name	AVG	AB	R	H	HR	RBI	BB	SO	SB
Vargas, Imanol	.327	49	19	16	5	16	12	11	0
Maiben, Derek	.294	85	11	25	0	10	14	8	11
Rey, Brian	.293	338	49	99	15	51	30	35	10
OKeefe, Brian	.288	160	22	46	8	24	21	24	1
Stuart, Daunte	.288	396	49	114	6	45	34	47	24
Rojas Jr., Freddy	.277	112	20	31	2	11	16	27	0
Roskam, Luke	.270	282	34	76	6	35	44	83	9
Aviles Jr., Luis	.257	109	11	28	2	12	5	26	10
Zuberer III, Ray	.257	296	48	76	11	44	39	85	17
Blackford, Braedon	.250	12	3	3	0	2	2	4	0
Hernandez, Ryan	.249	334	48	83	18	50	38	66	1
Perez, Eury	.242	33	4	8	1	2	1	4	1
Clark, Tripp	.238	21	3	5	0	1	1	4	1
Cootway, Adam	.234	64	14	15	1	12	10	21	1
Matthews, Dave	.231	13	2	3	0	0	4	3	1
Hill, Aaron	.227	313	55	71	12	37	40	91	31
Dunhurst, Hayden	.216	167	16	36	2	20	16	53	0
Northcut, Nicholas	.209	91	9	19	1	7	8	20	1
Sims, Demetrius	.195	215	27	42	9	26	29	75	12
Young, Chavez	.194	93	11	18	3	12	5	23	7
Gray, Joe	.176	51	2	9	0	5	9	14	7
Pelc, Eddy	.107	28	3	3	0	0	7	12	0

Name	W	L	ERA	G	SV	IP	H	BB	SO
Torres, Eric	2	1	1.59	39	16	40	13	29	64
Fenlong, Connor	2	5	2.15	22	0	59	50	13	50
Philip, Beau	2	2	3.29	26	1	27	24	8	40
Gsellman, Robert	3	2	3.38	36	8	40	38	9	40
Hansel, Luke	9	5	3.48	19	0	116	103	29	99
Bonnin, Bryce	3	3	3.51	30	1	33	24	15	41

Name	W	L	ERA	G	SV	IP	H	BB	SO
Riley, Trey	2	1	3.82	36	0	33	29	20	32
Cancellieri, Dominic	4	2	3.96	8	0	39	41	13	28
Aguilera, Gabriel	3	2	4.00	7	0	36	31	13	26
Nix, Jacob	2	1	4.04	10	0	56	52	10	65
Conine, Brett	3	1	4.17	20	0	110	115	41	101
Dillard, Trey	0	1	4.20	13	0	15	14	10	18
Moeller, JT	4	0	4.21	22	0	26	21	5	22
Jefferson, Chris	2	2	4.26	19	0	68	71	22	40
Sandy, Will	2	0	5.24	24	1	22	23	17	35
Lobstein, Kyle	3	1	5.34	6	0	30	30	9	27
Pilot, Kelvan	6	6	5.79	19	0	79	100	33	78
Cantleberry, Jake	2	1	6.63	18	2	19	14	11	29

LINCOLN SALTDOGS

Name	AVG	AB	R	H	HR	RBI	BB	SO	SB
Dragum, Jack	.301	113	13	34	0	6	16	12	0
Bautista Jr., Danny	.299	391	67	117	5	44	41	53	17
DeVine, Drew	.295	275	47	81	2	31	30	62	15
Kane, Mikey	.279	111	17	31	0	17	12	11	2
Hewitt, Max	.264	144	18	38	2	25	19	17	3
Castillo, Neyfy	.258	322	53	83	9	62	37	110	10
Fahr, Brody	.256	356	59	91	4	45	45	73	21
Diaz, Yusniel	.253	198	25	50	9	44	22	43	1
Maiben, Derek	.250	20	4	5	0	1	1	2	0
Henson, Spencer	.243	177	23	43	11	32	10	42	0
Coulter, Clint	.238	122	18	29	3	15	11	34	1
Sosa, Gustavo	.236	89	10	21	1	13	8	29	4
Espinosa, Rolando	.218	325	60	71	17	63	37	114	20
Battle, Kyle	.216	296	51	64	11	45	42	114	20
Phipps, Matt	.212	33	2	7	0	3	1	12	0
Denning, Connor	.211	57	7	12	0	6	5	21	0
Cone, Jack	.206	175	28	36	0	9	37	40	9
Everitt, Griffin	.185	81	11	15	1	6	8	31	0
Stroh, Parker	.143	35	1	5	0	1	1	14	0

Name	W	L	ERA	G	SV	IP	H	BB	SO
Ray, Johnny	1	1	1.27	5	0	21	11	15	28
Landis, Dutch	0	3	2.87	16	5	16	19	7	8
Cariaco, Peyton	3	2	2.87	28	0	31	22	13	19
Cobos, Franny	6	2	3.97	29	1	68	59	23	49
Castaneda, Dylan	4	4	4.35	18	0	81	70	52	44
Blain, Sean	5	4	4.50	19	0	86	103	43	63
Loukinen, Greg	7	9	5.32	20	0	108	120	45	87
Beck, Dylan	2	0	5.62	34	0	50	49	30	43
Blake, Johnny	3	6	5.83	21	0	88	96	45	82
Langrell, Connor	0	5	6.07	29	3	30	22	22	24
Roberts, Jacob	1	3	6.10	37	1	38	24	31	49
Vargas, Jhon	4	3	6.62	13	0	67	79	26	50
Shaw, David	1	3	7.07	15	1	14	11	12	13
Mullen, Sean	0	1	7.11	14	0	13	12	9	7
Patel, Karan	1	3	7.54	18	0	43	50	42	50
Viney, Gaylon	0	2	7.84	18	0	21	25	18	20
Mullenbach, Matt	3	5	8.17	35	2	40	51	20	30

MILWAUKEE MILKMEN

Name	AVG	AB	R	H	HR	RBI	BB	SO	SB
Ostberg, Erik	.309	256	48	79	16	54	40	49	5
Estep, Chase	.307	387	66	119	9	54	40	89	20
Lester, Parker	.281	139	21	39	1	19	25	28	1
Hollow, Kaden	.277	65	7	18	2	15	9	10	0
Santiago, Glenn	.277	249	29	69	3	35	14	43	1
Perez, Delvin	.265	325	45	86	9	31	39	85	17
Ota, Scott	.264	352	47	93	10	40	28	53	8
Gray, Joe	.261	264	34	69	4	30	24	54	14
Olund, Alec	.258	66	8	17	0	5	8	13	6
Blake, Andy	.256	328	63	84	13	42	38	80	17
Radcliff, Baron	.244	131	16	32	7	22	20	47	0
Adolfo, Micker	.238	147	14	35	2	19	11	42	0
Amaya, Carlos	.233	60	6	14	0	6	3	17	2
Sanford, Mitchell	.216	97	12	21	2	16	10	24	1
Escala, Willie	.200	175	27	35	1	17	12	44	3
Marte, Jefry	.195	113	9	22	4	19	8	14	1
Davis, Jaylin	.167	78	6	13	0	6	6	25	2
Sundean, Andrew	.158	38	1	6	0	2	1	4	0
Stroh, Zach	.115	87	11	10	0	0	16	26	0

Name	W	L	ERA	G	SV	IP	H	BB	SO
Johnson, Jordan	0	1	2.35	20	4	23	13	8	18
Bentley, Denny	5	4	2.49	36	13	43	30	9	48
Givin, Matt	4	2	3.42	28	0	53	55	14	56
Busse, Terry	3	1	3.55	13	0	13	11	4	12
Diaz, Juan	5	5	3.83	19	0	87	86	32	66
Puckett, Brady	0	4	4.02	41	0	47	37	25	63
Mezquita, Jhordany	7	6	4.20	19	0	109	97	47	83
Chalus, Eric	2	7	4.47	15	0	56	64	17	46
Purnell, Blake	1	5	4.73	36	1	51	58	17	45
Walker, Matt	7	3	5.22	14	0	71	72	25	60
Thomas, Tahnaj	0	0	5.23	28	0	31	33	20	34
Welch, Davis	3	4	5.36	18	0	94	109	40	51
Bartow, Frankie	2	1	5.54	5	0	26	31	7	14
Gearing, Chase	3	6	6.82	17	0	67	84	22	58
Snow, Logan	0	1	8.06	18	1	22	34	8	21
Mishoulam, Aaron	1	2	8.41	33	0	35	42	26	40
Hernandez, Nyan	2	2	8.47	16	0	17	22	10	20

Name	W	L	ERA	G	SV	IP	H	BB	SO
Cosby, Christian	4	2	0.76	25	6	24	12	10	31
Stover, Brady	1	1	1.46	12	6	12	9	2	18
Richardson, Ryan	4	2	2.47	47	0	47	31	10	32
Culley, Nathan	0	0	2.61	13	0	21	16	11	13
Dorminy, Thomas	11	1	2.90	20	0	121	96	32	108
Levine, Will	3	0	3.19	36	1	37	26	19	39
Hasty, Charlie	2	3	3.25	28	13	28	27	10	11
Brown, Tanner	6	5	3.69	20	0	122	109	33	134
LaLonde, Cole	5	5	3.78	33	1	52	57	23	53
Solter, Matt	1	1	4.50	3	0	16	19	7	14
Veen, Zach	0	0	4.66	11	0	10	7	9	9
Knoll, Brendan	6	3	5.66	17	0	70	80	37	30
Dalen, Kody	2	1	6.08	29	0	27	28	14	28
Zimmerman, Ryan	4	5	6.12	24	0	90	92	35	64
Miller, Seth	3	6	7.19	23	0	96	122	48	63
Torgerson, Cade	6	6	8.29	22	0	76	110	49	42
Johnson, Christian	0	0	8.38	9	0	10	18	3	8

SIOUX CITY EXPLORERS

Name	AVG	AB	R	H	HR	RBI	BB	SO	SB
Quinones, Michael	.379	58	9	22	0	5	6	9	0
Alvarez, Armando	.333	12	4	4	1	4	5	0	0
Vooletich, Zac	.291	320	43	93	6	48	42	48	41
George, Henry	.291	344	65	100	9	43	62	53	43
Knowles, DShawn	.286	304	62	87	9	54	47	49	53
Day, Joshua	.285	351	50	100	6	63	34	87	20
Montgomery, Torin	.260	281	45	73	7	41	27	62	12
Davis, Austin	.257	343	71	88	5	25	31	56	60
Castro, Carlos	.238	42	5	10	0	4	1	15	1
Layer, Abdiel	.234	346	45	81	14	65	20	91	16
Toribio, Luis	.230	152	20	35	3	19	21	63	2
Tovalin, Osvaldo	.225	111	14	25	1	9	7	18	0
Byrne, Kurtis	.214	234	25	50	2	31	21	65	1
Shumpert, Nick	.209	239	38	50	7	38	28	87	21
Meyer, Jake	.208	24	5	5	0	1	6	11	0
Barns, Landen	.176	17	2	3	0	2	1	4	0
Escotto, Maikol	.170	53	6	9	1	8	4	10	2
Rose, Nathan	.160	25	4	4	0	2	1	8	2
Gomez, Dario	.158	19	1	3	0	2	0	9	1

Name	W	L	ERA	G	SV	IP	H	BB	SO
Cepeda, Felix	6	3	1.42	44	24	51	33	28	63
DeTaeye, Ben	2	0	1.45	22	0	31	17	20	32
Matthews, Brett	1	1	1.61	23	0	22	11	24	18
Jessee, Chase	8	1	2.01	42	1	54	38	29	85
Willeman, Zach	4	2	2.34	8	0	50	31	22	65
Marman, Kyle	8	3	3.07	19	0	123	117	35	140
Wetherbee, Jared	9	4	3.29	19	0	107	86	40	125
Gercken, Nate	7	2	3.32	35	1	38	35	18	22
Drury, Austin	7	4	3.81	20	0	125	108	60	106
Macuare, Angel	2	2	4.24	8	0	34	38	6	39
Jackson, Jaren	2	2	5.29	28	1	48	55	17	37
Otano, Peniel	2	7	6.72	21	0	82	104	56	58
Scholten, J.D.	1	1	6.75	8	0	21	31	11	5
Goins, Jeremy	2	3	6.81	33	3	41	42	38	54
Murray, Joey	1	1	6.88	4	0	17	20	10	16

SIOUX FALLS CANARIES

Name	AVG	AB	R	H	HR	RBI	BB	SO	SB
Estrada, Calvin	.352	366	71	129	20	88	31	51	20
Rehwaldt, Josh	.315	343	74	108	16	61	70	91	11
Bottcher, Matt	.313	67	14	21	1	14	9	12	2
Barth, Jordan	.303	396	71	120	19	66	20	63	9
Zimmermann, Peter	.264	269	31	71	11	44	42	52	9
Henry, Jabari	.262	294	69	77	22	61	74	93	0
Ruiz, Matt	.255	314	51	80	7	36	20	69	34
Vos, Joe	.246	183	24	45	3	17	24	45	9
Combs, Scott	.241	228	26	55	3	27	9	45	0
Hart, Mike	.227	300	57	68	17	45	52	98	9
Ordonez, Ernny	.213	61	9	13	3	9	5	18	6
Achenbach, Trevor	.199	282	45	56	3	26	40	96	6
Clanin, Hunter	.176	102	15	18	4	14	12	39	1
Dirksen, Drey	.176	176	22	31	3	13	28	77	5

WINNIPEG GOLDEYES

Name	AVG	AB	R	H	HR	RBI	BB	SO	SB
Bramasco, Ramon	.289	374	56	108	7	51	63	64	20
Enriquez, Roby	.280	243	30	68	0	22	21	35	4
Clark, Tripp	.278	72	10	20	0	7	6	14	2
Murphy, Max	.277	364	52	101	15	62	29	111	10
Lynch, Keshawn	.267	266	39	71	1	27	42	58	10
Robson, Jacob	.257	370	57	95	14	52	46	94	30
Warkentin, Matthew	.256	328	51	84	15	54	28	101	1
Garcia, Kevin	.248	214	19	53	4	27	16	43	2
Armstrong, Andy	.245	188	22	46	1	19	8	35	7
Sosa, Gustavo	.218	101	9	22	1	13	11	32	4
OTremba, Tanner	.215	246	35	53	6	31	29	74	11
Didder, Ray-Patrick	.199	282	43	56	10	30	55	79	11
Emery, Rob	.196	51	3	10	1	5	5	8	0
Alexander, Evan	.162	68	16	11	2	5	13	20	5
Simington, Miles	.158	57	3	9	0	10	4	8	3
Guenther, Jake	.151	53	4	8	1	5	4	6	3
Turner, Braxton	.097	31	3	3	0	2	11	0	

Name	W	L	ERA	G	SV	IP	H	BB	SO
Omana, Henry	0	0	1.50	9	0	12	7	8	9
Lombard, Weston	1	0	1.80	6	0	10	5	8	7
Yakel, Ryder	2	5	2.70	43	8	67	53	11	82
Brigden, Trevor	2	5	3.07	27	2	29	22	17	33
Onyshko, Ben	1	2	3.51	34	1	33	28	12	29
Kowalski, Ben	3	1	3.58	7	0	33	31	9	22
Strobel, Tasker	3	5	3.60	46	1	75	64	32	48
Cherry, Derrick	3	1	4.09	40	0	66	62	22	62
Bourassa, Landen	6	6	4.20	15	0	86	91	10	55
Boyd, Luke	5	5	4.53	17	0	95	94	43	61
Bradwell, James	1	3	4.61	7	0	41	38	19	26
Lambson, Mitchell	8	6	4.86	20	0	130	138	27	83
Galindo, Jesse	2	5	5.09	17	0	74	79	49	42
Rose, Zan	4	6	5.66	22	0	68	72	33	51
Sierra, Will	0	0	6.40	11	0	13	15	13	8
Jaco, Joe	0	0	7.45	10	0	10	11	8	3
Leach, Landon	0	0	10.97	9	0	11	14	12	7

ATLANTIC LEAGUE

York won its second consecutive title and its fifth overall, as it knocked off High Point in the league championship series. It continued the Revolution's perfect record as the team is now 5-for-5 on winning titles when it makes it to the championship series.

Jalen Miller hit .452/.500/.613 during the playoffs for York, while Kyle Martin and Jaylin Davis each hit three home runs. Chris Vallimont went 1-0, 1.22 in two postseason starts, allowing just four hits and four walks while striking out 22 in 14.2 innings.

North Division	W	L	PCT	
York Revolution*	74	52	.587	--
Long Island Ducks	72	54	.571	2
Lancaster Stormers &	71	55	.563	3
Staten Island Ferry Hawks	56	70	.444	18
Hagerstown Flying Boxcars	31	95	.246	43

South Division	W	L	PCT	
High Point Rockers*	74	52	.587	--
Gastonia Ghost Peppers &	68	58	.540	6
Southern Maryland Blue Crabs	68	58	.540	6
Lexington Legends	64	62	.508	10
Charleston Dirty Birds	52	74	.413	22

*First-half champion. & Second-half champion.

Playoffs—Semifinals: York defeated Lancaster 3-0 and High Point defeated Gastonia 3-2 in best-of-5 series. **Finals:** York defeated High Point 3-1 in best-of-5 series.

Attendance: Long Island Ducks 292,467; Lancaster Stormers 248,683; York Revolution 174,949; Charleston Dirty Birds 167,222; Hagerstown Flying Boxcars 159,653; Southern Maryland Blue Crabs 147,651; Lexington Legends 130,704; High Point Rockers 99,309; Gastonia Ghost Peppers 87,634; Staten Island Ferry Hawks 71,448.

All-Star Team: C: Matthew Scheffler, Staten Island. **1B:** Mason Martin, Lancaster. **2B:** Jalen Miller, York. **SS:** Joseph Rosa, Charleston. **3B:** James Nelson, Charleston. **DH:** Brady Whalen, Lexington. **OF:** Ben Aklinski, High Point; River Town, Long Island; Justin Wylie, Gastonia; Luis Gonzalez, High Point. **SP:** Noah Skirrow, Lancaster. **RP:** Scott Engler, Lancaster. **Closer:** Cam Robinson, York.

Player of the Year: James Nelson, Charleston. **Pitcher of the Year:** Noah Skirrow, Lancaster. **Defensive Player of the Year:** Ben Alinski, High Point. **Manager of the Year:** Jamie Keefe, High Point.

BATTING LEADERS

Name	AVG	AB	R	H	HR	RBI	BB	SO	SB
Matthew Scheffler, SI	.347	303	58	105	15	61	49	68	1
Frankie Tostado, YRK	.337	362	59	122	11	73	21	45	2
Brady Whalen, LEX	.331	399	89	132	26	84	74	64	31
Nick Ward, LAN	.329	422	95	139	20	84	53	72	20
River Town, LI	.326	439	92	143	13	71	74	61	42
Dalton Guthrie, GAS	.325	422	84	137	18	88	38	50	20
James Nelson, CWV	.315	501	102	158	34	89	61	117	53
Brett Barrera, SMD	.312	433	68	135	8	76	42	63	5
Eddy Diaz, SI	.311	415	77	129	7	57	24	62	40
Shayne Fontana, YRK	.310	439	105	136	16	88	55	99	24

PITCHING LEADERS

Player, Team	W	L	ERA	G	IP	H	BB	SO
Shawn Semple, SMD	6	7	3.95	22	130	133	30	101
Noah Skirrow, LAN	15	3	3.99	25	138	130	47	143
David Griffin, LI	6	4	4.03	22	103	106	27	92
Mike Kickham, YRK	11	8	4.38	25	148	171	34	145
Wesley Scott, SI	7	9	4.74	23	118	100	78	128
Juan Hillman, LI	9	6	4.88	24	127	130	49	106
Andrew Thurman, SMD	7	2	4.94	25	126	128	56	128
Colton Eastman, LEX	11	7	5.04	22	114	116	35	128
Nic Laio, LEX	9	5	5.49	22	121	135	46	111
Noah Bremer, LAN	10	4	5.60	22	116	124	36	122

CHARLESTON DIRTY BIRDS

Name	AVG	AB	R	H	HR	RBI	BB	SO	SB
Nelson, James	.315	501	102	158	34	89	61	117	53
Sedio, Chad	.300	270	38	81	17	47	30	85	0
Womack, Alsander	.297	495	66	147	16	63	30	66	33
Blackwell, Benjamin	.278	396	62	110	2	26	51	102	42
Rosa, Joseph	.274	398	71	109	22	71	62	116	14
Matijevic, JJ	.273	99	14	27	8	20	16	26	4
Daniels, Zach	.272	474	77	129	23	63	39	154	23
Smith, Jaylen	.271	59	8	16	3	9	7	8	5
Barnum, Keon	.270	200	25	54	17	50	21	77	0
Amezquita, Carlos	.256	43	6	11	0	8	7	14	11
Demeritte, Travis	.232	297	36	69	8	33	30	89	10
Bradley, Bobby	.219	64	6	14	2	8	14	24	0
DeLuca, Joe	.207	116	22	24	9	24	25	45	1
Alonso, Alan	.207	135	22	28	4	6	15	51	8
Hill, Tyler	.205	83	13	17	4	13	10	34	2
Lopez, BJ	.204	98	8	20	1	8	7	29	0
Moorer, Demetrius	.193	254	47	49	4	25	62	87	40
Pestano Jr., Ariel	.174	92	11	16	2	14	9	36	4
Soto, Jonathan	.158	146	10	23	0	15	13	53	2

Name	W	L	ERA	G	SV	IP	H	BB	SO
Record, Joe	2	0	0.00	13	4	19	6	11	24
Alesandro, Ronaldo	1	0	1.64	21	5	22	17	13	31
Sampson, Keyvius	3	1	3.00	5	0	24	17	10	26
Corona, Reibyn	2	1	3.18	12	3	11	7	5	9
McGowin, Kyle	2	6	3.39	12	0	64	71	28	51
Lusk, Lance	4	4	3.86	52	8	54	49	34	45
Lebron, David	8	4	3.88	21	0	118	110	38	125
Van Gurp, Franklin	1	0	3.93	18	0	18	17	17	23
Lugo, Alejandro	0	0	4.24	14	0	17	16	14	17
Reyes, Samuel	4	4	4.39	48	0	53	50	23	58
Demurias, Eddy	5	4	4.71	36	3	73	64	35	96
de Avila, Luis	4	4	5.45	13	0	71	66	28	60
Hill, Jamison	2	1	6.20	5	24	0	118	128	61	125
Moscatiello, Frank	1	2	6.30	60	3	60	53	52	73
Davis, Marc	0	4	6.75	7	0	21	21	23	29
Romero, Luis	0	2	6.75	5	0	24	28	15	23
Diaz, Anthony	3	5	6.85	10	0	47	51	32	34
Del Prado, Nick	2	1	7.13	10	0	18	22	13	20
Medoro, Brendan	1	1	7.71	19	0	30	39	14	17
Henriquez, Jonh	2	5	7.74	18	0	57	70	39	64
Suriel, Edison	2	3	7.82	35	0	63	64	65	53
Alvarez, Manuel	0	1	8.64	17	0	17	20	22	16
Campbell, Maceo	0	2	9.21	6	0	15	20	12	12
Meza, Carlos	2	0	10.44	24	0	25	25	34	26
Endersby, Jimmy	0	2	11.32	3	0	10	21	4	7

GASTONIA GHOST PEPPERS

Name	AVG	AB	R	H	HR	RBI	BB	SO	SB
McKeithan, Aaron	.369	65	14	24	1	15	8	8	0
Long Jr., Shed	.340	47	12	16	0	9	4	8	4
OGrady, Brian	.339	124	25	42	10	25	21	28	4
Guthrie, Dalton	.325	422	84	137	18	88	38	50	20
Martin, Richie	.318	85	20	27	7	16	8	19	7
Wylie, Justin	.304	438	125	133	29	101	89	90	37
Scantlin, Nate	.299	294	59	88	14	56	34	74	21
Aldrete, Carter	.289	187	35	54	17	56	23	38	2
De La Rosa, Eric	.286	370	81	106	22	78	52	150	50
Crook, Narciso	.278	352	67	98	19	70	49	101	28
Skender, Ethan	.268	287	54	77	13	58	21	50	18
Roederer, Cole	.258	419	85	108	20	70	80	90	26
Barditch, Jonny	.255	55	8	14	1	8	7	6	2
Perez, Henderson	.246	122	21	30	1	16	16	31	0
Reinheimer, Jack	.246	419	63	103	12	64	67	101	27
Grullon, Francis	.238	21	4	5	0	2	4	7	2
Watson Jr., Kevin	.220	286	66	63	12	44	54	84	32
Mazeika, Patrick	.218	124	17	27	2	15	12	19	1
Meyer, Jake	.182	66	6	12	1	8	13	21	1
Alonso, Alan	.175	40	4	7	1	2	3	17	1
Olmeda, Alexis	.149	74	8	11	1	7	11	32	1
Aviles, Luis	.143	14	3	2	1	1	1	5	0

Name	W	L	ERA	G	SV	IP	H	BB	SO
Silber, Cas	1	0	1.59	5	0	11	5	5	12
Snyder, Nick	0	2	2.17	27	6	29	19	10	30
Thompson, Cory	3	2	3.27	37	3	41	37	14	40
Hartman, Matt	5	1	3.42	21	0	92	79	42	89
Warren, Art	3	0	3.60	18	1	20	18	14	28
Westcott, Zac	3	0	3.95	4	0	14	11	3	7
Underwood Jr., Duane	5	2	3.97	32	0	68	73	15	58
Wilson, John	6	3	3.98	25	0	61	66	18	52
Hasler, Kent	1	4	4.07	36	2	42	35	20	57
Hennen, Ryan	5	3	4.42	42	1	57	55	15	56
Grey, Ronald	1	3	4.46	17	0	73	69	31	79
Newsome, Ljay	4	3	5.05	14	0	66	89	12	47
Horvath, Nick	2	5	5.14	55	3	68	74	32	78
Benoit, Donovan	1	2	5.21	12	0	19	19	6	25
Myatt, Tanner	2	3	5.24	15	0	22	26	29	29
Sheffield, Justus	5	5	5.27	15	0	43	47	24	33
Blanton, Bryan	2	5	5.49	50	3	61	46	46	82
Stem, Craig	5	1	5.58	12	0	60	67	22	47
Wells, Nick	7	9	6.27	22	0	98	117	47	99
King, Thomas	5	0	6.50	18	0	44	42	28	50

Name	AVG	AB	R	H	HR	RBI	BB	SO	SB
Miednik, Jake	0	0	6.52	9	0	10	10	10	8
Espinal, Raynel	0	0	6.75	5	0	17	23	5	20
Smith, Kevin	0	2	6.97	5	0	21	25	19	19
Boss, Jackson	0	0	12.19	12	0	10	17	15	4
Scott, Adam	1	2	13.03	6	0	10	13	13	7

HAGERSTOWN FLYING BOXCARS

Name	AVG	AB	R	H	HR	RBI	BB	SO	SB
Walker, Mason	.333	18	2	6	0	0	1	7	0
Dotel, Welington	.311	103	9	32	4	15	4	33	2
Takacs, Aaron	.310	145	20	45	3	19	24	33	1
Mattis, Gary	.306	408	56	125	6	35	30	99	19
Williams, Tyler	.293	341	50	100	10	40	25	80	27
Semo, Andrew	.270	37	2	10	0	3	4	8	0
Lujano, Jesus	.268	149	19	40	2	6	8	26	2
Arbolida, Cary	.266	331	39	88	12	45	30	113	1
Alonso, Alan	.264	53	5	14	1	8	8	14	3
Cannon, Bryce	.263	266	27	70	10	53	19	78	0
Escanio, Brenny	.260	50	4	13	0	2	2	17	0
Black, Mark	.251	195	14	49	3	17	22	36	0
Martinez, Roidel	.245	143	13	35	0	9	16	32	0
Campagna, Joe	.243	144	23	35	4	13	24	28	3
Abreu, Osvaldo	.239	415	54	99	15	53	40	97	6
DeLuca, Joe	.233	176	32	41	10	29	32	69	1
Robinson, Errol	.226	93	9	21	2	15	9	29	2
Saenz Jr., Kevin	.222	27	4	6	1	1	5	10	0
Sedio, Chad	.217	60	7	13	2	7	4	25	0
Quiroz, Isaias	.209	67	3	14	3	11	7	24	0
Leach, Dante	.203	153	17	31	1	14	6	44	5
Kwitzer, Chris	.201	144	12	29	2	12	9	48	0
Schield, Slater	.196	56	8	11	0	2	6	13	0
Tovalin, Osvaldo	.195	41	2	8	0	2	2	7	0
Acal, Justin	.195	190	23	37	3	19	26	58	1
Barham, Robby	.176	34	1	6	0	2	3	13	0
Williams, Miles	.176	102	12	18	5	10	14	42	0
Costes, Marty	.154	13	0	2	0	0	0	2	0
Chung, Patrick	.150	20	2	3	0	1	7	7	1
Mayberry, Blake	.146	41	3	6	0	2	6	9	0
Gomez, Daniel	.109	46	4	5	0	0	6	21	0
Rosario, Dilan	.080	25	3	2	0	0	8	11	1
Colon, Rabel	.077	13	3	1	0	1	3	8	2
Johnson, Tyler	.056	18	0	1	0	1	1	10	0

Name	W	L	ERA	G	SV	IP	H	BB	SO
Reyes, Carlo	3	0	2.96	22	0	24	14	9	30
Kelly, Rafael	4	5	3.13	52	14	60	50	20	54
Picone, Domenic	2	5	4.56	10	0	47	42	23	56
Kickham, Mike	4	8	4.57	17	0	102	117	22	98
Henriquez, Jonh	2	3	4.89	9	0	39	39	20	33
Martinez, Quinton	1	8	5.44	33	0	91	97	42	105
Weisenburger, Jack	1	1	5.66	132	0	103	111	54	106
Saturria, Michael	0	2	6.32	25	0	31	35	22	43
Richardson, David	2	8	6.52	12	0	48	59	27	39
Noriega, Branden	1	1	6.67	47	0	54	52	46	51
Conklin, MacCallan	1	4	6.75	27	0	32	41	24	24
Simone, Andrew	1	2	6.92	22	0	26	34	12	20
Reitz, Matt	1	2	6.92	16	0	40	55	3	22
Imhoff, Anthony	2	8	6.97	15	0	71	94	33	46
Minaya, Julian	0	1	7.16	018	0	83	113	45	50
Martinez, Jorge	0	4	7.36	5	0	22	33	9	19
Paulino, Franklin	0	1	7.71	9	0	14	17	6	8
Shapley, Jake	0	0	8.56	12	0	14	20	11	10
Marshalwitz, Casey	0	0	9.99	14	0	24	37	17	8
Brown, Ethan	0	0	10.39	12	0	13	17	13	6
Robbins, Zane	1	2	10.45	12	0	10	11	9	8
Corcino, Daniel	1	4	10.58	6	0	25	31	17	17
Quesada, Rogelio	0	2	11.91	8	0	11	21	10	9
Maruskin, Jack	1	0	15.50	16	0	18	23	24	15

HIGH POINT ROCKERS

Name	AVG	AB	R	H	HR	RBI	BB	SO
Napleton, Luke	.407	113	17	46	6	29	14	25	1
Edwards, Evan	.328	229	48	75	21	73	41	53	5
Gonzalez, Luis	.297	435	110	129	21	73	72	72	36
Mendoza, Drew	.293	460	86	135	19	96	71	90	11
Aklinski, Ben	.283	448	112	127	32	96	75	94	31
Amezquita, Carlos	.269	52	7	14	0	6	5	21	5
Longhi, Nick	.265	113	12	30	3	19	6	26	0
Dickerson, Alex	.265	294	45	78	19	68	44	71	2
Viera, Max	.261	357	64	93	5	53	47	73	17
Luplow, Jordan	.255	47	9	12	4	13	8	11	0
Parks, Bryson	.250	16	3	4	0	0	1	9	1
Conley, Jack	.247	170	23	42	4	28	26	45	11
Burt, D.J.	.241	340	58	82	3	31	52	68	33
Mirabal, Isaiah	.232	'95	17	22	2	12	16	37	0
Brewer, Aidan	.230	383	65	88	13	46	51	128	21
Wilson, Cody	.222	117	23	26	2	14	12	29	12
Davidson, Braxton	.220	227	37	50	11	31	61	109	0
Logan, Michael	.200	10	2	2	0	0	1	4	1
Watson, Nolan	.186	113	16	21	2	14	20	45	5
Yetsko, Ian	.179	168	15	30	3	16	17	65	5

Name	W	L	ERA	G	SV	IP	H	BB	SO
Klobosits, Gabe	3	0	1.64	13	1	22	17	8	28
Hess, David	2	0	1.82	15	1	30	22	11	29
Cotter, Cam	0	2	2.51	14	1	14	13	2	9
McGrane, Jameson	1	2	2.63	37	16	38	27	16	43
Emanuel, Kent	6	1	3.41	10	0	58	60	14	48
Solter, Matt	7	2	3.50	10	0	62	50	21	59
Barraclough, Kyle	5	0	3.51	8	0	41	33	19	38
Wereski, Ben	4	4	3.76	12	0	55	47	20	64
Del Bonta-Smith, Fin	2	3	3.77	15	0	57	50	7	42
Uelmen, Erich	6	4	3.83	17	0	80	72	23	65
Edwards, Jacob	2	1	3.86	6	0	12	7	4	11
Halbohn, Kyle	1	0	3.95	34	5	41	38	6	38
Doyle, Tommy	1	3	4.03	16	5	38	34	19	43
Gilbert, Jake	1	3	4.04	10	0	49	34	29	50
Scott, Win	3	0	4.22	16	0	21	19	10	17
Rouse, Scott	1	3	4.26	17	0	25	32	10	23
Devine, Mike	2	1	4.75	6	0	30	29	9	13
Backman, Brandon	2	2	4.89	8	0	35	34	15	44
Blair, Daniel	3	1	5.26	31	1	50	52	21	43
Branche, Stevie	2	2	5.65	29	3	29	28	15	45
Casad, Cooper	3	2	6.10	9	0	38	54	4	21
Lewis, Justin	2	1	6.91	15	0	14	16	4	11
Scolaro, Jonah	9	6	6.96	31	0	98	109	54	81
Vennora, Zach	0	1	7.62	44	1	41	45	29	53
Gardner, Pat	0	1	7.86	6	0	26	33	8	12
Frisbee, Matt	2	1	10.13	9	0	13	22	2	14
Ogle, Braeden	0	1	10.90	16	0	17	18	20	18

LANCASTER STORMERS

Name	AVG	AB	R	H	HR	RBI	BB	SO	SB
Mayberry, Blake	.360	25	1	9	0	5	1	5	0
Campagna, Joe	.331	160	34	53	9	29	28	29	9
Ward, Nick	.329	422	95	139	20	84	53	72	20
Lucky, Nick	.293	430	82	126	17	87	55	107	28
Kelly, Scott	.292	48	5	14	0	6	6	15	5
Martin, Mason	.291	453	98	132	36	92	70	116	16
Carpenter, Joseph	.279	362	57	101	14	58	31	85	12
Sandoval, Ariel	.276	185	29	51	7	39	20	39	16
Coca, Yeison	.262	370	71	97	1	40	62	89	28
Watson Jr., Kevin	.254	114	20	29	5	25	14	35	14
Castro, Luis	.252	103	17	26	4	16	5	25	8
Dugan, Kelly	.250	32	2	8	0	8	3	10	0
Isola, Alex	.243	379	64	92	12	58	61	52	2
Schield, Slater	.241	174	28	42	0	23	31	33	11
Amaral, Daniel	.235	255	37	60	2	36	33	57	36
Semo, Andrew	.231	117	16	27	2	14	26	36	5
Clark, LeDarious	.224	85	9	19	2	6	11	26	10
Alexander, Evan	.222	185	36	41	8	24	36	57	9
Mercedes, Kevin	.204	98	17	20	0	12	21	14	5
Wagner, Brandon	.182	44	7	8	2	8	9	21	0
Matthews, Dave	.179	78	13	14	5	16	11	31	3
Hamilton, Quincy	.170	47	7	8	3	8	9	12	1

Name	W	L	ERA	G	SV	IP	H	BB	SO
Engler, Scott	6	2	1.90	59	6	62	42	23	63
Stashak, Cody	2	0	1.99	21	6	23	12	5	31
Gilliam, Ryley	2	2	2.66	21	8	20	12	10	33
Rees, Jackson	5	3	2.90	52	2	59	55	25	72
Moreno, Gerson	1	1	3.26	20	5	19	15	4	33
Diehl, Phillip	3	4	3.74	52	7	55	53	9	63
Sullivan, Billy	2	2	3.78	34	1	33	27	20	46
Brennan, Tim	3	2	3.79	7	0	38	46	9	23
Skirrow, Noah	15	3	3.99	25	0	138	130	47	143
Killgore, Keylan	2	6	4.74	17	0	68	80	29	64
Green, Max	5	8	5.22	24	0	79	97	20	71
Bell, Brock	0	0	5.27	4	0	14	18	5	10
Johnson, Kyle	3	0	5.35	36	1	37	30	25	41
White, Brendan	2	0	5.59	10	0	10	9	6	9
Bremer, Noah	10	4	5.60	22	0	116	124	36	122
McCollough, Luke	0	4	5.63	12	0	54	63	23	41
Lacey, Steven	1	2	5.68	22	1	51	59	29	52
McAvene, Michael	7	4	5.72	38	2	102	123	19	87
Scafidi, Christian	0	1	7.56	12	0	17	21	11	25
Swarmer, Matt	2	4	7.91	13	0	47	73	14	54
Alexy, A.J.	0	2	12.38	30	0	40	61	42	36

LEXINGTON LEGENDS

Name	AVG	AB	R	H	HR	RBI	BB	SO	SB
Ellis, Drew	.373	51	11	19	5	11	9	11	0
Dixon, Brenden	.344	61	13	21	6	15	13	12	4
Cumbo, EJ	.331	260	38	86	6	52	10	61	10
Whalen, Brady	.331	399	89	132	26	84	74	64	31
Terry, Curtis	.309	411	76	127	25	97	46	59	4
Briggs, Lamar	.294	17	3	5	0	3	1	8	0
Atwood, Andy	.278	418	77	116	17	62	31	102	26
Rock, Dylan	.277	382	96	106	22	65	57	95	25
Fuentes, Brian	.265	392	68	104	16	79	59	106	10
Washington, Xane	.261	383	65	100	6	44	31	94	26
Bates, Austin	.259	58	6	15	0	4	2	12	0
Winland Jr., Paul	.257	74	12	19	2	13	7	28	1
Riddle, JT	.252	115	21	29	2	14	9	36	1
Pike, Garret	.250	36	9	9	1	4	3	7	4
Gonzalez, Pedro	.245	249	46	61	12	30	27	86	16
Burgess, Colin	.236	55	6	13	1	9	4	9	1
McCarthy, Ryan	.230	291	45	67	8	29	37	95	37
Dinesen, Mason	.217	60	5	13	0	8	4	25	2
Huntzinger, Jerry	.210	257	39	54	6	30	32	66	7
Dawson, Ronnie	.209	43	5	9	2	7	4	21	0
Cottam, Kole	.206	68	11	14	2	7	6	17	0
Quiroz, Isaias	.180	111	18	20	6	12	18	51	0
Toetz, Paul	.176	34	3	6	0	2	2	11	0
Williams, Justin	.095	21	1	2	0	0	3	3	0

Name	W	L	ERA	G	SV	IP	H	BB	SO
Armstrong, John	2	1	2.25	16	0	20	15	10	24
Zeldin, Brian	0	0	2.61	15	0	21	18	12	25
Sophy, Kaleb	0	0	3.97	8	0	11	9	3	11
Lambert, Carson	3	1	4.07	19	0	24	24	5	27
Tully, Tanner	2	3	4.26	6	0	32	34	4	30
Loper, Jimmy	5	2	4.26	44	5	61	49	35	84
Dilone, Julio	0	0	4.63	33	0	35	33	33	36
Haab, Jonathan	2	6	4.98	50	17	56	50	35	77
Ferrer, Ben	4	4	5.03	18	0	91	101	32	67
Eastman, Colton	11	7	5.04	22	0	114	116	35	128
Beggs, Dustin	6	2	5.38	17	0	84	93	24	58
Laio, Nic	9	7	5.49	22	0	121	135	46	111
Acosta, Jose	1	3	5.61	25	0	34	34	20	37
Gregersen, Simon	0	2	5.85	13	1	20	19	7	25
Lynch, Jack	0	3	6.06	41	0	55	50	39	61
Edwards, Christian	1	2	6.64	42	0	62	71	39	52
Wicklander, Patrick	11	8	6.71	22	0	109	128	54	83
Castillo, Wilton	5	8	7.13	16	0	77	88	43	62
Ross, Dalton	1	1	8.23	28	0	27	39	10	30
Feltman, Durbin	0	0	10.13	11	6	11	13	16	5

LONG ISLAND DUCKS

Name	AVG	AB	R	H	HR	RBI	BB	SO	SB
Castillo, Ivan	.341	232	46	79	4	36	23	27	13
Flores, Ronaldo	.341	249	30	85	12	51	18	42	3
Town, River	.326	439	92	143	13	71	74	61	42
Beer, Seth	.303	231	32	70	10	58	32	47	1
Kelly, Scott	.300	10	1	3	0	0	4	0	2
Kohlwey, Taylor	.291	409	73	119	10	64	53	70	15
Antonini, Aaron	.277	137	15	38	5	21	10	28	2
Viola, Troy	.276	460	76	127	17	87	37	119	21
Kaler, Kole	.268	355	48	95	3	46	35	76	34
Johnson, Ed	.265	151	21	40	0	17	20	23	10
Dennis, Austin	.263	38	6	10	0	2	2	7	5
Encarnacion, JC	.262	252	58	66	5	37	28	97	31
Roller, Chris	.251	415	94	104	14	42	52	131	37
OConner, Justin	.247	215	30	53	4	35	22	69	2
Baldwin, Roldani	.244	45	6	11	3	15	1	11	0
Cabrera, Leobaldo	.241	83	12	20	1	12	6	17	3
Thomas, Cody	.233	386	74	90	18	70	50	117	15
Pike, Chad	.175	114	15	20	5	16	15	52	2
Lynch, Jack	.128	47	2	6	1	2	5	19	1
Bates, Austin	.125	24	2	3	0	0	1	3	0

Name	W	L	ERA	G	SV	IP	H	BB	SO
Santos, Ramon	4	1	0.47	19	6	19	7	11	37
Gant, John	2	1	1.71	4	0	21	10	5	27
Clenney, Nolan	4	1	1.72	21	0	31	16	10	41
Romano, Sal	1	1	2.25	20	0	20	20	11	20
Williams, Peyton	1	2	2.33	18	8	19	13	8	15
Plesac, Zach	4	1	2.84	7	0	38	27	16	33
Case, Brad	5	3	3.22	54	0	45	39	19	48
Nelson, Braydon	4	2	3.60	51	6	50	51	19	36
Sandberg, Ryan	5	3	3.83	19	0	92	81	44	73
Griffin, David	6	4	4.03	22	0	103	106	27	92
Dominguez, Michael	1	0	4.08	6	0	18	14	10	14
Dipoto, Jonah	3	5	4.26	26	2	57	50	34	69
Pike, Chad	0	0	4.44	2	1	2	6	2	10	17
Asa, Jacob	4	3	4.57	44	2	45	31	19	45
Hillman, Juan	9	6	4.88	24	0	127	130	49	106
Langford, Ryan	0	0	4.97	23	0	38	38	22	35
Reed, Michael	0	1	5.06	23	5	21	19	13	21
Melville, Tim	5	5	5.36	10	0	82	88	39	74
Washington, Mark	1	2	5.40	23	2	23	30	11	28
Beede, Tyler	2	1	5.48	5	0	21	22	11	26
Alintoff, Justin	4	5	6.19	21	0	73	94	18	57
Senger, Mitchell	0	2	6.30	10	0	40	28	40	23
Flores, Bernardo	2	2	6.75	24	1	37	47	29	21
Sharp, Sterling	0	1	14.40	3	0	10	17	8	10

SOUTHERN MARYLAND BLUE CRABS

Name	AVG	AB	R	H	HR	RBI	BB	SO	SB
Barrera, Brett	.312	433	68	135	8	76	42	63	5
Baylor, Jamari	.303	330	73	100	21	77	54	114	19
Taylor, John	.288	191	49	55	8	28	40	51	13
Loftin, Jackson	.279	469	88	131	21	63	39	111	60
Hubbard, Dondrei	.273	198	22	54	7	30	15	51	0
Dexter, Sam	.270	381	53	103	15	66	22	77	2
Digiacomo, Giovanni	.266	402	67	107	14	65	58	122	34
Wilson, Ethan	.261	433	73	113	14	70	33	84	21
Racusin, Zach	.260	154	21	40	1	16	22	27	2
Howard, Pearce	.257	362	49	93	11	44	30	84	5
De Aza, Alejandro	.253	371	73	94	12	67	53	89	11
McCarthy, Ryan	.247	247	41	61	4	30	38	79	0
Weiss, Cooper	.226	31	5	7	0	1	3	7	0
Estrada, Willie	.220	77	7	17	9	2	4	4	10	0
Valdes, Andy	.158	38	3	6	2	2	4	17	0
Chatham, Cael	.154	39	6	6	0	3	8	21	0
Lin, Lyle	.153	72	6	11	0	4	7	16	0

Name	W	L	ERA	G	SV	IP	H	BB	SO
Briceno, Endrys	3	0	0.47	15	6	19	11	8	34
Blanchard, Jason	0	0	1.45	8	0	31	17	12	40
Carr, Jordan	1	0	2.25	13	0	12	7	9	10
Virbitsky, Kyle	1	1	2.84	5	0	32	28	7	36
McCabe, Brandon	5	4	3.70	46	2	49	46	43	73
Semple, Shawn	6	7	3.95	22	0	130	133	30	101

Kahaloa, Ian	7	2	4.11	12	0	66	61	16	67
Miller, Jalen	9	6	4.26	32	0	93	84	47	103
Hennessey, Joey	4	3	4.73	24	1	51	48	29	40
Scrubb, Andre	3	2	4.78	33	12	32	34	21	30
Thurman, Andrew	7	2	4.94	25	0	126	128	56	128
Thompson, Cody	5	6	5.03	45	2	54	46	23	54
Vazquez, Rafi	4	3	5.06	37	1	48	53	18	45
Overton, Connor	2	5	5.46	11	0	66	79	20	76
Chatham, Cael	1	2	6.05	9	0	19	14	14	12
Ross, Dalton	0	1	7.04	14	0	15	20	15	15
Campbell, Maceo	2	4	7.16	22	0	60	72	38	71
Martin, Garrett	4	5	7.26	12	0	66	95	19	45
Wright, Jarod	1	1	7.84	23	0	31	37	16	30
Willamson, Noah	0	0	7.94	21	0	23	23	24	20
Kelly, John	0	3	8.60	7	0	30	35	19	22
Florez, Santiago	0	0	10.13	10	0	11	16	20	12

STATEN ISLAND FERRYHAWKS

Name	AVG	AB	R	H	HR	RBI	BB	SO	SB
Scheffler, Matthew	.347	303	58	105	15	61	49	68	1
Dearden, Tyler	.341	173	29	59	7	38	20	32	0
Dues, Damon	.331	154	36	51	5	20	28	26	23
Johnson, Kolby	.313	246	43	77	8	37	22	44	17
Diaz, Eddy	.311	415	77	129	7	57	24	62	40
Brown, Vaun	.307	166	28	51	5	15	14	35	8
Takacs, Aaron	.305	220	40	67	5	40	34	59	4
Contreras, Mark	.288	451	88	130	18	94	58	97	14
Rodriguez, Cristhian	.279	269	49	75	16	55	33	102	6
Martorano, Brandon	.277	300	48	83	10	37	34	46	5
Osuna, Alberto	.253	158	26	40	4	27	31	49	1
Maggi, Drew	.249	289	43	72	7	28	28	71	4
Fontana, Shayne	.243	202	41	49	6	41	22	50	9
Borden, Tim	.231	91	14	21	2	15	18	31	0
Sandoval, Pablo	.230	405	37	93	13	63	34	117	0
Jones, Amani	.208	24	4	5	0	0	2	4	0
Decker, Nicholas	.207	121	14	25	5	15	17	52	0
Scantlin, Nate	.168	113	23	19	3	9	18	34	8
Espinosa, Albert	.136	22	4	3	0	0	5	12	0
Melfi, David	.101	89	8	9	1	3	6	36	0
Abbatine, Anthony	.100	20	1	2	0	1	2	4	0

Name	W	L	ERA	G	SV	IP	H	BB	SO
Andrews, Tanner	2	0	0.00	15	3	14	5	2	25
Snead, Kirby	0	3	1.80	37	0	35	36	8	41
McKenna, Brian	3	0	2.63	14	0	14	14	1	12
McSweeney, Morgan	4	2	3.00	10	0	54	48	18	41
Baker, Robbie	6	3	3.66	56	15	59	46	36	80
Dunaway, Matt	4	1	3.75	11	1	36	37	9	37
Peralta, Ofelky	0	5	4.24	5	0	17	22	17	12
Meeker, James	1	2	4.25	33	0	36	39	11	48
Helvey, Clay	3	0	4.53	35	2	44	35	23	59
Higgins, Connor	0	2	4.61	14	0	14	7	19	18
Roe, Nate	0	2	4.68	19	0	33	30	23	28
Allegretti, Christia	6	4	4.69	18	0	86	87	35	75
Feltman, Durbin	1	0	4.91	20	1	18	18	14	16
Scott, Wesley	3	6	5.23	12	0	62	56	38	67
Mahoney, Jack	1	2	5.46	6	0	33	29	12	41
Kaminsky, Rob	0	3	5.60	6	0	18	39	0	11
Reitz, Matt	2	3	5.91	9	0	32	41	5	18
Guzman, Luis	1	0	6.30	32	1	30	35	21	22
Kehoe, Ryan	3	3	6.35	11	0	45	63	17	21
Williamson, Ryan	0	5	7.04	15	0	55	65	45	50
Mack, Alex	4	5	7.21	17	0	54	67	28	48
Mejia, Adalberto	1	5	7.68	12	0	41	58	21	41
Kubo, Trayson	0	2	7.91	42	0	80	83	60	59
Barringer, Shane	2	4	8.41	9	0	35	46	24	35
Capuano, Christian	0	2	9.00	4	0	18	20	8	16
Zguro, Matt	0	0	10.34	10	0	16	25	15	13
Hernandez, Leandro	2	0	10.50	12	0	18	30	18	11
Parra, Reinier	3	1	10.50	19	0	24	43	24	14
Lepard, Taylor	0	2	14.40	3	0	10	16	8	5

YORK REVOLUTION

Name	AVG	AB	R	H	HR	RBI	BB	SO	SB
Otosaka, Tomo	.405	37	11	15	1	8	7	10	4
Fontana, Shayne	.367	237	64	87	10	47	33	49	15
Costes, Marty	.341	214	35	73	9	44	30	24	6
Tostado, Frankie	.337	362	59	122	11	73	21	45	2
Martin, Kyle	.333	39	11	13	2	7	3	6	1
Connell, Justin	.316	98	20	31	7	19	28	24	3
Peralta, Elvis	.297	37	7	11	1	7	1	9	1
Miller, Jalen	.297	508	113	151	19	80	43	76	60
Higgins, Ryan	.293	314	69	92	21	65	46	89	5
McNeely, Caleb	.292	113	24	33	7	21	15	34	9
Simoneit, William	.286	287	67	82	17	61	39	57	0
Arocho, Jeremy	.283	293	51	83	3	39	51	38	35
Wehler, Jeffrey	.281	374	58	105	13	64	48	86	21
Alleyne, Bubba	.257	237	49	61	7	35	26	43	36
Lewis, Brandon	.255	385	58	98	15	69	38	104	9
Davis, Jaylin	.238	214	47	51	17	48	43	66	11
Tovalin, Osvaldo	.229	48	8	11	2	8	3	8	0
Williams, Chris	.229	118	16	27	10	19	10	39	0
Olmeda, Alexis	.222	45	6	10	2	5	6	15	0
Soularie, Alerick	.203	79	8	16	3	15	8	18	6
Simington, Miles	.178	45	4	8	2	6	2	11	0
Berglund, Michael	.174	92	12	16	1	10	14	33	2
Richards, Jairus	.171	35	7	6	1	4	2	12	5
Veloz, Omar	.100	10	2	1	0	1	2	5	0
McRae, Blake	.091	22	8	2	0	0	9	10	0
Acal, Justin	.077	13	4	1	0	1	2	4	1

Name	W	L	ERA	G	SV	IP	H	BB	SO
Robinson, Cam	5	4	0.61	42	16	44	26	26	49
Burnette, Jimmy	1	2	1.69	14	0	11	6	5	19
Mikolajchak, Nick	0	1	1.93	19	1	19	11	8	27
Cellucci, Brendan	1	2	1.96	18	9	18	8	7	32
Scott, Braden	2	0	3.32	4	0	22	22	9	19
Mollerus, Josh	1	0	3.50	15	0	18	11	4	26
Valverde, Alex	1	2	3.81	14	0	50	50	23	47
Kickham, Mike	7	0	3.94	8	0	46	54	12	47
Scott, Wesley	4	3	4.20	11	0	56	44	40	61
Dula, Hunter	4	1	4.25	30	0	30	24	20	24
Thurman, Grayson	4	1	4.38	13	0	12	14	4	11
Denoyer, Noah	3	0	4.57	22	0	22	18	8	36
Palm, Tyler	3	4	4.82	21	1	62	69	20	63
Denz, Danny	1	2	4.95	26	0	56	51	21	72
Vallimont, Chris	9	4	4.96	18	0	98	99	27	119
Horrell, Michael	3	4	5.02	8	0	43	55	6	32
Llovera, Mauricio	4	1	5.34	30	1	29	28	11	37
Churchill, Ian	3	5	5.40	44	1	40	32	34	60
Pace, Foster	8	3	5.58	18	0	90	116	22	61
Morales, Jordan	1	1	5.69	29	0	62	79	22	65
Bustamante, Alex	0	0	5.82	17	0	22	16	15	23
Firoved, Ethan	1	1	6.11	10	0	18	25	9	15
Coles, Chad	1	0	6.28	8	0	14	9	6	16
Miranda, Kevin	4	3	6.32	11	0	41	60	10	33
Galdoni, Lukas	2	1	6.33	15	0	21	16	14	22
Walker, Matt	0	1	6.46	7	0	31	39	10	36
Sanabia, Alex	0	1	6.75	3	0	12	14	6	9
Ramirez, J.C.	1	2	7.13	9	0	35	40	18	24
Bugg, Parker	0	0	7.78	16	0	20	27	8	20
Woolfolk, Dallas	1	1	9.87	20	0	17	31	8	9

FRONTIER LEAGUE

The Frontier League has now entered its fourth decade of sustained operations, and in all of that time, it's never seen a level of domination like this. The Quebec Capitales won their fourth consecutive league title in 2025, knocking off Schaumburg 3-1 in the championship series. The Capitales have now won 11 league titles across two different leagues (having won seven Can-Am League titles as well).

Atlantic Conference - East Div.	W	L	PCT	GB
Sussex County Miners *	53	43	.552	-
New York Boulders †	52	43	.547	0.5
Down East Bird Dawgs	37	58	.389	15.5
New Jersey Jackals	28	65	.301	23.5

Atlantic Conference - North Div.	W	L	PCT	GB
Quebec Capitales *	67	29	.698	-
Tri-City ValleyCats †	62	34	.646	5
Ottawa Titans	51	45	.531	16
Brockton Rox	38	54	.413	27
Trois-Rivieres Aigles	38	57	.400	28.5

Midwest Conference - Central Div.	W	L	PCT	GB
Washington Wild Things †	54	42	.563	-
Lake Erie Crushers †	52	42	.553	1
Florence Yalls	43	53	.448	11
Evansville Otters	40	56	.417	14

Midwest Conference - West Div.	W	L	PCT	GB
Schaumburg Boomers *	58	38	.604	-
Gateway Grizzlies †	56	40	.583	2
Mississippi Mud Monsters	49	47	.510	9
Joliet Slammers	44	52	.458	14
Windy City ThunderBolts	36	60	.375	22

Division Champ. †Wild Card

Playoffs—Wild Card: Schaumburg defeated Lake Erie 2-0; Quebec defeated New York 2-0; Tri-City defeated Sussex County 2-0 and Gateway defeated Washington 2-0 in best-of-three series. **Semifinals:** Schaumburg defeated Gateway 3-0 and Quebec defeated Tri-City 3-1 in best-of-five series. **Finals:** Quebec defeated Schaumburg 3-1 in best-of-five series.

Attendance: Schaumburg Boomers 234,226; Quebec Capitales 181,942; Tri-City ValleyCats 131,108; New York Boulders 113,094; Lake Erie Crushers 112,194; Florence Yalls 110,021; Evansville Otters 105,527; Ottawa Titans 99,004; Washington Wild Things 96,495; Gateway Grizzlies 92,195; Sussex County Miners 90,516; Mississippi Mud Monsters 90,473; Windy City ThunderBolts 90,383; Joliet Slammers 86,779; Trois-Rivieres Aigles 75,362; New Jersey Jackals 72,635; Down East Bird Dawgs 59,988; Brockton Rox 55,736.

All-Star Team: SP: Braeden Allemann, Québec. **RP:** Tyler Vail, New York. **C:** Jason Agresti, New York. **1B:** Hank Zeisler, Florence. **2B:** Fritz Genther, New York. **3B:** Sean Roby, Jr, Sussex County. **SS:** Kyle Crowl, Québec. **OF:** Mathieu Vallée, Trois-Rivières; Dom Johnson, Sussex County; Victor Castillo, Gateway. **DH:** Anthony Calarco, Schaumburg.

Most Valuable Player: Anthony Calarco, Schaumburg. **Pitcher of the Year:** Braeden Allemann, Québec. **Rookie of the Year:** Ian Battipaglia, Joliet. **Manager of the Year:** Patrick Scalabrini, Quebec.

BATTING LEADERS

Name	AVG	AB	R	H	HR	RBI	BB	SO	SB
Ruben Castro, QC	.396	217	42	86	1	24	36	27	13
Gabriel Maciel, SC	.385	247	46	95	5	40	26	30	10
Brandon Hylton, 3R	.354	336	60	119	9	64	38	65	12
Mathieu Vallee, 3R	.352	361	75	127	1	41	47	42	83
Anthony Calarco, SCH	.347	378	82	131	24	116	54	70	3
Austin Dennis, NY	.342	407	97	139	8	65	39	40	43
Oscar Campos, T-C	.340	244	57	83	10	60	29	20	6
Dom Johnson, SC	.340	347	68	118	6	57	26	60	23
Jose Alvarez, GAT	.332	289	51	96	2	38	25	42	12
Josh Leslie, T-C	.330	276	56	91	2	46	24	51	12

PITCHING LEADERS

Player, Team	W	L	ERA	G	IP	H	BB	SO
Jack Eisenbarger, LE	10	4	2.37	19	110	73	56	107
Dylan Spain, LE	7	5	2.39	23	106	99	23	94
Brandon Kaminer, DE	3	4	2.51	23	79	54	30	72
CJ Blowers, JOL	3	3	2.71	17	93	71	46	53
Anthony Escobar, LE	9	6	2.95	19	116	99	25	106
Braeden Allemann, QC	6	2	3.05	20	100	68	35	144
Connor Wilford, T-C	10	2	3.25	15	91	92	18	63
Braden Scott, EVV	8	4	3.29	20	129	119	54	157
Greg Duncan, QC	5	8	3.33	19	103	88	48	103
Brian Williams, MIS	3	6	3.48	18	106	107	34	84

BROCKTON ROX

Name	AVG	AB	R	H	HR	RBI	BB	SO	SB
Kretzler, Tommy	.314	331	54	104	17	64	31	74	6
White, Austin	.306	353	72	108	1	20	60	52	52
Rosario, Hemmanuel	.299	345	43	103	10	60	21	66	10
Bender, Derek	.282	330	55	93	11	54	42	57	2
Giordano, Evan	.277	328	60	91	10	46	40	59	7
Wold, Jack Thomas	.258	124	22	32	4	26	9	25	1
Calero, Keagan	.256	180	19	46	1	22	24	33	9
Ybarra, Jeter	.233	86	12	20	2	11	13	15	1
Eldred, Zach	.230	122	13	28	2	11	6	34	1
Logan, Michael	.222	36	4	8	2	3	1	11	4
DiSarcina, JR	.216	324	43	70	5	31	25	87	3
Ciulla Hall, Trey	.214	173	21	37	4	25	24	76	2
Smart, Jamey	.213	127	5	27	1	12	7	15	1
Johnson, Tyler	.188	16	2	3	0	2	3	11	1
Young, Brett	.178	45	8	8	0	4	0	8	2
Marola, Nick	.176	68	4	12	0	6	5	23	0
Caufield, Andrew	.077	13	0	1	0	2	0	4	0

Name	W	L	ERA	G	SV	IP	H	BB	SO
Saturria, Michael	1	1	0.93	10	0	10	5	5	13
Eldred, Zach	1	3	3.06	15	1	65	69	20	39
Bell, Brendan	1	0	3.60	20	2	20	21	11	25
O'Donnell, Brendan	2	1	3.67	23	1	27	24	12	28
Majick, Eli	1	1	3.82	7	0	38	36	13	33
McKenna, Mike	4	4	3.94	28	10	30	25	16	46
Ryan, Dillon	6	4	4.42	26	0	39	31	22	47
Bedder, Dylan	2	0	4.50	32	0	36	20	33	50
Williams, Pierce	3	3	4.71	11	0	57	57	23	46
Anibal, Trevor	2	3	4.75	32	2	30	39	10	34
Melendez, Omar	1	3	4.86	9	0	46	48	26	33
Bobo, Ethan	0	1	5.51	12	0	16	20	6	12
Baro, Heisell	3	4	5.53	24	0	57	72	21	43
Kemlage, Joe	3	3	6.15	14	0	53	72	24	44
Maloney, Matthew	2	3	6.39	38	1	44	43	38	50
Nelson, Thomas	1	3	7.01	13	0	35	31	36	20
Ramirez, Santiago	0	5	7.30	12	0	37	33	41	36
Sprake, Joe	0	2	7.71	4	0	14	19	12	9
Quigley, Michael	0	4	7.96	10	0	37	43	44	30
Henry, Jared	3	5	8.02	12	0	34	41	25	27
DeGaetano, Chic	1	0	8.86	17	0	21	28	15	19

DOWN EAST BIRD DAWGS

Name	AVG	AB	R	H	HR	RBI	BB	SO	SB
Parks, Pavin	.301	306	47	92	5	36	24	52	16
Pino, Yassel	.289	350	67	101	15	52	25	70	20
LaPread, Ali	.287	261	32	75	3	31	27	69	12
Laboy, Yeniel	.286	84	15	24	4	17	8	22	0
Harlan, Trotter	.266	301	38	80	2	35	29	53	17
Adams, Christian	.255	47	8	12	3	7	6	16	0
Harrison, Kalae	.253	95	15	24	3	12	5	15	6
Stevens, Elias	.246	126	19	31	8	18	19	36	0
Law, Trey	.246	228	26	56	0	13	22	24	5
Smith, Jaylen	.245	298	47	73	7	49	22	51	17
Tapia, Emmanuel	.217	304	49	66	20	56	54	136	6
Masterman, Cameron	.213	230	30	49	10	37	28	75	4
Blaum, Tyler	.208	149	16	31	1	23	18	31	2
Johnson, Joe	.205	44	8	9	1	5	7	14	0
Hill, Cole	.203	197	25	40	1	22	26	52	18
Ebel, Gehrig	.120	50	8	6	0	3	7	13	0
Backus, Colby	.118	17	2	2	0	0	1	3	1
Guidry, Kam	.075	40	3	3	0	4	9	21	3

Name	W	L	ERA	G	SV	IP	H	BB	SO
Blaum, Tyler	0	0	0.87	7	0	10	13	1	1
Kaminer, Brandon	3	4	2.51	23	0	79	54	30	72
Trueman, Luke	1	1	3.09	21	1	23	22	16	12
LaCour, Andrew	0	1	4.50	11	0	14	13	11	18
Hicks, Jackson	1	1	4.57	15	4	22	15	9	21
Tiburcio, David	2	2	4.62	22	0	25	27	11	17
Johnston, Spencer	9	7	4.70	18	0	103	114	31	64
Martinez, Greg	0	0	4.73	11	4	13	11	6	22
Henderson, Drew	4	5	5.13	25	1	79	80	38	66
Beal, Danny	5	4	5.55	21	0	99	103	55	78
Andueza, Axel	2	3	6.04	20	0	57	56	36	36
Durst, Drew	1	7	6.39	17	1	49	52	31	46
Baker, Andrew	2	4	7.34	23	0	31	32	20	16
Czyz, TJ	0	8	8.02	15	0	49	25	23	9

Grace, Zach	1	4	8.53	7	0	25	24	23	26
Waldichuk, Eric	0	4	8.87	12	0	23	36	18	14
Roof, Nate	4	0	9.13	22	4	23	32	19	16
Lamb, Nate	1	3	9.51	7	0	35	51	15	19
O'Brien, Caden	1	0	14.50	16	0	18	23	37	14

EVANSVILLE OTTERS

Name	AVG	AB	R	H	HR	RBI	BB	SO	SB
Taylor, Keenan	.299	334	58	100	15	62	26	73	11
Mendham, David	.295	146	25	43	2	18	36	27	2
Benson, JT	.295	285	59	84	10	40	45	67	24
Pierce, Dennis	.286	245	48	70	17	39	25	56	1
Brown, Logan	.284	215	24	61	3	33	9	32	1
Jones, LJ	.279	362	41	101	10	58	30	80	4
Brown, Graham	.279	369	70	103	12	53	34	85	15
Wilbanks, Cohen	.277	83	17	23	1	8	18	23	1
Parks, Pavin	.268	228	41	61	8	37	38	77	12
Waddell, Chase	.267	15	4	4	0	0	2	4	0
Schwartz, Ellis	.244	90	15	22	1	10	12	19	4
Taveras, Crix	.236	55	3	13	0	6	2	17	0
Cruz, JJ	.236	296	42	70	11	50	13	80	8
Jackson, Darryl	.233	30	6	7	0	2	2	5	2
Gil, Raymond	.216	51	5	11	1	6	8	16	2
Camou, Alain	.208	125	15	26	0	14	12	18	3
Crittenberger, Ty	.184	38	5	7	0	5	6	18	3
Paolini, Stephen	.153	59	6	9	2	6	5	22	6
White, Mason	.143	21	1	3	0	1	1	9	1
Felix, Justin	.132	106	11	14	4	15	19	57	1
Campbell, Jared	.100	20	2	2	1	1	2	13	1
Bouck, Parks	.071	14	3	1	0	0	4	1	0
Callil, George	.063	16	2	1	0	1	1	6	0

Name	W	L	ERA	G	SV	IP	H	BB	SO
Dennis, Gunnar	0	0	2.03	14	0	13	8	2	21
Crowley, Garrett	0	0	2.31	10	5	12	9	1	20
Hughes, Grif	4	2	2.89	13	0	19	13	3	28
Thebiay, Nolan	1	1	2.89	34	1	44	43	19	48
McAuliffe, Nick	2	5	3.11	39	3	38	36	18	54
Scott, Braden	8	4	3.29	20	0	129	119	54	157
Valdez, Alex	4	7	3.40	39	6	45	35	16	52
Canney, Alex	4	1	3.67	7	0	34	31	20	45
Malouf, Jackson	2	1	4.79	12	0	21	29	7	18
Willeman, Landon	1	1	5.14	3	0	14	17	3	7
Gonzalez, Joan	6	3	5.42	26	0	86	86	44	74
Montilva, Adrian	0	2	6.00	8	0	24	23	12	21
Brahms, Parker	2	9	6.05	18	0	94	115	34	70
Wiltse, Ryan	0	5	6.38	24	0	72	83	26	64
Beymer, Jon	3	5	7.71	17	0	47	61	17	59
Simpson, Garret	0	3	7.86	7	0	26	35	13	15
Backer, CJ	0	1	8.35	4	0	18	23	14	12
Murphy, Colin	0	0	9.90	6	0	10	15	9	8
Patterson, Anthony	0	1	11.49	4	0	16	25	10	9
Parks, Pavin	0	1	13.50	4	0	10	19	5	10
Bradford, Ethan	1	1	14.81	8	0	10	20	5	9

FLORENCE Y'ALLS

Name	AVG	AB	R	H	HR	RBI	BB	SO	SB
Saben, Blaze	.438	32	10	14	1	3	10	6	10
Davis, Dalton	.327	55	8	18	0	4	6	7	4
Quinones, Michael	.318	107	7	34	1	15	13	20	0
Smith, Armani	.316	133	23	42	5	27	16	34	2
Zeisler, Hank	.312	340	78	106	22	80	68	91	20
Shaneyfelt, Tyler	.301	249	65	75	0	24	50	54	46
Reeves, TJ	.297	384	70	114	16	77	40	88	6
Bobo, Brendan	.295	261	57	77	15	60	23	67	12
Hauge, Jackson	.294	68	5	20	0	9	6	11	0
Elvir, Josh	.288	52	8	15	3	11	2	13	0
Thompson, Dalen	.286	119	15	34	1	8	6	33	1
Massey, Craig	.281	135	29	38	0	10	29	23	3
Ballard, Michael	.276	192	28	53	5	27	14	33	2
Brocato, Anthony	.276	199	36	55	17	55	26	63	3
Hrustich, Stephen	.265	34	7	9	3	8	3	6	2
Hunter, Henry	.260	73	10	19	0	8	9	19	2

Moreno, Heladio	.238	101	23	24	1	13	12	22	4
Baker, Dillon	.237	93	4	22	0	6	7	22	2
Richardson, Zade	.234	235	41	55	6	29	22	57	1
Javier Jr, Eddie	.212	66	10	14	4	12	9	18	1
Nieves, Hector	.204	250	37	51	8	39	33	110	1
Butcher, Will	.185	27	4	5	0	2	3	9	0
McClure, Norris	.167	36	7	6	0	4	5	11	0
Morris, Sam	.143	14	1	2	0	3	0	1	0

Name	W	L	ERA	G	SV	IP	H	BB	SO
Mattox, Seth	4	1	2.03	12	3	13	8	4	8
Villalobos, Jonaiker	2	1	2.05	8	0	44	36	14	28
Whitesell, Max	0	2	2.19	17	3	25	19	14	18
Westcott, Zac	6	2	2.58	9	0	59	43	17	30
Lotito, Chris	0	1	3.60	7	0	10	8	3	8
Carsten, Will	1	1	3.71	25	2	34	28	25	34
Martinez, Edgar	0	2	4.08	10	0	18	17	11	10
Webster, Evan	7	4	4.22	19	0	98	97	24	63
Hines, Carter	3	2	4.26	34	0	51	48	27	47
Souza, August	1	0	4.60	10	1	16	19	6	15
Lodes, Jett	1	5	5.12	25	6	32	36	24	24
Wilson, Bradley	1	4	5.12	15	0	46	56	14	30
Gamelin, Shaun	4	8	6.53	21	0	101	136	28	87
Mackay, Conner	2	2	6.85	26	1	43	55	18	38
Miranda, Agnel	0	1	6.92	6	0	26	28	13	21
Majick, Eli	3	1	7.09	10	0	39	57	14	37
Barker, Michael	5	5	7.12	15	1	49	61	26	48
Robbins, Zane	0	1	7.54	12	0	14	21	8	10
Fernandez, Matt	2	5	7.94	12	1	40	68	12	27
Hutchison, Rodney	0	1	8.22	5	0	15	20	14	5
Alfonseca, Pedro	0	0	10.92	13	1	16	18	18	10

GATEWAY GRIZZLIES

Name	AVG	AB	R	H	HR	RBI	BB	SO	SB
Alvarez, Jose	.332	289	51	96	2	38	25	42	12
Stewart, DJ	.305	357	74	109	18	80	43	76	35
Holt, Gabe	.301	316	56	95	3	31	37	23	2
Castillo, Victor	.298	359	77	107	11	65	58	53	24
Mateo, Edwin	.291	316	42	92	6	59	21	46	11
Smith, Sawyer	.284	74	14	21	1	8	8	18	2
Thomas, Dale	.283	318	67	90	16	72	45	77	17
Shallenberger, Mark	.280	254	65	71	15	55	49	66	9
Diaz, Abdiel	.279	215	42	60	8	39	19	32	16
Wallace, Paxton	.273	88	12	24	2	9	7	16	1
Brannen, Cole	.253	300	57	76	12	53	42	84	22
Halvorson, Calyn	.250	12	1	3	0	1	0	3	0
Garrison, Tanner	.250	84	12	21	1	9	6	25	0
Wargo, Tate	.229	35	11	8	0	2	8	11	4
Friedrick, Ross	.227	66	8	15	2	17	5	21	0
Lee, Matthew	.154	39	3	6	1	3	8	17	0
Shaw, Corbin	.143	28	1	4	0	2	1	8	0
Young, Tyler	.136	22	4	3	0	1	1	6	0
Parks, Pavin	.000	10	1	0	0	1	3	2	0

Name	W	L	ERA	G	SV	IP	H	BB	SO
Rochard, Sam	3	1	1.17	4	0	23	9	11	23
Collett, Keegan	2	3	1.21	35	11	30	14	25	47
Galva, Claudio	7	1	2.94	28	1	61	57	27	49
Peguero, Francis	4	4	3.00	39	2	42	31	18	40
Whaley, Alec	5	2	3.02	56	3	51	41	19	41
Hickey, Matt	1	2	3.20	49	1	51	48	18	54
Veinbergs, Lukas	7	5	4.17	18	0	99	101	44	103
Lovin, Xander	1	0	4.54	14	0	38	44	22	22
Stice, Bennett	2	4	4.73	11	1	51	50	9	28
Vailes, Gage	5	3	4.75	18	0	89	101	44	57
De La Cruz, Leoni	2	1	4.84	23	2	22	19	18	30
De Los Santos, Alver	5	0	5.27	32	0	68	75	36	71
Treece, Zac	4	4	5.37	12	0	59	62	23	47
Conrad, Teague	1	1	5.40	4	0	22	27	3	24
Burcham, Jake	0	0	5.52	4	0	15	17	5	18
Burke, Donovan	2	5	5.79	10	0	23	28	12	15
Harris, Ben	5	2	6.13	10	0	47	43	28	49
Fuller, Brady	0	0	9.22	4	0	14	17	11	11

JOLIET SLAMMERS

Name	AVG	AB	R	H	HR	RBI	BB	SO	SB
Battipaglia, Ian	.298	363	61	108	3	32	40	89	41
Marine, Braylin	.297	344	45	102	4	60	31	70	12
McArthur, Liam	.283	371	54	105	2	35	51	55	10
Contreras, Jose	.279	183	28	51	7	40	13	68	7
Flete, Bryant	.271	118	19	32	1	8	25	30	4
Carricato, Sal	.268	41	3	11	0	5	1	12	0
Valdez, Antonio	.259	355	52	92	8	50	34	49	17
Davis, Chris	.235	268	33	63	1	36	43	67	5
Berry, Blake	.231	281	33	65	4	30	37	51	3
Goldstein, Dylan	.225	129	19	29	1	22	18	24	0
Heidal, Brandon	.225	204	26	46	3	27	30	54	0
Smart, Jamey	.217	129	17	28	1	12	12	28	2
Corliss, Craig	.211	19	4	4	0	1	4	6	0
Wuestenfeld, Dan	.204	54	5	11	1	6	4	19	0
Ordonez, Ernny	.197	66	5	13	0	5	2	19	2
Iannantone, Nick	.194	31	3	6	0	4	8	6	0
Stengren, Drew	.184	103	12	19	0	2	16	15	0
Belo, Bryan	.172	29	2	5	0	3	2	7	0
Robertson, Dylan	.143	14	7	2	0	1	5	6	0
Ewell, Kendal	.095	21	2	2	0	0	4	5	0
De La Cruz, Jeissy	.094	32	4	3	0	2	8	7	1

Name	W	L	ERA	G	SV	IP	H	BB	SO
Rybarczyk, Ty	1	2	2.33	33	1	46	34	9	46
Blowers, CJ	3	3	2.71	17	0	93	71	46	53
Grogan, Mychal	4	3	2.72	29	1	40	35	10	34
Morin, Jacob	2	2	3.57	42	1	40	37	11	46
Daly, Ryan	3	4	3.65	10	0	57	54	17	45
Plesac, Frank	3	1	4.26	26	0	51	63	15	33
McEvoy, Aidan	6	4	4.47	19	0	95	89	42	94
Sanchez, Brett	1	2	4.66	8	0	37	38	7	25
Kines, Gunnar	5	8	4.67	19	0	108	109	19	107
Smith, Cameron	3	3	4.73	42	0	40	42	11	31
Hopewell, Chase	4	5	4.93	38	0	38	37	14	22
Linderman, Greyson	4	5	5.30	40	17	37	30	13	32
Westcott, Zac	2	3	6.02	10	0	46	56	20	28
Pena, Bryan	2	2	7.80	7	0	30	43	18	17
Powell, Jordan	0	5	9.93	9	0	29	26	33	25

LAKE ERIE CRUSHERS

Name	AVG	AB	R	H	HR	RBI	BB	SO	SB
Gomez, Dario	.303	337	61	102	7	47	37	53	27
Alexander, Sebastian	.292	106	27	31	1	9	11	26	11
Vegas, Derek	.291	237	29	69	5	41	23	55	0
Franco, Sam	.291	282	47	82	10	38	26	74	10
Morgan, Davie	.284	306	48	87	7	36	34	57	9
Irizarry, Kenen	.282	131	20	37	5	22	7	20	5
Gonzalez, Alfredo	.280	286	51	80	10	41	36	66	12
Watkins, Jarrod	.268	220	20	59	4	31	19	32	0
Dixon, Burle	.256	308	48	79	7	43	43	75	13
Campbell, Zach	.252	119	17	30	0	9	22	33	3
Knotts, Scout	.252	302	51	76	11	46	56	65	2
Wright, Joey	.250	32	3	8	0	8	6	3	1
Thomason, Logan	.227	97	19	22	2	11	27	19	9
Harrison Dudley, Jor	.216	51	8	11	3	8	4	28	1
Strong, Seth	.209	91	10	19	1	13	13	21	1
Briggs, Lamar	.200	15	3	3	0	3	1	4	0
Quinn, Jaidan	.177	113	21	20	6	13	36	54	2
Huckstorf, Kyle	.167	12	3	2	0	1	3	1	3
Byrd Jr, Vincent	.133	90	5	12	1	11	8	24	0
Harrell, Alex	.130	23	1	3	0	1	4	2	0
Corson, Jacob	.100	10	0	1	0	1	0	4	0

Name	W	L	ERA	G	SV	IP	H	BB	SO
Eisenbarger, Jack	10	4	2.37	19	0	110	73	56	107
Spain, Dylan	7	5	2.39	23	0	106	99	23	94
Brewer, Michael	2	1	2.68	38	15	37	30	21	53
Escobar, Anthony	9	6	2.95	19	0	116	99	25	106
Sittinger, Brandyn	3	1	3.33	39	4	73	50	22	88

Spinozzi, Michael	0	1	4.18	25	0	32	29	19	29
Rodriguez, Leonardo	3	3	4.36	37	3	43	40	27	42
Smith, Ethan	7	5	4.61	18	0	84	76	41	76
Ragins, Darrien	6	7	4.75	18	0	78	76	46	56
Reinoso, Dayan	1	1	5.22	35	1	40	34	36	42
Pierson, Kenny	3	2	6.45	33	0	38	44	23	27
Zapata, Juan	0	1	6.52	7	0	10	12	3	4
Scheurer, Brandon	0	0	8.03	9	0	12	14	7	17
Saldana, Enrique	0	2	8.22	5	0	15	16	11	7

MISSISSIPPI MUD MONSTERS

Name	AVG	AB	R	H	HR	RBI	BB	SO	SB
Bradshaw, Davis	.402	107	22	43	1	19	9	11	6
Holman, Jack	.303	33	3	10	0	5	5	8	0
Paz, Karrell	.299	87	17	26	2	20	11	21	9
Booker, Kyle	.297	353	66	105	4	34	54	68	27
Skinner, Brayland	.294	357	62	105	3	44	37	71	49
De La Rosa, Samil	.293	191	27	56	5	21	17	35	6
Furr, Kasten	.289	180	36	52	1	22	39	21	13
Diaz, Victor	.273	253	34	69	7	39	10	46	1
Holt, Travis	.264	367	56	97	11	61	28	51	13
Cash, Ryan	.236	203	24	48	2	19	26	46	11
Paz, Karell	.233	210	32	49	5	36	23	42	13
Gonzalez, Roberto	.229	170	14	39	1	19	13	22	5
Updegrave, Charlie	.217	46	5	10	0	5	4	22	0
Rijo, Nilo	.211	166	31	35	2	22	32	38	21
Hassan, Nick	.201	214	28	43	3	27	22	28	3
Forbes, TiQuan	.186	86	11	16	2	14	8	27	1
Stayte, Angus	.167	12	0	2	0	0	0	7	0
Lantigua, Andriel	.108	83	11	9	0	3	11	32	0

Name	W	L	ERA	G	SV	IP	H	BB	SO
Reed, Michael	0	1	1.83	15	2	20	10	8	28
Barraza, Chris	1	1	2.80	33	8	45	24	39	54
Smith, Jackson	1	1	3.15	19	1	34	29	3	25
Williams, Brian	6	6	3.48	18	0	106	107	34	84
Morris, Zack	0	1	3.86	8	0	16	15	3	29
Thompson, Tyree	6	3	4.10	21	0	75	70	34	55
Mitchell, Brandon	7	5	4.12	17	0	90	105	35	91
Devers, Luis	8	6	4.76	18	0	106	117	45	94
Sanchez, Sergio	2	6	4.94	29	14	31	20	21	34
Theophile, Rodney	6	4	5.03	12	0	63	86	34	49
Joven, Art	0	0	5.25	6	0	12	14	12	10
Bihm, Gage	4	2	5.40	34	3	53	59	39	49
Forsyth, Braden	1	1	5.50	11	1	18	21	11	18
Peguero, Jeremy	2	4	5.95	23	0	56	61	29	54
Boeree, James	1	2	7.13	11	0	35	32	33	31
Paulina, Joshua	2	3	9.79	6	0	27	33	21	23

NEW JERSEY JACKALS

Name	AVG	AB	R	H	HR	RBI	BB	SO	SB
Bellony, Isaac	.321	81	12	26	6	20	7	27	1
Acevedo, Luis	.306	268	44	82	5	25	33	35	9
Parks, Bryson	.303	277	58	84	9	33	28	71	26
Costin, Jimmy	.286	168	25	48	2	23	36	44	0
Cipion, Arbert	.260	296	43	77	9	35	36	64	31
Ford, Ryan	.255	318	49	81	11	53	37	94	17
Torres, Gilberto	.254	71	8	18	1	5	4	13	0
Angelo, Sam	.234	128	19	30	5	20	19	38	0
DeLeo, Jake	.231	199	21	46	5	27	22	48	10
Mueller, Sebastian	.218	133	12	29	3	10	7	43	0
Gomez, Miguel	.218	156	13	34	4	27	10	8	0
Sanchez, Patrick	.205	220	20	45	2	23	27	63	4
Jimenez, Kenneth	.203	69	11	14	0	7	19	17	5
Reeder, Chris	.190	21	2	4	0	2	0	8	0
Del Rosario, Richel	.186	70	9	13	2	7	5	31	6
Brady, Chris	.182	22	2	4	0	2	3	8	0
Espinal, Walner	.182	44	1	8	0	5	5	15	0
Sheehan, Trevor	.180	122	16	22	0	10	18	36	7
Ortiz, Jorge	.167	12	1	2	1	2	1	5	0
Seeker, Sam	.167	48	8	8	0	5	5	18	0
Davis, Ryan	.157	70	11	11	1	4	5	21	5
Olmstead, Taylor	.133	30	2	4	0	0	0	13	1

Name	AVG	AB	R	H	HR	RBI	BB	SO	SB
Ortiz, Jankel	.133	30	5	4	0	4	3	19	2
Nigro, Anthony	.118	17	1	2	0	2	2	5	0
Vargas, Xavier	.118	17	2	2	0	0	3	7	0
Velez, Sebastian	.095	21	1	2	0	0	3	10	0

Name	W	L	ERA	G	SV	IP	H	BB	SO
Trabacchi, Nick	0	1	0.73	8	1	12	8	1	20
Fauci, Sonny	1	0	1.50	3	0	12	4	7	24
Long, Jalon	4	5	2.51	13	0	61	54	19	59
Testa, Joe	1	5	3.49	12	2	49	48	8	27
Martzolf, Max	1	3	3.86	15	0	28	20	12	24
Barker, Alex	6	6	4.39	14	0	82	68	28	56
Baird, Dustin	3	4	4.72	34	1	48	51	22	46
Ferguson, Francis	2	8	5.22	15	0	78	83	49	59
Leak, Anthony	2	3	5.44	27	4	50	41	29	35
Rodriguez, Joe Joe	2	5	6.02	10	0	46	56	23	41
Giuliano, Frankie	1	4	7.43	29	2	27	28	21	24
Waltz, Logan	0	3	7.71	19	0	47	63	26	39
Zarnoch, Kevin	0	2	7.86	4	0	18	22	7	13
Lawrence, Tommy	1	3	7.94	5	0	23	24	11	7
Webb, Colt	1	1	8.46	23	0	33	43	23	29
Esposito, Michael	0	0	9.00	13	0	11	14	14	12
Timpanelli, Nick	1	7	9.00	10	0	53	73	29	29
Kiritsis, Dan	0	0	12.21	13	0	14	18	13	21

NEW YORK BOULDERS

Name	AVG	AB	R	H	HR	RBI	BB	SO	SB
Hess, Kyle	.356	149	45	53	4	24	38	19	13
McCoy, Ryan	.346	188	48	65	11	38	37	58	34
Dennis, Austin	.342	407	97	139	8	65	39	40	43
Agresti, Jason	.319	310	60	99	11	78	22	53	2
Genther, Fritz	.311	367	64	114	13	83	39	96	17
Rosso, Santino	.295	244	45	72	6	49	24	25	14
Apodaca, Enzo	.283	99	17	28	2	11	13	19	3
Marte, Alfredo	.261	330	39	86	6	62	45	53	7
Vogel, Ryan	.258	248	55	64	2	19	46	59	17
Higgins, Kevin	.246	65	7	16	0	4	4	18	2
Zurbrugg, Zane	.243	70	6	17	0	12	9	24	7
Ficca, Christian	.234	290	47	68	9	51	44	65	3
Bellony, Isaac	.233	176	33	41	3	23	30	49	3
Scanlon, Jack	.198	202	26	40	6	29	20	69	0
Dolbashian, Braydon	.094	32	8	3	0	1	3	14	0

Name	W	L	ERA	G	SV	IP	H	BB	SO
Vail, Tyler	5	2	0.81	40	15	45	28	21	39
Gorgen, Grady	1	0	1.08	15	0	17	12	8	10
Olson, Mason	3	0	2.57	8	0	42	34	15	42
Kruglewicz, Parker	0	5	3.18	31	0	34	29	20	25
Reeves, Cobe	0	1	3.66	12	1	20	16	12	29
Traxel, Blaine	2	2	4.41	7	0	35	40	12	28
Patten, Cole	0	1	4.50	7	0	14	15	9	12
Sleeper, Ryan	1	3	4.58	5	0	20	22	14	17
Harper, Scott	2	1	4.66	50	1	56	69	22	55
Cooper, Garrett	9	2	4.78	17	0	96	122	22	61
Bradford, Ethan	7	0	5.24	24	0	34	38	14	36
Senger, Mitchell	3	1	5.32	9	0	44	57	23	31
Risse, Aidan	4	5	5.50	12	1	52	57	22	39
Bice, Emmett	3	6	5.63	16	0	86	98	41	65
Rohde, Isaac	3	3	5.90	12	0	58	74	18	59
LaMere, Nolan	2	0	6.29	36	1	34	39	14	28
Coe, Garrett	1	4	6.82	8	0	32	38	21	28
Luciano, Jordy	0	0	7.20	12	0	10	6	16	11
Stock, Erik	1	3	8.13	9	0	28	35	14	15
Miceli, Joe	4	1	10.62	22	0	20	20	23	24
DeSanti, Mike	0	0	11.12	11	0	11	9	20	17
Phelps, Holden	0	1	11.46	3	0	11	19	4	5

OTTAWA TITANS

Name	AVG	AB	R	H	HR	RBI	BB	SO	SB
Fuhrman, Michael	.342	38	9	13	1	7	8	12	3
Fogel, Justin	.338	207	43	70	2	35	19	18	1
McCarthy, Nolan	.320	100	24	32	3	20	12	19	15
Martin, Tyler	.318	22	5	7	1	5	4	4	1
Inoa, Cristian	.315	73	12	23	3	16	6	12	0

Name	AVG	AB	R	H	HR	RBI	BB	SO	SB
Cerny, Victor	.309	282	33	87	6	53	11	46	1
Cardoso, Kaiden	.296	179	37	53	4	25	47	52	9
Oyama, Jo	.273	44	6	12	0	8	4	8	4
Piatkiewicz, Jeremy	.265	83	8	22	0	7	5	26	2
Sanford, Jake	.257	237	36	61	4	35	25	48	1
Wright, Taylor	.254	189	42	48	3	24	29	31	18
Urbaez, Jackie	.254	334	69	85	9	52	58	74	8
Briggs, Lamar	.250	72	12	18	2	11	9	16	6
Casillas, Aaron	.248	270	36	67	2	30	19	36	0
Wright, AJ	.245	326	60	80	10	55	64	85	2
Mugan, Michael	.221	95	8	21	2	14	3	15	4
Driver, Dylan	.221	104	16	23	1	10	9	11	6
Chayka, Robert	.219	64	15	14	0	6	16	11	1
Zdunich, Tucker	.217	46	4	10	0	4	8	15	0
Hale, Damone	.216	37	4	8	1	9	1	13	0
Sebring, Jonah	.212	66	8	14	1	4	7	19	6
Abbott, Sam	.204	49	5	10	1	4	11	20	0
Guida, Ryne	.200	15	1	3	0	1	1	2	1
Preap, Bradlee	.200	30	3	6	0	3	3	15	0
McGarry Doyle, Noel	.182	22	2	4	0	0	3	12	1
Valerio, Felix	.182	33	0	6	0	2	3	7	2
Holyk, Tim	.181	94	9	17	3	14	8	23	0
Frett, Kishon	.167	24	2	4	1	2	4	14	1
Rowland, Parker	.111	36	0	4	0	0	2	13	0

Name	W	L	ERA	G	SV	IP	H	BB	SO
Beymer, Jon	0	0	1.74	13	0	10	3	7	10
Duby, Billy	0	2	2.81	36	3	48	45	14	34
Hill, Kaleb	6	3	3.61	29	1	72	67	40	60
Larson, Grant	8	7	4.20	18	0	94	100	19	61
Gray, Shane	2	4	4.29	31	12	92	93	39	80
Villa, Alfredo	10	4	4.34	19	0	93	99	42	98
Marklund, Brandon	2	0	4.39	36	0	39	43	26	34
Grills, Evan	4	4	4.90	9	0	57	66	22	48
Powell, Luke	0	0	5.21	15	0	19	21	11	17
Garcia, Brett	2	2	5.75	11	3	16	13	3	22
Telfer, Shane	8	7	6.73	20	0	91	126	42	75
Lardner, Mac	4	6	6.87	16	0	55	63	25	35
Cameron, Zach	1	2	7.01	36	1	44	53	23	37
Pinales, Erasmo	1	1	7.11	12	4	13	14	7	11
Cole, Dazon	1	0	7.89	20	0	22	26	20	15
Rembisz, Ryan	0	1	9.26	3	0	12	15	6	11

QUEBEC CAPITALES

Name	AVG	AB	R	H	HR	RBI	BB	SO	SB
Castro, Ruben	.396	217	42	86	1	24	36	27	13
Mendham, David	.361	72	12	26	1	13	10	12	1
Simmons, Kendall	.318	66	16	21	3	8	10	14	2
Belbin, Jarrod	.318	343	63	109	10	66	46	58	17
Crowl, Kyle	.302	308	84	93	23	74	70	77	16
Valentin, Jesmuel	.297	239	46	71	4	39	38	32	3
Lebreux, Marc Antoin	.296	338	66	100	12	79	49	91	8
Inoa, Cristian	.292	195	29	57	5	32	22	34	0
Gideon, Justin	.283	336	70	95	14	79	61	61	4
Riley, Will	.265	272	45	72	5	24	44	51	15
Quirion, Anthony	.259	332	58	86	9	57	54	76	9
Tobol, Vance	.250	16	2	4	0	1	2	7	1
Boucher, Pier Olivie	.239	67	22	16	2	12	13	20	8
Boies, Emiles	.223	139	13	31	1	22	20	36	0
De Freitas, Arturo	.208	168	30	35	5	25	18	48	0
Wright, Joshwan	.191	47	8	9	0	4	4	5	1
Irizarry, Kenen	.129	31	4	4	1	4	1	4	0
Porcellato, Matteo	.071	28	7	2	0	1	7	11	1

Name	W	L	ERA	G	SV	IP	H	BB	SO
Roland, Cole	5	1	0.87	38	7	41	20	13	58
Duncan, Greg	3	0	0.89	3	0	20	10	5	18
Kohigashi, Ryo	3	1	1.69	16	0	27	16	9	30
Boies, Emiles	3	0	1.91	17	0	28	17	7	20
Crowley, Garrett	1	0	2.05	24	1	26	19	17	34
Chu, Gilberto	4	1	2.09	30	0	43	33	13	28
Perez, Cleiverth	7	1	2.49	10	0	54	38	11	51
Allemann, Braeden	6	2	3.05	20	0	100	68	35	144
Cortijo, Harold	2	3	3.38	32	15	35	33	12	33

Sepulveda, Hector	3	0	3.65	5	0	25	21	14	14
Sakurai, Masatoshi	6	2	3.82	22	1	99	92	18	98
Parra, Franklin	0	1	4.21	23	0	26	20	22	28
Rodriguez, Kevin	1	1	4.59	29	1	35	36	11	26
Quiroga, Ulises	2	0	5.06	5	0	16	18	3	14
Gollert, Harley	5	5	5.14	20	0	98	113	35	78
Ito, Ryusuke	1	0	5.28	12	0	15	15	10	17
Cooper-Vassalakis, Brodie	8	4	5.68	24	0	44	52	15	42
Buckner, Ty	5	5	6.05	15	0	74	82	24	67
Garabitos, Pablo	0	0	6.23	3	0	13	14	4	7

SCHAUMBURG BOOMERS

Name	AVG	AB	R	H	HR	RBI	BB	SO	SB
Calarco, Alex	.383	47	10	18	3	11	16	10	0
Calarco, Anthony	.347	378	82	131	24	116	54	70	3
Gould, Michael	.330	282	60	93	7	48	21	45	12
Tolley, Banks	.313	262	53	82	12	65	38	60	2
Sojka, Andrew	.312	279	68	87	17	65	44	52	23
Podkul, Nick	.295	112	35	33	3	23	20	33	3
Fitzgerald, Kyle	.281	303	70	85	10	55	44	78	11
Fedko, Christian	.279	365	81	102	7	63	59	46	11
Simmons, Aaron	.275	258	47	71	9	41	32	64	9
Prater, Will	.274	237	41	65	3	31	25	50	7
Craig, Alec	.258	194	47	50	2	29	56	35	11
Spillane, Bren	.255	137	25	35	5	26	19	67	0
Gonzalez, Alec	.231	13	3	3	0	3	1	5	0
Dawson, Chase	.211	109	20	23	4	15	10	18	9
Kuchinski, Sam	.196	138	14	27	5	21	28	47	1
Norman, Satchell	.163	92	23	15	3	12	20	25	5
Fiorenza, John	.149	47	4	7	2	5	4	21	0
Livermore, Tony	.148	27	3	4	0	2	2	9	0

Name	W	L	ERA	G	SV	IP	H	BB	SO
Riedel, Caleb	0	1	0.84	8	3	11	3	4	14
Glickstein, Aaron	4	2	2.95	34	2	58	53	18	62
Kirkeby, Dylan	2	1	3.43	4	0	21	22	14	15
White, Mitch	3	2	3.77	33	11	31	28	20	33
Matos, Dwayne	3	1	3.86	6	0	35	32	12	26
Johnson, Christian	4	3	3.86	8	0	47	47	14	31
Stutsman, Dylan	6	2	4.08	39	1	40	29	13	44
Pindel, Buddie	3	0	4.50	4	0	28	34	0	13
Cook, Cole	9	4	4.52	20	0	123	142	24	119
Paciorek, Nick	3	1	4.70	33	4	38	35	22	50
Thompson, Ross	1	1	5.58	11	0	31	36	10	23
Turner, Eric	7	2	5.67	16	0	79	87	48	60
Lopez, Cristian	1	1	5.68	4	0	19	21	11	18
Oliver, Hambleton	0	1	5.84	15	0	25	22	19	12
Woolfolk, Dallas	0	1	6.60	15	0	15	17	8	14
Salata, Derek	6	6	6.12	19	0	93	114	41	88
Wiley, Quinlan	3	3	7.44	9	0	42	49	24	23
Rivera, Isaiah	1	0	8.60	17	0	30	38	34	39
Taylor, Kai	1	3	9.53	12	0	23	39	11	22
Parra, Deretd	0	1	10.27	19	0	24	33	22	26

SUSSEX COUNTY MINERS

Name	AVG	AB	R	H	HR	RBI	BB	SO	SB
Sleight, Evan	.417	24	6	10	0	5	3	4	1
Maciel, Gabriel	.385	247	46	95	5	40	26	30	10
Johnson, Dom	.340	347	68	118	6	57	26	60	23
Backstrom, Mahki	.323	257	58	83	12	58	44	67	11
Roby Jr, Sean	.319	295	47	94	16	88	40	56	1
Smith, Jordan	.307	303	51	93	6	45	31	55	4
Guadalupe, Abdel	.302	199	20	60	1	28	23	31	0
D Amato, Hunter	.286	374	87	107	2	36	53	60	26
Sayre, Alec	.249	313	52	78	6	56	43	83	14
Zimmerman, Will	.221	213	58	47	6	31	50	61	24
O Brien, Keenan	.219	260	37	57	4	37	36	62	5
Turner, Gionti	.214	168	29	36	1	19	15	44	17
Seeker, Scott	.188	32	3	6	1	5	6	12	1
Gilligan, Ty	.169	71	11	12	0	6	4	19	1
Singer, Kyle	.103	68	6	7	0	6	9	27	1

Name	W	L	ERA	G	SV	IP	H	BB	SO
Primeaux, Parker	2	1	2.60	10	2	17	11	5	16

Gartland, Chad	1	0	2.77	10	0	13	13	3	9
Parsons, Billy	9	4	3.52	22	2	92	90	40	77
Hensey, Rob	7	6	3.71	19	0	112	115	22	116
Stil, Matt	2	2	3.86	19	5	28	20	7	42
Luneke, Tyler	1	4	4.13	29	9	33	23	20	35
Kelly, Colin	0	0	4.36	7	0	10	9	6	7
Balzan, Jackson	7	6	4.37	18	0	103	104	41	75
Thornton, Tyler	8	3	4.45	21	0	87	93	37	55
Reagan, Mike	5	5	4.50	21	0	82	86	28	70
Brothers, Kellen	8	5	4.50	18	0	104	113	35	80
Huter, Blayne	2	0	5.23	16	0	43	46	24	33
Kiritsis, Dan	0	0	5.79	14	0	14	10	17	14
Ariza, JC	1	3	6.16	19	0	38	29	24	24
Voacolo, Ronnie	0	2	6.67	22	1	28	40	10	34
Curry, Bobby	0	1	6.75	11	0	16	24	10	9

TRI-CITY VALLEYCATS

Name	AVG	AB	R	H	HR	RBI	BB	SO	SB
Burgess, Chris	.392	79	16	31	5	24	16	18	0
Campos, Oscar	.340	244	57	83	10	60	29	20	6
Useche, Miguel	.333	45	9	15	0	7	5	7	0
Stevanovic, Ranko	.333	108	18	36	2	15	5	23	0
Leslie, Josh	.330	276	56	91	2	46	24	51	31
Boyd, Julian	.319	144	27	46	1	22	16	32	15
Larry, Amani	.300	200	31	60	2	24	33	23	15
Walters, Ian	.288	323	61	93	17	76	52	68	6
Reinisch, Jake	.279	276	55	77	20	57	48	92	3
Jones, Cam	.271	210	42	57	1	37	34	29	9
Urdaneta, Josue	.262	149	29	39	0	17	20	35	11
McHenry, John	.260	104	12	27	0	7	16	21	7
Jimerson, Demias	.260	169	32	44	7	27	20	43	9
Rosso, Santino	.259	27	5	7	0	4	1	5	1
Novak, Kyle	.251	167	30	42	1	19	9	12	3
Glancy, David	.245	208	38	51	7	30	26	44	8
Broderick, Dylan	.231	169	36	39	6	27	25	36	4
Williams, Javeyan	.224	214	34	48	2	31	29	47	14
Colon, JanCarlos	.174	23	2	4	0	1	1	5	0

Name	W	L	ERA	G	SV	IP	H	BB	SO
Thompson, Ross	1	0	1.32	5	0	14	8	2	9
Fuenmayor, Liu	0	2	2.08	31	13	39	24	12	36
Nabholz, Nate	0	2	2.61	21	0	31	30	9	30
Morrill, Dylan	1	0	2.70	8	0	10	7	9	8
Maryncak, Arlo	3	1	3.05	12	0	62	57	25	51
Wilford, Connor	10	2	3.25	15	0	91	92	18	63
Klein, Easton	8	4	3.80	17	0	104	102	39	61
Still, Stephen	13	3	3.89	19	0	109	114	44	97
Dill, Austin	3	1	4.03	20	2	29	23	17	27
Albert, Wes	5	2	4.25	13	0	53	43	26	29
Brotherton, Duke	4	2	5.04	22	1	55	50	29	35
Trueman, Luke	3	2	5.06	13	0	21	22	11	14
Manzano, Mikell	6	4	5.35	18	0	101	113	31	59
Barreto, Brayhans	1	3	5.60	16	2	27	30	24	25
Sabatine, Gino	2	2	5.94	19	3	33	46	10	16

TROIS RIVIERES AIGLES

Name	AVG	AB	R	H	HR	RBI	BB	SO	SB
Lopez, Gabe	.360	50	8	18	0	6	3	12	3
Hylton, Brandon	.354	336	60	119	9	64	38	65	12
Vallee, Mathieu	.352	361	75	127	1	41	47	42	83
Pelletier, Louis-Philippe	.309	337	75	104	8	54	39	62	20
Burgess, Chris	.278	151	27	42	2	20	31	35	3
Farmer, Justin	.272	313	57	85	5	50	44	61	18
Montes, John	.251	279	42	70	11	61	29	54	4
Negret, Juan Carlos	.248	222	31	55	16	52	19	73	1
Vinsky, David	.246	191	31	47	4	33	33	49	2
Garcia, Manny	.239	71	9	17	1	9	3	11	1
Curbelo, Luis	.233	189	37	44	12	38	29	50	0
Meregildo, Omar	.229	201	33	46	5	27	19	58	5
Espinal, Walner	.222	18	2	4	1	3	1	6	0
Smibert, James	.208	183	29	38	5	28	25	38	3
Lopez, Joshua	.200	40	8	8	1	8	8	14	0
Hicks, Connor	.195	41	3	8	0	3	2	7	0

Sanchez, Victor	.174	121	17	21	1	11	10	31	1
Marrero, Alan	.160	106	20	17	0	9	18	37	18
Sanchez, Edward	.133	15	0	2	0	2	0	7	0

Name	W	L	ERA	G	SV	IP	H	BB	SO
Vega, Lucas	1	0	3.33	16	0	27	27	7	22
Kramer, Cameron	4	0	3.51	20	0	26	21	15	25
Del Prado, Nick	1	1	3.63	24	0	22	14	12	39
Therrien, Jesen	7	4	4.05	18	0	111	105	30	111
Hansell, Mike	5	7	4.28	18	0	95	118	30	79
Floranus, Wendell	1	1	4.50	13	0	12	11	6	20
Chapple, Bronson	3	4	4.77	8	0	45	53	15	33
Castro, Alexander	5	6	4.84	43	5	45	42	25	48
Carver, Cal	0	1	4.97	35	1	29	33	26	29
Lefebvre, Charles	1	2	5.11	31	1	44	53	20	29
Knoll, Halen	0	0	6.30	2	0	10	13	4	3
Waldichuk, Eric	0	0	6.35	8	0	17	21	9	16
Gorgas, Marvin	0	2	6.53	4	0	21	23	12	11
Rosales, Gavino	1	4	6.86	8	0	39	51	18	15
Villar, Brayan	0	4	6.87	4	0	18	25	8	10
Rodriguez, Luis Manu	1	0	6.99	32	3	28	22	32	46
Seward, Jack	0	0	7.15	7	0	11	16	8	13
Petric, Ethan	0	0	8.18	8	0	11	15	9	11
Ramirez, Jose	4	8	8.28	18	0	79	102	43	54
Rutkowski, Harry	2	3	9.46	19	0	32	42	27	26
Fernandez, Ronalda	0	3	10.05	14	0	14	19	12	19
Peaden, Jacob	0	3	10.47	13	0	43	72	20	22
Landry, Nathan	0	2	15.63	5	0	13	22	17	7

WASHINGTON WILD THINGS

Name	AVG	AB	R	H	HR	RBI	BB	SO	SB
Parks, Pavin	.351	57	13	20	2	12	11	19	1
Fowler, Cole	.341	82	12	28	4	20	6	20	0
Watson, Ben	.326	135	22	44	2	14	10	17	4
Caufield, Tommy	.321	268	51	86	8	41	35	55	17
Lagrange, Wagner	.319	326	52	104	6	37	16	62	7
Hacopian, Eddie	.317	101	17	32	0	10	17	9	6
Orrico, AJ	.313	16	3	5	0	0	4	3	0
Chayka, Robert	.294	153	32	45	1	12	41	34	5
Infante, Sammy	.292	72	7	21	1	14	2	21	5
McNeely, Caleb	.286	35	9	10	2	6	10	15	5
Wilder, Ethan	.278	295	47	82	2	42	41	70	6
Morton, Kadon	.275	120	21	33	2	18	14	34	6
Amezquita, Carlos	.269	26	6	7	1	8	2	4	2
Czech, Andrew	.265	321	73	85	25	80	66	100	3
Liquori, Jeff	.256	320	57	82	9	50	35	45	6
Young, Tyler	.250	12	5	3	0	0	1	6	0
Roberts, Brett	.250	64	9	16	1	14	6	15	4
Edwards, Kyle	.250	72	11	18	0	11	10	14	5
Estrada, Willie	.242	62	5	15	0	6	4	14	0
Hillier, Three	.242	128	14	31	1	17	9	23	0
Reed, Tyreque	.230	274	53	63	13	67	51	64	0
Hernandez, Jommer	.212	66	7	14	0	5	4	19	0
Chatham, Cael	.200	90	12	18	0	10	13	24	0
Mack, Charles	.184	38	4	7	1	5	3	9	0
DeLeo, Jake	.091	11	1	1	0	0	1	4	0
Del Valle, Francisco	.087	23	1	2	0	1	0	6	0
Awtry, Marshall	.000	11	1	0	0	0	1	2	0
Wilson, Nolan	.000	12	0	0	0	2	2	1	0

Name	W	L	ERA	G	SV	IP	H	BB	SO
Coles, Chad	2	2	2.19	31	0	37	20	18	42
Rodriguez, Sebastian	5	2	2.57	14	0	67	60	20	46
Foster, Kobe	5	2	2.76	12	0	72	66	20	47
Garcia, Hector	3	3	2.81	40	3	48	35	19	62
Grace, Regi	4	2	3.54	11	0	61	52	18	47
DiValerio, Jordan	10	4	3.93	21	0	117	103	25	101
Diaz, Christian	1	1	4.08	20	0	29	27	13	22
Herbert, Andrew	7	3	4.08	30	12	40	36	19	35
Chasse, Ryan	1	0	4.15	19	0	22	21	22	30
Kirby, Zach	7	5	4.62	20	1	109	117	40	61
Puccetti, Dominic	2	5	5.00	9	0	45	51	31	22
McCaskey, Jacob	0	2	6.11	18	4	18	18	19	21
Nahas, Joe	1	1	6.23	11	2	13	13	3	16

Carroll, Jake	2	0	6.30	14	0	20	18	11	13
Kirkeby, Dylan	0	0	7.02	4	0	17	20	5	14
Perez, Marlon	2	3	7.04	6	0	31	43	15	25
Oviedo, Ivan	0	3	9.00	3	0	13	15	7	10
Hicks, Jackson	0	2	9.00	18	0	24	30	13	21

WINDY CITY THUNDERBOLTS

Name	AVG	AB	R	H	HR	RBI	BB	SO	SB
Dunlap, James	.316	250	33	79	1	27	21	31	11
Ruiz, Daryl	.313	198	21	62	6	40	8	40	0
Maberry, David	.278	205	24	57	5	30	26	38	1
Sandle, Michael	.275	327	75	90	16	58	50	82	19
Phelts, Cam	.268	246	39	66	0	15	26	63	45
Curpa, Jose	.241	87	6	21	0	9	7	20	7
Greer, Jalen	.237	173	21	41	2	19	13	42	16
Diaz, Winder	.233	43	4	10	0	2	3	14	2
Thoroman, Grant	.230	122	11	28	2	18	12	29	7
Gibson, Josh	.227	198	27	45	1	12	20	58	18
Harbison, Kyle	.225	89	9	20	1	9	8	23	2
Pena, Carlos	.224	49	10	11	3	10	5	14	2
Beadle, Zach	.212	179	15	38	0	12	12	88	2
Serratos, Oscar	.206	262	34	54	5	28	25	69	25
Kuzemka, Christian	.199	201	20	40	8	35	6	39	1
Kotowski, Dakota	.195	205	27	40	13	38	16	79	6
Broussard, Garrett	.186	247	20	46	2	16	24	69	0
Herron Jr., Anthony	.167	12	1	2	0	0	3	5	0
Roberts, Ethan	.167	24	11	4	0	2	7	7	5
Corliss, Craig	.156	32	3	5	0	1	3	12	0

Name	W	L	ERA	G	SV	IP	H	BB	SO
Milburn, Isaac	4	2	1.53	6	0	35	31	11	37
Riedel, Caleb	2	3	2.59	29	8	56	33	27	71
Wehrle, Tyler	0	1	3.20	7	0	25	21	8	24
Pindel, Buddie	6	6	3.50	16	0	93	113	19	56
Reynolds, Trevin	5	6	3.91	31	10	48	44	19	41
Duncan, Greg	2	8	3.94	16	0	82	78	43	85
Evers, Aaron	2	4	4.14	12	0	59	57	23	55
Evans, Jalen	2	0	4.43	21	2	22	17	17	19
LaMere, Nolan	0	0	4.66	13	0	10	14	6	8
Newman, Jacob	0	3	4.73	5	1	13	16	8	15
Maietta, Dante	4	4	4.87	15	0	65	59	42	53
Hellgeth, Bryce	1	5	5.03	29	1	91	94	43	67
Kirkeby, Dylan	3	5	5.19	10	0	43	44	25	35
Plumadore, Carsen	2	4	5.93	25	0	41	30	27	28
Stants, Noah	0	1	6.55	10	0	11	8	11	10
Savino, Dylan	1	0	7.63	12	0	15	18	14	16
Cook, Avery	1	0	8.03	7	0	12	15	8	8
Turner, Eric	0	2	8.53	4	0	13	17	12	11
Vath, Bobby	0	2	9.00	4	0	15	26	6	4
Dominguez, Ronny	1	0	11.65	22	0	34	45	27	37

PIONEER LEAGUE

In the same year that the Athletics left Oakland, the Oakland Ballers brought the city a championship. In only their second year of existence, the Ballers were clearly the class of the Pioneer League. They won both the first and second half titles. The playoffs were a bit tougher. Idaho Falls won the first two games of the championship series, but Oakland rallied to win three eliminaton games. The deciding Game 5 8-1 win came in front of 4,100 Oakland fans.

Team	W	L	PCT	GB
Oakland Ballers*%	73	23	.760	-
Missoula PaddleHeads*	64	32	.667	9
Idaho Falls Chukars^	54	41	.568	18.5
Ogden Raptors^	52	43	.547	20.5
Yuba-Sutter High Wheelers	50	46	.521	23
Boise Hawks	48	48	.500	25
Rocky Mountain Vibes	47	47	.500	25
Billings Mustangs	46	48	.490	26
Grand Junction Jackalopes	41	55	.427	32
Glacier Range Riders	40	56	.417	33
Great Falls Voyagers	33	61	.354	39
Colorado Springs Sky Sox	23	71	.245	49

*First-half Champ. %Second-half Champ. ^Wild Card

Playoffs—Semifinals: Oakland defeated Ogden 2-1 and Idaho Falls defeated Missoula 2-1 in best-of-3 series. **Finals:** Oakland defeated Idaho Falls 3-1 in best-of-5 series.

Attendance: Ogden Raptors 160,192; Boise Hawks 159,440; Rocky Mountain Vibes 114,679; Oakland Ballers 110,502; Billings Mustangs 109,610; Glacier Range Riders 104,285; Idaho Falls Chukars 96,731; Missoula PaddleHeads 79,159; Great Falls Voyagers 65,457; Grand Junction Jackalopes 62,077; Yuba-Sutter High Wheelers 53,985.

Most Valuable Player: Christopher Sargent, Ogden. **Pitcher of the Year:** Matthew Sox, Missoula. **Rookie of the Year:** Taylor Darden, Boise. **International Player of the Year:** Roberto Pena, Missoula. **Reliever of the Year:** Reese Miller, Grand Junction. **Manager of the Year:** Aaron Miles, Oakland.

BATTING LEADERS

Player, Team	AVG	OBP	SLG	AB	H	HR	RBI	BB	SO
Benjamin Rosengard, IF	.463	.558	.716	229	106	10	57	49	43
Taylor Darden, Boise	.429	.524	.685	371	159	18	125	68	58
Sam Linscott, R. Mountain	.395	.447	.586	382	151	14	87	31	36
Adam Fogel, Missoula	.388	.463	.784	320	124	34	108	38	63
Christopher Sargent, Ogden	.384	.443	.741	352	135	35	130	36	57
Mike Rosario, Missoula	.382	.431	.583	374	143	13	75	29	41
Damian Stone, Ogden	.382	.478	.519	314	120	5	52	48	42
Spence Coffman, GJ	.381	.436	.571	333	127	12	90	53	37
Brett Roberts, Colo. Springs	.380	.429	.679	287	109	20	65	27	41
Trevor Rogers, Idaho Falls	.379	.478	.705	383	145	28	104	61	68

PITCHING LEADERS

Player, Team	W	L	ERA	G	IP	H	BB	SO
Reese Miller, GJ	3	0	1.33	46	54	37	17	83
Jacob Hasty, GR	1	1	1.45	45	43	33	27	56
Noah Millikan, Oakland	7	1	2.12	14	85	65	12	96
Conner Richardson, Oakland	6	0	2.54	39	50	41	8	36
Matthew Taubensee, Missoula	3	0	2.78	32	36	26	23	64
Zac Lampton, Missoula	4	2	2.90	47	50	32	25	83
Gabe Tanner, Oakland	9	0	3.26	17	77	70	24	47
Brett Wozniak, Y-S	10	3	3.45	17	104	114	30	80
Luke Short, Oakland	7	1	3.58	15	65	62	23	79
Luke Cooper, GR	2	3	3.60	45	50	41	25	74

BILLINGS MUSTANGS

Name	AVG	OBP	SLG	AB	R	H	HR	RBI	SB
Dylan Leach	.386	.517	.750	44	20	17	3	13	3
Cameron Bowen	.344	.378	.496	393	82	135	10	63	28
Sean Lynch	.333	.400	.556	36	10	12	2	9	0
Jack O'Dowd	.333	.449	.642	324	73	108	22	91	2
John McHenry	.319	.408	.440	182	35	58	3	29	6
Patrick Mills	.315	.411	.477	279	54	88	9	49	2
Chase Hanson	.307	.399	.400	140	30	43	2	19	2
Casey Sorg	.305	.367	.415	82	13	25	0	14	1
AJ Shaver	.299	.403	.477	264	71	79	10	39	32
Xavier Casserilla	.284	.338	.403	352	43	100	9	51	1
Zane Denton	.274	.384	.321	84	14	23	0	10	1
Briley Knight	.273	.409	.423	286	68	78	7	59	22
Efrain Manzo	.272	.366	.400	195	29	53	3	16	0
Tyler Shelnut	.272	.397	.497	316	70	86	15	72	13
Jacob Kline	.268	.344	.348	138	30	37	1	18	0
Bodee Wright	.250	.397	.375	48	11	12	0	12	6
Colby Seltzer	.244	.312	.427	82	15	20	2	17	1
Ronnie Allen Jr	.239	.400	.261	46	7	11	0	10	0
Charlie Muniz	.230	.336	.349	126	16	29	4	26	0
Justin Williams	.222	.317	.222	36	8	8	0	3	1
Kyle Micklus	.217	.362	.365	115	26	25	5	15	2
CJ Colyer	.185	.324	.370	27	4	5	1	7	0

Name	W	L	ERA	G	SV	IP	H	BB	SO
Jaden Harris	2	1	2.08	6	0	26	16	13	21
Garrett Ouellette	0	0	2.30	15	7	16	15	8	24
CJ Colyer	3	2	2.30	25	0	27	23	15	21
Justin Fuson	6	0	3.63	14	0	69	60	31	70
Cole Calnon	4	0	3.68	7	0	29	29	1	15
Hudson Boncal	4	5	3.92	19	0	64	68	34	66
Julian Garcia	4	6	4.41	15	0	86	98	23	64

Ritter Steinmann	3	0	4.88	17	0	28	29	19	42
Cole Chimenti	0	3	5.19	14	4	17	23	5	11
Devyn Lopez	1	1	5.32	21	2	24	30	13	23
Arturo Alvarez	0	2	5.77	11	0	44	68	20	23
Chase Hanson	0	0	6.07	23	2	27	22	13	22
EJ Johnson	2	4	7.46	21	0	66	100	27	52
Daniel Foster	7	3	7.61	21	0	73	108	18	56
Jack Maruskin	2	1	7.84	18	2	21	23	21	24
Chris Hardin	1	1	8.44	13	0	16	26	11	17
Sam Schmitt	1	2	8.73	8	0	33	51	14	22
Hollis Fanning	0	2	12.06	8	0	16	32	7	7
Thomas Wilhite	0	1	15.19	14	0	11	19	12	8

BOISE HAWKS

Name	AVG	OBP	SLG	AB	R	H	HR	RBI	SB
Taylor Darden	.429	.524	.685	371	109	159	18	125	24
Max Jung-Goldberg	.361	.476	.678	360	98	130	26	130	10
Noah Marcelo	.351	.421	.552	424	119	149	12	75	64
Paul Myro IV	.345	.449	.465	325	87	112	2	72	24
Coleton Horner	.341	.492	.500	44	9	15	1	9	0
Jake Hjelle	.338	.381	.635	394	91	133	26	102	18
Ethan Underwood	.337	.463	.453	309	95	104	6	68	23
Jaylon Lee	.322	.361	.461	115	30	37	1	21	3
Jeremiah Begora	.315	.395	.505	305	59	96	14	64	10
Dakota Conners	.314	.368	.371	35	2	11	0	4	0
Ryan Grabosch	.314	.357	.510	51	11	16	2	9	0
Drew Woodcox	.308	.383	.497	169	29	52	9	32	4
Joseph Kalafut	.283	.406	.434	113	25	32	2	19	0
Ethan Crawford	.278	.371	.500	54	12	15	3	13	1
JC Santini	.268	.360	.380	213	35	57	3	22	7
Xavier Croxton	.246	.358	.304	69	13	17	1	10	6
Braxton Turner	.214	.299	.320	103	13	22	2	13	2

Name	W	L	ERA	G	SV	IP	H	BB	SO
Chaney Trout	2	2	3.96	41	2	36	38	15	19
Blake McFadden	0	1	4.68	24	0	25	23	13	27
Bryan Perez	1	1	4.80	4	0	15	10	16	14
Trey Jones	1	2	5.06	14	2	32	34	21	38
Graham Edwards	6	3	5.15	15	0	80	73	38	86
Hylan Hall	1	1	5.40	12	0	22	25	12	16
Joe Skapinetz	3	1	6.29	6	0	24	27	17	18
Bryson Vaughn	0	0	6.32	8	0	16	29	7	6
Cameron Dayton	7	1	6.44	23	0	88	115	48	73
Jacob Hughes	5	3	6.56	13	0	60	65	32	69
Jaykob Acosta	2	1	6.75	11	0	17	22	7	20
Quinn Waterhouse	1	2	7.65	26	5	42	63	22	38
Richard Dell	2	1	7.78	22	1	20	20	13	20
Tony Roca	1	1	8.14	10	0	24	34	17	25
Jeremiah Locklear	1	3	8.51	38	1	49	56	24	40
Murphy Gienger	2	2	8.68	27	0	28	34	21	31
Cole Tremain	0	0	9.24	7	0	13	15	9	4
Oscar Fernandez	1	2	9.26	9	0	12	11	19	6
Carter Gannaway	3	2	9.38	15	0	24	26	25	28
Gabriel Pacheco	0	3	9.61	9	0	35	60	21	28
Christian Marrufo	1	1	9.95	12	0	13	18	13	11
Brady Gilmore	1	1	10.13	10	0	11	13	8	9
Braden Carmichael	3	3	10.61	6	0	28	46	15	22
Jack Leary	1	0	12.34	5	0	12	22	7	5
Noah McBride	0	2	12.90	28	3	22	37	29	32
Nolan George	0	1	13.14	3	0	12	21	10	10

COLORADO SPRINGS SKY SOX

Name	AVG	OBP	SLG	AB	R	H	HR	RBI	SB
Brett Roberts	.380	.429	.679	287	81	109	20	65	23
Kai Moody	.336	.442	.529	274	60	92	8	69	4
Marquis Jackson	.333	.500	.444	27	7	9	0	2	0
Quintt Landis	.333	.464	.494	255	72	85	8	31	8
Zane Denton	.319	.430	.543	188	45	60	9	37	0
Edwin Martinez Pagani	.289	.353	.401	152	30	44	2	15	4
Justin Johnson	.283	.354	.504	240	48	68	12	59	3
Anthony Abbatine	.282	.378	.308	39	6	11	0	7	1
Matt Fabian	.280	.405	.355	200	35	56	2	26	3
Omar Veloz	.277	.317	.398	264	24	73	7	56	1

Name	AVG	OBP	SLG	AB	R	H	HR	RBI	SB
Zachary Chamizo	.259	.310	.370	27	3	7	1	2	0
Manny Jackson	.233	.273	.233	30	4	7	0	3	0
Gordon Richardson	.233	.282	.282	103	15	24	0	13	1
William Brassil	.230	.319	.344	61	7	14	1	14	0
Gianni Horvat	.230	.319	.377	61	11	14	1	9	4
Anthony Torreullas	.219	.390	.281	32	11	7	0	1	0
Maury Weaver	.189	.225	.216	37	3	7	0	5	1
Josiah Chavez	.186	.269	.200	70	10	13	0	6	0
Marco Martinez	.171	.264	.276	76	7	13	2	9	1
Dreylin Holmes	.160	.311	.180	50	6	8	0	4	2

Name	W	L	ERA	G	SV	IP	H	BB	SO
Max Maarleveld	0	0	4.38	4	0	12	15	12	6
Alain Lopez	0	4	4.62	26	5	25	26	21	34
Jose Ochoa	2	1	6.34	27	0	33	42	30	38
Chase Martinez	3	4	7.05	14	0	52	71	42	42
Johan Castillo	5	7	8.91	19	0	104	159	49	82
Ethan Ross	1	3	9.25	32	0	48	72	38	46
Maikol Lopez	0	3	9.50	16	1	36	58	26	37
Adam Wibert	2	1	10.44	27	0	25	33	29	30
D'Anthony Beckman	0	0	11.77	10	0	13	14	15	11
Matthew Lauria	1	4	11.79	10	0	47	78	30	36
Kenny Carrillo	0	2	12.10	13	0	29	51	34	20
Joe Kinsky	0	1	12.38	22	0	32	46	42	29
Charlie Adamson	0	4	13.32	5	0	24	43	15	14
Noel Soto	0	7	15.40	9	0	45	103	28	39
Andres Alonso	0	1	16.50	5	0	12	23	17	5
Trey Watson	0	5	17.05	5	0	25	61	19	17
Ubaldo Romo	0	5	17.21	10	0	27	60	26	15
Danny Fox	0	1	17.23	10	0	35	63	40	27
Breyln Jones	0	6	17.89	8	0	27	39	57	14
Eldridge Armstrong III	1	2	18.16	11	0	18	48	13	16

GLACIER RANGE RIDERS

Name	AVG	OBP	SLG	AB	R	H	HR	RBI	SB
JD McLaughlin	.350	.412	.500	60	12	21	2	9	6
Eli Paton	.330	.434	.557	115	22	38	4	27	2
John Mabry	.328	.363	.354	189	23	62	0	23	3
Donovan Ratfield	.314	.453	.471	51	11	16	1	15	0
TJ Clarkson	.299	.405	.486	364	77	109	14	60	4
Kingston Liniak	.280	.350	.442	346	44	97	13	66	3
Kenneth Levari	.271	.335	.347	199	30	54	1	12	4
Jack Lynch	.269	.351	.490	245	40	66	12	49	7
Logan Beard	.249	.350	.393	305	42	76	10	52	0
Jake Millan	.248	.321	.384	125	23	31	4	20	0
Angel Mendoza	.247	.344	.434	219	34	54	8	32	4
Kyle Ashworth	.242	.335	.295	190	31	46	1	23	5
Gabe Howell	.238	.304	.352	281	44	67	6	21	8
Gavin Tonkel	.167	.318	.194	36	7	6	0	0	1
Carson Garner	.154	.241	.179	78	9	12	0	4	1

Name	W	L	ERA	G	SV	IP	H	BB	SO
Jacob Hasty	1	1	1.45	45	2	43	33	27	56
Luke Cooper	2	3	3.60	45	3	50	41	25	74
Luke Schafer	9	2	4.18	18	0	108	119	40	108
Nick Zegna	0	2	4.24	37	6	40	38	14	50
Davis Pratt	2	1	4.70	40	0	44	41	21	40
Grant Taylor	7	7	4.71	19	0	115	127	30	117
Ty Bothwell	4	6	5.40	19	0	105	109	42	130
Jason Franks	1	2	5.93	27	1	27	37	17	35
Rayne Supple	2	6	6.58	29	5	52	54	30	56
Nicholas Ferazzi	1	1	6.75	18	0	20	27	5	20
Cam Cowan	0	3	7.15	21	1	23	21	18	33
Eldridge Armstrong III	1	1	7.24	17	0	27	31	12	31
Jared Engman	1	6	7.35	14	0	67	84	28	56
Sean Brennan	1	7	7.38	12	0	46	56	29	41
Noah Owen	0	1	9.00	7	0	26	40	4	29
Trevor Baker	0	1	9.24	3	0	13	27	2	3

GRAND JUNCTION JACKALOPES

Name	AVG	OBP	SLG	AB	R	H	HR	RBI	SB
Calyn Halvorson	.383	.460	.551	167	41	64	5	41	4
Spence Coffman	.381	.436	.571	333	85	127	12	90	12
Evan Scavotto	.358	.480	.604	369	111	132	22	104	10
Christian Castaneda	.344	.422	.527	279	62	96	11	54	6
Isaac Nunez	.344	.463	.543	326	101	112	17	70	29
Zeb Roos	.341	.466	.572	355	110	121	14	75	52
Alex Pimentel	.329	.449	.591	313	89	103	17	75	26
Mason Minzey	.327	.439	.636	324	77	106	24	106	3
Damon Maynard	.324	.463	.400	105	25	34	0	15	5
Preston Shelton	.312	.391	.413	138	36	43	2	15	6
Kendal Ewell	.309	.434	.617	81	19	25	7	16	4
Diego Aragon	.291	.443	.436	110	26	32	2	22	1
Kendall Foster	.276	.350	.490	294	59	81	15	67	13
Matt Piotrowski	.233	.267	.233	43	4	10	0	2	2
Robin Fernandez	.225	.296	.394	71	10	16	3	11	0
Luis Hernandez	.192	.333	.192	26	3	5	0	4	1

Name	W	L	ERA	G	SV	IP	H	BB	SO
Reese Miller	3	0	1.33	46	16	54	37	17	83
Riley Egloff	4	2	5.61	7	0	34	55	5	32
Tristan Wolf	3	2	6.12	31	0	32	38	18	26
Jacob McCaskey	0	1	6.43	12	0	14	18	9	12
Brock Gillis	3	3	8.14	40	0	63	78	55	83
Albert Bobadilla	4	3	8.39	16	0	59	86	47	41
Evan Massie	4	6	9.23	18	0	79	115	69	66
Ethan Brown	0	1	9.82	12	0	15	19	22	10
Joe Cuomo	1	2	10.25	6	0	26	43	12	14
Zach Zaborowski	4	6	10.74	17	0	62	109	27	65
Alec Rodriguez	3	1	11.23	29	0	34	41	35	35
Mason Longoria	1	1	11.51	5	0	20	32	11	10
Zach DeVito	0	2	11.52	23	0	27	34	15	29
Maddux Hoaglund	1	1	12.41	10	0	29	51	19	22
Aydan Alger	3	6	12.60	51	0	55	93	29	48
Coley Kilpatrick	0	1	13.22	5	0	16	32	15	11
Tai Atkins	1	0	14.34	13	0	11	17	6	10
Blake Barquin	3	4	14.80	19	0	35	75	24	31
Parker Wakeman	1	1	15.19	7	0	21	47	21	9

GREAT FALLS VOYAGERS

Name	AVG	OBP	SLG	AB	R	H	HR	RBI	SB
Brock Watkins	.364	.458	.556	99	21	36	4	18	0
Luis Carlos Moreno	.347	.508	.449	49	13	17	1	10	2
Kyle Schmack	.336	.482	.555	128	28	43	6	26	0
Trey Cruz	.333	.410	.507	219	30	54	1	12	6
Emilio Corona	.332	.361	.548	283	59	94	11	52	33
AJ Fritz	.329	.403	.542	286	59	94	12	67	23
Anthony Swenda	.312	.423	.500	234	53	73	7	39	6
Tommy Specht	.306	.368	.468	372	62	114	9	65	6
Frank Podkul	.280	.340	.491	218	28	61	11	46	1
Jedier Hernandez	.274	.413	.384	73	10	20	1	9	1
Armando Albert	.274	.452	.333	117	24	32	0	17	3
Devon Dixon	.269	.363	.397	78	20	21	2	10	0
Jeff Nicol	.264	.360	.401	182	30	48	3	25	0
Aidan Redahan	.256	.330	.333	78	12	20	0	10	3
Antonio Barranca	.256	.368	.556	90	23	23	7	27	4
Cooper Vest	.254	.373	.462	130	29	33	6	30	1
Ryley Preece	.253	.351	.434	83	13	21	1	17	4
Freddy Rojas Jr	.252	.314	.340	159	19	40	3	23	0
Roman Kuntz	.247	.341	.519	162	20	40	11	36	0
Christian Hall	.238	.347	.357	42	7	10	1	5	1
Alec Patino	.225	.354	.275	40	4	9	0	2	0
Sebastian Mueller	.214	.313	.286	28	4	6	0	2	0
Kody Putnam	.214	.270	.397	126	23	27	6	20	4
Devin Hurdle	.175	.327	.275	40	9	7	1	3	0

Name	W	L	ERA	G	SV	IP	H	BB	SO
Cam Cowan	0	0	1.64	11	0	11	6	15	9
Wyatt Cameron	1	1	3.93	34	8	34	29	15	44
Zach Voelker	1	1	4.09	11	1	11	6	10	14
Mitchell Grannan	1	0	4.11	30	0	35	36	13	34
Jordan Hamberg	0	2	4.41	4	0	16	16	15	15
Robert Kelley	3	2	4.91	30	0	33	34	19	36
Tariq Bacon	0	2	5.47	24	2	26	24	25	27
Nolan Pender	2	2	5.74	39	3	53	74	25	54
CJ Czerwinski	4	8	7.31	16	0	89	121	50	82
Sam Lavin	3	6	7.88	12	0	64	90	26	62

Name	W	L	ERA	G	SV	IP	H	BB	SO
Nick Marshall	5	7	8.19	16	0	86	122	45	65
Josh Collett	1	0	8.47	27	0	39	45	27	50
Brendan Moody	2	5	8.57	11	0	49	82	20	26
Danny Galvan	3	3	8.67	25	0	72	118	29	62
Daniel Batcher	4	5	9.83	13	0	54	101	29	36
Luke Helton	1	7	9.95	10	0	44	79	21	29
AJ Fritz	1	2	10.65	7	0	24	40	13	19
Kelvin Perez	0	0	12.23	18	2	18	34	2	16
Braden Forsyth	0	0	14.21	8	0	13	25	7	8
Jason Pineda	2	2	15.92	3	0	13	30	8	12
Nate Madej	0	2	17.61	4	0	15	29	19	13

IDAHO FALLS CHUKARS

Name	AVG	OBP	SLG	AB	R	H	HR	RBI	SB
Benjamin Rosengard	.463	.558	.716	229	80	106	10	57	9
Spencer Rich	.385	.455	.630	192	51	74	13	58	20
Trevor Rogers	.379	.478	.705	383	97	145	28	104	1
Johnny Pappas	.371	.484	.580	224	63	83	13	65	2
Garret Ostrander	.371	.478	.540	315	102	117	9	51	6
Simon Baumgardt	.361	.444	.653	285	67	103	19	77	1
Anthony Mata	.346	.393	.500	280	69	97	5	57	18
Tyler Wyatt	.335	.416	.562	331	96	111	15	94	7
Thomas McCaffrey	.332	.393	.524	208	41	69	8	48	0
Eddie Pelc	.316	.438	.406	187	37	59	3	36	7
Jacob Jablonski	.314	.436	.603	242	66	76	18	67	6
Grady Morgan	.307	.432	.447	179	49	55	4	37	2
Jacob Shanks	.300	.435	.564	140	47	42	10	33	3
Kirkland Banks	.288	.366	.356	250	59	72	3	42	20
Gabriel Vasquez	.272	.362	.533	195	40	53	12	44	1

Name	W	L	ERA	G	SV	IP	H	BB	SO
Ricky Tibbett	2	0	4.35	14	1	21	28	5	18
Robert Hughes	1	4	4.84	33	1	35	36	22	43
Gary Grosjean	11	6	5.45	21	2	112	130	38	102
Steven Ordorica	1	0	5.57	34	1	42	53	16	28
Jake Dixon	2	0	5.76	29	0	30	46	6	23
Julien Hernandez	1	0	6.14	29	1	29	44	22	39
Nathan Hemmerling	8	4	6.43	16	0	84	121	43	60
Ryan Faulks	2	0	6.63	14	0	19	23	8	26
Shane Spencer	6	3	6.73	23	1	104	137	41	75
Jean Reyes	0	0	7.20	20	1	25	31	4	18
Nathan Shinn	3	4	7.23	22	0	80	115	39	63
Nicolo Pinazzi	1	1	8.13	29	2	31	40	17	42
Luke Hempel	0	1	8.37	21	0	24	27	21	25
Connor Harrison	7	8	8.58	19	0	93	155	26	74
Garrett Van Deventer	5	5	8.89	15	0	55	91	22	32
Dylan Porter	0	3	9.20	6	0	15	17	8	9
Jorge Romero	0	1	10.64	6	0	11	19	9	6
Dante Zamudio	1	1	10.71	16	0	21	39	14	17
Tyler Curtis	0	4	10.93	12	0	28	60	11	22
Bennett Flynn	1	1	14.66	6	0	12	23	6	15
Reed Garland	0	1	25.36	7	1	11	26	15	8

MISSOULA PADDLEHEADS

Name	AVG	OBP	SLG	AB	R	H	HR	RBI	SB
Adam Fogel	.388	.463	.784	320	86	124	34	108	5
Mike Rosario	.382	.431	.583	374	98	143	13	75	12
Roberto Pena	.358	.452	.789	388	125	139	46	129	36
Nich Klemp	.340	.433	.642	212	53	72	14	47	1
Evan Sleight	.334	.418	.580	305	68	102	16	66	2
Colby Wilkerson	.326	.406	.452	383	76	125	7	56	5
Carlos Perez	.316	.376	.482	228	49	72	9	50	7
Colin Gordon	.307	.418	.486	358	84	110	12	67	11
Kishon Frett	.304	.417	.493	69	16	21	3	14	1
Alec Sanchez	.293	.361	.495	307	59	90	12	68	9
Kamron Willman	.290	.357	.471	276	53	80	11	50	2
Leyton Barry	.274	.373	.456	226	45	62	7	36	19
Taylor Smith	.234	.351	.438	201	31	47	11	27	1
Jeremy Piatkiewicz	.214	.372	.316	117	23	25	2	16	5

Name	W	L	ERA	G	SV	IP	H	BB	SO
Taylor Smith	0	0	1.64	8	0	11	6	5	8
Noah Owen	2	0	2.66	19	0	20	21	5	28

Name	W	L	ERA	G	SV	IP	H	BB	SO
Matthew Taubensee	3	0	2.78	32	0	36	26	23	64
Zac Lampton	4	2	2.90	47	9	50	32	25	83
Matthew Sox	12	3	3.83	17	0	99	86	34	114
Dawson Day	5	0	3.94	17	0	62	53	33	74
Nick Bautista	1	1	5.19	18	0	17	14	13	20
Andrew Armstrong	3	1	5.36	33	0	45	46	22	53
Ryan Wentz	7	7	5.56	17	0	100	112	31	121
Brendan Beard	5	3	5.60	17	0	92	106	31	96
Reece Fields	6	2	5.67	25	1	54	61	30	64
Arman Sabouri	0	0	6.30	30	8	30	28	25	29
Pablo Garabitos	0	0	7.20	10	0	10	19	3	2
Cale Mathison	1	0	7.71	18	0	16	18	14	17
Nick Parker	3	3	8.94	12	0	54	68	33	50
Michael Peterson	5	6	9.23	16	0	78	135	18	63

OAKLAND BALLERS

Name	AVG	OBP	SLG	AB	R	H	HR	RBI	SB
Cam Bufford	.349	.403	.597	347	79	121	21	76	27
Dillon Tatum	.338	.455	.684	225	55	76	23	75	0
Michael O'Hara	.336	.388	.436	110	27	37	1	14	1
Lou Helmig	.326	.411	.473	273	46	89	8	63	7
Jake Allgeyer	.322	.408	.452	146	26	47	2	25	3
Christian Almanza	.315	.394	.653	352	89	111	31	105	4
Daniel Harris IV	.314	.370	.477	373	80	117	13	67	9
Tyler Lozano	.306	.348	.468	173	26	53	5	38	2
TJ McKenzie	.299	.393	.511	331	84	99	16	68	37
Tremayne Cobb Jr	.296	.389	.419	372	85	110	8	46	16
Davis Drewek	.291	.422	.578	268	77	78	19	68	12
Esai Santos	.289	.428	.488	256	66	74	11	46	11
Nick Leehey	.280	.382	.543	186	40	52	14	48	1
Darryl Buggs	.253	.355	.373	225	54	57	5	30	35
Ryan Pierce	.250	.317	.278	36	8	9	0	4	1
Pat Monteith	.216	.367	.352	88	19	19	2	9	4

Name	W	L	ERA	G	SV	IP	H	BB	SO
Carson Lambert	2	0	0.69	22	0	26	18	3	34
Noah Millikan	7	1	2.12	14	0	85	65	12	96
Conner Richardson	6	0	2.54	39	2	50	41	8	36
Gabe Tanner	9	2	3.26	17	0	77	70	24	47
Luke Short	7	1	3.58	15	0	65	62	23	79
James Colyer	3	0	3.77	36	2	43	42	18	55
Caleb Franzen	3	0	4.26	35	0	44	46	8	47
Brody Eglite	3	0	4.28	10	0	27	28	13	27
Connor Sullivan	2	1	4.81	42	19	43	38	16	47
Reed Butz	9	5	5.30	17	0	90	106	45	70
Adam Bogosian	3	0	5.33	31	2	49	59	14	53
Zach St Pierre	8	4	5.36	22	1	97	126	38	73
Alec Rodriguez	0	0	6.55	9	0	11	12	12	14
Dylan Matsuoka	5	1	7.46	19	0	57	75	29	45
Sean Kelby	0	0	7.50	7	0	12	18	5	11
Dylan Delvecchio	1	2	7.53	10	0	35	41	16	29
Malik Binns	1	2	12.34	6	1	12	13	8	9

OGDEN RAPTORS

Name	AVG	OBP	SLG	AB	R	H	HR	RBI	SB
Christopher Sargent Jr	.384	.443	.741	352	94	135	35	130	2
Damian Stone	.382	.478	.519	314	81	120	5	52	12
Sebastian Greico	.378	.440	.689	45	12	17	4	13	1
Bradley Pelle	.360	.418	.540	50	13	18	2	11	1
Connor Bagnieski	.354	.463	.611	339	92	120	23	110	7
Carmine Lane	.352	.413	.491	395	69	139	8	88	4
Kenneth Oyama	.351	.438	.409	350	96	123	0	59	23
Cole Jordan	.346	.425	.520	373	99	129	12	82	21
True Fontenot	.341	.407	.500	370	85	126	7	68	10
Elliot Good	.329	.443	.459	331	88	109	10	75	6
Christian Hall	.324	.434	.608	222	51	72	17	57	0
Carson Tucker	.323	.469	.452	62	16	20	1	12	6
Dylan Wilkinson	.317	.440	.426	183	52	58	2	53	17
Kyler Stancato	.312	.417	.497	157	47	49	6	36	10
Evan Blum	.282	.364	.641	39	8	11	3	13	1
Charles Updegrave	.214	.306	.357	42	5	9	1	6	0
Carter Mize	.205	.289	.282	39	5	8	1	9	0

Name	W	L	ERA	G	SV	IP	H	BB	SO
Jestin Jones	1	1	3.06	17	0	18	14	12	15
Nik Cardinal	5	4	5.04	43	12	45	43	26	47
Cole Stasio	7	1	5.29	12	0	65	77	19	65
Ryan Velazquez	3	2	5.73	36	3	44	51	39	44
Nico Saltaformaggio	8	1	5.94	47	0	86	104	35	72
Chase Chatman	8	3	5.95	20	0	88	101	49	75
Cameron Edmonson	2	1	6.06	48	1	49	58	24	58
Bryson Van Sickle	0	0	6.32	3	0	16	22	7	12
Christian Ciuffetelli	0	2	6.83	29	0	29	40	23	31
Christian Griffin	0	1	6.97	21	0	21	24	17	20
Jonah Montes	1	0	7.24	11	0	14	20	8	15
Eli Elliott	6	4	7.41	16	0	68	102	26	55
Kyler Stancato	1	0	7.52	15	0	26	40	14	25
Shawn Triplett	0	1	7.53	12	0	14	27	10	18
Rolando Gutierrez Rosario	2	4	7.66	10	0	47	66	26	37
Dylan Gardner	1	1	8.51	18	0	24	34	18	28
Shane Gustafson	5	4	9.04	19	0	80	120	34	49
Jose Moreno	1	1	9.53	5	0	23	41	11	17
Brett Erwin	0	1	9.75	7	0	12	20	6	6
Austyn Coleman	3	5	11.29	21	0	81	139	32	40
Miguel Hernandez	1	3	12.79	4	0	13	21	15	13
Nick Agacki	1	0	13.11	10	0	12	16	13	11

YUBA-SUTTER HIGH WHEELERS

Name	AVG	OBP	SLG	AB	R	H	HR	RBI	SB
Evan Berkey	.355	.480	.656	273	73	97	21	80	15
River Orsak	.349	.424	.562	372	89	130	19	84	25
Gio Brusa	.326	.409	.635	353	82	115	28	91	4
Parker Coddou	.318	.451	.430	242	64	77	6	43	29
Josh Duarte	.317	.402	.379	145	30	46	2	19	7
Cooper Hext	.312	.386	.516	343	74	107	16	77	22
Bobby Lada	.312	.370	.532	391	94	122	21	75	39
Cuba Bess	.295	.427	.608	288	81	85	26	94	8
Landon Wallace	.290	.444	.511	186	54	54	10	34	7
Mike Campagna	.284	.420	.406	155	23	44	4	27	2
Garret Pike	.276	.337	.471	87	16	24	3	9	2
Randy Flores	.271	.340	.396	48	7	13	0	6	1
Adam Juran	.264	.331	.400	110	18	29	3	28	1
Connor Denning	.233	.409	.422	223	52	52	9	42	5
Tyler Young	.222	.323	.296	54	10	12	0	4	3

Name	W	L	ERA	G	SV	IP	H	BB	SO
Brandon McPherson	2	0	2.38	2	0	11	11	2	16
Ty Buckner	0	1	3.00	11	3	12	8	2	17
Brett Wozniak	10	3	3.45	17	0	104	114	30	80
Garrett Martin	2	0	3.79	4	0	19	17	12	21
Logan Snow	1	0	4.50	10	0	12	8	4	7
Mason Bryant	2	3	4.87	38	1	44	44	20	52
Kris Anglin	1	0	5.17	4	0	16	23	7	20
Ethan Bates	3	3	5.60	32	4	35	41	13	31
Scott Ellis	0	2	5.64	26	0	53	54	24	47
Zach Voelker	0	1	5.94	13	0	17	18	11	22
Andrew Garcia	0	4	6.12	36	3	43	43	32	58
Jonah Jenkins	3	6	6.26	16	0	82	108	34	74
Sam Drumheller	0	4	6.32	32	0	37	40	17	30
Jayden Drake	4	2	6.34	13	0	50	54	18	34
Cole Cressend	3	2	7.26	21	0	62	61	42	73
Christian Womble	6	4	7.33	15	0	77	98	37	54
Nate Madej	2	3	7.36	8	0	33	31	37	31
Matthew Kavanaugh	5	3	7.40	14	0	62	81	22	49
Jack Martin	1	0	9.00	10	0	12	19	5	11
Andrew LaCour	0	2	10.13	19	0	21	31	14	27

ROCKY MOUNTAIN VIBES

Name	AVG	OBP	SLG	AB	R	H	HR	RBI	SB
Sam Linscott	.395	.447	.586	382	97	151	14	87	15
Joskar Feliciano	.378	.549	.405	37	14	14	0	9	0
Kellum Clark	.377	.471	.628	239	79	90	12	70	7
Tristin Garcia	.376	.444	.495	287	61	108	4	70	4
Christian Pregent	.371	.452	.571	35	9	13	2	9	0
Austin Chouinard	.370	.441	.529	189	39	70	4	46	0
Dane Tofteland	.345	.450	.562	354	83	122	15	103	3
Ty Dooley	.341	.455	.421	164	42	56	0	19	3
Carter Booth	.333	.422	.462	381	97	127	8	62	29
Gary Lora Gonzalez	.329	.402	.523	325	66	107	16	72	3
Hank Himrich	.317	.381	.433	104	27	33	1	21	3
Alex Adams	.311	.432	.403	119	29	37	2	14	0
Garrett Kueber	.311	.416	.412	296	68	92	5	63	6
Will Butcher	.281	.370	.400	160	27	45	4	32	2
Alonzo Zuniga	.267	.300	.307	75	3	20	0	10	0
Otto Jones	.250	.364	.411	56	12	14	1	10	3
Stephen Wilmer	.202	.315	.367	109	29	22	6	17	1

Name	W	L	ERA	G	SV	IP	H	BB	SO
Doug Olcese	1	0	1.10	7	0	16	13	10	7
Nate Varnier	2	0	3.00	7	0	12	16	5	5
Quinn Waterhouse	0	2	3.86	12	1	12	12	7	12
Caden Kratz	1	2	5.54	30	0	37	47	24	41
Wyatt Tucker	2	4	5.57	31	0	52	53	36	65
Nick Powers	8	4	5.61	19	0	101	116	48	76
Malik Binns	2	2	5.91	14	0	64	66	48	62
Cregg Scherrer	5	4	6.16	16	0	69	102	46	51
Hunter Bryan	2	4	6.18	37	10	44	47	19	57
Hunter Belton	2	1	6.29	5	0	24	27	20	13
Gabe White	0	1	6.57	21	0	25	21	28	35
Trey Morrill	6	3	6.75	43	8	48	61	35	53
Anthony Imhoff	2	0	7.33	5	0	23	29	16	23
Gabriel Courtright	1	1	7.42	7	0	13	14	14	4
Thomas Peltier	6	5	7.48	33	0	65	94	35	52
Caleb Strack	1	0	7.94	7	0	11	14	8	15
Evan Kowalski	1	2	8.36	15	1	66	103	35	49
John Walsh	2	1	9.24	12	0	13	20	10	8

U.S. PRO BASEBALL LEAGUE

East Division	W	L	PCT	GB
Westside Woolly Mammoths	26	18	.591	--
Utica Unicorns	22	22	.500	4
Eastside Diamond Hoppers	21	22	.488	4.5
Birmingham Bloomfield Beavers	18	25	.419	7.5

Playoffs—First Round: Birmingham defeated Utica. **Semifinals:** Eastside defeated Birmingham. **Finals:** Eastside defeated Westside 16-5 in championship game.

All-Star Team: C: Hank Dodson. 1B: Chase Maifield. 2B: Dante Morton. 3B: Jared Weber SS: Gio Ferraro. OF: Anthony Sharkas, Andrew Bergeron, Pablo Ruiz, Sam Schner. DH: Ryan Maka. UT: DJ Butler, Thomas Collins, Matt Piotrowski.

SP-SP: Pierce Banks, Guillermo Garcia Jr., Cam Vieaux. RP: Dyson Johnson, Ryan DuSang, Deion Walker.

Most Valuable Player: Anthony Sharkas. . **Pitcher of the Year:** Pierce Banks.

Team USA bounces back with pair of Cup wins

Team USA beat Japan 7-1 in the Gold Medal game of the 12U World Cup.

BY J.J. COOPER

In 2025, Team USA found its footing.

The last couple of years had been rough for the U.S. on the international stage. A nail-biting loss to Japan in the WBC championship game was quite explainable, as Japan's stars rose to the moment.

But Team USA also finished fourth in the 18U World Cup that same year, which was an event that the U.S. had dominated over the years. Team USA then didn't participate in the 15U America's qualifier and was therefore left out of the 15U World Cup. Team USA never participates in the 23U World Cup, so after dominating at all levels for much of the 2017-2019 stretch, Team USA had very few recent medals.

In 2025 that changed, as Team USA won gold in the two biggest tournaments of the year. At the 12U World Cup, Team USA was clearly the dominant team, their 8-1 record was the tournament best and the U.S. cruised past Japan 7-1 in the Gold Medal game.

Team USA outfielder Christopher Chikodroff hit .553/.563/.700 with 16 hits and 10 RBIs to earn MVP honors.

The story was very similar at the 18U World Cup. Team USA and Japan both went 8-1 and Japan had beaten the U.S. in the Super Round, but when they had a rematch in the Gold Medal Game, Team USA shut out Japan 2-0.

Team USA RHP/1B Coleman Borthwick was named the tournament MVP. He hit .300/.417.333 while also going 1-0, 0.00 in 10 innings over two starts.

Borthwick threw a three-hit complete game shutout in the gold medal game. He needed only 82 pitches, and after the U.S. took the lead in the fourth, he allowed only two baserunners the rest of the way. He retired the final seven batters in order.

A swinging bunt by Jaden Jackson drove in Brody Schumacher in the fourth for Team USA. Schumaker then drove in Aiden Ruiz in the fifth inning with a sacrifice fly.

The win was Team USA's 11th gold medal in 32 editions of the 18U World Cup. The U.S. has medaled 28 times.

Team USA also ensured that it will return to the 15U World Cup, as it swept the 15U Baseball Central and North American qualifier. Team USA outscored its opponents 42-6 across four games.

Team USA's pair of titles helps set the stage for

what should be a fascinating 2026. Team USA and Japan will be joined by 14 other teams battling for the World Baseball Classic title in venues across Asia and the U.S.

The commitments for players for the 2026 WBC seems to indicate that it should be the most talented lineups in WBC history. Aaron Judge, Cal Raleigh, Paul Skenes and Corbin Carroll are among early U.S. commitments, while Shohei Ohtani is expected to once again play for Samurai Japan.

The Women's World Cup group stage is also set to be held in 2026. One of the two groups will be played at Rockford, Ill.'s Rivets Stadium from July 22-26, 2026. That's significant because Rockford was the home of the Rockford Peaches of the All-American Girls Professional Baseball League. ■

Team USA shut out Japan 2-0 to win the 18U Baseball World Cup.

WBSC MEN'S RANKINGS

Rk.	Team	Points	2025 Points
1	Japan	6676	1071
2	Taiwan	5112	946
3	United States	4283	920
4	South Korea	4192	877
5	Venezuela	3612	0
6	Mexico	3605	177
7	Puerto Rico	3536	336
8	Panama	2899	423
9	Cuba	2858	408
10	Netherlands	2690	433
11	Australia	2591	354
12	Dominican Republic	2254	202
13	Colombia	1927	0
14	Italy	1729	625
15	Czech Republic	1532	592
16	Nicaragua	1455	45
17	China	1136	248
18	Germany	996	611
19	Great Britain	975	359
20	Canada	744	0

WBSC WOMEN'S RANKINGS

Rk.	Team	Points	2025 Points
1	Japan	6676	1071
2	Taiwan	5112	946
3	United States	4283	920
4	South Korea	4192	877
5	Venezuela	3612	0
6	Mexico	3605	177
7	Puerto Rico	3536	336
8	Panama	2899	423
9	Cuba	2858	408
10	Netherlands	2690	433
11	Australia	2591	354
12	Dominican Republic	2254	202
13	Colombia	1927	0
14	Italy	1729	625
15	Czech Republic	1532	592
16	Nicaragua	1455	45
17	China	1136	248
18	Germany	996	611
19	Great Britain	975	329
20	Canada	744	0

12U WORLD CUP

FINAL STANDINGS

Team	W	L	Team	W	L
United States	8	1	Cuba	5	3
Japan	6	3	Panama	3	4
South Korea	7	2	Australia	2	5
Taiwan	6	3	Czech Republic	2	6
Dominican Republic	4	4	Germany	1	6
Mexico	4	4	South Africa	0	7

Top six teams advanced to Super Round, while other six teams continued in consolation round.
Gold Medal Game: United States defeated Japan 7-1.
Bronze Medal Game: South Korea defeated Taiwan 2-0.
MVP: Christopher Chikodroff (United States).
All-World Team: P: Shotaro Hashimoto, Japan. C: Gaston Gaxiola, Mexico. 1B: Riku Sahashi, Japan. 2B: Jose Armenta, Mexico. SS: Cheng Hsieh, Taiwan. 3B: Kristian Valdez, USA. OF: Chris Chikodroff, USA; Cheng-en Hu, Taiwan; Sean Garcia, Cuba.

18U WORLD CUP

STANDINGS

Team	W	L	Team	W	L
United States	8	1	Cuba	5	3
Japan	8	1	Australia	4	4
Taiwan	6	3	Italy	3	5
South Korea	6	3	Germany	2	6
Puerto Rico	4	4	China	1	7
Panama	2	6	South Africa	1	7

Format: Top six teams advanced to Super Round, while the other six teams continued in consolation round.
Gold Medal Game: Team USA defeated Japan 2-0.
Bronze Medal Game: Taiwan defeated South Korea 3-2.
Most Valuable Player: Coleman Borthwick, United States.

18U ALL-WORLD TEAM

P: Gio Rojas, USA. **C:** Will Brick, USA. **1B:** Sheng-En Zen, Taiwan. **2B:** Ryota Okumura, Japan. **3B:** Grady Emerson, USA. **SS:** Aiden Ruiz, USA. **OF:** Jiho Park, South Korea; Luis Rivera, Panama; Kai-Qi Li, Taiwan. **DH:** Carlos Castillo, Panama.

12U LEADERS

BATTING LEADERS

PLAYER	TEAM	AVG	AB	R	H	2B	3B	HR	RBI	SB
Christopher Chikodroff	USA	.533	.563	.700	30	11	16	0	10	0
Nolan Hatch	USA	.522	.593	.522	23	12	12	0	4	1
Erick Claudio	DOM	.500	.538	.583	24	7	12	0	1	0
Yassith Concepcion	PAN	.500	.500	.864	22	7	11	2	8	0
Cheng-Chun Hsieh	TPE	.500	.643	.600	20	7	10	0	7	0
Qi-Sheng Chen	TPE	.481	.516	.593	27	6	13	0	10	0
Sean Garcia	CUB	.478	.520	1.043	23	8	11	4	10	0
Russell Mcgee	USA	.381	.440	.476	21	7	8	0	5	0
Jaxon Baker Spray	USA	.381	.458	.381	21	4	8	0	4	0
Luis Parra	DOM	.375	.483	.667	24	12	9	1	9	0
Cheng-En Hu	TPE	.370	.514	.741	27	12	10	3	11	0
Taiki Toyama	JPN	.370	.393	.667	27	9	10	2	7	0
Denis Rambousek	CZE	.364	.417	.500	22	4	8	0	4	0
Jeongwoo Ha	KOR	.348	.448	.391	23	6	8	0	6	1
Maykol Lluch	CUB	.333	.379	.381	21	4	7	0	8	0
Emiliano Felix	MEX	.304	.385	.391	23	5	7	0	2	0
Maxwell Montilla	PAN	.300	.440	.350	20	8	6	0	4	0
Sojiro Ohara	JPN	.286	.444	.333	21	8	6	0	4	0
David Štěpaník	CZE	.273	.385	.273	22	7	6	0	4	0
Cyuan-En Li	TPE	.261	.452	.304	23	7	6	0	4	0

PITCHING LEADERS

PLAYER	TEAM	W	L	ERA	G	IP	H	BB	SO
Shotaro Hashimoto	JPN	2	0	0.00	12	4	0	1	8
Denis Zamora	CUB	1	1	0.58	10	8	0	2	14
Barret Schell	USA	1	0	0.64	9	4	1	0	10
Duncan Mount	USA	1	0	0.75	8	4	0	6	13
Kristian Valadez	USA	1	0	0.82	7	1	0	6	8
Iker Calvillo	MEX	2	0	0.86	7	4	1	4	6
Ding-Xu Zhong	TPE	1	1	0.95	13	11	0	2	14
Yunseo Kwon	KOR	2	0	1.17	15	10	0	4	14
Brock Bliss	USA	3	1	1.29	9	6	0	2	7
Jaeseung Lee	KOR	2	0	1.59	11	7	0	3	13
Jeongan Seo	KOR	0	0	1.64	7	7	1	1	7
Yan Ramirez	CUB	1	1	2.18	11	11	0	4	7
Khaled Grajales	PAN	1	0	2.25	8	3	0	2	4
Craifer Montero	DOM	0	0	2.35	8	5	1	6	8
Xavier Garcia	CUB	1	0	2.45	7	6	0	4	4
Kosei Fukuyama	JPN	0	0	2.77	9	10	0	6	9
Felix Kaneko	GER	1	1	3.75	8	11	0	4	6
Jeroným Bartulík	CZE	1	1	3.91	8	5	0	7	10
Cheng-Chun Hsieh	TPE	1	1	3.91	8	11	0	5	7
Adriana Salabová	CZE	0	2	4.34	10	13	0	5	5
Preston Taylor	AUS	1	1	4.34	10	8	0	4	6
Eduardo Miranda	MEX	1	1	5.14	7	6	0	5	9

18U LEADERS

BATTING LEADERS

PLAYER	TEAM	AVG	AB	R	H	2B	3B	HR	RBI	SB
Hyuma Okabe	JPN	.400	.559	.440	25	7	10	0	6	7
Aiden Ruiz	USA	.379	.471	.379	29	5	11	0	6	2
Kazuki Takahata	JPN	.360	.346	.440	25	3	9	0	2	0
Alessandro Carrasquilla Romero	GER	.346	.452	.538	26	4	9	0	6	0
Grady Emerson	USA	.346	.526	.423	26	6	9	0	4	1
William Nicholas Hardy	AUS	.346	.406	.385	26	7	9	0	6	2
Yitong Li	CHN	.346	.370	.346	26	2	9	0	0	1
Kai-Qi Li	TPE	.320	.346	.400	25	2	8	0	8	0
Ryota Okumura	JPN	.320	.379	.400	25	4	8	0	7	0
Yota Abe	JPN	.308	.357	.346	26	6	8	0	3	2
Coleman Borthwick	USA	.300	.417	.333	30	6	9	0	5	1
Jaewon Oh	KOR	.286	.412	.429	28	6	8	0	6	3
Hikaru Tamenaga	JPN	.269	.367	.308	26	5	7	0	4	0
Anthony Murphy	USA	.259	.394	.296	27	8	7	0	2	6

PITCHING LEADERS

PLAYER	TEAM	W	L	ERA	G	IP	H	BB	SO
Edenis Cruz	CUB	2	0	0	16	6	6	10	0
Joel Kim	KOR	1	0	0	14	8	2	19	0
Shih-Chan Chen	TPE	0	0	0	13	5	0	8	0
Carson Bolemon	USA	1	0	0	11	2	2	17	0
Richard De Jesus	PUR	1	0	0	11	3	2	12	0
Giovanni Rojas	USA	2	0	0	11	5	3	13	0
Coleman Borthwick	USA	1	0	0	10	3	1	12	0
Keniel Miranda	PUR	2	0	0	9	3	5	13	0
Matthew Sharman	USA	2	0	0.7	10	6	2	8	0
Marlon Garcia	CUB	0	1	0.78	9	4	2	5	0

BASEBALL CHAMPIONS LEAGUE

SITE: MEXICO CITY, MEXICO

Team	W	L
Mexico Red Devils	4	0
Las Tunas	3	2
Kane County	2	1
Santa Maria	1	3
Chinandega	1	2
Florida	0	3

Championship: Mexico defeated Las Tunas 6-1
MVP: Robinson Cano, Mexico

MEXICO

Diablos Rojos Repeat As Champs

The Mexico Diablos Rojos (Red Devils) are clearly back. After winning its first title in a decade in 2024, the Diablos cruised a second-straight title (and their 18th overall).

Mexico had the best record in the regular season. They then went 12-2 in the postseason, sweeping through the quarterfinals and sweeping Jalisco in the Series Del Rey.

Jose Marmeolejos hit .667 with two home runs in the Series Del Rey, while Allen Cordoba hit .412 with two homers and Carlos Perez hit .412 with a pair of homers as well.

The Diablos outscored Jalisco 34-10 in the championship series. They trailed for only one inning in the entire series.

Mexico's Carlos Sepulveda led all hitters with a .395 batting average, while teammate Robinson Cano hit .372/.426/.573 as he went over 4,000 career hits across all levels. Aderlin Rodriguez had a dominating year as well, as he led all hitters with 35 home runs in just 89 games.

STANDINGS

Northern Division

Team	W	L	PCT	GB
Monterrey	55	37	.598	-
Tijuana	54	38	.587	1
Monclova	51	39	.567	3
Dos Laredos	51	42	.548	4.5
Laguna	50	42	.543	5
Jalisco	46	46	.500	9
Chihuahua	43	49	.467	12
Saltillo	43	49	.467	12
Durango	39	54	.419	16.5
Aguascalientes	37	53	.411	17

Southern Division

Team	W	L	PCT	GB
Mexico	63	25	.716	-
Oaxaca	53	39	.576	12
Campeche	47	43	.522	17
Puebla	44	47	.484	20.5
Veracruz	44	48	.478	21
Yucatan	42	50	.457	23
Tabasco	42	50	.457	23
Leon	40	50	.444	24
Queretaro	35	55	.389	29
Quintana Roo	35	58	.376	30.5

Playoffs—Quarterfinals: Jalisco defeated La Guaira 4-3, Mexico defeated Puebla 4-0, Campeche defeated Oaxaca 4-3 and Monterrey defeated Dos Laredos 4-0 in best-of-seven series. **Semifinals:** Jalisco defeated Monterey 4-1 and Mexico defeated Campeche 4-2 in best-of-seven series. **Finals:** Mexico defeated Jalisco 4-0 in best-of-seven series.

BATTING LEADERS

Player, Team	AVG	OBP	SLG	AB	R	H	HR	RBI	SB
Carlos Sepulveda, MEX	.395	.503	.515	233	78	92	2	38	12
Jose Gaitan, 2 Teams	.380	.459	.534	350	76	133	6	66	11
Alexi Amarista, OAX	.376	.426	.633	319	67	120	16	71	0
Juan Carlos Gamboa, MEX	.376	.440	.595	237	61	89	10	52	12
Brandon Villarreal, SLT	.373	.460	.459	279	57	104	2	30	8
Santiago Chavez, MVA	.373	.432	.594	217	46	81	10	41	2
Robinson Cano, MEX	.372	.426	.573	368	71	137	14	86	0
Andretty Cordero, AGS	.368	.407	.611	383	68	141	22	100	0
Connor Hollis, CAM	.366	.451	.457	322	72	118	4	30	17
Michael Wielansky, JAL	.365	.438	.483	230	55	84	3	47	27
Orlando Martinez, AGS	.364	.415	.689	225	60	82	16	48	2
Yadir Drake, YUC	.362	.431	.593	351	74	127	20	72	7
Harold Ramirez, LAR	.359	.412	.496	395	90	142	9	51	30
Yonathan Daza, OAX	.359	.414	.490	359	75	129	5	47	7
Reynaldo Rodriguez, OAX	.357	.405	.559	345	68	123	11	75	5
Alen Hanson, QRO	.355	.438	.625	301	75	107	18	58	6
Cristhian Adames, PUE	.354	.457	.566	274	63	97	11	63	3
Allen Cordoba, 2 Teams	.352	.437	.463	307	76	108	6	39	48
Carlos Perez, 2 Teams	.351	.405	.573	316	56	111	18	74	4
Estamy Urena, PUE	.350	.396	.537	337	67	118	14	77	6
Samar Leyva, PUE	.349	.423	.560	232	45	81	10	41	5
Magneuris Sierra, MVA	.348	.395	.403	293	44	102	1	29	13
Yurisbel Gracial, QRO	.348	.431	.567	247	48	86	15	49	0
Nicholas Torres, LAG	.347	.425	.730	326	82	113	27	79	6
Kelvin Gutierrez, QRO	.345	.418	.595	304	60	105	19	67	3
Jose Peraza, 2 Teams	.343	.366	.503	324	51	111	8	57	4
Sandber Pimentel, LEO	.341	.489	.616	302	61	103	21	84	1
Gustavo Nunez, MTY	.341	.410	.530	279	68	95	7	40	23
J.P. Martinez, SLT	.341	.461	.626	270	77	92	15	49	30
Yadiel Hernandez, LAR	.340	.444	.627	335	75	114	24	96	10
Johneshwy Fargas, JAL	.339	.389	.548	336	77	114	14	55	38
Julian Ornelas, MEX	.339	.420	.581	327	72	111	19	80	12
Eric Filia, QRO	.338	.448	.486	296	56	100	9	41	0
Aderlin Rodriguez, 2 Teams	.336	.369	.696	375	80	126	35	96	1
Angel Reyes, AGS	.336	.406	.644	351	75	118	31	79	15

PITCHING LEADERS

Player, Team	W	L	ERA	IP	H	HR	BB	SO
Julio Robaina, TIG	4	6	3.17	71	68	5	33	72
Carl Edwards, TIG	5	2	3.38	75	68	6	24	60
Tyler Danish, TAB	4	3	3.53	92	83	9	47	39
Daniel Mengden, LAR	8	5	4.00	90	96	9	33	67
Grant Gavin, LAG	4	3	4.11	70	60	10	29	64
Miller Hogan, CAM	5	5	4.31	88	87	13	19	74
David Reyes, 2 Teams	6	3	4.35	97	108	15	21	65
Yoanner Negrin, YUC	6	6	4.43	83	90	9	26	53
Wilmer Rios, MVA	10	6	4.49	104	108	18	22	81
Darel Torres, 2 Teams	7	9	4.50	90	76	11	58	84
Yoennis Yera, TAB	6	6	4.50	90	102	10	26	72
Junior Guerra, LAR	5	3	4.51	106	107	7	54	93
Travis Lakins, LAG	9	3	4.72	95	105	10	28	75
Domingo Acevedo, CAM	4	4	4.76	85	76	20	32	82
Jaime Barria, LAG	6	3	4.80	84	112	8	22	46
Manny Banuelos, MTY	7	4	4.83	82	84	6	34	74
Nate Antone, LAR	6	2	4.90	86	104	8	33	70
Christian Lindsay-Young, MVA	4	3	4.98	85	88	14	31	62
Dinelson Lamet, VER	7	5	5.01	88	74	11	44	88
Vladimir Gutierrez, PUE	5	3	5.03	88	102	9	32	66
Zach Mort, SLT	4	6	5.08	96	101	10	28	81
Alemao Hernandez, OAX	5	1	5.12	84	102	9	29	51
Devin Smeltzer, CHI	4	4	5.17	78	94	9	24	60
Nolan Kingham, MTY	6	4	5.21	85	97	9	35	55
Deylen Miley, AGS	7	7	5.26	91	91	12	59	100
Elniery Garcia, AGS	2	6	5.47	72	95	11	28	55
Zac Grotz, 2 Teams	5	6	5.51	85	98	11	36	80
Caleb Smith, CHI	3	9	5.52	93	87	21	60	95
Stephen Tarpley, MTY	4	4	5.74	78	92	11	28	66
Faustino Carrera, LEO	6	7	5.75	88	110	8	42	62

JAPAN

Fukuoka Extends NPB Dominance

In the 21st century, there is a new dominant team in the NPB.

The Fukuoka SoftBank Hawks won their eighth title in the past 15 seasons as Fukuoka blitzed the Hanshin Tigers needing just five games to claim the Japan Series.

Yuki Yanagita's two run homer in the eighth tied Game 5 while Ismai Nomura hit an 11th-inning homer to give the Hawks the 3-2 clinching win.

Yanagita had 10 hits in the Japan Series to win the outstanding player of the series award.

The Hawks had been shockingly upset in the 2024 Japan Series by Yokohama. This year, the erased any drama quickly. Hanshin won the opener 2-1, but Fukuoka won four straight after that.

The Hawks relied on their strong starting pitching all year with a trio of aces. Livan Moinelo (12-3, 1.46) was the ERA champ, but Koki Kitayama (9-5, 1.63) and Tomohisa Ohzeki (13-5, 1.66) were equally impressive.

The Japan Series loss capped a still excellent season for Hanshin. After snapping a 38-year title drought in 2023, Hanshin won its second pennant in three seasons, blitzing the rest of the Central League to win the league by 13 games.

Pitching has dominated the NPB in recent years, the Pacific League's hitters hit only .246/.307/.352 as a whole while the Central League was an ever worse .242/.302/.350. Only two hitters topped 30 home runs: Franmil Reyes and Teruaki Sato, who led the NPB with 40 homers.

After the season Munetaka Murakami and Tatsyua Imai both announced their intention to be posted. Imai is coming off of an excellent 10-5, 1.92 season that further established himself as one of the best pitchers in Japan.

For Murakami, the posting comes after an injury-plagued season. He hit 22 home runs in just 56 games but also struck out 28.5% of the time.

Among foreign players, Monielo, Reyes, Anthony Kay (9-6, 1.74), Luke Voit (.300/.384/.498) stood out.

Carter Stewart, a first round pick in the U.S. who opted to head to Japan after failing to come to agreement with the Braves, did not pitch in 2025. After a strong 2024 season, Stewart had a core abdominal muscle injury that sidelined him for the entirety of the season.

Trevor Bauer's return to the NPB did not go as he had hoped. He struggled, going 4-10, 4.51 in a league where the average ERA was 3.26.

The NPB's Central League has announced that it will adopt the designated hitter in 2027. That will mark the end of what was effectively the final holdout of a major league that didn't use the DH.

CENTRAL LEAGUE

Team	W	L	T	PCT	GB
Hanshin Tigers	85	54	4	.612	--
Yokohama DeNA BayStars	71	66	6	.518	13
Yomiuri Giants	70	69	4	.504	15
Chunichi Dragons	63	78	2	.447	23
Hiroshima Toyo Carp	59	79	5	.428	25.5
Tokyo Yakult Swallows	57	79	7	.419	26.5

Playoffs—First round: Yokohama defeated Yomiuri 2-0 in best-of-three series. **Climax Series:** Hanshin defeated Yokohama 4-0 in best-of-seven series. **Japan Series:** Fukuoka defeated Hanshin 4-1 in best-of-7 series.

CENTRAL LEAGUE BATTING LEADERS

Player, Team	AVG	OBP	SLG	AB	R	H	HR	RBI	SB
Kaito Kozono, Hiro.	.309	.365	.388	521	51	161	3	47	12
Yuta Izuguchi, Yomi.	.301	.362	.393	512	67	154	6	39	4
Yuki Okabayashi, Chun.	.291	.348	.382	578	71	168	5	35	17
Masayuki Kuwahara, DeNA	.284	.348	.382	398	48	113	6	27	10
Takumu Nakano, Hansh.	.282	.339	.328	531	65	150	0	30	19
Koji Chikamoto, Hansh.	.279	.348	.353	573	76	160	3	34	32
Teruaki Sato, Hansh.	.277	.345	.579	537	83	149	40	102	10
Naoki Yoshikawa, Yomi.	.277	.349	.351	404	33	112	3	32	8
Sandro Fabian, Hiro.	.276	.315	.427	539	60	149	17	65	2
Shota Morishita, Hansh.	.275	.350	.463	549	82	151	23	89	5
Keita Sano, DeNA	.274	.322	.406	525	47	144	15	70	0
Seiji Uebayashi, Chun.	.270	.303	.434	486	52	131	17	52	27
Trey Cabbage, Yomi.	.267	.331	.450	431	50	115	17	51	5
Yusuke Ohyama, Hansh.	.264	.363	.396	503	52	133	13	75	6
Souma Uchiyama, Tokyo	.262	.326	.385	423	50	111	8	48	8
Jason Vosler, Chun.	.261	.312	.429	452	37	118	13	58	0
Jose Osuna, Tokyo	.256	.307	.377	528	38	135	14	67	4
Shota Suekane, Hiro.	.243	.296	.373	437	40	106	11	62	2

OTHER NOTABLE HITTERS

Player, Team	AVG	OBP	SLG	AB	R	H	HR	RBI	SB
Kazuma Okamoto, Yomi.	.327	.416	.598	251	38	82	15	49	1
Yukinori Kishida, Yomi.	.293	.355	.417	266	25	78	8	39	0
Tatsuo Ebina, DeNA	.284	.355	.420	348	53	99	8	41	5
Shosei Nakamura, Hiro.	.282	.321	.439	344	43	97	9	33	2
Yudai Koga, Tokyo	.280	.319	.345	264	16	74	2	16	2
Toshiro Miyazaki, DeNA	.277	.335	.389	321	25	89	6	39	0
Shugo Maki, DeNA	.277	.325	.475	364	48	101	16	49	3
Naoki Yoshikawa, Yomi.	.277	.349	.351	404	33	112	3	32	8
Sandro Fabian, Hiro.	.276	.315	.427	539	60	149	17	65	2
Domingo Santana, Tokyo	.274	.358	.368	212	25	58	3	15	1
Munetaka Murakami, Tokyo	.273	.379	.663	187	34	51	22	47	4
Tyler Austin, DeNA	.269	.350	.484	219	35	59	11	28	0
Dayan Viciedo, DeNA	.259	.322	.383	81	8	21	2	6	0
Elehuris Montero, Hiro.	.255	.301	.391	368	23	94	9	41	0
Louis Okoye, Yomi.	.246	.291	.310	126	12	31	0	5	1
Ramon Hernandez, Hans.	.229	.257	.292	96	3	22	1	8	0
Orlando Calixte, Chun.	.227	.272	.307	176	13	40	1	14	1
Richard Sunagawa, Yomi.	.211	.269	.384	232	17	49	11	39	1
Michael Chavis, Chun.	.171	.267	.352	105	7	18	5	8	0

CENTRAL LEAGUE PITCHING LEADERS

Pitcher, Team	W	L	ERA	IP	H	HR	BB	SO
Hiroto Saiki, Hans.	12	6	1.55	157	123	6	44	122
Anthony Kay, DeNA	9	6	1.74	155	111	8	41	130
Iori Yamasaki, Yomi.	11	4	2.07	156	124	9	36	131
Shoki Murakami, Hans.	14	4	2.10	175	131	9	25	144
Katsuki Azuma, DeNA	14	8	2.19	160	142	15	26	123
Andre Jackson, DeNA	10	7	2.33	151	134	9	55	109
Masato Morishita, Hiro.	6	14	2.48	152	140	6	37	92
Takahiro Matsuba, Chun.	7	11	2.72	146	136	9	37	61
Hiroto Takahashi, Chun.	8	10	2.83	172	145	11	50	138
Hiroki Tokoda, Hiro.	9	12	3.15	171	158	13	42	102

OTHER NOTABLE PITCHERS

Pitcher, Team	W	L	ERA	IP	H	HR	BB	SO
Nash Walters, Chun.	0	0	0.00	5	3	0	5	5
Rowan Wick, Yoko.	4	1	0.84	43	25	0	11	49
Raidel Martinez, Yomi.	3	2	1.11	57	32	3	11	65
Jon Duplantier, Hans.	6	3	1.39	91	53	1	20	113
Foster Griffin, Yomi.	6	1	1.62	78	56	1	18	77
Rafael Dolis, Hans.	2	2	1.93	19	14	1	5	16
Nick Nelson, Hans.	2	1	1.93	33	29	2	9	25
Yunior Marte, Chun.	1	4	1.95	32	21	2	11	25
Yudai Ohno, Chun.	11	4	2.10	120	95	6	26	72
Takato Ihara, Hans.	5	7	2.29	110	95	4	25	81
Yuji Akahoshi, Yomi.	6	9	2.68	121	110	12	19	88
Takahiro Matsuba, Chun.	7	11	2.72	146	136	9	37	61
Kojiro Yoshimura, Tokyo	8	6	3.05	130	132	14	27	85
Kyle Keller, Yomi.	1	1	3.11	46	27	5	22	49
Hiroki Tokoda, Hiro.	9	12	3.15	171	158	13	42	102
Humberto Mejia, Chun.	2	2	3.35	46	35	6	14	28
Taylor Hearn, Hiro.	1	2	3.35	51	54	3	17	54
Daichi Ohsera, Hiro.	7	9	3.48	135	131	11	38	88
Kyle Muller, Chun.	4	9	3.54	102	102	7	28	86
Shohei Mori, Hiro.	7	8	3.55	132	129	14	32	101
Haruto Inoue, Yomi.	4	8	3.70	107	115	15	19	100
Johan Dominguez, Hiro.	1	1	3.71	27	18	2	17	20
Pedro Avila, Tokyo	7	8	4.04	82	70	4	30	61
Shosei Togo, Yomi.	8	9	4.14	111	124	8	46	87
Mike Baumann, Tokyo	0	2	4.20	15	17	3	12	19
Peter Lambert, Tokyo	3	11	4.26	116	123	11	52	104
Trevor Bauer, Yoko.	4	10	4.51	134	135	15	48	119
Jeremy Beasley, Hans.	1	3	4.60	29	35	0	12	25
Javy Guerra, Hans.	0	1	13.50	5	10	0	5	4

PACIFIC LEAGUE

Team	W	L	T	PCT	GB
Fukuoka SoftBank Hawks	87	52	4	.626	—
Hokkaido Nippon-Ham Fighters	83	57	3	.593	4.5
Orix Buffaloes	74	66	3	.529	13.5
Tokoku Rakuten Golden Eagles	67	74	2	.475	21
Saitama Seibu Liomns	63	77	3	.450	24.5
Chiba Lotte Marines	56	84	3	.400	31.5

Playoffs: First round: Hokkaido defeated Orix 2-0 in best-of-three series. **Climax Series:** Fukuoka defeated Hokkaido 4-3 in best-of-seven series. **Japan Series:** Fukuoka defeated Hanshin 4-1 in best-of-7 series..

PACIFIC LEAGUE BATTING LEADERS

Player, Team	AVG	OBP	SLG	AB	R	H	HR	RBI	SB
Taisei Makihara, Fuku.	.304	.317	.409	418	44	127	5	49	12
Tatsuru Yanagimachi, Fuku.	.292	.384	.376	442	54	129	6	50	2
Keita Nakagawa, Orix	.284	.314	.432	433	54	123	12	53	10
Ryo Ohta, Orix	.283	.337	.373	448	42	127	10	52	0
Itsuki Murabayashi, Toho.	.281	.320	.326	513	41	144	3	51	6
Misho Nishikawa, C.L.	.281	.318	.381	417	42	117	3	37	1
Franmil Reyes, Hokk.	.277	.347	.515	476	62	132	32	90	0
Tyler Nevin, Seibu	.277	.346	.448	509	51	141	21	63	2
Kotaro Kiyomiya, Hokk.	.272	.329	.392	525	63	143	12	65	8
Kyota Fujiwara, C.L.	.271	.335	.359	409	38	111	4	24	15
Daisuke Nakashima, Toho.	.265	.294	.351	462	51	123	6	31	22
Manaya Nishikawa, Seibu	.264	.318	.387	507	64	134	10	38	25
Rui Muneyama, Toho.	.260	.289	.340	430	32	112	3	27	7
Kotaro Kurebayashi, Orix	.260	.321	.383	400	36	104	9	43	1
Yutaro Sugimoto, Orix	.259	.332	.426	401	48	104	16	53	1
Seiya Watanabe, Seibu	.259	.299	.395	425	42	110	12	43	2
Ryusei Terachi, C.L.	.256	.299	.331	414	33	106	5	33	0
Taishi Hirooka, Orix	.254	.317	.348	402	43	102	7	34	9
Yuma Tongu, Orix	.249	.316	.374	473	41	118	13	54	1
Chusei Mannami, Hokk.	.229	.302	.431	420	48	96	20	56	3
Hotaka Yamakawa, Fuku.	.226	.300	.402	443	45	100	23	62	0
Shinya Hasegawa, Seibu	.225	.286	.325	400	42	90	6	36	9

OTHER NOTABLE HITTERS

Player, Team	AVG	OBP	SLG	AB	R	H	HR	RBI	SB
Ryoma Nishikawa, Orix	.310	.343	.413	387	29	120	5	40	4
Kensuke Kondoh, Fuku.	.301	.410	.492	256	28	77	10	41	0
Luke Voit, Toho.	.300	.384	.498	243	29	73	13	39	0
Fumiya Kurokawa, Toho.	.299	.372	.372	301	32	90	4	33	1
Yuya Gunji, Hokk.	.297	.379	.420	364	46	108	10	42	0
Masahiro Nishino, Orix	.287	.333	.443	230	27	66	7	35	0
Akito Takabe, C.L.	.286	.314	.384	357	49	102	2	34	20
Ukyo Shuto, Fuku.	.286	.357	.354	384	45	110	3	36	35
Shun Mizutani, Hokk.	.277	.322	.473	296	45	82	12	41	6
Neftali Soto, C.L.	.230	.302	.391	330	31	76	13	44	0
Oscar Gonzalez, Toho.	.229	.250	.323	201	18	46	4	19	0
Jordan Diaz, Orix	.228	.290	.307	127	6	29	2	6	0
Leandro Cedeno, Seibu	.228	.280	.357	224	13	51	7	26	0
Jeter Downs, Fuku.	.226	.315	.418	146	21	33	4	18	4
Jonathan Davis, Seibu	.204	.313	.310	113	8	23	3	9	0
Gregory Polanco, C.L.	.201	.273	.331	139	13	28	5	13	0

PACIFIC LEAGUE PITCHING LEADERS

Pitcher, Team	W	L	ERA	IP	H	HR	BB	SO
Livan Moinelo, Fuku.	12	3	1.46	167	112	10	42	172
Koki Kitayama, Fuku.	9	5	1.63	149	112	7	45	143
Tomohisa Ohzeki, Fuku.	13	5	1.66	147	107	11	35	97
Tatsuya Imai, Seibu	10	5	1.92	164	101	6	45	178
Hiroya Miyagi, Orix	7	3	2.39	150	135	6	30	165
Allen Kuri, Orix	11	8	2.41	164	155	7	48	114
Hiromi Itoh, Hokk.	14	8	2.52	197	179	15	29	195
Chihiro Sumida, Seibu	10	10	2.59	160	142	12	34	149
Atsuki Taneichi, Hokk.	9	8	2.63	161	134	13	50	161
Naoyuki Uwasawa, Fuku.	12	6	2.74	145	113	12	36	115
Kohei Arihara, Fuku.	14	9	3.03	175	167	10	41	121
Kona Takahashi, Seibu	8	9	3.04	148	141	10	41	88
Kazuya Ojima, C.L.	8	10	3.72	145	144	20	54	92

OTHER NOTABLE PITCHERS

Pitcher, Team	W	L	ERA	IP	H	HR	BB	SO
Emmanuel Ramirez, Seibu	1	0	1.01	27	16	1	12	28
Trey Wingenter, Seibu	1	4	1.74	47	26	2	20	69
Kota Tatsu, Hokk.	8	2	2.09	108	80	7	20	94
Spencer Howard, Toho.	5	1	2.22	49	42	1	11	36
Sachiya Yamasaki, Hokk.	7	5	2.27	111	105	11	18	51
Andres Machado, Orix	3	6	2.28	55	50	0	16	68
Nao Higashihama, Fuku.	4	2	2.51	32	30	2	5	19
Yutaro Watanabe, Seibu	7	9	2.69	134	127	9	38	81
Anderson Espinoza, Orix	5	8	2.98	130	131	3	47	119
Daiki Tajima, Orix	7	7	3.13	106	106	8	24	57
Luis Perdomo, Orix	2	4	3.17	48	50	1	16	27
Masaru Fujii, Toho.	6	7	3.20	110	121	9	43	58
Darwinzon Hernandez, Fuku.	1	2	3.35	40	34	1	12	43
Takayuki Katoh, Hokk.	9	6	3.40	119	125	15	13	56
Tatsuki Kojo, Toho.	7	7	3.70	107	118	8	27	76
Bryan Sammons, C.L.	5	5	3.78	86	75	12	40	73
Aneurys Zabala, Hokk.	0	0	3.86	2	1	0	1	2
Austin Voth, C.L.	3	9	3.96	125	129	8	28	92
Ryuhei Sotani, Orix	8	8	4.01	114	125	7	25	102
Roberto Osuna, Fuku.	3	1	4.15	26	23	2	6	16
Takayuki Kishi, Toho.	6	6	4.38	109	125	10	22	55
Miguel Yajure, Toho.	2	6	4.48	64	80	1	23	30
Shuta Ishikawa, C.L.	4	7	4.62	103	110	11	37	56
Drew VerHagen, Hokk.	3	3	6.08	27	28	4	6	22
Tayron Guerrero, C.L.	1	3	6.41	20	22	4	8	15
Nik Turley, Toho.	0	0	6.75	1	2	0	1	1

NETHERLANDS

Neptunus Rolls

Curaçao Neptunus had made winning almost routine in recent years.

For the second consecutive season, Neptunus won the Holland Series. It was the team's sixth Holland Series title since 2015.

The team's regular season dominance is even more noteworthy. Neptunus has had the best record in the regular season for six straight seasons.

Neptunus ace Tom De Block was named the MVP of the Holland Series. He threw a 10-inning complete game shutout in the Game 1 opener, and followed it up by throwing a complete-game three-hitter, allowing one run in the 3-1 Game 6 clincher.

The Netherlands also won the European Baseball Championships.

STANDINGS

Team	W	L	T	PCT	GB
Curaçao Neptunus	44	7	0	.863	--
HCAW	37	14	0	.725	7
Oosterhout Twins	26	20	1	.565	13.5
Amsterdam Pirates	24	23	0	.511	18
Hoofddorp Pioniers	23	29	1	.442	22.5
Kinheim	20	32	0	.385	24.5
UVV	15	34	2	.306	28
RCH-Pinguins	10	40	0	.200	33.5

Playoffs—Semifinals: Neptunus defeated Amsterdam 3-0 and HCAW defeated Oosterhout 3-0 in best-of-five series. **Holland Series:** Neptunus defeated HCAW 4-2 in best-of-seven series.

BATTING LEADERS

Player, Team	AVG	OBP	SLG	AB	R	H	HR	RBI	SB
Marnix Ruben, HCA	.411	.452	.596	141	40	58	2	29	18
Delano Selassa, HCA	.391	.410	.562	169	43	66	3	39	17
Kevin Dirksen, NEP	.357	.500	.464	112	26	40	0	29	1
Tommy Van De Sanden, AMS	.355	.464	.454	141	28	50	2	28	7
Alex Madera, HCA	.349	.396	.396	149	29	52	0	24	13
Railison Bentura, TWI	.342	.452	.432	146	25	50	0	26	10
Luca Van Gorkum, PIO	.336	.446	.414	140	23	47	0	36	12
Christian Diaz, NEP	.333	.418	.424	144	34	48	1	33	3
Thijmen Peters, TWI	.331	.399	.386	127	21	42	1	23	7
Dwayne Kemp, NEP	.331	.374	.488	166	35	55	2	25	20
Stijn Van Der Meer, NEP	.328	.444	.423	137	35	45	1	20	8
Darryl Collins, NEP	.322	.399	.428	152	30	49	2	31	7
Jair Van Borkulo, HCA	.320	.459	.475	122	27	39	3	22	6
Drew Janssen, NEP	.320	.405	.469	147	27	47	3	30	4
Jules Cremer, UVV	.307	.376	.417	127	24	39	1	24	9

PITCHING LEADERS

Player, Team	W	L	ERA	IP	H	HR	BB	SO
Tom De Blok, NEP	11	0	0.78	81	53	1	18	57
Nelmerson Angela, HCA	8	4	1.12	88	46	0	27	86
Dennis Burgersdijk, HCA	9	1	1.29	70	61	1	11	52
Shairon Martis, NEP	12	2	1.55	93	70	0	9	70
Rick Rizvić, HCA	6	3	1.79	60	54	3	28	45
Noah Zavolas, PIO	7	2	2.23	61	46	0	22	61
Misja Harcksen, TWI	8	2	2.99	81	71	0	24	74
Wyatt Lankford, TWI	6	3	3.00	81	63	1	43	88
Martijn Schoonderwoerd, AMS	4	4	3.00	63	54	3	19	68
Tijn Fredrikze, KIN	2	9	3.90	60	65	0	27	76

ITALY

San Marino Wins SerieA

When the SerieA season begins, it's reasonable to expect to see San Marino in the Italian Series. It's happened for eight straight seasons. San Marino once again won the title in 2025, and this year they got some revenge while doing so. They knocked off Parma, which had beaten them for the title in 2024.

Gabriel Lino went 3-for-4 with a double and a triple to drive in two runs in San Marino's clinching Game 5 win. Ortwin Pieternella was 8-for-12 (.667) for the series.

In the regular season, Senago's Wanner Mateo hit .507/.584/.571 in 20 games. Parma's Manuel Geraldo hit a league-best eight homers while Grosseto's Brandon McIlwain hit six while hitting .344/.410/.656.

STANDINGS

Group A	W	L	T	PCT	GB
Parma	22	6	0	.786	0
San Marino	19	9	0	.679	3
Fortitudo Bologna	16	12	0	.571	6
Hotsand Macerata	15	13	0	.536	7
Nettuno	14	14	0	.500	8
Big Mat Grosseto	10	18	0	.357	12
BBC Grosseto	9	19	0	.321	13
Reggio Emilia	7	21	0	.250	15

Group B	W	L	T	PCT	GB
Codogno	14	6	0	.700	0
Milano	12	8	0	.600	2
Senago	12	8	0	.600	2
Settimo	9	11	0	.450	5
Reale Mutua	8	12	0	.400	6
Cagliari	5	17	0	.227	10

Group C	W	L	T	PCT	GB
Ronchi	14	6	0	.700	0
Verona	11	9	0	.550	3
Buttrio	10	10	0	.500	4
Rovigo	9	11	0	.450	5
Padova	8	12	0	.400	6
Junior Alpina	8	14	0	.364	7

Group D	W	L	T	PCT	GB
Crocetta	11	1	0	.917	0
Collecchio	9	3	0	.750	2
Poviglio	3	9	0	.250	8
Oltretorrente	1	11	0	.083	10
Sicily Red Sox	0	0	0	.000	5

Group E	W	L	T	PCT	GB
Modena	13	6	0	.684	0
Athletics Bologna	13	7	0	.650	0.5
Fiorentina	11	9	0	.550	2.5
New Rimini	10	10	0	.500	3.5
Godo	7	13	0	.350	6.5
Pedrera	5	14	0	.263	8

Playoffs—Semifinals: Parma defeated Macerata 3-1 and San Marino defeated Bologna 3-1 in best-of-7 series **Finals**: San Marino defeated Parma 3-1 in best-of-5 series.

SOUTH KOREA

LG Twins Claim KBO Series

The LG Twins are champions again. For the second time in three years, the Twins cruised past Hanwha in the Korea Series. Only a six-run Hanwha comeback in Game 3 kept the Twins from a sweep.

This is the Twins' fourt title overall. Kim Hyun-Soo was named the Korea Series MVP. He has the go-ahead RBI hit in Game 4, and he hit .529 overall in the series with 8 RBIS in five games.

Kim also became the all-time KBO postseason hits leader. He has a record 105 postseason hits and a record 149 total bases. His 63 RBIs and 51 walks also are KBO postseason records.

Cody Ponce

Cody Ponce was the league's pitching star, as he authored one of the most dominant seasons in recent memory. Ponce led the league in wins, ERA and a league-record 245 strikeouts, going an exceptional 17-1, 1.89.

Ponce was unanimously named the Choi Dong-Won Award winner as the league's best pitcher.

Ponce worked at least five innings in every outing of his season. He struck out a KBO record 18 in a May 17 win over SSG.

Ponce shut down Samsung in a deciding Game 5 of the playoff final, earning Hanwha a spot in the Korea Series.

Ponce was not the only import to have a breakout season. Lewin Diaz, the former Twins and Marlins first baseman, hit 50 home runs, the most ever by a foreigner in the KBO. He led the league in slugging (.644) and OPS (1.025). His 158 RBIs were a league record.

Drew Anderson, the former Phillies righthander, finished second in the league in strikeouts (245) while going 12-7, 2.25.

Catcher Yang Eu Ji won his second batting title. Third baseman Choi Jeong became the first player to hit 500 career home runs.

The KBO's popularity continues to grow. The league drew 12,312,519 fans, which was an attendance record for a second consecutive season.

Outfielder Ahn Hyun Min was the standout rookie, as he finished second in the league with s .334 batting average to go with a league-best .448 on-base percentage.

STANDINGS

Team	W	L	T	PCT	GB
LG Twins	85	56	3	.603	0
Hanwha Eagles	83	57	4	.593	1.5
SSG Landers	75	65	4	.536	9.5
Samsung Lions	74	68	2	.521	11.5
NC Dinos	71	67	6	.514	12.5
KT Wiz	71	68	5	.511	13
Lotte Giants	66	72	6	.478	17.5
Kia Tigers	65	75	4	.464	19.5
Doosan Bears	61	77	6	.442	22.5
Kiwoom Heroes	47	93	4	.336	37.5

Playoffs—Wild Card: Samsung defeated NC Dinos 2-1 in best-of-3 series. **Semifinal Series:** Samsung defeated SSG 3-1 in best-of-five series. **Playoff Final:** Hanwha defeated Samsung 3-2 in best-of-5 series. **Korea Series:** LG Twins defeated Hanwha 4-1 in best-of-7 series.

INDVIDUAL BATTING LEADERS

Player, Team	AVG	OBP	SLG	AB	R	H	HR	RBI	SB
Yang Eui Ji, Doosan	.337	.406	.533	454	56	153	20	89	4
Ahn Hyun Min, KT	.334	.448	.570	395	72	132	22	80	7
Kim Seong Yoon, Samsung	.331	.419	.474	456	92	151	6	61	26
Victor Reyes, Lotte	.326	.386	.475	573	75	187	13	107	7
Moon Hyun Bin, Hanwha	.320	.370	.453	528	71	169	12	80	17
Koo Ja Wook, Samsung	.319	.402	.516	529	106	169	19	96	4
Song Sung Mun, Kiwoom	.315	.387	.530	574	103	181	26	90	25
Lewin Diaz, Samsung	.314	.381	.644	551	93	173	50	158	1
Shin Min Jae, LG	.313	.395	.382	463	87	145	1	61	15
Dean Austin, LG	.313	.393	.595	425	82	133	31	95	3
Choi Hyoung Woo, Kia	.307	.399	.529	469	74	144	24	86	1
Moon Sung Ju, LG	.305	.375	.375	475	57	145	3	70	4
Park Min Woo, NC	.302	.384	.426	404	64	122	3	67	28
Jake Cave, Doosan	.299	.351	.463	538	72	161	16	87	17
Kim Hyun Soo, LG	.298	.384	.422	483	66	144	12	90	4
Jeon Jun Woo, Lotte	.293	.369	.420	410	50	120	8	70	2
Kim Ju Won, NC	.289	.379	.451	539	98	156	15	65	44
Chae Eun Seong, Hanwha	.288	.347	.467	480	54	138	19	88	1
Park Chan Ho, Kia	.287	.363	.359	516	75	148	5	42	27
Choi Ji Hoon, SSG	.284	.342	.371	517	66	147	7	45	28

INDIVIDUAL PITCHING LEADERS

Player	W	L	ERA	IP	H	HR	BB	SO
Cody Ponce, Hanwha	17	1	1.89	181	128	10	41	252
James Naile, Kia	8	4	2.25	164	135	6	41	152
Drew Anderson, SSG	12	7	2.25	172	121	13	51	245
Ariel Jurado, Samsung	15	8	2.60	197	177	17	36	142
Zach Logue, Doosan	10	8	2.81	176	146	8	39	156
Ryan Weiss, Hanwha	16	5	2.87	179	127	13	56	207
Im Chan Kyu, LG	11	7	3.03	160	163	9	40	107
Won Tae In, Samsung	12	4	3.24	167	157	20	27	108
Ko Young Pyo, KT	11	8	3.30	161	170	10	30	154
So Hyeong Jun, KT	10	7	3.30	147	155	6	29	123
Yonny Chirinos, LG	13	6	3.31	177	173	5	36	137
Son Ju Young, LG	11	6	3.41	153	153	8	49	132
Thompson Riley, NC	17	7	3.45	172	136	18	56	216
Song Seung Ki, LG	11	6	3.50	144	149	15	49	125
Adam Oller, Kia	11	7	3.62	149	125	8	47	169
Enmanuel De Jesus, KT	9	9	3.96	164	173	17	44	165
Cole Irvin, Doosan	8	12	4.48	145	142	9	79	128
Logan Allen, NC	7	12	4.53	173	180	18	67	149
Park Se Woong, Lotte	11	13	4.93	161	183	15	54	156
Ha Yeong Min, Kiwoom	7	14	4.99	153	169	13	41	134

TAIWAN

Fernandez Stars In CPBL

The rules of the CPBL playoffs are heavily favored toward regular season winners. But that wasn't enough to slow down the Rakuten Monkeys, who had advanced as a wild card.

Rakuten won three straight elimination games in the semifinals and then cruised past the CTBC Brothers Elephant to win the Taiwan Series. The last time a wild card team won the title was 2007.

It was the eighth Taiwan Series title for the Monkeys.

It was quite the effort for the Monkeys to get to the Series. They entered the semifinal one game down thanks to the ruls that gave the Uni-Lions a one-game advantage because they won the first half title. Uni-President then won the opening Game 2 of the series, and led in Game 3.

Pedro Fernandez

But the Monkeys rallied to win Game 3, tied the series with a 9-3 win in Game 4 and then got an RBI single from Lin Li in the 10th inning to win Game 5 4-3.

Pedro Fernandez was named the Taiwan Series MVP. He allowed just one run in 13 innings in two starts in the chamoionship series. He struck out five and threw seven scoreless in his first start of the series, then followed it up by striking out 10 while allowing one run in six innings in Game 4.

Fernandez was also named the regular seasom MVP, becoming the first foreign-born player to claim the award. Fernandez is only the fourth player to win both the regular season MVP and the Taiwan Series MVP in the same season.

In his second year in the league, Fernandez led the league with 168 strikeouts and 15 wins while finishing fourth in ERA (2.01).

Rakuten manager Kenji Fuukubo was named Manager of the Year after winning the title, but the team's ownership surprisingly announced soon afterward that he would not return for the 2026 season.

Lin Shi Xiang was named the rookie of the year, as the TSG Hawks closer had a 2.76 ERA over 56 appearances.

The CPBL is planning to adopt an ABS challenge system for balls and strikes beginning in 2027. The league will experiment with the system in 2026 in preparation for the rollout in 2027.

STANDINGS

First Half	W	L	T	GB
Uni-Preisdent Lions	36	24	.600	
Brothers Elephant	34	26	.567	2
Rakuten Monkeys	30	30	.500	6
TSG Hawks	30	30	.500	6
Wei Chuan Dragons	29	31	.483	7
Fubon Guardians	21	39	.350	15

Second Half	W	L	PCT	GB
Brothers Elephant	36	24	.600	
Rakuten Monkeys	32	27	.542	3.5
Uni-Preisdent Lions	30	30	.500	6
TSG Hawks	29	29	.500	6
Wei Chuan Dragons	26	33	.441	9.5
Fubon Guardians	25	35	.417	11

Playoffs—Semifinals: Monkeys defeated Lions 3-2 in best-of-5 series. **Taiwan Series:** Monkeys defeated the Elephants 4-1 in best-of-seven series.

INDIVIDUAL BATTING LEADERS

Player, Team	AVG	AB	R	H	2B	3B	HR	RBI	SB
Wu Nien Ting, TSG	.328	.400	.407	332	49	109	2	50	5
Lin An Ko, U-Lions	.318	.397	.603	330	65	105	23	73	4
Chen Chen Wei, Monkeys	.307	.366	.411	433	72	133	4	37	27
Lin Hung Yu, Monkeys	.307	.345	.415	388	43	119	9	60	0
Steven Moya, TSG	.305	.387	.589	331	59	101	25	68	0
Li Kai Wei, Dragons	.300	.388	.338	447	65	134	0	40	28
Lin Chih Ping, Monkeys	.294	.343	.368	361	32	106	2	51	3
Chu Yu Hsien, Dragons	.293	.355	.476	338	36	99	15	61	2
Hsu Chi Hung, Brothers	.292	.390	.525	343	58	100	19	77	0
Wang Po Hsuan, TSG	.284	.348	.351	436	57	124	3	40	21
Kuo Tian Shin, Dragons	.280	.334	.351	436	58	122	4	45	17
Lin Chia Wei, U-Lions	.275	.322	.408	461	60	127	6	50	11
Kungkuan Giljegiljaw, Dragons	.274	.337	.525	453	54	124	24	86	4
Tseng Tzu Yu, TSG	.273	.319	.323	461	60	126	0	37	6
Chiang Kun Yu, Brothers	.272	.357	.317	382	61	104	1	44	7
Pan Chieh Kai, U-Lions	.266	.332	.336	354	41	94	2	27	17
Liu Ji Hong, Dragons	.258	.293	.372	414	45	107	10	51	1
Chiu Chih Cheng, U-Lions	.258	.340	.400	345	49	89	6	30	14
Sung Cheng Jui, Brothers	.257	.302	.398	412	44	106	12	62	17
Jhang Jhao Yuan, TSG	.250	.315	.376	348	35	87	10	45	0
Yueh Tung Hua, Brothers	.239	.318	.299	355	43	85	1	37	11
Wang Po Jung, Tsg	.239	.307	.316	389	33	93	4	57	10
Chen Tzu Hao, Dragons	.237	.347	.310	342	32	81	4	34	3

INDIVIDUAL PITCHING LEADERS

Player, Team	W	L	ERA	IP	H	HR	BB	SO
Nivaldo Rodriguez, Brot.	11	7	1.84	156	128	3	35	142
Bradin Hagens, TSG	13	3	1.89	152	136	5	38	109
Felix Pena, U-Lions	10	3	1.91	127	101	4	34	95
Pedro Fernandez, Monk.	15	2	2.01	170	123	6	32	168
Eric Stout, TSG	11	4	2.23	141	124	9	30	124
Marcelo Martinez, Monk.	13	8	2.51	158	140	6	31	98
Andrew Gagnon, Drag.	11	5	2.77	146	132	6	40	120
Shawn Morimando, Guard.	10	10	2.98	139	130	6	44	111
Humberto Castellanos, Brot.	10	7	3.15	123	135	8	34	96
Yohander Mendez, U-Lions	10	6	3.51	121	118	4	50	97
Roenis Elias, Guard.	8	12	3.75	144	149	7	33	114
Brock Dykxhoorn, U-Lions	7	9	4.13	122	136	8	24	89

CUBA

Serie Nacional Swaps Sked

After moving the Serie Nacional season to the summer in 2022, the league moved back to its more traditional winter ball schedule in 2025, beginning in September and wrapping up in January.

That meant that there was a much longer than normal gap between the Serie Nacional seasons.

The Cuban Elite League has seen its scheduled swapped as well to fill the void. The CEL had become the winter ball league, bringing the best players together to play for six teams. The goal of the league was to help centralize the talent, which has been diminished by players leaving the country to play in the U.S., Japan and elsewhere.

Now it's the summer ball league, filling the void left by moving the Serie Nacional back to the winter.

Ciego de Avila, led by manager Danny Miranda, won its first Elite League title in 2025 sweeping Las Tunas in the championship series after going 4-1 in the semifinals. Ciego de Avila also had the best record in the regular season.

The Tigers were the third different champion in the three years of the CEL. In fact, no team has yet managed to make it the championship series twice.

STANDINGS

Team	W	L	PCT	GB
Ciego De Avila	24	16	.600	-
Las Tunas	23	17	.575	1
Santiago de Cuba	20	20	.500	4
Industriales	20	20	.500	4
Granma	17	23	.425	7
Pinar del Rio	16	24	.400	8

Playoffs: Semifinals: Ciego de Avila defeated Industriales 4-1, Las Tunas defeated Santiago de Cuba 4-2 in best-of-7 series. **Finals:** Ciego de Avila defeated Las Tunas 4-0 in best-of-7 series.

BATTING LEADERS

Player, Team	AVG	AB	R	H	2B	3B	HR	RBI
Jeison Martinez, SCU	.415	.497	.577	130	45	54	3	24	3
William Saavedra, PRI	.411	.455	.680	197	37	81	14	55	0
Yosvani Alarcon, LTU	.396	.456	.638	265	65	105	12	69	4
Raico Santos, GRA	.394	.494	.574	188	44	74	7	40	4
Lázaro Emilio Blanco, PRI	.383	.466	.452	115	17	44	1	20	1
Yasiel Agete, PRI	.378	.460	.547	148	35	56	5	25	4
Alfredo Despaigne, GRA	.378	.575	.744	172	55	65	20	59	0
Jorge Yoan Rojas, PRI	.372	.420	.575	226	41	84	9	52	3
Héctor Adriel Labrada, CAV	.366	.466	.519	183	34	67	4	49	5
Osvaldo Abreu, GRA	.360	.436	.498	267	61	96	4	34	1
Leonel Moas, LTU	.358	.427	.568	95	26	34	3	21	1
Yosvani Peñalver, IND	.358	.457	.415	106	22	38	0	12	3
Leonardo Adrián Alarcón, GRA	.358	.466	.450	109	38	39	1	20	0
Alexei Ramírez, PRI	.357	.461	.580	269	59	96	14	70	2
Luis Vicente Mateo, LTU	.354	.414	.472	127	22	45	2	21	4
Guillermo José Avilés, GRA	.354	.470	.559	254	56	90	11	69	0
Yudier Rondón, PRI	.351	.437	.494	231	53	81	2	33	2
Dennis Laza, IND	.350	.463	.552	143	34	50	6	24	7
Juan Carlos Arencibia, PRI	.348	.404	.396	250	69	87	0	33	14
Yulieski Miguel Remón, GRA	.348	.408	.465	282	47	98	3	59	5
Yasiel Santoya, IND	.347	.461	.477	239	45	83	4	44	0
Roberto Suliban Baldoquín, LTU	.346	.464	.622	185	48	64	10	41	6
Yoelquis Guibert, SCU	.343	.492	.626	230	63	79	15	68	15
Yordanys Alarcón, LTU	.340	.370	.445	265	29	90	4	48	2
Denis Peña, LTU	.338	.408	.579	240	47	81	13	55	1
Ariel Hechavarría, IND	.337	.409	.535	187	41	63	9	34	8
Francisco J. Martínez, SCU	.337	.441	.446	285	62	96	3	37	22
Rafael Ramon Viñales, LTU	.336	.450	.642	232	50	78	18	68	0
Oscar Valdés, IND	.336	.463	.536	235	46	79	11	57	4
Fernando De La Paz, CAV	.335	.452	.441	188	39	63	4	27	1
Hubert Sánchez, GRA	.335	.389	.476	191	34	64	6	38	1
Darian Palma, GRA	.335	.388	.481	233	42	78	6	47	2
Ronaldo Castillo, CAV	.332	.391	.445	211	35	70	5	31	1
Yaser Julio González, PRI	.328	.373	.577	265	47	87	17	60	3
Yoasán Guillén, CAV	.327	.359	.445	110	16	36	0	12	3
Rubén Valdés, CAV	.327	.373	.504	284	46	93	11	60	0
Eduardo A. García, SCU	.324	.399	.641	142	23	46	12	52	0
Ángel Alfredo Hechavarría, IND	.320	.403	.475	181	40	58	5	35	1
Tailon Sánchez, PRI	.320	.377	.448	259	51	83	7	47	3
Yuniesky Larduert, LTU	.319	.407	.370	238	54	76	0	35	15

PITCHING LEADERS

Player	W	L	ERA	IP	H	HR	BB	SO
Ediel Ponce La, CAV	8	2	2.15	71	56	3	39	43
Danny Betancourt, SCU	6	1	2.60	79	83	3	14	39
Andy Vargas, IND	7	5	2.81	93	93	6	25	61
Yosiel Serrano, SCU	6	1	2.82	54	58	3	17	33
Ariel Ernesto Zerquera, CAV	7	2	2.88	59	56	2	24	29
Rafael Orlando Perdomo, IND	4	0	2.91	56	48	3	23	37
Yadier Zamora, LTU	4	2	3.05	44	42	0	25	14
Yunieski García, PRI	2	4	3.27	41	48	1	7	34
Mario Alejandro Valle, PRI	5	2	3.42	71	67	4	23	46
Leandro Francisco Martinez, GRA	6	2	3.65	81	81	4	12	49
Albert Valladares, LTU	3	2	3.65	37	39	4	15	25
Dachel Duquesne, CAV	9	5	3.83	120	136	4	35	72
Maikel Taylor, IND	4	2	3.86	47	63	2	17	25
Lismay Ferrales, GRA	8	2	3.92	57	51	5	31	37
Luis Alberto Marrero, CAV	5	5	3.97	90	103	10	24	42
Branlis Rodríguez, PRI	5	1	4.11	81	82	7	28	55
Diosvel Ernesto Nápoles, IND	6	2	4.11	57	41	4	38	40
Geonel Gutiérrez, PRI	2	2	4.19	43	51	2	22	34
Bladimir Baños, PRI	5	3	4.20	55	71	3	16	26
Randy Roman Martínez, PRI	5	2	4.21	57	68	4	40	50
César Raúl García, GRA	7	3	4.28	80	85	9	26	44
Eliander Bravo, LTU	4	2	4.48	62	72	2	30	24
José Isais Grandales, CAV	3	4	4.56	49	48	2	26	35
Kevin Soto, CAV	6	3	4.73	83	98	8	31	40
José Ernesto Pérez, IND	3	3	4.89	53	66	3	13	14
Sammy Enrique Benítez, GRA	6	2	5.04	64	70	5	32	20
Rubén Rodríguez, LTU	7	5	5.14	61	78	3	31	23
Osvaldo Acuña, SCU	8	3	5.31	79	88	5	55	50
Yunier Castillo, GRA	7	5	5.40	76	88	6	52	54
Leandro Grabiel Cañada, LTU	4	0	5.62	57	70	7	33	22
Carlos Michel Benavides, SCU	1	1	5.67	27	35	3	16	17
Jenier Alvarez, PRI	6	3	5.76	70	79	10	36	43
Yoelkis Cruz, LTU	0	1	6.38	37	48	3	22	16
Alberto Bisset, SCU	1	7	6.68	64	96	8	25	24
Wilber Reyna, SCU	4	5	7.62	69	96	16	29	24
Denis Quesada, IND	1	1	7.79	17	20	0	16	10
Alejandro Meneses, LTU	1	1	8.10	17	30	3	6	3
Marcos Ortega Del, IND	0	3	8.17	25	25	3	25	22
Alexei Ricardo, GRA	1	4	8.29	42	48	9	38	16
Alain Sánchez, GRA	1	1	8.34	23	35	3	5	18

WINTER BASEBALL

Players from Liga Dominican Republica celebrate their Caribbean Series title. Albert Pujols managed the D.R. to the title.

Dominican Republic Wins 23rd Caribbean Series Title

Junior Lake walked, stole second, advanced to third on a Manny Banuelos wild pitch and then scored on a Robinson Cano double play, providing the only run as the Dominican Republic topped Mexico in the Caribbean Series championshp game 1-0.

Esmil Rogers allowed just one hit in six scoreless innings, and three relievers held Mexico hitless. Mexico did get a runner into scoring position in the bottom of the ninth thanks to a hit-by-pitch and stolen base, but he was stranded there.

CARIBBEAN SERIES

Team	W	L	PCT	GB
Mexico	5	1	.833	-
Dominican Republic	4	2	.667	1
Puerto Rico	3	3	.500	2
Venezuela	2	4	.333	3
Japan	0	4	.000	4

Playoffs—Finals: Dominican Republic defeated Mexico 1-0 in the championship game.

AUSTRALIAN BASEBALL LEAGUE

Team	W	L	PCT	GB
Sydney Blue Sox	18	9	.667	-
Adelaide Giants	16	12	.571	2.5
Canberra Cavalry	14	14	.500	4.5
Perth Heat	13	15	.464	5.5
Melbourne Aces	12	15	.444	6.0
Brisbane Bandits	10	18	.357	8.5

Playoffs—Semifinals: Canberra defeated Sydney 2-0 and Perth defeated Adelaide 2-0 in best-of-three series. **Finals:** Canberra defeated Perth 2-0 in best-of-three series.

INDIVIDUAL BATTING LEADERS

Player	AVG	OBP	SLG	AB	R	H	HR	RBI	BB	SO	SB
Dale, Jarryd, Melbourne	.381	.428	.508	126	26	48	3	19	10	22	8
Whitefield, Aaron, Melb.	.348	.390	.525	141	37	49	5	15	10	16	8
Williams, Jess, Perth	.324	.395	.476	105	13	34	3	17	12	34	2
Perkins, Robbie, Can.	.315	.396	.508	124	23	39	6	21	17	38	1
Riley, Will, Brisbane	.315	.374	.484	124	18	39	6	13	12	20	4
Knight, Briley, Adelaide	.315	.413	.500	92	19	29	4	13	13	15	3
Bird, Greg, Melb.	.309	.410	.496	139	17	43	5	27	20	24	1
Edwards, Mitchell, Melb.	.305	.359	.411	95	14	29	1	6	8	14	0
Hulsizer, Niko, Adel.	.300	.384	.582	110	21	33	8	22	14	42	2
Glendinning, Robbie, Melb.	.299	.387	.465	127	18	38	4	22	17	45	0

INDIVIDUAL PITCHING LEADERS

Player, Team	W	L	ERA	G	SV	IP	H	BB	SO	AVG
Wells, Alex, Sydney	6	1	1.55	10	58	55	4	12	57	.248
Ferrer, Ben, Sydney	4	2	1.94	9	46	45	4	11	37	.256
Mahoney, Jack, Canb.	5	2	1.99	10	59	54	1	15	63	.248
Kyomoto, Makoto, Ade.	2	2	2.06	6	35	24	1	4	43	.185
Wynne, Coen, Sydney	3	2	2.35	15	38	29	4	7	32	.213
Osterberg, Matt, Ade.	3	3	2.62	10	45	44	2	16	40	.260
Kines, Gunnar, Brisbane	4	3	2.66	10	51	39	2	13	53	.211
MacDonald, Connor, Bris.	5	2	2.68	11	50	52	3	13	34	.260
Davis, Colten, Canberra	4	3	3.00	8	39	29	1	17	31	.203
Morimando, Shawn, Melb.	3	2	3.11	9	46	47	3	7	46	.263

DOMINICAN LEAGUE

Team	W	L	PCT	GB
Estrellas Orientales	30	20	.600	0.0
Aguilas Cibaenas	28	22	.560	2.0
Tigres del Licey	27	22	.551	2.5
Leones del Escogido	24	25	.490	5.5
Gigantes del Cibao	22	27	.449	7.5
Toros del Este	17	32	.347	12.5

Playoffs—Round Robin: Escogido and Licey advance. **Finals:** Escogido defeated Licey 4-3 in best-of-seven series.

INDIVIDUAL BATTING LEADERS

Player	AVG	OBP	SLG	AB	R	H	HR	RBI	BB	SO	SB
Escarra, J.C., Aguilas	.363	.467	.558	113	22	41	3	14	18	16	1
Rosario, Eguy, Estrellas	.336	.395	.509	116	14	39	4	20	12	19	4

WINTER BASEBALL

Rodriguez, Aderlin, Agu. .323 .375 .581 124 22 40 8 28 8 28 1
Encarnacion, Jerar, Agu. .297 .391 .469 145 22 43 4 24 20 31 3
Gutierrez, Kelvin, Gig. .296 .385 .393 135 17 40 2 20 19 28 3
Gonzalez, Erik, Esc. .295 .364 .331 139 19 41 0 15 15 10 12
Bonifacio, Emilio, Lic. .291 .369 .386 189 33 55 1 9 24 26 13
Mejia, Erick, Aguilas .289 .344 .451 142 21 41 5 22 12 34 4
Munguia, Ismael, Est. .289 .374 .364 121 18 35 0 15 12 11 13
Segura, Jean, Escogido .287 .324 .377 167 19 48 2 23 6 28 8

INDIVIDUAL PITCHING LEADERS

Player, Team	W	L	ERA	G	IP	H	HR	BB	SO	AVG
Romero, Enny, Agu.	6	1	1.24	10	51	36	0	19	47	.202
Liz, Radhames, Licey	3	1	1.64	9	38	22	1	18	33	.173
Moreno, Luis, Estr.	2	2	1.83	11	39	23	0	15	37	.176
Crismatt, Nabil, Gig.	5	2	2.65	11	54	45	2	11	49	.223
Peralta, Wily, Gig.	2	5	2.85	10	41	41	1	17	30	.268
Rogers, Esmil, Toros	3	2	3.04	10	47	43	4	13	29	.244
Dermody, Matt, Toros	1	3	3.05	10	41	47	2	11	39	.281
De La Cruz, Oscar, Est.	2	2	3.40	10	49	29	5	10	38	.197
Valdez, Cesar, Licey	1	3	3.60	7	35	35	4	0	20	.259
Gutierrez, Vladimir, Agu.	3	3	4.23	11	45	39	4	14	40	.232

MEXICAN PACIFIC LEAGUE

Team	W	L	PCT	GB
Tomateros de Culiacan	43	25	.632	—
Naranjeros de Hermosillo	42	26	.618	1.0
Caneros de Los Mochis	37	31	.544	6.0
Charros de Jalisco	37	31	.544	6.0
Algodoneros de Guasave	35	33	.515	8.0
Aguilas de Mexicali	34	33	.507	8.5
Yaquis de Obregon	32	35	.478	10.5
Venados de Mazatlan	30	38	.441	13.0
Mayos de Navojoa	25	43	.368	18.0
Sultanes de Monterrey	24	44	.353	19.0

Playoffs—Semifinals: Jalisco defeated Hermosillo 4-1 and Culiacan defeated Los Mochis 4-2 in best-of-seven series. **Finals:** Jalisco defeated Culiacan 4-2 in best-of-seven series.

INDIVIDUAL BATTING LEADERS

Player	AVG	OBP	SLG	AB	R	H	HR	RBI	BB	SO	SB
Atondo, Jasson, Herm.	.355	.405	.447	217	33	77	0	28	18	18	2
Filia, Eric, Los Moc.	.329	.413	.483	234	40	77	8	41	30	28	2
Wielansky, Michael, Jal.	.329	.434	.502	213	41	70	4	26	37	31	11
Cardona, Jose, Herm.	.325	.403	.481	206	38	67	4	21	26	31	17
Mendoza, Victor, Obre.	.322	.397	.441	236	22	76	6	30	27	38	5
Meneses, Joey, Culia.	.320	.385	.511	231	35	74	10	58	25	21	4
Garcia, Reivaj, Herm.	.313	.353	.443	176	23	55	1	19	11	33	2
Mayfield, Jack, Jali.	.311	.354	.437	190	29	59	4	30	13	33	9
Stewart, Joe, Navo.	.311	.369	.400	180	23	56	1	17	16	32	8
Sepulveda, Carlos, Mont.	.304	.447	.402	194	26	59	0	20	49	30	12

INDIVIDUAL PITCHING LEADERS

Player, Team	W	L	ERA	G	SV	IP	H	BB	SO	AVG
Stock, Robert, Herm.	10	2	1.60	14	84	53	2	37	78	.181
Reyes, David, Mexi.	8	3	1.86	14	87	69	1	14	71	.215
Cessa, Luis, Obr.	4	2	2.09	10	52	39	2	9	35	.211
Mendoza, Damian, Navo.	2	3	2.14	14	55	39	2	18	56	.203
Araujo, Omar, LM	4	3	2.15	13	63	49	1	32	46	.221
Torres, Darel, LM	10	2	2.43	13	67	39	5	47	62	.173
Carrillo, Raul, Mazatlan	2	4	2.57	11	56	55	3	13	39	.259
Perez, Jorge, Guas.	5	8	2.65	10	58	55	1	11	22	.266
Despaigne, Odrisamer, Obre.	5	2	2.93	14	83	79	2	30	58	.256
Barreda, Manny, Culi.	8	3	3.01	12	69	69	2	36	46	.258

PUERTO RICAN LEAGUE

Team	W	L	PCT	GB
Indios de Mayaguez	22	15	.595	—
Senadores de San Juan	20	17	.541	2.0
Cangrejeros de Santurce	19	18	.514	3.0
Criollos de Caguas	18	19	.486	4.0
Gigantes de Carolina	16	21	.432	6.0
Leones de Ponce	16	21	.432	6.0

Playoffs—Semifinals: Mayaguez defeated Caguas 4-2 and San Juan defeated Santurce 4-1 in best-of-7 series. **Finals:** Mayaguez defeated San Juan 5-1 in a best-of-nine series.

INDIVIDUAL BATTING LEADERS

Player	AVG	OBP	SLG	AB	R	H	HR	RBI	BB	SO	SB
Castro, Ruben, Sant.	.328	.465	.372	137	22	45	0	13	29	18	6
Garcia, Anthony, Maya.	.311	.434	.513	119	21	37	5	20	24	31	3
Torres, Bryan, Carolina	.308	.462	.358	120	25	37	0	8	34	9	22
Ramos, Henry, Sant.	.291	.372	.449	127	17	37	4	26	15	24	2
Morales, Roy, Sant.	.288	.400	.341	132	14	38	0	15	20	14	0
Feliciano, Mario, Maya.	.286	.343	.374	91	5	26	0	12	4	13	0
Hernandez, Jan, Caro.	.271	.340	.343	140	18	38	1	15	16	38	6
MacKinnon, David, Maya.	.269	.351	.369	130	20	35	1	16	17	20	0
Machin, Vimael, Cag.	.268	.381	.331	142	20	38	2	10	26	17	4
Rivera, Yadiel, Santurce	.255	.293	.274	106	11	27	0	14	3	28	3

INDIVIDUAL PITCHING LEADERS

Player, Team	W	L	ERA	G	SV	IP	H	BB	SO	AVG
Diaz, Jhonathan, Sant.	4	0	0.49	6	37	16	0	7	26	.133
Cruz, Luis Leroy, Maya.	2	1	0.95	8	38	30	1	9	33	.224
Rivera, Eduardo, Sant.	2	1	1.15	11	39	25	0	12	56	.180
Martinez, Miguel, SJ	1	3	1.52	8	41	29	0	6	14	.199
Mataki, Teppei, Sant.	1	0	1.72	7	31	19	0	6	19	.176
Vargas, Jhon, Caro.	1	0	1.93	11	33	24	1	12	26	.202
Adams, Derrick, Cag.	3	2	1.99	8	32	20	1	20	25	.182
Lakins, Travis, Cag.	3	2	2.10	9	34	28	0	9	34	.222
Rodriguez, Dereck, Cag.	1	1	2.12	7	34	27	1	6	21	.225
Garcia, Julian, SJ	2	3	2.35	9	38	21	2	14	37	.159

VENEZUELAN LEAGUE

Team	W	L	PCT	GB
Cardenales de Lara	33	23	.589	—
Bravos de Margarita	31	25	.554	2.0
Aguilas del Zulia	30	26	.536	3.0
Navegantes del Magallanes	29	27	.518	4.0
Tigres de Aragua	27	29	.482	6.0
Leones del Caracas	27	30	.474	6.5
Tiburones de La Guaira	26	31	.456	7.5
Caribes de Anzoategui	22	34	.393	11.0

Playoffs—Round Robin: Margarita and Lara advance. **Finals:** Lara defeated Margarita 4-2 in best-of-7 series.

INDIVIDUAL BATTING LEADERS

Player	AVG	OBP	SLG	AB	R	H	HR	RBI	BB	SO	SB
Cedrola, Lorenzo, Arag.	.395	.451	.557	210	47	83	4	33	20	19	11
Castillo, Ali, Zulia	.359	.399	.438	217	34	78	1	23	14	9	5
Santana, Juan, Marg.	.358	.382	.524	212	31	76	5	27	10	32	1
Herrera, Odubel, Ara.	.349	.399	.500	146	23	51	4	23	10	16	9
Perez, Carlos, Marg.	.338	.380	.539	154	26	52	5	22	11	8	0
Alfonzo, Eliezer, Mag.	.338	.425	.554	130	17	44	6	33	18	8	1
Castro, Harold, Car.	.332	.394	.627	193	37	64	15	41	16	41	6
Rodriguez, Carlos D., Maga.	.329	.382	.406	170	30	56	2	17	13	11	3
Rodriguez, Keyber, Ara.	.327	.389	.517	147	31	48	5	20	11	26	3
Torrealba, Eduardo, Zul.	.322	.391	.423	149	27	48	2	21	15	18	8

INDIVIDUAL PITCHING LEADERS

Player, Team	W	L	ERA	G	SV	IP	H	BB	SO	AVG
Guerra, Junior, Maga.	8	1	2.63	12	68	65	4	26	48	.249
Endersby, Jimmy, Lara	5	0	2.72	11	56	47	6	14	35	.225
Rodriguez, Jose, Caribes	5	1	3.45	13	60	67	8	14	29	.288
Castillo, Max, Lara	6	2	3.51	9	49	48	6	8	26	.265
Vargas, Jesus, Caracas	2	2	3.83	9	40	43	4	8	25	.285
Ogando, Cristofer, Maga.	3	3	4.33	12	52	49	6	23	53	.244
Sampson, Keyvius, Lara	2	3	4.53	11	44	46	4	24	31	.271
Morales, Osmer, Marg.	5	5	5.07	12	55	51	7	25	44	.246
Saldana, Abdiel, Marg.	2	2	5.15	12	51	50	5	28	34	.260
Casanova, Erly, La G.	1	1	5.15	12	44	51	2	20	21	.290

COLLEGE

LSU has now won two of the past three College World Series titles and eight overall.

LSU Edges Toward Dynasty Status

BY JACOB RUDNER

LSU returned to college baseball's mountaintop in Omaha, beating Coastal Carolina 5-3 to win its eighth national championship and second in three years.

The Tigers' 2023 title showed that the program had returned under head coach Jay Johnson to the heights that it had last reached under Paul Mainieri when it won the CWS title in 2009.

With this win, LSU looks to be edging closer to its status as the dominant program of college baseball, much as it did under Skip Bertman, when LSU won five titles from 1991-2000.

The Tigers are the only program to win multiple championships in the transfer portal era (since 2018) and Johnson becomes the sixth coach in the super regional era (since 1999) to win multiple titles.

LSU largely cruised to its series-clinching win. Designated hitter Ethan Frey tied the game with an RBI double in the third inning, and the Tigers took a lead they never relinquished in the fourth, with two-run singles from center fielder Chris Stanfield and left fielder Derek Curiel.

That four-run inning chased Coastal Carolina ace Jacob Morrison, who joined Paul Skenes as the only Division I pitchers in the last five years to record 10 or more starts of six-plus innings with one or fewer runs allowed.

LSU starting pitcher Anthony Eyanson offered a strong performance, limiting the Chanticleers to three runs on seven hits with nine strikeouts over

COACHING CAROUSEL

School	In (Previous Job)	Out (Reason/New Job)
Bradley	Justin Dedman (LMU assistant coach)	Elvis Dominguez (retired)
Brown	Frank Holbrook (Northeastern assistant coach)	Grant Achilles (fired)
Creighton	Mark Kingston (Creighton associate head coach)	Ed Servais (retired)
Dartmouth	*Blake McFadden (Dartmouth assistant coach)	Bob Whalen (retired)
Dayton	Jayson King (Vanderbilt assistant coach)	Scott Loiseau (Duke associate head coach)
Duke	Corey Muscara (Wake Forest assistant coach)	Chris Pollard (hired by Virginia)
Eastern Kentucky	Jan Weisberg (Valdosta State head coach)	Walt Jones (fired)
Eastern Michigan	*Trevor Beerman (Eastern Michigan assistant coach)	Robbie Britt (hired by Boston Red Sox)
Georgia Tech	James Ramsey (Georgia Tech associate head coach)	Danny Hall (retired)
Incarnate Word	Nick Zaleski (Tarleton State assistant coach)	Ryan Shotzberger (fired)
Massachusetts	*Brandon Shileikis and Max Weir (Mass. assistant coaches)	Matt Reynolds (hired by Wesleyan)
Louisiana-Monroe	Ford Pemberton (Memphis assistant coach)	Mike Federico (fired)
Mississippi State	Brian O'Connor (Virginia head coach)	Chris Lemonis (fired)
New Orleans	Andrew Gipson (Belhaven head coach)	Blake Dean (resigned)
Norfolk State	M.L. Morgan (Tampa Bay Rays Mid-Atlantic area scout)	Keith Shumate (resigned)
Ohio	Andrew See (Liberty associate head coach)	Craig Moore (fired)
Prairie View A&M	Daniel Dulin (Illinois-Chicago assistant coach)	Auntwan Riggins (fired)
Saint Louis	*Miles Miller (Saint Louis assistant coach)	Darin Hendrickson (fired)
Saint Peter's	TJ Ward (Hartford assistant coach)	Grant Neary (resigned)
San Diego State	Kevin Vance (assistant coach)	Shaun Cole (fired)
Stonehill	Sean Callahan (Stonehill associate head coach)	Pat Boen (retired)
Stony Brook	Jim Martin (Stony Brook associate head coach)	Matt Senk (retired)
Tennessee	Josh Elander (Tennessee associate head coach)	Tony Vitello (hired by San Francisco Giants)
UNC Asheville	*Alex Raburn (UNC Asheville assistant coach)	Scott Friedholm (resigned)
Virginia	Chris Pollard (Duke head coach)	Brian O'Connor (hired by Mississippi State)

6.1 innings. Reliever Chase Shores closed out the game with 2.2 spotless innings.

The game wasn't without controversy. Chanticleers head coach Kevin Schnall and first base coach Matt Schilling were ejected in the bottom of the first inning by home-plate umpire Angel Campos after the two argued balls and strikes. The NCAA issued a statement after the game supporting the ejections and adding that Schnall and Schilling would be suspended two and three games, respectively. Their suspensions will be enforced to start the 2026 season.

LSU put together a spectacular and largely unchallenged run through the College World Series, winning all of its games behind historic performances from lefty Kade Anderson, who threw 16 innings of one-run ball in Omaha, including the third-ever complete game shutout in championship series history on Saturday night.

The Tigers will go down in history as the college equivalent of a dynasty—and under Johnson, they should be positioned to compete again in 2026.

"I could coach this team forever," Johnson said repeatedly throughout his stay in Omaha. "I'll say it over and over."

Summer Ball's Fight For Survival

The email landed in midwinter, polite and plain. It was the kind of request the summer league official had read a hundred times before.

"Dear [league official]," it began. "My name is [redacted] and I was wondering if you had any spots available for me to pitch this summer. I would love to send you some film for you to watch and put you in touch with my college coach."

The official replied within minutes. No openings, he explained, but a reserve slot was possible. The player didn't hesitate to jump at the chance.

"Of course," he responded.

What followed were the familiar calls, texts and emails that go into summer roster building. Only this time, the league official's communications went unanswered by the player's coach, a departure from typical workflow. Weeks passed. Eventually, the official broke the news—he couldn't sign the player to a summer league contract.

That's when the player made his next move.

"I'm entering the transfer portal," he said. "Can I join now?"

With no coach to block his summer plans, the process moved fast. Flights were booked, housing was secured and introductions were made. Hours later, the phone rang again. The player had verbally committed to a new school, and his new coach didn't want him playing.

In the churn of summer baseball, nothing stays settled for long.

"I said, 'Listen,'" the summer league director of player personnel told Baseball America, "'I'm just telling you right now, any good baseball person who tells you that not playing baseball is good for you doesn't have your best interest in mind.'"

Still, no minds were changed. Plans—or the lack thereof—remained firm. The player stayed home that summer, joining a growing list of college players who did the same.

Few college coaches who spoke with Baseball America on the condition of anonymity denied that reality. In a landscape where loyalty to programs can be fickle at best, summer ball has become less an opportunity to improve than it is a showcase for coaches looking to pluck talent from other teams to bolster their own.

"Ever since the transfer portal picked up and became what it is, I think coaches started operating under the belief that home is the safest place for their players to be and train," the summer league official said. "College coaches want summer ball to exist as a place to find talent, not a place to send talent. To them, sending talent out is a risk."

This notion is at the core of growing frustration for summer league managers, officials and team personnel, many of whom have served in their respective roles long enough to see the transition firsthand.

Players who once spent full seasons in wood bat leagues now only pass through briefly, if they go at all. It's a trend that, in the eyes of several league administrators and scouts, has eroded the quality of what was once a fertile proving ground while also putting significant strain on teams scrambling to fill and maintain rosters throughout a season.

The numbers back it up. In some of the country's most tradition-rich leagues, officials say roster volatility has never been higher. Players sign, report, make a handful of appearances and then vanish back home on the word of a coach, personal trainer or private pitching guru.

One league general manager charted his team's trend over the last decade and found that rosters that used to turn over nine or 10 players in a summer now routinely shuffle through 20.

"It's survival mode," another league official said. "You're not building a team anymore. You're patching a boat."

College coaches insist they still want their players competing in the summer, but few shied away from the fact that they wanted it to be on their terms.

Many request ultra-specific pitch counts or innings limits. A few avoid summer ball entirely for returning pitchers, especially those who could

COLLEGE WORLD SERIES CHAMPIONS

Year	Champion	Coach	Record	Runner-Up	Most Outstanding Player
1948	Southern California	Sam Barry	40-12	Yale	None selected
1949	Texas*	Bibb Falk	23-7	Wake Forest	Charles Teague, 2B, Wake Forest
1950	Texas	Bibb Falk	27-6	Washington State	Ray VanCleef, OF, Rutgers
1951	Oklahoma*	Jack Baer	19-9	Tennessee	Sid Hatfield, 1B/P, Tennessee
1952	Holy Cross	Jack Barry	21-3	Missouri	Jim O'Neill, P, Holy Cross
1953	Michigan	Ray Fisher	21-9	Texas	J.L. Smith, P, Texas
1954	Missouri	Hi Simmons	22-4	Rollins	Tom Yewcic, C, Michigan State
1955	Wake Forest	Taylor Sanford	29-7	Western Michigan	Tom Borland, P, Oklahoma State
1956	Minnesota	Dick Siebert	33-9	Arizona	Jerry Thomas, P, Minnesota
1957	California*	George Wolfman	35-10	Penn State	Cal Emery, 1B/P, Penn State
1958	Southern California	Rod Dedeaux	35-7	Missouri	Bill Thom, P, Southern California
1959	Oklahoma State	Toby Greene	27-5	Arizona	Jim Dobson, 3B, Oklahoma State
1960	Minnesota	Dick Siebert	34-7	Southern California	John Erickson, 2B, Minnesota
1961	Southern California*	Rod Dedeaux	43-9	Oklahoma State	Littleton Fowler, P, Oklahoma State
1962	Michigan	Don Lund	31-13	Santa Clara	Bob Garibaldi, P, Santa Clara
1963	Southern California	Rod Dedeaux	37-16	Arizona	Bud Hollowell, C, Southern California
1964	Minnesota	Dick Siebert	31-12	Missouri	Joe Ferris, P, Maine
1965	Arizona State	Bobby Winkles	54-8	Ohio State	Sal Bando, 3B, Arizona State
1966	Ohio State	Marty Karow	27-6	Oklahoma State	Steve Arlin, P, Ohio State
1967	Arizona State	Bobby Winkles	53-12	Houston	Ron Davini, C, Arizona State
1968	Southern California*	Rod Dedeaux	45-14	Southern Illinois	Bill Seinsoth, 1B, Southern California
1969	Arizona State	Bobby Winkles	56-11	Tulsa	John Dolinsek, OF, Arizona State
1970	Southern California	Rod Dedeaux	51-13	Florida State	Gene Ammann, P, Florida State
1971	Southern California	Rod Dedeaux	53-13	Southern Illinois	Jerry Tabb, 1B, Tulsa
1972	Southern California	Rod Dedeaux	50-13	Arizona State	Russ McQueen, P, Southern California
1973	Southern California*	Rod Dedeaux	51-11	Arizona State	Dave Winfield, OF/P, Minnesota
1974	Southern California	Rod Dedeaux	50-20	Miami	George Milke, P, Southern California
1975	Texas	Cliff Gustafson	56-6	South Carolina	Mickey Reichenbach, 1B, Texas
1976	Arizona	Jerry Kindall	56-17	Eastern Michigan	Steve Powers, DH/P, Arizona
1977	Arizona State	Jim Brock	57-12	South Carolina	Bob Horner, 3B, Arizona State
1978	Southern California*	Rod Dedeaux	54-9	Arizona State	Rod Boxberger, P, Southern California
1979	Cal State Fullerton	Augie Garrido	60-14	Arkansas	Tony Hudson, P, Cal State Fullerton
1980	Arizona	Jerry Kindall	45-21	Hawaii	Terry Francona, OF, Arizona
1981	Arizona State	Jim Brock	55-13	Oklahoma State	Stan Holmes, OF, Arizona State
1982	Miami	Ron Fraser	57-18	Wichita State	Dan Smith, P, Miami
1983	Texas	Cliff Gustafson	66-14	Alabama	Calvin Schiraldi, P, Texas

shoulder heavy workloads in the spring. As one SEC assistant put it, "I don't need my Friday guy trying to prove something in a wood bat league in July."

At the same time, coaches are watching everyone else's players closely.

Several summer league administrators told Baseball America they now send weekly stat sheets directly to college coaches, some of whom use the information less to track their own rosters than to identify potential transfer targets.

"It's kind of the worst-kept secret," a Power Four recruiting coordinator said. "You go to the Cape now and half the time you're not watching your own kid. You're watching someone else's and (hoping) he jumps in the portal."

As such, some coaches feel the need to play defense.

"I went out to (watch several of my players) this summer and, as much as I was there to see how they were doing, I was also there to make sure my guys stayed my guys," one mid-major head coach said.

That protective mindset has produced a squeeze that has been particularly apparent even in the Cape Cod Baseball League, which has long been considered the gold standard of summertime amateur development. In 2018, 53 players logged at least 100 at-bats on the Cape. That number cratered to 25 in 2023 and ticked up only slightly to 29 in 2025. On the mound, the downturn has been even more severe: 58 pitchers reached 20 innings in 2018 while just 25 did the same this summer.

The dip in participation is reflected at the sport's highest levels, too. Just 60% of Division I first-round picks in 2025 played in a summer league the year before their draft season compared to 77% in 2018, the year the transfer portal was installed.

"We have successfully convinced baseball play-

Year	Champion	Coach	Record	Runner-Up	MOST OUTSTANDING PLAYER
1984	Cal State Fullerton	Augie Garrido	66-20	Texas	John Fishel, OF, Cal State Fullerton
1985	Miami*	Ron Fraser	64-16	Texas	Greg Ellena, DH, Miami
1986	Arizona	Jerry Kindall	49-19	Florida State	Mike Senne, OF, Arizona
1987	Stanford	Mark Marquess	53-17	Oklahoma State	Paul Carey, OF, Stanford
1988	Stanford	Mark Marquess	46-23	Arizona State	Lee Plemel, P, Stanford
1989	Wichita State	Gene Stephenson	68-16	Texas	Greg Brummett, P, Wichita State
1990	Georgia	Steve Webber	52-19	Oklahoma State	Mike Rebhan, P, Georgia
1991	Louisiana State*	Skip Bertman	55-18	Wichita State	Gary Hymel, C, Louisiana State
1992	Pepperdine*	Andy Lopez	48-11	Cal State Fullerton	Phil Nevin, 3B, Cal State Fullerton
1993	Louisiana State	Skip Bertman	53-17	Wichita State	Todd Walker, 2B, Louisiana State
1994	Oklahoma*	Larry Cochell	50-17	Georgia Tech	Chip Glass, OF, Oklahoma
1995	Cal State Fullerton*	Augie Garrido	57-9	Southern California	Mark Kotsay, OF/P, Cal State Fullerton
1996	Louisiana State*	Skip Bertman	52-15	Miami	Pat Burrell, 3B, Miami
1997	Louisiana State*	Skip Bertman	57-13	Alabama	Brandon Larson, SS, Louisiana State
1998	Southern California	Mike Gillespie	49-17	Arizona State	Wes Rachels, 2B, Southern California
1999	Miami*	Jim Morris	50-13	Florida State	Marshall McDougall, 2B, Florida State
2000	Louisiana State*	Skip Bertman	52-17	Stanford	Trey Hodges, P, Louisiana State
2001	Miami*	Jim Morris	53-12	Stanford	Charlton Jimerson, OF, Miami
2002	Texas*	Augie Garrido	57-15	South Carolina	Huston Street, P, Texas
2003	Rice	Wayne Graham	58-12	Stanford	John Hudgins, P, Stanford
2004	Cal State Fullerton	George Horton	47-22	Texas	Jason Windsor, P, Cal State Fullerton
2005	Texas*	Augie Garrido	56-16	Florida	David Maroul, 3B, Texas
2006	Oregon State	Pat Casey	50-16	North Carolina	Jonah Nickerson, P, Oregon State
2007	Oregon State*	Pat Casey	49-18	North Carolina	Jorge Reyes, P, Oregon State
2008	Fresno State	Mike Batesole	47-31	Georgia	Tommy Mendonca, 3B, Fresno State
2009	Louisiana State	Paul Mainieri	56-17	Texas	Jared Mitchell, OF, Louisiana State
2010	South Carolina	Ray Tanner	54-16	UCLA	Jackie Bradley Jr., OF, South Carolina
2011	South Carolina*	Ray Tanner	55-14	Florida	Scott Wingo, 2B, South Carolina
2012	Arizona*	Andy Lopez	48-17	South Carolina	Robert Refsnyder, OF, Arizona
2013	UCLA*	John Savage	49-17	Mississippi State	Adam Plutko, P, UCLA
2014	Vanderbilt	Tim Corbin	51-21	Virginia	Dansby Swanson, 2B, Vanderbilt
2015	Virginia	Brian O'Connor	44-24	Vanderbilt	Josh Sborz, P, Virginia
2016	Coastal Carolina	Gary Gilmore	55-18	Arizona	Andrew Beckwith, P, Coastal Carolina
2017	Florida	Kevin O'Sullivan	52-19	Louisiana State	Alex Faedo, P, Florida
2018	Oregon State	Pat Casey	55-12-1	Arkansas	Adley Rutschman, C, Oregon State
2019	Vanderbilt	Tim Corbin	59-12	Michigan	Kumar Rocker, RHP, Vanderbilt
2020	Canceled due to pandemic				
2021	Mississippi State	Chris Lemonis	50-18	Vanderbilt	Will Bednar, RHP, Mississippi State
2022	Ole Miss	Mike Bianco	42-23	Oklahoma	Dylan DeLucia, RHP, Ole Miss
2023	Louisiana State	Jay Johnson	54-17	Florida	Paul Skenes, RHP, Louisiana State
2024	Tennessee	Tony Vitello	60-13	Texas A&M	Dylan Dreiling, OF, Tennessee
2025	Louisiana State	Jay Johnson	53-15	Coastal Carolina	Kade Anderson, LHP, Louisiana State

ers that playing baseball is no longer good for them," one league official said. "Kids come here looking to showcase themselves for the portal. They get the offer, the love, the NIL promise—and they go home."

Added an official from another league: "The carousel of players is pretty much unprecedented in the last few years. It's a completely different product than it's ever been."

The concern, administrators say, extends far beyond entertainment value—it's an existential business problem. Summer leagues are built on nightly gates, community sponsors and the promise of stability to host families and local operators. When talent flees early—sometimes in waves—the quality of baseball drops, teams slump toward sub-.500 records with replacement players and crowds thin. One official described July attendance this year as "the quietest I can remember," attributing it largely to recognizable names disappearing before the stretch run.

"You take away the best players, you take away the draw," another general manager said. "And once fans stop showing up, everything else starts to wobble—concessions, merchandise, sponsorships, even host family willingness the next summer. It's not just wins and losses. It's the whole ecosystem."

To combat the churn, leagues have begun experimenting with drastic fixes. One director said his schedule has already been slashed from 58 games down to 48—a deliberate psychological ploy.

"My sell to all the coaches and the players is, 'You'll be home the very first few days of August,'" he said. "We purposely keep it just June and July so the player doesn't have to hear the word August."

Still, coaches are pushing for even shorter summers.

Others have floated the potential for reserving summer roster spots only for hitters while pulling back on pitching altogether, an idea met with skepticism.

"Schools want to send out their hitters—they all want their hitters to get better—but no one wants to send out quality pitching, because they're afraid the quality pitching won't come back," a summer league head coach said. "But you need someone to throw to the hitters."

At this point, even administrators admit they're running out of answers.

"They know there is a very real problem, and they are at a loss for what to do," a league director said. "We want to come fish, but we don't necessarily want to give you the fish to help everyone else."

The consequences, officials warn, may arrive sooner than most realize. Smaller wood bat leagues

RPI RANKINGS

The Ratings Percentage Index is an important tool used by the NCAA in selecting at-large teams for the 64-team Division I tournament. These were the top 100 finishers for 2025. These RPI Ratings are compiled by WarrenNolan.com.

Team	Record	Team	Record
1. Arkansas	50-15	51. SE Louisiana	37-16
2. Coastal Carolina	56-13	52. Stanford	27-25
3. Vanderbilt	43-18	53. Nebraska	33-29
4. LSU	53-15	54. Pittsburgh	28-27
5. Auburn	41-20	55. East Carolina	35-27
6. Texas	44-14	56. Virginia Tech	31-25
7. Georgia	43-17	57. Murray State	43-17
8. Oregon State	48-16-1	58. Kennesaw State	31-27
9. North Carolina	46-15	59. Hawaii	31-21
10. UCLA	48-18	60. Jacksonville St.	37-25
11. Florida State	42-16	61. Lamar	40-17
12. Ole Miss	43-21	62. BYU	28-27
13. Clemson	45-18	63. Columbia	30-19
14. Tennessee	46-19	64. Stetson	41-22
15. Alabama	41-18	65. FAU	37-21
16. TCU	39-20	66. Virginia	32-18
17. Florida	39-22	67. Charlotte	36-22
18. UTSA	47-15	68. Indiana	32-24
19. Georgia Tech	41-19	69. Boston College	28-29
20. Oregon	42-16	70. Michigan	33-23
21. Miss	47-16	71. Mercer	35-25
22. Dallas Baptist	41-18	72. UCSB	36-18
23. UC Irvine	43-17	73. Fairfield	39-19
24. Oklahoma	38-22	74. UCF	29-26
25. Arizona	44-21	75. South Carolina	28-29
26. Northeastern	49-11	76. UNCW	34-24
27. Louisville	42-24	77. Rhode Island	38-22
28. West Virginia	44-16	78. Washington	28-27
29. Wake Forest	39-22	79. Baylor	33-22
30. Kansas	43-17	80. Iowa	31-22-1
31. Cal Poly	43-19	81. South Florida	31-25
32. Duke	41-21	82. Miami	35-23
33. Miss. State	36-23	83. NW State	31-21
34. Miami	35-27	84. McNeese	29-16
35. NC State	35-21	85. Penn State	33-23
36. Kentucky	31-26	86. Rutgers	29-28
37. Cincinnati	33-26	87. Saint Mary's	36-26
38. Creighton	43-16	88. Wright State	40-21
39. USC	37-23	89. Samford	30-27
40. Kansas State	32-26	90. Austin Peay	45-14
41. Connecticut	38-21	91. South Caro. Up.	36-25
42. Xavier	32-27	92. Houston Christ.	32-25
43. UTRGV	36-18	93. Texas Tech	20-33
44. Western Ky.	46-14	94. High Point	39-19
45. East Tenn. State	41-17	95. Houston	30-25
46. Okla. State	30-25	96. Liberty	30-27
47. Troy	39-21	97. California	24-31
48. Notre Dame	32-21	98. Marshall	33-26
49. Arizona State	36-24	99. Charleston	37-22
50. Texas A&M	30-26	100. Rider	34-18

without significant financial backing are already bracing for what comes next.

If college programs continue to "fish" from summer leagues without supplying players of their own and continue to pull talent out midseason or refuse to send it at all, it threatens to destabilize the entire model. The nightly show summer leagues have put on for decades becomes tougher to stage.

As one long-time administrator put it, if coaches

COLLEGE ALL-AMERICA TEAM

FIRST TEAM

Pos.	Name	Year	AVG	OBP	SLG	AB	R	H	HR	RBI	BB	SO	SB
C	Carson Tinney, Notre Dame	So.	.348	.498	.753	158	52	55	17	53	34	40	1
1B	Andrew Fischer, Tennessee	Jr.	.341	.497	.760	217	70	74	25	65	63	42	4
2B	Gavin Kilen, Tennessee	Jr.	.357	.441	.671	210	60	75	15	46	30	27	6
3B	Daniel Cuvet, Miami	So.	.372	.450	.708	226	56	84	18	84	30	51	6
SS	Roch Cholowsky, UCLA	So.	.353	.480	.710	252	80	89	23	74	45	30	7
OF	Ike Irish, Auburn	Jr.	.364	.469	.710	214	65	78	19	58	53	37	11
OF	Devin Taylor, Indiana	Jr.	.374	.494	.706	214	63	80	18	66	52	30	12
OF	James Quinn-Irons, George Mason	Jr.	.419	.523	.734	241	74	101	16	85	39	46	36
DH	Alex Lodise, FSU	Jr.	.394	.462	.705	241	62	95	17	68	27	55	6
UT	Evan Dempsey, Florida Gulf Coast	So.	.309	.393	.435	230	43	71	3	30	16	23	14

Pos.	Name	Year	W	L	ERA	G	CG	SV	IP	H	BB	SO	AVG
SP	Liam Doyle, Tennessee	Jr.	10	4	3.20	19	1	96	63	10	32	164	.184
SP	Kade Anderson, LSU	So.	12	1	3.18	19	0	119	91	16	35	180	.211
SP	Anthony Eyanson, LSU	Jr.	12	2	3.00	20	2	108	88	8	36	152	.218
SP	Kyson Witherspoon, Oklahoma	Jr.	10	4	2.65	16	0	95	73	9	23	124	.207
RP	Dylan Voltantis, Texas	Fr.	4	1	1.94	23	12	51	33	3	12	74	.185
RP	Gabe Craig, Baylor	Sr.	3	0	0.56	24	10	32	13	0	3	51	.124
UT	Evan Dempsey, Florida Gulf Coast	So.	5	1	1.97	15	0	69	57	3	20	75	.225

SECOND TEAM

Pos.	Name	Year	AVG	OBP	SLG	AB	R	H	HR	RBI	BB	SO	SB
C	Boston Smith, Wright State	Sr.	.330	.498	.770	209	70	69	26	70	57	52	16
1B	Jared Jones, LSU	Jr.	.323	.414	.613	279	66	90	22	76	38	85	5
2B	Ryan Daniels, UConn	Jr.	.365	.476	.744	203	69	74	18	75	40	41	10
3B	Ace Reese, Mississippi State	So.	.352	.422	.718	227	58	80	21	66	26	52	1
SS	Aiva Arquette, Oregon State	So.	.354	.461	.654	254	73	90	19	66	39	51	7
OF	Sawyer Strosnider, TCU	Fr.	.350	.420	.650	220	52	77	11	51	20	47	10
OF	Ryan Wideman, Western Kentucky	Jr.	.398	.466	.652	244	71	97	10	68	23	47	45
OF	Gavin Turley, Oregon State	Jr.	.351	.472	.649	245	56	86	20	69	50	68	5
DH	Wehiwa Aloy, Arkansas	Jr.	.350	.434	.673	266	81	93	21	68	32	64	9
UT	Bryce Calloway, New Orleans	Sr.	.390	.484	.722	205	63	80	18	63	31	60	1

Pos.	Name	Year	W	L	ERA	G	CG	SV	IP	H	BB	SO	AVG
SP	Jacob Morrison, Coastal Carolina	Jr.	12	1	2.42	19	0	108	79	7	23	104	.202
SP	Zane Taylor, UNC Wilmington	Sr.	11	2	1.98	15	0	96	62	8	11	105	.181
SP	Blake Gillespie, Charlotte	Jr.	7	4	2.42	15	0	100	69	9	19	131	.193
SP	Jamie Arnold, Florida State	Jr.	8	2	2.98	15	0	85	63	7	27	119	.208
RP	Tony Pluta, Arizona	Jr.	3	0	1.46	30	14	37	28	0	7	34	.219
RP	Antoine Jean, Houston	Sr.	5	1	2.55	21	5	67	40	4	20	110	.167
UT	Bryce Calloway, New Orleans	Sr.	2	2	4.26	20	11	25	24	0	11	23	.247

THIRD TEAM

Pos.	Name	Year	AVG	OBP	SLG	AB	R	H	HR	RBI	BB	SO	SB
C	Easton Carmichael, Oklahoma	Jr.	.329	.398	.613	243	51	80	17	62	25	43	14
1B	Mulivai Levu, UCLA	So.	.320	.389	.522	272	61	87	12	85	24	48	4
2B	Nick Monistere, Southern Miss	Jr.	.323	.410	.623	257	59	83	21	72	27	53	7
3B	Bobby Boser, Florida	Sr.	.336	.437	.613	238	72	80	18	67	28	72	19
SS	Marek Houston, Wake Forest	Jr.	.354	.458	.597	243	61	86	15	66	46	46	19
OF	Mason Neville, Oregon	Jr.	.290	.429	.724	217	67	63	26	57	53	66	9
OF	Drew Burress, Georgia Tech	So.	.333	.469	.693	228	77	76	19	62	53	42	10
OF	Korbyn Dickerson, Indiana	Jr.	.314	.381	.632	242	57	76	19	77	24	51	5
DH	Justin Lebron, Alabama	So.	.316	.421	.636	231	60	73	18	72	35	68	17
UT	Noah Sullivan, Mississippi State	Jr.	.345	.475	.645	203	63	70	15	46	35	42	1

Pos.	Name	Year	W	L	ERA	G	CG	SV	IP	H	BB	SO	AVG
SP	Jake Knapp, North Carolina	Sr.	14	0	2.02	16	0	102	72	6	16	88	.196
SP	Jack Ohman, Yale	Fr.	8	1	1.34	12	0	74	45	4	20	87	.174
SP	Joseph Dzierwa, Michigan State	Jr.	11	3	1.42	18	0	119	77	4	22	137	.179
SP	JB Middleton, Southern Miss	Jr.	10	1	2.31	16	0	105	65	8	25	122	.174
RP	Ty Van Dyke, Stetson	Sr.	7	0	1.52	27	9	47	30	3	16	71	.175
RP	Dylan Crooks, Oklahoma	Sr.	2	1	1.69	26	16	32	23	1	10	33	.195
UT	Noah Sullivan, Mississippi State	Jr.	0	0	1.96	7	0	18	17	0	3	15	.246

keep treating summer ball solely as a place to scout talent rather than develop it, "the pond simply won't survive."

"I think you're going to see some (leagues) say they can't live like this because they have to put on a show every night," one official said. "You need

Tony Vitello Shocks The World

Shock isn't rare in college baseball, but this was different. When word broke that Tony Vitello had emerged as the leading candidate to manage the Giants, the reaction from coaches, agents and scouts was immediate and unanimous: disbelief.

Phones were abuzz within minutes in a cascade of texts from people trying to process how the sport's most magnetic figure could suddenly be headed for a major league dugout.

But the disbelief didn't last. It never does when the logic is this clear. Soon after the uproar, the tone shifted from confusion to clarity.

Of course it's Vitello. Of course it makes sense.

"It's brilliant," one SEC coach told Baseball America.

The more you think about it, the more obvious it becomes.

Vitello's charisma, relentlessness and player-first intensity have long belonged to a higher tier. He built Tennessee like a pro franchise, recruited like a front office with ample financial backing and coached like he was sure college baseball was merely the sport's next great developmental frontier.

And maybe that's exactly what it is. In an era when college players reach the majors faster than ever and with the draft possibly shrinking again in 2027, the distance between the SEC and the show has never been smaller. Someone was bound to cross it. It's fitting that the one to do it is the coach who blurred that line more than anyone else.

Vitello will get his chance now. He'll replace Bob Melvin as the Giants' manager, becoming the first skipper ever to job directly from college to the pros.

From the moment he arrived in Knoxville in the summer of 2017, Vitello began building Tennessee as if it were a major league organization disguised as a college program. His first step was assembling a staff fluent in analytics and data—long before that became standard across the college game. Tennessee's recruiting classes were sculpted with information and precision, and the results spoke for themselves: high-round draft picks, immediate contributors and a roster that played with the polish of a professional system.

The success came fast and kept building.

After taking the Volunteers to Omaha in 2021 and 2023, he captured the first national championship in program history in 2024 and won Baseball America's College Coach of the Year Award. He was rewarded for his accomplishments with a record five-year deal that made him one of the highest-paid coaches in the game.

During his rise to success, Vitello's rosters weren't just talented, they were balanced, modern, built through every avenue available. From prep recruits and portal transfers to returning veterans who believed in his vision, Vitello gathered like minds and talented players. That blend became his blueprint, proof that Tennessee's rise wasn't accidental or cyclical. It was structural. ∎

COLLEGE WORLD SERIES

STANDINGS

Bracket One	W	L
Coastal Carolina	3	0
Louisville	2	2
Oregon State	1	2
Arizona	0	2
Bracket Two		
LSU	3	0
Arkansas	2	2
UCLA	1	2
Murray State	0	2

CWS FINALS (BEST OF THREE)
June 21: LSU 1, Coastal Carolina 0
June 22: LSU 5, Coastal Carolina 3

ALL-TOURNAMENT TEAM
C: Adonys Guzman, Arizona. **1B:** Jared Jones, LSU. **2B:** Kamau Neighbors, Louisville. **3B:** Jake Munroe, Louisville. **SS:** Steven Milam, LSU. **OF:** Derek Curiel, LSU; Eddie King Jr., Louisville; Justin Thomas Jr., Arkansas. **DH:** Dean Mihos, Coastal Carolina. **P:** Gage Wood, Arkansas. **P:** Kade Anderson, LSU*
Named Most Outstanding Player.

BATTING
(Minimum 8 PA)

Player	AVG	R	H	2B	3B	HR	RBI	SB
Kamau Neighbors, LOU	.615	2	8	0	0	0	4	0
Justin Thomas Jr., ARK	.571	1	8	1	0	0	3	2
Adonys Guzman, ARIZ	.556	3	5	1	0	1	2	0
Tommy Splaine, ARIZ	.500	0	4	1	0	0	0	0
Dean Mihos, CCU	.450	3	9	1	1	1	4	0
Eddie King Jr., LOU	.429	2	6	1	0	0	3	0
Turley, Gavin, OSU	.429	2	6	1	0	1	3	1
Dean West, UCLA	.417	2	5	0	0	0	1	1
Jake Brown, LSU	.385	2	5	0	0	0	4	0
Wehiwa Aloy, ARK.	.375	3	6	1	1	1	4	1

PITCHING
(Minimum 6 IP)

Pitcher	W-L	ERA	G	SV	IP	H	BB	SO
Gage Wood, ARK.	1-0	0.00	1	0	9	0	0	19
Kade Anderson, LSU.	2-0	0.56	2	0	16	6	7	17
Isaac Silva, MUR.	0-1	1.50	1	0	6	6	2	7
Gabe Gaeckle, ARK.	0-0	2.00	2	0	9	7	3	14
Cameron Flukey, CCU.	1-1	2.70	2	0	10	6	3	12
Smith Bailey, ARIZ.	0-0	3.00	1	0	6	7	2	4
Chase Shores, LSU.	0-0	3.86	4	2	7	5	0	8
Zach Root, ARK.	1-1	4.05	2	0	7	5	4	7
Jacob Morrison, CCU.	1-1	4.76	2	0	11	11	1	9
Riley Eikhoff, CCU.	1-0	4.82	2	0	9	13	1	8

THE ROAD TO OMAHA

REGIONALS

MAY 30-JUNE 2
64 teams, 16 four-team, double-elimination tournaments. Winners advance to super regionals.

NASHVILLE, TENN.
Host: Vanderbilt (No. 1 national seed)
Participants: No. 1 Vanderbilt. No. 2. Louisville. No. 3 East Tennessee State. No. 4 Wright State.
Champion: Louisville (3-0).
Runner-Up: Wright State.
Outstanding Player: Vanderbilt 3B Brodie Johnston

HATTIESBURG REGIONAL
Host: Southern Miss (No. 16 national seed)
Participants: No. 1 Southern Miss. No. 2 Alabama. No. 3 Miami. No. 4 Columbia.
Champion: Miami (3-1)
Runner-Up: Southern Miss.
Outstanding Player: Miami 3B Daniel Cuvet

TALLAHASSEE REGIONAL
Host: Florida State (No. 9 national seed)
Participants: No. 1 Florida State. No. 2 Northeastern. No. 3 Mississippi State. No. 4 Bethune-Cookman.
Champion: FSU (3-0)
Runner-Up: Mississippi State
Outstanding Player: FSU LHP Jamie Arnold

CORVALLIS REGIONAL
Host: Oregon State (No. 8 national seed)
Participants: No. 1 Oregon State. No. 2 TCU. No. 3 Southern California. No. 4 Saint Mary's.
Champion: Oregon State (4-1)
Runner-Up: Southern California
Outstanding Player: Oregon State 3B Trent Caraway

CHAPEL HILL REGIONAL
Host: North Carolina (No. 5 national seed)
Participants: No. 1 North Carolina. No. 2 Oklahoma. No. 3 Nebraska. No. 4 Holy Cross.
Champion: North Carolina (3-1)
Runner-Up: Oklahoma
Outstanding Player: North Carolina 3B Gavin Gallaher

EUGENE REGIONAL
Host: Oregon (No. 12 national seed)
Participants: No. 1 Oregon. No. 2 Arizona. No. 3 Cal Poly. No. 4 Utah Valley.
Champion: Arizona (3-0)
Runner-Up: Cal Poly
Outstanding Player: Arizona SS Mason White

CONWAY REGIONAL
Host: Coastal Carolina (No. 13 national seed)
Participants: No. 1 Coastal Carolina. No. 2 Florida. No. 3 East Carolina. No. 4 Fairfield.
Champion: Coastal Carolina (3-0)
Runner-Up: East Carolina
Outstanding Player: Coastal Carolina 1B Colby Thorndyke

AUBURN REGIONAL
Host: Auburn (No. 4 national seed)
Participants: No. 1 Auburn. No. 2 N.C. State. No. 3 Stetson. No. 4 Central Connecticut.
Champion: Auburn (3-0)
Runner-Up: N.C. State
Outstanding Player: Auburn 1B Bub Terrell

AUSTIN REGIONAL
Host: Texas (No. 2 national seed)
Participants: No. 1 Texas. No. 2 UTSA. No. 3 Kansas State. No. 4 Houston Christian.
Champion: UTSA (3-0)
Runner-Up: Texas
Outstanding Player: UTSA OF James Taussig

LOS ANGELES REGIONAL
Host: UCLA (No. 15 national seed)
Participants: No. 1 UCLA. No. 2 UC Irvine. No. 3 Arizona State. No. 4 Fresno State.
Champion: UCLA (3-0)
Runner-Up: UC Irvine
Outstanding Player: UCLA 3B Roman Martin

OXFORD REGIONAL
Host: Ole Miss (No. 10 national seed)
Participants: No. 1 Ole Miss. No. 2 Georgia Tech. No. 3 Western Kentucky. No. 4 Murray State.
Champion: Murray State (3-1)
Runner-Up: Ole Miss
Outstanding Player: Murray State OF Dustin Mercer

ATHENS REGIONAL
Host: Georgia (No. 7 national seed)
Participants: No. 1 Georgia. No. 2 Duke. No. 3 Oklahoma State. No. 4 Binghamton.
Champion: Duke (3-0)
Runner-Up: Oklahoma State
Outstanding Player: Duke SS Wallace Clark

BATON ROUGE REGIONAL
Host: LSU (No. 6 national seed)
Participants: No. 1 LSU. No. 2 Dallas Baptist. No. 3 Rhode Island. No. 4 Little Rock.
Champion: LSU (3-1)
Runner-Up: Little Rock
Outstanding Player: Little Rock 1B Angel Cano.

CLEMSON REGIONAL
Host: Clemson (No. 11 national seed)
Participants: No. 1 Clemson. No. 2 West Virginia. No. 3 Kentucky. No. 4 SC-Upstate.
Champion: West Virginia (3-0)
Runner-Up: Kentucky
Outstanding Player: West Virginia OF Armani Guzman

KNOXVILLE REGIONAL
Host: Tennessee (No. 14 national seed)
Participants: No. 1 Tennessee. No. 2 Wake Forest. No. 3 Cincinnati. No. 4 Miami (Ohio).
Champion: Tennessee (3-1)
Runner-Up: Wake Forest
Outstanding Player: Tennessee LHP Liam Doyle

FAYETTEVILLE REGIONAL
Host: Arkansas (No. 3 national seed)
Participants: No. 1 Arkansas, No. 2 Kansas. No. 3 Creighton. No. 4 North Dakota State.
Champion: Arkansas (3-0)
Runner-Up: Creighton
Outstanding Player: Arkansas C Ryder Helfrick

SUPER REGIONALS

JUNE 6-9
16 teams, best-of-three series. Winners advance to College World Series.

MIAMI AT LOUISVILLE
Site: Louisville, Ky.
Louisville wins 2-1, advances to World Series

NO. 9 FLORIDA STATE AT NO. 8 OREGON STATE
Site: Corvallis, Ore.
Oregon State wins 2-1, advances to World Series

ARIZONA AT NO. 5 NORTH CAROLINA
Site: Chapel Hill, N.C.
Arizona wins 2-1, advances to World Series

NO. 13 COASTAL CAROLINA AT NO. 4 AUBURN
Site: Auburn, Ala.
Coastal Carolina wins 2-0, advances to World Series

UTSA AT NO. 15 UCLA
Site: Los Angeles
UCLA wins 2-0, advances to World Series

MURRAY STATE AT DUKE
Site: Durham, N.C.
Murray State wins 2-1, advances to World Series

WEST VIRGINIA AT NO. 6 LSU
Site: Baton Rouge, La.
LSU wins 2-0, advances to World Series

NO. 14 TENNESSEE AT NO. 3 ARKANSAS
Site: Fayetteville, Ark.
Arkansas wins 2-0, advances to World Series

Cholowsky Stands Out

PLAYER OF THE YEAR

BY JACOB RUDNER

John Savage still remembers the phone call vividly.

It was June 2020. Shortstop Roch Cholowsky had just finished ninth grade at his suburban Phoenix high school. Savage had been tracking him for months—long before other programs had even started looking.

It's a moment the UCLA head coach still believes changed the future of the Bruins' program.

"I committed on the spot," Cholowsky said. "I would have just turned 15."

There wasn't a parade of suitors. No national buzz. But Savage didn't need consensus. He saw the makeup, the athleticism and the respect for the game. He remembers the feeling washing over him as he watched Cholowsky play: The Bruins needed the budding middle infielder.

"We just knew he had a chance to be special," Savage said.

By the time Cholowsky stepped into the UCLA lineup as a freshman in 2024, he had already lived up to the projection. But what came next defied even the earliest expectations. He became the engine of a national power's revival, the face of a program that collapsed one season and returned to the College World Series the next.

And this June, he became something else entirely.

Cholowsky is the Baseball America College Player of the Year and joins an exclusive group. He is just the sixth POY to be honored prior to his draft year in the 44-year history of the award. His name now sits beside Robin Ventura, John Olerud, Mike Kelly, Mark Teixeira and Anthony Rendon.

Rare as it might be for an underclassman to win Baseball America's highest individual honor for a collegiate player, Cholowsky was more than deserving.

He hit .353/.480/.710 with 23 home runs and 74 RBIs in 66 games. He paced the Big Ten Conference in slugging and with a 1.190 OPS. His defensive value as a shortstop set him apart from other POY contenders.

Cholowsky's 80 runs scored fell just one shy of Chase Utley's UCLA program record. His 179 total bases are second-most by a Bruins player in the 64-team era.

In addition to Utley, other Bruins infielders who forged long, productive MLB careers include Troy Glaus and Brandon Crawford.

Cholowsky's freshman year didn't go according to plan—at least not for the team. UCLA won just 19 games, a historic low under Savage. Cholowsky played every day at third base and grinded through a tough season while staying tethered to the larger goal.

Cholowsky stayed. Not out of inertia or comfort, but conviction.

Roch Cholowsky

PREVIOUS WINNERS

1982: Jeff Ledbetter, OF/LHP, Florida St.
1983: Dave Magadan, 1B, Alabama
1984: Oddibe McDowell, OF, Arizona St.
1985: Pete Incaviglia, OF, Oklahoma State
1986: Casey Close, OF, Michigan
1987: Robin Ventura, 3B, Oklahoma State
1988: John Olerud, 1B/LHP, Washington St.
1989: Ben McDonald, RHP, Louisiana State
1990: Mike Kelly, OF, Arizona State
1991: David McCarthy, 1B, Stanford
1992: Phil Nevin, 3B, Cal State Fullerton
1993: Brooks Kieschnick, DH/RHP, Texas
1994: Jason Varitek, C, Georgia Tech
1995: Todd Helton, 1B/LHP, Tennessee
1996: Kris Benson, RHP, Clemson
1997: J.D. Drew, OF, Florida State
1998: Jeff Austin, RHP, Stanford
1999: Jason Jennings, RHP, Baylor
2000: Mark Teixeira, 3B, Georgia Tech
2001: Mark Prior, RHP, S. California
2002: Khalil Greene, SS, Clemson
2003: Rickie Weeks, 2B, Southern
2004: Jered Weaver, RHP, Long Beach St.
2005: Alex Gordon, 3B, Nebraska
2006: Andrew Miller, LHP, North Carolina
2007: David Price, LHP, Vanderbilt
2008: Buster Posey, C/RHP, Florida State
2009: Stephen Strasburg, RHP, San Diego St.
2010: Anthony Rendon, 3B, Rice
2011: Trevor Bauer, RHP, UCLA
2012: Mike Zunino, C, Florida
2013: Kris Bryant, 3B, San Diego
2014: A.J. Reed, 1B/LHP, Kentucky
2015: Andrew Benintendi, OF, Arkansas
2016: Klye Lewis, OF, Mercer
2017: Brendan McKay, LHP/1B, Louisville
2018: Brady Singer, RHP, Florida
2019: Adley Rutschman, C, Oregon State
2021: Kumar Rocker, RHP, Vanderbilt
2022: Ivan Melendez, 1B, Texas
2023: Paul Skenes, RHP, LSU
2024: Charlie Condon,

Schnall Took Coastal To CWS Finals

BY JACOB RUDNER

Kevin Schnall's instructions weren't printed on paper.

They were passed down in bus rides, in batting cage conversations, in quiet late-night moments after losses. Gary Gilmore didn't hand Schnall a manual when he retired as Coastal Carolina head coach last summer.

Instead, he handed Schnall something heavier: A program. A culture. A standard.

"Put together the best team," Schnall said Gilmore taught him. "Sometimes money doesn't always buy that."

This spring, Schnall built that team and took it all the way to the College World Series championship series.

In his first year as a head coach, Schnall guided Coastal Carolina to 56 wins, a Sun Belt title, a sweep at Auburn in super regionals and a 26-game winning streak that carried the Chanticleers to the national championship series for the second time in program history. And now, he's Baseball America's 2025 College Coach of the Year—the first ever to receive the honor in his debut season as a head coach.

But that's not what anyone inside the program talks about first.

COACH OF THE YEAR

"He really trusts in us," said Jacob Morrison, one of the team's rotation anchors. "Especially a lot of us at our low points. I'm one of the biggest examples of that."

When Morrison got hurt, Schnall stuck with him. He rewarded that belief by becoming the only Division I pitcher besides Paul Skenes in the last five years to post 10 or more outings of six-plus innings with one or fewer runs allowed in a season. Cameron Flukey and Riley Eikhoff, Morrison's partners in what became one of the most dominant rotations in the country, also dazzled.

The group's collective success was emblematic of the program's transformation under Schnall. It also reflected the trust he placed in Matt Williams, the first-year pitching coach whose fingerprints were all over Coastal's historic season.

"(Schnall) finds what each guy does well, then builds on it," Morrison said. "It's incredible. He's there for our catch play, for everything. And it's not just me. He knows what works for each guy."

A year ago, Coastal pitched to a 5.83 ERA. In 2025, that number dropped to 3.22. It wasn't just improved—it was unrecognizable.

So was the win column. Coastal went 36-25 in 2024 and bowed out in the Clemson Regional. Gilmore's retirement closed a nearly three-decade era redefined what mid-major baseball. He'd won a national title. He'd built Coastal into a destination. And his exit could've marked the end of the program's golden age.

Kevin Schnall

PREVIOUS WINNERS

1982: Gene Stephenson, Wichita State
1983: Barry Shollenberger, Alabama
1984: Augie Garrido, Cal State Fullerton
1985: Ron Polk, Mississippi State
1986: Skip Bertman, LSU/Dave Snow, LMU
1987: Mark Marquess, Stanford
1988: Jim Brock, Arizona State
1989: Dave Snow, Long Beach State
1990: Steve Webber, Georgia
1991: Jim Hendry, Creighton
1992: Andy Lopez, Pepperdine
1993: Gene Stephenson, Wichita State
1994: Jim Morris, Miami
1995: Pat Murphy, Arizona State
1996: Skip Bertman, Louisiana State
1997: Jim Wells, Alabama
1998: Pat Murphy, Arizona State
1999: Wayne Graham, Rice
2000: Ray Tanner, South Carolina
2001: Dave Van Horn, Nebraska
2002: Augie Garrido, Texas
2003: George Horton, Cal State Fullerton
2004: David Perno, Georgia
2005: Rick Jones, Tulane
2006: Pat Casey, Oregon State
2007: Dave Serrano, UC Irvine
2008: Mike Fox, North Carolina
2009: Paul Mainieri, Louisiana State
2010: Ray Tanner, South Carolina
2011: Kevin O'Sullivan, Florida
2012: Mike Martin, Florida State
2013: John Savage, UCLA
2014: Tim Corbin, Vanderbilt
2015: Brian O'Connor, Virginia
2016: Jim Schlossnagle, Texas Christian
2017: Dan McDonnell, Louisville
2018: David Pierce, Texas
2019: Mike Martin, Florida State
2021: Chris Lemonis, Mississippi State
2022: Mike Bianco, Mississippi
2023: Jay Johnson, LSU
2024: Tony Vitello, Tennessee

Volantis Makes Presence Felt

FRESHMAN OF THE YEAR

BY JACOB RUDNER

There were moments in 2025 when watching Dylan Volantis pitch didn't feel like baseball. It felt like ballet. Like choreography, if the dancers flung 94 mph sinkers from six-foot-six frames and painted the edges of the strike zone with sweeping breaking balls.

From the dugout steps, Texas pitching coach Max Weiner whispered into the pitch call system. On the mound, Volantis listened. The freshman lefthander nodded, exhaled and executed. Over and over. Out after out.

"It's like they're both painting the same picture," Texas head coach Jim Schlossnagle said. "One's doing it from the dugout, and one's doing it from the mound. And they're in sync."

That synchronization was the heartbeat of one of the nation's most dominant pitching performances in 2025. And after a freshman season that reset records and recalibrated expectations, Volantis has been named Baseball America's Freshman of the Year.

Volantis, who ranks third in BA's 2027 MLB Draft prospect rankings, earned the award with a 1.94 ERA, 74 strikeouts and only 12 walks across 51 innings. He converted 12 saves. Facing the sport's deepest lineups Southeastern Conference play, Volantis was otherworldly: a 1.59 ERA, 0.85 WHIP, a .160 opponent batting average and 11 saves. The save total was most ever by an SEC freshman, breaking a 22-year-old record set by Ole Miss' Steven Head.

But to Schlossnagle, Volantis' brilliance was never about raw numbers. It was about presence, poise and the unteachable heartbeat of a cold-blooded closer.

Dylan Volantis

PREVIOUS WINNERS

- **1993:** Brett Laxton, RHP, Louisiana State
- **1994:** R.A. Dickey, RHP, Tennessee
- **1995:** Kyle Peterson, RHP, Stanford
- **1996:** Pat Burrell, 3B, Miami
- **1997:** Brian Roberts, SS, North Carolina
- **1998:** Xavier Nady, 2B, California
- **1999:** James Jurries, 2B, Tulane
- **2000:** Kevin Howard, 3B, Miami
- **2001:** Michael Aubrey, OF/LHP, Texas
- **2002:** Stephen Drew, SS, Florida State
- **2003:** Ryan Braun, SS, Miami
- **2004:** Wade LeBlanc, LHP, Alabama
- **2005:** Joe Savery, LHP, Rice
- **2006:** Pedro Alvarez, 3B, Vanderbilt
- **2007:** Dustin Ackley, 1B, North Carolina
- **2008:** Chris Hernandez, LHP, Miami
- **2009:** Anthony Rendon, 3B, Rice
- **2010:** Matt Purke, LHP, Texas Christian
- **2011:** Colin Moran, 3B, North Carolina
- **2012:** Carlos Rodon, LHP, N.C. State
- **2013:** Alex Bregman, SS, Louisiana State
- **2014:** Zack Collins, C, Miami
- **2015:** Brendan McKay, LHP/1B, Louisville
- **2016:** Seth Beer, OF, Clemson
- **2017:** Matt Wallner, OF/RHP, Southern Miss
- **2018:** Kevin Abel, RHP, Oregon State
- **2019:** Kumar Rocker, RHP, Vanderbilt
- **2021:** Jack Leiter, RHP, Vanderbilt
- **2022:** Tommy White, 3B/DH, N.C. State
- **2023:** Charlie Condon, 1B/OF, Georgia
- **2024:** Drew Burress, OF, Georgia Tech

FRESHMAN ALL-AMERICA TEAMS

FIRST TEAM

Pos.		AVG	OBP	SLG	AB	R	H	HR	RBI	SB
C	Chase Fralick, Auburn	.335	.426	.472	212	36	71	4	41	0
1B	Myles Bailey, FSU	.327	.441	.663	202	50	66	19	56	4
2B	Chris Rembert, Auburn	.344	.467	.555	209	49	72	10	46	6
3B	Dalton Wentz, Wake Forest	.316	.393	.566	212	48	67	13	50	3
SS	Tyler Bell, Kentucky	.296	.385	.522	226	51	67	10	46	11
OF	Sawyer Strosnider, TCU	.350	.420	.650	220	52	77	11	51	10
OF	Derek Curiel, LSU	.345	.470	.519	258	67	89	7	55	3
OF	Nate Savoie, Loyola Marymount	.300	.384	.675	203	42	61	20	61	7
DH	Brendan Lawson, Florida	.317	.417	.522	224	48	71	10	61	8
UT	Alex Hernandez, Georgia Tech	.335	.415	.609	230	47	77	16	69	5

Pos.		W	L	ERA	G	GS	SV	IP	H	BB	SO
SP	Jack Ohman, Yale	8	1	1.34	12	0	74	45	4	20	87
SP	Adian King, Florida	7	2	2.58	17	0	73	58	3	23	79
SP	Dax Whitney, Oregon State	6	3	3.40	17	0	77	61	5	37	120
SP	Cam Bagwell, UNCW	9	2	3.07	15	0	85	72	6	17	62
RP	Dylan Volantis, Texas	4	1	1.94	23	12	51	33	3	12	74
RP	Casan Evans, LSU	5	1	2.05	19	7	53	44	0	19	71
UT	Alex Hernandez, Georgia Tech	0	1	6.14	6	2	7	4	2	3	3

SECOND TEAM

C: Jacob Lee, VCU. **1B:** Tague Davis, Louisville. **2B:** Tyler Smith, North Carolina A&T. **3B:** Sean Yamaguchi, Nevada. **SS:** Nate Castellon, Cal Poly. **OF:** Tatum Marsh, Stanford; Caleb Daniel, Georgia Tech; AJ Evasco, Kansas State. **DH:** Jake Hanley, Indiana. **SP:** AJ Ciscar, Miami; Landon Mack, Rutgers; Austin Nye, Vanderbilt; Smith Bailey, Arizona. **RP:** Walker McDuffie, North Carolina; Ryan Lynch, North Carolina. **TWP:** Noah Franco, TCU.

NCAA DIVISION I LEADERS

HITTING (MINIMUM 140 AT-BATS)

BATTING AVERAGE

Rk.	Player, Team	Class	AVG	OBP	SLG	G	AB	2B	3B	HR	RBI	BB	SO	SB
1.	Aidan Redahan, Central Conn. St.	Sr	.455	.511	.695	48	200	17	2	9	69	25	12	10
2.	Cardell Thibodeaux, Southern U.	So	.439	.544	.847	49	189	13	5	18	71	39	27	24
3.	Konni Durschlag, High Point	Sr	.434	.546	.751	56	221	23	1	15	59	39	34	4
4.	Logen Devenport, Northern Ky.	Jr	.423	.533	.786	46	168	19	0	14	54	32	41	19
5.	Cameron Nickens, Austin Peay	Sr	.422	.520	.768	59	237	24	2	18	71	47	28	8
6.	Aiden Robbins, Seton Hall	So	.422	.537	.652	53	204	19	5	6	38	44	32	20
7.	James Quinn-Irons, George Mason	Jr	.419	.523	.734	61	241	24	2	16	85	39	46	36
8.	Juan Cruz, Alabama St.	Jr	.416	.478	.682	60	255	22	2	14	73	33	22	6
9.	Ben Parker, William & Mary	Sr	.407	.498	.684	56	231	23	4	11	50	30	33	17
10.	Drew Wyers, Bryant	Jr	.407	.521	.710	45	145	11	0	11	50	26	17	9
11.	Matt King, Arizona St.	Sr	.403	.464	.593	56	216	18	1	7	55	20	20	8
12.	Michael DiMartini, Dayton	So	.403	.465	.685	55	238	11	7	14	65	27	51	37
13.	Jayce Tharnish, St. Bonaventure	Jr	.403	.461	.597	46	196	11	3	7	29	17	27	32
14.	Benny Casillas, Michigan	Sr	.401	.483	.585	55	207	21	1	5	41	28	26	6
15.	Dylan Palmer, Hofstra	Jr	.400	.449	.536	53	220	13	7	1	32	16	18	32
16.	Mason Wolf, NJIT	Sr	.400	.475	.593	44	150	10	2	5	42	21	21	9
17.	Khalil Walker, New Mexico	Sr	.399	.457	.591	53	198	16	5	4	34	18	23	2
18.	Bryce Phelps, Wagner	Sr	.399	.482	.489	51	188	14	0	1	33	18	26	4
19.	Ryan Wideman, Western Ky.	Jr	.398	.466	.652	60	244	20	6	10	68	23	47	45
20.	Kent Schmidt, Georgia Tech	So	.397	.464	.596	40	156	16	0	5	43	17	22	4
21.	Garrett Wright, Bowling Green	So	.396	.506	.644	54	202	20	3	8	48	24	23	6
22.	Jayden Smith, Utah Valley	Sr	.396	.504	.517	54	207	17	4	0	42	28	42	14
23.	Kerrington Cross, Cincinnati	Sr	.396	.526	.647	56	207	10	3	12	50	50	35	15
24.	Bryce Cermenelli, Central Ark.	Sr	.395	.461	.474	38	152	7	1	1	23	16	17	2
25.	Alex Lodise, Florida St.	Jr	.394	.462	.705	58	241	18	3	17	68	27	55	6
26.	Jacob French, California	So	.390	.440	.564	53	195	12	5	4	36	8	20	2
27.	Bryce Calloway, New Orleans	Sr	.390	.484	.722	54	205	10	2	18	63	31	60	1
28.	Brayden Simpson, High Point	Jr	.389	.477	.774	58	234	24	0	22	78	24	46	14
29.	Bradley Garner, VMI	So	.389	.496	.672	52	198	20	3	10	59	40	39	23
30.	Nolan Sailors, Creighton	Sr	.389	.485	.584	59	226	18	4	6	44	33	41	27
31.	Isaiah Barkett, Stetson	Jr	.389	.461	.498	54	221	16	1	2	33	25	9	32
32.	Braden Burress, East Carolina	Fr	.389	.488	.498	61	211	11	0	4	33	31	26	18
33.	Jordy Oriach, New Mexico	Jr	.388	.470	.748	52	214	25	2	16	63	29	29	1
34.	Damian Ruiz, Lamar University	So	.388	.511	.607	56	214	22	2	7	46	50	27	14
35.	Dyrenson Wouters, Dayton	So	.388	.470	.566	46	152	12	0	5	34	16	12	5
36.	Scott Campbell, USC Upstate	Jr	.388	.498	.622	55	188	11	0	11	54	20	25	21
37.	Trevor Cohen, Rutgers	Jr	.387	.460	.523	57	235	24	1	2	36	30	15	19
38.	Luke Nowak, UIC	Sr	.387	.455	.559	53	222	17	3	5	37	28	37	28
39.	Matt Ineich, Ohio	Fr	.387	.467	.514	36	142	9	0	3	25	21	11	9
40.	Owen Prince, VMI	Jr	.385	.504	.474	53	213	13	0	2	44	46	25	46
41.	Lukas Cook, Purdue	Sr	.385	.428	.490	40	143	10	1	1	21	11	26	7
42.	Armani Raygoza, UTRGV	So	.384	.474	.706	53	211	17	0	17	60	27	40	2
43.	Henry Zipay, Omaha	Sr	.384	.475	.551	48	185	15	5	2	25	23	46	3
44.	Kyle Fossum, Youngstown St.	Sr	.382	.496	.777	57	220	18	0	23	62	46	53	9
45.	Kelton Phillips, Texas Southern	Jr	.380	.479	.557	49	158	11	1	5	36	23	12	22
46.	Tyler Howard, Portland	Jr	.379	.481	.497	39	153	9	0	3	27	29	23	0
47.	Colby Shelton, Florida	Jr	.377	.458	.606	45	175	19	0	7	35	21	24	6
48.	Joe Tiroly, Rider	So	.377	.481	.749	52	199	16	2	18	70	36	25	6
49.	CJ Moran, San Diego St.	Fr	.377	.458	.484	44	159	15	1	0	36	20	22	1
50.	Tatum Marsh, Stanford	Fr	.377	.459	.526	50	175	13	2	3	25	11	24	4
51.	Dean Toigo, UNLV	Sr	.377	.445	.682	54	220	13	0	18	74	20	40	5
52.	Hayden Jatczak, Kent St.	Sr	.376	.491	.770	56	213	28	4	16	81	46	37	10
53.	Chris Baillargeon, Holy Cross	Sr	.376	.490	.507	58	205	18	0	3	52	38	48	5
54.	Kade Lewis, Wake Forest	So	.376	.482	.602	60	226	18	0	11	59	45	45	4
55.	Dylan Grego, Ball St.	Jr	.376	.429	.624	58	242	14	2	14	55	22	44	14
56.	Ahmar Donatto, Prairie View	Fr	.376	.448	.646	51	178	14	5	8	35	18	37	13
57.	Zandt Payne, Abilene Christian	Sr	.376	.490	.550	45	149	12	1	4	39	20	21	10
58.	Jordan McCladdie, Jackson St.	Sr	.376	.521	.564	51	181	12	5	4	32	44	22	49
59.	Chris Hacopian, Maryland	So	.375	.502	.656	52	192	12	0	14	61	40	19	1
60.	Trey Fenderson, Presbyterian	Sr	.374	.477	.521	51	163	16	1	2	24	27	25	14
61.	Dean Ferrara, Fairfield	Sr	.374	.435	.517	58	265	14	0	8	57	28	28	20
62.	Devin Taylor, Indiana	Jr	.374	.494	.706	55	214	13	2	18	66	52	30	12
63.	Daniel Cuvet, Miami (FL)	So	.372	.450	.708	61	226	20	1	18	84	30	51	6
64.	Jack Moroknek, Butler	Jr	.372	.443	.702	54	218	16	1	18	57	26	41	2
65.	Cider Canon, Davidson	So	.371	.460	.733	48	202	16	3	17	52	28	47	10
66.	Jack Gurevitch, San Diego	Jr	.371	.477	.681	56	229	16	2	17	56	35	43	5

COLLEGE

Alex Lodise was one of the most productive hitters in the ACC

Miami's Daniel Cuvet hit .372/.450/.708 in 61 games

67.	Roberto Gonzalez, CSUN	Sr	.371	.478	.617	45	167	10	8	5	30	21	28	9
68.	LeTrey McCollum, UC Santa Barbara	Sr	.371	.472	.540	54	213	10	4	6	40	26	29	17
69.	Aidan Paradine, Siena	Fr	.370	.474	.536	53	192	11	0	7	41	23	18	0
70.	Ryland Zaborowski, Georgia	Sr	.370	.500	.788	45	146	10	0	17	61	29	40	0
71.	Michael O'Shaughnessy, Davidson	Jr	.369	.482	.691	56	217	19	0	17	70	29	49	1
72.	Landon Williams, Prairie View	So	.369	.465	.667	51	168	12	1	12	51	27	37	3
73.	James Layman, Wofford	Jr	.369	.493	.484	49	157	11	2	1	33	26	43	23
74.	Tyler Bickers, Milwaukee	Sr	.369	.482	.498	58	225	11	3	4	42	46	45	7
75.	Nick Rodriguez, Missouri St.	Sr	.368	.444	.702	55	228	22	0	18	56	33	36	2
76.	Eric Becker, Virginia	So	.368	.453	.617	50	201	21	1	9	52	21	41	5
77.	Eddie Madrigal, Saint Mary's (CA)	Sr	.368	.462	.698	62	242	13	2	21	78	28	35	9
78.	Josh McAlister, New Mexico	Sr	.368	.452	.731	47	171	9	1	17	43	21	49	14
79.	Jon LeGrande, St. John's (NY)	Jr	.368	.443	.578	52	185	8	5	7	48	23	26	33
80.	Logan Sutter, Purdue	Sr	.367	.471	.709	54	196	22	0	15	62	36	47	3
81.	Eddie King Jr., Louisville	Sr	.367	.435	.750	55	188	19	1	17	63	21	38	4
82.	Ryan Kroepel, Utah Tech	So	.367	.442	.546	55	207	15	2	6	35	24	39	4
83.	Owen Hull, George Mason	So	.367	.474	.557	61	237	15	3	8	63	41	46	42
84.	Harrison Feinberg, Northeastern	Sr	.367	.455	.715	58	207	14	2	18	67	35	42	37
85.	Kyle McDaniel, Utah Tech	Sr	.367	.464	.481	55	210	10	1	4	21	35	21	10
86.	Jake Schaffner, North Dakota St.	So	.367	.435	.467	55	229	9	4	2	21	22	27	18
87.	Mason Lytle, UTSA	Sr	.366	.424	.560	62	268	22	0	10	68	24	23	17
88.	Carlos Vasquez, Western Ky.	Jr	.366	.435	.532	57	235	22	1	5	40	24	27	8
89.	Brady O'Brien, Richmond	Gr.	.366	.422	.777	50	202	19	2	20	72	22	44	2
90.	Mason Strong, Utah Valley	Jr	.366	.432	.609	58	238	19	3	11	67	23	27	12
91.	Keaton Grady, DBU	Sr	.366	.449	.531	47	175	13	2	4	25	26	21	18
92.	Lucas Carmichael, William & Mary	Sr	.366	.415	.571	56	238	13	0	12	47	15	34	8
93.	Ryan Fenn, Cal Poly	Sr	.365	.390	.482	58	249	19	2	2	42	9	22	16
94.	Aidan Cohall, Stonehill	Jr	.365	.430	.702	46	181	19	0	14	60	16	27	4
95.	Robin Villeneuve, Texas Tech	Sr	.365	.447	.661	52	189	18	1	12	49	26	50	3
96.	Cole Kitchens, Southern Ind.	Jr	.365	.414	.617	53	222	18	1	12	60	14	35	1
97.	Ryan Daniels, UConn	Jr	.365	.476	.744	54	203	15	4	18	75	40	41	10
98.	Jim Kemp, Iona	Sr	.365	.478	.625	52	200	12	2	12	57	33	40	2
99.	Chris McHugh, NC State	So	.365	.462	.533	53	197	12	0	7	48	23	40	1
100.	Brian Heckelman, Towson	Jr	.365	.442	.588	53	170	10	2	8	42	20	22	3

COLLEGE

ON-BASE PERCENTAGE
Rank Player, Pos., Team	OBP
1. Trey Rutledge, Alabama A&M	.567
2. Konni Durschlag, High Point	.546
3. Cardell Thibodeaux, Southern U.	.544
4. Jordan Ballin, UTSA	.541
5. Aiden Robbins, Seton Hall	.537
6. Logen Devenport, Northern Ky.	.533
7. Miggy Echazarreta, High Point	.530
8. Kerrington Cross, Cincinnati	.526
9. James Quinn-Irons, George Mason	.523
10. Jordan McCladdie, Jackson St.	.521

SLUGGING PERCENTAGE
Rank Player, Pos., Team	SLG
1. Landen Johnson, High Point	.847
2. James Quinn-Irons, George Mason	.788
3. Mulivai Levu, UCLA	.786
4. Daniel Cuvet, Miami (FL)	.777
5. Jack Hopko, Rhode Island	.777
6. Johnny Sweeney, USC Upstate	.774
7. Hayden Jatczak, Kent St.	.770
8. Matt Schark, Southern Ill.	.770
9. Kaden Smith, Charleston So.	.769
10. Brayden Simpson, High Point	.768

RUNS BATTED IN
Rank Player, Pos., Team	RBI
1. Landen Johnson, High Point	86
2. James Quinn-Irons, George Mason	85
2. Mulivai Levu, UCLA	85
4. Daniel Cuvet, Miami (FL)	84
5. Jack Hopko, Rhode Island	83
6. Johnny Sweeney, USC Upstate	82
7. Hayden Jatczak, Kent St.	81
8. Matt Schark, Southern Ill.	80
9. Kaden Smith, Charleston So.	79
10. Brayden Simpson, High Point	78
10. Eddie Madrigal, Saint Mary's (CA)	78

HOME RUNS
Rank Player, Pos., Team	HR
1. Boston Smith, Wright St.	26
2. Mason Neville, Oregon	26
3. Andrew Fischer, Tennessee	25
4. Matt Schark, Southern Ill.	24
5. Kyle Fossum, Youngstown St.	23
5. Cooper Torres, ETSU	23
5. Roch Cholowsky, UCLA	23
8. Seven tied	22

DOUBLES
Rank Player, Pos., Team	2B
1. Hayden Jatczak, Kent St.	28
1. Kaleb Freeman, Georgia St.	28
3. Jonathan Hogart, Murray St.	26
4. Jordy Oriach, New Mexico	25
4. Dillon Baker, Miami (OH)	25
6. Brayden Simpson, High Point	24
6. Cameron Nickens, Austin Peay	24
6. James Quinn-Irons, George Mason	24
6. Alex Ungar, Sacred Heart	24
6. Jared Beebe, St. John's (NY)	24
6. Jarrett Pokrovsky, Penn	24
6. Trevor Cohen, Rutgers	24

TRIPLES
Rank Player, Pos., Team	3B
1. Sawyer Strosnider, TCU	10
2. Broedy Poppell, Florida A&M	9
2. Connor Westenburg, McNeese	9
4. Mason White, Arizona	8
4. AJ Soldra, Seton Hall	8
4. Roberto Gonzalez, CSUN	8
6. Benjamin Greer, Abilene Christian	7
6. Kane Kepley, North Carolina	7
6. Dylan Palmer, Hofstra	7
6. Michael DiMartini, Dayton	7
6. Tyson Drake, Tarleton St.	7

STOLEN BASES
Rank Player, Pos., Team	SB
1. Lucas Moore, Louisville	53
2. Jordan McCladdie, Jackson St.	49
3. Owen Prince, VMI	46
4. Kane Kepley, North Carolina	45
4. Ryan Wideman, Western Ky.	45
6. Kazuya Jordan, VMI	44
6. Bryce Hughes, Texas Southern	44
8. Dariyan Pendergrass, C. of Charleston	43
8. Caleb Shpur, UConn	43
10. Owen Hull, George Mason	42
10. Jermel Ford, Alcorn	42

RUNS
Rank Player, Pos., Team	R
1. John Bay, Austin Peay	94
2. Lucas Moore, Louisville	85
2. Anthony DePino, Rhode Island	85
2. Owen Hull, George Mason	83
5. Wehiwa Aloy, Arkansas	81
6. Jonathan Hogart, Murray St.	80
6. Roch Cholowsky, UCLA	80
6. Eric Genther, Rhode Island	80
9. Konni Durschlag, High Point	79
9. Hayden Jatczak, Kent St.	79

HITS
Rank Player, Pos., Team	H
1. Juan Cruz, Alabama St.	106
2. James Quinn-Irons, George Mason	101
3. Cameron Nickens, Austin Peay	100
4. Dean Ferrara, Fairfield	99
5. Mason Lytle, UTSA	98
6. Ryan Wideman, Western Ky.	97
7. Konni Durschlag, High Point	96
7. Michael DiMartini, Dayton	96
9. Alex Lodise, Florida St.	95
10. Ben Parker, William & Mary	94

TOTAL BASES
Rank Player, Pos., Team	TB
1. Cameron Nickens, Austin Peay	182
1. Jonathan Hogart, Murray St.	182
3. Brayden Simpson, High Point	181
4. Wehiwa Aloy, Arkansas	179
4. Roch Cholowsky, UCLA	179
6. James Quinn-Irons, George Mason	177
6. Mason White, Arizona	177
8. Juan Cruz, Alabama St.	174
9. John Bay, Austin Peay	173
10. Matt Schark, Southern Ill.	172

WALKS
Rank Player, Pos., Team	BB
1. Grant Gallagher, ETSU	66
1. Miggy Echazarreta, High Point	66
3. Blake Cavill, Troy	65
4. Andrew Fischer, Tennessee	63
5. Easton Talt, Oregon St.	62
6. Kaleb Freeman, Georgia St.	61
7. Carson Garner, Murray St.	60
8. Luke Stevenson, North Carolina	59
8. Brayden Martin, Maryland	59
10. Four tied	57

TOUGHEST TO STRIKE OUT
Rank Player, Pos., Team	AB/SO
1. Casey Kleinman, VCU	34.5
2. Elliot Krewson, Dartmouth	26.2
3. Isaiah Barkett, Stetson	24.6
4. Andy Cisneros, Morehead St.	23.9
5. Irivn Escobar, Bethune-Cookman	22.0
6. Carson Schrack, Southeast Mo. St.	19.9
7. Julian Swift, SFA	17.4
8. Aidan Redahan, Central Conn.	16.7
9. Alejandro Garza, Cal Poly	16.4
10. Erik Paulsen, Stony Brook	16.1

HIT BY PITCH
Rank Player, Pos., Team	HBP
1. Gabe Natividad, Winthrop	34
1. Charlie Scholvin, Toledo	34
3. Evan Cloyd, CSU Bakersfield	33
4. Walker Mitchell, Coastal Carolina	32
5. Dominic Listi, Clemson	30
5. Will Brown, Florida A&M	30
7. Luke Iverson, Utah Valley	29
7. Alex Richter, Ball St.	29
7. Steven Meier, Troy	29
10. Five tied	28

SACRIFICE BUNTS
Rank Player, Pos., Team	SAC
1. Cody Kashimoto, Saint Mary's (CA)	23
2. Jeff Pierantoni, Yale	20
3. Ledy Alvarez, Jackson St.	16
3. Matt Heavner, NC State	16
5. Michael Perazzo, Sacramento St.	15
6. Tanner Griffith, Saint Mary's (CA)	14
6. Ethan Rossi, Eastern Ill.	14
6. Tommy Markey, Fordham	14
6. Cam Burdick, Cal St. Fullerton	14
10. Four tied	13

SACRIFICE FLIES
Rank Player, Pos., Team	SF
1. Joseph Eichelberger, Jackson St.	10
1. Ben Slanker, Ohio	10
1. AJ Havrilla, Marshall	10
4. Jake Butler, George Mason	9
4. Luke Gaffney, Clemson	9
4. Ryan Rivera, LIU	9
4. Harrison Feinberg, Northeastern	9
4. Nate Vargas, UC Santa Barbara	9
4. Ben Zeigler-Namoa, Hawaii	9
10. 14 tied	8

COLLEGE

Sawyer Hawks went 4-0, 1.60 as a reliever in the Vanderbilt bullpen

Dominic Carbone was a key member of an effective Coastal Carolina bullpen

PITCHING (MINIMUM 40 INNINGS PITCHED)

Rk. Pitcher, Team	Class	W	L	ERA	G	GS	SV	IP	H	R	ER	BB	SO
1. Charlie Walker, Northeastern	Jr	4	0	1.29	16	2	7	48.2	30	8	7	5	56
2. Jack Ohman, Yale	Fr	8	1	1.34	12	11	0	73.2	45	15	11	20	87
3. Ty VanDyke, Stetson	Sr	7	0	1.52	27	0	9	47.1	30	10	8	16	71
4. Sawyer Hawks, Vanderbilt	Sr	4	0	1.60	18	0	8	45	25	8	8	11	59
5. Jake Gorelick, Stetson	So	4	0	1.74	16	1	3	41.1	29	10	8	8	23
6. Drew Horn, Middle Tenn.	So	3	1	1.75	8	8	0	46.1	24	11	9	25	57
7. Cal Higgins, Western Ky.	Sr	3	2	1.87	22	0	6	43.1	28	12	9	11	52
8. Dylan Volantis, Texas	Fr	4	1	1.94	23	1	12	51	33	13	11	12	74
9. Evan Dempsey, FGCU	So	5	1	1.97	15	10	0	68.2	57	19	15	20	75
10. Wyatt Cameron, Central Conn. St.	Sr	3	2	1.98	22	0	5	41	26	13	9	21	47
11. Zane Taylor, UNCW	Sr	11	2	1.98	15	15	0	95.2	62	24	21	11	105
12. MJ Bollinger, Fla. Atlantic	So	3	3	2.01	28	0	10	44.2	37	10	10	13	39
13. Jake Knapp, North Carolina	Sr	14	0	2.02	16	15	0	102.1	72	27	23	16	88
14. Easton Rakers, Lindenwood	Jr	1	2	2.03	23	0	4	44.1	40	13	10	15	43
15. Casan Evans, LSU	Fr	5	1	2.05	19	3	7	52.2	44	13	12	19	71
16. Donovann Jackson, UC Santa Barbara	Jr	4	0	2.06	21	0	2	43.2	28	11	10	20	43
17. Sean Youngerman, Oklahoma St.	Jr	3	1	2.08	20	6	4	52	37	15	12	8	59
18. Brodie Purcell, Southern California	So	3	2	2.11	27	0	4	42.2	26	12	10	19	51
19. Jonathan Gonzalez, Stetson	Sr	10	2	2.11	15	15	0	93.2	70	23	22	21	105
20. Michael Lombardi, Tulane	Jr	4	1	2.14	23	6	11	42	20	16	10	21	73
21. Ryan Bilka, Richmond	Jr	6	2	2.18	18	0	3	62	43	18	15	13	57
22. Clay Edmondson, UNC Asheville	Jr	5	2	2.20	13	13	0	81.2	66	25	20	26	87
23. Bennett Stice, Lindenwood	Sr	4	1	2.21	17	1	5	40.2	32	10	10	2	34
24. Trace Baker, UNCW	Jr	4	1	2.24	18	2	5	52.1	36	22	13	16	54
25. Jordan Gottesman, Northeastern	Sr	9	2	2.27	16	12	1	83.1	55	24	21	17	97
26. Logan Reddemann, San Diego	So	3	1	2.29	11	9	0	55	44	17	14	12	53
27. Dominic Cancellieri, Creighton	Sr	2	1	2.29	13	13	0	55	47	28	14	23	59
28. Bryce Riggs, Eastern Ill.	So	3	4	2.30	19	4	2	47	35	29	12	18	45
29. Jake Schweitzer, Louisville	Fr	4	3	2.34	25	0	3	42.1	31	14	11	19	23
30. Cade Montgomery, Utah Tech	So	4	2	2.35	10	10	0	57.1	46	18	15	19	48
31. Dominick Carbone, Coastal Carolina	So	6	0	2.36	28	0	6	42	37	13	11	9	52
32. Andrew Wright, Cal St. Fullerton	So	3	2	2.40	27	0	10	41.1	35	16	11	13	49
33. Blake Gillespie, Charlotte	Jr	7	4	2.42	15	15	0	100.1	69	28	27	19	131
34. Jacob Morrison, Coastal Carolina	Jr	12	2	2.42	19	18	0	107.2	79	29	29	23	104
35. Caleb Granger, Florida A&M	Sr	3	1	2.47	8	8	0	43.2	37	19	12	14	35
36. Riely Hunsaker, Lamar University	Jr	4	3	2.47	14	14	0	76.2	72	26	21	16	70
37. Max Gitlin, Northeastern	Sr	8	1	2.49	11	8	1	50.2	38	16	14	12	30
38. Connor Fennell, Vanderbilt	So	6	0	2.53	17	7	2	53.1	33	16	15	11	84
39. Dom Velazquez, Delaware	Sr	1	3	2.53	17	0	4	46.1	32	18	13	18	50
40. Antoine Jean, Houston	Sr	5	1	2.55	21	0	5	67	40	21	19	20	110
41. Bryan Green, UC Davis	Sr	3	5	2.55	15	15	0	81.1	82	27	23	23	69
42. Ian Umlandt, Oregon	Jr	6	2	2.55	18	5	1	60	66	23	17	16	44
43. Charlie West, UConn	So	6	0	2.58	15	8	0	52.1	30	21	15	34	59
44. Aidan King, Florida	Fr	7	2	2.58	17	12	0	73.1	58	28	21	23	79
45. Richard Long, Jacksonville	Sr	8	4	2.59	15	15	0	93.2	72	37	27	20	66
46. Liam O'Brien, Hawaii	Sr	4	3	2.60	17	9	0	52	20	20	15	38	59
47. Carson Byers, Miami (OH)	Jr	2	2	2.61	23	2	6	76	59	27	22	24	72
48. Braylon Myers, Alabama	Sr	3	1	2.63	23	0	2	41	27	13	12	14	58
49. Will Jones, Northeastern	Sr	11	1	2.63	15	15	0	72	55	26	21	19	75
50. Josh Morano, Cal Poly	So	3	0	2.64	19	0	0	47.2	50	19	14	14	36

COLLEGE

WINS

Rank	Pitcher, Team	W
1.	Jake Knapp, North Carolina	14
2.	Ricky Ojeda, UC Irvine	13
3.	Jacob Morrison, Coastal Carolina	12
3.	Kade Anderson, LSU	12
3.	Anthony Eyanson, LSU	12
3.	Michael Barnett, UCLA	12
7.	Mason Patel, Georgia Tech	11
7.	Cooper Katskee, Miami (OH)	11
7.	Will Jones, Northeastern	11
7.	Zane Taylor, UNCW	11

SAVES

Rank	Pitcher, Team	SV
1.	Carson Ozmer, Alabama	17
2.	Dylan Crooks, Oklahoma	16
3.	Lucas Mahlstedt, Clemson	15
4.	Tony Pluta, Arizona	14
4.	Kade Brown, Sacramento St.	14
4.	Max Martin, UC Irvine	14
4.	Davis Aiken, Col. of Charleston	14
8.	Garrett Langrell, Creighton	13
8.	Luke Broderick, Nebraska	13
10.	Connar Penrod, Bowling Green	12
10.	Dylan Volantis, Texas	12

STRIKEOUTS

Rank	Pitcher, Team	SO
1.	Kade Anderson, LSU	180
2.	Liam Doyle, Tennessee	164
3.	Anthony Eyanson, LSU	152
4.	Blake Gillespie, Charlotte	131
5.	Zach Root, Arkansas	126
6.	Kyson Witherspoon, Oklahoma	124
7.	Colton Book, Saint Joseph's	122
7.	JD Thompson, Vanderbilt	122
9.	Dax Whitney, Oregon St.	120
9.	Ben Jacobs, Arizona St.	120

STRIKEOUTS PER NINE

Rank	Pitcher, Team	SO/9
1.	Liam Doyle, Tennessee	15.43
2.	Antoine Jean, Houston	14.78
3.	Patrick Forbes, Louisville	14.76
4.	Max Bayles, Santa Clara	14.18
5.	Dax Whitney, Oregon St.	14.09
6.	Kaden Echeman, Northern Ky.	13.98
7.	Kade Anderson, LSU	13.61
8.	James Ellwanger, DBU	13.50
9.	Tyler Bremner, UC Santa Barbara	12.92
10.	Ben Jacobs, Arizona St.	12.91

FEWEST HITS PER NINE

Rank	Pitcher, Team	H/9
1.	Albert Roblez, Long Beach St.	5.25
2.	Antoine Jean, Houston	5.37
3.	Truman Pauley, Harvard	5.37
4.	Jack Ohman, Yale	5.50
5.	JB Middleton, Southern Miss	5.55
6.	Jackson Phipps, Jacksonville St.	5.59
7.	Brian Curley, Georgia	5.73
8.	Ryan Piech, Xavier	5.73
9.	Brady Frederick, ETSU	5.79
10.	Zane Taylor, UNCW	5.83

FEWEST WALKS PER NINE

Rank	Pitcher, Team	BB/9
1.	Nathan Mertens, Southeast Mo. St.	0.91
2.	Zane Taylor, UNCW	1.03
3.	Kenton Deverman, Evansville	1.07
4.	Riley Eikhoff, Coastal Carolina	1.10
5.	Connor Harris, Winthrop	1.11
6.	Jack Anker, Fresno St.	1.12
7.	Jack Nedrow, South Fla.	1.25
8.	Luc Fladda, Tulane	1.29
9.	Caden Aoki, Southern California	1.30
10.	Colton Cosper, Mercer	1.32

TEAM LEADERS

SCORING

Rank	Team	G	R	R/G
1.	High Point	58	619	10.7
2.	Austin Peay	59	567	9.6
3.	USC Upstate	61	579	9.5
4.	Kent St.	56	531	9.5
5.	Grambling	54	506	9.4
6.	Charleston So.	53	491	9.3
7.	VMI	53	491	9.3
8.	New Mexico	53	490	9.2
9.	Rhode Island	60	539	9.0
10.	Winthrop	60	528	8.8
11.	UConn	59	519	8.8
12.	Southern Ill.	57	500	8.8
13.	Wright St.	61	532	8.7
14.	ETSU	58	501	8.6
15.	Murray St.	61	525	8.6
16.	George Mason	61	524	8.6
17.	UTSA	62	530	8.5
18.	Georgia	60	509	8.5
19.	Arkansas	65	550	8.5
20.	Wake Forest	61	515	8.4
21.	Utah Valley	62	523	8.4
22.	Georgia Tech	60	506	8.4
23.	DBU	59	494	8.4
24.	Duke	62	516	8.3
25.	Bethune-Cookman	60	499	8.3
26.	Davidson	56	463	8.3
27.	Arizona St.	60	492	8.2
28.	Indiana	56	459	8.2
29.	Miami (OH)	58	474	8.2
30.	Tennessee	65	531	8.2
31.	Maryland	56	457	8.2
32.	Western Caro.	58	473	8.2
33.	Fairfield	58	470	8.1
34.	UC Irvine	60	484	8.1
35.	Oregon	58	465	8.0
36.	Kansas	60	481	8.0
37.	UCLA	66	524	7.9
38.	Western Ky.	60	476	7.9
39.	LSU	68	536	7.9
40.	North Carolina	61	479	7.9
41.	West Virginia	60	470	7.8
42.	Ole Miss	64	498	7.8
43.	Louisville	66	512	7.8
44.	Alabama St.	60	465	7.8
45.	Mississippi St.	59	456	7.7
46.	Florida	61	465	7.6
47.	Saint Mary's (CA)	62	471	7.6
48.	Auburn	61	455	7.5
49.	Oregon St.	65	481	7.4
50.	Coastal Carolina	69	509	7.4

BATTING AVERAGE

Rank	Team	AVG
1.	New Mexico	.337
2.	Austin Peay	.333
3.	High Point	.331
4.	Central Conn. St.	.329
5.	George Mason	.326
6.	UCF	.319
7.	Alabama St.	.317
8.	Cal Poly	.316
9.	Richmond	.316
10.	USC Upstate	.315

HOME RUNS

Rank	Team	HR
1.	Georgia	144
2.	High Point	131
2.	Tennessee	131
4.	Arkansas	127
5.	Ole Miss	124
6.	ETSU	121
7.	Wake Forest	116
8.	Duke	115
8.	Oregon	115
10.	Southern Ill.	113

DOUBLES

Rank	Team	2B
1.	Arizona St.	149
1.	Georgia Tech	149
1.	High Point	149
4.	Murray St.	148
4.	New Mexico	148
6.	Austin Peay	141
7.	USC Upstate	140
8.	Arizona	137
9.	Cal Poly	136
9.	LSU	136

TRIPLES

Rank	Team	3B
1.	Arizona	36
2.	Kent St.	29
2.	TCU	29
4.	Tarleton St.	26
5.	San Jose St.	25
6.	Central Conn. St.	24
6.	Prairie View	24
6.	Rhode Island	24
6.	Southern U.	24
10.	Air Force	23

SLUGGING PERCENTAGE

Rank	Team	SLG
1.	High Point	.607
2.	Austin Peay	.585
3.	New Mexico	.574
4.	ETSU	.565
5.	Georgia	.564
6.	Southern Ill.	.555
7.	Missouri St.	.548
8.	Arkansas	.547
9.	Tennessee	.546
10.	Wake Forest	.540

STOLEN BASES

Rank	Team	SB
1.	VMI	209
2.	Northeastern	196
3.	Southern U.	191
4.	Mount St. Mary's	181
5.	George Mason	167
6.	Louisville	162
7.	Wofford	158

WALKS

Rank	Team	BB
8.	Alcorn	153
9.	Oakland	147
10.	Longwood	139
1.	Duke	408
2.	Wake Forest	390
3.	Oregon St.	377
4.	Kansas	367
5.	Fairfield	365
5.	High Point	365
7.	LSU	360
8.	Clemson	359
9.	Tennessee	357
10.	Murray St.	355

PITCHING

EARNED RUN AVERAGE

Rank	Team	ERA
1.	Northeastern	3.06
2.	Coastal Carolina	3.20
3.	North Carolina	3.47
4.	Western Ky.	3.50
5.	Yale	3.59
6.	Texas	3.71
7.	LSU	3.73
8.	Vanderbilt	3.73
9.	Southeastern La.	3.76
10.	Arkansas	3.84
11.	UC Santa Barbara	3.92
12.	UNCW	3.93
13.	Southern Miss.	4.03
14.	Tennessee	4.06
15.	Oregon	4.10
16.	Iowa	4.16
17.	Oregon St.	4.24
18.	Hawaii	4.25
19.	UCF	4.29
20.	Texas A&M	4.30
21.	Creighton	4.33
22.	Lamar University	4.33
23.	Stetson	4.39
24.	TCU	4.43
25.	Arkansas St.	4.44
26.	Mississippi St.	4.44
27.	Oklahoma	4.47
28.	Charlotte	4.49
29.	Baylor	4.52
30.	UCLA	4.53
31.	ETSU	4.54
32.	Kentucky	4.55
33.	Oklahoma St.	4.55
34.	UC Davis	4.56
35.	McNeese	4.56
36.	West Virginia	4.60
37.	Liberty	4.64
38.	Ole Miss	4.65
39.	George Mason	4.65
40.	Bryant	4.66
41.	Southeast Mo. St.	4.67
42.	Virginia	4.68
43.	Auburn	4.70
44.	Fla. Atlantic	4.71
45.	Southern California	4.75
46.	Mercer	4.75
47.	Florida St.	4.76
48.	Northwestern St.	4.77
49.	Eastern Ill.	4.82
50.	Washington	4.85

STRIKEOUTS PER NINE

Rank	Team	SO/9
1.	Vanderbilt	11.9
2.	Tennessee	11.9
3.	Mississippi St.	11.8
4.	LSU	11.7
5.	Florida	11.4
6.	Arkansas	11.3
7.	Arizona St.	11.3
8.	Wake Forest	11.1
9.	Georgia	11.1
10.	Florida St.	10.9

FEWEST WALKS PER NINE

Rank	Team	BB/9
1.	Northeastern	2.44
2.	Texas A&M	2.89
3.	Coastal Carolina	3.05
4.	Southeast Mo. St.	3.09
5.	Arkansas	3.11
6.	Southern Miss.	3.23
7.	Baylor	3.23
8.	Arizona	3.27
9.	UT Arlington	3.29
10.	Nevada	3.30

FIELDING

FIELDING PERCENTAGE

Rank	Team	PCT
1.	Charlotte	.984
2.	Arkansas	.983
3.	Liberty	.983
4.	Ball St.	.983
5.	Vanderbilt	.983
6.	Georgia	.983
7.	UCLA	.982
8.	Auburn	.982
9.	Cal Poly	.981
10.	LSU	.981
11.	Florida St.	.981
12.	Texas	.980
13.	Northeastern	.980
14.	Michigan	.980
15.	Oregon St.	.980
16.	DBU	.979
17.	UC Davis	.979
18.	UTRGV	.979
19.	Murray St.	.979
20.	Cincinnati	.979
21.	Arizona St.	.978
22.	BYU	.978
23.	Northwestern	.978
24.	Duke	.978
25.	Rutgers	.978
26.	UTSA	.978
27.	Arizona	.978
28.	Fresno St.	.977
29.	Stanford	.977
30.	Washington	.977
31.	Stetson	.977
32.	Kentucky	.977
33.	Nevada	.977
34.	Binghamton	.977
35.	Coastal Carolina	.977
36.	Abilene Christian	.977
37.	UC Santa Barbara	.977
38.	Kansas	.977
39.	NC State	.977
40.	Oregon	.977
41.	Southern California	.976
42.	Notre Dame	.976
43.	North Carolina	.976
44.	Missouri St.	.976
45.	Toledo	.976
46.	Richmond	.976
47.	Tulane	.976
48.	Alabama	.976
49.	Cornell	.976
50.	San Francisco	.975

DOUBLE PLAYS

Rank	Team	DP
1.	UCLA	66
2.	Arizona	57
3.	Coastal Carolina	57
4.	San Jose St.	55
5.	Utah Tech	55
6.	Louisville	54
6.	New Mexico St.	54
6.	Tulane	54
9.	Four tied	526

COLLEGE TOP 25

1. LSU
Coach: Jay Johnson. **Overall:** 53-15

Player, Pos, Yr	AVG	OBP	SLG	AB	R	H	2B	3B	HR	RBI	SB
Derek Curiel, OF, Fr	.345	.470	.519	258	67	89	20	2	7	55	3
Ethan Frey, OF, Jr	.331	.420	.641	181	43	60	15	1	13	50	4
Jared Jones, 1B, Jr	.323	.414	.613	279	66	90	15	0	22	76	5
Jake Brown, UT, So	.320	.407	.528	178	45	57	9	2	8	48	11
Daniel Dickinson, INF, Jr	.315	.458	.525	238	67	75	14	0	12	49	9
Chris Stanfield, OF, Jr	.298	.414	.404	208	53	62	15	2	1	31	5
Steven Milam, INF, So	.295	.398	.506	241	50	71	14	2	11	57	2
Josh Pearson, OF, Sr	.289	.434	.496	135	37	39	7	0	7	33	5
Luis Hernandez, C, Sr	.270	.348	.500	174	32	47	11	1	9	33	5
Tanner Reaves, INF, Jr	.262	.372	.446	65	18	17	3	0	3	12	0
Ashton Larson, OF, So	.256	.423	.487	39	7	10	3	0	2	12	1
Cade Arrambide, C, Fr	.242	.351	.484	62	11	15	3	0	4	14	0
John Pearson, INF, Fr	.238	.346	.571	21	5	5	1	0	2	7	0
Michael Braswell, INF, So	.189	.309	.270	148	20	28	6	0	2	18	0

Pitcher, Year	W	L	ERA	G	GS	SV	IP	H	BB	SO
Cooper Williams, Fr	0	1	1.80	21	0	0	20	13	13	21
Casan Evans, Fr	5	1	2.05	19	3	7	52	44	19	71
Zac Cowan, Jr	3	3	2.94	22	2	6	52	44	12	60
Anthony Eyanson, Jr	12	2	3.00	20	18	2	108	88	36	152
Kade Anderson, So	12	1	3.18	19	19	0	119	91	35	180
DJ Primeaux, So	0	0	3.86	22	0	0	14	11	8	13
Jaden Noot, So	2	1	4.13	20	5	1	32	28	15	44
William Schmidt, Fr	7	0	4.73	17	6	0	32	28	22	41
Mavrick Rizy, Fr	0	0	4.74	24	0	0	24	22	19	29
Jacob Mayers, Jr	2	0	4.80	17	0	0	15	4	20	26
Chase Shores, So	5	3	5.09	23	9	2	63	62	31	70
Conner Ware, Jr	4	1	5.48	16	6	0	21	13	18	23
Connor Benge, Jr	1	1	6.75	17	0	0	16	11	13	15

2. Coastal Carolina
Coach: Kevin Schnall. **Overall:** 56-13

Player, Pos, Yr	AVG	OBP	SLG	AB	R	H	2B	3B	HR	RBI	SB
Dean Mihos, INF, Jr	.332	.418	.453	190	50	63	12	1	3	22	8
Sebastian Alexander, OF, Sr	.318	.426	.521	217	59	69	12	1	10	54	28
Caden Bodine, C, Jr	.318	.454	.461	245	55	78	18	1	5	42	2
Chad Born, OF, Sr	.317	.431	.383	60	12	19	4	0	0	10	2
Colby Thorndyke, 1B, Fr	.303	.395	.445	211	41	64	18	0	4	48	7
Wells Sykes, OF, Jr	.291	.377	.397	189	38	55	8	0	4	39	18
Ty Dooley, INF, Sr	.289	.434	.452	166	43	48	9	0	6	37	5
Blake Barthol, INF, Jr	.274	.387	.468	252	55	69	13	0	12	53	13
Walker Mitchell, INF, So	.270	.443	.373	204	49	55	5	2	4	45	11
Blagen Pado, OF, Fr	.267	.364	.543	116	34	31	6	1	8	31	3
Domenico Tozzi, C, Fr	.264	.374	.453	148	25	39	7	0	7	39	0
Ty Barrango, INF, Sr	.241	.373	.354	79	21	19	1	1	2	19	6
Brice Estep, C, So	.227	.346	.455	22	2	5	2	0	1	5	1
Kaleb Huffman, OF, Jr	.188	.333	.313	32	4	6	4	0	0	3	0
Freddy Rodriguez, INF, So	.185	.405	.407	27	18	5	3	0	1	6	5
Jake Books, INF, Jr	.175	.313	.300	40	3	7	2	0	1	5	0

Pitcher, Year	W	L	ERA	G	GS	SV	IP	H	BB	SO
Ryan Lynch, Sr	2	1	0.56	28	0	9	32	23	10	36
Cullen McKay, So	1	1	1.46	3	3	0	12	7	10	18
Dominick Carbone, So	6	0	2.36	28	0	6	42	37	9	52
Jacob Morrison, Jr	12	1	2.42	19	18	0	107	79	23	104
Matthew Potok, Sr	4	1	2.52	21	1	1	35	33	8	33
Darin Horn, Sr	5	1	2.73	19	0	0	26	18	19	34
Hayden Johnson, So	5	0	2.82	24	0	1	38	28	18	55
Riley Eikhoff, Sr	7	2	3.10	17	17	0	90	91	11	71
Cameron Flukey, So	8	2	3.19	18	17	0	101	78	24	118
Luke Jones, Fr	4	2	3.51	17	10	1	48	39	22	38
Scott Doran, Fr	1	0	4.15	18	0	2	17	12	13	25

Derek Curiel led LSU hitters in batting average as a freshman.

3. Arkansas
Coach: Dave Van Horn. **Overall:** 47-15

Player, Pos, Yr	AVG	OBP	SLG	AB	R	H	2B	3B	HR	RBI	SB
Logan Maxwell, OF, Sr	.356	.454	.605	177	46	63	5	0	13	38	1
Wehiwa Aloy, INF, Jr	.350	.434	.673	266	81	93	19	2	21	68	9
Charles Davalan, OF, So	.346	.433	.561	269	71	93	12	2	14	60	10
Cam Kozeal, INF, So	.333	.386	.606	231	49	77	18	0	15	62	2
Kuhio Aloy, UT, So	.317	.424	.539	243	52	77	15	0	13	70	0
Carson Boles, OF, Sr	.310	.475	.500	58	18	18	5	0	2	16	0
Ryder Helfrick, C, So	.305	.420	.616	190	47	58	10	2	15	38	3
Justin Thomas Jr., OF, Jr	.303	.438	.515	165	47	50	6	1	9	38	7
Brent Iredale, INF, Sr	.286	.450	.544	206	63	59	11	0	14	57	9
Reese Robinett, INF, So	.260	.400	.438	73	16	19	4	0	3	13	1
Zane Becker, C, Fr	.258	.425	.452	31	5	8	3	0	1	6	1
Gabe Fraser, INF, Fr	.250	.339	.365	52	14	13	1	1	1	12	2
Nolan Souza, INF, So	.250	.374	.427	96	24	24	5	0	4	22	9
Rocco Peppi, UT, Sr	.217	.351	.261	46	7	10	2	0	0	9	0
Kendall Diggs, OF, Sr	.159	.264	.317	63	10	10	2	1	2	7	2

Pitcher, Year	W	L	ERA	G	GS	SV	IP	H	BB	SO
Parker Coil, Jr	3	0	1.27	14	0	1	21	22	2	24
Dylan Carter, Sr	6	0	2.18	20	0	0	33	23	12	36
Will McEntire, Sr	1	0	2.84	17	0	2	25	16	4	29
Carson Wiggins, Fr	1	1	3.21	14	0	3	14	7	9	20
Aiden Jimenez, So	4	1	3.40	22	2	1	42	41	13	40
Zach Root, Jr	9	6	3.62	19	19	0	99	82	35	126
Gage Wood, Jr	4	1	3.82	10	10	0	37	27	7	69
Cole Gibler, Fr	3	2	3.99	20	0	1	29	25	12	57
Christian Foutch, Jr	1	0	4.09	21	0	4	22	14	10	31
Ben Bybee, Jr	3	0	4.38	18	3	0	37	38	15	42
Gabe Gaeckle, So	4	2	4.42	19	9	2	71	63	31	92
Tate McGuire, So	3	2	4.55	14	4	1	27	23	9	24
Colin Fisher, So	3	0	4.62	16	5	0	25	20	12	31
Landon Beidelschies, Jr	4	0	4.82	16	13	0	61	59	20	70

4. Louisville

Coach: Dan McConnell. **Overall:** 42-24

Player, Pos, Yr	AVG	OBP	SLG	AB	R	H	2B	3B	HR	RBI	SB
Eddie King Jr., OF, Sr	.367	.435	.750	188	46	69	19	1	17	63	4
Jake Munroe, INF, Jr	.346	.451	.593	243	68	84	13	4	13	61	2
Lucas Moore, OF, So	.339	.430	.454	271	85	92	10	3	5	49	53
Bayram Hot, INF, So	.326	.382	.457	92	16	30	3	0	3	22	2
Matt Klein, C, Jr	.310	.431	.509	116	26	36	6	1	5	31	1
Zion Rose, OF, So	.310	.396	.552	252	64	78	16	3	13	67	31
Alex Alicea, INF, So	.307	.444	.401	202	50	62	10	3	1	25	34
Garret Pike, OF, Sr	.297	.343	.455	209	36	62	19	1	4	40	9
Tagger Tyson, C, So	.296	.370	.481	81	12	24	10	1	1	14	1
Kamau Neighbors, INF, Sr	.283	.381	.345	145	22	41	5	2	0	20	13
Tague Davis, UT, Fr	.283	.390	.571	219	46	62	9	0	18	52	2
Nate Earley, 1B, Jr	.250	.404	.550	40	7	10	3	0	3	12	0
Michael Lippe, OF, Jr	.212	.344	.308	52	15	11	3	1	0	6	7
Tanner Shiver, INF, Sr	.174	.240	.304	23	8	4	0	0	1	4	3
Collin Mowry, C, Fr	.162	.200	.216	37	4	6	2	0	0	5	0
George Baker, C, So	.111	.231	.222	45	6	5	2	0	1	5	0

Pitcher, Year	W	L	ERA	G	GS	SV	IP	H	BB	SO
Jake Schweitzer, Fr	4	3	2.34	25	0	3	42	31	19	23
Wyatt Danilowicz, Jr	0	1	2.70	28	0	3	33	19	25	52
Tucker Biven, Jr	5	0	3.71	23	5	4	43	47	22	36
Parker Detmers, So	1	1	3.94	4	4	0	16	16	4	15
Patrick Forbes, Jr	4	2	4.42	15	15	0	71	59	34	117
Ethan Eberle, Fr	6	2	4.65	20	10	0	62	62	25	59
Peter Michael, Jr	4	3	4.83	14	13	0	50	39	37	52
Brennyn Cutts, Sr	3	1	4.97	26	2	2	38	30	19	46
TJ Schlageter, So	3	2	5.04	17	6	0	30	26	16	17
Justin West, Jr	2	2	5.59	25	2	0	37	36	20	52
Jack Brown, Fr	5	5	6.59	26	2	0	42	60	27	27
Jared Lessman, Sr	0	0	7.84	9	1	0	10	13	11	9
Ty Starke, So	1	0	8.35	23	0	0	18	18	14	21
Casen Murphy, Fr	0	1	8.64	14	2	0	16	24	12	12
Colton Hartman, So	2	1	11.65	17	4	0	17	27	17	20

5. Oregon State

Coach: Mitch Canham. **Overall:** 48-17-1

Player, Pos, Yr	AVG	OBP	SLG	AB	R	H	2B	3B	HR	RBI	SB
Aiva Arquette, INF, So	.354	.461	.654	254	73	90	17	1	19	66	7
Gavin Turley, OF, Jr	.351	.472	.649	245	56	86	13	0	20	69	5
Wilson Weber, C, Sr	.326	.407	.565	230	45	75	15	2	12	58	2
AJ Singer, INF, Jr	.312	.409	.393	234	38	73	10	0	3	39	2
Canon Reeder, OF, Jr	.293	.402	.489	188	38	55	11	1	8	37	4
Tyce Peterson, INF, Jr	.288	.388	.469	160	39	46	10	2	5	20	1
Trent Caraway, INF, So	.267	.350	.470	251	51	67	15	0	12	47	5
Easton Talt, OF, Jr	.261	.433	.460	211	57	55	12	3	8	36	10
Jacob Krieg, INF, Jr	.245	.360	.500	200	41	49	9	0	14	37	1
Levi Jones, OF, So	.240	.406	.360	25	4	6	3	0	0	5	0
Carson McEntire, OF, Fr	.238	.360	.548	42	12	10	1	0	4	10	1
Bryce Hubbard, C, Jr	.200	.485	.200	20	5	4	0	0	0	3	0
Dallas Macias, INF, Jr	.159	.305	.243	107	19	17	3	0	2	12	0

Pitcher, Year	W	L	ERA	G	GS	SV	IP	H	BB	SO
Laif Palmer, So	2	0	2.03	18	1	2	31	17	14	19
Wyatt Queen, So	3	1	3.21	21	5	2	47	40	19	61
Dax Whitney, Fr	6	3	3.40	17	17	0	76	61	37	120
Ethan Kleinschmit, So	8	5	3.56	17	17	0	91	63	36	113
Kellan Oakes, Jr	5	1	3.68	20	4	1	36	32	18	47
Nelson Keljo, Jr	3	2	4.01	17	11	2	58	46	33	63
Zach Kmatz, Fr	2	0	4.05	18	0	1	26	30	9	29
AJ Hutcheson, Jr	3	0	4.28	24	0	3	48	44	14	38
Eric Segura, So	8	2	4.63	19	5	0	58	50	38	78
James DeCremer, Fr	3	0	5.34	14	3	0	28	34	11	30
Zach Edwards, Fr	1	0	5.89	16	0	1	18	17	9	22
Joey Mundt, Sr	1	1	6.00	15	0	1	15	13	12	23
Tanner Douglas, Jr	1	1	13.85	14	0	0	13	21	9	20

Oregon State's Aiva Arquette hit .354/.461/.654 with 19 home runs

EDDIE KELLY

6. UCLA

Coach: John Savage. **Overall:** 48-18

Player, Pos, Yr	AVG	OBP	SLG	AB	R	H	2B	3B	HR	RBI	SB
Roch Cholowsky, INF, So	.353	.480	.710	252	80	89	19	1	23	74	7
Dean West, OF, So	.320	.470	.425	247	76	79	12	1	4	41	13
Mulivai Levu, 1B, So	.320	.389	.522	272	61	87	15	2	12	85	4
Roman Martin, INF, So	.316	.450	.502	237	60	75	15	1	9	61	6
A.J. Salgado, INF, Sr	.312	.418	.581	234	58	73	19	4	12	56	14
Payton Brennan, OF, Jr	.303	.381	.487	195	41	59	10	4	6	41	11
Aidan Espinoza, OF, So	.286	.400	.333	21	3	6	1	0	0	7	0
Cameron Kim, INF, So	.286	.345	.306	49	6	14	1	0	0	10	0
Cashel Dugger, C, So	.279	.421	.360	172	35	48	5	0	3	25	0
Phoenix Call, INF, So	.256	.349	.342	199	41	51	8	0	3	31	2
Blake Balsz, C, So	.239	.415	.291	134	25	32	4	0	1	25	1
Grant Gray, UT, So	.207	.314	.310	29	5	6	0	0	1	3	1
Jarrod Hocking, OF, Jr	.206	.282	.321	131	22	27	3	0	4	22	2

Pitcher, Year	W	L	ERA	G	GS	SV	IP	H	BB	SO
Jack O'Connor, Jr	3	0	1.67	27	0	1	27	21	6	18
Luke Rodriguez, So	2	0	2.11	11	1	0	21	15	13	21
Wylan Moss, Fr	2	1	2.98	19	9	2	48	46	16	49
Cal Randall, So	2	1	3.08	28	0	0	26	17	15	31
Ryan Rissas, Sr	1	2	3.50	20	0	0	18	10	14	19
Michael Barnett, Jr	12	1	3.98	19	14	0	86	98	22	75
Easton Hawk, Fr	1	1	4.50	26	0	8	24	25	7	31
Josh Alger, Sr	1	0	4.76	17	0	0	17	13	21	16
Chris Grothues, Jr	4	1	4.96	21	0	0	32	25	15	31
Ian May, Jr	8	3	4.97	27	12	0	70	64	27	47
CJ Bott, Jr	2	1	5.00	21	3	0	27	27	12	17
Landon Stump, So	6	2	5.02	18	18	0	75	74	39	62
August Souza, Sr	0	0	6.04	30	0	1	28	20	17	28
Justin Lee, So	3	0	6.75	30	0	5	32	28	27	28
Cody Delvecchio, Jr	1	4	6.81	8	8	0	37	43	12	39

7. Arizona
Coach: Chip Hale. **Overall:** 44-21

Player, Pos, Yr	AVG	OBP	SLG	AB	R	H	2B	3B	HR	RBI	SB
Brendan Summerhill, OF, Jr	.343	.459	.556	169	35	58	12	6	4	34	11
Adonys Guzman, C, Jr	.328	.411	.496	232	43	76	12	0	9	44	0
Mason White, INF, Jr	.327	.412	.689	257	63	84	17	8	20	73	4
Aaron Walton, OF, Jr	.320	.437	.589	253	71	81	22	2	14	49	19
Tommy Splaine, C, Sr	.298	.390	.447	215	40	64	13	2	5	25	0
Maddox Mihalakis, INF, Jr	.279	.354	.421	240	36	67	13	3	5	37	6
Garen Caulfield, INF, Sr	.262	.349	.434	244	36	64	12	3	8	45	2
Andrew Cain, INF, So	.247	.350	.487	154	30	38	13	3	6	22	0
Mathis Meurant, INF, Jr	.245	.295	.402	102	16	25	6	2	2	15	0
Easton Breyfogle, OF, So	.244	.320	.419	172	27	42	5	5	5	31	2
Gunner Geile, OF, Fr	.219	.282	.313	64	7	14	4	1	0	9	1
Dom Rodriguez, OF, Jr	.208	.269	.292	24	4	5	2	0	0	1	0
TJ Adams, OF, So	.167	.301	.283	60	13	10	5	1	0	7	2
Richie Morales, INF, Sr	.162	.244	.189	37	3	6	1	0	0	3	3

Pitcher, Year	W	L	ERA	G	GS	SV	IP	H	BB	SO
Tony Pluta, Jr	3	0	1.46	30	0	14	37	28	7	34
Raul Garayzar, Sr	2	0	2.81	21	8	0	57	49	19	46
Hunter Alberini, Jr	1	0	3.48	18	0	0	20	27	7	33
Smith Bailey, Fr	3	3	3.94	18	18	0	89	92	32	80
Collin McKinney, So	0	2	3.98	15	13	0	54	47	35	60
Julian Tonghini, Jr	5	2	4.26	22	0	0	25	23	14	44
Matthew Martinez, Jr	3	0	4.42	17	0	1	18	16	7	18
Eric Orloff, Sr	1	0	5.14	16	0	0	14	20	6	11
Owen Kramkowski, So	9	6	5.48	18	18	0	92	116	18	90
Casey Hintz, Jr	7	4	5.56	24	0	2	55	55	21	53
Garrett Hicks, Jr	5	2	6.11	34	0	2	45	49	13	49
Michael Hilker Jr., Jr	2	1	6.45	13	2	1	22	22	4	27
Carson Johnson, Fr	2	0	8.03	12	0	0	12	15	5	7

8. Murray State
Coach: Dan Skirka. **Overall:** 44-17

Player, Pos, Yr	AVG	OBP	SLG	AB	R	H	2B	3B	HR	RBI	SB
Dustin Mercer, OF, Sr	.355	.437	.483	259	57	92	23	5	0	39	5
Dom Decker, 2B, So	.351	.496	.464	211	48	74	18	3	0	48	3
Jonathan Hogart, OF, Sr	.338	.446	.700	260	80	88	26	1	22	65	7
Luke Mistone, INF, Jr	.335	.399	.476	248	56	83	17	3	4	53	2
Will Vierling, C, Jr	.312	.415	.532	234	48	73	17	2	10	51	1
Nico Bermeo, INF, So	.286	.403	.381	63	16	18	3	0	1	7	1
Brady Grabowski, PH/LF, Fr	.283	.382	.413	46	7	13	3	0	1	12	1
Carson Garner, INF, So	.276	.429	.573	225	64	62	14	1	17	60	14
Dan Tauken, LF, Sr	.255	.348	.455	231	44	59	9	2	11	77	1
Conner Cunningham, SS, Fr	.247	.388	.432	190	49	47	10	2	7	39	3
Charlie Jury, RF, Jr	.182	.270	.485	33	7	6	4	0	2	10	0
Jackson McCoy, OF, Jr	.178	.312	.300	90	18	16	2	0	3	9	1

Pitcher, Year	W	L	ERA	G	GS	SV	IP	H	BB	SO
Jackson Ugo, Fr	1	0	3.55	9	1	0	12	14	10	11
Dylan Zentko, Jr	4	1	4.15	22	0	3	52	59	19	54
Kane Elmy, Sr	6	2	4.40	16	10	0	57	64	23	29
Graham Kelham, Jr	4	1	4.50	24	0	9	46	39	13	64
Ethan Lyke, Jr	2	1	4.64	9	7	0	33	37	17	24
Preston Chaudoin, Jr	0	0	4.76	8	1	0	11	12	6	14
Isaac Silva, Jr	9	3	4.84	18	16	0	87	84	36	81
Jacob Hustedde, So	2	0	5.09	16	5	0	40	37	28	40
Nic Schutte, Jr	8	5	5.16	18	16	0	96	83	55	97
Reese Oakley, Fr	3	0	5.56	15	0	2	22	25	11	25
Jack Wajda, So	2	3	5.73	13	0	2	22	29	9	16
Derek Lebron, Jr	2	0	6.14	13	0	1	14	16	10	12
Harper McLendon, Jr	1	0	7.36	10	0	3	11	17	7	8
Matt Parenteau, Jr	0	1	11.34	10	5	0	19	21	17	15

9. North Carolina
Coach: Scott Forbes. **Overall:** 46-15

Player, Pos, Yr	AVG	OBP	SLG	AB	R	H	2B	3B	HR	RBI	SB
Alex Madera, INF, Sr	.332	.432	.403	226	44	75	8	1	2	38	13
Hunter Stokley, 1B, Sr	.325	.410	.620	237	53	77	13	0	14	65	4
Gavin Gallaher, INF, So	.325	.409	.603	237	54	77	13	1	17	68	5
Jackson Van De Brake, INF, Sr	.306	.411	.504	232	57	71	16	3	8	58	4

Sawyer Black, OF, Fr	.297	.409	.568	37	7	11	1	0	3	6	1
Tyson Bass, OF, Sr	.292	.393	.485	233	48	68	10	1	11	47	12
Kane Kepley, OF, So	.291	.451	.444	234	74	68	13	7	3	30	45
Carter French, OF, Jr	.280	.357	.280	100	21	28	0	0	0	12	2
Luke Stevenson, C, So	.251	.414	.552	223	61	56	10	0	19	58	2
Sam Angelo, INF, Jr	.238	.344	.448	105	17	25	4	0	6	22	0
Rom Kellis, OF, Jr	.225	.291	.338	71	10	16	5	0	1	10	4
Perry Hargett, OF, Fr	.214	.333	.400	70	20	15	5	1	2	15	2
Macaddin Dye, C, So	.081	.239	.162	37	3	3	0	0	1	4	0

Pitcher, Year	W	L	ERA	G	GS	SV	IP	H	BB	SO
Tom Chmielewski, Sr	0	0	0.87	13	0	1	10	7	4	7
Jake Knapp, Sr	14	0	2.02	16	15	0	102	72	16	88
Ryan Lynch, Fr	5	1	2.93	27	3	2	61	44	25	72
Olin Johnson, So	2	1	3.56	17	2	0	30	25	14	20
Aidan Haugh, Sr	5	4	3.72	17	14	0	75	70	33	85
Walker McDuffie, Fr	3	3	3.74	28	1	7	55	35	25	72
Jason DeCaro, So	9	3	3.78	16	16	0	83	79	26	70
Folger Boaz, So	3	0	3.90	23	4	0	30	30	18	30
Matthew Matthijs, Jr	1	1	4.34	17	0	2	18	20	8	30
Camron Seagraves, Fr	2	1	4.56	18	1	0	23	21	23	34
Cameron Padgett, Jr	2	1	4.88	13	4	0	27	34	8	19

10. Auburn
Coach: Butch Thompson. **Overall:** 41-20

Player, Pos, Yr	AVG	OBP	SLG	AB	R	H	2B	3B	HR	RBI	SB
Ike Irish, C, Jr	.364	.469	.710	214	65	78	13	2	19	58	11
Chris Rembert, INF, Fr	.344	.467	.555	209	49	72	14	0	10	46	6
Chase Fralick, UT, Fr	.335	.426	.472	212	36	71	17	0	4	41	0
Eric Guevara, INF, So	.331	.388	.556	124	28	41	11	1	5	29	2
Cooper McMurray, INF, Sr	.326	.431	.588	233	50	76	19	0	14	59	0
Eric Snow, INF, Jr	.307	.403	.493	215	54	66	14	1	8	34	4
Bub Terrell, OF, Sr	.300	.372	.458	203	38	61	17	0	5	41	4
Cade Belyeu, OF, So	.278	.450	.444	126	34	35	4	1	5	20	12
Lucas Steele, C, Jr	.270	.411	.491	159	28	43	8	0	9	45	2
Bristol Carter, OF, Sr	.243	.331	.336	140	24	34	7	0	2	13	14
Deric Fabian, INF, So	.234	.339	.360	197	39	46	8	1	5	33	9

Pitcher, Year	W	L	ERA	G	GS	SV	IP	H	BB	SO
Carson Myers, Sr	3	2	2.77	22	1	3	52	48	10	67
Ryan Hetzler, So	2	1	3.86	19	0	8	35	38	4	25
Parker Carlson, Sr	3	1	4.28	17	0	1	27	22	5	29
Samuel Dutton, Sr	7	3	4.31	16	16	0	85	86	19	95
Alex Petrovic, So	1	0	4.34	7	5	0	18	13	4	25
Christian Chatterton, Fr	4	1	4.47	14	14	0	52	37	18	60
Griffin Graves, So	4	1	4.63	13	0	0	23	17	11	24
Cade Fisher, So	1	3	4.68	14	10	2	42	38	23	54
Jett Johnston, So	4	0	4.76	11	0	1	11	7	8	11
Andreas Alvarez, Fr	3	1	4.80	14	9	0	45	47	18	34
Jackson Sanders, Fr	.1	1	5.29	15	0	0	17	20	13	10
Cam Tilly, So	3	3	5.48	19	6	1	46	33	29	58
John Armstrong, Sr	2	1	5.75	18	0	0	20	30	7	25
Dylan Watts, Jr	2	1	7.39	17	0	2	28	32	11	28

11. Florida State
Coach: Link Jarrett. **Overall:** 42-16

Player, Pos, Yr	AVG	OBP	SLG	AB	R	H	2B	3B	HR	RBI	SB
Alex Lodise, INF, Jr	.394	.462	.705	241	62	95	18	3	17	68	6
Chase Williams, OF, So	.342	.394	.474	114	17	39	5	2	2	20	18
Gage Harrelson, OF, Jr	.339	.444	.462	236	63	80	10	2	5	43	15
Myles Bailey, INF, Fr	.327	.441	.663	202	50	66	11	0	19	56	4
Max Williams, OF, Jr	.316	.383	.598	234	47	74	9	0	19	53	2
Drew Faurot, INF, Jr	.307	.388	.564	218	51	67	8	0	16	51	8
Cal Fisher, INF, So	.303	.411	.489	188	32	57	11	0	8	37	2
Hunter Carns, C, Fr	.286	.379	.481	133	34	38	8	0	6	15	2
James Hankerson Jr., 1B, Fr	.261	.414	.457	46	7	12	3	0	2	9	0
Nathan Cmeyla, C, Sr	.259	.385	.370	54	13	14	3	0	1	8	3
Brody DeLamielleure, OF, Fr	.245	.280	.464	110	24	27	6	0	6	21	1
BJ Gibson, OF, Fr	.242	.409	.333	33	11	8	3	0	0	4	4
Jaxson West, C, Jr	.236	.370	.311	148	26	35	5	0	2	17	3
Carter McCulley, INF, Jr	.207	.415	.379	29	7	6	2	0	1	6	2

Pithcer, Year	W	L	ERA	G	GS	SV	IP	H	BB	SO
Evan Chrest, Jr	2	1	2.70	4	4	0	16	15	5	11
Jamie Arnold, Jr	8	2	2.98	15	15	0	84	63	27	119
Joey Volini, So	8	5	3.50	16	15	0	87	76	25	105
Brady Louck, So	0	0	3.86	9	0	0	11	5	7	10
John Abraham, So	4	1	4.64	22	1	1	33	32	24	42
Chris Knier, So	1	1	4.75	23	0	2	30	23	22	31
Joe Charles, Sr	2	0	4.84	22	0	4	35	26	19	49
Peyton Prescott, So	5	0	5.15	24	1	3	36	42	17	46
Wes Mendes, So	7	3	5.42	16	16	0	78	70	39	90
Maison Martinez, Jr	1	2	5.55	14	0	2	24	21	13	33
Payton Manca, Fr	2	1	6.56	13	4	0	23	17	16	24
Jacob Marlowe, Jr	1	0	9.28	8	1	0	10	17	5	11
Ben Barrett, Jr	0	0	11.57	13	0	2	11	14	12	17

12. Tennessee
Coach: Tony Vitello. **Overall:** 46-19

Player, Pos, Yr	AVG	OBP	SLG	AB	R	H	2B	3B	HR	RBI	SB
Gavin Kilen, INF, Jr	.357	.441	.671	210	60	75	13	4	15	46	6
Chris Newstrom, INF, Fr	.351	.433	.684	57	15	20	4	0	5	19	3
Andrew Fischer, INF, Jr	.341	.497	.760	217	70	74	16	0	25	65	4
Hunter Ensley, OF, Sr	.336	.418	.531	241	46	81	17	0	10	62	7
Blake Grimmer, INF, Fr	.318	.464	.591	44	14	14	0	0	4	15	1
Dean Curley, INF, So	.315	.435	.531	241	67	76	8	1	14	51	8
Levi Clark, C, Fr	.289	.459	.594	128	30	37	9	0	10	34	1
Stone Lawless, C, Fr	.288	.468	.644	59	17	17	4	1	5	20	1
Manny Marin, INF, Fr	.283	.356	.401	152	23	43	9	0	3	23	2
Jay Abernathy, UT, Fr	.282	.409	.340	103	38	29	3	0	1	11	8
Reese Chapman, OF, Jr	.273	.344	.523	216	44	59	11	2	13	53	4
Dalton Bargo, UT, Jr	.272	.366	.559	202	47	55	14	1	14	40	3
Cannon Peebles, C, Jr	.253	.335	.483	178	31	45	8	0	11	41	0
Ariel Antigua, INF, So	.192	.302	.205	73	15	14	1	0	0	11	3

Pitcher, Year	W	L	ERA	G	GS	SV	IP	H	BB	SO
Thomas Crabtree, Jr	2	0	3.00	12	2	0	15	8	5	20
Michael Sharman, Jr	3	1	3.18	17	3	0	22	19	10	25
Liam Doyle, Jr	10	4	3.20	19	17	1	95	63	32	164
Austin Breedlove, Jr	3	0	3.42	25	2	0	23	20	8	31
AJ Russell, Jr	2	1	3.55	12	6	0	25	23	11	36
Marcus Phillips, Jr	4	5	3.90	17	17	0	83	75	34	98
Dylan Loy, So	4	0	3.97	33	1	2	34	22	11	36
Brandon Arvidson, So	2	0	4.19	30	2	1	38	28	22	70
Nate Snead, Jr	4	2	4.53	23	1	5	49	56	21	42
Brayden Krenzel, Fr	3	0	4.68	21	2	0	32	35	19	41
Tanner Franklin, Jr	1	2	4.89	27	1	2	38	40	9	52
Andrew Behnke, Jr	2	0	5.11	14	0	0	12	10	3	6
Tegan Kuhns, Fr	2	4	5.40	15	10	0	36	43	16	40
Ryan Combs, Jr	0	0	7.36	13	0	1	11	12	6	20

13. West Virginia
Coach: Steven Sabins. **Overall:** 44-16

Player, Pos, Yr	AVG	OBP	SLG	AB	R	H	2B	3B	HR	RBI	SB
Sam White, INF, Jr	.361	.426	.529	191	47	69	17	0	5	46	9
Kyle West, INF, Jr	.339	.487	.601	183	43	62	15	0	11	38	6
Armani Guzman, UT, So	.327	.403	.449	107	27	35	5	1	2	22	17
Jace Rinehart, OF, Sr	.320	.395	.567	194	43	62	21	0	9	53	4
Chase Swain, INF, Jr	.319	.404	.452	135	40	43	6	3	2	30	1
Gavin Kelly, C, Fr	.299	.402	.395	167	38	50	6	2	2	37	16
Skylar King, OF, Jr	.291	.415	.398	206	42	60	9	2	3	32	13
Spencer Barnett, INF, So	.278	.336	.443	115	24	32	5	1	4	26	3
Brodie Kresser, INF, Sr	.278	.373	.378	209	50	58	12	0	3	41	13
Logan Sauve, C, Jr	.276	.385	.457	210	46	58	12	1	8	36	8
Alex Marot, UT, So	.273	.385	.333	33	4	9	2	0	0	6	0
Grant Hussey, 1B, Jr	.272	.360	.451	195	36	53	12	1	7	35	7
Michael Perazza, OF, So	.233	.250	.302	43	6	10	0	0	1	5	3
Ben Lumsden, INF, Jr	.160	.300	.300	50	11	8	1	0	2	15	1

Pitcher, Year	W	L	ERA	G	GS	SV	IP	H	BB	SO
David Hagen, Fr	2	0	2.35	11	7	0	23	17	13	13
Griffin Kim, Sr	5	3	3.36	18	17	1	99	86	30	103
Ben McDougal, JR	1	1	3.63	19	0	2	22	14	8	17
Jack Kartsonas, Sr	6	4	3.66	20	9	1	66	63	20	77
Chase Meyer, So	9	2	3.94	22	3	1	48	32	38	63

Tennessee's Liam Doyle struck out 164 batters in just 95 innings pitched.

Pitcher, Year (cont.)	W	L	ERA	G	GS	SV	IP	H	BB	SO
Benjamin Hudson, Fr	3	1	3.95	18	1	0	27	25	12	30
Reese Bassinger, Jr	7	1	4.23	30	0	5	61	63	12	43
Robby Porco, Jr	0	0	4.64	12	4	0	21	16	20	24
Mac Stiffler, Fr	2	1	4.95	15	2	0	20	10	20	20
Tyler Hutson, Jr	2	1	4.97	14	1	0	25	25	9	29
Gavin Van Kempen, Jr	2	0	6.13	14	13	0	39	41	26	37
Carson Estridge, Jr	3	1	6.14	23	3	5	48	54	18	48

14. Duke
Coach: Chris Pollard. **Overall:** 41-21

Player, Pos, Yr	AVG	OBP	SLG	AB	R	H	2B	3B	HR	RBI	SB
Noah Murray, INF, So	.342	.500	.632	38	7	13	2	0	3	10	0
Ben Miller, INF, Sr	.314	.413	.624	245	59	77	13	0	21	63	1
Wallace Clark, INF, Sr	.307	.478	.507	225	65	69	18	0	9	37	5
Ben Rounds, OF, Sr	.300	.433	.519	210	53	63	15	2	9	39	4
Tyler Albright, OF, Jr	.298	.435	.502	225	63	67	10	3	10	45	15
Sam Harris, 1B, So	.297	.385	.563	128	27	38	7	0	9	42	1
AJ Gracia, UT, So	.293	.449	.558	215	57	63	10	1	15	54	8
Jake Hyde, INF, Sr	.288	.403	.539	219	48	63	13	3	12	67	1
Macon Winslow, C, So	.278	.391	.490	198	43	55	13	1	9	48	3
Andrew Yu, C, Fr	.260	.400	.481	77	15	20	2	0	5	11	2
Jake Berger, INF, Sr	.243	.404	.432	206	47	50	13	1	8	45	3
Kyle Johnson, UT, So	.220	.343	.508	59	11	13	5	0	4	19	2

Pitcher, Year	W	L	ERA	G	GS	SV	IP	H	BB	SO
Reid Easterly, Sr	9	3	3.04	37	0	5	74	64	17	66
Gavin Brown, So	1	0	3.31	16	1	0	16	15	6	14
James Tallon, Jr	1	2	3.96	21	3	2	36	27	19	50
Max Stammel, Fr	0	1	4.09	18	1	0	22	19	12	25
Gabriel Nard, Jr	6	2	4.62	29	2	0	50	49	17	45
Mark Hindy, Sr	1	0	4.66	26	0	0	29	24	15	38
Owen Proksch, Jr	4	3	4.68	19	12	1	65	54	28	91
Henry Zatkowski, Fr	5	2	4.83	21	11	0	59	65	12	58
Aidan Weaver, Jr	2	0	4.91	10	2	0	14	12	12	10
Edward Hart, Jr	1	0	5.06	14	0	0	10	9	4	9
Ryan Higgins, Sr	1	1	6.12	15	5	0	25	26	15	35
Ryan Calvert, Sr	3	0	6.35	27	0	0	34	36	10	30

| Kyle Johnson, So | 4 | 4 | 7.19 | 19 | 11 | 0 | 41 | 43 | 26 | 43 |
| Andrew Healy, Jr | 3 | 3 | 7.29 | 13 | 13 | 0 | 42 | 45 | 18 | 37 |

15. UTSA
Coach: Pat Hallmark. **Overall:** 47-15

Player, Pos, Yr	AVG	OBP	SLG	AB	R	H	2B	3B	HR	RBI	SB
Mason Lytle, OF, Sr	.366	.424	.560	268	75	98	22	0	10	68	17
Norris McClure, INF, Sr	.352	.419	.493	213	51	75	10	1	6	42	9
James Taussig, OF, Sr	.344	.441	.579	195	45	67	14	1	10	65	4
Jordan Ballin, INF, Fr	.333	.541	.373	126	47	42	5	0	0	22	6
Andrew Stucky, C, Sr	.324	.467	.514	173	40	56	15	0	6	40	1
Drew Detlefsen, OF, Jr	.310	.418	.559	229	61	71	18	0	13	70	7
Nathan Hodge, UT, Fr	.308	.410	.433	120	33	37	6	0	3	26	3
Tye Odom, OF, Jr	.294	.294	.412	34	2	10	2	1	0	9	0
Ty Hodge, INF, Jr	.292	.400	.446	195	49	57	12	0	6	41	6
Caden Miller, UT, Fr	.280	.453	.487	189	56	53	13	1	8	41	9
Lorenzo Morresi, C, Sr	.277	.317	.372	94	16	26	4	1	1	11	4
Broc Parmer, C, Jr	.273	.365	.455	44	8	12	3	1	1	10	0
Garrett Gruell, OF, Sr	.270	.342	.381	63	10	17	4	0	1	15	0
Cade Sadler, 1B, Jr	.267	.382	.289	45	6	12	1	0	0	5	2
Diego Diaz, UT, So	.212	.384	.318	66	21	14	1	0	2	15	5

Pitcher, Year	W	L	ERA	G	GS	SV	IP	H	BB	SO
Connor Kelley, Jr	3	1	2.72	24	0	1	36	24	15	49
Robert Orloski, Sr	8	0	3.36	27	0	9	72	55	27	77
Christian Okerholm, Jr	3	1	3.95	14	0	0	27	29	5	18
Braylon Owens, Sr	7	2	4.47	21	14	3	90	75	40	100
Conor Myles, Sr	5	2	4.86	17	17	0	74	87	22	61
Zach Royse, Jr	9	5	5.17	19	17	0	94	104	34	83
Mike DeBattista, Jr	3	0	5.28	8	1	0	15	19	4	13
Kendall Dove, So	3	0	5.47	17	0	0	26	31	11	26
James Hubbard, Jr	1	2	6.29	10	6	0	24	26	7	23
Gunnar Brown, Sr	4	2	7.32	14	4	0	35	33	22	35
Sam Simmons, Jr	1	0	7.77	14	3	0	22	35	6	18

Outfielder Max Belyeu hit .303/.410/.576 for the Longhorns.

16. Miami (FL)
Coach: J.D Arteaga. **Overall:** 35-27

Player, Pos, Yr	AVG	OBP	SLG	AB	R	H	2B	3B	HR	RBI	SB
Daniel Cuvet, INF, So	.372	.450	.708	226	56	84	20	1	18	84	6
Jake Ogden, INF, Jr	.336	.402	.500	250	63	84	14	0	9	36	13
Derek Williams, OF, Jr	.317	.396	.590	139	34	44	11	0	9	22	10
Max Galvin, OF, Jr	.313	.372	.496	230	52	72	18	0	8	37	9
Jake Kulikowski, OF, So	.276	.447	.379	29	6	8	3	0	0	3	0
Todd Hudson, OF, Jr	.259	.368	.328	58	8	15	1	0	1	8	2
Dorian Gonzalez Jr., INF, Sr	.257	.338	.457	230	40	59	13	0	11	56	7
Tanner Smith, C, Sr	.253	.385	.416	166	26	42	10	1	5	25	3
Bobby Marsh, OF, Sr	.245	.304	.457	151	22	37	9	1	7	39	0
Fabio Peralta, OF, Fr	.238	.316	.302	172	26	41	5	0	2	13	10
Michael Torres, OF, Jr	.231	.350	.276	134	28	31	3	0	1	14	1
Renzo Gonzalez, UT, Jr	.230	.341	.274	113	17	26	2	0	1	11	0
Gaby Gutierrez, OF, Sr	.156	.250	.375	32	4	5	1	0	2	6	0
Evan Taveras, C, Fr	.141	.282	.338	71	11	10	5	0	3	9	0
Ethan Puig, INF, Fr	.100	.296	.100	20	2	2	0	0	0	1	0
Brandon DeGoti, INF, Fr	.094	.275	.313	32	4	3	1	0	2	4	1

Pitcher, Year	W	L	ERA	G	GS	SV	IP	H	BB	SO
Jake Dorn, So	0	0	1.98	11	0	0	13	12	7	8
Griffin Hugus, Jr	6	7	4.16	17	17	0	93	84	35	95
Will Smith, Sr	3	1	4.30	25	0	2	29	24	17	45
Jackson Cleveland, Sr	0	0	4.44	19	0	0	24	15	10	25
AJ Ciscar, Fr	6	2	4.46	21	10	0	66	56	16	65
Rob Evans, Jr	0	0	4.70	17	0	0	15	16	9	14
Brian Walters, Jr	2	3	4.94	21	7	11	51	58	19	56
Reese Lumpkin, Sr	4	2	5.31	15	12	0	57	59	20	51
Carson Fischer, Sr	5	1	5.40	30	0	0	36	35	19	29
Tate DeRias, Fr	2	3	5.77	18	7	0	43	43	16	30
Alex Giroux, Sr	5	2	6.50	22	3	1	36	38	11	27
Lazaro Collera, Fr	0	1	7.07	12	0	0	14	18	12	15
Nick Robert, So	2	4	7.14	8	6	0	29	34	11	38
Michael Fernandez, Fr	0	1	7.88	16	0	0	16	15	13	19

17. Vanderbilt
Coach: Tim Corbin. **Overall:** 43-18

Player, Pos, Yr	AVG	OBP	SLG	AB	R	H	2B	3B	HR	RBI	SB
Riley Nelson, INF, Jr	.344	.450	.526	215	48	74	13	1	8	47	7
Jacob Humphrey, INF, Sr	.279	.400	.442	154	39	43	5	4	4	22	19
Braden Holcomb, INF, So	.275	.378	.503	153	32	42	4	2	9	34	2
Jonathan Vastine, INF, Sr	.270	.358	.449	196	44	53	6	1	9	35	9
Mike Mancini, INF, Jr	.269	.398	.393	145	32	39	4	1	4	24	18
Brodie Johnston, INF, Fr	.260	.297	.354	223	40	58	14	1	15	55	2
Rustan Rigdon, INF, Fr	.259	.431	.346	162	44	42	6	1	2	25	19
RJ Austin, UT, Jr	.257	.353	.383	230	45	59	15	4	2	42	22
Colin Barczi, C, So	.253	.307	.439	198	33	50	11	1	8	39	2
Mac Rose, C, Jr	.250	.393	.326	132	19	33	4	0	2	25	1
Jayden Davis, INF, Jr	.203	.297	.297	64	5	13	3	0	1	6	0
David Mendez, INF, So	.167	.259	.292	24	4	4	0	0	1	4	1
Chris Maldonado, INF, Jr	.086	.250	.143	35	3	3	2	0	0	2	0

Pitcher, Year	W	L	ERA	G	GS	SV	IP	H	BB	SO
Luke Guth, So	4	0	0.93	19	0	0	19	9	7	22
Sawyer Hawks, Sr	4	0	1.60	18	0	8	45	25	11	59
Brennan Seiber, So	1	1	2.28	16	2	0	23	13	13	28
Connor Fennell, So	6	0	2.53	17	7	2	53	33	11	84
Levi Huesman, Jr	1	0	2.81	18	0	0	16	13	4	20
Austin Nye, Fr	2	1	3.55	15	15	0	50	41	22	58
Alex Kranzler, So	6	1	3.62	18	0	3	37	34	7	40
Miller Green, So	1	2	3.80	20	0	5	23	25	11	28
JD Thompson, Jr	6	5	4.00	16	16	0	90	79	30	122
Tommy O'Rourke, Sr	3	0	4.02	15	0	2	15	12	6	18
England Bryan, Fr	0	0	4.15	15	0	0	13	10	12	25
Cody Bowker, Jr	3	5	4.38	16	16	0	72	61	28	99
Matthew Shorey, Fr	2	0	5.27	14	0	0	13	10	4	12
Ethan McElvain, So	2	3	7.24	16	5	1	27	31	28	45

18. Texas
Coach: Jim Schlossnagle. **Overall:** 44-14

Player, Pos, Yr	AVG	OBP	SLG	AB	R	H	2B	3B	HR	RBI	SB
Ethan Mendoza, INF, So	.333	.437	.476	225	53	75	9	4	5	34	15
Jonah Williams, OF, Fr	.327	.383	.382	55	8	18	3	0	0	10	3
Adrian Rodriguez, INF, Fr	.313	.410	.516	182	35	57	14	1	7	23	15
Kimble Schuessler, C, Sr	.312	.377	.489	231	48	72	15	1	8	45	7
Max Belyeu, OF, Jr	.303	.410	.576	132	26	40	7	1	9	29	4
Rylan Galvan, C, Jr	.296	.452	.613	186	54	55	14	0	15	47	9
Casey Borba, INF, So	.278	.410	.574	162	26	45	10	1	12	47	3
Easton Winfield, OF, So	.250	.328	.385	52	11	13	4	0	1	8	1
Tommy Farmer IV, OF, So	.249	.371	.339	177	31	44	13	0	1	25	7
Will Gasparino, OF, So	.242	.339	.512	211	44	51	14	2	13	49	5
Jalin Flores, INF, Jr	.239	.317	.491	234	48	56	18	1	13	54	4
Jayden Duplantier, INF, Jr	.163	.345	.233	43	9	7	3	0	0	4	6
Jaquae Stewart, INF, So	.149	.273	.255	47	5	7	2	0	1	5	0
Cole Chamberlain, C, Fr	.135	.407	.189	37	9	5	2	0	0	3	0

Pitcher, Year	W	L	ERA	G	GS	SV	IP	H	BB	SO
Dylan Volantis, Fr	4	1	1.94	23	1	12	51	33	12	74
Jason Flores, Fr	4	2	2.78	14	5	0	32	23	10	27
Max Grubbs, Jr	6	2	2.84	22	1	5	57	50	14	61
Luke Harrison, Jr	5	1	3.06	15	15	0	70	63	24	72
Kade Bing, So	3	0	3.15	12	10	0	40	30	9	23
Jared Spencer, Sr	4	1	3.27	10	10	0	52	41	23	66
Hudson Hamilton, So	0	1	3.45	9	1	2	15	9	7	16
Thomas Burns, So	1	2	3.71	19	0	4	26	17	16	40
Grayson Saunier, Jr	2	0	3.86	12	1	1	25	22	10	17
Ethan Walker, So	1	0	4.40	10	2	0	14	10	2	14
Andre Duplantier II, Sr	2	0	4.68	16	0	0	25	16	10	20
Cody Howard, Jr	1	0	5.02	9	0	0	14	10	12	13
Ruger Riojas, Jr	9	3	5.61	18	10	0	69	68	21	62

19. Ole Miss
Coach: Mike Bianco. **Overall:** 43-21

Player, Pos, Yr	AVG	OBP	SLG	AB	R	H	2B	3B	HR	RBI	SB
Luke Hill, INF, Jr	.336	.459	.488	244	66	82	9	2	8	40	18
Mitchell Sanford, OF, Sr	.317	.423	.606	249	66	79	13	4	17	47	13
Will Furniss, INF, Jr	.305	.424	.517	203	46	62	7	0	12	47	0
Collin Reuter, C, Jr	.300	.404	.575	40	9	12	2	0	3	6	0
Judd Utermark, INF, Jr	.294	.376	.599	252	57	74	11	0	22	69	7
Brayden Randle, INF, So	.286	.378	.386	70	14	20	4	0	1	10	4
Isaac Humphrey, OF, Sr	.286	.396	.560	234	53	67	17	4	13	60	6
Campbell Smithwick, C, So	.282	.410	.464	110	20	31	5	0	5	23	2
Ryan Moerman, OF, Sr	.274	.385	.498	215	46	59	15	0	11	48	6
Austin Fawley, C, So	.256	.386	.648	176	40	45	6	0	21	53	0
Hayden Federico, INF, Fr	.243	.389	.343	181	33	44	6	0	4	23	12
Owen Paino, SS, Fr	.236	.348	.345	55	13	13	3	0	1	7	1
Luke Cheng, INF, Sr	.236	.394	.382	110	23	26	4	0	4	17	0

Pitcher, Year	W	L	ERA	G	GS	SV	IP	H	BB	SO
Connor Spencer, Sr	0	1	1.82	20	0	8	24	16	10	27
Hunter Elliott, Jr	10	3	2.94	17	16	0	85	59	40	102
Mason Morris, Jr	5	1	3.29	19	0	1	54	45	21	78
Will McCausland, Jr	3	1	4.32	24	1	2	41	42	11	55
Taylor Rabe, Fr	0	1	4.41	15	2	0	16	22	2	8
Walker Hooks, Fr	1	2	4.82	22	2	1	37	43	12	43
Gunnar Dennis, Sr	4	1	4.97	18	4	0	29	34	16	32
Alex Canney, Jr	1	1	5.09	15	1	0	17	25	10	22
Hudson Calhoun, So	3	0	5.11	21	0	0	24	15	18	37
Ryne Rodriguez, Jr	1	1	5.40	19	0	0	15	16	6	16
Mason Nichols, Sr	3	2	5.40	16	14	0	53	59	26	56
Brayden Jones, Jr	1	2	5.50	18	0	1	18	24	6	30
Riley Maddox, Sr	6	5	5.56	17	16	0	69	71	30	69
Landon Waters, Jr	2	0	6.27	17	0	1	18	16	10	24
Cade Townsend, Jr	1	0	6.35	15	8	0	34	28	20	43

20. Georgia
Coach: Wes Johnson. **Overall:** 43-17

Player, Pos, Yr	AVG	OBP	SLG	AB	R	H	2B	3B	HR	RBI	SB
Ryland Zaborowski, INF, Sr	.370	.500	.788	146	41	54	10	0	17	61	0
Slate Alford, INF, Sr	.331	.440	.649	242	71	80	16	2	19	63	2
Tre Phelps, INF, So	.318	.409	.547	201	45	64	14	1	10	44	4
Robbie Burnett, UT, So	.307	.477	.693	192	62	59	12	1	20	66	17
Kolby Branch, INF, Jr	.303	.398	.537	218	46	66	10	1	13	41	6
Christian Adams, INF, Jr	.293	.400	.537	123	24	36	7	1	7	23	0

Player, Pos, Yr	AVG	OBP	SLG	AB	R	H	2B	3B	HR	RBI	SB
Ryan Black, INF, Jr	.276	.390	.500	116	23	32	5	0	7	18	3
Nolan McCarthy, OF, Sr	.276	.376	.480	221	56	61	10	1	11	42	8
Daniel Jackson, C, So	.240	.365	.612	121	28	29	3	0	14	36	12
Henry Hunter, C, Sr	.237	.371	.480	173	35	41	9	0	11	28	1
Devin Obee, OF, Jr	.221	.388	.462	145	42	32	5	0	10	33	11
Brennan Hudson, C, Jr	.219	.457	.625	32	8	7	4	0	3	13	0
Cade Brown, INF, Fr	.171	.216	.314	35	3	6	2	0	1	5	0

Pitcher, Year	W	L	ERA	G	GS	SV	IP	H	BB	SO
JT Quinn, Jr	1	1	2.75	17	7	1	36	23	17	49
Brian Curley, Jr	4	4	3.55	17	10	2	66	42	27	85
Justin Byrd, Jr	0	0	3.74	18	0	0	21	15	6	26
Jordan Stephens, So	4	0	3.92	18	0	3	20	11	19	27
Eric Hammond, Jr	0	0	4.15	15	0	0	17	14	7	23
Tyler McLoughlin, Sr	4	0	4.19	16	1	1	19	16	10	24
Paul Farley, Fr	1	0	4.30	12	0	0	14	16	12	9
DJ Radtke, Jr	4	0	4.45	22	0	2	30	28	15	30
Zachary Harris, Jr	3	1	4.55	21	5	4	27	25	9	31
Leighton Finley, Jr	3	2	4.85	16	14	0	68	56	25	83
Davis Chastain, Jr	3	0	4.97	13	0	0	12	11	5	15
Kolten Smith, Sr	5	3	5.23	15	6	1	41	37	19	58
Brian Zeldin, Sr	2	1	5.68	19	2	0	31	31	21	36
Matthew Hoskins, Jr	1	2	5.93	18	2	2	27	24	23	39
Zach Brown, So	3	1	7.45	10	1	0	19	25	9	15
Charlie Goldstein, Sr	0	2	7.66	15	11	0	24	22	23	30
Alton Davis II, Jr	5	0	8.14	19	1	0	21	29	12	27

21. Southern Miss
Coach: Christian Ostrander. **Overall:** 47-16

Player, Pos, Yr	AVG	OBP	SLG	AB	R	H	2B	3B	HR	RBI	SB
Jake Cook, OF, So	.350	.436	.468	237	57	83	13	3	3	32	5
Joey Urban, OF, Jr	.333	.417	.552	174	36	58	9	1	9	27	2
Tucker Stockman, C, So	.332	.414	.474	190	41	63	9	0	6	33	0
Ben Higdon, OF, Jr	.323	.398	.513	158	45	51	9	0	7	22	2
Nick Monistere, P, Jr	.323	.410	.623	257	59	83	12	1	21	72	7
Ozzie Pratt, INF, Sr	.311	.404	.468	222	39	69	11	0	8	53	3
Matthew Russo, INF, Jr	.290	.407	.563	245	49	71	11	1	18	57	0
Seth Smith, INF, So	.278	.365	.315	54	9	15	2	0	0	7	0
Carson Paetow, OF, Sr	.268	.378	.561	239	47	64	18	2	16	64	0
Braden Luke, INF, Sr	.261	.393	.435	23	3	6	1	0	1	5	0
Drey Barrett, INF, Fr	.254	.359	.446	177	32	45	5	1	9	30	0
Davis Gillespie, INF, So	.242	.365	.464	153	27	37	10	0	8	30	0
Lawson Odom, C, Sr	.172	.351	.241	29	5	5	2	0	0	1	0

Pitcher, Year	W	L	ERA	G	GS	SV	IP	H	BB	SO
JB Middleton	10	1	2.31	16	16	0	105	65	25	122
Landen Payne	2	1	2.76	20	0	5	33	26	6	47
Grayden Harris	5	3	3.39	16	15	0	58	63	25	46
Colby Allen	7	4	3.63	29	2	12	67	53	17	77
Camden Sunstrom	3	0	4.00	17	2	0	27	32	11	18
Kros Sivley	7	1	4.14	22	8	0	72	73	20	58
Matthew Adams	6	4	4.31	18	17	0	79	78	22	89
Josh Och	2	0	4.71	24	0	1	36	24	22	41
Chandler Best	1	1	4.91	21	0	0	18	22	10	18
Brooks Willoughby	3	0	5.03	17	0	1	20	17	9	22
Ty Long	1	0	7.00	6	2	0	9	14	2	6
Micah Wascom	0	0	7.94	6	0	0	6	4	5	5
Michael Fowler	0	0	9.39	10	0	0	8	10	8	9

22. Oregon
Coach: Mark Wasikowski. **Overall:** 42-16

Player, Pos, Yr	AVG	OBP	SLG	AB	R	H	2B	3B	HR	RBI	SB
Ryan Cooney, INF, So	.335	.445	.500	182	45	61	12	0	6	49	15
Jacob Walsh, 1B, Sr	.332	.435	.651	232	54	77	17	0	19	60	8
Dominic Hellman, INF, Jr	.326	.426	.567	187	42	61	6	0	13	44	1
Drew Smith, INF, Jr	.313	.423	.487	115	23	36	3	1	5	25	6
Maddox Molony, INF, So	.309	.403	.565	207	41	64	8	0	15	45	10
Mason Neville, OF, Jr	.290	.429	.724	217	67	63	16	0	26	57	9
Jeffery Heard, OF, Sr	.289	.409	.500	90	18	26	4	0	5	17	4
Anson Aroz, C, Jr	.281	.417	.583	199	54	56	9	0	17	53	6
Carter Garate, INF, Jr	.272	.403	.417	180	48	49	12	1	4	36	6
Burke-Lee Mabeus, C, Fr	.257	.379	.376	109	27	28	5	1	2	23	6
Chase Meggers, C, Jr	.245	.290	.316	98	12	24	4	0	1	11	0
Coen Niclai, C, Fr	.242	.324	.455	33	3	8	4	0	1	4	0
Parker Stinson, OF, Sr	.200	.370	.350	20	7	4	0	0	1	3	0
Jack Brooks, UT, So	.182	.341	.242	33	11	6	2	0	0	7	3

Pitcher, Year	W	L	ERA	G	GS	SV	IP	H	BB	SO
Seth Mattox, Sr	2	1	2.41	21	0	8	18	10	8	16
Ian Umlandt, Jr	6	2	2.55	18	5	1	60	66	16	44
Michael Meckna, Fr	3	0	2.61	7	0	0	10	8	5	4
Jaxon Jordan, Sr	1	0	2.92	14	0	0	12	6	5	16
Grayson Grinsell, Jr	9	3	3.01	16	16	0	98	72	28	101
Cole Stokes, So	1	2	3.10	24	0	2	20	9	16	39
Jason Reitz, Jr	5	1	3.50	16	11	1	64	50	29	73
Santiago Garcia, So	3	0	4.20	24	0	4	30	18	19	40
Collin Clarke, So	5	2	4.59	13	13	0	68	60	21	60
Will Sanford, Fr	2	2	6.39	11	10	0	38	27	39	42
Ryan Featherston, So	2	0	7.08	18	0	2	34	34	21	31
Julien Hernandez, Sr	1	1	7.20	8	2	0	10	9	8	12
Kellan Knox, Fr	1	2	9.22	12	0	0	13	13	4	10

23. Florida
Coach: Kevin O'Sullivan. **Overall:** 39-22

Player, Pos, Yr	AVG	OBP	SLG	AB	R	H	2B	3B	HR	RBI	SB
Colby Shelton, INF, Jr	.377	.458	.606	175	40	66	19	0	7	35	6
Bobby Boser, UT, Sr	.336	.437	.613	238	72	80	12	0	18	67	19
Brendan Lawson, INF, Fr	.317	.417	.522	224	48	71	14	1	10	61	8
Cade Kurland, INF, Jr	.316	.490	.605	38	9	12	2	0	3	15	1
Brody Donay, C, Jr	.303	.418	.646	198	45	60	10	2	18	41	8
Luke Heyman, C, Jr	.301	.397	.578	173	37	52	7	1	13	44	0
Justin Nadeau, INF, Jr	.283	.421	.409	159	38	45	11	0	3	22	7
Landon Stripling, INF, So	.264	.397	.368	125	34	33	7	0	2	20	1
Ty Evans, OF, Sr	.263	.322	.451	133	25	35	11	1	4	30	2
Hayden Yost, OF, So	.259	.380	.392	189	39	49	13	0	4	38	14
Blake Cyr, INF, Jr	.254	.358	.429	205	45	52	9	0	9	34	8
Ashton Wilson, UT, Jr	.222	.368	.350	117	28	26	6	0	3	19	13

Pitcher, Year	W	L	ERA	G	GS	SV	IP	H	BB	SO
Pierce Coppola, Jr	3	1	2.53	7	7	0	21	12	9	43
Aidan King, Fr	7	2	2.58	17	12	0	73	58	23	79
Blaine Rowland, Fr	1	0	3.21	8	0	0	14	14	4	10
Jake Clemente, So	2	1	3.46	21	5	7	54	36	25	77
Liam Peterson, So	8	4	4.28	16	15	0	69	67	32	96
Jackson Barberi, Fr	2	1	4.45	20	5	0	32	37	19	41
Luke McNeillie, So	5	2	4.82	28	2	1	52	44	24	72
Caden McDonald, Fr	4	0	5.14	20	0	0	28	30	14	29
Christian Rodriguez, Fr	1	0	5.32	22	0	1	23	24	11	31
McCall Biemiller, Fr	1	0	5.93	11	1	0	13	11	17	18
Billy Barlow, Sr	1	4	6.26	22	7	1	46	55	23	46
Alex Philpott, So	3	4	7.30	22	3	2	37	41	18	44
Matthew Jenkins, So	0	2	9.64	9	4	0	14	15	11	24

24. Clemson
Coach: Erik Bakich. **Overall:** 45-18

Player, Pos, Yr	AVG	OBP	SLG	AB	R	H	2B	3B	HR	RBI	SB
Cam Cannarella, OF, Jr	.353	.479	.530	232	62	82	22	2	5	52	6
Dominic Listi, OF, Sr	.310	.507	.468	203	62	63	15	1	5	47	3
Jarren Purify, INF, So	.298	.417	.462	208	54	62	10	3	6	35	29
Tryston McCladdie, UT, So	.287	.393	.511	94	23	27	4	1	5	19	9
Jack Crighton, UT, Jr	.287	.370	.378	143	27	41	6	2	1	19	5
Luke Gaffney, UT, So	.271	.357	.388	188	26	51	7	0	5	39	2
Andrew Ciufo, INF, Sr	.263	.378	.418	194	38	51	10	1	6	33	7
Jacob Jarrell, C, Jr	.263	.387	.515	198	45	52	5	0	15	41	0
Josh Paino, INF, Sr	.249	.354	.426	237	47	59	10	1	10	47	10
Collin Priest, INF, So	.240	.407	.480	196	36	47	11	0	12	52	0
Tristan Bissetta, UT, Jr	.227	.358	.373	75	13	17	2	0	3	16	2
TP Wentworth, UT, Fr	.220	.350	.280	50	8	11	3	0	0	7	2

Pitcher, Year	W	L	ERA	G	GS	SV	IP	H	BB	SO
Reed Garris, Sr	3	0	1.57	18	0	3	28	18	8	30
Joe Allen, Jr	5	0	1.84	23	0	0	29	20	17	32
Lucas Mahlstedt, Sr	4	1	3.00	27	0	15	48	48	8	61
Jacob McGovern, So	3	1	3.86	20	2	2	35	20	12	44
Aidan Knaak, Jr	9	1	4.18	16	16	0	90	71	29	110
Drew Titsworth, So	5	1	4.28	10	7	2	54	57	19	50
B.J. Bailey, Sr	2	5	5.46	21	6	0	61	65	22	60
Talan Bell, Fr	0	2	5.56	9	8	0	22	22	15	22
Hudson Lee, So	0	0	5.79	15	0	0	14	10	13	19
Ethan Darden, Fr	4	2	6.08	9	9	0	40	46	16	34
Nathan Dvorsky, Jr	4	0	6.75	22	1	0	25	23	19	32

Cam Cannarella hit .453 and continued to be Clemson's spark plug.

Pitcher, Year	W	L	ERA	G	GS	SV	IP	H	BB	SO
Chance Fitzgerald, So	4	0	7.71	17	1	0	28	35	9	24
Justin LeGuernic, So	0	3	9.12	12	6	0	24	30	14	33
Chayce Kieck, Fr	2	0	9.75	9	0	0	12	19	5	11

25. Georgia Tech
Coach: Danny Hall. **Overall:** 41-19

Player, Pos, Yr	AVG	OBP	SLG	AB	R	H	2B	3B	HR	RBI	SB
Kent Schmidt, INF, So	.397	.464	.596	156	39	62	16	0	5	43	4
Vahn Lackey, C, So	.347	.421	.500	222	45	77	14	1	6	42	18
Alex Hernandez, INF, Fr	.335	.415	.609	230	47	77	11	2	16	69	5
Drew Burress, OF, So	.333	.469	.693	228	77	76	23	1	19	62	10
Kyle Lodise, INF, Jr	.329	.429	.667	219	68	72	20	3	16	61	13
Carson Kerce, INF, So	.313	.411	.475	198	48	62	20	0	4	40	6
Caleb Daniel, UT, Fr	.312	.397	.507	205	51	64	15	2	7	32	4
Tyler Neises, INF, Jr	.273	.393	.386	88	16	24	5	1	1	15	4
Drew Rogers, C, Fr	.269	.427	.612	67	13	18	3	1	6	18	0
Connor Shouse, UT, Fr	.265	.432	.559	34	15	9	4	0	2	8	3
Will Baker, INF, Fr	.263	.336	.495	99	19	26	5	0	6	26	0
John Giesler, INF, Sr	.259	.347	.376	85	18	22	4	0	2	16	0
Nathan Waugh, C, Sr	.237	.408	.368	38	12	9	2	0	1	7	0
Parker Brosius, OF, Jr	.234	.376	.323	124	31	29	6	1	1	20	14

Pitcher, Year	W	L	ERA	G	GS	SV	IP	H	BB	SO
Jaylen Paden, Sr	5	1	2.91	15	5	2	43	32	25	51
Mason Patel, Sr	11	2	3.34	23	0	5	70	57	18	64
Caden Spivey, Jr	2	1	4.05	14	5	0	33	32	22	32
Kayden Campbell, Jr	2	1	4.42	17	0	0	18	18	9	28
Tate McKee, So	8	3	4.84	16	16	0	80	82	38	83
Brady Jones, Jr	7	3	4.92	16	16	0	67	60	38	73
Riley Stanford, So	0	0	5.08	12	7	0	28	31	21	34
Connor Chicoli, Fr	1	1	5.46	14	5	0	28	33	5	18
Carson Ballard, So	1	3	5.70	17	1	1	36	39	6	38
Brett Barfield, Jr	0	0	5.93	20	1	1	13	16	8	14
Jake Lankie, So	0	1	6.10	8	0	0	10	13	4	12
Sam Swygert, Sr	1	1	6.27	14	3	0	18	20	8	17

CONFERENCE STANDINGS & LEADERS

NCAA regional teams in bold.

AMERICA EAST CONFERENCE

	Conference		Overall	
	W	L	W	L
Bryant	18	6	36	18
NJIT	14	10	27	26
Binghamton	13	11	28	26
Maine	13	11	20	31
UAlbany	10	14	22	32
UMBC	8	16	18	28
UMass Lowell	8	16	18	35

ALL-CONFERENCE TEAM: SP: Dylan Banner, Jr., UAlbany; Michael Belcher, Fr., Bryant; Nate DeSchryver, Gr., NJIT; Caleb Leys, Jr., Maine. **RP:** Nick Remy, Sr., UMBC. **C:** Mason Wolf, Gr., NJIT. **1B:** Freddy Forgione, Gr., Binghamton. **2B:** Zac Zyons, Jr., Bryant. **SS:** Drew Wyers, Jr., Bryant. **3B:** Devan Bade, Sr., Binghamton. **OF:** Matt Bolton, Fr., Binghamton; Brody Rasmussen, Jr., Maine; Ty Sallie, Jr., NJIT. **DH:** Evin Sullivan, Sr., Binghamton. **UTIL:** Zach Rogacki, Sr., Binghamton.

Player of the Year: Drew Wyers, Bryant. **Pitcher of the Year:** Caleb Leys, Maine. **Rookie of the Year:** Michael Belcher, Bryant. **Coach of the Year:** Ryan Klosterman, Bryant.

INDIVIDUAL BATTING LEADERS

	AVG	OBP	SLG	AB	2B	3B	HR	RBI	SB
Wyers, Drew, Bryant	.407	.521	.710	145	11	0	11	50	9
Wolf, Mason, NJIT	.400	.475	.593	150	10	2	5	42	9
Eppinger, Andrew, NJIT	.361	.406	.503	147	15	0	2	19	2
Rogacki, Zach, Binghamton	.361	.437	.600	205	17	4	8	43	5
Bade, Devan, Binghamton	.352	.430	.598	219	15	0	13	61	4
Forgione, Freddy, Binghamton	.348	.454	.637	201	13	0	15	48	0
Bolton, Matt, Binghamton	.347	.446	.498	225	13	0	7	33	11
Evan Menzel, Maine	.342	.447	.530	117	10	0	4	18	6
Myles Sargent, Maine	.339	.397	.570	165	12	1	8	42	4
Ortiz, Ray, NJIT	.324	.423	.623	207	17	3	13	40	4
Brandon Fish, Umass Lowell	.313	.363	.462	182	17	2	2	34	3
Jesiah Carpenter, UMBC	.312	.411	.393	173	8	0	2	25	16
Noriega, Gavin, Bryant	.311	.394	.514	212	16	0	9	50	4
Aidan Bardi, Maine	.310	.445	.380	100	4	0	1	14	0
Levi Mcallister, UAlbany	.310	.432	.589	158	15	1	9	55	3
Brody Rasmussen, Maine	.307	.366	.495	202	13	2	7	32	6
Sullivan, Evin, Binghamton	.307	.420	.579	202	16	0	13	50	1
Danny Orr, UMBC	.307	.367	.513	150	10	0	7	25	2
Sallie, Ty, NJIT	.305	.417	.416	197	14	1	2	29	7
Anthony Mascuilli, UMBC	.303	.460	.402	132	6	2	1	21	6
Campbell, Cole, NJIT	.302	.389	.405	215	10	3	2	24	17
Carlos Martinez, UMass Lowell	.299	.350	.456	204	12	1	6	27	1
Damon Gaither, Maine	.298	.402	.543	94	5	0	6	25	0
Conor Kelly, UMass Lowell	.296	.398	.370	135	10	0	0	14	9
Kyle Stephens, UAlbany	.293	.389	.488	82	9	2	1	14	0

INDIVIDUAL PITCHING LEADERS

	W	L	ERA	G	SV	IP	H	BB	SO
Caleb Leys, Maine	5	2	2.69	14	0	67	56	27	74
Nick Remy, UMBC	7	2	3.19	3	4	48	36	14	43
Dylan Banner, UAlbany	5	5	3.82	14	0	94	100	14	68
Matthew Mariano, UAlbany	5	6	4.38	3	2	64	70	30	60
Belcher, Michael, Bryant	3	1	4.52	13	0	66	63	18	60
Gianni Gambardella, Maine	5	4	4.88	10	0	63	66	24	51
Morrissey, MT, NJIT	6	6	5.03	14	1	82	83	33	77
DeSchryver, Nate, NJIT	4	4	5.43	10	2	60	40	46	72
Tarsia, Hayden, Binghamton	4	4	5.43	12	0	70	75	19	57
Colin Fitzgerald, Maine	5	6	5.68	14	0	89	106	33	78
Eddie Sargent, UMBC	3	3	5.75	8	0	56	71	15	52
Alfred Mucciarone, UMass Lowell	1	7	6.78	14	0	73	94	20	62
Peterson, Brandon, NJIT	4	4	6.97	12	0	61	68	39	39
Brendan Holland, UMass Lowell	3	6	7.09	14	0	72	89	22	71
Packard, Ryan, Binghamton	3	5	7.88	14	0	62	65	31	38
Bouchard, Brady, Binghamton	3	5	9.69	7	1	57	89	18	47

AMERICAN ATHLETIC CONFERENCE

	Conference		Overall	
	W	L	W	L
UTSA	23	4	47	15
Charlotte	18	9	36	22
South Florida	16	11	31	25
Florida Atlantic	15	12	37	21
Tulane	13	14	33	25
East Carolina	13	14	35	27
Wichita State	11	16	20	36
Rice	10	17	17	40
UAB	8	19	24	30
Memphis	8	19	22	33

ALL-CONFERENCE TEAM: P: Blake Gillespie, Jr., Charlotte; **P:** Trey Beard, So., Florida Atlantic; **P:** Corey Braun, R-Jr., South Florida. **RP:** Michael Lombardi, Tulane; **RP:** Robert Orloski, So., UTSA. **C:** Andrew Stucky, Sr., UTSA. **1B:** Cody Gunderson, Jr., Charlotte. **2B:** Connor Rasmussen, Jr., Tulane. **SS:** Ty Hodge, R-Jr., UTSA. **3B:** Dawson Bryce, So., Charlotte. **OF:** Marshall Lipsey, Jr., Florida Atlantic; Mason Lytle, Sr., UTSA; James Taussig, Sr., UTSA. **DH:** Blaine Brown, Fr., Rice. **UTL:** Colby Wallace, So., East Carolina.

Player of the Year & Defensive Player of the Year: Mason Lytle, Sr., OF, UTSA. **Pitcher of the Year & Newcomer Pitcher of the Year:** Blake Gillespie, Jr., P, Charlotte. **Newcomer Position Players of the Year:** Todd Clay, Jr., 3B, UAB; Drew Detlefsen, Jr., OF, UTSA. **Coach of the Year:** Pat Hallmark, UTSA.

INDIVIDUAL BATTING LEADERS

	AVG	OBP	SLG	AB	2B	3B	HR	RBI	SB
Braden Burress, East Carolina	.389	.488	.498	211	11	0	4	33	18
Mason Lytle, UTSA	.369	.429	.558	260	22	0	9	67	17
Todd Clay, UAB	.361	.473	.539	191	13	0	7	51	6
James Taussig, UTSA	.358	.457	.604	187	14	1	10	65	4
Norris McClure, UTSA	.356	.424	.498	205	9	1	6	42	9
Jordan Ballin, UTSA	.347	.554	.388	121	5	0	0	22	6
Spencer Nolan, Charlotte	.340	.398	.388	103	2	0	1	19	5
Dawson Bryce, Charlotte	.340	.389	.600	235	17	1	14	53	2
Jason Wachs, Tulane	.335	.457	.479	167	14	2	2	25	4
Connor Rasmussen, Tulane	.333	.427	.484	213	15	1	5	45	3
Cody Gunderson, Charlotte	.331	.462	.548	157	8	1	8	30	0
Brodil, Marcus, South Florida	.330	.448	.443	194	13	0	3	38	9
Andrew Stucky, Utsa	.325	.466	.521	169	15	0	6	40	1
Camden Johnson, Wichita State	.325	.402	.433	231	17	1	2	35	9
Rose, Matt, South Florida	.322	.398	.409	149	7	0	2	19	3
Logan Braunschweig, UAB	.319	.437	.500	204	14	1	7	31	27
Brando Leroux, Florida Atlantic	.319	.393	.454	185	10	0	5	32	10
Marshall Lipsey, Florida Atlantic	.318	.488	.573	192	7	3	12	43	17
Drew Detlefsen, UTSA	.316	.424	.569	225	18	0	13	70	7
Theo Bryant, Tulane	.311	.411	.567	90	5	0	6	21	23

INDIVIDUAL PITCHING LEADERS

	W	L	ERA	G	SV	IP	H	BB	SO
Blake Gillespie, Charlotte	7	4	2.42	15	0	100	69	19	131
Trey Beard, Florida Atlantic	7	1	3.14	15	1	86	61	32	118
Colin Daniel, UAB	6	5	3.15	14	0	91	81	15	80
Robert Orloski, UTSA	8	0	3.23	0	9	70	54	26	76
Braun, Corey, South Florida	8	4	3.71	15	0	97	83	24	97
Nedrow, Jack, South Florida	5	3	3.75	8	1	72	68	10	47
Norby, Ethan, East Carolina	8	5	3.80	14	0	90	74	22	119
Davion Hickson, Rice	2	7	3.82	11	1	73	59	35	90
Young, Ethan, East Carolina	5	0	3.84	1	3	70	57	34	92
Andrew Kribbs, Charlotte	3	2	4.15	15	0	65	63	28	61
Garner, Seth, Memphis	3	8	4.28	14	0	76	83	24	54
Braylon Owens, UTSA	7	2	4.38	14	3	88	72	38	97
Conor Myles, UTSA	5	1	4.93	16	0	69	80	21	58
James Litman, Florida Atlantic	3	3	5.04	15	0	61	61	20	50
Jenkins, Sean, East Carolina	4	4	5.12	12	1	70	73	20	52

Zach Royse, UTSA	9	4	5.16	16	0	89	95	31	80
Case, David, Memphis	1	7	5.28	14	0	60	74	31	63
Pruett, Brad, East Carolina	5	6	5.32	5	3	66	54	34	70
Chase Ingram, UAB	2	5	5.37	11	0	57	76	18	41
Hamilton, Brady, Wichita State	2	7	5.38	16	0	79	71	43	63
Tyler Murphy, Florida Atlantic	4	3	5.57	13	0	63	78	22	50
J.D. McCracken, Rice	4	5	6.46	14	0	71	74	36	37
Cole Cheatham, UAB	3	5	6.48	10	0	67	69	30	65
Adler, Grant, Wichita State	5	6	6.67	15	0	80	87	34	74
Luc Fladda, Tulane	4	6	6.69	15	0	77	97	11	62

ATLANTIC COAST CONFERENCE

	Conference		Overall	
	W	L	W	L
Georgia Tech	19	11	41	19
Florida State	17	10	42	16
North Carolina	18	11	46	15
NC State	17	11	35	21
Clemson	18	12	45	18
Virginia	16	11	32	18
Duke	17	13	41	21
Wake Forest	16	14	39	22
Miami	15	14	35	27
Louisville	15	15	42	24
Notre Dame	14	16	32	21
Virginia Tech	12	18	31	25
Stanford	11	19	27	25
Boston College	11	19	28	29
Pitt	10	20	28	27
California	9	21	24	31

ALL-CONFERENCE TEAM: C: Luke Stevenson, North Carolina; Carson Tinney, Notre Dame. **1B:** Hunter Stokely, North Carolina. **2B:** Drew Faurot, Florida State. **3B:** Ben Miller, Duke; Daniel Cuvet, Miami. **SS:** Alex Lodise, Florida State. **OF:** Drew Burress, Georgia Tech; Lucas Moore, Louisville; Zion Rose, Louisville. **DH/UTIL:** Alex Hernandez, Georgia Tech. **SP:** Aidan Knaak, Clemson; Jamie Arnold, Florida State; Jake Knapp, North Carolina; Blake Morningstar, Wake Forest. **RP:** Lucas Mahlstedt, Clemson.

Player of the Year: Alex Lodise, SS, Florida State. **Pitcher of the Year:** Jake Knapp, SP, North Carolina. **Freshman of the Year:** Alex Hernandez, 3B/RP, Georgia Tech. **Defensive Player of the Year:** Alex Lodise, SS, Florida State. **Coach of the Year:** Danny Hall, Georgia Tech.

Florida State's Jamie Arnold was named to the ACC all-conference team

INDIVIDUAL BATTING LEADERS

	AVG	OBP	SLG	AB	2B	3B	HR	RBI	SB
Kent Schmidt, Georgia Tech	.397	.464	.596	156	16	0	5	43	4
Alex Lodise, Florida State	.396	.467	.727	227	18	3	17	67	6
French, Jacob, California	.390	.440	.564	195	12	5	4	36	2
Chris McHugh, NC State	.377	.473	.552	183	11	0	7	47	1
Marsh, Tatum, Stanford	.377	.459	.526	175	13	2	3	25	4
Kade Lewis, Wake Forest	.376	.482	.602	226	18	0	11	59	4
Daniel Cuvet, Miami	.374	.451	.703	222	20	1	17	80	5
Eric Becker, Virginia	.368	.453	.617	201	21	1	9	52	5
King Jr, Louisville	.367	.435	.750	188	19	1	17	63	4
Henry Ford, Virginia	.362	.420	.575	207	9	1	11	46	4
Gage Harrelson, Florida State	.356	.463	.486	222	10	2	5	43	15
Marek Houston, Wake Forest	.354	.458	.597	243	14	0	15	66	19
Cam Cannarella, Clemson	.353	.479	.530	232	22	2	5	52	6
Carson Tinney, Notre Dame	.348	.498	.753	158	13	0	17	53	1
Vahn Lackey, Georgia Tech	.347	.421	.500	222	14	1	6	42	18
Jake Munroe, Louisville	.346	.451	.593	243	13	4	13	61	2
Advincula, Jarren, California	.342	.410	.506	237	17	2	6	33	13
Hott, Ethan, Stanford	.342	.414	.504	117	8	1	3	25	3
Lucas Moore, Louisville	.339	.430	.454	271	10	3	5	49	53
Caden Dulin, Pitt	.337	.421	.478	184	14	0	4	29	2
Myles Bailey, Florida State	.337	.453	.695	190	11	0	19	55	4
Alex Hernandez, Georgia Tech	.335	.415	.609	230	11	2	16	69	5
Drew Burress, Georgia Tech	.333	.469	.693	228	23	1	19	62	10
Jake Ogden, Miami	.333	.399	.500	246	14	0	9	36	12
Jacob Ference, Virginia	.333	.465	.595	126	6	0	9	29	9
Alex Madera, North Carolina	.332	.432	.403	226	8	1	2	38	13
Becerra, Temo, Stanford	.330	.384	.427	185	11	2	1	37	4

Kyle Lodise, Georgia Tech	.329	.429	.667	219	20	3	16	61	13
Haskins, Trevor, Stanford	.326	.370	.575	221	13	0	14	42	0
Gavin Gallaher, North Carolina	.325	.409	.603	237	13	1	17	68	5
Hunter Stokely, North Carolina	.325	.410	.557	237	13	0	14	65	4
A.J. Nessler, Pitt	.324	.439	.454	207	10	1	5	44	8
Max Galvin, Miami	.323	.378	.511	229	19	0	8	38	9
Max Williams, Florida State	.321	.391	.615	221	8	0	19	53	2
Luke Cantwell, Pitt	.320	.482	.510	200	18	1	6	45	6
Josiah Ragsdale, Boston College	.319	.418	.498	207	12	5	5	30	30
Derek Williams, Miami	.317	.396	.590	139	11	0	9	22	10
Bino Watters, Notre Dame	.317	.436	.549	164	9	1	9	39	3
Connor Hincks, Notre Dame	.317	.392	.509	161	13	3	4	39	0
Aiden Teel, Virginia	.317	.442	.538	186	20	0	7	40	9

INDIVIDUAL PITCHING LEADERS

	W	L	ERA	G	SV	IP	H	BB	SO
Jake Knapp, North Carolina	14	0	2.02	15	0	102	72	16	88
Ryan Lynch, North Carolina	5	1	2.93	3	2	61	44	25	73
Easterly, Reid, Duke	9	3	3.04	0	5	74	64	17	66
Jamie Arnold, Florida State	7	2	3.09	14	0	79	57	25	110
Joey Volini, Florida State	8	4	3.17	14	0	82	69	22	102
Mason Patel, Georgia Tech	11	2	3.34	0	5	70	57	18	64
Jack Radel, Notre Dame	7	4	3.58	13	0	70	56	18	60
Rory Fox, Notre Dame	4	4	3.58	14	0	65	44	27	64
Ryan Marohn, NC State	7	3	3.72	13	0	77	74	19	81
Aidan Haugh, North Carolina	5	4	3.72	14	0	75	70	33	85
Jason DeCaro, North Carolina	9	3	3.78	16	0	83	79	26	70
Blake Morningstar, Wake Forest	6	2	3.87	14	0	79	71	32	93
Brett Renfrow, Virginia Tech	7	3	3.89	15	0	74	78	34	84
Griffin Hugus, Miami	6	7	4.16	17	0	93	84	35	95
Dominic Fritton, NC State	5	5	4.17	16	0	86	90	36	106
Aidan Knaak, Clemson	9	1	4.18	16	0	90	71	29	110
Brady Miller, Boston College	4	1	4.27	12	0	59	60	26	41
Patrick Forbes, Louisville	4	2	4.42	15	0	71	59	34	117
AJ Ciscar, Miami	6	2	4.52	10	0	66	56	16	63
Tomas Valincius, Virginia	6	1	4.59	12	0	65	64	17	70
Proksch, Owen, Duke	4	3	4.68	12	1	65	54	28	91

	W	L	ERA	G	0	IP	H	BB	SO
Jay Woolfolk, Virginia	4	3	4.73	13	0	65	63	24	75
Tate McKee, Georgia Tech	8	3	4.84	16	0	80	82	38	83
A.J. Colarusso, Boston College	1	6	4.89	15	1	74	79	31	58
Brady Jones, Georgia Tech	7	3	4.92	16	0	68	60	38	73
Ryan Reed, Pitt	5	4	5.01	14	0	74	84	24	67
Wes Mendes, Florida State	3	5	5.67	15	0	73	67	36	86
Eddy,Gavin, California	4	4	5.74	9	0	58	52	32	50
Heath Andrews, NC State	4	3	5.97	13	0	60	69	22	50
Volchko, Joey, Stanford	3	4	6.01	15	0	70	79	34	56
Scott, Matt, Stanford	5	2	6.02	11	0	52	67	22	56
Jake Marciano, Virginia Tech	4	2	6.08	14	0	61	70	18	71
Patrick Gardner, Pitt	4	6	7.15	14	0	73	81	29	59

ATLANTIC SUN CONFERENCE

	Conference		Overall	
Gold Division	W	L	W	L
Austin Peay	26	4	45	14
Lipscomb	17	13	25	30
North Alabama	16	14	24	31
Central Arkansas	12	18	20	34
Bellarmine	11	19	17	38
EKU	8	22	11	44
Graphite Division	W	L	W	L
Stetson	24	6	41	22
Jacksonville	17	13	30	26
FGCU	16	14	31	29
North Florida	15	15	27	29
West Georgia	11	19	20	31
Queens	7	23	9	44

ALL-CONFERENCE TEAM: SP: Evan Dempsey, FGCU; Richard Long, Jacksonville; Jonathan Gonzalez, Stetson. **RP:** Ty Van Dyke, Stetson. **C:** Trevor Conley, Austin Peay. **1B:** Josh Steidl, Jacksonville. **2B:** Kyler Proctor, Austin Peay. **3B:** Ray Velazquez, Austin Peay. **SS:** Lorenzo Meola, Stetson. **OF:** John Bay, Austin Peay; Cameron Nickens, Austin Peay; Jaden Bastian, Jacksonville. **DH:** Cole Johnson, Austin Peay.

Player of the Year: Cameron Nickens, Austin Peay. **Defensive Player of the Year:** Lorenzo Meola, Stetson. **Pitcher of the Year:** Jonathan Gonzalez, Stetson. **Freshman of the Year:** Cole Johnson, Austin Peay. **Coach of the Year:** Roland Fanning, Austin Peay.

INDIVIDUAL BATTING LEADERS

	AVG	OBP	SLG	AB	2B	3B	HR	RBI	SB
Nickens, Cameron, Austin Peay	.422	.520	.768	237	24	2	18	71	8
Cermenelli, Bryce, C. Arkansas	.395	.461	.474	152	7	1	1	23	2
Barkett, Isaiah, Stetson	.389	.461	.498	221	16	1	2	33	32
Velazquez, Ray, Austin Peay	.364	.479	.728	173	9	0	18	57	8
Bay, John, Austin Peay	.360	.507	.769	225	16	5	22	66	12
Shields, Jonah, Jacksonville	.359	.441	.445	209	10	1	2	36	24
Johnson, Cole, Austin Peay	.356	.438	.587	225	23	1	9	70	3
Landon Kenealy Jr, Lipscomb	.356	.399	.511	225	15	1	6	24	16
Petey Craska, North Alabama	.344	.500	.550	189	18	0	7	35	0
Parks Bouck, Lipscomb	.339	.427	.471	189	10	0	5	40	3
Monile, Nick, North Florida	.338	.482	.460	198	11	5	1	26	13
Meola, Lorenzo, Stetson	.329	.406	.536	222	9	2	11	43	10
Cooper Prince, West Georgia	.325	.425	.461	191	7	5	3	22	10
Moore, Connor, North Florida	.324	.380	.498	219	23	3	3	34	16
Taylor, Jordan, Stetson	.322	.359	.504	242	16	2	8	43	22
McKee,Jake, FGCU	.321	.396	.457	162	9	2	3	27	2
Proctor, Kyler, Austin Peay	.320	.388	.462	253	14	2	6	42	14
Bush, Cade, North Florida	.316	.388	.449	158	9	0	4	35	6
Damian Kenealy Jr, Lipscomb	.316	.391	.492	187	9	0	8	37	6
Steidl,Josh, Jacksonville	.314	.461	.479	188	7	0	8	37	2
Moya,Robert, FGCU	.314	.397	.371	172	6	0	7	29	0
Freeman, Gus, Austin Peay	.313	.477	.529	208	15	0	10	51	13
Negre, Nathan, Central Arkansas	.310	.377	.410	210	10	4	1	40	8
Dempsey,Evan, FGCU	.309	.393	.435	230	18	1	3	30	14
Collins, Mitchell, North Florida	.307	.428	.402	179	11	0	2	28	16

INDIVIDUAL PITCHING LEADERS

	W	L	ERA	G	SV	IP	H	BB	SO
Dempsey, Evan, FGCU	5	1	1.97	10	0	69	57	20	75
Gonzalez, Jonathan, Stetson	10	2	2.11	15	0	94	70	22	105

Long,Richard, Jacksonville	8	4	2.59	15	0	94	72	20	66
Cole O'Brien, Lipscomb	4	3	3.14	12	0	63	62	35	51
Landry Jurecka, Queens	3	7	3.21	10	0	84	89	20	88
Glidewell, Lyndon, Austin Peay	8	0	3.36	13	1	78	61	34	64
Hendry, Clay, North Florida	6	5	3.92	11	0	60	53	22	64
Walsh, Alex, Jacksonville	1	3	3.99	13	0	68	58	30	51
Rothermel, Colin, Jacksonville	6	4	4.02	15	0	72	52	37	79
Lane Pearson, West Georgia	5	5	4.02	14	0	81	81	24	86
Braunecker, Gavin, Austin P.	10	0	4.24	6	1	70	70	17	62
Anthony Pingeton, N. Alabama	3	3	4.76	14	0	70	75	24	56
Diaz, Chris, FGCU	6	3	4.80	12	0	75	73	21	81
Seth Dudley, West Georgia	4	6	4.90	14	0	72	76	23	56
Tripp Patterson, North Ala.	5	6	4.98	15	0	85	78	28	50
ROSS, Will, North Florida	5	3	5.02	13	0	66	81	13	50
Treichel, Bryson, North Florida	4	5	5.25	14	0	62	69	24	74
Dylan Morrill, North Alabama	3	2	5.37	2	4	55	53	24	49
Weaver, Jacob, Austin Peay	5	2	5.37	15	0	70	70	30	56
Adrian Quezada, Queens	0	5	5.40	5	0	57	67	14	37
Sam Cole, West Georgia	2	6	5.58	12	1	61	81	24	42
Ryan Brown, Queens	1	4	5.61	7	1	59	78	16	45
Rigo Ramos, Lipscomb	3	5	5.74	15	0	63	65	35	65
Christensen, Charlie, C. Arkans.	4	5	5.85	15	0	80	102	33	74
Lawson, Nathan, EKU	1	2	6.33	3	1	58	73	17	55

ATLANTIC 10 CONFERENCE

	Conference		Overall	
	W	L	W	L
Rhode Island	23	8	39	20
George Mason	20	10	40	21
Davidson	19	12	28	29
Saint Louis	18	12	33	26
Saint Joseph's	17	13	24	28
Fordham	15	15	25	33
Richmond	14	16	33	19
George Washington	14	16	27	27
Dayton	14	16	27	31
St. Bonaventure	11	19	20	29
VCU	10	21	17	38
UMass	7	25	14	36

ALL-CONFERENCE TEAM: C: Jack Arcamone, Richmond. **1B:** Jordan Jaffe, Richmond. **2B:** Eli Putnam, Davidson. **SS:** Owen Clyne, George Mason. **3B:** Anthony DePino, Rhode Island. **OF:** Cider Canon, Davidson; Michael DiMartini, Dayton; James Quinn-Irons, George Mason. **DH:** Jack Hopko, Rhode Island. **SP:** Brandon Cassedy, George Mason; Connor O'Hara, George Mason; Colton Book, Saint Joseph's. **RP:** Ryan Bilka, Richmond.

Player of the Year: James Quinn-Irons, George Mason. **Pitcher of the Year:** Colton Book, Saint Joseph's. **Defensive Player of the Year:** Ethan Sitzman, Saint Louis. **Rookie of the Year:** Jacob Lee, VCU. **Coach of the Year:** Raphael Cerrato, Rhode Island.

INDIVIDUAL BATTING LEADERS

	AVG	OBP	SLG	AB	2B	3B	HR	RBI	SB
James Quinn-Irons, G. Mason	.419	.523	.734	241	24	2	16	85	36
Jayce Tharnish, St. Bona.	.403	.461	.597	196	11	3	7	29	32
Michael DiMartini, Dayton	.399	.461	.687	243	11	7	15	68	37
Dyrenson Wouters, Dayton	.387	.471	.561	155	12	0	5	34	5
Cider Canon, Davidson	.371	.460	.733	202	16	3	17	52	10
Michael O'Schaugnessy, David.	.369	.482	.691	217	19	0	17	70	1
Owen Hull, George Mason	.367	.474	.557	237	15	3	8	63	42
Brady O'Brien, Richmond	.366	.422	.777	202	19	2	20	72	2
Jordan Jaffe, Richmond	.364	.429	.599	217	19	1	10	59	5
Rylan Lujo, Dayton	.363	.418	.567	245	16	2	10	57	17
Eric Genther, Rhode Island	.361	.478	.584	238	17	3	10	53	6
Reece Moroney, Rhode Island	.356	.464	.462	225	12	3	2	42	24
Jack Arcamone, Richmond	.355	.463	.675	197	22	1	13	62	1
Anthony DePino, Rhode Island	.354	.505	.730	226	21	2	20	61	21
Anthony Torreso, Davidson	.351	.462	.649	131	10	1	9	39	0
Andrew Kanellis, Fordham	.349	.448	.509	212	10	0	8	50	15
Eli Putnam, Davidson	.349	.419	.660	241	18	0	19	62	13
Sam Gates, G. Washington	.346	.457	.532	188	11	0	8	37	11
Ellis Schwartz, G. Washington	.346	.454	.582	208	16	3	9	45	9
David Marshall, St. Bona.	.342	.404	.520	202	12	0	8	45	0

	AVG	OBP	SLG	AB	R	H	2B	3B	HR	RBI	SB
Riley Iffrig, Saint Louis	.341	.456	.551	214	19			1	8	65	6
Jack Hopko, Rhode Island	.341	.446	.606	226	8			2	16	83	8
Owen Clyne, George Mason	.341	.429	.447	246	10			2	4	60	20
Taylor Kirk, Fordham	.338	.421	.425	228	11			3	1	31	30
Lucas Alberti, George Mason	.335	.455	.464	233	15			0	5	47	16
Aaron Whitley, Richmond	.333	.434	.540	213	18			1	8	36	36
Root, Beau, UConn	.341	.442	.504	123	3			1	5	26	4
McMillan, Shaun, St. John's	.341	.410	.590	173	12			2	9	49	2
Tucker, Nolan, Xavier	.338	.429	.480	148	8			2	3	24	10
Dougherty, Aidan, UConn	.333	.417	.447	150	11			0	2	31	11
Leonard, Brayden, Villanova	.333	.417	.486	177	9			0	6	37	7
Soldra, AJ, Seton Hall	.330	.426	.514	218	12			8	4	28	15
Misch, Connor, Xavier	.326	.488	.472	178	10			2	4	44	4
Rispoli, Rob, UConn	.324	.473	.412	216	5			1	4	30	19
Solomon, AJ, Butler	.316	.466	.392	158	9			0	1	23	2
Whooley, Michael, Villanova	.314	.420	.541	185	9			3	9	32	5
Kavi Caster, Georgetown	.312	.384	.541	205	14			3	9	45	20

INDIVIDUAL PITCHING LEADERS

	W	L	ERA	G	SV	IP	H	BB	SO
Ryan Bilka, Richmond	6	2	2.18	0	3	62	43	13	57
Connor O'Hara, George Mason	7	4	2.81	16	0	90	76	26	86
Brandon Cassedy, G. Mason	8	2	3.32	15	0	84	76	30	78
Trystan Levesque, Rhode Island	8	2	3.49	16	0	95	92	23	95
Book, Colton, Saint Joseph's	6	3	3.53	14	0	87	66	20	122
Tappy, Owen, VCU	5	2	4.01	8	1	76	89	15	58
Josh Cunningham, Saint Louis	6	2	4.48	12	0	68	67	20	56
Rabayda, Mike, Fordham	2	6	4.59	15	0	84	86	31	72
Owen Kelly, Saint Louis	6	2	4.61	15	0	80	79	29	78
Ciccone, Frank, Saint Joseph's	5	5	4.70	14	0	75	74	35	69
Esteban Rodriguez, Richmond	3	5	5.15	14	0	58	58	25	44
Sam Lavin, George Mason	5	0	5.29	8	1	65	68	28	55
Powers, Callen, UMass	3	5	5.38	14	0	72	79	29	52
Jeremy Urena, Rhode Island	6	2	5.69	15	0	81	90	21	48
J.J. Gatti, Dayton	5	4	6.06	15	0	65	68	35	62
Chance Moore, St. Bonaventure	3	5	6.22	11	0	72	96	20	46
Foltz Jr, George Washington	2	8	6.51	14	0	76	91	36	60
Chris Peguero, Dayton	5	5	6.52	15	0	90	106	28	102
Stein, Nathan, Saint Joseph's	1	5	6.68	13	0	61	76	32	51
Wilson Perkins, Davidson	6	5	6.94	15	0	83	101	30	74
Isaac Fix, Davidson	7	5	6.98	15	0	70	79	45	61
O'Connor, Robbie, UMass	2	9	7.71	14	0	68	90	38	37
David James, St. Bonaventure	2	6	7.92	10	0	50	60	28	47
Wilson Magers, Creighton	6	2	3.09	13	0	67	45	36	50
Pudvar, Oliver, UConn	6	1	3.60	12	0	70	61	32	73
JT Raab, Georgetown	4	3	3.63	14	0	74	81	35	77
Piech, Ryan, Xavier	4	1	4.12	12	0	55	33	44	60
Weber, Ben, Xavier	6	2	4.13	11	0	81	87	25	42
Mccollough, Luke, Villanova	5	2	4.21	12	0	73	75	17	50
Sachais, Alec, Villanova	4	6	4.86	0	6	54	47	22	56
Andrew Williams, Georgetown	3	5	5.13	14	0	74	86	30	60
Hansen, Cole, Seton Hall	2	5	5.43	14	0	71	64	23	56
Ian Koosman, Creighton	6	4	5.58	9	1	50	43	21	55
Rodriguez, David, St. John's	3	3	5.65	11	0	51	57	34	27
Schmidt, Logan, Xavier	2	5	5.85	9	0	65	72	22	57
Frederick, Victor, St. John's	4	2	5.98	10	0	53	60	19	43
Olsen, Bobby, Villanova	1	5	6.19	11	0	57	67	28	59
Ellisen, Tommy, UConn	6	3	6.45	14	0	67	84	31	66
Francis, Jake, Creighton	5	5	6.60	12	2	61	84	15	34
Goodpaster, Marcus, Butler	3	6	7.41	13	0	75	109	23	41
Chaffee, Evan, St. John's	1	4	7.83	13	0	56	53	54	47

BIG EAST CONFERENCE

	Conference		Overall	
	W	L	W	L
Creighton	17	4	43	16
UConn	17	4	38	21
Xavier	14	7	32	27
St. John's	13	8	29	24
Seton Hall	10	11	24	30
Villanova	6	15	22	28
Butler	4	17	15	39
Georgetown	3	18	16	40

ALL-CONFERENCE TEAM: C: Owen Carapellotti, Sr., Georgetown. **1B:** Connor Misch, Jr., Xavier. **2B:** Ryan Daniels, Jr., UConn. **SS:** Rob Rispoli, R-Fr., UConn. **3B:** Jayder Raifstanger, So., St. John's. **OF:** Jon LeGrande, Jr., St. John's; Aiden Robbins, So., Seton Hall; Caleb Shpur, Gr., UConn. **DH:** Shaun McMillan, Fr., St. John's. **SP:** Steven Svenson, Fr., Seton Hall; Dominic Cancellieri, Gr., Creighton; JT Raab, Gr., Georgetown; Wilson Magers, Fr., Creighton. **RP:** Garrett Langrell, Gr., Creighton.

Player of the Year: Ryan Daniels, UConn, Jr., 2B. **Pitcher of the Year:** Dominic Cancellieri, Creighton, Gr., RHP. **Freshman of the Year:** Wilson Magers, Creighton, Fr., RHP. **Coaching Staff of the Year:** Creighton, Ed Servais

INDIVIDUAL BATTING LEADERS

	AVG	OBP	SLG	AB	R	H	2B	3B	HR	RBI	SB
Robbins, Aiden, Seton Hall	.422	.537	.652	204	19	5	6	38	20		
Nolan Sailors, Creighton	.392	.489	.540	189	13	3	3	33	26		
Moroknek, Jack, Butler	.379	.448	.715	214	16	1	18	57	2		
Daniels, Ryan, UConn	.365	.476	.744	203	15	4	18	75	10		
Bello, Jack, Butler	.365	.403	.583	192	17	2	7	45	2		
Shpur, Caleb, UConn	.363	.430	.529	240	10	3	8	44	43		
LeGrande, Jon, St. John's	.360	.432	.560	175	7	5	6	43	29		
Minick, Tyler, UConn	.355	.437	.734	214	11	2	22	74	15		
Raifstanger, Jayder, St. John's	.352	.470	.477	199	12	2	3	35	0		
Beebe, Jared, St. John's	.352	.414	.540	213	22	3	4	48	0		
Connor Capece, Creighton	.350	.400	.490	143	9	1	3	35	1		
Sackett, Connor, Butler	.349	.439	.430	86	4	0	1	17	5		
Blake Schaaf, Georgetown	.344	.442	.476	189	11	1	4	35	31		
Lemon, Austin, Villanova	.343	.455	.373	134	4	0	0	21	2		

BIG SOUTH CONFERENCE

	Conference		Overall	
	W	L	W	L
USC Upstate	19	5	36	25
High Point	18	6	39	19
Charleston Southern	14	10	31	22
Radford	13	11	28	28
Winthrop	13	11	31	29
Presbyterian	9	15	17	35
Longwood	8	16	14	38
UNC Asheville	8	16	15	35
Gardner-Webb	6	18	17	36

ALL-CONFERENCE TEAM: C: Preston Lucas, USC Upstate. **INF:** Brayden Simpson, High Point; Vance Sheahan, USC Upstate; Gabe Natividad, Winthrop; Hunter Keen, Radford. **OF:** Konni Durschlag, High Point; Miggy Echazarreta, High Point; Scott Campbell, USC Upstate. **DH:** Johnny Sweeney, USC Upstate. **UTL:** Myles Webb, Longwood. **SP:** Clay Edmondson, UNC Asheville; Wade Walton, High Point; Amp Phillips, USC Upstate. **RP:** Ryan DuSang, Charleston Southern; Adam Grintz, USC Upstate.

Player Of The Year: Konni Durschlag, OF, High Point. **Pitcher Of The Year:** Clay Edmondson, UNC Asheville. **Newcomer Of The Year:** Amp Phillips, SP, USC Upstate. **Freshman Of The Year:** Wade Walton, SP, High Point. **Coach Of The Year:** Kane Sweeney, USC Upstate. **Scholar-Athlete Of The Year:** Aidan Mcaskie, Charleston Southern.

INDIVIDUAL BATTING LEADERS

	AVG	OBP	SLG	AB	R	H	2B	3B	HR	RBI	SB
Durschlag, Konni, High Point	.434	.546	.751	221	23	1	15	59	4		
Simpson, Brayden, High Point	.389	.477	.774	234	24	0	22	78	14		
Campbell, Scott, USC Upstate	.388	.498	.622	188	11	0	11	54	21		
Trey Fenderson, Presbyterian	.374	.477	.521	163	16	1	2	24	14		
Johnson, Landen, High Point	.362	.449	.656	224	18	0	16	86	2		
Breckin Nace, Radford	.359	.470	.538	184	12	3	5	42	6		
Zenor, Henry, USC Upstate	.358	.450	.550	229	21	1	7	40	5		
Echazarreta, Miggy, High Point	.355	.530	.525	183	17	1	4	42	19		
James Ward, Radford	.353	.448	.618	207	17	1	12	56	5		
Smith, Kaden, Charleston So.	.348	.453	.652	184	17	0	13	73	5		
Melton, Jackson, High Point	.346	.456	.601	188	14	2	10	54	9		

COLLEGE

Player	AVG	OBP	SLG	AB	2B	3B	HR	RBI
Collins, Kain, Charleston So.	.345	.458	.390	177	6	1	0	17 19
Sweeney, Johnny, USC Upstate	.345	.500	.701	194	15	0	18	82 3
Nativitad, Gabe, Winthrop	.344	.484	.514	218	13	3	6	43 10
Rylen Stockton, UNC Asheville	.343	.421	.543	175	12	1	7	33 1
Rice, Lew, Charleston Southern	.341	.480	.600	135	7	5	6	33 11
Lucas, Preston, USC Upstate	.337	.439	.526	190	19	1	5	63 3
Macias, Garrett, Gardner-Webb	.331	.404	.450	151	6	0	4	21 0
Jake Randolph, Presbyterian	.329	.400	.410	173	6	1	2	32 6
Blaize Johnson, UNC Asheville	.328	.396	.555	137	13	0	6	29 1
Sheahan, Vance, USC Upstate	.328	.399	.522	268	16	0	12	57 25
Eli Hudgins, Radford	.324	.399	.466	176	16	0	3	38 20
Nelson, James, Longwood	.323	.406	.545	189	16	1	8	49 6
Smith, Christian, High Point	.321	.452	.628	196	9	3	15	62 8
Rhogue Wallace, Presbyterian	.319	.379	.571	91	8	0	5	23 4

INDIVIDUAL PITCHING LEADERS

Player	W	L	ERA	G	SV	IP	H	BB	SO
Clay Edmondson, UNC Asheville	5	1	2.20	13	0	82	66	26	87
Phillips, Amp, USC Upstate	7	2	3.64	12	2	84	63	29	81
Torres, Chris, USC Upstate	8	4	4.76	16	0	81	94	29	78
Tyrell Williams, Presbyterian	3	3	4.85	8	0	56	57	27	35
Sarna, Owen, Winthrop	4	3	5.04	10	0	64	77	22	58
Walton, Wade, High Point	8	3	5.18	15	0	83	80	27	91
Cole, Ryan, Charleston Southern	1	2	6.33	10	0	58	65	28	36
Pfeffer, John, Gardner-Webb	3	6	6.55	3	1	55	66	27	38
Story, Dylan, High Point	7	3	6.78	15	0	76	87	44	55
Garcia, Guillermo, Longwood	5	5	6.94	13	0	71	77	33	72
Harris, Connor, Winthrop	6	4	7.18	15	0	73	99	9	70
Andrew Steinhaus, Radford	4	6	7.46	8	0	57	63	40	48
Drew Stanley, Radford	4	4	7.90	8	1	63	86	27	47
Bertram, Reid, Gardner-Webb	1	6	8.67	13	0	55	78	25	37
Tristan McGregor, Presbyterian	2	7	8.67	13	0	55	79	22	42
Elges, Alek, Longwood	1	5	8.95	5	0	58	97	23	45

BIG 12 CONFERENCE

	Conference		Overall	
	W	L	W	L
West Virginia	19	9	44	16
Kansas	20	10	43	17
TCU	19	11	39	20
Arizona	18	12	44	21
Arizona State	18	12	36	24
Kansas State	17	13	32	26
Oklahoma State	15	12	30	25
Cincinnati	16	14	33	26
Texas Tech	13	17	20	33
Baylor	13	17	33	22
Houston	12	17	30	25
BYU	10	20	28	27
UCF	9	21	29	26
Utah	8	22	21	29

ALL CONFERENCE TEAM: C: Logan Sauve, West Virginia. **IF:** Matt King, Arizona State; Tyriq Kemp, Baylor; Kerrington Cross, Cincinnati; Brady Ballinger, Kansas; Core Jackson, Utah. **OF:** Isaiah Jackson, Arizona State; Sawyer Strosnider, TCU; Damian Bravo, Texas Tech; Logan Hughes, Texas Tech. **DH:** Noah Franco, TCU. **UT:** Landon Hairston, Arizona State. **SP:** Harrison Bodendorf, Oklahoma State; Tommy LaPour, TCU; Colter McAnelly, Utah; Griffin Kirn, West Virginia. **RP:** Cole Carlon, Arizona State; Gabe Craig, Baylor; Antoine Jean, Houston.

Player of the Year: Kerrington Cross, Cincinnati. **Pitcher of the Year:** Antoine Jean, Houston. **Co-Newcomers of the Year:** Matt King, Arizona State & Harrison Bodendorf, Oklahoma St. **Freshman of the Year:** Sawyer Strosnider, TCU. **Scholar-Athlete of the Year:** Tony Pluta, Arizona. **Coach of the Year:** Dan Fitzgerald, Kansas.

INDIVIDUAL BATTING LEADERS

Player	AVG	OBP	SLG	AB	2B	3B	HR	RBI
King, Matt, Arizona State	.403	.464	.593	216	18	1	7	55 8
Cross, Kerrington, Cincinnati	.396	.526	.647	207	10	3	12	50 15
Villeneuve Robin, Texas Tech	.365	.447	.661	189	18	1	12	49 3
Jackson, Core, Utah	.364	.445	.641	206	19	1	12	44 20
White, Sam, West Virginia	.361	.426	.529	191	17	0	5	46 9
Ross, DeAmez, UCF	.359	.429	.466	234	15	2	2	35 14
Kemp, Tyriq, Baylor	.358	.446	.542	201	14	1	7	41 9
Vu, Kien, Arizona State	.354	.458	.601	178	12	1	10	35 21
Ballinger, Brady, Kansas	.353	.495	.670	224	21	1	16	56 0
Williamson, Andrew, UCF	.352	.448	.662	213	19	4	13	53 13
Walker, Kyle, Arizona State	.352	.449	.526	216	19	1	7	30 22
Strosnider, Sawyer, TCU	.350	.420	.650	220	13	10	11	51 10
Hurdsman, Bryker, BYU	.342	.434	.532	190	18	3	4	36 8
Roellig, Austen, Utah	.341	.391	.441	211	16	1	1	35 8
Sundean, Andrew, UCF	.340	.421	.569	144	12	0	7	42 0
West, Kyle, West Virginia	.339	.487	.601	183	15	0	11	38 6
Natili, Jack, Cincinnati	.338	.451	.556	198	14	1	9	53 4
Sanders, Travis, Baylor	.335	.425	.549	164	9	1	8	25 8
Espinal, Edian, UCF	.335	.434	.470	185	13	0	4	37 11
Bowen, Karson, TCU	.333	.425	.516	159	11	3	4	28 3
Hairston, Landon, Arizona State	.333	.441	.467	195	12	1	4	37 4
Panaro, Santino, Utah	.331	.420	.470	151	9	3	2	18 12
Bravo, Damian, Texas Tech	.330	.384	.580	224	13	2	13	51 18
Jimenez, Antonio, UCF	.329	.407	.575	207	14	2	11	51 11
Guzman, Adonys, Arizona	.328	.411	.496	232	12	0	9	44 0
White, Mason, Arizona	.327	.412	.689	257	17	8	20	73 4
Hughes, Logan, Texas Tech	.327	.411	.697	211	13	4	19	58 3
Guzman, Armani, West Virginia	.327	.403	.449	107	5	1	2	22 17
Traeger, Nolan, TCU	.327	.429	.472	159	8	3	3	17 2
Dardar, Seth, Kansas State	.326	.429	.636	184	18	0	13	45 6
King, Dylan, UCF	.326	.442	.652	135	13	2	9	34 1
Osoria, Dariel, Kansas	.324	.421	.539	204	13	2	9	47 0
Martin, Maximus, Kansas State	.320	.420	.612	206	18	0	14	54 5
Walton, Aaron, Arizona	.320	.437	.589	253	22	2	14	49 19
Rinehart, Jace, West Virginia	.320	.395	.567	194	21	0	9	53 4
Cramer, Cole, TCU	.320	.433	.419	222	9	2	3	43 9
O'Connor, Keegan, Kansas State	.319	.376	.647	204	14	1	17	60 4
Swain, Chase, West Virginia	.319	.404	.452	135	6	3	2	30 11
Brunson, Chase, TCU	.317	.395	.554	224	13	2	12	46 9
Franco, Noah, TCU	.313	.396	.548	217	16	1	11	49 4

INDIVIDUAL PITCHING LEADERS

Player	W	L	ERA	G	SV	IP	H	BB	SO
Jean, Antoine, Houston	5	1	2.55	0	5	67	40	20	110
LaPour, Tommy, TCU	8	3	3.09	16	0	90	78	27	88
Bodendorf, Harrison, Okla. St.	10	1	3.30	16	0	93	69	28	102
Kirn, Griffin, West Virginia	5	3	3.36	17	1	99	86	30	103
Cebert, Jack, Texas Tech	7	3	3.45	2	0	60	62	20	54
Kartsonas, Jack, West Virginia	6	4	3.66	9	1	66	63	20	77
McAnelly, Colter, Utah	4	4	3.79	14	0	93	82	34	92
Taylor, Nathan, Cincinnati	7	2	3.93	15	0	87	83	36	91
Bailey, Smith, Arizona	3	3	3.94	18	0	89	92	32	80
Moore, Cooper, Kansas	7	3	3.96	14	1	89	91	19	85
Brassfield, Mason, TCU	5	2	4.09	7	0	62	59	23	68
Bassinger, Reese, West Virginia	7	1	4.23	0	5	62	63	12	43
Pesca, Mario, Oklahoma State	7	3	4.45	8	0	67	67	18	60
Jacobs, Ben, Arizona State	4	3	4.95	16	0	84	71	45	120
Calder, Ethan, Baylor	3	6	5.18	15	0	73	75	18	64
O'Connor, Kellen, Cincinnati	3	3	5.22	12	2	71	69	25	60
Watkins, Hunter, Okla. State	5	4	5.43	11	1	65	78	23	70
Sheffield, Lincoln, Kansas St.	7	4	5.45	15	0	74	96	19	70
Martinez, Jack, Arizona State	6	4	5.47	15	0	77	66	33	110
Kramkowski, Owen, Arizona	9	6	5.48	18	0	92	116	18	90
Schmitz, Paul, Houston	4	5	5.58	14	0	60	65	26	49
Voegele, Dominic, Kansas	7	5	5.70	16	0	96	93	36	89
Petty, Zane, Texas Tech	2	4	5.92	12	0	62	66	26	46
Frost, Jacob, Kansas State	1	5	5.97	15	0	66	62	40	75
Gubler, Payton, BYU	3	3	5.98	9	0	56	55	33	41

BIG TEN CONFERENCE

	Conference		Overall	
	W	L	W	L
Oregon	22	8	42	16
UCLA	22	8	48	18
Iowa	21	9	33	22
USC	18	12	37	23
Washington	17	13	29	28

Indiana	16	14		32	24
Michigan	16	14		33	23
Nebraska	15	15		33	29
Penn State	15	15		33	23
Rutgers	15	15		29	28
Illinois	14	16		30	24
Michigan State	13	17		28	27
Northwestern	13	17		25	27
Maryland	12	18		27	29
Purdue	11	19		31	23
Minnesota	10	20		24	28
Ohio State	5	25		13	37

ALL-CONFERENCE TEAM: SP: Cade Obermueller, Jr., Iowa; Aaron Savary, Jr., Iowa; Joseph Dzierwa, Jr., Michigan State; Grayson Grinsell, Jr., Oregon. **RP:** Will Rogers, Sr., Michigan; Seth Mattox, Sr., Oregon; Isaac Yeager, Jr., Washington. **C:** Alex Calarco, Sr., Maryland. **1B:** Jacob Walsh, Sr., Oregon. **2B:** Mitch Voit, Jr., Michigan. **SS:** Roch Cholowsky, So., UCLA. **3B:** Ethan Hedges, Jr., USC. **OF:** Korbyn Dickerson, So., Indiana; Devin Taylor, Jr., Indiana; Mason Neville, Jr., Oregon. **UTL:** Reese Moore, So., Iowa. **At-Large:** Ryan Cooney, So., Oregon. **At-Large:** Paxton Kling, Jr., Penn State.

Player Of The Year: Roch Cholowsky, So., SS, UCLA. **Pitcher Of The Year:** Joseph Dzierwa, Jr., SP, Michigan State. **Defensive Player Of The Year:** Roch Cholowsky, So., SS, UCLA. **Freshman Of The Year:** Jake Hanley, Fr., 1B, Indiana. **Coach Of The Year:** Mark Wasikowski, Oregon.

INDIVIDUAL BATTING LEADERS

	AVG	OBP	SLG	AB	2B	3B	HR	RBI	SB
Benny Casillas, Michigan	.401	.483	.585	207	21	1	5	41	6
Trevor Cohen, Rutgers	.387	.460	.523	235	24	1	2	36	19
Chris Hacopian, Maryland	.375	.502	.656	192	12	0	14	61	1
Devin Taylor, Indiana	.374	.494	.706	214	13	2	18	66	12
Logan Sutter, Purdue	.367	.471	.709	196	22	0	15	62	3
Caleb Wulf, Iowa	.364	.420	.414	140	4	0	1	27	5
Paxton Kling, Penn St.	.358	.470	.632	212	15	2	13	54	15
Roch Cholowsky, UCLA	.353	.480	.710	252	19	1	23	74	7
Ty Doucette, Rutgers	.350	.431	.557	237	10	0	13	54	2
Vytas Valincius, Illinois	.348	.434	.520	204	14	0	7	58	11
Mitch Voit, Michigan	.346	.471	.668	208	17	4	14	60	14
Ethan Hedges, Southern Calif.	.346	.462	.619	231	11	5	14	58	10
Ryan Cooney, Oregon	.335	.445	.500	182	12	0	6	49	15
Jake Hanley, Indiana	.333	.429	.575	219	9	1	14	52	1
Jacob Walsh, Oregon	.332	.435	.651	232	17	0	19	60	8
Adrian Lopez, Southern Calif.	.329	.400	.550	222	21	2	8	52	4
Gable Mitchell, Iowa	.329	.421	.476	225	18	0	5	44	12
Will Moore, Indiana	.328	.514	.389	131	5	0	1	19	6
Casen Taggart, Washington	.326	.469	.494	172	11	0	6	32	10
Dominic Hellman, Oregon	.326	.426	.567	187	6	0	13	44	1
Nick Groves, Illinois	.324	.493	.385	148	9	0	0	18	15
Brayden Dowd, Southern Calif.	.324	.446	.524	225	15	0	10	36	3
AJ Guerrero, Washington	.321	.413	.532	218	16	0	10	39	5
Cooper Malamazian, Indiana	.320	.394	.512	172	17	2	4	40	3
Dean West, UCLA	.320	.470	.425	247	12	1	4	41	13

INDIVIDUAL PITCHING LEADERS
(Minimum 40 innings pitched)

	W	L	ERA	G	SV	IP	H	BB	SO
Joseph Dzierwa, Michigan State	8	3	2.36	15	0	92	68	22	104
Ian Umlandt, Oregon	6	2	2.55	18	1	60	66	16	44
Grayson Grinsell, Oregon	9	3	3.01	16	0	99	72	28	101
Cade Obermueller, Iowa	5	3	3.02	15	0	83	62	32	117
Reece Beuter, Iowa	6	0	3.14	13	0	63	45	22	66
Kyle McCoy, Maryland	6	3	3.32	14	0	84	91	21	71
Jason Reitz, Oregon	5	1	3.50	16	1	64	50	29	73
Cole Gilley, Indiana	10	3	3.54	18	0	69	55	20	75
Tate Carey, Michigan	9	0	3.63	18	0	57	51	18	51
Jackson Brockett, Nebraska	4	4	3.66	16	0	64	73	23	45
Michael Vallone, Purdue	4	1	3.86	21	1	58	49	16	70
Max Banks, Washington	7	4	3.86	13	0	75	60	28	65
Ryan DeSanto, Penn St.	8	2	3.96	15	0	73	52	30	72
Michael Barnett, UCLA	12	1	3.98	19	0	86	98	22	75
Caden Aoki, Southern California	6	4	3.99	17	0	97	93	14	90

Landon Mack, Rutgers	6	5	4.03	15	0	80	81	17	70
Dylan Vigue, Michigan	1	4	4.25	16	1	59	47	42	51
Jackson Thomas, Washington	5	4	4.27	15	0	72	78	28	48
Cole Van Assen, Purdue	4	3	4.28	15	1	67	76	21	48
Ben Grable, Indiana	4	3	4.31	17	1	56	54	17	65
Ryan Kraft, Indiana	3	2	4.31	20	2	63	64	15	55
Will Rogers, Michigan	5	3	4.32	23	8	58	54	23	44
Aaron Savary, Iowa	7	2	4.37	15	0	80	67	33	82
Collin Clarke, Oregon	5	2	4.59	13	0	69	60	21	60
Kurt Barr, Michigan	6	5	4.65	16	0	70	72	34	74

BIG WEST CONFERENCE

	Conference		Overall	
	W	L	W	L
UC Irvine	24	6	43	17
Cal Poly	23	7	43	19
Cal State Fullerton	19	11	29	27
Hawai'i	16	14	35	21
UC Santa Barbara	16	14	36	18
UC San Diego	15	15	26	25
Long Beach State	15	15	22	31
UC Davis	13	17	27	28
CSUN	10	20	15	34
Cal State Bakersfield	9	21	18	38
UC Riverside	5	25	16	36

ALL-CONFERENCE TEAM: C: Blake Penso, Sr., UC Irvine. **1B:** Zach Daudet, Sr., Cal Poly. **2B:** Ryan Fenn, R-Sr., Cal Poly. **3B:** J.C. Allen, Jr., UC San Diego; Alejandro Garza, So., Cal Poly; Carter Johnstone, Fr., Cal State Fullerton. **SS:** Maddox Latta, Sr., Cal State Fullerton; Colin Yeaman, Jr., UC Irvine. **OF:** Michael Crossland, So., UC San Diego; LeTrey McCollum, Sr., UC Santa Barbara; Jacob McCombs, So., UC Irvine. **DH:** Gabe Camacho, So., UC San Diego. **UTL:** Itsuki Takemoto, So., Hawai'i. **SP:** Tyler Bremner, Jr., UC Irvine; Griffin Naess, So., Cal Poly. **RP:** Ricky Ojeda, So., UC Irvine. **CL:** Isaiah Magdaleno, So., Hawai'i; Andrew Wright, So., Cal State Fullerton.

Player Of The Year: Konni Durschlag, OF, High Point. **Pitcher Of The Year:** Clay Edmondson, UNC Asheville. **Newcomer Of The Year:** Amp Phillips, SP, USC Upstate. **Freshman Of The Year:** Wade Walton, SP, High Point. **Coach Of The Year:** Kane Sweeney, USC Upstate. **Scholar-Athlete Of The Year:** Aidan Mcaskie, Charleston Southern.

INDIVIDUAL BATTING LEADERS

	AVG	OBP	SLG	AB	2B	3B	HR	RBI	SB
LeTrey McCollum, UCSB	.371	.472	.540	213	10	4	6	40	17
Gonzalez, Roberto, CSUN	.371	.478	.617	167	10	8	5	30	9
Fenn, Ryan, Cal Poly	.365	.390	.482	249	19	2	2	42	16
Latta, Maddox, Cal St. Fullerton	.362	.486	.503	199	15	2	3	27	14
Daudet, Zach, Cal Poly	.360	.465	.593	189	15	1	9	26	4
Castellon, Nate, Cal Poly	.356	.413	.476	225	14	2	3	50	2
Rowan Kelly, UC Santa Barbara	.355	.424	.418	110	7	0	0	17	6
McCombs, Jacob, UC Irvine	.352	.446	.635	230	16	5	13	54	1
Garza, Alejandro, Cal Poly	.351	.408	.481	262	16	0	6	54	4
Johnstone, Carter, Cal St. Fullerton	.344	.431	.535	215	14	3	7	42	5
Crossland, Michael, UCSD	.341	.435	.644	205	15	1	15	44	6
Matthew Miura, Hawai'i	.338	.454	.460	213	13	2	3	35	18
Yeaman, Colin, UC Irvine	.336	.447	.591	247	16	4	13	56	3
Hoiland, Cam, Cal Poly	.333	.392	.522	159	8	2	6	24	0
Ben Zeigler-Namoa, Hawai'i	.333	.409	.509	216	17	0	7	54	1
Carney, Frankie, UC Irvine	.331	.431	.402	169	8	2	0	22	2
Ashworth, Kyle, LBSU	.330	.456	.443	194	12	2	2	35	6
Abel, Trent, CSUN	.326	.366	.395	129	3	0	2	18	3
Bardowell, Matthew, Cal St. Fullerton	.325	.411	.529	206	16	1	8	53	2
Pitts, Robert, UC Riverside	.325	.385	.450	209	15	1	3	26	22
Becker, Andrew, CSUN	.324	.376	.445	182	12	2	2	31	7
Potestio, Anthony, UCSD	.323	.450	.476	164	6	2	5	30	9
Linberg, Will, CSUN	.322	.425	.463	121	8	3	1	20	7
Martinez, Anthony, UC Irvine	.316	.387	.451	215	14	0	5	58	0
Call, Chase, UC Irvine	.315	.472	.582	184	12	2	11	49	1

INDIVIDUAL PITCHING LEADERS

	W	L	ERA	G	SV	IP	H	BB	SO
Bryan Green, UC Davis	3	5	2.55	15	0	81	82	23	69
Isaiah Magdaleno, Hawai'i	4	1	2.70	0	9	60	46	11	77
Roblez, Albert, LBSU	4	3	2.78	3	4	58	34	28	79
Hansen, Trevor, UC Irvine	9	3	3.30	16	0	95	87	31	95
Naess, Griffin, Cal Poly	7	3	3.41	16	0	95	85	30	62
Tyler Bremner, UCSB	5	4	3.49	14	0	77	60	19	111
Ojeda, Ricky, UC Irvine	13	1	3.55	2	2	66	49	29	83
Jackson Flora, UCSB	6	3	3.60	11	0	75	58	17	86
Noel Valdez, UC Davis	7	3	3.72	14	0	82	88	20	65
Cooper Walls, Hawai'i	3	3	3.73	13	0	60	69	15	45
Kelly, Riley, UC Irvine	4	1	3.78	12	0	67	66	32	70
Calvin Proskey, UCSB	5	4	3.78	13	0	67	65	17	71
Sebastian Gonzalez, Hawai'i	3	1	4.26	10	0	57	62	19	37
Dalquist, Matthew, UCSD	6	5	4.43	14	0	81	86	13	67
King, Ryan, CSB	0	6	4.78	13	0	70	72	25	62
Seid, Spencer, UC San Diego	3	1	4.79	5	3	56	51	22	71
Geiss, Owen, Long Beach State	6	8	4.90	11	1	68	75	25	44
Montgomery, Kellan, LBSU	9	4	4.97	14	0	76	93	29	60
Brooks, Ryder, UC Irvine	7	3	5.09	12	0	69	59	31	72
Leary, Jack, CSB	2	4	5.45	8	1	73	80	23	47
Negrete, Mikiah, CSF	5	3	5.58	15	0	81	94	33	80
Itsuki Takemoto, Hawai'i	2	6	5.75	14	0	67	80	22	57
Marmie, Ethan, Cal Poly	4	4	5.91	14	0	70	74	31	52
McAlinden, Shane, CSB	1	7	5.93	14	0	61	68	20	26
Volmerding, Josh, Cal Poly	5	5	6.02	17	0	84	98	29	83

COASTAL ATHLETIC ASSOCIATION

	Conference		Overall	
	W	L	W	L
Northeastern	25	2	49	11
UNCW	19	8	34	24
Charleston	15	12	37	22
Campbell	15	12	25	31
William & Mary	14	13	21	35
Elon	13	14	25	32
Delaware	12	15	28	25
Stony Brook	11	16	25	27
Towson	11	16	21	35
Monmouth	10	17	24	30
N.C. A&T	9	18	15	37
Hofstra	8	19	18	36

ALL-CONFERENCE TEAM: C: Brian Heckelman, Towson, Jr. **IF:** Jack Goodman, Northeastern, Jr.; Joey Morton, Campbell, Jr.; Erik Paulsen, Stony Brook, So.; Dylan Palmer, Hofstra, Jr.; Tanner Thach, UNCW, Jr. **OF:** Harrison Feinberg, Northeastern, Jr.; Aaron Graeber, Delaware, Sr.; Cam Maldonado, Northeastern, Jr.; Ben Parker, William & Mary, Gr. **UT:** Ryan Sprock, Elon, Jr. **DH:** Nico Azpilcueta, Stony Brook, Jr. **SP:** Aiven Cabral, Northeastern, Jr.; Will Jones, Northeastern, Gr.; Zane Taylor, UNCW, Sr. **RP:** Trace Baker, UNCW, Jr.; Charlie Walker, Northeastern, Jr.

Co-Players Of The Year: Harrison Feinberg, OF, Northeastern and Ben Parker, OF, William & Mary. **Pitcher Of The Year:** Zane Taylor, RHP, UNCW. **Defensive Player Of The Year:** Erik Paulsen, 1B, Stony Brook. **Rookie Of The Year:** Cam Bagwell, SP, UNCW. **Coach Of The Year:** Mike Glavine, Northeastern.

INDIVIDUAL BATTING LEADERS

	AVG	OBP	SLG	AB	2B	3B	HR	RBI	SB
Ben Parker, W&M	.414	.502	.700	237	24	4	12	52	18
Palmer, Dylan, Hofstra	.400	.449	.536	220	13	7	1	32	32
Feinberg, Harrison, NE	.367	.455	.715	207	14	2	18	67	37
Brian Heckelman, Towson	.365	.439	.588	170	10	2	8	42	3
Lucas Carmichael, W&M	.362	.414	.568	243	14	0	12	47	8
Jamie Laskoski, W&M	.360	.423	.467	214	11	3	2	42	12
Erik Paulsen, Stony Brook	.358	.452	.585	193	17	0	9	44	8
Maldonado, Cam, NE	.351	.467	.631	222	17	0	15	59	29
Aaron Graeber, Delaware	.351	.401	.609	225	12	2	14	52	14
Duffey, Alex, Elon	.349	.463	.479	192	13	0	4	54	5
Simpson, Joe, Campbell	.345	.439	.608	148	7	1	10	31	21
Caufield, Casey, Monmouth	.341	.446	.454	185	15	3	0	27	13

Goodman, Jack, NE	.335	.406	.547	203	11	1	10	51	20
Bant, Jay, Monmouth	.333	.394	.538	195	17	1	7	58	1
Thompson, Dalen, Campbell	.330	.384	.524	206	10	0	10	46	21
Aiden Stewart, Delaware	.326	.465	.579	190	17	2	9	48	8
Tanner Thach, UNCW	.325	.409	.538	240	11	2	12	46	5
Derek Holmes, W&M	.324	.387	.400	210	13	0	1	45	3
Matthew Jackson, Stony Brook	.324	.434	.528	108	7	0	5	18	16
Smith, Tyler, N.C. A&T	.323	.414	.542	201	13	2	9	36	8
Sprock, Ryan, Elon	.321	.411	.593	221	16	1	14	50	3
Yaghoubi, Tank, Elon	.321	.404	.352	193	4	1	0	26	4
Nico Azpilcueta, Stony Brook	.320	.390	.711	194	14	1	20	61	3
Will Baumhofer, Charleston	.319	.431	.432	213	13	4	1	42	17
LT Cockrill, Delaware	.314	.415	.564	156	12	0	9	37	5

INDIVIDUAL PITCHING LEADERS

	W	L	ERA	G	SV	IP	H	BB	SO
Zane Taylor, UNCW	11	2	1.98	15	0	96	62	11	105
Gottesman, Jordan, NE	9	2	2.27	12	1	83	55	17	97
Jones, Will, NE	11	1	2.63	15	0	72	55	19	75
Cabral, Aiven, NE	10	3	2.92	16	0	89	77	14	74
Cam Bagwell, UNCW	9	2	3.07	15	0	85	72	17	62
Alex Lyon, Charleston	10	1	3.47	0	0	60	63	13	34
Connor Marshburn, UNCW	4	3	3.51	15	0	74	53	37	68
Mealy, Ryan, Monmouth	5	2	3.56	9	0	68	75	14	53
Jake Brink, Charleston	6	6	3.58	15	0	93	88	32	82
Mitrovich, Justin, Elon	6	4	4.23	15	0	89	73	35	81
Daniel Brooks, Charleston	6	4	4.44	14	0	75	66	24	74
Brown, Peyton, Campbell	3	2	4.47	5	2	58	59	30	42
Murray, Jake, Campbell	4	2	4.68	15	0	60	50	34	82
Lavelle, Declan, Elon	3	6	5.53	15	0	81	89	20	63
Opanel, Kevin, Monmouth	2	6	5.61	10	0	59	63	25	47
Smith, Mason, Campbell	2	6	5.61	12	0	61	64	35	60
Halford, Jacob, N.C. A&T	1	6	5.83	1	5	54	68	20	46
Max Simpson, Towson	2	9	5.91	14	1	67	74	28	51
Nicholas Rizzo, Stony Brook	5	4	6.54	12	0	65	75	18	51
Nemjo, Tristan, Hofstra	2	6	6.56	15	0	73	86	35	38
Kent, Tommy, Monmouth	3	7	6.64	11	0	60	75	31	49
Eddie Smink, Stony Brook	1	5	6.83	14	0	59	87	27	50
Straniero, Nolan, Elon	4	4	7.10	14	0	71	85	32	69
Dutch DeProspero, Towson	2	5	7.34	14	0	58	69	18	38
Ortiz, Angel, N.C. A&T	6	2	8.40	14	0	70	101	17	47
Bauer, Jackson, Hofstra	4	6	8.41	14	1	71	89	36	56

CONFERENCE USA

	Conference		Overall	
	W	L	W	L
Dallas Baptist	21	6	41	18
WKU	18	9	46	14
Kennesaw State	17	9	31	27
Jax State	15	12	37	25
LA Tech	14	12	32	25
FIU	13	13	31	27
NM State	11	15	23	33
Liberty	10	17	30	27
MTSU	8	19	23	32
Sam Houston	6	21	12	43

ALL-CONFERENCE TEAM: C: Grant Jay, DBU. **INF:** Keaton Grady, DBU; Chayton Krauss, DBU; Brylan West, FIU; Brandon Forrester, NM State. **OF:** Nathan Humphreys, DBU; Eston Snider, MTSU; Ryan Wideman, WKU. **DH:** Steve Solorzano, NM State. **UT:** Donovan Cash, Kennesaw State. **SP:** Ryan Borberg, DBU; Easton Marks, FIU; Ben Blair, Liberty; Drew Whalen, WKU. **RP:** Bo Rhudy, Kennesaw State; Lucas Hartman, WKU.

Player & Newcomer of the Year: Ryan Wideman, WKU. **Pitcher of the Year:** Drew Whalen, WKU. **Defensive Player of the Year:** Nathan Humphreys, DBU. **Freshman of the Year:** Brooks Roberson, LA Tech. **Coach of the Year:** Marc Rardin, WKU. **Assistant Coach of the Year:** Dillon Napoleon, WKU.

INDIVIDUAL BATTING LEADERS

	AVG	OBP	SLG	AB	2B	3B	HR	RBI	SB
Ryan Wideman, WKU	.398	.466	.652	244	20	6	10	68	45
Grady, Keaton, Dallas Baptist	.377	.459	.551	167	13	2	4	25	16

Player	AVG	OBP	SLG	AB	2B	3B	HR	RBI	SB
Carlos Vasquez, WKU	.366	.435	.532	235	22	1	5	40	8
Kyle Hayes, WKU	.363	.472	.673	168	16	3	10	56	5
Humphreys, Nathan, DBU	.352	.457	.690	216	18	2	17	68	21
Poole, Tom, Dallas Baptist	.347	.503	.605	124	11	0	7	21	8
Eston Snider, MTSU	.341	.445	.509	214	16	1	6	34	22
Javier Crespo, FIU	.340	.454	.476	147	6	1	4	35	3
Mitch Namie, NM State	.340	.436	.530	215	16	2	7	46	5
Brylan West, FIU	.338	.432	.547	225	9	1	12	29	0
Ethan Lizama, WKU	.336	.407	.646	229	18	4	15	60	6
Steve Solorzano, NM State	.335	.470	.551	185	14	1	8	41	6
Brett Rogers, MTSU	.331	.383	.453	172	10	1	3	26	10
Donovan Cash, Kenne. State	.326	.419	.661	230	23	0	18	69	4
Hunter Autrey, Sam Houston	.325	.425	.524	206	12	1	9	43	14
Dattalo, Michael, DBU	.324	.441	.444	216	15	1	3	35	4
Krauss, Chayton, DBU	.324	.392	.616	219	19	0	15	70	6
Brandon Forrester, NM State	.323	.416	.419	217	9	3	2	23	16
Austin Haller, WKU	.321	.457	.457	140	10	0	3	27	7
Grayson Ashe, Jax State	.321	.440	.571	168	9	0	11	42	4
Jay, Grant, Dallas Baptist	.321	.448	.679	212	17	1	19	59	14
Nate Anderson, Kenne. State	.317	.429	.529	227	11	2	11	45	26
Mexico, Sebastian, LA Tech	.315	.395	.602	181	12	2	12	57	3
Brett Vondohlen, MTSU	.314	.363	.591	220	10	0	17	49	2
Wesley Alig, Kennesaw State	.312	.401	.457	199	10	2	5	37	3
Matt Wolfe, MTSU	.310	.433	.424	158	10	1	2	21	5
Ryan Franden, Sam Houston	.309	.365	.395	152	8	1	1	23	8
Cooper Williams, Kenne. State	.306	.388	.512	170	10	2	7	33	4
Camden Ross, WKU	.305	.449	.404	141	6	1	2	30	3
Drew Collins, Jax State	.305	.410	.502	223	13	5	7	38	20
Andrew Ildefonso, FIU	.304	.393	.497	161	11	1	6	37	3
Tyler Minnick, MTSU	.302	.391	.493	205	12	0	9	41	1
Troyer, Camden, Liberty	.300	.406	.524	210	11	3	10	44	7
Colton Hegwood, Jax State	.299	.368	.407	194	12	3	1	26	13
Carson Hornung, Jax State	.296	.441	.464	196	12	0	7	29	3

INDIVIDUAL PITCHING LEADERS

Player	W	L	ERA	G	SV	IP	H	BB	SO
Jack Bennett, WKU	7	1	3.13	14	0	63	62	20	49
Jackson Phipps, Jax State	4	2	3.33	15	0	76	47	43	83
Borberg, Ryan, Dallas Baptist	9	4	3.38	15	0	80	75	20	79
Easton Marks, FIU	3	3	3.49	14	0	67	59	35	72
Drew Whalen, WKU	9	3	3.53	16	0	82	71	31	90
Blair, Ben, Liberty	6	4	3.67	15	0	83	76	30	94
Smith Pinson, Kennesaw State	8	2	3.80	10	1	64	63	16	71
Ellwanger, James, Dallas Baptist	4	2	3.98	14	0	63	58	39	95
Steven Cash, Jax State	5	2	4.59	16	0	86	73	33	63
Buckmann, Micah, Dallas Baptist	6	2	4.62	13	0	62	54	25	80
Harry Cain, Kennesaw State	4	3	4.67	10	0	62	58	19	46
Roberson, Brooks, LA Tech	5	4	4.90	11	0	72	62	32	64
Cooley, Luke, LA Tech	7	2	4.95	13	0	64	68	29	65
Mathiesen, Dylan, Liberty	2	4	5.07	17	0	66	62	31	84
Chandler Alderman, MTSU	4	7	5.50	14	0	69	83	36	48
Nichols, Luke, LA Tech	5	6	6.29	6	2	59	71	22	53
Ryan Peterson, Sam Houston	2	9	6.29	14	0	73	86	32	75
Logan Runde, FIU	4	5	6.63	12	1	58	81	19	50
Connor Wylde, NM State	4	2	7.31	7	0	64	77	27	54

HORIZON LEAGUE

	Conference		Overall	
	W	L	W	L
Wright State	25	5	40	21
Northern Kentucky	18	12	31	25
Milwaukee	16	13	24	35
Youngstown State	11	19	15	42
Oakland	10	20	19	41
Purdue Fort Wayne	9	20	11	42

ALL-CONFERENCE TEAM: C: Boston Smith, Wright State. **1B:** Gabe Miranda, Northern Kentucky. **2B:** Braylen Blomquist, Wright State. **3B:** Tyler Bickers, Milwaukee. **SS:** Gabe Roessler, Milwaukee. **SS:** Camden Karczewski, Purdue Fort Wayne. **OF:** Logen Devenport, Northern Kentucky; JP Peltier, Wright State; Kyle Fossum, Youngstown State. Flex: Hunter Warren, Wright State. **SP:** Gavin Theis, Milwaukee. Kaden Echeman, Northern Kentucky; Cam Allen, Wright State. **RP:** Logan Snow, Milwaukee.

Player of the Year: Kyle Fossum, Youngstown State. **Pitcher of the Year:** Gavin Theis, Milwaukee. **Reliever of the Year:** Logan Snow, Milwaukee. **Freshman of the Year:** Hunter Warren, Wright State. **Coach of the Year:** Alex Sogard, Wright State. **Sportsmanship Award:** Brooks Sailors, Purdue Fort Wayne

INDIVIDUAL BATTING LEADERS

Player	AVG	OBP	SLG	AB	2B	3B	HR	RBI	SB
Devenport, Logen, No. Ky.	.423	.533	.786	168	19	0	14	54	19
Fossum, Kyle, Young. State	.382	.496	.777	220	18	0	23	62	9
Bickers, Tyler, Milwaukee	.369	.482	.498	225	11	3	4	42	7
John Lauinger, Oakland	.357	.480	.448	210	12	2	2	39	28
Gus Gregory, Wright State	.344	.424	.564	163	15	3	5	48	9
Miranda, Gabe, No. Kentucky	.338	.471	.610	213	14	4	12	69	11
Braylen Blomquist, Wright State	.333	.420	.494	162	10	5	2	35	9
Boston Smith, Wright State	.332	.500	.774	208	10	2	26	71	16
Patrick Fultz, Wright State	.332	.446	.468	235	11	0	7	45	12
Justin Osterhouse, Purdue FW	.328	.453	.636	195	10	1	16	46	13
Rover, Tommy, Young. State	.328	.475	.598	174	7	2	12	40	4
Hunter Warren, Wright State	.328	.423	.408	250	15	1	1	45	8
Matthew McGann, Oakland	.326	.405	.527	184	13	0	8	48	3
Shaneyfelt, Tyler, No. Kentucky	.324	.453	.423	222	4	3	4	30	34
Camden Karczewski, Purdue FW	.324	.391	.422	185	7	1	3	28	6
Taylor Tomlin, Oakland	.322	.419	.384	177	9	1	0	23	12
Wrona, Jay, Youngstown State	.313	.444	.393	112	7	1	0	13	2
Cam Gilkerson, Wright State	.305	.397	.567	210	12	2	13	53	12
JP Peltier, Wright State	.303	.391	.628	234	14	1	20	69	24
Kuriger, Brayden, Young. St.	.301	.385	.530	183	10	4	8	43	12
Beckley, Nathan, Young. St.	.301	.399	.468	173	15	1	4	42	6
Hausser, Justin, Milwaukee	.301	.365	.485	229	20	2	6	40	6
Kevin Hall, Purdue Fort Wayne	.298	.361	.448	181	8	2	5	28	9
Smith, Cole, Youngstown State	.291	.424	.487	199	21	0	6	41	7
Roessler, Gabe, Milwaukee	.288	.410	.476	233	15	1	9	38	24

INDIVIDUAL PITCHING LEADERS
(Minimum 40 innings pitched)

Player	W	L	ERA	G	SV	IP	H	BB	SO
Echeman, Kaden, N. Kentucky	3	3	4.34	8	0	56	45	23	87
Theis, Gavin, Milwaukee	9	1	4.38	16	0	88	89	37	74
Cam Allen, Wright State	7	3	4.95	13	0	67	60	41	71
Boster, Aaron, No. Kentucky	4	2	5.54	15	0	65	61	47	60
Zane Danielson, Purdue FW	0	6	5.82	10	0	56	56	30	40
Grant Garman, Oakland	3	5	5.83	15	0	79	84	46	68
Hunter Pidek, Oakland	2	5	6.25	15	0	81	81	35	61
Gehring, Jacob, Young. State	1	5	6.60	12	0	61	76	28	56
Dillon Fischer, Purdue FW	1	8	7.41	15	0	85	101	43	67
Linn, Conner, No. Kentucky	2	4	7.48	15	0	61	76	28	56
Mikos, Brandon, Youngst. State	5	3	7.60	11	0	58	75	29	42
Ehmke, Aric, Milwaukee	1	6	8.70	11	0	60	68	30	33

IVY LEAGUE

	Conference		Overall	
	W	L	W	L
Yale	16	5	31	14
Columbia	16	5	30	19
Penn	13	8	21	20
Harvard	9	12	14	28
Dartmouth	8	13	11	25
Princeton	8	13	12	31
Cornell	7	14	12	12
Brown	7	15	11	29

ALL-CONFERENCE TEAM: SP: Jacob Faulkner, Princeton; Jack Ohman, Yale; Colton Shaw, Yale. **RP:** Marty Coyne, Penn. **C:** Mark Quatrani, Cornell. **1B:** Gio Colasante, Harvard. **2B:** Jack Kail, Columbia. **3B:** Jack Dauer,

Yale. **SS**: Sam Miller, Columbia. **OF**: Mika Petersen, Brown; Cole Fellows, Columbia; Gavin Collins, Penn. **UTL**: Jarrett Pokrovsky, Penn. **UTL/P**: Gio Colasante, Harvard. **DH**: Alec Atkinson, Yale.

Player Of The Year: Sam Miller, Columbia. **Pitcher Of The Year:** Jack Ohman, Yale. **Rookie Of The Year:** Jack Dauer, Yale. **Coaching Staff Of The Year:** Yale.

INDIVIDUAL BATTING LEADERS

	AVG	OBP	SLG	AB	2B	3B	HR	RBI	SB
Mika Petersen, Brown	.355	.401	.467	152	21	54	2	20	9
Cooper, George, Harv	.350	.405	.509	163	30	57	5	29	2
Miller, Sam, Col	.338	.407	.606	216	50	73	16	57	1
Rodriguez, Taer, Dart	.336	.453	.391	128	24	43	0	17	1
Collins, Gavin, Penn	.335	.442	.484	155	36	52	4	29	3
Pokrovsky, Jarrett, Penn	.335	.394	.533	167	25	56	3	33	4
Kaiden Dossa, Yale	.329	.424	.514	173	49	57	6	30	12
Fellows, Cole, Col	.326	.411	.497	181	40	59	5	39	3
Ryan Porter, Cor	.324	.373	.647	102	20	33	7	23	3
Jake Williams, Yale	.321	.424	.479	165	35	53	3	38	10
Max Imhoff, Yale	.320	.447	.432	125	30	40	2	27	4
Alec Atkinson, Yale	.319	.405	.475	141	33	45	4	29	14
Mark Quatrani, Cor	.318	.436	.530	132	29	42	6	24	1
Colasante, Gio, Harv	.314	.383	.564	156	31	49	10	33	10
Kail, Jack, Col	.312	.372	.508	199	44	62	7	45	7
Jack Dauer, Yale	.306	.371	.468	173	27	53	5	39	10
Snyder, Hunter, Col	.306	.412	.430	121	26	37	2	19	2
Tommy Martin, Yale	.305	.503	.527	131	39	40	5	40	3
Garrett Larsen, Col	.305	.409	.402	174	47	53	0	31	16
Christian Butera, Brown	.303	.391	.504	119	21	36	4	17	5
Vogler, Tate, Col	.297	.382	.483	118	27	35	3	20	2
Spaventa, Nick, Penn	.293	.386	.446	157	30	46	5	29	0
Shulman, Tyler, Harv	.291	.377	.410	117	17	34	3	20	4
Giberti, Matt, Harv	.288	.351	.366	153	30	44	1	19	21
Lazits, Anton, Col	.287	.400	.612	188	47	54	14	46	9

INDIVIDUAL PITCHING LEADERS

	W	L	ERA	G	SV	IP	H	BB	SO
Jack Ohman, Yale	8	1	1.34	11	0	74	45	20	87
Colton Shaw, Yale	6	2	3.13	12	0	78	64	24	80
Tate Evans, Yale	3	3	3.19	0	4	48	45	18	53
Coyne, Marty, Penn	4	2	3.89	2	0	44	45	17	49
Faulkner, Jacob, Pri	2	4	4.14	5	2	67	76	17	55
Daniel Cohen, Yale	4	3	4.23	12	0	62	60	28	50
Carson Mayfield, Cor	2	2	4.26	11	0	61	41	26	56
Fang, Callan, Harv	3	3	4.36	11	0	64	68	20	62
Pauley, Truman, Harv	4	6	4.61	12	1	70	42	48	91
Edwards, Jagger, Col	4	3	5.13	13	0	60	68	21	47
D'Alessio, Andrew, Pri	4	4	5.25	9	0	48	59	16	33
Kim, Justin, Pri	2	6	5.26	2	3	50	53	22	42
Millikan, Noah, Penn	0	3	5.31	10	0	61	64	21	53
Tobin, Will, Penn	2	3	5.73	11	0	44	50	24	45
Kinneen, Liam, Pri	3	5	5.80	11	0	50	52	32	45
Santana, Thomas, Col	5	4	5.84	13	0	62	64	26	60
Santhosh Gottam, Brown	3	4	6.08	11	0	64	71	19	58
Sheets, Joe, Col	3	5	6.26	13	0	65	80	44	55
Loeger, Bryce, Dart	1	8	6.61	9	1	48	58	23	29
Isler, Nate, Dart	1	4	6.67	10	0	55	70	20	36
Huxley Holcombe, Cor	3	2	6.90	9	0	59	65	28	40
Katz, Josh, Penn	4	4	7.42	9	1	47	69	14	53
Albert, Eddie, Dart	1	3	7.69	10	0	50	64	29	51
Luke Trout, Brown	0	6	7.71	10	0	47	48	32	39
Christian Keel, Brown	1	7	8.33	10	1	54	72	27	51

METRO ATLANTIC ATHLETIC CONFERENCE

	Conference		Overall	
	W	L	W	L
Rider	23	6	40	18
Fairfield	23	10	43	22
Sacred Heart	17	13	28	26
Siena	17	13	22	33
Quinnipiac	17	13	30	26
Mount St. Mary's	15	13	24	28
Marist	14	14	26	29
Niagara	14	16	19	28
Manhattan	12	15	20	28
Iona	13	17	19	33
Merrimack	11	19	16	34
Canisius	10	19	14	31
Saint Peter's	5	24	11	37

ALL-CONFERENCE TEAM: C: Ashby Vining, Saint Peter's. **1B:** James Kemp, Iona. **2B:** Joe Tiroly, Rider. **3B:** Dean Ferrara, Fairfield. **SS:** Luke Nomura, Fairfield. **OF:** Matt Bucciero, Fairfield; CJ Willis, Quinnipiac; Kyle Neri, Rider. **P:** Ben Alekson, Fairfield; Brian Young, Rider; Alistair Morin, Siena. **DH:** Christian Smith, Quinnipiac. **UTIL:** Trent Rumley, Canisius.

Player of the Year: Joe Tiroly, Rider. **Pitcher of the Year:** Brian Young, Rider. **Relief Pitcher of the Year:** Gavin Hawkes, Rider. **Rookie of the Year:** Sean Stephenson, Iona. **Coach of the Year:** Lee Lipinski, Rider.

INDIVIDUAL BATTING LEADERS

	AVG	OBP	SLG	AB	2B	3B	HR	RBI	SB
Joe Tiroly, Rider	.377	.481	.749	199	16	2	18	70	6
Ferrara, Dean, Fairfield	.374	.435	.517	265	14	0	8	57	21
Paradine, Aidan, Siena	.370	.474	.536	192	11	0	7	41	0
Kemp, James, Iona	.365	.478	.625	200	12	2	12	57	2
Mendes, Alex, Mount St. Mary's	.364	.504	.421	107	6	0	0	22	27
Ungar, Alex, Sacred Heart	.359	.443	.708	192	24	2	13	52	31
Tommy Kendrick, Saint Peter's	.356	.457	.444	180	6	2	2	40	11
Erich Hartmann, Rider	.351	.418	.460	202	9	2	3	29	4
Jack Andrews, Merrimack	.347	.423	.510	98	7	0	3	13	5
Rumley, Trent, Canisius	.347	.430	.612	170	13	1	10	43	9
Bucciero, Matt, Fairfield	.345	.462	.633	229	13	4	15	67	21
Stephenson, Sean, Iona	.341	.410	.517	205	15	0	7	39	5
Ashby Vining, Saint Peter's	.335	.387	.534	191	8	0	10	51	4
CJ Willis, Quinnipiac	.333	.422	.607	219	13	4	13	65	15
Nomura, Luke, Fairfield	.332	.443	.578	244	16	1	14	52	16
Kyle Garbows, Quinnipiac	.331	.392	.404	245	12	0	2	37	4
Alex Irizarr, Quinnipiac	.330	.390	.642	215	22	0	15	50	6
Christian Sm, Quinnipiac	.329	.435	.612	219	13	2	15	67	3
Lordier, Ryan, Manhattan	.329	.440	.399	158	8	0	1	20	16
Claiborn, Jason, Marist	.328	.461	.423	201	9	2	2	44	21
Donohue, Gavin, Sacred Heart	.327	.397	.520	223	12	5	7	42	11
Book, Nolan, Mount St. Mary's	.326	.417	.429	184	10	0	3	37	15
Kyle Neri, Rider	.324	.414	.493	213	14	2	6	43	9
Zwirecki, Thomas, Canisius	.322	.451	.595	121	12	0	7	32	4
Sebastian Mu, Quinnipiac	.321	.451	.606	218	11	3	15	54	4
Taclas, Aidan, Manhattan	.321	.386	.554	184	17	1	8	35	7
Sparks, Jake, Siena	.319	.395	.601	213	16	1	14	51	1
Nick Shuet, Rider	.317	.424	.497	189	8	1	8	57	4
Harry Painte, Merrimack	.315	.371	.638	127	6	1	11	28	1
Charley Magoulic, Rider	.315	.396	.503	165	9	2	6	31	3

INDIVIDUAL PITCHING LEADERS

	W	L	ERA	G	SV	IP	H	BB	SO
Brian Young, Rider	9	0	2.83	14	0	89	83	29	73
Alekson, Ben, Fairfield	9	2	3.34	16	0	94	81	25	84
Taylor, Will, Marist	5	4	3.36	15	0	78	81	15	60
Baker, Bowen, Fairfield	8	2	3.47	15	0	80	76	21	71
Sarre, Serigne, Mount St. Mary's	5	6	3.50	10	0	72	77	29	86
Lesler, Kyle, Fairfield	5	1	3.86	11	0	58	56	28	52
Morin, Alistair, Siena	5	4	3.90	15	0	83	75	48	80
Payamps, Andrelys, Iona	4	5	4.52	13	0	66	57	34	72
Duffield, Joseph, Manhattan	4	5	4.58	13	0	53	44	40	44

Andrew Heffe, Merrimack	3	8	4.71	13	0	80	86	14	42
DelVecchio Matthew, Niagara	6	7	4.83	15	0	82	86	35	40
Trombley, Joey, Sacred Heart	5	7	4.89	15	0	85	97	34	52
Gialloreto, Eric, Iona	4	3	5.02	14	0	84	104	19	56
DeRossi, Eli, Mount St. Mary's	3	1	5.48	8	0	66	58	36	63
Foster, Elijah, Sacred Heart	5	3	5.61	14	0	67	57	51	68
Andrew Rubay, Quinnipiac	6	1	6.00	0		57	78	21	22
James Nichol, Merrimack	2	7	6.09	8	0	55	63	26	22
Matt Alduino, Quinnipiac	3	3	6.14	11	4	59	59	38	42
Morin, Felix, Canisius	2	4	6.16	6	0	57	78	29	39
Consigli, Peyton, Canisius	1	4	6.28	5	0	62	69	42	71
Parker, Ryan, Sacred Heart	3	4	6.52	14	0	58	66	32	33
Phelps, Holden, Siena	2	4	6.61	13	0	65	73	39	60
Rodriguez, Noah, Siena	3	8	6.67	16	0	81	103	22	59
Hartley, Tyler, Marist	1	6	6.86	13	0	60	65	39	54
Nick Balcom, Quinnipiac	3	4	7.05	11	0	60	78	39	51

MID-AMERICAN CONFERENCE

Team	Conference		Overall	
	W	L	W	L
Kent State	23	7	38	18
Miami	23	7	35	23
Ball State	21	9	36	22
Bowling Green	19	11	33	22
Toledo	17	13	32	29
Eastern Michigan	12	18	21	30
Western Michigan	12	18	19	32
Central Michigan	11	19	20	35
Northern Illinois	9	21	21	33
Akron	9	21	20	34
Ohio	9	21	14	37

ALL-CONFERENCE TEAM: C: Garrett Wright, Bowling Green. **1B:** Evan Appelwick, Miami. **2B:** Nick Husovsky, Ball State. **3B:** Hayden Jatczak, Kent State. **SS:** Dylan Grego, Ball State. **OF:** Jake Casey, Kent State; Ben Slanker, Ohio; Blake Bevis, Ball State. **DH:** Sawyer Solitaria, Kent State. **SP:** Cooper Katskee, Miami; Jacob Bean, Kent State; Jacob Tabor, Toledo; Keegan Johnson, Ball State. **RP:** Connar Penrod, Bowling Green. **At-Large:** Dillon Baker, Miami.

Coach of the Year: Brian Smiley, Miami. **Player of the Year:** Hayden Jatczak, Kent State. **Pitcher of the Year:** Cooper Katskee, Miami. **Freshman of the Year:** Sawyer Solitaria, Kent State. **Freshman Pitcher of the Year:** Brady Sasse, Toledo. **Defensive Player of the Year:** Garrett Wright, Bowling Green.

INDIVIDUAL BATTING LEADERS

	AVG	OBP	SLG	AB	2B	3B	HR	RBI	SB
Wright, Garrett, Bowling Green	.401	.510	.658	202	20	4	8	48	6
Ineich, Matt, Ohio	.387	.467	.514	142	9	0	3	25	9
Jatczak, Hayden, Kent State	.376	.491	.770	213	28	4	16	81	10
Dylan Grego, Ball State	.376	.429	.624	242	14	2	14	55	15
Covas, Alejandro, Kent State	.357	.429	.513	115	8	2	2	29	13
Casey, Jake, Kent State	.356	.500	.736	208	20	4	17	55	20
Mally, Tanner, Western Michigan	.356	.444	.439	205	11	3	0	20	16
Matthews, Luke, Kent State	.354	.438	.476	164	9	4	1	30	18
Andrew Horvath, Akron	.350	.424	.475	200	14	1	3	29	2
Dominic Krupinski, Miami	.348	.496	.552	201	17	3	6	43	7
Aydin Wright, Central Michigan	.345	.429	.459	148	12	1	1	30	3
Anthony Zarlingo, Miami	.344	.460	.493	221	13	4	4	38	10
Antillon, Gunner, Bowling Green	.344	.442	.479	192	13	2	3	27	8
Williams, Brody, Kent State	.341	.457	.535	185	13	1	7	53	9
Dillon Baker, Miami	.339	.442	.639	227	25	2	13	49	6
Zirwas, Devan, Eastern Michigan	.337	.436	.561	205	20	1	8	53	2
Nick Husovsky, Ball State	.336	.397	.556	232	17	2	10	59	2
Logan Gregorio, Ball State	.332	.400	.639	229	19	1	18	69	0
Stecko, Ty, Eastern Michigan	.325	.424	.591	154	8	0	11	37	3
Seidel, Sam, Bowling Green	.324	.414	.486	142	6	1	5	35	11
Cole Kwiatkowski, Central Michigan	.323	.364	.398	93	4	0	1	7	6
Gavin Baldwin, Northern Illinois	.322	.415	.644	202	18	1	15	57	0
Evan Appelwick, Miami	.322	.458	.673	214	10	1	21	74	3
Aaron Piasecki, Central Michigan	.319	.399	.464	207	15	3	3	33	13
Birchmier, Brady, Bowling Green	.318	.409	.558	154	10	0	9	50	0

Reed, Blake, Ohio	.317	.408	.467	120	9	0	3	26	0
Garrett Arnold, Ball State	.316	.407	.386	158	11	0	0	23	1
Evan Bottone, Akron	.315	.390	.404	213	11	1	2	27	14
Max Bowman, Akron	.315	.437	.500	200	17	1	6	35	7
Mikey Murphy, Central Michigan	.311	.414	.565	161	11	3	8	36	11
Houston King, Ball State	.311	.383	.387	106	5	0	1	15	0
Travis, Harrison, Eastern Michigan	.309	.373	.570	165	10	0	11	38	0
Solitaria, Sawyer, Kent State	.308	.402	.478	201	8	1	8	62	10
Horky, Zack, Bowling Green	.308	.383	.421	133	10	1	1	33	3
Hugo, Logan, Eastern Michigan	.308	.416	.563	208	13	2	12	62	17

INDIVIDUAL PITCHING LEADERS

	W	L	ERA	G	SV	IP	H	BB	SO
Carson Byers, Miami	2	2	2.61	2	6	76	59	24	72
Cooper Katskee, Miami	11	2	3.08	10	1	85	60	30	70
Bean, Jacob, Kent State	6	2	4.20	15	0	75	72	22	72
Jared Schaeffer, Akron	2	7	4.31	14	0	86	84	20	79
Keegan Johnson, Ball State	7	3	4.46	14	0	71	59	39	75
McKinstry, Ty, W. Michigan	3	7	5.02	14	0	72	67	36	51
Jacob Hartlaub, Ball State	6	2	5.09	15	0	81	88	29	69
Adam Brouwer, No. Illinois	4	3	5.14	13	0	68	76	26	67
Jack Kelley, Akron	4	2	5.17	11	0	56	49	28	52
Boncal, Hudson, Ohio	3	6	5.35	11	0	79	83	37	68
Beckner, Drew, E. Michigan	3	2	5.45	15	0	79	84	42	83
Jared Hanson, C. Michigan	2	4	5.46	10	0	58	72	12	32
Bergman Jackson, Toledo	3	3	5.65	16	0	65	62	25	31
Jones, Gavin, Kent State	6	2	6.25	15	0	72	67	44	56
Clayton Burke, Miami	6	3	6.45	12	0	67	68	34	52
Gaber, Reese, W. Michigan	3	3	6.71	11	0	54	48	45	38
Turner, Jacob, Bowl. Green	4	5	6.75	13	0	59	80	31	51
Kapa, Tyler, E. Michigan	5	7	6.82	14	0	66	87	37	90
Wizceb, Joey, W. Michigan	3	8	6.95	14	0	69	89	19	27
Hayden Bailey, C. Michigan	3	3	7.60	10	0	56	73	28	39
Alejandro Espinoza, C. Michigan	2	8	7.65	12	0	62	98	28	25
Gaskey, Blake, Ohio	4	5	7.80	14	0	73	95	30	48
Ty Brachbill, No. Illinois	1	8	8.10	13	0	70	93	31	75
Max Vaisvila, No. Illinois	3	5	9.00	11	0	58	102	18	58

MISSOURI VALLEY CONFERENCE

Team	Conference		Overall	
	W	L	W	L
Murray State	17	8	44	17
Missouri State	17	8	30	25
Southern Illinois	16	11	37	20
UIC	16	11	22	33
Illinois State	15	12	28	28
Belmont	13	14	26	34
Indiana State	12	15	24	31
Bradley	12	15	16	35
Evansville	10	17	17	37
Valparaiso	5	22	10	40

ALL-CONFERENCE TEAM: C: Will Vierling, Murray State. **1B:** Carlos Pena, Indiana State. **2B:** Nick Rodriguez, Missouri State. **3B:** Pete Daniel, Belmont. **SS:** Luke Nowak, UIC. **OF:** Daniel Pacella, Illinois State; Carter Beck, Indiana State; Jake McCutcheon, Missouri State; Jonathan Hogart, Murray State. **UT:** Max Knight, Missouri State. **SP:** Joe Ruzicka, Belmont; Nic Schutte, Murray State; Isaac Silva, Murray State. **RP:** Gavin Morris, Indiana State; Sam Frizzi, Southern Illinois.

Player of the Year: Nick Rodriguez, Missouri State. **Pitcher of the Year:** Joe Ruzicka, Belmont. **Defensive Player of the Year:** Tyler Epstein, Missouri State. **Co-Newcomer of the Year:** Luke Nowak, UIC; Max Knight, Missouri State. **Co-Freshmen of the Year:** Jeremy Martinez, Indiana State; Conner Cunningham, Murray State. **Coach of the Year:** Dan Skirka, Murray State.

INDIVIDUAL BATTING LEADERS

	AVG	OBP	SLG	AB	2B	3B	HR	RBI	SB
Nowak, Luke, UIC	.387	.455	.559	222	17	3	5	37	28
Rodriguez, Nick, Missouri State	.368	.444	.702	228	22	0	18	56	2
Daniel, Pete, Belmont	.360	.423	.521	211	15	2	5	32	21
McCutcheon, Jake, Missouri State	.358	.444	.647	218	14	2	15	54	10
Mercer, Dustin, Murray State	.355	.437	.483	259	23	5	0	39	5

COLLEGE

Player	AVG	OBP	SLG	AB	R	H	2B	3B	HR	RBI	SB
Pacella, Daniel, Illinois State	.355	.429	.714	231	19	2	20			59	1
Decker, Dom, Murray State	.351	.496	.464	211	18	3	0			48	9
Tim Simay, Southern Illinois	.351	.452	.539	191	16	1	6			31	10
Matt Schark, Southern Illinois	.340	.419	.732	235	18	1	24			80	9
Hogart, Jonathan, Murray State	.338	.446	.700	260	26	1	22			65	7
Beck, Carter, Indiana State	.335	.417	.564	227	15	2	11			56	11
Mistone, Luke, Murray State	.335	.399	.476	248	17	3	4			53	2
Smith, Lucas, UIC	.335	.456	.445	200	12	2	2			29	10
Rumsey Ty, Evansville	.333	.426	.455	213	10	2	4			37	31
Mcginnis Cal, Evansville	.333	.391	.448	192	10	0	4			36	2
Bobby Atkinson, Bradley	.332	.457	.582	184	19	3	7			43	2
Jaxon Holder, Southern Illinois	.329	.436	.521	167	10	2	6			40	13
Pena, Carlos, Indiana State	.327	.444	.624	205	12	2	15			50	8
Allen, Ty, Belmont	.323	.402	.534	232	13	0	12			48	8
Epstein,Tyler, Missouri State	.321	.432	.472	159	9	0	5			29	15
Gollert, Taeg, Missouri State	.319	.409	.541	185	22	2	5			44	2
Harris, James, UIC	.315	.404	.457	162	9	1	4			27	0
Davis, Charlie, Belmont	.315	.374	.421	254	14	2	3			30	25
Bakes, Brayden, Illinois State	.313	.407	.542	166	10	2	8			38	5
Vierling, Will, Murray State	.312	.415	.530	234	17	2	10			52	1

INDIVIDUAL PITCHING LEADERS

Player	W	L	ERA	G	SV	IP	H	BB	SO
Ruzicka, Joe, Belmont	6	4	3.56	15	0	81	56	44	70
Morris, Gavin, Indiana State	6	3	3.68	1	4	59	49	21	50
Chadwick, Tyrelle, Illinois State	6	2	4.23	11	0	72	70	23	43
McEwen, Max, Indiana State	6	3	4.63	10	0	58	50	31	64
Silva, Isaac, Murray State	9	3	4.84	16	0	87	84	36	81
Alec Nigut, Southern Illinois	7	4	5.10	13	0	60	66	16	60
Schutte, Nic, Murray State	8	5	5.16	16	0	96	83	55	97
Schueler, Dillon, UIC	6	7	5.53	15	0	83	89	33	62
Deverman Kenton, Evansville	3	7	5.61	12	0	67	88	8	51
Schaaf,Jason, Missouri State	5	2	5.74	11	0	69	74	29	57
Yusypchuk,Michael, Missouri St.	4	3	5.83	14	0	71	80	22	63
Perry, Tanner, Illinois State	4	6	6.18	15	0	71	83	28	76
Brooks, Ty, Indiana State	3	5	6.51	11	0	55	60	30	45
Lockwood, Connor, Valparaiso	3	8	6.59	14	0	96	116	20	80
Monke, Carter, Illinois State	4	6	6.60	12	0	59	79	15	38
Charlton,Tyler, Missouri State	5	2	6.75	14	0	57	67	21	82
Reed Kevin, Evansville	3	6	7.25	14	0	72	92	25	62
Gavin Thompson, Bradley	3	6	8.68	8	0	56	80	29	43
Deliyannis, Harry, Valparaiso	3	9	10.16	11	0	59	85	26	42

MOUNTAIN WEST CONFERENCE

	Conference		Overall	
	W	L	W	L
Nevada	19	11	34	23
Fresno State	18	12	31	29
New Mexico	17	13	30	23
UNLV	16	14	31	23
San Diego State	14	16	20	39
San José State	13	17	29	30
Air Force	12	18	20	34
Washington State	11	19	18	36

ALL-CONFERENCE TEAM: C: Jake Harvey, Jr., Nevada; Justin Stransky, Sr., Fresno State. **INF:** Ethan Ott, Sr., New Mexico; Jayce Dobie, Jr., Nevada; Josh McAlister, Sr., New Mexico; Murf Gray, Jr., Fresno State. **INF/OF:** Dean Toigo, Sr., UNLV. **OF:** Khalil Walker, Sr., New Mexico; Logan Johnstone, Jr., Washington State. **P:** Aidan Cremarosa, Jr., Fresno State; Alessandro Castro, So., Nevada; Carson Lane, So., UNLV; Jack Anker, Jr., Fresno State.

Co-Players Of The Year: Murf Gray, Jr., INF, Fresno State and Dean Toigo, Sr., INF/OF, UNLV. **Pitcher Of The Year:** Aidan Cremarosa, Jr., Fresno State. **Freshman Of The Year:** Sean Yamaguchi, INF, Nevada. **Coach Of The Year:** Jake McKinley, Nevada.

INDIVIDUAL BATTING LEADERS

Player	AVG	OBP	SLG	AB	2B	3B	HR	RBI	SB
Khalil Walker, New Mexico	.399	.457	.591	198	16	5	4	34	2
Jordy Oriach, New Mexico	.388	.470	.748	214	25	2	16	63	1
Dean Toigo, UNLV	.377	.445	.682	220	13	0	18	74	5
Josh McAlister, New Mexico	.368	.452	.731	171	9	1	17	43	14
Cole Koniarsky, UNLV	.363	.441	.549	204	15	1	7	47	3
Ethan Ott, New Mexico	.363	.456	.742	190	22	1	16	58	0
Max Hartman, Washington State	.363	.438	.518	168	9	1	5	29	7
Alex Fernandes, San Jose State	.361	.447	.509	216	11	6	3	28	14
Nevan Noonan, San Diego State	.356	.421	.558	233	18	1	9	52	5
Zach Peters, Air Force	.347	.427	.602	196	20	3	8	48	8
Billy Ham, Nevada	.345	.458	.562	194	21	0	7	46	0
Will Asby, New Mexico	.341	.415	.618	220	20	1	13	55	1
Akili Carris, New Mexico	.341	.382	.447	170	13	1	1	44	1
Jayce Dobie, Nevada	.339	.413	.531	192	16	0	7	36	3
Logan Johnstone, Washington State	.337	.439	.571	196	17	1	9	40	3
Zach Chamizo, San Jose State	.335	.388	.507	215	10	6	5	40	0
Griffen Sotomayor, Fresno State	.330	.393	.519	206	16	1	7	41	8
Walker Zapp, Air Force	.330	.420	.579	197	18	5	7	43	8
Will Cresswell, Washington State	.329	.404	.523	155	13	1	5	43	2
Murf Gray, Fresno State	.324	.398	.639	241	22	0	18	73	1

INDIVIDUAL PITCHING LEADERS

Player	W	L	ERA	G	SV	IP	H	BB	SO
Marko Sipila, San Diego	4	3	3.91	12	0	71	71	25	74
Carson Lane, UNLV	6	4	4.23	15	0	79	71	38	85
Aidan Cremarosa, Fresno State	6	6	4.34	17	0	95	89	27	112
Sam Simon, UNLV	3	4	4.53	13	0	60	63	31	33
Nolan George, San Jose State	4	4	4.82	21	2	71	80	18	56
Casey Burfield, UNLV	4	3	4.86	14	0	70	83	23	48
Luke Meyers, Washington St.	5	4	5.27	15	2	67	78	21	50
Alessandro Castro, UNLV	5	3	5.33	15	0	73	90	18	43
Griffin Smith, Washington St.	5	6	5.73	16	0	82	97	18	41
Peyton Fosher, UNLV	5	4	5.75	15	0	77	88	21	77
Jack Anker, Fresno State	9	5	5.98	16	0	96	122	12	109
David Thomas, San Jose State	2	5	6.27	14	0	75	102	21	51
Nick Lewis, Washington St.	4	7	6.69	16	0	74	98	21	47
Daxton Purser, New Mexico	3	5	6.94	17	1	71	84	31	80
Win Scott, San Jose State	4	5	6.97	14	0	71	86	28	59

NORTHEAST CONFERENCE

	Conference		Overall	
	W	L	W	L
LIU	24	6	35	23
Central Connecticut	23	7	31	17
Wagner	23	7	31	22
Stonehill	18	12	20	32
Le Moyne	17	13	20	28
FDU	16	14	16	37
Mercyhurst	15	15	17	35
Coppin State	13	17	15	34
Delaware State	6	24	7	34
Maryland Eastern Shore	6	24	7	41
Norfolk State	4	26	4	38

ALL-CONFERENCE TEAM: C: Aidan Sengenberger, Stonehill. **1B:** Jack Thorbahn, Stonehill. **2B:** Aidan Redahan, CCSU. **3B:** Chris Brown, CCSU. **SS:** Ryan Rivera, LIU. **OF:** Justin Journette, Norfolk State; Bryce Phelps, Wagner, Grayson Sparr, Stonehill. DH: Aidan Cohall, Stonehill. **SP:** Vincent Borghese, CCSU; Jake Toporek, Wagner; Garrett Yawn, LIU. **RP:** Wyatt Cameron, CCSU.

Player of the Year: Aidan Redahan, CCSU. **Pitcher of the Year:** Garrett Yawn, LIU. **Rookie of the Year:** Grayson Sparr, Stonehill. **Coach of the Year:** Charlie Hickey, CCSU.

INDIVIDUAL BATTING LEADERS

Player	AVG	OBP	SLG	AB	2B	3B	HR	RBI	SB
Redahan Aidan, Central Conn.	.455	.511	.695	200	17	2	9	69	10
Bryce Phelps, Wagner	.399	.482	.489	188	14	0	1	33	4
Cohall, Aidan, Stonehill	.365	.430	.702	181	19	0	14	60	4
Ryan Rivera, LIU	.357	.419	.489	221	14	3	3	51	16
Lukas Torres, Wagner	.351	.455	.455	202	15	0	2	41	13
Ducatelli Antonio, Central Conn.	.348	.451	.546	141	12	2	4	48	9
Sparr, Grayson, Stonehill	.345	.461	.583	168	8	1	10	48	0
Anderson, Indy, Coppin State	.339	.440	.411	180	7	0	2	34	0
Benji Ries, Le Moyne	.336	.494	.545	134	7	0	7	31	1

	AVG	OBP	SLG	AB	2B	3B	HR	RBI	SB
Nicholas Mazzotta, Wagner	.335	.419	.430	221	16	1	1	31	20
Journette, Justin, Norfolk State	.331	.429	.645	166	7	0	15	45	5
Jonathan Gon, Md. Eastern Shore	.331	.362	.408	142	11	0	0	26	1
Brown Chris, Central Conn.	.331	.473	.494	172	17	1	3	49	8
Moore, Daniel, Coppin State	.330	.415	.441	179	12	1	2	36	1
Thorbahn, Jack, Stonehill	.326	.473	.647	187	12	0	16	42	1
Gomez, Johnathan, FDU	.324	.463	.548	188	12	3	8	36	12
Diego Tavarez, Wagner	.324	.448	.514	185	11	3	6	39	8
Connor Roche, Wagner	.324	.360	.459	207	17	1	3	32	0
Short Brady, Central Connecticut	.324	.473	.434	182	17	0	1	18	8
Eric Chorba, Mercyhurst	.321	.430	.472	193	9	1	6	20	11
Jones, Jalan, Norfolk State	.320	.396	.537	175	10	2	8	33	12
Sengenberger, Aidan, Stonehill	.320	.435	.473	150	6	1	5	34	4
Matteo Matthews, Wagner	.319	.440	.541	135	9	0	7	42	0
Grutzmacher, Gavin, Coppin St.	.317	.481	.482	164	9	3	4	27	7
Jayden Walker, Mercyhurst	.314	.408	.562	194	10	1	12	40	2
Ritter, Jamal, Norfolk State	.313	.429	.563	160	12	2	8	27	24
Ryan Davis, Md. Eastern Shore	.312	.400	.475	141	9	1	4	31	7
Hassan Turner, Delaware State	.306	.353	.331	157	4	0	0	20	10
Diego Aponte, Md. Eastern Shore	.304	.381	.421	171	14	0	2	29	1
Matt Sutera, Wagner	.302	.372	.475	162	15	2	3	36	8

INDIVIDUAL PITCHING LEADERS

	W	L	ERA	G	SV	IP	H	BB	SO
Jake Toporek, Wagner	8	1	3.49	14	0	88	72	24	69
Garrett Yawn, LIU	10	2	3.93	16	0	105	101	33	113
Jacob Bazala, Mercyhurst	7	4	4.09	10	1	81	81	25	85
Ritz, Justin, Coppin State	3	2	4.11	0	6	57	46	13	36
Justin DeCastro, LIU	8	5	4.32	15	0	94	100	24	60
Borghese Vincent, Central Conn.	10	3	4.42	15	0	90	96	25	93
Nicholas Finarelli, LIU	9	5	4.66	15	0	87	100	42	97
Rivera, Reagan, Coppin State	5	4	4.91	14	0	81	72	38	97
Colin Trizuto, Wagner	4	3	4.96	15	0	62	65	19	41
Gilleran, Jimmy, Stonehill	6	4	5.02	14	0	75	81	43	55
Munn Drew, Central Conn.	8	3	5.02	14	0	81	85	38	55
Heitaro Hayashi, Wagner	6	2	5.14	10	0	56	50	21	34
Savinon, Jordan, FDU	3	4	5.19	10	0	61	54	37	69
Max Parker, Le Moyne	4	7	5.36	13	0	82	96	24	71
Aiden Kelly, Mercyhurst	2	4	5.86	14	0	71	79	41	72
AJ Petraitis, Le Moyne	3	3	6.08	12	0	74	80	32	47
Hampton, Parker, Norfolk State	2	4	6.29	9	0	54	79	33	39
Daniel Thomas, Mercyhurst	3	8	6.31	12	0	61	80	33	53
Varnier, Nathaniel, Norfolk St.	2	5	6.37	12	0	65	69	53	77
Bell, Hunter, Stonehill	4	2	6.67	12	0	57	60	28	43
Straily, Kaden, Coppin State	3	9	7.66	13	0	69	66	52	49
E. Del Valle, Delaware State	0	10	8.89	12	0	53	72	47	51
Nathan Vidmar, Delaware State	2	8	10.14	12	0	58	100	35	55
Corcoran, Luke, Coppin State	3	5	10.32	4	0	52	74	29	29
Blakeney, Ethan, Norfolk State	0	5	10.47	9	0	49	73	36	48

OHIO VALLEY CONFERENCE

	Conference W	L	Overall W	L
Eastern Illinois	17	7	31	22
SIUE	18	8	26	28
Tennessee Tech	18	9	37	20
Southeast Missouri	16	11	30	25
Southern Indiana	15	12	27	29
Lindenwood	14	12	30	30
UT Martin	11	14	20	34
Little Rock	8	16	27	34
Western Illinois	9	18	18	32
Morehead State	14	39		

ALL-CONFERENCE TEAM: C: Mack Whitcomb, Tennessee Tech. **2B:** Mack Mitchell, SIUE. **SS:** Chase Bloomer, SIUE. **3B:** Mike O'Conor, Eastern Illinois. **OF:** Cole Warehime, Southeast Missouri; Daniel Gierer, SIUE; Khi Holiday, Southern Indiana. **DH:** Cole Kitchens, Southern Indiana. **UT:** Jorsixt Jimenez, Tennessee Tech. **SP:** Josh Newell, Lindenwood; Nathan Mertens, Southeast Missouri; Tyler Kapraun, Eastern Illinois. **RP:** Jackson Kranawetter, Southeast Missouri; Juan Vargas, Tennessee Tech.

Player of the Year: Mack Whitcomb, Tennessee Tech. **Pitcher of the Year:** Josh Newell Lindenwood. **Freshman of the Year:** Charlie Isom-McCall, Lindenwood. **Coach of the Year:** Jason Anderson, Eastern Illinois.

INDIVIDUAL BATTING LEADERS

	AVG	OBP	SLG	AB	2B	3B	HR	RBI	SB
Kitchens, Cole, S. Indiana	.365	.413	.617	230	20	1	12	63	1
Grines, TJ, UT Martin	.364	.423	.557	88	7	2	2	19	15
Whitcomb, Mack, Tenn. Tech	.360	.485	.649	211	12	2	15	55	1
Gierer, Daniel, SIUE	.355	.390	.500	186	6	0	7	36	22
Peak, Austyn, Morehead State	.344	.447	.344	32	0	0	0	3	5
Coakley, Kannon, S. Indiana	.344	.445	.433	157	14	0	0	29	2
Townsend, Arderrius, UT Martin	.343	.444	.669	166	10	1	14	36	12
Liam Bushey, Western Illinois	.340	.436	.450	191	10	1	3	38	0
Dutton, JJ, Morehead State	.340	.423	.474	209	11	4	3	28	1
Holiday, Khi, S. Indiana	.336	.458	.409	220	6	2	2	37	24
Martin, Parker, S. Indiana	.336	.430	.463	214	9	0	6	43	1
Wiese, Sam, E. Illinois	.333	.383	.333	42	0	0	0	7	0
Niedzwiedz, Ryan, SIUE	.332	.434	.538	199	13	2	8	46	3
Ottensmeier, Jake, Eastern Illinois	.329	.354	.461	76	4	3	0	17	5
Goodwin, Zak, Eastern Illinois	.328	.474	.394	137	3	0	2	30	3
Krayton Morse, Western Illinois	.328	.412	.414	186	11	1	1	19	0
Edwards, Kam, Lindenwood	.328	.444	.470	198	10	3	4	35	14
Thomas, Hunter, Morehead State	.325	.407	.623	231	12	0	19	55	0
Goeke, Kade, Little Rock	.321	.424	.321	56	0	0	0	5	4
Green, Jackson, Tenn. Tech	.319	.448	.521	163	8	2	7	33	19
O'Conor, Mike, Eastern Illinois	.318	.379	.588	170	10	3	10	41	5
Umbach, Anthony, S. Indiana	.316	.349	.342	155	4	0	0	11	10
Jimenez, Jorsixt, Tenn. Tech	.315	.423	.506	178	14	1	6	35	0
Smelser, Landon, Tenn. Tech	.310	.375	.388	129	4	0	2	16	3
Melton, Luke, Eastern Illinois	.310	.408	.452	42	1	1	1	8	1

INDIVIDUAL PITCHING LEADERS

	W	L	ERA	G	SV	IP	H	BB	SO
Newell, Josh, Lindenwood	10	2	3.15	15	0	97	91	19	58
Dow, Haden, SE Missouri	5	4	3.33	14	0	78	62	14	67
Mertens, Nathan, SE Missouri	7	3	3.53	13	1	79	71	8	67
Conklin, Tyler, E. Illinois	5	1	3.94	11	0	64	57	16	45
Smith, Ethan, Lindenwood	4	4	4.16	15	0	76	71	39	53
Brown, Eli, Lindenwood	4	8	4.38	15	0	86	83	27	73
Kapraun, Tyler, E. Illinois	6	5	4.52	16	0	84	94	21	67
Pease, Jaxson, Tenn. Tech	5	3	4.64	14	0	66	78	25	52
Gonzalez, Andres, S. Indiana	3	4	4.79	13	0	73	59	40	55
Jorge Romero, Western Illinois	3	2	5.00	6	4	54	68	11	37
Wells, Jackson, Little Rock	3	7	5.02	15	0	84	88	35	90
Sitton, Jacob, UT Martin	3	3	5.03	15	0	77	85	43	53
Cline, Jack, Little Rock	8	5	5.06	16	0	84	83	33	64
Boruff, Dalton, E. Illinois	1	5	5.17	1	5	56	63	28	39
Wager, Zach, UT Martin	5	8	5.23	11	0	64	79	25	35
Heyman, Sam, SE Missouri	6	6	5.51	14	0	64	74	29	40
Max Tripure, Western Illinois	4	7	5.72	14	0	72	75	34	39
Solis, Anthony, E. Illinois	5	3	5.79	12	2	70	82	23	36
Stearns, Spencer, Siue	3	5	5.79	13	0	61	68	25	62
Teixeira, Tim, Siue	3	5	6.20	15	0	70	75	33	64
Hawks, Kamden, Morehead St.	1	5	6.21	10	0	58	53	57	57
Frederick Romano, W. Illinois	4	4	6.52	12	0	59	75	20	49
Kimball, Blake, S. Indiana	6	5	6.57	12	1	74	84	29	46
Poynter, Bradley, Morehead St.	2	4	9.69	12	0	57	96	17	23

PATRIOT LEAGUE

	Conference W	L	Overall W	L
Holy Cross	17	8	31	27
Navy	14	11	26	25
Army West Point	14	11	25	25
Lehigh	11	14	24	26
Bucknell	10	15	18	27
Lafayette	9	16	14	35

ALL-CONFERENCE TEAM: SP: Jaden Wywoda, Holy Cross, Jr.; Tyler O'Neill, Bucknell, Sr.; Andrew Berg, Army West Point, Jr. **RP:** Landon Kruer, Navy, Sr. **C:** Ethan Swidler, Lafayette, Jr. **IF:** Thomas Schreck, Army West Point, Sr.; Tyler Dunn, Bucknell, Sr.; Jimmy King, Holy Cross, Sr.; Chris

Baillargeon, Holy Cross, Sr.; Aidan Quinn, Lehigh, Jr.; **OF**: Chris Barr, Army West Point, Jr.; CJ Egrie, Holy Cross, Jr.; Easton Brenner, Lafayette, Sr. **At-Large**: William Parker, Army West Point, Jr.

Player of the Year: CJ Egrie, Holy Cross, Jr., OF. **Pitcher of the Year**: Jaden Wywoda, Holy Cross, Jr., RHP. **Rookie of the Year**: Ty DePerno, Navy, Fr., C. **Defensive Player of the Year:** Jake Whitlinger, Lehigh, Sr., OF. **Coach of the Year:** Ed Kahovec, Holy Cross.

INDIVIDUAL BATTING LEADERS

	AVG	OBP	SLG	AB	2B	3B	HR	RBI	SB
Chris Baillargeon, Holy Cross	.376	.490	.507	205	18	0	3	52	5
Quinn, Aidan, Lehigh	.345	.438	.536	168	12	1	6	49	3
Easton Brenner, Lafayette	.340	.498	.480	150	8	2	3	30	6
Thomas Schreck, Army	.335	.449	.494	158	14	1	3	35	2
Jimmy King, Holy Cross	.332	.402	.459	220	19	3	1	41	20
Ethan Swidler, Lafayette	.331	.462	.494	178	14	0	5	33	0
John Calabrese, Bucknell	.330	.465	.407	91	7	0	0	14	3
Tyler Dunn, Bucknell	.325	.503	.492	126	10	1	3	30	2
Jack Quinlan, Army	.319	.449	.533	135	12	1	5	32	1
Justin Lehman, Army	.316	.403	.449	136	13	1	1	24	1
Chris Barr, Army	.308	.388	.447	208	10	5	3	38	32
C.J. Egrie, Holy Cross	.308	.459	.485	198	14	3	5	28	35
DePerno, Ty, Navy	.307	.439	.438	153	5	0	5	32	5
Gianni Royer, Holy Cross	.307	.387	.468	205	18	3	3	40	24
William Parker, Army	.301	.391	.500	166	15	0	6	40	11
Walewander, Owen, Lehigh	.300	.407	.429	140	9	0	3	27	3
Alex Barrist, Lafayette	.298	.365	.433	171	7	5	2	31	4
Addison Ainsworth, Army	.293	.405	.457	188	14	1	5	40	10
Brown, Evan, Navy	.292	.354	.416	185	10	2	3	30	2
John LaFleur, Holy Cross	.292	.405	.484	161	8	1	7	48	6
Michael Zarrillo, Lafayette	.289	.365	.444	187	11	0	6	37	4
Whitlinger, Jake, Lehigh	.282	.396	.431	181	9	0	6	27	21
Manning, Andrew, Navy	.277	.379	.452	177	11	1	6	28	5
Murtha, Brock, Navy	.272	.408	.402	169	11	1	3	28	22
John McKillop, Army	.271	.343	.339	118	8	0	0	20	0

INDIVIDUAL PITCHING LEADERS

	W	L	ERA	G	SV	IP	H	BB	SO
Tyler O'Neill, Bucknell	4	4	3.14	12	0	83	63	22	68
Danny Macchiarola, Holy Cross	9	5	3.27	16	0	94	81	28	92
Jaden Wywoda, Holy Cross	9	3	3.63	16	0	84	76	28	79
Andrew Berg, Army	5	3	3.91	12	0	76	80	29	61
Bendik, Brady, Navy	4	4	3.95	13	0	73	62	26	62
Justin Lehman, Army	5	4	4.02	13	0	78	103	21	46
Grenn, Tyler, Navy	2	3	4.81	13	0	73	84	19	37
Ben Magovern, Bucknell	4	3	5.13	11	0	53	58	21	40
Joe Skapinetz, Lafayette	1	7	5.83	12	0	63	72	24	79
Trace Florio, Lafayette	1	7	6.41	11	0	60	85	18	56
Tristan Helmick, Lafayette	3	4	6.44	10	0	50	61	27	49

SOUTHEASTERN CONFERENCE

	Conference		Overall	
	W	L	W	L
Texas	22	8	44	14
Arkansas	20	10	50	15
LSU	19	11	53	15
Vanderbilt	19	11	43	18
Georgia	18	12	43	17
Auburn	17	13	41	20
Ole Miss	16	14	43	21
Tennessee	16	14	46	19
Alabama	16	14	41	18
Florida	15	15	39	22
Mississippi State	15	15	36	23
Oklahoma	14	16	38	22
Kentucky	13	17	31	26
Texas A&M	11	19	30	26
South Carolina	6	24	28	29
Missouri	3	27	16	39

ALL-CONFERENCE TEAM: C: Rylan Galvan, Texas; Luke Heyman, Florida. **1B:** Andrew Fischer, Tennessee. **2B:** Gavin Kilen, Tennessee. **3B:** Ace Reese, Mississippi State; Slate Alford, Georgia. **SS:** Wehiwa Aloy,

Anthony Eyanson gave LSU a second ace in the starting rotation.

Arkansas. **OF**: Ike Irish, Auburn; Charles Davalan, Arkansas; Kade Snell, Alabama. **DH/Util**: Kuhio Aloy, Arkansas. **SP**: Liam Doyle, Tennessee; Kade Anderson, LSU; Kyson Witherspoon, Oklahoma; Zach Root, Arkansas. **RP**: Dylan Volantis, Texas; Zac Cowan, LSU; Carson Ozmer, Alabama.

Player of the Year: Wehiwa Aloy, Arkansas. Pitcher of the Year: Liam Doyle, Tennessee. **Freshman of the Year:** Dylan Volantis, Texas. **Newcomer of the Year:** Ace Reese, Mississippi State. **Scholar-Athlete of the Year**: Ryan Prager, Texas A&M. **Coach of the Year:** Jim Schlossnagle, Texas.

INDIVIDUAL BATTING LEADERS

	AVG	OBP	SLG	AB	2B	3B	HR	RBI	SB
Colby Shelton, Florida	.377	.458	.606	175	40	6	6	7	35	6
Ryland Zaborowski, Georgia	.370	.500	.788	146	41	54	17	61	0
Ike Irish, Auburn	.364	.469	.710	214	65	78	19	58	11
Kade Snell, Alabama	.363	.464	.575	212	49	77	10	52	0
Gavin Kilen, Tennessee	.357	.441	.671	210	60	75	15	46	6
Jackson Lovich, Missouri	.357	.430	.622	185	39	66	12	51	7
Logan Maxwell, Arkansas	.356	.454	.605	177	46	63	13	38	1
Ace Reese, Mississippi St.	.352	.422	.718	227	58	80	21	66	1
Wehiwa Aloy, Arkansas	.350	.434	.673	266	81	93	21	68	9
Charles Davalan, Arkansas	.346	.433	.561	269	71	93	14	60	10
Derek Curiel, LSU	.345	.470	.519	258	67	89	7	55	3
Gehrig Frei, Mississippi St.	.345	.404	.586	145	33	50	8	17	2
Noah Sullivan, Mississippi St.	.345	.475	.645	203	63	70	15	46	1
Chris Rembert, Auburn	.344	.467	.555	209	49	72	10	46	6
Riley Nelson, Vanderbilt	.344	.450	.526	215	48	74	8	47	7
Andrew Fischer, Tennessee	.341	.497	.760	217	70	74	25	65	4
Caden Sorrell, Texas A&M	.337	.430	.789	95	23	32	12	32	0
Bobby Boser, Florida	.336	.437	.613	238	72	80	18	67	19
Hunter Ensley, Tennessee	.336	.418	.531	241	46	81	10	62	7
Luke Hill, Ole Miss	.336	.459	.488	244	66	82	8	40	18
Chase Fralick, Auburn	.335	.426	.472	212	36	71	4	41	0
Ethan Mendoza, Texas	.333	.437	.476	225	53	75	5	34	15
Blake Simpson, Missouri	.333	.333	.583	12	1	4	1	1	0
Cam Kozeal, Arkansas	.333	.386	.606	231	49	77	15	62	2

INDIVIDUAL PITCHING LEADERS

	W	L	ERA	G	SV	IP	H	BB	SO
Aidan King, Florida	7	2	2.58	17	0	73	58	23	79
Kyson Witherspoon, Oklahoma	10	4	2.65	16	0	95	73	23	124
Max Grubbs, Texas	6	2	2.84	22	5	57	50	14	61
Hunter Elliott, Ole Miss	10	3	2.94	17	0	86	59	40	102
Anthony Eyanson, LSU	12	2	3.00	20	2	108	88	36	152
Luke Harrison, Texas	5	1	3.06	15	0	71	63	24	72
Kade Anderson, LSU	12	1	3.18	19	0	119	91	35	180
Liam Doyle, Tennessee	10	4	3.20	19	1	96	63	32	164
Ben Cleaver, Kentucky	6	3	3.25	15	0	83	54	30	92
Justin Lamkin, Texas A&M	5	7	3.42	15	0	84	74	19	98
Brian Curley, Georgia	4	4	3.55	17	2	66	42	27	85
Zach Root, Arkansas	9	6	3.62	19	0	99	82	35	126
Ben Davis, Mississippi St.	4	2	3.77	23	1	57	52	24	61
Marcus Phillips, Tennessee	4	5	3.90	17	0	83	75	34	98
Riley Quick, Alabama	8	3	3.92	14	0	62	62	24	70
JD Thompson, Vanderbilt	6	5	4.00	16	0	90	79	30	122
Ryan Prager, Texas A&M	4	4	4.21	15	0	83	84	21	73
Nate Harris, Kentucky	5	2	4.25	13	0	59	54	26	45
Liam Peterson, Florida	8	4	4.28	16	0	69	67	32	96
Samuel Dutton, Auburn	7	3	4.31	16	0	86	86	19	95
Cody Bowker, Vanderbilt	3	5	4.38	16	0	72	61	28	99
Gabe Gaeckle, Arkansas	4	2	4.42	19	2	71	63	31	92
Nic McCay, Kentucky	5	0	4.50	15	0	72	53	41	71
Tyler Fay, Alabama	1	2	4.69	20	0	56	60	12	44
Pico Kohn, Mississippi St.	5	4	4.73	15	0	80	69	29	114
Landon Beidelschies, Arkansas	4	0	4.82	16	0	62	59	20	70
Leighton Finley, Georgia	3	2	4.85	16	0	69	56	25	83
Chase Shores, LSU	5	3	5.09	23	2	64	62	31	70
Malachi Witherspoon, Oklahoma	4	8	5.09	15	0	74	78	32	91

SOUTHERN CONFERENCE

	Conference W L	Overall W L
ETSU	14 7	41 17
Samford	13 8	30 27
Mercer	12 9	35 25
The Citadel	12 9	31 26
Western Carolina	10 11	30 28
UNC Greensboro	9 12	21 33
Wofford	8 13	33 27
VMI	6 15	27 26

ALL-CONFERENCE TEAM: SP: Carter Fink, ETSU; Jace Hyde, ETSU; Colton Cosper, Mercer. **RP:** Maddox Webb, The Citadel; Danny Thompson Jr., UNCG; Brady Frederick, ETSU. **C:** Jack Spyke, Western Carolina. **1B:** Grayson Fitzwater, VMI. **2B:** Cooper Torres, ETSU. **SS:** Bradley Frye, Mercer. **3B:** Parker McDonald, Samford. **OF:** Jamie Palmese, ETSU; Ty Dalley, Mercer; Michael Gupton, Samford. **DH:** Wyatt Stanley, Western Carolina.

Player of the Year: Cooper Torres, ETSU. **Pitcher of the Year:** Brady Frederick, ETSU. **Coach of the Year:** Joe Pennucci, ETSU. **Freshman of the Year:** Axel Melendez, ETSU. **Defensive Player of the Year:** Bradley Frye, Mercer.

INDIVIDUAL BATTING LEADERS

	AVG	OBP	SLG	AB	2B	3B	HR	RBI	SB
Bradley Garner, VMI	.389	.496	.672	198	20	3	10	59	23
Owen Prince, VMI	.385	.504	.474	213	13	0	2	44	46
James Layman, Wofford	.369	.493	.484	157	11	2	1	33	23
Cooper Torres, ETSU	.364	.463	.756	225	15	2	23	72	9
Tanner Hardin, Wofford	.346	.430	.379	153	5	0	0	29	17
Jack Spyke, Western Caro.	.340	.431	.560	191	19	1	7	41	1
Boston Torres, VMI	.337	.465	.580	193	14	0	11	67	19
Bradley Frye, Mercer	.337	.393	.552	252	18	0	12	54	16
Anthony Hausner, The Citadel	.336	.447	.464	125	7	0	3	25	1
Hayden Friese, Western Caro.	.335	.436	.511	227	11	1	9	47	1
Michael Gupton, Samford	.333	.401	.630	192	10	1	15	51	10
Blake Jacklin, ETSU	.332	.424	.474	190	8	2	5	27	15
Cade Carr, Samford	.332	.422	.531	154	11	1	8	61	0
Jackson Harris, Samford	.332	.402	.477	214	16	0	5	46	3
Wyatt Stanley, Western Caro.	.331	.466	.534	148	18	3	2	45	0

	AVG	OBP	SLG	AB	2B	3B	HR	RBI	SB
Cody Miller, ETSU	.331	.430	.623	236	15	0	18	58	27
Ryan Wynn, Wofford	.331	.413	.492	242	18	3	5	45	16
Jeffrey Ince, Samford	.330	.446	.552	221	17	1	10	34	20
Trent Turner, Western Caro.	.329	.402	.585	234	14	2	14	58	5
Jake Souders, Samford	.327	.391	.502	223	13	1	8	46	14
Tyler Bak, Wofford	.325	.427	.427	157	10	0	2	20	15
Ely Brown, Mercer	.320	.459	.401	222	9	0	3	32	10
Brant Baughcum, Mercer	.320	.415	.502	225	15	1	8	46	6
Brantley Truitt, UNC Greensboro	.318	.409	.442	154	6	2	3	21	9
Kazuya Jordan, VMI	.316	.420	.466	174	6	4	4	47	44

INDIVIDUAL PITCHING LEADERS

	W	L	ERA	G	SV	IP	H	BB	SO
Brady Frederick, ETSU	8	2	2.67	24	4	78	50	19	76
Mason Blasche, Samford	10	0	3.24	16	1	72	72	13	56
Colton Cosper, Mercer	7	2	3.57	16	0	88	88	13	80
Jace Hyde, ETSU	7	0	3.72	14	0	68	66	21	55
Daniel Thompson, UNCG	2	4	3.79	23	4	62	54	24	87
Dusty Revis, Western Caro.	7	5	4.04	15	0	82	73	31	78
Miller Riggins, Samford	5	2	4.31	15	0	79	63	31	85
Carter Fink, ETSU	6	5	4.48	16	0	72	88	19	60
Davis Wright, Western Caro.	5	7	4.50	15	0	86	90	26	88
Jess Ackerman, Mercer	4	4	4.73	18	0	70	62	40	84
Michael Harpster, ETSU	7	3	4.94	16	0	75	69	18	69
Sam Murchison, UNCG	6	5	4.97	15	0	80	84	28	79
Jay Miller, UNCG	2	5	4.98	11	0	60	55	21	69
Andrew Stanley, The Citadel	5	3	5.07	17	1	71	74	28	64
Noah Chapman, UNC Greensboro	5	3	5.14	21	1	68	71	16	76
George Derrick Floyd, The Citadel	6	3	5.42	14	0	73	86	17	45
Jeb Johnson, Mercer	4	5	5.43	21	1	61	70	14	58
Caden Plummer, VMI	4	4	5.55	14	1	60	66	16	50
Cameron Keshock, Samford	5	4	5.73	15	0	77	83	33	74
Marcus Van Alstine, VMI	3	1	6.75	22	3	56	78	19	53
Jaxon Lloyd, VMI	4	4	7.48	16	0	61	74	24	73
Branton Little, Wofford	4	8	8.29	16	0	67	95	20	50

SOUTHLAND CONFERENCE

	Conference W L	Overall W L
Southeastern	22 8	38 16
UTRGV	22 8	36 18
Lamar	20 10	40 17
Northwestern State	19 11	35 21
McNeese	19 11	31 17
HCU	17 13	32 23
A&M-Corpus Christi	12 18	21 31
New Orleans	12 18	28 26
Nicholls	10 20	17 32
SFA	9 21	17 32
UIW	3 27	17 33

ALL-CONFERENCE TEAM: C: Steven Lancia, UTRGV. **1B:** Rob Liddington, UIW. **2B:** Matt Ryan, Lamar. **SS:** TJ Salvaggio, Southeastern. **3B:** Easton Moomau, UTRGV. **OF:** Damian Ruiz, Lamar; Conner Westenburg, McNeese; Dane Watts, Southeastern. **DH:** Armani Raygoza, UTRGV. **UT:** Bryce Calloway, New Orleans. **SP:** Brennan Stuprich, Southeastern; Riely Hunsaker, Lamar; Victor Loa, UTRGV. **RP:** Brady St. Pierre, Southeastern.

INDIVIDUAL BATTING LEADERS

	AVG	OBP	SLG	AB	2B	3B	HR	RBI	SB
Calloway, Bryce, New Orleans	.390	.484	.722	205	10	2	18	63	1
Raygoza, Armani, UTRGV	.389	.477	.716	208	17	0	17	60	2
Ruiz, Damian, Lamar	.388	.511	.607	214	22	2	7	46	14
Easton Dowell, McNeese	.360	.412	.581	172	15	1	7	37	9
Liddington, Rob, UIW	.359	.448	.675	206	10	5	15	50	13
BLAND, Cemodrick, SFA	.356	.455	.458	118	6	0	2	23	24
Brome, Isaiah, Southeastern	.355	.475	.690	155	12	2	12	36	1
Lopez, Isaac, UTRGV	.347	.421	.491	216	13	0	6	41	11
Watts, Dane, Southeastern	.342	.438	.542	190	11	3	7	34	4
Lancia, Steven, UTRGV	.335	.436	.506	176	11	2	5	45	4
Moreno, Heladio, Lamar	.335	.409	.425	200	11	2	1	32	11
Woods, Peyton, Southeastern	.333	.379	.474	114	10	0	2	24	0
Calabrese, Daniel, UIW	.332	.397	.479	190	11	1	5	33	6

	AVG	OBP	SLG	AB	2B	3B	HR	RBI	SB
Moomau, Easton, UTRGV	.332	.420	.424	217	11	0	3	49	5
IBE, Josh, SFA	.331	.446	.675	157	10	1	14	46	3
Conner Westenburg, McNeese	.328	.429	.561	198	7	9	7	32	26
Sanchez, Jacob, UTRGV	.327	.437	.485	196	7	0	8	31	4
Marcus Heusohn, McNeese	.327	.450	.464	168	15	1	2	29	1
Jenkins, Carter, Nicholls	.326	.383	.402	132	5	1	1	20	0
Lipoma, Reese, NW State	.324	.451	.402	219	10	2	1	30	11

INDIVIDUAL PITCHING LEADERS

	W	L	ERA	GS	SV	IP	H	BB	SO
Hunsaker, Riely, Lamar	4	3	2.47	14	0	77	72	16	70
White, Carter, NW State	4	1	2.65	5	1	58	42	27	45
Havard, Peyton, Lamar	7	2	2.73	5	5	63	52	15	79
Sergio Lopez, McNeese	7	1	2.89	5	3	53	42	16	51
Stuprich, Brennan, SE	9	5	2.90	14	0	90	68	28	109
Olivier, Chris, Lamar	6	3	3.39	14	0	66	61	22	62
Loa, Victor, UTRGV	5	1	3.54	14	0	56	39	39	52
Sparks, Alec, Nicholls	4	3	3.63	12	0	72	59	28	66
Parache, Nuno, Nicholls	4	1	3.81	9	0	54	54	18	45
Edwards, Parker, HCU	3	5	3.83	17	0	89	78	36	71
Templeton, Cody, SFA	6	4	3.90	13	0	88	103	13	63
Lobell, Blake, Southeastern	7	1	3.90	13	0	65	68	17	42
Garcia, Zach, A&M-CCi	7	4	4.00	14	0	90	90	23	60
Edwards, Grant, New Orleans	3	5	4.23	15	0	77	72	29	92
Shea, Bryson, A&M-CC	1	5	4.64	9	0	64	67	13	48
Cooper Golden, McNeese	3	3	4.71	14	0	65	67	17	46
Dean, David, A&M-CCi	2	5	4.78	8	0	53	66	18	26
Bryan, Tyler, NW State	2	7	5.01	14	0	74	76	40	53
Hillen, Trent, NW State	7	1	5.54	14	0	76	84	30	63
Caravalho, Joshua, HCU	9	4	5.76	16	0	86	106	28	64

SOUTHWESTERN ATHLETIC CONFERENCE

	Conference		Overall	
	W	L	W	L
Bethune-Cookman	24	5	37	23
Florida A&M	24	6	33	25
Alabama State	23	9	32	28
Arkansas-Pine Bluff	17	9	19	34
Grambling State	18	11	26	28
Jackson State	16	12	30	21
Southern	15	14	26	28
Texas Southern	15	15	22	31
Prairie View A&M	13	14	17	36
Mississippi Valley State	6	24	11	30
Alabama A&M	2	27	10	40
Alcorn State	1	29	6	43

ALL-CONFERENCE TEAM: C: Broedy Poppell, Florida A&M. **1B:** Juan Cruz, Alabama State. **2B:** Jesus Vanegas, Bethune-Cookman. **3B:** Jay Campbell, Florida A&M. **SS:** Bryce Hughes, Texas Southern. **DH:** Taj Bates, Southern. **OF:** Cardell Thibodeaux, Southern; Andrey Martinez, Bethune-Cookman; Kameron Douglas, Alabama State. **SP:** Eric Elliott, Jackson State; Kenney Fabian, Arkansas-Pine Bluff. **RP:** Jean Carlos Zambrano, Bethune-Cookman.

INDIVIDUAL BATTING LEADERS

	AVG	OBP	SLG	AB	2B	3B	HR	RBI	SB
Cardell Thibodeaux, Southern	.439	.544	.847	189	13	5	18	71	24
Juan Cruz, Alabama State	.418	.479	.693	251	23	2	14	73	5
Kelton Phillips, Texas Southern	.394	.495	.576	165	10	1	6	40	23
Trey Rutledge, Alabama A&M	.392	.568	.515	130	7	3	1	13	35
Huerta, Arjun, Jackson State	.382	.489	.549	102	5	3	2	28	6
Davis Kanious, Alcorn State	.379	.475	.424	66	3	0	0	6	19
McCladdie, Jordan, Jackson St.	.375	.521	.571	184	12	6	4	35	49
Daniel Figueroa, B-Cookman	.375	.473	.466	88	8	0	0	25	17
Landon Williams, Prairie View	.373	.469	.663	166	13	1	11	50	3
Ford Jermel, Alcorn State	.370	.445	.496	127	8	4	0	20	42
Ahmar Donatto, Prairie View	.369	.441	.675	179	15	5	7	34	11
Andrey Martinez, B-Cookman	.367	.438	.777	215	14	1	24	75	7
Kylan Duncan, Alabama A&M	.361	.430	.443	158	7	0	2	46	10

	AVG	OBP	SLG	AB	2B	3B	HR	RBI	SB
Taj Bates, Southern	.358	.445	.625	176	12	1	11	65	10
Trey Bridges, Grambling State	.356	.479	.571	205	15	1	9	82	15
Miles Jackson, Alabama A&M	.356	.446	.470	149	9	1	2	20	5
Jorge Rodriguez, B-Cookman	.353	.440	.695	167	15	0	14	47	0
Damian Garcia, Texas Southern	.352	.462	.753	162	10	5	15	60	2
Ethan Miller, Florida A&M	.351	.429	.518	114	7	0	4	24	1
Jaden Jones, Texas Southern	.349	.430	.453	212	10	0	4	50	6
Tanner Aoki, Miss. Valley St.	.349	.485	.403	129	7	0	0	14	20
Kj White, Southern	.347	.463	.389	167	5	1	0	26	29
Torres, Hederick, Jackson State	.346	.437	.406	133	4	2	0	20	6
Jacoby Radcliffe, Southern	.346	.497	.586	133	3	4	7	30	35
Gamez Nathan, Alcorn State	.344	.418	.433	157	11	0	1	40	2

INDIVIDUAL PITCHING LEADERS

	W	L	ERA	GS	SV	IP	H	BB	SO
Edwin Sanchez, B-Cookman	9	1	3.08	18	0	88	85	34	105
Elliott, Eric, Jackson State	7	1	3.22	14	2	81	56	50	108
Leonardo Bravo, Prairie View	6	1	3.40	7	1	77	68	37	61
Kenney Fabian, Ark.-Pine Bluff	7	6	3.48	14	0	85	84	24	62
Garrett Workman, Florida A&M	9	4	3.66	15	0	86	83	30	71
Jorhan Laboy, Alabama State	8	2	3.90	12	0	92	97	25	79
Jesus Campa, Florida A&M	3	2	4.05	15	0	60	68	27	43
Carson Kelly, Florida A&M	7	2	4.15	1	3	69	72	33	54
Cody Williams, Florida A&M	5	3	4.69	1	3	63	61	28	64
Haston, Brandon, Jackson State	4	7	4.94	13	1	78	96	31	66
Esaid Pena, Alabama State	2	3	4.96	15	0	65	68	30	56
Joel Core, B-Cookman	6	2	5.15	14	0	80	79	32	83
Nick Luckett, Southern	10	4	5.15	15	0	93	109	32	51
Gonzalez, Erick, Jackson State	8	3	5.23	15	1	84	76	49	99
Tanner Boccabello, B-Cookman	7	2	5.25	12	0	72	77	25	52
Ethan Bates, Grambling State	6	0	5.55	2	4	60	76	18	45
Calvin McClendon, Texas So.	3	5	5.90	17	0	82	104	31	52
Logan Darnell, Miss. Valley St.	3	6	6.44	7	1	57	78	20	49
Randy Reyes, Grambling State	4	4	6.64	12	0	61	63	47	44
Mason Martinez, Grambling St.	5	6	6.89	17	0	82	106	43	66

SUMMIT LEAGUE

	Conference		Overall	
	W	L	W	L
St. Thomas	21	9	29	21
Oral Roberts	21	9	37	22
North Dakota State	13	15	21	34
Omaha	12	16	20	30
South Dakota State	12	18	16	36
Northern Colorado	9	21	18	33

ALL-CONFERENCE TEAM: C: Wailele Kane-Yates, Oral Roberts. **1B:** Tyler Bishop, Omaha. **2B:** Jack Schark, Oral Roberts. **3B:** Henry Zipay, Omaha. **SS:** Jake Schaffner, North Dakota State. **OF:** Will Edmunson, Oral Roberts; Jackson Trout, Omaha; Owen Siegert, South Dakota State. **UT:** Matthew Maulik, St. Thomas. **SP:** Easton Teel, Oral Roberts; Nolan Johnson, North Dakota State; Marcus Kruzan, St. Thomas. **RP:** Danny Lachenmayer, North Dakota State.

Player of the Year: Henry Zipay, Omaha. **Pitcher of the Year:** Nolan Johnson, North Dakota State. **Newcomer of the Year:** Easton Teel, Oral Roberts. **Defensive Player of the Year:** Jake Schaffner, North Dakota State. **Coach of the Year:** Ryan Folmar, Oral Roberts.

INDIVIDUAL BATTING LEADERS

	AVG	OBP	SLG	AB	2B	3B	HR	RBI	SB
Henry Zipay, Omaha	.384	.475	.551	185	15	5	2	25	3
Jake Schaffner, N. Dakota State	.367	.435	.467	229	9	4	2	21	18
Carter Sintek, S. Dakota State	.358	.407	.468	218	9	3	3	30	0
Nolan Grawe, S. Dakota State	.347	.414	.437	199	12	0	2	32	3
Wailele Kane-Yates, O. Roberts	.341	.425	.576	217	15	0	12	50	0
Jake King, Northern Colorado	.340	.430	.456	206	14	2	2	42	2
Luke Luskey, S. Dakota State	.336	.401	.691	149	9	1	14	52	2
Owen Siegert, S. Dakota State	.329	.414	.500	164	11	1	5	33	12
Jackson Trout, Omaha	.328	.404	.451	204	8	1	5	37	7
Max Moris, St. Thomas	.328	.414	.481	189	13	2	4	46	4
Kai Wagner, Northern Colorado	.327	.432	.571	205	6	2	10	57	2
Joe Vos, St. Thomas	.326	.388	.539	178	13	2	7	38	9
Tanner Recchio, St. Thomas	.324	.418	.415	188	12	1	1	23	30
Will Edmunson, Oral Roberts	.319	.394	.466	251	10	0	9	33	5

	AVG	OBP	SLG	AB	R	H	HR	RBI	SB
Matthew Maulik, St. Thomas	.315	.399	.485	165	7	0	7	39	0
Davis Hamilton, N. Dakota State	.314	.402	.473	207	12	3	5	42	12
Bryce Ronken, S. Dakota State	.314	.448	.474	156	13	0	4	36	5
Brett Barber, Northern Colorado	.310	.386	.386	145	6	1	1	19	13
Drew Borner, Omaha	.308	.390	.433	120	6	0	3	24	1
Jake Bullard, Northern Colorado	.306	.424	.429	147	5	2	3	23	2
Jack Schark, Oral Roberts	.306	.399	.500	222	14	1	9	40	3
Tyler Palmer, Omaha	.304	.405	.384	125	3	2	1	20	10
Dante Smith, N. Dakota State	.303	.383	.394	165	8	2	1	22	11
Joe Roder, St. Thomas	.303	.393	.491	175	16	1	5	53	1
Tyler Bishop, Omaha	.299	.380	.490	194	10	0	9	51	2

INDIVIDUAL PITCHING LEADERS

	W	L	ERA	G	SV	IP	H	BB	SO
Easton Teel, Oral Roberts	7	2	2.95	10	0	82	75	15	54
Jake Goble, S. Dakota State	2	2	3.69	--	--	54	52	16	51
Ben Weber, Omaha	3	5	3.92	14	0	80	68	42	68
Nathan Love, Oral Roberts	6	7	4.01	15	0	76	71	24	54
Walker Retz, St. Thomas	6	1	4.02	12	0	69	70	19	59
Riane Ritter, St. Thomas	6	1	4.08	7	0	64	59	29	63
Nolan Johnson, N. Dakota State	4	6	4.52	16	0	88	85	23	79
Logan Knight, N. Dakota State	5	6	4.54	15	0	83	89	28	68
Marcus Kruzan, St. Thomas	8	1	5.01	13	0	74	75	37	58
Murphy Gienger, No. Colorado	1	4	5.90	13	0	79	101	31	78
Caleb Duerr, South Dakota State	4	4	6.36	12	0	58	59	29	47
Jake Storey, Northern Colorado	2	4	8.47	14	0	63	104	22	45

SUN BELT CONFERENCE

	Conference		Overall	
	W	L	W	L
Coastal Carolina	26	4	56	13
Southern Miss	24	6	47	16
Troy	18	12	39	21
Marshall	16	14	33	26
Louisiana	16	14	27	31
Old Dominion	15	15	22	31
Arkansas State	14	16	26	28
Texas State	14	16	27	31
Georgia Southern	13	17	28	31
App State	13	17	23	31
South Alabama	12	18	23	28
Georgia State	11	19	26	30
James Madison	10	20	17	38
ULM	8	22	22	33

ALL-CONFERENCE TEAM: P: Cameron Flukey, Coastal Carolina; Jacob Morrison, Coastal Carolina; JB Middleton, Southern Miss. **RP** Colby Allen, Southern Miss. **C:** Caden Bodine, Coastal Carolina. **1B:** Blake Cavill, Troy. **2B:** Nick Monistere, Southern Miss. **SS:** Tyler Lichtenberger, App State. **3B:** Jesse Donohoe, Georgia State **OF:** Josh Tate, Georgia Southern; Conor Higgs, Louisiana; Carson Paetow, Southern Miss. **DH:** Kameron Miller, App State. **UT:** Austin Eaton, Texas State.
Player of the Year: Nick Monistere, Southern Miss. **Pitcher of the Year:** Jacob Morrison, Coastal Carolina. **Newcomer of the Year:** Kaleb Freeman, Georgia State. **Freshman of the Year:** Tyler Lichtenberger, App State. **Leadership Award:** Carson Paetow, Southern Miss. **Coach of the Year:** Kevin Schnall, Coastal Carolina.

INDIVIDUAL BATTING LEADERS

	AVG	OBP	SLG	AB	2B	3B	HR	RBI	SB
Tate, Josh, Georgia Southern	.362	.437	.606	246	18	3	12	46	7
Conor Higgs, Louisiana	.355	.472	.680	197	12	2	16	46	7
Smith, Sean, Georgia Southern	.352	.458	.599	162	9	2	9	36	6
Cook, Jake, Southern Miss	.350	.436	.468	237	13	3	3	32	3
Freeman, Kaleb, Georgia State	.349	.504	.732	209	28	2	16	46	15
Walker, Isaiah, ULM	.343	.415	.534	204	13	4	6	34	27
Leite, Zach, Old Dominion	.343	.461	.497	169	15	1	3	34	1
Tyler Lichtenberger, App State	.341	.410	.468	205	13	2	3	37	7
Lucas Ismaili, South Alabama	.337	.450	.554	166	10	1	8	34	2
Duncan Mathews, S. Alabama	.336	.486	.416	137	5	0	2	28	1
Urban, Joey, Southern Miss	.333	.417	.574	174	9	1	9	27	2
Dean Mihos, Coastal Carolina	.332	.418	.453	190	12	1	3	22	8
Stockman, Tucker, So.	.332	.414	.474	190	9	0	6	33	0

	AVG	OBP	SLG	AB	R	H	HR	RBI	SB
Rett Johnson, South Alabama	.327	.401	.439	171	8	1	3	23	9
Higdon, Ben, Southern Miss	.323	.398	.513	158	9	0	7	22	2
Monistere, Nick, So.	.323	.410	.623	257	12	1	21	72	7
Cavill, Blake, Troy	.320	.516	.562	194	12	1	11	50	2
Quiller, Ashton, Arkansas State	.318	.371	.479	192	12	5	3	30	13
Caden Bodine, C. Carolina	.318	.454	.461	245	18	1	5	42	2
Sebastian Alexander, C. Caro.	.318	.426	.521	217	12	1	10	54	28
John Smith, South Alabama	.314	.412	.466	191	8	0	7	30	2
Kameron Miller, App State	.311	.464	.569	167	7	0	12	50	2
Pratt, Ozzie, Southern Miss	.311	.404	.468	222	11	0	8	53	3
Morales, Efrain, Old Dominion	.308	.376	.385	130	7	0	1	16	1
Joseph Zamora, App State	.305	.393	.394	203	8	2	2	32	5

INDIVIDUAL PITCHING LEADERS

	W	L	ERA	G	SV	IP	H	BB	SO
JB Middleton, Southern Miss	10	1	2.31	16	0	105	65	25	122
Jacob Morrison, Coastal Caro.	12	1	2.42	18	0	108	79	23	104
Riley Eikhoff, Coastal Carolina	7	2	3.10	17	0	90	91	11	71
Cameron Flukey, Coastal Caro.	7	2	3.19	17	0	102	78	24	118
Griffin Miller, Marshall	7	4	3.46	15	0	83	68	46	71
JR Tollett, Louisiana	6	4	3.51	11	0	77	76	12	63
Chase Morgan, Louisiana	4	3	3.52	13	0	61	60	24	74
Logar, Jackson, James Madison	4	5	3.53	14	0	74	50	41	72
Mitchell Heer, South Alabama	7	2	3.53	9	0	66	60	15	39
Allen, Colby, Southern Miss	7	4	3.63	2	12	67	53	17	77
Richter, Chase, Arkansas State	3	4	3.67	1	8	54	39	22	53
Kuhle, Max, James Madison	2	4	4.02	5	3	56	52	21	62
Brown, Dylan, Old Dominion	5	2	4.06	15	0	82	76	26	102
Sivley, Kros, Southern Miss	7	1	4.14	8	0	72	73	20	58
Caleb Cross, App State	7	4	4.19	14	0	77	77	33	64
Adams, Matthew, So. Miss	6	4	4.31	17	0	79	78	22	89
Bradley Wilson, App State	3	2	4.35	0	1	68	69	24	53
Jaxon Shineflew, S. Alabama	3	4	4.50	6	3	56	44	29	59
Zach Willingham, S. Alabama	3	6	4.52	12	1	72	72	39	61
Morgan, Blake, Old Dominion	5	4	4.62	15	0	86	96	28	68
Roberts, Cole, Georgia State	6	4	4.69	10	0	71	61	26	62
Hibbard, Jack, Arkansas State	5	4	4.95	12	0	56	57	12	45
Andrew Herrmann, Louisiana	3	5	4.99	12	2	70	84	27	53
Brady Pendley, Ga. Southern	3	4	5.03	6	1	63	70	27	54
Edders, Noah, Troy	5	2	5.12	14	0	65	59	27	67

WEST COAST CONFERENCE

	Conference		Overall	
	W	L	W	L
San Diego	19	5	26	29
Gonzaga	16	8	26	25
Saint Mary's	15	9	36	26
LMU	14	10	27	27
Portland	13	11	22	29
San Francisco	9	15	26	30
Pacific	8	16	20	36
Santa Clara	7	17	20	30
Pepperdine	7	17	12	42

ALL-CONFERENCE TEAM: C: Robbie Ayers, LMU. **C/OF:** Eddie Madrigal, Saint Mary's; **C/OF:** Nate Savoie, LMU. **INF:** Beau Ankeney, LMU; Mikey Bell, Gonzaga; Jack Gurevitch, San Diego; Jonas Salk, Portland; Patrick Keighran, San Francisco. **P:** Erik Hoffberg, Gonzaga; Finbar O'Brien, Gonzaga; Cal Scolari, San Diego. **P/UTIL:** Austin Smith, San Diego; Logan Reddemann, San Diego.
Player of the Year: Mikey Bell, Gonzaga. **Pitcher of the Year:** Cal Scolari, San Diego. **Freshman of the Year:** Nate Savoie, LMU. **Defensive Player of the Year:** Jayden Lobliner, San Diego. **Coach of the Year:** Brock Ungricht, San Diego.

INDIVIDUAL BATTING LEADERS

	AVG	OBP	SLG	AB	2B	3B	HR	RBI	SB
Gurevitch, Jack, San Diego	.381	.491	.699	239	18	2	18	58	5
Howard, Tyler, Portland	.379	.481	.497	153	9	0	3	27	0
Eddie Madrigal, Saint Mary's	.375	.476	.723	256	18	4	21	88	9
Mikey Bell, Gonzaga	.360	.440	.616	203	17	1	11	45	5
Beau Ankeney, LMU	.358	.453	.712	229	13	1	22	69	5
Gage Mestas, Gonzaga	.352	.443	.448	105	8	1	0	22	7
Smith, Austin, San Diego	.351	.406	.510	239	18	1	6	53	6
Ian Armstrong, Saint Mary's	.350	.395	.554	157	11	3	5	40	5
Patrick Keighran, San Francisco	.348	.472	.671	155	14	0	12	48	13

INDIVIDUAL BATTING LEADERS

	AVG	OBP	SLG	AB	2B	3B	HR	RBI	SB
Upstill, Nick, Pepperdine	.345	.395	.468	171	11	2	2	19	5
Cam Hassert, LMU	.335	.444	.472	218	8	2	6	34	18
Lane, Isaiah, San Diego	.330	.460	.517	209	11	2	8	29	8
Hudson Shupe, Gonzaga	.329	.382	.417	228	5	3	3	36	4
JT Waldon, Pacific	.326	.394	.464	181	9	2	4	32	9
Aiden Taurek, Saint Mary's	.322	.407	.555	245	20	2	11	48	7
Diego Castellanos, Saint Mary's	.321	.419	.496	224	13	1	8	41	8
Robbie Ayers, LMU	.321	.455	.532	156	14	2	5	27	6
TJ Rogers, San Francisco	.314	.431	.519	185	15	1	7	43	13
Joyce, Dylan, Santa Clara	.314	.414	.580	188	11	0	13	49	3
Eddison Esquivel, San Francisco	.313	.379	.626	163	13	1	12	48	1
Bean, Brady, Portland	.310	.410	.493	213	12	0	9	48	11
Zion Williams, LMU	.310	.381	.478	184	13	0	6	39	21
Jared Mettam, Saint Mary's	.309	.419	.436	204	14	0	4	41	13
John-Howard Bobo, Pacific	.306	.417	.398	108	4	0	2	15	8
Jake Tandy, Pacific	.304	.370	.440	184	10	0	5	26	1
Cleary, Ben, Santa Clara	.302	.406	.401	182	12	0	2	16	5
Nitowitz, Cody, Portland	.300	.423	.344	160	5	1	0	12	4
Nate Savoie, LMU	.300	.454	.687	203	14	1	20	61	7
Cody Kashimoto, Saint Mary's	.295	.425	.386	210	7	0	4	24	16
Drake Bicknell, Pacific	.295	.361	.410	139	7	0	3	31	2
Smith, Jayden, UVU	.396	.504	.517	207	17	4	0	42	14
Payne, Zandt, ACU	.376	.490	.550	149	12	1	4	39	10
Ryan Kroepel, UTU	.367	.442	.546	207	15	2	6	35	4
Kyle McDaniel, UTU	.367	.464	.481	210	10	1	4	21	10
Strong, Mason, UVU	.366	.432	.609	238	19	3	11	67	12
Nick Dumesnil, CBU	.360	.442	.598	239	21	3	10	57	27
Barreras, Emilio, GCU	.358	.462	.484	159	11	0	3	31	3
McCloud, Slade, TSU	.358	.415	.541	218	12	2	8	45	20
Guerra, Sergio, TSU	.354	.439	.729	144	14	2	12	42	4
Pimentel-Guerrero, L, SAC	.351	.475	.479	194	14	1	3	37	4
Chris Ramirez, CBU	.350	.424	.414	203	9	2	0	29	7
Wakefield, Josh, GCU	.349	.436	.405	195	8	0	1	21	18
Yorke, Zach, GCU	.339	.447	.632	174	10	1	13	46	0
Bubba Rocha, GCU	.333	.462	.474	156	13	0	3	26	7
X. Melendez, UTA	.330	.386	.536	194	8	1	10	45	1
Aaron Perez, UTU	.330	.408	.492	191	7	0	8	42	0
Cardenas, Diego, ACU	.328	.454	.687	198	14	1	20	61	7
Andrew Walters, CBU	.325	.468	.544	169	8	1	9	41	5
C. Dodson, UTA	.324	.387	.479	213	16	1	5	28	16
Shirey, Ike, TSU	.319	.422	.436	188	4	3	4	38	13
T. Armstrong, UTA	.319	.415	.556	207	13	0	12	46	0
Ishikawa, Kenny, SU	.318	.420	.562	201	23	1	8	32	0
White, Tyler, SAC	.318	.418	.466	236	13	5	4	43	10
Peery, Cannon, GCU	.317	.381	.479	167	16	1	3	38	2
Heinrich, Rayner, TSU	.314	.394	.515	204	19	2	6	38	9
Portunak, Jakob, SAC	.309	.357	.541	233	13	1	13	52	0
Perazzo, Michael, SAC	.308	.376	.391	169	8	0	2	28	4
Perez, Jaime, TSU	.306	.422	.388	170	5	0	3	36	9
Dominic Longo II, UVU	.306	.397	.537	242	17	3	11	60	22

INDIVIDUAL PITCHING LEADERS

	W	L	ERA	G	SV	IP	H	BB	SO
Reddemann, Logan, San Diego	3	1	1.22	9	0	59	44	10	57
Erik Hoffberg, Gonzaga	2	4	4.00	0	7	54	45	24	71
Scolari, Cal, San Diego	5	3	4.22	15	0	70	54	39	77
Bayles, Max, Santa Clara	3	6	4.45	11	1	67	60	31	105
Avery Laine, Lmu	5	1	4.81	13	0	67	78	29	58
Dylan Delvecchio, Saint Mary's	7	3	4.90	14	0	79	69	31	87
Rembisz, Ryan, Portland	4	4	4.93	12	1	73	73	15	58
Gabriel Barrett, San Francisco	1	3	4.97	10	0	58	67	27	59
Aidan Risse, San Francisco	5	3	5.25	13	0	70	81	26	59
Smith, Austin, San Diego	7	5	5.26	5	4	63	52	39	56
Scavone, Tommy, Pepperdine	1	5	5.37	12	0	57	58	21	47
Segel, Kaden, Portland	4	4	5.37	6	3	62	73	14	53
Finbar O'Brien, Gonzaga	6	1	5.78	11	0	72	75	31	83
Gomez, Brandon, Santa Clara	3	8	5.81	12	0	70	69	34	71
Stewart,Dylan, Pepperdine	1	4	6.31	13	0	56	62	28	46
Kenji Pallares, Lmu	3	5	6.34	14	0	65	70	35	80
Miles Gosztola, Gonzaga	5	8	6.40	15	0	77	100	30	74
Jakob Guardado, Pacific	2	3	6.60	8	0	59	66	20	40
Gaston, Carter, Portland	3	8	6.61	13	0	67	80	24	57
Joe Soberon, San Francisco	2	5	6.86	9	0	62	61	35	34
Adan Perez, Pacific	4	5	6.98	13	0	68	85	38	56
Justin Feld, Gonzaga	3	5	7.29	11	0	54	59	27	38
Littledike, Cooper, UVU	3	1	2.27	4	0	63	32	28	12 30
Cade Montgomery, UTU	4	2	2.35	10	0	57	46	19	48
Brown, Kade, SAC	3	2	2.93	0	14	43	32	20	49
Reid, Dominick, ACU	6	3	3.26	15	0	88	71	27	112
Quinn, Walter, GCU	2	5	3.46	0	11	39	31	24	40
Cody New, CBU	6	3	3.49	15	1	80	65	31	98
Lay, Ethan, SAC	5	3	3.55	13	0	76	78	16	66
Hagler, Micah, SU	3	3	3.66	9	1	59	72	12	35
Panneton, Brian, TSU	6	3	3.69	14	0	78	85	16	65
C. Dygert, UTA	7	4	4.04	15	0	85	97	15	61
C. Noah, UTA	1	4	4.06	4	5	38	31	15	46
Lyon, Isaac, GCU	3	4	4.19	15	0	86	101	23	88
Gibbons, Evan, SAC	10	2	4.19	15	0	88	91	23	63
Ishikawa, Kenny, SU	5	6	4.21	9	1	66	82	22	73
Higginbottom, Elijah, GCU	6	0	4.32	1	1	50	58	9	42
Ryan Kittredge, CBU	4	4	4.62	11	0	76	59	34	54
Dakoda West, UTU	3	6	4.64	12	0	64	63	27	38
Andrew Rudd, CBU	2	2	4.68	7	3	67	71	11	55
Benson, Chandler, ACU	3	1	4.69	4	1	63	65	17	50
Monson, Andrew, SAC	2	2	4.91	0	2	33	36	13	28
Madariaga, Reid, SU	2	2	4.98	2	2	47	54	26	53
Tyler Ray, UTU	3	2	5.05	3	0	52	48	34	40
Ryan Martinez, UTU	2	4	5.08	14	0	83	102	19	57
Stewart, Tyler, SAC	1	4	5.10	11	0	42	42	10	40
Hardin, Andrew, TSU	0	3	5.22	0	2	29	27	20	32
Mattison, Connor, GCU	2	1	5.40	5	1	33	38	10	41
T. Zahradnik, UTA	1	3	5.40	0	2	32	40	14	41
N. Robb, UTA	4	6	5.54	15	0	80	109	20	32
J. Orozco, CBU	2	3	5.54	2	1	39	42	26	45
Lucchesi, Noah, SAC	5	2	5.56	0	1	34	38	10	44
Cameron Teper, CBU	4	6	5.66	6	1	41	46	20	37
Jaques, Ethan, TSU	4	0	5.71	0	1	35	40	10	29
Kirk, Corbin, UVU	5	4	5.74	16	0	78	96	32	69
J. Steeber, UTA	4	5	5.75	12	0	72	95	21	41
Olson, Tyler, TSU	3	2	5.79	5	0	28	40	9	19
Burcham, Jake, TSU	3	6	5.83	15	0	66	92	19	47
Jacob Wilson, CBU	2	3	5.86	8	2	35	47	13	40
Herman, Carston, UVU	5	4	5.87	1	2	61	59	32	57
Lucas, Aden, TSU	3	2	6.08	0	1	37	42	19	22
Latimer, Carson, SAC	2	3	6.14	7	0	37	41	26	28
McGarrh, Cade, ACU	4	5	6.19	15	0	77	84	30	70

WESTERN ATHLETIC CONFERENCE

	Conference W	L	Overall W	L
Sacramento State	15	9	32	26
Abilene Christian	15	9	34	23
Utah Valley	13	11	33	29
Grand Canyon	13	11	31	27
California Baptist	12	12	30	27
Tarleton State	12	12	24	32
UT Arlington	11	13	21	33
Utah Tech	9	15	24	31
Seattle U	8	16	20	32

ALL-CONFERENCE TEAM: SP: Dominick Reid, Jr., Abilene Christian; **SP**: Cody New, So., California Baptist; Evan Gibbons, Sr., Sacramento State. **RP:** Kade Brown, R-So., Sacramento State. **C:** Mason Strong, R-Jr., Utah Valley. **1B:** JP Smith, Jr., Sacramento State. **2B:** Slade McCloud, Sr., Tarleton State. **3B:** Ryan Kroepel, So., Utah Tech. **SS:** Zandt Payne, Sr., Abilene Christian; Chris Ramirez, Fr., California Baptist. **OF:** Nick Dumesnil, Jr., California Baptist; Luis Pimentel-Guerrero, Jr., Sacramento State; Jayden Smith, Sr., Utah Valley. **DH/UTL**: Kenny Ishikawa, So., Seattle U.

Player of the Year: Nick Dumesnil, Jr., OF, California Baptist. **Pitcher of the Year:** Evan Gibbons, Sr., RHP, Sacramento State. **Freshman of the Year**: Chris Ramirez, SS, California Baptist. **Defensive Player of the Year:** Chris Ramirez, Fr., SS, California Baptist. **Coach of the Year:** Reggie Christiansen, Sacramento State.

SMALL COLLEGES

NCAA DIVISION II

After cruising through the regular season, Tampa managed to survive to win its second straight D-II title.

Tampa lost its second game in the World Series, which meant that it had to claw its way through the loser's bracket. That meant that to win the title, Tampa needed to play seven games in seven days.

Somehow the Spartans found enough pitching, beating Central Missouri 11-5 in the deciding Game 3 of the championship series.

It gave Tampa and head coach Joe Urso back-to-back national titles. The Spartans were the preseason No. 1 team, and they carried that ranking through the year, winning a school record 55 games.

Tampa now has 10 national titles, including seven since 2000. They are the only school with 10 D-II titles.

DIVISION II WORLD SERIES
Site: Cary, N.C.
Participants: 1. Tampa. 2. Central Missouri. 3. Lenoir-Rhyne (N.C.). 4. UT Tyler. 5. Northwest Nazarene (Calif.). 6. East Stroudsburg (Pa.). 7. Northwood (Mich.). 8. Felcian (N.J.).
Champion: Tampa.
Runner-up: Cemtral Missiouri.

LEADERS: BATTING AVERAGE
(Minimum 140 at bats)

Rk. Player, Pos., Team	Class	AVG	OBP	SLG
1. Cameron Cartwright, Colorado Mesa	Jr.	.468	.558	.968
2. Adam Paniagua, Regis (Colo.)	Sr.	.448	.534	.970
3. Kendal Spencer, Savannah St.	Sr.	.446	.568	.662
4. Andrew Graham, MSU Denver	Jr.	.446	.537	.832
5. Noah Blythe, Hawaii Pacific	So.	.443	.508	.788
6. Christian Castaneda, CSU Pueblo	Sr.	.443	.544	.770
7. Jack Hines, Augustana (SD)	Sr.	.441	.502	.629
8. Jacob Houtz, Mansfield	Sr.	.439	.552	.856
9. Thomas Matuszewski, Jefferson	Fr.	.438	.534	.744
10. Cole Fowler, Lynn	Sr.	.438	.472	.810

EARNED RUN AVERAGE
(Minimum 40 innings pitched)

Rk. Pitcher, Team	Class	W	L	ERA
1. James Sill, Molloy	So.	5	2	1.52
2. Ian Korn, Seton Hill	Jr.	11	2	1.81
3. Dax Sharp, Central Okla.	Sr.	7	2	1.88
4. Dawson Montesa, Adelphi	So.	8	1	1.99
5. Ernesto Lugo-Canchola, NW Nazarene	Sr.	13	0	2.00
6. Miles Justin, Spring Hill	Sr.	7	2	2.08
7. Jake Nightingale, Purdue Northwest	Sr.	3	2	2.09
8. JJ Arbini, Saginaw Valley	Sr.	7	3	2.10
9. Sam Schmitt, Salem (WV)	Sr.	6	4	2.13
10. Maddox Long, Harding	Sr.	11	3	2.16

CATEGORY LEADERS: BATTING
*Minimum 140 at bats

Dept.	Player, Pos., Team	Class	G	Total
OBP*	Juan Guardado, Benedict	Jr.	38	.628
SLG*	Adam Paniagua, Regis (Colo.)	Jr.	51	.970
R	Mackenzie Wainwright, Lenoir-Rhyne	So.	65	102
H	Mackenzie Wainwright, Lenoir-Rhyne	So.	65	121
2B	Luke Hatcher, Young Harris	Sr.	57	28
3B	Josh Sharp, USC Aiken	Sr.	52	12
HR	Easton Amundson, MSU Denver	Sr.	57	34
RBI	Adam Paniagua, Regis (Colo.)	Sr.	51	100
SB	Jordan Williams, Tampa	Sr.	63	81

CATEGORY LEADERS: PITCHING
*Minimum 40 innings

Dept.	Pitcher, Team	Class	Total
W	C.J. Williams, Tampa	Sr.	15
SV	Hayden Simmersen, Catawba	Sr.	17
G	Hayden Simmersen, Catawba	Sr.	31
GS	Skylar Gonzalez, Tampa	Sr.	19
SO	Andrew Harlow, Lenoir-Rhyne	Sr.	125
SO/9*	Kolby Dougan, Pittsburg State	Sr.	13.81
BB/9*	Cade Barton, Emporia State	Sr.	0.42
WHIP*	Kolby Dougan, Pittsburg State	Sr.	0.87

NCAA Division III

In 2024, Wisconsin-Whitewater fell one win short of a national title. They responded in 2025 by making sure that they eliminated any drama or doubt.

The Warhawks trounced Messiah (Pa.) 18-3 in Game 1 and 21-5 in Game 2 of the College World Series championship series. The Warhawks had also won 17-4 to advance to the finals. They won every game at the CWS by four or more runs.

Adam Cootway was named the Most Outstanding Player. He hit .615 with 10 RBIS and 12 runs scored while hitting four home runs and two triples.

Wisconsin-Whitewater set an NCAA record with 75 runs scored in the CWS. It was the school's third national title and first since 2014.

DIVISION III WORLD SERIES
Site: Eastlake, Ohio.
Participants: 1. John Hopkins (Md.). 2. Deinson (Ohio). 3. Wisconsin-Whitewater. 4. Endicott (Mass.). 5. Kean (N.J.). 6. Trinity (Texas). 7. Rowan (N.J.). 8. Messiah (Pa.).
Champion: Wisconsin-Whitewater.
Runner-up: Messiah (Pa.).

LEADERS: BATTING AVERAGE
(Minimum 120 at bats)

RK. Player, Pos., Team	Class	AVG	OBP	SLG
1. Andrew Mazzone, Claremont-M-S	Sr.	.496	.623	.979
2. James Domer, Pitt.-Greensburg	Jr.	.496	.554	.815
3. Liam Daly, Purchase	Jr.	.496	.555	.803
4. Ethan Tuttle, Spalding	Sr.	.494	.564	.708
5. Alex Trinh, St. Thomas (TX)	Jr.	.476	.524	.687
6. Kanta Ueno, Houghton	Sr.	.464	.538	.618
7. Joseph Cocozza, Baruch	Sr.	.459	.540	.730
8. Joel Kennedy, Manchester	Jr.	.453	.524	.615
9. Mac Ciocco, Penn St.-Behrend	Sr.	.452	.527	.611
10. Hunter Strong, Spalding	Sr.	.452	.559	.845

EARNED RUN AVERAGE
(Minimum 30 innings pitched)

Rk. Pitcher, Team	Class	W	L	ERA
1. Nolan Romanowski, Salve Regina	Fr.	5	1	0.57
2. Dante DiMatteo, Wash. & Jeff.	Sr.	9	0	0.83
3. Nolan Reiman, Millikin	Fr.	1	2	1.39
4. Jackson Malouf, TCNJ	Sr.	8	2	1.52
5. Cam Scholl, Macalester	Sr.	5	3	1.62

6. Jackson Dorsey, Coast Guard	So.	2	0	1.69
7. Drew Grumbles, Johns Hopkins	So.	8	0	1.75
8. Matt Forrest, St. Scholastica	Sr.	6	4	1.75
9. Kolton Banfi, Westminster (PA)	Sr.	5	1	1.79
10. Brayden Clark, Salve Regina	Sr.	11	2	1.81

CATEGORY LEADERS: BATTING
*Minimum 120 at bats

Dept.	Player, Pos., Team	Class	G	Total
OBP*	Andrew Mazzone, Claremont-M-S	Sr.	42	.623
SLG*	Harry Genth, Haverford	Sr.	39	1.034
R	Matt Scolan, Wisconsin-Whitewater	Sr.	55	82
H	Aaron Holland, Wisconsin-Whitewater	So.	54	94
2B	Justin Gadomski, Ill. Wesleyan	Sr.	44	26
	Evan Taylor, Buena Vista	Sr.	44	26
3B	Carter Betts, Neb. Wesleyan	Sr.	46	12
HR	Harry Genth, Haverford	Sr.	39	23
RBI	Erik Sundgren, Denison	Jr.	48	81
SB	Joey Dwyer, SUNY Oneonta	Sr.	43	48

CATEGORY LEADERS: PITCHING
*Minimum 30 innings

Dept.	Pitcher, Team	Class	Total
W	Jason Gilman, Kean	Sr.	14
SV	Joel Arsenault, Webster	Sr.	12
GS	Kyle Molivas, Methodist	Sr.	16
SO	Jason Gilman, Kean	Sr.	150
SO/9*	Alex Kuntz, Concordia Wisconsin	So.	15.35
BB/9*	Chase Burrows, Babson	Fr.	0.38
WHIP*	Nolan Romanowski, Salve Regina	Fr.	0.70

NAIA

LSU Shreveport completed arguably the best season in college baseball history, winning the NAIA World Series without a blemish to cap off an unprecedented 59-0 season.

It was the Piots' first national title in any sport. Shreveport pitcher Isaac Rohde was named the tournament MVP.

NAIA WORLD SERIES
Site: Lewiston, Idaho.
Participants: 1. LSU Shreveport. 2. Georgia Gwinett. 3. Tennessee Wesleyan. 4. Hope International (Calif.). 5. Webber International (Fla.). 6. Southeastern (Fla.). 7. Cumberlands (Ky.). 8. Loyola (La.). 9. British Columbia. 10. Grand View (Iowa).
Champion: LSU Shreveport
Runner-up: Hope International (Calf.).
All-Americans: C: Charlie Muniz, Cumberlands (Ky.); Daniel Stewart, Tennessee Wesleyan. **1B:** Miguel Oropeza, Talladega (Ala.). **2B:** Braxton Meguiar, Georgia Gwinnett. **3B:** Josh Gibson, LSU Shreveport (La.). **SS:** Alfonso Villalobos, Southeastern (Fla.). **INF:** Brayden McGinnis, Columbia (Mo.). **OF:** Alex Harrell, Georgia Gwinnett; Simon Grinberg, Keiser (Fla.); James Jett, Missouri Baptist; Kolton Reynolds, Tennessee Wesleyan. **DH:** Scott Seeker, Georgia Gwinnett. **RP:** Noah Palmese, Webber International (Fla.). **SP:** Trey Seeley, Hope International (Calif.); Isaac Rohde, LSU Shreveport (La.); Draven Zeigler, LSU Shreveport (La.); Blayne Huter, Webber International (Fla.).

LEADERS: BATTING AVERAGE
(Minimum 120 at bats)

RK. Player, Team	AVG	OBP	SLG
1. McGinnis, Brayden, Columbia (MO)	.466	.524	.933
2. Jett, James, Missouri Baptist	.451	.547	.903
2. Broekemeier, Erik, Grand View	.451	.506	.704
4. Romero, Fabian, Northwestern Ohio	.442	.572	.533
5. Chang, Aidan, Mount Marty	.440	.546	.769

EARNED RUN AVERAGE
(Minimum 40 innings pitched)

Rk. Pitcher, Team	W	L	ERA
1. Trey Seeley, Hope International	12	1	1.72
2. Draven Zeigler, LSU Shreveport (La.)	13	0	1.76
3. Andrew Herbert, Reinhardt (Ga.)	12	0	1.88
4. Aaron Robertson, Southeastern (Fla.)	11	2	1.99
5. Owen Clark, Columbia (Mo.)	9	0	1.99

CATEGORY LEADERS: BATTING
*Minimum 140 at bats

Dept.	Player, Pos., Team	Class	G	Total
OBP*	Tyler Favretto, Kansas Wesleyan	Jr.	56	.579
SLG*	Charlie Muniz, Cumberlands (Ky.)	Sr.	62	.970
HR	Charlie Muniz, Cumberlands (Ky.)	Sr.	62	36
RBI	Charlie Muniz, Cumberlands (Ky.)	Sr.	62	961
SB	Jon Ponder, Georgia Gwinnett	Sr..	60	65

CATEGORY LEADERS: PITCHING

Dept.	Pitcher, Team	Class	Total
W	Isaac Rohde, LSU Shreveport	Sr.	13
SV	Noah Palmese, Webber International (Fla.)	Sr.	13
IP	Isaac Rohde, LSU Shreveport	Sr.	120
SO	Isaac Rohde, LSU Shreveport	Sr.	146

NJCAA Division I

Salt Lake (Utah) JC won three straight elimination games and then knocked off No. 1 seed Walters State (Tenn.) JC 9-6 in the championship game to win its first ever national title.

NJCAA DIVISION I WORLD SERIES
Site: Grand Junction, Colo.
Participants: 1. Walters State (Tenn.) JC. 2. Blinn (Texas) JC. 3. Florida Southwestern JC. 4. Johnson County (Kan.) JC. 5. Shelton State (Ala.). 6. Florence Darlington Tech (S.C.) JC. 7. McLennan (Texas) JC. 8. Salt Lake (Utah) JC. 9. Lake Land (Ill.) JC. 10. Eastern Okla. State JC.
Champion: Salt Lake (Utah) J.C.
Runner-up: Walters State (Tenn.) JC.

LEADERS: BATTING AVERAGE
Minimum 140 at bats)

RK. Player, Pos., Team	Class	AVG	OBP	SLG
1. Tyler Myatt, Walters State (Tenn.)	So.	.484	.583	1.014
2. Caleb Rhodes, Olive-Harvey (Ill.)	Fr.	.464	.591	.679
3. Brendan Brock, Southwestern Ill.	So.	.462	.565	.870
4. Isiah Padilla, Colby (Kan.)	So.	.458	.552	.869
5. Jack Barker, Southern Idaho	So.	.456	.543	.750

EARNED RUN AVERAGE
(Minimum 40 innings pitched)

Rk. Pitcher, Team	Class	W	L	ERA
1. Evan Brandt, Weatherford (Texas)	So.	14	1	1.88
2. Garett Blanchard, Bossier Parish (La.)	So.	5	2	1.92
3. Kai Fyke, Central Arizona	Fr.	4	2	2.07
4. Caleb Reed, Kansas City (Kan.)	So.	9	0	2.16
5. Giancarlos Arencibia, Delgado (La.)	Fr.	5	2	2.22

CATEGORY LEADERS: BATTING
*Minimum 140 at bats

Dept. Pos., Team	Player, Class	G	Total
OBP*	Caleb Rhodes, Olive-Harvey (Ill.)	Fr.	38	.591
SLG*	Tyler Myatt, Walters State (Tenn.)	So.	66	1.014
HR	Tyler Myatt, Walters State (Tenn.)	So.	66	31
RBI	Tyler Myatt, Walters State (Tenn.)	So.	66	110
SB	Sam Robertson, NW-Shoals (Ala.)	So.	55	60

CATEGORY LEADERS: PITCHING

Dept.	Pitcher, Team	Class	Total
W	Evan Brandt, Weatherford (Texas)	So.	14
SV	Darius Henderson, Salt Lake (Utah)	Fr.	12
IP	Evan Brandt, Weatherford (Texas)	So.	91
SO	Aiden Robertson, Walters State (Tenn.)	So.	130

NJCAA Division II

Trailing by four runs heading into the seventh, Pasco-Hernando (Fla.) JC got a grand slam from Grant Jordan followed by a second grand slam from Brandon Durfee to come from behind to knock off Pearl River (Miss.) JC 11-7 in the Division II national championship game. The win was Pasco-Hernando's first national title.

NJCAA DIVISION II WORLD SERIES
Site: Enid, Okla.
Participants: 1. Pasco-Hernando (Fla.) JC. 2. Pearl River (Miss.) JC. 3. South Mountain (Ariz.) JC. 4. Heartland (Ill.). 5. Madison (Wisc.). 6. East Central (Miss.). 7. Southeastern (Iowa). 8. Frederick (Md.). 9. Iowa Central. 10. Kellogg (Mich.). 11. Catawba Valley (N.C.). 12. Lackawanna (Penn.)
Champion: Pasco-Hernando (Fla.).
Runner-up: Pearl River (Miss.)

LEADERS: BATTING AVERAGE
(Minimum 120 at bats)

RK.	Player, Pos., Team	Class	AVG	OBP	SLG
1.	Austin Haley, Murray State (Okla.)	Fr.	.503	.594	.857
2.	Ian McCubbin, South Arkansas	Fr.	.467	.585	.820
3.	Joey Bruno, Lansing (Mich.)	So.	.460	.537	.708
4.	Spencer Mounce, Ark. State Mountain Home	So.	.481	.481	.746
5.	Byson Arthur, Edison State (Ohio)	So.	.469	.469	.755

EARNED RUN AVERAGE
(Minimum 40 innings pitched)

Rk.	Pitcher, Team	Class	W	L	ERA
1.	Josh Caccia, Eglin (Ill.)	So.	10	0	1.27
2.	Nick Falla, Allegany JC of Maryland	Fr.	10	2	1.33
3.	Peyton Niksch, Kankakee (Ill.)	So.	8	2	1.36
4.	Michael Savarese, Pasco-Hernando (Fla.)	So.	14	0	1.71
5.	Cole Martz, Kankakee (Ill.)	So.	6	0	1.75

CATEGORY LEADERS: BATTING
*Minimum 120 at bats

Dept.	Player, Pos., Team	Class	G	Total
OBP*	Ausitn Haley, Murray State (Okla.)	Fr.	53	.594
SLG*	Blade Carver, Northern Okla. JC-Tonkawa	So.	58	.898
HR	Blade Carver, Northern Okla. JC-Tonkawa	So.	58	23
RBI	Jake Busson, Iowa Central	So.	65	87
SB	Clay Thompson, Pasco-Hernando (Fla.)	Fr.	62	58

CATEGORY LEADERS: PITCHING

Dept.	Pitcher, Team	Class	Total
W	Michael Savarese, Pasco-Hernando (Fla.)	So.	14
SV	N Sturdivant, Copiah-Lincoln (Miss.)	Fr.	9
IP	Blake Lobell, LSU Eunice	So.	102
SO	Michael Savarese, Pasco-Hernando (Fla.)	So.	144

NJCAA Division III

Rowan Gloucester (N.J.) JC beat Century (Minn.) JC 16-1 to win its 10th NJCAA World Series title and its thrid in a row. This is back-to-back titles for the Roadrunners.

RJ Mustaro was named the World Series MVP.

NJCAA DIVISION III WORLD SERIES
Site: Auburn, N.Y.
Participants: 1. SUNY Niagara JC 2. Rowan Gloucester (N.J.) JC. 3. Brookdale (N.J.) JC. 4. Dallas-Richland (Texas) JC. 5. Northern Essex (Mass.) JC. 6. Surry (N.C.) JC. 7. Oakton (Ill.) JC. 8. Century (Minn.) JC
Champion: Rowan Gloucester (N.J.).
Runner-up: Century (Minn).

LEADERS: BATTING AVERAGE
(Minimum 120 at bats)

RK.	Player, Pos., Team	Class	AVG	OBP	SLG
1.	Hayden Frank, St. Cloud (Minn.)	So.	.514	.609	.740
2.	RJ Mustaro, Rowan (N.J.)	So	.503	.584	.849
3.	Mason Johnson, Terra State (Ohio)	Fr.	.494	.584	.963
4.	Jaxon Kenning, Minnesota North-Itasca	Fr.	.492	.582	.828
5.	Jameson Balich, Hudson Valley (N.Y.)	Fr.	.492	.616	.831

EARNED RUN AVERAGE
(Minimum 40 innings pitched)

Rk.	Pitcher, Team	Class	W	L	ERA
1.	Dylan Kinney, Jamestown (N.Y)	So.	1	3	0.89
2.	Brendan Ruscnack, Herkimer (N.Y.)	Fr.	7	0	1.57
3.	Michael Jayylo, Nassau (N.Y.)	Fr.	4	0	1.72
4.	Matt Barr, SUNY Niagara	Fr.	10	0	1.74
5.	Yamato Onozaki, Genesee (N.Y.)	So.	3	2	1.93

California Junior Colleges

Terell Jackson Jr. singled in the go-ahead run and a Ty Thomas' two-run single gave Mt. San Antonio (Calif.) JC some insurance, as the Mounties held on to beat West Valley (Calif.) JC 8-5 in 13 innings to win the California Community College state title.

CALIFORNIA CC ATHLETIC ASSOCIATION
Site: Walnut.
Participants: Mt. San Antonio (Calif.) JC, West Valley (Calif.) JC, Sierra (Calif.) JC, Cypress (Calif.) JC
Champion: Mt. San Antonio (Calif.) JC
Runner-up: West Valley (Calif.) JC.

LEADERS: BATTING AVERAGE
(Minimum 140 at bats)

RK.	Player, Pos., Team	AVG	OBP	SLG
1.	Landon White, Mt. San Antonio	.481	.537	.705
2.	Kai Smith, Los Medanos	.478	.504	.748
3.	Ryder Young, Chaffey	.447	.515	.807
4.	Will Anderson, Ohlone	.446	.545	.802
5.	Leonardo Veliz, Imperial Valley	.439	.491	.658

EARNED RUN AVERAGE
(Minimum 40 innings pitched)

Rk.	Pitcher, Team	W	L	ERA
1.	Luke Schat, Santa Rosa	8	1	0.71
2.	Joseph Talarico, Santa Barbara	9	2	1.46
3.	Nolan Patterson, Cerritos	10	1	1.48
4.	Derek Valdez, Cerritos	12	3	1.63
5.	Raul Valdivia, Santa Rosa	3	1	1.69

COLLEGE SUMMER BASEBALL

COLLEGIATE NATIONAL TEAM STATS

INTERNATIONAL FRIENDSHIP SERIES

Year indicates 2024-25 class standing

Player, Pos.	Year	School	AVG	OBP	SLG	G	AB	R	H	2B	3B	HR	RBI	BB	SO	SB
Chris Rembert, INF	Fr.	Auburn	.278	.278	.333	4	18	1	5	1	0	0	2	0	1	2
A.J. Gracia, OF	So.	Virginia	.263	.333	.368	5	19	2	5	2	0	0	1	2	5	0
Zion Rose, OF	So.	Louisville	.250	.400	.250	5	16	3	4	0	0	0	2	2	4	3
Ace Reeese, INF/OF	Fr.	Mississippi St.	.250	.357	.333	4	12	0	3	1	0	0	1	2	3	1
Vahn Lackey, C	So.	Georgia Tech	.250	.333	.625	4	8	1	2	0	0	1	1	1	1	1
Drew Burress, OF	So.	Georgia Tech	.231	.375	.385	4	13	1	3	2	0	0	1	2	7	1
Eric Becker, INF/OF	So.	Virginia	.222	.300	.222	5	18	1	4	0	0	0	1	2	8	1
Tyler Bell, INF	Fr.	Kentucky	.222	.385	.222	3	9	1	2	0	0	0	1	2	5	0
Lucas Moore, OF	So.	Louisville	.167	.167	.250	3	12	1	2	1	0	0	0	0	4	0
Mulivai Levu, INF	So.	UCLA	.143	.250	.214	4	14	0	2	1	0	0	0	1	6	0
Roch Cholowsky, INF	So.	UCLA	.059	.111	.235	5	17	1	1	0	0	1	1	1	9	0
Ryder Helfrick, C	So.	Arkansas	.000	.100	.000	3	8	0	0	0	0	0	1	1	4	0

Pitcher, Pos.	Year	School	W	L	ERA	G	SV	IP	H	R	ER	BB	SO	AVG
Ricky Ojeda	So.	UC Irvine	0	0	0.00	3	0	4	0	0	0	3	9	.000
Blake Morningstar	So.	Wake Forest	0	1	0.00	2	0	3	5	3	0	2	4	.333
Jacob Dudan	So.	N.C. State	0	0	0.00	2	0	3	1	0	0	0	1	.125
Jason DeCaro	So.	North Carolina	0	0	0.00	1	0	3	2	0	0	0	2	.222
Liam Peterson	So.	Florida	0	0	0.00	1	0	1	2	0	0	0	0	.400
Dax Whitney	Fr.	Oregon State	0	1	2.08	1	0	4	5	2	1	1	4	.294
Brett Renfrow	Fr.	Auburn	0	1	3.00	1	0	3	5	2	1	1	3	.357
Ethan Norby	So.	ECU	0	0	3.60	2	0	5	8	2	2	0	6	.381
Ryan McPherson	So.	Mississippi St.	0	0	6.00	2	0	3	4	2	2	2	3	.333
Gabe Gaeckle	So.	Arkansas	0	0	6.75	2	0	1	5	1	1	2	2	.556
Ryan Marohn	So.	N.C. State	0	0	9.00	1	0	2	4	2	2	1	2	.400
Ryan Lynch	Fr.	North Carolina	0	1	10.80	2	0	3	5	4	4	0	2	.313
Ethan Kleinschmit	So.	Oregon State	0	0	13.50	1	0	3	4	4	3	3	3	.364
Cole Gibler	Fr.	Arkansas	0	0	14.73	2	0	4	6	6	6	2	6	.333

Team USA Swept By Japan In Friendly Series

The 2025 summer friendship series against Japan is not one that the Collegiate National Team will want to remember.

For the first time since 2004, Team USA went winless in a five-game series against Japan.

This was the 45th edition of the U.S. vs. Japan All-Star Series. Stretching back to 1983, this is only the third time ever that Team USA has gone winless in a series against Japan.

Team USA's bats were baffled by Japan's pitching. Team USA struck out 57 times over the five games, and hit only .201/.289/.287 as a team. Roch Cholowsky, expected to be the No. 1 pick in the 2026 MLB draft, hit .059/.111/.235.

But the pitching also struggled for the U.S. Team USA's ERA was 4.90, and Japan hit .318 as a team.

Dax Whitney (2.08 ERA) allowed only one run in 4.1 innings, but five different U.S. relievers posted ERAs of 6.00 or higher.

COLLEGE SUMMER LEAGUES

For players who played for multiple teams: 1: Stats with first team. 2: Stats with second team. 3: Stats with third team. T: combined stats.

CAPE COD LEAGUE

ECCBL East	W	L	T	PTS
#-Orleans	24	12	4	52
@-Harwich	20	20	0	40
@-Brewster	16	24	0	32
@-Yarmouth-Dennis	15	25	0	30
Chatham	13	25	2	28

CCBL West	W	L	T	PTS
#-Bourne	24	14	2	50
@-Wareham	22	17	1	45
@-Cotuit	22	17	1	45
@-Hyannis	21	16	3	45
Falmouth	16	23	1	33

#-Clinched Division @-Clinched Playoff Berth

PLAYOFFS: First Round: Bourne defeated Hyannis 2-1; Yarmouth-Dennis defeated Orleans 2-0; Harwich defeated Brewster 2-1 and Cotuit defeated Wareham 2-0 best-of-3 series. **Semifinals:** Bourne defeated Cotuit 2-1 and Yarmouth-Dennis defeated Harwich 2-1 in best-of-3 series. **Finals:** Bourne defeated Yarmouth-Dennis 2-0 in best-of-three championship series.

MOST VALUABLE PLAYER: Maika Niu, OF, Falmouth. **OUTSTANDING PITCHER:** Tyler Pitzer, Yarmouth-Dennis. **OUTSTANDING RELIEF PITCHER:** Steele Murdock, Orleans. **OUTSTANDING PRO PROSPECT:** Jarren Advincula, 2B, Cotuit. **PLAYOFF MVP:** Jon LeGrande, OF, Bourne. **MANAGER OF THE YEAR:** Kelly Nicholson, Orleans.

INDIVIDUAL BATTING LEADERS

Player, Team	AVG	AB	R	H	2B	3B	HR	RBI	SB
Aiden Robbins, HAR	.307	101	16	31	6	0	6	14	2
Chase Krewson, WAR	.306	98	12	30	6	0	0	8	12
Ryan McKay, HYA	.300	130	12	39	7	0	0	10	8
Alejandro Garza, ORL	.298	114	5	34	3	0	1	16	2
Camden Johnson, COT	.292	144	24	42	7	1	0	11	18
Jon LeGrande, BOU	.288	132	23	38	8	1	0	16	21
Ryker Waite, BOU	.287	108	26	31	4	2	2	17	13
Kent Schmidt, FAL	.287	129	12	37	6	0	2	24	6
Braden Holcomb, BOU	.285	137	15	39	6	0	0	17	11
Carl Schmidt, FAL	.284	141	26	40	9	0	1	14	6

INDIVIDUAL PITCHING LEADERS

Player, Team	W	L	ERA	G	SV	IP	H	BB	SO
Tyler Pitzer, Y-D	3	0	0.34	8	0	26	15	9	36
Josh Butler, WAR	1	1	1.03	8	0	26	17	12	23
Cole Tryba, ORL	3	0	1.07	11	1	25	21	7	28
Brady Hamilton, Y-D	2	1	1.48	7	0	30	25	5	22
Ryan Oshinskie, ORL	1	1	1.93	13	1	28	20	7	38
Wyatt Halvorson, COT	1	1	1.95	11	0	28	15	21	26
Matthew Shorey, BOU	2	1	2.37	8	0	30	23	13	30
Troy Dressler, HAR	2	1	2.39	6	0	26	22	10	25
Cooper Consiglio, WAR	1	1	2.55	6	0	25	18	11	21
Gianni Gambardella, HAR	2	1	2.55	6	0	25	21	8	13

BOURNE

Batting	AVG	AB	R	H	2B	3B	HR	RBI	SB
Sefcik, C	.400	60	9	24	2	0	0	7	2
Aloy, K	.333	54	13	18	3	0	2	13	0
Neels, W	.303	33	4	10	3	0	0	3	1
Mexico, S	.300	10	1	3	1	0	0	4	1
LeGrande, J	.288	132	23	38	8	1	0	16	21
Waite, R	.287	108	26	31	4	2	2	17	13
Holcomb, B	.285	137	15	39	6	0	0	17	11
Kelly, G	.277	94	10	26	1	0	1	16	9
Quatrani, M	.276	29	8	8	2	0	1	4	1
Lewis, K	.267	135	19	36	7	0	1	17	0
Hughes, L	.265	83	13	22	3	0	2	9	2
Smithwick, C	.261	46	6	12	2	0	0	2	0
Wyers, D	.233	43	10	10	1	0	2	6	0
Cooney, R	.227	88	12	20	1	0	0	8	1
Fink, N	.214	14	2	3	2	0	0	0	0
Groves, N	.194	31	4	6	1	1	0	4	1
Keenan, J	.167	36	3	6	1	0	0	1	0
Kozeal, C	.159	44	2	7	1	0	1	5	0
Torres, J	.147	34	4	5	1	0	0	2	0
Franco, N	.111	18	3	2	0	0	1	2	0
Krieg, J	.100	10	1	1	0	0	0	1	0
Molinaro, B	.100	20	0	2	0	0	0	2	0

Pitching	W	L	ERA	G	SV	IP	H	BB	SO
Bayles, M	0	0	0.00	3	1	4	3	2	7
Bowie, R	1	0	0.00	1	0	5	0	1	11
Lawson, T	0	0	0.00	1	0	1	1	1	1
Roberts, S	0	0	0.00	1	0	2	1	1	2
Stevens, J	0	0	0.60	7	1	15	8	6	16
Whelan, W	3	1	1.31	9	1	21	12	7	20
Shorey, M	2	1	2.37	8	0	30	23	13	30
Mauro, D	0	1	2.38	6	2	11	9	2	18
Holt, Q	1	0	3.24	3	0	8	8	4	9
Marinaro, L	0	0	3.38	3	0	5	5	4	7
Konstantinovsky, Z	0	2	3.68	6	0	15	15	8	11
Bevis, L	1	0	3.93	8	1	18	18	8	20
Bradley-Cooney, P	1	0	4.00	5	1	9	5	2	14
Potok, M	0	0	4.15	2	0	4	3	0	3
Whysong, N	1	0	4.15	8	0	22	19	23	23
Petty, Z	2	1	4.41	4	0	16	15	13	17
Colucci, J	2	1	4.76	8	0	28	35	13	16
Reed, J	0	0	4.91	3	0	4	4	5	3
Sapienza, M	0	0	4.91	2	0	4	4	2	3
Brown, J	2	0	5.56	5	1	11	10	4	8
Seagraves, C	0	0	5.68	4	0	6	4	4	9
Boaz, F	0	2	5.75	6	0	20	28	14	21
Fisher, C	1	1	6.11	5	0	18	13	11	21
White, L	2	1	6.50	10	1	18	15	9	19
Valentin, A	0	2	6.55	3	0	11	16	9	7
Hartman, C	1	0	6.75	6	1	8	6	8	13
Smith, D	0	1	6.75	5	0	9	7	11	12
Gunther, J	0	2	15.95	5	1	7	11	9	11
Franco, N	0	1	21.00	2	0	3	11	4	3
Baker, J	0	0	27.00	3	0	3	4	7	5

BREWSTER

Batting	AVG	AB	R	H	2B	3B	HR	RBI	SB
Ragsdale, J	.373	51	10	19	4	0	0	11	15
Lawson, B	.333	81	12	27	3	0	4	13	1
Cyr, B	.308	39	8	12	4	0	1	5	2
DeLamielleure, B	.300	40	4	12	3	0	1	2	1
Cuvet, D	.289	38	7	11	4	0	0	2	2
Wentz, D	.283	120	15	34	6	0	3	24	6
Mihalakis, M	.265	34	5	9	1	0	1	4	1
Coates, C	.241	54	8	13	0	0	0	3	2
Kerce, C	.235	85	14	20	3	2	1	10	3
Sosa, A	.230	87	9	20	5	0	2	15	0
Magpoc, A	.223	94	22	21	5	0	1	11	26
Fisher, C	.222	81	14	18	0	0	2	16	2
Anderson, M	.212	33	4	7	2	0	2	4	0
Newman, S	.194	36	10	7	1	1	0	3	4
Priest, C	.185	81	16	15	5	1	1	4	0
Martin, R	.179	56	7	10	3	0	2	14	2
Jarrell, J	.174	23	5	4	0	0	0	2	0
Rogers, D	.167	24	2	4	0	0	1	3	0
Tinney, C	.165	79	7	13	4	0	4	10	0
Head, T	.133	30	5	4	0	0	0	2	4
McCombs, J	.095	21	0	2	1	0	0	1	0
Marin, M	.059	17	2	1	0	0	0	0	1

Pitching	W	L	ERA	G	SV	IP	H	BB	SO
DeTienne, J	1	0	0.00	4	1	7	2	2	6
Foster, E	0	0	0.00	1	0	3	1	3	1
James, D	0	0	0.00	1	0	1	0	1	2

COLLEGE

Kipp, K	1	0	0.00	14	2	17	14	5	17
Piech, R	0	0	0.00	3	0	6	6	1	7
Rizy, M	2	0	0.00	4	1	6	1	0	12
Shadek, J	0	0	0.00	3	2	2	0	1	3
Kuhns, T	1	0	1.35	3	0	13	13	1	20
Dudan, J	1	0	1.64	3	0	11	10	4	11
Dye, M	0	0	2.08	5	0	8	7	1	12
Bates, Z	4	0	2.41	11	1	18	10	8	19
Seid, S	0	0	2.53	4	0	10	12	5	9
Alicea, E	1	0	2.70	4	0	13	13	4	13
Barlow, W	0	0	2.70	3	0	13	9	6	13
Marsten, D	1	0	3.33	8	0	24	18	19	17
Davis, C	1	0	3.38	2	0	2	0	3	3
Hansen, T	1	2	3.65	3	0	12	13	7	12
Brittain, N	1	1	3.86	10	0	16	17	4	13
Schmitt, T	0	1	3.86	2	0	7	7	5	7
Davis, L	2	1	4.08	7	0	17	16	4	24
DeCremer, J	1	1	4.15	3	0	8	8	4	10
Proksch, O	0	1	4.66	3	0	9	9	5	7
Knier, C	1	1	4.91	8	1	11	9	3	7
Leffew, H	2	0	5.50	7	0	18	19	6	22
Philpott, A	0	2	5.65	7	1	14	18	2	16
Wimbish, C	1	1	6.00	8	0	12	13	4	13
Hilburger, K	0	0	6.23	1	0	4	6	2	3
Payamps, A	0	0	7.20	3	0	5	4	5	4
O'Donnell, L	0	1	7.94	6	3	5	5	6	9
Bauer, D	0	1	9.00	5	0	7	8	6	5
Louck, B	2	2	10.13	7	1	10	13	4	12
Bailey, C	0	0	10.80	1	0	1	2	5	1
Hartley, T	0	1	22.50	2	0	2	8	1	0
Jenkins, M	0	1	23.82	6	1	5	15	7	4

CHATHAM

Batting	AVG	AB	R	H	2B	3B	HR	RBI	SB
Reese, A	.303	33	3	10	0	0	2	7	0
Mendoza, E	.288	73	11	21	2	0	1	13	3
Gallaher, G	.278	90	17	25	2	0	0	1	3
Ford, H	.267	75	8	20	6	0	3	18	1
Larson, A	.263	76	9	20	2	0	1	11	0
Freeman, J	.259	143	19	37	7	1	2	15	2
Jackson, D	.256	125	31	32	7	0	4	17	12
Fralick, C	.248	121	18	30	6	0	0	16	2
Lane, I	.248	121	16	30	2	0	1	20	3
Martin, R	.247	77	10	19	2	0	1	8	3
Hanley, J	.231	108	16	25	5	1	1	18	3
Stallman, R	.208	53	4	11	2	0	1	5	2
Mazon, T	.206	34	2	7	0	0	0	2	3
Arrambide, C	.154	52	5	8	1	0	0	2	1
Miller, N	.146	41	5	6	1	0	0	6	1
Johnson, C	.053	19	1	1	0	0	0	1	0
Mathews, D	.000	17	2	0	0	0	0	0	0
Pitching	**W**	**L**	**ERA**	**G**	**SV**	**IP**	**H**	**BB**	**SO**
Freeman, C	0	0	0.00	5	1	6	6	5	5
Girardi, W	2	0	0.00	3	0	9	8	10	8
Godard, I	0	0	0.00	2	0	2	0	0	0
McMannis, J	0	0	0.00	3	0	3	2	2	4
Powell, L	1	0	0.00	3	0	3	2	3	2
Langley, C	0	0	1.17	5	1	7	5	4	10
Sharman, M	2	0	1.80	2	0	5	2	3	4
Breedlove, A	0	0	2.16	2	0	8	4	4	7
Davis, G	0	0	2.25	2	0	8	3	6	10
Jackson, L	0	1	2.45	3	0	11	10	5	9
Quinn, J	1	2	2.57	3	0	14	11	2	25
Swink, J	1	1	2.63	10	0	24	20	6	21
Taylor, N	0	1	2.93	4	0	15	10	4	22
Calder, E	0	0	3.00	3	0	9	4	4	5
Stone, D	2	1	3.33	9	0	27	20	6	35
Smith, K	1	1	3.55	10	2	25	24	16	19
Marshburn, C	0	0	3.60	2	0	5	4	3	3
Jones, G	1	1	3.91	7	1	25	32	9	14
Burns, D	2	0	4.50	5	0	14	12	8	17
Carey, T	1	1	4.50	5	0	16	15	11	12

Turner, J	0	3	5.40	3	0	10	15	3	7
Smith, K	0	0	5.68	2	0	6	5	3	4
Borberg, R	0	2	6.43	2	0	7	11	3	5
Barr, P	0	0	6.75	3	0	4	6	2	4
Johnson, C	0	0	6.75	6	0	9	3	13	13
Foster, C	0	3	7.32	7	0	19	20	15	24
Peters, M	1	0	7.45	3	0	9	15	3	6
Bixby, M	1	2	7.94	5	1	11	15	6	18
Glasscock, J	1	1	9.17	6	0	17	18	18	27
Patterson, W	0	0	9.82	3	0	3	6	2	3

COTUIT

Batting	AVG	AB	R	H	2B	3B	HR	RBI	SB
Von Schlegell, Z	.410	39	3	16	4	0	0	4	1
Beaver, L	.400	10	1	4	1	0	0	5	0
Advincula, J	.360	75	14	27	5	0	0	6	11
Johnson, C	.292	144	24	42	7	1	0	11	18
Farber, R	.278	151	27	42	5	0	2	17	9
Sanderson, C	.267	86	8	23	3	1	0	10	0
Wiggins, A	.255	51	6	13	2	0	1	8	2
West, D	.254	71	14	18	0	1	0	7	3
Natili, J	.248	129	21	32	6	0	6	24	0
Matthews, L	.247	73	12	18	2	1	0	13	5
Winfield, E	.245	49	6	12	1	1	0	5	0
Bogenpohl, C	.242	91	14	22	4	0	3	20	2
Stevens, N	.238	126	17	30	4	0	2	14	4
French, A	.194	36	2	7	1	0	0	1	0
Lavin, L	.170	53	6	9	1	0	0	4	0
Moutzouridis, P	.167	18	2	3	1	0	0	0	1
Tyson, T	.161	31	4	5	1	0	0	3	0
Jaros, R	.143	14	0	2	0	0	0	0	0
Sasaki, R	.107	28	2	3	1	0	2	6	0
Martinez, S	.077	13	1	1	0	0	0	2	0
Pitching	**W**	**L**	**ERA**	**G**	**SV**	**IP**	**H**	**BB**	**SO**
Deschenes, L	1	0	0.00	1	0	2	2	0	1
Gray, M	0	0	0.00	3	0	5	2	1	7
Langley, B	1	0	0.00	2	0	3	0	0	4
Mitchell, J	0	0	0.00	1	0	1	1	1	1
Newell, W	0	0	0.00	1	0	0	0	1	0
Tyler, D	0	0	0.00	1	0	3	4	0	2
Wimberly, N	0	0	0.00	1	0	5	2	1	4
Scudder, D	1	0	0.77	9	0	11	11	6	8
Remington, K	0	0	0.79	5	1	11	1	5	9
Evans, R	0	0	1.32	3	0	13	10	3	13
Carlon, C	1	0	1.42	3	0	6	3	2	8
Sampson, B	1	0	1.50	4	0	12	12	5	15
Halvorson, W	1	1	1.95	11	0	27	15	21	26
Walker, C	0	0	2.08	8	0	13	9	4	12
Davenport, M	0	1	2.25	3	0	4	1	2	2
Crowl, P	0	0	2.35	3	0	7	1	6	4
Albanese, T	1	2	2.45	10	4	22	14	7	20
Pirko, L	1	0	2.45	1	0	3	1	1	3
Swift, C	0	0	2.45	2	0	3	2	5	5
Buckler, R	3	0	2.63	10	0	27	22	5	14
Manca, P	2	2	2.70	7	0	30	26	11	25
Deverman, K	0	1	3.07	4	0	14	18	2	11
Adelmann, J	1	1	3.97	7	1	11	9	6	14
Moring, R	2	2	3.97	3	0	11	12	5	11
Haug, M	0	1	4.30	9	0	23	21	6	19
Coppersmith, Z	0	0	5.06	7	0	10	9	2	12
Carson, C	1	1	5.59	7	0	9	11	6	11
Adetuyi, K	0	0	6.00	2	0	3	3	1	5
Greaney, N	1	0	7.11	5	0	6	9	2	6
May, L	0	1	7.94	3	0	5	14	2	6
Hays, J	1	2	8.10	4	0	13	16	5	16
Volchko, J	0	1	8.10	2	0	6	5	10	8
Starling, Z	0	1	9.00	5	0	5	12	1	5
Egan, R	0	1	13.50	4	0	4	6	3	4
Jones, G	0	2	13.50	5	0	7	10	7	4

FALMOUTH

Batting	AVG	AB	R	H	2B	3B	HR	RBI	SB
Moroney, R	.400	15	3	6	0	0	0	6	3
Schmidt, K	.287	129	12	37	6	0	2	24	6
Schmidt, C	.284	141	26	40	9	0	1	14	6
Niu, M	.280	132	28	37	4	1	8	23	15
Harrison, B	.277	83	9	23	4	0	3	14	1
Osterhouse, J	.258	124	16	32	4	1	1	12	16
Zuckerman, R	.255	51	6	13	1	1	2	7	0
Quatrani, M	.250	32	4	8	2	0	1	9	0
Morales, A	.239	134	22	32	1	2	0	13	9
Brumbaugh, C	.238	21	2	5	1	0	0	3	2
Lopez, A	.215	107	20	23	5	0	0	8	10
Greger, G	.200	15	1	3	0	0	0	1	2
Wilson, A	.189	37	3	7	0	0	1	5	2
Moran, L	.182	22	2	4	2	0	1	5	0
Morrison, K	.171	35	6	6	1	0	1	3	2
McCann, D	.162	37	7	6	0	0	2	3	0
Salinas, T	.158	19	2	3	1	0	0	0	1
Royo, B	.143	21	1	3	0	0	0	0	0
Eckelman, M	.125	16	1	2	0	0	0	0	1
Newstrom, C	.122	82	8	10	0	1	1	4	6
Smith III, J	.056	18	2	1	0	0	0	0	1

Pitching	W	L	ERA	G	SV	IP	H	BB	SO
Estridge, C	0	0	0.00	2	0	3	2	1	3
Lavigueur, L	0	0	0.00	1	0	1	2	1	0
Marcum, R	1	0	0.00	4	0	6	2	2	5
McCarthy, D	0	0	0.00	1	0	1	1	2	1
Garber, E	1	0	0.82	3	1	11	6	5	10
Baumler, T	0	1	0.92	5	0	19	14	5	18
Dorn, J	1	0	1.00	2	0	9	2	3	6
Urena, J	1	1	1.00	3	0	9	8	1	4
Echeman, K	0	0	2.25	4	0	16	8	8	24
Schulz, J	0	0	2.35	14	1	15	14	9	23
Sabbath, J	1	3	2.37	13	5	19	14	8	26
Saunier, G	1	0	3.00	4	0	15	12	6	18
Rogan, P	0	0	3.38	5	1	8	3	6	6
Dallas, M	0	0	4.38	4	0	12	6	7	10
Sheerin, D	1	1	4.38	8	0	12	11	8	12
Coats, T	1	2	4.41	8	0	32	29	11	40
Berg, J	0	1	4.50	2	0	4	3	5	5
Barrett, E	3	1	4.57	6	0	21	18	9	25
Vanesko, J	2	0	4.80	8	1	15	20	9	7
Marchetti, M	0	0	5.40	1	0	1	3	2	0
Linn, C	2	1	5.59	6	0	19	22	8	22
Sauser, M	1	1	6.61	5	0	16	19	3	7
Johnston, Z	0	1	8.31	6	0	4	4	1	4
Palmer, L	0	2	8.36	5	0	14	20	7	13
Humphrey, K	0	0	9.00	4	1	5	6	3	3
Wywoda, J	0	2	9.39	4	0	7	14	5	4
Porco, R	0	1	10.00	5	1	9	9	7	13
Meert, G	0	1	10.38	7	0	8	12	6	8
Cullen, J	0	0	11.37	5	0	6	6	5	5
Stiffler, M	0	1	12.46	5	0	8	15	7	7
O'Harran, T	0	2	21.60	2	0	3	9	5	1
Rogovic, A	0	0	21.60	1	0	1	0	3	2
Gillen, M	0	1	54.00	1	0	0	3	1	1

HARWICH

Batting	AVG	AB	R	H	2B	3B	HR	RBI	SB
Moroney, R	.400	15	3	6	0	0	0	6	3
Schmidt, K	.287	129	12	37	6	0	2	24	6
Schmidt, C	.284	141	26	40	9	0	1	14	6
Niu, M	.280	132	28	37	4	1	8	23	15
Harrison, B	.277	83	9	23	4	0	3	14	1
Osterhouse, J	.258	124	16	32	4	1	1	12	16
Zuckerman, R	.255	51	6	13	1	1	2	7	0
Quatrani, M	.250	32	4	8	2	0	1	9	0
Morales, A	.239	134	22	32	1	2	0	13	9
Brumbaugh, C	.238	21	2	5	1	0	0	3	2
Lopez, A	.215	107	20	23	5	0	0	8	10
Greger, G	.200	15	1	3	0	0	0	1	2
Wilson, A	.189	37	3	7	0	0	1	5	2
Moran, L	.182	22	2	4	2	0	1	5	0
Morrison, K	.171	35	6	6	1	0	1	3	2
McCann, D	.162	37	7	6	0	0	2	3	0
Salinas, T	.158	19	2	3	1	0	0	0	1
Royo, B	.143	21	1	3	0	0	0	0	0
Eckelman, M	.125	16	1	2	0	0	0	0	1
Newstrom, C	.122	82	8	10	0	1	1	4	6
Smith III, J	.056	18	2	1	0	0	0	0	1
Fultz, P	.350	20	4	7	1	0	0	2	1
Bell, T	.316	19	3	6	3	0	0	2	2
Robbins, A	.307	101	16	31	6	0	6	14	2
Dempsey, E	.300	10	4	3	0	0	0	1	0
Wells, T	.300	20	2	6	0	0	0	2	0
Broussard, T	.296	71	9	21	2	0	0	7	10
Marsh, T	.277	101	20	28	3	0	0	7	8
Conte, M	.258	93	13	24	5	0	0	12	2
Kennedy, D	.253	99	12	25	6	0	1	18	3
Wolff, K	.250	80	8	20	3	0	1	11	1
Molony, M	.240	104	16	25	3	0	2	11	3
Becker, E	.238	21	2	5	0	0	0	3	0
Brini, N	.233	120	20	28	6	2	1	14	12
Inoue, S	.222	54	7	12	3	0	1	10	1
Carter, B	.218	78	12	17	3	0	2	8	17
Koonin, J	.190	100	15	19	4	0	3	13	9
DeCarlo, S	.188	32	4	6	2	0	0	4	4
Harris, S	.157	70	7	11	0	0	0	8	0
Swidler, E	.125	16	1	2	1	0	0	0	0
Feinberg, H	.100	20	4	2	0	0	0	0	3
Winslow, M	.100	10	1	1	1	0	0	1	0
Jaffe, J	.000	15	1	0	0	0	0	1	0

Pitching	W	L	ERA	G	SV	IP	H	BB	SO
Dillhoff, P	1	0	0.00	2	0	4	3	1	6
Friedman, P	1	0	0.00	1	0	6	0	2	6
Gray, M	0	0	0.00	2	0	2	2	3	1
Matuschat, B	0	0	0.00	1	0	4	2	1	1
Wilson, H	0	0	0.00	1	0	1	1	2	2
Harrington, C	1	1	0.93	7	1	9	7	1	11
Rodriguez, C	1	0	0.93	12	3	19	9	9	26
McCoy, J	0	1	1.46	3	0	12	13	3	25
Bilka, R	2	0	2.19	5	1	12	12	3	15
Heiberger, M	3	0	2.28	7	0	23	15	7	22
Dressler, T	2	1	2.39	6	0	26	22	10	25
Doran, S	2	0	2.51	5	0	14	8	8	11
Shurtleff, T	2	1	2.53	10	1	21	13	6	21
Gambardella, G	2	1	2.55	6	0	24	21	8	13
Nevills, E	0	0	2.84	3	0	6	3	4	5
Muscar, T	0	0	3.00	2	0	3	2	0	3
Arther, A	0	1	3.06	10	1	17	21	9	20
Rodriguez, F	0	0	3.71	4	0	17	16	3	12
Twist, T	0	1	3.86	4	0	11	11	8	11
Reich, R	0	1	4.70	8	0	15	17	8	16
Chmielewski, T	1	1	4.91	6	0	18	22	5	16
Donegan, J	0	1	4.91	5	0	11	12	2	16
Dempsey, E	0	1	5.00	2	0	9	9	1	7
Johnson, O	3	2	5.40	7	0	18	20	10	10
Simmerson, H	0	0	5.40	1	1	1	1	1	1
McNeillie, L	0	2	5.68	4	0	12	12	8	14
Butler, T	0	0	5.91	5	2	10	7	3	18
Duke, T	0	1	6.23	6	0	8	10	7	7
Feser, C	0	0	6.43	4	0	7	6	5	8
Volo, J	0	0	9.00	2	0	2	4	3	1

HYANNIS

Batting	AVG	AB	R	H	2B	3B	HR	RBI	SB
Rembert, C	.429	21	5	9	2	0	3	8	2
Willits, J	.366	41	16	15	2	0	1	6	5
Miura, M	.309	68	6	21	4	0	1	12	7
McKay, R	.300	130	12	39	7	0	0	10	8
Lougee, J	.288	80	7	23	6	2	0	16	1

Batting	AVG	AB	R	H	2B	3B	HR	RBI	SB
Schaffner, J	.281	89	16	25	3	1	1	10	3
Lawless, S	.280	25	5	7	1	0	1	2	0
Lachance, D	.269	52	7	14	4	0	2	11	0
Williamson, A	.265	49	13	13	3	0	3	12	6
Black, S	.256	39	5	10	2	0	2	7	2
Camacho, G	.253	91	9	23	1	1	0	4	3
Walk, J	.235	51	6	12	2	0	0	5	4
Federico, H	.234	47	6	11	1	0	2	6	5
Bailey, M	.219	32	3	7	2	0	1	6	0
Prince, O	.212	52	6	11	3	0	0	5	4
Bates, C	.196	102	11	20	2	1	0	6	4
Dobie, J	.195	41	8	8	2	0	0	2	0
Velazquez, R	.176	74	10	13	4	0	0	7	2
Mitchell, D	.171	35	5	6	0	0	1	2	1
Brosius, P	.160	25	2	4	1	0	0	4	2
Briggs, B	.143	56	9	8	0	0	2	8	0
Davis, M	.132	38	3	5	1	0	0	4	0
Lackey, V	.120	25	1	3	1	0	0	1	1
Pitching	**W**	**L**	**ERA**	**G**	**SV**	**IP**	**H**	**BB**	**SO**
Beard, T	0	0	0.00	2	0	8	4	2	9
Garcia, S	2	0	0.00	5	0	11	4	5	15
Hoffberg, E	0	0	0.00	3	0	4	0	1	6
Kelley, C	0	1	0.00	5	2	6	2	1	6
Minaberry, J	0	0	0.00	4	0	3	3	3	4
Wertz, A	0	0	0.00	2	0	2	3	3	3
Diaz, C	0	0	1.00	4	0	9	5	2	9
Blanco, E	1	0	1.50	3	0	12	8	6	7
Edwards, Z	2	1	1.65	8	0	16	11	5	16
Speshyock, R	2	2	1.96	11	3	18	16	8	22
Crabtree, T	0	2	2.70	4	0	13	13	10	13
Stammel, M	1	1	3.10	7	0	20	15	9	22
Libbert, W	0	0	3.12	2	0	8	12	0	11
Garewal, S	0	0	3.24	6	0	8	5	8	13
August, T	0	4	3.38	8	0	18	20	10	23
Lanman, B	0	1	3.60	3	0	10	11	4	11
Dorsey, C	2	1	4.11	8	0	15	15	10	23
Kinneen, L	0	0	4.15	2	0	4	5	1	3
Jasa, C	1	2	4.67	9	0	27	17	25	34
O'Rourke, T	1	0	4.91	5	1	7	7	2	10
Tomii, T	2	4	4.95	8	0	20	15	8	20
Roman, R	0	0	5.21	5	0	19	15	7	15
Olivera, B	0	0	5.40	4	0	6	9	3	9
Copper III, E	0	1	5.79	11	1	23	26	11	24
Russell, M	0	1	7.80	7	0	15	16	11	8
Dietz, H	0	0	8.49	7	0	11	14	12	13
Graves, G	0	1	8.64	5	0	8	10	4	13
Troy, A	0	0	9.00	4	0	5	8	5	5
Williams, I	1	0	12.27	2	0	3	4	5	7
Chabot, H	0	0	22.50	2	0	2	5	2	1
Jenkins, J	0	1	27.00	4	0	4	14	5	4
Plog, E	0	0	33.75	1	0	1	5	1	2

ORLEANS

Batting	AVG	AB	R	H	2B	3B	HR	RBI	SB
Myatt, T	.302	43	6	13	4	0	4	8	0
Garza, A	.298	114	5	34	3	0	1	16	2
Pisacreta, S	.292	24	2	7	2	0	1	3	0
Ickes, E	.282	131	26	37	6	0	5	21	3
Potestio, A	.274	95	19	26	9	0	0	9	8
Lavey, R	.262	122	13	32	5	0	1	18	1
Bryce, D	.233	103	17	24	4	0	3	16	10
O'Shaughnessy, M	.232	69	19	16	2	0	1	4	1
Dugger, C	.225	71	6	16	3	0	1	7	1
Williams, J	.225	71	12	16	0	1	0	8	14
Taylor, J	.200	25	3	5	0	0	1	1	3
Mendez, J	.182	44	6	8	0	0	0	3	2
Covarrubias, A	.162	37	4	6	0	0	0	6	1
Nixon, L	.161	56	10	9	3	0	1	4	2
Kucherak, R	.158	57	10	9	2	0	1	8	5
Wagner, K	.143	21	3	3	1	0	0	0	0
Salinas, T	.125	16	1	2	1	0	0	3	2
Crossland, M	.123	73	8	9	2	0	0	5	4

Batting	AVG	AB	R	H	2B	3B	HR	RBI	SB
Barr, C	.118	17	1	2	0	0	1	3	0
Bastian, J	.100	30	3	3	2	0	0	2	3
Johnson, K	.077	26	3	2	1	0	0	2	1
Pitching	**W**	**L**	**ERA**	**G**	**SV**	**IP**	**H**	**BB**	**SO**
Koenig, N	0	0	0.00	1	0	1	0	1	1
Morris, B	2	0	0.00	5	0	7	6	2	7
Tryba, C	3	0	1.07	11	1	25	21	7	28
Brown, D	1	0	1.29	7	0	7	1	5	12
Gosztola, M	0	0	1.35	2	0	6	6	4	7
Foley, E	3	0	1.62	10	0	16	10	5	25
Leckszas, K	0	0	1.64	9	1	11	6	1	9
Raab, J	0	2	1.80	5	0	20	16	7	18
Oshinskie, R	1	1	1.93	13	1	28	20	7	38
Kelly, O	0	0	2.08	2	0	8	5	1	7
Murdock, S	0	3	2.16	15	8	16	16	8	24
Fox, B	1	0	2.70	5	0	6	7	2	3
Koch, M	2	0	2.93	14	0	15	20	3	18
Hart, E	3	0	3.18	11	0	11	12	5	10
Reddemann, L	0	1	3.22	8	1	22	18	3	25
Magdaleno, I	0	0	3.78	7	1	16	18	4	22
Takemoto, I	0	2	4.05	5	0	13	9	10	7
Krenzel, B	1	1	4.76	4	0	11	6	13	7
Guy, C	0	0	5.40	4	0	3	4	4	1
Pettitte, L	1	1	5.55	7	1	24	27	4	33
Bean, J	1	1	5.73	4	0	11	12	4	6
Pauley, T	2	1	5.87	6	0	15	18	7	16
Scolari, C	0	0	7.62	4	0	13	14	7	13
Gonzalez, S	0	2	8.05	7	0	19	24	9	12
Gladden, J	0	0	9.00	1	0	1	1	1	0
Johnson, K	0	0	10.97	4	0	10	15	11	7
Morello, M	0	0	21.60	1	0	1	5	0	0
Litteral, L	1	0	40.50	2	0	1	3	5	0

WAREHAM

Batting	AVG	AB	R	H	2B	3B	HR	RBI	SB
Ramirez, C	.380	50	9	19	3	0	0	8	7
Clark, L	.333	75	19	25	2	1	4	10	1
Carns, H	.327	52	15	17	4	0	3	11	1
Krewson, R	.306	98	12	30	6	0	0	8	12
Dalley, T	.294	51	5	15	4	1	0	3	0
Randle, B	.258	120	18	31	11	1	1	14	13
McDonald, C	.256	86	15	22	1	0	6	18	1
Yost, H	.252	107	13	27	4	1	3	9	4
Apple, F	.250	12	2	3	0	0	1	1	1
Gargett, K	.250	44	6	11	0	1	2	10	4
McDuffie, S	.250	16	1	4	1	0	0	1	2
McHugh, C	.250	104	20	26	7	0	5	15	3
Turner, C	.229	109	18	25	6	0	4	19	3
Breyfogle, E	.222	36	4	8	1	1	0	4	2
Kail, J	.217	23	1	5	0	0	0	1	1
Lujo, R	.214	14	1	3	0	0	0	1	1
Ritchie, K	.186	59	8	11	2	0	4	12	1
Agresti, A	.176	17	3	3	0	0	0	1	0
Sheahan, V	.160	106	15	17	1	1	1	8	9
Cain, A	.150	20	0	3	0	0	0	3	0
Stripling, L	.143	35	1	5	1	0	0	2	0
Rogers, D	.105	38	5	4	2	0	1	3	0
Rose, M	.100	20	2	2	1	0	0	2	0
Pitching	**W**	**L**	**ERA**	**G**	**SV**	**IP**	**H**	**BB**	**SO**
Aikens, P	0	0	0.00	1	0	1	1	1	0
Clayton, C	0	0	0.00	2	0	2	0	2	1
Egan, T	1	0	0.00	1	0	2	0	0	3
Koshy, J	0	0	0.00	1	0	2	1	2	5
Melendy, J	0	0	0.00	1	0	1	3	0	1
Schlageter, T	3	0	0.57	9	0	15	11	6	12
McGuire, T	0	1	0.96	5	0	18	10	4	9
Butler, E	1	1	1.03	8	0	26	17	12	23
Galle, P	2	2	1.04	8	2	8	3	10	8
Mayfield, C	0	0	1.13	3	0	8	8	5	7
Applebey, K	2	1	1.20	7	1	15	7	6	11
Jones, E	0	0	1.59	6	0	5	3	4	4
Pluta, T	0	0	2.25	4	2	4	2	5	3

Richter, C	0	0	2.25	3	0	12	8	6	15
Consiglio, C	1	1	2.55	6	0	24	18	11	21
Starke, T	1	0	2.63	12	1	13	5	5	15
McDonald, C	3	1	3.51	8	1	25	27	7	17
Turner, B	0	1	3.52	5	1	7	7	1	12
Rowan, H	3	1	3.66	8	0	19	11	15	20
Faulkner, J	0	0	4.00	6	0	9	15	3	7
O'Connor, G	0	0	5.54	7	0	13	13	8	13
Powell, D	0	2	5.74	9	0	26	24	16	26
Baisley, L	0	1	6.43	10	2	21	25	13	18
Stephens, J	1	0	7.30	5	0	12	12	7	17
Wendt, S	1	1	7.41	12	0	17	17	20	13
Campbell, K	0	2	7.71	5	0	4	1	5	9
McDevitt, J	0	1	7.71	2	0	2	2	1	3
Collera, L	1	1	8.56	10	0	13	19	6	9
Skelding, T	0	3	9.24	9	0	12	16	9	12
Black, G	0	0	27.00	3	0	1	0	3	1

YARMOUTH-DENNIS

Batting	AVG	AB	R	H	2B	3B	HR	RBI	SB
Yamaguchi, S	.417	12	1	5	0	0	0	1	0
Briseno, A	.339	62	4	21	4	0	1	9	1
Soldra, A	.321	56	9	18	1	0	4	9	2
Tharnish, J	.315	54	8	17	2	0	1	4	4
Hernandez, A	.290	31	5	9	2	0	1	7	1
Arcamone, J	.273	44	8	12	1	0	2	11	0
Carpentier, D	.273	66	16	18	5	0	3	9	4
Miller, C	.261	69	14	18	4	0	3	10	8
Carreras, Y	.258	97	12	25	4	0	0	10	2
Hacopian, C	.258	132	15	34	6	1	2	17	4
Bold, J	.250	28	6	7	1	0	0	4	1
Ortiz, A	.250	28	3	7	2	0	0	3	2
Traeger, N	.250	32	4	8	2	0	0	0	0
Brunson, C	.231	13	1	3	0	0	0	0	1
Dowd, B	.219	114	18	25	1	1	2	9	7
Baker, W	.209	110	12	23	5	0	3	12	6
Wright, G	.203	74	8	15	3	0	0	7	2
McAndrews, T	.200	10	0	2	0	0	0	3	0
Gasparino, W	.195	41	4	8	0	0	0	6	2
Capece, C	.194	36	4	7	3	0	0	5	3
Nessler, A	.190	42	7	8	2	0	0	8	1
Bell, J	.159	63	6	10	2	0	1	5	3
Canon, C	.118	17	4	2	1	0	0	0	1
Costello, N	.114	35	4	4	0	0	2	3	1
Crosland, J	.091	11	0	1	0	0	0	0	1
Pitching	W	L	ERA	G	SV	IP	H	BB	SO
Koenen, D	0	0	0.00	2	0	2	1	2	3
Ojeda, R	1	0	0.00	4	0	6	3	3	11
Tabor, J	0	0	0.00	1	0	2	1	0	4
Zaslaw, S	0	0	0.00	1	0	1	0	3	1
Pitzer, T	3	0	0.34	8	0	26	15	9	36
Harris, Z	0	0	1.23	4	1	7	5	4	7
Hamilton, B	2	1	1.48	7	0	30	25	5	22
Marsh, C	1	0	1.69	4	0	5	3	5	8
Downs, C	1	2	1.83	9	2	19	19	8	18
Watkins, H	2	1	1.96	4	0	18	12	4	20
Carpentier, D	0	0	2.08	4	0	4	3	3	6
Malki, M	1	0	2.45	1	0	3	2	2	5
Rhudy, B	0	0	2.45	9	5	11	6	2	12
Ballard, C	0	1	3.38	5	0	18	19	7	18
Desch, D	1	0	3.38	9	2	13	14	3	13
Landry, J	1	0	3.86	4	1	14	10	5	16
Schaefer, D	2	1	3.86	8	0	28	23	18	23
Brooks, R	1	1	4.00	7	1	9	7	7	12
Frize, D	0	0	4.05	5	0	6	7	5	7
Hendry, C	0	1	4.76	4	0	11	10	5	11
Nobe, J	0	1	4.91	9	0	14	8	13	8
Renfroe, R	1	1	5.40	3	0	3	2	2	4
Pena, R	0	0	6.35	5	0	5	8	8	7
Catalano, M	1	2	6.75	9	0	25	32	15	36
Bentley, N	0	2	7.00	4	0	9	11	7	11
Lee, J	0	1	7.30	7	0	12	14	14	11

Tate, D	0	1	7.71	3	0	9	13	4	4
Overbay, A	0	1	8.10	4	0	3	4	0	1
New, C	1	2	14.00	5	0	9	13	13	9
Bayer, T	1	0	15.26	5	0	7	15	7	4
Lawrence, T	0	0	81.00	1	0	0	1	4	1

ALASKA LEAGUE

	W	L	PCT	GB
Mat-Su Miners	24	7	.774	-
Anchorage Bucs	16	16	.500	8.5
Chugiak-Eagle River Chinooks	11	18	.379	12
Anchorage Glacier Pilots	10	20	.333	13.5

CHAMPIONSHIP: Mat-Su defeated Anchorage 9-8.

INDIVIDUAL BATTING LEADERS

	AVG	AB	R	H	2B	3B	HR	RBI	SB
A Berghult, Anchorage	.364	.472	.534	88	32	7	1	2	14
J McGee, Mat-Su	.355	.420	.474	76	27	3	0	2	20
R Erickson, MatOSu	.353	.435	.451	102	36	2	1	2	22
C Geffre, Mat-Su	.347	.493	.525	101	35	7	1	3	14
S Togher, Anchorage	.329	.372	.457	70	23	3	0	2	8
E Bilter, Mat-Su	.323	.394	.417	96	31	4	1	1	19
G Pierantoni, MatOSu	.308	.368	.365	104	32	6	0	0	20
I Parido, Chugiak-Eagle	.306	.405	.337	98	30	1	1	0	9
J Ruby, Anchorage	.303	.446	.348	66	20	1	1	0	8
A Becker, Anchorage	.297	.354	.423	111	33	6	1	2	24

INDIVIDUAL PITCHING LEADERS

	W	L	ERA	G	SV	IP	H	BB	SO
M Malki, Mat-Su	4	1	1.20	8	2	30	14	19	54
C Foltz, Chugiak-Eagle	3	2	1.55	5	0	29	21	18	28
G Blachowicz, Mat-Su	1	0	2.22	6	0	28	21	12	27
E Buxton, Anchorage	2	1	2.49	6	0	25	15	5	27
L Rolland, Chugiak-Eagle	2	1	2.63	6	0	27	13	18	21
K Arn, Mat-Su	3	1	2.70	13	1	27	20	4	19
K Finazzo, Anchorage	2	2	2.73	9	0	33	28	11	25
J Robertson, Anchorage	3	1	2.74	5	0	23	20	7	17
T Hartman, Anchorage	2	1	2.77	7	0	26	23	13	18
J Jansen, Mat-Su	3	0	3.46	6	0	26	26	8	23

ATLANTIC COLLEGIATE LEAGUE

Kaiser Division	W	L	PCT	GB
East Coast Sandhogs	22	9	.703	-
LIB Neptunes	21	10	.677	1
Old Town Road Patriots	12	12	.500	6.5
Atlantic Whitecaps	13	15	.467	7.5
New York Crush	12	22	.353	11.5
Hitters Club Hawkeyes	9	21	.313	12.5
Wolff Division	W	L	PCT	GB
Essex Legends	22	8	.733	-
New Brunswick MATRIX	17	9	.643	3
Jersey Shore Stallions	15	15	.500	7
New York Phenoms	12	14	.464	8
Ocean Ospreys	10	17	.379	10.5
Bergen Metros	5	18	.229	13.5

INDIVIDUAL BATTING LEADERS

	AVG	AB	R	H	2B	3B	HR	RBI	SB
Alvarez, J, NBM	.386	70	21	27	7	0	2	17	10
Govea, T, JSS	.379	95	28	36	5	1	1	12	15
Manzella, J, NEP	.365	74	19	27	2	0	0	11	2
Johnston, B, JSS	.352	71	20	25	4	0	4	19	13
Robinson, B, NBM	.345	58	15	20	4	2	1	15	6
Sais, C, ECS	.329	76	13	25	5	1	1	10	3
Cumiskey, C, NBM	.318	66	17	21	7	0	1	22	5
LaFroscia, D, AW	.316	76	15	24	3	0	1	10	5
Villani, M, NYP	.296	71	15	21	7	0	0	11	5
Rosario, F, JSS	.290	69	22	20	4	0	0	7	14

INDIVIDUAL PITCHING LEADERS

	W	L	ERA	G	SV	IP	H	BB	SO
Dawson, M, NEP	4	0	0.00	8	0	25	13	12	26
Flack, T, LEG	4	0	0.89	9	1	30	12	15	27
Hayes, D, BM	2	2	1.64	6	0	22	16	8	24
Santos, J, NEP	0	1	2.08	10	0	26	19	14	31
Mattaliano, J, JSS	3	0	2.08	10	0	26	18	15	18
Ackerman, J, NEP	5	0	2.10	9	0	30	18	13	36
Mohr, E, NYC	2	1	2.25	6	0	32	28	10	26
Kielty, A, NYP	2	0	2.52	6	0	25	22	11	26
Craig, E, JSS	5	1	3.09	10	1	35	34	18	26
Kovach, M, JSS	1	2	3.81	10	1	26	21	21	32

APPALACHIAN LEAUE

East	W	L	PCT	GB
Burlington	29	17	.630	-
Bluefield	25	22	.532	4.5
Pulaski	23	22	.511	5.5
Danville	18	28	.391	11
Tri-State	16	28	.364	12
West	**W**	**L**	**PCT**	**GB**
Kingsport	31	15	.674	-
Greeneville	25	20	.556	5.5
Elizabethton	23	25	.479	9
Johnson City	22	24	.478	9
Bristol	18	29	.383	13.5

CHAMPIONSHIP: Conejo.

INDIVIDUAL BATTING LEADERS

	AVG	AB	R	H	2B	3B	HR	RBI	SB
Antigua, A, BUR	.442	77	20	34	6	1	1	19	2
Durnin, K, KNG	.407	145	44	59	15	2	6	56	10
Gillen, P, BRS	.403	129	23	52	13	2	2	36	0
Majette, T, JC	.357	140	37	50	6	2	2	27	10
McNaughton, E, GRN	.345	139	38	48	9	1	12	46	16
Kelsey, A, KNG	.342	114	29	39	4	0	0	23	13
Crosland, J, ELZ	.341	135	29	46	11	0	6	38	9
Tryon, B, KNG	.336	119	35	40	8	2	4	32	1
Ricketts, B, PUL	.333	132	31	44	10	0	4	35	0
Fyffe, L, JC	.326	141	30	46	15	1	1	36	7

INDIVIDUAL PITCHING LEADERS

	W	L	ERA	G	SV	IP	H	BB	SO
Thacker, B, JC	0	1	1.88	10	0	29	14	19	34
Bradle, T, BUR	3	1	1.95	8	0	32	27	13	29
DeLisle, T, TS	1	0	2.28	8	0	28	20	16	33
Jones, C, KNG	3	1	2.35	11	0	31	30	7	25
Vicenti, R, KNG	2	0	2.57	8	0	28	23	10	30
Lewis, A, DAN	2	1	3.23	12	0	31	34	11	22
Steinhaus, A, BUR	1	3	3.24	6	0	25	20	16	20
Downing, J, KNG	3	1	3.33	12	1	24	21	14	23
Collins, K, TS	2	2	3.60	8	0	40	31	17	47
Osbolt, M, JC	2	1	3.82	7	0	33	25	9	4

CAL RIPKEN COLLEGIATE LEAGUE

North	W	L	PCT	GB
Bethesda Big Train	27	8	.771	0
Olney Cropdusters	22	14	.611	5.5
SS-T Thunderbolts	14	20	.412	12.5
Gaithersburg Giants	13	24	.351	15
South	**W**	**L**	**PCT**	**GB**
Alexandria Aces	22	14	.611	0
Southern Maryland Senators	19	16	.543	2.5
D.C. Grays	17	20	.459	5.5
Metro South County Braves	9	27	.250	13

CHAMPIONSHIP: Bethesda defeated Alexandria 2-0 in best-of-3 series.

INDIVIDUAL BATTING LEADERS

	AVG	AB	R	H	2B	3B	HR	RBI	SB
Gonzalez, E, BT	.418	122	37	51	11	0	5	41	2
Tribble, L, SMD	.380	100	23	38	8	0	1	21	15
Wright, B, BT	.371	124	35	46	4	0	0	27	11

	AVG	AB	R	H	2B	3B	HR	RBI	SB
Almeda, D, ACES	.365	115	25	42	6	1	1	22	14
Gill, T, SST	.363	80	16	29	3	0	0	5	5
Soong, R, DC	.363	102	25	37	3	2	1	19	33
Gomez Jr, F, BR	.355	110	30	39	5	0	1	21	8
Hawton-Henley, N, GG	.350	80	24	28	7	1	0	9	15
Peltier, A, BT	.342	120	35	41	7	2	0	22	21
Adelman, T, BR	.337	86	13	29	7	1	0	14	5

INDIVIDUAL PITCHING LEADERS

	W	L	ERA	G	SV	IP	H	BB	SO
Adetuyi, A, BT	5	0	0.31	8	1	29	12	12	32
Christopher, M, ACES	2	2	1.95	7	0	32	25	11	23
Domaracki, J, SST	2	0	1.99	7	0	32	27	6	23
Smith, G, CDB	1	1	2.67	8	1	27	24	9	25
Wimberly, N, SMD	2	1	2.67	6	0	27	13	13	43
Bellis, D, BT	5	1	2.84	8	0	32	24	17	61
Morris, T, DC	2	5	3.10	9	0	41	38	21	20
Danielczyk, Z, SST	2	2	4.32	6	0	25	29	11	14
Davis, K, DC	1	1	4.59	7	0	35	36	17	20
Hutchinson, C, ACES	3	2	4.96	7	0	33	28	13	26

CALIFORNIA COLLEGIATE LEAGUE

North	W	L	PCT	GB
Walnut Creek Crawdads	23	14	.622	--
Sonoma Stompers	24	15	.615	1
San Luis Obispo Blues	24	17	.585	2
Menlo Park Legends	15	22	.405	8
San Francisco Seagulls	10	27	.270	13
South	**W**	**L**	**PCT**	
Santa Barbara Foresters	23	9	.719	--
Conejo Oaks	23	13	.639	2
Orange County Riptide	23	15	.605	3
Arroyo Seco Saints	17	20	.459	8.5
Academy Barons	13	21	.382	11
Affiliates	**W**	**L**	**PCT**	
Alameda Merchants	17	14	.548	
San Diego Waves	5	7	.417	
San Diego Bombers	6	13	.316	
Philippines Baseball Group	4	20	.167	

CHAMPIONSHIP: Conejo.

INDIVIDUAL BATTING LEADERS

	AVG	OBP	SLG	AB	H	HR	RBI
J Donnelly, Walnut Creek	.369	.435	.427	103	38	2	24
Q Medin, Sonoma	.312	.438	.312	125	39	0	28
N Sebastiani, Sonoma	.301	.396	.446	83	25	4	17
T Williams, San Diego	.270	.370	.270	63	17	0	5
L Bonham, San Diego	.259	.306	.259	58	15	0	3
J Brewer, San Francisco	.255	.342	.255	98	25	0	15
A Ramirez, San Francisco	.234	.344	.234	107	25	0	13
P Lizzul, Sonoma	.232	.382	.305	82	19	2	14
D Waldvogel, San Francisco	.226	.323	.226	84	19	0	11
A Balentine, Sonoma	.225	.344	.225	111	25	0	14

COASTAL PLAIN LEAGUE

East	W	L	PCT	GB
Peninsula Pilots	32	16	.667	--
Wilson Tobs	30	16	.652	1
Wilmington Sharks	25	20	.556	5.5
Morehead City Marlins	21	24	.467	9.5
Holly Springs Salamanders	22	26	.458	10
Greenville Yard Gnomes	20	26	.435	11
Tri-City Chili Peppers	17	30	.362	14.5
West	**W**	**L**	**PCT**	**GB**
Forest City Owls	31	15	.674	--
Lexington County Blowfish	27	18	.600	3.5
Boone Bigfoots	26	22	.542	6
Asheboro ZooKeepers	24	24	.500	8
Martinsville Mustangs	21	27	.438	11
Macon Bacon	17	27	.386	13.5
HP Thomasville HiToms	18	29	.383	13.5
Florence Flamingos	16	37	.372	13.5

CHAMPIONSHIP: Wilson defeated Forest City 2-0 in best-of-3 series.

INDIVIDUAL BATTING LEADERS

	AVG	AB	R	H	2B	3B	HR	RBI	SB
Anderson, N, MHC	.402	132	32	53	12	3	3	29	19
Pena, C, PEN	.387	150	54	58	8	0	15	40	21
Young, M, BBF	.384	172	50	66	11	2	4	35	3
Whitaker, D, BBF	.384	125	26	48	18	1	1	27	2
Waddell, C, WLS	.372	148	36	55	10	0	8	41	3
Ray, K, TRI	.370	135	28	50	9	0	6	34	6
Cowart, Z, LEX	.356	101	21	36	4	1	0	22	8
DiCarlo, N, LEX	.355	124	28	44	6	0	0	23	8
Diaz, Y, ASH	.344	131	29	45	9	0	2	26	2
Bussey, C, WLS	.336	149	57	50	8	0	4	26	23

INDIVIDUAL PITCHING LEADERS

	W	L	ERA	G	SV	IP	H	BB	SO
Morris, B, FOR	4	1	3.24	11	1	42	36	14	32
Jones, J, FOR	3	0	3.29	8	0	38	31	16	33
Harrison, D, BBF	5	0	3.29	7	0	41	25	15	51
Knowles, A, HYS	1	4	4.73	9	0	40	36	19	32
Boland, J, GRE	2	2	4.82	9	1	37	39	15	38
Yamada, H, ASH	1	5	4.85	8	1	43	36	21	30
Finch, D, FOR	3	1	5.27	11	0	43	47	23	42
Bazala, J, MAR	2	4	5.72	9	0	46	50	14	32
Murphy, Z, MAC	1	4	6.37	10	0	35	38	23	18

MLB DRAFT LEAGUE

Team	W	L	PCT	GB
West Virginia	45	28	.616	-
State College	38	36	.514	7.5
Mahoning Valley	38	38	.500	8.5
Trenton	37	39	.487	9.5
Frederick	36	41	.468	11
Williamsport	31	43	.419	14.5

CHAMPIONSHIP: West Virginia defeated State College 12-5.

INDIVIDUAL BATTING LEADERS

	AVG	AB	R	H	2B	3B	HR	RBI	SB
Rinehart, J, WV	.391	133	28	52	10	0	1	28	11
Mayo, J, WIL	.357	171	39	61	13	1	3	24	24
Nixon, C, MV	.351	148	26	52	13	0	2	16	5
Maryniak, C, TRN	.331	163	27	54	6	2	4	27	7
Hassert, C, FRE	.329	158	38	52	14	1	3	30	10
Collura, J, 2 Teams	.329	143	21	47	7	0	1	25	4
Roche, P, MV	.325	154	27	50	9	0	1	20	10
Hornung, C, MV	.317	167	27	53	10	1	3	39	3
Collins, D, WV	.315	143	33	45	6	5	2	19	21
Ungar, A, WV	.312	138	36	43	13	2	4	21	24

INDIVIDUAL PITCHING LEADERS

	W	L	ERA	G	SV	IP	H	BB	SO
Quevedo, M, SC	3	0	1.53	7	0	35	22	13	40
Holjes, C, SC	3	2	2.17	18	0	50	40	16	72
Hunter, J, FRE	4	0	2.62	13	0	55	45	18	69
Sparks, A, SC	2	1	2.63	8	0	41	37	18	37
Rudis, B, WIL	3	5	3.05	17	2	56	54	11	69
Hults, C, TRN	4	2	3.38	8	0	37	27	29	28
Boyle, J, WIL	2	1	3.55	21	4	38	31	19	44
Weaver, J, WV	2	2	3.76	7	0	41	46	13	31
Morrissey, M, TRN	3	0	3.94	8	0	46	37	17	38
Swygert, S, WIL	2	1	4.14	22	1	41	41	20	43

FLORIDA COLLEGIATE SUMMER LEAGUE

	W	L	PCT	GB
Sanford River Rats	26	3	.897	-
Orlando Snappers	19	13	.594	8.5
Leesburg Lightning	18	14	.563	9.5
DeLand Suns	14	19	.424	14
Winter Garden Squeeze	13	20	.394	15
Winter Park Diamond Dawgs	7	28	.200	22

CHAMPIONSHIP: Orlando defeated Sanford 2-0 in best-of-3 series.

INDIVIDUAL BATTING LEADERS

	AVG	AB	R	H	2B	3B	HR	RBI	SB
Calise, B, SAN	.408	76	20	31	4	0	1	12	17
Mock, D, SAN	.405	74	34	30	6	0	2	15	36
Fields, B, ORL	.387	75	18	29	4	1	2	13	5
Farner, M, ORL	.376	109	29	41	8	2	3	17	18
Puckett, S, SAN	.352	91	20	32	8	1	1	22	8
Harman, D, SAN	.347	72	16	25	2	3	2	20	7
Comeaux, G, ORL	.337	86	17	29	4	1	2	19	6
Young, G, WP	.333	63	13	21	4	0	0	11	1
Barrow, B, WP	.333	57	9	19	1	0	1	9	4
OBrien, M, DEL	.324	71	20	23	1	0	0	7	13

INDIVIDUAL PITCHING LEADERS

	W	L	ERA	G	SV	IP	H	BB	SO
Wright, B, SAN	2	0	1.00	5	0	18	10	7	24
Meeks, M, DEL	1	3	1.39	8	0	26	26	4	27
Tipmore, B, LEE	3	0	1.71	14	1	21	12	9	27
Clinton, T, SAN	2	0	1.90	7	0	19	12	9	14
Batson, B, ORL	1	0	2.21	6	0	20	10	9	18
Bozenhard, R, SAN	3	0	2.52	6	0	25	16	8	36
Waring, A, SAN	2	1	2.70	8	1	20	18	4	20
Happel, R, ORL	1	1	2.75	7	2	20	15	12	16
Janeczko, P, DEL	2	2	3.03	11	0	30	21	17	25
Furey, A, WG	2	4	3.10	8	0	29	29	5	24

FUTURES COLLEGIATE LEAGUE

	W	L	PCT	GB
Worcester Bravehearts	45	16	.738	--
Vermont Lake Monsters	40	22	.645	5.5
New Britain Bees	29	32	.484	16
Norwich Sea Unicorns	28	33	.467	17
Nashua Silver Knights	24	36	.400	20.5
Westfield Starfires	17	44	.295	28

CHAMPIONSHIP: Norwich defeated New Britain 2-0 in best-of-3 series.

INDIVIDUAL BATTING LEADERS

	AVG	AB	R	H	2B	3B	HR	RBI	SB
Shrake, P, NSK	.342	187	28	64	2	0	0	16	13
Cavossa, S, VER	.330	209	42	69	10	3	0	34	4
Richman, B, VER	.316	177	35	56	5	0	0	16	3
McMillan, S, VER	.313	192	40	60	16	0	11	52	8
Crowley, C, NBB	.310	187	30	58	8	3	0	23	7
Marshall, J, WOR	.306	183	39	56	16	0	9	44	1
Woodward, K, WOR	.303	152	38	46	5	2	0	16	25
Ruggiero, A, WES	.299	177	24	53	5	0	6	33	16
Staubley, B, NBB	.292	192	17	56	13	0	0	25	4
Kingsbury, H, VER	.291	179	31	52	8	4	2	26	5

INDIVIDUAL PITCHING LEADERS

	W	L	ERA	G	SV	IP	H	BB	SO
Wootton, M, NOR	5	1	2.70	9	0	50	49	5	47

GREAT LAKES LEAGUE

North	W	L	PCT	GB
Lima Locos	27	12	.692	--
Michigan Monarchs	21	19	.525	6.5
Muskegon Clippers	22	20	.524	6.5
Flag City Sluggers	20	20	.500	7.5

South	W	L	PCT	
Xenia Scouts	24	18	.571	--
Hamilton Joes	23	18	.561	0.5
S Ohio Copperheads	14	24	.368	8
Grand Lake Mariners	11	31	.262	13

CHAMPIONSHIP: Lima defeated Hamilton 2-1 in best-of-3 series.

INDIVIDUAL BATTING LEADERS

	AVG	AB	R	H	2B	3B	HR	RBI	SB
Franks, C, FCS	.364	88	29	32	4	2	2	16	18
Vercruysse, C, LL	.364	88	17	32	3	1	0	21	8
Engskov, H, FCS	.346	136	38	47	10	3	5	32	13
Wang, J, HJ	.345	139	30	48	11	0	3	32	14
Epple, W, MM	.341	123	35	42	10	1	0	15	17
Christ, J, HJ	.330	109	32	36	7	0	3	21	8
Kersey, B, LL	.327	98	23	32	8	1	6	23	6
Powell, T, FCS	.324	111	26	36	3	2	0	23	17
Rowley, R, SOC	.322	118	32	38	3	7	1	29	27
Smith, C, FCS	.322	121	14	39	5	0	1	27	6

INDIVIDUAL PITCHING LEADERS

	W	L	ERA	G	SV	IP	H	BB	SO
Bilo, M, HJ	5	1	1.01	7	0	36	21	9	25
Hayes, A, LL	2	0	1.93	8	0	33	27	11	36
Coddington, T, GLM	1	2	3.31	10	1	35	36	23	19
Hubbard, M, MM	1	1	3.41	8	1	34	26	9	31
Betancourt, B, FCS	3	2	3.62	8	0	37	31	10	38
Lopez, T, XS	1	2	4.93	9	0	35	34	17	32
Freeman, C, MSC	2	2	5.26	9	0	39	40	13	36

INDIVIDUAL BATTING LEADERS

	AVG	AB	R	H	2B	3B	HR	RBI	SB
D Cobb, Clarinda	.459	146	43	67	10	2	3	42	15
G Gonzalez, Carroll	.385	130	27	50	9	4	5	33	5
J Mosh, St. Joseph	.370	119	39	44	9	3	0	19	5
D Freeman, St. Joseph	.366	134	37	49	11	1	4	42	22
T Homolar, Clarinda	.338	130	20	44	4	1	2	34	4
A DiGiacinto, Jefferson City	.330	109	21	36	5	0	0	20	10
B Luikart, St. Joseph	.316	114	40	36	6	0	2	33	19
M Smith, Carroll	.313	96	19	30	4	2	0	14	10
C Knight, Clarinda	.306	144	35	44	4	0	0	27	26
J Roberts, Sedalia	.302	96	21	29	3	1	2	16	22

INDIVIDUAL PITCHING LEADERS

	W	L	ERA	G	SV	IP	H	BB	SO
L Chapman, St. Joseph	0	0	0.89	11	1	20	9	10	21
D Torpey, Sedalia	1	1	0.95	12	1	19	20	8	19
A Nance, St. Joseph	3	0	1.32	7	0	27	13	8	20
R Hirayana, Chillicothe	6	0	1.50	19	1	30	16	10	33
J Guck, St. Joseph	4	1	1.62	9	0	39	24	7	48
J Johnson, St. Joseph	2	0	1.66	18	3	22	8	9	34
E Harsell, Jefferson City	0	0	1.84	9	0	15	8	10	8
D Mccaskill, Nevada	1	1	1.84	4	1	15	12	1	17
Z Turpin, Carroll	2	0	1.88	10	0	14	6	13	14
T Graham, Jefferson City	2	0	1.96	6	1	23	20	4	27

HAMPTONS COLLEGIATE LEAGUE

	W	L	T	PTS
North Fork Ospreys	21	13	1	43
Southampton Breakers	18	15	2	38
South Shore Clippers	18	16	1	37
Shelter Island Bucks	16	19	0	32
Sag Harbor Whalers	15	16	4	34
Westhampton Aviators	13	22	0	26

CHAMPIONSHIP: South Shores defeated North Fork 2-0.

INDIVIDUAL BATTING LEADERS

	AVG	AB	R	H	2B	3B	HR	RBI	SB
Matuszewski, T, NF	.403	77	15	31	4	1	3	24	7
Pratt, N, NF	.398	88	13	35	3	1	2	27	1
Quintano, C, SH	.382	89	26	34	2	0	9	37	0
Slogik, N, SH	.350	80	22	28	7	0	3	24	1
Brunetti, M, WH	.337	89	22	30	6	0	4	18	5
Armenia, A, SSC	.333	84	19	28	6	1	3	25	11
Hotaling, L, SSC	.330	97	24	32	5	0	1	22	18
Fluharty, B, SI	.327	104	26	34	3	2	0	9	26
Sirchia, T, SAG	.324	74	15	24	0	0	2	17	3
Cimino, R, NF	.323	93	24	30	2	1	1	18	11

INDIVIDUAL PITCHING LEADERS

	W	L	ERA	G	SV	IP	H	BB	SO
Sliwkowski, D, SH	5	0	0.78	6	0	23	11	19	29
Travaglia, G, SH	1	0	1.64	8	2	22	9	17	21
Houghton, A, SH	3	0	2.05	6	0	26	19	16	27
Sarabia, D, SI	3	1	2.27	6	0	30	18	17	38
Soroca, A, SH	2	0	3.18	5	0	28	24	15	26
Onorato, D, SI	2	1	3.22	4	0	22	12	10	24
Mitchell, A, NF	3	2	3.38	8	0	27	16	26	31
Campanella, C, NF	2	1	3.38	5	0	21	15	23	25
Joseph, D, SI	3	1	3.55	7	0	33	20	20	51
Perez, S, NF	3	2	3.91	5	0	25	20	17	24

JAYHAWK COLLEGIATE LEAGUE

	W	L	PCT	GB
St. Joseph Mustangs	38	8	.826	--
Clarinda A's	27	18	.600	10.5
Chillicothe Mudcats	21	18	.538	13.5
Jefferson City Renegades	21	22	.488	15.5
Carroll Merchants	18	19	.486	15.5
Nevada Griffons	11	26	.297	23.5
Sedalia Bombers	8	27	.229	24.5

MINK LEAGUE

North Division

	W	L	PCT	GB
Keene SwampBats	32	12	.727	-
Sanford Mainers	22	22	.500	10
North Adams SteepleCats	21	23	.477	11
Upper Valley Nighthawks	18	26	.409	14
Vermont Mountaineers	16	28	.364	15
North Shore Navigators	16	28	.364	16

South Division

	W	L	PCT	GB
Newport Gulls	29	15	.659	-
Bristol Blues	27	17	.614	2
Marthas Vineyard Sharks	25	19	.568	4
Mystic Schooners	22	22	.500	7
Danbury Westerners	21	22	.488	7.5
Valley Blue Sox	20	23	.465	8.5
Ocean State Waves	16	28	.364	13

CHAMPIONSHIP: Keene defeated Martha's Vineyard 2-0 in best-of-3 series.

INDIVIDUAL BATTING LEADERS

	AVG	AB	R	H	2B	3B	HR	RBI	SB
Mainolfi, T, KSB	.383	115	27	44	8	0	1	28	9
Mexico, S, VAL	.375	112	13	42	8	2	6	27	1
Fellows, C, UVNH	.329	149	23	49	4	2	2	31	2
Lutte, J, DAN	.324	108	26	35	6	0	5	23	5
Hernandez, J, VM	.323	99	20	32	6	0	4	16	21
Herring, J, KSB	.322	146	33	47	8	0	8	33	1
Cha, E, MSC	.312	125	23	39	5	0	3	25	10
Bolton, M, NG	.311	151	34	47	9	1	6	34	10
Lipsey, M, KSB	.310	100	28	31	4	0	2	14	17
Martin, B, MVS	.309	110	26	34	8	0	0	22	16

INDIVIDUAL PITCHING LEADERS

	W	L	ERA	G	SV	IP	H	BB	SO
Kieck, C, MVS	3	1	2.13	9	0	38	36	8	37
Ruggiero Jr, J, NSC	2	1	2.82	10	0	38	32	21	22
Elarton, K, DAN	3	2	3.89	8	0	39	42	10	24
Brown, R, VM	1	3	4.29	14	2	36	34	24	39

NORTHWOODS LEAGUE

Great Lakes East

	W	L	PCT	GB
Traverse City Pit Spitters	28	9	.757	-
Kalamazoo GrowlersZ	20	17	.541	8
Royal Oak Leprechauns	18	18	.500	9.5
Kenosha Kingfish	17	19	.472	10.5
Battle Creek Battle Jacks	13	24	.351	15
Rockford Rivets	13	24	.351	15

Great Lakes West	W	L	PCT	GB
Wausau Woodchucks	25	9	.729	-
Madison Mallards	25	10	.708	0.5
Green Bay Rockers	20	17	.541	6.5
Lakeshore Chinooks	15	21	.417	11
Fond du Lac Dock Spiders	15	23	.395	12
Wisconsin Rapids Rafters	9	27	.250	17
Great Plains East	**W**	**L**	**PCT**	**GB**
Duluth Huskies	23	14	.622	-
Waterloo Bucks	21	17	.553	2.5
Thunder Bay Border Cats	19	17	.528	3.5
Eau Claire Express	19	19	.500	4.5
La Crosse Loggers	16	22	.421	7.5
Rochester Honkers	10	26	.278	12.5
Great Plains West	**W**	**L**	**PCT**	**GB**
Mankato MoonDogs	23	11	.676	-
St. Cloud Rox	22	14	.611	2
Badlands Big Sticks	21	16	.568	3.5
Willmar Stingers	21	18	.538	4.5
Minot Hot Tots	18	18	.500	6
Bismarck Larks	7	29	.194	17.5

CHAMPIONSHIP: Green Bay defeated Duluth 10-8..

INDIVIDUAL BATTING LEADERS

	AVG	AB	R	H	2B	3B	HR	RBI	SB
Piasecki, Aaron, TVC	.406	207	50	49	84	6	2	2	21
Surowiec, Ethan, DUL	.387	204	53	48	79	23	3	17	15
Malone, Noah, WAU	.381	202	55	66	77	15	1	14	12
Algarin, Joshua, BC	.366	235	61	53	86	11	2	2	18
Allen, Henry, MOT	.366	191	47	42	70	8	2	14	4
Coy, Noah, KZO	.363	182	52	50	66	9	4	1	26
Guzman, Armani, WIL	.361	155	40	38	56	12	2	2	28
Shimao, Tate, RFD	.346	162	46	39	56	11	1	2	1
Ohland, Carson, LAC	.345	200	54	42	69	13	0	3	16
Rodriguez, Dom, WAU	.340	162	43	38	55	9	0	7	2

INDIVIDUAL PITCHING LEADERS

	W	L	ERA	G	SV	IP	H	BB	SO
Crittendon, Jack, KZO	8	2	4.40	11	0	59	53	35	39
Day, Hunter, STC	5	5	4.80	11	0	60	69	16	41
Retz, Walker, EC	5	3	4.82	11	0	62	61	25	56
Alazaus, Beau, ROC	2	3	5.62	13	0	58	66	18	35
Spencer, Seth, WIR	2	7	5.88	15	0	60	65	47	46

PERFECT GAME COLLEGIATE LEAGUE

East Division	W	L	PCT	GB
Amsterdam Mohawks	31	11	.727	-
Saugerties Stallions	28	13	.679	2.5
Utica Blue Sox	23	18	.560	7.5
Boonville Lumberjacks	20	20	.500	10
Mohawk Valley Diamond Dawgs	21	22	.489	10.5
Glens Falls Dragons	12	28	.300	18
Oneonta Outlaws	9	32	.220	21.5
West Division	**W**	**L**	**PCT**	**GB**
Batavia Muckdogs	31	13	.700	-
Jamestown Tarp Skunks	29	14	.674	1.5
Niagara Falls Americans	30	16	.652	2
Auburn Doubledays	25	15	.611	4
Elmira Pioneers	23	20	.534	7.5
Newark Pilots	17	24	.420	12.5
Niagara Ironbacks	10	35	.222	21.5
Geneva Red Wings	7	35	.182	23

CHAMPIONSHIP: Saguerties defeated Batavia 2-0 in best-of-3 series.

INDIVIDUAL BATTING LEADERS

	AVG	AB	H	2B	3B	HR	RBI
G Moore, Niagara Falls	.388	121	47	4	4	0	26
T Gramesty, Elmira	.366	134	49	8	6	2	25
C Shin, Niagara	.364	129	47	12	0	0	25
C McKay, Boonville	.358	109	39	8	2	4	24
J Haynes, Jamestown	.355	107	38	9	1	5	27

	AVG	AB	H	2B	3B	HR	RBI
B Touchstone, Amsterdam	.350	143	50	13	1	5	44
T Jones, Mohawk Valley	.343	108	37	6	2	2	25
B Horton, Batavia	.342	114	39	11	3	1	19
B Marshall, Jamestown	.339	118	40	2	1	0	25
T Castrataro, Batavia	.338	145	49	7	1	0	31

INDIVIDUAL PITCHING LEADERS

	W	L	ERA	G	SV	IP	H	BB	SO
G Chandler, Batavia	4	1	1.40	8	0	39	45	7	20
L Rising, Batavia	3	1	1.85	16	1	39	20	8	47
H Boring, Niagara Falls	3	0	2.45	15	5	40	35	12	35
L Baker, Utica	4	1	2.74	8	0	43	29	19	21
O Birchard, Auburn	2	1	2.82	7	0	38	28	13	52
K Bazinet, Niagara Falls	3	4	3.05	8	0	38	39	16	21
G Rochon, Elmira	2	4	3.32	11	0	41	23	34	40
C Pencek, Jamestown	4	1	3.35	8	0	38	31	9	30
L Blandino, Niagara Falls	4	0	3.38	8	0	40	29	27	27
C Burkholder, Newark	4	4	4.22	9	0	43	47	14	35
B Hayes, Elmira	4	3	4.27	8	0	40	42	17	43

PROSPECT LEAGUE

Eastern Conference

Northeast	W	L	PCT	GB
Lafayette Aviators	35	21	.625	--
Chillicothe Paints	25	27	.481	8
Johnstown Mill Rats	26	29	.473	8.5
Champion City Kings	20	35	.364	14.5
Central	**W**	**L**	**PCT**	**GB**
REX Baseball	35	18	.660	--
Normal CornBelters	24	31	.436	12
Dubois County Bombers	21	30	.412	13
Danville Dans	18	33	.353	16.5
Springfield Lucky Horseshoes	13	38	.255	21

Western Conference

Northwest	W	L	PCT	GB
Clinton LumberKings	34	19	.642	--
Burlington Bees	33	21	.611	1.5
Illinois Valley Pistol Shrimp	31	23	.574	3.5
Quincy Doggy Paddlers	16	38	.296	18.5
South	**W**	**L**	**PCT**	**GB**
O'Fallon Hoots	41	15	.732	--
Cape Catfish	36	20	.643	5
Thrillville Thrillbillies	27	26	.509	12.5
Alton River Dragons	25	30	.455	15.5
Jackson Rockabillys	23	29	.442	16

CHAMPIONSHIP: Cape defeated Lafayette 2-0 in best-of-three championship series.

INDIVIDUAL BATTING LEADERS

	AVG	AB	H	2B	3B	HR	RBI	BB
C Yearsley, Burlington	.416	113	47	7	0	3	28	30
W Geary, O'Fallon	.390	159	62	11	2	1	29	28
B White, Clinton	.370	138	51	7	1	4	27	17
J Love, Illinois Valley	.366	142	52	8	2	1	31	25
L Keilen, Champion City	.359	131	47	10	1	8	35	25
K Schulte, Burlington	.341	185	63	11	5	4	48	20
W Diaz, REX	.338	157	53	9	4	14	48	14
M Bonczkowski, O'Fallon	.337	163	55	14	2	4	50	24
F Polanco, REX	.337	181	61	9	1	4	51	9
K Campbell, Alton River	.336	140	47	7	0	5	28	41

INDIVIDUAL PITCHING LEADERS

	W	L	ERA	G	SV	IP	H	BB	SO
S Guadamuz, REX	7	1	2.24	9	0	52	31	12	56
Z Cabell, Champion City	4	1	2.60	12	0	52	37	27	51
I Espiritusanto, Johnstown Mill	4	2	2.76	10	0	42	36	29	47
T Markezich, Alton River	3	1	2.79	17	4	42	41	6	42
A Pesci, Danville	3	3	3.12	9	1	40	35	11	43
C Kendall, Dubois County	1	3	3.24	10	0	42	48	15	21
W Culley, Lafayette	6	1	3.32	9	0	43	40	13	39
A Moss, REX	5	2	3.40	8	0	45	37	11	36
D Swanson, REX	4	0	3.40	9	0	42	32	8	47
C McDaniel, Lafayette	5	2	3.88	11	0	53	48	9	41

SOUTH FLORIDA COLLEGIATE LEAGUE

North Division	W	L	PCT	GB
Palm Beach Xtreme	29	9	.763	-
Boca Raton Beach Boys	25	12	.676	3.5
Delray Beach Lightning	22	16	.579	7
Palm Beach Gardens Matadors	19	18	.514	9.5
Boynton Beach Buccaneers	13	22	.371	14.5
Hialeah Gardens Lions	10	23	.303	16.5
West Palm Beach Iguanas	6	24	.200	19

South Division	W	L	T	GB
West Boca Snappers	29	11	.725	-
Boca Raton Blazers	23	13	.639	4
Coconut Creek Diamond Ducks	18	18	.500	9
Coconut Creek X Team	15	17	.469	10
Fort Lauderdale Hooks	13	17	.433	11
Pompano Beach Wave	11	21	.344	14
Miami Gardens Makos	9	21	.300	15

CHAMPIONSHIP: West Boca Snappers defeated Boca Raton Beach Boys 2-0 in best-of-3 series.

INDIVIDUAL BATTING LEADERS

	AVG	AB	R	H	2B	3B	HR	RBI	SB
Marshall, E. PBX	.409	132	27	54	12	1	5	47	2
Lindsey, J. PBW	.400	70	20	28	3	0	0	13	16
Benestad, N. DBL	.395	81	29	32	5	1	5	24	4
Cloud, C. BRB	.385	117	35	45	11	1	6	30	10
Martinez, S. PBX	.382	102	41	39	4	0	0	16	27
Potter, B. CCX	.375	88	24	33	6	1	3	21	19
Ebbs, L. CCD	.367	90	23	33	6	2	1	29	15
Cooke, L. PBX	.350	103	17	36	7	0	2	27	6
Strikowski, E. WBS	.350	103	26	36	7	0	2	28	4
Freeman, J. PBI	.347	72	19	25	7	2	2	19	15

INDIVIDUAL PITCHING LEADERS

	W	L	ERA	G	SV	IP	H	BB	SO
James, P, FLH	1	2	2.76	7	0	29	25	12	27
Ortiz, H, BRB	7	0	2.89	9	0	44	38	14	29
Koorse, N, CCD	3	1	3.31	8	0	35	30	25	39
Phillips, C, DBL	4	1	3.64	13	0	35	35	18	45
Sanchez, R, HI	1	5	4.73	11	0	32	36	30	26
Cardenas, A, DBL	1	3	5.20	12	0	36	39	18	41
Coffey, B, FLH	3	2	6.59	8	0	27	35	25	20

WEST COAST LEAGUE

North Division	W	L	PCT	GB
Edmonton Riverhawks	34	20	.630	-
Bellingham Bells	33	21	.611	1
Victoria HarbourCats	32	22	.593	2
Wenatchee AppleSox	31	23	.574	3
Kamloops NorthPaws	25	29	.463	9
Nanaimo NightOwls	23	31	.426	11
Port Angeles Lefties	20	34	.370	14
Kelowna Falcons	19	35	.352	15

South Division	W	L	PCT	GB
Portland Pickles	43	11	.796	-
Corvallis Knights	39	15	.722	4
Bend Elks	28	26	.519	15
Marion Berries	28	26	.519	15
Walla Walla Sweets	24	30	.444	19
Ridgefield Raptors	24	30	.444	19
Springfield Drifters	22	32	.407	21
Cowlitz Black Bears	20	34	.370	23
Yakima Valley Pippins	14	40	.259	29

CHAMPIONSHIP: Bellingham defeated Portland 2-1.

INDIVIDUAL BATTING LEADERS

	AVG	AB	R	H	2B	3B	HR	RBI	SB
Miller, J, BEN	.383	149	41	57	14	0	4	40	10
Wright, J, POR	.364	118	39	43	3	0	0	28	11
Wilson, B, COR	.348	138	44	48	9	3	3	25	15
Karliner, N, RID	.345	139	32	48	9	1	13	40	1
Chavez, C, SPR	.341	138	25	47	5	1	0	18	16
Estrella, A, RID	.340	144	27	49	11	1	9	41	5
Otis, T, POR	.333	135	39	45	14	0	4	40	18
Stagg, M, EDM	.329	167	43	55	6	3	4	33	19
Ketelsen, B, COR	.328	131	48	43	5	3	2	27	35
Miller, N, SPR	.326	184	33	60	9	0	0	31	3

INDIVIDUAL PITCHING LEADERS

	W	L	ERA	G	SV	IP	H	BB	SO
De Graauw, G, KEL	3	1	0.94	10	0	48	23	18	54
Verespey, S, MAR	4	0	1.45	7	0	43	37	12	21
Haythorn, M, WEN	4	2	3.33	10	0	46	33	32	54
Johnson, Z, COR	4	1	3.48	10	1	44	34	13	36
Wrightstone, S, PAL	2	2	3.52	11	0	46	38	18	36
Puodziunas, E, BEN	4	2	3.60	9	0	50	46	15	37
Holpuch, G, PAL	2	3	3.78	8	0	48	45	13	35
Pangborn, T, YVP	2	3	4.53	10	0	48	53	24	36
Boice, A, NAN	1	3	4.84	9	0	45	54	14	33

HIGH SCHOOL

To Be The Best Prep, It Takes A Holliday

Ethan Holliday is Baseball America's 2025 High School Player of the Year

PLAYER OF THE YEAR

BY JASON ELMQUIST

As a first-year third baseman for Stillwater (Okla.) High, he got to play alongside the best high school player in America. He also called that shortstop his brother.

He watched as MLB scouts dissected every grounder fielded and analyzed every at-bat taken by Jackson Holliday, who was on his way to a national-record 89 hits in a single season. Jackson was the Baseball America High School Player of the Year in 2022.

Now, three years later, Ethan finds himself in a similar situation. Scouts, crosscheckers and MLB decision-makers descended on Stillwater to watch the 18-year-old shortstop.

Like his brother before him, Ethan Holliday is the Baseball America High School Player of the Year. Jackson and Ethan are the first high school brother tandem to each be honored as POY.

"It's awesome, getting to share something like that with your brother, who you are super close with—and we actually got to play together," Ethan said. "We've got a family business in Stillwater, and baseball is kind of just what we love to do. So it's a real honor to share that with him."

PREVIOUS WINNERS

1992: Preston Wilson, OF/RHP, Bamberg-Ehrhardt (S.C.) HS
1993: Trot Nixon, OF/LHP, New Hanover HS, Wilmington, N.C.
1994: Doug Million, LHP, Sarasota (Fla.) HS
1995: Ben Davis, C, Malvern (Pa.) Prep
1996: Matt White, RHP, Waynesboro Area (Pa.) HS
1997: Darnell McDonald, OF, Cherry Creek HS, Englewood, Colo.
1998: Drew Henson, 3B/RHP, Brighton (Mich.) HS
1999: Josh Hamilton, OF/LHP, Athens Drive HS, Raleigh, N.C.
2000: Matt Harrington, RHP, Palmdale (Calif.) HS
2001: Joe Mauer, C, Cretin-Derham Hall HS, St. Paul, Minn.
2002: Scott Kazmir, LHP, Cypress Falls HS, Houston
2003: Jeff Allison, RHP, Veterans Memorial HS, Peabody, Mass.
2004: Homer Bailey, RHP, LaGrange (Texas) HS
2005: Justin Upton, SS, Great Bridge HS, Chesapeake, Va.
2006: Adrian Cardenas, SS/2B, Mons. Pace HS, Opa Locka, Fla.
2007: Mike Moustakas, SS, Chatsworth (Calif.) HS
2008: Ethan Martin, RHP/3B, Stephens County HS, Toccoa, Ga.
2009: Bryce Harper, C, Las Vegas HS
2010: Kaleb Cowart, RHP/3B, Cook HS, Adel, Ga.
2011: Dylan Bundy, RHP, Owasso (Okla.) HS
2012: Byron Buxton, OF, Appling County HS, Baxley, Ga.
2013: Clint Frazier, OF, Loganville (Ga.) HS
2014: Alex Jackson, OF, Rancho Bernardo (Calif.) HS
2015: Kyle Tucker, OF, Plant HS, Tampa
2016: Mickey Moniak, OF, La Costa Canyon HS, Carlsbad, Calif.
2017: MacKenzie Gore, LHP, Whiteville (N.C.) HS
2018: Cole Winn, RHP, Orange (Calif.) Lutheran HS
2019: Bobby Witt Jr., SS, Colleyville (Texas) Heritage HS
2020: No award given in truncated season
2021: Jackson Jobe, RHP/SS, Heritage Hall HS, Oklahoma City
2022: Jackson Holliday, SS, Stillwater (Okla.) HS
2023: Max Clark, OF, Franklin (Ind.) Community HS
2024: Konnor Griffin, SS, Jackson Prep, Flowood, Miss.

The historic achievement is surreal for their father Matt Holliday, who remembers reading Baseball America while in the coaches' offices at Allie P. Reynolds Stadium while his father Tom was an assistant coach for Oklahoma State.

"I remember (BA) was one of the early on—or I'd guess probably the original publication—that was really honing in on high school players, ranking high school players and giving these kinds of awards," the seven-time MLB all-star said. "So going back to me growing up with Baseball America—and my family has been in those magazines—and now for the boys to win Baseball America (High School) Player of the Year … it's quite an honor for them and exciting for the family."

Family friend and former Stillwater High baseball coach Marty Lees, who ran the program in Holliday's last two years before recently accepting a job to return to coaching in the college ranks with Wichita State, worked extensively with Ethan to help further mold his mechanics in the field, while Ethan's father could help with his swing.

But the one aspect Lees saw the senior shortstop take his greatest leap in the two years coaching him was something neither coach nor father could force.

"Leadership," Lees said. "I think that sometimes it takes time for kids to develop that … This year, he was always getting our kids together, always trying to make them believe that they're better than what they were, and he was coaching them."

Unprompted, the longtime coach gave his own ranking for the top prep prospect in the country.

"He'll be the best player I ever coached, and I've coached some big leaguers in my life—had several kids drafted—but there's going to be nobody better than Ethan Holliday as a player and as a person," Lees said.

"I've had some really good ones, but I'm excited for his future."

Holliday hit .611 batting average with 19 home runs this season—understandably high school teams were afraid of pitching to him.

In important games late in the season, including games against Bixby that would decide the district championship, Ethan was constantly being intentionally walked. It was understandable given that his first at-bat in both games of the series against the Spartans resulted in home runs.

He also was never given a chance to help his team in all three plate appearances in Stillwater's loss to Piedmont in the first round of the Oklahoma state tournament.

"That's a sign of respect. It's one of those things where, when that happens, you find a way on defense to make a play, or you encourage your teammates," Matt said. "He's very outgoing with his teammates. And so I think he handled all that really well."

HIGH SCHOOL TOP 50

Rank	School	Coach	Record
1	Stoneman Douglas HS, Parkland, Fla.	Todd Fitz-Gerald	31-2
2	Calallen HS, Corpus Christi, Texas	Steve Chapman	34-2
3	St. John Bosco HS, Long Beach, Calif.	Andy Rojo	27-4
4	Corona (Calif.) HS	Andy Wise	28-3
5	St. Johns College HS, Washington D.C.	Mark Gibbs	30-1
6	Magnolia Heights HS, Senatobia, Miss.	Chris McMinn	39-5
7	James Island Charter, Charleston, S.C.	Matt Spivey	30-4
8	Grapevine (Texas) HS	Jimmy Webster	35-3
9	Puyallup (Wash.) HS	Marc Wiese	28-1
10	South Walton HS, South Rosa Beach, Fla.	Nick Borthwick	31-4
11	Aquinas HS, San Bernardino, Calif.	Mike Carpentier	25-3
12	Owasso (Okla.) HS	Larry Turner	39-3
13	Walton HS, Marietta, Ga.	Russ Wright	33-8
14	Staley HS, Kansas City	Diondre Josenberger	37-3
15	Corona del Sol HS, Tempe, Ariz.	Dave Webb	27-6
16	Trinity HS, Louisville	Rick Arnold	34-3
17	Miller School, Charlottsville, Va.	Billy Wagner	34-6
18	Newnan (Ga.) HS	MarcGilmor	32-5
19	South Salem HS, Salem, Ore.	Max Price	29-1
20	Kingwood (Texas) HS	Michael Oros	38-4
21	Crespi Carmelite HS, Encino, Calif.	Mike Glendenning	24-3
22	Governor Livingston HS, Berkeley Heights, N.J.	Chris Roof	24-0
23	Madison HS, Vienna, Va.	Mark Gjormand	22-3
24	The First Academy, Orlando, Fla.	Alan Kunkel	30-4
25	Howell HS, St. Charles, Mo.	Tony Perkins	34-4
26	Catholic HS, Baton Rouge, La.	Brad Bass	37-5
27	Huntington Beach (Calif.) HS	Benji Medure	24-5
28	Trinity Christian Academy, Jacksonville	Jonathan Murphy	30-5
29	American Fork (Utah) HS	Jarod Ingersoll	28-4
30	Memorial HS, Houston	Jeremy York	29-5
31	Gloucester Catholic HS, Gloucester City, N.J.	Dennis Barth	21-3
32	Andrean HS, Merrillville, Ind.	Dave Pishkur	30-3
33	Miami Springs (Fla.) HS	David Fanshawe	28-3
34	Lincoln (Neb.) East HS	Mychal Lanik	33-3
35	Center Grove HS, Greenwood, Ill.	Keith Hartfield	25-4
36	Archbishop Moeller HS, Cincinnati	Tim Held	25-3
37	Arcadia (Calif.) HS	Nick Lemas	26-4
38	Cherry Creek HS, Greenwood Village, Colo.	Joe Smith	23-5
39	Thurston HS, Springfield, Ore.	Dennis Minium	26-3
40	Roberson HS, Asheville, N.C.	Eric Filipek	27-6
41	American Heritage HS, Plantation, Fla.	Bruce Aven	28-6
42	Live Oak HS, Watson, La.	Jesse Cassard	33-8
43	De La Salle HS, Concord, Calif.	David Jeans	26-4
44	Blessed Trinity HS, Roswell, Ga.	Jamie Wagner	32-5
45	Owyhee HS, Meridian, Idaho	Russ Wright	28-4
46	Hartselle (Ala.) HS	Brad Phillips	35-9
47	Ketchem HS, Wappingers Falls, N.Y.	Pat Mealy	20-4
48	Lawrence (Kan.) Free State HS	Mike Hill	28-2
49	Olathe (Kansas) West HS	Mike Zegunis	25-2
50	Brother Rice HS, Chicago	Sean McBride	33-3

2025 HIGH SCHOOL ALL-AMERICA TEAM

Xavier Neyens

Eli Willits

Taitn Gray, C, Dallas Center-Grimes Comm. HS, Dallas Center, Iowa
Gray is an explosive, switch-hitting catcher with plus raw power and a physical, 6-foot-3, 215-pound frame. He generates gaudy top-end exit velocities for a prep and has a chance to stick behind the plate with a strong arm. Gray was a home run machine this spring in Iowa, and he'll still be 17 years old on draft day.

Gavin Fien, CI, Great Oak HS, Temecula, Calif.
Fien was arguably the most impressive hitter on the 2024 showcase circuit and led Team USA with five extra-base hits and a .680 slugging percentage. He's got plenty of strength in his 6-foot-3, 200-pound frame and has both all-fields power and a knack for the barrel that could lead to an above-average pure hit tool.

Xavier Neyens, CI, Mount Vernon HS, Mount Vernon, Wash.
Neyens is an imposing, 6-foot-4 lefthanded slugger with loud tools led by his power and arm strength. A shortstop now, many scouts expect Neyens to slide to third base, where he could be a strong defender with 30+ home run upside and great batting eye that leads to lots of walks and a steady floor of on-base ability.

Ethan Holliday, MI, Stillwater HS, Stillwater, Okla.
Holliday has led the 2025 prep class for years as a famous slugger from a big league family. He has the tools and ability to back up the hype, with towering lefthanded power and an advanced approach. He has more risk to slide to a corner than his brother Jackson, but with more than enough impact to profile anywhere.

Eli Willits, MI, Fort Cobb-Broxton HS, Fort Cobb, Okla.
Willits has the most well-rounded set of tools and skills in the 2025 draft. He's a savvy switch-hitter with great contact skills and burgeoning power, he can pick it at shortstop with instincts and arm strength and he's also a plus runner. Big league bloodlines and extreme youth for the class are bonuses.

Tate Southisene, OF, Basic HS, Basic, Nev.
Southisene is an instinctual gamer who does everything on the field at a high level. The surprising torque and power he generates in his swing leads to sneaky pop, and he pairs it with an advanced feel for the barrel. He could become an above-average defender at either shortstop or center field.

Slater de Brun, OF, Summit HS, Bend, Ore.
De Brun has a Slade Caldwell starter kit as an undersized, speedy center fielder with top-of-the-lineup tools and a shot to go in the first round. He's a double-plus runner who should provide a plus glove up the middle. He makes a ton of contact, though it might be singles and doubles more than home runs.

Brock Sell, OF, Tokay HS, , Lodi, Calif.
Sell is a high-end athlete and plus runner who pairs great speed and defensive instincts in center field. He has a contact-oriented swing that allows him to collect hits in all areas of the field. Power is his lone question mark, but he has the tools and skills to impact the game as a hitter, runner and defender.

JoJo Parker, DH, Purvis HS, Purvis, Miss.
Parker has one of the better hit/power combos in the 2025 class. His smooth lefthanded swing combines bat speed and power. He's a big-bodied shortstop who could slide off the position, but he has the athleticism to handle a number of defensive spots and has turned in quicker run times this spring.

Seth Hernandez

Kruz Schoolcraft

Uli Fernsler, SP, Novi HS, Novi, Mich.
Fernsler is a fast-rising lefthander who pairs great control and command with a deceptive, low-slot release that amplifies his entire mix. While he currently tops out in the low 90s, the pitch jumps over barrels at the top of the zone. Fernsler also has a quality slider and changeup to create a high-probability starter kit.

Seth Hernandez, SP, Corona HS, Corona, Calif.
This is what a top-of-the-rotation arm looks like in high school. Hernandez pairs tremendous pure stuff with advanced control and athleticism. He's been up to 100 mph with his fastball, throws a 70-grade changeup that is among the best secondaries in the class and also has two distinct breaking balls.

Mason Pike, SP, Puyallup HS, Puyallup, Wash.
Pike is an athletic two-way player who could be a shortstop at the next level but might have more upside on the mound. He has a high-spin pitch mix with a fastball in the 90-95 mph range that touches 97, as well as a two-plane slider and a mid-80s changeup. He dominated Washington hitters with improved control.

Kruz Schoolcraft, SP, Sunset HS, Portland, Ore.
The 6-foot-8 Schoolcraft is a giant on the mound with elite extension that makes a fastball touching 97 mph a nightmare for opponents. He shows the makings of two real secondaries in his changeup and slider. If he weren't a giant lefthander with excellent stuff, he'd also be a pro prospect as a powerful first baseman.

Aaron Watson, SP, Trinity Christian academy, Jacksonville, Fla.
Watson has an ideal pitcher's frame at 6-foot-5, 205 pounds and screams starter thanks to a loose, easy delivery and a high-quality four-pitch mix. His fastball and slider are his bread and butter—with the slider showing a rare power/movement combo for a prep—but he can also mix in a quality curveball and changeup.

Second Team

Pos.	Player	School
C	Brayden Jaksa	Irvington HS, Fremont, Calif.
CI	Josh Hammond	Wesleyan Christian, High Point, N.C.
CI	Quentin Young	Oaks Christian HS, Westlake Village, Calif.
MI	Billy Carlson	Corona (Calif.) HS
MI	Steele Hall	Hewitt-Trussville (Ala.) HS
OF	Dean Moss	IMG Academy, Bradenton, Fla.
OF	Sean Gamble	IMG Academy, Bradenton, Fla.
OF	Blaine Bullard	Klein Cain HS, Houston
DH	Kayson Cunningham	Johnson HS, San Antonio
Position		**Player & School**
SP	Landon Harmon	East Union HS, Blue Springs, Miss.
SP	Briggs McKenzie	Corinth Holders HS, Wendell, N.C.
SP	Jack Bauer	Lincoln-Way East HS, Frankfort, Ill.
SP	Angel Cervantes	Warren HS, Downey, Calif.
SP	Talon Haley	Lewisburg HS, Olive Branch, Miss.

AMATEUR/YOUTH CHAMPIONS 2025

AMERICAN LEGION BASEBALL

Event	Site	Champion	Runner-up
World Series (19U)	Shelby, N.C.	Chesapeake (Va.).	League City (Texas)

BABE RUTH BASEBALL

Event	Site	Champion	Runner-up
Cal Ripken (9U)	Florence, Ala.	Tulare 9U	Hilo, Hawaii 9U
Cal Ripken 11-year-old (70 feet)	Florence, Ala.	South Lexington 11U	Marlton, N.J. 11U
13-year-old	Jamestown, N.Y.	Tallahassee Fla. 13U	Samford, Conn. 13U.
14-year-olds	Hot Springs, Ark.	Tallahassee-Leon 14U	Mexico 14U
13-to-16-year-olds	Branson, Mo.	Branson BRL 16U	West End BRL 16U
16-to-18-year-olds	Ocala, Fla.	Hanford Calif. 18U	Gulf Coast Ala 18U

LITTLE LEAGUE BASEBALL

Event	Site	Champion	Runner-up
Little League (11-12)	South Williamsport, Pa.	Taiwan	Las Vegas, Nevada
Junior League (12-14)	Taylor, Mich.	Taiwan	Macon, Ga.
Senior League (13-16)	Easley, S.C.	Puerto Rico	Easley, S.C.
Intermediate (50-70)	Livermore, Calif.	Venezuela	Waiuku, Hawaii.

REVIVING BASEBALL IN INNER CITIES (RBI)

Event	Site	Champion
Junior (13-15)	Vero Beach, Fla.	Dodgers Dreamtown RBI
Senior (16-18)	Vero Beach, Fla.	Arizona Diamondbacks RBI

Taiwan won both the Little League World Series (shown here) and the Junior World Series.

DRAFT

Eli Willits Becomes Youngest No. 1 Pick Ever

BY CARLOS COLLAZO

In the history of the event before 2025, a dozen players selected with the first overall pick were 17 years old on draft day.

By selecting Eli Willits with the No. 1 pick in the Nationals made it a baker's dozen. This time, though, was a little bit different.

The Oklahoma high school shortstop became the youngest 1-1 player in draft history in terms of baseball age at 17 years, six months and 21 days.

Another 15 players drafted first overall were 18 years old, and three were 19. All told, half of all No. 1 overall picks in history—30 out of 60—were teenagers on draft day.

The concept of "draft day" is fluid. Over the years, MLB has conducted its draft on dates ranging from June 1 to July 14. So players with birthdates in June or July could be aged up or down arbitrarily, simply because their birthdays fall on one side or the other of a moving line of demarcation.

To get around this, Baseball America has determined the "baseball age" of every first-round draft pick ever. This is calculated as the player's age as of June 30 of his draft year. This is the cutoff used to denote player age by resources such as Baseball Reference and FanGraphs.

Willits is the son of former big league outfielder Reggie Willits, who serves as associate head coach at Oklahoma. Eli's older brother Jaxon Willits is the Sooners' shortstop.

None of this would be possible if not for a deci-

Eli Willits was drafted No. 1 overall

FIRST-ROUND BONUS PROGRESSION

After dipping during the coronavirus pandemic and its after effects, MLB draft spending is once again growing at a relatively dramatic rate. This is to be expected, as the collective bargaining agreement mandates that as MLB revenues rise, draft bonus spending allotments rise at the same rate. But the nature of recent growth has made up for the stagnation that existed in the 2019-2022 range. These past four drafts are the first time that the draft has shown first round bonus growth for four straight years since 1998-2001. The average first round bonus has more than doubled since the draft bonus pool rules were implemented for the 2012 MLB Draft. This year's increase was smaller than that of the past two years, but the past two years were the biggest back-to-back increases since the 1990s.

Year	Average	Change	Year	Average	Change	Year	Average	Change	Year	Average	Change
1965	$42,516	—	1981	$78,573	6.10%	1997	$1,325,536	40.40%	2013	$2,641,538	6.70%
1966	$44,430	4.50%	1982	$82,615	5.10%	1998	$1,637,667	23.10%	2014	$2,612,109	-1.10%
1967	$42,898	-3.40%	1983	$87,236	5.60%	1999	$1,809,767	10.50%	2015	$2,774,945	6.23%
1968	$43,850	2.20%	1984	$105,391	20.80%	2000	$1,872,586	3.50%	2016	$2,897,557	4.42%
1969	$43,504	-0.80%	1985	$118,415	12.10%	2001	$2,154,280	15.00%	2017	$3,880,723	25.4%
1970	$45,230	3.90%	1986	$116,300	-1.60%	2002	$2,106,793	-2.20%	2018	$3,754,123	-3.37%
1971	$45,197	-0.10%	1987	$128,480	10.50%	2003	$1,765,644	-16.20%	2019	$3,791,729	1.01%
1972	$44,952	-0.50%	1988	$142,540	10.90%	2004	$1,958,448	10.90%	2020	$4,080,307	7.61%
1973	$48,832	8.60%	1989	$176,008	23.50%	2005	$2,018,000	3.00%	2021	$4,009,424	-1.74%
1974	$53,333	9.20%	1990	$252,577	43.50%	2006	$1,933,333	-4.20%	2022	$4,074,268	1.62%
1975	$49.33	-7.50%	1991	$365,396	44.70%	2007	$2,098,083	8.50%	2023	$4,561,460	12.0%
1976	$49,631	0.60%	1992	$481,893	31.90%	2008	$2,458,714	17.20%	2024	$5,036,544	10.4%
1977	$48,813	-1.60%	1993	$613,437	27.20%	2009	$2,434,800	-1.00%	2025	$5,334,019	5.9%
1978	$67,892	39.10%	1994	$790,357	28.90%	2010	$2,220,966	-8.80%			
1979	$68,094	0.20%	1995	$918,019	16.10%	2011	$2,653,375	19.50%			
1980	$74,025	8.70%	1996*	$944,404	2.90%	2012	$2,475,167	-6.70%			

sion Eli Willits made in May 2024. That's when he announced that he was reclassifying for the 2025 draft. He finished his course work at Fort Cobb-Broxton High in three years rather than four in order to be eligible for the draft a year early.

Through the 2024 draft, the youngest player ever selected No. 1 overall was California prep shortstop Tim Foli in 1968. His baseball age was 17 years, six months and 24 days—three days older than Willits—when the Mets made him the top pick in his draft.

Among the youngest players ever drafted at 1-1 are superstars Ken Griffey Jr. (1987), Bryce Harper (2010) and Alex Rodriguez (1993). Multi-time all-stars Carlos Correa (2012) and Justin Upton (2005) both were 17 and had notably young baseball ages when drafted.

The list of the five youngest top-five overall draft picks in history looks like this with Willits now included. Remember, the age listed here is as of June 30 of the player's draft year.

1. Expos SS Condredge Holloway (1971, fourth overall) at 17 years, five months and six days

2. Mets LHP Jon Matlack (1967, fourth overall) at 17 years, five months and 11 days

3. Phillies OF Jeff Jackson (1989, fourth overall) at 17 years, five months and 28 days

4. Oklahoma prep SS Eli Willits (2025, first overall) at 17 years, six months and 21 days

5. Mets SS Tim Foli (1968, first overall) at 17 years, six months and 24 days

While Holloway was the youngest top-five overall pick in draft history, he never played professional baseball. He did not sign with Montreal in 1971 or when drafted by the Braves in 1975 or '76. Instead, Holloway played football at Tennessee and was the first Black quarterback in SEC history. He later starred in the Canadian Football League.

In any case, not many elite draft talents have ever been as young as Willits, who immediately became the top prospect in the Nationals' farm system.

Eight More Notable 2025 Draft Themes

While the 2025 draft is unlikely to go down as one of the most talented of all time, it had numerous intriguing storylines. In addition to Willits making draft history, here are were eight other notables:

1. Ethan And Jackson Holliday Become Latest First-Round Brothers

Three years ago, the Orioles made Jackson Holliday the first pick in the 2022 draft. This year, the Rockies made younger brother Ethan Holliday the fourth pick in the draft.

The Hollidays tie Dmitri and Delmon Young with a cumulative draft position of five. Only BJ and Justin Upton have ever fared better in terms of the lowest sum of overall selection numbers.

The Uptons are also one of the most productive first-round brother tandems in MLB history. Only JD and Stephen Drew accumulated more WAR.

BONUS SPENDING BY TEAM

In the span of three drafts, draft bonus spending has climbed from $350 million to over $400 million. After the 2024 draft saw a $24 million increase on 2023, this year's draft saw a $27 million jump from 2024, as MLB teams spent a record $401,382,911 on bonuses for 2025 MLB draft picks.

This year didn't see any records for the highest bonus for a player, but the overall spending continued to grow.

The average team spent $13.4 million in 2025, up from $12.5 million in 2022. The Orioles $21.6 million broke the Guardians' bonus record of $20.4 million set in 2024.

The CBA that went into effect in 2012 curtailed spending by instituting harsh penalties for teams that exceeded their bonus pools by more than five percent. It also ended the practice of awarding major league contracts to draftees. But as revenues within the game have increased, so too have the bonus pools MLB allocates to teams for the first 10 rounds. No team has yet been willing to exceed the five percent mark.

The new CBA that added the draft lottery system also included a $25,000 bump in the maximum bonus that teams could spend after the 10th round without counting toward a team's bonus allotment.

TEAM	2025	2024	2023
Angels	$19,016,725	$13,990,500	$10,015,225
Athletics	$12,288,800	$16,908,900	$15,882,600
Blue Jays	$12,759,900	$10,356,050	$7,856,185
Braves	$11,288,000	$9,453,100	$9,988,500
Brewers	$14,623,250	$12,504,900	$12,498,100
Cardinals	$15,362,600	$11,739,100	$7,618,500
Cubs	$11,470,725	$11,481,900	$10,695,000
D-backs	$11,605,626	$13,462,000	$12,055,000
Dodgers	$10,584,425	$7,418,800	$8,583,000
Giants	$9,676,600	$8,927,350	$11,433,525
Guardians	$11,958,005	$20,416,100	$10,221,275
Mariners	$18,280,000	$10,479,900	$13,990,500
Marlins	$16,242,400	$11,360,000	$13,692,400
Mets	$7,418,190	$11,018,000	$9,869,850
Nationals	$18,630,000	$15,925,200	$16,150,000
Orioles	$21,585,840	$12,691,800	$11,414,800
Padres	$8,807,100	$11,014,600	$7,161,600
Phillies	$9,611,700	$8,784,400	$6,761,100
Pirates	$13,308,700	$15,370,525	$17,123,300
Rangers	$12,955,825	$8,252,600	$11,442,900
Rays	$15,513,000	$9,727,600	$12,172,100
Red Sox	$14,521,300	$12,250,000	$11,851,200
Reds	$13,030,200	$17,665,800	$15,321,500
Rockies	$17,063,000	$18,206,100	$13,192,450
Royals	$15,038,500	$14,594,600	$14,002,200
Tigers	$13,025,200	$13,712,500	$17,677,450
Twins	$14,085,500	$13,136,650	$15,245,600
White Sox	$14,157,100	$16,292,500	$10,967,800
Yankees	$7,838,100	$9,688,190	$6,970,900
TOTAL	$401,382,911	$374,345,077	$350,089,060
AVERAGE	$13,379,430	$12,478,169	$11,669,635

2. Seth Hernandez And Billy Carlson Are The First High School Teammates Both Drafted Top 10 Overall

Seven drafts previously have featured high school teammates selected in the first round of the same draft, but never before had prep teammates both been top 10 overall picks. That changed this year when Corona High teammates Seth Hernandez, drafted sixth by the Pirates, and Billy Carlson, drafted 10th by the White Sox, both were top 10 overall picks.

Only one high school teammate tandem has a lower cumulative draft position that the Corona duo of Hernandez and Carlson. That distinction belongs to 2007 first-rounders Mike Moustakas and Matt Dominguez of Chatsworth High. They were drafted second and 12th overall.

3. And Brady Ebel Makes Three For Corona High

Corona High teammates Seth Hernandez and Billy Carlson established a standard for high school teammates by both being top 10 overall picks. Their teammate Brady Ebel followed soon after when the Brewers drafted him 32nd overall with

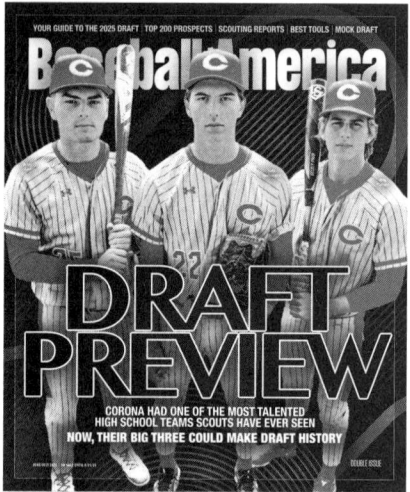

California's Corona High made history as the first high school with two top 10 picks, and they added a third top 40 pick as well.

HIGHEST BONUSES EVER

No 2025 draftee topped ther $9.25 million bonuses Chase Burns and Charlie Condon signed in 2024.

Player, Pos.	Team, Year (Pick)	Bonus
Chase Burns, RHP	Reds, 2024 (No. 2)	$9,250,000
Charlie Condon, OF	Rockies, 2024 (No. 3)	$9,250,000
Paul Skenes, RHP	Pirates, 2023 (No. 1)	$9,200,000
Dylan Crews, OF	Nationals, 2023 (No. 2)	$9,000,000
Ethan Holliday, SS	Rockies, 2025 (No. 4)	$9,000,000
Travis Bazzana, 2B	Guardians, 2024 (No. 1)	$8,950,000
Kade Anderson, LHP	Mariners, 2025 (No. 3)	$8,800,000
Spencer Torkelson, 1B	Tigers, 2020 (No. 1)	$8,416,300
Eli Willits, SS	Nationals, 2025 (No. 1)	$8,200,000
Jackson Holliday, SS	Orioles, 2022 (No. 1)	$8,190,000
Druw Jones, OF	D-backs, 2022 (No. 2)	$8,189,400
Adley Rutschman, C	Orioles, 2019 (No. 1)	$8,100,000
Gerrit Cole, RHP	Pirates, 2011 (No. 1)	$8,000,000
Wyatt Langford, OF	Rangers, 2023 (No. 4)	$8,000,000
Hagen Smith, LHP	White Sox, 2024 (No. 5)	$8,000,000
Jack Leiter, RHP	Rangers, 2021 (No. 2)	$7,922,000
Bobby Witt Jr., SS	Royals, 2019 (No. 2)	$7,787,400
Max Clark, OF	Tigers, 2023 (No. 3)	$7,767,500
Tyler Bremner, RHP	Angels, 2025 (No. 2)	$7,689,525
Stephen Strasburg, RHP	Nationals, 2009 (No. 1)*	$7,500,000
Bubba Starling, OF	Royals, 2011 (No. 5)	$7,500,000
Casey Mize, RHP	Tigers, 2018 (No. 1)	$7,500,000
Jac Caglianone, TWP	Royals, 2024 (No. 5)	$7,497,500
Liam Doyle, LHP	Cardinals, 2025 (No. 5)	$7,250,000
Seth Hernandez, RHP	Pirates, 2025 (No. 6)	$7,250,000
Hunter Greene, RHP/SS	Reds, 2017 (No. 2)	$7,230,000
Andrew Vaughn, 1B	White Sox, 2019 (No. 3)	$7,221,200
Termarr Johnson, SS	Pirates, 2022 (No. 4)	$7,219,000
Avia Arquette, SS	Marlins, 2025 (No. 7)	$7,149,900
Walker Jenkins, OF	Twins, 2023 (No. 5)	$7,144,200
Joey Bart, C	Giants, 2018 (No. 2)	$7,025,000
Brendan McKay, 1B/LHP	Rays, 2017 (No. 4)	$7,005,000
Austin Martin, SS	Blue Jays, 2020 (No. 5)	$7,000,825
Kyle Wright, RHP	Braves, 2017 (No. 5)	$7,000,000

a first-round compensatory pick. No high school had ever had three teammates drafted that high in one draft class.

Corona made draft history for its top trio—and did so by a wide margin. The highest trio before this was Moses Lake (Wash.)'s 1999 class of BJ Garbe (No. 5 pick), Ryan Doumit (No. 59), Jason Cooper (No. 63). Cooper did not sign.

The other top trio is the 2019 IMG Academy (Fla.) class that saw Brennan Malone (No. 33), Rece Hinds (No. 49) and Kendall Williams (No. 52).

The quality of Hernandez, Carlson and Ebel was a big reason why area scouts regarded Corona as perhaps the most talented high school team they had ever seen.

4. A Historic Year For Shortstops

No matter how you slice it, the 2025 draft was a historic one for shortstops. Six of the top 10 players drafted were announced as shortstops, as were 11 of the top 20 and 15 of the top 30. Each established a high-water mark for shortstops drafted among the top 10, 20 or 30 picks.

The previous record for most shortstops drafted among the top 30 picks was 10. That number was reached first in 2021 and then again in 2023.

5. Kyson And Malachi Witherspoon Are Highest-Drafted Twins Ever

Kyson and Malachi Witherspoon of Oklahoma made history as the highest-drafted twin brothers in one class. The Red Sox drafted Kyson 15th overall, while the Tigers selected Malachi 62nd overall in the second round. The previous record for twins in one draft class is believed to be Brian and Blake Doyle, who both were fourth-rounders in 1972.

If we extend the search to include discontinued phases of the draft, then Tom and Tim Brookens were both first-round picks in the January phase of the 1975 draft.

6. Eight Tennessee Players Were Drafted In The Top Three Rounds

When the Angels selected righthander Nate Snead with pick No. 105 to end the supplemental third round, it marked the eighth Tennessee player drafted in the top three rounds. That established a record for players drafted from one college program through the first three rounds, bettering the mark set by Arkansas and Florida, which both had six players drafted in the top three rounds in 2016.

A special thank you to the Pramana SHIFT AI tool, which output the data for this Tennessee note.

7. Liam Doyle, Gavin Kilen And Andrew Fischer Are The Ninth Trio Of College Teammates Drafted In The First Round

The Cardinals drafted lefthander Liam Doyle fifth overall. The Giants followed with shortstop Gavin Kilen at No. 13, and the Brewers selected third baseman Andrew Fischer 20th overall. All three players were Tennessee teammates this year—though only this year after each had transferred from other schools—marking just the ninth time a trio of college teammates had all been first-round picks.

It happened most recently in 2024, when Wake Forest teammates Chase Burns, Nick Kurtz and Seaver King were all drafted with top 10 overall picks.

Burns and King were also transfers from other schools, and this phenomenon of concentrated first-round college talent on one team is likely to continue in the age of the transfer portal.

8. Pirates Extend Their Streak Of Drafting High-End Two-Way Talents

The Pirates chose Corona High righthander Seth Hernandez with the sixth pick in this year's draft. He has the highest upside among pitchers in this draft class. He's also a terrific hitter who regularly DHed for Corona

NO. 1 OVERALL PICKS

Yr Team: Player, Pos., School	Bonus
1965 **Athletics:** Rick Monday, OF, Arizona State	$100,000
1966 **Mets:** Steve Chilcott, C, Antelope Valley HS, Lancaster, Calif.	$75,000
1967 **Yankees:** Ron Blomberg, 1B, Druid Hills HS, Atlanta	$65,000
1968 **Mets:** Tim Foli, SS, Notre Dame HS, Sherman Oaks, Calif.	$74,000
1969 **Senators:** Jeff Burroughs, OF, Centennial HS, Long Beach	$88,000
1970 **Padres:** Mike Ivie, C, Walker HS, Atlanta	$75,000
1971 **White Sox:** Danny Goodwin, C, Peoria (Ill.) HS	Did not sign
1972 **Padres:** Dave Roberts, 3B, Oregon	$70,000
1973 **Rangers:** David Clyde, LHP, Westchester HS, Texas	*$65,000
1974 **Padres:** Bill Almon, SS, Brown	*$90,000
1975 **Angels:** Danny Goodwin, C, Southern	*$125,000
1976 **Astros:** Floyd Bannister, LHP, Arizona State	$100,000
1977 **White Sox:** Harold Baines, OF, St. Michaels (Md.) HS	$32,000
1978 **Braves:** Bob Horner, 3B, Arizona State	*$162,000
1979 **Mariners:** Al Chambers, 1B, Harris HS, Harrisburg, Pa.	$60,000
1980 **Mets:** Darryl Strawberry, OF, Crenshaw HS, Los Angeles	$152,500
1981 **Mariners:** Mike Moore, RHP, Oral Roberts	$100,000
1982 **Cubs:** Shawon Dunston, SS, Jefferson HS, New York	$135,000
1983 **Twins:** Tim Belcher, RHP, Mount Vernon Nazarene (Ohio)	Did not sign
1984 **Mets:** Shawn Abner, OF, Mechanicsburg (Pa.) HS	$150,500
1985 **Brewers:** B.J. Surhoff, C, North Carolina	$150,000
1986 **Pirates:** Jeff King, 3B, Arkansas	$180,000
1987 **Mariners:** Ken Griffey Jr., OF, Moeller HS, Cincinnati	$160,000
1988 **Padres:** Andy Benes, RHP, Evansville	$235,000
1989 **Orioles:** Ben McDonald, RHP, Louisiana State	*$350,000
1990 **Braves:** Chipper Jones, SS, The Bolles School, Jacksonville	$275,000
1991 **Yankees:** Brien Taylor, LHP, East Carteret HS, Beaufort, N.C.	$1,550,000
1992 **Astros:** Phil Nevin, 3B, Cal State Fullerton	$700,000
1993 **Mariners:** Alex Rodriguez, SS, Westminster Christian HS, Miami	*$1,000,000
1994 **Mets:** Paul Wilson, RHP, Florida State	$1,550,000
1995 **Angels:** Darin Erstad, OF, Nebraska	$1,575,000
1996 **Pirates:** Kris Benson, RHP, Clemson	$2,000,000
1997 **Tigers:** Matt Anderson, RHP, Tigers	$2,505,000
1998 **Phillies:** Pat Burrell, 3B, Miami	*$3,150,000
1999 **Devil Rays:** Josh Hamilton, OF, Athens Drive HS, Raleigh	$3,960,000
2000 **Marlins:** Adrian Gonzalez, 1B, Eastlake HS, Chula Vista, Calif.	$3,000,000
2001 **Twins:** Joe Mauer, C, Cretin-Derham Hall, St. Paul	$5,150,000
2002 **Pirates:** Bryan Bullington, RHP, Ball State	$4,000,000
2003 **Devil Rays:** Delmon Young, OF, Camarillo (Calif.) HS	*$3,700,000
2004 **Padres:** Matt Bush, SS, Mission Bay HS, San Diego	$3,150,000
2005 **D-backs:** Justin Upton, SS, Great Bridge HS, Chesapeake, Va.	$6,100,000
2006 **Royals:** Luke Hochevar, RHP, Fort Worth (American Assoc.)	*$3,500,000
2007 **Devil Rays:** David Price, LHP, Vanderbilt	*$5,600,000
2008 **Rays:** Tim Beckham, SS, Griffin (Ga.) HS	$6,150,000
2009 **Nationals:** Stephen Strasburg, RHP, San Diego State	*$7,500,000
2010 **Nationals:** Bryce Harper, OF, JC of Southern Nevada	*$6,250,000
2011 **Pirates:** Gerrit Cole, RHP, UCLA	$8,000,000
2012 **Astros:** Carlos Correa, SS, Puerto Rico Baseball Acad., Gurabo, P.R.	$4,800,000
2013 **Astros:** Mark Appel, RHP, Stanford	$6,350,000
2014 **Astros:** Brady Aiken, LHP, Cathedral Catholic, San Diego	Did not sign
2015 **D-backs:** Dansby Swanson, SS, Vanderbilt	$6,500,000
2016 **Phillies:** Mickey Moniak, OF, La Costa Canyon HS, Carlsbad, Calif.	$6,100,000
2017 **Twins:** Royce Lewis, SS, JSerra Catholic HS, San Juan Capistrano, Calif.	$6,750,000
2018 **Tigers:** Casey Mize, RHP, Auburn	$7,500,000
2019 **Orioles:** Adley Rutschman, C, Oregon State	$8,100,000
2020 **Tigers:** Spencer Torkelson, 3B, Arizona State	$8,416,300
2021 **Pirates:** Henry Davis, C, Louisville	$6,500,000
2022 **Orioles:** Jackson Holliday, SS, Stillwater (Okla.) HS	$8,190,000
2023 **Pirates:** Paul Skenes, RHP, Louisiana State	$9,200,000
2024 **Guardians:** Travis Bazzana, Oregon State	$8,950,000
2025 **Nationals:** Eli Willits, SS, Fort Cobb-Broxton (Okla.) HS	$8,200,000

*Part of major league contract

and hit .300 with seven home runs and 30 RBIs in 31 games this season.

Pittsburgh's selection of Hernandez follows Konnor Griffin at No. 9 overall last year and Paul Skenes first overall in 2023. All three of the Pirates' most recent first-rounders were standout two-way players as amateurs. The same is true of 2021 third-rounder Bubba Chandler, who played shortstop initially in pro ball before focusing solely on the mound in the second half of 2022.

Griffin was the 2024 BA High School Player of the Year as a shortstop/righthander for Jackson Prep in Mississippi. This year he was one of the most electric prospects in the minor leagues and finished the season ranked No. 1 overall among the Top 100 Prospects.

Skenes' two-way background helped make him a three-time All-America first team selection for BA as a righthander/DH. He converted to pitching full-time at LSU in 2023, when he won BA College Player of the Year honors and won a College World Series championship with the Tigers.

While Hernandez did not win High School Player of the Year in 2025—that honor went to Ethan Holliday—he was certainly in the discussion.

Orioles Cash On Historic Draft Pool

The Orioles had seven picks inside the first 100, and their $19,144,500 bonus pool is the largest in the history of the bonus pool era of the draft. The team signed all of its picks in the first 10 rounds, went to the full 5% overage and ultimately spent $20,100,840 in total signing bonuses on its 2025 draft class.

On top of spending a lot, Baltimore got great value with many of their top picks based on rankings of the BA 500.

The Orioles seemingly got value at every pick, landing players we expected to go higher on draft day. When we talk about players slipping to teams with a lot of pool money, this is the exact sort of dynamic we mean.

At the top, Ike Irish ranked as the No. 13 player in the class and was the second-best college bat. Yes, it was a down group for the position, but Irish has one of the more enticing hit/power combos in the class. He was viewed as a potential top 10 pick, and the Orioles scooped him up at 19.

Baltimore followed suit with two more hitters who were expected to go in the middle of the first round, Caden Bodine and Wehiwa Aloy, at 30 and 31 respectively.

For those worried about the Orioles not diversifying their hitting profiles, they did so

THE BONUS RECORD

Rick Monday, the No. 1 overall pick in baseball's first draft in 1965, signed with the Athletics for $100,000—a figure that no draftee bettered for a decade. The record has been broken many times since, including in 2019, when Adley Rutschman signed with the Orioles as the No. 1 overall pick for $8,100,000. Spencer Torkelson broke in 2020. Paul Skenes set a new record in 2023, but it was then eclipsed by Chase Burns and Charlie Condon in 2024.

The longest bonus record stretch dates back to Todd Demeter, whose $208,000 bonus in 1979 held the mark for nine years until 1988 when Andy Benes topped him.

The list below represents only cash bonuses and doesn't include guaranteed money from major league deals, college scholarship plans or incentives. It doesn't include draft picks who signed after being granted free agency.

Year	Player, Pos., Club (Round)	Bonus
1965	Rick Monday, OF, Athletics (1)	$100,000
1975	Danny Goodwin, C, Angels (1)	$125,000
1978	Kirk Gibson, OF, Tigers (1)	$150,000
	*Bob Horner, 3B, Braves (1)	$162,000
1979	Todd Demeter, 1B, Yankees (2)	$208,000
1988	Andy Benes, RHP, Padres (1)	$235,000
1989	Tyler Houston, C, Braves (1)	$241,500
	*Ben McDonald, RHP, Orioles (1)	$350,000
	*John Olerud, 1B, Blue Jays (3)	$575,000
1991	Mike Kelly, OF, Braves (1)	$575,000
	Brien Taylor, LHP, Yankees (1)	$1,550,000
1994	Paul Wilson, RHP, Mets (1)	$1,550,000
	Josh Booty, 3B, Marlins (1)	$1,600,000
1996	Kris Benson, RHP, Pirates (1)	$2,000,000
1997	Rick Ankiel, LHP, Cardinals (2)	$2,500,000
	Matt Anderson, RHP, Tigers (1)	$2,505,000
1998	*J.D. Drew, OF, Cardinals (1)	$3,000,000
	*Pat Burrell, 3B, Phillies (1)	$3,150,000
	Mark Mulder, LHP, Athletics (1)	$3,200,000
	Corey Patterson, OF, Cubs (1)	$3,700,000
1999	Josh Hamilton, OF, Devil Rays (1)	$3,960,000
2000	Joe Borchard, OF, White Sox (1)	$5,300,000
2005	Justin Upton, SS, D-backs (1)	$6,100,000
2008	Tim Beckham, SS, Rays (1)	$6,150,000
	Buster Posey, C, Giants (1)	$6,200,000
2009	Donavan Tate, OF, Padres (1)	$6,250,000
	*Stephen Strasburg, RHP, Nationals (1)	$7,500,000
2011	Gerrit Cole, RHP, Pirates (1)	$8,000,000
2019	Adley Rutschman, C, Orioles (1)	$8,100,000
2020	Spencer Torkelson, 3B, Tigers (1)	$8,416,300
2023	Paul Skenes, RHP, Pirates (1)	$9,200,000
2024	Chase Burns, RHP, Reds (2)	$9,250,000
	Charlie Condon, OF, Rockies (3)	$9,250,000

*Part of major league contract.

here with Bodine's excellent contact skills and questionable power tied right beside Aloy, who has tons of bat speed and juice but some work to do with swing decisions and recognizing spin. Both should also provide value at up-the-middle positions.

Before the draft, the Orioles acquired the 37th overall pick from the Rays. On draft day they used that to select Slater de Brun, a top-of-the-order table-setting outfielder who we consistently expected to go in the late 20s. Aside from standout power, de Brun checks all the boxes we're looking for: a savvy hitter (and bunter), a double-plus runner and a plus defender in center with a strong arm as well.

BONUSES VS. PICK VALUES

For the first time in MLB draft history, the total bonus pool for 2025 topped $350 million. The Washington Nationals won the draft lottery, which meant they were handed the No. 1 pick in the 2025 draft, which carried a slot value of $11,075,900, a 4.78% increase from the $10,570,600 slot value for the Guardians No. 1 pick in 2024. In a balanced draft at the top, Ethan Holliday's bonus of $9 million led the draft, but that fell short of the 2024 record setting contracts of Chase Burns and Charlie Condon who received $9,250,000 apiece.

The slot values for the draft are determined each year by matching the growth in revenues in baseball.

The total bonus pool value for all clubs in the 2025 draft checked in at $350,357,700, which is more than $15 million more than the total bonus pool value from the 2024 draft—$334,375,000.

Player, Pos., Team (Round/Overall Pick)	Bonus	Pick Value
1. Ethan Holliday, SS, Stillwater HS (1st round/No. 4)	$9,000,000	$8,770,900
2. Kade Anderson, LHP, LSU (1st round/No. 3)	$8,800,000	$9,504,400
3. Eli Willits, SS, Fort Cobb-Broxton HS (1st round/No. 1)	$8,200,000	$11,075,900
4. Tyler Bremner, RHP, UC Santa Barbara (1st round/No. 2)	$7,689,525	$10,252,700
5. Liam Doyle, LHP, Tennessee (1st round/No. 5)	$7,250,000	$8,134,800
6. Seth Hernandez, RHP, Corona HS (1st round/No. 6)	$7,250,000	$7,558,600
7. Aiva Arquette, SS, Oregon State (1st round/No. 7)	$7,149,900	$7,149,900
8. Billy Carlson, SS, Corona HS (1st round/No. 10)	$6,235,900	$6,238,400
9. Joseph Parker, SS, Purvis HS (1st round/No. 8)	$6,197,500	$6,813,600
10. Jamie Arnold, LHP, Florida State (1st round/No. 11)	$5,985,100	$5,985,100
11. Steele Hall, SS, Hewitt-Trussville HS (1st round/No. 9)	$5,747,500	$6,513,800
12. Gavin Kilen, SS, Tennessee (1st round/No. 13)	$5,247,500	$5,524,300
13. Kyson Witherspoon, RHP, Oklahoma (1st round/No. 15)	$5,000,000	$5,114,200
14. Gavin Fien, SS, Great Oak HS (1st round/No. 12)	$4,800,000	$5,746,800
15. Kayson Cunningham, SS, Lady Bird Johnson HS (1st round/No. 18)	$4,581,900	$4,581,900
16. Marek Houston, SS, Wake Forest (1st round/No. 16)	$4,497,500	$4,929,600
17. Ike Irish, C, Auburn (1st round/No. 19)	$4,418,400	$4,420,900
18. Daniel Pierce, SS, Mill Creek HS (1st round/No. 14)	$4,310,600	$5,313,100
19. Xavier Neyens, SS, Mt. Vernon HS (1st round/No. 21)	$4,120,000	$4,122,500
20. Jace LaViolette, OF, Texas A&M (1st round/No. 27)	$4,000,000	$3,382,600
21. Slater de Brun, OF, Summit HS (1st supp. round/No. 37)	$4,000,000	$2,631,400
22. Sean Gamble, OF, IMG Academy (1st round/No. 23)	$3,997,500	$3,852,100
23. Kruz Schoolcraft, LHP, Sunset HS (1st round/No. 25)	$3,606,600	$3,606,600
24. Ethan Conrad, OF, Wake Forest (1st round/No. 17)	$3,563,100	$4,750,800
25. Andrew Fischer, 3B, Tennessee (1st round/No. 20)	$3,500,000	$4,268,100
26. Jordan Yost, SS, Sickles HS (1st round/No. 24)	$3,247,500	$3,726,300
27. Josh Hammond, SS, Wesleyan Christian Academy (1st supp. round/No. 28)	$3,197,500	$3,282,200
28. Caden Bodine, C, Coastal Carolina (1st supp. round/No. 30)	$3,110,800	$3,113,300
29. Wehiwa Aloy, SS, Arkansas (1st supp. round/No. 31)	$3,040,300	$3,042,800
30. Gage Wood, RHP, Arkansas (1st round/No. 26)	$3,000,000	$3,492,200
31. Patrick Forbes, RHP, Louisville (1st round/No. 29)	$3,000,000	$3,191,100
32. Jaden Fauske, OF, Nazareth Academy (2nd round/No. 44)	$2,997,500	$2,223,600
33. Briggs McKenzie, LHP, Corinth Holders HS (4th round/No. 127)	$2,997,500	$588,900
34. Luke Stevenson, C, North Carolina (1st supp. round/No. 35)	$2,800,000	$2,758,300
35. Dax Kilby, SS, Newnan HS (1st round/No. 39)	$2,797,500	$2,509,500
36. Brady Ebel, SS, Corona HS (1st supp. round/No. 32)	$2,750,000	$2,970,900
37. Nick Becker, SS, Don Bosco Prep HS (2nd round/No. 57)	$2,750,000	$1,636,800
38. Aaron Watson, RHP, Trinity Christian Academy (2nd round/No. 51)	$2,747,500	$1,891,200
39. Riley Quick, RHP, Alabama (1st supp. round/No. 36)	$2,692,000	$2,692,000
40. Tate Southisene, SS, Basic HS (1st round/No. 22)	$2,622,500	$3,983,900
41. A.J. Russell, RHP, Tennessee (2nd round/No. 52)	$2,600,000	$1,846,700
42. Marcus Phillips, RHP, Tennessee (1st supp. round/No. 33)	$2,500,000	$2,898,300
43. Devin Taylor, OF, Indiana (2nd round/No. 48)	$2,500,000	$2,031,500
44. Landon Harmon, RHP, East Union Attendance Center HS (3rd round/No. 80) $1,010,600	$2,500,000	
45. Coy James, SS, Davie HS (5th round/No. 142)	$2,500,000	$508,900
46. Johnny Slawinski, LHP, Lyndon B. Johnson HS (3rd round/No. 79)	$2,497,500	$1,027,200
47. Michael Oliveto, C, Hauppauge HS (1st supp. round/No. 34)	$2,447,500	$2,827,300
48. Cooper Flemming, SS, Ganesha HS (2nd round/No. 53)	$2,297,500	$1,803,500
49. Cam Cannarella, OF, Clemson (1st supp. round/No. 43)	$2,277,425	$2,276,700
50. Ryan Mitchell, OF, Houston HS (2nd round/No. 55)	$2,250,000	$1,720,300

After de Brun, the Orioles did start to grab a few pitchers—though Mike Elias has still never taken a pitcher inside the first 50 picks since he's been running the ship with Baltimore—with No. 50-ranked Joseph Dzierwa at No. 58 overall, and No. 144-ranked righthander JT Quinn at No. 127 overall.

They rounded out the draft with another college bat in RJ Austin with the 93rd overall pick. We had Austin ranked 189th, so this selection is the most questionable decision for us because we have some concerns about his offensive profile. Still, the first four (or five) look like easy slam dunks on draft night. ∎

DRAFT 2025 TOP 100 PICKS

Team, Player, Pos., School — **Bonus**

1. WSH, Eli Willits, SS, Fort Cobb-Broxton HS $8,200,000
2. LAA, Tyler Bremner, RHP, UC Santa Barbara $7,689,525
3. SEA, Kade Anderson, LHP, LSU $8,800,000
4. COL, Ethan Holliday, SS, Stillwater HS $9,000,000
5. STL, Liam Doyle, LHP, Tennessee $7,250,000
6. PIT, Seth Hernandez, RHP, Corona HS $7,250,000
7. MIA, Aiva Arquette, SS, Oregon State $7,149,900
8. TOR, Joseph Parker, SS, Purvis HS $6,197,500
9. CIN, Steele Hall, SS, Hewitt-Trussville HS.......... $5,747,500
10. CWS, Billy Carlson, SS, Corona HS $6,235,900
11. ATH, Jamie Arnold, LHP, Florida State $5,985,100
12. TEX, Gavin Fien, SS, Great Oak HS $4,800,000
13. SF, Gavin Kilen, SS, Tennessee $5,247,500
14. TB, Daniel Pierce, SS, Mill Creek HS $4,310,600
15. BOS, Kyson Witherspoon, RHP, Oklahoma $5,000,000
16. MIN, Marek Houston, SS, Wake Forest $4,497,500
17. CHC, Ethan Conrad, OF, Wake Forest............... $3,563,100
18. AZ, Kayson Cunningham, SS, Johnson HS $4,581,900
19. BAL, Ike Irish, C, Auburn $4,418,400
20. MIL, Andrew Fischer, 3B, Tennessee............... $3,500,000
21. HOU, Xavier Neyens, SS, Mt. Vernon HS.......... $4,120,000
22. ATL, Tate Southisene, SS, Basic HS $2,622,500
23. KC, Sean Gamble, OF, IMG Academy................ $3,997,500
24. DET, Jordan Yost, SS, Sickles HS..................... $3,247,500
25. SD, Kruz Schoolcraft, LHP, Sunset HS.............. $3,606,600
26. PHI, Gage Wood, RHP, Arkansas $3,000,000
27. CLE, Jace LaViolette, OF, Texas A&M $4,000,000
28. KC, Josh Hammond, SS, Wesleyan Christ.HS $3,197,500
29. AZ, Patrick Forbes, RHP, Louisville $3,000,000
30. BAL, Caden Bodine, C, Coastal Carolina........... $3,110,800
31. BAL, Wehiwa Aloy, SS, Arkansas..................... $3,040,300
32. MIL, Brady Ebel, SS, Corona HS $2,750,000
33. BOS, Marcus Phillips, RHP, Tennessee $2,500,000
34. DET, Michael Oliveto, C, Hauppauge HS $2,447,500
35. SEA, Luke Stevenson, C, North Carolina $2,800,000
36. MIN, Riley Quick, RHP, Alabama $2,692,500
37. BAL, Slater de Brun, OF, Summit HS $4,000,000
38. NYM, Mitch Voit, TWP, Michigan $1,750,000
39. NYY, Dax Kilby, SS, Newnan HS $2,797,500
40. LAD, Zach Root, LHP, Arkansas....................... $2,197,500
41. LAD, Charles Davalan, OF, Arkansas................ $1,997,500
42. TB, Brendan Summerhill, OF, Arizona $1,997,500
43. MIA, Cam Cannarella, OF, Clemson $2,277,425
44. CWS, Jaden Fauske, OF, Nazareth Academy..... $2,997,500
45. COL, J.B. Middleton, RHP, Southern Mississippi $2,071,900
46. MIA, Brandon Compton, OF, Arizona State $2,000,000
47. LAA, Chase Shores, RHP, LSU $2,077,200
48. ATH, Devin Taylor, OF, Indiana $2,500,000
49. WSH, Ethan Petry, OF, South Carolina $2,090,000
50. PIT, Angel Cervantes, RHP, Warren HS...........Did Not Sign
51. CIN, Aaron Watson, RHP, Trinity Christian HS .. $2,747,500
52. TEX, A.J. Russell, RHP, Tennessee.................... $2,600,000
53. TB, Cooper Flemming, SS, Ganesha HS............ $2,297,500
54. MIN, Quentin Young, SS, Oaks Christian HS $1,761,600
55. STL, Ryan Mitchell, OF, Houston HS $2,250,000
56. CHC, Kane Kepley, OF, North Carolina $1,400,000
57. SEA, Nick Becker, SS, Don Bosco Prep HS $2,750,000
58. BAL, Joseph Dzierwa, LHP, Michigan State...... $1,497,500
59. MIL, JD Thompson, LHP, Vanderbilt................ $1,560,200
60. ATL, Alex Lodise, SS, Florida State................... $1,297,500
61. KC, Michael Lombardi, RHP, Tulane................. $1,297,500
62. DET, Malachi Witherspoon, RHP, Oklahoma $1,448,700
63. PHI, Cade Obermueller, LHP, Iowa.................. $1,197,500
64. CLE, Dean Curley, SS, Tennessee $1,733,905
65. LAD, Cam Leiter, RHP, Florida State $1,346,500
66. CLE, Aaron Walton, OF, Arizona...................... $1,100,000
67. TB, Dean Moss, OF, IMG Academy $2,097,500
68. MIL, Frank Cairone, LHP, Delsea Reg HS.......... $1,097,500
69. BAL, J.T. Quinn, RHP, Georgia......................... $1,147,500
70. CLE, Will Hynes, RHP, Lorne Park SS $950,000
71. KC, Justin Lamkin, LHP, Texas A&M $1,161,200
72. STL, Tanner Franklin, RHP, Tennessee............. $1,145,900
73. PIT, Murf Gray, 3B, Fresno State $997,500
74. COL, Max Belyeu, OF, Texas $1,111,000
75. BOS, Henry Godbout, SS, Virginia................... $1,093,800
76. CWS, Kyle Lodise, SS, Georgia Tech................... $922,500
77. COL, Ethan Hedges, 3B, USC............................. $950,000
78. MIA, Max Williams, OF, Florida State................ $897,500
79. LAA, Johnny Slawinski, LHP, Johnson HS......... $2,497,500
80. WSH, Landon Harmon, RHP, E. Union Attendance Center HS $2,500,000
81. TOR, Jake Cook, OF, Southern Mississippi $922,500
82. PIT, Easton Carmichael, C, Oklahoma $977,000
83. CIN, Mason Morris, RHP, Ole Miss $897,500
84. TEX, Josh Owens, TWP, Providence Academy ... $1,100,000
85. SF, Trevor Cohen, OF, Rutgers.......................... $847,500
86. TB, Taitn Gray, C, Dallas Center-Grimes HS $918,300
87. BOS, Anthony Eyanson, RHP, LSU $1,750,000
88. MIN, James Ellwanger, RHP, Dallas Baptist..... $1,000,000
89. STL, Jack Gurevitch, 1B, University Of San Diego $879,000
90. CHC, Dominick Reid, RHP, Abilene Christian $649,125
91. SEA, Griffin Hugus, RHP, Miami $640,000
92. AZ, Brian Curley, RHP, Georgia $700,000
93. BAL, RJ Austin, OF, Vanderbilt......................... $823,900
94. MIL, Jacob Morrison, RHP, Coastal Carolina...... $697,500
95. HOU, Ethan Frey, OF, LSU $997,500
96. ATL, Cody Miller, SS, East Tennessee State $297,500
97. KC, Cameron Millar, RHP, Alhambra HS.......... $1,497,500
98. DET, Ben Jacobs, LHP, Arizona State................. $722,500
99. SD, Ryan Wideman, OF, Western Kentucky $650,000
100. PHI, Cody Bowker, RHP, Vanderbilt................ $700,000

Kade Anderson went third overall.

2025 CLUB-BY-CLUB SELECTIONS

Order Of Selection In Parentheses | Players Signed In Bold

ARIZONA DIAMONDBACKS (18)
1. Kayson Cunningham, SS, Lady Bird Johnson HS
1s. Patrick Forbes, RHP, Louisville
3. Brian Curley, RHP, Georgia
4. Dean Livingston, RHP, Hebron Christian Academy
5. Nathan Hall, OF, South Carolina
6. Sawyer Hawks, RHP, Vanderbilt
7. Joe Ariola, LHP, Wake Forest
8. Jack Martinez, RHP, Arizona State
9. Wallace Clark, SS, Duke
10. Brady Counsell, SS, Kansas
11. Luke Dotson, LHP, Mississippi State
12. Tayler Montiel, LHP, Tulane
13. Alex Galvan, RHP, Central Florida
14. Blake Fields, OF, The First Academy
15. Hayden Murphy, RHP, Auburn
16. Collin Rothermel, RHP, Jacksonville University
17. Joel Sarver, RHP, UNC Charlotte
18. Raul Garayzar, RHP, Arizona
19. Jacob Parker, OF, Purvis HS
20. Ethin Bingaman, RHP, Corona HS

ATHLETICS (11)
1. Jamie Arnold, LHP, Florida State
2. Devin Taylor, OF, Indiana
4. Gavin Turley, OF, Oregon State
5. Zane Taylor, RHP, UNC Wilmington
6. Grant Richardson, LHP, Grand Canyon University
7. Logan Sauve, C, West Virginia
8. Corey Braun, LHP, South Florida
9. Daniel Bucciero, 3B, Fordham
10. Samuel Dutton, RHP, Auburn
11. Bobby Boser, SS, Florida
12. Alex Barr, LHP, Kankakee Valley HS
13. Bryan Arendt, C, UNC Wilmington
14. Griffin Kirn, LHP, West Virginia
15. Diego Rosa, C, International Baseball Academy
16. Jackson Phipps, LHP, Jacksonville State
17. Jared Davis, SS, Virginia Tech
18. Jay Dill, RHP, Troy University
19. Itsuki Takemoto, RHP, Hawaii
20. Kade Brown, RHP, Sacramento State

ATLANTA BRAVES (22)
1. Tate Southisene, SS, Basic HS
2. Alex Lodise, SS, Florida State
3. Cody Miller, SS, East Tennessee State
4. Briggs McKenzie, LHP, Corinth Holders HS
4s. Dixon Williams, 2B, East Carolina
5. Conor Essenburg, OF, Lincoln-Way West HS
6. Landon Beidelschies, LHP, Arkansas
7. Zach Royse, RHP, UTSA
8. Carter Lovasz, RHP, William & Mary
9. Logan Braunschweig, OF, UAB
10. Kade Woods, RHP, LSU
11. Colin Daniel, RHP, U Alabama Birmingham
12. Jay Woolfolk, RHP, Virginia
13. Logan Forsythe, RHP, Louisiana Tech
14. Mathieu Curtis, RHP, Virginia Tech
15. Dallas Macias, OF, Oregon State
16. Nico Wagner, RHP, West Valley College
17. Brody Fowler, RHP, North Greenville U
18. Aiven Cabral, RHP, Northeastern
19. Ryan Heppner, RHP, U British Columbia
20. Hayden Friese, OF, Western Carolina

BALTIMORE ORIOLES (19)
1. Ike Irish, C, Auburn
1s. Caden Bodine, C, Coastal Carolina
1s. Wehiwa Aloy, SS, Arkansas
1s. Slater de Brun, OF, Summit HS
2. Joseph Dzierwa, LHP, Michigan State
2s. J.T. Quinn, RHP, Georgia
3. RJ Austin, OF, Vanderbilt
4. Colin Yeaman, SS, University Of California - Irvine
5. Jaiden Lo Re, SS, Corona Del Sol HS
6. Caden Hunter, LHP, USC
7. Hunter Allen, RHP, Ashland University
8. Kailen Hamson, LHP, University of the Cumberlands
9. Cam Lee, OF, Mineral Area JC
10. Dalton Neuschwander, RHP, University Of West Florida
11. Holden deJong, LHP, New Jersey Institute of Technology
12. Daniel Lopez, RHP, Odessa College
13. Brayden Smith, 2B, Oklahoma State
14. Brayan Orrantia, RHP, New Mexico JC
15. KK Clark, RHP, Pearl River CC
16. Denton Biller, RHP, Johnson County CC
17. Braeden Sloan, LHP, TCU
18. William Johnson, OF, Oconee County HS
19. Jimmy Anderson, SS, Heartland CC
20. Connor Gehr, RHP, Meridian CC

BOSTON RED SOX (15)
1. Kyson Witherspoon, RHP, Oklahoma
1s. Marcus Phillips, RHP, Tennessee
2s. Henry Godbout, SS, Virginia
3. Anthony Eyanson, RHP, LSU
4. Mason White, SS, Arizona
5. Christian Foutch, RHP, Arkansas
6. Leighton Finley, RHP, Georgia
7. Myles Patton, LHP, Texas A&M
8. Dylan Brown, LHP, Old Dominion
9. Jacob Mayers, RHP, LSU
10. Maximus Martin, SS, Kansas State
11. Barrett Morgan, RHP, Cowley County CC
12. Ethan Walker, LHP, Kentucky
13. Jack Winnay, 3B, Wake Forest
14. Carter Rasmussen, RHP, Wofford
15. Skylar King, OF, West Virginia
16. Jason Gilman, LHP, Kean University
17. Patrick Galle, RHP, Ole Miss
18. Cade Fisher, LHP, Auburn
19. Fabian Bonilla, OF, Christian Military Academy
20. Garrison Sumner, RHP, Brigham Young

CHICAGO CUBS (17)
1. Ethan Conrad, OF, Wake Forest
2. Kane Kepley, OF, North Carolina
3. Dominick Reid, RHP, Abilene Christian
4. Kaleb Wing, RHP, Scotts Valley HS
5. Kade Snell, OF, Alabama
6. Josiah Hartshorn, OF, Orange Lutheran HS
7. Pierce Coppola, LHP, Florida
8. Jake Knapp, RHP, North Carolina
9. Colton Book, LHP, Saint Joseph's
10. Justin Stransky, C, Fresno State
11. Eli Jerzembeck, RHP, South Carolina
12. Connor Spencer, RHP, Ole Miss
13. Nathan Williams, RHP, Mississippi State
14. Kaemyn Franklin, RHP, Victory Christian
15. Noah Edders, RHP, Troy University
16. Riely Hunsaker, RHP, Lamar
17. Logan Poteet, C, UNC Charlotte

18. Connor Knox, RHP, George Mason
19. Caleb Barnett, 3B, Mountain Brook HS
20. Freddy Rodriguez, RHP, U Hawaii

CHICAGO WHITE SOX (10)
1. Billy Carlson, SS, Corona HS
2. Jaden Fauske, OF, Nazareth Academy
3. Kyle Lodise, SS, Georgia Tech
4. Landon Hodge, C, Crespi Carmelite HS
5. Gabe Davis, RHP, Oklahoma State
6. Colby Shelton, SS, Florida
7. Anthony DePino, 3B, University Of Rhode Island
8. Blaine Wynk, RHP, Ohio State
9. Riley Eikhoff, RHP, Coastal Carolina
10. Dan Wright, RHP, Iowa
11. Matthew Boughton, SS, Covenant HS
12. Ely Brown, OF, Mercer U
13. Rylan Galvan, C, Texas
14. Max Banks, RHP, Washington
15. Caedmon Parker, RHP, TCU
16. Kaleb Freeman, UT, Georgia State
17. Derek Cerda, OF, Kansas
18. Landen Payne, RHP, Southern Mississippi
19. Nicholas Weyrich, RHP, Marshall
20. Andrew Sentlinger, LHP, Virginia Tech

CINCINNATI REDS (9)
1. Steele Hall, SS, Hewitt-Trussville HS
2. Aaron Watson, RHP, Trinity Christian Academy
3. Mason Morris, RHP, Ole Miss
4. Mason Neville, OF, Oregon
5. Eli Pitts, OF, North Atlanta HS
6. Braden Osbolt, RHP, Kennesaw State
7. Justin Henschel, RHP, Florida Gulf Coast University
8. Kyle McCoy, LHP, Maryland
9. Kien Vu, OF, Arizona State
10. Ty Doucette, 1B, Rutgers
11. Jake Brink, RHP, College of Charleston
12. Carson Latimer, RHP, Sacramento State
13. Brady Afthim, RHP, Connecticut
14. Bryce Archie, RHP, South Florida
15. Andrew Shaffner, RHP, NC State
16. Maison Martinez, RHP, Florida State
17. Dylan King, C, Central Florida
18. Ethan Moore, SS, Oak Park and River Forest HS
19. Myles Upchurch, RHP, St. Albans HS
20. Leamsi Montanez, C, Leadership Christian Academy

CLEVELAND GUARDIANS (27)
1. Jace LaViolette, OF, Texas A&M
2. Dean Curley, SS, Tennessee
2s. Aaron Walton, OF, Arizona
2s. Will Hynes, RHP, Lorne Park SS
3. Nolan Schubart, OF, Oklahoma State
4. Luke Hill, 3B, Ole Miss
5. Riley Nelson, 1B, Vanderbilt
6. Nelson Keljo, LHP, Oregon State
7. Will McCausland, RHP, Ole Miss
8. Anthony Martinez, 1B, University Of California - Irvine
9. Ryan Prager, LHP, Texas A&M
10. Harrison Bodendorf, LHP, Oklahoma State
11. Tyler Howard, C, University of Portland
12. Ryan DeSanto, LHP, Penn State
13. Aaron Savary, RHP, Iowa
14. Anthony Silva, SS, TCU
15. Evan Chrest, RHP, Florida State
16. Luke Fernandez, RHP, Wallace State CC
17. Cannon Peebles, C, Tennessee
18. Zane Petty, RHP, Texas Tech
19. Derek Munoz, RHP, Miami Christian School
20. Vaughn Neckar, RHP, Vista Murrieta HS

COLORADO ROCKIES (4)
1. Ethan Holliday, SS, Stillwater HS
2. J.B. Middleton, RHP, Southern Mississippi
2s. Max Belyeu, OF, Texas
3. Ethan Hedges, 3B, USC
4. Riley Kelly, RHP, University Of California - Irvine
5. Cameron Nelson, OF, Wake Forest
6. Matt Klein, C, Louisville
7. Antoine Jean, LHP, Houston
8. Tanner Thach, 1B, UNC Wilmington
9. Zach Rogacki, C, SUNY Binghamton
10. Austin Newton, RHP, South Florida
11. Zach Harris, RHP, Georgia
12. Brady Parker, LHP, Houston-Victoria
13. Izeah Muniz, RHP, Mt. San Antonio College
14. Luke Broderick, RHP, Nebraska
15. Dylan Crooks, RHP, Oklahoma
16. Seth Clausen, RHP, Minnesota
17. Derrick Smith, RHP, NC State
18. Tyrelle Chadwick, RHP, Illinois State
19. Easton Marks, RHP, Florida International
20. Ethan Cole, LHP, Augustana U

DETROIT TIGERS (24)
1. Jordan Yost, SS, Sickles HS
1s. Michael Oliveto, C, Hauppauge HS
2. Malachi Witherspoon, RHP, Oklahoma
3. Ben Jacobs, LHP, Arizona State
4. Caleb Leys, LHP, University Of Maine
5. Ryan Hall, RHP, North Gwinnett HS
6. Grayson Grinsell, LHP, Oregon
7. Cale Wetwiska, RHP, Northern Oklahoma College-Enid
8. Nick Dumesnil, OF, California Baptist University
9. Trevor Heishman, LHP, St. John Bosco HS
10. Edian Espinal, C, Central Florida
11. River Hamilton, RHP, Sam Barlow HS
12. Cash Kuiper, RHP, Murray State College
13. Jack Goodman, SS, Northeastern
14. Beau Ankeney, 1B, Loyola Marymount University
15. Charlie Christensen, RHP, U Central Arkansas
16. Joe Ruzicka, RHP, Belmont University
17. Joey Wimpelberg, RHP, College of Central Florida
18. Ethan Rogers, LHP, Lone Jack HS
19. Meridian Leffew, SS, Gaston Christian School
20. Kameron Douglas, OF, Alabama St U

HOUSTON ASTROS (21)
1. Xavier Neyens, SS, Mt. Vernon HS
3. Ethan Frey, OF, LSU
4. Nick Monistere, IF, Southern Mississippi
5. Nick Potter, RHP, Wichita State
6. Gabel Pentecost, RHP, Taylor University
7. Jase Mitchell, C, Cape Henlopen HS
8. Kyle Walker, 2B, Arizona State
9. Kellan Oakes, RHP, Oregon State
10. Zach Daudet, SS, Cal Poly San Luis Obispo
11. Justin Thomas, OF, Arkansas
12. Elijah Farley, OF, Navarro HS
13. Aubrey Smith, RHP, UNC Wilmington
14. Josh Wakefield, OF, Grand Canyon University
15. DJ Newman, TWP, Bowling Green
16. Chase Call, OF, University Of California - Irvine
17. Grayson Saunier, RHP, Texas
18. Landon Arroyos, SS, Grayson HS
19. Joey McLaughlin, OF, Harrah HS
20. Curtis Hebert, SS, University Of Portland

KANSAS CITY ROYALS (23)
1. Sean Gamble, OF, IMG Academy
1s. Josh Hammond, SS, Wesleyan Christian Academy

2. Michael Lombardi, RHP, Tulane
2s. Justin Lamkin, LHP, Texas A&M
3. Cameron Millar, RHP, Alhambra HS
4. Nolan Sailors, OF, Creighton
5. Aiden Jimenez, RHP, Arkansas
6. Tyriq Kemp, SS, Baylor
7. Bryson Dudley, RHP, Texas State
8. Brooks Bryan, C, Troy University
9. Shane Van Dam, RHP, NC State
10. Max Martin, RHP, University Of California - Irvine
11. Hunter Alberini, RHP, Arizona
12. Matthew Hoskins, RHP, Georgia
13. Tyson Moran, SS, No School
14. JC Vanek, 1B, Chipola College
15. Connor Rasmussen, SS, Tulane
16. Randy Ramnarace, RHP, University Of New Haven
17. Luke Nowak, OF, University Of Illinois At Chicago
18. Grayson Boles, RHP, St. Augustine HS
19. Dylan Wood, RHP, Franklin HS
20. Kamden Edge, RHP, Northern Oklahoma JC

LOS ANGELES ANGELS (2)
1. Tyler Bremner, RHP, UC Santa Barbara
2. Chase Shores, RHP, LSU
3. Johnny Slawinski, LHP, Lyndon B. Johnson HS
3s. Nate Snead, RHP, Tennessee
4. Jake Munroe, 3B, Louisville
5. CJ Gray, RHP, A.L. Brown HS
6. Luke LaCourse, RHP, Bay City Western HS
7. Lucas Mahlstedt, RHP, Clemson
8. Isaiah Jackson, OF, Arizona State
9. Slate Alford, 3B, Georgia
10. Nick Rodriguez, 2B, Missouri State
11. Alton Davis, LHP, Georgia
12. Talon Haley, LHP, Lewisburg HS
13. Robert Mitchell, LHP, Prestonwood Christian Academy
14. TJ Ford, OF, Trinity Christian School
15. Mikey Cascino, RHP, A3 Academy
16. Gage Harrelson, OF, Florida State
17. Cole Raymond, RHP, Avon Old Farms School
18. Angelo Smith, RHP, Central Florida
19. Ivan Tatis, SS, Georgia Premier Academy
20. Sam Tookoian, RHP, Ole Miss

LOS ANGELES DODGERS (40)
1. Zach Root, LHP, Arkansas
1s. Charles Davalan, OF, Arkansas
2. Cam Leiter, RHP, Florida State
3. Landyn Vidourek, OF, Cincinnati
4. Aidan West, SS, Long Reach HS
5. Davion Hickson, RHP, Rice
6. Mason Ligenza, OF, Tamaqua Area HS
7. Mason Estrada, RHP, MIT
8. Jack O'Connor, RHP, Virginia
9. Conner O'Neal, C, Southeastern Louisiana U
10. Jacob Frost, LHP, Kansas State
11. Dylan Tate, RHP, Oklahoma
12. Logan Lunceford, RHP, Wake Forest
13. Robby Porco, RHP, West Virginia
14. Davis Chastain, RHP, U Georgia
15. Matt Lanzendorfer, LHP, Virginia
16. AJ Soldra, OF, Seton Hall
17. Sam Horn, RHP, Missouri
18. Finn Edwards, RHP, Iowa Western CC
19. Anson Aroz, C, Oregon
20. Shane Brinham, LHP, Handsworth SS

MIAMI MARLINS (7)
1. Aiva Arquette, SS, Oregon State
1s. Cam Cannarella, OF, Clemson
2. Brandon Compton, OF, Arizona State

3. Max Williams, OF, Florida State
4. Drew Faurot, SS, Florida State
5. Chris Arroyo, 1B, Virginia
6. Joey Volini, LHP, Florida State
7. Jake Clemente, RHP, Florida
8. Emilio Barreras, SS, Grand Canyon University
9. Kaiden Wilson, LHP, Texas A&M
10. Jake McCutcheon, 2B, Missouri State
11. Jadon Williamson, RHP, Lewis-Clark State College
12. Wilson Weber, C, Oregon State
13. Chase Renner, RHP, Penn State
14. Carson Laws, RHP, Texas State
15. Josh Hogue, 3B, NC State
16. RJ Shunck, LHP, Toledo
17. Xavier Cardenas, RHP, San Diego State
18. Hayden Cuthbertson, LHP, Miami (OH)
19. Peyton Fosher, RHP, Nevada
20. Cannon Pickell, RHP, Western Carolina

MILWAUKEE BREWERS (20)
1. Andrew Fischer, 3B, Tennessee
1s. Brady Ebel, SS, Corona HS
2. JD Thompson, LHP, Vanderbilt
2s. Frank Cairone, LHP, Delsea Reg HS
3. Jacob Morrison, RHP, Coastal Carolina
4. Joshua Flores, RHP, Lake Central HS
5. Sean Episcope, RHP, Princeton
6. Daniel Dickinson, SS, LSU
7. Josiah Ragsdale, OF, Boston College
8. Hayden Vucinovich, RHP, Bloomington Jefferson HS
9. Andrew Healy, LHP, Duke
10. Braylon Owens, RHP, UTSA
11. CJ Hughes, SS, Junipero Serra HS
12. Cooper Underwood, LHP, Allatoona HS
13. Gavin Lauridsen, RHP, Foothill HS
14. Brendan Brock, C, Southwestern Illinois College
15. Dominic Cadiz, 3B, Notre Dame HS
16. Parker Coil, LHP, Arkansas
17. Luke Roupe, RHP, Grace Christian School
18. Rylan Mills, C, Oran HS
19. Chase Bentley, RHP, IMG Academy
20. Ma'Kale Holden, RHP, Thompson HS

MINNESOTA TWINS (16)
1. Marek Houston, SS, Wake Forest
1s. Riley Quick, RHP, Alabama
2. Quentin Young, SS, Oaks Christian HS
3. James Ellwanger, RHP, Dallas Baptist
4. Jason Reitz, RHP, Oregon
5. Matt Barr, RHP, SUNY Niagara CC
6. Bruin Agbayani, SS, Saint Louis School
7. Jacob McCombs, OF, University Of California - Irvine
8. Ryan Sprock, 3B, Elon University
9. Justin Mitrovich, RHP, Elon University
10. Shai Robinson, SS, Illinois State
11. Ryan Daniels, 2B, Connecticut
12. Kolten Smith, RHP, Georgia
13. Callan Fang, RHP, Harvard
14. Merit Jones, RHP, Utah
15. Reed Moring, RHP, UC Santa Barbara
16. Jonathan Stevens, RHP, U Alabama
17. JP Smith, 3B, Sacramento State
18. Matthew Dalquist, RHP, UC San Diego
19. Matthew Becker, LHP, South Carolina
20. Michael Hilker, RHP, U Arizona

NEW YORK METS (38)
1. Mitch Voit, TWP, Michigan
3. Antonio Jimenez, SS, Central Florida
4. Peter Kussow, RHP, Arrowhead Union HS
5. Peyton Prescott, RHP, Florida State

6. Nathan Hall, RHP, University Of Central Missouri
7. Cam Tilly, RHP, Auburn
8. Camden Lohman, RHP, Ft. Zumwalt North HS
9. Anthony Frobose, SS, Lakeland HS
10. Tyler McLoughlin, RHP, Georgia
11. Wyatt Vincent, OF, Nixa HS
12. Truman Pauley, RHP, Harvard
13. Frank Camarillo, RHP, UC Santa Barbara
14. James Smith, RHP, University Of Memphis
15. Conner Ware, LHP, LSU
16. Zack Mack, RHP, Loyola Marymount University
17. Sam Robertson, SS, Northwest Shoals CC
18. Dillon Stiltner, RHP, Trinity Christian School
19. Joe Scarborough, RHP, Jacksonville State
20. Garrett Stratton, RHP, Rice

NEW YORK YANKEES (39)
1. Dax Kilby, SS, Newnan HS
3. Kaeden Kent, SS, Texas A&M
4. Pico Kohn, LHP, Mississippi State
5. Core Jackson, SS, Utah
6. Rory Fox, RHP, Notre Dame
7. Richie Bonomolo, OF, Alabama
8. Mac Heuer, RHP, Texas Tech
9. Blake Gillespie, RHP, UNC Charlotte
10. Connor McGinnis, 2B, Houston
11. Ben Grable, RHP, Indiana
12. Camden Troyer, OF, Liberty University
13. Kyle West, 1B, West Virginia
14. Brennan Stuprich, RHP, Southeastern Louisiana University
15. Jack Cebert, RHP, Texas Tech
16. Jackson Lovich, SS, Missouri
17. Ryan Osinski, RHP, Virginia
18. Justin West, LHP, Louisville
19. Hayden Morris, RHP, Blinn College
20. Bryce Martin-Grudzielanek, SS, USC

PHILADELPHIA PHILLIES (26)
1. Gage Wood, RHP, Arkansas
2. Cade Obermueller, LHP, Iowa
3. Cody Bowker, RHP, Vanderbilt
4. Sean Youngerman, RHP, Oklahoma State
5. Gabe Craig, RHP, Baylor
6. James Tallon, LHP, Duke
7. Matthew Fisher, RHP, Memorial HS
8. Brian Walters, RHP, Miami
9. Matthew Ferrara, SS, Toms River HS East
10. Cole Gilley, RHP, Indiana
11. Will Vierling, C, Murray State University
12. Tyler Bowen, RHP, Lander University
13. Jack Barker, OF, Col of Southern Idaho
14. Jonathan Gonzalez, LHP, Stetson
15. Jacob Pruitt, RHP, Mississippi State
16. Logan Dawson, SS, Eastern HS
17. Richie Cortese, RHP, Lander University
18. Matthew Potok, RHP, Coastal Carolina
19. Robert Phelps, RHP, Reinhardt University
20. Landon Schaefer, SS, Fayetteville Sr HS

PITTSBURGH PIRATES (6)
1. Seth Hernandez, RHP, Corona HS
2. Angel Cervantes, RHP, Warren HS
2s. Murf Gray, 3B, Fresno State
3. Easton Carmichael, C, Oklahoma
4. Gustavo Melendez, SS, Colegio Nuestra Señora de la Merced
5. Adonys Guzman, C, Arizona
6. Jack Anker, RHP, Fresno State
7. Brent Iredale, 3B, Arkansas
8. Josh Tate, OF, Georgia Southern
9. Jared Jones, 1B, LSU

10. Matt King, SS, Arizona State
11. Dylan Palmer, 2B, Hofstra
12. Cameron Keshock, RHP, Samford University
13. Dylan Mathiesen, RHP, Liberty University
14. Connor Hamilton, RHP, Montgomery Bell Academy
15. McLane Moody, RHP, Northside Senior HS
16. Eddie King, OF, Louisville
17. Carter Gwost, OF, Little Falls HS
18. Canon Reeder, OF, Oregon State
19. Brandon Cain, RHP, Oklahoma
20. Nicholas Frusco, LHP, Miller Place HS

SAN DIEGO PADRES (25)
1. Kruz Schoolcraft, LHP, Sunset HS
3. Ryan Wideman, OF, Western Kentucky
4. Michael Salina, RHP, St. Bonaventure
5. Ty Harvey, C, Inspiration Academy
6. Jaxon Dalena, RHP, Shippensburg University
7. Kerrington Cross, 3B, Cincinnati
8. James Hitt, LHP, Oklahoma
9. Will Koger, RHP, Arizona State
10. Justin DeCriscio, SS, NC State
11. Truitt Madonna, C, Ballard HS
12. George Bilecki, OF, Lewis U
13. Dylan Grego, SS, Ball State
14. Clay Edmondson, RHP, UNC Asheville
15. Ryan Reed, LHP, Pittsburgh
16. Cardell Thibodeaux, OF, Southern
17. Tyler Schmitt, RHP, Illinois
18. Landry Jurecka, RHP, Queens University Of Charlotte
19. Jonathan Vastine, SS, Vanderbilt
20. Luke Cantwell, 1B, Pittsburgh

SAN FRANCISCO GIANTS (13)
1. Gavin Kilen, SS, Tennessee
3. Trevor Cohen, OF, Rutgers
4. Lorenzo Meola, SS, Stetson
6. Jordan Gottesman, LHP, Northeastern
7. Cam Maldonado, OF, Northeastern
8. Ben Bybee, RHP, Arkansas
9. Reid Worley, RHP, Cherokee HS
10. Isaiah Barkett, 2B, Stetson
11. Rod Barajas, C, Saddleback College
12. Cody Delvecchio, RHP, UCLA
13. Broedy Poppell, C, Florida A&M
14. Trey Seeley, RHP, Hope International University
15. Damian Bravo, OF, Texas Tech
16. Garrett Langrell, RHP, Creighton U
17. Luke Mensik, RHP, Lincoln-Way Central HS
18. Cooper McGrath, RHP, Northeastern
19. Braydon Risley, LHP, Grayson College
20. Elijah McNeal, SS, Dublin HS

SEATTLE MARINERS (3)
1. Kade Anderson, LHP, LSU
1s. Luke Stevenson, C, North Carolina
2. Nick Becker, SS, Don Bosco Prep HS
3. Griffin Hugus, RHP, Miami
4. Mason Peters, LHP, Dallas Baptist
5. Korbyn Dickerson, OF, Indiana
6. Lucas Kelly, RHP, Arizona State
7. Colton Shaw, RHP, Yale
8. Danny Macchiarola, RHP, Holy Cross
9. Jackson Steensma, RHP, Appalachian State
10. Isaac Lyon, RHP, Grand Canyon University
11. Dusty Revis, RHP, Western Carolina
12. Grant Jay, C, Dallas Baptist
13. Aiden Taurek, OF, Saint Mary's
14. Luke Heyman, C, Florida
15. Brayden Corn, OF, Western Carolina U
16. Casey Hintz, RHP, Arizona

17. Anthony Karoly, RHP, Nova Southeastern
18. Griffin Stieg, RHP, Virginia Tech
19. Cameron Appenzeller, LHP, Glenwood HS
20. Estevan Moreno, SS, Notre Dame

ST. LOUIS CARDINALS (5)
1. Liam Doyle, LHP, Tennessee
2. Ryan Mitchell, OF, Houston HS
2s. Tanner Franklin, RHP, Tennessee
3. Jack Gurevitch, 1B, University Of San Diego
4. Cade Crossland, LHP, Oklahoma
5. Ethan Young, RHP, East Carolina
6. Matthew Miura, OF, Hawaii
7. Payton Graham, RHP, Gonzaga
8. Ryan Weingartner, SS, Penn State
9. Michael Dattalo, 3B, Dallas Baptist
10. Ty Van Dyke, RHP, Stetson
11. Jalin Flores, SS, Texas
12. Kaden Echeman, RHP, Northern Kentucky
13. Jake Shelagowski, RHP, Saginaw Valley State
14. Anthony Watts, RHP, Iowa
15. Trevor Haskins, SS, Stanford
16. Alex Breckheimer, RHP, Kansas
17. Cameron Nickens, OF, Austin Peay
18. Dylan Driessen, RHP, South Dakota State
19. Liam Best, RHP, Appalachian State
20. Chase Heath, C, U Central Missouri

TAMPA BAY RAYS (14)
1. Daniel Pierce, SS, Mill Creek HS
1s. Brendan Summerhill, OF, Arizona
2. Cooper Flemming, SS, Ganesha HS
2s. Dean Moss, OF, IMG Academy
3. Taitn Gray, C, Dallas Center-Grimes HS
4. Dominic Fritton, LHP, NC State
5. James Quinn-Irons, OF, George Mason
6. Aidan Haugh, RHP, North Carolina
7. Jacob Kuhn, RHP, Midland College
8. Aidan Cremarosa, RHP, Fresno State
9. Mason Nichols, RHP, Ole Miss
10. Trendan Parish, RHP, Texas Tech
11. Luke Jackson, RHP, Texas A&M
12. Brady Jones, RHP, Georgia Tech
13. Ethan Storm, RHP, Rock Valley College
14. Jacob Hartlaub, RHP, Ball State
15. Alex Wallace, RHP, Mclennan CC
16. Riley Stanford, OF, Georgia Tech
17. Brody Donay, C, Florida
18. Brayden Jones, RHP, Ole Miss
19. Blake Morgan, LHP, Old Dominion
20. Ike Young, RHP, Monticello HS

TEXAS RANGERS (12)
1. Gavin Fien, SS, Great Oak HS
2. A.J. Russell, RHP, Tennessee
3. Josh Owens, TWP, Providence Academy
4. Mason McConnaughey, RHP, Nebraska
5. Ben Abeldt, LHP, TCU
6. Jack Wheeler, 3B, Morris HS
7. Paxton Kling, OF, Penn State
8. Evan Siary, RHP, Mississippi State
9. Owen Proksch, LHP, Duke
10. J.D. McReynolds, RHP, University Of Central Missouri
11. Jacob Johnson, RHP, Pearl River CC
12. Jake Barbee, RHP, Jay M Robinson HS
13. Aiden Robertson, RHP, Walters State CC
14. Landon Manzi, RHP, Killingly HS
15. Luke Hanson, SS, Virginia
16. Jaxon Grossman, RHP, Salt Lake CC
17. Noah Franklin, C, TNXL Academy
18. Julius Sanchez, RHP, Illinois

19. Cory Geinzer, RHP, Col of Central Florida
20. Jamaurion McQueen, OF, Brandon HS

TORONTO BLUE JAYS (8)
1. Joseph Parker, SS, Purvis HS
3. Jake Cook, OF, Southern Mississippi
4. Micah Bucknam, RHP, Dallas Baptist
5. Tim Piasentin, 3B, Foothills Composite HS
6. Eric Snow, SS, Auburn
7. Dylan Watts, RHP, Auburn
8. Danny Thompson, RHP, UNC Greensboro
9. Karson Ligon, RHP, Mississippi State
10. Austin Smith, OF, University Of San Diego
11. Jared Spencer, LHP, Texas
12. Blaine Bullard, OF, Klein Cain HS
13. Trace Baker, RHP, UNC Wilmington
14. Noah Palmese, RHP, Webber International University
15. Casey Jake, OF, Kent State
16. Jaxson West, C, Florida State
17. Jordan Rich, OF, American Heritage School
18. Will Cresswell, C, Washington State
19. Luke Kovach, LHP, Cal Poly
20. Ty Peeples, OF, Franklin County HS

WASHINGTON NATIONALS (17)
1. Eli Willits, SS, Fort Cobb-Broxton HS
2. Ethan Petry, OF, South Carolina
3. Landon Harmon, RHP, East Union Attendance Center HS
4. Miguel Sime, RHP, Poly Prep Country Day School
5. Coy James, SS, Davie HS
6. Boston Smith, C, Wright State
7. Julian Tonghini, RHP, Arizona
8. Riley Maddox, RHP, Ole Miss
9. Wyatt Henseler, 3B, Texas A&M
10. Hunter Hines, 1B, Mississippi State
11. Jack Moroknek, OF, Butler
12. Ben Moore, LHP, Old Dominion
13. Tucker Biven, RHP, Louisville
14. Nick Hollifield, C, UAB
15. Jacob Walsh, 1B, Oregon
16. Levi Huesman, LHP, Vanderbilt
17. Bryce Molinaro, 3B, Penn State
18. Owen Puk, RHP, Florida International
19. Mason Pike, RHP, Puyallup HS
20. Juan Cruz, 1B, Alabama State University

APPENDIX

OBITUARIES

Sandy Alomar, a longtime major league player and coach and the father of big league stars Sandy Jr. and Roberto Alomar, died on Oct. 13 in Salinas, P.R. He was 81.

Alomar spent 15 seasons in MLB as a slick-fielding, light-hitting second baseman. The switch-hitter played for six teams, but is best known for his time for his six seasons for the Angels—he was an American League all-star in 1970—and three seasons for the Yankees, for whom he was a utility infielder for the 1976 AL pennant winners.

Alomar batted .245/.290/.288 with 13 home runs and 227 stolen bases in 1,481 career games.

After his playing days, Alomar coached in the minor leagues and MLB for the Padres, Cubs, Rockies and Mets. In 1985, he coached both his sons at the Padres' Low-A Charleston affiliate.

Alomar signed professionally in 1960 and coached his last game in 2009, a span of 50 seasons.

Tony Blanco was a heralded Red Sox prospect who cracked the back of the Top 100 Prospects list in both 2001 and 2002.

The young Dominican third baseman showcased elite arm strength and bat speed he used to crack 13 home runs in the Gulf Coast League, a league record at the time, and then 17 more in the Low-A South Atlantic League as a 19-year-old in 2001.

Boston would trade Blanco to the Reds after the 2002 season to acquire Todd Walker, who played second base every day for a 95-win Red Sox team in 2003. Blanco continued to show power as a Reds farmhand, only now as a first baseman. Still, Cincinnati left him unprotected for the 2004 Rule 5 draft, and the Nationals selected him.

Blanco appeared in 56 games for Washington in 2005, the debut season for the franchise that had relocated from Montreal. In his lone season in MLB, Blanco hit one home run and collected seven RBIs.

Blanco made a name for himself in Japan beginning in 2009. In eight NPB seasons, Blanco made four all-star teams and was given the Best Nine Award three times. The Best Nine is given annually to the best player at each position in NPB.

Blanco, along with Octavio Dotel, was a victim of the April 8 roof collapse at the Jet Set nightclub in Santo Domingo. It was reported that Blanco saved the life of former big leaguer Esteban German by pushing him out of the way as the roof began to collapse. Blanco was 44.

Blanco's legacy lives on through his son Tony Blanco Jr., a first base prospect who began the season on the injured list with the Pirates' Low-A Bradenton affiliate.

Righthander **Jim Clancy** was a workhorse starter for the ascending 1980s Blue Jays. He died on July 12 at his home in Dunedin, Fla. He was 69.

Toronto chose Clancy from the Rangers in the 1976 expansion draft. He made 13 starts for the Blue Jays in their inaugural season of 1977 and continued taking the ball throughout his Toronto tenure. No pitcher started more games for the Blue Jays through his final season in Toronto in 1988.

Clancy made the 1982 American League all-star team in a season in which he made 40 starts and went 16-14 with a 3.71 ERA for a mediocre Blue Jays team that was building toward AL East division titles in 1985 and 1989.

In 15 MLB seasons for three clubs, Clancy went 140-167 with a 4.23 ERA that was right around league average.

He made one relief appearance for Toronto in the 1985 ALCS and later relieved for the National League pennant-winning 1991 Braves.

When the Braves drafted a home-state Georgia high school player under scouting director **Roy Clark**, they often struck gold.

Examples include Adam Wainwright in 2000, Jeff Francoeur and Brian McCann in 2002 and Jason Heyward in 2007.

Clark served as Atlanta scouting director from 2000 to 2009. The Braves hired him as an area scout in 1989. He worked his way up to crosschecker and then scouting director before leaving to become the Nationals' assistant GM in 2010.

Clark returned to the Braves in 2015 as a special assistant and senior advisor to scouting director Brian Bridges. The duo's 2015 draft is the most notable for yielding Austin Riley and Michael Soroka.

Clark died on Aug. 22 in Marietta, Ga. He was 68.

Just 18 players in MLB history have homered four times in one game. Cleveland right fielder **Rocky Colavito** was one of them.

Colavito showed immense promise early in his career. He launched 21 home runs in 1956, finish-

OBITUARIES

ing second in the American League Rookie of the Year voting. In 1958, Colavito delivered one of the finest performances of his career, batting .303, crushing 41 home runs and earning a third-place finish in the MVP race.

The following year, in 1959, he achieved his first all-star selection and led the AL with a career-best 42 home runs. In his 14-year career, he tallied 374 home runs and nine all-star selections.

That offseason, the Indians traded Colavito to the Tigers for batting champion Harvey Kuenn. Cleveland's fortunes immediately went into a tailspin. From 1960 until 1994, the Indians never finished within 11 games of first place. The dry spell became known colloquially as the "Curse of Rocky Colavito."

After retiring, Colavito took on a role as a TV analyst for WJW in Cleveland during 1972 and again from 1975 to '76. He also joined Cleveland's coaching staff, serving in 1973 and then from '76 to '78.

Colavito died on Dec. 10 in Bernville, Pa. He was 91.

Outfielder **Jason Conti** was a member of the Diamondbacks' first-ever draft class in 1996. Arizona selected him in the 32nd round out of Pittsburgh.

Conti spent parts of five seasons in the big leagues from 2000 to 2004, playing for the D-backs, Rays, Brewers and Rangers. He played professionally for 11 seasons and hit .301 in more than 1,000 minor league games.

After his playing career, Conti worked his way up to executive chef. He suffered a stroke while on the job and later died on May 17 in Phoenix. He was 50.

To say **Octavio Dotel** had been everywhere would be an understatement.

When Dotel signed with the Mets out of the Dominican Republic in 1993, it was the beginning of a 21-year pro odyssey for the righthander. He played for 13 teams in 15 major league seasons, which was the all-time record for individual teams before Edwin Jackson surpassed him with 14 in 2019.

Dotel climbed as high as No. 45 on the 1999 Top 100 Prospects ranking and made his MLB debut as a 25-year-old that season, appearing in 19 games for the Mets, including 14 starts. New York dealt him to the Astros after the season as a key piece for lefthander Mike Hampton, who had finished runner-up for the National League

Octavio Dotel

Cy Young Award in 1999 but was one year away from free agency.

In Houston, Dotel emerged as a lights-out setup man for Hall of Fame closer Billy Wagner. Dotel spent five seasons with the Astros and, counting his relief work only, recorded a 2.40 ERA and 1.02 WHIP with 442 strikeouts in 337 innings. Houston sent him to the Athletics at the 2004 trade deadline in a three-team deal that imported another star and pending free agent: Carlos Beltran.

Dotel worked as a closer for Oakland down the stretch in 2004 but lost most of the 2005 season after having Tommy John surgery. He returned in 2006 and hung on for eight more seasons, adding the Yankees, Royals, Braves, White Sox, Pirates, Dodgers, Rockies, Blue Jays, Cardinals and Tigers to his career register.

Dotel finished his career with 758 appearances. He pitched to a 3.78 ERA with 1,143 strikeouts and 109 saves in 951 innings.

Dotel won his first and only World Series with the Cardinals in 2011 and returned to the Fall Classic with the 2012 Tigers, who came up short against the Giants. Dotel added more hardware by winning the 2013 World Baseball Classic with his native Dominican Republic.

Dotel died on April 8 at the Jet Set nightclub in Santo Domingo after the roof collapsed, claiming the lives of 232 people and injuring 225. He was 51.

Photographer **Morris Fostoff** contributed many images to Baseball America over the years.

An accountant by trade, he started a successful sports photography business and contributed his work to BA, among other outlets. Fostoff published two books of his photography. Fostoff served honorably as a World War II Army veteran. He died on May 17 in Boca Raton, Fla. He was 100.

Two-time Red Sox all-star left fielder **Mike Greenwell** died of thyroid cancer on Oct. 9 in Boston. He was 62.

Greenwell played his entire 12-year MLB career with the Red Sox and spent one season with Hanshin in Japan in 1997 before retiring.

Boston drafted Greenwell in the third round in 1982 out of high school in North Fort Myers, Fla., and his Florida upbringing helped earn him the nickname "Gator."

Greenwell received MLB cups of coffee in 1985 and '86 before earning a regular role for the 1987 Red Sox, alongside fellow rookie phenom outfielder Ellis Burks.

As a 23-year-old rookie, Greenwell batted .328/.386/.570 with 19 home runs and 31 doubles in the supercharged 1987 offensive environment. He struck out just 40 times in 125 games and finished fourth in American League Rookie of the Year voting.

Greenwell upped the ante in 1988, when he finished second in AL MVP voting to the Athletics' Jose Canseco, who had authored the first 40-40 season in MLB history. The sweet-swinging Greenwell hit .325/.416/.531 with 22 homers, 39 doubles, 16 stolen bases and 119 RBIs as the primary cleanup hitter for the AL East division-winning Red Sox.

Greenwell made the AL all-star team in both 1988 and '89, helping to reinforce the incredible line of succession in front of Fenway Park's Green Monster. From 1939 to 1996, left field in Boston was patrolled by Hall of Famers Ted Williams, Carl Yastrzemski and Jim Rice, followed by Greenwell.

He appeared in the postseason for four Red Sox teams: the 1986 AL pennant winners and the division-winning 1988, 1990 and 1995 teams. In 12 seasons, he batted .303/.368/.463 with 130 home runs in 1,269 games. He drew 460 walks against 364 strikeouts and was renowned for his sweet lefthanded swing.

After his playing career, Greenwell was involved briefly as a coach in the Reds system and also raced stock cars and pickup trucks competitively. Greenwell's son Bo was drafted by Cleveland in the sixth round in 2007 and played his way to Double-A before calling it a career. His other son Garrett played collegiately. Both played for their father at Riverdale High in Fort Myers.

From roaming the hallways at Oakland Technical High to breaking records down the road at the Oakland Coliseum, left fielder **Rickey Henderson** personified the heart and grit of his home city.

Henderson used his speed to swipe an all-time major league record 1,406 bases across a 25-year career that included 10 All-Star Game appearances, an American League MVP Award in 1990 and World Series championships with the 1989 Athletics and 1993 Blue Jays.

His one-of-a-kind career made him a first-ballot Hall of Famer in 2009 with 94.8% of the vote. He had his No. 24 retired by the A's.

Henderson excelled as a three-sport athlete at Oakland Tech and dreamed of playing football for the Raiders. However, he stuck to baseball, and it's safe to say it was one of the best investments he could have made.

He was drafted in the fourth round in 1976 by his hometown team and then rose quickly through Oakland's minor league system. He suited up with short-season Boise to make his pro debut and was donning his beloved green and gold by the 1979 all-star break. Through his three years in the minor leagues, Henderson swiped 249 bases and recorded 434 hits.

While his career is heavily associated with the A's, Henderson played for nine teams. Over his career, he hit .279/.401/.419 and accumulated 3,055 hits, 510 doubles, 66 triples, 297 home runs, 1,115 RBIs and an MLB-record 2,205 runs scored. Henderson walked 2,190 times and held that all-time record before Barry Bonds passed him—though Henderson drew more unintentional walks than Bonds.

Henderson also holds the record for leadoff home runs with 81 and the single-season record for steals, which he set with 130 in 1982.

Henderson achieved an .820 OPS and a 127 OPS+ across his playing years. In his 1990 MVP season, he slashed .325/.439/.577 with 65 stolen bases and tied his career high with 18 home runs.

Henderson's place in history is assured. His stolen base record outpaces Lou Brock by 467. His runs scored tally surpasses Ty Cobb by 50.

Henderson died on Dec. 20 in Oakland, just five days shy of his birthday. He was 65.

OBITUARIES

Rickey Henderson

Bobby Jenks has one of the most amazing success stories of the 21st century.

A fifth-round pick of the Angels in 2000, Jenks didn't play high school ball in rural Washington, but scouts saw him touch 93-94 mph with a power curve in American Legion action and in showcases. The 6-foot-4 righthander was touching 100 mph in minor league games just a year later, but he also had little idea of where his pitches were going.

Jenks was soon touching 102 mph, but the Angels eventually dropped him from the 40-man roster after he got into an altercation with a teammate. The White Sox claimed him on waivers in December 2004 and he blossomed.

Jenks went from waiver bait to closing games in the World Series in the span of a year. He made his MLB debut for the White Sox as a 24-year-old on July 5, 2005. He earned Chicago's closer job by September. In the World Series, he picked up two saves in four appearances for the champions, who bullied the postseason field with an 11-1 October record.

Jenks made all-star appearances in each of the next two seasons. He was the White Sox's closer from late in 2005 until 2010, notching 173 saves. He pitched for the Red Sox in 2011, but a back injury ended his career. It also affected the rest of his life. An infection he suffered during a back surgery was found to be life-threatening.

Jenks became a pitching coach and eventually a manager in the Pioneer League with Grand Junction, and his team won the title in 2022.

Jenks was diagnosed with stomach cancer in 2025. The disease claimed his life on July 4 at the age of 44. He was living in Sintra, Portugal, to be closer to his wife's family.

General manager **Walt Jocketty** molded the Cardinals into one of the most successful franchises of the 2000s. St. Louis won the National League pennant in 2004 and then the World Series in 2006.

Only the Yankees and Red Sox won more games than the Cardinals from 2000 to 2009. While Jocketty wasn't running the club in 2008 and 2009, St. Louis continued winning with all-stars he had acquired, including Albert Pujols, Yadier Molina, Adam Wainwright and Chris Carpenter.

Jocketty is most strongly associated with the Cardinals, but he made his mark in baseball with the Athletics and Reds as well. It was with Oakland in the 1980s that he got his start.

Hired as A's director of minor league operations and scouting in 1980, Jocketty helped build Oakland into an American League power. The Athletics were BA Organization of the Year in 1982, had BA Minor League Player of the Year Jose Canseco in 1985 and then produced successive AL Rookies of the Year Canseco, Mark McGwire and Walt Weiss from 1986 to 1988.

The A's won three straight American League pennants from 1988 to 1990, taking the World Series in 1989. By this time, Jocketty had been promoted to director of baseball administration, setting the stage for a stopover as Rockies assistant GM of player personnel in 1994.

The Cardinals hired Jocketty as GM on Oct. 14, 1994, against the backdrop of the most contentious work stoppage in MLB history, one that resulted in the cancellation of the World Series. Jocketty installed future Hall of Famer manager Tony La Russa as manager in 1996. The two had worked together for nearly a decade in Oakland.

With Jocketty running baseball operations and La Russa managing the team on the field, the Cardinals embarked on one of their most successful periods. Between 1996 and 2007, St. Louis won six NL Central division titles, a wild card, a pennant, a World Series and a total of 1,055 games. The Braves were the only National League team with more wins in this window.

Despite Jocketty's success in St. Louis, a power struggle led to his ouster after the 2007 season. The Reds quickly hired him and elevated him to GM early in the 2008 season.

Jocketty oversaw one of the more successful recent periods in Reds history—two NL

Central division titles, a wild card and a nod as Organization of the Year in 2012—during his time at the helm of Cincinnati baseball operations, which ran through 2015.

Jocketty died on April 25 in Phoenix. He was 74.

Davey Johnson had a front-row seat to perhaps the most innovative manager in history when Earl Weaver took the helm in Baltimore midway through the 1968 season. Johnson himself would later join Weaver as one of the most successful skippers of all-time.

Unlike Weaver, Johnson had a decorated big league playing career that saw him make four all-star teams, win three Gold Gloves at second base and win two World Series rings before he became a manager.

Johnson's pro baseball journey began when the Orioles signed him in 1962 following one season at Texas A&M. He became the Orioles' regular second baseman in 1966 as a 23-year-old after the club traded Jerry Adair in June. He hit .257 with seven home runs in 501 at-bats but shined defensively and finished third in American League Rookie of the Year voting.

The 1966 Orioles won the World Series with future Hall of Famers Frank Robinson, Brooks Robinson and Luis Aparicio in their primes and young stars Jim Palmer, Dave McNally, Boog Powell, Paul Blair and Johnson on their way up.

The best was yet to come for Baltimore. The 1969–71 Orioles won the AL pennant each year, posting 109 wins in 1969 and defeating the Reds in the 1970 World Series. The Orioles' three-year stretch is one of the most dominant of the expansion era, and during it Johnson trailed only Joe Morgan in WAR among second basemen.

Johnson lost playing time to top prospect Bobby Grich down the stretch in 1972 and was traded to the Braves that offseason. In a much friendlier Atlanta home park in 1973, a 30-year-old Johnson smashed 43 home runs, 42 of them while in the lineup at second base. That tied Rogers Hornsby for the single-season record for homers by a second baseman, one that has not been surpassed.

The Mets hired Johnson to manage their Double-A Jackson affiliate in 1981. He moved to Triple-A Tidewater in 1983 and then up to New York in 1984. As good as he was as a player, Johnson is most famous for his time as Mets manager.

In seven seasons in Queens, he guided the

Davey Johnson

Mets to a .588 winning percentage, including 108 wins and a World Series championship in 1986. From 1984 to 1990, the Mets had 666 wins, the most in MLB.

Johnson managed the Reds from 1993–95, winning the NL Central in '95. He managed the Orioles in 1996 and '97, advancing to the AL Championship Series both times. He led the Dodgers in 1999 and 2000.

He managed the U.S. team at the 2008 Olympics and 2009 World Baseball Classic, setting the stage for his next gig. The Nationals hired Johnson in June 2011. He won NL East division titles the next two seasons and retired after the 2013 season.

Johnson led the Mets, Reds, Orioles and Nationals to the playoffs, just as Billy Martin led four different teams to October. Only Dusty Baker, with five, has a higher total.

Johnson managed one World Series champion and six total playoff teams—just as Weaver had on both counts—while finishing with a .562 winning percentage that ranks 15th highest among managers with at least 1,000 games.

Johnson died on Sept. 5 in Sarasota, Fla. He was 82.

Few center fielders of the 1970s and '80s were more accomplished than **Chet Lemon**. Just a handful of them recorded more starts or more putouts in center in those two decades.

Lemon developed into a star with the White

OBITUARIES

Sox and a World Series champion with the Tigers, but his pro journey began with the Athletics.

Oakland drafted Lemon out of high school in Los Angeles with the 22nd overall pick in 1972. The A's traded him to the White Sox in June 1975, and he made his MLB debut that September.

Lemon made American League all-star teams for Chicago in 1978 and '79. While he didn't record gaudy totals for home runs or stolen bases, he was a frequent .300 hitter who drew walks, hit for above-average power and shined defensively in center field.

Traded to the Tigers after the 1981 season, Lemon hit his stride in Detroit. The Tigers won more games in the 1980s than any team but the Yankees. No team hit more home runs than Detroit during the decade.

Lemon played a key role in the club's success, particularly for the World Series-champion 1984 Tigers. That season he hit .287/.357/.495 with 20 home runs and 76 RBIs in 141 games, while rounding out a lineup core that also included Alan Trammell, Lou Whitaker, Kirk Gibson and Lance Parrish.

A rare blood disorder called polycythemia vera cut Lemon's playing career short. He retired at age 35 in 1990. In 16 MLB seasons, Lemon batted .273/.355/.442 with 215 home runs and 1,875 hits in 1,988 games. He started 1,411 of those games in center field.

In 1993, he established the Chet Lemon Baseball School in Lake Mary, Fla., and built his Chet Lemon's Juice travel team into a power. He also coached baseball at Eustis High, where his son Marcus starred before he was drafted by the Rangers in the fourth round in 2006.

Rangers scout **Scott Littlefield** was part of a distinguished baseball family. His brother Dave is a longtime exec who was a former Pirates GM, and his brother Mark is on the medical staff with the Yankees. Scott was a scout for 34 years, including stops with San Diego, Pittsburgh and Atlanta. He won scout of the year honors with San Diego in 2007 and again with Texas in 2019. He died suddenly on Sept. 19. He was 59.

Félix Mantilla was the last living member of the 1957 World Series-champion Milwaukee Braves, and the shortstop's loyalty to the city remained rooted even after his playing career.

Born in Isabela, Puerto Rico, Mantilla took steps toward his future career as a 9-year-old, when he went from playing in police-sponsored city leagues to playing for the Puerto Rican national team that won the Amateur World Series in 1951, beating Cuba 6-5.

Mantilla also broke racial barriers throughout his career. In 1953, with the Jacksonville Braves, he and Hank Aaron were among the first players of color on the team.

Mantilla's impact went beyond the field. He faced and overcame challenges such as limited English proficiency and being one of the few non-white players in the major leagues during his time.

Mantilla's career continued with various teams, including the Mets and Red Sox, where he earned an all-star appearance in 1964. He went on to become a beloved figure in Milwaukee, working with the police department and mentoring youth after retirement.

Mantilla was 90 when he died of prostate cancer on Jan. 10.

At St. Mary's High in Phoenix, a young lefthander dominated the Arizona prep scene in the mid 2000s. **Brian Matusz** went 8-1 with a 0.50 ERA and was drafted by the Angles in the fourth round in 2005. He elected to attend the University of San Diego instead.

There, his dominance continued. Matusz became the most accomplished pitcher in Toreros history. As a junior in 2008, he compiled a nation-leading 141 strikeouts and a remarkable 1.71 ERA. He set the USD career standard with 396 strikeouts.

That standout season helped coax the Orioles to make Matusz the fourth overall pick in the 2008 draft.

Matusz pitched in 19 games between High-A and Double-A, posting a combined 2.36 ERA with 122 strikeouts before being called up for his MLB debut on Aug. 4, 2009. He had a 4.63 ERA in eight starts and followed that up with a fifth-place finish for American League Rookie of the Year Award in 2010.

Matusz struggled the following year with a 10.69 ERA in 12 starts in 2011 and a 5.42 ERA in 16 starts in 2012. His time as a starter came to an end, but the beginning of a new chapter was about to begin. The shift in role would extend his career.

Midway through the 2012 season, Matusz began pitching out of the bullpen and finished with a 1.35 ERA in 18 relief outings as the Orioles ended a 15-year playoff drought. He concluded an eight-year MLB career with a 4.92 ERA and 462 strikeouts in 529 innings.

Matusz died on Jan. 7 in Phoenix. He was 37.

Lefthander **Rob Mallicoat**, who made 51 career relief appearances for the 1987, 1991 and 1992 Astros, died Oct. 19. He was 60.

The Astros drafted Mallicoat in the first round of the 1984 January secondary draft out of Taft Junior College in California. He ranked as Houston's No. 1 prospect heading into 1986.

Bill Melton spent his prime years in a pitcher's era playing third base for White Sox teams that typically finished in the second division.

Melton debuted as a 22-year-old in 1968, the Year of the Pitcher, and performed well. In his first full season in 1969 he hit 23 home runs with 87 RBIs, which was a sign of things to come.

"Beltin' Melton" emerged as an impact regular in 1970 with a 33-homer, 96-RBI campaign, which set the stage for a career year. Melton made the American League all-star team in 1971, when he hit .269/.352/.492 with a league-leading 33 home runs. He finished 13th in AL MVP voting.

Two herniated disks in his back short-circuited his encore season in 1972, and Melton was never quite the same player again. Still, when he retired after the 1977 season he held the White Sox franchise record with 154 home runs. Harold Baines surpassed that total in 1987, but Melton still ranks ninth in franchise history.

Melton continued to associate with the White Sox after his playing days. He served as a hitting instructor for Michael Jordan when the NBA great tried his hand at baseball with Double-A Birmingham in 1994. Melton later worked as a pre- and postgame television analyst for the White Sox.

Melton died on Dec. 5, 2024 in Phoenix. He was 79.

Righthander **Randy Moffitt** spent 12 seasons as a major league reliever, primarily for the 1970s Giants. He died Aug. 28 in Long Beach. He was 76.

The Giants drafted Moffitt out of Long Beach State in the first round of the January phase of the 1970 draft. He reached San Francisco two years later as a reliever, appearing in 40 games. Moffitt spent his first 10 seasons with the Giants and still ranks among the franchise's top 10 all time with 83 saves and 459 appearances.

Moffitt's sister is tennis icon Billie Jean King.

Jesus Montero ranked as the No. 3 prospect

Dave Parker

in baseball heading into the 2011 season. Scouts thought that the powerful, righthanded-hitting catcher had the type of opposite-field power that would play in Yankee Stadium.

While Montero popped 18 home runs as a 21-year-old at Triple-A that season, and then four more for the Yankees as a September callup, it wasn't enough to keep him in pinstripes.

Traded to the Mariners in January 2012 for Michael Piñeda, Montero ranked No. 6 overall heading into that season. It would be his first—and only—full season in the big leagues. He batted .260/.298/.386 with 15 homers in 135 games for Seattle, but he started more games at DH than catcher, the first sign that he would need to really hit to have staying power.

Montero struggled with all facets of catching, due in part to his bulky 6-foot-3 frame, and he started just 83 games behind the plate in parts of five MLB seasons. He spent most of his time at DH and first base, batting .253/.295/.398 with 28 homers in 226 games.

Montero spent partial seasons with the Mariners in 2013, 2014 and 2015. Seattle waived him during spring training 2016. The Blue Jays claimed him and sent him to Triple-A for the season.

He served 50-game suspensions in 2013 for his link to Biogenesis and again in 2016 when he tested positive for a banned substance.

The Yankees signed Montero out of Venezuela in 2006. He died in his home country on Oct. 19

OBITUARIES

when he was involved in a motorcycle collision. He was 35.

Righthander **Rod Nichols** spent seven seasons in the big leagues, primarily with Cleveland, the team that drafted him out of New Mexico in the fifth round in 1985. He also pitched in Japan and later spent the better part of two decades as a coach.

Nichols' best season was 1991, when he logged 137.1 innings and pitched to a 3.54 ERA while making 16 of his 31 appearances as a starter. Cleveland at this time was building toward its mid-1990s dynasty period, but in 1991 it was a 105-game loser. That year, young players such as Jim Thome, Albert Belle and Sandy Alomar Jr. were finding their footing in MLB.

After his playing career, Nichols worked as a minor league pitching coach for the Phillies and Cubs from 2002 to 2019. In 2013, he served as big league bullpen coach for the Phillies.

Nichols went 11-31, 4.43 in 100 career MLB appearances. He died May 14 in Helena, Mont. He was 60.

Dave Parker died less than a month before his induction into the Hall of Fame, but the 74-year-old experienced the satisfaction of knowing that he had made it after years of waiting.

Anyone who watched Parker with the Pirates in the 1970s knew his Hall of Fame induction seemed like a foregone conclusion. In his 20s, he was one of the brightest stars in the game.

Parker was National League MVP in 1978, when he led baseball with a .334 average and led the NL with a .585 slugging percentage while hitting 30 homers and stealing 20 bases.

From 1975 to '79, Parker hit .321/.377/.532 with 23 home runs and 17 steals a season. He was a crucial part of the Pirates' 1979 World Series championship.

As impressive as his power, speed and athleticism were, his left arm was the showstopper. After watching Roberto Clemente demonstrate arguably the best arm ever seen from a right fielder, Pirates fans saw Parker produce a close facsimile.

He reached double digits in assists every year from 1976 to '80, and he had 26 assists in 1977. That number has not been equaled since, and it was just one shy of the figure Clemente produced in 1961, which stands as the integration era record. Famously, Parker threw out two baserunners in the 1979 All-Star Game to earn the event's

Ryne Sandberg

MVP award.

Parker's career took a dip in the early 1980s, as he battled a knee injury and gained weight. When healthy, however, he could still mash, as shown by the .312/.365/.551 season for the Reds in 1985. He finished second in MVP voting that year. Parker won a second World Series ring in 1989 with the Oakland Athletics before retiring after the 1991 season, which he spent playing for the Angels and Blue Jays. He finished his career as a .290 hitter with 339 home runs and 152 outfield assists.

Ryne Sandberg was synonymous with Cubs baseball in the 1980s and '90s. Millions watched his hitting exploits and masterful defense at second base on the cable superstation WGN.

Despite his iconic status in Chicago and in MLB as a whole, amplified by all those Wrigley Field day games, Sandberg did not want news of his failing health to overshadow Hall of Fame induction weekend.

His passing from prostate cancer was announced on Monday, July 29, one day after CC Sabathia, Ichiro Suzuki and Billy Wagner were enshrined. Sandberg was 65.

Superstardom was not preordained for Sandberg. Drafted by the Phillies in the 20th round in 1978, he was a star shortstop and quarterback at North Central High in Spokane, Wash.

Sandberg spent just three full seasons in the minor leagues before he made his MLB debut as a 21-year-old September callup in 1981. He appeared in 13 games, going 1-for-6.

In one of the most regrettable trades in franchise history, the Phillies traded Sandberg, along with 36-year-old shortstop Larry Bowa, to the Cubs for 29-year-old shortstop Ivan De Jesus in January 1982.

Sandberg didn't provide much offense for Chicago initially but did steal 30-plus bases in 1982 and 1983 and won a Gold Glove after switching from third base to second base. That '83 season was a sign of things to come. Sandberg won nine straight Gold Gloves, which was a record until it was eclipsed by Roberto Alomar.

Then, in 1984, Sandberg broke through. He won the National League MVP award with a brilliant all-around season in which he batted .314/.367/.520 with 19 home runs, 36 doubles and 32 stolen bases. He led the NL with 114 runs and 19 triples. He helped drive the Cubs to 96 wins and an NL East division title.

Sandberg would propel the Cubs to the NLCS in 1989 as well, starring as the best player on a division-winner for a franchise that went nearly 40 years in between playoff appearances.

The accolades continued to mount for Sandberg. He made 10 NL all-star teams, starting nine times at second base. He won seven Silver Sluggers, tied for most at the position with Jose Altuve. He finished fourth in MVP voting in both 1989 and 1990, slugging 40 homers for the first time in the latter season.

Sandberg initially retired at age 34 in June 1994, before the players' strike wiped out the World Series, but returned in 1997 for two more seasons.

Sandberg hit 282 career home runs, with 277 of them coming while in the lineup at second base. That was the record until Jeff Kent surpassed it. Only Joe Morgan turned in more 20-homer, 20-steal seasons as a second baseman than Sandberg's three.

Sandberg was inducted to the Hall of Fame on his third ballot in 2005.

A four-year letter winner at Miami (Ohio), lefthander **Scott Sauerbeck** was drafted in the 23rd round by the Mets in 1994.

The Pirates selected Sauerbeck in the 1998 Rule 5 draft, and he made his MLB debut with the 1999 club. He made 65 relief appearances as a rookie and quickly became one of Pittsburgh's most reliable bullpen pieces.

In 2002 he appeared in 78 games, setting a Pirates single-season franchise record for the most appearances by a lefthander.

Sauerbeck's big league career lasted seven seasons and included stops in Boston, Cleveland and Oakland. He had a 3.82 ERA with 389 strikeouts in 386.1 innings, serving primarily as a left-on-left matchup reliever, a role that has been phased out of the game by the three-batter rule.

Sauerbeck held lefthanded batters to a career .196 average over 616 at-bats. Just 12 lefties in the Wild Card Era allowed a lower average in a career of at least 500 left-on-left at-bats.

Sauerbeck was 53 when he died of a heart attack in Bradenton, Fla., on Feb. 18.

Cuban righthander **Diego Segui** pitched for 15 seasons in the major leagues, winning the 1970 American League ERA title. He died on July 24 in Kansas City, Kan. He was 87.

Segui pitched for six MLB franchises, primarily the Athletics in both Kansas City and Oakland. He began his MLB career in 1962, working mostly as a starter. By 1972 he entered his mid 30s and transitioned to journeyman reliever status. He was famous for throwing a forkball.

Segui made 639 career appearances, 171 of them starts, and recorded a 3.81 ERA in 1,807.2 innings. He pitched from 1962 until 1977, ending with the Mariners in their inaugural season.

His son David Segui was a switch-hitting first baseman who logged 15 MLB seasons.

At Rutgers, **Jeff Torborg** earned All-America honors, setting a single-season batting record with a .537 average in 1963.

Torborg's 10-year major league career spanned from 1964 to 1973. He served as a catcher for the Dodgers and Angels. He won a World Series with the Dodgers in 1965 and caught three no-hitters during his career: Sandy Koufax's perfect game on June 9, 1965; Bill Singer's no-hitter on July 20, 1970; and Nolan Ryan's first no-hitter on May 15, 1973.

Torborg later transitioned to managing, leading teams such as the Cleveland Indians (1977-79), White Sox (1989-91), Mets (1992-93), Montreal Expos (2001) and Marlins (2002-03). His most notable managerial achievement came in 1990, when he guided the White Sox to a 94-68 record and was named the American League Manager of the Year.

Torborg was 83 when he died on Jan. 19 in Port Orange, Fla.

OBITUARIES

Bob Uecker

There were dominant lefthanders in the 1960s, and then there was **Bob Veale**.

Veale cemented his place in Pirates history by striking out 276 batters in a single season, the most by any pitcher in Pittsburgh's modern era. He surpassed 200 strikeouts in both 1966 and 1969, establishing himself as one of the premier southpaws of the 1960s.

Veale still holds the Pirates' club modern era record for strikeouts in a season. Over his 13-year career, the flame-throwing southpaw racked up 120 victories and capped his legacy with a World Series title in 1971.

Veale worked as a scout and minor league pitching coach for the Braves and the Yankees.

Veale died on Jan. 7 in Birmingham, Ala. He was 91.

Francis Thomas "Fay" Vincent's short tenure as MLB commissioner changed the position for the long term.

Vincent served as deputy commissioner to longtime friend A. Bartlett Giamatti and ascended to the role of commissioner when Giamatti died suddenly of a heart attack in September 1989.

Vincent served as commissioner until September 1992, when the owners gave him a vote of no confidence and he resigned his post. The owners were angry that Vincent had intervened during the 1990 lockout to broker a Basic Agreement that included a higher minimum salary for players but did not include revenue sharing among teams.

With Vincent's ouster, Bud Selig became acting commissioner and eventually rose to commissioner. Because Selig was an owner himself, the role of commissioner shifted to one completely beholden to the interest of the owners. No lip service was paid to acting in the "best interests of baseball," as was the responsibility of Kenesaw Mountain Landis when he was installed as baseball's first commissioner in 1920.

Vincent remained active in baseball post commissionership. He served as president of the New England Collegiate Baseball League, a summer wood-bat league, from 1998 to 2004.

Vincent remained vocal about baseball issues ranging from collusion, the 1994 strike and suspected steroid use in the game.

In a press release, MLB commissioner Rob Manfred credited Vincent with ensuring the 1989 World Series was completed following the Loma Prieta earthquake that rocked Northern California and also for initiating the process for the National League to add the Marlins and Rockies in 1993.

Vincent died from bladder cancer at age 86 on Feb. 1 in Vero Beach, Fla.

Bob Uecker was never afraid to laugh at himself. His sense of humor endeared him to millions and earned him a place of reverence in the game, making his Mr. Baseball moniker entirely fitting.

So there was an outpouring of love for Uecker when his death at age 90 was announced on Jan. 16. Born and raised in Milwaukee, he died in nearby Menomonee Falls, Wis.

"Bob was the genuine item: always the funniest person in any room he was in, and always an outstanding ambassador for our national pastime," MLB commissioner Rob Manfred said in a statement.

Uecker signed with the Milwaukee Braves in 1956 and reached MLB as a 28-year-old in 1962.

A light-hitting catcher with a strong defensive reputation, Uecker spent six seasons in the big leagues as a backup. He picked up a World Series ring with the 1964 Cardinals.

He retired as a player in 1967 and embarked on a 56-year run as a broadcaster, actor, comedian and overall storyteller. Uecker worked as a color analyst on TV in the 1970s, '80s and '90s but was most familiar as the radio voice of the Brewers.

Uecker spent 54 seasons on the air, the second-longest continuous tenure with one MLB team, trailing only the Royals' Denny Matthews.

STATISTICS INDEX

MAJOR LEAGUES

AMERICAN LEAGUE
Team	Page
Athletics	55
Baltimore	74
Boston	87
Chicago	107
Cleveland	127
Detroit	145
Houston	156
Kansas City	167
Los Angeles	177
Minnesota	217
New York	238
Seattle	298
Tampa Bay	306
Texas	317
Toronto	328

NATIONAL LEAGUE
Team	Page
Arizona	45
Atlanta	65
Chicago	97
Cincinnati	117
Colorado	136
Los Angeles	186
Miami	196
Milwaukee	207
New York	227
Philadelphia	248
Pittsburgh	258
St. Louis	269
San Diego	278
San Francisco	288
Washington	339

TRIPLE-A

INTERNATIONAL LEAGUE
Team	Page
Buffalo	329
Charlotte	108
Columbus	128
Durham	308
Gwinnett	66
Indianapolis	259
Iowa	98
Jacksonville	197
Lehigh Valley	249
Louisville	118
Memphis	270
Nashville	208
Norfolk	75
Omaha	168
Rochester	340
Scranton/W-B	239
St. Paul	218
Syracuse	228
Toledo	146
Worcester	88

PACIFIC COAST LEAGUE
Team	Page
Albuquerque	137
El Paso	279
Las Vegas	56
Oklahoma City	187
Reno	46
Round Rock	318
Sacramento	289
Salt Lake	178
Sugar Land	157
Tacoma	299

DOUBLE-A

EASTERN LEAGUE
Team	Page
Akron	129
Altoona	261
Binghamton	230
Chesapeake	77
Erie	148
Harrisburg	341
Hartford	138
New Hampshire	331
Portland	89
Reading	250
Richmond	290
Somerset	240

SOUTHERN LEAGUE
Team	Page
Biloxi	209
Birmingham	110
Chattanooga	119
Columbus	68
Knoxville	99
Montgomery	309
Pensacola	197
Rocket City	179

TEXAS LEAGUE
Team	Page
Amarillo	48
Arkansas	300
Corpus Christi	159
Frisco	320
Midland	58
NW Arkansas	169
San Antonio	280
Springfield	271
Tulsa	188
Wichita	220

HIGH-A

NORTHWEST LEAGUE
Team	Page
Eugene	291
Everett	301
Hillsboro	49
Spokane	139
Tri-City	181
Vancouver	332

SOUTH ATLANTIC LEAGUE
Team	Page
Aberdeen	79
Asheville	160
Bowling Green	310
Brooklyn	231
Greensboro	262
Greenville	91
Hub City	321
Hudson Valley	242
Jersey Shore	251
Rome	69
Wilmington	343
Winston-Salem	111

MIDWEST LEAGUE
Team	Page
Beloit	200
Dayton	120
Cedar Rapids	221
Fort Wayne	282
Great Lakes	190
Lake County	130
Lansing	59
Peoria	272
Quad Cities	171
South Bend	100
West Michigan	149
Wisconsin	210

LOW-A

CALIFORNIA LEAGUE
Team	Page
Fresno	140
Inland Empire	182
Lake Elsinore	283
Modesto	302
Rancho Cucamonga	191
San Jose	293
Stockton	60
Visalia	50

CAROLINA LEAGUE
Team	Page
Augusta	70
Carolina	212
Charleston	311
Columbia	159
Delmarva	80
Fayetteville	161
Fredericksburg	344
Hickory	322
Kannapolis	112
Lynchburg	131
Myrtle Beach	102
Salem	92

FLORIDA STATE LEAGUE
Team	Page
Bradenton	263
Clearwater	253
Daytona	121
Dunedin	333
Fort Myers	222
Jupiter	201
Lakeland	150
Palm Beach	273
St. Lucie	232
Tampa	243

ROOKIE

ARIZONA COMPLEX LEAGUE
Team	Page
ACL Angels	183
ACL Athletics	61
ACL Brewers	213
ACL Cubs	103
ACL D-backs	51
ACL Dodgers	192
ACL Giants	294
ACL Guardians	132
ACL Mariners	303
ACL Padres	284
ACL Rangers	324
ACL Reds	123
ACL Rockies	141
ACL Royals	173
ACL White Sox	114

FLORIDA COMPLEX LEAGUE
Team	Page
FCL Astros	163
FCL Blue Jays	335
FCL Braves	71
FCL Cardinals	275
FCL Marlins	203
FCL Mets	234
FCL Nationals	345
FCL Orioles	82
FCL Phillies	254
FCL Pirates	265
FCL Rays	313
FCL Red Sox	93
FCL Tigers	151
FCL Twins	223
FCL Yankees	244

DOMINICAN SUMMER LEAGUE
Team	Page
Angels	184
Astros	164
Athletics	62
Blue Jays	336
Braves	72
Brewers	214
Cardinals	276
Cubs	104
D-backs	53
Dodgers	193
Giants	295
Guardians	133
Mariners	304
Marlins	204
Mets	235
Nationals	346
Orioles	83
Padres	285
Phillies	255
Pirates	266
Rangers	325
Rays	314
Red Sox	94
Reds	124
Rockies	143
Royals	174
Tigers	152
Twins	225
White Sox	115
Yankees	245